D0495219

Cassell's

Concise
German-English
English-German
Dictionary

Deutsch-Englisches
Englisch-Deutsches
Taschenwörterbuch

Compiled by

H.-C. SASSE, M.A. (Adel.), M.Litt. (Cantab.)

Lecturer in German in the University of Newcastle upon Tyne

DR. J. HORNE

Formerly Lecturer in German in the University of Birmingham

DR. CHARLOTTE DIXON

CASSELL
London

Cassell Publishers Limited
Artillery House, Artillery Row
London SW1P 1RT

Copyright © Cassell Ltd. 1966
Copyright © Macmillan Publishing Company, 1982
a division of Macmillan, Inc.

All rights reserved. No part of this book may be reproduced
or transmitted in any form or by any means, electronic or
mechanical, including photocopying, recording or by any
information storage and retrieval system, without
permission in writing from the Publisher.

CASSELL'S COMPACT GERMAN - ENGLISH
ENGLISH - GERMAN DICTIONARY
First edition 1966
Second edition, tenth impression (title
changed to CASSELL'S CONCISE GERMAN -
ENGLISH ENGLISH - GERMAN DICTIONARY) 1977
Second edition, fifteenth impression 1987

Printed in Great Britain by The Bath Press

ISBN 0 304 52265 1

Contents

Preface

Among the difficulties that arise in the compilation of a Concise Dictionary that of the selection of words is undoubtedly the most formidable one. The decision as to what to include and, much more difficult, what to exclude, must to a considerable extent depend on the type of student of a foreign language who is most likely to use it. Primarily a dictionary of this kind is intended for the student in the earlier stages of learning German, whether at school or university. As the study of German, even at an early stage, is likely to include the reading of literary texts from the eighteenth century onwards, it was felt that some attention at least must be paid to the inclusion of words no longer in common use today but frequently found in the prescribed texts, whether poetry, drama or prose. That in this respect severe limitations are imposed by the very concept of a 'Concise' Dictionary is of course obvious, but an attempt has been made to include at least some of the most common literary and poetical terms. However, the main emphasis throughout must of course be on straightforward contemporary German. In addition to the needs of the student, those of the traveller and the tourist, of the reader of contemporary literature and of newspapers and magazines, have been kept in mind. It is hoped that the student of science and technology too will find the dictionary useful, though in his case additional reference must of course be made to one of the growing number of specialized works dealing with the technical vocabulary of his particular discipline.

The aim of a Concise Dictionary must be to achieve some kind of viable compromise between conciseness on the one hand and completeness on the other. To make the dictionary as helpful as possible—given only a limited amount of space—certain economies were called for. Omissions were inevitable. What is similarly inevitable is that, except in the most obvious cases, no two experts are likely to agree as to what may safely be omitted unless (as was attempted here) one makes frequency of usage and general usefulness the main criteria.

It should be remembered, lastly, that this is a concise dictionary which cannot remotely hope to do justice to all the finer meanings and nuances of two highly developed and complex languages. But it is hoped that the student and reader of German, especially in the earlier stages of learning the language, will find here all the help he needs.

For more detailed reference the user will find Cassell's New German Dictionary (ed. Dr. H. T. Betteridge) of considerable help, while the Duden works of reference on German are regarded as the authoritative last word on matters of controversy. In the final analysis there will always be areas of doubt and dispute. That is the prerogative of a living and developing language.

Finally, thanks are due on behalf of the publishers to Prof. W. E. Collinson, late of the University of Liverpool, who acted in a consultative capacity.

H.-C. Sasse

Advice to the User

As a guide to the nature of words which have inevitably been omitted from a dictionary of this size, it may be helpful to state that, when a German *Fremdwort* is identical with the corresponding English term and possesses no grammatical peculiarities, it appears only in the English–German section. For example, it was felt that the word *Atom* (and *a fortiori* derivative compounds such as *Atomphysik*) was unlikely to perplex any English reader and it has therefore been omitted from the German–English, but included in the English–German, section. For the same reason, a somewhat similar plan has been followed with regard to the names of countries. These have mostly been given in German–English only, whereas the corresponding nouns and adjectives of nationality or race are given in English–German only.

Arrangement of Entries

Strict alphabetical order seemed to be most helpful in a dictionary intended primarily for readers in the earlier stages of acquiring a knowledge of German. Within the entries themselves literal meanings and frequency of usage determine the sequence of definitions. Admittedly the second criterion is to a considerable extent a matter of personal linguistic judgment, indeed of *Sprachgefühl*, but it is hoped that in most cases the reader will thereby more readily discover the meaning of any particular word. It can generally be assumed that definitions separated by commas have much the same meaning, whereas differences in meaning or usage are marked by semicolons. Where it was thought desirable and feasible to include idiomatic phrases, relative frequency of usage appeared a more helpful criterion than strict alphabetic sequence.

Words which are spelt alike but are etymologically distinct

Zur Benutzung des Wörterbuches

Ein Hinweis auf die Art der Wörter, auf die in einem Taschenwörterbuch unweigerlich verzichtet werden muss, wird dem Leser die Anwendung dieses Nachschlagwerkes gewiss erleichtern: Ein deutsches Fremdwort, das mit dem entsprechenden englischen Ausdruck identisch ist und keine grammatikalischen Besonderheiten aufweist, erscheint als Stichwort nicht in beiden Sprachen, sondern wird nur im englisch–deutschen Teil aufgeführt. Man darf wohl annehmen, dass ein Wort wie z.B. *Atom* (und *a fortiori* abgeleitete Zusammensetzungen wie *Atomphysik*) einen englischen Leser kaum verwirren wird, weshalb es denn auch im deutsch–englischen Teil weggelassen, indessen im englisch–deutschen Teil berücksichtigt wurde. Aus dem gleichen Grunde wurde bei den Namen von Ländern ein ähnliches Prinzip beachtet. Diese wurden in der Regel nur im deutsch–englischen Teil aufgeführt, während die entsprechenden Substantive und Adjektive der Nationalität oder Rasse nur im englisch–deutschen Teil erscheinen.

Anordnung der Stichwörter

Die strikte alphabetische Reihenfolge schien vorteilhaft für ein Nachschlagwerk, das in erster Linie für Lernende gedacht ist, die die deutsche Sprache noch nicht völlig beherrschen. Bei den gegebenen Übersetzungen eines Stichwortes bestimmen die wörtliche Übertragung sowie die Häufigkeit des Gebrauches die Folge der Definitionen. Gewiss ist das zweite Kriterium weitgehend eine Angelegenheit der persönlichen linguistischen Beurteilung, in der Tat des Sprachgefühls. Doch ist zu hoffen, dass der Leser in den meisten Fällen gerade dadurch der Bedeutung eines Begriffes näher kommt. Allgemein gilt, dass durch ein Komma getrennte Wörter eine annähernd gleiche Bedeutung haben, während Unterschiede in Bedeutung oder Anwendung

Advice to the User

have been given separate, numbered entries for the sake of clarity.

A word should be added on the subject of compounds. Most students of German come to realize before long that the notoriously long German nouns, far from complicating the understanding of the language, are merely a matter of syntactical and grammatical convenience, a device for structural conciseness within a given sentence construction. In a 'Concise' Dictionary only such compounds can be given which have a meaning which can be arrived at only with difficulty or not at all. Where a compound is not given, the constituent parts of the word should be looked up. The meaning should then become self-evident.

Grammar

Parts of Speech. These are indicated by abbreviations in italics (*adj.*, *v.a.* etc.), the meaning of which will be found in the List of Abbreviations. It has not been felt necessary to indicate the nature of English proper names.

Genders. In the German-English section nouns are denoted by their gender (*m.*, *f.* or *n.*). In the English-German section gender is shown by the definite article preceding the noun; in a series of nouns the gender is sometimes omitted when it is the same as that of the preceding noun or nouns.

Declension. The Genitive singular and Nominative plural of German nouns are given in parentheses after the gender. The plurals of English nouns are not given, except for certain very irregular forms. The cases governed by prepositions have been included.

Verbs. In both German and English the indication *irr.* refers the user to the tables of Irregular Verbs. Where a compound irregular verb is not given, its forms are identical with those of the simple irregular verb in the table. "To" is omitted from English infinitives throughout. German inseparable verbs are described as such only when there is any possibility of doubt, *e.g.* in the case of prepositional prefixes. Where prefixes are axiomatically always part of an

Zur Benutzung des Wörterbuches

durch ein Semikolon markiert sind. Wo es als notwendig und durchführbar erachtet wurde, idiomatische Redewendungen zu zitieren, schien die relative Häufigkeit der Anwendung ein nützlicheres Kriterium als die strenge alphabetische Folge. Orthographisch gleiche Wörter, die sich durch ihre etymologische Herkunft unterscheiden, wurden um der Klarheit willen als einzelne Stichwörter aufgeführt und mit Ziffern versehen. Noch ein Wort zum Thema der Wortzusammensetzungen: Die meisten Deutschlernenden werden bald erkennen, dass die berüchtigt langen deutschen Substantive das Verständnis der Sprache keineswegs erschweren. Sie sind lediglich eine Sache syntaktischer und grammatikalischer Vereinfachung, ein Hilfsmittel zu struktureller Kürze und Prägnanz innerhalb einer gegebenen Satzbildung. In einem Taschenwörterbuch können allein solche Wortverbindungen berücksichtigt werden, die nur mit Mühe oder überhaupt nicht abzuleiten sind. Ist eine Wortverbindung nicht angeführt, so sollten die einzelnen Bestandteile nachgesehen werden. Auf diese Weise wird sich der Sinn der Zusammensetzung von selbst ergeben.

Grammatik

Wortarten. Sie sind in abgekürzter Form durch Kursivschrift gekennzeichnet (*adj., v.a.* etc.). Eine Erläuterung der Abkürzungen findet sich im Verzeichnis der Abkürzungen. Es wurde nicht für nötig befunden, die Zugehörigkeit von Eigennamen anzuzeigen.

Geschlecht. Im deutsch–englischen Teil sind die Substantive mit ihrem Geschlecht (*m., f.* oder *n.*) gekennzeichnet. Im englisch–deutschen Teil ist das Geschlecht durch den bestimmten Artikel vor dem Substantiv angegeben. In einer Reihe aufeinanderfolgender Definitionen wurde der Artikel dort weggelassen, wo er mit dem vorhergehenden übereinstimmt.

Deklination. Die Endungen des Genitiv Singular und des Nominativ Plural deutscher Substantive sind in Klammern nach der Bezeichnung des Geschlechtes eingefügt. Der

Advice to the User

inseparable verb (*be-*, *ent-*, *zer-* etc.) no such information is given, as it is assumed that the student will be familiar with the function of these prefixes long before he comes to use a dictionary.

Phonetics. Phonetic transcriptions, using the symbols of the International Phonetic Association, are given throughout for all entries in both sections of the dictionary as a help to correct pronunciation. The mark ' precedes the syllable which carries the stress. The glottal stop is not indicated.

Numbers. Only the most common numerals appear in the body of the dictionary. However, fuller coverage is given in the separate Numerical Tables.

Zur Benutzung des Wörterbuches

Plural englischer Substantive wurde nicht berücksichtigt ausser bei einigen stark unregelmässigen Formen. Fälle, die von Präpositionen regiert werden, wurden aufgenommen.

Verben. Im Deutschen wie im Englischen weist die Anmerkung *irr.* den Leser auf die Tabellen unregelmässiger Verben hin. Ist ein zusammengesetztes Verb nicht angeführt, so sind seine Formen mit denen des einfachen Verbs in der Tabelle identisch. "To" vor englischen Infinitivformen wurde durchgehend weggelassen. Deutsche untrennbare Verben werden nur dort als solche gekennzeichnet, wo Zweifel möglich sind, also bei Verben mit präpositionalen Vorsilben. Wo Vorsilben grundsätzlich Teile eines untrennbaren Verbes (*be-, ent-, zer-* etc.) bilden, ist kein solcher Hinweis angebracht, da angenommen werden darf, dass der Lernende die Funktion dieser Vorsilben kennt, lange bevor er dazu kommt, ein Wörterbuch zu konsultieren.

Phonetik. Jedes einzelne Stichwort ist auch in seiner phonetischen Transkription wiedergegeben. Dabei wurden die phonetischen Symbole der *International Phonetic Association* benutzt. Der Akzent ' steht jeweils unmittelbar vor der betonten Silbe. Der Knacklaut ist indessen nicht markiert.

Zahlwörter. Nur die gebräuchlichsten Zahlen erscheinen im Hauptteil des Wörterbuches. Eine ausführliche Zusammenstellung findet sich in den besonderen Zahlentabellen.

Key to Pronunciation

Vowels

Phonetic Symbol	German Example	Phonetic Symbol	English Example
a	lassen ['lasən]	i:	seat [si:t]
a:	haben ['ha:bən], Haar [ha:r]	i	finish ['finiʃ], physic ['fizik]
ɛ	häßlich ['hɛslıç], Geld [gɛlt]	e	neck [nek]
ɛ:	Märchen ['mɛ:rçən], Zähne ['tsɛ:nə]	æ	man [mæn], malefactor ['mælifæktə]
e	Medizin [medi'tsi:n]	ɑ:	father ['fɑ:ðə], task [tɑ:sk]
e:	leben ['le:bən], See [ze:], lehnen ['le:nən]	ɔ	block [blɔk], waddle ['wɔdl]
ə	rufen ['ru:fən]	ɔ:	shawl [ʃɔ:l], tortoise ['tɔ:təs]
ı	Fisch [fıʃ], Mystik ['mıstık]	o	domain [do'mein]
i	Militär [mili'tɛ:r]	u	good [gud], July [dʒu'lai]
i:	Berlin [bɛr'li:n], Liebe ['li:bə], ihm [i:m]	u:	moon [mu:n], tooth [tu:θ]
ɔ	Kopf [kɔpf]	ʌ	cut [kʌt], somewhere ['sʌmwɛə]
o	mobil [mo'bi:l]	ə:	search [sə:tʃ], surgeon ['sə:dʒən]
o:	Rose ['ro:zə], Boot [bo:t], ohne ['o:nə]	ə	cathedral [kə'θi:drəl], never ['nevə]
œ	Mörder ['mœrdər]		
ø	möblieren [mø'bli:rən]		
ø:	Löwe ['lø:və], Röhre ['rø:rə]		
u	Hund [hunt]		
u:	gut [gu:t], Uhr [u:r]		
y	fünf [fynf], Symbol [zym'bo:l]		
y:	Lübeck ['ly:bɛk], Mühe ['my:ə]		

Diphthongs

aı	Eis [aıs], Waise ['vaızə]	ei	great [greit]
au	Haus [haus]	ou	show [ʃou]
ɔy	Beute ['bɔytə], Gebäude [gə'bɔydə]	ai	high [hai]
		au	crowd [kraud]
		ɔi	boy [bɔi]
		iə	steer [stiə]
		ɛə	hair [hɛə]
		uə	moor [muə]

Key to Pronunciation

Consonants

Phonetic Symbol	German Example	Phonetic Symbol	English Example
ç	Blech [blɛç], ich [ɪç]	p	paper ['peipə]
f	Vater ['fa:tər]	b	ball [bɔ:l]
j	ja [ja:]	t	tea [ti:], train [trein]
ŋ	bringen ['brɪŋən]	d	deed [di:d]
s	beißen ['baɪsən], wißen ['vɪsən], los [lo:s]	k	cake [keik], quest [kwest]
ʃ	schon [ʃo:n]	g	game [geim]
ts	Cäcilie [tsɛ'tsi:ljə], Zimmer ['tsɪmər]	m	mammoth ['mæməθ]
v	weiß [vaɪs]	n	nose [nouz], nanny ['næni]
x	Bach [bax], kochen ['kɔxən], ruchbar ['ru:xba:r]	ŋ	bring [briŋ], finger ['fiŋgə]
z	lesen ['le:zən]	f	fair [fɛə], far [fɑ:]
b	Biene ['bi:nə]	v	vine [vain]
d	Dach [dax]	θ	thin [θin], bath [bɑ:θ]
g	geben ['ge:bən]	ð	thine [ðain], bathe [beið]
h	hier [hi:r]	s	since [sins]
k	Koch [kɔx], quartieren [kwar'ti:rən]	z	busy ['bizi]
l	Lied [li:t]	l	land [lænd], hill [hil]
m	Mirakel [mi'ra:kəl]	ʃ	shield [ʃi:ld], sugar ['ʃugə]
n	Nase ['na:zə]	ʒ	vision ['viʒən]
p	Probe ['pro:bə]	r	rat [ræt], train [trein]
r	rot [ro:t]	h	here [hiə], horse [hɔ:s]
t	Tisch [tɪʃ]	x	coronach ['kɔrənæx], loch [lɔx]

Semi-Consonants

j	yellow ['jelou], yes [jes]
w	wall [wɔ:l]

List of Abbreviations

abbr.	abbreviation (of), abbreviated	*m.*	masculine
Acc.	Accusative	*Maths.*	Mathematics
adj.	adjective	*Meas.*	Measurement
adv.	adverb	*Mech.*	Mechanics
Agr.	agriculture	*Med.*	Medicine
Am.	American(ism)	*Met.*	Meteorology
Anat.	Anatomy	*Metall.*	Metallurgy
Archæol.	Archæology	*Mil.*	Military
Archit.	Architecture	*Min.*	Mining
Arith.	Arithmetic	*Motor.*	Motoring
art.	article	*Mount.*	Mountaineering
Astrol.	Astrology	*Mus.*	Music
Astron.	Astronomy	*Myth.*	Mythology
Austr.	Austrian	*n.*	neuter
aux.	auxiliary	*Naut.*	Nautical
Aviat.	Aviation	*Nav.*	Navigation
Bibl.	Biblical	*o.('s)*	one('s)
Bot.	Botany	*o.s.*	oneself
Br.	British	*obs.*	obsolete
Build.	Building	*Orn.*	Ornithology
Carp.	Carpentry	*p.*	person
Chem.	Chemistry	*Parl.*	Parliament
coll.	colloquial	*part.*	particle
collec.	collective	*pej.*	pejorative
Comm.	Commerce	*pers.*	person(al)
comp.	comparative	*Phil.*	Philosophy
conj.	conjunction	*Phonet.*	Phonetics
Cul.	Culinary	*Phot.*	Photography
Dat.	Dative	*Phys.*	Physics
def.	definite	*Physiol.*	Physiology
defect.	defective	*pl.*	plural
dem.	demonstrative	*Poet.*	Poetical
dial.	dialect	*Pol.*	Political
Eccl.	Ecclesiastical	*poss.*	possessive
Econ.	Economics	*p.p.*	past participle
Elec.	Electricity	*prec.*	preceded
em.ph.	emphatic	*pred.*	predicative
Engin.	Engineering	*prep.*	preposition
Ent.	Entomology	*pron.*	pronoun
excl.	exclamation	*Psych.*	Psychology
f.	feminine	*r.*	reflexive
fig.	figurative	*Rad.*	Radio
Fin.	Finance	*Railw.*	Railways
Footb.	Football	*reg.*	regular
Genit.	Genitive	*Rel.*	Religion
Geog.	Geography	*rel.*	relative
Geol.	Geology	*s.*	substantive
Geom.	Geometry	*Sch.*	School
Gram.	Grammar	*Scot.*	Scottish
Gymn.	Gymnastics	*sing.*	singular
Her.	Heraldry	*sl.*	slang
Hist.	History	*s.th.*	something
Hunt.	Hunting	*Tail.*	Tailoring
imper.	imperative	*Tech.*	Technical
impers.	impersonal	*Teleph.*	Telephone
Ind.	Industry	*temp.*	temporal
indecl.	indeclinable	*Text.*	Textiles
indef.	indefinite	*Theat.*	Theatre
infin.	infinitive	*Theol.*	Theology
insep.	inseparable	*Transp.*	Transport
int.	interjection	*Typ.*	Typography
interr.	interrogative	*Univ.*	University
intim.	intimate	*us.*	usually
iron.	ironical	*v.a.*	active *or* transitive verb
irr.	irregular	*v.n.*	neuter *or* intransitive verb
Ling.	Linguistics	*v.r.*	reflexive verb
Lit.	Literary	*Vet.*	Veterinary Science
Log.	Logic	*vulg.*	vulgar
		Zool.	Zoology

Cassell's German-English Dictionary

A

A, a [a:], *n. das A* (*des* —**s**, *die* —**s**) the letter A; (*Mus.*) the note A; *A Dur*, A major; *A Moll*, A minor.

Aal [a:l], *m.* (—**s**, *pl.* —**e**) eel.

Aas [a:s], *n.* (—**es**, *pl.* **Äser** *or* —**e**) carcass, carrion.

ab [ap], *adv.* off; down; away; (*Theat.*) exit *or* exeunt, — *und zu*, now and again, occasionally; *auf und* —, up and down, to and fro. — *prep.* from; — *Hamburg*, from Hamburg.

abändern [ˈapɛndərn], *v.a.* alter.

Abart [ˈapaːrt], *f.* (—, *pl.* —**en**) variety, species.

Abbau [ˈapbau], *m.* (—**s**, *no pl.*) demolition, dismantling; reduction (of staff).

abberufen [ˈapbəruːfən], *v.a. irr.* recall.

abbestellen [ˈapbəʃtɛlən], *v.a.* countermand, annul, cancel (an order).

Abbild [ˈapbɪlt], *n.* (—**es**, *pl.* —**er**) copy, image.

Abbildung [ˈapbɪlduŋ], *f.* (—, *pl.* —**en**) illustration.

Abbitte [ˈapbɪtə], *f.* (—, *pl.* —**n**) apology; — *leisten*, — *tun*, apologise.

abblenden [ˈapblɛndən], *v.a.* dim (lights).

Abbruch [ˈapbrux], *m.* (—**s**, *pl.* ˙**e**) breaking off; demolition; *einer Sache* — *tun*, damage s.th.

abdanken [ˈapdaŋkən], *v.n.* resign, abdicate, retire (from office).

abdecken [ˈapdɛkən], *v.a.* uncover, unroof; clear (the table).

Abdruck [ˈapdruk], *m.* (—**s**, *pl.* —**e**) impression, copy, reprint, cast.

Abend [ˈaːbənt], *m.* (—**s**, *pl.* —**e**) evening, eve.

Abendbrot [ˈaːbəntbroːt], *n.* (—**s**, *no pl.*) evening meal, (*Am.*) supper.

Abendland [ˈaːbəntlant], *n.* (—**es**, *no pl.*) occident, west.

Abendmahl [ˈaːbəntmaːl], *n.* (—**s**, *no pl.*) supper; *das heilige* —, Holy Communion, the Lord's Supper.

abends [ˈaːbənts], *adv.* in the evening, of an evening.

Abenteuer [ˈaːbəntɔyər], *n.* (—**s**, *pl.* —) adventure.

aber [ˈaːbər], *conj.* but, however; (*emphatic*) — *ja!* yes, indeed! of course! — *prefix.* again, once more.

Aberglaube [ˈaːbərglaubə], *m.* (—**ns**, *no pl.*) superstition.

abermals [ˈaːbərmaːls], *adv.* again, once more.

Abessinien [abɛˈsiːnjən], *n.* Abyssinia.

abfahren [ˈapfaːrən], *v.n. irr.* (*aux.* sein) set out, depart, drive off.

Abfall [ˈapfal], *m.* (—**s**, *pl.* ˙**e**) scrap, remnant; secession; slope; (*pl.*) waste, refuse.

abfallen [ˈapfalən], *v.n. irr.* (*aux.* sein) fall off; desert; slope.

abfällig [ˈapfɛlɪç], *adj.* derogatory.

abfangen [ˈapfaŋən], *v.a. irr.* intercept, catch.

abfärben [ˈapfɛrbən], *v.n.* (*colours*) run; stain; lose colour.

abfassen [ˈapfasən], *v.a.* compose, draft.

abfertigen [ˈapfɛrtɪgən], *v.a.* despatch; deal with, serve (a customer *or* client).

abfeuern [ˈapfɔyərn], *v.a.* fire (off), launch (rocket, missile).

abfinden [ˈapfɪndən], *v.a. irr.* indemnify, compound with (o.'s creditors). — *v.r. sich* — *mit*, put up with, come to terms with.

Abflug [ˈapfluːk], *m.* (—**s**, *pl.* ˙**e**) take-off, departure (by air).

Abfluß [ˈapflus], *m.* (—**sses**, *pl.* ˙**sse**) flowing off; drain.

Abfuhr [ˈapfuːr], *f.* (—, *pl.* —**en**) removal, collection (of refuse); (*coll.*) rebuff.

abführen [ˈapfyːrən], *v.a.* arrest, lead away. — *v.n.* (*Med.*) act as a purgative.

Abführmittel [ˈapfyːrmɪtəl], *n.* (—**s**, *pl.* —) purgative, laxative.

Abgabe [ˈapgaːbə], *f.* (—, *pl.* —**n**) delivery, tax, duty, levy.

abgabepflichtig [ˈapgaːbəpflɪçtɪç], *adj.* taxable, subject to duty.

Abgang [ˈapgaŋ], *m.* (—(**e**)**s**, *pl.* ˙**e**) wastage, loss; departure; *Schul*—, school-leaving.

abgängig [ˈapgɛnɪç], *adj.* lost, missing; (*of goods*) saleable.

abgeben [ˈapgeːbən], *v.a. irr.* deliver, cede; give (an opinion). — *v.r. sich mit etwas*, — concern o.s. with s.th.

abgedroschen [ˈapgədrɔʃən], *adj.* (*phrases etc.*) trite, hackneyed.

abgefeimt [ˈapgəfaImt], *adj.* cunning, crafty.

abgegriffen [ˈapgəgrɪfən], *adj.* well thumbed, worn.

abgehen [ˈapgeːən], *v.n. irr.* (*aux.* sein) leave, retire; branch off; (*Theat.*) make an exit.

abgelebt [ˈapgəleːpt], *adj.* (*of humans*) decrepit, worn out.

abgelegen [ˈapgəleːgən], *adj.* remote, distant.

abgemacht [ˈapgəmaxt], *adj., int.* agreed! done!

abgeneigt [ˈapgənaIkt], *adj.* disinclined, averse.

Abgeordnete [ˈapgəɔrdnətə], *m., f.* (—**n**, *pl.* —**n**) political representative, deputy, Member of Parliament.

Abgesandte [ˈapgəzantə], *m., f.* (—**n**, *pl.* —**n**) delegate, ambassador.

abgeschieden

abgeschieden [ˈapgəʃiːdən], *adj.* secluded, remote; deceased.
abgeschmackt [ˈapgəʃmakt], *adj.* insipid.
abgesehen [ˈapgəzeːən], *adv.* — *von*, apart from, except for.
abgespannt [ˈapgəʃpant], *adj.* worn out, run down, exhausted.
abgestorben [ˈapgəʃtɔrbən], *adj.* dead, numb.
abgetan [ˈapgətaːn], *adj.* finished, over, done with; *damit ist die Sache* —, that finishes the matter.
abgetragen [ˈapgətraːgən], *adj.* (*clothes*) shabby, threadbare.
abgewöhnen [ˈapgəvøːnən], *v.a. einem etwas* —, free (rid) s.o. from (of) a habit, wean from.
abgrasen [ˈapgraːzən], *v.a.* (*animals*) graze.
Abgrund [ˈapgrunt], *m.* (**-es**, *pl.* ⁓e) abyss, precipice.
Abguss [ˈapgus], *m.* (**-es**, *pl.* ⁓e) cast, plaster-cast, mould.
abhalten [ˈaphaltən], *v.a. irr.* restrain, hold back; hold (meeting etc.).
abhandeln [ˈaphandəln], *v.a. einem etwas* —, bargain for s.th.
abhanden [apˈhandən], *adv.* mislaid; — *kommen*, get lost.
Abhandlung [ˈaphandluŋ], *f.* (—, *pl.* **-en**) treatise, dissertation; (*pl.*) proceedings.
Abhang [ˈaphaŋ], *m.* (**-es**, *pl.* ⁓e) slope; declivity.
abhängen [ˈaphɛŋən], *v.a. irr.* take off, unhook; *von etwas* oder *jemandem* —, depend on s.th. or s.o.
abhärten [ˈaphɛrtən], *v.a.* inure against rigours, toughen.
abheben [ˈapheːbən], *v.a. irr.* draw (money from bank).
abhold [ˈaphɔlt], *adj.* averse to (*Dat.*).
abholen [ˈaphoːlən], *v.a. etwas* —, fetch, collect s.th.; *einen* —, meet s.o. (at the station etc.).
Abitur [abiˈtuːr], *n.* (**-s**, *no pl.*) matriculation examination.
Abiturient [abituˈrjɛnt], *m.* (**-en**, *pl.* **-en**) matriculation candidate.
Abkehr [ˈapkeːr], *f.* (—, *no pl.*) turning away, renunciation.
abklären [ˈapklɛːrən], *v.a.* (*Chem.*) filter, clear.
Abkommen [ˈapkɔmən], *n.* (**-s**, *pl.* —) treaty, agreement, contract.
Abkömmling [ˈapkœmliŋ], *m.* (**-s**, *pl.* **-e**) descendant.
abkühlen [ˈapkyːlən], *v.a.* cool, chill.
Abkunft [ˈapkunft], *f.* (—, *no pl.*) descent, origin.
abkürzen [ˈapkyrtsən], *v.a.* shorten, abridge, curtail.
abladen [ˈapladən], *v.a. irr.* unload, dump.
Ablaß [ˈaplas], *m.* (**-sses**, *pl.* ⁓sse) (*Eccl.*) indulgence.
ablassen [ˈaplasən], *v.n. irr. von etwas* —, desist from, refrain from s.th.— *v.a. einem etwas billig* —, reduce the

price of s.th. for s.o.
Ablauf [ˈaplauf], *m.* (**-es**, *no pl.*) (*water*) drainage; (*ticket*) expiration; lapse (of time); (*bill*) maturity.
ablaufen [ˈaplaufən], *v.n. irr.* (*aux.* sein) (*water*) run off; (*ticket*) expire; *gut* —, turn out well.
Ableben [ˈapleːbən], *n.* (**-s**, *no pl.*) decease, death.
ablegen [ˈapleːgən], *v.a.* (*clothes*) take off; (*documents*) file; *Rechenschaft* —, account for; *eine Prüfung* —, take an examination.
Ableger [ˈapleːgər], *m.* (**-s**, *pl.* —) (*Hort.*) cutting.
Ablegung [ˈapleːguŋ], *f.* (—, *no pl.*) making (of a vow); taking (of an oath).
ablehnen [ˈapleːnən], *v.a.* refuse, decline.
ableiten [ˈaplaitən], *v.a.* divert, draw off; (*water*) drain; (*words*) derive from.
ablenken [ˈaplɛŋkən], *v.a.* (*aux.* haben) *einen von etwas* —, divert s.o.'s attention from s.th., distract.
ablesen [ˈapleːzən], *v.a. irr.* (*meter*) read off; (*field*) glean.
abliefern [ˈapliːfərn], *v.a.* deliver.
ablösen [ˈapløːzən], *v.a. einen* —, take the place of s.o., (*Mil.*) relieve; detach (a stamp from a letter etc.).
abmachen [ˈapmaxən], *v.a.* undo, detach; settle, arrange.
abmagern [ˈapmaːgərn], *v.n.* (*aux.* sein) get thinner, waste away.
Abmarsch [ˈapmarʃ], *m.* (**-es**, *no pl.*) (*Mil.*) marching off.
abmelden [ˈapmɛldən], *v.r. sich* —, give notice of departure.
abmessen [ˈapmɛsən], *v.a. irr.* measure (off), gauge.
abmühen [ˈapmyːən], *v.r. sich* —, exert o.s., strive.
Abnahme [ˈapnaːmə], *f.* (—, *pl.* **-n**) decline, loss of weight; (*moon*) waning; (*goods*) taking delivery.
abnehmen [ˈapneːmən], *v.n. irr.* lose weight; (*moon*) wane. — *v.a.* (*hat*) take off; *einem etwas* —, relieve s.o. (of trouble *or* work).
Abneigung [ˈapnaiguŋ], *f.* (—, *pl.* **-en**) antipathy, dislike.
abnutzen [ˈapnutsən], *v.a.* wear out by use.
Abonnement [abɔnəˈmaŋ], *n.* (**-s**, *pl.* **-s**) (*newspaper*) subscription; (*railway*) season-ticket.
Abonnent [abɔˈnɛnt], *m.* (**-en**, *pl.* **-en**) subscriber.
abonnieren [abɔˈniːrən], *v.a.* subscribe to (a paper).
Abordnung [ˈapɔrdnuŋ,] *f.* (—, *pl.* **-en**) delegation, deputation.
Abort [aˈbɔrt], *m.* (**-s**, *pl.* **-e**) lavatory, toilet.
Abortus [aˈbɔrtus], *m.* (**-us**, *no pl.*) (*Med.*) abortion.
abplagen [ˈaplaːgən], *v.r. sich* —, slave, toil.
abprallen [ˈapralən], *v.n.* (*aux.* sein) *von etwas* —, bounce off, rebound.

absprechen

abquälen ['apkvɛ:lən], *v.r. sich —*, toil, make o.s. weary (*mit*, with).

abraten ['apra:tən], *v.n. irr. einem von etwas —*, dissuade s.o. from, advise *or* warn s.o. against.

abräumen ['aprɔymən], *v.a.* remove; *den Tisch —*, clear the table.

abrechnen ['aprɛçnən], *v.a.* reckon up. *— v.n. mit einem —*, settle accounts with s.o., (*coll.*) get even with s.o.

Abrede ['apre:də], *f.* (*—, pl. —n*) agreement, arrangement; *in — stellen*, deny.

abreißen ['apraɪsən], *v.a. irr.* tear off.

abrichten ['aprıçtən], *v.a.* (*dogs*) train, (*horses*) break in.

abriegeln ['apri:gəln], *v.a.* bolt, bar.

Abriß ['aprıs], *m.* (*—sses, pl. —sse*) sketch; summary, synopsis.

abrollen ['aprɔlən], *v.a.* uncoil. *— v.n.* (*aux.* sein) roll off.

abrücken ['aprʏkən], *v.a.* move away. *—v.n.* (*aux.* sein) (*Mil.*) march off.

Abruf ['apru:f], *m.* (*—es, no pl.*) recall (from a post).

abrunden ['aprundən], *v.a.* round off.

abrupfen ['aprupfən], *v.a.* (*feathers*) pluck; (*flowers*) pluck off.

abrüsten ['aprʏstən], *v.n.* disarm.

Abrüstung ['aprʏstuŋ], *f.* (*—, no pl.*) disarmament.

abrutschen ['aprutʃən], *v.n.* (*aux.* sein) slide, slither down.

Absage ['apza:gə], *f.* (*—, pl. —n*) cancellation, refusal.

absagen ['apza:gən], *v.n.* refuse, beg to be excused, decline (an invitation).

Absatz ['apzats], *m.* (*—es, pl. ⸚e*) (*shoe*) heel; (*letter*) paragraph; (*Comm.*) *guter —*, ready sale.

abschaffen ['apʃafən], *v.a.* abolish, do away with.

abschälen ['apʃɛ:lən], *v.a.* peel. *— v.r. sich —*, peel off.

abschätzen ['apʃɛtsən], *v.a.* estimate, appraise; (*taxes*) assess.

Abschaum ['apʃaum], *m.* (*—es, no pl.*) scum.

Abscheu ['apʃɔy], *m.* (*—s, no pl.*) abhorrence, detestation, loathing.

abscheulich ['apʃɔylıç], *adj.* abominable, repulsive.

abschieben ['apʃi:bən], *v.a. irr.* shove off, push off; *schieb ab!* scram!

Abschied ['apʃi:t], *m.* (*—s, pl. —e*) leave, departure, farewell; discharge; resignation.

abschießen ['apʃi:sən], *v.a. irr.* shoot off; discharge; (*gun*) fire; *den Vogel —*, win the prize.

abschinden ['apʃındən], *v.r. irr. sich —*, exhaust o.s. with hard work.

abschirren ['apʃırən], *v.a.* unharness.

abschlagen ['apʃla:gən], *v.a. irr.* (*attack*) beat off; (*branches*) lop off; *einem etwas —*, deny s.o. s.th.; *eine Bitte —*, refuse a request.

abschlägig ['apʃlɛgıç], *adj.* negative.

Abschlagszahlung ['apʃlakstsa:luŋ], *f.* (*—, pl. —en*) payment by instalments.

abschleifen ['apʃlaɪfən], *v.a. irr.* grind off.

abschleppen ['apʃlɛpən], *v.a.* (*car*) tow (away). *— v.r. sich —*, wear o.s. out by carrying heavy loads.

abschließen ['apʃli:sən], *v.a. irr.* lock up; (*work*) conclude; (*accounts*) balance; *einen Vertrag —*, conclude an agreement.

Abschluß ['apʃlus], *m.* (*—sses, pl. ⸚sse*) settlement, winding-up.

abschneiden ['apʃnaɪdən], *v.a. irr.* cut off. *— v.n. gut —*, come off well.

Abschnitt ['apʃnıt], *m.* (*—es, pl. —e*) section; (*book*) paragraph.

abschnüren ['apʃny:rən], *v.a.* lace up, tie up.

abschrecken ['apʃrɛkən], *v.a.* deter, frighten.

abschreiben ['apʃraɪbən], *v.a. irr.* copy, transcribe; crib; *eine Schuld —*, write off a debt.

Abschrift ['apʃrıft], *f.* (*—, pl. —en*) copy, transcript, duplicate; *beglaubigte —*, certified copy.

Abschuß ['apʃus], *m.* (*—sses, pl. ⸚sse*) act of firing (a gun), shooting down (aircraft).

abschüssig ['apʃysıç], *adj.* steep.

abschütteln ['apʃytəln], *v.a.* shake off, cast off.

abschwächen ['apʃvɛçən], *v.a.* weaken, diminish.

abschweifen ['apʃvaɪfən], *v.n.* (*aux.* sein) digress (from), deviate.

abschwenken ['apʃvɛŋkən], *v.n.* (*aux.* sein) wheel off (*or* aside).

abschwören ['apʃvø:rən], *v.a. irr.* abjure, renounce by oath.

absehbar ['apze:ba:r], *adj.* imaginable, conceivable, foreseeable.

absehen ['apze:ən], *v.a., v.n. irr. einem etwas —*, copy s.th. from s.o.; *auf etwas —*, aim at s.th.; *von etwas —*, waive s.th.; refrain from s.th.

abseits ['apzaɪts], *adv., prep.* (*Genit.*) aside; *— von*, away from.

Absender ['apzɛndər], *m.* (*—s, pl.—*) sender; (*Comm.*) consigner.

absetzen ['apzɛtsən], *v.a.* set down; dismiss, deprive of office; depose; (*Comm.*) sell, dispose of.

Absicht ['apzıçt], *f.* (*—, pl. —en*) intention, purpose, aim.

absondern ['apzɔndərn], *v.a.* separate, set apart; (*Med.*) secrete. *— v.r. sich —*, seclude o.s. from.

abspannen ['apʃpanən], *v.a.* unharness.

absparen ['apʃpa:rən], *v.n. sich etwas vom Munde —*, stint o.s. for s.th.

abspenstig ['apʃpɛnstıç], *adj. — machen*, alienate s.o.'s affections, entice s.o. away; *— werden*, desert.

absperren ['apʃpɛrən], *v.a.* (*door*) lock, shut up; (*street*) close, barricade; (*gas, water*) turn off.

absprechen ['apʃprɛçən], *v.a. irr. einem das Recht —*, deprive s.o. of the right to do s.th.

3

abspülen [ˈapʃpyːlən], v.a. wash up, rinse.

abstammen [ˈapʃtamən], v.n. (aux. sein) descend from, originate from.

Abstand [ˈapʃtant], m. (—es, pl. ⸚e) distance; von etwas — nehmen, refrain from doing s.th.

abstatten [ˈapʃtatən], v.a. einen Besuch —, pay a visit; einen Bericht —, report on; Dank —, return thanks.

abstechen [ˈapʃteçən], v.a. irr. Tiere —, slaughter animals. — v.n. von etwas —, contrast with s.th.

Abstecher [ˈapʃteçər], m. (—s, pl. —) short trip, excursion; detour.

abstecken [ˈapʃtekən], v.a. mark off, peg out.

absteigen [ˈapʃtaɪɡən], v.n. irr. (aux. sein) descend, alight, dismount.

abstellen [ˈapʃtelən], v.a. put s.th. down; (gas, water) turn off.

absterben [ˈapʃterbən], v.n. irr. (aux. sein) wither; die.

Abstieg [ˈapʃtiːk], m. (—es, no pl.) descent.

Abstimmung [ˈapʃtɪmuŋ], f. (—, pl. —en) (Parl.) division; referendum, voting.

abstoßen [ˈapʃtoːsən], v.a. irr. push off, kick off. —v.n. (Naut.) set sail.

abstoßend [ˈapʃtoːsənt], adj. repulsive, repugnant.

abstreifen [ˈapʃtraɪfən], v.a. irr. strip off, pull off; cast, shed.

abstufen [ˈapʃtuːfən], v.a. grade.

abstumpfen [ˈapʃtumpfən], v.a. blunt, dull, take the edge off.

abstürzen [ˈapʃtyrtsən], v.n. (aux. sein) (person) fall; fall down; (Aviat.) crash.

Abt [apt], m. (—es, pl. ⸚e) abbot.

Abtei [ˈaptaɪ], f. (—, pl. —en) abbey.

Abteil [ˈaptaɪl], n. (—s, pl. —e) compartment.

abteilen [ˈaptaɪlən], v.a. divide, partition.

Abteilung [apˈtaɪluŋ], f. (—, pl. —en) section, department.

Äbtissin [ɛpˈtɪsɪn], f. (—, pl. —nen) abbess.

abtöten [ˈaptøːtən], v.a. mortify, deaden.

abtragen [ˈaptraːɡən], v.a. irr. carry away; (building) demolish; (dress, shoes) wear out; eine Schuld —, pay a debt.

abtreiben [ˈaptraɪbən], v.a. irr. (cattle) drive off; procure an abortion. — v.n. (aux. sein) (ship) drift off.

Abtreibung [ˈaptraɪbuŋ], f. (—, pl. —en) abortion.

abtrennen [ˈaptrenən], v.a. (s.th. sewn) unpick; separate.

Abtretung [ˈaptreːtuŋ], f. (—, pl. —en) cession; conveyance.

Abtritt [ˈaptrɪt], m. (—es, pl. —e) W.C. (Theat.) exit or exeunt.

abtrocknen [ˈaptrɔknən], v.a. dry.

abtrünnig [ˈaptrynɪç], adj. disloyal, faithless.

aburteilen [ˈapurtaɪlən], v.a. pass judgment on.

abwägen [ˈapvɛːɡən], v.a. gegeneinander —, weigh against each other.

abwälzen [ˈapvɛltsən], v.a. etwas von sich —, clear o.s. from s.th.

abwandeln [ˈapvandəln], v.a. change; (verbs) conjugate; (nouns) decline.

abwärts [ˈapvɛrts], prep., adv. downward.

abwaschen [ˈapvaʃən], v.a. irr. wash up.

abwechseln [ˈapvɛksəln], v.a. vary, alternate.

Abweg [ˈapveːk], m. (—es, pl. —e) wrong way; auf —e geraten, go astray.

abwehren [ˈapveːrən], v.a. ward off, parry.

abweichen [ˈapvaɪçən], v.n. irr. (aux. sein) — von, deviate from.

abweisen [ˈapvaɪzən], v.a. irr. refuse admittance to, rebuff.

abwenden [ˈapvendən], v.a. irr. avert, prevent. — v.r. sich —, turn away from.

abwesend [ˈapveːzənt], adj. absent.

Abwesenheit [ˈapveːzənhaɪt], f. (—, pl. —en) absence.

abwickeln [ˈapvɪkəln], v.a. uncoil; (business) wind up.

abwischen [ˈapvɪʃən], v.a. wipe clean; sich die Stirn —, mop o.'s brow.

abzahlen [ˈaptsaːlən], v.a. pay off; pay by instalments.

abzehren [ˈaptseːrən], v.n. (aux. sein) waste away.

Abzeichen [ˈaptsaɪçən], n. (—s, pl. —) badge, insignia.

abzeichnen [ˈapsaɪçnən], v.a. sketch, draw from a model. — v.r. sich —, become clear.

abziehen [ˈaptsiːən], v.a. irr. deduct, subtract; (knife) sharpen; strip (a bed). — v.n. (aux. sein) depart; (Mil.) march off.

Abzug [ˈaptsuːk], m. (—es, pl. ⸚e) retreat, departure; photographic copy; — der Kosten, deduction of charges; (steam, air) outlet.

abzweigen [ˈaptsvaɪɡən], v.n. (aux. sein) fork off, branch off.

Achsel [ˈaksəl], f. (—, pl. —n) shoulder; die —n zucken, shrug o.'s shoulders.

Acht [axt], f. (—, no pl.) attention, care, caution, heed; acht geben, pay attention; sich in — acht nehmen, be careful; ban, excommunication, outlawry; in — und Bann tun, outlaw, proscribe.

acht [axt], num. adj. eight; in — Tagen, in a week; vor — Tagen, a week ago.

achtbar [ˈaxtbaːr], adj. respectable.

achten [ˈaxtən], v.a. hold in esteem, value; — auf, pay attention to, keep an eye on.

ächten [ˈɛxtən], v.a. ban, outlaw, proscribe.

achtlos [ˈaxtloːs], adj. inattentive, negligent.

achtsam [ˈaxtzaːm], adj. attentive, careful.

Achtung [ˈaxtuŋ], f. (—, no pl.) esteem, regard; (Mil.) attention!

Ächtung [ˈɛxtuŋ], f. (—, no pl.) ban, proscription.

achtzehn [ˈaxtseːn], num. adj. eighteen.

Alpdrücken

achtzig ['axtsɪç], *num. adj.* eighty.
ächzen ['ɛçtsən], *v.n.* groan.
Acker ['akər], *m.* (—s, *pl.* ⸚) field, arable land; *den — bestellen*, till the soil.
ackern ['akərn], *v.n.* till (the land).
addieren [a'di:rən], *v.a.* add, add up.
Adel ['a:dəl], *m.* (—s, *no pl.*) nobility, aristocracy.
ad(e)lig ['a:dlɪç], *adj.* of noble birth, aristocratic.
Ader ['a:dər], *f.* (—, *pl.* —n) vein; *zu — lassen*, bleed s.o.
Adler ['a:dlər], *m.* (—s, *pl.* —) eagle.
Adresse [a'drɛsə], *f.* (—, *pl.* —n) address.
adrett [a'drɛt], *adj.* neat, adroit, smart.
Affe ['afə], *m.* (—n, *pl.* —n) ape, monkey; *(fig.)* fool.
affektiert [afɛk'ti:rt], *adj.* affected, giving o.s. airs.
äffen ['ɛfən], *v.a.* ape, mimic.
Afghanistan [af'ganistan], *n.* Afghanistan.
Afrika ['a:frika], *n.* Africa.
After ['aftər], *m.* (—s, *pl.* —) anus.
Agentur [agɛn'tu:r], *f.* (—, *pl.* —en) agency.
Agraffe [a'grafə], *f.* (—, *pl.* —n) brooch, clasp.
Agrarier [a'gra:rjər], *m.* (—s, *pl.* —) landed proprietor.
Ägypten [ɛ'gyptən], *n.* Egypt.
Ahle ['a:lə], *f.* (—, *pl.* —n) awl, bodkin.
Ahn [a:n], *m.* (—en, *pl.* —en) ancestor, forefather.
ahnden ['a:ndən], *v.a.* avenge, punish.
Ahne ['a:nə] *see* **Ahn**.
ähneln ['ɛ:nəln], *v.a.* resemble, look like.
ahnen ['a:nən], *v.a., v.n.* have a presentiment, foresee, have a hunch.
ähnlich ['ɛ:nlɪç], *adj.* resembling, like, similar.
Ahnung ['a:nuŋ], *f.* (—, *pl.* —en) foreboding, presentiment, idea, *(Am.)* hunch.
Ahorn ['a:hɔrn], *m.* (—s, *pl.* —e) *(Bot.)* maple.
Ähre ['ɛ:rə], *f.* (—, *pl.* —n) ear of corn.
Akademiker [aka'de:mɪkər], *m.* (—s, *pl.* —) university graduate.
akademisch [aka'de:mɪʃ], *adj.* academic; — *gebildet*, with a university education.
Akazie [a'ka:tsjə], *f.* (—, *pl.* —n) *(Bot.)* acacia.
akklimatisieren [aklimati'zi:rən], *v.r. sich* —, become acclimatised.
Akkord [a'kɔrt], *m.* (—es, *pl.* —e) *(Mus.)* chord; *in — arbeiten*, work on piece-rates.
Akt [akt], *m.* (—es, *pl.* —e) deed, action; *(Theat.)* act; *(Art)* (depiction of) the nude.
Akte ['aktə], *f.* (—, *pl.* —n) document, deed; *(pl.)* records, files; *zu den —n legen*, pigeonhole, shelve.
Aktenstück ['aktənʃtyk], *n.* (—es, *pl.* —e) official document, file.
Aktie ['aktsjə], *f.* (—, *pl.* —n) *(Comm.)* share, *(Am.)* stock.

Aktiengesellschaft ['aktsjəngəzɛlʃaft], *f.* (—, *pl.* —en) joint stock company.
Aktionär [aktsjo'nɛ:r], *m.* (—s, *pl.* —e) shareholder, *(Am.)* stockholder.
Aktiv ['akti:f], *n.* (—s, *pl.* —e) *(Gram.)* active voice.
Aktiva [ak'ti:va], *n. pl. (Comm.)* assets.
aktuell [aktu'ɛl], *adj.* topical.
akzentuieren [aktsɛntu'i:rən], *v.a.* accentuate, stress, emphasize.
Albanien [al'ba:njən], *n.* Albania.
albern ['albərn], *adj.* silly, foolish.
Aliment [ali'mɛnt], *n.* (—es, *pl.* —e) *(usually pl.*—e) alimony, maintenance.
Alkali [al'ka:li], *n.* (—s, *pl.* —en) alkali.
Alkohol ['alkoho:l], *m.* (—s, *no pl.*) alcohol.
Alkoholiker [alko'ho:lɪkər], *m.* (—s, *pl.* —) drunkard, alcoholic.
All [al], *n.* (—s, *no pl.*) the universe, (outer) space.
all [al], *adj.* all, entire, whole; every, each, any.
alle ['alə], *adj.* all, everybody; — *beide*, both of them.
Allee [a'le:], *f.* (—, *pl.* —n) tree-lined walk, avenue.
allein [a'laɪn], *adj.* alone, sole. — *adv.* solely, only, merely. —*conj. (obs.)* only, but, however.
alleinig [a'laɪnɪç], *adj.* sole, only, exclusive.
allenfalls [alən'fals], *adv.* possibly, perhaps, if need be.
allenthalben [alənt'halbən], *adv.* everywhere, in all places.
allerdings [alər'dɪŋs], *adv.* of course, indeed, nevertheless.
allerhand [alər'hant], *adj.* of all sorts or kinds, various; *das ist ja* —*!* I say!
Allerheiligen [alər'haɪlɪgən], *pl.* All Saints' Day.
allerlei [alər'laɪ], *adj.* miscellaneous, various.
allerliebst [alər'li:pst], *adj. (Am.)* cute; charming.
allerseits ['alərzaɪts], *adv.* generally, on all sides, universally.
alles ['aləs], *adj.* everything, all.
allgemein [algə'maɪn], *adj.* universal, common, general.
alliieren [ali'i:rən], *v.a., v.n.* ally (o.s.).
allmächtig [al'mɛçtɪç], *adj.* omnipotent.
allmählich [al'mɛ:lɪç], *adj.* by degrees, gradual.
allseitig ['alzaɪtɪç], *adj.* universal, *(Am.)* all-round.
Alltag ['alta:k], *m.* (—s, *pl.*—e) working day, week-day.
allwissend [al'vɪsənt], *adj.* omniscient.
allzu ['altsu:], *adv.* too, much too.
Alm [alm], *f.* (—, *pl.* —en) Alpine meadow.
Almosen ['almo:zən], *n.* (—s, *pl.* —) alms, charity.
Alp [alp], *f.* (—, *pl.* —en) *(mostly pl.)* mountain(s), Alps.
Alpdrücken ['alpdrykən], *n.* (—s, *no pl.*) nightmare.

5

als

als [als], *conj.* than; *(after comparatives)* than; as, like; but; *er hat nichts — Schulden,* he has nothing but debts; *(temp.)* when, as.

alsbald [als'balt], *adv.* forthwith.

also ['alzo:], *adv.* thus, so, in this manner. — *conj.* consequently, therefore.

Alt [alt], *m.* (—s, *pl.* —e) *(Mus.)* alto.

alt [alt], *adj.* old, ancient; aged; antique.

Altan [al'ta:n], *m.* (—s, *pl.* —e) balcony, gallery.

Altar [al'ta:r], *m.* (—s, *pl.* ⁻e) altar.

altbacken ['altbakən], *adj.* stale.

Alter ['altər], *n.* (—s, *no pl.*) age, old age; epoch.

altern ['altərn], *v.n. (aux.* sein) grow old.

Altertum ['altərtu:m], *n.* (—s, *pl.* ⁻er) antiquity.

Altistin [al'tıstın], *f.* (—, *pl.* —nen) *(Mus.)* contralto.

altklug ['altklu:k], *adj.* precocious.

ältlich ['ɛltlıç], *adj.* elderly.

Altweibersommer [alt'vaıbərzɔmər], *m.* (—s, *pl.* —) Indian summer.

Amboß ['ambɔs], *m.* (—sses, *pl.* —sse) anvil.

Ameise ['a:maızə], *f.* (—, *pl.* —n) *(Ent.)* ant.

Amerika [a'me:rika], *n.* America.

Amme ['amə], *f.* (—, *pl.* —n) wet nurse.

Ammoniak [amon'jak], *n.* (—s, *no pl.*) ammonia.

Ampel ['ampəl], *f.* (—, *pl.* —n) (hanging) light, lamp, lantern; traffic light.

Ampfer ['ampfər], *m.* (—s, *pl.* —) *(Bot.)* sorrel, dock.

Amsel ['amzəl], *f.* (—, *pl.* —n) *(Orn.)* blackbird.

Amt [amt], *n.* (—es, *pl.* ⁻er) office, post, employment; administration, domain, jurisdiction; place of public business.

amtlich ['amtlıç], *adj.* official.

Amtmann ['amtman], *m.* (—s, *pl.* ⁻er) bailiff.

Amtsblatt ['amtsblat], *n.* (—es, *pl.* ⁻er) official gazette.

Amtsgericht ['amtsgərıçt], *n.* (—s, *pl.* —e) county court; *(Am.)* district court.

amüsieren [amy'zi:rən], *v.a.* amuse.— *v.r. sich —,* enjoy o.s.

an [an], *prep. (Dat. or Acc.),* at, to, on.

analog [ana'lo:k], *adj.* analogous.

Ananas ['ananas], *f.* (—, *pl.* —) pineapple.

Anatom [ana'to:m], *m.* (—en, *pl.* —en) anatomist.

anbahnen ['anba:nən], *v.a.* initiate, open up, pave the way for.

anbändeln ['anbɛndəln], *v.n.* — *mit,* flirt with, make up to.

Anbau ['anbau], *m.* (—s, *pl.* —ten) *(grain)* cultivation; annex(e), wing (of building).

anbauen ['anbauən], *v.a.* cultivate; add to a building.

anbei [an'baı], *adv.* enclosed (in letter).

anbeißen ['anbaısən], *v.a. irr.* bite at,

take a bite of. — *v.n. (fish)* bite; *(coll.)* take the bait.

anbelangen ['anbəlaŋən], *v.a.* concern.

anberaumen ['anbəraumən], *v.a.* fix (a date).

anbeten ['anbe:tən], *v.a.* worship, adore, idolise.

anbiedern ['anbi:dərn], *v.r. sich mit einem —,* chum up with s.o.

anbieten ['anbi:tən], *v.a. irr.* offer.

anbinden ['anbındən], *v.a. irr.* tie on, bind to; *kurz angebunden sein,* be curt.

Anblick ['anblık], *m.* (—s, *no pl.*) view, sight, aspect, spectacle.

anbrechen ['anbreçən], *v.a. irr.* begin; break; start on. —*v.n.* dawn.

anbrennen ['anbrɛnən], *v.a. irr.* light, set fire to, burn. — *v.n. (aux.* sein) catch fire; burn.

anbringen ['anbrıŋən], *v.a. irr.* fit to, place.

Anbruch ['anbrux], *m.* (—s, *no pl.*) beginning; — *der Nacht,* night-fall.

anbrüllen ['anbrylən], *v.a.* roar at.

Andacht ['andaxt], *f.* (—, *pl.* —en) *(Eccl.)* devotion(s).

andächtig ['andɛxtıç], *adj.* devout.

andauern ['andauərn], *v.n.* last, continue.

Andenken ['andɛŋkən], *n.* (—s, *pl.* —) memory; keepsake; souvenir.

anderer ['andərər], *adj.* other, different; *ein —,* another.

andermal ['andərma:l], *adv. ein —,* another time.

ändern ['ɛndərn], *v.a.* alter, change.

andernfalls ['andərnfals], *adv.* otherwise, or else.

anders ['andərs], *adv.* differently, in another manner, otherwise.

anderthalb ['andərthalp], *adj.* one and a half.

anderweitig ['andərvaıtıç], *adj.* elsewhere.

andeuten ['andɔytən], *v.a.* hint at, intimate, indicate.

Andrang ['andraŋ], *m.* (—es, *no pl.*) throng, crowd.

aneignen ['anaıgnən], *v.r. sich etwas —,* appropriate s.th.; *(an opinion)* adopt.

anekeln ['ane:kəln], *v.a.* disgust.

Anerbieten ['anɛrbi:tən], *n.* (—s, *pl.* —) offer.

anerkennen ['anɛrkɛnən], *v.a. irr.* acknowledge, appreciate, recognize, accept.

anfachen ['anfaxən], *v.a.* kindle (a flame).

Anfahrt ['anfa:rt], *f.* (—, *pl.* —en) drive; *(down a mine)* descent; *(Am.)* drive-way.

Anfall ['anfal], *m.* (—s, *pl.* ⁻e) attack, assault; *(Med.)* seizure, fit; *(mood)* fit, burst.

anfallen ['anfalən], *v.a. irr. einen —,* attack s.o.

Anfang ['anfaŋ], *m.* (—s, *pl.* ⁻e) beginning, start, commencement.

6

anfangen [ˈanfaŋən], *v.a. irr.* begin, start. — *v.n.* begin, originate.

Anfänger [ˈanfɛŋər], *m.* (—**s**, *pl.* —) beginner, novice.

anfänglich [ˈanfɛŋlɪç], *adv.* in the beginning, at first, initially.

anfassen [ˈanfasən], *v.a.* take hold of; touch; seize.

anfechtbar [ˈanfɛçtbaːr], *adj.* disputable, refutable, debatable.

anfechten [ˈanfɛçtən], *v.a.* (*a will, a verdict*) contest; (*jurors*) challenge.

anfeinden [ˈanfaɪndən], *v.a.* show enmity to.

anfertigen [ˈanfɛrtɪgən], *v.a.* make, manufacture, prepare; (*a list*) draw up.

anflehen [ˈanfleːən], *v.a.* implore, beseech.

Anflug [ˈanfluːk], *m.* (—**s**, *pl.* ⁻e) (*Aviat.*) approach; (*beard*) down; touch.

anfordern [ˈanfɔrdərn], *v.a.* demand, claim.

Anfrage [ˈanfraːgə], *f.* (—, *pl.* —**n**) enquiry.

anfügen [ˈanfyːgən], *v.a.* join to, annex.

anführen [ˈanfyːrən], *v.a.* lead; adduce, quote (examples), cite; *einen* —, dupe s.o., take s.o. in.

Anführungszeichen [ˈanfyːruŋstsaɪçən], *n.* (—**s**, *pl.* —) inverted commas, quotation marks.

anfüllen [ˈanfylən], *v.a. wieder* —, replenish.

Angabe [ˈanɡaːbə], *f.* (—, *pl.* —**n**) declaration, statement; data; instruction; bragging.

angeben [ˈanɡeːbən], *v.a. irr.* declare, state; *den Ton* —, lead the fashion; *den Wert* —, declare the value of.— *v.n. groß* —, brag, show off.

Angeber [ˈanɡeːbər], *m.* (—**s**, *pl.* —) informer; braggart.

Angebinde [ˈanɡəbɪndə], *n.* (—**s**, *pl.* —) (*obs.*) present, gift.

angeblich [ˈanɡeːplɪç], *adj.* ostensible, alleged, so-called.

angeboren [ˈanɡəboːrən], *adj.* innate, inborn.

Angebot [ˈanɡəboːt], *n.* (—**es**, *pl.* —**e**) offer, tender, bid; (*Comm.*) — *und Nachfrage*, supply and demand.

angebracht [ˈanɡəbraxt], *adj.* apt, appropriate, opportune.

angedeihen [ˈanɡədaɪən], *v.n. einem etwas* — *lassen*, bestow s.th. on s.o.

angegossen [ˈanɡəɡɔsən], *adj. das sitzt wie* —, it fits like a glove.

angehen [ˈanɡeːən], *v.a. irr. einen um etwas* —, apply to s.o. for s.th.; *das geht Dich nichts an*, that is none of your business.

angehören [ˈanɡəhøːrən], *v.n.* belong to.

Angehörige [ˈanɡəhøːrɪgə], *m., f.* (—**n**, *pl.* —**n**) near relative; next of kin.

Angeklagte [ˈanɡəklaːktə], *m., f.* (—**n**, *pl.* —**n**) the accused, defendant, prisoner at the bar.

Angel [ˈaŋəl], *f.* (—, *pl.* —**n**) fishing-rod;

(*door*) hinge, pivot; *zwischen Tür und* —, in passing.

angelegen [ˈanɡələːgən], *adj. sich etwas* — *sein lassen*, interest o.s. in s.th.; *concern o.s. in s.th.; ich werde es mir* — *sein lassen*, I shall make it my business.

Angelegenheit [ˈanɡələːgənhaɪt], *f.* (—, *pl.* —**en**) concern, matter, affair.

angeln [ˈaŋəln], *v.a.* fish, angle.

angemessen [ˈanɡəmɛsən], *adj.* proper, suitable, appropriate.

angenehm [ˈanɡəneːm], *adj.* acceptable, agreeable, pleasing, pleasant.

angenommen [ˈanɡənɔmən], *conj.* — *daß*, given that, supposing that, say.

Anger [ˈaŋər], *m.* (—**s**, *pl.* —) grass-plot; green, common.

angesehen [ˈanɡəzeːən], *adj.* respected, esteemed, distinguished.

Angesicht [ˈanɡəzɪçt], *n.* (—**s**, *pl.* —**er**) face, countenance.

angestammt [ˈanɡəʃtamt], *adj.* ancestral, hereditary.

Angestellte [ˈanɡəʃtɛltə], *m., f.* (—**n**, *pl.* —**n**) employee; (*pl.*) staff.

Angler [ˈaŋlər], *m.* (—**s**, *pl.* —) angler, fisherman.

angliedern [ˈanɡliːdərn], *v.a.* annex, attach.

Anglist [aŋˈɡlɪst], *m.* (—**en**, *pl.* —**en**) (*Univ.*) professor *or* student of English.

angreifen [ˈanɡraɪfən], *v.a. irr.* handle, touch; (*capital*) break into; attack, assail; *es greift mich an*, it taxes my strength.

angrenzen [ˈanɡrɛntsən], *v.n.* border upon, adjoin.

Angriff [ˈanɡrɪf], *m.* (—**s**, *pl.* —**e**) offensive, attack, assault.

Angst [aŋst], *f.* (—, *pl.* ⁻e) anxiety; fear; anguish.

ängstigen [ˈɛŋstɪgən], *v.a.* alarm, frighten. — *v.r. sich* —, feel uneasy, be afraid.

angucken [ˈanɡukən], *v.a.* look at.

anhaben [ˈanhaːbən], *v.a. irr.* have on, be dressed in, wear; *einem etwas* —, hold s.th. against s.o.

anhaften [ˈanhaftən], *v.n.* stick to, adhere to.

Anhalt [ˈanhalt], *m.* (—**es**, *no pl.*) support, basis.

anhalten [ˈanhaltən], *v.a. irr. einen* —, stop s.o. — *v.n.* stop, pull up, halt; *um ein Mädchen* —, ask for a girl's hand in marriage. — *v.r. sich an etwas halten*, cling to, hang on to s.th.

Anhaltspunkt [ˈanhaltspuŋkt], *m.* (—**es**, *pl.* —**e**) clue, (*Am.*) lead.

Anhang [ˈanhaŋ], *m.* (—**s**, *pl.* ⁻e) appendix, supplement.

anhängen [ˈanhɛŋən], *v.a. irr.* hang on, fasten to, attach.

Anhänger [ˈanhɛŋər], *m.* (—**s**, *pl.* —) follower, adherent; (*Footb.*) supporter; pendant (on a necklace); label; (*Transp.*) trailer.

anhänglich [ˈanhɛŋlɪç], *adj.* attached, affectionate.

7

Anhängsel

Anhängsel ['anhɛŋsəl], *n.* (—s, *pl.* —) appendage.

anhauchen ['anhauxən], *v.a.* breathe upon.

anhäufen ['anhɔyfən], *v.a.* heap up, pile up, amass. —*v.r. sich* —, accumulate.

anheben ['anhe:bən], *v.a. irr.* lift. — *v.n.* (*obs.*) begin.

anheim [an'haɪm], *adv.* — *stellen*, leave to s.o.'s discretion.

anheimeln ['anhaɪməln], *v.a.* remind one of home.

anheischig ['anhaɪʃɪç], *adj. sich* — *machen*, undertake, pledge o.s.

Anhieb ['anhi:p], *m.* (—s, *pl.* —e) (*fencing*) first stroke; *auf* —, at the first attempt.

Anhöhe ['anhø:ə], *f.* (—, *pl.* —n) hill, rising ground.

anhören ['anhø:rən], *v.a.* listen to; tell by s.o.'s voice *or* accent.

animieren [ani'mi:rən], *v.a.* instigate, egg on.

ankämpfen ['ankɛmpfən], *v.n. gegen etwas* —, struggle against s.th.

ankaufen ['ankaufən], *v.a.* purchase, buy. — *v.r. sich irgendwo* —, buy land somewhere.

Anker ['aŋkər], *m.* (—s, *pl.* —) (*Naut.*) anchor; *den* — *auswerfen*, cast anchor.

ankern ['aŋkərn], *v.a., v.n.* anchor, cast anchor.

Anklage ['ankla:gə], *f.* (—, *pl.* —n) accusation; *gegen einen* — *erheben*, bring a charge against s.o.

Ankläger ['anklɛ:gər], *m.* (—s, *pl.* —) accuser, prosecutor; plaintiff.

Anklang ['anklaŋ], *m.* (—s, *pl.* ̈e) reminiscence; — *finden*, please, meet with approval.

ankleben ['ankle:bən], *v.a.* stick to, glue to, paste on.

ankleiden ['anklaɪdən], *v.a.* dress. — *v.r. sich* —, dress o.s., get dressed.

anklingeln ['anklɪŋəln], *v.a.* (*coll.*) *einen* —, ring s.o. up (on the telephone.)

anklopfen ['anklɔpfən], *v.n.* knock.

anknüpfen ['anknypfən], *v.a.* tie; join on to; *ein Gespräch* —, start a conversation; *wieder* —, resume.

ankommen ['ankɔmən], *v.n. irr.* (*aux.* sein) arrive; *es kommt darauf an*, it depends upon.

ankreiden ['ankraɪdən], *v.a.* chalk up.

ankündigen ['ankyndɪgən], *v.a.* announce, advertise, give notice of, proclaim.

Ankunft ['ankunft], *f.* (—, *no pl.*) arrival.

ankurbeln ['ankurbəln], *v.a.* (*Motor.*) crank up.

Anlage ['anla:gə], *f.* (—, *pl.* —n) (*capital*) investment; enclosure (*with a letter*); (*industrial*) plant; (*building*) lay-out; *öffentliche* —, pleasure grounds; talent.

anlangen ['anlaŋən], *v.n.* (*aux.* sein) arrive; concern; *was das anlangt*, as far as this is concerned.

Anlaß ['anlas], *m.* (—sses, *pl.* ̈sse) cause, occasion, motive.

anlassen ['anlasən], *v.a. irr.* keep on; (*Motor.*) start. — *v.r. sich gut* —, promise well.

Anlasser ['anlasər], *m.* (—s, *pl.* —) (*Motor.*) starter.

anläßlich ['anlɛslɪç], *prep.* (*Genit.*) à propos of, on the occasion of.

Anlauf ['anlauf], *m.* (—s, *pl.* ̈e) start, run, (*Aviat.*) take-off run.

anlaufen ['anlaufən], *v.n. irr.* tarnish; call at (port).

anlegen ['anle:gən], *v.a. Geld* —, invest money; *Kleider* —, don clothes; *einen Garten* —, lay out a garden; *Hand* —, give a helping hand; *auf einen* —, take aim at s.o.; (*Naut.*) land, dock.

Anlegestelle ['anle:gəʃtɛlə], *f.* (—, *pl.* —n) landing place.

anlehnen ['anle:nən], *v.r. sich an etwas* —, lean against s. th.

Anleihe ['anlaɪə], *f.* (—, *pl.* —n) loan, *öffentliche* —, government loan; *eine* — *machen*, raise a loan.

anleiten ['anlaɪtən], *v.a.* train, instruct.

anlernen ['anlɛrnən], *v.a. einen* —, train, apprentice s.o. (in a craft).

Anliegen ['anli:gən], *n.* (—s, *pl.* —) request, petition, concern.

anmachen ['anmaxən], *v.a.* fix, fasten; light (a fire).

anmaßen ['anma:sən], *v.a. sich etwas* —, arrogate s.th.

anmaßend ['anma:sənt], *adj.* arrogant.

anmelden ['anmɛldən], *v.a.* announce, (*claim*) give notice of. — *v.r. sich* —, notify o.'s arrival, make an appointment; *sich* — *lassen*, send in o.'s name.

Anmeldungsformular [an'mɛlduŋsformula:r], *n.* (—s, *pl.* —e) registration form.

Anmerkung ['anmɛrkuŋ], *f.* (—, *pl.* —en) remark, annotation, footnote.

anmessen ['anmɛsən], *v.a. irr.* measure (s.o. for a garment).

Anmut ['anmu:t], *f.* (—, *no pl.*) grace, charm.

annähen ['annɛ:ən], *v.a.* sew on (to).

annähern ['annɛ:ərn], *v.r. sich* —, approach, draw near; (*Maths.*) approximate.

Annäherung ['annɛ:əruŋ], *f.* (—, *pl.* —en) approach; (*Maths.*) approximation.

Annahme ['anna:mə], *f.* (—, *pl.* —n) acceptance; assumption, hypothesis.

annehmbar ['anne:mba:r], *adj.* acceptable; *ganz* —, passable.

annehmen ['anne:mən], *v.a. irr.* take, accept, take delivery of; suppose, assume, presume; *an Kindes Statt* —, adopt.

Annehmlichkeit ['anne:mlɪçkaɪt], *f.* (—, *pl.* —en) amenity, comfort.

Annonce [an'nɔ̃:sə], *f.* (—, *pl.* —n) (classified) advertisement (in newspaper).

anordnen ['anɔrdnən], *v.a.* arrange, regulate; order, direct.

ansspringen

anorganisch ['anɔrgaːnɪʃ], *adj.* inorganic.

anpacken ['anpakən], *v.a.* get hold of, seize, grasp.

anpassen ['anpasən], *v.a.* fit, suit. — *v.r. sich* —, adapt o.s.

anpflanzen ['anpflantsən], *v.a.* plant, grow.

Anprall ['anpral], *m.* (—s, *no pl.*) impact, bounce, shock.

anpumpen ['anpumpən], *v.a.* (*coll.*) *einen* —, borrow money from s.o.

anrechnen ['anrɛçnən], *v.a.* *einem etwas* —, charge s.o. with s.th.; *einem etwas hoch* —, think highly of a person for s.th.

Anrecht ['anrɛçt], *n.* (—es, *no pl.*) — *auf*, title to, claim to.

Anrede ['anreːdə], *f.* (—, *pl.* —n) (form of) address, title.

anreden ['anreːdən], *v.a.* address (s.o.).

anregen ['anreːgən], *v.a.* stimulate (s.o.); suggest (s.th.).

Anregung ['anreːguŋ], *f.* (—, *pl.* —en) suggestion, hint.

Anreiz ['anraɪts], *m.* (—es, *no pl.*) incentive; impulse.

Anrichte ['anrɪçtə], *f.* (—, *pl.* —n) dresser, sideboard.

anrichten ['anrɪçtən], *v.a.* (*meal*) prepare, serve (up); *Unheil* —, make mischief.

anrüchig ['anry:çɪç], *adj.* disreputable.

anrücken ['anrykən], *v.a.* bring near to. — *v.n.* (*aux.* sein) approach.

Anruf ['anruːf], *m.* (—s, *pl.* —e) (by *sentry*) challenge; telephone call.

anrufen ['anruːfən], *v.a. irr.* call to, challenge; implore; ring up; *Gott* —, invoke God.

anrühren ['anry:rən], *v.a.* handle, touch; (*Cul.*) mix.

Ansage ['anzaːgə], *f.* (—, *pl.* —n) announcement.

ansagen ['anzaːgən], *v.a.* announce, notify.

Ansager ['anzaːgər], *m.* (—s, *pl.* —) announcer; compere.

ansammeln ['anzaməln], *v.a.* accumulate, gather. — *v.r. sich* —, gather, foregather, congregate, collect.

ansässig ['anzɛsɪç], *adj.* domiciled, resident; *sich* — *machen*, settle.

Ansatz ['anzats], *m.* (—es, *pl.* ⁓e) start; (*Maths.*) construction; disposition (to), tendency (to).

anschaffen ['anʃafən], *v.a.* buy, purchase, get.

anschauen ['anʃauən], *v.a.* look at, view.

anschaulich ['anʃaulɪç], *adj.* clear; *einem etwas* — *machen*, give s.o. a clear idea of s.th.

Anschauung ['anʃauuŋ], *f.* (—, *pl.* —en) view, perception; *nach meiner* —, in my opinion.

Anschein ['anʃaɪn], *m.* (—s, *no pl.*) appearance, semblance.

anscheinend ['anʃaɪnənt], *adj.* apparent, ostensible, seeming.

anschicken ['anʃɪkən], *v.r. sich* — *zu*, prepare for, get ready for.

anschirren ['anʃɪrən], *v.a.* (*horses*) harness.

Anschlag ['anʃlaːk], *m.* (—s, *pl.* ⁓e) poster, placard; — *auf das Leben*, attempt at assassination.

Anschlagbrett ['anʃlaːkbrɛt], *n.* (—es, *pl.* —er) notice-board.

anschlagen ['anʃlaːgən], *v.a. irr.* (*keys of piano or typewriter*) strike, touch; (*knitting*) cast on; *zu hoch* —, overestimate.

anschließen ['anʃliːsən], *v.a. irr.* fasten with a lock. — *v.r. sich* —, join in; (*club*) join.

Anschluß ['anʃlus], *m.* (—sses, *pl.* ⁓sse) (*Railw., telephone*) connection; (*Pol.*) annexation.

Anschlußpunkt ['anʃluspuŋkt], *m.* (—es, *pl.* —e) junction; (*Elec.*) inlet point, power point.

anschmiegen ['anʃmiːgən], *v.r. sich* —, nestle closely to.

anschmieren ['anʃmiːrən], *v.a. einen* —, (*coll.*) deceive, cheat s.o.

anschnallen ['anʃnalən], *v.a.* buckle on.

anschnauzen ['anʃnautsən], *v.a.* snarl at, snap at.

anschneiden ['anʃnaɪdən], *v.a. irr.* cut into; *ein Thema* —, broach a subject.

Anschrift ['anʃrɪft], *f.* (—, *pl.* —en) address.

anschwellen ['anʃvɛlən], *v.n.* (*aux.* sein) swell.

Ansehen ['anzeːən], *n.* (—s, *no pl.*) respect; reputation; authority.

ansehen ['anzeːən], *v.a. irr.* look at *or* upon, consider, regard.

ansehnlich ['anzeːnlɪç], *adj.* considerable, appreciable.

anseilen ['anzaɪlən], *v.a.* (*Mount.*) rope together.

ansetzen ['anzɛtsən], *v.a.* join to; (*Maths.*) start, write out (an equation).

Ansicht ['anzɪçt], *f.* (—, *pl.* —en) opinion; view; (*Comm.*) approval.

ansichtig ['anzɪçtɪç], *adj.* — *werden*, get a glimpse of.

Ansichts(post)karte ['anzɪçts(pɔst)kartə], *f.* (—, *pl.* —n) picture postcard.

ansiedeln ['anziːdəln], *v.r. sich* —, settle (down), colonize.

Ansinnen ['anzɪnən], *n.* (—s, *pl.* —) demand, suggestion.

anspannen ['anʃpanən], *v.a.* tighten yoke, stretch; harness.

anspielen ['anʃpiːlən], *v.n.* (*Game, Sport*) lead off; *auf etwas* —, allude to s.th.

Ansporn ['anʃpɔrn], *m.* (—s, *no pl.*) spur, incentive.

Ansprache ['anʃpraːxə], *f.* (—, *pl.* —n) address, speech, talk.

ansprechen ['anʃprɛçən], *v.a. irr.* address, accost; please.

anspringen ['anʃprɪŋən], *v.a. irr.* leap at. — *v.n.* (*Motor.*) start.

9

Anspruch ['anʃprux], *m.* (**—s**, *pl.* ˙̈e) (*Law*) claim, title.

anspruchsvoll ['anʃpruxsfɔl], *adj.* demanding, hard to please.

anstacheln ['anʃtaxəln], *v.a.* goad, prod.

Anstalt ['anʃtalt], *f.* (—, *pl.* **—en**) institution, establishment; *—en treffen*, make arrangements (for).

Anstand ['anʃtant], *m.* (**—es**, *no pl.*) propriety; politeness, good manners, good grace; decency; (*Hunt.*) stand, butts.

anständig ['anʃtɛndɪç], *adj.* decent, proper, respectable.

Anstandsbesuch ['anʃtantsbəzu:x], *m.* (**—es**, *pl.* **—e**) formal visit.

anstandshalber ['anʃtantshalbər], *adv.* for decency's sake.

anstandslos ['anʃtantslo:s], *adv.* unhesitatingly.

anstarren ['anʃtarən], *v.a.* stare at.

anstatt [an'ʃtat], *prep.* (*Genit.*), *conj.* instead of, in lieu of, in the place of.

anstecken ['anʃtɛkən], *v.a.* pin on; set fire to; infect.

Ansteckung ['anʃtɛkuŋ], *f.* (—, *pl.* **—en**) infection, contagion.

anstehen ['anʃte:ən], *v.n. irr.* stand in a queue; *— lassen*, put off, delay.

ansteigen ['anʃtaɪgən], *v.n. irr.* (*aux.* sein) rise, increase.

anstellen ['anʃtɛlən], *v.a. einen —*, appoint s.o. to a post; employ; *Betrachtungen —*, speculate. *— v.r. sich —*, form a queue, line up.

anstellig ['anʃtɛlɪç], *adj.* able, skilful, adroit.

Anstellung ['anʃtɛluŋ], *f.* (—, *pl.* **—en**) appointment, employment.

anstiften ['anʃtɪftən], *v.a.* instigate.

anstimmen ['anʃtɪmən], *v.a.* intone.

Anstoß ['anʃto:s], *m.* (**—es**, *pl.* ˙̈e) (*Footb.*) kick-off; *— erregen*, give offence; *den — geben zu*, initiate, give an impetus to; *Stein des —es*, stumbling block; *— nehmen*, take offence.

anstoßen ['anʃto:sən], *v.a. irr.* knock against, push against; give offence; clink (glasses); border on; *mit der Zunge —*, lisp.

anstößig ['anʃtø:sɪç], *adj.* shocking, offensive.

anstreichen ['anʃtraɪçən], *v.a. irr.* paint; *Fehler —*, mark wrong.

Anstreicher ['anʃtraɪçər], *m.* (**—s**, *pl.* **—**) house-painter.

anstrengen ['anʃtrɛŋən], *v.a.* strain exert; *eine Klage gegen einen —*, bring an action against s.o. *— v.r. sich —*, exert o.s.

Anstrengung ['anʃtrɛŋuŋ], *f.* (—, *pl.* **—en**) exertion, effort.

Anstrich ['anʃtrɪç], *m.* (**—s**, *pl.* **—e**) coat of paint.

Ansturm ['anʃturm], *m.* (**—s**, *no pl.*) attack, assault, charge.

Ansuchen ['anzu:xən], *n.* (**—s**, *pl.* **—**) application, request, petition.

ansuchen ['anzu:xən], *v.n. bei einem um etwas —*, apply to s.o. for s.th.

Anteil ['antaɪl], *m.* (**—s**, *pl.* **—e**) share, portion; sympathy.

Anteilnahme ['antaɪlna:mə], *f.* (—, *no pl.*) sympathy.

Antenne [an'tɛnə], *f.* (—, *pl.* **—n**) aerial; antenna.

antik [an'ti:k], *adj.* antique, ancient, classical.

Antike [an'ti:kə], *f.* (—, *pl.* **—en**) (classical) antiquity; ancient work of art (statue etc.).

Antiquar [anti'kva:r], *m.* (**—s**, *pl.* **—e**) second-hand dealer; antiquary.

Antiquariat [antikva'rja:t], *n.* (**—s**, *pl.* **—e**) second-hand bookshop.

antiquarisch [anti'kva:rɪʃ], *adj.* antiquarian, second-hand.

Antlitz ['antlɪts], *n.* (**—es**, *pl.* **—e**) countenance, (*Poet.*) face.

Antrag ['antra:k], *m.* (**—s**, *pl.* ˙̈e) proposition, proposal, application; *einen — stellen*, bring in a motion; make application.

antragen ['antra:gən], *v.a. irr.* propose, make a proposal, offer to.

Antragsformular ['antra:ksfɔrmula:r], *n.* (**—s**, *pl.* **—e**) (*Insurance*) proposal form; application form.

Antragsteller ['antra:kʃtɛlər], *m.* (**—s**, *pl.* **—**) applicant, mover of a resolution.

antreten ['antre:tən], *v.a. irr. ein Amt —*, enter upon an office; *eine Reise —*, set out on a journey. *— v.n.* (*aux.* sein) (*Mil.*) fall in.

Antrieb ['antri:p], *m.* (**—s**, *pl.* **—e**) impulse, motive; incentive; *aus eigenem —*, voluntarily.

Antritt ['antrɪt], *m.* (**—s**, *no pl.*) start, commencement.

Antrittsvorlesung ['antrɪtsforle:zuŋ], *f.* (*Univ.*) inaugural lecture.

antun ['antu:n], *v.a. irr. einem etwas —*, do s.th. to s.o.

Antwort ['antvɔrt], *f.* (—, *pl.* **—en**) answer, reply; *abschlägige —*, refusal, rebuff.

antworten ['antvɔrtən], *v.a.* answer, reply to.

anvertrauen ['anfɛrtrauən], *v.a. einem etwas —*, entrust s.o. with s.th.; confide in s.o.

anverwandt ['anfɛrvant] *see* **verwandt**.

Anwalt ['anvalt], *m.* (**—s**, *pl.* ˙̈e) lawyer, barrister, solicitor, attorney, advocate.

anwandeln ['anvandəln], *v.a.* befall.

Anwandlung ['anvandluŋ], *f.* (—, *pl.* **—en**) fit, turn.

Anwartschaft ['anvartʃaft], *f.* (—, *pl.* **—en**) (*Law*) reversion; candidacy.

anweisen ['anvaɪzən], *v.a. irr.* instruct, direct; *angewiesen sein auf*, depend upon.

Anweisung ['anvaɪzuŋ], *f.* (—, *pl.* **—en**) instruction, advice, method; (*Comm.*) voucher, credit voucher, cheque.

anwenden ['anvɛndən], *v.a. irr.* use, make use of, apply.

armselig

anwerben ['anvɛrbən], *v.a. irr.* (*Mil.*) recruit; *sich — lassen,* enlist.

anwesend ['anve:zənt], *adj.* at hand, present.

Anwesenheit ['anve:zənhaɪt], *f.* (—, *no pl.*) presence, attendance.

anwidern ['anvi:dərn], *v.a.* disgust.

Anzahl ['antsa:l], *f.* (—, *no pl.*) number, quantity.

anzahlen ['antsa:lən], *v.a.* pay a deposit.

Anzahlung ['antsa:luŋ], *f.* (—, *pl.* **—en**) deposit.

Anzeichen ['antsaɪçən], *n.* (—s, *pl.* —) indication, omen.

Anzeige ['antsaɪgə], *f.* (—, *pl.* **—n**) notice, (classified) advertisement; denunciation; — *erstatten,* to lay information.

anzeigen ['antsaɪgən], *v.a.* point out, indicate; announce; notify; advertise; denounce.

Anzeiger ['antsaɪgər], *m.* (—s, *pl.* —) indicator; (*newspaper*) advertiser.

anzetteln ['antsɛtəln], *v.a.* plot, contrive.

anziehen ['antsi:ən], *v.a. irr.* pull, draw tight, give a tug; attract; stretch; dress; (*screws*) tighten. —, *v.r. sich* —, dress, put on o.'s clothes.

anziehend ['antsi:ənt], *adj.* attractive.

Anziehung ['antsi:uŋ], *f.* (—, *no pl.*) attraction.

Anzug ['antsu:k], *m.* (—s, *pl.* **-e**) (man's) suit; approach.

anzüglich ['antsy:klɪç], *adj.* allusive; suggestive; — *werden,* become offensive.

anzünden ['antsyndən], *v.a.* kindle, ignite.

apart [a'part], *adj.* charming, delightful; (*Am.*) cute.

Apfel ['apfəl], *m.* (—s, *pl.* **-**) apple.

Apfelmost ['apfəlmɔst], *m.* (—s, *no pl.*) cider.

Apfelsine [apfəl'zi:nə], *f.* (—, *pl.* **—n**) orange.

Apostel [a'pɔstəl], *m.* (—s, *pl.* —) apostle.

Apotheke [apo'te:kə], *f.* (—, *pl.* **—n**) dispensary, pharmacy, chemist's shop; (*Am.*) drugstore.

Apparat [apa'ra:t], *m.* (—(e)s, *pl.* **—e**) apparatus; radio *or* television set; telephone.

appellieren [apɛ'li:rən], *v.n.* — *an,* appeal to.

appetitlich [ape'ti:tlɪç], *adj.* appetising, dainty.

Aprikose [aprɪ'ko:zə], *f.* (—, *pl.* **—en**) apricot.

Aquarell [akva'rɛl], *n.* (—s, *pl.* **—e**) water-colour (painting).

Ära ['ɛ:ra], *f.* (—, *no pl.*) era.

Arabien [a'ra:bjən], *n.* Arabia.

Arbeit ['arbaɪt], *f.* (—, *pl.* **—en**) work, labour; job; employment; workmanship; *an die — gehen,* set to work.

arbeiten ['arbaɪtən], *v.a., v.n.* work, labour, toil.

Arbeiter ['arbaɪtər], *m.* (—s, *pl.* —) worker, workman, labourer, hand.

Arbeiterschaft ['arbaɪtərʃaft], *f.* (—, *no pl.*) working men; workers.

arbeitsam ['arbaɪtza:m], *adj.* industrious, diligent.

Arbeitsamt ['arbaɪtsamt], *n.* (—s, *pl.* **-er**) labour exchange.

arbeitsfähig ['arbaɪtsfɛ:ɪç], *adj.* capable of working, able-bodied.

arbeitslos ['arbaɪtslo:s], *adj.* unemployed, out of work.

Arbeitslosigkeit ['arbaɪtslo:zɪçkaɪt], *f.* (—, *no pl.*) unemployment.

Arbeitsnachweis ['arbaɪtsnaxvaɪs], *m.* (—es, *no pl.*) labour exchange; (*Am.*) labour registry-office.

Arbeitssperre ['arbaɪtsʃpɛrə], *f.* (—, *pl.* **—n**) (*Ind.*) lock-out.

Archäologe [arçeo'lo:gə], *m.* (—n, *pl.* **—n**) archaeologist.

Arche ['arçə], *f.* (—, *pl.* **—n**) ark.

Archipel [arçi'pe:l], *m.* (—s, *pl.* **—e**) archipelago.

architektonisch [arçɪtɛk'to:nɪʃ], *adj.* architectural.

Archivar [arçi'va:r], *m.* (—s, *pl.* **—e**) keeper of archives.

arg [ark], *adj.* bad, wicked, mischievous.

Argentinien [argən'ti:njən], *n.* Argentina.

Ärger ['ɛrgər], *m.* (—s, *no pl.*) anger, annoyance.

ärgerlich ['ɛrgərlɪç], *adj.* annoying, aggravating, vexing; angry.

ärgern ['ɛrgərn], *v.a.* annoy, vex, make angry. — *v.r. sich* —, get annoyed.

Ärgernis ['ɛrgərnɪs], *n.* (—ses, *pl.* **—se**) scandal, nuisance.

arglistig ['arklɪstɪç], *adj.* crafty, sly.

arglos ['arklo:s], *adj.* unsuspecting, guileless, naive.

Argwohn ['arkvo:n], *m.* (—s, *no pl.*) mistrust, suspicion.

argwöhnisch ['arkvø:nɪʃ], *adj.* suspicious, distrustful.

Arie ['a:rjə], *f.* (—, *pl.* **—n**) (*Mus.*) aria.

Arm [arm], *m.* (—s, *pl.* **—e**) arm.

arm [arm], *adj.* poor, indigent, needy.

Armaturenbrett [arma'tu:rənbrɛt], *n.* (—s, *no pl.*) dashboard.

Armband ['armbant], *n.* (—s, *pl.* **-er**) bracelet.

Armbanduhr ['armbantu:r], *f.* (—, *pl.* **—en**) wrist-watch.

Armbrust ['armbrust], *f.* (—, *pl.* **—e**) cross-bow.

Ärmel ['ɛrməl], *m.* (—s, *pl.* —) sleeve.

Ärmelkanal ['ɛrməlkana:l], *m.* (—s, *no pl.*) English Channel.

Armenien [ar'me:njən], *n.* Armenia.

Armenhaus ['armənhaus], *n.* (—es, *pl.* **-er**) poor-house, almshouse.

Armenpfleger ['armənpfle:gər], *m.* (—s, *pl.* —) almoner.

Armesündermiene [armə'zyndərmi:nə], *f.* (—, *pl.* **—n**) hangdog look.

ärmlich ['ɛrmlɪç], *adj.* poor, shabby, scanty.

armselig ['armze:lɪç], *adj.* poor, miserable, wretched; paltry.

11

Armut ['armuːt], *f.* (—, *no pl.*) poverty; *in — geraten*, be reduced to penury.

Arsch [arʃ], *m.* (—es, ⁀e) (*vulg.*) arse.

Arsen(ik) [ar'zeːn(ɪk)], *n.* (—s, *no pl.*) arsenic.

Art [aːrt], *f.* (—, *pl.* —en) kind, species; race; sort; method, way, manner.

artig ['aːrtɪç], *adj.* well-behaved, civil, polite.

Artigkeit ['aːrtɪçkaɪt], *f.* (—, *pl.* —en) politeness, courtesy.

Artikel [ar'tiːkəl], *m.* (—s, *pl.* —) article; commodity.

Artist [ar'tɪst], *m.* (—en, *pl.* —en) artiste (circus, variety).

Arznei [arts'naɪ], *f.* (—, *pl.* —en) medicine.

Arzneimittel [arts'naɪmɪtəl], *n.* (—s, *pl.*—) medicine, drug.

Arzt [artst], *m.* (—es, *pl.* ⁀e) doctor, physician; *praktischer —,* general practitioner.

ärztlich ['ɛrtstlɪç], *adj.* medical.

As (1) [as], *n.* (—ses, *pl.* —se) (*Mus.*) A flat; *— Dur,* A flat major, *— Moll,* A flat minor.

As (2) [as], *n.* (—sses, *pl.* —sse) (*Sport, cards*) ace.

Asbest [as'best], *m.* (—s, *no pl.*) asbestos.

Asche ['aʃə], *f.* (—, *no pl.*) ashes.

Aschenbecher ['aʃənbɛçər], *m.* (—s, *pl.* —) ash-tray.

Aschenbrödel ['aʃənbrøːdəl]or**Aschenputtel** ['aʃənputəl], *n.* Cinderella.

Aschkraut ['aʃkraut], *n.* (—s, *pl.* ⁀er) (*Bot.*) cineraria.

Askese [as'keːzə], *f.* (—, *no pl.*) asceticism.

Asket [as'keːt], *m.* (—en, *pl.* —en) ascetic.

Assessor [a'sesɔr], *m.* (—s, *pl.* —en) assistant; assistant judge.

Ast [ast], *m.* (—es, *pl.* ⁀e) branch, bough.

Aster ['astər], *f.* (—, *pl.* —n) (*Bot.*) aster.

Astronaut [astro'naut], *m.* (—en, *pl.* —en) astronaut.

Astronom [astro'noːm], *m.* (—en, *pl.* —en) astronomer.

Asyl [a'zyːl], *n.* (—s, *pl.* —e) asylum, sanctuary.

Atem ['aːtəm], *m.* (—s, *no pl.*) breath, breathing, respiration.

Atemzug ['aːtəmtsuːk], *m.* (—s, *pl.* ⁀e) breath.

Äthiopien [ɛti'oːpjən], *n.* Ethiopia.

Atlas (1) ['atlas], *m.* (—sses, *pl.* —sse *and* **Atlanten**) atlas, book of maps.

Atlas (2) ['atlas], *m.* (—sses, *pl.* —sse) satin.

atmen ['aːtmən], *v.n.* breathe.

atomar [ato'maːr], *adj.* atomic.

Attentat [atɛn'taːt], *n.* (—s, *pl.* —e) attempt on s.o.'s life.

Attest [a'test], *n.* (—s, *pl.* —e) (*Med.*) certificate.

ätzen ['ɛtsən], *v.a.* corrode; (*Art*) etch; (*Med.*) cauterise.

auch [aux], *conj., adv.* also, too, likewise, as well.

Au(e) ['au(ə)], *f.* (—, *pl.* —en) green meadow, pasture.

auf [auf], *prep.* on, upon; *— der Straße,* in the road; *— deine Gefahr,* at your own risk; *— Befehl,* by order; *— einige Tage,* for a few days; *— dem Lande,* in the country; *— keinen Fall,* on no account.

aufatmen ['aufaːtmən], *v.n.* breathe a sigh of relief.

Aufbau ['aufbau], *m.* (—s, *no pl.*) building; (*Lit.*) composition, structure.

aufbauen ['aufbauən], *v.a.* erect, build, construct.

aufbäumen ['aufbɔymən], *v.r. sich —,* (*horses*) rear.

aufbewahren ['aufbəvaːrən], *v.a.* keep, store; (*luggage*) take charge of.

Aufbewahrung ['aufbəvaːruŋ], *f.* (—, *pl.* —en) storage, safe keeping.

aufbieten ['aufbiːtən], *v.a. irr.* call up for service; exert (*energies*).

aufbinden ['aufbɪndən], *v.a. irr.* untie; *einem einen Bären —,* to hoax s.o.

aufblähen ['aufblɛːən], *v.a.* puff up, swell, inflate.

aufblühen ['aufblyːən], *v.n.* (*aux.* sein) flourish, unfold.

aufbrausen ['aufbrauzən], *v.n.* (*aux.* sein) fly into a rage.

aufbringen ['aufbrɪŋən], *v.a. irr.* bring up; afford; annoy (s.o.).

Aufbruch ['aufbrux], *m.* (—s, *no pl.*) departure.

aufbürden ['aufbyrdən], *v.a. einem eine Last —,* burden s.o. with a thing.

aufdecken ['aufdɛkən], *v.a.* uncover, unveil.

aufdonnern ['aufdɔnərn], *v.r. sich —,* dress up showily.

aufdrängen ['aufdrɛŋən], *v.a. einem etwas —,* press s.th. upon s.o. *— v.r. sich —,* force o.'s company on.

aufdrehen ['aufdreːən], *v.a.* (*tap*) turn on.

aufdringlich ['aufdrɪŋlɪç], *adj.* importunate, officious, obtrusive.

Aufdruck ['aufdruk], *m.* (—s, *pl.* —e) imprint.

aufdrücken ['aufdrykən], *v.a.* press open; press on s.th.

Aufenthalt ['aufɛnthalt], *m.* (—s, *pl.* —e) stay, sojourn; delay; stop.

auferlegen ['auferleːgən], *v.a.* impose; enjoin.

auferstehen ['auferʃteːən], *v.n. irr.* (*aux.* sein) (*Rel.*) rise from the dead.

auffahren ['aufaːrən], *v.n. irr.* (*aux.* sein) start (from o.'s sleep); mount; flare up (in anger).

Auffahrt ['aufaːrt], *f.* (—, *pl.* —en) ascent; approach to a house, drive.

auffallen ['aufalən], *v.n. irr.* (*aux.* sein) strike the ground; *einem —,* strike s.o., astonish.

auffangen ['aufaŋən], *v.a. irr.* (*ball*) catch; (*blow*) parry, ward off; (*letter*) intercept.

auffassen ['aufasən], *v.a.* take in, comprehend.

auflodern

Auffassung ['auffasuŋ], *f.* (—, *pl.* —**en**) conception, interpretation; view.

aufflackern ['aufflakərn],*v.n.* (*aux.* sein) flare up, flicker.

auffordern ['auffɔrdərn], *v.a.* summon, request, ask, invite.

aufforsten ['auffɔrstən], *v.a.* afforest.

auffressen ['auffrɛsən], *v.a. irr.* devour; (*of animals*) eat up.

auffrischen ['auffrɪʃən], *v.a.* renew, redecorate; (*fig.*) brush up.

aufführen ['auffy:rən], *v.a.* (*Theat.*) perform; *einzeln* —, specify, particularise. — *v.r. sich* —, behave, conduct o.s.

Aufführung ['auffy:ruŋ], *f.* (—, *pl.* —**en**) (*Theat.*) performance.

Aufgabe ['aufga:bə], *f.* (—, *pl.* —**n**) giving up, abandonment; (*letters, telegrams*) posting, despatch; (*work*) task; (*Sch.*) exercise; (*Maths.*) problem.

aufgabeln ['aufga:bəln], *v.a.* (*sl.*) pick up.

Aufgang ['aufgaŋ], *m.* (—**s**, *pl.* ⸚**e**) ascent, stairs.

aufgeben ['aufge:bən], *v.a. irr.* give up, abandon, relinquish; (*Am.*) quit; (*luggage*) check.

aufgeblasen ['aufgəbla:zən], *adj.* conceited, stuck up.

Aufgebot ['aufgəbo:t], *n.* (—**s**, *pl.* —**e**) (*marriage*) banns; (*Mil.*) levy; *mit aller Kräfte*, with the utmost exertion.

aufgebracht ['aufgəbraxt], *adj.* angry, annoyed.

aufgedunsen ['aufgədunzən], *adj.* bloated, sodden.

aufgehen ['aufge:ən], *v.n. irr.* (*aux.* sein) (*knot*) come undone; (*sun*) rise; (*dough*) swell, rise; (*Maths.*) leave no remainder, cancel out.

aufgehoben ['aufgəho:bən], *adj. gut* — *sein*, be in good hands.

aufgelegt ['aufgəle:kt], *adj.* disposed, inclined.

aufgeräumt ['aufgərɔymt], *adj.* merry, cheerful, in high spirits.

aufgeweckt ['aufgəvɛkt], *adj.* bright, clever, intelligent.

aufgießen ['aufgi:sən], *v.a. irr. Kaffee* —, make coffee.

aufgreifen ['aufgraɪfən], *v.a. irr.* seize.

Aufguß ['aufgus], *m.* (—**sses**, *pl.* ⸚**sse**) infusion.

aufhalsen ['aufhalzən], *v.a. einem etwas* —, (*coll.*) saddle s.o. with s.th.

aufhalten ['aufhaltən], *v.a. irr.* (*door*) hold open; *einen* —, delay s.o. — *v.r. sich an einem Ort* —, stay at a place; *sich über etwas* —, find fault with s.th.

aufhängen ['aufhɛŋən], *v.a. irr.* hang (up).

aufhäufen ['aufhɔyfən], *v.a.* pile up. — *v.r. sich* —, accumulate.

Aufheben ['aufhe:bən], *n.* (—**s**, *no pl.*) lifting up; ado; *viel* —*s machen*, make a great fuss.

aufheben ['aufhe:bən], *v.a. irr.* lift (up), pick up; keep, preserve; (*laws*) repeal, abolish; (*agreements*) rescind, annul.

Aufhebung ['aufhe:buŋ], *f.* (—, *pl.* —**en**) abolition, abrogation, annulment, repeal.

aufheitern ['aufhaɪtərn], *v.a.* cheer up; amuse. — *v.r. sich* —, (*weather*) brighten, clear up.

aufhelfen ['aufhɛlfən], *v.n. irr. einem* —, help s.o. up.

aufhellen ['aufhɛlən], *v.r. sich* —, (*weather*) clear up; (*face*) brighten up.

aufhetzen ['aufhɛtsən],*v.a.* rouse (s.o.); *einen* — *gegen*, incite s.o. against.

aufhorchen ['aufhɔrçən], *v.n.* prick up o.'s ears.

aufhören ['aufhø:rən], *v.n.* cease, stop; (*Am.*) quit; *ohne aufzuhören*, incessantly; *da hört sich doch alles auf!* that is the limit!

aufklären ['aufklɛ:rən], *v.a.* enlighten; clear up; *einen* —, enlighten s.o. —*v.r. sich* —, (*weather*) brighten.

Aufklärung ['aufklɛ:ruŋ], *f.* (—, *no pl.*) (age of) Enlightenment.

aufknacken ['aufknakən], *v.a.* crack (open).

aufknöpfen ['aufknœpfən], *v.a.* unbutton; *aufgeknöpft sein*, be in a talkative mood.

aufkommen ['aufkɔmən], *v.n. irr.* (*aux.* sein) come into use, spring up; *für etwas* —, pay for s.th.; *einen nicht* — *lassen*, give s.o. no chance.

aufkrempeln ['aufkrɛmpəln], *v.a.* (*coll.*) roll up (o.'s sleeves).

aufkündigen ['aufkyndɪgən], *v.a.* (*money*) recall; *einem die Freundschaft* —, break with s.o.

Auflage ['aufla:gə], *f.* (—, *pl.* —**n**) (*tax*) impost, duty, levy; (*book*) edition, impression; circulation.

auflassen ['auflasən], *v.a. irr.* leave open; (*Law*) cede.

auflauern ['auflauərn], *v.n. einem* —, lie in wait for s.o., waylay s.o.

Auflauf ['auflauf], *m.* (—**s**, *pl.* ⸚**e**) tumult, noisy street gathering; soufflé.

auflaufen ['auflaufən], *v.n. irr.* (*aux.* sein) swell, increase; (*ship*) run aground.

aufleben ['aufle:bən], *v.n.* (*aux.* sein) *wieder* —, revive.

auflegen ['aufle:gən], *v.a. irr.* lay upon, put on; (*book*) publish; (*tax, punishment*) impose, inflict.

auflehnen ['aufle:nən], *v.r. sich gegen einen* (or *etwas*) —, rebel against, mutiny, oppose.

auflesen ['aufle:zən], *v.a. irr.* pick up, gather.

aufleuchten ['auflɔyçtən], *v.n.* light up; (*eyes*) shine.

auflockern ['auflɔkərn], *v.a.* loosen.

auflodern ['auflo:dərn], *v.n.* (*aux.* sein) flare up, blaze up.

auflösen [ˈaʊfløːzən], v.a. dissolve, loosen; (puzzle) solve, guess; (meeting) break up; (business) wind up; (partnership) dissolve; (army) disband. — v.r. sich —, melt, dissolve, be broken up.

aufmachen [ˈaʊfmaxən], v.a. (door, packet) open; (knot) undo; gut —, pack nicely. — v.r. sich —, get going, set out for.

Aufmachung [ˈaʊfmaxuŋ], f. (—, pl. —en) outward appearance, make-up, get-up.

Aufmarsch [ˈaʊfmarʃ], m. (—es, pl. ⸚e) (Mil.) parade.

aufmerksam [ˈaʊfmɛrkzaːm], adj. attentive, observant; civil, kind; einen — machen auf, draw s.o.'s attention to.

aufmuntern [ˈaʊfmuntərn], v.a. encourage, cheer up.

Aufnahme [ˈaʊfnaːmə], f. (—, pl. —n) reception; (Phot.) snap, photograph; (Geog.) mapping out, survey; (Mus.) recording.

aufnehmen [ˈaʊfneːmən], v.a. irr. take up; receive, give shelter to; (Phot.) photograph, film; (Mus.) record; (money) raise, borrow; (minutes) draw up; den Faden wieder —, take up the thread; die Arbeit wieder —, return to work, resume work; die Fährte —, (Hunt.) recover the scent; es mit einem —, be a match for s.o.; (Comm.) Inventar —, take stock, draw up an inventory.

aufnötigen [ˈaʊfnøːtɪgən], v.a. einem etwas —, force s.th. upon s.o.

aufpassen [ˈaʊfpasən], v.n. attend to, pay attention to, take notice of, take care of.

aufpeitschen [ˈaʊfpaɪtʃən], v.a. whip up.

aufpflanzen [ˈaʊfpflantsən], v.a. mount, erect. — v.r. sich vor einem —, plant o.s. in front of s.o.; mit aufgepflanztem Bajonett, with bayonets fixed.

Aufputz [ˈaʊfputs], m. (—es, no pl.) finery, trimmings.

aufraffen [ˈaʊfrafən], v.a. snatch up, rake up. — v.r. sich wieder —, pull o.s. together.

aufräumen [ˈaʊfrɔʏmən], v.a. put in order, clear away; (room) tidy up; mit etwas —, make a clean sweep of s.th.; aufgeräumt sein, be in a jolly mood.

aufrechnen [ˈaʊfrɛçnən], v.a. reckon up; set off against.

aufrecht [ˈaʊfrɛçt], adj. upright, erect; etwas — erhalten, maintain s.th.; (opinion) stick to, adhere to, uphold.

Aufrechterhaltung [ˈaʊfrɛçtərhaltuŋ], f. (—, no pl.) maintenance, preservation.

aufregen [ˈaʊfreːgən], v.a. excite, enrage.

aufreiben [ˈaʊfraɪbən], v.a. irr. rub sore; (Mil.) destroy, wipe out. — v.r. sich —, exhaust o.s. with worry (or work).

aufreizen [ˈaʊfraɪtsən], v.a. incite, provoke.

aufrichten [ˈaʊfrɪçtən], v.a. raise, erect, set upright; (fig.) comfort, console. — v.r. sich —, rise, sit up.

aufrichtig [ˈaʊfrɪçtɪç], adj. sincere, frank.

aufriegeln [ˈaʊfriːgəln], v.a. unbolt.

Aufriß [ˈaʊfrɪs], m. (—sses, pl. —sse) sketch, draft; (Archit.) elevation, section.

aufrücken [ˈaʊfrʏkən], v.n. (aux. sein) rise, be promoted (in rank), advance.

Aufruf [ˈaʊfruːf], m. (—s, pl. —e) summons, proclamation, appeal; (Law) citation.

aufrufen [ˈaʊfruːfən], v.a. irr. summons; (Sch.) call upon.

Aufruhr [ˈaʊfruːr], m. (—s, pl. —e) uproar, riot, tumult, rebellion, mutiny.

aufrühren [ˈaʊfryːrən], v.a. stir up, agitate, rouse to rebellion.

Aufrüstung [ˈaʊfrʏstuŋ], f. (—, no pl.) (Mil.) (re-)armament.

aufrütteln [ˈaʊfrʏtəln], v.a. rouse, shake s.o. out of his lethargy.

aufsagen [ˈaʊfzaːgən], v.a. recite.

aufsässig [ˈaʊfzɛsɪç], adj. refractory, rebellious.

Aufsatz [ˈaʊfzats], m. (—es, pl. ⸚e) top, head-piece, table centre-piece; (Sch.) composition, essay; (newspaper) article.

aufscheuchen [ˈaʊfʃɔʏçən], v.a. flush (game), startle.

aufschichten [ˈaʊfʃɪçtən], v.a. stack, pile up in layers.

aufschieben [ˈaʊfʃiːbən], v.a. irr. push open; delay, postpone, adjourn; (Parl.) prorogue.

Aufschlag [ˈaʊfʃlaːk], m. (—s, pl. ⸚e) impact, striking; (sleeve) cuff; turn-up; (uniform) facings; (Comm.) increase in price; (Tennis) service.

aufschlagen [ˈaʊfʃlaːgən], v.n. irr. (aux. sein) hit, strike (open); (Tennis) serve. — v.a. die Augen —, open o.'s eyes; ein Lager —, pitch camp; ein Buch —, open a book.

aufschlitzen [ˈaʊfʃlɪtsən], v.a. rip open, slit open.

Aufschluß [ˈaʊfʃlus], m. (—sses, pl. ⸚sse) disclosure, information.

aufschneiden [ˈaʊfʃnaɪdən], v.a. irr. cut open. — v.n. brag, boast.

Aufschneider [ˈaʊfʃnaɪdər], m. (-s, pl. —) swaggerer, braggart.

Aufschnitt [ˈaʊfʃnɪt], m. (—s, no pl.) slice of cold meat or sausage.

aufschnüren [ˈaʊfʃnyːrən], v.a. unlace, untie.

Aufschrei [ˈaʊfʃraɪ], m. (—s, pl. —e) outcry, screech, scream, shout, shriek.

Aufschrift [ˈaʊfʃrɪft], f. (—, pl. —en) inscription, address; heading.

Aufschub [ˈaʊfʃuːp], m. (—s, pl. ⸚e) delay, adjournment, postponement.

aufschütten [ˈaʊfʃʏtən], v.a. (liquid) pour upon; (dam) raise.

aufzeichnen

aufschwingen [ˈaufʃvɪŋən], *v.r. irr.*
sich —, soar, rise; *ich kann mich dazu nicht* —, I cannot rise to that.
Aufschwung [ˈaufʃvuŋ], *m.* (—s, *no pl.*) flight, rising; (*Comm.*) improvement, boom.
Aufsehen [ˈaufzeːən], *n.* (—s, *no pl.*) sensation, stir.
Aufseher [ˈaufzeːər], *m.* (—s, *pl.* —) overseer, inspector.
aufsein [ˈaufzaɪn], *v.n. irr.* (*aux.* sein) be out of bed, be up and about.
aufsetzen [ˈaufzɛtsən], *v.a.* (*hat*) put on; (*letter, essay*) draft.
Aufsicht [ˈaufzɪçt], *f.* (—, *no pl.*) inspection, supervision, control.
Aufsichtsrat [ˈaufzɪçtsraːt], *m.* (—s, *pl.* ⁻e) (*Comm.*) board of directors.
aufsitzen [ˈaufzɪtsən], *v.n. irr.* sit up, wait up at night; (*horse*) mount.
aufspannen [ˈaufʃpanən], *v.a.* (*umbrella*) put up; (*tent*) pitch.
aufspeichern [ˈaufʃpaɪçərn], *v.a.* store (up), warehouse.
aufsperren [ˈaufʃpɛrən], *v.a.* open wide, unlock.
aufspielen [ˈaufʃpiːlən], *v.n. zum Tanz* —, play music for dancing. — *v.r. sich groß* —, give o.s. airs.
aufspießen [ˈaufʃpiːsən], *v.a.* pierce on a spit; (*joint*) skewer.
aufspringen [ˈaufʃprɪŋən], *v.n. irr.* (*aux.* sein) leap up, jump up; (*door*) fly open; (*hands in winter*) chap.
aufspüren [ˈaufʃpyːrən], *v.a.* track, trace.
aufstacheln [ˈaufʃtaxəln], *v.a.* goad, incite.
Aufstand [ˈaufʃtant], *m.* (—s, *pl.* ⁻e) insurrection, revolt, sedition.
aufstapeln [ˈaufʃtaːpəln], *v.a.* pile up, stack, store.
aufstechen [ˈaufʃtɛçən], *v.a. irr.* (*Med.*) lance.
aufstehen [ˈaufʃteːən], *v.n. irr.* (*aux.* sein) (*door*) stand open; stand up; get up (from bed); rise (from a chair).
aufstellen [ˈaufʃtɛlən], *v.a.* set up, arrange; erect; (*Pol.*) put forward (candidate).
Aufstellung [ˈaufʃtɛluŋ], *f.* (—, *pl.* —en) arrangement; statement; inventory; (*Pol.*) nomination.
aufstemmen [ˈaufʃtɛmən], *v.a.* prise open.
Aufstieg [ˈaufʃtiːk], *m.* (—s, *pl.* —e) ascent, rise.
aufstöbern [ˈaufʃtøːbərn], *v.a.* stir (up); start; (*fig.*) discover, ferret out.
aufstoßen [ˈaufʃtoːsən], *v.a. irr.* push open; bump against. — *v.n.* belch.
aufstreben [ˈaufʃtreːbən], *v.n.* soar; (*fig.*) aspire.
aufstreichen [ˈaufʃtraɪçən], *v.a. irr.* (*paint*) lay on; (*butter*) spread.
aufstülpen [ˈaufʃtylpən], *v.a.* turn up; (*hat*) clap on o.'s head.
auftakeln [ˈauftaːkəln], *v.a.* (*Naut.*) rig.
Auftakt [ˈauftakt], *m.* (—s, *pl.* —e) (*Mus.*) arsis; (*fig.*) opening, prelude.

auftauchen [ˈauftauxən], *v.n.* (*aux.* sein) appear, emerge, surface.
auftauen [ˈauftauən], *v.n.* (*aux.* sein) thaw; (*fig.*) lose o.'s reserve.
auftischen [ˈauftɪʃən], *v.a.* dish up.
Auftrag [ˈauftraːk], *m.* (—s, *pl.* ⁻e) assignment, commission, errand; *im* — *von*, on behalf of.
auftragen [ˈauftraːgən], *v.a. irr.* (*food*) serve up; (*paint*) apply; *einem etwas* —, charge s.o. with a job; *stark* —, lay it on thick.
auftreiben [ˈauftraɪbən], *v.a. irr.* raise (*money*); procure, obtain. — *v.n.* (*aux.* sein) (*ship*) run aground.
auftrennen [ˈauftrɛnən], *v.a.* unstitch; (*hem*) unpick.
Auftreten [ˈauftreːtən], *n.* (—s, *no pl.*) (*Theat.*) appearance; behaviour.
auftreten [ˈauftreːtən], *v.n. irr.* (*aux.* sein) tread upon, step upon; (*Theat.*) appear, come on; *energisch* —, take strong measures, put o.'s foot down.
Auftritt [ˈauftrɪt], *m.* (—s, *pl.* —e) (*Theat.*) scene; altercation, row.
auftun [ˈauftuːn], *v.a. irr.* open; *den Mund* —, speak. — *v.r. sich* —, (*abyss*) yawn.
auftürmen [ˈauftyrmən], *v.a.* pile up, heap up. — *v.r. sich* —, tower.
aufwachen [ˈaufvaxən], *v.n.* (*aux.* sein) awake, wake up.
aufwallen [ˈaufvalən], *v.n.* (*aux.* sein) boil up, bubble up, rage.
Aufwand [ˈaufvant], *m.* (—s, *no pl.*) expense, expenditure; sumptuousness.
aufwarten [ˈaufvartən], *v.n.* wait upon, attend on.
aufwärts [ˈaufvɛrts], *adv.* upward(s), aloft.
Aufwartung [ˈaufvartuŋ], *f.* (—, *pl.* —en) attendance; *seine* — *machen*, pay a (formal) visit.
aufwaschen [ˈaufvaʃən], *v.a. irr.* wash the dishes.
aufweisen [ˈaufvaɪzən], *v.a. irr.* show, produce.
aufwenden [ˈaufvɛndən], *v.a. irr.* spend upon, expend upon.
aufwickeln [ˈaufvɪkəln], *v.a.* wind up; unwind.
aufwiegeln [ˈaufviːgəln], *v.a.* stir up, incite to rebellion.
aufwiegen [ˈaufviːgən], *v.a. irr.* outweigh, counter-balance, make up for.
aufwischen [ˈaufvɪʃən], *v.a.* wipe away, mop up.
aufwühlen [ˈaufvyːlən], *v.a.* dig, root up, (*fig.*) stir.
aufzählen [ˈauftsɛːlən], *v.a.* count up, enumerate, list.
aufzäumen [ˈauftsɔymən], *v.a.* bridle (horses).
aufzehren [ˈauftseːrən], *v.a.* eat up, consume.
aufzeichnen [ˈauftsaɪçnən], *v.a.* write down, take a note of, record.

15

aufziehen

aufziehen ['auftsi:ən], *v.a. irr.* draw up, pull up; pull open; (*pennant*) hoist; (*clock*) wind up; (*child*) bring up, rear; *einen —,* tease s.o.; *gelindere Saiten —,* be more lenient.

Aufzucht ['auftsuxt], *f.* (—, *no pl.*) breeding, rearing.

Aufzug ['auftsu:k], *m.* (—**s**, *pl.* ⸚e) lift; (*Am.*) elevator; (*Theat.*) act; dress, array, attire.

aufzwingen ['auftsvɪŋən], *v.a. irr. einem etwas —,* force s.th. on s.o.

Augapfel ['aukapfəl], *m.* (—**s**, *pl.* ⸚) eye-ball; (*fig.*) apple of o.'s eye.

Auge ['augə], *n.* (—**s**, *pl.* —**n**) eye; *aus den —n, aus dem Sinn,* out of sight, out of mind; *mit einem blauen — davonkommen,* escape by the skin of o.'s teeth, get off cheaply; *es wird mir schwarz vor den —n,* I feel faint.

Augenblick ['augənblɪk], *m.* (—**s**, *pl.* —e) moment, instant; *jeden —,* at any moment.

augenblicklich [augən'blɪklɪç], *adj.* momentary, instantaneous.— *adv.* at present, for the moment, immediately.

Augenbraue ['augənbrauə], *f.* (—, *pl.* —**n**) eye-brow.

augenfällig ['augənfɛlɪç], *adj.* visible, evident, conspicuous.

Augenglas ['augənglas], *n.* (—**es**, *pl.* ⸚er) eye-glass.

Augenhöhle ['augənhø:lə], *f.* (—, *pl.* —**n**) eye-socket.

Augenlicht ['augənlɪçt], *n.* (—**s**, *no pl.*) eye-sight.

Augenlid ['augənli:t], *n.* (—**s**, *pl.* —**er**) eye-lid.

Augenmaß ['augənma:s], *n.* (—**es**, *no pl.*) *gutes —,* good measuring ability with the eye, a sure eye.

Augenmerk ['augənmɛrk], *n.* (—**s**, *no pl.*) attention; *sein — auf etwas richten,* focus o.'s attention on s.th.

Augenschein ['augənʃaɪn], *m.* (—**s**, *no pl.*) appearance; *in — nehmen,* view.

augenscheinlich ['augənʃaɪnlɪç], *adj.* apparent, evident.

Augenweide ['augənvaɪdə], *f.* (—, *pl.* —**n**) delight to the eye, s.th. lovely to look at.

Augenwimper ['augənvɪmpər], *f.* (—, *pl.* —**n**) eye-lash.

Augenzeuge ['augəntsoygə], *m.* (—**n**, *pl.* —**n**) eye-witness.

August [au'gust], *m.* (—**s**, *no pl.*) (*month*) August.

Augustiner [augus'ti:nər], *m.* (—**s**, *pl.* —) (*Eccl.*) Augustinian.

auktionieren [auktsjo'ni:rən], *v.a.* auction(eer), sell by auction.

Aula ['aula], *f.* (—, *pl.* —**len**) (*Sch., Univ.*) great hall; auditorium maximum.

Aurikel [au'ri:kəl], *f.* (—, *pl.* —**n**) (*Bot.*) auricula.

aus [aus], *prep.* (*Dat.*) from, out of, of, off. — *adv.* out, over, finished, done with, spent; *es ist alles —,* it is over and done with; *ich weiß weder ein noch —,* I am at my wits' end.

ausarten ['ausartən], *v.n.* (*aux.* sein) degenerate; (*fig.*) deteriorate.

Ausbau ['ausbau], *m.* (—**s**, *no pl.*) enlargement, extension.

ausbauen ['ausbauən], *v.a.* enlarge (a house); improve on.

ausbedingen ['ausbədɪŋən], *v.a. sich etwas —,* stipulate.

ausbessern ['ausbɛsərn], *v.a.* (*garment*) mend, repair.

Ausbeute ['ausbɔytə], *f.* (—, *no pl.*) gain, profit, produce.

Ausbeutung ['ausbɔytuŋ], *f.* (—, *no pl.*) exploitation, sweating; (*Min.*) working.

ausbezahlen ['ausbətsa:lən], *v.a.* pay in full.

ausbilden ['ausbɪldən], *v.a.* develop, train; (*Mil.*) drill.

Ausbildung ['ausbɪlduŋ], *f.* (—, *pl.* —en) training, education.

ausbleiben ['ausblaɪbən], *v.n. irr.* (*aux.* sein) fail to appear, be absent.

Ausblick ['ausblɪk], *m.* (—**s**, *pl.* —e) view (from window); (*fig.*) prospect, outlook.

ausborgen ['ausbɔrgən], *v.a.* (*sich*) *etwas —,* borrow s.th. from.

ausbreiten ['ausbraɪtən], *v.a.* spread (things); stretch out (o.'s arms). — *v.r. sich —,* spread, extend.

Ausbreitung ['ausbraɪtuŋ], *f.* (—, *no pl.*) spreading, extension, distribution, expansion.

ausbringen ['ausbrɪŋən], *v.a. irr. einen Toast auf einen —,* drink s.o.'s health.

Ausbruch ['ausbrux], *m.* (—**s**, *pl.* ⸚e) breaking out, outbreak, eruption, burst (of laughter).

ausbrüten ['ausbry:tən], *v.a.* hatch; (*fig.*) plot.

Ausbund ['ausbunt], *m.* (—**s**, *pl.* ⸚e) paragon, embodiment.

Ausdauer ['ausdauər], *f.* (—, *no pl.*) perseverance, persistence, stamina.

ausdehnen ['ausde:nən], *v.a.* extend, stretch, distend; (*fig.*) prolong, protract. — *v.r. sich —,* expand, extend, stretch.

Ausdehnung ['ausde:nuŋ], *f.* (—, *pl.* —en) extension, expansion; dilation; (*Phys.*) dimension.

ausdenken ['ausdɛŋkən], *v.a. irr.* think out. — *v.r. sich etwas —,* devise s.th., invent s.th.; *das ist gar nicht auszudenken,* that is unimaginable, inconceivable.

Ausdeutung ['ausdɔytuŋ], *f.* (—, *pl.* —en) interpretation, explanation.

ausdörren ['ausdœrən], *v.a.* parch, dry (up).

ausdrehen ['ausdre:ən], *v.a.* (gas, light, water) turn off, switch off.

Ausdruck ['ausdruk], *m.* (—**s**, *pl.* ⸚e) expression, phrase.

ausdrücken ['ausdrykən], *v.a.* squeeze out, press out; (*fig.*) express.

ausdrücklich ['ausdryklɪç], *adj.* express, explicit.

Ausdrucksweise ['ausdruksvaɪzə], *f.* (—, *pl.* —n) enunciation, manner of speech, (mode of) expression, style.

ausdünsten ['ausdynstən], *v.a.* exhale, perspire.

auseinander [ausaɪn'andər], *adv.* asunder, apart.

Auseinandersetzung [ausaɪn'andər-zɛtsuŋ], *f.* (—, *pl.* —en) altercation; discussion, explanation.

auserkoren ['ausɛrkoːrən], *adj.* elect, chosen, selected.

auserlesen ['ausɛrleːzən], *adj.* choice, picked, excellent, first class.

auserwählen ['ausɛrvɛːlən], *v.a.* choose, select.

Ausfahrt ['ausfaːrt], *f.* (—, *pl.* —en) drive; gateway; exit.

Ausfall ['ausfal], *m.* (—s, *pl.* ¨e) falling out; (*radioactivity*) fall-out; sortie, sally; deficiency, loss, cancellation; result, outcome.

ausfallen ['ausfalən], *v.n. irr.* (*aux.* sein) drop out, fall out; be cancelled, be omitted, fail to take place; turn out (well etc.).

ausfallend ['ausfalənt], *adj.* offensive, abusive; — *werden*, become insulting.

ausfertigen ['ausfɛrtɪgən], *v.a.* despatch, draw up, make out, issue.

ausfindig ['ausfɪndɪç], *adj.* — *machen*, find out, locate, discover.

ausflicken ['ausflɪkən], *v.a.* mend, patch.

Ausflucht ['ausfluxt], *f.* (—, *pl.* ¨e) evasion, excuse, subterfuge.

Ausflug ['ausfluːk], *m.* (—s, *pl.* ¨e) trip, excursion, outing.

Ausfluß ['ausflus], *m.* (—sses, *pl.* ¨sse) (*Engin.*) outflow, outlet; (*Med.*) discharge, suppuration.

ausfragen ['ausfraːgən], *v.a. einen —*, question, quiz s.o.

Ausfuhr ['ausfuːr], *f.* (—, *pl.* —en) export.

ausführbar ['ausfyːrbaːr], *adj.* practicable, feasible; exportable.

ausführen ['ausfyːrən], *v.a.* take out; lead out; export; carry out, perform, fulfil; point out.

ausführlich [aus'fyːrlɪç], *adj.* detailed, full.

Ausführung ['ausfyːruŋ], *f.* (—, *pl.* —en) execution, carrying out; finish; workmanship.

ausfüllen ['ausfylən], *v.a.* (*forms*) fill up, fill in, complete.

ausfüttern ['ausfytərn], *v.a.* line (a dress).

Ausgabe ['ausgaːbə], *f.* (—, *pl.* —en) issue, distribution; (*goods*) dispatch, issuing counter; delivery; (*book*) edition; (*pl.*) expenses, expenditure.

Ausgang ['ausgaŋ], *m.* (—s, *pl.* ¨e) going out; exit; result, upshot; end, conclusion; time off (from duty).

Ausgangspunkt ['ausgaŋspuŋkt], *m.* (—s, *pl.* —e) starting-point; point of departure.

ausgären ['ausgɛːrən], *v.n. irr.* (*aux.* sein) ferment; *ausgegoren sein*, have fermented.

ausgeben ['ausgeːbən], *v.a. irr.* (*work*) give out, distribute; (*money*) expend, spend; (*tickets*) issue. —*v.r. sich — für*, pass o.s. off as.

ausgebreitet ['ausgəbraɪtət], *adj.* extensive, widespread.

Ausgeburt ['ausgeburt], *f.* (—, *pl.* —en) monstrosity; — *des Hirns*, figment of the imagination.

ausgefahren ['ausgəfaːrən], *adj.* (*street*) rutted, well-worn.

ausgehen ['ausgeːən], *v.n. irr.* (*aux.* sein) go out; (*hair*) to fall out; (*colour*) come off, fade; (*breath, patience, money*) become exhausted; result, end in.

ausgelassen ['ausgəlasən], *adj.* boisterous, exuberant, frolicsome, merry, jolly, unbridled.

ausgemacht ['ausgəmaxt], *adj.* arranged, settled, decided; *eine —e Sache*, a matter of course, a foregone conclusion; *ein —er Schurke*, a downright scoundrel.

ausgeschlossen ['ausgəʃlɔsən], *p.p. das ist —*, that is impossible, out of the question.

ausgewachsen ['ausgəvaksən], *adj.* full-grown, fully grown.

ausgezeichnet ['ausgətsaɪçnət], *adj.* excellent, first rate, distinguished.

ausgiebig ['ausgiːbɪç], *adj.* abundant, plentiful; (*soil*) fertile, rich.

ausgießen ['ausgiːsən], *v.a. irr.* pour out.

Ausgleich ['ausglaɪç], *m.* (—s, *no pl.*) settlement, compromise, compensation, equalisation.

ausgleichen ['ausglaɪçən], *v.a. irr.* make even, balance, equalise, compensate; (*sport*) equalise, draw.

ausgraben ['ausgraːbən], *v.a. irr.* dig out, dig up, excavate, exhume.

Ausguck ['ausguk], *m.* (—s, *pl.* —e) look-out; (*Naut.*) crow's nest.

Ausguß ['ausgus], *m.* (—sses, *pl.* ¨sse) sink, gutter.

aushalten ['aushaltən], *v.a. irr.* sustain, endure, bear, stand.

aushändigen ['aushɛndɪgən], *v.a.* deliver up, hand over.

Aushang ['aushaŋ], *m.* (—s, *pl.* ¨e) sign, sign-board, placard.

ausharren ['ausharən], *v.n.* persevere, hold out, wait patiently.

aushecken ['aushɛkən], *v.a.* hatch (a plot).

aushelfen ['aushɛlfən], *v.n. irr.* help out.

Aushilfe ['aushɪlfə], *f.* (—, *pl.* —n) help, aid, assistance.

aushilfsweise ['aushɪlfsvaɪzə], *adv.* temporarily, as a stop-gap.

aushöhlen ['aushøːlən], *v.a.* hollow out, excavate.

ausholen ['ausho:lən], *v.a.* pump, sound s.o. — *v.n.* strike out; *weit —*, go far back (in a narration).

auskehren

auskehren [ˈauskeːrən], v.a. sweep out.
auskennen [ˈauskɛnən], v.r. irr. sich in etwas —, know all about s.th.
auskleiden [ˈausklaɪdən], v.a. undress.
ausklingen [ˈausklɪŋən], v.n. irr. (aux. sein) (sound) die away.
ausklügeln [ˈauskly:gəln], v.a. puzzle out, contrive.
auskneifen [ˈausknaɪfən], v.n. irr. (aux. sein) (coll.) bolt, run away.
Auskommen [ˈauskɔmən], n. (—s, no pl.) sufficiency, subsistence, livelihood; mit dem ist kein —, there is no getting on with him.
auskommen [ˈauskɔmən], v.n. irr. (aux. sein) mit etwas —, have enough or sufficient of s.th., manage; mit einem gut —, be on good terms with s.o., get on well with s.o.
auskömmlich [ˈauskœmlɪç], adj. sufficient.
auskosten [ˈauskɔstən], v.a. taste or enjoy to the full.
auskramen [ˈauskraːmən], v.a. rummage out; (fig.) reminisce; talk freely.
auskundschaften [ˈauskuntʃaftən], v.a. spy out, reconnoitre, explore.
Auskunft [ˈauskunft], f. (—, pl. ⁻e) information; (Tel.) enquiries; (Mil.) intelligence, enquiry.
auslachen [ˈauslaxən], v.a. laugh at, deride.
ausladen [ˈauslaːdən], v.a. irr. unload, discharge; cancel (invitation).
Auslage [ˈauslaːgə], f. (—, pl. —n) outlay, expenses, advance; shop-window display.
Ausland [ˈauslant], n. (—s, no pl.) foreign country; ins — fahren, go abroad.
Ausländer [ˈauslɛndər], m. (—s, pl. —) foreigner, alien.
auslassen [ˈauslasən], v.a. irr. let off (steam); let out (a dress); melt (butter); leave off, omit. — v.r. sich über etwas —, speak o.'s mind about s.th.
Auslassung [ˈauslasuŋ], f. (—, pl. —en) utterance; omission.
auslaufen [ˈauslaufən], v.n. irr. (aux. sein) run out, leak out; (ship) put to sea; (result) turn out.
Ausläufer [ˈauslɔyfər], m. (—s, pl. —) errand boy; (mountain) spur.
Auslaut [ˈauslaut], m. (—s, pl. —e) (Phonet.) final sound.
auslegen [ˈausleːgən], v.a. lay out, spread out, display; interpret; (money) advance.
ausleihen [ˈauslaɪən], v.a. irr. lend, hire out. — v.r. sich etwas —, borrow s.th.
auslernen [ˈauslɛrnən], v.n. end o.'s apprenticeship.
ausliefern [ˈausliːfərn], v.a. hand over, deliver; surrender, give up, extradite.
auslöschen [ˈauslœʃən], v.a. extinguish, put out (fire).
auslosen [ˈauslozən], v.a. raffle, draw lots for.

auslösen [ˈausløːzən], v.a. redeem, ransom, recover; (fig.) produce; arouse.
Auslosung [ˈauslozuŋ], f. (—, pl. —en) raffle, draw.
Auslösung [ˈausløːzuŋ], f. (—, pl. —en) ransom.
auslüften [ˈauslyftən], v.a. air, ventilate.
ausmachen [ˈausmaxən], v.a. decide, settle; amount to; etwas mit einem —, arrange s.th. with s.o.; es macht nichts aus, it does not matter; wieviel macht das aus? how much is this? würde es Ihnen etwas —? would you mind?
Ausmaß [ˈausmaːs], n. (—es, pl. —e) dimension, amount, extent, scale.
ausmeißeln [ˈausmaɪsəln], v.a. chisel out, carve out.
ausmerzen [ˈausmertsən], v.a. expunge, eradicate.
ausmisten [ˈausmɪstən], v.a. clean, clear up (mess).
ausmustern [ˈausmustərn], v.a. eliminate, reject; (Mil.) discharge.
Ausnahme [ˈausnaːmə], f. (—, pl. —n) exception.
ausnehmen [ˈausneːmən], v.a. irr. except, exclude; (poultry) draw; (fish) clean.
ausnutzen [ˈausnutsən], v.a. make the most of s.th.; take advantage of s.th.
ausnützen [ˈausnytsən], v.a. exploit.
auspacken [ˈauspakən], v.a. unpack. — v.n. talk freely; (coll.) open up.
auspfeifen [ˈauspfaɪfən], v.a. irr. (Theat.) hiss at, cat-call.
auspolstern [ˈauspɔlstərn], v.a. stuff.
ausprägen [ˈausprɛːgən], v.a. stamp, impress, coin.
ausprobieren [ˈausprobiːrən], v.a. try out.
Auspuff [ˈauspuf], m. (—s, no pl.) (Motor.) exhaust.
auspusten [ˈauspuːstən], v.a. blow out.
ausputzen [ˈausputsən], v.a. clean out; adorn.
ausquartieren [ˈauskvartiːrən], v.a. (Mil.) billet out.
ausquetschen [ˈauskvɛtʃən], v.a. squeeze out.
ausradieren [ˈausradiːrən], v.a. erase.
ausrangieren [ˈausraŋʒiːrən], v.a. cast off, sort out.
ausräuchern [ˈausrɔyçərn], v.a. fumigate.
ausraufen [ˈausraufən], v.a. (obs.) tear or pull out (hair).
ausräumen [ˈausrɔymən], v.a. clear out, clear away.
ausrechnen [ˈausrɛçnən], v.a. reckon, compute, calculate; ausgerechnet du, (emph.) you of all people.
ausrecken [ˈausrɛkən], v.a. sich den Hals —, crane o.'s neck.
Ausrede [ˈausreːdə], f. (—, pl. —n) evasion, excuse, subterfuge.
ausreden [ˈausreːdən], v.a. einem etwas —, dissuade s.o. from s.th. — v.n. finish speaking; einen — lassen, allow s.o. to finish speaking.

ausreichen ['ausraɪçən], *v.n.* suffice.

ausreißen ['ausraɪsən], *v.a. irr.* pluck, pull out. — *v.n.* (*aux.* sein) run away, bolt.

ausrenken ['ausrɛŋkən], *v.a.* dislocate, sprain.

ausrichten ['ausrɪçtən], *v.a.* adjust, make straight; deliver (a message); accomplish; (*Mil.*) dress.

ausrotten ['ausrɔtən], *v.a.* root up; exterminate, extirpate.

ausrücken ['ausrykən], *v.n.* (*aux.* sein) (*Mil.*) march out; (*coll.*) decamp.

Ausruf ['ausru:f], *m.* (—s, *pl.* —e) exclamation, interjection, outcry; (*public*) proclamation.

Ausruf(ungs)zeichen ['ausru:f(uŋs)-tsaɪçən], *n.* (—s, *pl.* —) exclamation mark.

ausruhen ['ausru:ən], *v.r. sich* —, rest, take a rest.

ausrüsten ['ausrystən], *v.a.* furnish, fit out, equip.

Ausrutschen ['ausrutʃən], *v.n.* (*aux.* sein) slip.

Aussage ['ausza:gə], *f.* (—, *pl.* —n) declaration, statement, evidence; (*Law*) deposition, affidavit; (*Gram.*) predicate.

aussagen ['ausza:gən], *v.a.* say, state, utter, declare; (*Law*) depose, give evidence.

Aussatz ['auszats], *m.* (—es, *no pl.*) leprosy.

Aussätzige ['auszɛtsɪgə], *m.* (—n, *pl.* —n) leper.

aussaugen ['auszaugən], *v.a.* suck dry.

ausschalten ['ausʃaltən], *v.a.* switch off.

Ausschank ['ausʃaŋk], *m.* (—s, *no pl.*) pub, bar.

Ausschau ['ausʃau], *f.* (—, *no pl.*) watch; — *halten*, look out for.

ausscheiden ['ausʃaɪdən], *v.a. irr.* separate; (*Med.*) secrete. — *v.n.* (*aux.* sein) withdraw from, retire, secede.

Ausscheidung ['ausʃaɪduŋ], *f.* (—, *pl.* —en) retirement, withdrawal; (*Med.*) secretion.

Ausschlag ['ausʃla:k], *m.* (—s, *pl.* ‿e) turn (of the scales); deflection (of the magnetic needle); (*Med.*) rash, eczema; *den* — *geben*, clinch the matter; give the casting vote.

ausschlagen ['ausʃla:gən], *v.a. irr.* knock out; refuse, decline (an invitation); *das schlägt dem Faß den Boden aus*, that is the last straw. — *v.n.* (*aux.* sein) (*Hort.*) bud, shoot; *gut* —, turn out well.

auschlaggebend ['ausʃla:kge:bənt], *adj.* decisive; (*vote*) casting.

ausschließen ['ausʃli:sən], *v.a. irr.* lock out; exclude.

ausschließlich ['ausʃli:slɪç], *adj.* exclusive, sole.

ausschlüpfen ['ausʃlypfən], *v.n.* (*aux.* sein) hatch out.

Ausschluß ['ausʃlus], *m.* (—sses, *pl.* ‿sse) exclusion; *unter* — *der Öffentlichkeit*, in camera.

ausschmücken ['ausʃmykən], *v.a.* adorn, decorate, embellish.

Ausschnitt ['ausʃnɪt], *m.* (—s, *pl.* —e) cutting out; (*newspaper*) cutting; (*dress*) neck (line).

ausschreiben ['ausʃraɪbən], *v.a. irr.* write down in full; make out a bill; advertise (post) as vacant.

ausschreiten ['ausʃraɪtən], *v.n. irr.* (*aux.* sein) step out, stride along.

Ausschreitungen ['ausʃraɪtuŋən], *f. pl.* rioting; excesses.

Ausschuß ['ausʃus], *m.* (—sses, *pl.* ‿sse) dross, refuse, rejects, low quality goods; committee, commission, board.

ausschweifend ['ausʃvaɪfənt], *adj.* extravagant; licentious, dissolute.

aussehen ['ausze:ən], *v.n. irr.* look; look like, appear.

außen ['ausən], *adv.* outside, abroad, outward, without.

Außenhandel ['ausənhandəl], *m.* (—s, *no pl.*) export trade.

Außenministerium .['ausənmɪnɪste:rjum], *n.* (—s, *pl.* —terien) Ministry of Foreign Affairs; (*U.K.*) Foreign Office, (*U.S.*) State Department.

Außenstände ['ausənʃtɛndə], *m. pl.* outstanding claims, liabilities.

außer ['ausər], *prep.* (*Dat.*) in addition to, besides, apart from; out of, at the outside of, beside, without; — *Dienst*, retired. — *conj.* except, save, but.

außerdem ['ausərde:m], *adv.* besides, moreover, furthermore.

Äussere ['ɔysərə], *n.* (—n, *no pl.*) exterior.

außerehelich ['ausəre:əlɪç], *adj.* illegitimate.

außergewöhnlich ['ausərgəvø:nlɪç], *adj.* unusual, exceptional.

außerhalb ['ausərhalp], *prep.* outside.

äußerlich ['ɔysərlɪç], *adj.* external.

Äußerlichkeit ['ɔysərlɪçkaɪt], *f.* (—, *pl.* —en) formality.

äußern ['ɔysərn], *v.a.* utter, express. — *v.r. sich zu etwas* —, give o.'s opinion on some question; express o.s. on some subject.

außerordentlich [ausər'ɔrdəntlɪç], *adj.* extraordinary, unusual; (*Univ.*) —*er Professor*, senior lecturer *or* reader; (*Am.*) associate professor.

äußerst ['ɔysərst], *adj.* outermost, most remote; extreme, utmost.

außerstande ['ausərʃtandə], *adj.* unable.

Äußerung ['ɔysəruŋ], *f.* (—, *pl.* —en) utterance, remark, observation.

aussetzen ['auszɛtsən], *v.a.* set out, put out; offer (a reward); suspend; *etwas an einer Sache* —, find fault with s.th.; *sich einer Gefahr* —, expose o.s. to danger, run a risk. — *v.n.* pause, discontinue; (*Motor.*) stop, misfire.

Aussicht ['auszɪçt], *f.* (—, *pl.* —en) view, panorama; prospect, chance; *etwas in* — *stellen*, hold out the prospect of s.th.; *in* — *nehmen*, intend.

19

aussinnen

aussinnen [ˈauszɪnən],*v. a. irr.* imagine, invent, devise.

aussöhnen [ˈauszøːnən], *v.r. sich mit einem —,* become reconciled with s.o.

aussondern [ˈauszɔndərn], *v.a.* single out.

ausspannen [ˈausʃpanən], *v.a. (animals)* unharness. — *v.n. (coll.)* relax.

ausspeien [ˈausʃpaɪən], *v.a.* spit out, vomit.

aussperren [ˈausʃpɛrən], *v.a.* shut out; *(industrial)* lock out.

ausspielen [ˈausʃpiːlən], *v.n.* finish playing; *(Sport, Game)* lead (off).

Aussprache [ˈausʃpraːxə], *f.* (—, *no pl.*) pronunciation; discussion; confidential talk.

aussprechen [ˈausʃprɛçən], *v.a. irr.* have o.'s say; utter; pronounce. — *v.r. sich —,* speak o.'s mind.

Ausspruch [ˈausʃprux], *m.* (—s, *pl.* ˙-e) utterance, dictum.

ausspüren [ˈausʃpyːrən], *v.a.* (*Hunt.*) track down.

ausstaffieren [ˈausʃtafiːrən],*v.a.*furnish, equip.

Ausstand [ˈausʃtant], *m.* (—s, *pl.* ˙-e) *(industry)* strike; *(pl.)* outstanding debts, arrears.

ausständig [ˈausʃtɛndɪç], *adj.* outstanding; on strike.

ausstatten [ˈausʃtatən], *v.a.* endow with, provide with, equip.

Ausstattung [ˈausʃtatuŋ], *f.* (—, *pl.* —en) outfit; (bridal) trousseau; *(coll.)* get-up.

ausstechen [ˈausʃtɛçən],*v.a. irr.* pierce; *einen —,* (*fig.*) excel s.o.

ausstehen [ˈausʃteːən], *v.n. irr.* stand out; *(money)* be overdue. — *v.a.* endure, suffer, bear, undergo; *ich kann ihn nicht —,* I cannot stand him.

aussteigen [ˈausʃtaɪgən], *v.n. irr.* *(aux. sein)* get out, alight; disembark.

ausstellen [ˈausʃtɛlən], *v.a.* exhibit; display; make out (bill etc.).

Aussteller [ˈausʃtɛlər], *m.* (—s, *pl.* —) drawer (of a cheque); exhibitor.

Ausstellung [ˈausʃtɛluŋ], *f.* (—, *pl.* —en) exhibition; (*Am.*) exposition.

Aussteuer [ˈausʃtɔyər], *f.* (—, *pl.* —n) trousseau.

ausstopfen [ˈausʃtɔpfən], *v.a.* stuff.

ausstoßen [ˈausʃtoːsən], *v.a. irr.* push out, expel; utter.

Ausstrahlung [ˈausʃtraːluŋ], *f.* (—, *pl.* —en) radiation.

ausstrecken [ˈausʃtrɛkən], *v.a.* stretch out, reach out, extend.

ausstreichen [ˈausʃtraɪçən], *v.a. irr.* strike out, erase, delete; smoothe.

ausstreuen [ˈausʃtrɔyən], *v.a.* scatter, spread, sprinkle; *Gerüchte —,* circulate rumours.

ausstudieren [ˈausʃtudiːrən], *v.n.* finish o.'s studies; graduate.

aussuchen [ˈauszuːxən], *v.a.* select.

Austausch [ˈaustauʃ], *m.* (—es, *pl.* —e) barter, exchange; *(thoughts, letters)* interchange.

austauschen [ˈaustauʃən], *v.a.* barter, exchange; *(thoughts, letters)* interchange.

austeilen [ˈaustaɪlən], *v.a.* distribute, allocate.

Auster [ˈaustər], *f.* (—, *pl.* —n) oyster.

Austerbank [ˈaustərbaŋk], *f.* (—, *pl.* ˙-e) oyster-bed.

austilgen [ˈaustɪlgən], *v.a.* exterminate, eradicate, extirpate.

Australien [auˈstraːljən], *n.* Australia.

austreiben [ˈaustraɪbən], *v.a. irr.* drive out, expel; exorcise.

austreten [ˈaustreːtən], *v.a. irr.* tread out; stretch (shoes) by walking; *ausgetretene Stufen,* worn steps. — *v.n. (aux. sein)* retire (from business); withdraw (from a club); *(coll.)* go to the lavatory.

Austritt [ˈaustrɪt], *m.* (—s, *pl.* —e) withdrawal, retirement.

ausüben [ˈausyːbən], *v.a.* exercise, practise; exert, commit.

Ausverkauf [ˈausfɛrkauf], *m.* (—s, *pl.* ˙-e) selling-off, clearance sale.

Auswahl [ˈausvaːl], *f.* (—, *pl.* —en) choice, selection.

Auswanderer [ˈausvandərər], *m.* (—s, *pl.* —) emigrant.

auswärtig [ˈausvɛrtɪç], *adj.* foreign, away.

auswärts [ˈausvɛrts], *adv.* outward(s), away from home.

auswechseln [ˈausvɛksəln], *v.a.* exchange; fit (spare parts).

Ausweg [ˈausveːk], *m.* (—s, *pl.* —e) expedient; way out; *ich weiß keinen —,* I am at my wits' end.

ausweichen [ˈausvaɪçən], *v.n. irr. (aux. sein)* give way; evade, parry.

Ausweis [ˈausvaɪs], *m.* (—es, *pl.* —e) proof of identity, identity card.

ausweisen [ˈausvaɪzən], *v.a. irr.* turn out, banish, exile, deport. — *v.r. (aux. haben) sich —,* show proof of o.'s identity.

auswendig [ˈausvɛndɪç], *adj.* by heart.

auswirken [ˈausvɪrkən], *v.r. sich gut —,* work out well, have a good effect.

Auswuchs [ˈausvuːks], *m.* (—es, *pl.* ˙-e) sprouting, outgrowth, (*fig.*) excrescence.

Auswurf [ˈausvurf], *m.* (—s, *pl.* ˙-e) excretion; expectoration; — *der Menschheit,* scum of the earth.

auszählen [ˈaustsɛːlən], *v.n.* count, number. — *v.a.* count out.

Auszahlung [ˈaustsaːluŋ], *f.* (—, *pl.* —en) payment.

auszanken [ˈaustsaŋkən], *v.a.* scold, chide.

auszehren [ˈaustseːrən], *v.n. (aux. sein)* waste away, be consumed.

auszeichnen [ˈaustsaɪçnən], *v.a.* mark out, honour, decorate. — *v.r. sich —,* distinguish o.s.

Auszeichnung [ˈaustsaɪçnuŋ], *f.* (—, *pl.* —en) distinction, medal.

Baltikum

ausziehen ['austsi:ən], *v.a. irr.* undress,
take off (clothes); (*Chem.*) extract;
stretch. — *v.n.* (*aux.* sein) move out.
— *v.r. sich* —, undress.

auszischen ['austsɪʃən], *v.a.* (*Theat.*)
hiss, cat-call.

Auszug ['austsu:k], *m.* (—s, *pl.* ⁻e)
removal (from home); marching off;
exodus; extract (from a book),
abstract (from a deed).

Auto ['auto], *n.* (—s, *pl.* —s) motor-
car, (*Am.*) automobile.

Autogramm [auto'gram], *n.* (—s, *pl.*
—e) autograph.

Automat [auto'ma:t], *m.* (—en, *pl.* —en)
slot machine.

Autor ['autɔr], *m.* (—s, *pl.* —en) author,
writer.

Autorität [autori'tɛ:t], *f.* (—, *pl.* —en)
authority.

avisieren [avi'zi:rən], *v.a.* notify, advise.

Axt [akst], *f.* (—, *pl.* ⁻e) axe.

Azur [a'tsu:r], *m.* (—s, *no pl.*) azure.

B

B [be:], *n.* (—s, *pl.*—s) the letter B;
(*Mus.*) B flat; — *Dur,* B flat major;
— *Moll,* B flat minor.

Bach [bax], *m.* (—es, *pl.* ⁻e) brook,
rivulet.

Bachstelze ['baxʃtɛltsə], *f.* (—, *pl.*
—n) wagtail.

Backe ['bakə], *f.* (—, *pl.* —n) cheek.

backen ['bakən], *v.a.* bake.

Backenstreich ['bakənʃtraɪç], *m.* (—s,
pl. —e) box on the ear.

Bäcker ['bɛkər], *m.* (—s, *pl.* —) baker.

Backfisch ['bakfɪʃ], *m.* (—es, *pl.* —e)
(*fig.*) teenage girl.

Backhuhn ['bakhu:n], *n.* (—s, *pl.* ⁻er)
fried chicken.

Backobst ['bakopst], *n.* (—es, *no pl.*)
dried fruit.

Backpfeife ['bakpfaɪfə], *f.* (—, *pl.* —n)
box on the ear.

Backpflaume ['bakpflaumə], *f.* (—, *pl.*
—n) prune.

Backstein ['bakʃtaɪn], *m.* (—s, *pl.* —e)
brick.

Backwerk ['bakvɛrk], *n.* (—s, *no pl.*)
pastry.

Bad [ba:t], *n.* (—es, *pl.* ⁻er) bath; spa,
watering-place.

Badeanstalt ['ba:dəanʃtalt], *f.* (—, *pl.*
—en) public baths.

baden ['ba:dən], *v.n.* bathe, have a bath.

Badewanne ['ba:dəvanə], *f.* (—, *pl.*
—n) bath-tub.

Bagage [ba'ga:ʒə], *f.* (—, *no pl.*) luggage; (*Am.*) baggage; (*sl.*) mob, rabble.

Bagger ['bagər], *m.* (—s, *pl.* —)
dredger, dredging-machine.

baggern ['bagərn], *v.a.* dredge.

Bahn [ba:n], *f.* (—, *pl.* —en) road, path,
course; (*Astr.*) orbit; railway(-line);
— *brechen,* open a path.

bahnbrechend ['ba:nbrɛçənt], *adj.*
pioneering, epoch-making.

bahnen ['ba:nən], *v.a.* make passable;
pave (the way).

Bahngleis ['ba:nglaɪs], *n.* (—es, *pl.*
—e) railway-line, railway-track; (*Am.*)
railroad-line, railroad-track.

Bahnhof ['ba:nho:f], *m.* (—s, *pl.* ⁻e)
railway-station, (*Am.*) depot.

Bahnsteig ['ba:nʃtaɪk], *m.* (—s, *pl.* —e)
platform.

Bahnwärter ['ba:nvɛrtər], *m.* (—s, *pl.*
—) signal-man.

Bahre ['ba:rə], *f.* (—, *pl.* —n) litter,
stretcher; bier.

Bahrtuch ['ba:rtu:x], *n.* (—s, *pl.* ⁻er)
pall, shroud.

Bai [baɪ], *f.* (—, *pl.* —en) bay, cove.

Baisse ['bɛsə], *f.* (—, *pl.* —n) (*Comm.*)
fall in share prices.

Bakkalaureat [bakalaure'a:t], *n.* (—s,
pl. —e) bachelor's degree.

Bakterie [bak'te:rjə], *f.* (—, *pl.* —n)
bacterium.

bald [balt], *adv.* soon, shortly, directly,
presently.

Baldachin ['baldaxɪn], *m.* (—s, *pl.* —e)
canopy.

baldig ['baldɪç], *adj.* quick, speedy; *auf
—es Wiedersehen,* see you again soon.

Baldrian ['baldria:n], *m.* (—s, *no pl.*)
valerian.

Balearen, die [balɛ'a:rən, di:], *pl.*
Balearic Islands.

Balg (1) [balk], *m.* (—s, *pl.* ⁻e) skin,
slough, husk; bellows (of organ *or*
forge).

Balg (2) [balk], *n.* (—s, *pl.* ⁻er) brat;
naughty child.

balgen ['balgən], *v.r. sich* —, (*children*)
fight, romp.

Balgerei ['balgəraɪ], *f.* (—, *pl.* —en)
scuffle, scrimmage.

Balken ['balkən], *m.* (—s, *pl.* —) beam,
joist, rafter.

Balkenwerk ['balkənvɛrk], *n.* (—s, *no
pl.*) building-frame, timbers, woodwork.

Balkon [bal'kɔ̃], *m.* (—s, *pl.* —s, —e)
balcony.

Ball [bal], *m.* (—s, *pl.* ⁻e) ball; globe;
sphere; dance.

ballen ['balən], *v.a.* form into a ball;
clench (o.'s fist).

Ballen ['balən], *m.* (—s, *pl.* —) bale,
bundle, package; ball (of the hand *or*
foot).

ballförmig ['balfœrmɪç], *adj.* spherical.

Ballistik [ba'lɪstɪk], *f.* (—, *no pl.*)
ballistics.

Ballon [ba'lɔ̃], *m.* (—s, *pl.* —s, —e)
balloon.

Balsam ['balza:m], *m.* (—s, *pl.* —e)
balm, balsam.

Baltikum ['baltɪkum], *n.* (—s, *no pl.*)
the Baltic countries.

21

Bambusrohr

Bambusrohr ['bambusro:r], *n.* (—**s**, *pl.* —**e**) bamboo (cane).

Banane [ba'na:nə], *f.* (—, *pl.* —**n**) banana.

Banause [ba'nauzə], *m.* (—**n**, *pl.* —**n**) narrow-minded person, philistine.

Band (1) [bant], *n.* (—**s**, *pl.* ∙er) ribbon, riband, tape; string; (*Bot.*) band; hoop (*for a cask*); (*Anat.*) ligament, tendon.

Band (2) [bant], *n.* (—**s**, *pl.* —**e**) (*fig.*) bond, fetter, chain, (*pl.*) bonds, ties (*of friendship*).

Band (3) [bant], *m.* (—**es**, *pl.* ∙e) volume.

Bändchen ['bentçən], *n.* (—**s**, *pl.* —) small ribbon, small piece of string; (*book*) small volume.

Bande ['bandə], *f.* (—, *pl.* —**n**) horde, gang, set.

bändigen ['bendɪgən], *v.a.* tame, subdue.

Bandmaß ['bantma:s], *n.* (—**es**, *pl.* —**e**) tape-measure.

Bandwurm ['bantvurm], *m.* (—**s**, *pl.* ∙er) (*Zool.*) tape-worm.

bange ['baŋə], *adj.* afraid, worried, alarmed.

Bangigkeit ['baŋɪçkaɪt], *f.* (—, *no pl.*) uneasiness, anxiety.

Bank (1) [baŋk], *f.* (—, *pl.* ∙e) bench, seat (in a park); *auf die lange — schieben,* delay, shelve; *durch die —,* without exception.

Bank (2) [baŋk], *f.* (—, *pl.* —**en**) bank; *die — sprengen,* break the bank.

Bänkelsänger ['beŋkəlzeŋər], *m.* (—**s**, *pl.* —) ballad singer.

bank(e)rott [baŋk'rɔt], *adj.* bankrupt.

Bankett [baŋ'ket], *n.* (—**s**, *pl.* —**e**) banquet.

Bankkonto ['baŋkkɔnto], *n.* (—**s**, *pl.* —**ten**) bank-account.

Bann [ban], *m.* (—**s**, *no pl.*) ban, exile; (*Eccl.*) excommunication; *in den — tun,* outlaw, (*Eccl.*) excommunicate; (*fig.*) charm, spell.

bannen ['banən], *v.a.* banish, exile, cast out.

Banner ['banər], *n.* (—**s**, *pl.* —) banner, standard.

Bannmeile ['banmaɪlə], *f.* (—, *pl.* —**n**) boundary.

bar [ba:r], *adv.* in cash, ready money.

Bar [ba:r], *f.* (—, *pl.* —**s**) bar (for selling drinks etc.).

Bär [be:r], *m.* (—**en**, *pl.* —**en**) (*Zool.*) bear; *einem einen —en aufbinden,* to lead s.o. up the garden-path.

Barauslagen ['barausla:gən], *f. pl.* cash expenses.

Barbar [bar'ba:r], *m.* (—**en**, *pl.* —**en**) barbarian, vandal.

barbarisch [bar'ba:rɪʃ], *adj.* barbarous.

Barbestand [bar'rbəʃtant], *m.* (—**s**, *pl.* ∙e) cash reserve, cash balance.

bärbeißig ['be:rbaɪsɪç], *adj.* surly, morose.

Barchent ['barçənt], *m.* (—**s**, *no pl.*) fustian.

Barde ['bardə], *m.* (—**n**, *pl.* —**n**) bard, minstrel.

Bärenfell ['be:rənfel], *n.* (—**s**, *pl.* —**e**) bear-skin.

Bärenmütze ['be:rənmytsə], *f.* (—, *pl.* —**n**) (*Mil.*) busby.

Bärenzwinger ['be:rəntsvɪŋər], *m.* (—**s**, *pl.* —) bear-garden.

Barett [ba'ret], *n.* (—**s**, *pl.* —**e**) cap, beret; (*Eccl.*) biretta.

barfuß ['barfus], *adj.* barefoot(ed).

Bargeld ['bargelt], *n.* (—(**e**)**s**, *no pl.*) cash.

barhäuptig ['barhɔyptɪç], *adj.* bareheaded.

Barkasse [bar'kasə], *f.* (—, *pl.* —**n**) launch.

Barke ['barkə], *f.* (—, *pl.* —**n**) barge, lighter.

barmherzig [barm'hertsɪç], *adj.* merciful, charitable, compassionate.

Barock [ba'rɔk], *n.* (—**s**, *no pl.*) Baroque.

Baronin [ba'ro:nɪn], *f.* (—, *pl.* —**nen**) baroness.

Barren ['barən], *m.* (—**s**, *pl.* —) parallel bars.

Barsch [barʃ], *m.* (—**es**, *pl.* —**e**) (*Zool.*) perch.

barsch [barʃ], *adj.* rough, harsh, sharp, abrupt, unfriendly.

Barschaft ['ba:rʃaft], *f.* (—, *pl.* —**en**) ready money.

Bart [ba:rt], *m.* (—**s**, *pl.* ∙e) beard; (*key*) ward.

Bartflechte ['ba:rtfleçtə], *f.* (—, *pl.* —**n**) barber's itch.

bärtig ['be:rtɪç], *adj.* bearded.

Basalt [ba'zalt], *m.* (—**s**, *pl.* —**e**) (*Min.*) basalt.

Base ['ba:zə], *f.* (—, *pl.* —**n**) female cousin; (*Chem.*) base.

Basis ['ba:zɪs], *f.* (—, *pl.* **Basen**) base, foundation.

Baskenmütze ['baskənmytsə], *f.* (—, *pl.* —**n**) tam-o'-shanter, beret.

Baß [bas], *m.* (—**sses**, *pl.* ∙**sse**) (*Mus.*) bass.

Baßschlüssel ['basʃlysəl], *m.* (—**s**, *pl.* —) (*Mus.*) bass-clef.

Bassin [ba'sɛ̃], *n.* (—**s**, *pl.* —**s**) basin, reservoir.

Bast [bast], *m.* (—**es**, *pl.* —**e**) inner bark, fibre (*of trees etc.*); bast.

basta ['basta], *int.* and that's that!

Bastei [bas'taɪ], *f.* (—, *pl.* —**en**) bastion.

basteln ['bastəln], *v.a.* work on a hobby, tinker.

Batist [ba'tɪst], *m.* (—**s**, *pl.* —**e**) cambric.

Bau [bau], *m.* (—**es**, *pl.* —**ten**) building, structure, edifice; act of building; *im — begriffen,* in course of construction.

Bauart ['bauart], *f.* (—, *pl.* —**en**) (architectural) style, structure.

Bauch [baux], *m.* (—**es**, *pl.* ∙e) belly, stomach.

Bauchfell ['bauxfel], *n.* (—**s**, *pl.* —**e**) peritoneum.

bauchig ['bauçtç], *adj.* bulgy.
Bauchredner ['bauxre:dnər], *m.* (—s, *pl.* —) ventriloquist.
bauen ['bauən], *v.a.* build, construct, erect. — *v.n. auf etwas* —, (*fig.*) rely on s.th., count on s.th.
Bauer (1) ['bauər], *m.* (—n, *pl.* —n) farmer, peasant; (*chess*) pawn.
Bauer (2) ['bauər], *n.* (—s, *pl.* —) (*bird*) cage.
Bauernfänger ['bauərnfeŋər], *m.* (—s, *pl.* —) sharper, rook, confidence-trickster.
Bäuerin ['bɔyərɪn], *f.* (—, *pl.* —nen) farmer's wife.
Bauernstand ['bauərnftant], *m.* (—s, *pl.* ⁻e) peasantry.
baufällig ['baufɛlɪç], *adj.* dilapidated, ramshackle.
Baugerüst ['baugəryst], *n.* (—s, *pl.* —e) scaffolding.
Baugewerbe ['baugəverbə], *n.* (—s, *no pl.*) building trade.
Baukunst ['baukunst], *f.* (—, *no pl.*) architecture.
Baum [baum], *m.* (—(e)s, *pl.* ⁻e) tree.
Baumeister ['baumaɪstər], *m.* (—s, *pl.* —) architect, master-builder.
baumeln ['bauməln], *v.n.* dangle.
Baumkuchen ['baumku:xən], *m.* (—s, *pl.* —) pyramid-cake.
Baumschule ['baumfu:lə], *f.* (—, *pl.* —n) plantation of trees, orchard, tree nursery.
Baumstamm ['baumftam], *m.* (—s, *pl.* ⁻e) stem, trunk.
Baumwolle ['baumvɔlə], *f.* (—, *pl.* —n) cotton.
Bauriß ['baurɪs], *m.* (—sses, *pl.* —sse) plan, architect's drawing.
Bausch [bauf], *m.* (—es, *pl.* ⁻e) pad, bolster; *in* — *und Bogen*, in the lump: all at once.
bauschig ['baufɪç], *adj.* baggy.
Bauwerk ['bauverk] *see* **Gebäude**.
Bayern ['baɪərn], *n.* Bavaria.
Bazar [ba'za:r], *m.* (—s, *pl.* —e) bazaar, fair, emporium.
beabsichtigen [bə'apzɪçtɪgən], *v.a.* aim at, intend, have in view.
beachten [bə'axtən], *v.a.* observe, pay attention to.
Beamte [bə'amtə], *m.* (—n, *pl.* —n) official, officer, civil servant.
Beamtin [bə'amtɪn], *f.* (—, *pl.* —nen) female official, female civil servant.
beängstigen [bə'ɛŋstɪgən], *v.a.* alarm, make afraid.
beanspruchen [bə'anfpruxən], *v.a.* demand, claim, lay claim to.
beanstanden [bə'anftandən], *v.a.* object to, raise objections to, query.
beantragen [bə'antra:gən], *v.a.* move, apply, lodge an application.
beantworten [bə'antvɔrtən], *v.a.* answer, reply to.
bearbeiten [bə'arbaɪtən], *v.a.* work (on); (*book, play*) adapt, arrange, revise; (*Agr.*) cultivate; (*fig.*) *einen* —, try to influence s.o., try to convince s.o.

Bearbeitung [bə'arbaɪtuŋ], *f.* (—, *pl.* —en) working, manipulation, operation; (*Agr.*) culture, cultivation; (*book, play*) adaptation, revision, arrangement.
beargwöhnen [bə'arkvø:nən], *v.a.* suspect, view with suspicion.
beaufsichtigen [bə'aufzɪçtɪgən], *v.a.* control, supervise, superintend.
beauftragen [bə'auftra:gən], *v.a.* commission, charge, authorize.
bebauen [bə'bauən], *v.a.* build upon; (*Agr.*) cultivate.
beben ['be:bən], *v.n.* shake, quake, tremble; *vor Kälte* —, shiver with cold.
Becher ['bɛçər], *m.* (—s, *pl.* —) beaker, cup, goblet, mug; (*dice*) box.
Becken ['bɛkən], *n.* (—s, *pl.* —) basin, bowl; (*Anat.*) pelvis; (*Mus.*) cymbal.
Bedacht [bə'daxt], *m.* (—s, *no pl.*) consideration; *mit* —, deliberately; *ohne* —, thoughtlessly.
bedächtig [bə'dɛçtɪç], *adj.* circumspect, deliberate, cautious, slow.
bedanken [bə'daŋkən], *v.r. sich für etwas* —, thank s.o. for s.th., decline with thanks (*also iron.*).
Bedarf [bə'darf], *m.* (—s, *no pl.*) need, requirement, demand.
bedauerlich [bə'dauərlɪç], *adj.* regrettable, deplorable.
bedauern [bə'dauərn], *v.a.* pity, commiserate, regret; *ich bedaure, daß*, I am sorry that . . .
bedecken [bə'dɛkən], *v.a.* cover (up); *sich mit Ruhm* —, cover o.s. with glory.
bedeckt [bə'dɛkt], *adj.* (*sky*) overcast.
bedenken [bə'dɛŋkən], *v.a. irr.* consider, bear in mind. — *v.r. sich* —, deliberate, hesitate; *sich anders* —, change o.'s mind.
bedenklich [bə'dɛŋklɪç], *adj.* (*persons*) doubtful, dubious; (*things*) risky, delicate, precarious; (*illness*) serious, grave.
Bedenkzeit [bə'dɛŋktsaɪt], *f.* (—, *pl.* —en) time to consider, respite.
bedeuten [bə'dɔytən], *v.a.* signify, mean, imply; direct, order.
bedeutend [bə'dɔytənt], *adj.* important, eminent, considerable, outstanding.
bedeutsam [bə'dɔytza:m], *adj.* significant.
Bedeutung [bə'dɔytuŋ], *f.* (—, *pl.* —en) significance, meaning; consequence, importance; *nichts von* —, nothing to speak of.
bedienen [bə'di:nən], *v.a.* serve, attend to, wait on; (*machine*) operate; (*Cards*) follow suit. —*v.r. sich* —, help o.s., make use of.
Bediente [bə'di:ntə], *m.* (—n, *pl.* —n) servant, attendant, footman, lackey.
Bedienung [bə'di:nuŋ], *f.* (—, *pl.* —en) service, attendance.
bedingen [bə'dɪŋən], *v.a.* stipulate, postulate, condition, cause.

23

bedingt

bedingt [bə'dıŋkt], *adj.* conditional.
Bedingung [bə'dıŋuŋ], *f.* (—, *pl.* —en) stipulation, condition, term; *unter keiner* —, on no account.
bedingungsweise [bə'dıŋuŋsvaızə], *adv.* on condition, conditionally.
bedrängen [bə'drɛŋən], *v.a.* oppress; press hard, afflict.
Bedrängnis [bə'drɛŋnıs], *n.* (—ses, *pl.* —se) oppression, distress.
bedrohen [bə'dro:ən], *v.a.* threaten, menace.
bedrohlich [bə'dro:lıç], *adj.* threatening, menacing, ominous.
bedrücken [bə'drykən], *v.a.* oppress, harass, depress.
Beduine [bedu'i:nə], *m.* (—n, *pl.* —n) Bedouin.
bedünken [bə'dyŋkən], *v.a.* appear, seem; *es bedünkt mich,* methinks.
bedürfen [bə'dyrfən], *v.n. irr.* want, need, be in need of.
Bedürfnis [bə'dyrfnıs], *n.* (—ses, *pl.* —se) want, need, requirement, necessity; *es ist mir ein* —, I cannot but; *einem dringenden* — *abhelfen,* meet an urgent want *or* need; *ein* — *haben, (coll.)* need to relieve o.s.
Bedürfnisanstalt [bə'dyrfnısanʃtalt], *f.* (—, *pl.* —en) public lavatory, public convenience.
bedürftig [bə'dyrftıç], *adj.* needy, indigent, poor.
beeidigen [bə'aıdıgən], *v.a.* confirm by oath, swear in.
beeifern [bə'aıfərn], *v.r. sich* —, exert o.s., strive, be zealous.
beeilen [bə'aılən], *v.r. sich* —, hurry, hasten, make haste.
beeindrucken [bə'aındrukən], *v.a.* impress.
beeinflussen [bə'aınflusən], *v.a.* influence.
beeinträchtigen [bə'aıntrɛçtıgən], *v.a.* injure, lessen, diminish, detract from, curtail.
beenden [bə'ɛndən], *v.a.* end, finish, terminate, conclude.
beendigen [bə'ɛndıgən], *v.a.* end, finish, terminate, conclude.
beengen [bə'ɛŋən], *v.a.* cramp, narrow.
beerben [bə'ɛrbən], *v.a. einen* —, inherit from s.o.
beerdigen [bə'e:rdıgən], *v.a.* bury, inter.
Beere ['be:rə], *f.* (—, *pl.* —n) berry.
Beet [be:t], *n.* (—es, *pl.* —e) (flower) bed.
befähigen [bə'fɛ:ıgən], *v.a.* fit, enable, qualify.
Befähigung [bə'fɛ:ıguŋ], *f.* (—, *pl.* —en) qualification, capacity, aptitude.
befahren [bə'fa:rən], *v.a. irr.* pass over, travel over; *(Naut.)* navigate.
befallen [bə'falən], *v.a. irr.* befall, fall on; *von Traurigkeit* — *sein,* be overcome by sadness.
befangen [bə'faŋən], *adj.* biased, prejudiced; bashful, embarrassed.

befassen [bə'fasən], *v.a.* touch, handle. — *v.r. sich mit etwas* —, occupy o.s. with s.th.
befehden [bə'fe:dən], *v.a.* make war upon, show enmity towards.
Befehl [bə'fe:l], *m.* (—s, *pl.* —e) order, command; *(Mil.) zu* —, very good, sir; *(Mil.) den* — *führen über,* command.
befehlen [bə'fe:lən], *v.a. irr.* order, command.
befehligen [bə'fe:lıgən], *v.a. (Mil.)* command, head.
Befehlshaber [bə'fe:lsha:bər], *m.* (—s, *pl.* —) commander, commanding officer, chief.
befehlswidrig [bə'fe:lsvi:drıç], *adj.* contrary to orders.
befestigen [bə'fɛstıgən], *v.a.* fasten, fix, attach, affix; *(Mil.)* fortify; strengthen.
befeuchten [bə'fɔyçtən], *v.a.* wet, moisten, dampen.
Befinden [bə'fındən], *n.* (—s, *no pl.*) state of health.
befinden [bə'fındən], *v.a. irr.* think, deem, find. — *v.r. sich an einem Ort* —, be in some place; *sich wohl* —, feel well.
befindlich [bə'fıntlıç], *adj.* existing — *sein,* be contained in.
beflecken [bə'flɛkən], *v.a.* stain, spot, blot; defile, pollute.
befleißigen [bə'flaısıgən], *v.r. sich* —, devote o.s. to, take pains to.
beflissen [bə'flısən], *adj.* eager to serve, assiduous.
beflügeln [bə'fly:gəln], *v.a.* give wings; *(fig.)* accelerate, animate.
befolgen [bə'fɔlgən], *v.a.* follow, obey; *einen Befehl* —, comply with an order.
befördern [bə'fœrdərn], *v.a.* despatch, forward, send, post, mail, transmit; promote, advance.
Beförderung [bə'fœrdəruŋ], *f.* (—, *pl.* —en) forwarding, transmission; *(office)* promotion, advancement.
Beförderungsmittel [bə'fœrdəruŋsmıtəl], *n.* (—s, *pl.* —) conveyance, means of transport.
befragen [bə'fra:gən], *v.a.* question, interrogate, examine.
befreien [bə'fraıən], *v.a.* free, liberate.
befremden [bə'frɛmdən], *v.a.* appear strange, astonish, surprise.
befreunden [bə'frɔyndən], *v.a.* befriend. — *v.r. sich mit einem* —, make friends with s.o.
befriedigen [bə'fri:dıgən], *v.a.* content, satisfy; appease, calm.
befruchten [bə'fruxtən], *v.a.* fertilise; impregnate.
Befugnis [bə'fu:knıs], *f.* (—, *pl.* —se) authority, right, warrant.
Befund [bə'funt], *m.* (—s, *pl.* —e) *(Med.)* diagnosis, findings.
befürchten [bə'fyrçtən], *v.a.* fear, be afraid of.
befürworten [bə'fy:rvɔrtən], *v.a.* support, second.

24

begabt [bəˈgaːpt], *adj.* gifted, talented, able.

Begabung [bəˈgaːbuŋ], *f.* (—, *pl.* —en) ability, talent, gift.

begaffen [bəˈgafən], *v.a.* stare at, gape at.

begatten [bəˈgatən], *v.r. sich* —, (*Zool.*) copulate.

begeben [bəˈgeːbən], *v.r. irr. sich an einen Ort* —, go to a place, betake o.s. to a place; happen, occur.

Begebenheit [bəˈgeːbənhaɪt], *f.* (—, *pl.* —en) happening, event, occurrence.

begegnen [bəˈgeːgnən], *v.n.* (*aux.* sein) meet, meet with, encounter, befall, happen.

begehen [bəˈgeːən], *v.a. irr.* (*road*) walk along, go over; (*festival*) celebrate; (*crime*) commit, perpetrate.

begehren [bəˈgeːrən], *v.a.* desire, wish, covet, want.—*v.n. nach etwas* —, long for s.th.

begehrlich [bəˈgeːrlɪç], *adj.* covetous, greedy, desirous.

begeifern [bəˈgaɪfərn], *v.a.* spit at; (*fig.*) vilify, besmirch.

begeistern [bəˈgaɪstərn], *v.a.* inspire, fill with enthusiasm, enrapture.—*v.r. sich für etwas* —, become enthusiastic about s.th.

Begier(de) [bəˈgiːr(də)], *f.* (—, *pl.* —den) desire, lust, appetite.

begierig [bəˈgiːrɪç], *adj.* desirous, lustful; anxious; curious (for news).

begießen [bəˈgiːsən], *v.a. irr.* (*plants*) water; (*meat etc.*) baste; *etwas festlich* —, celebrate s.th. by drinking; *sich die Nase* —, (*coll.*) get tight.

Beginn [bəˈgɪn], *m.* (—s, *no pl.*) beginning, commencement, start.

beginnen [bəˈgɪnən], *v.a.,v.n. irr.* begin, commence, start.

beglaubigen [bəˈglaubɪgən], *v.a.* attest; certify, verify; accredit (an ambassador).

Beglaubigungsschreiben [bəˈglaubɪguŋsʃraibən], *n.* (—s, *pl.* —) credentials.

begleichen [bəˈglaɪçən], *v.a. irr.* (*bill*) pay, settle.

begleiten [bəˈglaɪtən], *v.a.* accompany, escort, see s.o. off, home etc.

Begleiter [bəˈglaɪtər], *m.* (—s, *pl.* —) companion, escort; (*Mus.*) accompanist.

Begleiterscheinung [bəˈglaɪtərʃaɪnuŋ], *f.* (—, *pl.* —en) concomitant; (*Med.*) complication, attendant symptom.

Begleitung [bəˈglaɪtuŋ], *f.* (—, *pl.* —en) company; (*Mus.*) accompaniment.

beglücken [bəˈglykən], *v.a.* make happy.

beglückwünschen [bəˈglykvynʃən], *v.a.* congratulate.

begnadet [bəˈgnaːdət], *adj.* highly talented.

begnadigen [bəˈgnaːdiːgən], *v.a.* pardon, reprieve.

begnügen [bəˈgnyːgən], *v.r. sich mit etwas* —, content o.s. with s.th.

Begonie [bəˈgoːnjə], *f.* (—, *pl.* —n) (*Bot.*) begonia.

begraben [bəˈgraːbən], *v.a. irr.* bury, inter.

Begräbnis [bəˈgrɛːpnɪs], *n.* (—ses, *pl.* —se) burial, funeral, interment.

begreifen [bəˈgraɪfən], *v.a. irr.* understand, comprehend, conceive.

begreiflich [bəˈgraɪflɪç], *adj.* comprehensible, conceivable, understandable.

begrenzen [bəˈgrɛntsən], *v.a.* bound, border, limit.

Begriff [bəˈgrɪf], *m.* (—s, *pl.* —e) notion, concept, idea, conception; *im — sein*, be about to . . . .

begriffen [bəˈgrɪfən], *adj.* — *sein in*, be engaged in.

begriffsstutzig [bəˈgrɪfsʃtutsɪç], *adj.* obtuse, dense, slow in the uptake.

begründen [bəˈgryndən], *v.a.* base on, justify; found, establish.

begrüßen [bəˈgryːsən], *v.a.* greet, salute, welcome.

begünstigen [bəˈgynstɪgən], *v.a.* favour, prefer.

Begutachter [bəˈguːtaxtər], *m.* (—s, *pl.* —) expert; (*Sch.*) assessor, second examiner.

Begutachtung [bəˈguːtaxtuŋ], *f.* (—, *pl.* —en) expert opinion, assessment, report.

begütert [bəˈgyːtərt], *adj.* wealthy, rich, well-to-do.

behaart [bəˈhaːrt], *adj.* covered with hair, hairy.

behäbig [bəˈhɛːbɪç], *adj.* comfortable; corpulent, portly.

behaften [bəˈhaftən], *v.a.* charge, burden.

behagen [bəˈhaːgən], *v.n.* please, be agreeable; *es behagt mir nicht*, I do not like it.

behaglich [bəˈhaːklɪç], *adj.* cosy, comfortable, snug.

behalten [bəˈhaltən], *v.a. irr.* retain, keep.

Behälter [bəˈhɛltər], *m.* (—s, *pl.* —) container; box, bin; (*water*) reservoir; tank.

behandeln [bəˈhandəln], *v.a.* treat, use; (*Med.*) treat; (*subject*) treat; handle.

Behandlung [bəˈhandluŋ], *f.* (—, *pl.* —en) treatment, use; (*Med.*) treatment.

Behang [bəˈhaŋ], *m.* (—es, *pl.* ⸚e) hanging(s); appendage.

behängen [bəˈhɛŋən], *v.a. irr.* festoon with, drape.

beharren [bəˈharən], *v.n.* persevere, persist, insist.

beharrlich [bəˈharlɪç], *adj.* persevering, persistent, constant, firm.

behauen [bəˈhauən], *v.a.* (*stones*) hew, cut.

behaupten [bəˈhauptən], *v.a.* claim, assert, affirm, maintain.

Behauptung

Behauptung [bə'hauptuŋ], *f.* (—, *pl.* —en) claim, assertion, affirmation.

Behausung [bə'hauzuŋ], *f.* (—, *pl.* —en) habitation, housing.

behelfen [bə'hɛlfən], *v.r. irr. sich — mit*, make do with.

behelfsmäßig [bə'hɛlfsmɛ:sɪç], *adj.* makeshift, temporary.

behelligen [bə'hɛlɪgən], *v.a.* trouble, molest, disturb.

behend(e) [bə'hɛndə], *adj.* quick, nimble, agile.

beherbergen [bə'hɛrbergən], *v.a.* give shelter to, put up, harbour.

beherrschen [bə'hɛrʃən], *v.a.* rule, govern, dominate; *eine Sache —*, master a subject. *— v.r. sich —*, control o.s.

Beherrschung [bə'hɛrʃuŋ], *f.* (—, *pl.* (*rare*) —en) domination, sway; (*subject*) grasp; (*languages*) command.

beherzigen [bə'hɛrtsɪgən], *v.a.* take to heart, follow, heed.

Beherztheit [bə'hɛrtsthaɪt], *f.* (—, *no pl.*) courage, spirit.

behexen [bə'hɛksən], *v.a.* bewitch.

behilflich [bə'hɪlflɪç], *adj.* helpful, useful.

behindern [bə'hɪndərn], *v.a.* hinder, hamper.

Behörde [bə'hœrdə], *f.* (—, *pl.* —n) the authorities.

behufs [bə'hu:fs], *prep.* (*Genit.*) in order to, with a view to.

behüten [bə'hy:tən], *v.a.* guard, protect; *Gott behüte!* Heaven forbid!

behutsam [bə'hu:tza:m], *adj.* careful, cautious.

bei [baɪ], *prep.* (*Dat.*) (*locally*) near by, close by, next to, at.

beibehalten ['baɪbəhaltən], *v.a. irr.* keep, retain.

Beiblatt ['baɪblat], *n.* (—s, *pl.* ⁀er) supplement (to a newspaper).

beibringen ['baɪbrɪŋən], *v.a. irr.* adduce (proof); produce (witnesses); (*fig.*) teach; impart to.

Beichte ['baɪçtə], *f.* (—, *pl.* —n) confession.

Beichtstuhl ['baɪçtʃtu:l], *m.* (—s, *pl.* ⁀e) confessional.

beide ['baɪdə], *adj.* both, either, the two.

beiderlei ['baɪdərlaɪ], *adj.* of both kinds.

beidrehen ['baɪdre:ən], *v.n.* (*Naut.*) heave to.

Beifall ['baɪfal], *m.* (—s, *no pl.*) (*verbal*) approbation; (*shouting*) acclamation, acclaim; (*clapping*) applause.

beifällig ['baɪfɛlɪç], *adj.* favourable, approving, assenting.

beifügen ['baɪfy:gən], *v.a.* enclose, attach.

Beifuß ['baɪfu:s], *m.* (—es, *no pl.*) (*Bot.*) mugwort.

beigeben ['baɪge:bən], *v.a. irr.* add, join to. *— v.n. klein —*, give in.

Beigeschmack ['baɪgəʃmak], *m.* (—s, *no pl.*) aftertaste, tang.

beigesellen ['baɪgəzɛlən], *v.r. sich —*, associate with.

Beihilfe ['baɪhɪlfə], *f.* (—, *pl.* —n) aid, assistance, subsidy.

beikommen ['baɪkɔmən], *v.n. irr.* (*aux.* sein) *einer Sache —*, to grapple with s.th.; *ich kann ihm nicht —*, I cannot catch him out, get at him.

Beil [baɪl], *n.* (—s, *pl.* —e) hatchet, axe.

Beilage ['baɪla:gə], *f.* (—, *pl.* —n) enclosure (with a letter); supplement (to a newspaper); *Braten mit —*, joint with vegetables.

beiläufig ['baɪlɔyfɪç], *adv.* by the way, incidentally.

beilegen ['baɪle:gən], *v.a.* add, join; enclose (in letter).

beileibe [baɪ'laɪbə], *int. — nicht!* on no account!

Beileid ['baɪlaɪt], *n.* (—s, *no pl.*) condolence, sympathy.

beiliegen ['baɪli:gən], *v.n. irr.* be enclosed with.

beimengen ['baɪmɛŋən], *v.a.* (*Cul.*) mix with, add.

beimessen ['baɪmɛsən], *v.a. irr. einem etwas —*, impute s.th. to s.o.; *einem Glauben —*, credit s.o., give credence to.

Bein [baɪn], *n.* (—s, *pl.* —e) leg; *einem auf die —e helfen*, give a helping hand to s.o.

beinahe [baɪ'na:ə], *adv.* almost, nearly.

Beiname ['baɪna:mə], *m.* (—ns, *pl.* —n) surname; nickname.

Beinbruch ['baɪnbrux], *m.* (—s, *pl.* ⁀e) fracture of the leg; (*coll.*) *Hals- und Beinbruch!* good luck!

Beinkleider ['baɪnklaɪdər], *n. pl.* (*obs.*) pants, trousers.

beipflichten ['baɪpflɪçtən], *v.n. einem —*, agree with s.o.

beirren [bə'ɪrən], *v.a. sich nicht — lassen*, not let o.s. be dissuaded or put off.

beisammen [baɪ'zamən], *adv.* together.

Beischlaf ['baɪʃla:f], *m.* (—s, *no pl.*) cohabitation, coition.

Beisein ['baɪzaɪn], *n.* (—s, *no pl.*) *im — von*, in the presence of.

beiseite [baɪ'zaɪtə], *adv.* apart, aside; (*Theat.*) aside.

beisetzen ['baɪzɛtsən], *v.a.* bury, inter, entomb.

Beispiel ['baɪʃpi:l], *n.* (—s, *pl.* —e) example, instance; *zum —* (*abbr.* z.B.), for instance, for example.

beißen ['baɪsən], *v.a. irr.* bite; (*pepper, smoke*) burn, sting.

Beißzange ['baɪstsaŋə], *f.* (—, *pl.* —n) pair of pincers or nippers.

Beistand ['baɪʃtant], *m.* (—s, *pl.* ⁀e) assistance, help; (*Law*) counsel; *— leisten*, give assistance.

beistehen ['baɪʃte:ən], *v.n. irr. einem —*, stand by s.o., help s.o.

beisteuern ['baɪʃtɔyərn], *v.a. zu etwas —*, contribute to s.th.

beistimmen ['baɪʃtɪmən], *v.n.* agree with, assent.

Beistrich ['baɪʃtrɪç], *m.* (—(e)s, *pl.* —e) comma.

beitragen ['baɪtra:gən], *v.a. irr.* contribute; be conducive to.

beitreten ['baɪtre:tən], *v.n. irr.* (*aux.* sein) join (a club); enter into partnership with (a firm).

Beitritt ['baɪtrɪt], *m.* (—s, *no pl.*) accession, joining.

Beiwagen ['baɪva:gən], *m.* (—s, *pl.* —) trailer, sidecar (on motor cycle).

beiwohnen ['baɪvo:nən], *v.n.* be present at, attend.

Beiwort ['baɪvɔrt], *n.* (—s, *pl.* ˫er) adjective, epithet.

Beize ['baɪtsə], *f.* (—, *pl.* —n) caustic fluid; (*wood*) stain.

beizeiten [baɪ'tsaɪtən], *adv.* betimes, early, in good time.

beizen ['baɪtsən], *v.a.* cauterise; (*wood*) stain.

bejahen [bə'ja:ən], *v.a.* answer in the affirmative.

bejahrt [bə'ja:rt], *adj.* aged, elderly, old.

bejammern [bə'jamərn], *v.a.* bemoan, bewail.

bekannt [bə'kant], *adj.* known, well-known; — *mit,* acquainted with.

Bekannte [bə'kantə], *m.* (—n, *pl.* —n) acquaintance.

bekanntlich [bə'kantlɪç], *adv.* as is well known.

Bekanntmachung [bə'kantmaxuŋ], *f.* (—, *pl.* —en) publication, announcement.

Bekanntschaft [bə'kantʃaft], *f.* (—, *pl.* —en) — *mit einem machen,* strike up an acquaintance with s.o.

bekehren [bə'ke:rən], *v.a.* convert. — *v.r. sich* —, be converted *or* become a convert (to); reform.

bekennen [bə'kɛnən], *v.a. irr.* confess, profess; admit, own up to.

Bekenner [bə'kɛnər], *m.* (—s, *pl.* —) Confessor (as title).

Bekenntnis [bə'kɛntnɪs], *n.* (—ses, *pl.* —se) confession (of faith), avowal, creed.

beklagen [bə'kla:gən], *v.a.* lament, bewail, deplore. — *v.r. sich* — *über,* complain of.

Beklagte [bə'kla:ktə], *m.* (—n, *pl.* —n) (*Law*) defendant.

bekleiden [bə'klaɪdən], *v.a.* clothe, dress, cover; (*office*) hold.

Bekleidung [bə'klaɪduŋ], *f.* (—, *no pl.*) clothing, clothes; (*office*) administration, holding, exercise.

beklemmen [bə'klɛmən], *v.a. irr.* oppress.

Beklemmung [bə'klɛmuŋ], *f.* (—, *pl.* —en) oppression, anguish.

beklommen [bə'klɔmən], *adj.* anxious, uneasy.

bekommen [bə'kɔmən], *v.a. irr.* obtain, get, receive.

bekömmlich [bə'kœmlɪç], *adj.* beneficial; digestible, wholesome.

beköstigen [bə'kœstɪgən], *v.a.* board; feed.

bekräftigen [bə'krɛftɪgən], *v.a.* aver, corroborate, confirm.

bekränzen [bə'krɛntsən], *v.a.* wreathe, crown (with a garland).

bekreuzigen [bə'krɔytsɪgən], *v.r. sich* —, make the sign of the cross, cross o.s.

bekriegen [bə'kri:gən], *v.a.* make war on.

bekritteln [bə'krɪtəln], *v.a.* criticise, carp at, find fault with.

bekritzeln [bə'krɪtsəln], *v.a.* scrawl on, doodle on.

bekümmern [bə'kymərn], *v.a.* grieve, distress, trouble. — *v.r.* trouble o.s. about, grieve over.

bekunden [bə'kundən], *v.a.* manifest, show; declare.

beladen [bə'la:dən], *v.a. irr.* load.

Belag [bə'la:k], *m.* (—s, *pl.* ˫e) covering, layer; spread (on sandwiches); fur (on the tongue).

belagern [bə'la:gərn], *v.a.* besiege.

Belang [bə'laŋ], *m.* (—s, *pl.* —e) importance; *von* —, of great moment *or* consequence; (*pl.*) concerns, interests.

belangen [bə'laŋən], *v.a.* (*Law*) sue, prosecute.

belanglos [bə'laŋlo:s], *adj.* of small account; irrelevant, unimportant.

belassen [bə'lasən], *v.a. irr. es dabei* —, leave things as they are.

belasten [bə'lastən], *v.a.* load, burden; (*Comm.*) debit, charge; (*Law*) incriminate.

belästigen [bə'lɛstɪgən], *v.a.* bother, pester, molest.

Belastung [bə'lastuŋ], *f.* (—, *pl.* —en) load, burden; (*Comm.*) debiting; (*house*) mortgage; *erbliche* —, hereditary disposition.

Belastungszeuge [bə'lastuŋstsɔygə], *m.* (—n, *pl.* —n) witness for the prosecution.

belaubt [bə'laupt], *adj.* covered with leaves, leafy.

belaufen [bə'laufən], *v.r. irr. sich* — *auf,* amount to, come to.

belauschen [bə'lauʃən], *v.a.* eavesdrop, overhear.

beleben [bə'le:bən], *v.a.* animate, enliven.

Belebtheit [bə'le:pthaɪt], *f.* (—, *no pl.*) animation, liveliness.

Beleg [bə'le:k], *m.* (—s, *pl.* —e) document, proof, receipt, voucher.

belegen [bə'le:gən], *v.a.* cover, overlay; reserve, book (*seat*); support by documents, authenticate, prove.

Belegschaft [bə'le:kʃaft], *f.* (—, *pl.* —en) workers, personnel, staff; (*Min.*) gang, shift.

belegt [bə'le:kt], *adj.* (*tongue*) furred; —*es Brot,* sandwich.

belehnen [bə'le:nən], *v.a.* enfeoff; invest (with a fief).

belehren [bə'le:rən], *v.a.* instruct, advise, inform.

27

Belehrung [bə'le:ruŋ], *f.* (—, *pl.* —en) information, instruction, advice.

beleibt [bə'laɪpt], *adj.* stout, corpulent, obese.

beleidigen [bə'laɪdɪgən], *v.a.* insult, offend, give offence to.

belesen [bə'le:zən], *adj.* well-read.

beleuchten [bə'lɔyçtən], *v.a.* illumine, illuminate; (*fig.*) throw light on, elucidate.

Beleuchtungskörper [bə'lɔyçtuŋskœr-pər], *m.* (—s, *pl.* —) lighting fixture, lamp.

Belgien ['bɛlgjən], *n.* Belgium.

belichten [bə'lɪçtən], *v.a.* (*Phot.*) expose.

belieben [bə'li:bən], *v.a.*, *v.n.* please, like, choose.

beliebig [bə'li:bɪç], *adj.* optional; any, whatever.

beliebt [bə'li:pt], *adj.* popular, well-liked.

Beliebtheit [bə'li:pthaɪt], *f.* (—, *no pl.*) popularity.

bellen ['bɛlən], *v.n.* bark.

beloben [bə'lo:bən], *v.a.* praise, approve.

belohnen [bə'lo:nən], *v.a.* reward, recompense.

belügen [bə'ly:gən], *v.a. irr. einen* —, tell lies to s.o., deceive s.o. by lying.

belustigen [bə'lustɪgən], *v.a.* amuse, divert, entertain.

bemächtigen [bə'mɛçtɪgən], *v.r. sich einer Sache* —, take possession of s.th.

bemäkeln [bə'mɛ:kəln], *v.a.* find fault with.

bemalen [bə'ma:lən], *v.a.* paint (over).

bemängeln [bə'mɛŋəln], *v.a.* find fault with.

bemannen [bə'manən], *v.a.* man.

bemänteln [bə'mɛntəln], *v.a.* cloak, hide.

bemeistern [bə'maɪstərn], *v.a.* master.

bemerkbar [bə'mɛrkba:r], *adj.* perceptible, noticeable.

bemerken [bə'mɛrkən], *v.a.* observe, perceive, notice.

Bemerkung [bə'mɛrkuŋ], *f.* (—, *pl.* —en) remark, observation, note.

bemessen [bə'mɛsən], *v.a. irr.* measure; curtail.

bemitleiden [bə'mɪtlaɪdən], *v.a.* pity, be sorry for.

bemittelt [bə'mɪtəlt], *adj.* well-off, well-to-do.

bemoost [bə'mo:st], *adj.* mossy.

bemühen [bə'my:ən], *v.a.* trouble, give trouble (to). — *v.r. sich* —, take pains, strive, endeavour.

bemüht [bə'my:t], *adj.* studious; — *sein*, endeavour, try to.

bemuttern [bə'mutərn], *v.a.* mother.

benachbart [bə'naxba:rt], *adj.* neighbouring, adjacent.

benachrichtigen [bə'naxrɪçtɪgən], *v.a.* inform, give notice of, notify.

benachteiligen [bə'naxtaɪlɪgən], *v.a.* prejudice, discriminate against, handicap.

benagen [bə'na:gən], *v.a.* gnaw at.

benebeln [bə'ne:bəln], *v.a.* befog, cloud; (*fig.*) dim, intoxicate.

benedeien [bene'daɪən], *v.a.* bless, glorify.

Benediktiner [benedɪk'ti:nər], *m.* (—s, *pl.* —) (monk) Benedictine; Benedictine liqueur.

Benefiz [bene'fi:ts], *n.* (—es, *pl.* —e) benefit; benefit performance.

Benehmen [bə'ne:mən], *n.* (—s, *no pl.*) conduct, behaviour.

benehmen [bə'ne:mən], *v.r. irr. sich* —, behave, conduct o.s.

beneiden [bə'naɪdən], *v.a. einen* — *um*, envy s.o. (s.th.).

benennen [bə'nɛnən], *v.a.* name.

benetzen [bə'nɛtsən], *v.a.* moisten.

Bengel ['bɛŋəl], *m.* (—s, *pl.* —) naughty boy, scamp; rascal, lout.

benommen [bə'nɔmən], *adj.* dazed, giddy.

benötigen [bə'nø:tɪgən], *v.a.* be in need of, require.

benutzen [bə'nutsən], *v.a.* make use of, utilise.

Benzin [bɛnt'si:n], *n.* (—s, *no pl.*) benzine; (*Motor.*) petrol; (*Am.*) gas, gasoline.

beobachten [bə'o:baxtən], *v.a.* watch, observe.

bequem [bə'kve:m], *adj.* comfortable, easy; convenient; indolent, lazy.

bequemen [bə'kve:mən], *v.r. sich* —, condescend (to), comply (with).

Bequemlichkeit [bə'kve:mlɪçkaɪt], *f.* (—, *pl.* —en) convenience, ease; indolence.

beraten [bə'ra:tən], *v.a. irr.* advise, assist with advice, counsel. — *v.r. sich* — *mit*, confer with, consult with.

beratschlagen [bə'ra:tʃla:gən], *v.n.* deliberate with.

Beratung [bə'ra:tuŋ], *f.* (—, *pl.* —en) council, deliberation, consultation.

berauben [bə'raubən], *v.a.* rob, deprive (s.o.) of (s.th.).

berauschen [bə'rauʃən], *v.a.* intoxicate.

berechnen [bə'rɛçnən], *v.a.* compute, charge, calculate, estimate.

berechtigen [bə'rɛçtɪgən], *v.a. einen zu etwas* —, entitle s.o. to s.th.; authorise s.o. to have or do s.th.

beredsam [bə're:tza:m], *adj.* eloquent.

beredt [bə're:t], *adj.* eloquent.

Bereich [bə'raɪç], *m. & n.* (—s, *pl.* —e) extent, realm, sphere, scope.

bereichern [bə'raɪçərn], *v.a.* enrich, enlarge.

bereisen [bə'raɪzən], *v.a.* travel over or through, tour (a country).

bereit [bə'raɪt], *adj.* ready, prepared.

bereiten [bə'raɪtən], *v.a.* prepare, get ready.

bereits [bə'raɪts], *adv.* already.

Bereitschaft [bə'raɪtʃaft], *f.* (—, *no pl.*) readiness, preparedness.

bereitwillig [bə'raɪtvɪlɪç], *adj.* willing, ready, obliging.

bereuen [bə'rɔyən], *v.a.* repent, be sorry for, regret.

Berg [bɛrk], *m.* (—es, *pl.* —e) mountain, hill.

bergab [bɛrk'ap], *adj.* downhill.

Bergamt ['bɛrkamt], *n.* (—s, *pl.* ⁓er) mining-office, mine authority.

bergan [bɛrk'an], *adj.* uphill.

Bergarbeiter ['bɛrkarbaɪtər], *m.* (—s, *pl.* —) miner, collier.

bergauf [bɛrk'auf], *adj.* uphill.

Bergbau ['bɛrkbau], *m.* (—s, *no pl.*) mining, mining industry.

bergen ['bɛrgən], *v.a. irr.* shelter, protect, save; (*flotsam*) save, recover, salvage.

bergig ['bɛrgɪç], *adj.* mountainous, hilly.

Bergkristall ['bɛrkkrɪstal], *m.* (—s, *pl.* —e) rock-crystal.

Bergleute ['bɛrklɔytə], *pl.* miners, colliers.

Bergmann ['bɛrkman], *m.* (—s, *pl.* **Bergleute**) miner, collier.

Bergpredigt ['bɛrkpre:dɪçt], *f.* (—, *no pl.*) Sermon on the Mount.

Bergschlucht ['bɛrkʃluxt], *f.* (—, *pl.* —en) ravine, gorge.

Bergsteiger ['bɛrkʃtaɪgər], *m.* (—s, *pl.* —) mountaineer.

Bergstock ['bɛrkʃtɔk], *m.* (—s, *pl.* ⁓e) alpenstock.

Bergsturz ['bɛrkʃturts], *m.* (—es, *pl.* ⁓e) landslip, landslide.

Bergung ['bɛrguŋ], *f.* (—, *pl.* —en) sheltering, salvaging; rescue operation.

Bergwerk ['bɛrkvɛrk], *n.* (—s, *pl.* —e) mine, pit.

Bericht [bə'rɪçt], *m.* (—s, *pl.* —e) report, account, statement;—*erstatten*, report, give an account of.

Berichterstatter [bə'rɪçtərʃtatər], *m.* (—s, *pl.* —) reporter.

berichtigen [bə'rɪçtɪgən], *v.a.* set right, correct, rectify, amend.

berieseln [bə'ri:zəln], *v.a.* irrigate.

beritten [bə'rɪtən], *adj.* mounted on horseback.

Berlin [bɛr'li:n], *n.* Berlin; —*er Blau*, Prussian blue.

Bern [bɛrn], *n.* Berne.

Bernhardiner [bɛrnhar'di:nər], *m.* (—s, *pl.* —) Cistercian monk; Newfoundland dog, St. Bernard dog.

Bernstein ['bɛrnʃtaɪn], *m.* (—s, *no pl.*) amber.

bersten ['bɛrstən], *v.n. irr.* (*aux.* sein) burst.

berüchtigt [bə'ryçtɪçt], *adj.* notorious, infamous.

berücken [bə'rykən], *v.a.* enchant, fascinate.

berücksichtigen [bə'rykzɪçtɪgən], *v.a.* have regard to, take into consideration, allow for.

Beruf [bə'ru:f], *m.* (—s, *pl.* —e) profession, occupation, calling, trade.

berufen [bə'ru:fən], *v.a. irr.* (*meeting*) call, convene; appoint (to an office). — *v.r. sich* — *auf*, appeal to, refer to. — *adj.* competent, qualified.

berufsmäßig [bə'ru:fsmɛːsɪç], *adj.* professional.

Berufung [bə'ru:fuŋ], *f.* (—, *pl.* —en) call, vocation, appointment; (*Law*) appeal.

beruhen [bə'ru:ən], *v.n. auf etwas* —, be based on, be founded on.

beruhigen [bə'ru:gən], *v.a.* calm, pacify; comfort, console, set at rest.

Beruhigung [bə'ru:ɪguŋ], *f.* (—, *pl.* —en) reassurance, quieting, calming.

berühmt [bə'ry:mt], *adj.* famous, celebrated, illustrious, renowned.

berühren [bə'ry:rən], *v.a.* touch, handle; (*subject*) mention, touch upon; *peinlich berührt*, unpleasantly affected.

berußt [bə'ru:st], *adj.* sooty.

Beryll [be'ryl], *m.* (—s, *pl.* —e) beryl.

besagen [bə'za:gən], *v.a.* mean, signify.

besagt [bə'za:kt], *adj.* aforesaid, above-mentioned.

besaiten [bə'zaɪtən], *v.a.* fit with strings.

Besan [bə'za:n], *m.* (—s, *pl.* —e) (*Naut.*) miz(z)en.

besänftigen [bə'zɛnftɪgən], *v.a.* calm, appease, pacify.

Besatz [bə'zats], *m.* (—es, *pl.* ⁓e) trimming, border.

Besatzung [bə'zatsuŋ], *f.* (—, *pl.* —en) crew; (*Mil.*) garrison, occupation.

besaufen [bə'zaufən], *v.r. irr.* (*vulg.*) *sich* —, get drunk.

beschädigen [bə'ʃɛ:dɪgən], *v.a.* damage.

beschaffen [bə'ʃafən], *v.a.* procure, get. — *adj.* conditioned, constituted.

Beschaffenheit [bə'ʃafənhaɪt], *f.* (—, *no pl.*) nature, kind, quality, condition.

beschäftigen [bə'ʃɛftɪgən], *v.a.* occupy, employ.

beschämen [bə'ʃɛ:mən], *v.a.* make ashamed, shame.

beschatten [bə'ʃatən], *v.a.* shade, shadow; follow (s.o.).

Beschau [bə'ʃau], *f.* (—, *no pl.*) examination; inspection.

beschauen [bə'ʃauən], *v.a.* view, look at.

beschaulich [bə'ʃaulɪç], *adj.* tranquil, contemplative.

Beschaulichkeit [bə'ʃaulɪçkaɪt], *f.* (—, *pl.* —en) tranquillity, contemplation.

Bescheid [bə'ʃaɪt], *m.* (—s, *pl.* —e) answer, information; (*Law*) decision; — *wissen*, know o.'s way about; know what's what.

bescheiden [bə'ʃaɪdən], *v.a. irr.* inform (s.o.); *einen zu sich* —, send for s.o. — *adj.* modest, unassuming.

Bescheidenheit [bə'ʃaɪdənhaɪt], *f.* (—, *no pl.*) modesty.

bescheinen [bə'ʃaɪnən], *v.a. irr.* shine upon.

bescheinigen [bə'ʃaɪnɪgən], *v.a. einem etwas* —, attest, certify.

beschenken [bə'ʃɛŋkən], *v.a.* give a present to.

bescheren

bescheren [bə'ʃe:rən], v.a. give (a present to), bestow (s.th. on s.o.).
Bescherung [bə'ʃe:ruŋ], f. (—, pl. —en) giving (of present); das ist eine schöne —, (fig.) this is a nice mess!
beschicken [bə'ʃikən], v.a. eine Ausstellung —, contribute to an exhibition.
beschießen [bə'ʃi:sən], v.a. irr. shoot at, fire upon, bombard.
beschiffen [bə'ʃifən], v.a. navigate, sail.
beschimpfen [bə'ʃimpfən], v.a. insult, abuse, revile.
beschirmen [bə'ʃirmən], v.a. protect, shelter, defend.
Beschlag [bə'ʃla:k], m. (—s, pl. ⸚e) mounting; metal fitting; (on stick) ferrule; etwas mit — belegen, or in — nehmen, sequestrate, confiscate, seize.
beschlagen [bə'ʃla:gən], v.a. irr. shoe (a horse). — v.n. (window) mist over.
Beschlagnahme [bə'ʃla:kna:mə], f. (—, pl. —n) confiscation, seizure.
beschleunigen [bə'ʃlɔynigən], v.a. hasten, speed up, accelerate.
beschließen [bə'ʃli:sən], v.a. irr. shut, lock up; close, conclude, finish; decide, resolve upon.
Beschluß [bə'ʃlus], m. (—sses, pl. ⸚sse) determination, resolution, decree.
beschmieren [bə'ʃmi:rən], v.a. soil, smear.
beschmutzen [bə'ʃmutsən], v.a. soil, dirty, foul.
beschneiden [bə'ʃnaidən], v.a. irr. cut, clip; (Hort.) lop, prune; (animals) crop; circumcise.
Beschneidung [bə'ʃnaiduŋ], f. (—, pl. —en) lopping, pruning; circumcision.
beschönigen [bə'ʃø:nigən], v.a. palliate, excuse.
beschränken [bə'ʃrɛnkən], v.a. limit, restrict.
beschränkt [bə'ʃrɛŋkt], adj. limited; etwas —, a little stupid; Gesellschaft mit —er Haftung, limited (liability) company.
Beschränkung [bə'ʃrɛŋkuŋ], f. (—, pl. —en) limitation, restriction.
beschreiben [bə'ʃraibən], v.a. irr. describe; write upon.
beschreiten [bə'ʃraitən], v.a. irr. tread on.
beschuldigen [bə'ʃuldigən], v.a. charge (s.o.), accuse.
beschützen [bə'ʃytsən], v.a. protect, shelter, guard.
Beschützer [bə'ʃytsər], m. (—s, pl. —) protector, defender.
Beschwerde [bə'ʃve:rdə], f. (—, pl. —en) trouble, hardship, difficulty; complaint, grievance.
beschweren [bə'ʃve:rən], v.a. make heavier, weight. — v.r. sich über etwas —, complain of s.th.
beschwerlich [bə'ʃve:rliç], adj. burdensome, hard, troublesome.

beschwichtigen [bə'ʃviçtigən], v.a. soothe, appease, still.
beschwindeln [bə'ʃvindəln], v.a. cheat, swindle (s.o.).
beschwingt [bə'ʃviŋkt], adj. winged, light-footed.
beschwipst [bə'ʃvipst], adj. (coll.) tipsy.
beschwören [bə'ʃvø:rən], v.a. irr. testify on oath; einen —, implore s.o.; conjure (up) (ghosts etc.); exorcize.
beseelen [bə'ze:lən], v.a. animate.
besehen [bə'ze:ən], v.a. irr. look at, inspect.
beseitigen [bə'zaitigən], v.a. remove.
beseligt [bə'ze:liçt], adj. enraptured, beatified.
Besen ['be:zən], m. (—s, pl. —) broom, besom.
Besenstiel ['be:zənʃti:l], m. (—s, pl. —e) broom-stick.
besessen [bə'zɛsən], adj. possessed, obsessed, mad.
besetzen [bə'zɛtsən], v.a. (dress) trim, lace; (Mil.) occupy, garrison; (office) fill; (Theat.) cast; (seat) occupy, take; besetzt, engaged.
Besetzung [bə'zɛtsuŋ], f. (—, pl. —en) lacing, trimming; appointment (to post); (Theat.) cast.
besichtigen [bə'ziçtigən], v.a. view, go over, inspect, examine.
besiedeln [bə'zi:dəln], v.a. colonise.
besiegeln [bə'zi:gəln], v.a. seal, set o.'s seal to.
besiegen [bə'zi:gən], v.a. vanquish, conquer, overcome.
besinnen [bə'zinən], v.r. irr. reflect; sich auf etwas —, recollect, remember, think of.
besinnungslos [bə'zinuŋslo:s], adj. insensible, unconscious.
Besitz [bə'zits], m. (—es, no pl.) possession, property.
besitzanzeigend [bə'zitsantsaigənt], adj. (Gram.) possessive.
besitzen [bə'zitsən], v.a. irr. possess, own, have.
Besitzergreifung [bə'zitsɛrgraifuŋ], f. (—, no pl.) occupation, taking possession (of).
besoffen [bə'zɔfən], adj. (vulg.) drunk.
besohlen [bə'zo:lən], v.a. sole (shoes).
besolden [bə'zɔldən], v.a. give a salary to, pay.
besonder [bə'zɔndər], adj. special, particular.
Besonderheit [bə'zɔndərhait], f. (—, pl. —en) particularity, peculiarity, strangeness.
besonders [bə'zɔndərs], adv. especially.
besonnen [bə'zɔnən], adj. prudent, cautious, collected, circumspect.
besorgen [bə'zɔrgən], v.a. take care of, provide, procure.
Besorgnis [bə'zɔrknis], f. (—, pl. —se) care, concern, anxiety, fear.
besorgt [bə'zɔrkt], adj. apprehensive, anxious, worried.

Besorgung [bəˈzɔrguŋ], *f.* (—, *pl.* —en) care, management; purchase, commission; —*en machen*, go shopping.

bespannen [bəˈʃpanən], *v.a.* string (a musical instrument); put horses (to a carriage).

bespötteln [bəˈʃpœtəln], *v.a.* ridicule.

besprechen [bəˈʃprɛçən], *v.a. irr.* discuss, talk over; (book) review. — *v.r. sich — mit*, confer with.

bespritzen [bəˈʃprɪtsən], *v.a.* sprinkle, splash.

besser [ˈbɛsər], *adj.* better; *um so —*, so much the better; *je mehr desto —*, the more the better; — *sein als*, be better than; be preferable to; — *werden*, (*weather*) clear up; (*health*) improve.

bessern [ˈbɛsərn], *v.a.* better, improve. — *v.r. sich —*, reform, improve, mend o.'s ways.

Besserung [ˈbɛsəruŋ], *f.* (—*pl.* —en) improvement, amendment, reform; (*Med.*) recovery; *gute —*, get well soon.

Besserungsanstalt [ˈbɛsəruŋsanʃtalt], *f.* (—, *pl.* —en) reformatory.

best [ˈbɛst], *adj.* best.

bestallen [bəˈʃtalən], *v.a.* appoint.

Bestand [bəˈʃtant], *m.* (—s, *pl.* ⸚e) continuance, duration; stock; balance of cash; — *haben*, endure.

Bestandaufnahme [bəˈʃtantaufnaːmə], *f.* (—, *pl.* —n) (*Comm.*) stocktaking.

beständig [bəˈʃtɛndɪç], *adj.* continual, perpetual; (*persons*) steady, steadfast, constant.

Bestandteil [bəˈʃtanttail], *m.* (—s, *pl.* —e) constituent part, component, ingredient, essential part.

bestärken [bəˈʃtɛrkən], *v.a.* confirm, strengthen.

bestätigen [bəˈʃtɛːtɪɡən], *v.a.* confirm, ratify, bear out, sanction; *den Empfang eines Briefes —*, acknowledge receipt of a letter.

bestatten [bəˈʃtatən], *v.a.* bury, inter.

bestäuben [bəˈʃtɔybən], *v.a.* cover with dust, spray; (*Bot.*) pollinate.

bestechen [bəˈʃtɛçən], *v.a. irr.* bribe, corrupt; (*fig.*) captivate.

bestechlich [bəˈʃtɛçlɪç], *adj.* corruptible.

Bestechung [bəˈʃtɛçuŋ], *f.* (—, *pl.* —en) corruption, bribery.

Besteck [bəˈʃtɛk], *n.* (—s, *pl.* —e) set of knife, fork and spoon; set *or* case (of instruments).

Bestehen [bəˈʃteːən], *n.* (—s, *no pl.*) existence.

bestehen [bəˈʃteːən], *v.a. irr.* undergo, endure, pass (an examination). — *v.n.* exist; *aus etwas —*, consist of s.th.; be composed of s.th.; *auf* (*Dat.*) —, insist upon s.th.

besteigen [bəˈʃtaiɡən], *v.a. irr.* ascend, mount, climb.

bestellen [bəˈʃtɛlən], *v.a.* order, book; appoint; put in order; (*letter, message*) deliver; (*field*) till.

Bestellung [bəˈʃtɛluŋ], *f.* (—, *pl.* —en) order, commission, delivery (of letter); tilling (of field); appointment; *auf —*, to order.

bestens [ˈbɛstəns], *adv.* in the best manner.

besteuern [bəˈʃtɔyərn], *v.a.* tax.

bestialisch [bɛstiˈaːlɪʃ], *adj.* beastly, bestial.

Bestie [ˈbɛstjə], *f.* (—, *pl.* —n) beast, brute.

bestimmen [bəˈʃtɪmən], *v.a.* fix, settle; decide (s.th.); determine, define.

bestimmt [bəˈʃtɪmt], *adj.* decided, fixed, appointed; *ganz —*, positively, most decidedly.

Bestimmtheit [bəˈʃtɪmthait], *f.* (—, *no pl.*) certainty.

Bestimmung [bəˈʃtɪmuŋ], *f.* (—, *pl.* —en) settlement, decision, determination; provision; destiny.

bestrafen [bəˈʃtraːfən], *v.a.* punish, chastise.

bestrahlen [bəˈʃtraːlən], *v.a.* irradiate; (*Med.*) treat by radiotherapy.

bestreben [bəˈʃtreːbən], *v.r. sich —*, exert o.s., strive (for), endeavour.

Bestrebung [bəˈʃtreːbuŋ], *f.* (—, *pl.* —en) effort, endeavour, exertion.

bestreichen [bəˈʃtraiçən], *v.a. irr.* spread.

bestreiten [bəˈʃtraitən], *v.a. irr.* contest, deny, dispute; defray (costs).

bestreuen [bəˈʃtrɔyən], *v.a.* sprinkle, strew, powder.

bestricken [bəˈʃtrɪkən], *v.a.* ensnare, entangle.

bestürmen [bəˈʃtyrmən], *v.a.* storm, assail; (*fig.*) importune.

bestürzen [bəˈʃtyrtsən], *v.a.* dismay, confound, perplex.

Besuch [bəˈzuːx], *m.* (—s, *pl.* —e) visit; (*person*) visitor.

besuchen [bəˈzuːxən], *v.a.* visit, call on; attend; frequent.

besudeln [bəˈzuːdəln], *v.a.* soil, foul.

betagt [bəˈtaːkt], *adj.* aged, elderly.

betätigen [bəˈtɛːtɪɡən], *v.a.* practise, operate. — *v.r. sich —*, take an active part, work, participate (in).

betäuben [bəˈtɔybən], *v.a.* deafen; stun, benumb, anaesthetize.

Betäubung [bəˈtɔybuŋ], *f.* (—, *pl.* —en) stupor, stupefaction; *örtliche —*, local anaesthetic.

beteiligen [bəˈtailɪɡən], *v.a. einen an etwas —*, give s.o. a share of s.th. — *v.r. sich an etwas —*, participate in s.th.; (*Comm.*) have shares in s.th.

Beteiligte [bəˈtailɪçtə], *m.* (—n, *pl.* —n) person concerned.

Beteiligung [bəˈtailɪɡuŋ], *f.* (—, *pl.* —en) participation, interest.

beten [ˈbeːtən], *v.n.* pray, say o.'s prayers.

beteuern [bəˈtɔyərn], *v.a.* aver, affirm solemnly.

betiteln [bəˈtiːtəln], *v.a.* entitle, name.

Beton [beˈtɔ̃], *m.* (—s, *no pl.*) concrete.

betonen

betonen [bə'to:nən], *v.a.* accentuate, stress, emphasise.

Betonung [bə'to:nuŋ], *f.* (—, *pl.* —en) accentuation, emphasis, stress.

betören [bə'tø:rən], *v.a.* delude, infatuate.

Betracht [bə'traxt], *m.* (—s, *no pl.*) consideration, respect, regard.

betrachten [bə'traxtən], *v.a.* consider, look at, view; *etwas aufmerksam —,* contemplate s.th.

beträchtlich [bə'trɛçtlɪç], *adj.* considerable.

Betrachtung [bə'traxtuŋ], *f.* (—, *pl.* —en) contemplation, consideration.

Betrag [bə'tra:k], *m.* (—s, *pl.* ⁻e) amount, sum total.

betragen [bə'tra:gən], *v.a. irr.* amount to, come to. — *v.r. sich —,* behave, conduct o.s.

Betragen [bə'tra:gən], *n.* (—s, *no pl.*) behaviour, conduct, demeanour.

betrauen [bə'trauən], *v.a. einen mit etwas —,* entrust s.o. with s.th.

betrauern [bə'trauərn], *v.a.* mourn for, bemoan.

Betreff [bə'trɛf], *m.* (—s, *no pl.*) reference; *in —,* with regard to.

betreffen [bə'trɛfən], *v.a. irr.* concern, affect, relate to.

Betreiben [bə'traibən], *n.* (—s, *no pl.*) *auf — von,* at the instigation of.

betreiben [bə'traibən], *v.a. irr.* (*business*) carry on; (*factory*) run; (*trade*) follow, practise.

Betreten [bə'tre:tən], *n.* (—s, *no pl.*) entry, entering.

betreten [bə'tre:tən], *v.a. irr.* step upon, set foot on, enter. — *adj.* disconcerted, embarrassed.

betreuen [bə'trɔyən], *v.a.* care for, attend to.

Betrieb [bə'tri:p], *m.* (—s, *pl.* —e) management, business, factory, plant; *den — einstellen,* close down; *in — sein,* be in operation; *in — setzen,* start working.

betriebsam [bə'tri:pza:m], *adj.* active, busy, industrious, diligent.

Betriebsamkeit [bə'tri:pza:mkait], *f.* (—, *pl.* —en) activity, industry, bustle.

betriebsfertig [bə'tri:psfɛrtiç], *adj.* ready for service; operational.

Betriebsmaterial [bə'tri:psmaterja:l], *n.* (—s, *pl.* —ien) (*Railw.*) rolling-stock; (*factory*) working-stock.

Betriebspersonal [bə'tri:psperzona:l], *n.* (—s, *no pl.*) workmen, employees, staff.

betrinken [bə'trɪŋkən], *v.r. irr. sich —,* get drunk.

betroffen [bə'trɔfən], *adj.* perplexed, confounded.

betrüben [bə'try:bən], *v.a.* afflict, grieve.

Betrübnis [bə'trypnɪs], *f.* (—ses, *pl.* ⁻se) affliction, grief, distress, sorrow.

betrübt [bə'try:pt], *adj.* sad, grieved.

Betrug [bə'tru:k], *m.* (—s, *pl.* ⁻ereien) fraud, deceit, deception, imposture; *einen — begehen,* commit a fraud.

betrügen [bə'try:gən], *v.a. irr.* cheat, deceive.

Betrüger [bə'try:gər], *m.* (—s, —) swindler, cheat, deceiver, impostor.

betrunken [bə'truŋkən], *adj.* drunk, drunken, tipsy.

Bett [bɛt], *n.* (—(e)s, *pl.* —en) bed; (*river*) bed, channel.

Bettdecke ['bɛtdɛkə], *f.* (—, *pl.* —n) counterpane; (*Am.*) bedspread; *wollene —,* blanket; *gesteppte —,* quilt.

Bettel ['bɛtəl], *m.* (—s, *no pl.*) trash, trifle.

bettelarm ['bɛtəlarm], *adj.* destitute.

Bettelei [bɛtə'lai], *f.* (—, *pl.* —en) begging, beggary, penury.

betteln ['bɛtəln], *v.a.* beg, ask alms.

betten ['bɛtən], *v.a.* bed, lay to rest. — *v.r.* (*fig.*) *sich —,* make o.'s bed.

bettlägerig ['bɛtlɛgəriç], *adj.* bedridden.

Bettlaken ['bɛtla:kən], *n.* (—s, *pl.* —) sheet.

Bettler ['bɛtlər], *m.* (—s, *pl.* —) beggar.

Bettstelle ['bɛtʃtɛlə], *f.* (—, *pl.* —n) bedstead.

Bettvorleger ['bɛtfo:rle:gər], *m.* (—s, *pl.* —) bedside-carpet *or* rug.

Bettwäsche ['bɛtvɛʃə], *f.* (—, *no pl.*) bed linen, bed clothes.

Bettzeug ['bɛttsɔyk], *n.* (—s, *no pl.*) bedding.

beugen ['bɔygən], *v.a.* bend, bow. — *v.r. sich —,* bend down, stoop.

Beugung ['bɔyguŋ], *f.* (—, *pl.* —en) (*Gram.*) inflection.

Beule ['bɔylə], *f.* (—, *pl.* —n) bruise, bump, swelling, boil.

beunruhigen [bə'unru:igən], *v.a.* alarm, trouble, disquiet.

beurkunden [bə'u:rkundən], *v.a.* authenticate, verify.

beurlauben [bə'u:rlaubən], *v.a.* grant leave of absence. — *v.r. sich —,* take leave.

beurteilen [bə'urtailən], *v.a.* judge, criticise.

Beute ['bɔytə], *f.* (—, *no pl.*) booty, loot; (*animals*) prey; (*Hunt.*) bag.

Beutel ['bɔytəl], *m.* (—s, *pl.* —) bag; (*money*) purse; (*Zool.*) pouch.

Beuteltier ['bɔytəlti:r], *n.* (—s, *pl.* —e) marsupial.

bevölkern [bə'fœlkərn], *v.a.* people, populate.

Bevölkerung [bə'fœlkəruŋ], *f.* (—, *pl.* —en) population.

bevollmächtigen [bə'fɔlmɛçtigən], *v.a.* empower, authorise.

bevor [bə'fo:r], *conj.* before, ere, beforehand.

bevormunden [bə'fo:rmundən], *v.a. insep.* act as guardian to; (*fig.*) browbeat.

bevorrechtigt [bə'fo:rrɛçtiçt], *adj.* privileged.

beziehungsweise

bevorstehen [bə'fo:rʃteːən], *v.n. irr.*
impend, lie ahead, be imminent;
einem —, be in store for s.o.
bevorzugen [bə'fo:rtsuːgən], *v.a. insep.*
prefer, favour.
bewachen [bə'vaxən], *v.a.* watch over,
guard.
bewachsen [bə'vaksən], *adj.* overgrown.
bewaffnen [bə'vafnən], *v.a.* arm,
supply with arms.
Bewahranstalt [bə'va:ranʃtalt], *f.* (—
pl. —**en**) kindergarten, nursery.
bewahren [bə'va:rən], *v.a.* preserve,
keep, take care of.
bewähren [bə'vɛːrən], *v.r. sich —,*
prove o.s.
bewahrheiten [bə'va:rhaItən], *v.r. sich*
—, come true.
bewährt [bə'vɛːrt], *adj.* proved.
Bewährung [bə'vɛːruŋ], *f.* (—, *no pl.*)
proof, verification.
Bewährungsfrist [bə'vɛːruŋsfrɪst], *f.*
(—, *no pl.*) probation.
bewaldet [bə'valdət], *adj.* wooded,
woody.
bewältigen [bə'vɛltɪgən], *v.a.* overcome; manage, master; cope *or* deal
with.
bewandert [bə'vandərt], *adj.* versed,
skilled, experienced, conversant.
bewandt [bə'vant], *adj.* such; *damit ist
es so —*, it is like this.
Bewandtnis [bə'vantnɪs], *f.* (—, *pl.*
—**se**) circumstance, condition, state;
es hat damit folgende —, the circumstances are as follows.
bewässern [bə'vɛsərn], *v.a.* water,
irrigate.
bewegen [bə've:gən], *v.a., v.r.* move,
stir; take exercise. — *v.a. irr.* persuade, induce.
Beweggrund [bə've:kgrunt], *m.* (—**es**,
pl. **-e**) motive, reason, motivation.
beweglich [bə've:klɪç], *adj.* movable;
agile, brisk, sprightly.
Bewegung [bə've:guŋ], *f.* (—, *pl.* —**en**)
motion, movement; (*mind*) emotion,
agitation.
beweinen [bə'vaInən], *v.a.* lament,
bemoan, deplore.
Beweis [bə'vaIs], *m.* (—**es**, *pl.* —**e**)
proof, evidence; (*Maths.*) demonstration.
beweisen [bə'vaIzən], *v.a. irr.* prove,
show, demonstrate.
Beweiskraft [bə'vaIskraft], *f.* (—, *no
pl.*) (*Law*) probative force.
Beweismittel [bə'vaIsmItəl], *n.* (—**s**,
pl. —) evidence, proof.
Bewenden [bə'vɛndən], *n.* (—**s**, *no pl.*)
es hat damit sein —, there the matter
rests.
bewenden [bə'vɛndən], *v.n. irr. es
dabei — lassen*, leave it at that.
bewerben [bə'vɛrbən], *v.r. irr. sich um
etwas —*, apply for s.th.
Bewerber [bə'vɛrbər], *m.* (—**s**, *pl.* —)
applicant, candidate; (*marriage*)
suitor.

Bewerbung [bə'vɛrbuŋ], *f.* (—, *pl.*
—**en**) application, candidature; (*marriage*) courtship.
bewerkstelligen [bə'vɛrkʃtɛlɪgən], *v.a.*
perform, bring about.
bewerten [bə'vɛrtən], *v.a.* estimate,
value.
bewilligen [bə'vɪlɪgən], *v.a.* grant,
allow, permit.
bewillkommnen [bə'vɪlkɔmnən], *v.a.*
welcome.
bewirken [bə'vɪrkən], *v.a.* effect, bring
about.
bewirten [bə'vɪrtən], *v.a.* entertain,
act as host (to).
bewirtschaften [bə'vɪrtʃaftən], *v.a.*
manage.
bewohnen [bə'vo:nən], *v.a.* inhabit,
occupy.
Bewohner [bə'vo:nər], *m.* (—**s**, *pl.* —)
inhabitant, tenant, resident.
bewölken [bə'vœlkən], *v.r. sich —,*
become overcast, become cloudy.
bewundern [bə'vundərn], *v.a.* admire.
bewundernswert [bə'vundərnsvɛrt],
adj. admirable.
bewußt [bə'vust], *adj.* conscious, aware;
es war mir nicht —, I was not aware of.
bewußtlos [bə'vustloːs], *adj.* unconscious; — *werden*, faint, lose consciousness.
Bewußtsein [bə'vustzaIn], *n.* (—**s**, *no
pl.*) consciousness; *einem etwas zum —
bringen*, bring s.th. home to s.o.
bezahlbar [bə'tsa:lba:r], *adj.* payable.
bezahlen [bə'tsa:lən], *v.a.* pay; (*bill*)
settle.
bezähmen [bə'tsɛ:mən], *v.a.* tame,
restrain. — *v.r. sich —*, restrain o.s.,
control o.s.
bezaubern [bə'tsaubərn], *v.a.* bewitch,
enchant, fascinate.
bezeichnen [bə'tsaIçnən], *v.a.* mark,
denote, indicate, designate.
bezeichnend [bə'tsaIçnənt], *adj.* indicative, characteristic, significant.
bezeigen [bə'tsaIgən], *v.a.* manifest,
show.
bezeugen [bə'tsɔygən], *v.a.* attest, bear
witness, testify.
bezichtigen [bə'tsɪçtɪgən], *v.a.* accuse
(s.o.) of (s.th.).
beziehbar [bə'tsi:ba:r], *adj.* (*goods*)
obtainable; (*house*) ready for occupation.
beziehen [bə'tsi:ən], *v.a. irr.* cover;
(*house etc.*) move into; (*instrument*)
string; make up (a bed); *die Wache —,*
mount guard. — *v.r. sich —*, (*sky*)
cloud over; *sich auf etwas —*, refer to
s.th.
Bezieher [bə'tsi:ər], *m.* (—**s**, *pl.* —)
customer; (*newspaper*) subscriber.
Beziehung [bə'tsi:uŋ], *f.* (—, *pl.* —**en**)
relation, connection; reference, bearing; *in dieser —*, in this respect;
(*Comm.*) *unter — auf*, with reference
to.
beziehungsweise [bə'tsi:uŋsvaIzə], *adv.*
respectively, as the case may be, or.

beziffern [bə'tsɪfərn], *v.a.* number.
Bezirk [bə'tsɪrk], *m.* (—s, *pl.* —e)
district; (*Am.*) precinct; (*Parl.*)
constituency; (*Law*) circuit.
Bezirksgericht [bə'tsɪrksgərɪçt], *n.*
(—s, *pl.* —e) county court.
Bezug [bə'tsu:k], *m.* (—s, *pl.* ‒e)
(*pillow*) case, cover; (*goods*) order,
purchase; (*fig.*) relation; — haben auf,
refer to; *mit* — *auf*, referring to;
(*pl.*) emoluments, income.
bezüglich [bə'tsy:klɪç], *adj.* with regard
to, regarding.
Bezugnahme [bə'tsu:kna:mə], *f.* (—,
pl. —n) reference; *unter* — *auf*, with
reference to.
Bezugsbedingung [bə'tsu:ksbədɪŋuŋ],
f. (—, *pl.* —en) (*usually pl.*) (*Comm.*)
conditions *or* terms of delivery.
Bezugsquelle [bə'tsu:kskvɛlə], *f.* (—,
pl. —n) source of supply.
bezwecken [bə'tsvɛkən], *v.a.* aim at,
intend.
bezweifeln [bə'tsvaɪfəln], *v.a.* doubt,
question.
bezwingen [bə'tsvɪŋən], *v.a. irr.* subdue,
conquer. — *v.r. sich* —, restrain o.s.
Bibel ['bi:bəl], *f.* (—, *pl.* —n) Bible.
Bibelauslegung ['bi:bəlauslɛ:guŋ], *f.*
(—, *pl.* —en) (Biblical) exegesis.
Biber ['bi:bər], *m.* (—s, *pl.* —) (*Zool.*)
beaver.
Bibliothek [biblio'te:k], *f.* (—, *pl.* —en)
library.
Bibliothekar [bibliote'ka:r], *m.* (—s,
pl. —e) librarian.
biblisch ['bi:blɪʃ], *adj.* biblical, scrip-
tural.
Bickbeere ['bɪkbe:rə], *f.* (—, *pl.* —n)
bilberry.
bieder ['bi:dər], *adj.* upright, honest,
decent.
Biederkeit ['bi:dərkaɪt], *f.* (—, *no pl.*)
uprightness, probity.
Biedermann ['bi:dərman], *m.* (—s, *pl.*
‒er) honourable man; (*iron.*) Philistine.
biegen ['bi:gən], *v.a. irr.* bend, bow.
— *v.n.* (*aux.* sein) *um die Ecke* —,
turn the corner. — *v.r. sich* —, curve;
— *oder brechen*, by hook or by
crook.
biegsam ['bi:kza:m], *adj.* flexible,
supple, pliant.
Biegung ['bi:guŋ], *f.* (—, *pl.* —en)
curve, bend; (*Gram.*) inflexion.
Biene ['bi:nə], *f.* (—, *pl.* —n) bee.
Bienenhaus ['bi:nənhaus], *n.* (—es,
pl. ‒er) apiary.
Bienenkorb ['bi:nənkɔrp], *m.* (—s, *pl.*
‒e) beehive.
Bienenzüchter ['bi:nəntsyçtər], *m.*
(—s, *pl.* —) apiarist, bee-keeper.
Bier ['bi:r], *n.* (—(e)s, *pl.* —e) beer.
Bierkanne ['bi:rkanə], *f.* (—, *pl.* —n)
tankard.
Biest [bi:st], *n.* (—es, *pl.* —er) brute,
beast.
bieten ['bi:tən], *v.a. irr.* offer; (*auction*)
bid.

Bieter ['bi:tər], *m.* (—s, *pl.* —) (*auction*)
bidder.
Bigotterie [bɪgɔtə'ri:], *f.* (—, *no pl.*)
bigotry.
Bijouterie [bɪʒutə'ri:], *f.* (—, *pl.* —n)
trinkets, dress-jewellery.
Bilanz [bi'lants], *f.* (—, *pl.* —en)
(*Comm.*) balance; (financial) statement.
Bild [bɪlt], *n.* (—es, *pl.* —er) picture,
painting, portrait, image; idea; (*coins*)
effigy; (*Cards*) court card; (*books*)
illustration; (*speech*) figure of speech,
metaphor.
bilden ['bɪldən], *v.c.* form, shape;
(*mind*) cultivate. — *v.r. sich* —,
improve o.'s mind, educate o.s.
bildend ['bɪldənt], *adj.* instructive,
civilising; *die —en Künste*, the fine
arts.
bilderreich ['bɪldəraɪç], *adj.* —e
Sprache, flowery language, figurative
style.
Bilderschrift ['bɪldərʃrɪft], *f.* (—, *pl.*
—en) hieroglyphics.
Bilderstürmer ['bɪldərʃtyrmər], *m.*
(—s, *pl.* —) iconoclast.
Bildhauer ['bɪlthauər], *m.* (—s, *pl.*
—) sculptor.
bildhübsch ['bɪlthypʃ], *adj.* as pretty
as a picture.
bildlich ['bɪltlɪç], *adj.* figurative.
Bildnis ['bɪltnɪs], *n.* (—ses, *pl.* —se)
portrait, figure, image, effigy.
bildsam ['bɪltza:m], *adj.* plastic, ductile.
bildschön ['bɪltʃø:n], *adj.* very beautiful.
Bildseite ['bɪltzaɪtə], *f.* (—, *pl.* —n)
(*coin*) face, obverse.
Bildung ['bɪlduŋ], *f.* (—, *pl.* (*rare*)
—en) formation; (*mind*) education,
culture; knowledge, learning, accom-
plishments, attainments.
Billard ['bɪljart], *n.* (—s, *pl.* —s)
billiards.
Billett [bɪl'jɛt], *n.* (—s, *pl.* —s)
ticket.
billig ['bɪlɪç], *adj.* cheap, inexpensive;
equitable, just, fair, reasonable.
billigen ['bɪlɪgən], *v.a.* sanction,
approve of, consent to.
Billigkeit ['bɪlɪçkaɪt], *f.* (—, *no pl.*)
cheapness; fairness, equitableness,
reasonableness.
Billigung ['bɪliguŋ], *f.* (—, *no pl.*)
approbation, approval, sanction.
Bilsenkraut ['bɪlzənkraut], *n.* (—s, *pl.*
‒er) henbane.
bimmeln ['bɪməln], *v.n.* (*coll.*) tinkle.
Bimsstein ['bɪmsʃtaɪn], *m.* (—s, *pl.*
—e) pumice stone.
Binde ['bɪndə], *f.* (—, *pl.* —n) band,
bandage; tie; ligature; sanitary towel.
Bindeglied ['bɪndegli:t], *n.* (—s, *pl.*
—er) connecting link.
Bindehaut ['bɪndəhaut], *f.* (—, *pl.* ‒e)
(*Anat.*) conjunctiva.
Bindehautentzündung ['bɪndəhaut-
ɛntsynduŋ], *f.* (—, *pl.* —en) conjunctivitis.

binden ['bɪndən], *v.a. irr.* bind, tie, fasten.

Bindestrich ['bɪndeʃtrɪç], *m.* (—(e)s, *pl.* —e) hyphen.

Bindewort ['bɪndəvɔrt], *n.* (—s, *pl.* ꞏer) conjunction.

Bindfaden ['bɪntfaːdən], *m.* (—s, *pl.* ꞏ) string, twine.

Bindung ['bɪnduŋ], *f.* (—, *pl.* —en) binding, bond; obligation; (*Mus.*) ligature.

binnen ['bɪnən], *prep.* (*Genit. & Dat.*), *adv.* within.

Binnenhafen ['bɪnənhaːfən], *m.* (—s, *pl.* ꞏ) inland harbour.

Binnenhandel ['bɪnənhandəl], *m.* (—s, *no pl.*) inland trade.

Binse ['bɪnzə], *f.* (—, *pl.* —n) (*Bot.*) rush, reed.

Biographie [biograˈfiː], *f.* (—, *pl.* —n) biography.

Birke ['bɪrkə], *f.* (—, *pl.* —n) (*Bot.*) birch, birch-tree.

Birma ['bɪrmaː], *n.* Burma.

Birnbaum ['bɪrnbaum], *m.* (—s, *pl.* ꞏe) pear-tree.

Birne ['bɪrnə], *f.* (—, *pl.* —n) pear; (*Elec.*) bulb.

birnförmig ['bɪrnfœrmɪç], *adj.* pear-shaped.

bis [bɪs], *prep.* (*time*) till, until; by; (*place*) to, up to; — *auf*, with the exception of. — *conj.* till, until.

Bisam ['biːzam], *m.* (—s, *pl.* —e) musk.

Bischof ['bɪʃɔf], *m.* (—s, *pl.* ꞏe) bishop.

bischöflich ['bɪʃœflɪç], *adj.* episcopal.

Bischofsstab ['bɪʃɔfsʃtaːp], *m.* (—s, *pl.* ꞏe) crosier.

bisher ['bɪsheːr], *adv.* hitherto, till now.

bisherig [bɪsˈheːrɪç], *adj.* up to this time, hitherto existing.

Biskayischer Meerbusen [bɪsˈkaːɪʃər ˈmeːrbuːzən]. Bay of Biscay.

Biß [bɪs], *m.* (—sses, *pl.* —sse) bite, sting.

Bißchen ['bɪsçən], *n.* (—s, *pl.* —) morsel; little bit.

Bissen ['bɪsən], *m.* (—s, *pl.* —) bite, morsel.

bissig ['bɪsɪç], *adj.* biting, cutting; sharp, vicious; sarcastic.

Bistum ['bɪstum], *n.* (—s, *pl.* ꞏer) bishopric, diocese; see.

bisweilen [bɪsˈvaɪlən], *adv.* sometimes, now and then, occasionally.

Bitte ['bɪtə], *f.* (—, *pl.* —n) request, entreaty.

bitte ['bɪtə], *int.* please.

bitten ['bɪtən], *v.a. irr.* ask; request.

bitter ['bɪtər], *adj.* bitter.

Bitterkeit ['bɪtərkaɪt], *f.* (—, *no pl.*) bitterness.

bitterlich ['bɪtərlɪç], *adv.* (*fig.*) bitterly.

Bittersalz ['bɪtərzalts], *n.* (—es, *no pl.*) Epsom salts.

Bittgang ['bɪtgaŋ], *m.* (—(e)s, *pl.* ꞏe) (*Eccl.*) procession.

Bittsteller ['bɪtʃtɛlər], *m.* (—s, *pl.* —) petitioner, suppli(c)ant.

Biwak ['biːvak], *m.* (—s, *pl.* —s) bivouac.

blähen ['blɛːən], *v.a.* inflate, puff up, swell.

Blähung ['blɛːuŋ], *f.* (—, *pl.* —en) (*Med.*) flatulence.

blaken ['blaːkən], *v.n.* smoulder; smoke.

Blamage [blaˈmaːʒə], *f.* (—, *pl.* —n) shame, disgrace.

blamieren [blaˈmiːrən], *v.a.*, *v.r.* make (o.s.) ridiculous, make a fool of o.s.

blank [blaŋk], *adj.* shining, bright, smooth, polished.

Bläschen ['blɛːsçən], *n.* (—s, *pl.* —) little bubble, blister; (*Med.*) vesicle.

Blase ['blaːzə], *f.* (—, *pl.* —n) (*soap*) bubble; (*skin*) blister; (*Anat.*) bladder.

Blasebalg ['blaːzəbalk], *m.* (—s, *pl.* ꞏe) pair of bellows.

blasen ['blaːzən], *v.a. irr.* blow; (*Mus.*) sound.

Bläser ['blɛːzər], *m.* (—s, *pl.* —) (*glass*) blower; (*Mus.*) wind player.

blasiert [blaˈziːrt], *adj.* blasé, haughty.

Blasrohr ['blaːsroːr], *n.* (—s, *pl.* —e) blow-pipe, pea-shooter.

blaß [blas], *adj.* pale, wan, pallid.

Blässe ['blɛsə], *f.* (—, *no pl.*) paleness, pallor.

Blatt [blat], *n.* (—s, *pl.* ꞏer) leaf; (*paper*) sheet; blade.

Blatter ['blatər], *f.* (—, *pl.* —n) pustule; (*pl.*) smallpox.

blättern ['blɛtərn], *v.a.* turn the leaves (of a book).

Blätterteig ['blɛtərtaɪk], *m.* (—s, *no pl.*) puff pastry.

Blattgold ['blatgɔlt], *n.* (—es, *no pl.*) gold-leaf.

Blattlaus ['blatlaus], *f.* (—, *pl.* ꞏe) (*Ent.*) plant-louse.

Blattpflanze ['blatpflantsə], *f.* (—, *pl.* —n) leaf-plant.

blau [blau], *adj.* blue; *—en Montag machen*, stay away from work; *sein —es Wunder erleben*, be amazed.

blauäugig ['blauɔygɪç], *adj.* blue-eyed.

Blaubeere ['blaubeːrə], *f.* (—, *pl.* —n) bilberry, blueberry.

blaublütig ['blaublyːtɪç], *adj.* aristocratic.

bläuen ['blauən], *v.a.* dye blue, rinse in blue.

bläulich ['blɔylɪç], *adj.* pale blue, bluish.

Blausäure ['blauzɔyrə], *f.* (—, *no pl.*) prussic acid.

Blaustrumpf ['blauʃtrumpf], *m.* (—s, *pl.* ꞏe) blue-stocking.

Blech [blɛç], *n.* (—s, *pl.* —e) tinplate, sheet metal.

blechen ['blɛçən], *v.n.* (*coll.*) fork out money.

blechern ['blɛçərn], *adj.* made of tin, tinny.

Blechinstrument ['blɛçɪnstrumɛnt], *n.* (—s, *pl.* —e) (*Mus.*) brass instrument.

Blei [blaɪ], *n.* (—s, *no pl.*) lead.
bleiben ['blaɪbən], *v.n. irr.* (*aux.* sein) remain, stay.
bleich [blaɪç], *adj.* pale, wan, pallid.
Bleiche ['blaɪçə], *f.* (—, *pl.* —n) pallor; (*laundry*) bleaching-place.
bleichen ['blaɪçən], *v.a. irr.* bleach, whiten.
Bleichsucht ['blaɪçzuxt], *f.* (—, *no pl.*) chlorosis, anaemia.
bleiern ['blaɪərn], *adj.* leaden.
Bleiglanz ['blaɪglants], *m.* (—es, *no pl.*) (*Min.*) lead sulphide.
Bleisoldat ['blaɪzɔldaːt], *m.* (—en, *pl.* —en) tin soldier.
Bleistift ['blaɪʃtɪft], *m.* (—s, *pl.* —e) pencil.
Blende ['blɛndə], *f.* (—, *no pl.*) blind; (*Min.*) blende; (*Phot.*) shutter.
blenden ['blɛndən], *v.a.* dazzle, blind.
Blendlaterne ['blɛntlatɛrnə], *f.* (—, *pl.* —n) dark-lantern.
Blendung ['blɛnduŋ], *f.* (—, *pl.* —en) blinding, dazzling.
Blendwerk ['blɛntvɛrk], *n.* (—s, *no pl.*) (optical) illusion, false show.
Blick [blɪk], *m.* (—s, *pl.* —e) glance, look, glimpse.
blicken ['blɪkən], *v.n.* look, glance.
blind [blɪnt], *adj.* blind, sightless; —*er Passagier*, stowaway.
Blinddarm ['blɪntdarm], *m.* (—s, *pl.* ‒e) appendix.
Blinddarmentzündung ['blɪntdarm-ɛntsynduŋ], *f.* (—, *pl.* —en) appendicitis.
Blindekuh [blɪndə'kuː], *f.* (—, *no pl.*) blind man's buff.
Blindgänger ['blɪntgɛŋər], *m.* (—s, *pl.* —) misfire, dud, blind.
Blindheit ['blɪnthaɪt], *f.* (—, *no pl.*) blindness.
blindlings ['blɪntlɪŋs], *adv.* blindly; at random.
Blindschleiche ['blɪntʃlaɪçə], *f.* (—, *pl.* —n) (*Zool.*) blind-worm.
blinken ['blɪŋkən], *v.n.* blink, flash, glitter, gleam.
blinzeln ['blɪntsəln], *v.n.* blink.
Blitz [blɪts], *m.* (—es, *pl.* —e) lightning, flash.
Blitzableiter ['blɪtsaplaɪtər], *m.* (—s, *pl.* —) lightning-conductor.
blitzblank ['blɪtsblaŋk], *adj.* as bright as a new pin; shining.
blitzen ['blɪtsən], *v.n.* flash; *es blitzt*, it is lightning; glitter, shine.
Blitzesschnelle ['blɪtsəsʃnɛlə], *f.* (—, *no pl.*) lightning-speed.
Blitzlicht ['blɪtslɪçt], *n.* (—s, *no pl.*) flashlight.
Blitzschlag ['blɪtsʃlaːk], *m.* (—s, *pl.* ‒e) flash of lightning.
Blitzstrahl ['blɪtsʃtraːl], *m.* (—s, *pl.* —en) flash of lightning.
Block [blɔk], *m.* (—s, *pl.* ‒e) block, log; pad.
Blockhaus ['blɔkhaus], *n.* (—es, *pl.* ‒er) log-cabin.

blockieren [blɔ'kiːrən], *v.a.* block (up); (*Mil.*) blockade.
blöde ['bløːdə], *adj.* stupid, dull, thick-headed, dim.
Blödsinn ['bløːtsɪn], *m.* (—s, *no pl.*) nonsense, idiocy.
blöken ['bløːkən], *v.n.* bleat; (*cows*) low.
blond [blɔnt], *adj.* blond, fair, fair-headed.
bloß [bloːs], *adj.* naked, uncovered; bare, mere.
Blöße ['bløːsə], *f.* (—, *pl.* —n) nakedness, bareness; (*fig.*) weak point.
bloßlegen ['bloːsleːgən], *v.a.* uncover, lay bare; (*fig.*) reveal, expose.
bloßstellen ['bloːsʃtɛlən], *v.a.* compromise, show up. — *v.r. sich* —, compromise o.s.
blühen ['blyːən], *v.n.* bloom, blossom, flower, flourish.
Blümchen ['blyːmçən], *n.* (—s, *pl.* —) small flower.
Blume ['bluːmə], *f.* (—, *pl.* —n) flower, bloom; (*wine*) bouquet; (*beer*) froth.
Blumenblatt ['bluːmənblat], *n.* (—s, *pl.* ‒er) petal.
Blumenerde ['bluːməneːrdə], *f.* (—, *no pl.*) garden mould.
Blumenkelch ['bluːmənkɛlç], *m.* (—es, *pl.* —e) calyx.
Blumenkohl ['bluːmənkoːl], *m.* (—s, *pl.* —e) cauliflower.
Blumenstaub ['bluːmənʃtaup], *m.* (—s, *no pl.*) pollen.
Blumenstrauß ['bluːmənʃtraus], *m.* (—es, *pl.* ‒e) bunch of flowers, posy, nosegay.
Blumenzucht ['bluːməntsuxt], *f.* (—, *no pl.*) floriculture.
Bluse ['bluːzə], *f.* (—, *pl.* —n) blouse.
Blut [bluːt], *n.* (—es, *no pl.*) blood.
blutarm ['bluːtarm], *adj.* anaemic; (*fig.*) very poor.
Blutbad ['bluːtbaːt], *n.* (—es, *pl.* ‒er) massacre.
blutdürstig ['bluːtdyrstɪç], *adj.* blood-thirsty.
Blüte ['blyːtə], *f.* (—, *pl.* —n) blossom, flower, bloom.
Blutegel ['bluːteːgəl], *m.* (—s, *pl.* —) leech.
bluten ['bluːtən], *v.n.* bleed.
Bluterguß ['bluːtɛrgus], *m.* (—es, *pl.* ‒e) effusion of blood.
Blutgefäß ['bluːtgəfɛːs], *n.* (—es, *pl.* —e) blood-vessel.
blutig ['bluːtɪç], *adj.* bloody; cruel.
blutjung ['bluːtjuŋ], *adj.* very young.
Blutkörperchen ['bluːtkœrpərçən], *n.* (—s, *pl.* —) blood-corpuscle.
Blutlassen ['bluːtlasən], *n.* (—s, *no pl.*) (*Med.*) bloodletting.
Blutrache ['bluːtraxə], *f.* (—, *no pl.*) vendetta.
Blutsauger ['bluːtzaugər], *m.* (—s, *pl.* —) vampire.
Blutschande ['bluːtʃandə], *f.* (—, *no pl.*) incest.

blutstillend ['blu:ʃtɪlənt], *adj.* styptic, blood-stanching.

Blutsturz ['blu:tʃturts], *m.* (—es, *no pl.*) haemorrhage; *einen* — *haben*, burst a blood-vessel.

Blutsverwandte ['blu:tsfɛrvantə], *m. or f.* (—n, *pl.* —n) blood-relation.

Blutvergießen ['blu:tfɛrgi:sən], *n.* (—s, *no pl.*) bloodshed.

Blutvergiftung ['blu:tfɛrgɪftuŋ], *f.* (—, *pl.* —en) blood poisoning.

Blutwurst ['blu:tvurst], *f.* (—, *pl.* ̇e) black-pudding.

Blutzeuge ['blu:ttsɔygə], *m.* (—n, *pl.* —n) martyr.

Bö [bø:], *f.* (—, *pl.* —en) (*Naut.*) squall, gust of wind.

Bock [bɔk], *m.* (—s, *pl.* ̇e) buck; he-goat; (*Gymn.*) horse; (*horse-drawn carriage*) box seat.

bockbeinig ['bɔkbaɪnɪç], *adj.* bow-legged; pigheaded, obstinate.

Bockbier ['bɔkbi:r], *n.* (—s, *no pl.*) bock beer.

bocken ['bɔkən], *v.n.* kick, be refractory; sulk.

Bockfell ['bɔkfɛl], *n.* (—s, *pl.* —e) buckskin.

bockig ['bɔkɪç], *adj.* pigheaded, obstinate.

Bocksbeutel ['bɔksbɔytəl], *m.* (—s, *pl.* —) leather bag; Franconian wine (bottle).

Bockshorn ['bɔkshɔrn], *n.* (—s, *pl.* ̇er) buck horn; *einen ins* — *jagen*, intimidate s.o.

Boden ['bo:dən], *m.* (—s, *pl.* ̇) ground, bottom, soil, floor; garret, loft.

Bodenfenster ['bo:dənfɛnstər], *n.* (—s, *pl.* —) attic window.

Bodenkammer ['bo:dənkamər], *f.* (—, *pl.* —n) garret, attic.

bodenlos ['bo:dənlo:s], *adj.* bottomless; (*fig.*) unimaginable, enormous.

Bodensatz ['bo:dənzats], *m.* (—es, *pl.* ̇e) sediment, dregs, deposit.

Bodensee ['bo:dənze:], *m.* Lake Constance.

Bogen ['bo:gən], *m.* (—s, *pl.* —, ̇) arch, vault, curve; (*Maths.*) arc; (*violin*) bow; (*paper*) sheet; (*Mus.*) ligature.

bogenförmig ['bo:gənfœrmɪç], *adj.* arch-shaped, arched.

Bogenführung ['bo:gənfy:ruŋ], *f.* (—, *no pl.*) (*Mus.*) bowing (technique).

Bogengang ['bo:gəngaŋ], *m.* (—es, *pl.* ̇e) arcade.

Bogenlampe ['bo:gənlampə], *f.* (—, *pl.* —n) arc-lamp.

Bogenschütze ['bo:gənʃytsə], *m.* (—n, *pl.* —n) archer.

bogig ['bo:gɪç], *adj.* bent, curved, arched.

Bohle ['bo:lə], *f.* (—, *pl.* —n) board, plank.

Böhmen ['bø:mən], *n.* Bohemia.

Bohne ['bo:nə], *f.* (—, *pl.* —n) bean; *grüne* —*n*, French (*Am.* string) beans; *dicke* —*n*, broad beans; *blaue* —*n*, (*fig.*) bullets.

Bohnenstange ['bo:nənʃtaŋə], *f.* (—, *pl.* —n) bean-pole.

Bohnerbürste ['bo:nərbyrstə], *f.* (—, *pl.* —n) polishing-brush.

bohnern ['bo:narn], *v.a.* polish, wax.

bohren ['bo:rən], *v.a.* bore, pierce, drill.

Bohrer ['bo:rər], *m.* (—s, *pl.* —) gimlet; drill.

Bohrturm ['bo:rturm], *m.* (—s, *pl.* ̇e) derrick.

Boje ['bo:jə], *f.* (—, *pl.* —n) (*Naut.*) buoy.

Bolivien [bɔ'li:vjən], *n.* Bolivia.

Böller ['bœlər], *m.* (—s, *pl.* —) (*Mil.*) small mortar.

Bollwerk ['bɔlvɛrk], *n.* (—s, *pl.* —e) bulwark.

Bolzen ['bɔltsən], *m.* (—s, *pl.* —) bolt, arrow, pin; (*smoothing iron*) heater.

Bombe ['bɔmbə], *f.* (—, *pl.* —n) bomb, bomb-shell.

Bombenerfolg ['bɔmbənɛrfɔlk], *m.* (—(e)s,*pl.* —e) (*Theat.*) smash hit.

Bonbon [bɔ̃'bɔ̃], *m.* (—s, *pl.* —s) sweet(s), bonbon; (*Am.*) candy.

Bonbonniere [bɔ̃bɔ'njɛ:rə], *f.* (—, *pl.* —n) box of sweets.

Bonze ['bɔntsə], *m.* (—n, *pl.* —n) (*coll.*) bigwig, (*Am.*) big shot.

Boot [bo:t], *n.* (—es, *pl.* —e) boat.

Bootsanker ['bo:tsaŋkər], *m.* (—s, *pl.* —) grapnel.

Bootsleine ['bo:tslaɪnə], *f.* (—, *pl.* —n) tow-rope.

Bor [bo:r], *n.* (—s, *no pl.*) (*Chem.*) boron.

Bord [bɔrt], *m.* (—s, *pl.* —e) rim; (*Naut.*) board.

Bordell [bɔr'dɛl], *n.* (—s, *pl.* —e) brothel.

borgen ['bɔrgən], *v.a., v.n.* borrow; borrow (*von*, from); lend (*Dat.*, to).

Borke ['bɔrkə], *f.* (—, *pl.* —n) bark, rind.

Born [bɔrn], *m.* (—es, —e) (*Poet.*) bourn, spring, well, source.

borniert [bɔr'ni:rt], *adj.* narrow-minded

Borsäure ['bo:rzɔyrə], *f.* (—, *no pl.*) boric acid.

Börse ['bœrzə], *f.* (—, *pl.* —n) purse; (*Comm.*) stock-exchange, bourse.

Börsenbericht ['bœrzənbərɪçt]. *m.* (—s, *pl.* —e) stock-market report.

Borste ['bɔrstə], *f.* (—, *pl.* —n) bristle.

borstig ['bɔrstɪç], *adj.* bristly; (*fig.*) irritable.

Borte ['bɔrtə], *f.* (—, *pl.* —n) order, trimming.

bösartig ['bø:sartɪç], *adj.* malevolent, malicious, vicious; (*disease*) malignant.

Böschung ['bøʃuŋ], *f.* (—, *pl.* —en) slope, scarp.

böse ['bø:zə], *adj.* bad, wicked; evil; angry, cross (with, *Dat.*); — *auf* (*Acc.*), angry with s.o., (*Am.*) mad at s.o.

Bösewicht ['bø:zəvɪçt], *m.* (—s, *pl.* —er) villain, ruffian; wretch.

boshaft ['bo:ʃaft], *adj.* spiteful, malicious.

Bosheit ['bo:ʃaɪt], *f.* (—, *pl.* —en) malice.

böswillig ['bø:svɪlɪç], *adj.* malevolent.

Botanik [bo'ta:nɪk], *f.* (—, *no pl.*) botany.

Botaniker [bo'ta:nɪkər], *m.* (—s, *pl.* —) botanist.

Botanisiertrommel [botanɪ'zi:rtrɔmməl], *f.* (—, *pl.* —n) specimen-box.

Bote ['bo:tə], *m.* (—n, *pl.* —n) messenger.

Botengang ['bo:təŋaŋ], *m.* (—s, *pl.* ⁓e) errand.

botmäßig [bo:tmɛ:sɪç], *adj.* subject, subordinate.

Botschaft ['bo:tʃaft], *f.* (—, *pl.* —en) message; (*Pol.*) embassy; *gute* —, glad tidings.

Botschafter ['bo:tʃaftər], *m.* (—s, *pl.* —) ambassador.

Böttcher ['bœtçər], *m.* (—s, *pl.* —) cooper.

Bottich [bɔtɪç], *m.* (—s, *pl.* —e) vat, tub.

Bouillon [bul'jɔ̃], *f.* (—, *no pl.*) broth, meat soup.

Bowle ['bo:lə], *f.* (—, *no pl.*) bowl; spiced wine.

boxen ['bɔksən], *v.n.* box.

brach [bra:x], *adj.* fallow, unploughed, untilled.

Brand [brant], *m.* (—es, *pl.* ⁓e) burning, fire, combustion, conflagration; (*Med.*) gangrene.

Brandblase ['brantbla:zə], *f.* (—, *pl.* —n) blister.

branden ['brandən], *v.n.* surge, break (waves).

brandig ['brandɪç], *adj.* blighted; (*Med.*) gangrenous.

Brandmal ['brantma:l], *n.* (—s, *pl.* —e) burn mark; brand (cattle); (*fig.*) stigma.

brandmarken ['brantmarkən], *v.a.* brand; (*fig.*) stigmatise.

Brandmauer ['brantmauər], *f.* (—, *pl.* —n) fire-proof wall.

brandschatzen ['brantʃatsən], *v.a.* levy contributions (from); pillage, plunder.

Brandsohle ['brantzo:lə], *f.* (—, *pl.* —n) inner sole, welt (of shoe).

Brandstifter ['brantʃtɪftər], *m.* (—s, *pl.* —) incendiary, fire-raiser.

Brandstiftung ['brantʃtɪftuŋ], *f.* (—, *pl.* —en) arson.

Brandung ['branduŋ], *f.* (—, *pl.* —en) breakers, surf, surge (of sea).

Branntwein ['brantvaɪn], *m.* (—s, *pl.* —e) brandy.

Brasilien [bra'zi:ljən], *n.* Brazil.

Braten ['bra:tən], *m.* (—s, *pl.* —) roast (meat), joint.

braten ['bra:tən], *v.a. reg. & irr.* roast, broil, bake, fry, grill. — *v.n.* (*coll.*) bask (in sun), roast.

Brathering ['bra:the:rɪŋ], *m.* (—s, *pl.* —e) grilled herring.

Brathuhn ['bra:thu:n], *n.* (—s, *pl.* ⁓er) roast chicken.

Bratkartoffeln ['bra:tkartɔfəln], *f. pl.* roast *or* fried potatoes.

Bratpfanne ['bra:tpfanə], *f.* (—, *pl.* —n) frying pan.

Bratsche ['bratʃə], *f.* (—, *pl.* —n) (*Mus.*) viola.

Bratspieß ['bra:tʃpi:s], *m.* (—es, *pl.* —e) spit (roasting).

Bratwurst ['bra:tvurst], *f.* (—, *pl.* ⁓e) sausage for frying; fried sausage.

Brau [brau], **Bräu,** [brɔy], *n. & m.* (—s, *no pl.*) brew.

Brauch [braux], *m.* (—es, *pl.* ⁓e) usage, custom, habit.

brauchbar ['brauxba:r], *adj.* useful, serviceable.

brauchen ['brauxən], *v.a.* make use of, employ; need, require, want; (*time*) take.

Braue ['brauə], *f.* (—, *pl.* —n) brow, eye-brow.

brauen ['brauən], *v.a.* brew.

Brauer ['brauər], *m.* (—s, *pl.* —) brewer.

Brauerei ['brauəraɪ], *f.* (—, *pl.* —en) brewery.

Brauhaus ['brauhaus], *n.* (—es, *pl.* ⁓er) brewery.

braun [braun], *adj.* brown.

bräunen ['brɔynən], *v.a.* make brown, tan.

Braunkohl ['braunko:l], *m.* (—s, *no pl.*) (*Bot.*) broccoli.

Braunschweig ['braunʃvaɪk], *n.* Brunswick.

Braus [braus], *m.* (—es, *no pl.*) bustle, tumult; *in Saus und — leben,* lead a riotous life.

Brause ['brauzə], *f.* (—, *pl.* —n) shower (bath); effervescence, (*coll.*) fizzy drink.

Brausekopf ['brauzəkɔpf], *m.* (—es, *pl.* ⁓e) hothead.

Brauselimonade ['brauzəlimona:də], *f.* (—, *pl.* —n) effervescent *or* fizzy lemonade.

brausen ['brauzən], *v.n.* roar, bluster, rush; effervesce.

Brausepulver ['brauzəpulvər], *n.* (—s, *pl.* —) effervescent powder.

Braut [braut], *f.* (—, *pl.* ⁓e) bride, betrothed, fiancée.

Brautführer ['brautfy:rər], *m.* (—s, *pl.* —) best man.

Bräutigam ['brɔytɪgam], *m.* (—s, *pl.* —e) bridegroom, betrothed, fiancé.

Brautjungfer ['brautjuŋfər], *f.* (—, *pl.* —n) bridesmaid.

bräutlich ['brɔytlɪç], *adj.* bridal.

Brautpaar ['brautpa:r], *n.* (—es, *pl.* —e) engaged couple.

Brautschau ['brautʃau], *f.* (—, *no pl.*) (*obs.*) search for a wife.

brav [bra:f], *adj.* honest, upright, worthy, honourable; well-behaved, good.

bravo! ['bra:vo], *int.* well done!

Bravourstück [bra'vu:rʃtyk], *n.* (—s, *pl.* —e) feat of valour.

Brechbohnen ['brɛçbo:nən], *f. pl.* kidney-beans.

Brecheisen ['brɛçaɪzən], *n.* (—s, *pl.* —) jemmy.

brechen ['brɛçən], *v.a. irr.* break; (*flowers*) pluck, pick; vomit. — *v.n.* (*aux.* sein) break.

Brechmittel ['brɛçmɪtəl], *n.* (—s, *pl.* —) emetic.

Brechruhr ['brɛçru:r], *f.* (—, *no pl.*) cholera.

Brechstange ['brɛçʃtaŋə], *f.* (—, *pl.* —n) crow-bar.

Brechung ['brɛçuŋ], *f.* (—, *pl.* —en) breaking; (*Phys.*) refraction.

Brei [braɪ], *m.* (—s, *pl.* —e) pap, pulp, porridge.

breiartig ['braɪa:rtɪç], *adj.* pulpy.

breiig ['braɪɪç], *adj.* pappy.

breit [braɪt], *adj.* broad, wide.

breitbeinig ['braɪtbaɪnɪç], *adj.* straddle-legged.

Breite ['braɪtə], *f.* (—, *pl.* —n) breadth, width; (*Geog.*) latitude.

Breitengrad ['braɪtəngra:t], *m.* (—es, *pl.* —e) (*Geog.*) degree of latitude.

Breitenkreis ['braɪtənkraɪs], *m.* (—es, *pl.* —e) (*Geog.*) parallel.

breitschultrig ['braɪtʃultrɪç], *adj.* broad-shouldered.

Bremse ['brəmzə], *f.* (—. *pl.* —n) (*Ent.*) gad-fly; (*Motor.*) brake; (*horse*) barnacle.

bremsen ['brɛmzən], *v.a.* brake, pull up.

brennbar ['brɛnba:r], *adj.* combustible.

Brenneisen ['brɛnaɪzən], *n.* (—s, *pl.* —) branding iron.

brennen ['brɛnən], *v.a. irr.* burn; (*Med.*) cauterise; (*alcohol*) distil; (*hair*) curl; (*coffee*) roast; (*coal*) char; (*bricks*) bake. — *v.n.* burn; (*fig.*) sting; (*eyes*) smart.

Brenner ['brɛnər], *m.* (—s, *pl.* —) (*person*) distiller; (*Tech.*) burner.

Brennerei [brɛnə'raɪ], *f.* (—, *pl.* —en) distillery.

Brennessel ['brɛnnɛsəl], *f.* (—, *pl.* —n) stinging nettle.

Brennholz ['brɛnhɔlts], *n.* (—es, *no pl.*) firewood.

Brennmaterial ['brɛnmatərja:l], *n.* (—s, *pl.* —ien) fuel.

Brennofen ['brɛno:fən], *m.* (—s, *pl.* ∸n) kiln.

Brennpunkt ['brɛnpuŋkt], *m.* (—s, *pl.* —e) focus.

Brennschere ['brɛnʃe:rə], *f.* (—, *pl.* —n) curling-irons.

Brennstoff ['brɛnʃtɔf], *m.* (—(e)s, *pl.* —e) fuel.

brenzlich ['brɛntslɪç], *adj.* smelling (or tasting) of burning; (*fig.*) ticklish.

Bresche ['brɛʃə], *f.* (—, *pl.* —n) breach, gap.

Brett [brɛt], *n.* (—s, *pl.* —er) board, plank, shelf.

Brettspiel ['brɛtʃpi:l], *n.* (—s, *pl.* —e) table-game.

Brevier [bre'vi:r], *n.* (—s, *pl.* (*rare*) —e) breviary.

Brezel ['bre:tsəl], *f.* (—, *pl.* —n) cracknel, pretzel.

Brief [bri:f], *m.* (—es, *pl.* —e) letter; epistle.

Briefanschrift ['bri:fanʃrɪft], *f.* (—, *pl.* —en) address.

Briefbeschwerer ['bri:fbəʃve:rər], *m.* (—s, *pl.* —) letter-weight, paper-weight.

Briefbogen ['bri:fbo:gən], *m.* (—s, *pl.* —) sheet of notepaper.

Briefkasten ['bri:fkastən], *m.* (—s, *pl.* ∸) (*house*) letter-box; (*street*) pillar-box, (*Am.*) post-box.

brieflich ['bri:flɪç], *adv.* by letter, in writing.

Briefmarke ['bri:fmarkə], *f.* (—, *pl.* —n) postage stamp.

Briefpapier ['bri:fpapi:r], *n.* (—s, *no pl.*) notepaper.

Briefporto ['bri:fpɔrto], *n.* (—s, *pl.* —ti) postage.

Brieftasche ['bri:ftaʃə], *f.* (—, *pl.* —n) portfolio, wallet; (*Am.*) pocket-book.

Brieftaube ['bri:ftaubə], *f.* (—, *pl.* —n) carrier pigeon.

Briefträger ['bri:ftrɛ:gər], *m.* (—s, *pl.* —) postman.

Briefumschlag ['bri:fumʃla:k], *m.* (—s, *pl.* ∸e) envelope.

Briefwechsel ['bri:fvɛksəl], *m.* (—s, *no pl.*) correspondence.

Brillant [bril'jant], *m.* (—en, *pl.* —en) brilliant, diamond. — *adj.* brilliant.

Brille ['brɪle], *f.* (— *pl.* —n) spectacles, glasses.

Brillenschlange ['brɪlənʃlaŋə], *f.* (—, *pl.* —n) (*Zool.*) hooded cobra.

bringen ['brɪŋən], *v.a. irr.* bring, fetch, carry to, take to, conduct to.

Brise ['bri:zə], *f.* (—, *pl.* —n) breeze, light wind.

Britannien [brɪ'tanjən], *n.* Britain.

bröckeln ['brœkəln], *v.a., v.n.* crumble.

Brocken ['brɔkən], *m.* (—s, *pl.* —) bit, piece, fragment, scrap; (*bread*) crumb.

bröcklig ['brœklɪç], *adj.* crumbling.

brodeln ['bro:dəln], *v.n.* bubble, simmer.

Brodem ['bro:dəm], *m.* (—s, *no pl.*) (*Poet.*) steam, vapour, exhalation.

Brokat [bro'ka:t], *m.* (—s, *pl.* —e) brocade.

Brom [bro:m], *n.* (—s, *no pl.*) (*Chem.*) bromine.

Brombeere ['brɔmbe:rə], *f.* (—, *pl.* —n) blackberry, bramble.

Bronze ['brɔ̃:sə], *f.* (—, *pl.* —n) bronze.

Brosamen ['bro:za:mən], *pl.* crumbs.

Brosche ['brɔʃə], *f.* (—, *pl.* —n) brooch.

Broschüre [brɔ'ʃy:rə], *f.* (—, *pl.* —n) pamphlet, brochure, folder.

Brösel ['brø:zəl], *m.* (—s, *pl.* —) crumb.

Brot [bro:t], *n.* (—es, *pl.* —e) bread, loaf; (*fig.*) livelihood.

Brötchen ['brø:tçən], *n.* (—s, *pl.* —) roll, bread-roll.

Broterwerb

Broterwerb ['bro:tərvɛrp], *m.* (—s, *no pl.*) livelihood.

Brotgeber ['bro:tge:bər], *m.* (—s, *pl.* —) employer, master.

Brotherr ['bro:thɛr], *m.* (—n, *pl.* —en) employer, master.

Brotkorb ['bro:tkɔrp], *m.* (—s, *pl.* ⁀e) bread-basket.

brotlos ['bro:tlo:s], *adj.* unemployed; (*fig.*) unprofitable.

Brotneid ['bro:tnaɪt], *m.* (—s, *no pl.*) professional jealousy.

Bruch [brux], *m.* (—s, *pl.* ⁀e) breakage; rupture; (*Med.*) fracture, rupture, hernia; (*Maths.*) fraction.

Bruchband ['bruxbant], *f.* (—es, *pl.* ⁀er) abdominal belt, truss.

brüchig ['bryçɪç], *adj.* brittle, full of flaws.

Bruchlandung ['bruxlanduŋ], *f.* (—, —en) (*Aviat.*) crash-landing.

Bruchrechnung ['bruxrɛçnuŋ], *f.* (—, *pl.* —en) (*Arith.*) fractions.

Bruchstück ['bruxʃtyk], *n.* (—s, *pl.* —e) fragment, scrap.

Bruchteil ['bruxtaɪl], *m.* (—s, *pl.* —e) fraction.

Brücke ['brykə], *f.* (—, *pl.* —n) bridge.

Brückenpfeiler ['brykənpfaɪlər], *m.* (—s, *pl.* —) pier.

Bruder ['bru:dər], *m.* (—s, *pl.* ⁀) brother; (*Eccl.*) friar.

brüderlich ['bry:dərlɪç], *adj.* fraternal, brotherly.

Bruderschaft ['bru:dərʃaft], *f.* (—, *pl.* —en) fraternity, brotherhood.

Brügge ['brygə], *n.* Bruges.

Brühe ['bry:ə], *f.* (—, *pl.* —n) broth, meat-soup.

brühen ['bry:ən], *v.a.* scald.

Brühkartoffeln ['bry:kartɔfəln], *f. pl.* potatoes cooked in broth.

brüllen ['brylən], *v.n.* roar, howl, yell; (*cows*) low, bellow.

Brummbaß ['brumbas], *m.* (—sses, *pl.* ⁀sse) (*Mus.*) double-bass.

Brummeisen ['brumaɪzən], *n.* (—s, *pl.* —) Jew's harp.

brummen ['brumən], *v.n.* growl, grumble, hum.

Brummer ['brumər], *n.* (—s, *pl.* —) (*Ent.*) blue-bottle.

Brunnen ['brunən], *m.* (—s, *pl.* —) well, fountain, spring.

Brunnenkur ['brunənku:r], *f.* (—, *pl.* —en) taking of mineral waters.

Brunst [brunst], *f.* (—, *pl.* ⁀e) (*Zool.*) rut, heat.

Brust [brust], *f.* (—, *pl.* ⁀e) breast; chest; bosom.

Brustbein ['brustbaɪn], *n.* (—s, *pl.* —e) breastbone, sternum.

Brustbild ['brustbɪlt], *n.* (—s, *pl.* —er) half-length portrait.

brüsten ['brystən], *v.r. sich* —, boast, brag, plume o.s.

Brustfell ['brustfɛl], *n.* (—s, *pl.* —e) pleura.

Brustfellentzündung ['brustfɛlɛntsyn-duŋ], *f.* (—, *no pl.*) pleurisy.

Brusthöhle ['brusthø:lə], *f.* (—, *pl.* —n) thoracic cavity.

Brustkasten ['brustkastən], *m.* (—s, *pl.* ⁀n) chest.

Brusttee ['brustte:], *m.* (—s, *no pl.*) pectoral (herbal) tea.

Brüstung ['brystuŋ], *f.* (—, *pl.* —en) parapet.

Brustwarze ['brustvartsə], *f.* (—, *pl.* —n) nipple.

Brustwehr ['brustve:r], *f.* (—, *pl.* —en) breastwork, parapet.

Brut [bru:t], *f.* (—, *no pl.*) brood; (*fish*) fry.

brutal [bru'ta:l], *adj.* brutal.

brüten ['bry:tən], *v.a.* brood, hatch.

Brutofen ['bru:to:fən], *m.* (—s, *pl.* ⁀) incubator.

brutto ['bruto], *adj.* (*Comm.*) gross.

Bube ['bu:bə], *m.* (—n, *pl.* —n) boy, lad; (*cards*) knave, (*Am.*) jack; rogue, rascal.

Bubenstreich ['bu:bənʃtraɪç], *m.* (—s, *pl.* —e) boyish prank; knavish trick.

Bubikopf ['bu:bɪkɔpf], *m.* (—(e)s, *pl.* ⁀e) bobbed hair.

Buch [bu:x], *n.* (—s, *pl.* ⁀er) book; quire (of paper).

Buchdruckerei ['bu:xdrukəraɪ], *f.* (—, —en) printing works, printing office.

Buche ['bu:xə], *f.* (—, *pl.* —n) beech (tree).

buchen ['bu:xən], *v.a.* book, enter, reserve; (*fig.*) score.

Bücherei [by:çə'raɪ], *f.* (—, *pl.* —en) library.

Buchesche ['bu:xɛʃə], *f.* (—, *pl.* —n) hornbeam.

Buchfink ['bu:xfɪŋk], *m.* (—en, *pl.* —en) (*Orn.*) chaffinch.

Buchhalter ['bu:xhaltər], *m.* (—s, *pl.* —) book-keeper.

Buchhändler ['bu:xhɛndlər], *m.* (—s, *pl.* —) bookseller.

Buchmarder ['bu:xmardər], *m.* (—s, *pl.* —) (*Zool.*) pine-marten.

Buchsbaum ['buksbaum], *m.* (—s, *pl.* ⁀e) (*Bot.*) box-tree.

Büchse ['byksə], *f.* (—, *pl.* —n) box, case; tin, can; rifle, gun.

Büchsenfleisch ['byksənflaɪʃ], *n.* (—es, *no pl.*) tinned meat.

Büchsenlauf ['byksənlauf], *m.* (—s, *pl.* ⁀e) gun-barrel.

Büchsenöffner ['byksənœfnər], *m.* (—s, *pl.*—) tin-opener.

Buchstabe ['bu:xʃta:bə], *m.* (—n, *pl.* —n) letter, character; *großer* —, capital (letter).

Buchstabenrätsel ['bu:xʃta:bənrɛtsəl], *n.* (—s, *pl.* —) anagram.

buchstabieren [bu:xʃta'bi:rən], *v.a.* spell (out).

buchstäblich ['bu:xʃtɛplɪç], *adj.* literal.

Bucht [buxt], *f.* (—, *pl.* —en) inlet, bay, creek, bight.

Buchung ['bu:xuŋ], *f.* (—, *pl.* —en) (*Comm.*) entry (in a book); booking (of tickets).

40

Buchwissen ['bu:xvɪsən], n. (—s, no pl.) book-learning.

Buckel ['bukəl], m. (—s, pl. —) hump, humpback; boss, stud; (coll.) back.

bücken ['bykən], v.r. sich —, stoop, bow.

bucklig ['buklɪç], adj. humpbacked.

Bückling ['byklɪŋ], m. (—s, pl. —e) smoked herring; kipper.

buddeln ['budəln], v.n. (coll.) dig.

Bude ['bu:də], f. (—, pl. —n) shack, stall; (coll.) room; (student's) digs.

Büfett [by'fɛt], n. (—s, pl. —s) sideboard; buffet.

Büffel ['byfəl], m. (—s, pl. —) buffalo.

büffeln ['byfəln], v.n. (coll.) cram (for an examination), swot.

Bug [bu:k], m. (—s, pl. ⁻e, —e) (Naut.) bow, (Aviat.) nose.

Buganker ['bu:kaŋkər], m. (—s, pl. —) bow-anchor.

Bügel ['bygəl], m. (—s, pl. —) coat-hanger; (trigger) guard; (horse) stirrup.

bügeln ['bygəln], v.a. iron, smoothe, press.

bugsieren [buk'si:rən], v.a. tow.

Bugspriet ['bu:kʃpri:t], n. (—s, pl. —e) bowsprit.

Buhle ['bu:lə], m. or f. (—n, pl. —n) (Poet.) paramour, lover.

buhlen ['bu:lən], v.n. (Poet.) woo, make love (to).

buhlerisch ['bu:lərɪʃ], adj. (Poet.) amorous, wanton, lewd.

Bühne ['by:nə], f. (—, pl. —n) (Theat.) stage; scaffold, platform.

Bühnenbild ['by:nənbɪlt], n. (—es, pl. —er) scenery.

Bukett [bu'kɛt], n. (—s, pl. —s) bunch of flowers, bouquet; bouquet (wine).

Bulgarien [bul'ga:rjən], n. Bulgaria.

Bulldogge ['buldɔgə], f. (—, pl. —n) bulldog.

Bulle (1) ['bulə], m. (—n, pl. —n) bull, bullock.

Bulle (2) ['bulə], f. (—, pl. —n) (Eccl.) (Papal) Bull.

bumm [bum], int. boom! bang!

Bummel ['buməl], m. (—s, pl. —) stroll.

Bummelei [bumə'laɪ], f. (—, pl. —en) idleness, negligence, casualness, carelessness.

bummeln ['buməln], v.n. lounge, waste o.'s time, dawdle; stroll.

Bummelzug ['buməltsu:k], m. (—s, pl. ⁻e) slow train.

bums [bums], int. bang! crash!

Bund (1) [bunt], m. (—es, pl. ⁻e) bond, tie, league, alliance, federation, confederacy; (Eccl.) covenant.

Bund (2) [bunt], n. (—es, pl. —e) bundle, bunch (of keys).

Bündel ['byndəl], n. (—s, pl. —) bundle, package.

Bundesgenosse ['bundəsgənɔsə], m. (—n, pl. —n) confederate, ally.

Bundesstaat ['bundəsʃta:t], m. (—es, pl. —en) federal state; federation.

Bundestag ['bundəsta:k], m. (—es, pl. —e) federal parliament.

Bundeswehr ['bundəsve:r], f. (—, no pl.) federal defence; armed forces.

bündig ['byndɪç], adj. binding; kurz und —, concise, terse, to the point.

Bündnis ['byntnɪs], n. (—ses, pl. —se) alliance.

Bundschuh ['buntʃu:], m. (—s, pl. —e) clog, sandal.

bunt [bunt], adj. many-coloured, chequered, variegated, motley; das ist mir zu —, this is going too far.

buntscheckig ['buntʃekɪç], adj. dappled, spotted.

Buntspecht ['buntʃpeçt], m. (—s, pl. —e) (Orn.) (spotted) woodpecker.

Bürde ['byrdə], f. (—, pl. —n) load, burden.

Bure ['bu:rə], m. (—n, pl. —n) Boer.

Burg [burk], f. (—, pl. —en) castle, fortress, citadel, stronghold.

Bürge ['byrgə], m. (—n, pl. —n) surety, bail, guarantee; einen —n stellen, offer bail.

bürgen ['byrgən], v.n. give security, vouch (for), go bail (for).

Bürger ['byrgər], m. (—s, pl. —) citizen, townsman, bourgeois, commoner.

bürgerlich ['byrgərlɪç], adj. civic; middle-class, bourgeois; —e Küche, plain cooking.

Bürgermeister ['byrgərmaɪstər], m. (—s, pl. —) burgomaster, mayor.

Burggraf ['burkgra:f], m. (—en, pl. —en) burgrave.

Bürgschaft ['byrkʃaft], f. (—, pl. —en) bail, surety, guarantee; — leisten, provide security.

Burgund [bur'gunt], n. Burgundy.

Burgvogt ['burkfo:kt], m. (—s, pl. —e) (obs.) castellan, bailiff.

Burgwarte ['burkvartə], f. (—, pl. —n) watch-tower.

Büro [by'ro:], n. (—s, pl. —s) office, bureau, (professional) chambers.

Bursche ['burʃə], m. (—n, pl. —n) lad, boy, fellow; student; (Mil.) batman.

Burschenschaft ['burʃənʃaft], f. (—, pl. —en) students' association.

Bürste ['byrstə], f. (—, pl. —n) brush.

Burundi [bu'rundi], n. Burundi.

Busch [buʃ], m. (—es, pl. ⁻e) bush, shrub, copse, thicket.

Büschel ['byʃəl], n. (—s, pl. —) bunch; (hair) tuft.

buschig ['buʃɪç], adj. bushy, tufted.

Buschklepper ['buʃklepər], m. (—s, pl. —) bushranger.

Busen ['bu:zən], m. (—s, pl. —) bosom, breast; (Geog.) bay, gulf.

Bussard ['busart], m. (—s, pl. —e) (Orn.) buzzard.

Buße ['bu:sə], f. (—, pl. —n) penance; repentance; penalty.

büßen ['by:sən], v.a., v.n. repent, atone, expiate, make amends.

bußfertig ['bu:sfɛrtɪç], adj. penitent, repentant.

Büste

Büste ['bystə], *f.* (—, *pl.* —**n**) bust.
Büstenhalter ['bystenhaltər], *m.* (—**s**, *pl.* —) brassière.
Bütte ['bytə], *f.* (—, *pl.* —**n**) tub.
Büttel ['bytəl], *m.* (—**s**, *pl.* —) beadle; bailiff.
Büttenpapier ['bytənpapi:r], *n.* (—**s**, *no pl.*) hand-made paper.
Butter ['butər], *f.* (—, *no pl.*) butter.
Butterblume ['butərblu:mə], *f.* (—, *pl.* —**n**) buttercup.
Butterbrot ['butərbro:t], *n.* (—**s**, *pl.* —**e**) bread and butter.
buttern ['butərn], *v.a.*, *v.n.* smear with butter; churn.
Butterteig ['butərtaik], *m.* (—**es**, *pl.* —**e**) puff-pastry.
Butzenscheibe ['butsənʃaibə], *f.* (—, *pl.* —**n**) bull's-eyed pane.
Byzanz [by'tsants], *n.* Byzantium, Constantinople.

C

C [tse:], *n.* (—**s**, *pl.* —**s**) the letter C; (*Mus.*) *C dur*, C major; *C Moll*, C minor; *C-Schlüssel*, C clef.
Cäsar ['tse:zar], *m.* Cæsar.
Ceylon ['tseilon], *n.* Ceylon.
Chaiselongue [ʃɛ:zə'lɔ̃:g], *f.* (—, *pl.* —**s**) couch, settee, sofa.
Champagner [ʃam'panjər], *m.* (—**s**, *pl.* —) champagne.
Champignon [ʃampin'jɔ̃], *m.* (—**s**, *pl.* —**s**) mushroom.
chaotisch [ka'o:tiʃ], *adj.* chaotic.
Charakter [ka'raktər], *m.* (—**s**, *pl.* —**e**) character; mental make-up, disposition.
Charakteristik [karaktər'istik], *f.* (—, *pl.* —**en**) characterisation.
charakteristisch [karaktər'istiʃ], *adj.* characteristic; typical.
Charge ['ʃarʒə], *f.* (—, *pl.* —**n**) office, appointment; (*pl.*) (*Mil.*) non-commissioned officers.
Chaussee [ʃɔ'se:], *f.* (—, *pl.* —**n**) main road, highway.
Chef [ʃɛf], *m.* (—**s**, *pl.* —**s**) chief, head, employer; (*coll.*) boss.
Chefredakteur ['ʃɛfredaktø:r], *m.* (—**s**, *pl.* —**e**) editor-in-chief.
Chemie [çe'mi:], *f.* (—, *no pl.*) chemistry.
Chemikalien [çemi'ka:ljən], *f. pl.* chemicals.
Chemiker ['çe:mikər], *m.* (—**s**, *pl.* —) (analytical) chemist.
chemisch ['çe:miʃ], *adj.* chemical; — *gereinigt*, dry-cleaned.
Chiffre ['ʃifər], *f.* (—, *pl.* —**n**) cipher.
chiffrieren [ʃi'fri:rən], *v.a.* encipher.
Chile ['tʃi:lə, 'çi:lə], *n.* Chile.

China ['çi:na], *n.* China.
Chinarinde [çi:na'rində], *f.* (—, *no pl.*) Peruvian bark.
Chinin [çi'ni:n], *n.* (—**s**, *no pl.*) quinine.
Chirurg [çi'rurk], *m.* (—**en**, *pl.* —**en**) surgeon.
Chirurgie [çirur'gi:], *f.* (—, *no pl.*) surgery.
Chlor [klo:r], *n.* (—**s**, *no pl.*) chlorine.
Chlorkalk ['klo:rkalk], *m.* (—**s**, *no pl.*) chloride of lime.
Chlornatrium [klo:r'na:trjum], *n.* (—**s**, *no pl.*) sodium chloride.
Choleriker [ko'le:rikər], *m.* (—**s**, *pl.* —) irascible person.
Chor [ko:r], *m.* (—**s**, *pl.* ¨**e**) chorus; choir; (*Archit.*) choir, chancel.
Choral [ko'ra:l], *m.* (—**s**, *pl.* ¨**e**) hymn, chorale.
Choramt ['ko:ramt], *n.* (—**s**, *pl.* ¨**er**) cathedral service.
Chorgesang ['ko:rgəsaŋ], *m.* (—**s**, *pl.* ¨**e**) chorus, choral singing.
Chorhemd ['ko:rhɛmt], *n.* (—**s**, *pl.* —**en**) surplice.
Chorherr ['ko:rhɛr], *m.* (—**n**, *pl.* —**en**) canon, prebendary.
Christ [krist], *m.* (—**en**, *pl.* —**en**) Christian.
Christbaum ['kristbaum], *m.* (—**s**, *pl.* ¨**e**) Christmas tree.
Christentum ['kristəntu:m], *n.* (—**s**, *no pl.*) Christendom, Christianity.
Christkind ['kristkint], *n.* (—**s**, *no pl.*) Infant Christ, Christ child.
christlich ['kristliç], *adj.* Christian.
Christmette ['kristmɛtə], *f.* (—, *pl.* —**n**) Christmas matins; midnight mass.
Christus ['kristus], *m.* (—**i**) Christ; *vor* —, B.C.; *nach* —, A.D.
Chrom [kro:m], *n.* (—**s**, *no pl.*) chrome.
chromatisch [kro'ma:tiʃ], *adj.* chromatic.
chromsauer ['kro:mzauər], *adj.* chromate of; —*es Salz*, chromate.
Chronik ['kro:nik], *f.* (—, *pl.* —**en**) chronicle.
chronisch ['kro:niʃ], *adj.* chronic.
Chronist [kro'nist], *m.* (—**en**, *pl.* —**en**) chronicler.
Chrysantheme [kryzan'te:mə], *f.* (—, *pl.* —**n**) chrysanthemum.
Cis [tsis], *n.* (*Mus.*) C sharp.
Clique ['klikə], *f.* (—, *pl.* —**n**) clique, set.
Coeur [kø:r], *n.* (*Cards*) hearts.
coulant [ku'lant], *adj.* polite, friendly; (*Comm.*) fair, obliging.
Couleur [ku'lø:r], *f.* (—, *pl.* —**en**) colour; students' corporation.
Coupé [ku'pe:], *n.* (—**s**, *pl.* —**s**) (*train*) compartment.
Couplet [ku'ple:], *n.* (—**s**, *pl.* —**s**) comic song.
Coupon [ku'põ], *m.* (—**s**, *pl.* —**s**) coupon, check, dividend voucher.
Cour [ku:r], *f.* (—, *no pl.*) *einem Mädchen die* — *machen*, court a girl.

Danzig

Courtage [kur'ta:ʒə], *f.* (—, *pl.* —n) brokerage.
Cousin [ku'zɛ̃], *m.* (—s, *pl.* —s) cousin.
Cousine [ku'zi:nə], *f.* (—, *pl.* —n) (female) cousin.
Cutaway ['katave:], *m.* (—s, *pl.* —s) morning coat.
Czar [tsa:r], *m.* (—en, *pl.* —en) Tsar, Czar.

D

D [de:], *n.* (—s, *pl.* —s) the letter D; (*Mus.*) D *dur*, D major; D *moll*, D minor; *D-Zug*, express train.
da [da:], *adv.* (*local*) there; here; (*temporal*) then, at that moment; (*Mil.*) *wer* —? who goes there? (*Poet. obs.*) where. — *conj.* (*temporal*) when, as; (*causal*) as, because, since.
dabei [da'baɪ], *adv.* nearby; besides, moreover; as well; —*sein*, be present, be about to (*infin.*); — *bleiben*, persist in.
Dach [dax], *n.* (—es, *pl.* ⁻er) roof.
Dachboden ['daxbo:dən], *m.* (—s, *pl.* ⁻) loft.
Dachdecker ['daxdɛkər], *m.* (—s, *pl.* —) slater, tiler.
Dachgiebel ['daxgi:bəl], *m.* (—s, *pl.* —) gable.
Dachluke ['daxlu:kə], *f.* (—, *pl.* —n) dormer window.
Dachpappe ['daxpapə], *f.* (—, *pl.* —n) roofing felt.
Dachrinne ['daxrɪnə], *f.* (—, *pl.* —n) gutter.
Dachs [daks], *m.* (—es, *pl.* —e) badger.
Dachstube ['daxʃtu:bə], *f.* (—, *pl.* —n) garret, attic (room).
Dachtraufe ['daxtraufə], *f.* (—, *pl.* —n) eaves.
dadurch [da'durç], *adv.* (*local*) through it; in that way; (*causal*) thereby.
dafür [da'fy:r], *adv.* for it; instead of it, in return for it; *ich kann nichts* —, it is not my fault, I can't help it.
Dafürhalten [da'fy:rhaltən], *n.* (—s, *no pl.*) opinion.
dagegen [da'ge:gən], *adv.* against it, compared to it. — *conj.* on the other hand.
daheim [da'haɪm], *adv.* at home.
daher [da'he:r], *adv.* thence, from that. — *conj.* therefore, for that reason.
dahin [da'hɪn], *adv.* thither, to that place; there; *bis* —, (*local*) thither; (*temporal*) till then; over, past, lost, gone.
dahinbringen [da'hɪnbrɪŋən], *v.a. irr.* *jemanden* —, induce s.o. to; *es* —, succeed in, manage to.

dahinsiechen [da'hɪnzi:çən], *v.n.* (*aux. sein*) pine away, be failing (in health).
dahinter [da'hɪntər], *adv.* behind that.
Dahlie ['da:ljə], *f.* (—, *pl.* —n) (*Bot.*) dahlia.
Dahome ['daome:], *n.* Dahomey.
damalig ['da:malɪç], *adj.* then; of that time; past.
damals ['da:mals], *adv.* then, at that time.
Damast [da'mast], *m.* (—s, *no pl.*) damask.
Damaszener [damas'tse:nər], *m.* (—s, *pl.* —) Damascene. — *adj.* — *Stahl*, Damascus steel, dagger.
Dame ['da:mə], *f.* (—, *pl.* —n) lady; (*cards, chess*) queen; draughts (*game*).
damit [da'mɪt], *adv.* therewith, with that, with it; *und* — *basta!* and that's all there is to it. — *conj.* in order that, so that; — *nicht*, lest.
dämlich ['dɛ:mlɪç], *adj.* (*coll.*) foolish, silly.
Damm [dam], *m.* (—es, *pl.* ⁻e) dam, dyke, mole; (*street*) roadway, causeway; (*rail*) embankment.
dämmen ['dɛmən], *v.a.* dam; (*fig.*) stop, restrain.
dämmerig ['dɛmərɪç], *adj.* dusky.
dämmern ['dɛmərn], *v.n.* grow dusky; dawn.
dämonisch [dɛ'mo:nɪʃ], *adj.* demoniac(-al), demonlike.
Dampf [dampf], *m.* (—es, *pl.* ⁻e) vapour, steam, mist, fume; smoke, steam.
dampfen ['dampfən], *v.n.* smoke, fume, steam.
dämpfen ['dɛmpfən], *v.a.* damp, smother, steam; subdue, deaden, muffle, soften down.
Dampfer ['dampfər], *m.* (—s, *pl.* —) steamer.
Dämpfer ['dɛmpfər], *m.* (—s, *pl.* —) damper; (*Mus.*) mute.
Dampfkessel ['dampfkɛsəl], *m.* (—s, *pl.* —) boiler.
Dämpfung ['dɛmpfuŋ], *f.* (—, *pl.* —en) damping, smothering, suppression; (*Aviat.*) stabilization.
danach [da'na:x], *adv.* after that, thereafter; accordingly, according to that.
daneben [da'ne:bən], *adv.* near it, by it, close by; *es geht* —, it goes amiss. — *conj.* besides.
Dänemark ['dɛ:nəmark], *n.* Denmark.
Dank [daŋk], *m.* (—es, *no pl.*) thanks, gratitude; reward; *Gott sei* —, thank heaven!
dank [daŋk], *prep.* (*Dat.*) owing to, thanks to.
dankbar ['daŋkba:r], *adj.* grateful; thankful.
danken ['daŋkən], *v.n.* (*Dat.*) thank. — *v.a.* owe.
Dankgebet ['daŋkgəbe:t], *n.* (—s, *pl.* —e) (prayer of) thanksgiving.
dann [dan], *adv.* then, at that time, in that case; — *und wann*, now and then, occasionally.
Danzig ['dantsɪç], *n.* Dantzig.

43

daran

daran, dran [da'ran, dran], *adv.* on it, at it, near that; thereon, thereby; *was liegt —?* what does it matter?

darauf, drauf [da'rauf, drauf], *adv.* (*local*) upon it, on it; (*temporal*) thereupon, thereafter.

daraufhin [darauf'hɪn], *adv.* thereupon; on the strength of that.

daraus, draus [da'raus, draus], *adv.* therefrom, hence, from that; *ich mache mir nichts —*, I do not care for it.

darben ['darbən], *v.n.* suffer want, go short; famish.

darbieten ['da:rbi:tən], *v.a. irr.* offer, tender, present.

Darbietung ['da:rbi:tuŋ], *f.* (—, *pl.* —en) offering, presentation, performance.

darbringen ['da:rbrɪŋən], *v.a. irr.* bring, present, offer.

darein, drein [da'raɪn, draɪn], *adv.* into it, therein.

darin, drin [da'rɪn, drɪn], *adv.* therein, in it, within.

darinnen, drinnen [da'rɪnən, 'drɪnən], *adv.* inside, in there.

darlegen ['da:rle:gən], *v.a.* demonstrate, explain; expound.

Darlehen ['da:rle:ən], *n.* (—s, *pl.* —) loan.

Darm [darm], *m.* (—s, *pl.* ⸚e) gut; (*pl.*) intestines, bowels.

Darmsaite ['darmzaɪtə], *f.* (—, *pl.* —n) catgut, gut-string.

darob [da'rɔp], *adv.* (*obs.*) on that account, on account of it.

darreichen ['da:raɪçən], *v.a.* offer, tender, present; (*Eccl.*) administer (sacraments).

darstellen ['da:rʃtɛlən], *v.a.* represent, delineate; (*Theat.*) perform.

Darstellung ['da:rʃtɛluŋ], *f.* (—, *pl.* —en) representation, exhibition, presentation; (*Theat.*) performance.

dartun ['da:rtu:n], *v.a. irr.* prove, demonstrate.

darüber, drüber [dar'y:bər, 'dry:bər], *adv.* over that, over it; concerning that.

darum, drum [da'rum, drum], *adv.* around it, around that, thereabout; therefore, for that reason.

darunter, drunter [da'runtər, 'druntər], *adv.* under that; thereunder; among; — *und drüber*, topsy-turvy.

das [das], *def. art. n.* the. — *dem. pron.*, *dem. adj.* that, this. —*rel. pron.* which.

Dasein ['da:zaɪn], *n.* (—s, *no pl.*) presence, being, existence.

daselbst [da:'zɛlpst], *adv.* there, in that very place.

daß [das], *conj.* that; *es sei denn —*, unless; — *nicht*, lest.

dastehen ['da:ʃte:ən], *v.n. irr.* stand (there).

datieren [da'ti:rən], *v.a.* date, put a date to.

Dativ ['da:ti:f], *m.* (—s, *pl.* —e) dative.

dato ['da:to], *adv. bis —*, till now, hitherto.

Dattel ['datəl], *f.* (—, *pl.* —n) (*Bot.*) date.

Datum ['da:tum], *n.* (—s, *pl.* **Daten**) date (*calendar*).

Dauer ['dauər], *f.* (—, *no pl.*) duration, length of time; continuance; permanence.

dauerhaft ['dauərhaft], *adj.* durable, lasting; (*colours*) fast.

Dauerkarte ['dauərkartə], *f.* (—, *pl.* —n) season ticket; (*Am.*) commutation ticket.

dauern ['dauərn], *v.n.* continue, last, endure.— *v.a.* move to pity; *er dauert mich*, I am sorry for him.

Dauerpflanze ['dauərpflantsə], *f.* (—, *pl.* —n) perennial plant.

Dauerwelle ['dauərvɛlə], *f.* (—, *pl.* —n) permanent wave, (*coll.*) perm.

Daumen ['daumən], *m.* (—s, *pl.* —) thumb; *einem den — halten*, wish s.o. well, keep o.'s fingers crossed for s.o.

Daune ['daunə], *f.* (—, *pl.* —n) down.

davon [da'fɔn], *adv.* thereof, therefrom, from that; off, away.

davonkommen [da'fɔnkɔmən], *v.n. irr.* (*aux.* sein) get off; *mit einem blauen Auge —*, get off lightly.

davor [da'fo:r], *adv.* before that, before it.

dawider [da'vi:dər], *adv.* against it.

dazu [da'tsu:], *adv.* thereto, to that, to it; in addition to that; for that purpose; *noch —*, besides.

dazumal ['da:tsuma:l], *adv.* then, at that time.

dazwischen [da'tsvɪʃən], *adv.* between, among; — *kommen*, intervene, interfere; — *treten*, intervene.

debattieren [deba'ti:rən], *v.a.*, *v.n.* debate.

Debet ['de:bɛt], *n.* (—s, *pl.* —s) debit.

Debüt [de'by:], *n.* (—s, *pl.* —s) first appearance, début.

Dechant [de'çant], *m.* (—en, *pl.* —en) (*Eccl.*) dean.

dechiffrieren [deʃɪf'ri:rən], *v.a.* decode, decipher.

Deck [dɛk], *n.* (—s, *pl.* —e) (*Naut.*) deck.

Deckbett ['dɛkbɛt], *n.* (—s, *pl.* —en) coverlet.

Deckblatt ['dɛkblat], *n.* (—s, *pl.* ⸚er) (*Bot.*) bractea; (*cigar*) wrapper.

Decke ['dɛkə], *f.* (—, *pl.* —n) cover; blanket, rug; (*bed*) coverlet; (*room*) ceiling.

Deckel ['dɛkəl], *m.* (—s, *pl.* —) lid, top; (*book*) cover; (*coll.*) hat.

decken ['dɛkən], *v.a.* cover; (*Comm.*) secure, reimburse. — *v.r. sich* (*Maths.*) coincide; (*fig.*) square, tally.

Deckfarbe ['dɛkfarbə], *f.* (—, *pl.* —n) body colour.

Deckmantel ['dɛkmantəl], *m.* (—s, *pl.* ⸚) cloak, disguise.

Deckung ['dɛkuŋ], *f.* (—, *pl.* —en) covering, protection; (*Comm.*) reimbursement; security; (*Mil.*) cover.

dedizieren [dedɪ'tsi:rən], *v.a.* dedicate.

deduzieren [dedu'tsi:rən], *v.a.* deduce.

defekt [de'fɛkt], *adj.* defective, incomplete, imperfect.

defilieren [defi'li:rən], *v.n.* (*Mil.*) pass in review, march past.

definieren [defi'ni:rən], *v.a.* define.

Degen ['de:gən], *m.* (—s, *pl.* —) sword; (*fig.*) brave warrior.

degradieren [degra'di:rən], *v.a.* degrade, demote.

dehnbar ['de:nba:r], *adj.* extensible, ductile.

dehnen ['de:nən], *v.a.* extend, expand, stretch. — *v.r. sich* —, stretch o.s.

Deich [daɪç], *m.* (—es, *pl.* —e) dike, dam, embankment.

Deichsel ['daɪksəl], *f.* (—, *pl.* —n) thill, shaft, pole.

deichseln ['daɪksəln], *v.a.* (*fig.*) engineer; (*coll.*) manage; wangle.

dein [daɪn], *poss. adj.* your; (*Poet.*) thy. — *poss. pron.* yours; (*Poet.*) thine.

deinesgleichen [daɪnəs'glaɪçən], *adj. pron.* the like of you, such as you.

deinethalben ['daɪnəthalbən], *adv.* on your account, for your sake, on your behalf.

deinetwegen ['daɪnətve:gən], *adv.* because of you, on your account, for your sake, on your behalf.

deinetwillen ['daɪnətvɪlən], *adv. um* —, on your account, for your sake, on your behalf.

deinige ['daɪnɪgə], *poss. adj.* your; (*Poet.*) thy. — *poss. pron.* yours; (*Poet.*) thine.

Dekan [de'ka:n], *m.* (—s, *pl.* —e) (*Eccl., Univ.*) dean.

Dekanat [deka'na:t], *n.* (—s, *pl.* —e) (*Eccl., Univ.*) deanery, office of dean.

deklamieren [dekla'mi:rən], *v.a., v.n.* recite, declaim.

deklarieren [dekla'ri:rən], *v.a.* declare (for customs duty).

Deklination [deklina'tsjo:n], *f.* (—, *pl.* —en) (*Gram.*) declension; (*Phys.*) declination.

deklinieren [deklɪ'ni:rən], *v.a.* (*Gram.*) decline.

dekolletiert [dekɔle'ti:rt], *adj.* décolleté, low-necked.

Dekret [de'kre:t], *n.* (—s, *pl.* —e) decree, edict, official regulation.

dekretieren [dekre'ti:rən], *v.a.* decree, ordain.

delegieren [dele'gi:rən], *v.a.* delegate.

Delegierte [dele'gi:rtə], *m.* (—n, *pl.* —n) delegate.

delikat [deli'ka:t], *adj.* subtle, dainty; tasty; (*coll.*) tricky, difficult.

Delikatesse [delɪka'tɛsə], *f.* (—, *pl.* —n) delicacy, dainty; (*pl.*) (*Am.*) delicatessen.

Delikt [de'lɪkt], *n.* (—s, *pl.* —e) (*Law*) crime; misdemeanour.

Delle ['dɛlə], *f.* (—, *pl.* —n) dent.

Delphin [dɛl'fi:n], *m.* (—s, *pl.* —e) dolphin.

deltaförmig ['dɛltafœrmɪç], *adj.* deltoid.

dem [de:m], *def. art. Dat.* to the. — *dem. adj.* to this, to that: — *dem. pron.* to this, to that; *wie — auch sei,* however that may be. — *rel. pron.* to whom, to which.

demarkieren [demar'ki:rən], *v.a.* mark, demarcate.

Dementi [de'mɛnti], *n.* (—s, *pl.* —s) (*official*) denial.

dementieren [demɛn'ti:rən], *v.a.* (*Pol.*) deny, contradict.

demgemäß ['de:mgəmɛ:s], *adv.* accordingly.

demnach ['de:mnax], *conj.* therefore, consequently, in accordance with that.

demnächst ['de:mnɛ:çst], *adv.* shortly, soon, in the near future.

demokratisch [demo'kra:tɪʃ], *adj.* democratic.

demolieren [demo'li:rən], *v.a.* demolish.

demonstrieren [demɔn'stri:rən], *v.a., v.n.* demonstrate.

Demut ['de:mu:t], *f.* (—, *no pl.*) humility, meekness.

demütig ['de:mytɪç], *adj.* humble, meek, submissive.

demütigen ['de:mytɪgən], *v.a.* humble, humiliate, subdue.

Denkart ['dɛŋka:rt], *f.* (—, *pl.* —en) way of thinking.

denken ['dɛŋkən], *v.a., v.n. irr.* think, reflect (upon); imagine; (*coll.*) guess.

Denker ['dɛŋkər], *m.* (—s, *pl.* —) thinker, philosopher.

Denkmal ['dɛŋkma:l], *n.* (—s, *pl.* ⁔er) monument.

Denkmünze ['dɛŋkmyntsə], *f.* (—, *pl.* —n) (commemorative) medal.

Denkschrift ['dɛŋkʃrɪft], *f.* (—, *pl.* —en) memorandum, memoir.

Denkspruch ['dɛŋkʃprux], *m.* (—s, *pl.* ⁔e) aphorism, maxim, motto.

Denkungsart ['dɛŋkuŋsart], *f.* (*pl.* —en) *see* **Denkart**.

Denkweise ['dɛŋkvaɪzə], *f.* (—, *pl.* —n) *see* **Denkart**.

denkwürdig ['dɛŋkvyrdɪç], *adj.* memorable.

Denkzettel ['dɛŋktsɛtəl], *m.* (—s, *pl.* —) (*fig.*) reminder, punishment, lesson; *einem einen — geben,* give s.o. s.th. to think about *or* a sharp reminder.

denn [dɛn], *conj.* for. — *adv.* then; (*after comparatives*) than; *es sei — dass,* unless.

dennoch ['dɛnɔx], *conj.* yet, nevertheless, notwithstanding.

Denunziant [denun'tsjant], *m.* (—en, *pl.* —en) informer.

denunzieren [denun'tsi:rən], *v.a.* inform against, denounce.

Depesche [de'pɛʃə], *f.* (—, *pl.* —n) dispatch; telegram, wire.

deponieren [depo'ni:rən], *v.a.* deposit; (*Law*) depose.

Depositenbank [depo'zi:tənbaŋk], *f.* (—, *pl.* —en) deposit-bank.

deprimieren

deprimieren [depri'mi:rən], *v.a.* depress.

Deputierte [depu'ti:rtə], *m.* (—n, *pl.* —n) deputy.

der [de:r], *def. art. m.* the. — *dem. adj.*, *dem. pron.* this, that. — *rel. pron.* who, which, that.

derart ['de:ra:rt], *adv.* so, in such a manner.

derartig ['de:ra:rtiç], *adj.* such.

derb [dɛrp], *adj.* firm, solid, coarse, blunt, uncouth; strong, robust.

dereinst [de:r'aɪnst], *adv.* one day (in future).

derenthalben ['de:rənthalbən], *adv.* for her (their) sake, on her (their) account, on whose account.

derentwegen ['de:rəntve:gən], *adv. see* **derenthalben**.

derentwillen ['de:rəntvilən], *adv. see* **derenthalben**.

dergestalt ['de:rgəʃtalt], *adv.* in such a manner; so.

dergleichen [de:r'glaɪçən], *adv.* such, such as, suchlike.

derjenige ['de:rje:nɪgə], *dem. adj., dem. pron.* that, this; — *welcher*, he who.

derlei ['de:rlaɪ], *adj.* of that sort.

dermaßen ['de:rma:sən], *adv.* to such an extent, to such a degree.

derselbe [de:r'zɛlbə], *pron.* the same.

derweilen [de:r'vaɪlən], *adv.* meanwhile.

Derwisch ['dɛrvɪʃ], *m.* (—(e)s, *pl.* —e) dervish.

derzeit ['de:rtsaɪt], *adv.* at present.

Des [dɛs], *n.* (—, *pl.* —) (*Mus.*) D flat; — *Dur*, D flat major; — *Moll*, D flat minor.

des [dɛs], *def. art. m. & n. Genit. sing.* of the.

desgleichen [dɛs'glaɪçən], *adj.* such, suchlike. — *adv.* likewise, ditto.

deshalb ['dɛshalp], *adv., conj.* therefore.

desinfizieren [dɛsɪnfit'si:rən], *v.a.* disinfect.

dessen ['dɛsən], *dem. pron. m & n. Genit. sing.* of it, of that. — *rel. pron. m. & n. Genit. sing.* whose, of whom, of which, whereof.

dessenungeachtet [dɛsənungə'axtət], *conj.* notwithstanding that, for all that, despite all that.

Destillateur [dɛstɪla'tø:r], *m.* (—s, *pl.* —e) distiller.

destillieren [dɛstɪ'li:rən], *v.a.* distil.

desto ['dɛsto], *adv.* the; — *besser*, so much the better; *je* . . . —, the . . . the.

deswegen ['dɛsve:gən], *adv., conj.* therefore.

Detaillist [deta'jɪst], *m.* (—en, *pl.* —en) retailer.

deucht [dɔyçt] *see* **dünken**; (*obs.*) *mich deucht*, methinks.

deuten ['dɔytən], *v.a.* point to, show; explain, interpret.

deutlich ['dɔytlɪç], *adj.* clear, distinct; evident, plain.

deutsch [dɔytʃ], *adj.* German.

Deutschland ['dɔytʃlant], *n.* Germany.

Deutschmeister ['dɔytʃmaɪstər], *m.* (—s, *pl.* —) Grand Master of the Teutonic Order.

Deutschtum ['dɔytʃtu:m], *n.* (—s, *no pl.*) German nationality, German customs, German manners.

Deutung ['dɔytuŋ], *f.* (—, *pl.* —en) explanation, interpretation.

Devise [de'vi:zə], *f.* (—, *pl.* —n) device, motto; (*pl.*) foreign currency

devot [de'vo:t], *adj.* submissive, respectful, humble.

Dezember [de'tsɛmbər], *m.* December

dezent [de'tsɛnt], *adj.* modest, decent unobtrusive.

Dezernent [detsɛr'nɛnt], *m.* (—en, *pl.* —en) head of section in ministry or city administration.

dezimieren [detsi'mi:rən], *v.a.* decimate, reduce.

Diagramm [dia'gram], *n.* (—s, *pl.* —e) diagram, graph.

Diakon [dia'ko:n], *m.* (—s, *pl.* —e) (*Eccl.*) deacon.

Diakonisse, Diakonissin [diako'nɪsə, diako'nɪsɪn], *f.* (—, *pl.* —nen) deaconess.

Dialektik [dia'lɛktɪk], *f.* (—, *no pl.*) dialectics.

Diamant [dia'mant], *m.* (—en, *pl.* —en) diamond.

diametral [diame'tra:l], *adj.* diametrical.

Diapositiv [diapozi'ti:f], *n.* (—s, *pl.* —e) (*lantern, Phot.*) slide.

Diät [di'ɛ:t], *f.* (—, *pl.* —en) diet; (*pl.*) daily allowance.

dich [dɪç], *pers. pron.* you. — *refl. pron.* yourself.

dicht [dɪçt], *adj.* tight; impervious (to water); dense, compact, solid, firm; — *bei*, hard by, close to.

Dichte ['dɪçtə], *f.* (—, *no pl.*) density.

dichten ['dɪçtən], *v.a., v.n.* write poetry, compose (*verses etc.*); (*Tech.*) tighten; (*Naut.*) caulk.

Dichter ['dɪçtər], *m.* (—s, *pl.* —) poet.

dichterisch ['dɪçtərɪʃ], *adj.* poetic(al).

Dichtigkeit ['dɪçtɪçkaɪt], *f.* (—, *no pl.*) closeness, compactness, thickness, density.

Dichtkunst ['dɪçtkunst], *f.* (—, *no pl.*) (art of) poetry.

Dichtung ['dɪçtuŋ], *f.* (—, *pl.* —en) poetry, poem; fiction; (*Tech.*) caulking; washer, gasket.

dick [dɪk], *adj.* thick; fat; (*books*) bulky; voluminous, stout, obese, corpulent.

Dicke ['dɪkə], *f.* (—, *no pl.*) thickness, stoutness.

dickfellig ['dɪkfɛlɪç], *adj.* thick-skinned.

Dickicht ['dɪkɪçt], *n.* (—s, *pl.* —e) thicket.

die [di:], *def. art. f. & pl.* the. — *dem. adj.*, *dem. pron. f. & pl.* this, these. — *rel. pron. f. & pl.* who, that which.

Dieb [di:p], *m.* (—s, *pl.* —e) thief.

Diebstahl ['di:pʃta:l], *m.* (—s, *pl.* ⸚e) theft.

Diele ['di:lə], *f.* (—, *pl.* —n) floor;
(entrance) hall; plank.
dielen ['di:lən], *v.a.* board, floor.
dienen ['di:nən], *v.n. einem —*, serve
(s.o.); help (s.o.).
Diener ['di:nər], *m.* (—s, *pl.* —) servant, attendant; (*coll.*) bow.
dienlich ['di:nlɪç], *adj.* serviceable,
useful; *für — halten*, think fit.
Dienst [di:nst], *m.* (—es, *pl.* —e)
service, employment, duty; — *haben*,
be on duty.
Dienstag ['di:nsta:k], *m.* (—s, *pl.* —e)
Tuesday.
Dienstalter ['di:nstaltər], *n.* (—s, *pl.*
—) seniority.
dienstbar ['di:nstba:r], *adj.* subject,
subservient.
Dienstbarkeit ['di:nstba:rkaɪt], *f.* (—,
no pl.) bondage, servitude.
dienstbeflissen ['di:nstbəflɪsən], *adj.*
assiduous.
Dienstbote ['di:nstbo:tə], *m.* (—n,
pl. —n) domestic servant.
dienstfertig ['di:nstfɛrtɪç], *adj.* obliging, ready to serve.
Dienstleistung ['di:nstlaɪstuŋ], *f.* (—,
pl. —en) service.
dienstlich ['di:nstlɪç], *adj.* official.
Dienstmädchen ['di:nstmɛ:tçən], *n.*
(—s, *pl.* —) maidservant.
Dienstmann ['di:nstman], *m.* (—s, *pl.*
-er) commissionaire, porter.
Dienstpflicht ['di:nstpflɪçt], *f.* (—, *no
pl.*) official duty, liability to serve;
(*Mil.*) (compulsory) military service.
Dienststunden ['di:nstʃtundən], *f. pl.*
office hours.
diensttauglich ['di:nsttauklɪç], *adj.*
(*Mil.*) fit for service.
Dienstverhältnis ['di:nstferhɛltnɪs], *n.*
(—ses, *pl.* —se) (*pl.*) terms of service.
dies [di:s], *abbr. dieses.*
diesbezüglich ['di:sbətsy:klɪç], *adj.*
concerning this, relating to this
matter.
diese ['di:zə], *dem. adj., dem. pron. f. &
pl.* this, these.
dieser ['di:zər], *dem. adj., dem. pron. m.*
this.
dieses ['di:zəs], *dem. adj., dem. pron. n.*
this.
diesjährig ['di:sjɛ:rɪç], *adj.* of this year,
this year's.
diesmal ['di:sma:l], *adv.* this time, for
this once.
Dietrich (1) ['di:trɪç], *m.* Derek.
Dietrich (2) ['di:trɪç], *m.* (—s, *pl.* —e)
pick lock, master-key, skeleton key.
Differentialrechnung [dɪfərɛnts'ja:l-
rɛçnuŋ], *f.* (—, *pl.* —en) differential
calculus.
Differenz [dɪfə'rɛnts], *f.* (—, *pl.* —en)
difference; quarrel.
Diktat [dɪk'ta:t], *n.* (—s, *pl.* —e)
dictation.
diktatorisch [dɪkta'to:rɪʃ], *adj.* dicta-
torial.
Diktatur [dɪkta'tu:r], *f.* (—, *pl.* —en)
dictatorship.

diktieren [dɪk'ti:rən], *v.a.* dictate.
Ding [dɪŋ], *n.* (—s, *pl.* —e) thing,
object, matter.
dingen ['dɪŋən], *v.a.* hire, engage (a
manual worker).
dingfest ['dɪŋfɛst], *adj.* — *machen*,
arrest.
dinglich ['dɪŋlɪç], *adj.* real.
dinieren [di'ni:rən], *v.n.* dine.
Diözese [diø'tse:zə], *f.* (—, *pl.* —n)
diocese.
Diphtherie [dɪftə'ri:], *f.* (—, *no pl.*)
diphtheria.
Diplom [di'plo:m], *n.* (—s, *pl.* —e)
diploma.
Diplomatie [dɪploma'ti:], *f.* (—, *no pl.*)
diplomacy.
dir [di:r], *pers. pron. Dat.* to you.
direkt [di'rɛkt], *adj.* direct; —*er Wagen*,
(*railway*) through carriage; — *danach*,
immediately afterwards.
Direktion [dirɛkt'sjo:n], *f.* (—, *pl.*
—en) direction, management.
Direktor [di'rɛktɔr], *m.* (—s, *pl.* —en)
(managing) director, manager; headmaster, principal.
Direktorium [dirɛk'to:rjum], *n.* (—s
pl. —rien) directorate, board of
directors.
Direktrice [dirɛk'tri:sə], *f.* (—, *pl.* —n)
manageress.
Dirigent [diri'gɛnt], *m.* (—en, *pl.*
—en) (*Mus.*) conductor; (*Austr.
Admin.*) head of section in Ministry.
dirigieren [diri'gi:rən], *v.a.* direct,
manage; (*Mus.*) conduct.
Dirndl ['dɪrndl], *n.* (—s, *pl.* —) (*dial.*)
young girl, country wench; (*fig.*)
peasant dress, dirndl.
Dirne ['dɪrnə], *f.* (—, *pl.* —n) (*Poet.*)
girl; prostitute.
Dis [dɪs], *n.* (—, *no pl.*) (*Mus.*) D sharp.
disharmonisch [dɪshar'mo:nɪʃ], *adj.*
discordant.
Diskant [dɪs'kant], *m.* (—s, *pl.* —e)
(*Mus.*) treble, soprano.
Diskont [dɪs'kɔnt], *m.* (—(e)s, *pl.* —e)
discount, rebate.
diskret [dɪs'kre:t], *adj.* discreet.
Diskurs [dɪs'kurs], *m.* (—es, *pl.* —e)
discourse.
diskutieren [dɪsku'ti:rən], *v.a.* discuss,
debate.
Dispens [dɪs'pɛns], *m.* (—es, *pl.* —e)
dispensation.
dispensieren [dɪspɛn'zi:rən], *v.a.* dispense (from); exempt (from).
disponieren [dɪspo'ni:rən], *v.n.* —
über, dispose of; make plans about.
Dissident [dɪsi'dɛnt], *m.* (—en, *pl.*
—en) dissenter, nonconformist.
distanzieren [dɪstan'tsi:rən], *v.r. sich
— von*, keep o.'s distance from; dissociate o.s. from.
Distel ['dɪstəl], *f.* (—, *pl.* —n) thistle.
Distelfink ['dɪstəlfɪŋk], *m.* (—s, *pl.*
—e) (*Orn.*) gold-finch.
disziplinarisch [dɪstsipli'na:rɪʃ], *adj.*
diciplinary.
dito ['di:to], *adv.* ditto.

dividieren

dividieren [dıvı'di:rən], *v.a.* divide.

Diwan ['di:van], *m.* (—s, *pl.* —e) divan, sofa, couch.

doch [dɔx], *adv.*, *conj.* however, though, although, nevertheless, yet, but; after all, (*emphatic*) yes.

Docht [dɔxt], *m.* (—es, *pl.* —e) wick.

Dock [dɔk], *n.* (—s, *pl.* —s, —e) dock.

Dogge ['dɔgə], *f.* (—, *pl.* —n) bulldog, mastiff; Great Dane.

Dogmatiker [dɔg'ma:tıkər], *m.* (—s, *pl.* —) dogmatist.

dogmatisch [dɔg'ma:tıʃ], *adj.* dogmatic, doctrinal.

Dohle ['do:lə], *f.* (—, *pl.* —n) (*Orn.*) jackdaw.

Doktor ['dɔktɔr], *m.* (—s, *pl.* —en) doctor; physician, surgeon.

Dolch [dɔlç], *m.* (—es, *pl.* —e) dagger, dirk.

Dolde ['dɔldə], *f.* (—, *pl.* —n) (*Bot.*) umbel.

Dolmetscher ['dɔlmɛtʃər], *m.* (—s, *pl.* —) interpreter.

dolmetschen ['dɔlmɛtʃən], *v.a.* interpret.

Dolomiten [dolo'mi:tən], *pl.* Dolomites.

Dom [do:m], *m.* (—s, *pl.* —e) cathedral; dome, cupola.

Domherr ['do:mhɛr], *m.* (—n, *pl.* —en) canon, prebendary.

dominieren [domi'ni:rən], *v.a.* dominate, domineer.

Dominikaner [domini'ka:nər], *m.* (—s, *pl.* —) Dominican friar.

dominikanische Republik [domini-'ka:nıʃə repu'bli:k], *f.* Dominican Republic.

Domizil [domi'tsi:l], *n.* (—s, *pl.* —e) domicile, residence, address.

Domkapitel ['do:mkapıtəl], *n.* (—s, *pl.* —) dean and chapter.

Dompfaff ['do:mpfaf], *m.* (—s, *pl.* —en) (*Orn.*) bullfinch.

Dompropst ['do:mpro:pst], *m.* (—es, *pl.* -e) provost.

Donau ['do:nau], *f.* (—, *no pl.*) Danube.

Donner ['dɔnər], *m.* (—s, *no pl.*) thunder.

donnern ['dɔnərn], *v.n.* thunder; (*fig.*) storm, rage.

Donnerschlag ['dɔnərʃla:k], *m.* (—s, *pl.* -e) thunderclap.

Donnerstag ['dɔnərsta:k], *m.* (—s, *pl.* —e) Thursday; *Grün* —, Maundy Thursday.

Donnerwetter ['dɔnərvɛtər], *n.* (—s, *pl.* —) thunderstorm; *zum* — (*nochmal*)! hang it all, confound it!

doppeldeutig ['dɔpəldɔytıç], *adj.* ambiguous.

Doppelgänger ['dɔpəlgɛŋər], *m.* (—s, *pl.* —) double.

Doppellaut ['dɔpəllaut], *m.* (—s, *pl.* —e) diphthong.

doppeln ['dɔpəln] *see* **verdoppeln**.

doppelsinnig ['dɔpəlzınıç] *see* **doppeldeutig**.

doppelt ['dɔpəlt], *adj.* double, twofold.

Doppelzwirn ['dɔpəltsvırn], *m.* (—s, *no pl.*) double-thread.

Dorf [dɔrf], *n.* (—es, *pl.* ˙er) village.

dörflich ['dœrflıç], *adj.* rural, rustic.

dorisch ['do:rıʃ], *adj.* Doric.

Dorn [dɔrn], *m.* (—s, *pl.* —en) thorn, prickle; (*Bot.*) spine; (*buckle*) tongue.

dornig ['dɔrnıç], *adj.* thorny.

Dornröschen ['dɔrnro:sçən], *n.* (—s, *pl.* —) Sleeping Beauty.

Dorothea [doro'te:a], *f.* Dorothea, Dorothy.

dorren ['dɔrən] *see* **verdorren**.

dörren ['dœrən], *v.a.* dry, make dry, parch.

Dörrobst ['dœrrobst], *n.* (—es, *no pl.*) dried fruit.

Dorsch [dɔrʃ], *m.* (—es, *pl.* —e) cod, codfish.

dort [dɔrt], (*Austr.*) **dorten** ['dɔrtən], *adv.* there, yonder; *von* — *aus*, from that point, from there.

dorther ['dɔrthe:r], *adv.* from there, therefrom, thence.

dorthin ['dɔrthın], *adv.* to that place, thereto, thither.

dortig ['dɔrtıç], *adj.* of that place, local.

Dose ['do:zə], *f.* (—, *pl.* —n) box, tin, can.

dösen ['dø:zən], *v.n.* doze, daydream.

Dosis ['do:zıs], *f.* (—, *pl.* **Dosen**) dose.

Dotter ['dɔtər], *n.* (—s, *pl.* —) yolk (of egg).

Dozent [do'tsɛnt], *m.* (—en, *pl.* —en) university lecturer; (*Am.*) Assistant Professor.

dozieren [do'tsi:rən], *v.n.* lecture.

Drache ['draxə], *m.* (—n, *pl.* —n) dragon; kite; (*fig.*) termagant, shrew.

Dragoner [dra'go:nər], *m.* (—s, *pl.* —) dragoon.

Draht [dra:t], *m.* (—es, *pl.* ˙e) wire.

drahten ['dra:tən], *v.a.* wire, telegraph.

Drahtgewebe ['dra:tgəve:bə], *n.* (—s, *pl.* —) wire-gauze.

Drahtgitter ['dra:tgıtər], *m.* (—s, *pl.* —) wire grating.

drahtlos ['dra:tlo:s], *adj.* wireless.

Drahtseilbahn ['dra:tzaılba:n], *f.* (—, *pl.* —en) cable (funicular) railway.

Drahtzange ['dra:ttsaŋə], *f.* (—, *pl.* —n) pliers.

drall [dral], *adj.* buxom, plump.

Drama ['dra:ma], *n.* (—s, *pl.* —men) drama.

Dramatiker [dra'ma:tıkər], *m.* (—s, *pl.* —) dramatist.

dramatisch [dra'ma:tıʃ], *adj.* dramatic.

dran [dran] *see* **daran**.

Drang [draŋ], *m.* (—s, *no pl.*) urge; rush; throng; pressure; impulse.

drängeln ['drɛŋəln], *v.a.* jostle.

drängen ['drɛŋən], *v.a.* press, urge; *die Zeit drängt*, time presses; *es drängt mich*, I feel called upon.

Drangsal ['draŋza:l], *f.* or *n.* (—s, *pl.* —e or —en) distress, misery.

drapieren [dra'pi:rən], *v.a.* drape.

drastisch [ˈdrastiʃ], *adj.* drastic.
drauf [drauf] *see* **darauf.**
Draufgänger [ˈdraufgɛŋər], *m.* (—s, *pl.* —) daredevil.
draußen [ˈdrausən], *adv.* outside, without, out of doors.
drechseln [ˈdrɛksəln], *v.a.* turn (on a lathe); *Phrasen* —, turn phrases.
Drechsler [ˈdrɛkslər], *m.* (—s, *pl.* —) turner.
Dreck [drɛk], *m.* (—s, *no pl.*) dirt, mire, dust, filth, dung.
dreckig [ˈdrɛkɪç], *adj.* dirty, filthy, muddy.
drehbar [ˈdreːbaːr], *adj.* revolving, swivelling.
Drehbuch [ˈdreːbuːx], *n.* (—s, *pl.* ˙er) (*film*) script.
drehen [ˈdreːən], *v.a.* turn; (*film*) shoot. — *v.n.* turn round, veer.
Drehorgel [ˈdreːɔrgəl], *f.* (—, *pl.* —n) barrel-organ.
Drehrad [ˈdreːraːt], *n.* (—s, *pl.* ˙er) fly-wheel.
Drehung [ˈdreːuŋ], *f.* (—, *pl.* —en) rotation, turn, revolution.
drei [drai], *num. adj.* three.
dreiblätterig [ˈdraiblɛtərɪç], *adj.* trifoliate.
Dreieck [ˈdraiɛk], *n.* (—s, *pl.* —e) triangle.
dreieckig [ˈdraiɛkɪç], *adj.* triangular, three-cornered.
dreieinig [draiˈainɪç], *adj.* (*Theol.*) triune.
dreifach [ˈdraifax], *adj.* threefold, triple.
Dreifaltigkeit [draiˈfaltɪçkait], *f.* (—, *no pl.*) (*Theol.*) Trinity.
Dreifuß [ˈdraifuːs], *m.* (—es, *pl.* ˙e) tripod.
dreijährlich [ˈdraijɛrlɪç], *adj.* triennial.
Dreikönigsfest [draiˈkøːnɪksfɛst], *n.* (—es, *no pl.*) Epiphany.
dreimonatlich [ˈdraimoːnatlɪç], *adj.* quarterly.
Dreirad [ˈdrairaːt], *n.* (—s, *pl.* ˙er) tricycle.
dreiseitig [ˈdraizaitɪç], *adj.* trilateral.
dreißig [ˈdraisɪç], *num. adj.* thirty.
dreist [draist], *adj.* bold, audacious; impudent.
dreistellig [ˈdraiʃtɛlɪç], *adj.* —*e Zahl,* number of three figures.
dreistimmig [ˈdraiʃtɪmɪç], *adj.* for three voices.
Dreistufenrakete [ˈdraiʃtuːfənraˈkeːtə], *f.* (—, *pl.* —n) three-stage rocket.
dreistündig [ˈdraiʃtyndɪç], *adj.* lasting three hours.
dreitägig [ˈdraitɛːgɪç], *adj.* lasting three days.
dreiteilig [ˈdraitailɪç], *adj.* tripartite; three-piece.
dreizehn [ˈdraitseːn], *num. adj.* thirteen.
Drell [drɛl], *m.* (—s, *no pl.*) *see* **Drillich.**
Dresche [ˈdrɛʃə], *f.* (—, *no pl.*) thrashing, beating.
dreschen [ˈdrɛʃən], *v.a. irr.* (*corn*) thresh; (*person*) thrash.

Dreschflegel [ˈdrɛʃfleːgəl], *m.* (—s, *pl.* —) flail.
dressieren [drɛˈsiːrən], *v.a.* (*animal*) train; break in.
Dressur [drɛˈsuːr], *f.* (—, *pl.* —en) training, breaking-in.
Drillbohrer [ˈdrɪlboːrər], *m.* (—s, *pl.* —) drill.
drillen [ˈdrɪlən], *v.a.* (*a hole*) bore; (*soldiers*) drill.
Drillich [ˈdrɪlɪç], *m.* (—s, *pl.* —e) drill, canvas.
Drilling [ˈdrɪlɪŋ], *m.* (—s, *pl.* —e) three-barrelled gun; (*pl.*) triplets.
drin [drɪn] *see* **darin.**
dringen [ˈdrɪŋən], *v.n. irr.* penetrate, force o.'s way through; *auf etwas* —, insist on s.th.
dringlich [ˈdrɪŋlɪç], *adj.* urgent, pressing.
drinnen [ˈdrɪnən], *adv.* inside, within.
drittens [ˈdrɪtəns], *adv.* thirdly.
droben [ˈdroːbən], *adv.* up there, above, aloft, overhead.
Droge [ˈdroːgə], *f.* (—, *pl.* —n) drug.
Drogerie [droːgəˈriː], *f.* (—, *pl.* —n) druggist's shop, chemist's; (*Am.*) drugstore.
drohen [ˈdroːən], *v.a., v.n.* threaten, menace.
Drohne [ˈdroːnə], *f.* (—, *pl.* —n) drone.
dröhnen [ˈdrøːnən], *v.n.* boom, roar.
Drohung [ˈdroːuŋ], *f.* (—, *pl.* —en) threat, menace.
drollig [ˈdrɔlɪç], *adj.* droll, odd, quaint.
Dromedar [drɔməˈdaːr], *n.* (—s, *pl.* —e) dromedary.
Droschke [ˈdrɔʃkə], *f.* (—, *pl.* —n) cab, hansom, taxi.
Drossel [ˈdrɔsəl], *f.* (—, *pl.* —n) thrush.
Drosselader [ˈdrɔsəladər], *f.* (—, *pl.* —n) jugular vein.
Drosselbein [ˈdrɔsəlbain], *n.* (—s, *pl.* —e) collar-bone.
drosseln [ˈdrɔsəln], *v.a.* throttle. *See also* **erdrosseln.**
drüben [ˈdryːbən], *adv.* over there, on the other side.
drüber [ˈdryːbər] *see* **darüber.**
Druck [druk], *m.* (—s, *pl.* ˙e, —e) pressure, squeeze; (*Phys.*) compression; (*Typ.*) impression, print; (*fig.*) hardship.
Druckbogen [ˈdrukboːgən], *m.* (—s, *pl.* —) proof-sheet, proof.
Druckbuchstabe [ˈdrukbuːxʃtaːbə], *m.* (—n, *pl.* —n) letter, type.
Drückeberger [ˈdrykəbɛrgər], *m.* (—s, *pl.* —) slacker, shirker.
drucken [ˈdrukən], *v.a.* print.
drücken [ˈdrykən], *v.a.* press, squeeze; trouble, oppress. — *v.r. sich* —, sneak away, shirk.
Drucker [ˈdrukər], *m.* (—s, *pl.* —) printer.
Drücker [ˈdrykər], *m.* (—s, *pl.* —) (*door*) handle, latch; (*gun*) trigger.
Druckerei [ˈdrukərai], *f.* (—, *pl.* —en) printing shop.

Druckerschwärze

Druckerschwärze ['drukərʃvɛrtsə], *f.* (—, *no pl.*) printing-ink.

Druckfehler ['drukfe:lər], *m.* (—s, *pl.* —) misprint, printer's error.

druckfertig ['drukfɛrtɪç], *adj.* ready for press.

Drucksache ['drukzaxə], *f.* (—, *pl.* —n) (*Postal*) printed matter.

drum [drum] *see* **darum.**

drunten ['druntən], *adv.* down there, below.

drunter ['druntər] *see* **darunter.**

Drüse ['dry:zə], *f.* (—, *pl.* —n) gland.

Dschungel ['dʒuŋəl], *m.* or *n.* (—s, *pl.* —) jungle.

du [du:], *pers. pron.* thou, you.

ducken ['dukən], *v.a.* bring down, humble. — *v.r. sich* —, duck, stoop, crouch.

dudeln ['du:dəln], *v.n.* play the bagpipes; tootle.

Dudelsack ['du:dəlzak], *m.* (—s, *pl.* ⁝e) bagpipe(s).

Duft [duft], *m.* (—s, *pl.* ⁝e) scent, odour, fragrance, aroma, perfume.

duften ['duftən], *v.n.* be fragrant.

duftig ['duftɪç], *adj.* fragrant, odoriferous, perfumed.

dulden ['duldən], *v.a.* suffer, endure, bear, tolerate.

duldsam ['dultza:m], *adj.* tolerant, indulgent, patient.

dumm [dum], *adj.* stupid, foolish, dull.

Dummheit ['dumhaɪt], *f.* (—, *pl.* —en) stupidity, folly.

dumpf [dumpf], *adj.* musty; (*air*) close; (*sound*) hollow; (*fig.*) gloomy.

dumpfig ['dumpfɪç], *adj.* damp, musty, stuffy.

Düne ['dy:nə], *f.* (—, *pl.* —n) dune, sand-hill.

Düngemittel ['dyŋəmɪtəl], *n.* (—s, *pl.* —) fertilizer.

düngen ['dyŋən], *v.a.* manure, fertilize.

Dünger ['dyŋər], *m.* (—s, *no pl.*) compost, artificial manure.

dunkel ['duŋkəl], *adj.* dark; (*fig.*) obscure, mysterious.

Dünkel ['dyŋkəl], *m.* (—s, *no pl.*) conceit, arrogance.

dünkelhaft ['dyŋkəlhaft], *adj.* conceited, arrogant.

Dunkelheit ['duŋkəlhaɪt], *f.* (—, *no pl.*) darkness, obscurity.

dunkeln ['duŋkəln], *v.n.* grow dark.

dünken ['dyŋkən], *v.n.* (*rare*) seem, appear. — *v.r. sich* —, fancy o.s., imagine o.s.

dünn [dyn], *adj.* thin, slim, weak.

Dunst [dunst], *m.* (—es, *pl.* ⁝e) vapour, fume; exhalation; haze; *einem blauen* — *vormachen*, humbug a p.

dünsten ['dynstən], *v.a.* stew.

dunstig ['dunstɪç], *adj.* misty, hazy.

Dunstkreis ['dunstkraɪs], *m.* (—es, *pl.* —e) atmosphere.

Dunstobst ['dunsto:pst], *n.* (—es, *no pl.*) stewed fruit.

duodez [duo'de:ts], *adj.* (*Typ.*) duodecimo (12mo).

Duodezfürst [duo'de:tsfyrst], *m.* (—en, *pl.* —en) petty prince, princeling.

Dur [du:r], *n.* (*Mus.*) major; sharp.

durch [durç], *prep.* (*Acc.*) (*local*) through, across; (*temporal*) during, throughout; (*manner*) by means of, by. — *adv.* thoroughly, through.

durchaus [durç'aus], *adv.* throughout, quite, by all means, absolutely.

Durchblick ['durçblɪk], *m.* (—s, *pl.* —e) vista, view.

durchbohren [durç'bo:rən], *v.a. insep.* perforate, pierce.

durchbrennen ['durçbrɛnən], *v.n. irr.* (*aux.* sein) abscond, bolt.

durchbringen ['durçbrɪŋən], *v.a. irr.* bring through, get through; squander (money); pull (a sick person) through. — *v.r. sich redlich* —, make an honest living.

Durchbruch ['durçbrux], *m.* (—s, *pl.* ⁝e) breach, break-through.

durchdrängen ['durçdrɛŋən], *v.r. sich* —, force o.'s way through.

durchdringen ['durçdrɪŋən], *v.n. irr. sep.* (*aux.* sein) get through. — [durç'drɪŋən], *v.a. irr. insep.* penetrate, pierce, permeate, pervade.

durchdrücken ['durçdrykən], *v.a.* press through; (*fig.*) carry through.

durcheilen [durç'aɪlən], *v.a. insep.* hurry through.

Durcheinander [durçaɪn'andər], *n.* (—s, *no pl.*) confusion, muddle.

durcheinander [durçaɪn'andər], *adv.* in confusion, pell-mell.

Durchfall ['durçfal], *m.* (—s, *no pl.*) diarrhoea; (*exams etc.*) failure.

durchfallen ['durçfalən], *v.n. irr.* (*aux.* sein) fall through, come to nought; (*exams etc.*) fail.

durchflechten [durç'flɛçtən], *v.a. irr.* interweave, intertwine.

durchfliegen [durç'fli:gən], *v.a. irr.* fly through; read superficially, skim through.

durchforschen [durç'fɔrʃən], *v.a. insep.* explore, scrutinise, examine thoroughly.

Durchfuhr ['durçfu:r], *f.* (—, *pl.* —en) passage, transit.

durchführbar ['durçfy:rba:r], *adj.* practicable, feasible.

durchführen ['durçfy:rən], *v.a.* escort through; (*fig.*) execute, bring about, carry through.

Durchgang ['durçgaŋ], *m.* (—s, *pl.* ⁝e) passage, thoroughfare; (*Comm.*) transit.

Durchgänger ['durçgɛŋər], *m.* (—s, *pl.* —) runaway horse, bolter; (*fig.*) hothead.

durchgängig ['durçgɛŋɪç], *adj.* general, universal.

durchgehen ['durçge:ən], *v.n. irr.* (*aux.* sein) go through; (*fig.*) abscond; (*horse*) bolt; (*proposal*) be carried. — *v.a. irr.* (*aux.* sein) peruse, review, go over.

ebenbürtig

durchgreifen [ˈdurçgraıfən], *v.n. irr.*
act decisively, take strong action.
durchhauen [ˈdurçhauən], *v.a.* cut
through; *einen* —, flog s.o.
durchkommen [ˈdurçkɔmən], *v.n. irr.*
(*aux.* sein) get through; (*exams etc.*)
pass.
durchkreuzen [durçˈkrɔytsən], *v.a.*
insep. cross out; (*fig.*) thwart.
durchlassen [ˈdurçlasən], *v.a. irr.* let
pass.
Durchlaucht [ˈdurçlauxt], *f.* (— *pl.*
—en) Highness.
durchleuchten [durçˈlɔyçtən], *v.a.*
insep. (*Med.*) X-ray.
durchlöchern [durçˈlœçərn], *v.a. insep.*
perforate, riddle.
durchmachen [ˈdurçmaxən], *v.a.* go
through, suffer.
Durchmesser [ˈdurçmɛsər], *m.* (—s,
pl. —) diameter.
durchnässen [durçˈnɛsən], *v.a. insep.*
wet to the skin, soak.
durchnehmen [ˈdurçneːmən], *v.a. irr.*
go over *or* cover (a subject).
durchpausen [ˈdurçpauzən], *v.a.* trace,
copy.
durchqueren [durçˈkveːrən], *v.a. insep.*
cross, traverse.
Durchsage [ˈdurçzaːgə], *f.* (—, *pl.* —n)
(radio) announcement.
durchschauen [durçˈʃauən], *v.a. insep.*
einen —, see through s.o.
durchscheinend [ˈdurçʃaınənt], *adj.*
transparent, translucent.
Durchschlag [ˈdurçʃlaːk], *m.* (—s,
pl. ˙e) strainer, sieve, colander, filter;
carbon copy.
durchschlagen [ˈdurçʃlaːgən], *v.a. irr.*
insep. strain, filter. — *v.r. irr. sich* —,
fight o.'s way through.
durchschlagend [ˈdurçʃlaːgənt], *adj.*
thorough, complete, effective.
Durchschnitt [ˈdurçʃnıt], *m.* (—s, *pl.*
—e) average; (*Med. etc.*) cross section.
durchschnittlich [ˈdurçʃnıtlıç], *adj.*
average; ordinary.
durchschossen [durçˈʃɔsən], *adj.* inter-
leaved; interwoven.
durchseihen [ˈdurçzaıən], *v.a. see*
durchsieben.
durchsetzen [durçˈzɛtsən], *v.a. insep.*
intersperse; [ˈdurçzɛtsən], *v.a. sep.*
have o.'s way (with s.o.). — *v.r. sep.*
sich —, make o.'s way successfully,
succeed.
Durchsicht [ˈdurçzıçt], *f.* (—, *no pl.*)
revision, inspection, perusal.
durchsichtig [ˈdurçzıçtıç], *adj.* transparent.
durchsickern [ˈdurçzıkərn], *v.n.* (*aux.*
sein) trickle through, ooze through.
durchsieben [ˈdurçziːbən], *v.a.* strain,
filter, sift.
durchsprechen [ˈdurçʃprɛxən], *v.a.*
irr. talk over, discuss.
durchstöbern [durçˈʃtøːbərn], *v.a.*
insep. rummage through.
durchstreichen [ˈdurçʃtraıçən], *v.a.*
irr. cross out, delete.

durchstreifen [durçˈʃtraıfən], *v.a*
insep. roam (through).
durchströmen [durçˈʃtrøːmən], *v.a.*
insep. flow through, permeate.
durchsuchen [durçˈzuːxən], *v.a. insep.*
search thoroughly, examine closely.
durchtrieben [durçˈtriːbən], *adj.* artful,
sly, cunning, crafty.
durchweben [durçˈveːbən], *v.a.* interweave.
durchweg(s) [ˈdurçvɛk(s)], *adv.* without exception, every time, throughout.
durchwühlen [durçˈvyːlən], *v.a. insep.*
search; ransack.
durchziehen [durçˈtsiːən], *v.a. irr.*
insep. wander through, traverse;
[ˈdurçtsiːən], *v.a. irr. sep.* interlace
(with threads); draw through.
durchzucken [durçˈtsukən], *v.a. insep.*
flash through, convulse.
Durchzug [ˈdurçtsuːk], *m.* (—s, *no pl.*)
passage, march through; (*air*)
draught.
dürfen [ˈdyrfən], *v.n. irr.* be permitted;
be allowed; dare; be likely.
dürftig [ˈdyrftıç], *adj.* paltry, insufficient, poor.
dürr [dyr], *adj.* dry, arid, withered;
(*wood*) dead; (*persons*) thin, gaunt.
Dürre [ˈdyrə], *f.* (—, *pl.* —n) aridity,
dryness; drought; (*persons*) thinness.
Durst [durst], *m.* (—es, *no pl.*) thirst.
dürsten [ˈdyrstən], *v.n.* thirst.
durstig [ˈdurstıç], *adj.* thirsty.
Dusche [ˈduːʃə], *f.* (—, *pl.* —n) shower
(bath).
Düse [ˈdyːzə], *f.* (—, *pl.* —n) jet.
duselig [ˈduːzəlıç], *adj.* drowsy; silly.
düster [ˈdyːstər], *adj.* dark, gloomy;
sad, mournful; sombre.
Dutzend [ˈdutsənt], *n.* (—s, *pl.* —e)
dozen.
Duzbruder [ˈduːtsbruːdər], *m.* (—s,
pl. ˙) crony, chum; close friend.
duzen [ˈduːtsən], *v.a.* be on close terms
with.
dynamisch [dyˈnaːmıʃ], *adj.* dyna-
mic(al).

E

E [eː], *n.* (—s, *pl.* —s) the letter E;
(*Mus.*) *E Dur*, E major; *E Moll*, E
minor.
Ebbe [ˈɛbə], *f.* (—, *pl.* —n) ebb, low
tide; — *und Flut*, the tides.
ebben [ˈɛbən], *v.n.* ebb.
eben [ˈeːbən], *adj.* even, level, plane;
(*fig.*) plain. — *adv.* precisely, exactly.
Ebenbild [ˈeːbənbılt], *n.* (—es, *pl.* —er)
likeness, image.
ebenbürtig [ˈeːbənbyrtıç], *adj.* of equal
birth *or* rank; equal.

51

ebenda

ebenda ['e:bəndɑ:], *adv.* in the same place.

ebendeswegen ['e:bəndɛsve:gən], *adv.* for that very reason.

Ebene ['e:bənə], *f.* (—, *pl.* —n) plain; level ground; (*Maths.*) plane; *schiefe* —, inclined plane.

ebenfalls ['e:bənfals], *adv.* likewise, also, too, as well.

Ebenholz ['e:bənhɔlts], *n.* '(—es, *no pl.*) ebony.

Ebenmaß ['e:bənmɑ:s], *n.* (—es, *pl.* —e) symmetry.

ebenmäßig ['e:bənmɛ:sɪç], *adj.* symmetrical.

ebenso ['e:bənzo:], *adv.* in the same way; — *wie*, just as . . .

Eber ['e:bər], *m.* (—s, *pl.* —) (*Zool.*) boar.

Eberesche ['e:bərɛʃə], *f.* (—, *pl.* —n) (*Bot.*) mountain ash, rowan.

ebnen ['e:bnən], *v.a.* even out, level; smoothe.

echt [ɛçt], *adj.* genuine, real, true, authentic, pure.

Ecke ['ɛkə], *f.* (—, *pl.* —en) corner, nook.

eckig ['ɛkɪç], *adj.* angular.

Eckzahn ['ɛktsɑ:n], *m.* (—s, *pl.* ⁖e) eye tooth; canine tooth.

Eckziegel ['ɛktsi:gəl], *m.* (—s, *pl.* —) (*Build.*) header.

edel ['e:dəl], *adj.* noble; well-born, aristocratic; (*metal*) precious.

Edelmann ['e:dəlman], *m.* (—s, *pl.* **Edelleute**) nobleman, aristocrat.

Edelmut ['e:dəlmu:t], *m.* (—s, *no pl.*) generosity, magnanimity.

Edelstein ['e:dəlʃtain], *m.* (—s, *pl.* —e) precious stone, jewel.

Edeltanne ['e:dəltanə], *f.* (—, *pl.* —n) (*Bot.*) silver fir.

Edelweiß ['e:dəlvais], *n.* (—sses, *no pl.*) (*Bot.*) edelweiss; lion's foot.

Eduard ['e:duart], *m.* Edward.

Efeu ['e:fɔy], *m.* (—s, *no pl.*) (*Bot.*) ivy.

Effekten [e'fɛktən], *m. pl.* goods and chattels; effects; stocks, securities.

Effektenbörse [e'fɛktənbœrzə], *f.* (—, *pl.* —n) Stock Exchange.

Effekthascherei [e'fɛkthaʃərai], *f.* (—, *pl.* —en) sensationalism, clap-trap.

effektuieren [efɛktu'i:rən], *v.a.* (*Comm.*) execute, effectuate.

egal [e'ga:l], *adj.* equal; all the same.

Egge ['ɛgə], *f.* (—, *pl.* —n) harrow.

Egoismus [ego'ismus], *m.* (—, *no pl.*) selfishness, egoism.

egoistisch [ego'istiʃ], *adj.* selfish, egoistic(al).

Ehe ['e:ə,] *f.* (—, *pl.* —n) marriage.

ehe ['e:ə], *conj.* before; *adv.* formerly; *je* —r, *desto besser*, the sooner, the better.

Ehebrecher ['e:əbrɛçər], *m.* (—s, *pl.* —) adulterer.

Ehebruch ['e:əbrux], *m.* (—s, *pl.* ⁖e) adultery.

Ehefrau ['e:əfrau], *f.* (—, *pl.* —en) wife, spouse, consort.

Ehegatte ['e:əgatə], *m.* (—n, *pl.* —n) husband, spouse.

ehelich ['e:əlɪç], *adj.* matrimonial; (*children*) legitimate.

Ehelosigkeit ['e:əlo:zɪçkait], *f.* (—, *no pl.*) celibacy.

ehemalig ['e:əma:lɪç], *adj.* former, late.

ehemals ['e:əma:ls], *adv.* formerly, once, of old.

Ehemann ['e:əman], *m.* (—s, *pl.* ⁖er) husband.

ehern ['e:ərn], *adj.* brazen; of brass, of bronze.

Ehestand ['e:əʃtant], *m.* (—s, *no pl.*) matrimony.

ehestens ['e:əstəns], *adv.* as soon as possible.

Ehre ['e:rə], *f.* (—, *pl.* —n) honour, reputation, respect, distinction, glory.

ehren ['e:rən], *v.a.* honour, respect, esteem; *sehr geehrter Herr*, dear Sir.

Ehrenbezeigung ['e:rənbətsaigun], *f.* (—, *pl.* —en) mark of respect; (*Mil.*) salute.

Ehrenbürger ['e:rənbyrgər], *m.* (—s, *pl.* —) honorary citizen *or* freeman.

Ehrendame ['e:randa:mə], *f.* (—, *pl.* —n) maid of honour.

Ehrenerklärung ['e:rənɛrklɛ:run], *f.* (—, *pl.* —en) reparation, apology.

Ehrengericht ['e:rəngərɪçt], *n.* (—s, *pl.* —e) court of honour.

ehrenhaft ['e:rənhaft], *adj.* honourable, worthy.

Ehrenpreis ['e:rənprais], *m.* (—s, *pl.* —e) prize; (*no pl.*) (*Bot.*) speedwell.

Ehrenrettung ['e:rənrɛtun], *f.* (—, *pl.* —en) vindication.

ehrenrührig ['e:rənry:rɪç], *adj.* defamatory, calumnious.

ehrenvoll ['e:rənfɔl], *adj.* honourable.

ehrenwert ['e:rənvɛrt], *adj.* honourable, respectable.

ehrerbietig ['e:rərbi:tɪç], *adj.* reverential, respectful.

Ehrfurcht ['e:rfurçt], *f.* (—, *no pl.*) reverence, awe.

Ehrgefühl ['e:rgəfy:l], *n.* (—s, *no pl.*) sense of honour.

Ehrgeiz ['e:rgaits], *m.* (—es, *no pl.*) ambition.

ehrlich ['e:rlɪç], *adj.* honest; — *währt am längsten*, honesty is the best policy.

ehrlos ['e:rlo:s], *adj.* dishonourable, infamous.

ehrsam ['e:rza:m], *adj.* respectable, honourable.

Ehrwürden ['e:rvyrdən], *m. & f.* (*form of address*) *Euer* —, Reverend Sir, Your Reverence.

ehrwürdig ['e:rvyrdɪç], *adj.* venerable, reverend.

Ei [ai], *n.* (—s, *pl.* —er) egg, ovum.

ei [ai], *int.* ay, indeed.

Eibe ['aibə], *f.* (—, *pl.* —n) (*Bot.*) yew.

Eichamt ['aiçamt], *n.* (—s, *pl.* ⁖er) office of weights and measures; (*Am.*) bureau of standards.

Eichapfel ['aɪçapfəl], *m.* (—s, *pl.* ∵) oak apple.

Eiche ['aɪçə], *f.* (—, *pl.* —n) (*Bot.*) oak.

Eichel ['aɪçəl], *f.* (—, *pl.* —n) acorn; (*Anat.*) glans; (*Cards*) clubs.

eichen ['aɪçən], *v.a.* gauge, calibrate. — *adj.* made of oak.

Eichhörnchen ['aɪçhœrnçən] or **Eichkätzchen** ['aɪçkɛtsçən], *n.* (—s, *pl.* —) squirrel.

Eid [aɪt], *m.* (—es, *pl.* —e) oath; *falscher* —, perjury.

Eidam ['aɪdam], *m.* (—s, *pl.* —e) (*obs.*) son-in-law.

eidbrüchig ['aɪtbryçɪç], *adj.* guilty of perjury.

Eidechse ['aɪdɛksə], *f.* (—, *pl.* —n) lizard.

Eidesleistung ['aɪdəslaɪstuŋ], *f.* (—, *pl.* —en) affidavit.

Eidgenosse ['aɪtgənɔsə], *m.* (—n, *pl.* —n) confederate.

Eidgenossenschaft ['aɪtgənɔsənʃaft], *f.* (—, *pl.* —en) confederacy.

eidlich ['aɪtlɪç], *adj.* by oath, sworn.

Eidotter ['aɪdɔtər], *m. & n.* (—s, *pl.* —) yolk of an egg.

Eierbecher ['aɪərbɛçər], *m.* (—s, *pl.* —) egg cup.

Eierkuchen ['aɪərku:xən], *m.* (—s, *pl.* —) omelet(te), pancake.

Eierschale ['aɪərʃa:lə], *f.* (—, *pl.* —n) egg shell.

Eierspeise ['aɪərʃpaɪzə], *f.* (—, *pl.* —n) dish prepared with eggs.

Eierstock ['aɪərʃtɔk], *m.* (—s, *pl.* ∵e) ovary.

Eifer ['aɪfər], *m.* (—s, *no pl.*) zeal, eagerness, ardour, haste, passion, vehemence.

Eiferer ['aɪfərər], *m.* (—s, *pl.* —) zealot.

eifern ['aɪfərn], *v.n.* be zealous; *gegen einen* —, inveigh against s.o.

eiförmig ['aɪfœrmɪç], *adj.* oval, egg-shaped.

eifrig ['aɪfrɪç], *adj.* zealous, ardent, eager.

Eigelb ['aɪgɛlp], *n.* (—s, *no pl.*) yolk of (an) egg.

eigen ['aɪgən], *adj.* own; particular, peculiar.

Eigenart ['aɪgəna:rt], *f.* (—, *pl.* —en) peculiarity; idiosyncrasy.

eigenhändig ['aɪgənhɛndɪç], *adj.* with o.'s own hand.

Eigenheit ['aɪgənhaɪt], *f.* (—, *pl.* —en) peculiarity; idiosyncrasy.

eigenmächtig ['aɪgənmɛçtɪç], *adj.* arbitrary, autocratic, high-handed.

Eigenname ['aɪgənna:mə], *m.* (—ns, *pl.* —n) proper name.

Eigennutz ['aɪgənnuts], *m.* (—es, *no pl.*) self-interest, selfishness.

eigennützig ['aɪgənnytsɪç], *adj.* selfish, self-interested, self-seeking.

eigens ['aɪgəns], *adv.* particularly, specially.

Eigenschaft ['aɪgənʃaft], *f.* (—, *pl.* —en) quality, peculiarity; property.

Eigenschaftswort ['aɪgənʃaftsvɔrt], *n.* (—s, *pl.* ∵er) (*Gram.*) adjective.

Eigensinn ['aɪgənzɪn], *m.* (—s, *no pl.*) obstinacy.

eigentlich ['aɪgəntlɪç], *adj.* true, real; exact, literal.

Eigentum ['aɪgəntu:m], *n.* (—s, *pl.* ∵er) property, possession, estate.

Eigentümer ['aɪgənty:mər], *m.* (—s, *pl.* —) owner, proprietor.

eigenwillig ['aɪgənvɪlɪç], *adj.* self-willed.

eignen ['aɪgnən], *v.r. sich* — *für* (*zu*), suit, fit, be suitable *or* fit for (to).

Eilbote ['aɪlbo:tə], *m.* (—n, *pl.* —n) special messenger.

Eile ['aɪlə], *f.* (—, *no pl.*) haste, hurry.

eilen ['aɪlən], *v.n.* (*aux.* sein), *v.r.* (*sich* —), hasten, hurry; be urgent.

eilends ['aɪlənts], *adv.* hastily.

eilfertig ['aɪlfɛrtɪç], *adj.* hasty.

Eilgut ['aɪlgu:t], *n.* (—s, *pl.* ∵er) express goods.

eilig ['aɪlɪç], *adj.* hasty, speedy; pressing, urgent.

Eilzug ['aɪltsu:k], *m.* (—s, *pl.* ∵e) fast train.

Eimer ['aɪmər], *m.* (—s, *pl.* —) pail, bucket.

ein(e) ['aɪn(ə)], *indef. art,* a, an; *was für* —; what kind of a(n). — *num. adj.* one; — *jeder,* each one.

einander [aɪn'andər], *adv.* each other, one another.

einarbeiten ['aɪnarbaɪtən], *v.a.* train, familiarise s.o. with. —*v.r.* (*aux.* haben) *sich* —, familiarize o.s.

einäschern ['aɪnɛʃərn], *v.a.* reduce to ashes, incinerate; cremate.

einatmen ['aɪna:tmən], *v.a.* breathe in, inhale.

einätzen ['aɪnɛtsən], *v.a.* etch in.

einäugig ['aɪnɔygɪç], *adj.* one-eyed.

Einbahnstraße ['aɪnba:nʃtra:sə], *f.* (—, *pl.* —n) one-way street.

Einband ['aɪnbant], *m.* (—s, *pl.* ∵e) binding, cover of book.

einbändig ['aɪnbɛndɪç], *adj.* in one volume.

einbauen ['aɪnbauən], *v.a.* build in.

einbegreifen ['aɪnbəgraɪfən], *v.a. irr.* include, comprise.

einberufen ['aɪnbəru:fən], *v.a. irr.* convene, convoke; (*Mil.*) call up.

einbeziehen ['aɪnbətsi:ən], *v.a. irr.* include.

einbiegen ['aɪnbi:gən], *v.n. irr.* turn into (road).

einbilden ['aɪnbɪldən], *v.r. sich* —, imagine, fancy.

Einbildung ['aɪnbɪlduŋ], *f.* (—, *no pl.*) imagination, fancy, delusion; conceit.

einbinden ['aɪnbɪndən], *v.a. irr.* (*book*) bind.

Einblick ['aɪnblɪk], *m.* (—s, *no pl.*) insight.

Einbrecher ['aɪnbrɛçər], *m.* (—s, *pl.* —) burglar; intruder.

Einbrenne

Einbrenne [ˈaɪnbrɛnə], *f.* (—, *pl.* —n) thickening of soup.

einbringen [ˈaɪnbrɪŋən], *v.a. irr.* bring in, yield, fetch (a price); *wieder* —, retrieve.

einbrocken [ˈaɪnbrɔkən], *v.a.* crumble; *einem etwas* —, (*fig.*) get s.o. into trouble.

Einbruch [ˈaɪnbrux], *m.* (—s, *pl.* ⁒e) breaking-in; burglary, house-breaking.

Einbuchtung [ˈaɪnbuxtuŋ], *f.* (—, *pl.* —en) bight, bay.

einbürgern [ˈaɪnbyrgərn], *v.a.* naturalise.

Einbuße [ˈaɪnbuːsə], *f.* (—, *pl.* —n) loss.

einbüßen [ˈaɪnbyːsən], *v.a.* suffer a loss from, lose, forfeit.

eindämmen [ˈaɪndɛmən], *v.a.* dam in (*or* up).

Eindecker [ˈaɪndɛkər], *m.* (—s, *pl.* —) (*Aviat.*) monoplane.

eindeutig [ˈaɪndɔytɪç], *adj.* unequivocal, unambiguous.

eindrängen [ˈaɪndrɛŋən], *v.r. sich* —, intrude (into), force o.'s way in(to), interfere.

eindrillen [ˈaɪndrɪlən], *v.a. einem etwas* —, drum s.th. into s.o.

eindringen [ˈaɪndrɪŋən], *v.n. irr.* (*aux.* sein) enter, intrude; invade; penetrate.

eindringlich [ˈaɪndrɪŋlɪç], *adj.* forceful, urgent; impressive.

Eindruck [ˈaɪndruk], *m.* (—s, *pl.* ⁒e) impression.

eindrücken [ˈaɪndrykən], *v.a.* press in, squeeze in.

eindrucksfähig [ˈaɪndruksfɛːɪç], *adj.* impressionable.

einengen [ˈaɪnɛŋən], *v.a.* compress, limit, confine, cramp.

Einer [ˈaɪnər], *m.* (—s, *pl.* —) (*Maths.*) digit, unit.

einerlei [ˈaɪnərlaɪ], *adj.* the same, all the same.

einerseits [ˈaɪnərzaɪts], *adv.* on the one hand.

einfach [ˈaɪnfax], *adj.* single; simple, plain, uncomplicated; modest, homely.

einfädeln [ˈaɪnfɛːdəln], *v.a.* thread.

einfahren [ˈaɪnfaːrən], *v.n. irr.* (*aux.* sein) drive in, enter. — *v.a.* run in (new car).

Einfahrt [ˈaɪnfaːrt], *f.* (—, *pl.* —en) entrance, gateway, drive; (*Min.*) descent.

Einfall [ˈaɪnfal], *m.* (—-s, *pl.* ⁒e) falling-in, downfall, fall; (*Mil.*) invasion; (*fig.*) idea, inspiration.

einfallen [ˈaɪnfalən], *v.n. irr.* (*aux.* sein) fall in, fall into; (*Mil.*) invade; (*fig.*) occur to s.o.

Einfalt [ˈaɪnfalt], *f.* (—, *no pl.*) simplicity; silliness.

Einfaltspinsel [ˈaɪnfaltspɪnzəl], *m.* (—s, *pl.* —) simpleton, dunce.

einfangen [ˈaɪnfaŋən], *v.a. irr.* catch, get hold of.

einfarbig [ˈaɪnfarbɪç], *adj.* of one colour; monochrome.

einfassen [ˈaɪnfasən], *v.a.* border, trim; (*diamonds*) set.

Einfassung [ˈaɪnfasuŋ], *f.* (—, *pl.* —en) bordering, trimming, edging, framing.

einfetten [ˈaɪnfɛtən], *v.a.* grease, lubricate.

einfinden [ˈaɪnfɪndən], *v.r. irr. sich* —, appear, be present.

einflechten [ˈaɪnflɛctən], *v.a. irr.* plait; (*fig.*) insert.

einfließen [ˈaɪnfliːsən], *v.n. irr.* (*aux.* sein) flow in; — *lassen*, (*fig.*) mention casually, slip in (a word).

einflößen [ˈaɪnfløːsən], *v.a.* infuse; (*fig.*) instil, inspire with.

Einfluß [ˈaɪnflus], *m.* (—sses, *pl.* ⁒sse) influx; (*fig.*) influence.

einflußreich [ˈaɪnflusraɪç], *adj.* influential.

einflüstern [ˈaɪnflystərn], *v.n.* suggest, insinuate.

einförmig [ˈaɪnfœrmɪç], *adj.* uniform; monotonous.

einfriedigen [ˈaɪnfriːdɪgən], *v.a.* fence in, enclose.

einfügen [ˈaɪnfyːgən], *v.a.* insert, include, fit in. — *v.r. sich* —, adapt o.s., become a part of.

Einfühlungsvermögen [ˈaɪnfyːluŋsfɛrmøːgən], *n.* (—s, *no pl.*) (*Phil.*) empathy, sympathetic understanding.

Einfuhr [ˈaɪnfuːr], *f.* (—, *pl.* —en) importation, import.

einführen [ˈaɪnfyːrən], *v.a.* introduce; (*goods*) import.

Einführung [ˈaɪnfyːruŋ], *f.* (—, *pl.* —en) introduction; (*goods*) importation.

einfüllen [ˈaɪnfylən], *v.a.* fill in, pour into, bottle.

Eingabe [ˈaɪngaːbə], *f.* (—, *pl.* —n) petitition; application.

Eingang [ˈaɪngaŋ], *m.* (—s, *pl.* ⁒e) entry, entrance; arrival.

eingangs [ˈaɪngaŋs], *adv.* in *or* at the beginning.

eingeben [ˈaɪngeːbən], *v.a. irr.* inspire (with); (*petition*) present, deliver; (*claim*) file; (*complaint*) bring; (*medicine*) administer.

eingeboren [ˈaɪngəboːrən], *adj.* native; (*Theol.*) only-begotten.

Eingeborene [ˈaɪngəboːrənə], *m.* (—n, *pl.* —n) native.

Eingebrachte [ˈaɪngəbraxtə], *n.* (—n, *no pl.*) dowry.

Eingebung [ˈaɪngəbuŋ], *f.* (—, *pl.* —en) inspiration.

eingedenk [ˈaɪngədɛŋk], *prep.* (*Genit.*) mindful of, remembering.

eingefleischt [ˈaɪngəflaɪʃt], *adj.* inveterate, confirmed.

eingehen [ˈaɪngeːən], *v.n. irr.* (*aux.* sein) (*Comm.*) arrive; *auf etwas* —, enter into s.th., agree to s.th.; *auf etwas näher* —, enter into the details of s.th.; (*animals, plants*) die; (*cloth*) shrink.

eingehend [ˈaɪngeːənt], *adj.* thorough, exhaustive.

Eingemachte [ˈaɪngəmaxtə], *n.* (—n, *no pl.*) preserve.

eingenommen [ˈaɪngənɔmən], *adj.* enthusiastic for, infatuated with; — *von sich*, conceited.

Eingeschlossenheit [ˈaɪngəʃlɔsənhaɪt], *f.* (—, *no pl.*) isolation, seclusion.

eingeschrieben [ˈaɪngəʃriːbən], *adj.* registered (letter).

eingesessen [ˈaɪngəzɛsən], *adj.* old-established; resident.

Eingeständnis [ˈaɪngəʃtɛntnɪs], *n.* (—ses, *pl.* —se) confession.

eingestehen [ˈaɪngəʃteːən], *v.a. irr.* confess to, avow.

Eingeweide [ˈaɪngəvaɪdə], *n. pl.* bowels, intestines.

eingewöhnen [ˈaɪngəvøːnən], *v.r. sich* —, accustom o.s. to, get used to.

eingießen [ˈaɪngiːsən], *v.a. irr.* pour in; pour out.

eingleisig [ˈaɪnglaɪzɪç], *adj.* single-track.

eingliedern [ˈaɪngliːdərn], *v.r. sich* —, adapt o.s., fit in.

eingreifen [ˈaɪngraɪfən], *v.n. irr.* intervene in; interfere with, encroach on.

Eingriff [ˈaɪngrɪf], *m.* (—s, *pl.* —e) intervention, encroachment, infringement; (*Med.*) operation.

Einguß [ˈaɪngus], *m.* (—sses, *pl.* ⁻sse) infusion; enema.

einhaken [ˈaɪnhaːkən], *v.a.* hook in. — *v.r. sich* —, (*fig.*) take a p.'s arm.

Einhalt [ˈaɪnhalt], *m.* (—s, *no pl.*) stop, check, prohibition, cessation; — *gebieten*, check, suppress.

einhalten [ˈaɪnhaltən], *v.a. irr.* observe, adhere to.

einhändigen [ˈaɪnhɛndɪgən], *v.a.* hand in, deliver.

einhauen [ˈaɪnhauən], *v.a.* hew in, break open.

Einhebung [ˈaɪnheːbuŋ], *f.* (—, *pl.* —en) (*taxes*) collection.

einheften [ˈaɪnhɛftən], *v.a.* sew in, stitch in; (*papers*) file.

einhegen [ˈaɪnheːgən], *v.a.* fence in, hedge in.

einheimisch [ˈaɪnhaɪmɪʃ], *adj.* native; (*Bot.*) indigenous.

einheimsen [ˈaɪnhaɪmzən], *v.a.* reap.

Einheit [ˈaɪnhaɪt], *f.* (—, *pl.* —en) unit, unity.

einheitlich [ˈaɪnhaɪtlɪç], *adj.* uniform, consistent.

einheizen [ˈaɪnhaɪtsən], *v.a., v.n.* heat the stove, light the fire.

einhellig [ˈaɪnhɛlɪç], *adj.* unanimous, harmonious.

einher [aɪnˈheːr], *adv.* forth, along, on.

einholen [ˈaɪnhoːlən], *v.a.* obtain; catch up with. — *v.n.* go shopping.

Einhorn [ˈaɪnhɔrn], *n.* (—s, *pl.* ⁻er) unicorn.

einhüllen [ˈaɪnhylən], *v.a.* wrap up, cover, envelop.

einig [ˈaɪnɪç], *adj.* at one. — *adv.* in agreement.

einige [ˈaɪnɪgə], *adj.* some, several.

einigemal [ˈaɪnɪgəmaːl], *adv.* several times.

einigen [ˈaɪnɪgən], *v.a.* unite. — *v.r. sich* — *mit*, come to an agreement with.

einigermaßen [aɪnɪgərˈmaːsən], *adv.* to a certain extent.

Einigkeit [ˈaɪnɪçkaɪt], *f.* (—, *no pl.*) union; unity, unanimity, harmony.

Einigung [ˈaɪnɪguŋ], *f.* (—, *no pl.*) agreement.

einimpfen [ˈaɪnɪmpfən], *v.a.* inoculate, vaccinate.

einjährig [ˈaɪnjɛːrɪg], *adj.* one-year-old, annual.

einkassieren [ˈaɪnkasiːrən], *v.a.* cash (*cheque*), collect (*money*).

Einkauf [ˈaɪnkauf], *m.* (—s, *pl.* ⁻e) purchase, buy.

einkaufen [ˈaɪnkaufən], *v.a.* purchase, buy. — *v.n.* go shopping.

Einkäufer [ˈaɪnkɔyfər], *m.* (—s, *pl.* —) (*Comm.*) purchaser, buyer.

Einkehr [ˈaɪnkeːr], *f.* (—, *no pl.*) stopping (at an inn); (*fig.*) meditation.

einkehren [ˈaɪnkeːrən], *v.n.* (*aux.* sein) stop *or* put up (at an inn).

einkerkern [ˈaɪnkɛrkərn], *v.a.* imprison.

einklagen [ˈaɪnklaːgən], *v.a.* (*Law*) sue for (*money*).

einklammern [ˈaɪnklamərn], *v.a.* bracket, enclose in brackets.

Einklang [ˈaɪnklaŋ], *m.* (—s, *no pl.*) accord, unison, harmony.

einkleben [ˈaɪnkleːbən], *v.a.* paste in.

einkleiden [ˈaɪnklaɪdən], *v.a.* clothe; (*fig.*) invest; *sich* — *lassen*, (*Eccl.*) take the veil.

einklemmen [ˈaɪnklɛmən], *v.a.* squeeze in, jam in.

einkochen [ˈaɪnkɔxən], *v.a.* preserve. — *v.n.* (*aux.* sein) boil down.

Einkommen [ˈaɪnkɔmən], *n.* (—s, *no pl.*) income, revenue.

einkommen [ˈaɪnkɔmən], *v.n. irr.* (*aux.* sein) *bei einem wegen etwas* —, apply to s.o. for s.th.

einkreisen [ˈaɪnkraɪzən], *v.a.* encircle, isolate.

Einkünfte [ˈaɪnkynftə], *pl.* income, revenue; emoluments.

einladen [ˈaɪnlaːdən], *v.a. irr.* load in; invite.

Einlage [ˈaɪnlaːgə], *f.* (—, *pl.* —en) (*letter*) enclosure; (*Theat.*) addition to programme; (*game*) stake; (*Comm.*) investment.

einlagern [ˈaɪnlaːgərn], *v.a.* (*goods*) store, warehouse; (*Mil.*) billet, quarter.

Einlaß [ˈaɪnlas], *m.* (—sses, *no pl.*) admission, admittance; (*water*) inlet.

einlassen [ˈaɪnlasən], *v.a. irr.* admit, allow in; let in. — *v.r. sich auf etwas* —, engage in s.th., enter into s.th.

Einlauf [ˈaɪnlauf], *m.* (—s, *no pl.*) entering; (*Med.*) enema.

einlaufen ['aɪnlaufən], *v.n. irr.* (*aux.* sein) (*Naut.*) enter harbour, put into port; (*materia!*) shrink.

einleben ['aɪnleːbən], *v.r. sich* —, grow accustomed to, settle down, acclimatise o.s.

einlegen ['aɪnleːgən], *v.a.* put in, lay in; enclose; (*money*) deposit; (*food*) pickle, preserve; *Fürbitte* —, intercede; *eingelegte Arbeit*, inlaid work.

einleiten ['aɪnlaɪtən], *v.a.* begin, introduce; institute.

Einleitung ['aɪnlaɪtuŋ], *f.* (—, *pl.* —en) introduction; (*book*) preface; (*Mus.*) prelude; (*Law*) institution.

einlenken ['aɪnlɛŋkən], *v.n.* turn in; give in, come round.

einleuchten ['aɪnlɔyçtən], *v.n.* become clear.

einlösen ['aɪnløːzən], *v.a.* redeem; (*bill*) honour; (*cheque*) cash.

einmachen ['aɪnmaxən], *v.a.* preserve.

einmal ['aɪnmaːl], *adv.* once; *es war* —, once upon a time; *auf* —, suddenly; *noch* —, once more; *nicht* —, not even.

Einmaleins ['aɪnmaːlaɪns], *n.* (—es, *no pl.*) multiplication table.

einmalig ['aɪnmaːlɪç], *adv.* unique, unrepeatable.

Einmaster ['aɪnmastər], *m.* (—s, *pl.* —) (*Naut.*) brigantine, cutter.

einmauern ['aɪnmauərn], *v.a.* wall in, immure.

einmengen ['aɪnmɛŋən], *v.r. sich* —, meddle with, interfere.

einmieten ['aɪnmiːtən], *v.r. sich* —, take lodgings.

einmischen ['aɪnmɪʃən], *v.r. sich* —, meddle (with), interfere.

einmütig ['aɪnmyːtɪç], *adj.* unanimous, in harmony, united.

Einnahme ['aɪnnaːmə], *f.* (—, *pl.* —n) income, revenue; receipts; (*Mil.*) occupation, capture.

einnehmen ['aɪnneːmən], *v.a. irr.* take in; (*money*) receive; (*medicine*) take; (*taxes*) collect; (*place*) take up, occupy; (*Mil.*) occupy, conquer; (*fig.*) captivate, fascinate.

einnehmend ['aɪnneːmənt], *adj.* fetching, engaging, charming.

einnicken ['aɪnnɪkən], *v.n.* (*aux.* sein) nod *or* doze off.

einnisten ['aɪnnɪstən], *v.r. sich* —, nestle down; (*fig.*) settle in a place.

Einöde ['aɪnøːdə], *f.* (—, *pl.* —n) desert, solitude.

einordnen ['aɪnɔrdnən], *v.a.* place in order, file, classify.

einpauken ['aɪnpaukən], *v.a.* cram.

einpferchen ['aɪnpfɛrçən], *v.a.* pen in, coop up.

einpökeln ['aɪnpøːkəln], *v.a.* salt, pickle.

einprägen ['aɪnprɛːgən], *v.a.* imprint; impress.

einquartieren ['aɪnkvartiːrən], *v.a.* (*Mil.*) quarter, billet.

einrahmen ['aɪnraːmən], *v.a.* frame.

einräumen ['aɪnrɔymən], *v.a.* stow (things) away; *einem etwas* —, concede s.th. to s.o.

Einrede ['aɪnreːdə], *f.* (—, *pl.* —n) objection.

einreden ['aɪnreːdən], *v.a. einem etwas* —, persuade s.o. to. — *v.r. sich etwas* —, get s.th. into o.'s head.

einreichen ['aɪnraɪçən], *v.a.* hand in, deliver; tender.

einreihen ['aɪnraɪən], *v.a.* place in line, arrange.

einreihig ['aɪnraɪɪç], *adj.* consisting of a single row; (*Tail.*) single-breasted (suit).

einreißen ['aɪnraɪsən], *v.a. irr.* make a tear in; (*houses*) pull down. — *v.n.* (*fig.*) gain ground.

einrenken ['aɪnrɛŋkən], *v.a.* (*Med.*) set; (*fig.*) settle.

einrichten ['aɪnrɪçtən], *v.a.* put in order, arrange; equip, set up; furnish.

Einrichtung ['aɪnrɪçtuŋ], *f.* (—, *pl.* —en) arrangement, management; furnishing; (*pl.*) facilities; equipment, amenities.

einrücken ['aɪnrykən], *v.n.* (*aux.* sein) march in. — *v.a.* insert (in the newspaper).

Eins [aɪns], *f.* (—, *pl.* —en, —er) one; (*Sch.*) top marks.

eins [aɪns], *num.* one; *es ist mir alles* —, it is all the same to me.

einsalzen ['aɪnzaltsən], *v.a.* salt, pickle, cure.

einsam ['aɪnzaːm], *adj.* lonely, solitary, secluded.

Einsamkeit ['aɪnzaːmkaɪt], *f.* (—, *no pl.*) loneliness, solitude, seclusion.

Einsatz ['aɪnzats], *m.* (—es, *pl.* ⁻e) (*game*) stake, pool; (*dress*) lace inset; (*Mus.*) entry (of a voice), starting intonation; (*Mil.*) sortie, mission.

einsaugen ['aɪnzaugən], *v.a.* suck in; (*fig.*) imbibe.

einsäumen ['aɪnzɔymən], *v.a.* hem (in).

einschalten ['aɪnʃaltən], *v.a.* insert, interpolate; switch on; put in gear.

einschärfen ['aɪnʃɛrfən], *v.a.* impress s.th. on s.o.

einschätzen ['aɪnʃɛtsən], *v.a.* assess.

einschenken ['aɪnʃɛŋkən], *v.a.* pour in *or* out, fill.

einschieben ['aɪnʃiːbən], *v.a.* push in; interpolate, insert.

Einschiebsel ['aɪnʃiːpsəl], *n.* (—s, *pl.* —) interpolation; interpolated part.

einschiffen ['aɪnʃɪfən], *v.a.* embark; (*goods*) ship. — *v.r. sich* —, go aboard, embark.

einschlafen ['aɪnʃlaːfən], *v.n. irr.* (*aux.* sein) fall asleep, go to sleep.

einschläfern ['aɪnʃlɛːfərn], *v.a.* lull to sleep.

Einschlag ['aɪnʃlaːk], *m.* (—s, *pl.* ⁻e) cover, envelope; (*weaving*) woof, weft; explosion; strike; (*fig.*) streak (of character); touch.

einschlagen ['aɪnʃlaːgən], v.a. irr. knock in; (nail) drive in; (parcel) wrap up; (road) take. — v.n. (lightning) strike; be a success.

einschlägig ['aɪnʃlɛːgɪç], adj. bearing on (the subject), pertinent.

einschleppen ['aɪnʃlɛpən], v.a. (disease) bring in, introduce.

einschließen ['aɪnʃliːsən], v.a. irr. lock in or up; (enemy) surround; (fig.) include.

einschlummern ['aɪnʃlumərn], v.n. (aux. sein) doze off, fall asleep.

Einschluß ['aɪnʃlus], m. (—sses, pl. ⁓sse) inclusion; mit — von, inclusive of.

einschmeicheln ['aɪnʃmaɪçəln], v.r. sich bei einem —, ingratiate o.s. with s.o.

einschmelzen ['aɪnʃmɛltsən], v.a. irr. melt down.

einschmieren ['aɪnʃmiːrən], v.a. smear, grease, oil; (sore) put ointment on.

einschneidend ['aɪnʃnaɪdənt], adj. important, sweeping, incisive, trenchant.

einschneidig ['aɪnʃnaɪdɪç], adj. single-edged.

Einschnitt ['aɪnʃnɪt], m. (—s, pl. —e) incision, cut, notch; (nerve) caesura.

einschnüren ['aɪnʃnyːrən], v.a. lace up; (parcel) tie up.

einschränken ['aɪnʃrɛŋkən], v.a. confine, limit, restrict. — v.r. sich —, curtail o.'s expenses, economize.

einschrauben ['aɪnʃraubən], v.a. screw in.

einschreiben ['aɪnʃraɪbən], v.a. irr. write in or down, inscribe; (letter) register. — v.r. sich —, enter o.'s name; enrol.

Einschreibesendung ['aɪnʃraɪbəzenduŋ], f. (—, pl. —en) registered letter, registered parcel.

einschreiten ['aɪnʃraɪtən], v.n. irr. (aux. sein) step in, intervene.

einschrumpfen ['aɪnʃrumpfən], v.n. (aux. sein) shrink, shrivel.

einschüchtern ['aɪnʃyçtərn], v.a. intimidate, overawe.

Einschuß ['aɪnʃus], m. (—sses, pl. ⁓sse) share, advance of capital; (weaving) woof, weft.

einsegnen ['aɪnzeːgnən], v.a. consecrate, bless; (Eccl.) confirm.

Einsehen ['aɪnzeːən], n. (—s, no pl.) realisation; ein — haben, be reasonable.

einsehen ['aɪnzeːən], v.a. irr. look into, glance over; (fig.) comprehend, realise.

einseifen ['aɪnzaɪfən], v.a. soap, lather; (fig.) take s.o. in.

einseitig ['aɪnzaɪtɪç], adj. one-sided; (fig.) one-track (mind).

Einsenkung ['aɪnzeŋkuŋ], f. (—, pl. —en) depression (of the ground).

einsetzen ['aɪnzɛtsən], v.a. put in, set in; institute, establish; (money) stake; (Hort.) plant; (office) install s.o. — v.n. begin.

Einsetzung ['aɪnzɛtsuŋ], f. (—, pl. —en) (office) investiture, installation; institution.

Einsicht ['aɪnzɪçt], f. (—, no pl.) inspection, examination; insight, understanding.

einsichtig ['aɪnzɪçtɪç], adj. intelligent, sensible, judicious.

Einsichtnahme ['aɪnzɪçtnaːmə], f. zur —, (Comm.) on approval, for inspection.

Einsiedler ['aɪnziːdlər], m. (—s, pl. —) hermit, recluse.

einsilbig ['aɪnzɪlbɪç], adj. monosyllabic; (fig.) taciturn, laconic.

einspannen ['aɪnʃpanən], v.a. stretch in a frame; harness; (coll.) put to work.

Einspänner ['aɪnʃpɛnər], m. (—s, pl. —) one-horse vehicle; one-horse cab, fiacre.

einsperren ['aɪnʃpɛrən], v.a. lock in, shut up, imprison.

einspinnen ['aɪnʃpɪnən], v.r. irr. sich —, spin a cocoon.

einsprengen ['aɪnʃprɛŋən], v.a. sprinkle.

einspringen ['aɪnʃprɪŋən], v.n. irr. (aux. sein) auf einen —, leap at; (lock) catch, snap; für einen —, deputize for s.o.

Einspruch ['aɪnʃprux], m. (—s, pl. ⁓e) objection, protest; — erheben, protest; (Law) appeal (against).

einspurig ['aɪnʃpuːrɪç], adj. (Railw.) single-track line.

einst [aɪnst], adv. (past) once, once upon a time; (future) some day.

Einstand ['aɪnʃtant], m. (—s, no pl.) (Tennis) deuce.

einstecken ['aɪnʃtɛkən], v.a. put in; pocket; post (a letter).

einstehen ['aɪnʃteːən], v.a. irr. zu etwas —, answer for s.th.; für einen —, stand security for s.o.

einsteigen ['aɪnʃtaɪgən], v.n. irr. (aux. sein) get in, climb on; board.

einstellen ['aɪnʃtɛlən], v.a. put in; (persons) engage, hire; adjust; (work) stop, strike; (payments) stop; (hostilities) suspend, cease fire. — v.r. sich —, turn up, appear.

einstellig ['aɪnʃtɛlɪç], adj. (Maths.) of one digit.

Einstellung ['aɪnʃtɛluŋ], f. (—, pl. —en) putting in; (persons) engagement, hiring; adjustment; (work) stoppage, strike; (payments) suspension; (hostilities) suspension, cessation; (fig.) opinion, attitude.

einstig ['aɪnstɪç], adj. (past) former, late, erstwhile; (future) future, to be, to come.

einstimmen ['aɪnʃtɪmən], v.n. join in, chime in.

einstimmig ['aɪnʃtɪmɪç], adj. (Mus.) (for) one voice, unison; (fig.) unanimous.

einstmals ['aɪnstmaːls], adv. once, formerly.

einstöckig

einstöckig [ˈaɪnʃtœkɪç], *adj.* one-storied.

einstreichen [ˈaɪnʃtraɪçən], *v.a. irr.* (*money*) take in, pocket.

einstreuen [ˈaɪnʃtrɔyən], *v.a.* strew; (*fig.*) intersperse.

einstudieren [ˈaɪnʃtudiːrən], *v.a.* study; (*Theat., Mus.*) rehearse.

einstürmen [ˈaɪnʃtyrmən], *v.n.* (*aux.* sein) *auf einen* —, rush at, fall upon.

Einsturz [ˈaɪnʃturts], *m.* (—es, *pl.* ⁻e) fall, crash; subsidence, collapse.

einstürzen [ˈaɪnʃtyrtsən], *v.n.* (*aux.* sein) fall in, fall into ruin, fall to pieces, collapse.

einstweilen [ˈaɪnstvaɪlən], *adv.* in the meantime, meanwhile, for the time being, provisionally.

einstweilig [ˈaɪnstvaɪlɪç], *adj.* temporary, provisional.

eintägig [ˈaɪntɛːgɪç], *adj.* one-day, ephemeral.

Eintagsfliege [ˈaɪntaːksfliːgə], *f.* (—, *pl.* —n) dayfly.

eintauschen [ˈaɪntauʃən], *v.a.* — *gegen*, exchange for, barter for.

einteilen [ˈaɪntaɪlən], *v.a.* divide; distribute; classify.

eintönig [ˈaɪntøːnɪç], *adj.* monotonous.

Eintracht [ˈaɪntraxt], *f.* (—, *no pl.*) concord, harmony.

einträchtig [ˈaɪntrɛçtɪç], *adj.* united, harmonious.

Eintrag [ˈaɪntraːk], *m.* (—s, *pl.* ⁻e) entry (in a book); prejudice, damage, detriment.

eintragen [ˈaɪntraːgən], *v.a. irr.* enter (in a book), register; bring in, yield.

einträglich [ˈaɪntrɛklɪç], *adj.* profitable, lucrative.

Eintragung [ˈaɪntraːguŋ], *f.* (—, *pl.* —en) entry (in a book); enrolment.

einträufeln [ˈaɪntrɔyfəln], *v.a.* instil.

eintreffen [ˈaɪntrɛfən], *v.n. irr.* (*aux.* sein) arrive; happen, come true.

eintreiben [ˈaɪntraɪbən], *v.a. irr.* drive home (*cattle*); collect (debts etc.).

eintreten [ˈaɪntreːtən], *v.n. irr.* (*aux.* sein) step in, enter; happen, take place; *in einen Verein* —, join a club; *für einen* —, speak up for s.o.

eintrichtern [ˈaɪntrɪçtərn], *v.a. einem etwas* —, cram s.th. into s.o.

Eintritt [ˈaɪntrɪt], *m.* (—s, *no pl.*) entry, entrance; beginning; *kein* —, no admission.

eintrocknen [ˈaɪntrɔknən], *v.n.* (*aux.* sein) shrivel, dry up.

einüben [ˈaɪnyːbən], *v.a.* practise, exercise.

einverleiben [ˈaɪnfɛrlaɪbən], *v.a.* incorporate in, embody in.

Einvernahme [ˈaɪnfɛrnaːmə], *f.* (—, *pl.* —n) (*Austr.*) *see* **Vernehmung**.

Einvernehmen [ˈaɪnfɛrneːmən], *n.* (—s, *no pl.*) understanding; *im besten* —, on the best of terms.

einvernehmen [ˈaɪnfɛrneːmən], *v.a.* (*aux.* haben) (*Austr.*) *see* **vernehmen**.

einverstanden [ˈaɪnfɛrʃtandən], (*excl.*) agreed! — *adj.* — *sein*, agree.

Einverständnis [ˈaɪnfɛrʃtɛntnɪs], *n.* (—ses, *no pl.*) consent, agreement, accord.

Einwand [ˈaɪnvant], *m.* (—s, *pl.* ⁻e) objection, exception; — *erheben*, raise objections.

einwandern [ˈaɪnvandərn], *v.n.* (*aux.* sein) immigrate.

einwandfrei [ˈaɪnvantfraɪ], *adj.* irreproachable, unobjectionable.

einwärts [ˈaɪnvɛrts], *adv.* inward(s).

einwechseln [ˈaɪnvɛksəln], *v.a.* change, exchange.

einweichen [ˈaɪnvaɪçən], *v.a.* steep in water, soak.

einweihen [ˈaɪnvaɪən], *v.a.* dedicate; (*Eccl.*) consecrate; open (formally), inaugurate; initiate (into).

Einweihung [ˈaɪnvaɪuŋ], *f.* (—, *pl.* —en) (*Eccl.*) consecration; inauguration, formal opening; initiation.

einwenden [ˈaɪnvɛndən], *v.a. irr.* object to, raise objections, urge against.

einwerfen [ˈaɪnvɛrfən], *v.a. irr.* throw in; smash in; interject.

einwickeln [ˈaɪnvɪkəln], *v.a.* wrap up, envelop.

einwilligen [ˈaɪnvɪlɪgən], *v.n.* consent, assent, agree, accede.

einwirken [ˈaɪnvɪrkən], *v.n. auf einen* —, influence s.o.

Einwohner [ˈaɪnvoːnər], *m.* (—s, *pl.* —) inhabitant.

Einwohnerschaft [ˈaɪnvoːnərʃaft], *f.* (—, *no pl.*) population, inhabitants.

Einwurf [ˈaɪnvurf], *m.* (—s, *pl.* ⁻e) (*letter box*) opening, slit; slot; objection.

einwurzeln [ˈaɪnvurtsəln], *v.r. sich* —, take root; *eingewurzelt*, deep-rooted.

Einzahl [ˈaɪntsaːl], *f.* (—, *no pl.*) singular.

einzahlen [ˈaɪntsaːlən], *v.a.* pay in, deposit.

einzäunen [ˈaɪntsɔynən], *v.a.* fence in.

einzeichnen [ˈaɪntsaɪçnən], *v.a.* draw in, sketch in. — *v.r. sich* —, enter o.'s name, sign.

Einzelhaft [ˈaɪntsəlhaft], *f.* (—, *no pl.*) solitary confinement.

Einzelheit [ˈaɪntsəlhaɪt], *f.* (—, *pl.* —en) detail, particular.

einzeln [ˈaɪntsəln], *adj.* single; isolated; detached, apart.

einziehen [ˈaɪntsiːən], *v.a. irr.* draw in, retract; (*Law*) confiscate, impound; (*debts*) collect, call in; (*bill of sight*) discount, cash; (*money*) withdraw (from circulation); (*sails*) furl; (*Mil.*) call up.

einzig [ˈaɪntsɪç], *adj.* sole, single; unique, only.

Einzug [ˈaɪntsuːk], *m.* (—s, *pl.* ⁻e) entry, entrance; move (into new house).

einzwängen [ˈaɪntsvɛŋən], *v.a.* force in, squeeze in.

Eis [aɪs], *n.* (—es, *no pl.*) ice; ice-cream.

E-is [ˈeːɪs], *n.* (—, *pl.* —) (*Mus.*) E sharp.

Ende

Eisbahn ['aɪsbaːn], *f.* (—, *pl.* —en) ice-rink, skating-rink.
Eisbär ['aɪsbɛːr], *m.* (—en, *pl.* —en) polar bear, white bear.
Eisbein ['aɪsbaɪn], *n.* (—s, *pl.* —e) pig's trotters.
Eisberg ['aɪsbɛrk], *m.* (—s, *pl.* —e) iceberg.
Eisblumen ['aɪsbluːmən], *f. pl.* frost patterns (*on glass*).
Eisen ['aɪzən], *n.* (—s, *pl.* —) iron; *altes* —, scrap iron.
Eisenbahn ['aɪzənbaːn], *f.* (—, *pl.* —en) railway.
Eisenfleck ['aɪzənflɛk], *m.* (—s, *pl.* —e) iron mould.
Eisengießerei ['aɪzəngiːsəraɪ], *f.* (—, *pl.* —en) iron foundry, iron forge.
Eisenguß ['aɪzəngus], *m.* (—sses, *pl.* ⸗sse) cast-iron.
Eisenhändler ['aɪzənhɛndlər], *m.* (—s, *pl.* —) ironmonger.
Eisenhütte ['aɪzənhytə], *f.* (—, *pl.* —n) *see* **Eisengießerei**.
Eisenschlacke ['aɪzənʃlakə], *f.* (—, *no pl.*) iron dross, iron slag.
eisern ['aɪzərn], *adj.* made of iron; (*coll. & fig.*) strong; strict.
Eisgang ['aɪsgaŋ], *m.* (—s, *pl.* ⸗e) drift of ice.
eisgrau ['aɪsgrau], *adj.* hoary.
eiskalt ['aɪskalt], *adj.* icy cold.
Eislauf ['aɪslauf], *m.* (—s, *no pl.*) ice-skating.
Eismeer ['aɪsmeːr], *n.* (—s, *pl.* —e) polar sea; *nördliches* —, Arctic Ocean; *südliches* —, Antarctic Ocean.
Eispickel ['aɪspɪkəl], *m.* (—s, *pl.* —) ice axe.
Eisvogel ['aɪsfoːgəl], *m.* (—s, *pl.* ⸗) (*Orn.*) kingfisher.
Eiszapfen ['aɪstsapfən], *m.* (—s, *pl.* —) icicle.
eitel ['aɪtəl], *adj.* vain, frivolous, conceited; (*obs.*) pure.
Eiter ['aɪtər], *m.* (—s, *no pl.*) (*Med.*) pus, matter.
Eitergeschwür ['aɪtərgəʃvyːr], *n.* (—s, *pl.* —e) abscess.
eitern ['aɪtərn], *v.n.* suppurate.
Eiterung ['aɪtəruŋ], *f.* (—, *pl.* —en) suppuration.
eitrig ['aɪtrɪç], *adj.* purulent.
Eiweis ['aɪvaɪs], *n.* (—es, *no pl.*) white of egg; albumen.
Ekel ['eːkəl], *m.* (—s, *no pl.*) nausea, disgust, distaste, aversion.
ekelhaft ['eːkəlhaft], *adj.* loathsome, disgusting, nauseous.
ekeln ['eːkəln], *v.r. sich — vor*, be disgusted (by), feel sick, loathe.
Ekuador [ɛkuaˈdɔr], *n.* Ecuador.
Elan [eˈlaː], *m.* (—s, *no pl.*) verve, vigour.
elastisch [eˈlastɪʃ], *adj.* elastic, flexible, buoyant.
Elastizität [elastɪtsɪˈtɛːt], *f.* (—, *no pl.*) elasticity; (*mind*) buoyancy.
Elch [ɛlç], *m.* (—s, *pl.* —e) (*Zool.*) elk.
Elegie [eleˈgiː], *f.* (—, *pl.* —n) elegy.

elektrisieren [elɛktriˈziːrən], *v.a.* electrify.
Elektrizität [elɛktritsɪˈtɛːt], *f.* (—, *no pl.*) electricity.
Elend ['eːlɛnt], *n.* (—s, *no pl.*) misery, distress, wretchedness.
elend ['eːlɛnt], *adj.* miserable, wretched, pitiful; weak; *sich — fühlen*, feel poorly.
elendiglich ['eːlɛndɪklɪç], *adv.* miserably, wretchedly.
Elentier ['eːlɛntiːr], *n.* (—s, *pl.* —e) (*Zool.*) elk.
elf [ɛlf], *num. adj.* eleven.
Elfe ['ɛlfə], *f.* (—, *pl.* —n) fairy.
Elfenbein ['ɛlfənbaɪn], *n.* (—s, *no pl.*) ivory.
Elisabeth [eˈliːzabɛt], *f.* Elizabeth.
Ellbogen ['ɛlboːgən], *m.* (—s, *pl.* —) elbow.
Elle ['ɛlə], *f.* (—, *pl.* —n) yard, ell.
Elritze ['ɛlrɪtsə], *f.* (—, *pl.* —n) minnow.
Elsaß ['ɛlzas], *n.* Alsace.
Elster ['ɛlstər], *f.* (—, *pl.* —n) magpie.
Eltern ['ɛltərn], *pl.* parents.
Emaille [eˈmaːj], *n.* (—s, *no pl.*) enamel.
emailliert [ema(l)ˈjiːrt], *adj.* covered with vitreous enamel, enamelled.
Empfang [ɛmˈpfaŋ], *m.* (—s, *pl.* ⸗e) receipt; reception.
empfangen [ɛmˈpfaŋən], *v.a. irr.* receive, accept, take.
Empfänger [ɛmˈpfɛŋər], *m.* (—s, *pl.* —) recipient, receiver.
empfänglich [ɛmˈpfɛŋlɪç], *adj.* susceptible, impressionable.
Empfängnis [ɛmˈpfɛŋnɪs], *f.* (—, *no pl.*) conception.
empfehlen [ɛmˈpfeːlən], *v.a. irr.* commend, recommend; give compliments to. — *v.r. sich* —, take leave.
empfinden [ɛmˈpfɪndən], *v.a. irr.* feel, perceive.
empfindlich [ɛmˈpfɪntlɪç], *adj.* sensitive, susceptible; touchy, thin-skinned.
empfindsam [ɛmˈpfɪntsaːm], *adj.* sentimental.
Empfindung [ɛmˈpfɪnduŋ], *f.* (—, *pl.* —en) sensation, feeling, sentiment.
empor [ɛmˈpoːr], *adv.* upward(s), up.
Empore [ɛmˈpoːrə], *f.* (—, *pl.* —n) gallery (*in church*).
empören [ɛmˈpøːrən], *v.a.* excite, enrage, shock. — *v.r. sich* —, revolt, rebel.
Emporkömmling [ɛmˈpoːrkœmlɪŋ], *m.* (—s, *pl.* —e) upstart.
empört [ɛmˈpøːrt], *adj.* furious, shocked, disgusted.
Empörung [ɛmˈpøːruŋ], *f.* (—, *pl.* —en) rebellion, revolt, mutiny, insurrection; indignation, disgust.
emsig ['ɛmzɪç], *adj.* assiduous, industrious, busy.
Emsigkeit ['ɛmzɪçkaɪt], *f.* (—, *no pl.*) assiduity, diligence.
Ende ['ɛndə], *n.* (—s, *pl.* —n) end, conclusion.

enden

enden ['ɛndən], *v.n.* end, finish, conclude. — *v.a.* terminate, put an end to.
endgültig ['ɛntɡyltɪç], *adj.* definitive, final.
Endivie [ɛn'diːvjə], *f.* (—, *pl.* —n) (*Bot.*) endive.
endlich ['ɛntlɪç], *adj.* finite, final, ultimate. — *adv.* at last, at length, finally.
endlos ['ɛntloːs], *adj.* endless, never-ending, boundless.
Endung ['ɛnduŋ], *f.* (—, *pl.* —en) (*Gram.*) ending, termination.
Endziel ['ɛntsiːl], *n.* (—s, *pl.* —e) final aim.
Energie [enɛr'ɡiː], *f.* (—, *pl.* —n) energy.
energisch [e'nɛrɡɪʃ], *adj.* energetic.
eng [ɛŋ], *adj.* narrow, tight; tight-fitting.
engagieren [ãɡa'ʒiːrən], *v.a.* engage, hire.
Enge ['ɛŋə], *f.* (—, *pl.* —n) narrowness, lack of space; *einen in die* — *treiben* drive s.o. into a corner.
Engel ['ɛŋəl], *m.* (—s, *pl.* —) angel.
engelhaft ['ɛŋəlhaft], *adj.* angelic.
Engelschar ['ɛŋəlʃaːr], *f.* (—, *pl.* —en) angelic host.
Engelwurzel ['ɛŋəlvurtsəl], *f.* (—, *pl.* —n) angelica.
engherzig ['ɛŋhɛrtsɪç], *adj.* narrow-minded.
England ['ɛŋlant], *n.* England.
englisch (1) ['ɛŋlɪʃ], *adj.* (*obs.*) angelic.
englisch (2) ['ɛŋlɪʃ], *adj.* English; —e *Krankheit*, rickets.
Engpaß ['ɛŋpas], *m.* (—sses, *pl.* ⁓e) defile, narrow pass; (*fig.*) bottleneck.
engros [ã'ɡroː], *adj.* wholesale.
engstirnig ['ɛŋʃtɪrnɪç], *adj.* narrow-minded.
Enkel ['ɛŋkəl], *m.* (—s, *pl.* —) grand-child, grandson.
enorm [e'nɔrm], *adj.* enormous; (*coll.*) terrific.
entarten [ɛnt'artən], *v.n.* (*aux.* sein) degenerate.
entäußern [ɛnt'ɔysərn], *v.r. sich einer Sache* —, part with s.th.
entbehren [ɛnt'beːrən], *v.a.* lack, be in want of; spare.
entbehrlich [ɛnt'beːrlɪç], *adj.* dispensable, unnecessary, superfluous.
Entbehrung [ɛnt'beːruŋ], *f.* (—, *pl.* —en) privation, want.
entbieten [ɛnt'biːtən], *v.a. irr. Grüße* —, send o.'s respects.
entbinden [ɛnt'bɪndən], *v.a. irr. einen von etwas* —, release *or* dispense s.o. from s.th.; (*Med.*) deliver (a woman of a child).
Entbindung [ɛnt'bɪnduŋ], *f.* (—, *pl.* —en) (*Med.*) delivery, child-birth.
entblättern [ɛnt'blɛtərn], *v.a.* strip of leaves.
entblößen [ɛnt'bløːsən], *v.a.*, *v.r.* (*sich*) —, uncover (o.s.), bare (o.s.).
entdecken [ɛnt'dɛkən], *v.a.* discover, detect.

Ente ['ɛntə], *f.* (—, *pl.* —n) duck; *junge* —, duckling; (*fig.*) hoax, fictitious newspaper report.
entehren [ɛnt'eːrən], *v.a.* dishonour, disgrace; deflower, ravish.
enterben [ɛnt'ɛrbən], *v.a.* disinherit.
Enterich ['ɛntərɪç], *m.* (—s, *pl.* —e) drake.
entfachen [ɛnt'faxən], *v.a.* set ablaze, kindle.
entfahren [ɛnt'faːrən], *v.n. irr.* (*aux.* sein) slip off, escape.
entfallen [ɛnt'falən], *v.n. irr.* (*aux.* sein) escape o.'s memory; be left off.
entfalten [ɛnt'faltən], *v.a.* unfold; display. — *v.r. sich* —, develop, open up, expand.
entfärben [ɛnt'fɛrbən], *v.r. sich* —, lose colour, grow pale.
entfernen [ɛnt'fɛrnən], *v.a.* remove. — *v.r. sich* —, withdraw.
Entfernung [ɛnt'fɛrnuŋ], *f.* (—, *pl.* —en) removal; distance.
entfesseln [ɛnt'fɛsəln], *v.a.* unfetter; let loose.
Entfettungskur [ɛnt'fɛtuŋskuːr], *f.* (—, —en) slimming-cure.
entflammen [ɛnt'flamən], *v.a.* inflame.
entfliegen [ɛnt'fliːɡən], *v.n. irr.* (*aux.* sein) fly away.
entfliehen [ɛnt'fliːən], *v.n. irr.* (*aux.* sein) run away, escape, flee.
entfremden [ɛnt'frɛmdən], *v.a.* estrange, alienate.
entführen [ɛnt'fyːrən], *v.a.* abduct, carry off; kidnap; elope with.
entgegen [ɛnt'ɡeːɡən], *prep.* (*Dat.*), *adv.* against, contrary to; towards.
Entgegenkommen [ɛnt'ɡeːɡənkɔmən], *n.* (—s, *no pl.*) obliging behaviour, courtesy.
entgegenkommen [ɛnt'ɡeːɡənkɔmən], *v.n. irr.* (*aux.* sein) come towards s.o., come to meet s.o.; do a favour, oblige.
entgegennehmen [ɛnt'ɡeːɡənneːmən], *v.a. irr.* receive, accept.
entgegensehen [ɛnt'ɡeːɡənzeːən], *v.n. irr.* await, look forward to.
entgegnen [ɛnt'ɡeːɡnən], *v.a.* reply, retort.
Entgegnung [ɛnt'ɡeːɡnuŋ], *f.* (—, *pl.* —en) reply, retort, rejoinder.
entgehen [ɛnt'ɡeːən], *v.n. irr.* (*aux.* sein) (*Dat.*) escape; — *lassen*, let slip.
Entgelt [ɛnt'ɡɛlt], *n.* (—s, *no pl.*) remuneration, recompense.
entgelten [ɛnt'ɡɛltən], *v.a. irr. einen etwas* — *lassen*, make s.o. pay for s.th. *or* suffer.
entgleisen [ɛnt'ɡlaɪzən], *v.n.* (*aux.* sein) run off the rails, be derailed.
enthaaren [ɛnt'haːrən], *v.a.* depilate.
enthalten [ɛnt'haltən], *v.a. irr.* hold, contain. — *v.r. sich* —, abstain from, refrain from.
enthaltsam [ɛnt'haltzaːm], *adj.* abstinent, abstemious, temperate.
Enthaltung [ɛnt'haltuŋ], *f.* (—, *no pl.*) abstention.

60

enthaupten [εnt'hauptən], *v.a.* behead, decapitate.

entheben [εnt'he:bən], *v.a. irr. einen einer Sache* —, exempt *or* dispense from, suspend from, relieve of.

entheiligen [εnt'haılıgən], *v.a.* profane, desecrate.

enthüllen [εnt'hylən], *v.a.* unveil; (*fig.*) reveal.

entkleiden [εnt'klaıdən], *v.a.* unclothe, undress, strip.

entkommen [εnt'kɔmən], *v.n. irr.* (*aux. sein*) escape, get off.

entkräften [εnt'krεftən], *v.a.* enfeeble, debilitate, weaken; (*fig.*) refute (an argument).

entladen [εnt'la:dən], *v.a. irr.* unload, discharge. — *v.r. sich* —, burst; (*gun*) go off.

Entladung [εnt'la:duŋ], *f.* (—, *pl.* —en) unloading, discharge, explosion.

entlang [εnt'laŋ], *prep.* along.

entlarven [εnt'larfən], *v.a.* unmask; expose.

Entlarvung [εnt'larfuŋ], *f.* (—, *pl.* —en) unmasking, exposure.

entlassen [εnt'lasən], *v.a. irr.* dismiss; (*Am.*) fire; discharge; pension off.

Entlastung [εnt'lastuŋ], *f.* (—, *no pl.*) exoneration; credit (to s.o.'s bank account).

entlaufen [εnt'laufən], *v.n. irr.* (*aux. sein*) run away.

entlausen [εnt'lauzən], *v.a.* delouse.

entledigen [εnt'le:dıgən], *v.r. sich einer Sache* —, rid o.s. of *or* get rid of a thing; *sich einer Aufgabe* —, perform a task, discharge a commission.

entleeren [εnt'le:rən], *v.a.* empty.

entlegen [εnt'le:gən], *adj.* remote, distant, far off.

entlehnen [εnt'le:nən], *v.a.* borrow from.

entleihen [εnt'laıən], *v.a. irr.* borrow.

entlocken [εnt'lɔkən], *v.a.* elicit from.

entmannen [εnt'manən], *v.a.* castrate, emasculate.

entmündigen [εnt'myndıgən], *v.a.* place under care of a guardian *or* (*Law*) trustees.

Entmündigung [εnt'myndıguŋ], *f.* (—, *no pl.*) placing under legal control.

entmutigen [εnt'mu:tıgən], *v.a.* discourage, dishearten.

Entnahme [εnt'na:mə], *f.* (—, *pl.* —n) (*money*) withdrawal.

entnehmen [εnt'ne:mən], *v.a. irr.* (*money*) withdraw; understand, gather *or* infer from.

entnerven [εnt'nεrfən], *v.a.* enervate.

entpuppen [εnt'pupən], *v.r. sich* —, burst from the cocoon; (*fig.*) turn out to be.

enträtseln [εnt'rε:tsəln], *v.a.* decipher, make out.

entreißen [εnt'raısən], *v.a. irr.* snatch away from; *einer Gefahr* —, save *or* rescue from danger.

entrichten [εnt'rıçtən], *v.a.* pay (off).

entrinnen [εnt'rınən], *v.n. irr.* (*aux. sein*) escape from.

entrückt [εnt rykt], *adj.* enraptured.

entrüsten [εnt'rystən], *v.a.* make angry, exasperate. — *v.r. sich* —, become angry, fly into a passion.

entsagen [εnt'za:gən], *v.n.* renounce; waive; abdicate.

Entsatz [εnt'zats], *m.* (—es, *no pl.*) (*Mil.*) relief.

entschädigen [εnt'ʃε:dıgən], *v.a.* indemnify, compensate.

entscheiden [εnt'ʃaıdən], *v.a. irr.* decide. — *v.r. sich* — *für*, come to a decision for, decide in favour of.

Entscheidung [εnt'ʃaıduŋ], *f.* (—, *pl.* —en) decision; verdict.

entschieden [εnt'ʃi:dən], *adj.* decided, determined, resolute, determination.

Entschiedenheit [εnt'ʃi:dənhaıt], *f.* (—, *no pl.*) resolution, firmness, determination.

entschlafen [εnt'ʃla:fən], *v.n. irr.* (*aux. sein*) fall asleep; (*fig.*) die, depart this life.

entschleiern [εnt'ʃlaıərn], *v.a.* unveil.

entschließen [εnt'ʃli:sən], *v.r. irr. sich* —, decide (upon), resolve, make up o.'s mind.

Entschlossenheit [εnt'ʃlɔsənhaıt], *f.* (—, *no pl.*) resoluteness, determination.

entschlummern [εnt'ʃlumərn], *v.n.* (*aux. sein*) fall asleep.

entschlüpfen [εnt'ʃlypfən], *v.n.* (*aux. sein*) slip away; escape.

Entschluß [εnt'ʃlus], *m.* (—sses, *pl.* ⸚sse) resolution; *einen* — *fassen*, resolve (to).

entschuldigen [εnt'ʃuldıgən], *v.a.* excuse. — *v.r. sich* —, apologise.

entschwinden [εnt'ʃvındən], *v.n. irr.* (*aux. sein*) disappear, vanish.

entseelt [εnt'ze:lt], *adj.* inanimate, lifeless.

entsenden [εnt'zεndən], *v.a. irr.* send off, despatch.

Entsetzen [εnt'zεtsən], *n.* (—s, *no pl.*) horror, terror.

entsetzen [εnt'zεtsən], *v.a.* (*Mil.*) relieve; frighten, shock, fill with horror. — *v.r. sich* — *über*, be horrified at.

entsetzlich [εnt'zεtslıç], *adj.* horrible, terrible, dreadful, awful.

entsiegeln [εnt'zi:gəln], *v.a.* unseal.

entsinnen [εnt'zınən], *v.r. sich einer Sache* —, recollect, remember, call s.th. to mind.

entspannen [εnt'ʃpanən], *v.a., v.r.* (*sich*) —, relax.

entspinnen [εnt'ʃpınən], *v.r. irr. sich* —, arise, begin.

entsprechen [εnt'ʃprεçən], *v.n. irr.* respond to, correspond to, meet, suit.

entsprechend [εnt'ʃprεçənt], *adj.* corresponding, suitable.

entsprießen [εnt'ʃpri:sən], *v.n. irr.* (*aux. sein*) spring up, sprout.

entspringen [εnt'ʃprıŋən], *v.n. irr.* (*aux. sein*) escape, originate from; (*river*) have its source at, rise.

entstammen

entstammen [ɛnt'ʃtamən], *v.n.* (*aux.* sein) spring from, originate from.

entstehen [ɛnt'ʃteːən], *v.n. irr.* (*aux.* sein) arise, originate, begin, result, spring from.

Entstehung [ɛnt'ʃteːuŋ], *f.* (—, *no pl.*) origin, rise.

entstellen [ɛnt'ʃtɛlən], *v.a.* disfigure, deform, distort; (*fig.*) garble.

entsühnen [ɛnt'zyːnən], *v.a.* free from sin, purify, purge.

enttäuschen [ɛnt'tɔyʃən], *v.a.* disappoint.

entthronen [ɛnt'troːnən], *v.a.* dethrone.

entvölkern [ɛnt'fœlkərn], *v.a.* depopulate.

entwachsen [ɛnt'vaksən], *v.n. irr.* (*aux.* sein) grow out of, outgrow.

entwaffnen [ɛnt'vafnən], *v.a.* disarm.

entwässern [ɛnt'vɛsərn], *v.a.* drain.

entweder [ɛnt'veːdər], *conj.* either; — ......*oder*, either ...... or.

entweichen [ɛnt'vaɪçən], *v.n. irr.* escape, run away.

entweihen [ɛnt'vaɪən], *v.a.* profane, desecrate.

entwenden [ɛnt'vɛndən], *v.a.* take away, steal, embezzle.

entwerfen [ɛnt'vɛrfən], *v.a. irr.* design, sketch, plan, draw up.

entwerten [ɛnt'vɛrtən], *v.a.* reduce in value, depreciate; (*stamps*) cancel.

entwickeln [ɛnt'vɪkəln], *v.a.* unfold, develop; (*ideas*) explain, explicate. — *v.r. sich —*, develop (into), evolve.

Entwicklung [ɛnt'vɪkluŋ], *f.* (—, *pl.* —en) unfolding, development, evolution.

entwinden [ɛnt'vɪndən], *v.a. irr.* wrench from, wrest from.

entwirren [ɛnt'vɪrən], *v.a.* unravel, disentangle.

entwischen [ɛnt'vɪʃən], *v.n.* (*aux.* sein) slip away, escape.

entwöhnen [ɛnt'vøːnən], *v.a.* disaccustom; break off a habit; (*baby*) wean.

entwürdigen [ɛnt'vyrdɪgən], *v.a.* disgrace, degrade.

Entwurf [ɛnt'vurf], *m.* (—s, *pl.* ∶e) sketch, design, draft, plan, project.

entwurzeln [ɛnt'vurtsəln], *v.a.* uproot.

entziehen [ɛnt'tsiːən], *v.a. irr.* withdraw, take away, deprive of.

entziffern [ɛnt'tsɪfərn], *v.a.* decipher.

entzücken [ɛnt'tsykən], *v.a.* enchant, delight, charm.

entzündbar [ɛnt'tsyntbaːr], *adj.* inflammable.

entzünden [ɛnt'tsyndən], *v.a.* set on fire, light the fire; (*fig.*) inflame. — *v.r. sich —*, catch fire, ignite; (*Med.*) become inflamed.

Entzündung [ɛnt'tsynduŋ], *f.* (—, *pl.* —en) kindling, setting on fire; (*Med.*) inflammation.

entzwei [ɛnt'tsvaɪ], *adv.* in two, broken.

entzweien [ɛnt'tsvaɪən], *v.a.* disunite.

Enzian ['ɛntsian], *m.* (—s, *pl.* —e) (*Bot.*) gentian.

Enzyklopädie [ɛntsyklopɛ'diː], *f.* (—, *pl.* —n) encyclopædia.

Epidemie [epɪde'miː], *f.* (—, *pl.* —en) epidemic.

epidemisch [epɪ'deːmɪʃ], *adj.* epidemic(al).

Epik ['eːpɪk], *f.* (—, *no pl.*) epic poetry.

episch ['eːpɪʃ], *adj.* epic.

Epos ['eːpɔs], *n.* (—, *pl.* **Epen**) epic poem.

Equipage [ekvi'paːʒə], *f.* (—, *pl.* —n) carriage.

er [eːr], *pers. pron.* he.

Erachten [ɛr'axtən], *n.* (—s, *no pl.*) opinion, judgment: *meines —s*, in my opinion.

erachten [ɛr'axtən], *v.a.* think, consider.

erarbeiten [ɛr'arbaɪtən], *v.a.* gain *or* achieve by working.

erb ['ɛrb], *adj.* (*in compounds*) hereditary.

erbarmen [ɛr'barmən], *v.r. sich —*, have mercy (on), take pity (on).

erbärmlich [ɛr'bɛrmlɪç], *adj.* miserable, pitiful; contemptible.

erbauen [ɛr'bauən], *v.a.* build, erect; (*fig.*) edify.

erbaulich [ɛr'baulɪç], *adj.* edifying.

Erbauung [ɛr'bauuŋ], *f.* (—, *no pl.*) building, erection; (*fig.*) edification.

Erbbesitz ['ɛrpbəzɪts], *m.* (—es, *pl.* —e) hereditary possession.

Erbe ['ɛrbə], *m.* (—n, *pl.* —n) heir. *n.* (—s, *no pl.*) inheritance; heritage.

erbeben [ɛr'beːbən], *v.n.* (*aux.* sein) shake, tremble, quake.

erbeigen ['ɛrbaɪgən], *adj.* inherited.

erben ['ɛrbən], *v.a.* inherit.

erbeten [ɛr'beːtən], *v.a. sich etwas —*, ask for s.th. by prayer; request.

erbetteln [ɛr'bɛtəln], *v.a.* obtain by begging.

erbeuten [ɛr'bɔytən], *v.a.* take as booty.

Erbfeind ['ɛrpfaɪnt], *m.* (—s, *pl.* —e) sworn enemy.

Erbfolge ['ɛrpfɔlgə], *f.* (—, *no pl.*) succession.

erbieten [ɛr'biːtən], *v.r. irr. sich —*, offer to do s.th.; volunteer; *Ehre —*, do homage.

Erbin ['ɛrbɪn], *f.* (—, *pl.* —nen) heiress.

erbitten [ɛr'bɪtən], *v.a. irr.* beg, request, ask for, gain by asking.

erbittern [ɛr'bɪtərn], *v.a.* embitter, anger, exasperate.

erblassen [ɛr'blasən], *v.n.* (*aux.* sein) turn pale.

Erblasser ['ɛrblasər], *m.* (—s, *pl.* —) testator.

erbleichen [ɛr'blaɪçən], *v.n. irr.* (*aux.* sein) turn pale, lose colour.

erblich ['ɛrplɪç], *adj.* hereditary, congenital.

erblicken [ɛr'blɪkən], *v.a.* perceive, behold, catch sight of.

erblinden [ɛr'blɪndən], *v.n.* (*aux.* sein) turn blind.

erblos ['ɛrploːs], *adj.* disinherited: without an heir.

erblühen [ɛr'bly:ən], *v.n.* (*aux.* sein) blossom (out).

Erbmasse ['ɛrpmasə], *f.* (—, *no pl.*) estate.

erbosen [ɛr'bo:zən], *v.a.* make angry. — *v.r. sich —,* become angry.

erbötig [ɛr'bø:tıç], *adj.* — *sein,* be willing, be ready.

Erbpacht ['ɛrppaxt], *f.* (—, *pl.* —en) hereditary tenure.

erbrechen [ɛr'brɛçən], *v.a. irr.* break open, open by force. — *v.r. sich —,* vomit.

Erbrecht ['ɛrprɛçt], *n.* (—s, *no pl.*) law (*or* right) of succession.

Erbschaft ['ɛrpʃaft], *f.* (—, *pl.* —en) inheritance, heritage, legacy.

Erbse ['ɛrpsə], *f.* (—, *pl.* —n) pea.

Erbstück ['ɛrpʃtyk], *n.* (—s, *pl.* —e) heirloom.

Erbsünde ['ɛrpzyndə], *f.* (—, *no pl.*) original sin.

Erbteil ['ɛrptaıl], *n.* (—s, *pl.* —e) portion of inheritance.

Erdapfel ['e:rtapfəl], *m.* (—s, *pl.* :) (*Austr.*) potato.

Erdbahn ['e:rtba:n], *f.* (—, *no pl.*) orbit of the earth.

Erdball ['e:rtbal], *m.* (—s, *no pl.*) terrestrial globe.

Erdbeben ['e:rtbe:bən], *n.* (—s, *pl.* —) earthquake.

Erdbeere ['e:rtbe:rə], *f.* (—, *pl.* —n) strawberry.

Erde ['e:rdə], *f.* (—, *pl.* —n) earth, soil ground.

erden ['e:rdən], *v.a.* (*Rad.*) earth.

erdenken [ɛr'dɛŋkən], *v.a. irr.* think out; invent. — *v.r. sich etwas —,* invent s.th., devise s.th.

erdenklich [ɛr'dɛŋklıç], *adj.* imaginable, conceivable.

Erdenleben ['e:rdənle:bən], *n.* (—s, *no pl.*) life on this earth.

Erdfall ['e:rtfal], *m.* (—s, *pl.* :e) landslip.

Erdfläche ['e:rtflɛçə], *f.* (—, *no pl.*) surface of the earth.

Erdgeschoß ['e:rtgəʃəs], *n.* (—sses, *pl.* —sse) ground floor.

Erdhügel ['e:rthy:gəl], *m.* (—s, *pl.* —) mound of earth.

erdichten [ɛr'dıçtən], *v.a.* think out, invent, feign.

Erdkunde ['e:rtkundə], *f.* (—, *no pl.*) geography.

Erdleitung ['e:rtlaıtuŋ], *f.* (—, *pl.* —en) earth circuit, earth connexion.

Erdmaus ['e:rtmaus], *f.* (—, *pl.* :e) field mouse.

Erdmolch ['e:rtmɔlç], *m.* (—s, *pl.* —e) salamander.

Erdnuß ['e:rtnus], *f.* (—, *pl.* :sse) groundnut, peanut.

Erdöl ['e:rtø:l], *n.* (—s, *no pl.*) petroleum, mineral oil.

erdolchen [ɛr'dɔlçən], *v.a.* stab (with a dagger).

Erdpech ['e:rtpɛç], *n.* (—s, *no pl.*) bitumen.

erdreisten [ɛr'draıstən], *v.r. sich —,* dare, have the audacity.

erdrosseln [ɛr'drɔsəln], *v.a.* strangle, throttle.

erdrücken [ɛr'drykən], *v.a.* crush to death.

Erdrutsch ['e:rtrutʃ], *m.* (—es, *no pl.*) landslip, landslide.

Erdschicht ['e:rtʃıçt], *f.* (—, *pl.* —en) (*Geol.*) layer, stratum.

Erdschnecke ['e:rtʃnɛkə], *f.* (—, *pl.* —n) slug, snail.

Erdscholle ['e:rtʃɔlə], *f.* (—, *pl.* —n) clod (of earth).

Erdsturz ['e:rtʃturts], *m.* (—es, *no pl.*) landslide.

erdulden [ɛr'duldən], *v.a.* suffer, endure.

Erdumseg(e)lung ['e:rtumze:g(ə)luŋ], *f.* (—, *pl.* —en) circumnavigation of the earth.

ereifern [ɛr'aıfərn], *v.r. sich —,* become heated, get excited.

ereignen [ɛr'aıgnən], *v.r. sich —,* happen, come to pass.

Ereignis [ɛr'aıknıs], *n.* (—ses, *pl.* —se) event, occurrence, happening.

ereilen [ɛr'aılən], *v.a.* overtake, befall.

Eremit [ere'mi:t], *m.* (—en, *pl.* —en) hermit, recluse.

erfahren [ɛr'fa:rən], *v.a. irr.* learn, hear; experience. — *adj.* experienced, practised; conversant with, versed in.

Erfahrenheit [ɛr'fa:rənhaıt], *f.* (—, *no pl.*) experience, skill.

Erfahrung [ɛr'fa:ruŋ], *f.* (—, *pl.* —en) experience, knowledge, expertness, skill; *in — bringen,* ascertain, come to know.

erfahrungsgemäß [ɛr'fa:ruŋsgəmɛ:s], *adj.* based on *or* according to experience.

erfahrungsmäßig [ɛr'fa:ruŋsmɛ:sıç], *adj.* based on experience; empirical.

erfassen [ɛr'fasən], *v.a.* get hold of, seize, comprehend, grasp.

erfinden [ɛr'fındən], *v.a. irr.* invent, contrive.

erfinderisch [ɛr'fındərıʃ], *adj.* inventive, ingenious.

Erfindung [ɛr'fınduŋ], *f.* (—, *pl.* —en) invention; contrivance.

Erfolg [ɛr'fɔlk], *m.* (—s, *pl.* —e) success; result; effect; — *haben,* succeed, be successful; *keinen — haben,* fail.

erfolgen [ɛr'fɔlgən], *v.n.* (*aux.* sein) ensue, follow, result.

erfolgreich [ɛr'fɔlkraıç], *adj.* successful.

erforderlich [ɛr'fɔrdərlıç], *adj.* necessary, required.

erfordern [ɛr'fɔrdərn], *v.a.* demand, require.

Erfordernis [ɛr'fɔrdərnıs], *n.* (—ses, *pl.* —se) necessity, requirement, requisite.

erforschen [ɛr'fɔrʃən], *v.a.* explore, investigate, conduct research into.

erfragen [ɛr'fra:gən], *v.a.* find out by asking, ascertain.

erfreuen [ɛr'frɔyən], *v.a.* gladden, cheer, delight. — *v.r. sich — an,* enjoy, take pleasure in.

erfreulich [ɛrˈfrɔylɪç], *adj.* pleasing, gratifying.

erfrieren [ɛrˈfriːrən], *v.n. irr. (aux. sein)* freeze to death, die of exposure; become numb.

erfrischen [ɛrˈfrɪʃən], *v.a.* refresh.

erfüllen [ɛrˈfylən], *v.a.* fulfil, keep (promise); comply with; perform; *seinen Zweck* —, serve its purpose. — *v.r. sich* —, come true, be fulfilled.

Erfüllung [ɛrˈfylʊŋ], *f.* (—, *no pl.*) fulfilment; granting; performance; *in* — *gehen*, come true, be realised.

ergänzen [ɛrˈgɛntsən], *v.a.* complete, complement.

Ergänzung [ɛrˈgɛntsʊŋ], *f.* (—, *pl.* —en) completion; complement, supplement.

ergattern [ɛrˈgatərn], *v.a.* pick up.

ergeben [ɛrˈgeːbən], *v.a. irr.* give, yield, prove, show. — *v.r. sich* —, surrender (to), acquiesce (in); happen, result, follow. — *adj.* devoted, submissive, humble, obedient.

Ergebenheit [ɛrˈgeːbənhaɪt], *f.* (—, *no pl.*) devotion, obedience, humility, fidelity.

ergebenst [ɛrˈgeːbənst], *adj. Ihr* —*er* (*letter ending*), yours very truly, your obedient servant. — *adv.* respectfully.

Ergebnis [ɛrˈgeːpnɪs], *n.* (—ses, *pl.* —se) outcome, result; (*Agr.*) yield.

Ergebung [ɛrˈgeːbʊŋ], *f.* (—, *no pl.*) submission, resignation; surrender.

Ergehen [ɛrˈgeːən], *n.* (—s, *no pl.*) health, condition, well-being.

ergehen [ɛrˈgeːən], *v.n. irr. (aux. sein)* be promulgated *or* issued; — *lassen*, issue, publish; *etwas über sich* — *lassen*, submit to *or* suffer s.th. patiently. — *v.r. sich* —, (*obs.*) take a stroll.

ergiebig [ɛrˈgiːbɪç], *adj.* rich, productive, fertile, profitable.

ergießen [ɛrˈgiːsən], *v.r. irr. sich* —, discharge, flow into.

erglänzen [ɛrˈglɛntsən], *v.n. (aux. sein)* shine forth, sparkle.

erglühen [ɛrˈglyːən], *v.n. (aux. sein)* glow; blush.

ergötzen [ɛrˈgœtsən], *v.a.* (*obs.*) amuse, delight. — *v.r. sich* — *an*, delight in.

ergrauen [ɛrˈgrauən], *v.n. (aux. sein)* become grey; grow old.

ergreifen [ɛrˈgraɪfən], *v.a. irr.* seize, grasp, get hold of; move, touch, affect; *Maßnahmen* —, take measures.

Ergreifung [ɛrˈgraɪfʊŋ], *f.* (—, *no pl.*) seizure; (*measure*) adoption.

ergriffen [ɛrˈgrɪfən], *adj.* moved, touched, impressed.

Ergriffenheit [ɛrˈgrɪfənhaɪt], *f.* (—, *no pl.*) emotion.

ergrimmen [ɛrˈgrɪmən], *v.n. (aux. sein)* grow angry, be enraged.

ergründen [ɛrˈgryndən], *v.a.* get to the bottom of, investigate, fathom.

Erguß [ɛrˈgus], *m.* (—sses, *pl.* ‑sse) outpouring; (*fig.*) effusion.

erhaben [ɛrˈhaːbən], *adj.* sublime, exalted; majestic, elevated.

Erhabenheit [ɛrˈhaːbənhaɪt], *f.* (—, *no pl.*) majesty, sublimity.

erhalten [ɛrˈhaltən], *v.a. irr.* receive, obtain, get, preserve; maintain, keep up. — *v.r. sich* — *von*, subsist on.

erhältlich [ɛrˈhɛltlɪç], *adj.* obtainable.

Erhaltung [ɛrˈhaltʊŋ], *f.* (—, *no pl.*) preservation, conservation; (*family*) maintenance.

erhärten [ɛrˈhɛrtən], *v.a.* make hard; (*fig.*) prove, confirm.

erhaschen [ɛrˈhaʃən], *v.a.* catch, snatch.

erheben [ɛrˈheːbən], *v.a. irr.* lift up, raise; (*fig.*) elevate, exalt; *Klage* —, bring an action; *Geld* —, raise money; *Steuern* —, levy taxes. — *v.r. sich* —, rise, stand up.

erheblich [ɛrˈheːplɪç], *adj.* considerable, weighty, appreciable.

Erhebung [ɛrˈheːbʊŋ], *f.* (—, *pl.* —en) elevation; (*taxes*) levying; revolt, rebellion, rising.

erheischen [ɛrˈhaɪʃən], *v.a.* (*rare*) require, demand.

erheitern [ɛrˈhaɪtərn], *v.a.* cheer, exhilarate.

erhellen [ɛrˈhɛlən], *v.a.* light up, illuminate; (*fig.*) enlighten. — *v.n.* become evident.

erhitzen [ɛrˈhɪtsən], *v.a.* heat; (*fig.*) inflame, excite. — *v.r. sich* —, grow hot; grow angry.

erhöhen [ɛrˈhøːən], *v.a.* heighten, raise, intensify, increase; (*value*) enhance.

erholen [ɛrˈhoːlən], *v.r. sich* —, recover, get better; relax (after work); take a rest.

erholungsbedürftig [ɛrˈhoːlʊŋsbədyrftɪç], *adj.* in need of a rest.

erhören [ɛrˈhøːrən], *v.a.* hear, vouchsafe, grant.

Erich [ˈeːrɪç], *m.* Eric.

erinnerlich [ɛrˈɪnərlɪç], *adj.* remembered; *soweit mir* — *ist*, as far as I can remember.

erinnern [ɛrˈɪnərn], *v.a.* remind. — *v.r. sich* —, remember, recollect, recall, call to mind.

Erinnerung [ɛrˈɪnərʊŋ], *f.* (—, *pl.* —en) remembrance; recollection; reminiscences.

erjagen [ɛrˈjaːgən], *v.a.* hunt (down), chase.

erkalten [ɛrˈkaltən], *v.n. (aux. sein)* grow cold.

erkälten [ɛrˈkɛltən], *v.r. sich* —, catch cold.

Erkältung [ɛrˈkɛltʊŋ], *f.* (—, *pl.* —en) cold, chill.

erkämpfen [ɛrˈkɛmpfən], *v.a.* obtain by fighting; obtain by great exertion.

erkaufen [ɛrˈkaufən], *v.a.* purchase; bribe, corrupt.

erkennen [ɛrˈkɛnən], *v.a. irr.* recognise; perceive, distinguish, discern; (*Comm.*) credit; *zu* — *geben*, give to understand; *sich zu* — *geben*, make o.s. known. — *v.n.* (*Law*) judge; — *auf*, (*Law*) announce verdict, pass sentence.

erkenntlich [ɛrˈkɛntlɪç], *adj.* grateful; (*fig.*) *sich — zeigen*, show o.s. grateful.
Erkenntlichkeit [ɛrˈkɛntlɪçkaɪt], *f.* (—, *no pl.*) gratitude.
Erkenntnis [ɛrˈkɛntnɪs], *f.* (—, *pl.* —**e**) perception, knowledge, comprehension, understanding; realisation, (*Phil.*) cognition.
Erkennung [ɛrˈkɛnuŋ], *f.* (—, *no pl.*) recognition.
Erker [ˈɛrkər], *m.* (—**s**, *pl.* —) alcove, bay, turret.
Erkerfenster [ˈɛrkərfɛnstər], *n.* (—**s**, *pl.* —) bay-window.
erklären [ɛrˈklɛːrən], *v.a.* explain, expound, account for; make a statement on, declare, state.
erklärlich [ɛrˈklɛːrlɪç], *adj.* explicable.
Erklärung [ɛrˈklɛːruŋ], *f.* (—, *pl.* —**en**) explanation; declaration, statement; (*income tax*) return.
erklecklich [ɛrˈklɛklɪç], *adj.* considerable.
erklettern [ɛrˈklɛtərn], *v.a.* climb.
erklimmen [ɛrˈklɪmən], *v.a. irr.* climb.
erklingen [ɛrˈklɪŋən], *v.n. irr.* (*aux.* sein) sound, resound.
erkoren [ɛrˈkoːrən], *adj.* select, chosen.
erkranken [ɛrˈkraŋkən], *v.n.* (*aux.* sein) fall ill.
erkühnen [ɛrˈkyːnən], *v.r. sich —*, dare, make bold, venture.
erkunden [ɛrˈkundən], *v.a.* explore, find out; (*Mil.*) reconnoitre.
erkundigen [ɛrˈkundɪgən], *v.r. sich —*, enquire (about), make enquiries.
erlaben [ɛrˈlaːbən], *v.r. sich —*, (*obs.*) refresh o.s.
erlahmen [ɛrˈlaːmən], *v.n.* (*aux.* sein) become lame; lose o.'s drive; grow tired.
erlangen [ɛrˈlaŋən], *v.a.* reach, gain, obtain; acquire; attain.
Erlaß [ɛrˈlas], *m.* (—**sses**, *pl.* ¨**sse**) remission, exemption, release, dispensation; (*Comm.*) deduction; (*Law, Pol.*) proclamation, edict, decree, writ; (*Eccl.*) indulgence; remission.
erlassen [ɛrˈlasən], *v.a. irr.* remit, release, let off; (*Law, Pol.*) enact, promulgate.
erläßlich [ɛrˈlɛslɪç], *adj.* remissible, dispensable, venial.
erlauben [ɛrˈlaubən], *v.a.* permit, allow; *sich etwas —*, take the liberty of, make bold to; have the impertinence to.
Erlaubnis [ɛrˈlaupnɪs], *f.* (—, *no pl.*) permission, leave, permit; *die — haben*, be permitted; *um — bitten*, beg leave; *mit Ihrer —*, by your leave.
erlaucht [ɛrˈlauxt], *adj.* illustrious, noble.
erlauschen [ɛrˈlauʃən], *v.a.* overhear.
erläutern [ɛrˈlɔytərn], *v.a.* explain, illustrate, elucidate.
Erle [ˈɛrlə], *f.* (—, *pl.* —**n**) (*Bot.*) alder.
erleben [ɛrˈleːbən], *v.a.* live to see; go through, experience.
Erlebnis [ɛrˈleːpnɪs], *n.* (—**sses**, *pl.* —**sse**) experience, adventure, occurrence.

erledigen [ɛrˈleːdɪgən], *v.a.* settle, finish off, clear up; dispatch; execute (commission etc.).
erledigt [ɛrˈleːdɪçt], *adj.* (*coll.*) worn-out; exhausted.
erlegen [ɛrˈleːgən], *v.a.* slay; pay down.
erleichtern [ɛrˈlaɪçtərn], *v.a.* lighten, ease, facilitate.
erleiden [ɛrˈlaɪdən], *v.a. irr.* suffer, endure, bear, undergo.
erlernen [ɛrˈlɛrnən], *v.a.* learn, acquire.
erlesen [ɛrˈleːzən], *v.a. irr.* select, choose. — *adj.* select, choice.
erleuchten [ɛrˈlɔyçtən], *v.a.* illumine, illuminate, floodlight; (*fig.*) enlighten, inspire.
erliegen [ɛrˈliːgən], *v.n. irr.* (*aux.* sein) succumb.
Erlkönig [ˈɛrlkøːnɪç], *m.* (—**s**, *pl.* —**e**) fairy-king, elf-king.
erlogen [ˈːrˈloːgən], *adj.* false, untrue; trumped-up.
Erlös [ɛrˈløːs], *m.* (—**es**, *no pl.*) proceeds.
erlöschen [ɛrˈlœʃən], *v.n. irr.* (*aux.* sein) be extinguished, die out; (*fire*) go out; (*contract*) expire.
erlösen [ɛrˈløːzən], *v.a.* redeem; release, save, deliver.
ermächtigen [ɛrˈmɛçtɪgən], *v.a.* empower; authorise.
ermahnen [ɛrˈmaːnən], *v.a.* admonish, exhort, remind.
ermäßigen [ɛrˈmɛːsɪgən], *v.a.* reduce.
ermatten [ɛrˈmatən], *v.a.* weaken, weary, tire. — *v.n.* (*aux.* sein) grow weak, become tired.
Ermessen [ɛrˈmesən], *n.* (—**s**, *no pl.*) judgment, opinion.
ermitteln [ɛrˈmɪtəln], *v.a.* ascertain, find out.
ermöglichen [ɛrˈmoːklɪçən], *v.a.* make possible.
ermorden [ɛrˈmɔrdən], *v.a.* murder.
ermüden [ɛrˈmyːdən], *v.a.* tire, fatigue. — *v.n.* (*aux.* sein) get tired, grow weary.
ermuntern [ɛrˈmuntərn], *v.a.* encourage, cheer up.
ermutigen [ɛrˈmuːtɪgən], *v.a.* encourage.
ernähren [ɛrˈnɛːrən], *v.a.* nourish, feed.
ernennen [ɛrˈnɛnən], *v.a. irr.* nominate, appoint.
erneuern [ɛrˈnɔyərn], *v.a.* renew, repair, renovate.
erniedrigen [ɛrˈniːdrɪgən], *v.a.* humble, humiliate, degrade. — *v.r. sich —*, humble o.s., abase o.s.
Ernst (1) [ɛrnst], *m.* Ernest.
Ernst (2) [ɛrnst], *m.* (—**es**, *no pl.*) earnestness, seriousness.
ernst [ɛrnst], *adj.* earnest, serious.
Ernte [ˈɛrntə], *f.* (—, *pl.* —**n**) harvest, crop.
ernüchtern [ɛrˈnyçtərn], *v.a.* sober; (*fig.*) disenchant, disillusion.
erobern [ɛrˈoːbərn], *v.a.* (*Mil.*) conquer; take, win.
eröffnen [ɛrˈœfnən], *v.a.* open, inaugurate; inform, reveal.
erörtern [ɛrˈœrtərn], *v.a.* discuss, debate, argue.

erpicht [ɛr'pɪçt], *adj.* eager for, bent on.

erpressen [ɛr'prɛsən], *v.a.* extort, blackmail.

erquicken [ɛr'kvɪkən], *v.a.* refresh.

erraten [ɛr'raːtən], *v.a. irr.* guess.

erregen [ɛr're:gən], *v.a.* cause; stir up, excite, agitate; provoke.

erreichen [ɛr'raɪçən], *v.a.* reach, arrive at; (*fig.*) attain, reach.

erretten [ɛr'rɛtən], *v.a.* save, rescue.

errichten [ɛr'rɪçtən], *v.a.* erect, raise, build.

erringen [ɛr'rɪŋən], *v.a. irr.* obtain (by exertion), achieve.

erröten [ɛr'rø:tən], *v.n.* (*aux.* sein) blush, redden.

Errungenschaft [ɛr'ruŋənʃaft], *f.* (—, *pl.* —en) achievement, acquisition.

Ersatz [ɛr'zats], *m.* (—es, *no pl.*) substitute; compensation, amends: (*Mil. etc.*) replacement.

erschallen [ɛr'ʃalən], *v.n.* (*aux.* sein) resound, sound.

erschaudern [ɛr'ʃaudərn], *v.n.* (*aux.* sein) be seized with horror.

erscheinen [ɛr'ʃaɪnən], *v.n. irr.* (*aux.* sein) appear, make o.'s appearance; seem; be published.

erschießen [ɛr'ʃi:sən], *v.a. irr.* shoot dead.

erschlaffen [ɛr'ʃlafən], *v.n.* (*aux.* sein) flag, slacken.

erschlagen [ɛr'ʃla:gən], *v.a. irr.* slay, kill.

erschließen [ɛr'ʃli:sən], *v.a. irr.* open up.

erschöpfen [ɛr'ʃœpfən], *v.a.* exhaust.

erschrecken [ɛr'ʃrɛkən], *v.a. irr.* startle, shock, terrify. — *v.n.* (*aux.* sein) be startled, be frightened, be terrified.

erschüttern [ɛr'ʃytərn], *v.a.* shake; (*fig.*) move, affect strongly.

erschweren [ɛr'ʃve:rən], *v.a.* (*fig.*) aggravate, make more difficult.

erschwingen [ɛr'ʃvɪŋən], *v.a. irr.* afford, be able to pay.

erschwinglich [ɛr'ʃvɪŋlɪç], *adj.* attainable, within o.'s means.

ersehen [ɛr'zɛ:ən], *v.a. irr.* — *aus*, gather (from).

ersehnen [ɛr'ze:nən], *v.a.* long for, yearn for.

ersetzen [ɛr'zɛtsən], *v.a.* replace, take the place of; restore, make good; repair; (*money*) refund.

ersichtlich [ɛr'zɪçtlɪç], *adj.* evident.

ersinnen [ɛr'zɪnən], *v.a. irr.* think out; imagine, devise, contrive.

ersparen [ɛr'ʃpa:rən], *v.a.* save.

ersprießlich [ɛr'ʃpri:slɪç], *adj.* useful, profitable, beneficial.

erst [e:rst], *num. adj.* first. — *adv.* first, at first, only, but; — *jetzt*, only now; *nun* — *recht*, now more than ever.

erstatten [ɛr'ʃtatən], *v.a.* reimburse, compensate, repay; *Bericht* —, report.

Erstattung [ɛr'ʃtatuŋ], *f.* (—, *pl.* —en) reimbursement, restitution.

Erstaufführung ['e:rstauffy:ruŋ], *f.* (—, *pl.* —en) (*Theat.*) first night; première.

Erstaunen [ɛr'ʃtaunən], *n.* (—s, *no pl.*) amazement, astonishment, surprise.

erstechen [ɛr'ʃtɛçən], *v.a. irr.* stab.

erstehen [ɛr'ʃte:ən], *v.n. irr.* (*aux.* sein) rise, arise. — *v.a.* buy, purchase.

ersteigen [ɛr'ʃtaɪgən], *v.a. irr.* climb, mount, ascend.

ersticken [ɛr'ʃtɪkən], *v.a. irr.* choke, stifle, suffocate. — *v.n.* (*aux.* sein) choke, suffocate.

erstmalig ['e:rstma:lɪç], *adj.* first. — *adv.* for the first time.

erstreben [ɛr'ʃtre:bən], *v.a.* strive after.

erstrecken [ɛr'ʃtrɛkən], *v.r. sich* —, extend, reach to.

ersuchen [ɛr'zu:xən], *v.a.* request, ask.

ertappen [ɛr'tapən], *v.a.* catch, detect.

erteilen [ɛr'taɪlən], *v.a.* bestow, impart; *einen Auftrag* —, issue an order; *Unterricht* —, instruct; *die Erlaubnis* —, give permission.

ertönen [ɛr'tø:nən], *v.n.* (*aux.* sein) sound, resound.

Ertrag [ɛr'tra:k], *m.* (—s, *pl.* ⁻e) produce; returns, yield; output; (*sale*) proceeds.

ertragen [ɛr'tra:gən], *v.a. irr.* bear, suffer, endure.

ertränken [ɛr'trɛnkən], *v.a.* drown.

ertrinken [ɛr'trɪŋkən], *v.n. irr.* (*aux.* sein) drown, be drowned.

erübrigen [ɛr'y:brɪgən], *v.a.* save, spare.

erwachen [ɛr'vaxən], *v.n.* (*aux.* sein) awake, wake up.

erwachsen [ɛr'vaksən], *adj.* grown-up, adult. — *v.n. irr.* grow up; ensue, follow, arise.

erwägen [ɛr've:gən], *v.a. irr.* weigh, ponder, consider.

erwähnen [ɛr've:nən], *v.a.* mention.

erwärmen [ɛr'vɛrmən], *v.a.* warm (up), make warm.

erwarten [ɛr'vartən], *v.a.* expect, await.

Erwartung [ɛr'vartuŋ], *f.* (—, *pl.* —en) expectation.

erwecken [ɛr'vɛkən], *v.a.* wake up, awaken, raise; rouse.

erwehren [ɛr've:rən], *v.r. sich* — (*Genit.*), defend o.s.; *ich kann mich des Lachens nicht* —, I cannot help laughing.

erweichen [ɛr'vaɪçən], *v.a.* soften.

erweisen [ɛr'vaɪzən], *v.a. irr.* prove, show; demonstrate.

erweitern [ɛr'vaɪtərn], *v.a.* widen, enlarge, expand.

erwerben [ɛr'vɛrbən], *v.a. irr.* acquire.

erwidern [ɛr'vi:dərn], *v.a.* reply, answer; return.

erwirken [ɛr'vɪrkən], *v.a.* effect, secure.

erwischen [ɛr'vɪʃən], *v.a. see* **ertappen**.

erwünschen [ɛr'vynʃən], *v.a.* desire, wish for.

erwürgen [ɛr'vyrgən], *v.a.* strangle, throttle.

Erz [ɛrts], (—es, *pl.* —e) ore; brass, bronze.

erzählen [ɛrˈtsɛːlən], *v.a.* narrate, relate, tell.

Erzbischof [ˈɛrtsbɪʃɔf], *m.* (**—s**, *pl.* ⸚e) archbishop.

erzeugen [ɛrˈtsɔygən], *v.a.* engender; beget; produce; (*Elec.*) generate.

Erzherzog [ˈɛrtshɛrtsoːk], *m.* (**—s**, *pl.* ⸚e) archduke.

erziehen [ɛrˈtsiːən], *v.a. irr.* educate, train, bring up, rear.

Erziehungsanstalt [ɛrˈtsiːuŋsanʃtalt], *f.* (**—**, *pl.* **—en**) approved school, reformatory.

erzielen [ɛrˈtsiːlən], *v.a.* obtain; fetch, realize (a price); *Gewinn* **—**, make a profit.

erzittern [ɛrˈtsɪtərn], *v.n.* (*aux.* sein) tremble, shake.

Erzofen [ˈɛrtsoːfən], *m.* (**—s**, *pl.* ⸚n) furnace.

erzürnen [ɛrˈtsyrnən], *v.a.* make angry. **—** *v.r. sich* **—**, grow angry.

Erzvater [ˈɛrtsfaːtər], *m.* (**—s**, *pl.* ⸚) patriarch.

erzwingen [ɛrˈtsvɪŋən], *v.a. irr.* enforce, force, compel.

es [ɛs], *pron.* it; **—** *gibt*, there is; **—** *sind*, there are; **—** *lebe*, long live!

Es [ɛs], *n.* (**—**, *pl.* **—**) (*Mus.*) E flat.

Esche [ˈɛʃə], *f.* (**—**, *pl.* **—n**) (*Bot.*) ash, ashtree.

Esel [ˈeːzəl], *m.* (**—s**, *pl.* **—**) ass, donkey.

Eselsohr [ˈeːzəlsoːr], *n.* (**—s**, *pl.* **—en**) (*fig.*) dog's ear.

Eskadron [ɛskaˈdroːn], *f.* (**—**, *pl.* **—en**) squadron.

Espe [ˈɛspə], *f.* (**—**, *pl.* **—n**) (*Bot.*) asp, aspen.

eßbar [ˈɛsbaːr], *adj.* edible.

Esse [ˈɛsə], *f.* (**—**, *pl.* **—n**) chimney, forge.

Essen [ˈɛsən], *n.* (**—s**, *no pl.*) meal; eating.

essen [ˈɛsən], *v.a. irr.* eat, have a meal.

Essenz [ɛˈsɛnts], *f.* (**—**, *pl.* **—en**) essence.

Essig [ˈɛsɪç], *m.* (**—s**, *no pl.*) vinegar.

Eßlöffel [ˈɛslœfəl], *m.* (**—s**, *pl.* **—**) table-spoon.

Estland [ˈɛstlant], *n.* Estonia.

Estrade [ɛˈstraːdə], *f.* (**—**, *pl.* **—n**) platform.

Estrich [ˈɛstrɪç], *m.* (**—s**, *no pl.*) floor, flooring, plaster-floor.

etablieren [etaˈbliːrən], *v.a.* establish, set up (business).

Etagenwohnung [eˈtaːʒənvoːnuŋ], *f.* (**—**, *pl.* **—en**) flat; (*Am.*) apartment.

Etappe [eˈtapə], *f.* (**—**, *pl.* **—n**) stage; (*Mil.*) lines of communication.

Etat [eˈtaː], *m.* (**—s**, *pl.* **—s**) (*Parl.*) estimates, budget; (*Comm.*) statement, balance sheet.

ethisch [ˈeːtɪʃ], *adj.* ethical.

Etikett [etiˈkɛt], *n.* (**—s**, *pl.* **—s**) label, ticket, tag.

Etikette [etiˈkɛtə], *f.* (**—**, *no pl.*) etiquette; ceremonial.

etikettieren [etikɛˈtiːrən], *v.a.* label.

etliche [ˈɛtlɪçə], *pl. adj. & pron.* some, several, sundry.

Etui [eˈtviː], *n.* (**—s**, *pl.* **—s**) small case, small box.

etwa [ˈɛtva], *adv.* nearly, about; perhaps, perchance, in some way.

etwaig [ˈɛtvaɪç], *adj.* possible, any, eventual.

etwas [ˈɛtvas], *indef. pron.* some, something. **—** *adj.* some, any. **—** *adv.* a little, somewhat.

Etzel [ˈɛtsəl], *m.* Attila.

euch [ɔyç], *pers. pron. pl. Dat. & Acc.* you, yourselves.

euer [ˈɔyər], *poss. adj.* your. **—** *poss. pron.* yours.

Eule [ˈɔylə], *f.* (**—**, *pl.* **—n**) owl.

eurige [ˈɔyrɪgə], *poss. pron. der, die, das* **—**, yours.

Europa [ɔyˈroːpa], *n.* Europe.

Euter [ˈɔytər], *n.* (**—s**, *pl.* **—**) udder.

evangelisch [evanˈgeːlɪʃ], *adj.* Evangelical, Protestant.

Evangelium [evanˈgeːljum], *n.* (**—s**, *pl.* **—lien**) gospel.

eventuell [evɛntuˈɛl], *adj.* possible.

ewig [ˈeːvɪç], *adj.* eternal; perpetual.

Ewigkeit [ˈeːvɪçkaɪt], *f.* (**—**, *pl.* **—en**) eternity.

explodieren [ɛksploˈdiːrən], *v.n.* explode; detonate.

exponieren [ɛkspoˈniːrən], *v.a.* set forth, explain at length.

Extemporale [ɛkstɛmpoˈraːlə], *n.* (**—s**, *pl.* **—lien**) unprepared exercise.

extrahieren [ɛkstraˈhiːrən], *v.a.* extract.

Extremitäten [ɛkstremɪˈtɛːtən], *f. pl.* extremities.

F

F [ɛf], *n.* (**—s**, *pl.* **—s**) the letter F; (*Mus.*) F *Dur*, F major; F *Moll*, F minor.

Fabel [ˈfaːbəl], *f.* (**—**, *pl.* **—n**) fable; (*fig.*) tale, fiction; (*drama*) plot, story.

fabelhaft [ˈfaːbəlhaft], *adj.* fabulous; phenomenal, gorgeous.

fabeln [ˈfaːbəln], *v.n.* tell fables; talk nonsense.

Fabrik [faˈbriːk], *f.* (**—**, *pl.* **—en**) factory; plant, works.

Fabrikant [fabrɪˈkant], *m.* (**—en**, *pl.* **—en**) manufacturer.

fabrizieren [fabrɪˈtsiːrən], *v.a.* manufacture, make.

fabulieren [fabuˈliːrən], *v.n.* tell fables; (*fig.*) tell tall stories.

Fach [fax], *n.* (**—s**, *pl.* ⸚er) compartment; pigeon-hole, drawer; (*fig.*) subject of study, department, branch.

Fachausdruck [ˈfaxausdruk], *m.* (**—s**, *pl.* ⸚e) technical term.

Fächer

Fächer ['fɛçər], *m.* (**—s**, *pl.* **—**) fan.
Fächertaube ['fɛçərtaubə], *f.* (**—**, *pl.* **—n**) fantail.
Fachmann ['faxman], *m.* (**—s**, *pl.* ¨er *or* **Fachleute**) expert, specialist.
Fachschule ['faxʃuːlə], *f.* (**—**, *pl.* **—n**) technical school.
fachsimpeln ['faxzɪmpəln], *v.n.* talk shop.
Fachwerk ['faxvɛrk], *n.* (**—s**, *no pl.*) timbered framework.
Fackel ['fakəl], *f.* (**—**, *pl.* **—n**) torch.
fade ['faːdə], *adj.* tasteless; boring, insipid.
Faden ['faːdən], *m.* (**—s**, *pl.* ¨) thread; (*measure*) fathom.
fadenscheinig ['faːdənʃaɪnɪç], *adj.* threadbare.
Fagott [faˈgɔt], *n.* (**—s**, *pl.* ¨e) (*Mus.*) bassoon.
fähig ['fɛːɪç], *adj.* able, capable; talented, gifted, competent.
fahl [faːl], *adj.* pale, sallow.
Fähnchen ['fɛˈnçən], *n.* (**—s**, *pl.* **—**) small banner; pennon; (*Mil.*) (*obs.*) small troop.
fahnden ['faːndən], *v.a.* search for (officially).
Fahne ['faːnə], *f.* (**—**, *pl.* **—n**) flag, banner, standard, colours; (*weather*) vane; (*Typ.*) galley proof.
Fahnenflucht ['faːnənfluxt], *f.* (**—**, *no pl.*) (*Mil.*) desertion.
Fähnrich ['fɛːnrɪç], *m.* (**—s**, *pl.* **—e**) ensign.
Fahrbahn ['faːrbaːn], *f.* (**—**, *pl.* **—en**) traffic lane, roadway.
fahrbar ['faːrbaːr], *adj.* passable, navigable, negotiable.
Fähre ['fɛːrə], *f.* (**—**, *pl.* **—n**) ferry, ferry-boat.
fahren ['faːrən], *v.a. irr.* drive. — *v.n.* (*aux.* sein) (*vehicle*) ride (in), be driven; (*vessel*) sail; go, travel.
Fahrer ['faːrər], *m.* (**—s**, *pl.* **—**) driver, chauffeur.
Fahrgast ['faːrgast], *m.* (**—s**, *pl.* ¨e) passenger.
fahrig ['faːrɪç], *adj.* absent-minded, giddy, thoughtless.
Fahrkarte ['faːrkartə], *f.* (**—**, *pl.* **—n**) ticket.
fahrlässig ['faːrlɛsɪç], *adj.* negligent, careless.
Fährmann ['fɛːrman], *m.* (**—s**, *pl.* ¨er) ferry-man.
Fahrplan ['faːrplaːn], *m.* (**—s**, *pl.* ¨e) timetable, railway-guide.
fahrplanmäßig ['faːrplanmɛːsɪç], *adj.* according to the timetable, scheduled.
Fahrpreis ['faːrpraɪs], *m.* (**—es**, *pl.* **—e**) cost of ticket, fare.
Fahrrad ['faːrraːt], *n.* (**—s**, *pl.* ¨er) cycle, bicycle.
Fahrschein ['faːrʃaɪn], *m.* (**—s**, *pl.* **—e**) ticket.
Fahrstraße ['faːrʃtrasə], *f.* (**—**, *pl.* **—n**) roadway.
Fahrstuhl ['faːrʃtuːl], *m.* (**—s**, *pl.* ¨e) lift; (*Am.*) elevator.

Fahrt [faːrt], *f.* (**—**, *pl.* **—en**) drive, ride, journey; (*sea*) voyage, cruise.
Fährte ['fɛːrtə], *f.* (**—**, *pl.* **—n**) track, trace, trail.
Fahrzeug ['faːrtsɔyk], *n.* (**—s**, *pl.* **—e**) vehicle, conveyance; vessel, craft.
faktisch ['faktɪʃ], *adj.* real, actual.
Faktor ['faktɔr], *m.* (**—s**, *pl.* **—en**) foreman, overseer, factor; (*Maths.*) factor, component part.
Faktura [fakˈtuːra], *f.* (**—**, *pl.* **—ren**) (*Comm.*) invoice.
fakturieren [faktuˈriːrən], *v.a.* (*Comm.*) invoice.
Fakultät [fakulˈtɛːt], *f.* (**—**, *pl.* **—en**) (*Univ.*) faculty.
fakultativ [fakultaˈtiːf], *adj.* optional.
Falbel ['falbəl], *f.* (**—**, *pl.* **—n**) flounce, furbelow.
Falke ['falkə], *m.* (**—n**, *pl.* **—n**) (*Orn.*) falcon, hawk.
Fall [fal], *m.* (**—s**, *pl.* ¨e) fall, falling; case; (*Geog.*) decline, incline, gradient; (*fig.*) fall, decline, downfall, failure.
Fallbaum ['falbaum], *m.* (**—s**, *pl.* ¨e) tollbar, turnpike.
Fallbeil ['falbaɪl], *n.* (**—s**, *pl.* **—e**) guillotine.
Fallbrücke ['falbrykə], *f.* (**—**, *pl.* **—n**) draw-bridge.
Falle ['falə], *f.* (**—**, *pl.* **—n**) trap, snare.
fallen ['falən], *v.n. irr.* (*aux.* sein) fall, drop; (*Mil.*) be killed.
fällen ['fɛlən], *v.a.* fell, cut down, hew down; *ein Urteil* **—**, (*Law*) pronounce judgment.
Fallensteller ['falənʃtɛlər], *m.* (**—s**, *pl.* **—**) trapper.
fallieren [faˈliːrən], *v.n.* become bankrupt.
fällig ['fɛlɪç], *adj.* due, payable.
Fälligkeit ['fɛlɪçkaɪt], *f.* (**—**, *pl.* **—en**) (*Comm.*) maturity.
Fallobst ['falɔpst], *n.* (**—es**, *no pl.*) windfall (of fruit).
falls [fals], *conj.* in case, if.
Fallschirm ['falʃɪrm], *m.* (**—s**, *pl.* **—e**) parachute.
Fallstrick ['falʃtrɪk], *m.* (**—s**, *pl.* **—e**) snare, trap.
Fallsucht ['falzuxt], *f.* (**—**, *no pl.*) (*Med.*) epilepsy.
Falltür ['faltyːr], *f.* (**—**, *pl.* **—en**) trap-door.
Fällung ['fɛluŋ], *f.* (**—**, *pl.* **—en**) cutting down.
falsch [falʃ], *adj.* false, incorrect, wrong; disloyal; counterfeit.
fälschen ['fɛlʃən], *v.a.* falsify, forge, tamper with.
Falschheit ['falʃhaɪt], *f.* (**—**, *pl.* **—en**) falsehood, deceit, disloyalty.
fälschlich ['fɛlʃlɪç], *adv.* wrongly, falsely.
Fälschung ['fɛlʃuŋ], *f.* (**—**, *pl.* **—en**) falsification, forgery.
Falte ['faltə], *f.* (**—**, *pl.* **—n**) fold, pleat; (*face*) wrinkle.
falten ['faltən], *v.a.* fold, plait, pleat; wrinkle.

Falter ['faltər], *m.* (—s, *pl.* —) (*Ent.*) butterfly.

-fältig [fɛltɪç], *suffix* (*following numbers*). -fold (*e.g.* vierfältig, fourfold).

Falz [falts], *m.* (—es, *pl.* —e) groove, notch; joint.

Falzbein ['faltsbain], *n.* (—s, *pl.* —e) paper-folder, paper-knife.

Falzmaschine ['faltsmaʃiːnə], *f.* (—, *pl.* —n) folding-machine.

familiär [famil'jɛːr], *adj.* familiar, intimate.

Familie [fa'miːljə], *f.* (—, *pl.* —n) family.

famos [fa'moːs], *adj.* (*coll.*) excellent, splendid.

fanatisch [fa'naːtɪʃ], *adj.* fanatic(al), bigoted.

Fanatismus [fana'tɪsmus], *m.* (—, *no pl.*) fanaticism.

Fang [faŋ], *m.* (—es, *pl.* ⁻e) catch, capture; (*bird*) talon, claw.

fangen ['faŋən], *v.a. irr.* catch, seize.

Fangzahn ['faŋtsaːn], *m.* (—s, *pl.* ⁻e) fang, tusk.

Fant [fant], *m.* (—s, *pl.* —e) fop, cockscomb.

Farbe ['farbə], *f.* (—, *pl.* —n) colour, hue, paint, dye.

färben ['fɛrbən], *v.a.* dye, stain.

Farbenbrett ['farbənbrɛt], *n.* (—s, *pl.* —er) palette.

Farb(en)druck ['farpdruk, farbəndruk], *m.* (—s, *pl.* —e) colour-printing.

Farbenspiel ['farbənʃpiːl], *n.* (—s, *no pl.*) iridescence.

Färber ['fɛrbər], *m.* (—s, *pl.* —) dyer.

farbig ['farbɪç], *adj.* coloured.

Farbstift ['farpʃtɪft], *m.* (—s, *pl.* —e) crayon.

Farbstoff ['farpʃtɔf], *m.* (—es, *pl.* —e) dye.

Farbton ['farptoːn], *m.* (—s, *pl.* ⁻e) hue, tone, tinge, shade.

Farn [farn], *m.* (—s, *pl.* —e) (*Bot.*) fern.

Färse ['fɛrzə], *f.* (—, *pl.* —n) (*Zool.*) heifer.

Fasan [fa'zaːn], *m.* (—s, *pl.* —e) (*Orn.*) pheasant.

Fasching ['faʃɪŋ], *m.* (—s, *no pl.*) (Shrovetide) carnival.

Faschismus [fa'ʃɪsmus], *m.* (—s, *no pl.*) fascism.

Faselei [fazə'lai], *f.* (—, *pl.* —en) silly talk, drivel.

faseln ['faːzəln], *v.n.* drivel.

Faser ['faːzər], *f.* (—, *pl.* —n) thread; string; fibre, filament.

fasern ['faːzərn], *v.n.* fray.

Faß [fas], *n.* (—sses, *pl.* ⁻sser) barrel, vat, tun, tub, cask, keg; Bier vom —, draught beer; Wein vom —, wine from the wood.

Fassade [fa'saːdə], *f.* (—, *pl.* —n) façade.

faßbar ['fasbaːr], *adj.* tangible.

Faßbinder ['fasbɪndər], *m.* (—s, *pl.* —) cooper.

fassen ['fasən], *v.a.* seize, take hold of, grasp; (*jewels*) set; contain, hold. — *v.r.* (*aux.* haben) *sich* —, compose o.s.; *sich kurz* —, be brief.

faßlich ['faslɪç], *adj.* comprehensible, understandable.

Fasson [fa'sõ], *f.* (—, *pl.* —s) fashion; (*fig.*) cut, style.

Fassung ['fasuŋ], *f.* (—, *pl.* —en) (*jewels*) setting; (*speech*) wording, version; (*fig.*) composure.

fassungslos ['fasuŋsloːs], *adj.* bewildered, disconcerted; distraught, speechless.

fast [fast], *adv.* almost, nearly.

fasten ['fastən], *v.n.* fast.

Fastenzeit ['fastəntsait], *f.* (—, *pl.* —en) time of fasting; Lent.

Fastnacht ['fastnaxt], *f.* (—, *pl.* —e) Shrove Tuesday; Shrovetide.

fauchen ['fauxən], *v.n.* spit, hiss.

faul [faul], *adj.* (*food*) rotten, putrid, decayed; (*persons*) lazy, idle.

Fäule ['fɔylə], *f.* (—, *no pl.*) rot.

faulen ['faulən], *v.n.* (*aux.* sein) rot.

faulenzen ['faulɛntsən], *v.n.* laze, idle.

Faulenzer ['faulɛntsər], *m.* (—s, *pl.* —) idler, sluggard, lazybones.

Faulenzerei ['faulɛntsərai], *f.* (—, *pl.* —en) idleness, laziness.

Faulheit ['faulhait], *f.* (—, *no pl.*) idleness, laziness, sluggishness.

faulig ['faulɪç], *adj.* putrid, rotten.

Fäulnis ['fɔylnɪs], *f.* (—, *no pl.*) rottenness, putridity.

Faust [faust], *f.* (—, *pl.* ⁻e) fist.

Fäustchen ['fɔystçən], *n.* (—s, *pl.* —) small fist; *sich ins* — *lachen*, laugh in o.'s sleeve.

Faustkampf ['faustkampf], *m.* (—es, *pl.* ⁻e) boxing (match).

Faxen ['faksən], *f. pl.* foolery; — *machen*, play the buffoon.

Fazit ['fatsɪt], *n.* (—s, *no pl.*) sum, amount.

Februar ['feːbruaːr], *m.* (—s, *no pl.*) February.

fechten ['fɛçtən], *v.n. irr.* fight; fence; (*fig.*) beg.

Feder ['feːdər], *f.* (—, *pl.* —n) (*bird*) feather; (*hat*) plume; (*writing*) pen; (*antique*) quill; (*Tech.*) spring.

Federball ['feːdərbal], *m.* (—s, *pl.* ⁻e) shuttle-cock.

federig ['feːdərɪç], *adj.* feathery; (*Tech.*) springy, resilient.

Federlesen(s) ['feːdərleːzən(s)], *n.* (—s, *no pl.*) *nicht viel* — *machen*, make short work of.

Fee [feː], *f.* (—, *pl.* —n) fairy.

feenhaft ['feːənhaft], *adj.* fairy-like, magical.

Fegefeuer ['feːgəfɔyər], *n.* (—s, *no pl.*) purgatory.

fegen ['feːgən], *v.a.* clean, sweep. — *v.n.* (*aux.* sein) tear along.

Fehde ['feːdə], *f.* (—, *pl.* —n) feud, quarrel.

Fehdehandschuh ['feːdəhantʃuː], *m.* (—s, *pl.* —e) gauntlet.

fehlbar

fehlbar ['feːlbaːr], *adj.* fallible.
Fehlbetrag ['feːlbətraːk], *m.* (—s, *pl.* ∸e) deficit.
fehlen ['feːlən], *v.a.* miss. — *v.n.* err, do wrong; be absent; be wanting; *er fehlt mir*, I miss him.
Fehler ['feːlər], *m.* (—s, *pl.* —) fault, defect; mistake, error.
Fehlgeburt ['feːlgəburt], *f.* (—, *pl.* —en) miscarriage.
Fehlschlag ['feːlʃlaːk], *m.* (—s, *pl.* ∸e) failure, disappointment.
feien ['faɪən], *v.a.* einen — gegen, charm s.o. against; *gefeit*, proof.
Feier ['faɪər], *f.* (—, *pl.* —n) celebration, festival, holiday, festive day.
Feierabend ['faɪəraːbənt], *m.* (—s, —e) time for leaving off work; — *machen*, knock off (work).
feierlich ['faɪərlɪç], *adj.* festive, solemn, stately.
feiern ['faɪərn], *v.a.* celebrate; honour, praise. — *v.n.* rest from work.
Feiertag ['faɪərtaːk], *m.* (—s, *pl.* —e) holiday, festive day.
feig [faɪk], *adj.* cowardly.
Feige ['faɪgə], *f.* (—, *pl.* —n) (*Bot.*) fig.
Feigheit ['faɪkhaɪt], *f.* (—, *pl.* —en) cowardice, cowardliness.
Feigling ['faɪklɪŋ], *m.* (—s, *pl.* —e) coward.
Feigwurz ['faɪkvurts], *m.* (—es, *no pl.*) (*Bot.*) fennel.
feil [faɪl], *adj.* (*obs.*) for sale; venal.
feilbieten ['faɪlbiːtən], *v.a.* offer for sale.
Feile ['faɪlə], *f.* (—, *pl.* —n) file.
feilen ['faɪlən], *v.a.* file.
feilhalten ['faɪlhaltən], *v.a.* have for sale, be ready to sell.
feilschen ['faɪlʃən], *v.n.* bargain, haggle.
Feilspäne ['faɪlʃpɛːnə], *m. pl.* filings.
fein [faɪn], *adj.* fine; neat, pretty, nice; delicate; (*clothes*) elegant; (*behaviour*) refined, polished.
Feinbäckerei ['faɪnbɛkəraɪ], *f.* (—, *pl.* —en) confectioner's shop.
Feind [faɪnt], *m.* (—es, *pl.* —e) enemy, foe, adversary.
Feindschaft ['faɪntʃaft], *f.* (—, *pl.* —en) enmity, hostility.
feindselig ['faɪntzeːlɪç], *adj.* hostile, malignant.
feinfühlend ['faɪnfyːlənt], *adj.* delicate, sensitive.
Feinheit ['faɪnhaɪt], *f.* (—, *pl.* —en) fineness, elegance, politeness, delicacy.
Feinschmecker ['faɪnʃmɛkər], *m.* (—s, *pl.* —), gourmet.
Feinsliebchen ['faɪnsˈliːpçən], *n.* (—s, *pl.* —) (*Poet. obs.*) sweetheart.
feist [faɪst], *adj.* fat, obese.
Feld [fɛlt], *n.* (—es, *pl.* —er) field, plain; (*chess*) square; (*fig.*) sphere, province.
Feldbett ['fɛltbɛt], *n.* (—s, *pl.* —en) camp-bed.
Feldherr ['fɛlthɛr], *m.* (—n, *pl.* —en) commander, general.

Feldmesser ['fɛltmɛsər], *m.* (—s, *pl.* —) land-surveyor.
Feldscher ['fɛltʃeːr], *m.* (—s, *pl.* —e) army-surgeon.
Feldstecher ['fɛltʃtɛçər], *m.* (—s, *pl.* —) field-glass(es).
Feldwebel ['fɛltveːbəl], *m.* (—s, *pl.* —) sergeant-major.
Feldzug ['fɛlttsuːk], *m.* (—es, *pl.* ∸e) campaign, expedition.
Felge ['fɛlgə], *f.* (—, *pl.* —n) (*wheel*) felloe, felly, rim.
Fell [fɛl], *n.* (—s, *pl.* —e) hide, skin, pelt.
Felsabhang ['fɛlsaphaŋ], *m.* (—s, *pl.* ∸e) rocky slope.
Felsen ['fɛlzən], *m.* (—s, *pl.* —) rock, cliff.
Felsengebirge ['fɛlzəngəbɪrgə], *n.* Rocky Mountains.
Felsenriff ['fɛlzənrɪf], *n.* (—s, *pl.* —e) reef.
felsig ['fɛlzɪç], *adj.* rocky.
Feme ['feːmə], *f.* (—, *pl.* —n) secret tribunal.
Fenchel ['fɛnçəl], *m.* (—s, *no pl.*) (*Bot.*) fennel.
Fenster ['fɛnstər], *n.* (—s, *pl.* —) window.
Fensterbrett ['fɛnstərbrɛt], *n.* (—s, *pl.* —er) window-sill.
Fensterflügel ['fɛnstərflyːgəl], *m.* (—s, *pl.* —) (window) casement.
Fensterladen ['fɛnstərlaːdən], *m.* (—s, *pl.* ∸) shutter.
Fensterscheibe ['fɛnstərʃaɪbə], *f.* (—, *pl.* —n) pane.
Ferien ['feːrjən], *pl.* holidays.
Ferkel ['fɛrkəl], *n.* (—s, *pl.* —) young pig, piglet.
Fermate [fɛrˈmaːtə], *f.* (—, *pl.* —n) (*Mus.*) pause, fermata.
fern [fɛrn], *adj.* far, distant, remote.
Fernbleiben ['fɛrnblaɪbən], *n.* (—s, *no pl.*) absence.
Ferne ['fɛrnə], *f.* (—, *pl.* —n) distance, remoteness.
ferner ['fɛrnər], *adv.* further, furthermore, moreover.
fernerhin ['fɛrnərhɪn], *adv.* henceforth.
Ferngespräch ['fɛrngəʃprɛx], *n.* (—s, *pl.* —e) long-distance telephone call, trunk call.
Fernglas ['fɛrnglaːs], *n.* (—es, *pl.* ∸er) binoculars.
fernhalten ['fɛrnhaltən], *v.a.* *irr.* keep away.
fernher ['fɛrnheːr], *adv.* von —, from afar.
fernliegen ['fɛrnliːgən], *v.n.* *irr.* be far from.
Fernrohr ['fɛrnroːr], *n.* (—s, *pl.* —e) telescope.
Fernschreiber ['fɛrnʃraɪbər], *m.* (—s, *pl.* —) teleprinter.
Fernsehen ['fɛrnzeːən], *n.* (—s, *no pl.*) television.
fernsehen ['fɛrnzeːən], *v.n.* *irr.* watch television.

Fernsehgerät ['fɛrnzeːgərɛːt], n. (—s, —e) television set.

Fernsprechamt ['fɛrnʃprɛçamt], n. (—s, pl. ⁻er) telephone exchange.

Fernsprecher ['fɛrnʃprɛçər], m. (—s, pl. —) telephone.

Fernstehende ['fɛrnʃteːəndə], m. (—n, pl. —n) outsider.

Fernverkehr ['fɛrnfɛrkeːr], m. (—s, no pl.) long-distance traffic.

Ferse ['fɛrzə], f. (—, pl. —n) heel.

Fersengeld ['fɛrzəngɛlt], n. (—s, no pl.) — geben, take to o.'s heels.

fertig ['fɛrtɪç], adj. ready, finished: (coll.) worn-out, ruined, done for.

Fertigkeit ['fɛrtɪçkaɪt], f. (—, pl. —en) dexterity, skill.

Fes [fɛs], n. (—, pl. —) (Mus.) F flat.

fesch [fɛʃ], adj. smart, stylish; (dial.) good-looking.

Fessel ['fɛsəl], f. (—, pl. —n) fetter, shackle.

Fesselballon ['fɛsəlbalɔ̃], m. (—s, pl. —s) captive balloon.

Fesselbein ['fɛsəlbaɪn], n. (—s, pl. —e) pastern-joint.

fesseln ['fɛsəln], v.a. fetter, shackle, chain; (fig.) captivate.

Fest [fɛst], n. (—es, pl. —e) feast, festival.

fest [fɛst], adj. fast, firm; solid, hard; sound; fixed; constant, steadfast.

Feste ['fɛstə], f. (—, pl. —n) fortress, stronghold.

festigen ['fɛstɪgən], v.a. make firm; strengthen.

Festland ['fɛstlant], n. (—es, pl. ⁻er) continent.

festlich ['fɛstlɪç], adj. festive, solemn.

festmachen ['fɛstmaxən], v.a. fasten.

Festnahme ['fɛstnaːmə], f. (—, no pl.) apprehension, arrest.

festnehmen ['fɛstneːmən], v.a. irr. seize, arrest.

Festrede ['fɛstreːdə], f. (—, pl. —n) formal address.

festschnallen ['fɛstʃnalən], v.a. buckle on, fasten.

Festschrift ['fɛstʃrɪft], f. (—, pl. —en) commemorative volume (in honour of a person or an occasion).

festsetzen ['fɛstzɛtsən], v.a. fix, decree.

Festspiel ['fɛstʃpiːl], n. (—s, pl. —e) festival (play).

feststehen ['fɛstʃteːən], v.n. irr. stand firm; es steht fest, it is certain.

feststellen ['fɛstʃtɛlən], v.a. ascertain; state; find; determine; diagnose; establish.

Festtag ['fɛstaːk], m. (—s, pl. —e) feast-day, holiday.

Festung ['fɛstuŋ], f. (—, pl. —en) fortress, stronghold, citadel.

festziehen ['fɛsttsiːən], v.a. irr. tighten.

Festzug ['fɛsttsuːk], m. (—s, pl. ⁻e) procession.

Fett [fɛt], n. (—s, pl. —e) fat, grease, lard.

fett [fɛt], adj. fat, greasy.

fettartig ['fɛtartɪç], adj. fatty.

fetten ['fɛtən], v.a. oil, grease.

Fettfleck ['fɛtflɛk], m. (—s, pl. —e) spot of grease.

fettgedruckt ['fɛtgədrukt], adj. in heavy type.

fetthaltig ['fɛthaltɪç], adj. greasy; adipose.

fettig ['fɛtɪç], adj. greasy.

fettleibig ['fɛtlaɪbɪç], adj. corpulent, obese.

Fetzen ['fɛtsən], m. (—s, pl. —) piece, rag, tatter, shred.

feucht [fɔyçt], adj. moist; (weather) muggy, wet; (room) damp.

Feuchtigkeit ['fɔyçtɪçkaɪt], f. (—, no pl.) moisture, humidity, dampness, wetness.

feudal [fɔyˈdaːl], adj. feudal; (coll.) distinguished, magnificent.

Feuer ['fɔyər], n. (—s, pl. —) fire; (jewels) brilliancy; (fig.) ardour, passion.

feuerbeständig ['fɔyərbəʃtɛndɪç], adj. fire-proof.

Feuerbestattung ['fɔyərbəʃtatuŋ], f. (—, pl. —en) cremation.

Feuereifer ['fɔyəraɪfər], m. (—s, no pl.) ardour.

feuerfest ['fɔyərfɛst], adj. fire-proof, incombustible.

feuergefährlich ['fɔyərgəfɛːrlɪç], adj. inflammable.

Feuerlilie ['fɔyərliːljə], f. (—, pl. —n) tiger lily.

Feuermal ['fɔyərmaːl], n. (—s, pl. —e) burn, burn-mark.

Feuermauer ['fɔyərmauər], f. (—, pl. —n) fire-proof wall, party-wall.

Feuermelder ['fɔyərmɛldər], m. (—s, pl. —) fire-alarm.

feuern ['fɔyərn], v.a. (Mil.) fire, discharge; (coll.) fire, sack.

Feuerprobe ['fɔyərproːbə], f. (—, pl. —n) ordeal by fire.

Feuerrad ['fɔyəraːt], n. (—s, pl. ⁻er) Catherine wheel.

Feuerrohr ['fɔyərɔːr], n. (—s, pl. —e) gun, matchlock.

Feuersbrunst ['fɔyərsbrunst], f. (—, pl. ⁻e) (rare) fire, conflagration.

Feuerspritze ['fɔyərʃprɪtsə], f. (—, pl. —n) fire-engine.

Feuerstein ['fɔyərʃtaɪn], m. (—s, no pl.) flint.

Feuertaufe ['fɔyərtaufə], f. (—, pl. —n) baptism of fire.

Feuerwarte ['fɔyərvartə], f. (—, pl. —en) beacon; lighthouse.

Feuerwehr ['fɔyərveːr], f. (—, no pl.) fire-brigade.

Feuerwerk ['fɔyərvɛrk], n. (—, no pl.) fireworks.

Feuerwerkskunst ['fɔyərvɛrkskunst], f. (—, no pl.) pyrotechnics.

Feuerzange ['fɔyərtsaŋə], f. (—, pl. —n) fire-tongs.

Feuerzeug ['fɔyərtsɔyk], n. (—s, pl. —e) match-box; cigarette-lighter.

feurig ['fɔyrɪç], adj. fiery, burning; (fig.) ardent, impassioned, fervent; (wine) heady.

Fiaker [fi'akər], *m.* (**—s**, *pl.* **—**) (*Austr.*) cab, hansom; (*Am.*) coach.

Fiasko [fi'asko:], *n.* (**—s**, *pl.* **—s**) failure.

Fibel ['fi:bəl], *f.* (**—**, *pl.* **—n**) primer, spelling-book.

Fiber ['fi:bər], *f.* (**—**, *pl.* **—n**) fibre.

Fichte ['fıçtə], *f.* (**—**, *pl.* **—n**) (*Bot.*) pine, pine-tree.

fidel [fi'de:l], *adj.* merry, jolly.

Fidibus ['fi:dibus], *m.* (**—ses**, *pl.* **—se**) spill, fidibus.

Fidschi ['fıdʒi:], Fiji.

Fieber ['fi:bər], *n.* (**—s**, *no pl.*) fever.

fieberhaft ['fi:bərhaft], *adj.* feverish, vehement.

fieberig ['fi:bərıç], *adj.* feverish, racked by fever.

Fieberkälte ['fi:bərkɛltə], *f.* (**—**, *no pl.*) chill, shivering (fit).

fiebern ['fi:bərn], *v.n.* have a fever; (*fig.*) rave.

fiebrig ['fi:brıç], *see* **fieberig**.

Fiedel ['fi:dəl], *f.* (**—**, *pl.* **—n**) (*Mus.*) fiddle, violin.

Figur [fi'gu:r], *f.* (**—**, *pl.* **—en**) figure, statue, sculpture; chessman.

figürlich [fi'gy:rlıç], *adj.* figurative.

Filet [fi'le:], *n.* (**—s**, *pl.* **—s**) netting, net-work; (*meat*) fillet.

Filiale [fil'ja:lə], *f.* (**—**, *pl.* **—n**) branch, branch-establishment, branch-office.

Filigran [fili'gra:n], *n.* (**—s**, *no pl.*) filigree.

Film [fılm], *m.* (**—s**, *pl.* **—e**) film; (motion) picture.

Filter ['fıltər], *m.* (**—s**, *pl.* **—**) filter.

filtrieren [fıl'tri:rən], *v.a.* filter.

Filz [fılts], *m.* (**—es**, *pl.* **—e**) felt; (*fig.*) niggard, miser, skinflint.

Filzlaus ['fıltslaus], *f.* (**—**, *pl.* ⁼e) crab-louse.

Finanzamt [fi'nantsamt], *n.* (**—s**, *pl.* ⁼er) income-tax office; revenue-office.

Finanzen [fi'nantsən], *f. pl.* finances, revenue.

Findelkind ['fındəlkınt], *n.* (**—s**, *pl.* **—er**) foundling.

finden ['fındən], *v.a. irr.* find. — *v.r. sich* **—**, *das wird sich* **—**, we shall see.

Finder ['fındər], *m.* (**—s**, *pl.* **—**) finder.

findig ['fındıç], *adj.* resourceful, ingenious.

Findling ['fıntlıŋ], *m.* (**—s**, *pl.* **—e**) foundling.

Finger ['fıŋər], *m.* (**—s**, *pl.* **—**) finger.

Fingerabdruck ['fıŋərapdruk], *m.* (**—s**, *pl.* ⁼e) finger-print.

fingerfertig ['fıŋərfɛrtıç], *adj.* nimble-fingered.

Fingerhut ['fıŋərhu:t], *m.* (**—s**, *pl.* ⁼e) thimble; (*Bot.*) foxglove.

fingern ['fıŋərn], *v.a.* touch with the fingers, finger.

Fingersatz ['fıŋərzats], *m.* (**—es**, *pl.* ⁼e) (*Mus.*) fingering.

Fingerspitze ['fıŋərʃpıtsə], *f.* (**—**, *pl.* **—n**) finger-tip.

Fingerzeig ['fıŋərtsaık], *m.* (**—s**, *pl.* **—e**) hint.

fingieren [fıŋ'gi:rən], *v.a.* sham.

fingiert [fıŋ'gi:rt], *adj.* fictitious.

Fink [fıŋk], *m.* (**—en**, *pl.* **—en**) (*Orn.*) finch.

Finne (1) ['fınə], *m.* (**—n**, *pl.* **—n**) Finn.

Finne (2) ['fınə], *f.* (**—**, *pl.* **—n**) pimple; (*fish*) fin.

finnig ['fınıç], *adj.* pimpled; (*fish*) finny.

Finnland ['fınlant], *n.* Finland.

finster ['fınstər], *adj.* dark, obscure; (*fig.*) gloomy, sinister.

Finsternis ['fınstərnıs], *f.* (**—**, *no pl.*) darkness, gloom.

Finte ['fıntə], *f.* (**—**, *pl.* **—n**) feint; (*fig.*) pretence, trick.

Firlefanz ['fırləfants], *m.* (**—es**, *no pl.*) foolery.

Firma ['fırma], *f.* (**—**, *pl.* **—men**) (*business*) firm, company.

Firmung ['fırmuŋ], *f.* (**—**, *pl.* **—en**) (*Eccl.*) confirmation.

Firnis ['fırnıs], *m.* (**—ses**, *pl.* **—se**) varnish.

firnissen ['fırnısən], *v.a.* varnish.

First [fırst], *m.* (**—es**, *pl.* **—e**) (*house*) roof-ridge; (*mountain*) top.

Fis [fıs], *n.* (**—**, *pl.* **—**) (*Mus.*) F sharp.

Fisch [fıʃ], *m.* (**—es**, *pl.* **—e**) fish.

Fischadler ['fıʃa:dlər], *m.* (**—s**, *pl.* **—**) osprey, sea-eagle.

Fischbein ['fıʃbaın], *n.* (**—s**, *no pl.*) whalebone.

fischen ['fıʃən], *v.a., v.n.* fish, angle.

Fischer ['fıʃər], *m.* (**—s**, *pl.* **—**) fisherman, fisher.

Fischerei [fıʃə'raı], *f.* (**—**, *no pl.*) fishing; fishery.

Fischergerät ['fıʃərgərɛ:t], *n.* (**—s**, *pl.* **—e**) fishing-tackle.

Fischgräte ['fıʃgrɛ:tə], *f.* (**—**, *pl.* **—n**) fish-bone.

Fischkelle ['fıʃkɛlə], *f.* (**—**, *pl.* **—n**) fish-slice.

Fischlaich ['fıʃlaıç], *m.* (**—s**, *no pl.*) spawn.

Fischmilch ['fıʃmılç], *f.* (**—**, *no pl.*) soft roe, milt.

Fischotter ['fıʃɔtər], *m.* (**—**, *pl.* **—n**) common otter.

Fischreiher ['fıʃraıər], *m.* (**—s**, *pl.* **—**) (*Orn.*) heron.

Fischreuse ['fıʃrɔyzə], *f.* (**—**, *pl.* **—n**) bow-net; weir.

Fischrogen ['fıʃro:gən], *m.* (**—s**, *no pl.*) roe.

Fischschuppe ['fıʃʃupə], *f.* (**—**, *pl.* **—n**) scale.

Fischtran ['fıʃtra:n], *m.* (**—s**, *no pl.*) train-oil.

Fischzucht ['fıʃtsuxt], *f.* (**—**, *no pl.*) fish-breeding, pisciculture.

Fiskus ['fıskus], *m.* (**—**, *pl.* **—ken**) Treasury, Exchequer.

Fisole [fi'zo:lə], *f.* (**—**, *pl.* **—n**) (*Austr.*) French bean.

Fistelstimme ['fɪstəlʃtɪmə], *f.* (—, *no pl.*) (*Mus.*) falsetto.
Fittich ['fɪtɪç], *m.* (—es, *pl.* —e) (*Poet.*) wing, pinion.
fix [fɪks], *adj.* quick, sharp; — *und fertig*, quite ready.
Fixum ['fɪksum], *n.* (—s, *pl.* —xa) fixed amount; regular salary.
flach [flax], *adj.* flat, plain, smooth, level; (*water*) shallow.
Fläche ['flɛçə], *f.* (—, *pl.* —n) plain; (*Maths.*) plane; (*crystal*) face.
Flächeninhalt ['flɛçənɪnhalt], *m.* (—s, *no pl.*) area.
Flächenmaß ['flɛçənmaːs], *n.* (—es, *pl.* —e) square-measure.
Flächenraum ['flɛçənraum], *m.* (—es, *no pl.*) surface area.
Flachheit ['flaxhaɪt], *f.* (—, *no pl.*) flatness; (*fig.*) shallowness.
Flachs [[flaks], *m.* (—es, *no pl.*) flax.
flackern ['flakərn], *v.n.* flare, flicker.
Fladen ['flaːdən], *m.* (—s, *pl.* —) flat cake; cow-dung.
Flagge ['flagə], *f.* (—, *pl.* —n) flag.
Flame ['flaːmə], *m.* (—n, *pl.* —n) Fleming.
flämisch ['flɛːmɪʃ], *adj.* Flemish.
Flamme ['flamə], *f.* (—, *pl.* —n) flame; blaze.
flammen ['flamən], *v.n.* flame, blaze, sparkle.
Flammeri ['flaməriː], *m.* (—s, *pl.* —s) blanc-mange.
Flandern ['flandərn], *n.* Flanders.
Flanell [fla'nɛl], *m.* (—s, *pl.* —e) flannel.
Flaneur [fla'nøːr], *m.* (—s, *pl.* —e) lounger, stroller.
flanieren [fla'niːrən], *v.n.* lounge, stroll.
Flanke ['flaŋkə], *f.* (—, *pl.* —n) flank; *in die — fallen*, (*Mil.*) attack in the flank.
Flasche ['flaʃə], *f.* (—, *pl.* —en) bottle, flask.
Flaschenzug ['flaʃəntsuːk], *m.* (—es, *pl.* ⁻e) pulley.
flatterhaft ['flatərhaft], *adj.* fickle, inconstant, flighty.
flattern ['flatərn], *v.n.* flutter.
flau [flau], *adj.* insipid, stale; (*fig.*) dull.
Flaum [flaum], *m.* (—s, *no pl.*) down.
Flausch [flauʃ], *m.* (—es, *no pl.*) pilot-cloth.
Flaute ['flautə], *f.* (—, *pl.* —n) (*Nav.*) calm; (*fig.*) (*Comm.*) depression.
Flechte ['flɛçtə], *f.* (—, *pl.* —n) twist, plait, braid; (*Med.*) eruption, ring-worm; (*Bot.*) lichen.
flechten ['flɛçtən], *v.a. irr.* plait; wreathe.
Flechtwerk ['flɛçtvɛrk], *n.* (—s, *no pl.*) wicker-work, basketry.
Fleck [flɛk], *m.* (—s, *pl.* —e) spot; place, piece (of ground); (*fig.*) stain, blemish.
Flecken ['flɛkən], *m.* (—s, *pl.* —) market town, small town.

fleckenlos ['flɛkənloːs], *adj.* spotless.
fleckig ['flɛkɪç], *adj.* spotted, speckled.
Fledermaus ['fleːdərmaus], *f.* (—, *pl.* ⁻e) (*Zool.*) bat.
Flederwisch ['fleːdərvɪʃ], *m.* (—es, *pl.* —e) feather-duster.
Flegel ['fleːgəl], *m.* (—s, *pl.* —) flail; (*fig.*) boor.
flegelhaft ['fleːgəlhaft], *adj.* boorish, churlish, rude.
Flegeljahre ['fleːgəljaːrə], *n. pl.* years of indiscretion; teens, adolescence.
flehen ['fleːən], *v.a., v.n.* implore, supplicate, entreat.
Fleisch [flaɪʃ], *n.* (—es, *no pl.*) (raw) flesh; (*for cooking*) meat; (*fruit*) pulp.
Fleischbrühe ['flaɪʃbryːə], *f.* (—, *pl.* —n) broth, beef-tea.
Fleischer ['flaɪʃər], *m.* (—s, *pl.* —) butcher.
fleischfressend ['flaɪʃfrɛsənt], *adj.* carnivorous.
Fleischhacker ['flaɪʃhakər], **Fleischhauer** ['flaɪʃhauər], *m.* (—s, *pl.* —) butcher.
fleischlich ['flaɪʃlɪç], *adj.* fleshly, carnal.
fleischlos ['flaɪʃloːs], *adj.* vegetarian.
Fleischpastete ['flaɪʃpasteːtə], *f.* (—, *pl.* —n) meat-pie.
Fleiß [flaɪs], *m.* (—es, *no pl.*) diligence, assiduity, industry.
fleißig ['flaɪsɪç], *adj.* diligent, assiduous, industrious, hard-working.
fletschen ['flɛtʃən], *v.a. die Zähne* —, show o.'s teeth.
Flicken ['flɪkən], *m.* (—s, *pl.* —) patch.
flicken ['flɪkən], *v.a.* patch, repair, mend; (*shoes*) cobble; (*stockings*) darn.
Flieder ['fliːdər], *m.* (—s, *pl.* —) (*Bot.*) elder, lilac.
Fliege ['fliːgə], *f.* (—, *pl.* —n) (*Ent.*) fly; (*beard*) imperial.
fliegen ['fliːgən], *v.n. irr.* (*aux.* sein) fly; (*coll.*) get the sack, be fired. — *v.a.* fly, pilot (an aircraft).
Flieger ['fliːgər], *m.* (—s, *pl.* —) airman, aviator; pilot.
fliehen ['fliːən], *v.n. irr.* (*aux.* sein) flee, run away; *zu einem* —, take refuge with s.o. — *v.a. irr.* avoid, shun (s.o.).
Fliehkraft ['fliːkraft], *f.* (—, *no pl.*) centrifugal force.
Fliese ['fliːzə], *f.* (—, *pl.* —n) floor-tile, flagstone.
Fließband ['fliːsbant], *n.* (—(e)s, *pl.* ⁻er) (*Ind.*) assembly line.
fließen ['fliːsən], *v.n. irr.* (*aux.* sein) flow.
Fließpapier ['fliːspapiːr], *n.* (—s, *no pl.*) blotting-paper.
Flimmer ['flɪmər], *m.* (—s, *no pl.*) glittering, sparkling, glimmer.
flimmern ['flɪmərn], *v.n.* glisten, glitter.
flink [flɪŋk], *adj.* brisk, agile, quick, sharp, nimble.

Flinte

Flinte ['flɪntə], f. (—, pl. —n) gun, musket, rifle.

Flitter ['flɪtər], m. (—s, no pl.) tinsel, spangle, frippery.

Flitterwochen ['flɪtərvɔxən], f. pl. honeymoon.

flitzen ['flɪtsən], v.n. (aux. sein) vorbei —, flit or rush past, dash along.

Flocke ['flɔkə], f. (—, pl. —n) (snow) flake; (wool) flock.

Floh [flo:], m. (—s, pl. ⁼e) (Ent.) flea.

Flor [flo:r], m. (—s, pl. —e) bloom; gauze, crape; in —, blossoming, blooming.

Florenz [flo'rɛnts], n. Florence.

Florett [flo'rɛt], n. (—s, pl. —e) (fencing) foil.

florieren [flo'ri:rən], v.n. flourish.

Florstrumpf ['flo:rʃtrumpf], m. (—s, pl. ⁼e) lisle stocking.

Floskel ['flɔskəl], f. (—, pl. —n) rhetorical ornament; oratorical flourish; phrase.

Floß [flo:s], n. (—es, pl. ⁼e) raft.

Flosse ['flɔsə], f. (—, pl. —n) fin.

flößen ['flø:sən], v.a. float.

Flößer ['flø:sər], m. (—s, pl. —) raftsman.

Flöte ['flø:tə], f. (—, pl. —n) (Mus.) flute.

Flötenzug ['flø:təntsu:k], m. (—es, pl. ⁼e) (organ) flute-stop.

flott [flɔt], adj. (Naut.) afloat, floating; (fig.) gay, jolly, lively, smart; — leben, lead a fast life.

Flotte ['flɔtə], f. (—, pl. —n) fleet, navy.

Flottille [flɔ'tɪljə], f. (—, pl. —n) flotilla, squadron.

Flöz [flø:ts], n. (—es, pl. —e) layer, stratum; (coal) seam.

Fluch [flu:x], m. (—es, pl. ⁼e) curse, spell; (verbal) curse, oath, swear-word.

fluchen ['flu:xən], v.n. curse, swear.

Flucht [fluxt], f. (—, pl. —en) flight, fleeing; suite (of rooms).

flüchten ['flyçtən], v.n. (aux. sein), v.r. flee, run away, escape.

flüchtig ['flyçtɪç], adj. fugitive; (Chem.) volatile; (fig.) superficial; evanescent; hasty; slight.

Flüchtling ['flyçtlɪŋ], m. (—s, pl. —e) fugitive, refugee.

Flug [flu:k], m. (—s, pl. ⁼e) (Aviat.) flight.

Flugblatt ['flu:kblat], n. (—s, pl. ⁼er) broadsheet, leaflet.

Flügel ['fly:gəl], m. (—s, pl. —) wing; (Mus.) grand piano; (door) leaf.

Flügelschlag ['fly:gəlʃla:k], m. (—s, pl. ⁼e) wing-stroke.

Flügeltür ['fly:gəlty:r], f. (—, pl. —en) folding-door.

flügge ['flygə], adj. fledged.

Flughafen ['flu:kha:fən], m. (—s, pl. ⁼) airport; aerodrome.

Flugpost ['flu:kpɔst], f. (—, no pl.) air mail.

flugs [fluks], adv. quickly, instantly; (Lit., obs.) anon.

Flugsand ['flu:kzant], m. (—s, no pl.) quicksand, drifting sand.

Flugzeug ['flu:ktsɔyk], n. (—s, pl. —e) aeroplane; (Am.) airplane.

Flugzeugführer ['flu:ktsɔykfy:rər], m. (—s, pl. —) (Aviat.) pilot.

Fluidum ['flu:idum], n. (—s, pl. —da) fluid; (fig.) atmosphere.

Flunder ['flundər], f. (—, pl. —n) (fish) flounder.

Flunkerer ['fluŋkərər], m. (—s, pl. —) (coll.) fibber, story-teller.

Flur (1) [flu:r], f. (—, pl. —en) field, plain; auf weiter —, in the open.

Flur (2) [flu:r], m. (—s, pl. —e) (house) hall, vestibule; corridor.

Flurschaden ['flu:rʃa:dən], m. (—s, pl. ⁼) damage to crops.

Fluß [flus], m. (—sses, pl. ⁼sse) river, stream; flow, flowing; flux.

Flußbett ['flusbɛt], n. (—s, pl. —en) channel, riverbed.

flüssig ['flysɪç], adj. fluid, liquid; —e Gelder, ready cash; liquid assets.

flüstern ['flystərn], v.a. whisper.

Flut [flu:t], f. (—, pl. —en) flood; high-tide, high water; torrent; deluge.

fluten ['flu:tən], v.n. flow.

Focksegel ['fɔkze:gəl], n. (—s, pl. —) foresail.

Fockmast ['fɔkmast], m. (—s, pl. —en) foremast.

Föderalismus [fø:dəra'lɪsmus], m. (—, no pl.) federalism.

Fohlen ['fo:lən], n. (—s, pl. —) foal.

fohlen ['fo:lən], v.n. foal.

Föhn [fø:n], m. (—s, pl. —e) (warm) Alpine wind.

Föhre ['fø:rə], f. (—, pl. —n) (Bot.) fir, fir-tree.

Folge ['fɔlgə], f. (—, pl. —n) succession; series, sequence; continuation; consequence.

folgen ['fɔlgən], v.n. (aux. sein) follow; succeed; result from, be the consequence of; obey.

folgendermaßen ['fɔlgəndərma:sən], adv. as follows.

folgenschwer ['fɔlgənʃve:r], adj. momentous, portentous.

folgerichtig ['fɔlgərɪçtɪç], adj. consistent, logical.

folgern ['fɔlgərn], v.a. draw a conclusion, infer, conclude, deduce.

Folgerung ['fɔlgəruŋ], f. (—, pl. —en) induction, deduction, inference.

folglich ['fɔlklɪç], conj. consequently, therefore.

folgsam ['fɔlkza:m], adj. obedient.

Foliant [fo:l'jant], m. (—en, pl. —en) folio-volume, tome.

Folie ['fo:ljə], f. (—, pl. —n) foil.

Folter ['fɔltər], f. (—, pl. —n) rack, torture.

Folterbank ['fɔltərbaŋk], f. (—, pl. ⁼e) rack.

Fond [fɔ:], m. (—s, pl. —s) back seat.

Fontäne [fɔ̃'tɛ:nə], *f.* (—, *pl.* —n) fountain.

foppen ['fɔpən], *v.a.* chaff, banter, tease.

Fopperei [fɔpə'rai], *f.* (—, *pl.* —en) chaff, banter, teasing.

forcieren [fɔr'si:rən], *v.a.* strain, overdo.

Förderer ['fœrdərər], *m.* (—s, *pl.* —) promoter, backer.

Förderkarren ['fœrdərkarən], *m.* (—s, *pl.* —) (*Min.*) truck, trolley.

förderlich ['fœrdərlɪç], *adj.* useful, conducive (to).

Fördermaschine ['fœrdərmaʃi:nə], *f.* (—, *pl.* —n) hauling-machine.

fordern ['fɔrdərn], *v.a.* demand, claim, ask for; (*duel*) challenge.

fördern ['fœrdərn], *v.a.* further, advance, promote, back; hasten; (*Min.*) haul.

Förderschacht ['fœrdərʃaxt], *m.* (—s, *pl.* ⁼e) (*Min.*) winding shaft.

Forderung ['fɔrdəruŋ], *f.* (—, *pl.* —en) demand, claim; (*duel*) challenge.

Förderung ['fœrdəruŋ], *f.* (—, *no pl.*) furtherance, promotion, advancement: (*Min.*) hauling.

Forelle [fo'rɛlə], *f.* (—, *pl.* —n) trout.

Forke ['fɔrkə], *f.* (—, *pl.* —n) pitch-fork, garden-fork.

Form [fɔrm], *f.* (—, *pl.* —en) form, shape, figure; manner; condition; (*casting*) mould; (*grammar*) form, voice.

Formalien [fɔr'ma:ljən], *pl.* formalities.

Formalität [fɔrmali'tɛ:t], *f.* (—, *pl.* —en) formality, form.

Format [fɔr'ma:t], *n.* (—s, *pl.* —e) (*book, paper*) size; format; (*fig.*) stature.

Formel ['fɔrməl], *f.* (—, *pl.* —n) formula.

formell [fɔr'mɛl], *adj.* formal.

Formfehler ['fɔrmfe:lər], *m.* (—s, *pl.* —) faux pas, breach of etiquette.

formieren [fɔr'mi:rən], *v.a.* form. — *v.r. sich* —, fall into line.

förmlich ['fœrmlɪç], *adj.* formal: downright.

formlos ['fɔrmlo:s], *adj.* shapeless: (*fig.*) unconventional, informal, unceremonious.

Formular [fɔrmu'la:r], *n.* (—s, *pl.* —e) (printed) form, schedule.

formulieren [fɔrmu'li:rən], *v.a.* formulate, word.

formvollendet ['fɔrmfɔlɛndət], *adj.* well-rounded, well-finished.

forsch [fɔrʃ], *adj.* dashing.

forschen ['fɔrʃən], *v.n.* search, enquire (after), do research.

Forschung ['fɔrʃuŋ], *f.* (—, *pl.* —en) research, investigation; search, exploration.

Forst [fɔrst], *m.* (—es, *pl.* —e) forest.

Förster ['fœrstər], *m.* (—s, *pl.* —) forester, forest-keeper; (*Am.*) ranger.

Forstfrevel ['fɔrstfre:fəl], *m.* (—s, *no pl.*) infringement of forest-laws.

Forstrevier ['fɔrstrevi:r], *n.* (—s, *pl.* —e) section of forest.

Forstwesen ['fɔrstve:zən], *n.* (—s, *no pl.*) forestry.

Forstwirtschaft ['fɔrstvɪrtʃaft], *f.* (—, *no pl.*) forestry.

fort [fɔrt], *adv.* away; lost, gone, forth, forward.

Fort [fo:rt], *n.* (—s, *pl.* —s) fort.

fortan [fɔrt'an], *adv.* henceforth.

fortbilden ['fɔrtbɪldən], *v.r. sich* —, improve o.s., receive further education.

fortbleiben ['fɔrtblaibən], *v.n. irr.* (*aux.* sein) stay away.

Fortdauer ['fɔrtdauər], *f.* (—, *no pl.*) continuance, duration.

fortfahren ['fɔrtfa:rən], *v.n. irr.* (*aux.* sein) drive off: (*Naut.*) set sail; (*fig.*) continue, go on.

Fortgang ['fɔrtgaŋ], *m.* (—s, *no pl.*) going away, departure; (*fig.*) continuation, progress.

Fortkommen ['fɔrtkɔmən], *n.* (—s, *no pl.*) advancement, progress; (*fig.*) livelihood.

fortkommen ['fɔrtkɔmən], *v.n. irr.* (*aux.* sein) *gut* —, prosper, succeed.

fortlassen ['fɔrtlasən], *v.a. irr.* allow to go; leave out, omit; *nicht* —, detain.

fortlaufen ['fɔrtlaufən], *v.n. irr.* (*aux.* sein) run away.

fortpflanzen ['fɔrtpflantsən], *v.r. sich* —, propagate, multiply; (*sickness*) spread.

forträumen ['fɔrtrɔymən], *v.a.* clear away, remove.

fortschaffen ['fɔrtʃafən], *v.a.* carry away, get rid of.

fortscheren ['fɔrtʃe:rən], *v.r. sich* — (*coll.*) beat it, go away.

fortscheuchen ['fɔrtʃɔyçən], *v.a.* scare away.

fortschreiten ['fɔrtʃraitən], *v.n. irr.* (*aux.* sein) progress, advance.

Fortschritt ['fɔrtʃrɪt], *m.* (—s, *pl.* —e) progress, advancement, proficiency.

fortsetzen ['fɔrtzɛtsən], *v.a.* continue, carry on.

fortwährend ['fɔrtvɛ:rənt], *adj.* continual, perpetual, unceasing.

Fracht [fraxt], *f.* (—, *pl.* —en) freight, cargo, load.

Frack [frak], *m.* (—s, *pl.* —s, ⁼e) dress-suit, evening dress.

Frage ['fra:gə], *f.* (—, *pl.* —n) question, query.

Fragebogen ['fra:gəbo:gən], *m.* (—s, *pl.* —) questionnaire.

fragen ['fra:gən], *v.a.* ask, enquire, question.

Fragesteller ['fra:gəʃtɛlər], *m.* (—s, *pl.* —) interrogator, questioner.

fraglich ['fra:klɪç], *adj.* questionable, problematic(al).

fragwürdig ['fra:kvyrdɪç], *adj.* doubtful, questionable.

Fraktion [frak'tsjo:n], *f.* (—, *pl.* —en) (*Pol.*) party group.

Frakturschrift [frak´tuːrʃrɪft], *f.* (—, *no pl.*) (*lettering*) Gothic type, Old English type, Black Letter type.

Frank [fraŋk], *m.* (—en, *pl.* —en) (*money*) franc.

Franke [´fraŋkə], *m.* (—n, *pl.* —n) Frank, Franconian.

frankieren [fraŋ´kiːrən], *v.a.* (*post*) prepay, frank.

franko [´fraŋko], *adj.* post-paid; *gratis und* —, gratuitously.

Frankreich [´frankraɪx], *n.* France.

Franse [´franzə], *f.* (—, *pl.* —n) fringe.

Franzose [fran´tsoːzə], *m.* (—n, *pl.* —n) Frenchman.

französisch [fran´tsøːzɪʃ], *adj.* French.

frappant [fra´pant], *adj.* striking.

frappieren [fra´piːrən], *v.a.* strike, astonish.

Fraß [fraːs], *m.* (—es, *no pl.*) (*animals*) feed, fodder; (*sl.*) grub.

Fratz [frats], *m.* (—es, *pl.* —en) brat, little monkey.

Fratze [´fratsə], *f.* (—, *pl.* —en) grimace, caricature.

Frau [frau], *f.* (—, *pl.* —en) woman, wife, lady; (*title*) Mrs.; *gnädige* —, Madam.

Frauenkirche [´frauənkɪrçə], *f.* (—, *no pl.*) Church of Our Lady.

Frauenzimmer [´frauəntsɪmər], *n.* (—s, *pl.* —) (*pej.*) woman, female.

Fräulein [´froylaɪn], *n.* (—s, *pl.* —) young lady; (*title*) Miss.

frech [frɛç], *adj.* insolent, impudent, cheeky, pert, saucy.

Frechheit [´frɛçhaɪt], *f.* (—, *pl.* —en) insolence, impudence.

Fregatte [fre´gatə], *f.* (—, *pl.* —n) frigate.

frei [fraɪ], *adj.* free, exempt, unhampered, independent, disengaged; vacant; candid, frank.

Freibeuter [´fraɪboytər], *m.* (—s, *pl.* —) freebooter, pirate.

Freibrief [´fraɪbriːf], *m.* (—s, *pl.* —e) patent, licence; permit.

freien [´fraɪən], *v.a.* woo, court.

Freier [´fraɪər], *m.* (—s, *pl.* —) (*obs.*) suitor.

Freigabe [´fraɪgaːbə], *f.* (—, *no pl.*) release.

freigeben [´fraɪgeːbən], *v.a. irr.* release.

freigebig [´fraɪgeːbɪç], *adj.* liberal, generous.

Freigebigkeit [´fraɪgeːbɪçkaɪt], *f.* (—, *no pl.*) liberality, munificence, generosity.

Freigut [´fraɪguːt], *n.* (—s, *pl.* ̶er) freehold.

Freiheit [´fraɪhaɪt], *f.* (—, *pl.* —en) freedom, liberty, immunity, privilege.

Freiherr [´fraɪhɛr], *m.* (—n, *pl.* —en) baron.

Freikorps [´fraɪkoːr], *n.* (—, *no pl.*) volunteer-corps.

Freilauf [´fraɪlauf], *m.* (—s, *no pl.*) (*bicycle*) free-wheel.

freilich [´fraɪlɪç], *adv.* to be sure, it is true, indeed, of course.

Freilicht- [´fraɪlɪxt], *adj.* (*in compounds*) open-air.

Freimarke [´fraɪmarkə], *f.* (—, *pl.* —n) postage stamp.

freimütig [´fraɪmyːtɪç], *adj.* frank, open, candid.

Freisprechung [´fraɪʃprɛçuŋ], *f.* (—, *no pl.*) acquittal; absolution.

Freistätte [´fraɪʃtɛtə], *f.* (—, *pl.* —n) refuge, asylum.

Freistoß [´fraɪʃtoːs], *m.* (—es, *pl.* ̶e) (*Footb.*) free-kick.

Freitag [´fraɪtaːk], *m.* (—s, *pl.* —e) Friday.

Freitreppe [´fraɪtrɛpə], *f.* (—, *pl.* —n) outside staircase.

Freiübung [´fraɪyːbuŋ], *f.* (—, *pl.* —en) (*mostly pl.*) physical exercises, gymnastics.

freiwillig [´fraɪvɪlɪç], *adj.* voluntary, of o.'s own accord; spontaneous.

Freiwillige [´fraɪvɪlɪgə], *m.* (—n, *pl.* —n) (*Mil.*) volunteer.

fremd [frɛmt], *adj.* strange, foreign, outlandish; odd.

fremdartig [´frɛmtartɪç], *adj.* strange, odd.

Fremde (1) [´frɛmdə], *f.* (—, *no pl.*) foreign country; *in die* — *gehen*, go abroad.

Fremde (2) [´frɛmdə], *m.* (—n, *pl.* —n) stranger, foreigner.

Fremdheit [´frɛmthaɪt], *f.* (—, *no pl.*) strangeness.

Freßbeutel [´frɛsboytəl], *m.* (—s, *pl.* —) nose-bag.

Fresse [´frɛsə], *f.* (—, *pl.* —n) (*vulg.*) mouth, snout.

fressen [´frɛsən], *v.a. irr.* (*animals*) eat; (*also fig.*) devour.

Fresserei [´frɛsəraɪ], *f.* (—, *no pl.*) gluttony.

Frettchen [´frɛtçən], *n.* (—s, *pl.* —) (*Zool.*) ferret.

Freude [´froydə], *f.* (—, *pl.* —n) joy, joyfulness, gladness, enjoyment, delight, pleasure.

Freudenfest [´froydənfɛst], *n.* (—s, *pl.* —e) feast, jubilee.

Freudenhaus [´froydənhaus], *n.* (—es, *pl.* ̶er) brothel.

Freudenmädchen [´froydənmɛːtçən], *n.* (—s, *pl.* —) prostitute.

freudig [´froydɪç], *adj.* joyful, cheerful, glad.

freudlos [´froytloːs], *adj.* joyless.

freuen [´froyən], *v.r. sich* —, rejoice (at), be glad (of); *sich auf etwas* —, look forward to s.th.

Freund [froynt], *m.* (—es, *pl.* —e) friend.

freundlich [´froyntlɪç], *adj.* friendly, kind, affable, pleasing, cheerful, pleasant, genial.

Freundschaft [´froyntʃaft], *f.* (—, *pl.* —en) friendship.

Frevel [´freːfəl], *m.* (—s, *pl.* —) crime, misdeed, offence.

Fühler

freveln ['fre:fəln], *v.n.* do wrong, trespass, commit an outrage.
Friede(n) ['fri:də(n)], *m.* (—ns, *no pl.*) peace.
friedfertig ['fri:tfɛrtɪç], *adj.* peaceable.
Friedhof ['fri:tho:f], *m.* (—s, *pl.* ⁻e) churchyard, cemetery.
friedlich ['fri:tlɪç], *adj.* peaceful.
friedliebend ['fri:tli:bənt], *adj.* peaceable, peace-loving.
Friedrich ['fri:drɪç], *m.* Frederic(k).
friedselig ['fri:tze:lɪç], *adj.* peaceable.
frieren ['fri:rən], *v.n. irr.* feel cold, freeze.
Fries [fri:s], *m.* (—es, *pl.* —e) frieze.
Friese ['fri:zə], *m.* (—n, *pl.* —n) Frisian.
frisch [frɪʃ], *adj.* fresh; new; (*weather*) crisp; (*fig.*) lively, brisk, gay.
Frische ['frɪʃə], *f.* (—, *no pl.*) freshness, liveliness, gaiety.
Friseur [fri'zo:r], *m.* (—s, *pl.* —e) hairdresser, barber.
Friseuse [fri'zo:zə], *f.* (—, *pl.* —n) female hairdresser.
frisieren [fri'zi:rən], *v.a.* dress (s.o.'s) hair.
Frist [frɪst], *f.* (—, *pl.* —en) time, term, period; (fixed) term; delay, respite.
fristen ['frɪstən], *v.a. das Leben —,* gain a bare living.
Frisur [fri'zu:r], *f.* (—, *pl.* —en) coiffure, hair-style.
frivol [fri'vo:l], *adj.* frivolous.
Frivolität [frivo:li'tɛ:t], *f.* (—, *pl.* —en) frivolity.
froh [fro:], *adj.* glad, joyful, joyous.
frohgelaunt ['fro:gəlaunt], *adj.* good-humoured, cheerful.
fröhlich ['frø:lɪç], *adj.* gay, merry.
frohlocken [fro:'lɔkən], *v.n.* (*rare*) exult.
Frohsinn ['fro:zɪn], *m.* (—s, *no pl.*) good humour, gaiety.
fromm [frɔm], *adj.* pious, religious, devout.
frommen ['frɔmən], *v.n.* (*obs.*) be of advantage (to s.o.).
Frömmigkeit ['frœmɪçkaɪt], *f.* (—, *no pl.*) piety, devoutness.
Fron [fro:n], *f.* (—, *no pl.*) (feudal) service; statute labour.
frönen ['frø:nən], *v.n.* (*fig.*) be a slave to; indulge in (*Dat.*).
Fronleichnam [fro:n'laɪxna:m], *m.* (*Eccl.*) (feast of) Corpus Christi.
Front [frɔnt], *f.* (—, *pl.* —en) front, forepart; (*building*) elevation; (*Mil.*) front line.
Frosch [frɔʃ], *m.* (—es, *pl.* ⁻e) (*Zool.*) frog.
Frost [frɔst], *m.* (—es, *pl.* ⁻e) frost; coldness, chill.
Frostbeule ['frɔstbɔylə], *f.* (—, *pl.* —n) chilblain.
frösteln ['frœstəln], *v.n.* feel a chill, shiver.
frostig ['frɔstɪç], *adj.* frosty; cold, chilly.
frottieren [frɔ'ti:rən], *v.a.* rub (down).

Frottiertuch [frɔ'ti:rtu:x], *n.* (—s, *pl.* ⁻er) Turkish towel, bath towel.
Frucht [fruxt], *f.* (—, *pl.* ⁻e) fruit; (*fig.*) result, effect; (*Med.*) foetus.
fruchtbar ['fruxtba:r], *adj.* fruitful, productive, fertile.
fruchten ['fruxtən], *v.n.* produce fruit; (*fig.*) be effectual.
Fruchtknoten ['fruxtkno:tən], *m.* (—s, *pl.* —) (*Bot.*) seed-vessel.
früh(e) [fry:(ə)], *adj.* early.
Frühe ['fry:ə], *f.* (—, *no pl.*) early morning, dawn.
früher ['fry:ər], *adv.* earlier (on), formerly.
frühestens ['fry:əstəns], *adv.* at the earliest (possible moment).
Frühjahr ['fry:ja:r], *n.*, **Frühling** ['fry:lɪn], *m.* (—s, *pl.* —e) spring.
frühreif ['fry:raɪf], *adj.* precocious.
Frühschoppen ['fry:ʃɔpən], *m.* (—s, *pl.* —) morning pint (beer *or* wine).
Frühstück ['fry:ʃtyk], *n.* (—s, *pl.* —e) breakfast; *zweites —,* lunch.
Fuchs [fuks], *m.* (—es, *pl.* ⁻e) fox; chestnut (horse); (*fig.*) cunning chap; (*student*) freshman.
Fuchsbau ['fuksbau], *m.* (—s, *pl.* —e) fox-hole.
Fuchseisen ['fuksaɪzən], *n.* (—s, *pl.* —) fox-trap.
fuchsen ['fuksən], *v.r. sich — über,* be annoyed about.
Fuchsie ['fuksjə], *f.* (—, *pl.* —n) (*Bot.*) fuchsia.
fuchsig ['fuksɪç], *adj.* (*coll.*) very angry.
Füchsin ['fyksɪn], *f.* (—, *pl.* —innen) vixen.
fuchsrot ['fuksro:t], *adj.* fox-coloured, sorrel.
Fuchsschwanz ['fuksʃvants], *m.* (—es, *pl.* ⁻e) fox-brush; pad saw.
Fuchtel ['fuxtəl], *f.* (—, *pl.* —e) sword blade; rod, whip.
Fuder ['fu:dər], *n.* (—s, *pl.* —) load, cart-load; wine measure (c. 270 gallons).
Fug ['fu:k], *m.* (—s, *no pl.*) (*rare*) right, justice; *mit — und Recht,* with every right.
Fuge (1) ['fu:gə], *f.* (—, *pl.* —n) joint, groove.
Fuge (2) ['fu:gə], *f.* (—, *pl.* —n) (*Mus.*) fugue.
fügen ['fy:gən], *v.a.* fit together, join, dovetail. — *v.r. sich —,* submit (to), accommodate o.s. (to).
fügsam ['fy:kza:m], *adj.* pliant, submissive, yielding.
Fügung ['fy:gun], *f.* (—, *pl.* —en) coincidence; dispensation (of Providence); Providence).
fühlbar ['fy:lba:r], *adj.* perceptible; tangible; *sich — machen,* make o.s. felt.
fühlen ['fy:lən], *v.a.* feel, touch, sense, be aware of.
Fühler ['fy:lər], *m.* (—s, *pl.* —) tentacle, feeler.

77

Fühlhorn

Fühlhorn [ˈfyːlhɔrn], *n.* (—s, *pl.* ˙er) feeler, antenna, tentacle.

Fühlung [ˈfyːluŋ], *f.* (—, *no pl.*) — *haben mit*, be in touch with.

Fuhre [ˈfuːrə], *f.* (—, *pl.* —n) conveyance, vehicle, cart-load.

führen [ˈfyːrən], *v.a.* lead, guide, conduct, command; (*pen*) wield; (*law-suit*) carry on; (*conversation*) have, keep up; (*name, title*) bear; (*goods*) stock, deal in; *Krieg* —, wage war; *etwas im Schilde* —, have a plan; *das Wort* —, be spokesman; *einen hinters Licht* —, cheat s.o.

Führer [ˈfyːrər], *m.* (—s, *pl.* —) leader, guide; head, manager; conductor; driver, pilot.

Führerschaft [ˈfyːrərʃaft], *f.* (—, *no pl.*) leadership.

Führerschein [ˈfyːrərʃain], *m.* (—s, *pl.* —e) driving-licence.

Führersitz [ˈfyːrərzits], *m.* (—es, *pl.* —e) driver's seat; pilot's cockpit.

Fuhrlohn [ˈfuːrloːn], *m.* (—s, *no pl.*) cartage, carriage.

Fuhrmann [ˈfuːrman], *m.* (—s, *pl.* ˙er) carter, carrier.

Führung [ˈfyːruŋ], *f.* (—, *no pl.*) guidance; leadership; conducted tour; management, direction; behaviour, conduct.

Führungszeugnis [ˈfyːruŋstsɔyknis], *n.* (—sses, *pl.* —sse) certificate of good conduct.

Fuhrwerk [ˈfuːrvɛrk], *n.* (—s, *pl.* —e) carriage, vehicle, waggon.

Fuhrwesen [ˈfuːrveːzən], *n.* (—s, *no pl.*) transport services, transportation.

Fülle [ˈfylə], *f.* (—, *no pl.*) fullness; abundance, plenty.

Füllen [ˈfylən], *n.* (—s, *pl.* —) foal.

füllen [ˈfylən], *v.a.* fill, fill up; stuff.

Füllfederhalter [ˈfylfeːdərhaltər], *m.* (—s, *pl.* —) fountain-pen.

Füllung [ˈfyluŋ], *f.* (—, *pl.* —en) filling; stuffing; (*door*) panel.

fummeln [ˈfuməln], *v.n.* fumble.

Fund [funt], *m.* (—es, *pl.* —e) find; discovery.

Fundbüro [ˈfuntbyroː], *n.* (—s, *pl.* —s) lost property office.

Fundgrube [ˈfuntgruːbə], *f.* (—, *pl.* —n) gold-mine, source, treasure-house.

fundieren [funˈdiːrən], *v.a.* found; establish.

fünf [fynf], *num. adj.* five.

Fünfeck [ˈfynfɛk], *n.* (—s, *pl.* —e) pentagon.

Fünffüßler [ˈfynffyːslər], *m.* (—s, *pl.* —) (*Poet.*) pentameter.

fünfjährig [ˈfynfjɛːriç], *num. adj.* five-year-old.

fünfjährlich [ˈfynfjɛːrliç], *num. adj.* quinquennial, five-yearly.

fünfzehn [ˈfynftseːn], *num. adj.* fifteen.

fünfzig [ˈfynftsiç], *num. adj.* fifty.

fungieren [fuŋˈgiːrən], *v.n.* — *als*, act as, officiate as.

Funk [fuŋk], *m.* (—s, *no pl.*) radio; wireless; telegraphy.

Funke [ˈfuŋkə], *m.* (—n, *pl.* —n) spark, sparkle.

funkeln [ˈfuŋkəln], *v.n.* sparkle, glitter; (*stars*) twinkle.

funkelnagelneu [ˈfuŋkəlnaːgəlnɔy], *adj.* (*coll.*) brand-new.

funken [ˈfuŋkən], *v.a.* flash (messages); telegraph, broadcast.

Funker [ˈfuŋkər], *m.* (—s, *pl.* —) wireless operator.

Funksender [ˈfuŋkzɛndər], *m.* (—s, *pl.* —) radio-transmitter.

Funkspruch [ˈfuŋkʃprux], *m.* (—s, *pl.* ˙e) wireless-message.

Funktelegramm [ˈfuŋktelegram], *n.* (—s, *pl.* —e) radio telegram.

für [fyːr], *prep.* (*Acc.*) for, instead of; *ein — allemal*, once and for all; *an und — sich*, in itself.

Fürbitte [ˈfyːrbitə], *f.* (—, *pl.* —n) intercession.

Furche [ˈfurçə], *f.* (—, *pl.* —n) furrow; (*face*) wrinkle.

furchen [ˈfurçən], *v.a.* furrow; (*face*) wrinkle.

Furcht [furçt], *f.* (—, *no pl.*) fear, worry, anxiety; dread, fright, terror, apprehension.

furchtbar [ˈfurçtbaːr], *adj.* dreadful, terrible, frightful.

fürchten [ˈfyrçtən], *v.a.* fear, be afraid of. — *v.r. sich — vor*, be afraid of.

fürchterlich [ˈfyrçtərliç], *adj.* terrible, horrible, awful.

furchtsam [ˈfurçtzaːm], *adj.* timid, fearful, apprehensive.

Furie [ˈfuːriə], *f.* (—, *pl.* —n) fury, virago.

fürlieb [fyrˈliːp], *adv.* *mit etwas* — *nehmen*, put up with, be content with s.th.

Furnier [furˈniːr], *n.* (—s, *pl.* —e) veneer, inlay.

Furore [fuˈroːrə], *n.* (—s, *no pl.*) — *machen*, cause a sensation, create an uproar.

Fürsorge [ˈfyːrzɔrgə], *f.* (—, *no pl.*) solicitude; provision; welfare.

fürsorglich [ˈfyːrzɔrgliç], *adj.* thoughtful, with loving care.

Fürsprache [ˈfyːrʃpraːxə], *f.* (—, *no pl.*) advocacy, intercession.

Fürst [fyrst], *m.* (—en, *pl.* —en) prince, sovereign.

Furt [furt], *f.* (—, *pl.* —en) ford.

Furunkel [fuˈruŋkəl], *m.* (—s, *pl.* —) furuncle, boil.

Fürwort [ˈfyːrvɔrt], *n.* (—s, *pl.* ˙er) pronoun.

Fusel [ˈfuːzəl], *m.* (—s, *no pl.*) bad liquor, (*Am.*) hooch (*sl.*).

Fuß [fuːs], *m.* (—es, *pl.* ˙e) (*human*) foot; (*object*) base.

Fußangel [ˈfuːsaŋəl], *f.* (—, *pl.* —n) man-trap.

Fußball [ˈfuːsbal], *m.* (—s, *pl.* ˙e) football.

Fußboden ['fu:sbo:dən], *m.* (—s, *pl.* ⁻) floor.
fußen ['fu:sən], *v.n.* — *auf*, be based upon.
fußfrei ['fu:sfraɪ], *adj.* ankle-length.
Fußgänger ['fu:sgɛŋər], *m.* (—s, *pl.* —) pedestrian.
Fußgestell ['fu:sgəʃtɛl], *n.* (—s, *pl.* —e) pedestal.
Fußpflege ['fu:spfle:gə], *f.* (—, *no pl.*) chiropody.
Fußpunkt ['fu:spuŋkt], *m.* (—s, *no pl.*) nadir.
Fußtritt ['fu:strɪt], *m.* (—s, *pl.* —e) kick.
futsch [futʃ], *excl.* (*coll.*) gone, lost.
Futter ['futər], *n.* (—s, *no pl.*) (*dress*) lining; (*animals*) fodder, feed.
Futteral [futə'ra:l], *n.* (—s, *pl.* —e) case; sheath.
Futterkräuter ['futərkrɔytər], *n. pl.* herbage.
futtern ['futərn], *v.n.* (*coll.*) feed, stuff o.s.
füttern ['fytərn], *v.a.* feed; (*garment*) line.

G

G [ge:], *n.* (—s, *pl.* —s) the letter G; (*Mus.*) *G Dur*, G major; (*Mus.*) *G Moll*, G minor; (*Mus.*) — *-Saite*, G string.
Gabe ['ga:bə], *f.* (—, *pl.* —n) gift, present; donation; *barmherzige* —, alms; (*fig.*) gift, talent.
Gabel ['ga:bəl], *f.* (—, *pl.* —n) fork; (*deer*) antler; (*cart*) shafts.
gabelig ['ga:bəlɪç], *adj.* forked.
Gabelung ['ga:bəluŋ], *f.* (—, *pl.* —en) bifurcation, branching (of road).
Gabelzinke ['ga:bəltsɪŋkə], *f.* (—, *pl.* —n) prong, tine.
Gabun [ga'bu:n], *n.* Gaboon.
gackern ['gakərn], *v.n.* cackle; (*fig.*) chatter.
gaffen ['gafən], *v.n.* gape (at), stare.
Gage ['ga:ʒə], *f.* (—, *pl.* —n) salary, pay, fee.
gähnen ['gɛ:nən], *v.n.* yawn, gape.
Galan [ga'la:n], *m.* (—s, *pl.* —e) lover, gallant.
galant [ga'lant], *adj.* polite, courteous; *—es Abenteuer*, love affair.
Galanterie [galantə'ri:], *f.* (—, *pl.* —n) courtesy.
Galanteriewaren [galantə'ri:va:rən], *f. pl.* fancy goods.
Galeere [ga'le:rə], *f.* (—, *pl.* —n) galley.
Galerie [galə'ri:], *f.* (—, *pl.* —n) gallery.
Galgen ['galgən], *m.* (—s, *pl.* —) gallows, gibbet; scaffold.

Galgenfrist ['galgənfrɪst], *f.* (—, *no pl.*) short delay, respite.
Galgenhumor ['galgənhumo:r], *m.* (—s, *no pl.*) wry *or* grim humour.
Galgenvogel ['galgənfo:gəl], *m.* (—s, *pl.* ⁻) gallows-bird.
Galizien [ga'li:tsjən], *n.* Galicia.
Gallapfel ['galapfəl], *m.* (—s, *pl.* ⁻) gall-nut.
Galle ['galə], *f.* (—, *pl.* —n) gall, bile.
Gallenblase ['galənbla:zə], *f.* (—, *pl.* —n) gall-bladder.
Gallert ['galərt], *n.* (—s, *no pl.*) jelly.
Gallien ['galjən], *n.* Gaul.
gallig ['galɪç], *adj.* bilious.
galvanisieren [galvanı'zi:rən], *v.a.* galvanize.
Gamaschen [ga'maʃən], *f. pl.* spats, gaiters.
Gang [gaŋ], *m.* (—es, *pl.* ⁻e) walk, gait; (*horse*) pace; (*house*) passage, corridor; (*meal*) course, dish; (*action*) progress, course; (*sport*) round, bout; (*machine*) motion; stroke; (*Motor.*) gear.
gang [gaŋ], *adj.* — *und gäbe*, customary, usual, common.
Gangart ['gaŋa:rt], *f.* (—, *pl.* —en) gait; (*horse*) pace.
gangbar ['gaŋba:r], *adj.* marketable, saleable; (*road*) passable; practicable.
Gans [gans], *f.* (—, *pl.* ⁻e) (*Orn.*) goose.
Gänseblümchen ['gɛnzəbly:mçən], *n.* (—s, *pl.*—) daisy.
Gänsefüßchen ['gɛnzəfy:sçən], *n. pl.* (*coll.*) inverted commas, quotation marks.
Gänsehaut ['gɛnzəhaut], *f.* (—, *no pl.*) goose-flesh, goose-pimples.
Gänserich ['gɛnzərɪç], *m.* (—s, *pl.* —e) (*Orn.*) gander.
ganz ['gants], *adj.* whole, entire, all; complete, total.
gänzlich ['gɛntslɪç], *adj.* whole, total, entire, full, complete.
gar [ga:r], *adj.* sufficiently cooked, done. — *adv.* very, quite.
garantieren [garan'ti:rən], *v.a.* guarantee, warrant.
Garaus ['ga:raus], *m.* (—, *no pl.*) *einem den* — *machen*, finish s.o., kill s.o.
Garbe ['garbə], *f.* (—, *pl.* —n) sheaf.
Garde ['gardə], *f.* (—, *pl.* —n) guard, guards.
Garderobe [gardə'ro:bə], *f.* (—, *pl.* —n) wardrobe; cloak-room; (*Theat.*) dressing-room.
Gardine [gar'di:nə], *f.* (—, *pl.* —n) curtain.
Gardist [gar'dɪst], *m.* (—en, *pl.* —en) guardsman.
gären ['gɛ:rən], *v.n.* ferment; effervesce.
Garn [garn], *n.* (—s, *pl.* —e) yarn, thread.
Garnele [gar'ne:lə], *f.* (—, *pl.* —n) (*Zool.*) shrimp; *große* —, prawn.
garnieren [gar'ni:rən], *v.a.* trim, garnish.
Garnison [garni'zo:n], *f.* (—, *pl.* —en) garrison.

Garnitur

Garnitur [garni'tuːr], *f.* (—, *pl.* **—en**) trimming; set.

Garnröllchen ['garnrœlçən], *n.* (—s, *pl.* —) reel of thread.

garstig ['garstɪç], *adj.* nasty, loathsome, ugly.

Garten ['gartən], *m.* (—s, *pl.* ⸚) garden.

Gartenlaube ['gartənlaubə], *f.* (—, *pl.* —n) bower, arbour.

Gärtner ['gɛrtnər], *m.* (—s, *pl.* —) gardener.

Gärtnerei [gɛrtnə'raɪ], *f.* (—, *pl.* —en) horticulture; market-garden; (plant) nursery.

Gärung ['gɛːruŋ], *f.* (—, *pl.* —en) fermentation, effervescence.

Gas [gaːs], *n.* (—es, —e) gas; — *geben*, (*Motor.*) accelerate.

gasartig ['gaːsartɪç], *adj.* gaseous.

Gäßchen ['gɛsçən], *n.* (—s, *pl.* —) narrow alley; lane.

Gasse ['gasə], *f.* (—, *pl.* —n) alleyway, lane; (*rare*) street.

Gassenbube ['gasənbuːbə] *see* **Gassenjunge**.

Gassenhauer ['gasənhauər], *m.* (—s, *pl.* —), street-song, vulgar ballad; pop song.

Gassenjunge ['gasənjuŋə], *m.* (—n, *pl.* —n) street-urchin.

Gast [gast], *m.* (—s, *pl.* ⸚e) guest, visitor.

gastfrei ['gastfraɪ], *adj.* hospitable.

Gastfreund ['gastfrɔynt], *m.* (—s, *pl.* —e) guest; host.

Gastfreundschaft ['gastfrɔyntʃaft], *f.* (—, *no pl.*) hospitality.

Gastgeber ['gastgeːbər], *m.* (—s, *pl.* —) host.

Gasthaus ['gasthaus], *n.* (—es, *pl.* ⸚er), **Gasthof** ['gasthoːf], *m.* (—es, *pl.* ⸚e) inn, hotel, public house.

gastieren [gas'tiːrən], *v.n.* (*Theat.*) appear as a guest artist; star.

gastlich ['gastlɪç], *adj.* hospitable.

Gastmahl ['gastmaːl], *n.* (—s, *pl.* —e) banquet, feast.

Gastrecht ['gastrɛçt], *n.* (—s, *no pl.*) right of hospitality.

Gastspiel ['gastʃpiːl], *n.* (—s, *pl.* —e) (*Theat.*) performance by visiting company.

Gaststätte ['gaststɛtə], *f.* (—, *pl.* —n) restaurant.

Gaststube ['gastʃtuːbə], *f.* (—, *pl.* —n) hotel lounge; guest room.

Gastwirt ['gastvɪrt], *m.* (—s, *pl.* —e) landlord.

Gastwirtin ['gastvɪrtɪn], *f.* (—, *pl.* —nen) landlady.

Gastzimmer ['gasttsɪmər], *n.* (—s, *pl.* —) *see* **Gaststube**; spare bedroom.

Gatte ['gatə], *m.* (—n, *pl.* —n) husband, spouse, consort.

Gatter ['gatər], *n.* (—s, *pl.* —) grate, lattice, grating.

Gattin ['gatɪn], *f.* (—, *pl.* —nen) wife, spouse, consort.

Gattung ['gatuŋ], *f.* (—, *pl.* —en) kind, species, sort, class; breed, genus; (*Lit.*) genre.

Gau [gau], *m.* (—s, *pl.* —e) district, province.

gaukeln ['gaukəln], *v.n.* juggle. — *v.a.* dazzle.

Gaul [gaul], *m.* (—s, *pl.* ⸚e) (old) horse, nag; *einem geschenkten — sieht man nicht ins Maul*, never look a gift horse in the mouth.

Gaumen ['gaumən], *m.* (—s, *pl.* —) palate.

Gauner ['gaunər], *m.* (—s, *pl.* —) rogue, sharper, swindler, cheat.

gaunern ['gaunərn], *v.n.* cheat, trick, swindle.

Gaunersprache ['gaunərʃpraːxə], *f.* (—, *no pl.*) thieves' slang.

Gaze ['gaːzə], *f.* (—, *pl.* —n) gauze.

Gazelle [ga'tsɛlə], *f.* (—, *pl.* —n) (*Zool.*) gazelle, antelope.

Geächtete [gə'ɛçtətə], *m.* (—n, *pl.* —n) outlaw.

Geächze [gə'ɛçtsə], *n.* (—s, *no pl.*) moaning, groaning.

Geäder [gə'ɛːdər], *n.* (—s, *no pl.*) veins, arteries; veining.

geädert [gə'ɛdərt], *adj.* veined, streaked; grained.

-geartet [gə'aːrtət], *adj.* (*suffix in compounds*) —natured.

Gebäck [gə'bɛk], *n.* (—s, *no pl.*) pastry, rolls, cakes.

Gebälk [gə'bɛlk], *n.* (—s, *no pl.*) timberwork, timber-frame.

Gebärde [gə'bɛːrdə], *f.* (—, *pl.* —n) gesture.

gebärden [gə'bɛːrdən], *v.r. sich* —, behave.

Gebaren [gə'baːrən], *n.* (—s, *no pl.*) demeanour.

gebären [gə'bɛːrən], *v.a. irr.* bear, bring forth, give birth to, be delivered of.

Gebärmutter [gə'bɛːrmutər], *f.* (—, *no pl.*) womb, uterus.

Gebäude [gə'bɔydə], *n.* (—s, *pl.* —) building, edifice.

Gebein [gə'baɪn], *n.* (—s, *pl.* —e) bones, skeleton; (*fig.*) remains.

Gebell [gə'bɛl], *n.* (—s, *no pl.*) barking.

geben ['geːbən], *v.a. irr.* give, present; confer, bestow; yield; (*cards*) deal. — *v.r. sich* —, show o.s., behave; abate; *das gibt sich*, that won't last long; *es gibt . . .*, there is . . .; *was gibt's?* what's the matter?

Geber ['geːbər], *m.* (—s, *pl.* —) giver, donor.

Gebet [gə'beːt], *n.* (—s, *pl.* —e) prayer; *sein — verrichten*, say o.'s prayers; *ins — nehmen*, question s.o. thoroughly.

Gebiet [gə'biːt], *n.* (—s, *pl.* —e) district, territory; (*Am.*) precinct; jurisdiction; (*fig.*) province, field, sphere, domain.

gebieten [gə'biːtən], *v.a. irr.* command, order.

Gebieter [gə'biːtər], *m.* (—s, *pl.* —) lord, master, ruler.

Gefährte

Gebilde [gə'bɪldə], *n.* (—s, *pl.* —) form, thing; formation, structure; figment.
gebildet [gə'bɪldət], *adj.* educated, cultured, refined.
Gebirge [gə'bɪrgə], *n.* (—s, *pl.* —) mountains.
Gebirgskamm [gə'bɪrkskam], *m.* (—s, *pl.* ¨e) mountain-ridge.
Gebiß [gə'bɪs], *n.* (—sses, *pl.* —sse) set of (false) teeth, denture; (*horse*) bit.
Gebläse [gə'blɛ:zə], *n.* (—s, *pl.* —) bellows; blower.
Gebläsemaschine [gə'blɛ:zəmaʃi:nə], *f.* (—, *pl.* —n) blower.
Gebläseofen [gə'blɛ:zɔɔ:fən], *m.* (—s, *pl.* ¨) blast-furnace.
geblümt [gə'bly:mt], *adj.* flowered.
Geblüt [gə'bly:t], *n.* (—s, *no pl.*) blood; race, line, lineage, stock.
geboren [gə'bo:rən], *adj.* born.
geborgen [gə'bɔrgən], *adj.* saved, hidden, sheltered, rescued.
Gebot [gə'bo:t], *n.* (—s, *pl.* —e) order, decree, command; (*Bibl.*) Commandment.
geboten [gə'bo:tən], *adj.* necessary, advisable.
Gebräu [gə'brɔy], *n.* (—s, *no pl.*) brew, concoction, mixture.
Gebrauch [gə'braux], *m.* (—s, *pl.* ¨e) use; employment; custom, usage, habit, practice; (*rare*) rite.
gebrauchen [gə'brauxən], *v.a.* use, make use of, employ.
gebräuchlich [gə'brɔyçlɪç], *adj.* usual, customary, common.
Gebrauchsanweisung [gə'brauxsanvaɪzuŋ], *f.* (—, *pl.* —en) directions for use.
gebraucht [gə'brauxt], *adj.* used, second-hand.
Gebrechen [gə'brɛçən], *n.* (—s, *pl.* —) infirmity.
gebrechen [gə'brɛçən], *v.n. irr. es gebricht mir an,* I am in want of, I lack.
gebrechlich [gə'brɛçlɪç], *adj.* infirm, frail, weak.
gebrochen [gə'brɔxən], *adj.* broken; —*es Deutsch,* broken German.
Gebrüder [gə'bry:dər], *m. pl.* (*Comm.*) brothers.
Gebrüll [gə'bryl], *n.* (—s, *no pl.*) roaring; (*cows*) lowing.
Gebühr [gə'by:r], *f.* (—, *pl.* —en) charge, due; fee; tax, duty.
gebühren [gə'by:rən], *v.n.* be due to s.o. — *v.r. sich* —, *wie es sich gebührt,* as it ought to be, as is right and proper.
gebunden [gə'bundən], *adj.* (*fig.*) bound, committed; (*Poet.*) metrical.
Geburt [gə'burt], *f.* (—, *pl.* —en) birth.
gebürtig [gə'byrtɪç], *adj.* a native of.
Geburtsfehler [gə'burtsfe:lər], *m.* (—s, *pl.* —) congenital defect.
Geburtshelfer [gə'burtshɛlfər], *m.* (—s, *pl.* —) obstetrician.
Geburtshelferin [gə'burtshɛlfərɪn], *f.* (—, *pl.* —nen) midwife.

Geburtsort [gə'burtsɔrt], *m.* (—s, *pl.* —e) birthplace.
Geburtsschein [gə'burtsʃaɪn], *m.* (—(e)s, *pl.* —e) birth certificate.
Geburtswehen [gə'burtsve:ən], *f. pl.* birthpangs; labour pains.
Gebüsch [gə'byʃ], *n.* (—es, *pl.* —e) bushes, thicket; underwood.
Geck [gɛk], *m.* (—en, *pl.* —en) fop, dandy; (*carnival*) fool.
geckenhaft ['gɛkənhaft], *adj.* foppish, dandyish.
Gedächtnis [gə'dɛçtnɪs], *n.* (—ses, *no pl.*) memory; remembrance, recollection; *im* — *behalten,* keep in mind.
Gedanke [gə'daŋkə], *m.* (—ns, *pl.* —n) thought, idea.
Gedankenfolge [gə'daŋkənfɔlgə], *f.* (—, *no pl.*), **Gedankengang** [gə'daŋkəngaŋ], *m.* (—s, *pl.* ¨e) sequence of thought, train of thought.
Gedankenstrich [gə'daŋkənʃtrɪç], *m.* (—s, *pl.* —e) dash; hyphen.
Gedärm [gə'dɛrm], *n.* (—s, *pl.* —e) bowels, intestines, entrails.
Gedeck [gə'dɛk], *n.* (—s, *pl.* —e) cover; menu; place laid at a table.
gedeihen [gə'daɪən], *v.n. irr.* (*aux. sein*) thrive, prosper; progress.
gedeihlich [gə'daɪlɪç], *adj.* thriving, salutary.
gedenken [gə'dɛŋkən], *v.n. irr.* (*Genit.*) think of, remember; — *etwas zu tun,* intend to do s.th.
Gedenken [gə'dɛŋkən], *n.* (—s, *no pl.*) remembrance.
Gedenkfeier [gə'dɛŋkfaɪər], *f.* (—, *pl.* —n) commemoration.
Gedicht [gə'dɪçt], *n.* (—s, *pl.* —e) poem.
gediegen [gə'di:gən], *adj.* solid, sound, genuine, true, honourable, sterling.
Gedränge [gə'drɛŋə], *n.* (—s, *no pl.*) crowd, throng; crush.
Gedrängtheit [gə'drɛnkthaɪt], *f.* (—, *no pl.*) conciseness.
gedrungen [gə'druŋən], *adj.* thick-set, stocky; compact; concise (style).
Geduld [gə'dult], *f.* (—, *no pl.*) patience, forbearance.
gedulden [gə'duldən], *v.r. sich* —, be patient.
geduldig [gə'duldɪç], *adj.* patient, forbearing, indulgent.
Geduld(s)spiel [gə'dult(s)ʃpi:l], *n.* (—s, *pl.* —e) puzzle; (*Cards*) patience.
gedunsen [gə'dunzən], *adj.* bloated.
geeignet [gə'aɪgnet], *adj.* suitable, fit, appropriate, apt.
Gefahr [gə'fa:r], *f.* (—, *pl.* —en) danger, peril, hazard, risk; — *laufen,* run the risk.
gefährden [gə'fɛ:rdən], *v.a.* endanger, imperil, jeopardize.
gefährlich [gə'fɛ:rlɪç], *adj.* dangerous, perilous.
Gefährt [gə'fɛ:rt], *n.* (—s, *pl.* —e) (*obs.*) vehicle, conveyance.
Gefährte [gə'fɛ:rtə], *m.* (—en, *pl.* —en) comrade, companion, fellow.

81

Gefälle

Gefälle [gə'fɛlə], *n.* (**—s**, *pl.* **—e**) fall, descent, incline, gradient.

Gefallen [gə'falən], *m.* (**—s**, *no pl.*) pleasure, liking; favour, kindness.

gefallen (1) [gə'falən], *v.n. irr.* please; *es gefällt mir,* I like it; *wie gefällt Ihnen . . .;* how do you like . . ..

gefallen (2) [gə'falən], *adj.* (*Mil.*) fallen, killed in action.

gefällig [gə'fɛlɪç], *adj.* pleasing, accommodating, obliging, anxious to please; *was ist* —? what can I do for you?

Gefälligkeit [gə'fɛlɪçkaɪt], *f.* (**—**, *pl.* **—en**) courtesy; favour, service, good turn.

gefälligst [gə'fɛlɪçst], *adv.* if you please.

Gefallsucht [gə'falzuxt], *f.* (**—**, *no pl.*) coquetry.

gefallsüchtig [gə'falzyçtɪç], *adj.* coquettish.

gefangen [gə'faŋən], *adj.* in prison, imprisoned, captive.

Gefangene [gə'faŋənə], *m.* (**—n**, *pl.* **—n**) prisoner, captive.

Gefangennahme [gə'faŋənnɑːmə], *f.* (**—**, *no pl.*) arrest, capture.

Gefangenschaft [gə'faŋənʃaft], *f.* (**—**, *no pl.*) captivity, imprisonment, detention; *in — geraten,* be taken prisoner.

Gefängis [gə'fɛŋnɪs], *n.* (**—sses**, *pl.* **—sse**) prison, gaol.

Gefäß [gə'fɛːs], *n.* (**—es**, *pl.* **—e**) vessel.

gefaßt [gə'fast], *adj.* collected, composed, ready; calm; *sich auf etwas — machen,* prepare o.s. for s.th.

Gefecht [gə'fɛçt], *n.* (**—s**, *pl.* **—e**) fight, battle, combat; action, engagement.

gefeit [gə'faɪt], *adj.* proof against.

Gefieder [gə'fiːdər], *n.* (**—s**, *no pl.*) plumage, feathers.

Gefilde [gə'fɪldə], *n.* (**—s**, *pl.* **—**) (*Poet.*) fields, plain.

Geflecht [gə'flɛçt], *n.* (**—s**, *no pl.*) wicker-work, texture.

geflissentlich [gə'flɪsəntlɪç], *adj.* intentional, wilful, with a purpose.

Geflügel [gə'flyːgəl], *n.* (**—s**, *no pl.*) fowls, poultry.

geflügelt [gə'flyːgəlt], *adj.* winged; *—e Worte,* household word, familiar quotation.

Geflüster [gə'flystər], *n.* (**—s**, *no pl.*) whispering, whisper.

Gefolge [gə'fɔlgə], *n.* (**—s**, *no pl.*) retinue, following.

gefräßig [gə'frɛːsɪç], *adj.* voracious, gluttonous.

Gefreite [gə'fraɪtə], *m.* (**—n**, *pl.* **—n**) (*Mil.*) lance-corporal.

gefrieren [gə'friːrən], *v.n. irr.* (*aux.* sein) freeze; congeal.

Gefrierpunkt [gə'friːrpuŋkt], *m.* (**—s**, *no pl.*) freezing point, zero.

Gefrorene [gə'froːrənə], *n.* (**—n**, *no pl.*) ice-cream.

Gefüge [gə'fyːgə], *n.* (**—s**, *no pl.*) joints, structure, construction; frame.

gefügig [gə'fyːgɪç], *adj.* pliant; docile; *einen — machen,* make s.o. amenable, persuade s.o.

Gefühl [gə'fyːl], *n.* (**—s**, *pl.* **—e**) feeling, sense, sensation.

gegen ['geːgən], *prep.* (*Acc.*) against; towards; about, near; in comparison with; in the direction of; opposed to; in exchange for; — *Quittung,* against receipt. — *adv., prefix.* counter, opposing, contrary.

Gegend ['geːgənt], *f.* (**—**, *pl.* **—en**) region, country, part.

Gegengewicht ['geːgəngəvɪçt], *n.* (**—s**, *pl.* **—e**) counterweight, counterpoise.

Gegengift ['geːgəngɪft], *n.* (**—s**, *pl.* **—e**) antidote.

Gegenleistung ['geːgənlaɪstuŋ], *f.* (**—**, *pl.* **—en**) return; service in return; *Leistung und —,* give and take.

Gegenrede ['geːgənreːdə], *f.* (**—**, *pl.* **—n**) contradiction; objection.

Gegensatz ['geːgənzats], *m.* (**—es**, *pl.* **—e**) contrast, opposition, antithesis.

gegensätzlich ['geːgənzɛtslɪç], *adj.* contrary, adverse.

Gegenseite ['geːgənzaɪtə], *f.* (**—**, *pl.* **—n**) opposite side; (*coin*) reverse.

gegenseitig ['geːgənzaɪtɪç], *adj.* reciprocal, mutual.

Gegenstand ['geːgənʃtant], *m.* (**—s**, *pl.* **—e**) object; subject, matter.

gegenstandslos ['geːgənʃtantsloːs], *adj.* superfluous, irrelevant.

Gegenstück ['geːgənʃtyk], *n.* (**—s**, *pl.* **—e**) counterpart.

Gegenteil ['geːgəntaɪl], *n.* (**—s**, *no pl.*) contrary; *im —,* on the contrary.

gegenüber [geːgən'yːbər], *prep.* (*Dat.*) opposite to, facing. — *adv.* opposite.

Gegenüberstellung [geːgən'yːbərʃtɛluŋ], *f.* (**—**, *pl.* **—en**) confrontation.

Gegenwart ['geːgənvart], *f.* (**—**, *no pl.*) presence; (*Gram.*) present tense.

Gegenwehr ['geːgənveːr], *f.* (**—**, *no pl.*) defence, resistance.

Gegenwirkung ['geːgənvɪrkuŋ], *f.* (**—**, *pl.* **—en**) reaction, counter-effect.

gegenzeichnen ['geːgəntsaɪçnən], *v.a.* countersign.

Gegner ['geːgnər], *m.* (**—s**, *pl.* **—**) opponent, adversary, antagonist.

gegnerisch ['geːgnərɪʃ], *adj.* adverse, antagonistic.

Gegnerschaft ['geːgnərʃaft], *f.* (**—**, *no pl.*) antagonism; opposition.

Gehalt (1) [gə'halt], *m.* (**—s**, *no pl.*) contents; (*fig.*) value, standard.

Gehalt (2) [gə'halt], *n.* (**—s**, *pl.* **—er**) salary, stipend; pay.

Gehaltszulage [gə'haltstsuːlaːgə], *f.* (**—**, *pl.* **—n**) rise (in salary); increment; (*Am.*) raise.

gehaltvoll [gə'haltfɔl], *adj.* substantial.

Gehänge [gə'hɛŋə], *n.* (**—s**, *pl.* **—**) slope; festoon, garland.

geharnischt [gə'harnɪʃt], *adj.* armoured, steel-clad; (*fig.*) severe.

gehässig [gə'hɛsɪç], *adj.* malicious, spiteful.

Gehäuse [gə'hɔyzə], *n.* (—s, *pl.* —) casing, case; (*snail*) shell.

Gehege [gə'he:gə], *n.* (—s, *pl.* —) enclosure; *einem ins* — *kommen*, trespass on s.o.'s preserves.

geheim [gə'haɪm], *adj.* secret, clandestine.

Geheimnis [gə'haɪmnɪs], *n.* (—ses, *pl.* —se) secret, mystery.

geheimnisvoll [gə'haɪmnɪsfɔl], *adj.* mysterious.

Geheimrat [gə'haɪmra:t], *m.* (—s, *pl.* ⁻e) Privy Councillor.

Geheimschrift [gə'haɪmʃrɪft], *f.* (—, *pl.* —en) cryptography.

Geheimsprache [gə'haɪmʃpra:xə], *f.* (—, *pl.* —en) cipher.

Geheiß [gə'haɪs], *n.* (—es, *no pl.*) command, order, bidding.

gehen ['ge:ən], *v.n. irr.* (*aux.* sein) go, walk; (*Mach.*) work, function; (*goods*) sell; (*dough*) rise; *er lässt sich* —, he lets himself go; *er lässt es sich gut* —, he enjoys himself; *einem an die Hand* —, lend s.o. a hand, assist s.o.; *in Erfüllung* —, come true; *in sich* —, reflect; *wie geht es dir?* how are you? *es geht mir gut*, I am well.

geheuer [gə'hɔyər], *adj.* (*only in neg.*) *nicht ganz* —, creepy, eerie, uncanny; (*coll.*) fishy.

Gehilfe [gə'hɪlfə], *m.* (—n, *pl.* —n) assistant, helper.

Gehirn [gə'hɪrn], *n.* (—s, *pl.* —e) brain, brains.

Gehirnhautentzündung [gə'hɪrnhautɛntsyndun], *f.* (—, *pl.* —en) meningitis, cerebral inflammation.

Gehirnschlag [gə'hɪrnʃla:k], *m.* (—s, *pl.* ⁻e) apoplexy.

Gehöft [gə'hœft], *n.* (—es, *pl.* —e) farmstead.

Gehör [gə'hø:r], (—s, *no pl.*) hearing; *gutes* —, musical ear.

gehorchen [gə'hɔrçən], *v.n.* obey; *nicht* —, disobey.

gehören [gə'hø:rən], *v.n.* belong. — *v.r. sich* —, be the proper thing to do.

gehörig [gə'hø:rɪç], *adj. dazu* —, belonging to, referring to; due, fit, proper, thorough; (*fig.*) sound.

Gehörn [gə'hœrn], *n.* (—s, *pl.* —e) horns, antlers.

gehörnt [gə'hœrnt], *adj.* horned; (*fig.*) duped (husband).

Gehorsam [gə'ho:rza:m], *m.* (—s, *no pl.*) obedience; — *leisten*, show obedience; *den* — *verweigern*, refuse to obey.

gehorsam [gə'ho:rza:m], *adj.* obedient, dutiful, submissive.

Gehrock ['ge:rɔk], *m.* (—s, *pl.* ⁻e) frock-coat.

Geier ['gaɪər], *m.* (—s, *pl.* —) (*Orn.*) vulture.

Geifer ['gaɪfər], *m.* (—s, *no pl.*) saliva, drivel; (*animals*) foam; (*fig.*) venom, rancour.

geifern ['gaɪfərn], *v.n.* slaver, drivel; (*fig.*) foam at the mouth; give vent to o.'s anger.

Geige ['gaɪgə], *f.* (—, *pl.* —n) violin, fiddle.

Geigenharz ['gaɪgənha:rts], *n.* (—es, *no pl.*) colophony; rosin.

Geigensteg ['gaɪgənʃte:k], *m.* (—s, *pl.* —e) bridge of a violin.

Geiger ['gaɪgər], *m.* (—s, *pl.* —) violinplayer, violinist.

geil [gaɪl], *adj.* rank; lecherous, lascivious.

Geisel ['gaɪzəl], *f.* (—, *pl.* —n) hostage.

Geiß [gaɪs], *f.* (—, *pl.* —en) goat, she-goat.

Geißblatt ['gaɪsblat], *n.* (—s, *no pl.*) (*Bot.*) honeysuckle.

Geißbock ['gaɪsbɔk], *m.* (—s, *pl.* ⁻e) billy-goat.

Geißel ['gaɪsəl], *f.* (—, *pl.* —n) scourge.

geißeln ['gaɪsəln], *v.a.* scourge, whip, flagellate.

Geist [gaɪst], *m.* (—es, *pl.* —er) spirit, mind; brains, intellect; wit; apparition, ghost.

Geisterbeschwörung ['gaɪstərbəʃvø:-run], *f.* (—, *pl.* —en) evocation (of spirits); necromancy; exorcism.

geisterhaft ['gaɪstərhaft], *adj.* ghostly, spectral, weird.

Geisterwelt ['gaɪstərvɛlt], *f.* (—, *no pl.*) world of spirits.

geistesabwesend ['gaɪstəsapve:zənt], *adj.* absent-minded.

Geistesfreiheit ['gaɪstəsfraɪhaɪt], *f.* (—, *no pl.*) freedom of thought.

Geistesgegenwart ['gaɪstəsge:gənvart], *f.* (—, *no pl.*) presence of mind.

Geisteskraft ['gaɪstəskraft], *f.* (—, *pl.* ⁻e) faculty of the mind.

Geistesstörung ['gaɪstəsʃtø:run], *f.* (—, *pl.* —en) mental aberration.

Geistesverfassung ['gaɪstəsfɛrfasun], *f.* (—, *no pl.*) state of mind.

geistesverwandt ['gaɪstəsfɛrvant], *adj.* congenial.

Geistesverwirrung ['gaɪstəsfɛrvɪrun], *f.* (—, *no pl.*) bewilderment.

Geisteswissenschaften ['gaɪstəsvɪsənʃaftən], *f.pl.* (*Univ.*) Arts, Humanities.

Geisteszerrüttung ['gaɪstəstsɛrytun], *f.* (—, *no pl.*) mental derangement, insanity.

geistig ['gaɪstɪç], *adj.* intellectual, mental; spiritual; —*e Getränke*, alcoholic liquors.

geistlich ['gaɪstlɪç], *adj.* spiritual; religious; ecclesiastical, clerical; —*er Orden*, religious order; —*er Stand*, holy orders, the Clergy.

Geistliche ['gaɪstlɪçə], *m.* (—n, *pl.* —n) priest, clergyman, cleric; minister of religion.

Geistlichkeit ['gaɪstlɪçkaɪt], *f.* (—, *no pl.*) clergy.

geistlos ['gaɪstlo:s], *adj.* dull, stupid.

geistreich ['gaɪstraɪç], *adj.* clever, witty.

Geiz [gaɪts], *m.* (—es, *no pl.*) avarice, covetousness.

geizen ['gaɪtsən], *v.n.* be miserly.

Geizhals ['gaɪtshals], *m.* (—es, *pl.* ⸚e) miser, niggard.

Geizkragen ['gaɪtskra:gən], *m.* (—s, *pl.* —) *see* **Geizhals**.

Gekreisch [gə'kraɪʃ], *n.* (—es, *no pl.*) screaming, shrieks.

Gekritzel [gə'krɪtsəl], *n.* (—s, *no pl.*) scrawling, scribbling.

Gekröse [gə'krø:zə], *n.* (—s, *no pl.*) tripe; (*Anat.*) mesentery.

gekünstelt [gə'kynstəlt], *adj.* artificial, affected.

Gelächter [gə'lɛçtər], *n.* (—s, *no pl.*) laughter.

Gelage [gə'la:gə], *n.* (—s, *pl.* —) (*obs.*) feast, banquet.

Gelände [gə'lɛndə], *n.* (—s, *pl.* —) terrain, region; landscape.

Geländer [gə'lɛndər], *n.* (—s, *pl.* —) railing, balustrade, banister.

gelangen [gə'laŋən], *v.n.* (*aux.* sein) arrive, come (to).

Gelaß [gə'las], *n.* (—sses, *pl.* —sse) (*obs.*) room, chamber.

gelassen [gə'lasən], *adj.* calm, composed, collected.

geläufig [gə'lɔyfɪç], *adj.* fluent.

gelaunt [gə'launt], *adj.* disposed.

Geläute [gə'lɔytə], *n.* (—s, *no pl.*) ringing, chiming; bells.

geläutert [gə'lɔytərt], *adj.* purified, cleansed.

gelb [gɛlp], *adj.* yellow, amber.

Gelbschnabel ['gɛlpʃna:bəl], *m.* (—s, *pl.* ⸚) (*Orn.*) fledg(e)ling; greenhorn.

Gelbsucht ['gɛlpzuxt], *f.* (—, *no pl.*) jaundice.

Geld [gɛlt], *n.* (—es, *pl.* —er) money, currency, coin; *bares* —, ready money, hard cash; *kleines* —, small change.

Geldanweisung ['gɛltanvaɪzuŋ], *f.* (— *pl.* —en) money-order.

Geldbuße ['gɛltbu:sə], *f.* (—, *pl.*—n) fine.

Geldkurs ['gɛltkurs], *m.* (—es, *pl.* —e) rate of exchange.

Geldmittel ['gɛltmɪtəl], *n. pl.* pecuniary resources, financial resources.

Geldschrank ['gɛltʃraŋk], *m.* (—s, *pl.* ⸚e) safe.

Geldstrafe ['gɛltʃtra:fə], *f.* (—, *pl.* —n) fine.

Geldverlegenheit ['gɛltfɛrle:gənhaɪt], *f.* (—, *pl.* —en) pecuniary embarrassment, financial difficulty.

Geldwährung ['gɛltvɛ:ruŋ], *f.* (—, *pl.* —en) currency.

Geldwechsel ['gɛltvɛksəl], *m.* (—s, *no pl.*) exchange.

Gelee [ʒə'le:], *n.* (—s, *pl.* —s) jelly.

gelegen [gə'le:gən], *adj.* situated, situate; *das kommt mir gerade* —, that suits me; *mir ist daran* —, *dass*, I am anxious that.

Gelegenheit [gə'le:gənhaɪt], *f.* (—, *pl.* —en) occasion, chance, opportunity; facility; *bei* —, one of these days.

Gelegenheitskauf [gə'le:gənhaɪtskauf], *m.* (—s, *pl.* ⸚e) bargain.

gelegentlich [gə'le:gəntlɪç], *adj.* occasional.

gelehrig [gə'le:rɪç], *adj.* docile, tractable.

Gelehrsamkeit [gə'le:rzamkaɪt], *f.* (—, *no pl.*) learning, erudition.

gelehrt [gə'le:rt], *adj.* learned, erudite.

Gelehrte [gə'le:rtə], *m.* (—n, *pl.* —n) scholar, man of learning, savant.

Geleise [gə'laɪzə], *n.* (—s, *pl.* —) *see* **Gleis**.

Geleit [gə'laɪt], *n.* (—s, *no pl.*) escort, accompaniment; (*Naut.*) convoy; *sicheres* —, safe conduct.

geleiten [gə'laɪtən], *v.a.* accompany, conduct, escort.

Gelenk [gə'lɛŋk], *n.* (—s, *pl.* —e) (*human*) joint; (*chain*) link.

Gelenkentzündung [gə'lɛŋkɛnttsynduŋ], *f.* (—, *pl.* —en) (*Med.*) arthritis.

gelenkig [gə'lɛŋkɪç], *adj.* flexible, pliant, nimble, supple.

Gelenkrheumatismus [gə'lɛŋkrɔymatɪsmus], *m.* (—, *no pl.*) (*Med.*) rheumatoid arthritis, rheumatic gout.

Gelichter [gə'lɪçtər], *n.* (—s, *no pl.*) riff-raff.

Geliebte [gə'li:ptə], *m.* (—n, *pl.* —n) lover, sweetheart, beloved. — *f.* (—n, *pl.* —n) mistress; beloved.

gelinde [gə'lɪndə], *adj.* soft, smooth, gentle, mild; — *gesagt*, to say the least.

Gelingen [gə'lɪŋən], *n.* (—s, *no pl.*) success.

gelingen [gə'lɪŋən], *v.n. irr.* (*aux.* sein) succeed; *es gelingt mir*, I succeed.

gellen ['gɛlən], *v.n.* yell; shrill.

geloben [gə'lo:bən], *v.a.* (*aux.* haben) promise solemnly, vow; *das Gelobte Land*, the Promised Land.

Gelöbnis [gə'lø:pnɪs], *n.* (—ses, *pl.* —se) vow, promise.

gelt [gɛlt], *inter.* (*coll.*) isn't it? don't you think so?

gelten ['gɛltən], *v.a. irr.* be worth, cost. — *v.n.* count (as), be valid.

Geltung ['gɛltuŋ], *f.* (—, *no pl.*) value, importance.

Gelübde [gə'lypdə], *n.* (—s, *pl.* —) vow, solemn promise *or* undertaking.

gelungen [gə'luŋən], *adj.* (*coll.*) funny, capital.

Gelüst [gə'lyst], *n.* (—s, *pl.* —e) appetite, desire.

gelüsten [gə'lystən], *v.a.* — *nach*, long for, covet.

Gemach [gə'ma:x], *n.* (—es, *pl.* ⸚er) (*Poet.*) chamber, room; apartment.

gemach [gə'ma:x], *adv.* slowly, softly, by degrees.

gemächlich [gə'mɛçlɪç], *adj.* slow, soft, easy, unhurried, leisurely.

Gemahl [gə'ma:l], *m.* (—s, *pl.* —e) spouse, husband, consort.

Gemahlin [gə'ma:lɪn], *f.* (—, *pl.* —nen) spouse, wife, consort.

Gemälde [gə'mɛ:ldə], *n.* (—s, *pl.* —) picture, painting, portrait.

gemäß [gə'mɛ:s], *prep.* (*Dat.*) in accordance with, according to.

gemäßigt [gə'mɛːsɪçt], *adj.* temperate, moderate; **—es** *Klima*, temperate climate.

Gemäuer [gə'mɔyər], *n.* (**—s**, *no pl.*) ancient walls, ruins.

gemein [gə'maɪn], *adj.* common, mean, low, vulgar, base.

Gemeinde [gə'maɪndə], *f.* (**—**, *pl.* **—n**) community, parish, municipality; (*Eccl.*) congregation.

Gemeindevorstand [gə'maɪndeforʃtant], *m.* (**—es**, *no pl.*) town *or* borough council.

gemeingefährlich [gə'maɪngəfɛːrlɪç], *adj.* dangerous to the public.

Gemeinheit [gə'maɪnhaɪt], *f.* (**—**, *pl.* **—en**) meanness; baseness; dirty trick.

gemeinhin [gə'maɪnhɪn], *adv.* commonly.

Gemeinplatz [gə'maɪnplats], *m.* (**—es**, *pl.* ¨**e**) commonplace, truism.

gemeinsam [gə'maɪnzaːm], *adj.* common, joint; *der* **—** *Markt*, (*Pol.*) Common Market; **—e** *Sache machen*, make common cause. **—** *adv.* together.

Gemeinschaft [gə'maɪnʃaft], *f.* (**—**, *pl.* **—en**) community; association; *in* **—** *mit*, jointly; *in* **—** *haben*, hold in common.

gemeinschaftlich [gə'maɪnʃaftlɪç], *adj.* common. **—** *adv.* in common, together.

Gemeinsinn [gə'maɪnzɪn], *m.* (**—s**, *no pl.*) public spirit.

Gemeinwesen [gə'maɪnveːzən], *n.* (**—s**, *no pl.*) community.

Gemeinwohl [gə'maɪnvoːl], *n.* (**—s**, *no pl.*) common weal; common good.

Gemenge [gə'mɛŋə], *n.* (**—s**, *no pl.*) mixture; (*fig.*) scuffle.

Gemengsel [gə'mɛŋsəl], *n.* (**—s**, *no pl.*) medley, hotchpotch.

gemessen [gə'mɛsən], *adj.* deliberate.

Gemessenheit [gə'mɛsənhaɪt], *f.* (**—**, *no pl.*) precision, deliberation.

Gemetzel [gə'mɛtsəl], *n.* (**—s**, *no pl.*) slaughter, massacre.

Gemisch [gə'mɪʃ], *n.* (**—es**, *pl.* **—e**) mixture, motley.

Gemme ['gɛmə], *f.* (**—**, *pl.* **—n**) gem, cameo.

Gemse ['gɛmzə], *f.* (**—**, *pl.* **—n**) chamois.

Gemüse [gə'myːzə], *n.* (**—s**, *pl.* **—**) vegetables, greens.

Gemüsehändler [gə'myːzəhɛndlər], *m.* (**—s**, *pl.* **—**) greengrocer.

gemustert [gə'mustərt], *adj.* patterned, figured; (*Comm.*) **—e** *Sendung*, delivery as per sample.

Gemüt [gə'myːt], *n.* (**—s**, *pl.* **—er**) mind, soul, heart; disposition, nature, spirit, temper; feeling.

gemütlich [gə'myːtlɪç], *adj.* cosy, snug, comfortable; genial, friendly, pleasant.

Gemütlichkeit [gə'myːtlɪçkaɪt], *f.* (**—**, *no pl.*) cosiness, snugness; *da hört die* **—** *auf*, that is more than I will stand for.

gemütlos [gə'myːtloːs], *adj.* unfeeling.

Gemütsart [gə'myːtsaːrt], *f.* (**—**, *no pl.*) disposition; character.

Gemütsbewegung [gə'myːtsbəveːguŋ], *f.* (**—**, *pl.* **—en**) emotion.

gemütskrank [gə'myːtskraŋk], *adj.* sick in mind; melancholy.

Gemütsleben [gə'myːtsleːbən], *n.* (**—s**, *no pl.*) emotional life.

Gemütsmensch [gə'myːtsmɛnʃ], *m.* (**—en**, *pl.* **—en**) man of feeling *or* sentiment; (*pej.*) sentimentalist.

gemütvoll [gə'myːtfɔl], *adj.* full of feeling, sympathetic.

gen [gɛn], *prep. contraction* of **gegen**, (*Poet.*) towards, to (*Acc.*).

Genannte [gə'nantə], *m.* (**—n**, *pl.* **—n**) named person, aforesaid.

genäschig [gə'nɛʃɪç], *adj.* fond of sweets, sweet-toothed.

genau [gə'nau], *adj.* precise, exact, accurate; strict, parsimonious.

Genauigkeit [gə'nauɪçkaɪt], *f.* (**—**, *no pl.*) accuracy, exactitude, precision.

Gendarm [ʒãˈdarm], *m.* (**—en**, *pl.* **—en**) policeman, constable.

genehm [gə'neːm], *adj.* agreeable, acceptable, convenient.

genehmigen [gə'neːmɪgən], *v.a.* approve of, agree to, permit; (*contract*) ratify.

geneigt [gə'naɪkt], *adj.* inclined (to), disposed (to), prone (to); *einem* **—** *sein*, be well disposed towards s.o.; (*Lit.*) *der* **—e** *Leser*, gentle reader.

Geneigtheit [gə'naɪkthaɪt], *f.* (**—**, *no pl.*) inclination, proneness, propensity; favour, kindness.

General [genə'raːl], *m.* (**—s**, *pl.* **—e**, ¨**e**) general.

Generalfeldmarschall [genə'raːlfɛltmarʃal], *m.* (**—s**, *pl.* ¨**e**) field marshal.

Generalkommando [genə'raːlkɔmando], *n.* (**—s**, *pl.* **—s**) general's headquarters; (corps) headquarters.

Generalkonsul [genə'raːlkɔnzul], *m.* (**—s**, *pl.* **—e**) consul-general.

Generalnenner [genə'raːlnɛnər], *m.* (**—s**, *pl.* **—**) (*Maths.*) common denominator.

Generalprobe [genə'raːlproːbə], *f.* (**—**, *pl.* **—n**) dress-rehearsal.

Generalvollmacht [genə'raːlfɔlmaxt], *f.* (**—**, *pl.* **—en**) (*Law*) general power of attorney.

generell [genə'rɛl], *adj.* general, common.

generös [genə'røːs], *adj.* generous, magnanimous.

genesen [gə'neːzən], *v.n. irr.* (*aux.* sein) recover, be restored to health; convalesce.

Genf [gɛnf], *n.* Geneva.

genial [gen'jaːl], *adj.* ingenious; extremely gifted.

Genick [gə'nɪk], *n.* (**—s**, *pl.* **—e**) nape, neck.

Genickstarre [gə'nɪkʃtarə], *f.* (**—**, *no pl.*) (*Med.*) (cerebrospinal) meningitis.

Genie [ʒe'niː], *n.* (**—s**, *pl.* **—s**) genius.

genieren

genieren [ʒeˈniːrən], *v.a.* trouble, embarrass, disturb. — *v.r. sich* —, feel embarrassed; *sich nicht* —, make o.s. at home.

genießbar [gəˈniːsbaːr], *adj.* eatable, edible, palatable; drinkable; (*fig.*) pleasant, agreeable.

genießen [gəˈniːsən], *v.a. irr.* enjoy; have the use of; (*food*) eat, partake of; *Ansehen* —, enjoy respect.

Geniestreich [ʒeˈniːʃtraiç], *m.* (—s, *pl.* —e) stroke of genius.

Genitiv [ˈgeːnitiːf], *m.* (—s, *pl.* —e) (*Gram.*) genitive.

Genosse [gəˈnɔsə], *m.* (—n, *pl.* —n) comrade, mate, colleague; (*crime*) accomplice.

Genossenschaft [gəˈnɔsənʃaft], *f.* (—, *pl.* —en) association, company, confederacy, co-operative, union.

Genre [ˈʒãrə], *n.* (—s, *pl.* —s) genre; style, kind.

Gent [gɛnt], *n.* Ghent.

Genua [ˈgeːnua], *n.* Genoa.

genug [gəˈnuːk], *indecl. adj.* enough, sufficient; —*!* that will do!

Genüge [gəˈnyːgə], *f.* (—, *no pl.*) *zur* —, sufficiently; *einem* — *leisten*, give satisfaction to s.o.

genügen [gəˈnyːgən], *v.n.* be enough, suffice; *sich etwas* — *lassen*, be content with s.th.

genügsam [gəˈnyːkzaːm], *adj.* easily satisfied; temperate, sober.

Genügsamkeit [gəˈnyːkzaːmkait], *f.* (—, *no pl.*) contentedness, moderation; temperateness, sobriety.

Genugtuung [gəˈnuːktuːuŋ], *f.* (—, *no pl.*) satisfaction; reparation; atonement.

Genuß [gəˈnus], *m.* (—sses, *pl.* ˙sse) enjoyment; use; (*food*) consumption.

Genußmittel [gəˈnusmitəl], *n.* (—s, *pl.* —) (*mostly pl.*) luxuries; (*Am.*) delicatessen.

genußreich [gəˈnusraiç], *adj.* enjoyable, delightful.

Genußsucht [gəˈnuszuxt], *f.* (—, *no pl.*) thirst for pleasure.

Geograph [geoˈgraːf], *m.* (—en, *pl.* —en) geographer.

Geographie [geograˈfiː], *f.* (—, *no pl.*) geography.

Geologe [geoˈloːgə], *m.* (—n, *pl.* —n) geologist.

Geologie [geoloˈgiː], *f.* (—, *no pl.*) geology.

Geometer [geoˈmeːtər], *m.* (—s, *pl.* —) geometrician; land-surveyor.

Geometrie [geomeˈtriː], *f.* (—, *no pl.*) geometry.

Georg [geˈɔrk], *m.* George.

Georgine [geɔrˈgiːnə], *f.* (—, *pl.* —n) (*Bot.*) dahlia.

Gepäck [gəˈpɛk], *n.* (—s, *no pl.*) luggage; (*Am.*) baggage.

Gepäckaufbewahrung [gəˈpɛkaufbəvaːruŋ], *f.* (—, *pl.* —en) left luggage office.

Gepäckträger [gəˈpɛktrɛːgər], *m.* (—s, *pl.* —) porter.

Gepflogenheit [gəˈpfloːgənhait], *f.* (—, *pl.* —en) habit, custom, wont.

Geplänkel [gəˈplɛŋkəl], *n.* (—s, *pl.* —) (*rare*) skirmish.

Geplärr [gəˈplɛr], *n.* (—s, *no pl.*) bawling.

Geplauder [gəˈplaudər], *n.* (—s, *no pl.*) chatting; small talk.

Gepräge [gəˈprɛːgə], *n.* (—s, *no pl.*) impression, stamp.

Gepränge [gəˈprɛŋə], *n.* (—s, *no pl.*) pomp, ceremony, splendour.

Ger [geːr], *m.* (—s, *pl.* —e) (*rare*) spear, javelin.

Gerade [gəˈraːdə], *f.* (—n, *pl.* —n) (*Maths.*) straight line.

gerade [gəˈraːdə], *adj.* straight, direct, erect, even; (*fig.*) upright, honest. — *adv.* quite, just; *jetzt* —, now more than ever; *fünf* — *sein lassen*, stretch a point; — *heraus*, in plain terms.

geradeaus [gəˈraːdaus], *adv.* straight on.

gerädert [gəˈrɛːdərt], *adj.* (*fig.*) fatigued, exhausted, worn out.

geradeswegs [gəˈraːdəsveːks], *adv.* straightaway, immediately.

geradezu [gəˈraːdətsuː], *adv.* frankly, downright; *das ist* — *scheußlich*, this is downright nasty.

Geradheit [gəˈraːthait], *f.* (—, *no pl.*) straightness; (*fig.*) straightforwardness.

geradlinig [gəˈraːtliniç], *adj.* rectilinear.

geradsinnig [gəˈraːtziniç], *adj.* honest, upright.

gerändert [gəˈrɛndərt], *adj.* with a milled edge.

Geranie [geˈraːnjə], *f.* (—, *pl.* —n) (*Bot.*) geranium.

Gerät [gəˈrɛːt], *n.* (—s, *pl.* —e) tool, implement, device; appliance; (radio, television) set; apparatus.

geraten [gəˈraːtən], *v.n. irr.* (*aux.* sein) turn out; *gut* —, turn out well; — *auf*, come upon.

Geräteturnen [gəˈrɛːtəturnən], *n.* (—s, *no pl.*) gymnastics with apparatus.

Geratewohl [gəˈraːtəvoːl], *n.* (—s, *no pl.*) *aufs* —, at random.

geraum [gəˈraum], *adj.* —*e Zeit*, a long time.

geräumig [gəˈrɔymiç], *adj.* spacious, large, wide, roomy.

Geräusch [gəˈrɔyʃ], *n.* (—es, *pl.* —e) noise; sound.

gerben [ˈgɛrbən], *v.a.* tan, taw; *einem die Haut* —, give s.o. a hiding.

Gerber [ˈgɛrbər], *m.* (—s, *pl.* —) tanner.

Gerbsäure [ˈgɛrpsɔyrə], *f.* (—, *no pl.*) tannin.

gerecht [gəˈrɛçt], *adj.* just, fair; (*Bibl.*) righteous; *einem* — *werden*, do justice to s.o.

Gerechtigkeit [gəˈrɛçtiçkait], *f.* (—, *no pl.*) justice, fairness; (*Bibl.*) righteousness.

Gerede [gə're:də], *n.* (—**s,** *no pl.*) talk, rumour, gossip.

gereichen [gə'raɪçən], *v.n.* turn out to be; *einem zur Ehre* —, redound to s.o.'s honour.

gereizt [gə'raɪtst], *adj.* irritated, annoyed.

gereuen [gə'rɔyən] *see* **reuen.**

Gerhard ['ge:rhart], *m.* Gerard, Gerald.

Gericht [gə'rɪçt], *n.* (—**s,** *pl.* —**e**) court of justice, tribunal; (*food*) course, dish; *das Jüngste* —, Last Judgment.

gerichtlich [gə'rɪçtlɪç], *adj.* judicial, legal; *einen* — *belangen,* sue s.o.

Gerichtsbarkeit [gə'rɪçtsbarkaɪt], *f.* (—, *no pl.*) jurisdiction.

Gerichtsdiener [gə'rɪçtsdi:nər], *m.* (—**s,** *pl.* —) (*law court*) usher.

Gerichtshof [gə'rɪçtsho:f], *m.* (—**es,** *pl.* ¨e) court of justice.

Gerichtskanzlei [gə'rɪçtskantslaɪ], *f.* (—, *pl.* —**en**) record office.

Gerichtskosten [gə'rɪçtskɔstən], *f. pl.* (*Law*) costs.

Gerichtsordnung [gə'rɪçtsɔrdnuŋ], *f.* (—, *pl* —**en**) legal procedure.

Gerichtstermin [gə'rɪçtstermi:n], *m.* (—**s,** *pl.* —**e**) day fixed for a hearing.

Gerichtsverhandlung [gə'rɪçtsferhandluŋ], *f.* (—, *pl.* —**en**) hearing; trial.

Gerichtsvollzieher [gə'rɪçtsfɔltsi:ər], *m.* (—**s,** *pl.* —) bailiff.

gerieben [gə'ri:bən], *adj.* ground; crafty, cunning.

gering [gə'rɪŋ], *adj.* small, little, mean, petty, unimportant, of little value, trifling; low, base.

geringfügig [gə'rɪŋfy:gɪç], *adj.* small, petty, insignificant.

geringschätzig [gə'rɪŋʃɛtsɪç], *adj.* contemptuous, disdainful, supercilious; derogatory.

gerinnen [gə'rɪnən], *v.n. irr.* (*aux.* sein) coagulate, clot; curdle.

Gerinnsel [gə'rɪnzəl], *n.* (—**s,** *pl.* —) embolism (of the blood); clot.

Gerippe [gə'rɪpə], *n.* (—**s,** *pl.* —) skeleton; frame; (*Aviat.*) air-frame.

gerippt [gə'rɪpt], *adj.* ribbed, fluted.

gerissen [gə'rɪsən], *adj.* (*coll.*) sharp, cunning.

Germane [ger'ma:nə], *m.* (—**n,** *pl.* —**n**) Teuton.

Germanist ['germanɪst], *m.* (—**en,** *pl.* — **en**) (*Univ.*) student of *or* expert in German language and/or literature.

gern [gern], *adv.* gladly, willingly, readily, with pleasure; — *haben,* like.

Geröll [gə'rœl], *n.* (—**s,** *no pl.*) boulders, rubble.

Gerste ['gerstə], *f.* (—, *no pl.*) (*Bot.*) barley.

Gerstenschleim ['gerstənʃlaɪm], *m.* (—**s,** *no pl.*) barley water.

Gerte ['gertə], *f.* (—, *pl.* —**n**) whip, switch, rod.

Geruch [gə'ru:x], *m.* (—**s,** *pl.* ¨e) smell, odour, scent; *guter* —, fragrance, aroma.

geruchlos [gə'ru:xlo:s], *adj.* scentless, odourless, without smell.

Geruchsinn [gə'ru:xzɪn], *m.* (—**es,** *no pl.*) sense of smell.

Gerücht [gə'ryçt], *n.* (—**s,** *pl.* —**e**) rumour, report.

Gerümpel [gə'rympəl], *n.* (—**s,** *no pl.*) lumber, trash.

Gerundium [gə'rundjum], *n.* (—**s,** *pl.* —**dien**) (*Gram.*) gerund.

Gerüst [gə'ryst], *n.* (—**es,** *pl.* —**e**) scaffolding.

Ges [ges], *n.* (—, *pl.* —) (*Mus.*) G flat.

gesamt [gə'zamt], *adj.* entire, all, complete.

Gesamtheit [gə'zamthaɪt], *f.* (—, *no pl.*) totality.

Gesandte [gə'zantə], *m.* (—**n,** *pl.* —**n**) messenger; ambassador, envoy; *päpstlicher* —, papal nuncio.

Gesandtschaft [gə'zantʃaft], *f.* (—, *pl.* —**en**) embassy, legation.

Gesang [gə'zaŋ], *m.* (—**s,** *pl.* ¨e) song, air; hymn; (*Lit.*) canto.

Gesangbuch [gə'zaŋbu:x], *n.* (—**s,** *pl.* ¨er) hymnal, hymn-book.

Gesäß [gə'zɛ:s], *n.* (—**es,** *pl.* —**e**) seat, buttocks.

Geschäft [gə'ʃɛft], *n.* (—**s,** *pl.* —**e**) business; trade, commerce; affairs; occupation; shop; (*Am.*) store.

geschäftig [gə'ʃɛftɪç], *adj.* active, bustling, busy.

geschäftlich [gə'ʃɛftlɪç], *adj.* concerning business. — *adv.* on business.

Geschäftsführer [gə'ʃɛftsfy:rər], *m.* (—**s,** *pl.* —) manager.

Geschäftshaus [gə'ʃɛftshaus], *n.* (—**es,** *pl.* ¨er) firm; business premises.

geschäftskundig [gə'ʃɛftskundɪç], *adj.* experienced in business.

Geschäftslokal [gə'ʃɛftsloka:l], *n.* (—**s,** *pl.* —**e**) business premises, shop.

Geschäftsordnung [gə'ʃɛftsɔrdnuŋ], *f.* (—, *pl.* —**en**) standing orders; agenda.

Geschäftsträger [gə'ʃɛftstrɛ:gər], *m.* (—**s,** *pl.* —) (*Comm.*) agent; (*Pol.*) chargé d'affaires.

Geschäftsverkehr [gə'ʃɛftsferke:r], *m.* (—**s,** *no pl.*) business dealings.

Geschehen [gə'ʃe:ən], *n.* (—**s,** *no pl.*) happening.

geschehen [gə'ʃe:ən], *v.n. irr.* (*aux.* sein) happen, occur; take place; be done; *das geschieht dir recht,* it serves you right.

gescheit [gə'ʃaɪt], *adj.* clever, intelligent.

Geschenk [gə'ʃɛŋk], *n.* (—**s,** *pl.* —**e**) gift, present, donation.

Geschichte [gə'ʃɪçtə], *f.* (—, *pl.* —**n**) tale; story; history.

Geschichtenbuch [gə'ʃɪçtənbu:x], *n.* (—**es,** *pl.* ¨er) story-book.

geschichtlich [gə'ʃɪçtlɪç], *adj.* historical.

Geschichtsschreiber [gə'ʃɪçtsʃraɪbər], *m.* (—**s,** *pl.* —) historian.

Geschick [gə'ʃɪk], *n.* (—**es,** *no pl.*) fate, destiny; dexterity, skill, knack, aptitude.

Geschicklichkeit

Geschicklichkeit [gəˈʃɪklɪçkaɪt], *f.* (—, *pl.* —en) dexterity, adroitness, skill.

geschickt [gəˈʃɪkt], *adj.* skilled, skilful, clever, able.

Geschirr [gəˈʃɪr], *n.* (—s, *no pl.*) crockery, plates and dishes; (*horses*) harness.

Geschlecht [gəˈʃlɛçt], *n.* (—s, *pl.* —er) sex; kind, race, species, extraction, family; (*Gram.*) gender.

geschlechtlich [gəˈʃlɛçtlɪç], *adj.* sexual; generic.

Geschlechtsart [gəˈʃlɛçtsaːrt], *f.* (—, *pl.* —en) generic character.

Geschlechtskrankheit [gəˈʃlɛçtskraŋkhaɪt], *f.* (—, *pl.* —en) venereal disease.

Geschlechtskunde [gəˈʃlɛçtskundə], *f.* (—, *no pl.*) genealogy.

Geschlechtsreife [gəˈʃlɛçtsraɪfə], *f.* (—, *no pl.*) puberty.

Geschlechtsteile [gəˈʃlɛçtstaɪlə], *m. pl.* genitals.

Geschlechtstrieb [gəˈʃlɛçtstriːp], *m.* (—s, *no pl.*) sexual instinct.

Geschlechtswort [gəˈʃlɛçtsvɔrt], *n.* (—s, *pl.* ⁓er) (*Gram.*) article.

geschliffen [gəˈʃlɪfən], *adj.* polished; (*glass*) cut.

Geschmack [gəˈʃmak], *m.* (—s, *pl.* ⁓er) taste, flavour.

geschmacklos [gəˈʃmakloːs], *adj.* tasteless, insipid; in bad taste.

Geschmacksrichtung [gəˈʃmaksrɪçtuŋ], *f.* (—, *pl.* —en) prevailing taste; vogue; tendency.

Geschmeide [gəˈʃmaɪdə], *n.* (—s, *pl.* —) jewels, jewellery; trinkets.

geschmeidig [gəˈʃmaɪdɪç], *adj.* flexible, pliant, supple; (*Tech.*) malleable.

Geschmeiß [gəˈʃmaɪs], *n.* (—es, *no pl.*) dung; vermin; (*fig.*) rabble.

Geschnatter [gəˈʃnatər], *n.* (—s, *no pl.*) cackling.

geschniegelt [gəˈʃniːgəlt], *adj.* spruce, dressed up.

Geschöpf [gəˈʃœpf], *n.* (—es, *pl.* —e) creature.

Geschoß [gəˈʃɔs], *n.* (—sses, *pl.* —sse) shot, shell, projectile, missile; (*house*) storey.

geschraubt [gəˈʃraupt], *adj.* (*style*) stilted, affected.

Geschrei [gəˈʃraɪ], *n.* (—s, *no pl.*) shrieking, shouting, screaming; (*fig.*) stir, great noise.

Geschreibsel [gəˈʃraɪpsəl], *n.* (—s, *no pl.*) scrawl, scribbling.

Geschütz [gəˈʃʏts], *n.* (—es, *pl.* —e) artillery, guns; *schweres — auffahren*, bring o.'s. guns into play.

Geschützweite [gəˈʃʏtsvaɪtə], *f.* (—, *no pl.*) calibre.

Geschwader [gəˈʃvaːdər], *n.* (—s, *pl.*—) squadron.

Geschwätz [gəˈʃvɛts], *n.* (—es, *no pl.*) chatter, gossip, prattle, tittle-tattle.

geschweige [gəˈʃvaɪgə], *adv.* let alone, to say nothing of.

geschwind [gəˈʃvɪnt], *adj.* quick, nimble, fast, swift, fleet.

Geschwindigkeitsmesser [gəˈʃvɪndɪçkaɪtsmɛsər], *m.* (—s, *pl.* —) (*Motor.*) speedometer.

Geschwister [gəˈʃvɪstər], *pl.* brothers and sisters.

geschwollen [gəˈʃvɔlən], *adj.* stilted, turgid, pompous.

Geschworene [gəˈʃvoːrənə], *m.* (—n, *pl.* —n), juror, juryman; (*pl.*) jury.

Geschwulst [gəˈʃvulst], *f.* (—, *pl.* ⁓e) swelling, tumour.

Geschwür [gəˈʃvyːr], *n.* (—s, *pl.* —e) sore, ulcer, abscess.

Geselle [gəˈzɛlə], *m.* (—n, *pl.* —n) journeyman; companion, comrade, mate.

gesellen [gəˈzɛlən], *v.a., v.r.* join, associate with, keep company with.

gesellig [gəˈzɛlɪç], *adj.* sociable, companionable; gregarious.

Gesellschaft [gəˈzɛlʃaft], *f.* (—, *pl.* —en) society; community; (formal) party; company, club; *geschlossene —*, private party; *einem — leisten*, keep s.o. company; (*Comm.*) — *mit beschränkter Haftung*, (abbr.) *GmbH*, limited company, (*abbr.*) Ltd.

gesellschaftlich [gəˈzɛlʃaftlɪç], *adj.* social.

Gesellschaftsanzug [gəˈzɛlʃaftsantsuːk], *m.* (—s, *pl.* ⁓e) evening dress.

Gesellschaftsspiel [gəˈzɛlʃaftsʃpiːl], *n.* (—s, *pl.* —e) round game, party game.

Gesellschaftsvertrag [gəˈzɛlʃaftsfɛrtraːk], *m.* (—es, *pl.* ⁓e) (*Law*) partnership agreement; deed of partnership.

Gesellschaftszimmer [gəˈzɛlʃaftstsɪmər], *n.* (—s, *pl.* —) drawing-room, reception room.

Gesetz [gəˈzɛts], *n.* (—es, *pl.* —e) law, statute, regulation.

Gesetzbuch [gəˈzɛtsbuːx], *n.* (—es, *pl.* ⁓er) code of laws; statute book.

Gesetzentwurf [gəˈzɛtsɛntvurf], *m.* (—es, *pl.* ⁓er) (*Parl.*) draft bill.

gesetzgebend [gəˈzɛtsgeːbənt], *adj.* legislative.

gesetzlich [gəˈzɛtslɪç], *adj.* lawful, legal.

Gesetzlichkeit [gəˈzɛtslɪçkaɪt], *f.* (—, *no pl.*) lawfulness, legality.

gesetzlos [gəˈzɛtsloːs], *adj.* lawless, anarchical.

gesetzmäßig [gəˈzɛtsmɛːsɪç], *adj.* conforming to law, lawful, legitimate.

gesetzt [gəˈzɛtst], *adj.* steady, sedate, staid; *von —em Alter*, of mature age; — *daß*, supposing that.

Gesetztheit [gəˈzɛtsthaɪt], *f.* (—, *no pl.*) sedateness, steadiness.

gesetzwidrig [gəˈzɛtsviːdrɪç], *adj.* illegal, unlawful.

Gesicht (1) [gəˈzɪçt], *n.* (—s, *pl.* —er) face, physiognomy, look.

Gesicht (2) [gəˈzɪçt], *n.* (—s, *pl.* —e) sight; vision, apparition.

Gesichtsausdruck [gəˈzɪçtsausdruk], *m.* (—s, *no pl.*) face, mien; expression.

Gesichtsfeld [gə'zɪçtsfɛlt], *n.* (—es, *pl.* —er) field of vision.

Gesichtskreis [gə'zɪçtskraɪs], *m.* (—es, *pl.* —e) horizon.

Gesichtspunkt [gə'zɪçtspuŋkt], *m.* (—es, *pl.* —e) point of view.

Gesichtszug [gə'zɪçtstsu:k], *m.* (—s, *pl.* ̇e) feature.

Gesims [gə'zɪms], *n.* (—es, *pl.* —e) cornice, moulding, ledge.

Gesinde [gə'zɪndə], *n.* (—s, *no pl.*) (domestic) servants.

Gesindel [gə'zɪndəl], *n.* (—s, *no pl.*) mob, rabble.

gesinnt [gə'zɪnt], *adj.* disposed.

Gesinnung [gə'zɪnuŋ], *f.* (—, *pl.* —en) disposition, sentiment; conviction.

gesinnungslos [gə'zɪnuŋslo:s], *adj.* unprincipled.

gesinnungstreu [gə'zɪnuŋstrɔy], *adj.* loyal, staunch.

Gesinnungswechsel [gə'zɪnuŋsvɛksəl], *m.* (—s, *no pl.*) change of opinion, volte-face.

gesittet [gə'zɪtət], *adj.* civilised, well-mannered.

Gesittung [gə'zɪtuŋ], *f.* (—, *no pl.*) (*rare*) civilisation, good manners.

gesonnen [gə'zɔnən] *see* **gesinnt**.

Gespann [gə'ʃpan], *n.* (—s, *pl.* —e) team, yoke (oxen etc.).

gespannt [gə'ʃpant], *adj.* stretched; intense, thrilled; tense; filled with suspense.

Gespanntheit [gə'ʃpanthaɪt], *f.* (—, *no pl.*) tension, strain, suspense.

Gespenst [gə'ʃpɛnst], *n.* (—es, *pl.* —er) ghost, spectre, apparition.

gespenstisch [gə'ʃpɛnstɪʃ], *adj.* ghostly, spectral.

Gespiele [gə'ʃpi:lə], *m.* (—n, *pl.* —n) playmate.

Gespielin [gə'ʃpi:lɪn], *f.* (—, *pl.* —innen) (girl) playmate.

Gespinst [gə'ʃpɪnst], *n.* (—es, *pl.* —e) web.

Gespött [gə'ʃpœt], *n.* (—s, *no pl.*) mocking, mockery, jeering, derision; (*fig.*) laughing stock.

Gespräch [gə'ʃprɛ:ç], *n.* (—s, *pl.* —e) conversation, discourse, talk; (*phone*) call; *ein — anknüpfen*, start a conversation.

gesprächig [gə'ʃprɛ:çɪç], *adj.* talkative, communicative.

gespreizt [gə'ʃpraɪtst], *adj.* wide apart; (*fig.*) affected, pompous.

gesprenkelt [gə'ʃprɛŋkəlt], *adj.* speckled.

gesprungen [gə'ʃpruŋən], *adj.* cracked (glass etc.).

Gestade [gə'ʃta:də], *n.* (—s, *pl.* —) shore, coast, bank.

Gestalt [gə'ʃtalt], *f.* (—, *pl.* —en) form, figure, shape; configuration; stature; fashion; manner, way.

gestalten [gə'ʃtaltən], *v.a.* form, shape, fashion, make. — *v.r. sich —*, turn out.

Gestaltung [gə'ʃtaltuŋ], *f.* (—, *pl.* —en) formation; arrangement; planning.

geständig [gə'ʃtɛndɪç], *adj.* confessing; — *sein,* confess.

Geständnis [gə'ʃtɛntnɪs], *n.* (—ses, *pl.* —se) confession, admission.

Gestank [gə'ʃtaŋk], *m.* (—s, *no pl.*) stink, stench.

gestatten [gə'ʃtatən], *v.a.* permit, allow, grant; *wir — uns,* we beg leave to; — *Sie !* pardon me, excuse me.

Geste ['gɛstə], *f.* (—, *pl.* —n) gesture, gesticulation.

gestehen [gə'ʃte:ən], *v.a. irr.* confess, admit, own; *offen gestanden,* quite frankly.

Gestein [gə'ʃtaɪn], *n.* (—s, *pl.* —e) (*Poet.*) rock; (*Geol.*) rocks, minerals.

Gestell [gə'ʃtɛl], *n.* (—s, *pl.* —e) rack, frame; (*table*) trestle; (*books*) stand.

Gestellung [gə'ʃtɛluŋ], *f.* (—, *no pl.*) (*Mil.*) reporting for service.

gestern ['gɛstərn], *adv.* yesterday; — *abend,* last night.

gestiefelt [gə'ʃti:fəlt], *adj.* booted; *der —e Kater,* Puss in Boots.

gestielt [gə'ʃti:lt], *adj.* (*axe*) helved; (*Bot.*) stalked, stemmed.

gestikulieren [gɛstiku'li:rən], *v.n.* gesticulate.

Gestirn [gə'ʃtɪrn], *n.* (—s, *pl.* —e) star, constellation.

gestirnt [gə'ʃtɪrnt], *adj.* starred, starry.

Gestöber [gə'ʃtø:bər], *n.* (—s, *pl.* —) (*snow, dust*) drift, storm, blizzard.

Gesträuch [gə'ʃtrɔyç], *n.* (—es, *no pl.*) bushes, shrubs; thicket.

gestreift [gə'ʃtraɪft], *adj.* striped.

gestreng [gə'ʃtrɛŋ], *adj.* (*obs.*) strict, severe.

gestrig ['gɛstrɪç], *adj.* of yesterday.

Gestrüpp [gə'ʃtryp], *n.* (—s, *no pl.*) bushes, underwood, shrubs, shrubbery.

Gestüt [gə'ʃty:t], *n.* (—s, *pl.* —e) stud (-farm).

Gestüthengst [gə'ʃty:thɛŋst], *m.* (—es, *pl.* —e) stallion.

Gesuch [gə'zu:x], *n.* (—s, *pl.* —e) petition, request, application.

gesucht [gə'zu:xt], *adj.* in demand; (*style*) far-fetched; affected; studied.

gesund [gə'zunt], *adj.* healthy, wholesome; *der —e Menschenverstand,* common sense.

Gesundbrunnen [gə'zuntbrunən], *m.* (—s, *pl.* —) mineral waters; spa.

gesunden [gə'zundən], *v.n.* (*aux.* sein) recover o.'s health.

Gesundheit [gə'zunthaɪt], *f.* (—, *no pl.*) health.

Gesundheitslehre [gə'zunthaɪtsle:rə], *f.* (—, *no pl.*) hygiene.

Getäfel [gə'tɛ:fəl], *n.* (—s, *no pl.*) wainscot, wainscoting, panelling.

Getändel [gə'tɛndəl], *n.* (—s, *no pl.*) (*rare*) flirting, dallying.

Getier [gə'ti:r], *n.* (—s, *no pl.*) (*collective term*) animals.

Getöse [gə'tø:zə], *n.* (—s, *no pl.*) loud noise, din.

Getränk

Getränk [gə'trɛŋk], *n.* (—s, *pl.* —e) drink, beverage.

getrauen [gə'trauən], *v.r. sich* —, dare, venture.

Getreide [gə'traɪdə], *n.* (—s, *pl.* —) corn, grain.

getreu [gə'trɔy], *adj.* faithful, true, loyal.

getreulich [gə'trɔylɪç], *adv.* faithfully, truly, loyally.

Getriebe [gə'tri:bə], *n.* (—s, *pl.* —) machinery; (*Motor.*) gear; drive; *das — der Welt*, the bustle of life.

getrieben [gə'tri:bən], *adj.* (*Tech.*) chased (work.)

Getrödel [gə'trø:dəl], *n.* (—s, *no pl.*) dawdling.

getrost [gə'tro:st], *adj.* confident, cheerful; *— sein*, be of good cheer.

Getto ['gɛto], *n.* (—s, *pl.* —s) ghetto.

Getue [gə'tu:ə], *n.* (—s, *no pl.*) pretence, fuss.

Getümmel [gə'tyməl], *n.* (—s, *no pl.*) bustle, turmoil.

geübt [gə'y:pt], *adj.* skilled, versed.

Geübtheit [gə'y:pthaɪt], *f.* (—, *no pl.*) skill, experience, dexterity.

Gevatter [gə'fatər], *m.* (—s, *pl.* —) (*obs.*) godfather.

gevierteilt [gə'fi:rtaɪlt], *adj.* quartered.

Gewächs [gə'vɛks], *n.* (—es, *pl.* —e) plant, growth; (*Med.*) excrescence.

gewachsen [gə'vaksən], *adj. einem* (*einer Sache*) — *sein*, be equal to s.o. (s.th.).

Gewächshaus [gə'vɛkshaus], *n.* (—es, *pl.* —er) green-house, hot-house, conservatory.

gewagt [gə'va:kt], *adj.* risky, hazardous; daring.

gewählt [gə've:lt], *adj.* choice, select.

gewahr [gə'va:r], *adj. einer Sache — werden*, become aware of s.th., perceive s.th.

Gewähr [gə've:r], *f.* (—, *no pl.*) surety; guarantee; warranty; *— leisten*, guarantee.

gewahren [gə'va:rən], *v.a.* perceive, see, become aware of.

gewähren [gə've:rən], *v.a.* allow, grant; *einen — lassen*, let s.o. do as he pleases, let be.

Gewährleistung [gə've:rlaɪstuŋ], *f.* (—, *pl.* —en) grant of security (*or* bail); guarantee.

Gewahrsam [gə'va:rza:m], *m.* (—s, *no pl.*) safe-keeping, custody.

Gewährsmann [gə've:rsman], *m.* (—es, *pl.* —er) authority; informant.

Gewährung [gə've:ruŋ,] *f.* (—, *no pl.*) granting (of request).

Gewalt [gə'valt], *f.* (—, *pl.* —en) power, force, might; authority; violence; *höhere —*, (*Law*) act of God, force majeure; *sich in der — haben*, have control over o.s.

Gewalthaber [gə'valtha:bər], *m.* (—s, *pl.* —) tyrant; despot, autocrat; person in authority.

gewaltig [gə'valtɪç], *adj.* powerful, mighty, enormous, stupendous.

gewaltsam [gə'valtza:m], *adj.* forcible, violent.

Gewaltstreich [gə'valtʃtraɪç], *m.* (—s, *pl.* —e) bold stroke; coup d'état.

Gewalttat [gə'valtta:t], *f.* (—, *pl.* —en) violent action, violence, outrage.

gewalttätig [gə'valttɛ:tɪç], *adj.* violent, fierce, outrageous.

Gewand [gə'vant], *n.* (—es, *pl.* —er) (*Lit.*) garment, dress; (*Eccl.*) vestment.

gewandt [gə'vant], *adj.* nimble, deft, clever; (*mind*) versatile.

gewärtig [gə'vɛrtɪç], *adj. einer Sache — sein*, expect s.th. to happen.

Gewäsch [gə'vɛʃ], *n.* (—es, *no pl.*) stuff and nonsense; rubbish.

Gewässer [gə'vɛsər], *n.* (—s, *pl.* —) waters.

Gewebe [gə've:bə], *n.* (—s, *pl.* —) (*Physiol.*, *Text.*) tissue; web, weft, texture.

geweckt [gə'vɛkt], *adj.* smart, wide-awake.

Gewehr [gə've:r], *n.* (—s, *pl.* —e) gun, fire-arm, rifle.

Gewehrlauf [gə've:rlauf], *m.* (—s, *pl.* —e) barrel.

Geweih [gə'vaɪ], *n.* (—s, *pl.* —e) horns, antlers.

geweiht [gə'vaɪt], *adj.* consecrated; holy.

gewellt [gə'vɛlt], *adj.* corrugated, wavy.

Gewerbe [gə'vɛrbə], *n.* (—s, *pl.* —) trade, profession, business; calling; industry.

Gewerbekunde [gə'vɛrbəkundə], *f.* (—, *no pl.*) technology.

Gewerbeschein [gə'vɛrbəʃaɪn], *m.* (—s, *pl.* —e) trade-licence.

gewerblich [gə'vɛrplɪç], *adj.* industrial.

gewerbsmäßig [gə'vɛrpsmɛ:sɪç], *adj.* professional.

Gewerkschaft [gə'vɛrkʃaft], *f.* (—, *pl.* —en) trade union.

Gewicht [gə'vɪçt], *n.* (—s, *pl.* —e) weight; *schwer ins — fallen*, carry great weight, weigh heavily.

gewichtig [gə'vɪçtɪç], *adj.* weighty, ponderous; (*fig.*) momentous, important, strong.

gewiegt [gə'vi:kt], *adj.* experienced, clever.

gewillt [gə'vɪlt], *adj.* willing.

Gewimmel [gə'vɪməl], *n.* (—s, *no pl.*) milling crowd, swarm, throng.

Gewinde [gə'vɪndə], *n.* (—s, *pl.* —) (*screw*) thread; (*flowers*) garland.

Gewinn [gə'vɪn], *m.* (—s, *pl.* —e) gain, profit; (*lottery*) prize; (*gambling*) winnings.

gewinnen [gə'vɪnən], *v.a. irr.* win, gain, obtain, get, earn.

gewinnend [gə'vɪnənt], *adj.* prepossessing; engaging.

Gewinnung [gə'vɪnuŋ], *f.* (—, *no pl.*) (*Ind.*, *Chem.*) extraction; output, production.

Gewinsel [gə'vɪnzəl], *n.* (—s, *no pl.*) whimpering.

Gewinst [gə'vɪnst], *m.* (—es, *pl.* —e) (*obs.*) gain, profit.

Gewirr [gə'vɪr], *n.* (—s, *no pl.*) entanglement, confusion.

gewiß [gə'vɪs], *adj.* (*Genit.*) certain, sure. — *adv.* indeed.

Gewissen [gə'vɪsən], *n.* (—s, *no pl.*) conscience.

gewissenhaft [gə'vɪsənhaft], *adj.* conscientious, scrupulous.

gewissenlos [gə'vɪsənlo:s], *adj.* unscrupulous.

Gewissensbiß [gə'vɪsənsbɪs],*m.*(—sses, *pl.* —sse) (*mostly pl.*) pangs of conscience.

gewissermaßen [gə'vɪsərma:sən], *adv.* to a certain extent, so to speak.

Gewißheit [gə'vɪshaɪt], *f.* (—, *no pl.*) certainty.

gewißlich [gə'vɪslɪç], *adv.* surely.

Gewitter [gə'vɪtər], *n.* (—s, *pl.* —) thunderstorm.

gewittern [gə'vɪtərn], *v.n.* thunder.

gewitzigt, gewitzt [gə'vɪtsɪçt, gə'vɪtst], *adj.* knowing, clever; shrewd.

gewogen [gə'vo:gən], *adj.* kindly disposed, favourable; *einem — sein*, be favourably inclined towards s.o.

Gewogenheit [gə'vo:gənhaɪt], *f.* (—, *no pl.*) kindness, favour.

gewöhnen [gə'vø:nən], *v.a.* accustom to. — *v.r. sich — an*, get used to, accustom o.s. to.

Gewohnheit [gə'vo:nhaɪt], *f.* (—, *pl.* —en) (*general*) custom, usage; (*personal*) habit.

gewohnheitsmäßig [gə'vo:nhaɪtsmɛ:sɪç], *adj.* habitual. — *adv.* by force of habit.

Gewohnheitsrecht [gə'vo:nhaɪtsrɛçt], *n.* (—s, *no pl.*) common law.

gewöhnlich[gə'vø:nlɪç],*adj.* customary, usual; (*fig.*) common, mean, vulgar.

gewohnt [gə'vo:nt], *adj.* accustomed to, used to.

Gewöhnung [gə'vø:nuŋ], *f.* (—, *no pl.*) habit, use, habituation.

Gewölbe [gə'vœlbə], *n.* (—s, *pl.* —) vault, arch.

Gewölk [gə'vœlk], *n.* (—s, *no pl.*) clouds, cloud formation.

Gewühl [gə'vy:l], *n.* (—s, *no pl.*) crowd, throng, bustle.

gewunden [gə'vundən], *adj.* tortuous.

Gewürm [gə'vyrm], *n.* (—s, *no pl.*) reptiles, worms; vermin.

Gewürz [gə'vyrts], *n.* (—es, *pl.* —e) spice.

Gewürznelke [gə'vyrtsnɛlkə], *f.* (—, *pl.* —n) clove.

Gezänk [gə'tsɛŋk], *n.* (—s, *no pl.*) quarrelling, bickering.

Gezeiten [gə'tsaɪtən], *f. pl.* tides.

Gezeter [gə'tse:tər], *n.* (—s, *no pl.*) screaming, yelling; (*fig.*) outcry.

geziemen [gə'tsi:mən], *v.r. sich für einen —*, befit *or* become s.o.

geziert [gə'tsi:rt], *adj.* affected.

Gezischel [gə'tsɪʃəl], *n.* (—s, *no pl.*) whispering.

Gezücht [gə'tsyçt], *n.* (—s, *no pl.*) brood, breed.

Gezweig [gə'tsvaɪk], *n.* (—s, *no pl.*) branches, boughs.

Gezwitscher [gə'tsvɪtʃər], *n.* (—s, *no pl.*) chirping.

Gezwungenheit [gə'tsvuŋənhaɪt], *f.* (—, *no pl.*) constraint.

Gicht [gɪçt], *f.* (—, *no pl.*) (*Med.*) gout.

gichtbrüchig ['gɪçtbryçɪç], *adj.* (*obs.*) paralytic; gouty.

gichtig ['gɪçtɪç], *adj.* gouty.

Giebel ['gi:bəl], *m.* (—s, *pl.* —) gable.

Giebelfenster ['gi:bəlfɛnstər], *n.* (—s, *pl.*—) gable-window, dormer-window.

gieb(e)lig ['gi:b(ə)lɪç], *adj.* gabled.

Gier [gi:r], *f.* (—, *no pl.*) greediness, eagerness.

gieren ['gi:rən], *v.n.* (*rare*) — *nach*, thirst for, yearn for.

gierig ['gi:rɪç], *adj.* eager, greedy.

Gießbach ['gi:sbax], *m.* (—s, *pl.* ⸚e) mountain-torrent.

gießen ['gi:sən], *v.a. irr.* (*liquids*) pour, shed; (*metal*) cast, found.

Gießer ['gi:sər], *m.* (—s, *pl.* —) founder.

Gießerei [gi:sə'raɪ], *f.* (—, *pl.* —en) foundry.

Gießform ['gi:sfɔrm], *f.* (—, *pl.* —en) casting-mould.

Gießkanne ['gi:skanə], *f.* (—, *pl.* —n) watering-can.

Gift [gɪft], *n.* (—es, *pl.* —e) poison, venom; (*fig.*) virulence; (*coll.*) *darauf kannst du — nehmen*, you can bet your life on it.

Giftbaum ['gɪftbaum], *m.* (—s, *pl.* ⸚e) upas-tree.

Giftdrüse ['gɪftdry:zə], *f.* (—, *pl.* —n) poison-gland.

giftig ['gɪftɪç], *adj.* poisonous; (*fig.*) venomous; (*Med.*) toxic.

Giftlehre ['gɪftle:rə], *f.* (—, *no pl.*) toxicology.

Giftpilz ['gɪftpɪlts], *m.* (—es, *pl.* —e) poisonous toadstool.

Giftschlange ['gɪftʃlaŋə], *f.* (—, *pl.* —n) poisonous snake.

Giftstoff ['gɪftʃtɔf], *m.* (—es, *pl.* —e) poison, virus.

Gigant [gɪ'gant], *m.* (—en, *pl.* —en) giant.

Gigerl ['gi:gərl], *m.* (—s, *pl.* —) (*Austr. dial.*) fop, coxcomb.

Gilde ['gɪldə], *f.* (—, *pl.* —n) guild, corporation.

Gimpel ['gɪmpəl], *m.* (—s, *pl.* —) (*Orn.*) bullfinch, chaffinch; (*fig.*) simpleton.

Ginster ['gɪnstər], *m.* (—s, *no pl.*) (*Bot.*) gorse, furze, broom.

Gipfel ['gɪpfəl], *m.* (—s, *pl.* —) summit, peak; (*fig.*) acme, culmination, height.

gipfeln ['gɪpfəln], *v.n.* culminate.

Gips [gɪps], *m.* (—es, *no pl.*) gypsum, stucco, plaster of Paris.

Gipsabdruck ['gɪpsapdruk], *m.* (—s, *pl.* ⸚e) plaster-cast.

Gipsbild

Gipsbild ['gɪpsbɪlt], *n.* (—s, *pl.* —er) plaster-figure.

Gipsverband ['gɪpsfɛrbant], *m.* (—es, *pl.* -̈e) (*Med.*) plaster of Paris dressing.

girieren [ʒɪ'riːrən], *v.a.* (*Comm.*) endorse (a bill).

Girlande [gɪr'landə], *f.* (—, *pl.* —n) garland.

Girobank ['ʒiːrobaŋk], *f.* (—, *pl.* —en) transfer *or* clearing bank.

Gis [gɪs], *n.* (—, *pl.* —) (*Mus.*) G sharp; — *Moll*, G sharp minor.

gischen ['gɪʃən], *v.n.* foam, froth.

Gischt [gɪʃt], *f.* (—, *pl.* —e) foam, froth; spray.

Gitarre [gi'tarə], *f.* (—, *pl.* —n) guitar.

Gitter ['gɪtər], *n.* (—s, *pl.* —) trellis, grate, fence; railing; lattice; (*colour-printing*) screen.

Gitterwerk ['gɪtərvɛrk], *n.* (—s, *no pl.*) trellis-work.

Glacéhandschuh [gla'seː:hantʃuː], *m.* (—s, *pl.* —e) kid-glove.

Glanz [glants], *m.* (—es, *no pl.*) brightness, lustre, gloss; polish, sheen; (*fig.*) splendour.

glänzen ['glɛntsən], *v.n.* shine, glitter, glisten; (*fig.*) sparkle.

glänzend ['glɛntsənt], *adj.* glossy; (*fig.*) splendid, magnificent.

Glanzfirnis ['glantsfɪrnɪs], *m.* (—ses, *pl.* —se) glazing varnish.

Glanzleder ['glantsleːdər], *n.* (—s, *no pl.*) patent leather.

Glanzleinwand ['glantslaɪnvant], *f.* (—, *no pl.*) glazed linen.

glanzlos ['glantsloːs], *adj.* lustreless, dull.

glanzvoll ['glantsfɔl], *adj.* splendid, brilliant.

Glanzzeit ['glantstsaɪt], *f.* (—, *pl.* —en) golden age.

Glas [glaːs], *n.* (—es, *pl.* -̈er) glass, tumbler.

glasartig ['glaːsaːrtɪç], *adj.* vitreous, glassy.

Glaser ['glaːzər], *m.* (—s, *pl.* —) glazier.

Glaserkitt ['glaːzərkɪt], *m.* (—s, *no pl.*) putty.

gläsern ['glɛːzərn], *adj.* vitreous, glassy, made of glass.

Glashütte ['glaːshytə], *f.* (—, *pl.* —n) glass-works.

glasieren [gla'ziːrən], *v.a.* glaze; (*cake etc.*) ice.

glasiert [gla'ziːrt], *adj.* glazed; (*Cul.*) frosted, iced; (*Art.*) varnished.

Glasröhre ['glaːsrøːrə], *f.* (—, *pl.* —n) glass-tube.

Glasscheibe ['glaːsʃaɪbə], *f.* (—, *pl.* —n) glass-pane, sheet of glass.

Glassplitter ['glaːsʃplɪtər], *m.* (—s, *pl.* —) splinter of glass.

Glasur [gla'zuːr], *f.* (—, *pl.* —en) (*potter's*) glaze, glazing; enamel, varnish; (*cake*) icing.

glatt [glat], *adj.* smooth, sleek; even, plain, glossy; glib; downright. — *adv.* entirely; — *rasiert*, close-shaven.

Glätte ['glɛtə], *f.* (—, *no pl.*) smoothness, evenness, slipperiness; polish.

Glatteis ['glataɪs], *n.* (—es, *no pl.*) slippery ice; sheet ice; (*Am.*) glaze; *einen aufs — führen*, lead s.o. up the garden path.

glätten ['glɛtən], *v.a.* smooth; (*dial.*) iron.

Glatze ['glatsə], *f.* (—, *pl.* —n) bald head.

glatzköpfig ['glatskœpfɪç], *adj.* bald, bald-pated.

Glaube(n) ['glaubə(n)], *m.* (—ns, *no pl.*) faith, belief; creed, religion.

glauben ['glaubən], *v.a.* believe; think, suppose. — *v.n. an etwas* (*Acc.*) —, believe in s.th.

Glaubensbekenntnis ['glaubənsbəkɛntnɪs], *n.* (—ses, *pl.* —se) confession of faith; creed.

Glaubensgericht ['glaubənsgərɪçt], *n.* (—es, *no pl.*) inquisition.

Glaubersalz ['glaubərzalts], *n.* (—es, *no pl.*) phosphate of soda, Glauber's salts.

glaubhaft ['glauphaft], *adj.* credible, authentic.

gläubig ['glɔybɪç], *adj.* believing, faithful; (*Eccl.*) *die Gläubigen*, the faithful.

Gläubiger ['glɔybɪgər], *m.* (—s, *pl.* —) creditor.

glaublich ['glauplɪç], *adj.* credible, believable.

glaubwürdig ['glaupvyrdɪç], *adj.* authentic, worthy of belief; plausible.

gleich [glaɪç], *adj.* same, like, equal, even; *auf —e Weise*, likewise; *es ist mir ganz —*, it is all the same to me. — *adv.* alike, at once; almost; just as; *ich komme —*, I shall be there in a moment; — *und — gesellt sich gern*, birds of a feather flock together.

gleichaltrig ['glaɪçaltrɪç], *adj.* of the same age.

gleichartig ['glaɪça:rtɪç], *adj.* of the same kind, homogeneous.

gleichberechtigt ['glaɪçbərɛçtɪçt], *adj.* entitled to equal rights.

Gleiche ['glaɪçə], *n.* (—n, *pl.* —n) the like; the same; *etwas ins — bringen*, straighten s.th. out.

gleichen ['glaɪçən], *v.n. irr.* be like, resemble, be equal to.

gleichermaßen ['glaɪçərmaːsən], *adv.* in a like manner, likewise.

gleichfalls ['glaɪçfals], *adv.* likewise, equally, as well; *danke —*, thanks, the same to you.

gleichförmig ['glaɪçfœrmɪç], *adj.* uniform; monotonous.

gleichgesinnt ['glaɪçgəzɪnt], *adj.* congenial, of the same mind.

Gleichgewicht ['glaɪçgəvɪçt], *n.* (—s, *no pl.*) balance, equilibrium.

gleichgültig ['glaɪçgyltɪç], *adj.* indifferent; *es ist mir —*, it's all the same to me.

Gleichheit ['glaɪçhaɪt], *f.* (—, *pl.* —en) equality, likeness.

Gleichklang ['glaɪçklaŋ], *m.* (—s, *pl.* ˸e) consonance.

gleichmachen ['glaɪçmaxən], *v.a.* level, equate; *dem Erdboden* —, raze to the ground.

Gleichmaß ['glaɪçmaːs], *n.* (—es, *no pl.*) proportion, symmetry.

gleichmäßig ['glaɪçmɛːsɪç], *adj.* proportionale, symmetrical.

Gleichmut ['glaɪçmuːt], *m.* (—s, *no pl.*) equanimity, calm.

gleichmütig ['glaɪçmyːtɪç], *adj.* even-tempered, calm.

gleichnamig ['glaɪçnaːmɪç], *adj.* homonymous.

Gleichnis ['glaɪçnɪs], *n.* (—ses, *pl.* —se) simile; (*Bibl.*) parable.

gleichsam ['glaɪçzaːm], *adv.* as it were, as if.

gleichschenklig ['glaɪçʃɛŋklɪç], *adj.* (*Maths.*) isosceles.

gleichseitig ['glaɪçzaɪtɪç], *adj.* (*Maths.*) equilateral.

Gleichsetzung ['glaɪçzɛtsuŋ], *f.* (—, *no pl.*), **Gleichstellung** ['glaɪçʃtɛluŋ], *f.* (—, *pl.* —en) equalisation.

Gleichstrom ['glaɪçʃtroːm], *m.* (—s, *no pl.*) (*Elec.*) direct current.

gleichtun ['glaɪçtuːn], *v.a. irr. es einem* —, emulate s.o.

Gleichung ['glaɪçuŋ], *f.* (—, *pl.* —en) (*Maths.*) equation.

gleichwohl ['glaɪçvoːl], *adv., conj.* nevertheless, however, yet.

gleichzeitig ['glaɪçtsaɪtɪç], *adj.* simultaneous, contemporary.

Gleis [glaɪs], *n.* (—es, *pl.* —e) (*Railw.*) track; rails; (*Am.*) track.

gleiten ['glaɪtən], *v.n. irr.* (*aux.* sein) glide, slide, slip.

Gleitflug ['glaɪtfluːk], *m.* (—es, *pl.* ˸e) (*Aviat.*) gliding.

Gletscher ['glɛtʃər], *m.* (—s, *pl.* —) glacier.

Gletscherspalte ['glɛtʃərʃpaltə], *f.* (—, *pl.* —n) crevasse.

Glied [gliːt], *n.* (—es, *pl.* —er) limb, joint; member; link; rank, file.

Gliederlähmung ['gliːdərlɛːmuŋ], *f.* (—, *no pl.*) paralysis.

gliedern ['gliːdərn], *v.a.* articulate, arrange, form.

Gliederreißen ['gliːdərraɪsən], *n.* (—s, *no pl.*) pain in the limbs, rheumatism, arthritis etc.

Gliederung ['gliːdəruŋ], *f.* (—, *pl.* —en) articulation, disposition, structure, arrangement, organisation.

Gliedmaßen ['gliːtmaːsən], *f. pl.* limbs.

glimmen ['glɪmən], *v.n. irr.* glimmer, glow, burn faintly; —*de Asche*, embers.

Glimmer ['glɪmər], *m.* (—s, *no pl.*) (*Min.*) mica.

glimpflich ['glɪmpflɪç], *adj.* gentle.

glitschen ['glɪtʃən], *v.n.* (*aux.* sein) (*coll.*) slide.

glitschig ['glɪtʃɪç], *adj.* (*coll.*) slippery.

glitzern ['glɪtsərn], *v.n.* glisten, glitter.

Globus ['gloːbus], *m.* (—ses, *pl.* —se) globe.

Glöckchen ['glœkçən], *n.* (—s, *pl.* —) small bell; hand-bell.

Glocke ['glɔkə], *f.* (—, *pl.* —n) bell; *etwas an die große* — *hängen*, make a great fuss about s.th.

Glockenblume ['glɔkənbluːmə], *f.* (—, *pl.* —n) (*Bot.*) bluebell.

Glockengießer ['glɔkəngiːsər], *m.* (—s, *pl.* —) bell-founder.

glockenklar ['glɔkənklaːr], *adj.* as clear as a bell.

Glockenläuter ['glɔkənlɔytər], *m.* (—s, *pl.* —) bell-ringer.

Glockenspiel ['glɔkənʃpiːl], *n.* (—s, *pl.* —e) chime; (*Mus.*) glockenspiel, carillon.

Glockenstuhl ['glɔkənʃtuːl], *m.* (—s, *pl.* ˸e) belfry.

Glockenzug ['glɔkəntsuːk], *m.* (—s, *pl.* ˸e) bell-rope; (*Mus.*) bell-stop.

Glöckner ['glœkner], *m.* (—s, *pl.* —) bellringer, sexton.

glorreich ['gloːraɪç], *adj.* glorious.

Glosse ['glɔsə], *f.* (—, *pl.* —n) gloss, comment, annotation; — *n machen über*, comment upon; find fault with; scoff at.

glotzen ['glɔtsən], *v.n.* stare wide-eyed; gape.

Glück [glyk], *n.* (—s, *no pl.*) luck, good luck, fortune, happiness; — *haben*, be in luck; *auf gut* —, at random; *zum* —, fortunately, luckily; *viel* —, good luck.

Glucke ['glukə], *f.* (—, *pl.* —n) (sitting) hen.

glücken ['glykən], *v.n.* succeed; *es ist mir geglückt*, I have succeeded in.

glücklich ['glyklɪç], *adj.* fortunate, lucky, happy.

glückselig [glyk'zeːlɪç], *adj.* blissful, happy.

glucksen ['gluksən], *v.n.* gurgle.

Glücksfall ['glyksfal], *m.* (—es, *pl.* ˸e) lucky chance, windfall, stroke of good fortune.

Glückspilz ['glykspɪlts], *m.* (—es, *pl.* —e) (*coll.*) lucky dog.

glückverheißend ['glykferhaɪsənt], *adj.* auspicious, propitious.

Glückwunsch ['glykvunʃ], *m.* (—es, *pl.* ˸e) congratulation; felicitation.

glühen ['glyːən], *v.a.* make red-hot; (*wine*) mull. — *v.n.* glow, be red-hot.

glühend ['glyːənt], *adj.* glowing, burning; red-hot; (*coal*) live; (*fig.*) ardent, fervent.

Glühstrumpf ['glyːʃtrumpf], *m.* (—es, *pl.* ˸e) incandescent mantle.

Glühwein ['glyːvaɪn], *m.* (—s, *no pl.*) mulled wine.

Glut [gluːt], *f.* (—, *no pl.*) glowing fire; heat; (*fig.*) ardour.

glutrot ['gluːtroːt], *adj.* fiery red.

Glyzerin ['glytsəriːn], *n.* (—s, *no pl.*) glycerine.

Gnade

Gnade ['gna:də], f. (—, pl. —n) grace; favour; pardon, clemency, mercy; kindness; *Euer* —n, Your Grace.

Gnadenakt ['gna:dənakt], m. (—s, pl. —e) act of grace.

Gnadenbrot ['gna:dənbro:t], n. (—s, no pl.) *das* — *essen*, live on charity.

Gnadenfrist ['gna:dənfrıst], f. (—, pl. —en) respite.

Gnadenort ['gna:dənɔrt], m. (—(e)s, pl. —e) place of pilgrimage.

Gnadenstoß ['gna:dənʃto:s], m. (—es, pl. ⁝e) finishing stroke, coup de grâce, death-blow.

gnadenvoll ['gna:dənfɔl], adj. merciful, gracious.

Gnadenweg ['gna:dənve:k], m. (—es, no pl.) act of grace; *auf dem* —, by reprieve (as an act of grace).

gnädig ['gnɛ:dɪç], adj. gracious, merciful, kind; —*e Frau*, Madam; —*er Herr*, Sir.

Gnostiker ['gnɔstıkər], m. (—s, pl. —) gnostic.

Gnu [gnu:], n. (—s, pl. —s) (*Zool.*) gnu.

Gold [gɔlt], n. (—(e)s, no pl.) gold.

Goldammer ['gɔltamər], f. (—, pl. —n) (*Orn.*) yellow-hammer.

Goldamsel ['gɔltamzəl], f. (—, pl. —n) (*Orn.*) yellow-thrush.

Goldarbeiter ['gɔltarbaıtər], m. (—s, pl. —) goldsmith.

Goldbarren ['gɔltbarən], m. (—s, pl. —) ingot of gold.

Goldbergwerk ['gɔltberkverk], n. (—s, pl.—e) gold-mine.

Goldfisch ['gɔltfıʃ], m. (—es, pl. —e) goldfish.

Goldgewicht ['gɔltgəvıçt], n. (—s, no pl.) gold-weight, troy-weight.

Goldgrube ['gɔltgru:bə], f. (—, pl. —n) gold-mine.

goldig ['gɔldıç], adj. golden; (*fig.*) sweet, cute, charming.

Goldklumpen ['gɔltklumpən], m. (—s, pl. —) nugget (of gold).

Goldlack ['gɔltlak], m. (—s, no pl.) gold-coloured varnish; (*Bot.*) wallflower.

Goldmacher ['gɔltmaxər], m. (—s, pl. —) alchemist.

Goldregen ['gɔltre:gən], m. (—s, pl. —) (*Bot.*) laburnum.

Goldscheider ['gɔltʃaıdər], m. (—s, pl. —) gold-refiner.

Goldschmied ['gɔltʃmi:t], m. (—s, pl. —e) goldsmith.

Goldschnitt ['gɔltʃnıt], m. (—s, no pl.) gilt edge.

Golf (1) [gɔlf], m. (—s, pl. —e) gulf.

Golf (2) [gɔlf], n. (—s, no pl.) golf.

Gondel ['gɔndəl], f. (—, pl. —n) gondola.

gondeln ['gɔndəln], v.n. (*aux.* sein) ride in a gondola; (*coll.*) travel, get about.

gönnen ['gœnən], v.a. *einem etwas* —, not grudge s.o. s.th.; *wir* — *es ihm*, we are happy for him.

Gönner ['gœnər], m. (—s, pl. —) patron, protector.

gönnerhaft ['gœnərhaft], adj. patronising.

Gönnerschaft ['gœnərʃaft], f. (—, no pl.) patronage.

gordisch ['gɔrdıʃ], adj. Gordian; *der* —*e Knoten*, the Gordian knot.

Göre ['gø:rə], f. (—, pl. —n) (*coll.*) brat; (*Am.*) kid.

Gosse ['gɔsə], f. (—, pl. —n) gutter.

Gote ['go:tə], m. (—n, pl. —n) Goth.

Gotik ['go:tık], f. (—, no pl.) Gothic style (architecture etc.).

gotisch ['go:tıʃ], adj. Gothic.

Gott [gɔ:t], m. (—es, pl. ⁝er) God, god; — *befohlen*, goodbye; *grüß* —! (*Austr.*) good day; — *sei Dank*, thank God, thank heaven.

gottbegnadet ['gɔtbəgna:dət], adj. favoured by God, inspired.

Götterbild ['gœtərbılt], n. (—es, pl. —er) image of a god.

gottergeben ['gɔterge:bən], adj. submissive to God's will, devout.

Götterlehre ['gœtərle:rə], f. (—, pl. —n) mythology.

Götterspeise ['gœtərʃpaızə], f. (—, pl. —n) ambrosia.

Götterspruch ['gœtərʃprux], m. (—s, no pl.) oracle.

Göttertrank ['gœtərtraŋk], m. (—s, pl. ⁝e) nectar.

Gottesacker ['gɔtəsakər], m. (—s, pl. —) God's acre, churchyard.

Gottesdienst ['gɔtəsdi:nst], m. (—es, pl. —e) divine service, public worship.

gottesfürchtig ['gɔtəsfyrçtıç], adj. God-fearing, pious.

Gottesgelehrsamkeit ['gɔtəsgəle:rza:mkaıt], f. (—, no pl.) (*rare*) theology, divinity.

Gottesgericht ['gɔtəsgərıçt], n. (—s, pl. —e) ordeal.

Gotteshaus ['gɔtəshaus], n. (—es, pl. ⁝er) house of God; (*rare*) church.

Gotteslästerer ['gɔtəslestərər], m. (—s, pl. —) blasphemer.

Gottesleugner ['gɔtəslɔygnər], m. (—s, pl. —) atheist.

Gottfried ['gɔtfri:t], m. Godfrey, Geoffrey.

gottgefällig ['gɔtgəfɛlıç], adj. pleasing to God.

Gottheit ['gɔthaıt], f. (—, pl. —en) deity, divinity.

Göttin ['gœtın], f. (—, pl. —nen) goddess.

göttlich ['gœtlıç], adj. divine, godlike; (*fig.*) heavenly.

gottlob! [gɔt'lo:p], excl. thank God!

gottlos ['gɔtlo:s], adj. godless, ungodly, impious; (*fig.*) wicked.

gottvergessen ['gɔtfergesən], adj. reprobate, impious.

gottverlassen ['gɔtferlasən], adj. God-forsaken.

Götze ['gœtsə], m. (—n, pl. —n) idol, false deity.

Götzenbild ['gœtsənbɪlt], *n.* (—es, *pl.* —er) idol.
Götzendienst ['gœtsəndi:nst], *m.* (—es, *no pl.*) idolatry.
Gouvernante [guvɛr'nantə], *f.* (—, *pl.* —n) governess.
Gouverneur [guvɛr'nø:r], *m.* (—s, *pl.* —e) governor.
Grab [gra:p], *n.* (—s, *pl.* ⁻er) grave, tomb; sepulchre.
Graben ['gra:bən], *m.* (—s, *pl.* ⁻) ditch, trench.
graben ['gra:bən], *v.a. irr.* dig.
Grabgeläute ['gra:pgəlɔytə], *n.* (—s, *no pl.*) death-knell.
Grabhügel ['gra:phy:gəl], *m.* (—s, *pl.* —) tumulus, mound.
Grablegung ['gra:ple:guŋ], *f.* (—, *no pl.*) *(rare)* burial, interment.
Grabmal ['gra:pma:l], *n.* (—s, *pl.* —e, ⁻er) tomb, sepulchre, monument.
Grabschrift ['gra:pʃrɪft], *f.* (—, *pl.* —n) epitaph.
Grabstichel ['gra:pʃtɪçəl], *m.* (—s, *pl.* —) graving-tool.
Grad [gra:t], *m.* (—s, *pl.* —e) degree; rank; grade; extent; point; *in gewissem —e,* to a certain degree; *im höchsten —e,* in the highest degree, extremely.
Gradeinteilung ['gra:taɪntaɪluŋ], *f.* (—, *pl* —en) gradation, graduation.
Gradmesser ['gra:tmesər], *m.* (—s, *pl.* —) graduator; *(fig.)* index.
gradweise ['gra:tvaɪzə], *adv.* gradually, by degrees.
Graf [gra:f], *m.* (—en, *pl.* —en) count, earl.
Gräfin ['grɛfɪn], *f.* (—, *pl.* —en) countess.
gräflich ['grɛflɪç], *adj.* belonging to a count *or* earl.
Grafschaft ['gra:fʃaft], *f.* (—, *pl.* —en) county, shire.
Gral [gra:l], *m.* (—s, *no pl.*) Holy Grail.
Gram [gra:m], *m.* (—s, *no pl.*) grief, sorrow.
grämen ['grɛ:mən], *v.a.* grieve. — *v.r. sich —,* grieve, fret, worry.
gramgebeugt ['gra:mgəbɔykt], *adj.* prostrate with grief.
grämlich ['grɛ:mlɪç], *adj.* sullen, morose, ill-humoured.
Gramm [gram], *n.* (—s, *pl.* —e) gramme (15.438 grains); *(Am.)* gram.
Grammatik [gra'matɪk], *f.* (—, *pl.* —en) grammar.
grammatikalisch, grammatisch [gramatɪ'ka:lɪʃ, gra'matɪʃ], *adj.* grammatical.
Gran [gra:n], *n.* (—s, *pl.* —e) *(weight)* grain.
Granat [gra'na:t], *m.* (—s, *pl.* —e) garnet.
Granatapfel [gra'na:tapfəl], *m.* (—s, *pl.* ⁻e) *(Bot.)* pomegranate.
Granate [gra'na:tə], *f.* (—, *pl.* —n) shell, grenade.
Grande ['grandə], *m.* (—n, *pl.* —n) grandee.

Grandezza [gran'dɛtsa], *f.* (—, *no pl.*) grandeur; sententiousness; pomposity.
grandios [grandi'o:s], *adj.* grand.
Granit [gra'ni:t], *m.* (—s, *pl.* —e) granite.
Granne ['granə], *f.* (—, *pl.* —n) *(corn)* awn, beard.
graphisch ['gra:fɪʃ], *adj.* graphic.
Graphit [gra'fi:t], *m.* (—s, *no pl.*) blacklead.
Gras [gra:s], *n.* (—es, *pl.* ⁻er) grass; *ins — beißen,* bite the dust.
grasartig ['gra:sa:rtɪç], *adj.* gramineous.
grasen ['gra:zən], *v.n.* graze.
Grasfleck ['gra:sflɛk], *m.* (—s, *pl.* —e) grass-stain.
Grashalm ['gra:shalm], *m.* (—s, *pl.* —e) grass-blade.
Grashüpfer ['gra:shypfər], *m.* (—s, *pl.* —) *(Ent.)* grass-hopper.
grasig ['gra:zɪç], *adj.* grassy.
Grasmäher ['gra:smɛ:ər], *m.* (—s, *pl.* —) lawn-mower.
Grasmücke ['gra:smykə], *f.* (—, *pl.* —n) *(Orn.)* hedge-sparrow.
grassieren [gra'si:rən], *v.n.* *(epidemics etc.)* spread, rage.
gräßlich ['grɛslɪç], *adj.* hideous, horrible, ghastly.
Grasweide ['gra:svaɪdə], *f.* (—, *pl.* —n) pasture.
Grat [gra:t], *m.* (—s, *pl.* —e) edge, ridge.
Gräte ['grɛ:tə], *f.* (—, *pl.* —n) fish-bone.
Grätenstich ['grɛ:tənʃtɪç], *m.* (—s, *pl.* —e) *(embroidery)* herring-bone stitch.
grätig ['grɛ:tɪç], *adj.* full of fishbones; *(fig.)* grumpy.
gratis ['gra:tɪs], *adj.* gratis; — *und franko,* for nothing.
Gratulation [gratula'tsjo:n], *f.* (—, *pl.* —en) congratulation.
gratulieren [gratu'li:rən], *v.n.* *einem zu etwas —,* congratulate s.o. on s.th.
grau [grau], *adj.* grey; *(Am.)* gray; *vor —en Zeiten,* in times of yore.
Grauen ['grauən], *n.* (—s, *no pl.*) horror, aversion.
grauen ['grauən], *v.n.* *(morning)* dawn; *es graut mir vor,* I shudder at.
grauenhaft ['grauənhaft], *adj.* horrible, awful, ghastly.
graulen ['graulən], *v.r. sich —,* shudder, be afraid (of ghosts etc.).
graulich ['graulɪç], *adj.* *mir ist ganz —,* I shudder.
Graupe ['graupə], *f.* (—, *pl.* —n) groats, peeled barley.
graupeln ['graupəln], *v.n. imp.* *(coll.)* drizzle, sleet.
Graus [graus], *m.* (—es, *no pl.*) horror, dread.
grausam ['grauza:m], *adj.* cruel.
Grauschimmel ['grauʃɪməl], *m.* (—s, *pl.* —) grey (horse).
grausen ['grauzən], *v.n. es graust mir vor,* I shudder at.
grausig ['grauzɪç], *adj.* dread. gruesome, horrible.

Graveur

Graveur [gra'vøːr], *m.* (—s, *pl.* —e) engraver.

gravieren [gra'viːrən], *v.a.* engrave.

Gravität [graviˈtɛːt], *f.* (—, *no pl.*) gravity.

gravitätisch [graviˈtɛːtiʃ], *adj.* grave, solemn.

Grazie ['graːtsjə], *f.* (—, *pl.* —n) grace, charm; (*goddess*) Grace.

graziös [graˈtsjøːs], *adj.* graceful.

Greif [graif], *m.* (—(e)s, *pl.* —e) griffin.

greifbar ['graifbaːr], *adj.* to hand; (*fig.*) tangible, palpable.

greifen ['graifən], *v.a. irr.* grasp, seize, touch, handle; *etwas aus der Luft* —, invent s.th.; *um sich* —, gain ground.

greinen ['grainən], *v.n.* (*dial. & coll.*) cry, blubber.

Greis [grais], *m.* (—es, *pl.* —e) old man.

greisenhaft ['graizənhaft], *adj.* senile.

grell [grɛl], *adj.* (*colour*) glaring; (*light*) dazzling; (*tone*) shrill, sharp.

Grenadier [grenaˈdiːr], *m.* (—s, *pl.* —e) grenadier.

Grenadiermütze [grenaˈdiːrmytsə], *f.* (—, *pl.* —n) busby, bearskin.

Grenze ['grɛntsə], *f.* (—, *pl.* —n) boundary; frontier; borders; (*fig.*) limit.

grenzen ['grɛntsən], *v.n.* — *an*, border on; (*fig.*) verge on.

Grenzlinie ['grɛntsliːnjə], *f.* (—, *pl.* —n) boundary-line, line of demarcation.

Greuel ['grɔyəl], *m.* (—s, *pl.* —) horror, abomination; *das ist mir ein* —, I abominate it.

Greueltat ['grɔyəltaːt], *f.* (—, *pl.* —en) atrocity.

greulich ['grɔylɪç], *adj.* horrible, dreadful, shocking, heinous.

Griebe ['griːbə], *f.* (—, *pl.* —n) (*mostly pl.*) greaves.

Griebs ['griːps], *m.* (—es, *pl.* —e) (*dial.*) (*apple*) core.

Grieche ['griːçə], *m.* (—n, *pl.* —n) Greek.

Griechenland ['griːçənlant], *n.* Greece.

Griesgram ['griːsgraːm], *m.* (—s, *pl.* —e) grumbler.

griesgrämig ['griːsgrɛːmɪç], *adj.* morose, grumbling.

Grieß ['griːs], *m.* (—es, *no pl.*) groats, semolina.

Grießbrei ['griːsbrai], *m.* (—s, *pl.* —e) gruel.

Griff [grɪf], *m.* (—s, *pl.* —e) grip, hold, handle.

griffbereit ['grɪfbərait], *adj.* handy.

Grille ['grɪlə], *f.* (—, *pl.* —n) (*Ent.*) cricket; (*fig.*) whim; —*n haben*, be capricious; —*n fangen*, be crotchety, be depressed.

grillenhaft ['grɪlənhaft], *adj.* whimsical; capricious.

Grimasse [griˈmasə], *f.* (—, *pl.* —n) grimace.

Grimm [grɪm], *m.* (—s, *no pl.*) fury, rage, wrath.

Grimmen ['grɪmən], *n.* (—s, *no pl.*) gripes; (*Med.*) colic.

grimmig ['grɪmɪç], *adj.* fierce, furious; grim.

Grind [grɪnt], *m.* (—s, *pl.* —e) scab, scurf.

grinsen ['grɪnzən], *v.n.* grin.

Grippe ['grɪpə], *f.* (—, *pl.* —n) influenza, grippe.

Grips [grɪps], *m.* (—es, *no pl.*) (*coll.*) sense, brains; *einen beim* — *nehmen*, take s.o. by the scruff of his neck.

grob [grɔp], *adj.* coarse; rough; gross; rude, crude, uncouth, impolite; (*jewels*) rough, unpolished.

Grobheit ['grɔphait], *f.* (—, *pl.* —en) rudeness; abusive language.

Grobian ['groːbjaːn], *m.* (—s, *pl.* —e) boor, rude fellow.

Grobschmied ['grɔpʃmiːt], *m.* (—s, *pl.* —e) blacksmith.

Grog [grɔk], *m.* (—s, *pl.* —s) grog, toddy.

grölen ['grøːlən], *v.n.* (*coll.*) scream, squall, bawl.

Groll [grɔl], *m.* (—s, *no pl.*) resentment, anger, rancour; *einen* — *gegen einen haben*, bear s.o. a grudge.

grollen ['grɔlən], *v.n.* (*thunder*) rumble; *einem* —, bear s.o. ill-will; (*Poet.*) be angry (with).

Grönland ['grøːnlant], *n.* Greenland.

Gros (1) [grɔs], *n.* (—ses, *pl.* —se) gross; twelve dozen.

Gros (2) [groː], *n.* (—s, *no pl.*) bulk, majority; *en* —, wholesale.

Groschen ['grɔʃən], *m.* (—s, *pl.* —) small coin, penny; one 100th of an Austrian shilling; ten-pfennig piece; *einen schönen* — *verdienen*, make good money.

groß [groːs], *adj.* great, big, large; tall; vast; eminent, famous; intense; —*e Augen machen*, stare; *Grosser Ozean*, Pacific (Ocean).

großartig ['groːsaːrtɪç], *adj.* grand, sublime, magnificent, splendid.

Großbetrieb ['groːsbətriːp], *m.* (—s, *pl.* —e) large business; large (industrial) concern.

Großbritannien [groːsbriˈtanjən], *n.* Great Britain.

Größe ['grøːsə], *f.* (—, *pl.* —n) size, largeness, greatness; height; quantity; power; celebrity, star; importance.

Großeltern ['groːsɛltərn], *pl.* grandparents.

Großenkel ['groːsɛnkəl], *m.* (—s, *pl.* —) great-grandson.

Größenverhältnis ['grøːsənfɛrhɛltnɪs], *n.* (—ses, *pl.* —se) proportion, ratio.

Größenwahn ['grøːsənvaːn], *m.* (—s, *no pl.*) megalomania; delusion of grandeur.

Großfürst ['groːsfyrst], *m.* (—en, *pl.* —en) grand-duke.

Großfürstin ['gro:sfyrstɪn], *f.* (—, *pl.* —nen) grand-duchess.

Großgrundbesitz ['gro:sgruntbəzɪts], *m.* (—es, *pl.* —e) large landed property, estates.

Großhandel ['gro:shandəl], *m.* (—s, *no pl.*) wholesale business.

großherzig ['gro:shɛrtsɪç], *adj.* magnanimous.

Grossist [grɔ'sɪst], *m.* (—en, *pl.* —en) wholesale merchant.

großjährig ['gro:sjɛːrɪç], *adj.* of age; — werden, come of age.

großmächtig ['gro:smɛçtɪç], *adj.* (*fig.*) high and mighty.

großmäulig ['gro:smɔylɪç], *adj.* bragging, swaggering.

Großmut ['gro:smu:t], *f.* (—, *no pl.*) magnanimity, generosity.

Großmutter ['gro:smutər], *f.* (—, *pl.* ⁙) grandmother.

Großsiegelbewahrer [gro:s'zi:gəlbəva:rər], *m.* (—s, *pl.* —) Lord Chancellor; Keeper of the Great Seal.

Großstadt ['gro:sʃtat], *f.* (—, *pl.* ⁙e) large town, city, metropolis.

Großtat ['gro:sta:t], *f.* (—, *pl.* —en) achievement, exploit, feat.

Großtuer ['gro:stu:ər], *m.* (—s, *pl.* —) boaster, braggart.

großtun ['gro:stu:n], *v.r. irr. sich — mit*, brag of; show off, parade.

Großvater ['gro:sfa:tər], *m.* (—s, *pl.* ⁙) grandfather.

großziehen ['gro:stsi:ən], *v.a. irr.* bring up, rear.

großzügig ['gro:stsy:gɪç], *adj.* boldly conceived; grand, generous.

Grotte ['grɔtə], *f.* (—, *pl.* —n) grotto.

Grübchen ['gry:pçən], *n.* (—s, *pl.* —) dimple.

Grube ['gru:bə], *f.* (—, *pl.* —n) hole, pit; (*Min.*) mine; *in die — fahren,* (*Bibl.*) go down to the grave.

Grübelei ['gry:bəlaɪ], *f.* (—, *pl.* —en) brooding, musing.

grübeln ['gry:bəln], *v.n.* brood (over s.th.).

Grubenarbeiter ['gru:bənarbaɪtər], *m.* (—s, *pl.* —) miner.

Grubengas ['gru:bənga:s], *n.* (—es, *pl.* —e) fire-damp.

Grubenlampe ['gru:bənlampə], *f.* (—, *pl.* —n) miner's lamp.

Gruft [gruft], *f.* (—, *pl.* ⁙e) tomb, sepulchre; vault, mausoleum.

grün [gry:n], *adj.* green; *grüne Bohnen,* French beans, runner beans; (*fig.*) unripe, immature, inexperienced; *am —en Tisch,* at the conference table; (*fig.*) in theory; *auf einen —en Zweig kommen,* thrive, get on in the world; *einem nicht — sein,* dislike s.o.

Grund [grunt], *m.* (—s, *pl.* ⁙e) ground, soil; earth; land; bottom; foundation, basis; valley; reason, cause, argument; motive.

Grundbedeutung ['gruntbədɔytuŋ], *f.* (—, *pl.* —en) primary meaning, basic meaning.

Grundbesitz ['gruntbəzɪts], *m.* (—es, *no pl.*) landed property.

Grundbuch ['gruntbu:x], *n.* (—s, *pl.* ⁙er) land register.

grundehrlich ['grunte:rlɪç], *adj.* thoroughly honest.

Grundeigentum ['gruntaɪgəntu:m], *n.* (—s, *pl.* ⁙er) landed property.

Grundeis ['gruntaɪs], *n.* (—es, *no pl.*) ground-ice.

gründen ['gryndən], *v.a.* found, establish, float (a company). — *v.r. sich — auf,* be based on.

grundfalsch ['gruntfalʃ], *adj.* radically false.

Grundfarbe ['gruntfarbə], *f.* (—, *pl.* —n) primary colour.

Grundfläche ['gruntflɛçə], *f.* (—, *pl.* —n) basis, base.

Grundherr ['grunther], *m.* (—n, *pl.* —en) lord of the manor, freeholder.

grundieren [grun'di:rən], *v.a.* prime, size, paint the undercoat.

Grundkapital ['gruntkapita:l], *n.* (—s, *no pl.*) original stock.

Grundlage ['gruntla:gə], *f.* (—, *pl.* —n) foundation, basis.

Grundlegung ['gruntle:guŋ], *f.* (— *no pl.*) laying the foundation.

gründlich ['gryntlɪç], *adj.* thorough, solid.

grundlos ['gruntlo:s], *adj.* bottomless; groundless, unfounded, without foundation.

Grundmauer ['gruntmauər], *f.* (—, *pl.* —n) foundation wall.

Gründonnerstag [gry:n'dɔnərsta:k], *m.* (—s, *pl.* —e) Maundy Thursday.

Grundpfeiler ['gruntpfaɪlər], *m.* (—s, *pl.* —) (main) pillar.

Grundriß ['gruntrɪs], *m.* (—sses, *pl.* —sse) design, groundplan; compendium, elements; blueprint.

Grundsatz ['gruntzats], *m.* (—es, *pl.* ⁙e) principle, maxim; axiom.

grundschlecht ['gruntʃlɛçt], *adj.* thoroughly bad.

Grundschuld ['gruntʃult], *f.* (—, *pl.* —en) mortgage (on land).

Grundstein ['gruntʃtaɪn], *m.* (—s, *pl.* —e) foundation-stone.

Grundsteuer ['gruntʃtɔyər], *f.* (—, *pl.* —n) land-tax.

Grundstoff ['gruntʃtɔf], *m.* (—es, *pl.* —e) raw material.

Grundstück ['gruntʃtyk], *n.* (—s, *pl.* —e) real estate; plot of land; lot.

Grundtugend ['gruntu:gənt], *f.* (— *pl.* —en) cardinal virtue.

Gründung ['grynduŋ], *f.* (—, *pl.* —en) foundation, establishment.

grundverschieden ['gruntfɛrʃi:dən], *adj.* radically different.

Grundwasser ['gruntvasər], *n.* (—s, *no pl.*) underground water.

Grundzahl ['gruntsa:l], *f.* (—, *pl.* —en) cardinal number.

Grundzug ['grunttsu:k], *m.* (—s, *pl.* ⁙e) characteristic; distinctive feature.

Grüne ['gry:nə], *n.* (—n, *no pl.*) greenness, verdure; *ins — gehen*, take a walk in the open country.

grünen ['gry:nən], *v.n.* become green; (*fig.*) flourish.

Grünfutter ['gry:nfutər], *n.* (—s, *no pl.*) green food.

Grünkohl ['gry:nko:l], *m.* (—s, *no pl.*) green kale.

Grünkramhändler ['gry:nkra:mhɛndlər], *m.* (—s, *pl.* —) greengrocer.

Grünschnabel ['gry:nʃna:bəl], *m.* (—s, *pl.* ˙̈) greenhorn.

Grünspan ['gry:nʃpa:n], *m.* (—s, *no pl.*) verdigris.

Grünspecht ['gry:nʃpɛçt], *m.* (—s, *pl.* —e) (*Orn.*) green woodpecker.

grunzen ['gruntsən], *v.n.* grunt.

Grünzeug ['gry:ntsɔyk], *n.* (—s, *no pl.*) greens, herbs.

Gruppe ['grupə], *f.* (—, *pl.* —n) group.

gruppieren [gru'pi:rən], *v.a.* group.

gruselig ['gru:zəlɪç], *adj.* creepy, uncanny.

gruseln ['gru:zəln], *v.a. es gruselt mir* I shudder, it gives me the creeps.

Gruß [gru:s], *m.* (—es, *pl.* ˙̈e) salutation, greeting; (*pl.*) regards; *mit herzlichem —,* with kind regards; *einen — ausrichten,* convey s.o.'s regards.

grüßen ['gry:sən], *v.a.* greet; *einen — lassen,* send o.'s regards to s.o.; — *Sie ihn von mir,* remember me to him.

Grütze ['grytsə], *f.* (—, *pl.* —n) peeled grain, groats; (*fig.*) (*coll.*) gumption, brains.

Guatemala [guata'ma:la], *n.* Guatemala.

gucken ['gukən], *v.n.* look, peep.

Guinea [gɪ'ne:a], *n.* Guinea.

Gulasch ['gulaʃ], *n.* (—s, *no pl.*) goulash.

Gulden ['guldən], *m.* (—s, *pl.* —) florin, guilder.

gülden ['gyldən], *adj.* (*Poet.*) golden.

gültig ['gyltɪç], *adj.* valid; (*money*) current, legal (tender).

Gummi ['gumi:], *m.* (—s, *no pl.*) gum, rubber.

Gummiarabikum [gumia'ra:bɪkum], *n.* gum arabic.

gummiartig ['gumia:rtɪç], *adj.* gummy; like rubber.

Gummiball ['gumibal], *m.* (—s, *pl.* ˙̈e) rubber-ball.

Gummiband ['gumibant], *n.* (—s, *pl.* ˙̈er) rubber-band, elastic.

Gummielastikum [gumie'lastɪkum], *n.* indiarubber.

gummieren [gu'mi:rən], *v.a.* gum.

Gummireifen ['gumiraifən], *m.* (—s, *pl.* —) tyre; (*Am.*) tire.

Gummischuhe ['gumiʃu:ə], *m. pl.* galoshes; (*Am.*) rubbers.

Gunst [gunst], *f.* (—, *no pl.*) favour; *zu seinen —en,* in his favour.

Gunstbezeigung ['gunstbətsaigun], *f.* (—, *pl.* —en) favour, kindness, goodwill.

günstig ['gynstɪç], *adj.* favourable, propitious.

Günstling ['gynstlɪŋ], *m.* (—s, *pl.* —e) favourite.

Gurgel ['gurgəl], *f.* (—, *pl.* —n) gullet, throat.

gurgeln ['gurgəln], *v.n.* gargle; gurgle.

Gurke ['gurkə], *f.* (—, *pl.* —n) (*Bot.*) cucumber; (*pickled*) gherkin.

Gurt [gurt], *m.* (—es, *pl.* —e) belt; strap; harness.

Gürtel ['gyrtəl], *m.* (—s, *pl.* —) girdle, belt; (*Geog.*) zone.

Guß [gus], *m.* (—sses, *pl.* ˙̈sse) gush, downpour; founding, cast; (*Cul.*) icing.

Gut [gu:t], *n.* (—(e)s, *pl.* ˙̈er) good thing, blessing; property, possession; country seat; estate; (*pl.*) goods.

gut [gu:t], *adj.* good; beneficial; kind; virtuous. — *adv.* well; *es — haben,* be well off; *—er Dinge sein,* be of good cheer; *kurz und —,* in short.

Gutachten ['gu:taxtən], *n.* (—s, *pl.* —) expert opinion, expert evidence.

gutartig ['gu:ta:rtɪç], *adj.* good-natured; benign.

Güte ['gy:tə], *f.* (—, *no pl.*) goodness, kindness, quality.

Güterabfertigung ['gy:tərapfɛrtɪguŋ], *f.* (—, *pl.* —en) (*Railw.*) goods-depot, goods-office.

Güterabtretung ['gy:təraptre:tuŋ], *f.* (—, *pl.* —en) cession of goods; (*Law*) surrender of an estate.

gutgelaunt ['gu:tgəlaunt], *adj.* in good spirits, good-humoured.

gutgemeint ['gu:tgəmaint], *adj.* well-meant, well-intentioned.

gutgesinnt ['gu:tgəzɪnt], *adj.* well-intentioned.

Guthaben ['gu:tha:bən], *n.* (—s, *pl.* —) credit-balance, assets.

gutheißen ['gu:thaisən], *v.a. irr.* approve.

gütig ['gy:tɪç], *adj.* kind, benevolent.

gütlich ['gy:tlɪç], *adj.* amicable, friendly; *—er Vergleich,* amicable settlement; *sich — tun,* indulge o.s.

gutmachen ['gu:tmaxən], *v.a. etwas wieder —,* make amends for s.th., compensate.

gutmütig ['gu:tmy:tɪç], *adj.* good-natured, good-tempered.

Gutsbesitzer ['gu:tsbəzitsər], *m.* (—s, *pl.* —) landowner; proprietor of an estate.

gutschreiben ['gu:tʃraibən], *v.a. irr. einem etwas —,* enter a sum to s.o.'s credit.

Gutsverwalter ['gu:tsfɛrvaltər], *m.* (—s, *pl.* —) land-steward, agent, bailiff.

gutwillig ['gu:tvilɪç], *adj.* willing, of o.'s own free will.

Gymnasialbildung [gymnaz'ja:lbɪlduŋ], *f.* (—, *no pl.*) classical *or* grammar school education.

Gymnasiast [gymnaz'jast], *m.* (—en, *pl.* —en) grammar-school pupil.

Gymnasium [gym'na:zjum], *n.* (**—s**, *pl.* **—sien**) high school.
Gymnastik [gym'nastɪk], *f.* (**—**, *no pl.*) gymnastics.
gymnastisch [gym'nastɪʃ], *adj.* gymnastic(al); *—e Übungen*, physical exercises.

H

H [ha:], *n.* (**—s**, *pl.* **—s**) the letter H; (*Mus.*) *H Dur*, B major; *H Moll*, B minor.
ha! [ha:], *excl.* ha!
Haag, Den [ha:k, de:n], *m.* The Hague.
Haar [ha:r], *n.* (**—s**, *pl.* **—e**) hair; wool; nap; *aufs —*, exactly, to a hair; *um ein —*, very nearly, within a hair's breadth.
haaren ['ha:rən], *v.r. sich —*, shed o.'s hair.
haargenau ['ha:rgənau], *adj.* (very) exactly; to a nicety.
haarig ['ha:rɪç], *adj.* hairy.
Haarlocke ['ha:rlɔkə], *f.* (**—**, *pl.* **—n**) curl, ringlet.
Haarnadel ['ha:rna:dəl], *f.* (**—**, *pl.* **—n**) hairpin.
Haaröl ['ha:røːl], *n.* (**—s**, *no pl.*) hair-oil.
Haarpinsel ['ha:rpɪnzəl], *m.* (**—s**, *pl.* **—**) camel-hair brush.
Haarröhrchen ['ha:rrø:rçən], *n.* (**—s**, *pl.* **—**) capillary tube.
Haarschleife ['ha:rʃlaifə], *f.* (**—**, *pl.* **—en**) bow in the hair.
Haarschnitt ['ha:rʃnɪt], *m.* (**—s**, *pl.* **—e**) hair-cut.
Haarschuppen ['ha:rʃupən], *f. pl.* dandruff.
Haarspalterei ['ha:rʃpaltəraɪ], *f.* (**—**, *pl.* **—en**) hair-splitting.
haarsträubend ['ha:rʃtrɔybənt], *adj.* hair-raising, monstrous.
Haarwäsche ['ha:rvɛʃə], *f.* (**—**, *no pl.*) shampooing.
Haarwickel ['ha:rvɪkəl], *m.* (**—s**, *pl.* **—**) curler.
Haarzange ['ha:rtsaŋə], *f.* (**—**, *pl.* **—n**) tweezers.
Habe ['ha:bə], *f.* (**—**, *no pl.*) property, belongings, effects; *Hab und Gut*, all o.'s belongings, goods and chattels.
Haben ['ha:bən], *n.* (**—s**, *no pl.*) credit: *Soll und —*, debit and credit.
haben ['ha:bən], *v.a. irr.* have, possess; *da hast du's*, there you are; *es ist nicht zu —*, it is not available.
Habenichts ['ha:bənɪçts], *m.* (**—es**, *no pl.*) have-not.
Habgier ['ha:pgi:r], *f.* (**—**, *no pl.*) greediness, avarice, covetousness.

habhaft ['ha:phaft], *adj. einer Sache — werden*, get possession of a thing.
Habicht ['ha:bɪçt], *m.* (**—s**, *pl.* **—e**) (*Orn.*) hawk.
Habichtsinseln ['ha:bɪçtsɪnzəln], *f. pl.* the Azores.
Habichtsnase ['ha:bɪçtsna:zə], *f.* (**—**, *pl.* **—n**) hooked nose, aquiline nose.
Habilitation [habilita'tsjo:n], *f.* (**—**, *pl.* **—en**) admission *or* inauguration as a university lecturer.
habilitieren [habili'ti:rən], *v.r. sich —*, qualify as a university lecturer.
Habseligkeiten ['ha:pzelɪçkaɪtən], *f. pl.* property, effects, chattels.
Habsucht ['ha:pzuxt], *f.* (**—**, *no pl.*) avarice, greediness.
Hackbeil ['hakbaɪl], *n.* (**—s**, *pl.* **—e**) cleaver, chopping-knife.
Hackbrett ['hakbrɛt], *n.* (**—s**, *pl.* **—er**) chopping-board.
Hacke ['hakə], *f.* (**—**, *pl.* **—n**) hoe, mattock; heel.
Hacken ['hakən], *m.* (**—s**, *pl.* **—**) heel; *sich auf die — machen*, be off, take to o.'s heels.
hacken ['hakən], *v.a.* hack, chop, hoe; mince; (*birds*) peck.
Hacker ['hakər], *m.* (**—s**, *pl.* **—**) chopper.
Häckerling ['hɛkərlɪŋ], *m.* (**—s**, *no pl.*) chopped straw.
Hackfleisch ['hakflaɪʃ], *n.* (**—es**, *no pl.*) minced meat.
Häcksel ['hɛksəl], *m.* (**—s**, *no pl.*) chopped straw.
Hader ['ha:dər], *m.* (**—s**, *no pl.*) quarrel, dispute.
hadern ['ha:dərn], *v.n.* quarrel, have a dispute.
Hafen ['ha:fən], *m.* (**—s**, *pl.* ⁓) harbour, port; refuge, haven.
Hafendamm ['ha:fəndam], *m.* (**—s**, *pl.* ⁓e) jetty, mole, pier.
Hafensperre ['ha:fɛnʃpɛrə], *f.* (**—**, *pl.* **—n**) embargo, blockade.
Hafenzoll ['ha:fəntsɔl], *m.* (**—s**, *no pl.*) anchorage, harbour due.
Hafer ['ha:fər], *m.* (**—s**, *no pl.*) oats; *es sticht ihn der —*, he is getting cheeky, insolent.
Haferbrei ['ha:fərbraɪ], *m.* (**—s**, *no pl.*) porridge.
Hafergrütze ['ha:fərgrytsə], *f.* (**—**, *no pl.*) ground-oats, oatmeal.
Haferschleim ['ha:fərʃlaɪm], *m.* (**—s**, *no pl.*) oat-gruel, porridge.
Haff [haf], *n.* (**—s**, *pl.* **—e**) bay, lagoon.
Haft [haft], *f.* (**—**, *no pl.*) custody, imprisonment, arrest.
haftbar ['haftba:r], *adj.* answerable; (*Law*) liable.
Haftbefehl ['haftbəfe:l], *m.* (**—s**, *pl.* **—e**) warrant for arrest.
haften ['haftən], *v.n.* stick, cling, adhere; *für einen —*, go bail for s.o.; *für etwas —*, answer for, be liable for s.th.

99

Häftling [ˈhɛftlɪŋ], *m.* (—s, *pl.* —e) prisoner.

Haftpflicht [ˈhaftpflɪçt], *f.* (—, *no pl.*) liability.

Haftung [ˈhaftuŋ], *f.* (—, *no pl.*) liability, security; (*Comm.*) *Gesellschaft mit beschränkter —,* limited liability company, (*abbr.*) Ltd.

Hag [haːk], *m.* (—es, *pl.* —e) hedge, enclosure.

Hagebuche [ˈhaːgəbuːxə], *f.* (—, *pl.* —n) hornbeam.

Hagebutte [ˈhaːgəbutə], *f.* (—, *pl.* —n) (*Bot.*) hip, haw.

Hagedorn [ˈhaːgədɔrn], *m.* (—s, *no pl.*) (*Bot.*) hawthorn.

Hagel [ˈhaːgəl], *m.* (—s, *no pl.*) hail.

hageln [ˈhaːgəln], *v.n.* hail.

Hagelschauer [ˈhaːgəlʃauər], *m.* (—s, *pl.* —) hailstorm.

hager [ˈhaːgər], *adj.* thin, lean, lank, gaunt.

Häher [ˈhɛːər], *m.* (—s, *pl.* —) (*Orn.*) jay.

Hahn [haːn], *m.* (—s, *pl.* ⸚e) (*Orn.*) cockerel, cock; (*water*, *gas*) cock, tap, faucet; — *im Korbe sein,* rule the roost; *da kräht kein — danach,* nobody cares two hoots about it.

Hahnenbalken [ˈhaːnənbalkən], *m.* (—s, *pl.* —) cock-loft; hen-roost.

Hahnenfuß [ˈhaːnənfuːs], *m.* (—es, *no pl.*) (*Bot.*) crow-foot.

Hahnensporn [ˈhaːnənʃpɔrn], *m.* (—s, *no pl.*) cockspur.

Hahnentritt [ˈhaːnəntrɪt], *m.* (—s, *no pl.*) cock's tread.

Hahnrei [ˈhaːnraɪ], *m.* (—s, *pl.* —e) cuckold; *einen zum — machen,* cuckold s.o.

Hai [haɪ], *m.* (—s, *pl.* —e) (*Zool.*) shark.

Haifisch [ˈhaɪfɪʃ], *m.* (—es, *pl.* —e) (*Zool.*) shark.

Hain [haɪn], *m.* (—s, *pl.* —e) (*Poet.*) grove, thicket.

Haiti [haˈɪtɪ], *n.* Haiti.

Häkchen [ˈhɛːkçən], *n.* (—s, *pl.* —) small hook, crotchet; apostrophe.

häkeln [ˈhɛːkəln], *v.a. v.n.* crochet; (*fig.*) tease; (*Am.*) needle (*coll.*).

Haken [ˈhaːkən], *m.* (—s, *pl.* —) hook, clasp; (*fig.*) hitch, snag.

Hakenkreuz [ˈhaːkənkrɔyts], *n.* (—es, *pl.* —e) swastika.

halb [halp], *adj.* half; *halb neun,* half past eight.

halbieren [halˈbiːrən], *v.a.* halve, divide into halves; (*Maths.*) bisect.

Halbinsel [ˈhalpɪnzəl], *f.* (—, *pl.* —n) peninsula.

Halbmesser [ˈhalpmɛsər], *m.* (—s, *pl.* —) radius.

halbpart [ˈhalppart], *adj.* — *mit einem machen,* go halves with s.o.

halbstündig [ˈhalpʃtyndɪç], *adj.* lasting half an hour.

halbstündlich [ˈhalpʃtyntlɪç], *adj.* half-hourly, every half-hour.

halbwegs [ˈhalpveːks], *adv.* (*coll.*) reasonably, tolerably.

Halbwelt [ˈhalpvɛlt], *f.* (—, *no pl.*) demi-monde.

halbwüchsig [ˈhalpvyːksɪç], *adj.* teen-age.

Halde [ˈhaldə], *f.* (—, *pl.* —n) declivity, hill; (*Min.*) waste-heap, slag-heap.

Hälfte [ˈhɛlftə], *f.* (—, *pl.* —n) half; (*obs.*) moiety.

Halfter [ˈhalftər], *f.* (—, *pl.* —n) halter.

Hall [hal], *m.* (—s, *no pl.*) sound, echo.

Halle [ˈhalə], *f.* (—, *pl.* —n) hall, vestibule; portico; porch.

hallen [ˈhalən], *v.n.* sound, resound; clang.

Halm [halm], *m.* (—es, *pl.* —e) stalk; (*grass*) blade.

Hals [hals], *m.* (—es, *pl.* ⸚e) neck, throat; — *über Kopf,* head over heels, hastily, hurriedly.

Halsader [ˈhalsaːdər], *f.* (—, *pl.* —n) jugular vein.

Halsbinde [ˈhalsbɪndə], *f.* (—, *pl.* —n) scarf, tie.

Halsentzündung [ˈhalsɛntsynduŋ], *f.* (—, *pl.* —en) inflammation of the throat.

Halskrause [ˈhalskrauzə], *f.* (—, *pl.* —n) frill, ruff.

halsstarrig [ˈhalsʃtarɪç], *adj.* stubborn, obstinate.

Halsweh [ˈhalsveː], *n.* (—s, *no pl.*) sore throat.

Halt [halt], *m.* (—es, *no pl.*) halt; stop; hold; (*also fig.*) support.

haltbar [ˈhaltbaːr], *adj.* durable, strong; tenable, valid.

halten [ˈhaltən], *v.a. irr.* hold; keep; detain; deliver (speech, lecture); observe, celebrate. — *v.n.* stop; stand firm; insist; *halt!* stop! stop it! — *v.r. sich —,* hold out, keep, behave.

haltlos [ˈhaltloːs], *adj.* unprincipled; floundering, unsteady.

Haltung [ˈhaltuŋ], *f.* (—, *pl.* —en) carriage, posture, attitude; (*fig.*) behaviour, demeanour; attitude.

Halunke [haˈluŋkə], *m.* (—n, *pl.* —n) scoundrel, rascal, scamp.

hämisch [ˈhɛːmɪʃ], *adj.* malicious, spiteful.

Hammel [ˈhaməl], *m.* (—s, *pl.* —) (*meat*) mutton.

Hammelkeule [ˈhaməlkɔylə], *f.* (—, *pl.* —n) leg of mutton.

Hammer [ˈhamər], *m.* (—s, *pl.* ⸚) hammer; *unter den — kommen,* be sold by auction.

Hämorrhoiden [hɛmoˈriːdən], *f. pl.* (*Med.*) piles, haemorrhoids.

Hand [hant], *f.* (—, *pl.* ⸚e) hand.

Handarbeit [ˈhantarbaɪt], *f.* (—, *pl.* —en) manual labour; needlework.

Handel [ˈhandəl], *m.* (—s, *no pl.*) trade, commerce; — *treiben,* carry on trade, do business.

Händel [ˈhɛndəl], *m. pl.* quarrel, difference, dispute.

handeln ['handəln], *v.n.* act; — *in*, deal in; *es handelt sich um* . . . it is a question of . . . ; *es handelt von* . . ., it deals with . . . .

handelseinig ['handəlsaınıç], *adj.* — *werden*, come to terms.

Handelsgenossenschaft ['handəls-gənɔsənʃaft], *f.* (—, *pl.* —**en**) trading company.

Handelsgeschäft ['handəlsgəʃeft], *n.* (—**es**, *pl.* —**e**) commercial transaction.

Handelsgesellschaft ['handəlsgəzel-ʃaft], *f.* (—, *pl.* —**en**) trading company; joint-stock company.

Handelskammer ['handəlskamər], *f.* (—, *pl.* —**n**) chamber of commerce.

Handelsmarke ['handəlsmarkə], *f.* (—, *pl.* —**n**) trade-mark.

Handelsreisende ['handəlsraızəndə], *m.* (—**n**, *pl.* —**n**) commercial traveller.

händelsüchtig ['hendəlzyçtıç], *adj.* quarrelsome; litigious.

Handelsvertrag ['handəlsfertra:k], *m.* (—**es**, *pl.* —**e**) commercial treaty; contract.

Handelszweig ['handəlstsvaık], *m.* (—**es**, *pl.* —**e**) branch of trade.

Handfeger ['hantfe:gər], *m.* (—**s**, *pl.* —) hand-broom, handbrush.

Handfertigkeit ['hantfertıçkaıt], *f.* (—, *no pl.*) dexterity, manual skill; handicrafts.

Handfessel ['hantfesəl], *f.* (—, *pl.* —**n**) handcuff.

handfest ['hantfest], *adj.* robust, strong.

Handgeld ['hantgelt], *n.* (—**es**, *no pl.*) earnest; (*money*) advance.

Handgelenk ['hantgələŋk], *n.* (—**s**, *pl.* —**e**) wrist.

handgemein ['haŋgəmaın], *adj.* — *werden*, come to blows.

Handgemenge ['hantgəmeŋə], *n.* (—**s**, *no pl.*) fray, scuffle.

handgreiflich ['hantgraıflıç], *adj.* palpable; evident, plain.

Handgriff ['hantgrıf], *m.* (—**es**, *pl.* —**e**) handle; (*fig.*) knack.

Handhabe ['hantha:bə], *f.* (—, *pl.* —**n**) (*fig.*) hold, handle.

handhaben ['hantha:bən], *v.a.* handle, manage; operate.

Handlanger ['hantlaŋər], *m.* (—**s**, *pl.* —) helper, carrier.

Händler ['hendlər], *m.* (—**s**, *pl.* —) dealer, merchant.

handlich ['hantlıç], *adj.* handy, manageable.

Handlung ['handluŋ], *f.* (—, *pl.* —**en**) shop; (*Am.*) store; commercial house, mercantile business; action, act, deed; (*Lit.*) plot.

Handrücken ['hantrykən], *m.* (—**s**, *pl.* —) back of the hand.

Handschelle ['hantʃelə], *f.* (—, *pl.* —**n**) manacle, handcuff.

Handschlag ['hantʃla:k], *m.* (—**s**, *pl.* —**e**) handshake.

Handschuh ['hantʃu:], *m.* (—**s**, *pl.* —**e**) glove; (*of iron*) gauntlet.

Handstreich ['hantʃtraıç], *m.* (—**es**, *pl.* —**e**) (*Mil.*) surprise attack, coup de main.

Handtuch ['hanttu:x], *n.* (—**es**, *pl.* —**er**) towel.

Handumdrehen ['hantumdre:ən], *n.* (—**s**, *no pl.*) *im* —, in no time, in a jiffy.

Handwerk ['hantverk], *n.* (—**s**, *pl.* —**e**) handicraft, trade, craft.

Handwörterbuch ['hantvœrtərbu:x], *n.* (—**es**, *pl.* —**er**) compact dictionary.

Handwurzel ['hantvurtsəl], *f.* (—, *pl.* —**n**) wrist.

Hanf [hanf], *m.* (—**es**, *no pl.*) hemp.

Hänfling ['henflıŋ], *m.* (—**s**, *pl.* —**e**) (*Orn.*) linnet.

Hang [haŋ], *m.* (—**es**, *pl.* —**e**) slope, declivity; (*fig.*) (*no pl.*) inclination, propensity.

Hängematte ['heŋəmatə], *f.* (—, *pl.* —**n**) hammock.

hängen ['heŋən], *v.a.* *irr.* hang, suspend. — *v.r. sich* —, hang o.s. — *v.n.* hang, be suspended; be hanged (*execution*).

Hannover [ha'no:fər], *n.* Hanover.

Hänselei ['henzəlaı], *f.* (—, *pl.* —**en**) chaffing, leg-pulling, teasing.

hänseln ['henzəln], *v.a.* tease, chaff.

Hantel ['hantəl], *f.* (—, *pl.* —**n**) dumb-bell.

hantieren [han'ti:rən], *v.n.* busy o.s., work, occupy o.s. (with).

hapern ['ha:pərn], *v.n.* lack, be deficient; *da hapert es*, that's the snag.

Häppchen ['hepçən], *n.* (—**s**, *pl.* —) morsel.

Happen ['hapən], *m.* (—**s**, *pl.* —) mouthful.

happig ['hapıç], *adj.* greedy; excessive.

Härchen ['he:rçən], *n.* (—**s**, *pl.* —) short hair.

Harfe ['harfə], *f.* (—, *pl.* —**n**) (*Mus.*) harp.

Harke ['harkə], *f.* (—, *pl.* —**n**) rake.

Harm [harm], *m.* (—**es**, *no pl.*) grief, sorrow; injury, wrong.

härmen ['hermən], *v.r. sich* — *um*, grieve over.

harmlos ['harmlo:s], *adj.* harmless, innocuous.

Harmonielehre [harmo'ni:le:rə], *f.* (—, *pl.* —**n**) (*Mus.*) harmonics; harmony.

harmonieren [harmo'ni:rən], *v.n. mit einem* —, be in concord with s.o., agree with s.o.

Harmonika [har'mo:nıka], *f.* (—, *pl.* —**ken**) (*Mus.*) accordion, concertina; mouth-organ.

Harn [harn], *m.* (—**s**, *no pl.*) urine.

Harnisch ['harnıʃ], *m.* (—**es**, *pl.* —**e**) harness, armour; *in* — *bringen*, enrage.

Harpune [har'pu:nə], *f.* (—, *pl.* —**n**) harpoon.

harren ['harən], *v.n.* wait for, hope for.

harsch [harʃ], *adj.* harsh; rough; unfriendly.

hart [hart], *adj.* hard, severe, cruel, austere.

Härte [ˈhɛrtə], *f.* (—, *pl.* —n) hardness, severity.

härten [ˈhɛrtən], *v.a.* harden.

hartleibig [ˈhartlaɪbɪç], *adj.* constipated.

hartnäckig [ˈhartnɛkɪç], *adj.* stubborn, obstinate; undaunted.

Harz (1) [harts], *m.* (*Geog.*) (—es, *no pl.*) the Hartz mountains.

Harz (2) [harts], *n.* (—es, *pl.* —e) resin, rosin.

harzig [ˈhartsɪç], *adj.* resinous.

Hasardspiel [haˈzartʃpiːl], *n.* (—es, *pl.* —e) game of chance, gamble.

Haschee [haˈʃeː], *n.* (—s, *pl.* —s) puree, hash, mash.

haschen [ˈhaʃən], *v.a.* catch, snatch, seize. — *v.n.* — *nach*, strain after, snatch at.

Häschen [ˈhɛːsçən], *n.* (—s, *pl.* —) (*Zool.*) small hare, leveret.

Häscher [ˈhɛʃər], *m.* (—s, *pl.* —) bailiff.

Hase [ˈhaːzə], *m.* (—n, *pl.* —n) (*Zool.*) hare.

Haselrute [ˈhaːzəlruːtə], *f.* (—, *pl.* —n) hazel-switch.

Hasenfuß [ˈhaːzənfuːs], *m.* (—es, *no pl.*) coward.

Hasenklein [ˈhaːzənklaɪn], *n.* (—s, *no pl.*) jugged hare.

Hasenscharte [ˈhaːzənʃartə], *f.* (—, *pl.* —n) hare-lip.

Haspe [ˈhaspə], *f.* (—, *pl.* —n) hasp, hinge.

Haspel [ˈhaspəl], *f.* (—, *pl.* —n) reel.

haspeln [ˈhaspəln], *v.a.* wind on a reel; (*fig.*) rattle off.

Haß [has], *m.* (—sses, *no pl.*) hatred, hate, detestation.

hassen [ˈhasən], *v.a.* hate, detest.

haßerfüllt [ˈhasərfylt], *adj.* full of spite, full of hatred.

häßlich [ˈhɛslɪç], *adj.* ugly, repulsive; (*fig.*) unpleasant, unkind; unseemly.

Hast [hast], *f.* (—, *no pl.*) haste, hurry, hastiness, rashness.

hastig [ˈhastɪç], *adj.* hasty, hurried.

hätscheln [ˈhɛtʃəln], *v.a.* pamper, caress, fondle.

Hatz [hats], *f.* (—, *pl.* —en) baiting; hunt; revelry.

Haube [ˈhaubə], *f.* (—, *pl.* —n) bonnet, cap; (*Motor.*) bonnet, (*Am.*) hood.

Haubenlerche [ˈhaubənlɛrçə], *f.* (—, *pl.* —n) (*Orn.*) crested lark.

Haubitze [hauˈbɪtsə], *f.* (—, *pl.* —n) howitzer.

Hauch [haux], *m.* (—es, *no pl.*) breath, whiff; (*fig.*) touch, tinge.

hauchdünn [ˈhauxˈdyn], *adj.* extremely thin.

hauchen [ˈhauxən], *v.n.* breathe.

Hauchlaut [ˈhauxlaut], *m.* (—es, *pl.* —e) (*Phonet.*) aspirate.

Haudegen [ˈhaudeːgən], *m.* (—s, *pl.* —) broad-sword; *ein alter* —, an old bully.

Haue [ˈhauə], *f.* (—, *no pl.*) (*coll.*) thrashing.

hauen [ˈhauən], *v.a.* hew; cut; strike; hit; give a hiding to. — *v.n. über die Schnur* —, kick over the traces.

Hauer [ˈhauər], *m.* (—s, *pl.* —) hewer, cutter; (*animal*) fang, tusk.

Häuer [ˈhɔyər], *m.* (—s, *pl.* —) miner.

Haufen [ˈhaufən], *m.* (—s, *pl.* —) heap, pile.

häufen [ˈhɔyfən], *v.a.* heap, pile. — *v.r. sich* —, accumulate, multiply, increase.

häufig [ˈhɔyfɪç], *adj.* frequent, abundant. — *adv.* frequently, often.

Häufung [ˈhɔyfuŋ], *f.* (—, *pl.* —en) accumulation.

Haupt [haupt], *n.* (—es, *pl.* ⸗er) head; leader; chief, principal; (*compounds*) main—; *aufs* — *schlagen*, inflict a total defeat on; *ein bemoostes* —, an old student.

Hauptaltar [ˈhauptaltaːr], *m.* (—s, *pl.* —e) (*Eccl.*) high altar.

Hauptbuch [ˈhauptbuːx], *n.* (—es, *pl.* ⸗er) ledger.

Häuptling [ˈhɔyptlɪŋ], *m.* (—s, *pl.* —e) chieftain.

Hauptmann [ˈhauptman], *m.* (—s, *pl.* ⸗er, **Hauptleute**) (*Mil.*) captain.

Hauptnenner [ˈhauptnɛnər], *m.* (—s, *pl.* —) (*Maths.*) common denominator.

Hauptquartier [ˈhauptkvartiːr], *n.* (—es, *pl.* —e) headquarters.

Hauptsache [ˈhauptzaxə], *f.* (—, *pl.* —n) main thing, substance, main point; *in der* —, in the main.

hauptsächlich [ˈhauptzɛçlɪç], *adj.* chief, main, principal, essential.

Hauptsatz [ˈhauptzats], *m.* (—es, *pl.* ⸗e) (*Gram.*) principal sentence.

Hauptschriftleiter [ˈhauptʃrɪftlaɪtər], *m.* (—s, *pl.* —) editor-in-chief.

Hauptschule [ˈhauptʃuːlə], *f.* (—, *pl.* —n) intermediate school.

Hauptstadt [ˈhauptʃtat], *f.* (—, *pl.* ⸗e) capital, metropolis.

Hauptton [ˈhauptoːn], *m.* (—s, *pl.* ⸗e) (*Mus.*) key-note; (*Phonet.*) primary accent.

Haupttreffer [ˈhaupttrefər], *m.* (—s, *pl.* —) first prize; jackpot.

Hauptverkehrsstunden [ˈhauptfɛrkeːrsʃtundən], *f. pl.* (*traffic etc.*) rush-hour.

Hauptwache [ˈhauptvaxə], *f.* (—, *pl.* —n) central guardroom.

Hauptwort [ˈhauptvɔrt], *n.* (—es, *pl.* ⸗er) noun, substantive.

Hauptzahl [ˈhauptsaːl], *f.* (—, *pl.* —en) cardinal number.

Haus [haus], *n.* (—es, *pl.* ⸗er) house, home; household; firm; *zu* —e, at home; *nach* —e, home.

Hausarbeit [ˈhausarbaɪt], *f.* (—, *pl.* —en) housework, domestic work; homework.

Hausarrest ['hausarɛst], *m.* (**—es,** *no pl.*) house arrest.

Hausarzt ['hausartst], *m.* (**—es,** *pl.* ⸚**e**) family doctor.

hausbacken ['hausbakən], *adj.* homemade; homely; humdrum.

Häuschen ['hɔysçən], *n.* (**—s,** *pl.* **—**) small house, cottage; *ganz aus dem — sein,* be beside o.s.

Hausen ['hauzən], *m.* (**—s,** *pl.* **—**) sturgeon.

hausen ['hauzən], *v.n.* reside, be domiciled; *übel —,* play havoc among.

Hausflur ['hausflu:r], *m.* (**—s,** *pl.* **—e**) entrance hall (of a house), vestibule.

Hausfrau ['hausfrau], *f.* (**—,** *pl.* **—en**) housewife, mistress of the house.

Hausfriedensbruch ['hausfri:dənsbrux], *m.* (**—es,** *pl.* ⸚**e**) (*Law*) intrusion, trespass.

Hausgenosse ['hausgənɔsə], *m.* (**—n,** *pl.* **—n**) fellow-lodger.

Haushalt ['haushalt], *m.* (**—es,** *no pl.*) household.

Haushaltung ['haushaltuŋ], *f.* (**—,** *no pl.*) housekeeping.

Hausherr ['hausher], *m.* (**—n,** *pl.* **—en**) master of the house, householder.

Haushofmeister ['haushofmaistər], *m.* (**—s,** *pl.* **—**) steward; butler.

hausieren [hau'zi:rən], *v.n.* peddle, hawk.

Hauslehrer ['hausle:rər], *m.* (**—s,** *pl.* **—**) private tutor.

Häusler ['hɔyslər], *m.* (**—s,** *pl.* **—**) cottager.

häuslich ['hɔyslɪç], *adj.* domestic, domesticated.

Hausmädchen ['hausmɛdçən], *n.* (**—s,** *pl.* **—**) housemaid.

Hausmannskost ['hausmanskɔst], *f.* (**—,** *no pl.*) plain fare.

Hausmeister ['hausmaistər], *m.* (**—s,** *pl.* **—**) house-porter, caretaker.

Hausmittel ['hausmɪtəl], *n.* (**—s,** *pl.* **—**) household remedy.

Hausrat ['hausra:t], *m.* (**—s,** *no pl.*) household furnishings, household effects.

Hausschlüssel ['hausʃlysəl], *m.* (**—s,** *pl.* **—**) latch-key.

Hausschuh ['hausʃu:], *m.* (**—s,** *pl.* **—e**) slipper.

Hausstand ['hausʃtant], *m.* (**—es,** *pl.* ⸚**e**) household.

Haustier ['hausti:r], *n.* (**—s,** *pl.* **—e**) domestic animal.

Hausvater ['hausfa:tər], *m.* (**—s,** *pl.* ⸚) paterfamilias.

Hausverwalter ['hausfɛrvaltər], *m.* (**—s,** *pl.* **—**) steward, caretaker; (*Am.*) janitor.

Hauswesen ['hausve:zən], *n.* (**—s,** *no pl.*) household management *or* affairs.

Hauswirt ['hausvɪrt], *m.* (**—es,** *pl.* **—e**) landlord.

Hauswirtin ['hausvɪrtɪn], *f.* (**—,** *pl.* **—nen**) landlady.

Hauswirtschaft ['hausvɪrtʃaft], *f.* (**—,** *no pl.*) housekeeping, domestic economy.

Haut [haut], *f.* (**—,** *pl.* ⸚**e**) (*human*) skin; (*animal*) hide; (*fruit*) peel; (*on liquid*) skin; membrane; film; *aus der — fahren,* flare up.

Hautausschlag ['hautausʃla:k], *m.* (**—s,** *pl.* ⸚**e**) rash, eczema.

Häutchen ['hɔytçən], *n.* (**—s,** *pl.* **—**) cuticle, pellicle, membrane.

häuten ['hɔytən], *v.a.* skin, flay, strip off the skin. — *v.r. sich —,* cast off (skin) *or* slough.

Hebamme ['he:pamə], *f.* (**—,** *pl.* **—n**) midwife.

Hebel ['he:bəl], *m.* (**—s,** *pl.* **—**) lever.

heben ['he:bən], *v.a. irr.* raise, lift, hoist, heave; elevate; improve; *aus der Taufe —,* be godfather (godmother) to (s.o.).

Heber ['he:bər], *m.* (**—s,** *pl.* **—**) siphon.

Hebräer [he'brɛ:ər], *m.* (**—s,** *pl.* **—**) Hebrew.

Hechel ['hɛçəl], *f.* (**—,** *pl.* **—n**) hackle, flax-comb.

hecheln ['hɛçəln], *v.a.* dress flax; hackle; (*fig.*) taunt, heckle.

Hecht [hɛçt], *m.* (**—es,** *pl.* **—e**) (*Zool.*) pike; (*swimming*) dive.

Hechtsprung ['hɛçtʃpruŋ], *m.* header.

Heck [hɛk], *n.* (**—s,** *pl.* **—e**) (*Naut.*) stern; (*Motor.*) rear; (*Aviat.*) tail.

Heckbord ['hɛkbɔrt], *m.* (**—s,** *pl.* **—e**) (*Naut.*) taffrail.

Hecke ['hɛkə], *f.* (**—,** *pl.* **—n**) hedge.

hecken ['hɛkən], *v.n.* breed, bring forth.

Heckpfennig ['hɛkpfɛnɪç], *m.* (**—s,** *pl.* **—e**) lucky sixpence.

heda! ['he:da:], *excl.* hey, you!

Heer [he:r], *m.* (**—es,** *pl.* **—e**) army; multitude; *stehendes —,* regular army.

Heeresmacht ['he:rəsmaxt], *f.* (**—,** *pl.* ⸚**e**) armed forces, troops.

Heerschar ['he:rʃa:r], *f.* (**—,** *pl.* **—en**) host; corps, legion; (*Bibl.*) *der Herr der —en,* the Lord of Hosts.

Heerschau ['he:rʃau], *f.* (**—,** *pl.* **—en**) review, muster, parade.

Heerstraße ['he:rʃtra:sə], *f.* (**—,** *pl.* **—en**) military road; highway; (*Am.*) highroad.

Heerwesen ['he:rve:zən], *n.* (**—s,** *no pl.*) military affairs.

Hefe ['he:fə], *f.* (**—,** *no pl.*) yeast; dregs, sediment.

Hefeteig ['he:fətaɪk], *m.* (**—s,** *pl.* **—e**) leavened dough.

Heft [hɛft], *n.* (**—es,** *pl.* **—e**) exercise-book, copy-book; haft, handle, hilt.

heften ['hɛftən], *v.a.* fasten; baste, stitch, fix, pin.

heftig ['hɛftɪç], *adj.* vehement, violent.

Heftnadel ['hɛftna:dəl], *f.* (**—,** *pl.* **—n**) stitching-needle.

hegen ['he:gən], *v.a.* enclose, protect, preserve; (*fig.*) cherish; entertain; hold; *— und pflegen,* nurse carefully.

Hehl [he:l], *n.* (—**es**, *no pl.*) concealment, secret.

hehlen [ˈheːlən], *v.n.* receive stolen goods.

Hehler [ˈhəːlər], *m.* (—**s**, *pl.* —) receiver of stolen goods, (*sl.*) fence.

hehr [heːr], *adj.* (*Lit.*) exalted, august, sublime.

Heide (1) [ˈhaɪdə], *m.* (—**n**, *pl.* —**n**) heathen, pagan.

Heide (2) [ˈhaɪdə], *f.* (—, *pl.* —**n**) heath.

Heidekraut [ˈhaɪdəkraut], *n.* (—**es**, *no pl.*) heath, heather.

Heidelbeere [ˈhaɪdəlbeːrə], *f.* (—, *pl.* —**n**) (*Bot.*) bilberry; (*Am.*) blueberry.

Heidenangst [ˈhaɪdənaŋst], *f.* (—, *no pl.*) (*coll.*) mortal fear.

Heidenlärm [ˈhaɪdənlɛrm], *m.* (—**es**, *no pl.*) hullaballoo.

Heidenröschen [ˈhaɪdənrøːsçən], *n.* (—**s**, *pl.* —) (*Bot.*) sweet-briar.

Heidentum [ˈhaɪdəntuːm], *n.* (—**s**, *no pl.*) paganism.

heidnisch [ˈhaɪdnɪʃ], *adj.* pagan, heathen.

Heidschnuke [ˈhaɪtʃnuːkə], *f.* (—, *pl.* —**n**) moorland sheep.

heikel [ˈhaɪkəl], *adj.* delicate, sensitive, critical.

Heil [haɪl], *n.* (—(**e**)**s**, *no pl.*) safety, welfare; (*Theol.*) salvation; *sein* — *versuchen*, have a try, try o.'s luck. — *int.* hail! — *der Königin*, God save the Queen.

heil [haɪl], *adj.* unhurt, intact.

Heiland [ˈhaɪlant], *m.* (—**s**, *no pl.*) Saviour, Redeemer.

Heilanstalt [ˈhaɪlanʃtalt], *f.* (—, *pl.* —**en**) sanatorium, convalescent home; (*Am.*) sanitarium.

heilbar [ˈhaɪlbaːr], *adj.* curable.

heilbringend [ˈhaɪlbrɪŋənt], *adj.* salutary.

heilen [ˈhaɪlən], *v.a.* cure, heal. — *v.n.* (*aux.* sein) heal.

heilig [ˈhaɪlɪç], *adj.* holy, sacred; *der Heilige Abend*, Christmas Eve; — *sprechen*, canonise; (*before name*) *der, die —e*, Saint.

Heiligenschein [ˈhaɪlɪɡənʃaɪn], *m.* (—**s**, *pl.* —**e**) halo; (*clouds*) nimbus.

Heiligkeit [ˈhaɪlɪçkaɪt], *f.* (—, *no pl.*) holiness, sanctity, sacredness.

Heiligtum [ˈhaɪlɪçtuːm], *n.* (—**s**, *pl.* —**er**) sanctuary, shrine; holy relic.

Heiligung [ˈhaɪlɪɡuŋ], *f.* (—, *pl.* —**en**) sanctification, consecration.

heilkräftig [ˈhaɪlkrɛftɪç], *adj.* curative, salubrious.

Heilkunde [ˈhaɪlkundə], *f.* (—, *no pl.*) therapeutics.

heillos [ˈhaɪlloːs], *adj.* wicked, mischievous; (*fig.*) awful.

Heilmittel [ˈhaɪlmɪtəl], *n.* (—**s**, *pl.* —) remedy.

heilsam [ˈhaɪlzaːm], *adj.* salubrious, salutary.

Heilsamkeit [ˈhaɪlzaːmkaɪt], *f.* (—, *no pl.*) salubrity; salubriousness.

Heilsarmee [ˈhaɪlsarmeː], *f.* (—, *no pl.*) Salvation Army.

Heilslehre [ˈhaɪlsleːrə], *f.* (—, *pl.* —**n**) doctrine of salvation.

Heiltrank [ˈhaɪltraŋk], *m.* (—**es**, *no pl.*) (medicinal) potion.

Heim [haɪm], *n.* (—**es**, *pl.* —**e**) home.

heim [haɪm], *adv. prefix* (*to verbs*) home.

Heimat [ˈhaɪmat], *f.* (—, *no pl.*) native place, home, homeland.

Heimatschein [ˈhaɪmatʃaɪn], *m.* (—**es**, *pl.* —**e**) certificate of origin *or* domicile.

Heimchen [ˈhaɪmçən], *n.* (—**s**, *pl.* —) (*Ent.*) cricket.

heimführen [ˈhaɪmfyːrən], *v.a.* bring home (a bride); (*fig.*) marry.

Heimgang [ˈhaɪmgaŋ], *m.* (—**es**, *no pl.*) going home; (*fig.*) decease, death.

heimisch [ˈhaɪmɪʃ], *adj.* native, indigenous; *sich — fühlen*, feel at home.

heimkehren [ˈhaɪmkeːrən], *v.n.* return (home).

heimleuchten [ˈhaɪmlɔyçtən], *v.n. einem —*, tell s.o. the plain truth, give s.o. a piece of o.'s mind.

heimlich [ˈhaɪmlɪç], *adj.* secret, clandestine, furtive.

heimsuchen [ˈhaɪmzuːxən], *v.a.* visit; afflict, punish.

Heimtücke [ˈhaɪmtykə], *f.* (—, *no pl.*) malice.

heimwärts [ˈhaɪmvɛrts], *adv.* homeward.

Heimweh [ˈhaɪmveː], *n.* (—**s**, *no pl.*) homesickness; nostalgia.

heimzahlen [ˈhaɪmtsaːlən], *v.a.* pay back, retaliate.

Hein [haɪn], *m.* (*coll.*) *Freund* —, Death.

Heinzelmännchen [ˈhaɪntsəlmɛnçən], *n.* (—**s**, *pl.* —) goblin, brownie, imp.

Heirat [ˈhaɪraːt], *f.* (—, *pl.* —**en**) marriage, wedding.

heiraten [ˈhaɪraːtən], *v.a.* marry, wed.

Heiratsgut [ˈhaɪraːtsguːt], *n.* (—**es**, *pl.* —**er**) dowry.

heischen [ˈhaɪʃən], *v.a.* (*Poet.*) ask, demand.

heiser [ˈhaɪzər], *adj.* hoarse.

heiß [haɪs], *adj.* hot; (*fig.*) ardent; (*climate*) torrid.

heißen [ˈhaɪsən], *v.a. irr.* bid, command. — *v.n.* be called; be said; signify, mean; *es heißt*, it is said; *das heißt (d.h.)*, that is to say; *wie — Sie?* what is your name?

heißgeliebt [ˈhaɪsɡəliːpt], *adj.* dearly beloved.

heiter [ˈhaɪtər], *adj.* clear; serene; cheerful.

Heiterkeit [ˈhaɪtərkaɪt], *f.* (—, *no pl.*) serenity; cheerfulness.

heizen [ˈhaɪtsən], *v.a. v.n.* heat.

Heizkissen [ˈhaɪtskɪsən], *n.* (—**s**, *pl.* —) electric pad *or* blanket.

Heizkörper [ˈhaɪtskœrpər], *m.* (—**s**, *pl.* —) radiator; heater.

Heizung [ˈhaɪtsuŋ], *f.* (—, *pl.* —**en**) heating.

hektisch [ˈhɛktɪʃ], *adj.* hectic.

hektographieren [hɛktograˈfiːrən], *v.a.* stencil, duplicate.

Hektoliter [ˈhɛktoliːtər], *m.* (—s, *pl.* —) hectolitre (22 gallons).

Held [hɛlt], *m.* (—en, *pl.* —en) hero.

Heldengedicht [ˈhɛldəngədɪçt], *n.* (—es, *pl.* —e) heroic poem, epic.

heldenhaft [ˈhɛldənhaft], *adj.* heroic. — *adv.* heroically.

Heldenmut [ˈhɛldənmuːt], *m.* (—es, *no pl.*) heroism.

helfen [ˈhɛlfən], *v.n. irr.* (*Dat.*) help, aid, assist.

Helfershelfer [ˈhɛlfərshɛlfər], *m.* (—s, *pl.* —) accomplice, accessory.

Helgoland [ˈhɛlgolant], *n.* Heligoland.

hell [hɛl], *adj.* clear, bright, light; (*coll.*) clever, wide awake.

Helldunkel [ˈhɛlduŋkəl], *n.* (—s, *no pl.*) twilight; (*Art*) chiaroscuro.

Helle [ˈhɛlə], *f.* (—, *no pl.*) clearness; brightness; daylight.

Heller [ˈhɛlər], *m.* (—s, *pl.* —) small coin, farthing.

hellhörig [ˈhɛlhøːrɪç], *adj.* keen of hearing.

Helligkeit [ˈhɛlɪçkaɪt], *f.* (—, *no pl.*) clearness; daylight.

Hellseher [ˈhɛlzeːər], *m.* (—s, *pl.* —) clairvoyant.

hellsichtig [ˈhɛlzɪxtɪç], *adj.* clairvoyant; clear-sighted.

Helm [hɛlm], *m.* (—es, *pl.* —e) helmet.

Helmbusch [ˈhɛlmbuʃ], *m.* (—es, *pl.* ⁒e) crest (of helmet).

Helmgitter [ˈhɛlmgɪtər], *n.* (—s, *pl.* —) eye-slit (in helmet).

Helsingfors [ˈhɛlzɪŋfɔrs], *n.* Helsinki.

Helsingör [hɛlzɪŋˈøːr], *n.* Elsinore.

Hemd [hɛmt], *n.* (—es, *pl.* —en) shirt; vest.

Hemdenstoff [ˈhɛmdənʃtɔf], *m.* (—es, *pl.* —e) shirting.

hemmen [ˈhɛmən], *v.a.* stop, hamper, hinder, restrain; (*fig.*) inhibit.

Hemmschuh [ˈhɛmʃuː], *m.* (—s, *pl.* —e) brake; (*fig.*) drag, obstruction.

Hemmung [ˈhɛmuŋ], *f.* (—, *pl.* —en) stoppage, hindrance, restraint; (*watch*) escapement; (*fig.*) inhibition, reluctance.

Hengst [hɛŋkst], *m.* (—es, *pl.* —e) stallion.

Henkel [ˈhɛŋkəl], *m.* (—s, *pl.* —) handle.

henken [ˈhɛŋkən], *v.a* hang (s.o.).

Henker [ˈhɛŋkər], *m.* (—s, *pl.* —) hangman, executioner.

Henne [ˈhɛnə], *f.* (—, *pl.* —n) (*Zool.*) hen; *junge* —, pullet.

her [heːr], *adv.* hither, here, to me; (*temp.*) since, ago; *von alters* —, from olden times; *von je* —, from time immemorial; *wo kommst du* —? where do you come from? *wie lange ist es* —? how long ago was it?

herab [hɛˈrap], *adv.* downwards, down to; *die Treppe* —, downstairs.

herablassen [hɛˈraplasən], *v.r. irr. sich — etwas zu tun*, condescend to do s.th.

herabsehen [hɛˈrapzeːən], *v.n. irr.* look down; (*fig.*) look down upon s.o.

herabsetzen [hɛˈrapzɛtsən], *v.a.* put down; degrade; (*value*) depreciate; (*price*) reduce, lower; (*fig.*) disparage.

herabwürdigen [hɛˈrapvyrdɪgən], *v.a.* degrade, abase.

herabziehen [hɛˈraptsiːən], *v.a. irr.* pull down.

Heraldik [heˈraldɪk], *f.* (—, *no pl.*) heraldry.

heran [hɛˈran], *adv.* up to, on, near.

heranbilden [hɛˈranbɪldən], *v.a.* train. — *v.r. sich* —, train, qualify.

herangehen [hɛˈrangeːən], *v.n. irr.* (*aux.* sein) approach, sidle up (to); *an etwas* —, set to work on s.th.

heranmachen [hɛˈranmaxən], *v.r. sich an etwas* —, set to work on s.th., set about s.th.

herannahen [hɛˈrannaːən], *v.n.* (*aux.* sein) approach, draw near.

heranrücken [hɛˈranrykən], *v.a.* move near. — *v.n.* (*aux.* sein) advance, draw near.

heranschleichen [hɛˈranʃlaɪçən], *v.r. irr. sich — an*, sneak up to.

heranwachsen [hɛˈranvaksən], *v.n. irr.* (*aux.* sein) grow up.

heranwagen [hɛˈranvaːgən], *v.r. sich* —, venture near.

heranziehen [hɛˈrantsiːən], *v.a. irr.* draw near; *als Beispiel* —, cite as an example; (*fig.*) enlist (s.o.'s aid). — *v.n.* (*aux.* sein) draw near, approach.

herauf [hɛˈrauf], *adv.* up, upwards.

heraufbeschwören [hɛˈraufbəʃvøːrən], *v.a.* conjure up.

heraus [hɛˈraus], *adv.* out, out of.

herausfordern [hɛˈrausfɔrdərn], *v.a.* challenge.

Herausgabe [hɛˈrausgaːbə], *f.* (—, *pl.* —n) delivery; (*book*) publication; editing.

herausgeben [hɛˈrausgeːbən], *v.a. irr.* give out, deliver; (*money*) give change; (*book*) publish, edit.

Herausgeber [hɛˈrausgeːbər], *m.* (—s, *pl.* —) publisher; editor.

heraushaben [hɛˈrausha:bən], *v.a. irr. etwas* —, have the knack of s.th.

herausputzen [hɛˈrausputsən], *v.r. sich* —, dress up.

herausrücken [hɛˈrausrykən], *v.n. mit Geld* —, fork out money; *mit der Sprache* —, speak out, come out with.

herausschlagen [hɛˈrausʃlaːgən], *v.a. irr. die Kosten* —, recover expenses; *viel* —, make the most of; profit by.

herausstellen [hɛˈrausʃtɛlən], *v.a.* put out, expose. — *v.r. sich — als*, turn out to be.

herausstreichen [hɛˈrausʃtraɪçən], *v.a. irr.* extol, praise.

heraussuchen [hɛˈrausuːxən], *v.a.* pick out.

herauswollen

herauswollen [hɛ'rausvɔlən], *v.n. nicht mit der Sprache* —, hesitate to speak out.

herb [hɛrp], *adj.* sour, sharp, tart, acrid; (*fig.*) austere, harsh, bitter; (*wine*) dry.

herbei [hɛr'baɪ], *adv.* hither, near.

herbeischaffen [hɛr'baɪʃafən], *v.a.* procure.

herbeiströmen [hɛr'baɪʃtrøːmən], *v.n.* (*aux.* sein) crowd, flock.

Herberge ['hɛrbɛrgə], *f.* (—, *pl.* —n) shelter, lodging, inn.

Herbst [hɛrpst], *m.* (—es, *pl.* —e) autumn; (*Am.*) fall.

Herbstrose ['hɛrpstroːzə], *f.* (—, *pl.* —n) (*Bot.*) hollyhock.

Herbstzeitlose ['hɛrpsttsaɪtloːzə], *f.* (—, *pl.* —n) (*Bot.*) meadow-saffron.

Herd [heːrt], *m.* (—es, *pl.* —e) hearth, fireplace; cooking-stove; (*fig.*) focus.

Herde [heːrdə], *f.* (—, *pl.* —n) flock, herd; (*fig.*) troop.

herein [hɛ'raɪn], *adv.* in, inside. — *int.* —*!* come in!

hereinbrechen [hɛ'raɪnbrɛçən], *v.n. irr.* (*aux.* sein) *über einen* —, befall s.o., overtake s.o.; (*night*) close in.

hereinfallen ['hɛ'raɪnfalən], *v.n. irr.* (*aux.* sein) (*fig.*) be taken in, fall for s.th.

herfallen ['heːrfalən], *v.n. irr.* (*aux.* sein) *über einen* —, go for s.o., set upon s.o.

Hergang ['heːrgaŋ], *m.* (—es, *no pl.*) proceedings, course of events; circumstances; story, plot.

hergeben ['heːrgeːbən], *v.a. irr.* give up, surrender.

hergebracht ['heːrgəbraxt], *adj.* traditional, time-honoured.

hergehen ['heːrgeːən], *v.n. irr.* (*aux.* sein) proceed; *es geht lustig her*, they are having a gay time.

hergelaufen ['heːrgəlaufən], *adj. ein —er Kerl*, an adventurer, an upstart.

herhalten ['heːrhaltən], *v.n. irr.* suffer, serve (as a butt).

Hering ['heːrɪŋ], *m.* (—s, *pl.* —e) (*Zool.*) herring; *geräucherter* —, smoked herring, bloater; *gesalzener* —, pickled herring.

herkommen ['heːrkɔmən], *v.n. irr.* (*aux.* sein) come here; be derived from, descend from.

herkömmlich ['heːrkœmlɪç], *adj.* traditional, customary, usual.

Herkunft ['heːrkunft], *f.* (—, *no pl.*) descent, extraction; origin.

herleiern ['heːrlaɪərn], *v.a.* recite monotonously; reel off.

herleiten ['heːrlaɪtən], *v.a.* derive from.

Hermelin [hɛrmə'liːn], *n.* (—s, *no pl.*) ermine (*fur*).

hermetisch [hɛr'meːtɪʃ], *adj.* hermetical.

hernach [hɛr'naːx], *adv.* after, afterwards; hereafter.

hernehmen ['heːrneːmən], *v.a. irr.* take, get (from); take (s.o.) to task.

hernieder [hɛr'niːdər], *adv.* down.

Herr [hɛr], *m.* (—n, *pl.* —en) master; lord; nobleman; gentleman; (*Theol.*) Lord; principal, governor; *mein* —, Sir; *meine Herren*, gentlemen; — *Schmidt*, Mr. Smith; *einer Sache* — *werden*, master s.th.

Herrenhaus ['hɛrənhaus], *n.* (—es, *pl.* ⸚er) mansion, manor house; (*Parl.*) House of Lords.

Herrenhof ['hɛrənhoːf], *m.* (—es, *pl.* ⸚e) manor, country-seat.

Herrenstand ['hɛrənʃtant], *m.* (—es, *no pl.*) nobility, gentry.

Herrenzimmer ['hɛrəntsɪmər], *n.* (—s, *pl.* —) study.

Herrgott ['hɛrgɔt], the Lord God.

herrichten ['heːrrɪçtən], *v.a.* prepare, fix up.

Herrin ['hɛrɪn], *f.* (—, *pl.* —innen) mistress, lady.

herrisch ['hɛrɪʃ], *adj.* imperious, lordly.

herrlich ['hɛrlɪç], *adj.* magnificent, splendid, glorious, excellent.

Herrnhuter ['hɛrnhuːtər], *m.* (—s, *pl.* —) Moravian; (*pl.*) Moravian brethren.

Herrschaft ['hɛrʃaft], *f.* (—, *pl.* —en) mastery, rule, dominion; master, mistress; *meine* —*en!* ladies and gentlemen!

herrschaftlich ['hɛrʃaftlɪç], *adj.* belonging to a lord; (*fig.*) elegant, fashionable, distinguished.

herrschen ['hɛrʃən], *v.n.* rule, govern, reign.

Herrscher ['hɛrʃər], *m.* (—s, *pl.* —) ruler.

herrühren ['heːrryːrən], *v.n.* come from, originate in.

hersagen ['heːrzaːgən], *v.a.* recite, reel off.

herschaffen ['heːrʃafən], *v.a.* procure.

herstammen ['heːrʃtamən], *v.n.* come from, stem from, originate from; be derived from.

herstellen ['heːrʃtɛlən], *v.a.* place here; manufacture; *wieder* —, restore; (*sick person*) restore to health.

Herstellung ['heːrʃtɛluŋ], *f.* (—, *no pl.*) manufacture, production.

herstürzen ['heːrʃtyrtsən], *v.n.* (*aux.* sein) *über einen* —, rush at s.o.

herüber [hɛ'ryːbər], *adv.* over, across; — *und hinüber*, there and back.

herum [hɛ'rum], *adv.* round, about; around.

herumbalgen [hɛ'rumbalgən], *v.r. sich* —, scrap; scuffle.

herumbekommen [hɛ'rumbəkɔmən], *v.a. irr.* (*coll.*) talk s.o. over, win s.o. over.

herumbummeln [hɛ'rumbumən], *v.n.* loaf about.

herumstreichen [hɛ'rumʃtraɪçən], *v.n. irr.* (*aux.* sein) gad about.

herumtreiben [hɛ'rumtraɪbən], *v.r. irr. sich* —, loaf about, gad about.

herumzanken [hɛ'rumtsaŋkən], *v.r. sich* —, squabble, quarrel; live like cat and dog.

herumziehen [hɛ'rumtsi:ən], *v.a. irr.* drag about. — *v.n.* (*aux.* sein) wander about, move from place to place.

herunter [hɛ'runtər], *adj.* down, downward; *ich bin ganz* —, I feel poorly.

heruntergekommen [hɛ'runtərgəkɔmən], *adj.* decayed, broken down; in straitened circumstances; depraved.

herunterhandeln [hɛ'runtərhandəln], *v.a. einem etwas* —, beat s.o. down (in price).

herunterwürgen [hɛ'runtervyrgən], *v.a.* swallow s.th. with dislike.

hervor [hɛr'fo:r], *adv.* forth, forward, out.

hervorheben [hɛr'fo:rhe:bən], *v.a. irr.* emphasize, stress.

hervorragen [hɛr'fo:rra:gən], *v.n.* stand out, project; (*fig.*) be distinguished, excel.

hervorragend [hɛr'fo:rra:gənt], *adj.* prominent; (*fig.*) outstanding, excellent.

hervorrufen [hɛr'fo:rru:fən], *v.a. irr.* call forth; (*fig.*) evoke, bring about, create, cause.

hervorstechen [hɛr'fo:rʃteçən], *v.n. irr.* be predominant, stand out.

hervortun [hɛr'fo:rtu:n], *v.r. irr. sich* —, distinguish o.s.

Herz [hɛrts], *n.* (—**ens**, *pl.* —**en**) heart; courage; mind; spirit; feeling; core; (*Cards*) hearts; (*coll.*) darling; *einem etwas ans* — *legen*, impress s.th. upon s.o.; *von* —*en gern*, with all my heart; *sich etwas zu* —*en nehmen*, take s.th. to heart.

herzählen ['he:rtsɛ:lən], *v.a.* enumerate.

Herzanfall ['hɛrtsanfal], *m.* (—**s**, *pl.* ⸚**e**) (*Med.*) heart attack.

Herzbube ['hɛrtsbu:bə], *m.* (—**n**, *pl.* —**n**) (*Cards*) knave *or* jack of hearts.

Herzdame ['hɛrtsda:mə], *f.* (—, *pl.* —**n**) (*Cards*) queen of hearts.

Herzeleid ['hɛrtsəlaɪt], *n.* (—**es**, *no pl.*) heartbreak, sorrow, anguish, grief.

herzen ['hɛrtsən], *v.a.* hug.

Herzenseinfalt ['hɛrtsənsaɪnfalt], *f.* (—, *no pl.*) simple-mindedness.

Herzensgrund ['hɛrtsənsgrunt], *m.* (—**es**, *no pl.*) *aus* —, with all my heart.

Herzenslust ['hɛrtsənslust], *f.* (—, *no pl.*) heart's delight; *nach* —, to o.'s heart's content.

Herzfehler ['hɛrtsfe:lər], *m.* (—**s**, *pl.* —) (*Med.*) cardiac defect; organic heart disease.

Herzfell ['hɛrtsfɛl], *n.* (—**s**, *pl.* —**e**) pericardium.

herzförmig ['hɛrtsfœrmɪç], *adj.* heart-shaped.

herzhaft ['hɛrtshaft], *adj.* stout-hearted; courageous, bold; resolute; hearty.

herzig ['hɛrtsɪç], *adj.* lovely, charming, sweet; (*Am.*) cute.

Herzkammer ['hɛrtskamər], *f.* (—, *pl.* —**n**) ventricle (of the heart).

Herzklappe ['hɛrtsklapə], *f.* (—, *pl.* —**n**) valve of the heart.

Herzklopfen ['hɛrtsklɔpfən], *n.* (—**s**, *no pl.*) palpitations.

herzlich ['hɛrtslɪç], *adj.* hearty, cordial, affectionate; — *gern*, with pleasure; —*e Grüße*, kind regards.

Herzog ['hɛrtso:k], *m.* (—**s**, *pl.* ⸚**e**) duke.

Herzogtum ['hɛrtso:ktu:m], *n.* (—**s**, *pl.* ⸚**er**) duchy, dukedom.

Herzschlag ['hɛrtsʃla:k], *m.* (—**es**, *pl.* ⸚**e**) heartbeat; (*Med.*) heart attack, cardiac failure.

Hetäre [he'tɛ:rə], *f.* (—, *pl.* —**n**) courtesan.

Hetzblatt ['hɛtsblat], *n.* (—**s**, *pl.* ⸚**er**) gutter press.

Hetze ['hɛtsə], *f.* (—, *pl.* —**n**) chase, hunt, hurry, rush; agitation.

hetzen ['hɛtsən], *v.a.* bait, fluster, chase, hunt, incite. — *v.n. herum* —, rush around.

Hetzer ['hɛtsər], *m.* (—**s**, *pl.* —) instigator, rabble-rouser.

Heu [hɔy], *n.* (—**s**, *no pl.*) hay.

Heuboden ['hɔybo:dən], *m.* (—**s**, *pl.* ⸚) hayloft.

Heuchelei [hɔyçə'laɪ], *f.* (—, *pl.* —**en**) hypocrisy.

heucheln ['hɔyçəln], *v.n.* play the hypocrite, dissemble. — *v.a.* simulate, affect, feign.

Heuchler ['hɔyçlər], *m.* (—**s**, *pl.* —) hypocrite.

Heuer ['hɔyər], *f.* (—, *pl.* —**n**) (*Naut.*) engagement; hire, wages.

heuer ['hɔyər], *adv.* (*dial.*) this year, this season.

heuern ['hɔyərn], *v.a.* (*Naut.*) engage, hire.

Heugabel ['hɔyga:bəl], *f.* (—, *pl.* —**n**) pitchfork.

heulen ['hɔylən], *v.n.* howl; roar; cry, yell, scream.

Heupferd ['hɔypfert], *n.* (—**es**, *pl.* —**e**) (*Ent.*) grasshopper.

heurig ['hɔyrɪç], *adj.* of this year, this year's (*wine etc.*).

Heuschnupfen ['hɔyʃnupfən], *m.* (—**s**, *no pl.*) hay-fever.

Heuschober ['hɔyʃo:bər], *m.* (—**s**, *pl.* —) hayrick.

Heuschrecke ['hɔyʃrɛkə], *f.* (—, *pl.* —**n**) (*Ent.*) locust.

heute ['hɔytə], *adv.* today, this day; — *in acht Tagen*, today week, a week today; — *abend*, tonight.

heutig ['hɔytɪç], *adj.* today's, this day's; modern.

heutzutage ['hɔytsuta:gə], *adv.* nowadays.

Hexe ['hɛksə], *f.* (—, *pl.* —**n**) witch, sorceress, hag.

hexen ['hɛksən], *v.n.* use witchcraft; practise sorcery.

Hexenschuß ['hɛksənʃus], *m.* (—**sses**, *no pl.*) (*Med.*) lumbago.

107

Hexerei

Hexerei [hɛksə'raɪ], *f.* (—, *pl.* —en) witchcraft, sorcery, juggling.

hie [hiː], *adv.* (*dial.*) here.

Hieb [hiːp], *m.* (—es, *pl.* —e) cut, stroke; hit, blow; (*pl.*) a thrashing.

hienieden [hiːˈniːdən], *adv.* here below, down here.

hier [hiːr], *adv.* here, in this place.

Hiersein ['hiːrzaɪn], *n.* (—s, *no pl.*) presence, attendance.

hiesig ['hiːzɪç], *adj.* of this place, of this country, local.

Hifthorn ['hɪfthɔrn], *n.* (—s, *pl.* ⁻er) hunting-horn.

Hilfe ['hɪlfə], *f.* (—, *pl.* —n) help, aid, assistance, succour, relief.

hilflos ['hɪlfloːs], *adj.* helpless.

hilfreich ['hɪlfraɪç], *adj.* helpful.

Hilfsmittel ['hɪlfsmɪtəl], *n.* (—s, *pl.* —) expedient, remedy.

Hilfsschule ['hɪlfsʃuːlə], *f.* (—, *pl.* —n) school for backward children.

Hilfszeitwort ['hɪlfstsaɪtvɔrt], *n.* (—s, *pl.* ⁻er) (*Gram.*) auxiliary verb.

Himbeere ['hɪmbeːrə], *f.* (—, *pl.* —n) raspberry.

Himmel ['hɪməl], *m.* (—s, *pl.* —) heaven, heavens; sky; firmament.

himmelan [hɪməlˈan], *adv.* heavenward.

himmelangst ['hɪmələŋkst], *adv. ihm war —*, he was panic-stricken.

Himmelbett ['hɪməlbet], *n.* (—s, *pl.* —en) fourposter.

himmelblau ['hɪməlblau], *adj.* sky-blue.

Himmelfahrt ['hɪməlfaːrt], *f.* (—, *no pl.*) Ascension.

Himmelschlüssel ['hɪməlʃlysəl], *m.* (—s, *pl.* —) (*Bot.*) primrose.

himmelschreiend ['hɪməlʃraɪənt], *adj.* atrocious, revolting.

Himmelsgewölbe ['hɪməlsgəvœlbə], *n.* (—s, *pl.* —) firmament.

Himmelsstrich ['hɪməlsʃtrɪç], *m.* (—s, *pl.* —e) climate, zone.

Himmelszeichen ['hɪməlstsaɪçən], *n.* (—s, *pl.* —) sign of the zodiac.

himmelweit ['hɪməlvaɪt], *adj.* enormous; *— entfernt*, poles apart.

himmlisch ['hɪmlɪʃ], *adj.* celestial, heavenly.

hin [hɪn], *adv.* there, towards that place; finished, gone; ruined; *— und her*, to and fro.

hinab [hɪnˈap], *adv.* down.

hinan [hɪnˈan], *adv.* up.

hinarbeiten ['hɪnarbaɪtən], *v.n. auf etwas —*, work towards s.th.

hinauf [hɪnˈauf], *adv.* up, up to.

hinaus [hɪnˈaus], *adv.* out, out of; *es kommt auf dasselbe —*, it comes to the same thing.

hinauswollen [hɪnˈausvɔlən], *v.n.* wish to go out; (*fig.*) *hoch —*, aim high.

hinausziehen [hɪnˈaustsiːən], *v.a. irr.* draw out; drag on; (*fig.*) protract.

Hinblick ['hɪnblɪk], *m.* (—es, *no pl.*) *im — auf*, in consideration of, with regard to.

hinbringen ['hɪnbrɪŋən], *v.a. irr.* bring to; escort; *Zeit —*, while away time.

hinderlich ['hɪndərlɪç], *adj.* obstructive, cumbersome.

hindern ['hɪndərn], *v.a.* hinder, obstruct, hamper, impede.

hindeuten ['hɪndɔytən], *v.n. auf etwas —*, point to s.th., hint at s.th.

Hindin ['hɪndɪn], *f.* (—, *pl.* —innen) (*Poet.*) hind.

hindurch [hɪnˈdurç], *adv.* through; throughout; *die ganze Zeit —*, all the time.

hinein [hɪnˈaɪn], *adv.* in, into; *in den Tag — leben*, live for the present, lead a life of carefree enjoyment.

hineinfinden [hɪnˈaɪnfɪndən], *v.r. irr. sich in etwas —*, reconcile *or* adapt o.s. to s.th.

hinfällig ['hɪnfɛlɪç], *adj.* frail, feeble, weak; shaky, void, invalid.

Hingabe ['hɪngaːbə], *f.* (—, *no pl.*) surrender; (*fig.*) devotion.

hingeben ['hɪngeːbən], *v.a. irr.* give up, surrender. — *v.r. sich einer Sache —*, devote o.s. to a task.

hingegen [hɪnˈgeːgən], *adv.* on the other hand.

hinhalten ['hɪnhaltən], *v.a. irr.* (*thing*) hold out; (*person*) keep in suspense, put off.

hinken ['hɪnkən], *v.n.* limp.

hinlänglich ['hɪnlɛŋlɪç], *adj.* sufficient.

hinlegen ['hɪnleːgən], *v.a.* lay down, put away. — *v.r. sich —*, lie down, go to bed.

hinnehmen ['hɪnneːmən], *v.a. irr.* take, submit to, accept.

hinreichen ['hɪnraɪçən], *v.a.* pass to. — *v.n.* suffice, be sufficient.

Hinreise ['hɪnraɪzə], *f.* (—, *pl.* —n) outward journey.

hinreißen ['hɪnraɪsən], *v.r. irr. sich — lassen*, allow o.s. to be carried away.

hinreißend ['hɪnraɪsənt], *adj.* charming, ravishing, enchanting.

hinrichten ['hɪnrɪçtən], *v.a.* execute, put to death.

hinscheiden ['hɪnʃaɪdən], *v.n. irr.* die, pass away.

hinschlängeln ['hɪnʃlɛŋəln], *v.r. sich —*, meander, wind along.

Hinsicht ['hɪnzɪçt], *f.* (—, *no pl.*) view, consideration, regard.

hinsichtlich ['hɪnzɪçtlɪç], *prep.* (*Genit.*) with regard to.

hinstellen ['hɪnʃtelən], *v.a.* put down; make out to be.

hinten ['hɪntən], *adv.* behind; *von —*, from behind.

hinter ['hɪntər], *prep.* (*Dat.*) behind, after.

Hinterachse ['hɪntəraksə], *f.* (—, *pl.* —n) (*Motor.*) rear-axle.

Hinterbein ['hɪntərbaɪn], *n.* (—s, *pl.* —e) hind-leg; (*fig.*) *sich auf die —e stellen*, get up on o.'s hind-legs.

108

hochachtungsvoll

Hinterbliebene [hɪntər'bli:bənə], *m.* (**—n**, *pl.* **—n**) survivor; mourner; (*pl.*) the bereaved.
hinterbringen [hɪntər'brɪŋən], *v.a. irr.* give information about, (*coll.*) tell on.
Hinterdeck ['hɪntərdɛk], *n.* (**—s**, *no pl.*) (*Naut.*) quarter deck.
hinterdrein ['hɪntərdraɪn], *adv.* afterwards, after; behind.
hintereinander [hɪntəraɪn'andər], *adv.* in succession, one after another.
Hintergedanke ['hɪntərgədaŋkə], *m.* (**—n**, *pl.* **—n**) mental reservation, ulterior motive.
hintergehen [hɪntər'ge:ən], *v.a. irr.* deceive, circumvent.
Hintergrund ['hɪntərgrunt], *m.* (**—es**, *pl.* ⁖e) background; (*Theat.*) back-cloth, back-drop.
Hinterhalt ['hɪntərhalt], *m.* (**—s**, *pl.* **—e**) ambush; (*fig.*) reserve.
hinterhältig ['hɪntərhɛltɪç], *adj.* furtive, secretive; insidious.
hinterher [hɪntər'he:r], *adv.* behind; in the rear; afterwards.
Hinterindien ['hɪntərɪndjən], *n.* Indo-China.
Hinterkopf ['hɪntərkɔpf], *m.* (**—es**, *pl.* ⁖e) occiput, back of the head.
Hinterlader ['hɪntərla:dər], *m.* (**—s**, *pl.* —) breech-loader.
hinterlassen [hɪntər'lasən], *v.a. irr.* leave (a legacy), bequeath; leave (word).
Hinterlassenschaft [hɪntər'lasənʃaft], *f.* (**—**, *pl.* **—en**) inheritance, bequest.
Hinterlegung [hɪntər'le:guŋ], *f.* (**—**, *pl.* **—en**) deposition.
Hinterlist ['hɪntərlɪst], *f.* (**—**, *no pl.*) fraud, deceit; cunning.
hinterrücks [hɪntər'ryks], *adv.* from behind; (*fig.*) treacherously, behind s.o.'s back.
Hintertreffen ['hɪntərtrɛfən], *n.* (**—s**, *no pl.*) *ins — geraten*, be left out in the cold, fall behind.
hintertreiben [hɪntər'traɪbən], *v.a. irr.* prevent, frustrate.
Hintertreppe ['hɪntərtrɛpə], *f.* (**—**, *pl.* **—n**) back-stairs.
Hintertreppenroman ['hɪntərtrɛpənroma:n], *m.* (**—s**, *pl.* **—e**) (*Lit.*) cheap thriller.
hinterziehen ['hɪntərtsi:ən], *v.a. irr. insep.* defraud.
hinträumen ['hɪntrɔymən], *v.n. vor sich —*, daydream.
hinüber [hɪn'y:bər], *adv.* over, across.
hinunter [hɪn'untər], *adv.* down; *den Berg —*, downhill.
hinweg [hɪn'vɛk], *adv.* away, off.
hinwegsetzen [hɪn'vɛkzetsən], *v.r. sich über etwas —*, make light of s.th.
Hinweis ['hɪnvaɪs], *m.* (**—es**, *pl.* **—e**) hint, indication, reference; *unter — auf*, with reference to.
hinweisen ['hɪnvaɪzən], *v.a. irr. auf etwas —*, refer to, point to s.th.

hinwerfen ['hɪnvɛrfən], *v.a. irr.* throw down; *hingeworfene Bemerkung*, casual remark.
hinziehen ['hɪntsi:ən], *v.a. irr.* draw along; attract. — *v.n.* (*aux.* sein) march along. — *v.r. sich —*, drag on.
hinzielen ['hɪntsi:lən], *v.n. auf etwas —*, aim at s.th., have s.th. in mind.
hinzu [hɪn'tsu:], *adv.* to, near; besides, in addition.
hinzufügen [hɪn'tsu:fy:gən], *v.a.* add.
hinzukommen [hɪn'tsu:kɔmən], *v.n. irr.* (*aux.* sein) be added.
hinzuziehen [hɪn'tsutsi:ən], *v.a. irr.* include, add; call in (expert).
Hiobsbotschaft ['hi:ɔpsbo:tʃaft], *f.* (**—**, *no pl.*) bad news.
Hirn [hɪrn], *n.* (**—es**, *pl.* **—e**) brain, brains. *See also* **Gehirn**.
Hirngespinst ['hɪrngəʃpɪnst], *n.* (**—es**, *pl.* **—e**) fancy, chimera, illusion, figment of the imagination.
hirnverbrannt ['hɪrnfɛrbrant], *adj.* crazy, insane, mad; (*coll.*) crack-brained.
Hirsch [hɪrʃ], *m.* (**—es**, *pl.* **—e**) (*Zool.*) stag, hart.
Hirschbock ['hɪrʃbɔk], *m.* (**—s**, *pl.* ⁖e) (*Zool.*) stag.
Hirschfänger ['hɪrʃfɛŋər], *m.* (**—s**, *pl.* —) hunting-knife.
Hirschgeweih ['hɪrʃgəvaɪ], *n.* (**—s**, *pl.* **—e**) horns, antlers.
Hirschhorn ['hɪrʃhɔrn], *n.* (**—s**, *no pl.*) (*Chem.*) hartshorn.
Hirschkäfer ['hɪrʃkɛ:fər], *m.* (**—s**, *pl.* —) (*Ent.*) stag beetle.
Hirschkeule ['hɪrʃkɔylə], *f.* (**—**, *pl.* **—n**) haunch of venison.
Hirschkuh ['hɪrʃku:], *f.* (**—**, *pl.* ⁖e) (*Zool.*) hind, doe.
Hirse ['hɪrzə], *f.* (**—**, *no pl.*) (*Bot.*) millet.
Hirt [hɪrt], *m.* (**—en**, *pl.* **—en**) shepherd, herdsman.
Hirtenbrief ['hɪrtənbri:f], *m.* (**—s**, *pl.* **—e**) (*Eccl.*) pastoral letter.
His [hɪs], *n.* (**—**, *pl.* —) (*Mus.*) B sharp.
hissen ['hɪsən], *v.a.* hoist (the flag).
Historiker [hɪ'sto:rɪkər], *m.* (**—s**, *pl.* —) historian.
historisch [hɪ'sto:rɪʃ], *adj.* historical.
Hitzblase ['hɪtsbla:zə], *f.* (**—**, *pl.* **—n**) blister, heat-rash.
Hitze ['hɪtsə], *f.* (**—**, *no pl.*) heat, hot weather.
hitzig ['hɪtsɪç], *adj.* hot-headed, hasty, passionate.
Hitzschlag ['hɪtsʃla:k], *m.* (**—es**, *pl.* ⁖e) sunstroke, heat-stroke.
Hobel ['ho:bəl], *m.* (**—s**, *pl.* —) (*tool*) plane.
Hoch [ho:x], *n.* (**—s**, *no pl.*) toast (*drink*); (*Met.*) high.
hoch, hoh [ho:x, ho:], *adj.* high; (*fig.*) eminent, sublime.
Hochachtung ['ho:xaxtuŋ], *f.* (**—**, *no pl.*) esteem, regard, respect.
hochachtungsvoll ['ho:xaxtuŋsfɔl], *adj., adv.* (*letters*) yours faithfully.

109

Hochamt

Hochamt ['hoːxamt], *n.* (**—es**, *pl.* ¨**er**) (*Eccl.*) High Mass.

Hochbau ['hoːxbau], *m.* (**—s**, *pl.* **—ten**) superstructure.

hochbetagt ['hoːxbətaːkt], *adj.* advanced in years.

Hochburg ['hoːxburk], *f.* (**—**, *pl.* **—en**) (*fig.*) stronghold, citadel.

Hochebene ['hoːxeːbənə], *f.* (**—**, *pl.* **—n**) table-land, plateau.

hochfahrend ['hoːxfaːrənt], *adj.* haughty, high-flown; (*coll.*) stuck-up.

Hochgefühl ['hoːxgəfyːl], *n.* (**—s**, *no pl.*) exaltation.

Hochgenuß ['hoːxgənus], *m.* (**—sses**, *pl.* ¨**sse**) exquisite enjoyment; treat.

Hochgericht ['hoːxgərɪçt], *n.* (**—s**, *pl.* **—e**) place of execution, scaffold.

hochherzig ['hoːxhɛrtsɪç], *adj.* magnanimous.

Hochmeister ['hoːxmaɪstər], *m.* (**—s**, *pl.* **—**) Grand Master.

Hochmut ['hoːxmuːt], *m.* (**—s**, *no pl.*) haughtiness, pride.

hochnäsig ['hoːxnɛːzɪç], *adj.* supercilious, stuck-up.

hochnotpeinlich ['hoːxnoːtpaɪnlɪç], *adj.* (*obs.*) penal, criminal; **—es** *Verhör*, criminal investigation.

Hochofen ['hoːxoːfən], *m.* (**—s**, *pl.* ¨) blast-furnace.

Hochschule ['hoːxʃuːlə], *f.* (**—**, *pl.* **—n**) academy; university.

Hochschüler ['hoːxʃyːlər], *m.* (**—s**, *pl.* **—**) student, undergraduate.

höchst [høːçst], *adj.* highest, most. **—** *adv.* most, extremely.

Hochstapler ['hoːxstaːplər], *m.* (**—s**, *pl.* **—**) confidence trickster, swindler.

höchstens ['høːçstəns], *adv.* at most, at best.

hochtrabend ['hoːxtraːbənt], *adj.* (*horse*) high-stepping; (*fig.*) high-sounding, bombastic.

hochverdient ['hoːxfɛrdiːnt], *adj.* highly meritorious.

Hochverrat ['hoːxfɛraːt], *m.* (**—s**, *no pl.*) high treason.

Hochwild ['hoːxvɪlt], *n.* (**—es**, *no pl.*) deer; big game.

hochwohlgeboren ['hoːxvoːlgəboːrən], *adj.* (*obs.*) noble; *Euer Hochwohlgeboren*, Right Honourable Sir.

hochwürden ['hoːxvyrdən], *adj. Euer Hochwürden*, Reverend Sir.

Hochzeit ['hoːxtsaɪt], *f.* (**—**, *pl.* **—en**) wedding; nuptials.

hochzeitlich ['hoːxtsaɪtlɪç], *adj.* nuptial, bridal.

Hochzeitsreise ['hoːxtsaɪtsraɪzə], *f.* (**—**, *pl.* **—n**) honeymoon.

Hocke ['hɔkə], *f.* (**—**, *pl.* **—n**) squatting posture; shock, stook.

hocken ['hɔkən], *v.n.* crouch, squat; *zu Hause* **—**, be a stay-at-home.

Hocker ['hɔkər], *m.* (**—s**, *pl.* **—**) stool.

Höcker ['hœkər], *m.* (**—s**, *pl.* **—**) hump.

höckerig ['hœkərɪç], *adj.* hump-backed, hunch-backed.

Hode ['hoːdə], *f.* (**—**, *pl.* **—n**) testicle.

Hof [hoːf], *m.* (**—es**, *pl.* ¨**e**) yard, courtyard; farm(stead); (*royal*) court; (*moon*) halo; *einem den* **—** *machen*, court s.o.

Hofarzt ['hoːfartst], *m.* (**—es**, *pl.* ¨**e**) court physician.

hoffähig ['hoːfɛːɪç], *adj.* presentable at court.

Hoffart ['hɔfart], *f.* (**—**, *no pl.*) pride, arrogance.

hoffärtig ['hɔfɛrtɪç], *adj.* proud, arrogant.

hoffen ['hɔfən], *v.n.* hope; *fest auf etwas* **—**, trust.

hoffentlich ['hɔfəntlɪç], *adv.* as I hope, I trust that.

Hoffnung ['hɔfnuŋ], *f.* (**—**, *pl.* **—en**) hope, expectation, anticipation, expectancy; *guter* **—** *sein*, be full of hope; be expecting a baby; *sich* **—** *machen auf*, cherish hopes of.

hoffnungslos ['hɔfnuŋsloːs], *adj.* hopeless, past hope.

hofieren [hoˈfiːrən], *v.a.* court.

höfisch ['høːfɪʃ], *adj.* courtlike, courtly.

höflich ['høːflɪç], *adj.* courteous, civil, polite.

Hoflieferant ['hoːfliːfərant], *m.* (**—en**, *pl.* **—en**) purveyor to His *or* Her Majesty.

Höfling ['høːflɪŋ], *m.* (**—s**, *pl.* **—e**) courtier.

Hofmarschall ['hoːfmarʃal], *m.* (**—s**, *pl.* **—e**) Lord Chamberlain.

Hofmeister ['hoːfmaɪstər], *m.* (**—s**, *pl.* **—**) (*obs.*) steward; tutor.

Hofnarr ['hoːfnar], *m.* (**—en**, *pl.* **—en**) court jester, court fool.

Hofrat ['hoːfraːt], *m.* (**—s**, *pl.* ¨**e**) Privy Councillor.

Hofschranze ['hoːfʃrantsə], *m.* (**—n**, *pl.* **—n**) courtier; flunkey.

Hofsitte ['hoːfzɪtə], *f.* (**—**, *pl.* **—n**) court etiquette.

Höhe ['høːə], *f.* (**—**, *pl.* **—n**) height, altitude; *bis zur* **—** *von*, up to the level of; *in die* **—**, upwards; *in die* **—** *fahren*, give a start, get excited.

Hoheit ['hoːhaɪt], *f.* (**—**, *pl.* **—en**) grandeur; sovereignty; (*title*) Highness.

Hohelied [hoːəˈliːt], *n.* (**—s**, *no pl.*) Song of Solomon.

Höhenmesser ['høːənmɛsər], *m.* (**—s**, *pl.* **—**) (*Aviat.*) altimeter.

Höhensonne ['høːənzɔnə], *f.* (**—**, *pl.* **—n**) Alpine sun; (*Med.*) ultra-violet lamp.

Höhenzug ['høːəntsuːk], *m.* (**—s**, *pl.* ¨**e**) mountain range.

Höhepunkt ['høːəpuŋkt], *m.* (**—s**, *pl.* **—e**) climax, culmination, acme; peak.

höher ['høːər], *comp. adj.* higher.

hohl [hoːl], *adj.* hollow; (*tooth*) decayed, hollow.

Höhle ['høːlə], *f.* (**—**, *pl.* **—n**) cave, cavern, den.

Hörsaal

hohlgeschliffen [ˈhoːlgəʃlɪfən], *adj.* concave, hollow-ground.
Hohlheit [ˈhoːlhaɪt], *f.* (—, *no pl.*) hollowness.
Hohlleiste [ˈhoːllaɪstə], *f.* (—, *pl.* —n) groove, channel.
Hohlmaß [ˈhoːlmaːs], *n.* (—es, *pl.* —e) dry measure.
Hohlmeißel [ˈhoːlmaɪsəl], *m.* (—s, *pl.* —) gouge.
Hohlsaum [ˈhoːlzaum], *m.* (—s, *pl.* ⁻e) hemstitch.
Hohlspiegel [ˈhoːlʃpiːgəl], *m.* (—s, *pl.* —) concave mirror.
Höhlung [ˈhøːluŋ], *f.* (—, *pl.* —en) hollow, cavity.
Hohlziegel [ˈhoːltsiːgəl], *m.* (—s, *pl.* —) hollow brick.
Hohn [hoːn], *m.* (—s, *no pl.*) scorn, derision, mockery; sneer.
höhnen [ˈhøːnən], *v.a.* deride, sneer at; *see* **verhöhnen**.
Höker [ˈhøːkər], *m.* (—s, *pl.* —) hawker, huckster.
hold [hɔlt], *adj.* kind, friendly; gracious; graceful; sweet.
Holder [ˈhɔldər] *see* **Holunder**.
holdselig [ˈhɔltzeːlɪç], *adj.* sweet, charming, gracious.
holen [ˈhoːlən], *v.a.* fetch, collect, get.
Holland [ˈhɔlant], *n.* Holland.
Hölle [ˈhœlə], *f.* (—, *no pl.*) hell.
Holm [hɔlm], *m.* (—es, *pl.* —e) islet, holm; (*Gymn.*) bar.
holperig [ˈhɔlpərɪç], *adj.* rough, bumpy.
holpern [ˈhɔlpərn], *v.n.* jolt, stumble; (*fig.*) falter.
Holunder [hoˈlundər], *m.* (—s, *pl.* —) (*Bot.*) elder; *spanischer* —, lilac.
Holz [hɔlts], *n.* (—es, *pl.* ⁻er) wood, timber; (*Am.*) lumber; (*no pl.*) forest; bush.
Holzapfel [ˈhɔltsapfəl], *m.* (—s, *pl.* ⁻) (*Bot.*) crab-apple.
holzartig [ˈhɔltsartɪç], *adj.* woody, ligneous.
holzen [ˈhɔltsən], *v.a.* cut *or* gather wood.
hölzern [ˈhœltsərn], *adj.* wooden; (*fig.*) stiff.
Holzhändler [ˈhɔltshɛndlər], *m.* (—s, *pl.* —) timber-merchant; (*Am.*) lumber merchant.
Holzhauer [ˈhɔltshauər], *m.* (—s, *pl.* —) wood-cutter.
holzig [ˈhɔltsɪç], *adj.* woody, wooded; (*asparagus*) woody, hard; (*beans*) stringy.
Holzkohle [ˈhɔltskoːlə], *f.* (—, *no pl.*) charcoal.
Holzscheit [ˈhɔltsʃaɪt], *n.* (—s, *pl.* —e) log of wood.
Holzschlag [ˈhɔltsʃlaːk], *m.* (—es, *pl.* ⁻e) clearing; felling area.
Holzschnitt [ˈhɔltsʃnɪt], *m.* (—es, *pl.* —e) wood-cut.
Holzschuh [ˈhɔltsʃuː], *m.* (—s, *pl.* —e) clog.

Holzweg [ˈhɔltsveːk], *m.* (—s, *pl.* —e) timbertrack; (*fig.*) *auf dem — sein*, be on the wrong tack.
Holzwolle [ˈhɔltsvɔlə], *f.* (—, *no pl.*) wood shavings.
homogen [homoˈgeːn], *adj.* homogeneous.
homolog [homoˈloːg], *adj.* homologous.
honett [hɔˈnɛt], *adj.* (*obs.*) respectable, genteel.
Honig [ˈhoːnɪç], *m.* (—s, *no pl.*) honey.
Honigkuchen [ˈhoːnɪçkuːxən], *m.* (—s, *pl.* —) ginger-bread.
Honigwabe [ˈhoːnɪçvaːbə], *f.* (—, *pl.* —n) honeycomb.
Honorar [honoˈraːr], *n.* (—s, *pl.* —e) remuneration; (*professional*) fee; honorarium.
Honoratioren [honoraˈtsjoːrən], *m. pl.* people of rank; dignitaries.
honorieren [honoˈriːrən], *v.a.* pay a fee to, remunerate.
Hopfen [ˈhɔpfən], *m.* (—s, *no pl.*) (*Bot.*) hop, hops; *an dem ist — und Malz verloren*, he is beyond help.
Hopfenstange [ˈhɔpfənʃtaŋə], *f.* (—, *pl.* —n) hop-pole; (*fig.*) tall thin person.
hopsen [ˈhɔpsən], *v.n.* (*aux.* sein) (*coll.*) hop, jump.
hörbar [ˈhøːrbaːr], *adj.* audible.
horchen [ˈhɔrçən], *v.n.* listen, eavesdrop.
Horde [ˈhɔrdə], *f.* (—, *pl.* —n) horde.
hören [ˈhøːrən], *v.a., v.n.* hear.
Hörer [ˈhøːrər], *m.* (—s, *pl.* —) listener; (*Univ.*) student; (*telephone*) receiver.
Hörerin [ˈhøːrərɪn], *f.* (—, *pl.* —innen) female listener; (*Univ.*) woman student.
Hörerschaft [ˈhøːrərʃaft], *f.* (—, *no pl.*) audience.
Hörgerät [ˈhøːrgerɛːt], *n.* (—es, *pl.* —e) hearing aid.
hörig [ˈhøːrɪç], *adj.* in bondage, a slave to.
Horizont [horiˈtsɔnt], *m.* (—es, *pl.* —e) horizon.
Horizontale [horitsɔnˈtaːlə], *f.* (—, *pl.* —n) horizontal line.
Horn [hɔrn], *n.* (—s, *pl.* ⁻er) horn; (*Mus.*) French horn.
Hörnchen [ˈhœrnçən], *n.* (—s, *pl.* —) French roll, croissant.
hörnern [ˈhœrnərn], *adj.* horny, made of horn.
Hornhaut [ˈhɔrnhaut], *f.* (—, *pl.* ⁻te) horny skin; (*eye*) cornea.
Hornhautverpflanzung [ˈhɔrnhautfɛrpflantsuŋ], *f.* (—, *no pl.*) corneal graft.
hornig [ˈhɔrnɪç], *adj.* hard, horny.
Hornisse [hɔrˈnɪsə], *f.* (—, *pl.* —n) (*Ent.*) hornet.
horrend [hɔˈrɛnt], *adj.* exorbitant; stupendous.
Hörrohr [ˈhøːrroːr], *n.* (—s, *pl.* —e) ear trumpet.
Hörsaal [ˈhøːrzaːl], *m.* (—s, *pl.* —säle) auditorium, lecture room.

111

Hörspiel

Hörspiel ['hø:rʃpi:l], *n.* (—s, *pl.* —e) radio play.

Horst [hɔrst], *m.* (—es, *pl.* —e) eyrie.

Hort [hɔrt], *m.* (—es, *pl.* —e) (*Poet.*) treasure; stronghold.

Hortensie [hɔr'tɛnzjə], *f.* (—, *pl.* —n) (*Bot.*) hydrangea.

Hose ['ho:zə], *f.* (—, *pl.* —n) trousers, pants, breeches; (*women*) slacks.

Hosenband ['ho:zənbant], *n.* (—es, *pl.* ⁻er) garter.

Hosenträger ['ho:zəntrɛgər], *m. pl.* braces, suspenders.

Hospitant [hɔspi'tant], *m.* (—en, *pl.* —en) (*Univ.*) temporary student, non-registered student.

hospitieren [hɔspi'ti:rən], *v.n.* attend lectures as a visitor.

Hostie ['hɔstjə], *f.* (—, *pl.* —n) (*Eccl.*) the Host.

hüben ['hy:bən], *adv.* on this side; — *und drüben*, on either side.

hübsch [hypʃ], *adj.* pretty, attractive; handsome; good-looking.

Hubschrauber ['hu:pʃraubər], *m.* (—s, *pl.* —) (*Aviat.*) helicopter.

huckepack ['hukəpak], *adv.* — *tragen*, carry pick-a-back.

Huf [hu:f], *m.* (—es, *pl.* —e) hoof.

Hufe ['hu:fə], *f.* (—, *pl.* —n) hide (of land).

Hufeisen ['hu:faizən], *n.* (—s, *pl.* —) horseshoe.

Huflattich ['hu:flatiç], *m.* (—s, *pl.* —e) (*Bot.*) colt's foot.

Hufschlag ['hu:fʃla:k], *m.* (—s, *pl.* ⁻e) (*of a horse*) hoof-beat.

Hüfte ['hyftə], *f.* (—, *pl.* —n) (*Anat.*) hip; (*animals*) haunch.

Hügel ['hy:gəl], *m.* (—s, *pl.* —) hill, hillock.

hügelig ['hy:gəliç], *adj.* hilly.

Huhn [hu:n], *n.* (—s, *pl.* ⁻er) fowl; hen.

Hühnchen ['hy:nçən], *n.* (—s, *pl.* —) pullet, chicken.

Hühnerauge ['hy:nəraugə], *n.* (—s, *pl.* —n) corn (*on the foot*).

Huld [hult], *f.* (—, *no pl.*) grace, favour.

huldigen ['huldigən], *v.n.* pay homage.

huldvoll ['hultfɔl], *adj.* gracious.

Hülle ['hylə], *f.* (—, *pl.* —n) cover, covering; veil; *in — und Fülle*, in abundance, in profusion.

hüllen ['hylən], *v.a.* cover, veil, wrap.

Hülse ['hylzə], *f.* (—, *pl.* —n) hull, husk, shell; cartridge-case.

Hülsenfrucht ['hylzənfruxt], *f.* (—, *pl.* ⁻e) (*Bot.*) leguminous plant.

human [hu'ma:n], *adj.* humane.

humanistisch [huma'nistiʃ], *adj.* classical; humanistic.

Hummel ['huməl], *f.* (—, *pl.* —n) (*Ent.*) bumble-bee.

Hummer ['humər], *m.* (—s, *pl.* —) (*Zool.*) lobster.

Humor [hu'mo:r], *m.* (—s, *no pl.*) humour.

humoristisch [humo'ristiʃ], *adj.* humorous, witty.

humpeln ['humpəln], *v.n.* hobble, limp.

Humpen ['humpən], *m.* (—s, *pl.* —) deep drinking-cup, bowl, tankard.

Humus ['hu:mus], *m.* (—, *no pl.*) garden-mould, humus.

Hund [hunt], *m.* (—es, *pl.* —e) dog; (*hunting*) hound; (*fig.*) rascal, scoundrel.

Hundehaus ['hundəhaus], *n.* (—es, *pl.* ⁻er) dog-kennel.

hundert ['hundərt], *num. adj.* a hundred, one hundred.

Hündin ['hyndin], *f.* (—, *pl.* —innen) bitch.

Hundstage ['huntsta:gə], *m. pl.* dog days (July to August).

Hundszahn ['huntstsa:n], *m.* (—es, *pl.* ⁻e) (*Bot.*) dandelion.

Hüne ['hy:nə], *m.* (—n, *pl.* —n) giant, colossus; (*fig.*) tall man.

Hünengrab ['hy:nəngra:p], *n.* (—es, *pl.* ⁻er) tumulus, burial mound, barrow, cairn.

Hunger ['huŋər], *m.* (—s, *no pl.*) hunger; starvation.

hungern ['huŋərn], *v.n.* hunger, be hungry.

Hungertuch ['huŋərtu:x], *n.* (—es, *no pl.*) *am — nagen*, go without food; live in poverty.

hungrig ['huŋriç], *adj.* hungry; (*fig.*) desirous (of).

Hupe ['hu:pə], *f.* (—, *pl.* —n) motor-horn, hooter (of a car).

hüpfen ['hypfən], *v.n.* (*aux.* sein) hop, skip.

Hürde ['hyrdə], *f.* (—, *pl.* —n) hurdle.

Hure ['hu:rə], *f.* (—, *pl.* —n) whore, prostitute, harlot; (*coll.*) tart.

hurtig ['hurtiç], *adj.* nimble, agile; quick, speedy, swift.

Husar [hu'za:r], *m.* (—en, *pl.* —en) hussar.

husch! [huʃ], *excl.* quick!

huschen ['huʃən], *v.n.* (*aux.* sein) scurry, slip away.

hüsteln ['hy:stəln], *v.n.* cough slightly; clear o.'s throat.

husten ['hu:stən], *v.n.* cough.

Hut (1) [hu:t], *m.* (—es, *pl.* ⁻e) hat; *steifer —*, bowler.

Hut (2) [hu:t], *f.* (—, *no pl.*) guard, keeping, care.

hüten ['hy:tən], *v.a.* guard, tend, care for; *Kinder —*, baby-sit; *das Bett —*, be confined to o.'s bed, be ill in bed. — *v.r. sich — vor*, be on o.'s guard against, beware of.

Hüter ['hy:tər], *m.* (—s, *pl.* —) guardian, keeper; (*cattle*) herdsman.

Hutkrempe ['hu:tkrɛmpə], *f.* (—, *pl.* —n) hat-brim.

Hütte ['hytə], *f.* (—, *pl.* —n) hut, cottage; (*Tech.*) furnace, forge, foundry.

Hüttenarbeiter ['hytənarbaitər], *m.* (⁻s, *pl.* —) smelter, foundry worker.

Hyäne [hy'ɛ:nə], *f.* (—, *pl.* —n) (*Zool.*) hyena.

Individuum

Hyazinthe [hyat'sɪntə], *f.* (—, *pl.* —n) (*Bot.*) hyacinth.
Hyperbel [hy'pɛrbəl], *f.* (—, *pl.* —n) hyperbola.
hypnotisch [hyp'no:tɪʃ], *adj.* hypnotic.
hypnotisieren [hypnoti'zi:rən], *v.a.* hypnotise.
Hypochonder [hypo'xɔndər], *m.* (—s, *pl.* —) hypochondriac.
Hypothek [hypo'te:k], *f.* (—, *pl.* —en) mortgage.
Hysterie [hyste'ri:], *f.* (—, *no pl.*) hysterics, hysteria.
hysterisch [hys'te:rɪʃ], *adj.* hysterical.

I

I [i:], *n.* (—, *no pl.*) the letter I. — *excl. i wo!* (*dial.*) certainly not, of course not.
ich [ɪç], *pers. pron.* I, myself.
ideal [ide'a:l], *adj.* ideal.
idealisieren [ideali'zi:rən], *v.a.* idealise.
Idealismus [idea'lɪsmus], *m.* (—, *no pl.*) idealism.
Idee [i'de:], *f.* (—, *pl.* —n) idea, notion, conception.
identifizieren [idɛntifi'tsi:rən], *v.a.* identify.
identisch [i'dɛntɪʃ], *adj.* identical.
Identität [idɛnti'tɛ:t], *f.* (—, *no pl.*) identity.
idiomatisch [idio'ma:tɪʃ], *adj.* idiomatic.
Idyll [i'dyl], *n.* (—s, *pl.* —e) idyll.
Idylle [i'dylə], *f.* (—, *pl.* —n) idyll.
idyllisch [i'dylɪʃ], *adj.* idyllic.
Igel [i'gəl], *m.* (—s, *pl.* —) (*Zool.*) hedgehog.
ignorieren [ɪgno'ri:rən], *v.a.* ignore, take no notice of.
ihm [i:m], *pers. pron. Dat.* to him, it.
ihn [i:n], *pers. pron. Acc.*, him, it.
Ihnen [i:nən], *pers. pron. Dat.* you, to you.
ihnen [i:nən], *pers. pron. pl. Dat.* them, to them.
Ihr [i:r], *poss. adj.* your; of your. —, *poss. pron.* yours.
ihr [i:r], *pers. pron.* to her; (*pl.*) (*intim.*) you. — *poss. adj.* her, their. — *poss. pron.* hers, theirs.
Ihrer [i:rər], *pers. pron.* of you. — *poss. adj.* of your.
ihrer [i:rər], *pers. pron.* of her, of it; (*pl.*) of them. — *poss. adj* of her; to her; (*pl.*) of them.
ihresgleichen [i:rəsglaɪçən], *adv.* of her, its *or* their kind.
ihrethalben [i:rəthalbən], *adv.* for her sake, for their sake, on her account, on their account.

ihretwegen [i:rətve:gən] *see* **ihrethalben.**
ihretwillen [i:rətvɪlən] *see* **ihrethalben.**
Ihrige [i:rɪgə], *poss. pron.* yours.
ihrige [i:rɪgə], *poss. pron.* hers, its, theirs.
illegitim [ɪlegi'ti:m], *adj.* illegitimate.
illuminieren [ɪlumi'ni:rən], *v.a.* illuminate, floodlight.
illustrieren [ɪlu'stri:rən], *v.a.* illustrate.
Iltis [ɪltɪs], *m.* (—ses, *pl.* —se) (*Zool.*) polecat, fitchet.
im [ɪm], *contraction of* **in dem,** in the.
Imbiß [ɪmbɪs], *m.* (—sses, *pl.* —sse) snack, refreshment, light meal.
Imker [ɪmkər], *m.* (—s, *pl.* —) bee-keeper.
immatrikulieren [ɪmmatriku'li:rən], *v.a.* (*Univ.*) matriculate, enrol.
Imme [ɪmə], *f.* (—, *pl.* —n) (*dial., Poet.*) bee.
immer [ɪmər], *adv.* always, ever; — *mehr,* more and more; — *noch,* still; — *wieder,* time and again: — *größer,* larger and larger; *auf* —, for ever.
immerdar [ɪmərda:r], *adv.* for ever.
immerhin [ɪmərhɪn], *adv.* nevertheless, still, after all.
immerzu [ɪmərtsu:], *adv.* always, constantly.
Immobilien [ɪmo'bi:ljən], *pl.* real estate.
Immortelle [ɪmɔr'tɛlə], *f.* (—, *pl.* —n) (*Bot.*) everlasting flower.
immun [ɪ'mu:n], *adj.* immune.
impfen [ɪmpfən], *v.a.* vaccinate, inoculate; (*Hort.*) graft.
imponieren [ɪmpo'ni:rən], *v.n.* impress.
Import [ɪm'pɔrt], *m.* (—s, *pl.* —e) import, importation.
imposant [ɪmpo'zant], *adj.* imposing, impressive.
imstande [ɪm'ʃtandə], *adv.* capable, able; — *sein,* be able.
in [ɪn], *prep.* (*Dat., Acc.*) in, into; at; within.
Inangriffnahme [ɪn'angrɪfna:mə], *f.* (—, *no pl.*) start, beginning, inception.
Inbegriff [ɪnbəgrɪf], *m.* (—es, *no pl.*) essence, epitome.
inbegriffen [ɪnbəgrɪfən], *adv.* inclusive.
Inbrunst [ɪnbrunst], *f.* (—, *no pl.*) ardour, fervour.
indem [ɪn'de:m], *adv.* meanwhile. — *conj.* while, whilst; as, because, in that.
indessen [ɪn'dɛsən], *adv.* meanwhile, in the meantime. — *conj.* however, nevertheless, yet.
Indien [ɪndjən], *n.* India.
Individualität [ɪndividuali'tɛ:t], *f.* (—, *pl.* —en) individuality, personality.
individuell [ɪndividu'ɛl], *adj.* individual.
Individuum [ɪndi'vi:duum], *n.* (—s, *pl.* —duen) individual.

113

Indizienbeweis

Indizienbeweis [ɪnˈdiːtsjənbəvaɪs], *m.* (—es, *pl.* —e) (*Law*) circumstantial evidence *or* proof.

indossieren [ɪndɔˈsiːrən], *v.a.* endorse.

Industrie [ɪndusˈtriː], *f.* (—, *pl.* —n) industry; manufacture.

industriell [ɪndustriˈɛl], *adj.* industrial.

Industrielle [ɪndustriˈɛlə], *m.* (—n, *pl.* —n) manufacturer, industrialist.

ineinander [ɪnaɪˈnandər], *adv.* into each other, into one another.

infam [ɪnˈfaːm], *adj.* infamous.

Infantin [ɪnˈfantɪn], *f.* (—, *pl.* —en) Infanta.

infizieren [ɪnfiˈtsiːrən], *v.a.* infect.

infolge [ɪnˈfɔlgə], *prep.* (*Genit.*) in consequence of, owing to.

informieren [ɪnfɔrˈmiːrən], *v.a.* inform, advise.

Ingenieur [ɪnʒenˈjøːr], *m.* (—s, *pl.* —e) engineer.

Ingrimm [ˈɪngrɪm], *m.* (—s, *no pl.*) anger, rage, wrath.

Ingwer [ˈɪŋvər], *m.* (—s, *no pl.*) ginger.

Inhaber [ˈɪnhaːbər], *m.* (—s, *pl.* —) possessor, owner; proprietor; occupant.

inhaftieren [ɪnhafˈtiːrən], *v.a.* imprison; arrest.

inhalieren [ɪnhaˈliːrən], *v.a.* inhale.

Inhalt [ˈɪnhalt], *m.* (—(e)s, *no pl.*) content; contents; tenor.

Inhaltsverzeichnis [ˈɪnhaltsfertsaɪçnɪs], *n.* (—ses, *pl.* —se) (table of) contents; index.

inhibieren [ɪnhiˈbiːrən], *v.a.* inhibit, prevent.

Inkasso [ɪnˈkaso], *n.* (—s, *pl.* —s) encashment.

inklinieren [ɪnkliˈniːrən], *v.n.* be inclined to.

inklusive [ɪnkluˈziːvə], *adv.* inclusive of, including.

inkonsequent [ˈɪnkɔnzəkvɛnt], *adj.* inconsistent.

Inkrafttreten [ɪnˈkrafttreːtən], *n.* (—s, *no pl.*) enactment; coming into force.

Inland [ˈɪnlant], *n.* (—s, *no pl.*) inland, interior.

Inländer [ˈɪnlɛndər], *m.* (—s, *pl.* —) native.

Inlett [ˈɪnlɛt], *n.* (—s, *pl.* —e) bed-tick, ticking.

inliegend [ˈɪnliːgənt], *adj.* enclosed.

inmitten [ɪnˈmɪtən], *prep.* (*Genit.*) in the midst of.

innehaben [ˈɪnəhaːbən], *v.a. irr.* possess; occupy; hold.

innehalten [ˈɪnəhaltən], *v.a. irr.* (*conditions*) keep to, observe; (*time*) come promptly at. — *v.n.* stop, pause.

innen [ˈɪnən], *adv.* within; nach —, inwards; von —, from within.

Innenminister [ˈɪnənmɪnɪstər], *m.* (—s, *pl.* —) Minister for Internal Affairs; Home Secretary; (*Am.*) Secretary of the Interior.

inner [ˈɪnər], *adj.* inner, interior, internal; intrinsic.

innerhalb [ˈɪnərhalp], *prep.* (*Genit.*) within.

innerlich [ˈɪnərlɪç], *adj.* internal; inside o.s.; inward.

innerste [ˈɪnərstə], *adj.* inmost, innermost.

innewerden [ˈɪnəveːrdən], *v.a. irr.* (*aux.* sein) perceive, become aware of.

innewohnen [ˈɪnəvoːnən], *v.n.* be inherent in.

innig [ˈɪnɪç], *adj.* heartfelt, cordial.

Innung [ˈɪnuŋ], *f.* (—, *pl.* —en)guild, corporation.

Insasse [ˈɪnzasə], *m.* (—n, *pl.* —n) inmate; occupant.

insbesondere [ɪnsbəˈzɔndərə], *adv.* especially, particularly, in particular.

Inschrift [ˈɪnʃrɪft], *f.* (—, *pl.* —en) inscription.

Insel [ˈɪnzəl], *f.* (—, *pl.* —n) island.

Inserat [ɪnzəˈraːt], *n.* (—es, *pl.* —e) classified advertisement; (*coll.*) (small) ad.

inserieren [ɪnzəˈriːrən], *v.a.* advertise; insert.

insgeheim [ɪnsgəˈhaɪm], *adv.* privately, secretly.

insgesamt [ɪnsgəˈzamt], *adv.* altogether, in a body.

insofern [ɪnzoˈfɛrn], *conj.* — als, in so far as, inasmuch as, so far as.

inspirieren [ɪnspiˈriːrən], *v.a.* inspire.

installieren [ɪnstaˈliːrən], *v.a.* install, fit.

instandhalten [ɪnˈʃtanthaltən], *v.a. irr.* maintain, preserve, keep in repair.

inständig [ˈɪnʃtɛndɪç], *adj.* urgent; fervent.

instandsetzen [ɪnˈʃtantzɛtsən], *v.a.* restore, repair; *einen* — *etwas zu tun*, enable s.o. to do s.th.

Instanz [ɪnˈstants], *f.* (—, *pl.* —en) (*Law*) instance; *letzte* —, highest court of appeal, last resort.

Institut [ɪnstiˈtuːt], *n.* (—es, *pl.* —e) institute, institution, establishment; (*Univ.*) department.

instruieren [ɪnstruˈiːrən], *v.a.* instruct.

Insulaner [ɪnzuˈlaːnər], *m·* (—s, *pl.* —) islander.

inszenieren [ɪnstseˈniːrən], *v.a.* put on the stage, produce.

Inszenierung [ɪnstseˈniːruŋ], *f.* (—, *pl.* —en) (*Theat.*) production, staging.

intellektuell [ɪntɛlektuˈɛl], *adj.* intellectual.

Intendant [ɪntɛnˈdant], *m.* (—en, *pl.* —en) (*Theat.*) director.

interessant [ɪntərɛˈsant], *adj.* interesting.

Interesse [ɪntəˈrɛsə], *n.* (—s, *pl.* —n) interest.

Interessent [ɪntərɛˈsɛnt], *m.* (—en, *pl.* —en) interested party.

interessieren [ɪntərɛˈsiːrən], *v.a.* interest. — *v.r. sich* —, be interested (in).

intern [ɪnˈtɛrn], *adj.* internal.

Internat [ɪntɛrˈnaːt], *n.* (—es, *pl.* —e) boarding-school.

Interne [ɪn'tɛrnə], *m.* (—n, *pl.* —n) resident (pupil *or* doctor), boarder.

Internist [ɪntɛr'nɪst], *m.* (—en, *pl.* —en) specialist in internal diseases.

interpunktieren [ɪntərpuŋk'tiːrən], *v.a.* punctuate.

Interpunktion [ɪntərpuŋkts'joːn], *f.* (—, *pl.* —en) punctuation.

intim [ɪn'tiːm], *adj.* intimate; *mit einem — sein*, b : on close terms with s.o.

intonieren [ɪnto'niːrən], *v.n.* intone.

Intrigant [ɪntri'gant], *m.* (—en, *pl.* —en) intriguer, schemer.

intrigieren [ɪntri'giːrən], *v.n.* intrigue, scheme.

Inventar [ɪnvɛn'taːr], *n.* (—s, *pl.* —e) inventory; *ein — aufnehmen*, draw up an inventory.

Inventur [ɪnvɛn'tuːr], *f.* (—, *pl.* —en) stock-taking.

inwärts [ɪnvɛrts], *adv.* inwards.

inwendig ['ɪnvɛndɪç], *adj.* inward, internal, inner.

inwiefern [ɪnviːˈfɛrn], *adv.* to what extent.

inwieweit [ɪnviːˈvaɪt], *adv.* how far.

Inzucht ['ɪntsuxt], *f.* (—, *no pl.*) inbreeding.

inzwischen [ɪn'tsvɪʃən], *adv.* meanwhile, in the meantime.

Irak [iˈraːk], *m.*, *n.* Iraq.

Iran [iˈraːn], *n.* Iran.

irden ['ɪrdən], *adj.* earthen.

irdisch ['ɪrdɪʃ], *adj.* earthly, worldly; terrestrial, temporal.

irgend ['ɪrgənt], *adv.* any, some; *wenn es — geht*, if it can possibly be done.

irgendein [ɪrgənt'aɪn], *pron.* any, some.

Irland ['ɪrlant], *n.* Ireland.

ironisch [iˈroːnɪʃ], *adj.* ironic, ironical.

Irre (1) ['ɪrə], *f.* (—, *no pl.*) *in die — gehen*, go astray.

Irre (2) ['ɪrə], *m.* (—n, *pl.* —n) madman, lunatic.

irre ['ɪrə], *adj.* astray; wrong, confused; crazy, demented.

irren ['ɪrən], *v.n.* err, go astray, be wrong. — *v.r. sich —*, be mistaken.

Irrenarzt ['ɪrənartst], *m.* (—es, *pl.* ⁻e) psychiatrist.

Irrenhaus ['ɪrənhaus], *n.* (—es, *pl.* ⁻er) lunatic asylum, mental hospital.

Irrfahrt ['ɪrfaːrt], *f.* (—, *pl.* —en) wandering.

Irrglaube ['ɪrglaubə], *m.* (—ns, *no pl.*) heresy.

irrig ['ɪrɪç], *adj.* erroneous.

irritieren [ɪri'tiːrən], *v.a.* irritate.

Irrlicht ['ɪrlɪçt], *n.* (—s, *pl.* —er) will-o'-the-wisp.

Irrsinn ['ɪrzɪn], *m.* (—s, *no pl.*) madness, insanity, lunacy.

irrsinnig ['ɪrzɪnɪç], *adj.* insane, deranged.

Irrtum ['ɪrtuːm], *m.* (—s, *pl.* ⁻er) error, mistake, fault, oversight.

Irrweg ['ɪrveːk], *m.* (—s, *pl.* —e) wrong track.

Irrwisch ['ɪrvɪʃ], *m.* (—es, *pl.* —e) will-o'-the-wisp.

Ischias ['ɪsçias], *f.*, *m.* (*Med.*) sciatica.

Isegrim ['iːzəgrɪm], *m.* (—s, *pl.* —e) (*fable*) the wolf; a bear (with a sore head) (*also fig.*).

Island ['iːslant], *n.* Iceland.

isolieren [izo'liːrən], *v.a.* (*Electr.*) insulate; (*fig.*) isolate.

Isolierung [izo'liːruŋ], *f.* (—, *pl.* —en) (*Electr.*) insulation; (*fig.*) isolation.

Italien [i'taːljən], *n.* Italy.

J

J [jɔt], *n.* (—, *no pl.*) the letter J.

ja [jaː], *adv.*, *part.* yes; indeed, certainly; even; — *doch*, to be sure; — *freilich*, certainly.

Jacht [jaxt], *f.* (—, *pl.* —en) yacht.

Jacke ['jakə], *f.* (—, *pl.* —n) jacket, tunic.

Jackett [ja'kɛt], *n.* (—s, *pl.* —s) jacket, short coat.

Jagd [jaːkt], *f.* (—, *pl.* —en) hunt, hunting; shooting; chase.

Jagdhund ['jaːkthunt], *m.* (—es, *pl.* —e) retriever, setter; hound.

Jagdrevier ['jaːktreviːr], *n.* (—s, *pl.* —e) hunting-ground.

jagen ['jaːgən], *v.a.* hunt; chase; (*fig.*) tear along.

Jäger ['jɛːgər], *m.* (—s, *pl.* —) hunter, huntsman; game-keeper.

Jägerei [jɛːgə'raɪ], *f.* (—, *no pl.*) huntsmanship.

jäh [jɛː], *adj.* abrupt; steep, precipitous; (*fig.*) hasty, rash, sudden.

jählings ['jɛːlɪŋs], *adv.* abruptly, suddenly, hastily.

Jahr [jaːr], *n.* (—es, *pl.* —e) year.

jähren ['jɛːrən], *v.r. sich —*, (*anniversary*) come round.

Jahresfeier ['jaːrəsfaɪər], *f.* (—, *pl.* —n) anniversary.

Jahresrente ['jaːrəsrɛntə], *f.* (—, *pl.* —n) annuity.

Jahreszeit ['jaːrəstsaɪt], *f.* (—, *pl.* —en) season.

Jahrgang ['jaːrgaŋ], *m.* (—s, *pl.* ⁻e) age group; class; year of publication; vintage.

Jahrhundert [jaːr'hundərt], *n.* (—s, *pl.* —e) century.

jährig ['jɛːrɪç], *adj.* year-old.

jährlich ['jɛːrlɪç], *adj.* yearly, annual. — *adv.* every year.

Jahrmarkt ['jaːrmarkt], *m.* (—s, *pl.* ⁻e) annual fair.

Jahrtausend [jaːr'tauzənt], *n.* (—s, *pl.* —e) millennium.

Jahrzehnt [jaːr'tseːnt], *n.* (—s, *pl.* —e) decade.

Jähzorn ['jɛːtsɔrn], *m.* (—s, *no pl.*) irascibility.

Jalousie

Jalousie [ʒalu'ziː], *f.* (—, *pl.* —n) Venetian blind.

Jamaika [ja'maika], *n.* Jamaica.

Jambus ['jambus], *m.* (—, *pl.* —ben) (*Poet.*) iambic foot.

Jammer ['jamər], *m.* (—s, *no pl.*) lamentation; misery; (*fig.*) pity.

jämmerlich ['jɛmərlɪç], *adj.* lamentable, miserable, wretched, piteous.

jammerschade ['jamərʃaːdə], *adv.* a thousand pities.

Jänner ['jɛnər] (*Austr.*) *see* **Januar**.

Januar ['januaːr], *m.* (—s, *pl.* —e) January.

Japan ['jaːpan], *n.* Japan.

Jaspis ['jaspɪs], *m.* (—ses, *pl.* —se) jasper.

jäten ['jɛːtən], *v.a.* weed.

Jauche ['jauxə], *f.* (—, *pl.* —n) liquid manure.

jauchzen ['jauxtsən], *v.n.* exult, shout with joy.

Jauchzer ['jauxtsər], *m.* (—s, *pl.* —) shout of joy.

jawohl [ja'voːl], *int.* yes, indeed! certainly, of course.

je [jeː], *adv.* ever; at any time; at a time; each; *von — her*, always; — *nachdem*, it depends; — *zwei*, in twos; — *eher — besser*, the sooner the better.

jedenfalls ['jeːdənfals], *adv.* at all events, in any case, at any rate, anyway.

jeder, -e, -es ['jeːdər], *adj.* every, each; — *beliebige*, any. — *pron.* each, each one; everybody.

jederlei ['jeːdərlaɪ], *adj.* of every kind.

jedoch [je'dɔx], *adv.*, however, nevertheless, yet, notwithstanding.

jeglicher, -e, -es ['jeːklɪçər], *adj.* every, each. — *pron.* every man, each.

jemals ['jeːmals], *adv.* ever, at any time.

jemand ['jeːmant], *pron.* somebody, someone; anybody, anyone.

Jemen [je'meːn], *n.* Yemen.

jener, -e, -es ['jeːnər], *dem. adj.* that, (*Poet.*) yonder. — *dem. pron.* that one, the former.

Jenseits ['jɛnzaɪts], *n.* (—, *no pl.*) the next world, the hereafter, the life to come.

jenseits ['jɛnzaɪts], *prep.* (*Genit.*) on the other side, beyond.

jetzig ['jɛtsɪç], *adj.* present, now existing, current, extant.

jetzt [jɛtst], *adv.* now, at this time, at present.

jeweilig ['jeːvaɪlɪç], *adj.* momentary; actual, for the time being.

Joch [jɔx], *n.* (—es, *pl.* —e) yoke.

Jochbein ['jɔxbaɪn], *n.* (—s, *pl.* —e) cheek-bone.

Jockei ['jɔkaɪ], *m.* (—s, *pl.* —s) jockey.

Jod [joːt], *n.* (—s *no pl.*) iodine.

jodeln ['joːdəln], *v.n.* yodel.

Jodler ['joːdlər], *m.* (—s, *pl.* —) (*person*) yodeler; (*sound*) yodelling.

Johannisbeere [jo'hanɪsbeːrə], *f.* (—, *pl.* —n) (*Bot.*) red currant.

Johannisfest [jo'hanɪsfɛst], *n.* (—s, *pl.* —e) Midsummer Day, St. John the Baptist's Day (June 24th).

Johanniskäfer [jo'hanɪskɛːfər], *m.* (—s, *pl.* —) (*Ent.*) glow-worm.

Johannisnacht [jo'hanɪsnaxt], *f.* (—, *pl.* ⁝e) Midsummer Eve.

johlen ['joːlən], *v.n.* bawl.

Joppe ['jɔpə], *f.* (—, *pl.* —n) shooting jacket.

Jota ['joːta], *n.* (—s, *pl.* —s) iota, jot.

Journalismus [ʒurna'lɪsmus], *m. see* **Journalistik**.

Journalistik [ʒurna'lɪstɪk], *f.* (—, *no pl.*) journalism.

jubeln ['juːbəln], *v.n.* rejoice, exult.

Jubilar [juːbi'laːr], *m.* (—s, *pl.* —e) person celebrating a jubilee.

Jubiläum [juːbi'lɛːum], *n.* (—s, *pl.* —läen) jubilee.

jubilieren [juːbi'liːrən], *v.n.* exult, shout with glee.

juchhe [jux'heː], *excl.* hurrah!

Juchten ['juxtən], *m.* (—, *no pl.*) Russian leather.

jucken ['jukən], *v.a.* scratch. — *v.n.* itch.

Jude ['juːdə], *m.* (—n, *pl.* —n) Jew, Israelite.

Judentum ['juːdəntuːm], *n.* (—s, *no pl.*) Judaism.

Judenviertel ['juːdənfiːrtəl], *n.* (—s, *pl.* —) Jewish quarter, ghetto.

Jüdin ['jyːdɪn], *f.* (—, *pl.* —innen) Jewess.

jüdisch ['jyːdɪʃ], *adj.* Jewish.

Jugend ['juːgənt], *f.* (—, *no pl.*) youth.

jugendlich ['juːgəntlɪç], *adj.* youthful, juvenile.

Jugoslawien [juːgo'slaːvjən], *n.* Jugoslavia.

Julfest ['juːlfɛst], *n.* (—es, *pl.* —e) Yule.

Juli ['juːli], *m.* (—s, *pl.* —s) July.

jung [juŋ], *adj.* young.

Junge (1) ['juŋə], *m.* (—n, *pl.* —n) boy, lad.

Junge (2) ['juŋə], *n.* (—n, *pl.* —n) young animal.

jungenhaft ['juŋənhaft], *adj.* boyish.

Jünger ['jyŋər], *m.* (—s, *pl.* —) disciple, devotee, follower.

Jungfer ['juŋfər], *f.* (—, *pl.* —n) (*obs.*) virgin, maid, maiden; lady's maid.

jüngferlich ['jyŋfərlɪç], *adj.* maidenly, coy, prim.

Jungfrau ['juŋfrau], *f.* (—, *pl.* —en) virgin.

Junggeselle ['juŋgəzɛlə], *m.* (—n, *pl.* —n) bachelor; *eingefleischter —*, confirmed bachelor.

Jüngling ['jyŋlɪŋ], *m.* (—s, *pl.* —e) young man.

jüngst [jyŋst], *adv.* lately, recently.

Juni ['juːni], *m.* (—s, *pl.* —s) June.

Junker ['juŋkər], *m.* (—s, *pl.* —) country squire; titled landowner.

Jura ['juːra], *n. pl.* jurisprudence, law; (*Univ.*) — *studieren*, read law.

Jurisprudenz [juːrɪspru'dɛnts], *f.* (—, *no pl.*) jurisprudence.

Jurist [juː'rɪst], *m.* (—en, *pl.* —en) lawyer, jurist.

juristisch [ju:'rɪstɪʃ], *adj.* juridical; legal.
just [just], *adv.* just now.
Justiz [jus'ti:ts], *f.* (—, *no pl.*) administration of the law *or* of justice.
Justizrat [jus'ti:tsra:t], *m.* (—s, *pl.* ⁼e) (*Law*) Counsellor; King's (Queen's) Counsel.
Jute ['ju:tə], *f.* (—, *no pl.*) jute.
Juwel [ju've:l], *n.* (—s, *pl.* —en) jewel; (*pl.*) jewellery; (*Am.*) jewelry.
Juwelier [juvə'li:r], *m.* (—s, *pl.* —e) jeweller, goldsmith.

K

K [ka:], *n.* (—, *no pl.*) the letter K.
Kabel ['ka:bəl], *n.* (—s, *pl.* —) cable.
Kabeljau [kabəl'jau], *m.* (—s, *pl.* —e) (*Zool.*) cod, codfish.
kabeln ['ka:bəln], *v.n.* cable, send a cablegram.
Kabine [ka'bi:nə], *f.* (—, *pl.* —n) cabin, cubicle.
Kabinett [kabi'nɛt], *n.* (—s, *pl.* —e) closet; cabinet.
Kabinettsrat [kabi'nɛtsra:t], *m.* (—s, *pl.* ⁼e) cabinet *or* ministerial committee; political adviser.
Kabüse [ka'by:zə], *f.* (—, *pl.* —n) ship's galley.
Kachel ['kaxəl], *f.* (—, *pl.* —n) glazed tile.
Kadaver [ka'da:vər], *m.* (—s, *pl.* —) carrion, carcass; corpse.
Kadenz [ka'dɛnts], *f.* (—, *pl.* —en) (*Mus.*) cadenza.
Kadett [ka'dɛt], *m.* (—en, *pl.* —en) cadet.
Käfer ['kɛ:fər], *m.* (—s, *pl.* —) (*Ent.*) beetle, (*Am.*) bug.
Kaffee ['kafe], *m.* (—s, *no pl.*) coffee.
Käfig ['kɛ:fɪç], *m.* (—s, *pl.* —e) cage.
kahl [ka:l], *adj.* bald; (*trees*) leafless; (*landscape*) barren; — geschoren, close-cropped.
Kahn ['ka:n], *m.* (—s, *pl.* ⁼e) boat; punt.
Kai [kaɪ], *m.* (—s, *pl.* —s) quay, wharf, landing-place.
Kaimeister ['kaɪmaɪstər], *m.* (—s, *pl.* —) wharfinger.
Kaiser ['kaɪzər], *m.* (—s, *pl.* —) emperor; *um des —s Bart streiten*, quarrel about nothing.
kaiserlich ['kaɪzərlɪç], *adj.* imperial.
Kaiserschnitt ['kaɪzərʃnɪt], *m.* (—es, *pl.* —e) (*Med.*) Caesarean operation.
Kajüte [ka'jy:tə], *f.* (—, *pl.* —n) cabin.
Kakadu [ka'ka:du:], *m.* (—s, *pl.* —s) (*Orn.*) cockatoo.
Kakao [ka'ka:o], *m.* (—s, *no pl.*) cocoa.
Kalauer ['ka:lauər], *m.* (—s, *no pl.*)

pun; stale joke.
Kalb [kalp], *n.* (—es, *pl.* ⁼er) calf; (*roe*) fawn; (*fig.*) colt, calf.
Kalbfleisch ['kalpflaɪʃ], *n.* (—es, *no pl.*) veal.
Kälberei [kɛlbə'raɪ], *f.* (—, *pl.* —en) friskiness.
kälbern ['kɛlbərn], *v.n.* frisk, frolic.
Kalbsbraten ['kalpsbra:tən], *m.* (—s, *pl.* —) roast veal.
Kalbshaxe ['kalpshaksə], *f.* (—, *pl.* —n) knuckle of veal.
Kalbskeule ['kalpskɔylə], *f.* (—, *pl.* —n) leg of veal.
Kalbsmilch ['kalpsmɪlç], *f.* (—, *no pl.*) sweetbread.
Kaldaunen [kal'daunən], *f. pl.* (*dial.*) tripe.
Kalesche [ka'lɛʃə], *f.* (—, *pl.* —n) chaise, light carriage.
Kali ['ka:li], *n.* (—s, *no pl.*) potash.
Kaliber [ka'li:bər], *n.* (—s, *pl.* —) calibre; (*fig.*) sort, quality.
kalibrieren [kali'bri:rən], *v.a.* (*Tech.*) calibrate, graduate, gauge.
Kalifornien [kali'fɔrnjən], *n.* California.
Kalium ['ka:ljum], *n.* (—s, *no pl.*) (*Chem.*) potassium.
Kalk [kalk], *m.* (—s, *pl.* —e) lime; *gebrannter* —, quicklime; *mit* — *bewerfen*, rough-cast.
kalkartig ['kalka:rtɪç], *adj.* calcareous.
Kalkbewurf ['kalkbəvurf], *m.* (—es, *pl.* ⁼e) coat of plaster.
kalken ['kalkən], *v.a.* whitewash; (*Agr.*) lime.
kalkig ['kalkɪç], *adj.* limy, calcareous.
kalkulieren [kalku'li:rən], *v.n.* calculate, reckon.
kalt [kalt], *adj.* cold, frigid; *mir ist* —, I am cold.
kaltblütig ['kaltbly:tɪç], *adj.* cold-blooded, cool.
Kälte ['kɛltə], *f.* (—, *no pl.*) cold, coldness.
Kaltschale ['kaltʃa:lə], *f.* (—, *pl.* —n) cold beer (*or* wine) soup.
Kambodscha [kam'bɔtʃa], *f.* Cambodia.
Kamee [ka'me:], *f.* (—, *pl.* —n) cameo.
Kamel [ka'me:l], *n.* (—s, *pl.* —e) (*Zool.*) camel.
Kamelziege [ka'me:ltsi:gə], *f.* (—, *pl.* —n) (*Zool.*) Angora-goat, llama.
Kamerad [kamə'ra:t], *m.* (—en, *pl.* —en) comrade, companion, mate.
Kameradschaft [kamə'ra:tʃaft], *f.* (—, *pl.* —en) comradeship, fellowship.
Kamerun [kamə'ru:n], *n.* the Cameroons.
Kamille [ka'mɪlə], *f.* (—, *pl.* —n) camomile.
Kamin [ka'mi:n], *m.* (—s, *pl.* —e) chimney; funnel; fireplace, fireside.
Kaminaufsatz [ka'mi:naufzats], *m.* (—es, *pl.* ⁼e) mantel-piece, over-mantel.
Kaminfeger [ka'mi:nfe:gər], *m.* (—s, *pl.* —) chimney-sweep.

Kaminsims

Kaminsims [ka'mi:nzıms], *m.* or *n.* (—es, *pl.* —e) mantel-piece.

Kamm [kam], *m.* (—es, *pl.* ⁔e) comb; (*cock*) crest; (*mountains*) ridge.

kämmen ['kɛmən], *v.a.* comb; (*wool*) card.

Kammer ['kamər], *f.* (—, *pl.* —n) chamber, small room; (*Am.*) closet; (*authority*) board; (*Parl. etc.*) chamber.

Kammerdiener ['kamərdi:nər], *m.* (—s, *pl.* —) valet.

Kämmerer ['kɛmərər], *m.* (—s, *pl.* —) Chamberlain, Treasurer.

Kammergericht ['kamərgərıçt], *n.* (—s, *pl.* —e) Supreme Court of Justice.

Kammergut ['kamərgu:t], *n.* (—s, *pl.* ⁔er) domain, demesne; crown land.

Kammerherr ['kamərhɛr], *m.* (—n, *pl.* —en) chamberlain.

Kammersänger ['kamərzɛŋər], *m.* (—s, *pl.* —e) court singer; title given to prominent singers.

Kammgarn ['kamgarn], *n.* (—s, *no pl.*) worsted.

Kammwolle ['kamvɔlə], *f.* (—, *no pl.*) carded wool.

Kampagne [kam'panjə], *f.* (—, *pl.* —n) (*Mil.*) campaign.

Kämpe ['kɛmpe], *m.* (—n, *pl.* —n) (*Poet.*) champion, warrior; *alter* —, old campaigner.

Kampf [kampf], *m.* (—es, *pl.* ⁔e) combat, fight, struggle; (*fig.*) conflict.

kämpfen ['kɛmpfən], *v.n.* fight, combat, struggle.

Kampfer ['kampfər], *m.* (—s, *no pl.*) camphor.

Kämpfer ['kɛmpfər], *m.* (—s, *pl.* —) fighter, combatant.

kampfunfähig ['kampfunfɛ:ıç], *adj.* (*Mil.*) disabled; — *machen*, disable, put out of action.

kampieren [kam'pi:rən], *v.n.* be encamped, camp.

Kanada ['kanada], *n.* Canada.

Kanal [ka'na:l], *m.* (—s, *pl.* ⁔e) (*natural*) channel; (*artificial*) canal; sewer; *der Ärmelkanal*, the English Channel.

kanalisieren [kanali'zi:rən], *v.a.* canalise; (*streets*) drain by means of sewers.

Kanapee [kanape:], *n.* (—s, *pl.* —s) sofa, divan.

Kanarienvogel [ka'na:rjənfo:gəl], *m.* (—s, *pl.* ⁔) (*Orn.*) canary.

Kanarische Inseln [ka'na:rıʃə 'ınzəln], *f.pl.* Canary Islands.

Kandare [kan'da:rə], *f.* (—, *pl.* —n) bridle, bit.

Kandelaber [kandə'la:bər], *m.* (—s, *pl.* —) candelabrum, chandelier.

kandidieren [kandi'di:rən], *v.n.* be a candidate (for), apply (for) (*post*); (*Parl.*) stand (for), (*Am.*) run (for election).

kandieren [kan'di:rən], *v.a.* candy.

Kandiszucker ['kandıstsukər], *m.* (—, *no pl.*) sugar-candy.

Kanevas ['kanəvas], *m.* (—ses, *pl.* —se) canvas.

Känguruh ['kɛŋguru:], *n.* (—s, *pl.* —s) (*Zool.*) kangaroo.

Kaninchen [ka'ni:nçən], *n.* (—s, *pl.* —) (*Zool.*) rabbit.

Kaninchenbau [ka'ni:nçənbau], *m.* (—s, *pl.* —e) rabbit-warren, burrow.

Kanne ['kanə], *f.* (—, *pl.* —n) can, tankard, mug; jug; pot; quart.

Kannegießer ['kanəgi:sər], *m.* (—s, *pl.* —) pot-house politician.

kannelieren [kanə'li:rən], *v.a.* flute; channel.

Kannibale [kani'ba:lə], *m.* (—n, *pl.* —n) cannibal.

Kanoe [ka'nu:], *n. see* Kanu.

Kanone [ka'no:nə], *f.* (—, *pl.* —n) cannon, gun; *unter aller* —, beneath contempt; beneath criticism.

Kanonier [kano'ni:r], *m.* (—s, *pl.* —e) gunner.

Kanonikus [ka'no:nikus], *m.* (—, *pl.* —ker) canon, prebendary.

kanonisieren [kanoni'zi:rən], *v.a.* canonise.

Kante ['kantə], *f.* (—, *pl.* —n) edge, rim, brim, brink, ledge; (*cloth*) list, selvedge.

Kanten ['kantən], *m.* (—s, *pl.* —) (*bread*) crust.

kanten ['kantən], *v.a.* edge, tilt.

Kanthaken ['kantha:kən], *m.* (—s, *pl.* —) cant-hook; grapple; grappling hook.

kantig ['kantıç], *adj.* angular.

Kantine [kan'ti:nə], *f.* (—, *pl.* —n), canteen, mess.

Kanton [kan'to:n], *m.* (—s, *pl.* —e) (*Swiss*) canton; district, region.

Kantonist [kanto'nıst], *m.* (—en, *pl.* —en) *unsicherer* —, shifty fellow.

Kantor ['kantɔr], *m.* (—s, *pl.* —en) precentor; organist; cantor.

Kanu [ka'nu:], *n.* (—s, *pl.* —s) canoe.

Kanzel ['kantsəl], *f.* (—, *pl.* —n) pulpit; (*Aviat.*) cockpit.

Kanzlei [kants'laı], *f.* (—, *pl.* —en) office, secretariat; chancellery; chancery office; lawyer's office.

Kanzleipapier [kants'laıpapi:r], *n.* (—s, *no pl.*) foolscap (paper).

Kanzleistil [kants'laıʃti:l], *m.* (—s, *no pl.*) legal jargon.

Kanzler ['kantslər], *m.* (—s, *pl.* —) Chancellor.

Kanzlist [kants'lıst], *m.* (—en, *pl.* —en) chancery clerk; copying clerk.

Kap [kap], *n.* (—s, *pl.* —s) (*Geog.*) cape, promontory.

Kapaun [ka'paun], *m.* (—s, *pl.* —e) capon.

Kapazität [kapatsi'tɛ:t], *f.* (—, *pl.* —en) capacity; (*fig.*) (*person*) authority.

Kapelle [ka'pɛlə], *f.* (—, *pl.* —n) chapel; (*Mus.*) band.

Kapellmeister [ka'pɛlmaıstər], *m.* (—s, *pl.* —) (*Mus.*) band leader, conductor.

Kaper ['ka:pər], *f.* (—, *pl.* —n) (*Bot.*) caper.

kapern ['ka:pərn], v.a. capture, catch.
kapieren [ka'pi:rən], v.a. (coll.) understand, grasp.
Kapital [kapi'ta:l], n. (—s, pl. —ien) (money) capital, stock.
Kapitäl, Kapitell [kapɪ'tɛ:l, kapɪ'tɛl], n. (—s, pl. —e) (Archit.) capital.
Kapitalanlage [kapi'talanla:gə], f. (— pl. —n) investment.
kapitalisieren [kapitali'zi:rən], v.a. capitalise.
kapitalkräftig [kapi'ta:lkrɛftɪç], adj. wealthy, moneyed, affluent; (business, firm) sound.
Kapitalverbrechen [kapi'ta:lfɛrbrɛçən], n. (—s, pl. —) capital offence.
Kapitän [kapi'tɛ:n], m. (—s, pl. —e) captain (of a ship), master.
Kapitel [ka'pɪtəl], n. (—s, pl. —) chapter.
Kapitulation [kapitulats'jo:n], f. (—, pl. —en) surrender.
kapitulieren [kapitu'li:rən], v.n. surrender; capitulate.
Kaplan [kap'la:n], m. (—s, pl. ̈e) chaplain; assistant priest.
Kapotte [ka'pɔtə], f. (—, pl. —n) hood.
Kappe [kapə], f. (—, pl. —n) cap, bonnet; (shoe) toe-cap.
Käppi ['kɛpi], n. (—s, pl. —s) military cap.
Kapriole [kapri'o:lə], f. (—, pl. —n) caper.
kaprizieren [kapri'tsi:rən], v.r. sich auf etwas —, set o.'s heart on s.th., be obstinate about s.th.
kapriziös [kapri'tsjø:s], adj. whimsical, capricious.
Kapsel ['kapzəl], f. (—, pl. —n) capsule.
kaputt [ka'put], adj. broken, ruined, done for; — machen, break, ruin.
Kapuze [ka'pu:tsə], f. (—, pl. —n) hood; monk's cowl.
Kapuziner [kaput'si:nər], m. (—s, pl. —) Capuchin (friar); (coffee) cappuccino.
Kapuzinerkresse [kaput'si:nərkrɛsə], f. (—, no pl.) (Bot.) nasturtium.
Karabiner [kara'bi:nər], m. (—s, pl. —) (rifle) carbine.
Karaffe [ka'rafə], f. (—, pl. —n) carafe; decanter.
Karambolage [karambo'la:ʒə], f. (—, pl. —n) collision; (billiards) cannon.
Karawane [kara'va:nə], f. (—, pl. —n) convoy; caravan.
Karbol [kar'bo:l], n. (—s, no pl.) carbolic acid.
Karbunkel [kar'buŋkəl], m. (—s, pl. —) (Med.) carbuncle.
Karfreitag [kar'fraɪta:k], m. Good Friday.
Karfunkel [kar'fuŋkəl], m. (—s, pl. —) (Min.) carbuncle.
karg [kark], adj. scant; meagre; parsimonious.
kargen ['kargən], v.n. be stingy, be niggardly.
kärglich ['kɛrklɪç], adj. sparing, scanty, poor, paltry.

karieren [ka'ri:rən], v.a. checker.
kariert [ka'ri:rt], adj. checked, checkered.
Karikatur [karika'tu:r], f. (—, pl. —en) caricature, cartoon.
karikieren [kari'ki:rən], v.a. caricature, distort.
Karl [karl], m. Charles; — der Grosse, Charlemagne.
Karmeliter [karme'li:tər], m. (—s, pl. —) Carmelite (friar).
karminrot [kar'mi:nro:t], adj. carmine.
karmoisin [karmoa'zi:n], adj. crimson.
Karneol [karne'o:l], m. (—s, pl. —e) (Min.) cornelian, carnelian.
Karneval ['karnəval], m. (—s, pl. —s) carnival; Shrovetide festivities.
Karnickel [kar'nɪkəl], n. (—s, pl. —) rabbit; er war das —, he was to blame.
Kärnten ['kɛrntən], n. Carinthia.
Karo ['ka:ro], n. (—s, pl. —s) check, square; (cards) diamonds.
Karosse [ka'rɔsə], f. (—, pl. —n) state-coach.
Karosserie [karɔsə'ri:], f. (—, pl. —n) (Motor.) body(-work).
Karotte [ka'rɔtə], f. (—, pl. —n) (Bot.) carrot.
Karpfen ['karpfən], m. (—s, pl. —) (fish) carp.
Karre ['karə], f. (—, pl. —n) cart, wheelbarrow.
Karren ['karən], m. (—s, pl. —) cart, wheelbarrow, dray.
Karrete [ka're:tə], f. (—, pl. —n) (Austr.) rattletrap, rickety coach.
Karriere [ka'rjɛ:rə], f. (—, pl. —n) career; — machen, get on well.
Kärrner ['kɛrnər], m. (—s, pl. —) (obs.) carter.
Karst [karst], m. (—s, pl. —e) mattock.
Karthago [kar'ta:go], n. Carthage.
Kartätsche [kar'tɛ:tʃə], f. (—, pl. —n) grape-shot, shrapnel.
Kartäuser [kar'tɔyzər], m. (—s, pl. —) Carthusian (monk).
Karte ['kartə], f. (—, pl. —n) card; ticket; map; chart; (pl.) pack ((Am.) deck) of cards.
Kartei [kar'taɪ], f. (—, pl. —en) card index.
Kartell [kar'tɛl], n. (—s, pl. —e) cartel; ring; syndicate.
Kartoffel [kar'tɔfəl], f. (—, pl. —n) (Bot.) potato.
Kartoffelpuffer [kar'tɔfəlpufər], m. —s, pl. —) potato-pancake.
Karton [kar'tɔŋ], m. (—s, pl. —s) carton, cardboard-box; (material) cardboard, paste-board; cartoon.
Kartusche [kar'tuʃə], f. (—, pl. —n) cartridge.
Karussell [karu'sɛl], n. (—s, pl. —e) merry-go-round.
Karwoche ['ka:rvɔxə], f. Holy Week.
Karzer ['kartsər], m. (—s, pl. —) lock-up, prison.
Kaschmir ['kaʃmi:r], m. (—s, no pl.) cashmere.

Käse

Käse ['kɛːzə], *m.* (—**s**, *pl.* —) cheese.
käseartig ['kɛːzəaːrtɪç], *adj.* like cheese; caseous.
Kaserne [ka'zɛrnə], *f.* (—, *pl.* —**n**) barracks.
kasernieren [kazɛr'niːrən], *v.a.* put into barracks.
Käsestoff ['kɛːzəʃtɔf], *m.* (—**s**, *pl.* —**e**) casein.
käseweiß ['kɛːzəvaɪs], *adj.* deathly pale.
käsig ['kɛːzɪç], *adj.* cheese-like, cheesy, caseous; (*fig.*) sallow.
Kasperle ['kaspɛrlə], *n.* (—**s**, *pl.* —) Punch.
Kasperl(e)theater ['kaspɛrl(ə)teaːtər], *n.* (—**s**, *pl.* —) Punch-and-Judy show.
Kaspisches Meer ['kaspɪʃəsmeːr], *n.* Caspian Sea.
Kasse ['kasə], *f.* (—, *pl.* —**n**) money-box, till; cash-desk; box-office; cash, ready money.
Kassenanweisung ['kasənanvaɪzuŋ], *f.* (—, *pl.* —**en**) treasury-bill; cash voucher.
Kassenbuch ['kasənbuːx], *n.* (—**es**, *pl.* ̈er) cash-book.
Kassenschrank ['kasənʃraŋk], *m.* (—**s**, *pl.* ̈e) strong-box, safe.
Kasserolle [kasə'rɔlə], *f.* (—, *pl.* —**n**) stew-pot, casserole.
Kassette [ka'sɛtə], *f.* (—, *pl.* —**n**) deed-box; casket; (*Phot.*) plate-holder.
kassieren [ka'siːrən], *v.a.* cash, collect (money); cashier, annul, discharge.
Kastagnette [kastan'jɛtə], *f.* (—, *pl.* —**n**) castanet.
Kassierer [ka'siːrər], *m.* (—**s**, *pl.* —) cashier; teller.
Kastanie [ka'staːnjə], *f.* (—, *pl.* —**n**) (*Bot.*) chestnut, (*coll.*) conker; chest-nut-tree.
Kästchen ['kɛstçən], *n.* (—**s**, *pl.* —) casket, little box.
Kaste ['kastə], *f.* (—, *pl.* —**n**) caste.
kasteien [ka'staɪən], *v.r.* sich —, castigate *or* mortify o.s.
Kastell [ka'stɛl], *n.* (—**s**, *pl.* —**e**) citadel, small fort; castle.
Kastellan [kastɛ'laːn], *m.* (—**s**, *pl.* —**e**) castellan; caretaker.
Kasten ['kastən], *m.* (—**s**, *pl.* ̈) box, chest, case, crate.
Kastengeist ['kastəngaɪst], *m.* (—**es**, *no pl.*) exclusiveness; class consciousness.
Kastilien [ka'stiːljən], *n.* Castile.
Kastrat [ka'straːt], *m.* (—**en**, *pl.* —**en**) eunuch.
kastrieren [ka'striːrən], *v.a.* castrate.
Katafalk [kata'falk], *m.* (—**s**, *pl.* —**e**) catafalque.
katalogisieren [katalogi'ziːrən], *v.a.* catalogue.
Katarakt [kata'rakt], *m.* (—**es**, *pl.* —**e**) cataract; waterfall.
Katasteramt [ka'tastəramt], *n.* (—**es**, *pl.* ̈er) land-registry office.
katechisieren [kateçi'ziːrən], *v.a.* catechise, instruct.

kategorisch [kate'goːrɪʃ], *adj.* categorical, definite.
Kater ['kaːtər], *m.* (—**s**, *pl.* —) tom-cat; (*fig.*) hangover; *der gestiefelte* —, Puss-in-Boots.
Katheder [ka'teːdər], *m.* (—**s**, *pl.* —) desk; rostrum; lecturing-desk; (*fig.*) professorial chair.
Kathedrale [kate'draːlə], *f.* (—, *pl.* —**n**) cathedral.
Katholik [kato'liːk], *m.* (—**en**, *pl.* —**en**) (Roman) Catholic.
katholisch [ka'toːlɪʃ], *adj.* (Roman) Catholic.
Kattun [ka'tuːn], *m.* (—**s**, *pl.* —**e**) calico, cotton.
Kätzchen ['kɛtsçən], *n.* (—**s**, *pl.* —) kitten; (*Bot.*) catkin.
Katze ['katsə], *f.* (—, *pl.* —**n**) cat; *die* — *im Sack kaufen*, buy a pig in a poke; *für die* —, no good at all, useless.
katzenartig ['katsəna:rtɪç], *adj.* cat-like, feline.
Katzenauge ['katsənaugə], *n.* (—**s**, *pl.* —**n**) cat's-eye.
Katzenbuckel ['katsənbukəl], *m.* (—**s**, *pl.* —) arched back of a cat.
Katzenjammer ['katsənjamər], *m.* (—**s**, *pl.* —) hangover.
Katzenmusik ['katsənmuzi:k], *f.* (—, *no pl.*) caterwauling; cacophony, discordant music.
Katzensprung ['katsənʃpruŋ], *m.* (—**es**, *no pl.*) (*fig.*) stone's throw.
Kauderwelsch ['kaudərvɛlʃ], *n.* (—**s**, *no pl.*) gibberish, double-Dutch.
kauen ['kauən], *v.a.*, *v.n.* chew.
kauern ['kauərn], *v.n.* cower, squat, crouch.
Kauf [kauf], *m.* (—**es**, *pl.* ̈e) purchase, buy; bargain.
Kaufbummel ['kaufbuməl], *m.* (—**s**, *no pl.*) shopping-spree.
kaufen ['kaufən], *v.a.* (*things*) buy, purchase; (*persons*) bribe.
Käufer ['kɔyfər], *m.* (—**s**, *pl.* —) buyer, purchaser.
Kaufhaus ['kaufhaus], *n.* (—**es**, *pl.* ̈er) department store, emporium.
Kaufladen ['kaufla:dən], *m.* (—**s**, *pl.* ̈) shop.
käuflich ['kɔyflɪç], *adj.* (*things*) purchasable, marketable; (*persons*) open to bribery, venal.
Kaufmann ['kaufman], *m.* (—**s**, *pl.* **Kaufleute**) merchant; shopkeeper; (*Am.*) store-keeper.
kaufmännisch ['kaufmɛnɪʃ], *adj.* commercial, mercantile.
Kaugummi ['kaugumi], *m.* (—**s**, *no pl.*) chewing gum.
Kaukasus ['kaukazus], *m.* Caucasus (Mountains).
Kaulquappe ['kaulkvapə], *f.* (—, *pl.* —**n**) (*Zool.*) tadpole.
kaum [kaum], *adv.* scarcely, hardly; no sooner.
Kaurimuschel ['kaurimuʃəl], *f.* (—, *pl.* —**n**) (*Zool.*) cowrie shell.

Kautabak ['kautabak], m. (—s, no pl.) chewing-tobacco.
Kaution [kau'tsjo:n], f. (—, pl. —en) security, bail, surety; eine — stellen, go, give or stand bail.
Kautschuk ['kautʃuk], m. (—s, no pl.) caoutchouc, India-rubber.
Kauz [kauts], m. (—es, pl. ̈e) (Orn.) screech-owl; (fig.) komischer —, queer customer.
Käuzchen ['kɔytsçən], n. (—s, pl. —) little owl; (fig.) imp.
Kavalier [kava'li:r], m. (—s, pl. —e) gentleman; lady's man.
keck [kɛk], adj. bold, daring; pert, saucy.
Kegel ['ke:gəl], m. (—s, pl. —) ninepin, skittle; (Geom.) cone; mit Kind und —, bag and baggage.
Kegelbahn ['ke:gəlba:n], f. (—, pl. —en) skittle-alley, bowling-alley.
kegelförmig ['ke:gəlfœrmiç], adj. conical.
kegeln ['ke:gəln], v.n. bowl, play at ninepins.
Kehle ['ke:lə], f. (—, pl. —n) throat, windpipe.
Kehlkopf ['ke:lkɔpf], m. (—es, pl. ̈e) larynx.
Kehllaut ['ke:llaut], m. (—es, pl. —e) (Phonet.) guttural sound.
Kehlung ['ke:luŋ], f. (—, pl. —en) channel, flute, groove.
Kehraus ['ke:raus], m. (—, no pl.) last dance; (fig.) break-up, end.
kehren ['ke:rən], v.a. sweep; turn; den Rücken —, turn o.'s back. — v.r. sich — an, pay attention to, regard.
Kehricht ['ke:riçt], m. (—s, no pl.) sweepings; rubbish.
Kehrreim ['ke:rraIm], m. (—s, pl. —e) refrain.
Kehrseite ['ke:rzaItə], f. (—, pl. —n) reverse.
kehrtmachen ['ke:rtmaxən], v.n. turn around; (Mil.) face about; turn back.
keifen ['kaIfən], v.n. scold, nag.
Keil [kaIl], m. (—s, pl. —e) wedge.
Keile ['kaIlə], f. (—, no pl.) blows; (coll.) hiding; — kriegen, get a thrashing.
keilen ['kaIlən], v.a. wedge; (coll.) thrash.
Keilerei [kaIlə'raI], f. (—, pl. —en) brawl, fight.
keilförmig ['kaIlfœrmiç], adj. wedge-shaped.
Keilschrift ['kaIlʃrIft], f. (—, pl. —en) cuneiform writing.
Keim [kaIm], m. (—es, pl. —e) germ, seed.
keimen ['kaImən], v.n. germinate.
keimfrei ['kaImfraI], adj. sterile, germ-free.
keiner, -e, -es [kaInər], adj. no, not a, not any. — pron. no one, none.
keinerlei ['kaInərlaI], adj. no, of no sort, no … whatever.
keineswegs ['kaInəsve:ks], adv. by no means, on no account.

Keks [ke:ks], m. (—es, pl. —e) biscuit.
Kelch [kɛlç], m. (—es, pl. —e) cup; (Eccl.) chalice; (Bot.) calyx.
Kelchblatt ['kɛlçblat], n. (—es, pl. ̈er) sepal.
kelchförmig ['kɛlçfœrmiç], adj. cup-shaped.
Kelle ['kɛlə], f. (—, pl. —n) ladle; (mason) trowel.
Keller ['kɛlər], m. (—s, pl. —) cellar, basement.
Kellergewölbe ['kɛlərgəvœlbə], n. (—s, pl. —) vault.
Kellner ['kɛlnər], m. (—s, pl. —) waiter.
keltern ['kɛltərn], v.a. press (grapes).
Kenia ['ke:nja], n. Kenya.
kennbar ['kɛnba:r], adj. recognisable, conspicuous.
kennen ['kɛnən], v.a. irr. know, be acquainted with.
Kenner ['kɛnər], m. (—s, pl. —) connoisseur, expert.
Kennkarte ['kɛnkartə], f. (—, pl. —n) identity card.
kenntlich ['kɛntliç], adj. distinguishable.
Kenntnis ['kɛntnIs], f. (—, pl. —se) knowledge; (language) command.
Kennzeichen ['kɛntsaIxən], n. (—s, pl. —) characteristic, distinguishing mark; sign; symptom; criterion.
Kenterhaken ['kɛntərha:kən], m. (—s, pl. —) grappling-iron.
kentern ['kɛntərn], v.n. (aux. sein) capsize.
keramisch [ke'ra:mIʃ], adj. ceramic.
Kerbe ['kɛrbə], f. (—, pl. —n) notch, indentation.
kerben ['kɛrbən], v.a. notch.
Kerbholz ['kɛrphɔlts], n. (—es, no pl.) tally; auf dem —, on o.'s conscience, charged against o.
Kerbtier ['kɛrpti:r], n. (—es, pl. —e) insect.
Kerker ['kɛrkər], m. (—s, pl. —) prison, jail, gaol; dungeon.
Kerl [kɛrl], m. (—s, pl. —e) fellow, chap; (Am.) guy (coll.).
Kern [kɛrn], m. (—es, pl. —e) (nut) kernel; (fruit) stone; (fig.) heart, crux; pith; (Phys.) nucleus.
kerngesund ['kɛrngəzunt], adj. hale and hearty, fit as a fiddle.
kernig ['kɛrniç], adj. solid, pithy.
Kernphysik ['kɛrnfyzi:k], f. (—, no pl.) nuclear physics.
Kernpunkt ['kɛrnpuŋkt], m. (—es, pl. —e) gist, essential point.
Kernwaffe ['kɛrnvafə], f. (—, pl. —n) nuclear weapon.
Kerze ['kɛrtsə], f. (—, pl. —n) candle.
Kessel ['kɛsəl], m. (—s, pl. —) kettle, cauldron; (steam) boiler.
Kesselschmied ['kɛsəlʃmi:t], m. (—s, pl. —e) boiler maker.
Kesselstein ['kɛsəlʃtaIn], m. (—s, no pl.) fur, deposit, scale (on boiler).
Kette ['kɛtə], f. (—, pl. —n) chain.
ketten ['kɛtən], v.a. chain, fetter.
Kettenstich ['kɛtənʃtIç], m. (—es, pl. —e) chain stitch; (Naut.) chain knot.

Ketzer

Ketzer ['kɛtsər], m. (—s, pl. —) heretic.
Ketzerei [kɛtsə'raɪ], f. (—, pl. —en) heresy.
ketzerisch ['kɛtsərɪʃ], adj. heretical.
keuchen ['kɔyçən], v.n. pant, puff, gasp.
Keuchhusten ['kɔyçhu:stən], m. (—s, no pl.) whooping-cough.
Keule ['kɔylə], f. (—, pl. —n) club; (meat) leg.
keusch [kɔyʃ], adj. chaste, pure.
kichern ['kɪçərn], v.n. titter, giggle.
Kiebitz ['ki:bɪts], m. (—es, pl. —e) (Orn.) lapwing, peewit; (fig.) on-looker; (coll.) rubber-neck (at chess or cards).
Kiefer (1) ['ki:fər], m. (—s, pl. —) jaw, jaw-bone.
Kiefer (2) ['ki:fər], f. (—, pl. —n) (Bot.) pine.
Kiel [ki:l], m. (—es, pl. —e) keel; (pen) quill.
Kielwasser ['ki:lvasər], n. (—s, no pl.) wake.
Kieme ['ki:mə], f. (—, pl. —n) (fish) gill.
Kien [ki:n], m. (—s, no pl.) pine-resin, resinous pinewood.
Kienspan ['ki:nʃpa:n], m. (—s, pl. ¨e) pine-splinter.
Kiepe ['ki:pə], f. (—, pl. —n) (dial.) creel, wicker basket.
Kies [ki:s], m. (—es, no pl.) gravel.
Kiesel ['ki:zəl], m. (—s, pl. —) pebble; flint.
Kieselsäure ['ki:zəlzɔyrə], f. (—, no pl.) silicic acid.
Kieselstein ['ki:zəlʃtaɪn], m. (—s, pl. —e) pebble.
Kilogramm ['ki:logram], n. (—s, pl. —e) kilogram (1000 grammes).
Kilometer ['ki:lome:tər], m. (—s, pl. —) kilometre; (Am.) kilometer (1000 metres).
Kimme ['kɪmə], f. (—, pl. —n) notch.
Kind [kɪnt], n. (—es, pl. —er) child; (law) infant; — und Kegel, bag and baggage.
Kind(e)l ['kɪnd(ə)l], n. (—s, pl. —) (dial.) small child, baby; Münchner —, Munich beer.
Kinderei [kɪndə'raɪ], f. (—, pl. —en) childishness; childish prank.
Kinderfräulein ['kɪndərfrɔylaɪn], n. (—s, pl. —) nurse, (coll.) nannie.
Kindergarten ['kɪndərgartən], m. (—s, pl. ¨) kindergarten, infant-school.
Kinderhort ['kɪndərhɔrt], m. (—s, pl. —e) crèche.
kinderleicht ['kɪndərlaɪçt], adj. extremely easy, child's play.
Kindermärchen ['kɪndərmɛ:rçən], n. (—s, pl. —) fairy-tale.
Kinderstube ['kɪndərʃtu:bə], f. (—, pl. —n) nursery; eine gute —, a good upbringing.
Kinderwagen ['kɪndərva:gən], m. (—s, pl. —) perambulator, pram.
Kindesbeine ['kɪndəsbaɪnə], n. pl. von —n an, from infancy.

Kindeskind ['kɪndəskɪnt], n. (—es, pl. —er) (obs.) grandchild.
Kindheit ['kɪnthaɪt], f. (—, no pl.) childhood, infancy.
kindisch ['kɪndɪʃ], adj. childish.
kindlich ['kɪntlɪç], adj. childlike; naïve.
Kinn [kɪn], n. (—s, pl. —e) chin.
Kinnbacken ['kɪnbakən], m. (—s, pl. —) (Anat.) jaw-bone.
Kinnbackenkrampf ['kɪnbakənkrampf], m. (—s, pl. ¨e) (Med.) lock-jaw.
Kinnlade ['kɪnla:də], f. (—, pl. —n) (Anat.) jaw-bone.
Kino ['ki:no], n. (—s, pl. —s) cinema; (coll.) pictures; (Am.) motion picture theatre; motion pictures, (coll.) movies.
Kipfel ['kɪpfəl], n. (—s, pl. —) (dial.) roll, croissant.
kippen ['kɪpən], v.a. tilt, tip over.
Kirche ['kɪrçə], f. (—, pl. —n) church.
Kirchenbann ['kɪrçənban], m. (—s, no. pl.) excommunication.
Kirchenbuch ['kɪrçənbu:x], n. (—es, pl. ¨er) parish-register.
Kirchengut ['kɪrçəngu:t], n. (—es, pl. ¨er) church-property.
Kirchenlicht ['kɪrçənlɪçt], n. (—es, pl. —er) (fig.) shining light, bright spark.
Kirchenrecht ['kɪrçənrɛçt], n. (—es, no pl.) canon law.
Kirchenschiff ['kɪrçənʃɪf], n. (—es, pl. —e) nave.
Kirchenstuhl ['kɪrçənʃtu:l], m. (—es, pl. ¨e) pew.
Kirchenversammlung ['kɪrçənfɛrzamluŋ], f. (—, pl. —en) synod; convocation.
Kirchenvorsteher ['kɪrçənforʃte:ər], m. (—s, pl. —) churchwarden.
kirchlich ['kɪrçlɪç], adj. ecclesiastic(al), religious.
Kirchspiel ['kɪrçʃpi:l], n. (—es, pl. —e) parish.
Kirchsprengel ['kɪrçʃprɛŋəl], m. (—s, pl. —) diocese.
Kirchturm ['kɪrçturm], m. (—es, pl. ¨e) steeple.
Kirchweih ['kɪrçvaɪ], f. (—, pl. —en) consecration (of a church); church fair.
Kirmes ['kɪrmɛs], f. (—, pl. —sen) see Kirchweih.
kirre ['kɪrə], adj. tame; (fig.) amenable.
kirren ['kɪrən], v.a. tame, allure. — v.n. coo.
Kirsch(branntwein) [kɪrʃ(brantvaɪn)], m. (—s, no pl.) cherry-brandy.
Kirsche ['kɪrʃə], f. (—, pl. —n) (Bot.) cherry; mit ihr ist nicht gut —n essen, she is hard to get on with or not pleasant to deal with.
Kirschsaft ['kɪrʃzaft], m. (—es, no pl.) cherry-juice.
Kirschwasser ['kɪrʃvasər], n. (—s, no pl.) cherry-brandy.
Kissen ['kɪsən], n. (—s, pl. —) cushion, pillow.

122

kleiden

Kiste ['kɪstə], *f.* (—, *pl.* —n) box, case, chest; crate; coffer.

Kitsch [kɪtʃ], *m.* (—es, *no pl.*) trash; rubbish.

Kitt [kɪt], *m.* (—s, *pl.* —e) cement; (*Glazing*) putty.

Kittel ['kɪtəl], *m.* (—s, *pl.* —) smock; overall, tunic; frock.

kitten ['kɪtən], *v.a.* cement, glue.

Kitzchen ['kɪtsçən], *n.* (—s, *pl.* —) kid; fawn; kitten.

Kitzel ['kɪtsəl], *m.* (—s, *no pl.*) tickling; titillation; itch; (*fig.*) desire, appetite.

kitzeln ['kɪtsəln], *v.a.* tickle, titillate.

kitzlich ['kɪtslɪç], *adj.* ticklish; (*fig.*) delicate.

Kladderadatsch ['kladəradatʃ], *m.* (—es, *no pl.*) bang; mess, muddle.

klaffen ['klafən], *v.n.* gape, yawn.

kläffen ['klɛfən], *v.n.* bark, yelp.

Klafter ['klaftər], *f.* (—, *pl.* —n) fathom; (*wood*) cord.

klagbar ['kla:kba:r], *adj.* (*Law*) actionable.

Klage ['kla:gə], *f.* (—, *pl.* —n) complaint; (*Law*) suit, action.

Klagelied ['kla:gəli:t], *n.* (—es, *pl.* —er) dirge, lamentation.

klagen ['kla:gən], *v.n.* complain, lament; (*Law*) sue.

Kläger ['klɛːgər], *m.* (—s, *pl.* —) complainant; (*Law*) plaintiff.

Klageschrift ['kla:gəʃrɪft], *f.* (—, *pl.* —en) bill of indictment; written complaint.

kläglich ['klɛːklɪç], *adj.* woeful, pitiful, deplorable.

klaglos ['kla:klo:s], *adj.* uncomplaining.

Klamm [klam], *f.* (—, *pl.* —en) gorge, ravine.

klamm [klam], *adj.* tight, narrow; numb; clammy.

Klammer ['klamər], *f.* (—, *pl.* —n) clamp, clasp, hook; peg; clip; bracket, parenthesis.

klammern ['klamərn], *v.a.* fasten, peg. — *v.r. sich — an*, cling to.

Klang [klaŋ], *m.* (—es, *pl.* e) sound, tone; *ohne Sang und —*, unheralded and unsung.

klanglos ['klaŋlo:s], *adj.* soundless.

klangnachahmend ['klaŋnaxa:mənt], *adj.* onomatopoeic.

klangvoll ['klaŋfɔl], *adj.* sonorous.

Klappe ['klapə], *f.* (—, *pl.* —en) flap; (*Tech.*) valve; (*vulg.*) *halt die —!* shut up!

klappen ['klapən], *v.n.* flap; (*fig.*) tally, square; *es hat geklappt*, it worked.

Klapper ['klapər], *f.* (—, *pl.* —n) rattle.

klappern ['klapərn], *v.n.* rattle; (*teeth*) chatter.

Klapperschlange ['klapərʃlaŋə], *f.* (—, *pl.* —n) (*Zool.*) rattle-snake.

Klapphut ['klaphu:t], *m.* (—es, *pl.* e) opera-hat; chapeau-claque.

Klapps [klaps], *m.* (—es, *pl.* e) slap, smack; (*fig.*) touch of madness, kink.

Klappstuhl ['klapʃtu:l], *m.* (—s, *pl.* e) camp-stool, folding-chair.

Klapptisch ['klaptɪʃ], *m.* (—es, *pl.* —e) folding-table.

klar [kla:r], *adj.* clear; bright; (*fig.*) evident; plain, distinct.

Kläranlage ['klɛːranla:gə], *f.* (—, *pl.* —n) sewage-farm; filter plant.

klären ['klɛːrən], *v.a.* clear.

Klarheit ['kla:rhaɪt], *f.* (—, *no pl.*) clearness, plainness.

Klarinette [klari'nɛtə], *f.* (—, *pl.* —n) (*Mus.*) clarinet.

Klärmittel ['klɛːrmɪtəl], *n.* (—s, *pl.* —) clarifier.

Klärung ['klɛːruŋ], *f.* (—, *pl.* —en) clarification; (*fig.*) elucidation.

Klasse ['klasə], *f.* (—, *pl.* —n) class, order; (*Sch.*) form.

klassifizieren [klasifi'tsi:rən], *v.a.* classify.

Klassiker ['klasɪkər], *m.* (—s, *pl.* —) classic.

klassisch ['klasɪʃ], *adj.* classic(al), standard.

Klatsch [klatʃ], *m.* (—es, *no pl.*) gossip, scandal.

klatschen ['klatʃən], *v.n.* clap; gossip; (*rain*) patter; *Beifall —*, applaud.

Klatscherei [klatʃə'raɪ], *f.* (—, *pl.* —en) gossip, scandalmongering.

klauben ['klaubən], *v.a.* pick.

Klaue ['klauə], *f.* (—, *pl.* —n) claw, talon; paw.

klauen ['klauən], *v.a.* steal, (*coll.*) pinch.

Klauenseuche ['klauənzɔyçə], *f.* (—, *pl.* —n) *Maul und —*, foot and mouth disease.

Klause ['klauzə], *f.* (—, *pl.* —n) cell, hermitage; (*coll.*) den.

Klausel ['klauzəl], *f.* (—, *pl.* —n) clause, paragraph.

Klausner ['klausnər], *m.* (—s, *pl.* —) hermit, recluse, anchorite.

Klausur [klau'zu:r], *f.* (—, *pl.* —en) seclusion; written examination.

Klaviatur [klavja'tu:r], *f.* (—, *pl.* —en) keyboard.

Klavier [kla'vi:r], *n.* (—s, *pl.* —e) piano, pianoforte.

Klavierstück [kla'vi:rʃtyk], *n.* (—s, *pl.* —e) piece of piano music.

Klebemittel ['kle:bəmɪtəl], *n.* (—s, *pl.* —) adhesive, glue.

kleben ['kle:bən], *v.a.* paste, stick, glue. — *v.n.* stick, adhere.

klebrig ['kle:brɪç], *adj.* sticky; clammy.

Klebstoff ['kle:pʃtɔf], *m.* (—es, *no pl.*) gum; glue.

Klecks [klɛks], *m.* (—es, *pl.* —e) blot; blotch.

Kleckser ['klɛksər], *m.* (—s, *pl.* —) scrawler; (*painter*) dauber.

Klee [kle:], *m.* (—s, *no pl.*) (*Bot.*) clover, trefoil.

Kleid [klaɪt], *n.* (—es, *pl.* —er) frock, garment, dress. gown; (*Poet.*) garb; (*pl.*) clothes; *—er machen Leute*, clothes make the man.

Kleidchen ['klaɪtçən], *n.* (—s, *pl.* —) child's dress.

kleiden ['klaɪdən], *v.a.* dress, clothe.

123

Kleiderbügel

Kleiderbügel [ˈklaɪdərbyːgəl], m. (—s, pl. —) coat-hanger.

Kleiderpuppe [ˈklaɪdərpupə], f. (—, pl. —n) tailor's dummy.

Kleiderschrank [ˈklaɪdərʃraŋk], m. (—s, pl. ⁻e) wardrobe.

kleidsam [ˈklaɪtzaːm], adj. becoming; well-fitting, a good fit.

Kleidung [ˈklaɪduŋ], f. (—, no pl.) clothing, clothes, dress.

Kleie [ˈklaɪə], f. (—, no pl.) bran.

klein [klaɪn], adj. little, small; minute; petty; ein — wenig, a little bit.

Kleinasien [klaɪnˈaːzjən], n. Asia Minor.

Kleinbahn [ˈklaɪnbaːn], f. (—, pl. —en) narrow-gauge railway.

kleinbürgerlich [ˈklaɪnbyrgərlɪç], adj. (petit) bourgeois.

Kleingeld [ˈklaɪngɛlt], n. (—(e)s, no pl.) small change.

kleingläubig [ˈklaɪnglɔybɪç], adj. faint-hearted.

Kleinhandel [ˈklaɪnhandəl], m. (—s, no pl.) retail-trade.

Kleinigkeit [ˈklaɪnɪçkaɪt], f. (—, pl. —en) trifle, small matter.

Kleinkram [ˈklaɪnkraːm], m. (—s, no pl.) trifles.

kleinlaut [ˈklaɪnlaut], adj. subdued, dejected, low-spirited.

kleinlich [ˈklaɪnlɪç], adj. petty; mean; narrow-minded; pedantic.

Kleinmut [ˈklaɪnmuːt], m. (—es, no pl.) faint-heartedness; dejection.

Kleinod [ˈklaɪnoːt], n. (—s, pl. —ien) jewel; trinket.

Kleinstadt [ˈklaɪnʃtat], f. (—, pl. ⁻e) small town.

Kleister [ˈklaɪstər], m. (—s, no pl.) paste.

Klemme [ˈklɛmə], f. (—, pl. —n) (Tech.) vice; clamp; (fig.) difficulty, straits; (coll.) fix, jam.

klemmen [ˈklɛmən], v.a. pinch, squeeze, jam.

Klemmer [ˈklɛmər], m. (—s, pl.—) (eye) glasses, pince-nez.

Klempner [ˈklɛmpnər], m. (—s, pl.—) tin-smith; plumber.

Klerus [ˈkleːrus], m. (—, no pl.) clergy.

Klette [ˈklɛtə], f. (—, pl. —n) burdock, bur(r); (fig.) hanger-on.

klettern [ˈklɛtərn], v.n. (aux. sein) climb, clamber.

Klima [ˈkliːma], n. (—s, pl. —s) climate.

Klimaanlage [ˈkliːmaːanlaːgə], f. (—, pl. —n) air conditioning plant.

Klimbim [ˈklɪmˈbɪm], m. (—s, no pl.) goings-on; festivity; fuss; der ganze —, the whole caboodle.

klimpern [ˈklɪmpərn], v.n. (piano) strum; (money) jingle.

Klinge [ˈklɪŋə], f. (—, pl. —n) blade.

Klingel [ˈklɪŋəl], f. (—, pl. —n) (door, telephone) bell.

Klingelbeutel [ˈklɪŋəlbɔytəl], m. (—s, pl.—) collecting-bag.

klingeln [ˈklɪŋəln], v.n. ring, tinkle.

Klingelzug [ˈklɪŋəltsuːk], m. . (—es, pl. ⁻e) bell-rope, bell-pull.

klingen [ˈklɪŋən], v.n. irr. sound; (metals) clang; (ears) tingle; —de Münze, hard cash, ready money.

Klinke [ˈklɪŋkə], f. (—, pl. —en) (door) handle, latch.

klipp [klɪp], adv. — und klar, as clear as daylight.

Klippe [ˈklɪpə], f. (—, pl. —n) cliff, crag, rock.

klirren [ˈklɪrən], v.n. clatter, rattle.

Klischee [kliˈʃeː], n. (—s, pl. —s) (Typ.) plate, printing-block; (fig.) cliché, hackneyed expression, tag.

Klistier [klɪˈstiːr], n. (—s, pl. —e) (Med.) enema.

Kloake [kloˈaːkə], f. (—, pl. —n) sewer, drain.

Kloben [ˈkloːbən], m. (—s, pl. —) log, block (of wood); pulley.

klopfen [ˈklɔpfən], v.a., v.n. knock, beat.

Klöppel [ˈklœpəl], m. (—s, pl. —) mallet; (bell) tongue, clapper; (drum) stick; (lace) bobbin.

klöppeln [ˈklœpəln], v.a make (bone) lace.

Klöppelspitze [ˈklœpəlʃpɪtsə], f. (—, no pl.) bone-lace.

Klops [klɔps], m. (—es, pl. —e) meat-dumpling.

Klosett [kloˈzɛt], n. (—s, pl. —e) lavatory, water-closet, toilet.

Kloß [kloːs], m. (—es, pl. ⁻e) dumpling.

Kloster [ˈkloːstər], n. (—s, pl. ⁻) cloister; monastery; convent.

Klostergang [ˈkloːstərgaŋ], m. (—es, pl. ⁻e) cloisters.

Klotz [klɔts], m. (—es, pl. ⁻e) block, trunk, stump; (fig.) ein grober —, a great lout.

klotzig [ˈklɔtsɪç], adj. cloddy; lumpish; (sl.) enormous.

Klub [klup], m. (—s, pl. —s) club.

Kluft [kluft], f. (—, pl. ⁻e) gap; gulf, chasm; (fig.) cleavage.

klug [kluːk], adj. clever, wise, prudent, judicious, sagacious; ich kann daraus nicht — werden, I cannot make head nor tail of it.

klügeln [ˈklyːgəln], v.n. ponder; quibble.

Klugheit [ˈkluːkhaɪt], f. (—, no pl.) cleverness, wisdom, prudence, judiciousness.

Klumpfuß [ˈklumpfuːs], m. (—es, pl. ⁻e) club-foot.

Klumpen [ˈklumpən], m. (—s, pl. —) lump, mass, clod; (blood) clot; (metal) ingot; (gold) nugget.

Klüngel [ˈklyŋəl], m. (—s, pl. —) clique, set.

knabbern [ˈknabərn], v.n. nibble.

Knabe [ˈknaːbə], m. (—n, pl. —n) boy.

Knäblein [ˈknɛːblaɪn], n. (—s, pl. —) (Poet.) baby boy, small boy.

knack [knak], int. crack! snap!

Knäckebrot [ˈknɛkəbroːt], n. (—es, no pl.) crispbread.

knacken [ˈknakən], v.a. crack.

Knackmandel ['knakmandəl], *f.* (—, *pl.* —n) shell-almond.

Knackwurst ['knakvurst], *f.* (—, *pl.* ⁻e) saveloy.

Knacks [knaks], *m.* (—es, *pl.* —e) crack.

knacksen ['knaksən], *v.n.* (*coll.*) crack.

Knall [knal], *m.* (—es, *pl.* —e) report, bang, detonation; — *und Fall*, quite suddenly, then and there.

Knallbüchse ['knalbyksə], *f.* (—, *pl.* —n) pop-gun.

Knalleffekt ['knalɛfɛkt], *m.* (—s, *pl.* —e) coup de théâtre; sensation.

knallen ['knalən], *v.n.* pop, explode, crack.

Knallgas ['knalga:s], *n.* (—es, *no pl.*) oxyhydrogen gas.

knallrot ['knalro:t], *adj.* scarlet; glaring red.

knapp [knap], *adj.* tight; scarce, insufficient; (*style*) concise; (*majority*) narrow, bare.

Knappe ['knapə], *m.* (—n, *pl.* —n) esquire, shield-bearer; miner.

Knappheit ['knaphaɪt], *f.* (—, *no pl.*) scarcity, shortage.

Knappschaft ['knapʃaft], *f.* (—, *pl.* —en) miners' association.

Knarre ['knarə], *f.* (—, *pl.* —n) rattle.

knarren ['knarən], *v.n.* rattle, creak.

Knaster ['knastər], *m.* (—s, *pl.* —) tobacco.

knattern ['knatərn], *v.n.* crackle.

Knäuel ['knɔyəl], *m.*, *n.* (—s, *pl.* —) skein, clew, ball.

Knauf [knauf], *m.* (—es, *pl.* ⁻e) (*stick*) knob, head; (*Archit.*) capital.

Knauser ['knauzər], *m.* (—s, *pl.* —) niggard, skinflint.

knausern ['knauzərn], *v.n.* be stingy, scrimp.

Knebel ['kne:bəl], *m.* (—s, *pl.* —) cudgel; gag.

knebeln ['kne:bəln], *v.a.* tie, bind; gag; (*fig.*) muzzle.

Knecht [knɛçt], *m.* (—es, *pl.* —e) servant, farm hand, menial; vassal, slave.

Knechtschaft ['knɛçtʃaft], *f.* (—, *no pl.*) servitude, slavery.

kneifen ['knaɪfən], *v.a. irr.* pinch. — *v.n.* (*fig. coll.*) back out (of), shirk.

Kneifer ['knaɪfər], *m.* (—s, *pl.* —) pince-nez.

Kneifzange ['knaɪftsaŋə], *f.* (—, *pl.* —n) pincers.

Kneipe ['knaɪpə], *f.* (—, *pl.* —n) pub; saloon.

kneten ['kne:tən], *v.a.* knead; massage.

knick(e)beinig ['knɪk(ə)baɪnɪç], *adj.* knock-kneed.

knicken ['knɪkən], *v.a.* crack, break.

Knicks [knɪks], *m.* (—es, *pl.* —e) curtsy.

knicksen ['knɪksən], *v.n.* curtsy.

Knie [kni:], *n.* (—s, *pl.* —) knee; *etwas übers* — *brechen*, make short work of.

Kniekehle ['kni:ke:lə], *f.* (—, *pl.* —n) hollow of the knee.

knien ['kni:ən], *v.n.* kneel.

Kniescheibe ['kni:ʃaɪbə], *f.* (—, *pl.* —n) knee-cap.

Kniff [knɪf], *m.* (—es, *pl.* —e) fold; (*fig.*) trick, knack, dodge.

knipsen ['knɪpsən], *v.a.* (*tickets*) clip, punch; (*Phot.*) take a snap of.

Knirps [knɪrps], *m.* (—es, *pl.* —e) pigmy; (*fig.*) urchin.

knirschen ['knɪrʃən], *v.n.* crunch, grate, gnash (teeth).

knistern ['knɪstərn], *v.n.* crackle.

knittern ['knɪtərn], *v.a.* rumple, wrinkle, crinkle, crease.

Knobel ['kno:bəl], *m. pl.* dice.

Knoblauch ['kno:blaux], *m.* (—s, *no pl.*) (*Bot.*) garlic.

Knöchel ['knœçəl], *m.* (—s, *pl.* —) knuckle, joint; ankle.

Knochen ['knɔxən], *m.* (—s, *pl.* —) bone.

Knochengerüst ['knɔxəngəryst], *n.* (—es, *pl.* —e) skeleton.

knöchern ['knœçərn], *adj.* made of bone.

knochig ['knɔxɪç], *adj.* bony.

Knödel ['knø:dəl], *m.* (—s, *pl.* —) dumpling.

Knollen ['knɔlən], *m.* (—s, *pl.* —) lump, clod; (*Bot.*) tuber, bulb.

knollig ['knɔlɪç], *adj.* knobby, bulbous.

Knopf [knɔpf], *m.* (—es, *pl.* ⁻e) button; stud; (*stick*) head, knob.

knöpfen ['knœpfən], *v.a.* button.

Knorpel ['knɔrpəl], *m.* (—s, *pl.* —) gristle, cartilage.

knorplig ['knɔrplɪç], *adj.* gristly.

knorrig ['knɔrɪç], *adj.* knotty, gnarled.

Knospe ['knɔspə], *f.* (—, *pl.* —n) bud.

Knote ['kno:tə], *m.* (—n, *pl.* —n) (*fig.*) bounder; lout.

Knoten ['kno:tən], *m.* (—s, *pl.* —) knot; (*fig.*) difficulty; (*Theat.*) plot.

Knotenpunkt ['kno:tənpuŋkt], *m.* (—es, *pl.* —e) (*Railw.*) junction.

Knotenstock ['kno:tənʃtɔk], *m.* (—es, *pl.* ⁻e) knotty stick.

knotig ['kno:tɪç], *adj.* knotty, nodular.

knüllen ['knylən], *v.a.* crumple.

knüpfen ['knypfən], *v.a.* tie; knot; form (a friendship etc.).

Knüppel ['knypəl], *m.* (—s, *pl.* —) cudgel.

knurren ['knurən], *v.n.* grunt, snarl; (*fig.*) growl, grumble.

knurrig ['knurɪç], *adj.* surly, grumpy.

knusprig ['knusprɪç], *adj.* crisp, crunchy.

Knute ['knu:tə], *f.* (—, *pl.* —n) knout.

knutschen ['knu:tʃən], *v.r. sich* —, (*coll.*) cuddle; (*Am.*) neck.

Knüttel [knytəl], *m.* (—s, *pl.* —) cudgel, bludgeon.

Knüttelvers ['knytəlfɛrs], *m.* (—es, *pl.* —e) doggerel, rhyme.

Kobalt ['ko:balt], *m.* (—s, *no pl.*) cobalt.

Kobaltblau ['ko:baltblau], *n.* (—s, *no pl.*) smalt.

Koben

Koben ['ko:bən], *m.* (—s, *pl.* —) pig-sty.

Kober ['ko:bər], *m.* (—s, *pl.* —) (*dial.*) basket, hamper.

Kobold ['ko:bɔlt], *m.* (—(e)s, *pl.* —e) goblin, hobgoblin.

Koch [kɔx], *m.* (—es, *pl.* ⁻e) cook, chef.

kochen ['kɔxən], *v.a.* cook, boil. — *v.n.* boil; (*fig.*) seethe.

Kocher ['kɔxər], *m.* (—s, *pl.* —) boiler.

Köcher ['kœçər], *m.* (—s, *pl.* —) quiver.

Köchin ['kœçɪn], *f.* (—, *pl.* —innen) (female) cook.

Kochsalz ['kɔxzalts], *n.* (—es, *no pl.*) common salt.

Köder ['kø:dər], *m.* (—s, *no pl.*) bait, lure; (*fig.*) decoy.

ködern ['kø:dərn], *v.a.* bait; (*fig.*) decoy.

Kodex ['ko:dɛks], *m.* (—es, *pl.* —e) codex; old MS.; (*Law*) code.

kodifizieren [ko:difi'tsi:rən], *v.a.* codify.

Koffein [kɔfə'i:n], *n.* (—s, *no pl.*) caffeine.

Koffer ['kɔfər], *m.* (—s, *pl.* —) box, trunk, suitcase, portmanteau.

Kofferradio ['kɔfarra:djo], *n.* (—s, *pl.* —s) portable radio.

Kofferraum ['kɔfərraum], *m.* (—s, *no pl.*) (*Motor.*) boot, (*Am.*) trunk.

Kohl [ko:l], *m.* (—s, *no pl.*) (*Bot.*) cabbage; (*fig.*) nonsense, rot.

Kohle ['ko:lə], *f.* (—, *pl.* —n) coal.

Kohlenflöz ['ko:lənflø:ts], *n.* (—es, *pl.* —e) coal-seam.

Kohlenoxyd ['ko:lənɔksy:t], *n.* (—s, *no pl.*) carbon monoxide.

Kohlensäure ['ko:lənzɔyrə], *f.* (—, *no pl.*) carbonic acid.

Kohlenstift ['ko:lənʃtɪft], *m.* (—es, *pl.* —e) charcoal-crayon.

Köhler ['kø:lər], *m.* (—s, *pl.* —) charcoal-burner.

Koje ['ko:jə], *f.* (—, *pl.* —n) (*Naut.*) berth, bunk.

Kokarde [ko'kardə], *f.* (—, *pl.* —n) cockade.

kokett [ko'kɛt], *adj.* coquettish.

Kokette [ko'kɛtə], *f.* (—, *pl.* —n) coquette, flirt.

kokettieren [kokɛ'ti:rən], *v.n.* flirt.

Kokon [ko'kɔ̃], *m.* (—s, *pl.* —s) cocoon.

Kokosnuß ['ko:kɔsnus], *f.* (—, *pl.* ⁻sse) (*Bot.*) coconut.

Koks [ko:ks], *m.* (—es, *no pl.*) coke.

Kolben ['kɔlbən], *m.* (—s, *pl.* —) club; (*rifle*) butt-end; (*engine*) piston; (*Chem.*) retort.

Kolbenstange ['kɔlbənʃtaŋə], *f.* (—, *pl.* —n) piston-rod.

Kolibri ['ko:libri:], *m.* (—s, *pl.* —s) (*Orn.*) humming-bird.

Kolkrabe ['kɔlkra:bə], *m.* (—n, *pl.* —n) (*Orn.*) raven.

Kolleg [kɔ'le:k], *n.* (—s, *pl.* —ien) course of lectures; lecture.

Kollege [kɔ'le:gə], *m.* (—n, *pl.* —n) colleague.

Kollekte [kɔ'lɛktə], *f.* (—, *pl.* —n) collection; (*Eccl.*) collect.

Koller ['kɔlər], *m.* (—s, *no pl.*) frenzy, rage.

kollidieren [kɔli'di:rən], *v.n.* collide.

Köln [kœln], *n.* Cologne.

kölnisch ['kœlnɪʃ], *adj.* of Cologne; —*Wasser*, eau de Cologne.

kolonisieren [koloni'zi:rən], *v.a.* colonise.

Kolonnade [kolo'na:də], *f.* (— *pl.* —n) colonnade.

Koloratur [kolora'tu:r], *f.* (—, *pl.* —n) coloratura.

kolorieren [kolo'ri:rən], *v.a.* colour.

Koloß [ko'lɔs], *m.* (—sses, *pl.* —sse) colossus.

Kolportage [kɔlpɔr'ta:ʒə], *f.* (—, *pl.* —n) colportage, door-to-door sale of books; sensationalism.

Kolportageroman [kɔlpɔr'ta:ʒəroma:n], *m.* (—s, *pl.* —e) penny dreadful, shocker.

kolportieren [kɔlpɔr'ti:rən], *v.a.* hawk; spread, disseminate.

Kombinationsgabe [kɔmbina'tsjo:nsga:bə], *f.* (—, *pl.* —en) power of deduction.

kombinieren [kɔmbi'ni:rən], *v.a.* combine; deduce.

Kombüse [kɔm'by:zə], *f.* (— *pl.* —n) galley, caboose.

Komik ['ko:mɪk], *f.* (—, *no pl.*) comicality; humour; funny side.

Komiker ['ko:mɪkər], *m.* (—s, *pl.* —) comedian.

komisch ['ko:mɪʃ], *adj.* comical, funny; peculiar, strange, odd.

Kommandantur [kɔmandan'tu:r], *f.* (—, *pl.* —en) commander's office; garrison headquarters.

kommandieren [kɔman'di:rən], *v.a.* command.

Kommanditgesellschaft [kɔman'di:tgəzɛlʃaft], *f.* (—, *pl.* —en) limited partnership.

Kommando [kɔ'mando], *n.* (—s, *pl.* —s) command.

kommen ['kɔmən], *v.n. irr.* (*aux.* sein) come, arrive; come about; *um etwas* —, lose s.th.; *zu etwas* —, come by s.th.; *zu sich* —, come to, regain consciousness.

Kommentar [kɔmen'ta:r], *m.* (—s, *pl.* —e) comment, commentary.

Kommers [kɔ'mɛrs], *m.* (—es, *pl.* —e) students' festivity; drinking party.

Kommersbuch [kɔ'mɛrsbu:x], *n.* (—es, *pl.* ⁻er) students' song-book.

kommerziell [kɔmɛrts'jɛl], *adj.* commercial.

Kommerzienrat [kɔ'mɛrtsjənra:t], *m.* (—s, *pl.* —e) Councillor to the Chamber of Commerce.

Kommilitone [kɔmili'to:nə], *m.* (—n, *pl.* —n) fellow-student.

Kommis [kɔ'mi:], *m.* (—, *pl.* —s) clerk.

Kommiß [kɔ'mɪs], *m.* (—sses, *pl.* —) military fatigue-dress; (*fig.*) military service.

126

können

Kommißbrot [kɔ'mɪsbroːt], *n.* (—es, *no pl.*) (coarse) army bread.

Kommissar [kɔmɪ'saːr], *m.* (—s, *pl.* —e) commissioner.

Kommissariat [kɔmɪsar'jaːt], *n.* (—s, *pl.* —e) commissioner's office.

Kommission [kɔmɪs'joːn], *f.* (—, *pl.* —en) commission, mission, committee.

kommod [kɔ'moːd], *adj.* (*coll.*) snug, comfortable.

Kommode [kɔ'moːdə], *f.* (—, *pl.* —n) chest of drawers.

Kommune [kɔ'muːnə], *f.* (—, *pl.* —n) (*coll.*) Communist Party; Reds.

Kommunismus [kɔmu'nɪsmus], *m.* (—, *no pl.*) Communism.

kommunistisch [kɔmu'nɪstɪʃ], *adj.* Communist.

Komödiant [kɔmød'jant], *m.* (—en, *pl.* —en) comedian, player; humbug.

Komödie [kɔ'møːdjə], *f.* (—, *pl.* —n) comedy, play; make-believe; — *spielen,* (*fig.*) sham, pretend, play-act.

Kompagnon ['kɔmpanjõ], *m.* (—s, *pl.* —s) partner, associate.

Kompanie [kɔmpa'niː], *f.* (—, *pl.* —n) (*Mil.*) company; (*Comm.*) partnership, company.

Kompaß ['kɔmpas], *m.* (—sses, *pl.* —sse) compass.

Kompaßrose ['kɔmpasroːzə], *f.* (—, *pl.* —n) compass-card.

kompensieren [kɔmpɛn'ziːrən], *v.a.* compensate.

komplementär [kɔmplemən'tɛːr], *adj.* complementary.

komplett [kɔm'plɛt], *adj.* complete.

komplimentieren [kɔmplimɛn'tiːrən], *v.a.* compliment, flatter.

Komplize [kɔm'pliːtsə], *m.* (—n, *pl.* —n) accomplice.

kompliziert [kɔmpli'tsiːrt], *adj.* complicated.

Komplott [kɔm'plɔt], *n.* (—s, *pl.* —e) plot, conspiracy.

Komponente [kɔmpo'nɛntə], *f.* (—, *pl.* —n) component part; constituent.

komponieren [kɔmpo'niːrən], *v.a.* compose, set to music.

Komponist [kɔmpo'nɪst], *m.* (—en, *pl.* —en) composer.

Kompositum [kɔm'poːzɪtum], *n.* (—s, *pl.* —ta) (*Gram.*) compound word.

Kompott [kɔm'pɔt], *n.* (—s, *pl.* —e) stewed fruit, compote; sweet, dessert.

Kompresse [kɔm'prɛsə], *f.* (—, *pl.* —n) compress.

komprimieren [kɔmpri'miːrən], *v.a.* compress.

Kompromiß [kɔmpro'mɪs], *m.* (—sses, *pl.* —sse) compromise, settlement.

kompromittieren [kɔmprɔmɪ'tiːrən], *v.a.* compromise; — *v.r. sich —,* compromise o.s.

kondensieren [kɔndɛn'ziːrən], *v.a.* condense.

Konditor [kɔn'diːtɔr], *m.* (—s, *pl.* —en) confectioner, pastry-cook.

Konditorei [kɔnditɔ'raɪ], *f.* (—, *pl.* —en) confectioner's shop, pastryshop; café.

kondolieren [kɔndo'liːrən], *v.n.* condole with s.o.

Kondukteur [kɔnduk'tøːr], *m.* (—s, *pl.* —e) (*Swiss & Austr. dial.*) guard (on train), conductor (on tram *or* bus).

Konfekt [kɔn'fɛkt], *n.* (—s, *pl.* —e) chocolates; (*Am.*) candy.

Konfektion [kɔnfɛk'tsjoːn], *f.* (—, *no pl.*) ready-made clothes; outfitting.

Konfektionär [kɔnfɛktsjo'nɛːr], *m.* (—s, *pl.* —e) outfitter.

Konferenz [kɔnfe'rɛnts], *f.* (—, *pl.* —en) conference.

konfessionell [kɔnfɛsjo'nɛl], *adj.* denominational, confessional.

Konfirmand [kɔnfɪr'mant], *m.* (—en, *pl.* —en) confirmation candidate.

konfirmieren [kɔnfɪr'miːrən], *v.a.* (*Eccl.*) confirm.

konfiszieren [kɔnfɪs'tsiːrən], *v.a.* confiscate.

Konfitüren [kɔnfɪ'tyːrən], *f. pl.* confectionery, candied fruit, preserves.

konform [kɔn'fɔrm], *adj.* in comformity (with).

konfus [kɔn'fuːs], *adj.* confused, puzzled, disconcerted.

Kongo ['kɔŋgo], *m.* Congo.

Kongruenz [kɔngru'ɛnts], *f.* (—, *no pl.*) congruity.

König ['køːnɪç], *m.* (—s, *pl.* —e) king.

Königin ['køːnɪgɪn], *f.* (—, *pl.* —nen) queen.

königlich ['køːnɪglɪç], *adj.* royal, regal, kingly, king-like.

Königreich ['køːnɪçraɪç], *n.* (—(e)s, *pl.* —e) kingdom.

Königsadler ['køːnɪçsaːdlər], *m.* (—s, *pl.* —) golden eagle.

Königsschlange ['køːnɪçsʃlaŋə], *f.* (—, *pl.* —n) (*Zool.*) boa constrictor.

Königstiger ['køːnɪçstiːgər], *m.* (—s, *pl.* —) (*Zool.*) Bengal tiger.

Königtum ['køːnɪçtuːm], *n.* (—s, *no pl.*) kingship.

Konjunktur [kɔnjuŋk'tuːr], *f.* (—, *pl.* —en) state of the market, (*coll.*) boom.

Konkordat [kɔnkɔr'daːt], *n.* (—s, *pl.* —e) concordat.

konkret [kɔn'kreːt], *adj.* concrete.

Konkurrent [kɔnku'rɛnt], *m.* (—en, *pl.* —en) competitor, (business) rival.

Konkurrenz [kɔnku'rɛnts], *f.* (—, *no pl.*) competition.

konkurrieren [kɔnku'riːrən], *v.n.* compete.

Konkurs [kɔn'kurs], *m.* (—es, *pl.* —e) bankruptcy.

Konkursmasse [kɔn'kursmasə], *f.* (—, *pl.* —n) bankrupt's estate, bankrupt's stock.

Können ['kœnən], *n.* (—s, *no pl.*) ability; knowledge.

können ['kœnən], *v.a., v.n. irr.* be able to, be capable of; understand; *ich kann,* I can; *er kann Englisch,* he speaks English.

127

konsequent

konsequent [kɔnze'kvɛnt], *adj.* consistent.

Konsequenz [kɔnze'kvɛnts], *f.* (—, *pl.* —en) (*characteristic*) consistency; (*result*) consequence.

Konservatorium [kɔnzɛrva'to:rjum], *n.* (—s, *pl.* —rien) (*Mus.*) conservatoire, conservatorium.

Konserve [kɔn'zɛrvə], *f.* (—, *pl.* —n) preserve; tinned, *or* (*Am.*) canned food.

konservieren [kɔnzɛr'vi:rən], *v.a.* preserve.

Konsistorium [kɔnzɪs'to:rjum], *n.* (—s, *pl.* —rien) (*Eccl.*) consistory.

Konsole [kɔn'zo:lə], *f.* (—, *pl.* —n) bracket.

konsolidieren [kɔnzoli'di:rən], *v.a.* consolidate.

Konsonant [kɔnzo'nant], *m.* (—en, *pl.* —en) (*Phonet.*) consonant.

Konsorte [kɔn'zɔrtə], *m.* (—n, *pl.* —n) associate, accomplice.

Konsortium [kɔn'zɔrtsjum], *n.* (—s, *pl.* —tien) syndicate.

konstatieren [kɔnsta'ti:rən], *v.a.* state, note, assert.

konsternieren [kɔnstɛr'ni:rən], *v.a.* dismay, disconcert.

konstituieren [kɔnstitu'i:rən], *v.a.* constitute.

konstitutionell [kɔnstitutsjo'nɛl], *adj.* constitutional.

konstruieren [kɔnstru'i:rən], *v.a.* construct; (*Gram.*) construe.

konsularisch [kɔnzu'la:rɪʃ], *adj.* consular.

Konsulat [kɔnzu'la:t], *n.* (—s, *pl.* —e) consulate.

Konsulent [kɔnzu'lɛnt], *m.* (—en, *pl.* —en) (*Law*) counsel; consultant.

konsultieren [kɔnzul'ti:rən], *v.a.* consult.

Konsum [kɔn'zu:m], *m.* (—s, *no pl.*) (*Econ.*) consumption.

Konsumverein [kɔn'zu:mfɛraɪn], *m.* (—s, *pl.* —e) cooperative society.

konsumieren [kɔnzu'mi:rən], *v.a.* consume.

Konterbande [kɔntər'bandə], *f.* (—, *no pl.*) contraband.

Konterfei [kɔntər'faɪ], *n.* (—s, *pl.* —e) (*obs.*) portrait, likeness.

Kontertanz ['kɔntərtants], *m.* (—es, *pl.* ⸚e) square dance, quadrille.

kontinuierlich [kɔntinu'i:rlɪç], *adj.* continuous.

Kontinuität [kɔntinui'tɛ:t], *f.* (—, *no pl.*) continuity.

Konto ['kɔnto], *n.* (—s, *pl.* —ten) (*bank*) account; à —, on account.

Kontokorrent [kɔntoko'rɛnt], *n.* (—s, *pl.* —e) current account.

Kontor [kɔn'to:r], *n.* (—s, *pl.* —e) (*obs.*) office.

Kontorist [kɔnto'rɪst], *m.* (—en, *pl.* —en) clerk.

Kontrabaß ['kɔntrabas], *m.* (—sses, *pl.* ⸚sse) double-bass.

Kontrapunkt ['kɔntrapuŋkt], *m.* (—es, *pl.* —e) (*Mus.*) counterpoint.

kontrastieren [kɔntras'ti:rən], *v.a., v.n.* contrast.

kontrollieren [kɔntro'li:rən], *v.a.* check, verify.

Kontroverse [kɔntro'vɛrzə], *f.* (—, *pl.* —n) controversy.

Kontur [kɔn'tu:r], *f.* (—, *pl.* —en) outline, (*pl.*) contours.

Konvent [kɔn'vɛnt], *m.* (—s, *pl.* —e) convention, assembly, congress.

konventionell [kɔnvɛntsjo'nɛl], *adj.* conventional, formal.

Konversationslexikon [kɔnvɛrza-'tsjo:nslɛksɪkɔn], *n.* (—s, *pl.* —s) encyclopaedia.

konvertieren [kɔnvɛr'ti:rən], *v.a., v.n.* convert.

Konvertit [kɔnvɛr'tɪt], *m.* (—en, *pl.* —en) convert.

Konvolut [kɔnvo'lu:t], *n.* (—s, *pl.* —e) bundle; scroll.

konvulsivisch [kɔnvul'zi:vɪʃ], *adj.* convulsive.

konzentrieren [kɔntsɛn'tri:rən], *v.a., v.r.* concentrate; *auf etwas* —, centre upon.

konzentrisch [kɔn'tsɛntrɪʃ], *adj.* concentric.

Konzept [kɔn'tsɛpt], *n.* (—es, *pl.* —e) rough draft, sketch; *aus dem* — *bringen*, unsettle, disconcert.

Konzeptpapier [kɔn'tsɛptpapi:r], *n.* (—s, *no pl.*) scribbling paper.

Konzern [kɔn'tsɛrn], *m.* (—s, *pl.* —e) (*Comm.*) combine.

Konzert [kɔn'tsɛrt], *n.* (—es, *pl.* —e) concert, (musical) recital.

Konzertflügel [kɔn'tsɛrtfly:gəl], *m.* (—s, *pl.* —) grand piano.

konzertieren [kɔntsɛr'ti:rən], *v.n.* give recitals; play in a concert.

Konzertmeister [kɔn'tsɛrtmaɪstər], *m.* (—s, *pl.* —) impresario.

Konzession [kɔntsɛ'sjo:n], *f.* (—, *pl.* —en) concession, licence.

konzessionieren [kɔntsɛsjo'ni:rən], *v.a.* license.

Konzil [kɔn'tsi:l], *n.* (—s, *pl.* —ien) (*Eccl.*) council.

konzipieren [kɔntsi'pi:rən], *v.a.* draft, plan.

Koordinierung [ko:ɔrdi'ni:ruŋ], *f.* (—, *pl.* —en) co-ordination.

Kopf [kɔpf], *m.* (—es, *pl.* ⸚e) head; top; heading; (*fig.*) mind, brains, judgment; *aus dem* —, by heart.

köpfen ['kœpfən], *v.a.* behead, decapitate; (*Bot.*) lop.

Kopfhaut ['kɔpfhaut], *f.* (—, *no pl.*) scalp.

Kopfhörer ['kɔpfhø:rər], *m.* (—s, *pl.* —s) headphone, receiver.

Kopfkissen ['kɔpfkɪsən], *n.* (—s, *pl.* —) pillow.

Kopfsalat ['kɔpfzala:t], *m.* (—s, *pl.* —e) (garden) lettuce.

kopfscheu ['kɔpfʃɔy], *adj.* afraid; alarmed, timid; — *machen*, scare; — *werden*, take fright, jib.

Kopfschmerz ['kɔpfʃmɛrts], m. (—es, pl. —en) (mostly pl.) headache.

Kopfsprung ['kɔpfʃpruŋ], m. (—s, pl. ⸚e) (diving) header.

kopfüber [kɔpf'y:bər], adv. head over heels; headlong.

Kopfweh ['kɔpfve:], n. (—s, no pl.) headache.

Kopfzerbrechen ['kɔpftsɛrbrɛçən], n. (—s, no pl.) racking o.'s brains.

Kopie [ko'pi:] f. (—, pl. —n) copy, duplicate.

kopieren [ko'pi:rən], v.a. copy, ape, mimic, take off.

Koppe ['kɔpə], f. see **Kuppe**.

Koppel ['kɔpəl], f. (—, pl. —n) (dogs) couple, leash; (ground) enclosure, paddock.

koppeln ['kɔpəln], v.a. couple, leash.

kopulieren [kopu'li:rən], v.a. (obs.) marry; pair; (Hort.) graft.

Koralle [ko'ralə], f. (—, pl. —n) coral.

Korallenriff [ko'ralənrif], n. (—es, pl. —e) coral-reef.

Korb [kɔrp], m. (—s, pl. ⸚e) basket, hamper; einen — geben, turn s.o. down, refuse an offer of marriage.

Korbweide ['kɔrpvaɪdə], f. (—, pl. —n) (Bot.) osier.

Kord [kɔrt], m. (—s, no pl.) corduroy.

Kordel ['kɔrdəl], f. (—, pl. —n) cord, twine, thread.

Korea [ko're:a], n. Korea.

Korinthe [ko'rintə], f. (—, pl. —n) (Bot.) currant.

Korken ['kɔrkən], m. (—s, pl. —) cork, stopper.

Korkenzieher ['kɔrkəntsi:ər], m. (—s, pl. —) cork-screw.

Korn [kɔrn], n. (—s, pl. —e, ⸚er) (Bot.) corn, grain, cereal, rye; (gun) sight, aufs — nehmen, take aim at.

Kornblume ['kɔrnblu:mə], f. (—, pl. —n) (Bot.) corn-flower.

Kornbranntwein ['kɔrnbrantvaɪn], m. (—s, no pl.) corn-brandy, whisky.

Kornett [kɔr'nɛt], m. (—s, pl. —e) (Mil., Mus.) cornet.

körnig ['kœrniç], adj. granular, granulous; grained.

Kornrade ['kɔrnra:də], f. (—, pl. —n) (Bot.) corn-cockle.

Kornspeicher ['kɔrnʃpaɪçər], m. (—s, pl. —) granary, corn-loft.

Körper ['kœrpər], m. (—s, pl. —) body; (Phys.) solid.

Körperbau ['kœrpərbau], m. (—s, no pl.) build, frame.

Köpergeruch ['kœrpərgəru:x], m. (—s, no pl.) body odour.

körperlich ['kœrpərliç], adj. bodily, physical; —e Züchtigung, corporal punishment.

Körpermaß ['kœrpərma:s], n. (—es, pl. —e) cubic measure.

Körperschaft ['kœrpərʃaft], f. (—, pl. —en) corporation.

Korps [ko:r], n. (—, pl. —) (Mil.) corps; students' corporation.

Korrektheit [kɔ'rɛkthaɪt], f. (—, no pl.) correctness.

Korrektionsanstalt [kɔrɛk'tsjo:nsanʃtalt], f. (—, pl. —en) penitentiary, Borstal institution.

Korrektor [kɔ'rɛktɔr], m. (—s, pl. —en) proof-reader.

Korrektur [kɔrɛk'tu:r], f. (—, pl. —en) correction; proof-correction; revision.

Korrekturbogen [kɔrɛk'tu:rbo:gən], m. (—s, pl. —) (Typ.) proof-sheet, galley.

Korrespondenzkarte [kɔrɛspɔn'dɛntskartə], f. (—, pl. —n) post-card.

korrigieren [kɔri'gi:rən], v.a. correct, revise; read (proofs).

Korsett [kɔr'zɛt], n. (—s, pl. —s) corset, bodice, stays.

Koryphäe [kɔri'fɛ:ə], m. (—n, pl. —n) celebrity, authority, master mind.

Koseform ['ko:zəfɔrm], f. (—, pl. —en) term of endearment, pet-name, diminutive.

kosen ['ko:zən], v.a., v.n. caress, fondle; make love (to).

Kosinus ['ko:zinus], m. (—, pl. —) (Maths.) cosine.

Kosmetik [kɔs'me:tik], f. (—, no pl.) cosmetics.

kosmetisch [kɔs'me:tiʃ], adj. cosmetic.

kosmisch ['kɔzmiʃ], adj. cosmic.

Kosmopolit [kɔsmopo'li:t], m. (—en, pl. —en) cosmopolitan.

kosmopolitisch [kɔsmopo'li:tiʃ], adj. cosmopolitan.

Kost [kɔst], f. (—, no pl.) food, fare; board.

Kostarika [kɔsta'rika], n. Costa Rica.

kostbar ['kɔstba:r], adj. valuable, precious, costly.

Kostbarkeit ['kɔstba:rkaɪt], f. (—, pl. —en) costliness, preciousness; (pl.) (goods) valuables.

Kosten ['kɔstən], pl. cost(s), expenses, charges; (Law) costs.

kosten ['kɔstən], v.a. taste; (money) cost; take, require; was kostet das? how much is this?

Kosten(vor)anschlag ['kɔstən(for)anʃla:k], m. (—s, pl. ⸚e) estimate.

Kostenaufwand ['kɔstənaufvant], m. (—s, pl. ⸚e) expenditure.

Kostenersatz ['kɔstənɛrzats], m. (—es, no pl.) refund of expenses, compensation.

kostenfrei ['kɔstənfraɪ], adj. free (of charge), gratis.

kostenlos ['kɔstənlo:s], see **kostenfrei**.

Kostgänger ['kɔstgɛŋər], m. (—s, pl. —) boarder.

Kostgeld ['kɔstgɛlt], n. (—es, no pl.) maintenance or board allowance.

köstlich ['kœstliç], adj. excellent, precious; delicious; ein —er Witz, a capital joke.

kostspielig ['kɔstʃpi:liç], adj. expensive, costly.

Kostüm [kɔ'sty:m], n. (—s, pl. —e) costume; fancy dress.

Kostümfest [kɔ'sty:mfɛst], n. (—s, pl. —e) fancy-dress ball.

kostümieren

kostümieren [kɔsty'miːrən], *v.a.* dress up.

Kot [koːt], *m.* (—es, *no pl.*) mud, dirt; filth, mire; excrement.

Kotelett [kɔt'let], *n.* (—s, *pl.* —s) cutlet.

Köter ['køːtər], *m.* (—s, *pl.* —) cur, mongrel.

Koterie [koːtə'riː], *f.* (—, *pl.* —n) clique, set, coterie.

Kotflügel ['koːtflyːgəl], *m.* (—s, *pl.* —) (*Motor.*) mudguard.

kotig ['koːtɪç], *adj.* dirty, miry.

kotzen ['kɔtsən], *v.n.* (*vulg.*) vomit.

Koweit ['kɔvaɪt], *n.* Kuwait.

Krabbe ['krabə], *f.* (—, *pl.* —n) (*Zool.*) crab; shrimp; (*fig.*) brat, imp.

krabbeln ['krabəln], *v.n.* crawl.

Krach [krax], *m.* (—es, *pl.* —e) crack, crash; din, noise; (*Comm.*) slump; quarrel, row.

krachen ['kraxən], *v.n.* crack, crash.

krächzen ['krɛçtsən], *v.n.* croak.

Kraft [kraft], *f.* (—, *pl.* ⁻e) strength, vigour; force; power, energy; intensity; *in — treten*, come into force.

kraft [kraft], *prep.* (*Genit.*) by virtue of, by authority of, on the strength of.

Kraftausdruck ['kraftausdruk], *m.* (—s, *pl.* ⁻e) forcible expression; expletive.

Kraftbrühe ['kraftbryːə], *f.* (—, *pl.* —n) meat-soup, beef-tea.

Kraftfahrer ['kraftfaːrər], *m.* (—s, *pl.* —) motorist.

kräftig ['krɛftɪç], *adj.* strong, powerful, vigorous, energetic; (*food*) nourishing.

Kraftlehre ['kraftleːrə], *f.* (—, *no pl.*) dynamics.

kraftlos ['kraftloːs], *adj.* weak, feeble.

Kraftwagen ['kraftvaːgən], *m.* (—s, *pl.* —) motor car, automobile, car; lorry, truck.

Kragen ['kraːgən], *m.* (—s, *pl.* —) collar; *es geht mir an den —*, it will cost me dearly.

Krähe ['krɛːə], *f.* (—, *pl.* —n) (*Orn.*) crow.

krähen ['krɛːən], *v.n.* crow.

Krähenfüße ['krɛːənfyːsə], *m. pl.* crow's feet (wrinkles).

Krakau ['kraːkau], *n.* Cracow.

krakeelen [kra'keːlən], *v.n.* (*coll.*) kick up a row.

Kralle ['kralə], *f.* (—, *pl.* —n) claw, talon.

Kram [kraːm], *m.* (—s, *no pl.*) small wares (trade); stuff, rubbish, litter; *es paßt mir nicht in den —*, it does not suit my purpose.

kramen ['kraːmən], *v.n.* rummage.

Krämer ['krɛːmər], *m.* (—s, *pl.* —) retailer, general dealer, shopkeeper.

Kramladen ['kraːmlaːdən], *m.* (—s, *pl.* ⁻) small retail-shop, general shop or store.

Krampe ['krampə], *f.* (—, *pl.* —n) staple.

Krampf [krampf], *m.* (—es, *pl.* ⁻) cramp, spasm, convulsion.

Krampfader ['krampfaːdər], *f.* (—, *pl.* —n) varicose vein.

krampfartig ['krampfaːrtɪç], *adj.* spasmodic.

krampfhaft ['krampfhaft], *adj.* convulsive.

Kran [kraːn], *m.* (—s, *pl.* ⁻e) (*Engin.*) crane.

Kranich ['kraːnɪç], *m.* (—s, *pl.* —e) (*Orn.*) crane.

krank [kraŋk], *adj.* sick, ill.

kränkeln ['krɛŋkəln], *v.n.* be ailing, be in poor health.

kranken ['kraŋkən], *v.n. an etwas —*, suffer from s.th., be afflicted with s.th.

kränken ['krɛŋkən], *v.a.* vex, grieve; offend, insult.

Krankenbahre ['kraŋkənbaːrə], *f.* (—, *pl.* —n) stretcher.

Krankenhaus ['kraŋkənhaus], *n.* (—es, *pl.* ⁻er) hospital.

Krankenkasse ['kraŋkənkasə], *f.* (—, *pl.* —n) sick-fund; health insurance.

Krankenkost ['kraŋkənkɔst], *f.* (—, *no pl.*) invalid diet.

Krankenschwester ['kraŋkənʃvestər], *f.* (—, *pl.* —n) nurse.

Krankenstuhl ['kraŋkənʃtuːl], *m.* (—s, *pl.* ⁻e) invalid chair.

Krankenversicherung ['kraŋkənferziçəruŋ], *f.* (—, *pl* —en) health insurance.

Krankenwärter ['kraŋkənvɛrtər], *m.* (—s, *pl.* —) attendant, male nurse.

krankhaft ['kraŋkhaft], *adj.* morbid.

Krankheit ['kraŋkhaɪt], *f.* (—, *pl.* —en) illness, sickness, disease, malady; complaint; *englische —*, rickets.

Krankheitserscheinung ['kraŋkhaɪtsɛrʃaɪnuŋ], *f.* (—, *pl.* —en) symptom.

kränklich ['krɛŋklɪç], *adj.* sickly, infirm, in poor health.

Kränkung ['krɛŋkuŋ], *f.* (—, *pl.* —en) grievance, annoyance; offence, insult.

Kranz [krants], *m.* (—es, *pl.* ⁻e) wreath, garland.

Kränzchen ['krɛntsçən], *n.* (—s, *pl.* —) little garland; (*fig.*) (ladies') weekly tea party; circle, club.

kränzen ['krɛntsən], *v.a.* garland, wreathe.

Krapfen ['krapfən], *m.* (—s, *pl.* —) doughnut.

kraß [kras], *adj.* crass, crude.

Krater ['kraːtər], *m.* (—s, *pl.* —) crater.

Kratzbürste ['kratsbyrstə], *f.* (—, *pl.* —n) scraper; (*fig.*) cross-patch, irritable person.

Krätze ['krɛtsə], *f.* (—, *no pl.*) (*Med.*) scabies, itch, mange.

kratzen ['kratsən], *v.a., v.n.* scratch, scrape, itch.

krauen ['krauən], *v.a.* scratch softly.

kraus [kraus], *adj.* frizzy, curly; crisp, fuzzy; creased; (*fig.*) abstruse; *die Stirn — ziehen*, frown, knit o.'s brow.

Krause ['krauzə], *f.* (—, *pl.* —n) ruff.

kräuseln ['krɔyzəln], *v.a., v.r.* crisp, curl; ripple.

Krauskohl ['krauskoːl], *m.* (—s, *no pl.*) Savoy cabbage.

Kraut [kraut], *n.* (**—es,** *pl.* ¨**er**) herb; plant; (*dial.*) cabbage; *wie — und Rüben,* higgledy-piggledy.

krautartig ['krauta:rtıç], *adj.* herbaceous.

Kräuterkäse ['krɔytərke:zə], *m.* (**—s,** *pl.* —) green cheese.

Kräutertee ['krɔytərte:], *m.* (**—s,** *no pl.*) herb-tea, infusion of herbs.

Krawall [kra'val], *m.* (**—s,** *pl.* **—e**) (*coll.*) row, uproar; shindy.

Krawatte [kra'vatə], *f.* (—, *pl.* **—n**) cravat, tie.

kraxeln ['kraksəln], *v.n.* (*coll.*) climb, clamber.

Krebs [kre:ps], *m.* (**—es,** *pl.* **—e**) (*Zool.*) crayfish, crab; (*Med.*) cancer, carcinoma; (*Geog.*) Tropic of Cancer.

krebsartig ['kre:psa:rtıç], *adj.* cancerous.

Krebsbutter ['kre:psbutər], *f.* (—, *no pl.*) crab-cheese.

Krebsgang ['kre:psgaŋ], *m.* (**—es,** *no pl.*) crab's walk, sidling; *den — gehen,* retrograde, decline.

Krebsschaden ['kre:psʃa:dən], *m.* (**—s,** *pl.* ¨) cancerous sore *or* affection; (*fig.*) canker, inveterate evil.

Kredenz [kre'dɛnts], *f.* (—, *pl.* **—en**) buffet, serving table, sideboard.

kredenzen [kre'dɛntsən], *v.a.* taste (*wine*); (*obs.*) present, offer.

kreditieren [kredi'ti:rən], *v.a. einem etwas —,* credit s.o. with s.th.

Kreide ['kraıdə], *f.* (—, *pl.* **—n**) chalk; (*Art*) crayon.

kreieren [kre'i:rən], *v.a.* create.

Kreis [kraıs], *m.* (**—es,** *pl.* **—e**) circle; (*Astron.*) orbit; district; range; sphere.

Kreisabschnitt ['kraısapʃnıt], *m.* (**—s,** *pl.* **—e**) segment.

Kreisausschnitt ['kraısausʃnıt], *m.* (**—s,** *pl.* **—e**) sector.

Kreisbogen ['kraısbo:gən], *m.* (**—s,** *pl.* ¨) arc.

kreischen ['kraıʃən], *v.n.* scream, shriek.

Kreisel ['kraızəl], *m.* (**—s,** *pl.* —) (*toy*) (spinning) top; gyroscope.

kreisen ['kraızən], *v.n.* circle, revolve; circulate.

Kreislauf ['kraıslauf], *m.* (**—es,** *pl.* ¨**e**) circular course; (*Astron.*) orbit; (*blood*) circulation.

kreißen ['kraısən], *v.n.* (*Med.*) be in labour.

Kreisstadt ['kraısʃtat], *f.* (—, *pl.* ¨**e**) county town.

Kreisumfang ['kraısumfaŋ], *m.* (**—s,** *pl.* ¨**e**) circumference.

Kreml [krɛml], *m.* (**—s,** *no pl.*) the Kremlin.

Krempe ['krɛmpə], *f.* (—, *pl.* **—n**) (*hat*) brim.

Krempel ['krɛmpəl], *m.* (**—s,** *no pl.*) (*coll.*) refuse, rubbish; stuff.

Kren [kre:n], *m.* (**—s,** *no pl.*) (*Austr.*) horse-radish.

krepieren [kre'pi:rən], *v.n.* (*aux.* sein) (*animals*) die; (*humans*) (*coll.*) perish miserably; explode.

Krepp [krɛp], *m.* (**—s,** *no pl.*) crape, crêpe.

Kresse ['krɛsə], *f.* (—, *pl.* **—n**) cress.

Kreta ['kre:ta], *n.* Crete.

Kreuz [krɔyts], *n.* (**—es,** *pl.* **—e**) cross, crucifix; (*Anat.*) small of the back; (*fig.*) calamity; affliction; *kreuz und quer,* in all directions.

Kreuzband ['krɔytsbant], *n.* (**—es,** *pl.* ¨**er**) wrapper (for printed matter).

kreuzbrav ['krɔytsbra:f], *adj.* as good as gold.

kreuzen ['krɔytsən], *v.a.* cross. — *v.r. sich —,* make the sign of the cross.

Kreuzfahrer ['krɔytsfa:rər], *m.* (**—s,** *pl.* —) crusader.

kreuzfidel ['krɔytsfide:l], *adj.* jolly, merry, as merry as a cricket.

Kreuzgang ['krɔytsgaŋ], *m.* (**—es,** *pl.* ¨**e**) cloisters.

kreuzigen ['krɔytsıgən], *v.a.* crucify.

Kreuzritter ['krɔıtsrıtər], *m.* (**—s,** *pl.* —) Knight of the Cross; crusader.

Kreuzschmerzen ['krɔytsʃmɛrtsən], *m. pl.* lumbago.

Kreuzstich ['krɔytsʃtıç], *m.* (**—es,** *no pl.*) (*Embroidery*) cross-stitch.

Kreuzung ['krɔytsuŋ], *f.* (—, *pl.* **—en**) (*road*) crossing; (*animals*) cross-breeding.

Kreuzverhör ['krɔytsfɛrhø:r], *n.* (**—s,** *pl.* **—e**) cross-examination.

Kreuzweg ['krɔytsve:k], *m.* (**—s,** *pl.* **—e**) crossroads; (*Eccl.*) Stations of the Cross.

Kreuzworträtsel ['krɔytsvɔrtrɛ:tsəl], *n.* (**—s,** *pl.* —) crossword-puzzle.

Kreuzzug ['krɔytstsu:k], *m.* (**—es,** *pl.* ¨**e**) crusade.

kriechen ['kri:çən], *v.n. irr.* (*aux.* sein) creep, crawl; (*fig.*) cringe, fawn.

kriecherisch ['kri:çərıʃ], *adj.* fawning, cringing.

Kriechtier ['kri:çti:r], *n.* (**—s,** *pl.* **—e**) reptile.

Krieg [kri:k], *m.* (**—es,** *pl.* **—e**) war.

kriegen ['kri:gən], *v.a.* get, obtain.

Krieger ['kri:gər], *m.* (**—s,** *pl.* —) warrior.

kriegerisch ['kri:gərıʃ], *adj.* warlike, martial.

kriegführend ['kri:kfy:rənt], *adj.* belligerent.

Kriegsfuß ['kri:ksfu:s], *m.* (**—es,** *no pl.*) *auf —,* at logger-heads.

Kriegsgewinnler ['kri:ksgəvınlər], *m.* (**—s,** *pl.* —) war-profiteer.

Kriegslist ['kri:kslıst], *f.* (—, *pl.* **—en**) stratagem.

Kriegsschauplatz ['kri:ksʃauplats], *m.* (**—es,** *pl.* ¨**e**) theatre of war.

Kriegsschiff ['kri:ksʃıf], *n.* (**—es,** *pl.* **—e**) man-of-war, warship.

Kriegswesen ['kri:ksve:zən], *n.* (**—s,** *no pl.*) military affairs.

Kriegszug ['kri:kstsu:k], *m.* (**—es,** *pl.* ¨**e**) campaign.

Krim [krım], *f.* the Crimea.

Kriminalbeamte [krımi'na:lbəamtə], *m.* (**—n,** *pl.* **—n**) crime investigator.

Kriminalprozeß [krɪmi'na:lprotsɛs], *m.* (—sses, *pl.* —sse) criminal procedure *or* trial.

Krimskrams ['krɪmskrams], *m.* (—, *no pl.*) whatnots, knick-knacks, medley.

Krippe ['krɪpə], *f.* (—, *pl.* —n) crib, manger; crèche.

Krise ['kri:zə], *f.* (—, *pl.* —n) crisis.

Kristall [krɪ'stal], *m.* (—s, *pl.* —e) crystal; cut glass.

kristallartig [krɪ'stala:rtɪç], *adj.* crystalline.

kristallisieren [krɪstali'zi:rən], *v.a., v.n.* (*aux.* sein), crystallise.

Kristallkunde [krɪ'stalkundə], *f.* (—, *no pl.*) crystallography.

Kriterium [kri'te:rjum], *n.* (—s, *pl.* —rien) criterion, test.

Kritik [kri'ti:k], *f.* (—, *pl.* —en) criticism, review; *unter aller* —, extremely bad.

Kritiker ['kri:tɪkər], *m.* (—s, *pl.* —) critic.

kritisch ['kri:tɪʃ], *adj.* critical; precarious, crucial.

kritisieren [kriti'zi:rən], *v.a.* criticise; review; censure.

kritteln ['krɪtəln], *v.n.* cavil (at), find fault.

Krittler ['krɪtlər], *m.* (—s, *pl.* —) caviller, fault-finder.

Kritzelei [krɪtsə'laɪ], *f.* (—, *pl.* —en) scrawling, scribbling.

kritzeln ['krɪtsəln], *v.a.* scrawl, scribble.

Kroatien [kro'a:tsjən], *n.* Croatia.

Krokodil [kroko'di:l], *m.* (—s, *pl.* —e) (*Zool.*) crocodile.

Kronbewerber ['kro:nbevɛrbər], *m.* (—s, *pl.* —) aspirant to the crown, pretender.

Krone ['kro:nə], *f.* (—, *pl.* —n) crown; (*Papal*) tiara; (*fig.*) head, top, flower.

krönen ['krø:nən], *v.a.* crown.

Kronerbe ['kro:nɛrbə], *m.* (—n, *pl.* —n) heir apparent.

Kronleuchter ['kro:nlɔyçtər], *m.* (—s, *pl.* —) chandelier.

Kronsbeere ['kro:nsbe:rə], *f.* (—, *pl.* —n) (*Bot.*) cranberry.

Krönung ['krø:nuŋ], *f.* (—, *pl.* —en) coronation.

Kropf [krɔpf], *m.* (—es, *pl.* ᵕe) (*human*) goitre, wen; (*birds*) crop, craw.

kropfartig ['krɔpfa:rtɪç], *adj.* goitrous.

kröpfen ['krœpfən], *v.a.* (*birds*) cram.

Kropftaube ['krɔpftaubə], *f.* (—, *pl.* —n) (*Orn.*) pouter-pigeon.

Kröte ['krø:tə], *f.* (—, *pl.* —n) toad.

Krücke ['krykə], *f.* (—, *pl.* —n) crutch; (*fig.*) rake.

Krückstock ['krykʃtɔk], *m.* (—s, *pl.* ᵕe) crutch.

Krug [kru:k], *m.* (—es, *pl.* ᵕe) jug, pitcher, mug; (*fig.*) pub, inn.

Krüger ['kry:gər], *m.* (—s, *pl.* —) pub-keeper, tapster.

Krume ['kru:mə], *f.* (—, *pl.* —n) crumb.

krüm(e)lig ['kry:m(ə)lɪç], *adj.* crumbly, crumby.

krümeln ['kry:meln], *v.n.* crumble.

krumm [krum], *adj.* crooked, curved; *etwas* — *nehmen*, take s.th. amiss.

krummbeinig ['krumbaɪnɪç], *adj.* bandy-legged.

krümmen ['krymən], *v.a.* crook, bend, curve. — *v.r. sich* —, (*fig.*) writhe, cringe.

Krummholz ['krumhɔlts], *n.* (—es, *no pl.*) (*Bot.*) dwarf-pine.

Krummschnabel ['krumʃna:bəl], *m.* (—s, *pl.* ᵕ) (*Orn.*) curlew, crook-bill.

Krümmung ['krymuŋ], *f.* (—, *pl.* —en) curve; turning, winding.

Krüppel ['krypəl], *m.* (—s, *pl.* —) cripple.

krüppelhaft ['krypəlhaft], *adj.* crippled, lame.

krüpp(e)lig ['kryp(ə)lɪç], *adj.* crippled, lame.

Kruste ['krustə], *f.* (—, *pl.* —n) crust.

Kübel ['ky:bəl], *m.* (—s, *pl.* —) tub, bucket.

Kubikfuß [ku'bi:kfu:s], *m.* (—es, *pl.* —) cubic foot.

Kubikinhalt [ku'bi:kɪnhalt], *m.* (—s, *no pl.*) cubic content.

Kubismus [ku'bɪsmus], *m.* (—, *no pl.*) cubism.

Küche ['kyçə], *f.* (—, *pl.* —n) (*room*) kitchen; (*food*) cooking, cookery, cuisine.

Kuchen ['ku:xən], *m.* (—s, *pl.* —) cake.

Küchengeschirr ['kyçəngəʃɪr], *n.* (—s, *no pl.*) kitchen utensils.

Küchenherd ['kyçənhe:rt], *m.* (—es, *pl.* —e) kitchen-range.

Küchenlatein ['kyçənlataɪn], *n.* (—s, *no pl.*) dog-Latin.

Küchenmeister ['kyçənmaɪstər], *m.* (—s, *pl.* —) chef, head cook.

Küchenschrank ['kyçənʃraŋk], *m.* (—s, *pl.* ᵕe) dresser.

Kuchenteig ['ku:xəntaɪk], *m.* (—s, *pl.* —e) dough (for cake).

Küchenzettel ['kyçəntsetəl], *m.* (—s, *pl.* —) bill of fare.

Küchlein ['ky:çlaɪn], *n.* (—s, *pl.* —) young chicken, pullet.

Kücken ['kykən], *n.* (—s, *pl.* —) young chicken, pullet.

Kuckuck ['kukuk], *m.* (—s, *pl.* —e) (*Orn.*) cuckoo; *scher Dich zum* — !'go to blazes!

Kufe ['ku:fə], *f.* (—, *pl.* —n) tub, vat; (*sleigh*) runner; (*cradle*) rocker.

Küfer ['ky:fər], *m.* (—s, *pl.* —) cooper.

Kugel ['ku:gəl], *f.* (—, *pl.* —n) ball, bullet, sphere; globe.

kugelfest ['ku:gəlfest], *adj.* bulletproof.

kugelförmig ['ku:gəlfœrmɪç], *adj.* spherical, globular.

Kugelgelenk ['ku:gəlgələŋk], *n.* (—s, *pl.* —e) ball and socket joint.

Kugellager ['ku:gəlla:gər], *n.* (—s, *pl.* —) ball-bearing.

Kugelmaß ['ku:gəlma:s], *n.* (—es, *pl.* —e) ball-calibre.

kugeln ['ku:gəln], *v.a.* roll; bowl.

Kugelregen [ˈkuːgəlreːgən], *m.* (—s, *no pl.*) hail of bullets.
kugelrund [ˈkuːgəlrunt], *adj.* round as a ball, well-fed.
Kugelschreiber [ˈkuːgəlʃraɪbər], *m.* (—s, *pl.* —) ball-point pen.
Kuh [kuː] *f.* (—, *pl.* ⁻e) cow; *junge* —, heifer.
Kuhblattern [ˈkuːblatərn], *f. pl.* cow-pox.
Kuhblume [ˈkuːbluːmə], *f.* (—, *pl.* —n) (*Bot.*) marigold.
Kuhfladen [ˈkuːflaːdən], *m.* (—s, *pl.* —) cow-dung.
Kuhhaut [ˈkuːhaut], *f.* (—, *pl.* ⁻e) cow-hide; *das geht auf keine* —, that defies description.
kühl [kyːl], *adj.* cool, fresh; (*behaviour*) reserved.
Kühle [ˈkyːlə], *f.* (—, *no pl.*) coolness, freshness; (*behaviour*) reserve.
kühlen [ˈkyːlən], *v.a.* cool, freshen.
Kühlraum [ˈkyːlraum], *m.* (—es, *pl.* ⁻e) refrigerating-chamber.
Kühlschrank [ˈkyːlʃraŋk], *m.* (—s, *pl.* ⁻e) refrigerator, (*coll.*) fridge.
Kühltruhe [ˈkyːltruːə], *f.* (—, *pl.* —n) deep freeze.
Kühlung [ˈkyːluŋ], *f.* (—, *pl.* —en) refrigeration.
Kuhmist [ˈkuːmɪst], *m.* (—s, *no pl.*) cow-dung.
kühn [kyːn], *adj.* bold, daring, audacious.
Kühnheit [ˈkyːnhaɪt], *f.* (—, *no pl.*) boldness, daring, audacity.
Kujon [kuˈjoːn], *m.* (—s, *pl.* —e) bully, scoundrel.
kujonieren [kujoˈniːrən], *v.a.* bully, exploit.
Kukuruz [ˈkukuruts], *m.* (—es, *no pl.*) (*Austr.*) maize.
kulant [kuˈlant], *adj.* obliging; (*terms*) easy.
Kulanz [kuˈlants], *f.* (—, *no pl.*) accommodating manner.
Kuli [ˈkuːliː], *m.* (—s, *pl.* —s) coolie.
kulinarisch [kuliˈnaːrɪʃ], *adj.* culinary.
Kulisse [kuˈlɪsə], *f.* (—, *pl.* —n) (*Theat.*) back-drop, side-scene, wings.
Kulissenfieber [kuˈlɪsənfiːbər], *n.* (—s, *no pl.*) stage-fright.
kulminieren [kulmiˈniːrən], *v.n.* culminate.
kultivieren [kultiˈviːrən], *v.a.* cultivate.
Kultur [kulˈtuːr], *f.* (—, *pl.* —en) (*Agr.*) cultivation; (*fig.*) culture, civilization.
Kultus [ˈkultus], *m.* (—, *pl.* **Kulte**) cult, worship.
Kultusministerium [ˈkultusmɪnɪsteːrjum], *n.* (—s, *pl.* —rien) Ministry of Education.
Kümmel [ˈkyməl], *m.* (—s, *no pl.*) caraway-seed; (*drink*) kümmel.
Kummer [ˈkumər], *m.* (—s, *no pl.*) grief, sorrow, trouble.
kümmerlich [ˈkymərlɪç], *adj.* miserable, pitiful.
kummerlos [ˈkumərloːs], *adj.* untroubled.

kümmern [ˈkymərn], *v.r. sich* — *um*, mind, look after, be worried about, care for.
Kümmernis [ˈkymərnɪs], *f.* (—, *pl.* —se) grief, sorrow.
kummervoll [ˈkumərfɔl], *adj.* sorrowful, painful, grievous.
Kumpan [kumˈpaːn], *m.* (—s, *pl.* —e) companion; mate; *lustiger* —, jolly fellow, good companion.
kund [kunt], *adj.* known, public; *etwas* — *tun*, make s.th. public; *und zu wissen sei hiermit,* (*obs.*) we hereby give notice.
kundbar [ˈkuntbaːr], *adj.* known; *etwas* — *machen*, announce s.th., make s.th. known.
kündbar [ˈkyntbaːr], *adj.* (*loan, capital etc.*) redeemable; capable of being called in, terminable.
Kunde (1) [ˈkundə], *m.* (—n, *pl.* —n) customer; *ein schlauer* —, an artful dodger.
Kunde (2) [ˈkundə], *f.* (—, *pl.* —n) news; information, notification; (*compounds*) science.
Kundgebung [ˈkuntgeːbuŋ], *f.* (—, *pl.* —en) publication; rally; demonstration.
kundig [ˈkundɪç], *adj.* versed in, conversant with.
Kundige [ˈkundɪgə], *m.* (—n, *pl.* —n) expert, initiate.
kündigen [ˈkyndɪgən], *v.n.* give notice (*Dat.*).
Kundmachung [ˈkuntmaxuŋ], *f.* (—, *pl.* —en) publication.
Kundschaft [ˈkuntʃaft], *f.* (—, *no pl.*) clientele, customers; information, reconnaissance.
kundschaften [ˈkuntʃaftən], *v.n.* reconnoitre, scout.
künftig [ˈkynftɪç], *adj.* future, prospective, to come.
Kunst [kunst], *f.* (—, *pl.* ⁻e) art; skill.
Kunstbutter [ˈkunstbutər], *f.* (—, *no pl.*) margarine.
Künstelei [kynstəˈlaɪ], *f.* (—, *pl.* —en) affectation, mannerism.
kunstfertig [ˈkunstfɛrtɪç], *adj.* skilled, skilful.
Kunstfreund [ˈkunstfrɔynt], *m.* (—es, *pl.* —e) art-lover.
kunstgerecht [ˈkunstgərɛçt], *adj.* workmanlike.
Kunstgewerbe [ˈkunstgəvɛrbə], *n.* (—s, *no pl.*) arts and crafts.
Kunstgriff [ˈkunstgrɪf], *m.* (—es, *pl.* —e) trick, dodge, artifice, knack.
Kunsthändler [ˈkunsthɛndlər], *m.* (—s, *pl.* —) art-dealer.
Kunstkenner [ˈkunstkɛnər], *m.* (—s, *pl.* —) connoisseur.
Künstler [ˈkynstlər], *m.* (—s, *pl.* —) artist, performer.
künstlerisch [ˈkynstlərɪʃ], *adj.* artistic, elaborate, ingenious.
künstlich [ˈkynstlɪç], *adj.* artificial.
kunstlos [ˈkunstloːs], *adj.* artless, unaffected.

kunstreich ['kunstraɪç], *adj.* ingenious.
Kunstseide ['kunstzaɪdə], *f.* (—, *no pl.*) artificial silk.
Kunststickerei ['kunstʃtɪkəraɪ], *f.* (—, *no pl.*) art needlework.
Kunststoff ['kunstʃtɔf], *m.* (—es, *pl.* —e) plastics.
Kunststopfen ['kunstʃtɔpfən], *n.* (—s, *no pl.*) invisible mending.
Kunststück ['kunstʃtyk], *n.* (—s, *pl.* —e) trick, feat.
Kunstverständige ['kunstfɛrʃtɛndɪgə], *m.* (—n, *pl.* —n) art expert.
Küpe ['ky:pə], *f.* (—, *pl.* —n) large tub; (dyeing) copper.
Kupfer ['kupfər], *n.* (—s, *no pl.*) copper.
Kupferblech ['kupfərblɛç], *n.* (—es, *no pl.*) copper-sheet.
Kupferdraht ['kupfərdra:t], *m.* (—es, *pl.* ¨e) copper-wire.
kupferhaltig ['kupfərhaltɪç], *adj.* containing copper.
Kupferrost ['kupfərrɔst], *m.* (—es, *no pl.*) verdigris.
Kupferstecher ['kupfərʃtɛçər], *m.* (—s, *pl.* —) (copperplate) engraver.
kupieren [ku'pi:rən], *v.a.* (*rare*) (ticket) punch; (*Austr.*) (horse) dock.
Kuppe ['kupə], *f.* (—, *pl.* —n) (hill) top, summit.
Kuppel ['kupəl], *f.* (—, *pl.* —n) cupola, dome.
kuppeln ['kupəln], *v.n.* procure, pimp; make a match.
Kuppler ['kuplər], *m.* (—s, *pl.* —) procurer, pimp; matchmaker.
Kupplung ['kupluŋ], *f.* (—, *pl.* —en) (*Railw.*) coupling, joint; (*Motor.*) clutch.
Kur [ku:r], *f.* (—. *pl.* —en) cure; *eine — machen*, undergo medical treatment.
Kuranstalt ['ku:ranʃtalt], *f.* (—, *pl.* —en) sanatorium; (*Am.*) sanitarium.
Küraß ['ky:ras], *m.* (—sses, *pl.* —sse) cuirass.
Kuratel [kura'tɛl], *f.* (—, *pl.* —en) guardianship, trusteeship.
Kuratorium [kura'to:rjum], *n.* (—s, *pl.* —rien) board of guardians *or* trustees; council, governing body.
Kurbel ['kurbəl], *f.* (—, *pl.* —n) crank, winch.
Kurbelstange ['kurbəlʃtaŋə], *f.* (—, *pl.* —n) connecting rod.
Kurbelwelle ['kurbəlvelə], *f.* (—, *pl.* —n) crankshaft.
Kürbis ['kyrbɪs], *m.* (—ses, *pl.* —se) (*Bot.*) pumpkin, gourd.
küren ['ky:rən], *v.a. irr.* (*Poet.*) choose, elect.
Kurfürst ['ku:rfyrst], *m.* (—en, *pl.* —en) Elector (of the Holy Roman Empire).
Kurhaus ['ku:rhaus], *n.* (—es, *pl.* ¨er) spa; hotel; pump room.
Kurie ['ku:rjə], *f.* (—, *pl.* —n) (*Eccl.*) Curia; Papal Court.

Kurier [ku'ri:r], *m.* (—s, *pl.* —e) courier.
kurieren [ku'ri:rən], *v.a.* cure.
kurios [kur'jo:s], *adj.* curious, queer, strange.
Kuriosität [kurjozi'tɛ:t], *f.* (—, *pl.* —en) curio, curiosity.
Kurort ['ku:rɔrt], *m.* (—es, *pl.* —e) spa, watering-place, health-resort.
Kurrentschrift [ku'rɛntʃrɪft], *f.* (—, *no pl.*) running hand, cursive writing.
Kurs [kurs], *m.* (—es, *pl.* —e) rate of exchange; quotation; circulation; course.
Kursaal ['ku:rza:l], *m.* (—s, *pl.* —säle) hall, (*spa*) pump-room, casino.
Kursbericht ['kursbarɪçt], *m.* (—es, *pl.* —e) market report.
Kursbuch ['kursbu:x], *n.* (—es, *pl.* ¨er) railway-guide, time-table.
Kürschner ['kyrʃnər], *m.* (—s, *pl.* —) furrier, skinner.
kursieren [kur'zi:rən], *v.n.* be current, circulate.
Kursivschrift [kur'zi:fʃrɪft], *f.* (—, *no pl.*) italics.
Kursstand ['kursʃtant], *m.* (—es, *no pl.*) rate of exchange.
Kursus ['kurzus], *m.* (—, *pl.* **Kurse**) course (of lectures).
Kurszettel ['kursʃtsetəl], *m.* (—s, *pl.* —) quotation-list.
Kurve ['kurvə], *f.* (—, *pl.* —n) curve.
kurz [kurts], *adj.* short, brief, concise; curt, abrupt.
kurzangebunden [kurts'angəbundən], *adj.* terse, abrupt, curt.
kurzatmig ['kurtsa:tmɪç], *adj.* short-winded, short of breath.
Kürze ['kyrtsə], *f.* (—, *no pl.*) shortness, brevity.
kürzen ['kyrtsən], *v.a.* shorten, abbreviate, condense; (*Maths.*) reduce.
kürzlich ['kyrtslɪç], *adv.* lately, recently, the other day.
Kurzschluß ['kurtsʃlus], *m.* (—sses, *pl.* ¨sse) short circuit.
Kurzschrift ['kurtsʃrɪft], *f.* (—, *no pl.*) shorthand.
kurzsichtig ['kurtszɪçtɪç], *adj.* short-sighted.
kurzum [kurts'um], *adv.* in short.
Kürzung ['kyrtsuŋ], *f.* (—, *pl.* —en) abbreviation, abridgment.
Kurzwaren ['kurtsva:rən], *f. pl.* haberdashery.
kurzweg [kurts've:k], *adv.* simply, off-hand, briefly.
Kurzweil ['kurtsvaɪl], *f.* (—, *no pl.*) pastime.
kurzweilig ['kurtsvaɪlɪç], *adj.* amusing, diverting, entertaining.
kusch! [kuʃ], *excl.* (*to dogs*) lie down!
kuschen ['kuʃən], *v.n., v.r.* crouch, lie down.
Kuß [kus], *m.* (—sses, *pl.* ¨sse) kiss.
küssen ['kysən], *v.a., v.n., v.r.* kiss.
Küste ['kystə], *f.* (—, *pl.* —n) coast, shore.

Küstenstadt ['kystənʃtat], *f.* (—, *pl.* ⸚e) seaside town.
Küster ['kystər], *m.* (—s, *pl.* —) sacristan, sexton, verger.
Kustos ['kustɔs], *m.* (—, *pl.* —oden) custodian; director of museum.
Kutschbock ['kutʃbɔk], *m.* (—s, *pl.* ⸚e) box(-seat).
Kutsche ['kutʃə], *f.* (—, *pl.* —n) coach, carriage.
kutschieren [kut'ʃiːrən], *v.n.* drive a coach.
Kutte ['kutə], *f.* (—, *pl.* —n) cowl.
Kutter ['kutər], *m.* (—s, *pl.* —) (*Naut.*) cutter.
Kuvert [ku've:r], *n.* (—s, *pl.* —s) envelope; (*dinner*) place laid.
kuvertieren [kuver'tiːrən], *v.a.* envelop, wrap.
Kux [kuks], *m.* (—es, *pl.* —e) share in a mining concern.
Kybernetik [kyːbɛr'neːtɪk], *f.* (—, *no pl.*) cybernetics.

L

L [ɛl], *n.* (—, *pl.* —) the letter L.
Lab [laːp], *n.* (—es, *pl.* —e) rennet.
labbern ['labərn], *v.a.*, *v.n.* dribble, slobber; blab.
Labe ['laːbə], *f.* (—, *no pl.*) (*Poet.*) refreshment; comfort.
laben ['laːbən], *v.a.* refresh, restore, revive.
labil [la'biːl], *adj.* unstable.
Laborant [labo'rant], *m.* (—en, *pl.* —en) laboratory assistant.
Laboratorium [labora'toːrjum], *n.* (—s, *pl.* —rien) laboratory.
laborieren [labo'riːrən], *v.n.* experiment; suffer (from).
Labsal ['laːpzaːl], *n.* (—s, *pl.* —e) restorative, refreshment.
Labung ['laːbuŋ], *f.* (—, *pl.* —en) refreshment, comfort.
Lache ['laxə], *f.* (—, *pl.* —n) pool, puddle.
Lächeln ['lɛçəln], *n.* (—s, *no pl.*) smile; *albernes* —, smirk; *höhnisches* —, sneer.
lächeln ['lɛçəln], *v.n.* smile.
Lachen ['laxən], *n.* (—s, *no pl.*) laugh, laughter.
lachen ['laxən], *v.n.* laugh.
lächerlich ['lɛçərlɪç], *adj.* laughable, ridiculous; preposterous; ludicrous; *sich* — *machen*, make a fool of o.s.; *etwas* — *machen*, ridicule s.th.
Lachgas ['laxgaːs], *n.* (—es, *no pl.*) nitrous oxide, laughing-gas.
lachhaft ['laxhaft], *adj.* laughable, ridiculous.

Lachkrampf ['laxkrampf], *m.* (—es, *pl.* ⸚e) hysterical laughter, a fit of laughter.
Lachs [laks], *m.* (—es, *pl.* —e) salmon.
Lachsalve ['laxzalvə], *f.* (—, *pl.* —n) peal of laughter.
Lack [lak], *m.* (—s, *pl.* —e) lac, lacquer, varnish.
lackieren [la'kiːrən], *v.a.* lacquer, varnish.
Lackmus ['lakmus], *n.* (—, *no pl.*) litmus.
Lackschuh ['lakʃuː], *m.* (—s, *pl.* —e) patent-leather shoe.
Lackwaren ['lakvaːrən], *f. pl.* japanned goods.
Lade ['laːdə], *f.* (—, *pl.* —n) box, chest, case, drawer.
Ladebaum ['laːdəbaum], *m.* derrick.
Ladefähigkeit ['laːdəfɛːɪçkait], *f.* (—, *pl.* —en), carrying capacity, loading capacity; tonnage.
Ladegeld ['laːdəgɛlt], *n.* (—es, *pl.* —er) loading charges.
Laden ['laːdən], *m.* (—s, *pl.* ⸚) (*window*) shutter; shop, store.
laden ['laːdən], *v.a. irr.* load; (*Elec.*) charge; (*Law*) summon, (*fig.*) incur.
Ladenhüter ['laːdənhyːtər], *m.* (—s, *pl.* —) unsaleable article.
Ladenpreis ['laːdənprais], *m.* (—es, *pl.* —e) retail-price.
Ladentisch ['laːdəntɪʃ], *m.* (—es, *pl.* —e) counter.
Ladeschein ['laːdəʃain], *m.* (—s, *pl.* —e) bill of lading.
Ladestock ['laːdəʃtɔk], *m.* (—es, *pl.* ⸚e) ramrod.
Ladung ['laːduŋ], *f.* (—, *pl.* —en) loading, lading, freight; shipment, cargo; (*gun*) charge; (*Law*) summons.
Laffe ['lafə], *m.* (—n, *pl.* —n) fop.
Lage ['laːgə], *f.* (—, *pl.* —n) site, position, situation; state, condition; stratum, layer.
Lager ['laːgər], *n.* (—s, *pl.* —) couch, bed, divan; (*Geol.*) seam, vein; (*Tech.*) bearing; (*Comm.*) warehouse, store; camp.
Lageraufnahme ['laːgəraufnaːmə], *f.* (—, *pl.* —n) stock-taking, inventory.
Lager(bier) ['laːgər(biːr)], *n.* (—s, *pl.* —e) lager.
Lagergeld ['laːgərgɛlt], *n.* (—es, *pl.* —er) storage charge.
Lagerist [laːgə'rɪst], *m.* (—en, *pl.* —en) warehouse-clerk.
lagern ['laːgərn], *v.a.* store, warehouse.
Lagerstätte ['laːgərʃtɛtə], *f.* (—, *pl.*—n) couch, resting-place; camp site.
Lagerung ['laːgəruŋ], *f.* (—, *pl.* —en) encampment; storage; stratification.
Lagune [la'guːnə], *f.* (—, *pl.* —n) lagoon.
lahm [laːm], *adj.* lame, paralysed, crippled.
lahmen ['laːmən], *v.n.* be lame, limp.
lähmen ['lɛːmən], *v.a.* paralyse.
lahmlegen ['laːmleːgən], *v.a.* paralyse.

135

Lähmung

Lähmung ['lɛːmuŋ], *f.* (—, *pl.* —en) paralysis.
Laib [laɪp], *m.* (—es, *pl.* —e) (*bread*) loaf.
Laich [laɪç], *m.* (—es, *pl.* —e) spawn.
laichen ['laɪçən], *v.n.* spawn.
Laie ['laɪə], *m.* (—n, *pl.* —n) layman, (*pl.*) laity.
Lakai [la'kaɪ], *m.* (—en, *pl.* —en) lackey, flunkey, footman.
Lake ['laːkə], *f.* (—, *pl.* —n) brine, pickle.
Laken ['laːkən], *n.* (—s, *pl.* —) (*bed*) sheet.
lakonisch [la'koːnɪʃ], *adj.* laconic.
Lakritze [la'krɪtsə], *f.* (—, *pl.* —n) liquorice.
lallen ['lalən], *v.a.*, *v.n.* stammer; babble.
Lama (1) ['laːmaː], *m.* (—s, *pl.* —s) (*animal*) llama.
Lama (2) ['laːmaː], *m.* (—s, *pl.* —s) (*priest*) lama.
lamentieren [lamɛn'tiːrən], *v.n.* lament, wail.
Lamm [lam], *n.* (—es, *pl.* ⁝er) (*Zool.*) lamb.
Lämmchen ['lɛmçən], *n.* (—s, *pl.* —) (*Zool.*) lambkin.
Lämmergeier ['lɛmərgaɪər], *m.* (—s, *pl.* —) (*Orn.*) great bearded vulture.
Lampe ['lampə], *f.* (—, *pl.* —n) lamp.
Lampenfieber ['lampənfiːbər], *n.* (—s, *no pl.*) stage-fright.
Lampenputzer ['lampənputsər], *m.* (—s, *pl.* —) lamplighter.
Lampenschirm ['lampənʃɪrm], *m.* (—s, *pl.* —e) lampshade.
Lampion [lam'pjɔ], *m. & n.* (—s, *pl.* —s) Chinese lantern.
lancieren [lã'siːrən], *v.a.* thrust; launch.
Land [lant], *n.* (—es, *pl.* —e (*Poet.*) and ⁝er) land, country; state; ground, soil; *das Gelobte* —, the Promised Land; *an* — *gehen*, go ashore; *aufs* — *gehen*, go into the country.
Landadel ['lantaːdəl], *m.* (—s, *no pl.*) landed gentry.
Landarbeiter ['lantarbaɪtər], *m.* (—s, *pl.* —) farm-worker.
Landauer ['landauər], *m.* (—s, *pl.* —) landau.
Landebahn ['landəbaːn], *f.* (—, *pl.* —en) (*Aviat.*) runway.
landen ['landən], *v.n.* (*aux. sein*) land, disembark; (*aircraft*) land, touch down.
Landenge ['lantɛŋə], *f.* (—, *pl.* —n) isthmus.
Ländereien ['lɛndəraɪən], *f. pl.* landed property, estate.
Landeserzeugnis ['landəsɛrtsɔyknɪs], *n.* (—sses, *pl.* —sse) home produce.
Landesfürst ['landəsfyrst], *m.* (—en, *pl.* —en) sovereign.
Landesherr ['landəshɛr], *m.* (—n, *pl.* —en) (reigning) prince; sovereign.
Landeshoheit ['landəshohaɪt], *f.* (—, *no pl.*) sovereignty.

Landeskirche ['landəskɪrçə], *f.* (—, *pl.* —n) established church; national church.
Landesschuld ['landəsʃult], *f.* (—, *no pl.*) national debt.
Landessprache ['landəsʃpraːxə], *f.* (—, *pl.* —n) vernacular.
Landestracht ['landəstraxt], *f.* (—, *pl.* —en) national costume.
landesüblich ['landəsyːplɪç], *adj.* conventional, usual, customary.
Landesverweisung ['landəsfɛrvaɪzuŋ], *f.* (—, *pl.* —en) exile, banishment.
landflüchtig ['lantflyçtɪç], *adj.* fugitive.
Landfrieden ['lantfriːdən], *m.* (—s, *no pl.*) King's (*or* Queen's) peace; (*medieval*) public peace.
Landgericht ['lantgərɪçt], *n.* (—es, *pl.* —e) district court; county court.
Landgraf ['lantgraːf], *m.* (—en, *pl.* —en) landgrave, count.
Landhaus ['lanthaus], *n.* (—es, *pl.* ⁝er) country house.
Landjunker ['lantjuŋkər], *m.* (—s, *pl.* —) country squire.
Landkarte ['lantkartə], *f.* (—, *pl.* —n) map.
landläufig ['lantlɔyfɪç], *adj.* customary, conventional.
ländlich ['lɛntlɪç], *adj.* rural, rustic.
Landmann ['lantman], *m.* (—es, *pl.* **Landleute**) rustic, peasant.
Landmesser ['lantmɛsər], *m.* (—s, *pl.* —) surveyor.
Landpartie ['lantparti:], *f.* (—, *pl.* —n) country excursion, picnic.
Landplage ['lantplaːgə], *f.* (—, *pl.* —n) scourge, calamity; *eine richtige* —, a public nuisance.
Landrat ['lantraːt], *m.* (—s, *pl.* ⁝e) district president *or* magistrate.
Landratte ['lantratə], *f.* (—, *pl.* —n) landlubber.
Landrecht ['lantreçt], *n.* (—es, *no pl.*) common law.
Landregen ['lantreːgən], *m.* (—s, *no pl.*) steady downpour; persistent rain.
Landschaft ['lantʃaft], *f.* (—, *pl.* —en) landscape.
landschaftlich ['lantʃaftlɪç], *adj.* scenic.
Landsknecht ['lantskneçt], *m.* (—es, *pl.* —e) mercenary; hired soldier.
Landsmann ['lantsman], *m.* (—es, *pl.* **Landsleute**) fellow-countryman, compatriot.
Landspitze ['lantʃpɪtsə], *f.* (—, *pl.* —n) cape, headland, promontory.
Landstraße ['lantʃtraːsə], *f.* (—, *pl.* —n) open road, main road, highway.
Landstreicher ['lantʃtraɪçər], *m.* (—s, *pl.* —) vagabond, tramp, (*Am.*) hobo.
Landstrich ['lantʃtrɪç], *m.* (—es, *pl.* —e) tract of land.
Landsturm ['lantʃturm], *m.* (—s, *no pl.*) (*Milit.*) militia; Home Guard.
Landtag ['lanttaːk], *m.* (—s, *pl.* —e) (*Parl.*) diet.
Landung ['landuŋ], *f.* (—, *pl.* —en) landing.
Landvermesser *see* **Landmesser.**

Landvogt ['lantfo:kt], *m.* (—es, *pl.* ˙⁻e) (provincial) governor.
Landweg ['lantve:k], *m.* (—s, *pl.* —e) overland route.
Landwehr ['lantve:r], *f.* (—, *pl.* —en) militia.
Landwirt ['lantvɪrt], *m.* (—s, *pl.* —e) farmer, husbandman.
Landwirtschaft ['lantvɪrtʃaft], *f.* (—, *no pl.*) agriculture.
Landzunge ['lanttsuŋə], *f.* (—, *pl.* —n) spit of land.
lang [laŋ], *adj.* long, tall. — *adv.*, *prep.* (*prec. by Acc.*) for, during, long.
langatmig ['laŋa:tmɪç], *adj.* long-winded.
lange ['laŋə], *adv.* a long time; *wie* —? how long? *so* — *wie*, as long as.
Länge ['lɛŋə], *f.* (—, *pl.* —n) length; (*Geog.*) longitude.
langen ['laŋən], *v.a.* reach, hand, give s.o. s.th. — *v.n.* suffice, be enough.
Längengrad ['lɛŋəngra:t], *m.* (—s, *pl.* —e) degree of longitude.
Längenkreis ['lɛŋənkraɪs], *m.* (—es, *pl.* —e) meridian.
Längenmaß ['lɛŋənma:s], *n.* (—es, *pl.* —e) linear measure.
Langeweile ['laŋəvaɪlə], *f.* (—, *no pl.*) boredom, ennui.
Langfinger ['laŋfɪŋər], *m.* (—s, *pl.* —) pickpocket.
langjährig ['laŋjɛ:rɪç], *adj.* of long standing.
Langlebigkeit ['laŋle:bɪçkaɪt], *f.* (—, *no pl.*) longevity.
länglich ['lɛŋlɪç], *adj.* oblong.
Langmut ['laŋmu:t], *f.* (—, *no pl.*) forbearance, patience.
längs [lɛŋs], *prep.* (*Genit.*, *Dat.*) along.
langsam ['laŋza:m], *adj.* slow; deliberate.
längst [lɛŋst], *adv.* long ago, long since.
längstens ['lɛŋstəns], *adv.* at the longest; at the latest.
Languste [laŋ'gustə], *f.* (—, *pl.* —n) (*Zool.*) spiny lobster.
langweilen ['laŋvaɪlən],*v.a.*(*insep.*) bore, tire. — *v.r. sich* —, feel bored, be bored.
langwierig ['laŋvi:rɪç], *adj.* lengthy, protracted, wearisome.
Lanze ['lantsə], *f.* (—, *pl.* —n) lance, spear; *eine* — *brechen*, take up the cudgels, stand up for (s.th. *or* s.o.).
Lanzenstechen ['lantsənʃteçən], *n.* (—s, *no pl.*) tournament.
Lanzette [lan'tsɛtə], *f.* (—, *pl.* —n) lancet.
Lanzknecht ['lantsknɛçt], *m.* (—s, *pl.* —e) *see* **Landsknecht**.
Laos ['la:ɔs], *n.* Laos.
Lappalie [la'pa:ljə], *f.* (—, *pl.* —n) trifle.
Lappen ['lapən], *m.* (—s, *pl.* —) rag, duster, patch; (*ear*) lobe.
Läpperschulden ['lɛpərʃuldən], *f. pl.* petty debts.
läppisch ['lɛpɪʃ], *adj.* silly, foolish, trifling.
Lappland ['lapland], *n.* Lapland.

Lärche ['lɛrçə], *f.* (—, *pl.* —n) (*Bot.*) larch.
Lärm [lɛrm], *m.* (—s, *no pl.*) noise, din.
lärmen ['lɛrmən], *v.n.* make a noise, brawl.
Larve ['larfə], *f.* (—, *pl.* —n) mask; (*Ent.*) grub, larva.
lasch [laʃ], *adj.* limp; insipid.
Lasche ['laʃə], *f.* (—, *pl.* —n) flap; (*shoe*) gusset, strip.
lassen ['lasən], *v.a.*, *v.n. irr.* let, allow, suffer, permit; leave; make, cause; order, command; desist.
läßlich ['lɛslɪç], *adj.* (*Eccl.*) venial (*sin*).
lässig ['lɛsɪç], *adj.* indolent, sluggish, inactive.
Lässigkeit ['lɛsɪçkaɪt], *f.* (—, *no pl.*) lassitude, inaction, indolence; negligence.
Last [last], *f.* (—, *pl.* —en) load, burden, weight, charge.
lasten ['lastən], *v.n.* be heavy; weigh (on).
lastenfrei ['lastənfraɪ], *adj.* unencumbered.
Laster ['lastər], *n.* (—s, *pl.* —) vice.
Lästerer ['lɛstərər], *m.* (—s, *pl.* —) slanderer, calumniator; blasphemer.
lasterhaft ['lastərhaft], *adj.* vicious, wicked; corrupt.
Lasterhöhle ['lastərhø:lə], *f.* (—, *pl.* —n) den of vice.
lästerlich ['lɛstərlɪç], *adj.* blasphemous.
lästern ['lɛstərn], *v.a.* slander, defame; blaspheme.
lästig ['lɛstɪç], *adj.* tiresome, troublesome.
Lasttier ['lasttiːr], *n.* (—es, *pl.* —e) beast of burden.
Lastwagen ['lastva:gən], *m.* (—s, *pl.* —) lorry, (*Am.*) truck.
Lasur [la'zu:r], *m.* (—s, *pl.* —e) lapis-lazuli; ultramarine.
Latein [la'taɪn], *n.* (—s, *no pl.*) Latin.
lateinisch [la'taɪnɪʃ], *adj.* Latin.
Laterne [la'tɛrnə], *f.* (—, *pl.* —n) lantern; (*street*) lamp.
latschen ['la:tʃən], *v.n.* shuffle along.
Latte ['latə], *f.* (—, *pl.* —n) lath, batten; *eine lange* —, lanky person.
Lattich ['latɪç], *m.* (—s, *pl.* —e) lettuce.
Latz [lats], *m.* (—es, *pl.* ˙⁻e) flap, bib; pinafore.
lau [lau], *adj.* tepid, lukewarm, insipid; (*fig.*) half-hearted.
Laub [laup], *n.* (—es, *no pl.*) foliage, leaves.
Laube ['laubə], *f.* (—, *pl.* —n) arbour, summer-house.
Laubengang ['laubəngaŋ], *m.* (—es, *pl.* ˙⁻e) arcade, covered walk.
Laubfrosch ['laupfrɔʃ], *m.* (—es, *pl.* ˙⁻e) (*Zool.*) tree-frog.
Laubsäge ['laupzɛ:gə], *f.* (—, *pl.* —n) fret-saw.
Lauch [laux], *m.* (—es, *no pl.*) (*Bot.*) leek.
Lauer ['lauər], *f.* (—, *no pl.*) ambush, hiding-place; *auf der* — *sein*, lie in wait.

lauern

lauern ['lauərn], *v.n.* lurk, lie in wait (for), watch (for).

Lauf [lauf], *m.* (**—es**, *pl.* ⁻e) course, run; running; operation; (*river*) current; (*gun*) barrel; (*fig.*) rein.

Laufbahn ['laufbaːn], *f.* (**—**, *pl.* **—en**) career, *die medizinische — einschlagen*, enter upon a medical career.

Laufband ['laufbant], *n.* (**—s**, *pl.* ⁻er) (*baby*) rein, leading-string; (*Tech.*) conveyor-belt.

Laufbrücke ['laufbrykə], *f.* (**—**, *pl.* **—n**) gangway.

Laufbursche ['laufburʃə], *m.* (**—n**, *pl.* **—n**) errand-boy.

laufen ['laufən], *v.n. irr.* (*aux.* sein) run; walk; (*wheel*) turn; flow, trickle down.

laufend ['laufənt], *adj.* current.

Läufer ['lɔyfər], *m.* (**—s**, *pl.* **—**) runner; (*carpet*) rug; (*Chess*) bishop; (*Footb.*) half-back.

Lauffeuer ['laufɔyər], *n.* (**—s**, *no pl.*) wildfire.

Laufgraben ['laufgraːbən], *m.* (**—s**, *pl.* ⁻) trench.

läufig ['lɔyfɪç], *adj.* (*animals*) ruttish.

Laufpaß ['laufpas], *m.* (**—sses**, *no pl.*) *den — geben*, give (s.o.) the sack.

Laufschritt ['laufʃrɪt], *m.* (**—es**, *pl.* **—e**) march; *im —*, at the double.

Laufzeit ['lauftsaɪt], *f.* (**—**, *pl.* **—en**) running-time; currency; (*animals*) rutting time.

Lauge ['laugə], *f.* (**—**, *pl.* **—en**) (*Chem.*) lye, alkali.

Lauheit ['lauhaɪt], *f.* (**—**, *no pl.*) tepidity, lukewarmness; (*fig.*) half-heartedness.

Laune ['launə], *f.* (**—**, *pl.* **—n**) humour, temper, mood, whim.

launenhaft ['launənhaft], *adj.* moody.

launig ['launɪç], *adj.* humorous.

launisch ['launɪʃ], *adj.* moody, fitful, bad-tempered.

Laus [laus], *f.* (**—**, *pl.* ⁻e) (*Zool.*) louse.

Lausbub ['lausbuːp], *m.* (**—en**, *pl.* **—en**) young scamp, rascal.

lauschen ['lauʃən], *v.n.* listen, eavesdrop.

Lausejunge ['lauzəjuŋə], *m.* (**—n**, *pl.* **—n**) rascal, lout.

lausig ['lauzɪç], *adj.* (*vulg.*) sordid, lousy.

laut [laut], *adj.* loud, noisy, audible, clamorous. *— prep.* (*Genit.*) as per, according to, in virtue of.

Laut [laut], *m.* (**—es**, *pl.* **—e**) sound.

lautbar ['lautbaːr], *adj. — machen*, make known.

Laute ['lautə], *f.* (**—**, *pl.* **—n**) (*Mus.*) lute.

lauten ['lautən], *v.n.* purport, run, read.

läuten ['lɔytən], *v.a., v.n.* ring; toll; *es läutet*, the bell is ringing.

lauter ['lautər], *adj.* clear, pure; (*fig.*) single-minded; genuine; nothing but. *— adv.* merely.

Lauterkeit ['lautərkaɪt], *f.* (**—**, *no pl.*) clearness, purity; (*fig.*) single-mindedness, integrity.

läutern ['lɔytərn], *v.a.* clear, purify; refine.

Läuterung ['lɔytəruŋ], *f.* (**—**, *pl.* **—en**) clearing, purification; refinement.

lautieren [lau'tiːrən], *v.a.* read phonetically.

Lautlehre ['lautleːrə], *f.* (**—**, *no pl.*) phonetics.

lautlich ['lautlɪç], *adj.* phonetic.

lautlos ['lautloːs], *adj.* mute, silent; noiseless.

Lautmalerei ['lautmaːləraɪ], *f.* (**—**, *no pl.*) onomatopoeia.

Lautsprecher ['lautʃprɛçər], *m.* (**—s**, *pl.* **—**) loudspeaker.

Lautverschiebung ['lautfɛrʃiːbuŋ], *f.* (**—**, *pl.* **—en**) sound shift.

lauwarm ['lauvarm], *adj.* lukewarm, tepid; (*fig.*) half-hearted.

Lava ['laːva], *f.* (**—**, *no pl.*) lava.

Lavendel [la'vɛndəl], *m.* (**—s**, *no pl.*) (*Bot.*) lavender.

lavieren [la'viːrən], *v.n.* tack; (*fig.*) wangle.

Lawine [la'viːnə], *f.* (**—**, *pl.* **—n**) avalanche.

lax [laks], *adj.* lax, loose.

Laxheit ['lakshaɪt], *f.* (**—**, *pl.* **—en**) laxity.

Laxiermittel [lak'siːrmɪtəl], *n.* (**—s**, *pl.* **—**) laxative, aperient.

Lazarett [latsa'rɛt], *n.* (**—s**, *pl.* **—e**) infirmary, military hospital.

Lebemann ['leːbəman], *m.* (**—es**, *pl.* ⁻er) man about town.

Leben ['leːbən], *n.* (**—s**, *pl.* **—**) life; (*fig.*) existence; activity; animation, bustle, stir.

leben ['leːbən], *v.n.* live, be alive.

lebend ['leːbənt], *adj.* alive, living; (*language*) modern.

lebendig [le'bɛndɪç], *adj.* living, alive, quick.

Lebensanschauung ['leːbənsanʃauuŋ], *f.* (**—**, *pl.* **—en**) conception of life, philosophy of life.

Lebensart ['leːbənsaːrt], *f.* (**—**, *no pl.*) way of living; (*fig.*) behaviour; *gute —*, good manners.

lebensfähig ['leːbənsfɛːɪç], *adj.* capable of living, viable.

lebensgefährlich ['leːbənsgəfɛːrlɪç], *adj.* perilous, extremely dangerous.

Lebensgeister ['leːbənsgaɪstər], *m. pl.* spirits.

lebensgroß ['leːbənsgroːs], *adj.* life-size.

lebenslänglich ['leːbənslɛnlɪç], *adj.* lifelong, for life; *—e Rente*, life annuity.

Lebenslauf ['leːbənslauf], *m.* (**—es**, *pl.* ⁻e) curriculum vitae.

Lebensmittel ['leːbənsmɪtəl], *n. pl.* food, provisions, victuals.

lebensmüde ['leːbənsmyːdə], *adj.* weary of life.

Lebensunterhalt ['leːbənsuntərhalt], *m.* (**—s**, *no pl.*) livelihood.

Lebenswandel ['leːbənsvandəl], *m.* (**—s**, *no pl.*) conduct, mode of life.

Lebensweise ['le:bənsvaɪzə], *f.* (—, *no pl.*) habits, way of life.
Leber ['le:bər], *f.* (—, *pl.* —**n**) liver; *frisch von der — weg*, frankly, without mincing matters.
Leberblümchen ['le:bərbly:mçən], *n.* (—**s**, *pl.* —) (*Bot.*) liverwort.
Leberfleck ['le:bərflɛk], *m.* (—**s**, *pl.* —**e**) mole.
Lebertran ['le:bərtra:n], *m.* (—**s**, *no pl.*) cod-liver oil.
Leberwurst ['le:bərvurst], *f.* (—, *pl.* ⸚e) liver sausage.
Lebewesen ['le:bəve:zən], *n.* (—**s**, *pl.* —) living creature.
Lebewohl ['le:bəvo:l], *n.*, *excl.* farewell, good-bye; — *sagen*, bid farewell.
lebhaft ['le:phaft], *adj.* lively, vivacious, brisk, animated.
Lebkuchen ['le:pku:xən], *m.* (—**s**, *pl.* —) gingerbread.
Lebzeiten ['le:ptsaɪtən], *f. pl. zu — von* (*Genit.*), in the lifetime of.
lechzen ['lɛçtsən], *v.n.* be parched with thirst; *nach etwas* —, (*fig.*) long for s.th., pine for s.th.
Leck [lɛk], *n.* (—**s**, *pl.* —**e**) leak; *ein — bekommen*, spring a leak.
leck [lɛk], *adj.* leaky.
lecken ['lɛkən], *v.a.* lick, lap.
lecker ['lɛkər], *adj.* delicate, delicious, dainty.
Leckerbissen ['lɛkərbɪsən], *m.* (—**s**, *pl.* —) delicacy; dainty, tit-bit.
Leckerei [lɛkə'raɪ], *f.* (—, *pl.* —**en**) delicacy.
Leder ['le:dər], *n.* (—**s**, *no pl.*) leather.
ledern ['le:dərn], *adj.* (of) leather, leathery; (*fig.*) dull, boring.
ledig ['le:dɪç], *adj.* unmarried, single; (*fig.*) rid of, free from.
lediglich ['le:dɪklɪç], *adv.* merely, only, solely.
leer [le:r], *adj.* empty, void; blank; (*fig.*) hollow, futile, empty, vain, inane.
Leere ['le:rə], *f.* (—, *no pl.*) emptiness, void, vacuum.
leeren ['le:rən], *v.a.* empty, evacuate.
Leerlauf ['le:rlauf], *m.* (—**s**, *no pl.*) (*Motor.*) idling; (*gear*) neutral.
legalisieren [legali'zi:rən], *v.a.* legalise, authenticate.
Legat (1) [le'ga:t], *m.* (—**en**, *pl.* —**en**) legate.
Legat (2) [le'ga:t], *n.* (—**s**, *pl.* —**e**) legacy, bequest.
Legationsrat [lega'tsjo:nsra:t], *m.* (—**s**, *pl.* ⸚**e**) counsellor in a legation.
legen ['le:gən], *v.a.* lay, put, place. — *v.r. sich* —, lie down; cease, subside.
Legende [le'gɛndə], *f.* (—, *pl.* —**n**) legend.
Legierung [lə'gi:ruŋ], *f.* (—, *pl.* —**en**) alloy.
Legion [le'gjo:n], *f.* (—, *pl.* —**en**) legion.
Legionär [le:gjo'nɛ:r], *m.* (—**s**, *pl.* —**e**) legionary.
legitim [legi'ti:m], *adj.* legitimate.
Legitimation [legitima'tsjo:n], *f.* (—, *pl.* —**en**) proof of identity.
legitimieren [legiti'mi:rən], *v.a.* legitimise. — *v.r. sich* —, prove o.'s identity.
Lehen ['le:ən], *n.* (—**s**, *pl.* —) fief; *zu — geben*, invest with, enfeoff; *zu — tragen*, hold in fee.
Lehensdienst *see* **Lehnsdienst**.
Lehenseid *see* **Lehnseid**.
Lehensmann *see* **Lehnsmann**.
Lehm [le:m], *m.* (—**s**, *no pl.*) loam, clay, mud.
lehmig ['le:mɪç], *adj.* clayey, loamy.
Lehne ['le:nə], *f.* (—, *pl.* —**n**) support, prop; (*chair*) back, arm-rest.
lehnen ['le:nən], *v.a.*, *v.n.* lean. — *v.r. sich — an*, lean against.
Lehnsdienst ['le:nsdi:nst], *m.* (—**es**, *pl.* —**e**) feudal service.
Lehnseid ['le:nsaɪt], *m.* (—**es**, *pl.* —**e**) oath of allegiance.
Lehnsmann ['le:nsman], *m.* (—**es**, *pl.* ⸚**er**) feudal tenant, vassal.
Lehnstuhl ['le:nʃtu:l], *m.* (—**s**, *pl.* ⸚**e**) armchair, easy chair.
Lehramt ['le:ramt], *n.* (—**es**, *pl.* ⸚**er**) professorship; teaching post *or* profession.
Lehrbrief ['le:rbri:f], *m.* (—**es**, *pl.* —**e**) apprentice's indentures; certificate of apprenticeship.
Lehrbuch ['le:rbu:x], *n.* (—**es**, *pl.* ⸚**er**) textbook, manual.
Lehre ['le:rə], *f.* (—, *pl.* —**n**) teaching, advice, rule, doctrine, dogma, moral; (*craft*) apprenticeship.
lehren ['le:rən], *v.a.* teach, inform, instruct; profess.
Lehrer ['le:rər], *m.* (—**s**, *pl.* —) teacher, instructor, schoolmaster.
Lehrgang ['le:rgaŋ], *m.* (—**es**, *pl.* ⸚**e**) course (of instruction).
Lehrgegenstand ['le:rge:gənʃtant], *m.* (—**es**, *pl.* ⸚**e**) subject of instruction; branch of study.
Lehrgeld ['le:rgɛlt], *n.* (—**es**, *pl.* —**er**) premium for apprenticeship; — *zahlen*, (*fig.*) pay for o.'s experience.
Lehrkörper ['le:rkø:rpər], *m.* (—**s**, *no pl.*) teaching staff; (*Univ.*) faculty.
Lehrling ['le:rlɪŋ], *m.* (—**s**, *pl.* —**e**) apprentice.
Lehrmädchen ['le:rmɛ:tçən], *n.* (—**s**, *pl.* —) girl apprentice.
Lehrmeister ['le:rmaɪstər], *m.* (—**s**, *pl.* —) teacher, instructor, master.
Lehrmittel ['le:rmɪtəl], *n.* (—**s**, *pl.* —) teaching appliance *or* aid.
lehrreich ['le:rraɪç], *adj.* instructive.
Lehrsatz ['le:rzats], *m.* (—**es**, *pl.* ⸚**e**) tenet, dogma, rule; (*Maths.*) theorem.
Lehrstuhl ['le:rʃtu:l], *m.* (—**s**, *pl.* ⸚**e**) (*Univ.*) chair; professorship.
Lehrzeit ['le:rtsaɪt], *f.* (—, *pl.* —**en**) apprenticeship.
Leib [laɪp], *m.* (—**es**, *pl.* —**er**) body; abdomen; womb.
Leibarzt ['laɪpa:rtst], *m.* (—**es**, *pl.* ⸚**e**) court surgeon.

Leibbinde

Leibbinde ['laɪpbɪndə], *f.* (—, *pl.* —n) abdominal belt.

Leibchen ['laɪpçən], *n.* (—s, *pl.* —) bodice, corset; vest.

leibeigen [laɪp'aɪɡən], *adj.* in bondage, in thraldom, in serfdom.

Leibeserbe ['laɪbəsɛrbə], *m.* (—n, *pl.* —n) heir, descendant, offspring; (*pl.*) issue.

Leibesfrucht ['laɪbəsfruxt], *f.* (—, *pl.* ⁓e) embryo, foetus.

Leibeskraft ['laɪbəskraft], *f.* (—, *pl.* ⁓e) bodily strength; *aus —en,* with might and main.

Leibesübung ['laɪbəsy:buŋ], *f.* (—, *pl.* —en) physical exercise; (*pl.*) gymnastic exercises.

Leibgericht ['laɪpɡərɪçt], *n.* (—s, *pl.* —e) favourite dish.

leibhaftig [laɪp'haftɪç], *adj.* real, incarnate, in person.

leiblich ['laɪplɪç], *adj.* bodily, corporeal.

Leibrente ['laɪprɛntə], *f.* (—, *pl.* —n) life-annuity.

Leibschmerzen ['laɪpʃmɛrtsən], *m. pl.* stomach-ache.

Leibspeise ['laɪpʃpaɪzə], *f.* (—, *pl.* —n) favourite dish.

Leibwache ['laɪpvaxə], *f.* (—, *no pl.*) body-guard.

Leibwäsche ['laɪpvɛʃə], *f.* (—, *no pl.*) underwear.

Leiche ['laɪçə], *f.* (—, *pl.* —n) (dead) body, corpse; (*dial.*) funeral.

Leichenbegängnis ['laɪçənbəɡɛŋnɪs], *n.* (—ses, *pl.* —se) funeral, burial, interment.

Leichenbeschauer ['laɪçənbəʃauər], *m.* (—s, *pl.* —) coroner.

Leichenbestatter ['laɪçənbəʃtater], *m.* (—s, *pl.* —) undertaker; (*Am.*) mortician.

leichenhaft ['laɪçənhaft], *adj.* corpse-like, cadaverous.

Leichenschau ['laɪçənʃau], *f.* (—, *no pl.*) post mortem (examination), (coroner's) inquest.

Leichentuch ['laɪçəntu:x], *n.* (—es, *pl.* ⁓er) shroud, pall.

Leichenverbrennung ['laɪçənfɛrbrɛnuŋ], *f.* (—, *pl.* —en) cremation.

Leichenwagen ['laɪçənva:ɡən], *m.* (—s, *pl.* —) hearse.

Leichenzug ['laɪçəntsu:k], *m.* (—es, *pl.* ⁓e) funeral procession.

Leichnam ['laɪçna:m], *m.* (—s, *pl.* —e) (dead) body, corpse.

leicht [laɪçt], *adj.* light; slight; weak; easy.

leichtfertig ['laɪçtfɛrtɪç], *adj.* frivolous, irresponsible.

leichtgläubig ['laɪçtɡlɔybɪç], *adj.* credulous, gullible.

leichthin ['laɪçthɪn], *adv.* lightly.

Leichtigkeit ['laɪçtɪçkaɪt], *f.* (—, *no pl.*) ease, facility.

Leichtsinn ['laɪçtzɪn], *m.* (—s, *no pl.*) thoughtlessness, carelessness; frivolity.

Leid [laɪt], *n.* (—es, *no pl.*) sorrow, grief; harm, hurt; *einem etwas zu —e tun,* harm s.o.

leid [laɪt], *adj. es tut mir —,* I am sorry; *du tust mir —,* I am sorry for you.

Leiden ['laɪdən], *n.* (—s, *pl.* —) suffering, misfortune; (*illness*) affliction, complaint; *das — Christi,* the Passion.

leiden ['laɪdən], *v.a.,v.n. irr.* suffer, bear, endure, undergo.

Leidenschaft ['laɪdənʃaft], *f.* (—, *pl.* —en) passion.

leider ['laɪdər], *adv.* unfortunately.

leidig ['laɪdɪç], *adj.* tiresome, unpleasant.

leidlich ['laɪtlɪç], *adj.* tolerable, moderate.

leidtragend ['laɪttra:ɡənt], *adj.* in mourning.

Leidtragende ['laɪttra:ɡəndə], *m.* or *f.* (—n, *pl.* —n) mourner.

Leidwesen ['laɪtve:zən], *n.* (—s, *no pl.*) *zu meinem —,* to my regret.

Leier ['laɪər], *f.* (—, *pl.* —n) lyre.

Leierkasten ['laɪərkastən], *m.* (—s, *pl.* ⁓) barrel organ.

leiern ['laɪərn], *v.n.* drone, drawl on.

leihen ['laɪən], *v.a. irr. einem etwas —,* lend s.o. s.th.; *von einem etwas —,* borrow s.th. from s.o.

Leim [laɪm], *m.* (—s, *no pl.*) glue; *einem auf den — gehen,* be taken in by s.o., fall for s.th.

Leimfarbe ['laɪmfarbə], *f.* (—, *pl.* —en) water-colour, distemper.

Lein [laɪn], *m.* (—s, *pl.* —e) linseed, flax.

Leine ['laɪnə], *f.* (—, *pl.* —n) line, cord.

Leinen ['laɪnən], *n.* (—s, *no pl.*) linen.

Leinöl ['laɪnø:l], *n.* (—s, *no pl.*) linseed oil.

Leintuch ['laɪntu:x], *n.* (—es, *pl.* ⁓er) linen sheet, sheeting.

Leinwand ['laɪnvant], *f.* (—, *no pl.*) linen, sheeting; (*Art*) canvas; (*film*) screen.

leise ['laɪzə], *adj.* low, soft, gentle, faint, slight; delicate.

Leiste ['laɪstə], *f.* (—, *pl.* —n) ledge, border; groin.

Leisten ['laɪstən], *m.* (—s, *pl.* —) (*shoe*) last, form.

leisten ['laɪstən], *v.a.* do, perform; accomplish; *ich kann es mir nicht —,* I cannot afford it.

Leistenbruch ['laɪstənbrux], *m.* (—es, *pl.* ⁓e) hernia, rupture.

Leistung ['laɪstuŋ], *f.* (—, *pl.* —en) performance, accomplishment, achievement.

leistungsfähig ['laɪstuŋksfe:ɪç], *adj.* efficient.

leiten ['laɪtən], *v.a.* lead, guide, manage; preside over.

Leiter (1) ['laɪtər], *m.* (—s, *pl.* —) leader, manager; conductor; head.

Leiter (2) ['laɪtər], *f.* (—, *pl.* —n) ladder.

Leiterwagen ['laɪtərva:ɡən], *m.* (—s, *pl.* —) rack-wagon; (*Austr.*) small hand-cart.

Leitfaden ['laɪtfa:dən], *m.* (—s, *pl.* ∵) (*book*) manual, textbook, guide.

Leitstern ['laɪtʃtɛrn], *m.* (—s, *pl.* —e) pole-star; (*fig.*) lodestar, guiding star.

Leitung ['laɪtuŋ], *f.* (—, *pl.* —en) management, direction; (*Elec.*) lead, connection; line; (water- *or* gas-) main(s); pipeline; *eine lange — haben*, be slow in the uptake.

Leitungsvermögen ['laɪtuŋsfɛrmø:-gən], *n.* (—s, *no pl.*) conductivity.

Leitwerk ['laɪtvɛrk], *n.* (—s, *no pl.*) (*Aviat.*) tail unit.

Lektion [lɛkts'jo:n], *f.* (—, *pl.* —en) lesson; *einem eine — geben*, lecture s.o.

Lektor ['lɛktɔr], *m.* (—s, *pl.* —en) publisher's reader; teacher, lector.

Lektüre [lɛk'ty:rə], *f.* (—, *pl.* —n) reading matter, books.

Lende ['lɛndə], *f.* (—, *pl.* —n) (*Anat.*) loin.

lendenlahm ['lɛndənla:m], *adj.* weak-kneed, lame.

lenkbar ['lɛŋkba:r], *adj.* dirigible, manageable, tractable, governable.

lenken ['lɛŋkən], *v.a.* drive, steer; (*fig.*) direct, rule, manage.

Lenkstange ['lɛŋkʃtaŋə], *f.* (—, *pl.* —n) connecting-rod; (*bicycle*) handle-bar.

Lenz [lɛnts], *m.* (—es, *pl.* —e) (*Poet.*) spring.

Lepra ['le:pra], *f.* (—, *no pl.*) leprosy.

Lerche ['lɛrçə], *f.* (—, *pl.* —n) (*Orn.*) lark, skylark.

lernbegierig ['lɛrnbəgi:rɪç], *adj.* studious, eager to learn.

lernen ['lɛrnən], *v.a.* learn; study; *einen kennen —*, make s.o.'s acquaintance; *auswendig —*, learn by heart.

Lesart ['le:sa:rt], *f.* (—, *pl.* —en) reading, version.

lesbar ['le:sba:r], *adj.* legible; readable.

Lese ['le:zə], *f.* (—, *pl.* —n) gathering (of fruit); vintage.

lesen ['le:zən], *v.a. irr.* gather; glean; read; *die Messe —*, celebrate *or* say mass; *über etwas —*, (*Univ.*) lecture on s.th.

lesenswert ['le:zənsvɛrt], *adj.* worth reading.

Leser ['le:zər], *m.* (—s, *pl.* —) gatherer, gleaner; reader.

leserlich ['le:zərlɪç], *adj.* legible.

Lettland ['lɛtlant], *n.* Latvia.

letzen ['lɛtsən], *v.a.* (*Poet.*) comfort, cheer, refresh.

letzt [lɛtst], *adj.* last, extreme, ultimate, final.

letztens ['lɛtstəns], *adv.* lastly, in the end.

letztere ['lɛtstərə], *adj.* latter.

letzthin ['lɛtsthɪn], *adv.* (*rare*) lately, the other day, recently.

Leu [lɔy], *m.* (—en, *pl.* —en) (*Poet.*) lion.

Leuchte ['lɔyçtə], *f.* (—, *pl.* —n) light, lamp, lantern; (*fig.*) luminary, star.

leuchten ['lɔyçtən], *v.n.* light, shine.

leuchtend ['lɔyçtənt], *adj.* shining, bright; luminous.

Leuchter ['lɔyçtər], *m.* (—s, *pl.* —) candlestick, candelabrum.

Leuchtrakete ['lɔyçtrake:tə], *f.* (—, *pl.* —n) Roman candle; flare.

Leuchtturm ['lɔyçtturm], *m.* (—s, *pl.* ∵e) lighthouse.

leugnen ['lɔygnən], *v.a.* deny, disclaim; *nicht zu —*, undeniable.

Leumund ['lɔymunt], *m.* (—es, *no pl.*) renown, reputation.

Leute ['lɔytə], *pl.* persons, people, men; servants, domestic staff.

Leutnant ['lɔytnant], *m.* (—s, *pl.* —s) lieutenant.

leutselig ['lɔytze:lɪç], *adj.* affable, friendly; condescending.

Levkoje [lɛf'ko:jə], *f.* (—, *pl.* —n) (*Bot.*) stock.

Lexikon ['lɛksɪkɔn], *n.* (—s, *pl.* —s, —ka) dictionary, lexicon, encyclopaedia.

Libanon ['li:banɔn], *m.* Lebanon.

Libelle [li'bɛlə], *f.* (—, *pl.* —n) (*Ent.*) dragonfly.

Liberia [li'be:rja], *n.* Liberia.

Libyen ['li:bɪən], *n.* Libya.

Licht [lɪçt], *n.* (—es, *pl.* —er) light, candle; luminary.

licht [lɪçt], *adj.* light, clear, open.

Lichtbild ['lɪçtbɪlt], *n.* (—es, *pl.* —er) photograph.

Lichtbrechung ['lɪçtbrɛçuŋ], *f.* (—, *pl.* —en) refraction of light.

lichten ['lɪçtən], *v.a.* clear, thin; *den Anker —*, weigh anchor.

lichterloh ['lɪçtərlo:], *adj.* blazing, ablaze.

Lichthof ['lɪçtho:f], *m.* (—s, *pl.* ∵e) well of a court, quadrangle.

Lichtmeß ['lɪçtmɛs], *f.* (—, *no pl.*) (*Eccl.*) Candlemas.

Lichtschirm ['lɪçtʃɪrm], *m.* (—s, *pl.* —e) screen, lamp-shade.

Lichtspieltheater ['lɪçtʃpi:ltea:tər], *n.* (—s, *pl.* —) cinema.

Lichtung ['lɪçtuŋ], *f.* (—, *pl.* —en) glade, clearing.

Lid [li:t], *n.* (—s, *pl.* —er) eye-lid.

lieb [li:p], *adj.* dear; beloved; good; *das ist mir —*, I am glad of it; *der —e Gott*, God; *unsere —e Frau*, Our Lady; *bei einem — Kind sein*, be a favourite with s.o., curry favour with s.o.

liebäugeln ['li:pɔygəln], *v.n. insep.* ogle.

Liebchen ['li:pçən], *n.* (—s, *pl.* —) sweetheart, love, darling.

Liebe ['li:bə], *f.* (—, *no pl.*) love.

Liebelei [li:bə'laɪ], *f.* (—, *pl.* —en) flirtation.

lieben ['li:bən], *v.a.* love, like, be fond of.

liebenswürdig ['li:bənsvyrdɪç], *adj.* amiable, kind, charming.

lieber ['li:bər], *adv.* rather, better, sooner; *etwas — tun*, prefer to do s.th.

Liebhaber ['li:pha:bər], *m.* (—s, *pl.* —) lover; (*fig.*) amateur, dilettante; (*Theat.*) leading man.

Liebhaberin ['li:phabərɪn], *f.* leading lady.

141

liebkosen ['li:pko:zən], *v.a. insep.* fondle, caress.

lieblich ['li:pliç], *adj.* lovely, charming, sweet.

Liebling ['li:pliŋ], *m.* (—s, *pl.* —e) darling, favourite.

lieblos ['li:plo:s], *adj.* hard-hearted; unkind.

Liebreiz ['li:praɪts], *m.* (—es, *no pl.*) charm, attractiveness.

liebreizend ['li:praɪtsənt], *adj.* charming.

Liebschaft ['li:pʃaft], *f.* (—, *pl.* —en) love affair.

Lied [li:t], *n.* (—es, *pl.* —er) song, air, tune; *geistliches* —, hymn.

liederlich ['li:dərliç], *adj.* careless, slovenly; dissolute, debauched; —*es Leben*, profligacy.

Lieferant [li:fə'rant], *m.* (—en, *pl.* —en) supplier, purveyor, contractor; *Eingang für* —*en*, tradesmen's entrance.

liefern ['li:fərn], *v.a.* deliver, furnish, supply.

Lieferschein ['li:fərʃaɪn], *m.* (—s, *pl.* —e) delivery note.

liegen ['li:gən], *v.n. irr.* lie; be situated; *es liegt mir daran*, it is of importance to me, I have it at heart; *es liegt mir nichts daran*, it is of no consequence to me.

Liegenschaft ['li:gənʃaft], *f.* (—, *pl.* —en) landed property, real estate.

Liga ['li:ga:], *f.* (—, *pl.* —**gen**) league.

Liguster [li'gustər], *m.* (—s, *no pl.*) privet.

liieren [li:'i:rən], *v.r.* (*aux.* haben) *sich* — *mit*, unite with, combine with.

Likör [li'kø:r], *m.* (—s, *pl.* —e) liqueur.

lila ['li:la:] *adj.* (*colour*) lilac.

Lilie ['li:ljə], *f.* (—, *pl.* —n) (*Bot.*) lily.

Limonade [limo'na:də], *f.* (—, *pl.* —n) lemonade.

lind [lɪnt], *adj.* soft, gentle, mild.

Linde ['lɪndə], *f.* (—, *pl.* —n) (*Bot.*) lime-tree, linden.

lindern ['lɪndərn], *v.a.* soften, assuage, mitigate, soothe, allay.

Lindwurm ['lɪntvurm], *m.* (—s, *pl.* —er) (*Poet.*) dragon.

Lineal [line'a:l], *n.* (—s, *pl.* —e) ruler, rule.

Linie ['li:njə], *f.* (—, *pl.* —n) line; lineage, descent; *in erster* —, in the first place.

Linienschiff ['li:njənʃɪf], *n.* (—es, *pl.* —e) (*Naut.*) liner.

lin(i)ieren [lin'(j)i:rən], *v.a.* rule.

linkisch ['lɪŋkɪʃ], *adj.* awkward, clumsy.

links [lɪŋks], *adv.* to the left, on the left-hand side; —*um!* left about turn!

Linnen ['lɪnən], *n.* (—s, *no pl.*) (*Poet.*) linen.

Linse ['lɪnzə], *f.* (—, *pl.* —n) (*vegetable*) lentil; (*optical*) lens.

linsenförmig ['lɪnzənfœrmiç], *adj.* lens-shaped.

Linsengericht ['lɪnzəngəriçt], *n.* (—s, *pl.* —e) (*Bibl.*) mess of pottage.

Lippe ['lɪpə], *f.* (—, *pl.* —n) lip; (*coll.*) *eine* — *riskieren*, be cheeky.

Lippenlaut ['lɪpənlaut], *m.* (—s, *pl.* —e) (*Phonet.*) labial.

Lippenstift ['lɪpənʃtɪft], *m.* (—s, *pl.* —e) lipstick.

liquidieren [lɪkvi'di:rən], *v.a.* liquidate, wind up, settle; charge.

lispeln ['lɪspəln], *v.n.* lisp.

Lissabon [lɪsa'bɔn], *n.* Lisbon.

List [lɪst], *f.* (—, *pl.* —en) cunning, craft; trick, stratagem, ruse.

Liste ['lɪstə], *f.* (—, *pl.* —n) list, roll, catalogue.

listig ['lɪstiç], *adj.* cunning, crafty, sly.

Listigkeit ['lɪstiçkaɪt], *f.* (—, *no pl.*) slyness, craftiness.

Litanei [lita'naɪ], *f.* (—, *pl.* —en) litany.

Litauen ['lɪtauən], *n.* Lithuania.

Liter ['li:tər], *m. & n.* (—s, *pl.* —) litre.

literarisch [litə'ra:rɪʃ], *adj.* literary.

Literatur [litəra'tu:r], *f.* (—, *pl.* —en) literature, letters.

Litfaßsäule ['lɪtfaszɔylə], *f.* (—, *pl.* —n) advertisement pillar.

Liturgie [litur'gi:], *f.* (—, *pl.* —n) liturgy.

Litze ['lɪtsə], *f.* (—, *pl.* —n) lace, braid, cord; (*Elec.*) flex.

Livland ['li:flant], *n.* Livonia.

Livree [li'vre:], *f.* (—, *pl.* —n) livery.

Lizenz [li'tsɛnts], *f.* (—, *pl.* —en) licence.

Lob [lo:p], *n.* (—es, *no pl.*) praise, commendation.

loben ['lo:bən], *v.a.* praise, commend.

lobesam ['lo:bəza:m], *adj.* (*Poet.*) worthy, honourable.

Lobgesang ['lo:pgəzaŋ], *m.* (—s, *pl.* —e) hymn of praise.

Lobhudelei [lo:phu:də'laɪ], *f.* (—, *pl.* —en) adulation, flattery, toadying.

löblich ['lø:pliç], *adj.* laudable, commendable, meritorious.

lobpreisen ['lo:ppraɪzən], *v.a. insep.* eulogise, extol.

Lobrede ['lo:pre:də], *f.* (—, *pl.* —n) panegyric, eulogy.

Loch [lɔx], *n.* (—es, *pl.* —er) hole.

Lochbohrer ['lɔxbo:rər], *m.* (—s, *pl.*—) auger.

lochen ['lɔxən], *v.a.* perforate, punch.

Locher ['lɔxər], *m.* (—s, *pl.* —) perforator, punch.

löcherig ['lœçəriç], *adj.* full of holes.

Lochmeißel ['lɔxmaɪsəl], *m.* (—s, *pl.* —) mortice-chisel.

Locke ['lɔkə], *f.* (—, *pl.* —n) curl, lock, ringlet, tress.

locken ['lɔkən], *v.a.* allure, decoy, entice.

locker ['lɔkər], *adj.* loose; slack; spongy; dissolute; *nicht* — *lassen*, stick to o.'s guns.

lockern ['lɔkərn], *v.a.* loosen.

lockig ['lɔkiç], *adj.* curled, curly.

Lockmittel ['lɔkmɪtəl], *n.* (—s, *pl.* —) inducement, lure, bait.

Lockspeise ['lɔkʃpaɪzə], *f.* (—, *pl.* —n) lure, bait.

Lotrechtstarter

Lockung ['lɔkuŋ], *f.* (—, *pl.* —en) allurement, enticement.

Lockvogel ['lɔkfo:gəl], *m.* (—s, *pl.* ̈) decoy-bird.

Loden ['lo:dən], *m.* (—s, *pl.* —) coarse cloth, frieze.

lodern ['lo:dərn], *v.n.* blaze, flame.

Löffel ['lœfəl], *m.* (—s, *pl.* —) spoon; (*animal*) ear; *einen über den — barbieren*, take s.o. in.

Logarithmus [loga'rɪtmʊs], *m.* (—, *pl.* —men) logarithm.

Logbuch ['lɔkbu:x], *n.* (—es, *pl.* ̈er) logbook.

Loge ['lo:ʒə], *f.* (—, *pl.* —n) (*Theat.*) box; (*Freemasonry*) lodge.

Logenschließer ['lo:ʒənʃli:sər], *m.* (—s, *pl.* —) (*Theat.*) attendant.

logieren [lo'ʒi:rən], *v.n.* board (with).

Logis [lo'ʒi:], *n.* (—, *pl.* —) lodgings.

logisch ['lo:gɪʃ], *adj.* logical.

Lohe ['lo:hə], *f.* (—, *pl.* —n) tanning bark; flame.

Lohgerber ['lo:gɛrbər], *m.* (—s, *pl.* —) tanner.

Lohn [lo:n], *m.* (—s, *pl.* ̈e) wages, pay; reward; recompense.

lohnen ['lo:nən], *v.a.* reward, recompense, remunerate; pay wages to; *es lohnt sich nicht*, it is not worth while.

Lohnstopp ['lo:nʃtɔp], *m.* (—s, *pl.* —s) pay pause, wage freeze.

Löhnung ['lø:nuŋ], *f.* (—, *pl.* —en) pay, payment.

Lokal [lo'ka:l], *n.* (—s, *pl.* —e) locality, premises; inn, pub, café.

lokalisieren [lokali'zi:rən], *v.a.* localise.

Lokalität [lokali'tɛ:t], *f.* (—, *pl.* —en) *see* Lokal.

Lokomotive [lokomo'ti:və], *f.* (—, *pl.* —n) (*Railw.*) locomotive, engine.

Lokomotivführer [lokomo'ti:ffy:rər], *m.* (—s, *pl.* —) (*Railw.*) engine-driver.

Lombard [lɔm'bart], *m.* (—s, *pl.* —e) deposit-bank, loan bank.

Lombardei [lɔmbar'daɪ], *f.* Lombardy.

Lorbeer ['lɔrbe:r], *m.* (—s, *pl.* —en) laurel.

Lorbeerbaum ['lɔrbe:rbaum], *m.* (—s, *pl.* ̈e) laurel-tree, bay-tree.

Lorbeerspiritus ['lɔrbe:rʃpi:ritus], *m.* (—, *no pl.*) bay rum.

Lorgnon [lɔrn'jʃ], *n.* (—s, *pl.* —s) monocle, eye-glass.

Los [lo:s], *n.* (—es, *pl.* —e) share, ticket; lot, fate; *das große —*, first prize.

los [lo:s], *adj.* loose, untied; free from, released from, rid of; (*Am.*) quit of; *was ist los?* what is going on? what's the matter? *etwas — werden*, get rid of s.th.; *schieß los!* fire away!

lösbar ['lø:sba:r], *adj.* (*question, riddle*) soluble.

losbinden ['lo:sbɪndən], *v.a. irr.* untie, unbind, loosen.

losbrechen ['lo:sbrɛçən], *v.a. irr.* break off. — *v.n.* (*aux.* sein) break loose.

Löschblatt ['lœʃblat], *n.* (—es, *pl.* ̈er) blotting-paper.

Löscheimer ['lœʃaɪmər], *m.* (—s, *pl.* —) fire-bucket.

löschen ['lœʃən], *v.a.* put out; extinguish; (*debt*) cancel; (*writing*) efface, blot; (*freight*) (*Naut.*) unload; (*thirst*) quench.

Löschpapier ['lœʃpapi:r], *n.* (—s, *no pl.*) blotting-paper.

Löschung ['lœʃuŋ], *f.* (—, *pl.* —en) (*freight*) (*Naut.*) discharging, landing, unloading.

losdrücken ['lo:sdrykən], *v.n.* discharge, fire.

lose ['lo:zə], *adj.* loose, slack; (*fig.*) dissolute; *—s Maul*, malicious tongue.

Lösegeld ['lø:zəgɛlt], *n.* (—es, *pl.* —er) ransom.

losen ['lo:zən], *v.n.* draw lots.

lösen ['lø:zən], *v.a.* loosen, untie; absolve, free, deliver; dissolve; solve; (*relations*) break off; (*tickets*) take, buy.

losgehen ['lo:sge:ən], *v.n. irr.* (*aux.* sein) begin; (*gun*) go off; *auf einen —*, go for s.o.; *jetzt kann's —*, now for it.

loskaufen ['lo:skaufən], *v.a.* redeem, ransom.

loskommen ['lo:skɔmən], *v.n. irr.* (*aux.* sein) come loose; *von etwas —*, get rid of s.th.

löslich ['lø:slɪç], *adj.* (*Chem.*) soluble.

loslösen ['lo:slø:zən], *v.a.* detach.

losmachen ['lo:smaxən], *v.a.* free from. — *v.r. sich — von*, disengage o.s. from.

losreißen ['lo:sraɪsən], *v.a. irr.* pull away, separate. — *v.n.* (*aux.* sein), break loose. — *v.r. sich — von*, tear o.s. away from.

lossagen ['lo:sza:gən], *v.r. sich — von*, renounce s.th., dissociate o.s. from s.th.

losschlagen ['lo:sʃla:gən], *v.a.* knock loose; let fly; (*fig.*) sell, dispose of.

lossprechen ['lo:sʃprɛçən], *v.a. irr.* (*Eccl.*) absolve; (*Law*) acquit.

lossteuern ['lo:sʃtɔyərn], *v.n. — auf*, make for.

Losung ['lo:zuŋ], *f.* (—, *pl.* —en) watchword, motto, password, slogan.

Lösung ['lø:zuŋ], *f.* (—, *pl.* —en) loosening; solution.

losziehen ['lo:stsi:ən], *v.n. irr.* (*Mil.*) set out; *gegen einen —*, inveigh against s.o.; (*fig., coll.*) run s.o. down.

Lot [lo:t], *n.* (—es, *pl.* —e) lead, plummet; (*weight*) half an ounce; (*Maths.*) perpendicular (line).

Löteisen ['lø:taɪzən], *n.* (—s, *pl.* —) soldering iron.

loten ['lo:tən], *v.a., v.n.* (*Naut.*) take soundings, plumb.

löten ['lø:tən], *v.a.* solder.

Lothringen ['lo:triŋən], *n.* Lorraine.

Lötkolben ['lø:tkɔlbən], *m.* (—s, *pl.* —) soldering iron.

Lotleine ['lo:tlaɪnə], *f.* (—, *pl.* —n) sounding-line.

Lotrechtstarter ['lo:trɛçtʃtartər], *m.* (—s, *pl.* —) (*Aviat.*) vertical take-off plane (V.T.O.L.).

143

Lötrohr

Lötrohr ['løːtroːr], *n.* (—s, *pl.* —e) soldering-pipe.

Lotse ['loːtsə], *m.* (—n, *pl.* —n) (*Naut.*) pilot.

Lotterbett ['lɔtərbɛt], *n.* (—es, *pl.* —en) bed of idleness; (*obs.*) couch.

Lotterie [lɔtə'riː], *f.* (—, *pl.* —n) lottery, sweep-stake.

Lotterleben ['lɔtərleːbən], *n.* (—s, *no pl.*) dissolute life.

Löwe ['løːvə], *m.* (—n, *pl.* —n) (*Zool.*) lion.

Löwenbändiger ['løːvənbɛndɪgər], *m.* (—s, *pl.*—) lion tamer.

Löwengrube ['løːvəngruːbə], *f.* (—, *pl.* —n) lion's den.

Löwenmaul ['løːvənmaul], *n.* (—s, *no pl.*) (*Bot.*) snapdragon.

Löwenzahn ['løːvəntsaːn], *m.* (—s, *no pl.*) (*Bot.*) dandelion.

Löwin ['løːvɪn], *f.* (—, *pl.* —nen) (*Zool.*) lioness.

Luchs [luks], *m.* (—es, *pl.* —e) lynx.

Lücke ['lykə], *f.* (—, *pl.* —n) gap, breach; (*fig.*) omission, defect, blank.

Lückenbüßer ['lykənbyːsər], *m.* (—s, *pl.* —) stop-gap, stand-in.

lückenhaft ['lykənhaft], *adj.* fragmentary, incomplete, imperfect.

Luder ['luːdər], *n.* (—s, *pl.* —) (*rare*) carrion; (*vulg.*) beast, trollop; *dummes* —, silly ass, fathead.

Luderleben ['luːdərleːbən], *n.* (—s, *no pl.*) dissolute life.

ludern ['luːdərn], *v.n.* lead a dissolute life.

Luft [luft], *f.* (—, *pl.* ̈e) air.

Luftbrücke ['luftbrykə], *f.* (—, *no pl.*) air-lift.

Lüftchen ['lyftçən], *n.* (—s, *pl.* —) gentle breeze.

luftdicht ['luftdɪçt], *adj.* airtight.

Luftdruck ['luftdruk], *m.* (—s, *no pl.*) air pressure, atmospheric pressure; blast.

Luftdruckmesser ['luftdrukmɛsər], *m.* (—s, *pl.* —) barometer, pressure-gauge.

lüften ['lyftən], *v.a.* air, ventilate.

luftförmig ['luftfœrmɪç], *adj.* gaseous.

luftig ['luftɪç], *adj.* airy, windy.

Luftklappe ['luftklapə], *f.* (—, *pl.* —n) air-valve.

Luftkurort ['luftkuːrɔrt], *m.* (—s, *pl.* —e) health resort.

Luftlinie ['luftliːnjə], *f.* (—, *pl.*—n) bee-line; *in der* —, as the crow flies; (*Aviat.*) airline.

Luftloch ['luftlɔx], *m.* (—s, *pl.* ̈er) air-pocket.

Luftraum ['luftraum], *m.* (—s, *no pl.*) atmosphere; air space.

Luftröhre ['luftrøːrə], *f.* (—, *pl.* —n) windpipe.

Luftschiff ['luftʃɪf], *n.* (—es, *pl.* —e) air-ship.

Luftschiffahrt ['luftʃɪfaːrt], *f.* (—, *no pl.*) aeronautics.

Luftspiegelung ['luftʃpiːgəluŋ], *f.* (—, *pl.* —en) mirage.

Luftsprung ['luftʃpruŋ], *m.* (—s, *pl.* ̈e) caper, gambol; ̈*e machen*, caper, gambol.

Lüftung ['lyftuŋ], *f.* (—, *no pl.*) airing, ventilation.

Lug [luːk], *m.* (—s, *no pl.*) (*obs.*) lie; — *und Trug*, a pack of lies.

Lüge ['lyːgə], *f.* (—, *pl.* —n) lie, falsehood, fib; *einen* — *strafen*, give s.o. the lie.

lügen ['lyːgən], *v.n. irr.* lie, tell a lie.

lügenhaft ['lyːgənhaft], *adj.* lying, false, untrue.

Lügner ['lyːgnər], *m.* (—s, *pl.* —) liar.

Luke ['luːkə], *f.* (—, *pl.* —n) dormer-window; (*ship*) hatch.

Lümmel ['lymǝl], *m.* (—s, *pl.* —) lout; hooligan.

Lump [lump], *m.* (—s, —en, *pl.* —e, —en) scoundrel, blackguard.

Lumpen ['lumpən], *m.* (—s, *pl.* —) rag, tatter.

Lumpengesindel ['lumpəngəzɪndəl], *n.* (—s, *no pl.*) rabble, riffraff.

Lumpenpack ['lumpənpak], *n.* (—s, *no pl.*) rabble, riffraff.

Lumpensammler ['lumpənzamlər], *m.* (—s, *pl.* —) rag-and-bone-man.

Lumperei [lumpə'rat], *f.* (—, *pl.* —en) shabby trick; meanness; trifle.

lumpig ['lumpɪç], *adj.* ragged; (*fig.*) shabby, mean.

Lunge ['luŋə], *f.* (—, *pl.* —n) (*human*) lung; (*animals*) lights.

Lungenentzündung ['luŋənɛntsynduŋ], *f.* (—, *pl.* —en) pneumonia.

Lungenkrankheit ['luŋənkraŋkhaɪt], *f.* (—, *pl.* —en) pulmonary disease.

Lungenkraut ['luŋənkraut], *n.* (—s, *pl.* ̈er) lungwort.

Lungenschwindsucht ['luŋənʃvɪntzuxt], *f.* (—, *no pl.*) pulmonary consumption, tuberculosis.

lungern ['luŋərn], *v.n.* idle, loiter.

Lunte ['luntə], *f.* (—, *pl.* —n) fuse, slow-match; — *riechen*, smell a rat.

Lupe ['luːpə], *f.* (—, *pl.* —n) magnifying glass, lens; *etwas durch die* — *besehen*, examine s.th. closely, scrutinise s.th.; *unter die* — *nehmen*, examine closely.

lüpfen ['lypfən], *v.a.* lift.

Lupine [lu'piːnə], *f.* (—, *pl.* —n) (*Bot.*) lupin.

Lust [lust], *f.* (—, *pl.* ̈e) enjoyment, pleasure, delight; desire, wish, inclination, liking; — *bekommen zu*, feel inclined to; — *haben auf*, have a mind to, feel like; *nicht übel* — *haben*, have half a mind to.

Lustbarkeit ['lustbaːrkaɪt], *f.* (—, *pl.* —en) amusement, diversion, entertainment, pleasure.

Lustdirne ['lustdɪrnə], *f.* (—, *pl.* —n) prostitute.

lüstern ['lystərn], *adj.* lustful, lascivious.

lustig ['lustɪç], *adj.* gay, merry, cheerful, amusing, funny; — *sein*, make merry; *sich über einen* — *machen*, poke fun at s.o.

Mahlzahn

Lüstling ['lystlɪŋ], m. (—s, pl. —e) libertine, lecher.
Lustmord ['lustmɔrt], m. (—es, pl. —e) sex murder.
Lustreise ['lustraɪzə], f. (—, pl. —n) pleasure trip.
Lustschloß ['lustʃlɔs], n. (—sses, pl. ⁓sser) country house, country seat.
Lustspiel ['lustʃpiːl], n. (—s, pl. —e) comedy.
lustwandeln ['lustvandəln], v.n. insep. (aux. sein) stroll, promenade.
Lutherisch ['lutərɪʃ], adj. Lutheran.
lutschen ['lutʃən], v.a. suck.
Lüttich ['lytɪç], n. Liège.
Luxus ['luksus], m. (—, no pl.) luxury.
Luzern [lu'tsɛrn], n. Lucerne.
Luzerne [lut'sɛrnə], f. (—, pl. —n) (Bot.) lucerne.
Lymphe ['lymfə], f. (—, pl. —n) lymph.
lynchen ['lynçən], v.a. lynch.
Lyrik ['lyːrɪk], f. (—, no pl.) lyric poetry.
lyrisch ['lyːrɪʃ], adj. lyric(al).
Lyzeum [ly'tseːum], n. (—s, pl. Lyzeen) lyceum, grammar school or high school for girls.

M

M [ɛm], n. (—s, pl. —s) the letter M.
Maas [maːs], f. River Meuse.
Maat [maːt], m. (—s, pl. —s, —en) (Naut.) mate.
Mache ['maxə], f. (—, no pl.) put-up job, humbug, sham, eyewash.
machen ['maxən], v.a. make, do, produce, manufacture; cause; amount to; mach schon, be quick; das macht nichts, it does not matter; mach's kurz, cut it short; etwas — lassen, have s.th. made; sich auf den Weg —, set off; sich viel (wenig) aus etwas —, care much (little) for s.th.; mach, daß du fortkommst! get out! scram!
Macherlohn ['maxərloːn], m. (—es, pl. ⁓e) charge for making s.th.
Macht [maxt], f. (—, pl. ⁓e) might, power; force, strength; authority; mit aller —, with might and main.
Machtbefugnis ['maxtbəfuːknɪs], f. (—, pl. —se) competence.
Machtgebot ['maxtgəboːt], n. (—s, pl. —e) authoritative order.
Machthaber ['maxthaːbər], m. (—s, pl. —) potentate, ruler.
mächtig ['mɛçtɪç], adj. mighty, powerful; einer Sache — sein, to have mastered s.th.
machtlos ['maxtloːs], adj. powerless.
Machtspruch ['maxtʃprux], m. (—s, pl. ⁓e) authoritative dictum; command; decree.

Machtvollkommenheit ['maxtfɔlkəmənhaɪt], f. (—, pl. —en) absolute power; sovereignty; aus eigner —, of o.'s own authority.
Machtwort ['maxtvɔrt], n. (—es, pl. —e) word of command, fiat; ein — sprechen, bring o.'s authority to bear, speak with authority.
Machwerk ['maxvɛrk], n. (—s, pl. —e) shoddy product; bad job; concoction; (story) pot-boiler.
Madagaskar [mada'gaskar], n. Madagascar.
Mädchen ['mɛːtçən], n. (—s, pl. —) girl; (servant) maid; — für alles, maid-of-all-work.
mädchenhaft ['mɛːtçənhaft], adj. girlish, maidenly.
Mädchenhandel ['mɛːtçənhandəl], m. (—s, no pl.) white slave trade.
Made ['maːdə], f. (—, pl. —n) maggot, mite.
Mädel ['mɛːdəl], n. (—s, pl. —) (coll.) see Mädchen.
madig ['maːdɪç], adj. maggoty.
Magazin [maga'tsiːn], n. (—s, pl. —e) warehouse, storehouse; journal.
Magd [maːkt], f. (—, pl. ⁓e) maid, maidservant; (Poet.) maiden.
Magen ['maːgən], m. (—s, pl. —) (human) stomach; (animals) maw.
Magengrube ['maːgəngruːbə], f. (—, pl. —n) pit of the stomach.
Magensaft ['maːgənzaft], m. (—es, pl. ⁓e) gastric juice.
mager ['maːgər], adj. lean, thin, slender, slim; (fig.) meagre.
Magerkeit ['maːgərkaɪt], f. (—, no pl.) leanness, thinness, slenderness.
Magie [ma'giː], f. (—, no pl.) magic.
Magier ['maːgjər], m. (—s, pl. —) magician.
Magister [ma'gɪstər], m. (—s, pl. —) schoolmaster; (Univ.) Master; — der freien Künste, Master of Arts.
Magistrat [magɪs'traːt], m. (—s, pl. —e) municipal board, local authority.
magnetisch [mag'neːtɪʃ], adj. magnetic.
magnetisieren [magneti'ziːrən], v.a. magnetise.
Magnetismus [magne'tɪsmus], m. (—, pl. —men) magnetism; (person) mesmerism; Lehre vom —, magnetics.
Magnifizenz [magnifi'tsɛnts], f. (—, pl. —en) magnificence; seine —, (Univ.) title of Vice-Chancellor.
Mahagoni [maha'goːni], n. (—s, no pl.) mahogany.
Mahd [maːt], f. (—, pl. —en) mowing.
mähen ['mɛːən], v.a. mow.
Mäher ['mɛːər], m. (—s, pl. —) mower.
Mahl [maːl], n. (—s, pl. —e, ⁓er) meal, repast.
mahlen ['maːlən], v.a. grind.
Mahlstrom ['maːlʃtroːm], m. (—s, no pl.) maelstrom, whirlpool, eddy.
Mahlzahn ['maːltsaːn], m. (—s, pl. ⁓e) molar, grinder.

145

Mahlzeit [ˈmaːltsaɪt], *f.* (—, *pl.* —en) meal, repast.

Mähmaschine [ˈmɛːmaʃinə], *f.* (—, *pl.* —n) reaping-machine; lawn-mower.

Mähne [ˈmɛːnə], *f.* (—, *pl.* —n) mane.

mahnen [ˈmaːnən], *v.a.* remind, admonish, warn; (*debtor*) demand payment, dun.

Mähre [ˈmɛːrə], *f.* (—, *pl.* —n) mare.

Mähren [ˈmɛːrən], *n.* Moravia.

Mai [maɪ], *m.* (—s, *pl.* —e) May.

Maid [maɪt], *f.* (—, *no pl.*) (*Poet.*) maiden.

Maiglöckchen [ˈmaɪɡlœkçən], *n.* (—s, *pl.* —) (*Bot.*) lily of the valley.

Maikäfer [ˈmaɪkɛːfər], *m.* (—s, *pl.* —) (*Ent.*) cockchafer.

Mailand [ˈmaɪlant], *n.* Milan.

Mais [maɪs], *m.* (—es, *no pl.*) (*Bot.*) maize, Indian corn.

Majestät [majɛsˈtɛːt], *f.* (—, *pl.* —en) majesty.

majestätisch [majɛsˈtɛːtiʃ], *adj.* majestic.

Major [maˈjoːr], *m.* (—s, *pl.* —e) (*Mil.*) major.

Majoran [majoˈraːn], *m.* (—s, *no pl.*) (*Bot.*) marjoram.

Majorat [majoˈraːt], *n.* (—s, *pl.* —e) primogeniture; entail.

majorenn [majoˈrɛn], *adj.* (*obs.*) of age, over twenty-one.

Majorität [majoriˈtɛːt], *f.* (—, *pl.* —en) majority.

Makel [ˈmaːkəl], *m.* (—s, *pl.* —) spot, blot; (*fig.*) blemish, flaw, defect.

Mäkelei [mɛːkəˈlaɪ], *f.* (—, *pl.* —en) fault-finding, carping; fastidiousness.

makellos [ˈmaːkəlloːs], *adj.* spotless, immaculate.

mäkeln [ˈmɛːkəln], *v.n.* find fault (with), cavil (at).

Makkabäer [makaˈbɛːər], *m.* Maccabee.

Makler [ˈmaːklər], *m.* (—ø, *pl.* —) broker.

Mäkler [ˈmɛːklər], *m.* (—s, *pl.* —) fault-finder, caviller.

Maklergebühr [ˈmaːklərɡəbyːr], *f.* (—, *pl.* —e) brokerage.

Makrele [maˈkreːla], *f.* (—, *pl.* —n) (*Zool.*) mackerel.

Makrone [maˈkroːnə], *f.* (—, *pl.* —n) macaroon.

Makulatur [makulaˈtuːr], *f.* (—, *no pl.*) waste paper.

Mal [maːl], *n.* (—s, *pl.* —e) mark, sign, token; monument; mole, birthmark; stain; time; *dieses* —, this time, this once; *manches* —, sometimes; *mehrere* —*e*, several times; *mit einem* —, all of a sudden.

mal [maːl], *adv. & part.* once; *noch*—, once more; (*coll.*) *hör* —, I say.

Malaya [maˈlaɪa], *n.* Malaya.

malen [ˈmaːlən], *v.a.* paint.

Maler [ˈmaːlər], *m.* (—s, *pl.* —) painter.

Malerei [maːləˈraɪ], *f.* (—, *pl.* —en) painting; picture.

malerisch [ˈmaːləriʃ], *adj.* picturesque.

Malerleinwand [ˈmaːlərlaɪnvant], *f.* (—, *no pl.*) canvas.

Malheur [maˈløːr], *n.* (—s, *pl.* —e) misfortune, mishap.

Mali [ˈmaːli] *n.* Mali.

maliziös [maliˈtsjøːs], *adj.* malicious.

Malkasten [ˈmaːlkastən], *m.* (—s, *pl.* ⸚) paint-box.

Malstein [ˈmaːlʃtaɪn], *m.* (—s, *pl.* —e) monument; boundary stone.

Malstock [ˈmaːlʃtɔk], *m.* (—s, *pl.* ⸚e) maulstick, mahlstick.

Malteserorden [malˈteːzərɔrdən], *m.* (—s, *no pl.*) Order of the Knights of Malta.

malträtieren [maltrɛˈtiːrən], *v.a.* illtreat.

Malve [ˈmalvə], *f.* (—, *pl.* —n) (*Bot.*) mallow.

Malz [malts], *n.* (—es, *no pl.*) malt; *an ihm ist Hopfen und — verloren*, he is hopeless.

Malzbonbon [ˈmaltsbɔ̃bɔ̃], *m.* (—s, *pl.* —s) cough-lozenge, malt drop.

Mälzer [ˈmɛltsər], *m.* (—s, *pl.* —) maltster.

Mama [maˈmaː], *f.* (—, *pl.* —s) (*fam.*) mummy, mum, (*Am.*) ma.

Mammon [ˈmamɔn], *m.* (—s, *no pl.*) mammon; *schnöder* —, filthy lucre.

Mammut [ˈmamut], *n.* (—s, *pl.* —e) mammoth.

Mamsell [mamˈzɛl], *f.* (—, *pl.* —en) housekeeper.

man [man], *indef. pron.* one, they, people, men; — *sagt*, they say.

manch [manç], *pron.* (—er, —e, —es) many a, some, several.

mancherlei [mançərˈlaɪ], *adj.* several; of several kinds.

Manchester [manˈçɛstər], *m.* (—s, *no pl.*) corduroy.

manchmal [ˈmançmaːl], *adv.* sometimes.

Mandant [manˈdant], *m.* (—en, *pl.* —en) client.

Mandantin [manˈdantin], *f.* (—, *pl.* —innen) female client.

Mandarine [mandaˈriːnə], *f.* (—, *pl.* —n) mandarin (orange), tangerine.

Mandat [manˈdaːt], *n.* (—s, *pl.* —e) mandate.

Mandel [ˈmandəl], *f.* (—, *pl.* —n) almond; (*Anat.*) tonsil; (*quantity*) fifteen; *eine* — *Eier*, fifteen eggs.

Mandoline [mandoˈliːnə], *f.* (—, *pl.* —n) mandolin.

Mangan [maŋˈɡaːn], *n.* (—s, *no pl.*) (*Chem.*) manganese.

Mangel (1) [ˈmaŋəl], *f.* (—, *pl.* —n) mangle, wringer.

Mangel (2) [ˈmaŋəl], *m.* (—s, *pl.* ⸚) deficiency, defect; blemish; lack, shortage, want; *aus* — *an*, for want of; — *haben an*, be short of, lack (s.th.).

mangelhaft [ˈmaŋəlhaft], *adj.* defective, imperfect.

mangeln (1) [ˈmaŋəln], *v.a.* (*laundry*) mangle.

mangeln (2) ['maŋəln], *v.n.* be in want of, be short of; *es —t uns an . . .*, we lack . . . .

mangels ['maŋəls], *prep.* (*Genit.*) for lack of, for want of.

Mangold ['maŋɔlt], *m.* (**—s**, *no pl.*) (*Bot.*) beet, mangel-wurzel.

Manie [ma'ni:], *f.* (**—**, *pl.* **—n**) mania, craze.

Manier [ma'ni:r], *f.* (**—**, *pl.* **—en**) manner, habit; *gute —en haben*, have good manners.

maniert [ma'ni:rt], *adj.* affected; (*Art*) mannered.

manierlich [ma'ni:rliç], *adj.* well behaved, civil, polite.

manipulieren [manipu'li:rən], *v.a.* manipulate.

Manko ['maŋko:], *n.* (**—s**, *pl.* **—s**) deficit, deficiency.

Mann [man], *m.* (**—(e)s**, *pl.* ̈er, (*Poet.*) **—en**) man; husband; *etwas an den — bringen*, get s.th. off o.'s hands, dispose of s.th.; *seinen — stellen*, hold o.'s own; *bis auf den letzten —*, to a man.

Mannbarkeit ['manba:rkaɪt], *f.* (**—**, *no pl.*) puberty; marriageable age.

Männchen ['mɛnçən], *n.* (**—s**, *pl.* **—**) little man, manikin; (*Zool.*) male; *mein —*, (*coll.*) my hubby; *— machen*, (*dogs*) sit on the hindlegs, beg.

mannhaft ['manhaft], *adj.* manly, stout, valiant.

mannigfaltig ['manɪçfaltɪç], *adj.* manifold, multifarious.

männlich ['mɛnlɪç], *adj.* male; (*fig.*) manly; (*Gram.*) masculine.

Mannsbild ['mansbɪlt], *n.* (**—es**, *pl.* **—er**) (*coll.*) man, male person.

Mannschaft ['manʃaft], *f.* (**—**, *pl.* **—en**) men; crew, team.

mannstoll ['manstɔl], *adj.* man-mad.

Mannszucht ['manstsuxt], *f.* (**—**, *no pl.*) discipline.

Manöver [ma'nø:vər], *n.* (**—s**, *pl.* **—**) manoeuvre.

manövrieren [manø'vri:rən], *v.a.* manoeuvre.

Mansarde [man'zardə], *f.* (**—**, *pl.* **—n**) garret, attic.

manschen ['manʃən], *v.a.*, *v.n.* dabble; splash (about).

Manschette [man'ʃɛtə], *f.* (**—**, *pl.* **—n**) cuff.

Mantel ['mantəl], *m.* (**—s**, *pl.* ̈) cloak, overcoat, coat, mantle, wrap; *den — nach dem Winde hängen*, be a timeserver.

Manufaktur [manufak'tu:r], *f.* (**—**, *pl.* **—en**) manufacture.

Mappe ['mapə], *f.* (**—**, *pl.* **—n**) portfolio, case, file.

Mär [mɛːr], *f.* (**—**, *pl.* **—en**) (*Poet.*) tale, tidings, legend.

Märchen ['mɛːrçən], *n.* (**—s**, *pl.* **—**) fairy-tale, fable; fib.

märchenhaft ['mɛːrçənhaft], *adj.* fabulous, legendary; (*coll.*) marvellous.

Marder ['mardər], *m.* (**—s**, *pl.* **—**) (*Zool.*) marten.

Maria [ma'ri:a], *f.* Mary; *die Jungfrau —*, the Virgin Mary.

Marienbild [ma'ri:ənbɪlt], *n.* (**—es**, *pl.* **—er**) image of the Virgin Mary.

Marienblume [ma'ri:ənblu:mə], *f.* (**—**, *pl.* **—n**) (*Bot.*) daisy.

Marienglas [ma'ri:ənglas], *n.* (**—es**, *no pl.*) mica.

Marienkäfer [ma'ri:ənkɛfər], *m.* (**—s**, *pl.* **—**) (*Ent.*) lady-bird.

Marine [ma'ri:nə], *f.* (**—**, *pl.* **—n**) navy.

marinieren [mari'ni:rən], *v.a.* pickle.

Marionette [mario'nɛtə], *f.* (**—**, *pl.* **—n**) puppet, marionette.

Mark (1) [mark], *n.* (**—s**, *no pl.*) (*bone*) marrow; (*fruit*) pith, pulp.

Mark (2) [mark], *f.* (**—**, *pl.* **—en**) boundary, frontier province.

Mark (3) [mark], *f.* (**—**, *pl.* **—**) (*coin*) mark.

markant [mar'kant], *adj.* striking, prominent; (*remark*) pithy.

Marke ['markə], *f.* (**—**, *pl.* **—n**) (*trade*) mark, brand; (*postage*) stamp; (*game*) counter.

markieren [mar'ki:rən], *v.a.* mark.

markig ['markɪç], *adj.* marrowlike; (*fig.*) pithy, strong.

Markise [mar'ki:zə], *f.* (**—**, *pl.* **—n**) (sun)blind, awning.

Markt [markt], *m.* (**—es**, *pl.* ̈e) market, market-square, fair.

Marktflecken ['marktflɛkən], *m.* (**—s**, *pl.* **—**) borough; (small) market town.

Marktschreier ['marktʃraɪər], *m.* (**—s**, *pl.* **—**) cheap-jack, quack, charlatan.

Markus ['markus], *m.* Mark.

Marmel ['marmǝl], *f.* (**—**, *pl.* **—n**) (*obs.*) marble.

Marmelade [marmǝ'la:də], *f.* (**—**, *pl.* **—n**) marmalade, jam.

Marmor ['marmor], *m.* (**—s**, *no pl.*) marble.

Marokko [ma'rɔko], *n.* Morocco.

Marone [ma'ro:nə], *f.* (**—**, *pl.* **—n**) sweet chestnut.

Maroquin [maro'kē], *n.* (**—s**, *no pl.*) Morocco leather.

Marotte [ma'rɔtə], *f.* (**—**, *pl.* **—n**) whim; fad.

Marquise [mar'ki:zə], *f.* (**—**, *pl.* **—n**) marchioness.

Marsch (1) [marʃ], *m.* (**—es**, *pl.* ̈e) march; *sich in — setzen*, set out; march off.

Marsch (2) [marʃ], *f.* (**—**, *pl.* **—en**) fen, marsh.

marsch! [marʃ], *int.* march! be off! get out!

Marschboden ['marʃbo:dən], *m.* (**—s**, *no pl.*) marshy soil, marshland.

marschieren [mar'ʃi:rən], *v.n.* (*aux.* sein) march.

Marstall ['marʃtal], *m.* (**—s**, *pl.* ̈e) royal stud.

Marter ['martər], *f.* (**—**, *pl.* **—n** torture, torment.

martern

martern [ˈmartərn], *v.a.* torture, torment.

Märtyrer [ˈmɛrtyrər], *m.* (—s, *pl.* —) martyr.

Martyrium [marˈtyːrjum], *n.* (—s, *pl.* —rien) martyrdom.

März [mɛrts], *m.* (—es, *pl.* —e) (*month*) March.

Masche [ˈmaʃə], *f.* (—, *pl.* —n) mesh; (*knitting*) stitch; (*dial.*) bow tie; (*coll.*) racket.

Maschine [maˈʃiːnə], *f.* (—, *pl.* —n) machine; engine; *mit der* — *geschrieben*, typewritten.

Maschinengarn [maˈʃiːnəngarn], *n.* (—s, *no pl.*) twist.

Maschinerie [maʃinəˈriː], *f.* (—, *pl.* —en) machinery.

Maser [ˈmaːzər], *f.* (—, *pl.* —n) (*wood*) vein, streak.

Masern [ˈmaːzərn], *f. pl.* measles.

Maske [ˈmaskə], *f.* (—, *pl.* —n) mask, visor.

Maskerade [maskəˈraːdə], *f.* (—, *pl.* —n) masquerade.

maskieren [masˈkiːrən], *v.a.* mask. — *v.r. sich* —, put on a mask.

Maß (1) [maːs], *n.* (—es, *pl.* —e) measure, size; moderation, propriety; degree, extent; proportion; — *halten*, be moderate; *einem* — *nehmen*, measure s.o. (for); *in starkem* —, to a high degree; *mit* —, in moderation; *nach* —, to measure; *ohne* — *und Ziel*, immoderately, with no holds barred; *über alle* —en, exceedingly.

Maß (2) [maːs], *m. & f.* (—, *pl.* —e) (*drink*) quart.

massakrieren [masaˈkriːrən], *v.a.* massacre, slaughter.

Maßarbeit [ˈmaːsarbaɪt], *f.* (—, *pl.* —en) (*work*) made to measure; bespoke tailoring.

Masse [ˈmasə], *f.* (—, *pl.* —n) mass, bulk; multitude; *eine* —, a lot.

Maßeinheit [ˈmaːsaɪnhaɪt], *f.* (—, *pl.* —n) measuring-unit.

massenhaft [ˈmasənhaft], *adj.* abundant.

Maßgabe [ˈmaːsgaːbə], *f.* (—, *pl.* —n) *nach* —, according to, in proportion to.

maßgebend [ˈmaːsgeːbənt], *adj.* standard; (*fig.*) authoritative.

massieren [maˈsiːrən], *v.a.* massage.

mäßig [ˈmɛːsɪç], *adj.* moderate, temperate, frugal.

Mäßigkeit [ˈmɛːsɪçkaɪt], *f.* (—, *no pl.*) moderation, temperance, frugality.

Mäßigung [ˈmɛːsɪguŋ], *f.* (—, *no pl.*) moderation.

Massiv [maˈsiːf], *n.* (—s, *pl.* —e) (*mountains*) massif, range.

Maßliebchen [ˈmaːsliːpçən], *n.* (—s, *pl.* —) (*Bot.*) daisy.

maßlos [ˈmaːsloːs], *adj.* immoderate; (*fig.*) extravagant.

Maßnahme [ˈmaːsnaːmə], *f.* (—, *pl.* —n) measure; —*n ergreifen*, take steps.

Maßregel [ˈmaːsreːgəl], *f.* (—, *pl.* —n) measure.

maßregeln [ˈmaːsreːgəln], *v.a.* reprove, reprimand.

Maßstab [ˈmaːsʃtaːp], *m.* (—es, *pl.* —e) standard; (*maps*) scale; *in kleinem* (*großem*) —, on a small (large) scale.

maßvoll [ˈmaːsfɔl], *adj.* moderate.

Mast (1) [mast], *m.* (—es, *pl.* —e) mast; pylon.

Mast (2) [mast], *f.* (—, *no pl.*) fattening.

Mastbaum [ˈmastbaum], *m.* (—s, *pl.* —e) mast.

Mastdarm [ˈmastdarm], *m.* (—s, *pl.* —e) rectum.

mästen [ˈmɛstən], *v.a.* feed, fatten.

Mastkorb [ˈmastkɔrp], *m.* (—s, *pl.* —e) masthead.

Mästung [ˈmɛstuŋ], *f.* (—, *no pl.*) fattening, cramming.

Materialwaren [mateˈrjalvaːrən], *f. pl.* groceries; household goods.

materiell [mateˈrjɛl], *adj.* material, real; materialistic.

Mathematik [matemaˈtiːk], *f.* (—, *no pl.*) mathematics.

mathematisch [mateˈmaːtiʃ], *adj.* mathematical.

Matratze [maˈtratsə], *f.* (—, *pl.* —n) mattress.

Matrikel [maˈtriːkəl], *f.* (—, *pl.* —n) register, roll.

Matrize [maˈtriːtsə], *f.* (—, *pl.* —n) matrix, die, stencil.

Matrose [maˈtroːzə], *m.* (—n, *pl.* —n) sailor, seaman.

Matsch [matʃ], *m.* (—es, *no pl.*) slush; mud.

matt [mat], *adj.* tired, exhausted, spent; languid; weak, feeble; (*light*) dim; (*gold*) dull; (*silver*) tarnished; (*Chess*) (check-)mate; — *setzen*, (*Chess*) to (check-)mate.

Matte [ˈmatə], *f.* (—, *pl.* —n) mat, matting.

Matthäus [maˈtɛːus], *m.* Matthew.

Mattheit [ˈmathaɪt], *f.* (—, *no pl.*) tiredness, exhaustion, languor, feebleness; (*light*) dimness; (*gold*) dullness.

mattherzig [ˈmathɛrtsɪç], *adj.* poorspirited, faint-hearted.

Matura [maˈtuːra], *f.* (—, *pl.* —en) (*Austr.*) school-leaving *or* matriculation examination.

Mätzchen [ˈmɛtsçən], *n.* (—s, *pl.* —) nonsense; trick; *mach keine* —, don't be silly.

Mauer [ˈmauər], *f.* (—, *pl.* —n) wall.

Mauerkelle [ˈmauərkɛlə], *f.* (—, *pl.* —n) trowel.

mauern [ˈmauərn], *v.a.* build. — *v.n.* lay bricks, construct a wall.

Mauerwerk [ˈmauərvɛrk], *n.* (—s, *no pl.*) brick-work.

Maul [maul], *n.* (—es, *pl.* —er) (*animals*) mouth, muzzle; (*vulg.*) mouth; *das* — *halten*, shut up, hold o.'s tongue; *ein loses* — *haben*, have a loose tongue; *nicht aufs* — *gefallen sein*, have a quick tongue; (*vulg.*) *halt's* —, shut up.

Maulaffe ['maulafə], *m.* (**—n**, *pl.* **—n**) booby; *—n feilhalten*, stand gaping.
Maulbeere ['maulbe:rə], *f.* (**—**, *pl.* **—n**) (*Bot.*) mulberry.
maulen ['maulən], *v.n.* pout, sulk.
Maulesel ['maule:zəl], *m.* (**—s**, *pl.* **—**) (*Zool.*) mule.
maulfaul ['maulfaul], *adj.* tongue-tied; taciturn.
Maulheld ['maulhɛlt], *m.* (**—en** *pl.* **—en**) braggart.
Maulkorb ['maulkɔrp], *m.* (**—s**, *pl.* -e) muzzle.
Maulschelle ['maulʃɛlə], *f.* (**—**, *pl.* **—n**) box on the ear.
Maultier ['maulti:r], *n.* (**—s**, *pl.* **—e**) (*Zool.*) mule.
Maulwerk ['maulvɛrk], *n.* (**—s**, *no pl.*) *ein großes — haben*, (*coll.*) have the gift of the gab.
Maulwurf ['maulvurf], *m.* (**—s**, *pl.* -e) (*Zool.*) mole.
Maurer ['maurər], *m.* (**—s**, *pl.* **—**) mason, bricklayer.
Maus [maus], *f.* (**—**, *pl.* -e) mouse.
Mausefalle ['mauzəfalə], *f.* (**—**, *pl.* **—n**) mouse-trap.
mausen ['mauzən], *v.n.* catch mice. *— v.a.* (*fig.*) pilfer, pinch.
Mauser ['mauzər], *f.* (**—**, *no pl.*) moulting.
mausern ['mauzərn], *v.r. sich —*, moult.
mausetot ['mauzəto:t], *adj.* dead as a door-nail.
mausig ['mauzɪç], *adj. sich — machen*, put on airs.
Maxime [mak'si:mə], *f.* (**—**, *pl.* **—n**) maxim, motto, device.
Mazedonien [matsə'do:njən], *n.* Macedonia.
Mäzen [mɛ'tse:n], *m.* (**—s**, *pl.* **—e**) patron of the arts, Maecenas.
Mechanik [me'ça:nɪk], *f.* (**—**, *no pl.*) mechanics.
Mechaniker [me'ça:nɪkər], *m.* (**—s**, *pl.* **—**) mechanic.
mechanisch [me'ça:nɪʃ], *adj.* mechanical.
meckern ['mɛkərn], *v.n.* bleat; (*fig.*) grumble, complain.
Medaille [me'daljə], *f.* (**—**, *pl.* **—n**) medal.
Medaillon [medal'jõ], *n.* (**—s**, *pl.* **—s**) locket.
meditieren [medi'ti:rən], *v.n.* meditate.
Medizin [medi'tsi:n], *f.* (**—**, *pl.* **—en**) medicine, physic.
Mediziner [medi'tsi:nər], *m.* (**—s**, *pl.* **—**) physician, medical practitioner, student of medicine.
medizinisch [medi'tsi:nɪʃ], *adj.* medical, medicinal.
Meer [me:r], *n.* (**—es**, *pl.* **—e**) sea, ocean; *offnes —*, high seas; *am —*, at the seaside; *auf dem —*, at sea; *übers —*, overseas.
Meerbusen ['me:rbu:zən], *m.* (**—s**, *pl.* **—**) bay, gulf, bight.

Meerenge ['me:rɛŋə], *f.* (**—**, *pl.* **—n**) straits.
Meeresspiegel ['me:rəsʃpi:gəl], *m.* (**—s**, *no pl.*) sea-level.
Meerkatze ['me:rkatsə], *f.* (**—**, *pl.* **—n**) long-tailed monkey.
Meerrettich ['me:rrɛtɪç], *m.* (**—s**, *pl.* **—e**) (*Bot.*) horse-radish.
Meerschaum ['me:rʃaum], *m.* (**—s**, *no pl.*) sea-foam; (*pipe*) meerschaum.
Meerschwein ['me:rʃvain], *n.* (**—s**, *pl.* **—e**) (*Zool.*) porpoise.
Meerschweinchen ['me:rʃvainçən], *n.* (**—s**, *pl.* **—**) (*Zool.*) guinea-pig.
Mehl [me:l], *n.* (**—es**, *no pl.*) flour; meal; dust, powder.
Mehlkleister ['me:lklaistər], *m.* (**—s**, *no pl.*) flour paste.
Mehlspeise ['me:lʃpaizə], *f.* (**—**, *pl.* **—n**) (*dial.*) pudding, sweet.
mehr [me:r], *indecl. adj., adv.* more; *umso —*, all the more; *immer —*, more and more; *— als genug*, enough and to spare.
Mehrbetrag ['me:rbətra:k], *m.* (**—s**, *pl.* -e) surplus.
mehrdeutig ['me:rdɔytɪç], *adj.* ambiguous.
mehren ['me:rən], *v.r. sich —*, multiply, increase in numbers.
mehrere ['me:rərə], *pl. adj.* several.
mehrfach ['me:rfax], *adj.* repeated.
Mehrheit ['me:rhait], *f.* (**—**, *pl.* **—en**) majority.
mehrmals ['me:rma:ls], *adv.* several times.
Mehrzahl ['me:rtsa:l], *f.* (**—**, *no pl.*) (*Gram.*) plural; majority, bulk.
meiden ['maidən], *v.a. irr.* shun, avoid.
Meierei [maiə'rai], *f.* (**—**, *pl.* **—en**) (*dairy*) farm.
Meile ['mailə], *f.* (**—**, *pl.* **—n**) mile; league.
Meiler ['mailər], *m.* (**—s**, *pl.* **—**) charcoal-kiln, charcoal-pile.
mein(e) ['main(ə)], *poss. adj.* my. *— poss. pron.* mine.
Meineid ['mainait], *m.* (**—s**, *pl.* **—e**) perjury; *einen — schwören*, perjure o.s.
meineidig ['mainaidɪç], *adj.* perjured, forsworn.
meinen ['mainən], *v.a.* mean, intend, think.
meinerseits ['mainərzaits], *adv.* I, for my part.
meinethalben ['mainəthalbən], *adv.* on my account, speaking for myself, for my sake; I don't care, I don't mind.
meinetwegen ['mainətve:gən], *adv. see* meinethalben.
meinetwillen ['mainətvilən], *adv. um —*, for my sake, on my behalf.
meinige ['mainigə], *poss. pron.* mine.
Meinung ['mainuŋ], *f.* (**—**, *pl.* **—en**) opinion; meaning; notion; *öffentliche —*, public opinion; *der — sein*, be of the opinion, hold the opinion; *einem die — sagen*, give s.o. a piece of o.'s mind; *meiner — nach*, in my opinion.

Meinungsverschiedenheit [′maɪnuŋs-fɛrʃi:dənhaɪt], *f.* (—, *pl.* —en) difference of opinion, disagreement.
Meise [′maɪzə], *f.* (—, *pl.* —n) (*Orn.*) titmouse.
Meißel [′maɪsəl], *m.* (—s, *pl.* —) chisel.
meißeln [′maɪsəln], *v.a.* chisel, sculpt.
meist [maɪst], *adj.* most. — *adv.* usually, generally.
meistens [′maɪstəns], *adv.* mostly.
Meister [′maɪstər], *m.* (—s, *pl.* —) (*craft*) master; (*sport*) champion; *seinen — finden*, meet o.'s match.
meisterhaft [′maɪstərhaft], *adj.* masterly.
meisterlich [′maɪstərlɪç], *adj.* masterly.
meistern [′maɪstərn], *v.a.* master.
Meisterschaft [′maɪstərʃaft], *f.* (—, *pl.* —en) mastery; (*sport*) championship.
Mekka [′mɛka], *n.* Mecca.
Meldeamt [′mɛldəamt], *n.* (—s, *pl.* ⁚er) registration office.
melden [′mɛldən], *v.a.* announce, inform, notify; (*Mil.*) report. — *v.r. sich —*, answer the phone; *sich — lassen*, send in o.'s name, have o.s. announced; *sich zu etwas —*, apply for s.th.
Meldezettel [′mɛldətsetəl], *m.* (—s, *pl.* —) registration form.
meliert [me′li:rt], *adj.* mixed; (*hair*) iron grey, streaked with grey.
melken [′mɛlkən], *v.a. irr.* milk.
Melodie [melo′di:], *f.* (—, *pl.* —n) melody, tune.
Melone [me′lo:nə], *f.* (—, *pl.* —n) (*Bot.*) melon; (*coll.*) bowler hat.
Meltau [′me:ltau], *m.* (—s, *no pl.*) mildew.
Membrane [mɛm′bra:nə], *f.* (—, *pl.* —n) membrane, diaphragm.
Memme [′mɛmə], *f.* (—, *pl.* —n) coward, poltroon.
memorieren [memo′ri:rən], *v.a.* memorise, learn by heart.
Menage [me′na:ʒə], *f.* (—, *pl.* —n) household.
Menge [′mɛŋə], *f.* (—, *pl.* —n) quantity, amount; multitude, crowd; *eine —*, a lot.
mengen [′mɛŋən], *v.a.* mix. — *v.r. sich —*, interfere in.
Mensch (1) [mɛnʃ], *m.* (—en, *pl.* —en) human being; man; person; *kein —*, nobody.
Mensch (2) [mɛnʃ], *n.* (—es, *pl.* —er) (*vulg.*) wench.
Menschenfeind [′mɛnʃənfaɪnt], *m.* (—es, *pl.* —e) misanthropist.
Menschenfreund [′mɛnʃənfrɔynt], *m.* (—es, *pl.* —e) philanthropist.
Menschengedenken [′mɛnʃəngədeŋkən], *n.* (—s, *no pl.*) *seit —*, from time immemorial.
Menschenhandel [′mɛnʃənhandəl], *m.* (—s, *no pl.*) slave-trade.
Menschenkenner [′mɛnʃənkɛnər], *m.* (—s, *pl.* —) judge of character.

Menschenmenge [′mɛnʃənmɛŋə], *f.* (—, *no pl.*) crowd.
Menschenraub [′mɛnʃənraup], *m.* (—s, *no pl.*) kidnapping.
Menschenverstand [′mɛnʃənfɛrʃtant], *m.* (—es, *no pl.*) human understanding; *gesunder —*, commonsense.
Menschheit [′mɛnʃhaɪt], *f.* (—, *no pl.*) mankind, human race.
menschlich [′mɛnʃlɪç], *adj.* human.
Menschwerdung [′mɛnʃverduŋ], *f.* (—, *no pl.*) incarnation.
Mensur [mɛn′zu:r], *f.* (—, *pl.* —en) students' duel.
Mergel [′mɛrgəl], *m.* (—s, *no pl.*) marl.
merkbar [′mɛrkba:r], *adj.* perceptible, noticeable.
merken [′mɛrkən], *v.a.* note, perceive, observe, notice; *sich etwas —*, bear in mind; *sich nichts — lassen*, show no sign.
merklich [′mɛrklɪç], *adj.* perceptible, appreciable.
Merkmal [′mɛrkma:l], *n.* (—s, *pl.* —e) mark, characteristic, feature.
merkwürdig [′mɛrkvyrdɪç], *adj.* remarkable, curious, strange.
Merle [′mɛrlə], *f.* (—, *pl.* —n) (*dial.*) blackbird.
Mesner [′mɛsnər], *m.* (—s, *pl.* —) sexton, sacristan.
meßbar [′mɛsba:r], *adj.* measurable.
Meßbuch [′mɛsbu:x], *n.* (—es, *pl.* ⁚er) missal.
Messe [′mɛsə], *f.* (—, *pl.* —n) (*Eccl.*) Mass; *stille —*, Low Mass; (*Comm.*) fair; (*Mil.*) mess.
messen [′mɛsən], *v.a. irr.* measure, gauge. — *v.r. sich mit einem —*, pit oneself against s.o.
Messer (1) [′mɛsər], *m.* (—s, *pl.* —) gauge, meter.
Messer (2) [′mɛsər], *n.* (—s, *pl.* —) knife.
Messerheld [′mɛsərhɛlt], *m.* (—en, *pl.* —en) cut-throat, hooligan, rowdy.
Messias [mɛ′si:as], *m.* Messiah.
Meßgewand [′mɛsgəvant], *n.* (—es, *pl.* ⁚er) chasuble, vestment.
Meßkunst [′mɛskunst], *f.* (—, *no pl.*) surveying.
Messing [′mɛsɪŋ], *n.* (—s, *no pl.*) brass; *aus —*, brazen.
Metall [me′tal], *n.* (—s, *pl.* —e) metal; *unedle —e*, base metals.
Metallkunde [me′talkundə], *f.* (—, *no pl.*) metallurgy.
meteorologisch [meteoro′lo:gɪʃ], *adj.* meteorological.
Meter [′me:tər], *n. & m.* (—s, *pl.* —) (*linear measure*) metre; (*Am.*) meter; (*Poet.*) metre.
methodisch [me′to:dɪʃ], *adj.* methodical.
Metrik [′me:trɪk], *f.* (—, *no pl.*) prosody, versification.
Mette [′mɛtə], *f.* (—, *pl.* —n) (*Eccl.*) matins.

Metze ['mɛtsə], *f.* (—, *pl.* —n) (*obs.*) prostitute.

Metzelei [mɛtsə'laɪ], *f.* (—, *pl.* —en) slaughter, massacre.

metzeln ['mɛtsəln], *v.a.* massacre, butcher.

Metzger ['mɛtsgər], *m.* (—s, *pl.* —) butcher.

Meuchelmörder ['mɔyçəlmœrdər], *m.* (—s, *pl.* —) assassin.

meucheln ['mɔyçəln], *v.a.* assassinate.

meuchlings ['mɔyçlɪŋs], *adv.* treacherously, insidiously.

Meute ['mɔytə], *f.* (—, *pl.* —n) pack of hounds; (*fig.*) gang.

Meuterei [mɔytə'raɪ], *f.* (—, *pl.* —en) mutiny, sedition.

meutern ['mɔytərn], *v.n.* mutiny.

Mezzanin ['mɛtsanɪn], *n.* (—s, *pl.* —e) half-storey, mezzanine.

miauen [mi'auən], *v.n.* mew.

mich [mɪç], *pers. pron.* me, myself.

Michaeli(s) [mɪça'e:li(s)], *n.* Michaelmas.

Michel ['mɪçəl], *m.* Michael; *deutscher* —, plain honest German.

Mieder ['mi:dər], *n.* (—s, *pl.* —) bodice.

Miene ['mi:nə], *f.* (—, *pl.* —n) mien, air; (*facial*) expression.

Miete ['mi:tə], *f.* (—, *pl.* —n) rent; hire; (*corn*) rick, stack.

mieten ['mi:tən], *v.a.* rent, hire.

Mieter ['mi:tər], *m.* (—s, *pl.* —) tenant, lodger.

Mietskaserne ['mi:tskazɛrnə], *f.* (—, *pl.* —en) tenement house.

Mietszins ['mi:tstsɪns], *m.* (—es, *pl.* —e) rent.

Milbe ['mɪlbə], *f.* (—, *pl.* —n) mite.

Milch [mɪlç], *f.* (—, *no pl.*) milk; (*fish*) soft roe; *abgerahmte* —, skim(med) milk; *geronnene* —, curdled milk.

Milchbart ['mɪlçba:rt], *m.* (—s, *pl.* ⁻e) milksop.

Milchbruder ['mɪlçbru:dər], *m.* (—s, *pl.* ⁻) foster-brother.

milchen ['mɪlçən], *v.n.* yield milk.

Milcher ['mɪlçer], *m.* (—s, *pl.* —) (*fish*) milter.

Milchgesicht ['mɪlçgəzɪçt], *n.* (—s, *pl.* —er) baby face; smooth complexion.

Milchglas ['mɪlçglas], *n.* (—es, *no pl.*) opalescent glass, frosted glass.

Milchstraße ['mɪlçʃtra:sə], *f.* (—, *no pl.*) Milky Way.

Milde ['mɪldə], *f.* (—, *no pl.*) mildness, softness; (*fig.*) gentleness, (*rare*) charity, generosity.

mildern ['mɪldərn], *v.a.* soften, alleviate, mitigate, soothe, allay; —*de Umstände*, extenuating circumstances.

Milderung ['mɪldərʊŋ], *f.* (—, *pl.* —en) mitigation, mellowing; soothing.

mildtätig ['mɪlttɛːtɪç], *adj.* charitable, benevolent, munificent.

Militär [mili'tɛːr], *n.* (—s, *no pl.* military, army ; *beim* — *sein*, serve in the army.

Miliz [mi'li:ts], *f.* (—, *no pl.*) militia.

Milliarde [mɪl'jardə], *f.* (—, *pl.* —n) a thousand millions; (*Am.*) billion.

Million [mɪl'jo:n], *f.* (—, *pl.* —en) million.

Millionär [mɪljo'nɛːr], *m.* (—s, *pl.* —e) millionaire.

Milz [mɪlts], *f.* (—, *pl.* —en) spleen.

Mime ['mi:mə], *m.* (—n, *pl.* —n) mime, actor.

Mimik ['mi:mɪk], *f.* (—, *no pl.*) mime, miming.

Mimiker ['mi:mɪkər], *m.* (—s, *pl.* —) mimic.

Mimose [mi'mo:zə], *f.* (—, *pl.* —n) (*Bot.*) mimosa.

minder ['mɪndər], *adj.* lesser, smaller, minor, inferior.

Minderheit ['mɪndərhaɪt], *f.* (—, *pl.* —en) minority.

minderjährig ['mɪndərjɛːrɪç], *adj.* (*Law*) under age.

mindern ['mɪndərn], *v.a.* diminish, lessen.

minderwertig ['mɪndərvɛrtɪç], *adj.* inferior, of poor quality.

Minderwertigkeitskomplex ['mɪndərvɛrtɪçkaɪtskɔmplɛks], *m.* (—es, *pl.* —e) inferiority complex.

mindest ['mɪndəst], *adj.* least, smallest, minimum, lowest; *nicht im* —*en*, not in the least, not at all.

mindestens ['mɪndəstəns], *adv.* at least.

Mine ['mi:nə], *f.* (—, *pl.* —n) mine; (*ball point pen*) refill; (*pencil*) lead.

minimal [mini'ma:l], *adj.* infinitesimal, minimum.

Ministerialrat [minister'ja:lra:t], *m.* (—s, *pl.* ⁻e) senior civil servant.

ministeriell [mɪnister'jɛl], *adj.* ministerial.

Ministerium [mini'ste:rjum], *n.* (—s, *pl.* —rien) ministry.

Ministerpräsident [mi'nɪstərprɛ:zidɛnt], *m.* (—en, *pl.* —en) prime minister; premier.

Ministerrat [mi'nɪstərra:t], *m.* (—s, *pl.* ⁻e) cabinet, council of ministers.

Ministrant [mini'strant], *m.* (—en, *pl.* —en) acolyte; sacristan.

Minne ['mɪnə], *f.* (—, *no pl.*) (*obs.*, *Poet.*) love.

Minnesänger [mɪnə'zɛŋər], *m.* (—s, *pl.* —) minnesinger; troubadour, minstrel.

Minus ['mi:nus], *n.* (—, *no pl.*) deficit.

Minze ['mɪntsə], *f.* (—, *pl.* —n) (*Bot.*) mint.

mir [mi:r], *pers. pron.* to me.

Mirakel [mi'ra:kəl], *n.* (—s, *pl.* —) miracle, marvel, wonder.

mischen ['mɪʃən], *v.a.* mix; (*Cards*) shuffle; (*coffee, tea*) blend.

Mischling ['mɪʃlɪŋ], *m.* (—s, *pl.* —e) mongrel, hybrid.

Mischrasse

Mischrasse ['mɪʃrasə], f. (—, pl. —n) cross-breed.

Mischung ['mɪʃuŋ], f. (—, pl. —en) mixture, blend.

Misere [mi'zeːrə], f. (—, no pl.) unhappiness, misery.

Mispel ['mɪspəl], f. (—, pl. —n) (Bot.) medlar (tree).

mißachten [mɪs'axtən], v.a. disregard, despise.

mißarten [mɪs'aːrtən], v.n. (aux. sein) degenerate.

Mißbehagen ['mɪsbəhaːgən], n. (—s, no pl.) displeasure, uneasiness.

mißbilligen [mɪs'bɪlɪgən], v.a. object (to), disapprove (of).

Mißbrauch ['mɪsbraux], m. (—s, pl. ⁓e) abuse, misuse.

missen ['mɪsən], v.a. lack, be without, feel the lack of.

Missetat ['mɪsətaːt], f. (—, pl. —en) misdeed, felony.

mißfallen [mɪs'falən], v.n. irr. displease.

mißförmig ['mɪsfœrmɪç], adj. deformed, misshapen.

Mißgeburt ['mɪsgəburt], f. (—, pl. —en) abortion; monster.

mißgelaunt ['mɪsgəlaunt], adj. ill-humoured.

Mißgeschick ['mɪsgəʃɪk], n. (—s, no pl.) mishap, misfortune.

mißgestimmt ['mɪsgəʃtɪmt], adj. grumpy, out of sorts.

mißglücken [mɪs'glykən], v.n. (aux. sein) fail, be unsuccessful.

Mißgriff ['mɪsgrɪf], m. (—s, pl. —e) blunder, mistake.

Mißgunst ['mɪsgunst], f. (—, no pl.) jealousy, envy.

mißhandeln [mɪs'handəln], v.a. illtreat.

Missionar [mɪsjo'naːr], m. (—s, pl. —e) missionary.

mißlich ['mɪslɪç], adj. awkward; difficult, unpleasant.

mißliebig ['mɪsliːbɪç], adj. unpopular, odious.

mißlingen [mɪs'lɪŋən], v.n. irr. (aux. sein) miscarry, go wrong, misfire, prove a failure, turn out badly.

mißraten [mɪs'raːtən], v.n. irr. (aux. sein) miscarry, turn out badly.

Mißstand ['mɪsʃtant], m. (—es, pl. ⁓e) grievance, abuse.

Mißton ['mɪstoːn], m. (—s, pl. ⁓e) dissonance.

mißtrauen [mɪs'trauən], v.n. distrust, mistrust.

Mißverhältnis ['mɪsfɛrhɛltnɪs], n. (—ses, no pl.) disproportion.

Mißverständnis ['mɪsfɛrʃtɛntnɪs], n. (—ses, pl. —se) misunderstanding.

Mist [mɪst], m. (—es, no pl.) dung, manure, muck; (fig.) rubbish.

Mistel ['mɪstəl], f. (—, pl. —n) (Bot.) mistletoe.

Mistfink ['mɪstfɪŋk], m. (—s, pl. —e) (fig.) dirty child; mudlark.

mit [mɪt], prep. (Dat.) with. — adv. also, along with.

mitarbeiten ['mɪtarbaɪtən], v.n. collaborate, cooperate; (lit. work) contribute.

mitbringen ['mɪtbrɪŋən], v.a. irr. bring along.

Mitbürger ['mɪtbyrgər], m. (—s, pl. —) fellow-citizen.

mitempfinden ['mɪtɛmpfɪndən], v.a. irr. sympathise with.

Mitesser ['mɪtɛsər], m. (—s, pl. —) (Med.) blackhead.

mitfahren ['mɪtfaːrən], v.n. irr. (aux. sein) ride with s.o.; einen — lassen, give s.o. a lift.

mitfühlen ['mɪtfyːlən], v.n. sympathise.

mitgehen ['mɪtgeːən], v.n. irr. (aux. sein) go along (with), accompany (s.o.); etwas — heißen or lassen, pilfer, pocket, pinch.

Mitgift ['mɪtgɪft], f. (—, no pl.) dowry.

Mitglied ['mɪtgliːt], n. (—s, pl. —er) member, fellow, associate.

mithin [mɪt'hɪn], adv., conj. consequently, therefore.

Mitläufer ['mɪtlɔyfər], m. (—s, pl. —) (Polit.) fellow-traveller.

Mitlaut ['mɪtlaut], m. (—s, pl. —e) (Phonet.) consonant.

Mitleid ['mɪtlaɪt], n. (—s, no pl.) compassion, sympathy, pity; mit einem — haben, take pity on s.o.

Mitleidenschaft ['mɪtlaɪdənʃaft], f. (—, no pl.) einen in — ziehen, involve s.o., implicate s.o.

mitmachen ['mɪtmaxən], v.a., v.n. join in, participate (in), do as others do; go through, suffer.

Mitmensch ['mɪtmɛnʃ], m. (—en, pl. —en) fellow-man; fellow-creature.

mitnehmen ['mɪtneːmən], v.a. irr. take along, take with o.; strain, take it out of o., weaken.

mitnichten [mɪt'nɪçtən], adv. by no means.

mitreden ['mɪtreːdən], v.n. join in a conversation; contribute.

mitsamt [mɪt'zamt], prep. (Dat.) together with.

Mitschuld ['mɪtʃult], f. (—, no pl.) complicity.

Mitschüler ['mɪtʃyːlər], m. (—s, pl. —) schoolfellow, fellow-pupil, fellow-student, classmate.

Mittag ['mɪtaːk], m. (—s, pl. —e) midday, noon, noontide; zu — essen, have dinner or lunch.

Mittagessen ['mɪtaːkɛsən], n. (—s, pl. —) lunch, luncheon.

Mittagsseite ['mɪtaːkszaɪtə], f. (—, no pl.) south side.

Mittäter ['mɪttɛːtər], m. (—s, pl. —) accomplice.

Mitte ['mɪtə], f. (—, no pl.) middle, midst.

mitteilen ['mɪttaɪlən], v.a. (Dat.) communicate, inform, impart.

moll

mitteilsam ['mɪttaɪlzaːm], *adj.* communicative.
Mitteilung ['mɪttaɪluŋ], *f.* (—, *pl.* —en) communication.
Mittel ['mɪtəl], *n.* (—s, *pl.*) means, expedient, way, resource; remedy; (*pl.*) money, funds; *als — zum Zweck*, as a means to an end; *sich ins — legen*, mediate, intercede.
Mittelalter ['mɪtəlaltər], *n.* (—s, *no pl.*) Middle Ages.
mittelbar ['mɪtəlbaːr], *adj.* indirect.
Mittelding ['mɪtəldɪŋ], *n.* (—s, *pl.* —e) medium; something in between.
Mittelgebirge ['mɪtəlgəbɪrgə], *n.* (—s, *pl.* —) hills; (subalpine) mountains.
mittelländisch ['mɪtəllendɪʃ], *adj.* Mediterranean.
mittellos ['mɪtəlloːs], *adj.* penniless, impecunious.
Mittelmaß ['mɪtəlmaːs], *n.* (—es, *pl.* —e) average.
mittelmäßig ['mɪtəlmɛːsɪç], *adj.* mediocre.
Mittelmeer ['mɪtəlmeːr], *n.* (—s, *no pl.*) Mediterranean.
Mittelpunkt ['mɪtəlpuŋkt], *m.* (—s, *pl.* —e) centre; focus.
mittels ['mɪtəls], *prep.* (*Genit.*) by means of.
Mittelschule ['mɪtəlʃuːlə], *f.* (—, *pl.* —n) secondary (intermediate) school; (*Austr.*) grammar school; (*Am.*) high school.
Mittelstand ['mɪtəlʃtant], *m.* (—es, *no pl.*) middle class.
mittelste ['mɪtəlstə], *adj.* middlemost, central.
Mittelstürmer ['mɪtəlʃtyrmər], *m.* (—s, *pl.* —) (*Footb.*) centre-forward.
Mittelwort ['mɪtəlvɔrt], *n.* (—es, *pl.* ⁓er) (*Gram.*) participle.
mitten ['mɪtən], *adv.* in the midst; — *am Tage*, in broad daylight.
Mitternacht ['mɪtərnaxt], *f.* (—, *no pl.*) midnight.
Mittler ['mɪtlər], *m.* (—s, *pl.* —) mediator.
mittlere ['mɪtlərə], *adj.* middle; average; mean.
Mittwoch ['mɪtvɔx], *m.* (—s, *pl.* —e) Wednesday.
mitunter [mɪt'untər], *adv.* now and then, occasionally, sometimes.
mitunterzeichnen ['mɪtuntərtsaɪçnən], *v.a., v.n.* countersign; add o.'s signature (to).
Miturheber ['mɪtuːrheːbər], *m.* (—s, *pl.* —) co-author.
Mitwelt ['mɪtvɛlt], *f.* (—, *no pl.*) the present generation, contemporaries, our own times; the world outside.
mitwirken ['mɪtvɪrkən], *v.n.* cooperate.
Mnemotechnik [mneːmoˈtɛçnɪk], *f.* (—, *no pl.*) mnemonics.
Möbel ['møːbəl], *n.* (—s, *pl.* —) piece of furniture; (*pl.*) furniture.
mobil [moˈbiːl], *adj.* mobile, active, quick; — *machen*, mobilise, put in motion.

Mobiliar [mobilˈjaːr], *n.* (—s, *pl.* Mobilien) furniture, movables.
mobilisieren [mobiliˈziːrən], *v.a.* mobilise.
möblieren [møˈbliːrən], *v.a.* furnish; *neu —*, refurnish.
Mode ['moːdə], *f.* (—, *pl.* —n) mode, fashion; custom, use; *in der —*, in fashion, in vogue.
Modell [moˈdɛl], *n.* (—s, *pl.* —e) model; — *stehen*, model; (*fig.*) be the prototype.
modellieren [modɛˈliːrən], *v.a.* (*dresses*) model; (*Art*) mould.
Moder ['moːdər], *m.* (—s, *no pl.*) mould.
moderig ['moːdrɪç] *see* **modrig**.
modern(1) ['moːdərn], *v.n.* moulder, rot.
modern(2) [moˈdɛrn], *adj.* modern, fashionable, up-to-date.
modernisieren [modɛrniˈziːrən], *v.a.* modernise.
modifizieren [modifiˈtsiːrən], *v.a.* modify.
modisch ['moːdɪʃ], *adj.* stylish, fashionable.
Modistin [moˈdɪstɪn], *f.* (—, *pl.* —nen) milliner.
modrig ['moːdrɪç], *adj.* mouldy.
modulieren [moduˈliːrən], *v.a.* modulate.
Modus ['moːdus], *m.* (—, *pl.* Modi) (*Gram.*) mood; mode, manner.
mogeln ['moːgəln], *v.n.* cheat.
mögen ['møːgən], *v.n. irr.* like, desire, want, be allowed, have a mind to; (*modal auxiliary*) may, might; *ich möchte gern*, I should like to.
möglich ['møːklɪç], *adj.* possible, practicable; feasible; *sein —stes tun*, do o.'s utmost; *nicht —!* you don't say (so)!
Möglichkeit ['møːklɪçkaɪt], *f.* (—, *pl.* —en) possibility, feasibility, practicability; (*pl.*) potentialities; contingencies, prospects (of career).
Mohn [moːn], *m.* (—es, *no pl.*) poppy(seed).
Mohr [moːr], *m.* (—en, *pl.* —en) Moor; negro.
Möhre ['møːrə], *f.* (—, *pl.* —n) carrot.
Mohrenkopf ['moːrənkɔpf], *m.* (—es, *pl.* ⁓e) chocolate éclair.
Mohrrübe ['moːrryːbə], *f.* (—, *pl.* —n) carrot.
mokieren [moˈkiːrən], *v.r. sich — über*, sneer at, mock at, be amused by.
Mokka ['mɔka], *m.* (—s, *no pl.*) Mocha coffee.
Molch [mɔlç], *m.* (—es, *pl.* —e) (*Zool.*) salamander.
Moldau ['mɔldau], *f.* Moldavia.
Mole ['moːlə], *f.* (—, *pl.* —n) breakwater, jetty, pier.
Molekül [moleˈkyːl], *n.* (—s, *pl.* —e) molecule.
Molke ['mɔlkə], *f.* (—, *pl.* —n) whey.
Molkerei [mɔlkeˈraɪ], *f.* (—, *pl.* —en) dairy.
moll [mɔl], *adj.* (*Mus.*) minor.

Molluske

Molluske [mɔˈluskə], *f.* (—, *pl.* —**n**) (*Zool.*) mollusc.

Moment (1) [moˈmɛnt], *m.* (—**s**, *pl.* —**e**) moment, instant.

Moment (2) [moˈmɛnt], *n.* motive, factor; (*Phys.*) momentum.

Momentaufnahme [moˈmɛntaufnaːmə], *f.* (—, *pl.* —**n**) snapshot.

momentan [momɛnˈtaːn], *adv.* at the moment, for the present, just now.

Monarch [moˈnarç], *m.* (—**en**, *pl.* —**en**) monarch.

Monarchie [monarˈçiː], *f.* (—, *pl.* —**n**) monarchy.

Monat [ˈmoːnat], *m.* (—**s**, *pl.* —**e**) month.

monatlich [ˈmoːnatlɪç], *adj.* monthly.

Monatsfluß [ˈmoːnatsflus], *m.* (—**sses**, *pl.* ⸚**sse**) menses.

Monatsschrift [ˈmoːnatsʃrɪft], *f.* (—, *pl.* —**en**) monthly (*journal*).

Mönch [mœnç], *m.* (—**es**, *pl.* —**e**) monk, friar.

Mönchskappe [ˈmœnçskapə], *f.* (—⸗, *pl.* —**n**) cowl, monk's hood.

Mönchskutte [ˈmœnçskutə], *f.* (—, *pl.* —**n**) cowl.

Mond [moːnt], *m.* (—**es**, *pl.* —**e**) moon; *zunehmender* —, waxing moon; *abnehmender* —, waning moon.

Mondfinsternis [ˈmoːntfɪnstɛrnɪs], *f.* (—, *pl.* —**se**) eclipse of the moon.

mondsüchtig [ˈmoːntzyçtɪç], *adj.* given to sleep-walking; (*fig.*) moon-struck.

Mondwandlung [ˈmoːntvandluŋ], *f.* (—, *pl.* —**en**) phase of the moon.

Moneten [moˈneːtən], *pl.* (*sl.*) money, cash, funds.

Mongolei [mɔŋgoˈlaɪ], *f.* Mongolia.

monieren [moˈniːrən], *v.a.* remind (a debtor); censure.

monogam [monoˈgaːm], *adj.* monogamous.

Monopol [monoˈpoːl], *n.* (—**s**, *pl.* —**e**) monopoly.

monoton [monoˈtoːn], *adj.* monotonous.

Monstrum [ˈmɔnstrum], *n.* (—**s**, *pl.* **Monstra**) monster, monstrosity.

Monsun [mɔnˈzuːn], *m.* (—**s**, *pl.* —**e**) monsoon.

Montag [ˈmoːntaːk], *m.* (—**s**, *pl.* —**e**) Monday; *blauer* —, Bank Holiday Monday.

Montage [mɔnˈtaːʒə], *f.* (—, *pl.* —**n**) fitting (up), setting up, installation, assembling.

Montanindustrie [mɔnˈtaːnɪndustriː], *f.* (—, *no pl.*) mining industry.

Montanunion [mɔnˈtaːnunjoːn], *f.* (—, *no pl.*) (*Pol.*) European Coal and Steel Community.

Monteur [mɔnˈtøːr], *m.* (—**s**, *pl.* —**e**) fitter.

montieren [mɔnˈtiːrən], *v.a.* fit (up), set up, mount, install.

Montur [mɔnˈtuːr], *f.* (—, *pl.* —**en**) uniform, livery.

Moor [moːr], *n.* (—**es**, *pl.* —**e**) swamp, fen, bog.

Moos [moːs], *n.* (—**es**, *pl.* —**e**) moss; (*sl.*) cash.

Moped [ˈmoːpɛt], *n.* (—**s**, *pl.* —**s**) moped, motorised pedal cycle.

Mops [mɔps], *m.* (—**es**, *pl.* ⸚**e**) pug (dog).

mopsen [ˈmɔpsən], *v.r. sich* —, feel bored.

Moral [moˈraːl], *f.* (—, *no pl.*) moral, morals.

moralisch [moˈraːlɪʃ], *adj.* moral.

Morast [moˈrast], *m.* (—**es**, *pl.* ⸚**e**) morass, bog, fen, mire.

Moratorium [moraˈtoːrjum], *n.* (—**s**, *pl.* —**rien**) (*payments etc.*) respite.

Morchel [ˈmɔrçəl], *f.* (—, *pl.* —**n**) (*Bot.*) morel (edible fungus).

Mord [mɔrt], *m.* (—**es**, *pl.* —**e**) murder.

morden [ˈmɔrdən], *v.a.*, *v.n.* murder.

Mörder [ˈmœrdər], *m.* (—**s**, *pl.* —) murderer.

Mordsgeschichte [ˈmɔrtsgəʃɪçtə], *f.* (—, *pl.* —**n**) (*coll.*) cock-and-bull story.

Mordskerl [ˈmɔrtskɛrl], *m.* (—**s**, *pl.* —**e**) devil of a fellow; (*Am.*) great guy.

Mordtat [ˈmɔrttaːt], *f.* (—, *pl.* —**en**) murder.

Morelle [moˈrɛlə], *f.* (—, *pl.* —**n**) (*Bot.*) morello cherry.

Morgen [ˈmɔrgən], *m.* (—**s**, *pl.* —) morning, daybreak; (*Poet.*) east; measure of land; *eines* —**s**, one morning.

morgen [ˈmɔrgən], *adv.* tomorrow; — *früh*, tomorrow morning; *heute* —, this morning.

Morgenblatt [ˈmɔrgənblat], *n.* (—**s**, *pl.* ⸚**er**) morning paper.

morgendlich [ˈmɔrgəntlɪç], *adj.* of or in the morning; matutinal.

Morgenland [ˈmɔrgənlant], *n.* (—**es**, *pl.* —) orient, east.

Morgenrot [ˈmɔrgənroːt], *n.* (—**s**, *no pl.*) dawn, sunrise.

morgens [ˈmɔrgəns], *adv.* in the morning.

morgig [ˈmɔrgɪç], *adj.* tomorrow's.

Morphium [ˈmɔrfjum], *n.* (—**s**, *no pl.*) morphia, morphine.

morsch [mɔrʃ], *adj.* brittle, rotten, decayed.

Mörser [ˈmœrzər], *m.* (—**s**, *pl.* —) mortar.

Mörserkeule [ˈmœrzərkɔylə], *f.* (—, *pl.* —**n**) pestle.

Mörtel [ˈmœrtəl], *m.* (—**s**, *no pl.*) mortar, plaster.

Mörtelkelle [ˈmœrtəlkɛlə], *f.* (—, *pl.* —**n**) trowel.

Mosaik [mozaˈiːk], *n.* (—**s**, *pl.* —**e**) mosaic (work); inlaid work.

mosaisch [moˈzaːɪʃ], *adj.* Mosaic.

Moschee [moˈʃeː], *f.* (—, *pl.* —**n**) mosque.

Moschus [ˈmɔʃus], *m.* (—, *no pl.*) musk.

Mosel [ˈmoːzəl], *f.* Moselle.

Moskau [ˈmɔskau], *n.* Moscow.

Moskito [mɔs'ki:to], *m.* (—s, *pl.* —s) (*Ent.*) mosquito.

Most [mɔst], *m.* (—es, *no pl.*) new wine, cider.

Mostrich ['mɔstrɪç], *m.* (—s, *no pl.*) mustard.

Motiv [mo'ti:f], *n.* (—es, *pl.* —e) motive; (*Mus.*, *Lit.*) motif, theme.

motivieren [moti'vi:rən], *v.a.* motivate.

Motorrad ['mo:tɔrra:t], *n.* (—es, *pl.* ⁼er) motor-cycle.

Motte ['mɔtə], *f.* (—, *pl.* —n) (*Ent.*) moth.

moussieren [mu'si:rən], *v.n.* effervesce, sparkle.

Möwe ['mø:və], *f.* (—, *pl.* —n) (*Orn.*) seagull.

Mucke ['mukə], *f.* (—, *pl.* —n) whim, caprice; obstinacy.

Mücke ['mykə], *f.* (—, *pl.* —n) (*Ent.*) gnat, fly, mosquito.

Muckerei [mukə'raɪ], *f.* (—, *pl.* —en) cant.

mucksen ['muksən], *v.n.* stir, move, budge.

müde ['my:də], *adj.* tired, weary; — *machen*, tire.

Muff [muf], *m.* (—es, *pl.* —e) muff.

muffig ['mufɪç], *adj.* musty, fusty, stuffy.

Mühe ['my:ə], *f.* (—, *pl.* —n) trouble, pains; effort, labour, toil; *sich* — *geben*, take pains.

mühelos ['my:əlo:s], *adj.* effortless, easy.

mühen ['my:ən], *v.r. sich* —, exert o.s., take pains.

Mühewaltung ['my:əvaltuŋ], *f.* (—, *pl.* —en) exertion, effort.

Mühle ['my:lə], *f.* (—, *pl.* —n) (*flour*) mill; (*coffee*) grinder; game.

Muhme ['mu:mə], *f.* (—, *pl.* —n) (*obs.*) aunt.

Mühsal ['my:za:l], *f.* (—, *pl.* —e) hardship, misery, toil.

mühsam ['my:za:m], *adj.* troublesome, laborious.

mühselig ['my:ze:lɪç], *adj.* painful, laborious; miserable.

Mulatte [mu'latə], *m.* (—n, *pl.* —n) mulatto.

Mulde ['muldə], *f.* (—, *pl.* —n) trough.

muldenförmig ['muldənfœrmɪç], *adj.* trough-shaped.

Mull [mul], *m.* (—s, *no pl.*) Indian muslin.

Müll [myl], *m.* (—s, *no pl.*) dust, rubbish; (*Am.*) garbage.

Müller ['mylər], *m.* (—s, *pl.* —) miller.

mulmig ['mulmɪç], *adj.* dusty, mouldy, decayed.

multiplizieren [multipli'tsi:rən], *v.a.* multiply.

Mumie ['mu:mjə], *f.* (—, *pl.* —n) (*Archæol.*) mummy.

Mummenschanz ['mumənʃants], *m.* (—es, *no pl.*) mummery, masquerade.

München ['mynçən], *n.* Munich.

Mund [munt], *m.* (—es, *pl.* —e, ⁼er) mouth; *den* — *halten*, keep quiet; *einen großen* — *haben*, talk big; *sich den* — *verbrennen*, put o.'s foot in it.

Mundart ['munta:rt], *f.* (—, *pl.* —en) (local) dialect.

Mündel ['myndəl], *m.*, *f. & n.* (—s, *pl.* —) ward, minor, child under guardianship.

mündelsicher ['myndəlzɪçər], *adj.* gilt-edged.

munden ['mundən], *v.n. es mundet mir*, I like the taste, I relish it.

münden ['myndən], *v.n.* discharge (into), flow (into).

mundfaul ['muntfaul], *adj.* tongue-tied; taciturn.

mundgerecht ['muntgəreçt], *adj.* palatable; (*fig.*) suitable.

Mundharmonika ['muntharmo:nɪka], *f.* (—, *pl.* —kas, —ken) mouth organ.

mündig ['myndɪç], *adj.* of age; — *werden*, come of age.

mündlich ['myntlɪç], *adj.* verbal, oral, by word of mouth; (*examination*) viva voce.

Mundschenk ['muntʃɛŋk], *m.* (—s, *pl.* —e) cupbearer.

mundtot ['muntto:t], *adj.* — *machen*, silence, gag.

Mündung ['mynduŋ], *f.* (—, *pl.* —en) (*river*) estuary, mouth; (*gun*) muzzle.

Mundvorrat ['muntforra:t], *m.* (—s, *pl.* ⁼e) provisions, victuals.

Mundwerk ['muntvɛrk], *n.* (—s, *no pl.*) mouth; (*fig.*) gift of the gab.

Munition [muni'tsjo:n], *f.* (—, *no pl.*) ammunition.

munkeln ['muŋkəln], *v.n.* whisper; *man munkelt*, it is rumoured.

Münster ['mynstər], *n.* (—s, *pl.* —) minster, cathedral.

munter ['muntər], *adj.* awake; lively, active, sprightly, vivacious, cheerful, gay.

Münze ['myntsə], *f.* (—, *pl.* —n) coin.

Münzeinheit ['myntsaɪnhaɪt], *f.* (—, *no pl.*) monetary unit.

Münzfälscher ['myntsfɛlʃər], *m.* (—s, *pl.* —) (counterfeit) coiner.

Münzkunde ['myntskundə], *f.* (—, *no pl.*) numismatics.

Münzprobe ['myntspro:bə], *f.* (—, *pl.* —n) assay of a coin.

mürbe ['myrbə], *adj.* mellow; (*meat*) tender; (*cake*) crisp; brittle; *einen* — *machen*, soften s.o. up, force s.o. to yield.

Murmel ['murməl], *f.* (—, *pl.* —n) (*toy*) marble.

murmeln ['murməln], *v.n.* murmur, mutter.

Murmeltier ['murməlti:r], *n.* (—s, *pl.* —e) (*Zool.*) marmot; *wie ein* — *schlafen*, sleep like a log.

murren ['murən], *v.n.* grumble, growl.

mürrisch ['myrɪʃ], *adj.* morose, surly, sulky, peevish, sullen.

Mus [mu:s], *n.* (**—es**, *no pl.*) purée, (apple) sauce; pulp.

Muschel ['muʃəl], *f.* (—, *pl.* **—n**) mussel, shell; (*telephone*) ear-piece.

Muse ['mu:zə], *f.* (—, *pl.* **—n**) muse.

Muselman ['mu:zəlman], *m.* (**—en**, *pl.* **—en**) Muslim, Moslem.

Musik [mu'zi:k], *f.* (—, *no pl.*) music.

musikalisch [muzi'ka:lɪʃ], *adj.* musical.

Musikant [muzi'kant], *m.* (**—en**, *pl.* **—en**) musician; performer.

Musiker ['mu:zɪkər], *m.* (**—s**, *pl.* —) musician.

musizieren [muzi'tsi:rən], *v.n.* play music.

Muskateller [muska'tɛlər], *m.* (**—s**, *no pl.*) muscatel (wine).

Muskatnuß [mus'ka:tnus], *f.* (—, *pl.* **⸗sse**) nutmeg.

Muskel ['muskəl], *m.* (**—s**, *pl.* **—n**) muscle.

muskelig ['musklɪç] *see* **musklig**.

Muskete [mus'ke:tə], *f.* (—, *pl.* **—n**) musket.

Musketier [muske'ti:r], *m.* (**—s**, *pl.* **—e**) musketeer.

musklig ['musklɪç], *adj.* muscular.

muskulös [musku'lø:s], *adj.* muscular.

Muße ['mu:sə], *f.* (—, *no pl.*) leisure; *mit* —, leisurely, at leisure.

Musselin [musə'li:n], *m.* (**—s**, *pl.* **—e**) muslin.

müssen ['mysən], *v.n. irr.* have to, be forced, be compelled, be obliged; *ich muß,* I must, I have to.

müßig ['my:sɪç], *adj.* idle, lazy, unemployed.

Müßiggang ['my:sɪçɡaŋ], *m.* (**—s**, *no pl.*) idleness, laziness, sloth.

Muster ['mustər], *n.* (**—s**, *pl.* —) sample; pattern; (proto-)type; (*fig.*) example.

Musterbild ['mustərbɪlt], *n.* (**—s**, *pl.* **—er**) paragon.

mustergültig ['mustərgyltɪç], *adj.* exemplary; standard; excellent.

musterhaft ['mustərhaft], *adj.* exemplary.

mustern ['mustərn], *v.a.* examine, muster, scan; (*troops*) review, inspect.

Musterung ['mustərun], *f.* (—, *pl.* **—en**) review; examination, inspection.

Mut ['mu:t], *m.* (**—es**, *no pl.*) courage, spirit; *— fassen,* take heart, muster up courage.

Mutation [muta'tsjo:n], *f.* (—, *pl.* **—en**) change.

mutieren [mu'ti:rən], *v.n.* change; (*voice*) break.

mutig ['mu:tɪç], *adj.* courageous, brave.

mutlos ['mu:tlo:s], *adj.* discouraged, dejected, despondent.

mutmaßen ['mu:tma:sən], *v.a. insep.* surmise, suppose, conjecture.

Mutter ['mutər], *f.* (—, *pl.* **⸗**) mother; (*screw*) nut.

Mutterkorn ['mutərkɔrn], *n.* (**—s**, *no pl.*) ergot.

Mutterkuchen ['mutərku:xən], *m.* (**—s**, *pl.* —) placenta, after-birth.

Mutterleib ['mutərlaɪp], *m.* (**—s**, *no pl.*) womb, uterus.

Muttermal ['mutərma:l], *n.* (**—s**, *pl.* **—e**) birth-mark.

Mutterschaft ['mutərʃaft], *f.* (—, *no pl.*) motherhood, maternity.

mutterseelenallein ['mutərze:lənalaɪn], *adj.* quite alone; (*coll.*) all on o.'s own.

Muttersöhnchen ['mutərzø:nçən], *n.* (**—s**, *pl.* —) mother's darling, spoilt child.

Mutterwitz ['mutərvɪts], *m.* (**—es**, *no pl.*) mother-wit, native wit, common sense.

Mutwille ['mu:tvɪlə], *m.* (**—ns**, *no pl.*) mischievousness, wantonness.

Mütze ['mytsə], *f.* (—, *pl.* **—n**) cap; bonnet; beret.

Myrrhe ['mɪrə], *f.* (—, *pl.* **—n**) myrrh.

Myrte ['mɪrtə], *f.* (—, *pl.* **—n**) (*Bot.*) myrtle.

Mysterium [mɪs'te:rjum], *n.* (**—s**, *pl.* **—rien**) mystery.

Mystik ['mɪstɪk], *f.* (—, *no pl.*) mysticism.

Mythologie [mytolo'gi:], *f.* (—, *pl.* **—n**) mythology.

Mythus ['mytus], *m.* (—, *pl.* **Mythen**) myth.

N

N [ɛn], *n.* (**—s**, *pl.* **—s**) the letter N.

na [na], *int.* well, now; *—nu!* well, I never! — *und?* so what?

Nabe ['na:bə], *f.* (—, *pl.* **—n**) hub.

Nabel ['na:bəl], *m.* (**—s**, *pl.* —) navel.

Nabelschnur ['na:bəlʃnu:r], *f.* (—, *pl.* **⸗e**) umbilical cord.

nach [na:x], *prep.* (*Dat.*) after, behind, following; to, towards; according to, in conformity *or* accordance with; in imitation of. — *adv.*, *prefix.* after, behind; afterwards, later; — *und* —, little by little, by degrees, gradually.

nachäffen ['na:xɛfən], *v.a.* ape, mimic, imitate; (*coll.*) take off.

nachahmen ['na:xa:mən], *v.a.* imitate, copy; counterfeit.

nacharbeiten ['na:xarbaɪtən], *v.n.* work after hours *or* overtime. — *v.a.* copy (*Dat.*).

nacharten ['na:xa:rtən], *v.n.* (*aux. sein*) resemble, (*coll.*) take after.

Nachbar ['naxba:r], *m.* (**—s**, *pl.* **—n**, *pl.* **—n**) neighbour.

Nachbarschaft ['naxba:rʃaft], *f.* (—, *no pl.*) neighbourhood, vicinity; (*people*) neighbours.

nachbestellen ['na:xbəʃtɛlən], *v.a.* order more, re-order.

nachbilden ['na:xbɪldən], v.a. copy, reproduce.

nachdem [na:x'de:m], adv. afterwards, after that. — conj. after, when; je —, according to circumstances, that depends.

nachdenken ['na:xdɛŋkən], v.n. irr. think (over), meditate, muse, ponder.

nachdenklich ['na:xdɛŋklɪç], adj. reflective, pensive, wistful; — stimmen, set thinking.

Nachdruck ['na:xdruk], m. (—s, pl. —e) reprint; stress, emphasis.

nachdrucken ['na:xdrukən], v.a. reprint.

nachdrücklich ['na:xdryklɪç], adj. emphatic; — betonen, emphasise.

nacheifern ['na:xaɪfərn], v.n. einem —, emulate s.o.

nacheinander ['na:xaɪnandər], adv. one after another.

nachempfinden ['na:xɛmpfɪndən], v.a. irr. sympathize with, feel for.

Nachen ['naxən], m. (—s, pl. —) (Poet.) boat, skiff.

Nachfolge ['na:xfɔlgə], f. (—, pl. —n) succession.

nachfolgend ['na:xfɔlgənt], adj. following, subsequent.

Nachfolger ['na:xfɔlgər], m. (—s, pl. —) successor.

nachforschen ['na:xfɔrʃən], v.a. search after; enquire into, investigate.

Nachfrage ['na:xfra:gə], f. (—, no pl.) enquiry; (Comm.) demand; Angebot und —, supply and demand.

nachfühlen ['na:xfy:lən], v.a. einem etwas —, enter into s.o.'s feelings, sympathize with s.o.

nachfüllen ['na:xfylən], v.a. replenish, fill up.

nachgeben ['na:xge:bən], v.n. irr. relax, slacken, yield; give in, relent, give way.

nachgehen ['na:xge:ən], v.n. irr. (aux. sein) einem —, follow s.o., go after s.o.; (clock) be slow; follow up, investigate.

nachgerade ['na:xgəra:də], adv. by this time, by now; gradually.

nachgiebig ['na:xgi:bɪç], adj. yielding, compliant.

nachgrübeln ['na:xgry:bəln], v.n. speculate.

Nachhall ['na:xhal], m. (—s, no pl.) echo, resonance.

nachhaltig ['na:xhaltɪç], adj. lasting, enduring.

nachhängen ['na:xhɛŋən], v.n. irr. seinen Gedanken —, muse.

nachher ['na:xhe:r], adv. afterwards, later on.

nachherig ['na:xhe:rɪç], adj. subsequent, later.

Nachhilfestunde ['na:xhɪlfəʃtundə], f. (—, pl. —n) private coaching.

nachholen ['na:xho:lən], v.a. make good; make up for.

Nachhut ['na:xhu:t], f. (—, no pl.) (Mil.) rearguard.

nachjagen ['na:xja:gən], v.n. (aux sein) pursue.

Nachklang ['na:xklaŋ], m. (—s, pl. ⁻e) echo; (fig.) after-effect, reminiscence.

Nachkomme ['na:xkɔmə], m. (—n, pl. —n) descendant, offspring.

nachkommen ['na:xkɔmən], v.n. irr. (aux. sein) come after, follow; seiner Pflicht —, do o.'s duty; comply with; einem Versprechen —, keep a promise; seinen Verpflichtungen nicht — können, be unable to meet o.'s commitments.

Nachkommenschaft ['na:xkɔmənʃaft], f. (—, no pl.) descendants, offspring, issue, progeny.

Nachlaß ['na:xlas], m. (—sses, pl. ⁻sse) inheritance, estate, bequest; remission, discount, allowance.

nachlassen ['na:xlasən], v.a. irr. leave behind, bequeath; (trade) give a discount of. — v.n. abate, subside, slacken.

nachlässig ['na:xlɛsɪç], adj. negligent, remiss, careless.

nachlaufen ['na:xlaufən], v.n. irr. (aux. sein) einem —, run after s.o.

Nachlese ['na:xle:zə], f. (—, pl. —n) gleaning.

nachliefern ['na:xli:fərn], v.a. supply subsequently, complete delivery of.

nachmachen ['na:xmaxən], v.a. copy, imitate; counterfeit, forge.

nachmals ['na:xma:ls], adv. afterwards, subsequently.

Nachmittag ['na:xmɪta:k], m. (—s, pl. —e) afternoon.

Nachnahme ['na:xna:mə], f. (—, no pl.) per —, cash or (Am.) collect (payment) on delivery (abbr. C.O.D.).

nachplappern ['na:xplapərn], v.a. repeat mechanically.

Nachrede ['na:xre:də], f. (—, pl. —n) epilogue; üble —, slander.

Nachricht ['na:xrɪçt], f. (—, pl. —en) news, information; (Mil.) intelligence; — geben, send word.

nachrücken ['na:xrykən], v.n. (aux. sein) move up.

Nachruf ['na:xru:f], m. (—s, pl. —e) obituary.

nachrühmen ['na:xry:mən], v.a. einem etwas —, speak well of s.o.

Nachsatz ['na:xzats], m. (—es, pl. ⁻e) concluding clause; postscript.

nachschauen ['na:xʃauən], v.n. jemandem —, gaze after s.o.

nachschlagen ['na:xʃla:gən], v.a. irr. look up, consult (a book).

Nachschlagewerk ['na:xʃla:gəvɛrk], n. (—s, pl. —e) work of reference, reference book.

Nachschlüssel ['na:xʃlysəl], m. (—s, pl. —) master-key, skeleton-key.

Nachschrift ['na:xʃrɪft], f. (—, pl. —en) postscript, (abbr. P.S.).

Nachschub ['na:xʃu:p], m. (—s, pl. ⁻e) (fresh) supply; (Mil.) reinforcements.

Nachsehen ['na:xze:ən], n. (—s, no pl.) das — haben, be left out in the cold.

157

nachsehen

nachsehen ['na:xze:ən], *v.a., v.n. irr.* look for, look s.th. up, refer to s.th.; *einem etwas* —, be indulgent with s.o.

Nachsicht ['na:xzıçt], *f.* (—, *no pl.*) forbearance, indulgence.

Nachsilbe ['na:xzılbə], *f.* (—, *pl.* —n) suffix.

nachsinnen ['na:xzınən], *v.n.* muse, reflect.

nachsitzen ['na:xzıtsən], *v.n.* be kept in after school.

Nachsommer ['na:xzɔmər], *m.* (—s, *pl.* —) Indian summer.

Nachspeise ['na:xʃpaızə], *f.* (—, *pl.* —n) dessert.

nachspüren ['na:xʃpy:rən], *v.n. einem* —, trace, track.

nächst [nɛːçst], *prep.* (*Dat.*) next to, nearest to. — *adj.* next.

Nächste ['nɛːçstə], *m.* (—n, *pl.* —n) fellow-man, neighbour.

nachstehen ['na:xʃte:ən], *v.n. irr. einem* —, be inferior to s.o.; *keinem* —, be second to none.

nachstehend ['na:xʃte:ənt], *adv.* below, hereinafter. — *adj.* following.

nachstellen ['na:xʃtɛlən], *v.n. einem* —, lie in wait for s.o.

Nachstellung ['na:xʃtɛluŋ], *f.* (—, *pl.* —en) persecution, ambush; (*Gram.*) postposition.

nächstens ['nɛːçstəns], *adv.* soon, shortly.

nachstöbern ['na:xʃtø:bərn], *v.n.* rummage.

nachströmen ['na:xʃtrø:mən], *v.n.* (*aux.* sein) crowd after.

Nacht [naxt], *f.* (—, *pl.* ⁻e) night; *die ganze* — *hindurch*, all night; *bei* —, at night; *gute* — *wünschen*, bid goodnight; *über* —, overnight; *in der* —, during the night; *bei* — *und Nebel*, in the dead of night.

Nachteil ['na:xtaıl], *m.* (—s, *pl.* —e) disadvantage, damage.

Nachtessen ['naxtɛsən], *n.* (—s, *pl.* —) supper; evening meal.

Nachtfalter ['naxtfaltər], *m.* (—s, *pl.* —) (*Ent.*) moth.

Nachtgeschirr ['naxtgəʃır], *n.* (—s, *pl.* —e) chamber-pot.

Nachtgleiche ['naxtglaıçə], *f.* (—, *pl.* —n) equinox.

Nachthemd ['naxthɛmt], *n.* (—es, *pl.* —en) night-dress, night-gown.

Nachtigall ['naxtıgal], *f.* (—, *pl.* —en) (*Orn.*) nightingale.

nächtigen ['nɛçtıgən], *v.n.* spend the night.

Nachtisch ['naxtıʃ], *m.* (—es, *pl.* —e) dessert.

Nachtlager ['naxtla:gər], *n.* (—s, *pl.* —) lodgings for the night; (*Mil.*) bivouac.

Nachtmahl ['naxtma:l], *n.* (—s, *pl.* —e) (*Austr.*) supper.

nachtönen ['na:xtø:nən], *v.n.* resound.

Nachtrag ['na:xtra:k], *m.* (—s, *pl.* ⁻e) supplement, postscript, addition; (*pl.*) addenda.

nachtragen ['na:xtra:gən], *v.a. irr.* carry after; add; (*fig.*) *einem etwas* —, bear s.o. a grudge.

nachträglich ['na:xtrɛːklıç], *adj.* subsequent; supplementary; additional; further; later.

Nachtrupp ['na:xtrup], *m.* (—s, *no pl.*) rearguard.

Nachtschwärmer ['naxtʃvɛrmər], *m.* (—s, *pl.* —) night-reveller.

Nachttisch ['naxttıʃ], *m.* (—es, *pl.* —e) bedside-table.

nachtun ['na:xtu:n], *v.a. irr. einem etwas* —, imitate s.o., emulate s.o.

Nachtwächter ['naxtvɛçtər], *m.* (—s, *pl.* —) night-watchman.

Nachtwandler ['naxtvandlər], *m.* (—s, *pl.* —) sleep-walker, somnambulist.

Nachwahl ['na:xva:l], *f.* (—, *pl.* —en) by(e)-election.

Nachwehen ['na:xve:ən], *f. pl.* after-math; unpleasant consequences.

Nachweis ['na:xvaıs], *m.* (—es, *pl.* —e) proof; (*Lit.*) reference; agency.

nachweisen ['na:xvaızən], *v.a. irr.* prove, establish; (*Lit.*) refer.

Nachwelt ['na:xvɛlt], *f.* (—, *no pl.*) posterity.

Nachwort ['na:xvɔrt], *n.* (—es, *pl.* —e) epilogue.

Nachwuchs ['na:xvu:ks], *m.* (—es, *no pl.*) coming generation; recruits.

Nachzahlung ['na:xtsa:luŋ], *f.* (—, *pl.* —en) additional payment, supplementary payment.

Nachzählung ['na:xtsɛːluŋ], *f.* (—, *pl.* —en) recount.

nachziehen ['na:xtsi:ən], *v.a. irr.* drag, tow; tighten; trace, pencil. — *v.n.* follow.

Nachzügler ['na:xtsy:glər], *m.* (—s, *pl.* —) straggler.

Nacken ['nakən], *m.* (—s, *pl.* —) nape, scruff of the neck.

nackend ['nakənt], *adj.* naked.

nackt [nakt], *adj.* nude, naked; (*bird*) callow; (*fig.*) bare; *sich* — *ausziehen*, strip.

Nadel ['na:dəl], *f.* (—, *pl.* —n) needle, pin; *wie auf* —n *sitzen*, be on tenterhooks.

Nadelöhr ['na:dələ:r], *n.* (—s, *pl.* —e) eye of a needle.

Nagel ['na:gəl], *m.* (—s, *pl.* ⁻) nail; (*wooden*) peg; (*ornament*) stud; *etwas an den* — *hängen*, lay s.th. aside, give s.th. up.

nagelneu ['na:gəlnɔy], *adj.* brand new.

nagen ['na:gən], *v.a., v.n.* gnaw; (*fig.*) rankle.

Näharbeit ['nɛːarbaıt], *f.* (—, *pl.* —en) sewing, needlework.

nahe ['na:ə], *adj., adv.* near, close, nigh; — *bei*, close to; — *daran sein*, be on the point of; *es geht mir* —, it grieves me, it touches me; *einem zu* — *treten*, hurt s.o.'s feelings; *es liegt* —, it is obvious, it suggests itself.

Nähe ['nɛːə], *f.* (—, *no pl.*) nearness, proximity; *in der* —, at hand, close by.

Naturlehre

nahen ['na:ən], *v.n.* (*aux.* sein) draw near, approach.
nähen ['nɛ:ən], *v.a.* sew, stitch.
Nähere ['nɛ:ərə], *n.* (—n, *no pl.*) details, particulars.
Näherin ['nɛ:ərɪn], *f.* (—, *pl.* — innen) seamstress, needlewoman.
nähern ['nɛ:ərn], *v.r. sich* —, draw near, approach.
nahestehen ['na:əʃte:ən], *v.n.* be closely connected *or* friendly (with s.o.).
Nährboden ['nɛ:rbo:dən], *m.* (—s, *pl.* ⁼) rich soil; (*Med.*, *Biol.*) culture-medium.
nähren ['nɛ:rən], *v.a.* nourish, feed. — *v.r. sich — von*, feed on; (*fig.*) gain a livelihood.
nahrhaft ['na:rhaft], *adj.* nourishing, nutritive, nutritious.
Nährstand ['nɛ:rʃtant], *m.* (—es, *no pl.*) peasants, producers.
Nahrung ['na:ruŋ], *f.* (—, *no pl.*) nourishment.
Nahrungsmittel ['na:ruŋsmɪtəl], *n.* (—s, *pl.* —) food, provisions, victuals.
Naht [na:t], *f.* (—, *pl.* ⁼e) seam.
Nähzeug ['nɛ:tsɔyk], *n.* (—s, *no pl.*) sewing kit, work box.
naiv [na'i:f], *adj.* naïve, artless, guileless.
Naivität [naivi'tɛ:t], *f.* (—, *no pl.*) artlessness, guilelessness, naïveté.
Name ['na:mə], *m.* (—ns, *pl.* —n) name; *guter* —, good name, renown, reputation; *dem —n nach*, by name; *etwas beim rechten —n nennen*, call a spade a spade.
namens ['na:məns], *adv.* called; by the name of.
Namensvetter ['na:mənsfɛtər], *m.* (—s, *pl.* —n) namesake.
namentlich ['na:məntlɪç], *adj.* by name; particularly.
Namenverzeichnis ['na:menfɛrtsaɪç-nɪs], *n.* (—ses, *pl.* —se) list of names; (*scientific*) nomenclature.
namhaft ['na:mhaft], *adj.* distinguished, renowned; considerable; *— machen*, name.
nämlich ['nɛ:mlɪç], *adv.* namely, to wit.
Napf [napf], *m.* (—es, *pl.* ⁼e) bowl, basin.
Napfkuchen ['napfku:xən], *m.* (—s, *pl.* —) pound-cake, large cake.
Narbe ['narbə], *f.* (—, *pl.* —n) scar; (*leather*) grain.
Narkose [nar'ko:zə], *f.* (—, *pl.* —n) anaesthesia; narcosis.
Narr [nar], *m.* (—en, *pl.* —en) fool; jester, buffoon; *einen zum —en haben*, make a fool of s.o.; *an einem einen —en gefressen haben*, dote on, be infatuated with s.o.
Narrheit ['narhaɪt], *f.* (—, *pl.* —en) foolishness, folly.
närrisch ['nɛrɪʃ], *adj.* foolish, comical; odd; merry; eccentric, mad; *werden*, go mad.
Narzisse [nar'tsɪsə], *f.* (—, *pl.* —n) (*Bot.*) narcissus; *gelbe* —, daffodil.

naschen ['naʃən], *v.a.*, *v.n.* pilfer titbits; nibble at, eat sweets.
Näscherei [nɛʃər'aɪ], *f.* (—, *pl.* —en) sweets, dainties, sweetmeats.
naschhaft ['naʃhaft], *adj.* sweet-toothed.
Naschkatze ['naʃkatsə], *f.* (—, *pl.* —n) sweet tooth.
Nase ['na:zə], *f.* (—, *pl.* —n) nose; (*animal*) snout; scent; *stumpfe* —, snub nose; *gebogene* —, Roman nose; *immer der — nach*, follow your nose; *die — hoch tragen*, be stuck-up; *eine feine (gute) — haben*, be good at; *nicht miss much*; *die — rümpfen*, turn up o.'s nose; *seine — in alles stecken*, poke o.'s nose into everything; *einem etwas unter die — reiben*, bring s.th. home to s.o.
näseln ['nɛ:zəln], *v.n.* speak with a twang.
Nasenbein ['na:zənbaɪn], *n.* (—s, *pl.* —e) nasal bone.
Nasenbluten ['na:zənblu:tən], *n.* (—s, *no pl.*) nose-bleed.
Nasenflügel ['na:zənfly:gəl], *m.* (—s, *pl.* —) side of the nose; nostril.
naseweis ['na:zəvaɪs], *adj.* pert, saucy.
Nashorn ['na:shɔrn], *n.* (—s, *pl.* ⁼er) (*Zool.*) rhinoceros.
Naß [nas], *n.* (—sses, *no pl.*) (*Poet.*) fluid.
naß [nas], *adj.* wet, moist, damp.
Nässe ['nɛsə], *f.* (—, *no pl.*) wetness, dampness, moisture, humidity.
nationalisieren [natsjonali'zi:rən], *v.a.* nationalise.
Nationalität [natsjonali'tɛ:t], *f.* (—, *pl.* —en) nationality.
Natrium ['na:trjum], *n.* (—s, *no pl.*) sodium.
Natron ['natrɔn], *n.* (—s, *no pl.*) sodium carbonate; *doppelkohlensaures* —, sodium bicarbonate; bi-carbonate of soda.
Natter ['natər], *f.* (—, *pl.* —n) (*Zool.*) adder, viper.
Natur [na'tu:r], *f.* (—, *pl.* —en) nature; (*body*) constitution; (*mind*) disposition; *von* —, by nature, constitutionally; *nach der — zeichnen*, draw from nature.
naturalisieren [naturali'zi:rən], *v.a.* naturalise.
Naturalleistung [natu'ra:llaɪstuŋ], *f.* (—, *pl.* —en) payment in kind.
Naturell [natu'rɛl], *n.* (—s, *pl.* —e) natural disposition, temper.
Naturforscher [na'tu:rfɔrʃər], *m.* (—s, *pl.* —) naturalist.
naturgemäß [na'tu:rgəmɛ:s], *adj.* natural.
Naturgeschichte [na'tu:rgəʃɪçtə], *f.* (—, *no pl.*) natural history.
naturgetreu [na'tu:rgətrɔy], *adj.* true to nature, lifelike.
Naturkunde [na'tu:rkundə], *f.* (—, *no pl.*) natural history.
Naturlehre [na'tu:rle:rə], *f.* (—, *no pl.*) natural philosophy; physics.

natürlich

natürlich [na'ty:rlɪç], *adj.* natural; innate, inherent; unaffected, artless. — *adv.* of course, naturally.

Naturspiel [na'tu:rʃpi:l], *n.* (—s, *pl.* —e) freak of nature.

Naturtrieb [na'tu:rtri:p], *m.* (—s, *no pl.*) natural impulse, instinct.

naturwidrig [na'tu:rvi:drɪç], *adj.* contrary to nature, unnatural.

Naturwissenschaft [na'tu:rvɪsənʃaft], *f.* (—, *pl.* —en) (natural) science.

naturwüchsig [na'tu:rvy:ksɪç], *adj.* original; unsophisticated.

Nautik ['nautɪk], *f.* (—, *no pl.*) nautical science.

nautisch ['nautɪʃ], *adj.* nautical.

Nazi ['na:tsi], *abbr.* National Socialist.

Neapel [ne'a:pəl], *n.* Naples.

Nebel ['ne:bəl], *m.* (—s, *pl.* —) fog; *leichter* —, haze, mist; *dichter* —, (*London*) pea-souper; (*with soot*) smog.

Nebelschicht ['ne:bəlʃɪçt], *f.* (—, *pl.* —n) fog-bank.

neben ['ne:bən], *prep.* (*Dat., Acc.*) near, by, beside, besides, close to, next to; (*in compounds*) secondary, subsidiary, side-. — *adv.* beside, besides.

nebenan [ne:bən'an], *adv.* next door, nearby.

nebenbei [ne:bən'baɪ], *adv.* besides, by the way, incidentally.

Nebenbuhler ['ne:bənbu:lər], *m.* (—s, *pl.* —) rival.

nebeneinander [ne:bənaɪn'andər], *adv.* side by side, abreast.

Nebenfluß ['ne:bənflus], *m.* (—sses, *pl.* ⸚sse) tributary, affluent.

nebenher [ne:bən'he:r], *adv.* by the side of, along with.

Nebenmensch ['ne:bənmɛnʃ], *m.* (—en, *pl.* —en) fellow creature.

Nebensatz ['ne:bənzats], *m.* (—es, *pl.* ⸚e) (*Gram.*) subordinate clause.

Nebenzimmer ['ne:bəntsɪmər], *n.* (—s, *pl.* —) adjoining room.

neblig ['ne:blɪç], *adj.* foggy, misty, hazy.

nebst [ne:pst], *prep.* (*Dat.*) together with, including.

necken ['nɛkən], *v.a.* tease, chaff, banter.

neckisch ['nɛkɪʃ], *adj.*, droll, playful, arch.

Neffe ['nɛfə], *m.* (—n, *pl.* —n) nephew.

Neger ['ne:gər], *m.* (—s, *pl.* —) Negro.

negerartig ['ne:gəra:rtɪç], *adj.* Negroid.

negieren [ne'gi:rən], *v.a.* deny, negate, negative.

nehmen ['ne:mən], *v.a. irr.* take, seize; receive, accept; *einem etwas* —, take s.th. from s.o.; *das lasse ich mir nicht* —, I insist on that, I am not to be done out of that; *ein Ende* —, come to an end; *etwas in die Hand* —, take s.th. in hand; *Schaden* —, suffer damage; *einen beim Wort* —, take s.o. at his word; *sich in acht* —, take care.

Nehrung ['ne:ruŋ], *f.* (—, *pl.* —en) narrow tongue of land, spit.

Neid [naɪt], *m.* (—es, *no pl.*) envy, grudge.

Neidhammel ['naɪthaməl], *m.* (—s, *pl.* —) dog in the manger.

neidisch ['naɪdɪʃ], *adj.* envious, grudging, jealous.

Neige ['naɪgə], *f.* (—, *pl.* —n) remnant, sediment; *zur* — *gehen*, be on the decline, run short, dwindle.

neigen ['naɪgən], *v.a., v.n.* incline, bow, bend; *zu etwas* —, be inclined to, be prone to. — *v.r. sich* —, bow.

Neigung ['naɪguŋ], *f.* (—, *pl.* —en) inclination, proneness; affection; (*ground*) dip, slope, gradient; (*ship*) list.

Neigungsfläche ['naɪguŋsflɛçə], *f.* (—, *pl.* —n) inclined plane.

nein [naɪn], *adv.* no.

Nekrolog [nekro'lo:k], *m.* (—(e)s, *pl.* —e) obituary.

Nelke ['nɛlkə], *f.* (—, *pl.* —n) (*Bot.*) pink, carnation; (*condiment*) clove.

nennen ['nɛnən], *v.a. irr.* name, call by name, term, style.

Nenner ['nɛnər], *m.* (—s, *pl.* —) denominator.

Nennung ['nɛnuŋ], *f.* (—, *pl.* —en) naming, mentioning.

Nennwert ['nɛnve:rt], *m.* (—s, *pl.* —e) nominal value.

Nepal ['ne:pal], *n.* Nepal.

Nerv [nɛrf], *m.* (—s, *pl.* —en) nerve, sinew; *einem auf die* —en *gehen*, get on s.o.'s nerves.

Nervenlehre ['nɛrfənle:rə], *f.* (—, *no pl.*) neurology.

nervig ['nɛrvɪç], *adj.* strong; (*fig.*) pithy.

nervös [nɛr'vø:s], *adj.* nervous, irritable, fidgety.

Nerz [nɛrts], *m.* (—es, *pl.* —e) mink.

Nessel ['nɛsəl], *f.* (—, *pl.* —n) nettle.

Nesseltuch ['nɛsəltu:x], *n.* (—es, *no pl.*) muslin.

Nest [nɛst], *n.* (—es, *pl.* —er) nest; (*eagle*) eyrie; *kleines* —, small town.

Nesthäkchen ['nɛsthɛ:kçən], *n.* (—s, *pl.* —) youngest child.

nett [nɛt], *adj.* nice, kind, friendly; neat, trim.

netto ['nɛto], *adv.* (*Comm.*) net, clear.

Netz [nɛts], *n.* (—es, *pl.* —e) net; (*Electr.*) grid; *Eisenbahn* —, railway network *or* system.

netzen ['nɛtsən], *v.a.* (*obs., Poet.*) wet, moisten.

Netzhaut ['nɛtshaut], *f.* (—, *pl.* ⸚e) retina.

neu [nɔy], *adj.* new, fresh; modern; recent; *aufs* —e, *von* —em, anew, afresh; —e *Sprachen*, modern languages.

Neuenburg ['nɔyənburk], *n.* Neuchâtel.

neuerdings ['nɔyərdɪŋs], *adv.* newly, lately.

Neuerer ['nɔyərər], *m.* (—s, *pl.* —) innovator.

Nixe

neuerlich ['nɔyərlɪç], *adj.* late, repeated.
Neufundland [nɔy'funtlant], *n.* Newfoundland.
Neugier(de) ['nɔygiːr(də)], *f.* (—, *no pl.*) inquisitiveness, curiosity.
neugierig ['nɔygiːrɪç], *adj.* curious, inquisitive.
Neuheit ['nɔyhaɪt], *f.* (—, *pl.* —en) novelty.
Neuigkeit ['nɔyɪçkaɪt], *f.* (—, *pl.* —en) piece of news.
neulich ['nɔylɪç], *adv.* lately, recently.
Neuling ['nɔylɪŋ], *m.* (—s, *pl.* —e) novice, beginner, tyro, newcomer; (*Am.*) greenhorn.
neumodisch ['nɔymoːdɪʃ], *adj.* newfangled, in vogue.
Neumond ['nɔymoːnt], *m.* (—s, *pl.* —e) new moon.
neun [nɔyn], *num. adj.* nine.
Neunauge ['nɔynaugə], *n.* (—s, *pl.* —n) river lamprey.
neunzehn ['nɔyntseːn], *num. adj.* nineteen.
neunzig ['nɔyntsɪç], *num. adj.* ninety.
Neuregelung ['nɔyreːgəluŋ], *f.* (—, *pl.* —en) rearrangement.
Neuseeland [nɔy'zeːlant], *n.* New Zealand.
neutralisieren [nɔytrali'ziːrən], *v.a.* neutralise.
Neutralität [nɔytrali'tɛːt], *f.* (—, *no pl.*) neutrality.
Neutrum ['nɔytrum], *n.* (—s, *pl.* —ren) (*Gram.*) neuter.
Neuzeit ['nɔytsaɪt], *f.* (—, *no pl.*) modern times.
nicht [nɪçt], *adv.* not; *auch* —, nor; — *doch*, don't; — *einmal*, not even; *durchaus* —, not at all, by no means; — *mehr*, no more, no longer; not any more; *noch* —, not yet; — *wahr?* isn't it? aren't you? (*in compounds*) non-, dis-, a- (*negativing*).
Nichte ['nɪçtə], *f.* (—, *pl.* —n) niece.
nichten ['nɪçtən], *adv.* (*obs.*) *mit*—, by no means, not at all.
nichtig ['nɪçtɪç], *adj.* null, void, invalid.
Nichtigkeit ['nɪçtɪçkaɪt], *f.* (—, *no pl.*) invalidity, nullity.
nichts [nɪçts], *pron.* nothing, nought; — *als*, nothing but.
nichtsdestoweniger [nɪçtsdesto'veːnɪgər], *adv.* nevertheless.
Nichtsnutz ['nɪçtsnuts], *m.* (—es, *pl.* —e) good for nothing.
Nickel ['nɪkəl], *n.* (—s, *no pl.*) (*metal*) nickel.
nicken ['nɪkən], *v.n.* nod.
nie [niː], *adv.* never, at no time.
nieder ['niːdər], *adj.* low, lower, nether; mean, inferior. — *adv.* down.
niedergeschlagen ['niːdərgəʃlaːgən], *adj.* dejected, low-spirited, depressed.
niederkommen ['niːdərkɔmən], *v.n. irr.* (*aux.* sein) (*rare*) be confined.
Niederkunft ['niːdərkunft], *f.* (—, *no pl.*) confinement, childbirth.

Niederlage ['niːdərlaːgə], *f.* (—, *pl.* —n) (*enemy*) defeat, overthrow; (*goods*) depot, warehouse; agency.
Niederlande ['niːdərlandə], *n. pl.* the Netherlands.
niederlassen ['niːdərlasən], *v.a. irr.* let down. — *v.r. sich* —, sit down, take a seat; settle; establish o.s. in business.
Niederlassung ['niːdərlasuŋ], *f.* (—, *pl.* —en) establishment; settlement, colony; branch, branch establishment.
niederlegen ['niːdərleːgən], *v.a.* lay down, put down; (*office*) resign, abdicate. — *v.r. sich* —, lie down.
Niederschlag ['niːdərʃlaːk], *m.* (—s, *pl.* ⁻e) precipitation, sediment, deposit; rain.
niederschlagen ['niːdərʃlaːgən], *v.a. irr.* strike down; (*fig.*) depress, discourage; (*Law*) quash, cancel; (*eyes*) cast down; (*Chem.*) precipitate; (*Boxing*) knock out.
Niedertracht ['niːdərtraxt], *f.* (—, *no pl.*) baseness, meanness, villainy, beastliness.
Niederung ['niːdəruŋ], *f.* (—, *pl.* —en) low ground, marsh.
niedlich ['niːtlɪç], *adj.* pretty, dainty; (*Am.*) cute.
niedrig ['niːdrɪç], *adj.* low; (*fig.*) base, vile.
niemals ['niːmaːls], *adv.* never, at no time.
niemand ['niːmant], *pron.* nobody, no one.
Niere ['niːrə], *f.* (—, *pl.* —n) kidney.
Nierenbraten ['niːrənbraːtən], *m.* (—s, *no pl.*) roast loin.
Nierenfett ['niːrənfɛt], *n.* (—s, *no pl.*) suet.
nieseln ['niːzəln], *v.n. imp.* drizzle.
niesen ['niːzən], *v.n.* sneeze.
Nießbrauch ['niːsbraux], *m.* (—s, *no pl.*) usufruct, benefit.
Niete ['niːtə], *f.* (—, *pl.* —n) blank; (*Engin.*) rivet; failure.
Niger ['niːgər], *n.* Niger.
Nigeria [niˈgeːrja], *n.* Nigeria.
Nikaragua [nikaˈraˑgua], *n.* Nicaragua.
Nikolaus ['niːkolaus], *m.* Nicholas; *Sankt* —, Santa Claus.
Nil [niːl], *m.* (—s, *no pl.*) Nile.
Nilpferd ['niːlpfeːrt], *n.* (—s, *pl.* —e) (*Zool.*) hippopotamus.
nimmer (mehr) ['nɪmər (meːr)], *adv.* never, never again.
nippen ['nɪpən], *v.a., v.n.* sip, (take a) nip (of).
Nippsachen ['nɪpzaxən], *f. pl.* knickknacks.
nirgends ['nɪrgənts], *adv.* nowhere.
Nische ['niːʃə], *f.* (—, *pl.* —n) niche.
Nisse ['nɪsə], *f.* (—, *pl.* —n) nit.
nisten ['nɪstən], *v.n.* nest.
Niveau [niˈvoː], *n.* (—s, *pl.* —s) level, standard.
nivellieren [nivɛˈliːrən], *v.a.* level.
Nixe ['nɪksə], *f.* (—, *pl.* —n) water-nymph, mermaid, water-sprite.

161

Nizza

Nizza ['nɪtsa], *n.* Nice.
nobel ['no:bəl], *adj.* noble, smart; (*Am.*) swell; munificent, open-handed, magnanimous.
noch [nɔx], *adv.* still, yet; — *einmal*, — *mals*, once more; *weder* . . . — . . ., neither . . . nor . . .; — *nicht*, not yet; — *nie*, never yet, never before.
nochmalig ['nɔxma:lɪç], *adj.* repeated.
Nomade [no'ma:də], *m.* (—**n**, *pl.* —**n**) nomad.
nominell [nomi'nɛl], *adj.* nominal.
nominieren [nomi'ni:rən], *v.a.* nominate.
Nonne ['nɔnə], *f.* (—, *pl.* —**n**) nun.
Noppe ['nɔpə], *f.* (—, *pl.* —**n**) nap.
Norden ['nɔrdən], *m.* (—**s**, *no pl.*) north.
nördlich ['nœrtlɪç], *adj.* northern, northerly.
Nordsee ['nɔrtze:], *f.* North Sea.
nörgeln ['nœrgəln], *v.n.* find fault, cavil, carp, nag.
Norm ['nɔrm], *f.* (—, *pl.* —**en**) standard, rule, norm.
normal [nɔr'ma:l], *adj.* normal, standard.
Norwegen ['nɔrve:gən], *n.* Norway.
Not [no:t], *f.* (—, *pl.* ⁻**e**) need, necessity; misery, want, trouble, distress; (*in compounds*) emergency.
not [no:t], *pred. adj.* — *tun*, be necessary.
Nota ['no:ta], *f.* (—, *pl.* —**s**) bill, statement.
Notar [no'ta:r], *m.* (—**s**, *pl.* —**e**) notary.
Notdurft ['notdurft], *f.* (—, *pl.* ⁻**e**) want, necessaries, necessity; *seine* — *verrichten*, ease o.s.
notdürftig ['no:tdyrftɪç], *adj.* scanty, makeshift.
Note ['no:tə], *f.* (—, *pl.* —**n**) note; (*Mus.*) note; (*School*) mark(s); *nach* —*n*, (*fig.*) with a vengeance.
Notenbank ['no:tənbaŋk], *f.* (—, *pl.* —**en**) bank of issue.
Notenblatt ['no:tənblat], *n.* (—**s**, *pl.* ⁻**er**) sheet of music.
notgedrungen ['no:tgədruŋən], *adj.* compulsory, forced; perforce.
Nothelfer ['no:thɛlfər], *m.* (—**s**, *pl.* —) helper in time of need.
notieren [no'ti:rən], *v.a.* note, book; (*Comm.*) quote.
notifizieren [notifi'tsi:rən], *v.a.* notify.
nötig ['nø:tɪç], *adj.* necessary; — *haben*, want, need.
nötigen ['nø:tɪgən], *v.a.* compel, press, force, urge; necessitate; *sich* — *lassen*, stand upon ceremony.
Notiz [no'ti:ts], *f.* (—, *pl.* —**en**) note, notice; — *nehmen von*, take notice of; (*pl.*) notes, jottings.
notleidend ['no:tlaɪdənt], *adj.* financially distressed, indigent, needy.
notorisch [no'to:rɪʃ], *adj.* notorious.
Notstand ['no:tʃtant], *m.* (—**s**, *no pl.*) state of distress; emergency.

Notverband ['no:tfɛrbant], *m.* (—**es**, *pl.* ⁻**e**) first-aid dressing.
Notwehr ['no:tve:r], *f.* (—, *no pl.*) self-defence.
notwendig ['no:tvɛndɪç], *adj.* necessary, essential, needful.
Notzucht ['no:ttsuxt], *f.* (—, *no pl.*) rape, violation.
Novelle [no'vɛlə], *f.* (—, *pl.* —**n**) (*Lit.*) novella, short story, short novel.
Novize [no'vi:tsə], *m.* (—**n**, *pl.* —**n**) or *f.* (—, *pl.* —**n**) novice.
Nu [nu:], *m. & n.* (—, *no pl.*) moment; *im* —, in no time, in an instant.
Nubien ['nu:bjən], *n.* Nubia.
nüchtern ['nʏçtərn], *adj.* fasting; sober; jejune; (*fig.*) dry, matter-of-fact, realistic.
Nüchternheit ['nʏçtərnhaɪt], *f.* (—, *no pl.*) sobriety; (*fig.*) dryness.
Nudel ['nu:dəl], *f.* (—, *pl.* —**n**) noodles, macaroni, vermicelli; *eine komische* —, a funny person.
Null [nul], *f.* (—, *pl.* —**en**) nought, zero; (*fig.*) nonentity.
null [nul], *adj.* null; nil; — *und nichtig*, null and void; *etwas für* — *und nichtig erklären*, annul.
numerieren [nume'ri:rən], *v.a.* number.
Nummer ['numər], *f.* (—, *pl.* —**n**) number, size, issue.
nun [nu:n], *adv., conj.* now, at present; since; —*!* now! well! *von* — *an*, henceforth; — *und nimmermehr*, nevermore; *was* —? what next?
nunmehr ['nu:nme:r], *adv.* now, by this time.
Nunzius ['nuntsjus], *m.* (—, *pl.* —**zien**) (Papal) nuncio.
nur [nu:r], *adv.* only, solely, merely, but; *wenn* —, if only, provided that; — *das nicht*, anything but that; — *zu*, go to it!
Nürnberg ['nʏrnbɛrk], *n.* Nuremberg.
Nuß [nus], *f.* (—, *pl.* ⁻**sse**) nut.
Nußhäher ['nushɛ:ər], *m.* (—**s**, *pl.* —) (*Orn.*) jay.
Nüster ['nystər], *f.* (—, *pl.* —**n**) (*horse*) nostril.
Nutzanwendung ['nutsanvɛnduŋ], *f.* (—, *pl.* —**en**) practical application.
nutzbar ['nutsba:r], *adj.* useful, usable, productive.
nütze ['nytsə], *adj.* useful, of use.
Nutzen ['nutsən], *m.* (—**s**, *pl.* —) use, utility; profit, gain, advantage, benefit; — *bringen*, yield profit; — *ziehen aus*, derive profit from.
nützen ['nytsən], *v.a.* make use of, use. — *v.n.* be of use, serve, be effective, work.
nützlich ['nytslɪç], *adj.* useful.
nutzlos ['nutslo:s], *adj.* useless.
Nutznießer ['nutsni:sər], *m.* (—**s**, *pl.* —) beneficiary, usufructuary.
Nymphe ['nymfə], *f.* (—, *pl.* —**en**) nymph.

O

O [o:], *n*, (**—s**, *pl.* **—s**) the letter O.
o! [o:], *excl.* oh!
Oase [o'a:zə], *f.* (**—**, *pl.* **—n**) oasis.
ob [ɔp], *conj.* whether; if; *als* **—**, as if; *und* **—**! rather! yes, indeed! — *prep.* (*Genit.*, *Dat.*) on account of; upon, on.
Obacht ['o:baxt], *f.* (**—**, *no pl.*) heed, care; — *geben*, pay attention, look out.
Obdach ['ɔpdax], *n.* (**—es**, *no pl.*) shelter, lodging.
Obduktion ['ɔpdukts'jo:n], *f.* (**—**, *pl.* **—en**) post-mortem examination.
oben [o:bən], *adv.* above, aloft, on top; (*house*) upstairs; (*water*) on the surface; *von* — *bis unten*, from top to bottom; *von* — *herab*, from above; (*fig.*) haughtily, superciliously.
obendrein [o:bən'draɪn], *adv.* besides, into the bargain.
obengenannt ['o:bəngənant], *adj.* above-mentioned.
Ober ['o:bər], *m.* (**—s**, *pl.* **—**) head waiter; *Herr* — *!*, waiter!; (*in compounds*) upper, chief.
ober ['o:bər], *adj.* upper, higher; chief; superior.
Oberfläche ['o:bərflɛçə], *f.* (**—**, *pl.* **—n**) surface.
oberflächlich ['o:bərflɛçlɪç], *adj.* superficial, casual.
oberhalb ['o:bərhalp], *adv.*, *prep.* (*Genit.*) above.
Oberin ['o:bərɪn], *f.* (**—**, *pl.* **—innen**) (*Eccl.*) Mother Superior; hospital matron.
Oberschule ['o:bərʃu:lə], *f.* (**—**, *pl.* **—n**) high school, secondary school.
Oberst ['o:bərst], *m.* (**—en**, *pl.* **—en**) colonel.
Oberstaatsanwalt ['o:bərʃta:tsanvalt], *m.* (**—s**, *pl.* **-̈e**) Attorney-General.
oberste ['o:bərstə], *adj.* uppermost, highest, supreme.
Oberstimme ['o:bərʃtɪmə], *f.* (**—**, *pl.* **—n**) (*Mus.*) treble, soprano.
Oberstübchen ['o:bərʃty:pçən], *n.* (**—s**, *pl.* **—**) (*fig.*) *nicht richtig im* — *sein*, have bats in the belfry.
Obervolta ['o:bərvɔlta], *n.* Upper Volta.
obgleich [ɔp'glaɪç], *conj.* though, although.
Obhut ['ɔphu:t], *f.* (**—**, *no pl.*) keeping, care, protection.
obig ['o:bɪç], *adj.* foregoing, above-mentioned, aforementioned, aforesaid.
objektiv [ɔpjɛk'ti:f], *adj.* objective, impartial, unprejudiced.
Oblate [o'bla:tə], *f.* (**—**, *pl.* **—n**) wafer; (*Eccl.*) Host.

obliegen ['ɔpli:gən], *v.n. irr.* be incumbent upon s.o.; be o.'s duty; apply o.s. to.
Obmann ['ɔpman], *m.* (**—es**, *pl.* *-̈*er) chairman; (*jury*) foreman.
Obrigkeit ['o:brɪçkaɪt], *f.* (**—**, *pl.* **—en**) authorities.
obschon [ɔp'ʃo:n] *see under* **obwohl**.
Observatorium ['ɔpzɛrva'to:rjum], *n.* (**—s**, *pl.* **—rien**) observatory.
obsiegen ['ɔpzi:gən], *v.n.* (*rare*) be victorious.
Obst [o:pst], *n.* (**—es**, *no pl.*) fruit.
obszön [ɔps'tsø:n], *adj.* obscene.
obwalten ['ɔpvaltən], *v.n.* (*rare*) exist, prevail, obtain; *unter den* **—den** *Umständen*, in the circumstances, as matters stand.
obwohl [ɔp'vo:l] (also **obschon** [ɔp'ʃo:n], **obzwar** [ɔp'tsva:r]), *conj.* though, although.
Ochse ['ɔksə], *m.* (**—n**, *pl.* **—n**) (*Zool.*) ox; bullock; (*fig.*) blockhead.
ochsen ['ɔksən], *v.n.* (*sl.*) swot, cram.
Ochsenauge ['ɔksənaugə], *n.* (**—s**, *pl.* **—n**) ox-eye, bull's eye; (*Archit.*) oval dormer window; porthole light.
Ochsenziemer ['ɔksəntsi:mər], *m.* (**—s**, *pl.* **—**) (*obs.*) horse-whip.
Ocker ['ɔkər], *m.* (**—s**, *no pl.*) ochre.
Öde ['ø:də], *f.* (**—**, *pl.* **—n**) wilderness.
öde ['ø:də], *adj.* desolate, bleak, dreary.
Odem ['o:dəm], *m.* (**—s**, *no pl.*) (*Poet.*) breath.
oder ['o:dər], *conj.* or; — *aber*, or else; — *auch*, or rather.
Ofen ['o:fən], *m.* (**—s**, *pl.* *-̈*) stove; oven, furnace.
Ofenpest [o:fən'pɛst], *n.* Budapest.
offen ['ɔfən], *adj.* open; (*fig.*) candid, sincere, frank; — *gestanden*, frankly speaking.
offenbar [ɔfən'ba:r], *adj.* obvious, manifest, evident.
offenbaren [ɔfən'ba:rən], *v.a. insep.* make known, reveal, disclose. — *v.r. sich einem* —, open o.'s heart to s.o.; unbosom o.s.
Offenheit ['ɔfənhaɪt], *f.* (**—**, *pl.* **—en**) frankness, candour.
offenkundig ['ɔfənkundɪç], *adj.* obvious, manifest.
offensichtlich ['ɔfənzɪçtlɪç], *adj.* obvious; apparent.
öffentlich ['œfəntlɪç], *adj.* public.
offerieren [ɔfe'ri:rən], *v.a.* offer.
Offerte [ɔ'fɛrtə], *f.* (**—**, *pl.* **—n**) offer, tender.
offiziell [ɔfi'tsjɛl], *adj.* official.
Offizier [ɔfi'tsi:r], *m.* (**—s**, *pl.* **—e**) officer, lieutenant.
Offizierspatent [ɔfi'tsi:rspatɛnt], *n.* (**—s**, *pl.* **—e**) (*Mil.*) commission.
offiziös [ɔfi'tsjø:s], *adj.* semi-official.
öffnen ['œfnən], *v.a.* open.
oft [ɔft], **oftmals** ['ɔftma:ls], *adv.* often, frequently.
öfters ['œftərs], *adv.* often, frequently.

163

Oheim

Oheim ['o:haɪm], *m.* (—s, *pl.* —e) (*Poet.*) uncle.

ohne ['o:nə], *prep.* (*Acc.*) without, but for, except.

ohnehin ['o:nəhɪn], *adv.* as it is.

Ohnmacht ['o:nmaxt], *f.* (—, *pl.* —en) fainting-fit, swoon; impotence; *in — fallen*, faint.

Ohr [o:r], *n.* (—es, *pl.* —en) ear; *bis über beide —en*, head over heels; *die —en spitzen*, prick up o.'s ears.

Ohrenbläser ['o:rənblɛ:zər], *m.* (—s, *pl.* —) tale-bearer.

Ohrensausen ['o:rənzauzən], *n.* (—s, *no pl.*) humming in the ears.

Ohrenschmaus ['o:rənʃmaus], *m.* (—es, *no pl.*) musical treat.

Ohrfeige ['o:rfaɪgə], *f.* (—, *pl.* —n) box on the ear.

Ohrläppchen ['o:rlɛpçən], *n.* (—s, *pl.* —) lobe of the ear.

Ohrmuschel ['o:rmuʃəl], *f.* (—, *pl.* —n) auricle.

oktav [ɔk'ta:f], *adj.* octavo.

Oktober [ɔk'to:bər], *m.* (—s, *pl.* —) October.

oktroyieren [ɔktroa'ji:rən], *v.a.* dictate, force s.th. upon s.o.

okulieren [oku'li:rən], *v.a.* (*trees*) graft.

Öl [ø:l], *n.* (—s, *pl.* —e) oil; (*rare*) olive-oil.

Ölanstrich ['ø:lanʃtrɪç], *m.* (—s, *pl.* —e) coat of oil-paint.

ölen ['ø:lən], *v.a.* oil, lubricate; (*rare*) anoint.

Ölgemälde ['ø:lgəmɛ:ldə], *n.* (—s, *pl.* —) oil painting.

Ölung ['ø:luŋ], *f.* (—, *pl.* —en) oiling; anointing; (*Eccl.*) *die letzte —*, Extreme Unction.

Olymp [o'lymp], *m.* Mount Olympus.

olympisch [o'lympɪʃ], *adj.* Olympian.

Omelett [ɔmə'lɛt], *n.* (—s, *pl.* —s) omelette.

Onkel ['ɔŋkəl], *m.* (—s, *pl.* —) uncle.

Oper ['o:pər], *f.* (—, *pl.* —n) opera.

operieren [opə'ri:rən], *v.a., v.n.* operate (on); *sich — lassen*, be operated on; undergo an operation.

Opfer ['ɔpfər], *n.* (—s, *pl.* —) sacrifice; victim.

opfern ['ɔpfərn], *v.a., v.n.* offer (up), sacrifice, immolate.

opponieren [ɔpo'ni:rən], *v.n.* oppose.

Optiker ['ɔptɪkər], *m.* (—s, *pl.* —) optician.

oratorisch [ora'to:rɪʃ], *adj.* oratorical.

Orchester [ɔr'kɛstər], *n.* (—s, *pl.* —) orchestra, band.

orchestrieren [ɔrkɛs'tri:rən], *v.a.* orchestrate, score for orchestra.

Orchidee [ɔrçi'de:], *f.* (—, *pl.* —n) (*Bot.*) orchid

Orden ['ɔrdən], *m.* (—s, *pl.* —) medal; (*Eccl.*) (religious) order.

ordentlich ['ɔrdəntlɪç], *adj.* orderly, tidy, methodical, neat; regular; respectable, steady; sound; *—er Professor*, (full) professor.

Order ['ɔrdər], *f.* (—, *pl.* —s) (*Comm.*) order.

Ordinarius [ɔrdi'na:rjus], *m.* (—, *pl.* —ien) (*Univ.*) professor; (*Eccl.*) ordinary.

ordinär [ɔrdi'nɛ:r], *adj.* common, vulgar.

ordnen ['ɔrdnən], *v.a.* put in order, tidy, arrange, dispose.

Ordnung ['ɔrdnuŋ], *f.* (—, *pl.* —en) order, arrangement, disposition, routine; tidiness; class, rank; *in —*, all right, in good trim; *nicht in —*, out of order, wrong.

ordnungsgemäß ['ɔrdnuŋsgəmɛ:s], *adv.* duly.

ordnungsmäßig ['ɔrdnuŋsmɛsɪç], *adj.* regular.

ordnungswidrig ['ɔrdnuŋsvi:drɪç], *adj.* irregular.

Ordnungszahl ['ɔrdnuŋstsa:l], *f.* (—, *pl.* —en) ordinal number.

Ordonnanz [ɔrdɔ'nants], *f.* (—, *pl.* —en) ordinance; (*Mil.*) orderly.

Organ [ɔr'ga:n], *n.* (—s, *pl.* —e) organ.

organisieren [ɔrgani'zi:rən], *v.a.* organise.

Orgel ['ɔrgəl], *f.* (—, *pl.* —n) (*Mus.*) organ.

Orgelzug ['ɔ:rgəltsu:k], *m.* (—s, *pl.* ⁓e) organ-stop.

Orgie ['ɔrgjə], *f.* (—, *pl.* —n) orgy.

orientalisch [orjɛn'ta:lɪʃ], *adj.* oriental, eastern.

orientieren [orjɛn'ti:rən], *v.a.* inform, orientate; set s.o. right. — *v.r. sich — über*, orientate o.s., find out about; get o.'s bearings.

Orkan [ɔr'ka:n], *m.* (—s, *pl.* —e) hurricane, gale, typhoon.

Ornat [ɔr'na:t], *m.* (—es, *pl.* —e) official robes; vestments.

Ort [ɔrt], *m.* (—es, *pl.* —e, ⁓er) place, spot; region; (*in compounds*) local.

örtlich ['œrtlɪç], *adj.* local.

Ortschaft ['ɔrtʃaft], *f.* (—, *pl.* —en) place, township, village.

Öse ['ø:zə], *f.* (—, *pl.* —n) loop; *Haken und —n*, hooks and eyes.

Ostasien ['ɔsta:zjən], *n.* Eastern Asia, the Far East.

Ost(en) ['ɔst(ən)], *m.* (—s, *no pl.*) east.

ostentativ [ɔstɛnta'ti:f], *adj.* ostentatious.

Osterei ['o:stəraɪ], *n.* (—s, *pl.* —er) Easter egg.

Ostern ['o:stərn], *f. pl.* (*used as n. sing.*) Easter.

Österreich ['ø:stərraɪç], *n.* Austria.

Ostindien ['ɔstɪndjən], *n.* the East Indies.

östlich ['œstlɪç], *adj.* eastern, easterly.

Oxyd [ɔk'sy:t], *n.* (—es, *pl.* —e) oxide.

oxydieren [ɔksy'di:rən], *v.a., v.n.* oxidise.

Ozean ['o:tsea:n], *m.* (—s, *pl.* —e) ocean, sea; *Grosser —*, Pacific (Ocean).

Ozon [o'tso:n], *n.* (—s, *no pl.*) ozone.

P

P [pe:], *n.* (—s, *pl.* —s) the letter P.
Paar [pa:r], *n.* (—es, *pl.* —e) pair, couple.
paar [pa:r], *adj.* ein —, a few, some.
Pacht [paxt], *f.* (—, *pl.* —en) lease; *in — nehmen*, take on lease.
Pachthof ['paxtho:f], *m.* (—s, *pl.* ⁻e) leasehold estate, farm.
Pack (1) [pak], *m.* (—s, *pl.* ⁻e) pack, bale, packet; *mit Sack und —*, (with) bag and baggage.
Pack (2) [pak], *n.* (—s, *no pl.*) rabble, mob.
Päckchen ['pɛkçən], *n.* (—s, *pl.* —) pack, packet; (small) parcel.
packen ['pakən], *v.a.* pack; seize; (*fig.*) —d, thrilling; *pack dich!* be off! scram!
pädagogisch [pɛ:da'go:giʃ], *adj.* educational, pedagogic(al).
paddeln ['padəln], *v.n.* paddle.
paff [paf], *excl.* bang! *ich bin ganz —*, I am astounded.
paffen ['pafən], *v.n.* puff; draw (at a pipe).
Page ['pa:ʒə], *m.* (—n, *pl.* —n) page-boy.
Paket [pa'ke:t], *n.* (—s, *pl.* —e) packet, package, parcel.
paktieren [pak'ti:rən], *v.n.* come to terms.
Palast [pa'last], *m.* (—es, *pl.* ⁻e) palace.
Palästina [palɛ'sti:na], *n.* Palestine.
Paletot ['paləto:], *m.* (—s, *pl.* —s) overcoat.
Palisanderholz [pali'zandərhɔlts], *n.* (—es, *no pl.*) rosewood.
Palme ['palmə], *f.* (—, *pl.* —n) (*Bot.*) palm-tree.
Palmkätzchen ['palmkɛtsçən], *n.* (—s, *pl.* —) (*Bot.*) catkin.
Palmwoche ['palmvɔxə], *f.* Holy Week.
Pampelmuse ['pampəlmu:zə], *f.* (—, *pl.* —n) (*Bot.*) grapefruit.
Panama ['pa:nama], *n.* Panama.
Panier [pa'ni:r], *n.* (—s, *pl.* —e) standard, banner.
panieren [pa'ni:rən], *v.a.* dress (*meat etc.*), roll in bread-crumbs.
Panne ['panə], *f.* (—, *pl.* —n) puncture; (*Motor.*) break-down; mishap.
panschen ['panʃən], *v.n.* splash about in water. — *v.a.* adulterate.
Pantoffel [pan'tɔfəl], *m.* (—s, *pl.* —n) slipper; *unter dem — stehen*, be henpecked.
Pantoffelheld [pan'tɔfəlhɛlt], *m.* (—en, *pl.* —en) henpecked husband.

Panzer ['pantsər], *m.* (—s, *pl.* —) armour, breast-plate, coat of mail; (*Mil.*) tank.
Papagei [papa'gai], *m.* (—s, *pl.* —en) (*Orn.*) parrot.
Papier [pa'pi:r], *n.* (—s, *pl.* —e) paper; (*Comm.*) stocks; (*pl.*) papers, documents; *ein Bogen —*, a sheet of paper.
Papierkrieg [pa'pi:rkri:k], *m.* (—s, *no pl.*) (*coll.*) red tape.
Papierwaren [pa'pi:rva:rən], *f. pl.* stationery.
Pappdeckel ['papdɛkəl], *m.* (—s, *pl.* —) pasteboard.
Pappe ['papə], *f.* (—, *no pl.*) paste, cardboard, pasteboard.
Pappel ['papəl], *f.* (—, *pl.* —n) poplar.
pappen ['papən], *v.a.* stick; glue, paste.
Pappenstiel ['papənʃti:l], *m.* (—s, *pl.* —e) trifle.
papperlapapp ['papərlapap], *excl.* fiddlesticks! nonsense!
Papst [pa:pst], *m.* (—es, *pl.* ⁻e) Pope.
päpstlich ['pɛ:pstlɪç], *adj.* papal; *—er als der Papst*, fanatically loyal, outheroding Herod; over-zealous.
Parabel [pa'ra:bəl], *f.* (—, *pl.* —n) parable; (*Maths.*) parabola.
paradieren [para'di:rən], *v.n.* parade, make a show.
Paradies [para'di:s], *n.* (—es, *pl.* —e) paradise.
paradox [para'dɔks], *adj.* paradoxical.
Paragraph [para'gra:f], *m.* (—en, *pl.* —en) paragraph, article, clause, section.
Paraguay ['paragvai, para'gua:i], *n.* Paraguay.
Paralyse [para'ly:zə], *f.* (—, *pl.* —n) paralysis.
parat [pa'ra:t], *adj.* prepared, ready.
Pardon [par'dõ], *m.* (—s, *no pl.*) pardon, forgiveness.
Parfüm [par'fy:m], *n.* (—s, *pl.* —e) perfume, scent.
pari ['pa:ri], *adv.* at par.
parieren [pa'ri:rən], *v.a.* parry, keep off. — *v.n.* obey; *aufs Wort —*, obey implicitly *or* to the letter.
Parität [pari'tɛ:t], *f.* (—, *no pl.*) parity; (*religious*) equality.
Parkanlagen [park'anla:gən], *f. pl.* parks; public gardens.
parken ['parkən], *v.a.* park.
Parkett [par'kɛt], *n.* (—s, *pl.* —e) parquet flooring; (*Theat.*) stalls.
Parkuhr [park'u:r], *f.* (—, *pl.* —en) parking-meter.
Parlament [parla'mɛnt], *n.* (—s, *pl.* —e) parliament.
Parlamentär [parlamɛn'tɛ:r], *m.* (—s, *pl.* —e) officer negotiating a truce.
Parlamentarier [parlamɛn'ta:rjər], *m.* (—s, *pl.* —) parliamentarian, member of a parliament.
Parole [pa'ro:lə], *f.* (—, *pl.* —n) watchword, cue, motto, slogan, password.

Partei

Partei [par'taɪ], *f.* (—, *pl.* —en) party, faction; — *nehmen für*, side with.

Parteigänger [par'taɪgɛŋər], *m.* (—s, *pl.* —) partisan.

Parteigenosse [par'taɪgənɔsə], *m.* (—n, *pl.* —n) party member (especially National Socialist); comrade.

parteiisch [par'taɪɪʃ], *adj.* partial, biased, prejudiced.

Parteinahme [par'taɪnaːmə], *f.* (—, *no pl.*) partisanship.

Parteitag [par'taɪtaːk], *m.* (—s, *pl.* —e) party conference; congress.

Parterre [par'tɛrə], *n.* (—s, *pl.* —s) ground floor; (*Theat.*) pit; stalls.

Partie [par'tiː], *f.* (—, *pl.* —n) (*Comm.*) parcel; (*marriage*) match; (*chess etc.*) game; (*bridge*) rubber; outing, excursion, trip.

Partitur [parti'tuːr], *f.* (—, *pl.* —en) (*Mus.*) score.

Partizip [parti'tsiːp], *n.* (—s, *pl.* —e, —ien) (*Gram.*) participle.

Parzelle [par'tsɛlə], *f.* (—, *pl.* —n) allotment, lot, parcel.

paschen ['paʃən], *v.a.* smuggle.

Paß [pas], *m.* (—sses, *pl.* ⸚sse) (*mountain*) pass; (*travelling*) passport; (*horse*) amble.

Passagier [pasa'ʒiːr], *m.* (—s, *pl.* —e) passenger; *blinder* —, stowaway.

Passant [pa'sant], *m.* (—en, *pl.* —en) passer-by.

Passatwind [pa'saːtvɪnt], *m.* (—s, *pl.* —e) trade-wind.

passen ['pasən], *v.n.* fit, suit, be suitable, be convenient; (*Cards*) pass.

passieren [pa'siːrən], *v.a.* sieve; (*road*) pass, cross, negotiate. — *v.n.* (*aux.* sein) pass; happen, take place, come about.

Passif, Passivum [pa'siːf *or* 'pasiːf, pa'siːvum], *n.* (—s, *pl.* —e, —, —va) (*Gram.*) passive voice; (*Comm.*) (*pl.*) debts, liabilities.

Passus ['pasus], *m.* (—, *pl.* —) passage (in book).

Pasta, Paste ['pasta, 'pastə], *f.* (—, *pl.* —ten) paste.

Pastell [pa'stɛl], *m.* (—s, *pl.* —e) pastel, crayon; — *malen*, draw in pastel.

Pastete [pa'steːtə], *f.* (—, *pl.* —n) pie, pastry.

Pastille [pa'stɪlə], *f.* (—, *pl.* —n) lozenge, pastille.

Pastor ['pastɔr], *m.* (—s, *pl.* —en) minister, pastor; parson; vicar, rector.

Pate ['paːtə], *m.* (—n, *pl.* —n) godparent; — *stehen*, be godfather to.

patent [pa'tɛnt], *adj.* fine, grand, (*sl.*) smashing.

Patent [pa'tɛnt], *n.* (—(e)s, *pl.* —e) patent; charter, licence.

patentieren [patɛn'tiːrən], *v.a.* patent, license.

pathetisch [pa'teːtɪʃ], *adj.* elevated, solemn, moving.

Patin ['paːtɪn], *f.* (—, *pl.* —innen) godmother.

patriotisch [patri'oːtɪʃ], *adj.* patriotic.

Patrone [pa'troːnə], *f.* (—, *pl.* —n) cartridge; stencil, pattern.

Patrouille [pa'truljə], *f.* (—, *pl.* —n) (*Mil.*) patrol.

Patsche ['patʃə], *f.* (—, *pl.* —n) (*dial.*) hand; (*fig.*) mess, pickle; *in eine — geraten*, get into a jam.

patschen ['patʃən], *v.n.* (*aux.* sein) splash.

Patt [pat], *n.* (—s, *pl.* —s) (*Chess*) stalemate.

patzig ['patsɪç], *adj.* rude; cheeky, saucy.

Pauke ['paukə], *f.* (—, *pl.* —n) kettledrum; *mit* —*n und Trompeten*, with drums beating and colours flying.

pauken ['paukən], *v.n.* beat the kettledrum; (*coll.*) swot, plod, grind; fight a duel.

pausbackig ['pausbakɪç], *adj.* chubby-faced, bonny.

Pauschale [pau'ʃaːlə], *f.* (—, *pl.* —n) lump sum.

Pause ['pauzə], *f.* (—, *pl.* —n) pause, stop; (*Theat.*) interval; (*Sch.*) playtime, break; (*Tech.*) tracing.

pausen ['pauzən], *v.a.* trace.

pausieren [pau'ziːrən], *v.n.* pause.

Pavian ['paːvjaːn], *m.* (—s, *pl.* —e) (*Zool.*) baboon.

Pech [pɛç], *n.* (—es, *no pl.*) pitch; (*shoemaker's*) wax; (*fig.*) bad luck, rotten luck.

pechschwarz ['pɛçʃvarts], *adj.* black as pitch.

Pechvogel ['pɛçfoːgəl], *m.* (—s, *pl.* ⸚) unlucky fellow.

Pedell [pe'dɛl], *m.* (—s, *pl.* —e) beadle; porter, caretaker; (*Univ. sl.*) bulldog.

Pegel ['peːgəl], *m.* (—s, *pl.* —) water-gauge.

peilen ['paɪlən], *v.a.*, *v.n.* sound, measure, take bearings (of).

Pein [paɪn], *f.* (—, *no pl.*) pain, torment.

peinigen ['paɪnɪgən], *v.a.* torment; harass, distress.

peinlich ['paɪnlɪç], *adj.* painful, disagreeable; embarrassing; delicate; strict, punctilious; (*Law*) capital, penal.

Peitsche ['paɪtʃə], *f.* (—, *pl.* —n) whip.

pekuniär [pekun'jɛːr], *adj.* financial.

Pelerine [pelə'riːnə], *f.* (—, *pl.* —n) cape.

Pelle ['pɛlə], *f.* (—, *pl.* —n) peel, husk.

Pellkartoffeln ['pɛlkartɔfəln], *f. pl.* potatoes in their jackets.

Pelz [pɛlts], *m.* (—es, *pl.* —e) pelt, fur; fur coat.

pelzig ['pɛltsɪç], *adj.* furry.

Pendel ['pɛndəl], *n.* (—s, *pl.* —) pendulum.

pendeln ['pɛndəln], *v.n.* swing, oscillate; commute.

pennen ['pɛnən], *v.n.* (*sl.*) sleep.

Pension [pã'sjo:n], *f.* (—, *pl.* —en) pension; boarding-house; board and lodging.
Pensionat [pãsjo'na:t], *n.* (—s, *pl.* —e) boarding-school.
pensionieren [pãsjo'ni:rən], *v.a.* pension off; *sich — lassen*, retire.
Pensum ['pɛnzum], *n.* (—s, *pl.* —sen) task; curriculum, syllabus.
per [pɛr], *prep.* — *Adresse*, care of.
Perfekt [pɛr'fɛkt], *n.* (—s, *pl.* —e) *(Gram.)* perfect (tense).
perforieren [pɛrfo'ri:rən], *v.a.* perforate, punch.
Pergament [pɛrga'mɛnt], *n.* (—s, *pl.* —e) parchment, vellum.
Perle ['pɛrlə], *f.* (—, *pl.* —n) pearl; *(glass)* bead; *(fig.)* gem, treasure.
perlen ['pɛrlən], *v.n.* sparkle.
Perlgraupe ['pɛrlgraupə], *f.* (—, *no pl.*) *(Bot.)* pearl-barley.
Perlhuhn ['pɛrlhu:n], *n.* (—s, *pl.* ⁻er) *(Zool.)* guinea-fowl.
Perlmutter ['pɛrlmutər], *f.* (—, *no pl.*) mother-of-pearl.
Perpendikel [pɛrpən'di:kəl], *m. & n.* (—s, *pl.* —) pendulum.
Perser ['pɛrzər], *m.* (—s, *pl.* —) Persian; *echter —*, genuine Persian carpet.
Persien ['pɛrzjən], *n.* Persia.
Personal [pɛrzo'na:l], *n.* (—s, *no pl.*) personnel, staff.
Personalien [pɛrzo'na:ljən], *n. pl.* particulars (of a person).
Personenverkehr [pɛr'zo:nənfɛrke:r], *m.* (—s, *no pl.*) passenger-traffic.
Personenzug [pɛr'zo:nəntsu:k], *m.* (—s, *pl.* ⁻e) (slow) passenger train.
personifizieren [pɛrzonifi'tsi:rən], *v.a.* personify, embody, impersonate.
Persönlichkeit [pɛr'zø:nlɪçkaɪt], *f.* (—, *pl.* —en) personality, person.
perspektivisch [pɛrspɛk'ti:vɪʃ], *adj.* perspective.
Peru [pe'ru:], *n.* Peru.
Perücke [pe'rykə], *f.* (—, *pl.* —n) wig.
Pest [pɛst], *f.* (—, *no pl.*) plague, pestilence.
pestartig ['pɛsta:rtɪç], *adj.* pestilential.
Petersilie [pe:tər'zi:ljə], *f.* (—, *no pl.*) *(Bot.)* parsley.
petitionieren [petitsjo'ni:rən], *v.a.* petition.
Petschaft ['pɛtʃaft], *n.* (—s, *pl.* —e) seal, signet.
Petz [pɛts], *m.* (—es, *pl.* —e) *Meister —*, Bruin (the bear).
petzen ['pɛtsən], *v.n.* tell tales (about), sneak.
Pfad [pfa:t], *m.* (—es, *pl.* —e) path.
Pfadfinder ['pfa:tfɪndər], *m.* (—s, *pl.* —) Boy Scout.
Pfaffe ['pfafə], *m.* (—n, *pl.* —n) *(pej.)* cleric, priest.
Pfahl [pfa:l], *m.* (—s, *pl.* ⁻e) post, stake.
Pfahlbauten ['pfa:lbautən], *m. pl.* lake dwellings.

pfählen ['pfɛ:lən], *v.a.* fasten with stakes; impale.
Pfand [pfant], *n.* (—s, *pl.* ⁻er) pawn, pledge; security; *(game)* forfeit; *ein — einlösen*, redeem a pledge.
pfänden ['pfɛndən], *v.a.* take in pledge; seize.
Pfänderspiel ['pfɛndərʃpi:l], *n.* (—s, *pl.* —e) game of forfeits.
Pfandgeber ['pfantge:bər], *m.* (—s, *pl.* —) pawner.
Pfandleiher ['pfantlaɪər], *m.* (—s, *pl.* —) pawnbroker.
Pfandrecht ['pfantrɛçt], *n.* (—s, *no pl.*) lien.
Pfändung ['pfɛnduŋ], *f.* (—, *pl.* —en) seizure, attachment, distraint.
Pfanne ['pfanə], *f.* (—, *pl.* —n) pan, frying-pan.
Pfannkuchen ['pfanku:xən], *m.* (—s, *pl.* —) pancake; *Berliner —*, doughnut.
Pfarre ['pfarə], *f.* (—, *pl.* —n) living, parish; *(house)* vicarage, parsonage, manse.
Pfarrer ['pfarər], *m.* (—s, *pl.* —) parson; vicar, (parish) priest.
Pfau [pfau], *m.* (—en, *pl.* —en) *(Orn.)* peacock.
Pfauenauge ['pfauənaugə], *n.* (—s, *pl.* —n) *(Ent.)* peacock butterfly.
Pfeffer ['pfɛfər], *m.* (—s, *no pl.*) pepper; *spanischer —*, red pepper, cayenne.
Pfefferkuchen ['pfɛfərku:xən], *m.* (—s, *pl.* —) gingerbread, spiced cake.
Pfefferminz ['pfɛfərmɪnts], *n.* (—, *no pl.*) peppermint.
Pfeife ['pfaɪfə], *f.* (—, *pl.* —n) whistle, fife; pipe.
pfeifen ['pfaɪfən], *v.a., v.n. irr.* whistle, play the fife; *(Theat.)* boo, hiss; *(bullets)* whiz(z).
Pfeifenrohr ['pfaɪfənro:r], *n.* (—s, *pl.* —e) pipe-stem.
Pfeil [pfaɪl], *m.* (—es, *pl.* —e) arrow, dart, bolt.
Pfeiler ['pfaɪlər], *m.* (—s, *pl.* —) pillar.
Pfeilwurz ['pfaɪlvurts], *f.* (—, *no pl.*) *(Bot.)* arrow root.
Pfennig ['pfɛnɪç], *m.* (—s, *pl.* —e) one hundredth of a mark; *(loosely)* penny.
Pferch [pfɛrç], *m.* (—es, *pl.* —e) fold, pen.
Pferd [pfe:rt], *n.* (—es, *pl.* —e) horse; *zu —*, on horseback; *vom — steigen*, dismount.
Pferdeknecht ['pfe:rdəknɛçt], *m.* (—es, *pl.* —e) groom.
Pferdestärke ['pfe:rdəʃtɛrkə], *f.* (—, *no pl.*) horse-power *(abbr. PS)*.
Pfiff [pfɪf], *m.* (—es, *pl.* —e) whistle.
Pfifferling ['pfɪfərlɪŋ], *m.* (—s, *pl.* —e) *(Bot.)* mushroom; chanterelle; *einen — wert*, worthless.
pfiffig ['pfɪfɪç], *adj.* cunning, sly, crafty.
Pfiffikus ['pfɪfɪkus], *m.* (—, *pl.* —se) *(coll.)* sly dog.

Pfingsten

Pfingsten ['pfiŋkstən], *n.* Whitsun (-tide), Pentecost.

Pfingstrose ['pfiŋkstro:zə], *f.* (—, *pl.* (*Bot.*) peony.

Pfirsich ['pfirziç], *m.* (—s, *pl.* —e) (*Bot.*) peach.

Pflanze ['pflantsə], *f.* (—, *pl.* —n) plant.

pflanzen ['pflantsən], *v.a.* plant.

Pflanzer ['pflantsər], *m.* (—s, *pl.* —) planter.

pflanzlich ['pflantsliç], *adj.* vegetable, botanical.

Pflänzling ['pflɛntsliŋ], *m.* (—s, *pl.* —e) seedling, young plant.

Pflanzung ['pflantsuŋ], *f.* (—, *pl.* —en) plantation.

Pflaster ['pflastər], *n.* (—s, *pl.* —) (*Med.*) plaster; (*street*) pavement; *ein teures* —, an expensive place to live in.

Pflaume ['pflaumə], *f.* (—, *pl.* —n) plum; *getrocknete* —, prune.

Pflege ['pfle:gə], *f.* (—, *no pl.*) care, attention, nursing, fostering.

Pflegeeltern ['pfle:gəɛltərn], *pl.* foster-parents.

pflegen ['pfle:gən], *v.a.* nurse, look after, take care of; *Umgang* — *mit*, associate with. — *v.n.* be used to, be in the habit of.

Pflegling ['pfle:kliŋ], *m.* (—s, *pl.* —e) foster-child, ward.

Pflicht [pfliçt], *f.* (—, *pl.* —en) duty, obligation.

Pflichtgefühl ['pfliçtgəfy:l], *n.* (—s, *no pl.*) sense of duty.

pflichtgemäß ['pfliçtgəmɛ:s], *adj.* dutiful.

pflichtschuldig ['pfliçtʃuldiç], *adj.* in duty bound.

Pflock [pflɔk], *m.* (—s, *pl.* ⸚e) plug, peg.

pflücken ['pflykən], *v.a.* pluck, pick, gather.

Pflug [pflu:k], *m.* (—es, *pl.* ⸚e) plough.

Pflugschar ['pflu:kʃa:r], *f.* (—, *pl.* —en) ploughshare.

Pforte ['pfɔrtə], *f.* (—, *pl.* —n) gate, door, porch.

Pförtner ['pfœrtnər], *m.* (—s, *pl.* —) door-keeper, porter.

Pfosten ['pfɔstən], *m.* (—s, *pl.* —) post, stake; (*door*) jamb.

Pfote ['pfo:tə], *f.* (—, *pl.* —n) paw.

Pfriem [pfri:m], *m.* (—es, *pl.* —e) awl.

Pfropf(en) ['pfrɔpf(ən)], *m.* (—s, *pl.* —en) cork, stopper; (*gun*) wad.

pfropfen ['pfrɔpfən], *v.a.* graft; cork.

Pfründe ['pfryndə], *f.* (—, *pl.* —n) living, benefice.

Pfuhl [pfu:l], *m.* (—es, *pl.* —e) pool, puddle.

Pfühl [pfy:l], *m.* (—es, *pl.* —e) (*Poet.*) bolster, pillow, cushion.

pfui! [pfui], *excl.* shame! ugh! — *Teufel!* shame! a damned shame!

Pfund [pfunt], *n.* (—es, *pl.* —e) pound.

pfuschen ['pfuʃən], *v.n.* botch; *einem ins Handwerk* —, poach on s.o. else's preserve.

Pfütze ['pfytsə], *f.* (—, *pl.* —n) puddle.

Phänomen [fɛːnoˈmeːn], *n.* (—s, *pl.* —e) phenomenon.

Phantasie [fantaˈziː], *f.* (—, *pl.* —n) fancy, imagination; (*Mus.*) fantasia.

phantasieren [fantaˈziːrən], *v.n.* indulge in fancies; (*sick person*) rave, wander, be delirious; (*Mus.*) improvise.

Phantast [fanˈtast], *m.* (—en, *pl.* —en) dreamer, visionary.

Pharisäer [fariˈzɛːər], *m.* (—s, *pl.* —) Pharisee.

Phase ['faːzə], *f.* (—, *pl.* —n) phase, stage (of process *or* development).

Philippinen [filiˈpiːnən], *f. pl.* Philippines.

Philister [fiˈlistər], *m.* (—s, *pl.* —) Philistine.

philisterhaft [fiˈlistərhaft], *adj.* philistine, narrow-minded, conventional.

Philologie [filoloˈgiː], *f.* (—, *no pl.*) philology; study of languages.

Philosoph [filoˈzoːf], *m.* (—en, *pl.* —en) philosopher.

Philosophie [filozoˈfiː], *f.* (—, *pl.* —n) philosophy.

Phiole [fiˈoːlə], *f.* (—, *pl.* —n) phial, vial.

Phlegma ['flɛgma], *n.* (—s, *no pl.*) phlegm.

Phonetik [foˈneːtik], *f.* (—, *no pl.*) phonetics.

photogen [fotoˈgeːn], *adj.* photogenic.

Photograph [fotoˈgraːf], *m.* (—en, *pl.* —en) photographer.

Photographie [fotograˈfiː], *f.* (—, *pl.* —n) photograph, photo; (*Art*) photography.

photographieren [fotograˈfiːrən], *v.a.* photograph.

Physik [fyˈziːk], *f.* (—, *no pl.*) physics (of physics).

physikalisch [fyziˈkaːliʃ], *adj.* physical (of physics).

Physiker ['fyːzikər], *m.* (—s, *pl.* —) physicist.

Physiologe [fyːzjoˈloːgə], *m.* (—en, *pl.* —en) physiologist.

physiologisch [fyːzjoˈloːgiʃ], *adj.* physiological.

physisch ['fyːziʃ], *adj.* physical.

Picke ['pikə], *f.* (—, *pl.* —n) pickaxe, axe.

Pickel ['pikəl], *m.* (—s, *pl.* —) pimple.

Piedestal ['pjeːdɛsta:l], *n.* (—s, *pl.* —e) pedestal.

piepen ['piːpən], *v.n.* squeak, chirp.

piepsen ['piːpsən], *v.n.* squeak, chirp.

Pietät [pieˈtɛːt], *f.* (—, *no pl.*) piety, reverence.

Pik [piːk], *n.* (—s, *pl.* —s) (*cards*) spades.

pikant [piˈkant], *adj.* piquant, spicy; (*fig.*) risqué.

Pikee [piˈkeː], *m.* (—s, *pl.* —s) piqué.

pikiert [piˈkiːrt], *adj.* irritated, annoyed, piqued.

Pikkolo ['pikolo], *m.* (—s, *pl.* —s) apprentice waiter, boy (waiter); (*Mus.*) piccolo, flute.

Pilger ['pɪlgər], *m.* (—s, *pl.* —) pilgrim.
Pille ['pɪlə], *f.* (—, *pl.* —n) pill.
Pilz [pɪlts], *m.* (—es, *pl.* —e) fungus, mushroom.
Piment [pi'mɛnt], *n.* (—s, *pl.* —e) pimento, Jamaican pepper, all-spice.
pimplig ['pɪmplɪç], *adj.* effeminate.
Pinguin [pɪŋgu'i:n], *m.* (—s, *pl.* —e) (*Orn.*) penguin.
Pinie ['pi:njə], *f.* (—, *pl.* —n) (*Bot.*) stone-pine.
Pinne ['pɪnə], *f.* (—, *pl.* —n) drawing-pin; peg.
Pinscher ['pɪnʃər], *m.* (—s, *pl.* —) terrier.
Pinsel ['pɪnzəl], *m.* (—s, *pl.* —) (*Painting*) brush, pencil; (*fig.*) simpleton.
Pinzette [pɪn'tsɛtə], *f.* (—, *pl.* —n) pincers, tweezers.
Pirsch [pɪrʃ], *f.* (—, *no pl.*) (deer-) stalking.
Piste ['pɪstə], *f.* (—, *pl.* —n) track; (*Aviat.*) runway.
pittoresk [pɪto'rɛsk], *adj.* picturesque.
placken ['plakən], *v.r. sich* —, toil, drudge.
plädieren [plɛ'di:rən], *v.n.* plead.
Plädoyer [plɛ:doa'je:], *n.* (—s, *pl.* —s) speech for the prosecution *or* the defence (in a court of law), plea, pleading.
Plage ['pla:gə], *f.* (—, *pl.* —n) torment, trouble; calamity; plague.
plagen ['pla:gən], *v.a.* plague, trouble, torment, vex. — *v.r. sich* —, toil.
Plagiat [plag'ja:t], *n.* (—es, *pl.* —e) plagiarism.
Plaid [plɛ:t], *n.* (—s, *pl.* —s) travelling-rug.
Plakat [pla'ka:t], *n.* (—(e)s, *pl.* —e) poster, placard, bill.
Plan [pla:n], *n.* (—es, *pl.* ⁛e) plan, scheme, plot; map, ground-plan.
Plane ['pla:nə], *f.* (—, *pl.* —n) awning, cover.
planieren [pla'ni:rən], *v.a.* level, plane down; bulldoze, flatten.
Planke ['plaŋkə], *f.* (—, *pl.* —n) plank, board.
Plänkelei [plɛnkə'laɪ], *f.* (—, *pl.* —en) skirmish.
planmäßig ['pla:nmɛ:sɪç], *adj.* according to plan.
planschen ['planʃən], *v.n.* splash; paddle.
Plantage [plan'ta:ʒə], *f.* (—, *pl.* —n) plantation.
planvoll ['pla:nfɔl], *adj.* systematic, well-planned.
Planwagen ['pla:nva:gən], *m.* (—s, *pl.* —) tilt-cart.
plappern ['plapərn], *v.n.* prattle, chatter.
plärren ['plɛrən], *v.n.* blubber, bawl.
Plastik ['plastɪk], *f.* (—, *pl.* —en) plastic art; plastic (material).
Platane [pla'ta:nə], *f.* (—, *pl.* —n) plane-tree.

Platin ['pla:ti:n], *n.* (—s, *no pl.*) platinum.
platonisch [pla'to:nɪʃ], *adj.* platonic.
plätschern ['plɛtʃərn], *v.n.* splash about.
platt [plat], *adj.* flat, level, even; insipid; downright; —*e Redensart*, commonplace, platitude; (*coll.*) *ich bin ganz* —, I am astonished *or* dumbfounded.
Plättbrett ['plɛtbrɛt], *n.* (—es, *pl.* —er) ironing board.
plattdeutsch ['platdɔytʃ], *adj.* Low German.
Platte ['platə], *f.* (—, *pl.* —n) plate; dish; board; slab; sheet; ledge; (*fig.*) bald head; (*Mus.*) (gramophone) record.
plätten ['plɛtən], *v.a.* iron (clothes).
Plattfisch ['platfɪʃ], *m.* (—es, *pl.* —e) (*Zool.*) plaice.
Plattfuß ['platfu:s], *n.* (—es, *pl.* ⁛e) flat foot.
Plattheit ['plathaɪt], *f.* (—, *pl.* —en) flatness; (*fig.*) platitude.
Platz [plats], *m.* (—es, *pl.* ⁛e) place, town, spot, site; space, room; (*town*) square; seat; — *nehmen*, take a seat, be seated.
Platzanweiserin ['platsanvaɪzərɪn], *f.* —, *pl.* —nen) usherette.
Plätzchen ['plɛtsçən], *n.* (—s, *pl.* —) small place; drop; biscuit.
platzen ['platsən], *v.n.* (*aux.* sein) burst, explode.
Platzregen ['platsre:gən], *m.* (—s, *no pl.*) downpour, heavy shower.
Plauderei [plaudə'raɪ], *f.* (—, *pl.* —en) chat.
Plaudertasche ['plaudərtaʃə], *f.* (—, *pl.* —n) chatterbox.
Pleite ['plaɪtə], *f.* (—, *pl.* —n) (*coll.*) bankruptcy; — *machen*, go bankrupt.
Plenum ['ple:num], *n.* (—s, *no pl.*) plenary session.
Pleuelstange ['plɔyəlʃtaŋə], *f.* (—, *pl.* —n) connecting-rod.
Plinsen ['plɪnzən], *f. pl.* (*Austr.*) fritters.
Plissee [plɪ'se:], *n.* (—s, *pl.* —s) pleating.
Plombe ['plɔmbə], *f.* (—, *pl.* —n) lead, seal; (*teeth*) filling.
plombieren [plɔm'bi:rən], *v.a.* seal with lead; (*teeth*) fill.
plötzlich ['plœtslɪç], *adj.* sudden.
plump [plump], *adj.* clumsy, ungainly, awkward; crude, coarse.
plumps [plumps], *excl.* bump! oops!
Plunder ['plundər], *m.* (—s, *no pl.*) lumber, trash.
plündern ['plyndərn], *v.a.* plunder, pillage.
Plüsch [ply:ʃ], *m.* (—es, *no pl.*) plush.
pneumatisch [pnɔy'ma:tɪʃ], *adj.* pneumatic.
Pöbel ['pø:bəl], *m.* (—s, *no pl.*) mob, rabble.
pochen ['pɔxən], *v.a., v.n.* knock, beat, throb.

Pocke

Pocke ['pɔkə], *f.* (—, *pl.* —n) pockmark; (*pl.*) smallpox.
pockennarbig ['pɔkənnarbɪç], *adj.* pockmarked.
Podagra ['po:dagra:], *n.* (—s, *no pl.*) (*Med.*) gout.
Pointe [po'ɛ̃tə], *f.* (—, *pl.* —n) (*of a story*) point.
Pokal [po'ka:l], *m.* (—s, *pl.* —e) goblet, cup; trophy.
Pökelfleisch ['pø:kəlflaɪʃ], *n.* (—es, *no pl.*) salted meat.
Pol [po:l], *m.* (—s, *pl.* —e) pole.
polemisch [po'le:mɪʃ], *adj.* polemic(al), controversial.
Polen ['po:lən], *n.* Poland.
Police [po'li:sə], *f.* (—, *pl.* —n) insurance policy.
polieren [po'li:rən], *v.a.* polish, furbish, burnish.
Poliklinik ['po:likli:nɪk], *f.* (—, *pl.* —en) (*Med.*) out-patients' department.
Politik [poli'ti:k], *f.* (—, *no pl.*) politics; policy.
politisieren [politi'zi:rən], *v.n.* talk politics.
Politur [poli'tu:r], *f.* (—, *no pl.*) polish, gloss.
Polizei [poli'tsaɪ], *f.* (—, *no pl.*) police.
polizeilich [poli'tsaɪlɪç], *adj.* of the police.
Polizeistunde [poli'tsaɪʃtundə], *f.* (—, *no pl.*) closing time.
Polizeiwache [poli'tsaɪvaxə], *f.* (—, *pl.* —n) police station.
Polizist [poli'tsɪst], *m.* (—en, *pl.* —en) policeman, constable.
Polizze [po'lɪtsə], *f.* (—, *pl.* —n) (*Austr. dial.*) insurance policy.
polnisch ['pɔlnɪʃ], *adj.* Polish.
Polster ['pɔlstər], *n.* (—s, *pl.* —) cushion, bolster.
Polterabend ['pɔltəra:bənt], *m.* (—s, *pl.* —e) wedding-eve party.
Poltergeist ['pɔltərgaɪst], *m.* (—es, *pl.* —er) poltergeist, hobgoblin.
poltern ['pɔltərn], *v.n.* rumble; make a noise; bluster.
Polyp [po'ly:p], *m.* (—en, *pl.* —en) (*Zool.*) polyp; (*Med.*) polypus.
Pomeranze [pomə'rantsə], *f.* (—, *pl.* —n) (*Bot.*) orange.
Pommern ['pɔmərn], *n.* Pomerania.
Pope ['po:pə], *m.* (—n, *pl.* —n) Greek Orthodox priest.
Popo [po'po:], *m.* (—s, *pl.* —s) (*coll.*) backside, bottom.
populär [popu'lɛ:r], *adj.* popular.
porös [po'rø:s], *adj.* porous.
Porree ['pɔre:], *m.* (—s, *no pl.*) leek.
Portefeuille [pɔrt'fœj], *n.* (—s, *pl.* —s) portfolio.
Portier [pɔr'tje:], *m.* (—s, *pl.* —s) doorkeeper, caretaker; porter.
Porto ['pɔrto:], *n.* (—s, *pl.* **Porti**) postage.
Porzellan [pɔrtsɛ'la:n], *n.* (—s, *pl.* —e) china, porcelain; *Meißner* —, Dresden china.

Posamenten [poza'mɛntən], *n. pl.* trimmings.
Posaune [po'zaunə], *f.* (—, *pl.* —n) (*Mus.*) trombone.
Positur [pozi'tu:r], *f.* (—, *pl.* —en) posture; *sich in — setzen*, strike an attitude.
Posse ['pɔsə], *f.* (—, *pl.* —n) (*Theat.*) farce, skit.
Possen ['pɔsən], *m.* (—s, *pl.* —) trick; *einem einen — spielen*, play a trick on s.o.
possierlich [pɔ'si:rlɪç], *adj.* droll, funny, comic(al).
Post [pɔst], *f.* (—, *pl.* —en) post, mail; (*building*) post-office.
Postament [pɔsta'mɛnt], *n.* (—s, *pl.* —e) plinth, pedestal.
Postanweisung ['pɔstanvaɪzuŋ], *f.* (—, *pl.* —en) postal order, money order.
Posten ['pɔstən], *m.* (—s, *pl.* —) post, station; place; (*goods*) parcel, lot, job lot; (*Comm.*) item; (*Mil.*) outpost; *— stehen*, stand sentry; *nicht auf dem — sein*, be unwell.
Postfach ['pɔstfax], *n.* (—es, *pl.* ⁻er) post-office box.
postieren [pɔs'ti:rən], *v.a.* post, place, station.
postlagernd ['pɔstla:gərnt], *adj.* poste restante, to be called for.
Postschalter ['pɔstʃaltər], *m.* (—s, *pl.* —) post-office counter.
postulieren [pɔstu'li:rən], *v.a.* postulate.
postwendend ['pɔstvɛndənt], *adj.* by return of post.
Postwertzeichen ['pɔstve:rttsaɪçən], *n.* (—s, *pl.* —) stamp.
Potenz [po'tɛnts], *f.* (—, *pl.* —en) (*Maths.*) power; *zur dritten —*, cubed, to the power of three.
potenzieren [potɛn'tsi:rən], *v.a.* (*Math.*) raise; intensify.
Pottasche ['pɔtaʃə], *f.* (—, *no pl.*) potash.
potzblitz ['pɔtsblɪts], *excl.* good Heavens! good gracious!
potztausend ['pɔtstauzənt], *excl.* great Scott! good Heavens!
Pracht [praxt], *f.* (—, *no pl.*) splendour, magnificence; (*in compounds*) de luxe.
prächtig ['prɛçtɪç], *adj.* splendid, magnificent, sumptuous.
prachtvoll ['praxtfɔl], *adj.* gorgeous, magnificent.
Prädikat [prɛ:di'ka:t], *n.* (—s, *pl.* —e) mark; (*Gram.*) predicate.
Prag [pra:k], *n.* Prague.
prägen ['prɛ:gən], *v.a.* coin, mint, stamp.
prägnant [prɛg'nant], *adj.* meaningful, precise.
prahlen ['pra:lən], *v.n.* boast, brag, talk big, show off.
Praktikant [praktɪ'kant], *m.* (—en, *pl.* —en) probationer; apprentice.
Praktiken ['praktɪkən], *f. pl.* machinations.

praktisch ['praktıʃ], *adj.* practical; —*er Arzt,* general practitioner.
praktizieren [prakti'tsi:rən], *v.a.* practise.
Prall [pral], *m.* (—es, *pl.* —e) impact.
prall [pral], *adj.* tense, tight; (*cheeks*) chubby.
prallen ['pralən], *v.n.* (*aux.* sein) *auf etwas* —, bounce against s.th.
Prämie ['prɛ:mjə], *f.* (—, *pl.* —n) prize; (*insurance*) premium; (*dividend*) bonus.
prangen ['praŋən], *v.n.* shine, glitter, make a show.
Pranger ['praŋər], *m.* (—s, *pl.* —) pillory; *etwas an den* — *stellen,* expose s.th., pillory.
präparieren [prɛpa'ri:rən], *v.a., v.r.* prepare.
Präsens ['prɛ:zɛns], *n.* (—, *pl.* —ntia) (*Gram.*) present tense.
präsentieren [prɛzɛn'ti:rən], *v.a.* present; *präsentiert das Gewehr!* present arms!
prasseln ['prasəln], *v.n.* (*fire*) crackle; rattle.
prassen ['prasən], *v.n.* revel, gorge (o.s.), guzzle, feast.
Prätendent [prɛtɛn'dɛnt], *m.* (—en, *pl.* —en) pretender, claimant.
Präteritum [prɛ'tɛ:ritum], *n.* (—s, *pl.* —ta) (*Gram.*) preterite, past tense.
Praxis ['praksis], *f.* (—, *no pl.*) practice.
präzis [prɛ'tsi:s], *adj.* precise, exact.
präzisieren [prɛtsi'zi:rən], *v.a.* define exactly.
predigen ['pre:dıgən], *v.a., v.n.* preach.
Predigt ['pre:dıçt], *f.* (—, *pl.* —en) sermon; (*fig.*) homily, lecture.
Preis [praıs], *m.* (—es, *pl.* —e) price, rate, value; (*reward*) prize; praise; *um jeden* —, at any price, at all costs; *um keinen* —, not for all the world; *feste* —*e,* fixed prices; no rebate, no discount.
Preisausschreiben ['praısausʃraıbən], *n.* (—s, *pl.* —) prize competition.
Preiselbeere ['praızəlbe:rə], *f.* (—, *pl.* —n) (*Bot.*) bilberry, cranberry.
preisen ['praızən], *v.a.* *irr.* praise, laud; glorify.
preisgeben ['praısgɛ:bən], *v.a.* *irr.* give up, abandon, part with; *dem Spott preisgegeben sein,* become a laughing-stock.
Preisunterbietung ['praısuntərbi:-tuŋ], *f.* (—, *pl.* —en) under-cutting.
Prellbock ['prɛlbɔk], *m.* (—s, *pl.* ⸚e) buffer (-block).
prellen ['prɛlən], *v.a.* cheat, defraud.
Prellstein ['prɛlʃtaın], *m.* (—s, *pl.* —e) kerbstone.
pressant [prɛ'sant], *adj.* (*Austr*). urgent.
Presse ['prɛsə], *f.* (—, *pl.* —n) press; newspapers; (*coll.*) coaching establishment, crammer.
pressieren [prɛ'si:rən], *v.n.* be urgent.
Preßkohle ['prɛsko:lə], *f.* (—, *no pl.*) briquette(s).

Preßkolben ['prɛskɔlbən], *m.* (—s, *pl.* —) piston.
Preßluft ['prɛsluft], *f.* (—, *no pl.*) compressed air.
Preußen ['prɔysən], *n.* Prussia.
prickeln ['prıkəln], *v.n.* prick, prickle, sting, tickle.
Prieme ['pri:mə], *f.* (—, *pl.* —n) chew, quid.
Priester ['pri:stər], *m.* (—s, *pl.* —) priest; *zum* — *weihen,* ordain to the priesthood.
Prima ['pri:ma:], *f.* (—, *pl.* **Primen**) highest form at a grammar school (sixth form).
prima ['pri:ma:], *adj.* excellent, splendid, first-rate.
Primaner [pri'ma:nər], *m.* (—s, *pl.* —) pupil in the highest form at a grammar school, sixth form boy.
Primel ['pri:məl], *f.* (—, *pl.* —n) (*Bot.*) primrose, primula.
Primus ['pri:mus], *m.* (—, *no pl.*) (*School*) head boy, captain of the school.
Prinzip [prın'tsi:p], *n.* (—s, *pl.* —ien) principle.
Priorität [priori'tɛ:t], *f.* (—, *no pl.*) priority, precedence.
Prise ['pri:zə], *f.* (—, *pl.* —n) pinch of snuff.
Prisma ['prısma:], *n.* (—s, *pl.* —men) prism.
Pritsche ['prıtʃə], *f.* (—, *pl.* —n) plank-bed.
Privatdozent [pri'va:tdotsɛnt], *m.* (—en, *pl.* —en) (*Univ.*) (unsalaried) lecturer.
privatisieren [privati'zi:rən], *v.n.* have private means.
Probe ['pro:bə], *f.* (—, *pl.* —n) experiment, trial, probation, test; (*Theat., Mus.*) rehearsal; sample, pattern; *auf* —, on trial; *auf die* — *stellen,* put to the test *or* on probation.
Probeabzug ['pro:bəaptsu:k], *m.* (—s, *pl.* ⸚e) (*Printing*) proof.
proben ['pro:bən], *v.a.* rehearse.
probieren [pro'bi:rən], *v.a.* try, attempt; taste.
Probst [pro:pst], *m.* (—es, *pl.* ⸚e) provost.
Produzent [produ'tsɛnt], *m.* (—en, *pl.* —en) producer (of goods), manufacturer.
produzieren [produ'tsi:rən], *v.a.* produce (goods). — *v.r. sich* —, perform, show off.
profanieren [profa'ni:rən], *v.a.* desecrate, profane.
Professur [profɛ'su:r], *f.* (—, *pl.* —en) (*Univ.*) professorship, Chair.
profitieren [profi'ti:rən], *v.a., v.n.* profit (by), take advantage (of).
projizieren [proji'tsi:rən], *v.a.* project.
Prokura [pro'ku:ra:], *f.* (—, *no pl.*) (*Law*) power of attorney.
Prokurist [proku'rıst], *m.* (—en, *pl.* —en) confidential clerk; company secretary.

171

prolongieren

prolongieren [prolɔn'giːrən], *v.a.* prolong, extend.

promenieren [promə'niːrən], *v.n.* take a stroll.

Promotion [promo'tsjoːn], *f.* (—, *pl.* —en) graduation, degree ceremony.

promovieren [promo'viːrən], *v.n.* graduate, take a degree.

promulgieren [promul'giːrən], *v.a.* promulgate.

Pronomen [pro'noːmən], *n.* (—s, *pl.* —mina) (*Gram.*) pronoun.

prophezeien [profe'tsaɪən], *v.a.* prophesy, predict, forecast.

prophylaktisch [profy'laktɪʃ], *adj.* preventive, prophylactic.

Propst [proːpst], *m.* (—es, *pl.* ⁻e) provost.

Prosa ['proːzaː], *f.* (—, *no pl.*) prose.

prosit ['proːzɪt], *excl.* cheers! here's to you! your health!

Prospekt [pro'spɛkt], *m.* (—es, *pl.* —e) prospect; (*booklet*) prospectus.

Prostituierte [prostitu'iːrtə], *f.* (—n, *pl.* —n) prostitute; (*coll.*) tart.

protegieren [prote'ʒiːrən], *v.a.* favour, patronize.

Protektion [protɛk'tsjoːn], *f.* (—, *no pl.*) patronage, favouritism.

protestieren [protɛs'tiːrən], *v.n.* make a protest, protest (against s.th.).

Protokoll [proto'kɔl], *n.* (—s, *pl.* —e) minutes, record; protocol; regulations.

Protokollführer [proto'kɔlfyːrər], *m.* (—s, *pl.* —) recorder, clerk of the minutes.

Protz [prɔts], *m.* (—en, *pl.* —en) snob, upstart; show-off.

Proviant [pro'vjant], *m.* (—s, *no pl.*) provisions, stores.

provinziell [provɪn'tsjɛl], *adj.* provincial.

Provinzler [pro'vɪntsler], *m.* (—s, *pl.* —) provincial.

Provision [provi'zjoːn], *f.* (—, *pl.* —en) (*Comm.*) commission, brokerage.

Provisor [pro'viːzɔr], *m.* (—s, *pl.* —en) dispenser.

provisorisch [provi'zoːrɪʃ], *adj.* provisional, temporary.

provozieren [provo'tsiːrən], *v.a.* provoke.

Prozedur [protse'duːr], *f.* (—, *pl.* —en) proceedings, procedure.

Prozent [pro'tsɛnt], *m. & n.* (—s, *pl.* —e) per cent.

Prozentsatz [pro'tsɛntzats], *m.* (—es, *pl.* ⁻e) percentage, rate of interest.

Prozeß [pro'tsɛs], *m.* (—es, *pl.* —e) process; lawsuit, litigation; trial; *mit etwas kurzen — machen*, deal summarily with.

Prozeßwesen [pro'tsɛsveːzən], *n.* (—s, *no pl.*) legal procedure.

prüde ['pryːdə], *adj.* prudish, prim.

prüfen ['pryːfən], *v.a.* test, examine.

Prüfung ['pryːfuŋ], *f.* (—, *pl.* —en) trial, test; examination; (*fig.*) temptation, affliction.

Prügel ['pryːgəl], *m.* (—s, *pl.*—) cudgel; (*pl.*) thrashing; *eine Tracht —*, a good hiding.

prügeln ['pryːgəln], *v.a.* beat, give a hiding to.

Prunk [pruŋk], *m.* (—(e)s, *no pl.*) splendour, ostentation, pomp.

prusten ['pruːstən], *v.n.* snort.

Psalm [psalm], *m.* (—es, *pl.* —e) psalm.

Psalter ['psaltər], *m.* (—s, *pl.* —) (*book*) psalter; (*instrument*) psaltery.

Psychiater [psyçi'aːtər], *m.* (—s, *pl.* —) psychiatrist.

Psychologe [psyço'loːgə], *m.* (—n, *pl.* —n) psychologist.

Pubertät [pubɛr'tɛːt], *f.* (—, *no pl.*) puberty.

Publikum ['puːblɪkum], *n.* (—s, *no pl.*) public; (*Theat.*) audience.

publizieren [publi'tsiːrən], *v.a.* publish; promulgate.

Pudel ['puːdəl], *m.* (—s, *pl.* —) poodle; *des —s Kern*, the gist of the matter.

Puder ['puːdər], *m.* (—s, *no pl.*) powder, face-powder.

pudern ['puːdərn], *v.a.* powder.

Puff [puf], *m.* (—es, *pl.* ⁻e) cuff, thump.

puffen ['pufən], *v.a.* cuff, thump.

Puffer ['pufər], *m.* (—s, *pl.* —) buffer.

Puffspiel ['pufʃpiːl], *n.* (—s, *pl.* —e) backgammon.

pullen ['pulən], *v.n.* rein in (a horse); (*coll.*) piddle.

Pulsader ['pulsaːdər], *f.* (—, *pl.* —n) artery; aorta.

pulsieren [pul'ziːrən], *v.n.* pulsate; pulse, throb.

Pulsschlag ['pulsʃlaːk], *m.* (—s, *pl.* ⁻e) pulse-beat; pulsation.

Pult [pult], *n.* (—es, *pl.* —e) desk, writing-table; lectern.

Pulver ['pulvər], *n.* (—s, *pl.* —) powder.

Pump [pump], *m.* (—s, *no pl.*) (*sl.*) credit; *auf —*, on tick.

pumpen ['pumpən], *v.a., v.n.* pump; (*fig.*) (*sl.*) *sich etwas —*, borrow s.th., touch s.o. for s.th.; lend.

Pumpenschwengel ['pumpənʃvɛŋəl], *m.* (—s, *pl.* —) pump-handle.

Pumpernickel ['pumpərnɪkəl], *m.* (—s, *pl.* —) black bread, Westphalian rye-bread.

Pumphosen ['pumphoːzən], *f. pl.* plusfours.

Punkt [puŋkt], *m.* (—es, *pl.* —e) point, dot, spot; (*Gram.*) full stop.

punktieren [puŋk'tiːrən], *v.a.* dot; punctuate.

pünktlich ['pyŋktlɪç], *adj.* punctual.

punktum ['puŋktum], *excl. und damit —*, that's the end of it; that's it.

Puppe ['pupə], *f.* (—, *pl.* —n) doll; (*Ent.*) pupa, chrysalis.

pur [puːr], *adj.* pure, sheer; (*drink*) neat.

Puritaner [puri'ta:nər], m. (—s, pl. —) puritan.

Purpur ['purpur], m. (—s, no pl.) purple.

Purzelbaum ['purtsəlbaum], m. (—s, pl. ⸚e) somersault.

purzeln ['purtsəln], v.n. tumble.

Pustel ['pustəl], f. (—, pl. —n) pustule.

pusten ['pu:stən], v.n. puff, blow.

Pute ['pu:tə], f. (—, pl. —n) (Orn.) turkey-hen; dumme —, silly goose.

Puter ['pu:tər], m. (—s, pl. —) turkeycock.

puterrot ['pu:tərro:t], adj. as red as a turkey-cock.

Putsch [putʃ], m. (—es, pl. —e) coup de main, insurrection, riot.

Putz [puts], m. (—es, no pl.) finery; cleaning; rough-cast.

putzen ['putsən], v.a. polish, shine; clean. — v.r. sich —, dress up.

Putzfrau ['putsfrau], f. (—, pl. —en) charwoman.

Putzmacherin ['putsmaxərIn], f. (—, pl. —nen) milliner.

Pyramide [pyra'mi:də], f. (—, pl. —n) pyramid.

Pyrenäen [pyrə'nɛ:ən], pl. Pyrenees; —halbinsel, Iberian Peninsula.

Q

Q [ku:], n. (—s, pl. —s) the letter Q.

quabbeln ['kvabəln], v.n. shake, wobble.

Quacksalber ['kvakzalbər], m. (—s, pl. —) quack, mountebank.

Quacksalberei [kvakzalbə'raI], f. (—, pl. —en) quackery.

Quaderstein ['kva:dərʃtaIn], m. (—s, pl. —e) ashlar, hewn stone.

Quadrat [kva'dra:t], n. (—es, pl. —e) square; zum (or ins) — erheben, square (a number).

Quadratur [kvadra'tu:r], f. (—, pl. —en) quadrature; die — des Kreises finden, square the circle.

quadrieren [kva'dri:rən], v.a. square.

quaken ['kva:kən], v.n. (frog) croak; (duck) quack.

quäken ['kvɛ:kən], v.n. squeak.

Quäker ['kvɛ:kər], m. (—s, pl. —) Quaker.

Qual [kva:l], f. (—, pl. —en) anguish, agony, torment.

quälen ['kvɛ:lən], v.a. torment, torture, vex. — v.r. sich —, toil.

qualifizieren [kvalifi'tsi:rən], v.a. qualify.

Qualität [kvali'tɛ:t], f. (—, pl. —en) quality.

Qualle ['kvalə], f. (—, pl. —n) (Zool.) jelly-fish.

Qualm [kvalm], m. (—es, no pl.) dense smoke.

Quantität [kvanti'tɛ:t], f. (—, pl. —en) quantity.

Quantum ['kvantum], n. (—s, pl. —ten) portion, quantity.

Quappe ['kvapə], f. (—, pl. —n) (Zool.) tadpole.

Quarantäne [kvaran'tɛ:nə], f. (—, no pl.) quarantine.

Quark [kvark], m. (—s, no pl.) curds; cream-cheese; (fig.) trash, rubbish, nonsense, bilge.

Quarta ['kvarta:], f. (—, no pl.) fourth form.

Quartal [kvar'ta:l], n. (—s, pl. —e) quarter of a year; term.

Quartier [kvar'ti:r], n. (—s, pl. —e) quarters, lodging; (Mil.) billet.

Quarz [kvarts], m. (—es, no pl.) quartz.

Quaste ['kvastə], f. (—, pl. —n) tassel.

Quatember [kva'tembər], m. (—s, pl. —) quarter day; (Eccl.) Ember Day.

Quatsch [kvatʃ], m. (—es, no pl.) nonsense, drivel.

Quecke ['kvɛkə], f. (—, pl. —n) couch-grass, quick-grass.

Quecksilber ['kvɛkzIlbər], n. (—s, no pl.) quicksilver, mercury.

Quelle ['kvɛlə], f. (—, pl. —n) well, spring, fountain; (fig.) source; aus sicherer —, on good authority.

Quentchen ['kvɛntçən], n. (—s, pl. —) small amount, dram.

quer [kve:r], adj. cross, transverse, oblique, diagonal. — adv. across; kreuz und —, in all directions.

Querbalken ['kve:rbalken], m. (—s, pl. —) cross-beam.

querdurch ['kve:rdurç], adv. across.

querfeldein ['kve:rfɛltaIn], adv. crosscountry.

Querkopf ['kve:rkopf], m. (—es, pl. ⸚e) crank.

Quersattel ['kve:rzatəl], m. (—s, pl. ⸚) side-saddle.

Querschiff ['kve:rʃIf], n. (—es, pl. —e) (church) transept.

Querschnitt ['kve:rʃnIt], m. (—s, pl. —e) cross-section; (fig.) average.

Querulant [kveru'lant], m. (—en, pl. —en) grumbler.

quetschen ['kvɛtʃən], v.a. squeeze, crush, mash; bruise.

Queue [kø:], n. (—s, pl. —s) (Billiards) cue.

quieken ['kvi:kən], v.n. squeak.

Quinta ['kvInta:], f. (—, no pl.) fifth form.

Quinte ['kvIntə], f. (—, pl. —n) (Mus.) fifth.

Quirl [kvIrl], m. (—s, pl. —e) whisk; (Bot.) whorl.

quitt [kvIt], adj. — sein, be quits.

Quitte ['kvItə], f. (—, pl. —n) (Bot.) quince.

quittegelb ['kvɪtəgɛlp], *adj.* bright yellow.

quittieren [kvɪ'ti:rən], *v.a.* receipt; give a receipt; *den Dienst —,* leave the service.

Quittung ['kvɪtuŋ], *f.* (—, *pl.* —en) receipt.

Quodlibet ['kvɔdlɪbɛt], *n.* (—s, *pl.* —s) medley.

Quote ['kvo:tə], *f.* (—, *pl.* —n) quota, share.

quotieren [kvo'ti:rən], *v.a.* (*stock exchange*) quote (prices).

R

R [ɛr], *n.* (—s, *pl.* —s) the letter R.

Rabatt [ra'bat], *m.* (—s, *pl.* —e) rebate, discount.

Rabatte [ra'batə], *f.* (—, *pl.* —n) flower-border.

Rabbiner [ra'bi:nər], *m.* (—s, *pl.* —) rabbi.

Rabe ['ra:bə], *m.* (—n, *pl.* —n) (*Orn.*) raven; *ein weißer —,* a rare bird.

Rabenaas ['ra:bəna:s], *n.* (—es, *pl.* —e) carrion.

rabiat [ra'bja:t], *adj.* furious, rabid.

Rache ['raxə], *f.* (—, *no pl.*) revenge, vengeance.

Rachen ['raxən], *m.* (—s, *pl.* —) jaws, throat.

rächen ['rɛ:çən], *v.a.* avenge. — *v.r. sich —,* avenge o.s., take vengeance.

Rachenbräune ['raxənbrɔynə], *f.* (—, *no pl.*) croup, quinsy.

Rachitis [ra'xi:tɪs], *f.* (—, *no pl.*) (*Med.*) rickets.

rachsüchtig ['raxzyçtɪç], *adj.* vindictive, vengeful.

rackern ['rakərn], *v.r. sich —,* (*coll.*) toil, work hard.

Rad [ra:t], *n.* (—es, *pl.* ⁻er) wheel; bicycle; *ein — schlagen,* turn a cart-wheel; (*peacock*) spread the tail.

Radau [ra'dau], *m.* (—s, *no pl.*) noise, din, shindy.

Rade ['ra:də], *f.* (—, *pl.* —n) corn-cockle.

radebrechen ['ra:dəbrɛçən], *v.a. insep.* murder a language.

radeln ['ra:dəln], *v.n.* (*aux.* sein) (*coll.*) cycle.

Rädelsführer ['rɛ:dəlsfy:rər], *m.* (—s, *pl.* —) ringleader.

rädern ['rɛ:dərn], *v.a.* break on the wheel; *gerädert sein,* (*fig.*) ache in all o.'s bones, be exhausted.

Radfahrer ['ra:tfa:rər], *m.* (—s, *pl.* —) cyclist.

radieren [ra'di:rən], *v.n.* erase; etch.

Radierung [ra'di:ruŋ], *f.* (—, *pl.* —en) etching.

Radieschen [ra'di:sçən], *n.* (—s, *pl.* —) (*Bot.*) radish.

Radio ['ra:djo], *n.* (—s, *pl.* —s) wireless, radio.

raffen ['rafən], *v.a.* snatch up, gather up.

Raffinade [rafi'na:də], *f.* (—, *no pl.*) refined sugar.

Raffinement [rafinə'mã], *n.* (—s, *no pl.*) elaborateness.

raffinieren [rafi'ni:rən], *v.a.* refine.

raffiniert [rafi'ni:rt], *adj.* refined; elaborate, crafty, wily, cunning.

ragen ['ra:gən], *v.n.* tower, soar.

Rahm [ra:m], *m.* (—es, *no pl.*) cream; *den — abschöpfen,* skim; (*fig.*) skim the cream off.

Rahmen ['ra:mən], *m.* (—s, *pl.* —) frame; milieu, limit, scope, compass; *im — von,* within the framework of.

rahmig ['ra:mɪç], *adj.* creamy.

raisonnieren [rɛzɔ'ni:rən], *v.n.* reason, argue; (*fig.*) grumble, answer back.

Rakete [ra'ke:tə], *f.* (—, *pl.* —n) rocket, sky-rocket.

Rakett [ra'kɛt], *n.* (—s, *pl.* —s) (*tennis*) racket.

rammen ['ramən], *v.a.* ram.

Rampe ['rampə], *f.* (—, *pl.* —n) ramp, slope; platform; (*Theat.*) apron.

ramponiert [rampo'ni:rt], *adj.* battered, damaged.

Ramsch [ramʃ], *m.* (—es, *pl.* ⁻e) odds and ends; (*Comm.*) job lot.

Rand [rant], *m.* (—es, *pl.* ⁻er) edge, border, verge, rim; (*book*) margin; (*hat*) brim; *am — des Grabes,* with one foot in the grave; *außer — und Band geraten,* get completely out of hand.

randalieren [randa'li:rən], *v.n.* kick up a row.

Randbemerkung ['rantbəmɛrkuŋ], *f.* (—, *pl.* —en) marginal note, gloss.

rändern [rɛndərn], *v.a.* border, edge, mill.

Ränftchen ['rɛnftçən], *n.* (—s, *pl.* —) crust (of bread).

Rang [raŋ], *m.* (—es, *pl.* ⁻e) rank, grade, rate; order, class; standing (in society); (*Theat.*) circle, tier, gallery.

Range ['raŋə], *m.* (—n, *pl.* —n) scamp, rascal. — *f.* (—, *pl.* —n) tom-boy, hoyden.

rangieren [rã'ʒi:rən], *v.a.* (*Railw.*) shunt. — *v.n.* rank.

Ranke ['raŋkə], *f.* (—, *pl.* —n) tendril, shoot.

Ränke ['rɛŋkə], *m. pl.* intrigues, tricks.

ranken ['raŋkən], *v.r.* (*aux.* haben) *sich —,* (*plant*) climb (with tendrils).

Ränkeschmied ['rɛŋkəʃmi:t], *m.* (—es, *pl.* —e) plotter, intriguer.

Ranzen ['rantsən], *m.* (—s, *pl.* —) satchel, knapsack, rucksack.

ranzig ['rantsɪç], *adj.* rancid, rank.

Rappe ['rapə], *m.* (—n, *pl.* —n) black horse.

Rappel ['rapəl], *m.* (—s, *no pl.*) (*coll.*) slight madness; rage, fit.

Rappen ['rapən], *m.* (—s, *pl.* —) small Swiss coin; centime.

rapportieren [rapɔr'tiːrən], *v.a.* report.

Raps [raps], *m.* (—es, *no pl.*) rapeseed.

rar [raːr], *adj.* rare, scarce; exquisite.

rasch [raʃ], *adj.* quick, swift.

rascheln ['raʃəln], *v.n.* rustle.

Rasen ['raːzən], *m.* (—s, *pl.* —) lawn, turf, sod.

rasen ['raːzən], *v.n.* rave, rage, be delirious; rush, speed; *in —der Eile*, in a tearing hurry.

Raserei [raːzə'raɪ], *f.* (—, *pl.* —en) madness; (*fig.*) fury.

Rasierapparat [ra'ziːrapara:t], *m.* (—s, *pl.* —e) (safety-)razor; shaver.

rasieren [ra'ziːrən], *v.a.* shave; *sich — lassen*, be shaved, get a shave.

Rasierzeug [ra'ziːrtsɔyk], *n.* (—s, *no pl.*) shaving-tackle.

Raspel ['raspəl], *f.* (—, *pl.* —n) rasp.

Rasse ['rasə], *f.* (—, *pl.* —n) race; breed; *reine —*, thoroughbred; *gekreuzte —*, cross-breed.

Rassel ['rasəl], *f.* (—, *pl.* —n) rattle.

rasseln ['rasəln], *v.n.* rattle, clank.

Rassendiskriminierung ['rasəndiskri-mini:ruŋ], *f.* (—, *no pl.*) racial discrimination.

Rast [rast], *f.* (—, *no pl.*) rest, repose.

rasten ['rastən], *v.n.* rest, take a rest; halt.

Raster ['rastər], *m.* (—s, *pl.* —) (*Phot.*) screen.

rastlos ['rastloːs], *adj.* restless.

Rat (1) [raːt], *m.* (—es, *pl.* —schläge) advice, counsel; deliberation.

Rat (2) [raːt], *m.* (—es, *pl.* ⁻e) council, councillor; *mit — und Tat*, with advice and assistance; *einem einen — geben*, give s.o. advice, counsel s.o.; *einen um — fragen*, consult s.o.; *— schaffen*, find ways and means.

Rate ['raːtə], *f.* (—, *pl.* —n) instalment, rate.

raten ['raːtən], *v.a., v.n. irr.* advise; guess, conjecture.

Ratgeber ['raːtgeːbər], *m.* (—s, *pl.* —) adviser, counsellor.

Rathaus ['raːthaus], *n.* (—es, *pl.* ⁻er) town-hall.

Ratifizierung [ratifi'tsiːruŋ], *f.* (—, *pl.* —en) ratification.

Ration [ra'tsjoːn], *f.* (—, *pl.* —en) ration, share, portion.

rationell [ratsjo'nɛl], *adj.* rational.

ratlos ['raːtloːs], *adj.* helpless, perplexed.

ratsam ['raːtzaːm], *adj.* advisable.

Ratschlag ['raːtʃlaːk], *m.* (—s, *pl.* ⁻e) advice, counsel.

Ratschluß ['raːtʃlus], *m.* (—sses, *pl.* ⁻sse) decision, decree.

Ratsdiener ['raːtsdiːnər], *m.* (—s, *pl.* —) beadle, tipstaff, summoner.

Rätsel ['rɛːtsəl], *n.* (—s, *pl.* —) riddle, puzzle, mystery, enigma, conundrum.

Ratsherr ['raːtshɛr], *m.* (—n, *pl.* —en) alderman, (town-)councillor, senator.

Ratte ['ratə], *f.* (—, *pl.* —n) (*Zool.*) rat.

Raub [raup], *m.* (—es, *no pl.*) robbery; booty, prey.

rauben ['raubən], *v.a.* rob, plunder; *es raubt mir den Atem*, it takes my breath away.

Räuber ['rɔybər], *m.* (—s, *pl.* —) robber, thief; highwayman; *— und Gendarm*, cops and robbers.

Raubgier ['raupgiːr], *f.* (—, *no pl.*) rapacity.

Rauch [raux], *m.* (—s, *no pl.*) smoke, vapour.

Rauchen ['rauxən], *n.* (—s, *no pl.*) smoking; *— verboten*, no smoking.

rauchen ['rauxən], *v.a., v.n.* smoke.

räuchern ['rɔyçərn], *v.a.* (*meat, fish*) smoke-dry, cure; (*disinfect*) fumigate. — *v.n.* (*Eccl.*) burn incense.

Rauchfang ['rauxfaŋ], *m.* (—s, *pl.* ⁻e) chimney-flue.

Räude ['rɔydə], *f.* (—, *no pl.*) mange.

Raufbold ['raufbɔlt], *m.* (—s, *pl.* —e) brawler, bully.

raufen ['raufən], *v.a.* (*hair*) tear out, pluck. — *v.n.* fight, brawl. — *v.r. sich — mit*, scuffle with, fight, have a scrap with.

rauh [rau], *adj.* rough; (*fig.*) harsh, rude; hoarse; (*weather*) raw, inclement.

Rauheit ['rauhaɪt], *f.* (—, *no pl.*) roughness; hoarseness; (*fig.*) harshness, rudeness; (*weather*) inclemency; (*landscape*) ruggedness.

rauhen ['rauən], *v.a.* (*cloth*) nap.

Raum [raum], *m.* (—es, *pl.* ⁻e) space, room; outer space; (*fig.*) scope; *dem Gedanken — geben*, entertain an idea.

räumen ['rɔymən], *v.a.* clear, empty; quit, leave; *das Feld —*, abandon the field, clear out.

Rauminhalt ['raumʔinhalt], *m.* (—s, *no pl.*) volume.

räumlich ['rɔymlɪç], *adj.* spatial; (*in compounds*) space-.

Räumlichkeiten ['rɔymlɪçkaɪtən], *f. pl.* premises.

Raumschiff ['raumʃɪf], *n.* (—es, *pl.* —e) spaceship, spacecraft.

Räumung ['rɔymuŋ], *f.* (—, *pl.* —en) evacuation.

raunen ['raunən], *v.a., v.n.* whisper.

Raupe ['raupə], *f.* (—, *pl.* —n) (*Ent.*) caterpillar.

Rausch [rauʃ], *m.* (—es, *pl.* ⁻e) intoxication; delirium, frenzy; *einen — haben*, be drunk, intoxicated; *seinen — ausschlafen*, sleep it off.

rauschen ['rauʃən], *v.n.* rustle, rush, roar.

Rauschgift ['rauʃgɪft], *n.* (—s, *pl.* —e) drug; narcotic.

Rauschgold ['rauʃgɔlt], *n.* (—es, *no pl.*) tinsel.

räuspern ['rɔyspərn], *v.r. sich —*, clear o.'s throat.

Raute ['rautə], *f.* (—, *pl.* —n) (*Maths.*) rhombus; lozenge; (*Bot.*) rue.

Razzia ['ratsja], *f.* (—, *pl.* —**zzien**) (police-)raid, swoop.

reagieren [rea'gi:rən], *v.n.* react (on).

realisieren [reali'zi:rən], *v.a.* convert into money, realise.

Realschule [re'a:lʃu:lə], *f.* (—, *pl.* —**n**) technical grammar school; secondary modern school.

Rebe ['re:bə], *f.* (—, *pl.* —**n**) vine.

Rebell [re'bɛl], *m.* (—**en**, *pl.* —**en**) rebel, mutineer, insurgent.

Rebensaft ['re:bənzaft], *m.* (—**s**, *pl.* ⸚**e**) grape-juice, wine.

Rebhuhn ['re:phu:n], *n.* (—**s**, *pl.* ⸚**er**) (*Orn.*) partridge.

Reblaus ['re:plaus], *f.* (—, *pl.* ⸚**e**) (*Ent.*) phylloxera.

Rechen ['rɛçən], *m.* (—**s**, *pl.* —) (*garden*) rake; (*clothes*) rack.

Rechenaufgabe ['rɛçənaufga:bə], *f.* (—, *pl.* —**n**) sum; mathematical *or* arithmetical problem.

Rechenmaschine ['rɛçənmaʃi:nə], *f.* (—, *pl.* —**n**) calculating machine, adding-machine.

Rechenschaft ['rɛçənʃaft], *f.* (—, *no pl.*) account; — *ablegen,* account for; *zur* — *ziehen,* call to account.

Rechenschieber ['rɛçənʃi:bər], *m.* (—**s**, *pl.* —) slide-rule.

Rechentabelle ['rɛçəntabɛlə], *f.* (—, *pl.* —**n**) ready reckoner.

rechnen ['rɛçnən], *v.a.,* *v.n.* reckon, calculate, do sums, compute; *auf etwas* —, count on s.th.; *auf einen* —, rely on s.o.

Rechnung ['rɛçnuŋ], *f.* (—, *pl.* —**en**) reckoning, account, computation; (*document*) invoice, bill, statement, account; *einer Sache* — *tragen,* make allowances for s.th.; take s.th. into account; *einem einen Strich durch die* — *machen,* put a spoke in s.o.'s wheel; *eine* — *begleichen,* settle an account.

Rechnungsabschluß ['rɛçnuŋsapʃlus], *m.* (—**sses**, *pl.* ⸚**sse**) balancing of accounts, balance-sheet.

Rechnungsprüfer ['rɛçnuŋspry:fər], *m.* (—**s**, *pl.* —) auditor.

Rechnungsrat ['rɛçnuŋsra:t], *m.* (—**s**, *pl.* ⸚**e**) member of the board of accountants, (senior government) auditor.

Recht [rɛçt], *n.* (—**es**, *pl.* —**e**) right, justice; claim on, title to; law, jurisprudence; *von* —**s** *wegen,* by right; — *sprechen,* administer justice; *die* —**e** *studieren,* study law.

recht [rɛçt], *adj.* right; just; real, true; suitable; proper; *zur* —**en** *Zeit,* in time; *es geht nicht mit* —**en** *Dingen zu,* there is s.th. queer about it; *was dem einen* —, *ist dem andern billig,* what is sauce for the goose is sauce for the gander; *einem* — *geben,* agree with s.o.; — *haben,* be (in the) right.

Rechteck ['rɛçtɛk], *n.* (—**s**, *pl.* —**e**) rectangle.

rechten ['rɛçtən], *v.n. mit einem* —, dispute, remonstrate with s.o.

rechtfertigen ['rɛçtfɛrtigən], *v.a. insep.* justify. — *v.r. sich* —, exculpate o.s.

rechtgläubig ['rɛçtglɔybiç], *adj.* orthodox.

rechthaberisch ['rɛçtha:bəriʃ], *adj.* stubborn, obstinate.

rechtlich ['rɛçtliç], *adj.* legal, lawful, legitimate; (*Law*) judicial, juridical.

rechtmäßig ['rɛçtmɛ:siç], *adj.* lawful, legitimate, legal.

rechts [rɛçts], *adv.* to the right, on the right.

Rechtsabtretung ['rɛçtsaptre:tuŋ], *f.* (—, *pl.* —**en**) cession, assignment.

Rechtsanwalt ['rɛçtsanvalt], *m.* (—**s**, *pl.* ⸚**e**) lawyer, solicitor, attorney.

Rechtsbeistand ['rɛçtsbaɪʃtant], *m.* (—**s**, *pl.* ⸚**e**) (legal) counsel.

rechtschaffen ['rɛçtʃafən], *adj.* upright, honest, righteous.

Rechtschreibung ['rɛçtʃraɪbuŋ], *f.* (—, *no pl.*) orthography, spelling.

Rechtshandel ['rɛçtshandəl], *m.* (—**s**, *pl.* ⸚) action, case, lawsuit.

rechtskräftig ['rɛçtskrɛftiç], *adj.* legal, valid.

Rechtslehre ['rɛçtsle:rə], *f.* (—, *pl.* —**n**) jurisprudence.

Rechtsspruch ['rɛçtsʃprux], *m.* (—(**e**)**s**, *pl.* ⸚**e**) verdict.

Rechtsverhandlung ['rɛçtsfɛrhand-luŋ], *f.* (—, *pl.* —**en**) legal proceedings.

Rechtsweg ['rɛçtsve:k], *m.* (—(**e**)**s**, *pl.* —**e**) course of law.

rechtswidrig ['rɛçtsvi:driç], *adj.* against the law, illegal.

Rechtszuständigkeit ['rɛçtstsu:ʃtendiçkaɪt], *f.* (—, *pl.* —**en**) (legal) competence.

rechtwinklig ['rɛçtviŋkliç], *adj.* rectangular.

rechtzeitig ['rɛçttsaɪtiç], *adj.* opportune. — *adv.* in time, at the right time.

Reck [rɛk], *n.* (—**s**, *pl.* —**e**) horizontal bar.

Recke ['rɛkə], *m.* (—**n**, *pl.* —**n**) (*Poet.*) hero.

recken ['rɛkən], *v.a.* stretch, extend.

Redakteur [redak'tø:r], *m.* (—**s**, *pl.* —**e**) editor (newspaper, magazine).

Redaktion [redak'tsjo:n], *f.* (—, *pl.* —**en**) editorship, editorial staff; (*room*) editorial office.

Rede ['re:də], *f.* (—, *pl.* —**n**) speech, oration; address; *es geht die* —, people say; *es ist nicht der* — *wert,* it is not worth mentioning; *eine* — *halten,* deliver a speech; *zur* — *stellen,* call to account.

reden ['re:dən], *v.a.* speak, talk, discourse; *einem nach dem Munde* —, humour s.o.; *in den Wind* —, speak in vain, preach to the winds; *mit sich* — *lassen,* be amenable to reason.

Redensart ['re:dənsa:rt], *f.* (—, *pl.* —en) phrase, idiom; cliché; *einen mit leeren —en abspeisen*, put s.o. off with fine words.

Redewendung ['re:dəvɛnduŋ], *f.* (—, *pl.* —en) turn of phrase.

redigieren [redi'gi:rən], *v.a.* edit.

redlich ['re:tlɪç], *adj.* honest, upright.

Redner ['re:dnər], *m.* (—s, *pl.* —) speaker, orator.

Reede ['re:də], *f.* (—, *pl.* —n) (*Naut.*) roadstead.

Reederei [re:də'raɪ], *f.* (—, *pl.* —en) shipping-business.

reell [re'ɛl], *adj.* honest, fair, sound, bona fide.

Reep [re:p], *n.* (—s, *pl.* —e) (*Naut.*) rope.

Referat [refe'ra:t], *n.* (—s, *pl.* —e) report; paper (to a learned society); lecture.

Referendar [referen'da:r], *m.* (—s, *pl.* —e) junior barrister *or* teacher.

Referent [refe'rɛnt], *m.* (—en, *pl.* —en) reporter, reviewer; lecturer; expert (adviser).

Referenz [refe'rɛnts], *f.* (—, *pl.* —en) reference (to s.o. *or* s.th.).

referieren [refe'ri:rən], *v.a., v.n.* report (on), give a paper (on).

reflektieren [reflɛk'ti:rən], *v.a.* reflect. — *v.n. auf etwas* —, be a prospective buyer of s.th., have o.'s eye on s.th.

Reformator [refor'ma:tor], *m.* (—s, *pl.* —en) reformer.

reformieren [refor'mi:rən], *v.a.* reform.

Regal [re'ga:l], *n.* (—s, *pl.* —e) shelf.

rege ['re:gə], *adj.* brisk, lively, animated.

Regel ['re:gəl], *f.* (—, *pl.* —n) rule, precept, principle; *in der* —, as a rule, generally.

regelmäßig ['re:gəlmɛ:sɪç], *adj.* regular.

regeln ['re:gəln], *v.a.* regulate, arrange, order.

Regelung ['re:gəluŋ], *f.* (—, *pl.* —en) regulation.

regelwidrig ['re:gəlvi:drɪç], *adj.* contrary to rule, irregular, foul.

Regen ['re:gən], *m.* (—s, *no pl.*) rain.

regen ['re:gən], *v.r. sich* —, move, stir.

Regenbogen ['re:gənbo:gən], *m.* (—s, *pl.* —) rainbow.

Regenbogenhaut ['re:gənbo:gənhaut], *f.* (—, *pl.* ¨e) (*eye*) iris.

Regenguß ['re:gəngus], *m.* (—sses, *pl.* ¨sse) downpour, violent shower.

Regenmantel ['re:gənmantəl], *m.* (—s, *pl.* ¨) waterproof, raincoat, mac.

Regenpfeifer ['re:gənpfaɪfər], *m.* (—s, *pl.* —) (*Orn.*) plover.

Regenrinne ['re:gənrɪnə], *f.* (—, *pl.* —n) eaves.

Regenschirm ['re:gənʃirm], *m.* (—s, *pl.* —e) umbrella.

Regentschaft [re'gɛntʃaft], *f.* (—, *pl.* —en) regency.

Regie [re'ʒi:], *f.* (—, *pl.* —n) stage management, production, direction.

regieren [re'gi:rən], *v.a.* rule, reign over, govern. — *v.n.* reign; (*fig.*) prevail, predominate.

Regierung [re'gi:ruŋ], *f.* (—, *pl.* —en) government; reign.

Regierungsrat [re'gi:ruŋsra:t], *m.* (—s, *pl.* ¨e) government adviser.

Regiment (1) [regi'mɛnt], *n.* (—s, *pl.* —e) rule, government.

Regiment (2) [regi'mɛnt], *n.* (—s, *pl.* —er) (*Mil.*) regiment.

Regisseur [reʒi'sø:r], *m.* (—s, *pl.* —e) stage-manager, producer, director.

Registrator [regɪs'tra:tor], *m.* (—s, *pl.* —en) registrar, recorder; registering machine.

Registratur [regɪstra'tu:r], *f.* (—, *pl.* —en) record office, registry; filing-cabinet.

registrieren [regɪs'tri:rən], *v.a.* register, record, file.

reglos ['re:klo:s], *adj.* motionless.

regnen ['re:gnən], *v.n.* rain; *es regnet in Strömen*, it is raining cats and dogs.

Regreß [re'grɛs], *m.* (—sses, *pl.* —sse) recourse, remedy.

regsam ['re:kza:m], *adj.* quick, alert, lively.

regulieren [regu'li:rən], *v.a.* regulate.

Regung ['re:guŋ], *f.* (—, *pl.* —en) movement; impulse.

Reh [re:], *n.* (—(e)s, *pl.* —e) doe, roe.

rehabilitieren [rehabili'ti:rən], *v.a.* rehabilitate.

Rehbock ['re:bok], *m.* (—s, *pl.* ¨e) (*Zool.*) roe-buck.

Rehkeule ['re:kɔylə], *f.* (—, *pl.* —n) haunch of venison.

reiben ['raɪbən], *v.a. irr.* rub, grate, grind; *einem etwas unter die Nase* —, throw s.th. in s.o.'s teeth, bring s.th. home to s.o.

Reibung ['raɪbuŋ], *f.* (—, *pl.* —en) friction.

Reich [raɪç], *n.* (—(e)s, *pl.* —e) kingdom, realm, empire, state.

reich [raɪç], *adj.* rich, wealthy, opulent.

reichen ['raɪçən], *v.a.* reach, pass, hand; *einem die Hand* —, shake hands with s.o. — *v.n.* reach, extend; be sufficient.

reichhaltig ['raɪçhaltɪç], *adj.* abundant, copious.

reichlich ['raɪçlɪç], *adj.* ample, plentiful.

Reichskammergericht [raɪçs'kamərgərɪçt], *n.* (—s, *no pl.*) Imperial High Court of Justice (*Holy Roman Empire*).

Reichskanzlei ['raɪçskantslaɪ], *f.* (—, *pl.* —en) (Imperial) Chancery.

Reichskanzler ['raɪçskantslər], *m.* (—s, *pl.* —) (Imperial) Chancellor.

Reichsstände ['raɪçsʃtɛndə], *m. pl.* Estates (of the Holy Roman Empire).

Reichstag ['raɪçsta:k], *m.* (—s, *pl.* —e) Imperial Parliament, Reichstag, Diet.

Reichtum

Reichtum [ˈraɪçtuːm], *m.* (—s, *pl.* -er) riches, wealth, opulence.
Reif (1) [raɪf], *m.* (—s, *no pl.*) hoar-frost.
Reif (2) [raɪf], *m.* (—s, *pl.* —e) ring.
reif [raɪf], *adj.* ripe, mature.
Reifen [ˈraɪfən], *m.* (—s, *pl.* —) hoop; tyre; — *schlagen*, trundle a hoop.
reifen [ˈraɪfən], *v.n.* (*aux.* sein) ripen, mature, grow ripe.
Reifeprüfung [ˈraɪfəpryːfuŋ], *f.* (—, *pl.* —en) matriculation examination.
reiflich [ˈraɪflɪç], *adj. sich etwas — überlegen*, give careful consideration to s.th.
Reigen [ˈraɪgən], *m.* (—s, *pl.* —) round-dance, roundelay.
Reihe [ˈraɪə], *f.* —, *pl.* —n) series; file; row; progression, sequence; (*Theat.*) tier; *in — und Glied*, in closed ranks; *nach der —*, in turns; *ich bin an der —*, it is my turn.
Reihenfolge [ˈraɪənfɔlgə], *f.* (—, *no pl.*) succession.
Reiher [ˈraɪər], *m.* (—s, *pl.* —) (*Orn.*) heron.
Reim [raɪm], *m.* (—(e)s, *pl.* —e) rhyme.
rein [raɪn], *adj.* clean, pure, clear, neat; —*e Wahrheit*, plain truth; *ins —e bringen*, settle, clear up; *ins —e schreiben*, make a fair copy of; *einem —en Wein einschenken*, have a straight talk with s.o.
Reineke [ˈraɪnəkə], *m.* (—, *no pl.*) — *Fuchs*, Reynard the Fox.
Reinertrag [ˈraɪnɛrtraːk], *m.* (—(e)s, *pl.* -e) net proceeds.
Reinfall [ˈraɪnfal], *m.* (—s, *pl.* -e) sell, wild-goose chase; disappointment.
reinfallen [ˈraɪnfalən], *v.n. irr.* (*aux.* sein) be unsuccessful.
Reingewinn [ˈraɪngəvɪn], *m.* (—s, *pl.* —e) net proceeds.
Reinheit [ˈraɪnhaɪt], *f.* (—, *no pl.*) purity.
reinigen [ˈraɪnɪgən], *v.a.* clean, cleanse; dry-clean; purge.
Reinigung [ˈraɪnɪguŋ], *f.* (—, *pl.* —en) cleaning; (*fig.*) purification, cleansing; *chemische —*, dry-cleaning.
reinlich [ˈraɪnlɪç], *adj.* clean, neat.
Reis (1) [raɪs], *m.* (—es, *no pl.*) rice.
Reis (2) [raɪs], *n.* (—es, *pl.* —er) twig, sprig; scion; cutting.
Reisbesen [ˈraɪsbeːzən], *m.* (—s, *pl.* —) birch-broom, besom.
Reise [ˈraɪzə], *f.* (—, *pl.* —n) tour, trip, journey, travels; voyage; *gute —!* bon voyage!
reisefertig [ˈraɪzəfɛrtɪç], *adj.* ready to start.
Reisegeld [ˈraɪzəgɛlt], *n.* (—es, *pl.* —er) travel allowance.
reisen [ˈraɪzən], *v.n.* (*aux.* sein) travel, tour, journey, take a trip.
Reisende [ˈraɪzəndə], *m.* (—n, *pl.* —n) traveller; commercial traveller.
Reisig [ˈraɪzɪç], *n.* (—s, *no pl.*) brush-wood.

Reisige [ˈraɪzɪgə], *m.* (—n, *pl.* —n) (*obs.*) trooper, horseman.
Reißaus [raɪsˈaus], *n.* (—, *no pl.*) — *nehmen*, take to o.'s heels.
Reißbrett [ˈraɪsbrɛt], *n.* (—es, *pl.* —er) drawing-board.
reißen [ˈraɪsən], *v.a. irr.* tear; rend; pull; snatch; *etwas an sich —*, seize s.th., usurp.
reißend [ˈraɪsənt], *adj.* rapid; ravening; carnivorous; (*Comm.*) brisk, rapid (sales).
Reißnagel [ˈraɪsnaːgəl], *m. see* **Reißzwecke**.
Reißschiene [ˈraɪsʃiːnə], *f.* (—, *pl.* —n) T-square.
Reißverschluß [ˈraɪsfɛrʃlus], *m.* (—sses, *pl.* -sse) zip-fastener.
Reißzwecke [ˈraɪstsvɛkə], *f.* (—, *pl.* —n) drawing-pin.
reiten [ˈraɪtən], *v.a. irr.* ride (a horse). — *v.n.* (*aux.* sein) ride, go on horse-back.
Reiterei [raɪtəˈraɪ], *f.* (—, *pl.* —en) cavalry.
Reitknecht [ˈraɪtknɛçt], *m.* (—es, *pl.* —e) groom.
Reiz [raɪts], *m.* (—es, *pl.* —e) charm, attraction, fascination, allure; stimulus; irritation; (*Phys.*) impulse.
reizbar [ˈraɪtsbaːr], *adj.* susceptible; irritable.
reizen [ˈraɪtsən], *v.a.* irritate; stimulate, charm, entice.
reizend [ˈraɪtsənt], *adj.* charming.
Reizmittel [ˈraɪtsmɪtəl], *n.* (—s, *pl.* —) stimulant; irritant.
rekeln [ˈreːkəln], *v.r.* (*dial.*) *sich —*, loll about.
Reklame [reˈklaːmə], *f.* (—, *pl.* —n) propaganda, advertisement, advertising, publicity.
reklamieren [reklaˈmiːrən], *v.a.* claim, reclaim. — *v.n.* complain.
rekognoszieren [rekɔgnɔsˈtsiːrən], *v.a.* reconnoitre.
rekommandieren [rekɔmanˈdiːrən], *v.a.* (*Austr.*) register (a letter).
Rekonvaleszent [rekɔnvalɛsˈtsɛnt], *m.* (—en, *pl.* —en) convalescent.
Rekrut [reˈkruːt], *m.* (—en, *pl.* —en) recruit.
rekrutieren [rekruˈtiːrən], *v.a.* recruit. — *v.r. sich — aus*, be recruited from.
rektifizieren [rɛktifiˈtsiːrən], *v.a.* rectify.
Rektor [ˈrɛktɔr], *m.* (—s, *pl.* —en) (school) principal; (*Univ.*) president.
Rektorat [rɛktoˈraːt], *n.* (—es, *pl.* —e) rectorship, presidency.
relativ [relaˈtiːf], *adj.* relative, comparative.
relegieren [releˈgiːrən], *v.a.* expel; (*Univ.*) send down, rusticate.
Relief [rɛlˈjef], *n.* (—s, *pl.* —s) (*Art*) relief.
religiös [reliˈgjøːs], *adj.* religious.
Reliquie [reˈliːkvjə], *f.* (—, *pl.* —n) (*Rel.*) relic.

178

Remise [re'mi:zə], *f.* (—, *pl.* —n) coach-house.

Remittent [remɪ'tɛnt], *m.* (—en, *pl.* —en) remitter.

Renegat [rene'ga:t], *m.* (—en, *pl.* —en) renegade.

Renette [rɛ'nɛtə], *f.* (—, *pl.* —n) rennet(-apple).

renken ['rɛŋkən], *v.a.* wrench, bend, twist.

Rennbahn ['rɛnba:n], *f.* (—, *pl.* —en) race-course; (cinder)-track; (*Motor.*) racing-circuit.

rennen ['rɛnən], *v.n. irr.* (*aux.* sein) run, race, rush.

Renommé [renɔ'me:], *n.* (—s, *no pl.*) renown, repute, reputation.

renommieren [renɔ'mi:rən], *v.n.* brag, boast.

renovieren [reno'vi:rən], *v.a.* renovate, restore, redecorate, renew.

rentabel [rɛn'ta:bəl], *adj.* profitable, lucrative.

Rente ['rɛntə], *f.* (—, *pl.* —n) pension, annuity.

Rentier [rɛn'tje:], *m.* (—s, *pl.* —s) rentier, person of independent means.

rentieren [rɛn'ti:rən], *v.r. sich* —, be profitable, be worthwhile, pay.

Rentner ['rɛntnər], *m.* (—s, *pl.* —) pensioner.

Reparatur [repara'tu:r], *f.* (—, *pl.* —en) repair.

reparieren [repa'ri:rən], *v.a.* repair.

Repräsentant [reprɛzɛn'tant], *m.* (—en, *pl.* —en) representative.

Repräsentantenkammer [reprɛzɛn-'tantənkamər], *f.* (—, *pl.* —n) (*Am.*) House of Representatives.

Repressalien [reprɛ'sa:ljən], *f. pl.* reprisals, retaliation.

reproduzieren [reprodu'tsi:rən], *v.a.* reproduce.

Republikaner [republi'ka:nər], *m.* (—s, *pl.* —) republican.

requirieren [rekvi'ri:rən], *v.a.* requisition.

Reseda [re'ze:da], *f.* (—, *pl.* —s) (*Bot.*) mignonette.

Reservat [rezɛr'va:t], *n.* (—es, *pl.* —e) reservation, reserve.

Residenz [rezi'dɛnts], *f.* (—, *pl.* —en) residence, seat of the Court.

residieren [rezi'di:rən], *v.n.* reside.

Residuum [re'zi:duum], *n.* (—s, *pl.* —duen) residue, dregs.

resignieren [rezɪg'ni:rən], *v.n., v.r.* resign; be resigned (to s.th.); give up.

Respekt [re'spɛkt], *m.* (—es, *no pl.*) respect, regard; *mit — zu sagen*, with all due respect.

respektieren [respɛk'ti:rən], *v.a.* respect, honour.

Ressort [rɛ'so:r], *n.* (—s, *pl.* —s) department, domain.

Rest [rɛst], *m.* (—es, *pl.* —e) rest, residue, remainder; remnant; (*money*) balance.

restaurieren [rɛsto'ri:rən], *v.a.* restore, renovate.

Resultat [rezul'ta:t], *n.* (—es, *pl.* —e) result, outcome.

Resümee [rezy'me:], *n.* (—s, *pl.* —s) résumé, précis, digest, summary, synopsis, abstract.

retten ['rɛtən], *v.a.* save, preserve; rescue, deliver; *die Ehre* —, vindicate o.'s honour.

Rettich ['rɛtɪç], *m.* (—s, *pl.* —e) radish.

Rettung ['rɛtuŋ], *f.* (—, *pl.* —en) saving, rescue, deliverance.

retuschieren [retu'ʃi:rən], *v.a.* retouch.

Reue ['rɔyə], *f.* (—, *no pl.*) repentance, remorse, contrition.

reuen ['rɔyən], *v.a., v.n.* repent, regret; *es reut mich*, I am sorry.

Reugeld ['rɔygɛlt], *n.* (—es, *pl.* —er) forfeit-money, penalty.

reüssieren [rey'si:rən], *v.n.* succeed.

Revanche [re'vã:ʃə], *f.* (—, *pl.* —n) revenge; (*fig.*) return.

revanchieren [revã'ʃi:rən], *v.r. sich* —, repay a service, have *or* take o.'s revenge.

Reverenz [reve'rɛnts], *f.* (—, *pl.* —en) bow, curtsy.

revidieren [revi'di:rən], *v.a.* revise, check.

Revier [re'vi:r], *n.* (—s, *pl.* —e) district, precinct, quarter; preserve.

Revisor [re'vi:zor], *m.* (—s, *pl.* —en) accountant, auditor.

revoltieren [revɔl'ti:rən], *v.n.* rise, revolt.

revolutionieren [revolutsjo'ni:rən], *v.a.* revolutionise.

Revolverblatt [re'vɔlvərblat], *n.* (—s, *pl.* ÷er) gutter press.

Revue [re'vy:], *f.* (—, *pl.* —n) revue; review; *— passieren lassen*, pass in review.

Rezensent [retsɛn'zɛnt], *m.* (—en, *pl.* —en) reviewer, critic.

rezensieren [retsɛn'zi:rən], *v.a.* review.

Rezept [re'tsɛpt], *n.* (—es, *pl.* —e) (*Med.*) prescription; (*Cul.*) recipe.

rezitieren [retsi'ti:rən], *v.a.* recite.

Rhabarber [ra'barbər], *m.* (—s, *no pl.*) (*Bot.*) rhubarb.

Rhein [rain], *m.* (—s, *no pl.*) (River) Rhine.

Rhodesien [ro'de:zjən], *n.* Rhodesia.

Rhodus ['ro:dus], *n.* Rhodes.

Rhythmus ['rytmus], *m.* (—, *pl.* —men) rhythm.

Richtbeil ['rɪçtbail], *n.* (—s, *pl.* —e) executioner's axe.

richten ['rɪçtən], *v.a., v.n.* direct, point at; prepare; *die Augen — auf*, fix o.'s eyes upon; *einen zugrunde —*, ruin s.o.; judge, try, pass sentence on, condemn. *—v.r. sich nach* (*Dat.*) —, be guided by.

Richter ['rɪçtər], *m.* (—s, *pl.* —) judge; justice.

richtig ['rɪçtɪç], *adj.* right, correct, exact, true; *nicht ganz — sein*, be not quite right in the head.

Richtlot

Richtlot ['rɪçtloːt], *n.* (—s, *pl.* —e) plumb-line.

Richtschnur ['rɪçtʃnuːr], *f.* (—, *pl.* —en) plumb-line; (*fig.*) rule, precept.

Richtung ['rɪçtuŋ], *f.* (—, *pl.* —en) direction.

riechen ['riːçən], *v.a., v.n. irr.* smell, scent, reek; *Lunte* —, smell a rat.

Riege ['riːgə], *f.* (—, *pl.* —n) row, section.

Riegel ['riːgəl], *m.* (—s, *pl.* —) bar, bolt; *ein* — *Schokolade,* a bar of chocolate.

Riemen ['riːmən], *m.* (—s, *pl.* —) strap, thong; oar.

Ries [riːs], *n.* (—es, *pl.* —e) (*paper*) ream.

Riese ['riːzə], *m.* (—n, *pl.* —n) giant.

rieseln ['riːzəln], *v.n.* murmur, babble, ripple, trickle; drizzle.

Riesenschlange ['riːzənʃlaŋə], *f.* (—, *pl.* —n) anaconda.

Riff [rɪf], *n.* (—es, *pl.* —e) reef.

rigoros [rigoˈroːs], *adj.* strict, rigorous.

Rille ['rɪlə], *f.* (—, *pl.* —n) groove, small furrow; (*Archit.*) flute, chamfer.

Rind [rɪnt], *n.* (—es, *pl.* —er) ox, cow; (*pl.*) cattle, horned cattle, head of cattle.

Rinde ['rɪndə], *f.* (—, *pl.* —n) rind, bark, peel; (*bread*) crust.

Rinderbraten ['rɪndərbraːtən], *m.* (—s, *pl.* —) roast beef.

Rindfleisch ['rɪntflaɪʃ], *n.* (—es, *no pl.*) beef.

Rindvieh ['rɪntfiː], *n.* (—s, *no pl.*) cattle; (*fig.*) blockhead, ass.

Ring [rɪŋ], *m.* (—(e)s, *pl.* —e) ring; (*chain*) link; (*under the eye*) dark circle; (*Comm.*) syndicate, trust.

Ringelblume ['rɪŋəlbluːmə], *f.* (—, *pl.* —n) (*Bot.*) marigold.

ringeln ['rɪŋəln], *v.r. sich* —, curl.

ringen ['rɪŋən], *v.a. irr.* wring — *v.n.* wrestle.

Ringer ['rɪŋər], *m.* (—s, *pl.* —) wrestler.

Ringmauer ['rɪŋmauər], *f.* (—, *pl.* —n) city *or* town wall.

rings [rɪŋs], *adv.* around.

ringsum(her) [rɪŋˈsum(heːr)], *adv.* round about.

Rinne ['rɪnə], *f.* (—, *pl.* —n) furrow, gutter; groove.

rinnen ['rɪnən], *v.n. irr.* (*aux,* sein) run, leak, drip.

Rinnsal ['rɪnzaːl], *n.* (—s, *pl.* —e) channel, water-course.

Rinnstein ['rɪnʃtaɪn], *m.* (—s, *pl.* —e) gutter.

Rippe ['rɪpə], *f.* (—, *pl.* —n) rib.

Rippenfellentzündung ['rɪpənfɛlɛnttsynduŋ], *f.* (—, *pl.* —en) pleurisy.

Rippenspeer ['rɪpənʃpeːr], *m.* (—s, *pl.* —e) (*Casseler*) —, spare-rib, ribs of pork.

Rippenstoß ['rɪpənʃtoːs], *m.* (—es, *pl.* ⁻e) dig in the ribs, nudge.

Rips [rɪps], *m.* (—es, *no pl.*) rep.

Risiko ['riːziko], *n.* (—s, *pl.* —ken) risk.

riskant [rɪsˈkant], *adj.* risky.

riskieren [rɪsˈkiːrən], *v.a.* risk.

Riß [rɪs], *m.* (—sses, *pl.* —sse) rent, tear; sketch, design, plan.

rissig ['rɪsɪç], *adj.* cracked, torn.

Ritt [rɪt], *m.* (—(e)s, *pl.* —e) ride.

Ritter ['rɪtər], *m.* (—s, *pl.* —) knight; *einen zum* — *schlagen,* dub s.o. a knight.

ritterlich ['rɪtərlɪç], *adj.* knightly; (*fig.*) chivalrous, valiant, gallant.

Ritterschlag ['rɪtərʃlaːk], *m.* (—(e)s, *pl.* ⁻e) accolade.

Rittersporn ['rɪtərʃpɔrn], *m.* (—s, *pl.* —e) (*Bot.*) larkspur.

rittlings ['rɪtlɪŋs], *adv.* astride.

Rittmeister ['rɪtmaɪstər], *m.* (—s, *pl.* —) captain (of cavalry).

Ritus ['riːtus], *m.* (—, *pl.* **Riten**) rite.

Ritz [rɪts], *m.* (—es, *pl.* —e) chink, fissure, cleft, crevice; (*glacier*) crevasse.

ritzen ['rɪtsən], *v.a.* scratch.

Rivale [riˈvaːlə], *m.* (—n, *pl.* —n) rival.

Rivalität [rivaliˈtɛːt], *f.* (—, *pl.* —en) rivalry.

Rizinusöl ['riːtsinusøːl], *n.* (—s, *no pl.*) castor oil.

Robbe ['rɔbə], *f.* (—, *pl.* —n) (*Zool.*) seal.

Robe ['roːbə], *f.* (—, *pl.* —n) dress, robe; gown.

röcheln ['rœçəln], *v.n.* rattle in o.'s throat.

rochieren [rɔˈxiːrən], *v.n.* (*Chess*) castle.

Rock [rɔk], *m.* (—(e)s, *pl.* ⁻e) (*woman*) skirt; (*man*) coat.

rodeln ['roːdəln], *v.n.* (*aux.* haben & sein) toboggan.

roden ['roːdən], *v.a.* clear, weed, thin out (plants).

Rogen ['roːgən], *m.* (—s, *no pl.*) (*fish*) roe, spawn.

Roggen ['rɔgən], *m.* (—s, *no pl.*) rye.

roh [roː], *adj.* raw; rough, rude, coarse, crude; *ein* —*er Mensch,* a brute; (*in compounds*) rough-; preliminary, unrefined.

Rohbilanz ['roːbilants], *f.* (—, *pl.* —en) trial balance.

Roheisen ['roːaɪzən], *n.* (—s, *no pl.*) pig-iron.

Roheit ['roːhaɪt], *f.* (—, *pl.* —en) coarseness, rudeness, crudity.

Rohr [roːr], *n.* (—es, *pl.* —e, ⁻en) tube, pipe; reed, cane; (*gun*) barrel.

Rohrdommel ['roːrdɔməl], *f.* (—, *pl.* —n) (*Orn.*) bittern.

Röhre ['røːrə], *f.* (—, *pl.* —n) tube, pipe; (*Radio*) valve.

Röhricht ['røːrɪçt], *n.* (—s, *pl.* —e) reeds.

Rohrpfeife ['roːrpfaɪfə], *f.* (—, *pl.* —n) reed-pipe.

Rohrpost ['roːrpɔst], *f.* (—, *no pl.*) pneumatic post.

Rohrzucker ['roːrtsukər], *m.* (—s, *no pl.*) cane-sugar.

Rolladen [ˈrɔladən], *m.* (**—s**, *pl.* ˙⃛) sliding shutter, roller blind.

Rollbahn [ˈrɔlbaːn], *f.* (**—**, *pl.* **—en**) (*Aviat.*) runway.

Rolle [ˈrɔlə], *f.* (**—**, *pl.* **—n**) reel, roll; pulley; (*Theat.*) part; rôle; (*laundry*) mangle.

rollen [ˈrɔlən], *v.a.* roll, reel; (*laundry*) mangle. — *v.n.* (*aux.* sein) roll (along); (*thunder*) roar, roll.

Roller [ˈrɔlər], *m.* (**—s**, *pl.* **—**) scooter.

Rollmops [ˈrɔlmɔps], *m.* (**—es**, *pl.* ˙⃛e) soused herring.

Rollschuh [ˈrɔlʃuː], *m.* (**—s**, *pl.* **—e**) roller-skate.

Rollstuhl [ˈrɔlʃtuːl], *m.* (**—s**, *pl.* ˙⃛e) wheel-chair, bath-chair.

Rolltreppe [ˈrɔltrɛpə], *f.* (**—**, *pl.* **—n**) escalator, moving staircase.

Rom [roːm], *n.* Rome.

Roman [roˈmaːn], *m.* (**—s**, *pl.* **—e**) novel.

romanisch [roˈmaːnɪʃ], *adj.* Romanesque.

Romanliteratur [roˈmaːnlitəratuːr], *f.* (**—**, *no pl.*) fiction.

Romanschriftsteller [roˈmaːnʃrɪftʃtelər], *m.* (**—s**, *pl.* **—**) novelist.

Römer [ˈrøːmər], *m.* (**—s**, *pl.* **—**) Roman; (*glass*) rummer.

Rondell [rɔnˈdɛl], *n.* (**—s**, *pl.* **—e**) circular flower-bed.

Röntgenstrahlen [ˈrœntgənʃtraːlən], *m. pl.* X-rays.

rosa [ˈroːzaː], *adj.* pink, rose-coloured.

Rose [ˈroːzə], *f.* (**—**, *pl.* **—n**) rose.

Rosenkranz [ˈroːzənkrants], *m.* (**—es**, *pl.* ˙⃛e) garland of roses; (*Eccl.*) rosary.

Rosenkreuzer [ˈroːzənkrɔytsər], *m.* (**—s**, *pl.* **—**) Rosicrucian.

Rosine [roˈziːnə], *f.* (**—**, *pl.* **—n**) sultana, raisin.

Rosmarin [ˈrɔsmariːn], *m.* (**—s**, *no pl.*) (*Bot.*) rosemary.

Roß [rɔs], *n.* (**—sses**, *pl.* **—sse**) horse, steed.

Roßbremse [ˈrɔsbrɛmzə], *f.* (**—**, *pl.* **—n**) (*Ent.*) horsefly, gadfly.

Rössel [ˈrœsəl], *n.* (**—s**, *pl.* **—**) (*Chess*) knight.

Roßhaarmatratze [ˈrɔshaːrmatratsə], *f.* (**—**, *pl.* **—n**) hair-mattress.

Roßkastanie [ˈrɔskastaːnjə], *f.* (**—**, *pl.* **—n**) (*Bot.*) horse-chestnut.

Rost (1) [rɔst], *m.* (**—es**, *no pl.*) rust.

Rost (2) [rɔst], *m.* (**—s**, *pl.* **—e**) grate; gridiron.

Rostbraten [ˈrɔstbraːtən], *m.* (**—s**, *pl.* **—**) roast meat.

rosten [ˈrɔstən], *v.n.* go rusty; rust; *alte Liebe rostet nicht*, love that's old rusts not away.

rösten [ˈrøːstən], *v.a.* toast, roast, grill.

rot [roːt], *adj.* red; **— werden**, redden, blush.

Rotauge [ˈroːtaugə], *n.* (**—s**, *pl.* **—n**) (*Zool.*) roach.

Röte [ˈrøːtə], *f.* (**—**, *no pl.*) redness, red colour.

Röteln [ˈrøːtəln], *m. pl.* (*Med.*) German measles, rubella.

Rotfink [ˈroːtfɪŋk], *m.* (**—en**, *pl.* **—en**) (*Orn.*) bullfinch.

Rotfuchs [ˈroːtfuks], *m.* (**—es**, *pl.* ˙⃛e) (*Zool.*) sorrel horse.

rotieren [roˈtiːrən], *v.n.* rotate.

Rotkäppchen [ˈroːtkɛpçən], *n.* Little Red Riding Hood.

Rotkehlchen [ˈroːtkeːlçən], *n.* (**—s**, *pl.* **—**) robin.

Rotlauf [ˈroːtlauf], *m.* (**—s**, *no pl.*) (*Med.*) erysipelas.

Rotschimmel [ˈroːtʃɪməl], *m.* (**—s**, *pl.* **—**) roan-horse.

Rotspon [ˈroːtʃpoːn], *m.* (**—s**, *no pl.*) (*dial.*) claret.

Rotte [ˈrɔtə], *f.* (**—**, *pl.* **—n**) band, gang, rabble; (*Mil.*) file, squad.

Rotwild [ˈroːtvɪlt], *n.* (**—s**, *no pl.*) red deer.

Rotz [rɔts], *m.* (**—es**, *no pl.*) (*vulg.*) mucus; snot.

Rouleau [ruˈloː], *n.* (**—s**, *pl.* **—s**) sun-blind, roller-blind.

routiniert [rutiˈnɪrt], *adj.* smart; experienced.

Rübe [ˈryːbə], *f.* (**—**, *pl.* **—n**) (*Bot.*) turnip; *rote* **—**, beetroot; *gelbe* **—**, carrot.

Rubel [ˈruːbəl], *m.* (**—s**, *pl.* **—**) rouble.

Rübenzucker [ˈryːbəntsukər], *m.* (**—s**, *no pl.*) beet-sugar.

Rubin [ruˈbiːn], *m.* (**—s**, *pl.* **—e**) ruby.

Rubrik [ruˈbriːk], *f.* (**—**, *pl.* **—en**) rubric; title, heading, category, column.

Rübsamen [ˈryːpzaːmən], *m.* (**—s**, *no pl.*) rape-seed.

ruchbar [ˈruːxbaːr], *adj.* manifest, known, notorious.

ruchlos [ˈruːxloːs], *adj.* wicked, profligate, vicious.

Ruck [ruk], *m.* (**—(e)s**, *pl.* **—e**) pull, jolt, jerk.

Rückblick [ˈrykblɪk], *m.* (**—s**, *pl.* **—e**) retrospect, retrospective view.

Rücken [ˈrykən], *m.* (**—s**, *pl.* **—**) back; (*mountains*) ridge; *einem den* **—** *kehren*, turn o.'s back upon o.a.

rücken [ˈrykən], *v.a.* move, push. — *v.n.* move along.

Rückenmark [ˈrykənmark], *n.* (**—s**, *no pl.*) spinal marrow.

Rückenwirbel [ˈrykənvɪrbəl], *m.* (**—s**, *pl.* **—**) dorsal vertebra.

rückerstatten [ˈrykərʃtatən], *v.a.* refund.

Rückfahrkarte [ˈrykfaːrkartə], *f.* (**—**, *pl.* **—n**) return ticket.

Rückfall [ˈrykfal], *m.* (**—s**, *pl.* ˙⃛e) relapse.

rückgängig [ˈrykgɛnɪç], *adj.* **— machen**, cancel, annul, reverse (a decision).

Rückgrat [ˈrykgraːt], *n.* (**—s**, *pl.* **—e**) backbone, spine.

Rückhalt [ˈrykhalt], *m.* (**—s**, *no pl.*) reserve; support, backing.

Rückkehr

Rückkehr ['rykke:r], *f.* (—, *no pl.*) return.

Rücklicht ['ryklıçt], *n.* (—s, *pl.* —er) (*Motor. etc.*) tail-light.

rücklings ['ryklıŋks], *adv.* from behind.

Rucksack ['rukzak], *m.* (—s, *pl.* ̈e) rucksack; knapsack.

Rückschritt ['rykʃrıt], *m.* (—es, *pl.* —e) step backward, retrograde step, regression.

Rücksicht ['rykzıçt], *f.* (—, *pl.* —en) consideration, regard.

Rücksprache ['rykʃpra:xə], *f.* (—, *pl.* —n) conference, consultation; — *nehmen mit,* consult, confer with.

rückständig ['rykʃtɛndıç], *adj.* outstanding; old-fashioned; backward.

Rücktritt ['ryktrıt], *m.* (—s, *no pl.*) resignation.

ruckweise ['rukvaızə], *adv.* by fits and starts; jerkily.

Rückwirkung ['rykvırkuŋ], *f.* (—, *pl.* —en) reaction, retroaction.

Rüde ['ry:də], *m.* (—n, *pl.* —n) male (dog, fox etc.).

Rudel ['ru:dəl], *n.* (—s, *pl.* —) flock, herd, pack.

Ruder ['ru:dər], *n.* (—s, *pl.* —) oar, rudder, paddle; *am — sein,* be at the helm; (*Pol.*) be in power.

rudern ['ru:dərn], *v.a., v.n.* row.

Ruf [ru:f], *m.* (—(e)s, *pl.* —e) call; shout; reputation, renown; *einen guten* (*schlechten*) — *haben,* have a good (bad) reputation, be well (ill) spoken of.

rufen ['ru:fən], *v.a., v.n. irr.* call, shout; *einen — lassen,* send for s.o.

Rüffel ['ryfəl], *m.* (—s, *pl.* —) (*coll.*) reprimand; (*sl.*) rocket.

Rüge ['ry:gə], *f.* (—, *pl.* —n) censure, blame, reprimand.

Ruhe ['ru:ə], *f.* (—, *no pl.*) rest, repose; quiet, tranquillity; *sich zur — setzen,* retire (from business etc.).

Ruhegehalt ['ru:əgəhalt], *n.* (—es, *pl.* ̈er) retirement pension, superannuation.

ruhen ['ru:ən], *v.n.* rest, repose, take a rest.

Ruhestand ['ru:əʃtant], *m.* (—es, *no pl.*) retirement.

ruhig ['ru:ıç], *adj.* quiet, tranquil, peaceful, calm; *sich — verhalten,* keep quiet.

Ruhm [ru:m], *m.* (—(e)s, *no pl.*) glory, fame, renown; *einem zum — gereichen,* be *or* redound to s.o.'s credit.

rühmen ['ry:mən], *v.a.* praise, extol, glorify. — *v.r. sich —,* boast.

Ruhr (1) [ru:r], *f.* (River) Ruhr.

Ruhr (2) [ru:r], *f.* (—, *no pl.*) dysentery.

Rührei ['ry:raɪ], *n.* (—s, *pl.* —er) scrambled egg.

rühren ['ry:rən], *v.a.* stir, move, touch. — *v.r. sich —,* move, stir; get a move on.

rührig ['ry:rıç], *adj.* active, alert.

rührselig ['ry:rze:lıç], *adj.* oversentimental; lachrymose.

Rührung ['ry:ruŋ], *f.* (—, *no pl.*) emotion.

Ruin [ru'i:n], *m.* (—s, *no pl.*) (*fig.*) ruin; decay; bankruptcy.

Ruine [ru'i:nə], *f.* (—, *pl.* —n) ruin(s).

rülpsen ['rylpsən], *v.n.* belch.

Rum [rum], *m.* (—s, *no pl.*) rum.

Rumänien [ru'mɛ:njən], *n.* Rumania.

Rummel ['ruməl], *m.* (—s, *no pl.*) tumult, row, hubbub.

Rumor [ru'mo:r], *m.* (—s, *no pl.*) noise; rumour.

rumoren [ru'mo:rən], *v.n.* make a noise.

Rumpelkammer ['rumpəlkamər], *f.* (—, *pl.* —n) lumber-room, junkroom.

rumpeln ['rumpəln], *v.n.* rumble.

Rumpf [rumpf], *m.* (—(e)s, *pl.* ̈e) (*Anat.*) trunk; (*ship*) hull; (*Aviat.*) fuselage.

rümpfen ['rympfən], *v.a. die Nase —,* turn up o.'s nose.

rund [runt], *adj.* round, rotund; — *heraus,* flatly; *etwas — abschlagen,* refuse s.th. flatly; — *herum,* round about.

Runde ['rundə], *f.* (—, *pl.* —n) round; (*Sport*) round, bout; *die — machen,* (*watchman*) patrol.

Rundfunk ['runtfuŋk], *m.* (—s, *no pl.*) broadcasting, wireless; radio.

Rundgang ['runtgaŋ], *m.* (—s, *pl.* ̈e) round, tour (of inspection).

rundlich ['runtlıç], *adj.* plump.

Rundschau ['runtʃau], *f.* (—, *no pl.*) panorama; review, survey.

Rundschreiben ['runtʃraıbən], *n.* (—s, *pl.* —) circular letter.

rundweg ['runtve:k], *adv.* flatly, plainly.

Rune ['ru:nə], *f.* (—, *pl.* —n) rune; runic writing.

Runkelrübe ['ruŋkəlry:bə], *f.* (—, *pl.* —n) beetroot.

Runzel ['runtsəl], *f.* (—, *pl.* —n) wrinkle, pucker.

Rüpel ['ry:pəl], *m.* (—s, *pl.* —) bounder, lout.

rupfen ['rupfən], *v.a.* pluck; *einen —,* (*fig.*) fleece s.o.

Rupie ['ru:pjə], *f.* (—, *pl.* —n) rupee.

ruppig ['rupıç], *adj.* unfriendly, rude; scruffy.

Ruprecht ['ru:prɛçt], *m. Knecht —,* Santa Claus.

Rüsche ['ry:ʃə], *f.* (—, *pl.* —n) ruche.

Ruß [ru:s], *m.* (—es, *no pl.*) soot.

Rüssel ['rysəl], *m.* (—s, *pl.* —) snout; (*elephant*) trunk.

Rußland ['ruslant], *n.* Russia.

rüsten ['rystən], *v.a.* prepare, fit (out); equip; (*Mil.*) arm, mobilise.

Rüster ['rystər], *f.* (—, *pl.* —) elm.

rüstig ['rystıç], *adj.* vigorous, robust.

Rüstung ['rystuŋ], *f.* (—, *pl.* —en) armour; preparation; (*Mil.*) armament.

Rüstzeug ['rʏsttsɔyk], *n.* (—s, *no pl.*) equipment.

Rute ['ru:tə], *f.* (—, *pl.* —n) rod, twig; (*fox*) brush.

Rutengänger ['ru:təŋɡɛŋər], *m.* (—s, *pl.* —) water-diviner.

rutschen ['rutʃən], *v.n.* (*aux.* sein) slip, slide, skid, slither.

rütteln ['rʏtəln], *v.a., v.n.* shake, jolt.

S

S [ɛs], *n.* (—s, *pl.* —s) the letter S.

Saal [za:l], *m.* (—(e)s, *pl.* **Säle**) hall, large room.

Saat [za:t], *f.* (—, *pl.* —en) seed; sowing; standing corn.

Sabbat ['zabat], *m.* (—s, *pl.* —e) sabbath.

sabbern ['zabərn], *v.n.* (*sl.*) slaver, drivel.

Säbel ['zɛ:bəl], *m.* (—s, *pl.* —) sabre; *krummer* —, falchion, scimitar.

säbeln ['zɛ:bəln], *v.a.* sabre, hack at.

sachdienlich ['zaxdi:nlɪç], *adj.* relevant, pertinent.

Sache ['zaxə], *f.* (—, *pl.* —n) thing, matter, affair; (*Law*) action, case; *die* — *ist* (*die*) *daß*, the fact is that; *das gehört nicht zur* —, that is beside the point; *bei der* — *sein*, pay attention to the matter in hand; *das ist meine* —, that is my business; *die* — *der Unterdrückten verteidigen*, take up the cause of the oppressed.

Sachlage ['zaxla:ɡə], *f.* (—, *no pl.*) state of affairs.

sachlich ['zaxlɪç], *adj.* pertinent; objective.

sächlich ['zɛçlɪç], *adj.* (*Gram.*) neuter.

Sachse ['zaksə], *m.* (—n, *pl.* —n) Saxon.

Sachsen ['zaksən], *n.* Saxony.

sachte ['zaxtə], *adj.* soft, slow, quiet, careful, gentle.

Sachverhalt ['zaxfɛrhalt], *m.* (—s, *no pl.*) facts (of a case), state of things, circumstances.

sachverständig ['zaxfɛrʃtɛndɪç], *adj.* expert, competent, experienced.

Sachwalter ['zaxvaltər], *m.* (—s, *pl.* —) manager, counsel, attorney.

Sack [zak], *m.* (—(e)s, *pl.* ⸚e) sack, bag; *mit* — *und Pack*, (with) bag and baggage.

Säckel ['zɛkəl], *m.* (—s, *pl.* —) purse.

Sackgasse ['zakɡasə], *f.* (—, *pl.* —n) cul-de-sac, blind alley; *einen in eine* — *treiben*, corner s.o.

Sackpfeife ['zakpfaɪfə], *f.* (—, *pl.* —n) bagpipe.

Sacktuch ['zaktu:x], *n.* (—es, *pl.* ⸚er) sacking; (*dial.*) pocket-handkerchief.

säen ['zɛ:ən], *v.a.* sow.

Saffian ['zafja:n], *m.* (—s, *no pl.*) morocco-leather.

Saft [zaft], *m.* (—(e)s, *pl.* ⸚e) juice; (*tree*) sap; (*meat*) gravy; *ohne* — *und Kraft*, insipid; *im eigenen* — *schmoren*, stew in o.'s own juice.

Sage ['za:ɡə], *f.* (—, *pl.* —n) legend, fable, myth; *es geht die* —, it is rumoured.

Säge ['zɛ:ɡə], *f.* (—, *pl.* —n) saw.

sagen ['za:ɡən], *v.a.* say, tell; *einem etwas* — *lassen*, send word to s.o.; *es hat nichts zu* —, it does not matter; *was Du nicht sagst!* you don't say (so)!

sägen ['zɛ:ɡən], *v.a., v.n.* saw; (*fig.*) snore.

sagenhaft ['za:ɡənhaft], *adj.* legendary, mythical; (*fig.*) fabulous.

Sahne ['za:nə], *f.* (—, *no pl.*) cream.

Saite ['zaɪtə], *f.* (—, *pl.* —n) string; *strengere* —n *aufziehen*, (*fig.*) take a stricter line.

Sakko ['zako], *m.* (—s, *pl.* —s) lounge jacket.

Sakristei [zakrɪ'staɪ], *f.* (—, *pl.* —en) vestry.

Salat [za'la:t], *m.* (—(e)s, *pl.* —e) salad; (*plant*) lettuce; (*sl.*) mess.

salbadern ['zalba:dərn], *v.n.* prate, talk nonsense.

Salbe ['zalbə], *f.* (—, *pl.* —n) ointment, salve.

Salbei ['zalbaɪ], *m.* (—s, *no pl.*) (*Bot.*) sage.

salben ['zalbən], *v.a.* anoint.

salbungsvoll ['zalbuŋsfɔl], *adj.* unctuous.

Saldo ['zaldo], *m.* (—s, *pl.* —s) balance.

Saline [za'li:nə], *f.* (—, *pl.* —n) salt-mine, salt-works.

Salkante ['za:lkantə], *f.* (—, *pl.* —n) selvedge, border.

Salm [zalm], *m.* (—s, *pl.* —e) (*Zool.*) salmon.

Salmiakgeist ['zalmjakɡaɪst], *m.* (—s, *no pl.*) ammonia.

Salon [za'lɔ̃], *m.* (—s, *pl.* —s) salon; saloon; drawing-room.

salonfähig [za'lɔ̃fɛ:ɪç], *adj.* presentable, socially acceptable.

salopp [za'lɔp], *adj.* careless, slovenly, shabby, sloppy.

Salpeter [zal'pe:tər], *m.* (—s, *no pl.*) nitre, saltpetre.

salutieren [zalu'ti:rən], *v.a., v.n.*, salute.

Salve ['zalvə], *f.* (—, *pl.* —n) volley, discharge, salute.

Salz [zalts], *n.* (—es, *pl.* —e) salt.

Salzfaß ['zaltsfas], *n.* (—sses, *pl.* ⸚sser) salt-cellar.

Salzlake ['zaltsla:kə], *f.* (—, *pl.* —n) brine.

Salzsäure ['zaltssɔyrə], *f.* (—, *no pl.*) hydrochloric acid.

Sämann ['zɛ:man], *m.* (—s, *pl.* ⸚ner) sower.

Sambia ['zambia], *n.* Zambia.

Same(n)

Same(n) ['za:mə(n)], *m.* (**—ns**, *pl.* **—n**)
seed; sperm; spawn.

Samenstaub ['za:mənʃtaup], *m.* (**—s**,
no pl.) pollen.

Sämereien [zɛ:mə'raɪən], *f. pl.* seeds,
grain.

sämisch ['zɛ:mɪʃ], *adj.* chamois.

Sammelband ['zaməlbant], *m.* (**—es**,
pl. **ⁿe**) miscellany, anthology.

sammeln ['zaməln], *v.a.* collect, gather.
— *v.r. sich* —, meet; collect o.'s
thoughts, compose o.s.

Sammler ['zamlər], *m.* (**—s**, *pl.* **—**)
collector; accumulator.

Samstag ['zamsta:k], *m.* (**—s**, *pl.* **—e**)
Saturday.

Samt [zamt], *m.* (**—(e)s**, *pl.* **—e**) velvet.

samt [zamt], *adv.* together, all together;
— *und sonders*, jointly and severally.—
prep. (*Dat.*) together with.

sämtlich ['zɛmtlɪç], *adj.* each and
every.

Sand [zant], *m.* (**—es**, *no pl.*) sand;
feiner —, grit; *grober* —, gravel.

Sandtorte ['zanttɔrtə], *f.* (**—**, *pl.* **—n**)
sponge-cake, madeira-cake.

Sanduhr ['zantu:r], (**—**, *pl.* **—en**) hour-
glass.

sanft [zanft], *adj.* soft, gentle.

Sänfte ['zɛnftə], *f.* (**—**, *pl.* **—n**) sedan-
chair.

Sang [zaŋ], *m.* (**—es**, *pl.* **Gesänge**)
song; *ohne* — *und Klang*, (*fig.*) un-
ostentatiously, without fuss, without
ceremony.

sanieren [za'ni:rən], *v.a.* cure; (*company*) reconstruct, put on a sound
financial basis.

sanitär [zani'tɛ:r], *adj.* sanitary.

Sanitäter [zani'tɛ:tər], *m.* (**—s**, *pl.*—)
medical orderly; ambulance man.

Sankt [zaŋkt], *indecl. adj.* Saint; (*abbr.*)
St.

sanktionieren [zaŋktsjo'ni:rən], *v.a.*
sanction.

Sansibar ['zanzɪba:r], *n.* Zanzibar.

Sardelle [zar'dɛlə], *f.* (**—**, *pl.* **—n**)
(*Zool.*) anchovy.

Sardinien [zar'di:njən], *n.* Sardinia.

Sarg [zark], *m.* (**—es**, *pl.* **ⁿe**) coffin.

sarkastisch [zar'kastɪʃ], *adj.* sarcastic.

Satellit [zatə'li:t], *m.* (**—en**, *pl.* **—en**)
satellite.

Satiriker [za'ti:rɪkər], *m.* (**—s**, *pl.* **—**)
satirist.

satt [zat], *adj.* sated, satiated, satisfied;
(*colours*) deep, rich; *sich* — *essen*,
eat o.'s fill; *einer Sache* — *sein*, be
sick of s.th., have had enough of s.th.

Sattel ['zatəl], *m.* (**—s**, *pl.* **ⁿ**) saddle;
einen aus dem — *heben*, (*fig.*) oust s.o.;
fest im — *sitzen*, (*fig.*) be master of a
situation; *in allen* **ⁿn** *gerecht*, versatile.

satteln ['zatəln], *v.a.* saddle.

Sattheit ['zathaɪt], *f.* (**—**, *no pl.*)
satiety.

sättigen ['zɛtɪgən], *v.a.* satisfy, sate,
satiate; (*Chem.*) saturate.

sattsam ['zatza:m], *adv.* enough, sufficiently.

saturieren [zatu'ri:rən], *v.a.* (*Chem.*)
saturate.

Satz [zats], *m.* (**—es**, *pl.* **ⁿe**) sentence;
proposition; thesis; (*Mus.*) movement;
(*Typ.*) composition; (*dregs*) sediment;
(*gambling*) stake; *mit einem* —, with
one leap (*or* jump *or* bound).

Satzbildung ['zatsbɪlduŋ], *f.* (**—**, *pl.*
—en) (*Gram.*) construction; (*Chem.*)
sedimentation.

Satzlehre ['zatsle:rə], *f.* (**—**, *no pl.*)
syntax.

Satzung ['zatsuŋ], *f.* (**—**, *pl.* **—en**)
statute.

Satzzeichen ['zatstsaɪçən], *n.* (**—s**,
pl. **—**) punctuation-mark.

Sau [zau], *f.* (**—**, *pl.* **ⁿe**) sow; (*vulg.*)
dirty person, slut.

sauber ['zaubər], *adj.* clean, neat, tidy.

säubern ['zɔybərn], *v.a.* clean, cleanse;
(*fig.*) purge.

Saubohne ['zaubo:nə], *f.* (**—**, *pl.* **—n**)
broad bean.

Saudiarabien ['zaudiara:bjən], *n.* Saudi
Arabia.

sauer ['zauər], *adj.* sour, acid; (*fig.*)
troublesome; morose.

Sauerbrunnen ['zauərbrunən], *m.* (**—s**,
pl. **—**) mineral water.

Sauerei [zauə'raɪ], *f.* (**—**, *pl.* **—en**)
(*sl.*) filthiness; mess.

Sauerkraut ['zauərkraut], *n.* (**—s**, *no
pl.*) pickled cabbage.

säuerlich ['zɔyərlɪç], *adj.* acidulous.

Sauerstoff ['zauərʃtɔf], *m.* (**—(e)s**, *no
pl.*) oxygen.

Sauerteig ['zauərtaɪk], *m.* (**—(e)s**, *pl.*
—e) leaven.

sauertöpfisch ['zauərtœpfɪʃ], *adj.* morose, peevish.

saufen ['zaufən], *v.a.*, *v.n. irr.* (*animals*)
drink; (*humans*) drink to excess.

Säufer ['zɔyfər], *m.* (**—s**, *pl.* **—**)
drunkard, drinker, alcoholic.

saugen ['zaugən], *v.a.*, *v.n.* suck.

säugen ['zɔygən], *v.a.* suckle.

Säugetier ['zɔygəti:r], *n.* (**—s**, *pl.* **—e**)
mammal.

Saugheber ['zaukhe:bər], *m.* (**—s**, *pl.*
—) suction-pump; siphon.

Säugling ['zɔyklɪŋ], *m.* (**—s**, *pl.* **—e**)
suckling, baby.

Saugwarze ['zaukvartsə], *f.* (**—**, *pl.*
—n) nipple.

Säule ['zɔylə], *f.* (**—**, *pl.* **—n**) pillar,
column.

Säulenbündel ['zɔylənbyndəl], *n.* (**—s**,
pl. **—**) (*Archit.*) clustered column.

Säulenfuß ['zɔylənfu:s], *m.* (**—es**,
pl. **ⁿe**) (*Archit.*) base, plinth.

Säulengang ['zɔyləngaŋ], *m.* (**—s**, *pl.*
ⁿe) colonnade.

Saum [zaum], *m.* (**—(e)s**, *pl.* **ⁿe**) seam,
hem, border, edge; selvedge.

saumäßig ['zaumɛ:sɪç], *adj.* (*sl.*)
beastly, filthy, piggish; enormous.

säumen (1) ['zɔymən], *v.a.* hem.

säumen (2) ['zɔymən], *v.n.* delay, tarry.

säumig ['zɔymɪç], *adj.* tardy, slow,
dilatory.

Saumpferd ['zaumpfe:rt], *n.* (—s, *pl.* —e) pack-horse.
saumselig ['zaumze:lɪç], *adj.* tardy, dilatory.
Säure ['zɔyrə], *f.* (—, *pl.* —n) acid; *(Med.)* acidity.
Saurier ['zaurjər], *m.* (—s, *pl.* —) saurian.
Saus [zaus], *m.* (—es, *no pl.*) rush; revel, riot; *in — und Braus leben*, live a wild life, live riotously.
säuseln ['zɔyzəln], *v.n.* rustle, murmur.
sausen ['zauzən], *v.n.* bluster, blow, howl, whistle; *(coll.)* rush, dash.
Saustall ['zauʃtal], *m.* (—s, *pl.* ⸚e) pigsty.
Schabe ['ʃa:bə], *f.* (—, *pl.* —n) *(Ent.)* cockroach.
schaben ['ʃa:bən], *v.a.* scrape, shave, rub.
Schabernack ['ʃa:bərnak], *m.* (—s, *pl.* —e) practical joke, trick.
schäbig ['ʃɛ:bɪç], *adj.* shabby.
Schablone [ʃa'blo:nə], *f.* (—, *pl.* —n) model, mould, pattern, stencil; *(fig.)* routine.
Schach [ʃax], *n.* (—(e)s, *no pl.*) chess; *— bieten*, check; *— spielen*, play chess; *in — halten*, keep in check.
Schacher ['ʃaxər], *m.* (—s, *no pl.*) haggling, bargaining, barter.
Schächer ['ʃɛçər], *m.* (—s, *pl.* —) wretch, felon, robber.
Schacht [ʃaxt], *m.* (—(e)s, *pl.* ⸚e) shaft.
Schachtel ['ʃaxtəl], *f.* (—, *pl.* —n) box, (cardboard) box, (small) case.
Schachtelhalm ['ʃaxtəlhalm], *m.* (—s, *pl.* —e) *(grass)* horse-tail.
Schächter ['ʃɛçtər], *m.* (—s, *pl.* —) (kosher) butcher.
schade ['ʃa:də], *int.* a pity, a shame, unfortunate; *wie —*, what a pity; *sehr —*, a great pity.
Schädel ['ʃɛ:dəl], *m.* (—s, *pl.* —) skull.
Schaden ['ʃa:dən], *m.* (—s, *pl.* ⸚) damage, injury, detriment; *zu — kommen*, come to grief.
schaden ['ʃa:dən], *v.n.* do harm, do damage, do injury; *es schadet nichts*, it does not matter.
Schadenersatz ['ʃa:dənɛrzats], *m.* (—es, *no pl.*) indemnity, compensation, indemnification; *(money)* damages.
Schadenfreude ['ʃa:dənfrɔydə], *f.* (—, *no pl.*) malicious pleasure.
Schadensforderung ['ʃa:dənsfordəruŋ], *f.* (—, *pl.* —en) claim (for damages).
schadhaft ['ʃa:thaft], *adj.* defective, faulty.
schädlich ['ʃɛ:tlɪç], *adj.* injurious, noxious, pernicious, noisome.
schadlos ['ʃa:tlo:s], *adj.* indemnified; *einen — halten*, indemnify s.o., compensate s.o.; *sich an einem — halten*, recoup o.s. from s.o.
Schadlosigkeit ['ʃa:tlo:zɪçkait], *f.* (—, *no pl.*) harmlessness.
Schaf [ʃa:f], *n.* (—(e)s, *pl.* —e) sheep.

Schafblattern ['ʃa:fblatərn], *f. pl.* *(Med.)* chicken-pox.
Schafdarm ['ʃa:fdarm], *m.* (—s, *pl.* ⸚e) sheep-gut.
Schäfer ['ʃɛ:fər], *m.* (—s, *pl.* —) shepherd.
Schäferstündchen ['ʃɛ:fərʃtyntçən], *n.* (—s, *pl.* —) tryst; rendezvous.
schaffen ['ʃafən], *v.a.*, *v.n. irr.* make, produce, create. — *v.a. reg.* provide; manage; *aus dem Wege —*, remove. — *v.n. reg.* work; *einem zu — machen*, give s.o. trouble.
Schaffner ['ʃafnər], *m.* (—s, *pl.* —) *(Railw. etc.)* guard, conductor.
Schafgarbe ['ʃa:fgarbə], *f.* (—, *pl.* —n) *(Bot.)* common yarrow.
Schafhürde ['ʃa:fhyrdə], *f.* (—, *pl.* —n) sheep-fold.
Schafott [ʃa'fɔt], *n.* (—(e)s, *pl.* —e) scaffold.
Schafschur ['ʃa:fʃu:r], *f.* (—, *pl.* —en) sheep-shearing.
Schaft [ʃaft], *m.* (—(e)s, *pl.* ⸚e) shaft; *(gun)* stock.
Schafwolle ['ʃa:fvɔlə], *f.* (—, *no pl.*) sheep's wool, fleece.
Schakal [ʃa'ka:l], *m.* (—s, *pl.* —e) *(Zool.)* jackal.
Schäkerei [ʃɛ:kə'rai], *f.* (—, *pl.* —en) playfulness, teasing, dalliance, flirtation.
Schal [ʃa:l], *m.* (—s, *pl.* —e) scarf, shawl.
schal [ʃa:l], *adj.* stale, flat, insipid.
Schale ['ʃa:lə], *f.* (—, *pl.* —n) *(nut, egg)* shell; *(fruit)* peel, rind; dish, bowl; *(Austr.)* cup; *(fig.)* outside.
schälen ['ʃɛ:lən], *v.a.* shell; peel.
Schalk [ʃalk], *m.* (—(e)s, *pl.* —e) knave, rogue; wag, joker.
Schall [ʃal], *m.* (—(e)s, *no pl.*) sound.
Schallbecken ['ʃalbɛkən], *n.* (—s, *pl.* —) cymbal.
Schallehre ['ʃalle:rə], *f.* (—, *no pl.*) acoustics.
schallen ['ʃalən], *v.n.* sound, reverberate.
Schalmei [ʃal'mai], *f.* (—, *pl.* —en) *(Poet., Mus.)* shawm.
Schallplatte ['ʃalplatə], *f.* (—, *pl.* —n) (gramophone) record.
schalten ['ʃaltən], *v.n.* rule; switch; *(Motor.)* change gear; *— und walten*, manage.
Schalter ['ʃaltər], *m.* (—s, *pl.* —) *(Elec.)* switch; booking-office; counter.
Schalthebel ['ʃalthe:bəl], *m.* (—s, *pl.* —) *(Motor.)* gear lever.
Schaltier ['ʃa:lti:r], *n.* (—s, *pl.* —e) *(Zool.)* crustacean.
Schaltjahr ['ʃaltja:r], *n.* (—s, *pl.* —e) leap year.
Schalttafel ['ʃalttafəl], *f.* (—, *pl.* —n) switch-board.
Scham [ʃa:m], *f.* (—, *no pl.*) shame, modesty; private parts.
schämen ['ʃɛ:mən], *v.r. sich —*, be ashamed (of).
schamlos ['ʃa:mlo:s], *adj.* shameless.
schamrot ['ʃa:mro:t], *adj.* blushing; *— werden*, blush.

schandbar [ˈʃantbaːr], *adj.* ignominious, infamous.

Schande [ˈʃandə], *f.* (—, *no pl.*) shame, disgrace; dishonour, ignominy.

schänden [ˈʃɛndən], *v.a.* dishonour, disgrace; violate, ravish.

Schandfleck [ˈʃantflɛk], *m.* (—s, *pl.* —e) stain, blemish.

schändlich [ˈʃɛntlɪç], *adj.* shameful, disgraceful, infamous.

Schändung [ˈʃɛnduŋ], *f.* (—, *pl.* —en) violation.

Schank [ˈʃaŋk], *m.* (—s, *no pl.*) sale of liquor.

Schanzarbeiter [ˈʃantsarbaɪtər], *m.* (—s, *pl.* —) sapper.

Schanze [ˈʃantsə], *f.* (—, *pl.* —n) redoubt, bulwark; *in die — schlagen*, risk, venture.

Schar [ʃaːr], *f.* (—, *pl.* —en) troop, band; host.

Scharade [ʃaˈraːdə], *f.* (—, *pl.* —n) charade.

scharen [ˈʃaːrən], *v.r. sich — um*, assemble, congregate, gather round.

Schären [ˈʃɛːrən], *f. pl.* reefs, skerries.

scharf [ʃarf], *adj.* sharp, keen, acute, acrid, pungent; piercing; (*fig.*) severe, rigorous.

Schärfe [ˈʃɛrfə], *f.* (—, *no pl.*) sharpness, keenness, acuteness; pungency, acridness; severity, rigour.

schärfen [ˈʃɛrfən], *v.a.* sharpen, whet; (*fig.*) strengthen, intensify.

Scharfrichter [ˈʃarfrɪçtər], *m.* (—s, *pl.* —) executioner.

scharfsichtig [ˈʃarfzɪçtɪç], *adj.* sharp-eyed, (*fig.*) penetrating, astute.

scharfsinnig [ˈʃarfzɪnɪç], *adj.* clear-sighted, sagacious, ingenious.

Scharlach [ˈʃarlax], *m.* (—s, *no pl.*) scarlet; (*Med.*) scarlet-fever.

Scharlatan [ˈʃarlataːn], *m.* (—s, *pl.* —e) charlatan, humbug.

scharmant [ʃarˈmant], *adj.* charming.

Scharmützel [ʃarˈmytsəl], *n.* (—s, *pl.* —) skirmish.

Scharnier [ʃarˈniːr], *n.* (—s, *pl.* —e) hinge, joint.

Schärpe [ˈʃɛrpə], *f.* (—, *pl.* —n) sash.

Scharpie [ʃarˈpiː], *f.* (—, *no pl.*) lint.

scharren [ˈʃarən], *v.a., v.n.* scrape, rake.

Scharte [ˈʃartə], *f.* (—, *pl.* —n) notch, crack; *eine — auswetzen*, repair a mistake, make up for s.th.

Scharteke [ʃarˈteːkə], *f.* (—, *pl.* —n) worthless book, trash; *eine alte —*, an old fuddy-duddy, frump.

scharwenzeln [ʃarˈvɛntsəln], *v.n.* dance attendance, be obsequious.

Schatten [ˈʃatən], *m.* (—s, *pl.* —) shade, shadow.

Schattenbild [ˈʃatənbɪlt], *n.* (—s, *pl.* —er) silhouette.

Schattenriß [ˈʃatənrɪs], *m.* (—sses, *pl.* —sse) silhouette.

schattieren [ʃaˈtiːrən], *v.a.* shade (drawing).

schattig [ˈʃatɪç], *adj.* shady.

Schatulle [ʃaˈtulə], *f.* (—, *pl.* —n) cash-box; privy purse.

Schatz [ʃats], *m.* (—es, *pl* ̈-e) treasure; (*fig.*) sweetheart, darling.

Schatzamt [ˈʃatsamt], *n.* (—s, *pl.* ̈-er) Treasury, Exchequer.

schätzbar [ˈʃɛtsbaːr], *adj.* estimable.

Schätzchen [ˈʃɛtsçən], *n.* (—s, *pl.* —) (*coll.*) sweetheart.

schätzen [ˈʃɛtsən], *v.a.* value, estimate; esteem; reckon at.

Schatzkammer [ˈʃatskamər], *f.* (—, *pl.* —n) treasury.

Schatzmeister [ˈʃatsmaɪstər], *m.* (—s, *pl.* —) treasurer.

Schätzung [ˈʃɛtsuŋ], *f.* (—, *pl.* —en) valuation, estimate; (*fig.*) esteem.

Schau [ʃau], *f.* (—, *pl.* —en) show, view, spectacle; *zur — stellen*, display; parade.

Schauder [ˈʃaudər], *m.* (—s, *pl.* —) shudder, shiver; horror.

schaudern [ˈʃaudərn], *v.n.* shudder, shiver.

schauen [ˈʃauən], *v.a.* see, view. — *v.n.* look, gaze (*auf*, at), *schau mal*, look here.

Schauer [ˈʃauər], *m.* (—s, *pl.* —) shiver, paroxysm; (*fig.*) thrill, awe; (*rain*) shower.

schauern [ˈʃauərn], *v.n.* shudder, shiver; (*rain*) shower.

Schauerroman [ˈʃauərromaːn], *m.* (—s, *pl.* —e) (*novel*) penny dreadful, thriller.

Schaufel [ˈʃaufəl], *f.* (—, *pl.* —n) shovel.

Schaufenster [ˈʃaufɛnstər], *n.* (—s, *pl.* —) shop-window.

Schaukel [ˈʃaukəl], *f.* (—, *pl.* —n) swing.

schaulustig [ˈʃaulustɪç], *adj.* curious.

Schaum [ʃaum], *m.* (—es, *pl.* ̈-e) foam, froth; bubbles; scum; *— schlagen*, whip cream.

schäumen [ˈʃɔymən], *v.n.* foam, froth, sparkle.

Schauplatz [ˈʃauplats], *m.* (—es, *pl.* ̈-e) scene, stage.

schaurig [ˈʃaurɪç], *adj.* grisly, horrid, horrible.

Schauspiel [ˈʃauʃpiːl], *n.* (—s, *pl.* —e) spectacle; drama, play.

Schauspieler [ˈʃauʃpiːlər], *m.* (—s, *pl.* —) actor, player.

Schaustellung [ˈʃauʃtɛluŋ], *f.* (—, *pl.* —en) exhibition.

Scheck [ʃɛk], *m.* (—s, *pl.* —s) cheque.

scheckig [ˈʃɛkɪç], *adj.* piebald, spotted, dappled.

scheel [ʃeːl], *adj.* squint-eyed; envious; *einen — ansehen*, look askance at s.o.

Scheffel [ˈʃɛfəl], *m.* (—s, *pl.* —) bushel.

scheffeln [ˈʃɛfəln], *v.a.* rake in; accumulate.

Scheibe [ˈʃaibə], *f.* (—, *pl.* —n) disc; (*window*) pane; (*shooting*) target; (*bread*) slice.

Scheibenhonig [ˈʃaibənhoːnɪç], *m.* (—s, *no pl.*) honey in the comb.

Scheibenschießen [ˈʃaɪbənʃiːsən], *n.* (—s, *no pl.*) target-practice.

Scheich [ʃaɪç], *m.* (—s, *pl.* —e) sheikh.

Scheide [ˈʃaɪdə], *f.* (—, *pl.* —n) sheath, scabbard; (*Anat.*) vagina.

Scheidemünze [ˈʃaɪdəmyntsə], *f.* (—, *pl.* —n) small coin, change.

scheiden [ˈʃaɪdən], *v.a. irr.* divide; separate, divorce; *sich — lassen*, obtain a divorce. — *v.n.* (*aux.* sein) part, depart; *aus dem Amte —*, resign office.

Scheidewand [ˈʃaɪdəvant], *f.* (—,*pl.* ⁻e) partition-wall.

Scheideweg [ˈʃaɪdəveːk], *m.* (—s, *pl.* —e) cross-roads; *am — stehen*, be at the parting of the ways.

Scheidung [ˈʃaɪduŋ], *f.* (—, *pl.* —en) divorce.

Schein [ʃaɪn], *m.* (—(e)s, *no pl.*) shine, sheen, lustre, splendour; semblance, pretence; *den — wahren*, keep up appearances; *der — trügt*, appearances are deceptive; (*in compounds*) mock, would-be, apparent; (*pl.* —e) (piece of) paper, chit, note; (*fig.*) attestation, certificate.

scheinbar [ˈʃaɪnbaːr], *adj.* apparent; ostensible, specious. — *adv.* seemingly.

scheinen [ˈʃaɪnən], *v.n. irr.* shine, sparkle; seem, appear.

scheinheilig [ˈʃaɪnhaɪlɪç], *adj.* hypocritical.

Scheinheiligkeit [ˈʃaɪnhaɪlɪçkaɪt], *f.* (—, *no pl.*) hypocrisy.

scheintot [ˈʃaɪntoːt], *adj.* in a cataleptic trance; seemingly dead.

Scheinwerfer [ˈʃaɪnverfər], *m.* (—s, *pl.* —) headlight; searchlight; floodlight.

Scheit [ʃaɪt], *n.* (—(e)s, *pl.* —e) piece of wood, billet.

Scheitel [ˈʃaɪtəl], *m.* (—s, *pl.* —) (*hair*) parting; top, vertex.

Scheiterhaufen [ˈʃaɪtərhaufən], *m.* (—s, *pl.* —) stake; funeral pyre.

scheitern [ˈʃaɪtərn], *v.n.* (*aux.* sein) (*ship*) founder, be wrecked; (*fig.*) miscarry, fail.

Schelle [ˈʃɛlə], *f.* (—, *pl.* —n) bell.

Schellen [ˈʃɛlən], *f. pl.* (*Cards*) diamonds.

schellen [ˈʃɛlən], *v.n.* ring the bell.

Schellfisch [ˈʃɛlfɪʃ], *m.* (—es, *pl.* —e) (*Zool.*) haddock.

Schelm [ʃɛlm], *m.* (—(e)s, *pl.* —e) rogue, knave, villain.

schelten [ˈʃɛltən], *v.a. irr.* scold, chide, rebuke, reprimand.

Schema [ˈʃeːma], *n.* (—s, *pl.* —s) schedule, model, plan, scheme.

Schemel [ˈʃeːməl], *m.* (—s, *pl.* —) foot-stool.

Schenk [ʃɛŋk], *m.* (—en, *pl.* —en) cupbearer; publican.

Schenke [ˈʃɛŋkə], *f.* (—, *pl.* —n) ale-house, tavern, pub.

Schenkel [ˈʃɛŋkəl], *m.* (—s, *pl.* —) thigh; (*Geom.*) side of triangle.

schenken [ˈʃɛŋkən], *v.a.* present s.o. with, donate, give.

Schenkstube [ˈʃɛŋkʃtuːbə], *f.* (—, *pl.* —n) tap-room.

Scherbe [ˈʃɛrbə], *f.* (—, *pl.* —n) potsherd; fragment of glass etc.

Schere [ˈʃeːrə], *f.* (—, *pl.* —n) scissors; (*garden*) shears; (*crab*) claw.

scheren [ˈʃeːrən], *v.a.* shave; clip, shear; bother, concern. — *v.r. sich —*, clear off; *scher dich zum Teufel!* go to blazes!

Scherereien [ʃeːrəˈraɪən], *f. pl.* vexation, bother, trouble.

Scherflein [ˈʃɛrflaɪn], *n.* (—s, *pl.* —) mite; *sein — beitragen*, contribute o.'s share.

Scherge [ˈʃɛrgə], *m.* (—n, *pl.* —n) (*obs.*) beadle.

Scherz [ʃɛrts], *m.* (—es, *pl.* —e) jest, joke; *— beiseite*, joking apart.

scheu [ʃɔy], *adj.* shy, bashful, timid; skittish.

scheuchen [ˈʃɔyçən], *v.a.* scare away.

scheuen [ˈʃɔyən], *v.a.* shun, avoid, fight shy of, fear. — *v.n.* take fright.

Scheuer [ˈʃɔyər], *f.* (—, *pl.* —n) barn.

scheuern [ˈʃɔyərn], *v.a.* scour, scrub.

Scheuklappe [ˈʃɔyklapə], *f.* (—, *pl.* —n) blinker.

Scheune [ˈʃɔynə], *f.* (—, *pl.* —n) barn.

Scheusal [ˈʃɔyzaːl], *n.* (—s, *pl.* —e) monster.

scheußlich [ˈʃɔyslɪç], *adj.* frightful, dreadful, abominable, hideous.

Schicht [ʃɪçt], *f.* (—, *pl.* —en) layer, stratum, seam; (*society*) class; (*work*) shift.

schick [ʃɪk], *adj.* stylish, chic.

schicken [ˈʃɪkən], *v.a.* send, despatch, convey. — *v.r. sich —*, be proper; *sich in etwas —*, put up with s.th., resign o.s. to s.th.

schicklich [ˈʃɪklɪç], *adj.* proper, becoming, suitable, seemly.

Schicksal [ˈʃɪkzaːl], *n.* (—s, *pl.* —e) fate, destiny, lot.

Schickung [ˈʃɪkuŋ], *f.* (—, *pl.* —en) Divine Will, Providence.

schieben [ˈʃiːbən], *v.a. irr.* shove, push; *die Schuld auf einen —*, put the blame on s.o.

Schieber [ˈʃiːbər], *m.* (—s, *pl.* —) bolt, slide; (*fig.*) profiteer, spiv.

Schiedsgericht [ˈʃiːtsgərɪçt], *n.* (—es, *pl.* —e) arbitration tribunal.

Schiedsrichter [ˈʃiːtsrɪçtər], *m.* (—s, *pl.* —) referee, umpire, arbiter.

schief [ʃiːf], *adj.* slanting, oblique, bent, crooked; wry; *—e Ebene*, inclined plane; *— gehen*, go wrong.

Schiefe [ˈʃiːfə], *f.* (—, *no pl.*) obliquity.

Schiefer [ˈʃiːfər], *m.* (—s, *no pl.*) slate.

schiefrig [ˈʃiːfrɪç], *adj.* slaty.

schielen [ˈʃiːlən], *v.n.* squint, be cross-eyed.

Schienbein [ˈʃiːnbaɪn], *n.* (—s, *pl.* —e) shin-bone, shin.

187

Schiene

Schiene ['ʃiːnə], f. (—, pl. —n) rail; (Med.) splint.

schier [ʃiːr], adj. (rare) sheer, pure. — adv. almost, very nearly.

Schierling ['ʃiːrlɪŋ], m. (—s, pl. —e) (Bot.) hemlock.

schießen ['ʃiːsən], v.a., v.n. irr. shoot, fire, discharge; (fig.) rush; etwas — lassen, let go of s.th.; die Zügel — lassen, loosen o.'s hold on the reins; ein Kabel — lassen, pay out a cable; das ist zum —, that's very funny.

Schiff [ʃɪf], n. (—(e)s, pl. —e) ship, vessel, boat; (church) nave.

schiffbar ['ʃɪfbaːr], adj. navigable.

Schiffbruch ['ʃɪfbrux], m. (—s, pl ⁓e) shipwreck.

Schiffbrücke ['ʃɪfbrykə], f. (—, pl. —n) pontoon-bridge.

schiffen ['ʃɪfən], v.n. sail; navigate.

Schiffsboden ['ʃɪfsboːdən], m. (—s, pl. ⁓) (ship's) hold.

Schiffsmaat ['ʃɪfsmaːt], m. (—s, pl. —e) shipmate.

Schiffsrumpf ['ʃɪfsrumpf], m. (—es, pl. ⁓e) hull.

Schiffsschnabel ['ʃɪfsʃnaːbəl], m. (—s, pl. ⁓) prow, bows.

Schiffsvorderteil ['ʃɪfsfɔrdərtaɪl], n. (—s, pl. —e) forecastle, prow.

Schiffszwieback ['ʃɪfstsviːbak], m. (—s, no pl.) ship's biscuit.

Schikane [ʃiˈkaːnə], f. (—, pl. —n) chicanery.

Schild (1) [ʃɪlt], m. (—(e)s, pl. —e) shield, buckler, escutcheon; etwas im — führen, have designs on s.th., plan s.th.

Schild (2) [ʃɪlt], n. (—s, pl. —er) signboard, plate.

Schilderhaus ['ʃɪldərhaus], n. (—es, pl. ⁓er) sentry-box.

Schildermaler ['ʃɪldərmaːlər], m. (—s, pl. —) sign-painter.

schildern ['ʃɪldərn], v.a. describe, depict.

Schildknappe ['ʃɪltknapə], m. (—n, pl. —n) shield-bearer, squire.

Schildkrot ['ʃɪltkroːt], n. (—s, no pl.) tortoise-shell.

Schildkröte ['ʃɪltkrøːtə], f. (—, pl. —n) (Zool.) turtle, tortoise.

Schildpatt ['ʃɪltpat], n. (—s, no pl.) tortoise-shell.

Schildwache ['ʃɪltvaxə], f. (—, pl. —n) sentinel, sentry; — stehen, be on sentry duty, stand guard.

Schilf(rohr) ['ʃɪlf(roːr)], n. (—(e)s, no pl.) (Bot.) reed, rush, sedge.

schillern ['ʃɪlərn], v.n. opalesce, glitter, change colour, be iridescent.

Schilling ['ʃɪlɪŋ], m. (—s, pl. —e) Austrian coin; shilling.

Schimmel (1) ['ʃɪməl], m. (—s, pl. —) white horse.

Schimmel (2) ['ʃɪməl], m. (—s, no pl.) mould, mustiness.

schimmeln ['ʃɪməln], v.n. (aux. sein) go mouldy, moulder.

Schimmer ['ʃɪmər], m. (—s, pl. —) glitter, gleam; ich habe keinen —, I haven't a clue.

schimmlig ['ʃɪmlɪç], adj. mouldy, musty, mildewed.

Schimpanse [ʃɪmˈpanzə], m. (—n, pl. —n) (Zool.) chimpanzee.

Schimpf [ʃɪmpf], m. (—es, no pl.) abuse, affront, insult; mit — und Schande, in disgrace.

schimpfen ['ʃɪmpfən], v.n. curse, swear; — auf, (fig.) run (s.o.) down. — v.a. insult (s.o.), call (s.o.) names; scold.

Schindel ['ʃɪndəl], f. (—, pl. —n) shingle.

schinden ['ʃɪndən], v.a. irr. flay; (fig.) grind, oppress, sweat. — v.r. sich —, slave, drudge.

Schindluder ['ʃɪntluːdər], n. (—s, pl. —) worn-out animal; mit einem — treiben, exploit s.o.

Schinken ['ʃɪŋkən], m. (—s, pl. —) ham.

Schinkenspeck ['ʃɪŋkənʃpɛk], m. (—s, no pl.) bacon.

Schippe ['ʃɪpə], f. (—, pl. —n) shovel, spade.

Schirm [ʃɪrm], m. (—(e)s, pl. —e) screen; umbrella; parasol, sunshade; lampshade; (fig.) shield, shelter, cover.

schirmen ['ʃɪrmən], v.a. protect (from), shelter.

Schirmherr ['ʃɪrmhɛr], m. (—n, pl. —en) protector, patron.

Schlacht [ʃlaxt], f. (—, pl. —en) battle; fight; eine — liefern, give battle; die — gewinnen, carry the day, win the battle.

Schlachtbank ['ʃlaxtbaŋk], f. (—, pl. ⁓e) shambles; zur — führen, lead to the slaughter.

schlachten ['ʃlaxtən], v.a. kill, butcher, slaughter.

Schlachtenbummler ['ʃlaxtənbumlər], m. (—s, pl. —) camp follower.

Schlachtfeld ['ʃlaxtfɛlt], n. (—s, pl. —er) battlefield.

Schlachtruf ['ʃlaxtruːf], m. (—s, pl. —e) battle-cry.

Schlacke ['ʃlakə], f. (—, pl. —n) slag, clinker, dross.

Schlackwurst ['ʃlakvurst], f. (—, pl. ⁓e) (North German) sausage.

Schlaf [ʃlaːf], m. (—(e)s, no pl.) sleep; slumber, rest; in tiefem —, fast asleep; in den — wiegen, rock to sleep.

Schläfchen ['ʃlɛːfçən], n. (—s, pl. —) nap; einen — machen, have forty winks.

Schläfe ['ʃlɛːfə], f. (—, pl. —n) temple.

schlafen ['ʃlaːfən], v.n. irr. sleep; schlaf wohl, sleep well; — gehen, go to bed.

schlaff [ʃlaf], adj. slack, loose, lax, flabby; weak; remiss.

schlaflos ['ʃlaːfloːs], adj. sleepless.

Schlafmittel ['ʃlaːfmɪtəl], n. (—s, pl. —) soporific, sleeping tablet, sleeping draught.

schläfrig ['ʃlɛːfrɪç], adj. drowsy, sleepy.

188

schleudern

Schlafrock [ˈʃlaːfrɔk], s. (—s, pl. ⸚e) dressing-gown; *Äpfel im —,* apple fritters.

schlafwandeln [ˈʃlaːfvandəln], v.n. (aux. sein) walk in o.'s sleep, sleep-walk.

Schlag [ʃlaːk], m. (—(e)s, pl. ⸚e) blow, stroke; beat; (*Elec.*) shock; *ein Mann von gutem —,* a good type of man; *vom — gerührt,* struck by apoplexy; *— fünf,* at five o'clock sharp.

Schlagader [ˈʃlaːkaːdər], f. (—, pl. —n) artery.

Schlaganfall [ˈʃlaːkanfal], m. (—s, pl. ⸚e) stroke, apoplexy.

Schlagballspiel [ˈʃlaːkbalʃpiːl], n. (—s, pl. —e) rounders.

Schlagbaum [ˈʃlaːkbaum], m. (—s, pl. ⸚e) turnpike.

schlagen [ˈʃlaːgən], v.a. irr. beat, strike, hit; (*tree*) fell; (*money*) coin; *Alarm —,* sound the alarm; *ans Kreuz —,* crucify; *ein Kreuz —,* make the sign of the cross. — v.n. (*clock*) strike; (*birds*) warble; *aus der Art —,* degenerate. — v.r. sich —, fight; *sich auf Säbel —,* fight with sabres; *sich an die Brust —,* beat o.'s breast.

Schlager [ˈʃlaːgər], m. (—s, pl. —) hit, pop song; (*fig.*) success.

Schläger [ˈʃleːgər], m. (—s, pl. —) rapier; bat; (tennis-)racket; (golf-) club.

Schlägerei [ʃleːgəˈraɪ], f. (—, pl. —en) fray, scuffle.

schlagfertig [ˈʃlaːkfɛrtiç], adj. quick-witted.

Schlagkraft [ˈʃlaːkkraft], f. (—, no pl.) striking power.

Schlaglicht [ˈʃlaːklɪçt], n. (—s, pl. —er) strong direct light.

Schlagsahne [ˈʃlaːkzaːnə], f. (—, no pl.) double cream, raw cream; whipped cream.

Schlagschatten [ˈʃlaːkʃatən], m. (—s, pl. —) deep shadow.

Schlagseite [ˈʃlaːkzaɪtə], f. (—, no pl.) — *bekommen,* (*Naut.*) list.

Schlagwort [ˈʃlaːkvɔrt], n. (—s, pl. ⸚er) catchword, slogan; trite saying.

Schlagzeile [ˈʃlaːktsaɪlə], f. (—, pl. —n) headline.

Schlamm [ʃlam], m. (—(e)s, no pl.) mud, mire.

Schlampe [ˈʃlampə], f. (—, pl. —n) slut.

Schlange [ˈʃlaŋə], f. (—, pl. —n) snake, serpent; (*fig.*) queue.

schlängeln [ˈʃlɛŋəln], v.r. sich —, wind, meander.

schlangenartig [ˈʃlaŋənaːrtiç], adj. snaky, serpentine.

schlank [ʃlaŋk], adj. slim, slender.

schlapp [ʃlap], adj. limp, tired, weak, slack; *— machen,* break down, collapse.

Schlappe [ˈʃlapə], f. (—, pl. —n) reverse, defeat; *eine — erleiden,* suffer a set-back.

Schlappschwanz [ˈʃlapʃvants], m. (—es, pl. ⸚e) weakling; milksop.

Schlaraffenland [ʃlaˈrafənlant], n. (—(e)s, pl. ⸚er) land of milk and honey.

schlau [ʃlau], adj. cunning, crafty, sly, shrewd.

Schlauch [ʃlaux], m. (—(e)s, pl. ⸚e) hose; tube.

Schlaukopf [ˈʃlaukɔpf], m. (—(e)s, pl. ⸚e) slyboots; (*Am.*) wiseacre.

schlecht [ʃlɛçt], adj. bad, evil, wicked; poor; *mir ist —,* I feel ill; *—e Zeiten,* hard times; *—es Geld,* base money.

schlechterdings [ˈʃlɛçtərdɪŋs], adv. simply, positively, absolutely.

schlechthin [ˈʃlɛçthɪn], adv. simply, plainly.

Schlechtigkeit [ˈʃlɛçtɪçkaɪt], f. (—, pl. —en) wickedness, baseness.

Schlegel [ˈʃleːgəl], m. (—s, pl. —) mallet; drumstick; (*bell*) clapper.

Schlehdorn [ˈʃleːdɔrn], m. (—s, pl. —e) blackthorn, sloe-tree.

schleichen [ˈʃlaɪçən], v.n. irr. (aux. sein) sneak, prowl, slink; *—de Krankheit,* lingering illness.

Schleichhandel [ˈʃlaɪçhandəl], m. (—s, pl. ⸚) smuggling, black marketeering.

Schleie [ˈʃlaɪə], f. (—, pl. —n) tench.

Schleier [ˈʃlaɪər], m. (—s, pl. —) veil.

Schleife [ˈʃlaɪfə], f. (—, pl. —n) bow, loop, noose.

schleifen [ˈʃlaɪfən], v.a. irr. drag along, trail; grind, polish, sharpen, whet, hone; cut.

Schleim [ʃlaɪm], m. (—(e)s, no pl.) slime, mucus, phlegm.

Schleimhaut [ˈʃlaɪmhaut], f. (—, pl. ⸚e) mucous membrane.

Schleimsuppe [ˈʃlaɪmzupə], f. (—, pl. —n) gruel.

schleißen [ˈʃlaɪsən], v.a. irr. split, slit; (*feathers*) strip.

schlemmen [ˈʃlɛmən], v.n. carouse, gormandise.

schlendern [ˈʃlɛndərn], v.n. (aux. sein) saunter along, stroll.

Schlendrian [ˈʃlɛndriaːn], m. (—s, no pl.) old jog-trot, routine.

schlenkern [ˈʃlɛŋkərn], v.a. dangle, swing.

Schleppdampfer [ˈʃlɛpdampfər], m. (—s, pl. —) steam-tug, tug-boat, tow-boat.

Schleppe [ˈʃlɛpə], f. (—, pl. —n) train (of a dress).

schleppen [ˈʃlɛpən], v.a. carry (s.th. heavy), drag, tow.

Schleppträger [ˈʃlɛpɛntrɛːgər], m. (—s, pl. —) train-bearer.

Schleppnetz [ˈʃlɛpnɛts], n. (—es, pl. —e) dragnet.

Schlesien [ˈʃleːzjən], n. Silesia.

Schleuder [ˈʃlɔydər], f. (—, pl. —n) sling; catapult.

schleudern [ˈʃlɔydərn], v.a. sling, throw, fling away. — v.n. (*Motor.*) skid; (*Comm.*) sell cheaply, undersell.

189

schleunigst

schleunigst [ˈʃlɔynɪçst], *adv.* very quickly, with the utmost expedition, promptly.
Schleuse [ˈʃlɔyzə], *f.* (—, *pl.* —n) sluice, flood-gate, lock.
Schlich [ʃlɪç], *m.* (—es, *pl.* —e) trick, dodge; *einem hinter seine —e kommen*, be up to s.o.'s tricks.
schlicht [ʃlɪçt], *adj.* plain, simple, homely; *—er Abschied*, curt dismissal.
schlichten [ˈʃlɪçtən], *v.a.* level; (*argument*) settle; adjust, compose.
Schlichtheit [ˈʃlɪçthaɪt], *f.* (—, *no pl.*) plainness, simplicity, homeliness.
schließen [ˈʃliːsən], *v.a. irr.* shut, close; contract; *etwas — aus*, conclude s.th. from; (*meeting*) close; *Frieden —*, make peace; *einen in die Arme —*, embrace s.o.; *etwas in sich —*, imply, entail.
Schließer [ˈʃliːsər], *m.* (—s, *pl.* —) doorkeeper; (*prison*) jailer, turnkey.
schließlich [ˈʃliːslɪç], *adv.* lastly, finally, in conclusion.
Schliff [ʃlɪf], *m.* (—(e)s, *no pl.*) polish, refinement.
schlimm [ʃlɪm], *adj.* bad, evil, ill; sad; serious, sore; disagreeable; naughty; *um so —er*, so much the worse, worse luck.
Schlinge [ˈʃlɪŋə], *f.* (—, *pl.* —n) loop, knot; noose, snare.
Schlingel [ˈʃlɪŋəl], *m.* (—s, *pl.* —) little rascal.
schlingen [ˈʃlɪŋən], *v.a. irr.* sling, wind; swallow, devour.
Schlips [ʃlɪps], *m.* (—es, *pl.* —e) (neck-)tie, cravat.
Schlitten [ˈʃlɪtən], *m.* (—s, *pl.* —) sledge, sled, sleigh.
Schlittschuh [ˈʃlɪtʃuː], *m.* (—s, *pl.* —e) skate; *— laufen*, skate.
Schlitz [ʃlɪts], *m.* (—es, *pl.* —e) slit.
schlohweiß [ˈʃloːvaɪs], *adj.* white as sloe-blossom, snow-white.
Schloß [ʃlɔs], *n.* (—sses, *pl.* ⸚sser) (*door*) lock, padlock; (*gun*) lock; palace, castle; *unter — und Riegel*, under lock and key.
Schloße [ˈʃloːsə], *f.* (—, *pl.* —n) hailstone.
Schlosser [ˈʃlɔsər], *m.* (—s, *pl.* —) locksmith.
Schlot [ʃloːt], *m.* (—(e)s, *pl.* —e) chimney, funnel.
schlottern [ˈʃlɔtərn], *v.n.* wobble, dodder; tremble.
Schlucht [ʃluxt], *f.* (—, *pl.* —en) deep valley, defile, cleft, glen, ravine, gorge.
schluchzen [ˈʃluxtsən], *v.n.* sob.
schlucken [ˈʃlukən], *v.a.* gulp down, swallow. *— v.n.* hiccup.
Schlucker [ˈʃlukər], *m.* (—s, *pl.* —) *armer —*, poor wretch.
Schlummer [ˈʃlumər], *m.* (—s, *no pl.*) slumber.
Schlumpe [ˈʃlumpə], *f.* (—, *pl.* —n) slut, slattern.

Schlund [ʃlunt], *m.* (—(e)s, *pl.* ⸚e) throat, gorge, gullet; gulf, abyss.
schlüpfen [ˈʃlypfən], *v.n.* (*aux.* sein) slip, slide, glide.
Schlüpfer [ˈʃlypfər], *m. pl.* knickers.
schlüpfrig [ˈʃlypfrɪç], *adj.* slippery; (*fig.*) obscene, indecent.
schlürfen [ˈʃlyrfən], *v.a.* drink noisily, lap up. *— v.n.* (*aux.* sein) (*dial.*) shuffle along.
Schluß [ʃlus], *m.* (—sses, *pl.* ⸚sse) end, termination; conclusion.
Schlüssel [ˈʃlysəl], *m.* (—s, *pl.* —) key; (*Mus.*) clef.
Schlüsselbein [ˈʃlysəlbaɪn], *n.* (—s, *pl.* —e) collar-bone.
Schlüsselblume [ˈʃlysəlbluːmə], *f.* (—, *pl.* —n) (*Bot.*) cowslip, primrose.
Schlußfolgerung [ˈʃlusfɔlgəruŋ], *f.* (—, *pl.* —en) conclusion, inference, deduction.
schlüssig [ˈʃlysɪç], *adj.* resolved, determined; sure; (*Law*) well-grounded; *sich — werden über*, resolve on.
Schmach [ʃmaːx], *f.* (—, *no pl.*) disgrace, ignominy.
schmachten [ˈʃmaxtən], *v.n.* languish, pine.
schmächtig [ˈʃmɛçtɪç], *adj.* slender, slim, spare.
schmackhaft [ˈʃmakhaft], *adj.* tasty, savoury.
schmähen [ˈʃmɛːən], *v.a.* revile, abuse, calumniate.
Schmähschrift [ˈʃmɛːʃrɪft], *f.* (—, *pl.* —en) lampoon.
schmal [ʃmaːl], *adj.* narrow.
schmälen [ˈʃmɛːlən], *v.a.* chide, scold.
schmälern [ˈʃmɛːlərn], *v.a.* lessen, diminish, curtail; detract from, belittle.
Schmalz [ʃmalts], *n.* (—es, *no pl.*) grease, lard, fat.
schmarotzen [ʃmaˈrɔtsən], *v.n.* sponge on others.
Schmarren [ˈʃmarən], *m.* (—s, *pl.* —) trash; (*dial.*) omelette.
Schmatz [ʃmats], *m.* (—es, *pl.* ⸚e) (*dial.*) smacking kiss.
schmauchen [ˈʃmauxən], *v.a., v.n.* smoke.
Schmaus [ʃmaus], *m.* (—es, *pl.* —e) feast, banquet.
schmecken [ˈʃmɛkən], *v.a.* taste. *— v.n.* taste; *es schmeckt mir*, I like it.
Schmeichelei [ʃmaɪçəˈlaɪ], *f.* (—, *pl.* —en) flattery, adulation.
schmeicheln [ˈʃmaɪçəln], *v.n.* flatter; fondle, pet.
schmeißen [ˈʃmaɪsən], *v.a. irr.* throw, hurl, fling; (*sl.*) *ich werde die Sache schon —*, I shall pull it off.
Schmeißfliege [ˈʃmaɪsfliːgə], *f.* (—, *pl.* —n) (*Ent.*) bluebottle.
Schmelz [ʃmɛlts], *m.* (—es, *no pl.*) enamel; melting; (*voice*) mellowness.
schmelzbar [ˈʃmɛltsbaːr], *adj.* fusible.
schmelzen [ˈʃmɛltsən], *v.a. irr.* smelt, melt. *— v.n.* (*aux.* sein) (*ice*) melt; (*fig.*) decrease, diminish.

schnellen

Schmelztiegel [ˈʃmɛltsti:gəl], *m.* (—s, *pl.* —) crucible; melting pot.
Schmelztopf [ˈʃmɛltstɔpf], *m. see* **Schmelztiegel.**
Schmerbauch [ˈʃme:rbaux], *m.* (—(e)s, *pl.* ⁻e) (*coll.*) paunch, belly.
Schmerz [ʃmɛrts], *m.* (—es, *pl.* —en) ache, pain; grief, sorrow; *einem —en verursachen*, give *or* cause s.o. pain.
schmerzlich [ˈʃmɛrtslɪç], *adj.* painful, distressing.
Schmetterling [ˈʃmɛtərlɪŋ], *m.* (—s, *pl.* —e) (*Ent.*) butterfly, moth.
schmettern [ˈʃmɛtərn], *v.n.* resound; (*trumpets*) blare; (*bird*) warble.
Schmied [ʃmi:t], *m.* (—s, *pl.* —e) (black)smith.
Schmiede [ˈʃmi:də], *f.* (—, *pl.* —n) forge, smithy.
schmiegen [ˈʃmi:gən], *v.r. sich —,* bend, yield; *sich an einen —,* cling to s.o., nestle against s.o.
Schmiere [ˈʃmi:rə], *f.* (—, *pl.* —n) grease, salve; (*Theat.*) troop of strolling players.
schmieren [ˈʃmi:rən], *v.a.* smear, grease, spread; (*fig.*) bribe; (*bread*) butter. — *v.n.* scrawl, scribble.
Schmierfink [ˈʃmi:rfɪŋk], *m.* (—en, *pl.* —en) dirty person; muckraker.
Schmiermittel [ˈʃmi:rmɪtəl], *n.* (—s, *pl.* —) lubricant.
Schmierseife [ˈʃmi:rzaɪfə], *f.* (—, *no pl.*) soft soap.
Schminke [ˈʃmɪŋkə], *f.* (—, *pl.* —n) greasepaint; rouge; make-up, cosmetics.
Schmirgel [ˈʃmɪrgəl], *m.* (—s, *no pl.*) emery.
Schmiß [ʃmɪs], *m.* (—sses, *pl.* —sse) cut in the face, (duelling) scar; (*fig.*) smartness, verve.
Schmöker [ˈʃmøːkər], *m.* (—s, *pl.* —) trashy book.
schmollen [ˈʃmɔlən], *v.n.* sulk, pout.
Schmorbraten [ˈʃmoːrbraːtən], *m.* (—s, *pl.* —) stewed meat.
Schmuck [ʃmuk], *m.* (—(e)s, *pl.* —stücke) ornament, jewels, jewellery; (*Am.*) jewelry.
schmuck [ʃmuk], *adj.* neat, spruce, dapper, smart.
schmücken [ˈʃmykən], *v.a.* adorn, embellish.
Schmucksachen [ˈʃmukzaxən], *f. pl.* jewels, finery, jewellery, articles of adornment; (*Am.*) jewelry.
schmuggeln [ˈʃmugəln], *v.a.* smuggle.
schmunzeln [ˈʃmuntsəln], *v.n.* smirk, grin.
Schmutz [ʃmuts], *m.* (—es, *no pl.*) dirt, filth.
schmutzen [ˈʃmutsən], *v.n.* get soiled, get dirty.
Schmutzkonkurrenz [ˈʃmutskɔnkurɛnts], *f.* (—, *no pl.*) unfair competition.
Schnabel [ˈʃnaːbəl], *m.* (—s, *pl.* ⁻) bill, beak; (*ship*) prow; *halt den —,* keep your mouth shut; *er spricht, wie ihm*

der — gewachsen ist, he calls a spade a spade.
Schnabeltier [ˈʃnaːbəltiːr], *n.* (—s, *pl.* —e) duck-bill, duck-billed platypus.
Schnaderhüpfel [ˈʃnaːdərhypfəl], *n.* (—s, *pl.* —) (*dial.*) Alpine folk-song.
Schnalle [ˈʃnalə], *f.* (—, *pl.* —n) buckle.
schnalzen [ˈʃnaltsən], *v.n.* click; snap.
schnappen [ˈʃnapən], *v.n.* snap; snatch at s.th.; *nach Luft —,* gasp for breath.
Schnaps [ʃnaps], *m.* (—es, *pl.* ⁻e) spirits, brandy, gin.
schnarchen [ˈʃnarçən], *v.n.* snore.
Schnarre [ˈʃnarə], *f.* (—, *pl.* —n) rattle.
schnattern [ˈʃnatərn], *v.n.* cackle; gabble; chatter.
schnauben [ˈʃnaubən], *v.n.* puff and blow; snort; *vor Zorn —,* fret and fume.
schnaufen [ˈʃnaufən], *v.n.* breathe heavily, pant.
Schnauze [ˈʃnautsə], *f.* (—, *pl.* —n) (*animals*) snout; (*vulg.*) mouth, trap; nozzle.
schnauzen [ˈʃnautsən], *v.n.* snarl, shout (at).
Schnecke [ˈʃnɛkə], *f.* (—, *pl.* —n), (*Zool.*) snail, slug.
Schnee [ʃne:], *m.* (—s, *no pl.*) snow.
Schneegestöber [ˈʃne:gəʃtøːbər], *n.* (—s, *pl.* —) snow-storm.
Schneeglöckchen [ˈʃne:glœkçən], *n.* (—s, *pl.* —) (*Bot.*) snowdrop.
Schneeschläger [ˈʃne:ʃlɛːgər], *m.* (—s, *pl.* —) whisk.
Schneetreiben [ˈʃne:traɪbən], *n.* (—s, *no pl.*) snow-storm, blizzard.
Schneewittchen [ˈʃne:vɪtçən], *n.* (—s, *no pl.*) Snow White.
Schneid [ʃnaɪt], *m.* (—s, *no pl.*) go, push, dash, courage.
Schneide [ˈʃnaɪdə], *f.* (—, *pl.* —n) edge.
Schneidebohne [ˈʃnaɪdəboːnə], *f.* (—, *pl.* —n) French bean, string-bean.
Schneidemühle [ˈʃnaɪdəmyːlə], *f.* (—, *pl.* —n) saw mill.
schneiden [ˈʃnaɪdən], *v.a. irr.* cut, trim, carve; (*fig.*) ignore, cut; *Gesichter —,* make faces. — *v.r. sich —,* cut o.s.; (*Maths.*) intersect; *sich die Haare — lassen,* have o.'s hair cut.
Schneider [ˈʃnaɪdər], *m.* (—s, *pl.* —) tailor.
Schneiderei [ʃnaɪdəˈraɪ], *f.* (—, *no pl.*) tailoring; dressmaking.
Schneidezahn [ˈʃnaɪdətsaːn], *m.* (—s, *pl.* ⁻e) incisor.
schneidig [ˈʃnaɪdɪç], *adj.* dashing.
schneien [ˈʃnaɪən], *v.n.* snow.
Schneise [ˈʃnaɪzə], *f.* (—, *pl.* —n) (*forest*) glade, cutting.
schnell [ʃnɛl], *adj.* quick, swift, speedy, fast, rapid; *mach —,* hurry up.
Schnelle [ˈʃnɛlə], *f.* (—, *pl.* —n) (*river*) rapids.
schnellen [ˈʃnɛlən], *v.n.* spring, jump.

191

Schnelligkeit [ˈʃnɛliçkaɪt], f. (—, no pl.) quickness, speed, swiftness, rapidity; (Tech.) velocity.

Schnepfe [ˈʃnɛpfə], f. (—, pl. —n) (Orn.) snipe, woodcock.

schneuzen [ˈʃnɔytsən], v.r. sich (die Nase) —, blow o.'s nose.

schniegeln [ˈʃniːɡəln], v.r. sich —, (coll.) dress up, deck out; geschniegelt und gebügelt, spick and span.

Schnippchen [ˈʃnɪpçən], n. (—s, pl. —) einem ein — schlagen, play a trick on s.o.

schnippisch [ˈʃnɪpɪʃ], adj. pert, perky.

Schnitt [ʃnɪt], m. (—(e)s, pl. —e) cut, incision; (beer) small glass; (dress) cut-out pattern; (book) edge.

Schnittbohne [ˈʃnɪtboːnə], f. (—, pl. —n) (Bot.) French bean.

Schnitte [ˈʃnɪtə], f. (—, pl. —n) slice (of bread).

Schnitter [ˈʃnɪtər], m. (—s, pl. —) reaper.

Schnittlauch [ˈʃnɪtlaux], m. (—s, no pl.) (Bot.) chives.

Schnittmuster [ˈʃnɪtmustər], n. (—s, pl. —) cut-out pattern.

Schnittwaren [ˈʃnɪtvaːrən], f. pl. dry goods, drapery.

Schnitzel [ˈʃnɪtsəl], n. (—s, pl. —) (Cul.) cutlet; Wiener —, veal cutlet; snip; (pl.) shavings.

schnitzen [ˈʃnɪtsən], v.a. carve (in wood).

schnodd(e)rig [ˈʃnɔd(ə)rɪç], adj. (coll.) cheeky, insolent.

schnöde [ˈʃnøːdə], adj. base, heinous, mean, vile; —r Mammon, filthy lucre; —r Undank, rank ingratitude.

Schnörkel [ˈʃnœrkəl], m. (—s, pl. —) (writing) flourish.

schnorren [ˈʃnɔrən], v.n. (rare) cadge, beg.

schnüffeln [ˈʃnyfəln], v.n. sniff; (fig.) pry, snoop.

Schnuller [ˈʃnulər], m. (—s, pl. —) baby's dummy; (Am.) pacifier.

Schnupfen [ˈʃnupfən], m. (—s, pl. —) cold (in the head); den — haben, have a (running) cold; den — bekommen, catch cold.

schnupfen [ˈʃnupfən], v.a., v.n. take snuff.

Schnupftuch [ˈʃnupftuːx], n. (—(e)s, pl. ˙er) (dial.) (pocket-) handkerchief.

schnuppe [ˈʃnupə], adj. (sl.) mir ist alles —, it is all the same to me, I don't care.

schnuppern [ˈʃnupərn], v.n. smell, snuffle.

Schnur [ʃnuːr], f. (—, pl. —en, ˙e) twine, cord, string; (Elec.) lead, extension cord.

Schnurrbart [ˈʃnurbaːrt], m. (—s, pl. ˙e) moustache; sich einen — wachsen lassen, grow a moustache.

Schnürchen [ˈʃnyːrçən], n. (—s, pl. —) wie am —, like clockwork.

schnüren [ˈʃnyːrən], v.a. lace, tie up; sein Ränzel —, pack o.'s bag.

Schnurre [ˈʃnurə], f. (—, pl. —n) funny story, yarn.

schnurren [ˈʃnurən], v.n. purr.

Schnürsenkel [ˈʃnyːrzɛŋkəl], m. (—s, pl. —) (shoe) lace.

schnurstracks [ˈʃnuːrʃtraks], adv. directly, immediately, on the spot.

Schober [ˈʃoːbər], m. (—s, pl. —) stack, rick.

Schock (1) [ʃɔk], n. (—(e)s, pl. —e) sixty, three score.

Schock (2) [ʃɔk], m. (—(e)s, pl. —s) shock; blow; stroke.

Schöffe [ˈʃœfə], m. (—n, pl. —n) (Law) juror; member of jury.

Schokolade [ʃokoˈlaːdə], f. (—, pl. —n) chocolate; eine Tafel —, a bar of chocolate.

Scholle [ˈʃɔlə], f. (—, pl. —n) plaice; (ice) floe; clod; soil.

schon [ʃoːn], adv. already; indeed; yet; na wenn —, so what; — gut, that'll do; — gestern, as early as yesterday.

schön [ʃøːn], adj. beautiful, fair, handsome, lovely; —e Literatur, belles-lettres, good books.

schonen [ˈʃoːnən], v.a. spare, save; treat considerately.

Schoner [ˈʃoːnər], m. (—s, pl. —) antimacassar; (Naut.) schooner.

Schönheit [ˈʃøːnhaɪt], f. (—, no pl.) beauty.

Schonung [ˈʃoːnuŋ], f. (—, pl. —en) forbearance, considerate treatment; (forest) plantation of young trees.

Schonzeit [ˈʃoːntsaɪt], f. (—, pl. —en) close season.

Schopf [ʃɔpf], m. (—es, pl. ˙e) tuft, head of hair; (bird) crest; das Glück beim —e fassen, take time by the forelock, make hay while the sun shines.

Schöpfbrunnen [ˈʃœpfbrunən], m. (—s, pl. —) (draw-)well.

schöpfen [ˈʃœpfən], v.a. (water) draw; derive; Verdacht —, become suspicious; frische Luft —, get a breath of fresh air; Mut —, take heart.

Schöpfer [ˈʃœpfər], m. (—s, pl. —) creator.

Schöpfkelle [ˈʃœpfkɛlə], f. (—, pl. —n) scoop.

Schopflerche [ˈʃɔpflɛrçə], f. (—, pl. —n) (Orn.) crested lark.

Schöpfung [ˈʃœpfuŋ], f. (—, pl. —en) creation.

Schoppen [ˈʃɔpən], m. (—s, pl. —) (approx.) half a pint.

Schöps [ʃœps], m. (—es, pl. —e) (Zool.) wether; (fig.) simpleton.

Schorf [ʃɔrf], m. (—(e)s, pl. —e) scab, scurf.

Schornstein [ˈʃɔrnʃtaɪn], m. (—s, pl. —e) chimney; (ship) funnel.

Schoß [ʃoːs], m. (—es, pl. ˙e) lap; (Poet.) womb; skirt, tail; die Hände in den — legen, be idle, fold o.'s arms, twiddle o.'s thumbs.

schuldig

Schößling ['ʃœslɪŋ], *m.* (—s, *pl.* —e) shoot, sprig.

Schote ['ʃoːtə], *f.* (—, *pl.* —n) pod, husk, shell; (*pl.*) green peas.

Schotter ['ʃɔtər], *m.* (—s, *no pl.*) road-metal, broken stones, gravel.

Schottland ['ʃɔtlant], *n.* Scotland.

schraffieren [ʃraˈfiːrən], *v.a.* (*Art*) hatch.

schräg [ʃrɛːk], *adj.* oblique, sloping, slanting, diagonal.

Schramme ['ʃramə], *f.* (—, *pl.* —n) scratch, scar.

Schrank [ʃraŋk], *m.* (—(e)s, *pl.* ⁻e) cupboard, wardrobe.

Schranken ['ʃraŋkən], *f. pl.* barriers, (level crossing) gates, limits, bounds; *in — halten*, limit, keep within bounds.

schränken ['ʃrɛŋkən], *v.a.* cross; fold.

Schranze ['ʃrantsə], *m.* (—n, *pl.* —n) sycophant, toady.

Schraube ['ʃraubə], *f.* (—, *pl.* —n) screw; bolt; propeller.

Schraubengewinde ['ʃraubəngəvɪndə], *n.* (—s, *pl.* —) thread of a screw.

Schraubenmutter ['ʃraubənmutər], *f.* (—, *pl.* —n) female screw, nut.

Schraubenzieher ['ʃraubəntsiːər], *m.* (—s, *pl.* —) screw-driver.

Schraubstock ['ʃraupʃtɔk], *m.* (—s, *pl.* ⁻e) (*tool*) vise.

Schreck(en) ['ʃrɛk(ən)], *m.* (—s, *pl.* —) fright, terror, alarm, horror; shock.

Schrecknis ['ʃrɛknɪs], *n.* (—ses, *pl.* —se) terror, horror.

Schrei [ʃraɪ], *m.* (—s, *pl.* —e) cry; scream.

Schreiben ['ʃraɪbən], *n.* (—s, *pl.* —) letter, missive.

schreiben ['ʃraɪbən], *v.a. irr.* write; *ins Reine —*, make a fair copy.

Schreibfehler ['ʃraɪpfeːlər], *m.* (—s, *pl.* —) slip of the pen.

Schreibkrampf ['ʃraɪpkrampf], *m.* (—(e)s, *pl.* ⁻e) writer's cramp.

Schreibmaschine ['ʃraɪpmaʃiːnə], *f.* (—, *pl.* —n) typewriter.

Schreibwaren ['ʃraɪpvaːrən], *f. pl.* stationery.

Schreibweise ['ʃraɪpvaɪzə], *f.* (— *pl.* —n) style; spelling.

schreien ['ʃraɪən], *v.a., v.n. irr.* cry, shout, scream, yell.

Schreihals ['ʃraɪhals], *m.* (—es, *pl.* ⁻e) cry-baby, noisy child.

Schrein [ʃraɪn], *m.* (—(e)s, *pl.* —e) box, chest; shrine.

schreiten ['ʃraɪtən], *v.n. irr.* (*aux.* sein) stride, step, pace.

Schrift [ʃrɪft], *f.* (—, *pl.* —en) writing; handwriting, calligraphy; publication; type; *Heilige —*, Holy Writ, Holy Scripture.

Schriftführer ['ʃrɪftfyːrər], *m.* (—s, *pl.* —) secretary.

Schriftgießerei ['ʃrɪftgiːsəraɪ], *f.* (—, *pl.* —en) type-foundry.

Schriftleiter ['ʃrɪftlaɪtər], *m.* (—s, *pl.* —) editor.

schriftlich ['ʃrɪftlɪç], *adj.* written. — *adv.* in writing, by letter.

Schriftsetzer ['ʃrɪftzetsər], *m.* (—s, *pl.* —) compositor.

Schriftsteller ['ʃrɪftʃtɛlər], *m.* (—s, *pl.* —) writer, author.

Schriftstück ['ʃrɪftʃtyk], *n.* (—s, *pl.* —e) document, deed.

Schriftwechsel ['ʃrɪftvɛksəl], *m.* (—s, *no pl.*) exchange of notes, correspondence.

Schriftzeichen ['ʃrɪftsaɪçən], *n.* (—s, *pl.* —) character, letter (of alphabet).

schrill [ʃrɪl], *adj.* shrill.

Schritt [ʃrɪt], *m.* (—(e)s, *pl.* —e) step, pace, move; *lange —e machen*, stride; *— halten*, keep pace; *— fahren*, drive slowly, drive at walking pace; *aus dem —*, out of step; *in einer Sache —e tun*, make a move or take steps about s.th.

schrittweise ['ʃrɪtvaɪzə], *adv.* step by step, gradually.

schroff ['ʃrɔf], *adj.* steep, precipitous; (*fig.*) gruff, blunt, rough, harsh.

schröpfen ['ʃrœpfən], *v.a.* (*Med.*) cup; (*fig.*) fleece.

Schrot [ʃroːt], *m. & n.* (—(e)s, *pl.* —e) grape-shot, small shot; *ein Mann vom alten —*, a man of the utmost probity.

Schrotbrot ['ʃroːtbroːt], *n.* (—es, *no pl.*) wholemeal bread.

Schrott [ʃrɔt], *m.* (—(e)s, *pl.* —e), old iron, scrap metal.

Schrulle ['ʃrulə], *f.* (—, *pl.* —n) fad, whim.

schrumpfen ['ʃrumpfən], *v.n.* (*aux.* sein) shrink, shrivel.

Schub [ʃup], *m.* (—s, *pl.* ⁻e) shove, push; batch.

Schubkarren ['ʃupkarən], *m.* (—s, *pl.* —) wheelbarrow.

Schublade ['ʃuplaːdə], *f.* (—, *pl.* —n) drawer.

schüchtern ['ʃyçtərn], *adj.* shy, bashful, timid.

Schuft [ʃuft], *m.* (—(e)s, *pl.* —e) blackguard, scoundrel.

schuften ['ʃuftən], *v.n.* work hard, toil.

Schufterei [ʃuftəˈraɪ], *f.* (—, *no pl.*) drudgery.

schuftig ['ʃuftɪç], *adj.* rascally, mean.

Schuh [ʃuː], *m.* (—s, *pl.* —e) shoe; *einem etwas in die —e schieben*, lay the blame at s.o.'s door.

Schuhwerk ['ʃuːvɛrk], *n.* (—s, *no pl.*) footwear.

Schuhwichse ['ʃuːvɪksə], *f.* (—, *no pl.*) shoe-polish.

Schuld [ʃult], *f.* (—, *pl.* —en) guilt, offence, sin; fault; blame; cause; (*money*) debt; *in —en geraten*, run into debt.

schuld [ʃult], *adj. ich bin —*, it is my fault, I am to blame.

schulden ['ʃuldən], *v.a.* owe, be indebted to.

schuldig ['ʃuldɪç], *adj.* guilty, culpable; *sich — bekennen*, plead guilty; *einen — sprechen*, pronounce s.o. guilty;

193

ihm ist Anerkennung —, appreciation is due to him.

Schuldigkeit [ˈʃuldɪçkaɪt], *f.* (—, *no pl.*) obligation, duty.

schuldlos [ˈʃultloːs], *adj.* innocent, guiltless.

Schuldner [ˈʃuldnər], *m.* (—s, *pl.* —) debtor.

Schule [ˈʃuːlə], *f.* (—, *pl.* —n) school; *in die — gehen,* go to school, attend school; *die — schwänzen,* play truant; *hohe —,* (*Riding*) advanced horsemanship.

schulen [ˈʃuːlən], *v.a.* train, instruct.

Schüler [ˈʃyːlər], *m.* (—s, *pl.* —) schoolboy, pupil, student, scholar.

Schulklasse [ˈʃuːlklasə], *f.* (—, *pl.* —n) class, form.

Schulleiter [ˈʃuːllaɪtər], *m.* (—s, *pl.* —) headmaster.

Schulrat [ˈʃuːlraːt], *m.* (—s, *pl.* ⁻e) school-inspector.

Schulter [ˈʃultər], *f.* (—, *pl.* —n) shoulder.

Schulterblatt [ˈʃultərblat], *n.* (—s, *pl.* ⁻er) shoulder-blade.

Schultheiß [ˈʃulthaɪs], *m.* (—en, *pl.* —en) village magistrate, mayor.

Schulunterricht [ˈʃuːluntərrɪçt], *m.* (—s, *no pl.*) school teaching, lessons.

schummeln [ˈʃuməln], *v.n.* (*coll.*) cheat.

Schund [ʃunt], *m.* (—(e)s, *no pl.*) trash.

Schuppe [ˈʃupə], *f.* (—, *pl.* —n) scale; (*pl.*) dandruff.

Schuppen [ˈʃupən], *m.* (—s, *pl.* —) shed.

Schuppentier [ˈʃupəntiːr], *n.* (—s, *pl.* —e) (*Zool.*) armadillo.

Schur [ʃuːr], *f.* (—, *pl.* —en) shearing.

schüren [ˈʃyːrən], *v.a.* (*fire*) poke, rake; (*fig.*) stir up, fan, incite.

schürfen [ˈʃyrfən], *v.a.* scratch. — *v.n.* (*Min.*) prospect.

schurigeln [ˈʃuːrɪgəln], *v.a.* bully, pester.

Schurke [ˈʃurkə], *m.* (—n, *pl.* —n) scoundrel, villain, blackguard.

Schurz [ʃurts], *m.* (—es, *pl.* —e) apron, overall.

Schürze [ˈʃyrtsə], *f.* (—, *pl.* —n) apron, pinafore.

schürzen [ˈʃyrtsən], *v.a.* tuck up, pin up.

Schürzenjäger [ˈʃyrtsənjɛːgər], *m.* (—s, *pl.* —) ladies' man.

Schurzfell [ˈʃurtsfɛl], *n.* (—s, *pl.* —e) leather apron.

Schuß [ʃus], *m.* (—sses, *pl.* ⁻sse) shot, report; dash; *weit vom —,* out of harm's way; wide of the mark.

Schüssel [ˈʃysəl], *f.* (—, *pl.* —n) dish.

Schußwaffe [ˈʃusvafə], *f.* (—, *pl.* —n) fire-arm.

Schuster [ˈʃuːstər], *m.* (—s, *pl.* —) shoemaker, cobbler; *auf —s Rappen,* on Shanks's pony.

schustern [ˈʃuːstərn], *v.n.* cobble, make or mend shoes.

Schutt [ʃut], *m.* (—(e)s, *no pl.*) rubbish, refuse; rubble; *— abladen,* dump refuse.

Schütte [ˈʃytə], *f.* (—, *pl.* —n) (*dial.*) bundle, truss.

schütteln [ˈʃytəln], *v.a.* shake, jolt.

schütten [ˈʃytən], *v.a.* shoot, pour; pour out.

schütter [ˈʃytər], *adj.* (*dial.*) (*hair*) thin; scarce.

Schutz [ʃuts], *m.* (—es, *no pl.*) protection, shelter, cover; *einen in — nehmen gegen,* defend s.o. against.

Schutzbefohlene [ˈʃutsbəfoːlənə], *m.* (—n, *pl.* —n) charge, person in o.'s care, ward.

Schutzbündnis [ˈʃutsbyntnɪs], *n.* (—ses, *pl.* —se) defensive alliance.

Schütze [ˈʃytsə], *m.* (—n, *pl.* —n) rifleman, sharpshooter, marksman; (*Astrol.*) Sagittarius.

schützen [ˈʃytsən], *v.a.* protect, shelter, defend. — *v.r. sich — vor,* guard o.s. against.

Schützengraben [ˈʃytsəngraːbən], *m.* (—s, *pl.* —) trench.

Schutzgebiet [ˈʃutsgəbiːt], *n.* (—s, *pl.* —e) protectorate.

Schutzgitter [ˈʃutsgɪtər], *n.* (—s, *pl.* —) grid, guard.

Schutzheilige [ˈʃutshaɪlɪgə], *m.* (—n, *pl.* —n) patron saint.

Schützling [ˈʃytslɪŋ], *m.* (—s, *pl.* —e) protégé, charge.

Schutzmann [ˈʃutsman], *m.* (—s, *pl.* ⁻er, **Schutzleute**) policeman, constable.

Schutzmarke [ˈʃutsmarkə], *f.* (—, *pl.* —n) trade-mark.

Schutzzoll [ˈʃutstsɔl], *m.* (—s, *pl.* ⁻e) protective duty, tariff.

Schwaben [ˈʃvaːbən], *n.* Swabia.

Schwabenstreich [ˈʃvaːbənʃtraɪç], *m.* (—s, *pl.* —e) tomfoolery.

schwach [ʃvax], *adj.* weak, frail, feeble; (*noise*) faint; (*pulse*) low; *—e Seite,* foible; *—e Stunde,* unguarded moment.

Schwäche [ˈʃvɛçə], *f.* (—, *pl.* —n) weakness, faintness; infirmity.

schwächen [ˈʃvɛçən], *v.a.* weaken, debilitate.

Schwächling [ˈʃvɛçlɪŋ], *m.* (—s, *pl.* —e) weakling.

Schwachsinn [ˈʃvaxzɪn], *m.* (—s, *no pl.*) feeble-mindedness.

Schwächung [ˈʃvɛçuŋ], *f.* (—, *pl.* —en) weakening, lessening.

Schwadron [ʃvaˈdroːn], *f.* (—, *pl.* —en) squadron.

Schwadroneur [ʃvadroˈnøːr], *m.* (—s, *pl.* —e) swaggerer.

schwadronieren [ʃvadroˈniːrən], *v.n.* talk big, swagger.

schwafeln [ˈʃvaːfəln], *v.n.* (*sl.*) talk nonsense, waffle.

Schwager [ˈʃvaːgər], *m.* (—s, *pl.* ⁻) brother-in-law.

Schwägerin [ˈʃvɛːgərɪn], *f.* (—, *pl.* —nen) sister-in-law.

Schwalbe [ˈʃvalbə], *f.* (—, *pl.* —n) (*Orn.*) swallow.

Schwellung

Schwalbenschwanz [ˈʃvalbənʃvants], *m.* (—es, *pl.* ⸚e) (*butterfly*) swallow's tail; (*joinery*) dovetail.

Schwall [ʃval], *m.* (—(e)s, *no pl.*) flood; (*fig.*) deluge, torrent.

Schwamm [ʃvam], *m.* (—(e)s, *pl.* ⸚e) sponge; fungus, mushroom; dry rot.

schwammig [ˈʃvamɪç], *adj.* spongy, fungous.

Schwan [ʃvaːn], *m.* (—(e)s, *pl.* ⸚e) swan; *junger* —, cygnet.

schwanen [ˈʃvaːnən], *v.n. imp.* es *schwant mir*, I have a foreboding.

Schwang [ʃvaŋ], *m. im* —e *sein*, be in fashion, be the rage.

schwanger [ˈʃvaŋər], *adj.* pregnant.

schwängern [ˈʃvɛŋərn], *v.a.* make pregnant, get with child; (*fig.*) impregnate.

Schwangerschaft [ˈʃvaŋərʃaft], *f.* (—, *pl.* —en) pregnancy.

Schwank [ʃvaŋk], *m.* (—(e)s, *pl.* ⸚e) funny story, joke; (*Theat.*) farce.

schwank [ʃvaŋk], *adj.* flexible, supple; *ein* —es *Rohr*, a reed shaken by the wind.

schwanken [ˈʃvaŋkən], *v.n.* totter, stagger; (*fig.*) waver, vacillate; (*prices*) fluctuate.

Schwanz [ʃvants], *m.* (—es, *pl.* ⸚e) tail.

schwänzeln [ˈʃvɛntsəln], *v.n.* (*animal*) wag the tail; (*fig.*) fawn, cringe.

schwänzen [ˈʃvɛntsən], *v.a. die Schule* —, play truant.

Schwären [ˈʃvɛːrən], *m.* (—s, *pl.* —) ulcer, abscess.

schwären [ˈʃvɛːrən], *v.n.* fester, suppurate.

Schwarm [ʃvarm], *m.* (—(e)s, *pl.* ⸚e) (*insects*) swarm; (*humans*) crowd; (*birds*) flight.

Schwärmerei [ʃvɛrməˈraɪ], *f.* (—, *pl.* —en) enthusiasm, passion, craze.

Schwarte [ˈʃvartə], *f.* (—, *pl.* —n) rind; crust; *alte* —, (*fig.*) old volume; tome.

schwarz [ʃvarts], *adj.* black.

Schwarzamsel [ˈʃvartsamzəl], *f.* (—, *pl.* —n) (*Orn.*) blackbird.

Schwarzdorn [ˈʃvartsdɔrn], *m.* (—s, *no pl.*) (*Bot.*) blackthorn, sloe.

Schwärze [ˈʃvɛrtsə], *f.* (—, *no pl.*) blackness; printer's ink.

schwärzen [ˈʃvɛrtsən], *v.a.* blacken.

Schwarzkünstler [ˈʃvartskynstlər], *m.* (—s, *pl.* —) magician, necromancer.

Schwarzwald [ˈʃvartsvalt], *m.* Black Forest.

Schwarzwild [ˈʃvartsvɪlt], *n.* (—(e)s, *no pl.*) wild boar.

schwatzen [ˈʃvatsən], *v.n.* chat, chatter, prattle.

Schwätzer [ˈʃvɛtsər], *m.* (—s, *pl.* —) chatterbox.

Schwatzhaftigkeit [ˈʃvatshaftɪçkaɪt], *f.* (—, *no pl.*) loquacity, talkativeness.

Schwebe [ˈʃveːbə], *f.* (—, *pl.* —n) suspense; suspension.

Schwebebaum [ˈʃveːbəbaum], *m.* (—s, *pl.* ⸚e) horizontal bar.

schweben [ˈʃveːbən], *v.n.* be suspended, hover; (*fig.*) be pending; *in Gefahr* —, be in danger; *es schwebt mir auf der Zunge*, it is on the tip of my tongue.

Schwede [ˈʃveːdə], *m.* (—n, *pl.* —n) Swede; *alter* —, (*fig.*) old boy.

Schweden [ˈʃveːdən], *n.* Sweden.

Schwedenhölzer [ˈʃveːdənhœltsər], *n. pl.* (*rare*) matches.

Schwefel [ˈʃveːfəl], *m.* (—s, *no pl.*) sulphur, brimstone.

Schwefelhölzchen [ˈʃveːfəlhœltsçən], *n.* (—s, *pl.* —) (*obs.*) match.

schwefeln [ˈʃveːfəln], *v.a.* impregnate with sulphur, fumigate.

Schwefelsäure [ˈʃveːfəlzɔyrə], *f.* (—, *no pl.*) sulphuric acid.

Schweif [ʃvaɪf], *m.* (—(e)s, *pl.* —e) tail.

schweifen [ˈʃvaɪfən], *v.n.* (*aux.* sein) ramble, stray, wander.

schweifwedeln [ˈʃvaɪfveːdəln], *v.n.* fawn.

Schweigegeld [ˈʃvaɪgəgɛlt], *n.* (—(e)s, *pl.* —er) (*coll.*) hush-money.

Schweigen [ˈʃvaɪgən], *n.* (—s, *no pl.*) silence.

schweigen [ˈʃvaɪgən], *v.n. irr.* be silent; be quiet; *ganz zu* — *von*, to say nothing of.

schweigsam [ˈʃvaɪkzaːm], *adj.* taciturn.

Schwein [ʃvaɪn], *n.* (—(e)s, *pl.* —e) pig, hog; swine; *wildes* —, boar; (*fig.*) luck, fluke; — *haben*, be lucky.

Schweinekoben [ˈʃvaɪnəkoːbən], *m.* (—s, *pl.* —) pigsty.

Schweinerei [ʃvaɪnəˈraɪ], *f.* (—, *pl.* —en) filth; (*fig.*) smut, filthiness, obscenity; mess.

Schweineschmalz [ˈʃvaɪnəʃmalts], *n.* (—es, *no pl.*) lard.

Schweinigel [ˈʃvaɪnɪgəl], *m.* (—s, *pl.* —) (*Zool.*) hedgehog, porcupine; (*fig.*) dirty pig, filthy wretch.

Schweinskeule [ˈʃvaɪnskɔylə], *f.* (—, *pl.* —n) leg of pork.

Schweiß [ʃvaɪs], *m.* (—es, *no pl.*) sweat, perspiration.

schweißen [ˈʃvaɪsən], *v.a.* weld, solder.

Schweiz [ʃvaɪts], *f.* Switzerland.

Schweizer [ˈʃvaɪtsər], *m.* (—s, *pl.* —) Swiss; (*fig.*) dairyman.

Schweizerei [ʃvaɪtsəˈraɪ], *f.* (—, *pl.* —en) dairy.

schwelen [ˈʃveːlən], *v.n.* burn slowly, smoulder.

schwelgen [ˈʃvɛlgən], *v.n.* carouse, revel.

Schwelgerei [ʃvɛlgəˈraɪ], *f.* (—, *pl.* —en) revelry.

schwelgerisch [ˈʃvɛlgərɪʃ], *adj.* luxurious, voluptuous.

Schwelle [ˈʃvɛlə], *f.* (—, *pl.* —n) threshold; (*Railw.*) sleeper, tie.

schwellen [ˈʃvɛlən], *v.n. irr.* (*aux.* sein) swell; (*water*) rise.

Schwellung [ˈʃvɛluŋ], *f.* (—, *pl.* —en) swelling.

195

schwemmen

schwemmen [ˈʃvɛmən], *v.a.* wash, soak, carry off.

Schwengel [ˈʃvɛnəl], *m.* (—s, *pl.* —) (*bell*) clapper; (*pump*) handle.

schwenken [ˈʃvɛnkən], *v.a.* swing; shake, brandish; (*glasses*) rinse.

Schwenkung [ˈʃvɛnkuŋ], *f.* (—, *pl.* —en) change; (*Mil.*) wheeling.

schwer [ʃveːr], *adj.* heavy; difficult, hard; ponderous; severe; — *von Begriff*, obtuse, slow in the uptake; —*e Speise*, indigestible food; *einem das Herz — machen*, grieve s.o.

schwerblütig [ˈʃveːrblyːtɪç], *adj.* phlegmatic.

Schwere [ˈʃveːrə], *f.* (—, *no pl.*) weight, heaviness; gravity.

Schwerenöter [ˈʃveːrənøːtər], *m.* (—s, *pl.* —) gay dog, ladies' man.

schwerfällig [ˈʃveːrfɛlɪç], *adj.* ungainly, cumbrous, unwieldy; (*fig.*) thick-headed, dense.

Schwergewicht [ˈʃveːrɡəvɪçt], *n.* (—s, *no pl.*) (*Sport*) heavyweight; (*fig.*) emphasis.

schwerhörig [ˈʃveːrhøːrɪç], *adj.* hard of hearing, deaf.

Schwerkraft [ˈʃveːrkraft], *f.* (—, *no pl.*) gravity.

schwerlich [ˈʃveːrlɪç], *adv.* hardly, scarcely.

schwermütig [ˈʃveːrmyːtɪç], *adj.* melancholy.

Schwerpunkt [ˈʃveːrpuŋkt], *m.* (—s, *pl.* —e) centre of gravity.

Schwert [ʃveːrt], *n.* (—(e)s, *pl.* —er) sword.

Schwertgriff [ˈʃveːrtɡrɪf], *m.* (—s, *pl.* —e) hilt.

Schwertlilie [ˈʃveːrtliːljə], *f.* (—, *pl.* —n) (*Bot.*) iris; fleur-de-lys.

Schwertstreich [ˈʃveːrtʃtraɪç], *m.* (—(e)s, *pl.* —e) sword-blow, sword-stroke.

schwerwiegend [ˈʃveːrviːɡənt], *adj.* weighty.

Schwester [ˈʃvɛstər], *f.* (—, *pl.* —n) sister; *barmherzige* —, sister of mercy.

Schwesternschaft [ˈʃvɛstərnʃaft], *f.* (—, *pl.* —en) sisterhood; (*Am.*) sorority.

Schwibbogen [ˈʃvɪpboːɡən], *m.* (—s, *pl.* —) (*Archit.*) flying buttress.

Schwiegersohn [ˈʃviːɡərzoːn], *m.* (—s, *pl.* ⁻e) son-in-law.

Schwiegertochter [ˈʃviːɡərtɔxtər], *f.* (—, *pl.* ⁻) daughter-in-law.

Schwiele [ˈʃviːlə], *f.* (—, *pl.* —n) hard skin, callus, weal.

schwielig [ˈʃviːlɪç], *adj.* callous, horny.

schwierig [ˈʃviːrɪç], *adj.* difficult, hard.

Schwierigkeit [ˈʃviːrɪçkaɪt], *f.* (—, *pl.* —en) difficulty; *auf —en stoßen*, meet with difficulties.

schwimmen [ˈʃvɪmən], *v.n. irr.* (*aux.* sein) swim, float.

Schwimmer [ˈʃvɪmər], *m.* (—s, *pl.* —) swimmer.

Schwimmgürtel [ˈʃvɪmɡyrtəl], *m.* (—s, *pl.* —) life-belt.

Schwindel [ˈʃvɪndəl], *m.* (—s, *pl.* —) giddiness, dizziness, vertigo; swindle, fraud.

Schwindelanfall [ˈʃvɪndəlanfal], *m.* (—s, *pl.* ⁻e) attack of giddiness, vertigo.

Schwindelei [ʃvɪndəˈlaɪ], *f.* (—, *pl.* —en) swindle, fraud, deceit.

schwindelhaft [ˈʃvɪndəlhaft], *adj.* fraudulent.

schwinden [ˈʃvɪndən], *v.n. irr.* (*aux.* sein) dwindle; disappear, vanish.

Schwindler [ˈʃvɪndlər], *m.* (—s, *pl.* —) swindler, humbug, cheat.

schwindlig [ˈʃvɪndlɪç], *adj.* dizzy, giddy.

Schwindsucht [ˈʃvɪntzuxt], *f.* (—, *no pl.*) (*Med.*) tuberculosis, consumption.

schwindsüchtig [ˈʃvɪntzyçtɪç], *adj.* (*Med.*) tubercular.

Schwinge [ˈʃvɪŋə], *f.* (—, *pl.* —n) wing.

schwingen [ˈʃvɪŋən], *v.a. irr.* brandish. — *v.n.* swing, vibrate. — *v.r. sich* —, vault; *sich auf den Thron* —, usurp *or* take possession of the throne.

Schwingung [ˈʃvɪŋuŋ], *f.* (—, *pl.* —en) vibration, oscillation.

Schwips [ʃvɪps], *m.* (—es, *pl.* —e) (*coll.*) tipsiness; *einen — haben*, be tipsy.

schwirren [ˈʃvɪrən], *v.n.* whir, buzz.

Schwitzbad [ˈʃvɪtsbaːt], *n.* (—es, *pl.* ⁻er) Turkish bath, steam-bath.

schwitzen [ˈʃvɪtsən], *v.n.* sweat, perspire.

schwören [ˈʃvøːrən], *v.a., v.n. irr.* swear, take an oath; *darauf kannst du* —, you can be quite sure of that, you bet; *falsch* —, forswear o.s., perjure o.s.

schwül [ʃvyːl], *adj.* sultry, close.

Schwüle [ˈʃvyːlə], *f.* (—, *no pl.*) sultriness.

Schwulst [ʃvulst], *m.* (—es, *no pl.*) bombast.

schwülstig [ˈʃvylstɪç], *adj.* bombastic, turgid.

Schwülstigkeit [ˈʃvylstɪçkaɪt], *f.* (—, *pl.* —en) bombastic style, turgidity.

Schwund [ʃvunt], *m.* (—(e)s, *no pl.*) dwindling, decline; shrinkage.

Schwung [ʃvuŋ], *m.* (—(e)s, *pl.* ⁻e) swing, leap, bound; (*fig.*) verve, élan; (*Poet.*) flight, soaring.

schwunghaft [ˈʃvuŋhaft], *adj.* flourishing, soaring.

Schwungkraft [ˈʃvuŋkraft], *f.* (—, *no pl.*) centrifugal force; (*mental*) resilience.

Schwungrad [ˈʃvuŋraːt], *n.* (—s, *pl.* ⁻er) fly-wheel.

schwungvoll [ˈʃvuŋfɔl], *adj.* spirited.

Schwur [ʃvuːr], *m.* (—(e)s, *pl.* ⁻e) oath.

Schwurgericht [ˈʃvuːrɡərɪçt], *n.* (—s, *pl.* —e) (*Law*) assizes.

sechs [zɛks], *num. adj.* six.

Sechseck [ˈzɛksɛk], *n.* (—s, *pl.* —e) hexagon.

sechseckig [ˈzɛksɛkɪç], *adj.* hexagonal.

Segen

Sechser ['zɛksər], *m.* (—s, *pl.* —) coin of small value.

sechsspännig ['zɛksʃpɛnɪç], *adj.* drawn by six horses.

sechzehn ['zɛçtseːn], *num. adj.* sixteen.

sechzig ['zɛçtsɪç], *num. adj.* sixty.

Sediment [zedi'mɛnt], *n.* (—s, *pl.* —e) sediment.

See (1) [zeː], *m.* (—s, *pl.* —n) lake, pool.

See (2) [zeː], *f.* (—, *no pl.*) sea, ocean; *hohe* —, high seas; *zur* — *gehen*, go to sea, become a sailor.

Seeadler ['zeːadlər], *m.* (—s, *pl.* —) (*Orn.*) osprey.

Seebad ['zeːbaːt], *n.* (—s, *pl.* ⁓er) seaside resort; bathe in the sea.

Seebär ['zeːbɛːr], *m.* (—en, *pl.* —en) (*fig.*) old salt.

Seefahrer ['zeːfaːrər], *m.* (—s, *pl.* —) mariner, navigator.

Seefahrt ['zeːfaːrt], *f.* (—, *pl.* —en) seafaring; voyage, cruise.

seefest ['zeːfɛst], *adj.* (*ship*) seaworthy; (*person*) a good sailor.

Seefischerei ['zeːfɪʃəraɪ], *f.* (—, *no pl.*) deep-sea fishing.

Seeflotte ['zeːflɔtə], *f.* (—, *pl.* —n) navy, fleet.

Seegang ['zeːɡaŋ], *m.* (—s, *no pl.*) swell.

Seegras ['zeːɡraːs], *n.* (—es, *no pl.*) seaweed.

Seehandel ['zeːhandəl], *m.* (—s, *no pl.*) maritime trade.

Seehund ['zeːhunt], *m.* (—s, *pl.* —e) (*Zool.*) seal.

Seeigel ['zeːiːɡəl], *m.* (—s, *pl.* —) (*Zool.*) sea-urchin.

Seejungfrau ['zeːjuŋfrau], *f.* (—, *pl.* —en) mermaid.

Seekadett ['zeːkadɛt], *m.* (—en, *pl.* —en) midshipman; (*naval*) cadet.

Seekarte ['zeːkartə], *f.* (—, *pl.* —n) chart.

seekrank ['zeːkraŋk], *adj.* seasick.

Seekrieg ['zeːkriːk], *m.* (—s, *pl.* —e) naval war.

Seeküste ['zeːkystə], *f.* (—, *pl.* —n) sea-coast, shore, beach.

Seele ['zeːlə], *f.* (—, *pl.* —n) soul; *mit ganzer* —, with all my heart.

Seelenamt ['zeːlənamt], *n.* (—s, *pl.* ⁓er) (*Eccl.*) office for the dead, requiem.

Seelenangst ['zeːlənaŋkst], *f.* (—, *pl.* ⁓e) anguish, agony.

Seelenheil ['zeːlənhaɪl], *n.* (—s, *no pl.*) (*Theol.*) salvation.

Seelenhirt ['zeːlənhɪrt], *m.* (—en, *pl.* —en) pastor.

seelenlos ['zeːlənloːs], *adj.* inanimate.

Seelenmesse ['zeːlənmɛsə], *f.* (—, *pl.* —n) requiem; Mass for the dead.

Seelenruhe ['zeːlənruːə], *f.* (—, *no pl.*) tranquillity of mind.

seelenruhig ['zeːlənruːɪç], *adj.* cool, calm, collected, unperturbed.

Seelenstärke ['zeːlənʃtɛrkə], *f.* (—, *no pl.*) fortitude; composure.

seelenvergnügt ['zeːlənfɛrɡnyːkt], *adj.* blissfully happy.

Seelenverwandtschaft ['zeːlənfɛrvantʃaft], *f.* (—, *pl.* —en) mental affinity, (mutual) understanding.

seelenvoll ['zeːlənfɔl], *adj.* wistful, soulful.

Seelenwanderung ['zeːlənvandəruŋ], *f.* (—, *no pl.*) transmigration of souls, metempsychosis.

Seeleute ['zeːlɔytə] *see under* **Seemann.**

seelisch ['zeːlɪʃ], *adj.* mental, psychological, psychic(al).

Seelsorge ['zeːlzɔrɡə], *f.* (—, *no pl.*) (*Eccl.*) cure of souls; pastoral duties or work.

Seemann ['zeːman], *m.* (—s, *pl.* ⁓er, **Seeleute**) sea·man, sailor, mariner.

Seemeile ['zeːmaɪlə], *f.* (—, *pl.* —n) knot, nautical mile.

Seemöwe ['zeːmøːvə], *f.* (—, *pl.* —n) (*Orn.*) seagull.

Seemuschel ['zeːmuʃəl], *f.* (—, *pl.* —n) sea-shell.

Seepflanze ['zeːpflantsə], *f.* (—, *pl.* —n) marine plant.

Seerabe ['zeːraːbə], *m.* (—n, *pl.* —n) (*Orn.*) cormorant.

Seeräuber ['zeːrɔybər], *m.* (—s, *pl.* —) pirate.

Seerose ['zeːroːzə], *f.* (—, *pl.* —n) (*Bot.*) water-lily.

Seesalz ['zeːzalts], *n.* (—es, *no pl.*) bay salt, sea salt.

Seeschlacht ['zeːʃlaxt], *f.* (—, *pl.* —en) naval engagement, naval battle.

Seestern ['zeːʃtɛrn], *m.* (—s, *pl.* —e) (*Zool.*) starfish.

Seestille ['zeːʃtɪlə], *f.* (—, *no pl.*) calm (at sea).

Seetang ['zeːtaŋ], *m.* (—s, *no pl.*) (*Bot.*) seaweed.

seetüchtig ['zeːtyçtɪç], *adj.* seaworthy.

Seeuhr ['zeːuːr], *f.* (—, *pl.* —en) marine chronometer.

Seeuntüchtigkeit ['zeːuntyçtɪçkaɪt], *f.* (—, *no pl.*) unseaworthiness.

Seewasser ['zeːvasər], *n.* (—s, *no pl.*) sea-water, brine.

Seewesen ['zeːvezən], *n.* (—s, *no pl.*) naval affairs.

Seezunge ['zeːtsuŋə], *f.* (—, *pl.* —n) sole (*fish*).

Segel ['zeːɡəl], *n.* (—s, *pl.* —) sail; *großes* —, mainsail; *unter* — *gehen*, set sail, put to sea; *die* — *streichen*, strike sail.

segelfertig ['zeːɡəlfɛrtɪç], *adj.* ready to sail; *sich* — *machen*, get under sail.

Segelflugzeug ['zeːɡəlfluːktsɔyk], *n.* (—s, *pl.* —e) glider(-plane).

Segelschiff ['zeːɡəlʃɪf], *n.* (—s, *pl.* —e) sailing-vessel.

Segelstange ['zeːɡəlʃtaŋə], *f.* (—, *pl.* —n) sail-yard.

Segen ['zeːɡən], *m.* (—s, *no pl.*) blessing, benediction; (*fig.*) abundance; — *sprechen*, give the blessing, say grace.

segensreich ['ze:gǝnsraɪç], *adj.* blessed, full of blessings; prosperous.

Segenswunsch ['ze:gǝnsvunʃ], *m.* (—es, *pl.* ⁻e) good wish.

segnen ['ze:gnǝn], *v.a.* bless.

sehen ['ze:ǝn], *v.a. irr.* see, behold, perceive; *etwas gern* —, like s.th., approve of s.th. — *v.n.* look, see; *sich lassen*, parade, show o.s., *wir werden* —, that remains to be seen, we shall see.

sehenswert ['ze:ǝnsve:rt], *adj.* worth seeing.

Sehenswürdigkeit ['ze:ǝnsvyrdɪçkaɪt], *f.* (—, *pl.* —en) curiosity, object of interest, tourist attraction; (*pl.*) sights.

Seher ['ze:ǝr], *m.* (—s, *pl.* —) seer, prophet.

Sehne ['ze:nǝ], *f.* (—, *pl.* —n) sinew, tendon; string.

sehnig ['ze:nɪç], *adj.* sinewy, muscular; (*meat*) tough.

sehnlich ['ze:nlɪç], *adj.* earnest, passionate, eager.

Sehnsucht ['ze:nzuxt], *f.* (—, *no pl.*) longing, yearning, desire.

sehr [ze:r], *adv.* very, much, greatly, very much; *zu* —, too much; — *gut*, very good; — *wohl*, very well.

Sehweite ['ze:vaɪtǝ], *f.* (—, *no pl.*) range of vision.

seicht [zaɪçt], *adj.* shallow, superficial.

Seide ['zaɪdǝ], *f.* (—, *pl.* —n) silk.

Seidel ['zaɪdǝl], *n.* (—s, *pl.* —) (*dial.*) mug, tankard; pint.

seiden ['zaɪdǝn], *adj.* silk, silken, silky.

Seidenpapier ['zaɪdǝnpapi:r], *n.* (—s, *no pl.*) tissue-paper.

Seidenraupe ['zaɪdǝnraupǝ], *f.* (—, *pl.* —n) (*Ent.*) silkworm.

Seidenstoff ['zaɪdǝnʃtɔf], *m.* (—es, *pl.* —e) spun silk.

Seife ['zaɪfǝ], *f.* (—, *pl.* —n) soap; *ein Stück* —, a cake of soap.

seifen ['zaɪfǝn], *v.a.* soap.

Seifenschaum ['zaɪfǝnʃaum], *m.* (—s, *no pl.*) lather.

Seifenwasser ['zaɪfǝnvasǝr], *n.* (—s, *no pl.*) soap-suds.

seifig ['zaɪfɪç], *adj.* soapy, saponaceous.

seihen ['zaɪǝn], *v.a.* strain, filter.

Seil [zaɪl], *n.* (—(e)s, *pl.* —e) rope; *straffes* —, taut rope, tight rope; *schlaffes* —, slack rope.

Seilbahn ['zaɪlba:n], *f.* (—, *pl.* —en) funicular railway; cable car.

Seilbrücke ['zaɪlbrykǝ], *f.* (—, *pl.* —n) rope bridge.

Seiltänzer ['zaɪltɛntsǝr], *m.* (—s, *pl.* —) tight-rope walker.

Seilziehen ['zaɪltsi:ǝn], *n.* (—s, *no pl.*) tug of war.

Seim [zaɪm], *m.* (—(e)s, *pl.* —e) strained honey.

Sein [zaɪn], *n.* (—s, *no pl.*) being, existence.

sein (1) [zaɪn], *v.n. irr.* (*aux.* sein) be, exist.

sein (2) [zaɪn], *poss. adj.* his, her, its; one's. — *pers. pron.* his.

seinerseits ['zaɪnǝrzaɪts], *adv.* for his part.

seinerzeit ['zaɪnǝrtsaɪt], *adv.* at that time, at the time, formerly.

seinesgleichen ['zaɪnǝsglaɪçǝn], *indecl. adj. & pron.* of his sort, such as he.

seinethalben ['zaɪnǝthalbǝn], *adv.* on his account, for his sake, on his behalf.

seinetwegen ['zaɪnǝtve:gǝn], *adv.* on his account, for his sake, on his behalf.

Seinige ['zaɪnɪgǝ], *n.* (—n, *pl.* —n) his, his property; (*pl.*) his family, his people; *das* — *tun*, do o.'s share.

seit [zaɪt], *prep.* (*Dat.*) since, for; *gestern*, since yesterday, from yesterday onwards; — *einiger Zeit*, for some time past. — *conj. see* **seitdem**.

seitdem [zaɪt'de:m], *adv.* since then, since that time. — *conj.* since.

Seite ['zaɪtǝ], *f.* (—, *pl.* —n) side, flank; (*book*) page; *etwas auf die* — *bringen*, put s.th. aside; *ich bin auf seiner* —, I side with him, I am on his side; *er hat seine guten* —n, he has his good points.

Seitenansicht ['zaɪtǝnanzɪçt], *f.* (—, *pl.* —en) profile.

Seitengleis ['zaɪtǝnglaɪs], *n.* (—es, *pl.* —e) (railway) siding.

Seitenhieb ['zaɪtǝnhi:p], *m.* (—s, *pl.* —e) innuendo, sly hit, dig.

seitens ['zaɪtǝns], *prep.* (*Genit.*) on the part of.

Seitensprung ['zaɪtǝnʃpruŋ], *m.* (—s, *pl.* ⁻e) side-leap, caper; (*fig.*) (amorous) escapade.

Seitenstraße ['zaɪtǝnʃtra:sǝ], *f.* (—, *pl.* —n) side-street.

Seitenstück ['zaɪtǝnʃtyk], *n.* (—s, *pl.* —e) companion-piece.

Seitenzahl ['zaɪtǝntsa:l], *f.* (—, *pl.* —en) page-number; number of pages.

seither ['zaɪthe:r], *adv.* since that time, since then.

seitlich ['zaɪtlɪç], *adj.* lateral.

Sekretär [zekre'tɛ:r], *m.* (—s, *pl.* —e) secretary.

Sekretariat [zekreta'rja:t], *n.* (—s, *pl.* —e) secretariat, secretary's office.

Sekt [zɛkt], *m.* (—s, *pl.* —e) champagne.

Sekte ['zɛktǝ], *f.* (—, *pl.* —n) sect.

Sektierer [zɛk'ti:rǝr], *m.* (—s, *pl.* —) sectarian.

Sektion [zɛk'tsjo:n] *f.* (—, *pl.* —en) section; (*Med.*) dissection.

Sekundaner [zekun'da:nǝr], *m.* (—s, *pl.* —) pupil in the second (highest) form.

Sekundant [zekun'dant], *m.* (—en, *pl.* —en) (*Duelling*) second.

sekundär [zekun'dɛ:r], *adj.* secondary.

Sekunde [ze'kundǝ], *f.* (—, *pl.* —n) (*time*) second.

Sekundenzeiger [ze'kundǝntsaɪgǝr], *m.* (—s, *pl.* —) (*clock*) second-hand.

sekundieren [zekun'di:rǝn], *v.n. einem* —, second s.o.

selber ['zɛlbǝr], *indecl. adj. & pron.* self.

selb(ig) ['zɛlb(ɪg)], *adj.* the same.

selbst [zɛlpst], *indecl. adj. & pron.* self; — *ist der Mann,* depend on yourself; *von —,* of its own accord, spontaneously. — *adv.* even; — *wenn,* even if, even though; — *dann nicht,* not even then.
selbständig ['zɛlpʃtɛndɪç], *adj.* independent.
Selbstbestimmung ['zɛlpstbəʃtɪmuŋ], *f.* (—, *no pl.*) self-determination, autonomy.
selbstbewußt ['zɛlpstbəvust], *adj.* self-assertive, self-confident, conceited.
selbstherrlich ['zɛlpstherlɪç], *adj.* autocratic, tyrannical.
Selbstlaut ['zɛlpstlaut], *m.* (—s, *pl.* —e) vowel.
selbstlos ['zɛlpstloːs], *adj.* unselfish, selfless, altruistic.
Selbstlosigkeit [zɛlpst'loːzɪçkaɪt], *f.* (—, *no pl.*) unselfishness, altruism.
Selbstmord ['zɛlpstmɔrt], *m.* (—s, *pl.* —e) suicide.
selbstredend ['zɛlpstreːdənt], *adj.* self-evident, obvious.
Selbstsucht ['zɛlpstzuxt], *f.* (—, *no pl.*) selfishness, ego(t)ism.
selbstsüchtig ['zɛlpstzyçtɪç], *adj.* selfish, ego(t)istic(al).
selbstverständlich ['zɛlpstferʃtɛntlɪç], *adj.* self-evident. — *adv.* of course, obviously.
Selbstzweck ['zɛlpsttsvɛk], *m.* (—s, *no pl.*) end in itself.
selig ['zeːlɪç], *adj.* blessed, blissful; (*fig.*) delighted; deceased, late; — *sprechen,* beatify.
Seligkeit ['zeːlɪçkaɪt], *f.* (—, *pl.* —en) bliss, blissfulness; (*Eccl.*) salvation, beatitude.
Seligsprechung ['zeːlɪçʃpreçuŋ], *f.* (—, *pl.* —en) beatification.
Sellerie ['zɛləriː], *m.* (—s, *pl.* —s) (*Bot.*) celery.
selten ['zɛltən], *adj.* rare, scarce; (*fig.*) remarkable. — *adv.* seldom, rarely, infrequently.
Seltenheit ['zɛltənhaɪt], *f.* (—, *pl.* —en) rarity, curiosity, scarcity; (*fig.*) remarkableness.
Selterwasser ['zɛltərvasər], *n.* (—s, *no pl.*) soda-water.
seltsam ['zɛltzaːm], *adj.* strange, unusual, odd, curious.
Semester [ze'mɛstər], *n.* (—s, *pl.* —) university term, semester.
Semit [ze'miːt], *m.* (—en, *pl.* —en) Semite, Jew.
semmelblond ['zɛməlblɔnt], *adj.* flaxen-haired.
Semmelkloß ['zɛməlkloːs], *m.* (—es, *pl.* ̈e) bread dumpling.
Senator [ze'naːtɔr], *m.* (—s, *pl.* —en) senator.
senden ['zɛndən], *v.a. irr.* send, despatch; (*money*) remit. — *v.a. reg.* (*Rad.*) broadcast.
Sender ['zɛndər], *m.* (—s, *pl.* —) sender; (*Rad.*) (broadcasting) station, transmitter.

Sendling ['zɛntlɪŋ], *m.* (—s, *pl.* —e) (*Poet.*) emissary.
Sendschreiben ['zɛntʃraɪbən], *n.* (—s, *pl.* —) epistle, missive.
Sendung ['zɛnduŋ], *f.* (—, *pl.* —en) (*Comm.*) shipment, consignment; (*fig.*) mission; (*Rad.*) broadcast, transmission.
Senegal ['zeːnəgal], *n.* Senegal.
Senf [zɛnf], *m.* (—s, *no pl.*) mustard.
sengen ['zɛŋən], *v.a.* singe, scorch; — *und brennen,* lay waste.
Senkblei ['zɛŋkblaɪ], *n.* (—s, *pl.* —e) plummet.
Senkel ['zɛŋkəl], *m.* (—s, *pl.* —) shoe-lace.
senken ['zɛŋkən], *v.a.* lower, sink. — *v.r. sich —,* sink, go down; dip, slope, subside.
senkrecht ['zɛŋkreçt], *adj.* perpendicular.
Senkung ['zɛŋkuŋ], *f.* (—, *pl.* —en) depression, dip, subsidence.
Senn(e) ['zɛn(ə)], *m.* (—n, *pl.* —(e)n) Alpine herdsman.
Sennerin ['zɛnərɪn], *f.* (—, *pl.* —nen) Alpine dairy-woman.
Senneschoten ['zɛnəʃoːtən], *f. pl.* senna pods.
Sennhütte ['zɛnhytə], *f.* (—, *pl.* —n) Alpine dairy; chalet.
sensationell [zɛnzatsjoˈnɛl], *adj.* sensational.
Sense ['zɛnzə], *f.* (—, *pl.* —n) scythe.
sensibel [zɛnˈziːbəl], *adj.* sensitive.
Sentenz [zɛnˈtɛnts], *f.* (—, *pl.* —en) aphorism.
sentimental [zɛntimɛnˈtaːl], *adj.* sentimental.
separat [zepaˈraːt], *adj.* separate, special.
September [zɛpˈtɛmbər], *m.* (—s, *pl.* —) September.
Serbien ['zɛrbjən], *n.* Serbia.
Serie ['zeːrjə], *f.* (—, *pl.* —n) series.
Service [zɛrˈviːs], *n.* (—s, *pl.* —) dinner-set, dinner-service.
servieren [zɛrˈviːrən], *v.a., v.n.* serve, wait at table.
Serviertisch [zɛrˈviːrtɪʃ], *m.* (—es, *pl.* —e) sideboard.
Sessel ['zɛsəl], *m.* (—s, *pl.* —) armchair, easy-chair; (*Austr. dial.*) chair.
seßhaft ['zɛshaft], *adj.* settled, domiciled.
setzen ['zɛtsən], *v.a.* set, put, place; (*monument*) erect; (*bet*) stake; (*Typ.*) compose. — *v.r. sich —,* sit down; (*coffee*) settle; *sich bei einem in Gunst —,* ingratiate o.s. with s.o.
Setzer ['zɛtsər], *m.* (—s, *pl.* —) compositor.
Setzling ['zɛtslɪŋ], *m.* (—s, *pl.* —e) young tree, young plant.
Seuche ['zɔyçə], *f.* (—, *pl.* —n) pestilence; epidemic.
seufzen ['zɔyftsən], *v.n.* sigh.
Seufzer ['zɔyftsər], *m.* (—s, *pl.* —) sigh.
Sexta ['zɛkstaː], *f.* (—, *pl.* —s) (*Sch.*) sixth form, lowest form.

Sextant

Sextant [zɛks'tant], *m.* (—en, *pl.* —en) sextant.

sexuell [zɛksu'ɛl], *adj.* sexual.

sezieren [zeˈtsiːrən], *v.a.* dissect.

Seziersaal [zeˈtsiːrzaːl], *m.* (—s, *pl.* —säle) dissecting-room.

Sibirien [ziˈbiːrjən], *n.* Siberia.

sich [zɪç], *pron.* oneself, himself, herself, itself, themselves; each other.

Sichel [ˈzɪçəl], *f.* (—, *pl.* —n) sickle.

sicher [ˈzɪçər], *adj.* certain, sure, secure, safe; confident, positive; *seiner Sache — sein*, be sure of o.'s ground; — *stellen*, secure.

Sicherheit [ˈzɪçərhaɪt], *f.* (—, *pl.* —en) certainty; security, safety; confidence, positiveness; *in — bringen*, secure.

sichern [ˈzɪçərn], *v.a.* secure, make secure; assure, ensure.

Sicherung [ˈzɪçəruŋ], *f.* (—, *pl.* —en) securing; (*Elec.*) fuse; (*gun*) safety-catch.

Sicht [zɪçt], *f.* (—, *no pl.*) sight.

sichtbar [ˈzɪçtbaːr], *adj.* visible; conspicuous.

sichten [ˈzɪçtən], *v.a.* sift, sort out; sight.

sichtlich [ˈzɪçtlɪç], *adv.* visibly.

Sichtwechsel [ˈzɪçtvɛksəl], *m.* (—s, *pl.* —) (*Banking*) sight-bill, bill payable on sight.

Sichtweite [ˈzɪçtvaɪtə], *f.* (—, *no pl.*) range of vision.

sickern [ˈzɪkərn], *v.n.* (*aux.* sein) leak, ooze, seep.

Sie [ziː], *pron.* (*formal*) you.

sie [ziː], *pers. pron.* she, her; they, them.

Sieb [ziːp], *n.* (—(e)s, *pl.* —e) sieve; riddle; colander.

sieben (1) [ˈziːbən], *v.a.* (*Cul.*) sift, strain.

sieben (2) [ˈziːbən], *num. adj.* seven; *meine — Sachen*, my belongings.

Siebeneck [ˈziːbənɛk], *n.* (—s, *pl.* —e) heptagon.

Siebengestirn [ˈziːbəngəʃtɪrn], *n.* (—s, *no pl.*) Pleiades.

siebenmal [ˈziːbənmaːl], *adv.* seven times.

Siebenmeilenstiefel [ziːbənˈmaɪlənʃtiːfəl], *m. pl.* seven-league boots.

Siebenschläfer [ˈziːbənʃlɛːfər], *m.* (—s, *pl.* —) lazy-bones.

siebzehn [ˈziːptseːn], *num. adj.* seventeen.

siebzig [ˈziːptsɪç], *num. adj.* seventy.

siech [ziːç], *adj.* (*rare*) sick, infirm.

siechen [ˈziːçən], *v.n.* be in bad health.

sieden [ˈziːdən], *v.a., v.n.* boil, seethe.

siedeln [ˈziːdəln], *v.n.* settle.

Siedlung [ˈziːdluŋ], *f.* (—, *pl.* —en) settlement; housing estate.

Sieg [ziːk], *m.* (—(e)s, *pl.* —e) victory; *den — davontragen*, win the day.

Siegel [ˈziːgəl], *n.* (—s, *pl.* —) seal; *Brief und* —, sign and seal.

Siegelbewahrer [ˈziːgəlbavaːrər], *m.* (—s, *pl.* —) Lord Privy Seal; keeper of the seal.

Siegellack [ˈziːgəllak], *n.* (—s, *no pl.*) sealing wax.

siegeln [ˈziːgəln], *v.a.* seal.

siegen [ˈziːgən], *v.n.* conquer, win, be victorious, triumph (over).

Sieger [ˈziːgər], *m.* (—s, *pl.* —) victor, conqueror.

Siegesbogen [ˈziːgəsboːgən], *m.* (—s, *pl.* ⸚) triumphal arch.

Siegeszeichen [ˈziːgəstsaɪçən], *n.* (—s, *pl.* —) sign of victory, trophy.

sieghaft [ˈziːkhaft], *adj.* victorious, triumphant.

siegreich [ˈziːkraɪç], *adj.* victorious, triumphant.

siehe! [ˈziːə], *excl.* see! look! lo and behold!

Sierra Leone [ˈsiɛra leˈoːnə], *f.* Sierra Leone.

Signal [zɪgˈnaːl], *n.* (—s, *pl.* —e) signal.

Signalement [zɪgnaləˈmã], *n.* (—s, *pl.* —s) personal description.

Signalglocke [zɪgˈnaːlgləkə], *f.* (—, *pl.* —n) warning-bell.

signalisieren [zɪgnaliˈziːrən], *v.a.* signal.

Signatarmacht [zɪgnaˈtaːrmaxt], *f.* (—, *pl.* ⸚e) signatory power.

signieren [zɪgˈniːrən], *v.a.* sign.

Silbe [ˈzɪlbə], *f.* (—, *pl.* —n) syllable.

Silbenmaß [ˈzɪlbənmaːs], *n.* (—es, *pl.* —e) (*Poet.*) metre.

Silbenrätsel [ˈzɪlbənrɛːtsəl], *n.* (—s, *pl.* —) charade.

Silber [ˈzɪlbər], *n.* (—s, *no pl.*) silver; plate.

Silberbuche [ˈzɪlbərbuːxə], *f.* (—, *pl.* —n) white beech(-tree).

Silberfuchs [ˈzɪlbərfuks], *m.* (—es, *pl.* ⸚e) (*Zool.*) silver fox.

silbern [ˈzɪlbərn], *adj.* made of silver, silvery.

Silberpappel [ˈzɪlbərpapəl], *f.* (—, *pl.* —n) (*Bot.*) white poplar(-tree).

Silberschimmel [ˈzɪlbərʃɪməl], *m.* (—s, *pl.* —) grey-white horse.

Silberzeug [ˈzɪlbərtsɔyk], *n.* (—s, *no pl.*) (silver) plate.

Silvester [zɪlˈvɛstər], *m.* (—s, *pl.* —) New Year's Eve.

Similistein [ˈziːmiliʃtaɪn], *m.* (—s, *pl.* —e) imitation *or* paste jewellery.

Sims [zɪms], *m.* (—es, *pl.* —e) cornice, moulding, shelf, ledge.

Simulant [zimuˈlant], *m.* (—en, *pl.* —en) malingerer.

simulieren [zimuˈliːrən], *v.a.* simulate.

simultan [zimulˈtaːn], *adj.* simultaneous.

Singapur [zɪŋgaˈpuːr], *n.* Singapore.

Singdrossel [ˈzɪŋdrɔsəl], *f.* (—, *pl.* —n) (*Orn.*) common thrush.

singen [ˈzɪŋən], *v.a., v.n. irr.* sing.

Singspiel [ˈzɪŋʃpiːl], *n.* (—s, *pl.* —e) musical comedy, light opera, opera buffa.

Singular [ˈzɪŋgulaːr], *m.* (—s, *pl.* —e) singular.

sinken ['zɪŋkən], *v.n. irr.* (*aux.* sein) sink; (*price*) decline, drop, fall; *den Mut — lassen,* lose heart.

Sinn [zɪn], *m.* (—(e)s, *pl.* —e) sense; intellect, mind; consciousness, memory; taste, meaning, purport; wish; *etwas im — haben,* have s.th. in mind, intend s.th.; *leichter —,* lightheartedness; *andern —es werden,* change o's mind; *das hat keinen —,* there is no sense in that; *von —en sein,* be out of o.'s senses; *seine fünf —e beisammen haben,* be in o.'s right mind; *sich etwas aus dem — schlagen,* dismiss s.th. from o.'s mind; *es kommt mir in den —,* it occurs to me.

Sinnbild ['zɪnbɪlt], *n.* (—s, *pl.* —er) symbol, emblem.

sinnen ['zɪnən], *v.n. irr.* meditate, reflect.

Sinnesänderung ['zɪnəsɛndərʊŋ], *f.* (—, *pl.* —en) change of mind.

Sinnesart ['zɪnəsa:rt], *f.* (—, *no pl.*) disposition, character.

Sinnesorgan ['zɪnəsɔrga:n], *n.* (—s, *pl.* —e) sense-organ.

Sinnestäuschung ['zɪnəstɔyʃʊŋ], *f.* (—, *pl.* —en) illusion, hallucination.

sinnfällig ['zɪnfɛlɪç], *adj.* obvious, striking.

Sinngedicht ['zɪngədɪçt], *n.* (—es, *pl.* —e) epigram.

sinnig ['zɪnɪç], *adj.* thoughtful, meaningful; judicious, fitting.

sinnlich ['zɪnlɪç], *adj.* sensual, sensuous.

Sinnlichkeit ['zɪnlɪçkaɪt], *f.* (—, *no pl.*) sensuality, sensuousness.

sinnlos ['zɪnlo:s], *adj.* senseless, meaningless, pointless.

sinnreich ['zɪnraɪç], *adj.* ingenious.

Sinnspruch ['zɪnʃprʊx], *m.* (—es, *pl.* —e) sentence, maxim, device, motto.

sinnverwandt ['zɪnfɛrvant], *adj.* synonymous.

sinnvoll ['zɪnfɔl], *adj.* meaningful, significant.

sinnwidrig ['zɪnvi:drɪç], *adj.* nonsensical, absurd.

Sintflut ['zɪntflu:t], *f.* (—, *no pl.*) (*Bibl.*) the Flood.

Sinus ['zi:nus], *m.* (—, *pl.* —se) (*Maths.*) sine.

Sippe ['zɪpə], *f.* (—, *pl.* —n) kin, tribe, family, clan.

Sippschaft ['zɪpʃaft], *f.* (—, *pl.* —en) kindred; *die ganze —,* the whole caboodle.

Sirene [zi're:nə], *f.* (—, *pl.* —n) siren.

Sirup ['zi:rup], *m.* (—s, *no pl.*) syrup, treacle.

Sitte ['zɪtə], *f.* (—, *pl.* —n) custom, mode, fashion; (*pl.*) manners, morals; *—n und Gebräuche,* manners and customs.

Sittengesetz ['zɪtəngəzɛts], *n.* (—es, *pl.* —e) moral law.

Sittenlehre ['zɪtənle:rə], *f.* (—, *no pl.*) moral philosophy, ethics.

sittenlos ['zɪtənlo:s], *adj.* immoral, profligate, licentious.

Sittenprediger ['zɪtənpre:dɪgər], *m.* (—s, *pl.* —) moraliser.

Sittich ['zɪtɪç], *m.* (—s, *pl.* —e) (*Orn.*) budgerigar; parakeet.

sittig ['zɪtɪç], *adj.* well-behaved.

sittlich ['zɪtlɪç], *adj.* moral.

Sittlichkeit ['zɪtlɪçkaɪt], *f.* (—, *no pl.*) morality, morals.

sittsam ['zɪtza:m], *adj.* modest, demure.

situiert [zitu'i:rt], *adj. gut* (*schlecht*) —, well (badly) off.

Sitz [zɪts], *m.* (—es, *pl.* —e) seat, chair; residence, location, place; (*Eccl.*) see.

Sitzarbeit ['zɪtsarbaɪt], *f.* (—, *pl.* —en) sedentary work.

Sitzbad ['zɪtsba:t], *n.* (—(e)s, *pl.* ⁻er) hip bath.

sitzen ['zɪtsən], *v.n. irr.* sit, be seated; (*fig.*) be in prison; (*dress*) fit; *— lassen,* throw over, jilt; *— bleiben,* remain seated; (*school*) stay in the same class, not be moved up; be a wallflower; remain unmarried.

Sitzfleisch ['zɪtsflaɪʃ], *n.* (—es, *no pl.*) (*coll.*) *kein — haben,* be restless, lack application.

Sitzplatz ['zɪtsplats], *m.* (—es, *pl.* ⁻e) seat.

Sitzung ['zɪtsʊŋ], *f.* (—, *pl.* —en) meeting, sitting, session.

Sitzungsprotokoll ['zɪtsʊŋsprotokɔl], *n.* (—s, *pl.* —e) minutes (of a meeting).

Sitzungssaal ['zɪtsʊŋssa:l], *m.* (—s, *pl.* —säle) board-room, conference room.

Sizilien [zi'tsi:ljən], *n.* Sicily.

Skala ['ska:la], *f.* (—, *pl.* —len) scale; (*Mus.*) gamut.

Skandal [skan'da:l], *m.* (—s, *pl.* —e) scandal; row, riot; *— machen,* kick up a row.

skandalös [skanda'lø:s], *adj.* scandalous.

skandieren [skan'di:rən], *v.a.* (*Poet.*) scan.

Skandinavien [skandɪ'na:vjən], *n.* Scandinavia.

Skelett [ske'lɛt], *n.* (—s, *pl.* —e) skeleton.

Skepsis ['skɛpsɪs], *f.* (—, *no pl.*) scepticism, doubt.

skeptisch ['skɛptɪʃ], *adj.* sceptical, doubtful.

Skizze ['skɪtsə], *f.* (—, *pl.* —n) sketch.

skizzieren [skɪ'tsi:rən], *v.a.* sketch.

Sklave ['skla:və], *m.* (—n, *pl.*—n) slave; *zum —n machen,* enslave.

Sklavendienst ['skla:vəndi:nst], *m.* (—es, *no pl.*) slavery.

Sklaverei [skla:və'raɪ], *f.* (—, *no pl.*) slavery, thraldom.

Skonto ['skɔnto], *m. & n.* (—s, *pl.* —s) discount.

Skrupel ['skru:pəl], *m.* (—s, *pl.* —) scruple; *sich — machen,* have scruples.

skrupulös [skrupu'lø:s], *adj.* scrupulous, meticulous.

Skulptur

Skulptur [skulp'tu:r], *f.* (—, *pl.* —en) sculpture.

skurril [sku'ri:l], *adj.* ludicrous.

Slawe ['sla:və], *m.* (—n, *pl.* —n) Slav.

slawisch ['sla:vɪʃ], *adj.* Slav, Slavonic.

Slowake [slo'va:kə], *m.* (—n, *pl.* —n) Slovakian.

Slowene [slo've:nə], *m.* (—n, *pl.* —n) Slovenian.

Smaragd [sma'rakt], *m.* (—(e)s, *pl.* —e) emerald.

smaragden [sma'raktən], *adj.* emerald.

Smoking ['smo:kɪŋ], *m.* (—s, *pl.* —s) dinner-jacket.

so [zo:], *adv.* so, thus, in this way, like this; —? really? — *ist es*, that is how it is; — *daß*, so that; — ... *wie*, as ... as; *na* — *was!* well, I never! — *conj.* then, therefore.

sobald [zo'balt], *conj.* as soon as, directly.

Socke ['zɔkə], *f.* (—, *pl.* —n) sock.

Sockel ['zɔkəl], *m.* (—s, *pl.* —) pedestal, plinth, stand, base.

Soda ['zo:da], *n.* (—s, *no pl.*) (carbonate of) soda.

sodann [zo'dan], *adv. conj.* then.

Sodbrennen ['zo:tbrɛnən], *n.* (—s, *no pl.*) heartburn.

soeben [zo'e:bən], *adv.* just now.

sofern [zo'fɛrn], *conj.* if, in case, so far as.

sofort [zo'fɔrt], *adv.* at once, immediately.

Sog [zo:k], *m.* (—(e)s, *pl.* —e) undertow, suction.

sogar [zo'ga:r], *adv.* even.

sogenannt [zogə'nant], *adj.* so-called, would-be.

sogleich [zo'glaɪç], *adv.* at once, immediately.

Sohle ['zo:lə], *f.* (—, *pl.* —n) sole; *(mine)* floor.

Sohn [zo:n], *m.* (—(e)s, *pl.* ⸚e) son; *der verlorene* —, the prodigal son.

solange [zo'laŋə], *conj.* as long as.

Solbad ['zo:lba:t], *n.* (—s, *pl.* ⸚er) saline bath.

solch [zɔlç], *adj., dem. pron.* such.

solcherlei ['zɔlçərlaɪ], *adj.* of such a kind, suchlike.

Sold [zɔlt], *m.* (—(e)s, *no pl.*) army pay.

Soldat [zɔl'da:t], *m.* (—en, *pl.* —en) soldier.

Soldateska [zɔlda'tɛska], *f.* (—, *pl.* —s) soldiery.

Söldner ['zœldnər], *m.* (—s, *pl.* —) mercenary, hireling.

Sole ['zo:lə], *f.* (—, *pl.* —n) salt-water, brine.

Solei ['zo:laɪ], *n.* (—s, *pl.* —er) pickled egg.

solidarisch [zoli'da:rɪʃ], *adj.* joint, jointly responsible; unanimous.

Solidarität [zolidari'tɛ:t], *f.* (—, *no pl.*) solidarity.

Solist [zo'lɪst], *m.* (—en, *pl.* —en) soloist.

Soll [zɔl], *n.* (—s, *no pl.*) debit; — *und Haben*, debit and credit.

sollen ['zɔlən], *v.n. irr.* be obliged, be compelled; have to; be supposed to; *(aux.)* shall, should etc.; *ich soll*, I must, I am to; *er soll krank sein*, he is said to be ill; *ich sollte eigentlich*, I really ought to.

Söller ['zœlər], *m.* (—s, *pl.* —) loft, garret, balcony.

Somali [zɔ'ma:li], *n.* Somalia.

somit [zo'mɪt], *adv.* consequently, therefore, accordingly.

Sommer ['zɔmər], *m.* (—s, *pl.* —) summer.

Sommerfäden ['zɔmərfɛ:dən], *m. pl.* gossamer.

Sommerfrische ['zɔmərfrɪʃə], *f.* (—, *pl.* —n) holiday resort.

Sommergetreide ['zɔmərgətraɪdə], *n.* (—s, *no pl.*) spring corn.

Sommersonnenwende ['zɔmərzɔnənvɛndə], *f.* (—, *pl.* —n) summer solstice.

Sommersprosse ['zɔmərʃprɔsə], *f.* (—, *pl.* —n) freckle.

sonach [zo'na:x], *adv.* therefore, consequently.

Sonate [zo'na:tə], *f.* (—, *pl.* —n) sonata.

Sonde ['zɔndə], *f.* (—, *pl.* —n) sounding-lead, plummet; probe.

sonder ['zɔndər], *(obs.)* prep. *(Acc.)* without.

Sonderausgabe ['zɔndərausga:bə], *f.* (—, *pl.* —n) separate edition; special edition.

Sonderausschuß ['zɔndərausʃus], *m.* (—sses, *pl.* ⸚sse) select committee.

sonderbar ['zɔndərba:r], *adj.* strange, odd, queer, singular, peculiar.

sonderlich ['zɔndərlɪç], *adj.* special, especial, particular. — *adv. nicht* —, not much.

Sonderling ['zɔndərlɪŋ], *m.* (—s, *pl.* —e) freak, odd character, crank.

sondern ['zɔndərn], *v.a.* separate, distinguish, differentiate. — *conj.* but; *nicht nur*, ... — *auch*, not only ... but also.

Sonderrecht ['zɔndərrɛçt], *n.* (—s, *pl.* —e) special privilege.

sonders ['zɔndərs], *adv. samt und* —, all and each, all and sundry.

Sonderstellung ['zɔndərʃtɛluŋ], *f.* (—, *no pl.*) exceptional position.

Sonderung ['zɔndəruŋ], *f.* (—, *pl.* —en) separation.

Sonderzug ['zɔndərtsu:k], *m.* (—s, *pl.* ⸚e) special train.

sondieren [zɔn'di:rən], *v.a.* *(wound)* probe; *(ocean)* plumb; *(fig.)* sound.

Sonett [zo'nɛt], *n.* (—(e)s, *pl.* —e) sonnet.

Sonnabend ['zɔna:bənt], *m.* (—s, *pl.* —e) Saturday.

Sonne ['zɔnə], *f.* (—, *pl.* —n) sun.

sonnen ['zɔnən], *v.r. sich* —, sun o.s., bask in the sun, sunbathe.

Sonnenaufgang ['zɔnənaufgaŋ], *m.* (—s, *pl.* ⸚e) sunrise.

Sonnenbrand ['zɔnənbrant], *m.* (—s, *pl.* ⸚e) sunburn.

Spannung

Sonnendeck [ˈzɔnəndɛk], n. (—s, pl. —e) awning.
Sonnenfinsternis [ˈzɔnənfɪnstərnɪs], f. (—, pl. —se) eclipse of the sun.
sonnenklar [ˈzɔnənklaːr], adj. very clear, as clear as daylight.
Sonnenschirm [ˈzɔnənʃɪrm], m. (—s, pl. —e) parasol, sunshade.
Sonnenstich [ˈzɔnənʃtɪç], n. (—(e)s, no pl.) sunstroke.
Sonnenuhr [ˈzɔnənuːr], f. (—, pl. —en) sundial.
Sonnenuntergang [ˈzɔnənuntərgaŋ], m. (—s, pl. ̈e) sunset.
Sonnenwende [ˈzɔnənvɛndə], f. (—, no pl.) solstice.
Sonntag [ˈzɔntaːk], m. (—s, pl. —e) Sunday.
sonntags [ˈzɔntaːks], adv. on Sundays, of a Sunday.
Sonntagsjäger [ˈzɔntaːksjɛːgər], m. (—s, pl. —) amateur sportsman.
sonor [zoˈnoːr], adj. sonorous.
sonst [zɔnst], adv. else, otherwise, besides, at other times; — noch etwas? anything else?
sonstig [ˈzɔnstɪç], adj. other, existing besides.
sonstwo [ˈzɔnstvo], adv. elsewhere, somewhere else.
Sopran [zoˈpraːn], m. (—s, pl. —e) soprano.
Sorbett [ˈzɔrbɛt], n. (—s, pl. —s) sherbet.
Sorge [ˈzɔrgə], f. (—, pl. —n) care; grief, worry; sorrow; anxiety; concern; (pl.) troubles, worries; — tragen dass..., see to it that ...; — tragen zu, take care of; — um, concern for.
sorgen [ˈzɔrgən], v.n. — für, care for, provide for, look after. — v.r. sich — um, worry about.
sorgenvoll [ˈzɔrgənfɔl], adj. uneasy, troubled, anxious.
Sorgfalt [ˈzɔrkfalt], f. (—, no pl.) care, attention.
sorgfältig [ˈzɔrkfɛltɪç], adj. careful, painstaking; elaborate.
sorglos [ˈzɔrkloːs], adj. careless, irresponsible, unconcerned, indifferent; carefree.
sorgsam [ˈzɔrkzaːm], adj. careful, heedful.
Sorte [ˈzɔrtə], f. (—, pl. —n) sort, kind, species, brand.
sortieren [zɔrˈtiːrən], v.a. sort (out).
Sortiment [zɔrtiˈmɛnt], n. (—s, pl. —e) assortment; bookshop.
Sortimentsbuchhändler [zɔrtiˈmɛntsbuːxhɛndlər], m. (—s, pl. —) retail bookseller.
Soße [ˈzoːsə], f. (—, pl. —n) sauce, gravy.
Souffleur [sufˈløːr], m. (—s, pl. —e) prompter.
Soutane [suˈtaːnə], f. (—, pl. —n) cassock, soutane.
Souterrain [suteˈrɛ̃], n. (—s, pl. —s) basement.
souverän [suvəˈrɛːn], adj. sovereign; (fig.) supremely good.

Souveränität [suːvərɛːniˈtɛːt], f. (—, no pl.) sovereignty.
soviel [zoˈfiːl], adv. so much; — wie, as much as. — conj. so far as; — ich weiß, as far as I know.
sowie [zoˈviː], conj. as, as well as, as soon as.
Sowjet [sɔvˈjɛt], m. (—s, pl. —s) Soviet.
sowohl [zoˈvoːl], conj. — wie, as well as.
sozial [zoˈtsjaːl], adj. social.
sozialisieren [zotsjaliˈziːrən], v.a. nationalise.
Sozialwissenschaft [zoˈtsjaːlvɪsənʃaft], f. (—, pl. —en) sociology; social science.
Sozietät [zotsjeˈtɛːt], f. (—, pl. —en) partnership.
Sozius [ˈzotsjus], m. (—, pl. —se, Socii) partner; pillion-rider; —sitz, (motor cycle) pillion (seat).
sozusagen [ˈzoːtsuzaːgən], adv. as it were, so to speak.
Spagat [ʃpaˈgaːt], m. (—(e)s, no pl.) (dial.) string, twine; (Dancing) the splits.
spähen [ˈʃpɛːən], v.n. look out, watch; (Mil.) scout; spy.
Späher [ˈʃpɛːər], m. (—s, pl. —) scout; spy.
Spalier [ʃpaˈliːr], n. (—s, pl. —e) trellis; — bilden, form a lane (of people).
Spalierobst [ʃpaˈliːroːpst], n. (—(e)s, no pl.) wall-fruit.
Spalt [ʃpalt], m. (—(e)s, pl. —e) crack, rift, cleft, rent; (glacier) crevasse.
Spalte [ˈʃpaltə], f. (—, pl. —n) (newspaper) column.
spalten [ˈʃpaltən], v.a. split, cleave, slit. — v.r. sich —, divide, break up, split up; (in two) bifurcate.
Spaltholz [ˈʃpalthɔlts], n. (—es, no pl.) fire-wood.
Spaltpilz [ˈʃpaltpɪlts], m. (—es, pl. —e) fission-fungus.
Spaltung [ˈʃpaltuŋ], f. (—, pl. —en) cleavage; (atomic) fission; (fig.) dissension, rupture; (Eccl.) schism.
Span [ʃpaːn], m. (—(e)s, pl. ̈e) chip, chippings, shavings.
Spange [ˈʃpaŋə], f. (—, pl. —n) clasp, buckle.
Spanien [ˈʃpaːnjən], n. Spain.
spanisch [ˈʃpaːnɪʃ], adj. Spanish; —e Wand, folding screen; es kommt mir — vor, it is Greek to me.
Spann [ʃpan], m. (—(e)s, pl. —e) instep.
Spanne [ˈʃpanə], f. (—, pl. —n) span; eine — Zeit, a short space of time.
spannen [ˈʃpanən], v.a. stretch, strain, span.
spannend [ˈʃpanənt], adj. thrilling, tense.
Spannkraft [ˈʃpankraft], f. (—, no pl.) elasticity.
Spannung [ˈʃpanuŋ], f. (—, pl. —en) tension, suspense, strain; (fig.) eager expectation, curiosity, suspense, close attention; (Elec.) voltage.

203

Sparbüchse

Sparbüchse [ˈʃpaːrbyksə], *f.* (—, *pl.* —n) money-box.

sparen [ˈʃpaːrən], *v.a.*, *v.n.* save, economise, put by, lay by.

Spargel [ˈʃpargəl], *m.* (—s, *pl.* —) asparagus.

Spargelder [ˈʃpaːrgɛldər], *n. pl.* savings.

Sparkasse [ˈʃpaːrkasə], *f.* (—, *pl.* —n) savings bank.

spärlich [ˈʃpɛːrlɪç], *adj.* scant, scanty, sparse.

Sparpfennig [ˈʃpaːrpfɛnɪç], *m.* (—s, *pl.* —e) nest-egg.

Sparren [ˈʃparən], *m.* (—s, *pl.* —) spar, rafter; *er hat einen —*, he has a screw loose.

sparsam [ˈʃpaːrzaːm], *adj.* economical, thrifty, frugal.

Spaß [ʃpaːs], *m.* (—es, *pl.* ⸚e) jest, fun, joke; *aus —, im —, zum —*, in fun; *— verstehen*, take a joke; *es macht mir —*, it amuses me, it is fun for me.

spaßen [ˈʃpaːsən], *v.n.* jest, joke.

spaßhaft [ˈʃpaːshaft], *adj.* funny, facetious, jocular.

Spaßverderber [ˈʃpaːsfɛrdɛrbər], *m.* (—s, *pl.* —) spoil-sport.

Spaßvogel [ˈʃpaːsfoːgəl], *m.* (—s, *pl.* ⸚) wag.

Spat [ʃpaːt], *m.* (—(e)s, *pl.* —e) (*Min.*) spar.

spät [ʃpɛːt], *adj.* late; *wie — ist es?* what is the time? *zu — kommen*, be late.

Spätabend [ˈʃpɛːtaːbənt], *m.* (—s, *pl.* —e) latter part of the evening, late evening.

Spatel [ˈʃpaːtəl], *m.* (—s, *pl.* —) spatula.

Spaten [ˈʃpaːtən], *m.* (—s, *pl.* —) spade.

Spatenstich [ˈʃpaːtənʃtɪç], *m.* (—(e)s, *pl.* —e) *den ersten — tun*, turn the first sod.

später [ˈʃpɛːtər], *adv.* later (on), afterwards.

spätestens [ˈʃpɛːtəstəns], *adv.* at the latest.

Spätling [ˈʃpɛːtlɪŋ], *m.* (—s, *pl.* —e) late arrival; late fruit.

Spätsommer [ˈʃpɛːtzɔmər], *m.* (—s, *pl.* —) Indian summer.

Spatz [ʃpats], *m.* (—en *pl.* —en) (*Orn.*) sparrow.

spazieren [ʃpaˈtsiːrən], *v.n.* (*aux.* sein) walk leisurely, stroll; *— gehen*, go for a walk, take a stroll; *— führen*, take for a walk.

Spazierfahrt [ʃpaˈtsiːrfaːrt], *f.* (—, *pl.* —en) (pleasure-)drive.

Spazierstock [ʃpaˈtsiːrʃtɔk], *m.* (—s, *pl.* ⸚e) walking-stick.

Spazierweg [ʃpaˈtsiːrveːk], *m.* (—s, *pl.* —e) walk, promenade.

Specht [ʃpɛçt], *m.* (—(e)s, *pl.* —e) (*Orn.*) woodpecker.

Speck [ʃpɛk], *m.* (—(e)s, *no pl.*) bacon; *eine Scheibe —*, a rasher of bacon.

speckig [ˈʃpɛkɪç], *adj.* fat.

Speckschwarte [ˈʃpɛkʃvartə], *f.* (—, *pl.* —n) bacon-rind.

Speckseite [ˈʃpɛkzaɪtə], *f.* (—, *pl.* —n) flitch of bacon.

spedieren [ʃpeˈdiːrən], *v.a.* forward; despatch.

Spediteur [ʃpediˈtøːr], *m.* (—s, *pl.* —e) forwarding agent, furniture-remover, carrier.

Spedition [ʃpediˈtsjoːn], *f.* (—, *pl.* —en) conveyance; forwarding agency.

Speer [ʃpeːr], *m.* (—(e)s, *pl.* —e) spear, lance.

Speiche [ˈʃpaɪçə], *f.* (—, *pl.* —n) spoke.

Speichel [ˈʃpaɪçəl], *m.* (—s, *no pl.*) spittle, saliva.

Speicher [ˈʃpaɪçər], *m.* (—s, *pl.* —) granary; warehouse, storehouse; loft.

speien [ˈʃpaɪən], *v.a.*, *v.n. irr.* spit; vomit, be sick.

Speise [ˈʃpaɪzə], *f.* (—, *pl.* —n) food, nourishment, dish.

Speisekammer [ˈʃpaɪzəkamər], *f.* (—, *pl.* —n) larder, pantry.

Speisekarte [ˈʃpaɪzəkartə], *f.* (—, *pl.* —n) bill of fare, menu.

speisen [ˈʃpaɪzən], *v.a.* feed, give to eat. — *v.n.* eat, dine, sup, lunch.

Speiseröhre [ˈʃpaɪzərøːrə], *f.* (—, *pl.* —n) gullet.

Speisewagen [ˈʃpaɪzəvaːgən], *m.* (—s, *pl.* —) (*Railw.*) dining-car.

Spektakel [ʃpɛkˈtaːkəl], *m.* (—s, *no pl.*) uproar, hubbub; shindy, rumpus; noise, row.

Spektrum [ˈʃpɛktrum], *n.* (—s, *pl.* Spektren) spectrum.

Spekulant [ʃpekuˈlant], *m.* (—en, *pl.* —en) speculator.

spekulieren [ʃpekuˈliːrən], *v.n.* speculate; theorise.

Spende [ˈʃpɛndə], *f.* (—, *pl.* —n) gift, donation; bounty.

spenden [ˈʃpɛndən], *v.a.* bestow, donate, contribute.

Spender [ˈʃpɛndər], *m.* (—s, *pl.* —) donor, giver, benefactor.

spendieren [ʃpɛnˈdiːrən], *v.a.* (give a) treat, pay for, stand.

Sperber [ˈʃpɛrbər], *m.* (—s, *pl.* —) (*Orn.*) sparrow-hawk.

Sperling [ˈʃpɛrlɪŋ], *m.* (—s, *pl.* —e) (*Orn.*) sparrow.

sperrangelweit [ˈʃpɛraŋəlvaɪt], *adv.* wide open.

Sperre [ˈʃpɛrə], *f.* (—, *pl.* —n) shutting, closing, blockade, blocking; closure; ban; (*Railw.*) barrier.

sperren [ˈʃpɛrən], *v.a.* spread out; (*Typ.*) space; shut, close, block; cut off; *ins Gefängnis —*, put in prison. — *v.r. sich — gegen*, offer resistance to.

Sperrhaken [ˈʃpɛrhaːkən], *m.* (—s, *pl.* —) catch, ratchet.

Sperrsitz [ˈʃpɛrzɪts], *m.* (—es, *pl.* —e) (*Theat.*) stall.

Sperrung [ˈʃpɛruŋ], *f.* (—, *pl.* —en) barring, obstruction, block, blockade; (*Comm.*) embargo.

Sperrzeit [ˈʃpɛrtsaɪt], *f.* (—, *pl.* —en) closing-time.

Spesen [ˈʃpeːzən], *f. pl.* charges, expenses.

spesenfrei [ˈʃpeːzənfraɪ], *adj.* free of charge; expenses paid.

Spezereien [ʃpeːtsəˈraɪən], *f. pl.* spices.

spezial [ʃpeˈtsjaːl], *adj.* special, particular.

spezialisieren [ʃpetsjaliˈziːrən], *v.a.* specify. — *v.r. sich* —, specialise.

Spezialist [ʃpetsjaˈlɪst], *m.* (—en, *pl.* —en) specialist, expert.

Spezialität [ʃpetsjaliˈtɛːt], *f.* (—, *pl.* —en) speciality, (*Am.*) specialty.

Spezies [ˈʃpeːtsjɛs], *f.* (—, *pl.* —) species; (*Maths.*) rule.

Spezifikation [ʃpetsifikaˈtsjoːn], *f.* (—, *pl.* —en) specification.

spezifisch [ʃpeˈtsiːfɪʃ], *adj.* specific.

spezifizieren [ʃpetsifiˈtsiːrən], *v.a.* specify.

Spezifizierung [ʃpetsifiˈtsiːruŋ], *f.* (—, *pl.* —en) specification.

Spezimen [ˈʃpeːtsimən], *n.* (—s, *pl.* —mina) specimen.

Sphäre [ˈsfɛːrə], *f.* (—, *pl.* —n) sphere.

sphärisch [ˈsfɛːrɪʃ], *adj.* spherical.

Spickaal [ˈʃpɪkaːl], *m.* (—s, *pl.* —e) smoked eel.

spicken [ˈʃpɪkən], *v.a.* lard; *den Beutel* —, fill o.'s purse.

Spiegel [ˈʃpiːgəl], *m.* (—s, *pl.* —) mirror, looking-glass.

spiegelblank [ˈʃpiːgəlblaŋk], *adj.* sparkling, shiny, polished.

Spiegelei [ˈʃpiːgəlaɪ], *n.* (—s, *pl.* —er) fried egg.

Spiegelfechterei [ˈʃpiːgəlfɛçtəraɪ], *f.* (—, *pl.* —en) shadow-boxing, make-believe.

Spiegelfenster [ˈʃpiːgəlfɛnstər], *n.* (—s, *pl.* —) plate-glass window.

spiegeln [ˈʃpiːgəln], *v.n.* glitter, shine. — *v.a.* reflect. — *v.r. sich* —, be reflected.

Spiegelscheibe [ˈʃpiːgəlʃaɪbə], *f.* (—, *pl.* —n) plate-glass pane.

Spiegelung [ˈʃpiːgəluŋ], *f.* (—, *pl.* —en) reflection; mirage.

Spiel [ʃpiːl], *n.* (—(e)s, *pl.* —e) play; game; sport; (*Theat.*) acting, performance; (*Mus.*) playing; *ehrliches (unehrliches)* —, fair (foul) play; *leichtes* —, walk-over; *auf dem* — *stehen,* be at stake; *aufs* — *setzen,* stake, risk; *die Hand im* — *haben,* have a finger in the pie; *gewonnenes* — *haben,* gain o.'s point; *ein gewagtes* — *treiben,* play a bold game; *sein* — *mit einem treiben,* trifle with s.o.

Spielart [ˈʃpiːlaːrt], *f.* (—, *pl.* —en) manner of playing; variety.

Spielbank [ˈʃpiːlbaŋk], *f.* (—, *pl.* —en) casino; gambling-table.

Spieldose [ˈʃpiːldoːzə], *f.* (—, *pl.* —n) musical box.

spielen [ˈʃpiːlən], *v.a., v.n.* play; gamble; (*Mus.*) play; (*Theat.*) act; *eine Rolle* —, play a part; *mit dem Gedanken* —, play with the idea.

spielend [ˈʃpiːlənt], *adv.* easily.

Spieler [ˈʃpiːlər], *m.* (—s, *pl.* —) player; gambler; gamester.

Spielerei [ʃpiːləˈraɪ], *f.* (—, *pl.* —en) child's play; trivialities.

Spielhölle [ˈʃpiːlhœlə], *f.* (—, *pl.* —n) gambling-den.

Spielmann [ˈʃpiːlman], *m.* (—s, *pl.* **Spielleute**) musician, fiddler; (*Middle Ages*) minstrel.

Spielmarke [ˈʃpiːlmarkə], *f.* (—, *pl.* —n) counter, chip.

Spielplan [ˈʃpiːlplaːn], *m.* (—s, *pl.* ⸚e) (*Theat.*) repertory.

Spielplatz [ˈʃpiːlplats], *m.* (—es, *pl.* ⸚e) playground.

Spielraum [ˈʃpiːlraum], *m.* (—s, *no pl.*) elbow-room; (*fig.*) scope; margin; clearance.

Spielsache [ˈʃpiːlzaxə], *f.* (—, *pl.* —n) toy, plaything.

Spielschule [ˈʃpiːlʃuːlə], *f.* (—, *pl.* —n) infant-school, kindergarten.

Spieltisch [ˈʃpiːltɪʃ], *m.* (—es, *pl.* —e) card-table.

Spieluhr [ˈʃpiːluːr], *f.* (—, *pl.* —en) musical clock.

Spielverderber [ˈʃpiːlfɛrdɛrbər], *m.* (—s, *pl.* —) spoilsport.

Spielwaren [ˈʃpiːlvaːrən], *f. pl.* toys.

Spielzeit [ˈʃpiːltsaɪt], *f.* (—, *pl.* —en) playtime; (*Theat.*) season.

Spielzeug [ˈʃpiːltsɔyk], *n.* (—s, *pl.* —e) plaything, toy.

Spieß [ʃpiːs], *m.* (—es, *pl.* —e) spear, pike; (*Cul.*) spit.

Spießbürger [ˈʃpiːsbyrgər], *m.* (—s, *pl.* —) Philistine.

spießen [ˈʃpiːsən], *v.a.* spear, pierce.

Spießer [ˈʃpiːsər], *m.* (—s, *pl.* —) Philistine.

Spießgeselle [ˈʃpiːsgəzɛlə], *m.* (—n, *pl.* —n) accomplice, companion *or* partner in crime.

spießig [ˈʃpiːsɪç], *adj.* (*coll.*) Philistine, uncultured, narrow-minded.

Spießruten [ˈʃpiːsruːtən], *f. pl.* — *laufen,* run the gauntlet.

Spinat [ʃpiˈnaːt], *m.* (—s, *no pl.*) spinach.

Spind [ʃpɪnt], *n.* (—(e)s, *pl.* —e) cupboard.

Spindel [ˈʃpɪndəl], *f.* (—, *pl.* —n) spindle; distaff; (*staircase*) newel.

spindeldürr [ˈʃpɪndəldyr], *adj.* as thin as a lath.

Spindelholz [ˈʃpɪndəlhɔlts], *n.* (—es, *no pl.*) spindle-tree wood.

Spinett [ʃpiˈnɛt], *n.* (—s, *pl.* —e) spinet.

Spinne [ˈʃpɪnə], *f.* (—, *pl.* —n) spider.

spinnefeind [ˈʃpɪnəfaɪnt], *adj. einander* — *sein,* hate each other like poison.

spinnen [ˈʃpɪnən], *v.a. irr.* spin. — *v.n.* (*coll.*) be off o.'s head, be crazy.

Spinnerei [ʃpɪnəˈraɪ], *f.* (—, *pl.* —en) spinning-mill.

Spinngewebe [ˈʃpɪngəveːbə], *n.* (—s, *pl.* —) cobweb.

Spinnrocken [ˈʃpɪnrɔkən], *m.* (—s, *pl.* —) distaff.

spintisieren [ʃpɪntiˈziːrən], *v.n.* muse, meditate.

Spion

Spion [ʃpi'oːn], *m.* (—s, *pl.* —e) spy.

spionieren [ʃpio'niːrən], *v.n.* spy, pry.

Spirale [ʃpi'raːlə], *f.* (—, *pl.* —n) spiral.

Spirituosen [ʃpirituˈoːzən], *pl.* spirits, liquors.

Spiritus ['ʃpiːritus], *m.* (—, *pl.* —se) alcohol, spirits of wine; *denaturierter* —, methylated spirits.

Spiritusbrennerei ['ʃpiːritusbrɛnəraɪ], *f.* (—, *pl.* —en) distillery.

Spiritusgehalt ['ʃpiːritusgəhalt], *m.* (—s, *pl.* —e) (*alcoholic*) strength, proof.

Spital [ʃpi'taːl], *n.* (—s, *pl.* ⁻er) infirmary; hospital.

Spitz [ʃpɪts], *m.* (—es, *pl.* —e) Pomeranian dog; *einen — haben*, (*coll.*) be slightly tipsy.

spitz [ʃpɪts], *adj.* pointed; (*fig.*) snappy, biting.

Spitzbart ['ʃpɪtsbaːrt], *m.* (—s, *pl.* ⁻e) imperial (beard), pointed beard.

Spitzbogen ['ʃpɪtsboːgən], *m.* (—s, *pl.* —) pointed arch, Gothic arch.

Spitzbogenfenster ['ʃpɪtsboːgənfɛnstər], *n.* (—s, *pl.* —) lancet window.

Spitzbube ['ʃpɪtsbuːbə], *m.* (—n, *pl.* —n) rogue; rascal; scamp.

Spitzbubenstreich ['ʃpɪtsbuːbənʃtraɪç], *m.* (—(e)s, *pl.* —e) act of roguery, knavery.

spitzbübisch ['ʃpɪtsbyːbɪʃ], *adj.* roguish.

Spitze ['ʃpɪtsə], *f.* (—, *pl.* —n) point; tip; top, peak; extremity; (*pipe*) mouthpiece; (*cigarette*) holder; (*pen*) nib; lace; *etwas auf die — treiben*, carry s.th. to extremes; *an der — stehen*, be at the head of.

Spitzel ['ʃpɪtsəl], *m.* (—s, *pl.* —) police-agent; informer.

spitzen ['ʃpɪtsən], *v.a.* sharpen; *die Ohren —*, prick up o.'s ears; *sich auf etwas —*, await s.th. eagerly, be all agog for s.th.

Spitzenbelastung ['ʃpɪtsənbəlastuŋ], *f.* (—, *pl.* —en) peak load.

Spitzenleistung ['ʃpɪtsənlaɪstuŋ], *f.* (—, *pl.* —en) maximum output; peak performance.

Spitzentuch ['ʃpɪtsəntuːx], *n.* (—(e)s, *pl.* ⁻er) lace scarf.

spitzfindig ['ʃpɪtsfɪndɪç], *adj.* subtle, crafty; hair-splitting.

Spitzhacke ['ʃpɪtshakə], *f.* (—, *pl.* —n) pickaxe.

spitzig ['ʃpɪtsɪç], *adj.* pointed, sharp; (*fig.*) biting, poignant.

Spitzmaus ['ʃpɪtsmaus], *f.* (—, *pl.* ⁻e) (*Zool.*) shrew.

Spitzname ['ʃpɪtsnaːmə], *m.* (—ns, *pl.* —n) nickname.

spitzwinklig ['ʃpɪtsvɪŋklɪç], *adj.* acute-angled.

spleißen ['ʃplaɪsən], *v.a. irr.* split, cleave.

Splitter ['ʃplɪtər], *m.* (—s, *pl.* —) splinter, chip.

splitternackt ['ʃplɪtərnakt], *adj.* stark naked.

splittern ['ʃplɪtərn], *v.n.* (*aux.* sein) splinter.

spontan [ʃpɔn'taːn], *adj.* spontaneous.

sporadisch [ʃpo'raːdɪʃ], *adj.* sporadic.

Spore ['ʃpoːrə], *f.* (—, *pl.* —n) spore.

Sporn [ʃpɔrn], *m.* (—s, *pl.* **Sporen**) spur.

spornstreichs ['ʃpɔrnʃtraɪçs], *adv.* post-haste, at once.

Sportler ['ʃpɔrtlər], *m.* (—s, *pl.* —) athlete, sportsman.

sportlich ['ʃpɔrtlɪç], *adj.* athletic; sporting.

sportsmäßig ['ʃpɔrtsmɛːsɪç], *adj.* sportsmanlike.

Spott [ʃpɔt], *m.* (—(e)s, *no pl.*) mockery; scorn; *Gegenstand des —s*, laughing-stock; — *treiben mit*, mock, deride; *zum Schaden den — hinzufügen*, add insult to injury.

spottbillig ['ʃpɔtbɪlɪç], *adj.* ridiculously cheap, dirt-cheap.

Spöttelei [ʃpœtə'laɪ], *f.* (—, *pl.* —en) sarcasm.

spötteln ['ʃpœtəln], *v.n.* mock, jeer.

spotten ['ʃpɔtən], *v.a., v.n.* deride, scoff (at); *es spottet jeder Beschreibung*, it defies description.

Spötter ['ʃpœtər], *m.* (—s, *pl.* —) mocker, scoffer.

Spötterei [ʃpœtə'raɪ], *f.* (—, *pl.* —en) mockery, derision.

Spottgedicht ['ʃpɔtgədɪçt], *n.* (—(e)s, *pl.* —e) satirical poem.

spöttisch ['ʃpœtɪʃ], *adj.* mocking, satirical, ironical, scoffing.

spottlustig ['ʃpɔtlustɪç], *adj.* flippant, satirical.

Spottschrift ['ʃpɔtʃrɪft], *f.* (—, *pl.* —en) satire, lampoon.

Sprache ['ʃpraːxə], *f.* (—, *pl.* —n) speech, language; tongue; expression, diction; discussion; *etwas zur — bringen*, bring a subject up; *zur — kommen*, come up for discussion; *heraus mit der —!* speak out!

Sprachfehler ['ʃpraːxfeːlər], *m.* (—s, *pl.* —) impediment in o.'s speech.

sprachfertig ['ʃpraːxfɛrtɪç], *adj.* having a ready tongue; a good linguist, fluent.

Sprachgebrauch ['ʃpraːxgəbraux], *m.* (—(e)s, *no pl.*) (linguistic) usage.

Sprachkenner ['ʃpraːxkɛnər], *m.* (—s, *pl.* —) linguist.

sprachkundig ['ʃpraːxkundɪç], *adj.* proficient in languages.

Sprachlehre ['ʃpraːxleːrə], *f.* (—, *no pl.*) grammar.

sprachlich ['ʃpraːxlɪç], *adj.* linguistic.

sprachlos ['ʃpraːxloːs], *adj.* speechless, tongue-tied; — *dastehen*, be dumb-founded.

Sprachrohr ['ʃpraːxroːr], *n.* (—s, *pl.* —e) megaphone, speaking-tube; (*fig.*) mouthpiece.

Sprachschatz ['ʃpraːxʃats], *m.* (—es, *no pl.*) vocabulary.

Sprachvergleichung ['ʃpraːxfɛrglaɪçuŋ], *f.* (—, *no pl.*) comparative philology.

Spürhund

Sprachwerkzeug ['ʃpraːxvɛrktsɔyk], *n.* (—s, *pl.* —e) organ of speech.
Sprachwissenschaft ['ʃpraːxvisənʃaft], *f.* (—, *pl.* —en) linguistics, philology.
sprechen ['ʃprɛçən], *v.a.,v.n. irr.* speak, declare, say; talk; *für einen* —, put in a good word for s.o., speak up for s.o.; *er ist nicht zu* —, he is not available; *auf einen gut zu* — *sein*, feel well disposed towards s.o.; *schuldig* —, pronounce guilty; *das Urteil* —, pass sentence.
sprechend ['ʃprɛçənt], *adj.* expressive; — *ähnlich*, strikingly alike.
Sprecher ['ʃprɛçər], *m.* (—s, *pl.* —) speaker, orator, spokesman; (*Rad.*) announcer.
Sprechstunde ['ʃprɛçʃtundə], *f.* (—, *pl.* —n) consulting hours, surgery hours; office hours.
Sprechzimmer ['ʃprɛçtsimər], *n.* (—s, *pl.*—) consulting-room.
spreizen ['ʃpraitsən], *v.a.* spread open; *die Beine* —, plant o.'s legs wide apart, straddle. — *v.r. sich* —, give o.s. airs.
Sprengbombe ['ʃprɛŋbɔmbə], *f.* (—, *pl.* —n) (high explosive) bomb.
Sprengel ['ʃprɛŋəl], *m.* (—s, *pl.* —) diocese.
sprengen ['ʃprɛŋən], *v.a.* sprinkle; water; blast, explode; burst open, blow up; *eine Versammlung* —, break up a meeting. — *v.n.* (*aux.* sein) ride at full speed, gallop.
Sprengpulver ['ʃprɛŋpulvər], *n.* (—s, *no pl.*) blasting-powder.
Sprengstoff ['ʃprɛŋʃtɔf], *m.* (—es, *pl.* —e) explosive.
Sprengwagen ['ʃprɛŋvaːgən], *m.* (—s, *pl.* —) sprinkler; water-cart.
sprenkeln ['ʃprɛŋkəln], *v.a.* speckle.
Spreu [ʃprɔy], *f.* (—, *no pl.*) chaff.
Sprichwort ['ʃpriçvɔrt], *n.* (—s, *pl.* ⁻er) proverb, adage, saying.
sprießen ['ʃpriːsən], *v.n. irr.* sprout, shoot, germinate.
Springbrunnen ['ʃpriŋbrunən], *m.* (—s, *pl.* —) fountain.
springen ['ʃpriŋən], *v.n. irr.* (*aux.* sein) spring, leap, jump; (*glass*) burst; *etwas* — *lassen*, (*coll.*) treat s.o. to s.th.
Springer ['ʃpriŋər], *m.* (—s, *pl.* —) jumper, acrobat; (*Chess*) knight.
Springflut ['ʃpriŋfluːt], *f.* (—, *pl.* —en) spring-tide.
Springtau ['ʃpriŋtau], *n.* (—s, *pl.* —e) skipping-rope; (*Naut.*) slip-rope.
Sprit [ʃprit], *m.* (—s, *pl.* —e) spirit alcohol; (*sl.*) fuel, petrol.
Spritze ['ʃpritsə], *f.* (—, *pl.* —n) squirt, syringe; fire-engine; (*coll.*) injection.
spritzen ['ʃpritsən], *v.a.* squirt, spout, spray, sprinkle; (*coll.*) inject. — *v.n.* gush forth.
Spritzkuchen ['ʃpritskuːxən], *m.* (—s, *pl.* —) fritter.
Spritztour ['ʃpritstuːr], *f.* (—, *pl.* —en) (*coll.*) pleasure trip, outing; (*coll.*) spin.

spröde ['ʃprøːdə], *adj.* (*material*) brittle; (*person*) stubborn; coy, prim, prudish.
Sprödigkeit ['ʃprøːdɪçkait], *f.* (—, *no pl.*) (*material*) brittleness; (*person*) stubbornness; coyness, primness, prudery.
Sproß [ʃprɔs], *m.* (—sses, *pl.* —sse) sprout, shoot, germ; (*fig.*) scion, offspring.
Sprosse ['ʃprɔsə], *f.* (—, *pl.* —n) (*ladder*) step, rung.
Sprößling ['ʃprœslɪŋ], *m.* (—s, *pl.* —e) scion, offspring.
Sprotte ['ʃprɔtə], *f.* (—, *pl.* —n) sprat.
Spruch [ʃprux], *m.* (—(e)s, *pl.* ⁻e) saying, aphorism; proverb; (*obs.*) saw; (*judge*) sentence, verdict.
spruchreif ['ʃpruxraif], *adj.* ripe for judgment; ready for a decision.
Sprudel ['ʃpruːdəl], *m.* (—s, *pl.* —) bubbling spring; (*coll.*) soda water.
sprudeln ['ʃpruːdəln], *v.n.* bubble, gush.
sprühen ['ʃpryːən], *v.a.* sprinkle, scatter, spray. — *v.n.* sparkle, emit sparks; (*rain*) drizzle.
sprühend ['ʃpryːənt], *adj.* (*fig.*) sparkling, scintillating, brilliant.
Sprühregen ['ʃpryːreːgən], *m.* (—s, *no pl.*) drizzling rain, drizzle.
Sprung [ʃpruŋ], *m.* (—(e)s, *pl.* ⁻e) leap, bound, jump; chink, crack; *nur auf einen* — *zu Besuch kommen*, pay a flying visit; *auf dem* — *sein zu*, be on the point of; *sich auf den* — *machen*, cut and run, (*coll.*) fly; *große* ⁻e *machen*, (*coll.*) live it up, cut a dash.
Sprungfeder ['ʃpruŋfeːdər], *f.* (—, *pl.* —n) spring.
Sprungkraft ['ʃpruŋkraft], *f.* (—, *no pl.*) springiness, elasticity, buoyancy.
Spucke ['ʃpukə], *f.* (—, *no pl.*) spittle, saliva.
spucken ['ʃpukən], *v.a., v.n.* spit.
Spuk [ʃpuːk], *m.* (—s, *pl.* —e) haunting; ghost, spectre, apparition; (*coll.*) spook.
spuken ['ʃpuːkən], *v.n.* haunt; be haunted.
spukhaft ['ʃpuːkhaft], *adj.* uncanny, phantom-like, ghost-like, spooky.
Spule ['ʃpuːlə], *f.* (—, *pl.* —n) spool; (*Elec.*) coil.
Spüleimer ['ʃpyːlaimər], *m.* (—s, *pl.* —) slop-pail.
spülen ['ʃpyːlən], *v.a.* rinse, wash.
Spülicht ['ʃpyːlɪçt], *n.* (—s, *no pl.*) dish-water.
Spund [ʃpunt], *m.* (—(e)s, *pl.* ⁻e) bung.
Spundloch ['ʃpuntlɔx], *n.* (—s, *pl.* ⁻er) bung-hole.
Spur [ʃpuːr], *f.* (—, *pl.* —en) footprint, track, trail; spoor; (*fig.*) trace, vestige; *frische* —, hot scent; *einer Sache auf die* — *kommen*, be on the track of s.th.; *keine* — *von*, not a trace of, not an inkling of.
spüren ['ʃpyːrən], *v.a.* trace, track (down); feel, sense, notice.
Spürhund ['ʃpyːrhunt], *m.* (—s, *pl.* —e) tracker dog, setter, beagle; (*fig.*) spy, sleuth.

207

spurlos

spurlos ['ʃpuːrloːs], *adj.* trackless, without a trace; *es ging — an ihm vorüber,* it left no mark on him; *— verschwinden,* vanish into thin air.
Spürsinn ['ʃpyːrzɪn], *m.* (—s, *no pl.*) scent; flair; sagacity, shrewdness.
Spurweite ['ʃpuːrvaɪtə], *f.* (—, *pl.* —n) gauge, width of track.
sputen ['ʃpuːtən], *v.r. sich —,* make haste, hurry.
Staat [ʃtaːt], *m.* (—(e)s, *pl.* —en) state; government; pomp, show, parade; *— machen,* make a show of.
Staatenbund ['ʃtaːtənbunt], *m.* (—(e)s, *pl.* ⸚e) confederacy, federation.
staatlich ['ʃtaːtlɪç], *adj.* belonging to the state, public, national.
Staatsangehörige ['ʃtaːtsangəhøːrɪgə], *m.* (—n, *pl.* —n) citizen (of a country), subject, national.
Staatsangehörigkeit ['ʃtaːtsangəhøːrɪçkaɪt], *f.* (—, *pl.* —en) nationality.
Staatsanwalt ['ʃtaːtsanvalt], *m.* (—s, *pl.* ⸚e) public prosecutor, Attorney-General.
Staatsbeamte ['ʃtaːtsbəamtə], *m.* (—n, *pl.* —n) civil servant, employee of the state.
Staatsbürger ['ʃtaːtsbyrgər], *m.* (—s, *pl.* —) citizen, national.
Staatsdienst ['ʃtaːtsdiːnst], *m.* (—(e)s, *pl.* —e) civil service, government service.
Staatseinkünfte ['ʃtaːtsaɪnkynftə], *f. pl.* public revenue.
Staatsgesetz ['ʃtaːtsgəzɛts], *n.* (—es, *pl.* —e) statute law.
Staatsgewalt ['ʃtaːtsgəvalt], *f.* (—, *no pl.*) executive power.
Staatshaushalt ['ʃtaːtshaushalt], *m.* (—s, *no pl.*) state finances, budget.
Staatshaushaltsanschlag ['ʃtaːtshaushaltsanʃlaːk], *m.* (—s, *pl.* ⸚e) budget estimates.
Staatskanzler ['ʃtaːtskantslər], *m.* (—s, *pl.* —) Chancellor.
Staatskasse ['ʃtaːtskasə], *f.* (—, *no pl.*) public exchequer, treasury.
Staatskörper ['ʃtaːtskœrpər], *m.* (—s, *pl.* —) body politic.
Staatskosten ['ʃtaːtskɔstən], *f. pl. auf —,* at (the) public expense.
Staatskunst ['ʃtaːtskunst], *f.* (—, *no pl.*) statesmanship; statecraft.
Staatsminister ['ʃtaːtsmɪnɪstər], *m.* (—s, *pl.* —) cabinet minister; minister of state.
Staatsrat ['ʃtaːtsraːt], *m.* (—s, *no pl.*) council of state; (*pl.* ⸚e) councillor of state.
Staatsrecht ['ʃtaːtsrɛçt], *n.* (—(e)s, *no pl.*) constitutional law.
Staatssiegel ['ʃtaːtsziːgəl], *n.* (—s, *pl.* —) Great Seal, official seal.
Staatsstreich ['ʃtaːtsʃtraɪç], *m.* (—(e)s, *pl.* —e) coup d'état.
Staatswirtschaft ['ʃtaːtsvɪrtʃaft], *f.* (—, *no pl.*) political economy.
Staatszimmer ['ʃtaːtstsɪmər], *n.* (—s, *pl.* —) state apartment.

Stab [ʃtaːp], *m.* (—(e)s, *pl.* ⸚e) staff; stick, rod, pole; crosier; mace; (*Mil.*) field-officers, staff; *den — über einen brechen,* condemn s.o. (to death).
stabil [ʃtaˈbiːl], *adj.* steady, stable, firm.
stabilisieren [ʃtabiliˈziːrən], *v.a.* stabilise.
Stabreim ['ʃtaːpraɪm], *m.* (—s, *no pl.*) alliteration.
Stabsarzt ['ʃtaːpsartst], *m.* (—es, *pl.* ⸚e) (*Mil.*) medical officer.
Stabsquartier ['ʃtaːpskvartiːr], *n.* (—s, *pl.* —e) (*Mil.*) headquarters.
Stachel ['ʃtaxəl], *m.* (—s, *pl.* —n) (*animal*) sting; (*plant*) prickle, thorn; (*fig.*) keen edge, sting; stimulus; *wider den — löcken,* kick against the pricks.
Stachelbeere ['ʃtaxəlbeːrə], *f.* (—, *pl.* —n) (*Bot.*) gooseberry.
Stachelschwein ['ʃtaxelʃvaɪn], *n.* (—s, *pl.* —e) (*Zool.*) hedgehog, porcupine.
stachlig ['ʃtaxlɪç], *adj.* prickly, thorny; (*fig.*) disagreeable.
Stadion ['ʃtaːdjon], *n.* (—s, *pl.* —dien) sports-arena, stadium.
Stadium ['ʃtaːdjum], *n.* (—s, *pl.* —dien) stage (of development), phase.
Stadt [ʃtat], *f.* (—, *pl.* ⸚e) town; city.
Stadtbahn ['ʃtatbaːn], *f.* (—, *pl.* —en) metropolitan railway.
Städtchen ['ʃtɛtçən], *n.* (—s, *pl.* —) small town, township.
Städter ['ʃtɛtər], *m.* (—s, *pl.* —) townsman.
Stadtgemeinde ['ʃtatgəmaɪndə], *f.* (—, *pl.* —n) municipality.
städtisch ['ʃtɛtɪʃ], *adj.* municipal.
Stadtmauer ['ʃtatmauər], *f.* (—, *pl.* —n) town wall, city wall.
Stadtrat ['ʃtatraːt], *m.* (—s, *no pl.*) town council; (*pl.* ⸚e) town councillor; alderman.
Stadtteil ['ʃtattaɪl], *m.* (—s, *pl.* —e) ward, district, part of a town.
Stadttor ['ʃtattoːr], *n.* (—(e)s, *pl.* —e) city-gate.
Stadtverordnete ['ʃtatfɛrɔrdnətə], *m.* (—n, *pl.* —n) town councillor.
Stafette [ʃtaˈfɛtə], *f.* (—, *pl.* —n) courier; relay.
Staffel ['ʃtafəl], *f.* (—, *pl.* —n) step, rundle, rung, round; relay; (*fig.*) degree; (*Aviat.*) squadron.
Staffelei [ʃtafəˈlaɪ], *f.* (—, *pl.* —en) easel.
staffeln ['ʃtafəln], *v.a.* grade; differentiate; stagger.
Staffelung ['ʃtafəluŋ], *f.* (—, *pl.* —en) gradation.
stagnieren [ʃtagˈniːrən], *v.n.* stagnate.
Stahl [ʃtaːl], *m.* (—(e)s, *pl.* ⸚e) steel.
stählen ['ʃtɛːlən], *v.a.* steel, harden, temper; brace.
stählern ['ʃtɛːlərn], *adj.* made of steel, steely.
Stahlquelle ['ʃtaːlkvɛlə], *f.* (—, *pl.* —n) chalybeate spring; mineral spring.
Stahlstich ['ʃtaːlʃtɪç], *m.* (—(e)s, *pl.* —e) steel-engraving.

Stählung ['ʃtɛːluŋ], *f.* (—, *no pl.*) steeling; (*fig.*) bracing.

Stahlwaren ['ʃtaːlvaːrən], *f. pl.* hardware, cutlery.

Stall [ʃtal], *m.* (—(e)s, *pl.* ⏑e) stable; (*pig*) sty; (*dog*) kennel.

Stallbursche ['ʃtalburʃə], *m.* (—n, *pl.* —n) stable-boy, groom.

Stallungen ['ʃtaluŋən], *f. pl.* stabling, stables.

Stambul ['stambul], *n.* Istanbul.

Stamm [ʃtam], *m.* (—(e)s, *pl.* ⏑e) (*tree*) trunk; (*people*) tribe, family, race; (*words*) stem; root.

Stammaktie ['ʃtamaktsjə], *f.* (—, *pl.* —n) (*Comm.*) original share.

Stammbaum ['ʃtambaum], *m.* (—s, *pl.* ⏑e) pedigree; family tree.

Stammbuch ['ʃtambuːx], *n.* (—(e)s, *pl.* ⏑er) album.

stammeln ['ʃtaməln], *v.a., v.n.* stammer, stutter; falter.

stammen ['ʃtamən], *v.n.* (*aux.* sein) be descended from, spring from, originate from, stem from; be derived from.

Stammesgenosse ['ʃtaməsgənɔsə], *m.* (—n, *pl.* —n) kinsman, clansman.

Stammgast ['ʃtamgast], *m.* (—es, *pl.* ⏑e) regular customer.

Stammgut ['ʃtamguːt], *n.* (—s, *pl.* ⏑er) family estate.

Stammhalter ['ʃtamhaltər], *m.* (—s, *pl.* —) son and heir; eldest son.

Stammhaus ['ʃtamhaus], *n.* (—es, *pl.* ⏑er) ancestral mansion; (*royalty*) dynasty; (*Comm.*) business headquarters, head office.

stämmig ['ʃtɛmiç], *adj.* sturdy, strong.

Stammler ['ʃtamlər], *m.* (—s, *pl.* —) stammerer, stutterer.

Stammsilbe ['ʃtamzilbə], *f.* (—, *pl.* —n) (*Ling.*) radical syllable.

Stammtafel ['ʃtamtaːfəl], *f.* (—, *pl.* —n) genealogical table.

Stammvater ['ʃtamfaːtər], *m.* (—s, *pl.* ⏑) ancestor, progenitor.

stammverwandt ['ʃtamfɛrvant], *adj.* cognate, kindred.

stampfen ['ʃtampfən], *v.a.* stamp, pound, ram down. — *v.n.* stamp, trample.

Stand [ʃtant], *m.* (—(e)s, *pl.* ⏑e) stand; (*market*) stall; situation, state (of affairs), condition; reading, position; rank, station (in life); (*pl.*) the classes, the estates.

Standarte [ʃtan'dartə], *f.* (—, *pl.* —n) standard, banner.

Standbild ['ʃtantbilt], *n.* (—(e)s, *pl.* —er) statue.

Ständchen ['ʃtɛntçən], *n.* (—s, *pl.* —) serenade; *einem ein — bringen*, serenade s.o.

Ständehaus ['ʃtɛndəhaus], *n.* (—es, *pl.* ⏑er) state assembly-hall.

Ständer ['ʃtɛndər], *m.* (—s, *pl.* —) stand, pedestal; post; (upright) desk.

Standesamt ['ʃtandəsamt], *n.* (—s, *pl.* ⏑er) registry office.

Standesbeamte ['ʃtandəsbəamtə], *m.* (—n, *pl.* —n) registrar (of births, marriages and deaths).

Standesbewußtsein ['ʃtandəsbəvustzain], *n.* (—s, *no pl.*) class-feeling, class-consciousness.

Standesperson ['ʃtandəsperzoːn], *f.* (—, *pl.* —en) person of rank.

Standgericht ['ʃtantgəriçt], *n.* (—es, *pl.* —e) court-martial; summary court of justice.

standhaft ['ʃtanthaft], *adj.* constant, firm, steadfast.

standhalten ['ʃtanthaltən], *v.n. irr.* bear up, stand o.'s ground, withstand, resist.

ständig ['ʃtɛndiç], *adj.* permanent.

ständisch ['ʃtɛndiʃ], *adj.* relating to the estates (of the realm).

Standort ['ʃtantɔrt], *m.* (—s, *pl.* —e) location; station.

Standpauke ['ʃtantpaukə], *f.* (—, *pl.* —n) (*coll.*) harangue; severe reprimand.

Standpunkt ['ʃtantpuŋkt], *m.* (—(e)s, *pl.* —e) standpoint; point of view; *den — vertreten*, take the line; *einem den — klar machen*, give s.o. a piece of o.'s mind.

Standrecht ['ʃtantrɛçt], *n.* (—(e)s, *no pl.*) martial law.

Standuhr ['ʃtantuːr], *f.* (—, *pl.* —en) grandfather-clock.

Stange ['ʃtaŋə], *f.* (—, *pl.* —n) stick, pole; *bei der — bleiben*, stick to the point, persevere.

Stank [ʃtaŋk], *m.* (—s, *no pl.*) (*dial.*) stench; discord, trouble.

Stänker ['ʃtɛŋkər], *m.* (—s, *pl.* —) (*coll.*) mischief-maker, quarrelsome person.

stänkern ['ʃtɛŋkərn], *v.n.* pick quarrels; ferret about, make trouble.

Stanniol [ʃta'njoːl], *n.* (—s, *no pl.*) tinfoil.

stanzen ['ʃtantsən], *v.a.* punch, stamp.

Stapel ['ʃtaːpəl], *m.* (—s, *pl.* —) pile, heap; (*Naut.*) slipway; *ein Schiff vom — lassen*, launch a ship.

Stapellauf ['ʃtaːpəllauf], *m.* (—s, *pl.* ⏑e) (*Naut.*) launch, launching.

stapeln ['ʃtaːpəln], *v.a.* pile up.

Stapelnahrung ['ʃtaːpəlnaːruŋ], *f.* (—, *no pl.*) staple diet.

Stapelplatz ['ʃtaːpəlplats], *m.* (—es, *pl.* ⏑e) mart, emporium.

Stapelware ['ʃtaːpəlvaːrə], *f.* (—, *pl.* —n) staple goods.

Stapfen ['ʃtapfən], *m.* or *f. pl.* footsteps.

Star (1) [ʃtaːr], *m.* (—(e)s, *pl.* —e) (*Med.*) cataract; *einem den — stechen*, operate for cataract; (*fig.*) open s.o.'s eyes.

Star (2) [ʃtaːr], *m.* (—(e)s, *pl.* —en) (*Orn.*) starling.

stark [ʃtark], *adj.* strong, stout; robust; vigorous; heavy; considerable; *—er Esser*, hearty eater. — *adv.* very much.

Stärke

Stärke [ˈʃtɛrkə], f. (—, no pl.) strength, vigour, robustness; strong point; starch.

Stärkekleister [ˈʃtɛrkəklaɪstər], m. (—s, no pl.) starch-paste.

Stärkemehl [ˈʃtɛrkəmeːl], n. (—s, no pl.) starch-flour.

stärken [ˈʃtɛrkən], v.a. strengthen; corroborate; starch. — v.r. sich —, take some refreshment.

stärkend [ˈʃtɛrkənt], adj. strengthening, restorative; —es Mittel, tonic.

starkleibig [ˈʃtarklaɪbɪç], adj. corpulent, stout, obese.

Stärkung [ˈʃtɛrkuŋ], f. (—, pl. —en) strengthening, invigoration; refreshment.

starr [ʃtar], adj. stiff, rigid; fixed; inflexible; stubborn; einen — ansehen, stare at s.o.

starren [ˈʃtarən], v.n. stare.

Starrheit [ˈʃtarhaɪt], f. (—, no pl.) stiffness, rigidity; fixedness; inflexibility; stubbornness.

starrköpfig [ˈʃtarkœpfɪç], adj. headstrong, stubborn, obstinate, pigheaded.

Starrkrampf [ˈʃtarkrampf], m. (—(e)s, no pl.) (Med.) tetanus.

Starrsinn [ˈʃtarzɪn], m. (—s, no pl.) stubbornness, obstinacy.

Station [ʃtaˈtsjoːn], f. (—, pl. —en) (Railw.) station; (main) terminus; stop, stopping-place; (hospital) ward; freie —, board and lodging found.

stationär [ʃtatsjoˈnɛːr], adj. stationary.

stationieren [ʃtatsjoˈniːrən], v.a. station.

Stationsvorsteher [ʃtatˈsjoːnsfɔrʃteːər], m. (—s, pl. —) station-master.

statisch [ˈʃtaːtɪʃ], adj. static.

Statist [ʃtaˈtɪst], m. (—en, pl. —en) (Theat.) extra, walking-on part; (pl.) supers.

Statistik [ʃtaˈtɪstɪk], f. (—, pl. —en) statistics.

Statistiker [ʃtaˈtɪstɪkər], m. (—s, pl. —) statistician.

Stativ [ʃtaˈtiːf], n. (—s, pl. —e) stand, tripod.

Statt [ʃtat], f. (—, no pl.) place, stead; an seiner —, in his place.

statt [ʃtat], prep. (Genit.) instead of, in lieu of.

Stätte [ˈʃtɛtə], f. (—, pl. —n) place, abode.

stattfinden [ˈʃtatfɪndən], v.n. irr. take place.

stattgeben [ˈʃtatgeːbən], v.n. irr. einer Bitte —, grant a request.

statthaft [ˈʃtathaft], adj. admissible, allowable, lawful.

Statthalter [ˈʃtathaltər], m. (—s, pl. —) governor.

stattlich [ˈʃtatlɪç], adj. stately, handsome, distinguished, comely; portly; considerable; eine —e Summe, a tidy sum.

statuieren [ʃtatuˈiːrən], v.a. decree; ein Exempel —, make an example of.

Statut [ʃtaˈtuːt], n. (—s, pl. —en) statute, regulation.

Staub [ʃtaup], m. (—(e)s, no pl.) dust, powder; sich aus dem — machen, take French leave; abscond.

Stäubchen [ˈʃtɔypçən], n. (—s, pl. —) mote, particle of dust.

stauben [ˈʃtaubən], v.n. es staubt, it is dusty.

Staubgefäß [ˈʃtaupgəfɛːs], n. (—es, pl. —e) stamen.

staubig [ˈʃtaubɪç], adj. dusty.

Staubkamm [ˈʃtaupkam], m. (—s, pl. ⸚e) fine-tooth comb.

Staublappen [ˈʃtauplapən], m. (—s, pl. —) duster.

Staubmantel [ˈʃtaupmantəl], m. (—s, pl. ⸚) overall, smock; dust(er)coat, (Am.) duster.

Staubsauger [ˈʃtaupzaugər], m. (—s, pl. —) vacuum cleaner.

Staubtuch [ˈʃtauptuːx], n. (—es, pl. ⸚er) duster.

Staubwedel [ˈʃtaupveːdəl], m. (—s, pl. —) feather duster.

Staubwolke [ˈʃtaupvɔlkə], f. (—, pl. —n) cloud of dust.

Staubzucker [ˈʃtauptsukər], m. (—s, no pl.) castor-sugar, icing-sugar.

Staudamm [ˈʃtaudam], m. (—s, pl. ⸚e) dam, dyke.

Staude [ˈʃtaudə], f. (—, pl. —n) shrub, bush.

stauen [ˈʃtauən], v.a. stow; (water) dam. — v.r. sich —, be congested.

staunen [ˈʃtaunən], v.n. be astonished, be surprised, wonder (at).

Staupe [ˈʃtaupə], f. (—, pl. —n) (animals) distemper.

stäupen [ˈʃtɔypən], v.a. (obs.) scourge, flog.

Stauung [ˈʃtauuŋ], f. (—, pl. —en) stowage; (water) damming-up, swell, rising; (blood) congestion; (traffic) jam, build-up.

stechen [ˈʃtɛçən], v.a. irr. prick, sting; stab; (cards) trump.

stechend [ˈʃtɛçənt], adj. pungent, biting.

Stechmücke [ˈʃtɛçmykə], f. (—, pl. —n) (Ent.) gnat, mosquito.

Stechpalme [ˈʃtɛçpalmə], f. (—, pl. —n) (Bot.) holly.

Steckbrief [ˈʃtɛkbriːf], m. (—s, pl. —e) warrant (for arrest).

stecken [ˈʃtɛkən], v.a. stick into, put, place, fix; (plants) set, plant; in Brand —, set on fire, set fire to. — v.n. irgendwo —, be about somewhere; — bleiben, get stuck, break down; er steckt dahinter, he is at the bottom of it. — v.r. sich hinter einen —, shelter behind s.o.

Stecken [ˈʃtɛkən], m. (—s, pl. —) stick, staff.

Stecker [ˈʃtɛkər], m. (—s, pl. —) (Elec.) plug.

Steckkontakt [ˈʃtɛkkɔntakt], m. (—(e)s, pl. —e) (Elec.) plug, point.

Stecknadel [ˈʃtɛknaːdəl], f. (—, pl. —n) pin.

Steg [ʃteːk], m. (—(e)s, pl. —e) plank, foot-bridge; jetty; (violin) bridge.

Stelzbein

Stegreif [′ʃte:kraɪf], *m.* (—s, *pl.* —e) (*obs.*) stirrup; *aus dem* — *sprechen,* extemporise, improvise.

stehen [′ʃte:ən], *v.n. irr.* stand; be; stand still; *einem gut* —, fit *or* suit s.o. well; *mit einem gut* —, be on good terms with s.o.; *gut* —, be in a fair way, look promising; *was steht zu Diensten?* what can I do for you? — *bleiben,* stand still, stop, pull up.

stehlen [′ʃte:lən], *v.a. irr.* steal.

Steiermark [′ʃtaɪərmark], *f.* Styria.

steif [ʃtaɪf], *adj.* stiff; (*grog*) strong; awkward; ceremonious, punctilious, formal. — *adv. etwas* — *und fest behaupten,* swear by all that's holy.

steifen [′ʃtaɪfən], *v.a.* stiffen, starch.

Steifheit [′ʃtaɪfhaɪt], *f.* (—, *no pl.*) stiffness; (*fig.*) formality.

Steifleinen [′ʃtaɪflaɪnən], *n.* (—s, *no pl.*) buckram.

Steig [ʃtaɪk], *m.* (—(e)s, *pl.* —e) path, (mountain) track.

Steigbügel [′ʃtaɪkby:gəl], *m.* (—s, *pl.* —) stirrup.

Steigen [′ʃtaɪgən], *n.* (—s, *no pl.*) rising, increase; (*price*) advance, rise; *im* —, on the increase.

steigen [′ʃtaɪgən], *v.n. irr.* (*aux. sein*) climb, mount, ascend; (*barometer*) rise; (*population*) increase; (*horse*) rear; (*price*) advance, rise.

Steiger [′ʃtaɪgər], *m.* (—s, *pl.* —) climber, mountaineer; mining-surveyor, overseer.

steigern [′ʃtaɪgərn], *v.a.* (*price*) raise; (*fig.*) enhance, increase. — *v.r. sich* —, increase.

Steigerung [′ʃtaɪgəruŋ], *f.* (—, *pl.* —en) raising; (*fig.*) enhancement; increase; (*Gram.*) comparison.

Steigung [′ʃtaɪguŋ], *f.* (—, *pl.* —en) gradient.

steil [ʃtaɪl], *adj.* steep.

Stein [ʃtaɪn], *m.* (—(e)s, *pl.* —e) stone, rock; flint; jewel, gem; monument; (*Chess*) piece, chessman; (*Draughts*) man; (*fruit*) stone, kernel; — *des Anstoßes,* stumbling block; *mir fällt ein* — *vom Herzen,* it is a load off my mind; *bei einem einen* — *im Brett haben,* be in s.o.'s good books; *einem* —*e in den Weg legen,* put obstacles in s.o.'s way; *der* — *des Weisen,* the philosopher's stone.

Steinadler [′ʃtaɪna:dlər], *m.* (—s, *pl.* —) (*Orn.*) golden eagle.

steinalt [′ʃtaɪnalt], *adj.* very old.

Steinbock [′ʃtaɪnbɔk], *m.* (—s, *pl.* ⸚e) ibex; (*Astrol.*) Capricorn.

Steinbruch [′ʃtaɪnbrux], *m.* (—s, *pl.* ⸚e) stone-pit, quarry.

Steinbutt [′ʃtaɪnbut], *m.* (—s, *pl.* —e) (*Zool.*) turbot.

Steindruck [′ʃtaɪndruk], *m.* (—s, *no pl.*) lithography.

steinern [′ʃtaɪnərn], *adj.* stony; built of stone.

Steingut [′ʃtaɪngu:t], *n.* (—s, *no pl.*) earthenware, stoneware, pottery.

Steinhagel [′ʃtaɪnha:gəl], *m.* (—s, *no pl.*) shower of stones.

Steinhaue [′ʃtaɪnhauə], *f.* (—, *pl.* —n) pickaxe.

Steinhügel [′ʃtaɪnhy:gəl], *m.* (—s, *pl.* —) cairn.

steinig [′ʃtaɪnɪç], *adj.* stony, rocky.

steinigen [′ʃtaɪnɪgən], *v.a.* stone.

Steinkalk [′ʃtaɪnkalk], *m.* (—s, *no pl.*) quicklime.

Steinkohle [′ʃtaɪnko:lə], *f.* (—, *no pl.*) pit-coal.

Steinkrug [′ʃtaɪnkru:k], *m.* (—s, *pl.* ⸚e) stone jar.

Steinmarder [′ʃtaɪnmardər], *m.* (—s, *pl.* —) (*Zool.*) stone-marten.

Steinmetz [′ʃtaɪnmɛts], *m.* (—es, *pl.* —e) stone-cutter, stone-mason.

Steinobst [′ʃtaɪno:pst], *n.* (—es, *no pl.*) stone-fruit.

Steinplatte [′ʃtaɪnplatə], *f.* (—, *pl.* —n) slab, flagstone.

steinreich [′ʃtaɪnraɪç], *adj.* as rich as Croesus.

Steinsalz [′ʃtaɪnzalts], *n.* (—es, *no pl.*) rock-salt, mineral-salt.

Steinwurf [′ʃtaɪnvurf], *m.* (—s, *pl.* ⸚e) *einen* — *entfernt,* within a stone's throw.

Steiß [ʃtaɪs], *m.* (—es, *pl.* —e) rump; (*coll.*) buttocks, posterior.

Stellage [ʃtɛ′la:ʒə], *f.* (—, *pl.* —n) stand, frame.

Stelldichein [′ʃtɛldɪçaɪn], *n.* (—s, *no pl.*) assignation, rendezvous, tryst; (*coll.*) date.

Stelle [′ʃtɛlə], *f.* (—, *pl.* —n) place, spot; job, position; situation; (*book*) passage; figure, digit; department; *offene* —, vacancy; *auf der* —, at once, immediately; *an deiner* —, if I were you; *nicht von der* — *kommen,* remain stationary; *zur* — *sein,* be at hand.

stellen [′ʃtɛlən], *v.a.* put, place, set; *richtig* —, regulate, correct, amend; (*clock*) set right; *seinen Mann* —, play o.'s part, pull o.'s weight. — *v.r. sich* —, come forward; pretend; *sich krank* —, feign illness, malinger, pretend to be ill.

Stellenbewerber [′ʃtɛlənbəvɛrbər], *m.* (—s, *pl.* —) applicant (for a job).

Stellengesuch [′ʃtɛləngəzu:x], *n.* (—s, *pl.* —e) application (for a job).

Stellenvermittlung [′ʃtɛlənfɛrmɪtluŋ], *f.* (—, *pl.* —en) employment office, employment exchange.

stellenweise [′ʃtɛlənvaɪzə], *adv.* in parts, here and there.

Stellmacher [′ʃtɛlmaxər], *m.* (—s, *pl.* —) wheelwright.

Stellung [′ʃtɛluŋ], *f.* (—, *pl.* —en) position, posture; attitude; situation; job; (*Mil.*) trenches; — *nehmen zu,* express o.'s views on.

Stellvertreter [′ʃtɛlfɛrtre:tər], *m.* (—s, *pl.* —) representative, deputy; substitute, supply, proxy, relief; (*doctor*) locum.

Stelzbein [′ʃtɛltsbaɪn], *n.* (—s, *pl.* —e) wooden leg.

Stemmeisen

Stemmeisen ['ʃtɛmaɪzən], *n.* (—s, *pl.* —) crowbar.

stemmen ['ʃtɛmən], *v.a.* (*water*) stem, dam; (*weight*) lift. — *v.r. sich* — *gegen*, resist fiercely.

Stempel ['ʃtɛmpəl], *m.* (—s, *pl.* —) stamp, rubber-stamp, die; pounder; (*Bot.*) pistil.

Stempelgebühr ['ʃtɛmpəlɡəbyːr], *f.* (—, *pl.* —en) stamp-duty.

stempeln ['ʃtɛmpəln], *v.a.* stamp, hallmark; brand; cancel (*postage stamp*). — *v.n.* (*coll.*) — *gehen*, be on the dole.

Stengel ['ʃtɛŋəl], *m.* (—s, *pl.* —) stalk.

Stenografie [ʃtɛnoɡraˈfiː], *f.* (—, *no pl.*) stenography, shorthand.

stenografisch [ʃtɛnoˈɡrafɪʃ], *adj.* in shorthand.

Stenogramm [ʃtɛnoˈɡram], *n.* (—s, *pl.* —e) shorthand-note.

Stenotypistin [ʃtɛnotyˈpɪstɪn], *f.* (—, *pl.* —nen) shorthand-typist.

Stephan ['ʃtɛfan], *m.* Stephen.

Steppdecke ['ʃtɛpdɛkə], *f.* (—, *pl.* —n) quilt.

Steppe ['ʃtɛpə], *f.* (—, *pl.* —n) steppe.

steppen ['ʃtɛpən], *v.a.* stitch, quilt.

Sterbeglocke ['ʃtɛrbəɡlɔkə], *f.* (—, *pl.* —n) passing bell, death bell.

Sterbehemd ['ʃtɛrbəhɛmt], *n.* (—(e)s, *pl.* —en) shroud, winding-sheet.

sterben ['ʃtɛrbən], *v.n. irr.* (*aux.* sein) die.

Sterbenswörtchen ['ʃtɛrbənsvœrtçən], *n.* (—s, *pl.* —) *nicht ein* —, not a syllable.

Sterbesakramente ['ʃtɛrbəzakramɛntə], *n. pl.* (*Eccl.*) last sacraments, last rites.

sterblich ['ʃtɛrplɪç], *adj.* mortal; *verliebt*, desperately in love.

Sterblichkeit ['ʃtɛrplɪçkaɪt], *f.* (—, *no pl.*) mortality.

stereotyp [stereoˈtyːp], *adj.* stereotyped.

sterilisieren [steriliˈziːrən], *v.a.* sterilise.

Sterilität [steriliˈtɛːt], *f.* (—, *no pl.*) sterility.

Stern [ʃtɛrn], *m.* (—(e)s, *pl.* —e) star; (*Typ.*) asterisk.

Sternbild ['ʃtɛrnbɪlt], *n.* (—s, *pl.* —er) constellation.

Sterndeuter ['ʃtɛrndɔytər], *m.* (—s, *pl.* —) astrologer.

Sterndeutung ['ʃtɛrndɔytuŋ], *f.* (—, *no pl.*) astrology.

Sternenschimmer ['ʃtɛrnənʃɪmər], *m.* (—s, *no pl.*) starlight.

sternförmig ['ʃtɛrnfœrmɪç], *adj.* star-like, star-shaped.

Sterngucker ['ʃtɛrnɡukər], *m.* (—s, *pl.* —) stargazer.

sternhagelvoll ['ʃtɛrnhaɡəlfɔl], *adj.* (*coll.*) as drunk as a lord.

Sternkunde ['ʃtɛrnkundə], *f.* (—, *no pl.*) astronomy.

Sternkundige ['ʃtɛrnkundɪɡə], *m.* (—n, *pl.* —n) astronomer.

Sternschnuppe ['ʃtɛrnʃnupə], *f.* *pl.* —n) falling star, shooting star, meteorite.

Sternwarte ['ʃtɛrnvartə], *f.* (—, *pl.* —n) observatory.

stetig ['ʃteːtɪç], *adj.* continual, continuous, constant.

stets [ʃteːts], *adv.* always, ever, continually.

Steuer (1) ['ʃtɔyər], *n.* (—s, *pl.* —) rudder, helm, steering wheel.

Steuer (2) ['ʃtɔyər], *f.* (—, *pl.* —n) tax; (*local*) rate; (*import*) customs duty.

Steueramt ['ʃtɔyəramt], *n.* (—s, *pl.* ⸚er) inland revenue office, tax office.

Steuerbeamte ['ʃtɔyərbəamtə], *m.* (—n, *pl.* —n) revenue officer, tax collector.

Steuerbord ['ʃtɔyərbɔrt], *n.* (—s, *no pl.*) starboard.

Steuereinnehmer ['ʃtɔyəraɪnneːmər], *m.* (—s, *pl.* —) tax collector.

steuerfrei ['ʃtɔyərfraɪ], *adj.* duty-free, exempt from taxes.

Steuerhinterziehung ['ʃtɔyərhɪntərtsiːuŋ], *f.* (—, *pl.* —en) tax evasion.

steuerlos ['ʃtɔyərloːs], *adj.* rudderless, adrift.

Steuermann ['ʃtɔyərman], *m.* (—s, *pl.* ⸚er) mate; helmsman.

steuern ['ʃtɔyərn], *v.a.* steer; *einem Unheil* —, avoid *or* steer clear of an evil.

steuerpflichtig ['ʃtɔyərpflɪçtɪç], *adj.* taxable, liable to tax, dutiable.

Steuerrad ['ʃtɔyərraːt], *n.* (—s, *pl.* ⸚er) steering-wheel.

Steuerung ['ʃtɔyəruŋ], *f.* (—, *no pl.*) steering, controls.

Steuerveranlagung ['ʃtɔyərfɛranlaɡuŋ], *f.* (—, *pl.* —en) tax-assessment.

stibitzen [ʃtiˈbɪtsən], *v.a.* (*coll.*) pilfer, filch.

Stich [ʃtɪç], *m.* (—(e)s, *pl.* —e) sting; prick; stitch; stab; (*Cards*) trick; (*Art*) engraving; *einen im* — *lassen*, leave s.o. in the lurch.

Stichel [ʃtɪçəl], *m.* (—s, *pl.* —) (*Art*) graver.

Stichelei [ʃtɪçəˈlaɪ], *f.* (—, *pl.* —en) taunt, sneer, gibe.

sticheln [ʃtɪçəln], *v.a.* taunt, nag.

stichhaltig ['ʃtɪçhaltɪç], *adj.* valid, sound.

Stichhaltigkeit ['ʃtɪçhaltɪçkaɪt], *f.* (—, *no pl.*) validity, cogency.

Stichprobe ['ʃtɪçproːbə], *f.* (—, *pl.* —n) sample taken at random, sampling.

Stichwahl ['ʃtɪçvaːl], *f.* (—, *pl.* —en) second ballot.

Stichwort ['ʃtɪçvɔrt], *n.* (—s, *pl.* —e) key-word; (*Theat.*) cue.

sticken [ʃtɪkən], *v.a., v.n.* embroider.

Stickerei [ʃtɪkəˈraɪ], *f.* (—, *pl.* —en) embroidery.

Stickgarn ['ʃtɪkɡarn], *n.* (—s, *pl.* —e) embroidery cotton or silk.

Stickhusten ['ʃtɪkhuːstən], *m.* (—s, *no pl.*) choking cough.

Stock

stickig ['ʃtɪkɪç], *adj.* stuffy.
Stickmuster ['ʃtɪkmustər], *n.* (—s, *pl.* —) embroidery-pattern.
Stickstoff ['ʃtɪkʃtɔf], *m.* (—(e)s, *no pl.*) nitrogen.
stieben ['ʃti:bən], *v.n.* (*aux.* sein) scatter, spray; *auseinander* —, disperse.
Stiefbruder ['ʃti:fbru:dər], *m.* (—s, *pl.* ⸚) step-brother.
Stiefel ['ʃti:fəl], *m.* (—s, *pl.* —) boot.
Stiefelknecht ['ʃti:fəlknɛçt], *m.* (—(e)s, *pl.* —e) boot-jack.
Stiefelputzer ['ʃti:fəlputsər], *m.* (—s, *pl.* —) shoe-black; (*Am.*) shoe-shine; (*hotel*) boots.
Stiefeltern ['ʃti:fɛltərn], *pl.* step-parents.
Stiefmütterchen ['ʃti:fmytərçən], *n.* (—s, *pl.* —) (*Bot.*) pansy.
stiefmütterlich ['ʃti:fmytərlɪç], *adj.* like a stepmother; niggardly.
Stiefsohn ['ʃti:fzo:n], *m.* (—s, *pl.* ⸚e) stepson.
Stiege ['ʃti:gə], *f.* (—, *pl.* —n) staircase.
Stieglitz ['ʃti:glɪts], *m.* (—es, *pl.* —e) goldfinch.
Stiel [ʃti:l], *m.* (—(e)s, *pl.* —e) handle; (*plant*) stalk.
Stier [ʃti:r], *m.* (—(e)s, *pl.* —e) bull; *junger* —, bullock; (*Astrol.*) Taurus.
stieren ['ʃti:rən], *v.n.* stare (at), goggle.
Stift (1) [ʃtɪft], *m.* (—(e)s, *pl.* —e) tack, pin, peg; pencil; (*coll.*) apprentice; young chap.
Stift (2) [ʃtɪft], *n.* (—(e)s, *pl.* —e) charitable *or* religious foundation.
stiften ['ʃtɪftən], *v.a.* establish, give, donate; found, set on foot, originate; *Frieden* —, bring about peace.
Stifter ['ʃtɪftər], *m.* (—s, *pl.* —) founder, originator, donor.
Stiftung ['ʃtɪftuŋ], *f.* (—, *pl.* —en) establishment, foundation; institution; charitable foundation; endowment, donation.
Stil [ʃti:l], *m.* (—(e)s, *pl.* —e) style; (*fig.*) manner.
stilisieren [ʃti:li'zi:rən], *v.a.* word, draft.
Stilistik [ʃti:'lɪstɪk], *f.* (—, *no pl.*) art of composition.
stilistisch [ʃti:'lɪstɪʃ], *adj.* stylistic.
still [ʃtɪl], *adj.* quiet, still, silent; calm; —*er Teilhaber*, sleeping partner; *im* —*en*, secretly, on the sly.
Stille ['ʃtɪlə], *f.* (—, *no pl.*) silence, quietness, tranquillity; calm, calmness; *in der* —, silently; *in der* — *der Nacht*, at dead of night.
stillen ['ʃtɪlən], *v.a.* allay; (*blood*) staunch; (*baby*) suckle, feed, nurse; (*thirst*) quench; (*hunger*) appease.
stillos ['ʃti:llo:s], *adj.* incongruous; in bad taste.
Stillung ['ʃtɪluŋ], *f.* (—, *no pl.*) allaying; (*blood*) staunching; (*baby*) suckling, feeding, nursing; (*thirst*) quenching; (*hunger*) appeasing.

stilvoll ['ʃti:lfɔl], *adj.* harmonious; stylish; in good taste.
Stimmband ['ʃtɪmbant], *n.* (—s, *pl.* ⸚er) vocal chord.
stimmberechtigt ['ʃtɪmbərɛçtɪçt], *adj.* entitled to vote, enfranchised.
Stimmbruch ['ʃtɪmbrux], *m.* (—s, *no pl.*) breaking of the voice.
Stimme ['ʃtɪmə], *f.* (—, *pl.* —n) voice; (*election*) vote, suffrage; *die* — *abgeben*, vote.
stimmen ['ʃtɪmən], *v.a.* (*piano*) tune; *einen günstig* —, dispose s.o. favourably towards s.th. — *v.n.* agree, tally (with), square (with), accord (with); vote.
Stimmeneinheit ['ʃtɪmənaɪnhaɪt], *f.* (—, *no pl.*) unanimity.
Stimmengleichheit ['ʃtɪmənglaɪçhaɪt], *f.* (—, *no pl.*) equality of votes, tie.
Stimmer ['ʃtɪmər], *m.* (—s, *pl.* —) (*piano*) tuner.
Stimmführer ['ʃtɪmfy:rər], *m.* (—s, *pl.* —) leader, spokesman.
Stimmgabel ['ʃtɪmga:bəl], *f.* (—, *pl.* —n) tuning fork.
stimmhaft ['ʃtɪmhaft], *adj.* (*Phonet.*) voiced.
Stimmlage ['ʃtɪmla:gə], *f.* (—, *pl.* —n) (*Mus.*) register.
stimmlos ['ʃtɪmlo:s], *adj.* voiceless; (*Phonet.*) unvoiced.
Stimmrecht ['ʃtɪmrɛçt], *n.* (—s, *no pl.*) suffrage, right to vote; *allgemeines* —, universal suffrage.
Stimmung ['ʃtɪmuŋ], *f.* (—, *no pl.*) tuning; (*fig.*) disposition, humour, mood; atmosphere; *in guter* —, in high spirits, *in gedrückter* —, in low spirits.
stimmungsvoll ['ʃtɪmuŋsfɔl], *adj.* impressive, full of atmosphere.
Stimmwechsel ['ʃtɪmvɛksəl], *m.* (—s, *no pl.*) breaking of the voice.
Stimmzettel ['ʃtɪmtsɛtəl], *m.* (—s, *pl.* —) ballot-paper.
stinken ['ʃtɪŋkən], *v.n. irr.* stink, reek, smell.
Stinktier ['ʃtɪŋkti:r], *n.* (—s, *pl.* —e) (*Zool.*) skunk.
Stipendium [ʃti'pɛndjum], *n.* (—s, *pl.* —dien) scholarship.
Stirn [ʃtɪrn], *f.* (—, *pl.* —en) forehead, brow; *die* — *runzeln*, frown, knit o.'s brow; *die* — *haben zu*, have the cheek to; *einem die* — *bieten*, face s.o., defy s.o.
Stirnhöhle ['ʃtɪrnhø:lə], *f.* (—, *pl.* —en) frontal cavity.
Stirnseite ['ʃtɪrnzaɪtə], *f.* (—, *pl.* —n) front.
stöbern ['ʃtø:bərn], *v.n.* rummage about; (*snow*) drift.
stochern ['ʃtɔxərn], *v.a., v.n.* (*food*) pick (at); (*teeth*) pick.
Stock (1) [ʃtɔk], *m.* (—(e)s, *pl.* ⸚e) stick, cane, walking-stick; *über* — *und Stein*, over hedges and ditches.
Stock (2) [ʃtɔk], *m.* (—es, *pl.* —werke) storey, floor.

213

stocken ['ʃtɔkən], v.n. stop; (blood) run cold; (linen) go mildewed; hesitate, falter; (conversation) flag.

stockfinster ['ʃtɔkfɪnstər], adj. pitch dark.

Stockfisch ['ʃtɔkfɪʃ], m. (—es, pl. —e) dried cod; dried fish.

stöckisch ['ʃtœkɪʃ], adj. obstinate, stubborn.

Stockrose ['ʃtɔkroːzə], f. (—, pl. —n) (Bot.) hollyhock.

Stockschnupfen ['ʃtɔkʃnupfən], m. (—s, no pl.) heavy or chronic cold.

stocksteif ['ʃtɔkʃtaɪf], adj. stiff as a poker.

stockstill ['ʃtɔkʃtɪl], adj. quite still, stock-still.

stocktaub ['ʃtɔktaup], adj. deaf as a post.

Stockung ['ʃtɔkuŋ], f. (—, pl. —en) stagnation; hesitation; block, blockage; stopping, standstill.

Stockwerk ['ʃtɔkvɛrk], n. (—s, pl. —e) storey, floor.

Stoff [ʃtɔf], m. (—(e)s, pl. —e) fabric, material; substance; subject matter.

Stoffwechsel ['ʃtɔfvɛksəl], m. (—s, no pl.) metabolism.

stöhnen ['ʃtøːnən], v.n. groan, moan.

Stoiker ['stoːɪkər], m. (—s, pl. —) stoic.

Stola ['stoːlaː], f. (—, pl. —len) (Eccl.) stole.

Stollen ['ʃtɔlən], m. (—s, pl. —) fruitcake; (Min.) gallery, adit.

stolpern ['ʃtɔlpərn], v.n. (aux. sein) stumble, trip.

Stolz [ʃtɔlts], m. (—es, no pl.) haughtiness, pride.

stolz [ʃtɔlts], adj. haughty, proud; stuck-up, conceited; (fig.) majestic.

stolzieren [ʃtɔl'tsiːrən], v.n. (aux. sein) strut; prance.

stopfen ['ʃtɔpfən], v.a. stuff; fill; darn, mend; einem den Mund —, cut s.o. short.

Stopfgarn ['ʃtɔpfgarn], n. (—s, pl. —e) darning-thread.

Stoppel ['ʃtɔpəl], f. (—, pl. —n) stubble.

stoppeln ['ʃtɔpəln], v.a. glean; etwas zusammen —, compile s.th. badly.

Stöpsel ['ʃtœpsəl], m. (—s, pl. —) stopper, cork; kleiner —, little mite.

stöpseln ['ʃtœpsəln], v.a. cork.

Stör [ʃtøːr], m. (—(e)s, pl. —e) (Zool.) sturgeon.

Storch [ʃtɔrç], m. (—(e)s, pl. ⁓e) (Orn.) stork.

Storchschnabel ['ʃtɔrçʃnaːbəl], m. (—s, pl. ⁓) stork's bill; (Tech.) pantograph.

stören ['ʃtøːrən], v.a. disturb, trouble; (Rad.) jam. — v.n. intrude, be in the way.

Störenfried ['ʃtøːrənfriːd], m. (—s, pl. —e) intruder, mischief-maker, nuisance.

Störer ['ʃtøːrər], m. (—s, pl. —) disturber.

stornieren [stɔr'niːrən], v.a. cancel, annul.

störrisch ['ʃtœrɪʃ], adj. stubborn, obstinate.

Störung ['ʃtøːruŋ], f. (—, pl. —en) disturbance, intrusion; (Rad.) jamming.

Stoß [ʃtoːs], m. (—es, pl. ⁓e) push, thrust; impact; blow, stroke, jolt; (papers) heap, pile; (documents) bundle.

Stoßdegen ['ʃtoːsdeːgən], m. (—s, pl. —) rapier.

Stößel ['ʃtøːsəl], m. (—s, pl. —) pestle; (Motor.) tappet.

stoßen ['ʃtoːsən], v.a. irr. thrust, push; pound; vor den Kopf —, offend. — v.n. bump, jolt; — an, border upon; auf etwas —, come across s.th., stumble on s.th.; ins Horn —, blow a horn. — v.r. sich —, hurt o.s.; sich an etwas —, take offence at s.th., take exception to s.th.

Stoßseufzer ['ʃtoːszɔyftsər], m. (—s, pl. —) deep sigh.

Stoßwaffe ['ʃtoːsvafə], f. (—, pl. —n) thrusting or stabbing weapon.

stoßweise ['ʃtoːsvaɪzə], adv. by fits and starts.

Stotterer ['ʃtɔtərər], m. (—s, pl. —) stutterer, stammerer.

stottern ['ʃtɔtərn], v.n. stutter, stammer.

stracks [ʃtraks], adv. straight away, directly.

Strafanstalt ['ʃtraːfanʃtalt], f. (—, pl. —en) penitentiary, prison.

Strafarbeit ['ʃtraːfarbaɪt], f. (—, pl. —en) (Sch.) imposition.

strafbar ['ʃtraːfbaːr], adj. punishable, criminal, culpable.

Strafbarkeit ['ʃtraːfbaːrkaɪt], f. (—, no pl.) culpability.

Strafe ['ʃtraːfə], f. (—, pl. —n) punishment; (money) fine, penalty; bei —, von, on pain of.

strafen ['ʃtraːfən], v.a. punish, rebuke; (money) fine.

Straferlaß ['ʃtraːfərlas], m. (—sses, pl. —sse) remission of penalty, amnesty.

straff [ʃtraf], adj. tight, tense, taut.

Strafgericht ['ʃtraːfgərɪçt], n. (—es, no pl.) punishment; judgment; (Law) Criminal Court.

Strafgesetzbuch ['ʃtraːfgəzɛtsbuːx], n. (—(e)s, pl. ⁓er) penal code.

sträflich ['ʃtrɛːflɪç], adj. punishable; culpable; reprehensible, blameworthy.

Sträfling ['ʃtrɛːflɪŋ], m. (—s, pl. —e) convict.

Strafporto ['ʃtraːfpɔrto], n. (—s, pl. —ti) excess postage.

Strafpredigt ['ʃtraːfpreːdɪçt], f. (—, pl. —en) severe admonition, stern reprimand.

Strafprozess ['ʃtraːfprɔtsɛs], m. (—es, pl. —e) criminal proceedings.

Strafrecht ['ʃtraːfrɛçt], n. (—(e)s, no pl.) criminal law.

Strafverfahren ['ʃtraːffɛrfaːrən], n. (—s, pl. —) criminal procedure.

Strahl [ʃtraːl], *m.* (—(e)s, *pl.* —en)
beam, ray; (*water etc.*) jet, spout;
(*lightning*) flash; —en *werfen*, emit
rays.
Strahlantrieb ['ʃtraːlantriːp], *m.* (—s,
no pl.) (*Aviat.*) jet propulsion.
strahlen ['ʃtraːlən], *v.n.* radiate, shine,
beam, emit rays; (*fig.*) beam (with
joy).
strählen ['ʃtrɛːlən], *v.a.* (*rare*) comb.
Strahlenbrechung ['ʃtraːlənbrɛçuŋ],
f. (—, *pl.* —en) refraction.
strahlenförmig ['ʃtraːlənfœrmɪç], *adj.*
radiate.
Strahlenkrone ['ʃtraːlənkroːnə], *f.* (—,
pl. —n) aureole, halo.
Strahlung ['ʃtraːluŋ], *f.* (—, *pl.* —en)
radiation; (*fig.*) radiance.
Strähne ['ʃtrɛːnə], *f.* (—, *pl.* —n)
skein, hank; *eine* — *Pech*, a spell of
bad luck.
Stramin [ʃtraˈmiːn], *m.* (—s, *pl.* —e)
embroidery canvas.
stramm [ʃtram], *adj.* tight; rigid;
sturdy, strapping.
strampeln ['ʃtrampəln], *v.n.* struggle;
(*baby*) kick.
Strand [ʃtrant], *m.* (—(e)s, *pl.* —e)
shore, beach, strand.
stranden ['ʃtrandən], *v.n.* be stranded,
founder.
Strandkorb ['ʃtrantkɔrp], *m.* (—s,
pl. ⁻e) beach-chair.
Strandwache ['ʃtrantvaxə], *f.* (—, *no
pl.*) coast-guard.
Strang [ʃtraŋ], *m.* (—(e)s, *pl.* ⁻e) rope,
cord; *über die* ⁻e *schlagen*, kick over
the traces; *zum* — *verurteilen*, condemn to be hanged.
strangulieren [ʃtraŋguˈliːrən], *v.a.*
strangle.
Strapaze [ʃtraˈpatsə], *f.* (—, *pl.* —n)
over-exertion, fatigue, hardship.
strapazieren [ʃtrapaˈtsiːrən], *v.a.* overexert, fatigue.
strapaziös [ʃtrapaˈtsjøːs], *adj.* fatiguing,
exacting.
Straße ['ʃtraːsə], *f.* (—, *pl.* —n) (*city*)
street; (*country*) road, highway; (*sea*)
strait; *auf der* —, in the street; *über
die* — *gehen*, cross the street.
Straßenbahn ['ʃtraːsənbaːn], *f.* (—,
pl. —en) tram; tramcar, (*Am.*) streetcar.
Straßendamm ['ʃtraːsəndam], *m.* (—s,
pl. ⁻e) roadway.
Straßendirne ['ʃtraːsəndɪrnə], *f.* (—,
pl. —n) prostitute, street-walker.
Straßenfeger ['ʃtraːsənfeːgər], *m.* (—s,
pl. —) roadman, road-sweeper,
scavenger, crossing-sweeper.
Straßenpflaster ['ʃtraːsənpflastər], *n.*
(—s, *no pl.*) pavement.
Straßenraub ['ʃtraːsənraup], *m.* (—s,
no pl.) highway-robbery.
Stratege [ʃtraˈteːgə], *m.* (—n, *pl.* —n)
strategist.
sträuben ['ʃtrɔybən], *v.r. sich* —,
bristle; (*fig.*) struggle (against),
oppose.

Strauch [ʃtraux], *m.* (—(e)s, *pl.* ⁻er)
bush, shrub.
straucheln ['ʃtrauxəln], *v.n.* (*aux.* sein)
stumble.
Strauchritter ['ʃtrauxrɪtər], *m.* (—s,
pl. —) footpad, vagabond, highwayman.
Strauß (1) [ʃtraus], *m.* (—es, *pl.* ⁻e)
(*Poet.*) fight, tussle; (*flowers*) bunch,
bouquet, nosegay.
Strauß (2) [ʃtraus], *m.* (—es, *pl.* —e)
(*Orn.*) ostrich.
Sträußchen ['ʃtrɔysçən], *n.* (—s,
pl. —) small bunch of flowers, nosegay.
Straußfeder ['ʃtrausfeːdər], *f.* (—,
pl. —n) ostrich-feather.
Strazze ['ʃtratsə], *f.* (—, *pl.* —n)
scrapbook.
Strebe ['ʃtreːbə], *f.* (—, *pl.* —n) buttress, prop, stay.
Strebebogen ['ʃtreːbəboːgən], *m.* (—s,
pl. —) (*Archit.*) arch, buttress; flying
buttress.
Streben ['ʃtreːbən], *n.* (—s, *no pl.*)
ambition, aspiration; effort, endeavour, striving.
streben ['ʃtreːbən], *v.n.* strive, aspire,
endeavour.
Streber ['ʃtreːbər], *m.* (—s, *pl.* —)
pushing person, (social) climber. (*Am.
coll.*) go-getter.
strebsam ['ʃtreːpzaːm], *adj.* ambitious,
assiduous, industrious.
streckbar ['ʃtrɛkbaːr], *adj.* ductile,
extensible.
Streckbett ['ʃtrɛkbɛt], *n.* (—s, *pl.* —en)
orthopaedic bed.
Strecke ['ʃtrɛkə], *f.* (—, *pl.* —n) stretch,
reach, extent; distance; tract; line;
zur — *bringen*, (*Hunt.*) bag, run to
earth.
strecken ['ʃtrɛkən], *v.a.* stretch, extend; (*metal*) hammer out, roll; make
(s.th.) last; *die Waffen* —, lay down
arms.
Streich [ʃtraɪç], *m.* (—(e)s, *pl.* —e)
stroke, blow; (*fig.*) prank; trick;
dummer —, piece of folly, lark.
streicheln ['ʃtraɪçəln], *v.a.* stroke,
caress.
streichen ['ʃtraɪçən], *v.a. irr.* stroke,
touch; paint, spread; cancel; strike;
(*sail*) lower. — *v.n.* move past, fly
past; wander.
Streichholz ['ʃtraɪçhɔlts], *n.* (—es,
pl. ⁻er) match.
Streichinstrument ['ʃtraɪçɪnstru-
mɛnt], *n.* (—s, *pl.* —e) stringed
instrument.
Streif [ʃtraɪf], *m.* (—(e)s, *pl.* —e)
stripe, strip, streak.
Streifband ['ʃtraɪfbant], *n.* (—s, *pl.*
⁻er) wrapper.
Streifblick ['ʃtraɪfblɪk], *m.* (—s, *pl.*
—e) glance.
Streife ['ʃtraɪfə], *f.* (—, *pl.* —n) raid;
patrol (*police etc.*).
Streifen ['ʃtraɪfən], *m.* (—s, *pl.* —)
stripe, streak; (*Mil.*) bar.

streifen

streifen [ˈʃtraɪfən], *v.a.* graze, touch in passing; take off (*remove*). — *v.n.* (*aux.* sein) ramble, roam, rove.

streifig [ˈʃtraɪfɪç], *adj.* striped, streaky.

Streik [ʃtraɪk], *m.* (—(e)s, *pl.* —s) strike; *in den — treten*, go on strike.

Streikbrecher [ˈʃtraɪkbrɛçər], *m.* (—s, *pl.* —) blackleg.

streiken [ˈʃtraɪkən], *v.n.* (*workers*) strike, be on strike.

Streit [ʃtraɪt], *m.* (—(e)s, *pl.* —e) dispute, quarrel, conflict; (*words*) argument; *einen — anfangen*, pick a quarrel.

Streitaxt [ˈʃtraɪtakst], *f.* (—, *pl.* ⸚e) battle-axe.

streitbar [ˈʃtraɪtbaːr], *adj.* warlike, martial.

streiten [ˈʃtraɪtən], *v.n. irr.* quarrel, fight; *—de Kirche*, Church Militant.

Streitfrage [ˈʃtraɪtfraːgə], *f.* (—, *pl.* —n) moot point, point at issue; controversy.

Streithammel [ˈʃtraɪthaməl], *m.* (—s, *pl.* —) squabbler.

Streithandel [ˈʃtraɪthandəl], *m.* (—s, *pl.* ⸚) law-suit.

streitig [ˈʃtraɪtɪç], *adj.* disputable, doubtful, at issue; *einem etwas — machen*, contest s.o.'s right to s.th.

Streitkräfte [ˈʃtraɪtkrɛftə], *f. pl.* (*Mil.*) forces.

streitlustig [ˈʃtraɪtlustɪç], *adj.* argumentative.

Streitschrift [ˈʃtraɪtʃrɪft], *f.* (—, *pl.* —en) pamphlet, polemical treatise.

Streitsucht [ˈʃtraɪtzuxt], *f.* (—, *no pl.*) quarrelsomeness; (*Law*) litigiousness.

streitsüchtig [ˈʃtraɪtzyçtɪç], *adj.* quarrelsome, litigious.

streng [ʃtrɛŋ], *adj.* severe, strict, rigorous; *—e Kälte*, biting cold; *im —sten Winter*, in the depth of winter. — *adv. —genommen*, strictly speaking.

Strenge [ˈʃtrɛŋə], *f.* (—, *no pl.*) severity, rigour.

strenggläubig [ˈʃtrɛŋɡlɔybɪç], *adj.* strictly orthodox.

Streu [ʃtrɔy], *f.* (—, *pl.* —en) litter, bed of straw.

Streubüchse [ˈʃtrɔybyksə], *f.* (—, *pl.* —n) castor.

streuen [ˈʃtrɔyən], *v.a.* strew, scatter, sprinkle.

streunen [ˈʃtrɔynən], *v.n.* roam (about).

Streuung [ˈʃtrɔyuŋ], *f.* (—, *pl.* —en) strewing; (*shot*) dispersion.

Streuzucker [ˈʃtrɔytsukər], *m.* (—s, *no pl.*) castor-sugar.

Strich [ʃtrɪç], *m.* (—(e)s, *pl.* —e) stroke, line, dash; (*land*) tract; (*Art*) touch; region; *gegen den —*, against the grain; *einem einen — durch die Rechnung machen*, put a spoke in s.o.'s wheel, frustrate s.o.

Strichpunkt [ˈʃtrɪçpuŋkt], *m.* (—s, *pl.* —e) semicolon.

Strichregen [ˈʃtrɪçreːgən], *m.* (—s, *pl.* —) passing shower.

Strick [ʃtrɪk], *m.* (—(e)s, *pl.* —e) cord, line, rope; *du —*, (*fig.*) you scamp! *einem einen — drehen*, give s.o. enough rope to hang himself, lay a trap for s.o.

stricken [ˈʃtrɪkən], *v.a., v.n.* knit.

Strickerei [ʃtrɪkəˈraɪ], *f.* (—, *pl.* —en) knitting; knitting business, workshop.

Strickleiter [ˈʃtrɪklaɪtər], *f.* (—, *pl.* —n) rope-ladder.

Strickzeug [ˈʃtrɪktsɔyk], *n.* (—s, *pl.* —e) knitting.

Striegel [ˈʃtriːɡəl], *m.* (—s, *pl.* —) curry-comb.

striegeln [ˈʃtriːɡəln], *v.a.* curry.

Strieme [ˈʃtriːmə], *f.* (—, *pl.* —n) weal, stripe.

Strippe [ˈʃtrɪpə], *f.* (—, *pl.* —n) strap, band, string; cord.

strittig [ˈʃtrɪtɪç], *adj.* contentious, debatable.

Stroh [ʃtroː], *n.* (—s, *no pl.*) straw; (*roof*) thatch; *mit — decken*, thatch; *leeres — dreschen*, beat the air.

Strohfeuer [ˈʃtroːfɔyər], *n.* (—s, *no pl.*) (*fig.*) flash in the pan; short-lived enthusiasm.

Strohhalm [ˈʃtroːhalm], *m.* (—s, *pl.* —e) straw.

Strohhut [ˈʃtroːhuːt], *m.* (—s, *pl.* ⸚e) straw-hat.

Strohkopf [ˈʃtroːkɔpf], *m.* (—(e)s, *pl.* ⸚e) (*coll.*) stupid person.

Strohmann [ˈʃtroːman], *m.* (—s, *pl.* ⸚er) (*coll.*) man of straw; (*Cards*) dummy.

Strohmatte [ˈʃtroːmatə], *f.* (—, *pl.* —n) straw-mat.

Strohwitwe [ˈʃtroːvɪtvə], *f.* (—, *pl.* —n) grass-widow.

Strolch [ʃtrɔlç], *m.* (—(e)s, *pl.* —e) vagabond; (*fig.*) scamp.

Strom [ʃtroːm], *m.* (—(e)s, *pl.* ⸚e) river, torrent; (*also fig.*) flood; stream; (*also Elec.*) current; (*coll.*) electricity; *gegen den — schwimmen*, swim against the current, be an individualist.

stromab [ˈʃtroːmap], *adv.* downstream.

stromauf [ˈʃtroːmauf], *adv.* upstream.

strömen [ˈʃtrøːmən], *v.n.* (*aux.* sein) flow, stream; (*rain*) pour; (*people*) flock.

Stromer [ˈʃtroːmər], *m.* (—s, *pl.* —) vagabond, tramp, vagrant.

Stromkreis [ˈʃtroːmkraɪs], *m.* (—es, *pl.* —e) (*Elec.*) circuit.

Stromschnelle [ˈʃtroːmʃnɛlə], *f.* (—, *pl.* —n) rapids.

Strömung [ˈʃtrøːmuŋ], *f.* (—, *pl.* —en) current; (*fig.*) tendency.

Strophe [ˈʃtroːfə], *f.* (—, *pl.* —n) verse, stanza.

strotzen [ˈʃtrɔtsən], *v.n.* be puffed up; overflow, burst, teem.

strotzend [ˈʃtrɔtsənt], *adj. vor Gesundheit —*, bursting with health.

Strudel [ˈʃtruːdəl], *m.* (—s, *pl.* —) whirl, whirlpool, vortex, eddy; pastry.

Struktur [ʃtrukˈtuːr], *f.* (—, *pl.* —en) structure.

Strumpf [ʃtrumpf], *m.* (—(e)s, *pl.* ⸚e) stocking; (*short*) sock.

Strumpfband [ʃtrumpfbant], *n.* (—(e)s, *pl.* ⸚er) garter.

Strumpfwaren [ʃtrumpfvaːrən], *f. pl.* hosiery.

Strumpfwirker [ʃtrumpfvɪrkər], *m.* (—s, *pl.* —) stocking-weaver.

Strunk [ʃtruŋk], *m.* (—(e)s, *pl.* ⸚e) (*tree*) stump, trunk; (*plant*) stalk.

struppig [ʃtrupɪç], *adj.* rough, unkempt, frowsy.

Stube [ʃtuːbə], *f.* (—, *pl.* —n) room, chamber; *gute* —, sitting-room.

Stubenarrest [ʃtuːbənarɛst], *m.* (—s, *pl.* —e) confinement to quarters.

Stubenhocker [ʃtuːbənhɔkər], *m.* (—s, *pl.* —) stay-at-home.

Stubenmädchen [ʃtuːbənmɛːtçən], *n.* (—s, *pl.* —) housemaid.

Stuck [ʃtuk], *m.* (—(e)s, no *pl.*) stucco, plaster.

Stück [ʃtyk], *n.* (—(e)s, *pl.* —e) piece; part; lump; (*Theat.*) play; *aus freien —en,* of o.'s own accord; *große —e auf einen halten,* think highly of s.o.

Stückarbeit [ʃtykarbaɪt], *f.* (—, *pl.* —en) piece-work.

Stückchen [ʃtykçən], *n.* (—s, *pl.* —) small piece, morsel, bit.

stückeln [ʃtykəln], *v.a.* cut in(to) pieces; patch, mend.

stückweise [ʃtykvaɪzə], *adv.* piecemeal.

Stückwerk [ʃtykvɛrk], *n.* (—s, no *pl.*) (*fig.*) patchy *or* imperfect work, a bungled job.

Stückzucker [ʃtyktsukər], *m.* (—s, no *pl.*) lump sugar.

Student [ʃtuˈdɛnt], *m.* (—en, *pl.* —en) (*Univ.*) student, undergraduate.

studentenhaft [ʃtuˈdɛntənhaft], *adj.* student-like.

Studentenverbindung [ʃtuˈdɛntənfɛrbɪnduŋ], *f.* (—, *pl.* —en) students' association *or* union.

Studie [ʃtuːdjə], *f.* (—, *pl.* —n) study, (*Art*) sketch; (*Lit.*) essay; (*pl.*) studies.

Studienplan [ʃtuːdjənplaːn], *m.* (—s, *pl.* ⸚e) curriculum.

Studienrat [ʃtuːdjənraːt], *m.* (—s, *pl.* ⸚e) grammar school teacher, assistant master.

studieren [ʃtuˈdiːrən], *v.a., v.n.* study, read (a subject); be at (the) university.

studiert [ʃtuˈdiːrt], *adj.* educated; (*fig.*) affected, deliberate, studied.

Studierte [ʃtuˈdiːrtə], *m.* (*coll.*) egghead.

Studium [ʃtuːdjum], *n.* (—s,) *pl.* —dien study, pursuit; university education.

Stufe [ʃtuːfə], *f.* (—, *pl.* —n) step; (*fig.*) degree; *auf gleicher — mit,* on a level with.

stufenweise [ʃtuːfənvaɪzə], *adv.* gradually, by degrees.

Stuhl [ʃtuːl], *m.* (—s, *pl.* ⸚e) chair, seat; *der Heilige —,* the Holy See.

Stuhlgang [ʃtuːlgaŋ], *m.* (—s, no *pl.*) (*Med.*) stool, evacuation (of the bowels), movement, motion.

Stukkatur [ʃtukaˈtuːr], *f.* (—, no *pl.*) stucco-work.

Stulle [ʃtulə], *f.* (—, *pl.* —n) (*dial.*) slice of bread and butter.

Stulpe [ʃtulpə], *f.* (—, *pl.* —n) cuff.

stülpen [ʃtylpən], *v.a.* turn up, invert.

Stulpnase [ʃtulpnaːzə], *f.* (—, *pl.* —n) turned-up nose, pug-nose.

Stulpstiefel [ʃtulpʃtiːfəl], *m.* (—s, *pl.* —) top-boot.

stumm [ʃtum], *adj.* mute, dumb, silent.

Stumme [ʃtumə], *m. & f.* (—n, *pl.* —n) dumb person, mute.

Stummel [ʃtuməl], *m.* (—s, *pl.* —) stump; (*cigarette*) end, butt.

Stummheit [ʃtumhaɪt], *f.* (—, no *pl.*) dumbness.

Stümper [ʃtympər], *m.* (—s, *pl.* —) bungler, botcher.

stümperhaft [ʃtympərhaft], *adj.* bungling, botchy.

stümpern [ʃtympərn], *v.a., v.n.* bungle, botch.

Stumpf [ʃtumpf], *m.* (—(e)s, *pl.* ⸚e) stump, trunk; *mit — und Stiel ausrotten,* destroy root and branch.

stumpf [ʃtumpf], *adj.* obtuse; (*angle*) obtuse; (*fig.*) dull; *— machen,* blunt, dull.

Stumpfsinn [ʃtumpfzɪn], *m.* (—s, no *pl.*) stupidity, dullness.

stumpfwinklig [ʃtumpfvɪŋklɪç], *adj.* obtuse-angled.

Stunde [ʃtundə], *f.* (—, *pl.* —n) hour; lesson.

stunden [ʃtundən], *v.a.* give a respite, allow time (to pay up).

Stundenglas [ʃtundənglas], *n.* (—es, *pl.* ⸚er) hour-glass.

Stundenplan [ʃtundənplaːn], *m.* (—s, *pl.* ⸚e) (*Sch.*) schedule.

Stundenzeiger [ʃtundəntsaɪgər], *m.* (—s, *pl.* —) hour-hand.

Stündlein [ʃtyntlaɪn], *n.* (—s, *pl.* —) *sein — hat geschlagen,* his last hour has come.

Stundung [ʃtunduŋ], *f.* (—, *pl.* —en) respite, grace.

stupend [ʃtuˈpɛnt], *adj.* stupendous.

stur [ʃtuːr], *adj.* obdurate, unwavering, stolid, dour, stubborn.

Sturm [ʃturm], *m.* (—(e)s, *pl.* ⸚e) storm, gale, tempest, hurricane; (*Mil.*) attack, assault; *— und Drang,* (*Lit.*) Storm and Stress; *— im Wasserglas,* storm in a teacup; *— laufen gegen,* storm against.

Sturmband [ʃturmbant], *n.* (—s, *pl.* ⸚er) chinstrap.

Sturmbock [ʃturmbɔk], *m.* (—s, *pl.* ⸚e) battering-ram.

stürmen [ʃtyrmən], *v.a.* storm, take by assault. *— v.n.* be violent, be stormy; (*Mil.*) advance.

Stürmer [ʃtyrmər], *m.* (—s, *pl.* —) assailant; (*football*) centre-forward.

Sturmglocke [ʃturmglɔkə], *f.* (—, *pl.* —n) tocsin, alarm-bell.

Sturmhaube

Sturmhaube ['ʃturmhaubə], *f.* (—, *pl.* —en) (*Mil.*) morion, helmet.

stürmisch ['ʃtyrmɪʃ], *adj.* stormy, tempestuous; (*fig.*) boisterous, turbulent, tumultuous, impetuous; —*er Beifall*, frantic applause; —*e Überfahrt*, rough crossing.

Sturmschritt ['ʃturmʃrɪt], *m.* (—s, *no pl.*) double march.

Sturmvogel ['ʃturmfoːgəl], *m.* (—s, *pl.* ̈) (*Orn.*) stormy petrel.

Sturz [ʃturts], *m.* (—es, *pl.* ̈e) fall, tumble; crash; collapse; (*Comm.*) failure, smash; (*government*) overthrow.

Sturzacker ['ʃturtsakər], *m.* (—s, *pl.* ̈) freshly ploughed field.

Sturzbach ['ʃturtsbax], *m.* (—(e)s, *pl.* ̈e) torrent.

Stürze ['ʃtyrtsə], *f.* (—, *pl.* —n) pot-lid, cover.

stürzen ['ʃtyrtsən], *v.a.* hurl, overthrow; ruin. — *v.n.* (*aux.* sein) (*person*) have a fall; (*object*) tumble down; (*business*) fail; crash; plunge; (*water*) rush. — *v.r.* throw oneself; *sich — auf*, rush at, plunge into.

Sturzhelm ['ʃturtshɛlm], *m.* (—s, *pl.* —e) crash-helmet.

Sturzsee ['ʃturtszeː], *f.* (—, *no pl.*) heavy sea.

Sturzwelle ['ʃturtsvɛlə], *f.* (—, *pl.* —n) breaker, roller.

Stute ['ʃtuːtə], *f.* (—, *pl.* —n) mare.

Stutzbart ['ʃtutsbaːrt], *m.* (—s, *pl.* ̈e) short beard.

Stütze ['ʃtytsə], *f.* (—, *pl.* —n) prop, support, stay.

Stutzen ['ʃtutsən], *m.* (—s, *pl.* —) short rifle, carbine.

stutzen ['ʃtutsən], *v.a.* (*hair*) clip, trim; (*horse*) dock, crop; (*tree*) prune, lop. — *v.n.* be taken aback, hesitate.

stützen ['ʃtytsən], *v.a.* prop, support; base *or* found (on). — *v.r. sich — auf*, lean upon; (*fig.*) rely upon.

Stutzer ['ʃtutsər], *m.* (—s, *pl.* —) dandy, fop, beau.

stutzerhaft ['ʃtutsərhaft], *adj.* dandified.

stutzig ['ʃtutsɪç], *adj.* startled, puzzled; — *werden*, be non-plussed, be taken aback *or* puzzled.

Stützmauer ['ʃtytsmauər], *f.* (—, *pl.* —n) buttress, retaining wall.

Stützpunkt ['ʃtytspuŋkt], *m.* (—s, *pl.* —e) point of support; foothold; (*Mil.*) base; (*Tech.*) fulcrum.

Subjekt [zup'jɛkt], *n.* (—s, *pl.* —e) subject; (*fig.*) creature.

subjektiv [zupjɛk'tiːf], *adj.* subjective, personal, prejudiced.

sublimieren [zubli'miːrən], *v.a.* sublimate.

Substantiv [zupstan'tiːf], *n.* (—(e)s, *pl.* —e) (*Gram.*) substantive, noun.

subtil [zup'tiːl], *adj.* subtle.

subtrahieren [zuptra'hiːrən], *v.a.* subtract.

Subvention [zupvɛn'tsjoːn], *f.* (—, *pl.* —en) subsidy, grant-in-aid.

Suche ['zuːxə], *f.* (—, *no pl.*) search, quest; *auf der — nach*, in quest of.

suchen ['zuːxən], *v.a., v.n.* seek, look for; attempt, endeavour.

Sucht [zuxt], *f.* (—, *pl.* ̈e) mania, addiction, passion.

süchtig ['zyxtɪç], *adj.* addicted (to).

Sud [zuːd], *m.* (—(e)s, *pl.* —e) boiling, brewing; suds.

Sudan ['zuːdan], *m.* the Sudan.

sudeln ['zuːdəln], *v.a., v.n.* smear, daub, make a mess (of).

Süden ['zyːdən], *m.* (—s, *no pl.*) south.

Südfrüchte ['zyːtfryçtə], *f. pl.* Mediterranean *or* tropical fruit.

südlich ['zyːtlɪç], *adj.* southern, southerly; *in —er Richtung*, southward.

Südosten [zyːt'ɔstən], *m.* (—s, *no pl.*) south-east.

Suff [zuf], *m.* (—(e)s, *no pl.*) (*sl.*) boozing, tippling.

suggerieren [zugɛ'riːrən], *v.a.* suggest.

Sühne ['zyːnə], *f.* (—, *no pl.*) expiation, atonement.

sühnen ['zyːnən], *v.a.* expiate, atone for.

Sühneopfer ['zyːnəɔpfər], *n.* (—s, *pl.* —) expiatory sacrifice; atonement.

Suite ['sviːtə], *f.* (—, *pl.* —n) retinue, train.

sukzessiv [zuktsɛ'siːf], *adj.* gradual, successive.

Sülze ['zyltsə], *f.* (—, *pl.* —n) brawn, aspic, jelly.

Summa [zu'maː], *f.* (—, *pl.* **Summen**) — *summarum*, sum total.

summarisch [zu'maːrɪʃ], *adj.* summary.

Summe ['zumə], *f.* (—, *pl.* —n) sum, amount.

summen ['zumən], *v.a.* hum. — *v.n.* buzz, hum.

summieren [zu'miːrən], *v.a.* sum up, add up. — *v.r. sich* —, mount up.

Sumpf [zumpf], *m.* (—(e)s, *pl.* ̈e) bog, morass, marsh, moor, swamp.

sumpfig ['zumpfɪç], *adj.* boggy, marshy.

Sund [zunt], *m.* (—(e)s, *pl.* —e) straits, sound.

Sünde ['zyndə], *f.* (—, *pl.* —n) sin.

Sündenbock ['zyndənbɔk], *m.* (—s, *pl.* ̈e) scapegoat.

Sündenfall ['zyndənfal], *m.* (—s, *no pl.*) (*Theol.*) the Fall (*of man*).

Sündengeld ['zyndəngɛlt], *n.* (—(e)s, *no pl.*) ill-gotten gains; (*coll.*) vast sum of money.

sündenlos ['zyndənloːs], *adj.* sinless, impeccable.

Sündenpfuhl ['zyndənpfuːl], *m.* (—s, *pl.* —e) sink of iniquity.

Sünder ['zyndər], *m.* (—s, *pl.* —) sinner; *armer* —, poor devil; *du alter* —, you old scoundrel.

sündhaft ['zynthaft], *adj.* sinful, iniquitous.

sündig ['zyndɪç], *adj.* sinful.

sündigen ['zyndɪgən], *v.n.* sin, err.

Sündigkeit ['zyndɪçkaɪt], *f.* (—, *no pl.*) sinfulness.

Superlativ ['zuːpərlatiːf], *m.* (—s, *pl.* —e) superlative (degree).

Suppe ['zupə], *f.* (—, *pl.* —n) soup; *eingebrannte* —, thick soup; *einem edi* — *versalzen*, spoil s.o.'s little game.
Suppenfleisch ['zupənflaiʃ], *n.* (—es, *no pl.*) stock-meat.
Suppenkelle ['zupənkɛlə], *f.* (—, *pl.* —n) soup ladle.
Suppenterrine ['zupəntɛri:nə], *f.* (—, *pl.* —n) tureen.
Surrogat [zuroˈga:t], *n.* (—s, *pl.* —e) substitute.
süß [zy:s], *adj.* sweet.
Süße ['zy:sə], *f.* (—, *no pl.*) sweetness.
süßen ['zy:sən], *v.a.* sweeten.
Süßholz ['zy:shɔlts], *n.* (—es, *no pl.*) liquorice; — *raspeln*, talk sweet nothings, pay compliments.
Süßigkeit ['zy:sɪçkaɪt], *f.* (—, *pl.* —en) sweetness; (*pl.*) sweets.
süßlich ['zy:slɪç], *adj.* sweetish; (*fig.*) fulsome, mawkish, cloying.
Süßspeise ['zy:sʃpaɪzə], *f.* (—, *pl.* —n) dessert.
Süßwasser ['zy:svasər], *n.* (—s, *no pl.*) fresh water.
Symbolik [zymˈbo:lɪk], *f.* (—, *no pl.*) symbolism.
symbolisch [zymˈbo:lɪʃ], *adj.* symbolic(al).
symbolisieren [zymbɔliˈzi:rən], *v.a.* symbolize.
symmetrisch [zyˈme:trɪʃ], *adj.* symmetrical.
Sympathie [zympaˈti:], *f.* (—, *no pl.*) sympathy.
sympathisch [zymˈpa:tɪʃ], *adj.* congenial, likeable.
Synagoge [zynaˈgo:gə], *f.* (—, *pl.* —n) synagogue.
synchronisieren [zynkroniˈzi:rən], *v.a.* synchronise.
Syndikus ['zyndikus], *m.* (—, *pl.* Syndizi) syndic.
Synode [zyˈno:də], *f.* (—, *pl.* —n) synod.
synthetisch [zynˈte:tɪʃ], *adj.* synthetic.
Syrien ['zyːrjən], *n.* Syria.
systematisch [zysteˈma:tɪʃ], *adj.* systematic(al).
Szenarium [stseˈna:rjum], *n.* (—s, *pl.* —rien) scenario, stage, scene.
Szene ['stse:nə], *f.* (—, *pl.* —n) scene; *in* — *setzen*, stage, produce; (*coll.*) get up; *sich in* — *setzen*, show off.
Szenerie [stsenəˈri:], *f.* (—, *pl.* —n) scenery.
szenisch ['stse:nɪʃ], *adj.* scenic.
Szepter ['stsɛptər], *n.* (—s, *pl.* —) sceptre, mace.

T

T [te:], *n.* (—, *pl.* —) the letter T.
Tabak ['ta:bak], *m.* (—s, *pl.* —e) tobacco.

Tabaksbeutel ['ta:baksbɔytəl], *m.* (—s, *pl.* —) tobacco-pouch.
Tabatiere [ta:baˈtjɛ:rə], *f.* (—, *pl.* —n) snuff-box.
tabellarisch [tabɛˈla:rɪʃ], *adj.* in tables, tabular.
Tabelle [taˈbɛlə], *f.* (—, *pl.* —n) table, index, schedule.
Tablett [taˈblɛt], *n.* (—s, *pl.* —s) tray.
Tablette [taˈblɛtə], *f.* (—, *pl.* —n) tablet, pill.
Tabulatur [tabulaˈtu:r], *f.* (—, *pl.* —en) tablature, tabling, index.
Tadel ['ta:dəl], *m.* (—s, *pl.* —) blame, censure, reproach; (*Sch.*) bad mark; *ohne* —, blameless.
tadellos ['ta:dəllo:s], *adj.* blameless, faultless, impeccable.
tadeln ['ta:dəln], *v.a.* blame, censure, find fault with; reprimand.
tadelnswert ['ta:dəlnsvɛrt], *adj.* blameworthy, culpable.
Tafel ['ta:fəl], *f.* (—, *pl.* —n) board; (*Sch.*) blackboard; slate; (*fig.*) (*obs.*) dinner, banquet; festive fare; (*chocolate*) slab, bar.
Täfelchen ['tɛ:fəlçən], *n.* (—s, *pl.* —) tablet.
tafelförmig ['ta:fəlfœrmɪç], *adj.* tabular.
tafeln ['ta:fəln], *v.n.* dine, feast.
täfeln ['tɛ:fəln], *v.a.* wainscot, panel.
Täfelung ['tɛ:fəluŋ], *f.* (—, *pl.* —en) wainscoting, panelling.
Taft, Taffet [taft, 'tafət], *m.* (—(e)s, *pl.* —e) taffeta.
Tag [ta:k], *m.* (—(e)s, *pl.* —e) day; (*fig.*) light; *der jüngste* —, Doomsday; *bei* —e, in the daytime, by daylight; *sich etwas bei* —e *besehen*, examine s.th. in the light of day; — *für* — day by day; *von* — *zu* —, from day to day; *dieser* —e, one of these days, shortly; *etwas an den* — *bringen*, bring s.th. to light; *in den* — *hinein leben*, live improvidently; —. *und Nachtgleiche*, equinox.
Tagbau ['ta:kbau], *m.* (—s, *no pl.*) opencast mining.
Tageblatt ['ta:gəblat], *n.* (—s, *pl.* ⸚er) daily paper.
Tagebuch ['ta:gəbu:x], *n.* (—(e)s, *pl.* ⸚er) diary, journal.
Tagedieb ['ta:gədi:p], *m.* (—(e)s, *pl.* —e) idler, wastrel.
Tagelöhner ['ta:gəlø:nər], *m.* (—s, *pl.* —) day-labourer.
tagen ['ta:gən], *v.n.* dawn; (*gathering*) meet; (*Law*) sit.
Tagesanbruch ['ta:gəsanbrux], *m.* (—s, *pl.* ⸚e) daybreak, dawn.
Tagesbericht ['ta:gəsbərɪçt], *m.* (—(e)s, *pl.* —e) daily report.
Tagesgespräch ['ta:gəsgəʃprɛ:ç], *n.* (—(e)s, *pl.* —e) topic of the day.
Tagesordnung ['ta:gəsɔrdnuŋ], *f.* (—, *pl.* —en) agenda.
Tagewerk ['ta:gəvɛrk], *n.* (—s, *no pl.*) day's work, daily round.
täglich ['tɛ:klɪç], *adj.* daily.

tagsüber

tagsüber ['ta:ksy:bər], *adv.* in the daytime, during the day.

Taille ['taljə], *f.* (—, *pl.* —n) waist.

takeln ['ta:kəln], *v.a.* tackle, rig.

Takelwerk ['ta:kəlvɛrk], *n.* (—s, *no pl.*) rigging.

Takt (1) [takt], *m.* (—es, *pl.* —e) (*Mus.*) time, measure, bar; — *schlagen*, beat time.

Takt (2) [takt], *m.* (—es, *no pl.*) tact, discretion.

taktfest ['taktfɛst], *adj.* (*Mus.*) good at keeping time; (*fig.*) firm.

taktieren [tak'ti:rən], *v.n.* (*Mus.*) beat time.

Taktik ['taktɪk], *f.* (—, *pl.* —en) tactics.

Taktiker ['taktɪkər], *m.* (—s, *pl.* —) tactician.

taktisch ['taktɪʃ], *adj.* tactical.

taktlos ['taktlo:s], *adj.* tactless.

Taktmesser ['taktmɛsər], *m.* (—s, *pl.* —) metronome.

Taktstock ['taktʃtɔk], *m.* (—s, *pl.* ⁻e) baton.

Tal [ta:l], *n.* (—(e)s, *pl.* ⁻er) valley, dale, glen.

talab [ta:l'ap], *adv.* downhill.

Talar [ta'la:r], *m.* (—s, *pl.* —e) gown.

Talent [ta'lɛnt], *n.* (—(e)s, *pl.* —e) talent, accomplishment, gift.

talentiert [talən'ti:rt], *adj.* talented, gifted, accomplished.

talentvoll [ta'lɛntfəl], *adj.* talented, gifted, accomplished.

Taler ['ta:lər], *m.* (—s, *pl.* —) old German coin; thaler.

Talfahrt ['ta:lfa:rt], *f.* (—, *pl.* —en) descent.

Talg [talk], *m.* (—(e)s, *no pl.*) tallow.

Talk [talk], *m.* (—(e)s, *no pl.*) talc.

Talkerde ['talke:rdə], *f.* (—, *no pl.*) magnesia.

Talkessel [ta:lkɛsəl], *m.* (—s, *pl.* —) (*Geog.*) hollow, narrow valley.

Talmulde ['ta:lmuldə], *f.* (—, *pl.* —n) narrow valley, trough.

Talschlucht ['ta:lʃluxt], *f.* (—, *pl.* —en) glen.

Talsohle ['ta:lzo:lə], *f.* (—, *pl.* —n) floor of a valley.

Talsperre ['ta:lʃpɛrə], *f.* (—, *pl.* —n) dam (across valley); barrage.

Tambour ['tambu:r], *m.* (—s, *pl.* —e) drummer.

Tamtam ['tamtam], *n.* (—s, *no pl.*) tom-tom; (*fig.*) palaver.

Tand [tant], *m.* (—(e)s, *no pl.*) knick-knack, trifle; rubbish.

Tändelei [tɛndə'laɪ], *f.* (—, *pl.* —en) trifling, toying; (*fig.*) flirting.

Tändelmarkt ['tɛndəlmarkt], *m.* (—s, *pl.* ⁻e) rag-fair.

tändeln ['tɛndəln], *v.n.* trifle, dally, toy; (*fig.*) flirt.

Tang [taŋ], *m.* (—s, *pl.* —e) (*Bot.*) seaweed.

Tanganjika [taŋga'nji:ka], *n.* Tanganyika.

Tangente [taŋ'gɛntə], *f.* (—, *pl.* —n) tangent.

Tanger ['taŋər], *n.* Tangier.

Tank [taŋk], *m.* (—(e)s, *pl.* —e) tank.

tanken ['taŋkən], *v.n.* refuel; fill up (with petrol).

Tankstelle ['taŋkʃtɛlə], *f.* (—, *pl.* —n) filling-station.

Tanne ['tanə], *f.* (—, *pl.* —n) (*Bot.*) fir.

Tannenbaum ['tanənbaum], *m.* (—s, *pl.* ⁻e) (*Bot.*) fir-tree.

Tannenholz ['tanənhɔlts], *n.* (—es, *no pl.*) (*timber*) deal.

Tannenzapfen ['tanəntsapfən], *m.* (—s, *pl.* —) (*Bot.*) fir-cone.

Tansania [tanza'ni:a], *n.* Tanzania.

Tante ['tantə], *f.* (—, *pl.* —n) aunt.

Tantieme [tã'tjɛːmə], *f.* (—, *pl.* —n) royalty, share (in profits), percentage.

Tanz [tants], *m.* (—es, *pl.* ⁻e) dance.

Tanzboden ['tantsbo:dən], *m.* (—s, *pl.* ⁻) ballroom, dance-hall.

tänzeln ['tɛntsəln], *v.n.* skip about, frisk; (*horses*) amble.

tanzen ['tantsən], *v.a., v.n.* dance.

tanzlustig ['tantslustɪç], *adj.* fond of dancing.

Tapet [ta'pe:t], *n.* (—s, *no pl.*) *aufs — bringen*, broach, bring up for discussion.

Tapete [ta'pe:tə], *f.* (—, *pl.* —n) wallpaper.

tapezieren [tapə'tsi:rən], *v.a.* paper.

Tapezierer [tapə'tsi:rər], *m.* (—s, *pl.* —) paperhanger; upholsterer.

tapfer ['tapfər], *adj.* brave, valiant, gallant, courageous.

Tapferkeit ['tapfərkaɪt], *f.* (—, *no pl.*) valour, bravery, gallantry.

Tapisserie [tapɪsə'ri:], *f.* (—, *no pl.*) needlework; tapestry.

tappen ['tapən], *v.n.* grope about.

täppisch ['tɛpɪʃ], *adj.* clumsy, awkward, unwieldy.

tarnen ['tarnən], *v.a.* camouflage.

Tasche ['taʃə], *f.* (—, *pl.* —n) pocket; bag, pouch; *in die — stecken*; *in die — greifen*, pay, fork out, put o.'s hand in o.'s pocket.

Taschendieb ['taʃəndi:p], *m.* (—(e)s, *pl.* —e) pickpocket; *vor —en wird gewarnt*, beware of pickpockets.

Taschenformat ['taʃənfɔrma:t], *n.* (—s, *no pl.*) pocket-size.

Taschenspieler ['taʃənʃpi:lər], *m.* (—s, *pl.* —) juggler, conjurer.

Taschentuch ['taʃəntu:x], *n.* (—s, *pl.* ⁻er) (pocket-)handkerchief.

Taschenuhr ['taʃənu:r], *f.* (—, *pl.* —en) pocket-watch.

Tasse ['tasə], *f.* (—, *pl.* —n) cup.

Tastatur [tasta'tu:r], *f.* (—, *pl.* —en) keyboard.

Taste ['tastə], *f.* (—, *pl.* —n) (*Mus.*) key.

tasten ['tastən], *v.n.* grope about, feel o.'s way.

Tastsinn ['tastzɪn], *m.* (—s, *no pl.*) sense of touch.

Tat [ta:t], *f.* (—, *pl.* —en) deed, act, action; feat, exploit; *in der* —, in fact, indeed; *auf frischer* —, in the very act; *einem mit Rat und* — *beistehen*, give s.o. advice and guidance, help by word and deed.

Tatbestand ['ta:tbəʃtant], *m.* (—es, *pl.* ⁀e) (*Law*) facts of the case.

Tatendrang ['ta:təndraŋ], *m.* —(e)s, *no pl.*) urge for action; impetuosity.

tatenlos ['ta:tənlo:s], *adj.* inactive.

Täter ['tɛ:tər], *m.* (—s, *pl.* —) perpetrator, doer; culprit.

tätig ['tɛ:tɪç], *adj.* active, busy.

Tätigkeit ['tɛ:tɪçkaɪt], *f.* (—, *pl.* —en) activity.

Tätigkeitswort ['tɛ:tɪçkaɪtsvɔrt], *n.* (—(e)s, *pl.* ⁀er) (*Gram.*) verb.

Tatkraft ['ta:tkraft], *f.* (—, *no pl.*) energy.

tätlich ['tɛ:tlɪç], *adj.* — *werden*, become violent.

tätowieren [tɛ:to'vi:rən], *v.a.* tattoo.

Tatsache ['ta:tzaxə], *f.* (—, *pl.* —en) fact, matter of fact.

tatsächlich ['ta:tzɛçlɪç], *adj.* actual. — *excl.* really!

tätscheln ['tɛ:tʃəln], *v.a.* fondle.

Tatterich ['tatərɪç], *m.* (—s, *no pl.*) (*coll.*) trembling, shakiness.

Tatze ['tatsə], *f.* (—, —n) paw.

Tau (1) [tau], *m.* (—s, *no pl.*) thaw; dew.

Tau (2) [tau], *n.* (—s, *pl.* —e) rope, cable.

taub [taup], *adj.* deaf; (*nut*) hollow, empty; — *machen*, deafen; — *sein gegen*, turn a deaf ear to.

Täubchen ['tɔypçən], *n.* (—s, *pl.* —) little dove; (*fig.*) sweetheart.

Taube ['taubə], *f.* (—, *pl.* —n) (*Orn.*) pigeon, dove.

Taubenschlag ['taubənʃla:k], *m.* (—s, *pl.* ⁀e) dovecote.

Taubenschwanz ['taubənʃvants], *m.* (—es, *pl.* ⁀e) (*Ent.*) hawkmoth.

Tauber ['taubər], *m.* (—s, *pl.* —) (*Orn.*) cock-pigeon.

Taubheit ['tauphaɪt], *f.* (—, *no pl.*) deafness.

Taubnessel ['taupnɛsəl], *f.* (—, *pl.* —n) (*Bot.*) deadnettle.

taubstumm ['taupʃtum], *adj.* deaf and dumb, deaf-mute.

tauchen ['tauçən], *v.n.* (*aux.* haben & sein) dive, plunge. — *v.a.* immerse, dip.

Tauchsieder ['tauçzi:dər], *m.* (—s, *pl.* —) (*Elec.*) immersion heater.

tauen ['tauən], *v.a., v.n.* thaw, melt.

Taufbecken ['taufbɛkən], *n.* (—s, *pl.* —) (baptismal) font.

Taufe ['taufə], *f.* (—, *pl.* —n) baptism, christening; *aus der* — *heben*, stand godparent.

taufen ['taufən], *v.a.* baptise, christen.

Taufkleid ['taufklaɪt], *n.* (—s, *pl.* —er) christening robe.

Täufling ['tɔyflɪŋ], *m.* (—s, *pl.* —e) infant presented for baptism; neophyte.

Taufname ['taufna:mə], *m.* (—ns, *pl.* —n) Christian name.

Taufpate ['taufpa:tə], *m.* (—n, *pl.* —n) godfather, godmother.

Taufstein ['taufʃtaɪn], *n.* (—s, *pl.* —e) (baptismal) font.

taugen ['taugən], *v.n.* be good for, be fit for; *nichts* —, be good for nothing.

Taugenichts ['taugənɪçts], *m.* (—, *pl.* —e) ne'er-do-well, scapegrace, good-for-nothing.

tauglich ['tauklɪç], *adj.* able; useful, fit, suitable.

Taumel ['tauməl], *m.* (—s, *no pl.*) giddiness, dizziness, staggering; (*fig.*) whirl; ecstasy, frenzy, delirium, intoxication.

taumeln ['tauməln], *v.n.* (*aux.* sein) reel, stagger.

Tausch [tauʃ], *m.* (—es, *no pl.*) exchange, barter.

tauschen ['tauʃən], *v.a.* exchange for, barter against, swop; *die Rollen* —, change places.

täuschen ['tɔyʃən], *v.a.* deceive, delude. — *v.r. sich* —, be mistaken.

Tauschhandel ['tauʃhandəl], *m.* (—s, *no pl.*) barter.

Tauschmittel ['tauʃmɪtəl], *n.* (—s, *pl.* —) medium of exchange.

Täuschung ['tɔyʃuŋ], *f.* (—, *pl.* —en) deceit, deception; illusion.

Täuschungsversuch ['tɔyʃuŋsfɛrzu:ç], *m.* (—es, *pl.* —e) attempt at deception; (*Mil.*) diversion.

tausend ['tauzənt], *num. adj.* a thousand.

tausendjährig ['tauzəntjɛ:rɪç], *adj.* millennial, of a thousand years; *das* —*e Reich*, the millennium.

Tausendsasa ['tauzəntzasa], *m.* (—s, *pl.* —) devil of a fellow.

Tautropfen ['tautrɔpfən], *m.* (—s, *pl.* —) dew-drop.

Tauwetter ['tauvɛtər], *n.* (—s, *no pl.*) thaw.

Taxameter [taksa'me:tər], *m.* (—s, *pl.* —) taximeter.

Taxe ['taksə], *f.* (—, *pl.* —n) set rate, tariff; (taxi)cab; *nach der* — *verkauft werden*, be sold *ad valorem*.

taxieren [tak'si:rən], *v.a.* appraise, value.

Taxus ['taksus,] *m.* (—, *pl.* —) (*Bot.*) yew(-tree).

Technik ['tɛçnɪk], *f.* (—, *pl.* —en) technology, engineering; technique; skill, execution.

Techniker ['tɛçnɪkər], *m.* (—s, *pl.* —) technician, technical engineer.

Technikum ['tɛçnɪkum], *n.* (—s, *pl.* —s) technical school, college.

technisch ['tɛçnɪʃ], *adj.* technical; —*er Ausdruck*, technical term; —*e Störung*, technical hitch *or* breakdown.

technologisch [tɛçno'lo:gɪʃ], *adj.* technological.

Techtelmechtel ['tɛçtəlmɛçtəl], n. (—s, pl. —) (coll.) love affair, flirtation.
Tee [te:], m. (—s, no pl.) tea.
Teedose ['te:do:zə], f. (—, pl. —n) tea-caddy.
Teekanne ['te:kanə], f. (—, pl. —n) tea-pot.
Teelöffel ['te:lœfəl], m. (—s, pl. —) tea-spoon.
Teemaschine ['te:maʃi:nə], f. (—, pl. —n) tea-urn.
Teer [te:r], m. (—(e)s, no pl.) tar.
Teerleinwand ['te:rlaInvant], f. (—, no pl.) tarpaulin.
Teerose ['te:ro:zə], f. (—, pl. —n) (Bot.) tea rose.
Teerpappe ['te:rpapə], f. (—, no pl.) roofing-felt.
teeren ['te:rən], v.a. tar.
Teesieb ['te:zi:p], n. (—(e)s, pl. —e) tea-strainer.
Teich [taIç], m. (—es, pl. —e) pond.
Teig [taIk], m. (—(e)s, pl. —e) dough, paste.
teigig ['taIgIç], adj. doughy.
Teigrolle ['taIkrolə], f. (—, pl. —n) rolling-pin.
Teil [taIl], m. & n. (—(e)s, pl. —e) part; portion; piece, component; share; edler —, vital part; zum —, partly; zu gleichen —en, share and share alike.
teilbar ['taIlba:r], adj. divisible.
Teilchen ['taIlçən], n. (—s, pl. —) particle.
teilen ['taIlən], v.a. divide; share; partition off. — v.r. sich —, share in; (road) fork.
Teiler ['taIlər], m. (—s, pl. —) divider; (Maths.) divisor.
teilhaben ['taIlha:bən], v.n. irr. (have a) share in, participate in.
Teilhaber ['taIlha:bər], m. (—s, pl. —) partner.
teilhaftig ['taIlhaftIç], adj. sharing, participating; einer Sache — werden, partake of s.th., come in for s.th.
Teilnahme ['taIlna:mə], f. (—, no pl.) participation; (fig.) sympathy, interest.
teilnahmslos ['taIlna:mslo:s], adj. unconcerned, indifferent.
Teilnahmslosigkeit ['taIlna:mslo:zIçkaIt], f. (—, no pl.) unconcern; listlessness, indifference.
teilnahmsvoll ['taIlna:msfɔl], adj. solicitous.
teilnehmen ['taIlne:mən], v.n. irr. take part (in), participate, partake; (fig.) sympathise.
Teilnehmer ['taIlne:mər], m. (—s, pl. —) member, participant; (telephone) subscriber.
teils [taIls], adv. partly.
Teilstrecke ['taIlʃtrɛkə], f. (—, pl. —n) section (of a railway).
Teilung ['taIluŋ], f. (—, pl. —en) division, partition; distribution.
Teilungszahl ['taIluŋstsa:l], f. (—, pl. —en) (Maths.) dividend; quotient.

teilweise ['taIlvaIzə], adv. partly, in part.
Teilzahlung ['taIltsa:luŋ], f. (—, pl. —en) part-payment, instalment.
Teint [tɛ̃], m. (—s, no pl.) complexion.
telephonieren [telefo'ni:rən], v.a., v.n. telephone.
Telegraphie [telegra'fi:], f. (—, no pl.) telegraphy.
telegraphisch [tele'gra:fIʃ], adj. telegraphic, by telegram.
Telegramm [tele'gram], n. (—s, pl. —e) telegram, wire, cable.
Telegrammadresse [tele'gramadrɛsə], f. (—, pl. —n) telegraphic address.
Telegrammformular [tele'gramformula:r], n. (—s, pl. —e) telegram-form.
Teleskop [teles'ko:p], n. (—s, pl. —e) telescope.
Teller ['tɛlər], m. (—s, pl. —) plate.
Tempel ['tɛmpəl], m. (—s, pl. —) temple.
Temperament [tɛmpəra'mɛnt], n. (—s, pl. —e) temperament, disposition; (fig.) spirits.
temperamentvoll [tɛmpəra'mɛntfɔl], adj. full of spirits, vivacious; lively.
Temperatur [tɛmpəra'tu:r], f. (—, pl. —en) temperature.
Temperenzler [tɛmpə'rɛntslər], m. (—s, pl. —) total abstainer, tee-totaller.
temperieren [tɛmpə'ri:rən], v.a. temper.
Tempo ['tɛmpo:], n. (—s, pl. —s, Tempi) time, measure, speed.
temporisieren [tɛmpori'zi:rən], v.n. temporise.
Tendenz [tɛn'dɛnts], f. (—, pl. —en) tendency.
tendenziös [tɛndɛn'tsjø:s], adj. biased, coloured, tendentious.
Tender ['tɛndər], m. (—s, pl. —) (Railw.) tender.
Tenne ['tɛnə], f. (—, pl. —n) threshing floor.
Tenor [te'no:r], m. (—s, pl. ⁚e) (Mus.) tenor.
Teppich ['tɛpIç], m. (—s, pl. —e) carpet.
Termin [tɛr'mi:n], m. (—s, pl. —e) time, date, appointed day; einen — ansetzen, fix a day (for a hearing, examination etc.).
Termingeschäft [tɛr'mi:ngəʃɛft], n. (—s, pl. —e) (business in) futures.
Terminologie [tɛrminolo'gi:], f. (—, pl. —n) terminology.
Terpentin [tɛrpɛn'ti:n], n. (—s, no pl.) turpentine.
Terrain [tɛ'rɛ̃], n. (—s, pl. —s) ground, terrain.
Terrasse [tɛ'rasə], f. (—, pl. —n) terrace.
Terrine [tɛ'ri:nə], f. (—, pl. —n) tureen.
territorial [tɛrIto'rja:l], adj. territorial.
Territorium [tɛrI'to:rjum], n. (—s, pl. —torien) territory.

Tierschutzverein

tertiär [tɛr'tsjɛ:r], *adj.* tertiary.
Terzett [tɛr'tsɛt], *n.* (—s, *pl.* —e) trio.
Testament [tɛsta'mɛnt], *n.* (—s, *pl.* —e) testament, will; (*Bibl.*) Testament; *ohne* —, intestate.
testamentarisch [tɛstamɛn'ta:rɪʃ], *adj.* testamentary.
Testamentseröffnung [tɛsta'mɛntsɛrœfnuŋ], *f.* (—, *pl.* —en) reading of the will.
Testamentsvollstrecker [tɛsta'mɛntsfɔlʃtrɛkər], *m.* (—s, *pl.* —) executor.
teuer ['tɔyər], *adj.* dear; costly, expensive; *einem — zu stehen kommen,* cost s.o. dear.
Teuerung ['tɔyəruŋ], *f.* (—, *pl.* —en) scarcity, dearth.
Teufel ['tɔyfəl], *m.* (—s, *pl.* —) devil, fiend; *armer* —, poor devil; *scher dich zum —,* go to blazes; *den — an die Wand malen,* talk of the devil.
Teufelei [tɔyfə'laɪ], *f.* (—, *pl.* —en) devilry, devilish trick.
teuflisch ['tɔyflɪʃ], *adj.* devilish, diabolical.
Thailand ['taɪlant], *n.* Thailand.
Theater [te'a:tər], *n.* (—s, *pl.* —) theatre, stage.
Theaterkarte [te'a:tərkartə], *f.* (—, *pl.* —n) theatre-ticket.
Theaterkasse [te'a:tərkasə], *f.* (—, *pl.* —n) box-office.
Theaterstück [te'a:tərʃtyk], *n.* (—(e)s, *pl.* —e) play, drama.
Theatervorstellung [te'a:tərfo:rʃtɛluŋ], *f.* (—, *pl.* —en) theatre performance.
Theaterzettel [te'a:tərtsɛtəl], *m.* (—s, *pl.* —) play-bill.
theatralisch [tea'tra:lɪʃ], *adj.* theatrical; dramatic; histrionic.
Thema ['te:ma:], *n.* (—s, *pl.* —men, **Themata**) theme, subject, topic.
Themse ['tɛmzə], *f.* Thames.
Theologe [teo'lo:gə], *m.* (—n, *pl.* —n) theologian.
Theologie [teolo'gi:], *f.* (—, *no pl.*) theology, divinity.
theoretisch [teo're:tɪʃ], *adj.* theoretical.
theoretisieren [teoreti'zi:rən], *v.n.* theorise.
Theorie [teo'ri:], *f.* (—, *pl.* —n) theory.
Therapie [tera'pi:], *f.* (—, *no pl.*) therapy.
Therme ['tɛrmə], *f.* (—, *pl.* —n) hot spring.
Thermometer [tɛrmo'me:tər], *n.* (—s, *pl.* —) thermometer.
Thermosflasche ['tɛrmɔsflaʃə], *f.* (—, *pl.* —n) thermos-flask.
These ['te:zə], *f.* (—, *pl.* —n) thesis.
Thron [tro:n], *m.* (—(e)s, *pl.* —e) throne; *auf den — setzen,* place on the throne, enthrone; *vom — stoßen,* dethrone, depose.
Thronbesteigung ['tro:nbəʃtaɪguŋ], *f.* (—, *pl.* —en) accession (to the throne).
Thronbewerber ['tro:nbəvɛrbər], *m.* (—s, *pl.* —) claimant to the throne, pretender.
thronen ['tro:nən], *v.n.* sit enthroned.

Thronerbe ['tro:nɛrbə], *m.* (—n, *pl.* —n) heir apparent, crown prince.
Thronfolge ['tro:nfɔlgə], *f.* (—, *no pl.*) line *or* order of succession.
Thronfolger ['tro:nfɔlgər], *m.* (—s, *pl.* —) heir to the throne, heir apparent.
Thronhimmel ['tro:nhɪməl], *m.* (—s, *pl.* —) canopy.
Thronrede ['tro:nre:də], *f.* (—, *pl.* —n) speech from the throne.
Thunfisch ['tu:nfɪʃ], *m.* (—es, *pl.* —e) (*Zool.*) tunny, (*Am.*) tuna.
Thüringen ['ty:rɪŋən], *n.* Thuringia.
Thymian ['ty:mja:n], *m.* (—s, *no pl.*) (*Bot.*) thyme.
ticken ['tɪkən], *v.n.* tick.
tief [ti:f], *adj.* deep, profound, low; far; extreme; (*voice*) bass; (*fig.*) profound; *in —ster Nacht,* in the dead of night; *aus —stem Herzen,* from the bottom of o.'s heart. — *adv.* — *atmen,* take a deep breath; — *in Schulden,* head over ears in debt; — *verletzt,* cut to the quick.
Tiefbau ['ti:fbau], *m.* (—s, *no pl.*) underground workings.
tiefbedrückt ['ti:fbədrykt], *adj.* deeply distressed; very depressed.
tiefbewegt ['ti:fbəve:kt], *adj.* deeply moved.
Tiefe ['ti:fə], *f.* (—, *pl.* —en) depth; (*fig.*) profundity.
tiefgebeugt ['ti:fgəbɔykt], *adj.* bowed down.
tiefgreifend ['ti:fgraɪfənt], *adj.* radical, sweeping.
tiefschürfend ['ti:fʃyrfənt], *adj.* profound; thoroughgoing.
Tiefsee ['ti:fze:], *f.* (—, *no pl.*) deep sea.
Tiefsinn ['ti:fzɪn], *m.* (—s, *no pl.*) pensiveness, melancholy.
tiefsinnig ['ti:fzɪnɪç], *adj.* pensive, melancholy, melancholic(al).
Tiegel ['ti:gəl], *m.* (—s, *pl.* —) crucible; saucepan.
Tier [ti:r], *n.* (—(e)s, *pl.* —e) animal, beast; *ein großes —,* (*coll.*) a V.I.P., a bigwig; (*Am.*) a swell, a big shot.
Tierart ['ti:ra:rt], *f.* (—, *pl.* —en) (*Zool.*) species.
Tierarzt ['ti:ra:rtst], *m.* (—es, *pl.* —e) veterinary surgeon.
Tierbändiger ['ti:rbɛndɪgər], *m.* (—s, *pl.* —) animal-tamer.
Tiergarten ['ti:rgartən], *m.* (—s, *pl.* —) zoological gardens, zoo.
tierisch ['ti:rɪʃ], *adj.* animal, brute, brutal, bestial.
Tierkreis ['ti:rkraɪs], *m.* (—es, *no pl.*) zodiac.
Tierkunde ['ti:rkundə], *f.* (—, *no pl.*) zoology.
Tierquälerei ['ti:rkvɛ:ləraɪ], *f.* (—, *pl.* —en) cruelty to animals.
Tierreich ['ti:rraɪç], *n.* (—(e)s, *no pl.*) animal kingdom.
Tierschutzverein ['ti:rʃutsfəraɪn], *m.* (—s, *pl.* —e) society for the prevention of cruelty to animals.

223

Tierwärter

Tierwärter ['ti:rvɛrtər], *m.* (—s, *pl.* —) keeper (at a zoo).
Tiger ['ti:gər], *m.* (—s, *pl.* —) (*Zool.*) tiger.
Tigerin ['ti:gərɪn], *f.* (—, *pl.* —nen) (*Zool.*) tigress.
tilgbar ['tɪlkba:r], *adj.* extinguishable; (*debt*) redeemable.
tilgen ['tɪlgən], *v.a.* strike out, efface, annul; (*debt*) discharge; (*sin*) expiate, atone for.
Tilgung ['tɪlguŋ], *f.* (—, *pl.* —en) striking out, obliteration; annulment, payment; redemption.
Tilgungsfonds ['tɪlguŋsfɔ], *m.* (—, *pl.* —) sinking fund.
Tingeltangel ['tɪŋəltaŋəl], *m. & n.* (—s, *pl.* —) (*coll.*) music-hall.
Tinktur [tɪŋk'tu:r], *f.* (—, *pl.* —en) tincture.
Tinte ['tɪntə], *f.* (—, *pl.* —n) ink; *in der — sein*, be in a jam, be in the soup.
Tintenfaß ['tɪntənfas], *n.* (—sses, *pl.* ⸚sser) ink-pot, ink-stand.
Tintenfisch ['tɪntənfɪʃ], *m.* (—es, *pl.* —e) (*Zool.*) cuttle-fish.
Tintenfleck ['tɪntənflɛk], *m.* (—s, *pl.* —e) blot, ink-spot.
Tintenklecks ['tɪntənklɛks], *m.* (—es, *pl.* —e) blot.
Tintenstift ['tɪntənʃtɪft], *m.* (—s, *pl.* —e) indelible pencil.
Tintenwischer ['tɪntənvɪʃər], *m.* (—s, *pl.* —) pen-wiper.
tippen ['tɪpən], *v.a.* tap; (*coll.*) type.
Tirol [ti'ro:l], *n.* Tyrol.
Tisch [tɪʃ], *m.* (—es, *pl.* —e) table, board; *den — decken*, lay the table; *zu — gehen*, sit down to dinner.
Tischdecke ['tɪʃdɛkə], *f.* (—, *pl.* —n) tablecloth.
Tischgebet ['tɪʃgəbe:t], *n.* (—s, *pl.* —e) grace.
Tischler ['tɪʃlər], *m.* (—s, *pl.* —) joiner, cabinet-maker, carpenter.
Tischlerei [tɪʃlə'raɪ], *f.* (—, *no pl.*) joinery, cabinet-making, carpentry.
Tischrede ['tɪʃre:də], *f.* (—, *pl.* —n) after-dinner speech.
Tischrücken ['tɪʃrykən], *n.* (—s, *no pl.*) table-turning.
Tischtennis ['tɪʃtenɪs], *n.* (—, *no pl.*) table-tennis, ping-pong.
Tischtuch ['tɪʃtu:x], *n.* (—(e)s, *pl.* ⸚er) tablecloth.
Tischzeit ['tɪʃtsaɪt], *f.* (—, *pl.* —en) mealtime.
Titane [ti'ta:nə], *m.* (—n, *pl.* —n) Titan.
titanenhaft [ti'ta:nənhaft], *adj.* titanic.
Titel ['ti:təl], *m.* (—s, *pl.* —) title; claim; heading, headline.
Titelbild ['ti:təlbɪlt], *n.* (—(e)s, *pl.* —er) frontispiece.
Titelblatt ['ti:təlblat], *n.* (—(e)s, *pl.* ⸚er) title page.
Titelrolle ['ti:təlrɔlə], *f.* (—, *pl.* —n) title role.
titulieren [titu'li:rən], *v.a.* style, address.

toben ['to:bən], *v.n.* rave; rage, roar; be furious; be wild.
tobsüchtig ['to:pzyçtɪç], *adj.* raving, mad.
Tochter ['tɔxtər], *f.* (—, *pl.* ⸚) daughter.
töchterlich ['tœçtərlɪç], *adj.* filial, daughterly.
Tod [to:t], *m.* (—es, *pl.* —esfälle *or* (*rare*) —e) death, decease, demise; *dem — geweiht*, doomed; *Kampf auf — und Leben*, fight to the death; *zum — verurteilen*, condemn to death.
Todesangst ['to:dəsaŋst], *f.* (—, *pl.* ⸚e) agony, mortal terror.
Todesanzeige ['to:dəsantsaɪgə], *f.* (—, *pl.* —n) announcement of death; obituary notice.
Todesfall ['to:dəsfal], *m.* (—(e)s, *pl.* ⸚e) death, decease; fatality.
Todesgefahr ['to:dəsgəfa:r], *f.* (—, *pl.* —en) mortal danger.
Todeskampf ['to:dəskampf], *m.* (—(e)s, *pl.* ⸚e) death agony.
todesmutig ['to:dəsmu:tɪç], *adj.* death-defying.
Todesstoß ['to:dəsʃto:s], *m.* (—es, *pl.* ⸚e) death-blow.
Todesstrafe ['to:dəsʃtra:fə], *f.* (—, *no pl.*) capital punishment.
Todfeind ['to:tfaɪnt], *m.* (—es, *pl.* —e) mortal enemy.
todkrank ['to:tkraŋk], *adj.* sick unto death, dangerously *or* mortally ill.
tödlich ['tœ:tlɪç], *adj.* mortal, deadly, fatal.
todmüde ['to:tmy:də], *adj.* tired to death.
Todsünde ['to:tzyndə], *f.* (—, *pl.* —n) mortal sin.
Togo ['to:go], *n.* Togo.
Toilette [toa'lɛtə], *f.* (—, *pl.* —n) lavatory, toilet; (*fig.*) dress.
tolerant [tolə'rant], *adj.* tolerant.
Toleranz [tolə'rants], *f.* (—, *no pl.*) toleration; tolerance.
tolerieren [tolə'ri:rən], *v.a.* tolerate.
toll [tɔl], *adj.* mad, frantic; wild; —er *Streich*, mad prank; *zum — werden*, enough to drive o. mad.
Tolle ['tɔlə], *f.* (—, *pl.* —n) (*dial.*) forelock, tuft of hair, top-knot.
Tollhaus ['tɔlhaus], *n.* (—es, *pl.* ⸚er) madhouse, lunatic asylum.
Tollheit ['tɔlhaɪt], *f.* (—, *pl.* —en) foolhardiness, mad prank.
Tollkirsche ['tɔlkɪrʃə], *f.* (—, *pl.* —n) belladonna, deadly nightshade.
Tollwut ['tɔlvu:t], *f.* (—, *no pl.*) frenzy; rabies.
Tolpatsch ['tɔlpatʃ], *m.* (—es, *pl.* —e) clumsy person.
Tölpel ['tœlpəl], *m.* (—s, *pl.* —) blockhead, lout, hobbledehoy.
Tölpelei [tœlpə'laɪ], *f.* (—, *pl.* —en) clumsiness, awkwardness.
tölpelhaft ['tœlpəlhaft], *adj.* clumsy, doltish, loutish.
Tomate [to'ma:tə], *f.* (—, *pl.* —n) tomato.

Ton (1) [to:n], *m.* (—(e)s, *pl.* ⸚e)
sound, tone, accent, note; shade;
manners; *guter (schlechter)* —, good
(bad) form, etiquette; *den — angeben,*
set the fashion.

Ton (2) [to:n], *m.* (—s, *no pl.*) clay,
potter's earth.

Tonabnehmer ['to:nabne:mər], *m.*
(—s, *pl.* —) *(gramophone)* pick-up.

tonangebend ['to:nange:bənt], *adj.*
leading in fashion, setting the pace;
leading, fashionable.

Tonart ['to:na:rt], *f.* (—, *pl.* —en)
(Mus.) key.

Tonbandgerät ['to:nbantgɛrɛ:t], *n.*
(—s, *pl.* —e) tape-recorder.

tönen ['tø:nən], *v.n.* sound.

Tonerde ['to:ne:rdə], *f.* (—, *no pl.*)
clay.

tönern ['tø:nərn], *adj.* earthen.

Tonfall ['to:nfal], *m.* (—s, *no pl.*)
cadence, intonation (of voice).

Tonfolge ['to:nfɔlgə], *f.* (—, *pl.* —n)
(Mus.) succession of notes.

Tonführung ['to:nfy:ruŋ], *f.* (—, *no pl.*)
modulation.

Tonkunst ['to:nkunst], *f.* (—, *no pl.*)
music.

Tonkünstler ['to:nkynstlər], *m.* (—s,
pl. —) musician.

Tonleiter ['to:nlaitər], *f.* (—, *pl.* —n)
scale, gamut.

Tonne ['tɔnə], *f.* (—, *pl.* —n) tun, cask,
barrel; ton.

Tonnengewölbe ['tɔnəngəvœlbə], *n.*
(—s, *pl.* —) cylindrical vault.

Tonpfeife ['to:npfaifə], *f.* (—, *pl.* —n)
clay-pipe.

Tonsatz ['to:nzats], *m.* (—es, *pl.* ⸚e)
(Mus.) composition.

Tonsur [tɔn'zu:r], *f.* (—, *pl.* —en)
tonsure.

Tonwelle ['to:nvɛlə], *f.* (—, *pl.* —n)
sound-wave.

Topas [to'pa:s], *m.* (—es, *pl.* —e) topaz.

Topf [tɔpf], *m.* (—(e)s, *pl.* ⸚e) pot;
alles in einen — werfen, lump everything together.

Topfblume ['tɔpfblu:mə], *f.* (—, *pl.*
—n) pot-plant.

Topfdeckel ['tɔpfdɛkəl], *m.* (—s, *pl.* —)
lid of a pot.

Töpfer ['tœpfər], *m.* (—s, *pl.* —)
potter.

Töpferarbeit ['tœpfərarbait], *f.* (—, *pl.*
—en) pottery.

Töpferscheibe ['tœpfərʃaibə], *f.* (—,
pl. —n) potter's wheel.

Töpferware ['tœpfərva:rə], *f.* (—, *pl.*
—n) pottery, earthenware.

Topfgucker ['tɔpfgukər], *m.* (—s, *pl.*
—) busybody; inquisitive person.

Topographie [topogra'fi:], *f.* (—, *no
pl.*) topography.

Tor (1) [to:r], *m.* (—en, *pl.* —en)
(obs.) fool, simpleton.

Tor (2) [to:r], *n.* (—(e)s, *pl.* —e) gate;
(Footb.) goal.

Torangel ['to:raŋəl], *f.* (—, *pl.* —n)
hinge.

Tor(es)schluß ['to:r(əs)ʃlus], *m.* (—es,
no pl.) shutting of the gate; *noch
gerade vor —,* at the eleventh hour.

Torf [tɔrf], *m.* (—(e)s, *no pl.*) peat,
turf.

Torfgrube ['tɔrfgru:bə], *f.* (—, *pl.*
—n) turf-pit.

Torfmoor ['tɔrfmo:r], *n.* (—s, *pl.* —e)
peat-bog.

Torfstecher ['tɔrfʃtɛçər], *m.* (—s, *pl.*
—) peat-cutter.

Torheit ['to:rhait], *f.* (—, *pl.* —en)
foolishness, folly.

Torhüter ['to:rhy:tər], *m.* (—s, *pl.* —)
gate-keeper.

töricht ['tø:rɪçt], *adj.* foolish, silly.

Törin ['tø:rɪn], *f.* (—, *pl.* —nen) *(rare)*
foolish woman.

torkeln ['tɔrkəln], *v.n.* *(aux.* sein)
(coll.) stagger, reel.

Tornister [tɔr'nɪstər], *m.* (—s, *pl.* —)
knapsack, satchel.

Torpedo [tɔr'pe:do], *m.* (—s, *pl.* —s)
torpedo.

Torso ['tɔrzo], *m.* (—s, *pl.* —s) trunk,
torso.

Tort [tɔrt], *m.* (—s, *no pl.*) injury,
wrong; *einem einen — antun,* wrong
s.o.; play a trick on s.o.

Torte ['tɔrtə], *f.* (—, *pl.* —n) cake,
pastry, tart.

Tortur [tɔr'tu:r], *f.* (—, *pl.* —en)
torture.

Torwächter ['to:rvɛçtər], *m.* (—s, *pl.*
—) gate-keeper; porter.

tosen ['to:zən], *v.n.* roar.

tot [to:t], *adj.* dead, deceased.

total [to'ta:l], *adj.* total, complete.

Totalisator [totali'za:tɔr], *m.* (—s, *pl.*
—en) totalisator; *(coll.)* tote.

Totalleistung [to'ta:llaistuŋ], *f.* (—,
pl. —en) full effect; total output.

Tote ['to:tə], *m., f.* (—n, *pl.* —n) dead
person, the deceased.

töten ['tø:tən], *v.a.* kill, put to death.

Totenacker ['to:tənakər], *m.* (—s, *pl.*
⸚) churchyard, cemetery.

Totenamt ['to:tənamt], *n.* (—s, *no pl.*)
office for the dead, requiem, Mass for
the dead.

Totenbahre ['to:tənba:rə], *f.* (—, *pl.*
—n) bier.

Totengräber ['to:təngrɛ:bər], *m.* (—s,
pl. —) grave-digger.

Totenhemd ['to:tənhɛmt], *n.* (—(e)s,
pl. —en) shroud, winding-sheet.

Totenklage ['to:tənkla:gə], *f.* (—, *no
pl.*) lament.

Totenschein ['to:tənʃain], *m.* (—(e)s,
pl. —e) death-certificate.

Totenstille ['to:tənʃtilə], *f.* (—, *no pl.*)
dead calm.

Totenwache ['to:tənvaxə], *f.* (—, *no
pl.*) wake.

totgeboren ['to:tgəbo:rən], *adj.* still-
born, born dead.

Totschlag ['to:tʃla:k], *m.* (—s, *no pl.*)
manslaughter.

totschlagen ['to:tʃla:gən], *v.a.* *irr.*
kill, strike dead.

Totschläger

Totschläger ['to:tʃlɛ:gər], m. (—s, pl. —) loaded cane, cudgel.

totschweigen ['to:tʃvaɪgən], v.a. irr. hush up.

Tötung ['tø:tuŋ], f. (—, pl. —en) killing.

Tour [tu:r], f. (—, pl. —en) tour, excursion; in einer —, ceaselessly; auf —en bringen,(coll.) (Motor.) rev up.

Tournee [tur'ne:], f. (—, pl. —n) (Theat.) tour.

Trab [tra:p], m. (—(e)s, no pl.) trot.

Trabant [tra'bant], m. (—en, pl. —en) satellite.

traben ['tra:bən], v.n. (aux. sein) trot.

Trabrennen ['tra:prɛnən], n. (—s, pl. —) trotting-race.

Tracht [traxt], f. (—, pl. —en) dress, costume; national costume; native dress; eine — Prügel, a good hiding.

trachten ['traxtən], v.n. strive, aspire, endeavour; einem nach dem Leben —, seek to kill s.o.

trächtig ['trɛçtɪç], adj. (animal) pregnant, with young.

Trafik [tra'fɪk], m. (—s, pl. —s) (Austr.) tobacco-kiosk.

Tragbahre ['tra:kba:rə], f. (—, pl. —n) stretcher.

Tragbalken ['tra:kbalkən], m. (—s pl., —) girder.

tragbar ['tra:kba:r], adj. portable; tolerable.

träge ['trɛ:gə], adj. lazy, indolent, inert, sluggish.

tragen ['tra:gən], v.a. irr. bear, carry; (dress) wear; (fig.) bear, endure; Bedenken —, hesitate, have doubts; Zinsen —, yield interest; einen auf Händen —, care lovingly for s.o.

Träger ['trɛ:gər], m. (—s, pl. —) porter, carrier; girder.

Trägheit ['trɛ:khaɪt], f. (—, no pl.) indolence, laziness, inertia.

tragisch ['tra:gɪʃ], adj. tragic(al).

Tragkraft ['tra:kkraft], f. (—, no pl.) carrying or load capacity; lifting power.

Tragödie [tra'gø:djə], f. (—, pl. —n) tragedy.

Tragsessel ['tra:kzɛsəl], m. (—s, pl. —) sedan-chair.

Tragweite ['tra:kvaɪtə], f. (—, no pl.) significance, importance, range.

trainieren [trɛ'ni:rən], v.a. train.

Traktat [trak'ta:t], n. (—s, pl. —e) treatise, tract.

Traktätchen [trak'tɛ:tçən], n. (—s, pl. —) (short) tract.

traktieren [trak'ti:rən], v.a. treat; treat badly.

trällern ['trɛlərn], v.n. trill, hum.

Trambahn ['tramba:n], f. (—, pl. —en) tram; (Am.) streetcar.

Trampel ['trampəl], n. (—s, pl. —) clumsy person, bumpkin; (Am.) hick.

trampeln ['trampəln], v.n. trample.

Trampeltier ['trampəlti:r], n. (—s, pl. —e) camel; (fig.) clumsy person.

Tran [tra:n], m. (—(e)s,no pl.) whale-oil.

tranchieren [trã'ʃi:rən], v.a. carve.

Tranchiermesser [trã'ʃi:rmɛsər], n. (—s, pl. —) carving-knife.

Träne ['trɛ:nə], f. (—, pl. —n) tear, teardrop; zu —n gerührt, moved to tears.

tränen ['trɛ:nən], v.n. (eyes) water.

Tränendrüse ['trɛ:nəndry:zə], f. (—, pl. —n) lachrymal gland.

tränenleer ['trɛ:nənle:r], adj. tearless.

Tränenstrom ['trɛ:nənʃtro:m], m. (—s, pl. ̈e) flood of tears.

tränenvoll ['trɛ:nənfɔl], adj. tearful.

tranig ['tra:nɪç], adj. dull, slow.

Trank [traŋk], m. (—(e)s, pl. ̈e) drink, beverage, potion.

Tränke ['trɛŋkə], f. (—, pl. —n) (horse) watering-place.

tränken ['trɛŋkən], v.a. give to drink, water; impregnate, saturate.

transitiv ['tranziti:f], adj. transitive.

Transitlager ['tranzitla:gər], n. (—s, pl. —) bonded warehouse; transit camp.

transitorisch [tranzi'to:rɪʃ], adj. transitory.

transpirieren [transpi'ri:rən], v.n. perspire.

transponieren [transpo'ni:rən], v.a. transpose.

Transportkosten [trans'pɔrtkɔstən], f. pl. shipping charges.

Transportmittel [trans'pɔrtmɪtəl], n. (—s, pl. —) means of carriage, conveyance, transport.

Trapez [tra'pe:ts], n. (—es, pl. —e) trapeze; (Maths.) trapezoid.

Tratsch [tra:tʃ], m. (—es, no pl.) (coll.) gossip, tittle-tattle.

tratschen ['tra:tʃən], v.n. (coll.) gossip.

Tratte ['tratə], f. (—, pl. —n) (Comm.) draft, bill of exchange.

Traube ['traubə], f. (—, pl. —n) (Bot.) grape, bunch of grapes.

Traubensaft ['traubənzaft], m. (—s, pl. ̈e) grape-juice; (Poet.) wine.

traubig ['traubɪç], adj. clustered, grape-like.

trauen ['trauən], v.a. marry; join in marriage; sich — lassen, get married. — v.n. einem —, trust s.o., confide in s.o. — v.r. sich —, dare, venture.

Trauer ['trauər], f. (—, no pl.) mourning; sorrow, grief.

Trauermarsch ['trauərmarʃ], m. (—es, pl. ̈e) funeral march.

trauern ['trauərn], v.n. mourn, be in mourning.

Trauerspiel ['trauərʃpi:l], n. (—s, pl. —e) tragedy.

Trauerweide ['trauərvaɪdə], f. (—, pl. —n) (Bot.) weeping willow.

Traufe ['traufə], f. (—, pl. —n) eaves; vom Regen in die —, out of the frying pan into the fire.

träufeln ['trɔyfəln], v.a. drip, drop.

Traufröhre ['traufrø:rə], f. (—, pl. —n) gutter-pipe.

traulich ['traulıç], *adj.* familiar, homely, cosy.
Traum [traum], *m.* (—(e)s, *pl.* ⸚e) dream; *das fällt mir nicht im —e ein,* I should not dream of it.
Traumbild ['traumbılt], *n.* (—s, *pl.* —er) vision.
Traumdeutung ['traumdɔytuŋ], *f.* (—, *no pl.*) interpretation of dreams.
träumen ['trɔymən], *v.n.* dream; *sich etwas nicht — lassen,* have no inkling of, not dream of s.th.; not believe s.th.
Träumer ['trɔymər], *m.* (—s, *pl.* —) dreamer; (*fig.*) visionary.
Träumerei [trɔymə'rai], *f.* (—, *pl.* —en) dreaming, reverie.
traumhaft ['traumhaft], *adj.* dream-like.
traurig ['trauriç], *adj.* sad, mournful, sorrowful.
Traurigkeit ['trauriçkait], *f.* (—, *no pl.*) sadness, melancholy.
Trauring ['trauriŋ], *m.* (—s, *pl.* —e) wedding-ring.
Trauschein ['trauʃain], *m.* (—s, *pl.* —e) marriage certificate.
traut [traut], *adj.* dear, beloved; cosy; *—es Heim Glück allein,* east, west, home's best; there's no place like home.
Trauung ['trauuŋ], *f.* (—, *pl.* —en) marriage ceremony.
Trauzeuge ['trautsɔygə], *m.* (—n, *pl.* —n) witness to a marriage.
trecken ['trɛkən], *v.a.* (*dial.*) draw, drag, tug.
Trecker ['trɛkər], *m.* (—s, *pl.* —) tractor.
Treff [trɛf], *n.* (—s, *no pl.*) (*Cards*) clubs.
Treffen ['trɛfən], *n.* (—s, *pl.* —) action, battle, fight; meeting, gathering; *etwas ins — führen,* put s.th. forward, urge s.th.
treffen ['trɛfən], *v.a. irr.* hit, meet; *nicht —,* miss; *wie vom Donner getroffen,* thunderstruck; *ins Schwarze —,* hit the mark, score a bull's eye. *— v.r. sich —,* happen.
treffend ['trɛfənt], *adj.* appropriate, pertinent.
Treffer ['trɛfər], *m.* (—s, *pl.* —) (*lottery*) win, prize; (*Mil.*) hit.
trefflich ['trɛfliç], *adj.* excellent.
Treffpunkt ['trɛfpuŋkt], *m.* (—s, *pl.* —e) meeting-place.
Treffsicherheit ['trɛfsıçərhait], *f.* (—, *no pl.*) accurate aim.
Treibeis ['traipais], *n.* (—es, *no pl.*) floating-ice, ice floe.
treiben ['traibən], *v.a. irr.* drive, urge; incite; (*trade*) carry on, ply; *Studien —,* study; *was treibst du?* what are you doing? *etwas zu weit —,* carry s.th. too far; *einen in die Enge —,* drive s.o. into a corner. *— v.n.* be adrift, drift.
Treiben ['traibən], *n.* (—s, *no pl.*) driving; doings; bustle.

Treiber ['traibər], *m.* (—s, *pl.* —) (*Hunt.*) driver; beater.
Treibhaus ['traiphaus], *n.* (—es, *pl.* ⸚er) hothouse, greenhouse.
Treibkraft ['traipkraft], *f.* (—, *no pl.*) impulse, driving power.
Treibriemen ['traipri:mən], *m.* (—s, *pl.* —) driving-belt.
Treibsand ['traipzant], *m.* (—s, *no pl.*) quicksand, shifting sand.
Treibstange ['traipʃtaŋə], *f.* (—, *pl.* —en) main rod, connecting-rod.
Treibstoff ['traipʃtɔf], *m.* (—(e)s, *pl.* —e) fuel.
treideln ['traidəln], *v.a.* (*Naut.*) tow.
Treidelsteig ['traidəlʃtaik], *m.* (—s, *pl.* —e) towpath.
trennbar ['trɛnbaːr], *adj.* separable.
trennen ['trɛnən], *v.a.* separate, sever. *— v.r. sich —,* part.
Trennung ['trɛnuŋ], *f.* (—, *pl.* —en) separation, segregation; parting; division.
Trennungsstrich ['trɛnuŋsʃtriç], *m.* (—es, *pl.* —e) hyphen, dash.
treppab [trɛp'ap], *adv.* downstairs.
treppauf [trɛp'auf], *adv.* upstairs.
Treppe ['trɛpə], *f.* (—, *pl.* —n) stairs, staircase, flight of stairs.
Treppenabsatz ['trɛpənapzats], *m.* (—es, *pl.* ⸚e) (*staircase*) landing.
Treppengeländer ['trɛpəngəlɛndər], *n.* (—s, *pl.* —) balustrade, banisters.
Treppenhaus ['trɛpənhaus], *n.* (—es, *pl.* ⸚er) stair-well, staircase.
Treppenläufer ['trɛpənlɔyfər], *m.* (—s, *pl.* —) stair-carpet.
Treppenstufe ['trɛpənʃtuːfə], *f.* (—, *pl.* —n) step, stair.
Treppenwitz ['trɛpənvits], *m.* (—es, *no pl.*) afterthought, esprit de l'escalier.
Tresor [tre'zoːr], *m.* (—s, *pl.* —e) safe, strongroom.
Tresse ['trɛsə], *f.* (—, *pl.* —n) braid, lace, galloon.
treten ['treːtən], *v.a., v.n. irr.* tread, step, trample upon; go; *— Sie näher,* step this way; *in Verbindung — mit,* make contact with; *in den Ehestand —,* get married; *einem zu nahe —,* offend s.o., tread on s.o.'s toes.
treu [trɔy], *adj.* faithful, loyal, true; conscientious.
Treubruch ['trɔybrux], *m.* (—(e)s, *pl.* ⸚e) breach of faith, disloyalty.
Treue ['trɔyə], *f.* (—, *no pl.*) faithfulness, loyalty, fidelity; *meiner Treu!* upon my soul! *auf Treu und Glauben,* on trust.
Treueid ['trɔyait], *m.* (—s, *pl.* —e) oath of allegiance.
Treuhänder ['trɔyhɛndər], *m.* (—s, *pl.* —) trustee.
treuherzig ['trɔyhɛrtsiç], *adj.* guileless, trusting.
treulich ['trɔyliç], *adv.* faithfully.
treulos ['trɔyloːs], *adj.* faithless, perfidious; unfaithful.

227

Treulosigkeit ['trɔylo:zɪçkaɪt], f. (—, no pl.) faithlessness, perfidy, disloyalty.

Tribüne [tri'by:nə], f. (—, pl. —n) tribune, platform; (racing) grandstand.

Tribut [tri'bu:t], m. (—s, pl. —e) tribute.

tributpflichtig [tri'bu:tpflɪçtɪç], adj. tributary.

Trichter ['trɪçtər], m. (—s, pl. —) funnel.

trichterförmig ['trɪçtərfœrmɪç], adj. funnel-shaped.

Trieb [tri:p], m. (—(e)s, pl. —e) (plant) shoot, growth; instinct, bent, propensity, inclination; (Psych.) drive.

Triebfeder ['tri:pfe:dər], f. (—, pl. —n) mainspring; (fig.) motive, guiding principle.

Triebkraft ['tri:pkraft], f. (—, pl. ⁓e) motive power.

Triebwagen ['tri:pva:gən], m. (—s, pl. —) rail-car.

Triebwerk ['tri:pvɛrk], n. (—s, pl. —e) power unit, drive.

triefen ['tri:fən], v.n. irr. & reg. trickle, drip; be wet through, be soaking wet.

Trient [tri'ɛnt], n. Trent.

Trier [tri:r], n. Treves.

Triest [tri'ɛst], n. Trieste.

Trift [trɪft], f. (—, pl. —en) pasture, pasturage, common, meadow.

triftig ['trɪftɪç], adj. weighty, valid, conclusive, cogent.

Trikot [tri'ko:], m. & n. (—s, pl. —s) stockinet; (circus, ballet) tights.

Triller ['trɪlər], m. (—s, pl. —) (Mus.) trill, shake.

trillern ['trɪlərn], v.n. trill, quaver, shake; warble.

Trinität ['trini'tɛ:t], f. (—, no pl.) Trinity.

trinkbar ['trɪŋkba:r], adj. drinkable.

Trinkbecher ['trɪŋkbeçər], m. (—s, pl. —) drinking-cup.

trinken ['trɪŋkən], v.a., v.n. irr. drink.

Trinker ['trɪŋkər], m. (—s, pl. —) drinker, drunkard.

Trinkgelage ['trɪŋkgəla:gə], n. (—s, pl. —) drinking-bout.

Trinkgeld ['trɪŋkgɛlt], n. (—s, pl. —er) tip, gratuity.

Trinkhalle ['trɪŋkhalə], f. (—, pl. —n) (spa) pump-room.

Trinkspruch ['trɪŋkʃprux], m. (—(e)s, pl. ⁓e) toast.

Trinkstube ['trɪŋkʃtu:bə], f. (—, pl. —n) tap-room.

Tripolis ['tri:polɪs], n. Tripoli.

trippeln ['trɪpəln], v.n. trip (daintily), patter.

Tripper ['trɪpər], m. (—s, no pl.) (Med.) gonorrhoea.

Tritt [trɪt], m. (—(e)s, pl. —e) step, pace; kick.

Trittbrett ['trɪtbrɛt], n. (—s, pl. —er) foot-board; carriage-step; (organ) pedal.

Triumph [tri'umf], m. (—(e)s, pl. —e) triumph.

Triumphzug [tri'umftsu:k], m. (—(e)s, pl. ⁓e) triumphal procession.

Trivialität [trivjali'tɛ:t], f. (—, pl. —en) triviality, platitude.

trocken ['trɔkən], adj. dry, arid; (fig.) dull, dry as dust; (wine) dry.

Trockenfäule ['trɔkənfɔylə], f., **Trockenfäulnis** ['trɔkənfɔylnɪs], f. (—, no pl.) dry rot.

Trockenboden ['trɔkənbo:dən], m. (—s, pl. ⁓) drying-loft.

Trockenfutter ['trɔkənfutər], n. (—s, no pl.) fodder.

Trockenfütterung ['trɔkənfytəruŋ], f. (—, pl. —en) dry feeding.

Trockenhaube ['trɔkənhaubə], f. (—, pl. —n) hair drier.

Trockenheit ['trɔkənhaɪt], f. (—, no pl.) dryness; drought.

Trockenschleuder ['trɔkənʃlɔydər], f. (—, pl. —n) spin-drier.

trocknen ['trɔknən], v.a., v.n. dry, air.

Troddel ['trɔdəl], f. (—, pl. —n) tassel.

Trödel ['trø:dəl], m. (—s, no pl.) junk, lumber, rubbish.

Trödelladen ['trø:dalla:dən], m. (—s, pl. ⁓) junk-shop.

Trödelmarkt ['trø:dəlmarkt], m. (—s, no pl.) kettle market, jumble sale.

trödeln ['trø:dəln], v.n. dawdle, loiter.

Trödler ['trø:dlər], m. (—s, pl. —) second-hand dealer; (coll.) dawdler, loiterer.

Trog [tro:k], m. (—(e)s, pl. ⁓e) trough.

Troja ['tro:ja], n. Troy.

trollen ['trɔlən], v.r. sich —, decamp, toddle off, make o.s. scarce.

Trommel ['trɔməl], f. (—, pl. —n) drum; cylinder, barrel; tin box; die — rühren, beat the big drum.

Trommelfell ['trɔməlfɛl], n. (—s, pl. —e) drum-skin; ear-drum.

trommeln ['trɔməln], v.n. drum, beat the drum.

Trommelschlegel ['trɔməlʃle:gəl], m. (—s, pl. —) drumstick.

Trommelwirbel ['trɔməlvɪrbəl], m. (—s, pl. —) roll of drums.

Trommler ['trɔmlər], m. (—s, pl. —) drummer.

Trompete [trɔm'pe:tə], f. (—, pl. —n) trumpet; die — blasen, blow the trumpet.

trompeten [trɔm'pe:tən], v.n. trumpet, sound the trumpet.

Trompetengeschmetter [trɔm'pe:təngəʃmɛtər], n. (—s, no pl.) flourish of trumpets.

Tropen ['tro:pən], f. pl. the tropics.

Tropenfieber ['tro:pənfi:bər], n. (—s, no pl.) tropical fever.

tröpfeln ['trœpfəln], v.a., v.n. trickle, sprinkle.

Tropfen ['trɔpfən], m. (—s, pl. —) drop; steter — höhlt den Stein, constant dripping wears away a stone.

tropfen ['trɔpfən], v.n. drop, drip.

Trophäe [tro'fɛə], f. (—, pl. —n) trophy.

tropisch ['tro:pɪʃ], adj. tropical, tropic.

Troß [trɔs], m. (—sses, pl. -sse) (Mil.) baggage-train; (fig.) hangers-on, camp-followers.

Troßpferd ['trɔspfe:rt], n. (—s, pl. —e) pack-horse.

Trost [tro:st], m. (—es, no pl.) consolation, comfort; geringer —, cold comfort; du bist wohl nicht bei —? have you taken leave of your senses?

trösten ['trø:stən], v.a. comfort, console; tröste dich, cheer up.

Tröster ['trø:stər], m. (—s, pl. —) comforter, consoler; (Theol.) Holy Ghost, Comforter.

tröstlich ['trø:stlɪç], adj. consoling, comforting.

trostlos ['tro:stlo:s], adj. disconsolate, inconsolable; desolate, bleak.

Trostlosigkeit ['tro:stlo:zɪçkaɪt], f. (—, no pl.) disconsolateness; (fig.) wretchedness; dreariness.

Trott [trɔt], m. (—s, no pl.) trot.

Trottel ['trɔtəl], m. (—s, pl. —) (coll.) idiot.

Trottoir [trɔto'a:r], n. (—s, pl. —e) pavement, footpath; (Am.) sidewalk.

trotz [trɔts], prep. (Genit., Dat.) in spite of, despite; — alledem, all the same.

Trotz [trɔts], m. (—es, no pl.) defiance, obstinacy, refractoriness; einem — bieten, defy s.o.; einem etwas zum — machen, do s.th. in defiance of s.o.

trotzdem [trɔts'de:m], conj. notwithstanding that, albeit, although. — adv. nevertheless.

trotzen ['trɔtsən], v.n. defy; sulk, be obstinate; Gefahren —, brave dangers.

trotzig ['trɔtsɪç], adj. defiant; sulky, refractory; headstrong, stubborn, obstinate.

Trotzkopf ['trɔtskɔpf], m. (—(e)s, pl. —e) obstinate child; pig-headed person.

trübe ['try:bə], adj. dim, gloomy; (weather) dull, cloudy, overcast; (water) troubled; (glass) misted; —s Lächeln, wan smile.

Trubel ['tru:bəl], m. (—s, no pl.) tumult, turmoil, disturbance.

trüben ['try:bən], v.a. darken, sadden, trouble; (glass) mist; (metal) tarnish; (fig.) obscure.

Trübsal ['try:pza:l], f. (—, pl. —e), n. (—s, pl. —e) misery, trouble, distress; — blasen, mope.

trübselig ['try:pze:lɪç], adj. woeful, lamentable; woebegone, forlorn.

Trübsinn ['try:pzɪn], m. (—s, no pl.) sadness, dejection.

trübsinnig ['try:pzɪnɪç], adj. sad, dejected.

Trüffel ['tryfəl], f. (—, pl. —n) truffle.

Trug [tru:k], m. (—(e)s, no pl.) deceit, fraud; Lug und —, a pack of lies.

Trugbild ['tru:kbɪlt], n. (—es, pl. —er) phantom.

trügen ['try:gən], v.a. irr. deceive.

trügerisch ['try:gərɪs], adj. deceptive, illusory, fallacious.

Truggewebe ['tru:kgəve:bə], n. (—s, pl. —) tissue of lies.

Trugschluß ['tru:kʃlus], m. (—sses, pl. ⸚sse) fallacy, false deduction.

Truhe ['tru:ə], f. (—, pl. —n) chest, trunk, coffer.

Trumm [trum], m. (—s, pl. ⸚er) lump, broken piece.

Trümmer ['trymər], m. pl. fragments, debris, ruins; in — gehen, go to wrack and ruin; in — schlagen, wreck.

Trümmerhaufen ['trymərhaufən], m. (—s, pl. —) heap of ruins, heap of rubble.

Trumpf [trumpf], m. (—(e)s, pl. ⸚e) trump, trump-card.

trumpfen ['trumpfən], v.a. trump.

Trumpffarbe ['trumpffarbə], f. (—, pl. —n) trump-suit.

Trunk [truŋk], m. (—(e)s, pl. ⸚e) draught, potion, drinking; sich dem — ergeben, take to drink.

trunken ['truŋkən], adj. drunk, intoxicated; (fig.) elated.

Trunkenbold ['truŋkənbɔlt], m. (—s, pl. —e) drunkard.

Trunkenheit ['truŋkənhaɪt], f. (—, no pl.) drunkenness, intoxication.

Trunksucht ['truŋkzuxt], f. (—, no pl.) dipsomania, alcoholism.

trunksüchtig ['truŋkzyçtɪç], adj. dipsomaniac, addicted to drinking.

Trupp [trup], m. (—s, pl. —s) troop, band.

Truppe ['trupə], f. (—, pl. —n) (Mil.) company, troops, forces; (actors) troupe.

Truppengattung ['trupəngatuŋ], f. (—, pl. —en) branch of the armed forces.

Truthahn ['tru:tha:n], m. (—s, pl. ⸚e) (Orn.) turkey cock.

Truthenne ['tru:thɛnə], f. (—, pl. —n) (Orn.) turkey hen.

Trtuhühner ['tru:thy:nər], n. pl. (Orn.) turkey-fowl.

Trutz [truts], m. (—es, no pl.) (Poet.) defiance; zum Schutz und —, offensively and defensively.

Tschad [tʃat], n. Chad.

Tschechoslowakei [tʃɛçoslova'kaɪ], f. Czechoslovakia.

Tuch (1) [tu:x], n. (—(e)s, pl. ⸚er) shawl, wrap.

Tuch (2) [tu:x], n. (—s, pl. —e) cloth, fabric.

Tuchhändler ['tu:xhɛndlər], m. (—s, pl. —) draper, clothier.

tüchtig ['tyçtɪç], adj. able, competent, efficient. — adv. largely, much, heartily.

Tüchtigkeit ['tyçtɪçkaɪt], f. (—, no pl.) ability, competence, efficiency.

Tücke ['tykə], f. (—, pl. —n) malice, spite.

tückisch

tückisch ['tykɪʃ], *adj.* malicious, insidious.

Tugend ['tu:gənt], *f.* (—, *pl.* —en) virtue.

Tugendbold ['tu:gəntbɔlt], *m.* (—s, *pl.* —e) paragon.

tugendhaft ['tu:gənthaft], *adj.* virtuous.

Tugendlehre ['tu:gəntle:rə], *f.* (—, *no pl.*) ethics, morals.

Tüll [tyl], *m.* (—s, *pl.* —e) tulle.

Tulpe ['tulpə], *f.* (—, *pl.* —n) (*Bot.*) tulip.

Tulpenzwiebel ['tulpəntsvi:bəl], *f.* (—, *pl.* —n) tulip-bulb.

tummeln ['tuməln], *v.r. sich* —, romp about; make haste.

Tummelplatz ['tuməlplats], *m.* (—es, *pl.* ⁓e) playground, fairground.

Tümpel ['tympəl], *m.* (—s, *pl.* —) pond, pool, puddle.

Tun [tu:n], *n.* (—s, *no pl.*) doing; *sein — und Lassen,* his conduct.

tun [tu:n], *v.a. irr.* do, make; put; *tut nichts,* it does not matter; *viel zu — haben,* have a lot to do, be busy; *Not —,* be necessary; *Buße —,* repent.

Tünche ['tynçə], *f.* (—, *pl.* —n) whitewash.

tünchen ['tynçən], *v.a.* whitewash.

Tunichtgut ['tu:nɪçtgu:t], *m.* (—s, *no pl.*) ne'er-do-well, scamp.

Tunke ['tuŋkə], *f.* (—, *pl.* —n) sauce, gravy.

tunken ['tuŋkən], *v.a.* dip, steep; (*Am.*) dunk.

tunlich ['tu:nlɪç], *adj.* feasible, practicable, expedient.

tunlichst ['tu:nlɪçst], *adv.* if possible, possibly.

Tunnel ['tunəl], *m.* (—s, *pl.* —) tunnel.

Tunnelbau ['tunəlbau], *m.* (—s, *no pl.*) tunnelling.

tüpfeln ['typfəln], *v.a.* dot, spot.

Tupfen ['tupfən], *m.* (—s, *pl.* —) dot, polka-dot.

Tür [ty:r], *f.* (—, *pl.* —en) door; *einem die — weisen,* show s.o. the door; *vor der — stehen,* be imminent; *kehr vor deiner eigenen —,* mind your own business; put your own house in order; *offene —en einrennen,* flog a willing horse; *zwischen — und Angel stecken,* be undecided.

Türangel ['ty:raŋəl], *f.* (—, *pl.* —n) door-hinge.

Türhüter ['ty:rhy:tər], *m.* (—s, *pl.* —) doorkeeper.

Türkei [tyr'kai], *f.* Turkey.

Türkensäbel ['tyrkənze:bəl], *m.* (—s, *pl.* —) scimitar.

Türkis [tyr'ki:s], *m.* (—es, *pl.* —e) turquoise.

Türklinke ['ty:rklɪŋkə], *f.* (—, *pl.* —n) door-handle.

Turm [turm], *m.* (—(e)s, *pl.* ⁓e) tower; spire, steeple; belfry; (*Chess*) castle.

Turmalin [turma'li:n], *m.* (—s, *pl.* —e) tourmaline.

Türmchen ['tyrmçən], *n.* (—s, *pl.* —) turret.

türmen ['tyrmən], *v.a.* pile up. — *v.n.* (*coll.*) bolt, run away. — *v.r. sich* —, rise high, be piled high.

Turmspitze ['turmʃpɪtsə], *f.* (—, *pl.* —n) spire.

turnen ['turnən], *v.n.* do exercises *or* gymnastics.

Turnen ['turnən], *n.* (—s, *no pl.*) gymnastics, physical training.

Turner ['turnər], *m.* (—s, *pl.* —) gymnast.

Turngerät ['turngəre:t], *n.* (—es, *pl.* —e) gymnastic apparatus.

Turnhalle ['turnhalə], *f.* (—, *pl.* —n) gymnasium.

Turnier [tur'ni:r], *n.* (—s, *pl.* —e) tournament.

Turnübung ['turny:buŋ], *f.* (—, *pl.* —en) gymnastic exercise.

Turnverein ['turnfərain], *m.* (—s, *pl.* —e) athletics club, gymnastics club.

Türpfosten ['ty:rpfɔstən], *m.* (—s, *pl.* —) door-post.

Türriegel ['ty:rri:gəl], *m.* (—s, *pl.* —) bolt.

Türschild ['ty:rʃɪlt], *n.* (—(e)s, *pl.* —e) (door)plate.

Türschloß ['ty:rʃlɔs], *n.* (—sses, *pl.* ⁓sser) lock.

Türschlüssel ['ty:rʃlysəl], *m.* (—s, *pl.* —) door-key, latch-key.

Türschwelle ['ty:rʃvelə], *f.* (—, *pl.* —n) threshold.

Tusch [tuʃ], *m.* (—es, *pl.* —e) (*Mus.*) flourish.

Tusche ['tuʃə], *f.* (—, *pl.* —n) water-colour; Indian ink.

tuscheln ['tuʃəln], *v.n.* whisper.

tuschen ['tuʃən], *v.a.* draw in Indian ink.

Tuschkasten ['tuʃkastən], *m.* (—s, *pl.* ⁓) paint-box.

Tüte ['ty:tə], *f.* (—, *pl.* —n) paper bag.

Tutel [tu'te:l], *f.* (—, *no pl.*) guardianship.

tuten ['tu:tən], *v.n.* hoot, honk, blow a horn.

Tütendreher ['ty:təndre:ər], *m.* (—s, *pl.* —) (*sl.*) small shopkeeper.

Typ [ty:p], *m.* (—s, *pl.* —en) type.

Type ['ty:pə], *f.* (—, *pl.* —n) (*Typ.*) type; (*fig.*) queer fish.

Typhus ['ty:fus], *m.* (—, *no pl.*) (*Med.*) typhoid (fever).

typisch ['ty:pɪʃ], *adj.* typical.

Typus ['ty:pus], *m.* (—, *pl.* Typen) type.

Tyrann [ty'ran], *m.* (—en, *pl.* —en) tyrant.

Tyrannei [tyra'nai], *f.* (—, *pl.* —en) tyranny, despotism.

tyrannisch [ty'ranɪʃ], *adj.* tyrannical, despotic.

tyrannisieren [tyrani'zi:rən], *v.a.* tyrannize over, oppress, bully.

U

U [u:], *n.* (—s, *pl.* —s) the letter U.
U-Bahn ['u:ba:n], *f.* (—, *no pl.*)
underground (railway) (*Am.*) subway.
Übel ['y:bəl], *n.* (—s, *pl.* —) evil,
trouble; misfortune; disease.
übel ['y:bəl], *adj.* evil, ill, bad; *mir
ist* —, I feel sick; *nicht* —, not too
bad; — *daran sein*, be in a bad way,
be in a mess.
übelgesinnt ['y:bəlgəzınt], *adj.* evil-
minded; ill-disposed; *einem* — *sein*,
bear s.o. a grudge.
Übelkeit ['y:bəlkaıt], *f.* (—, *pl.* —en)
nausea, sickness.
übellaunig ['y:bəllaunıç], *adj.* ill-
humoured, bad-tempered.
übelnehmen ['y:bəlne:mən], *v.a. irr.*
take amiss, resent, be offended at.
übelnehmerisch ['y:bəlne:mərıʃ], *adj.*
touchy, easily offended.
Übelstand ['y:bəlʃtant], *m.* (—(e)s,
pl. ⸚e) inconvenience, drawback; (*pl.*)
abuses.
Übeltat ['y:bəlta:t], *f.* (—, *pl.* —en)
misdeed.
Übeltäter ['y:bəltɛ:tər], *m.* (—s, *pl.*
—) evildoer, malefactor.
übelwollend ['y:bəlvɔlənt], *adj.* malevolent.
üben ['y:bən], *v.a.* practise, exercise;
Rache —, wreak vengeance.
über ['y:bər], *prep.* (*Dat., Acc.*) over,
above; across; about; more than,
exceeding; via, by way of; concerning, on. — *adv.* over, above;
— *und* —, all over; — *kurz oder lang*,
sooner or later; *heute* —s *Jahr*, a year
from today.
überall ['y:bəral], *adv.* everywhere,
anywhere.
überanstrengen [y:bər'anʃtrɛŋən], *v.a.
insep.* overtax s.o.'s strength, strain.
— *v.r. sich* —, overtax o.'s strength,
overexert o.s.
Überanstrengung [y:bər'anʃtrɛŋuŋ],
f. (—, *pl.* —en) over-exertion,
strain.
überantworten [y:bər'antvɔrtən], *v.a.
insep.* deliver up, surrender.
überarbeiten [y:bər'arbaıtən], *v.a.
insep.* revise, do again. — *v.r. sich* —,
overwork o.s.
überarbeitet [y:bər'arbaıtət], *adj.* overwrought, overworked.
überaus ['y:bəraus], *adv.* exceedingly,
extremely.
überbauen [y:bər'bauən], *v.a. insep.*
build over.
überbieten [y:bər'bi:tən], *v.a. irr.
insep.* outbid (s.o.); (*fig.*) surpass.

Überbleibsel ['y:bərblaıpsəl], *n.* (—s,
pl. —) remainder, remnant, residue,
rest.
Überblick ['y:bərblık], *m.* (—(e)s, *pl.*
—e) survey, general view.
überblicken [y:bər'blıkən], *v.a. insep.*
survey, look over.
überbringen [y:bər'brıŋən], *v.a. irr.
insep.* bear, deliver, hand in.
Überbringung [y:bər'brıŋuŋ], *f.* (—,
no pl.) delivery.
überbrücken [y:bər'brykən], *v.a.
insep.* bridge, span.
überdachen [y:bər'daxən], *v.a. insep.*
roof (over).
überdauern [y:bər'dauərn], *v.a. insep.*
outlast; tide over.
überdenken [y:bər'dɛŋkən], *v.a. irr.
insep.* think over, consider.
überdies [y:bər'di:s], *adv.* besides,
moreover.
überdrucken [y:bər'drukən], *v.a. insep.*
overprint.
Überdruß ['y:bərdrus], *m.* (—sses, *no
pl.*) weariness; disgust; *zum* —, ad
nauseam.
überdrüssig ['y:bərdrysıç], *adj.* weary of.
Übereifer ['y:bəraıfər], *m.* (—s, *no pl.*)
excessive zeal.
übereifrig ['y:bəraıfrıç], *adj.* excessively zealous, officious.
übereilen [y:bər'aılən], *v.r. insep.
sich* —, hurry too much, overshoot the
mark.
übereilt [y:bər'aılt], *adj.* overhasty,
rash.
übereinkommen [y:bər'aınkomən],
v.n. irr. (*aux.* sein) agree.
Übereinkunft [y:bər'aınkunft], *f.* (—,
pl. ⸚e) agreement, convention.
übereinstimmen [y:bər'aınʃtımən],
v.n. agree, concur, harmonize, be of
one mind, be of the same opinion;
(*things*) tally, square.
Übereinstimmung [y:bər'aınʃtımuŋ],
f. (—, *no pl.*) accord, agreement,
conformity, harmony.
überfahren (1) [y:bər'fa:rən], *v.a. irr.
insep.* traverse, pass over; run over
(s.o.).
überfahren (2) ['y:bərfa:rən], *v.a. irr.*
ferry across. — *v.n.* (*aux.* sein)
cross.
überfahren (3) ['y:bərfa:rən], *v.n.* (*aux.*
sein) cross.
Überfahrt ['y:bərfa:rt], *f.* (—, *pl.* —en)
passage, crossing.
Überfall ['y:bərfal], *m.* (—s, *pl.* ⸚e)
sudden attack, raid.
überfallen (1) ['y:bərfalən], *v.n. irr.*
(*aux.* sein) (*p.p.* übergefallen) fall
over.
überfallen (2) [y:bər'falən], *v.a. irr.,
insep.* (*p.p.* überfallen) attack suddenly, raid.
überfliegen [y:bər'fli:gən], *v.a. irr.
insep.* fly over; (*fig.*) glance over,
skim.
überfließen ['y:bərfli:sən], *v.n. irr.*
(*aux.* sein) overflow.

überflügeln

überflügeln [y:bər'fly:gəln], *v.a. insep.* surpass, outstrip.

Überfluß ['y:bərflus], *m.* (**—sses,** *no pl.*) abundance, plenty, profusion; surplus; — *haben an,* abound in, have too much of.

überflüssig ['y:bərflysıç], *adj.* superfluous, unnecessary.

überfluten [y:bər'flu:tən], *v.a. insep.* overflow, flood.

überführen (1) ['y:bərfy:rən], *v.a.* convey, conduct (across).

überführen (2) [y:bər'fy:rən], *v.a. insep.* convict; transport a coffin.

Überführung [y:bər'fy:ruŋ], *f.* (—, *pl.* **—en**) conviction (for a crime); transport (of a coffin).

Überfüllung [y:bər'fyluŋ], *f.* (—, *no pl.*) overcrowding.

Übergabe ['y:bərga:bə], *f.* (—, *no pl.*) surrender, yielding up; delivery, handing over.

Übergang ['y:bərgaŋ], *m.* (**—s,** *pl.* **ːe**) passage; (*Railw.*) crossing; (*fig.*) change-over, transition.

übergeben [y:bər'ge:bən], *v.a. irr. insep.* deliver up, hand over. — *v.r. sich* —, vomit.

übergehen (1) ['y:bərge:ən], *v.n. irr.* (*aux.* sein) (*p.p.* übergegangen) go over, change over, turn (into); *zum Feinde* —, go over to the enemy; *in andre Hände* —, change hands.

übergehen (2) [y:bər'ge:ən], *v.a. irr. insep.* (*p.p.* übergangen) pass over, pass by.

Übergehung [y:bər'ge:uŋ], *f.* (—, *no pl.*) omission; passing over.

übergeordnet ['y:bərgəɔrdnət], *adj.* superior.

Übergewicht ['y:bərgəvıçt], *n.* (**—(e)s,** *no pl.*) overweight; (*fig.*) preponderance, superiority.

übergießen [y:bər'gi:sən], *v.a. irr. insep.* pour over, douse with.

überglücklich ['y:bərglyklıç], *adj.* overjoyed.

übergreifen ['y:bərgraıfən], *v.n. irr.* overlap; encroach (upon); spread.

Übergriff ['y:bərgrıf], *m.* (**—(e)s,** *pl.* **—e**) encroachment.

übergroß ['y:bərgro:s], *adj.* excessively large, overlarge.

überhaben ['y:bərha:bən], *v.a. irr.* have enough of, be sick of.

überhandnehmen [y:bər'hantne:mən], *v.n. irr.* gain the upper hand; run riot.

überhangen ['y:bərhaŋən], *v.n. irr.* hang over.

überhängen ['y:bərhɛŋən], *v.a. irr.* cover, hang upon.

überhäufen [y:bər'hɔyfən], *v.a. insep.* overwhelm.

überhaupt [y:bər'haupt], *adv.* in general, altogether, at all.

überheben [y:bər'he:bən], *v.r. insep. sich* —, strain o.s. by lifting; (*fig.*) be overbearing.

überheblich [y:bər'he:plıç], *adj.* overbearing, arrogant.

überheizen [y:bər'haıtsən], *v.a. insp.* overheat.

überhitzt [y:bər'hıtst], *adj.* overheated; impassioned.

überholen [y:bər'ho:lən], *v.a. insep.* overtake, out-distance; (*fig.*) overhaul.

überhören [y:bər'hø:rən], *v.a. insep.* hear s.o.'s lessons; ignore, miss (s.th.).

überirdisch ['y:bərırdıʃ], *adj.* celestial, superterrestrial.

Überkleid ['y:bərklaıt], *n.* (**—(e)s,** *pl.* **—er**) outer garment; overall.

überklug ['y:bərklu:k], *adj.* too clever by half, conceited.

überkochen ['y:bərkɔxən], *v.n.* (*aux.* sein) boil over.

überkommen [y:bər'kɔmən], *adj.* — *sein von,* be seized with.

überladen [y:bər'la:dən], *v.a. irr. insep.* overload. — *adj.* overdone, too elaborate; bombastic.

überlassen [y:bər'lasən], *v.a irr. insep.* leave, relinquish, give up, yield.

überlasten [y:bər'lastən], *v.a. insep.* overburden.

überlaufen (1) ['y:bərlaufən], *v.a. irr.* run over; (*to the enemy*) desert.

überlaufen (2) [y:bər'laufən], *v.a. insep.* (*p.p.* überlaufen) overrun.

Überläufer ['y:bərlɔyfər], *m.* (**—s,** *pl.* —) deserter, runaway.

überleben [y:bər'le:bən], *v.a. insep.* survive, outlive; (*fig.*) live (s.th.) down; *sich überlebt haben,* be out of date, be dated.

Überlebende [y:bər'le:bəndə], *m.* (**—n,** *pl.* **—n**) survivor.

überlegen (1) ['y:bərle:gən], *v.a.* lay over, cover.

überlegen (2) [y:bər'le:gən], *v.a. insep.* (*p.p.* überlegt) think over, consider, turn over in o.'s mind. — *adj.* superior; — *sein,* outdo, be superior to.

Überlegenheit [y:bər'le:gənhaıt], *f.* (—, *no pl.*) superiority.

Überlegung [y:bər'le:guŋ], *f.* (—, *pl.* **—en**) consideration, deliberation; *bei näherer* —, on second thoughts, on thinking it over.

überliefern [y:bər'li:fərn], *v.a. insep.* hand down (to posterity), hand on, pass on.

Überlieferung [y:bər'li:fəruŋ], *f.* (—, *pl.* **—en**) tradition.

überlisten [y:bər'lıstən], *v.a. insep.* outwit.

Übermacht ['y:bərmaxt], *f.* (—, *no pl.*) superiority, superior force.

übermalen [y:bər'ma:lən], *v.a. insep.* paint over.

übermangansauer [y:bərmaŋ'ga:nzauər], *adj.* permanganate of; —*saueres Kali,* permanganate of potash.

übermannen [y:bər'manən], *v.a. insep.* overpower.

Übermaß ['y:bərma:s], *n.* (**—es,** *no pl.*) excess; *im* —, to excess.

übermäßig [´y:bərmɛ:sɪç], adj. excessive, immoderate.

Übermensch [´y:bərmɛnʃ], m. (—en, pl. —en) superman.

übermenschlich [´y:bərmɛnʃlɪç], adj. superhuman.

übermitteln [y:bər´mɪtəln], v.a. insep. convey.

übermorgen [´y:bərmɔrgən], adv. the day after tomorrow.

Übermut [´y:bərmu:t], m. (—s, no pl.) wantonness; high spirits.

übermütig [´y:bərmy:tɪç], adj. wanton; full of high spirits.

übernachten [y:bər´naxtən], v.n. insep. pass or spend the night.

übernächtig [y:bər´nɛçtɪç], adj. haggard, tired by a sleepless night.

Übernahme [´y:bərna:mə], f. (—, no pl.) taking possession, taking charge.

übernatürlich [´y:bərnaty:rlɪç], adj. supernatural.

übernehmen [y:bər´ne:mən], v.a. irr. insep. take possession of, take upon o.s., take over. — v.r. sich —, overtax o.'s strength.

überordnen [´y:bərɔrdnən], v.a. place above.

überprüfen [y:bər´pry:fən], v.a. insep. examine, overhaul.

überquellen [´y:bərkvɛlən], v.n. irr. insep. (aux. sein) bubble over.

überqueren [y:bər´kve:rən], v.a. insep. cross.

überragen [y:bər´ra:gən], v.a. insep. tower above, overtop; (fig.) surpass, outstrip.

überraschen [y:bər´raʃən], v.a. insep. surprise, take by surprise.

Überraschung [y:bər´raʃuŋ], f. (—, pl. —en) surprise.

überreden [y:bər´re:dən], v.a. insep. persuade, talk s.o. into (s.th.).

Überredung [y:bər´re:duŋ], f. (—, no pl.) persuasion.

überreichen [y:bər´raɪçən], v.a. insep. hand over, present formally.

überreichlich [´y:bərraɪçlɪç], adj. superabundant.

Überreichung [y:bər´raɪçuŋ], f. (—, no pl.) formal presentation.

überreizen [y:bər´raɪtsən], v.a. insep. over-excite, over-stimulate.

überrennen [y:bər´rɛnən], v.a. irr. insep. take by storm, overrun.

Überrest [´y:bərrɛst], m. (—es, pl. —e) remainder, remnant, residue.

überrumpeln [y:bər´rumpəln], v.a. insep. catch unawares, surprise.

übersättigen [y:bər´zɛtɪgən], v.a. insep. saturate; surfeit, cloy.

Übersättigung [y:bər´zɛtɪguŋ], f. (—, no pl.) saturation; surfeit.

Überschallgeschwindigkeit [´y:bərʃalgəʃvɪndɪçkaɪt], f. (—, no pl.) supersonic speed.

überschatten [y:bər´ʃatən], v.a. insep. overshadow.

überschätzen [y:bər´ʃɛtsən], v.a. insep. overrate, over-estimate.

überschauen [y:bər´ʃauən], v.a. insep. survey.

überschäumen [´y:bərʃɔymən], v.n. (aux. sein) bubble over.

überschäumend [´y:bərʃɔymənt], adj. ebullient, exuberant.

Überschlag [´y:bərʃla:k], m. (—s, pl. ˝e) somersault; estimate.

überschlagen [y:bər´ʃla:gən], v.a. irr. insep. (pages) miss, skip; estimate, compute. — v.r. sich —, turn a somersault, overturn. — adj. tepid, lukewarm.

überschnappen [´y:bərʃnapən], v.n. (aux. sein) snap; (fig., coll.) go out of o.'s mind.

überschreiben [y:bər´ʃraɪbən], v.a. irr. insep. superscribe, entitle.

überschreiten [y:bər´ʃraɪtən], v.a. irr. insep. cross; go beyond, exceed.

Überschrift [´y:bərʃrɪft], f. (—, pl. —en) heading, headline.

Überschuß [´y:bərʃus], m. (—sses, pl. ˝sse) surplus.

überschüssig [´y:bərʃysɪç], adj. surplus, remaining.

überschütten [y:bər´ʃytən], v.a. insep. shower with, overwhelm with.

Überschwang [´y:bərʃvaŋ], m. (—s, no pl.) exaltation; rapture.

überschwemmen [y:bər´ʃvɛmən], v.a. insep. flood, inundate.

Überschwemmung [y:bər´ʃvɛmuŋ], f. (—, pl. —en) inundation, flood, deluge.

überschwenglich [y:bər´ʃvɛŋlɪç], adj. exuberant, exalted.

Übersee [´y:bərze:], f. (—, no pl.) overseas.

übersehen [y:bər´ze:ən], v.a. irr. insep. survey, look over; overlook, disregard.

übersenden [y:bər´zɛndən], v.a. irr. insep. send, forward, transmit; (money) remit.

Übersendung [y:bər´zɛnduŋ], f. (—, pl. —en) sending, forwarding, transmission; remittance.

übersetzen (1) [´y:bərzɛtsən], v.a. (p.p. übergesetzt) ferry across, cross (a river).

übersetzen (2) [y:bər´zɛtsən], v.a. insep. (p.p. übersetzt) translate.

Übersetzer [y:bər´zɛtsər], m. (—s, pl. —) translator.

Übersetzung [y:bər´zɛtsuŋ], f. (—, pl. —en) translation.

Übersicht [´y:bərzɪçt], f. (—, pl. —en) survey, summary; epitome.

übersichtlich [´y:bərzɪçtlɪç], adj. clearly arranged, readable at a glance, lucid.

übersiedeln [y:bər´zi:dəln], v.n. (aux. sein) remove, move, settle in a different place.

Übersiedlung [y:bər´zi:dluŋ], f. (—, pl. —en) removal.

überspannen [y:bər´ʃpanən], v.a. insep. overstretch.

überspannt [y:bər´ʃpant], adj. eccentric, extravagant.

Überspanntheit [y:bər'ʃpanthaɪt], *f.*
(—, *pl.* —en) eccentricity.
überspringen [y:bər'ʃprɪŋən], *v.a. irr.*
insep. jump over; (*fig.*) skip.
übersprudeln ['y:bərʃpru:dəln], *v.n.*
(*aux.* sein) bubble over.
überstechen [y:bər'ʃtɛçən], *v.a. irr.*
(*cards*) trump higher.
überstehen [y:bər'ʃte:ən], *v.a. irr.*
insep. overcome, endure, get over,
weather.
übersteigen [y:bər'ʃtaɪgən], *v.a. irr.*
insep. exceed, surpass.
überstrahlen [y:bər'ʃtra:lən], *v.a. insep.*
outshine, surpass in splendour.
überstreichen [y:bər'ʃtraɪçən], *v.a. irr.*
insep. paint over.
überströmen [y:bər'ʃtrø:mən], *v.a.*
insep. flood, overflow.
Überstunde ['y:bərʃtundə], *f.* (—, *pl.*
—n) extra working time, overtime.
überstürzen [y:bər'ʃtyrtsən], *v.r. insep.*
sich —, act in haste.
übertäuben [y:bər'tɔybən], *v.a. insep.*
deafen.
überteuern [y:bər'tɔyərn], *v.a. insep.*
overcharge.
übertölpeln [y:bər'tœlpəln], *v.a. insep.*
cheat.
übertönen [y:bər'tø:nən], *v.a. insep.*
(*sound*) drown.
übertragen [y:bər'tra:gən], *v.a. irr.*
insep. transfer, hand over; convey;
broadcast; translate; (*Comm.*) carry
over; *einem ein Amt* —, confer an
office on s.o.
Übertragung [y:bər'tra:guŋ], *f.* (—, *pl.*
—en) cession; transference; handing
over; (*Comm.*) carrying over; (*Rad.*)
transmission; (*Med.*) transfusion.
übertreffen [y:bər'trɛfən], *v.a. irr.*
insep. surpass, excel, outdo.
übertreiben [y:bər'traɪbən], *v.a. irr.*
insep. exaggerate.
Übertreibung [y:bər'traɪbuŋ], *f.* (—,
pl. —en) exaggeration.
übertreten (1) ['y:bərtre:tən], *v.n. irr.*
(*aux.* sein) go over to; (*river*) overflow; (*religion*) change to, join (*church,
party*).
übertreten (2) [y:bər'tre:tən], *v.a. irr.*
insep. transgress, trespass against,
infringe, violate.
Übertretung [y:bər'tre:tuŋ], *f.* (—, *pl.*
—en) transgression, trespass, violation, infringement.
übertrieben [y:bər'tri:bən], *adj.* excessive, immoderate, exaggerated.
Übertritt ['y:bərtrɪt], *m.* (—s, *no pl.*)
defection, going over; (*Rel.*) change,
conversion.
übertünchen [y:bər'tynçən], *v.a. insep.*
whitewash, rough-cast; (*fig.*) gloss
over.
Übervölkerung [y:bər'fœlkəruŋ], *f.*
(—, *no pl.*) overpopulation.
übervoll ['y:bərfɔl], *adj.* overful, brimful, chock-full.
übervorteilen [y:bər'fo:rtaɪlən], *v.a.*
insep. cheat, defraud.

überwachen [y:bər'vaxən], *v.a. insep.*
watch over, superintend, supervise.
Überwachung [y:bər'vaxuŋ], *f.* (—,
no pl.) superintendence, supervision.
überwachsen [y:bər'vaksən], *v.a. irr.*
insep. overgrow.
überwältigen [y:bər'vɛltɪgən], *v.a.*
insep. overcome, overpower, subdue.
überwältigend [y:bər'vɛltɪgənt], *adj.*
overwhelming.
Überwältigung [y:bər'vɛltɪguŋ], *f.*
(—, *no pl.*) overpowering.
überweisen [y:bər'vaɪzən], *v.a. irr.*
insep. assign; (*money*) remit.
Überweisung [y:bər'vaɪzuŋ], *f.* (—, *pl.*
—en) assignment; (*money*) remittance.
überwerfen (1) ['y:bərvɛrfən], *v.a. irr.*
throw over; (*clothes*) slip on.
überwerfen (2) [y:bər'vɛrfən], *v.r. irr.*
insep. sich — *mit*, fall out with s.o.
überwiegen [y:bər'vi:gən], *v.n. irr.*
insep. prevail.
überwiegend [y:bər'vi:gənt], *adj.* paramount, overwhelming, predominant.
überwinden [y:bər'vɪndən], *v.a. irr.*
insep. overcome, conquer. — *v.r.
sich* —, prevail upon o.s., bring o.s.
(to).
Überwindung [y:bər'vɪnduŋ], *f.* (—,
no pl.) conquest; reluctance.
überwintern [y:bər'vɪntərn], *v.n. insep.*
winter, hibernate.
Überwinterung [y:bər'vɪntəruŋ], *f.*
(—, *no pl.*) hibernation.
überwölkt [y:bər'vœlkt], *adj.* overcast.
Überwurf [y:bər'vurf], *m.* (—s, *pl.* ⸚e)
wrap, shawl, cloak.
Überzahl ['y:bərtsa:l], *f.* (—, *no pl.*) in
der —, in the majority.
überzählig [y:bər'tsɛ:lɪç], *adj.* super-
numerary, surplus.
überzeichnen ['y:bərtsaɪçnən], *v.a.*
insep. (*Comm.*) over-subscribe.
überzeugen [y:bər'tsɔygən], *v.a. insep.*
convince. — *v.r. sich*—, satisfy o.s.
Überzeugung [y:bər'tsɔyguŋ], *f.* (—,
no pl.) conviction.
überziehen (1) ['y:bərtsi:ən], *v.a. irr.*
put on (a garment).
überziehen (2) [y:bər'tsi:ən], *v.a. irr.*
insep. cover; (*bed*) put fresh linen on;
(*Bank*) overdraw.
Überzieher [y:bər'tsi:ər], *m.* (—s, *pl.*
—) overcoat.
Überzug ['y:bərtsu:k], *m.* (—s, *pl.* ⸚e)
case, cover; bed-tick; coating.
üblich ['y:plɪç], *adj.* usual, customary;
nicht mehr —, out of use, obsolete.
übrig ['y:brɪç], *adj.* remaining, left
over; *die* —*en*, the others; — *bleiben*,
be left, remain; — *haben*, have left;
— *sein*, be left; *im* —*en*, for the rest;
ein —*es tun*, stretch a point; *für
einen etwas* — *haben*, like s.o.
übrigens ['y:brɪgəns], *adv.* besides,
moreover; by the way.
Übung ['y:buŋ], *f.* (—, *pl.* —en)
exercise, practice.

234

Ufer ['u:fər], *n.* (—s, *pl.* —) (*river*) bank; (*sea*) shore, beach.

Uganda [u'ganda], *n.* Uganda.

Uhr [u:r], *f.* (—, *pl.* —en) clock; watch; *elf* —, eleven o'clock; *wieviel — ist es?* what is the time?

Uhrmacher ['u:rmaxər], *m.* (—s, *pl.* —) watchmaker, clockmaker.

Uhrwerk ['u:rvɛrk], *n.* (—s, *pl.* —e) clockwork.

Uhrzeiger ['u:rtsaɪɡər], *m.* (—s, *pl.* —) hand (of clock *or* watch).

Uhu ['u:hu:], *m.* (—s, *pl.* —s) (*Orn.*) eagle-owl.

uikig ['ulkɪç], *adj.* funny.

Ulme ['ulmə], *f.* (—, *pl.* —en) (*Bot.*) elm, elm-tree.

Ultrakurzwelle ['ultrakurtsvɛlə], *f.* (—, *pl.* —n) ultra-short wave.

ultrarot ['ultraro:t], *adj.* infra-red.

Ultrastrahlung ['ultraʃtra:lun], *f.* (—, *pl.* —en) cosmic radiation.

ultraviolett ['ultraviolet], *adj.* ultra-violet.

um [um], *prep.* (*Acc.*) about, around; approximately, near; for, because of; by; — *Geld bitten*, ask for money; — 5 *Uhr*, at five o'clock. — *conj.* to, in order to. — *adv.* up, past, upside down; round about; around.

umarbeiten ['umarbaɪtən], *v.a.* do again, remodel, revise; recast.

umarmen [um'armən], *v.a. insep.* embrace.

Umarmung [um'armun], *f.* (—, *pl.* —en) embrace.

umbauen (1) ['umbauən], *v.a.* rebuild.

umbauen (2) ['umbauən], *v.a. insep.* surround with buildings.

umbiegen ['umbi:ɡən], *v.a. irr.* bend.

umbilden ['umbɪldən], *v.a.* transform, reform, recast, remould.

umbinden ['umbɪndən], *v.a. irr. sich etwas —*, tie s.th. around o.s.

umblicken ['umblɪkən], *v.r. sich —*, look round.

umbringen ['umbrɪnən], *v.a. irr.* kill, slay, murder.

umdrehen ['umdre:ən], *v.a.* turn over, turn round, revolve. — *v.r. sich —*, turn round.

Umdrehung [um'dre:un], *f.* (—, *pl.* —en) revolution, rotation.

umfahren (1) [um'fa:rən], *v.a. irr. insep.* drive round, circumnavigate.

umfahren (2) ['umfa:rən], *v.a. irr.* run down.

umfallen ['umfalən], *v.n. irr.* (*aux.* sein) fall down, fall over.

Umfang ['umfan], *m.* (—s, *pl.* ⁀e) circumference; (*fig.*) extent.

umfangen [um'faŋən], *v.a. irr. insep.* encircle, embrace.

umfangreich ['umfaŋraɪç], *adj.* extensive, voluminous.

umfassen [um'fasən], *v.a. insep.* comprise, contain.

umfassend [um'fasənt], *adj.* comprehensive.

umfließen [um'fli:sən], *v.a. irr. insep.* surround by water.

umformen ['umfɔrmən], *v.a.* transform, remodel.

Umformung ['umfɔrmun], *f.* (—, *pl.* —en) transformation, remodelling.

Umfrage ['umfra:ɡə], *f.* (—, *pl.* —n) enquiry, poll, quiz.

Umfriedung [um'fri:dun], *f.* (—, *pl.* —en) enclosure.

Umgang ['umɡan], *m.* (—s, *pl.* ⁀e) circuit, procession; (*fig.*) acquaintance, association; relations, connection; — *haben mit*, associate with.

umgänglich ['umɡɛnlɪç], *adj.* sociable, companionable.

Umgangsformen ['umɡaŋsfɔrmən], *f. pl.* manners.

Umgangssprache ['umɡaŋsʃpra:xə], *f.* (— *pl.* —en) colloquial speech.

umgeben [um'ɡe:bən], *v.a. irr. insep.* surround.

Umgebung [um'ɡe:bun], *f.* (—, *pl.* —en) environment, surroundings.

umgehen (1) ['umɡe:ən], *v.n. irr.* (*aux.* sein) associate with s.o.; handle s.th.; — *in*, haunt.

umgehen (2) [um'ɡe:ən], *v.a. irr. insep.* go round; (*flank*) turn; (*fig.*) evade, shirk.

umgehend ['umɡe:ənt], *adv.* immediately; (*letter*) by return mail.

Umgehung [um'ɡe:un], *f.* (—, *pl.* —en) shirking, evasion; detour; (*Mil.*) flank movement, turning.

umgekehrt ['umɡəke:rt], *adj.* reverse. — *adv.* conversely.

umgestalten ['umɡəʃtaltən], *v.a.* transform, recast.

Umgestaltung ['umɡəʃtaltun], *f.* (—, *pl.* —en) transformation; recasting.

umgraben ['umɡra:bən], *v.a. irr.* dig up.

umgrenzen [um'ɡrɛntsən], *v.a. insep.* limit, set bounds to.

Umgrenzung [um'ɡrɛntsun], *f.* (—, *pl.* —en) boundary; limitation.

umgucken ['umɡukən], *v.r. sich —*, look about o.

umhalsen [um'halzən], *v.a. insep.* hug, embrace.

Umhang ['umhan], *m.* (—s, *pl.* ⁀e) shawl, cloak.

umher [um'he:r], *adv.* around, round, about.

umherblicken [um'he:rblɪkən], *v.n.* look round.

umherflattern [um'he:rflatərn], *v.n.* (*aux.* sein) flutter about.

umherlaufen [um'he:rlaufən], *v.n. irr.* (*aux.* sein) run about; roam about, ramble, wander.

umherziehend [um'he:rtsi:ənt], *adj.* itinerant.

umhüllen [um'hylən], *v.a. insep.* envelop, wrap up.

Umkehr ['umke:r], *f.* (—, *no pl.*) return; change; (*fig.*) conversion.

235

umkehren

umkehren ['umke:rən], *v.a.* turn (back), upset, overturn. — *v.n.* (*aux.* sein) turn back, return.

Umkehrung ['umke:ruŋ], *f.* (—, *pl.* —en) inversion.

umkippen ['umkɪpən], *v.a.* upset, overturn. — *v.n.* (*aux.* sein) capsize, tilt over.

umklammern [um'klamərn], *v.a. insep.* clasp; clutch; (*fig.*) cling to.

umkleiden (1) ['umklaɪdən], *v.r. sich* —, change o.'s clothes.

umkleiden (2) [um'klaɪdən], *v.a. insep.* cover.

umkommen ['umkɔmən], *v.n. irr.* (*aux.* sein) perish.

Umkreis ['umkraɪs], *m.* (—es, *pl.* —e) circumference, compass.

Umlauf ['umlauf], *m.* (—s, *no pl.*) circulation; *in* — *bringen*, put into circulation.

Umlaut ['umlaut], *m.* (—s, *pl.* —e) (*Phonet.*) modification of vowels.

umlegen ['umle:gən], *v.a.* lay down, move, shift, put about; (*sl.*) kill.

umleiten ['umlaɪtən], *v.a.* (*traffic*) divert.

umlernen ['umlɛrnən], *v.a., v.n.* relearn; retrain (for new job).

umliegend ['umli:gənt], *adj.* surrounding.

ummodeln ['ummo:dəln], *v.a.* remodel, recast, change, fashion differently.

Umnachtung [um'naxtuŋ], *f.* (—, *no pl.*) mental derangement.

umpacken ['umpakən], *v.a.* repack.

umpflanzen ['umpflantsən], *v.a.* transplant.

Umpflanzung ['umpflantsuŋ], *f.* (—, *pl.* —en) transplantation.

umrahmen ['umra:mən], *v.a. insep.* frame, surround.

umrändern [um'rɛndərn], *v.a. insep.* border, edge.

umrechnen ['umrɛçnən], *v.a.* (*figures*) reduce, convert.

umreißen (1) ['umraɪsən], *v.a. irr.* pull down, break up.

umreißen (2) [um'raɪsən], *v.a. irr. insep.* sketch, outline.

umrennen ['umrɛnən], *v.a. irr.* run down, knock over.

umringen [um'rɪŋən], *v.a. insep.* encircle, surround.

Umriß ['umrɪs], *m.* (—sses, *pl.* —sse) outline, contour.

umrühren ['umry:rən], *v.a.* (*Cul.*) stir.

umsatteln ['umzatəln], *v.n.* (*fig.*) change o.'s profession.

Umsatz ['umzats], *m.* (—es, *pl.* ⁻e) turnover.

umschalten ['umʃaltən], *v.a.* (*Elec.*) switch (over); reverse (current).

Umschau ['umʃau], *f.* (—, *no pl.*) review, survey; — *halten*, look round, muster, review.

umschauen ['umʃauən], *v.r. sich* —, look round.

umschichtig ['umʃɪçtɪç], *adv.* turn and turn about, in turns.

umschiffen (1) ['umʃɪfən], *v.a.* tranship, transfer (cargo, passengers).

umschiffen (2) [um'ʃɪfən], *v.a. insep.* sail round, circumnavigate.

Umschlag ['umʃla:k], *m.* (—(e)s, *pl.* ⁻e) (*weather*) break, sudden change; (*letter*) envelope; (*Med.*) poultice, compress.

umschlagen ['umʃla:gən], *v.n. irr.* (*aux.* sein) (*weather*) change suddenly; capsize; turn sour.

umschließen [um'ʃli:sən], *v.a. irr. insep.* enclose, surround; comprise.

umschlingen [um'ʃlɪŋən], *v.a. irr. insep.* embrace.

umschnallen ['umʃnalən], *v.a.* buckle on.

umschreiben (1) ['umʃraɪbən], *v.a. irr. insep.* rewrite, write differently.

umschreiben (2) [um'ʃraɪbən], *v.a. irr. insep.* circumscribe, paraphrase.

Umschreibung [um'ʃraɪbuŋ], *f.* (—, *pl.* —en) paraphrase.

Umschweife ['umʃvaɪfə], *m.pl.* fuss, talk; circumlocution; *ohne* —, point-blank.

Umschwung ['umʃvuŋ], *m.* (—s, *no pl.*) sudden change, revolution.

umsegeln [um'ze:gəln], *v.a. insep.* sail round.

umsehen ['umze:ən], *v.r. irr. sich* —, look round; look out (for), cast about (for).

Umsicht ['umzɪçt], *f.* (—, *no pl.*) circumspection.

umsichtig ['umzɪçtɪç], *adj.* cautious, circumspect.

umsinken ['umzɪŋkən], *v.n. irr.* (*aux.* sein) sink down.

umsonst [um'zɔnst], *adv.* without payment, gratis, for nothing; in vain, vainly, to no purpose.

umspannen (1) ['umʃpanən], *v.a.* change horses.

umspannen (2) [um'ʃpanən], *v.a. insep.* encompass, span.

umspringen ['umʃprɪŋən], *v.n. irr.* (*aux.* sein) (*wind*) change suddenly; *mit einem* —, (*fig.*) deal with s.o.

Umstand ['umʃtant], *m.* (—s, *pl.* ⁻e) circumstance; fact; factor; (*pl.*) fuss; *in anderen* ⁻*en sein*, be expecting a baby; *unter keinen* ⁻*en*, on no account.

umständlich ['umʃtɛntlɪç], *adj.* circumstantial, ceremonious; complicated, fussy.

Umstandswort ['umʃtantsvɔrt], *n.* (—es, *pl.* ⁻er) (*Gram.*) adverb.

umstehend ['umʃte:ənt], *adv.* on the next page.

Umstehenden ['umʃte:əndən], *pl.* bystanders.

umsteigen ['umʃtaɪgən], *v.n. irr.* (*aux.* sein) change (trains etc.).

umstellen (1) ['umʃtɛlən], *v.a.* place differently, transpose, change over.

umstellen (2) [um'ʃtɛlən], *v.a. insep.* surround, beset.

236

Umstellung [ˈumʃtɛluŋ], *f.* (—, *pl.* —en) transposition; (*Gram.*) inversion; change of position in team.

umstimmen [ˈumʃtɪmən], *v.a.* turn s.o. from his opinion, bring s.o. round to (s.th.).

umstoßen [ˈumʃtoːsən], *v.a. irr.* knock down, upset, overthrow; (*judgment*) reverse.

umstricken [umˈʃtrɪkən], *v.a. insep.* ensnare.

umstritten [umˈʃtrɪtən], *adj.* controversial, disputed.

umstülpen [ˈumʃtylpən], *v.a.* turn up, turn upside down.

Umsturz [ˈumʃturts], *m.* (—es, *no pl.*) downfall; subversion; revolution.

umstürzen [ˈumʃtyrtsən], *v.a.* upset, overturn; overthrow.

umtaufen [ˈumtaufən], *v.a.* rename, rechristen.

Umtausch [ˈumtauʃ], *m.* (—s, *no pl.*) exchange.

umtauschen [ˈumtauʃən], *v.a.* exchange, change.

Umtriebe [ˈumtriːbə], *m. pl.* plots, goings-on, intrigues.

umtun [ˈumtuːn], *v.r. irr. sich — nach,* look for, cast about for.

Umwälzung [ˈumvɛltsuŋ], *f.* (—, *pl.* —en) turning-about; (*fig.*) revolution.

umwandeln [ˈumvandəln], *v.a.* change, transform; (*Gram.*) inflect.

umwechseln [ˈumvɛksəln], *v.a.* exchange.

Umweg [ˈumveːk], *m.* (—s, *pl.* —e) roundabout way, detour.

Umwelt [ˈumvɛlt], *f.* (—, *no pl.*) environment, milieu.

umwenden [ˈumvɛndən], *v.a. irr.* turn round; turn over. — *v.r. sich —,* turn round.

umwerben [umˈvɛrbən], *v.a. irr. insep.* court.

umwerfen [ˈumvɛrfən], *v.a. irr.* overturn, knock over, upset.

umwickeln [umˈvɪkəln], *v.a. insep.* wrap round, wind round.

umwölken [umˈvœlkən], *v.r. insep. sich —,* (*sky*) darken, become overcast.

umzäunen [umˈtsɔynən], *v.a. insep.* hedge in, fence in, enclose.

umziehen (1) [ˈumtsiːən], *v.a. irr.* change (clothes). — *v.n.* (*aux. sein*) move (abode).— *v.r. sich —,* change o.'s clothes.

umziehen (2) [umˈtsiːən], *v.r. irr. insep. sich —,* get overcast, cloud over.

umzingeln [umˈtsɪŋəln], *v.a. insep.* surround.

Umzug [ˈumtsuːk], *m.* (—s, *pl.* ⁻e) procession; removal; move.

unabänderlich [unapˈɛndərlɪç], *adj.* unalterable, irrevocable.

Unabänderlichkeit [ˈunapɛndərlɪçkaɪt], *f.* (—, *no pl.*) unchangeableness, irrevocability.

unabhängig [ˈunaphɛŋɪç], *adj.* independent, autonomous; unrelated.

Unabhängigkeit [ˈunaphɛŋɪçkaɪt], *f.* (—, *no pl.*) independence, self-sufficiency.

unabkömmlich [ˈunapkœmlɪç], *adj.* indispensable.

unablässig [ˈunaplɛsɪç], *adj.* unceasing, continual, unremitting.

unabsehbar [ˈunapzeːbaːr], *adj.* immeasurable, immense; unfathomable.

unabsichtlich [ˈunapzɪçtlɪç], *adj.* unintentional, accidental.

unabwendbar [unapˈvɛntbaːr], *adj.* irremediable; unavoidable.

unachtsam [ˈunaxtzaːm], *adj.* inattentive, inadvertent, negligent, careless.

Unachtsamkeit [ˈunaxtzaːmkaɪt], *f.* (—, *pl.* —en) inadvertence, inattention, negligence, carelessness.

unähnlich [ˈunɛːnlɪç], *adj.* unlike, dissimilar.

unanfechtbar [ˈunanfɛçtbaːr], *adj.* indisputable, incontestable.

unangebracht [ˈunangəbraxt], *adj.* out of place, inapposite.

unangefochten [ˈunangəfɔxtən], *adj.* undisputed, uncontested.

unangemeldet [ˈunangəmɛldət], *adj.* unannounced, unheralded.

unangemessen [ˈunangəmɛsən], *adj.* unsuitable, inappropriate, inadequate.

unangenehm [ˈunangəneːm], *adj.* disagreeable, unpleasant; *einen — berühren,* jar, grate on s.o.

unangetastet [ˈunangətastət], *adj.* untouched.

unangreifbar [ˈunangraɪfbaːr], *adj.* unassailable, secure.

unannehmbar [ˈunanneːmbaːr], *adj.* unacceptable.

Unannehmlichkeit [ˈunanneːmlɪçkaɪt], *f.* (—, *pl.* —en) unpleasantness, annoyance.

unansehnlich [ˈunanzeːnlɪç], *adj.* insignificant, unattractive.

unanständig [ˈunanʃtɛndɪç], *adj.* improper, indecent.

Unanständigkeit [ˈunanʃtɛndɪçkaɪt], *f.* (—, *pl.* —en) indecency, immodesty, impropriety.

unantastbar [ˈunantastbaːr], *adj.* unimpeachable.

unappetitlich [ˈunapeti:tlɪç], *adj.* distasteful, unsavoury, unappetising.

Unart [ˈunaːrt], *f.* (—, *pl.* —en) bad habit, naughtiness.

unartig [ˈunaːrtɪç], *adj.* ill-behaved, naughty.

unästhetisch [ˈunɛsteːtɪʃ], *adj.* offensive, coarse; inartistic.

unauffällig [ˈunauffɛlɪç], *adj.* unobtrusive.

unaufgefordert [ˈunaufgəfɔrdərt], *adj.* unbidden.

unaufgeklärt [ˈunaufgəklɛːrt], *adj.* unexplained, unsolved.

unaufgeschnitten [ˈunaufgəʃnɪtən], *adj.* uncut.

unaufhaltsam [ˈunaufhaltzaːm], *adj.* incessant, irresistible.

237

unaufhörlich

unaufhörlich [ˈunaufhøːrlɪç], *adj.* incessant, continual.

unauflöslich [ˈunaufløːslɪç], *adj.* indissoluble.

unaufmerksam [ˈunaufmɛrkzaːm], *adj.* inattentive.

unaufrichtig [ˈunaufrɪçtɪç], *adj.* insincere.

unaufschiebbar [ˈunauffʃiːpbaːr], *adj.* urgent, pressing, brooking no delay.

unausbleiblich [ˈunausblaɪplɪç], *adj.* inevitable, unfailing.

unausführbar [ˈunausfyːrbaːr], *adj.* impracticable.

unausgebildet [ˈunausgəbɪldət], *adj.* untrained, unskilled.

unausgefüllt [ˈunausgəfylt], *adj.* not filled up; (*form*) blank.

unausgegoren [ˈunausgəgoːrən], *adj.* crude; (*wine*) unfermented.

unausgesetzt [ˈunausgəzɛtst], *adj.* continual, continuous.

unausgesprochen [ˈunausgəʃprɔxən], *adj.* unsaid; (*fig.*) implied.

unauslöschlich [ˈunausløːʃlɪç], *adj.* indelible, inextinguishable.

unaussprechlich [ˈunausʃpreçlɪç], *adj.* inexpressible, unspeakable.

unausstehlich [ˈunausʃteːlɪç], *adj.* insufferable.

unausweichlich [ˈunausvaɪçlɪç], *adj.* inevitable.

unbändig [ˈunbɛndɪç], *adj.* intractable, unmanageable; (*fig.*) extreme.

unbarmherzig [ˈunbarmhɛrtsɪç], *adj.* merciless.

unbeabsichtigt [ˈunbəapzɪçtɪçt], *adj.* unintentional.

unbeanstandet [ˈunbəanʃtandət], *adj.* unexceptionable; unopposed; with impunity.

unbeantwortlich [ˈunbəantvɔrtlɪç], *adj.* unanswerable.

unbeaufsichtigt [ˈunbəaufzɪçtɪçt], *adj.* unattended to, not looked after; without supervision.

unbebaut [ˈunbəbaut], *adj.* (*Agr.*) uncultivated; undeveloped (by building).

unbedacht [ˈunbədaxt], *adj.* thoughtless.

unbedenklich [ˈunbədɛŋklɪç], *adj.* harmless, innocuous. — *adv.* without hesitation.

unbedeutend [ˈunbədɔytənt], *adj.* insignificant.

unbedingt [ˈunbədɪŋkt], *adj.* unconditional, unlimited, absolute. — *adv.* quite definitely; without fail.

unbeeinflußt [ˈunbəaɪnflust], *adj.* uninfluenced.

unbefahrbar [ˈunbəfaːrbaːr], *adj.* impassable, impracticable.

unbefangen [ˈunbəfaŋən], *adj.* unbiased, unprejudiced; easy, unselfconscious, unembarrassed, uninhibited; natural.

Unbefangenheit [ˈunbəfaŋənhaɪt], *f.*

(—, *no pl.*) impartiality; ease of manner, unselfconsciousness, openness, naturalness.

unbefestigt [ˈunbəfɛstɪçt], *adj.* unfortified.

unbefleckt [ˈunbəflɛkt], *adj.* immaculate; —*e Empfängnis,* Immaculate Conception.

unbefriedigend [ˈunbəfriːdɪgənt], *adj.* unsatisfactory.

unbefriedigt [ˈunbəfriːdɪçt], *adj.* not satisfied, unsatisfied.

unbefugt [ˈunbəfuːkt], *adj.* unauthorised.

unbegreiflich [ˈunbəgraɪflɪç], *adj.* incomprehensible, inconceivable.

unbegrenzt [ˈunbəgrɛntst], *adj.* unlimited, unbounded.

unbegründet [ˈunbəgryndət], *adj.* unfounded, groundless.

Unbehagen [ˈunbəhaːgən], *n.* (—s, *no pl.*) uneasiness, discomfort.

unbehaglich [ˈunbəhaːklɪç], *adj.* uncomfortable; *sich — fühlen,* feel ill at ease.

unbehelligt [ˈunbəhɛlɪçt], *adj.* unmolested.

unbeholfen [ˈunbəhɔlfən], *adj.* awkward, clumsy.

unbeirrt [ˈunbəɪrt], *adj.* unswerving, uninfluenced, unperturbed.

unbekannt [ˈunbəkant], *adj.* unknown, unacquainted; *ich bin hier —,* I am a stranger here.

unbekümmert [ˈunbəkymərt], *adj.* unconcerned, careless, indifferent.

unbelehrt [ˈunbəleːrt], *adj.* uninstructed.

unbeliebt [ˈunbəliːpt], *adj.* unpopular.

unbemannt [ˈunbəmant], *adj.* without crew, unmanned.

unbemerkbar [ˈunbəmɛrkbaːr], *adj.* unnoticeable, imperceptible.

unbemerkt [ˈunbəmɛrkt], *adj.* unnoticed.

unbemittelt [ˈunbəmɪtəlt], *adj.* impecunious, poor.

unbenommen [ˈunbənɔmən], *adj. es bleibt dir —,* you are free to.

unbenutzt [ˈunbənutst], *adj.* unused.

unbequem [ˈunbəkveːm], *adj.* uncomfortable, inconvenient, troublesome.

Unbequemlichkeit [ˈunbəkveːmlɪçkaɪt], *f.* (—, *pl.* —**en**) inconvenience.

unberechenbar [ˈunbərɛçənbaːr], *adj.* incalculable; (*fig.*) erratic.

unberechtigt [ˈunbərɛçtɪçt], *adj.* unwarranted, unjustified.

unberücksichtigt [ˈunbərykzɪçtɪçt], *adj.* disregarded; — *lassen,* ignore.

unberufen [ˈunbəruːfən], *adj.* unauthorized. — *excl.* touch wood!

unbeschadet [ˈunbəʃaːdət], *prep.* (*Genit.*) without prejudice to.

unbeschädigt [ˈunbəʃeːdɪçt], *adj.* undamaged.

unbeschäftigt [ˈunbəʃɛftɪçt], *adj.* unemployed, disengaged.

unbescheiden [ˈunbəʃaɪdən], *adj.* presumptuous, greedy, immodest; unblushing; exorbitant; arrogant.

Unbescheidenheit [ˈunbəʃaɪdənhaɪt], *f.* (—, *no pl.*) presumptuousness, greed.

unbescholten [ˈunbəʃɔltən], *adj.* irreproachable, of unblemished character.

Unbescholtenheit [ˈunbəʃɔltənhaɪt], *f.* (—, *no pl.*) blamelessness, good character, unsullied reputation.

unbeschränkt [ˈunbəʃrɛŋkt], *adj.* unlimited, unbounded; —*e Monarchie*, absolute monarchy.

unbeschreiblich [ˈunbəʃraɪplɪç], *adj.* indescribable.

unbeschrieben [ˈunbəʃriːbən], *adj.* unwritten; *ein* —*es Papier*, a blank sheet of paper.

unbeschwert [ˈunbəʃveːrt], *adj.* unburdened; easy.

unbeseelt [ˈunbəzeːlt], *adj.* inanimate.

unbesiegbar [unbəˈziːkbaːr], *adj.* invincible.

unbesoldet [ˈunbəzɔldət], *adj.* unpaid, unsalaried.

unbesonnen [ˈunbəzɔnən], *adj.* thoughtless, rash.

Unbesonnenheit [ˈunbəzɔnənhaɪt], *f.* (—, *pl.* —en) thoughtlessness.

unbesorgt [ˈunbəzɔrkt], *adj.* unconcerned; *sei* —, never fear.

unbeständig [ˈunbəʃtɛndɪç], *adj.* fickle, inconstant; (*weather*) unsettled.

unbestechlich [ˈunbəʃtɛçlɪç], *adj.* incorruptible.

unbestellbar [ˈunbəʃtɛlbaːr], *adj.* not deliverable; (*letters etc.*) address(ee) unknown.

unbestellt [ˈunbəʃtɛlt], *adj.* not ordered; (*Agr.*) uncultivated, untilled.

unbestimmt [ˈunbəʃtɪmt], *adj.* uncertain, not settled; indefinite; irresolute; vague.

unbestraft [ˈunbəʃtraːft], *adj.* unpunished; without previous conviction.

unbestreitbar [ˈunbəʃtraɪtbaːr], *adj.* indisputable, incontestable.

unbestritten [ˈunbəʃtrɪtən], *adj.* uncontested, undoubted, undisputed.

unbeteiligt [ˈunbətaɪlɪçt], *adj.* unconcerned, indifferent.

unbeträchtlich [ˈunbətrɛçtlɪç], *adj.* inconsiderable, trivial.

unbetreten [ˈunbətreːtən], *adj.* untrodden, untouched.

unbeugsam [ˈunbɔykzaːm], *adj.* inflexible, unyielding.

unbewacht [ˈunbəvaxt], *adj.* unguarded.

unbewaffnet [ˈunbəvafnət], *adj.* unarmed; *mit* —*em Auge*, with the naked eye.

unbewandert [ˈunbəvandərt], *adj.* unversed in, unfamiliar with.

unbezahlt [ˈunbətsaːlt], *adj.* unpaid.

unbezähmbar [ˈunbətsɛːmbaːr], *adj.* uncontrollable; indomitable.

unbezwinglich [ˈunbətsvɪŋlɪç], *adj.* invincible, unconquerable.

Unbildung [ˈunbɪldun], *f.* (—, *no pl.*) lack of education or knowledge or culture.

Unbill [ˈunbɪl], *f.* (—, *pl.* **Unbilden**) injustice, wrong, injury; (*weather*) inclemency.

unbillig [ˈunbɪlɪç], *adj.* unreasonable, unfair.

Unbilligkeit [ˈunbɪlɪçkaɪt], *f.* (—, *no pl.*) unreasonableness, injustice, unfairness.

unbotmäßig [ˈunboːtmɛːsɪç], *adj.* unruly, insubordinate.

unbußfertig [ˈunbuːsfɛrtɪç], *adj.* impenitent, unrepentant.

und [unt], *conj.* and; — *nicht*, nor; — *so weiter* (abbr. *u.s.w.*), etc., and so on, and so forth; — *wenn*, even if.

Undank [ˈundaŋk], *m.* (—s, *no pl.*) ingratitude.

undankbar [ˈundaŋkbaːr], *adj.* ungrateful; *eine* —*e Aufgabe*, a thankless task.

Undankbarkeit [ˈundaŋkbaˈrkaɪt], *f.* (—, *no pl.*) ingratitude.

undenkbar [ˈundɛŋkbaːr], *adj.* unthinkable, unimaginable, inconceivable.

undenklich [ˈundɛŋklɪç], *adj. seit* —*en Zeiten*, from time immemorial.

undeutlich [ˈundɔytlɪç], *adj.* indistinct; inarticulate; (*fig.*) unintelligible.

Unding [ˈundɪŋ], *n.* (—s, *no pl.*) absurdity.

unduldsam [ˈundultzaːm], *adj.* intolerant.

undurchdringlich [ˈundurçdrɪŋlɪç], *adj.* impenetrable.

undurchführbar [ˈundurçfyˈrbaːr], *adj.* impracticable, unworkable.

undurchsichtig [ˈundurçzɪçtɪç], *adj.* opaque, not transparent.

uneben [ˈuneːbən], *adj.* uneven, rugged; (*coll.*) *nicht* —, not bad.

unecht [ˈunɛçt], *adj.* false, not genuine, spurious, counterfeit.

unedel [ˈuneːdəl], *adj.* (*metal*) base.

unehelich [ˈuneːəlɪç], *adj.* illegitimate.

Unehre [ˈuneːrə], *f.* (—, *no pl.*) dishonour, disgrace, discredit.

unehrlich [ˈuneːrlɪç], *adj.* dishonest

Unehrlichkeit [ˈuneːrlɪçkaɪt], *f.* (—, *pl.* —en) dishonesty.

uneigennützig [ˈunaɪɡənnytsɪç], *adj.* unselfish, disinterested, public-spirited.

uneingedenk [ˈunaɪŋɡədɛŋk], *adj.* (*Genit.*) unmindful, forgetful.

uneingeschränkt [ˈunaɪŋɡəʃrɛŋkt], *adj.* unrestrained, unlimited.

uneinig [ˈunaɪnɪç], **uneins** [ˈunaɪns], *adj.* disunited, divided; — *werden*, fall out; — *sein*, disagree.

Uneinigkeit [ˈunaɪnɪçkaɪt], *f.* (—, *pl.* —en) disharmony, discord.

uneinnehmbar [ˈunaɪnneːmbaːr], *adj.* unconquerable, impregnable.

uneins *see under* **uneinig**.
unempfänglich [ˈunɛmpfɛŋlɪç], *adj.*
insusceptible; unreceptive.
unempfindlich [ˈunɛmpfɪntlɪç], *adj.*
insensitive, indifferent; unfeeling.
unendlich [unˈɛntlɪç], *adj.* endless,
infinite.
unentbehrlich [unɛntbeːrlɪç], *adj.*
indispensable, (absolutely) essential.
unentgeltlich [unɛntˈgɛltlɪç], *adj.* free
(of charge).
unentschieden [ˈunɛntʃiːdən], *adj.* undecided, undetermined; irresolute;
(*game*) drawn, tied.
unentschlossen [ˈunɛntʃlɔsən], *adj.*
irresolute.
Unentschlossenheit [ˈunɛntʃlɔsən-
haɪt], *f.* (—, *no pl.*) irresolution,
indecision.
unentschuldbar [ˈunɛntʃultbaːr], *adj.*
inexcusable.
unentstellt [ˈunɛntʃtɛlt], *adj.* undis-
torted.
unentwegt [ˈunɛntveːkt], *adj.* steadfast, unflinching, unswerving.
unentwickelt [ˈunɛntvɪkəlt], *adj.* undeveloped; —*e Länder*, under-
developed countries.
unentwirrbar [ˈunɛntvɪrbaːr], *adj.* inextricable.
unentzifferbar [ˈunɛnttsɪfərbaːr], *adj.*
indecipherable.
unentzündbar [ˈunɛnttsyntbaːr], *adj.*
non-inflammable.
unerachtet [ˈunɛraxtət], *prep.* (*Genit.*)
(*obs.*) notwithstanding.
unerbeten [ˈunɛrbeːtən], *adj.* unsolicited.
unerbittlich [ˈunɛrbɪtlɪç], *adj.* inexorable.
unerfahren [ˈunɛrfaːrən], *adj.* inexperienced.
unerforschlich [ˈunɛrfɔrʃlɪç], *adj.* inscrutable.
unerfreulich [ˈunɛrfrɔylɪç], *adj.* unpleasant, displeasing, disagreeable.
unerfüllbar [ˈunɛrfylbaːr], *adj.* un-
realisable.
unerfüllt [ˈunɛrfylt], *adj.* unfulfilled.
unergründlich [ˈunɛrgryntlɪç], *adj.*
unfathomable, impenetrable.
unerheblich [ˈunɛrheːplɪç], *adj.*
trifling, unimportant.
unerhört [ˈunɛrhøːrt], *adj.* unpre-
cedented, unheard of, shocking, outrageous; not granted; turned
down.
unerkannt [ˈunɛrkant], *adj.* unrecog-
nised.
unerkennbar [ˈunɛrkɛnbaːr], *adj.* unrecognisable.
unerklärlich [ˈunɛrklɛːrlɪç], *adj.* inexplicable.
unerläßlich [ˈunɛrlɛslɪç], *adj.* indispensable.
unerlaubt [ˈunɛrlaupt], *adj.* unlawful,
illicit.
unermeßlich [ˈunɛrmɛslɪç], *adj.*
immense, vast.

unermüdlich [ˈunɛrmyːtlɪç], *adj.* untiring, indefatigable.
unerquicklich [ˈunɛrkvɪklɪç], *adj.* un-
edifying, disagreeable.
unerreichbar [ˈunɛrraɪçbaːr], *adj.* un-
attainable, inaccessible.
unerreicht [ˈunɛrraɪçt], *adj.* unequalled.
unersättlich [ˈunɛrzɛtlɪç], *adj.* insatiable, greedy.
unerschöpflich [ˈunɛrʃœpflɪç], *adj.*
inexhaustible.
unerschöpft [ˈunɛrʃœpft], *adj.* unexhausted.
unerschrocken [ˈunɛrʃrɔkən], *adj.* intrepid, undaunted.
unerschütterlich [ˈunɛrʃytərlɪç], *adj.*
imperturbable.
unerschüttert [ˈunɛrʃytərt], *adj.* un-
shaken, unperturbed.
unerschwinglich [ˈunɛrʃvɪŋlɪç], *adj.*
prohibitive, exorbitant, unattain-
able.
unersetzlich [ˈunɛrzɛtslɪç], *adj.* ir-
replaceable.
unersprießlich [ˈunɛrʃpriːslɪç], *adj.*
unprofitable.
unerträglich [ˈunɛrtrɛːklɪç], *adj.* intolerable, insufferable.
unerwartet [ˈunɛrvartət], *adj.* unexpected.
unerwidert [ˈunɛrviːdərt], *adj.* (*love*)
unrequited; (*letter*) unanswered.
unerwünscht [ˈunɛrvynʃt], *adj.* un-
desirable, unwelcome.
unerzogen [ˈunɛrtsoːgən], *adj.* un-
educated; ill-bred, unmannerly.
unfähig [ˈunfɛːɪç], *adj.* incapable,
unable, unfit.
Unfähigkeit [ˈunfɛːɪçkaɪt], *f.* (—, *no
pl.*) incapability, inability, unfit-
ness.
Unfall [ˈunfal], *m.* (—*s, pl.* ⸚e) accident.
unfaßbar [ˈunfasbaːr], *adj.* incomprehensible, inconceivable.
unfehlbar [ˈunfɛːlbaːr], *adj.* inevitable;
infallible.
Unfehlbarkeit [ˈunfɛːlbaːrkaɪt], *f.* (—,
no pl.) infallibility.
unfein [ˈunfaɪn], *adj.* indelicate, coarse,
impolite.
unfern [ˈunfɛrn], *prep.* (*Genit., Dat.*)
not far from.
unfertig [ˈunfɛrtɪç], *adj.* unfinished,
unready.
unflätig [ˈunflɛːtɪç], *adj.* obscene,
nasty, filthy.
unfolgsam [ˈunfɔlkzaːm], *adj.* disobedient, recalcitrant.
unförmig [ˈunfœrmɪç], *adj.* deformed,
ill-shaped, misshapen.
unförmlich [ˈunfœrmlɪç], *adj.* shapeless; free and easy, unceremonious.
unfrankiert [ˈunfraŋkiːrt], *adj.* (*letter*)
not prepaid, unstamped, unfranked.
unfrei [ˈunfraɪ], *adj.* not free; sub-
jugated; constrained.
unfreiwillig [ˈunfraɪvɪlɪç], *adj.* involuntary.

unfreundlich [′unfrɔyntlɪç], *adj.* unfriendly, unkind; (*weather*) inclement.
Unfreundlichkeit [′unfrɔyntlɪçkaɪt], *f.*
(—, *pl.* —en) unfriendliness, un-
kindness; (*weather*) inclemency.
Unfrieden [′unfri:dən], *m.* (—s, *no pl.*)
discord, dissension.
unfruchtbar [′unfruxtba:r], *adj.* barren,
sterile; (*fig.*) fruitless.
Unfug [′unfu:k], *m.* (—s, *no pl.*) disturbance, misconduct; mischief;
grober —, public nuisance.
unfühlbar [′unfy:lba:r], *adj.* imperceptible.
ungangbar [′unganba:r], *adj.* impassable.
Ungarn [′uŋgarn], *n.* Hungary.
ungastlich [′ungastlɪç], *adj.* inhospitable.
ungeachtet [′ungəaxtət], *prep.* (*Genit.*)
notwithstanding.
ungeahndet [′ungəa:ndət], *adj.* unpunished, with impunity.
ungeahnt [′ungəa:nt], *adj.* unexpected,
unsuspected, undreamt of.
ungebändigt [′ungəbendɪçt], *adj.* untamed.
ungebärdig [′ungəbɛrdɪç], *adj.* unmannerly, refractory.
ungebeten [′ungəbe:tən], *adj.* uninvited, unbidden.
ungebleicht [′ungəblaɪçt], *adj.* un-
bleached.
ungebraucht [′ungəbrauxt], *adj.* unused.
Ungebühr [′ungəby:r], *f.* (—, *no pl.*)
unseemliness, impropriety, excess.
ungebührlich [′ungəby:rlɪç], *adj.* unseemly.
ungebunden [′ungəbundən], *adj.* un-
bound, in sheets; unrestrained, loose;
unlinked; —*e Rede*, prose.
Ungeduld [′ungədult], *f.* (—, *no pl.*)
impatience.
ungeduldig [′ungəduldɪç], *adj.* impatient.
ungeeignet [′ungəaɪgnət], *adj.* unfit,
unsuitable.
ungefähr [′ungəfɛ:r], *adj.* approximate,
rough. — *adv.* approximately,
roughly, about, round.
ungefährlich [′ungəfɛ:rlɪç], *adj.* not
dangerous, harmless, safe.
ungefällig [′ungəfɛlɪç], *adj.* ungracious,
disobliging.
ungefärbt [′ungəfɛrpt], *adj.* un-
coloured; (*fig.*) unvarnished.
ungefüge [′ungəfy:gə], *adj.* clumsy.
ungehalten [′ungəhaltən], *adj.* indignant, angry.
ungeheißen [′ungəhaɪsən], *adj.* unbidden. — *adv.* of o.'s own accord.
ungehemmt [′ungəhɛmt], *adj.* un-
checked, uninhibited.
ungeheuchelt [′ungəhɔyçəlt], *adj.* un-
feigned.
Ungeheuer [′ungəhɔyər], *n.* (—s, *pl.*
—) monster, monstrosity.

ungeheuer [′ungəhɔyər], *adj.* huge,
immense; atrocious, frightful.
ungehobelt [′ungəho:bəlt], *adj.* un-
planed; (*fig.*) boorish, uncultured,
unpolished.
ungehörig [′ungəhø:rɪç], *adj.* unseemly, improper.
Ungehorsam [′ungəho:rza:m], *m.* (—s,
no pl.) disobedience.
ungehorsam [′ungəho:rza:m], *adj.*
disobedient; — *sein*, disobey.
Ungehorsamkeit [′ungəho:rza:mkaɪt],
f. (—, *pl.* —en) disobedience, insubordination.
ungekämmt [′ungəkɛmt], *adj.* unkempt.
ungekünstelt [′ungəkynstəlt], *adj.* artless, unstudied.
ungeladen [′ungəla:dən], *adj.* (*gun*)
unloaded, not charged; uninvited.
ungeläutert [′ungəlɔytərt], *adj.* unrefined; unpurified.
ungelegen [′ungəle:gən], *adj.* inconvenient, inopportune.
Ungelegenheit [′ungəle:gənhaɪt], *f.*
(—, *pl.* —en) inconvenience, trouble.
ungelehrig [′ungəle:rɪç], *adj.* intractable, unintelligent.
ungelenk [′ungəlɛŋk], *adj.* clumsy,
awkward; ungainly.
ungelöscht [′ungəlœʃt], *adj.* unquenched; (*lime*) unslaked; (*mortgage*) unredeemed.
Ungemach [′ungəma:x], *n.* (—(e)s,
no pl.) adversity, toil, privation.
ungemein [′ungəmaɪn], *adj.* uncommon, extraordinary. — *adv.* very
much, exceedingly.
ungemütlich [′ungəmy:tlɪç], *adj.* uncomfortable, cheerless, unpleasant.
ungeniert [′unʒeni:rt], *adj.* free and
easy, unceremonious, unabashed.
ungenießbar [′ungəni:sba:r], *adj.* un-
palatable, uneatable, inedible.
ungenügend [′ungənygənt], *adj.* insufficient, unsatisfactory.
ungenügsam [′ungəny:kza:m], *adj.*
insatiable, greedy.
ungeordnet [′ungəɔrdnət], *adj.* ill-
assorted, confused.
ungepflegt [′ungəpfle:kt], *adj.* un-
cared for, neglected.
ungerade [′ungəra:də], *adj.* uneven; —
Zahl, odd number.
ungeraten [′ungəra:tən], *adj.* abortive,
unsuccessful, spoiled; undutiful; ill-
bred.
ungerecht [′ungərɛçt], *adj.* unjust,
unfair.
ungerechtfertigt [′ungərɛçtfertɪçt],
adj. unwarranted, unjustified.
Ungerechtigkeit [′ungərɛçtɪçkaɪt], *f.*
(—, *pl.* —en) injustice.
ungeregelt [′ungəre:gəlt], *adj.* not
regulated, irregular.
ungereimt [′ungəraɪmt], *adj.* rhyme-
less; —*es Zeug*, nonsense, absurdity.
ungern [′ungɛrn], *adv.* unwillingly,
reluctantly.

ungerufen

ungerufen ['ungəru:fən], *adj.* unbidden.
ungerührt ['ungəry:rt], *adj.* unmoved.
ungesäumt ['ungəzɔymt], *adj.* unseamed, unhemmed; (*fig.*) immediate. — *adv.* immediately, without delay.
ungeschehen ['ungəʃe:ən], *adj.* undone; — *machen*, undo.
Ungeschick ['ungəʃɪk], *n.* (—s, *no pl.*) awkwardness, clumsiness.
Ungeschicklichkeit ['ungəʃɪklɪçkaɪt], *f.* (—, *pl.* —en) awkwardness, clumsiness.
ungeschickt ['ungəʃɪkt], *adj.* awkward, clumsy, unskilful.
ungeschlacht ['ungəʃlaxt], *adj.* uncouth, unwieldy; coarse, rude.
ungeschliffen ['ungəʃlɪfən], *adj.* unpolished; (*fig.*) coarse.
Ungeschliffenheit ['ungəʃlɪfənhaɪt], *f.* (—, *no pl.*) coarseness, uncouthness.
ungeschmälert ['ungəʃmɛːlərt], *adj.* undiminished, unimpaired.
ungeschminkt ['ungəʃmɪŋkt], *adj.* without cosmetics *or* make-up, not made up; (*truth*) plain, unvarnished.
ungeschoren ['ungəʃo:rən], *adj.* unshorn; *laß mich* —, leave me alone.
ungeschult ['ungəʃu:lt], *adj.* untrained.
ungeschwächt ['ungəʃvɛçt], *adj.* unimpaired.
ungesellig ['ungəzɛlɪç], *adj.* unsociable.
ungesetzlich ['ungəzetslɪç], *adj.* illegal, unlawful, illicit.
ungesetzmäßig ['ungəzetsmɛːsɪç], *adj.* illegitimate, lawless; exceptional; not regular.
ungesiegelt ['ungəzi:gəlt], *adj.* unsealed.
Ungestalt ['ungəʃtalt], *f.* (—, *no pl.*) deformity.
ungestalt ['ungəʃtalt], *adj.* misshapen, deformed.
ungestempelt ['ungəʃtempəlt], *adj.* unstamped, uncancelled, not postmarked.
ungestillt ['ungəʃtɪlt], *adj.* unquenched, unslaked; not fed, unsatisfied.
ungestört ['ungəʃtø:rt], *adj.* undisturbed.
ungestraft ['ungəʃtra:ft], *adj.* unpunished. — *adv.* with impunity.
ungestüm ['ungəʃty:m], *adj.* impetuous.
Ungestüm ['ungəʃty:m], *m. & n.* (—s, *no pl.*) impetuosity.
ungesund ['ungəzunt], *adj.* unwholesome, unhealthy, sickly; (*fig.*) unnatural, morbid.
ungetan ['ungəta:n], *adj.* not done, left undone.
ungetreu ['ungətrɔy], *adj.* disloyal, faithless.
ungetrübt ['ungətry:pt], *adj.* untroubled.
ungewandt ['ungəvant], *adj.* unskilful.
ungewaschen ['ungəvaʃən], *adj.* un-

washed; (*sl.*) —*es Mundwerk*, malicious tongue.
ungeweiht ['ungəvaɪt], *adj.* unconsecrated.
ungewiß ['ungəvɪs], *adj.* uncertain, doubtful.
Ungewißheit ['ungəvɪshaɪt], *f.* (—, *no pl.*) uncertainty, suspense.
Ungewitter ['ungəvɪtər], *n.* (—s, *pl.* —) storm, thunderstorm.
ungewöhnlich ['ungəvø:nlɪç], *adj.* unusual, uncommon.
Ungewohntheit ['ungəvo:nthaɪt], *f.* (—, *no pl.*) strangeness; want of practice.
ungezähmt ['ungətsɛːmt], *adj.* untamed; (*fig.*) uncurbed.
Ungeziefer ['ungətsi:fər], *n.* (—s, *pl.* —) vermin.
ungeziert ['ungətsi:rt], *adj.* unaffected, natural.
ungezogen ['ungətso:gən], *adj.* ill-mannered, naughty.
ungezügelt ['ungətsy:gəlt], *adj.* unbridled; (*fig.*) unruly.
ungezwungen ['ungətsvuŋən], *adj.* unforced; (*fig.*) unaffected.
Ungezwungenheit ['ungətsvuŋənhaɪt], *f.* (—, *no pl.*) naturalness, ease.
Unglaube ['unglaubə], *m.* (—ns, *no pl.*) disbelief.
unglaubhaft ['unglauphaft], *adj.* unauthenticated, incredible.
ungläubig ['unglɔybɪç], *adj.* incredulous, disbelieving.
Ungläubige ['unglɔybɪgə], *m.* (—n, *pl.* —n) unbeliever.
unglaublich ['unglauplɪç], *adj.* incredible, unbelievable.
unglaubwürdig ['unglaupvyrdɪç], *adj.* unauthenticated, incredible.
ungleichartig ['unglaɪçartɪç], *adj.* dissimilar, heterogeneous.
ungleichförmig ['unglaɪçfœrmɪç], *adj.* not uniform; dissimilar.
Ungleichheit ['unglaɪçhaɪt], *f.* (—, *pl.* —en) inequality; unlikeness, dissimilarity; unevenness.
ungleichmäßig ['unglaɪçmɛːsɪç], *adj.* unequal, irregular; changeable, fitful.
Unglimpf ['unglɪmpf], *m.* (—(e)s, *no pl.*) harshness; insult.
Unglück ['unglyk], *n.* (—s, *pl.* —sfälle) misfortune, adversity, ill-luck; accident, disaster; distress, sorrow, affliction.
unglückbringend ['unglykbrɪŋənt], *adj.* disastrous, unpropitious.
unglücklich ['unglyklɪç], *adj.* unfortunate, unhappy, unlucky; —*e Liebe*, unrequited love.
unglücklicherweise ['unglyklɪçərvaɪzə], *adv.* unfortunately, unluckily.
Unglücksbotschaft ['unglyksbo:tʃaft], *f.* (—, *pl.* —en) bad news.
unglückselig ['unglykze:lɪç], *adj.* luckless, wretched, unfortunate, calamitous.
Unglücksfall ['unglyksfal], *m.* (—(e)s, *pl.* ⸚e) accident.

242

Unglücksgefährte [ˈunglyksɡəfɛːrtə], m. (—n, pl. —n) companion in misfortune.

Ungnade [ˈungnaːdə], f. (—, no pl.) disgrace.

ungültig [ˈungyltɪç], adj. invalid, void; — machen, invalidate, annul.

Ungunst [ˈungunst], f. (—, no pl.) disfavour; unpropitiousness; (weather) inclemency.

ungünstig [ˈungynstɪç], adj. unfavourable, adverse.

ungut [ˈunguːt], adv. etwas für — nehmen, take s.th. amiss.

unhaltbar [ˈunhaltbaːr], adj. untenable.

Unheil [ˈunhaɪl], n. (—s, no pl.) mischief, harm; disaster.

unheilbar [ˈunhaɪlbaːr], adj. incurable.

unheilbringend [ˈunhaɪlbrɪŋənt], adj. ominous, unlucky; disastrous.

Unheilstifter [ˈunhaɪlʃtɪftər], m. (—s, pl. —) mischief-maker.

unheilvoll [ˈunhaɪlfɔl], adj. calamitous, disastrous.

unheimlich [ˈunhaɪmlɪç], adj. weird, eerie, uncanny.

unhöflich [ˈunhøːflɪç], adj. impolite, uncivil, discourteous.

Unhold [ˈunhɔlt], m. (—s, pl. —e) fiend, monster.

Unhörbarkeit [ˈunhøːrbaːrkaɪt], f. (—, no pl.) inaudibility.

Uniformität [uniformiˈtɛːt], f. (—, no pl.) uniformity.

Unikum [ˈuːnikum], n. (—s, pl. —s) unique thing or person; eccentric.

Universalmittel [univɛrˈzaːlmɪtəl], n. (—s, pl. —) panacea, universal remedy.

Universität [univɛrziˈtɛːt], f. (—, pl. —en) university.

Universitätsdozent [univɛrziˈtɛːtsdotsɛnt], m. (—en, pl. —en) university lecturer.

Universum [uniˈvɛrzum], n. (—s, no pl.) universe.

unkaufmännisch [ˈunkaufmɛnɪʃ], adj. unbusinesslike.

Unke [ˈuŋkə], f. (—, pl. —n) (Zool.) toad; (fig.) grumbler, pessimist.

unken [ˈuŋkən], v.n. grumble, grouse.

unkenntlich [ˈunkɛntlɪç], adj. indiscernible, unrecognisable.

Unkenntlichkeit [ˈunkɛntlɪçkaɪt], f. (—, no pl.) bis zur —, past recognition.

Unkenntnis [ˈunkɛntnɪs], f. (—, no pl.) ignorance.

unklug [ˈunkluːk], adj. imprudent.

Unkosten [ˈunkɔstən], f. pl. expenses, costs, charges; overheads.

Unkraut [ˈunkraut], n. (—s, no pl.) weed(s).

unkündbar [ˈunkyntbaːr], adj. irredeemable; irrevocable, permanent.

unkundig [ˈunkundɪç], adj. ignorant (of), unacquainted (with).

unlängst [ˈunlɛŋst], adv. recently, lately, not long ago.

unlauter [ˈunlautər], adj. sordid, squalid; unfair.

unleidlich [ˈunlaɪtlɪç], adj. intolerable.

unleserlich [ˈunleːzərlɪç], adj. illegible.

unleugbar [ˈunlɔykbaːr], adj. undeniable, indisputable.

unlieb [ˈunliːp], adj. disagreeable.

unliebenswürdig [ˈunliːbənsvyrdɪç], adj. sullen, surly.

unlösbar [ˈunløːsbaːr], adj. insoluble.

unlöslich [ˈunløːslɪç], adj. (substance) indissoluble, insoluble.

Unlust [ˈunlust], f. (—, no pl.) aversion, disinclination; slackness.

unlustig [ˈunlustɪç], adj. averse, disinclined.

unmanierlich [ˈunmaniːrlɪç], adj. ill-mannered.

unmännlich [ˈunmɛnlɪç], adj. unmanly, effeminate.

Unmaß [ˈunmaːs], n. (—es, no pl.) excess.

Unmasse [ˈunmasə], f. (—, pl. —n) vast quantity.

unmaßgeblich [ˈunmaːsɡeːplɪç], adj. unauthoritative, open to correction; (fig.) humble.

unmäßig [ˈunmɛːsɪç], adj. intemperate, excessive.

Unmenge [ˈunmɛŋə], f. (—, pl. —n) vast quantity.

Unmensch [ˈunmɛnʃ], m. (—en, pl. —en) brute.

unmenschlich [ˈunmɛnʃlɪç], adj. inhuman, brutal; (coll.) vast.

unmerklich [ˈunmɛrklɪç], adj. imperceptible.

unmeßbar [ˈunmɛsbaːr], adj. immeasurable.

unmittelbar [ˈunmɪtəlbaːr], adj. immediate, direct.

unmöglich [ˈunmøːklɪç], adj. impossible.

unmündig [ˈunmyndɪç], adj. under age, minor.

Unmündige [ˈunmyndɪɡə], m. (—n, pl. —n) (Law) minor.

Unmündigkeit [ˈunmyndɪçkaɪt], f. (—, no pl.) minority.

Unmut [ˈunmuːt], m. (—s, no pl.) ill-humour; displeasure, indignation, petulance.

unmutig [ˈunmuːtɪç], adj. ill-humoured, petulant, indignant.

unnachahmlich [ˈunnaxaːmlɪç], adj. inimitable.

unnachgiebig [ˈunnaxɡiːbɪç], adj. relentless, unyielding.

unnachsichtig [ˈunnaxzɪçtɪç], adj. unrelenting, relentless.

unnahbar [ˈunnaːbaːr], adj. unapproachable, stand-offish.

unnennbar [ˈunnɛnbaːr], adj. unutterable.

unnütz [ˈunnyts], adj. useless.

unordentlich [ˈunɔrdəntlɪç], adj. untidy, slovenly.

Unordnung [ˈunɔrdnuŋ], f. (—, no pl.) disorder, untidiness, muddle, confusion.

unparteiisch

unparteiisch [ˈunpartaɪɪʃ], *adj.* impartial, unbiased, objective.

unpassend [ˈunpasənt], *adj.* unsuitable, inappropriate; improper.

unpassierbar [ˈunpasiːrbaːr], *adj.* impassable.

unpäßlich [ˈunpɛslɪç], *adj.* indisposed, unwell, out of sorts.

Unpäßlichkeit [ˈunpɛslɪçkaɪt], *f.* (—, *pl.* **—en**) indisposition.

unproportioniert [ˈunprɔpɔrtsjoniːrt], *adj.* disproportionate; unshapely.

unqualifizierbar [ˈunkvalifitsiːrbaːr], *adj.* unspeakable, nameless.

Unrat [ˈunraːt], *m.* (—(e)s, *no pl.*) dirt, rubbish.

unratsam [ˈunraːtzaːm], *adj.* inadvisable.

Unrecht [ˈunrɛçt], *n.* (—(e)s, *no pl.*) wrong, injustice; — haben, be in the wrong.

unrecht [ˈunrɛçt], *adj.* wrong, unjust.

unrechtmäßig [ˈunrɛçtmɛːsɪç], *adj.* unlawful, illegal.

unredlich [ˈunreːtlɪç], *adj.* dishonest.

unregelmäßig [ˈunreːgəlmɛːsɪç], *adj.* irregular.

unreif [ˈunraɪf], *adj.* unripe, immature; (*fig.*) crude, raw.

Unreife [ˈunraɪfə], *f.* (—, *no pl.*) immaturity.

unrein [ˈunraɪn], *adj.* unclean; (*fig.*) impure.

Unreinheit [ˈunraɪnhaɪt], *f.* (—, *pl.* **—en**) impurity.

Unreinlichkeit [ˈunraɪnlɪçkaɪt], *f.* (—, *no pl.*) uncleanliness.

unrentabel [ˈunrɛntaːbəl], *adj.* unprofitable.

unrettbar [ˈunrɛtbaːr], *adj.* irretrievable, hopelessly lost.

unrichtig [ˈunrɪçtɪç], *adj.* incorrect, erroneous, wrong.

Unrichtigkeit [ˈunrɪçtɪçkaɪt], *f.* (—, *no pl.*) error, falsity, incorrectness.

Unruhe [ˈunruːə], *f.* (—, *pl.* **—en**) unrest, restlessness; disquiet, uneasiness; riot, disturbance; (*clock*) balance.

Unruhestifter [ˈunruːəʃtɪftər], *m.* (—s, *pl.* —) disturber (of the peace); troublemaker.

unruhig [ˈunruːɪç], *adj.* restless; troublesome, turbulent, uneasy (about), fidgety.

unrühmlich [ˈunryːmlɪç], *adj.* inglorious.

uns [uns], *pers. pron.* us, ourselves; to us.

unsachlich [ˈunzaxlɪç], *adj.* subjective; irrelevant.

unsagbar [ˈunzaːkbaːr], *adj.* unutterable, unspeakable.

unsanft [ˈunzanft], *adj.* harsh, violent.

unsauber [ˈunzaubər], *adj.* unclean, dirty; (*fig.*) squalid.

unschädlich [ˈunʃeːtlɪç], *adj.* harmless, innocuous.

unschätzbar [ˈunʃɛtsbaːr], *adj.* invaluable.

unscheinbar [ˈunʃaɪnbaːr], *adj.* plain, homely, insignificant.

unschicklich [ˈunʃɪklɪç], *adj.* unbecoming, indecent, improper, unseemly.

unschlüssig [ˈunʃlysɪç], *adj.* irresolute, undecided.

Unschuld [ˈunʃult], *f.* (—, *no pl.*) innocence; verfolgte —, injured innocence.

unschuldig [ˈunʃuldɪç], *adj.* innocent, guiltless; chaste; —es Vergnügen, harmless pleasure.

unschwer [ˈunʃveːr], *adv.* easily.

Unsegen [ˈunzeːgən], *m.* (—s, *no pl.*) misfortune; curse.

unselbständig [ˈunzɛlpʃtɛndɪç], *adj.* dependent.

unselig [ˈunzeːlɪç], *adj.* unfortunate, luckless, fatal.

unser [ˈunzər], *poss. adj.* our. — *pers. pron.* of us.

unsereiner [ˈunzəraɪnər], *pron.* s.o. in our position; one of us, people in our position.

unserthalben, unsertwegen [ˈunzərthalbən, unzərtveːgən], *adv.* for our sake, on our account.

unsertwillen [ˈunzərtvilən], *adv. um —*, for our sake, on our account.

unsicher [ˈunzɪçər], *adj.* unsafe; uncertain, doubtful; (*route*) precarious; (*hand*) unsteady; (*legs*) shaky.

unsichtbar [ˈunzɪçtbaːr], *adj.* invisible.

Unsinn [ˈunzɪn], *m.* (—s, *no pl.*) nonsense.

unsinnig [ˈunzɪnɪç], *adj.* nonsensical; mad, insane.

Unsitte [ˈunzɪtə], *f.* (—, *pl.* **—n**) abuse, nuisance; bad habit.

unsittlich [ˈunzɪtlɪç], *adj.* immoral.

unstät, unstet [ˈunʃtɛːt, ˈunʃteːt], *adj.* unsteady, inconstant; restless.

unstatthaft [ˈunʃtathaft], *adj.* illicit.

unsterblich [ˈunʃtɛrplɪç], *adj.* immortal.

Unsterblichkeit [ˈunʃtɛrplɪçkaɪt], *f.* (—, *no pl.*) immortality.

unstillbar [ˈunʃtɪlbaːr], *adj.* unappeasable, unquenchable.

unstreitig [ˈunʃtraɪtɪç], *adj.* indisputable, unquestionable.

Unsumme [ˈunzumə], *f.* (—, *pl.* **—n**) vast amount (of money).

unsympathisch [ˈunzympaːtɪʃ], *adj.* uncongenial, disagreeable; er ist mir —, I dislike him.

untadelhaft, untadelig [ˈuntaːdəlhaft, ˈuntaːdəlɪç], *adj.* blameless, irreproachable, unimpeachable.

Untat [ˈuntaːt], *f.* (—, *pl.* **—en**) misdeed, crime.

untätig [ˈunteːtɪç], *adj.* inactive, idle, supine.

untauglich [ˈuntauklɪç], *adj.* unfit, useless; incompetent; (*Mil.*) disabled.

unteilbar [ˈuntaɪlbaːr], *adj.* indivisible.

unten ['untən], *adv.* below, beneath; (*house*) downstairs.

unter ['untər], *prep.* (*Dat.*, *Acc.*) under, beneath, below, among, between.

Unterbau ['untərbau], *m.* (**—s**, *pl.* **—ten**) substructure, foundation.

Unterbewußtsein ['untərbəvustsaɪn], *n.* (**—s**, *no pl.*) subconscious mind, subconsciousness.

unterbieten [untər'bi:tən], *v.a. irr. insep.* underbid, undersell.

Unterbilanz ['untərbilants], *f.* (**—**, *pl.* **—en**) deficit.

unterbinden [untər'bɪndən], *v.a. irr. insep.* tie up, bind up; (*fig.*) prevent, check.

unterbleiben [untər'blaɪbən], *v.n. irr. insep.* (*aux.* sein) remain undone, be left undone, cease.

unterbrechen [untər'brɛçən], *v.a. irr. insep.* interrupt; (*journey*) break; (*speech*) cut short.

Unterbrechung [untər'brɛçuŋ], *f.* (**—**, *pl.* **—en**) interruption.

unterbreiten (1) ['untərbraɪtən], *v.a.* spread under.

unterbreiten (2) [untər'braɪtən], *v.a. insep.* submit, lay before.

unterbringen ['untərbrɪŋən], *v.a. irr.* provide (*a place*) for; (*goods*) dispose of; (*money*) invest; (*people*) accommodate, put up.

Unterbringung ['untərbrɪŋuŋ], *f.* (**—**, *no pl.*) provision for; (*goods*) disposal of; (*money*) investment; (*people*) accommodation.

unterdessen [untər'dɛsən], *adv.*, *conj.* in the meantime, meanwhile.

unterdrücken [untər'drykən], *v.a. insep.* suppress, curb, check; oppress.

Unterdrückung [untər'drykuŋ], *f.* (**—**, *no pl.*) oppression, suppression.

untereinander [untəraɪn'andər], *adv.* with each other, mutually, among themselves.

unterfangen [untər'faŋən], *v.r. irr. insep. sich* **—**, dare, venture, presume.

Untergang ['untərgaŋ], *m.* (**—s**, *pl.* **̈e**) (*sun*) setting; (*ship*) sinking; (*fig.*) decline.

untergeben [untər'ge:bən], *adj.* subject, subordinate.

Untergebene [untər'ge:bənə], *m.* (**—n**, *pl.* **—n**) subordinate.

untergehen ['untərge:ən], *v.n. irr.* (*aux.* sein) (*sun*) go down, set; (*ship*) sink; (*fig.*) perish; decline.

Untergeschoß ['untərgəʃɔs], *n.* (**—sses**, *pl.* **—sse**) ground floor; basement.

Untergestell ['untərgəʃtɛl], *n.* (**—s**, *pl.* **—e**) undercarriage, chassis.

untergraben [untər'gra:bən], *v.a. irr. insep.* undermine.

unterhalb ['untərhalp], *prep.* (*Genit.*) below, under.

Unterhalt ['untərhalt], *m.* (**—s**, *no pl.*) maintenance, support, livelihood.

unterhalten (1) ['untərhaltən], *v.a. irr.* hold under.

unterhalten (2) [untər'haltən], *v.a. irr. insep.* maintain, keep, support; entertain. — *v.r. sich* **—**, converse, make conversation; *sich gut* **—**, enjoy o.s.

unterhaltend [untər'haltənt], *adj.* entertaining, amusing, lively.

Unterhaltskosten ['untərhaltskɔstən], *f. pl.* maintenance; (*house*) cost of repairs.

Unterhaltung [untər'haltuŋ], *f.* (**—**, *pl.* **—en**) maintenance; conversation; amusement, entertainment.

Unterhaltungslektüre [untər'haltuŋslɛkty:rə], *f.* (**—**, *no pl.*) light reading, fiction.

unterhandeln [untər'handəln], *v.n. insep.* negotiate.

Unterhändler ['untərhɛndlər], *m.* (**—s**, *pl.* **—**) negotiator, mediator.

Unterhandlung [untər'handluŋ], *f.* (**—**, *pl.* **—en**) negotiation.

Unterhaus ['untərhaus], *n.* (**—es**, *pl.* **̈er**) ground floor; (*Parl.*) lower house; House of Commons.

Unterhemd ['untərhɛmt], *n.* (**—(e)s**, *pl.* **—en**) vest.

unterhöhlen [untər'hø:lən], *v.a. insep.* undermine.

Unterholz ['untərhɔlts], *n.* (**—es**, *no pl.*) undergrowth, underwood.

Unterhosen ['untərho:zən], *f. pl.* (*women*) briefs; (*men*) underpants.

unterirdisch ['untərɪrdɪʃ], *adj.* subterranean, underground.

unterjochen [untər'jɔxən], *v.a. insep.* subjugate, subdue.

Unterkiefer ['untərki:fər], *m.* (**—s**, *pl.* **—**) lower jaw.

Unterkleid ['untərklaɪt], *n.* (**—s**, *pl.* **—er**) under-garment.

unterkommen ['untərkɔmən], *v.n. irr.* (*aux.* sein) find accommodation *or* shelter; (*fig.*) find employment.

Unterkommen ['untərkɔmən], *n.* (**—s**, *no pl.*) shelter, accommodation; (*fig.*) employment, place.

Unterkörper ['untərkœrpər], *m.* (**—s**, *pl.* **—**) lower part of the body.

unterkriegen ['untərkri:gən], *v.a.* get the better of; *lass dich nicht* **—**, stand firm.

Unterkunft ['untərkunft], *f.* (**—**, *pl.* **̈e**) shelter, accommodation; employment.

Unterlage ['untərla:gə], *f.* (**—**, *pl.* **—n**) foundation, base; blotting pad; (*pl.*) documents, files.

unterlassen [untər'lasən], *v.a. irr. insep.* omit (to do), fail (to do), neglect; forbear.

Unterlassung [untər'lasuŋ], *f.* (**—**, *pl.* **—en**) omission, neglect.

Unterlassungssünde [untər'lasuŋszyndə], *f.* (**—**, *pl.* **—n**) sin of omission.

Unterlauf ['untərlauf], *m.* (**—(e)s**, *pl.* **̈e**) (*river*) lower course.

Unterlaufen

unterlaufen [untər'laufən], *v.n. irr.*
insep. (aux. sein) run under; *(mistake)*
creep in. — *adj.* suffused, blood-shot.
unterlegen (1) ['untərle:gən], *v.a.* lay
under; *einen anderen Sinn —,* put a
different construction upon.
unterlegen (2) [untər'le:gən], *adj.*
inferior.
Unterleib ['untərlaɪp], *m.* (—s, *no pl.*)
abdomen.
unterliegen [untər'li:gən], *v.n. irr.*
insep. (aux. sein) succumb, be
overcome; be subject (to).
Untermieter ['untərmi:tər], *m.* (—s,
pl. —) subtenant.
unterminieren [untərmi'ni:rən], *v.a.*
insep. undermine.
unternehmen [untər'ne:mən], *v.a. irr.*
insep. undertake, take upon o.s.,
attempt.
Unternehmen [untər'ne:mən], *n.* (—s,
pl. —) enterprise, undertaking.
unternehmend [untər'ne:mənt], *adj.*
bold, enterprising.
Unternehmer [untər'ne:mər], *m.* (—s,
pl. —) contractor, entrepreneur.
Unteroffizier ['untərɔfitsi:r], *m.* (—s,
pl. —e) *(army)* non-commissioned
officer; *(navy)* petty officer.
unterordnen ['untərɔrdnən], *v.a.*
subordinate. — *v.r. sich —,* submit
(to).
Unterordnung ['untərɔrdnuŋ], *f.* (—,
no pl.) subordination, submission;
(Biol.) sub-order.
Unterpacht ['untərpaxt], *f.* (—, *no pl.)*
sublease.
Unterpfand ['untərpfant], *n.* (—(e)s,
no pl.) (obs.) pawn, pledge.
Unterredung [untər're:duŋ], *f.* (—,
pl. —en) conference, interview, talk.
Unterricht ['untərrɪçt], *m.* (—(e)s, *no
pl.)* instruction, tuition, teaching.
unterrichten [untər'rɪçtən], *v.a. insep.*
instruct, teach.
Unterrichtsanstalt ['untərrɪçtsanʃtalt],
f. (—, *pl.* —en) educational establishment *or* institution.
Unterrichtsgegenstand ['untərrɪçts-
ge:gənʃtant], *m.* (—s, *pl.* ⁻e) subject
of instruction.
Unterrock ['untərrɔk], *m.* (—s, *pl.* ⁻e)
petticoat, slip; underskirt.
untersagen [untər'za:gən], *v.a. insep.*
forbid; *Rauchen untersagt,* smoking
prohibited.
Untersatz ['untərzats], *m.* (—es, *pl.*
⁻e) basis, holder, stand, trestle;
saucer.
unterschätzen [untər'ʃetsən], *v.a.*
insep. underrate, underestimate.
unterscheiden [untər'ʃaɪdən], *v.a. irr.*
insep. distinguish, discriminate,
discern, differentiate. — *v.r. sich —,*
differ; *ich kann sie nicht —,* I cannot
tell them apart.
Unterscheidung [untər'ʃaɪduŋ], *f.* (—,
pl. —en) distinction, differentiation.
Unterscheidungsmerkmal [untər-

'ʃaɪduŋsmerkma:l], *n.* (—s, *pl.* —e)
distinctive mark, characteristic.
Unterscheidungsvermögen [untər-
'ʃaɪduŋsfermø:gən], *n.* (—s, *no pl.)*
power of discrimination.
Unterscheidungszeichen [untər'ʃaɪ-
duŋstsaɪçən], *n.* (—s, *pl.* —) criterion.
Unterschenkel ['untərʃɛŋkəl], *m.* (—s,
pl. —) shank, lower part of the thigh.
Unterschicht ['untərʃɪçt], *f.* (—, *pl.*
—en) substratum, subsoil.
unterschieben (1) ['untərʃi:bən], *v.a.*
irr. substitute; interpolate; forge;
foist upon.
unterschieben (2) [untər'ʃi:bən], *v.a.*
irr. insep. (fig.) attribute falsely, pass
s.o. off as.
Unterschiebung [untər'ʃi:buŋ], *f.* (—,
pl. —en) substitution; forgery.
Unterschied ['untərʃi:t], *m.* (—(e)s,
pl. —e) difference.
unterschiedlich ['untərʃi:tlɪç], *adj.*
different, diverse.
unterschiedslos ['untərʃi:tslo:s], *adv.*
indiscriminately.
unterschlagen [untər'ʃla:gən], *v.a. irr.*
insep. embezzle, intercept.
Unterschlagung [untər'ʃla:guŋ], *f.*
(—, *pl.* —en) embezzlement.
Unterschlupf ['untərʃlupf], *m.* (—es,
pl. ⁻e) shelter, refuge.
unterschlüpfen ['untərʃlypfən], *v.n.*
(aux. sein) find shelter, slip away;
(fig.) hide.
unterschreiben [untər'ʃraɪbən], *v.a.*
irr. insep. sign, subscribe to.
Unterschrift ['untərʃrɪft], *f.* (—, *pl.*
—en) signature.
Unterseeboot ['untərze:bo:t], *n.* (—s,
pl. —e) submarine.
untersetzt [untər'zetst], *adj.* thickset,
dumpy.
untersinken ['untərzɪŋkən], *v.n. irr.*
(aux. sein) go down.
unterst ['untərst], *adj.* lowest, under-
most, bottom.
Unterstaatssekretär [untər'ʃta:tsse-
krete:r], *m.* (—s, *pl.* —e) under-
secretary of state.
unterstehen (1) ['untərʃte:ən], *v.n. irr.*
(aux. sein) find shelter (under).
unterstehen (2) [untər'ʃte:ən], *v.n. irr.*
insep. be subordinate. — *v.r. sich —,*
dare, venture.
unterstellen (1) ['untərʃtelən], *v.a.*
place under. — *v.r. sich —,* take
shelter (under).
unterstellen (2) [untər'ʃtelən], *v.a.*
insep. put under the authority of;
impute (s.th. to s.o.).
Unterstellung [untər'ʃteluŋ], *f.* (—,
pl. —en) imputation, insinuation.
unterstreichen [untər'ʃtraɪçən], *v.a.*
irr. insep. underline.
Unterstreichung [untər'ʃtraɪçuŋ], *f.*
(—, *pl.* —en) underlining.
Unterströmung [untər'ʃtrø:muŋ], *f.*
(—, *pl.* —en) undercurrent.
unterstützen [untər'ʃtytsən], *v.a. insep.*
support, assist, aid; *(fig.)* countenance.

unvereinbar

Unterstützung [untər'ʃtytsuŋ], *f.* (—, *pl.* —en) support, aid, assistance, relief.

Unterstützungsanstalt[untər'ʃtytsuŋs-anʃtalt], *f.* (—, *pl.* —en) charitable institution.

unterstützungsbedürftig [untər'ʃtyt-suŋsbədyrftiç], *adj.* indigent.

untersuchen [untər'zu:xən], *v.a. insep.* investigate, examine, look over.

Untersuchung [untər'zu:xuŋ], *f.* (—, *pl.* —en) investigation, inquiry; (*medical*) examination.

Untersuchungshaft [untər'zu:xuŋs-haft], *f.* (—, *no pl.*) imprisonment pending investigation.

Untersuchungsrichter [untər'zu:-xuŋsrıçtər], *m.* (—s, *pl.* —) examining magistrate.

Untertan ['untərta:n], *m.* (—s, *pl.* —en) subject, vassal.

untertan ['untərta:n], *adj.* subject.

untertänig ['untərte:nıç], *adj.* humble, obsequious, submissive, servile.

Untertasse ['untərtasə], *f.* (—, *pl.* —n) saucer.

untertauchen ['untərtauxən], *v.a.* dip, duck, submerge. — *v.n.* (*aux.* sein) dive.

unterwegs [untər've:ks], *adv.* on the way.

unterweisen [untər'vaɪzən], *v.a. irr. insep.* teach, instruct.

Unterweisung [untər'vaɪzuŋ], *f.* (—, *pl.* —en) instruction, teaching.

Unterwelt ['untərvɛlt], *f.* (—, *no pl.*) Hades, the underworld.

unterwerfen [untər'vɛrfən], *v.a. irr. insep.* subject, subdue. — *v.r. sich* —, submit (to), resign o.s. (to).

Unterwerfung [untər'vɛrfuŋ], *f.* (—, *no pl.*) subjection, submission.

unterwühlen [untər'vy:lən], *v.a. insep.* root up; (*fig.*) undermine.

unterwürfig [untər'vyrfıç], *adj.* submissive, subject; obsequious.

Unterwürfigkeit [untər'vyrfıçkaɪt], *f.* (—, *no pl.*) submissiveness; obsequiousness.

unterzeichnen [untər'tsaɪçnən], *v.a. insep.* sign.

Unterzeichner [untər'tsaɪçnər], *m.* (—s, *pl.* —) signatory; (*insurance*) underwriter.

Unterzeichnete [untər'tsaɪçnətə], *m.* (—n, *pl.* —n) undersigned.

Unterzeichnung [untər'tsaɪçnuŋ], *f.* (—, *pl.* —en) signature.

unterziehen [untər'tsi:ən], *v.r. irr. insep. sich* —, submit to, undertake; (*operation*) undergo.

Untiefe ['unti:fə], *f.* (—, *pl.* —n) shallow water, flat, shoal, sands.

Untier ['unti:r], *n.* (—s, *pl.* —e) monster.

untilgbar ['untılkba:r], *adj.* indelible; (*debt*) irredeemable.

untrennbar ['untrɛnba:r], *adj.* inseparable.

untreu ['untrɔy], *adj.* faithless, unfaithful, disloyal, perfidious.

Untreue ['untrɔyə], *f.* (—, *no pl.*) faithlessness, unfaithfulness, disloyalty, perfidy.

untröstlich ['untrø:stlıç], *adj.* inconsolable, disconsolate.

untrüglich ['untry:klıç], *adj.* unmistakable, infallible.

untüchtig ['untyçtıç], *adj.* inefficient; incompetent.

unüberlegt ['uny:bərle:kt], *adj.* inconsiderate, thoughtless; rash.

unübersehbar ['uny:bərze:ba:r], *adj.* immense, vast.

unübersteiglich ['uny:bərʃtaıklıç], *adj.* insurmountable.

unübertrefflich ['uny:bərtrɛflıç], *adj.* unsurpassable, unequalled, unrivalled.

unübertroffen ['uny:bərtrɔfən], *adj.* unsurpassed.

unüberwindlich ['uny:bərvıntlıç], *adj.* invincible, unconquerable.

unumgänglich ['unumgɛnlıç], *adj.* indispensable, unavoidable, inevitable.

unumschränkt ['unumʃrɛŋkt], *adj.* unlimited, absolute.

unumstößlich ['unumʃtø:slıç], *adj.* irrefutable.

unumwunden ['unumvundən], *adj.* frank, plain.

ununterbrochen ['ununtərbrɔxən], *adj.* uninterrupted, unremitting.

unveränderlich ['unfɛrɛndərlıç], *adj.* unchangeable, unalterable.

unverändert ['unfɛrɛndərt], *adj.* unchanged, unaltered.

unverantwortlich ['unfɛrantvɔrtlıç], *adj.* irresponsible, inexcusable, unjustifiable.

unveräußerlich ['unfɛrɔysərlıç], *adj.* not for sale; inalienable.

unverbesserlich ['unfɛrbɛsərlıç], *adj.* incorrigible.

unverbindlich ['unfɛrbɪntlıç], *adj.* not binding, without prejudice, without obligation.

unverblümt ['unfɛrblymt], *adj.* blunt, point-blank.

unverbrennlich ['unfɛrbrɛnlıç], *adj.* incombustible.

unverbrüchlich ['unfɛrbryçlıç], *adj.* inviolable.

unverbürgt ['unfɛrbyrkt], *adj.* unwarranted, unofficial; unconfirmed.

unverdaulich ['unfɛrdaulıç], *adj.* indigestible.

unverdaut ['unfɛrdaut], *adj.* undigested.

unverdient ['unfɛrdi:nt], *adj.* unmerited, undeserved.

unverdientermaßen ['unfɛrdi:ntərma:sən], *adv.* undeservedly.

unverdorben ['unfɛrdɔrbən], *adj.* unspoiled, uncorrupted, innocent.

unverdrossen ['unfɛrdrɔsən], *adj.* indefatigable.

unvereidigt ['unfɛraɪdıçt], *adj.* unsworn.

unvereinbar ['unfɛraɪnba:r], *adj.* incompatible, inconsistent.

247

Unvereinbarkeit

Unvereinbarkeit ['unfɛraɪnba:rkaɪt], *f.* (—, *no pl.*) incompatibility, inconsistency.

unverfälscht ['unfɛrfɛlʃt], *adj.* unadulterated, genuine, pure.

unverfänglich ['unfɛrfɛŋlɪç], *adj.* harmless.

unverfroren ['unfɛrfro:rən], *adj.* cheeky, impudent.

unvergeßlich ['unfɛrgɛslɪç], *adj.* memorable, not to be forgotten, unforgettable.

unvergleichlich ['unfɛrglaɪçlɪç], *adj.* incomparable.

unverhältnismäßig ['unfɛrhɛltnɪsmɛ:sɪç], *adj.* disproportionate.

unverheiratet ['unfɛrhaɪra:tət], *adj.* unmarried.

unverhofft ['unfɛrhɔft], *adj.* unexpected.

unverhohlen ['unfɛrho:lən], *adj.* unconcealed, undisguised, candid.

unverkennbar ['unfɛrkɛnba:r], *adj.* unmistakable.

unverlangt ['unfɛrlaŋkt], *adj.* unsolicited, not ordered.

unverletzlich ['unfɛrlɛtslɪç], *adj.* invulnerable; (*fig.*) inviolable.

unverletzt ['unfɛrlɛtst], *adj.* (*persons*) unhurt; (*things*) undamaged, intact.

unvermeidlich ['unfɛrmaɪtlɪç], *adj.* inevitable, unavoidable.

unvermindert ['unfɛrmɪndərt], *adj.* undiminished.

unvermittelt ['unfɛrmɪtəlt], *adj.* sudden, abrupt.

Unvermögen ['unfɛrmø:gən], *n.* (—s, *no pl.*) inability, incapacity.

unvermögend ['unfɛrmø:gənt], *adj.* incapable; impecunious.

unvermutet ['unfɛrmu:tət], *adj.* unexpected, unforeseen.

unverrichtet ['unfɛrrɪçtət], *adj. —er Sache,* empty-handed; unsuccessfully.

unverschämt ['unfɛrʃɛ:mt], *adj.* impudent, brazen.

unverschuldet ['unfɛrʃuldət], *adj.* not in debt, unencumbered; (*fig.*) undeserved.

unversehens ['unfɛrze:əns], *adv.* unexpectedly, unawares.

unversehrt ['unfɛrze:rt], *adv.* (*persons*) unhurt, safe; (*things*) undamaged.

unversiegbar ['unfɛrzi:kba:r], *adj.* inexhaustible.

unversiegt ['unfɛrzi:kt], *adj.* unexhausted.

unversöhnlich ['unfɛrzø:nlɪç], *adj.* implacable, irreconcilable.

unversöhnt ['unfɛrzø:nt], *adj.* unreconciled.

unversorgt ['unfɛrzɔrkt], *adj.* unprovided for.

Unverstand ['unfɛrʃtant], *m.* (—(e)s, *no pl.*) want of judgment, indiscretion.

unverständig ['unfɛrʃtɛndɪç], *adj.* foolish, unwise, imprudent.

unverständlich ['unfɛrʃtɛntlɪç], *adj.* unintelligible, incomprehensible.

unversteuert ['unfɛrʃtɔyərt], *adj.* with duty *or* tax unpaid.

unversucht ['unfɛrzu:xt], *adj.* untried; *nichts — lassen,* leave no stone unturned.

unverträglich ['unfɛrtrɛ:klɪç], *adj.* quarrelsome.

unverwandt ['unfɛrvant], *adj.* unrelated; fixed, constant; immovable.

unverwundbar ['unfɛrvuntba:r], *adj.* invulnerable.

unverwüstlich ['unfɛrvy:stlɪç], *adj.* indestructible.

unverzagt ['unfɛrtsa:kt], *adj.* undaunted, intrepid.

unverzeihlich ['unfɛrtsaɪlɪç], *adj.* unpardonable.

unverzinslich ['unfɛrtsɪnslɪç], *adj.* (*money*) gaining no interest.

unverzollt ['unfɛrtsɔlt], *adj.* duty unpaid.

unverzüglich ['unfɛrtsy:klɪç], *adj.* immediate.

unvollendet ['unfɔlɛndət], *adj.* unfinished.

unvollständig ['unfɔlʃtɛndɪç], *adj.* incomplete.

unvorbereitet ['unfo:rbəraɪtət], *adj.* unprepared.

unvordenklich ['unfo:rdɛŋklɪç], *adj. seit —en Zeiten,* from time immemorial.

unvorhergesehen ['unfo:rhe:rgəze:ən], *adj.* unforeseen, unlooked for.

unvorsichtig ['unfo:rzɪçtɪç], *adj.* imprudent, incautious, careless.

unvorteilhaft ['unfɔrtaɪlhaft], *adj.* unprofitable, disadvantageous; *— aussehen,* not look o.'s best.

unwägbar ['unve:kba:r], *adj.* imponderable.

unwahr ['unva:r], *adj.* untrue, false.

Unwahrhaftigkeit ['unva:rhaftɪçkaɪt], *f.* (—, *no pl.*) want of truthfulness, unreliability, dishonesty.

Unwahrheit ['unva:rhaɪt], *f.* (—, *pl.* —en) lie, untruth, falsehood.

unwegsam ['unve:kza:m], *adj.* impassable, impracticable.

unweigerlich ['unvaɪgərlɪç], *adj.* unhesitating, unquestioning. *— adv.* without fail.

unweit ['unvaɪt], *prep.* (*Genit.*) not far from, near.

Unwesen ['unve:zən], *n.* (—s, *no pl.*) nuisance; *sein — treiben,* be up to o.'s tricks.

Unwetter ['unvɛtər], *n.* (—s, *pl.* —) bad weather, thunderstorm.

unwichtig ['unvɪçtɪç], *adj.* unimportant; insignificant, of no consequence.

unwiderleglich ['unvi:dərle:klɪç], *adj.* irrefutable.

unwiderruflich ['unvi:dərru:flɪç], *adj.* irrevocable.

unwidersprechlich ['unvi:dərʃprɛçlɪç], *adj.* incontestable.

unwidersprochen ['unvi:dərʃprɔxən], *adj.* uncontradicted.

unwiderstehlich ['unvi:dərʃte:lIç], *adj.* irresistible.
unwiederbringlich ['unvi:dərbrɪŋlɪç], *adj.* irrecoverable, irretrievable.
Unwille ['unvɪlə], *m.* (**—ns**, *no pl.*) displeasure, indignation.
unwillkürlich ['unvɪlky:rlɪç], *adj.* involuntary; instinctive.
unwirsch ['unvɪrʃ], *adj.* petulant, testy; curt, uncivil.
unwirtlich ['unvɪrtlɪç], *adj.* inhospitable.
unwirtschaftlich ['unvɪrtʃaftlɪç], *adj.* not economic, uneconomic.
unwissend ['unvɪsənt], *adj.* illiterate, ignorant.
Unwissenheit ['unvɪsənhaɪt], *f.* (**—**, *no pl.*) ignorance.
unwissenschaftlich ['unvɪsənʃaftlɪç], *adj.* unscholarly; unscientific.
unwissentlich ['unvɪsəntlɪç], *adv.* unknowingly, unconsciously.
unwohl ['unvo:l], *adj.* unwell, indisposed.
Unwohlsein ['unvo:lzaɪn], *n.* (**—s**, *no pl.*) indisposition.
unwürdig ['unvyrdɪç], *adj.* unworthy, undeserving.
Unzahl ['untsa:l], *f.* (**—**, *no pl.*) vast number.
unzählbar [un'tsɛ:lba:r], *adj.* innumerable, numberless.
unzählig [un'tsɛ:lIç], *adj.* innumerable; *—e Male*, over and over again.
unzart ['untsa:rt], *adj.* indelicate, rude, rough; unceremonious.
Unzeit ['untsaɪt], *f.* (**—**, *no pl.*) *zur —*, out of season, inopportunely.
unzeitgemäß ['untsaɪtgəmɛ:s], *adj.* out of date, behind the times; unfashionable.
unzeitig ['untsaɪtɪç], *adj.* unseasonable; untimely, inopportune.
unziemlich ['untsi:mlɪç], *adj.* unseemly, unbecoming.
Unzier ['untsi:r], *f.* (**—**, *no pl.*) disfigurement; flaw.
Unzucht ['untsuxt], *f.* (**—**, *no pl.*) unchastity; lewdness; fornication.
unzüchtig ['untsyçtɪç], *adj.* unchaste, lascivious, lewd.
unzufrieden ['untsufri:dən], *adj.* discontented, dissatisfied.
unzugänglich ['untsugɛnlɪç], *adj.* inaccessible.
unzulänglich ['untsulɛŋlɪç], *adj.* inadequate, insufficient.
Unzulänglichkeit ['untsulɛŋlɪçkaɪt], *f.* (**—**, *no pl.*) inadequacy.
unzulässig ['untsulɛsɪç], *adj.* inadmissible.
unzurechnungsfähig ['untsurɛçnuŋsfɛ:ɪç], *adj.* not accountable (for o.'s actions), non compos mentis, insane.
Unzurechnungsfähigkeit ['untsurɛçnuŋsfɛ:ɪçkaɪt], *f.* (**—**, *no pl.*) irresponsibility; feeblemindedness.
unzusammenhängend ['untsuzamənhɛŋənt], *adj.* incoherent.
unzuständig ['untsuʃtɛndɪç], *adj.* incompetent, not competent (*Law etc.*).

unzuträglich ['untsutrɛ:klɪç], *adj.* unwholesome.
unzutreffend ['untsutrɛfənt], *adj.* inapposite; unfounded; inapplicable.
unzuverlässig ['untsufɛrlɛsɪç], *adj.* unreliable.
unzweckmäßig ['untsvɛkmɛ:sɪç], *adj.* inexpedient.
unzweideutig ['untsvaɪdɔytɪç], *adj.* unequivocal, explicit, unambiguous.
üppig ['yptɪç], *adj.* abundant; opulent; luxurious, luxuriant; voluptuous.
uralt ['u:ralt], *adj.* very old, old as the hills; ancient.
uranfänglich ['u:ranfɛŋlɪç], *adj.* primordial, primeval.
Uraufführung ['u:rauffy:ruŋ], *f.* (**—**, *pl.* **—en**) (*Theat.*) first night, première.
urbar ['u:rba:r], *adj.* arable, under cultivation; *— machen*, cultivate.
Urbarmachung ['u:rba:rmaxuŋ], *f.* (**—**, *no pl.*) cultivation.
Urbild ['u:rbɪlt], *n.* (**—(e)s**, *pl.* **—er**) prototype; (*fig.*) ideal.
ureigen ['u:raɪgən], *adj.* quite original; idiosyncratic.
Ureltern ['u:rɛltərn], *pl.* ancestors.
Urenkel ['u:rɛŋkəl], *m.* (**—s**, *pl.* **—**) great-grandson, great-grandchild.
Urenkelin ['u:rɛŋkəlɪn], *f.* (**—**, *pl.* **—nen**) great-granddaughter.
Urfehde ['u:rfe:də], *f.* (**—**, *no pl.*) oath to keep the peace.
Urform ['u:rfɔrm], *f.* (**—**, *pl.* **—en**) primitive form; original form; archetype.
Urgroßmutter ['u:rgro:smutər], *f.* (**—**, *pl.* ⸚) great-grandmother.
Urgroßvater ['u:rgro:sfa:tər], *m.* (**—s**, *pl.* ⸚) great-grandfather.
Urheber ['u:rhe:bər], *m.* (**—s**, *pl.* **—**) author, originator.
Urheberrecht ['u:rhe:bərrɛçt], *n.* (**—s**, *pl.* **—e**) copyright.
Urheberschaft ['u:rhe:bərʃaft], *f.* (**—**, *no pl.*) authorship.
Urin [u'ri:n], *m.* (**—s**, *no pl.*) urine.
Urkunde ['u:rkundə], *f.* (**—**, *pl.* **—n**) document, deed, charter; *zur dessen*, (*obs.*) in witness whereof.
Urkundenbeweis ['u:rkundənbavaɪs], *m.* (**—es**, *pl.* **—e**) documentary evidence.
urkundlich ['u:rkuntlɪç], *adj.* documentary.
Urlaub ['u:rlaup], *m.* (**—s**, *pl.* **—e**) leave of absence; vacation; (*Mil.*) furlough.
urplötzlich ['u:rplœtslɪç], *adj.* sudden. *— adv.* all at once, suddenly.
Urquell ['u:rkvɛl], *m.* (**—s**, *pl.* **—en**) fountain-head, original source.
Ursache ['u:rzaxə], *f.* (**—**, *pl.* **—n**) cause; *keine —*, don't mention it.
Urschrift ['u:rʃrɪft], *f.* (**—**, *pl.* **—en**) original text.
Ursprache ['u:rʃpra:xə], *f.* (**—**, *pl.* **—n**) original language.
Ursprung ['u:rʃpruŋ], *m.* (**—s**, *pl.* ⸚e) origin; extraction.

ursprünglich [ˈuːrʃpryŋlɪç], *adj.* original.

Urteil [ˈurtaɪl], *n.* (—s, *pl.* —e) opinion; (*Law*) judgment, verdict, sentence; *ein — fällen,* pass judgment on; *nach meinem —,* in my opinion.

urteilen [ˈurtaɪlən], *v.n.* judge.

Urteilsspruch [ˈurtaɪlsʃprux], *m.* (—s, *pl.* ¨e) judgment, sentence.

Uruguay [uruˈgwaːɪ], *n.* Uruguay.

Urureltern [ˈuːruːrɛltərn], *pl.* ancestors.

Urvater [ˈuːrfaːtər], *m.* (—s, *pl.* ¨) forefather.

Urvolk [ˈuːrfɔlk], *n.* (—(e)s, *pl.* ¨er) primitive people, aborigines.

Urwald [ˈuːrvalt], *m.* (—(e)s, *pl.* ¨er) primæval forest, virgin forest.

Urwelt [ˈuːrvɛlt], *f.* (—, *no pl.*) primæval world.

Urzeit [ˈuːrtsaɪt], *f.* (—, *pl.* —en) prehistoric times.

V

V [fau], *n.* (—s, *pl.* —s) the letter V.

Vagabund [vagaˈbunt], *m.* (—en, *pl.* —en) vagabond, tramp; (*Am.*) hobo.

vag [ˈvaːk], *adj.* vague.

Vakuumbremse [ˈvaːkuumbrɛmzə], *f.* (—, *pl.* —n) air-brake, vacuum-brake.

Vase [ˈvaːzə], *f.* (—, *pl.* —n) vase.

Vater [ˈfaːtər], *m.* (—s, *pl.* ¨) father.

Vaterland [ˈfaːtərlant], *n.* (—(e)s, *pl.* ¨er) mother-country, native country; —*sliebe,* patriotism.

vaterländisch [ˈfaːtərlendɪʃ], *adj.* patriotic.

vaterlandslos [ˈfaːtərlantsloːs], *adj.* having no mother country; unpatriotic.

väterlich [ˈfɛːtərlɪç], *adj.* fatherly, paternal. — *adv.* like a father.

vaterlos [ˈfaːtərloːs], *adj.* fatherless.

Vatermord [ˈfaːtərmɔrt], *m.* (—(e)s, *pl.* —e) parricide; patricide.

Vatermörder [ˈfaːtərmœrdər], *m.* (—s, *pl.* —) parricide; (*fig.*) high *or* stand-up collar.

Vaterschaft [ˈfaːtərʃaft], *f.* (—, *no pl.*) paternity.

Vatersname [ˈfaːtərsnaːmə], *m.* (—ns, *pl.* —n) surname, family name.

Vaterstadt [ˈfaːtərʃtat], *f.* (—, *pl.* ¨e) native town.

Vaterstelle [ˈfaːtərʃtelə], *f.* (—, *pl.* —n) — *vertreten,* act as a father, be a father (to).

Vaterunser [faːtərˈunzər], *n.* (—s, *pl.* —) Lord's Prayer.

Vatikan [vatiˈkaːn], *m.* (—s, *no pl.*) Vatican.

vegetieren [vegeˈtiːrən], *v.n.* vegetate.

Veilchen [ˈfaɪlçən], *n.* (—s, *pl.* — (*Bot.*) violet.

Vene [ˈveːnə], *f.* (—, *pl.* —n) vein.

Venezuela [vɛnətsuˈeːla], *n.* Venezuela.

Ventil [vɛnˈtiːl], *n.* (—s, *pl.* —e) valve.

ventilieren [vɛntiˈliːrən], *v.a.* ventilate, air; (*fig.*) discuss, ventilate.

verabfolgen [fɛrˈapfɔlgən], *v.a.* deliver, hand over, remit; serve.

Verabfolgung [fɛrˈapfɔlguŋ], *f.* (—, *no pl.*) delivery.

verabreden [fɛrˈapreːdən], *v.a.* agree (upon); stipulate; *etwas mit einem —,* agree on s.th. with s.o. — *v.r. sich mit einem —,* make an appointment with s.o.; (*coll.*) have a date.

Verabredung [fɛrˈapreːduŋ], *f.* (—, *pl.* —en) agreement, arrangement, appointment; (*coll.*) date.

verabreichen [fɛrˈapraɪçən], *v.a.* deliver, dispense.

verabsäumen [fɛrˈapzɔymən], *v.a.* neglect, omit.

verabscheuen [fɛrˈapʃɔyən], *v.a.* detest, loathe, abhor.

Verabscheuung [fɛrˈapʃɔyuŋ], *f.* (—, *no pl.*) abhorrence, detestation, loathing.

verabscheuungswürdig [fɛrˈapʃɔyuŋsvyrdɪç], *adj.* abominable, detestable.

verabschieden [fɛrˈapʃiːdən], *v.a.* dismiss, discharge. — *v.r. sich —,* take leave, say good-bye; (*Pol.*) pass (of an Act).

Verabschiedung [fɛrˈapʃiːduŋ], *f.* (—, *no pl.*) dismissal; discharge; (*Pol.*) passing (of an Act).

verachten [fɛrˈaxtən], *v.a.* despise, scorn.

verächtlich [fɛrˈɛçtlɪç], *adj.* despicable, contemptible; contemptuous, scornful.

Verachtung [fɛrˈaxtuŋ], *f.* (—, *no pl.*) contempt, disdain, scorn.

verallgemeinern [fɛralgəˈmaɪnərn], *v.a.*, *v.n.* generalise.

veralten [fɛrˈaltən], *v.n.* (*aux.* sein) become obsolete, date.

veraltet [fɛrˈaltət], *adj.* obsolete.

Veranda [veˈranda], *f.* (—, *pl.* —den) verandah, porch.

veränderlich [fɛrˈɛndərlɪç], *adj.* changeable, variable; (*fig.*) inconstant, fickle.

verändern [fɛrˈɛndərn], *v.a.* change, alter. — *v.r. sich —,* change, vary; change o.'s job.

verankern [fɛrˈaŋkərn], *v.a.* anchor.

veranlagt [fɛrˈanlaːkt], *adj.* inclined; gifted; having a propensity (to); *gut —,* talented; (*tax*) assessed.

Veranlagung [fɛrˈanlaːguŋ], *f.* (—, *pl.* —en) bent; talent: predisposition; (*tax*) assessment.

veranlassen [fɛrˈanlasən], *v.a.* bring about, cause, motivate; *einen —,* induce s.o., cause s.o.; *etwas —,* bring s.th. about, cause s.th.

Veranlassung [fɛr'anlasuŋ], *f.* (—, *no pl.*) cause, motive; occasion; inducement; *auf seine* —, at his suggestion; *ohne irgend eine* —, without the slightest provocation.

veranschaulichen [fɛr'anʃaulıçən], *v.a.* illustrate, make clear.

veranschlagen [fɛr'anʃlaːgən], *v.a.* estimate, assess.

Veranschlagung [fɛr'anʃlaːguŋ], *f.* (—, *pl.* —en) estimate.

veranstalten [fɛr'anʃtaltən], *v.a.* organise, arrange.

Veranstalter [fɛr'anʃtaltər], *m.* (—s, *pl.* —) organiser.

Veranstaltung [fɛr'anʃtaltuŋ], *f.* (—, *pl.* —en) arrangement; entertainment; show; event; (sporting) fixture.

verantworten [fɛr'antvɔrtən], *v.a.* account for. — *v.r. sich* —, answer (for), justify o.s.

verantwortlich [fɛr'antvɔrtlıç], *adj.* responsible, answerable, accountable.

Verantwortlichkeit [fɛr'antvɔrtlıçkaıt], *f.* (—, *no pl.*) responsibility.

Verantwortung [fɛr'antvɔrtuŋ], *f.* (—, *no pl.*) responsibility, justification, excuse; defence; *auf deine* —, at your own risk; *einen zur* — *ziehen*, call s.o. to account.

verantwortungsvoll [fɛr'antvɔrtuŋsfɔl], *adj.* responsible.

verarbeiten [fɛr'arbaıtən], *v.a.* manufacture, process; (*fig.*) digest.

Verarbeitung [fɛr'arbaıtuŋ], *f.* (—, *no pl.*) manufacture; process; finish; (*fig.*) digestion.

verargen [fɛr'argən], *v.a. einem etwas* —, blame *or* reproach s.o. for s.th.

verärgern [fɛr'ɛrgərn], *v.a.* annoy, make angry.

Verarmung [fɛr'armuŋ], *f.* (—, *no pl.*) impoverishment.

verausgaben [fɛr'ausgaːbən], *v.r. sich* —, overspend, run short of money; spend o.s., wear o.s. out.

veräußern [fɛr'ɔysərn], *v.a.* dispose of, sell.

Veräußerung [fɛr'ɔysəruŋ], *f.* (—, *no pl.*) sale; alienation.

Verband [fɛr'bant], *m.* (—s, *pl.* ⁻e) bandage, dressing; association, union; unit.

verbannen [fɛr'banən], *v.a.* banish, exile, outlaw.

Verbannte [fɛr'bantə], *m.* (—n, *pl.* —n) exile, outlaw.

Verbannung [fɛr'banuŋ], *f.* (—, *pl.* —en) banishment, exile.

verbauen [fɛr'bauən], *v.n.* obstruct; build up; use up *or* spend in building.

verbeißen [fɛr'baısən], *v.a. irr. sich etwas* —, suppress s.th.; *sich das Lachen* —, stifle a laugh. — *v.r. sich in etwas* —, stick doggedly to s.th.

verbergen [fɛr'bɛrgən], *v.a. irr.* conceal, hide.

verbessern [fɛr'bɛsərn], *v.a.* improve, correct, mend.

Verbesserung [fɛr'bɛsəruŋ], *f.* (—, *pl.* —en) improvement; correction.

verbeugen [fɛr'bɔygən], *v.r. sich* —, bow.

Verbeugung [fɛr'bɔyguŋ], *f.* (—, *pl.* —en) bow, obeisance.

verbiegen [fɛr'biːgən], *v.a. irr.* twist, distort, bend the wrong way.

verbieten [fɛr'biːtən], *v.a. irr.* forbid, prohibit.

verbilligen [fɛr'bıllıgən], *v.a.* cheapen, reduce the price of.

verbinden [fɛr'bındən], *v.a. irr.* tie up, bind up, connect; (*Med.*) dress, bandage; unite, join; *die Augen* —, blindfold. — *v.r. sich* —, unite, join; (*Chem.*) combine.

verbindlich [fɛr'bıntlıç], *adj.* binding; obligatory; obliging; —*en Dank*, my best thanks.

Verbindlichkeit [fɛr'bıntlıçkaıt], *f.* (—, *pl.* —en) liability, obligation; compliment.

Verbindung [fɛr'bınduŋ], *f.* (—, *pl.* —en) connexion, connection, junction; association; alliance; (*Railw.*) connection; (*Chem.*) compound.

Verbindungsglied [fɛr'bınduŋsgliːt], *n.* (—(e)s, *pl.* —er) connecting link.

Verbindungslinie [fɛr'bınduŋsliːnjə], *f.* (—, *pl.* —n) line of communication.

verbissen [fɛr'bısən], *adj.* obstinate, grim; soured. — *adv.* doggedly.

verbitten [fɛr'bıtən], *v.a. irr. sich etwas* —, forbid s.th. determinedly; insist on s.th. not being done, object to.

verbittern [fɛr'bıtərn], *v.a.* embitter.

Verbitterung [fɛr'bıtəruŋ], *f.* (—, *no pl.*) exasperation.

verblassen [fɛr'blasən], *v.n.* (*aux. sein*) turn pale.

Verbleib [fɛr'blaıp], *m.* (—(e)s, *no pl.*) whereabouts.

verbleiben [fɛr'blaıbən], *v.n. irr.* (*aux. sein*) remain.

verblenden [fɛr'blɛndən], *v.a.* dazzle, delude, blind.

Verblendung [fɛr'blɛnduŋ], *f.* (—, *no pl.*) infatuation; delusion.

verblüffen [fɛr'blyfən], *v.n.* amaze, stagger, dumbfound.

Verblüffung [fɛr'blyfuŋ], *f.* (—, *no pl.*) bewilderment.

verblühen [fɛr'blyːən], *v.n.* (*aux. sein*) wither, fade.

verblümt [fɛr'blyːmt], *adj.* veiled.

verbluten [fɛr'bluːtən], *v.n.* (*aux. sein*) bleed to death.

verborgen (1) [fɛr'bɔrgən], *v.a.* lend out.

verborgen (2) [fɛr'bɔrgən], *adj.* concealed, hidden; *im* —*en*, secretly.

Verborgenheit [fɛr'bɔrgənhaıt], *f.* (—, *no pl.*) concealment, seclusion.

Verbot [fɛr'boːt], *n.* (—(e)s, *pl.* —e) prohibition.

verboten [fɛr'boːtən], *adj.* forbidden, prohibited.

verbrämen [fɛr'brɛːmən], *v.a.* (*garment*) edge, border.

251

verbrauchen

verbrauchen [fɛr'brauxən], *v.a.* consume, use up; spend.

Verbraucher [fɛr'brauxər], *m.* (—s, *pl.* —) consumer.

Verbrechen [fɛr'brɛçən], *n.* (—s, *pl.* —) crime.

verbrechen [fɛr'brɛçən], *v.a. irr.* commit, perpetrate.

Verbrecher [fɛr'brɛçər], *m.* (—s, *pl.* —) criminal.

Verbrecheralbum [fɛr'brɛçəralbum], *n.* (—s, *no pl.*) rogues' gallery.

verbreiten [fɛr'braɪtən], *v.a.* spread, diffuse.

verbreitern [fɛr'braɪtərn], *v.a.* widen.

Verbreitung [fɛr'braɪtuŋ], *f.* (—, *no pl.*) spread(ing), propaganda, extension.

verbrennbar [fɛr'brɛnba:r], *adj.* combustible.

verbrennen [fɛr'brɛnən], *v.a. irr.* burn; cremate; *von der Sonne verbrannt*, sunburnt. — *v.n.* (*aux.* sein) get burnt. — *v.r.* scald o.s., burn o.s.

Verbrennung [fɛr'brɛnuŋ], *f.* (—, *pl.* —en) burning, combustion; cremation.

verbrieft [fɛr'bri:ft], *adj.* vested; documented.

verbringen [fɛr'brɪŋən], *v.a. irr.* (*time*) spend, pass.

verbrüdern [fɛr'bry:dərn], *v.r. sich* —, fraternise.

verbrühen [fɛr'bry:ən], *v.a.* scald.

verbummeln [fɛr'buməln], *v.a. die Zeit* —, fritter the time away.

verbunden [fɛr'bundən], *adj. einem* — *sein*, be obliged to s.o.

verbünden [fɛr'byndən], *v.r. sich* — *mit*, ally o.s. with.

Verbündete [fɛr'byndətə], *m.* (—n, *pl.* —n) ally, confederate.

verbürgen [fɛr'byrgən], *v.a.* warrant, guarantee. — *v.r. sich für etwas* —, vouch for s.th.; guarantee s.th.

Verdacht [fɛr'daxt], *m.* (—(e)s, *no pl.*) suspicion.

verdächtig [fɛr'dɛçtɪç], *adj.* suspicious, doubtful, questionable.

verdächtigen [fɛr'dɛçtɪgən], *v.a.* throw suspicion on, suspect.

verdammen [fɛr'damən], *v.a.* condemn, damn.

verdammenswert [fɛr'damənsvɛ:rt], *adj.* damnable.

Verdammung [fɛr'damuŋ], *f.* (—, *no pl.*) condemnation.

verdampfen [fɛr'dampfən], *v.n.* (*aux.* sein) evaporate.

verdanken [fɛr'daŋkən], *v.a. einem etwas* —, be indebted to s.o. for s.th.; owe s.th. to s.o.

verdauen [fɛr'dauən], *v.a.* digest.

verdaulich [fɛr'daulɪç], *adj.* digestible.

Verdauung [fɛr'dauuŋ], *f.* (—, *no pl.*) digestion.

Verdauungsstörung [fɛr'dauuŋsʃtø:-ruŋ], *f.* (—, *pl.* —en) indigestion.

Verdeck [fɛr'dɛk], *n.* (—s, *pl.* —e) awning; (*Naut.*) deck.

verdecken [fɛr'dɛkən], *v.a.* cover, hide.

verdenken [fɛr'dɛŋkən], *v.a. irr. einem etwas* —, blame s.o. for s.th.

Verderb [fɛr'dɛrp], *m.* (—s, *no pl.*) ruin, decay.

verderben [fɛr'dɛrbən], *v.a. irr.* spoil, corrupt, pervert. — *v.n.* (*aux.* sein) decay, go bad.

Verderben [fɛr'dɛrbən], *n.* (—s, *no pl.*) corruption, ruin.

Verderber [fɛr'dɛrbər], *m.* (—s, *pl.*—) corrupter, perverter.

verderblich [fɛr'dɛrplɪç], *adj.* ruinous, pernicious, destructive; (*goods*) perishable.

Verderbnis [fɛr'dɛrpnɪs], *f.* (—, *no pl.*) corruption, depravity; perversion; perdition.

Verderbtheit [fɛr'dɛrpthaɪt], *f.* (—, *no pl.*) corruption, perversion, depravity.

verdeutlichen [fɛr'dɔʏtlɪçən], *v.a.* illustrate, clarify.

verdichten [fɛr'dɪçtən], *v.a., v.r.* thicken, condense, liquefy.

Verdichtung [fɛr'dɪçtuŋ], *f.* (—, *no pl.*) condensation; solidification.

verdicken [fɛr'dɪkən], *v.a.* thicken; solidify.

verdienen [fɛr'di:nən], *v.a.* earn; deserve.

Verdienst (1) [fɛr'di:nst], *m.* (—es, *pl.* —e) profit, gain, earnings.

Verdienst (2) [fɛr'di:nst], *n.* (—es, *pl.* —e) merit, deserts.

verdienstvoll [fɛr'di:nstfɔl], *adj.* meritorious, deserving; distinguished.

verdient [fɛr'di:nt], *adj. sich* — *machen um*, deserve well of, serve well (a cause etc.).

verdientermaßen [fɛr'di:ntərmasən], *adv.* deservedly.

verdingen [fɛr'dɪŋən], *v.r. irr. sich* —, enter service (with), take a situation (with).

verdolmetschen [fɛr'dɔlmɛtʃən], *v.a.* interpret, translate.

verdoppeln [fɛr'dɔpəln], *v.a.* double.

verdorben [fɛr'dɔrbən], *adj.* spoilt; corrupted, depraved, debauched.

verdrängen [fɛr'drɛŋən], *v.a.* crowd out; (*Phys.*) displace; (*fig.*) supplant, supersede; (*Psych.*) inhibit, repress.

Verdrängung [fɛr'drɛŋuŋ], *f.* (—, *no pl.*) supplanting; (*Phys.*) displacement; (*Psych.*) inhibition, repression.

verdrehen [fɛr'dre:ən], *v.a.* twist (the wrong way); (*fig.*) misrepresent, distort.

verdreht [fɛr'dre:t], *adj.* cracked, cranky, crazy, queer.

Verdrehtheit [fɛr'dre:thaɪt], *f.* (—, *no pl.*) crankiness.

Verdrehung [fɛr'dre:uŋ], *f.* (—, *pl.* —en) distortion; (*fig.*) misrepresentation.

verdrießen [fɛr'dri:sən], *v.a. irr.* vex, annoy.

verdrießlich [fɛr'dri:slɪç], *adj.* (*thing*) vexatious, tiresome; (*person*) morose, peevish.

Verfälschung

verdrossen [fɛr'drɔsən], *adj.* annoyed; fretful, sulky.

Verdrossenheit [fɛr'drɔsənhaɪt], *f.* (—, *no pl.*) annoyance; fretfulness, sulkiness.

verdrücken [fɛr'drykən], *v.a.* (*sl.*) eat o.'s fill of. — *v.r.* (*coll.*) *sich* —, slink away; sneak away.

Verdruß [fɛr'drus], *m.* (**—sses**, *no pl.*) vexation, annoyance; — *bereiten*, give trouble, cause annoyance.

verduften [fɛr'duftən], *v.n.* (*aux.* sein) evaporate; (*fig.*) (*coll.*) take French leave, clear out.

verdummen [fɛr'dumən], *v.n.* (*aux.* sein) become stupid.

verdunkeln [fɛr'duŋkəln], *v.a.* blackout, obscure; (*fig.*) eclipse.

Verdunk(e)lung [fɛr'duŋk(ə)luŋ], *f.* (—, *no pl.*) darkening, eclipse; blackout.

Verdunk(e)lungsgefahr [ver'duŋk(ə)luŋsgəfa:r], *f.* (—, *no pl.*) (*Law*) danger of prejudicing the course *or* administration of justice.

verdünnen [fɛr'dynən], *v.a.* thin out, dilute.

Verdünnung [fɛr'dynuŋ], *f.* (—, *no pl.*) attenuation; dilution.

verdunsten [fɛr'dunstən], *v.n.* (*aux.* sein) evaporate.

verdursten [fɛr'durstən], *v.n.* (*aux.* sein) die of thirst, perish with thirst.

verdüstern [fɛr'dy:stərn], *v.a.* darken, make gloomy.

verdutzen [fɛr'dutsən], *v.a.* disconcert, bewilder, nonplus.

Veredlung [fɛr'e:dluŋ], *f.* (—, *no pl.*) improvement, refinement.

verehelichen [fɛr'e:əlɪçən], *v.r.* (*obs.*) *sich* —, get married.

verehren [fɛr'e:rən], *v.a.* respect, revere, esteem; worship, adore.

Verehrer [fɛr'e:rər], *m.* (**—s**, *pl.* —) admirer; lover.

verehrlich [fɛr'e:rlɪç], *adj.* venerable.

verehrt [fɛr'e:rt], *adj.* honoured; *sehr —er Herr*, dear Sir.

Verehrung [fɛr'e:ruŋ], *f.* (—, *no pl.*) reverence, veneration; worship, adoration.

verehrungswürdig [fɛr'e:ruŋsvyrdɪç], *adj.* venerable.

vereidigt [fɛr'aɪdɪçt], *adj.* sworn in, bound by oath, under oath; *—er Bücherrevisor*, chartered accountant.

Vereidigung [fɛr'aɪdɪguŋ], *f.* (—, *no pl.*) swearing in; oathtaking.

Verein [fɛr'aɪn], *m.* (**—s**, *pl.* **—e**) union, association, society; club.

vereinbar [fɛr'aɪnba:r], *adj.* compatible.

vereinbaren [fɛr'aɪnba:rən], *v.a.* agree upon, arrange.

Vereinbarung [fɛr'aɪnba:ruŋ], *f.* (—, *pl.* **—en**) arrangement, agreement.

vereinen [fɛr'aɪnən], *v.a.* unite.

vereinfachen [fɛr'aɪnfaxən], *v.a.* simplify.

vereinigen [fɛr'aɪnɪgən], *v.a.* unite. — *v.r. sich* — *mit*, associate o.s. with, join with.

Vereinigung [fɛr'aɪnɪguŋ], *f.* (—, *pl.* **—en**) union; association.

vereinnahmen [fɛr'aɪnna:mən], *v.a.* receive, take (*money*).

vereinsamen [fɛr'aɪnza:mən], *v.n.* (*aux.* sein) become isolated, become lonely.

vereint [fɛr'aɪnt], *adj.* united, joined. — *adv.* in concert, (all) together.

vereinzelt [fɛr'aɪntsəlt], *adj.* sporadic, isolated. — *adv.* here and there, now and then.

Vereinzelung [fɛr'aɪntsəluŋ], *f.* (—, *pl.* **—en**) isolation; individualization.

vereisen [fɛr'aɪzən], *v.n.* become frozen, freeze; congeal.

Vereisung [fɛr'aɪzuŋ], *f.* (—, *pl.* **—en**) freezing, icing (up).

vereiteln [fɛr'aɪtəln], *v.a.* frustrate, thwart.

Vereitelung [fɛr'aɪtəluŋ], *f.* (—, *pl.* **—en**) frustration, thwarting.

vereitern [fɛr'aɪtərn], *v.n.* suppurate.

Vereiterung [fɛr'aɪtəruŋ], *f.* (—, *pl.* **—en**) suppuration.

verenden [fɛr'ɛndən], *v.n.* (*aux.* sein) (*animal*) die.

verengen [fɛr'ɛŋən], *v.a.* narrow, straighten, constrict.

Verengung [fɛr'ɛŋuŋ], *f.* (—, *pl.* **—en**) narrowing, straightening, contraction.

vererben [fɛr'ɛrbən], *v.a.* leave (by will), bequeath. — *v.r. sich* — *auf*, devolve upon, be hereditary.

vererblich [fɛr'ɛrplɪç], *adj.* (in)heritable, hereditary.

Vererbung [fɛr'ɛrbuŋ], *f.* (—, *no pl.*) heredity.

verewigen [fɛr'e:vɪgən], *v.a.* immortalise.

Verewigte [fɛr'e:vɪçtə], *m.* (**—n**, *pl.* **—n**) (*Poet.*) deceased.

Verfahren [fɛr'fa:rən], *n.* (**—s**, *pl.* —) process; (*Law*) procedure; proceedings; *das — einstellen*, quash proceedings.

verfahren [fɛr'fa:rən], *v.n. irr.* (*aux.* sein) proceed, act, operate. — *v.a.* spend (*money etc.*) on travelling. — *v.r. sich* —, (*Motor.*) lose o.'s way.

Verfall [fɛr'fal], *m.* (**—s**, *no pl.*) decay, decline; downfall, ruin; (*Comm.*) expiration, maturity; *in — geraten*, fall into ruin, decay.

verfallen [fɛr'falən], *v.n. irr.* (*aux.* sein) decay; go to ruin; lapse; (*Comm.*) fall due, expire; (*pledge*) become forfeit; *einem —*, become the property of, accrue to, devolve upon s.o.; (*fig.*) become the slave of s.o.; (*health*) decline, fail; *auf etwas —*, hit upon an idea. — *adj.* decayed, ruined.

Verfalltag [fɛr'falta:k], *m.* (**—s**, *pl.* **—e**) day of payment; maturity.

verfälschen [fɛr'fɛlʃən], *v.a.* falsify; adulterate.

Verfälschung [fɛr'fɛlʃuŋ], *f.* (—, *pl.* **—en**) falsification; adulteration.

verfangen

verfangen [fɛrˈfaŋən], *v.r. irr. sich* —, get entangled; *sich in ein Lügennetz* —, entangle o.s. in a tissue of lies.

verfänglich [fɛrˈfɛŋlɪç], *adj.* risky; insidious.

verfärben [fɛrˈfɛrbən], *v.r. sich* —, change colour.

verfassen [fɛrˈfasən], *v.a.* compose, write, be the author of.

Verfasser [fɛrˈfasər], *m.* (—s, *pl.* —) author, writer.

Verfassung [fɛrˈfasuŋ], *f.* (—, *pl.* —en) composition; *(state)* constitution; state, condition, disposition.

verfassungsgemäß [fɛrˈfasuŋsgəmɛːs], *adj.* constitutional.

verfassungswidrig [fɛrˈfasuŋsviːdrɪç], *adj.* unconstitutional.

verfaulen [fɛrˈfaulən], *v.n. (aux.* sein) rot, putrefy.

verfechten [fɛrˈfɛçtən], *v.a. irr.* defend, advocate; maintain.

verfehlen [fɛrˈfeːlən], *v.a.* fail, miss; fail to meet; fail to do; *den Weg* —, lose o.'s way.

verfehlt [fɛrˈfeːlt], *adj.* unsuccessful, false, abortive; *eine* —*e Sache*, a failure.

Verfehlung [fɛrˈfeːluŋ], *f.* (—, *pl.* —en) lapse.

verfeinern [fɛrˈfainərn], *v.a.* refine, improve.

Verfeinerung [fɛrˈfainəruŋ], *f.* (—, *pl.* —en) refinement, polish.

verfertigen [fɛrˈfɛrtɪgən], *v.a.* make, manufacture.

verfilmen [fɛrˈfɪlmən], *v.a.* make a film of, film.

verfinstern [fɛrˈfɪnstərn], *v.r. sich* —, get dark; be eclipsed.

verflechten [fɛrˈflɛçtən], *v.a. irr.* interweave, interlace. — *v.r. sich* —, *(fig.)* become entangled, become involved.

verfließen [fɛrˈfliːsən], *v.n. irr. (aux.* sein) flow away; *(time)* elapse, pass.

verflossen [fɛrˈflɔsən], *adj.* past, bygone.

verfluchen [fɛrˈfluːxən], *v.a.* curse, execrate.

verflucht [fɛrˈfluːxt], *excl.* damn!

verflüchtigen [fɛrˈflyçtɪgən], *v.r. sich* —, become volatile; evaporate; *(coll.)* make off, make o.s. scarce.

Verfluchung [fɛrˈfluːxuŋ], *f.* (—, *pl.* —en) malediction, curse.

Verfolg [fɛrˈfɔlk], *m.* (—(e)s, *no pl.*) progress, course.

verfolgen [fɛrˈfɔlgən], *v.a.* pursue; persecute; prosecute.

Verfolger [fɛrˈfɔlgər], *m.* (—s, *pl.* —) pursuer; persecutor.

Verfolgung [fɛrˈfɔlguŋ], *f.* (—, *pl.* —en) pursuit; persecution; prosecution.

Verfolgungswahn [fɛrˈfɔlguŋsvaːn], *m.* (—s, *no pl.*) persecution mania.

verfrüht [fɛrˈfryːt], *adj.* premature.

verfügbar [fɛrˈfyːkbaːr], *adj.* available.

verfügen [fɛrˈfyːgən], *v.a.* decree, order. — *v.n.* — *über etwas*, have control of s.th, have s.th. at o.'s disposal.

Verfügung [fɛrˈfyːguŋ], *f.* (—, *pl.* —en) decree, ordinance; disposition, disposal; *einem zur* — *stehen*, be at s.o.'s service *or* disposal.

verführen [fɛrˈfyːrən], *v.a.* seduce.

verführerisch [fɛrˈfyːrərɪʃ], *adj.* seductive, alluring; *(coll.)* fetching.

Verführung [fɛrˈfyːruŋ], *f.* (—, *no pl.*) seduction.

vergällen [fɛrˈgɛlən], *v.a.* spoil, mar.

vergallopieren [fɛrgalɔˈpiːrən], *v.r. (coll.) sich* —, blunder, overshoot the mark.

vergangen [fɛrˈgaŋən], *adj.* past, gone, last.

Vergangenheit [fɛrˈgaŋənhait], *f.* (—, *no pl.*) past, time past; *(Gram.)* past tense.

vergänglich [fɛrˈgɛŋlɪç], *adj.* transient, transitory.

Vergaser [fɛrˈgaːzər], *m.* (—s, *pl.* —) *(Motor.)* carburettor.

vergeben [fɛrˈgeːbən], *v.a. irr.* give away; forgive, pardon; confer, bestow.

vergebens [fɛrˈgeːbəns], *adv.* in vain, vainly.

vergeblich [fɛrˈgeːplɪç], *adj.* vain, futile, fruitless. — *adv.* in vain.

Vergebung [fɛrˈgeːbuŋ], *f.* (—, *no pl.*) forgiveness, pardon; *(office)* bestowal.

vergegenwärtigen [fɛrgeːgənˈvɛrtɪgən], *v.a.* bring to mind, imagine.

Vergehen [fɛrˈgeːən], *n.* (—s, *pl.* —) offence lapse.

vergehen [fɛrˈgeːən], *v.n. irr. (aux.* sein) go away, pass (away); elapse; perish; *(time)* pass. — *v.r. sich* —, go wrong; offend; violate *(Law,* person).

vergelten [fɛrˈgɛltən], *v.a. irr.* repay, reward, recompense.

Vergeltung [fɛrˈgɛltuŋ], *f.* (—, *no pl.*) requital, retribution; reward, recompense.

vergessen [fɛrˈgɛsən], *v.a. irr.* forget; *bei einem* —, leave behind.

Vergessenheit [fɛrˈgɛsənhait], *f.* (— *no pl.*) oblivion.

vergeßlich [fɛrˈgɛslɪç], *adj.* forgetful.

vergeuden [fɛrˈgɔydən], *v.a.* waste, squander.

vergewaltigen [fɛrgəˈvaltɪgən], *v.a.* assault criminally, rape, violate; *(fig.)* coerce, force.

Vergewaltigung [fɛrgəˈvaltɪguŋ], *f.* (—, *no pl.*) criminal assault, rape; *(fig.)* coercion.

vergewissern [fɛrgəˈvɪsərn], *v.r. sich* —, ascertain, make sure.

vergießen [fɛrˈgiːsən], *v.a. irr.* spill; shed.

vergiften [fɛrˈgɪftən], *v.a.* poison.

Vergiftung [fɛrˈgɪftuŋ], *f.* (—, *pl.* —en) poisoning.

vergilbt [fɛrˈgɪlpt], *adj.* yellow with age.

Vergißmeinnicht [fɛrˈgɪsmainnɪçt], *n.* (—s, *pl.* —e) *(Bot.)* forget-me-not.

Vergleich [fɛrˈglaɪç], *m.* (—(e)s, *pl.* —e) comparison; agreement; (*Law*) compromise.

vergleichbar [fɛrˈglaɪçbaːr], *adj.* comparable.

vergleichen [fɛrˈglaɪçən], *v.a. irr.* compare.

vergleichsweise [fɛrˈglaɪçsvaɪzə], *adv.* by way of comparison; comparatively; (*Law*) by way of agreement.

Vergnügen [fɛrˈgnyːgən], *n.* (—s, *no pl.*) pleasure, enjoyment, fun.

vergnügen [fɛrˈgnyːgən], *v.a.* amuse, delight.

Vergnügung [fɛrˈgnyːguŋ], *f.* (—, *pl.* —en) entertainment, amusement.

vergönnen [fɛrˈgœnən], *v.a.* grant, allow; not (be)grudge.

vergöttern [fɛrˈgœtərn], *v.a.* idolise, worship.

vergraben [fɛrˈgraːbən], *v.a. irr.* hide in the ground, bury.

vergrämt [fɛrˈgrɛːmt], *adj.* careworn.

vergreifen [fɛrˈgraɪfən], *v.r. irr. sich — an*, lay violent hands on, violate.

vergriffen [fɛrˈgrɪfən], *adj.* out of stock, out of print.

vergrößern [fɛrˈgrøːsərn], *v.a.* enlarge, expand; increase; magnify; (*fig.*) exaggerate.

Vergrößerung [fɛrˈgrøːsəruŋ], *f.* (—, *pl.* —en) magnification, enlargement, increase.

Vergrößerungsglas [fɛrˈgrøːsəruŋsglas], *n.* (—es, *pl.* ⸚er) magnifying glass.

Vergünstigung [fɛrˈgynstɪguŋ], *f.* (—, *pl.* —en) privilege, favour, special facility, concession.

vergüten [fɛrˈgyːtən], *v.a. einem etwas —*, compensate s.o. for s.th.; reimburse s.o. for s.th.

Vergütung [fɛrˈgyːtuŋ], *f.* (—, *pl.* —en) indemnification, compensation, reimbursement.

verhaften [fɛrˈhaftən], *v.a.* arrest.

Verhaftung [fɛrˈhaftuŋ], *f.* (—, *pl.* —en) arrest.

verhallen [fɛrˈhalən], *v.n.* (*aux.* sein) (*sound*) fade, die away.

verhalten [fɛrˈhaltən], *v.r. irr. sich —*, act, behave.

Verhalten [fɛrˈhaltən], *n.* (—s, *no pl.*) behaviour, conduct, demeanour.

Verhältnis [fɛrˈhɛltnɪs], *n.* (—ses, *pl.* —se) (*Maths.*) proportion, ratio; relation; footing; love-affair, liaison; (*coll.*) mistress.

verhältnismäßig [fɛrˈhɛltnɪsmɛsɪç], *adj.* proportionate, comparative.

Verhältniswort [fɛrˈhɛltnɪsvɔrt], *n.* (—es, *pl.* ⸚er) preposition.

Verhältniszahl [fɛrˈhɛltnɪstsaːl], *f.* (—, *pl.* —en) proportional number.

Verhaltungsmaßregel [fɛrˈhaltuŋsmaːsreːgəl], *f.* (—, *pl.* —n) rule of conduct; instruction.

verhandeln [fɛrˈhandəln], *v.a.* discuss, transact. — *v.n.* negotiate.

Verhandlung [fɛrˈhandluŋ], *f.* (—, *pl.* —en) discussion, negotiation, transaction; (*Law*) proceedings.

verhängen [fɛrˈhɛŋən], *v.a.* cover with; decree; inflict (a penalty) on s.o.

Verhängnis [fɛrˈhɛŋnɪs], *n.* (—ses, *pl.* —se) fate, destiny; misfortune.

Verhängnisglaube [fɛrˈhɛŋnɪsglaubə], *m.* (—ns, *no pl.*) fatalism.

verhängnisvoll [fɛrˈhɛŋnɪsfɔl], *adj.* fateful, portentous; fatal.

verhärmt [fɛrˈhɛrmt], *adj.* careworn.

verharren [fɛrˈharən], *v.n.* remain; persist.

Verhärtung [fɛrˈhɛrtuŋ], *f.* (—, *pl.* —en) hardening, hardened state; (*skin*) callosity; (*fig.*) obduracy.

verhaßt [fɛrˈhast], *adj.* hated, odious.

verhätscheln [fɛrˈhɛtʃəln], *v.a.* pamper, coddle.

verhauen [fɛrˈhauən], *v.a.* beat, thrash.

Verheerung [fɛrˈheːruŋ], *f.* (—, *pl.* —en) devastation.

verhehlen [fɛrˈheːlən], *v.a.* conceal, hide.

verheilen [fɛrˈhaɪlən], *v.n.* (*aux.* sein) heal.

verheimlichen [fɛrˈhaɪmlɪçən], *v.a.* keep secret, hush up.

verheiraten [fɛrˈhaɪraːtən], *v.a.* give in marriage, marry off. — *v.r. sich —*, marry, get married.

verheißen [fɛrˈhaɪsən], *v.a. irr.* promise.

Verheißung [fɛrˈhaɪsuŋ], *f.* (—, *pl.* —en) promise.

verhelfen [fɛrˈhɛlfən], *v.n. irr. einem zu etwas —*, help s.o. to s.th.

Verherrlichung [fɛrˈhɛrlɪçuŋ], *f.* (—, *no pl.*) glorification.

Verhetzung [fɛrˈhɛtsuŋ], *f.* (—, *pl.* —en) incitement, instigation.

verhexen [fɛrˈhɛksən], *v.a.* bewitch.

verhindern [fɛrˈhɪndərn], *v.a.* hinder, prevent.

Verhinderung [fɛrˈhɪndəruŋ], *f.* (—, *pl.* —en) prevention, obstacle.

verhöhnen [fɛrˈhøːnən], *v.a.* deride, scoff at, jeer at.

Verhöhnung [fɛrˈhøːnuŋ], *f.* (—, *pl.* —en) derision.

Verhör [fɛrˈhøːr], *n.* (—s, *pl.* —e) hearing; (judicial) examination; *ins — nehmen*, question, interrogate, cross-examine.

verhören [fɛrˈhøːrən], *v.a.* examine judicially, interrogate. — *v.r. sich —*, misunderstand.

verhüllen [fɛrˈhylən], *v.a.* cover, wrap up, veil.

verhungern [fɛrˈhuŋərn], *v.n.* (*aux.* sein) starve.

verhungert [fɛrˈhuŋərt], *adj.* famished.

verhunzen [fɛrˈhuntsən], *v.a.* spoil, bungle.

verhüten [fɛrˈhyːtən], *v.a.* prevent, avert.

Verhütung [fɛrˈhyːtuŋ], *f.* (—, *no pl.*) prevention, warding off.

verirren [fɛrˈɪrən], *v.r. sich —*, go astray, lose o.'s way.

verirrt

verirrt [fɛrˈɪrt], adj. stray, straying, lost.
verjagen [fɛrˈjaːgən], v.a. drive away, chase away.
verjährt [fɛrˈjɛːrt], adj. statute-barred; prescriptive; obsolete; old.
verjubeln [fɛrˈjuːbəln], v.a. play ducks and drakes with; squander.
verjüngen [fɛrˈjyŋən], v.a. make younger; (Archit.) taper. — v.r. sich —, grow younger.
Verjüngung [fɛrˈjyŋuŋ], f. (—, pl. —en) rejuvenation.
verkannt [fɛrˈkant], adj. misunderstood.
verkappt [fɛrˈkapt], adj. disguised, secret, in disguise.
Verkauf [fɛrˈkauf], m. (—(e)s, pl. ⁝e) sale.
verkaufen [fɛrˈkaufən], v.a. sell.
Verkäufer [fɛrˈkɔyfər], m. (—s, pl. —) seller; shop assistant, salesman.
verkäuflich [fɛrˈkɔyflɪç], adj. for sale, saleable; mercenary.
Verkaufspreis [fɛrˈkaufsprais], m. (—es, pl. —e) selling-price.
Verkehr [fɛrˈkeːr], m. (—s, no pl.) traffic; commerce; intercourse; communication; — mit, association with; service (trains, buses etc.), transport.
verkehren [fɛrˈkeːrən], v.a. turn upside down; transform; pervert. — v.n. frequent (a place), visit, associate (with); run, operate.
Verkehrsstraße [fɛrˈkeːrsʃtraːsə], f. (—, pl. —n) thoroughfare.
Verkehrsstockung [fɛrˈkeːrsʃtɔkuŋ], f. (—, pl. —en) traffic jam.
verkehrt [fɛrˈkeːrt], adj. upside down; (fig.) wrong.
Verkehrtheit [fɛrˈkeːrthait], f. (—, pl. —en) absurdity, piece of folly.
Verkehrung [fɛrˈkeːruŋ], f. (—, pl. —en) turning; inversion; perversion; misrepresentation; (Gram.) inversion.
verkennen [fɛrˈkɛnən], v.a. irr. mistake, fail to recognize; misjudge (s.o.'s intentions).
verklagen [fɛrˈklaːgən], v.a. sue; accuse.
verklären [fɛrˈklɛːrən], v.a. transfigure, illumine.
verklärt [fɛrˈklɛːrt], adj. transfigured; radiant.
verkleben [fɛrˈkleːbən], v.a. paste over.
verkleiden [fɛrˈklaidən], v.a., v.r. disguise (o.s.).
Verkleidung [fɛrˈklaiduŋ], f. (— pl. —en) disguise.
verkleinern [fɛrˈklainərn], v.a. make smaller, diminish, reduce; belittle, disparage.
Verkleinerung [fɛrˈklainəruŋ], f. (—, pl. —en) diminution, reduction; belittling, detraction.
Verkleinerungswort [fɛrˈklainəruŋsvɔrt], n. (—s, pl. ⁝er) (Gram.) diminutive.
verkneifen [fɛrˈknaifən], v.r. irr. (coll.) sich etwas —, deny o.s. s.th.

verkniffen [fɛrˈknɪfən], adj. pinched; shrewd; hard-bitten.
verknöchern [fɛrˈknœçərn], v.n. (aux. sein) ossify; (fig.) become fossilised or inflexible.
Verknöcherung [fɛrˈknœçəruŋ], f. (—, pl. —en) ossification; (fig.) fossilisation.
verknüpfen [fɛrˈknypfən], v.a. tie, connect, link.
verkochen [fɛrˈkɔxən], v.n. (aux. sein) boil away.
verkommen [fɛrˈkɔmən], v.n. irr. (aux. sein) go from bad to worse, go to seed, decay, become depraved. — adj. demoralised, down and out, depraved.
Verkommenheit [fɛrˈkɔmənhait], f. (—, no pl.) demoralisation; depravity.
verkörpern [fɛrˈkœrpərn], v.a. embody.
verkrachen [fɛrˈkraxən], v.r. sich —, quarrel, (coll.) have a row.
verkriechen [fɛrˈkriːçən], v.r. irr. sich —, creep or crawl away; slink away, lie low.
verkümmern [fɛrˈkymərn], v.n. (aux. sein) wear away, waste away; pine away.
verkünden [fɛrˈkyndən], v.a. proclaim, announce, publish, prophesy.
Verkündigung [fɛrˈkyndiguŋ], f. (—, pl. —en) announcement, proclamation; prediction.
Verkündung [fɛrˈkynduŋ], f. (—, pl. —en) publication, proclamation.
Verkürzung [fɛrˈkyrtsuŋ], f. (—, pl. —en) shortening, curtailment.
verlachen [fɛrˈlaxən], v.a. laugh at, deride.
verladen [fɛrˈlaːdən], v.a. irr. load, ship, freight.
Verladung [fɛrˈlaːduŋ], f. (—, pl. —en) loading, shipping.
Verlag [fɛrˈlaːk], m. (—(e)s, pl. —e) publication; publishing-house, (firm of) publishers.
Verlagsrecht [fɛrˈlaːksrɛçt], n. (—s, pl. —e) copyright.
Verlangen [fɛrˈlaŋən], n. (—s, no pl.) demand, request; longing, desire.
verlangen [fɛrˈlaŋən], v.a. ask, demand, request.
verlängern [fɛrˈlɛŋərn], v.a. lengthen, prolong, extend.
Verlängerung [fɛrˈlɛŋəruŋ], f. (—, pl. —en) lengthening; (period) prolongation, extension.
verlangsamen [fɛrˈlaŋzaːmən], v.a. slow down, slacken, decelerate.
Verlaß [fɛrˈlas], m. (—sses, no pl.) es ist kein — auf dich, you cannot be relied on.
verlassen [fɛrˈlasən], v.a. irr. leave, abandon. — v.r. sich — auf, rely on, depend upon. — adj. forlorn, forsaken, deserted, desolate, lonely.
Verlassenheit [fɛrˈlasənhait], f. (—, no pl.) desolation, loneliness, solitude.
verläßlich [fɛrˈlɛslɪç], adj. reliable, trustworthy.

256

Verlauf [fɛr'lauf], *m.* (—(e)s, *no pl.*) lapse, expiration; course.

verlaufen [fɛr'laufən], *v.n. irr.* (*aux.* sein) (*time*) pass; (*period*) expire, elapse; develop(e), turn out. — *v.r. sich* —, lose o.'s way; (*colour*) run.

verlauten [fɛr'lautən], *v.n.* transpire.

verleben [fɛr'le:bən], *v.a.* pass, spend.

verlebt [fɛr'le:pt], *adj.* worn out; spent; (*Am.*) played out.

verlegen [fɛr'le:gən], *v.a.* (*domicile*) move, remove; (*things*) mislay; (*books*) publish; obstruct; adjourn; change to another date *or* place. — *v.r. sich auf etwas* —, devote o.s. to s.th. — *adj.* embarrassed, ill at ease.

Verlegenheit [fɛr'le:gənhaɪt], *f.* (—, *pl.* —en) embarrassment, perplexity; predicament, difficulty.

Verleger [fɛr'le:gər], *m.* (—s, *pl.* —) publisher.

verleiden [fɛr'laɪdən], *v.a. einem etwas* —, spoil s.th. for s.o.

verleihen [fɛr'laɪən], *v.a. irr.* lend; (*honour, title*) confer; bestow, award.

Verleiher [fɛr'laɪər], *m.* (—s, *pl.* —) lender.

Verleihung [fɛr'laɪuŋ], *f.* (—, *pl.* —en) lending, loan; (*medal, prize*) investiture; grant, conferring.

verleiten [fɛr'laɪtən], *v.a.* mislead, entice, induce; seduce.

Verleitung [fɛr'laɪtuŋ], *f.* (—, *no pl.*) misleading, enticement, inducement; seduction.

verlernen [fɛr'lɛrnən], *v.a.* unlearn; forget.

verlesen [fɛr'le:zən], *v.a. irr.* read aloud, read out, recite. — *v.r. sich* —, misread.

verletzen [fɛr'lɛtsən], *v.a.* injure, hurt, wound, violate.

verletzend [fɛr'lɛtsənt], *adj.* offensive, insulting; cutting.

verletzlich [fɛr'lɛtslɪç], *adj.* vulnerable.

Verletzlichkeit [fɛr'lɛtslɪçkaɪt], *f.* (—, *no pl.*) vulnerability.

Verletzung [fɛr'lɛtsuŋ], *f.* (—, *pl.* —en) hurt, wound; (*Law*) violation.

verleugnen [fɛr'lɔygnən], *v.a.* deny, renounce, disown.

Verleugnung [fɛr'lɔygnuŋ], *f.* (—, *pl.* —en) denial, abnegation.

verleumden [fɛr'lɔymdən], *v.a.* slander, calumniate, traduce.

Verleumdung [fɛr'lɔymduŋ], *f.* (—, *pl.* —en) slander, libel, calumny.

verlieben [fɛr'li:bən], *v.r. sich* — *in*, fall in love with.

Verliebte [fɛr'li:ptə], *m. or f.* (—n, *pl.* —n) person in love, lover.

Verliebtheit [fɛr'li:pthaɪt], *f.* (—, *no pl.*) infatuation, amorousness.

verlieren [fɛr'li:rən], *v.a. irr.* lose.

Verlierer [fɛr'li:rər], *m.* (—s, *pl.* —) loser.

Verlies [fɛr'li:s], *n.* (—(s)es, *pl.* —(s)e) dungeon.

verloben [fɛr'lo:bən], *v.r. sich* — *mit*, become engaged to.

Verlöbnis [fɛr'lø:pnɪs], *n.* (—ses, *pl.* —se) (*rare*) engagement.

Verlobte [fɛr'lo:ptə], *m.* (—n, *pl.* —n) and *f.* (—n, *pl.* —n) fiancé(e), betrothed.

Verlobung [fɛr'lo:buŋ], *f.* (—, *pl.* —en) engagement, betrothal.

verlocken [fɛr'lɔkən], *v.a.* tempt, entice.

verlogen [fɛr'lo:gən], *adj.* lying, mendacious.

Verlogenheit [fɛr'lo:gənhaɪt], *f.* (—, *no pl.*) mendacity.

verlohnen [fɛr'lo:nən], *v. impers.* be worth while.

verlöschen [fɛr'lœʃən], *v.a.* extinguish.

verlosen [fɛr'lo:zən], *v.a.* raffle; draw *or* cast lots for.

Verlosung [fɛr'lo:zuŋ], *f.* (—, *pl.* —en) raffle, lottery.

verlöten [fɛr'lø:tən], *v.a.* solder.

verlottern [fɛr'lɔtərn], *v.n.* (*aux.* sein) go to the dogs.

Verlust [fɛr'lust], *m.* (—es, *pl.* —e) loss; (*death*) bereavement; (*Mil.*) casualty.

verlustig [fɛr'lustɪç], *adj.* — *gehen*, lose s.th., forfeit s.th.

vermachen [fɛr'maxən], *v.a. einem etwas* —, bequeath s.th. to s.o.

Vermächtnis [fɛr'mɛçtnɪs], *n.* (—ses, *pl.* —sse) will; legacy, bequest; (*fig.*) *heiliges* —, sacred trust.

vermahlen [fɛr'ma:lən], *v.a.* grind (down).

Vermählung [fɛr'mɛ:luŋ], *f.* (—, *pl.* —en) marriage, wedding.

Vermahnung [fɛr'ma:nuŋ], *f.* (—, *pl.* —en) admonition, exhortation.

vermauern [fɛr'mauərn], *v.a.* wall up.

vermehren [fɛr'me:rən], *v.a.* augment, multiply, increase. — *v.r. sich* —, multiply.

Vermehrung [fɛr'me:ruŋ], *f.* (—, *pl.* —en) increase, multiplication.

vermeiden [fɛr'maɪdən], *v.a. irr.* avoid, shun, shirk.

vermeidlich [fɛr'maɪtlɪç], *adj.* avoidable.

Vermeidung [fɛr'maɪduŋ], *f.* (—, *no pl.*) avoidance.

vermeintlich [fɛr'maɪntlɪç], *adj.* supposed, alleged, pretended; (*heir*) presumptive.

vermelden [fɛr'mɛldən], *v.a.* announce, notify.

vermengen [fɛr'mɛŋən], *v.a.* mingle, mix.

Vermerk [fɛr'mɛrk], *m.* (—s, *pl.* —e) entry, notice, note.

vermerken [fɛr'mɛrkən], *v.a.* observe, jot down.

vermessen [fɛr'mɛsən], *v.a. irr.* measure; (*land*) survey. — *adj.* bold, daring, audacious; arrogant.

Vermessenheit [fɛr'mɛsənhaɪt], *f.* (—, *no pl.*) boldness, audacity; arrogance.

Vermesser [fɛr'mɛsər], *m.* (—s, *pl.* —) (*land*) surveyor.

Vermessung

Vermessung [fɛr'mɛsuŋ], *f.* (—, *pl.* —en) (*land*) survey; measuring.

vermieten [fɛr'mi:tən], *v.a.* let, lease, hire out.

Vermieter [fɛr'mi:tər], *m.* (—s, *pl.* —) landlord; hirer.

vermindern [fɛr'mɪndərn], *v.a.* diminish, lessen.

Verminderung [fɛr'mɪndəruŋ], *f.* (—, *pl.* —en) diminution, reduction, decrease, lessening.

vermischen [fɛr'mɪʃən], *v.a.* mix, mingle, blend.

vermissen [fɛr'mɪsən], *v.a.* miss; *vermißt sein*, be missing; *vermißt werden*, be missed.

vermitteln [fɛr'mɪtəln], *v.n.* mediate. — *v.a.* adjust; negotiate, secure.

Vermittler [fɛr'mɪtlər], *m.* (—s, *pl.* —) mediator; agent, middleman.

Vermittlung [fɛr'mɪtluŋ], *f.* (—, *pl.* —en) mediation, intervention.

vermöbeln [fɛr'mø:bəln], *v.a.* (*sl.*) *einen* —, thrash s.o.

vermodern [fɛr'mo:dərn], *v.n.* (*aux.* sein) moulder, rot.

vermöge [fɛr'mø:gə], *prep.* (*Genit.*) by virtue of, by dint of, on the strength of.

Vermögen [fɛr'mø:gən], *n.* (—s, *pl.* —) faculty, power; means, assets; fortune, wealth, riches; *er hat* —, he is a man of property; *nach bestem* —, to the best of o.'s ability.

vermögen [fɛr'mø:gən], *v.a. irr.* be able to, have the power to, be capable of.

vermögend [fɛr'mø:gənt], *adj.* wealthy.

Vermögensbestand [fɛr'mø:gənsbəʃtant], *m.* (—s, *pl.* ⸚e) assets.

Vermögenssteuer [fɛr'mø:gənsʃtɔyər], *f.* (—, *pl.* —n) property tax.

vermorscht [fɛr'mɔrʃt], *adj.* mouldering, rotten.

vermuten [fɛr'mu:tən], *v.a.* suppose, conjecture, surmise, presume; guess.

vermutlich [fɛr'mu:tlɪç], *adj.* likely, probable.

Vermutung [fɛr'mu:tuŋ], *f.* (—, *pl.* —en) guess, supposition, conjecture.

vernachlässigen [fɛr'naxlɛsɪgən], *v.a.* neglect.

Vernachlässigung [fɛr'naxlɛsɪguŋ], *f.* (—, *pl.* —en) neglect, negligence.

vernarren [fɛr'narən], *v.r. sich* — (*in, Acc.*), become infatuated (with).

vernarrt [fɛr'nart], *adj.* madly in love.

vernaschen [fɛr'naʃən], *v.a.* squander (money) on sweets.

vernehmbar [fɛr'ne:mba:r], *adj.* audible; *sich* — *machen*, make o.s. heard.

Vernehmen [fɛr'ne:mən], *n.* (—s, *no pl.*) *dem* — *nach*, from what o. hears.

vernehmen [fɛr'ne:mən], *v.a. irr.* hear, learn; (*Law*) examine, interrogate.

vernehmlich [fɛr'ne:mlɪç], *adj.* audible, distinct, clear.

Vernehmlichkeit [fɛr'ne:mlɪçkaɪt], *f.* (—, *no pl.*) audibility.

Vernehmung [fɛr'ne:muŋ], *f.* (—, *pl.* —en) (*Law*) interrogation, examination.

verneigen [fɛr'naɪgən], *v.r. sich* —, curts(e)y, bow.

Verneigung [fɛr'naɪguŋ], *f.* (—, *pl.* —en) curts(e)y, bow.

verneinen [fɛr'naɪnən], *v.a.* deny, answer in the negative.

Verneinung [fɛr'naɪnuŋ], *f.* (—, *pl.* —en) negation, denial; (*Gram.*) negation, negative.

vernichten [fɛr'nɪçtən], *v.a.* annihilate, destroy utterly, exterminate.

Vernichtung [fɛr'nɪçtuŋ], *f.* (—, *no pl.*) annihilation, extinction, destruction.

vernieten [fɛr'ni:tən], *v.a.* rivet.

Vernunft [fɛr'nunft], *f.* (—, *no pl.*) reason, sense, intelligence, judgment; *gesunde* —, common sense; — *annehmen*, listen to reason; *einen zur* — *bringen*, bring s.o. to his senses.

vernünftig [fɛr'nynftɪç], *adj.* sensible, reasonable, rational.

veröden [fɛr'ø:dən], *v.n.* (*aux.* sein) become desolate, become devastated.

Verödung [fɛr'ø:duŋ], *f.* (—, *no pl.*) devastation, desolation.

veröffentlichen [fɛr'œfəntlɪçən], *v.a.* publish.

Veröffentlichung [fɛr'œfəntlɪçuŋ], *f.* (—, *pl.* —en) publication.

verordnen [fɛr'ɔrdnən], *v.a.* order, command, ordain; (*Med.*) prescribe.

Verordnung [fɛr'ɔrdnuŋ], *f.* (—, *pl.* —en) order; (*Law*) decree, edict, statute; (*Med.*) prescription.

verpassen [fɛr'pasən], *v.a.* lose by delay, let slip; (*train etc.*) miss.

verpfänden [fɛr'pfɛndən], *v.a.* pawn, pledge.

Verpfänder [fɛr'pfɛndər], *m.* (—s, *pl.* —) mortgager.

Verpfändung [fɛr'pfɛnduŋ], *f.* (—, *pl.* —en) pawning, pledging.

verpflanzen [fɛr'pflantsən], *v.a.* transplant.

Verpflanzung [fɛr'pflantsuŋ], *f.* (—, *pl.* —en) transplantation.

verpflegen [fɛr'pfle:gən], *v.a.* board, provide food for, feed; nurse.

Verpflegung [fɛr'pfle:guŋ], *f.* (—, *no pl.*) board, catering; food.

Verpflegungskosten [fɛr'pfle:guŋskɔstən], *f. pl.* (cost of) board and lodging.

verpflichten [fɛr'pflɪçtən], *v.a.* bind, oblige, engage.

verpflichtend [fɛr'pflɪçtənt], *adj.* obligatory.

Verpflichtung [fɛr'pflɪçtuŋ], *f.* (—, *pl.* —en) obligation, duty; liability, engagement.

verplaudern [fɛr'plaudərn], *v.a.* spend (time) chatting.

verplempern [fɛr'plɛmpərn], *v.a.* (*coll.*) spend foolishly, fritter away.

verpönt [fɛr'pø:nt], *adj.* frowned upon; taboo.

verprassen [fɛr'prasən], *v.a.* squander (money) in riotous living.

verpuffen [fɛr'pufən], *v.n.* (*aux.* sein) (*coll.*) fizzle out.

verpulvern [fɛr'pulvərn], *v.a.* fritter away.

Verputz [fɛr'puts], *m.* (**—es**, *no pl.*) plaster.

verquicken [fɛr'kvɪkən], *v.a.* amalgamate; mix up.

Verrat [fɛr'ra:t], *m.* (**—(e)s**, *no pl.*) treachery, treason.

verraten [fɛr'ra:tən], *v.a. irr.* betray; disclose; *das verrät die Hand des Künstlers*, this proclaims the hand of the artist.

Verräter [fɛr'rɛːtər], *m.* (**—s**, *pl.* **—**) traitor.

verräterisch [fɛr'rɛːtərɪʃ], *adj.* treacherous, treasonable, perfidious; (*fig.*) tell-tale.

verrauchen [fɛr'rauxən], *v.n.* (*aux.* sein) evaporate; (*fig.*) blow over; cool down.

verräuchern [fɛr'rɔʏçərn], *v.a.* smoke, fill with smoke.

verräumen [fɛr'rɔʏmən], *v.a.* misplace, mislay.

verrauschen [fɛr'rauʃən], *v.n.* (*aux.* sein) (*sound*) die away; pass away.

verrechnen [fɛr'rɛçnən], *v.a.* reckon up. — *v.r. sich —*, miscalculate.

Verrechnung [fɛr'rɛçnuŋ], *f.* (**—**, *pl.* **— en**) reckoning-up.

Verrechnungsscheck [fɛr'rɛçnuŋsʃɛk], *m.* (**—s**, *pl.* **—e**, **—s**) crossed cheque, non-negotiable cheque.

verregnen [fɛr're:gnən], *v.a.* spoil by rain.

verreiben [fɛr'raɪbən], *v.a. irr.* rub away; rub hard.

verreisen [fɛr'raɪzən], *v.n.* (*aux.* sein) go on a journey.

verrenken [fɛr'rɛŋkən], *v.a.* sprain, dislocate.

Verrenkung [fɛr'rɛŋkuŋ], *f.* (**—**, *pl.* **—en**) sprain, dislocation.

verrichten [fɛr'rɪçtən], *v.a.* do, perform, acquit o.s. of; execute; (*prayer*) say.

verriegeln [fɛr'ri:gəln], *v.a.* bolt.

verringern [fɛr'rɪŋərn], *v.a.* reduce, diminish.

Verringerung [fɛr'rɪŋəruŋ], *f.* (**—**, *no pl.*) diminution, reduction.

verrinnen [fɛr'rɪnən], *v.n. irr.* (*aux.* sein) run off; (*fig.*) pass, elapse.

verrosten [fɛr'rɔstən], *v.n.* (*aux.* sein) rust.

verrottet [fɛr'rɔtət], *adj.* rotten.

verrucht [fɛr'ru:xt], *adj.* villainous, atrocious, heinous, infamous.

Verruchtheit [fɛr'ru:xthaɪt], *f.* (**—**, *no pl.*) villainy.

verrücken [fɛr'rykən], *v.a.* shift, displace.

verrückt [fɛr'rykt], *adj.* crazy, mad.

Verrückte [fɛr'ryktə], *m.* (**—n**, *pl.* **—n**) madman. — *f.* (**—n**, *pl.* **—n**) madwoman.

Verrücktheit [fɛr'rykthaɪt], *f.* (**—**, *pl.* **—en**) craziness; mad act.

Verruf [fɛr'ru:f], *m.* (**—s**, *no pl.*) discredit, ill repute.

verrufen [fɛr'ru:fən], *adj.* notorious, of ill repute.

Vers [fɛrs], *m.* (**—es**, *pl.* **—e**) verse.

versagen [fɛr'za:gən], *v.a. einem etwas —*, deny s.o. s.th., refuse s.o. s.th. — *v.n.* fail, break down; (*voice*) falter; *sich etwas —*, abstain from s.th., deny o.s. s.th.

Versager [fɛr'za:gər], *m.* (**—s**, *pl.* **—**) misfire; failure, unsuccessful person, flop.

versammeln [fɛr'zaməln], *v.a.* gather around, convene. — *v.r. sich —*, assemble, meet.

Versammlung [fɛr'zamluŋ], *f.* (**—**, *pl.* **—en**) assembly, meeting, gathering, convention.

Versand [fɛr'zant], *m.* (**—s**, *no pl.*) dispatch, forwarding, shipping, shipment.

versanden [fɛr'zandən], *v.n.* (*aux.* sein) silt up.

Versandgeschäft [fɛr'zantgəʃɛft], *n.* (**—s**, *pl.* **—e**) export business; mail order business.

Versatzamt [fɛr'zatsamt], *n.* (**—s**, *pl.* *̈*er) pawn-shop.

versauen [fɛr'zauən], *v.a.* (*sl.*) make a mess of.

versauern [fɛr'zauərn], *v.n.* (*aux.* sein) turn sour; (*fig.*) become morose.

versaufen [fɛr'zaufən], *v.a. irr.* (*sl.*) squander (money) on drink, drink away.

versäumen [fɛr'zɔʏmən], *v.a.* miss, omit, lose by delay; leave undone; neglect.

Versäumnis [fɛr'zɔʏmnɪs], *n.* (**—ses**, *pl.* **—se**) neglect, omission; (*time*) loss.

Versbau ['fɛrsbau], *m.* (**—s**, *no pl.*) versification; verse structure.

verschachern [fɛr'ʃaxərn], *v.a.* barter away.

verschaffen [fɛr'ʃafən], *v.a.* provide, procure, obtain, get.

verschämt [fɛr'ʃɛ:mt], *adj.* shamefaced, bashful.

verschanzen [fɛr'ʃantsən], *v.a.* fortify.

Verschanzung [fɛr'ʃantsuŋ], *f.* (**—**, *pl.* **—en**) fortification, entrenchment.

verschärfen [fɛr'ʃɛrfən], *v.a.* heighten, intensify, sharpen.

verscharren [fɛr'ʃarən], *v.a.* cover with earth; bury hurriedly.

verscheiden [fɛr'ʃaɪdən], *v.n. irr.* (*aux.* sein) die, pass away.

verschenken [fɛr'ʃɛŋkən], *v.a.* make a present of, give away.

verscherzen [fɛr'ʃɛrtsən], *v.a. sich etwas —*, forfeit s.th.

verscheuchen [fɛr'ʃɔʏçən], *v.a.* scare away, frighten away; *Sorgen —*, banish care.

verschicken [fɛr'ʃɪkən], *v.a.* send on, send out, forward, transmit; evacuate.

Verschickung [fɛr'ʃɪkuŋ], *f.* (**—**, *no pl.*) forwarding, transmission; evacuation; banishment, exile.

259

verschieben [fɛr'ʃiːbən], v.a. irr. shift, move; delay, put off, defer, postpone.
Verschiebung [fɛr'ʃiːbuŋ], f. (—, pl. —en) removal; postponement; (fig.) black marketeering.
verschieden [fɛr'ʃiːdən], adj. different, diverse; deceased, departed; (pl.) some, several, sundry.
verschiedenartig [fɛr'ʃiːdənaːrtɪç], adj. varied, various, heterogeneous.
verschiedenerlei [fɛr'ʃiːdənərlaɪ], indecl. adj. diverse, of various kinds.
Verschiedenheit [fɛr'ʃiːdənhaɪt], f. (—, pl. —en) difference; diversity, variety.
verschiedentlich [fɛr'ʃiːdəntlɪç], adv. variously, severally; repeatedly.
verschiffen [fɛr'ʃɪfən], v.a. export, ship.
verschimmeln [fɛr'ʃɪməln], v.n. (aux. sein) go mouldy.
verschlafen [fɛr'ʃlaːfən], v.a. irr. sleep through, sleep away. — v.r. sich —, oversleep. — adj. sleepy, drowsy.
Verschlag [fɛr'ʃlaːk], m. (—s, pl. ˙e) partition, box, cubicle.
verschlagen [fɛr'ʃlaːgən], v.a. irr. es verschlägt mir den Atem, it takes my breath away. — adj. cunning, crafty, sly.
verschlechtern [fɛr'ʃlɛçtərn], v.a. worsen, make worse. — v.r. sich —, deteriorate.
Verschlechterung [fɛr'ʃlɛçtəruŋ], f. (—, no pl.) deterioration.
verschleiern [fɛr'ʃlaɪərn], v.a. veil.
Verschleierung [fɛr'ʃlaɪəruŋ], f. (—, pl. —en) veiling, concealment; camouflage.
verschleißen [fɛr'ʃlaɪsən], v.a. irr. wear out, waste.
verschlemmen [fɛr'ʃlɛmən], v.a. squander on eating and drinking.
verschleppen [fɛr'ʃlɛpən], v.a. carry off, deport; kidnap; protract, spread; put off, procrastinate.
verschleudern [fɛr'ʃlɔydərn], v.a. waste; sell at cut prices.
verschließen [fɛr'ʃliːsən], v.a. irr. lock, lock up.
verschlimmern [fɛr'ʃlɪmərn], v.a. make worse. — v.r. sich —, get worse, worsen, deteriorate.
Verschlimmerung [fɛr'ʃlɪməruŋ], f. (—, no pl.) worsening, deterioration.
verschlingen [fɛr'ʃlɪŋən], v.a. irr. swallow up, devour.
verschlossen [fɛr'ʃlɔsən], adj. reserved, uncommunicative, withdrawn.
Verschlossenheit [fɛr'ʃlɔsənhaɪt], f. (—, no pl.) reserve.
verschlucken [fɛr'ʃlukən], v.a. swallow, gulp down; (fig.) suppress. — v.r. sich —, swallow the wrong way.
verschlungen [fɛr'ʃluŋən], adj. intricate, complicated.
Verschluß [fɛr'ʃlus], m. (—sses, pl. ˙sse) lock; clasp; fastening; unter — haben, keep under lock and key.
Verschlußlaut [fɛr'ʃluslaut], m. (—s, pl. —e) (Phon.) explosive, plosive, stop.

verschmachten [fɛr'ʃmaxtən], v.n. (aux. sein) languish, pine; be parched.
Verschmähung [fɛr'ʃmɛːuŋ], f. (—, no pl.) disdain, scorn, rejection.
Verschmelzung [fɛr'ʃmɛltsuŋ], f. (—, no pl.) coalescence, fusion, blending.
verschmerzen [fɛr'ʃmɛrtsən], v.a. get over; bear stoically, make the best of.
verschmitzt [fɛr'ʃmɪtst], adj. cunning, crafty, mischievous.
verschmutzen [fɛr'ʃmutsən], v.n. (aux. sein) get dirty.
verschnappen [fɛr'ʃnapən], v.r. sich —, blurt out a secret, give o.s. away, let the cat out of the bag.
verschneiden [fɛr'ʃnaɪdən], v.a. irr. (wings) clip; (trees) prune; (animals) castrate; (wine) blend.
verschneien [fɛr'ʃnaɪən], v.n. (aux. sein) be snowed up, be covered with snow, be snowbound.
Verschnitt [fɛr'ʃnɪt], m. (—s, no pl.) blended wine, blend.
Verschnittene [fɛr'ʃnɪtənə], m. (—n, pl. —n) eunuch.
verschnörkelt [fɛr'ʃnœrkəlt], adj. adorned with flourishes.
verschnupft [fɛr'ʃnupft], adj. — sein, have a cold in the head; (fig.) be vexed.
verschnüren [fɛr'ʃnyːrən], v.a. (shoes) lace up; (parcel) tie up.
verschonen [fɛr'ʃoːnən], v.a. spare, exempt from.
verschönern [fɛr'ʃøːnərn], v.a. embellish, beautify.
Verschönerung [fɛr'ʃøːnəruŋ], f. (—, pl. —en) embellishment, adornment.
Verschonung [fɛr'ʃoːnuŋ], f. (—, no pl.) exemption; forbearance.
verschossen [fɛr'ʃɔsən], adj. faded, discoloured; (fig.) madly in love.
verschreiben [fɛr'ʃraɪbən], v.a. irr. prescribe. — v.r. sich —, make a mistake in writing.
verschrien [fɛr'ʃriːən], adj. notorious.
verschroben [fɛr'ʃroːbən], adj. cranky, eccentric.
Verschrobenheit [fɛr'ʃroːbənhaɪt], f. (—, pl. —en) crankiness, eccentricity.
verschrumpfen [fɛr'ʃrumpfən], v.n. (aux. sein) shrivel up.
verschüchtern [fɛr'ʃyçtərn], v.a. intimidate.
verschulden [fɛr'ʃuldən], v.a. bring on, be the cause of; be guilty of.
verschuldet [fɛr'ʃuldət], adj. in debt.
Verschuldung [fɛr'ʃulduŋ], f. (—, no pl.) indebtedness.
verschütten [fɛr'ʃytən], v.a. spill; bury alive.
verschwägern [fɛr'ʃvɛːgərn], v.r. sich —, become related by marriage.
Verschwägerung [fɛr'ʃvɛːgəruŋ], (—, no pl.) relationship by marriage.
verschwatzen [fɛr'ʃvatsən], v.a. gossip (the time) away, spend o.'s time gossiping.
verschweigen [fɛr'ʃvaɪgən], v.a. irr. keep secret, keep (news) from, hush up.

Verständnis

verschwenden [fɛr'ʃvɛndən], *v.a.*
squander, waste.
verschwenderisch [fɛr'ʃvɛndəriʃ], *adj.*
prodigal, profuse, lavish; wasteful.
Verschwendung [fɛr'ʃvɛnduŋ], *f.* (—,
no pl.) waste, extravagance.
Verschwendungssucht [fɛr'ʃvɛnduŋs-
zuxt], *f.* (—, *no pl.*) prodigality;
extravagance.
verschwiegen [fɛr'ʃviːgən], *adj.* discreet, close, secretive.
Verschwiegenheit [fɛr'ʃviːgənhait], *f.*
(—, *no pl.*) discretion, secrecy.
verschwimmen [fɛr'ʃvimən], *v.n. irr.*
(*aux.* sein) become blurred.
verschwinden [fɛr'ʃvindən], *v.n. irr.*
(*aux.* sein) disappear, vanish.
verschwommen [fɛr'ʃvɔmən], *adj.*
vague, blurred.
verschwören [fɛr'ʃvøːrən], *v.r. irr.*
sich —, plot, conspire.
Verschwörer [fɛr'ʃvøːrer], *m.* (—s,
pl. —) conspirator.
Verschwörung [fɛr'ʃvøːruŋ], *f.* (—,
pl. —en) conspiracy.
Versehen [fɛr'zeːən], *n.* (—s, *pl.* —)
error, mistake, oversight.
versehen [fɛr'zeːən], *v.a. irr.* provide;
perform; fill (an office); *einen* — *mit*,
furnish s.o. with. — *v.r. sich* —, make
a mistake.
versehren [fɛr'zeːrən], *v.a.* wound,
disable.
versenden [fɛr'zɛndən], *v.a. irr.* forward, consign, send off.
Versender [fɛr'zɛndər], *m.* (—s, *pl.*—)
consigner, exporter.
Versendung [fɛr'zɛnduŋ], *f.* (—, *no
pl.*) transmission, shipping.
Versendungskosten [fɛr'zɛnduŋskɔs-
tən], *f. pl.* forwarding charges.
versengen [fɛr'zɛŋən], *v.a.* singe,
scorch.
versenken [fɛr'zɛŋkən], *v.a.* sink;
(*ship*) scuttle.
Versenkung [fɛr'zɛŋkuŋ], *f.* (—, *no
pl.*) sinking; hollow; (*ship*) scuttling;
(*Theat.*) trap-door.
versessen [fɛr'zɛsən], *adj.* — *sein auf*,
be bent upon, be mad on.
versetzen [fɛr'zɛtsən], *v.a.* transplant,
remove; give; pawn, pledge; transfer;
(*pupil*) promote to a higher form.
— *v.r. sich in die Lage eines anderen*
—, put o.s. in s.o. else's position.
versichern [fɛr'ziçərn], *v.a.* assert,
declare, aver, assure (s.o. of s.th);
insure (s.th.).
Versicherung [fɛr'ziçəruŋ], *f.* (—,
pl. —en) assurance, assertion; insurance.
Versicherungsgesellschaft [fɛr'ziçə-
ruŋsgəzɛlʃaft], *f.* (—, *pl.* —en)
insurance company.
Versicherungsprämie [fɛr'ziçəruŋs-
prɛːmjə], *f.* (—, *pl.* —n) insurance
premium.
versiegbar [fɛr'ziːkbaːr], *adj.* exhaustible.
versiegeln [fɛr'ziːgəln], *v.a.* seal (up).

versiegen [fɛr'ziːgən], *v.n.* (*aux.* sein)
dry up, be exhausted.
versilbern [fɛr'zilbərn], *v.a.* plate with
silver; (*fig.*) convert into money.
versinken [fɛr'ziŋkən], *v.n. irr.* sink;
(*ship*) founder; sink; *versunken sein*,
be absorbed (in s.th.).
Versmaß ['fɛrsmaːs], *n.* (—es, *pl.* —e)
metre.
versoffen [fɛr'zɔfən], *adj.* (*vulg.*)
drunken.
versohlen [fɛr'zoːlən], *v.a.* (*coll.*)
thrash (s.o.).
versöhnen [fɛr'zøːnən], *v.r. sich mit
einem* —, become reconciled with
s.o.
versöhnlich [fɛr'zøːnliç], *adj.* pro-
pitiatory, conciliatory.
Versöhnung [fɛr'zøːnuŋ], *f.* (—, *no
pl.*) reconciliation.
versorgen [fɛr'zɔrgən], *v.a.* provide
with; take care of; support, maintain.
Versorger [fɛr'zɔrgəi], *m.* (—s, *pl.* —)
provider.
Versorgung [fɛr'zɔrguŋ], *f.* (—, *no pl.*)
provision, maintenance.
verspäten [fɛr'ʃpɛːtən], *v.r. sich* —, be
late, be behind time; (*train*) be overdue.
Verspätung [fɛr'ʃpɛːtuŋ], *f.* (—, *no pl.*)
delay; lateness.
verspeisen [fɛr'ʃpaizən], *v.a.* eat up.
versperren [fɛr'ʃpɛrən], *v.a.* block up,
barricade, close.
verspielen [fɛr'ʃpiːlən], *v.a.* lose (at
play); gamble away. — *v.r. sich* —,
play wrong.
verspielt [fɛr'ʃpiːlt], *adj.* playful.
verspotten [fɛr'ʃpɔtən], *v.a.* deride,
scoff at.
versprechen [fɛr'ʃprɛçən], *v.a. irr.*
promise. — *v.r. sich* —, make a slip
of the tongue.
Versprechen [fɛr'ʃprɛçən], *n.* (—s,
pl. —) promise.
versprengen [fɛr'ʃprɛŋən], *v.a.* disperse.
verspüren [fɛr'ʃpyːrən], *v.a.* feel,
perceive.
verstaatlichen [fɛr'ʃtaːtliçən], *v.a.*
nationalise.
Verstand [fɛr'ʃtant], *m.* (—(e)s, *no pl.*)
intellect, intelligence, sense; understanding, reason, mind.
verstandesmäßig [fɛr'ʃtandəsmɛːsiç],
adj. rational, reasonable.
Verstandesschärfe [fɛr'ʃtandəsʃɛrfə],
f. (—, *no pl.*) penetration, acumen.
verständig [fɛr'ʃtɛndiç], *adj.* judicious,
sensible, reasonable.
verständigen [fɛr'ʃtɛndigən], *v.a.* inform, notify. — *v.r. sich mit einem* —,
come to an agreement with s.o.
Verständigung [fɛr'ʃtɛndiguŋ], *f.* (—,
pl. —en) understanding, agreement;
information; arrangement.
verständlich [fɛr'ʃtɛntliç], *adj.* intelligible, clear, understandable.
Verständnis [fɛr'ʃtɛntnis], (—ses, *no
pl.*) comprehension, understanding,
perception, insight.

261

verständnisinnig [fɛr'ʃtɛntnɪsɪnɪç], *adj.* sympathetic; having profound insight.

verstärken [fɛr'ʃtɛrkən], *v.a.* strengthen, reinforce, intensify.

Verstärker [fɛr'ʃtɛrkər], *m.* (—s, *pl.* —) amplifier; magnifier.

Verstärkung [fɛr'ʃtɛrkuŋ], *f.* (—, *pl.* —en) strengthening, intensification, amplification; (*Mil.*) reinforcements.

verstauben [fɛr'ʃtaubən], *v.n.* (*aux.* sein) get dusty.

verstauchen [fɛr'ʃtauxən], *v.a.* wrench, sprain, dislocate.

verstauen [fɛr'ʃtauən], *v.a.* stow away.

Versteck [fɛr'ʃtɛk], *n.* (—s, *pl.* —e) hiding-place; place of concealment; —(*en*) *spielen*, play hide-and-seek.

verstecken [fɛr'ʃtɛkən], *v.a.* hide, conceal.

versteckt [fɛr'ʃtɛkt], *adj.* indirect, veiled.

verstehen [fɛr'ʃte:ən], *v.a. irr.* understand, comprehend.

versteigen [fɛr'ʃtaɪɡən], *v.r. irr. sich* —, climb too high; (*fig.*) go too far.

versteigern [fɛr'ʃtaɪɡərn], *v.a.* sell by auction.

Versteigerung [fɛr'ʃtaɪɡəruŋ], *f.* (—, *pl.* —en) auction, public sale.

versteinern [fɛr'ʃtaɪnərn], *v.n.* (*aux.* sein) turn into stone, petrify.

verstellbar [fɛr'ʃtɛlba:r], *adj.* adjustable.

verstellen [fɛr'ʃtɛlən], *v.a.* adjust; (*voice*) disguise. — *v.r. sich* —, sham, pretend.

versterben [fɛr'ʃtɛrbən], *v.n. irr.* (*aux.* sein) die. (*Poet.*)

versteuern [fɛr'ʃtɔyərn], *v.a.* pay tax on.

verstiegen [fɛr'ʃti:ɡən], *adj.* eccentric, extravagant.

verstimmen [fɛr'ʃtɪmən], *v.a.* (*Mus.*) put out of tune; (*fig.*) put out of humour, annoy.

Verstimmtheit [fɛr'ʃtɪmthaɪt], *f.* (—, *no pl.*) ill-humour, ill-temper, pique.

Verstimmung [fɛr'ʃtɪmuŋ], *f.* (—, *pl.* —en) bad temper, ill-feeling.

verstockt [fɛr'ʃtɔkt], *adj.* stubborn, obdurate.

Verstocktheit [fɛr'ʃtɔkthaɪt], *f.* (—, *no pl.*) stubbornness, obduracy.

verstohlen [fɛr'ʃto:lən], *adj.* surreptitious, clandestine, furtive.

verstopfen [fɛr'ʃtɔpfən], *v.a.* stop up; block (up); *verstopft sein*, be constipated.

Verstopfung [fɛr'ʃtɔpfuŋ], *f.* (—, *pl.* —en) obstruction; constipation.

verstorben [fɛr'ʃtɔrbən], *adj.* deceased, late.

verstört [fɛr'ʃtø:rt], *adj.* troubled, worried; distracted.

Verstörtheit [fɛr'ʃtø:rthaɪt], *f.* (—, *no pl.*) consternation, agitation; distraction; haggardness.

Verstoß [fɛr'ʃto:s], *m.* (—es, *pl.* ⁀e) blunder, mistake; offence.

verstoßen [fɛr'ʃto:sən], *v.a. irr.* cast off, disown, repudiate. — *v.n.* —

gegen, offend against, act in a manner contrary to.

verstreichen [fɛr'ʃtraɪçən], *v.n. irr.* (*aux.* sein) (*time*) elapse, pass away.

verstricken [fɛr'ʃtrɪkən], *v.a.* entangle, ensnare.

Verstrickung [fɛr'ʃtrɪkuŋ], *f.* (—, *pl.* —en) entanglement.

verstümmeln [fɛr'ʃtyməln], *v.a.* mutilate, mangle.

verstummen [fɛr'ʃtumən], *v.n.* (*aux.* sein) grow silent; become speechless.

Verstümmlung [fɛr'ʃtymluŋ], *f.* (—, *pl.* —en) mutilation.

Versuch [fɛr'zu:x], *m.* (—s, *pl.* —e) attempt, trial, endeavour; (*science*) experiment; (*Lit.*) essay.

versuchen [fɛr'zu:xən], *v.a.* try, attempt, endeavour; (*food*) taste; *einen* —, tempt s.o.

Versucher [fɛr'zu:xər], *m.* (—s, *pl.* —) tempter.

Versuchskaninchen [fɛr'zu:xskani:nçən], *n.* (—s, *pl.* —) (*fig.*) guinea-pig.

Versuchung [fɛr'zu:xuŋ], *f.* (—, *pl.* —en) temptation.

versündigen [fɛr'zyndɪɡən], *v.r. sich* —, sin (against).

Versunkenheit [fɛr'zuŋkənhaɪt], *f.* (—, *no pl.*) absorption, preoccupation.

vertagen [fɛr'ta:ɡən], *v.a.* adjourn, prorogue.

Vertagung [fɛr'ta:ɡuŋ], *f.* (—, *pl.* —en) adjournment, prorogation.

vertauschen [fɛr'tauʃən], *v.a.* exchange, barter, mistake, confuse.

verteidigen [fɛr'taɪdɪɡən], *v.a.* defend, uphold, vindicate; (*fig.*) maintain.

Verteidiger [fɛr'taɪdɪɡər], *m.* (—s, *pl.* —) defender; (*Law*) counsel for the defence.

Verteidigung [fɛr'taɪdɪɡuŋ], *f.* (—, *no pl.*) defence; justification.

Verteidigungskrieg [fɛr'taɪdɪɡuŋskri:k], *m.* (—(e)s, *pl.* —e) defensive war.

verteilen [fɛr'taɪlən], *v.a.* distribute, allot, allocate.

Verteilung [fɛr'taɪluŋ], *f.* (—, *pl.* —en) distribution, apportionment.

verteuern [fɛr'tɔyərn], *v.a.* make dearer, raise the price of.

verteufelt [fɛr'tɔyfəlt], *adj.* devilish. — *adv.* (*coll.*) awfully, infernally.

vertiefen [fɛr'ti:fən], *v.a.* deepen.

vertieft [fɛr'ti:ft], *adj.* absorbed, deep in thought.

Vertiefung [fɛr'ti:fuŋ], *f.* (—, *pl.* —en) cavity, recess, hollow; (*knowledge*) deepening; (*fig.*) absorption.

vertilgen [fɛr'tɪlɡən], *v.a.* wipe out, exterminate; (*food*) (*coll.*) polish off.

Vertilgung [fɛr'tɪlɡuŋ], *f.* (—, *no pl.*) extermination, extirpation.

Vertrag [fɛr'tra:k], *m.* (—(e)s, *pl.* ⁀e) contract, agreement; (*Pol.*) treaty, pact, convention.

vertragen [fɛr'tra:ɡən], *v.a. irr.* suffer, endure; (*food*) digest. — *v.r. sich* — *mit*, get on well with.

Verwandlung

vertraglich [fɛrˈtraːklɪç], *adj.* as per contract, according to agreement.
verträglich [fɛrˈtrɛːklɪç], *adj.* accommodating, peaceable.
vertragsmäßig [fɛrˈtraːksmɛːsɪç], *adj.* according to contract.
vertragswidrig [fɛrˈtraːksviːdrɪç], *adj.* contrary to contract.
vertrauen [fɛrˈtrauən], *v.n.* rely (upon), trust (in).
Vertrauen [fɛrˈtrauən], *n.* (—s, *no pl.*) confidence, trust, reliance.
vertrauenerweckend [fɛrˈtrauənervɛkənt], *adj.* inspiring confidence.
Vertrauensbruch [fɛrˈtrauənsbrux], *m.* (—es, *pl.* ⁓e) breach of faith.
Vertrauensmann [fɛrˈtrauənsman], *m.* (—s, *pl.* ⁓er) confidant; delegate; person entrusted with s.th.; (*Ind.*) shop steward.
vertrauensselig [fɛrˈtrauənszeːlɪç], *adj.* confiding, trusting.
Vertrauensvotum [fɛrˈtrauənsvoːtum], *n.* (—s, *pl.* —ten) vote of confidence.
vertrauenswürdig [fɛrˈtrauənsvyrdɪç], *adj.* trustworthy.
vertraulich [fɛrˈtraulɪç], *adj.* confidential; familiar.
Vertraulichkeit [fɛrˈtraulɪçkaɪt], *f.* (—, *pl.* —en) familiarity.
verträumt [fɛrˈtrɔymt], *adj.* dreamy.
vertraut [fɛrˈtraut], *adj.* intimate, familiar; conversant.
Vertraute [fɛrˈtrautə], *m.* (—n, *pl.* —n) close friend, confidant.
Vertrautheit [fɛrˈtrauthaɪt], *f.* (—, *no pl.*) familiarity.
vertreiben [fɛrˈtraɪbən], *v.a. irr.* drive away, expel; eject; (*person*) banish; (*time*) pass, kill; (*goods*) sell.
Vertreibung [fɛrˈtraɪbuŋ], *f.* (—, *no pl.*) expulsion; banishment.
vertreten [fɛrˈtreːtən], *v.a. irr.* represent (s.o.), deputise for (s.o.).
Vertreter [fɛrˈtreːtər], *m.* (—s, *pl.* —) representative, deputy; (*Comm.*) agent.
Vertretung [fɛrˈtreːtuŋ], *f.* (—, *pl.* —en) representation, agency.
Vertrieb [fɛrˈtriːp], *m.* (—s, *pl.* —e) sale; distribution.
vertrinken [fɛrˈtrɪŋkən], *v.a. irr.* spend *or* waste money on drink.
vertrocknen [fɛrˈtrɔknən], *v.n.* (*aux.* sein) dry up, wither.
vertrödeln [fɛrˈtrøːdəln], *v.a.* fritter (o.'s time) away.
vertrösten [fɛrˈtrøːstən], *v.a.* console; put off; put (s.o.) off with fine words; fob (s.o.) off with vain hopes.
Vertröstung [fɛrˈtrøːstuŋ], *f.* (—, *pl.* —en) comfort; empty promises.
vertun [fɛrˈtuːn], *v.a. irr.* squander, waste.
vertuschen [fɛrˈtuʃən], *v.a.* hush up.
verübeln [fɛrˈyːbəln], *v.a.* take amiss.
verüben [fɛrˈyːbən], *v.a.* commit, perpetrate.
verunehren [fɛrˈuneːrən], *v.a.* dishonour, disgrace.

verunglimpfen [fɛrˈunglɪmpfən], *v.a.* bring into disrepute; defame, calumniate.
Verunglimpfung [fɛrˈunglɪmpfuŋ], *f.* (—, *pl.* —en) defamation, detraction, calumny.
verunglücken [fɛrˈunglykən], *v.n.* (*aux.* sein) (*person*) meet with an accident; be killed; (*thing*) misfire, fail.
verunreinigen [fɛrˈunraɪnɪgən], *v.a.* contaminate.
Verunreinigung [fɛrˈunraɪnɪguŋ], *f.* (—, *pl.* —en) contamination.
verunstalten [fɛrˈunʃtaltən], *v.a.* disfigure, deface.
Verunstaltung [fɛrˈunʃtaltuŋ], *f.* (—, *pl.* —en) disfigurement.
Veruntreuung [fɛrˈuntrɔyuŋ], *f.* (—, *pl.* —en) embezzlement, misappropriation.
verunzieren [fɛrˈuntsiːrən], *v.a.* disfigure, spoil.
verursachen [fɛrˈuːrzaxən], *v.a.* cause, occasion.
verurteilen [fɛrˈurtaɪlən], *v.a.* condemn; (*Law*) sentence.
Verurteilung [fɛrˈurtaɪluŋ], *f.* (—, *no pl.*) condemnation; (*Law*) sentence.
vervielfältigen [fɛrˈfiːlfɛltɪgən], *v.a.* multiply; duplicate, make copies of.
Vervielfältigung [fɛrˈfiːlfɛltɪguŋ], *f.* (—, *pl.* —en) multiplication; duplication, copying.
vervollkommnen [fɛrˈfɔlkɔmnən], *v.a.* improve, perfect.
Vervollkommnung [fɛrˈfɔlkɔmnuŋ], *f.* (—, *no pl.*) improvement, perfection.
vervollständigen [fɛrˈfɔlʃtɛndɪgən], *v.a.* complete.
Vervollständigung [fɛrˈfɔlʃtɛndɪguŋ], *f.* (—, *no pl.*) completion.
verwachsen [fɛrˈvaksən], *v.n. irr.* (*aux.* sein) grow together; be overgrown. — *adj.* deformed.
verwahren [fɛrˈvaːrən], *v.a.* take care of, preserve, secure. — *v.r. sich* — *gegen*, protest against.
verwahrlosen [fɛrˈvaːrloːzən], *v.a.* neglect. — *v.n.* (*aux.* sein) be in need of care and protection, be neglected.
Verwahrlosung [fɛrˈvaːrloːzuŋ], *f.* (—, *no pl.*) neglect.
Verwahrung [fɛrˈvaːruŋ], *f.* (—, *no pl.*) keeping; charge; *in — geben*, deposit, give into s.o.'s charge; *— einlegen gegen*, enter a protest against.
verwalten [fɛrˈvaltən], *v.a.* manage, administer.
Verwalter [fɛrˈvaltər], *m.* (—s, *pl.* —) administrator, manager; steward, bailiff.
Verwaltung [fɛrˈvaltuŋ], *f.* (—, *pl.* —en) administration, management; Civil Service.
Verwaltungsbezirk [fɛrˈvaltuŋsbətsɪrk], *m.* (—s, *pl.* —e) administrative district.
Verwandlung [fɛrˈvandluŋ], *f.* (—, *pl.* —en) alteration, transformation.

263

Verwandlungskünstler [fɛr'vandluŋs-kynstlər], *m.* (**—s**, *pl.* **—**) quick-change artist.

verwandt [fɛr'vant], *adj.* related; cognate; congenial.

Verwandte [fɛr'vantə], *m.* (**—n**, *pl.* **—n**) relative, relation; kinsman; *der nächste —*, next of kin.

Verwandtschaft [fɛr'vantʃaft], *f.* (**—**, *pl.* **—en**) relationship; relations, family; congeniality, sympathy.

verwarnen [fɛr'varnən], *v.a.* admonish, forewarn.

Verwarnung [fɛr'varnuŋ], *f.* (**—**, *pl.* **—en**) admonition.

Verwässerung [fɛr'vɛsəruŋ], *f.* (**—**, *pl.* **—en**) dilution.

verwechseln [fɛr'vɛksəln], *v.a.* confuse; mistake for.

Verwechslung [fɛr'vɛksluŋ], *f.* (**—**, *pl.* **—en**) confusion, mistake.

verwegen [fɛr've:gən], *adj.* bold, audacious.

Verwegenheit [fɛr've:gənhaɪt], *f.* (**—**, *pl.* **—en**) boldness, audacity.

verweichlichen [fɛr'vaɪçlɪçən], *v.a.* coddle. — *v.n.* (*aux.* sein) become effeminate.

verweigern [fɛr'vaɪgərn], *v.a.* refuse, deny; reject.

Verweigerung [fɛr'vaɪgəruŋ], *f.* (**—**, *pl.* **—en**) refusal, denial; rejection.

verweilen [fɛr'vaɪlən], *v.n.* remain; tarry; stay (with), dwell (on).

verweint [fɛr'vaɪnt], *adj.* (*eyes*) red with weeping.

Verweis [fɛr'vaɪs], *m.* (**—es**, *pl.* **—e**) reproof, reprimand, rebuke.

verweisen [fɛr'vaɪzən], *v.a. irr.* reprimand; banish, exile; — *auf etwas*, refer to s.th., hint at s.th.

Verweisung [fɛr'vaɪzuŋ], *f.* (**—**, *pl.* **—en**) banishment, exile; reference.

verweltlichen [fɛr'vɛltlɪçən], *v.a.* secularise, profane.

verwenden [fɛr'vɛndən], *v.a.* use, make use of; apply to, employ in, utilize.

Verwendung [fɛr'vɛnduŋ], *f.* (**—**, *pl.* **—en**) application, use, expenditure, employment.

verwerfen [fɛr'vɛrfən], *v.a. irr.* reject, disapprove of.

verwerflich [fɛr'vɛrflɪç], *adj.* objectionable.

Verwertung [fɛr've:rtuŋ], *f.* (**—**, *no pl.*) utilisation.

verwesen [fɛr've:zən], *v.a.* administer. — *v.n.* (*aux.* sein) rot, decompose, putrefy.

Verweser [fɛr've:zər], *m.* (**—s**, *pl.* **—**) administrator.

Verwesung [fɛr've:zuŋ], *f.* (**—**, *no pl.*) (*office*) administration; putrefaction, rotting.

verwickeln [fɛr'vɪkəln], *v.a.* entangle, involve.

verwickelt [fɛr'vɪkəlt], *adj.* intricate, complicated, involved.

Verwicklung [fɛr'vɪkluŋ], *f.* (**—**, *pl.* **—en**) entanglement, involvement, complication.

verwildern [fɛr'vɪldərn], *v.n.* (*aux.* sein) run wild.

verwildert [fɛr'vɪldərt], *adj.* wild, uncultivated, overgrown; (*fig.*) intractable.

Verwilderung [fɛr'vɪldəruŋ], *f.* (**—**, *no pl.*) running wild, growing wild.

verwirken [fɛr'vɪrkən], *v.a.* forfeit.

verwirklichen [fɛr'vɪrklɪçən], *v.a.* realise. — *v.r. sich —*, materialise, come true.

Verwirklichung [fɛr'vɪrklɪçuŋ], *f.* (**—**, *no pl.*) realisation, materialisation.

Verwirkung [fɛr'vɪrkuŋ], *f.* (**—**, *no pl.*) forfeiture.

verwirren [fɛr'vɪrən], *v.a.* disarrange, throw into disorder, entangle; puzzle, bewilder, confuse, disconcert.

Verwirrung [fɛr'vɪruŋ], *f.* (**—**, *pl.* **—en**) bewilderment, confusion.

verwischen [fɛr'vɪʃən], *v.a.* blot out, smudge, obliterate.

verwittern [fɛr'vɪtərn], *v.n.* (*aux.* sein) be weather-beaten.

verwöhnen [fɛr'vø:nən], *v.a.* spoil, pamper, coddle.

verworfen [fɛr'vɔrfən], *adj.* profligate; rejected, reprobate.

verworren [fɛr'vɔrən], *adj.* confused, perplexed; intricate; (*speech*) rambling.

verwundbar [fɛr'vuntba:r], *adj.* vulnerable.

verwunden [fɛr'vundən], *v.a.* wound, hurt, injure.

verwundern [fɛr'vundərn], *v.r. sich —*, be surprised, wonder, be amazed.

Verwunderung [fɛr'vundəruŋ], *f.* (**—**, *no pl.*) surprise, astonishment, amazement.

Verwundung [fɛr'vunduŋ], *f.* (**—**, *pl.* **—en**) wounding, wound, injury.

verwunschen [fɛr'vunʃən], *adj.* enchanted, spellbound, bewitched.

verwünschen [fɛr'vynʃən], *v.a.* curse; cast a spell on, bewitch.

verwünscht [fɛr'vynʃt], *excl.* confound it!

Verwünschung [fɛr'vynʃuŋ], *f.* (**—**, *pl.* **—en**) curse, malediction.

verwüsten [fɛr'vy:stən], *v.a.* devastate, ravage, lay waste.

Verwüstung [fɛr'vy:stuŋ], *f.* (**—**, *pl.* **—en**) devastation.

verzagen [fɛr'tsa:gən], *v.n.* (*aux.* sein) lose heart, lose courage.

verzagt [fɛr'tsa:kt], *adj.* fainthearted, discouraged.

Verzagtheit [fɛr'tsa:kthaɪt], *f.* (**—**, *no pl.*) faintheartedness.

verzählen [fɛr'tsɛ:lən], *v.r. sich —*, miscount.

verzapfen [fɛr'tsapfən], *v.a.* sell (liquor) on draught; (*fig.*) tell (a story), talk (nonsense).

verzärteln [fɛr'tsɛ:rtəln], *v.a.* pamper, coddle; spoil.

verzaubern [fɛr'tsaubərn], *v.a.* bewitch, charm, put a spell on.

verzehren [fɛr'tseːrən], *v.a.* consume, eat. — *v.r. sich — in*, pine away with, be consumed with.

Verzehrung [fɛr'tseːruŋ], *f.* (—, *no pl.*) (*obs.*) consumption, tuberculosis.

verzeichnen [fɛr'tsaɪçnən], *v.a.* draw badly; note down, register, record.

Verzeichnis [fɛr'tsaɪçnɪs], *n.* (—ses, *pl.* —se) catalogue, list, register.

verzeihen [fɛr'tsaɪən], *v.a. irr.* forgive, pardon.

verzeihlich [fɛr'tsaɪlɪç], *adj.* pardonable, forgivable, excusable, venial.

Verzeihung [fɛr'tsaɪuŋ], *f.* (—, *no pl.*) pardon, forgiveness; *ich bitte um —*, I beg your pardon.

verzerren [fɛr'tsɛrən], *v.a.* distort.

Verzerrung [fɛr'tsɛruŋ], *f.* (—, *pl.* —en) distortion; (*face*) grimace.

verzetteln [fɛr'tsɛtəln], *v.a.* disperse, scatter.

Verzicht [fɛr'tsɪçt], *m.* (—(e)s, *no pl.*) renunciation, resignation.

verzichten [fɛr'tsɪçtən], *v.n.* forgo, renounce.

verziehen [fɛr'tsiːən], *v.a. irr.* distort; spoil (*child*). — *v.n.* (*aux.* sein) go away, move away.

Verzierung [fɛr'tsiːruŋ], *f.* (—, *pl.* —en) decoration, ornament.

verzögern [fɛr'tsøːgərn], *v.a.* delay, defer, retard, protract, procrastinate. — *v.r. sich —*, be delayed.

Verzögerung [fɛr'tsøːgəruŋ], *f.* (—, *pl.* —en) delay, retardation, procrastination; time-lag.

verzollen [fɛr'tsɔlən], *v.a.* pay duty on.

Verzücktheit [fɛr'tsʏkthaɪt], *f.* (—, *no pl.*) ecstasy, rapture.

Verzug [fɛr'tsuːk], *m.* (—s, *no pl.*) delay.

verzweifeln [fɛr'tsvaɪfəln], *v.n.* despair, be desperate.

Verzweiflung [fɛr'tsvaɪfluŋ], *f.* (—, *no pl.*) despair.

verzwickt [fɛr'tsvɪkt], *adj.* complicated, intricate, tricky.

Vesuv [ve'zuːf], *m.* Mount Vesuvius.

Vetter ['vɛtər], *m.* (—s, *pl.* —n) cousin.

Vetternwirtschaft ['vɛtərnvɪrtʃaft], *f.* (—, *no pl.*) nepotism.

Vexierbild [vɛ'ksiːrbɪlt], *n.* (—s, *pl.* —er) picture-puzzle.

Vexierspiegel [vɛ'ksiːrʃpiːgəl], *m.* (—s, *pl.*—) distorting mirror.

vibrieren [vi'briːrən], *v.n.* vibrate.

Vieh [fiː], *n.* (—s, *no pl.*) cattle, livestock.

Viehfutter ['fiːfutər], *n.* (—s, *no pl.*) forage, fodder, feeding-stuff.

viehisch ['fiːɪʃ], *adj.* beastly, brutal.

Viehwagen ['fiːvaːgən], *m.* (—s, *pl.* —) cattle-truck.

Viehweide ['fiːvaɪdə], *f.* (—, *pl.* —n) pasture, pasturage.

Viehzüchter ['fiːtsʏçtər], *m.* (—s, *pl.* —) cattle-breeder.

viel [fiːl], *adv.* much, a great deal, a lot; (*pl.*) many.

vielartig ['fiːlartɪç], *adj.* multifarious.

vieldeutig ['fiːldɔytɪç], *adj.* ambiguous, equivocal.

Vieleck ['fiːlɛk], *n.* (—s, *pl.* —e) polygon.

vielerlei ['fiːlərlaɪ], *adj.* of many kinds, various.

vielfältig ['fiːlfɛltɪç], *adj.* manifold.

vielfarbig ['fiːlfarbɪç], *adj.* multicoloured, variegated.

Vielfraß ['fiːlfraːs], *m.* (—es, *pl.* —e) glutton.

vielgeliebt ['fiːlgəliːpt], *adj.* much loved.

vielgereist ['fiːlgəraɪst], *adj.* much travelled.

vielleicht [fi'laɪçt], *adv.* perhaps, maybe.

vielmals ['fiːlmaːls], *adv.* many times, frequently, much.

Vielmännerei [fiːlmɛnə'raɪ], *f.* (—, *no pl.*) polyandry.

vielmehr [fiːl'meːr], *adv.* rather, much more. — *conj.* rather, on the other hand.

vielsagend ['fiːlzaːgənt], *adj.* expressive, full of meaning.

vielseitig ['fiːlzaɪtɪç], *adj.* multilateral; (*fig.*) versatile.

Vielseitigkeit ['fiːlzaɪtɪçkaɪt], *f.* (—, *no pl.*) versatility.

vielverheißend ['fiːlfɛrhaɪsənt], *adj.* promising, auspicious.

Vielweiberei [fiːlvaɪbe'raɪ], *f.* (—, *no pl.*) polygamy.

vier [fiːr], *num. adj.* four.

Viereck ['fiːrɛk], *n.* (—s, *pl.* —e) square, quadrangle.

viereckig ['fiːrɛkɪç], *adj.* square.

vierfüßig ['fiːrfyːsɪç], *adj.* four-footed.

vierhändig ['fiːrhɛndɪç], *adj.* fourhanded; — *spielen*, (*piano*) play duets.

vierschrötig ['fiːrʃrøːtɪç], *adj.* robust, thick-set, stocky.

vierseitig ['fiːrzaɪtɪç], *adj.* quadrilateral.

vierstimmig ['fiːrʃtɪmɪç], *adj.* (*Mus.*) four-part; for four voices.

vierteilen ['fiːrtaɪlən], *v.a.* quarter, divide into four parts.

Viertel ['fɪrtəl], *n.* (—s, *pl.* —) quarter, fourth part.

Viertelstunde [fɪrtəl'ʃtundə], *f.* (—, *pl.* —n) quarter of an hour.

viertens ['fiːrtəns], *num. adv.* fourthly, in the fourth place.

Vierwaldstättersee [fiːr'valtʃtɛtərzeː], *m.* Lake Lucerne.

vierzehn ['fɪrtseːn], *num. adj.* fourteen; — *Tage*, a fortnight.

vierzig ['fɪrtsɪç], *num. adj.* forty.

Vietnam [viɛt'naːm], *n.* Vietnam.

Vikar [vi'kaːr], *m.* (—s, *pl.* —e) curate.

Violinschlüssel [vio'liːnʃlʏsəl], *m.* (—s, *pl.* —) (*Mus.*) treble clef.

Virtuosität [vɪrtuozi'tɛːt], *f.* (—, *no pl.*) mastery, virtuosity.

Visage [vi'zaːʒə], *f.* (—, *pl.* —n) (*coll.*) face.

Visier [vi'ziːr], *n.* (—, *pl.* —e) visor; (*gun*) sight.

Vision [vi'zjoːn], *f.* (—, *pl.* —en) vision.

Visionär

Visionär [vizjoˈnɛːr], *m.* (—s, *pl.* —e) visionary.

Visitenkarte [viˈziːtənkartə], *f.* (—, *pl.* —n) card, visiting card.

Visum [ˈviːzum], *n.* (—s, *pl.* **Visa**) visa.

Vizekönig [ˈviːtsəkøːnɪç], *m.* (—s, *pl.* —e) viceroy.

Vlies [fliːs], *n.* (—es, *pl.* —e) fleece.

Vogel [ˈfoːgəl], *m.* (—s, *pl.* ⁓) bird; (*coll.*) fellow; *einen* — *haben*, be off o.'s head.

Vogelbauer [ˈfoːgəlbauər], *n.* (—s, *pl.* —) bird-cage.

Vogelfänger [ˈfoːgəlfɛŋər], *m.* (—s, *pl.* —) fowler, bird-catcher.

vogelfrei [ˈfoːgəlfraɪ], *adj.* outlawed, proscribed.

Vogelfutter [ˈfoːgəlfutər], *n.* (—s, *no pl.*) bird-seed.

Vogelhändler [ˈfoːgəlhɛndlər], *m.* (—s, *pl.* —) bird-dealer.

Vogelhaus [ˈfoːgəlhaus], *n.* (—es, *pl.* ⁓er) aviary.

Vogelkenner [ˈfoːgəlkɛnər], *m.* (—s, *pl.* —) ornithologist.

Vogelkunde [ˈfoːgəlkundə], *f.* (—, *no pl.*) ornithology.

Vogelperspektive [ˈfoːgəlpɛrspɛktiːvə], *f.* (—, *no pl.*) bird's-eye view.

Vogelschau [ˈfoːgəlʃau], *f.* (—, *no pl.*) bird's-eye view.

Vogelsteller [ˈfoːgəlʃtɛlər], *m.* (—s, *pl.* —) fowler, bird-catcher.

Vogesen [voˈgeːzən], *pl.* Vosges Mountains.

Vogler [ˈfoːglər], *m.* (—s, *pl.* —) fowler.

Vogt [foːkt], *m.* (—(e)s, *pl.* ⁓e) prefect, bailiff, steward, provost.

Vogtei [foːkˈtaɪ], *f.* (—, *pl.* —en) prefecture, bailiwick.

Vokabel [voˈkaːbəl], *f.* (—, *pl.* —n) word, vocable.

Vokabelbuch [voˈkaːbəlbuːx], *n.* (—(e)s, *pl.* ⁓er) vocabulary (book).

Vokal [voˈkaːl], *m.* (—s, *pl.* —e) vowel.

Vokativ [vokaˈtiːf], *m.* (—s, *pl.* —e) (*Gram.*) vocative.

Volk [fɔlk], *n.* (—(e)s, *pl.* ⁓er) people, nation; *das gemeine* —, mob, the common people.

Völkerkunde [ˈfœlkərkundə], *f.* (—, *no pl.*) ethnology.

Völkerrecht [ˈfœlkərrɛçt], *n.* (—s, *no pl.*) international law.

Völkerschaft [ˈfœlkərʃaft], *f.* (—, *pl.* —en) tribe, people.

Völkerwanderung [ˈfœlkərvandəruŋ], *f.* (—, *pl.* —en) mass migration.

Volksabstimmung [ˈfɔlksapʃtɪmuŋ], *f.* (—, *pl.* —en) referendum.

Volksausgabe [ˈfɔlksausgaːbə], *f.* (—, *pl.* —n) popular edition.

Volksbeschluß [ˈfɔlksbəʃlus], *m.* (—sses, *pl.* ⁓sse) plebiscite.

Volksbibliothek [ˈfɔlksbiblioteːk], *f.* (—, *pl.* —en) public library.

Volkscharakter [ˈfɔlkskaraktər], *m.* (—s, *no pl.*) national character.

Volksentscheid [ˈfɔlksɛntʃaɪt], *m.* (—s, *pl.* —e) plebiscite.

Volksführer [ˈfɔlksfyːrər], *m.* (—s, *pl.* —) demagogue.

Volksheer [ˈfɔlksheːr], *n.* (—s, *pl.* —e) national army.

Volksherrschaft [ˈfɔlksherʃaft], *f.* (—, *no pl.*) democracy.

Volkshochschule [ˈfɔlkshoxʃuːlə], *f.* (—, *no pl.*) adult education (classes).

Volksjustiz [ˈfɔlksjustiːts], *f.* (—, *no pl.*) lynch-law.

Volkskunde [ˈfɔlkskundə], *f.* (—, *no pl.*) folklore.

Volkslied [ˈfɔlksliːt], *n.* (—s, *pl.* —er) folk-song.

Volksschicht [ˈfɔlksʃɪçt], *f.* (—, *pl.* —en) class.

Volksschule [ˈfɔlksʃuːlə], *f.* (—, *pl.* —n) primary school; elementary school.

Volkssitte [ˈfɔlkszɪtə], *f.* (—, *pl.* —n) national custom.

Volkssprache [ˈfɔlksʃpraːxə], *f.* (—, *pl.* —n) vernacular.

Volksstamm [ˈfɔlksʃtam], *m.* (—s, *pl.* ⁓e) tribe.

Volkstracht [ˈfɔlkstraxt], *f.* (—, *pl.* —en) national costume.

volkstümlich [ˈfɔlkstyːmlɪç], *adj.* national, popular.

Volksvertretung [ˈfɔlksfɛrtreːtuŋ], *f.* (—, *no pl.*) representation of the people, parliamentary representation.

Volkswirt [ˈfɔlksvɪrt], *m.* (—s, *pl.* —e) political economist.

Volkswirtschaft [ˈfɔlksvɪrtʃaft], *f.* (—, *no pl.*) political economy.

Volkszählung [ˈfɔlkstsɛːluŋ], *f.* (—, *pl.* —en) census.

voll [fɔl], *adj.* full, filled; whole, complete, entire.

vollauf [ˈfɔlauf], *adv.* abundantly.

Vollbart [ˈfɔlbaːrt], *m.* (—s, *pl.* ⁓e) beard.

vollberechtigt [ˈfɔlbərɛçtɪçt], *adj.* fully entitled.

Vollbild [ˈfɔlbɪlt], *n.* (—s, *pl.* —er) full-length portrait, full-page illustration.

Vollblut [ˈfɔlbluːt], *n.* (—s, *pl.* ⁓er) thoroughbred.

vollblütig [ˈfɔlblyːtɪç], *adj.* full-blooded, thoroughbred.

vollbringen [fɔlˈbrɪŋən], *v.a. irr.* accomplish, achieve, complete.

Vollbringung [fɔlˈbrɪŋuŋ], *f.* (—, *no pl.*) achievement.

Volldampf [ˈfɔldampf], *m.* (—es, *no pl.*) full steam.

vollenden [fɔlˈɛndən], *v.a.* finish, complete.

vollendet [fɔlˈɛndət], *adj.* finished; accomplished.

vollends [ˈfɔlɛnts], *adv.* quite, altogether, wholly, entirely, moreover.

Vollendung [fɔlˈɛnduŋ], *f.* (—, *no pl.*) completion; perfection.

Völlerei [fœləˈraɪ], *f.* (—, *pl.* —en) gluttony.

vollführen [fɔl'fy:rən], *v.a.* execute, carry out.

Vollgefühl ['fɔlgəfy:l], *n.* (—**s**, *no pl.*) consciousness, full awareness.

Vollgenuß ['fɔlgənus], *m.* (—**sses**, *no pl.*) full enjoyment.

vollgültig ['fɔlgyltɪç], *adj.* fully valid; unexceptionable.

Vollheit ['fɔlhaɪt], *f.* (—, *no pl.*) fullness, plenitude.

völlig ['fœlɪç], *adj.* entire, whole, complete.

vollinhaltlich ['fɔlɪnhaltlɪç], *adv.* to its full extent.

volljährig ['fɔljɛ:rɪç], *adj.* of age.

Volljährigkeit ['fɔljɛ:rɪçkaɪt], *f.* (—, *no pl.*) adult years, majority.

vollkommen ['fɔlkɔmən], *adj.* perfect. — *adv.* entirely.

Vollkommenheit [fɔl'kɔmənhaɪt], *f.* (—, *no pl.*) perfection.

Vollmacht ['fɔlmaxt], *f.* (—, *pl.* —**en**) authority; fullness of power; power of attorney.

vollsaftig ['fɔlzaftɪç], *adj.* juicy, succulent.

vollständig ['fɔlʃtɛndɪç], *adj.* complete, full. — *adv.* entirely.

vollstrecken [fɔl'ʃtrɛkən], *v.a.* execute, carry out.

Vollstrecker [fɔl'ʃtrɛkər], *m.* (—**s**, *pl.* —) executor.

volltönig ['fɔltø:nɪç], *adj.* sonorous.

vollwertig ['fɔlvɛrtɪç], *adj.* standard, sterling.

vollzählig ['fɔltsɛ:lɪç], *adj.* complete.

vollziehen [fɔl'tsi:ən], *v.a. irr.* execute, carry out, ratify.

vollziehend [fɔl'tsi:ənt], *adj.* executive.

Vollziehungsgewalt [fɔl'tsi:ʊŋsɡəvalt], *f.* (—, *no pl.*) executive power.

Vollzug [fɔl'tsu:k], *m.* (—**s**, *no pl.*) execution; fulfilment.

Volontär [vɔlɔ'tɛ:r], *m.* (—**s**, *pl.* —**e**) volunteer.

von [fɔn] (*von dem* becomes **vom**), *prep.* (*Dat.*) by, from; of; on; concerning, about; — *Shakespeare*, by Shakespeare; — *Beruf*, by profession; *er kommt — London*, he comes from London; — *fern*, from afar; — *jetzt an*, from now on; — *einem sprechen*, speak of s.o.; *dein Brief vom 15.*, your letter of the 15th.

vonnöten [fɔn'nø:tən], *adv.* — *sein*, be necessary.

vonstatten [fɔn'ʃtatən], *adv.* — *gehen*, progress; go off.

vor [fo:r], *prep.* (*Dat., Acc.*) (*place*) before, ahead of, in front of; (*time*) before, prior to, earlier than; from; of; with; above; in presence of, because of; more than; — *dem Hause*, in front of the house; — *Sonnenaufgang*, before sunrise; —*zwei Tagen*, two days ago; *sich — einem verstecken*, hide from s.o.; *sich hüten* —, beware of; *starr* — *Kälte*, stiff with cold; — *allem*, above all. — *adv.* before; *nach wie* —, now as before.

Vorabend ['fo:ra:bənt], *m.* (—**s**, *pl.* —**e**) eve.

Vorahnung ['fo:ra:nuŋ], *f.* (—, *pl.* —**en**) presentiment, foreboding.

voran [fo'ran], *adv.* before, in front, forward, on.

vorangehen [fo'range:ən], *v.n. irr.* (*aux.* sein) take the lead, go ahead.

Voranzeige ['fo:rantsaɪɡə], *f.* (—, *pl.* —**n**) advance notice; (*film*) trailer.

Vorarbeiter ['fo:rarbaɪtər], *m.* (—**s**, *pl.* —) foreman.

voraus [fo'raus], *adv.* before, in front, foremost; in advance; *im* or *zum* —, beforehand; (*thanks*) in anticipation.

vorauseilen [fo'rausaɪlən], *v.n.* (*aux.* sein) run ahead.

vorausgehen [fo'rausge:ən], *v.n. irr.* (*aux.* sein) walk ahead; *einem* —, go before; precede s.o.

voraushaben [fo'rausha:bən], *v.n. irr.* *etwas vor einem* —, have the advantage over s.o.

Voraussage [fo'rausza:ɡə], *f.* (—, *pl.* —**n**) prediction, prophecy; (*weather*) forecast.

voraussagen [fo'rausza:ɡən], *v.a.* predict, foretell; (*weather*) forecast.

voraussehen [fo'rausze:ən], *v.a. irr.* foresee.

voraussetzen [fo'rausetsən], *v.a.* presuppose, take for granted.

Voraussetzung [fo'rausetsuŋ], *f.* (—, *pl.* —**en**) supposition, presupposition; *unter der* —, on the understanding.

Voraussicht [fo'rauzɪçt], *f.* (—, *no pl.*) foresight, forethought; *aller* — *nach*, in all probability.

voraussichtlich [fo'rauzɪçtlɪç], *adj.* prospective, presumptive, probable, expected. — *adv.* probably, presumably.

Vorbau ['fo:rbau], *m.* (—**s**, *pl.* —**ten**) frontage.

Vorbedacht ['fo:rbədaxt], *m.* (—**s**, *no pl.*) premeditation; *mit* —, on purpose, deliberately.

vorbedacht ['fo:rbədaxt], *adj.* premeditated.

Vorbedeutung ['fo:rbədɔytuŋ], *f.* (—, *pl.* —**en**) omen.

Vorbehalt ['fo:rbəhalt], *m.* (—**s**, *pl.* —**e**) reservation, proviso.

vorbehalten ['fo:rbəhaltən], *v.a. irr.* reserve; make reservation that.

vorbehaltlich ['fo:rbəhaltlɪç], *prep.* (*Genit.*) with the proviso that.

vorbei [fo:r'baɪ], *adv.* by; along; past, over, finished, gone.

vorbeigehen [fo:r'baɪɡe:ən], *v.n. irr.* (*aux.* sein) pass by; go past; march past.

vorbeilassen [fo:r'baɪlasən], *v.a. irr.* let pass.

Vorbemerkung ['fo:rbəmɛrkuŋ], *f.* (—, *pl.* —**en**) preface, prefatory note.

vorbereiten ['fo:rbəraɪtən], *v.a.* prepare.

Vorbereitung ['fo:rbəraɪtuŋ], *f.* (—, *pl.* —**en**) preparation.

Vorbesitzer ['foːrbəzɪtsər], *m.* (**—s**, *pl.* **—**) previous owner.

Vorbesprechung ['foːrbəʃprɛçuŋ], *f.* (**—**, *pl.* **—en**) preliminary discussion.

vorbestimmen ['foːrbəʃtɪmən], *v.a.* predestine, predetermine.

Vorbestimmung ['foːrbəʃtɪmuŋ], *f.* (**—**, *no pl.*) predestination.

vorbestraft ['foːrbəʃtraːft], *adj.* previously convicted.

vorbeten ['foːrbeːtən], *v.n.* lead in prayer.

vorbeugen ['foːrbɔygən], *v.n.* prevent, preclude, obviate. — *v.r. sich —*, bend forward.

Vorbeugung ['foːrbɔyguŋ], *f.* (**—**, *no pl.*) prevention; prophylaxis.

Vorbeugungsmaßnahme ['foːrbɔyguŋsmaːsnaːmə], *f.* (**—**, *pl.* **—n**) preventive measure.

Vorbild ['foːrbɪlt], *n.* (**—s**, *pl.* **—er**) model, example, pattern, ideal.

vorbildlich ['foːrbɪltlɪç], *adj.* exemplary; typical; — *sein*, be a model.

Vorbildung ['foːrbɪlduŋ], *f.* (**—**, *no pl.*) preparatory training.

Vorbote ['foːrboːtə], *m.* (**—n**, *pl.* **—n**) herald, precursor, forerunner.

vorbringen ['foːrbrɪŋən], *v.a. irr.* produce, proffer; advance, utter, allege, assert, claim.

vordatieren ['foːrdatiːrən], *v.a.* antedate.

vordem [for'deːm], *adv.* (*obs.*) formerly, once.

Vorderachse ['fɔrdəraksə], *f.* (**—**, *pl.* **—n**) front axle.

Vorderansicht ['fɔrdəranzɪçt], *f.* (**—**, *pl.* **—en**) front view.

Vorderarm ['fɔrdərarm], *m.* (**—s**, *pl.* **—e**) forearm.

Vordergrund ['fɔrdərgrʊnt], *m.* (**—s**, *pl.* **-e**) foreground.

vorderhand ['fɔrdərhant], *adv.* for the present.

Vorderseite ['fɔrdərzaɪtə], *f.* (**—**, *pl.* **—n**) front.

vorderst ['fɔrdərst], *adj.* foremost, first.

Vordertür ['fɔrdərtyːr], *f.* (**—**, *pl.* **—en**) front door.

Vordertreffen ['fɔrdərtrɛfən], *n.* (**—s**, *no pl.*) *ins* — *kommen*, be in the vanguard, come to the fore.

vordrängen ['foːrdrɛŋən], *v.r. sich* —, press forward, jump the queue.

vordringen ['foːrdrɪŋən], *v.n. irr.* (*aux.* sein) advance, push forward.

vordringlich ['foːrdrɪŋlɪç], *adj.* urgent; forward, importunate.

Vordruck ['foːrdruk], *m.* (**—s**, *pl.* **—e**) (*printed*) form.

voreilen ['foːraɪlən], *v.n.* (*aux.* sein) rush forward.

voreilig ['foːraɪlɪç], *adj.* over-hasty, rash.

Voreiligkeit ['foːraɪlɪçkaɪt], *f.* (**—**, *no pl.*) hastiness, rashness.

voreingenommen ['foːraɪngənɔmən], *adj.* biased, prejudiced.

Voreingenommenheit ['foːraɪngənɔmənhaɪt], *f.* (**—**, *no pl.*) bias, prejudice.

Voreltern ['foːrɛltərn], *pl.* forefathers, ancestors.

vorenthalten ['foːrɛnthaltən], *v.a. irr. sep. & insep.* withhold.

Vorentscheidung ['foːrɛntʃaɪduŋ], *f.* (**—**, *pl.* **—en**) preliminary decision.

vorerst [foːr'eːrst], *adv.* first of all, firstly; for the time being.

vorerwähnt ['foːrɛrvɛːnt], *adj.* aforementioned.

Vorfahr ['foːrfaːr], *m.* (**—en**, *pl.* **—en**) ancestor.

vorfahren ['foːrfaːrən], *v.n. irr.* (*aux.* sein) drive up (to a house *etc.*).

Vorfall ['foːrfal], *m.* (**—s**, *pl.* **-e**) occurrence, incident.

vorfinden ['foːrfɪndən], *v.a. irr.* find, find present, meet with.

Vorfrage ['foːrfraːgə], *f.* (**—**, *pl.* **—n**) preliminary question.

vorführen ['foːrfyːrən], *v.a.* bring forward, produce.

Vorführung ['foːrfyːruŋ], *f.* (**—**, *pl.* **—en**) production, presentation; performance.

Vorgang ['foːrgaŋ], *m.* (**—s**, *pl.* **-e**) occurrence, event, happening; proceeding, precedent; procedure.

Vorgänger ['foːrgɛŋər], *m.* (**—s**, *pl.* **—**) predecessor.

Vorgarten ['foːrgartən], *m.* (**—s**, *pl.* **-**) front garden.

vorgeben ['foːrgeːbən], *v.a. irr.* pretend; allow (in advance).

Vorgebirge ['foːrgəbɪrgə], *n.* (**—s**, *no pl.*) cape, promontory.

vorgeblich ['foːrgeːplɪç], *adj.* pretended; ostensible.

vorgefaßt ['foːrgəfast], *adj.* preconceived.

Vorgefühl ['foːrgəfyːl], *n.* (**—s**, *pl.* **—e**) presentiment.

vorgehen ['foːrgeːən], *v.n. irr.* (*aux.* sein) advance, walk ahead; proceed; (*clock*) be fast, gain; (*fig.*) take precedence; occur, happen; *was geht hier vor?* what's going on here?

Vorgehen ['foːrgeːən], *n.* (**—s**, *no pl.*) (course of) action, (manner of) procedure.

vorgenannt ['foːrgənant], *adj.* aforenamed.

Vorgericht ['foːrgərɪçt], *n.* (**—s**, *pl.* **—e**) hors d'œuvre, entrée.

Vorgeschichte ['foːrgəʃɪçtə], *f.* (**—**, *no pl.*) prehistory; early history; antecedents.

vorgeschichtlich ['foːrgəʃɪçtlɪç], *adj.* prehistoric.

Vorgeschmack ['foːrgəʃmak], *m.* (**—s**, *no pl.*) foretaste.

Vorgesetzte ['foːrgəzɛtstə], *m.* (**—n**, *pl.* **—n**) superior, senior; boss.

vorgestern ['foːrgɛstərn], *adv.* the day before yesterday.

vorgreifen ['foːrgraɪfən], *v.n. irr.* anticipate, forestall.

Vorhaben ['fo:rha:bən], *m.* (**—s,** *no pl.*) intention, purpose, design.

vorhaben ['fo:rha:bən], *v.a. irr.* intend; be busy with; *etwas mit einem* —, have designs on s.o.; have plans for s.o.

Vorhalle ['fo:rhalə], *f.* (**—,** *pl.* **—n**) vestibule, hall, porch.

vorhalten ['fo:rhaltən], *v.a. irr.* hold s.th. before s.o.; (*fig.*) remonstrate (with s.o. about s.th.); reproach. — *v.n.* last.

Vorhaltungen ['fo:rhaltuŋən], *f. pl.* remonstrances, expostulations.

vorhanden [for'handən], *adj.* at hand, present, in stock, on hand.

Vorhandensein [for'handənzaın], *n.* (**—s,** *no pl.*) existence; availability.

Vorhang ['fo:rhaŋ], *m.* (**—s,** *pl.* ‐e) curtain.

Vorhängeschloß ['fo:rhɛŋəʃlɔs], *n.* (**—sses,** *pl.* ‐sser) padlock.

vorher ['fo:rhe:r], *adv.* before, beforehand, in advance.

vorhergehen [fo:r'he:rge:ən], *v.n. irr.* (*aux.* sein) go before, precede.

vorhergehend [fo:r'he:rge:ənt], *adj.* foregoing, aforesaid, preceding.

vorherig [fo:r'he:rıç], *adj.* preceding, previous, former.

vorherrschen ['fo:rhɛrʃən], *v.n.* prevail, predominate.

vorhersagen [fo:r'he:rza:gən], *v.a.* predict, foretell.

vorhersehen [fo:r'he:rze:ən], *v.a. irr.* foresee.

vorheucheln ['fo:rhɔyçəln], *v.a. einem etwas* —, pretend s.th. to s.o.

vorhin [fo:r'hın], *adv.* just before, a short while ago.

Vorhof ['fo:rho:f], *m.* (**—s,** *pl.* ‐e) forecourt.

Vorhölle ['fo:rhœlə], *f.* (**—,** *no pl.*) limbo.

Vorhut ['fo:rhu:t], *f.* (**—,** *no pl.*) vanguard.

vorig ['fo:rıç], *adj.* former, preceding.

Vorjahr ['fo:rja:r], *n.* (**—s,** *pl.* **—e**) preceding year.

vorjammern ['fo:rjamərn], *v.n. einem etwas* —, moan to s.o. about s.th.

Vorkämpfer ['fo:rkɛmpfər], *m.* (**—s,** *pl.* **—**) champion; pioneer.

vorkauen ['fo:rkauən], *v.a.* (*fig.*) predigest; spoon-feed.

Vorkaufsrecht ['fo:rkaufsrɛçt], *n.* (**—s,** *no pl.*) right of first refusal, right of pre-emption.

Vorkehrung ['fo:rke:ruŋ], *f.* (**—,** *pl.* **—en**) preparation; precaution; (*pl.*) arrangements.

Vorkenntnisse ['fo:rkɛntnısə], *f. pl.* rudiments, elements, grounding; previous knowledge.

vorkommen ['fo:rkɔmən], *v.n. irr.* (*aux.* sein) occur, happen; be found.

Vorkommnis ['fo:rkɔmnıs], *n.* (**—ses,** *pl.* **—se**) occurrence, event, happening.

Vorkriegs- ['fo:rkri:ks], *prefix.* pre-war.

Vorladung ['fo:rla:duŋ], *f.* (**—,** *pl.* **—en**) summons, writ, subpœna.

Vorlage ['fo:rla:gə], *f.* (**—,** *pl.* **—n**) pattern, master-copy.

vorlagern ['fo:rla:gərn], *v.n.* (*aux.* sein) extend (in front of).

Vorland ['fo:rlant], *n.* (**—s,** *pl.* ‐er) cape, foreland, foreshore.

vorlassen ['fo:rlasən], *v.a. irr.* give precedence to; admit, show in.

Vorläufer ['fo:rlɔyfər], *m.* (**—s,** *pl.* **—**) forerunner, precursor.

vorläufig ['fo:rlɔyfıç], *adj.* provisional, preliminary, temporary. — *adv.* for the time being.

vorlaut ['fo:rlaut], *adj.* pert, forward.

Vorleben ['fo:rle:bən], *n.* (**—s,** *no pl.*) antecedents, past life.

vorlegen ['fo:rle:gən], *v.a.* put before s.o.; submit, propose; (*food*) serve.

Vorleger ['fo:rle:gər], *m.* (**—s,** *pl.* **—**) rug, mat.

Vorlegeschloß ['fo:rle:gəʃlɔs], *n.* (**—sses,** *pl.* ‐sser) padlock.

vorlesen ['fo:rle:zən], *v.a. irr.* read aloud, read out.

Vorlesung ['fo:rle:zuŋ], *f.* (**—,** *pl.* **—en**) lecture.

vorletzte ['fo:rlɛtstə], *adj.* last but one, penultimate.

Vorliebe ['fo:rli:bə], *f.* (**—,** *no pl.*) predilection, partiality.

vorliebnehmen [for'li:pne:mən], *v.n.* — *mit etwas*, be content with s.th., take pot luck.

vorliegen ['fo:rli:gən], *v.n. irr.* (*aux.* sein) be under consideration.

vorlügen ['fo:rly:gən], *v.a. irr. einem etwas* —, tell lies to s.o.

vormachen ['fo:rmaxən], *v.a. einem etwas* —, show s.o. how a thing is done; (*fig.*) play tricks on s.o., deceive s.o.

vormalig ['fo:rma:lıç], *adj.* former, erstwhile, late.

vormals ['fo:rma:ls], *adv.* formerly.

Vormarsch ['fo:rmarʃ], *m.* (**—es,** *pl.* ‐e) (*Mil.*) advance.

vormerken ['fo:rmɛrkən], *v.a.* make a note of, take down; book.

Vormittag ['fo:rmıta:k], *m.* (**—s,** *pl.* **—e**) morning, forenoon.

vormittags ['fo:rmıta:ks], *adv.* in the morning; before noon.

Vormund ['fo:rmunt], *m.* (**—s,** *pl.* ‐er) guardian.

Vormundschaft ['fo:rmuntʃaft], *f.* (**—,** *pl.* **—en**) guardianship.

Vormundschaftsgericht ['fo:rmuntʃaftsgərıçt], *n.* (**—s,** *pl.* **—e**) Court of Chancery.

vorn [fɔrn], *adv.* before, in front of; in front; (*Naut.*) fore.

Vorname ['fo:rna:mə], *m.* (**—ns,** *pl.* **—n**) first name, Christian name.

vornehm ['fo:rne:m], *adj.* of noble birth, refined; distinguished, elegant.

vornehmen ['fo:rne:mən], *v.a. irr.* take in hand; *sich etwas* —, undertake s.th.; plan *or* intend to do s.th.

Vornehmheit ['fo:rne:mhaɪt], *f.* (—, *no pl.*) refinement, distinction.

vornehmlich ['fo:rne:mlɪç], *adv.* chiefly, principally, especially.

vornherein ['fɔrnhɛraɪn], *adv. von* —, from the first; from the beginning.

Vorort ['fo:rɔrt], *m.* (—s, *pl.* —e) suburb.

Vorortsbahn ['fo:rɔrtsba:n], *f.* (—, *pl.* —en) suburban (railway) line.

Vorplatz ['fo:rplats], *m.* (—es, *pl.* ⁃e) forecourt.

Vorposten ['fo:rpɔstən], *m.* (—s, *pl.* —) (*Mil.*) outpost, pickets.

Vorpostengefecht ['fo:rpɔstəngəfɛçt], *n.* (—s, *pl.* —e) outpost skirmish.

Vorprüfung ['fo:rpry:fuŋ], *f.* (—, *pl.* —en) preliminary examination.

Vorrang ['fo:rraŋ], *m.* (—s, *no pl.*) precedence, first place, priority.

Vorrat ['fo:rra:t], *m.* (—s, *pl.* ⁃e) store, stock, provision.

Vorratskammer ['fo:rra:tskamər], *f.* (—, *pl.* —n) store-room; larder.

Vorrecht ['fo:rrɛçt], *n.* (—s, *pl.* —e) privilege, prerogative.

Vorrede ['fo:rre:də], *f.* (—, *pl.* —n) preface; introduction.

Vorredner ['fo:rre:dnər], *m.* (—s, *pl.* —) previous speaker.

vorrichten ['fo:rrɪçtən], *v.a.* prepare, fix up, get ready.

Vorrichtung ['fo:rrɪçtuŋ], *f.* (—, *pl.* —en) appliance, device, contrivance.

vorrücken ['fo:rrykən], *v.a.* move forward, advance; (*clock*) put on. — *v.n.* (*aux.* sein) (*Mil.*) advance.

Vorsaal ['fo:rza:l], *m.* (—s, *pl.* —säle) hall, entrance hall.

Vorsatz ['fo:rzats], *m.* (—es, *pl.* ⁃e) purpose, design, intention.

vorsätzlich ['fo:rzɛtslɪç], *adj.* intentional, deliberate.

Vorschein ['fo:rʃaɪn], *m. zum* — *kommen*, turn up; appear.

vorschießen ['fo:rʃi:sən], *v.a. irr.* (*money*) advance, lend.

Vorschlag ['fo:rʃla:k], *m.* (—s, *pl.* ⁃e) proposal, offer, proposition.

vorschlagen ['fo:rʃla:gən], *v.a. irr.* put forward, propose, suggest; recommend.

vorschnell ['fo:rʃnɛl], *adj.* hasty, rash, precipitate.

vorschreiben ['fo:rʃraɪbən], *v.a. irr.* write out (for s.o.); (*fig.*) prescribe, order.

Vorschrift ['fo:rʃrɪft], *f.* (—, *pl.* —en) prescription, direction, order, command, regulation.

vorschriftsmäßig ['fo:rʃrɪftsmɛ:sɪç], *adj.* according to regulations.

vorschriftswidrig ['fo:rʃrɪftsvi:drɪç], *adj.* contrary to regulations.

Vorschub ['fo:rʃup], *m.* (—s, *no pl.*) aid, assistance; — *leisten*, countenance, encourage, abet.

Vorschule ['fo:rʃu:lə], *f.* (—, *pl.* —n) preparatory school.

Vorschuß ['fo:rʃus], *m.* (—sses, *pl.* ⁃sse) advance (of cash).

vorschützen ['fo:rʃytsən], *v.a.* use as a pretext, pretend, plead.

vorschweben ['fo:rʃve:bən], *v.n.* be present in o.'s mind.

vorsehen ['fo:rze:ən], *v.r. irr. sich* —, take heed, be careful, look out, beware.

Vorsehung ['fo:rze:uŋ], *f.* (—, *no pl.*) Providence.

vorsetzen ['fo:rzɛtsən], *v.a.* set before; serve; (*word*) prefix.

Vorsicht ['fo:rzɪçt], *f.* (—, *no pl.*) care, precaution, caution, circumspection.

vorsichtig ['fo:rzɪçtɪç], *adj.* cautious, careful, circumspect.

vorsichtshalber ['fo:rzɪçtshalbər], *adv.* as a precautionary measure.

Vorsichtsmaßnahme ['fo:rzɪçtsma:sna:mə], *f.* (—, *pl.* —n) precautionary measure, precaution.

Vorsilbe ['fo:rzɪlbə], *f.* (—, *pl.* —n) prefix.

vorsintflutlich ['fo:rzɪntflu:tlɪç], *adj.* antediluvian; (*fig.*) out-of-date.

Vorsitzende ['fo:rzɪtsəndə], *m.* (—n, *pl.* —n) chairman, president.

Vorsorge ['fo:rzɔrgə], *f.* (—, *no pl.*) care, precaution.

vorsorglich ['fo:rzɔrklɪç], *adj.* provident, careful.

vorspiegeln ['fo:rʃpi:gəln], *v.a. einem etwas* —, deceive s.o.; pretend.

Vorspiegelung ['fo:rʃpi:gəluŋ], *f.* (—, *pl.* —en) pretence; — *falscher Tatsachen*, false pretences.

Vorspiel ['fo:rʃpi:l], *n.* (—s, *pl.* —e) prelude; overture.

vorsprechen ['fo:rʃprɛçən], *v.n. irr. bei einem* —, call on s.o. — *v.a. einem etwas* —, say s.th. for s.o.; repeat.

vorspringen ['fo:rʃprɪŋən], *v.n. irr.* (*aux.* sein) leap forward; jut out, project.

Vorsprung ['fo:rʃpruŋ], *m.* (—s, *pl.* ⁃e) projection, prominence; (*fig.*) advantage (over), start, lead.

Vorstadt ['fo:rʃtat], *f.* (—, *pl.* ⁃e) suburb.

vorstädtisch ['fo:rʃtɛtɪʃ], *adj.* suburban.

Vorstand ['fo:rʃtant], *m.* (—s, *pl.* ⁃e) board of directors; director, principal.

Vorstandssitzung ['fo:rʃtantszɪtsuŋ], *f.* (—, *pl.* —en) board meeting.

vorstehen ['fo:rʃte:ən], *v.n. irr.* project, protrude; (*office*) administer, govern, direct, manage.

vorstehend ['fo:rʃte:ənt], *adj.* projecting, protruding; above-mentioned, foregoing.

Vorsteher ['fo:rʃte:ər], *m.* (—s, *pl.* —) director, manager; supervisor.

Vorsteherdrüse ['fo:rʃte:ərdry:zə], *f.* (—, *pl.* —n) prostate gland.

vorstellbar ['fo:rʃtɛlba:r], *adj.* imaginable.

vorstellen ['fo:rʃtɛlən], *v.a.* (*thing*) put forward; (*person*) present, introduce; (*Theat.*) impersonate; represent; (*clock*) put on; *sich etwas* —, visualise s.th., imagine s.th.

vorstellig ['fo:rʃtɛlɪç], adj. — werden, petition; lodge a complaint.

Vorstellung ['fo:rʃtɛluŋ], f. (—, pl. —en) (person) presentation, introduction; (Theat.) performance; idea, notion, image; representation.

Vorstellungsvermögen ['fo:rʃtɛluŋs-fɛr'mø:gən], n. (—s, no pl.) imagination, imaginative faculty.

Vorstoß ['fo:rʃto:s], m. (—es, pl. ⁔e) (Mil.) sudden advance, thrust.

vorstoßen ['fo:rʃto:sən], v.a. irr. push forward. — v.n. (aux. sein) (Mil.) advance suddenly.

Vorstrafe ['fo:rʃtra:fə], f. (—, pl. —n) previous conviction.

vorstrecken ['fo:rʃtrɛkən], v.a. stretch forward, protrude; (money) advance.

Vorstufe ['fo:rʃtu:fə], f. (—, pl. —n) first step.

Vortänzerin ['fo:rtɛntsərɪn], f. (—, pl. —nen) prima ballerina.

Vorteil ['fortaɪl], m. (—s, pl. —e) advantage, profit.

vorteilhaft ['fortaɪlhaft], adj. advantageous, profitable, lucrative.

Vortrag ['fo:rtra:k], m. (—s, pl. ⁔e) recitation, delivery, rendering; statement, report; talk, speech, lecture.

vortragen ['fo:rtra:gən], v.a. irr. make a report; (poem) recite, declaim; make a request; (Comm.) carry forward; lecture on.

Vortragskunst ['fo:rtra:kskunst], f. (—, no pl.) elocution; (art of) public speaking.

vortrefflich [for'trɛflɪç], adj. excellent, splendid.

Vortrefflichkeit [for'trɛflɪçkaɪt], f. (—, no pl.) excellence.

vortreten ['fo:rtre:tən], v.n. irr. (aux. sein) step forward.

Vortritt ['fo:rtrɪt], m. (—s, no pl.) precedence.

vorüber [for'y:bər], adv. past, gone, over, finished, done with.

vorübergehen [for'y:bərge:ən], v.n. irr. (aux. sein) pass by, pass, go past.

vorübergehend [for'y:bərge:ənt], adj. passing, temporary, transitory.

Vorübung ['fo:ry:buŋ], f. (—, pl. —en) preliminary exercise.

Voruntersuchung ['fo:runtərzu:xuŋ], f. (—, pl. —en) preliminary inquiry; trial in magistrate's court.

Vorurteil ['fo:rurtaɪl], n. (—s, pl. —e) bias, prejudice.

vorurteilslos ['fo:rurtaɪlslo:s], adj. impartial, unprejudiced, unbiased.

Vorvater ['fo:rfa:tər], m. (—s, pl. ⁔) progenitor, ancestor.

Vorverkauf ['fo:rfɛrkauf], m. (—s, pl. ⁔e) booking in advance, advance booking.

vorwagen ['fo:rva:gən], v.r. sich —, dare to go (or come) forward.

vorwaltend ['fo:rvaltənt], adj. prevailing, predominating.

Vorwand ['fo:rvant], m. (—s, pl. ⁔e) pretence, pretext; unter dem —, under pretence of.

vorwärts ['forvɛrts], adv. forward.

vorwärtskommen ['forvɛrtskɔmən], v.n. irr. (aux. sein) make headway, get on.

vorweg [for'vɛk], adv. before.

vorwegnehmen [for'vɛkne:mən], v.a. irr. anticipate.

vorweisen ['fo:rvaɪzən], v.a. irr. show, produce, exhibit.

Vorwelt ['fo:rvɛlt], f. (—, no pl.) primitive world; former ages.

vorweltlich ['fo:rvɛltlɪç], adj. primæval, prehistoric.

vorwerfen ['fo:rvɛrfən], v.a. irr. einem etwas —, blame s.o. for s.th.; charge s.o. with s.th., tax s.o. with s.th.

vorwiegen ['fo:rvi:gən], v.n. irr. prevail.

vorwiegend ['fo:rvi:gənt], adv. mostly, for the most part.

Vorwissen ['fo:rvɪsən], n. (—s, no pl.) foreknowledge, prescience.

Vorwitz ['fo:rvɪts], m. (—es, no pl.) pertness.

vorwitzig ['fo:rvɪtsɪç], adj. forward, pert, meddlesome.

Vorwort (1) ['fo:rvɔrt], n. (—s, pl. —e) preface.

Vorwort (2) ['fo:rvɔrt], n. (—s, pl. ⁔er) (Gram.) preposition.

Vorwurf ['fo:rvurf], m. (—s, pl. ⁔e) reproach; theme, subject.

vorwurfsfrei ['fo:rvurfsfraɪ], adj. free from blame, irreproachable.

vorwurfsvoll ['fo:rvurfsfɔl], adj. reproachful.

Vorzeichen ['fo:rtsaɪxən], n. (—s, pl. —) omen, token; (Maths.) sign.

vorzeigen ['fo:rtsaɪgən], v.a. show, produce, exhibit, display.

Vorzeit ['fo:rtsaɪt], f. (—, no pl.) antiquity, olden times.

vorzeiten [for'tsaɪtən], adv. (Poet.) in olden times, formerly.

vorzeitig ['fo:rtsaɪtɪç], adj. premature.

vorziehen ['fo:rtsi:ən], v.a. irr. prefer.

Vorzimmer ['fo:rtsɪmər], n. (—s, pl. —) anteroom, antechamber.

Vorzug ['fo:rtsu:k], m. (—s, pl. ⁔e) preference, advantage; excellence, superiority.

vorzüglich [for'tsy:klɪç], adj. superior, excellent, exquisite.

Vorzüglichkeit [for'tsy:klɪçkaɪt], f. (—, no pl.) excellence, superiority.

Vorzugsaktie ['fo:rtsu:ksaktsjə], f. (—, pl. —n) preference share.

vorzugsweise ['fo:rtsu:ksvaɪzə], adv. for choice, preferably.

vulgär [vul'gɛ:r], adj. vulgar.

Vulkan [vul'ka:n], m. (—s, pl. —e) volcano.

vulkanisch [vul'ka:nɪʃ], adj. volcanic.

W

W

W [ve:] *n.* (—**s**, *pl.* —**s**) the letter W.
Waage ['va:gə], *f.* (—, *pl.* —**n**) balance, pair of scales.
waag(e)recht ['va:g(ə)rɛçt], *adj.* horizontal.
Waagschale ['va:kʃa:lə], *f.* (—, *pl.* —**n**) pan of a balance.
Wabe ['va:bə], *f.* (—, *pl.* —**n**) honeycomb.
Waberlohe ['va:bərlo:ə], *f.* (—, *no pl.*) (*Poet.*) flickering flames, magic fire.
wach [vax], *adj.* awake; alert; *völlig* —, wide awake.
Wachdienst ['vaxdi:nst], *m.* (—**es**, *no pl.*) guard, sentry duty.
Wache ['vaxə], *f.* (—, *pl.* —**n**) guard, watch; (*person*) sentry, sentinel.
wachen ['vaxən], *v.n.* be awake; guard; — *über*, watch, keep an eye on.
Wacholder [va'xɔldər], *m.* (—**s**, *pl.* —) (*Bot.*) juniper.
wachrufen [vax'ru:fən], *v.a. irr.* (*fig.*) call to mind.
Wachs [vaks], *n.* (—**es**, *no pl.*) wax.
wachsam ['vaxza:m], *adj.* watchful, vigilant.
Wachsamkeit ['vaxza:mkaɪt], *f.* (—, *no pl.*) watchfulness, vigilance.
Wachsbild ['vaksbɪlt], *n.* (—**s**, *pl.* —**er**) waxen image.
wachsen ['vaksən], *v.n. irr.* (*aux.* sein) grow, increase.
wächsern ['vɛksərn], *adj.* waxen, made of wax.
Wachsfigur ['vaksfigu:r], *f.* (—, *pl.* —**en**) wax figure.
Wachsfigurenkabinett ['vaksfigu:rənkabinɛt], *n.* (—**s**, *pl.* —**e**) waxworks.
Wachsleinwand ['vakslaɪnvant], *f.* (—, *no pl.*) oil-cloth.
Wachstuch ['vakstu:x], *n.* (—(**e**)**s**, *no pl.*) oil-cloth; American cloth.
Wachstum ['vakstu:m], *n.* (—**s**, *no pl.*) growth, increase.
Wacht [vaxt], *f.* (—, *pl.* —**en**) watch, guard.
Wachtdienst ['vaxtdi:nst] *see* **Wachdienst.**
Wachtel ['vaxtəl], *f.* (—, *pl.* —**n**) (*Orn.*) quail.
Wachtelhund ['vaxtəlhunt], *m.* (—(**e**)**s**, *pl.* —**e**) (*Zool.*) spaniel.
Wächter ['vɛçtər], *m.* (—**s**, *pl.* —) watchman, warder, guard.
wachthabend ['vaxtha:bənt], *adj.* on duty.
Wachtmeister ['vaxtmaɪstər], *m.* (—**s**, *pl.* —) sergeant.

Wachtparade [vaxtpara:də], *f.* (—, *pl.* —**n**) mounting of the guard.
Wachtposten ['vaxtpɔstən], *m.* (—**s**, *pl.* —) guard, picket.
Wachtraum ['vaxtraum], *m.* (—**s**, *pl.* ⁻**e**) day-dream, waking dream.
Wachtturm ['vaxtturm], *m.* (—**s**, *pl.* ⁻**e**) watch-tower.
wackeln ['vakəln], *v.n.* totter, shake, wobble.
wacker ['vakər], *adj.* gallant, brave, valiant; upright.
wacklig ['vaklɪç], *adj.* tottering, shaky; (*furniture*) rickety; (*tooth*) loose.
Wade ['va:də], *f.* (—, *pl.* —**n**) calf (of the leg).
Wadenbein ['va:dənbaɪn], *n.* (—**s**, *pl.* —**e**) shin-bone.
Waffe ['vafə], *f.* (—, *pl.* —**n**) weapon, arm; *die —n strecken*, surrender.
Waffel ['vafəl], *f.* (—, *pl.* —**n**) wafer; waffle.
Waffeleisen ['vafəlaɪzən], *n.* (—**s**, *pl.* —) waffle-iron.
Waffenbruder ['vafənbru:dər], *m.* (—**s**, *pl.* ⁻) brother-in-arms, comrade.
waffenfähig ['vafənfɛ:ɪç], *adj.* able to bear arms.
Waffengewalt ['vafəngəvalt], *f.* (—, *no pl.*) *mit* —, by force of arms.
Waffenglück ['vafənglyk], *n.* (—**s**, *no pl.*) fortunes of war.
Waffenrock ['vafənrɔk], *m.* (—**s**, *pl.* ⁻**e**) tunic.
Waffenruf ['vafənru:f], *m.* (—**s**, *no pl.*) call to arms.
Waffenschmied [vafənʃmi:t], *m.* (—**s**, *pl.* —**e**) armourer.
Waffenstillstand ['vafənʃtɪlʃtant], *m.* (—**s**, *no pl.*) armistice, truce.
waffnen ['vafnən], *v.a.* arm.
Wage *see* **Waage.**
Wagebalken ['va:gəbalkən], *m.* (—**s**, *pl.* —) scale-beam.
Wagen ['va:gən], *m.* (—**s**, *pl.* —) vehicle, conveyance, carriage, coach, car, cab, wagon, cart, truck, van, dray.
wagen ['va:gən], *v.a., v.n.* dare, venture, risk.
wägen ['vɛ:gən], *v.a., irr.* weigh, balance; (*words*) consider.
Wagenverkehr ['va:gənfɛrke:r], *m.* (—**s**, *no pl.*) vehicular traffic.
wagerecht *see* **waagerecht.**
Waggon [va'gɔ̃], *m.* (—**s**, *pl.* —**s**) railway car, goods van, freight car.
waghalsig ['va:khalzɪç], *adj.* foolhardy, rash, daring.
Wagnis ['va:knɪs], *n.* (—**ses**, *pl.* —**se**) venture, risky undertaking; risk.
Wagschale *see* **Waagschale.**
Wahl [va:l], *f.* (—, *pl.* —**en**) choice; election; selection; alternative.
Wahlakt ['va:lakt], *m.* (—**s**, *pl.* —**e**) poll, election.
Wahlaufruf ['va:laufru:f], *m.* (—**s**, *pl.* —**e**) manifesto, election address.
wählbar ['vɛ:lba:r], *adj.* eligible.
Wählbarkeit ['vɛ:lba:rkaɪt], *f.* (—, *no pl.*) eligibility.

wahlberechtigt ['va:lbərɛçtɪçt], *adj.* entitled to vote.

wählen ['vɛ:lən], *v.a.* choose; (*Parl.*) elect; (*Telephone*) dial.

Wähler ['vɛ:lər], *m.* (—s, *pl.* —) elector; constituent.

wählerisch ['vɛ:lərɪʃ], *adj.* fastidious, particular.

Wählerschaft ['vɛ:lərʃaft], *f.* (—, *pl.* —en) constituency.

wahlfähig ['va:lfɛ:ɪç], *adj.* eligible.

Wahlliste ['va:llɪstə], *f.* (—, *pl.* —n) electoral list, register (of electors).

wahllos ['va:llo:s], *adj.* indiscriminate.

Wahlrecht ['va:lrɛçt], *n.* (—s, *no pl.*) franchise.

Wahlspruch ['va:lʃprux], *m.* (—s, *pl.* ⸚e) device, motto.

wahlunfähig ['va:lunfɛ:ɪç], *adj.* ineligible.

Wahlurne ['va:lurnə], *f.* (—, *pl.* —n) ballot-box.

Wahlverwandtschaft ['va:lfɛrvantʃaft], *f.* (—, *no pl.*) elective affinity, congeniality.

Wahlzettel ['va:ltsɛtəl], *m.* (—s, *pl.* —) ballot-paper.

Wahn [va:n], *m.* (—(e)s, *no pl.*) delusion.

Wahnbild ['va:nbɪlt], *n.* (—s, *pl.* —er) hallucination, delusion; phantasm.

wähnen ['vɛ:nən], *v.a.* fancy, believe.

Wahnsinn ['va:nzɪn], *m.* (—s, *no pl.*) madness, lunacy.

wahnsinnig ['va:nzɪnɪç], *adj.* insane, mad, lunatic; (*coll.*) terrific.

Wahnsinnige ['va:nzɪnɪgə], *m.* (—n, *pl.* —n) madman, lunatic.

Wahnwitz ['va:nvɪts], *m.* (—es, *no pl.*) madness.

wahnwitzig ['va:nvɪtsɪç], *adj.* mad.

wahr [va:r], *adj.* true, real, genuine.

wahren ['va:rən], *v.a.* guard, watch over.

während ['vɛ:rən], *v.n.* last.

während ['vɛ:rənt], *prep.* (*Genit.*) during. — *conj.* while, whilst; whereas.

wahrhaft ['va:rhaft], *adj.* truthful, veracious.

wahrhaftig [va:r'haftɪç], *adv.* truly, really, in truth.

Wahrhaftigkeit [va:r'haftɪçkaɪt], *f.* (—, *no pl.*) truthfulness, veracity.

Wahrheit ['va:rhaɪt], *f.* (—, *pl.* —en) truth; reality; *die — sagen*, tell the truth.

Wahrheitsliebe ['va:rhaɪtsli:bə], *f.* (—, *no pl.*) love of truth, truthfulness.

wahrlich ['va:rlɪç], *adv.* truly, in truth.

wahrnehmbar ['va:rnɛ:mba:r], *adj.* perceptible.

wahrnehmen ['va:rnɛ:mən], *v.a. irr.* perceive, observe.

Wahrnehmung ['va:rnɛ:muŋ], *f.* (—, *pl.* —en) perception, observation.

wahrsagen ['va:rza:gən], *v.n.* prophesy; tell fortunes.

Wahrsager ['va:rza:gər], *m.* (—s, *pl.* —) fortune-teller, soothsayer.

wahrscheinlich [va:r'ʃaɪnlɪç], *adj.* likely, probable; *es wird — regnen*, it will probably rain.

Wahrscheinlichkeit [va:r'ʃaɪnlɪçkaɪt], *f.* (—, *pl.* —en) likelihood, probability.

Wahrung ['va:ruŋ], *f.* (—, *no pl.*) protection, preservation, maintenance.

Währung ['vɛ:ruŋ], *f.* (—, *pl.* —en) currency, standard.

Wahrzeichen ['va:rtsaɪçən], *n.* (—s, *pl.* —) landmark; (*fig.*) sign, token.

Waibling(er) ['vaɪblɪŋ(ər)], *m.* Ghibelline.

Waidmann ['vaɪtman], *m.* (—s, *pl.* ⸚er) huntsman, hunter.

waidmännisch ['vaɪtmɛnɪʃ], *adj.* sportsmanlike.

Waise ['vaɪzə], *f.* (—, *pl.* —n) orphan.

Waisenhaus ['vaɪzənhaus], *n.* (—es, *pl.* ⸚er) orphanage.

Waisenmutter ['vaɪzənmutər], *f.* (—, *pl.* ⸚) foster-mother.

Waisenvater ['vaɪzənfa:tər], *m.* (—s, *pl.* ⸚) foster-father.

Wald [valt], *m.* (—es, *pl.* ⸚er) wood, forest; woodland.

Waldbrand ['valtbrant], *m.* (—s, *pl.* ⸚e) forest-fire.

Waldlichtung ['valtlɪçtuŋ], *f.* (—, *pl.* —en) forest glade, clearing.

Waldmeister ['valtmaɪstər], *m.* (—s, *no pl.*) (*Bot.*) woodruff.

Waldung ['valduŋ], *f.* (—, *pl.* —en) woods, woodland.

Waldwiese ['valtvi:zə], *f.* (—, *pl.* —en) forest-glade.

Walfisch ['va:lfɪʃ], *m.* (—es, *pl.* —e) whale.

Walfischfang ['va:lfɪʃfaŋ], *m.* (—s, *no pl.*) whaling.

Walfischfänger ['va:lfɪʃfɛŋər], *m.* (—s, *pl.* —) whaler, whale fisher.

Walfischtran ['va:lfɪʃtra:n], *m.* (—s, *no pl.*) train-oil.

Walküre [val'ky:rə], *f.* (—, *pl.* —n) Valkyrie.

Wall [val], *m.* (—(e)s, *pl.* ⸚e) rampart, dam, vallum; mound.

Wallach ['valax], *m.* (—s, *pl.* —e) castrated horse, gelding.

wallen ['valən], *v.n.* bubble, boil up; wave, undulate.

Wallfahrer ['valfa:rər], *m.* (—s, *pl.* —) pilgrim.

Wallfahrt ['valfa:rt], *f.* (—, *pl.* —en) pilgrimage.

wallfahrten ['valfa:rtən], *v.n.* (*aux.* sein) go on a pilgrimage.

Walnuß ['valnus], *f.* (—, *pl.* ⸚sse) (*Bot.*) walnut.

Walpurgisnacht [val'purgɪsnaxt], *f.* witches' sabbath.

Walroß ['valrɔs], *n.* (—sses, *pl.* —sse) sea-horse, walrus.

Walstatt ['valʃtat], *f.* (—, *pl.* ⸚en) (*Poet.*) battlefield.

walten ['valtən], *v.n.* rule; *seines Amtes —*, do o.'s duty, carry out o.'s duties.

Walze ['valtsə], *f.* (—, *pl.* —n) roller, cylinder.

walzen ['valtsən], *v.a.* roll. — *v.n.* waltz.

wälzen ['vɛltsən], *v.a.* roll, turn about.

walzenförmig ['valtsənfœrmɪç], *adj.* cylindrical.

Walzer ['valtsər], *m.* (—s, *pl.* —) waltz.

Wälzer ['vɛltsər], *m.* (—s, *pl.* —) tome; thick volume.

Walzwerk ['valtsvɛrk], *n.* (—s, *pl.* —e) rolling-mill.

Wams [vams], *n.* (—es, *pl.* ⁻e) (*obs.*) doublet, jerkin.

Wand [vant], *f.* (—, *pl.* ⁻e) wall; side.

Wandbekleidung ['vantbaklaidun], *f.* (—, *pl.* —en) wainscot, panelling.

Wandel ['vandəl], *m.* (—s, *no pl.*) mutation, change; behaviour, conduct; *Handel und* —, trade and traffic.

wandelbar ['vandəlba:r], *adj.* changeable, inconstant.

Wandelgang ['vandəlgaŋ], *m.* (—s, *pl.* ⁻e) lobby; lounge, foyer; (*in the open*) covered way, covered walk.

wandeln ['vandəln], *v.a.* (*aux.* haben) change. — *v.n.* (*aux.* sein) walk, wander. — *v.r. sich* —, change.

Wanderbursche ['vandərburʃə], *m.* (—n, *pl.* —n) travelling journeyman.

Wanderer ['vandərər], *m.* (—s, *pl.* —) wanderer, traveller; hiker.

Wanderleben ['vandərle:bən], *n.* (—s, *no pl.*) nomadic life.

Wanderlehrer ['vandərle:rər], *m.* (—s, *pl.* —) itinerant teacher.

Wanderlust ['vandərlust], *f.* (—, *no pl.*) urge to travel; call of the open.

wandern ['vandərn], *v.n.* (*aux.* sein) wander, travel; migrate.

Wanderschaft ['vandərʃaft], *f.* (—, *no pl.*) wanderings.

Wandersmann ['vandərsman], *m.* (—s, *pl.* ⁻er) wayfarer.

Wandertruppe ['vandərtrupə], *f.* (—, *pl.* —n) (*Theat.*) strolling players.

Wanderung ['vandəruŋ], *f.* (—, *pl.* —en) walking tour; hike.

Wandervolk ['vandərfɔlk], *n.* (— (e)s, *pl.* ⁻er) nomadic tribe.

Wandgemälde ['vantgəmɛ:ldə], *n.* (—s, *pl.* —) mural painting, mural.

Wandlung ['vandluŋ], *f.* (—, *pl.* —en) transformation; (*Theol.*) transubstantiation.

Wandspiegel ['vantʃpi:gəl], *m.* (—s, *pl.* —) pier-glass.

Wandtafel ['vantta:fəl], *f.* (—, *pl.* —n) blackboard.

Wange ['vaŋə], *f.* (—, *pl.* —n) cheek.

Wankelmut ['vaŋkəlmu:t], *m.* (—s, *no pl.*) fickleness, inconstancy.

wankelmütig ['vaŋkəlmy:tɪç], *adj.* inconstant, fickle.

wanken ['vaŋkən], *v.n.* totter, stagger; (*fig.*) waver, be irresolute.

wann [van], *adv.* when; *dann und* —, now and then, sometimes.

Wanne ['vanə], *f.* (—, *pl.* —n) tub, bath.

wannen ['vanən], *adv.* (*obs.*) *von* —, whence.

Wannenbad ['vanənba:t], *n.* (—s, *pl.* ⁻er) bath.

Wanst [vanst], *m.* (—es, *pl.* ⁻e) belly, paunch.

Wanze ['vantsə], *f.* (—, *pl.* —n) (*Ent.*) bug.

Wappen ['vapən], *n.* (—s, *pl.* —) crest, coat-of-arms.

Wappenbild ['vapənbɪlt], *n.* (—s, *pl.* —er) heraldic figure.

Wappenkunde ['vapənkundə], *f.* (—, *no pl.*) heraldry.

Wappenschild ['vapənʃɪlt], *m.* (—s, *pl.* —e) escutcheon.

Wappenspruch ['vapənʃprux], *m.* (—(e)s, *pl.* ⁻e) motto, device.

wappnen ['vapnən], *v.a.* arm.

Ware ['va:rə], *f.* (—, *pl.* —n) article, commodity; (*pl.*) merchandise, goods, wares.

Warenausfuhr ['va:rənausfu:r], *f.* (—, *no pl.*) exportation, export.

Warenbörse ['va:rənbœrzə], *f.* (—, *pl.* —n) commodity exchange.

Wareneinfuhr ['va:rənainfu:r], *f.* (—, *no pl.*) importation, import.

Warenhaus ['va:rənhaus], *n.* (—es, *pl.* ⁻er) department store, emporium; (*Am.*) store.

Warenlager ['va:rənla:gər], *n.* (—s, *pl.* —) magazine; stock; warehouse.

Warensendung ['va:rənzɛndun], *f.* (—, *pl.* —en) consignment of goods.

Warentausch ['va:rəntauʃ], *m.* (—es, *no pl.*) barter.

warm [varm], *adj.* warm, hot.

warmblütig ['varmbly:tɪç], *adj.* warm-blooded.

Wärme ['vɛrmə], *f.* (—, *no pl.*) warmth; heat.

Wärmeeinheit ['vɛrməainhait], *f.* (—, *pl.* —en) thermal unit; calorie.

Wärmegrad ['vɛrməgra:t], *m.* (—s, *pl.* —e) degree of heat; temperature.

Wärmeleiter ['vɛrmələitər], *m.* (—s, *pl.* —) conductor of heat.

Wärmemesser ['vɛrməmɛsər], *m.* (—s, *pl.* —) thermometer.

wärmen ['vɛrmən], *v.a.* warm, heat.

Wärmflasche ['vɛrmflaʃə], *f.* (—, *pl.* —n) hot-water bottle.

warnen ['varnən], *v.a.* warn; caution.

Warnung ['varnuŋ], *f.* (—, *pl.* —en) warning, caution, admonition; notice.

Warschau ['varʃau], *n.* Warsaw.

Warte ['vartə], *f.* (—, *pl.* —n) watch-tower, belfry, look-out.

Wartegeld ['vartəgɛlt], *n.* (—s, *pl.* —er) half pay; (*ship*) demurrage charges.

warten ['vartən], *v.n.* wait; — *auf* (*Acc.*), wait for, await. — *v.a.* tend, nurse.

Wärter ['vɛrtər], *m.* (—s, *pl.* —) keeper, attendant; warder; male nurse.

Wartesaal ['vartəza:l], *m.* (—s, *pl.* —säle) (*Railw.*) waiting-room.

Wartung ['vartuŋ], *f.* (—, *no pl.*) nursing, attendance; servicing; maintenance.

warum [va′rum], *adv.*, *conj.* why, for what reason.

Warze [′vartsə], *f.* (—, *pl.* —n) wart.

was [vas], *interr. pron.* what? — *rel. pron.* what, that which.

Waschanstalt [′vaʃanʃtalt], *f.* (—, *pl.* —en) laundry.

waschbar [′vaʃbaːr], ·*adj.* washable.

Waschbär [′vaʃbɛːr], *m.* (—en, *pl.* —en) (*Zool.*) raccoon.

Waschbecken [′vaʃbɛkən], *n.* (—s, *pl.* —) wash-basin.

Wäsche [′vɛʃə], *f.* (—, *no pl.*) washing, wash, laundry; linen.

waschecht [′vaʃeçt], *adj.* washable; (*fig.*) genuine.

waschen [′vaʃən], *v.a. irr.* wash.

Wäscherin [′vɛʃərin], *f.* (—, *pl.* —nen) washerwoman, laundress.

Waschhaus [′vaʃhaus], *n.* (—es, *pl.* ″er) wash-house, laundry; (*reg. trade name*) launderette.

Waschkorb [′vaʃkɔrp], *m.* (—s, *pl.* ″e) clothes-basket.

Waschküche [′vaʃkyçə], *f.* (—, *pl.* —en) wash-house.

Waschlappen [′vaʃlapən], *m.* (—s, *pl.* —) face-flannel, face-cloth, face-washer; (*fig.*) milksop.

Waschleder [′vaʃleːdər], *n.* (—s, *no pl.*) chamois leather, wash-leather.

Waschmaschine [′vaʃmaʃiːnə], *f.* (—, *pl.* —n) washing-machine.

Waschtisch [′vaʃtiʃ], *m.* (—es, *pl.* —e) wash-stand.

Waschwanne [′vaʃvanə], *f.* (—, *pl.* —n) wash-tub.

Wasser [′vasər], *n.* (—s, *pl.* —) water; *stille — sind tief,* still waters run deep.

wasserarm [′vasərarm], *adj.* waterless, dry, arid.

Wasserbehälter [′vasərbəhɛltər], *m.* (—s, *pl.* —) reservoir, cistern, tank.

Wasserblase [′vasərblaːzə], *f.* (—, *pl.* —en) bubble.

Wässerchen [′vɛsərçən], *n.* (—s, *pl.* —) brook, streamlet; *er sieht aus, als ob er kein — trüben könnte,* he looks as if butter would not melt in his mouth.

Wasserdampf [′vasərdampf], *m.* (—(e)s, *no pl.*) steam.

wasserdicht [′vasərdiçt], *adj.* water-proof.

Wasserdruck [′vasərdruk], *m.* (—s, *no pl.*) hydrostatic pressure, hydraulic pressure.

Wassereimer [′vasəraimər], *m.* (—s, *pl.* —) pail, water-bucket.

Wasserfall [′vasərfal], *m.* (—s, *pl.* ″e) waterfall, cataract, cascade.

Wasserfarbe [′vasərfarbə], *f.* (—, *pl.* —n) water-colour.

Wasserheilanstalt [′vasərhailanʃtalt], *f.* (—, *pl.* —en) spa.

wässerig [′vɛsəriç], *adj.* watery; (*fig.*) insipid, flat, diluted.

Wasserkanne [′vasərkanə], *f.* (—, *pl.* —n) pitcher, ewer.

Wasserkessel [′vasərkɛsəl], *m.* (—s, *pl.* —) boiler; kettle.

Wasserkopf [′vasərkɔpf], *m.* (—(e)s, *pl.* ″e) (*Med.*) hydrocephalus.

Wasserkur [′vasərkuːr], *f.* (—, *pl.* —en) hydropathic treatment.

Wasserleitung [′vasərlaituŋ], *f.* (—, *pl.* —en) aqueduct; water main.

Wasserlinsen [′vasərlinzən], *f. pl.* (*Bot.*) duck-weed.

Wassermann [′vasərman], *m.* (—s, *no pl.*) (*Astron.*) Aquarius.

wässern [′vɛsərn], *v.a.* water, irrigate, soak.

Wassernixe [′vasərniksə], *f.* (—, *pl.* —n) water nymph.

Wassernot [′vasərnoːt], *f.* (—, *no pl.*) drought, scarcity of water.

Wasserrabe [′vasərraːbə], *m.* (—n, *pl.* —n) (*Orn.*) cormorant.

Wasserrinne [′vasərrinə], *f.* (—, *pl.* —n) gutter.

Wasserröhre [′vasərrøːrə], *f.* (—, *pl.* —n) water-pipe.

Wasserscheide [′vasərʃaidə], *f.* (—, *pl.* —n) watershed.

Wasserscheu [′vasərʃɔy], *f.* (—, *no pl.*) hydrophobia.

Wasserspiegel [′vasərʃpiːgəl], *m.* (—s, *pl.* —) water-level.

Wasserspritze [′vasərʃpritsə], *f.* (—, *pl.* —n) squirt; sprinkler.

Wasserstand [′vasərʃtant], *m.* (—s, *no pl.*) water-level.

Wasserstiefel [′vasərʃtiːfəl], *m.* (—s, *pl.* —n) wader, gumboot.

Wasserstoff [′vasərʃtɔf], *m.* (—(e)s, *no pl.*) hydrogen.

Wassersucht [′vasərzuxt], *f.* (—, *no pl.*) dropsy.

Wassersuppe [′vasərzupə], *f.* (—, *pl.* —n) water-gruel.

Wässerung [′vɛsəruŋ], *f.* (—, *pl.* —en) watering, irrigation.

Wasserverdrängung [′vasərfɛrdrɛŋuŋ], *f.* (—, *no pl.*) displacement (of water).

Wasserwaage [′vasərvaːgə], *f.* (—, *pl.* —n) water-balance, water-level; hydrometer.

Wasserweg [′vasərveːk], *m.* (—s, *pl.* —e) waterway; *auf dem —,* by water, by sea.

Wasserzeichen [′vasərtsaiçən], *n.* (—s, *pl.* —) watermark.

waten [′vaːtən], *v.n.* (*aux.* sein) wade.

watscheln [′vaːtʃəln], *v.n.* (*aux.* sein) waddle.

Watt (1) [vat], *n.* (—s, *pl.* —e) sand-bank; (*pl.*) shallows.

Watt (2) [vat], *n.* (—s, *pl.* —) (*Elec.*) watt.

Watte [′vatə], *f.* (—, *no pl.*) wadding, cotton-wool.

wattieren [va′tiːrən], *v.a.* pad.

Webe [′veːbə], *f.* (—, *pl.* —n) web, weft.

weben [′veːbən], *v.a.* weave.

Weber [′veːbər], *m.* (—s, *pl.* —) weaver.

Weberei [veːbə′rai], *f.* (—, *pl.* —en) weaving-mill.

Weberschiffchen

Weberschiffchen [ˈveːbərʃɪfçən], n. (—s, pl. —) shuttle.

Wechsel [ˈvɛksəl], m. (—s, pl. —) change; turn, variation; vicissitude; (Comm.) bill of exchange.

Wechselbalg [ˈvɛksəlbalk], m. (—s, pl. ⁻e) changeling.

Wechselbank [ˈvɛksəlbaŋk], f. (—, pl. ⁻e) discount-bank.

Wechselbeziehung [ˈvɛksəlbətsiːuŋ], f. (—, pl. —en) reciprocal relation, correlation.

Wechselfälle [ˈvɛksəlfɛlə], m. pl. vicissitudes.

Wechselfieber [ˈvɛksəlfiːbər], n. (—s, pl. —) intermittent fever.

Wechselfolge [ˈvɛksəlfɔlɡə], f. (—, no pl.) rotation, alternation.

Wechselgeld [ˈvɛksəlɡɛlt], n. (—(e)s, no pl.) change.

wechseln [ˈvɛksəln], v.a. change, exchange. — v.n. change, alternate, change places.

wechselseitig [ˈvɛksəlzaıtıç], adj. reciprocal, mutual.

Wechselstrom [ˈvɛksəlʃtroːm], m. (—s, no pl.) alternating current.

Wechselstube [ˈvɛksəlʃtuːbə], f. (—, pl. —n) exchange office.

wechselvoll [ˈvɛksəlfɔl], adj. eventful, chequered; changeable.

wechselweise [ˈvɛksəlvaızə], adv. reciprocally, mutually; by turns, alternately.

Wechselwinkel [ˈvɛksəlvɪŋkəl], m. (—s, pl. —) alternate angle.

Wechselwirkung [ˈvɛksəlvɪrkuŋ], f. (—, pl. —en) reciprocal effect.

Wechselwirtschaft [ˈvɛksəlvɪrtʃaft], f. (—, no pl.) rotation of crops.

Wecken [ˈvɛkən], m. (—s, pl. —) (dial.) bread-roll.

wecken [ˈvɛkən], v.a. wake, rouse, awaken.

Wecker [ˈvɛkər], m. (—s, pl. —) alarm-clock.

Weckuhr [ˈvɛkuːr], f. (—, pl. —en) alarm-clock.

Wedel [ˈveːdəl], m. (—s, pl. —) feather-duster, fan; tail.

wedeln [ˈveːdəln], v.n. mit dem Schwanz —, wag its tail.

weder [ˈveːdər], conj. neither; — . . . noch, neither . . . nor.

Weg [veːk], m. (—(e)s, pl. —e) way, path, route, road; walk, errand; am —, by the wayside.

weg [vɛk], adv. away, gone, off, lost.

wegbegeben [ˈvɛkbəɡeːbən], v.r. irr. sich —, go away, leave.

wegbekommen [ˈvɛkbəkɔmən], v.a. irr. etwas —, get the hang of s.th.; get s.th. off or away.

Wegbereiter [ˈveːkbəraıtər], m. (—s, pl. —) forerunner, pathfinder, pioneer.

wegblasen [ˈvɛkblaːzən], v.a. irr. blow away; wie weggeblasen, without leaving a trace.

wegbleiben [ˈvɛkblaıbən], v.n. irr. (aux. sein) stay away.

wegblicken [ˈvɛkblɪkən], v.n. look the other way.

wegbringen [ˈvɛkbrıŋən], v.a. irr. einen —, get s.o. away.

wegdrängen [ˈvɛkdrɛŋən], v.a. push away.

Wegebau [ˈveːɡəbau], m. (—s, no pl.) road-making.

wegeilen [ˈvɛkaılən], v.n. (aux. sein) hasten away, hurry off.

wegelagern [ˈveːɡəlaɡərn], v.a. waylay.

wegen [ˈveːɡən], prep. (Genit., Dat.) because of, on account of, owing to, by reason of.

Wegfall [ˈvɛkfal], m. (—s, no pl.) omission.

wegfallen [ˈvɛkfalən], v.n. irr. (aux. sein) fall off; be omitted; cease.

Weggang [ˈvɛkɡaŋ], m. (—s, no pl.) departure, going away.

weggießen [ˈvɛkɡiːsən], v.a. irr. pour away.

weghaben [ˈvɛkhaːbən], v.a. irr. etwas —, understand how to do s.th, have the knack of doing s.th.

wegkommen [ˈvɛkkɔmən], v.n. irr. (aux. sein) get away; be lost.

wegkönnen [ˈvɛkkœnən], v.n. irr. nicht —, not be able to get away.

Weglassung [ˈvɛklasuŋ], f. (—, pl. —en) omission.

wegmachen [ˈvɛkmaxən], v.r. sich —, decamp, make off.

wegmüssen [ˈvɛkmysən], v.n. irr. be obliged to go; have to go.

Wegnahme [ˈvɛknaːmə], f. (—, no pl.) taking, seizure, capture.

Wegreise [ˈvɛkraızə], f. (—, no pl.) departure.

Wegscheide [ˈveːkʃaıdə], f. (—, pl. —n) crossroads, crossways.

wegscheren [ˈvɛkʃeːrən], v.a. clip; shave off. — v.r. sich —, be off.

wegschnappen [ˈvɛkʃnapən], v.a. snatch away.

wegsehnen [ˈvɛkzeːnən], v.r. sich —, wish o.s. far away; long to get away.

wegsein [ˈvɛkzaın], v.n. irr. (aux. sein) (person) be gone, be away; have gone off; (things) be lost; ganz —, (coll.) be beside o.s. or amazed.

wegsetzen [ˈvɛkzɛtsən], v.a. put away.

wegspülen [ˈvɛkʃpyːlən], v.a. wash away.

Wegstunde [ˈveːkʃtundə], f. (—, pl. —n) an hour's walk.

Wegweiser [ˈveːkvaızər], m. (—s, pl. —) signpost, road-sign.

wegwenden [ˈvɛkvɛndən], v.r. irr. sich —, turn away.

wegwerfen [ˈvɛkvɛrfən], v.a. irr. throw away.

wegwerfend [ˈvɛkvɛrfənt], adj. disparaging, disdainful.

Wegzehrung [ˈveːkʦeːruŋ], f. (—, no pl.) food for the journey; (Eccl.) viaticum.

Wein

wegziehen ['vɛktsiːən], *v.a. irr.* draw away, pull away. — *v.n.* (*aux.* sein) march away; (*fig.*) move, remove.

Wegzug ['vɛktsuːk], *m.* (—s, *no pl.*) removal; moving away.

Weh [veː], *n.* (—s, *no pl.*) pain; grief, pang; misfortune.

weh [veː], *adj.* painful, sore; *mir ist — ums Herz*, I am sick at heart; my heart aches. — *adv.* — *tun*, ache; pain, hurt, offend, distress, grieve. — *int.* — *mir !* woe is me!

Wehen ['veːən], *n. pl.* birth-pangs, labour-pains.

wehen ['veːən], *v.n.* (*wind*) blow.

Wehgeschrei ['veːgəʃraɪ], *n.* (—s, *no pl.*) wailings.

Wehklage ['veːklaːgə], *f.* (—, *pl.* —n) lamentation.

wehklagen ['veːklaːgən], *v.n. insep.* lament, wail.

wehleidig ['veːlaɪdɪç], *adj.* tearful; easily hurt; self-pitying.

wehmütig ['veːmyːtɪç], *adj.* sad, melancholy, wistful.

Wehr (1) [veːr], *n.* (—s, *pl.* —e) weir.

Wehr (2) [veːr], *f.* (—, *pl.* —en) defence, bulwark.

wehren ['veːrən], *v.r. sich* —, defend o.s., offer resistance.

wehrhaft ['veːrhaft], *adj.* capable of bearing arms, able-bodied.

wehrlos ['veːrloːs], *adj.* defenceless, unarmed; (*fig.*) weak, unprotected.

Wehrpflicht ['veːrpflɪçt], *f.* (—, *no pl.*) compulsory military service, conscription.

Wehrstand ['veːrʃtant], *m.* (—s, *no pl.*) the military.

Weib [vaɪp], *n.* (—(e)s, *pl.* —er) woman; (*Poet.*) wife.

Weibchen ['vaɪpçən], *n.* (—s, *pl.* —) (*animal*) female.

Weiberfeind ['vaɪbərfaɪnt], *m.* (—s, *pl.* —e) woman-hater, misogynist.

Weiberherrschaft ['vaɪbərhɛrʃaft], *f.* (—, *no pl.*) petticoat rule.

weibisch ['vaɪbɪʃ], *adj.* womanish, effeminate.

weiblich ['vaɪplɪç], *adj.* female, feminine; womanly.

Weiblichkeit ['vaɪplɪçkaɪt], *f.* (—, *no pl.*) womanliness, femininity.

Weibsbild ['vaɪpsbɪlt], *n.* (—s, *pl.* —er) (*sl.*) female; wench.

weich [vaɪç], *adj.* weak; soft; tender, gentle; effeminate; sensitive; — *machen*, soften; — *werden*, relent.

Weichbild ['vaɪçbɪlt], *n.* (—s, *no pl.*) precincts; city boundaries.

Weiche ['vaɪçə], *f.* (—, *pl.* —n) (*Railw.*) switch, points.

weichen (1) ['vaɪçən], *v.a.* steep, soak, soften.

weichen (2) ['vaɪçən], *v.n. irr.* (*aux.* sein) yield, make way, give ground.

Weichensteller ['vaɪçənʃtɛlər], *m.* (—s, *pl.* —) (*Railw.*) pointsman, signalman.

Weichheit ['vaɪçhaɪt], *f.* (—, *no pl.*) softness; (*fig.*) weakness, tenderness.

weichherzig ['vaɪçhɛrtsɪç], *adj.* softhearted, tender-hearted.

weichlich ['vaɪçlɪç], *adj.* soft; (*fig.*) weak, effeminate.

Weichling ['vaɪçlɪŋ], *m.* (—s, *pl.* —e) weakling.

Weichsel ['vaɪksəl], *f.* Vistula.

Weichselkirsche ['vaɪksəlkɪrʃə], *f.* (—, *pl.* —n) sour cherry; morello.

Weide ['vaɪdə], *f.* (—, *pl.* —n) pasture, pasturage; (*Bot.*) willow.

Weideland ['vaɪdəlant], *n.* (—s, *pl.* ⸚er) pasture-ground.

weiden ['vaɪdən], *v.a.,v.n.* pasture, feed.

Weidenbaum ['vaɪdənbaum], *m.* (—s, *pl.* ⸚e) willow-tree.

Weiderich ['vaɪdərɪç], *m.* (—s, *pl.* —e) willow-herb, loose-strife, rose bay.

Weidgenosse ['vaɪtgənɔsə], *m.* (—en, *pl.* —en) fellow huntsman.

weidlich ['vaɪtlɪç], *adv.* (*rare*) greatly, thoroughly.

Weidmann ['vaɪtman], *m.* (—s, *pl.* ⸚er) sportsman, huntsman.

Weidmannsheil! ['vaɪtmanshaɪl], *excl.* tally-ho!

weigern ['vaɪgərn], *v.r. sich* —, refuse, decline.

Weigerung ['vaɪgəruŋ], *f.* (—, *pl.* —en) refusal, denial.

Weih [vaɪ], *m.* (—s, *pl.* —en) (*Orn.*) kite.

Weihbischof ['vaɪbɪʃɔf], *m.* (—s, *pl.* ⸚e) suffragan bishop.

Weihe ['vaɪə], *f.* (—, *pl.* —en) consecration; (*priest*) ordination; initiation; (*fig.*) solemnity.

weihen ['vaɪən], *v.a.* bless, consecrate; ordain. — *v.r. sich* —, devote o.s. (to).

Weiher ['vaɪər], *m.* (—s, *pl.* —) pond, fishpond.

weihevoll ['vaɪəfɔl], *adj.* solemn.

Weihnachten ['vaɪnaxtən], *n. or f.* Christmas.

Weihnachtsabend ['vaɪnaxtsaːbənt], *m.* (—s, *pl.* ⸚e) Christmas Eve.

Weihnachtsfeiertag ['vaɪnaxtsfaɪərtaːk], *m.* (—s, *pl.* ⸚e) Christmas Day; *zweiter* —, Boxing Day.

Weihnachtsgeschenk ['vaɪnaxtsgəʃɛŋk], *n.* (—s, *pl.* ⸚e) Christmas box, Christmas present.

Weihnachtslied ['vaɪnaxtsliːt], *n.* (—(e)s, *pl.* —er) Christmas carol.

Weihnachtsmann ['vaɪnaxtsman], *m.* (—(e)s, *pl.* ⸚er) Santa Claus, Father Christmas.

Weihrauch ['vaɪraux], *m.* (—s, *no pl.*) incense.

Weihwasser ['vaɪvasər], *n.* (—s, *no pl.*) holy water.

weil [vaɪl], *conj.* because, as, since.

weiland ['vaɪlant], *adv.* (*obs.*) formerly, once.

Weile ['vaɪlə], *f.* (—, *no pl.*) while, short time; leisure.

weilen ['vaɪlən], *v.n.* tarry, stay, abide.

Wein [vaɪn], *m.* (—(e)s, *pl.* —e) wine; (*plant*) vine; *einem reinen — einschenken*, tell s.o. the truth.

277

Weinbau ['vaɪnbau], *m.* (—s, *no pl.*) vine growing, viticulture.

Weinbeere ['vaɪnbeːrə], *f.* (—, *pl.* —n) grape.

Weinberg ['vaɪnbɛrk], *m.* (—s, *pl.* —e) vineyard.

Weinbrand ['vaɪnbrant], *m.* (—s, *no pl.*) brandy.

weinen ['vaɪnən], *v.n.* weep, cry.

Weinernte ['vaɪnɛrntə], *f.* (—, *pl.* —n) vintage.

Weinessig ['vaɪnɛsɪç], *m.* (—s, *no pl.*) (wine) vinegar.

Weinfaß ['vaɪnfas], *n.* (—sses, *pl.* ‛sser) wine-cask.

Weingeist ['vaɪngaɪst], *m.* (—es, *no pl.*) spirits of wine, alcohol.

Weinhändler ['vaɪnhɛndlər], *m.* (—s, *pl.* —) wine merchant.

Weinkarte ['vaɪnkartə], *f.* (—, *pl.* —n) wine-list.

Weinkeller ['vaɪnkɛlər], *m.* (—s, *pl.* —) wine-cellar; wine-tavern.

Weinkellerei ['vaɪnkɛlərai], *f.* (—, *pl.* —en) wine-store.

Weinkelter ['vaɪnkɛltər], *f.* (—, *pl.* —n) wine-press.

Weinkneipe ['vaɪnknaɪpə], *f.* (—, *pl.* —n) wine-tavern.

Weinkoster ['vaɪnkɔstər], *m.* (—s, *pl.* —) wine-taster.

Weinlaub ['vaɪnlaup], *n.* (—s, *no pl.*) vine-leaves.

Weinlese ['vaɪnleːzə], *f.* (—, *pl.* —n) vintage, grape harvest.

Weinranke ['vaɪnraŋkə], *f.* (—, *pl.* —n) vine-branch, tendril.

Weinschenke ['vaɪnʃɛŋkə], *f.* (—, *pl.* —n) wine-house, tavern.

weinselig ['vaɪnzeːlɪç], *adj.* tipsy.

Weinstein ['vaɪnʃtaɪn], *m.* (—s, *no pl.*) tartar.

Weinsteinsäure ['vaɪnʃtaɪnzɔyrə], *f.* (—, *no pl.*) tartaric acid.

Weinstock ['vaɪnʃtɔk], *m.* (—s, *pl.* ‛e) vine.

Weintraube ['vaɪntraubə], *f.* (—, *pl.* —n) grape, bunch of grapes.

weinumrankt ['vaɪnumraŋkt], *adj.* vine-clad.

weise ['vaɪzə], *adj.* wise, prudent.

Weise (1) ['vaɪzə], *m.* (—n, *pl.* —n) wise man, sage.

Weise (2) ['vaɪzə], *f.* (—, *pl.* —n) manner, fashion; method, way; tune, melody.

weisen ['vaɪzən], *v.a. irr.* point to, point out, show.

Weiser ['vaɪzər], *m.* (—s, *pl.* —) signpost; indicator; (*clock*) hand.

Weisheit ['vaɪshaɪt], *f.* (—, *pl.* —en) wisdom, prudence.

Weisheitszahn ['vaɪshaɪtstsaːn], *m.* (—s, *pl.* ‛e) wisdom tooth.

weislich ['vaɪslɪç], *adv.* wisely, prudently, advisedly.

weismachen ['vaɪsmaxən], *v.a. einem etwas —,* (*coll.*) spin a yarn to s.o.; *laß dir nichts —,* don't be taken in.

weissagen ['vaɪszaːgən], *v.a. insep.* prophesy, foretell.

Weissager ['vaɪszaːgər], *m.* (—s, *pl.* —) prophet, soothsayer.

Weissagung ['vaɪszaːguŋ], *f.* (—, *pl.* —en) prophecy.

weiß [vaɪs], *adj.* white, clean, blank.

Weißbuche ['vaɪsbuːxə], *f.* (—, *pl.* —n) (*Bot.*) hornbeam.

Weiße ['vaɪsə], *f.* (—, *no pl.*) whiteness; (*fig.*) (*dial.*) pale ale.

weißglühend ['vaɪsglyːənt], *adj.* at white heat, incandescent, white hot.

Weißnäherin ['vaɪsnɛːrɪn], *f.* (—, *pl.* —nen) seamstress.

Weißwaren ['vaɪsvaːrən], *f. pl.* linen.

Weisung ['vaɪzuŋ], *f.* (—, *pl.* —en) order, direction, instruction; directive.

weit [vaɪt], *adj.* distant, far, far off; wide, broad, vast, extensive; (*clothing*) loose, too big.

weitab ['vaɪt'ap], *adv.* far away.

weitaus ['vaɪt'aus], *adv.* by far.

weitblickend ['vaɪtblɪkənt], *adj.* far-sighted.

Weite ['vaɪtə], *f.* (—, *pl.* —n) width, breadth; distance.

weiten ['vaɪtən], *v.a.* widen, expand.

weiter ['vaɪtər], *adj.* further, farther, wider.

weiterbefördern ['vaɪtərbəfœrdərn], *v.a.* send, forward, send on.

weiterbilden ['vaɪtərbɪldən], *v.a.* improve, develop(e), extend.

Weitere ['vaɪtərə], *n.* (—n, *no pl.*) rest, remainder.

weiterführen ['vaɪtərfyːrən], *v.a.* continue, carry on.

weitergeben ['vaɪtərgeːbən], *v.a. irr.* pass on.

weitergehen ['vaɪtərgeːən], *v.n. irr.* (*aux.* sein) walk on.

weiterhin ['vaɪtərhɪn], *adv.* furthermore; in time to come; in future.

weiterkommen ['vaɪtərkɔmən], *v.n. irr.* (*aux.* sein) get on, advance.

Weiterung ['vaɪtərun], *f.* (—, *pl.* —en) widening, enlargement.

weitgehend ['vaɪtgeːənt], *adj.* far-reaching, sweeping.

weitläufig ['vaɪtlɔyfɪç], *adj.* ample, large; detailed, elaborate; distant, widespread; diffuse, long-winded.

weitschweifig ['vaɪtʃvaɪfɪç], *adj.* prolix, diffuse, rambling.

weitsichtig ['vaɪtzɪçtɪç], *adj.* long-sighted.

weittragend ['vaɪttraːgənt], *adj.* portentous, far-reaching.

weitverbreitet ['vaɪtfɛrbraɪtət], *adj.* widespread.

Weizen ['vaɪtsən], *m.* (—s, *no pl.*) wheat.

Weizengrieß ['vaɪtsəngriːs], *m.* (—es, *no pl.*) semolina; grits.

welch [vɛlç], *pron.* what (a).

welcher, -e, -es ['vɛlçər], *interr. pron.* which? what? — *rel. pron.* who which, that; (*indef.*) (*coll.*) some.

welcherlei ['vɛlçərlaɪ], *indecl. adj.* of what kind.

Welfe ['vɛlfə], *m.*(**—n,** *pl.* **—n**) Guelph.

welk [vɛlk], *adj.* faded, withered; — *werden*, fade, wither.

welken ['vɛlkən], *v.n.* (*aux.* sein) wither, fade, decay.

Wellblech ['vɛlblɛç], *n.* (**—s,** *no pl.*) corrugated iron.

Welle ['vɛlə], *f.* (**—,** *pl.* **—n**) wave, billow.

wellen ['vɛlən], *v.a.* wave.

Wellenbewegung ['vɛlənbəve:guŋ], *f.* (**—,** *pl.* **—en**) undulation.

Wellenlinie ['vɛlənli:njə], *f.* (**—,** *pl.* **—n**) wavy line.

wellig ['vɛlɪç], *adj.* wavy, undulating.

welsch [vɛlʃ], *adj.* foreign; Italian; French.

Welschkohl ['vɛlʃko:l], *m.* (**—s,** *no pl.*) (*Bot.*) savoy cabbage.

Welschkorn ['vɛlʃkɔrn], *n.* (**—s,** *no pl.*) (*Bot.*) Indian corn.

Welt [vɛlt], *f.* (**—,** *pl.* **—en**) world, earth; universe; society.

Weltall ['vɛltal], *n.* (**—s,** *no pl.*) universe, cosmos; (outer) space.

Weltanschauung ['vɛltanʃauuŋ], *f.* (**—,** *pl.* **—en**) view of life, philosophy of life, ideology.

Weltbeschreibung ['vɛltbəʃraɪbuŋ], *f.* (**—,** *no pl.*) cosmography.

Weltbürger ['vɛltbyrgər], *m.* (**—s,** *pl.* **—**) cosmopolitan.

welterschütternd ['vɛltərʃytərnt], *adj.* world-shaking.

weltfremd ['vɛltfrɛmt], *adj.* unwordly, unsophisticated.

Weltgeschichte ['vɛltgəʃɪçtə], *f.* (**—,** *no pl.*) world history.

Weltherrschaft ['vɛlthɛrʃaft], *f.* (**—,** *no pl.*) world dominion.

Weltkenntnis ['vɛltkɛntnɪs], *f.* (**—,** *no pl.*) worldly wisdom.

weltklug ['vɛltklu:k], *adj.* astute, worldly-wise.

Weltkrieg ['vɛltkri:k], *m.* (**—es,** *pl.* **—e**) world war.

weltlich ['vɛltlɪç], *adj.* worldly; (*Eccl.*) temporal, secular.

Weltmacht ['vɛltmaxt], *f.* (**—,** *pl.* **⸚e**) world power, great power.

Weltmeer ['vɛltme:r], *n.* (**—s,** *pl.* **—e**) ocean.

Weltmeisterschaft ['vɛltmaɪstərʃaft], *f.* (**—,** *pl.* **—en**) world championship.

Weltordnung ['vɛltɔrdnuŋ], *f.* (**—** *pl.* **—en**) cosmic order.

Weltraum ['vɛltraum], *m.* (**—s,** *no pl.*) space.

Weltraumflug ['vɛltraumflu:k], *m.* (**—(e)s,** *pl.* **⸚e**) space flight.

Weltraumforschung ['vɛltraumfɔrʃuŋ], *f.* (**—,** *no pl.*) space exploration.

Weltraumgeschoss ['vɛltraumgəʃo:s], *n.* (**—es,** *pl.* **—e**) space rocket.

Weltruf ['vɛltru:f], *m.* (**—s,** *no pl.*) world-wide renown.

Weltschmerz ['vɛltʃmɛrts], *m.* (**—es,** *no pl.*) world-weariness, Wertherism; melancholy.

Weltsprache ['vɛltʃpra:xə], *f.* (**—,** *pl.* **—en**) universal language; world language.

Weltstadt ['vɛltʃtat], *f.* (**—,** *pl.* **⸚e**) metropolis.

Weltumseglung ['vɛltumze:gluŋ], *f.* (**—,** *pl.* **—en**) circumnavigation (of the globe).

Weltuntergang ['vɛltuntərgaŋ], *m.* **—s,** *no pl.*) end of the world.

Weltwirtschaft ['vɛltvɪrtʃaft], *f.* (**—,** *no pl.*) world trade.

wem [ve:m], *pers. pron.* (*Dat. of* **wer**) to whom — *interr. pron.* to whom?

wen [ve:n], *pers. pron.* (*Acc. of* **wer**) whom — *interr. pron.* whom?

Wende ['vɛndə], *f.* (**—,** *pl.* **—n**) turn, turning(point).

Wendekreis ['vɛndəkraɪs], *m.* (**—es,** *pl.* **—e**) tropic.

Wendeltreppe ['vɛndəltrɛpə], *f.* (**—,** *pl.* **—n**) spiral staircase.

wenden ['vɛndən], *v.a. reg. & irr.* turn.

Wendepunkt ['vɛndəpuŋkt], *m.* (**—es,** *pl.* **—e**) turning point; crisis.

Wendung ['vɛnduŋ], *f.* (**—,** *pl.* **—en**) turn, turning; crisis; (*speech*) phrase.

wenig ['ve:nɪç], *adj.* little, few; *ein* **—,** a little.

weniger ['ve:nɪgər], *adj.* less, fewer.

wenigstens ['ve:nɪçstəns], *adv.* at least.

wenn [vɛn], *conj.* if; when; whenever, in case; — *nicht,* unless.

wenngleich [vɛn'glaɪç], *conj.* though, although.

wer [ve:r], *rel. pron.* who, he who; — *auch,* whoever. — *interr. pron.* who? which? — *da?* who goes there?

Werbekraft ['vɛrbəkraft], *f.* (**—,** *no pl.*) (*Advertising*) attraction; appeal; publicity value.

werben ['vɛrbən], *v.n. irr.* advertise, canvass; court, woo. — *v.a.* (*soldiers*) recruit.

Werbung ['vɛrbuŋ], *f.* (**—,** *pl.* **—en**) advertising, publicity, propaganda; recruiting; courtship.

Werdegang ['ve:rdəgaŋ], *m.* (**—s,** *no pl.*) evolution, development.

werden ['ve:rdən], *v.n. irr.* (*aux.* sein) become, get; grow; turn; *Arzt* —, become a doctor; *alt* —, grow old; *bleich* —, turn pale.

werdend ['ve:rdənt], *adj.* becoming; nascent, incipient, budding.

werfen ['vɛrfən], *v.a. irr.* throw, cast.

Werft (1) [vɛrft], *m.* (**—(e)s,** *pl.* **—e**) warp.

Werft (2) [vɛrft], *f.* (**—,** *pl.* **—en**) dockyard, shipyard, wharf.

Werk [vɛrk], *n.* (**—(e)s,** *pl.* **—e**) work, action, deed; undertaking; (*Ind.*) works, plant, mill, factory.

Werkführer ['vɛrkfy:rər], *m.* (**—s,** *pl.* **—**) foreman.

Werkleute ['vɛrklɔytə], *pl.* workmen.

Werkmeister ['vɛrkmaɪstər], *m.* (**—s,** *pl.* **—**) overseer.

werktätig ['vɛrkte:tɪç], *adj.* active, practical; hard-working.

Werkzeug

Werkzeug ['vɛrktsɔyk], *n.* (—s, *pl.* —e) implement, tool, jig, instrument.

Wermut ['ve:rmu:t], *m.* (—s, *no pl.*) absinthe, vermouth.

Wert [ve:rt], *m.* (—(e)s, *pl.* —e) value, worth, price; use; merit; importance.

wert [ve:rt], *adj.* valuable; worth; dear, esteemed.

Wertangabe ['ve:rtaŋa:bə], *f.* (—, *pl.* —n) valuation; declared value.

Wertbestimmung ['ve:rtbəʃtɪmuŋ], *f.* (—, *no pl.*) appraisal, assessment, valuation.

Wertbrief ['ve:rtbri:f], *m.* (—s, *pl.* —e) registered letter.

werten ['ve:rtən], *v.a.* value.

Wertgegenstand ['ve:rtge:gənʃtant], *m.* (—s, *pl.* ⁝e) article of value.

Wertmesser ['ve:rtmɛsər], *m.* (—s, *pl.* —) standard.

Wertpapiere ['ve:rtpapi:rə], *n. pl.* securities.

Wertsachen ['ve:rtzaxən], *f. pl.* valuables.

wertschätzen ['ve:rtʃɛtsən], *v.a.* esteem (highly).

wertvoll ['ve:rtfɔl], *adj.* of great value, valuable.

Wertzeichen ['ve:rttsaɪçən], *n.* (—s, *pl.* —) stamp; coupon.

wes [vɛs], *pers. pron.* (*obs.*) whose.

Wesen ['ve:zən], *n.* (—s, *pl.* —) being, creature; reality; essence, nature, substance; character, demeanour; (*in compounds*) organisation, affairs.

wesenlos ['ve:zənlo:s], *adj.* disembodied, unsubstantial, shadowy; trivial.

wesensgleich ['ve:zənsglaɪç], *adj.* identical, substantially the same.

wesentlich ['ve:zəntlɪç], *adj.* essential, material.

weshalb [vɛs'halp], *conj., adv.* wherefore, why; therefore.

Wespe ['vɛspə], *f.* (—, *pl.* —n) (*Ent.*) wasp.

Wespennest ['vɛspənnɛst], *n.* (—s, *pl.* —er,) wasp's nest; *in ein — stechen,* stir up a hornet's nest.

wessen ['vɛsən], *pers .pron.* (*Genit. of* **wer**) whose. — *interr. pron.* whose?

Weste ['vɛstə], *f.* (—, *pl.* —n) waistcoat.

Westen ['vɛstən], *m.* (—s, *no pl.*) west; *nach —,* westward.

Westfalen [vɛst'fa:lən], *n.* Westphalia.

Westindien [vɛst'ɪndjən], *n.* the West Indies.

weswegen [vɛs've:gən] *see* **weshalb**.

Wettbewerb ['vɛtbəvɛrp], *m.* (—s, *pl.* —e) competition, rivalry; *unlauterer —,* unfair competition.

Wettbewerber ['vɛtbəvɛrbər], *m.* (—s, *pl.* —) rival, competitor.

Wette ['vɛtə], *f.* (—, *pl.* —n) bet, wager; *um die — laufen,* race one another.

Wetteifer ['vɛtaɪfər], *m.* (—s, *no pl.*) rivalry.

wetteifern ['vɛtaɪfərn], *v.n. insep.* vie (with), compete.

wetten ['vɛtən], *v.a., v.n.* bet, lay a wager, wager.

Wetter ['vɛtər], *n.* (—s, *pl.* —) weather; bad weather, storm; *schlagende —,* (*Min.*) fire-damp.

Wetterbeobachtung ['vɛtərbəobaxtuŋ], *f.* (—, *pl.* —en) meteorological observation.

Wetterbericht ['vɛtərbərɪçt], *m.* (—s, *pl.* —e) weather report *or* forecast.

Wetterfahne ['vɛtərfa:nə], *f.* (—, *pl.* —en) weather-cock, vane; (*fig.*) turncoat.

wetterfest ['vɛtərfɛst], *adj.* weather-proof.

Wetterglas ['vɛtərgla:s], *n.* (—es, *pl.* ⁝er) barometer.

Wetterhahn ['vɛtərha:n], *m.* (—s, *pl.* ⁝e) weather-cock.

Wetterkunde ['vɛtərkundə], *f.* (—, *no pl.*) meteorology.

Wetterleuchten ['vɛtərlɔyçtən], *n.* (—s, *no pl.*) summer lightning; sheet lightning.

wettern ['vɛtərn], *v.n.* be stormy; (*fig.*) curse, swear, thunder (against), storm.

Wettervorhersage ['vɛtərfo:rhe:rza:gə], *f.* (—, *pl.* —n) weather forecast.

wetterwendisch ['vɛtərvɛndɪʃ], *adj.* changeable; irritable, peevish.

Wettkampf ['vɛtkampf], *m.* (—(e)s, *pl.* ⁝e) contest, tournament.

Wettlauf ['vɛtlauf], *m.* (—s, *pl.* ⁝e) race.

wettmachen ['vɛtmaxən], *v.a.* make up for.

Wettrennen ['vɛtrɛnən], *n.* (—s, *pl.* —) racing, race.

Wettstreit ['vɛtʃtraɪt], *m.* (—s, *pl.* —e) contest, contention.

wetzen ['vɛtsən], *v.a.* whet, hone, sharpen.

Wichse ['vɪksə], *f.* (—, *pl.* —n) blacking, shoe-polish; (*fig.*) thrashing.

wichsen ['vɪksən], *v.a.* black, shine; (*fig.*) thrash.

Wicht [vɪçt], *m.* (—(e)s, *pl.* —e) creature; (*coll.*) chap.

Wichtelmännchen ['vɪçtəlmɛnçən], *n.* (—s, *pl.* —) pixie, goblin.

wichtig ['vɪçtɪç], *adj.* important; weighty; significant; *sich — machen,* put on airs.

Wichtigkeit ['vɪçtɪçkaɪt], *f.* (—, *no pl.*) importance; significance.

Wicke ['vɪkə], *f.* (—, *pl.* —n) (*Bot.*) vetch.

Wickel ['vɪkəl], *m.* (—s, *pl.* —) roller; (*hair*) curler; (*Med.*) compress.

Wickelkind ['vɪkəlkɪnt], *n.* (—s, *pl.* —er) babe in arms.

wickeln ['vɪkəln], *v.a.* roll, coil; wind; wrap (up); (*babies*) swaddle; (*hair*) curl.

Widder ['vɪdər], *m.* (—s, *pl.* —) ram; (*Astrol.*) Aries.

wider ['vi:dər], *prep.* (*Acc.*) against, in opposition to, contrary to.

widerfahren [viːdərˈfaːrən], *v.n. irr. insep.* (*aux.* sein) happen to s.o., befall s.o.; *einem Gerechtigkeit — lassen*, give s.o. his due.
Widerhaken [ˈviːdərhaːkən], *m.* (**—s**, *pl.* —) barb.
Widerhall [ˈviːdərhal], *m.* (**—s**, *pl.* —e) echo, resonance; (*fig.*) response.
widerlegen [viːdərˈleːgən], *v.a. insep.* refute, disprove, prove (s.o.) wrong.
Widerlegung [viːdərˈleːguŋ], *f.* (—, *pl.* —en) refutation, rebuttal.
widerlich [ˈviːdərliç], *adj.* disgusting, nauseating, repulsive.
widernatürlich [ˈviːdərnatyːrliç], *adj.* unnatural; perverse.
widerraten [viːdərˈraːtən], *v.a. irr. insep.* advise against; dissuade from.
widerrechtlich [ˈviːdərrɛçtliç], *adj.* illegal, unlawful.
Widerrede [ˈviːdərreːdə], *f.* (—, *pl.* —n) contradiction.
Widerruf [ˈviːdərruːf], *m.* (**—s**, *pl.* —e) revocation, recantation.
widerrufen [viːdərˈruːfən], *v.a. irr. insep.* recant, retract, revoke.
Widersacher [ˈviːdərzaxər], *m.* (**—s**, *pl.* —) adversary, antagonist.
Widerschein [ˈviːdərʃain], *m.* (**—s**, *no pl.*) reflection.
widersetzen [viːdərˈzɛtsən], *v.r. insep. sich —*, resist, (*Dat.*) oppose.
widersetzlich [viːdərˈzɛtsliç], *adj.* refractory, insubordinate.
Widersinn [ˈviːdərzin], *m.* (**—s**, *no pl.*) nonsense, absurdity; paradox.
widersinnig [ˈviːdərziniç], *adj.* nonsensical, absurd; paradoxical.
widerspenstig [ˈviːdərʃpɛnstiç], *adj.* refractory, rebellious, obstinate, stubborn.
widerspiegeln [viːdərˈʃpiːgəln], *v.a.* reflect, mirror.
widersprechen [viːdərˈʃprɛçən], *v.n. irr. insep.* (*Dat.*) contradict, gainsay.
Widerspruch [ˈviːdərʃprux], *m.* (**—es**, *pl.* ⁻e) contradiction.
widerspruchsvoll [ˈviːdərʃpruxsfɔl], *adj.* contradictory.
Widerstand [ˈviːdərʃtant], *m.* (**—s**, *pl.* ⁻e) resistance, opposition.
widerstandsfähig [ˈviːdərʃtantsfɛːiç], *adj.* resistant, hardy.
widerstehen [viːdərˈʃteːən], *v.n. irr. insep.* (*Dat.*) resist, withstand; be distasteful (to).
Widerstreben [viːdərˈʃtreːbən], *n.* (**—s**, *no pl.*) reluctance.
widerstreben [viːdərˈʃtreːbən], *v.n. insep.* (*Dat.*) strive against, oppose; be distasteful to a p.
Widerstreit [ˈviːdərʃtrait], *m.* (**—s**, *no pl.*) contradiction, opposition; conflict.
widerwärtig [ˈviːdərvɛrtiç], *adj.* unpleasant, disagreeable, repugnant, repulsive; hateful, odious.
Widerwille [ˈviːdərvilə], *m.* (**—ns**, *no pl.*) aversion (to).

widmen [ˈvidmən], *v.a.* dedicate.
Widmung [ˈvidmuŋ], *f.* (—, *pl.* —en) dedication.
widrig [ˈviːdriç], *adj.* contrary, adverse, inimical, unfavourable.
widrigenfalls [ˈviːdriɡənfals], *adv.* failing this, otherwise, else.
wie [viː], *adv.* how. — *conj.* as, just as, like; — *geht's?* how are you?
wieder [ˈviːdər], *adv.* again, anew, afresh; back, in return.
Wiederabdruck [ˈviːdərapdruk], *m.* (**—s**, *pl.* —e) reprint.
Wiederaufbau [viːdərˈaufbau], *m.* (**—s**, *no pl.*) rebuilding.
Wiederaufnahme [viːdərˈaufnaːmə], *f.* (—, *no pl.*) resumption.
Wiederbelebungsversuch [ˈviːdərbəleːbuŋsfɛrzuːx], *m.* (**—es**, *pl.* —e) attempt at resuscitation.
Wiederbezahlung [ˈviːdərbətsaːluŋ], *f.* (—, *pl.* —en) reimbursement.
wiederbringen [ˈviːdərbriŋən], *v.a. irr.* bring back, restore.
Wiedereinrichtung [ˈviːdərainriçtuŋ], *f.* (—, *no pl.*) reorganisation, re-establishment.
Wiedereinsetzung [ˈviːdərainzɛtsuŋ], *f.* (—, *pl.* —en) restoration, reinstatement, rehabilitation.
wiedererkennen [ˈviːdərɛrkɛnən], *v.a. irr.* recognise.
Wiedererstattung [ˈviːdərɛrʃtatuŋ], *f.* (—, *no pl.*) restitution.
Wiedergabe [ˈviːdərgaːbə], *f.* (—, *no pl.*) restitution, return; (*fig.*) rendering, reproduction.
wiedergeben [ˈviːdərgeːbən], *v.a. irr.* return, give back; (*fig.*) render.
Wiedergeburt [ˈviːdərgəbuːrt], *f.* (—, *no pl.*) rebirth, regeneration, renascence.
Wiedergutmachung [viːdərˈguːtmaxuŋ], *f.* (—, *no pl.*) reparation.
Wiederherstellung [viːdərˈheːrʃtɛluŋ], *f.* (—, *no pl.*) restoration; recovery.
Wiederherstellungsmittel [viːdərˈheːrʃtɛluŋsmitəl], *n.* (**—s**, *pl.* —) restorative, tonic.
wiederholen [viːdərˈhoːlən], *v.a. insep.* repeat, reiterate.
Wiederholung [viːdərˈhoːluŋ], *f.* (—, *pl.* —en) repetition.
Wiederkäuer [ˈviːdərkɔyər], *m.* (**—s**, *pl.* —) ruminant.
Wiederkehr [ˈviːdərkeːr], *f.* (—, *no pl.*) return; recurrence.
wiederkehren [ˈviːdərkeːrən], *v.n.* (*aux.* sein) return.
wiederklingen [ˈviːdərkliŋən], *v.n. irr.* reverberate.
wiederkommen [ˈviːdərkɔmən], *v.n. irr.* (*aux.* sein) return, come back.
Wiedersehen [ˈviːdərzeːən], *n.* (**—s**, *no pl.*) reunion, meeting after separation; *auf —*, good-bye; so long! see you again!
wiedersehen [ˈviːdərzeːən], *v.a. irr.* see again, meet again.

wiederum

wiederum [ˈviːdərum], *adv.* again, anew, afresh.

Wiedervereinigung [ˈviːdərfɛraɪnɪguŋ], *f.* (—, *pl.* —en) reunion, reunification.

Wiedervergeltung [ˈviːdərfɛrgɛltuŋ], *f.* (—, *no pl.*) requital, retaliation, reprisal.

Wiederverkauf [ˈviːdərfɛrkauf], *m.* (—s, *no pl.*) resale.

Wiederverkäufer [ˈviːdərfɛrkɔyfər], *m.* (—s, *pl.* —) retailer.

Wiederversöhnung [ˈviːdərfɛrzøːnuŋ], *f.* (—, *no pl.*) reconciliation.

Wiederwahl [ˈviːdərvaːl], *f.* (—, *no pl.*) re-election.

Wiege [ˈviːgə], *f.* (—, *pl.* —n) cradle.

wiegen [ˈviːgən], *v.a.* rock (the cradle). — *v.r. sich — in,* delude o.s. with. — *v.a., v.n. irr.* weigh.

Wiegenfest [ˈviːgənfɛst], *n.* (—es, *pl.* —e) (*Poet., Lit.*) birthday.

Wiegenlied [ˈviːgənliːt], *n.* (—s, *pl.* —er) cradle-song, lullaby.

wiehern [ˈviːərn], *v.n.* neigh.

Wien [viːn], *n.* Vienna.

Wiese [ˈviːzə], *f.* (—, *pl.* —n) meadow.

Wiesel [ˈviːzəl], *n.* (—s, *pl.* —) (*Zool.*) weasel.

wieso [viˈzoː] *adv.* why? how do you mean? in what way?

wieviel [viˈfiːl], *adv.* how much, how many; *den —ten haben wir heute?* what is the date today?

wiewohl [viˈvoːl], *conj.* although, though.

Wild [vɪlt], *n.* (—(e)s, *no pl.*) game; venison.

wild [vɪlt], *adj.* wild, savage, fierce; furious.

Wildbach [ˈvɪltbax], *m.* (—s, *pl.* ⁻e) (mountain) torrent.

Wilddieb [ˈvɪltdiːp], *m.* (—(e)s, *pl.* —e) poacher.

Wilde [ˈvɪldə], *m.* (—n, *pl.* —n) savage.

wildern [ˈvɪldərn], *v.n.* poach.

Wildfang [ˈvɪltfaŋ], *m.* (—s, *pl.* ⁻e) scamp, tomboy.

wildfremd [ˈvɪltfrɛmt], *adj.* completely strange.

Wildhüter [ˈvɪlthyːtər], *m.* (—s, *pl.* —) gamekeeper.

Wildleder [ˈvɪltleːdər], *n.* (—s, *no pl.*) suède, doeskin, buckskin.

Wildnis [ˈvɪltnɪs], *f.* (—, *pl.* —se) wilderness, desert.

Wildpark [ˈvɪltpark], *m.* (—s, *pl.* —s) game-reserve.

Wildpret [ˈvɪltprɛt], *n.* (—s, *no pl.*) game; venison.

Wildschwein [ˈvɪltʃvaɪn], *n.* (—s, *pl.* —e) wild boar.

Wille [ˈvɪlə], *m.* (—ns, *no pl.*) will, wish, design, purpose.

willenlos [ˈvɪlənloːs], *adj.* weak-minded.

willens [ˈvɪləns], *adv.* — *sein,* be willing, have a mind to.

Willenserklärung [ˈvɪlənsɛrklɛːruŋ], *f.* (—, *pl.* —en) (*Law*) declaratory act.

Willensfreiheit [ˈvɪlənsfraɪhaɪt], *f.* (—, *no pl.*) free will.

Willenskraft [ˈvɪlənskraft], *f.* (—, *no pl.*) strength of will, will-power.

willentlich [ˈvɪləntlɪç], *adv.* purposely, on purpose, intentionally, wilfully.

willfahren [vɪlˈfaːrən], *v.n. insep.* (*Dat.*) comply with, gratify.

willfährig [ˈvɪlfɛːrɪç], *adj.* compliant, complaisant.

willig [ˈvɪlɪç], *adj.* willing, ready, docile.

willkommen [vɪlˈkɔmən], *adj.* welcome; — *heißen,* welcome.

Willkür [ˈvɪlkyːr], *f.* (—, *no pl.*) free will; discretion; caprice, arbitrariness.

willkürlich [ˈvɪlkyːrlɪç], *adj.* arbitrary.

wimmeln [ˈvɪməln], *v.n.* swarm, teem (with).

wimmern [ˈvɪmərn], *v.n.* whimper.

Wimpel [ˈvɪmpəl], *m.* (—s, *pl.* —) pennon, pennant, streamer.

Wimper [ˈvɪmpər], *f.* (—, *pl.* —n) eyelash; *ohne mit der — zu zucken,* without turning a hair, without batting an eyelid.

Wind [vɪnt], *m.* (—(e)s, *pl.* —e) wind, breeze; *von etwas — bekommen,* get wind of.

Windbeutel [ˈvɪntbɔytəl], *m.* (—s, *pl.* —) cream puff; (*fig.*) windbag.

Windbüchse [ˈvɪntbyksə], *f.* (—, *pl.* —n) air-gun.

Winde [ˈvɪndə], *f.* (—, *pl.* —n) (*Tech.*) windlass; (*Bot.*) bindweed.

Windel [ˈvɪndəl], *f.* (—, *pl.* —n) (baby's) napkin; (*Am.*) diaper.

windelweich [ˈvɪndəlvaɪç], *adj.* very soft, limp; *einen — schlagen,* beat s.o. to a jelly.

winden [ˈvɪndən], *v.a. irr.* wind, reel; wring; (*flowers*) make a wreath of. — *v.r. sich —,* writhe.

Windeseile [ˈvɪndəsaɪlə], *f.* (—, *no pl.*) lightning speed.

Windfahne [ˈvɪntfaːnə], *f.* (—, *pl.* —n) weather-cock, vane.

windfrei [ˈvɪntfraɪ], *adj.* sheltered.

Windhund [ˈvɪnthunt], *m.* (—s, *pl.* —e) greyhound; (*fig.*) windbag.

windig [ˈvɪndɪç], *adj.* windy.

Windklappe [ˈvɪntklapə], *f.* (—, *pl.* —n) air-valve.

Windlicht [ˈvɪntlɪçt], *n.* (—s, *pl.* —er) torch; storm lantern.

Windmühle [ˈvɪntmyːlə], *f.* (—, *pl.* —n) windmill.

Windpocken [ˈvɪntpɔkən], *f. pl.* (*Med.*) chicken-pox.

Windrichtung [ˈvɪntrɪçtuŋ], *f.* (—, *pl.* —en) direction of the wind.

Windrose [ˈvɪntroːzə], *f.* (—, *pl.* —n) compass card; windrose.

Windsbraut [ˈvɪntsbraut], *f.* (—, *no pl.*) gust of wind, squall; gale.

windschief [ˈvɪntʃiːf], *adj.* warped, bent.

Windschutzscheibe [ˈvɪntʃutsʃaɪbə], *f.* (—, *pl.* —n) (*Motor.*) windscreen.

Windseite [ˈvɪntzaɪtə], *f.* (—, *pl.* —n) windward side.

Witterungsverhältnisse

Windspiel ['vɪntʃpiːl], *n.* (—s, *pl.* —e) greyhound.

windstill ['vɪntʃtɪl], *adj.* calm.

Windung ['vɪnduŋ], *f.* (—, *pl.* —en) winding; convolution; twist, loop; coil; meandering.

Wink [vɪŋk], *m.* (—(e)s, *pl.* —e) sign, nod; (*fig.*) hint, suggestion.

Winkel ['vɪŋkəl], *m.* (—s, *pl.* —) corner; (*Maths.*) angle.

Winkeladvokat ['vɪŋkəlatvokaːt], *m.* (—en, *pl.* —en) quack lawyer.

Winkelmaß ['vɪŋkəlmaːs], *n.* (—es, *pl.* —e) set-square.

Winkelmesser ['vɪŋkəlmɛsər], *m.* (—s, *pl.* —) protractor.

Winkelzug ['vɪŋkəltsuːk], *m.* (—s, *pl.* ːe) evasion, trick, shift.

winken ['vɪŋkən], *v.n.* signal, nod, beckon, wave.

winklig ['vɪŋklɪç], *adj.* angular.

winseln ['vɪnzəln], *v.n.* whimper, whine, wail.

Winter ['vɪntər], *m.* (—s, *pl.* —) winter.

Wintergarten ['vɪntərgartən], *m.* (—s, *pl.* ː) conservatory.

Wintergewächs ['vɪntərgəvɛks], *n.* (—es, *pl.* —e) perennial plant.

Wintergrün ['vɪntərgryːn], *n.* (—s, no *pl.*) evergreen; wintergreen.

wintern ['vɪntərn], *v.n.* become wintry.

Winterschlaf ['vɪntərʃlaːf], *m.* (—s, no *pl.*) hibernation; den — halten, hibernate.

Winzer ['vɪntsər], *m.* (—s, *pl.* —) vine-grower.

winzig ['vɪntsɪç], *adj.* tiny, diminutive.

Wipfel ['vɪpfəl], *m.* (—s, *pl.* —) top (of a tree), tree-top.

Wippe ['vɪpə], *f.* (—, *pl.* —n) seesaw.

wippen ['vɪpən], *v.n.* balance, see-saw.

wir [viːr], *pers. pron.* we.

Wirbel ['vɪrbəl], *m.* (—s, *pl.* —) (*water*) whirlpool, eddy; whirlwind; (*drum*) roll; (*head*) crown; (*back*) vertebra.

wirbeln ['vɪrbəln], *v.a., v.n.* whirl.

Wirbelsäule ['vɪrbəlzɔylə], *f.* (—, *pl.* —n) spine, vertebral column.

Wirbelwind ['vɪrbəlvɪnt], *m.* (—s, *pl.* —e) whirlwind.

Wirken ['vɪrkən], *n.* (—s, no *pl.*) activity.

wirken ['vɪrkən], *v.a.* effect, work; bring to pass; (*materials*) weave; (*dough*) knead. — *v.n.* work.

Wirker ['vɪrkər], *m.* (—s, *pl.* —) weaver.

wirklich ['vɪrklɪç], *adj.* real, actual; true, genuine.

Wirklichkeit ['vɪrklɪçkaɪt], *f.* (—, no *pl.*) reality.

wirksam ['vɪrkzaːm], *adj.* effective, efficacious.

Wirksamkeit ['vɪrkzaːmkaɪt], *f.* (—, no *pl.*) efficacy, efficiency.

Wirkung ['vɪrkuŋ], *f.* (—, *pl.* —en) working, operation; reaction; efficacy; effect, result, consequence; force, in-

fluence; eine — ausüben auf, have an effect on; influence s.o. or s.th.

Wirkungskreis ['vɪrkuŋskraɪs], *m.* (—es, *pl.* —e) sphere of activity.

wirkungslos ['vɪrkuŋsloːs], *adj.* ineffectual.

wirkungsvoll ['vɪrkuŋsfɔl], *adj.* effective, efficacious; (*fig.*) impressive.

wirr [vɪr], *adj.* tangled, confused; — durcheinander, higgledy-piggledy; mir ist ganz — im Kopf, my head is going round.

Wirren ['vɪrən], *f. pl.* troubles, disorders, disturbances.

wirrköpfig ['vɪrkœpfɪç], *adj.* muddle-headed.

Wirrsal ['vɪrzaːl], *n.* (—s, *pl.* —e) confusion, disorder.

Wirrwarr ['vɪrvar], *m.* (—s, no *pl.*) jumble, hurly-burly, hubbub.

Wirt [vɪrt], *m.* (—(e)s, *pl.* —e) host; innkeeper; landlord.

Wirtin ['vɪrtɪn], *f.* (—, *pl.* —innen) hostess, landlady, innkeeper's wife.

wirtlich ['vɪrtlɪç], *adj.* hospitable.

Wirtschaft ['vɪrtʃaft], *f.* (—, *pl.* —en) housekeeping; administration; economy; household; housekeeping; inn, ale-house; (*coll.*) mess.

wirtschaften ['vɪrtʃaftən], *v.n.* keep house, housekeep; administer, run; (*coll.*) rummage.

Wirtschafterin ['vɪrtʃaftərɪn], *f.* (—, *pl.* —innen) housekeeper.

wirtschaftlich ['vɪrtʃaftlɪç], *adj.* economical, thrifty.

Wirtschaftlichkeit ['vɪrtʃaftlɪçkaɪt], *f.* (—, no *pl.*) economy; profitability.

Wirtschaftsgeld ['vɪrtʃaftsgɛlt], *n.* (—s, *pl.* —er) housekeeping-money.

Wirtshaus ['vɪrtshaus], *n.* (—es, *pl.* ːer) inn.

Wisch [vɪʃ], *m.* (—es, *pl.* —e) scrap of paper, rag.

wischen ['vɪʃən], *v.a.* wipe.

wispern ['vɪspərn], *v.a., v.n.* whisper.

Wißbegier(de) ['vɪsbəgiːr(də)], *f.* (—, no *pl.*) craving for knowledge; curiosity.

Wissen ['vɪsən], *n.* (—s, no *pl.*) knowledge, learning, erudition.

wissen ['vɪsən], *v.a. irr.* know, be aware of (a fact); be able to.

Wissenschaft ['vɪsənʃaft], *f.* (—, *pl.* —en) learning, scholarship; science.

wissenschaftlich ['vɪsənʃaftlɪç], *adj.* learned, scholarly; scientific.

wissenswert ['vɪsənsveːrt], *adj.* worth knowing.

Wissenszweig ['vɪsənstsvaɪk], *m.* (—s, *pl.* —e) branch of knowledge.

wissentlich ['vɪsəntlɪç], *adj.* deliberate, wilful. — *adv.* knowingly.

wittern ['vɪtərn], *v.a.* scent, smell; (*fig.*) suspect.

Witterung ['vɪtəruŋ], *f.* (—, no *pl.*) weather; trail; scent.

Witterungsverhältnisse ['vɪtəruŋsfɛrhɛltnɪsə], *n. pl.* atmospheric conditions.

283

Witterungswechsel [ˈvɪtəruŋsvɛksəl], *m.* (—s, *no pl.*) change in the weather.
Witwe [ˈvɪtvə], *f.* (—, *pl.* —n) widow.
Witwer [ˈvɪtvər], *m.* (—s, *pl.* —) widower.
Witz [vɪts], *m.* (—es, *pl.* —e) wit, brains; joke, jest, witticism; funny story.
Witzblatt [ˈvɪtsblat], *n.* (—s, *pl.* ⸚er) satirical *or* humorous journal.
Witzbold [ˈvɪtsbɔlt], *m.* (—es, *pl.* —e) wag; wit.
witzeln [ˈvɪtsəln], *v.n.* poke fun (at).
witzig [ˈvɪtsɪç], *adj.* witty; funny, comical; bright.
wo [voː], *interr. adv.* where? — *conj.* when.
wobei [voːˈbaɪ], *adv.* by which, at which, in connection with which; whereby; in doing so.
Woche [ˈvɔxə], *f.* (—, *pl.* —n) week.
Wochenbericht [ˈvɔxənbərɪçt], *m.* (—s, *pl.* —e) weekly report.
Wochenbett [ˈvɔxənbɛt], *n.* (—s, *no pl.*) confinement.
Wochenblatt [ˈvɔxənblat], *n.* (—s, *pl.* ⸚er) weekly (paper).
Wochenlohn [ˈvɔxənloːn], *m.* (—s, *pl.* ⸚e) weekly wage(s).
Wochenschau [ˈvɔxənʃau], *f.* (—, *no pl.*) newsreel.
Wochentag [ˈvɔxəntaːk], *m.* (—s, *pl.* —e) week-day.
wöchentlich [ˈvœçəntlɪç], *adj.* weekly, every week.
wodurch [voːˈdurç], *adv.* whereby, by which, through which; (*interr.*) by what?
wofern [voːˈfɛrn], *conj.* if, provided that.
wofür [voːˈfyːr], *adv.* for what, for which, wherefore.
Woge [ˈvoːgə], *f.* (—, *pl.* —n) wave, billow.
wogegen [voːˈgeːgən], *adv.* against what, against which, in return for which.
wogen [ˈvoːgən], *v.n.* heave, sway; (*fig.*) fluctuate.
woher [voːˈheːr], *adv.* whence, from what place, how.
wohin [voːˈhɪn], *adv.* whither, where.
wohingegen [voːhɪnˈgeːgən], *conj.* (*obs.*) whereas.
Wohl [voːl], *n.* (—(e)s, *no pl.*) welfare, health; *auf dein* —, your health! cheers!
wohl [voːl], *adv.* well, fit; indeed, doubtless, certainly; *ja* —, to be sure.
wohlan! [voːlˈan], *excl.* well! now then!
wohlauf! [voːlˈauf], *excl.* cheer up! — *sein*, be in good health.
wohlbedacht [ˈvoːlbədaxt], *adj.* well considered.
Wohlbefinden [ˈvoːlbəfɪndən], *n.* (—s, *no pl.*) good health.
Wohlbehagen [ˈvoːlbəhaːgən], *n.* (—s, *no pl.*) comfort, ease, wellbeing.
wohlbehalten [ˈvoːlbəhaltən], *adj.* safe.
wohlbekannt [ˈvoːlbəkant], *adj.* well known.

wohlbeleibt [ˈvoːlbəlaɪpt], *adj.* corpulent, stout.
wohlbestallt [ˈvoːlbəʃtalt], *adj.* duly installed.
Wohlergehen [ˈvoːlɛrgeːən], *n.* (—s, *no pl.*) welfare, wellbeing.
wohlerhalten [ˈvoːlɛrhaltən], *adj.* well preserved.
wohlerzogen [ˈvoːlɛrtsoːgən], *adj.* well bred, well brought up.
Wohlfahrt [ˈvoːlfaːrt], *f.* (—, *no pl.*) welfare, prosperity.
wohlfeil [ˈvoːlfaɪl], *adj.* cheap, inexpensive.
Wohlgefallen [ˈvoːlgəfalən], *n.* (—s, *no pl.*) pleasure, delight, approval.
wohlgefällig [ˈvoːlgəfɛlɪç], *adj.* pleasant, agreeable.
Wohlgefühl [ˈvoːlgəfyːl], *n.* (—s, *no pl.*) comfort, ease.
wohlgelitten [ˈvoːlgəlɪtən], *adj.* popular.
wohlgemeint [ˈvoːlgəmaɪnt], *adj.* well meant.
wohlgemerkt [ˈvoːlgəmɛrkt], *adv.* mind you! mark my words!
wohlgemut [ˈvoːlgəmuːt], *adj.* cheerful, merry.
wohlgeneigt [ˈvoːlgənaɪkt], *adj.* well disposed (towards).
wohlgepflegt [ˈvoːlgəpfleːkt], *adj.* well kept.
wohlgeraten [ˈvoːlgəraːtən], *adj.* successful; well turned out; good, well behaved.
Wohlgeruch [ˈvoːlgəruːx], *m.* (—es, *pl.* ⸚e) sweet scent, perfume, fragrance.
Wohlgeschmack [ˈvoːlgəʃmak], *m.* (—s, *no pl.*) pleasant flavour, agreeable taste.
wohlgesinnt [ˈvoːlgəzɪnt], *adj.* well disposed.
wohlgestaltet [ˈvoːlgəʃtaltət], *adj.* well shaped.
wohlgezielt [ˈvoːlgətsiːlt], *adj.* well aimed.
wohlhabend [ˈvoːlhaːbənt], *adj.* well-to-do, wealthy, well off.
wohlig [ˈvoːlɪç], *adj.* comfortable, cosy.
Wohlklang [ˈvoːlklaŋ], *m.* (—s, *pl.* ⸚e) harmony, euphony.
wohlklingend [ˈvoːlklɪŋənt], *adj.* harmonious, euphonious, sweet-sounding.
Wohlleben [ˈvoːlleːbən], *n.* (—s, *no pl.*) luxurious living.
wohllöblich [ˈvoːlløːplɪç], *adj.* worshipful.
wohlmeinend [ˈvoːlmaɪnənt], *adj.* well-meaning.
wohlschmeckend [ˈvoːlʃmɛkənt], *adj.* savoury, tasty, delicious.
Wohlsein [ˈvoːlzaɪn], *n.* (—s, *no pl.*) good health, wellbeing.
Wohlstand [ˈvoːlʃtant], *m.* (—s, *no pl.*) prosperity.
Wohltat [ˈvoːltaːt], *f.* (—, *pl.* —en) benefit; kindness; (*pl.*) benefaction, charity; (*fig.*) treat.

Wohltäter ['vo:ltɛ:tər], *m.* (—s, *pl.* —) benefactor.

Wohltätigkeit ['vo:ltɛ:tɪçkaɪt], *f.* (—, *no pl.*) charity.

wohltuend ['vo:ltu:ənt], *adj.* soothing.

wohltun ['vo:ltu:n], *v.n. irr.* do good; be comforting.

wohlweislich ['vo:lvaɪslɪç], *adj.* wisely.

Wohlwollen ['vo:lvɔlən], *n.* (—s, *no pl.*) benevolence; favour, patronage.

wohnen ['vo:nən], *v.n.* reside, dwell, live.

wohnhaft ['vo:nhaft], *adj.* domiciled, resident; — *sein*, reside, be domiciled.

Wohnhaus ['vo:nhaus], *n.* (—es, *pl.* ⁓er) dwelling-house.

wohnlich ['vo:nlɪç], *adj.* comfortable; cosy.

Wohnort ['vo:nɔrt], *m.* (—s, *pl.* —e) place of residence.

Wohnsitz ['vo:nzɪts], *m.* (—es, *pl.* —e) domicile, abode, residence.

Wohnstätte ['vo:nʃtɛtə], *f.* (—, *pl.* —n) abode, home.

Wohnung ['vo:nuŋ], *f.* (—, *pl.* —en) residence, dwelling; house, flat, lodging; apartment.

Wohnungsmangel ['vo:nuŋsmaŋəl], *m.* (—s, *no pl.*) housing shortage.

Wohnwagen ['vo:nva:gən], *m.* (—s, *pl.* —) caravan.

Wohnzimmer ['vo:ntsɪmər], *n.* (—s, *pl.* —) sitting-room, living-room.

wölben ['vœlbən], *v.r. sich* —, vault, arch.

Wölbung ['vœlbuŋ], *f.* (—, *pl.* —en) vault, vaulting.

Wolf [vɔlf], *m.* (—(e)s, *pl.* ⁓e) wolf.

Wolke ['vɔlkə], *f.* (—, *pl.* —n) cloud.

Wolkenbruch ['vɔlkənbrux], *m.* (—s, *pl.* ⁓e) cloudburst, violent downpour.

Wolkenkratzer ['vɔlkənkratsər], *m.* (—s, *pl.* —) sky-scraper.

Wolkenkuckucksheim [vɔlkən'kukukshaɪm], *n.* (—s, *no pl.*) Utopia, cloud cuckoo land.

Wolldecke ['vɔldɛkə], *f.* (—, *pl.* —n) blanket.

Wolle ['vɔlə], *f.* (—, *pl.* —n) wool.

wollen (1) ['vɔlən], *v.a., v.n. irr.* wish, want to, be willing, intend; *was — Sie*, what do you want?

wollen (2) ['vɔlən], *ad .* woollen, made of wool.

Wollgarn ['vɔlgarn], *n.* (—s, *pl.* —e) woollen yarn.

Wollhandel ['vɔlhandəl], *m.* (—s, *no pl.*) wool-trade.

wollig ['vɔlɪç], *adj.* woolly.

Wollsamt ['vɔlzamt], *m.* (—s, *no pl.*) plush, velveteen.

Wollust ['vɔlust], *f.* (—, *pl.* ⁓e) voluptuousness; lust.

wollüstig ['vɔlystɪç], *adj.* voluptuous.

Wollwaren ['vɔlva:rən], *f. pl.* woollen goods.

Wollzupfen ['vɔltsupfən], *n.* (—s, *no pl.*) wool-picking.

womit [vo:'mɪt], *adv.* wherewith, with which; (*interr.*) with what?

womöglich [vo:'mø:klɪç], *adv.* if possible, perhaps.

wonach [vo:'na:x], *adv.* whereafter, after which; according to which.

Wonne ['vɔnə], *f.* (—, *pl.* —n) delight, bliss, rapture.

wonnetrunken ['vɔnətruŋkən], *adj.* enraptured.

wonnig ['vɔnɪç], *adj.* delightful.

woran [vo:'ran], *adv.* whereat, whereby; (*interr.*) by what? at what?

worauf [vo:'rauf], *adv.* upon which, at which; whereupon; (*interr.*) on what?

woraufhin [vo:rauf'hɪn], *conj.* whereupon.

woraus [vo:'raus], *adv.* (*rel. & interr.*) whence, from which; by *or* out of which.

worein [vo:'raɪn], *adv.* (*rel. & interr.*) into which; into what.

worin [vo:'rɪn], *adv.* (*rel.*) wherein; (*interr.*) in what?

Wort [vɔrt], *n.* (—(e)s, *pl.* ⁓er, —e) word, term; expression, saying.

wortarm ['vɔrtarm], *adj.* poor in words, deficient in vocabulary.

Wortarmut ['vɔrtarmu:t], *f.* (—, *no pl.*) paucity of words, poverty of language.

Wortbildung ['vɔrtbɪlduŋ], *f.* (—, *pl.* —en) word-formation.

wortbrüchig ['vɔrtbryçɪç], *adj.* faithless, disloyal.

Wörterbuch ['vœrtərbu:x], *n.* (—(e)s, *pl.* ⁓er) dictionary.

Worterklärung ['vɔrtɛrklɛ:ruŋ], *f.* (—, *pl.* —en) definition.

Wortforschung ['vɔrtfɔrʃuŋ], *f.* (—, *no pl.*) etymology.

Wortfügung ['vɔrtfy:guŋ], *f.* (—, *no pl.*) syntax.

Wortführer ['vɔrtfy:rər], *m.* (—s, *pl.* —) spokesman.

Wortgefecht ['vɔrtgəfɛçt], *n.* (—es, *pl.* —e) verbal battle.

wortgetreu ['vɔrtgətrɔy], *adj.* literal, verbatim.

wortkarg ['vɔrtkark], *adj.* laconic, sparing of words, taciturn.

Wortlaut ['vɔrtlaut], *m.* (—s, *pl.* —e) wording, text.

wörtlich ['vœrtlɪç], *adj.* verbal; literal; word for word.

wortlos ['vɔrtlo:s], *adj.* speechless. — *adv.* without uttering a word.

wortreich ['vɔrtraɪç], *adj.* (*language*) rich in words; (*fig.*) verbose, wordy.

Wortreichtum ['vɔrtraɪçtum], *m.* (—s, *no pl.*) (*language*) wealth of words; (*fig.*) verbosity, wordiness.

Wortschwall ['vɔrtʃval], *m.* (—s, *no pl.*) bombast; torrent of words.

Wortspiel ['vɔrtʃpi:l], *n.* (—s, *pl.* —e) pun.

Wortversetzung ['vɔrtfɛrzɛtsuŋ], *f.* (—, *pl.* —en) inversion (of words).

Wortwechsel ['vɔrtvɛksəl], *m.* (—s, *pl.* —) dispute, altercation.

worüber [vo:'ry:bər], *adv.* (*rel.*) about which, whereof; (*interr.*) about what?

worunter

worunter [vo'rʊntər], *adv.* (*rel.*) whereunder; (*interr.*) under what?

woselbst [vo:'zɛlpst], *adv.* where.

wovon [vo:'fɔn], *adv.* (*rel.*) whereof; (*interr.*) of what?

wovor [vo:'fo:r], *adv.* (*rel.*) before which; (*interr.*) before what?

wozu [vo:'tsu:], *adv.* (*rel.*) whereto; (*interr.*) why? for what purpose? to what end?

Wrack [vrak], *n.* (—s, *pl.* —s) wreck.

wringen ['vrɪŋən], *v.a.* wring.

Wringmaschine ['vrɪŋmaʃi:nə], *f.* (—, *pl.* —n) wringer, mangle.

Wucher ['vu:xər], *m.* (—s, *no pl.*) usury.

wucherisch ['vu:xəriʃ], *adj.* usurious, extortionate.

wuchern ['vu:xərn], *v.n.* practise usury; (*plants*) luxuriate, grow profusely.

Wucherungen ['vu:xərʊŋən], *f. pl.* (*Med.*) excrescence, growth.

Wuchs [vu:ks], *m.* (—es, *no pl.*) growth; shape, build.

Wucht [vuxt], *f.* (—, *no pl.*) power, force; weight; impetus.

wuchten ['vuxtən], *v.n.* (*Poet.*) press heavily. — *v.a.* prise up.

wuchtig ['vuxtɪç], *adj.* weighty, forceful.

Wühlarbeit ['vy:larbaɪt], *f.* (—, *pl.* —en) subversive activity.

wühlen ['vy:lən], *v.a., v.n.* dig, burrow; (*fig.*) agitate.

Wühler ['vy:lər], *m.* (—s, *pl.* —) agitator, demagogue.

Wühlmaus ['vy:lmaus], *f.* (—, *pl.* ⁻e) (*Zool.*) vole.

Wulst [vulst], *m.* (—es, *pl.* ⁻e) roll, pad; swelling.

wülstig ['vylstɪç], *adj.* padded, stuffed; swollen.

wund [vunt], *adj.* sore, wounded.

Wundarzt ['vuntartst], *m.* (—es, *pl.* ⁻e) (*obs.*) surgeon.

Wundbalsam ['vuntbalzam], *m.* (—s, *pl.* —e) balm.

Wunde ['vundə], *f.* (—, *pl.* —n) wound, hurt.

Wunder ['vundər], *n.* (—s, *pl.* —) marvel, wonder, miracle.

wunderbar ['vundərba:r], *adj.* wonderful, marvellous.

Wunderding ['vundərdɪŋ], *n.* (—s, *pl.* —e) marvel.

Wunderdoktor ['vundərdɔktər], *m.* (—s, *pl.* —en) quack doctor.

Wunderglaube ['vundərglaubə], *m.* (—ns, *no pl.*) belief in miracles.

wunderhübsch [vundər'hypʃ], *adj.* exceedingly pretty.

Wunderkind ['vundərkɪnt], *n.* (—s, *pl.* —er) infant prodigy.

Wunderlampe ['vundərlampə], *f.* (—, *pl.* —n) magic lantern.

wunderlich ['vundərlɪç], *adj.* strange, odd, queer.

wundern ['vundərn], *v.r. sich — über*, be surprised at, be astonished at.

wundersam ['vundərza:m], *adj.* wonderful, strange.

wunderschön ['vundərʃø:n], *adj.* lovely, gorgeous; exquisite.

Wundertat ['vundərta:t], *f.* (—, *pl.* —en) miraculous deed.

wundertätig ['vundərtɛ:tɪç], *adj.* miraculous.

Wundertier ['vundərti:r], *n.* (—s, *pl.* —e) monster; (*fig.*) prodigy.

Wunderwerk ['vundərvɛrk], *n.* (—s, *pl.* —e) miracle.

Wundmal ['vuntma:l], *n.* (—s, *pl.* —e) scar.

Wunsch [vunʃ], *m.* (—es, *pl.* ⁻e) wish, desire, aspiration.

Wünschelrute ['vynʃəlru:tə], *f.* (—, *pl.* —n) divining-rod.

wünschen ['vynʃən], *v.a.* wish, desire, long for.

wünschenswert ['vynʃənsvɛ:rt], *adj.* desirable.

Wunschform ['vunʃfɔrm], *f.* (—, *no pl.*) (*Gram.*) optative form.

wuppdich! ['vupdɪç], *excl.* here goes!

Würde ['vyrdə], *f.* (—, *pl.* —n) dignity, honour.

Würdenträger ['vyrdəntrɛ:gər], *m.* (—s, *pl.* —) dignitary.

würdevoll ['vyrdəfɔl], *adj.* dignified.

würdig ['vyrdɪç], *adj.* worthy (of), deserving, meritorious.

würdigen ['vyrdɪgən], *v.a.* honour; *ich weiss es zu —*, I appreciate it.

Würdigung ['vyrdɪguŋ], *f.* (—, *pl.* —en) appreciation.

Wurf [vurf], *m.* (—(e)s, *pl.* ⁻e) cast, throw.

Würfel ['vyrfəl], *m.* (—s, *pl.* —) die; (*Geom.*) cube; — *spielen*, play at dice.

würfelförmig ['vyrfəlfœrmɪç], *adj.* cubic, cubiform.

würfeln ['vyrfəln], *v.n.* play at dice.

Wurfgeschoß ['vurfgəʃo:s], *n.* (—sses, *pl.* —sse) missile, projectile.

Wurfmaschine ['vurfmaʃi:nə], *f.* (—, *pl.* —n) catapult.

Wurfscheibe ['vurfʃaɪbə], *f.* (—, *pl.* —n) discus, quoit.

Wurfspieß ['vurfʃpi:s], *m.* (—es, *pl.* —e) javelin.

würgen ['vyrgən], *v.a.* strangle, throttle. — *v.n.* choke.

Würgengel ['vyrgɛŋəl], *m.* (—s, *no pl.*) avenging angel.

Würger ['vyrgər], *m.* (—s, *pl.* —) strangler, murderer; (*Poet.*) slayer; (*Orn.*) shrike, butcher-bird.

Wurm [vurm], *m.* (—(e)s, *pl.* ⁻er) worm; (*apple*) maggot.

wurmen ['vurmən], *v.a.* vex.

wurmstichig ['vurmʃtɪçɪç], *adj.* worm-eaten.

Wurst [vurst], *f.* (—, *pl.* ⁻e) sausage.

wurstig ['vurstɪç], *adj.* (*sl.*) quite indifferent.

Wurstigkeit ['vurstɪçkaɪt], *f.* (—, *no pl.*) callousness, indifference.

Würze ['vyrtsə], *f.* (—, *pl.* —n) seasoning, spice, condiment.

Wurzel ['vurtsəl], *f.* (—, *pl.* —n) root.

wurzeln ['vurtsəln], *v.n.* be rooted.

würzen ['vyrtsən], *v.a.* season, spice.

würzig ['vyrtsɪç], *adj.* spicy, fragrant.

Wust [vust], *m.* (**—es**, *no pl.*) chaos, trash.
wüst [vy:st], *adj.* waste, desert; desolate; dissolute.
Wüste [ˈvy:stə], *f.* (**—**, *pl.* **—n**) desert, wilderness.
Wüstling [ˈvy:stlɪŋ], *m.* (**—s**, *pl.* **—e**) profligate, libertine.
Wut [vu:t], *f.* (**—**, *no pl.*) rage, fury, passion.
wüten [ˈvy:tən], *v.n.* rage, storm, fume.
wutentbrannt [ˈvu:təntbrant], *adj.* enraged, infuriated.
Wüterich [ˈvy:tərɪç], *m.* (**—s**, *pl.* **—e**) tyrant; ruthless fellow.
Wutgeschrei [ˈvu:tgəʃraɪ], *n.* (**—s**, *no pl.*) yell of rage.
wutschnaubend [ˈvu:tʃnaubənt], *adj.* foaming with rage.

X

X [ɪks], *n.* (**—s**, *pl.* **—s**) the letter X.
X-Beine [ˈɪksbaɪnə], *n. pl.* knock-knees.
x-beliebig [ˈɪksbəli:bɪç], *adj.* any, whatever (one likes).
Xenie [ˈkse:njə], *f.* (**—**, *pl.* **—n**) epigram.
Xereswein [ˈkse:rəsvaɪn], *m.* (**—s**, *pl.* **—e**) sherry.
x-mal [ˈɪksma:l], *adv.* (*coll.*) so many times, umpteen times.
X-Strahlen [ˈɪksʃtra:lən], *m. pl.* X-rays.
Xylographie [ksylograˈfi:], *f.* (**—**, *no pl.*) wood-engraving.
Xylophon [ksyloˈfo:n], *n.* (**—s**, *pl.* **—e**) (*Mus.*) xylophone.

Y

Y [ˈypsilɔn], *n.* (**—s**, *pl.* **—s**) the letter Y.
Yak [jak], *m.* (**—s**, *pl.* **—s**) (*Zool.*) yak.
Yamswurzel [ˈjamsvurtsəl], *f.* (**—**, *pl* **—n**) yam.
Ysop [yˈzo:p], *m.* (**—s**, *no pl.*) hyssop.

Z

Z [tsɛt], *n.* (**—s**, *pl.* **—s**) the letter Z.
Zabel [ˈtsa:bəl], *m.* (**—s**, *pl.* **—**) (*obs.*) chess-board.

Zacke [ˈtsakə], *f.* (**—**, *pl.* **—n**) tooth, spike; (*fork*) prong.
zackig [ˈtsakɪç], *adj.* pronged, toothed, indented; (*rock*) jagged; (*sl.*) smart.
zagen [ˈtsa:gən], *v.n.* quail, blench, be disheartened, be fainthearted.
zaghaft [ˈtsa:khaft], *adj.* faint-hearted.
Zaghaftigkeit [ˈtsa:khaftɪçkaɪt], *f.* (**—**, *no pl.*) faintheartedness, timidity.
zäh [tsɛ:], *adj.* tough.
Zähigkeit [ˈtsɛ:ɪçkaɪt], *f.* (**—**, *no pl.*) toughness.
Zahl [tsa:l], *f.* (**—**, *pl.* **—en**) number, figure.
zahlbar [ˈtsa:lba:r], *adj.* payable, due.
zählbar [ˈtsɛ:lba:r], *adj.* calculable.
zahlen [ˈtsa:lən], *v.a.* pay; *Ober!* **—**, waiter! the bill, please.
zählen [ˈtsɛ:lən], *v.a.*, *v.n.* count, number.
Zahlenfolge [ˈtsa:lənfɔlgə], *f.* (**—**, *no pl.*) numerical order.
Zahlenlehre [ˈtsa:lənle:rə], *f.* (**—**, *no pl.*) arithmetic.
Zahlenreihe [ˈtsa:lənraɪə], *f.* (**—**, *pl.* **—n**) numerical progression.
Zahlensinn [ˈtsa:lənzɪn], *m.* (**—s**, *no pl.*) head for figures.
Zahler [ˈtsa:lər], *m.* (**—s**, *pl.* **—**) payer.
Zähler [ˈtsɛ:lər], *m.* (**—s**, *pl.* **—**) counter, teller; meter; (*Maths.*) numerator.
Zahlkellner [ˈtsa:lkɛlnər], *m.* (**—s**, *pl.* **—**) head waiter.
Zahlmeister [ˈtsa:lmaɪstər], *m.* (**—s**, *pl.* **—**) paymaster, treasurer, bursar.
zahlreich [ˈtsa:lraɪç], *adj.* numerous.
Zahltag [ˈtsa:lta:k], *m.* (**—s**, *pl.* **—e**) pay-day.
Zahlung [ˈtsa:luŋ], *f.* (**—**, *pl.* **—en**) payment; *— leisten*, make payment; *die —en einstellen*, stop payment.
Zählung [ˈtsɛ:luŋ], *f.* (**—**, *pl.* **—en**) counting, computation; census.
Zahlungseinstellung [ˈtsa:luŋsaɪnʃtɛluŋ], *f.* (**—**, *pl.* **—en**) suspension of payment.
zahlungsfähig [ˈtsa:luŋsfɛ:ɪç], *adj.* solvent.
Zahlungsmittel [ˈtsa:luŋsmɪtəl], *n.* (**—s**, *pl.* **—**) means of payment; *gesetzliches —*, legal tender.
Zahlungstermin [ˈtsa:luŋstɛrmi:n], *m.* (**—s**, *pl.* **—e**) time of payment.
zahlungsunfähig [ˈtsa:luŋsunfɛ:ɪç], *adj.* insolvent.
Zahlwort [ˈtsa:lvɔrt], *n.* (**—s**, *pl.* **˙er**) (*Gram.*) numeral.
zahm [tsa:m], *adj.* tame; domestic(ated); *— machen*, tame.
zähmen [ˈtsɛ:mən], *v.a.* tame, domesticate.
Zähmer [ˈtsɛ:mər], *m.* (**—s**, *pl.* **—**) tamer.
Zahmheit [ˈtsa:mhaɪt], *f.* (**—**, *no pl.*) tameness.
Zähmung [ˈtsɛ:muŋ], *f.* (**—**, *no pl.*) taming, domestication.
Zahn [tsa:n], *m.* (**—(e)s**, *pl.* **˙e**) tooth; (*wheel*) cog.

Zahnarzt ['tsa:nartst], *m.* (—es, *pl.* ̈e)
dentist, dental surgeon.

Zahnbürste ['tsa:nbyrstə], *f.* (—, *pl.*
—n) tooth-brush.

Zähneklappern ['tsɛ:nəklapərn], *n.*
(—s, *no pl.*) chattering of teeth.

Zähneknirschen ['tsɛ:nəknirʃən], *n.*
(—s, *no pl.*) gnashing of teeth.

zahnen ['tsa:nən], *v.n.* teethe, cut o.'s
teeth.

zähnen ['tsɛ:nən], *v.a.* indent, notch.

Zahnfleisch ['tsa:nflaiʃ], *n.* (—es, *no
pl.*) gums.

Zahnfüllung ['tsa:nfyluŋ], *f.* (—, *pl.*
—en) filling, stopping (of tooth).

Zahnheilkunde ['tsa:nhailkundə], *f.*
(—, *no pl.*) dentistry, dental surgery.

Zahnlücke ['tsa:nlykə], *f.* (—, *pl.* —n)
gap in the teeth.

Zahnpaste ['tsa:npastə], *f.* (—, *no pl.*)
tooth-paste.

Zahnpulver ['tsa:npulvər], *n.* (—s, *no
pl.*) tooth-powder.

Zahnrad ['tsa:nra:t], *n.* (—s, *pl.* ̈er)
cog-wheel.

Zahnradbahn ['tsa:nra:tba:n], *f.* (—,
pl. —en) rack-railway.

Zahnschmerzen ['tsa:nʃmertsən], *m.
pl.* toothache.

Zahnstocher ['tsa:nʃtɔxər], *m.* (—s, *pl.*
—) tooth-pick.

Zähre ['tsɛ:rə], *f.* (—, *pl.* —n) (*Poet.*) tear.

Zander ['tsandər], *m.* (—s, *pl.* —)
(*fish*) pike.

Zange ['tsaŋə], *f.* (—, *pl.* —n) tongs;
pincers; tweezers; nippers; (*Med.*)
forceps.

Zank [tsaŋk], *m.* (—es, *pl.* ̈ereien)
quarrel, altercation, tiff.

Zankapfel ['tsaŋkapfəl], *m.* (—s, *pl.* ̈)
bone of contention.

zanken ['tsaŋkən], *v.r. sich* —, quarrel,
dispute.

zänkisch ['tsɛnkiʃ], *adj.* quarrelsome.

Zanksucht ['tsaŋkzuxt], *f.* (—, *no pl.*)
quarrelsomeness.

zanksüchtig ['tsaŋkzyçtiç], *adj.*
quarrelsome, cantankerous.

Zapfen ['tsapfən], *m.* (—s, *pl.* —)
pin, peg; (*cask*) bung, spigot; (*fir*)
cone.

zapfen ['tsapfən], *v.a.* tap, draw.

Zapfenstreich ['tsapfənʃtraiç], *m.* (—s,
no pl.) (*Mil.*) tattoo, retreat.

zapp(e)lig ['tsap(ə)liç], *adj.* fidgety.

zappeln ['tsapəln], *v.n.* kick, struggle,
wriggle.

Zar [tsa:r], *m.* (—en, *pl.* —en) Czar,
Tsar.

zart [tsart], *adj.* tender, sensitive,
delicate, gentle; — *besaitet*, (*iron.*)
sensitive, highly strung.

Zartgefühl ['tsartgəfy:l], *n.* (—s, *no
pl.*) delicacy, sensitivity.

Zartheit ['tsarthait], *f.* (—, *no pl.*)
tenderness, gentleness.

zärtlich ['tsɛ:rtliç], *adj.* loving,
amorous, tender.

Zärtlichkeit ['tsɛ:rtliçkait], *f.* (—, *pl.*
—en) tenderness; caresses.

Zartsinn ['tsartzin], *m.* (—s, *no pl.*)
delicacy.

Zauber ['tsaubər], *m.* (—s, *no pl.*) charm,
spell, enchantment; magic; fascination.

Zauberei [tsaubə'rai], *f.* (—, *pl.* —en)
magic, witchcraft, sorcery.

Zauberer ['tsaubərər], *m.* (—s, *pl.* —)
magician, sorcerer, wizard.

zauberisch ['tsaubəriʃ], *adj.* magical;
(*fig.*) enchanting.

Zauberkraft ['tsaubərkraft], *f.* (—, *no
pl.*) magic power, witchcraft.

Zaubermittel ['tsaubərmitəl], *n.* (—s,
pl. —) charm.

zaubern ['tsaubərn], *v.n.* practise
magic; conjure.

Zauberspruch ['tsaubərʃprux], *m.* (—s,
pl. ̈e) spell, charm.

Zauberstab ['tsaubərʃta:p], *m.* (—s,
pl. ̈e) magic wand.

Zauderer ['tsaudərər], *m.* (—s, *pl.* —)
loiterer, temporizer, procrastinator.

zaudern ['tsaudərn], *v.n.* delay; hesitate, procrastinate.

Zaum [tsaum], *m.* (—(e)s, *pl.* ̈e)
bridle; *im* — *halten*, check, restrain.

zäumen ['tsɔymən], *v.a.* bridle.

Zaun [tsaun], *m.* (—(e)s, *pl.* ̈e) hedge,
fence; *einen Streit vom* — *brechen*,
pick a quarrel.

Zaungast ['tsaungast], *m.* (—s, *pl.* ̈e)
onlooker, outsider; intruder.

Zaunkönig ['tsaunkø:niç], *m.* (—s,
pl. —e) (*Orn.*) wren.

Zaunpfahl ['tsaunpfa:l], *m.* (—s, *pl.*
̈e) pale, hedge-pole; *mit dem* —
winken, give s.o. a broad hint.

Zaunrebe ['tsaunre:bə], *f.* (—, *pl.* —n)
(*Bot.*) Virginia creeper.

zausen ['tsauzən], *v.a.* tousle; (*hair*)
disarrange, ruffle.

Zechbruder ['tsɛçbru:dər], *m.* (—s,
pl. ̈) tippler, toper.

Zeche ['tsɛçə], *f.* (—, *pl.* —n) bill (in a
restaurant); mine; *die* — *bezahlen*,
foot the bill, pay the piper.

Zeder ['tse:dər], *f.* (—, *pl.* —n) (*Bot.*)
cedar.

zedieren [tsɛ'di:rən], *v.a.* cede.

Zehe ['tse:ə], *f.* (—, *pl.* —n) toe.

Zehenspitze ['tse:ənʃpitsə], *f.* (—, *pl.*
—n) tip of the toe, tiptoe.

zehn [tse:n], *num. adj.* ten.

Zehneck ['tse:nɛk], *n.* (—s, *pl.* —e)
decagon.

Zehnte ['tse:ntə], *m.* (—n, *pl.* —n) tithe.

zehren ['tse:rən], *v.n. von etwas* —,
live on s.th., prey upon s.th.

Zehrfieber ['tse:rfi:bər], *n.* (—s, *no pl.*)
hectic fever.

Zehrgeld ['tse:rgɛlt], *n.* (—s, *pl.* —er)
subsistence, allowance.

Zehrvorrat ['tse:rfo:rra:t], *m.* (—s, *pl.*
̈e) provisions.

Zehrung ['tse:ruŋ], *f.* (—, *pl.* —en)
consumption; victuals; (*Eccl.*) *letzte*
—, viaticum.

Zeichen ['tsaiçən], *n.* (—s, *pl.* —) sign,
token, symptom, omen; indication;
badge; signal.

Zeichenbrett ['tsaɪçənbrɛt], *n.* (—s, *pl.* —er) drawing-board.
Zeichendeuter ['tsaɪçəndɔytər], *m.* (—s, *pl.* —) astrologer.
Zeichendeuterei [tsaɪçəndɔytə'raɪ], *f.* (—, *no pl.*) astrology.
Zeichenerklärung ['tsaɪçənɛrklɛːruŋ], *f.* (— *pl.*—en) legend, key.
Zeichensprache ['tsaɪçənʃpraːxə], *f.* (—, *no pl.*) sign-language.
Zeichentinte ['tsaɪçəntɪntə], *f.* (—, *no pl.*) marking ink.
zeichnen ['tsaɪçnən], *v.a.* draw; mark; (*money*) subscribe; (*letter*) sign.
Zeichner ['tsaɪçnər], *m.* (—s, *pl.* —) draughtsman, designer.
Zeichnung ['tsaɪçnuŋ], *f.* (—, *pl.* —en) drawing.
Zeigefinger ['tsaɪgəfɪŋər], *m.* (—s, *pl.* —) forefinger, index finger.
zeigen ['tsaɪgən], *v.a.* show, point to, prove.
Zeiger ['tsaɪgər], *m.* (—s, *pl.* —) indicator; hand (of watch, clock).
zeihen ['tsaɪən], *v.a. irr. einen einer Sache* —, tax s.o. with s.th.
Zeile ['tsaɪlə], *f.* (—, *pl.* —n) line; furrow; (*pl.*) letter.
Zeisig ['tsaɪzɪç], *m.* (—s, *pl.* —e) (*Orn.*) siskin.
Zeit [tsaɪt], *f.* (—, *pl.* —en) time; *zur* —, at present; *auf* —, on credit.
Zeitabschnitt ['tsaɪtapʃnɪt], *m.* (—s, *pl.* —e) period; epoch.
Zeitalter ['tsaɪtaltər], *n.* (—s, *pl.* —) age, era.
Zeitdauer ['tsaɪtdauər], *f.* (—, *no pl.*) space of time.
Zeitfrage ['tsaɪtfraːgə], *f.* (—, *pl.* —n) topical question; question of time.
Zeitgeist ['tsaɪtgaɪst], *m.* (—s, *no pl.*) spirit of the age.
zeitgemäß ['tsaɪtgəmɛːs], *adj.* timely, seasonable, opportune, modern.
Zeitgenosse ['tsaɪtgənɔsə], *m.* (—n, *pl.* —n) contemporary.
zeitig ['tsaɪtɪç], *adj.* early, timely.
zeitigen ['tsaɪtɪgən], *v.a.* engender, generate. — *v.n.* mature, ripen.
Zeitkarte ['tsaɪtkartə], *f.* (—, *pl.* —n) season ticket.
Zeitlauf ['tsaɪtlauf], *m.* (—s, *pl.* ⁻e) course of time, conjuncture.
zeitlebens ['tsaɪtleːbəns], *adv.* for life, (for) all his (*or* her) life.
zeitlich ['tsaɪtlɪç], *adj.* temporal, earthly; secular; temporary, transient.
zeitlos ['tsaɪtloːs], *adj.* lasting, permanent.
Zeitmangel ['tsaɪtmaŋəl], *m.* (—s, *no pl.*) lack of time.
Zeitmesser ['tsaɪtmɛsər], *m.* (—s, *pl.* —) chronometer, timepiece; metronome.
Zeitpunkt ['tsaɪtpuŋkt], *m.* (—s, *pl.* —e) moment, date; point of time.
zeitraubend ['tsaɪtraubənt], *adj.* time-consuming.
Zeitraum ['tsaɪtraum], *m.* (—s, *pl.* ⁻e) space of time, period.

Zeitschrift ['tsaɪtʃrɪft], *f.* (—, *pl.* —en) periodical, journal, magazine.
Zeitung ['tsaɪtuŋ], *f.* (—, *pl.* —en) newspaper.
Zeitungsente ['tsaɪtuŋsɛntə], *f.* (—, *pl.* —n) canard, newspaper hoax.
Zeitungskiosk ['tsaɪtuŋkiɔsk], *m.* (—s, *pl.* —e) newspaper-stall.
Zeitungsnachricht ['tsaɪtuŋsnaːxrɪçt], *f.* (—, *pl.* —en) newspaper report.
Zeitungswesen ['tsaɪtuŋsveːzən], *n.* (—s, *no pl.*) journalism.
Zeitverlust ['tsaɪtfɛrlust], *m.* (—s, *no pl.*) loss of time; *ohne* —, without delay.
Zeitvertreib ['tsaɪtfɛrtraɪp], *m.* (—s, *no pl.*) pastime, amusement; *zum* —, to pass the time.
zeitweilig ['tsaɪtvaɪlɪç], *adj.* temporary.
zeitweise ['tsaɪtvaɪzə], *adv.* from time to time.
Zeitwort ['tsaɪtvɔrt], *n.* (—s, *pl.* ⁻er) (*Gram.*) verb.
Zelle ['tsɛlə], *f.* (—, *pl.* —n) cell; booth.
Zelt [tsɛlt], *n.* (—(e)s, *pl.* —e) tent.
Zeltdecke ['tsɛltdɛkə], *f.* (—, *pl.* —n) awning, marquee.
Zement [tse'mɛnt], *m.* (—s, *no pl.*) cement.
Zenit [tse'niːt], *m.* (—s, *no pl.*) zenith.
zensieren [tsɛn'ziːrən], *v.a.* review, censure; (*Sch.*) mark.
Zensor ['tsɛnzɔr], *m.* (—s, *pl.* —en) censor.
Zensur [tsɛn'zuːr], *f.* (—, *pl.* —en) censure; (*Sch.*) report, mark; censorship.
Zentimeter ['tsɛntimeːtər], *m.* (—s, *pl.* —) centimetre.
Zentner ['tsɛntnər], *m.* (—s, *pl.* —) hundredweight.
zentral [tsɛn'traːl], *adj.* central.
Zentrale [tsɛn'traːlə], *f.* (—, *pl.* —n) control room; head office.
zentralisieren [tsɛntrali'ziːrən], *v.a.* centralise.
Zentrum ['tsɛntrum], *n.* (—s, *pl.* —tren) centre; (*Am.*) center.
Zephir ['tseːfiːr], *m.* (—s, *pl.* —e) zephyr.
Zepter ['tsɛptər], *m. & n.* (—s, *pl.* —) sceptre, mace.
zerbrechen [tsɛr'brɛçən], *v.a., v.n. irr.* (*aux.* sein) break to pieces; shatter; *sich den Kopf* —, rack o.'s brains.
zerbrechlich [tsɛr'brɛçlɪç], *adj.* brittle, fragile.
zerbröckeln [tsɛr'brœkəln], *v.a., v.n.* (*aux.* sein) crumble.
zerdrücken [tsɛr'drykən], *v.a.* crush, bruise.
Zeremonie [tseremo'niː], *f.* (—, *pl.* —n) ceremony.
zeremoniell [tseremo'njɛl], *adj.* ceremonial, formal.
Zerfahrenheit [tsɛr'faːrənhaɪt], *f.* (—, *no pl.*) absent-mindedness.
Zerfall [tsɛr'fal], *m.* (—s, *no pl.*) disintegration; decay.
zerfallen [tsɛr'falən], *v.n. irr.* (*aux.* sein) fall to pieces. — *adj.* in ruins.

zerfleischen

zerfleischen [tsɛr'flaɪʃən], *v.a.* lacerate, tear to pieces.

zerfließen [tsɛr'fli:sən], *v.n. irr. (aux.* sein) dissolve, melt.

zerfressen [tsɛr'frɛsən], *v.a. irr.* gnaw, corrode.

zergehen [tsɛr'ge:ən], *v.n. irr. (aux.* sein) dissolve, melt.

zergliedern [tsɛr'gli:dərn], *v.a.* dissect; (*fig.*) analyse.

zerhauen [tsɛr'hauən], *v.a.* hew in pieces, chop up.

zerkauen [tsɛr'kauən], *v.a.* chew.

zerkleinern [tsɛr'klaɪnərn], *v.a.* cut into small pieces; (*firewood*) chop.

zerklüftet [tsɛr'klyftət], *adj.* rugged.

zerknirscht [tsɛr'knɪrʃt], *adj.* contrite.

Zerknirschung [tsɛr'knɪrʃuŋ], *f.* (—, *no pl.*) contrition.

zerknittern [tsɛr'knɪtərn], *v.a.* crumple.

zerknüllen [tsɛr'knylən], *v.a.* rumple.

zerlassen [tsɛr'lasən], *v.a. irr.* melt, liquefy.

zerlegen [tsɛr'le:gən], *v.a.* resolve; take to pieces; cut up, carve; (*fig.*) analyse.

zerlumpt [tsɛr'lumpt], *adj.* ragged, tattered.

zermahlen [tsɛr'ma:lən], *v.a.* grind to powder.

zermalmen [tsɛr'malmən], *v.a.* crush.

zermartern [tsɛr'martərn], *v.a.* torment; *sich das Hirn* —, rack o.'s brains.

zernagen [tsɛr'na:gən], *v.a.* gnaw (away).

zerquetschen [tsɛr'kvɛtʃən], *v.a.* squash, crush.

zerraufen [tsɛr'raufən], *v.a.* dishevel.

Zerrbild ['tsɛrbɪlt], *n.* (—s, *pl.* —er) caricature.

zerreiben [tsɛr'raɪbən], *v.a. irr.* grind to powder, pulverise.

zerreißen [tsɛr'raɪsən], *v.a. irr.* tear, rend, tear up; break; rupture. — *v.n.* (*aux.* sein) be torn; (*clothes*) wear out.

zerren ['tsɛrən], *v.a.* pull, tug, drag; strain.

zerrinnen [tsɛr'rɪnən], *v.n. irr. (aux.* sein) dissolve, melt; (*fig.*) vanish.

zerrütten [tsɛr'rytən], *v.a.* unsettle, disorder, unhinge; ruin, destroy.

zerschellen [tsɛr'ʃɛlən], *v.n.* (*aux.* sein) be dashed to pieces, be wrecked.

zerschlagen [tsɛr'ʃla:gən], *v.a. irr.* break, smash to pieces, batter.

zerschmettern [tsɛr'ʃmɛtərn], *v.a.* dash to pieces, break, crush; shatter, overwhelm.

zersetzen [tsɛr'zɛtsən], *v.a., v.r.* break up; disintegrate.

zerspalten [tsɛr'ʃpaltən], *v.a.* cleave, split, slit.

zersprengen [tsɛr'ʃprɛŋən], *v.a.* explode, burst; (*crowd*) disperse; (*Mil.*) rout.

zerspringen [tsɛr'ʃprɪŋən], *v.n. irr.* (*aux.* sein) crack; fly to pieces, split.

zerstampfen [tsɛr'ʃtampfən], *v.a.* crush, pound.

zerstäuben [tsɛr'ʃtɔybən], *v.a.* spray, atomize.

zerstörbar [tsɛr'ʃtø:rba:r], *adj.* destructible.

zerstören [tsɛr'ʃtø:rən], *v.a.* destroy, devastate.

Zerstörer [tsɛr'ʃtø:rər], *m.* (—s, *pl.* —) destroyer.

Zerstörung [tsɛr'ʃtø:ruŋ], *f.* (—, *pl.* —en) destruction.

Zerstörungswut [tsɛr'ʃtø:ruŋsvu:t], *f.* (—, *no pl.*) vandalism.

zerstoßen [tsɛr'ʃto:sən], *v.a. irr.* bruise, pound.

zerstreuen [tsɛr'ʃtrɔyən], *v.a.* scatter, disperse; divert.

zerstreut [tsɛr'ʃtrɔyt], *adj.* absentminded.

Zerstreuung [tsɛr'ʃtrɔyuŋ], *f.* (—, *pl.* —en) dispersion; amusement, diversion, distraction.

zerstückeln [tsɛr'ʃtykəln], *v.a.* dismember.

Zerstückelung [tsɛr'ʃtykəluŋ], *f.* (—, *no pl.*) dismemberment.

zerteilen [tsɛr'taɪlən], *v.a.* divide, separate; disperse, dissipate. — *v.r. sich* —, dissolve.

Zertifikat [tsɛrtifi'ka:t], *n.* (—s, *pl.* —e) certificate, attestation.

zertrennen [tsɛr'trɛnən], *v.a.* rip up, unstitch.

zertrümmern [tsɛr'trymərn], *v.a.* destroy, break up, demolish.

Zerwürfnis [tsɛr'vyrfnɪs], *n.* (—ses, *pl.* —se) discord, dissension.

zerzausen [tsɛr'tsauzən], *v.a.* dishevel, tousle.

zerzupfen [tsɛr'tsupfən], *v.a.* pick to pieces, pluck.

Zession [tsɛs'jo:n], *f.* (—, *pl.* —en) cession, assignment, transfer.

Zetergeschrei ['tse:tərgəʃraɪ], *n.* (—s, *no pl.*) outcry, hullabaloo.

zetern ['tse:tərn], *v.n.* yell; (*coll.*) kick up a row.

Zettel ['tsɛtəl], *m.* (—s, *pl.* —) slip of paper; label, chit.

Zettelkasten ['tsɛtəlkastən], *m.* (—s, *pl.* ⁻) card-index, filing cabinet.

Zeug [tsɔyk], *n.* (—(e)s, *no pl.*) stuff, material; implements, kit, utensils; (*coll.*) things.

Zeuge ['tsɔygə], *m.* (—n, *pl.* —n) witness; *zum* —*n aufrufen*, call to witness.

zeugen ['tsɔygən], *v.a.* beget, generate, engender. — *v.n.* give evidence.

Zeugenaussage ['tsɔygənausza:gə], *f.* (—, *pl.* —n) evidence, deposition.

Zeugenbeweis ['tsɔygənbəvaɪs], *m.* (—es, *pl.* —e) evidence, proof.

Zeugeneid ['tsɔygənaɪt], *m.* (—s, *pl.* —e) oath of a witness.

Zeughaus ['tsɔykhaus], *n.* (—es, *pl.* ⁻er) (*obs.*) arsenal.

Zeugin ['tsɔygɪn], *f.* (—, *pl.* —innen) female witness.

Zeugnis ['tsɔyknɪs], *n.* (—ses, *pl.* —se) (*Law.*) deposition; testimonial, certificate, reference; character; school report; — *ablegen,* give evidence, bear witness; *einem ein gutes — ausstellen,* give s.o. a good reference.

Zeugung ['tsɔyguŋ], *f.* (—, *pl.* —en) procreation, generation.

Zeugungskraft ['tsɔyguŋskraft], *f.* (—, *no pl.*) generative power.

Zeugungstrieb ['tsɔyguŋstri:p], *m.* (—s, *no pl.*) procreative instinct.

Zichorie [tsɪ'ço:rjə], *f.* (—, *pl.* —n) chicory.

Zicke ['tsɪkə], *f.* (—, *pl.* —n) *dial.* for **Ziege.**

Ziege ['tsi:gə], *f.* (—, *pl.* —n) goat.

Ziegel ['tsi:gəl], *m.* (—s, *pl.* —) (*roof*) tile; (*wall*) brick.

Ziegelbrenner ['tsi:gəlbrɛnər], *m.* (—s, *pl.* —) tile-maker, tiler; brickmaker.

Ziegelbrennerei [tsi:gəlbrɛnə'raɪ], *f.* (—, *pl.* —en) tile-kiln; brickyard.

Ziegeldach ['tsi:gəldax], *n.* (—s, *pl.* ⁝er) tiled roof.

Ziegeldecker ['tsi:gəldɛkər], *m.* (—s, *pl.* —) tiler.

Ziegelei [tsi:gə'laɪ], *f.* (—, *pl.* —en) brickyard, brickworks.

Ziegelerde ['tsi:gəlɛrdə], *f.* (—, *no pl.*) brick-clay.

Ziegenbart ['tsi:gənba:rt], *m.* (—s, *pl.* ⁝e) goat's beard; (*human*) goatee.

Ziegenleder ['tsi:gənle:dər], *n.* (—s, *no pl.*) kid (leather).

Ziegenpeter ['tsi:gənpe:tər], *m.* (—s, *no pl.*) (*Med.*) mumps.

ziehen ['tsi:ən], *v.a. irr.* draw, pull, drag; pull out; cultivate; breed; (*game*) move. — *v.n.* draw, be an attraction; (*aux.* sein) go, move. — *v.r. sich —,* extend.

Ziehkind ['tsi:kɪnt], *n.* (—s, *pl.* —er) foster-child.

Ziehmutter ['tsi:mutər], *f.* (—, *pl.* ⁝) foster-mother.

Ziehung ['tsi:uŋ], *f.* (—, *pl.* —en) draw (in a lottery).

Ziehvater ['tsi:fa:tər], *m.* (—s, *pl.* ⁝) foster-father.

Ziel [tsi:l], *n.* (—s, *pl.* —e) goal, aim, purpose, intention, end; butt, target; (*Mil.*) objective; (*sports*) winning-post.

zielbewußt ['tsi:lbəvust], *adj.* purposeful; systematic.

zielen ['tsi:lən], *v.n.* aim (at), take aim (at).

Ziellosigkeit ['tsi:llo:zɪçkaɪt], *f.* (—, *no pl.*) aimlessness.

Zielscheibe ['tsi:lʃaɪbə], *f.* (—, *pl.* —en) target, butt.

ziemen ['tsi:mən], *v.r. sich —,* become s.o., behove s.o., be proper for, befit.

Ziemer ['tsi:mər], *n. & m.* (—s, *pl.* —) whip.

ziemlich ['tsi:mlɪç], *adj.* moderate, tolerable, middling, fairly considerable, fair. — *adv.* rather, fairly.

Zier [tsi:r], *f.* (—, *pl.* —den) ornament.

Zieraffe ['tsi:rafə], *m.* (—n, *pl.* —n) fop, affected person.

Zierat ['tsi:ra:t], *m.* (—s, *no pl.*) ornament, finery.

Zierde ['tsi:rdə], *f.* (—, *pl.* —n) decoration, embellishment; (*fig.*) credit, pride.

Ziererei [tsi:rə'raɪ], *f.* (—, *pl.* —en) affectation.

Ziergarten ['tsi:rgartən], *m.* (—s, *pl.* ⁝) flower-garden, ornamental garden.

zierlich ['tsi:rlɪç], *adj.* dainty, graceful, pretty.

Zierpflanze ['tsi:rpflantsə], *f.* (—, *pl.* —n) ornamental plant.

Zierpuppe ['tsi:rpupə], *f.* (—, *pl.* —n) overdressed woman.

Ziffer ['tsɪfər], *f.* (—, *pl.* —n) figure, numeral.

Zifferblatt ['tsɪfərblat], *n.* (—s, *pl.* ⁝er) dial, face.

ziffernmäßig ['tsɪfərnmɛ:sɪç], *adj.* statistical.

Ziffernschrift ['tsɪfərnʃrɪft], *f.* (—, *pl.* —en) code.

Zigarette [tsiga'rɛtə], *f.* (—, *pl.* —n) cigarette.

Zigarettenetui [tsiga'rɛtənɛtvi:], *n.* (—s, *pl.* —s) cigarette-case.

Zigarettenspitze [tsiga'rɛtənʃpɪtsə], *f.* (—, *pl.* —n) cigarette-holder.

Zigarettenstummel [tsiga'rɛtənʃtuməl], *m.* (—s, *pl.* —) cigarette-end.

Zigarre [tsi'garə], *f.* (—, *pl.* —n) cigar.

Zigarrenkiste [tsi'garənkɪstə], *f.* (—, *pl.* —n) cigar-box.

Zigarrenstummel [tsi'garənʃtuməl], *m.* (—s, *pl.* —) cigar-end.

Zigeuner [tsi'gɔynər], *m.* (—s, *pl.* —) gipsy.

Zikade [tsi'ka:də], *f.* (—, *pl.* —n) (*Ent.*) grasshopper.

Zimmer ['tsɪmər], *n.* (—s, *pl.* —) room.

Zimmermädchen ['tsɪmərmɛ:tçən], *n.* (—s, *pl.* —) chambermaid.

Zimmermann ['tsɪmərman], *m.* (—s, *pl.* **Zimmerleute**) carpenter, joiner.

zimmern ['tsɪmərn], *v.a.* carpenter, construct, build.

Zimmernachweis ['tsɪmərna:xvaɪs], *m.* (—es, *pl.* —e) accommodation bureau.

Zimmerreihe ['tsɪmərraɪə], *f.* (—, *pl.* —n) suite of rooms.

Zimmervermieter ['tsɪmərfɛrmi:tər], *m.* (—s, *pl.* —) landlord.

zimperlich ['tsɪmpərlɪç], *adj.* simpering; prim; finicky, hypersensitive.

Zimt [tsɪmt], *m.* (—(e)s, *no pl.*) cinnamon.

Zink [tsɪŋk], *n.* (—s, *no pl.*) zinc.

Zinke ['tsɪŋkə], *f.* (—, *pl.* —n) prong, tine.

Zinn [tsɪn], *n.* (—s, *no pl.*) tin; pewter.

Zinnblech ['tsɪnblɛç], *n.* (—s, *no pl.*) tin-plate.

Zinne ['tsɪnə], *f.* (—, *pl.* —n) battlement, pinnacle.

zinnern

zinnern ['tsɪnern], *adj.* made of pewter, of tin.

Zinnober [tsɪn'oːbər], *m.* (—s, *no pl.*) cinnabar; (*coll.*) fuss.

Zinnsäure ['tsɪnzɔyrə], *f.* (—, *no pl.*) stannic acid.

Zins [tsɪns], *m.* (—es, *pl.* —en) duty, tax; rent; (*pl.*) interest.

zinsbar ['tsɪnsbaːr], *adj.* tributary; — *anlegen*, invest at interest; — *machen*, force to pay a tribute.

Zinsen ['tsɪnzən], *m. pl.* interest.

zinsentragend ['tsɪnzəntraːgənt], *adj.* interest-bearing.

Zinseszins ['tsɪnzəstsɪns], *m.* (—, *no pl.*) compound interest.

Zinsfuß ['tsɪnsfuːs], *m.* (—es, *pl.* ⁼e) rate of interest.

zinspflichtig ['tsɪnspflɪçtɪç], *adj.* subject to tax.

Zinsrechnung ['tsɪnsrɛçnuŋ], *f.* (—, *pl.* —en) interest account, calculation of interest.

Zinsschein ['tsɪnsʃaɪn], *m.* (—s, *pl.* —e) coupon, dividend warrant.

Zipfel ['tsɪpfəl], *m.* (—s, *pl.* —) tassel, edge, point, tip.

Zipperlein ['tsɪpərlaɪn], *n.* (—s, *no pl.*) (*coll.*) gout.

zirka ['tsɪrka], *adv.* circa, about, approximately.

Zirkel ['tsɪrkəl], *m.* (—s, *pl.* —) circle; (*Maths.*) pair of compasses; gathering.

zirkulieren [tsɪrku'liːrən], *v.n.* circulate; — *lassen*, put in circulation.

Zirkus ['tsɪrkus], *m.* (—, *pl.* —se) circus.

zirpen ['tsɪrpən], *v.n.* chirp.

zischeln ['tsɪʃəln], *v.n.* whisper.

zischen ['tsɪʃən], *v.n.* hiss; sizzle.

Zischlaut ['tsɪʃlaut], *m.* (—s, *pl.* —e) (*Phon.*) sibilant.

Zisterne [tsɪs'tɛrnə], *f.* (—, *pl.* —n) cistern.

Zisterzienser [tsɪstɛr'tsjɛnzər], *m.* (—s, *pl.* —s) Cistercian (monk).

Zitadelle [tsɪta'dɛlə], *f.* (—, *pl.* —n) citadel.

Zitat [tsi'taːt], *n.* (—(e)s, *pl.* —e) quotation, reference; *falsches* —, misquotation.

Zither ['tsɪtər], *f.* (—, *pl.* —n) zither.

zitieren [tsi'tiːrən], *v.a.* cite, quote; *falsch* —, misquote.

Zitronat [tsitro'naːt], *n.* (—s, *no pl.*) candied lemon peel.

Zitrone [tsi'troːnə], *f.* (—, *pl.* —n) lemon.

Zitronenlimonade [tsi'troːnənlimonaːdə], *f.* (—, *pl.* —n) lemonade, lemon drink.

Zitronensaft [tsi'troːnənzaft], *m.* (—s, *pl.* ⁼e) lemon-juice.

Zitronensäure [tsi'troːnənzɔyrə], *f.* (—, *no pl.*) citric acid.

Zitronenschale [tsi'troːnənʃaːlə], *f.* (—, *pl.* —n) lemon-peel.

zitterig ['tsɪtərɪç], *adj.* shaky, shivery.

zittern ['tsɪtərn], *v.n.* tremble, shiver, quake.

Zitterpappel ['tsɪtərpapəl], *f.* (—, *pl.* —n) (*Bot.*) aspen-tree.

Zivil [tsi'viːl], *n.* (—s, *no pl.*) civilians, *in* —, in plain clothes; (*coll.*) in civvies *or* mufti.

Zivilbeamte [tsi'viːlbəamtə], *m.* (—n, *pl.* —n) civil servant.

Zivildienst [tsi'viːldiːnst], *m.* (—es, *no pl.*) civil service.

Zivilehe [tsi'viːleːə], *f.* (—, *pl.* —n) civil marriage.

Zivilgesetzbuch [tsi'viːlgəzɛtsbuːx], *n.* (—s, *pl.* ⁼er) code of civil law.

Zivilingenieur [tsi'viːlɪnʒenjøːr], *m.* (—s, *pl.* —e) civil engineer.

Zivilisation [tsiviliza'tsjoːn], *f.* (—, *pl.* —en) civilisation.

zivilisatorisch [tsiviliza'toːrɪʃ], *adj.* civilising.

zivilisieren [tsivili'ziːrən], *v.a.* civilise.

Zivilist [tsivi'lɪst], *m.* (—en, *pl.* —en) civilian.

Zivilkleidung [tsi'viːlklaɪduŋ], *f.* (—, *no pl.*) civilian dress, plain clothes.

Zobel ['tsoːbəl], *m.* (—s, *pl.* —) sable.

Zobelpelz ['tsoːbəlpɛlts], *m.* (—es, *pl.* —e) sable fur; sable-coat.

Zofe ['tsoːfə], *f.* (—, *pl.* —n) lady's maid.

zögern ['tsøːgərn], *v.n.* hesitate, tarry, delay.

Zögerung ['tsøːgəruŋ], *f.* (—, *pl.* —en) hesitation, delay.

Zögling ['tsøːklɪŋ], *m.* (—s, *pl.* —e) pupil, charge.

Zölibat [tsøːli'baːt], *m. & n.* (—s, *no pl.*) celibacy.

Zoll (1) [tsɔl], *m.* (—s, *no pl.*) inch.

Zoll (2) [tsɔl], *m.* (—s, *pl.* ⁼e) customs duty; (*bridge*) toll.

Zollabfertigung ['tsɔlapfɛrtɪguŋ], *f.* (—, *no pl.*) customs clearance.

Zollamt ['tsɔlamt], *n.* (—s, *pl.* ⁼er) custom house.

Zollaufschlag ['tsɔlaufʃlaːk], *m.* (—s, *pl.* ⁼e) additional duty.

Zollbeamte ['tsɔlbəamtə], *m.* (—n, *pl.* —n) customs officer.

zollbreit ['tsɔlbraɪt], *adj.* one inch wide.

zollen ['tsɔlən], *v.a. Ehrfurcht* —, pay o.'s respects; *Beifall* —, applaud; *Dank* —, show gratitude.

zollfrei ['tsɔlfraɪ], *adj.* duty-free, exempt from duty.

Zöllner ['tsœlnər], *m.* (—s, *pl.* —) tax-gatherer.

zollpflichtig ['tsɔlpflɪçtɪç], *adj.* liable to duty, dutiable.

Zollsatz ['tsɔlzats], *m.* (—es, *pl.* ⁼e) customs tariff.

Zollverein ['tsɔlfəraɪn], *m.* (—s, *no pl.*) customs union.

Zollverschluß ['tsɔlfɛrʃlus], *m.* (—sses, *pl.* ⁼sse) bond.

Zone ['tsoːnə], *f.* (—, *pl.* —n) zone.

Zoologe [tsoːo'loːgə], *m.* (—n, *pl.* —n) zoologist.

Zoologie [tsoːolo'giː], *f.* (—, *no pl.*) zoology.

Zuflucht

zoologisch [tso:o'lo:gɪʃ], *adj.* zoological; —er *Garten*, zoological gardens, zoo.

Zopf [tsɔpf], *m.* (—(e)s, *pl.* ˫e) plait, pigtail; (*coll.*) (old-fashioned) pedantry.

Zorn [tsɔrn], *m.* (—(e)s, *no pl.*) wrath, anger, indignation; *seinen* — *auslassen*, vent o.'s anger; *in* — *geraten*, get angry.

zornglühend ['tsɔrngly:ənt], *adj.* boiling with rage.

zornig ['tsɔrnɪç], *adj.* angry, wrathful, irate; — *werden*, get angry.

Zote ['tso:tə], *f.* (—, *pl.* —n) smutty story, ribaldry, bawdiness.

zotig ['tso:tɪç], *adj.* loose, ribald, smutty.

zottig ['tsɔtɪç], *adj.* shaggy.

zu [tsu:], *prep.* (*Dat.*) to, towards; in addition to; at, in, on; for; — *Anfang.* in the beginning; — *Fuß*, on foot; — *Hause*, at home; — *Wasser*, at sea, by sea; — *deinem Nutzen*, for your benefit. — *adv. & prefix*, to, towards; closed; too; — *sehr*, too; — *viel*, too much.

Zubehör ['tsu:bəhø:r], *n.* (—s, *no pl.*) accessory, appurtenance.

zubekommen ['tsu:bəkɔmən], *v.a. irr.* get in addition.

Zuber ['tsu:bər], *m.* (—s, *pl.* —) tub.

zubereiten ['tsu:bəraɪtən], *v.a.* prepare.

Zubereitung ['tsu:bəraɪtuŋ], *f.* (—, *no pl.*) preparation.

zubilligen ['tsu:bɪlɪgən], *v.a.* allow, grant.

zubleiben ['tsu:blaɪbən], *v.n. irr.* (*aux. sein*) remain shut.

zubringen ['tsu:brɪŋən], *v.a. irr. die Zeit* —, spend the time.

Zubringerdienst ['tsu:brɪŋərdi:nst], *m.* (—es, *pl.* —) shuttle-service, tender-service.

Zubuße ['tsu:bu:sə], *f.* (—, *pl.* —n) (additional) contribution.

Zucht [tsuxt], *f.* (—, *no pl.*) race, breed; discipline; breeding, rearing; education, discipline; (good) manners; *in* — *halten*, keep in hand.

züchten ['tsyçtən], *v.a.* cultivate; rear, breed; grow.

Züchter ['tsyçtər], *m.* (—s, *pl.* —) (*plants*) nurseryman; (*animals*) breeder.

Zuchthaus ['tsuxthaus], *n.* (—es, *pl.* ˫er) penitentiary, convict prison.

Zuchthäusler ['tsuxthɔyslər], *m.* (—s, *pl.* —) convict.

Zuchthengst ['tsuxthɛŋst], *m.* (—es, *pl.* —e) stallion.

züchtig ['tsyçtɪç], *adj.* modest, chaste.

züchtigen ['tsyçtɪgən], *v.a.* chastise, lash.

Züchtigkeit ['tsyçtɪçkaɪt], *f.* (—, *no pl.*) modesty, chastity.

Züchtigung ['tsyçtɪguŋ], *f.* (—, *pl.* —en) chastisement; *körperliche* —, corporal punishment.

Zuchtlosigkeit ['tsuxtlo:zɪçkaɪt], *f.* (—, *no pl.*) want of discipline.

Zuchtmeister ['tsuxtmaɪstər], *m.* (—s, *pl.* —) disciplinarian, taskmaster.

Zuchtochse ['tsuxtɔksə], *m.* (—n, *pl.* —n) bull.

Zuchtstute ['tsuxtʃtu:tə], *f.* (—, *pl.* —n) brood-mare.

Züchtung ['tsyçtuŋ], *f.* (—, *pl.* —en) (*plants*) cultivation; (*animals*) rearing, breeding.

Zuchtvieh ['tsuxtfi:], *n.* (—s, *no pl.*) breeding stock.

Zuchtwahl ['tsuxtva:l], *f.* (—, *no pl.*) (*breeding*) selection.

zucken ['tsukən], *v.n.* quiver, twitch; wince; start, jerk.

Zucken ['tsukən], *n.* (—s, *no pl.*) palpitation, convulsion, twitch, tic.

Zucker ['tsukər], *m.* (—s, *no pl.*) sugar.

Zuckerbäcker ['tsukərbɛkər], *m.* (—s, *pl.* —) confectioner.

Zuckerguß ['tsukərgus], *m.* (—es, *no pl.*) (sugar-)icing.

Zuckerkandis ['tsukərkandɪs], *m.* (—, *no pl.*) sugar-candy.

zuckerkrank ['tsukərkraŋk], *adj.* (*Med.*) diabetic.

Zuckerkrankheit ['tsukərkraŋkhaɪt], *f.* (—, *no pl.*) (*Med.*) diabetes.

zuckern ['tsukərn], *v.a.* sugar.

Zuckerpflanzung ['tsukərpflantsuŋ], *f.* (—, *pl.* —en) sugar-plantation.

Zuckerraffinerie ['tsukərrafinəri:], *f.* (—, *pl.* —n) sugar-refinery.

Zuckerrohr ['tsukərro:r], *n.* (—s, *no pl.*) sugar-cane.

Zuckerrübe ['tsukərry:bə], *f.* (—, *pl.* —n) sugar-beet.

Zuckerwerk ['tsukərvɛrk], *n.* (—s, *no pl.*) confectionery.

Zuckerzange ['tsukərtsaŋə], *f.* (—, *pl.* —n) sugar-tongs.

Zuckung ['tsukuŋ], *f.* (—, *pl.* —en) convulsion, spasm.

zudecken ['tsu:dɛkən], *v.a.* cover up.

zudem [tsu'de:m], *adv.* besides, moreover.

Zudrang ['tsu:draŋ], *m.* (—s, *no pl.*) crowd(ing); rush (on), run (on).

zudrehen ['tsu:dre:ən], *v.a.* turn off.

zudringlich ['tsu:drɪŋlɪç], *adj.* importunate; intruding.

zudrücken ['tsu:drykən], *v.a.* close (by pressing), shut.

zueignen ['tsu:aɪgnən], *v.a.* dedicate.

zuerkennen ['tsu:ɛrkɛnən], *v.a. irr.* award, adjudicate.

zuerst [tsu'e:rst], *adv.* at first, first, in the first instance.

Zufahrt ['tsu:fa:rt], *f.* (—, *no pl.*) approach, drive.

Zufall ['tsu:fal], *m.* (—s, *pl.* ˫e) chance, coincidence; *durch* —, by chance.

zufallen ['tsu:falən], *v.n. irr.* (*aux. sein*) close, fall shut; *einem* —, devolve upon s.o., fall to s.o.'s lot.

zufällig ['tsu:fɛlɪç], *adj.* accidental, casual, fortuitous. — *adv.* by chance.

Zuflucht ['tsu:fluxt], *f.* (—, *no pl.*) refuge, shelter, haven, recourse.

Zufluchtsort

Zufluchtsort ['tsu:fluxtsɔrt], *m.* (—(e)s, *pl.* —e) asylum, shelter, place of refuge.

Zufluß ['tsu:flus], *m.* (—sses, *pl.* ˙sse) supply; influx.

zuflüstern ['tsu:flystərn], *v.a. einem etwas —,* whisper s.th. to s.o.

zufolge [tsu'fɔlgə], *prep.* (*Genit.*, *Dat.*) in consequence of, owing to, due to, on account of.

zufrieden [tsu'fri:dən], *adj.* content, contented, satisfied; — *lassen,* leave alone.

zufriedenstellen [tsu'fri:dənʃtɛlən], *v.a.* satisfy.

zufügen ['tsu:fy:gən], *v.a.* add (to); inflict.

Zufuhr ['tsu:fu:r], *f.* (—, *pl.* —en) (*goods*) supplies.

Zug [tsu:k], *m.* (—(e)s, *pl.* ˙e) drawing, pull, tug; draught; march, procession; (*Railw.*) train; (*face*) feature; (*chess*) move; (*character*) trait; (*pen*) stroke; (*birds*) flight; migration; (*mountains*) range.

Zugabe ['tsu:ga:bə], *f.* (—, *pl.* —n) addition, make-weight, extra; (*concert*) encore; *als —,* into the bargain.

Zugang ['tsu:gaŋ], *m.* (—s, *pl.* ˙e) approach, entry, entrance, admittance, access.

zugänglich ['tsu:gɛŋlɪç], *adj.* accessible, available; (*person*) affable.

Zugbrücke ['tsu:kbrykə], *f.* (—, *pl.* —n) drawbridge.

zugeben ['tsu:ge:bən], *v.a. irr.* give in addition; concede, admit.

zugegen [tsu'ge:gən], *adv.* present.

zugehen ['tsu:ge:ən], *v.n. irr.* (*aux.* sein) (*door*) shut (of itself), close; happen; *auf einen —,* walk towards s.o.; *so geht es im Leben zu,* such is life; *das geht nicht mit rechten Dingen zu,* there is something uncanny about it.

zugehörig ['tsu:gəhø:rɪç], *adj.* belonging, appertaining.

zugeknöpft ['tsu:gəknœpft], *adj.* reserved, taciturn.

Zügel ['tsy:gəl], *m.* (—s, *pl.* —) rein, bridle.

zügeln ['tsy:gəln], *v.a.* bridle, curb, check.

zugesellen ['tsu:gəzɛlən], *v.r. sich —,* associate with, join.

Zugeständnis ['tsu:gəʃtɛntnɪs], *n.* (—sses, *pl.* —sse) admission; concession.

zugestehen ['tsu:gəʃte:ən], *v.a. irr.* admit; concede; *einem etwas —,* allow s.o. s.th.

zugetan ['tsu:gəta:n], *adj.* attached, devoted.

Zugführer ['tsu:kfy:rər], *m.* (—s, *pl.* —) (*Railw.*) guard; (*Mil.*) platoon commander.

zugießen ['tsu:gi:sən], *v.a. irr.* fill up, pour on.

zugig ['tsu:gɪç], *adj.* windy, draughty.

Zugkraft ['tsu:kkraft], *f.* (—, *no pl.*) tractive power, magnetic attraction;

(*fig.*) pull, attraction; publicity value.

zugleich [tsu'glaɪç], *adv.* at the same time; — *mit,* together with.

Zugluft ['tsu:kluft], *f.* (—, *no pl.*) draught (of air).

zugreifen ['tsu:graɪfən], *v.n. irr.* grab; lend a hand; (*at table*) help o.s.

Zugrolle ['tsu:krɔlə], *f.* (—, *pl.* —n) pulley.

zugrunde [tsu'grundə], *adv.* — *gehen,* perish, go to ruin, go to the dogs; — *legen,* base upon.

Zugstück ['tsu:kʃtyk], *n.* (—s, *pl.* —e) (*Theat.*) popular show; (*coll.*) success, hit.

zugucken ['tsu:gukən], *v.n.* look on, watch.

zugunsten [tsu'gunstən], *prep.* (*Genit.*) for the benefit of.

zugute [tsu'gu:tə], *adv.* — *halten,* make allowances.

Zugvogel ['tsu:kfo:gəl], *m.* (—s, *pl.* ˙) bird of passage.

zuhalten ['tsu:haltən], *v.a. irr.* keep closed.

Zuhälter ['tsu:hɛltər], *m.* (—s, *pl.* —) souteneur; pimp.

Zuhilfenahme [tsu'hɪlfəna:mə], *f.* (—, *no pl.*) *unter —,* with the help of, by means of.

zuhören ['tsu:hø:rən], *v.n.* listen to, attend to.

Zuhörerschaft ['tsu:hø:rərʃaft], *f.* (—, *pl.* —en) audience.

zujubeln ['tsu:ju:bəln], *v.n. einem —,* acclaim s.o., cheer s.o.

zukehren ['tsu:ke:rən], *v.a. einem den Rücken —,* turn o.'s back on s.o.

zuknöpfen ['tsu:knœpfən], *v.a.* button (up).

zukommen ['tsu:kɔmən], *v.n. irr.* (*aux.* sein) *auf einen —,* advance towards s.o.; *einem —,* be due to s.o.; become s.o.; reach s.o.

Zukost ['tsu:kɔst], *f.* (—, *no pl.*) (*food*) trimmings, extras.

Zukunft ['tsu:kunft], *f.* (—, *no pl.*) future; prospects.

zukünftig ['tsu:kynftɪç], *adj.* future, prospective.

Zukunftsmusik ['tsu:kunftsmuzi:k], *f.* (—, *no pl.*) daydreams, pipedreams.

zulächeln ['tsu:lɛçəln], *v.a. einem —,* smile at s.o.

Zulage ['tsu:la:gə], *f.* (—, *pl.* —n) addition; increase of salary, rise; (*Am.*) raise.

zulangen ['tsu:laŋən], *v.n.* be sufficient; (*at table*) help o.s.

zulänglich ['tsu:lɛŋlɪç], *adj.* sufficient, adequate.

zulassen ['tsu:lasən], *v.a. irr.* leave unopened; allow; admit; permit.

zulässig ['tsu:lɛsɪç], *adj.* admissible; *das ist nicht —,* that is not allowed.

Zulassung ['tsu:lasuŋ], *f.* (—, *pl.* —en) admission.

Zulauf ['tsu:lauf], *m.* (—s, *no pl.*) run (of customers); crowd, throng.

zulaufen ['tsu:laufən], *v.n. irr. (aux.* sein) *auf einen* —, run towards s.o.; *spitz* —, taper, come to a point.

zulegen ['tsu:le:gən], *v.a.* add; increase; *sich etwas* —, make o.s. a present of s.th.; get s.th.

zuletzt [tsu'lɛtst], *adv.* last, at last, lastly, finally, eventually, in the end.

zuliebe [tsu'li:bə], *adv. einem etwas* — *tun*, oblige s.o.; do s.th. for s.o.'s sake.

zum = **zu dem**.

zumachen ['tsu:maxən], *v.a.* shut, close.

zumal [tsu'ma:l], *adv.* especially, particularly. — *conj.* especially since.

zumeist [tsu'maɪst], *adv.* mostly, for the most part.

zumute [tsu'mu:tə], *adv. mir ist nicht gut* —, I don't feel well.

zumuten ['tsu:mu:tən], *v.a. einem etwas* —, expect *or* demand s.th. of s.o.

Zumutung ['tsu:mu:tuŋ], *f.* (—, pl. —en) unreasonable demand.

zunächst [tsu'nɛ:çst], *adv.* first, above all.

Zunahme ['tsu:na:mə], *f.* (—, pl. —n) increase.

Zuname ['tsu:na:mə], *m.* (—ns, pl. —n) surname, family name.

zünden ['tsyndən], *v.n.* catch fire, ignite.

Zunder ['tsundər], *m.* (—s, no pl.) tinder.

Zünder ['tsyndər], *m.* (—s, pl. —) lighter, detonator, fuse.

Zündholz ['tsynthɔlts], *n.* (—es, pl. ⁀er) match.

Zündkerze ['tsyntkɛrtsə], *f.* (—,pl.—n) (*Motor.*) sparking-plug.

Zündstoff ['tsyntʃtɔf], *m.* (—s, pl. —e) fuel.

Zündung ['tsynduŋ], *f.* (—, pl. —en) ignition; detonation.

zunehmen ['tsu:ne:mən], *v.n. irr.* increase, put on weight; (*moon*) wax.

zuneigen ['tsu:naɪgən], *v.r. sich* —, incline towards.

Zuneigung ['tsu:naɪguŋ], *f.* (—, pl. —en) affection, inclination.

Zunft [tsunft], *f.* (—, pl. ⁀e) company, guild, corporation; (*fig.*) brotherhood.

Zunftgenosse ['tsunftgənɔsə], *m.* (—n, pl. —n) member of a guild.

zünftig ['tsynftɪç], *adj.* professional; proper.

zunftmäßig ['tsunftmɛ:sɪç], *adj.* professional; competent.

Zunge ['tsuŋə], *f.* (—, pl. —n) tongue; (*buckle*) catch; (*fig.*) language; (*fish*) sole.

züngeln ['tsyŋəln], *v.n.* (*flame*) shoot out, lick.

Zungenband ['tsuŋənbant], *n.* (—s, pl. ⁀er) ligament of the tongue.

zungenfertig ['tsuŋənfɛrtɪç], *adj.* voluble, glib.

Zungenlaut ['tsuŋənlaut], *m.* (—s, pl. —e) (*Phon.*) lingual sound.

Zungenspitze ['tsuŋənʃpɪtsə], *f.* (—, pl. —n) tip of the tongue.

zunichte [tsu'nɪçtə], *adv.* — *machen*, ruin, undo, destroy; — *werden*, come to nothing.

zupfen ['tsupfən], *v.a.* pick, pluck.

zurechnungsfähig ['tsu:rɛçnuŋsfɛ:ɪç], *adj.* accountable, of sane mind, compos mentis.

zurecht [tsu'rɛçt], *adv.* aright, right(ly), in order.

zurechtfinden [tsu'rɛçtfɪndən], *v.r. irr. sich* —, find o.'s way about.

zurechtkommen [tsu'rɛçtkɔmən], *v.n. irr. (aux.* sein) arrive in (good) time; *mit einem gut* —, get on well with s.o.

zurechtlegen [tsu'rɛçtle:gən], *v.a.* put in order, get ready.

zurechtmachen [tsu'rɛçtmaxən], *v.a.* get s.th. ready, prepare s.th. — *v.r. sich*—, prepare o.s.; (*women*) make up; (*coll.*) put on o.'s face.

zurechtweisen [tsu'rɛçtvaɪzən], *v.a. irr.* reprove (s.o.), set (s.o.) right; direct.

Zurechtweisung [tsu'rɛçtvaɪzuŋ], *f.* (—, pl. —en) reprimand.

Zureden ['tsu:re:dən], *n.* (—s, no pl.) encouragement; entreaties.

zureden ['tsu:re:dən], *v.n.* encourage (s.o.), persuade (s.o.)

zureichen ['tsu:raɪçən], *v.a.* reach, hand. — *v.n.* be sufficient, be enough, suffice.

zurichten ['tsu:rɪçtən], *v.a. etwas* (*einen*) *übel* —, maltreat s.th. (s.o.).

zürnen ['tsyrnən], *v.n.* be angry (with).

zurück [tsu'ryk], *adv.* back; behind; backwards; — *excl.* stand back!

zurückbegeben [tsu'rykbəge:bən], *v.r. irr. sich* —, go back, return.

zurückbehalten [tsu'rykbəhaltən], *v.a. irr.* retain, keep back.

zurückbekommen [tsu'rykbəkɔmən], *v.a. irr.* get back, recover (s.th.).

zurückberufen [tsu'rykbəru:fən], *v.a. irr.* recall.

zurückfordern [tsu'rykfɔrdərn], *v.a.* demand back, demand the return of.

zurückführen [tsu'rykfy:rən], *v.a.* lead back; *auf etwas* —, attribute to; trace back to.

zurückgeblieben [tsu'rykgəbli:bən], *adj.* retarded, mentally deficient, backward.

zurückgezogen [tsu'rykgətso:gən], *adj.* secluded, retired.

zurückhalten [tsu'rykhaltən], *v.a. irr.* keep back, retain.

zurückhaltend [tsu'rykhaltənt], *adj.* reserved.

zurückkehren [tsu'rykke:rən], *v.n. (aux.* sein) return.

zurückkommen [tsu'rykkɔmən], *v.n. irr. (aux.* sein) come back.

zurücklassen [tsu'ryklasən], *v.a. irr.* leave behind, abandon.

zurücklegen [tsu′rykle:gən], v.a. lay aside, put by; *eine Strecke* —, cover a distance. — v.r. *sich* —, lean back; *zurückgelegter Gewinn*, undistributed profits.

zurückmüssen [tsu′rykmysən], v.n. irr. be obliged to return.

zurücknehmen [tsu′rykne:mən], v.a. irr. take back.

zurückschrecken [tsu′rykʃrɛkən], v.a. frighten away. — v.n. irr. (aux. sein) recoil (from).

zurücksehnen [tsu′rykze:nən], v.r. *sich* —, long to return, wish o.s. back.

zurücksetzen [tsu′rykzɛtsən], v.a. put back; slight; discriminate against; neglect.

Zurücksetzung [tsu′rykzɛtsuŋ], f. (—, pl. **—en**) slight, rebuff.

zurückstrahlen [tsu′rykʃtra:lən], v.a. reflect.

zurücktreten [tsu′ryktre:tən], v.n. irr. (aux. sein) stand back, withdraw; resign.

zurückverlangen [tsu′rykfɛrlaŋən], v.a. demand back, request the return of.

zurückversetzen [tsu′rykfɛrzɛtsən], v.a. (Sch.) put in a lower form. — v.r. *sich* —, turn o.'s thoughts back (to), hark back.

zurückweichen [tsu′rykvaɪçən], v.n. irr. (aux. sein) withdraw, retreat.

zurückweisen [tsu′rykvaɪzən], v.a. irr. refuse, reject, repulse.

zurückwollen [tsu′rykvɔlən], v.n. wish to return.

zurückziehen [tsu′ryktsi:ən], v.a. irr. (fig.) draw back; (fig.) withdraw, retract, countermand. — v.r. *sich* —, retire, withdraw.

Zuruf [′tsu:ru:f], m. (—s, pl. —e) call, acclaim, acclamation.

Zusage [′tsu:za:gə], f. (—, pl. —n) promise; acceptance.

zusagen [′tsu:za:gən], v.a. promise; *es sagt mir zu*, I like it. — v.n. accept.

zusagend [′tsu:za:gənt], adj. affirmative; agreeable.

zusammen [tsu′zamən], adv. together, jointly.

zusammenbeißen [tsu′zamənbaɪsən], v.a. irr. *die Zähne* —, set o.'s teeth.

zusammenbetteln [tsu′zamənbɛtəln], v.a. *sich etwas* —, collect (by begging).

zusammenbrechen [tsu′zamənbrɛçən], v.n. irr. (aux. sein) break down, collapse.

Zusammenbruch [tsu′zamənbrux], m. (—s, pl. ˝e) breakdown, collapse, débâcle.

zusammendrängen [tsu′zaməndrɛŋən], v.a. press together; (fig.) abridge, condense.

zusammendrücken [tsu′zaməndrykən], v.a. compress.

zusammenfahren [tsu′zamənfa:rən], v.n. irr. (aux. sein) collide; give a start.

zusammenfallen [tsu′zamənfalən], v.n. irr. (aux. sein) collapse.

zusammenfassen [tsu′zamənfasən], v.a. sum up, summarize.

Zusammenfassung [tsu′zamənfasuŋ], f. (—, no pl.) summing-up, summary.

zusammenfinden [tsu′zamənfɪndən], v.r. irr. *sich* —, discover a mutual affinity, come together.

Zusammenfluß [tsu′zamənflus], m. (—sses, pl. ˝sse) confluence.

zusammengeben [tsu′zamənge:bən], v.a. irr. join in marriage.

Zusammengehörigkeit [tsu′zaməngəhø:rɪçkaɪt], f. (—, no pl.) solidarity; (Am.) togetherness.

zusammengesetzt [tsu′zaməngəzɛtst], adj. composed (of), consisting (of); complicated; (Maths.) composite.

zusammengewürfelt [tsu′zaməngəvyrfəlt], adj. motley, mixed.

Zusammenhalt [tsu′zamənhalt], m. (—s, no pl.) holding together; unity.

Zusammenhang [tsu′zamənhaŋ], m. (—s, pl. ˝e) coherence; connection, context.

zusammenhängen [tsu′zamənhɛŋən], v.n. irr. hang together, cohere; (fig.) be connected (with).

Zusammenklang [tsu′zamənklaŋ], m. (—s, pl. ˝e) unison, harmony.

Zusammenkunft [tsu′zamənkunft], f. (—, pl. ˝e) meeting, convention, conference; reunion.

zusammenlaufen [tsu′zamənlaufən], v.n. irr. (aux. sein) crowd together, converge; flock together; (milk) curdle; (material) shrink.

zusammenlegen [tsu′zamənle:gən], v.a. put together; (money) collect; (letter) fold up.

zusammennehmen [tsu′zamənne:mən], v.a. irr. gather up. — v.r. *sich* —, get a firm grip on o.s., pull o.s. together.

zusammenpassen [tsu′zamənpasən], v.n. fit together, match; agree; be compatible.

zusammenpferchen [tsu′zamənpfɛrçən], v.a. pen up, crowd together in a small space.

zusammenpressen [tsu′zamənprɛsən], v.a. squeeze together.

zusammenraffen [tsu′zamənrafən], v.a. gather up hurriedly, collect. — v.r. *sich* —, pluck up courage; pull o.s. together.

zusammenrechnen [tsu′zamənrɛçnən], v.a. add up.

zusammenreimen [tsu′zamənraɪmən], v.a. *sich etwas* —, figure s.th. out.

zusammenrücken [tsu′zamənrykən], v.a. move together, draw closer. — v.n. move closer together, move up.

zusammenschießen [tsu′zamənʃi:sən], v.a. irr. shoot to pieces, shoot down; *Geld* —, club together, raise a subscription.

zusammenschlagen [tsu′zamənʃla:gən], v.a. irr. beat up; strike together; clap, fold.

zusammenschließen [tsu'zamənʃli:-sən], *v.r. irr. sich* —, join, unite, ally o.s. (with).

zusammenschweißen [tsu'zamənʃvaɪsən], *v.a.* weld together.

Zusammensein [tsu'zamənzaɪn], *n.* (—s, *no pl.*) meeting, social gathering.

Zusammensetzung [tsu'zamənzɛtsuŋ], *f.* (—, *no pl.*) construction; composition.

Zusammenspiel [tsu'zamənʃpi:l], *n.* (—s, *no pl.*) (*Theat.*, *Mus.*) ensemble.

zusammenstellen [tsu'zamənʃtɛlən], *v.a.* compose, concoct; put together, compile.

Zusammenstellung [tsu'zamənʃtɛluŋ], *f.* (—, *pl.* —en) combination, compilation; juxtaposition.

zusammenstoppeln [tsu'zamənʃtɔpəln], *v.a.* string together, patch up.

Zusammenstoß [tsu'zamənʃto:s], *m.* (—es, *pl.* ⁻e) clash, conflict; collision.

zusammenstoßen [tsu'zamənʃto:sən], *v.n. irr.* (*aux.* sein) clash; crash, come into collision, collide.

zusammentragen [tsu'zaməntra:gən], *v.a. irr.* collect, compile.

zusammentreffen [tsu'zam2əntrɛfən], *v.n. irr.* meet; coincide.

zusammentreten [tsu'zaməntre:tən], *v.n. irr.* (*aux.* sein) meet.

zusammentun [tsu'zamən tu:n], *v.r. irr. sich* — *mit*, associate with, join.

zusammenwirken [tsu'zamənvɪrkən], *v.n.* cooperate, collaborate.

zusammenwürfeln [tsu'zamənvyrfəln], *v.a.* jumble up.

zusammenzählen [tsu'zaməntsɛ:lən], *v.a.* add up.

zusammenziehen [tsu'zaməntsi:ən], *v.n. irr.* (*aux.* sein) move in together. — *v.a.* draw together, contract. — *v.r. sich* —, shrink; (*storm*) gather; *Zahlen* —, add up.

Zusammenziehung [tsu'zaməntsi:uŋ], *f.* (—, *no pl.*) contraction.

Zusatz [tsu:zats], *m.* (—es, *pl.* ⁻e) addition, supplement, admixture; (*will*) codicil.

zuschanzen [tsu:ʃantsən], *v.a. einem etwas* —, obtain s.th. for s.o.

zuschauen [tsu:ʃauən], *v.n.* look on, watch.

Zuschauer [tsu:ʃauər], *m.* (—s, *pl.* —) onlooker, spectator.

Zuschauerraum [tsu:ʃauərraum], *m.* (—s, *pl.* ⁻e) (*Theat.*) auditorium.

zuschaufeln [tsu:ʃaufəln], *v.a.* shovel in, fill up.

zuschieben [tsu:ʃi:bən], *v.a. irr.* push towards; shut; *einem etwas* —, shove (blame) on to s.o.

zuschießen [tsu:ʃi:sən], *v.a. irr. Geld* —, put money into (an undertaking).

Zuschlag [tsu:ʃla:k], *m.* (—s, *pl.* ⁻e) addition; (*Railw.*) excess fare.

zuschlagen [tsu:ʃla:gən], *v.a. irr.* add; (*door*) bang; (*auction*) knock down to (s.o.). — *v.n.* strike hard.

zuschlag(s)pflichtig [tsu:ʃla:k(s)pflɪç-tɪç], *adj.* liable to a supplementary charge.

zuschmeißen [tsu:ʃmaɪsən], *v.a. irr.* (*door*) slam to, bang.

zuschneiden [tsu:ʃnaɪdən], *v.a. irr.* (*pattern*) cut out; cut up.

Zuschneider [tsu:ʃnaɪdər], *m.* (—s, *pl.*—) (*Tail.*) cutter.

Zuschnitt [tsu:ʃnɪt], *m.* (—s, *no pl.*) (*clothing*) cut.

zuschreiben [tsu:ʃraɪbən], *v.a. irr. einem etwas* —, impute s.th. to s.o.; attribute *or* ascribe s.th. to s.o.

Zuschrift [tsu:ʃrɪft], *f.* (—, *pl.* —en) communication, letter.

Zuschuß [tsu:ʃus], *m.* (—sses, *pl.* ⁻sse) additional money, supplementary allowance, subsidy.

zuschütten [tsu:ʃytən], *v.a.* fill up.

Zusehen [tsu:ze:ən], *n.* (—s, *no pl.*) *das* — *haben*, be left out in the cold.

zusehen [tsu:ze:ən], *v.n. irr.* look on, watch; be a spectator; see to it.

zusehends [tsu:ze:ənts], *adv.* visibly.

zusetzen [tsu:zɛtsən], *v.a.* add to, admix; lose. — *v.n. einem* —, pester s.o.; attack s.o.

zusichern [tsu:zɪçərn], *v.a.* promise, assure.

Zusicherung [tsu:zɪçəruŋ], *f.* (—, *pl.* —en) promise, assurance.

Zuspeise [tsu:ʃpaɪzə], *f.* (—, *no pl.*) (*dial.*) (*food*) trimmings; vegetables.

zusperren [tsu:ʃpɛrən], *v.a.* shut, close, lock up.

zuspitzen [tsu:ʃpɪtsən], *v.a.* sharpen to a point. — *v.r. sich* —, come to a climax.

zusprechen [tsu:ʃprɛçən], *v.n. irr. dem Wein* —, drink heavily. — *v.a. Mut* —, comfort.

Zuspruch [tsu:ʃprux], *m.* (—s, *pl.* ⁻e) exhortation; consolation.

Zustand [tsu:ʃtant], *m.* (—s, *pl.* ⁻e) condition, state of affairs, situation.

zustande [tsu:ʃtandə], *adv.* — *kommen*, come off, be accomplished; — *bringen*, accomplish.

zuständig [tsu:ʃtɛndɪç], *adj.* competent; appropriate.

Zuständigkeit [tsu:ʃtɛndɪçkaɪt], *f.* (—, *no pl.*) competence.

zustecken [tsu:ʃtɛkən], *v.a.* pin up; *einem etwas* —, slip⸱ s.th. into s.o.'s hand.

zustehen [tsu:ʃte:ən], *v.n. irr.* be due to, belong to; be s.o.'s business to.

zustellen [tsu:ʃtɛlən], *v.a.* deliver, hand over; (*Law*) serve (a writ).

Zustellung [tsu:ʃtɛluŋ], *f.* (—, *pl.* —en) delivery; (*Law*) service.

zusteuern [tsu:ʃtɔyərn], *v.a.* contribute. — *v.n.* (*aux.* sein) steer for; (*fig.*) aim at.

zustimmen [tsu:ʃtɪmən], *v.n.* agree to.

Zustimmung [tsu:ʃtɪmuŋ], *f.* (—, *pl.* —en) assent, consent, agreement.

zustopfen

zustopfen ['tsu:ʃtɔpfən], *v.a.* fill up, stop up, plug; darn, mend.

zustoßen ['tsu:ʃtoːsən], *v.a. irr.* push to, shut.

zustürzen ['tsu:ʃtyrtsən], *v.n.* (*aux.* sein) *auf einen* —, rush at *or* towards s.o.

Zutaten ['tsu:taːtən], *f. pl.* ingredients, garnishings.

zuteil [tsu'taɪl], *adv.* — *werden,* fall to s.o.'s share.

zutragen ['tsu:traːgən], *v.a. irr.* report, tell. — *v.r. sich* —, happen.

Zuträger ['tsu:trɛ:gər], *m.* (—s, *pl.* —) informer, tale-bearer.

zuträglich ['tsu:trɛ:klɪç], *adj.* advantageous, wholesome.

Zutrauen ['tsu:trauən], *n.* (—s, *no pl.*) confidence.

zutrauen ['tsu:trauən], *v.a. einem etwas* —, credit s.o. with s.th.

zutraulich ['tsu:traulɪç], *adj.* trusting; familiar, intimate; tame.

zutreffen ['tsu:trɛfən], *v.n. irr.* prove correct, take place.

zutreffend ['tsu:trɛfənt], *adj.* apposite, pertinent.

Zutritt ['tsu:trɪt], *m.* (—s, *no pl.*) entry; access, admittance; — *verboten,* no admittance.

zutunlich ['tsu:tu:nlɪç], *adj.* confiding; obliging.

zuverlässig ['tsu:fɛrlɛsɪç], *adj.* reliable; authentic.

Zuversicht ['tsu:fɛrzɪçt], *f.* (—, *no pl.*) trust, confidence.

zuversichtlich ['tsu:fɛrzɪçtlɪç], *adj.* confident.

zuvor [tsu'fo:r], *adv.* before, first, formerly.

zuvorkommend [tsu'fo:rkɔmənt], *adj.* obliging, polite.

Zuwachs ['tsu:vaks], *m.* (—es, *no pl.*) increase, accretion, growth.

zuwachsen ['tsu:vaksən], *v.n. irr.* (*aux.* sein) become overgrown.

zuwandern ['tsu:vandərn], *v.n.* (*aux.* sein) immigrate.

zuwegebringen [tsu've:gəbrɪŋən], *v.a. irr.* bring about, effect.

zuweilen [tsu'vaɪlən], *adv.* sometimes, at times.

zuweisen ['tsu:vaɪzən], *v.a. irr.* assign, apportion.

zuwenden ['tsu:vɛndən], *v.a.* turn towards; give.

zuwerfen ['tsu:vɛrfən], *v.a. irr.* throw towards, cast; (*door*) slam.

zuwider ['tsu:vi:dər], *prep.* (*Dat.*) against, contrary to. — *adv.* repugnant.

Zuwiderhandlung [tsu'vi:dərhandluŋ], *f.* (—, *pl.* —en) contravention.

zuwiderlaufen [tsu'vi:dərlaufən], *v.n. irr.* (*aux.* sein) be contrary to, fly in the face of.

zuzählen ['tsu:tsɛ:lən], *v.a.* add to.

zuziehen ['tsu:tsi:ən], *v.a. irr.* draw together; hire; consult; (*curtain*) draw. — *v.r. sich eine Krankheit* —, catch a disease.

Zuzug ['tsu:tsu:k], *m.* (—s, *no pl.*) immigration; population increase.

zuzüglich ['tsu:tsy:klɪç], *prep.* (*Genit.*) in addition to, including, plus.

Zwang [tsvaŋ], *m.* (—s, *no pl.*) coercion, force; compulsion; (*fig.*) constraint; *sich* — *auferlegen,* restrain o.s.; *tu deinen Gefühlen keinen* — *an,* let yourself go.

zwanglos ['tsvaŋlo:s], *adj.* informal, free and easy.

Zwangsarbeit ['tsvaŋsarbaɪt], *f.* (—, *pl.* —en) forced labour.

Zwangsjacke ['tsvaŋsjakə], *f.* (—, *pl.* —en) strait-jacket.

Zwangsmaßnahme ['tsvaŋsma:sna:mə], *f.* (—, *pl.* —en) compulsory measure, compulsion.

Zwangsversteigerung ['tsvaŋsfɛrʃtaɪgəruŋ], *f.* (—, *pl.* —en) enforced sale.

Zwangsvollstreckung ['tsvaŋsfɔlʃtrekuŋ], *f.* (—, *pl.* —en) distraint.

zwangsweise ['tsvaŋsvaɪzə], *adv.* by force, compulsorily.

Zwangswirtschaft ['tsvaŋsvɪrtʃaft], *f.* (—, *no pl.*) price control, controlled economy.

zwanzig ['tsvantsɪç], *num. adj.* twenty.

zwar [tsva:r], *adv.* to be sure, indeed, it is true, true; (*Am.*) sure.

Zweck [tsvɛk], *m.* (—(e)s, *pl.* —e) end, object, purpose.

zweckdienlich ['tsvɛkdi:nlɪç], *adj.* useful, expedient.

Zwecke ['tsvɛkə], *f.* (—, *pl.* —n) tack, drawing-pin.

zweckentsprechend ['tsvɛkɛntʃpreçənt], *adj.* suitable, appropriate.

zweckmäßig ['tsvɛkmɛ:sɪç], *adj.* expedient, suitable, proper.

zwecks [tsvɛks], *prep.* (*Genit.*) for the purpose of.

zwei [tsvaɪ], *num. adj.* two.

zweibändig ['tsvaɪbɛndɪç], *adj.* in two volumes.

zweideutig ['tsvaɪdɔytɪç], *adj.* ambiguous, equivocal; (*fig.*) suggestive.

Zweideutigkeit ['tsvaɪdɔytɪçkaɪt], *f.* (—, *pl.* —en) ambiguity.

Zweifel ['tsvaɪfəl], *m.* (—s, *pl.* —) doubt, scruple; *ohne* —, no doubt.

zweifelhaft ['tsvaɪfəlhaft], *adj.* doubtful, dubious.

zweifellos ['tsvaɪfəllo:s], *adv.* doubtless.

zweifeln ['tsvaɪfəln], *v.n.* doubt, question; *ich zweifle nicht daran,* I have no doubt about it.

Zweifelsfall ['tsvaɪfəlsfal], *m.* (—s, *pl.* ÷e) doubtful matter; *im* —, in case of doubt.

Zweifler ['tsvaɪflər], *m.* (—s, *pl.* —) doubter, sceptic.

Zweig [tsvaɪk], *m.* (—(e)s, *pl.* —e) twig, bough, branch.

zweigen ['tsvaɪgən], *v.r. sich* —, bifurcate, fork, branch.

Zweigniederlassung ['tsvaɪkni:dərlasuŋ], *f.* (—, *pl.* —en) branch establishment.

zwitschern

zweihändig ['tsvaɪhɛndɪç], adj. two-handed; (keyboard music) solo.
Zweihufer ['tsvaɪhuːfər], m. (—s, pl. —) cloven-footed animal.
zweijährig ['tsvaɪjɛːrɪç], adj. two-year-old; of two years' duration.
zweijährlich ['tsvaɪjɛːrlɪç], adj. biennial. — adv. every two years.
Zweikampf ['tsvaɪkampf], m. (— (e)s, pl. ⁻e) duel.
zweimal ['tsvaɪmal], adv. twice; — soviel, twice as much.
zweimotorig ['tsvaɪmotoːrɪç], adj. twin- (or two-) engined.
Zweirad ['tsvaɪraːt], n. (—s, pl. ⁻er) bicycle.
zweireihig ['tsvaɪraɪɪç], adj. (suit) double-breasted.
zweischneidig ['tsvaɪʃnaɪdɪç], adj. two-edged.
zweiseitig ['tsvaɪzaɪtɪç], adj. two-sided, bilateral.
zweisprachig ['tsvaɪʃpraːxɪç], adj. bilingual, in two languages.
zweitälteste ['tsvaɪtɛltəstə], adj. second (eldest).
zweitbeste ['tsvaɪtbɛstə], adj. second best.
zweite ['tsvaɪtə], num. adj. second; aus —r Hand, secondhand; zu zweit, in twos, two of (us, them).
Zweiteilung ['tsvaɪtaɪluŋ], f. (—, pl. —en) bisection.
zweitens ['tsvaɪtəns], adv. secondly, in the second place.
zweitletzte ['tsvaɪtlɛtstə], adj. last but one, penultimate.
zweitnächste ['tsvaɪtnɛçstə], adj. next but one.
Zwerchfell ['tsvɛrçfɛl], n. (—s, pl. —e) diaphragm, midriff.
zwerchfellerschütternd ['tsvɛrçfɛlərʃtərnt], adj. side-splitting.
Zwerg [tsvɛrk], m. (—s, pl. —e) dwarf, pigmy.
zwerghaft ['tsvɛrkhaft], adj. dwarfish.
Zwetsche ['tsvɛtʃə], f. (—, pl. —n) (Bot.) damson.
Zwickel ['tsvɪkəl], m. (—s, pl. —) gusset; komische —, (coll.) queer fish.
zwicken ['tsvɪkən], v.a. pinch, nip.
Zwicker ['tsvɪkər], m. (—s, pl. —) pince-nez.
Zwickmühle ['tsvɪkmyːlə], f. (—, pl. —n) in der — sein, be on the horns of a dilemma, be in a jam.
Zwickzange ['tsvɪktsaŋə], f. (—, pl. —n) pincers.
Zwieback ['tsviːbak], m. (—s, pl. —e) rusk.
Zwiebel ['tsviːbəl], f. (—, pl. —n) onion; bulb.
zwiebelartig ['tsviːbəlaːrtɪç], adj. bulbous.
zwiebeln ['tsviːbəln], v.a. einen —, bully, torment s.o.
Zwielicht ['tsviːlɪçt], n. (—s, no pl.) twilight.
Zwiespalt ['tsviːʃpalt], m. (—s, pl. —e) difference, dissension; schism.

Zwiesprache ['tsviːʃpraːxə], f. (—, pl. —n) dialogue; discussion.
Zwietracht ['tsviːtraxt], f. (—, no pl.) discord, disharmony.
zwieträchtig ['tsviːtrɛçtɪç], adj. discordant, at variance.
Zwillich ['tsvɪlɪç], m. (—s, pl. —e) ticking.
Zwilling ['tsvɪlɪŋ], m. (—s, pl. —e) twin; (pl.) (Astron.) Gemini.
Zwingburg ['tsvɪŋburk], f. (—, pl. —en) stronghold.
Zwinge ['tsvɪŋə], f. (—, pl. —n) ferrule.
zwingen ['tsvɪŋən], v.a. irr. force, compel; master, overcome, get the better of. — v.r. sich —, force o.s. (to), make a great effort (to).
zwingend ['tsvɪŋənt], adj. cogent, imperative, convincing.
Zwinger ['tsvɪŋər], m. (—s, pl. —) keep, donjon, fort; bear-pit.
Zwingherrschaft ['tsvɪŋhɛrʃaft], f. (—, pl. —en) despotism, tyranny.
zwinkern ['tsvɪŋkərn], v.n. wink; (stars) twinkle.
Zwirn [tsvɪrn], m. (—(e)s, pl. —e) thread, sewing cotton.
Zwirnrolle ['tsvɪrnrɔlə], f. (—, pl. —n) ball of thread, reel of cotton.
zwischen ['tsvɪʃən], prep. (Dat., Acc.) between; among, amongst.
Zwischenakt ['tsvɪʃənakt], m. (—s, pl. —e) (Theat.) interval.
Zwischenbemerkung ['tsvɪʃənbəmɛrkuŋ], f. (—, pl. —en) interruption, digression.
Zwischendeck ['tsvɪʃəndɛk], n. (—s, pl. —e) (ship) steerage, between decks.
zwischendurch ['tsvɪʃəndurç], adv. in between, at intervals.
Zwischenfall ['tsvɪʃənfal], m. (—s, pl. ⁻e) incident; episode.
Zwischengericht ['tsvɪʃəngərɪçt], n. (—s, pl. —e) (food) entrée, entremets.
Zwischenglied ['tsvɪʃəngliːt], n. (—s, pl. —er) link.
Zwischenhändler ['tsvɪʃənhɛndlər], m. (—s, pl. —) middleman.
Zwischenpause ['tsvɪʃənpauzə], f. (—, pl. —n) interval; pause.
Zwischenraum ['tsvɪʃənraum], m. (—s, pl. ⁻e) intermediate space, gap.
Zwischenrede ['tsvɪʃənreːdə], f. (—, pl. —n) interruption.
Zwischenruf ['tsvɪʃənruːf], m. (—s, pl. —e) interruption, interjection.
Zwischensatz ['tsvɪʃənzats], m. (—es, pl. ⁻e) parenthesis; interpolation.
Zwischenspiel ['tsvɪʃənʃpiːl], n. (—s, pl. —e) interlude, intermezzo.
Zwischenzeit ['tsvɪʃəntsaɪt], f. (—, no pl.) interval, interim, meantime; in der —, meanwhile.
Zwist [tsvɪst], m. (—es, pl. —e) discord, quarrel, dispute.
Zwistigkeiten ['tsvɪstɪçkaɪtən], f. pl. hostilities.
zwitschern ['tsvɪtʃərn], v.n. chirp, twitter.

299

Zwitter

Zwitter ['tsvɪtər], *m.* (**—s**, *pl.* **—**) hybrid, cross-breed, mongrel; hermaphrodite.
zwitterhaft ['tsvɪtərhaft], *adj.* hybrid; bisexual.
zwölf [svœlf], *num. adj.* twelve.
Zwölffingerdarm ['tsvœlffɪŋərdarm], *m.* (**—s**, *pl.* **⁀e**) duodenum.
Zyankali [tsy:anˈkaːli], *n.* (**—s**, *no pl.*) potassium cyanide.
Zyklon [tsyˈkloːn], *m.* (**—s**, *pl.* **—e**) cyclone.
Zyklus ['tsyklus], *m.* (**—**, *pl.* **Zyklen**) cycle; course, series.

zylinderförmig [tsyˈlɪndərfœrmɪç], *adj.* cylindric(al).
Zylinderhut [tsyˈlɪndərhuːt], *m.* (**—s**, *pl.* **⁀e**) top-hat, silk-hat.
zylindrisch [tsyˈlɪndrɪʃ], *adj.* cylindric(al).
Zyniker ['tsyːnɪkər], *m.* (**—s**, *pl.* **—**) cynic.
zynisch ['tsyːnɪʃ], *adj.* cynical.
Zynismus [tsyˈnɪsmus], *m.* (**—**, *no pl.*) cynicism.
Zypern ['tsyːpərn], *n.* Cyprus.
Zypresse [tsyˈprɛsə], *f.* (**—**, *pl.* **—n**) (*Bot.*) cypress.

Cassell's English-German Dictionary

A

A [ei]. das A (*also Mus.*).
a [ə, ei] (**an** [ən, æn] *before vowel or silent* h), *indef. art.* ein, eine, ein; *two at a time*, zwei auf einmal; *many a*, mancher; *two shillings a pound*, zwei Schilling das Pfund.
abacus ['æbəkəs], *s.* das Rechenbrett.
abandon [ə'bændən], *v.a.* (*give up*) aufgeben; (*forsake*) verlassen; · (*surrender*) preisgeben.
abandonment [ə'bændənmənt], *s.* das Verlassen (*active*); das Verlassensein (*passive*); die Wildheit, das Sichgehenlassen.
abasement [ə'beismənt], *s.* die Demütigung, Erniedrigung.
abash [ə'bæʃ], *v.a.* beschämen.
abate [ə'beit], *v.n.* nachlassen.
abbess ['æbes], *s.* die Äbtissin.
abbey ['æbi], *s.* die Abtei.
abbot ['æbət], *s.* der Abt.
abbreviate [ə'bri:vieit], *v.a.* abkürzen.
abbreviation [əbri:vi'eiʃən], *s.* die Abkürzung.
abdicate ['æbdikeit], *v.a., v.n.* entsagen (*Dat.*), abdanken.
abdomen [æb'doumən, 'æbdəmən], *s.* (*Anat.*) der Unterleib, Bauch.
abdominal [æb'dɔminəl], *adj.* (*Anat.*) Bauch-, Unterleibs-.
abduct [æb'dʌkt], *v.a.* entführen.
abed [ə'bed], *adv.* zu Bett, im Bett.
aberration [æbə'reiʃən], *s.* die Abirrung; die Verirrung; (*Phys.*) die Strahlenbrechung.
abet [ə'bet], *v.a.* helfen (*Dat.*), unterstützen.
abeyance [ə'beiəns], *s.* die Unentschiedenheit, (der Zustand der) Ungewißheit; *in* —, unentschieden.
abhor [əb'hɔ:], *v.a.* verabscheuen.
abhorrence [əb'hɔrəns], *s.* die Abscheu (*of*, vor, *Dat.*).
abhorrent [əb'hɔrənt], *adj.* widerlich, ekelhaft.
abide [ə'baid], *v.n. irr.* bleiben, verweilen; (*last*) dauern. — *v.a.* aushalten.
ability [ə'biliti], *s.* die Fähigkeit, Tüchtigkeit; (*pl.*) die Geisteskräfte, *f. pl.*
abject ['æbdʒekt], *adj.* elend; (*submissive*) unterwürfig, verächtlich.
ablaze [ə'bleiz], *adj., adv.* in Flammen.
able [eibl], *adj.* fähig; (*clever*) geschickt; (*efficient*) tüchtig.
ablution [ə'blu:ʃən], *s.* die Abwaschung, Waschung.
abnormal [æb'nɔ:məl], *adj.* abnorm, ungewöhnlich.

abnormality [æbnɔ:'mæliti], *s.* die Ungewöhnlichkeit.
aboard [ə'bɔ:d], *adv.* an Bord.
abode [ə'boud], *s.* der Wohnsitz, Wohnort.
abolish [ə'bɔliʃ], *v.a.* aufheben, abschaffen.
abolition [æbo'liʃən], *s.* die Abschaffung, Aufhebung.
abominable [ə'bɔminəbl], *adj.* abscheulich, scheußlich.
abominate [ə'bɔmineit], *v.a.* verabscheuen.
abomination [əbɔmi'neiʃən], *s.* der Abscheu, Greuel.
aboriginal [æbə'ridʒinəl], *adj.* eingeboren, einheimisch. — *s.* der Eingeborene.
aborigines [æbə'ridʒini:z], *s. pl.* die Eingeborenen, Ureinwohner.
abortion [ə'bɔ:ʃən], *s.* die Fehlgeburt; die Abtreibung.
abortive [ə'bɔ:tiv], *adj.* mißlungen.
abound [ə'baund], *v.n.* wimmeln von (*Dat.*).
about [ə'baut], *prep.* um; (*toward*) gegen; *about 3 o'clock*, gegen drei; (*concerning*) über, betreffend. — *adv.* umher, herum; (*round*) rund herum; (*nearly*) etwa, ungefähr; (*everywhere*) überall; *to be* — *to*, im Begriffe sein or stehen zu . . .
above [ə'bʌv], *prep.* über; — *all things*, vor allen Dingen; *this is* — *me*, das ist mir zu hoch; — *board*, offen, ehrlich. — *adv.* oben, darüber, *over and* —, obendrein; — *mentioned*, obenerwähnt.
abrade [ə'breid], *v.a.* abschaben, abschürfen.
abrasion [ə'breiʒən], *s.* die Abschürfung; Abnutzung.
abreast [ə'brest], *adj., adv.* nebeneinander, Seite an Seite; *keep* —, (sich) auf dem Laufenden halten; Schritt halten (mit).
abridge [ə'bridʒ], *v.a.* (ab)kürzen.
abridgement [ə'bridʒmənt], *s.* die (Ab)kürzung; (*book etc.*) der Auszug.
abroad [ə'brɔ:d], *adv.* im Ausland, auswärts; *to go* —, ins Ausland reisen.
abrogate ['æbrogeit], *v.a.* abschaffen.
abrogation [æbro'geiʃən], *s.* (*Pol.*) die Abschaffung.
abrupt [ə'brʌpt], *adj.* plötzlich; (*curt*) schroff; kurz; jäh.
abruptness [ə'brʌptnis], *s.* (*speech*) die Schroffheit; (*suddenness*) die Plötzlichkeit; (*drop*) die Steilheit.
abscess ['æbses], *s.* das Geschwür, die Schwellung, der Abszeß.

abscond

abscond [əb'skɔnd], *v.n.* sich davonmachen.

absence ['æbsəns], *s.* die Abwesenheit; *leave of* —, der Urlaub.

absent (1) ['æbsənt], *adj.* abwesend; — *minded,* zerstreut.

absent (2) [æb'sent], *v.r.* — *oneself,* fehlen, fernbleiben; (*go away*) sich entfernen.

absentee [æbsən'ti:], *s.* der Abwesende.

absolute ['æbsɔlu:t], *adj.* absolut, unumschränkt.

absolve [əb'zɔlv], *v.a.* freisprechen (*from,* von), lossprechen, entbinden.

absorb [əb'sɔ:b], *v.a.* absorbieren, aufsaugen; (*attention*) in Anspruch nehmen.

absorbed [əb'sɔ:bd], *adj.* versunken.

absorbent [əb'sɔ:bənt], *adj.* absorbierend.

absorption [əb'sɔ:pʃən], *s.* (*Chem.*) die Absorption; (*attention*) das Versunkensein.

abstain [əb'stein], *v.n.* sich enthalten; — *from voting,* sich der Stimme enthalten.

abstainer [əb'steinə], *s.* der Abstinenzler, Antialkoholiker.

abstemious [əb'sti:miəs], *adj.* enthaltsam.

abstention [əb'stenʃən], *s.* die Enthaltung.

abstinence ['æbstinəns], *s.* die Enthaltsamkeit, das Fasten (*food*).

abstract [æb'strækt], *v.a.* abstrahieren, abziehen; (*summarize*) kürzen, ausziehen. —['æbstrækt], *adj.* abstrakt; (*Maths.*) rein. — *s.* der Auszug, Abriß (*of article, book, etc.*).

abstracted [æb'stræktid], *adj.* zerstreut, geistesabwesend.

abstraction [æb'strækʃən], *s.* die Abstraktion; der abstrakte Begriff.

abstruse [æb'stru:s], *adj.* schwerverständlich, tiefsinnig.

absurd [əb'sə:d], *adj.* absurd, töricht; (*unreasonable*) unvernünftig, gegen alle Vernunft; (*laughable*) lächerlich.

absurdity [əb'sə:diti], *s.* die Torheit, Unvernünftigkeit.

abundance [ə'bʌndəns], *s.* die Fülle, der Überfluß.

abundant [ə'bʌndənt], *adj.* reichlich.

abuse [ə'bju:z], *v.a.* mißbrauchen; (*insult*) beschimpfen; (*violate*) schänden. —[ə'bju:s], *s.* der Mißbrauch; (*language*) die Beschimpfung; (*violation*) die Schändung.

abusive [ə'bju:siv], *adj.* (*language*) grob; schimpfend, schmähend.

abut [ə'bʌt], *v.n.* anstoßen, angrenzen.

abysmal [ə'bizməl], *adj.* bodenlos.

abyss [ə'bis], *s.* der Abgrund, Schlund.

Abyssinian [æbi'sinjən], *adj.* abessinisch. — *s.* der Abessinier.

acacia [ə'keiʃə], *s.* (*Bot.*) die Akazie.

academic [ækə'demik], *adj.* akademisch. — *s.* der Akademiker.

academy [ə'kædəmi], *s.* die Akademie.

acajon ['ækəʒu:], *s.* (*Bot.*) der Nierenbaum.

accede [æk'si:d], *v.n.* beistimmen; einwilligen; — *to the throne,* den Thron besteigen.

accelerate [æk'seləreit], *v.a.* beschleunigen. — *v.n.* schneller fahren.

acceleration [ækselə'reiʃən], *s.* die Beschleunigung.

accelerator [æk'seləreitə], *s.* (*Motor.*) der Gashebel, das Gaspedal.

accent (1), **accentuate** [æk'sent, æk'sentjueit], *v.a.* akzentuieren, betonen.

accent (2) ['æksənt], *s.* (*Phon.*) der Ton, Wortton, die Betonung; der Akzent (*dialect*), die Aussprache.

accentuation [æksentju'eiʃən], *s.* die Aussprache, Akzentuierung, Betonung.

accept [æk'sept], *v.a.* annehmen.

acceptable [æk'septəbl], *adj.* angenehm, annehmbar, annehmlich.

acceptance [æk'septəns], *s.* die Annahme; (*Comm.*) das Akzept.

access ['ækses], *s.* der Zugang, Zutritt.

accessible [æk'sesibl], *adj.* erreichbar, zugänglich.

accession [æk'seʃən], *s.* der Zuwachs; — *to the throne,* die Thronbesteigung.

accessory [æk'sesəri], *adj.* zugehörig; hinzukommend; (*Law*) mitschuldig; (*subsidiary*) nebensächlich. — *s.* (*Law*) der Mitschuldige; (*pl.*) das Zubehör.

accidence ['æksidəns], *s.* (*Gram.*) die Flexionslehre.

accident ['æksidənt], *s.* (*chance*) der Zufall; (*mishap*) der Unfall, Unglücksfall.

accidental [æksi'dentəl], *adj.* zufällig; (*inessential*) unwesentlich; durch Unfall.

acclaim [ə'kleim], *v.a.* akklamieren, mit Beifall aufnehmen. — *v.n.* zujubeln. — *s.* der Beifall.

acclamation [æklə'meiʃən], *s.* der Beifall, Zuruf.

acclimatize [ə'klaimətaiz], *v.a., v.r.* akklimatisieren; sich anpassen, eingewöhnen.

accommodate [ə'kɔmədeit], *v.a.* (*adapt*) anpassen; (*lodge*) unterbringen, beherbergen, aufnehmen; einem aushelfen; (*with money*) jemandem Geld leihen. — *v.r.* — *oneself to,* sich an etwas anpassen, sich in etwas fügen.

accommodating [ə'kɔmədeitiŋ], *adj.* gefällig, entgegenkommend.

accommodation [əkɔmə'deiʃən], *s.* (*adaptation*) die Anpassung; (*dispute*) die Beilegung; (*room*) die Unterkunft.

accompaniment [ə'kʌmpənimənt], *s.* die Begleitung.

accompany [ə'kʌmpəni], *v.a.* begleiten.

accomplice [ə'kʌmplis *or* ə'kɔmplis], *s.* der Komplize, Mitschuldige, Mittäter.

accomplish [ə'kʌmpliʃ *or* ə'kɔmpliʃ], *v.a.* vollenden, zustandebringen, vollbringen; (*objective*) erreichen.

accomplished [ə'kʌmpliʃd *or* ə'kɔmpliʃd], *adj.* vollendet.

accomplishment [əˈkʌmpliʃmənt *or* əˈkɔmpliʃmənt], *s.* (*of project*) die Ausführung; (*of task*) die Vollendung; (*of prophecy*) die Erfüllung; (*pl.*) die Talente, *n. pl.*, Gaben, Kenntnisse, *f. pl.*

accord [əˈkɔːd], *s.* (*agreement*) die Übereinstimmung; (*unison*) die Eintracht. — *v.n.* übereinstimmen (*with*, mit) — *v.a.* bewilligen.

accordance [əˈkɔːdəns], *s.* die Übereinstimmung.

according [əˈkɔːdiŋ], *prep.* — *to*, gemäß, nach, laut.

accordingly [əˈkɔːdiŋli], *adv.* demgemäß, demnach, folglich.

accordion [əˈkɔːdiən], *s.* (*Mus.*) die Ziehharmonika, das Akkordeon.

accost [əˈkɔst], *v.a.* ansprechen, anreden.

account [əˈkaunt], *s.* die Rechnung; (*report*) der Bericht; (*narrative*) die Erzählung; (*importance*) die Bedeutung; (*Fin.*) das Konto, Guthaben; *cash* —, die Kassenrechnung; *on no* —, auf keinen Fall; *on his* —, seinetwegen, um seinetwillen; *on* — *of*, wegen (*Genit.*); *on that* —, darum; *of no* —, unbedeutend. — *v.n.* — *for*, Rechenschaft ablegen über (*Acc.*); (*explain*) erklären.

accountable [əˈkauntəbl], *adj.* verrechenbar (*item*); verantwortlich (*person*).

accountant [əˈkauntənt], *s.* der Bücherrevisor, Rechnungsführer; *junior* —, der Buchhalter.

accredit [əˈkredit], *v.a.* akkreditieren, beglaubigen; (*authorize*) ermächtigen, bevollmächtigen.

accretion [əˈkriːʃən], *s.* der Zuwachs.

accrue [əˈkruː], *v.n.* (*Comm.*) zuwachsen, erwachsen, zufallen.

accumulate [əˈkjuːmjuleit], *v.a., v.n.* anhäufen; sich anhäufen, zunehmen, sich ansammeln.

accumulation [əkjuːmjuˈleiʃən], *s.* die Ansammlung, Anhäufung.

accuracy [ˈækjurəsi], *s.* die Genauigkeit.

accurate [ˈækjurit], *adj.* genau, richtig.

accursed [əˈkəːsid], *adj.* verflucht, verwünscht.

accusation [ækjuˈzeiʃən], *s.* die Anklage.

accusative [əˈkjuːzətiv], *s.* (*Gram.*) der Akkusativ.

accuse [əˈkjuːz], *v.a.* anklagen, beschuldigen (*of*, Genit.).

accustom [əˈkʌstəm], *v.a.* gewöhnen (*to*, an, Acc.).

ace [eis], *s.* (*Cards*) das As, die Eins.

acerbity [əˈsəːbiti], *s.* die Rauheit, Herbheit; (*manner*) die Grobheit.

acetate [ˈæsiteit], *s.* das Azetat; essigsaures Salz.

acetic [əˈsiːtik, əˈsetik], *adj.* essigsauer.

acetylene [əˈsetiliːn], *s.* das Azetylen.

ache [eik], *s.* der Schmerz. — *v.n.* schmerzen, weh(e)tun.

achieve [əˈtʃiːv], *v.a.* erreichen, erlangen; (*accomplish*) vollenden; (*perform*) ausführen; (*gain*) erlangen, erwerben.

achievement [əˈtʃiːvmənt], *s.* (*accomplishment*) die Leistung, der Erfolg; die Errungenschaft; (*gain*) die Erwerbung.

achromatic [ækroˈmætik], *adj.* achromatisch, farblos.

acid [ˈæsid], *adj.* sauer, scharf. — *s.* (*Chem.*) die Säure.

acidulated [əˈsidjuleitid], *adj.* (*Chem.*) angesäuert.

acknowledge [əkˈnɔlidʒ], *v.a.* anerkennen; (*admit*) zugeben; (*confess*) bekennen; (*letter*) den Empfang bestätigen.

acknowledgement [əkˈnɔlidʒmənt], *s.* die Anerkennung, (*receipt*) Bestätigung, Quittung; (*pl.*) die Dankesbezeigung; die Erkenntlichkeit.

acme [ˈækmi], *s.* der Gipfel, Höhepunkt.

acorn [ˈeikɔːn], *s.* (*Bot.*) die Eichel.

acoustics [əˈkuːstiks], *s. pl.* die Akustik; (*subject, study*) die Schallehre.

acquaint [əˈkweint], *v.a.* bekanntmachen; (*inform*) mitteilen (*Dat.*), informieren; unterrichten.

acquaintance [əˈkweintəns], *s.* die Bekanntschaft; der Bekannte, die Bekannte (*person*); die Kenntnis (*with*, von).

acquiesce [ækwiˈes], *v.n.* einwilligen, sich fügen.

acquiescence [ækwiˈesəns], *s.* die Einwilligung (*in*, in, Acc.), Zustimmung (*in*, zu, Dat.)

acquiescent [ækwiˈesənt], *adj.* fügsam.

acquire [əˈkwaiə], *v.a.* erlangen, erwerben; (*language*) erlernen.

acquisition [ækwiˈziʃən], *s.* die Erlangung, Erwerbung.

acquit [əˈkwit], *v.a.* freisprechen.

acre [ˈeikə], *s.* der Acker (*appr.* 0.4 *Hektar*).

acrid [ˈækrid], *adj.* scharf, beißend.

acrimonious [ækriˈmouniəs], *adj.* scharf, bitter.

across [əˈkrɔs, əˈkrɔːs], *adv.* kreuzweise, (quer) hinüber. — *prep.* quer durch, über; *come* —, (zufällig) treffen, *come* — *a problem*, auf ein Problem stoßen.

act [ækt], *s.* (*deed*) die Tat; (*Theat.*) der Akt; (*Parl. etc.*) die Akte. — *v.a.* (*Theat.*) spielen. — *v.n.* handeln (*do something*); sich benehmen *or* tun, als ob (*act as if, pretend*); (*Theat.*) spielen; (*Chem.*) wirken (*react*).

action [ˈækʃən], *s.* die Handlung (*play, deed*); Wirkung (*effect*); (*Law*) der Prozeß; der Gang.

active [ˈæktiv], *adj.* (*person, Gram.*) aktiv; tätig; rührig (*industrious*); wirksam (*effective*).

activity [ækˈtiviti], *s.* die Tätigkeit; (*Chem.*) Wirksamkeit.

actor [ˈæktə], *s.* der Schauspieler.

actress [ˈæktrəs], die Schauspielerin.

actual [ˈæktjuəl], *adj.* tatsächlich, wirklich.

actuality [æktju'æliti], s. die Wirklichkeit.

actuary ['æktjuəri], s. der Aktuar, Versicherungsbeamte.

actuate ['æktjueit], v.a. betreiben, in Bewegung setzen.

acuity [ə'kju:iti], s. der Scharfsinn (mind), die Schärfe (vision etc.).

acute [ə'kju:t], adj. scharf, scharfsinnig (mind); spitz (angle); fein (sense); — accent, der Akut.

adage ['ædidʒ], s. das Sprichwort.

adamant ['ædəmənt], adj. sehr hart, unerbittlich (inexorable).

adapt [ə'dæpt], v.a. anpassen, angleichen; bearbeiten.

adaptable [ə'dæptəbl], adj. anpassungsfähig.

adaptation [ædæp'teiʃən], s. die Anpassung, die Bearbeitung (of book).

adaptive [ə'dæptiv], adj. anpassungsfähig.

add [æd], v.a. hinzufügen, (Maths.) addieren.

adder ['ædə], s. (Zool.) die Natter.

addict ['ædikt], s. der Süchtige.

addiction [ə'dikʃən], s. die Sucht.

addicted [ə'diktid], adj. verfallen.

addition [ə'diʃən], s. die Hinzufügung, Zugabe, (Maths.) Addition.

additional [ə'diʃənəl], adj. zusätzlich, nachträglich.

address [ə'dres], s. die Anschrift, Adresse (letter); die Ansprache (speech). — v.a. (letter) adressieren, richten an (Acc.).

addressee [ædre'si:], s. der Adressat, der Empfänger.

adduce [ə'dju:s], v.a. anführen (proof, Beweis).

adenoid ['ædinɔid], s. (usually pl.) (Med.) die Wucherung.

adept ['ædept], adj. geschickt, erfahren.

adequacy ['ædikwəsi], s. die Angemessenheit, das Gewachsensein, die Zulänglichkeit.

adequate ['ædikwət], adj. gewachsen (Dat.); angemessen, hinreichend (sufficient).

adhere [əd'hiə], v.n. haften, anhängen; — to one's opinion, bei seiner Meinung bleiben.

adherence [əd'hiərəns], s. das Festhalten (an, Dat.).

adhesion [əd'hi:ʒən], s. (Phys.) die Adhäsion; das Anhaften.

adhesive [əd'hi:ziv], adj. haftend, klebrig; — plaster, das Heftpflaster.

adipose ['ædipous], adj. fett, feist.

adjacent [ə'dʒeisənt], adj. naheliegend, benachbart, angrenzend.

adjective ['ædʒəktiv], s. (Gram.) das Adjektiv; Eigenschaftswort.

adjoin [ə'dʒɔin], v.a. anstoßen, angrenzen.

adjourn [ə'dʒə:n], v.a. vertagen, aufschieben.

adjudicate [ə'dʒu:dikeit], v.a. beurteilen, richten.

adjunct ['ædʒʌŋkt], s. der Zusatz.

adjust [ə'dʒʌst], v.a. ordnen; (adapt) anpassen; regulieren, einstellen.

adjustable [ə'dʒʌstəbl], adj. verstellbar, einstellbar.

adjustment [ə'dʒʌstmənt], s. die Einstellung, Anpassung; (Law) Schlichtung; Berichtigung.

administer [əd'ministə], v.a. verwalten (an enterprise); verabreichen (medicine); abnehmen (an oath, einen Eid).

administration [ədminis'treiʃən], s. die Verwaltung, Regierung; die Darreichung (sacraments).

administrative [əd'ministrətiv], adj. Verwaltungs-; verwaltend.

admirable ['ædmirəbl], adj. bewundernswert.

admiral ['ædmirəl], s. der Admiral.

Admiralty ['ædmirəlti], s. die Admiralität.

admiration [ædmi'reiʃən], s. die Bewunderung.

admire [əd'maiə], v.a. bewundern, verehren.

admirer [əd'maiərə], s. der Bewunderer, Verehrer.

admissible [əd'misibl], adj. zulässig.

admission [əd'miʃən], s. die Zulassung; (entry) der Eintritt; Zutritt; (confession) das Eingeständnis, Zugeständnis.

admit [əd'mit], v.a. zulassen; aufnehmen; zugeben (deed); gelten lassen (argument).

admittance [əd'mitəns], s. der Zugang, Eintritt, Zutritt.

admixture [əd'mikstʃə], s. die Beimischung, Beigabe.

admonish [əd'mɔniʃ], v.a. ermahnen, mahnen, warnen.

admonition [ædmə'niʃən], s. die Ermahnung, Warnung.

ado [ə'du:], s. der Lärm, das Tun, das Treiben; without further —, ohne weiteres.

adolescence [ædo'lesəns], s. die Adoleszenz, Jugend, Jugendzeit.

adolescent [ædo'lesənt], s. der Jugendliche. — adj. jugendlich.

adopt [ə'dɔpt], v.a. (Law) annehmen, adoptieren.

adoption [ə'dɔpʃən], s. (Law) die Annahme, Adoption.

adoptive [ə'dɔptiv], adj. Adoptiv-, angenommen.

adorable [ə'dɔ:rəbl], adj. anbetungswürdig; (coll.) wunderbar, schön.

adoration [ædo'reiʃən], s. die Anbetung.

adore [ə'dɔ:], v.a. anbeten; verehren.

adorn [ə'dɔ:n], v.a. (aus)schmücken, zieren.

Adriatic (Sea) [eidri'ætik (si:)]. das adriatische Meer.

adrift [ə'drift], adv. treibend; cut o.s. —, sich absondern.

adroit [ə'drɔit], adj. gewandt, geschickt.

adroitness [ə'drɔitnis], s. die Gewandtheit, die Geschicklichkeit.

afire

adulation [ædjuˈleiʃən], *s.* die Schmeichelei.

adulator [ˈædjuleitə], *s.* der Schmeichler.

adulatory [ˈædjuleitəri], *adj.* schmeichlerisch.

adult [əˈdʌlt *or* ˈædʌlt], *adj.* erwachsen. — *s.* der Erwachsene.

adulterate [əˈdʌltəreit], *v.a.* verfälschen; verwässern.

adulterer [əˈdʌltərə], *s.* der Ehebrecher.

adultery [əˈdʌltəri], *s.* der Ehebruch.

adumbrate [əˈdʌmbreit *or* ˈæd-], *v.a.* skizzieren, entwerfen, andeuten.

advance [ədˈvɑːns], *v.a.* fördern (*a cause*); vorschießen (*money*); geltend machen (*claim*). — *v.n.* vorrücken, vorstoßen; (*make progress, gain promotion*) aufsteigen. — *s.* der Fortschritt (*progress*); der Vorschuß (*money*); in —, im voraus.

advancement [ədˈvɑːnsmənt], *s.* der Fortschritt (*progress*), der Aufstieg, die Beförderung (*promotion*); die Förderung (*of a cause*).

advantage [ədˈvɑːntidʒ], *s.* der Vorteil, Nutzen; (*superiority*) die Überlegenheit.

Advent [ˈædvent]. (*Eccl.*) der Advent.

advent [ˈædvənt], *s.* die Ankunft.

adventitious [ædvenˈtiʃəs], *adj.* zufällig.

adventure [ədˈventʃə], *s.* das Abenteuer. — *v.n.* auf Abenteuer ausgehen, wagen.

adventurer [ədˈventʃərə], *s.* der Abenteurer.

adventurous [ədˈventʃərəs], *adj.* abenteuerlich, unternehmungslustig.

adverb [ˈædvəːb], *s.* (*Gram.*) das Adverb(ium), Umstandswort.

adverbial [ədˈvəːbiəl], *adj.* adverbial.

adversary [ˈædvəsəri], *s.* der Gegner, Widersacher.

adverse [ˈædvəːs], *adj.* widrig, feindlich, ungünstig.

adversity [ədˈvəːsiti], *s.* das Unglück, Mißgeschick; in —, im Unglück.

advert [ədˈvəːt], *v.n.* hinweisen.

advertise [ˈædvətaiz], *v.a.* anzeigen; annoncieren (*in press*), Reklame machen.

advertisement [ədˈvəːtizmənt], *s.* die Anzeige, Annonce; Reklame.

advertiser [ˈædvətaizə], *s.* der Anzeiger.

advice [ədˈvais], *s.* der Rat, Ratschlag; die Nachricht (*information*).

advise [ədˈvaiz], *v.a.* raten (*Dat.*), beraten; benachrichtigen (*inform*); verständigen.

advisable [ədˈvaizəbl], *adj.* ratsam.

advisedly [ədˈvaizidli], *adv.* absichtlich, mit Bedacht.

adviser [ədˈvaizə], *s.* der Berater.

advisory [ədˈvaizəri], *adj.* beratend, ratgebend, Rats-.

advocacy [ˈædvəkəsi], *s.* (*Law*) die Verteidigung; die Fürsprache (*championing of*, für, *Acc.*); die Vertretung (*of view*).

Aegean (**Sea**) [iːˈdʒiːən (siː)]. das ägäische Meer.

aerated [ˈɛəreitid], *adj.* kohlensauer.

aerial [ˈɛəriəl], *s.* (*Rad.*) die Antenne. — *adj.* luftig, Luft-.

aerie [ˈɛəri, ˈiəri], *s. see* **eyrie**.

aerodrome [ˈɛərodroum], *s.* der Flugplatz, Flughafen.

aeronautical [ɛəroˈnɔːtikəl], *adj.* aeronautisch.

aeronautics [ɛəroˈnɔːtiks], *s. pl.* die Aeronautik, Luftfahrt.

aeroplane, (*Am.*) **airplane** [ˈɛəroplein, ˈɛərplein], *s.* das Flugzeug.

aesthetic(al) [iːsˈθetik(əl)], *adj.* ästhetisch.

aesthetics [iːsˈθetiks], *s.* die Ästhetik.

afar [əˈfɑː], *adv.* fern, weit entfernt; *from* —, von weitem, (von) weit her.

affability [æfəˈbiliti], *s.* die Leutseligkeit, Freundlichkeit.

affable [ˈæfəbl], *adj.* freundlich, leutselig.

affair [əˈfɛə], *s.* die Affäre; die Angelegenheit (*matter*); das Anliegen (*concern*).

affect [əˈfekt], *v.a.* beeinflußen; rühren; wirken auf; vortäuschen (*pretend*); zur Schau tragen (*exhibit*).

affectation [æfekˈteiʃən], *s.* die Ziererei, das Affektieren, die Affektiertheit.

affected [əˈfektid], *adj.* affektiert, gekünstelt, geziert; befallen, angegriffen (*illness*).

affection [əˈfekʃən], *s.* die Zuneigung, Zärtlichkeit.

affectionate [əˈfekʃənit], *adj.* zärtlich, liebevoll; (*in letters*) *yours* —*ly*, herzlichst.

affinity [əˈfiniti], *s.* (*Chem.*) die Affinität; die Verwandtschaft (*relationship*).

affirm [əˈfəːm], *v.a.* behaupten, bestätigen, versichern; bekräftigen (*confirm*).

affirmation [æfəˈmeiʃən], *s.* die Behauptung, Bekräftigung.

affirmative [əˈfəːmətiv], *adj.* bejahend, positiv; *in the* —, bejahend.

affix [əˈfiks], *v.a.* anheften, aufkleben (*stick*); anbringen (*join to*, an, *Acc.*).

afflict [əˈflikt], *v.a.* quälen, plagen.

affliction [əˈflikʃən], *s.* die Plage, Qual; das Mißgeschick; die Not; das Leiden.

affluence [ˈæfluəns], *s.* der Überfluß (*abundance*); der Reichtum.

affluent [ˈæfluənt], *adj.* reich, wohlhabend. — *s.* der Nebenfluß (*tributary*).

afford [əˈfɔːd], *v.a.* geben, bieten; (*sich*) leisten (*have money for*); gewähren (*give*); hervorbringen (*yield*).

afforest [əˈfɔrist], *v.a.* aufforsten.

affray [əˈfrei], *s.* die Schlägerei.

African [ˈæfrikən], *adj.* afrikanisch. — *s.* der Afrikaner.

affront [əˈfrʌnt], *s.* die Beleidigung. — *v.a.* beleidigen.

Afghan [ˈæfgæn], *adj.* afghanisch. — *s.* der Afghane.

afield [əˈfiːld], *adj., adv.* im Felde; weit umher; weit weg.

afire [əˈfaiə], *adv., adv.* in Flammen.

aflame

aflame [ə'fleim], *adj.*, *adv.* in Flammen.
afloat [ə'flout], *adj.*, *adv.* schwimmend, dahintreibend.
afoot [ə'fut], *adj.*, *adv.* im Gange.
afore [ə'fɔ:], *adv.* vorher.
aforesaid [ə'fɔ:sed], *adj.* *the* —, das Obengesagte, der Vorhergenannte.
afraid [ə'freid], *adj.* ängstlich, furchtsam; *be* —, fürchten (*of s.th.*, etwas, *Acc.*); sich fürchten.
afresh [ə'freʃ], *adv.* von neuem.
aft [ɑ:ft], *adv.* (*Naut.*) achtern.
after ['ɑ:ftə], *prep.* nach (*time*); nach, hinter (*place*); *the day* — *tomorrow*, übermorgen. — *adj.* hinter, später. — *adv.* hinterher, nachher (*time*); darauf, dahinter (*place*). — *conj.* nachdem.
afternoon [ɑ:ftə'nu:n], *s.* der Nachmittag.
afterwards ['ɑ:ftəwədz], *adv.* nachher, daraufhin, später.
again [ə'gein], *adv.* wieder, abermals, noch einmal; zurück (*back*); dagegen (*however*); *as much* —, noch einmal soviel; — *and* —, immer wieder.
against [ə'geinst], *prep.* gegen, wider; nahe bei (*near*, *Dat.*); bis an (*up to*, *Acc.*); — *the grain*, wider *or* gegen den Strich.
agate ['ægeit], *s.* der Achat.
agave [ə'geivi], *s.* (*Bot.*) die Agave.
age [eidʒ], *s.* das Alter (*person*); das Zeitalter (*period*); die Reife; *come of* —, volljährig werden; mündig werden; *old* —, das Greisenalter; *for* —*s*, seit einer Ewigkeit. — *v.n.* altern, alt werden.
aged ['eidʒid], *adj.* bejahrt.
agency ['eidʒənsi], *s.* die Agentur (*firm*); die Mitwirkung (*participation*); die Hilfe (*assistance*); die Vermittlung (*mediation*).
agenda [ə'dʒendə], *s.* das Sitzungsprogramm; die Tagesordnung.
agent ['eidʒənt], *s.* der Agent, Vertreter.
agglomerate [ə'glɔmədreit], *v.a.* zusammenhäufen. — *v.n.* sich zusammenhäufen, sich ballen.
aggrandisement [ə'grændizmənt], *s.* die Überhebung, Übertreibung, Erweiterung.
aggravate ['ægrəveit], *v.a.* verschlimmern; ärgern.
aggravation [ægrə'veiʃən], *s.* die Verschlimmerung (*of condition*); der Ärger (*annoyance*).
aggregate ['ægrigit], *adj.* gesamt, vereinigt, vereint. — *s.* das Aggregat.
aggregation [ægri'geiʃən], *s.* (*Geol.*, *Chem.*) die Vereinigung, Anhäufung, Ansammlung.
aggression [ə'greʃən], *s.* der Angriff, Überfall.
aggressive [ə'gresiv], *adj.* aggressiv, angreifend.
aggressor [ə'gresə], *s.* der Angreifer.
aggrieve [ə'gri:v], *v.a.* kränken.

aghast [ə'gɑ:st], *adj.* bestürzt; sprachlos; entsetzt.
agile ['ædʒail], *adj.* behend, flink, beweglich.
agitate ['ædʒiteit], *v.a.* bewegen; beunruhigen; aufrühren; stören.
agitation [ædʒi'teiʃən], *s.* (*Pol.*) die Agitation; die Unruhe (*unrest*); der Aufruhr (*revolt*).
agitator ['ædʒiteitə], *s.* (*Pol.*) der Agitator; der Aufwiegler (*inciter*).
aglow [ə'glou], *adv.* glühend.
agnostic [æg'nɔstik], *s.* der Agnostiker.
ago [ə'gou], *adv.* vor; *long* —, vor langer Zeit; *not long* —, kürzlich; *a month* —, vor einem Monat.
agog [ə'gɔg], *adv.* erregt, gespannt, neugierig (*for*, auf, *Acc.*).
agonize ['ægənaiz], *v.a.* quälen, martern. — *v.n.* Qual erleiden; mit dem Tode ringen *or* kämpfen.
agonising ['ægənaiziŋ], *adj.* schmerzhaft, qualvoll.
agony ['ægəni], *s.* die Pein, Qual; der Todeskampf; — *column*, die Seufzerspalte.
agrarian [ə'greəriən], *adj.* landwirtschaftlich; — *party*, die Bauernpartei.
agree [ə'gri:], *v.n.* übereinstimmen (*be in agreement*); übereinkommen (*come to an agreement*), sich einigen.
agreeable [ə'gri:əbl], *adj.* angenehm, gefällig.
agreement [ə'gri:mənt], *s.* die Übereinstimmung, das Übereinkommen; der Vertrag, die Verständigung (*understanding*).
agricultural [ægri'kʌltʃərəl], *adj.* landwirtschaftlich.
agriculture ['ægrikʌltʃə], *s.* die Landwirtschaft.
aground [ə'graund], *adj.*, *adv.* (*Naut.*) gestrandet; *to run* —, stranden.
ague ['eigju:], *s.* (*Med.*) der Schüttelfrost.
ah! [ɑ:], *interj.* ach!; aha! (*surprise*).
aha! [ɑ'hɑ:], *interj.* ach so!
ahead [ə'hed], *adv.* vorwärts, voran (*movement*), voraus (*position*), *go* — (*carry on*), fortfahren; *go* — (*make progress*), vorwärtskommen.
ahoy! [ə'hɔi], *interj.* (*Naut.*) ahoi!
aid [eid], *v.a.* helfen (*Dat.*), unterstützen (*Acc.*), beistehen (*Dat.*). — *s.* die Hilfe, der Beistand.
aide-de-camp ['eiddə'kā], *s.* der Adjutant (eines Generals).
ail [eil], *v.n.* schmerzen; krank sein.
ailing ['eiliŋ], *adj.* kränklich, leidend.
ailment ['eilmənt], *s.* das Leiden.
aim [eim], *v.a.* (*weapon*, *blow etc.*) richten (*at*, auf). — *v.n.* zielen (auf, *Acc.*); trachten (nach, *strive for*). — *s*, das, Ziel, der Zweck (*purpose*); die Absicht (*intention*).
aimless ['eimlis], *adj.* ziellos, zwecklos.

306

air [ɛə], s. die Luft; die Melodie (tune);
die Miene (mien); air force, die Luftwaffe; air pocket, das Luftloch; air
raid, der Luftangriff; in the open —,
im Freien; on the —, im Rundfunk; to
give oneself —s, vornehm tun. — v.a.
lüften (room); trocknen (washing);
aussprechen (views).

airbase ['ɛəbeis], s. der Fliegerstützpunkt.

airconditioning ['ɛəkəndiʃəniŋ], s. die
Klimaanlage.

aircraft ['ɛəkrɑːft], s. das Luftfahrzeug,
Flugzeug.

airgun ['ɛəgʌn], s. die Windbüchse,
das Luftgewehr.

airiness ['ɛərinis], s. die Luftigkeit,
Leichtigkeit.

airletter ['ɛəletə], s. der Luftpostbrief.

airliner ['ɛəlainə], s. das Verkehrsflugzeug.

airmail ['ɛəmeil], s. die Luftpost.

airman ['ɛəmən], s. der Flieger.

airplane see aeroplane.

airport ['ɛəpɔːt], s. der Flughafen.

airtight ['ɛətait], adj. luftdicht.

airy ['ɛəri], adj. luftig.

aisle [ail], s. das Seitenschiff (church);
der Gang.

Aix-la-Chapelle ['eikslaʃæ'pel],Aachen,
n.

ajar [ə'dʒɑː], adv. angelehnt, halb
offen.

akimbo [ə'kimbou], adv. Hände an den
Hüften, Arme in die Seiten gestemmt.

akin [ə'kin], adj. verwandt (to, mit,
Dat.).

alack [ə'læk], interj. ach! oh, weh! alas
and —, ach und wehe!

alacrity [ə'lækriti], s. die Bereitwilligkeit; Munterkeit.

alarm [ə'lɑːm], s. der Alarm; Lärm
(noise); die Warnung; Angst, Bestürzung; — clock, der Wecker. — v.a.
erschrecken.

alas! [ə'læs], interj. ach, wehe!

Albanian [æl'beiniən], adj. albanisch.
— s. der Albanier.

album ['ælbəm], s. das Album.

albumen [æl'bjuːmən], s. das Eiweiß,
(Chem.) der Eiweißstoff.

albuminous [æl'bjuːminəs], adj. eiweißhaltig, Eiweiß-.

alchemist ['ælkimist], s. der Alchimist.

alchemy ['ælkimi], s. die Alchimie.

alcohol ['ælkəhɔl], s. der Alkohol.

alcoholic [ælkə'hɔlik], adj. alkoholisch.
— s. der Trinker, Alkoholiker.

alcove ['ælkouv], s. der Alkoven.

alder ['ɔːldə], s. (Bot.) die Erle.

alderman ['ɔːldəmən], s. der Ratsherr,
der Stadtrat.

ale [eil], s. englisches Bier.

alert [ə'ləːt], adj. wachsam, aufmerksam; on the —, auf der Hut.

algebra ['ældʒibrə], s. die Algebra.

Algerian [æl'dʒiəriən], adj. algerisch.
— s. der Algerier.

Algiers [æl'dʒiəz]. Algier, n.

alias ['eiliəs], adv. sonst genannt.

alien ['eiliən], adj. fremd, ausländisch.
— s. der Fremde, Ausländer.

alienate ['eiliəneit], v.a. entfremden.

alienation [eiliə'neiʃən], s. die Entfremdung; — of mind, die Geisteserkrankung, Geistesgestörtheit.

alienist ['eiliənist], s. der Irrenarzt.

alight (1) [ə'lait], v.n. absteigen (from
horse); aussteigen (from carriage etc.).

alight (2) [ə'lait], adj. brennend, in
Flammen.

alike [ə'laik], adj. gleich, ähnlich. —
adv. great and small —, sowohl große
wie kleine.

alimentary [æli'mentəri], adj. Nahrungs-, Verdauungs-; — canal, (Anat.)
der Darmkanal.

alimentation [ælimen'teiʃən], s. die
Beköstigung; (Law) der Unterhalt.

alimony ['æliməni], s. der Unterhaltsbeitrag; (pl.) Alimente., n.pl.

alive [ə'laiv], adj. lebendig; — and
kicking, wohlauf, munter; — to,
empfänglich für.

alkali ['ælkəlai], s. (Chem.) das Laugensalz, Alkali.

alkaline ['ælkəlain], adj. (Chem.) alkalisch, laugensalzig.

all [ɔːl], adj., pron. all, ganz (whole);
sämtliche, alle; above —, vor allem;
once and for —, ein für allemal; not
at —, keineswegs; All Saints, Allerheiligen; All Souls, Allerseelen. —
adv. ganz, gänzlich, völlig; — the
same, trotzdem; — the better, umso
besser.

allay [ə'lei], v.a. lindern, beruhigen,
unterdrücken.

allegation [æli'geiʃən], s. die Behauptung.

allege [ə'ledʒ],v.a. behaupten, aussagen.

allegiance [ə'liːdʒəns], s. die Treue,
Ergebenheit; Untertanenpflicht.

allegorical [æli'gɔrikəl], adj. allegorisch, sinnbildlich.

alleviate [ə'liːvieit], v.a. erleichtern,
mildern.

alleviation [əliːvi'eiʃən], s. die Erleichterung, Milderung.

alley ['æli], s. die Gasse; Seitenstraße;
bowling —, die Kegelbahn.

alliance [ə'laiəns], s. (Pol.) die Allianz,
das Bündnis (treaty); der Bund
(league).

allied [ə'laid, 'ælaid], adj. verbündet,
vereinigt; alliiert; verwandt.

alliteration [əlitə'reiʃən], s. die Alliteration, der Stabreim.

allocate ['ælokeit], v.a. zuweisen,
zuteilen.

allot [ə'lɔt], v.a. zuteilen (assign);
verteilen (distribute).

allotment [ə'lɔtmənt], s. der Anteil;
die Zuteilung; die Landparzelle; die
Laubenkolonie, der Schrebergarten
(garden).

allow [ə'lau], v.a. gewähren (grant);
erlauben (permit); zulassen (admit). —
v.n. — for, Rücksicht nehmen auf
(Acc.); in Betracht ziehen.

allowance

allowance [ə'lauəns], *s.* die Rente; das Taschengeld (*money*); die Erlaubnis (*permission*); die Genehmigung (*approval*); die Nachsicht (*indulgence*).

alloy [ə'lɔi, 'æləi], *s.* die Legierung. — *v.a.* (*Metall.*) legieren.

allude [ə'lu:d], *v.a.* anspielen (*to*, auf).

allure [ə'ljuə], *v.a.* locken, anlocken.

allurement [ə'ljuəmənt], *s.* der Reiz, die Lockung.

allusion [ə'lu:ʒən], *s.* die Anspielung.

alluvial [ə'lu:vial], *adj.* angeschwemmt.

alluvium [ə'lu:viam], *s.* das Schwemmgebiet, Schwemmland.

ally ['ælai], *s.* der Verbündete, Bundesgenosse, Alliierte. — [ə'lai], *v.a., v.r.* (sich) vereinigen, (sich) verbünden.

almanac ['ɔ:lmənæk], *s.* der Almanach.

almighty [ɔ:l'maiti], *adj.* allmächtig; *God Almighty!* allmächtiger Gott!

almond ['a:mənd], *s.* (*Bot.*) die Mandel.

almoner ['ælmənə], *s.* der Wohlfahrtsbeamte, die Fürsorgerin.

almost ['ɔ:lmoust], *adv.* fast, beinahe.

alms [a:mz], *s.* das Almosen.

aloe ['ælou], *s.* (*Bot.*) die Aloe.

aloft [ə'lɔft], *adv.* droben, (hoch) oben; empor.

alone [ə'loun], *adj., adv.* allein; *all —,* ganz allein; *leave —,* in Ruhe lassen; *let —,* geschweige (denn).

along [ə'lɔŋ], *adv.* längs, der Länge nach; entlang, weiter; *come —!* komm mit!; *get — (with),* auskommen. — *prep.* längs; entlang.

alongside [əlɔŋ'said], *adv.* nebenan. — [ə'lɔŋsaid], *prep.* neben.

aloof [ə'lu:f], *adj., adv.* fern, weitab; *keep —,* sich fernhalten.

aloofness [ə'lu:fnis], *s.* das Sichfernhalten; das Vornehmtun.

aloud [ə'laud], *adj., adv.* laut; hörbar.

alphabet ['ælfəbet], *s.* das Alphabet, Abc.

Alpine ['ælpain], *adj.* alpinisch, Alpen-.

Alps, The [ælps, ði]. die Alpen, *pl.*

already [ɔ:l'redi], *adv.* schon, bereits.

Alsatian [æl'seiʃən], *adj.* elsässisch. — *s.* der Elsässer; (*dog*) der Wolfshund, deutscher Schäferhund.

also ['ɔ:lsou], *adv.* (*likewise*) auch, ebenfalls; (*moreover*) ferner.

altar ['ɔ:ltə], *s.* der Altar.

alter ['ɔ:ltə], *v.a.* ändern, verändern. — *v.n.* sich (ver)ändern.

alterable ['ɔ:ltərəbl], *adj.* veränderlich.

alteration [ɔ:ltə'reiʃən], *s.* die Änderung, Veränderung.

altercation [ɔ:ltə'keiʃən], *s.* der Zank, Streit; Wortwechsel.

alternate ['ɔ:ltəneit], *v.a., v.n.* abwechseln lassen, abwechseln.

alternative [ɔ:l'tə:nətiv], *adj.* abwechselnd, alternativ, zur Wahl gestellt. — *s.* die Alternative, die Wahl.

although [ɔ:l'ðou], *conj.* obgleich, obwohl, obschon.

altimeter ['æltimi:tə], *s.* der Höhenmesser.

altitude ['æltitju:d], *s.* die Höhe.

alto ['æltou], *s.* (*Mus.*) die Altstimme, der Alt.

altogether [ɔ:ltu'geðə], *adv.* zusammen, zusammengenommen, allesamt; (*wholly*) ganz und gar, durchaus.

alum ['æləm], *s.* (*Chem.*) der Alaun.

aluminium [ælju'minjəm], (*Am.*) **aluminum** [ə'lu:minəm], *s.* das Aluminium.

always ['ɔ:lweiz], *adv.* immer, stets.

am [æm] *see* **be.**

amalgamate [ə'mælgəmeit], *v.a.* amalgamieren. — *v.n.* sich vereinigen, vermischen.

amalgamation [əmælgə'meiʃən], *s.* die Verbindung, Vereinigung.

amass [ə'mæs], *v.a.* anhäufen, zusammentragen.

amateur ['æmə'tə: *or* 'æmətjuə], *s.* der Amateur, Liebhaber.

amatory ['æmətəri], *adj.* Liebes-, verliebt, sinnlich.

amaze [ə'meiz], *v.a.* erstaunen, in Erstaunen versetzen; verblüffen (*baffle*).

amazement [ə'meizmənt], *s.* das Erstaunen, Staunen, die Verwunderung.

amazing [ə'meiziŋ], *adj.* erstaunlich, wunderbar.

Amazon (1) ['æməzən], *s.* (*Myth.*) die Amazone.

Amazon (2) ['æməzən], *s.* (*river*) der Amazonas.

ambassador [æm'bæsədə], *s.* der Botschafter.

ambassadorial [æmbæsə'dɔ:riəl], *adj.* Botschafts-, gesandtschaftlich.

amber ['æmbə], *s.* der Bernstein.

ambidextrous [æmbi'dekstrəs], *adj.* (mit beiden Händen gleich) geschickt.

ambiguity [æmbi'gju:iti], *s.* die Zweideutigkeit, der Doppelsinn.

ambiguous [æm'bigjuəs], *adj.* zweideutig; dunkel (*sense*).

ambit ['æmbit], *s.* der Umkreis, die Umgebung.

ambition [æm'biʃən], *s.* die Ambition, der Ehrgeiz.

ambitious [æm'biʃəs], *adj.* ehrgeizig.

amble [æmbl], *v.n.* schlendern, (gemächlich) spazieren.

ambulance ['æmbjuləns], *s.* der Krankenwagen.

ambush ['æmbuʃ], *v.a.* überfallen (*Acc.*), auflauern (*Dat.*). — *s.* die Falle, der Hinterhalt.

ameliorate [ə'mi:liəreit], *v.a.* verbessern.

amenable [ə'mi:nəbl], *adj.* zugänglich; unterworfen.

amend [ə'mend], *v.a.* verbessern, berichtigen; ändern.

amendment [ə'mendmənt], *s.* die Verbesserung; der Zusatz, die zusätzliche Änderung (*proposal*).

amends [ə'mendz], *s. pl.* der Schadenersatz; *make —,* Schadenersatz leisten; wiedergutmachen.

anise

amenity [ə'mi:niti or ə'meniti], s. die Behaglichkeit, Annehmlichkeit; (pl.) die Vorzüge, m pl.; die Einrichtungen, f. pl.

American [ə'merikən], adj. amerikanisch; — cloth, das Wachstuch. — s. der Amerikaner.

amiability [eimjə'biliti], s. die Liebenswürdigkeit.

amiable ['eimjəbl], adj. liebenswürdig.

amicable ['æmikəbl], adj. freundschaftlich.

amidst [ə'midst], prep. mitten in, mitten unter (Dat.), inmitten (Gen.).

amiss [ə'mis], adj., adv. übel; verkehrt; take —, übelnehmen.

amity ['æmiti], s. die Freundschaft.

ammonia [ə'mouniə], s. das Ammoniak; liquid —, der Salmiakgeist.

ammunition [æmju'niʃən], s. die Munition.

amnesty ['æmnisti], s. die Amnestie, Begnadigung.

among(st) [ə'mʌŋ(st)], prep. (mitten) unter, zwischen, bei.

amorous ['æmərəs], adj. verliebt.

amorphous [ə'mɔ:fəs], adj. amorph, gestaltlos, formlos.

amortization [əmɔ:ti'zeiʃən], s. die Amortisierung (debt); (Comm.) Tilgung, Abtragung.

amount [ə'maunt], s. der Betrag (sum of money); die Menge (quantity). — v.n. betragen; — to, sich belaufen auf (Acc.).

amphibian [æm'fibiən], adj. amphibisch. — s. (Zool.) die Amphibie.

amphibious [æm'fibiəs], adj. amphibienhaft.

ample [æmpl], adj. weit, breit (scope); voll, reichlich; ausgebreitet; genügend.

amplification [æmplifi'keiʃən], s. die Ausbreitung; Verbreiterung, Erklärung, Erweiterung; (Elec.) die Verstärkung (sound).

amplifier ['æmplifaiə], s. der Verstärker; der Lautsprecher.

amplify ['æmplifai], v.a. erweitern, ausführen, vergrößern; verstärken (sound).

amputate ['æmpjuteit], v.a. amputieren.

amputation [æmpju'teiʃən], s. die Amputation.

amuck [ə'mʌk], adv. amok.

amulet ['æmjulit], s. das Amulett.

amuse [ə'mju:z], v.a. unterhalten, amüsieren.

amusement [ə'mju:zmənt], s. die Unterhaltung, das Vergnügen.

an see under a.

Anabaptist [ænə'bæptist], s. der Wiedertäufer.

anachronism [ə'nækrənizm], s. der Anachronismus.

anaemia [ə'ni:miə], s. (Med.) die Blutarmut.

anaemic [ə'ni:mik], adj. (Med.) blutarm.

anaesthetic [ænəs'θetik], adj. schmerzbetäubend. — s. die Narkose.

analogous [ə'næləgəs], adj. analog.

analogy [ə'nælədʒi], s. die Analogie.

analyse ['ænəlaiz], v.a. analysieren.

analysis [ə'nælisis], s. die Analyse.

anarchic(al) [ə'na:kik(əl)], adj. anarchisch.

anarchy ['ænəki], s. die Anarchie.

anathema [ə'næθimə], s. (Eccl.) der Kirchenbann.

anatomical [ænə'tɔmikəl], adj. anatomisch.

anatomist [ə'nætəmist], s. der Anatom.

anatomize [ə'nætəmaiz], v.a. zergliedern, zerlegen.

anatomy [ə'nætəmi], s. die Anatomie.

ancestor ['ænsəstə], s. der Vorfahre, Ahnherr.

ancestry ['ænsəstri], s. die Ahnenreihe, Herkunft, der Stammbaum (family tree).

anchor ['æŋkə], s. der Anker. — v.a. verankern. — v.n. ankern.

anchorage ['æŋkəridʒ], s. die Verankerung; der Ankerplatz.

anchovy [æn'tʃouvi or 'æntʃəvi], s. (Zool.) die Sardelle.

ancient ['einʃənt], adj. alt, uralt, antik; althergebracht (traditional). — s. (pl.) die Alten (Griechen und Römer).

and [ænd], conj. und.

Andes, the ['ændi:z, ði]. die Anden, pl.

anecdote ['ænekdout], s. die Anekdote.

anemone [ə'neməni], s. (Bot.) die Anemone, das Windröschen; (Zool.) sea —, die Seeanemone.

anew [ə'nju:], adv. von neuem.

angel ['eindʒəl], s. der Engel.

angelic [æn'dʒelik], adj. engelhaft, engelgleich.

anger ['æŋgə], s. der Zorn, Unwille, Ärger. — v.a. erzürnen, verärgern, ärgerlich machen.

angle [æŋgl], s. (Geom.) der Winkel; die Angel (fishing). — v.n. angeln (for, nach).

Angles [æŋglz], s. pl. die Angeln, m. pl.

Anglo-Saxon [æŋglou'sæksən], adj. angelsächsisch. — s. der Angelsachse.

anglicism ['æŋglisizm], s. der Anglizismus (style).

anguish ['æŋgwiʃ], s. die Qual, Pein.

angular ['æŋgjulə], adj. winklig, eckig.

anhydrous [æn'haidrəs], adj. wasserfrei, (Chem.) wasserlos.

aniline ['ænilain], s. das Anilin. — adj. — dye, die Anilinfarbe.

animal ['æniməl], s. das Tier, Lebewesen.

animate ['ænimeit], v.a. beleben, beseelen; (fig.) anregen.

animated ['ænimeitid], adj. belebt; munter.

animation [æni'meiʃən], s. die Belebung.

animosity [æni'mɔsiti], s. die Feindseligkeit, Abneigung, Erbitterung.

anise ['ænis], s. (Bot.) der Anis.

ankle

ankle [æŋkl], *s.* (*Anat.*) der Fußknöchel;
— socks, kurze Socken.
anklet ['æŋklit], *s.* der Fußring.
annalist ['ænəlist], *s.* der Chronist,
Geschichtsschreiber.
annals ['ænəlz], *s. pl.* die Annalen
(*f. pl.*); die Chronik (*sing.*).
anneal [ə'ni:l], *v.a.* ausglühen.
annex [ə'neks], *v.a.* annektieren, angliedern, sich aneignen.
annex(e) ['æneks], *s.* der Anhang, der
Anbau.
annexation [ænek'seiʃən], *s.* die An-
gliederung, Aneignung.
annihilate [ə'naiileit], *v.a.* vernichten,
zerstören.
annihilation [ənaii'leiʃən], *s.* die
Vernichtung, Zerstörung.
anniversary [æni'və:səri], *s.* der Jah-
restag, die Jahresfeier.
annotate ['ænoteit], *v.a.* anmerken,
mit Anmerkungen versehen.
annotation [æno'teiʃən], *s.* die Anmerkung, Notiz.
announce [ə'nauns], *v.a.* melden,
ankündigen; anzeigen; (*Rad.*) ansagen.
announcement [ə'naunsmənt], *s.* die
Ankündigung,   Bekanntmachung;
(*Rad.*) die Ansage.
announcer [ə'naunsə], *s.* (*Rad.*) der
Ansager.
annoy [ə'nɔi], *v.a.* ärgern; belästigen.
annoyance [ə'nɔiəns], *s.* das Ärgernis;
die Belästigung.
annual ['ænjuəl], *adj.* jährlich, Jahres-.
— *s.* der Jahresband (*serial publication*);   das   Jahrbuch;   (*Bot.*)   die
einjährige Pflanze.
annuity [ə'nju:iti], *s.* die Jahresrente,
Lebensrente.
annul [ə'nʌl], *v.a.* annullieren, ungültig machen, für ungültig erklären.
annulment [ə'nʌlmənt], *s.* die Annul-
lierung, Ungültigkeitserklärung.
Annunciation [ənʌnsi'eiʃən], *s.* (*Eccl.*)
die Verkündigung.
anode ['ænoud], *s.* die Anode.
anodyne ['ænodain], *adj.* schmerz-
stillend.
anoint [ə'nɔint], *v.a.* salben.
anomalous [ə'nɔmələs], *adj.* abweichend, unregelmäßig, anomal.
anomaly [ə'nɔməli], *s.* die Anomalie,
Abweichung, Unregelmäßigkeit.
anon [ə'nɔn], *adv.* sogleich, sofort.
anonymous [ə'nɔniməs], *adj.* (*abbr.*
anon.) anonym; namenlos; unbekannt.
anonymity [æno'nimiti], *s.* die Anony-
mität.
another [ə'nʌðə], *adj. & pron.* ein
anderer; ein zweiter; noch einer; one
—, einander.
answer ['ɑ:nsə], *v.a.* beantworten. —
v.n. antworten. — *s.* die Antwort,
Erwiderung.
answerable ['ɑ:nsərəbl], *adj.* verantwortlich (*responsible*); beantwortbar
(*capable of being answered*).
ant [ænt], *s.* (*Ent.*) die Ameise.

antagonise [æn'tægənaiz], *v.a.* sich
(*Dat.*) jemanden zum Gegner machen.
antagonism [æn'tægənizm], *s.* der
Widerstreit, Konflikt; der Antagonis-
mus.
Antarctic [ænt'ɑ:ktik], *adj.* Südpol-,
antarktisch. — *s.* der südliche Polar-
kreis.
antecedence [ænti'si:dəns], *s.* der
Vortritt (*rank*).
antecedent [ænti'si:dənt], *s.* (*pl.*) das
Vorhergehende, die Vorgeschichte.
antedate ['æntideit], *v.a.* vordatieren.
antediluvian [æntidi'lu:viən], *adj.* vorsintflutlich; (*fig.*) überholt; altmodisch.
antelope ['æntiloup], *s.* (*Zool.*) die
Antilope.
antenna [æn'tenə], *s.* (*Ent.*) der
Fühler; (*Rad.*) die Antenne.
anterior [æn'tiəriə], *adj.* vorder (*in
space*), älter, vorherig, vorhergehend,
(*in time*).
anteroom ['æntiru:m], *s.* das Vorzimmer.
anthem ['ænθəm], *s.* die Hymne, der
Hymnus.
anther ['ænθə], *s.* (*Bot.*) der Staub-
beutel.
antic ['æntik], *s.* die Posse; (*pl.*)
komisches Benehmen.
anticipate [æn'tisipeit], *v.a.* vorwegnehmen;   zuvorkommen;   ahnen
(*guess*); erwarten (*await*); vorgreifen.
anticipation [æntisi'peiʃən], *s.* die
Vorwegnahme; die Erwartung.
antidote ['æntidout], *s.* das Gegengift.
antipathy [æn'tipəθi], *s.* die Antipathie,
der Widerwille.
antipodal [æn'tipədəl], *adj.* anti-
podisch; entgegengesetzt.
antiquarian [ænti'kwεəriən], *adj.* altertümlich; antiquarisch.
antiquary ['æntikwəri], *s.* der Alter-
tumsforscher, Antiquar.
antiquated ['æntikweitid], *adj.* überholt, unmodern, veraltet.
antique [æn'ti:k], *s.* die Antike; das
alte Kunstwerk. — *adj.* alt, antik;
altmodisch.
antiquity [æn'tikwiti], *s.* die Antike,
das Altertum; die Vorzeit (*period of
history*).
antiseptic [ænti'septik], *adj.* antisep-
tisch — *s.* das antiseptische Mittel.
antler ['æntlə], *s.* die Geweihsprosse;
(*pl.*) das Geweih.
anvil ['ænvil], *s.* der Amboß.
anxiety [æn'zaiəti], *s.* die Angst (*fear*);
Besorgnis (*uneasiness*); Unruhe.
anxious ['æŋkʃəs], *adj.* ängstlich
(*afraid*); besorgt (*worried*); eifrig
bemüht (*keen*, um, on, *Acc.*).
any ['eni], *adj. & pron.* jeder; irgendein;
etwas; (*pl.*) einige; (*neg.*) not —, kein.
anybody, anyone ['enibədi, 'eniwʌn],
pron. irgendeiner, jemand; jeder.
anyhow, anyway ['enihau, 'eniwei],
adv. irgendwie, auf irgendeine Weise;
auf alle Fälle.
anyone *see under* anybody.

anything ['eniθiŋ], s. irgend etwas; alles.

anyway see under **anyhow**.

anywhere ['enihwɛə], adv. irgendwo; überall; not —, nirgends.

apace [ə'peis], adv. geschwind, hurtig, flink.

apart [ə'pɑ:t], adv. für sich, abgesondert; einzeln; poles —, weit entfernt; take —, zerlegen; — from, abgesehen von.

apartment [ə'pɑ:tmənt], s. das Zimmer; (Am.) die Wohnung (flat).

apathy ['æpəθi], s. die Apathie, Interesselosigkeit, Gleichgültigkeit.

apathetic [æpə'θetik], adj. apathisch, uninteressiert; teilnahmslos.

ape [eip], s. (Zool.) der Affe. — v.a. nachäffen, nachahmen.

aperient [ə'piəriənt], adj. (Med.) abführend. — s. (Med.) das Abführmittel.

aperture ['æpətʃə], s. die Öffnung.

apex ['eipeks], s. die Spitze, der Gipfel.

aphorism ['æfərizm], s. der Aphorismus.

apiary ['eipiəri], s. das Bienenhaus.

apiece [ə'pi:s], adv. pro Stück, pro Person.

apologetic [əpɔlə'dʒetik], adj. entschuldigend, reumütig; verteidigend.

apologize [ə'pɔlədʒaiz], v.n. sich entschuldigen (for, wegen; to, bei).

apology [ə'pɔlədʒi], s. die Entschuldigung; Abbitte; Rechtfertigung.

apoplectic [æpə'plektik], adj. (Med.) apoplektisch.

apoplexy ['æpəpleksi], s. (Med.) der Schlagfluß, Schlaganfall (fit).

apostle [ə'pɔsl], s. der Apostel.

apostolic [æpəs'tɔlik], adj. apostolisch.

apostrophe [ə'pɔstrəfi], s. der Apostroph (punctuation); die Anrede (speech).

apostrophize [ə'pɔstrəfaiz], v.a. apostrophieren; anreden (speak to).

apotheosis [əpɔθi'ousis], s. die Apotheose.

appal [ə'pɔ:l], v.a. erschrecken.

appalling [ə'pɔ:liŋ], adj. schrecklich.

apparatus [æpə'reitəs], s. das Gerät, die Apparatur; (coll.) der Apparat.

apparel [ə'pærəl], s. die Kleidung.

apparent [ə'pærənt], adj. scheinbar; offensichtlich; augenscheinlich; heir —, der rechtmäßige Erbe.

apparition [æpə'riʃən], s. die Erscheinung; der Geist, das Gespenst (ghost).

appeal [ə'pi:l], v.n. appellieren (make an appeal); gefallen (please). — s. (public, Mil.) der Appell; die Bitte (request).

appear [ə'piə], v.n. erscheinen; scheinen; auftreten.

appearance [ə'piərəns], s. die Erscheinung; das Auftreten (stage, etc.); der Schein (semblance); keep up —s, den Schein wahren; to all —s, allem Anschein nach.

appease [ə'pi:z], v.a. besänftigen.

appeasement [ə'pi:zmənt], s. die Besänftigung, (Pol.) die Befriedung.

appellation [æpe'leiʃən], s. die Benennung.

append [ə'pend], v.a. anhängen, beifügen.

appendicitis [əpendi'saitis], s. (Med.) die Blinddarmentzündung.

appendix [ə'pendiks], s. der Anhang; (Med.) der Blinddarm.

appertain [æpə'tein], v.n. gehören (to, zu).

appetite ['æpitait], s. der Appetit.

appetizing ['æpitaiziŋ], adj. appetitlich, appetitanregend.

applaud [ə'plɔ:d], v.a., v.n. applaudieren, Beifall klatschen (Dat.).

applause [ə'plɔ:z], s. der Applaus, Beifall.

apple [æpl], s. der Apfel.

appliance [ə'plaiəns], s. das Gerät, die Vorrichtung.

applicable ['æplikəbl], adj. anwendbar, passend (to, auf).

applicant ['æplikənt], s. der Bewerber (for, um).

application [æpli'keiʃən], s. die Bewerbung (for, um); das Gesuch; die Anwendung (to, auf); letter of —, der Bewerbungsbrief; — form, das Bewerbungsformular.

apply [ə'plai], v.a. anwenden (auf, to, Acc.); gebrauchen. — v.n. sich bewerben (um, for, Acc.); (Dat.) this does not —, das trifft nicht zu; — within, drinnen nachfragen.

appoint [ə'pɔint], v.a. bestimmen, ernennen; ausrüsten.

appointment [ə'pɔintmənt], s. die Festsetzung; die Ernennung; die Bestellung, die Stellung (position); make an —, jemanden ernennen (fill a post), sich verabreden (arrange to meet); by —, Hoflieferant (to, Genit.).

apportion [ə'pɔ:ʃən], v.a. zuteilen, zuweisen, zumessen.

apposite ['æpəzit], adj. passend, angemessen.

appositeness ['æpəzitnis], s. die Angemessenheit.

appraise [ə'preiz], v.a. beurteilen.

appraisal [ə'preizəl], s. die Beurteilung, Abschätzung.

appreciable [ə'pri:ʃəbl], adj. merklich; nennenswert.

appreciate [ə'pri:ʃieit], v.a. würdigen, schätzen.

appreciation [əpri:ʃi'eiʃən], s. die Schätzung, Würdigung.

apprehend [æpri'hend], v.a. verhaften, ergreifen (arrest); befürchten (fear).

apprehension [æpri'henʃən], s. die Verhaftung (arrest); die Befürchtung (fear).

apprehensive [æpri'hensiv], adj. besorgt, in Furcht (for, um), furchtsam.

apprentice [ə'prentis], s. der Lehrling; Praktikant. — v.a. in die Lehre geben (with, bei, Dat.).

311

apprenticeship [əˈprentiʃip], s. die Lehre, Lehrzeit, Praktikantenzeit; *student* —, die Studentenpraxis.

apprise [əˈpraiz], v.a. benachrichtigen, informieren.

approach [əˈprəutʃ], v.a., v.n. sich nähern (*Dat.*). — s. die Annäherung, das Herankommen, Näherrücken.

approachable [əˈprəutʃəbl], adj. zugänglich, freundlich.

approbation [æproˈbeiʃən], s. die (offizielle) Billigung, Zustimmung.

appropriate [əˈprəupriit], adj. angemessen, gebührend, geeignet (*suitable*). — [əˈprəuprieit], v.a. requirieren, sich aneignen.

appropriation [əprəupriˈeiʃən], s. die Requisition, Aneignung, Übernahme, Besitznahme.

approval [əˈpruːvəl], s. die Billigung, der Beifall, die Zustimmung.

approve [əˈpruːv], v.a. loben, billigen; genehmigen; annehmen (*work*).

approved [əˈpruːvd], adj. anerkannt.

approximate [əˈprɔksimit], adj. ungefähr, annähernd. —v.n. & a.[əˈprɔksimeit], sich nähern.

approximation [əprɔksiˈmeiʃən], s. die Annäherung.

approximative [əˈprɔksimətiv], adj. annähernd.

appurtenance [əˈpəːtənəns], s. das (*or* der) Zubehör.

appurtenant [əˈpəːtənənt], adj. zugehörig.

apricot [ˈeiprikɔt], s. (*Bot.*) die Aprikose.

April [ˈeipril]. der April.

apron [ˈeiprən], s. die Schürze; der Schurz; — *stage*, die Vorbühne, das Proszenium.

apropos [ɑːprɔˈpou], adv. beiläufig; mit Bezug auf, diesbezüglich.

apse [æps], s. (*Archit.*) die Apsis.

apt [æpt], adj. geeignet, passend; fähig.

aptitude [ˈæptitjuːd], s. die Eignung, Fähigkeit.

aptness [ˈæptnis], s. die Angemessenheit, Eignung.

aquatic [əˈkwɔtik *or* əˈkwætik], adj. Wasser-, wasser-; — *display*, Wasserkünste. — s. (*pl.*) der Wassersport.

aqueduct [ˈækwidʌkt], s. die Wasserleitung; der Aquädukt.

aqueous [ˈeikwiəs], adj. (*Chem.*) wässerig.

aquiline [ˈækwilain], adj. adlerartig, Adler-.

Arab [ˈærəb], s. der Araber.

Arabian [əˈreibiən], adj. arabisch; — *Nights*, Tausend-und-eine-Nacht.

Arabic [ˈærəbik], adj. arabisch (*language, literature*).

arable [ˈærəbl], adj. pflügbar, bestellbar.

arbiter [ˈɑːbitə], s. der Schiedsrichter.

arbitrary [ˈɑːbitrəri], adj. willkürlich.

arbitrate [ˈɑːbitreit], v.n. vermitteln.

arbitration [ɑːbiˈtreiʃən], s. die Vermittlung; Entscheidung; (*Comm.*) Arbitrage.

arboriculture [ˈɑːbɔrikʌltʃə], s. die Baumzucht.

arbour [ˈɑːbə], s. die Laube, Gartenlaube.

arc [ɑːk], s. (*Geom.*) der Bogen; — *lamp*, die Bogenlampe; — *welding*, das Lichtschweißen.

arcade [ɑːˈkeid], s. die Arkade.

Arcadian [ɑːˈkeidiən], adj. arkadisch. — s. der Arkadier.

arch [ɑːtʃ], s. der Bogen, die Wölbung; —*way*, der Bogengang. — v.a., v.n. wölben, sich wölben. — adj. schelmisch, listig. — *prefix* oberst; erst Haupt-; —*enemy*, der Erzfeind.

archaeological [ɑːkiəˈlɔdʒikəl], adj. archäologisch.

archaeologist [ɑːkiˈɔlədʒist], s. der Archäologe.

archaeology [ɑːkiˈɔlədʒi], s. die Archäologie.

archaic [ɑːˈkeiik], adj. altertümlich.

archaism [ˈɑːkeiizm], s. der Archaismus (*style*).

archbishop [ɑːtʃˈbiʃəp], s. der Erzbischof.

archduke [ɑːtʃˈdjuːk], s. der Erzherzog.

archer [ˈɑːtʃə], s. der Bogenschütze.

archery [ˈɑːtʃəri], s. das Bogenschießen.

architect [ˈɑːkitekt], s. der Architekt, Baumeister.

architecture [ˈɑːkitektʃə], s. die Architektur, Baukunst.

archives [ˈɑːkaivz], s. pl. das Archiv.

Arctic [ˈɑːktik], adj. arktisch. — s. die Nordpolarländer, n. pl.

ardent [ˈɑːdənt], adj. heiß, glühend, brennend.

ardour [ˈɑːdə], s. die Hitze, die Inbrunst, der Eifer.

arduous [ˈɑːdjuəs], adj. schwierig; mühsam.

area [ˈɛəriə], s. das Areal (*measurement*); das Gebiet, die Zone; die Fläche (*region*).

arena [əˈriːnə], s. die Arena, der Kampfplatz.

Argentine [ˈɑːdʒəntain], adj. argentinisch. — (*Republic*), Argentinien, n.

Argentinian [ɑːdʒənˈtiniən], adj. argentinisch. — s. der Argentin(i)er.

argue [ˈɑːgjuː], v.n. disputieren, streiten; folgern, schließen.

argument [ˈɑːgjumənt], s. das Argument; (*Log.*) der Beweis; der Streit (*dispute*).

argumentative [ɑːgjuˈmentətiv], adj. streitsüchtig.

arid [ˈærid], adj. trocken, dürr.

aright [əˈrait], adv. richtig, zurecht.

arise [əˈraiz], v.n. irr. aufstehen; sich erheben; entstehen (*originate*); *arising from the minutes*, es ergibt sich aus dem Protokoll.

aristocracy [ærisˈtɔkrəsi], s. die Aristokratie, der Adel.

aristocratic [ærisˈoˈkrætik], adj. aristokratisch, adlig.

arithmetic [əˈriθmətik], s. die Arithmetik.

arithmetical [æriθ'metikəl], *adj.* arithmetisch.

ark [ɑːk], *s.* die Arche; — *of the Covenant*, die Bundeslade.

arm (1) [ɑːm], *s.* (*Anat.*) der Arm.

arm (2) [ɑːm], *s.* die Waffe; *up in —s*, in Aufruhr. — *v.a.*, *v.n.* bewaffnen, sich bewaffnen, rüsten, sich rüsten.

armament ['ɑːməmənt], *s.* die Rüstung, Bewaffnung.

armature ['ɑːmətiuə], *s.* die Armatur.

armchair ['ɑːmtʃɛə], *s.* der Lehnstuhl; der Sessel.

Armenian [ɑː'miːniən], *adj.* armenisch. — *s.* der Armenier.

armistice ['ɑːmistis], *s.* der Waffenstillstand.

armour ['ɑːmə], *s.* die Rüstung, der Harnisch; —*-plated*, gepanzert; —*ed car*, der Panzerwagen.

armourer ['ɑːmərə], *s.* der Waffenschmied.

armoury ['ɑːməri], *s.* die Rüstkammer, Waffenschmiede.

army ['ɑːmi], *s.* die Armee, das Heer.

aroma [ə'roumə], *s.* das Aroma, der Duft.

aromatic [ærə'mætik], *adj.* aromatisch. —*s.* (*Chem.*) das Aromat.

around [ə'raund], *adv.* herum, rund-, ringsherum, umher, im Kreise; *stand* —, herumstehen; *be* —, sich in der Nähe halten. — *prep.* um; bei, um . . . herum.

arouse [ə'rauz], *v.a.* aufwecken, aufrütteln.

arraignment [ə'reinmənt], *s.* die Anklage.

arrange [ə'reindʒ], *v.a.* anordnen, arrangieren, einrichten, vereinbaren.

arrangement [ə'reindʒmənt], *s.* die Anordnung; die Einrichtung; die Vereinbarung (*agreement*); (*Law*) die Vergleichung, der Vergleich.

arrant ['ærənt], *adj.* durchtrieben.

array [ə'rei], *v.a.* schmücken, aufstellen. — *s.* die Ordnung; Aufstellung.

arrears [ə'riəz], *s. pl.* der Rückstand, die Schulden.

arrest [ə'rest], *v.a.* (*Law*) festnehmen, verhaften; festhalten; aufhalten (*hinder*). — *s.* die Festnahme; die Festhaltung.

arrival [ə'raivəl], *s.* die Ankunft.

arrive [ə'raiv], *v.n.* ankommen.

arrogance ['ærəgəns], *s.* die Anmaßung, Überheblichkeit.

arrogant ['ærəgənt], *adj.* anmaßend, hochfahrend, überheblich.

arrow ['ærou], *s.* der Pfeil.

arrowroot ['ærouruːt], *s.* (*Bot.*) die Pfeilwurz.

arsenal ['ɑːsinəl], *s.* das Arsenal, Zeughaus.

arsenic ['ɑːsənik], *s.* das Arsen.

arson ['ɑːsən], *s.* die Brandstiftung.

art [ɑːt], *s.* die Kunst; *fine* —, schöne Kunst; (*Univ.*) —*s faculty*, die philosophische Fakultät; —*s* (*subject*), das humanistische Fach, die Geisteswissenschaften.

arterial [ɑː'tiəriəl], *adj.* Pulsader-, Schlagader-; — *road*, die Hauptverkehrsader, die Hauptstraße.

artery ['ɑːtəri], *s.* die Pulsader, Schlagader; der Hauptverkehrsweg.

artesian [ɑː'tiːʒən], *adj.* artesisch.

artful ['ɑːtful], *adj.* listig, schlau.

article ['ɑːtikl], *s.* (*Gram.*, *Law*, *Press*) der Artikel; der Posten (*item in list*). — *v.a. be —d to a solicitor*, bei einem Advokaten assistieren.

articulate [ɑː'tikjuleit], *v.a.* artikulieren (*pronounce clearly*). — [—lit], *adj.* deutlich (*speech*).

articulation [ɑːtikju'leiʃən], *s.* die Artikulation, deutliche Aussprache.

artifice ['ɑːtifis], *s.* der Kunstgriff, die List.

artificer [ɑː'tifisə], *s.* der Handwerker.

artificial [ɑːti'fiʃəl], *adj.* künstlich, Kunst-; — *silk*, die Kunstseide.

artillery [ɑː'tiləri], *s.* die Artillerie.

artisan [ɑːti'zæn], *s.* der Handwerker.

artist [ɑːtist], *s.* der Künstler, die Künstlerin.

artistic [ɑː'tistik], *adj.* künstlerisch.

artless ['ɑːtlis], *adj.* arglos, natürlich, naiv.

Aryan ['ɛəriən], *adj.* arisch. — *s.* der Arier.

as [æz], *adv.*, *conj.* so, als, wie, ebenso; als, während, weil; — *big* —, so groß wie; — *well* —, sowohl als auch; *such* —, wie; — *it were*, gleichsam.

asbestos [æz'bestəs], *s.* der Asbest.

ascend [ə'send], *v.a.*, *v.n.* ersteigen, besteigen; emporsteigen.

ascendancy, -ency [ə'sendənsi], *s.* der Aufstieg; der Einfluß; das Übergewicht.

ascendant, -ent [ə'sendənt], *s. in the* —, aufsteigend.

ascent [ə'sent], *s.* der Aufstieg, die Besteigung.

ascension [ə'senʃən], *s.* (*Astron.*) das Aufsteigen; *Ascension Day*, Himmelfahrt(stag).

ascertain [æsə'tein], *v.a.* in Erfahrung bringen, erkunden, feststellen.

ascertainable [æsə'teinəbl], *adj.* erkundbar, feststellbar.

ascetic [ə'setik], *adj.* asketisch.

asceticism [ə'setisizm], *s.* die Askese.

ascribe [ə'skraib], *v.a.* zuschreiben.

ascribable [ə'skraibəbl], *adj.* zuzuschreiben, zuschreibbar.

ash (1) [æʃ], *s.* (*Bot.*) die Esche.

ash (2) [æʃ], *s.* die Asche.

ashamed [ə'ʃeimd], *adj.* beschämt; *be* —, sich schämen.

ashcan ['æʃkæn] (*Am.*) *see* **dustbin**.

ashen ['æʃən], *adj.* aschgrau, aschfarben.

ashore [ə'ʃɔː], *adv.* am Land; am Ufer, ans Ufer *or* Land.

ashtray ['æʃtrei], *s.* der Aschenbecher.

Ash Wednesday [æʃ'wenzdei], *s.* der Aschermittwoch.

Asiatic [eiʃi'ætik], *adj.* asiatisch. — *s.* der Asiat.

aside [ə'said], *adv.* seitwärts, zur Seite; abseits.

ask [ɑːsk], *v.a.*, *v.n.* fragen (*question*); bitten (*request*); fordern (*demand*); einladen (*invite*).

asleep [ə'sliːp], *pred. adj.*, *adv.* schlafend, im Schlaf; eingeschlafen.

asp [æsp], *s.* (*Zool.*) die Natter.

asparagus [æs'pærəgəs], *s.* (*Bot.*) der Spargel.

aspect ['æspekt], *s.* der Anblick, die Ansicht (*view*, *angle*); der Gesichtspunkt.

aspen ['æspən], *s.* (*Bot.*) die Espe.

asperity [æs'periti], *s.* die Härte, Rauheit.

aspersion [æs'pəːʃən], *s.* die Verleumdung; Schmähung.

asphalt ['æsfælt], *s.* der Asphalt.

asphyxia [æs'fiksjə], *s.* (*Med.*) die Erstickung.

aspirant [ə'spaiərənt, 'æsp-], *s.* der Bewerber, Anwärter.

aspirate ['æspireit], *v.a.* (*Phon.*) aspirieren. — [—rit] *adj.* aspiriert. — *s.* der Hauchlaut.

aspiration [æspi'reiʃən], *s.* der Atemzug; das Streben (*striving*) ; (*Phon.*) die Aspiration.

aspire [ə'spaiə], *v.n.* streben, verlangen.

ass [æs], *s.* der Esel.

assail [ə'seil], *v.a.* angreifen, anfallen.

assailable [ə'seiləbl], *adj.* angreifbar.

assassin [ə'sæsin], *s.* der Meuchelmörder.

assassinate [ə'sæsineit], *v.a.* meuchlings ermorden.

assassination [əsæsi'neiʃən], *s.* der Meuchelmord, die Ermordung.

assault [ə'sɔːlt], *v.a.* angreifen, überfallen. — *s.* der Überfall, Angriff.

assay [ə'sei], *s.* die Metallprobe. — *v.a.* (auf Edelmetall hin) prüfen.

assemble [ə'sembl], *v.a.*, *v.n.* versammeln, sich versammeln.

assembly [ə'sembli], *s.* die Versammlung (*assemblage*); — *line*, das laufende Band, das Fließband.

assent [ə'sent], *v.n.* beistimmen (*Dat.*), billigen (*Acc.*). — *s.* die Zustimmung (zu, *Dat.*), Billigung (*Genit.*).

assert [ə'səːt], *v.a.* behaupten.

assertion [ə'səːʃən], *s.* die Behauptung.

assess [ə'ses], *v.a.* schätzen, beurteilen.

assessment [ə'sesmənt], *s.* die Beurteilung, Schätzung, Wertung.

assessor [ə'sesə], *s.* der Beurteiler, Einschätzer, Bewerter, Assessor; der Beisitzer (*second examiner*).

assets ['æsets], *s. pl.* (*Comm.*) die Aktiva; Vorzüge (*personal*).

assiduity [æsi'djuːiti], *s.* der Fleiß, die Emsigkeit.

assiduous [ə'sidjuəs], *adj.* fleißig, unablässig, emsig.

assign [ə'sain], *v.a.* zuteilen, anweisen, zuweisen (*apportion*), festsetzen (*fix*).

assignable [ə'sainəbl], *adj.* zuteilbar, bestimmbar.

assignation [æsig'neiʃən], *s.* die Zuweisung; (*Law*) die Übertragung; die Verabredung.

assignment [ə'sainmənt], *s.* die Zuweisung, Übertragung; die Aufgabe.

assimilate [ə'simileit], *v.a.*, *v.n.* assimilieren, angleichen; sich assimilieren, sich angleichen, ähnlich werden.

assist [ə'sist], *v.a.*, *v.n.* beistehen (*Dat.*), helfen (*Dat.*), unterstützen (*Acc.*).

assistance [ə'sistəns], *s.* der Beistand, die Hilfe; die Aushilfe; (*financial*) der Zuschuß.

assistant [ə'sistənt], *s.* der Assistent, Helfer.

assize [ə'saiz], *s.* die Gerichtssitzung; (*pl.*) das Schwurgericht.

associate [ə'souʃieit], *v.a.* verbinden (*link*). — *v.n.* verkehren (*company*); sich verbinden; (*Comm.*) sich vereinigen. — [—iit], *s.* (*Comm.*) der Partner.

association [əsousi'eiʃən], *s.* die Vereinigung, der Bund, Verein; die Gesellschaft; der Verkehr.

assonance ['æsənəns], *s.* (*Phon.*) die Assonanz, der Gleichlaut.

assort [ə'sɔːt], *v.a.* ordnen, aussuchen, sortieren; —*ed sweets*, gemischte Bonbons.

assortment [ə'sɔːtmənt], *s.* die Sammlung, Mischung, Auswahl.

assuage [ə'sweidʒ], *v.a.* mildern, besänftigen, stillen.

assume [ə'sjuːm], *v.a.* annehmen; übernehmen, ergreifen.

assuming [ə'sjuːmiŋ], *adj.* anmaßend; — *that*, angenommen daß . . ., gesetzt den Fall.

assumption [ə'sʌmpʃən], *s.* die Annahme (*opinion*); Übernahme (*taking up*); Aneignung (*appropriation*); *Assumption of the Blessed Virgin*, Mariä Himmelfahrt.

assurance [ə'ʃuərəns], *s.* die Versicherung; Sicherheit (*manner*).

assure [ə'ʃuə], *v.a.* versichern, sicher stellen, ermutigen.

assuredly [ə'ʃuəridli], *adv.* sicherlich, gewiß.

aster ['æstə], *s.* (*Bot.*) die Aster.

asterisk ['æstərisk], *s.* (*Typ.*) das Sternchen.

astern [ə'stəːn], *adv.* (*Naut.*) achteraus.

asthma ['æsθmə], *s.* das Asthma.

asthmatic [æsθ'mætik], *adj.* asthmatisch.

astir [ə'stəː], *adv.* wach, in Bewegung.

astonish [ə'stɔniʃ], *v.a.* in Erstaunen versetzen, verblüffen.

astonishment [ə'stɔniʃmənt], *s.* das Erstaunen, die Verwunderung; die Bestürzung.

astound [ə'staund], *v.a.* in Erstaunen versetzen, bestürzen.

astounding [ə'staundiŋ], *adj.* erstaunlich, verblüffend.

astral ['æstrəl], *adj.* Stern(en)-, gestirnt.

astray [ə'strei], *pred. adj., adv.* irre;
go —, sich verirren; (*fig.*) abschweifen.
astride[ə'straid],*pred.adj.,adv.*rittlings.
astringent [ə'strindʒənt], *adj.* zusam-
menziehend.
astrologer [ə'strɔlədʒə], *s.* der Sterndeuter, Astrolog(e).
astrological [æstrə'lɔdʒikəl], *adj.* astro-
logisch.
astrology [æ'strɔlədʒi], *s.* die Astrologie,
Sterndeuterei.
astronaut['æstrənɔ:t], *s.* der Astronaut.
astronomer [ə'strɔnəmə], *s.* der Astronom.
astronomical[æstrə'nɔmikəl],*adj.*astro-
nomisch.
astronomy [ə'strɔnəmi], *s.* die Astro-
nomie, Sternkunde.
astute [ə'stju:t], *adj.* listig, schlau.
astuteness [ə'stju:tnis], *s.* die Schlauheit, Listigkeit, der Scharfsinn.
asunder [ə'sʌndə], *adv.* auseinander,
entzwei.
asylum [ə'sailəm], *s.* das Asyl, der
Zufluchtsort (*refuge*); *lunatic* —, das
Irrenhaus.
at [æt], *prep.* an; auf; bei, für; in,
nach; mit, gegen; um, über; von,
aus, zu; — *my expense*, auf meine
Kosten; — *all*, überhaupt; — *first*,
zuerst; — *last*, zuletzt, endlich; —
peace, in Frieden; *what are you driving
—?* worauf wollen sie hinaus?
atheism ['eiθiizm], *s.* der Atheismus.
atheist ['eiθiist], *s.* der Atheist.
atheistic [eiθi'istik], *adj.* atheistisch,
gottlos.
Athens ['æθənz]. Athen, *n.*
Athenian [ə'θi:njən], *s.* der Athener.
— *adj.* athenisch.
athlete ['æθli:t], *s.* der Athlet.
athletic [æθ'letik], *adj.* athletisch.
athletics [æθ'letiks], *s. pl.* die Leicht-
athletik, Athletik.
Atlantic (Ocean) [ət'læntik ('ouʃən)].
der Atlantik.
atlas ['ætləs], *s.* der Atlas.
atmosphere ['ætməsfiə], *s.* die Atmo-
sphäre.
atmospheric(al) [ætməs'ferik(əl)], *adj.*
atmosphärisch. — *s.* (*pl.*) atmo-
sphärische Störungen, *f. pl.*
atoll[ə'tɔl], *s.* die Koralleninsel,dasAtoll.
atom ['ætəm], *s.* das Atom.
atomic [ə'tɔmik], *adj.* (*Phys.*) Atom-,
atomisch, atomar; (*theory*) atomi-
stisch; — *bomb*, die Atombombe; —
pile, der Atomreaktor; — *armament*,
die atomare Aufrüstung.
atone [ə'toun], *v.n.* sühnen, büßen.
atonement [ə'tounmənt], *s.* die Buße,
Sühne, Versöhnung.
atonic [ei'tonik], *adj.* tonlos, unbetont.
atrocious [ə'trouʃəs], *adj.* gräßlich,
schrecklich, entsetzlich.
atrocity [ə'trɔsiti], *s.* die Gräßlichkeit,
Grausamkeit, Greueltat.
atrophy ['ætrəfi], *s.* (*Med.*) die Abmagerung, Atrophie. — ['ætrəfai], *v.n.*
absterben, auszehren.

attach [ə'tætʃ], *v.a.* anheften, beilegen,
anhängen; (*fig.*) beimessen (*attribute*).
attachment [ə'tætʃmənt], *s.* das Anhaften (*sticking to*, an, *Acc.*); das
Anhängsel (*appendage*); die Freundschaft (*to*, für, *Acc.*); die Anhänglich-
keit (*loyalty*, an, *Acc.*).
attack [ə'tæk], *v.a.* angreifen. — *s.* die
Attacke, der Angriff; (*Med.*) der
Anfall.
attain [ə'tein], *v.a.* erreichen, erlangen.
attainable [ə'teinəbl], *adj.* erreichbar.
attainment [ə'teinmənt], *s.* die Erlangung, Erreichung; Errungenschaft;
(*pl.*) Kenntnisse, *f. pl.*
attempt [ə'tempt], *s.* der Versuch. —
v.a. versuchen.
attend [ə'tend], *v.a., v.n.* begleiten,
anwesend sein (*be present*, at, bei,
Dat.); beiwohnen (*be present as
guest*); zuhören (*listen to*); bedienen
(*customer*); behandeln (*patient*).
attendance [ə'tendəns], *s.* die Begleitung (*accompaniment*); die Anwesenheit (*presence*); die Zuhörerschaft
(*audience*); *to be in* —, Dienst tun
(*at*, bei); anwesend sein (*be present*).
attendant [ə'tendənt], *s.* der Diener,
Wärter.
attention [ə'tenʃən], *s.* die Aufmerksamkeit, Achtung.
attentive [ə'tentiv], *adj.* aufmerksam.
attenuate [ə'tenjueit], *v.a.* verdünnen
(*dilute*). — *v.n.* abmagern.
attest [ə'test], *v.a.* attestieren, bezeugen,
bescheinigen.
attestation [ætes'teiʃən], *s.* die Bescheinigung; das Zeugnis.
Attic ['ætik], *adj.* attisch, klassisch.
attic ['ætik], *s.* die Dachkammer, die
Dachstube.
attire [ə'taiə], *v.a.* ankleiden, kleiden.
— *s.* die Kleidung.
attitude ['ætitju:d], *s.* die Haltung,
Stellung (*toward*, zu), Einstellung.
attorney [ə'tə:ni], *s.* der Anwalt;
Attorney–General, der Kronanwalt;
(*Am.*) der Staatsanwalt; — *at law*,
Rechtsanwalt.
attract [ə'trækt], *v.a.* anziehen.
attraction [ə'trækʃən], *s.* die Anziehung; der Reiz (*appeal*); die Anzie-
hungskraft.
attractive [ə'træktiv], *adj.* anziehend,
reizvoll.
attribute [ə'tribju:t], *v.a.* zuschreiben,
beimessen. — *s.* ['ætribju:t], (*Gram.*)
das Attribut, die Eigenschaft.
attributive [ə'tribjutiv], *adj.* (*Gram.*)
attributiv; beilegend.
attrition [ə'triʃən], *s.* die Zermürbung,
Aufreibung, Reue.
attune [ə'tju:n], *v.a.* (*Mus.*) stimmen,
anpassen (*adapt to*, an, *Acc.*).
auburn ['ɔ:bə:n], *adj.* rotbraun.
auction ['ɔ:kʃən], *s.* die Auktion, die
Versteigerung.
auctioneer [ɔ:kʃə'niə], *s.* der Auk-
tionator, Versteigerer.

audacious

audacious [ɔ:'deiʃəs], *adj.* waghalsig, kühn, dreist.

audacity [ɔ:'dæsiti], *s.* die Kühnheit (*valour*); Frechheit (*impudence*).

audible ['ɔ:dibl], *adj.* hörbar.

audibility [ɔ:di'biliti], *s.* die Hörbarkeit, Vernehmbarkeit.

audience ['ɔ:djəns], *s.* die Audienz (*of the Pope*, beim Papst); (*Theat.*) das Publikum; (*listeners*) die Zuhörer.

audit ['ɔ:dit], *s.* die Rechnungsprüfung, Revision. — *v.a.* revidieren, prüfen.

auditor ['ɔ:ditə], *s.* der Rechnungsrevisor, Buchprüfer.

auditory ['ɔ:ditəri], *adj.* Gehör-, Hör-.

auditorium [ɔ:di'tɔ:riəm], *s.* der Hörsaal, Vortragssaal.

auger ['ɔ:gə], *s.* der (große) Bohrer.

aught [ɔ:t], *pron.* (*obs.*) irgend etwas (*opp. to naught*).

augment [ɔ:g'ment], *v.a., v.n.* vermehren, vergrößern; zunehmen.

augmentation [ɔ:gmen'teiʃən], *s.* die Vergrößerung, Erhöhung, Zunahme.

augur ['ɔ:gə], *v.a.* weissagen, prophezeien.

August ['ɔ:gəst]. der August.

august [ɔ:'gʌst], *adj.* erhaben.

aunt [ɑ:nt], *s.* die Tante.

aurora [ɔ:'rɔ:rə], *s.* die Morgenröte.

auscultation [ɔ:skəl'teiʃən], *s.* (*Med.*) die Auskultation, Untersuchung.

auspices ['ɔ:spisiz], *s.* die Auspizien.

auspicious [ɔ:'spiʃəs], *adj.* unter glücklichem Vorzeichen, verheißungsvoll, günstig.

austere [ɔ:s'tiə], *adj.* streng, ernst, schmucklos.

austerity [ɔ:s'teriti], *s.* die Strenge.

Australian [ə'streiljən], *adj.* australisch. — *s.* der Australier.

Austrian ['ɔ:striən], *adj.* österreichisch. — *s.* der Österreicher.

authentic [ɔ:'θentik], *adj.* authentisch, echt.

authenticity [ɔ:θen'tisiti], *s.* die Authentizität, Echtheit.

author, authoress ['ɔ:θə, ɔ:θər'es], *s.* der Autor, die Autorin; der Verfasser, die Verfasserin.

authoritative [ɔ:'θɒritətiv], *adj.* autoritativ, maßgebend.

authority [ɔ:'θɒriti], *s.* die Autorität, Vollmacht (*power of attorney*); das Ansehen; *the authorities*, die Behörden.

authorization [ɔ:θərai'zeiʃən], *s.* die Bevollmächtigung, Befugnis.

authorize ['ɔ:θəraiz], *v.a.* autorisieren, bevollmächtigen, berechtigen.

authorship ['ɔ:θəʃip], *s.* die Autorschaft.

autobiographical [ɔ:tobaiə'græfikl], *adj.* autobiographisch.

autobiography [ɔ:tobai'ɔgrəfi], *s.* die Autobiographie.

autocracy [ɔ:'tɔkrəsi], *s.* die Selbstherrschaft.

autocrat ['ɔ:tokræt], *s.* der Autokrat, Selbstherrscher.

autograph ['ɔ:togræf, -grɑ:f], *s.* die eigene Handschrift, Unterschrift; das Autogramm.

automatic [ɔ:to'mætik], *adj.* automatisch.

automatize [ɔ:'tɔmətaiz], *v.a.* automatisieren, auf Automation umstellen.

automation [ɔ:to'meiʃən], *s.* (*Engin.*) die Automation; Automatisierung.

automaton [ɔ:'tɔmətən], *s.* der Automat.

automobile ['ɔ:tomobi:l], *s.* der Kraftwagen, das Auto.

autonomous [ɔ:'tɔnəməs], *adj.* autonom, unabhängig.

autonomy [ɔ:'tɔnəmi], *s.* die Autonomie, Unabhängigkeit.

autopsy ['ɔ:tɔpsi], *s.* die Autopsie; Obduktion, Leichenschau.

autumn ['ɔ:təm], *s.* der Herbst.

autumnal [ɔ:'tʌmnəl], *adj.* herbstlich.

auxiliary [ɔ:g'ziljəri], *adj.* Hilfs-.

avail [ə'veil], *v.n.* nützen, helfen, von Vorteil sein. — *v.r.* — *o.s of a th.*, sich einer Sache bedienen. — *s.* der Nutzen; *of no* —, nutzlos.

available [ə'veiləbl], *adj.* vorrätig, verfügbar, zur Verfügung (stehend).

avalanche ['ævəlɑ:nʃ], *s.* die Lawine.

avarice ['ævəris], *s.* der Geiz, die Habsucht, Gier.

avaricious [ævə'riʃəs], *adj.* geizig, habsüchtig, habgierig.

avenge [ə'vendʒ], *v.a.* rächen.

avenue ['ævənju:], *s.* die Allee; der Zugang.

average ['ævəridʒ], *adj.* durchschnittlich; *not more than* —, mäßig. — *s.* der Durchschnitt; *on an* —, durchschnittlich, im Durchschnitt. — *v.a.* den Durchschnitt nehmen.

averse [ə'və:s], *adj.* abgeneigt (*to, Dat.*).

aversion [ə'və:ʃən], *s.* die Abneigung, der Widerwille.

avert [ə'və:t], *v.a.* abwenden.

aviary ['eiviəri], *s.* das Vogelhaus.

aviation [əivi'eiʃən], *s.* das Flugwesen.

aviator ['eivieitə], *s.* der Flieger.

avid ['ævid], *adj.* begierig (*of or for*, nach).

avidity [æ'viditi], *s.* die Begierde, Gier (*for*, nach).

avoid [ə'vɔid], *v.a.* vermeiden.

avoidable [ə'vɔidəbl], *adj.* vermeidlich, vermeidbar.

avoidance [ə'vɔidəns], *s.* die Vermeidung, das Meiden.

avow [ə'vau], *v.a.* eingestehen, anerkennen (*acknowledge*).

avowal [ə'vauəl], *s.* das Geständnis; die Erklärung.

await [ə'weit], *v.a.* erwarten, warten auf (*Acc.*).

awake(n) [ə'weik(ən)], *v.a., v.n. irr.* aufwecken, wecken; aufwachen (*wake up*). — *adj. wide awake*, schlau, auf der Hut.

award [ə'wɔːd], *s.* die Zuerkennung, Auszeichnung; Belohnung (*money*); (*Law*) das Urteil. — *v.a.* zuerkennen; — *damages*, Schadenersatz zusprechen; verleihen (*grant*).

aware [ə'weə], *adj.* gewahr, bewußt (*Genit.*).

away [ə'wei], *adv.* weg; hinweg, fort.

awe [ɔː], *s.* die Ehrfurcht; Furcht.

awful ['ɔːful], *adj.* furchtbar, schrecklich.

awhile [ə'wail], *adv.* eine Weile, eine kurze Zeit.

awkward ['ɔːkwəd], *adv.* ungeschickt, unbeholfen, ungelenk; unangenehm (*difficult*); — *situation*, peinliche Situation, Lage.

awkwardness ['ɔkwədnis], *s.* die Ungeschicklichkeit, Unbeholfenheit.

awl [ɔːl], *s.* die Ahle, der Pfriem.

awning ['ɔːniŋ], *s.* die Plane; das Sonnendach.

awry [ə'rai], *adj.* schief, verkehrt.

axe [æks], *s.* die Axt, das Beil.

axiom ['æksiəm], *s.* das Axiom, der Satz, Lehrsatz, Grundsatz.

axiomatic [æksiə'mætik], *adj.* axiomatisch, grundsätzlich; gewiß.

axis ['æksis], *s.* die Achse.

axle [æksl], *s.* die Achse.

ay(e) (1) [ai], *adv.* ja, gewiß.

ay(e) (2) [ei], *adv.* ständig, ewig.

azalea [ə'zeiliə], *s.* (*Bot.*) die Azalie.

azure ['æʒə, 'eiʒə], *adj.* himmelblau, azurblau.

B

B [biː]. das B; (*Mus.*) das H.

baa [baː], *v.n.* blöken.

babble [bæbl], *v.n.* schwatzen, schwätzen. — *s.* das Geschwätz; das Murmeln (*water*).

babe, baby [beib, 'beibi], *s.* der Säugling, das Baby, das kleine Kind, das Kindlein.

baboon [bə'buːn], *s.* (*Zool.*) der Pavian.

bachelor ['bætʃələ], *s.* der Junggeselle; (*Univ.*) Bakkalaureus.

back [bæk], *s.* der Rücken, die Rückseite. — *adj.* Hinter-, Rück-; — *door*, die Hintertür; — *stairs*, die Hintertreppe. — *adv.* rückwärts, zurück. — *v.a.* unterstützen; (*Comm.*) indossieren; gegenzeichnen; wetten auf (*Acc.*) (*bet on*).

backbone ['bækboun], *s.* (*Anat.*) das Rückgrat.

backfire ['bækfaiə], *s.* (*Motor.*) die Frühzündung; (*gun*) die Fehlzündung. — [bæk'faiə], *v.n.* (*Motor.*) frühzünden; (*gun*) fehlzünden.

backgammon [bæk'gæmən], *s.* das Bordspiel, das Puffspiel.

background ['bækgraund], *s.* der Hintergrund.

backhand ['bækhænd], *s.* (*Sport*) die Rückhand; *a* —*ed compliment*, eine verblümte Grobheit.

backside [bæk'said], *s.* (*vulg.*) der Hintere.

backslide [bæk'slaid], *v.n.* abfallen, abtrünnig werden.

backward ['bækwəd], *adj.* zurückgeblieben. **backward(s)** *adv.* rückwärts, zurück.

backwater ['bækwɔːtə], *s.* das Stauwasser.

backwoods ['bækwudz], *s. pl.* der Hinterwald.

bacon ['beikən], *s.* der Speck.

bad [bæd], *adj.* schlecht, schlimm; böse (*immoral*); (*coll.*) unwohl (*unwell*); *not too* —, ganz gut; *from* — *to worse*, immer schlimmer; — *language*, unanständige Worte, das Fluchen; — *luck*, Unglück, Pech; *want* —*ly*, nötig brauchen.

badge [bædʒ], *s.* das Abzeichen; Kennzeichen (*mark*).

badger (1) ['bædʒə], *s.* (*Zool.*) der Dachs.

badger (2) ['bædʒə], *v.a.* ärgern, stören, belästigen.

badness ['bædnis], *s.* die Schlechtigkeit, Bosheit, das schlechte Wesen, die Bösartigkeit.

baffle [bæfl], *v.a.* täuschen, verblüffen. — *s.* (*obs.*) die Täuschung; (*Build.*) Verkleidung; (*Elec.*) Verteilerplatte.

bag [bæg], *s.* der Sack, Beutel; die Tasche; *shopping* —, Einkaufstasche; *travelling* —, Reisehandtasche; *v.a.* einstecken, als Beute behalten (*hunt*).

bagatelle [bægə'tel], *s.* die Bagatelle, Lappalie, Kleinigkeit; das Kugelspiel (*pin-table ball-game*).

baggage ['bægidʒ], *s.* das Gepäck.

bagging ['bægiŋ], *s.* die Sackleinwand.

baggy ['bægi], *adj.* ungebügelt; bauschig.

bagpipe ['bægpaip], *s.* der Dudelsack.

bagpiper ['bægpaipə], *s.* der Dudelsackpfeifer.

bail [beil], *s.* der Bürge; die Bürgschaft; *stand* —, für einen bürgen; *allow* —, Bürgschaft zulassen. — *v.a.* Bürgschaft leisten; — *out*, (durch Kaution) in Freiheit setzen.

bailiff ['beilif], *s.* der Amtmann; Gerichtsvollzieher.

bait [beit], *s.* der Köder. — *v.a.* ködern, locken (*attract*).

baiter ['beitə], *s.* der Hetzer, Verfolger.

baiting ['beitiŋ], *s.* die Hetze.

bake [beik], *v.a., v.n.* backen.

baker ['beikə], *s.* der Bäcker; —*'s dozen*, 13 Stück.

bakery ['beikəri], *s.* die Bäckerei.

baking ['beikiŋ], *s.* das Backen.

balance

balance ['bæləns], s. die Waage (scales); die Bilanz (audit); das Gleichgewicht (equilibrium); (Comm.) der Saldo, der Überschuß (profit); die Unruhe (watch). — v.a., v.n. wägen, abwägen (scales); ausgleichen (— up), einen Saldo ziehen (— an account); ins Gleichgewicht bringen (bring into equilibrium).

balcony ['bælkəni], s. der Balkon, der Söller (castle); Altan (villa).

bald [bɔːld], adj. kahl, haarlos; (fig.) armselig, schmucklos.

baldness ['bɔːldnis], s. die Kahlheit (hairlessness); Nacktheit (bareness).

bale (1) [beil], s. der Ballen.

bale (2) [beil], v.n. — out, abspringen; aussteigen.

Balearic Islands [bæli'ærik ailəndz], s. pl. die Balearen, Balearischen Inseln. — adj. balearisch.

baleful ['beilful], adj. unheilvoll.

balk [bɔːk], v.a. aufhalten, hemmen. — v.n. scheuen, zurückscheuen (at, vor).

ball (1) [bɔːl], s. der Ball; die Kugel; — cock, der Absperrhahn; —point pen, der Kugelschreiber.

ball (2) [bɔːl], s. der Ball (dance).

ballad ['bæləd], s. die Ballade.

ballast ['bæləst], s. der Ballast.

ballet ['bælei], s. das Ballett.

balloon [bə'luːn], s. der Ballon.

ballot ['bælət], s. die geheime Wahl, Abstimmung; — -box, die Wahlurne; — -paper, der Stimmzettel. —v. n. wählen, abstimmen.

balm [baːm], s. der Balsam.

balsam ['bɔlsəm], s. der Balsam.

Baltic ['bɔːltik], adj. baltisch. — (Sea), die Ostsee; — Provinces, das Baltikum,

balustrade ['bæləstreid], s. die Balustrade, das Geländer.

bamboo [bæm'buː], s. (Bot.) der Bambus.

bamboozle [bæm'buːzl], v.a. verblüffen; beschwindeln (cheat).

ban [bæn], v.a. bannen, verbannen; verbieten. — s. der Bann, das Verbot.

banal [bæ'næl, 'beinəl], adj. banal.

banality [bæ'næliti], s. die Banalität, Trivialität.

banana [bə'naːnə], s. die Banane.

band [bænd], s. das Band (ribbon etc.); (Mus.) die Kapelle; die Bande (robbers). — v.n. — together, sich verbinden; sich zusammentun.

bandage ['bændidʒ], s. der Verband, die Bandage.

bandit ['bændit], s. der Bandit.

bandmaster ['bændmaːstə], s. der Kapellmeister.

bandstand ['bændstænd], s. der Musikpavillon.

bandy ['bændi], adj. — -legged, krummbeinig. — v.a. — words, Worte wechseln; streiten.

bane [bein], s. das Gift; (fig.) Verderben.

baneful ['beinful], adj. verderblich.

bang [bæŋ], s. der Knall (explosion), das Krachen (clap). — v.n. knallen, krachen lassen. — v.a. — a door, eine Türe zuwerfen.

banish ['bæniʃ], v.a. verbannen, bannen.

banisters ['bænistəz], s. pl. das Treppengeländer.

bank [bæŋk], s. (Fin.) die Bank; das Ufer (river); der Damm (dam). — v.a. einlegen, einzahlen, auf die Bank bringen (sum of money); eindämmen (dam up). — v.n. ein Konto haben (have an account, with, bei).

banker ['bæŋkə], s. der Bankier.

bankrupt ['bæŋkrʌpt], adj. bankrott; zahlungsunfähig; (coll.) pleite.

bankruptcy ['bæŋkrʌptsi], s. der Bankrott.

banns [bænz], s. pl. das Heiratsaufgebot.

banquet ['bæŋkwit], s. das Banquet, Festessen.

bantam ['bæntəm], s. das Bantamhuhn, Zwerghuhn; (Boxing) — -weight, das Bantamgewicht.

banter ['bæntə], v.n. scherzen, necken. — s. das Scherzen, der Scherz.

baptism ['bæptizm], s. die Taufe.

Baptist ['bæptist], s. der Täufer; Baptist.

baptize [bæp'taiz], v.a. taufen.

bar [baː], s. die Barre, Stange (pole); der Riegel; Balken; Schlagbaum (barrier); (fig.) das Hindernis; der Schanktisch (in public house); prisoner at the —, Gefangener vor (dem) Gericht; call to the —, zur Gerichtsadvokatur (or als Anwalt) zulassen; (Mus.) der Takt. — v.a. verriegeln (door); (fig.) hindern (from action); verbieten (prohibit); ausschließen (exclude).

barb [baːb], s. die Spitze (of wire); der Widerhaken (hook).

barbed [baːbd], adj. spitzig; — remark, die spitze Bemerkung; — wire, der Stacheldraht.

barbarian [baː'bɛəriən], s. der Barbar. — adj. barbarisch.

barbarism ['baːbərizm], s. die Roheit; der Barbarismus.

barber ['baːbə], s. der Barbier, Friseur.

barberry ['baːbəri], s. (Bot.) die Berberitze.

bard [baːd], s. der Barde, Sänger.

bare [bɛə], adj. nackt, bloß; — -headed, barhäuptig. — v.a. entblößen.

barefaced ['bɛəfeisd], adj. schamlos.

barely ['bɛəli], adv. kaum.

bargain ['baːgin], s. der Kauf, Gelegenheitskauf; der Handel (trading); das Geschäft; into the —, noch dazu, obendrein. — v.n. feilschen, handeln (haggle) (for, um).

barge [baːdʒ], s. der Lastkahn, die Barke. — v.n. (coll.) — in, stören.

bargee [baː'dʒiː], s. der Flußschiffer, Bootsmann.

baritone ['bæritoun], s. (Mus.) der Bariton.

bark (1) [baːk], s. die Rinde (of tree).
bark (2) [baːk], v.n. bellen (dog); — up the wrong tree, auf falscher Fährte sein. — s. das Gebell (dog).
barley ['baːli], s. (Bot.) die Gerste.
barmaid ['baːmeid], s. die Kellnerin.
barman ['baːmən], s. der Kellner.
barn [baːn], s. die Scheune; — owl, die Schleiereule.
barnacle ['baːnəkl], s. die Entenmuschel; die Klette.
barnstormer ['baːnstɔːmə], s. der Schmierenkomödiant.
barometer [bə'rɔmitə], s. das Barometer.
baron ['bærən], s. der Baron, Freiherr.
barony ['bærəni], s. die Baronswürde.
baroque [bə'rɔk], adj. barock. — s. das Barock.
barque [baːk], s. die Bark.
barracks ['bærəks], s. pl. die Kaserne.
barrage ['bæraːʒ, 'bæridʒ], s. das Sperrfeuer (firing); das Wehr, der Damm.
barrel ['bærəl], s. das Faß (vat), die Tonne (tun); der Gewehrlauf (rifle); die Trommel (cylinder); — organ, die Drehorgel.
barren ['bærən], adj. unfruchtbar, dürr.
barrenness ['bærənnis], s. die Unfruchtbarkeit.
barricade [bæri'keid], s. die Barrikade. — v.a. verrammeln, verschanzen.
barrier ['bæriə], s. die Barriere, der Schlagbaum; das Hindernis; (Railw.) die Schranke.
barrister ['bæristə], s. der Rechtsanwalt, Advokat.
barrow (1) ['bærou], s. der Schubkarren, Handkarren; — -boy, der Höker, Schnellverkäufer.
barrow (2) ['bærou], s. (Archaeol.) das Hünengrab, Heldengrab.
barter ['baːtə], v.a. tauschen, austauschen. — s. der Tauschhandel.
Bartholomew [baː'θɔləmjuː]. Bartholomäus, m.; Massacre of St. Bartholomew's Eve, Bartholomäusnacht, Pariser Bluthochzeit.
basalt ['bæsɔːlt, bæ'sɔːlt], s. der Basalt.
base [beis], s. die Basis, Grundlage; der Sockel; (Chem.) die Base. — adj. niedrig, gemein; (Metall.) unedel. — v.a. basieren, beruhen, fundieren (upon, auf).
baseless ['beislis], adj. grundlos.
basement ['beismənt], s. das Kellergeschoß.
baseness ['beisnis], s. die Gemeinheit, Niedrigkeit.
bashful ['bæfful], adj. verschämt, schamhaft, schüchtern.
basic ['beisik], adj. grundlegend.
basin ['beisən], s. das Becken.
basis ['beisis], s. die Basis, Grundlage.
bask [baːsk], v.n. sich sonnen.
basket ['baːskit], s. der Korb.
bass (1) [beis], s. (Mus.) der Baß, die Baßstimme.

bass (2) [bæs], s. (Zool.) der Barsch.
bassoon [bə'suːn], s. (Mus.) das Fagott.
bastard ['bæstəd], s. der Bastard.
baste [beist], v.a. mit Fett begießen (roast meat); (coll.) prügeln.
bastion ['bæstiən], s. die Bastion, Festung, das Bollwerk.
bat (1) [bæt], s. die Fledermaus.
bat (2) [bæt], s. der Schläger. — v.n. (den Ball) schlagen; (cricket) am Schlagen sein (be batting).
batch [bætʃ], s. der Stoß (pile); die Menge (people); (Mil.) der Trupp.
bath [baːθ], s. das Bad; (Am.) —robe, der Schlafrock, Bademantel; — tub, die Badewanne.
bathe [beið], v.n. baden; bathing pool, das Schwimmbad; bathing suit, der Badeanzug.
batman ['bætmən], s. der Offiziersbursche.
baton ['bætən], s. der Stab.
batsman ['bætsmən], s. der Schläger (cricket).
batten [bætn], s. die Holzlatte. — v.a. mästen, füttern. — v.n. fett werden.
batter ['bætə], s. der Schlagteig. — v.a. schlagen, zertrümmern; —ing ram, (Mil.) der Sturmbock.
battery ['bætəri], s. die Batterie.
battle [bætl], s. die Schlacht; — cruiser, der Schlachtkreuzer; —ship, das Schlachtschiff. — v.n. kämpfen (for, um).
Bavarian [bə'vɛəriən], adj. bayrisch. — s. der Bayer.
bawl [bɔːl], v.n. plärren, schreien.
bay (1) [bei], adj. rötlich braun.
bay (2) [bei], s. die Bucht, Bai; — window, das Erkerfenster.
bay (3) [bei], s. keep at —, in Schach halten, stand at —, sich zur Wehr setzen.
bay (4) [bei], s. (Bot.) der Lorbeer.
bay (5) [bei], v.n. bellen, heulen; — for the moon, das Unmögliche wollen.
bayonet ['beiənet], s. das Bajonett.
bazaar [bə'zaː], s. der Basar.
be [biː], v.n. irr. sein, existieren; sich befinden; vorhanden sein; — off, sich fortmachen (move); ungenießbar sein (meat, food); nicht mehr da sein (— off the menu).
beach [biːtʃ], s. der Strand, das Gestade.
beacon ['biːkən], s. das Leuchtfeuer; der Leuchtturm; das Lichtsignal.
bead [biːd], s. das Tröpfchen (drop); die Perle (pearl); (pl.) die Perlschnur; der Rosenkranz.
beadle [biːdl], s. (Univ.) der Pedell; (Eccl.) Kirchendiener.
beagle [biːgl], s. der Jagdhund, Spürhund.
beak [biːk], s. der Schnabel.
beaker ['biːkə], s. der Becher.
beam [biːm], s. der Balken (wood); der Strahl (ray), Glanz. — v.n. strahlen.

319

bean

bean [biːn], *s.* (*Bot.*) die Bohne; *not* ɹ —, keinen Heller *or* Pfennig.

bear (1) [bɛə], *s.* (*Zool.*) der Bär.

bear (2) [bɛə], *v.a. irr.* tragen, ertragen; gebären (*a child*); hegen (*sorrow etc.*). — *v.n.* — *upon*, drücken auf (*pressure*), Einfluß haben (*effect*); — *up*, geduldig sein.

bearable ['bɛərəbl], *adj.* tragbar, erträglich.

beard [biəd], *s.* der Bart. — *v.a.* trotzen (*Dat.*).

bearded ['biədid], *adj.* bärtig.

bearer ['bɛərə], *s.* der Träger, Überbringer.

bearing ['bɛəriŋ], *s.* das Benehmen, die Haltung (*manner*); (*pl.*) (*Geog.*) die Richtung; *lose o.'s* —*s*, sich verlaufen; *ball* —*s*, (*Engin.*) das Kugellager.

bearpit ['bɛəpit], *s.* der Bärenzwinger.

beast [biːst], *s.* das Tier; die Bestie.

beastliness ['biːstlinis], *s.* das tierische Benehmen; die Grausamkeit (*cruelty*); die Gemeinheit.

beastly ['biːstli], *adj.* grausam, (*coll.*) schrecklich.

beat [biːt], *s.* der Schlag, das Schlagen; (*Mus.*) der Takt; die Runde, das Revier (*patrol district*). — *v.a. irr.* schlagen; — *time*, den Takt schlagen; — *carpets*, Teppich klopfen. — *v.n.* — *it*, sich davonmachen.

beater ['biːtə], *s.* (*Hunt.*) der Treiber.

beatify [biːˈætifai], *v.a.* seligsprechen.

beau [bou], *s.* der Stutzer, Geck.

beautiful ['bjuːtiful], *adj.* schön.

beautify ['bjuːtifai], *v.a.* schön machen, verschönern.

beauty ['bjuːti], *s.* die Schönheit; — *salon*, der Schönheitssalon; *Sleeping Beauty*, das Dornröschen.

beaver ['biːvə], *s.* (*Zool.*) der Biber.

becalm [biˈkɑːm], *v.a.* besänftigen.

because [biˈkɔz], *conj.* weil, da; — *of*, wegen, um ... willen.

beck [bek], *s.* der Wink; *be at s.o.'s* — *and call*, jemandem zu Gebote stehen.

beckon ['bekən], *v.a., v.n.* winken, heranwinken, zuwinken (*Dat.*).

become [biˈkʌm], *v.n. irr.* werden. — *v.a.* anstehen, sich schicken, passen (*Dat.*).

becoming [biˈkʌmiŋ], *adj.* passend, kleidsam.

bed [bed], *s.* das Bett; Beet (*flowers*); (*Geol.*) das Lager, die Schicht. — *v.a.* betten, einbetten.

bedaub [biˈdɔːb], *v.a.* beflecken, beschmieren.

bedding ['bediŋ], *s.* das Bettzeug.

bedevil [biˈdevəl], *v.a.* behexen, verhexen.

bedew [biˈdjuː], *v.a.* betauen.

bedlam ['bedləm], *s.* (*coll.*) das Irrenhaus; *this is* —, die Hölle ist los.

Bedouin ['beduin], *s.* der Beduine.

bedpost ['bedpoust], *s.* der Bettpfosten.

bedraggle [biˈdrægl], *v.a.* beschmutzen.

bedridden ['bedridn], *adj.* bettlägerig, ans Bett gefesselt.

bedroom ['bedruːm], *s.* das Schlafzimmer.

bedtime ['bedtaim], *s.* die Schlafenszeit.

bee [biː], *s.* (*Ent.*) die Biene; *have a* — *in o.'s bonnet*, einen Vogel haben.

beech [biːtʃ], *s.* (*Bot.*) die Buche.

beef [biːf], *s.* das Rindfleisch; — *tea*, die Fleischbrühe.

beehive ['biːhaiv], *s.* der Bienenkorb.

beeline ['biːlain], *s.* die Luftlinie, gerade Linie; *make a* — *for s.th.*, schnurstracks auf etwas losgehen.

beer [biə], *s.* das Bier; *small* —, Dünnbier, (*fig.*) unbedeutend.

beet [biːt], *s.* (*Bot.*) die Runkelrübe; *sugar* —, die Zuckerrübe.

beetle [biːtl], *s.* (*Ent.*) der Käfer; — *brows*, buschige Augenbrauen.

beetroot ['biːtruːt], *s.* (*Bot.*) die rote Rübe.

befall [biˈfɔːl], *v.a. irr.* widerfahren (*Dat.*). — *v.n.* zustoßen (*happen*, *Dat.*).

befit [biˈfit], *v.a.* sich geziemen, sich gebühren.

befog [biˈfɔg], *v.a.* in Nebel hüllen; umnebeln.

before [biˈfɔː], *adv.* vorn; voraus, voran; (*previously*) vorher, früher; (*already*) bereits, schon. — *prep.* vor. — *conj.* bevor, ehe.

beforehand [biˈfɔːhænd], *adv.* im voraus, vorher.

befoul [biˈfaul], *v.a.* beschmutzen.

befriend [biˈfrend], *v.a.* befreunden, unterstützen (*support*).

beg [beg], *v.a., v.n.* betteln (um, *for*); ersuchen, bitten (*request*).

beget [biˈget], *v.a. irr.* zeugen.

beggar ['begə], *s.* der Bettler.

begin [biˈgin], *v.a., v.n. irr.* beginnen, anfangen.

beginner [biˈginə], *s.* der Anfänger.

beginning [biˈginiŋ], *s.* der Anfang.

begone! [biˈgɔn], *interj.* hinweg! fort! mach dich fort!

begrudge [biˈgrʌdʒ], *v.a.* nicht gönnen, mißgönnen.

beguile [biˈgail], *v.a.* bestricken, betrügen; — *the time*, die Zeit vertreiben.

behalf [biˈhɑːf], *s. on* — *of*, um ... (*Genit.*) willen; im Interesse von, im Namen von.

behave [biˈheiv], *v.n.* sich benehmen, sich betragen.

behaviour [biˈheivjə], *s.* das Benehmen, Gebaren.

behead [biˈhed], *v.a.* enthaupten.

behind [biˈhaind], *adv.* hinten, zurück, hinterher. — *prep.* hinter.

behindhand [biˈhaindhænd], *adj., adv.* im Rückstand (*in arrears*); zurück (*backward*).

behold [biˈhould], *v.a. irr.* ansehen; er blicken; *lo and* —! siehe da!

beholden [biˈhouldən], *adj.* verpflichtet (*to*, *Dat.*).

beholder [biˈhouldə], *s.* der Zuschauer.

behove [bi'houv], v.a. sich geziemen, ziemen, gebühren.

being ['bi:iŋ], pres. part for the time —, vorläufig, für jetzt. — s. das Sein, die Existenz; das Wesen (creature).

belated [bi'leitid], adj. verspätet.

belch [beltʃ], v.n. rülpsen, aufstoßen.

belfry ['belfri], s. der Glockenturm.

Belgian ['beldʒən], adj. belgisch. — s. der Belgier.

belie [bi'lai], v.a. täuschen, Lügen strafen.

belief [bi'li:f], s. der Glaube, die Meinung.

believable [bi'li:vəbl], adj. glaubhaft, glaublich.

believe [bi'li:v], v.a., v.n. glauben (an, Acc.), vertrauen (Dat.).

believer [bi'li:və], s. der Gläubige.

belittle [bi'litl], v.a. schmälern, verkleinern, verächtlich machen.

bell [bel], s. die Glocke; Schelle, Klingel; — -founder, der Glockengießer; — -boy, (Am.) — -hop, der Hotelpage.

belligerent [bi'lidʒərənt], adj. kriegführend. — s. der Kriegführende.

bellow ['belou], v.n. brüllen. — s. das Gebrüll.

bellows ['belouz], s. der Blasebalg.

belly ['beli], s. der Bauch.

belong [bi'lɔŋ], v.n. gehören (Dat.), angehören (Dat.).

belongings [bi'lɔŋiŋz], s. pl. die Habe, das Hab und Gut, der Besitz.

beloved [bi'lʌvd, -vid], adj. geliebt, lieb.

below [bi'lou], adv. unten. — prep. unterhalb (Genit.), unter (Dat.).

Belshazzar [bel'ʃæzə]. Belsazar, m.

belt [belt], s. der Gürtel, Gurt; der Riemen; (Tech.) Treibriemen; below the —, unfair. — v.a. umgürten; (coll.) prügeln.

bemoan [bi'moun], v.a. beklagen.

bench [bentʃ], s. die Bank; der Gerichtshof (court of law); Queen's Bench, der oberste Gerichtshof.

bend [bend], v.a., v.n. irr. biegen; beugen; sich krümmen. — s. die Biegung, Krümmung, Kurve.

bendable [bendəbl], adj. biegsam.

beneath [bi'ni:θ] see below.

Benedictine [beni'dikti:n], s. der Benediktiner.

benediction [beni'dikʃən], s. der Segensspruch, der Segen; die Segnung.

benefaction [beni'fækʃən], s. die Wohltat.

benefactor ['benifæktə], s. der Wohltäter.

benefactress ['benifæktris], s. die Wohltäterin.

beneficent [be'nefisənt], adj. wohltätig.

beneficial [beni'fiʃəl], adj. vorteilhaft, gut (for, für), wohltuend.

benefit ['benifit], s. der Vorteil, Nutzen. — v.n. Nutzen ziehen. — v.a. nützen.

benevolence [be'nevələns], s. das Wohlwollen.

benevolent [be'nevələnt], adj. wohlwollend; — society, der Unterstützungsverein; — fund, der Unterstützungsfond.

Bengali [ben'gɔ:li], adj. bengalisch. — s. der Bengale.

benign [bi'nain], adj. gütig, mild.

bent [bent], adj. gebogen, krumm; — on something, versessen auf etwas. — s. die Neigung, der Hang; — for, Vorliebe für.

benzene ['benzi:n], s. das Benzol, Kohlenbenzin.

benzine ['benzi:n], s. das Benzin.

bequeath [bi'kwi:θ], v.a. vermachen, hinterlassen.

bequest [bi'kwest], s. das Vermächtnis.

bereave [bi'ri:v], v.a. irr. berauben (durch Tod).

bereavement [bi'ri:vmənt], s. der Verlust (durch Tod).

beret ['berei], s. die Baskenmütze.

Bernard ['bə:nəd]. Bernhard, m.; St. — dog, der Bernhardiner.

berry ['beri], s. die Beere.

berth [bə:θ], s. (Naut.) der Ankerplatz; die Koje. — v.a., v.n. anlegen; vor Anker gehen (boat).

beseech [bi'si:tʃ], v.a. irr. bitten, anflehen.

beset [bi'set], v.a. irr. bedrängen, bedrücken, umringen.

beside [bi'said], prep. außer, neben, nahe bei; — the point, unwesentlich; quite — the mark, weit vom Schuß.

besides [bi'saidz], adv. überdies, außerdem.

besiege [bi'si:dʒ], v.a. belagern.

besmirch [bi'smə:tʃ], v.a. besudeln.

besom ['bi:zəm], s. der Besen.

bespatter [bi'spætə], v. a. bespritzen.

bespeak [bi'spi:k], v.a. irr. bestellen; (Tail.) bespoke, nach Maß gemacht or gearbeitet.

best [best], adj. (superl. of good) best; — adv. am besten. — s. want the — of both worlds, alles haben wollen; to the — of my ability, nach besten Kräften; to the — of my knowledge, soviel ich weiß.

bestial ['bestjəl], adj. bestialisch, tierisch.

bestow [bi'stou], v.a. verleihen, erteilen.

bet [bet], s. die Wette. — v.a., v.n. irr. wetten.

betray [bi'trei], v.a. verraten.

betrayal [bi'treiəl], s. der Verrat.

betrayer [bi'treiə], s. der Verräter.

betroth [bi'trouð], v.a. verloben.

betrothal [bi'trouðəl], s. die Verlobung.

better ['betə], adj. (comp. of good) besser. — adv. you had —, es wäre besser, Sie gingen; think — of it, sich eines Besseren besinnen, sich's überlegen. — s. get the — of, überwinden; so much the —, desto or umso besser. — v.a. verbessern; — oneself, seine Lage verbessern.

betterment

betterment ['betəmənt], *s.* die Verbesserung.
between [bi'twi:n], *adv.* dazwischen. — *prep.* zwischen; unter (*among*).
bevel ['bevəl], *s.* der Winkelpasser; die Schräge. — *v.a.* abkanten.
beverage ['bevəridʒ], *s.* das Getränk.
bevy ['bevi], *s.* die Schar (*of beauties, von Schönen*).
bewail [bi'weil], *v.a., v.n.* betrauern, beweinen; trauern um.
beware [bi'wɛə], *v.n.* sich hüten (*of, vor*).
bewilder [bi'wildə], *v.a.* verwirren.
bewitch [bi'witʃ], *v.a.* bezaubern.
beyond [bi'jɔnd], *adv.* jenseits, drüben. — *prep.* über ... hinaus; jenseits; außer.
biannual [bai'ænjuəl], *adj.* halbjährlich.
bias ['baiəs], *s.* die Neigung; das Vorurteil (*prejudice*). — *v.a.* beeinflussen.
bias(s)ed ['baiəsd], *adj.* voreingenommen.
bib [bib], *s.* der Schürzenlatz; das Lätzchen.
Bible [baibl], *s.* die Bibel.
Biblical ['biblikəl], *adj.* biblisch.
bibliography [bibli'ɔgrəfi], *s.* die Bibliographie.
bibliophile ['bibliɔfail], *s.* der Bücherfreund.
biceps ['baiseps], *s.* der Bizeps, Armmuskel.
bicker ['bikə], *v.n.* zanken, hadern.
bickering ['bikərin], *s.* das Gezänk, Hadern, der Hader.
bicycle ['baisikl], (*coll.*) **bike** [baik], *s.* das Fahrrad.
bicyclist ['baisiklist], *s.* der Radfahrer.
bid [bid], *v.a., v.n. irr.* gebieten, befehlen (*Dat.*) (*order*); bieten (*at auction*); — *farewell*, Lebewohl sagen. — *s.* das Gebot, Angebot (*at auction*).
bidding ['bidin], *s.* der Befehl (*order*); das Bieten (*at auction*); die Einladung (*invitation*).
bide [baid], *v.n. irr.* verbleiben, verharren (*in, by, bei*).
biennial [bai'eniəl], *adj.* zweijährig, alle zwei Jahre.
bier [biə], *s.* die Bahre, Totenbahre.
big [big], *adj.* groß, dick (*fat*); *talking* —, großsprecherisch; *talk* —, prahlen.
bigamy ['bigəmi], *s.* die Bigamie, die Doppelehe.
bigness ['bignis], *s.* die Größe, Dicke.
bigoted ['bigətid], *adj.* bigott, fanatisch.
bigotry ['bigətri], *s.* die Bigotterie.
bigwig ['bigwig], *s.* (*coll.*) die vornehme Person, der Würdenträger.
bike *see* **bicycle.**
bilberry ['bilbəri], *s.* (*Bot.*) die Heidelbeere.
bile [bail], *s.* die Galle.
bilge [bildʒ], *s.* die Bilge, der Schiffsboden; (*coll.*) Unsinn (*nonsense*).
bilious ['biljəs], *adj.* gallig.
bill (1) [bil], *s.* der Schnabel (*bird*).

bill (2) [bil], die Rechnung (*account*). — *of exchange*, der Wechsel; — *of entry*, die Zolldeklaration; — *of fare*, die Speisekarte; (*Parl.*) der Gesetzentwurf; das Plakat (*poster*). — *v.a.* anzeigen.
billboard ['bilbɔ:d], *s.* (*Am.*) das Anschlagbrett.
billet ['bilit], *s.* das Billett (*card*); das Quartier, die Unterkunft (*army*).
billfold ['bilfould], *s.* (*Am.*) die Brieftasche.
billhook ['bilhuk], *s.* die Hippe.
billiards ['biljədz], *s.* das Billardspiel.
billow ['bilou], *s.* die Woge. — *v.n.* wogen.
bin [bin], *s.* der Behälter.
bind [baind], *v.a. irr.* binden, verpflichten; (*Law*) — *over*, zu gutem Benehmen verpflichten.
binder ['baində], *s.* der Binder, Buchbinder.
bindery ['baindəri], *s.* die Buchbinderei, Binderwerkstatt.
binding ['baindin], *s.* der Einband.
binnacle ['binəkl], *s.* das Kompaßhäuschen.
binocular [bi'nɔkjulə], *adj.* für beide Augen. — *s.* (*pl.*) das Fernglas, der Feldstecher.
binomial [bai'noumiəl], *adj.* binomisch. — *s.* (*pl.*) (*Maths.*) das Binom, der zweigliedrige Ausdruck.
biochemical [baio'kemikəl], *adj.* biochemisch.
biochemistry [baio'kemistri], *s.* die Biochemie.
biographer [bai'ɔgrəfə], *s.* der Biograph.
biographical [baio'græfikəl], *adj.* biographisch.
biography [bai'ɔgrəfi], *s.* die Biographie, die Lebensbeschreibung.
biological [baio'lɔdʒikəl], *adj.* biologisch.
biology [bai'ɔlədʒi], *s.* die Biologie.
biometric(al) [baio'metrik(əl)], *adj.* biometrisch.
biometry [bai'ɔmitri], *s.* die Biometrie.
biophysical [baio'fizikəl], *adj.* biophysisch.
biophysics [baio'fiziks], *s.* die Biophysik.
biped ['baiped], *s.* der Zweifüßler.
biplane ['baiplein], *s.* (*Aviat.*) der Doppeldecker.
birch [bə:tʃ], *s.* (*Bot.*) die Birke; die Birkenrute, Rute (*cane*). — *v.a.* (mit der Rute) züchtigen.
bird [bə:d], *s.* der Vogel; — *of passage*, der Wandervogel, Zugvogel; —*cage*, der Vogelkäfig, das Vogelbauer; — *fancier*, der Vogelzüchter; —*'s-eye view*, die Vogelperspektive.
birth [bə:θ], *s.* die Geburt; — *certificate*, der Geburtsschein.
birthday ['bə:θdei], *s,* der Geburtstag.
biscuit ['biskit], *s.* der *or* das Keks; der Zwieback.

bisect [bai′sekt], *v.a.* entzweischneiden, halbieren.
bisection [bai′sekʃən], *s.* die Zweiteilung, Halbierung.
bishop [′biʃəp], *s.* der Bischof; (*Chess*) der Läufer.
bishopric [′biʃəprik], *s.* das Bistum.
bismuth [′bizməθ], *s.* der *or* das Wismut.
bison [′baisən], *s.* (*Zool.*) der Bison.
bit [bit], *s.* der Bissen (*bite*), das Bißchen (*little* —); das Gebiß (*bridle*); der Bart (*of key*).
bitch [bitʃ], *s.* die Hündin.
bite [bait], *v.a. irr.* beißen. — *s.* das Beißen (*mastication*); der Biß (*morsel*).
biting [′baitiŋ], *adj.* (*also fig.*) beißend, scharf. — *adv.* — *cold*, bitterkalt.
bitter [′bitə], *adj.* bitter.
bitterness [′bitənis], *s.* die Bitterkeit.
bittern [′bitə:n], *s.* (*Orn.*) die Rohrdommel.
bitumen [bi′tju:mən], *s.* der Bergteer, Asphalt.
bivouac [′bivuæk], *s.* (*Mil.*) das Biwak, Lager.
bizarre [bi′za:], *adj.* bizarr, wunderlich.
blab [blæb], *v.a., v.n.* schwatzen, ausplaudern (*give away*).
blabber [′blæbə], *s.* (*coll.*) der Schwätzer.
black [blæk], *adj.* schwarz; — *sheep*, der Taugenichts; — *pudding*, die Blutwurst; *Black Forest*, der Schwarzwald; *Black Maria*, der Polizeiwagen; (*coll.*) die grüne Minna; *Black Sea*, das schwarze Meer.
blackberry [′blækbəri], *s.* (*Bot.*) die Brombeere.
blackbird [′blækbə:d], *s.* (*Orn.*) die Amsel.
blackguard [′blæga:d], *s.* der Spitzbube, Schurke.
blackmail [′blækmeil], *v.a.* erpressen. — *s.* die Erpressung.
bladder [′blædə], *s.* (*Anat.*) die Blase.
blacksmith [′blæksmiθ], *s.* der Grobschmied.
blade [bleid], *s.* die Klinge (*razor*); der Halm (*grass*); *shoulder* —, das Schulterblatt.
blamable [′bleiməbl], *adj.* tadelnswert, tadelhaft.
blame [bleim], *s.* der Tadel, die Schuld. — *v.a.* tadeln, beschuldigen, die Schuld zuschreiben (*Dat.*).
blameless [′bleimlis], *adj.* tadellos, schuldlos.
blanch [bla:ntʃ], *v.n.* erbleichen, weiß werden. — *v.a.* weiß machen.
bland [blænd], *adj.* mild, sanft.
blandish [′blændiʃ], *v.a.* schmeicheln (*Dat.*).
blandishment [′blændiʃmənt], *s.* (*mostly in pl.*) die Schmeichelei.
blandness [′blændnis], *s.* die Milde, Sanftheit.
blank [blæŋk], *adj.* blank, leer; reimlos (*verse*); *leave a* —, einen Raum freilassen; — *cartridge*, die Platzpatrone.

blanket [′blæŋkit], *s.* die Decke; (*coll.*) *a wet* —, ein langweiliger Kerl, der Spielverderber.
blare [blɛə], *v.n.* schmettern.
blaspheme [blæs′fi:m], *v.a., v.n.* lästern, fluchen.
blasphemous [′blæsfiməs], *adj.* lästerlich.
blasphemy [′blæsfəmi], *s.* die Gotteslästerung.
blast [bla:st], *v.a.* sprengen, zerstören. — *s.* der Windstoß (*gust*); der Stoß (*trumpets*); die Explosion (*bomb*); — *furnace*, der Hochofen. — *excl.* (*sl.*) —! zum Teufel!
blasting [′bla:stiŋ], *s.* das Sprengen.
blatant [′bleitənt], *adj.* laut, lärmend; dreist.
blaze [bleiz], *s.* die Flamme (*flame*); das Feuer; der Glanz (*colour etc.*). — *v.n.* flammen; leuchten (*shine*). — *v.a.* ausposaunen, bekannt machen (*make known*).
blazer [′bleizə], *s.* die Sportjacke, Klubjacke.
blazon [′bleizən], *v.a.* verkünden.
bleach [bli:tʃ], *v.a.* bleichen. — *s.* das Bleichmittel.
bleak [bli:k], *adj.* öde, rauh; trübe, freudlos.
bleakness [′bli:knis], *s.* die Öde (*scenery*); Traurigkeit, Trübheit.
bleary [′bliəri], *adj.* trübe; — *eyed*, triefäugig.
bleat [bli:t], *v.n.* blöken.
bleed [bli:d], *v.n. irr.* bluten. — *v.a.* bluten lassen; erpressen (*blackmail*).
blemish [′blemiʃ], *s.* der Makel, der Fehler. — *v.a.* schänden, entstellen.
blench [blentʃ], *v.n.* zurückweichen, stutzen.
blend [blend], *v.a., v.n.* mischen, vermengen; sich mischen. — *s.* die Mischung, Vermischung.
bless [bles], *v.a.* segnen; beglücken; loben.
blessed [blest, ′blesid], *adj.* gesegnet, selig.
blessing [′blesiŋ], *s.* der Segen.
blight [blait], *s.* der Meltau. — *v.a.* verderben.
blind [blaind], *adj.* blind; — *man's buff*, Blinde Kuh; — *spot*, der schwache Punkt. — *s.* die Blende, das Rouleau; *Venetian* —, die Jalousie. — *v.a.* blind machen, täuschen.
blindfold [′blaindfould], *adj.* mit verbundenen Augen.
blindness [′blaindnis], *s.* die Blindheit.
blindworm [′blaindwə:m], *s.* (*Zool.*) die Blindschleiche.
blink [bliŋk], *s.* das Blinzeln. — *v.n.* blinzeln, blinken. — *v.a.* nicht sehen wollen.
blinkers [′bliŋkəz], *s. pl.* die Scheuklappen.
bliss [blis], *s.* die Wonne, Seligkeit.
blissful [′blisful], *adj.* wonnig, selig.
blister [′blistə], *s.* die Blase. — *v.n.* Blasen ziehen, Blasen bekommen.

blithe [blaiδ], *adj.* munter, lustig, fröhlich.
blitheness ['blaiδnis], *s.* die Munterkeit, Fröhlichkeit.
blizzard ['blizəd], *s.* der Schneesturm.
bloated ['bloutid], *adj.* aufgeblasen, aufgedunsen.
bloater ['bloutə], *s.* (*Zool.*) der Bückling.
blob [blɔb], *s.* der Kleks.
block [blɔk], *s.* der Block, Klotz (*wood*); Häuserblock (*houses*); — *letters*, große Druckschrift. — *v.a.* blockieren, hemmen (*hinder*); sperren (*road*).
blockade [blɔ'keid], *s.* die Blockade.
blockhead ['blɔkhed], *s.* der Dummkopf.
blonde [blɔnd], *adj.* blond. — *s.* die Blondine.
blood [blʌd], *s.* das Blut; — *vessel*, das Blutgefäß.
bloodcurdling ['blʌdkə:dliŋ], *adj.* haarsträubend.
bloodless ['blʌdlis], *adj.* blutlos, unblutig.
bloodthirsty ['blʌdθə:sti], *adj.* blutdürstig.
bloody ['blʌdi], *adj.* blutig; (*vulg.*) verflucht.
bloom [blu:m], *s.* die Blüte; die Blume. — *v.n.* blühen.
bloomers ['blu:məz], *s. pl.* altmodische Unterhosen für Damen.
blooming ['blu:miŋ], *adj.* blühend.
blossom ['blɔsəm], *s.* die Blüte. — *v.n.* blühen, Blüten treiben.
blot [blɔt], *s.* der Klecks; Fleck; (*fig.*) der Schandfleck. — *v.a.* beflecken; löschen (*ink*); — *out*, ausmerzen, austilgen; *blotting paper*, das Löschpapier.
blotch [blɔtʃ], *s.* der Hautfleck; die Pustel; der Klecks (*blot*).
blotter ['blɔtə], *s.* der Löscher.
blouse [blauz], *s.* die Bluse.
blow (1) [blou], *s.* der Schlag.
blow (2) [blou], *v.a.* irr. blasen; wehen; — *o.'s own trumpet*, prahlen; anfachen (*fire*); — *o.'s nose*, sich schneuzen. — *v.n.* schnaufen, keuchen; — *up*, in die Luft sprengen.
blower ['blouə], *s.* das Gebläse; der Bläser.
blowpipe ['bloupaip], *s.* das Lötrohr.
blubber ['blʌbə], *s.* der Walfischspeck, der Tran. — *v.n.* schluchzen, heulen, flennen.
bludgeon ['blʌdʒən], *s.* der Knüppel; die Keule (*club*). — *v.a.* niederschlagen.
blue [blu:], *adj.* blau; schwermütig (*sad*); — *blooded*, aus edlem Geblüte.
bluebell ['blu:bel], *s.* (*Bot.*) die Glockenblume.
bluebottle ['blu:bɔtl], *s.* (*Ent.*) die Schmeißfliege.
bluestocking ['blu:stɔkiŋ], *s.* der Blaustrumpf.

bluff [blʌf], *adj.* grob, schroff. — *s.* der Bluff, die Täuschung, der Trick. — *v.a., v.n.* vortäuschen (*pretend*), bluffen; verblüffen (*deceive*).
blunder ['blʌndə], *s.* der Fehler, Schnitzer. — *v.n.* einen Fehler machen.
blunderer ['blʌndərə], *s.* der Tölpel.
blunderbuss ['blʌndəbʌs], *s.* die Donnerbüchse.
blunt [blʌnt], *adj.* stumpf (*edge*); derb, offen (*speech*). — *v.a.* abstumpfen; verderben (*appetite*).
bluntness ['blʌntnis], *s.* die Stumpfheit (*edge*); die Derbheit (*speech*).
blur [blə:], *s.* der Fleck. — *v.a.* verwischen.
blurt [blə:t], *v.a.* — *out*, herausplatzen.
blush [blʌʃ], *v.n.* erröten. — *s.* die Schamröte, das Erröten.
bluster ['blʌstə], *s.* das Toben, Brausen. — *v.n.* toben, brausen.
blustering ['blʌstəriŋ], *adj.* lärmend, tobend.
boa ['bouə], *s.* (*Zool.*) die Boa.
boar [bɔ:], *s.* (*Zool.*) der Eber.
board [bɔ:d], *s.* das Brett (*wood*); die Tafel (*notice* —); die Verpflegung (*food*); — *and lodging*, die Vollpension; die Behörde, der Ausschuß (*officials*). — *v.a.* — *up*, vernageln, zumachen; — *someone*, verpflegen; — *a steamer*, an Bord gehen; — *ing school*, das Internat, das Pensionat.
boarder ['bɔ:də], *s.* der Internatsschüler; der Pensionär.
boast [boust], *v.n.* prahlen, sich rühmen. — *s.* der Stolz (*pride*).
boastful ['boustful], *adj.* prahlerisch.
boat [bout], *s.* das Boot; *rowing-* —, das Ruderboot; der Kahn.
bob [bɔb], *s.* der Knicks; (*coll.*) der Schilling. — *v.n.* baumeln; springen; *bobbed hair*, der Bubikopf.
bobbin ['bɔbin], *s.* die Spule, der Klöppel.
bobsleigh ['bɔbslei], *s.* der Bob(sleigh), Rennschlitten.
bodice ['bɔdis], *s.* das Mieder, Leibchen.
bodied ['bɔdid], *adj. suffix; able-* —, gesund, stark.
body ['bɔdi], *s.* der Körper; die Körperschaft (*organisation*).
bodyguard ['bɔdiga:d], *s.* die Leibwache.
Boer ['bouə], *s.* der Bure.
bog [bɔg], *s.* der Sumpf. — *v.a.* (*coll.*) — *down*, einsinken.
Bohemian [bo'hi:mjən], *s.* der Böhme. — *adj.* böhmisch; künstlerhaft.
boil (1) [bɔil], *v.a., v.n.* kochen, sieden. — *s.* das Kochen; — *ing point*, der Siedepunkt.
boil (2) [bɔil], *s.* (*Med.*) die Beule, der Furunkel.
boisterous ['bɔistərəs], *adj.* ungestüm; laut (*noisy*).
boisterousness ['bɔistərəsnis], *s.* die Heftigkeit, Lautheit.

bold [bould], *adj.* kühn, dreist; *make* —, sich erkühnen.
boldness ['bouldnis], *s.* die Kühnheit, Dreistigkeit.
Bolivian [bə'livjən], *adj.* bolivianisch. —*s.* der Bolivianer.
bolster ['boulstə], *s.* das Polster, Kissen.
bolt [boult], *s.* der Bolzen, Riegel (*on door*); der Pfeil (*arrow*). — *v.a.* verriegeln (*bar*); verschlingen (*devour*). — *v.n.* davonlaufen (*run away*), durchgehen (*abscond*).
bomb [bɔm], *s.* die Bombe. — *v.a.* bombardieren.
bombard [bɔm'bɑːd], *v.a.* bombardieren.
bombardment [bɔm'bɑːdmənt], *s.* die Beschießung.
bombastic [bɔm'bæstik], *adj.* schwülstig, bombastisch (*style*).
bombproof ['bɔmpruːf], *adj.* bombensicher.
bond [bɔnd], *s.* das Band (*link*); die Schuldverschreibung (*debt*); *in* —, unter Zollverschluß; (*pl.*) die Fesseln (*fetters*). — *v.a.* (*Chem.*) binden; (*Comm.*) zollpflichtig erklären (*declare dutiable*).
bondage ['bɔndidʒ], *s.* die Knechtschaft.
bone [boun], *s.* der Knochen; die Gräte (*fish*); — *china*, feines Geschirr, das Porzellan; — *of contention*, der Zankapfel; — *dry*, staubtrocken; — *idle*, stinkfaul; — *lace*, die Klöppelspitze. — *v.a.* Knochen oder Gräten entfernen.
bonfire ['bɔnfaiə], *s.* das Freudenfeuer.
bonnet ['bɔnit], *s.* die Haube, das Häubchen.
bonny ['bɔni], *adj.* hübsch, nett.
bony ['bouni], *adj.* beinern, knöchern.
book [buk], *s.* das Buch. — *v.a.* belegen (*seat*); eine Karte lösen (*ticket*); engagieren (*engage*).
bookbinder ['bukbaində], *s.* der Buchbinder.
bookcase ['bukkeis], *s.* der Bücherschrank.
bookie *see* bookmaker.
booking-office ['bukiɲɔfis], *s.* der Fahrkartenschalter; die Kasse (*Theat. etc.*)
book-keeper ['bukiːpə], *s.* der Buchhalter.
book-keeping ['bukiːpiɲ], *s.* die Buchhaltung; *double entry* —, doppelte Buchführung, *single entry* —, einfache Buchführung.
bookmaker ['bukmeikə] (*abbr.* bookie ['buki]), *s.* (*Racing*) der Buchmacher.
bookmark(er) ['bukmɑːk(ə)], *s.* das Lesezeichen.
bookseller ['buksələ], *s.* der Buchhändler.
bookshop ['bukʃɔp], *s.* die Buchhandlung.
bookstall ['bukstɔːl], *s.* der Bücherstand.

bookworm ['bukwəːm], *s.* der Bücherwurm.
boom (1) [buːm], *s.* der Aufschwung; Boom; (*Comm.*) die Konjunktur; Hausse.
boom (2) [buːm], *v.n.* dröhnen, (dumpf) schallen.
boon [buːn], *s.* die Wohltat.
boor [buə], *s.* der Lümmel.
boorish ['buəriʃ], *adj.* lümmelhaft.
boot [buːt], *s.* der Stiefel, hohe Schuh. — *v.a.* mit dem Stiefel stoßen, kicken.
booth [buːð], *s.* die Bude, Zelle (*Teleph.*).
bootlace ['buːtleis], *s.* der Schnürsenkel, der Schnürriemen.
booty ['buːti], *s.* die Beute.
booze [buːz], *v.n.* (*coll.*) saufen.
boozy ['buːzi], *adj.* (*coll.*) angeheitert, leicht betrunken.
border ['bɔːdə], *s.* der Rand; die Grenze. — *v.a., v.n.* angrenzen (*on*); einsäumen (*surround*).
borderer ['bɔːdərə], *s.* der Grenzbewohner.
bore [bɔː], *v.a.* bohren; langweilen (*be boring*). — *s.* das Bohrloch (*drill-hole*), die Bohrung (*drilling*); der langweilige Kerl (*person*).
boredom ['bɔːdəm], *s.* die Langeweile.
borer ['bɔːrə], *s.* der Bohrer (*drill*).
born [bɔːn], *adj.* geboren.
borrow ['bɔrou], *v.a.* borgen, entlehnen.
borrowing ['bɔrouiɲ], *s.* das Borgen, Entlehnen.
bosom ['buzəm], *s.* der Busen.
boss [bɔs], *s.* der Beschlag, der Buckel; (*coll.*) der Chef.
botanical [bə'tænikəl], *adj.* botanisch.
botanist ['bɔtənist], *s.* der Botaniker.
botany ['bɔtəni], *s.* die Botanik.
botch [bɔtʃ], *s.* das Flickwerk. — *v.a.* verderben, verhunzen.
both [bouθ], *adj., pron.* beide, beides; — *of them*, beide. — *conj.* — ... *and*, sowohl ... als auch.
bother ['bɔðə], *v.a.* plagen, stören, belästigen; — *it!* zum Henker damit! — *v.n.* sich bemühen. — *s.* die Belästigung, das Ärgernis.
bottle [bɔtl], *s.* die Flasche. — *v.a.* in Flaschen abfüllen.
bottom ['bɔtəm], *s.* der Boden, Grund (*ground*); die Ursache (*cause*); (*Naut.*) der Schiffsboden.
bottomless ['bɔtəmlis], *adj.* grundlos, bodenlos.
bough [bau], *s.* der Zweig, Ast.
boulder ['bouldə], *s.* der Felsblock.
bounce [bauns], *v.a.* aufprallen lassen (*ball*). — *v.n.* aufprallen. — *s.* der Rückprall, Aufprall.
bound (1) [baund], *s.* der Sprung; *by leaps and* —*s*, sehr schnell, sprunghaft. — *v.n.* springen, prallen.
bound (2) [baund], *v.a.* begrenzen, einschränken. — *adj.* verpflichtet; — *to* (*inf.*), wird sicherlich ...

bound (3) [baund], *adj.* — *for*, auf dem Wege nach.

boundary ['baundəri], *s.* die Grenzlinie, Grenze.

bounder ['baundə], *s.* der ungezogene Bursche.

boundless ['baundlis], *adj.* grenzenlos, unbegrenzt.

bounteous ['bauntiəs], *adj.* freigebig; reichlich (*plenty*).

bounty ['baunti], *s.* die Freigebigkeit (*generosity*); (*Comm.*) Prämie.

bouquet [bu'kei], *s.* das Bukett, der Blumenstrauß; die Blume (*wine*).

bourgeois ['buəӡwɑ:], *s.* der Bürger; Philister. — *adj.* kleinbürgerlich, philisterhaft.

bow (1) [bau], *s.* (*Naut.*) der Bug; —*sprit*, das Bugspriet.

bow (2) [bau], *s.* die Verbeugung, Verneigung. — *v.n.* sich verneigen, sich verbeugen. — *v.a.* neigen.

bow (3) [bou], *s.* (*Mus.*) der Bogen; die Schleife (*ribbon*). — *v.a.* streichen (*violin*).

bowel ['bauəl], *s.* der Darm; (*pl.*) die Eingeweide.

bowl (1) [boul], *s.* die Schale, der Napf, die Schüssel.

bowl (2) [boul], *s.* die Holzkugel; (*pl.*) das Rasenkugelspiel, Bowlingspiel. — *v.n.* (*Cricket*) den Ball werfen.

bowler (1) ['boulə], *s.* (*hat*) der steife Hut, die Melone.

bowler (2) ['boulə], *s.* (*Sport*) der Ballmann.

box (1) [bɔks], *s.* (*Bot.*) der Buchsbaum.

box (2) [bɔks], *s.* die Büchse, Dose, Schachtel, der Kasten; (*Theat.*) die Loge; — *office*, die Theaterkasse.

box (3) [bɔks], *s.* der Schlag; — *on the ear*, die Ohrfeige. — *v.n.* boxen.

boxer ['bɔksə], *s.* der Boxer; Boxkämpfer.

Boxing Day ['bɔksiŋ'dei], der zweite Weihnachtstag.

boy [bɔi], *s.* der Junge, Knabe; Diener (*servant*).

boyish ['bɔiiʃ], *adj.* knabenhaft.

boyhood ['bɔihud], *s.* das Knabenalter.

brace [breis], *s.* das Band; die Klammer (*clamp*); — *of partridges*, das Paar Rebhühner; die Spange (*denture*). — *v.a.* spannen, straffen. — *v.r.* — *yourself!* stähle dich!

bracelet ['breislit], *s.* das Armband.

braces ['breisiz], *s. pl.* die Hosenträger.

bracken ['brækən], *s.* (*Bot.*) das Farnkraut.

bracket ['brækit], *s.* die Klammer; *income* —, die Einkommensgruppe. — *v.a.* (ein-)klammern; (*Maths.*) in Klammern setzen.

brackish ['brækiʃ], *adj.* salzig.

brad [bræd], *s.* der kopflose Nagel; — *awl*, der Vorstechbohrer.

brag [bræg], *v.n.* prahlen.

braggart ['brægət], *s.* der Prahlhans.

Brahmin ['brɑ:min], *s.* der Brahmane.

braid [breid], *s.* die Borte; der Saumbesatz. — *v.a.* (mit Borten) besetzen.

Braille [breil], *s.* die Blindenschrift.

brain [brein], *s.* das Gehirn, Hirn; *scatter-* —*ed*, zerstreut.

brainwave ['breinweiv], *s.* der Geistesblitz.

brake [breik], *s.* die Bremse. — *v.a.* bremsen.

bramble ['bræmbl], *s.* der (*Bot.*) Brombeerstrauch.

bran [bræn], *s.* die Kleie.

branch [brɑ:ntʃ], *s.* der Ast, Zweig; (*Comm.*) die Zweigstelle, Filiale. — *v.n.* — *out*, sich verzweigen; — *out into*, sich ausbreiten, etwas Neues anfangen; — *off*, abzweigen.

brand [brænd], *s.* der (Feuer) Brand; das Brandmal (*on skin*); die Sorte, Marke (*make*); — *new*, funkelnagelneu. — *v.a.* brandmarken, kennzeichnen.

brandish ['brændiʃ], *v.a.* schwingen, herumschwenken.

brandy ['brændi], *s.* der Branntwein, Kognac, Weinbrand.

brass [brɑ:s], *s.* das Messing; — *band*, die Blechmusik, Militärmusikkapelle; — *founder*, Erzgießer, Gelbgießer; (*sl.*) die Frechheit (*impudence*).

brassiere ['bræsiɛə], *s.* der Büstenhalter.

brat [bræt], *s.* (*coll.*) das Kind, der Balg.

brave [breiv], *adj.* tapfer, kühn. — *v.a.* trotzen, standhalten (*Dat.*). — *s.* der Held, Krieger; der Indianer (*redskin*).

bravery ['breivəri], *s.* die Tapferkeit.

brawl [brɔ:l], *s.* der Krawall, die Rauferei. — *v.n.* zanken, lärmen.

brawn [brɔ:n], *s.* die Sülze; (*fig.*) die Körperkraft, Stärke.

brawny ['brɔ:ni], *adj.* stark, sehnig.

bray [brei], *v.n.* iah sagen, Eselslaute von sich geben (*donkey*). — *s.* das Iah des Esels, das Eselsgeschrei.

brazen [breizn], *adj.* (*Metall.*) aus Erz; unverschämt (*shameless*).

brazenfaced ['breiznfeisd], *adj.* unverschämt.

brazier ['breiziə], *s.* der Kupferschmied; die Kohlenpfanne.

Brazil [brə'zil]. Brasilien, *n.*; — *nut*, die Paranuß.

Brazilian [brə'ziliən], *adj.* brasilianisch. — *s.* der Brasilianer.

breach [bri:tʃ], *s.* die Bresche; der Bruch (*break*); die Verletzung; der Vertragsbruch (*of contract*); der Verstoß (*of*, gegen, *etiquette etc.*).

bread [bred], *s.* das Brot; *brown* —, das Schwarzbrot; — *and butter*, das Butterbrot.

breadth [bretθ], *s.* die Breite, Weite.

break [breik], *s.* der Bruch (*breach*); die Lücke (*gap*); die Chance (*chance*); *a lucky* —, ein glücklicher Zufall, ein Glücksfall; die Pause (*from work*). — *v.a., v.n. irr.* brechen; — *off,* Pause machen; — *in,* unterbrechen (*interrupt*); — *in,* (*horse*) einschulen, zureiten; — *up,* abbrechen (*school, work*); — *away,* sich trennen, absondern; — *down,* zusammenbrechen (*health*); (*Am.*) analysieren; auflösen.

breakage ['breikidʒ], *s.* der Bruch, der Schaden (*damage*).

breakdown ['breikdoun], *s.* der Zusammenbruch (*health*); die Panne (*car*); (*Am.*) die Analyse (*analysis*).

breaker ['breikə], *s.* die Brandungswelle, Brandung.

breakfast ['brekfəst], *s.* das Frühstück. *v.n.* frühstücken.

breast [brest], *s.* die Brust.

breath [breθ], *s.* der Atem; der Hauch (*exhalation*); *with bated* —, mit verhaltenem Atem.

breathe [bri:ð], *v.n.* atmen.

breathing ['bri:ðiŋ], *s.* die Atmung.

breathless ['breθlis], *adj.* atemlos.

breech [bri:tʃ], *s.* der Boden; (*pl.*) die Reithosen, *f. pl.*

breed [bri:d], *v.a. irr.* zeugen, züchten (*cattle, etc.*). — *v.n.* sich vermehren. — *s.* die Zucht, die Art (*type*); die Rasse (*race*).

breeder ['bri:də], *s.* der Züchter.

breeding ['bri:diŋ], *s.* die gute Kinderstube (*manners*); die Erziehung; das Züchten (*of plants, cattle etc.*).

breeze [bri:z], *s.* die Briese.

breezy ['bri:zi], *adj.* windig; lebhaft (*manner*), beschwingt (*tone*).

brethren ['breðrən], *s. pl.* (*obs.*) die Brüder.

Breton [bretn], *adj.* bretonisch. — *s.* der Bretagner, Bretone.

brevet ['brevit], *s.* das Patent.

breviary ['bri:viəri], *s.* das Brevier.

brevity ['breviti], *s.* die Kürze.

brew [bru:], *v.a.* brauen. — *s.* das Gebräu, Bräu (*beer*).

brewer ['bru:ə], *s.* der Brauer, Bierbrauer.

brewery ['bru:əri], *s.* die Brauerei, das Brauhaus.

briar, brier ['braiə], *s.* (*Bot.*) der Dornstrauch, die wilde Rose.

bribe [braib], *v.a.* bestechen. — *s.* das Bestechungsgeld.

bribery ['braibəri], *s.* die Bestechung.

brick [brik], *s.* der Ziegel, Backstein; *drop a* —, eine Taktlosigkeit begehen, einen Schnitzer machen.

bricklayer ['brikleiə], *s.* der Maurer.

bridal [braidl], *adj.* bräutlich.

bride [braid], *s.* die Braut.

bridegroom ['braidgru:m], *s.* der Bräutigam.

bridesmaid ['braidzmeid], *s.* die Brautjungfer.

bridge [bridʒ], *s.* die Brücke. — *v.a.* überbrücken; — *the gap,* die Lücke füllen.

bridle [braidl], *s.* der Zaum, Zügel. — *v.a.* aufzäumen. — *v.n.* sich brüsten.

brief [bri:f], *adj.* kurz, bündig, knapp. — *s.* der Schriftsatz, der Rechtsauftrag, die Instruktionen, *f. pl.* (*instructions*). — *v.a.* instruieren, beauftragen; informieren (*inform*).

brigade [bri'geid], *s.* die Brigade.

brigand ['brigənd], *s.* der Brigant, Straßenräuber.

bright [brait], *adj.* hell, glänzend (*shiny*); klug, intelligent (*clever*).

brighten [braitn], *v.a.* glänzend machen (*polish etc.*); erhellen, aufheitern (*cheer*).

brightness ['braitnis], *s.* der Glanz; die Helligkeit; die Klugheit (*cleverness*).

brill [bril], *s.* (*Zool.*) der Glattbutt.

brilliance, brilliancy ['briljəns, -jənsi], *s.* der Glanz, die Pracht.

brim [brim], *s.* der Rand (*glass*); die Krempe (*hat*). — *v.n.* — (*over*) *with,* überfließen von.

brimful ['brimful], *adj.* übervoll.

brimstone ['brimstoun], *s.* der Schwefel; — *butterfly,* der Zitronenfalter.

brindled ['brindld], *adj.* scheckig, gefleckt.

brine [brain], *s.* die Salzsole, das Salzwasser.

bring [briŋ], *v.a. irr.* bringen; — *about,* zustande bringen; — *forth,* hervorbringen; gebären; — *forward,* fördern; anführen; — *on,* herbeiführen; — *up,* erziehen, aufziehen.

brink [briŋk], *s.* (*fig.*) der Rand, — *of a precipice,* Rand eines Abgrundes.

briny ['braini], *adj.* salzig.

brisk [brisk], *adj.* frisch, munter, feurig (*horse*).

brisket ['briskit], *s.* die Brust (eines Tieres).

briskness ['brisknis], *s.* die Lebhaftigkeit.

bristle [brisl], *s.* die Borste. — *v.n.* sich sträuben.

British ['britiʃ], *adj.* britisch.

Britisher, Briton ['britiʃə, 'britən], *s.* der Brite.

brittle [britl], *adj.* zerbrechlich, spröde.

brittleness ['britlnis], *s.* die Sprödigkeit, Zerbrechlichkeit.

broach [broutʃ], *v.a.* anzapfen, anschneiden; — *a subject,* ein Thema berühren.

broad [brɔ:d], *adj.* breit, weit; ordinär, derb (*joke*); — *-minded,* duldsam, weitherzig.

broadcast ['brɔ:dkɑ:st], *v.a.* senden, übertragen (*radio*). — *s.* die Sendung, das Programm.

broadcaster ['brɔ:dkɑ:stə], *s.* der im Radio Vortragende *or* Künstler (*artist*); Ansager.

broadcasting ['brɔ:dkɑ:stiŋ], *s.* das Senden, der Rundfunk; — *station,* der Sender, die Rundfunkstation.

327

broadcloth

broadcloth ['brɔːdclɔθ], *s.* das feine Tuch.
broaden [brɔːdn], *v.a.* erweitern, verbreitern.
brocade [bro'keid], *s.* der Brokat.
brogue [broug], *s.* der grobe Schuh; der irische Akzent.
broil ['brɔil], *v.a.* braten, rösten.
broke [brouk], *adj. (coll.)* pleite.
broken ['broukən], *adj.* gebrochen; zerbrochen; unterbrochen (*interrupted*).
broker ['broukə], *s.* der Makler.
bronchial ['brɔŋkjəl], *adj.* (*Anat.*) bronchial, in *or* von der Luftröhre, Luftröhren-.
bronchitis [brɔŋ'kaitis], *s.* (*Med.*) die Luftröhrenentzündung, Bronchitis.
bronze [brɔnz], *s.* (*Metall.*) die Bronze, Bronzefarbe.
brooch [broutʃ], *s.* die Brosche.
brood [bruːd], *s.* die Brut. — *v.n.* brüten; grübeln (*meditate*).
brook (1) [bruk], *s.* der Bach.
brook (2) [bruk], *v.a.* ertragen, leiden.
brooklet ['bruklit], *s.* das Bächlein.
broom [bruːm], *s.* der Besen; (*Bot.*) der Ginster.
broth [brɔθ], *s.* die Brühe; *meat* —, Fleischbrühe.
brothel ['brɔθəl], *s.* das Bordell.
brother ['brʌðə], *s.* der Bruder; — *-in-law*, der Schwager.
brotherhood ['brʌðəhud], *s.* die Bruderschaft.
brotherly ['brʌðəli], *adj.* brüderlich.
brow [brau], *s.* die Braue, Augenbraue; der Kamm (*hill*); die Stirn(e) (*forehead*).
browbeat ['braubiːt], *v.a.* einschüchtern.
brown [braun], *adj.* braun; *in a — study*, in tiefem Nachsinnen.
browse [brauz], *v.n.* weiden (*cattle*); stöbern, (durch-)blättern (*in books etc.*).
Bruin ['bruːin]. Braun, Meister Petz, der Bär.
bruise [bruːz], *v.a.* quetschen, stoßen; (wund) schlagen. — *s.* die Quetschung.
Brunswick ['brʌnzwik]. Braunschweig, *n.*
brunt [brʌnt], *s.* der Anprall; *bear the* —, der Wucht ausgesetzt sein, den Stoß auffangen.
brush [brʌʃ], *s.* die Bürste (*clothes*); der Pinsel (*paint, painting*); — *stroke*, der Pinselstrich. — *v.a., v.n.* bürsten, abbürsten; — *against s.o.*, mit jemandem zusammenstoßen, streifen (*an, Acc.*); — *up one's English*, das Englisch auffrischen; — *off*, abschütteln.
brushwood ['brʌʃwud], *s.* das Gestrüpp.
brusque [brusk], *adj.* brüsk, barsch.
Brussels ['brʌsəlz]. Brüssel, *n.*; — *sprouts*, (*Bot.*) der Rosenkohl.
brutal [bruːtl], *adj.* brutal, grausam.
brutality [bruː'tæliti], *s.* die Brutalität.
brute [bruːt], *s.* der Unmensch.

bubble [bʌbl], *s.* die Blase; (*fig.*) der Schwindel (*swindle*). — *v.n.* sprudeln, wallen, schäumen.
buccaneer [bʌkə'niə], *s.* der Seeräuber.
buck [bʌk], *s.* (*Zool.*) der Bock; (*Am. sl.*) der Dollar. — *v.a.* — *up*, aufmuntern. — *v.n.* — *up*, sich zusammenraffen.
bucket ['bʌkit], *s.* der Eimer, Kübel.
buckle [bʌkl], *s.* die Schnalle. — *v.a.* zuschnallen; biegen. — *v.n.* sich krümmen.
buckler ['bʌklə], *s.* der Schild.
buckram ['bʌkrəm], *s.* die Steifleinwand.
buckskin ['bʌkskin], *s.* das Wildleder.
buckwheat ['bʌkwiːt], *s.* (*Bot.*) der Buchweizen.
bucolic [bjuː'kɔlik], *adj.* bukolisch, ländlich, Schäfer-.
bud [bʌd], *s.* (*Bot.*) die Knospe. — *v.n.* knospen.
buddy ['bʌdi], *s.(coll.Am.)* der Freund, Kamerad.
budge [bʌdʒ], *v.n.* sich rühren, sich regen.
budget ['bʌdʒit], *s.* das Budget; der Haushaltsplan; der Etat; *present the* —, den Staatsetat vorlegen. — *v.n.* voranschlagen (*for*), planen.
buff [bʌf], *adj.* ledergelb.
buffalo ['bʌfəlou], *s.* (*Zool.*) der Büffel.
buffer ['bʌfə], *s.* der Puffer.
buffet (1) ['bʌfit], *s.* der Puff, Faustschlag (*blow*). — *v.a.* schlagen, stoßen.
buffet (2) ['bufei], *s.* das Buffet, der Anrichtetisch.
buffoon [bʌ'fuːn], *s.* der Possenreißer.
buffoonery [bʌ'fuːnəri], *s.* die Possen, *f. pl.*; das Possenreißen.
bug [bʌg], *s.* (*Ent.*) die Wanze; (*Am.*) der Käfer; (*coll.*) das Insekt.
buggy ['bʌgi], *s.* der Einspänner.
bugle [bjuːgl], *s.* (*Mus.*) das Signalhorn, die Signaltrompete.
bugler ['bjuːglə], *s.* (*Mus.*) der Trompeter.
build [bild], *v.a., v.n. irr.* bauen; errichten; — *on*, sich verlassen auf (*rely on*). — *s.* die Statur, Figur (*figure*).
builder ['bildə], *s.* der Bauherr, Baumeister (*employer*); Bauarbeiter (*worker*).
building ['bildiŋ], *s.* das Gebäude, der Bau; — *site*, der Bauplatz.
bulb [bʌlb], *s.* (*Bot.*) der Knollen, die Zwiebel; *Dutch* —, die Tulpe; (*Elec.*) die Birne.
bulbous ['bʌlbəs], *adj.* zwiebelartig; dickbäuchig.
Bulgarian [bʌl'gɛəriən], *adj.* bulgarisch. — *s.* der Bulgare.
bulge [bʌldʒ], *s.* die Ausbauchung; die Ausbuchtung (*in fighting line*). — *v.n.* herausragen, anschwellen.
bulk [bʌlk], *s.* die Masse, Menge; *buy in* —, im Großen einkaufen.

bulky ['bʌlki], *adj.* schwer (*heavy*); massig (*stodgy*); unhandlich.

bull (1) [bul], *s.* (*Zool.*) der Bulle, Stier; —'s eye, das Schwarze (*target*).

bull (2) [bul], *s.* (*Papal*) die Bulle, der Erlass.

bulldog ['buldɔg], *s.* der Bullenbeißer.

bullet ['bulit], *s.* die Kugel, das Geschoß.

bulletin ['bulitin], *s.* das Bulletin, der Tagesbericht.

bullfight ['bulfait], *s.* der Stierkampf.

bullfinch ['bulfintʃ], *s.* (*Orn.*) der Dompfaff.

bullfrog ['bulfrɔg], *s.* (*Zool.*) der Ochsenfrosch.

bullion ['buljən], *s.* der Goldbarren, Silberbarren.

bullock ['bulək], *s.* (*Zool.*) der Ochse.

bully ['buli], *s.* der Raufbold, Angeber, Großtuer (*braggart*); der Tyrann. — *v.a.* tyrannisieren, einschüchtern.

bulrush ['bulrʌʃ], *s.* (*Bot.*) die Binse.

bulwark ['bulwək], *s.* das Bollwerk, die Verteidigung.

bump [bʌmp], *s.* der Schlag, der Stoß. — *v.a.* stoßen.

bun [bʌn], *s.* das Rosinenbrötchen; das süße Brötchen; (*hair*) der Knoten.

bunch [bʌntʃ], *s.* der Bund (*keys*); der Strauß (*flowers*); die Traube (*grapes*). — *v.a.* zusammenfassen, zusammenbinden, zusammenraffen.

bundle [bʌndl], *s.* das Bündel.

bung [bʌŋ], *s.* der Spund (*in barrel*).

bungle [bʌŋgl], *v.a.* verpfuschen, verderben.

bungler ['bʌŋglə], *s.* der Stümper.

bunion ['bʌnjən], *s.* die Fußschwiele.

bunk (1) [bʌŋk], *s.* die (Schlaf-)Koje.

bunk (2) [bʌŋk], *s.* (*coll.*) der Unsinn.

bunker ['bʌŋkə], *s.* der Kohlenraum, Bunker.

bunting ['bʌntiŋ], *s.* das Flaggentuch.

buoy [bɔi], *s.* die Boje.

buoyant ['bɔiənt], *adj.* schwimmend; lebhaft, heiter.

buoyancy ['bɔiənsi], *s.* die Schwimmkraft; die Schwungkraft.

burden (1) [bə:dn], *s.* die Bürde, Last. — *v.a.* belasten, beladen.

burden (2) [bə:dn], *s.* der Refrain; der Hauptinhalt.

burdensome ['bə:dnsəm], *adj.* beschwerlich.

bureau [bjuə'rou], *s.* der Schreibtisch; das Büro.

bureaucracy [bjuə'rɔkrəsi], *s.* die Bürokratie.

burgess ['bə:dʒis], *s.* der Bürger.

burglar ['bə:glə], *s.* der Einbrecher.

burglary ['bə:gləri], *s.* der Einbruch, der Diebstahl.

burgomaster ['bə:gomɑ:stə], *s.* der Bürgermeister.

Burgundian [bə:'gʌndiən], *adj.* burgundisch. —*s.* der Burgunder.

Burgundy (1) ['bə:gəndi], das Burgund.

Burgundy (2) ['bə:gəndi], *s.* der Burgunder(-wein).

burial ['beriəl], das Begräbnis; — ground, der Kirchhof, Friedhof; — service, die Totenfeier, Trauerfeier.

burlesque [bə:'lesk], *s.* die Burleske, Posse.

burly ['bə:li], *adj.* dick, stark.

Burmese [bə:'mi:z], *adj.* birmesisch. — *s.* der Birmese.

burn [bə:n], *v.a., v.n. irr.* brennen, verbrennen. — *s.* das Brandmal.

burner ['bə:nə], *s.* der Brenner.

burnish ['bə:niʃ], *v.a.* polieren.

burred [bə:d], *adj.* überliegend; (*Metall.*) ausgehämmert; — over, (*Metall.*) breitgeschmiedet.

burrow ['bʌrou], *s.* der Bau, (*rabbits etc.*). — *v.n.* sich eingraben; wühlen.

burst [bə:st], *v.a., v.n. irr.* bersten, platzen, explodieren (*explode*); — out laughing, laut auflachen; — into tears, in Tränen ausbrechen; — into flames, aufflammen; sprengen (*blow up*). — *s.* der Ausbruch; die Explosion.

bury ['beri], *v.a.* begraben; beerdigen.

bus [bʌs], *s.* der Autobus, Omnibus.

busby ['bʌzbi], *s.* (*Mil.*) die Bärenmütze.

bush [buʃ], *s.* der Busch.

bushel [buʃl], *s.* der Scheffel.

bushy ['buʃi], *adj.* buschig.

business ['biznis], *s.* das Geschäft; die Beschäftigung, die Tätigkeit (*activity*); Aufgabe, Obliegenheit; der Handel (*trade*); on —, geschäftlich.

businesslike ['biznislaik], *adj.* geschäftsmäßig, nüchtern, praktisch.

businessman ['biznismæn], *s.* der Geschäftsmann.

bust (1) [bʌst], *s.* die Büste.

bust (2) [bʌst], *v.a., v.n.* (*coll.*) sprengen; go —, bankrott machen.

bustard ['bʌstəd], *s.* (*Orn.*) die Trappe.

bustle [bʌsl], *s.* der Lärm, die Aufregung. — *v.n.* aufgeregt umherlaufen; rührig sein (*be active*).

busy ['bizi], *adj.* geschäftig (*active*); beschäftigt (*engaged*, mit, *in*); be —, zu tun haben.

but [bʌt], *conj.* aber, jedoch; sondern. — *adv.* nur, bloß; — yesterday, erst gestern. — *prep.* außer; all — two, alle außer zwei.

butcher ['butʃə], *s.* der Metzger, Fleischer; —'s knife, das Fleischmesser.

butchery ['butʃəri], *s.* die Schlächterei; das Blutbad, das Gemetzel.

butler ['bʌtlə], *s.* der oberste Diener; Kellermeister.

butt [bʌt], *s.* das dicke Ende; der Kolben (*rifle*); der Stoß (*blow*); die Zielscheibe (*target*). — *v.a.* stoßen, spießen.

butter ['bʌtə], *s.* die Butter. — *v.a.* mit Butter bestreichen. — up, schmeicheln (*Dat.*).

butterfly ['bʌtəflai], *s.* (*Ent.*) der Schmetterling.

buttery ['bʌtəri], *s.* die Speisekammer.

buttock(s)

buttock(s) ['bʌtək(s)], s. der Hintere, das Gesäß (usually pl.) (vulg.).
button [bʌtn], s. der Knopf. — v.a. — up, knöpfen, zumachen.
buttress ['bʌtris], s. der Strebepfeiler.
buxom ['bʌksəm], adj. drall, gesund.
buy [bai], v.a. irr. kaufen.
buzz [bʌz], s. das Summen. — v.n. summen.
buzzard ['bʌzəd], s. (Orn.) der Bussard.
by [bai], prep. (beside) neben, an; (near) nahe; (before) gegen, um, bei; (about) bei; (from, with) durch, von, mit; — the way, nebenbei bemerkt; — way of, mittels. — adv. (nearby) nahe; nebenan.
by-election ['baiilekʃən], s. die Nachwahl; Ersatzwahl.
bygone ['baigən], adj. vergangen.
bylaw, byelaw ['bailɔ:], s. die Bestimmung.
Byzantine [bai'zæntain], adj. byzantinisch.

C

C [si:]. das C (also Mus.).
cab [kæb], s. (horse-drawn) die Droschke, der Wagen; das Taxi; —stand, der Droschkenhalteplatz; (Motor.) der Taxiplatz, Taxistand.
cabaret ['kæbərei], s. das Kabarett, die Kleinbühne.
cabbage ['kæbidʒ], s. (Bot.) der Kohl.
cabin ['kæbin], s. die Kabine (boat); die Hütte (hut); — -boy, der Schiffsjunge.
cabinet ['kæbinet], s. das Kabinett (government); der Schrank (cupboard); das kleine Zimmer or Nebenzimmer (mainly Austr.); (Rad.) das Gehäuse; — maker, der Kunsttischler.
cable [keibl], s. das Kabel (of metal), das Seil (metal or rope); das Telegramm. — v.a. kabeln, telegraphieren.
cablegram ['keiblgræm], s. die (Am.) Depesche.
cabman ['kæbmən], s. der Taxichauffeur.
caboose [kə'bu:s], s. die Schiffsküche.
cabriolet [kæbrio'lei], s. das Kabriolett.
cackle [kækl], v.n. gackern (hens); schnattern (geese); (fig.) schwatzen.
cacophony [kə'kɔfəni], s. der Mißklang.
cad [kæd], s. der gemeine Kerl, Schuft.
cadaverous [kə'dævərəs], adj. leichenhaft.
caddie ['kædi], s. der Golfjunge.
caddy ['kædi], s. tea —, die Teebüchse, Teedose.
cadence ['keidəns], s. (Phonet.) der Tonfall; (Mus.) die Kadenz.
cadet [kə'det], s. (Mil.) der Kadett.
cadge [kædʒ], v.a. erbetteln.

Caesar ['si:zə]. Cäsar, m.
Caesarean [si'zɛəriən], adj. cäsarisch; — operation or section, (Med.) der Kaiserschnitt.
cafeteria [kæfə'tiəriə], s. das Selbstbedienungsrestaurant.
cage [keidʒ], s. (Zool.) der Käfig; (Orn.) das Vogelbauer. — v.a. einfangen, einsperren.
cagey ['keidʒi], adj. (coll.) argwöhnisch, zurückhaltend; schlau.
cairn [kɛən], s. (Archaeol.) der Steinhaufen, der Grabhügel.
caitiff ['keitif], adj. niederträchtig. — s. der Schuft.
cajole [kə'dʒoul],v.a.schmeicheln(Dat.).
cake [keik], s. der Kuchen; — of soap, das Stück Seife; have o.'s — and eat it, alles haben. — v.a., v.n. zusammenbacken; —d with dirt, mit Schmutz beschmiert.
calamity [kə'læmiti], s. das Unheil, Unglück; Elend.
calcareous [kæl'kɛəriəs], adj. (Geol.) kalkartig.
calculate ['kælkjuleit], v.a. berechnen.
calculation [kælkju'leiʃən], s. die Berechnung.
calendar ['kæləndə], s. der Kalender.
calf [ka:f], s. (Zool.) das Kalb; (Anat.) die Wade; — love, die Jugendliebe.
calibre ['kælibə], s. das Kaliber.
calico ['kælikou], s. der Kaliko, Kattun.
Caliph ['keilif], s. der Kalif.
calk (1) [kɔ:k], v.a. beschlagen (horse).
calk (2), caulk [kɔ:k], v.a. (Naut.) abdichten.
call [kɔ:l], v.a., v.n. rufen, herbeirufen; (Am.) antelefonieren, anrufen (ring up); (name) nennen; — to account, zur Rechenschaft ziehen; (summon) kommen lassen; — for, abholen; this —s for, das berechtigt zu. — s. der Ruf, Anruf; die (innere) Berufung, der Beruf.
callbox ['kɔ:lbɔks] see phone box.
calling ['kɔ:liŋ], s. der Beruf, das Gewerbe (occupation).
callous ['kæləs], adj. schwielig (hands); (fig.) unempfindlich, hart, gemein.
callow ['kælou], adj. ungefiedert (bird); (fig.) unerfahren.
calm [ka:m], adj. ruhig, still; gelassen. — s. die Ruhe; (Naut.) Windstille. — v.a. beruhigen. — v.n. — down, sich beruhigen, sich legen (storm etc.).
caloric [kæ'lɔrik], adj. Wärme-, warm; (Chem.) kalorisch.
calorie, calory ['kæləri], s. die Kalorie.
calumny ['kæləmni], s. die Verleumdung.
calve [ka:v], v.n. kalben, Kälber kriegen.
cambric ['kæmbrik],s.der Batist(textile).
camel ['kæməl], s. (Zool.) das Kamel.
cameo ['kæmiou], s. die Kamee.
camera ['kæmərə], s. (Phot.) die Kamera.
camomile ['kæməmail], s. (Bot.) die Kamille.

330

captain

camp [kæmp], *s.* das Lager; Zeltlager.
— *v.n.* sich lagern, ein Lager aufschlagen, zelten.
campaign [kæm'pein], *s.* der Feldzug.
— *v.n.* einen Feldzug mitmachen;
(*fig.*) Propaganda machen.
camphor ['kæmfə], *s.* der Kampfer.
camping ['kæmpiŋ], *s.* die Lagerausrüstung (*equipment*); das Lagern (*activity*), das Zelten.
can (1) [kæn], *s.* die Kanne; die Büchse;
watering —, die Gießkanne. — *v.a.*
(*Am.*) einmachen, einkochen (*fruit*).
can (2) [kæn], *v. aux. irr.* können,
imstande sein, vermögen.
Canadian [kə'neidiən] *adj.* kanadisch.
— *s.* der Kanadier.
canal [kə'næl], *s.* der Kanal; — *lock*,
die Kanalschleuse.
canalize ['kænəlaiz], *v.a.* kanalisieren,
leiten.
cancel ['kænsəl], *v.a.* widerrufen, absagen
(*show*); aufheben, ungültig machen.
cancellation [kænsə'leiʃən], *s.* die
Aufhebung, Absage, Widerrufung.
cancer ['kænsə], *s.* (*Med.*, *Astron.*) der
Krebs.
cancerous ['kænsərəs], *adj.* (*Med.*)
krebsartig.
candelabra [kændi'lɑ:brə], *s.* der
Kandelaber, Leuchter.
candid ['kændid], *adj.* offen, aufrichtig.
candidate ['kændideit], *s.* der Kandidat, Bewerber.
candidature ['kændiditʃə], *s.* die
Kandidatur, die Bewerbung.
candied ['kændid], *adj.* gezuckert,
kandiert (*fruit*).
candle [kændl], *s.* die Kerze, das Licht.
Candlemas ['kændlməs], (*Eccl.*)
Lichtmeß.
candlestick ['kændlstik], *s.* der Kerzenleuchter.
candlewick ['kændlwik], *s.* der Kerzendocht (*textile*).
candour ['kændə], *s.* die Offenheit,
Aufrichtigkeit.
candy ['kændi], *s.* (*Am.*) das Zuckerwerk, (*pl.*) Süßigkeiten. — *v.a.*
verzuckern.
cane [kein], *s.* (*Bot.*) das Rohr, der
Rohrstock; Spazierstock. — *v.a.* (mit
dem Stock) schlagen.
canine ['kænain], *adj.* Hunde-, hündisch; — *tooth*, der Eckzahn.
canister ['kænistə], *s.* die Blechbüchse,
der Kanister.
canker ['kæŋkə], *s.* (*Bot.*) der Brand;
(*Bot.*) der Pflanzenrost; (*fig.*) eine
zerfressende Krankheit.
cannibal ['kænibəl], *s.* der Kannibale,
Menschenfresser.
cannon ['kænən], *s.* die Kanone, das
Geschütz.
canoe [kə'nu:], *s.* das Kanu.
canon ['kænən], *s.* (*Mus.*, *Eccl.*) der
Kanon; die Regel; (*Eccl.*) der Domherr; — *law*, das kanonische Recht.
canonize ['kænənaiz], *v.a.* (*Eccl.*)
kanonisieren, heiligsprechen.

canopy ['kænəpi], *s.* der Baldachin.
cant [kænt], *s.* die Heuchelei.
can't, cannot [kɑ:nt,'kænɔt] see **can** (2).
cantankerous [kæn'tæŋkərəs], *adj.*
zänkisch, mürrisch.
cantata [kæn'tɑ:tə], *s.* (*Mus.*) die
Kantate.
canteen [kæn'ti:n], *s.* die Kantine (*restaurant*); die Besteckgarnitur (*set of cutlery*).
canter ['kæntə], *s.* der Galopp, der
Kurzgalopp.
canticle ['kæntikl], *s.* (*Eccl.*) der
Lobgesang, das Loblied.
canto ['kæntou], *s.* (*Lit.*) der Gesang.
canton ['kæntən], *s.* (*Pol.*) der Kanton,
der Bezirk.
canvas ['kænvəs], *s.* das Segeltuch;
(*Art*) die Malerleinwand; die Zeltplane (*tent*).
canvass ['kænvəs], *v.a.*, *v.n.* (*Pol.*)
um Stimmen werben.
canvasser ['kænvəsə], *s.* (*Pol.*) der
Werber, Stimmensammler.
cap [kæp], *s.* die Kappe, Mütze; die
Haube; der Deckel. — *v.a.* übertreffen.
capability [keipə'biliti], *s.* die Fähigkeit.
capable ['keipəbl], *adj.* fähig (*Genit.*),
imstande (*of*, zu); tüchtig.
capacious [kə'peiʃəs], *adj.* geräumig.
capacity [kə'pæsiti], *s.* der Inhalt, die
Geräumigkeit; die Fassungskraft
(*intellect*); die Leistungsfähigkeit
(*ability*); der Fassungsraum (*space*).
cape (1) [keip], *s.* (*Tail.*) der Kragenmantel.
cape (2) [keip], *s.* (*Geog.*) das Kap, das
Vorgebirge.
caper ['keipə], *s.* der Sprung, Luftsprung. — *v.n.* in die Luft springen.
capillary [kə'pilari], *adj.* haarfein; —
tubing, die Haarröhre, die Kapillarröhre.
capital ['kæpitl], *s.* (*Comm.*) das
Kapital; die Hauptstadt (*capital city*);
— *punishment*, die Todesstrafe; —
letter, der Großbuchstabe. — *adj.*
(*coll.*) ausgezeichnet, vorzüglich.
capitalize ['kæpitəlaiz], *v.a.* (*Comm.*)
kapitalisieren; ausnutzen.
capitation [kæpi'teiʃən], *s.* die Kopfsteuer.
capitulate [kə'pitjuleit], *v.n.* kapitulieren.
capon ['keipən], *s.* (*Zool.*) der Kapaun.
caprice [kə'pri:s], *s.* die Kaprize, Laune.
capricious [kə'priʃəs], *adj.* launenhaft,
eigensinnig.
Capricorn ['kæprikɔ:n]. (*Astron.*) der
Steinbock; *tropic of* —, der Wendekreis des Steinbocks.
capriole ['kæprioul], *s.* der Luftsprung.
capsize [kæp'saiz], *v.n.* umkippen,
kentern (*boat*).
capstan ['kæpstən], *s.* (*Engin.*) die
Ankerwinde; (*Mech.*) die Erdwinde;
(*Naut.*) das Gangspill.
capsular ['kæpsjulə], *adj.* kapselförmig.
capsule ['kæpsju:l], *s.* die Kapsel.
captain ['kæptin], *s.* (*Naut.*) der
Kapitän; (*Mil.*) der Hauptmann.

331

captious

captious ['kæpʃəs], *adj.* zänkisch, streitsüchtig; verfänglich.
captivate ['kæptiveit], *v.a.* einnehmen, gewinnen.
captive ['kæptiv], *s.* der Gefangene. — *adj.* gefangen.
capture ['kæptʃə], *s.* die Gefangennahme (*men*); Erbeutung (*booty*).
Capuchin ['kæputʃin], *s.* (*Eccl.*) der Kapuziner.
car [kɑː], *s.* (*Motor.*) der Wagen; das Auto; (*Am.*) der Eisenbahnwagen.
carafe [kæ'ræf], *s.* die Karaffe, Wasserflasche.
caravan ['kærəvæn], *s.* die Karawane; der Wohnwagen.
caraway ['kærəwei], *s.* (*Bot.*) der Kümmel.
carbine ['kɑːbain], *s.* der Karabiner.
carbolic [kɑː'bɔlik], *adj.* — *acid*, (*Chem.*) die Karbolsäure.
carbon ['kɑːbən], *s.* (*Chem.*) der Kohlenstoff.
carbonate ['kɑːbəneit], *s.* (*Chem.*) das kohlensaure Salz, Karbonat.
carbonize ['kɑːbənaiz], *v.a.* verkohlen. — *v.n.* (*Chem., Geol.*) zu Kohle werden.
carbuncle ['kɑːbʌnkl], *s.* (*Min.*) der Karfunkel; (*Med.*) der Karbunkel.
carburettor [kɑːbju'retə], *s.* (*Motor.*) der Vergaser.
carcase, carcass ['kɑːkəs], *s.* der Kadaver.
card (1) [kɑːd], *s.* die Karte, Postkarte; *playing* —, die Spielkarte; *put your* —*s on the table*, rück mit der Wahrheit heraus!
card (2) [kɑːd], *v.a.* krempeln (*wool*); kardätschen (*cotton*).
cardboard ['kɑːdbɔːd], *s.* die Pappe, der Pappendeckel.
cardiac ['kɑːdiæk], *adj.* (*Med.*) Herz–.
cardinal ['kɑːdinl], *s.* (*Eccl.*) der Kardinal. — *adj.* Kardinal–, grundlegend.
cardiogram ['kɑːdiogræm], *s.* (*Med.*) das Kardiogramm.
cardsharper ['kɑːdʃɑːpə], *s.* der Falschspieler.
care [kɛə], *s.* die Sorge (*anxiety*, um, *for*); *with* —, mit Sorgfalt, genau; *care of* (*abbr. c/o on letters*), bei; *take* —, sich in acht nehmen. — *v.n.* — *for*, sich interessieren, gern haben.
careen [kə'riːn], *v.a.* (*Naut.*) kielholen, umlegen.
career [kə'riə], *s.* die Karriere, Laufbahn.
careful ['kɛəful], *adj.* sorgfältig, vorsichtig, umsichtig.
carefulness ['kɛəfulnis], *s.* die Vorsicht, Sorgfalt, Umsicht.
careless ['kɛəlis], *adj.* unachtsam, nachlässig.
carelessness ['kɛəlisnis], *s.* die Nachlässigkeit, Unachtsamkeit.
caress [kə'res], *v.a.* liebkosen, herzen. — *s.* die Liebkosung, die Zärtlichkeit.
caretaker ['kɛəteikə], *s.* der Hausmeister.

careworn ['kɛəwɔːn], *adj.* abgehärmt, von Sorgen gebeugt.
cargo ['kɑːgou], *s.* die Fracht, die Ladung.
caricature [kærikə'tjuə *or* 'kærikətʃə], *s.* die Karikatur. — *v.a.* karikieren, verzerren.
Carinthian [kə'rinθjən], *adj.* kärntnerisch.
carmine ['kɑːmain], *s.* der Karmin.
carnage ['kɑːnidʒ], *s.* das Blutbad.
carnal ['kɑːnl], *adj.* fleischlich, sinnlich.
carnation [kɑː'neiʃən], *s.* (*Bot.*) die Nelke.
carnival ['kɑːnivl], *s.* der Karneval.
carnivorous [kɑː'nivərəs], *adj.* fleischfressend.
carol ['kærəl], *s. Christmas* —, das Weihnachtslied.
carotid [kə'rɔtid], *s.* (*Anat.*) die Halspulsader.
carousal [kə'rauzəl], *s.* das Gelage, das Gezeche.
carouse [kə'rauz], *v.n.* zechen, schmausen.
carp (1) [kɑːp], *s.* (*Zool.*) der Karpfen.
carp (2) [kɑːp], *v.n.* bekritteln, tadeln.
Carpathian Mountains [kɑː'peiθjən 'mauntinz]. die Karpathen, *f. pl.*
carpenter ['kɑːpəntə], *s.* der Zimmermann; Tischler.
carpentry ['kɑːpəntri], *s.* die Tischlerei, das Zimmerhandwerk.
carpet ['kɑːpit], *s.* der Teppich; — *bag*, die Reisetasche.
carriage ['kæridʒ], *s.* der Wagen, Waggon; das Verhalten, die Haltung (*bearing*); (*Comm.*) — *paid*, einschließlich Zustellung; — *way*, der Straßendamm.
carrier ['kæriə], *s.* der Fuhrmann, Fuhrunternehmer.
carrion ['kæriən], *s.* das Aas.
carrot ['kærət], *s.* (*Bot.*) die Mohrrübe; die Karotte.
carry ['kæri], *v.a.* tragen; bringen; führen (*on vehicle*), fahren (*convey*); — *interest*, Zinsen tragen; (*Comm.*) — *forward*, übertragen; — *two* (*in adding up*), zwei weiter; — *on*, weitermachen, fortfahren; — *through*, durchführen, durchhalten; — *v.n.* vernehmbar sein (*of sound*); — *on*, weiterarbeiten, weiterexistieren.
cart [kɑːt], *s.* der Karren, Frachtwagen.
cartel [kɑː'tel], *s.* (*Comm.*) das Kartell.
Carthage ['kɑːθidʒ]. Karthago, *n.*
carthorse ['kɑːthɔːs], *s.* das Zugpferd.
cartilage ['kɑːtilidʒ], *s.* der Knorpel.
carton ['kɑːtən], *s.* (*cardboard box*) der Karton, die Schachtel.
cartoon [kɑː'tuːn], *s.* die Karikatur; — *film*, der Trickfilm.
cartridge ['kɑːtridʒ], *s.* die Patrone.
cartwright ['kɑːtrait], *s.* der Stellmacher, Wagenbauer.
carve [kɑːv], *v.a.* schneiden (*cut*); schnitzen (*wood*), meißeln (*stone*), tranchieren (*meat*).

caustic

carver ['kɑːvə], *s.* der Schnitzer (*wood*); das Tranchiermesser (*carving knife*).
cascade [kæs'keid], *s.* der Wasserfall.
case (1) [keis], *s.* der Kasten, Behälter; das Futteral, Etui (*spectacles*); das Gehäuse (*watch*); die Kiste (*wooden box*); (*Typ.*) der Schriftkasten.
case (2) [keis], *s.* der Fall (*event*); (*Law*) der Rechtsfall, der Umstand (*circumstance*); *in* —, falls.
casement ['keismənt], *s.* der Fensterflügel, das Fenster (*frame*).
caseous ['keisjəs], *adj.* käsig.
cash [kæʃ], *s.* bares Geld; die Barzahlung; — *box*, die Kasse. — *v.a.* einlösen (*cheque*).
cashier [kæ'ʃiə], *s.* der Kassierer. — *v.a.* (*Mil.*) entlassen.
cashmere ['kæʃmiə], *s.* die Kaschmirwolle (*wool*).
casing ['keisiŋ], *s.* die Hülle; das Gehäuse (*case*); die Haut (*sausage skin*).
cask ['kɑːsk], *s.* das Faß.
casket ['kɑːskit], *s.* das Kästchen; (*Am.*) der Sarg.
Caspian (Sea) ['kæspiən (siː)], das kaspische Meer.
cassock ['kæsək], *s.* die Soutane.
cast [kɑːst], *v.a. irr.* werfen (*throw*); (*Metall.*) gießen; (*Theat.*) besetzen; (*plaster*) formen; — *off*, abwerfen; — *anchor*, ankern; — *o.'s skin*, sich häuten; — *down*, niederschlagen; — *a vote*, die Stimme abgeben. — *s.* der Wurf; (*Metall.*) der Guß; (*Theat.*) die Besetzung; der Abguß (plaster). — *adj.* — *iron*, das Gusseisen; — *steel*, der Gußstahl.
castanets [kæstə'nets], *s. pl.* (*Mus.*) die Kastagnetten, *f. pl.*
castaway ['kɑːstəwei], *adj.* weggeworfen; (*Naut.*) schiffbrüchig.
caste [kɑːst], *s.* die Kaste.
caster ['kɑːstə], *s.* der Streuer, die Streubüchse; — *sugar*, Streuzucker.
casting ['kɑːstiŋ], *s.* (*Metall.*) das Gießen, der Guß.
castle [kɑːsl], *s.* die Burg, das Schloß; (*Chess*) der Turm.
castor (1) ['kɑːstə], *s.* (*Zool.*) der Biber.
castor (2) ['kɑːstə] *see* **caster**.
castor (3) **oil** ['kɑːstər 'ɔil], *s.* das Rizinusöl.
castrate [kæs'treit], *v.a.* kastrieren.
castration [kæs'treiʃən], *s.* die Kastration.
casual ['kæʒjuəl], *adj.* zufällig; gelassen (*manner*); gelegentlich; flüchtig.
casualty ['kæʒjuəlti], *s.* der Unglücksfall; — *ward*, die Unfallstation; (*pl.*) die Verluste, *m. pl.*
cat [kæt], *s.* die Katze; *tom* —, der Kater; — *burglar*, der Fassadenkletterer; —'s *eye*, das Katzenauge, der Rückstrahler; der Reflektor.
cataclysm ['kætəklizm], *s.* die Sintflut, die Überschwemmung.
catacomb ['kætəkuːm], *s.* die Katakombe.

catalogue ['kætəlɔg], *s.* der Katalog, das Verzeichnis. — *v.a.* im Katalog verzeichnen, katalogisieren.
catapult ['kætəpult], *s.* die Schleuder (*hand*); (*Mil.*) die Wurfmaschine. — *v.a.* schleudern.
cataract ['kætərækt], *s.* der Wasserfall (*water*); (*Med.*) der Star.
catarrh [kə'tɑː], *s.* (*Med.*) der Katarrh.
catastrophe [kə'tæstrəfi], *s.* die Katastrophe, das Unglück.
catastrophic [kætəs'trɔfik], *adj.* katastrophal, unheilvoll.
catch [kætʃ], *v.a. irr.* fangen, auffangen, fassen; überfallen (— *unawares, ambush*); — *a cold*, sich einen Schnupfen zuziehen, sich erkälten; erreichen (*train, etc.*); — *redhanded*, bei frischer Tat ertappen. — *s.* der Fang (*fish*); die Beute (*prey, booty*); der Haken (*hook, also fig.*).
catchpenny ['kætʃpeni], *s.* der Flitterkram, Lockartikel. — *adj.* marktschreierisch.
catchphrase, catchword ['kætʃfreiz, 'kætʃwəːd], *s.* das (billige) Schlagwort.
catechism ['kætikizm], *s.* der Katechismus.
categorical [kæti'gɔrikəl], *adj.* kategorisch, entschieden.
category ['kætigəri], *s.* die Kategorie, Klasse, Gruppe, Gattung.
cater ['keitə], *v.n.* Lebensmittel einkaufen; verpflegen; (*fig.*) sorgen (*for, für*).
caterer ['keitərə], *s.* der Lebensmittellieferant.
catering ['keitəriŋ], *s.* die Verpflegung.
caterpillar ['kætəpilə], *s.* (*Ent.*) die Raupe; (*Mech.*) der Raupenschlepper.
caterwaul ['kætəwɔːl], *v.n.* miauen.
cathedral [kə'θiːdrəl], *s.* der Dom, die Kathedrale.
Catholic ['kæθəlik], *adj.* katholisch. — *s.* der Katholik.
catholic ['kæθəlik], *adj.* allumfassend.
Catholicism [kə'θɔlisizm], *s.* der Katholizismus.
catkin ['kætkin], *s.* (*Bot.*) das Kätzchen; *pussy-willow* —, das Palmkätzchen.
cattle [kætl], *s. pl.* das Vieh; — *plague*, die Rinderpest; — *show*, die Viehausstellung.
caucus ['kɔːkəs], *s.* die Wahlversammlung; der Wahlausschuß.
caul [kɔːl], *s.* das Haarnetz; (*Anat.*) die Eihaut.
cauldron ['kɔːldrən], *s.* der Kessel.
cauliflower ['kɔliflauə], *s.* (*Bot.*) der Blumenkohl.
caulk [kɔːk], *v.a.* kalfatern (*see under* **calk** (2)).
causal ['kɔːzəl], *adj.* ursächlich.
causality [kɔː'zæliti], *s.* der ursächliche Zusammenhang; (*Log.*) die Kausalität.
cause [kɔːz], *s.* die Ursache. — *v.a.* verursachen.
causeway ['kɔːzwei], *s.* der Damm.
caustic ['kɔːstik], *adj.* ätzend; beißend.

333

cauterize

cauterize ['kɔ:təraiz], v.a. (Med.) ätzen, ausbrennen.
caution ['kɔ:ʃən], s. die Vorsicht (care); die Warnung (warning). — v.a. (Law) ermahnen; warnen.
cautionary ['kɔ:ʃənəri], adj. warnend.
cautious ['kɔ:ʃəs], adj. vorsichtig, behutsam.
cautiousness ['kɔ:ʃəsnis], s. die Vorsicht, Behutsamkeit.
cavalcade [kævəl'keid], s. die Kavalkade; (Mil.) der Reiterzug.
cavalry ['kævəlri], s. die Kavallerie, die Reiterei.
cave [keiv], s. die Höhle. — v.a. aushöhlen. — v.n. — in, einstürzen, einfallen.
caveat ['keiviæt], s. (Law) die Warnung; der Vorbehalt.
cavern ['kævən], s. die Höhle.
cavernous ['kævənəs], adj. (Geog., Geol.) voll Höhlen.
caviare [kævi'ɑ:], s. der Kaviar.
cavil ['kævil], v.n. nörgeln (at, über), tadeln (Acc.).
cavity ['kæviti], s. die Höhlung.
caw [kɔ:], v.n. (Orn.) krächzen.
cease [si:s], v.a. einstellen. — v.n. aufhören.
ceaseless ['si:slis], adj. unaufhörlich.
cedar ['si:də], s. (Bot.) die Zeder.
cede [si:d], v.a. überlassen. — v.n. nachgeben.
ceiling ['si:lin], s. die Decke (room); (Comm.) die Preisgrenze.
celebrate ['selibreit], v.a. feiern; zelebrieren.
celebrated ['selibreitid], adj. berühmt.
celebration [seli'breiʃən], s. die Feier.
celebrity [si'lebriti], s. die Berühmtheit; der „Star".
celerity [si'leriti], s. die Behendigkeit, Schnelligkeit.
celery ['seləri], s. (Bot.) der Sellerie.
celestial [si'lestjəl], adj. himmlisch.
celibacy ['selibəsi], s. die Ehelosigkeit; (Eccl.) das Zölibat.
celibate ['selibit], adj. unverheiratet.
cell [sel], s. die Zelle.
cellar ['selə], s. der Keller; salt —, das Salzfaß.
cellarage ['seləridʒ], s. die Kellerei; die Einkellerung (storage).
cellarer ['selərə], s. der Kellermeister.
cellular ['seljulə], adj. zellartig, Zell-.
Celt [kelt, selt], s. der Kelte.
Celtic ['keltik, 'seltik], adj. keltisch.
cement [si'ment], s. der Zement, Mörtel. — v.a. auszementieren, verkitten.
cemetery ['semətri], s. der Kirchhof, der Friedhof.
cenotaph ['senotæf or -tɑ:f], s. das Ehrengrabmal, Ehrendenkmal.
censer ['sensə], s. (Eccl.) das Weihrauchfaß.
censor ['sensə], s. der Zensor.
censorious [sen'sɔ:riəs], adj. kritisch, tadelsüchtig.
censure ['senʃə], s. der Tadel, Verweis. — v.a. tadeln.

census ['sensəs], s. die Volkszählung.
cent [sent], s. (Am.) der Cent (coin); (Comm.) per —, das Prozent.
centenarian [senti'nɛəriən], adj. hundertjährig. — s. der Hundertjährige.
centenary [sen'ti:nəri], s. die Hundertjahrfeier.
centennial [sen'tenjəl], adj. alle hundert Jahre, hundertjährig.
centipede ['sentipi:d], s. (Zool.) der Tausendfüßler.
central ['sentrəl], adj. zentral.
centralize ['sentrəlaiz], v.a. zentralisieren.
centre ['sentə], s. das Zentrum, der Mittelpunkt; die Mitte.
centric(al) ['sentrik(əl)], adj. (Engin., Maths.) zentral.
centrifugal [sen'trifjugəl], adj. zentrifugal.
centrifuge [sen'trifju:dʒ], s. die Zentrifuge.
centripetal [sen'tripitl], adj. zentripetal, zum Mittelpunkt hinstrebend.
century ['sentʃuri], s. das Jahrhundert.
cereal ['siəriəl], adj. vom Getreide, Getreide—. — s. die Kornmehlspeise.
cerebral ['seribrəl], adj. Gehirn-.
ceremonial [seri'mounjəl], adj. feierlich, förmlich (formal). — s. das Zeremoniell.
ceremonious [seri'mounjəs], adj. feierlich, zeremoniell.
ceremony ['seriməni], s. die Zeremonie, die Feier.
certain ['sə:tin], adj. sicher, gewiß.
certainty ['sə:tinti], s. die Gewißheit.
certificate [sə'tifikit], s. das Zeugnis, die Bescheinigung.
certification [sə:tifi'keiʃən], s. die Bescheinigung, Bezeugung.
certify ['sə:tifai], v.a. bescheinigen, bezeugen, beglaubigen.
certitude ['sə:titju:d], s. die Gewißheit.
cerulean [si'ru:ljən], adj. himmelblau.
cesspool ['sespu:l], s. die Senkgrube.
cessation [se'seiʃən], s. das Aufhören; (of hostilities) der Waffenstillstand.
cession ['seʃən], s. die Abtretung, der Verzicht (of, auf).
chafe [tʃeif], v.a. wärmen, warmreiben; erzürnen (annoy); wundreiben (skin). — v.n. toben, wüten.
chafer ['tʃeifə], s. (Ent.) der Käfer.
chaff [tʃɑ:f], s. die Spreu; die Neckerei (teasing). — v.a. necken.
chaffer ['tʃæfə], v.n. handeln, schachern (haggle).
chaffinch ['tʃæfintʃ], s. (Orn.) der Buchfink.
chagrin [ʃæ'gri:n], s. der Verdruß, der Ärger.
chain [tʃein], s. die Kette. — v.a. anketten.
chair [tʃɛə], s. der Stuhl; (Univ.) Lehrstuhl. — v.a. vorsitzen (Dat.).
chairman ['tʃɛəmən], s. der Vorsitzende.
chalice ['tʃælis], s. (Eccl.) der Kelch.

chalk [tʃɔ:k], s. die Kreide. — v.a. — up, ankreiden, anschreiben.

chalky ['tʃɔ:ki], adj. (Geol.) kreidig, kreideartig.

challenge ['tʃælindʒ], v.a. herausfordern; in Frage stellen (question); anhalten (of a sentry). — s. die Herausforderung; das Anhalten (by a sentry); die Einwendung.

chalybeate [kə'libiət], adj. (Med.) eisenhaltig.

chamber ['tʃeimbə], s. das Zimmer, die Kammer.

chamberlain ['tʃeimbəlin], s. der Kammerherr.

chambermaid ['tʃeimbəmeid], s. das Zimmermädchen, Kammermädchen.

chameleon [kə'mi:ljən], s. (Zool.) das Chamäleon.

chamois ['ʃæmwa:], s. (Zool.) die Gemse.

champagne [ʃæm'pein], s. der Champagner, der Sekt.

champion ['tʃæmpjən], s. der Meister, Verteidiger. — v.a. vertreten (cause); beschützen (person).

chance [tʃa:ns], s. der Zufall; die Gelegenheit (opportunity); die Möglichkeit (possibility); take a —, es darauf ankommen lassen; by —, zufällig. — v.a. zufällig tun, geraten; riskieren (risk).

chancel ['tʃa:nsəl], s. (Eccl.) der Chor, der Altarplatz.

chancellor ['tʃa:nsələ], s. der Kanzler.

chancery ['tʃa:nsəri], s. das Kanzleigericht.

chandelier [ʃændə'liə], s. der Armleuchter, Kronleuchter.

chandler ['tʃa:ndlə], s. der Lichtzieher; Krämer; (corn merchant) der Kornhändler.

change [tʃeindʒ], s. die Änderung; das Umsteigen (trains); small —, das Kleingeld; die Veränderung; Abwechslung. — v.a. ändern (alter); wechseln (money); umsteigen (trains); eintauschen, umtauschen (exchange); sich umziehen (clothes). — v.n. sich (ver)ändern, anders werden, umschlagen; (Railw.) — for, umsteigen nach.

changeable ['tʃeindʒəbl], adj. veränderlich.

changeling ['tʃeindʒliŋ], s. der Wechselbalg.

changeover ['tʃeindʒouvə], s. der Wechsel; der Umschalter; die Umstellung.

channel ['tʃænəl], s. der Kanal. — v.a. leiten, kanalisieren.

chant [tʃa:nt], v.a., v.n. (Eccl.) singen. — s. (Mus.) der Kantus, der liturgische Gesang.

chaos ['keiɔs], s. das Chaos.

chaotic [kei'ɔtik], adj. chaotisch.

chap (1) [tʃæp], s. der Riss (skin etc.). — v.n. Risse bekommen.

chap (2) [tʃæp], s. (usually in pl.) der Kinnbacken.

chap (3) [tʃæp], s. (coll.) der Kerl, der Bursche.

chapel ['tʃæpəl], s. (Eccl.) die Kapelle.

chaperon ['ʃæpəroun], s. die Anstandsdame. — v.a. begleiten, bemuttern.

chaplain ['tʃæplin], s. der Kaplan.

chapter ['tʃæptə], s. das Kapitel.

char [tʃa:], v.a. verkohlen. — v.n. (coll.) putzen, Hausarbeit verrichten (do housework). — s. (coll.) die Haushilfe, die Hausgehilfin, Putzfrau.

character ['kærəktə], s. der Charakter (personality); das Zeichen (sign, symbol); (Maths.) die Ziffer; das Zeugnis (testimonial).

characteristic [kærəktə'ristik], adj. charakteristisch, typisch.

characterize ['kærəktəraiz], v.a. charakterisieren, kennzeichnen.

charade [ʃə'ra:d], s. die Scharade, das Silbenrätsel.

charcoal ['tʃa:koul], s. die Holzkohle; — burner, der Köhler.

charge [tʃa:dʒ], v.a. laden, aufladen; (Law) beschuldigen; (Mil.) angreifen; belasten (with a bill); — up to s.o., jemandem etwas anrechnen; verlangen (price). — s. die Ladung, der Auftrag (order); die Aufsicht; to be in —, die Aufsicht haben; (Law) die Beschuldigung, Anklage; die Mündel (of a guardian); (pl.) die Kosten, Spesen.

chargeable ['tʃa:dʒəbl], adj. anzurechnend; steuerbar (of objects).

charger ['tʃa:dʒə], s. das Schlachtroß.

chariness ['tʃɛərinis], s. die Behutsamkeit.

chariot ['tʃæriət], s. der Kriegswagen.

charioteer [tʃæriə'tiə], s. der Wagenlenker.

charitable ['tʃæritəbl], adj. wohltätig, mild, mildtätig.

charitableness ['tʃæritəblnis], s. die Wohltätigkeit, Milde.

charity ['tʃæriti], s. die Güte; Nächstenliebe; Mildtätigkeit (alms); die Barmherzigkeit (charitableness); die wohltätige Zweck (cause); sister of —, barmherzige Schwester.

charlatan ['ʃa:lətən], s. der Scharlatan, Pfuscher.

charm [tʃa:m], s. der Zauber (magic); der Reiz. — v.a. bezaubern.

chart [tʃa:t], s. (Geog.) die Karte. — v.a. auf die Karte einzeichnen.

charter ['tʃa:tə], s. die Urkunde; (Naut.) die Schiffsmiete. — v.a. mieten, chartern, heuern (ship, plane); ein Privileg geben, bevorrechtigen.

charwoman ['tʃa:wumən], s. die Putzfrau, Reinemacherin.

chary ['tʃɛəri], adj. behutsam; vorsichtig (cautious); sparsam (thrifty).

chase [tʃeis], v.a. jagen, verfolgen. — s. die Jagd (hunt); das Gehege (game preserve).

chaser ['tʃeisə], s. der Verfolger (pursuer); die Schiffskanone (gun).

chasm [kæzm], s. die Kluft; der Abgrund.

chassis ['ʃæsi], s. (Motor.) das Fahrgestell.

chaste

chaste [tʃeist], *adj.* keusch, züchtig.
chasten [tʃeisn], *v.a.* züchtigen; reinigen.
chastize [tʃæs'taiz], *v.a.* züchtigen.
chastity ['tʃæstiti], *s.* die Keuschheit, Züchtigkeit.
chasuble ['tʃæzjubl], *s.* (*Eccl.*) das Meßgewand.
chat [tʃæt], *v.n.* plaudern. — *s.* das Geplauder.
chattel [tʃætl], *s.* (*usually in pl.*) die Habe; *goods and —s,* Hab und Gut.
chatter ['tʃætə], *v.n.* schwätzen; schnattern. — *s.* das Geschwätz (*talk*).
chatterbox ['tʃætəbɔks], *s.* die Plaudertasche.
chatty ['tʃæti], *adj.* geschwätzig.
chauffeur ['ʃoufə, ʃou'fə:], *s.* (*Motor.*) der Fahrer.
chauffeuse [ʃou'fə:z], *s.* die Fahrerin.
chauvinism ['ʃouvinizm], *s.* der Chauvinismus.
cheap [tʃi:p], *adj.* billig.
cheapen ['tʃi:pən], *v.a.* herabsetzen, erniedrigen (*value*).
cheapness ['tʃi:pnis], *s.* die Billigkeit (*price*).
cheat [tʃi:t], *v.a., v.n.* betrügen. — *s.* der Betrüger.
cheating ['tʃi:tiŋ], *s.* das Betrügen; der Betrug.
check [tʃek], *s.* der Einhalt, der Halt; die Kontrolle; das Hindernis (*obstacle*); (*Chess*) Schach; (*Am.*) *see* cheque. — *v.a.* zurückhalten, aufhalten (*stop*); überprüfen. — *v.n.* Schach bieten (*Dat.*).
checker *see under* chequer.
checkmate ['tʃekmeit], *s.* das Schachmatt.
cheek [tʃi:k], *s.* die Wange, die Backe; die Unverschämtheit (*impertinence*). — *v.a.* unverschämt sein *or* handeln (*s.o.*), zu jemandem).
cheeky ['tʃi:ki], *adj.* frech, unverschämt.
cheer [tʃiə], *v.a.* anfeuern, anspornen; zujubeln; — *up,* aufmuntern. — *v.n.* — *up,* Mut fassen. — *s.* der Zuruf; der Beifallsruf (*acclaim*); *three —s,* ein dreifaches Hoch (*for,* auf).
cheerful ['tʃiəful], *adj.* fröhlich, froh.
cheerless ['tʃiəlis], *adj.* unfreundlich, freudlos.
cheese [tʃi:z], *s.* der Käse; — *straw,* die Käsestange.
cheesecloth ['tʃi:zklɔθ], *s.* (*Am.*) das Nesseltuch.
cheeseparing ['tʃi:zpɛəriŋ], *adj.* knauserig.
cheesy ['tʃi:zi], *adj.* käsig; (*sl.*) schlecht aussehend.
cheetah ['tʃi:itə], *s.* (*Zool.*) der Jagdleopard.
chemical ['kemikəl], *adj.* chemisch. — *s.* die Chemikalie, das chemische Element; das chemische Produkt.
chemise [ʃi'mi:z], *s.* das Frauenhemd.
chemist ['kemist], *s.* der Chemiker; Drogist; Apotheker (*dispenser*).

chemistry ['kemistri], *s.* die Chemie.
cheque, (*Am.*) check [tʃek], *s.* (*Fin.*) der Scheck.
chequer, checker ['tʃekə], *s.* das scheckige Muster, Würfelmuster. — *v.a.* würfelig machen, bunt machen.
cherish ['tʃeriʃ], *v.a.* hegen, wertschätzen, lieben.
cherry ['tʃeri], *s.* (*Bot.*) die Kirsche; — *brandy,* das Kirschwasser.
chess [tʃes], *s.* das Schachspiel; —*man,* die Schachfigur; —*board,* das Schachbrett.
chest [tʃest], *s.* die Truhe (*box*); die Kiste; (*Anat.*) Brust; — *of drawers,* die Kommode.
chestnut ['tʃestnʌt], *s.* (*Bot.*) die Kastanie; (*horse*) der Braune. — *adj.* kastanienbraun.
chew [tʃu:], *v.a.* kauen; —*ing gum,* der Kaugummi.
chic [ʃi:k], *adj.* elegant, schick.
chicanery [ʃi'keinəri], *s.* die Schikane, Haarspalterei, Kleinlichkeit.
chicken ['tʃikin], *s.* das Huhn, Kücken; — *soup,* die Hühnersuppe.
chickenpox ['tʃikinpɔks], *s.* (*Med.*) die Windpocken.
chicory ['tʃikəri], *s.* (*Bot.*) die Zichorie.
chide [tʃaid], *v.a. irr.* schelten.
chief [tʃi:f], *s.* der Häuptling (*of tribe*); (*Am. coll.*) der Chef (*boss*). — *adj.* hauptsächlich, Haupt-, oberst.
chieftain ['tʃi:ftin], *s.* der Häuptling (*of tribe*); Anführer (*leader*).
chilblain ['tʃilblein], *s.* die Frostbeule.
child [tʃaild], *s.* das Kind.
childbirth ['tʃaildbə:θ], *s.* die Niederkunft.
childhood ['tʃaildhud], *s.* die Kindheit.
childish ['tʃaildiʃ], *adj.* kindisch.
childlike ['tʃaildlaik], *adj.* kindlich, wie ein Kind.
Chilean ['tʃiliən], *adj.* chilenisch. — *s.* der Chilene.
chill [tʃil], *s.* die Kälte, der Frost; die Erkältung. — *v.a.* kalt machen (*freeze*); erstarren lassen (*make rigid*); entmutigen (*discourage*).
chilly ['tʃili], *adj.* frostig, eisig, eiskalt.
chime [tʃaim], *s.* das Glockengeläute. — *v.n.* klingen, läuten.
chimera [ki'miərə], *s.* das Hirngespinst, das Trugbild.
chimney ['tʃimni], *s.* der Kamin, der Schornstein; —*pot,* —*stack,* der Schornstein; —*sweep,* der Kaminfeger, Schornsteinfeger.
chimpanzee [tʃimpæn'zi:], *s.* (*Zool.*) der Schimpanse.
chin [tʃin], *s.* (*Anat.*) das Kinn.
china ['tʃainə], *s.* das Porzellan; —*ware,* das Küchengeschirr.
chine (1) [tʃain], *s.* das Rückgrat.
chine (2) [tʃain], *s.* (*Geog.*) der Kamm.
Chinaman ['tʃainəmən], *s.* (*obs.*) der Chinese.
Chinese [tʃai'ni:z], *adj.* chinesisch. — *s.* der Chinese.
chink [tʃink], *s.* die Ritze, der Spalt.

336

Circassian

chip [tʃip], *v.a.* schnitzeln (*wood*); ausbrechen (*stone*); in kleine Stücke schneiden. — *v.n.* — *off*, abbröckeln; — *in*, (*coll.*) sich hineinmischen. —*s.* der Span (*wood*); der Splitter (*glass, stone*); (*pl.*) Pommes frites (*pl.*) (*potatoes*).

chiromancy [ˈkaiərəmænsi], *s.* das Handlesen.

chiropodist [kiˈrɔpədist], *s.* der Fußpfleger.

chirp [tʃəːp], *v.n.* zwitschern (*birds*), zirpen (*crickets*).

chirping [ˈtʃəːpiŋ], *s.* das Gezwitscher (*birds*), das Gezirpe (*crickets*).

chisel [tʃizl], *s.* der Meißel. — *v.a.* meißeln.

chit [tʃit], *s.* das Stück Papier; (*coll.*) junges Ding; —*chat*, das Geplauder.

chivalrous [ˈʃivəlrəs], *adj.* ritterlich; tapfer (*brave*).

chivalry [ˈʃivəlri], *s.* die Ritterlichkeit (*courtesy*); Tapferkeit (*bravery*).

chive [tʃaiv], *s.* (*Bot.*) der Schnittlauch.

chlorate [ˈklɔːreit], *s.* (*Chem.*) das Chlorsalz.

chlorine [ˈklɔːriːn], *s.* (*Chem.*) das Chlor, Chlorgas.

chloroform [ˈklɔrəfɔːm], *s.* das Chloroform. — *v.a.* chloroformieren.

chocolate [ˈtʃɔkəlit], *s.* die Schokolade. — *adj.* schokoladefarben.

choice [tʃɔis], *s.* die Wahl; Auswahl (*selection*). — *adj.* auserlesen.

choir [ˈkwaiə], *s.* der Chor.

choke [tʃouk], *v.a., v.n.* ersticken; verstopfen (*block*). — *s.* (*Elec.*) die Drosselspule; (*Motor.*) die Starterklappe.

choler [ˈkɔlə], *s.* die Galle; (*fig.*) der Zorn (*anger*).

cholera [ˈkɔlərə], *s.* (*Med.*) die Cholera.

choleric [ˈkɔlərik], *adj.* jähzornig, cholerisch.

choose [tʃuːz], *v.a.* irr. wählen, auswählen (*select*).

choosy [ˈtʃuːzi], *adj.* wählerisch.

chop [tʃɔp], *v.a.* abhacken (*cut off*), hacken (*meat*). — *s.* das Kotelett (*meat*).

chopper [ˈtʃɔpə], *s.* das Hackbeil (*axe*); das Hackmesser (*knife*).

choppy [ˈtʃɔpi], *adj.* bewegt (*sea*), stürmisch.

chopstick [ˈtʃɔpstik], *s.* das Eßstäbchen.

choral [ˈkɔːrəl], *adj.* Chor-; — *society*, der Gesangverein.

chorale [kɔˈrɑːl], *s.* (*Eccl., Mus.*) der Choral.

chord [kɔːd], *s.* die Saite; (*Geom.*) die Sehne; (*Mus.*) der Akkord.

chorister [ˈkɔristə], *s.* der Chorknabe (*boy*), Chorsänger.

chorus [ˈkɔːrəs], *s.* der Chor (*opera*); der Refrain (*song*).

Christ [kraist], Christus, *m.*

christen [krisn], *v.a.* taufen (*baptize*); nennen (*name*).

Christendom [ˈkrisndəm], *s.* die Christenheit.

christening [ˈkrisniŋ], *s.* die Taufe.

Christian [ˈkristjən], *s.* der Christ (*believer in Christ*). — *adj.* christlich; — *name*, der Vorname.

Christianity [kristiˈæniti], *s.* die christliche Religion, das Christentum.

Christmas [ˈkrisməs], *s.* (die) Weihnachten; das Weihnachtsfest; — *Eve*, der heilige Abend.

chromatic [kroˈmætik], *adj.* (*Mus.*) chromatisch.

chrome [kroum], *s.* das Chrom.

chronic [ˈkrɔnik], *adj.* chronisch.

chronicle [ˈkrɔnikl], *s.* die Chronik. — *v.a.* (in einer Chronik) verzeichnen.

chronological [krɔnəˈlɔdʒikəl], *adj.* chronologisch.

chronology [krɔˈnɔlədʒi], *s.* die Chronologie.

chronometer [krɔˈnɔmitə], *s.* das Chronometer.

chrysalis [ˈkrisəlis], *s.* (*Ent.*) die Puppe.

chrysanthemum [kriˈzænθəməm], *s.* (*Bot.*) die Chrysantheme.

chub [tʃʌb], *s.* (*Zool.*) der Döbel.

chubby [ˈtʃʌbi], *adj.* pausbäckig, plump.

chuck [tʃʌk], *v.a.* (*coll.*) — *out*, hinauswerfen. — *v.n.* glucken (*chicken*).

chuckle [tʃʌkl], *v.n.* kichern. — *s.* das Kichern.

chum [tʃʌm], *s.* (*coll.*) der Freund, Kamerad. — *v.n.* (*coll.*) — *up*, sich befreunden (*with*, mit).

chump [tʃʌmp], *s.* der Klotz (*wood*).

chunk [tʃʌŋk], *s.* das große Stück (*meat etc.*).

church [tʃəːtʃ], *s.* die Kirche.

churchwarden [tʃəːˈtʃwɔːdn], *s.* der Kirchenvorsteher.

churchyard [ˈtʃəːtʃjɑːd], *s.* der Friedhof.

churl [tʃəːl], *s.* der Grobian, der grobe Kerl.

churlish [ˈtʃəːliʃ], *adj.* grob, unfein.

churn [tʃəːn], *s.* das Butterfaß. — *v.a.* mischen, schütteln (*butter etc.*); — *up*, aufwühlen (*stir up*).

chute [ʃuːt], *s.* die Gleitbahn.

cider [ˈsaidə], *s.* der Apfelmost.

cigar [siˈgɑː], *s.* die Zigarre; — *case*, das Zigarrenetui.

cigarette [sigəˈret], *s.* die Zigarette; — *holder*, die Zigarettenspitze; — *lighter*, das Feuerzeug.

cinder [ˈsində], *s.* (*usually in pl.*) die Asche (*fire*); die Schlacke (*furnace*).

Cinderella [sindəˈrelə], das Aschenbrödel, Aschenputtel.

cinema [ˈsinimə], *s.* das Kino.

cinematography [siniməˈtɔgrəfi], *s.* die Filmkunst.

Cingalese *see* **Singhalese**.

cinnamon [ˈsinəmən], *s.* der Zimt.

cipher [ˈsaifə], *s.* die Ziffer; die Geheimschrift (*code*). — *v.n.* rechnen. — *v.a.* chiffrieren (*code*).

Circassian [səːˈkæsiən], *adj.* tscherkessisch. — *s.* der Tscherkesse.

337

circle

circle [sə:kl], *s.* der Zirkel, Kreis; (*social*) Gesellschaftskreis; (*Theat.*) der Rang. — *v.a.* umringen. — *v.n.* umkreisen; sich drehen (*revolve*).

circuit ['sə:kit], *s.* der Kreislauf; (*Elec.*) der Stromkreis.

circuitous [sə:'kju:itəs], *adj.* weitschweifig, weitläufig.

circular ['sə:kjulə], *adj.* rund, kreisförmig, Rund-; — *tour*, die Rundreise. — *s.* das Rundschreiben (*letter*); der Werbebrief (*advertising*).

circulate ['sə:kjuleit], *v.a.* in Umlauf setzen. — *v.n.* umlaufen, kreisen, zirkulieren.

circulation [sə:kju'leifən], *s.* die Zirkulation, der Kreislauf (*blood*); die Verbreitung, Auflage (*newspaper*); der Umlauf (*banknotes*).

circumcise ['sə:kəmsaiz], *v.a.* beschneiden.

circumference [sə:'kʌmfərəns], *s.* der Umfang.

circumscribe ['sə:kəmskraib], *v.a.* beschränken, einengen (*narrow down*); umschreiben (*paraphrase*).

circumspect ['sə:kəmspekt], *adj.* umsichtig, vorsorglich.

circumspection [sə:kəm'spekfən], *s.* die Umsicht, Vorsicht.

circumstance ['sə:kəmstæns, -sta:ns], *s.* der Umstand; *pomp and* —, großer Aufmarsch.

circumstantial [sə:kəm'stænfəl], *adj.* umständlich; zu einem Umstand gehörig; eingehend; — *evidence*, der Indizienbeweis.

circumvent [sə:kəm'vent], *v.a.* überlisten, hintergehen.

circus ['sə:kəs], *s.* der Zirkus; der Platz.

cirrhus ['sirəs], *s.* die Federwolke.

Cistercian [sis'tə:fən], *s.* der Zisterzienser (*monk*).

cistern ['sistən], *s.* die Zisterne, der Wasserbehälter.

citadel ['sitədəl],*s.*die Zitadelle,die Burg.

citation [sai'teifən], *s.* das Zitat; (*Law*) die Zitierung, Vorladung; (*Mil.*) die rühmliche Erwähnung.

cite [sait], *v.a.* zitieren (*quote*); (*Law*) vorladen.

citizen ['sitizən], *s.* der Bürger, Staatsbürger (*national*); *fellow* —, der Mitbürger.

citizenship ['sitizənfip], *s.* das Bürgerrecht, die Staatsangehörigkeit.

citrate ['sitreit], *s.* (*Chem.*) das Zitrat.

citric ['sitrik], *adj.* (*Chem.*) Zitronen-.

citron ['sitrən], *s.* die Zitrone. — *adj.* zitronenfarben.

city ['siti], *s.* die Stadt; die Großstadt; die City. — *adj.* städtisch.

civic ['sivik], *adj.* Stadt-, städtisch (*ceremonial*); bürgerlich.

civil ['sivil], *adj.* zivil; höflich (*polite*); — *engineer*, der Zivilingenieur; — *service*, der Beamtendienst, die Beamtenlaufbahn, der Staatsdienst; — *war*, der Bürgerkrieg.

civilian [si'viljən], *s.* der Zivilist.

civility [si'viliti], *s.* die Höflichkeit.

civilization [sivilai'zeifən], *s.* die Zivilisation.

civilize ['sivilaiz], *v.a.* zivilisieren, verfeinern (*refine*).

clack [klæk], *v.n.* klappern (*wood etc.*); plaudern, plappern.

clad [klæd], *adj.* gekleidet.

claim [kleim], *v.a.* Anspruch erheben (*to, auf*); fordern (*demand*); behaupten (*assert*). — *s.* der Anspruch; die Forderung (*demand*); das Recht.

claimant ['kleimənt], *s.* der Beanspruchende, Ansprucherheber.

clairvoyance [klɛə'vɔiəns], *s.* das Hellsehen.

clairvoyant [klɛə'vɔiənt], *s.* der Hellseher.

clam [klæm], *s.* (*Zool.*) die Venusmuschel; *shut up like a* —, verschwiegen sein.

clamber ['klæmbə], *v.n.* klettern.

clamminess ['klæminis], *s.* die Feuchtigkeit, Klebrigkeit.

clammy ['klæmi], *adj.* feucht, klebrig.

clamorous ['klæmərəs], *adj.* lärmend, laut, ungestüm.

clamour ['klæmə], *s.* das Geschrei, der Lärm. — *v.n.* laut schreien (*for*, nach, *Dat.*).

clamp [klæmp], *s.* die Klammer, die Klampe. — *v.a.* festklammern.

clan [klæn], *s.* die Sippe, die Familie.

clandestine [klæn'destin], *adj.* heimlich, verstohlen.

clang [klæŋ], *s.* der Schall, das Geklirr. — *v.n.* erschallen. — *v.a.* erschallen lassen.

clangour ['klæŋə], *s.* das Getöse, der Lärm.

clank [klæŋk], *s.* das Geklirre, das Gerassel (*metal*).

clannish ['klænif], *adj.* stammesbewußt; engherzig (*narrow*).

clap [klæp], *v.a.* schlagen, zusammenschlagen (*hands*). — *v.n.* Beifall klatschen (*Dat.*).

clapperboard ['klæpəbɔ:d], *s.* (*Film*) das Klappbrett, die Klapptafel; der Klöppel (*beater, in lacemaking*).

claptrap ['klæptræp], *s.* der billige Effekt, das eitle Geschwätz (*gossip*).

claret ['klærit], *s.* der Rotwein.

clarification [klærifi'keifən], *s.* die Klarstellung, Aufklärung.

clarify ['klærifai], *v.a.* klarstellen.

clari(o)net [klæri(ə)'net], *s.* (*Mus.*) die Klarinette.

clarion ['klæriən], *s.* (*Mus.*) die Zinke, Trompete; — *call*, der laute Ruf.

clash [klæf], *v.a.* zusammenschlagen. — *v.n.* aufeinanderprallen, zusammenfallen (*dates*); widerstreiten (*views*). — *s.* (*fig.*) der Zusammenstoß, der Widerstreit.

clasp [kla:sp], *v.a.* ergreifen, festhalten. — *s.* der Haken (*hook*); die Schnalle, die Spange (*buckle, brooch*); — *knife*, das Taschenmesser.

cloisters

class [klɑ:s], *s.* die Klasse.
classic(al) [ˈklæsik(əl)], *adj.* klassisch.
classics [ˈklæsiks], *s. pl.* die Klassiker, *m. pl.*; die klassische Philologie (*subject of study*).
classification [klæsifiˈkeiʃən], *s.* die Klassifizierung.
classify [ˈklæsifai], *v.a.* klassifizieren.
clatter [ˈklætə], *s.* das Getöse, Geklirr. — *v.a., v.n.* klappern, klirren.
Claus [klɔ:z]. Claus, Nicholas, *m.*; *Santa* —, der heilige Nikolaus, Knecht Ruprecht, Weihnachtsmann.
clause [klɔ:z], *s.* (*Gram.*) der Nebensatz; die Klausel (*contract*); (*Law*) der Vertragspunkt.
claw [klɔ:], *s.* die Klaue, die Kralle. — *v.a.* kratzen.
clay [klei], *s.* der Ton, Lehm.
clayey [kleii], *adj.* lehmig, tonig.
clean [kli:n], *adj.* rein, reinlich (*habits*); sauber; — *shaven*, glattrasiert. — *v.a.* reinigen, putzen.
cleaner [ˈkli:nə], *s.* die Reinemacherin, die Putzfrau.
cleanliness [ˈklenlinis], *s.* die Reinlichkeit, Sauberkeit.
cleanse [klenz], *v.a.* reinigen.
clear [kliə], *adj.* klar, hell; deutlich (*meaning*); schuldlos (*not guilty*). — *s. in the* —, nicht betroffen, schuldlos. — *v.a.* (*Chem.*) klären; (*Law*) für unschuldig erklären; verzollen (*pass through customs*); springen (über, *Acc.*). — *v.n.* (— *up*), sich aufklären, aufhellen (*weather*).
clearance [ˈkliərəns], *s.* die Räumung; — *sale*, der Ausverkauf; die Verzollung (*customs*).
clearing [ˈkliəriŋ], *s.* die Lichtung (*in wood*); (*Comm.*) die Verrechnung.
clearness [ˈkliənis], *s.* die Deutlichkeit, die Klarheit, Helle.
cleave [kli:v], *v.a. irr.* spalten (*wood*). — *v.n.* sich spalten.
cleaver [ˈkli:və], *s.* das Hackmesser.
cleek [kli:k], *s.* der Golfschläger.
clef [klef], *s.* (*Mus.*) der Schlüssel.
cleft [kleft], *s.* der Spalt. — *adj.* — *palate*, die Gaumenspalte.
clemency [ˈklemənsi], *s.* die Milde, Gnade (*mercy*).
clement [ˈklemənt], *adj.* mild (*climate*); gnädig (*merciful*).
clench [klentʃ], *v.a.* zusammenpressen; ballen (*fist*).
clergy [ˈklə:dʒi], *s.* (*Eccl.*) die Geistlichkeit.
clergyman [ˈklə:dʒimən], *s.* (*Eccl.*) der Geistliche.
clerical [ˈklerikl], *adj.* (*Eccl.*) geistlich; beamtlich, Beamten-, Büro- (*office*); — *work*, die Büroarbeit.
clerk [klɑ:k], *s.* der Schreiber, der Bürogehilfe (*junior*), der Bürobeamte, Büroangestellte (*senior*); *bank* —, der Bankbeamte.
clever [ˈklevə], *adj.* klug; intelligent; geschickt (*deft*); gewandt, listig (*cunning*).

cleverness [ˈklevənis], *s.* die Klugheit (*intelligence*); die Schlauheit (*cunning*); die Begabung (*talent*); die Geschicklichkeit (*skill*).
clew [klu:] *see* **clue.**
click [klik], *v.a., v.n.* einschnappen (*lock*); zusammenschlagen (*o.'s heels*, die Hacken); schnalzen (*o.'s tongue*); (*sl.*) zusammenpassen (*of two people*). — *s.* das Einschnappen (*lock*); das Zusammenschlagen (*heels*); das Schnalzen (*tongue*).
client [ˈklaiənt], *s.* (*Law*) der Klient; (*Comm.*) der Kunde.
clientele [kli:ənˈtel], *s.* die Klientel, die Kundschaft.
cliff [klif], *s.* die Klippe.
climate [ˈklaimit], *s.* das Klima.
climatic [klaiˈmætik], *adj.* klimatisch.
climax [ˈklaimæks], *s.* der Höhepunkt.
climb [klaim], *v.a.* erklettern, erklimmen. — *v.n.* klettern, bergsteigen; (*Aviat.*) steigen. — *s.* der Aufstieg, die Ersteigung.
climber [ˈklaimə], *s.* der Bergsteiger (*mountaineer*); (*Bot.*) die Schlingpflanze.
clinch [klintʃ], *v.a.* vernieten, befestigen; — *a deal*, einen Handel abschließen. — *s.* der feste Griff; die Umklammerung (*boxing*).
cling [kliŋ], *v.n. irr.* sich anklammern, festhalten (*to*, an).
clinic [ˈklinik], *s.* die Klinik.
clinical [ˈklinikl], *adj.* klinisch.
clink [kliŋk], *s.* das Geklirre; (*coll.*) das Gefängnis. — *v.a.* — *glasses*, mit den Gläsern anstoßen.
clinker [ˈkliŋkə], *s.* der Backstein; die Schlacke.
clip (1) [klip], *v.a.* stutzen, beschneiden; lochen (*ticket*).
clip (2) [klip], *v.a.* befestigen. — *s. paper* —, die Büroklammer.
clippings [ˈklipiŋz], *s. pl.* die Abschnitte; die Schnitzel (*waste*); Zeitungsausschnitte, *m. pl.*
cloak [klouk], *s.* der Mantel, der Deckmantel (*cover*). — *v.a.* verbergen.
cloakroom [ˈkloukru:m], *s.* die Garderobe; — *free*, keine Garderobegebühr; (*Railw.*) die Gepäckaufbewahrung.
clock [klɔk], *s.* die (große) Uhr, Wanduhr; — *face*, das Zifferblatt. — *v.n.* — *in*, die Zeitkarte (Kontrollkarte) stempeln lassen, eintreffen (*arrive*).
clockwise [ˈklɔkwaiz], *adv.* im Uhrzeigersinne.
clod [klɔd], *s.* die Erdscholle, der Erdklumpen; (*sl.*) der Lümmel (*lout*).
clog [klɔg], *v.a.* belasten, hemmen, verstopfen. — *v.n.* sich verstopfen. — *s.* der Holzschuh.
cloisters [ˈklɔistəz], *s. pl.* (*Eccl., Archit.*) der Kreuzgang.

339

close

close [klouz], v.a. schließen, verschließen; beenden (meeting etc.). — v.n. — in on, über einen hereinbrechen, umzingeln. — s. das Ende, der Schluß; [klous] der Domplatz. — [klous], adj. nahe (near); knapp (narrow); nahestehend, vertraut (friend); schwül (weather); geizig (miserly).

closeness ['klousnis], s. die Nähe (nearness); die Schwüle (weather); die Vertrautheit (familiarity).

closet ['klɔzit], s. der Wandschrank (cupboard); das kleine Zimmer; das Klosett (W.C.). — v.r. — o.s. with, sich mit jemandem zurückziehen, sich vertraulich beraten.

closure ['klouʒə], s. der Schluß; der Abschluß (einer Debatte).

clot [klɔt], s. das Klümpchen. — v.n. sich verdicken, gerinnen; —ted cream, dicke Sahne.

cloth [klɔθ], s. das Tuch; der Stoff; die Leinwand (bookbinding); American —, das Wachstuch; — printing, der Zeugdruck.

clothe [klouð], v.a. kleiden. — v.r. sich kleiden.

clothes [klouðz], s. pl. die Kleider, n. pl.; die Kleidung; die Wäsche (washing); — basket, der Wäschekorb; — press, der Kleiderschrank.

clothier ['klouðiə], s. der Tuchmacher (manufacturer); der Tuchhändler (dealer).

clothing ['klouðiŋ], s. die Kleidung.

cloud [klaud], s. die Wolke; under a —, in Ungnade; —burst, der Wolkenbruch. — v.a. bewölken, verdunkeln. — v.n. — over, sich umwölken.

cloudiness ['klaudinis], s. die Umwölkung, der Wolkenhimmel.

cloudy ['klaudi], adj. wolkig, bewölkt, umwölkt.

clout [klaut], s. (obs.) der Lappen (rag); (coll.) der Schlag (hit). — v.a. schlagen (hit).

clove [klouv], s. die Gewürznelke (spice).

clove(n) [klouv(n)], adj. gespalten.

clover ['klouvə], s. (Bot.) der Klee; to be in —, Glück haben, es gut haben.

clown [klaun], s. der Hanswurst. — v.n. den Hanswurst spielen.

clownish ['klauniʃ], adj. tölpelhaft.

clownishness ['klauniʃnis], s. die Derbheit, Tölpelhaftigkeit.

cloy [klɔi], v.n. übersättigen, anwidern, anekeln.

club (1) [klʌb], s. die Keule (stick). — v.a. (einen) mit einer Keule schlagen.

club (2) [klʌb], s. der Klub, der Verein. — v.n. — together, zusammen beitragen, zusammensteuern (contribute jointly).

club (3) [klʌb], s. (cards) das Treff, die Eichel (German cards).

clubfoot ['klʌbfut], .. der Klumpfuß.

cluck [klʌk], v.n. glucken (hen).

clue [klu:], s. der Anhaltspunkt, Leitfaden, die Richtlinie, die Angabe (crossword); no —, keine blasse Ahnung.

clump [klʌmp], s. der Klumpen; die Gruppe.

clumsiness ['klʌmzinis], s. die Unbeholfenheit, Ungeschicklichkeit.

clumsy ['klʌmzi], adj. unbeholfen, schwerfällig, ungeschickt.

Cluniac ['klu:njæk]. (Eccl.) der Kluniazenser.

cluster ['klʌstə], s. die Traube (grapes), der Büschel. — v.n. in Büschen wachsen or stehen, dicht gruppiert sein.

clutch [klʌtʃ], v.a. ergreifen, packen (grip). — s. der Griff; (Motor.) der Kupplung.

coach [koutʃ], s. die Kutsche; der Wagen, der Autobus; der Privatlehrer (teacher). — v.a. unterrichten, vorbereiten (for examinations etc.).

coachman ['koutʃmən], s. der Kutscher.

coagulate [kou'ægjuleit], v.a. gerinnen lassen. — v.n. gerinnen.

coagulation [kouægju'leiʃən], s. das Gerinnen.

coal [koul], s. die Kohle; — mine, das Kohlenbergwerk; die Kohlengrube; — miner, der Bergmann.

coalesce [kouə'les], v.n. zusammenwachsen, sich vereinigen.

coalescence [kouə'lesəns], s. die Verschmelzung.

coalition [kouə'liʃən], s. (Pol.) die Koalition, das Bündnis.

coarse [kɔ:s], adj. grob; gemein (manner).

coarseness ['kɔ:snis], s. die Grobheit, Unfeinheit.

coast [koust], s. die Küste. — v.n. (an der Küste) entlangfahren; gleiten, rodeln.

coat [kout], s. der Mantel, Rock; die Jacke (jacket); das Fell (animal); — of arms, das Wappenschild; — of mail, das Panzerhemd; — of paint, der Anstrich. — v.a. überziehen, bemalen (paint).

coathanger ['kouthæŋə], s. der Kleiderbügel.

coating ['koutiŋ], s. der Überzug.

coax [kouks], v.a. beschwatzen; überreden (persuade).

cob (1) [kɔb], s. der Gaul.

cob (2) [kɔb], s. (Orn.) der Schwan.

cob (3) [kɔb], s. der (Mais)Kolben (corn on the —).

cobble [kɔbl], v.a. flicken (shoes).

cobbled ['kɔbld], adj. mit Kopfsteinen gepflastert.

cobbler ['kɔblə], s. der Schuhflicker.

cobble(stone) ['kɔbl(stoun)], s. das Kopfsteinpflaster.

cobweb ['kɔbweb], s. die Spinngewebe.

cock [kɔk], s. (Orn.) der Hahn; (Engin.) der Sperrhahn, Hahn; — sparrow, das Sperlingsmännchen; — -a-doodle-doo! kikeriki!

cockade [kɔ'keid], s. die Kokarde.

cockatoo [kɔkə'tu:], s. (Orn.) der Kakadu.

cockchafer ['kɔktʃeifə], s. (Ent.) der Maikäfer.

cockerel ['kɔkərəl], s. (Orn.) der junge Hahn.

cockswain [kɔksn] see coxswain.

cockle [kɔkl], s. (Zool.) die Herzmuschel.

cockney ['kɔkni], s. der geborene Londoner.

cockpit ['kɔkpit], s. (Aviat.) der Pilotensitz, die Kanzel, der Führerraum.

cockroach ['kɔkroutʃ], s. (Ent.) die Schabe.

cocksure ['kɔkʃuə], adj. zuversichtlich, allzu sicher.

cocoa ['koukou], s. der Kakao.

coconut ['koukonʌt], s. die Kokosnuß.

cocoon [kə'ku:n], s. der Kokon, die Puppe (of silkworm).

cod [kɔd], s. der Kabeljau, Dorsch; — liver oil, der Lebertran; dried —, der Stockfisch.

coddle [kɔdl], v.a. verhätscheln, verweichlichen.

code [koud], s. das Gesetzbuch, der Kodex; die Chiffre (cipher). — v.a. chiffrieren, schlüsseln.

codify ['koudifai], v.a. kodifizieren.

coerce [kou'ə:s], v.a. zwingen.

coercion [kou'ə:ʃən], s. der Zwang.

coercive [kou'ə:siv], adj. zwingend.

coeval [kou'i:vəl], adj. gleichaltrig, gleichzeitig.

coexist [kouig'zist], v.n. zugleich existieren, nebeneinander leben.

coffee ['kɔfi], s. der Kaffee; — grinder, die Kaffeemühle; — grounds, der Kaffeesatz; — pot, die Kaffeekanne; — set, das Kaffee service.

coffer ['kɔfə], s. der Kasten, die Truhe.

coffin ['kɔfin], s. der Sarg.

cog [kɔg], s. der Zahn (on wheel); — wheel, das Zahnrad.

cogency ['koudʒənsi], s. die zwingende Kraft, Triftigkeit.

cogent ['koudʒənt], adj. zwingend, triftig.

cogitate ['kɔdʒiteit], v.n. nachdenken.

cogitation [kɔdʒi'teiʃən], s. die Überlegung, das Nachdenken.

cognate ['kɔgneit], adj. verwandt.

cognisance ['kɔgnizəns], s. die Erkenntnis; die Kenntnisnahme; (Law) die gerichtliche Kenntnisnahme.

cognisant ['kɔgnizənt], adj. wissend, in vollem Wissen (of, Genit.).

cognition [kɔg'niʃən], s. die Kenntnis, das Erkennen.

cohabit [kou'hæbit], v.n. zusammenleben.

cohabitation [kouhæbi'teiʃən], s. das Zusammenleben.

coheir [kou'εə], s. der Miterbe.

cohere [kou'hiə], v.n. zusammenhängen.

coherence [kou'hiərəns], s. der Zusammenhang.

coherent [kou'hiərənt], adj. zusammenhängend.

cohesion [kou'hi:ʒən], s. (Phys.) die Kohäsion.

coiffure [kwæ'fjuə], s. die Frisur, die Haartracht.

coil [kɔil], s. (Elec.) die Spule; die Windung. — v.a. aufwickeln; umwickeln, (auf)spulen. — v.n. sich winden.

coin [kɔin], s. die Münze, das Geldstück. — v.a. münzen, prägen; — a phrase, eine Redewendung prägen.

coinage ['kɔinidʒ], s. die Prägung.

coincide [kouin'said], v.n. zusammenfallen, zusammentreffen.

coincidence [kou'insidəns], s. das Zusammenfallen, Zusammentreffen; der Zufall (chance).

coincident [kou'insidənt], adj. zusammentreffend.

coke [kouk], s. der Koks. — v.a. (Chem., Engin.) verkoken.

cold [kould], adj. kalt; gefühllos, kühl. — s. die Kälte (temperature); die Erkältung (indisposition).

coldish ['kouldiʃ], adj. kühl.

coldness ['kouldnis], s. die Kälte (temperature); die Kaltherzigkeit (heartlessness).

colic ['kɔlik], s. die Kolik.

collaborate [kə'læbəreit], v.n. zusammenarbeiten.

collaboration [kəlæbə'reiʃən], s. die Zusammenarbeit; die Mitwirkung, Mitarbeit (assistance).

collaborator [kə'læbəreitə], s. der Mitarbeiter.

collapse [kə'læps], s. der Zusammenbruch. — v.n. zusammenbrechen (disintegrate); zerfallen, einstürzen.

collapsible [kə'læpsibl], adj. zerlegbar, zusammenlegbar, zusammenklappbar.

collar ['kɔlə], s. der Kragen; —bone, das Schlüsselbein (Anat.); dog —, das Halsband; (coll.) der Priesterkragen; —stud, der Kragenknopf. — v.a. beim Kragen fassen, ergreifen.

collate [kɔ'leit], v.a. vergleichen (texts etc.).

collateral [kɔ'lætərəl], adj. Seiten-, von beiden Seiten. — s. (Am.) die Garantie, Bürgschaft.

collation [kɔ'leiʃən], s. die Vergleichung, der Vergleich (texts etc.); der Imbiß.

colleague ['kɔli:g], s. der Kollege, die Kollegin.

collect [kə'lekt], v.a. sammeln, zusammenbringen. — v.n. sich versammeln. — ['kɔlikt], s. (Eccl.) die Kollekte.

collection [kə'lekʃən], s. die Sammlung.

collective [kə'lektiv], adj. kollektiv, gemeinsam. — s. (Pol.) das Kollektiv.

collector [kə'lektə], s. der Sammler.

college ['kɔlidʒ], s. das Kollegium; das College; die Hochschule, Universität.

collide [kə'laid], v.n. zusammenstoßen.

collie ['kɔli], s. der Schäferhund.

collier ['kɔliə], s. der Kohlenarbeiter; das Kohlenfrachtschiff (boat).

collision

collision [kə'liʒən], s. der Zusammenstoß, Zusammenprall.
collocate ['kɔləkeit], v.a. ordnen.
collodion [kə'loudjən], s. (Chem.) das
Kollodium.
colloquial [kə'loukwiəl], adj. umgangssprachlich, Umgangs-.
colloquy ['kɔlekwi], s. die Unterredung,
das Gespräch (formal).
collusion [kə'lu:ʒən], s. das heimliche
Einverständnis, die unstatthafte Partnerschaft; die Verdunkelung.
collusive [kə'lu:ziv], adj. abgekartet.
Cologne [kə'loun], Köln, n.; eau de —,
Kölnisch Wasser.
Colombian [kɔ'lɔmbjən], adj. kolum-
bisch. — s. der Kolumbier.
colon (1) ['koulən], s. das Kolon, der
Doppelpunkt.
colon (2) ['koulən], s. (Med.) der
Dickdarm.
colonel [kə:nl], s. (Mil.) der Oberst; —
-in-chief, der Generaloberst, der oberste Befehlshaber; lieutenant- —, der
Oberstleutnant.
colonial [kə'lounjəl], adj. kolonial, aus
den Kolonien.
colonist ['kɔlənist], s. der Siedler;
Ansiedler.
colonization [kɔlənai'zeiʃən], s. die
Kolonisierung, Besiedelung.
colonize ['kɔlənaiz], v.a. besiedeln,
kolonisieren.
colonnade [kɔlə'neid], s. die Kolonnade,
der Säulengang.
colony ['kɔləni], s. die Kolonie.
colophony [kɔ'lɔfəni], s. das Kolo-
phonium (resin).
coloration [kʌlə'reiʃən], s. die Färbung,
Tönung.
colossal [kə'lɔsəl], adj. kolossal, riesig,
riesenhaft.
colour ['kʌlə], s. die Farbe; (complexion) die Gesichtsfarbe; (paint)
die Farbe, der Anstrich; (dye) die
Färbung. — v.a. färben; anstreichen
(paint house etc.).
colt [koult], s. das Füllen.
columbine ['kɔləmbain], s. (Bot.) die
Akelei.
column ['kɔləm], s. die Säule; die
Spalte (press); (also Mil.) die Kolonne.
colza ['kɔlzə], s. (Bot.) der Raps.
coma ['koumə], s. (Med.) das Koma,
die Schlafsucht.
comb [koum], s. der Kamm. — v.a.
kämmen; (fig.) genau untersuchen.
combat ['kʌmbət, 'kɔmbət], s. der
Kampf, das Gefecht; in single —, im
Duell, Zweikampf. — v.a. kämpfen,
bekämpfen.
combatant ['kʌmbətənt, 'kɔmb-], s. der
Kämpfer.
comber ['koumə], s. der Wollkämmer.
combination [kɔmbi'neiʃən], s. die
Kombination, die Verbindung.
combine [kəm'bain], v.a. kombinieren,
verbinden. — v.n. sich verbinden. —
['kɔmbain], s. (Comm.) der Trust,
Ring.

combustible [kəm'bʌstibl], adj. verbrennbar; feuergefährlich.
combustion [kəm'bʌstʃən], s. die
Verbrennung.
come [kʌm], v.n. irr. kommen; — about,
sich ereignen (event); — across,
stoßen auf (Acc.); — by (s.th.),
ergattern, erwerben; — for, abholen;
— forth, forward, hervorkommen,
hervortreten; — from, herkommen
von, — in, hereinkommen; — off, (of
object) loskommen, (succeed) glücken;
— out (appear), herauskommen;
— to o.s., zu sich kommen; — of age,
mündig werden; — to o.'s senses,
zur Besinnung or Vernunft kommen;
that is still to —, das steht uns noch
bevor.
comedian [kə'mi:djən], s. der Komödiant, Komiker (stage).
comedy ['kɔmədi], s. die Komödie, das
Lustspiel.
comeliness ['kʌmlinis], s. die Anmut,
Schönheit.
comely ['kʌmli], adj. anmutig, schön.
comestible [kə'mestibl], s. (usually pl.)
die Eßwaren, f. pl.
comet ['kɔmit], s. der Komet.
comfit ['kʌmfit], s. das Konfekt, die
Bonbons.
comfort ['kʌmfət], s. der Trost (solace);
der Komfort, die Bequemlichkeit. —
v.a. trösten.
comforter ['kʌmfətə], s. der Tröster;
(Am.) die Steppdecke.
comfortless ['kʌmfətlis], adj. trostlos,
unbehaglich.
comic ['kɔmik], adj. komisch; —
writer, humoristischer Schriftsteller.
— s. die Bilderzeitung (children's
paper).
comical ['kɔmikl], adj. lächerlich, zum
Lachen, komisch.
comma ['kɔmə], s. das Komma, der
Beistrich; inverted —s, die Anführungszeichen.
command [kə'ma:nd], v.a., v.n. (Mil.)
kommandieren; über jemanden verfügen (have s.o. at o.'s disposal). — s.
der Befehl.
commandant [kɔmən'dænt], s. der
Kommandant, Befehlshaber.
commander [kə'ma:ndə], s. der Befehlshaber.
commandment [kə'ma:ndmənt], s.
(Rel.) das Gebot.
commemorate [kə'meməreit], v.a.
feiern, gedenken (Genit.).
commemoration [kəmemə'reiʃən], s.
die Feier, die Gedächtnisfeier.
commemorative [kə'memərətiv], adj.
Gedächtnis-.
commence [kə'mens], v.a., v.n. beginnen, anfangen.
commencement [kə'mensmənt], s. der
Anfang, der Beginn.
commend [kə'mend], v.a. empfehlen,
loben (praise).
commendable [kə'mendəbl], adj. emp-
fehlenswert.

commendation [komen'deiʃən], s. die Empfehlung.

commensurable, commensurate [kə'menʃərəbl, kə'menʃərit], adj. kommensurabel, entsprechend; angemessen.

comment ['kɔment], v.n. kommentieren (on, zu, Dat.). — s. der Kommentar; die Bemerkung (remark).

commentary ['kɔməntəri], s. der Kommentar.

commentator ['kɔmənteitə], s. der Kommentator, Berichterstatter.

commerce ['kɔmə:s], s. der Handel; college of —, die Handelsschule.

commercial [kə'mə:ʃəl], adj. kommerziell, kaufmännisch, Handels-; — traveller, der Handelsreisende, Vertreter; — manager, der geschäftliche Leiter.

commingle [kə'miŋgl], v.a. vermischengefühl.

commiserate [kə'mizəreit], v.n. bemitleiden; — with s.o., mit einem Mitgefühl haben.

commissariat [komi'sɛəriət], s. (Pol.) das Kommissariat.

commissary ['kɔmisəri], s. der Kommissar. — adj. kommissarisch.

commission [kə'miʃən], s. die Kommission; (Mil.) der Offiziersrang; die Begehung (of crime); (Law) die (offizielle) Kommission; der Auftrag, die Bestellung (order).

commissionaire [kəmiʃən'ɛə], s. der Portier.

commissioned [kə'miʃənd], adj. bevollmächtigt.

commissioner [kə'miʃənə], s. (Pol.) der Kommissar, der Bevollmächtigte.

commit [kə'mit], v.a. begehen (do); übergeben (consign); anvertrauen (entrust). — v.r. sich verpflichten.

committal [kə'mitl], s. das Übergeben; die Überantwortung.

committee [kə'miti], s. das Kommitee, der Ausschuß.

commodious [kə'moudiəs], adj. bequem, geräumig.

commodity [kə'mɔditi], s. (Comm.) die Ware, der Artikel.

commodore ['kɔmədɔ:], s. (Naut.) der Kommodore, der Kommandant eines Geschwaders.

common ['kɔmən], adj. gewöhnlich (usual); gemein (vulgar); allgemein (general); in —, gemeinschaftlich; — sense, der gesunde Menschenverstand; the — man, der kleine Mann. — n. pl. House of Commons, das Unterhaus.

commoner ['kɔmənə], s. der Bürger; (Parl.) Mitglied des Unterhauses.

commonness ['kɔmənnis], s. die Gemeinheit (vulgarity); das häufige Vorkommen (frequency).

commonplace ['kɔmənpleis], adj. alltäglich. — s. der Gemeinplatz.

commonwealth ['kɔmənwelθ], s. die Staatengemeinschaft, der Staatenbund; das Commonwealth.

commotion [kə'mouʃən], s. die Erschütterung; der Aufruhr; der Lärm.

communal ['kɔmjunəl], adj. gemeinschaftlich, allgemein; (Pol.) Kommunal-.

commune ['kɔmju:n], s. (Pol.) die Kommune. — [kə'mju:n], v.n. sich unterhalten.

communicable [kə'mju:nikəbl], adj. mitteilbar; übertragbar.

communicate [kə'mju:nikeit], v.a. mitteilen; verkünden (proclaim); benachrichtigen. — v.n. in Verbindung stehen.

communication [kəmju:ni'keiʃən], s. die Mitteilung; Verlautbarung; die Verkündigung (proclamation); die Information; (Elec.) die Verbindung; (pl.), die Verbindungslinie; —s engineering, Fernmeldetechnik.

communion [kə'mju:njən], s. (Eccl.) die Kommunion; das heilige Abendmahl; die Gemeinschaft (fellowship).

Communism ['kɔmjunizm], s. (Pol.) der Kommunismus.

Communist ['kɔmjunist], s. der Kommunist. — adj. kommunistisch.

community [kə'mju:niti], s. die Gemeinschaft.

commutable [kə'mju:təbl], adj. umtauschbar, auswechselbar.

commutation [kɔmju'teiʃən], s. der Austausch; (Law) die Herabsetzung (of sentence).

commutator ['kɔmjuteitə], s. (Elec.) der Umschalter.

commute [kə'mju:t], v.n. hin und her fahren, pendeln, mit Zeitkarte fahren (travel). — v.a. herabsetzen (sentence).

compact ['kɔmpækt], adj. kompakt, fest; gedrängt (succinct); kurz, bündig (short).

companion [kəm'pænjən], s. der Gefährte, die Gefährtin.

companionable [kəm'pænjənəbl], adj. gesellig, freundlich.

companionship [kəm'pænjənʃip], s. die Geselligkeit; die Gesellschaft.

company ['kʌmpəni], s. die Gesellschaft; (Mil.) die Kompanie; der Freundeskreis (circle of friends); (Comm.) die Handelsgesellschaft; limited (liability) —, Gesellschaft mit beschränkter Haftung; public (private) —, Gesellschaft des öffentlichen (privaten) Rechtes.

comparative [kəm'pærətiv], adj. vergleichend, relativ. — s. (Gram.) der Komparativ.

compare [kəm'pɛə], v.a. vergleichen. — v.n. sich vergleichen lassen.

comparison [kəm'pærisən], s. der Vergleich; das Gleichnis (simile).

compartment [kəm'pɑ:tmənt], s. (Railw.) das Abteil; die Abteilung.

compass ['kʌmpəs], s. der Umkreis, Umfang (scope); (Naut.) der Kompaß; point of the —, der Kompaßstrich; (Engin.) der Zirkel.

compassion

compassion [kəm'pæʃən], *s.* die Barmherzigkeit, das Mitleid, das Erbarmen.

compassionate [kəm'pæʃənit], *adj.* mitleidig; (*Mil.*) — *leave*, der Sonderurlaub.

compatibility [kəmpæti'biliti], *s.* die Verträglichkeit, Vereinbarkeit.

compatible [kəm'pætibl], *adj.* verträglich, vereinbar.

compatriot [kəm'peitriət], *s.* der Landsmann.

compel [kəm'pel], *v.a.* zwingen, nötigen.

compendium [kəm'pendjəm], *s.* das Kompendium, die kurze Schrift, die kurze Darstellung.

compensate ['kɔmpənseit], *v.a.* kompensieren, einem Ersatz leisten.

compensation [kɔmpən'seiʃən], *s.* der Ersatz, die Wiedergutmachung.

compensatory [kɔmpən'seitəri], *adj.* ausgleichend, Ersatz-.

compete [kəm'pi:t], *v.n.* wetteifern, konkurrieren.

competence, competency ['kɔmpitəns, -nsi], *s.* die Kompetenz; Zuständigkeit; Befähigung (*capability*); Tüchtigkeit (*ability*).

competent ['kɔmpitənt], *adj.* kompetent; zuständig; fähig (*capable*); tüchtig (*able*).

competition [kɔmpi'tiʃən], *s.* die Konkurrenz; die Mitbewerbung (*for job*).

competitive [kəm'petitiv], *adj.* Konkurrenz-, konkurrierend.

competitor [kəm'petitə], *s.* (*Comm.*) der Konkurrent; der Mitbewerber (*fellow applicant*), Teilnehmer (*sport*).

complacent [kəm'pleisənt], *adj.* selbstzufrieden, selbstgefällig.

complain [kəm'plein], *v.n.* sich beklagen (*of*, über, *Acc.*).

complaint [kəm'pleint], *s.* die Klage; Beschwerde (*grievance*); das Leiden (*illness*).

complement ['kɔmplimənt], *s.* die Ergänzung, Gesamtzahl. — [-'ment], *v.a.* ergänzen.

complementary [kɔmpli'mentəri], *adj.* Ergänzungs-, ergänzend.

complete [kəm'pli:t], *adj.* komplett; voll (*full up*); vollkommen (*perfect*). — *v.a.* vollenden (*end*); ergänzen (*make whole*).

completeness [kəm'pli:tnis], *s.* die Vollendung (*condition*); Ganzheit (*wholeness*).

completion [kəm'pli:ʃən], *s.* die Vollendung (*fulfilment*); die Beendigung (*ending*); der Abschluß.

complex ['kɔmpleks], *adj.* (*Maths.*) komplex; kompliziert (*complicated*). — *s.* der Komplex (*Archit.*, *Psych.*).

complexion [kəm'plekʃən], *s.* die Gesichtsfarbe; (*fig.*) das Aussehen.

complexity [kəm'pleksiti], *s.* die Kompliziertheit; die Schwierigkeit.

compliance [kəm'plaiəns], *s.* die Willfährigkeit, Einwilligung.

compliant [kəm'plaiənt], *adj.* willig, willfährig.

complicate ['kɔmplikeit], *v.a.* komplizieren, erschweren.

complication [kɔmpli'keiʃən], *s.* die Komplikation, die Erschwerung.

complicity [kəm'plisiti], *s.* (*Law*) die Mitschuld.

compliment ['kɔmplimənt], *s.* das Kompliment. — [-'ment], *v.n.* Komplimente machen.

complimentary [kɔmpli'mentəri], *adj.* lobend; — *ticket*, die Freikarte.

comply [kəm'plai], *v.n.* einwilligen (*with*, in, *Acc.*); sich halten (*an*, *Acc.*).

compose [kəm'pouz], *v.a.*, *v.n.* (*Mus.*) komponieren; beruhigen (*the mind*); (*Lit.*) verfassen; (*Typ.*) setzen.

composed [kəm'pouzd], *adj.* ruhig, gefaßt.

composer [kəm'pouzə], *s.* (*Mus.*) der Komponist.

composite ['kɔmpəzit], *adj.* zusammengesetzt.

composition [kɔmpə'ziʃən], *s.* (*Mus. etc.*) die Komposition; Beschaffenheit Zusammensetzung.

compositor [kəm'pɔzitə], *s.* (*Typ.*) der Schriftsetzer.

compost ['kɔmpɔst], *s.* (*Agr.*) der Dünger, Kompost.

composure [kəm'pouʒə], *s.* die Gelassenheit, die Gemütsruhe, die Fassung.

compound ['kɔmpaund], *s.* (*Chem.*) die Verbindung; die Zusammensetzung. — *adj.* zusammengesetzt; kompliziert; (*Comm.*) — *interest*, die Zinseszinsen. — [əm'paund], *v.a.* (*Chem.*) mischen, zusammensetzen.

comprehend [kɔmpri'hend], *v.a.* verstehen (*understand*); einschließen (*include*).

comprehensible [kɔmpri'hensibl], *adj.* verständlich, begreiflich.

comprehension [kɔmpri'henʃən], *s.* das Verstehen, das Erfassen; (*Psych.*) — *tests*, die Verständnisprüfung.

comprehensive [kɔmpri'hensiv], *adj.* umfassend.

compress [kəm'pres], *v.a.* komprimieren; zusammendrücken (*press together*). — ['kɔmpres], *s.* (*Med.*) die Kompresse, der Umschlag (*poultice*).

compression [kəm'preʃən], *s.* der Druck; das Zusammendrücken (*pressing together*); die Kürzung (*abridgment*).

comprise [kəm'praiz], *v.a.* umfassen, einschließen.

compromise ['kɔmprəmaiz], *v.a.* kompromittieren. — *v.n.* einen Kompromiß schließen. — *s.* der *or* das Kompromiß.

compulsion [kəm'pʌlʃən], *s.* der Zwang.

compulsory [kəm'pʌlsəri], *adj.* zwingend; Zwangs-; — *subject*, das obligatorische Fach.

compunction [kəm'pʌŋkʃən], *s.* die Gewissensbisse, *m. pl.*

computation [kɔmpju'teiʃən], *s.* die Berechnung.

compute [kəm'pju:t], *v.a.*, *v.n.* berechnen.

computer [kəm'pju:tə], *s.* die automatische Rechenmaschine.

comrade ['kɔmrid], *s.* der Kamerad.

comradeship ['kɔmridʃip], *s.* die Kameradschaft.

con [kɔn], *v.a.* genau betrachten, studieren; (*ship*) steuern.

concave ['kɔnkeiv], *adj.* (*Phys.*) konkav.

conceal [kən'si:l], *v.a.* verbergen, verstecken.

concealment [kən'si:lmənt], *s.* die Verhehlung, die Verheimlichung (*act of concealing*); *place of* —, das Versteck.

concede [kən'si:d], *v.a.* zugestehen, einräumen.

conceit [kən'si:t], *s.* die Einbildung, der Eigendünkel (*presumption*); (*obs.*) die Idee; (*Lit.*) die (gedankliche) Spielerei.

conceited [kən'si:tid], *adj.* eingebildet, eitel.

conceivable [kən'si:vəbl], *adj.* denkbar; begreiflich (*understandable*).

conceive [kən'si:v], *v.a.*, *v.n.* empfangen (*become pregnant*); begreifen (*understand*).

concentrate ['kɔnsəntreit], *v.a.* konzentrieren. — *v.n.* sich konzentrieren (*on*, auf, *Acc.*). — *s.* (*Chem.*) das Konzentrat.

concentrated ['kɔnsəntreitid], *adj.* konzentriert.

concentration [kɔnsən'treiʃən], *s.* die Konzentration.

concentric [kɔn'sentrik], *adj.* (*Geom.*) konzentrisch.

conception [kən'sepʃən], *s.* die Vorstellung, der Begriff (*idea*); die Empfängnis (*of a child*).

concern [kən'sə:n], *v.a.* (*affect*) betreffen, angehen; *be concerned with*, zu tun haben (mit, *Dat.*). — *s.* die Angelegenheit (*affair*); die Sorge (*care*, *business*); das Geschäft, das Unternehmen; *cause grave* —, tiefe Besorgnis erregen.

concerned [kən'sə:nd], *adj.* (*worried*) besorgt; (*involved*) interessiert (*in*, an, *Dat.*).

concerning [kən'sə:niŋ], *prep.* betreffend (*Acc.*), hinsichtlich (*Genit.*).

concert ['kɔnsət], *s.* (*Mus.*) das Konzert; Einverständnis.

concerted [kən'sə:tid], *adj.* gemeinsam, gemeinschaftlich.

concertina [kɔnsə'ti:nə], *s.* (*Mus.*) die Ziehharmonika.

concerto [kən'tʃə:tou], *s.* (*Mus.*) das Konzert.

concession [kən'seʃən], *s.* die Konzession (*licence*); das Zugeständnis.

conch [kɔŋk], *s.* die (große) Muschel.

conciliate [kən'silieit], *v.a.* versöhnen.

conciliation [kənsili'eiʃən], *s.* die Versöhnung.

conciliatory [kən'siliətəri], *adj.* versöhnlich.

concise [kən'sais], *adj.* kurz, knapp.

conciseness [kən'saisnis], *s.* die Kürze, Knappheit.

conclave ['kɔnkleiv], *s.* (*Eccl.*) das Konklave.

conclude [kən'klu:d], *v.a.*, *v.n.* schließen, beenden (*speech etc.*); (*infer*) folgern (*from*, aus, *Dat.*); abschließen (*treaty*).

conclusion [kən'klu:ʒən], *s.* der Abschluß (*treaty*); die Folgerung (*inference*); der Beschluß (*decision*).

conclusive [kən'klu:siv], *adj.* entscheidend, überzeugend.

concoct [kən'kɔkt], *v.a.* zusammenbrauen, aushecken.

concoction [kən'kɔkʃən], *s.* das Gebräu, die Mischung.

concomitant [kɔn'kɔmitənt], *adj.* begleitend; Begleit-, Neben-. — *s.* der Begleitumstand.

concord ['kɔnkɔ:d], *s.* die Eintracht, die Harmonie.

concordance [kən'kɔ:dəns], *s.* die Übereinstimmung; die Konkordanz (*of Bible etc.*).

concordant [kən'kɔ:dənt], *adj.* in Eintracht (mit), übereinstimmend (mit) (*Dat.*).

concordat [kən'kɔ:dæt], *s.* (*Eccl.*, *Pol.*) das Konkordat.

concourse ['kɔnkɔ:s], *s.* das Gedränge (*crowd*).

concrete ['kɔnkri:t], *s.* (*Build.*) der Beton; (*Log.*) das Konkrete. — *adj.* konkret, wirklich.

concur [kən'kə:], *v.n.* übereinstimmen (*with*, mit, *Dat.*).

concurrence [kən'kʌrəns], *s.* die Übereinstimmung.

concurrent [kən'kʌrənt], *adj.* gleichzeitig (*simultaneous*); mitwirkend (*accompanying*).

concussion [kən'kʌʃən], *s.* (*Med.*) die (Gehirn)Erschütterung.

condemn [kən'dem], *v.a.* verurteilen, verdammen.

condemnable [kən'demnəbl], *adj.* verwerflich, verdammenswert.

condemnation [kɔndem'neiʃən], *s.* die Verurteilung, die Verdammung.

condensate ['kɔndenseit], *s.* (*Chem.*) das Kondensat, das Ergebnis der Kondensation.

condensation [kɔnden'seiʃən], *s.* die Kondensation; Verdichtung.

condensed [kən'densd], *adj.* (*Chem.*) kondensiert; (*Chem.*, *Engin.*) verdichtet; gekürzt (*abridged*).

condenser [kən'densə], *s.* (*Chem.*, *Engin.*) der Kondensator; (*Elec.*) der Verstärker.

condescend [kɔndi'send], *v.n.* sich herablassen.

condescending [kɔndi'sendiŋ], *adj.* herablassend.

condescension [kɔndi'senʃən], *s.* die Herablassung.

condiment ['kɔndimənt], *s.* die Würze.

condition [kən'diʃən], *s.* der Zustand; Umstand; die Bedingung (*proviso*); der Gesundheitszustand (*physical state*).

conditional

conditional [kən'diʃənəl], *adj.* bedingt; unter der Bedingung; konditionell.

conditioned [kən'diʃənd], *adj.* vorbereitet (*for action*); geartet.

condole [kən'doul], *v.n.* Beileid ausdrücken (*with, Dat.*), kondolieren (*with, Dat.*).

condolence [kən'douləns], *s.* das Beileid.

condone [kən'doun], *v.a.* verzeihen.

conducive [kən'dju:siv], *adj.* förderlich, dienlich, nützlich (*to, Dat.*).

conduct [kən'dʌkt], *v.a.* leiten, führen; (*Phys.*) ein Leiter sein; (*Mus.*) dirigieren. — *v.r.* sich aufführen, sich benehmen. — ['kɔndʌkt], *s.* das Benehmen (*behaviour*); — *of a war*, die Kriegsführung.

conductive [kən'dʌktiv], *adj.* (*Elec.*) leitend.

conductor [kən'dʌktə], *s.* der Leiter, Führer (*leader*); (*Phys., Elec.*) der Leiter; (*Am.*) der Schaffner (*train*); (*Mus.*) der Dirigent.

conduit ['kʌn-, 'kɔndit], *s.* die Leitung, die Röhre.

cone [koun], *s.* (*Geom.*) der Kegel; (*Bot.*) der Zapfen.

coney ['kouni], *s.* (*Zool.*) das Kaninchen.

confection [kən'fekʃən], *s.* das Konfekt.

confectioner [kən'fekʃənə], *s.* der Zuckerbäcker, Konditor.

confectionery [kən'fekʃənəri], *s.* die Zuckerwaren, *f.pl.* (*sweets*); Konditoreiwaren, *f.pl.* (*cakes*); die Zuckerbäckerei (*sweet shop*); die Konditorei.

confederacy [kən'fedərəsi], *s.* der Bund (*of states*); das Bündnis (*treaty*).

confederate [kən'fedərit], *s.* der Bundesgenosse, der Verbündete. — *adj.* verbündet; — *state*, der Bundesstaat. — [-reit], *v.n.* sich verbünden (*with*, mit, *Dat.*).

confederation [kɔnfedə'reiʃən], *s.* das Bündnis (*treaty*); der Bund (*state*).

confer [kən'fə:], *v.a.* verleihen (*degree, title*). — *v.n.* beraten (*with*, mit, *Dat.*), unterhandeln (*negotiate*).

conference ['kɔnfərəns], *s.* die Konferenz, die Besprechung, die Beratung, Tagung.

confess [kən'fes], *v.a.* bekennen; beichten (*sin*); zugestehen (*acknowledge*).

confession [kən'feʃən], *s.* das Bekenntnis; die Beichte (*sin*); das Glaubensbekenntnis (*creed*).

confessor [kən'fesə], *s.* der Bekenner; *father* —, der Beichtvater.

confidant [kɔnfi'dænt], *s.* der Vertraute.

confide [kən'faid], *v.a.* anvertrauen. — *v.n.* vertrauen (*Dat.*).

confidence ['kɔnfidəns], *s.* das Vertrauen; die Zuversicht; — *trick*, die Bauernfängerei, der Schwindel.

confident ['kɔnfidənt], *adj.* zuversichtlich; dreist (*bold*).

confidential [kɔnfi'denʃəl], *adj.* vertraulich, privat.

confine [kən'fain], *v.a.* einschränken (*hem in*); einsperren; *be* —*d to bed*, bettlägerig sein.

confinement [kən'fainmənt], *s.* die Einschränkung (*limitation*); das Wochenbett, die Niederkunft (*childbirth*).

confines ['kɔnfainz], *s. pl.* die Grenzen, *f. pl.* (*physical*); die Einschränkungen, *f. pl.* (*limitations*).

confirm [kən'fə:m], *v.a.* bestätigen, bekräftigen (*corroborate*); (*Eccl.*) firmen, konfirmieren.

confirmation [kɔnfə'meiʃən], *s.* die Bestätigung (*corroboration*); (*Eccl.*) die Firmung, Konfirmation.

confirmed [kən'fə:md], *adj.* eingefleischt; unverbesserlich.

confiscate ['kɔnfiskeit], *v.a.* konfiszieren, einziehen, beschlagnahmen.

confiscation [kɔnfis'keiʃən], *s.* die Konfiszierung, die Einziehung, die Beschlagnahme (*customs etc.*).

conflagration [kɔnflə'greiʃən], *s.* der (große) Brand.

conflict ['kɔnflikt], *s.* der Konflikt, der Zusammenstoß. — [kən'flikt], *v.n.* in Konflikt geraten; in Widerspruch stehen.

confluence ['kɔnfluəns], *s.* (*Geog.*) der Zusammenfluß.

confluent ['kɔnfluənt], *adj.* zusammenfließend. — *s.* der Nebenfluß (*tributary*).

conform [kən'fɔ:m], *v.n.* sich anpassen.

conformation [kɔnfɔ:'meiʃən], *s.* die Anpassung.

conformist [kən'fɔ:mist], *adj.* fügsam. — *s.* das Mitglied der Staatskirche.

conformity [kən'fɔ:miti], *s.* die Gleichförmigkeit; *in* — *with*, gerade so; gemäß (*Dat.*); die Gleichheit (*equality.*)

confound [kən'faund], *v.a.* verwirren (*confuse*); vernichten (*overthrow*).

confounded [kən'faundid], *adj.* — dammt, verwünscht.

confront [kən'frʌnt], *v.a.* (*Law*) — *s.o. with*, gegenüberstellen (*put in front of*); gegenüberstehen (*stand in front of*).

confrontation [kɔnfrʌn'teiʃən], *s.* die Gegenüberstellung.

confuse [kən'fju:z], *v.a.* verwirren (*muddle*); bestürzen (*perplex*); verwechseln (*mix up*).

confusion [kən'fju:ʒən], *s.* die Verwirrung, das Durcheinander (*muddle*); die Bestürzung (*astonishment*); die Verlegenheit (*dilemma*).

confutation [kɔnfju:'teiʃən], *s.* die Widerlegung.

confute [kən'fju:t], *v.a.* widerlegen.

congeal [kən'dʒi:l], *v.n.* gefrieren (*freeze*); gerinnen.

congenial [kən'dʒi:niəl], *adj.* geistesverwandt, geistig wesensbürtig, sympathisch.

congeniality [kəndʒi:ni'æliti], *s.* die Geistesverwandtschaft.

conger ['kɔŋgə], *s.* (*Zool.*) der Meeraal.

congest [kən'dʒest], *v.a.* anhäufen, überfüllen.

congestion [kən'dʒestʃən], *s.* die Überfüllung; Stauung; die Übervölkerung (*overpopulation*); (*Med.*) der Blutandrang.

conglomerate [kən'glɔməreit], *v.n.* sich zusammenballen. — [-rit], *s.* das Konglomerat, die Ballung.

conglomeration [kənglɔmə'reiʃən], *s.* die Zusammenhäufung, Zusammenballung.

Congolese [kɔŋgo'liːz], *adj.* kongolesisch. — *s.* der Kongolese.

congratulate [kən'grætjuleit], *v.n.* gratulieren (*on*, zu, *Dat.*).

congratulation [kəngrætju'leiʃən], *s.* (*usually pl.*) die Glückwünsche.

congratulatory [kən'grætjuleitəri], *adj.* Glückwunsch-.

congregate [kɔŋgrigeit], *v.a.* versammeln. — *v.n.* sich versammeln, sich scharen (*round*, um, *Acc.*).

congregation [kɔŋgri'geiʃən], *s.* die Versammlung, die Schar; (*Eccl.*) die Gemeinde.

congregational [kɔŋgri'geiʃənəl], *adj.* (*Eccl.*) Gemeinde-; *Congregational Church*, unabhängige Gemeindekirche.

congress [kɔŋgres], *s.* der Kongreß.

congruence [kɔŋgruəns], *s.* (*Geom.*) die Kongruenz.

congruent [kɔŋgruənt], *adj.* (*Geom.*) kongruent.

congruity [kɔŋ'gruːiti], *s.* (*Geom.*) die Übereinstimmung; die Kongruenz.

congruous [kɔŋgruəs], *adj.* übereinstimmend, angemessen.

conic(al) [kɔnik(əl)], *adj.* konisch, kegelförmig; (*Geom.*) — *section*, der Kegelschnitt.

conifer [kɔnifə], *s.* (*Bot.*) der Nadelbaum.

conjecture [kən'dʒəktʃə], *s.* die Mutmaßung, die Annahme. — *v.a.* mutmaßen, annehmen.

conjoin [kən'dʒɔin], *v.a.* (*Law*) verbinden.

conjugal [kɔndʒugəl], *adj.* ehelich.

conjugate [kɔndʒugeit], *v.a.* (*Gram.*) konjugieren.

conjugation [kɔndʒu'geiʃən], *s.* (*Gram.*) die Konjugation.

conjunction [kən'dʒʌŋkʃən], *s.* (*Gram.*) das Bindewort.

conjunctive [kən'dʒʌŋktiv], *adj.* verbindend; (*Gram.*) — *mood*, der Konjunktiv.

conjunctivitis [kən'dʒʌŋktivaitis], *s.* (*Med.*) die Bindehautentzündung.

conjuncture [kən'dʒʌŋktʃə], *s.* der Wendepunkt; die Krise (*of events*).

conjure [kʌndʒə], *v.a.* beschwören; — *up*, heraufbeschwören. — *v.n.* zaubern.

conjurer [kʌndʒərə], *s.* der Zauberer.

connect [kə'nekt], *v.a.* verbinden, in Zusammenhang bringen.

connection, connexion [kə'nekʃən], *s.* die Verbindung, der Zusammenhang.

connivance [kə'naivəns], *s.* die Nachsicht, das Gewährenlassen.

connive [kə'naiv], *v.n.* nachsichtig sein (*at*, bei, *Dat.*); gewähren lassen.

connoisseur [kɔne'səː], *s.* der Kenner.

connubial [kə'njuːbiəl], *adj.* ehelich.

conquer [kɔŋkə], *v.a.* besiegen (*foe*); erobern (*place*).

conqueror [kɔŋkərə], *s.* der Eroberer, der Sieger.

conquest [kɔŋkwest], *s.* der Sieg, die Eroberung.

consanguinity [kɔnsæŋ'gwiniti], *s.* die Blutsverwandtschaft.

conscience [kɔnʃəns], *s.* das Gewissen; *in all* — wahrhaftig.

conscientious [kɔnʃi'enʃəs], *adj.* gewissenhaft.

conscientiousness [kɔnʃi'enʃəsnis], *s.* die Gewissenhaftigkeit.

conscious [kɔnʃəs], *adj.* bewußt (*Genit.*).

consciousness [kɔnʃəsnis], *s.* das Bewußtsein.

conscript [kən'skript], *v.a.* (*Mil.*) einziehen, einberufen. — [kɔnskript], *s.* (*Mil.*) der Rekrut, der Dienstpflichtige.

conscription [kən'skripʃən], *s.* die allgemeine Wehrpflicht.

consecrate [kɔnsikreit], *v.a.* weihen, widmen.

consecrated [kɔnsikreitid], *adj.* geweiht (*Dat.*).

consecration [kɔnsi'kreiʃən], *s.* die Weihe, Einweihung (*of church*); die Weihung.

consecutive [kən'sekjutiv], *adj.* aufeinanderfolgend, fortlaufend.

consecutiveness [kən'sekjutivnis], *s.* die Aufeinanderfolge.

consent [kən'sent], *v.n.* zustimmen, beistimmen (*to*, *Dat.*). — *s.* die Zustimmung, die Einwilligung.

consequence [kɔnsikwəns], *s.* die Konsequenz; (*Log.*) Folgerung; die Folge; die Wichtigkeit (*importance*).

consequent [kɔnsikwənt], *adj.* folgend, nachfolgend.

consequential [kɔnsi'kwenʃəl], *adj.* wichtigtuend, anmaßend; (*Log.*) folgerichtig.

consequently [kɔnsikwəntli], *adv.* folglich, infolgedessen.

conservatism [kən'səː vətizm], *s.* (*Pol.*) der Konservatismus; die konservative Denkweise.

conservative [kən'səː vətiv], *adj.* (*Pol.*) konservativ.

conservatoire [kən'səː vətwɑː], *s.* (*Mus.*) das Konservatorium, die Musikhochschule.

conservatory [kən'səː vətəri], *s.* (*Bot.*) das Gewächshaus.

conserve [kən'səː v], *v.a.* konservieren, erhalten, einmachen. — *s.* (*fruit*) das Eingemachte.

consider [kən'sidə], *v.a.* betrachten, in Betracht ziehen (*think over*, *look at*); berücksichtigen (*have regard to*); nachdenken über (*Acc.*) (*ponder*).

considerable [kən'sidərəbl], *adj.* beträchtlich, ansehnlich.

considerate [kən'sidərit], *adj.* rücksichtsvoll (*thoughtful*).

consideration [kənsidə'reiʃən], *s.* die Betrachtung (*contemplation*); die Rücksicht (*regard*) (*for*, auf, *Acc.*); die Entschädigung (*compensation*); die Belohnung (*reward*).

considering [kən'sidəriŋ], *prep.* in Anbetracht (*Genit.*).

consign [kən'sain], *v.a.* überliefern (*hand over*); übersenden (*remit*).

consignee [kɔnsai'niː], *s.* (*Comm.*) der Empfänger, der Adressat (*recipient*).

consigner [kən'sainə], *s.* der Absender (*of goods*).

consignment [kən'sainmənt], *s.* die Sendung (*of goods*).

consist [kən'sist], *v.n.* bestehen (*of*, aus, *Dat.*).

consistency [kən'sistənsi], *s.* die Festigkeit, Dichtigkeit; (*Chem.*) die Konsistenz.

consistent [kən'sistənt], *adj.* konsequent; — *with*, übereinstimmend, gemäß (*Dat.*); (*Chem.*) dicht, fest.

consistory [kən'sistəri], *s.* (*Eccl.*) das Konsistorium.

consolable [kən'soulabl], *adj.* tröstlich, zu trösten.

consolation [kɔnso'leiʃən], *s.* der Trost; *draw* —, Trost schöpfen.

console (1) [kən'soul], *v.a.* trösten.

console (2) ['kɔnsoul], *s.* (*Archit.*) die Konsole.

consolidate [kən'sɔlideit], *v.a.* befestigen, konsolidieren. — *v.n.* fest werden.

consolidation [kənsɔli'deiʃən], *s.* die Befestigung; Festigung, Bestärkung (*confirmation*).

consonance ['kɔnsənəns], *s.* (*Phonet.*) die Konsonanz; der Einklang, die Harmonie.

consonant ['kɔnsənənt], *adj.* in Einklang (*with*, mit, *Dat.*). — *s.* der Konsonant.

consort ['kɔnsɔːt], *s.* der Gemahl, Gatte; die Gemahlin, die Gattin. — [kən'sɔːt], *v.n.* verkehren (*with*, mit, *Dat.*).

conspicuous [kən'spikjuəs], *adj.* auffallend, deutlich sichtbar, hervorragend.

conspiracy [kən'spirəsi], *s.* die Verschwörung.

conspirator [kən'spirətə], *s.* der Verschwörer.

conspire [kən'spaiə], *v.n.* sich verschwören.

constable ['kʌnstəbl], *s.* der Polizist, der Schutzmann.

Constance ['kɔnstəns]. Konstanze *f.* (*name*); Konstanz (*town*); *Lake* —, der Bodensee.

constancy ['kɔnstənsi], *s.* die Beständigkeit, Treue.

constant ['kɔnstənt], *adj.* (*Chem.*) konstant; treu, beständig.

constellation [kɔnste'leiʃən], *s.* die Konstellation; das Sternbild.

consternation [kɔnstə'neiʃən], *s.* die Bestürzung.

constipation [kɔnsti'peiʃən], *s.* die Verstopfung.

constituency [kən'stitjuənsi], *s.* der Wahlkreis (*electoral district*); die Wählerschaft (*voters*).

constituent [kən'stitjuənt], *adj.* wesentlich. — *s.* der Bestandteil (*component*); (*Pol.*) der Wähler.

constitute ['kɔnstitjuːt], *v.a.* ausmachen (*make up*); bilden (*form*); festsetzen (*establish*); (*Pol.*) errichten (*set up*).

constitution [kɔnsti'tjuːʃən], *s.* die Konstitution (*physique*); die Errichtung (*establishment*); die Beschaffenheit, Natur (*nature*); (*Pol.*) die Verfassung.

constitutional [kɔnsti'tjuːʃənəl], *adj.* körperlich bedingt; (*Pol.*) verfassungsmäßig.

constrain [kən'strein], *v.a.* nötigen, zwingen.

constraint [kən'streint], *s.* der Zwang.

constrict [kən'strikt], *v.a.* zusammenziehen.

constriction [kən'strikʃən], *s.* die Zusammenziehung, Beengtheit.

construct [kən'strʌkt], *v.a.* errichten, bauen, konstruieren.

construction [kən'strʌkʃən], *s.* die Errichtung, der Bau, die Konstruktion.

constructive [kən'strʌktiv], *adj.* (*Engin.*) konstruktiv; behilflich (*positive*).

constructor [kən'strʌktə], *s.* der Konstrukteur, der Erbauer (*builder*).

construe [kən'struː], *v.a.* konstruieren, deuten (*interpret*).

consul ['kɔnsul], *s.* der Konsul; — -*general*, der Generalkonsul.

consular ['kɔnsjulə], *adj.* konsularisch.

consulate ['kɔnsjulit], *s.* das Konsulat; — -*general*, das Generalkonsulat.

consult [kən'sʌlt], *v.a.* konsultieren, zu Rate ziehen; nachschlagen (*a book*). — *v.n.* sich beraten (*with*, mit, *Dat.*); (*Comm.*) als Berater hinzuziehen.

consultant [kən'sʌltənt], *s.* (*Med.*) der Facharzt; der Berater.

consultation [kɔnsəl'teiʃən], *s.* die Beratung (*advice*); die Besprechung (*discussion*); (*Med.*, *Engin.*) die Konsultation.

consume [kən'sjuːm], *v.a.* verzehren (*eat up*); verbrauchen (*use up*).

consumer [kən'sjuːmə], *s.* der Verbraucher; (*Comm.*) der Konsument.

consummate [kən'sʌmit], *adj.* vollendet. — ['kɔnsəmeit], *v.a.* vollenden, vollziehen.

consummation [kɔnsə'meiʃən], *s.* die Vollziehung, Vollendung.

consumption [kən'sʌmpʃən], *s.* (*Comm.*) der Verbrauch; (*Med.*) die Schwindsucht.

consumptive [kən'sʌmptiv], *adj.* (*Med.*) schwindsüchtig.

contact ['kɔntækt], *v.a.* berühren (*touch*); in Verbindung treten (mit) (*get into touch (with)*). — *s.* (*Elec.*) der Kontakt; die Berührung (*touch*); die Verbindung (*connexion*).

contagion [kən'teidʒən], *s.* (*Med.*) die Ansteckung.

contagious[kən'teidʒəs],*adj.*ansteckend.

contain [kən'tein], *v.a.* enthalten (*hold*); zurückhalten (*restrain*).

container [kən'teinə], *s.* der Behälter.

contaminate [kən'tæmineit], *v.a.* verunreinigen; vergiften.

contemplate ['kɔntəmpleit], *v.a.* betrachten (*consider*). — *v.n.* nachdenken (*ponder*).

contemplation [kɔntəm'pleiʃən], *s.* die Betrachtung (*consideration*); das Sinnen (*pondering*).

contemplative [kən'templətiv], *adj.* nachdenklich, kontemplativ.

contemporaneous [kəntempə'reiniəs], *adj.* gleichzeitig.

contemporary [kən'tempərəri], *adj.* zeitgenössisch. — *s.* der Zeitgenosse.

contempt [kən'tempt], *s.* die Verachtung; — *of court*, die Gerichtsbeleidigung.

contemptible [kən'temptibl], *adj.* verächtlich, verachtungswert.

contemptibleness [kən'temptiblnis], *s.* die Verächtlichkeit.

contemptuous [kən'temptjuəs], *adj.* höhnisch, verachtungsvoll.

contemptuousness [kən'temptjuəsnis], *s.* der Hohn, der verachtungsvolle Ton, der Hochmut.

contend [kən'tend], *v.n.* streiten; bestreiten, behaupten.

content [kən'tent], *adj.* zufrieden. — *v.a.* zufriedenstellen. — ['kɔntent], *s.* (*often pl.*) der Inhalt.

contented [kən'tentid], *adj.* zufrieden.

contentedness, contentment [kən'tentidnis, kən'tentmənt], *s.* die Zufriedenheit.

contention [kən'tenʃən], *s.* der Streit, die Behauptung.

contentious [kən'tenʃəs], *adj.* streitsüchtig (*person*); strittig (*question*).

contest ['kɔntest], *s.* der Streit, Wettstreit, Wettkampf. — [kən'test], *v.a.* um etwas streiten, bestreiten.

context ['kɔntekst], *s.* der Zusammenhang.

contexture [kən'tekstʃə], *s.* (*Engin.*) der Bau, die Zusammensetzung; das Gewebe (*textile*).

contiguity [kɔnti'gju:iti], *s.* die Berührung; die Nachbarschaft.

contiguous [kən'tigjuəs], *adj.* anstossend, anliegend.

continence ['kɔntinəns], *s.* die Mäßigung (*moderation*); die Enthaltsamkeit (*abstemiousness*).

continent (1) ['kɔntinənt], *adj.* enthaltsam, mässig.

continent (2) ['kɔntinənt], *s.* das Festland, der Kontinent.

contingency [kən'tindʒənsi], *s.* der Zufall; die Möglichkeit (*possibility*).

contingent [kən'tindʒənt], *s.* der Beitrag, das Kontingent (*share*). — *adj.* möglich.

continual [kən'tinjuəl], *adj.* fortwährend, beständig.

continuance [kən'tinjuəns], *s.* die Fortdauer.

continuation [kəntinju'eiʃən], *s.* die Fortsetzung.

continue [kən'tinju:], *v.a.* fortsetzen (*go on with*); verlängern (*prolong*). — *v.n.* weitergehen, weiterführen (*of story*).

continuity [kɔnti'nju:iti], *s.* der Zusammenhang, die ununterbrochene Folge, Kontinuität (*Film*); — *girl*, die Drehbuchsekretärin.

continuous [kən'tinjuəs], *adj.* zusammenhängend, ununterbrochen, andauernd.

contort [kən'tɔ:t], *v.a.* verdrehen.

contortion [kən'tɔ:ʃən], *s.* die Verdrehung, Verkrümmung, Verzerrung.

contortionist [kən'tɔ:ʃənist], *s.* der Schlangenmensch.

contour ['kɔntuə], *s.* die Kontur, der Umriß.

contraband ['kɔntrəbænd], *adj.* Schmuggel-, geschmuggelt. — *s.* die Bannware, Schmuggelware.

contract [kən'trækt], *v.a.* zusammenziehen (*pull together*); verengen (*narrow down*); verkürzen (*shorten*); sich eine Krankheit zuziehen (— *a disease*); Schulden machen (— *debts*). — *v.n.* sich zusammenziehen, kürzer werden; einen Kontrakt abschließen (*come to terms*). — ['kɔntrækt], *s.* der Vertrag (*pact*); (*Comm.*) der Kontrakt.

contraction [kən'trækʃən], *s.* die Zusammenziehung; (*Phonet.*) die Kürzung.

contractor [kən'træktə], *s.* (*Comm.*) der Kontrahent; der Lieferant (*supplier*); *building* —, der Bauunternehmer.

contradict [kɔntrə'dikt], *v.n.* widersprechen (*Dat.*).

contradiction [kɔntrə'dikʃən], *s.* der Widerspruch.

contradictory [kɔntrə'diktəri], *adj.* in Widerspruch stehend, widersprechend.

contrarily ['kɔntrərili], *adv.* im Gegensatz dazu, hingegen, dagegen.

contrary ['kɔntrəri], *adj.* entgegengesetzt, *on the* —, im Gegenteil; [kən'trɛəri], widersprechend.

contrast [kən'trɑ:st], *v.a.* einander entgegenstellen, gegenüberstellen. — *v.n.* einen Gegensatz darstellen *or* bilden. — ['kɔntrɑ:st], *s.* der Kontrast (*colours*); der Gegensatz.

contravene [kɔntrə'vi:n], *v.a.* übertreten, zuwiderhandeln (*Dat.*).

contribute [kən'tribju:t], *v.a.* beitragen; beisteuern (*money, energy*).

contribution [kɔntri'bju:ʃən], *s.* der Beitrag.

contributive

contributive, contributory [kən'tri-bjutiv, kən'tribjutəri], *adj.* beitragend, Beitrags-.

contributor [kən'tribjutə], *s.* der Beitragende, der Spender (*of money*); der Mitarbeiter (*journalist etc.*).

contrite ['kɔntrait], *adj.* zerknirscht, reuevoll.

contrition [kən'triʃən], *s.* die Zerknirschung, die Reue.

contrivance [kən'traivəns], *s.* die Vorrichtung, die Erfindung.

contrive [kən'traiv], *v.a.* ausdenken, erfinden; fertigbringen (*accomplish*).

control [kən'troul], *v.a.* kontrollieren (*check*); die Leitung haben (*have command of*); die Aufsicht führen (*supervise*). — *s.* die Kontrolle; die Aufsicht; die Leitung; (*pl.*) (*Motor.*) die Steuerung; (*Aviat.*) das Leitwerk.

controller [kən'troulə], *s.* der Aufseher (*supervisor*); der Direktor (*of corporation*); der Revisor (*examiner, auditor*).

controversial [kɔntro'və:ʃəl], *adj.* umstritten, strittig.

controversy ['kɔntrovə:si], *s.* die Kontroverse, die Streitfrage.

controvert ['kɔntrovə:t], *v.a.* bestreiten, widersprechen (*Dat.*).

contumacious [kɔntju'meiʃəs], *adj.* widerspenstig, halsstarrig.

contumacy ['kɔntjuməsi], *s.* die Widerspenstigkeit (*obstreperousness*); der Ungehorsam (*disobedience*).

contumelious [kɔntju'mi:liəs], *adj.* frech, unverschämt (*insolent*).

contuse [kən'tju:z], *v.a.* quetschen.

conundrum [kə'nʌndrəm], *s.* das Scherzrätsel.

convalescence [kɔnvə'lesəns], *s.* die Gesundung, die Genesung.

convalescent [kɔnvə'lesənt], *adj.* genesend. — *s.* der Genesende, der Rekonvaleszent.

convene [kən'vi:n], *v.a.* zusammenrufen, versammeln. — *v.n.* zusammentreten, sich versammeln.

convenience [kən'vi:niəns], *s.* die Bequemlichkeit; *at your early* —, umgehend; *public* —, öffentliche Bedürfnisanstalt.

convenient [kən'vi:niənt], *adj.* bequem, gelegen; passend (*time*).

convent ['kɔnvənt], *s.* das (Nonnen)-Kloster.

convention [kən'venʃən], *s.* die Konvention, der Kongress (*meeting*); der Vertrag (*treaty*); die Sitte (*tradition, custom*).

conventional [kən'venʃənəl], *adj.* herkömmlich, traditionell.

conventual [kən'ventjuəl], *adj.* klösterlich.

conversation [kɔnvə'seiʃən], *s.* die Konversation, Unterhaltung; das Gespräch.

conversational [kɔnvə'seiʃənəl], *adj.* gesprächig, umgangssprachlich.

converse (1) [kən'və:s], *v.n.* sich unterhalten (*with*, mit, *Dat.*).

converse (2) ['kɔnvə:s], *adj.* umgekehrt.

conversely ['kɔnvə:sli], *adv.* hingegen, dagegen.

conversion [kən'və:ʃən], *s.* die Umkehrung (*reversal*); (*Rel.*) die Bekehrung; (*Comm.*) die Umwechslung.

convert ['kɔnvə:t], *s.* (*Rel.*) der Bekehrte, die Bekehrte; der Konvertit. — [kən'və:t], *v.a.* (*Rel.*) bekehren; (*Comm.*) umwechseln.

converter [kən'və:tə], *s.* (*Rel.*) der Bekehrer; (*Metall.*, *Elec.*) der Umformer.

convertible [kən'və:tibl], *adj.* umwandelbar. — *s.* (*Motor.*) der or das Konvertible.

convex ['kɔnveks], *adj.* (*Phys.*) konvex.

convey [kən'vei], *v.a.* transportieren; führen (*bear, carry*); mitteilen (*impart*).

conveyance [kən'veiəns], *s.* die Beförderung (*transport*); das Fuhrwerk (*vehicle*); die Übertragung; (*Law*) das Übertragungsdokument.

conveyancing [kən'veiənsiŋ], *s.* (*Law*) die legale or rechtliche Übertragung.

convict ['kɔnvikt], *s.* der Sträfling. — [kən'vikt], *v.a.* für schuldig erklären.

conviction [kən'vikʃən], *s.* die Überzeugung; (*Law*) die Überführung, die Schuldigsprechung.

convince [kən'vins], *v.a.* überzeugen.

convivial [kən'viviəl], *adj.* gesellig (*sociable*).

conviviality [kənvivi'æliti], *s.* die Geselligkeit.

convocation [kɔnvə'keiʃən], *s.* die Zusammenberufung, Festversammlung; (*Eccl.*) die Synode.

convoke [kən'vouk], *v.a.* zusammenberufen.

convolvulus [kən'vɔlvjuləs], *s.* (*Bot.*) die Winde.

convoy ['kɔnvɔi], *s.* das Geleit, die Bedeckung; (*Mil.*) der Begleitzug. — [kən'vɔi], *v.a.* geleiten; (*Mil.*) im Geleitzug mitführen.

convulse [kən'vʌls], *v.a.* erschüttern.

convulsion [kən'vʌlʃən], *s.* der Krampf, die Zuckung.

convulsive [kən'vʌlsiv], *adj.* krampfhaft, zuckend.

coo [ku:], *v.n.* girren (*of birds*); *bill and* —, schnäbeln.

cook [kuk], *v.a.*, *v.n.* kochen; (*coll.*) — *the books*, die Bücher(Bilanz)fälschen or frisieren. — *s.* der Koch, die Köchin; *too many cooks* (*spoil the broth*), zu viele Köche (verderben den Brei).

cookery ['kukəri], *s.* die Kochkunst; — *school*, die Kochschule.

cool [ku:l], *adj.* kühl (*climate*); kaltblütig (*coldblooded*); unverschämt (*brazen*). — *s.* die Kühle. — *v.a.* abkühlen; (*fig.*) besänftigen. — *v.a.* sich abkühlen.

cooler ['ku:lə], *s.* (*Chem.*) das Kühlfaß; (*coll.*) das Gefängnis; (*sl.*) das Kittchen.

coop [ku:p], s. die Kufe; das Faß; *hen* —, der Hühnerkorb. — *v.a.* — *up*, einsperren.

cooper ['ku:pə], s. der Böttcher, der Faßbinder.

cooperate [kou'ɔpəreit], *v.n.* zusammenarbeiten; mitarbeiten, mitwirken.

cooperation [kouɔpə'reiʃən], s. die Zusammenarbeit, die Mitarbeit.

cooperative [kou'ɔpərətiv], *adj.* willig; mitwirkend. — s. die Konsumgenossenschaft, der Konsum.

coordinate [kou'ɔ:dineit], *v.a.* koordinieren, beiordnen. — [-nit], *adj.* (*Gram.*) koordiniert.

coordination [kouɔ:di'neiʃən], s. die Koordinierung.

coot [ku:t], s. (*Orn.*) das Wasserhuhn.

copartnership [kou'pa:tnəʃip], s. die Teilhaberschaft; die Partnerschaft in der Industrie.

cope (1) [koup], s. (*Eccl.*) das Pluviale, der Priesterrock; (*Build.*) die Decke.

cope (2) [koup], *v.n.* — *with s.th.*, mit etwas fertig werden, es schaffen.

coping ['koupiŋ], s. (*Build.*) die Kappe; — *-stone* or *copestone*, der Firststein, Schlußstein, Kappstein.

copious ['koupiəs], *adj.* reichlich; wortreich (*style*).

copiousness ['koupiəsnis], s. die Reichhaltigkeit, Fülle.

copper ['kɔpə], s. (*Metall.*) das Kupfer; (*sl.*) der Polizist; (*coll.*) der Penny, das Pennystück. — *adj.* kupfern.

copperplate ['kɔpəpleit], s. der Kupferstich (*etching*); (*Typ.*) die Kupferplatte.

coppery ['kɔpəri], *adj.* Kupfer-, kupfern, kupferfarben (*colour*).

coppice, copse ['kɔpis, kɔps], s. das Unterholz, das Dickicht.

copulate ['kɔpjuleit], *v.n.* sich paaren, begatten.

copulation [kɔpju'leiʃən], s. die Paarung; der Beischlaf (*human*).

copy ['kɔpi], *v.a.* kopieren, abschreiben (*write*); imitieren, nachahmen (*imitate*). — s. die Kopie; *carbon* —, die Durchschrift; Abschrift; die Nachahmung (*imitation*); die Fälschung (*forgery*).

copybook ['kɔpibuk], s. das Heft.

copyist ['kɔpiist], s. der Kopist.

coquet, coquette (1) [kɔ'ket], *v.n.* kokettieren.

coquette (2) [kɔ'ket], s. die Kokette.

coquettish [kɔ'ketiʃ], *adj.* kokett.

coral ['kɔrəl], s. die Koralle. — *adj.* Korallen-.

cord [kɔ:d], s. die Schnur, der Strick (*rope*); (*Am.*) der Bindfaden (*string*); die Klafter (*wood measure*); der Kordstoff (*textile*); *vocal* —, das Stimmband.

cordage ['kɔ:didʒ], s. (*Naut.*) das Tauwerk.

cordial (1) ['kɔ:diəl], *adj.* herzlich.

cordial (2) ['kɔ:diəl], s. der Fruchtsaft (konzentriert), Magenlikör.

cordiality [kɔ:di'æliti], s. die Herzlichkeit.

corduroy ['kɔ:djurɔi], s. der Kordsamt.

core [kɔ:], s. der Kern; das Innere (*innermost part*).

cork [kɔ:k], s. der Kork, der Korken. — *v.a.* verkorken.

corkscrew ['kɔ:kskru:], s. der Korkzieher.

cormorant ['kɔ:mərənt], s. (*Orn.*) der Kormoran, die Scharbe.

corn (1) [kɔ:n], s. das Korn, das Getreide (*wheat etc.*); (*Am.*) *sweet* —, der Mais.

corn (2) [kɔ:n], s. das Hühnerauge (*on foot*).

corned [kɔ:nd], *adj.* eingesalzt; — *beef*, das Pökelrindfleisch.

cornea ['kɔ:niə], s. (*Anat.*) die Hornhaut.

cornel-tree ['kɔ:nəltri:], s. (*Bot.*) der Kornelkirschbaum.

cornelian [kɔ:'ni:liən], s. (*Geol.*) der Karneol.

corner ['kɔ:nə], s. die Ecke; (*Footb.*) der Eckstoß. — *v.a.* in eine Ecke treiben; in die Enge treiben (*force*).

cornered ['kɔ:nəd], *adj.* eckig (*angular*); in die Enge getrieben, gefangen (*caught*).

cornet ['kɔ:nit], s. (*Mus.*) die Zinke, das Flügelhorn; (*Mil.*) der Kornett, der Fähnrich.

cornflower ['kɔ:nflauə], s. (*Bot.*) die Kornblume.

cornice ['kɔ:nis], s. (*Archit.*) das Gesims.

cornucopia [kɔ:nju'koupjə], s. das Füllhorn.

corollary [kə'rɔləri], s. (*Log.*) der Folgesatz; die Folgeerscheinung (*consequence*).

corona [kə'rounə], s. (*Astron.*) der Hof, Lichtkranz.

coronation [kɔrə'neiʃən], s. die Krönung.

coroner ['kɔrənə], s. der Leichenbeschauer.

coronet ['kɔrənet], s. die Adelskrone.

corporal (1) ['kɔ:pərəl], s. (*Mil.*) der Korporal, der Unteroffizier, Obergefreite.

corporal (2) ['kɔ:pərəl], *adj.* körperlich; — *punishment*, die Züchtigung.

corporate ['kɔ:pərit], *adj.* (*Law, Comm.*) als Körperschaft; gemeinschaftlich, einheitlich (*as a group or unit.*)

corporation [kɔ:pə'reiʃən], s. (*Law, Comm.*) die Körperschaft; die Korporation; die Gemeinde (*municipal*); (*sl.*) der Schmerbauch (*stoutness*).

corps [kɔ:], s. das Korps.

corpse [kɔ:ps], s. der Leichnam.

corpulence ['kɔ:pjuləns], s. die Korpulenz, die Beleibtheit.

corpulent ['kɔ:pjulənt], *adj.* korpulent, dick.

Corpus Christi ['kɔ:pəs 'kristi], (der) Fronleichnam, das Fronleichnamsfest.

corpuscle ['kɔ:pʌsl], s. (*Anat.*) das Körperchen.

351

correct

correct [kə'rekt], *v.a.* korrigieren (*remove mistakes*); verbessern; tadeln (*reprove*); berichtigen (*rectify*). — *adj.* korrekt, tadellos, richtig.

correction [kə'rekʃən], *s.* die Korrektur (*of mistakes*); die Verbesserung (*improvement*); die Richtigstellung (*restoration*); der Verweis (*censure*).

corrective [kə'rektiv], *adj.* zur Besserung. — *s.* das Korrektiv.

correctness [kə'rektnis], *s.* die Korrektheit (*of manner, action etc.*).

corrector [kə'rektə], *s.* der Korrektor (*proof reader etc.*).

correlate ['kɔrileit], *v.a.* in Beziehung setzen, aufeinander beziehen. — [-lit], *s.* (*Log.*) das Korrelat.

correlative [kɔ'relətiv], *adj.* in Wechselbeziehung stehend.

correspond [kɔris'pɔnd], *v.n.* korrespondieren (*exchange letters*); entsprechen (*to, Dat.*).

correspondence [kɔris'pɔndəns], *s.* die Korrespondenz; der Briefwechsel (*letters*); die Übereinstimmung (*harmony*).

correspondent [kɔris'pɔndənt], *s.* der Korrespondent (*letter-writer*); der Journalist, Berichterstatter (*newspaper*).

corridor ['kɔridɔ:], *s.* der Korridor; der Gang.

corrigible ['kɔridʒibl], *adj.* verbesserlich.

corroborate [kə'rɔbəreit], *v.a.* bestätigen (*confirm*); bestärken (*strengthen*).

corroboration [kərɔbə'reiʃən], *s.* die Bestätigung, die Bekräftigung.

corroborative [kə'rɔbərətiv], *adj.* bekräftigend.

corrode [kə'roud], *v.a.* zerfressen, zersetzen, ätzen (*acid*).

corrosion [kə'rouʒən], *s.* die Anfressung, Ätzung.

corrosive [kə'rouziv], *adj.* ätzend.

corrugated ['kɔrugeitid], *adj.* gewellt, Well-; — *iron*, das Wellblech; — *paper*, die Wellpappe.

corrupt [kə'rʌpt], *v.a.* verderben (*spoil*); bestechen (*bribe*). — *adj.* korrupt (*morals*); verdorben (*spoilt*).

corruptible [kə'rʌptibl], *adj.* verderblich; bestechlich.

corruption [kə'rʌpʃən], *s.* die Korruption; die Bestechung (*bribery*).

corruptness [kə'rʌptnis], *s.* die Verdorbenheit, der Verfall.

corsair ['kɔ:sɛə], *s.* der Korsar, der Seeräuber.

corset ['kɔ:sit], *s.* das Korsett.

coruscate ['kɔrəskeit], *v.n.* schimmern, leuchten.

corvette [kɔ:'vet], *s.* (*Naut.*) die Korvette.

cosine ['kousain], *s.* (*Maths.*) der Kosinus.

cosiness ['kouzinis], *s.* die Bequemlichkeit, die Behaglichkeit (*comfort*).

cosmetic [kɔz'metik], *adj.* kosmetisch. — *s.* (*pl.*) das *or* die (*pl.*) Schönheitsmittel.

cosmic ['kɔzmik], *adj.* kosmisch.

cosmopolitan [kɔzmo'pɔlitən], *adj.* kosmopolitisch, weltbürgerlich. — *s.* der Kosmopolit, der Weltbürger.

Cossack ['kɔsæk], *s.* der Kosak.

cost [kɔst], *v.a. irr.* kosten. — *v.n. irr.* zu stehen kommen. —*s.* die Kosten, *f. pl.* (*expenses*); *at all* —*s*, um jeden Preis.

costermonger ['kɔstəmʌŋgə], *s.* der Straßenhändler.

costly ['kɔstli], *adj.* kostspielig.

costume ['kɔstju:m], *s.* das Kostüm; — *play*, das Zeitstück.

cosy ['kouzi], *adj.* behaglich, bequem.

cot (1) [kɔt], *s.* das Bettchen, Kinderbett.

cot (2) [kɔt], *s.* (*obs.*) die Hütte (*hut*).

cottage ['kɔtidʒ], *s.* die Hütte, das Häuschen.

cottager ['kɔtidʒə], *s.* der Kleinhäusler.

cotton [kɔtn], *s.* die Baumwolle. — *v.n.* — *on to*, (*coll.*) sich anhängen, sich anschließen (*Dat.*); — *on*, folgen können (*understand*).

couch [kautʃ], *s.* die Chaiselongue; der Diwan. — *v.a.* (*express*) in Worte fassen.

cough [kɔf], *v.n.* husten. — *s.* der Husten; *whooping* —, der Keuchhusten.

council ['kaunsil], *s.* der Rat (*body*); die Ratsversammlung.

councillor ['kaunsilə], *s.* der Rat, das Ratsmitglied; der Stadtrat.

counsel ['kaunsəl], *s.* der Rat (*advice*); der Berater (*adviser*); der Anwalt (*lawyer*). — *v.a.* einen Rat geben, beraten (*Acc.*).

counsellor ['kaunsələ], *s.* der Ratgeber; der Ratsherr; (*Am.*) der Anwalt (*lawyer*).

count (1) [kaunt], *v.a.,v.n.* zählen; —*on s.o.*, sich auf jemanden verlassen. — *s.* die Zählung.

count (2) [kaunt], *s.* der Graf.

countenance ['kauntənəns], *s.* das Gesicht, die Miene. — *v.a.* begünstigen, unterstützen, zulassen.

counter (1) ['kauntə], *s.* der Rechner, der Zähler (*chip*); die Spielmarke; der Zahltisch (*desk*); Ladentisch (*in shop*); Schalter (*in office*).

counter (2) ['kauntə], *adv.* entgegen.

counteract [kauntə'rækt], *v.a.* entgegenwirken (*Dat.*).

counteraction [kauntə'rækʃən], *s.* die Gegenwirkung; der Widerstand (*resistance*).

counterbalance ['kauntəbæləns], *s.* das Gegengewicht. — [-'bæləns], *v.a.* ausbalancieren, ausgleichen.

countercharge ['kauntətʃɑ:dʒ], *s.* die Gegenklage.

counterfeit ['kauntəfi:t, -fit], *s.* die Fälschung (*forgery*); die Nachahmung (*imitation*). — *adj.* gefälscht, falsch.

352

counterfoil ['kauntəfɔil], s. das Kontrollblatt; der Kupon.
counter-intelligence ['kauntərintelidʒəns], s. die Spionageabwehr.
countermand [kauntə'mɑ:nd], v.a. widerrufen.
counterpane ['kauntəpein], s. die Steppdecke.
counterpart ['kauntəpɑ:t], s. das Gegenbild, das Gegenstück.
counterplot ['kauntəplɔt], s. der Gegenplan. — v.n. einen Gegenplan machen.
counterpoint ['kauntəpɔint], s. (Mus.) der Kontrapunkt.
counterpoise ['kauntəpɔiz], s. das Gegengewicht. — v.a. das Gleichgewicht halten.
countersign ['kauntəsain], v.a. gegenzeichnen, mitunterschreiben. — s. das Gegenzeichen.
countess ['kauntes], s. die Gräfin.
counting-house ['kauntiŋhaus], s. das Kontor.
countless ['kauntlis], adj. zahllos.
country ['kʌntri], s. das Land. — adj. Land-, ländlich, Bauern-.
county ['kaunti], s. die Grafschaft (British); der Landbezirk (U.S.A.).
couple [kʌpl], s. das Paar. — v.a. paaren, verbinden. — v.n. sich paaren (pair); sich verbinden.
couplet ['kʌplit], s. das Verspaar.
coupling ['kʌpliŋ], s. (Mech.) die Kupplung.
courage ['kʌridʒ], s. der Mut.
courageous [kə'reidʒəs], adj. mutig, tapfer.
courier ['kuriə], s. der Eilbote (messenger); der Reisebegleiter (tour leader).
course [kɔ:s], s. der Kurs; der Lauf (time); der Ablauf (lapse of a period etc.); die Bahn (racing track); in due —, zu gegebener Zeit; of —, natürlich.
courser ['kɔ:sə], s. das schnelle Pferd.
court [kɔ:t], s. der Hof (royal etc.); (Law) der Gerichtshof. — v.a. (a lady) den Hof machen (Dat.); — disaster, das Unglück herausfordern.
courteous ['kə:tiəs], adj. höflich.
courtesan ['kɔ:tizən or kɔ:ti'zæn], s. die Kurtisane, die Buhlerin.
courtesy ['kə:təsi], s. die Höflichkeit; by — of, mit freundlicher Erlaubnis von.
courtier ['kɔ:tiə], s. der Höfling.
courtly ['kɔ:tli], adj. höfisch, Hof-.
court-martial [kɔ:t'mɑ:ʃəl], s. das Kriegsgericht.
courtship ['kɔ:tʃip], s. das Werben, die Werbung, das Freien.
courtyard ['kɔ:tjɑ:d], s. der Hof, der Hofraum.
cousin [kʌzn], s. der Vetter (male); die Kusine (female).
cove [kouv], s. die (kleine) Bucht.
covenant ['kʌvənənt], s. (Bibl.) der Bund; (Comm.) der Vertrag.

cover ['kʌvə], v.a. decken, bedecken (table etc.); schützen (protect); — up, bemänteln. — s. die Decke (blanket); der Deckel (lid); der Einband (book); das Gedeck (table); (Comm.) die Deckung; — point, (Cricket) die Deckstellung; under —, (Mil.) verdeckt, unter Deckung; — girl, das Mädchen auf dem Titelblatt (einer Illustrierten.)
covering ['kʌvəriŋ], s. die Bedeckung, die Bekleidung (clothing).
coverlet, coverlid ['kʌvəlit, 'kʌvəlid], s. die Bettdecke.
covert ['kʌvə:t], s. der Schlupfwinkel (hideout); das Dickicht (thicket). — adj. verborgen, bedeckt (covered); heimlich (secret).
covet ['kʌvit], v.a., v.n. begehren (Acc.), gelüsten (nach (Dat.)).
covetous ['kʌvitəs], adj. begierig, habsüchtig.
covetousness ['kʌvitəsnis], s. die Begierde, die Habsucht.
covey ['kʌvi], s. der Flug or die Kette (Rebhühner, partridges).
cow (1) [kau], s. die Kuh; — —shed, der Kuhstall.
cow (2) [kau], v.a. einschüchtern.
coward ['kauəd], s. der Feigling.
cowardice ['kauədis], s. die Feigheit.
cower ['kauə], v.n. sich kauern.
cowherd ['kauhə:d], s. der Kuhhirt.
cowl [kaul], s. die Kappe (of monk), die Kapuze (hood).
cowslip ['kauslip], s. (Bot.) die Primel, die Schlüsselblume.
coxswain [kɔksn], s. (Naut.) der Steuermann.
coy [kɔi], adj. scheu, spröde, zurückhaltend.
coyness ['kɔinis], s. die Sprödigkeit.
crab [kræb], s. (Zool.) die Krabbe; — apple, (Bot.) der Holzapfel.
crabbed [kræbd], adj. mürrisch (temper); unleserlich (handwriting).
crack [kræk], s. der Riß (fissure); der Krach, Schlag; der Sprung; die komische Bemerkung (remark). — adj. (coll.) erstklassig; —shot, der Meisterschütze. — v.a. aufbrechen; aufknacken (nut, safe); — a joke, eine witzige Bemerkung machen. — v.n. — under strain, unter einer Anstrengung zusammenbrechen; bersten (break).
cracked, crackers [krækd, 'krækəz], adj. (coll.) verrückt.
cracker ['krækə], s. der Keks; der Frosch (firework).
crackle [krækl], v.n. knistern, prasseln (fire); knallen, platzen (rocket).
cracknel ['kræknəl], s. die Brezel.
crackpot ['krækpɔt], s. (coll.) der verrückte Kerl.
cradle [kreidl], s. die Wiege. — v.a. einwiegen.
craft [krɑ:ft], s. die Fertigkeit (skill); das Handwerk (trade); die List (cunning); arts and —s, die Handwerkskünste.

craftsman

craftsman ['krɑ:ftsmən], *s.* der (gelernte) Handwerker.
crafty ['krɑ:fti], *adj.* listig, schlau.
crag [kræg], *s.* die Klippe.
cragged, craggy [krægd, 'krægi], *adj.* felsig, schroff.
cram [kræm], *v.a.* vollstopfen (*stuff full*); (*coll.*) pauken (*coach*). — *v.n.* büffeln.
crammer ['kræmə], *s.* (*coll.*) der Einpauker, Privatlehrer (*tutor*).
cramp [kræmp], *s.* (*Med.*) der Krampf; die Klammer (*tool*). — *v.a.* einengen (*narrow*); verkrampfen.
cramped [kræmpd], *adj.* krampfhaft; eingeengt, beengt (*enclosed*).
cranberry ['krænbəri], *s.* (*Bot.*) die Preiselbeere.
crane [krein], *s.* (*Orn.*) der Kranich; (*Engin.*) der Kran. — *v.a.* *o.'s neck*, den Hals ausrecken.
crank (1) [kræŋk], *s.* (*Motor.*) die Kurbel; — *-handle*, die Andrehwelle; (*Motor., Engin.*) *—shaft*, die Kurbelwelle, die Kurbel.
crank (2) [kræŋk], *s.* der Sonderling, der sonderbare Kauz (*eccentric*).
cranky ['kræŋki], *adj.* sonderbar.
cranny ['kræni], *s.* der Spalt, der Riß; *nook and —*, Eck und Spalt.
crape [kreip], *s.* der Krepp, Flor.
crash [kræʃ], *s.* der Krach; (*Motor.*) Zusammenstoß; (*Aviat.*) Absturz. — *v.n.* krachen (*noise*); stürzen, abstürzen (*fall*).
crass [kræs], *adj.* derb, grob, kraß.
crate [kreit], *s.* der Packkorb (*basket*); die Kiste (*wood*).
crater ['kreitə], *s.* (*Geol.*) der Krater.
cravat [krə'væt], *s.* die breite Halsbinde, das Halstuch (*scarf*); die Krawatte.
crave [kreiv], *v.a.* (dringend) verlangen (*for*, nach, *Dat.*).
craven [kreivn], *adj.* feig, mutlos. — *s.* der Feigling.
craving ['kreiviŋ], *s.* das starke Verlangen.
craw [krɔ:], *s.* (*Zool.*) der Vogelkropf.
crawl [krɔ:l], *v.n.* kriechen; kraulen (*swim*).
crawling ['krɔ:liŋ], *s.* das Kriechen; das Kraulschwimmen.
crayon ['kreiən], *s.* der Farbstift, der Pastellstift.
craze [kreiz], *s.* die Manie; die verrückte Mode (*fashion*).
craziness ['kreizinis], *s.* die Verrücktheit.
crazy ['kreizi], *adj.* verrückt.
creak [kri:k], *v.n.* knarren.
cream [kri:m], *s.* der Rahm, die Sahne; *whipped —*, die Schlagsahne, (*Austr.*) der Schlagobers. — *v.a.* *— off*, (die Sahne) abschöpfen; (*fig.*) das Beste abziehen.
creamery ['kri:məri], *s.* die Molkerei.
creamy ['kri:mi], *adj.* sahnig.
crease [kri:s], *s.* die Falte (*trousers etc.*); *— -resistant*, knitterfrei. — *v.a.* falten (*fold*). — *v.n.* knittern.

create [kri'eit], *v.a.* erschaffen, schaffen.
creation [kri'eiʃən], *s.* die Schöpfung.
creative [kri'eitiv], *adj.* schöpferisch.
creator [kri'eitə], *s.* der Schöpfer.
creature ['kri:tʃə], *s.* das Geschöpf.
credence ['kri:dəns], *s.* der Glaube.
credentials [kri'denʃəlz], *s. pl.* das Zeugnis, das Beglaubigungsschreiben; die Legitimation (*proof of identity*).
credibility [kredi'biliti], *s.* die Glaubwürdigkeit.
credible ['kredibl], *adj.* glaubwürdig, glaublich.
credit ['kredit], *s.* (*Comm.*) der Kredit; der gute Ruf (*reputation*); das Guthaben (*assets*). — *v.a.* — *s.o. with s.th.*, jemandem etwas gutschreiben; glauben (*believe*).
creditable ['kreditəbl], *adj.* ehrenwert, lobenswert.
creditor ['kreditə], *s.* (*Comm.*) der Gläubiger.
credulity [kre'dju:liti], *s.* die Leichtgläubigkeit.
credulous ['kredjuləs], *adj.* leichtgläubig.
creed [kri:d], *s.* das Glaubensbekenntnis.
creek [kri:k], *s.* die kleine Bucht; das Flüßchen (*small river*).
creel [kri:l], *s.* der Fischkorb.
creep [kri:p], *s.* (*Geol.*) der Rutsch; (*pl., coll.*) *the —s*, die Gänsehaut, das Gruseln.—*v.n. irr.* kriechen; (*furtively*) sich einschleichen.
creeper ['kri:pə], *s.* die Schlingpflanze, das Rankengewächs, (*Sch.*) der Kriecher; *Virginia —*, der wilde Wein.
creepy ['kri:pi], *adj.* kriechend; gruselig (*frightening*).
cremate [kri'meit], *v.a.* einäschern.
cremation [kri'meiʃən], *s.* die Verbrennung, Einäscherung.
crematorium, (*Am.*) **crematory** [kremə'tɔ:riəm, 'kremətəri], *s.* das Krematorium.
Creole ['kri:oul], *s.* der Kreole.
crepuscular [kri'pʌskjulə], *adj.* dämmerig.
crescent ['kresənt], *adj.* wachsend, zunehmend. — *s.* der (zunehmende) Mond, die Mondsichel; das Hörnchen.
cress [kres], *s.* (*Bot.*) die Kresse; *mustard and —*, die Gartenkresse.
crest [krest], *s.* der Kamm (*cock*); der Gipfel (*hill*); der Kamm (*wave*); der Busch (*helmet*); das Wappenschild (*Heraldry*).
crestfallen ['krestfɔ:lən], *adj.* entmutigt, mutlos, niedergeschlagen.
Cretan ['kri:tən], *adj.* kretisch. — *s.* der Kreter, die Kreterin.
cretonne [kre'tɔn], *s.* die Kretonne.
crevasse [krə'væs], *s.* die Gletscherspalte.
crevice ['krevis], *s.* der Riß.
crew (1) [kru:], *s.* (*Naut., Aviat.*) die Besatzung; (*Naut.*) die Schiffsmannschaft; die Mannschaft (*team*); (*Am.*) *— cut*, die Bürstenfrisur.

crew (2) [kru:] *see* **crow**.

crib [krib], *s.* die Krippe (*Christmas*); die Wiege (*cradle*); (*Sch.*) die Eselsbrücke. — *v.a.* (*Sch.*) abschreiben (*copy*).

crick [krik], *s.* (*in neck*) der steife Hals.

cricket ['krikit], *s.* (*Ent.*) das Heimchen, die Grille; (*Sport*) das Cricket(spiel).

crime [kraim], *s.* das Verbrechen; — *fiction*, die Detektivromane, *m. pl.*

criminal ['kriminəl], *s.* der Verbrecher. — *adj.* — *case*, der Kriminalfall; verbrecherisch (*act*); — *investigation*, die Fahndung.

crimp [krimp], *v.a.* kräuseln (*hair*).

crimson ['krimzən], *adj.* karmesinrot.

cringe [krindʒ], *v.n.* kriechen.

crinkle [kriŋkl], *v.a., v.n.* kräuseln. — *s.* die Falte.

crinoline ['krinəlin], *s.* der Reifrock.

cripple [kripl], *s.* der Krüppel. — *v.a.* verkrüppeln; lahmlegen (*immobilize*).

crisis ['kraisis], *s.* die Krise, der Wendepunkt; die Notlage.

crisp [krisp], *adj.* kraus (*hair*); knusperig (*bread*); frisch.

criss-cross ['kriskrɔs], *adv.* kreuz und quer.

criterion [krai'tiəriən], *s.* das Kennzeichen, das Kriterium.

critic ['kritik], *s.* der Kritiker; Rezensent (*reviewer*).

critical ['kritikəl], *adj.* kritisch.

criticism ['kritisizm], *s.* die Kritik (*of, an, Dat.*); Rezension, Besprechung (*review*).

criticize ['kritisaiz], *v.a.* kritisieren.

croak [krouk], *v.n.* krächzen (*raven*); quaken (*frog*).

croaking ['kroukiŋ], *s.* das Krächzen, das Gekrächze (*raven*); das Quaken (*frog*).

Croat ['krouæt]. *s.* der Kroate.

Croatian [krou'eiʃən], *adj.* kroatisch.

crochet ['krouʃei], *s.* die Häkelei; — *hook*, die Häkelnadel. — *v.a., v.n.* häkeln.

crock [krɔk], *s.* der Topf, der irdene Krug; der alte Topf; (*coll.*) *old* —, der Invalide, Krüppel.

crockery ['krɔkəri], *s.* (*Comm.*) die Töpferware; das Geschirr (*household*).

crocodile ['krɔkədail], *s.* das Krokodil.

crocus ['kroukəs], *s.* (*Bot.*) der Krokus, die Safranblume.

croft [krɔft], *s.* das Kleinbauerngut.

crofter ['krɔftə], *s.* der Kleinbauer.

crone [kroun], *s.* das alte Weib; die Hexe (*witch*).

crony ['krouni], *s.* (*coll.*) *old* —, der alte Freund.

crook [kruk], *s.* der Krummstab (*staff*); der Schwindler (*cheat*). — *v.a.* krümmen, biegen.

crooked ['krukid], *adj.* krumm; (*fig.*) schwindlerisch, verbrecherisch.

crookedness ['krukidnis], *s.* die Krummheit; die Durchtriebenheit (*slyness*).

croon [kru:n], *v.n.* leise singen; (*Am.*) im modernen Stil singen.

crooner ['kru:nə], *s.* der Jazzsänger.

crop [krɔp], *s.* der Kropf (*bird*); die Ernte (*harvest*); der (kurze) Haarschnitt; *riding* —, die Reitpeitsche. — *v.a.* stutzen (*cut short*). — *v.n.* — *up*, auftauchen.

crosier ['krouziə], *s.* (*Eccl.*) der Bischofsstab.

cross [krɔs], *s.* das Kreuz. — *v.a.* (*Zool., Bot.*) kreuzen; überqueren (*road, on foot*); — *s.o.'s path*, einem in die Quere kommen. — *v.n.* überfahren (*übers Wasser*); hinübergehen; — *over*, übersetzen (*on boat or ferry*). — *v.r.* sich bekreuzigen. — *adj.* mürrisch (*grumpy*), verstimmt; *at* — *purposes*, ohne einander zu verstehen; *make* —, verstimmen. — *adv.* kreuzweise; — *-eyed*, schielend; — *-grained*, wider den Strich, schlecht aufgelegt.

crossbow ['krɔsbou], *s.* die Armbrust.

crossbreed ['krɔsbri:d], *s.* die Mischrasse, der Mischling.

cross-examine [krɔsig'zæmin], *v.a., v.n.* (*Law*) ins (Kreuz-)Verhör nehmen.

crossing ['krɔsiŋ], *s.* die Straßenkreuzung; (*Naut.*) die Überfahrt; der Straßenübergang; Kreuzweg.

crossroads ['krɔsroudz], *s.* der Kreuzweg, die Kreuzung.

crossword ['krɔswə:d], *s.* das Kreuzworträtsel.

crotch [krɔtʃ], *s.* der Haken.

crotchet ['krɔtʃit], *s.* (*Mus.*) die Viertelnote; die Grille (*mood*).

crotchety ['krɔtʃiti], *adj.* grillenhaft, verschroben.

crouch [krautʃ], *v.n.* sich ducken (*squat*); sich demütigen (*cringe*).

croup (1) [kru:p], *s.* (*Med.*) der Krupp.

croup (2) [kru:p], *s.* die Kruppe.

crow [krou], *s.* (*Orn.*) die Krähe; das Krähen (*of cock*). — *v.n. irr.* krähen (*cock*).

crowbar ['krouba:], *s.* das Brecheisen.

crowd [kraud], *s.* die Menge (*multitude*); das Gedränge (*throng*). — *v.n.* — *in*, sich hineindrängen, dazudrängen; — *around*, sich herumscharen um (*Acc.*).

crown [kraun], *s.* die Krone (*diadem or coin*); der Gipfel (*mountain*); (*Anat.*) der Scheitel; — *lands*, Krongüter (*n. pl.*), Landeigentum der Krone, *n.*; — *prince*, der Kronprinz; — *of thorns*, die Dornenkrone. — *v.a.* krönen.

crucial ['kru:ʃəl], *adj.* entscheidend, kritisch.

crucifix ['kru:sifiks], *s.* das Kruzifix.

crucify ['kru:sifai], *v.a.* kreuzigen.

crude [kru:d], *adj.* roh, ungekocht, unreif; grob (*manners*), ungeschliffen.

crudity ['kru:diti], *s.* die Rohheit; Grobheit (*manners*).

cruel ['kru:əl], *adj.* grausam.

cruelty ['kru:əlti], *s.* die Grausamkeit.

cruet ['kru:it], *s.* das Salz- *oder* Pfefferfäßchen; das Fläschchen.

cruise

cruise [kru:z], *v.n.* (*Naut.*) kreuzen. — *s.* die Seefahrt, die Seereise; *pleasure* —, die Vergnügungsreise (zu Wasser).

cruiser [ˈkru:zə], *s.* (*Naut.*) der Kreuzer; *battle* —, der Panzerkreuzer.

crumb [krʌm], *s.* die Krume. — *v.a.* zerbröckeln, zerkrümeln.

crumble [krʌmbl], *v.n.* zerfallen, zerbröckeln.

crumpet [ˈkrʌmpit], *s.* das Teebrötchen, das Teeküchlein.

crumple [krʌmpl], *v.a.* zerknittern (*material*). — *v.n.* — *up*, zusammenbrechen.

crunch [krʌntʃ], *v.a.* zerstoßen, zermalmen. — *v.n.* knirschen.

crusade [kru:ˈseid], *s.* der Kreuzzug.

crusader [kru:ˈseidə], *s.* der Kreuzfahrer.

crush [krʌʃ], *v.a.* zerdrücken; zerstoßen (*pulverize*); drängen (*crowd*); zertreten (*tread down*); (*fig.*) vernichten. — *s.* das Gedränge (*throng*); (*coll.*) *have a* — *on*, verknallt sein, in einen verliebt sein.

crust [krʌst], *s.* die Kruste, die Rinde (*bread*). — *v.a.* mit einer Kruste bedecken. — *v.n.* verkrusten.

crustaceous [krʌsˈteiʃəs], *adj.* (*Zool.*) krustenartig, Krustentier-.

crusty [ˈkrʌsti], *adj.* krustig, knusperig (*pastry, bread*); mürrisch (*grumpy*).

crutch [krʌtʃ], *s.* die Krücke.

crux [krʌks], *s.* der entscheidende Punkt, der springende Punkt, die Schwierigkeit.

cry [krai], *v.n.* schreien, rufen; weinen (*weep*). — *v.a.* — *down*, niederschreien. — *s.* der Schrei; der Zuruf (*call*).

crypt [kript], *s.* (*Eccl.*) die Krypta, die Gruft.

crystal [ˈkristəl], *s.* der Kristall.

crystallize [ˈkristəlaiz], *v.n.* sich kristallisieren, Kristalle bilden.

cub [kʌb], *s.* (*Zool.*) das Junge. — *v.n.* Junge haben, Junge werfen.

Cuban [ˈkju:bən], *adj.* kubanisch. — *s.* der Kubaner.

cube [kju:b], *s.* der Würfel; (*Maths.*) — *root*, die Kubikwurzel. — *v.a.* zur Dritten (Potenz) erheben; kubieren.

cubic(al) [ˈkju:bik(əl)], *adj.* kubisch, zur dritten Potenz.

cubit [ˈkju:bit], *s.* die Elle.

cuckoo [ˈkuku:], *s.* (*Orn.*) der Kuckuck.

cucumber [ˈkju:kʌmbə], *s.* (*Bot.*) die Gurke; *cool as a* —, ruhig und gelassen.

cud [kʌd], *s.* das wiedergekäute Futter; *chew the* —, wiederkauen (*also fig.*).

cuddle [kʌdl], *v.a.* liebkosen, an sich drücken. — *v.n.* sich anschmiegen.

cudgel [ˈkʌdʒəl], *s.* der Knüttel; *take up the* —*s for*, sich für etwas einsetzen.

cue (1) [kju:], *s.* (*Theat.*) das Stichwort. — *v.a.* einem (*Theat.*) das Stichwort *or* (*Mus.*) den Einsatz geben.

cue (2) [kju:], *s.* der Billardstock. — *v.a.* (*Billiards*) abschießen.

cuff (1) [kʌf], *s.* die Manschette, der Aufschlag (*shirt*); —*links*, die Manschettenknöpfe.

cuff (2) [kʌf], *s.* der Schlag. — *v.a.* schlagen, puffen.

culinary [ˈkju:linəri], *adj.* kulinarisch; Küchen-, Eß-, Speisen-.

cull [kʌl], *v.a.* auswählen, auslesen (*from books*).

culminate [ˈkʌlmineit], *v.n.* kulminieren, den Höhepunkt erreichen.

culpable [ˈkʌlpəbl], *adj.* schuldig; strafbar.

culprit [ˈkʌlprit], *s.* der Schuldige, Verbrecher.

cult [kʌlt], *s.* der Kult, die Verehrung; der Kultus.

cultivate [ˈkʌltiveit], *v.a.* kultivieren; (*Agr.*) anbauen; pflegen (*acquaintance*); bilden (*mind*).

cultivation [kʌltiˈveiʃən], *s.* (*Agr.*) der Anbau; die Bildung (*mind*).

culture [ˈkʌltʃə], *s.* die Kultur, die Bildung.

cumbersome [ˈkʌmbəsəm], *adj.* beschwerlich, lästig.

cunning [ˈkʌniŋ], *s.* die List, die Schlauheit. — *adj.* listig, schlau.

cup [kʌp], *s.* die Tasse (*tea*—); der Becher (*handleless*); (*Eccl.*) der Kelch; der Pokal (*sports*); — *final*, das Endspiel. — *v.a.* (*Med.*) schröpfen.

cupboard [ˈkʌbəd], *s.* der Schrank.

cupola [ˈkju:polə], *s.* (*Archit., Metall.*) die Kuppel.

cur [kə:], *s.* der Köter; (*fig.*). der Schurke.

curable [ˈkjuərəbl], *adj.* heilbar.

curate [ˈkjuərit], *s.* der Hilfsgeistliche.

curative [ˈkjuərətiv], *adj.* heilsam, heilend.

curator [kjuəˈreitə], *s.* der Kurator, Verwalter, Direktor.

curb [kə:b], *v.a.* zügeln, bändigen. — *s.* der Zaum (*bridle*).

curd [kə:d], *s.* der Rahmkäse, der Milchkäse; (*pl.*) der Quark.

curdle [kə:dl], *v.a.* gerinnen lassen. — *v.n.* gerinnen; erstarren.

cure [kjuə], *s.* die Kur, die Heilung. — *v.a.* kurieren, wieder gesundmachen; einpökeln (*foodstuffs*).

curfew [ˈkə:fju:], *s.* die Abendglocke (*bells*); das Ausgehverbot, die Polizeistunde (*police*).

curio [ˈkjuəriou], *s.* die Kuriosität, das Sammlerstück; die Rarität.

curiosity [kjuəriˈɔsiti], *s.* die Neugier; Merkwürdigkeit.

curious [ˈkjuəriəs], *adj.* neugierig (*inquisitive*); seltsam, sonderbar (*strange*).

curl [kə:l], *v.a.* kräuseln, (in Locken) wickeln. — *v.n.* sich kräuseln. — *s.* die Haarlocke.

curler [ˈkə:lə], *s.* der Lockenwickler.

curlew [ˈkə:lju:], *s.* (*Orn.*) der Brachvogel.

curly [ˈkə:li], *adj.* lockig.

currant [ˈkʌrənt], *s.* (*Bot.*) die Korinthe, die Johannisbeere.

currency [ˈkʌrənsi], *s.* die Währung (*money*); der Umlauf (*circulation*).

current [ˈkʌrənt], *adj.* im Umlauf; allgemein gültig, eben gültig; jetzig (*modern*). — *s.* (*Elect.*) der Strom; die Strömung (*river*); der Zug (*air*).

curry (1) [ˈkʌri], *v.a.* gerben (*tan*); — *comb,* der Pferdestriegel; — *favour,* sich einschmeicheln.

curry (2) [ˈkʌri], *s.* das indische Ragout. — *v.a.* würzen.

curse [kəːs], *v.a., v.n.* verfluchen; verwünschen. — *s.* der Fluch; die Verwünschung.

cursive [ˈkəːsiv], *adj.* kursiv, Kursiv-.

cursory [ˈkəːsəri], *adj.* kursorisch, oberflächlich.

curt [kəːt], *adj.* kurz angebunden (*speech, manner*).

curtail [kəːˈteil], *v.a.* stutzen, beschränken (*scope*); verkürzen (*time*).

curtain [ˈkəːtin], *s.* die Gardine; der Vorhang; (*Mil.*) — *fire,* das Sperrfeuer; — *lecture,* die Gardinenpredigt; — *speech,* die Ansprache vor dem Vorhang. — *v.a.* verhüllen (*hide*); mit Vorhängen versehen (*hang curtains*).

curtness [ˈkəːtnis], *s.* die Kürze; die Barschheit.

curts(e)y [ˈkəːtsi], *s.* der Knicks. — *v.n.* knicksen, einen Knicks machen.

curve [kəːv], *s.* die Krümmung; (*Geom.*) die Kurve. — *v.a.* krümmen, biegen. — *v.n.* sich biegen.

curved [kəːvd], *adj.* krumm, gebogen.

cushion [ˈkuʃən], *s.* das Kissen. — *v.a.* polstern.

custody [ˈkʌstədi], *s.* die Obhut; Bewachung, Haft.

custom [ˈkʌstəm], *s.* die Sitte, die Tradition; der Gebrauch, Brauch (*usage*); die Kundschaft (*trade*); (*pl.*) der Zoll (*duty*).

customary [ˈkʌstəməri], *adj.* gewohnt, althergebracht, gebräuchlich.

customer [ˈkʌstəmə], *s.* der Kunde, die Kundin.

cut [kʌt], *v.a. irr.* schneiden; — (*s.o.*), ignorieren; — *o.'s teeth,* zahnen; *this won't* — *any ice,* das wird nicht viel nützen; — *both ways,* das ist ein zweischneidiges Schwert; — *a lecture,* eine Vorlesung schwänzen; — *short,* unterbrechen. — *adj.* — *out for,* wie gerufen zu *or* für; — *to the quick,* aufs tiefste verletzt; — *glass,* das geschliffene Glas; — *price,* verbilligt. — *s.* der Schnitt (*section*); der Hieb (*gash*); (*Art*) der Stich; — *in salary,* eine Gehaltskürzung; die Abkürzung, die Kürzung (*abridgement*).

cute [kjuːt], *adj.* klug, aufgeweckt; (*Am.*) süß, niedlich.

cutler [ˈkʌtlə], *s.* der Messerschmied.

cutlery [ˈkʌtləri], *s.* das Besteck (*tableware*); (*Comm.*) die Messerschmiedwaren, *f. pl.*

cutlet [ˈkʌtlit], *s.* das Kotelett, das Rippchen.

cut-throat [ˈkʌtθrout], *s.* der Halsabschneider; — *competition,* Konkurrenz auf Leben und Tod.

cuttle [kʌtl], *s.* (*Zool.*) der Tintenfisch.

cyanide [ˈsaiənaid], *s.* (*Chem.*) zyanidsaures Salz; das Zyanid, die Blausäure.

cyclamen [ˈsikləmən], *s.* (*Bot.*) das Alpenveilchen.

cycle [saikl], *s.* (*Geom.*) der Kreis; (*Mus., Zool.*) der Zyklus; (*coll.*) das Fahrrad. — *v.n.* (*coll.*) radfahren; zirkulieren (*round,* um, *Acc.*).

cyclone [ˈsaikloun], *s.* der Wirbelwind, der Wirbelsturm.

cyclopaedia [saikloˈpiːdjə] *see* **encyclopædia.**

cylinder [ˈsilində], *s.* der Zylinder; die Walze.

cymbal [ˈsimbəl], *s.* (*Mus.*) die Zimbel, das Becken.

cynic [ˈsinik], *s.* der Zyniker.

cynical [ˈsinikəl], *adj.* zynisch.

cypress [ˈsaiprəs], *s.* (*Bot.*) die Zypresse.

Cypriot [ˈsipriət], *adj.* zyprisch. — *s.* der Zypriote.

czar [zaː], *s.* der Zar.

Czech, Czechoslovak(ian) [tʃek, tʃekoˈslouvæk, tʃekosloˈvækjən], *adj.* tschechisch. —*s.* der Tscheche.

D

D [diː], das D (*also Mus.*).

dab [dæb], *v.a.* leicht berühren. — *s.* der leichte Schlag (*blow*).

dabble [dæbl], *v.n.* sich in etwas versuchen, pfuschen (*in,* in, *Dat.*).

dabbler [ˈdæblə], *s.* der Pfuscher, Stümper.

dace [deis], *s.* (*Zool.*) der Weißfisch.

dad, daddy [dæd, ˈdædi], *s.* der Papa; Vati; *daddy longlegs,* die Bachmücke, die langbeinige Mücke.

dado [ˈdeidou], *s.* die Täfelung.

daffodil [ˈdæfədil], *s.* (*Bot.*) die Narzisse.

dagger [ˈdægə], *s.* der Dolch; *at* —*s drawn,* spinnefeind; *look* —*s,* mit Blicken durchbohren.

dahlia [ˈdeiliə], *s.* (*Bot.*) die Dahlie, die Georgine.

daily [ˈdeili], *adj.* täglich; Tages-. — *s.* (*newspaper*) die Tageszeitung; (*woman*) die Putzfrau.

dainties [ˈdeintiz], *s. pl.* das Backwerk, das kleine Gebäck, das Teegebäck.

daintiness [ˈdeintinis], *s.* die Feinheit; die Kleinheit; die Leckerhaftigkeit.

dainty [ˈdeinti], *adj.* fein, klein, zierlich; lecker (*food*).

dairy [ˈdɛəri], *s.* die Molkerei, die Meierei.

dairyman [ˈdɛərimən], *s.* der Milchmann; der Senne (*in Alps*).

dais [deis, ˈdeiis], *s.* das Podium.

daisy

daisy ['deizi], s. (Bot.) das Gänseblümchen, das Marienblümchen.
dale [deil], s. das Tal.
dalliance ['dæliəns], s. die Tändelei, Liebelei; Verzögerung.
dally ['dæli], v.n. die Zeit vertrödeln.
dam (1) [dæm], s. der Damm. — v.a. eindämmen, abdämmen.
dam (2) [dæm], s. (Zool.) die Tiermutter.
damage ['dæmidʒ], s. der Schaden; der Verlust (loss); (pl.) (Law) der Schadenersatz. — v.a. beschädigen.
damageable ['dæmidʒəbl], adj. leicht zu beschädigen.
damask ['dæməsk], s. der Damast (textile). — adj. damasten, aus Damast.
dame [deim], s. die Dame (title); (Am.) (coll.) die junge Dame, das Fräulein.
damn [dæm], v.a. verdammen.
damnable ['dæmnəbl], adj. verdammenswert, verdammt.
damnation [dæm'neiʃən], s. die Verdammung, Verdammnis.
damn(ed) [dæm(d)], adj. & adv. verwünscht, verdammt.
damp [dæmp], adj. feucht, dumpfig. — s. die Feuchtigkeit; (Build.) — course, die Schutzschicht. — v.a. dämpfen, befeuchten; — the spirits, die gute Laune verderben.
damsel ['dæmzəl], s. die Jungfer; das Mädchen.
damson ['dæmzən], s. (Bot.) die Damaszenerpflaume.
dance [dɑːns], v.a., v.n. tanzen. — s. der Tanz; lead s.o. a —, einem viel Mühe machen.
dandelion ['dændilaiən], s. (Bot.) der Löwenzahn.
dandle [dændl], v.a. hätscheln; schaukeln.
dandy ['dændi], s. der Geck, der Stutzer.
Dane [dein], s. der Däne.
dane [dein], s. great —, die Dogge.
Danish ['deiniʃ], adj. dänisch.
danger ['deindʒə], s. die Gefahr.
dangerous ['deindʒərəs], adj. gefährlich.
dangle [dæŋgl], v.a. baumeln lassen. — v.n. baumeln, hängen.
dank [dæŋk], adj. feucht, naßkalt.
Danube ['dænjuːb]. die Donau.
dapper ['dæpə], adj. schmuck; niedlich; elegant.
dappled [dæpld], adj. scheckig, bunt.
Dardanelles, The [dɑːdə'nelz]. die Dardanellen, pl.
dare [dɛə], v.n. irr. wagen; I — say, das meine ich wohl, ich gebe zu.
daredevil ['dɛədevl], s. der Wagehals, der Draufgänger.
daring ['dɛəriŋ], s. die Kühnheit.
dark [dɑːk], adj. dunkel, finster. — s. die Dunkelheit; shot in the —, ein Schuß aufs Geratewohl, ins Blaue.
darken ['dɑːkən], v.a. verdunkeln, verfinstern. — v.n. dunkel werden.

darkish ['dɑːkiʃ], adj. nahezu dunkel.
darkness ['dɑːknis], s. die Dunkelheit, Finsternis.
darkroom ['dɑːkruːm], s. die Dunkelkammer.
darling ['dɑːliŋ], s. der Liebling. — adj. lieb, teuer.
darn (1) [dɑːn], v.a. stopfen.
darn (2) [dɑːn], v.a. verdammen.
darn(ed) [dɑːn(d)], (excl.) verdammt.
darning ['dɑːniŋ], s. das Stopfen; — needle, die Stopfnadel.
dart [dɑːt], s. der Pfeil; der Spieß (spear); (pl.) das Pfeilwurfspiel. — v.n. losstürmen, sich stürzen.
dash [dæʃ], v.a. zerschmettern, zerstören (hopes). — v.n. stürzen. — s. der Schlag (blow); die Eleganz; (Typ.) der Gedankenstrich; (Motor.) —board, das Schaltbrett, Armaturenbrett.
dashing ['dæʃiŋ], adj. schneidig.
dastard ['dæstəd], s. der Feigling, die Memme.
dastardly ['dæstədli], adj., adv. feige.
data ['deitə], s. pl. (Science) die Angaben, die Daten.
date (1) [deit], s. das Datum; (Am.) die Verabredung; out of —, vertetal (antiquated), altmodisch (out of fashion). — v.a. datieren; (Am.) ausführen. — v.n. das Datum tragen.
date (2) [deit], s. (Bot.) die Dattel.
dative ['deitiv], s. (Gram.) der Dativ.
daub [dɔːb], v.a. bekleksen; (coll.) bemalen. — s. die Klekserei; (coll.) die Malerei.
daughter ['dɔːtə], s. die Tochter; —-in-law, die Schwiegertochter.
daunt [dɔːnt], v.a. einschüchtern.
dauphin ['dɔːfin], s. der Dauphin.
daw [dɔː], s. (Orn.) die Dohle.
dawdle [dɔːdl], v.n. trödeln, die Zeit vertrödeln.
dawdler ['dɔːdlə], s. der Trödler, Tagedieb, die Schlafmütze.
dawn [dɔːn], s. das Morgengrauen, die Morgendämmerung. — v.n. dämmern, tagen.
day [dei], s. der Tag; the other —, neulich; every —, täglich; one —, eines Tages; by —, bei or am Tage.
daybreak ['deibreik], s. der Tagesanbruch.
daytime ['deitaim], s. in the —, bei Tage.
daze [deiz], v.a. blenden (dazzle); betäuben (stupefy).
dazzle [dæzl], v.a. blenden.
deacon ['diːkən], s. (Eccl.) der Diakon.
deaconess ['diːkənes], s. (Eccl.) die Diakonisse.
dead [ded], adj. tot; stop —, plötzlich anhalten; as — as mutton, mausetot; — from the neck up, (coll.) dumm wie die Nacht. — adv. — beat, erschöpft; (Am.) — sure, ganz sicher. — s. in the — of night, in tiefster Nacht; (pl.) die Toten.

decompose

deaden [dedn], *v.a.* abschwächen (*weaken*); abtöten (*anæsthetise*).
deadly ['dedli], *adj.* tödlich.
deadness ['dednis], *s.* die Leblosigkeit; Mattheit (*tiredness*).
deaf [def], *adj.* taub; — *and dumb*, taubstumm.
deafen [defn], *v.a.* betäuben.
deafmute ['defmju:t], *s.* der Taubstumme.
deal (1) [di:l], *s.* das Geschäft; die Anzahl; *a fair* or *square* —, eine anständige Behandlung; *a good* —, beträchtlich; *a great* — *of*, sehr viel; *make a* —, ein Geschäft abschliessen; *it's a* —! abgemacht! — *v.a. irr.* austeilen; Karten geben (*cards*); — *a blow*, einen Schlag erteilen. — *v.n. irr.* — *with s.th.*, etwas behandeln.
deal (2) [di:l], *s.* (*Bot.*) das Kiefernholz, die Kiefer; — *board*, das Kiefernholzbrett.
dealer ['di:lə], *s.* der Händler.
dean [di:n], *s.* der Dekan.
dear [diə], *adj.* teuer, lieb (*beloved*); teuer, kostspielig (*expensive*); — *me!* ach, Du lieber Himmel! —, —! du liebe Zeit! — *John !* Lieber Hans!
dearness ['diənis], *s.* die Teuerung, das Teuersein.
dearth [də:θ], *s.* der Mangel (*of*, an, *Dat.*).
death [deθ], *s.* der Tod; der Todesfall; — *penalty*, die Todesstrafe; — *warrant*, das Todesurteil.
deathbed ['deθbed], *s.* das Totenbett, Sterbebett.
deathblow ['deθblou], *s.* der Todesstoß.
deathless ['deθlis], *adj.* unsterblich.
debar [di'bɑ:], *v.a.* ausschließen (*from*, von, *Dat.*).
debase [di'beis], *v.a.* erniedrigen, verschlechtern.
debatable [di'beitəbl], *adj.* strittig.
debate [di'beit], *s.* die Debatte. — *v.a., v.n.* debattieren.
debauch [di'bɔ:tʃ], *v.a., v.n.* verführen; verderben.
debauchee [di'bɔ:tʃi:], *s.* der Schwelger, der Wüstling.
debenture [di'bentʃə], *s.* der Schuldschein.
debilitate [di'biliteit], *v.a.* schwächen.
debit ['debit], *s.* die Schuldseite, das Soll (*in account*). — *v.a.* belasten.
debt [det], *s.* die Schuld; *run into* — or *incur* —, Schulden machen.
debtor ['detə], *s.* der Schuldner.
decade ['dekəd, 'dekeid], *s.* das Jahrzehnt; die Dekade.
decadence ['dekədəns], *s.* die Dekadenz, der Verfall.
decalogue ['dekəlɔg], *s.* (*Bibl.*) die zehn Gebote.
decamp [di:'kæmp], *v.n.* aufbrechen, ausreißen.
decant [di'kænt], *v.a.* abfüllen, abgießen.
decanter [di'kæntə], *s.* die Karaffe.

decapitate [di:'kæpiteit], *v.a.* enthaupten köpfen.
decapitation [di:kæpi'teiʃən], *s.* die Enthauptung.
decay [di'kei], *v.n.* in Verfall geraten. — *s.* der Verfall, die Verwesung.
decease [di'si:s], *s.* das Hinscheiden, der Tod. — *v.n.* sterben, dahinscheiden, verscheiden.
deceit [di'si:t], *s.* der Betrug; die List (*cunning*).
deceive [di'si:v], *v.a.* betrügen.
deceiver [di'si:və], *s.* der Betrüger.
December [di'sembə], der Dezember.
decency ['di:sənsi], *s.* der Anstand; die Anständigkeit, Ehrlichkeit; die Schicklichkeit.
decent ['di:sənt], *adj.* anständig.
decentralize [di:'sentrəlaiz], *v.a.* dezentralisieren.
deception [di'sepʃən], *s.* der Betrug.
deceptive [di'septiv], *adj.* trügerisch.
decide [di'said], *v.a., v.n.* entscheiden; bestimmen (*determine*).
decimal ['desiməl], *adj.* dezimal.
decimate ['desimeit], *v.a.* dezimieren, herabsetzen (*reduce*).
decipher [di'saifə], *v.a.* entziffern (*read*); dechiffrieren (*decode*).
decision [di'siʒən], *s.* die Entscheidung, der Beschluß (*resolution*); die Entschlossenheit (*decisiveness*).
decisive [di'saisiv], *adj.* entscheidend.
decisiveness [di'saisivnis], *s.* die Entschiedenheit.
deck [dek], *s.* (*Naut.*) das Deck; — *chair*, der Liegestuhl. — *v.a.* — (*out*), ausschmücken.
declaim [di'kleim], *v.a.* deklamieren.
declamation [deklə'meiʃən], *s.* die Deklamation.
declamatory [di'klæmətəri], *adj.* Deklamations-, deklamatorisch, Vortrags-.
declaration [deklə'reiʃən], *s.* die Erklärung; die Deklaration.
declare [di'kleə], *v.a.* erklären. — *v.n.* sich erklären.
declared [di'kleəd], *adj.* erklärt, offen.
declension [di'klenʃən], *s.* (*Gram.*) die Deklination, die Abwandlung.
declinable [di'klainəbl], *adj.* (*Gram.*) deklinierbar.
declination [dekli'neiʃən], *s.* (*Phys.*) die Abweichung, Deklination.
decline [di'klain], *v.n.* abweichen (*deflect*); abnehmen (*decrease*); sich weigern (*refuse*); fallen (*price*). — *v.a.* (*Gram.*) deklinieren; ablehnen (*turn down*). — *s.* die Abnahme (*decrease*); der Verfall (*decadence*); der Abhang (*slope*).
declivity [di'kliviti], *s.* der Abhang.
decode [di:'koud], *v.a.* entziffern, dechiffrieren.
decompose [di:kəm'pouz], *v.n.* verwesen; zerfallen, sich zersetzen. — *v.a.* auflösen.

359

decorate

decorate ['dekəreit], *v.a.* dekorieren (*honour*); ausschmücken (*beautify*); ausmalen (*paint*).

decoration [dekə'reiʃən], *s.* die Dekoration, der Orden (*medal*); die Ausschmückung (*ornamentation*); die Ausmalung (*décor*).

decorator ['dekəreitə], *s.* der Zimmermaler.

decorous ['dekərəs *or* di'kɔ:rəs], *adj.* anständig, sittsam.

decorum [di'kɔ:rəm], *s.* das Dekorum, das anständige Benehmen.

decoy [di'kɔi], *s.* der Köder (*bait*). — *v.a.* locken, verlocken.

decrease [di'kri:s], *v.a.* vermindern, verringern. — *v.n.* abnehmen. — ['di:kri:s], *s.* die Abnahme, die Verringerung.

decree [di'kri:], *s.* der Beschluß (*resolution*); (*Law*) das Urteil; — *nisi*, das provisorische Scheidungsurteil. — *v.a.*, *v.n.* eine Verordnung erlassen; beschließen (*decide*).

decrepit [di'krepit], *adj.* abgelebt; gebrechlich (*frail*).

decry [di'krai], *v.a.* verrufen; in Verruf bringen.

dedicate ['dedikeit], *v.a.* widmen, weihen, zueignen (*to, Dat.*).

dedication [dedi'keiʃən], *s.* die Widmung, Weihung; die Zueignung.

dedicatory ['dedikeitəri], *adj.* zueignend.

deduce [di'dju:s], *v.a.* schließen (*conclude*); ableiten (*derive*).

deduct [di'dʌkt], *v.a.* abziehen (*subtract*); abrechnen (*take off*).

deduction [di'dʌkʃən], *s.* der Abzug (*subtraction*); die Folgerung (*inference*); der Rabatt (*in price*).

deductive [di'dʌktiv], *adj.* (*Log.*) deduktiv.

deed [di:d], *s.* die Tat, die Handlung (*action*); (*Law*) die Urkunde, das Dokument.

deem [di:m], *v.a.* erachten, halten für.

deep [di:p], *adj.* tief; — *freeze*, die Tiefkühlung; (*fig.*) dunkel. — *s.* die Tiefe (*des Meeres*).

deepen [di:pn], *v.a.* vertiefen. — *v.n.* tiefer werden; sich vertiefen.

deer [diə], *s.* (*Zool.*) das Rotwild, der Hirsch; — *stalking*, die Pirsch.

deface [di'feis], *v.a.* entstellen, verunstalten.

defalcate [di'fælkeit], *v.n.* Gelder unterschlagen.

defamation [defə'meiʃən], *s.* die Verleumdung.

defamatory [di'fæmətəri], *adj.* verleumderisch.

defame [di'feim], *v.a.* verleumden.

default [di'fɔ:lt], *v.n.* (vor Gericht) ausbleiben. — *s.* der Fehler (*error*); die Unterlassung (*omission*).

defaulter [di'fɔ:ltə], *s.* der Pflichtvergessene; (*Law*) der Schuldige.

defeat [di'fi:t], *v.a.* schlagen, besiegen. — *s.* die Niederlage.

defect [di'fekt], *s.* der Fehler, Makel. — *v.n.* abfallen (*desert, from*, von, *Dat.*).

defection [di'fekʃən], *s.* der Abfall.

defective [di'fektiv], *adj.* fehlerhaft, mangelhaft.

defectiveness [di'fektivnis], *s.* die Mangelhaftigkeit, die Fehlerhaftigkeit.

defence [di'fens], *s.* die Verteidigung.

defenceless [di'fenslis], *adj.* wehrlos.

defencelessness [di'fenslisnis], *s.* die Wehrlosigkeit.

defend [di'fend], *v.a.* verteidigen.

defendant [di'fendənt], *s.* (*Law*) der Angeklagte.

defensive [di'fensiv], *adj.* verteidigend. — *s.* die Defensive; *be on the* —, sich verteidigen.

defer [di'fə:], *v.a.* aufschieben (*postpone*). — *v.n.* sich unterordnen, sich fügen (*to, Dat.*).

deference ['defərəns], *s.* der Respekt, die Achtung (*to*, vor, *Dat.*).

deferential [defə'renʃəl], *adj.* ehrerbietig, respektvoll.

defiance [di'faiəns], *s.* der Trotz, die Herausforderung.

defiant [di'faiənt], *adj.* trotzig, herausfordernd.

deficiency [di'fiʃənsi], *s.* die Unzulänglichkeit, der Mangel (*quantity*); die Fehlerhaftigkeit (*quality*).

deficient [di'fiʃənt], *adj.* unzulänglich (*quantity*); fehlerhaft (*quality*).

deficit ['defisit], *s.* das Defizit, der Fehlbetrag.

defile (1) [di'fail], *v.a.* schänden, beflecken.

defile (2) ['di:fail], *v.n.* vorbeimarschieren (*march past*) (an, *Dat.*). — *s.* der Engpaß.

defilement [di'failmənt], *s.* die Schändung.

define [di'fain], *v.a.* definieren, begrenzen; bestimmen (*determine*).

definite ['definit], *adj.* bestimmt (*certain*); klar, deutlich (*clear*); endgültig (*final*).

definition [defi'niʃən], *s.* die Definition, die Klarheit; (*Maths.*) die Bestimmung.

definitive [di'finitiv], *adj.* definitiv, endgültig (*final*); bestimmt (*certain*).

deflect [di'flekt], *v.a.* ablenken (*divert*). — *v.n.* abweichen (von, *Dat.*).

defoliation [di:fouli'eiʃən], *s.* der Blätterfall.

deform [di'fɔ:m], *v.a.* verunstalten, entstellen. — *v.n.* (*Metall.*) sich verformen.

deformity [di'fɔ:miti], *s.* die Entstellung; die Häßlichkeit (*ugliness*).

defraud [di'frɔ:d], *v.a.* betrügen.

defray [di'frei], *v.a.* bestreiten, bezahlen (*costs*).

deft [deft], *adj.* geschickt, gewandt.

deftness ['deftnis], *s.* die Gewandtheit, die Geschicktheit.

defunct [di'fʌŋkt], *adj.* verstorben. — *s.* der Verstorbene.

demerit

---

defy [di'fai], *v.a.* trotzen (*Dat.*).
degenerate [di'dʒenəreit], *v.n.* entarten; herabsinken (*sink low*). —[-rit], *adj.* degeneriert, entartet.
degradation [degri'deiʃən], *s.* die Absetzung, Entsetzung, Degradierung.
degrade [di'greid], *v.a.* (*Mil.*) degradieren; entwürdigen; vermindern.
degraded [di'greidid], *adj.* heruntergekommen.
degrading [di'greidiŋ], *adj.* entehrend.
degree [di'gri:], *s.* (*Meas., Univ.*) der Grad; (*Univ.*) die akademische Würde; die Stufe (*step, stage*); die Ordnung, die Klasse (*order, class*); by —s, nach und nach, allmählich.
deify ['di:ifai], *v.a.* vergöttern.
deign [dein], *v.n.* geruhen, belieben.
deity ['di:iti], *s.* die Gottheit.
dejected [di'dʒektid], *adj.* niedergeschlagen.
dejection [di'dʒekʃən], *s.* die Niedergeschlagenheit.
delay [di'lei], *v.a., v.n.* aufschieben (*put off*); verzögern (*retard*). — *s.* der Aufschub; die Verzögerung.
delectable [di'lektəbl], *adj.* erfreulich, köstlich.
delectation [delek'teiʃən], *s.* die Freude, das Ergötzen (*in*, an, *Dat.*).
delegate [deligit], *s.* der Delegierte, Abgeordnete; der Vertreter. — ['deligeit], *v.a.* delegieren, entsenden.
delegation [deli'geiʃən], *s.* die Delegation, die Abordnung.
delete [di'li:t], *v.a.* tilgen, (aus-)streichen, auslöschen (*writing*).
deletion [di'li:ʃən], *s.* die Tilgung, die Auslöschung.
deleterious [deli'tiəriəs], *adj.* schädlich.
delf [delf], *s.* das Delfter Porzellan.
deliberate [di'libərit], *adj.* absichtlich (*intentional*); vorsichtig (*careful*); bedächtig (*thoughtful*). — [-reit], *v.n.* beratschlagen, Rat halten. — *v.a.* überlegen, bedenken.
deliberateness [di'libəritnis], *s.* die Bedächtigkeit (*thoughtfulness*); die Absichtlichkeit (*intention*).
deliberation [diliba'reiʃən], *s.* die Überlegung, die Beratung.
delicacy ['delikəsi], *s.* die Feinheit, Zartheit (*manner*); der Leckerbissen (*luxury food*); die Schwächlichkeit (*health*).
delicate ['delikit], *adj.* fein (*manner*); schwächlich (*sickly*); kitzlig, heikel (*difficult*).
delicious [di'liʃəs], *adj.* köstlich (*food*).
deliciousness [di'liʃəsnis], *s.* die Köstlichkeit.
delight [di'lait], *s.* das Entzücken, das Vergnügen; *Turkish* —, türkisches Konfekt; *take* — *in*, an etwas Gefallen finden, sich freuen (an, über). — *v.a., v.n.* entzücken, erfreuen (*in*, an, *Dat.*).
delightful [di'laitful], *adj.* entzückend, bezaubernd.

delimit [di:'limit], *v.a.* abgrenzen, begrenzen.
delimitation [di:limi'teiʃən], *s.* die Begrenzung, Abgrenzung.
delineate [di'linieit], *v.a.* umreißen, entwerfen, skizzieren (*draft, sketch*); schildern, beschreiben (*describe*).
delineation [dilini'eiʃən], *s.* die Skizze, der Entwurf (*sketch, draft*); die Schilderung (*description*).
delinquency [di'liŋkwənsi], *s.* das Verbrechen.
delinquent [di'liŋkwənt], *adj.* verbrecherisch. — *s.* der Verbrecher, Missetäter (*criminal*).
deliquesce [deli'kwes], *v.n.* (*Chem.*) zergehen, zerschmelzen.
deliquescence [deli'kwesəns], *s.* das Zerschmelzen, die Schmelzbarkeit.
deliquescent [deli'kwesənt], *adj.* leicht schmelzbar (*melting*); leicht zerfliessend (*butter etc.*).
delirious [di'liriəs], *adj.* (*Med.*) phantasierend, wahnsinnig.
delirium [di'liriəm], *s.* (*Med.*) das Delirium; der Wahnsinn (*madness*); das Phantasieren (*raving*); — *tremens*, der Säuferwahnsinn.
deliver [di'livə], *v.a.* abliefern, überreichen (*hand over*); liefern (*goods*); befreien (*free*); erlösen (*redeem*); zustellen (*letters etc.*); entbinden (*woman of child*).
deliverance [di'livərəns], *s.* die Erlösung (*redemption*); die Befreiung (*liberation*); die Übergabe.
delivery [di'livəri], *s.* die Befreiung (*liberation*); (*Med.*) die Niederkunft, Entbindung; der Vortrag (*speech*); die Lieferung, die Zustellung (*goods*); — *man*, der Zustellbote; — *van*, der Lieferwagen.
dell [del], *s.* das enge Tal.
delude [di'lu:d], *v.a.* betrügen, täuschen.
deluge ['delju:dʒ], *s.* die Überschwemmung. — *v.a.* überschwemmen.
delusion [di'lu:ʒən], *s.* die Täuschung, das Blendwerk.
delusive, delusory [di'lu:ziv, di'lu:zəri], *adj.* täuschend, trügerisch.
delve [delv], *v.n.* graben.
demagogic(al) [demə'gɔdʒik(əl)], *adj.* demagogisch.
demagogue ['deməgɔg], *s.* der Demagoge, der Aufrührer.
demand [di'ma:nd], *v.a.* verlangen, fordern. — *s.* die Forderung; das Begehren (*desire*); *on* —, auf Verlangen; *in great* —, viel gefragt; *supply and* —, Angebot und Nachfrage.
demarcate [di:'ma:keit], *v.a.* abgrenzen; abstecken (*field*).
demarcation [di:ma:'keiʃən], *s.* die Abgrenzung; — *line*, die Grenzlinie.
demeanour [di'mi:nə], *s.* das Benehmen.
demented [di'mentid], *adj.* wahnsinnig, von Sinnen, toll.
demerit [di:'merit], *s.* der Fehler.

demesne [di'mi:n or -'mein], *s.* das Erbgut; die Domäne.

demi- ['demi], *prefix.* halb-.

demigod ['demigɔd], *s.* der Halbgott.

demijohn ['demidʒɔn], *s.* der Glasballon.

demise [di'maiz], *s.* der Tod, das Hinscheiden. — *v.a.* (*Law*) vermachen.

demisemiquaver ['demisemikweivə], *s.* (*Mus.*) die Zweiunddreißigstelnote.

demobilize [di:'moubilaiz], *v.a.* demobilisieren.

democracy [di'mɔkrəsi], *s.* die Demokratie.

democratic [demo'krætik], *adj.* demokratisch.

demolish [di'mɔliʃ], *v.a.* demolieren, zerstören, niederreißen.

demon ['di:mən], *s.* der Dämon, der Teufel; *a* — *for work*, ein unersättlicher Arbeiter.

demoniac [di'mouniæk], **demoniacal** [di:mə'naiəkl], *adj.* besessen, teuflisch.

demonstrable [di'mɔnstrəbl], *adj.* beweisbar, nachweislich (*verifiable*).

demonstrate ['demənstreit], *v.a.*, *v.n.* beweisen (*prove*); demonstrieren.

demonstration [demən'streiʃən], *s.* der Beweis (*theoretical*); die Demonstration (*practical*); (*Pol.*) Kundgebung.

demonstrative [di'mɔnstrətiv], *adj.* (*Gram.*) demonstrativ; überschwenglich (*emotional*).

demoralize [di:'mɔrəlaiz], *v.a.* demoralisieren.

demote [di:'mout], *v.a.* (*Mil.*, *official*) degradieren.

demotion [di:'mouʃən], *s.* (*Mil.*, *official*) die Degradierung.

demur [di'mə:], *v.n.* Anstand nehmen; Einwendungen machen (*raise objections*); zögern, zaudern (*hesitate*). — *s.* der Zweifel, der Skrupel.

demure [di'mjuə], *adj.* sittsam, zimperlich; spröde (*prim*).

demureness [di'mjuənis], *s.* die Sittsamkeit; die Sprödigkeit (*primness*).

den [den], *s.* die Höhle, Grube; *lion's* —, die Löwengrube.

denial [di'naiəl], *s.* die Verneinung, das Dementi (*negation*); das Ableugnen (*disclaimer*); die Absage (*refusal*).

denizen ['denizən], *s.* der Bürger, der Alteingesessene.

denominate [di'nɔmineit], *v.a.* nennen, benennen (*name*).

denomination [dinɔmi'neiʃən], *s.* die Bezeichnung; der Nennwert (*currency*); (*Rel.*) das Bekenntnis.

denominational [dinɔmi'neiʃənəl], *adj.* konfessionell.

denominator [di'nɔmineitə], *s.* (*Maths.*) der Nenner.

denote [di'nout], *v.a.* bezeichnen, kennzeichnen.

dénouement [dei'nu:mã], *s.* die Entwicklung, die Darlegung, die Lösung.

denounce [di'nauns], *v.a.* denunzieren, angeben; (*Law*) anzeigen.

dense [dens], *adj.* dicht; (*coll.*) beschränkt (*stupid*).

density ['densiti], *s.* die Dichte; — *of population*, die Bevölkerungsdichte.

dent (1) [dent], *s.* die Beule.

dent (2) [dent], *s.* die Kerbe (*in wood*); der Einschnitt (*cut*).

dental [dentl], *adj.* Zahn-; — *studies*, zahnärztliche Studien; — *treatment*, die Zahnbehandlung. — *s.* (*Phonet.*) der Zahnlaut.

dentist ['dentist], *s.* der Zahnarzt.

dentistry ['dentistri], *s.* die Zahnheilkunde.

denude [di'nju:d], *v.a.* entblößen; berauben (*of*, *Genit.*).

denunciation [dinʌnsi'eiʃən], *s.* die Denunzierung, die Anzeige.

deny [di'nai], *v.a.* verneinen (*negate*); abschlagen (*refuse*); verleugnen (*refuse to admit*).

deodorant, deodorizer [di:'oudərənt, di:'oudəraizə], *s.* der Geruchsentzieher (*apparatus*); der Deodorant.

deodorize [di:'oudəraiz], *v.a.* geruchlos machen.

depart [di'pa:t], *v.n.* abreisen, abfahren (*for*, nach, *Dat.*); scheiden.

department [di'pa:tmənt], *s.* die Abteilung; — *store*, das Kaufhaus.

departmental [di:pa:t'mentl], *adj.* Abteilungs-.

departure [di'pa:tʃə], *s.* die Abreise, die Abfahrt.

depend [di'pend], *v.n.* abhängen, abhängig sein (*upon*, von, *Dat.*); sich verlassen (*upon*, auf, *Acc.*); *that* —*s*, das kommt darauf an.

dependable [di'pendəbl], *adj.* verläßlich, zuverlässig.

dependant [di'pendənt], *s.* das abhängige Familienmitglied (*member of family*); der Angehörige, Abhängige.

dependence [di'pendəns], *s.* die Abhängigkeit (*need*); das Vertrauen, der Verlaß (*reliance*).

dependency [di'pendənsi], *s.* (*Pol.*) die abhängige Kolonie.

dependent [di'pendənt], *adj.* abhängig (*upon*, von, *Dat.*).

depict [di'pikt], *v.a.* schildern, beschreiben.

deplete [di'pli:t], *v.a.* entleeren (*make empty*); erschöpfen (*exhaust*).

depletion [di'pli:ʃən], *s.* die Entleerung.

deplorable [di'plɔ:rəbl], *adj.* bedauernswert, bedauerlich.

deplore [di'plɔ:], *v.a.* beklagen.

deploy [di'plɔi], *v.a.* entfalten. — *v.n.* sich entfalten; (*Mil.*) aufmarschieren.

deployment [di'plɔimənt], *s.* (*Mil.*) das Deployieren; die Entfaltung.

deponent [di'pounənt], *s.* (*Law*) der vereidigte Zeuge. — *adj.* (*Gram.*) (*verb*) das Deponens.

depopulate [di:'pɔpjuleit], *v.a.* entvölkern.

deport [di'pɔ:t], *v.a.* deportieren.

deportation [di:pɔ:'teiʃən], *s.* die Deportation.

design

deportment [di'pɔ:tmənt], *s.* die körperliche Haltung (*physical*); das Benehmen (*social*).

depose [di'pouz], *v.a.* absetzen (*remove from office*); (*Law*) zu Papier bringen (*write down*); schriftlich erklären (*declare in writing*).

deposit [di'pɔzit], *s.* (*Comm.*) die Anzahlung; (*Geol., Chem.*) der Niederschlag; (*Geol.*) die Ablagerung; (*Comm.*) — *account*, das Depositenkonto. — *v.a.* (*Geol., Chem.*) absetzen; (*Comm.*) anzahlen, einzahlen.

deposition [di:pə'ziʃən], *s.* die Niederschrift, die schriftliche Erklärung; die Absetzung (*removal from office*).

depositor [di'pɔzitə], *s.* (*Comm.*) der Einzahler.

depository [di'pɔzitəri], *s.* das Lagerhaus.

depot ['depou], *s.* das Depot, das Lagerhaus (*store*); (*Am.*) der Bahnhof.

deprave [di'preiv], *v.a.* verderben.

depraved [di'preivd], *adj.* (moralisch) verdorben.

depravity [di'præviti], *s.* die Verdorbenheit, die Verworfenheit.

deprecate ['deprikeit], *v.a.* mißbilligen (*disapprove of*; *Acc.*); sich verbitten.

deprecation [depri'keiʃən], *s.* die Abbitte; die Mißbilligung (*disapproval*).

depreciate [di'pri:ʃieit], *v.a.* abwerten, herabwürdigen. — *v.n.* an Wert verlieren, im Wert sinken.

depreciation [dipri:ʃi'eiʃən], *s.* die Abwertung; der Verlust (*loss*); (*Pol., Comm.*) die Entwertung.

depredation [depri'deiʃən], *s.* das Plündern, der Raub.

depress [di'pres], *v.a.* niederdrücken (*press down*); deprimieren (*morale*).

depressed [di'prest], *adj.* niedergeschlagen.

depression [di'preʃən], *s.* das Niederdrücken (*action*); (*Pol.*) die Depression; die Niedergeschlagenheit (*despondency*); das Tief (*weather*).

deprivation [depri'veiʃən], *s.* der Verlust (*lack*); die Beraubung (*robbery*).

deprive [di'praiv], *v.a.* berauben (*of, Genit.*); wegnehmen (*of, Acc.*).

depth [depθ], *s.* die Tiefe; — *charge*, die Unterwasserbombe; *in the* — *s of night*, in tiefster Nacht; (*Phys.*) — *of focus*, die Tiefenschärfe; *be out of o.'s* —, den Grund unter seinen Füßen verloren haben, ratlos sein (*be helpless*); — *sounder*, das Echolot.

deputation [depju'teiʃən], *s.* die Deputation, die Abordnung.

depute [di'pju:t], *v.a.* abordnen, entsenden.

deputize ['depjutaiz], *v.n.* vertreten (*for, Acc.*).

deputy ['depjuti], *s.* der Abgeordnete, der Deputierte (*delegate*); der Vertreter (*replacement*).

derail [di:'reil], *v.a.* zum Entgleisen bringen. — *v.n.* entgleisen.

derailment [di:'reilmənt], *s.* die Entgleisung.

derange [di'reindʒ], *v.a.* verwirren, stören.

derangement [di'reindʒmənt], *s.* die Verwirrung; die Geistesstörung (*madness*).

derelict ['derilikt], *adj.* verlassen.

dereliction [deri'likʃən], *s.* das Verlassen; — *of duty*, die Pflichtvergessenheit.

deride [di'raid], *v.a.* verlachen, verhöhnen.

derision [di'riʒən], *s.* die Verhöhnung.

derisive [di'raisiv], *adj.* höhnisch, spöttisch.

derivable [di'raivəbl], *adj.* ableitbar.

derivation [deri'veiʃən], *s.* die Ableitung.

derivative [di'rivətiv], *adj.* abgeleitet. — *s.* das abgeleitete Wort.

derive [di'raiv], *v.a., v.n.* ableiten, herleiten.

derogation [dero'geiʃən], *s.* die Herabsetzung.

derrick ['derik], *s.* der Ladebaum.

dervish ['də:viʃ], *s.* der Derwisch.

descant ['deskænt], *s.* (*Mus.*) der Diskant *or* der Sopran. — [dis'kænt], *v.n.* sich verbreiten (*on,* über, *Acc.*).

descend [di'send], *v.n.* hinab- *or* herabsteigen (*go down*); abstammen (*stem from*).

descendant [di'sendənt], *s.* der Nachkomme.

descent [di'sent], *s.* der Abstieg (*going down*); der Fall (*decline*); die Abstammung (*forebears*); der Abhang (*slope*); (*Aviat.*) die Landung.

describable [dis'kraibəbl], *adj.* zu beschreiben, beschreibbar.

describe [dis'kraib], *v.a.* beschreiben, schildern.

description [dis'kripʃən], *s.* die Beschreibung; *of any* —, jeder Art.

descriptive [dis'kriptiv], *adj.* schildernd, beschreibend.

desecrate ['desikreit], *v.a.* entweihen, entheiligen.

desecration [desi'kreiʃən], *s.* die Entweihung, die Schändung.

desert (1) ['dezət], *s.* die Wüste.

desert (2) [di'zə:t], *v.a.* verlassen, im Stiche lassen. — *v.n.* desertieren.

desert (3) [di'zə:t], *s.* (*usually pl.*) das Verdienst.

desertion [di'zə:ʃən], *s.* (*Mil.*) die Fahnenflucht.

deserve [di'zə:v], *v.a.* verdienen.

deserving [di'zə:viŋ], *adj.* verdienstvoll.

design [di'zain], *v.a.* entwerfen (*plan*); vorhaben (*intend*); bestimmen (*determine*). — *s.* der Entwurf (*sketch*), der Plan (*draft*); die Absicht, das Vorhaben (*intention*); das Muster (*pattern*).

363

designate

designate [´dezigneit], *v.a.* bezeichnen (*mark*); ernennen (*appoint*). — [–nit], *adj.* ernannt; *chairman* —, der künftige Vorsitzende.

designation [dezig´neiʃən], *s.* die Bestimmung, Ernennung (*appointment*); die Bezeichnung (*mark*).

designer [di´zainə], *s.* der Zeichner, der Graphiker (*artist*); der Ränkeschmied (*schemer*).

designing [di´zainiŋ], *adj.* hinterlistig, schlau.

desirable [di´zaiərəbl], *adj.* erwünscht, wünschenswert.

desire [di´zaiə], *s.* der Wunsch, die Begierde; das Verlangen, die Sehnsucht (*longing*). — *v.a.* verlangen, begehren.

desirous [di´zaiərəs], *adj.* begierig (*of, inf.*).

desist [di´zist], *v.n.* ablassen, aufhören.

desk [desk], *s.* der Schreibtisch; das Pult; — *lamp*, die Tischlampe *or* Bürolampe.

desolate [´desəlit], *adj.* verlassen, öde; trostlos (*sad*). — [–leit], *v.a.* verwüsten (*lay waste*).

desolation [desə´leiʃən], *s.* die Verwüstung (*of land*); die Trostlosigkeit (*sadness*).

despair [dis´pɛə], *v.n.* verzweifeln (*of, an, Dat.*). — *s.* die Verzweiflung.

despatch, dispatch [dis´pætʃ], *v.a.* absenden, befördern (*post*); abfertigen (*send*); erledigen (*deal with*); töten (*kill*). — *s.* die Abfertigung (*clearance*); die Eile (*speed*); die Depesche (*message*).

desperado [despə´reidou, -´rɑ:dou], *s.* der Wagehals, der Draufgänger.

desperate [´despərit], *adj.* verzweifelt.

desperation [despə´reiʃən], *s.* die Verzweiflung.

despicable [´despikəbl], *adj.* verächtlich.

despise [dis´paiz], *v.a.* verachten.

despite [dis´pait], *prep.* trotz (*Genit., Dat.*).

despoil [dis´pɔil], *v.a.* plündern, ausrauben.

despondency [dis´pɔndənsi], *s.* die Verzweiflung, Verzagtheit.

despondent [dis´pɔndənt], *adj.* verzagend, verzweifelnd, mutlos.

despot [´despɔt], *s.* der Despot, der Tyrann.

despotic [des´pɔtik], *adj.* despotisch.

despotism [´despətizm], *s.* (*Pol.*) der Despotismus.

dessert [di´zə:t], *s.* das Dessert, der Nachtisch.

destination [desti´neiʃən], *s.* die Bestimmung, das Ziel; der Bestimmungsort (*address*); das Reiseziel (*journey*).

destine [´destin], *v.a.* bestimmen.

destiny [´destini], *s.* das Geschick; das Schicksal, das Verhängnis (*fate*).

destitute [´destitju:t], *adj.* verlassen (*deserted*); hilflos, mittellos (*poor*); in bitterer Not (*in great distress*).

destitution [desti´tju:ʃən], *s.* die Notlage, die bittere Not.

destroy [dis´trɔi], *v.a.* zerstören (*buildings*); verwüsten; vernichten (*lives*).

destroyer [dis´trɔiə], *s.* der Zerstörer.

destructible [dis´trʌktibl], *adj.* zerstörbar.

destruction [dis´trʌkʃən], *s.* die Zerstörung (*of buildings*), die Verwüstung; die Vernichtung.

destructive [dis´trʌktiv], *adj.* zerstörend, verderblich.

destructiveness [dis´trʌktivnis], *s.* die Zerstörungswut, der Zerstörungssinn.

desultory [´dezəltəri], *adj.* unmethodisch, sprunghaft; oberflächlich (*superficial*).

detach [di´tætʃ], *v.a.* absondern, trennen.

detachment [di´tætʃmənt], *s.* die Absonderung (*separation*); (*Mil.*) das Kommando.

detail [di´teil], *v.a.* im einzelnen beschreiben (*describe minutely*); (*Mil.*) abkommandieren. — [´di:teil], *s.* die Einzelheit.

detailed [´di:teild], *adj.* ausführlich; detailliert, ins Einzelne gehend (*report etc.*); [di´teild], (*Mil.*) abkommandiert.

detain [di´tein], *v.a.* aufhalten, zurückhalten; festhalten (*in prison*).

detect [di´tekt], *v.a.* entdecken, aufdecken.

detection [di´tekʃən], *s.* die Entdeckung, die Aufdeckung.

detective [di´tektiv], *s.* der Detektiv.

detention [di´tenʃən], *s.* (*Law*) die Haft; die Vorenthaltung (*of articles*).

deter [di´tə:], *v.a.* abschrecken.

detergent [di´tə:dʒənt], *s.* das Reinigungsmittel.

deteriorate [di´tiəriəreit], *v.n.* sich verschlimmern, verschlechtern.

deterioration [ditiəriə´reiʃən], *s.* die Verschlimmerung.

determinable [di´tə:minəbl], *adj.* bestimmbar.

determinate [di´tə:minit], *adj.* festgesetzt, bestimmt.

determination [di´tə:mi´neiʃən], *s.* die Entschlossenheit (*resoluteness*); die Bestimmung (*identification*); der Entschluß (*resolve*).

determine [di´tə:min], *v.a.* bestimmen (*ascertain*); beschließen (*resolve*).

deterrent [di´terənt], *s.* das Abschreckungsmittel.

detest [di´test], *v.a.* verabscheuen.

detestable [di´testəbl], *adj.* abscheulich.

detestation [detes´teiʃən], *s.* der Abscheu (*of*, vor, *Dat.*).

dethrone [di:´θroun], *v.a.* entthronen, vom Thron verdrängen.

detonate [´di:- *or* ´detoneit], *v.n.* detonieren, explodieren. — *v.a.* explodieren, detonieren lassen, zum Detonieren bringen.

dice

detonation [deto'neiʃən], s. die Detonation, die Explosion.

detonator ['detoneitə], s. der Zünder, die Zündpatrone; (*Railw.*) die Knallpatrone.

detour ['deituə *or* di'tuə], s. der Umweg; (*Civil Engin.*) die Umleitung. — *v.n.* (*Am.*) einen Umweg machen. — *v.a.* (*Am.*) umleiten (*re-route*).

detract [di'trækt], *v.a.*, *v.n.* abziehen; schmälern.

detraction [di'trækʃən], s. die Schmälerung, die Verleumdung (*slander*).

detractive [di'træktiv], *adj.* verleumderisch.

detractor [di'træktə], s. der Verleumder.

detriment ['detrimənt], s. der Nachteil, der Schaden.

detrimental [detri'mentl], *adj.* nachteilig; abträglich; schädlich (*harmful*).

deuce (1) [dju:s], s. die Zwei (*game*); (*Tennis*) der Einstand.

deuce (2) [dju:s], s. (*coll.*) der Teufel.

devastate ['devəsteit], *v.a.* verwüsten, verheeren.

devastating ['devəsteitiŋ], *adj.* schrecklich, verheerend.

devastation [devəs'teiʃən], s. die Verheerung, die Verwüstung.

develop [di'veləp], *v.a.* entwickeln. — *v.n.* sich entwickeln; sich entfalten (*prove, turn out*).

developer [di'veləpə], s. (*Phot.*) das Entwicklungsmittel.

development [di'veləpmənt], s. die Entwicklung.

developmental [diveləp'mentl], *adj.* Entwicklungs-.

deviate ['di:vieit], *v.n.* abweichen.

deviation [di:vi'eiʃən], s. die Abweichung.

device [di'vais], s. die Vorrichtung (*equipment*); der Kungstgriff (*trick*).

devil [devl], s. der Teufel; der Lehrling, Laufbursche (*printer's, lawyer's*); *the — take the hindmost!* der Teufel hol was dann kommt! — *v.n.* in der Lehre sein (*for*, bei, *Dat.*).

devilish ['deviliʃ], *adj.* teuflisch.

devilment, devilry ['devəlmənt, 'devəlri], s. die Teufelei, die Teufelslaune.

devious ['di:viəs], *adj.* abweichend; abgelegen; abwegig.

deviousness ['di:viəsnis], s. die Abschweifung, Verirrung.

devise [di'vaiz], *v.a.* erfinden (*invent*); ersinnen (*think out*).

deviser, devisor [di'vaizə], s. der Erfinder (*inventor*); der Erblasser (*testator*).

devoid [di'vɔid], *adj.* frei (*of*, von, *Dat.*); ohne (*Acc.*).

devolve [di'vɔlv], *v.a.* übertragen (*transfer*); abwälzen (*pass on burden*) (*to*, auf, *Acc.*). — *v.n.* zufallen (*Dat.*).

devote [di'vout], *v.a.* widmen; aufopfern (*sacrifice*).

devoted [di'voutid], *adj.* ergeben (*affectionate*); geweiht (*consecrated*).

devotee [devo'ti:], s. der Anhänger; der Verehrer (*fan*).

devotion [di'vouʃən], s. die Hingabe; die Aufopferung (*sacrifice*); die Andacht (*prayer*).

devotional [di'vouʃənəl], *adj.* Andachts-.

devour [di'vauə], *v.a.* verschlingen.

devout [di'vaut], *adj.* andächtig, fromm.

devoutness [di'vautnis], s. die Frömmigkeit.

dew [dju:], s. der Tau.

dewy [dju:i], *adj.* betaut, taufeucht.

dexterity [deks'teriti], s. die Gewandtheit, die Fertigkeit.

dexterous ['dekstərəs], *adj.* gewandt, geschickt.

diabetes [daiə'bi:ti:z], s. (*Med.*) die Zuckerkrankheit.

diabetic [daiə'betik], s. (*Med.*) der Zuckerkranke. — *adj.* zuckerkrank.

diabolic(al) [daiə'bɔlik(əl)], *adj.* teuflisch.

diadem ['daiədem], s. das Diadem, das Stirnband.

diæresis [dai'iərəsis], s. die Diärese.

diagnose [daiəg'nouz], *v.a.* diagnostizieren, als Diagnose finden, befinden.

diagnosis [daiəg'nousis], s. die Diagnose, der Befund.

diagonal [dai'ægənəl], *adj.* diagonal, schräg. — s. (*Geom.*) die Diagonale.

diagram ['daiəgræm], s. das Diagramm.

dial ['daiəl], s. das Zifferblatt; (*Teleph.*) die Wählerscheibe. — *v.a.*, *v.n.* (*Teleph.*) wählen.

dialect ['daiəlekt], s. der Dialekt, die Mundart.

dialectic [daiə'lektik], s. (*Phil.*) die Dialektik.

dialektical [daiə'lektikəl], *adj.* dialektisch, logisch.

dialogue ['daiəlɔg], s. der Dialog, das Zwiegespräch.

diameter [dai'æmitə], s. der Durchmesser.

diametrical [daiə'metrikəl], *adj.* diametral; gerade entgegengesetzt.

diamond ['daiəmənd], s. der Diamant; (*Cards*) das Karo.

diaper ['daiəpə], s. (*Am.*) die Windel.

diaphragm ['daiəfræm], s. (*Anat.*) das Zwerchfell; (*Phys.*) die Membran.

diarrhœa [daiə'riə], s. (*Med.*) der Durchfall.

diary ['daiəri], s. das Tagebuch, der Kalender.

diatribe ['daiətraib], s. der Tadel, der Angriff (*verbal*), die Schmähschrift (*written*).

dibble [dibl], s. der Pflanzstock. — *v.n.* Pflanzen stecken, anpflanzen.

dice [dais], s. *pl.* die Würfel (*sing.* **die**). — *v.a.* würfeln, werfen.

365

dicker ['dikə], *v.n.* (*Am.*) feilschen, handeln.

dicky ['diki], *s.* das Vorhemd.

dictate [dik'teit], *v.a., v.n.* diktieren, vorschreiben.

dictation [dik'teiʃən], *s.* (*Sch.*) das Diktat.

dictator [dik'teitə], *s.* der Diktator.

dictatorship [dik'teitəʃip], *s.* die Diktatur.

diction ['dikʃən], *s.* die Ausdrucksweise (*speech*).

dictionary ['dikʃənri], *s.* das Wörterbuch.

didactic [di'dæktik], *adj.* lehrhaft, Lehr-.

die (1) [dai], *v.n.* sterben (*of*, an, *Dat.*); — *away*, verebben.

die (2) [dai], *s.* der Würfel (*cube*); die Gießform (*mould*); der Stempel (*punch*); (*Metall.*) das Gesenk (*swage*); — *casting*, der Spritzguß; — *castings*, die Spritzgußteile, Gußteile; — *forging*, das Gesenkschmiedestück.

die (3) [dai] *see under* dice.

dielectric [daii'lektrik], *adj.* dielektrisch.

diet (1) ['daiət], *s.* (*Pol.*) der Landtag, Reichstag.

diet (2) ['daiət], *s.* (*Med.*) die Diät. — *v.n.* (*Med.*) eine Diät halten. — *v.a.* (*Med.*) eine Diät vorschreiben.

dietary, dietetic ['daiətəri, daiə'tetik], *adj.* diätetisch.

differ ['difə], *v.n.* sich unterscheiden (*be different from*, von, *Dat.*); anderer Meinung sein (*be of different opinion*).

difference ['difərəns], *s.* (*Maths.*) die Differenz; der Unterschied (*discrepancy*); die Meinungsverschiedenheit (*divergence of opinion*).

different ['difərənt], *adj.* verschieden, verschiedenartig.

differentiate [difə'renʃieit], *v.n.* (*Maths.*) differenzieren; einen Unterschied machen (*between*, zwischen, *Dat.*).

difficult ['difikəlt], *adj.* schwierig, schwer.

difficulty ['difikəlti], *s.* die Schwierigkeit.

diffidence ['difidəns], *s.* die Schüchternheit.

diffident ['difidənt], *adj.* schüchtern.

diffraction [di'frækʃən], *s.* die Ablenkung, (*Phys.*, *Optics*) die Brechung.

diffuse [di'fju:z], *v.a.* ausgießen (*pour*); verbreiten (*spread*). — [di'fju:s], *adj.* verbreitet, weitschweifig (*style*); zerstreut.

diffuseness [di'fju:snis], *s.* die Weitläufigkeit (*style*).

diffusion [di'fju:ʒən], *s.* (*Phys.*) die Diffusion, die Zerstreuung, die Verbreitung.

dig (1) [dig], *v.a. irr.* graben; — *in the ribs*, in die Rippen stoßen. — *v.n.* (*coll.*) wohnen (*live in lodgings*).

dig (2) [dig], *v.a.* (*coll.*) verstehen.

digger ['digə], *s.* der Gräber; (*coll.*) der Australier.

digest [di'dʒest], *v.a.* (*Anat.*) verdauen. — ['daidʒest], *s.* (*Am.*) die Sammlung von Auszügen; (*pl.*) Pandekten.

digestibility [didʒesti'biliti], *s.* die Verdaulichkeit.

digestible [di'dʒestibl], *adj.* verdaulich.

digestion [di'dʒestʃən], *s.* die Verdauung.

digestive [di'dʒestiv], *adj.* Verdauungs-; — *biscuit*, das Kornmehlkeks; — *organs*, die Verdauungsorgane.

digit ['didʒit], *s.* (*Maths.*) die (einstellige) Zahl; der Zahlenwert.

digitalis [didʒi'teilis], *s.* (*Bot.*) der Fingerhut.

dignified ['dignifaid], *adj.* würdig, würdevoll.

dignify ['dignifai], *v.a.* ehren (*honour*); zieren (*decorate*).

dignitary ['dignitəri], *s.* der Würdenträger.

dignity ['digniti], *s.* die Würde.

digress [dai'gres], *v.n.* abweichen, abschweifen.

digression [dai'greʃən], *s.* die Abweichung, die Abschweifung.

digressive [dai'gresiv], *adj.* abschweifend (*style*).

digs [digz], *s. pl.* (*coll.*) das (möblierte) Zimmer, die Wohnung.

dike [daik], *s.* der Graben, der Deich. — *v.a.* eindeichen, eindämmen.

dilapidated [di'læpideitid], *adj.* baufällig.

dilapidation [diləpi'deiʃən], *s.* die Baufälligkeit, der Verfall.

dilate [d(a)i'leit], *v.a.* erweitern, ausdehnen. — *v.n.* sich ausdehnen; sich auslassen (*speak*) (*on*, über, *Acc.*).

dilation [d(a)i'leiʃən], *s.* die Erweiterung (*expansion*); die Auslassung (*speaking*).

dilatoriness ['dilətərinis], *s.* die Saumseligkeit.

dilatory ['dilətəri], *adj.* zögernd, aufschiebend, saumselig.

dilemma [d(a)i'lemə], *s.* das Dilemma, die Klemme.

diligence ['dilidʒəns], *s.* der Fleiß, die Emsigkeit.

diligent ['dilidʒənt], *adj.* fleißig, arbeitsam.

dilly-dally ['dili'dæli], *v.n.* tändeln, zaudern, Zeit vertrödeln.

dilute [d(a)i'lju:t], *v.a.* (*Chem.*) verdünnen; schwächen (*weaken*).

dilution [d(a)i'lju:ʃən], *s.* die Verdünnung.

diluvial, diluvian [d(a)i'lju:viəl, -iən], *adj.* Diluvial-, des Diluviums; sintflutlich.

dim [dim], *adj.* trübe, unklar; (*Phys.*) abgeblendet. — *v.a.* abdunkeln, abblenden.

dimension [d(a)i'menʃən], *s.* die Dimension, das Maß.

dimensional [d(a)i'menʃənəl], *adj.* dimensional.

diminish [di'miniʃ], *v.a.* vermindern. — *v.n.* sich vermindern.

diminution [dimi'nju:ʃən], *s.* die Verringerung, die Verminderung.

diminutive [di'minjutiv], *adj.* verkleinernd, klein. — *s.* (*Gram.*) das Verkleinerungswort.

dimness ['dimnis], *s.* die Trübheit; die Düsterkeit (*dark*).

dimple [dimpl], *s.* das Grübchen.

dimpled [dimpld], *adj.* mit einem Grübchen.

din [din], *s.* das Getöse, der Lärm.

dine [dain], *v.n.* speisen, essen.

dinginess ['dindʒinis], *s.* die Dunkelheit, die Schäbigkeit.

dingy ['dindʒi], *adj.* dunkel, schäbig.

dinner ['dinə], *s.* das Essen; das Festessen (*formal*); — *jacket*, der Smoking.

dint [dint], *s.* der Nachdruck, der Schlag; *by* — *of*, mittels (*Genit.*).

diocesan [dai'ɔsisən], *adj.* (*Eccl.*) einer Diözese angehörig, Diözesan–.

diocese ['daiəsis], *s.* (*Eccl.*) die Diözese.

dip [dip], *v.a.* eintauchen, eintunken; abblenden (*lights*). — *v.n.* (unter)tauchen; sinken; sich flüchtig einlassen (*into*, in). — *s.* die Senke; der Abhang (*slope*).

diphtheria [dif'θiəriə], *s.* (*Med.*) die Diphtherie.

diphthong ['difθɔŋ], *s.* (*Phonet.*) der Diphthong.

diploma [di'ploumə], *s.* das Diplom; *teaching* —, das Lehrerdiplom.

diplomacy [di'plouməsi], *s.* die Diplomatie.

diplomatic [diplo'mætik], *adj.* diplomatisch, taktvoll; urkundlich (*documents*). — *s.* (*pl.*) das Studium der Urkunden.

diplomat(ist) ['diplomæt, di'ploumətist], *s.* (*Pol.*) der Diplomat.

dipper ['dipə], *s.* der Taucher.

dire [daiə], *adj.* fürchterlich, schrecklich; — *necessity*, bittere Not.

direct [d(a)i'rekt], *adj.* direkt, unmittelbar. — *v.a.* leiten (*be in charge of*); hinweisen, den Weg zeigen (*tell the way to*); anordnen (*arrange for*).

direction [d(a)i'rekʃən], *s.* die Leitung (*management*); (*Geog.*) die Richtung, Himmelsrichtung; die Anordnung (*arrangement*, *order*); —*s for use*, die Gebrauchsanweisung.

director [d(a)i'rektə], *s.* der Direktor; der Leiter.

directory [d(a)i'rektəri], *s.* das Adreßbuch; das Telephonbuch.

dirge [də:dʒ], *s.* der Trauergesang.

dirigible ['diridʒibl], *adj.* lenkbar, leitbar.

dirt [də:t], *s.* der Schmutz, der Kot, Dreck. — *adj.* — *cheap*, spottbillig.

dirty ['də:ti], *adj.* schmutzig; gemein (*joke*).

disability [disə'biliti], *s.* die Unfähigkeit, das Unvermögen (*inability*); die Schädigung (*impairment of health*).

disable [dis'eibl], *v.a.* unfähig *or* untauglich machen.

disablement [dis'eiblmənt], *s.* die Versehrung, die Verkrüppelung.

disabuse [disə'bju:z], *v.a.* aufklären, eines Besseren belehren.

disaccustom [disə'kʌstəm], *v.a.* entwöhnen, abgewöhnen.

disadvantage [disəd'va:ntidʒ], *s.* der Nachteil.

disaffection [disə'fekʃən], *s.* die Abneigung; der Widerwille.

disagree [disə'gri:], *v.n.* nicht übereinstimmen, nicht einer Meinung sein.

disagreeable [disə'griəbl], *adj.* unangenehm, verdrießlich; unfreundlich.

disagreement [disə'gri:mənt], *s.* die Uneinigkeit (*disunity*); die Meinungsverschiedenheit (*difference of opinion*).

disallow [disə'lau], *v.a.* nicht gestatten; in Abrede stellen.

disappear [disə'piə], *v.n.* verschwinden.

disappearance [disə'piərəns], *s.* das Verschwinden.

disappoint [disə'pɔint], *v.a.* enttäuschen.

disappointment [disə'pɔintmənt], *s.* die Enttäuschung.

disapprobation [disæpro'beiʃən], *s.* die Mißbilligung.

disapproval [disə'pru:vəl], *s.* die Mißbilligung.

disapprove [disə'pru:v], *v.a.* mißbilligen (*of*, *Acc.*).

disarm [dis'a:m], *v.a.* entwaffnen. —*v.n.* abrüsten.

disarmament [dis'a:məmənt], *s.* die Abrüstung.

disarray [disə'rei], *v.a.* in Unordnung bringen. — *s.* die Unordnung (*disorder*); die Verwirrung (*confusion*).

disaster [di'za:stə], *s.* das Unglück; das Unheil, die Katastrophe.

disastrous [di'za:strəs], *adj.* unheilvoll, schrecklich.

disavow [disə'vau], *v.a.* ableugnen.

disavowal [disə'vauəl], *s.* das Ableugnen.

disband [dis'bænd], *v.a.* entlassen (*dismiss*); auflösen (*dissolve*).

disbar [dis'ba:], *v.a.* (*Law*) von der Rechtspraxis ausschließen.

disbelief [disbi'li:f], *s.* der Unglaube (*incredulity*); der Zweifel (*doubt*).

disbelieve [disbi'li:v], *v.a.* nicht glauben; bezweifeln.

disburse [dis'bə:s], *v.a.* auszahlen, ausgeben.

disbursement [dis'bə:smənt], *s.* die Auszahlung, die Ausgabe.

disc [disk], *s.* (*also Med.*) die Scheibe; die Platte (*record*).

discard [dis'ka:d], *v.a.* ablegen, beiseite legen, aufgeben.

discern [di'zə:n *or* di'sə:n], *v.a.* unterscheiden; wahrnehmen, bemerken.

discernment [di'sə:nmənt], *s.* die Urteilskraft (*powers of judgment*); die Einsicht.

discharge

discharge [dis'tʃɑːdʒ], *v.a.* entlassen (*dismiss*); abfeuern (*pistol*); abladen, ausladen (*cargo*); bezahlen (*debt*); tun, erfüllen (*duty*). — *s.* die Entladung (*gun*); die Entlassung (*dismissal*); die Bezahlung (*debt*); die Erfüllung (*duty*).

disciple [di'saipl], *s.* (*Bibl.*) der Jünger; der Schüler.

disciplinarian [disipli'nɛəriən], *s.* der Zuchtmeister.

disciplinary ['disiplinəri], *adj.* disziplinarisch.

discipline ['disiplin], *s.* die Disziplin, die Zucht. — *v.a.* disziplinieren, züchtigen.

disclaim [dis'kleim], *v.a.* verleugnen (*deny*); nicht anerkennen (*refuse to acknowledge*); verzichten (*renounce*).

disclaimer [dis'kleimə], *s.* der Widerruf.

disclose [dis'klouz], *v.a.* eröffnen, enthüllen.

disclosure [dis'klouʒə], *s.* die Eröffnung, die Enthüllung.

discoloration [diskʌlə'reiʃən], *s.* die Entfärbung, Verfärbung.

discomfiture [dis'kʌmfitʃə], *s.* die Verwirrung.

discomfort [dis'kʌmfət], *s.* das Unbehagen; die Beschwerde.

disconcert [diskən'səːt], *v.a.* außer Fassung bringen (*upset*); vereiteln (*frustrate*).

disconnect [diskə'nekt], *v.a.* trennen (*separate*); abstellen.

disconsolate [dis'kɔnsəlit], *adj.* trostlos, untröstlich.

discontent [diskən'tent], *s.* die Unzufriedenheit, das Mißvergnügen. — *v.a.* mißvergnügt stimmen.

discontinuance [diskən'tinjuəns], *s.* die Beendigung (*finish*); das Aufhören (*suspension*); die Unterbrechung (*interruption*).

discontinue [diskən'tinjuː], *v.a.* nicht fortsetzen; unterbrechen (*interrupt*); einstellen.

discord ['diskɔːd], *s.* die Zwietracht (*disagreement*); (*Mus.*) der Mißklang.

discordance [dis'kɔːdəns], *s.* die Uneinigkeit.

discordant [dis'kɔːdənt], *adj.* uneinig, widersprechend.

discount ['diskaunt], *s.* (*Comm.*) der Abzug, der Rabatt; *allow a —*, einen Rabatt gewähren; *be at a —*, unbeliebt sein, nicht geschätzt sein; *sell at a —*, unter dem Preis verkaufen. — [dis'kaunt], *v.a.* (*Comm.*) diskontieren, einen Rabatt gewähren; nur mit Vorsicht aufnehmen (*accept with doubt*).

discountable [dis'kauntəbl], *adj.* diskontierbar, in Abzug zu bringen.

discountenance [dis'kauntinəns], *v.a.* mißbilligen.

discourage [dis'kʌridʒ], *v.a.* entmutigen; abraten (*from*, von, *Dat.*).

discouragement [dis'kʌridʒmənt], *s.* die Entmutigung.

discourse [dis'kɔːs], *v.n.* einen Vortrag halten (*on*, über, *Acc.*); sprechen. — ['diskɔːs], *s.* der Vortrag; das Gespräch, die Rede.

discourteous [dis'kəːtiəs], *adj.* unhöflich.

discourtesy [dis'kəːtəsi], *s.* die Unhöflichkeit.

discover [dis'kʌvə], *v.a.* entdecken.

discovery [dis'kʌvəri], *s.* die Entdeckung.

discredit [dis'kredit], *s.* der üble Ruf; die Schande. — *v.a.* in schlechten Ruf bringen; diskreditieren.

discreditable [dis'kreditəbl], *adj.* schimpflich.

discreet [dis'kriːt], *adj.* diskret, verschwiegen; vorsichtig (*cautious*).

discrepancy [dis'krepənsi], *s.* die Diskrepanz, der Widerspruch; der Unterschied (*difference*).

discretion [dis'kreʃən], *s.* die Diskretion; die Klugheit; der Takt (*tact*); die Verschwiegenheit (*silence*); *at your —*, nach Ihrem Belieben; *use your —*, handle nach deinem Ermessen; handeln Sie nach Ihrem Ermessen.

discretionary [dis'kreʃənəri], *adj.* willkürlich, uneingeschränkt.

discriminate [dis'krimineit], *v.a.*, *v.n.* unterscheiden (*distinguish*); absondern (*separate*).

discriminating [dis'krimineitiŋ], *adj.* scharfsinnig; einsichtig.

discriminatory [dis'krimineitəri], *adj.* einen Unterschied machend; — *legislation*, das Ausnahmegesetz.

discursive [dis'kəːsiv], *adj.* diskursiv, ohne Zusammenhang.

discuss [dis'kʌs], *v.a.* besprechen, erörtern.

discussion [dis'kʌʃən], *s.* die Diskussion, das Gespräch.

disdain [dis'dein], *s.* die Verachtung. — *v.a.* verachten, verschmähen; herabsetzen (*belittle*).

disdainful [dis'deinful], *adj.* geringschätzig, verächtlich.

disease [di'ziːz], *s.* die Krankheit.

diseased [di'ziːzd], *adj.* krank.

disembark [disim'bɑːk], *v.n.* aussteigen, landen. — *v.a.* aussteigen lassen, ausschiffen.

disembarkation [disembɑː'keiʃən], *s.* die Ausschiffung; die Landung.

disenchant [disin'tʃɑːnt], *v.a.* ernüchtern.

disenchantment [disin'tʃɑːntmənt], *s.* die Ernüchterung.

disengage [disin'geidʒ], *v.a.* losmachen, befreien (*release*); freigeben. — *v.n.* (*Mil.*) sich absetzen.

disengaged [disin'geidʒd], *adj.* frei (*unoccupied*).

disentangle [disin'tæŋgl], *v.a.* entwirren; befreien (*free*).

~ **disentanglement** [disin'tæŋglmənt], *s.* die Entwirrung, die Befreiung.

dispel

disfavour [dis'feivə], s. die Ungunst, die Ungnade.
disfigure [dis'figə], v.a. entstellen, verunstalten.
disfiguration [disfigjuə'reiʃən], s. die Entstellung, die Verunstaltung.
disfranchise [dis'fræntʃaiz], v.a. das Wahlrecht entziehen (Dat.).
disgorge [dis'gɔːdʒ], v.a. ausspeien.
disgrace [dis'greis], v.a. entehren, Schande bringen. — s. die Ungnade, Schande (shame); die Entehrung (putting to shame).
disgraceful [dis'greisful], adj. schändlich, entehrend.
disgruntled [dis'grʌntld], adj. verstimmt, unzufrieden.
disguise [dis'gaiz], v.a. verkleiden (dress); (fig.) verstellen. — s. die Verkleidung, die Verstellung.
disgust [dis'gʌst], s. der Ekel, der Widerwille. — v.a. anekeln; be —ed, sehr ärgerlich sein; be —ed with s. th., etwas verabscheuen.
dish [diʃ], s. die Schüssel (bowl); das Gericht (food). — v.a. (coll.) abtun (frustrate); — up, auftragen (food).
dishcloth ['diʃklɔθ], s. das Wischtuch; der Abwaschlappen.
dishearten [dis'hɑːtn], v.a. entmutigen, verzagt machen.
dishevelled [di'ʃevəld], adj. aufgelöst (hair); zerzaust (hair, clothes).
dishonest [dis'ɔnist], adj. unehrlich.
dishonesty [dis'ɔnisti], s. die Unehrlichkeit.
dishonour [dis'ɔnə], s. die Schande. — v.a. schänden, Schande bringen (über, Acc.).
dishonourable [dis'ɔnərəbl], adj. ehrlos, schimpflich.
dishwater ['diʃwɔːtə], s. das Spülwasser.
disillusion [disi'luːʒən], s. die Enttäuschung, die Ernüchterung. — v.a. enttäuschen, ernüchtern.
disinclination [disinkli'neiʃən], s. die Abneigung.
disincline [disin'klain], v.a. abgeneigt machen (Dat.).
disinfect [disin'fekt], v.a. desinfizieren.
disinfectant [disin'fektənt], s. das Desinfektionsmittel.
disinfection [disin'fekʃən], s. die Desinfektion.
disingenuous [disin'dʒenjuəs], adj. unaufrichtig, unredlich.
disinherit [disin'herit], v.a. enterben.
disinter [disin'təː], v.a. exhumieren, ausgraben.
disinterested [dis'intrəstid], adj. uneigennützig.
disinterestedness [dis'intrəstidnis], s. die Selbstlosigkeit, die Uneigennützigkeit.
disjoin [dis'dʒɔin], v.a. trennen.
disjoint [dis'dʒɔint], v.a. zerlegen, zerstückeln.
disjointedness [dis'dʒɔintidnis], s. die Zerstücktheit, die Zusammenhangslosigkeit (style of writing etc.).

disjunction [dis'dʒʌŋkʃən], s. die Trennung, die Abtrennung.
disjunctive [dis'dʒʌŋktiv], adj. (Gram.) trennend, disjunktiv.
disk [disk] see disc.
dislike [dis'laik], v.a. nicht leiden mögen, nicht gerne haben. — s. die Abneigung (of, gegen, Acc.).
dislocate ['dislokeit], v.a. verrenken (bone); (fig.) in Unordnung bringen.
dislocation [dislo'keiʃən], s. (Med.) die Verrenkung; die Verwirrung (traffic etc.).
dislodge [dis'lɔdʒ], v.a. vertreiben (drive out); entfernen (remove).
disloyal [dis'lɔiəl], adj. ungetreu; verräterisch.
disloyalty [dis'lɔiəlti], s. die Untreue (sentiment); der Verrat (act).
dismal ['dizməl], adj. trostlos, traurig (mood); düster, trüb (weather).
dismantle [dis'mæntl], v.a. niederreißen, zerlegen; abbauen.
dismay [dis'mei], v.a. erschrecken, entmutigen. — s. die Furcht, der Schrecken, die Bangigkeit.
dismember [dis'membə], v.a. zerstücken.
dismemberment [dis'membəmənt], s. die Zerstückelung, die Aufteilung.
dismiss [dis'mis], v.a. entlassen (person); aufgeben (idea).
dismissal [dis'misəl], s. die Entlassung; (Law) die Abweisung.
dismount [dis'maunt], v.n. vom Pferd absteigen. — v.a. (die Truppen) absteigen lassen.
disobedience [diso'biːdjəns], s. der Ungehorsam.
disobedient [diso'biːdjənt], adj. ungehorsam.
disobey [diso'bei], v.a., v.n. nicht gehorchen.
disoblige [diso'blaidʒ], v.a. verletzen, unhöflich behandeln.
disorder [dis'ɔːdə], s. die Unordnung; der Aufruhr (riot). — v.a. verwirren, in Unordnung bringen.
disorderliness [dis'ɔːdəlinis], s. die Unordentlichkeit.
disorderly [dis'ɔːdəli], adj. unordentlich (unsystematic); aufrührerisch, liederlich.
disorganization [disɔːgəni'zeiʃən or -nai'zeiʃən], s. die Zerrüttung, die Auflösung (dissolution).
disorganize [dis'ɔːgənaiz], v.a. auflösen.
disown [dis'oun], v.a. verleugnen.
disparage [dis'pæridʒ], v.a. verunglimpfen (slight); herabsetzen (minimize).
disparagement [dis'pæridʒmənt], s. die Herabsetzung.
disparity [dis'pæriti], s. die Ungleichheit.
dispatch [dis'pætʃ] see despatch.
dispel [dis'pel], v.a. vertreiben, verscheuchen.

369

dispensable

dispensable [dis'pensəbl], *adj.* erläßlich, entbehrlich.
dispensation [dispen'seiʃən], *s.* die Austeilung; (*Eccl.*) die Dispensation.
dispensary [dis'pensəri], *s.* die Apotheke.
dispense [dis'pens], *v.a.* ausgeben, austeilen (*distribute*); — *with*, entbehren können, verzichten (auf, *Acc.*).
dispenser [dis'pensə], *s.* der Apotheker, der Pharmazeut.
dispersal [dis'pəːsəl], *s.* das Zerstreuen, die Verteilung.
disperse [dis'pəːs], *v.a.* zerstreuen. — *v.n.* sich zerstreuen, sich verteilen.
dispirit [dis'pirit], *v.a.* mutlos machen, entmutigen.
displace [dis'pleis], *v.a.* verlegen, versetzen; (*Phys.*) verdrängen; —*d person*, der Heimatlose, der Verschleppte, der Flüchtling.
displacement [dis'pleismənt], *s.* die Versetzung (*from one place to another*); die Entwurzelung (*uprooting*); (*Phys.*) die Verdrängung; (*Naut.*) das Deplacement.
display [dis'plei], *v.a.* entfalten, ausstellen, zur Schau stellen (*show*). — *s.* die Entfaltung (*showing*), die Schaustellung, Ausstellung (*exhibition*).
displease [dis'pliːz], *v.a.* mißfallen (*Dat.*).
displeased [dis'pliːzd], *adj.* ungehalten (*at*, über, *Acc.*).
displeasure [dis'pleʒə], *s.* das Mißvergnügen, das Mißfallen (— *at*, an, *Dat.*).
disposable [dis'pouzəbl], *adj.* (*Comm.*) disponibel; zur Verfügung stehend.
disposal [dis'pouzl], *s.* die Verfügung (*ordering*); die Übergabe (*handing over*); *at o.'s* —, zur Verfügung; *bomb* —, die Unschädlichmachung der Bomben.
dispose [dis'pouz], *v.a.* einrichten (*thing*); geneigt machen (*person*); — *of*, etwas loswerden (*Acc.*). — *v.n.* anordnen (*ordain*).
disposed [dis'pouzd], *adj.* geneigt; *be well — towards s.o.*, jemandem zugeneigt sein *or* wohlwollend gegenüberstehen; *well* —, (in) guter Laune.
disposition [dispə'ziʃən], *s.* (*Psych.*) die Anlage; die Gemütsart (*temperament*); die Anordnung (*sequence*); der Plan, die Anlage (*of book etc.*); die Verfügung (*arrangement*).
dispossess [dispə'zes], *v.a.* enteignen, (des Besitzes) berauben (*Genit.*).
disproof [dis'pruːf], *s.* die Widerlegung.
disproportion [disprə'pɔːʃən], *s.* das Mißverhältnis.
disproportionate [disprə'pɔːsənit], *adj.* unverhältnismäßig.
disprove [dis'pruːv], *v.a.* widerlegen.
disputable [dis'pjuːtəbl], *adj.* bestreitbar.

disputant ['dispjutənt], *s.* der Opponent, der Disputant.
disputation [dispju'teiʃən], *s.* der gelehrte Streit, die Disputation.
dispute [dis'pjuːt], *s.* der Disput, die Meinungsverschiedenheit. — *v.a.*, *v.n.* streiten, verschiedener Ansicht sein; disputieren (*debate*); mit Worten streiten (*argue*).
disqualification [diskwɔlifi'keiʃən], *s.* die Disqualifizierung.
disqualify [dis'kwɔlifai], *v.a.* disqualifizieren, ausschließen.
disquiet [dis'kwaiət], *v.a.* beunruhigen, stören. — *s.* die Unruhe, die Störung.
disquisition [diskwi'ziʃən], *s.* die (lange) Abhandlung *or* Rede.
disregard [disri'gɑːd], *v.a.* mißachten, nicht beachten. — *s.* die Außerachtlassung, die Mißachtung.
disreputable [dis'repjutəbl], *adj.* verrufen, in üblem Rufe stehend.
disrepute [disri'pjuːt], *s.* der schlechte Name, der üble Ruf.
disrespect [disris'pekt], *s.* die Geringschätzung, der Mangel an Respekt. — *v.a.* (*obs.*) mißachten, geringschätzen, respektlos behandeln.
disrespectful [disris'pektful], *adj.* respektlos, unhöflich.
disrobe [dis'roub], *v.a.* entkleiden. — *v.n.* sich entkleiden.
disrupt [dis'rapt], *v.a.* abreißen, unterbrechen, stören (*disturb*).
disruption [dis'rapʃən], *s.* die Störung, die Unterbrechung (*interruption*); der Bruch.
dissatisfaction [dissætis'fækʃən], *s.* die Unzufriedenheit.
dissatisfied [dis'sætisfaid], *adj.* unzufrieden, unbefriedigt.
dissatisfy [dis'sætisfai], *v.a.* unzufrieden lassen.
dissect [di'sekt], *v.a.* zergliedern, zerlegen; (*Anat.*) sezieren.
dissection [di'sekʃən], *s.* die Zergliederung; (*Anat.*) die Sektion.
dissemble [di'sembl], *v.a.*, *v.n.* heucheln; sich verstellen.
disseminate [di'semineit], *v.a.* verbreiten.
dissemination [disemi'neiʃən], *s.* die Verbreitung.
dissension [di'senʃən], *s.* die Uneinigkeit, der Zwist (*conflict*).
dissent [di'sent], *v.n.* anderer Meinung sein; abweichen (*from*, von, *Dat.*). — *s.* die Abweichung, die abweichende Meinung.
dissenter [di'sentə], *s.* der Dissenter, das Mitglied der Freikirche.
dissertation [disə'teiʃən], *s.* die Dissertation, die Abhandlung.
dissever [di'sevə], *v.a.* trennen (*separate*); zerteilen (*divide*).
dissidence ['disidəns], *s.* die Uneinigkeit.
dissident ['disidənt], *adj.* uneinig, anders denkend.

dissimilar [di'similə], *adj.* unähnlich, ungleichartig.

dissimilarity [disimi'læriti], *s.* die Unähnlichkeit, die Ungleichartigkeit.

dissimulate [di'simjuleit], *v.a.* verhehlen (*conceal*). — *v.n.* sich verstellen, heucheln.

dissimulation [disimju'leiʃən], *s.* die Verstellung, Heuchelei, das Vorgeben (*pretence*).

dissipate ['disipeit], *v.a.* zerstreuen (*spread*); verschwenden (*waste*).

dissipation [disi'peiʃən], *s.* die Zerstreuung, die Verschwendung; die Ausschweifung.

dissociate [di'souʃieit], *v.a.* trennen, lösen. — *v.r.* abrücken (von).

dissociation [disouʃi'eiʃən], *s.* die Trennung; die Dissoziation.

dissolubility [disɔlju'biliti], *s.* die Auflösbarkeit.

dissoluble [di'sɔljubl], *adj.* auflösbar.

dissolute ['disɔlju:t], *adj.* ausschweifend, lose, liederlich.

dissolution [disə'lju:ʃən], *s.* die Auflösung; der Tod (*death*).

dissolvable [di'zɔlvəbl], *adj.* auflösbar, löslich.

dissolve [di'zɔlv], *v.a.* auflösen; lösen. — *v.n.* sich auflösen, zergehen (*melt*).

dissonance ['disənəns], *s.* die Dissonanz, der Mißklang.

dissonant ['disənənt], *adj.* (*Mus.*) dissonant; mißhellig (*discordant*).

dissuade [di'sweid], *v.a.* abraten (*from*, von, *Dat.*).

dissuasion [di'sweiʒən], *s.* das Abraten.

dissuasive [di'sweisiv], *adj.* abratend.

distaff ['dista:f], *s.* der Spinnrocken (*spinning*); on the — side, auf der weiblichen Linie.

distance ['distəns], *s.* die Entfernung; die Ferne (*remoteness*). — *v.a.* hinter sich lassen, sich distanzieren(von,*Dat.*)

distant ['distənt], *adj.* entfernt, fern (*space*); kühl (*manner*).

distaste [dis'teist], *s.* die Abneigung (vor, *Dat.*); der Widerwille (gegen, *Acc.*).

distasteful [dis'teistful], *adj.* widerwärtig, zuwider.

distastefulness [dis'teistfulnis], *s.* die Widerwärtigkeit.

distemper (1) [dis'tempə], *s.* die Krankheit; die Staupe (*dogs*).

distemper (2) [dis'tempə]. *s.* die Wasserfarbe (*paint*). — *v.a.* mit Wasserfarbe streichen.

distend [dis'tend], *v.a.* (*Med.*) ausdehnen, strecken. — *v.n.* sich ausdehnen.

distension, distention [dis'tenʃən], *s.* das Dehnen; (*Med.*) die Ausdehnung, die Streckung.

distich ['distik], *s.* (*Poet.*) das Distichon.

distil [dis'til], *v.a.* destillieren. — *v.n.* (*Chem.*) destillieren, herauströpfeln.

distillation [disti'leiʃən], *s.* die Destillierung, (*Chem.*) der Destilliervorgang.

distiller [dis'tilə], *s.* der Branntweinbrenner.

distillery [dis'tiləri], *s.* die (Branntwein)brennerei.

distinct [dis'tiŋkt], *adj.* deutlich, klar; — from, verschieden von (*Dat.*).

distinction [dis'tiŋkʃən], *s.* der Unterschied, die Unterscheidung (*differentiation*); die Auszeichnung (*eminence*).

distinctive [dis'tiŋktiv], *adj.* unterscheidend (*differentiating*); deutlich (*clear*); leicht zu unterscheiden (*easy to distinguish*).

distinctiveness [dis'tiŋktivnis], *s.* die Deutlichkeit (*of voice etc.*); die Eigenart, Eigentümlichkeit (*peculiarity*).

distinguish [dis'tiŋgwiʃ], *v.a.* unterscheiden. — *v.r.* — o.s., sich auszeichnen.

distinguishable [dis'tiŋgwiʃəbl], *adj.* unterscheidbar.

distinguished [dis'tiŋgwiʃd], *adj.* berühmt, vornehm.

distort [dis'tɔ:t], *v.a.* verdrehen; verzerren, verrenken.

distortion [dis'tɔ:ʃən], *s.* die Verdrehung, Verzerrung; (*fig.*) die Entstellung (*of truth etc.*).

distract [dis'trækt], *v.a.* abziehen, ablenken (*divert*); stören (*disturb*).

distracted [dis'træktid], *adj.* zerstreut; verrückt (*mentally deranged*).

distraction [dis'trækʃən], *s.* die Ablenkung; die Störung (*disturbance*); to —, bis zur Raserei.

distrain [dis'trein], *v.a.* beschlagnahmen, in Beschlag nehmen.

distraint [dis'treint], *s.* die Beschlagnahme.

distress [dis'tres], *s.* die Not, die Trübsal. — *v.a.* betrüben (*sadden*); quälen (*torture*).

distribute [dis'tribju:t], *v.a.* verteilen, austeilen (*among*, unter, *Acc.*).

distribution [distri'bju:ʃən], *s.* die Verteilung; die Austeilung (*giving out*); (*Comm.*) der Vertrieb.

distributive [dis'tribjutiv], *adj.* (*Gram.*) distributiv; — trades, die Vertriebsgewerbe.

district ['distrikt], *s.* (*Geog., Pol.*) der Bezirk; die Gegend (*region*); der Kreis (*administrative*); — commissioner, der Kreisbeamte, Kreisvorsteher.

distrust [dis'trʌst], *v.a.* mißtrauen (*Dat.*). — *s.* das Mißtrauen (*of*, gegen, *Acc.*).

distrustful [dis'trʌstful], *adj.* mißtrauisch (*of*, gegen, *Acc.*).

disturb [dis'tə:b], *v.a.* stören (*trouble*); in Unordnung bringen (*disorder*).

disturbance [dis'tə:bəns], *s.* die Störung (*interruption etc.*); der Aufruhr (*riot*).

disunion [dis'ju:njən], *s.* die Entzweiung, die Zwietracht.

disunite [disju'nait], *v.a.* entzweien, Zwietracht säen zwischen. — *v.n.* sich trennen.

disuse

disuse [dis'ju:z], *v.a.* außer Gebrauch setzen. — [–'ju:s], *s.* der Nichtgebrauch (*abeyance*); die Entwöhnung (*cessation of practice*).

ditch [ditʃ], *s.* der Graben; *dull as —water*, uninteressant, langweilig. — *v.a.* mit einem Graben umgeben (*dig around*); graben.

ditto ['ditou], *adv.* desgleichen, dito.

ditty ['diti], *s.* das Liedchen.

diurnal [dai'ə:nəl], *adj.* täglich.

divan [di'væn], *s.* der Diwan.

dive [daiv], *v.n.* tauchen, springen (ins Wasser); (*Aviat.*) sturzfliegen, einen Sturzflug machen. — *s.* der Hechtsprung (ins Wasser); der Wassersprung; der Kopfsprung; (*Aviat.*) der Sturzflug.

diver ['daivə], *s.* (*Sport, Orn.*) der Taucher.

diverge [dai'və:dʒ], *v.n.* abweichen, auseinandergehen.

divergence [dai'və:dʒəns], *s.* die Abweichung, die Divergenz, Meinungsverschiedenheit.

divergent [dai'və:dʒənt], *adj.* auseinandergehend, abweichend.

divers ['daivəz], *adj. pl.* etliche, verschiedene.

diverse [dai'və:s], *adj.* verschieden, mannigfaltig.

diversify [dai'və:sifai], *v.a.* verschieden machen.

diversion [dai'və:ʃən], *s.* die Zerstreuung; (*Traffic*) die Umleitung.

diversity [dai'və:siti], *s.* die Verschiedenheit; die Ungleichheit (*disparity*).

divert [dai'və:t], *v.a.* ablenken, zerstreuen.

divest [di'vest *or* dai'-], *v.a.* entkleiden, berauben (*of office, eines Amtes*). — *v.r.* — *o.s. of,* auf etwas verzichten (*give up*).

divide [di'vaid], *v.a.* (*Maths.*) dividieren; teilen (*share*); aufteilen (*proportion*); sondern, trennen (*separate*). — *v.n.* sich teilen; (*Maths.*) sich dividieren lassen.

dividend ['dividənd], *s.* (*Comm.*) die Dividende; (*Maths.*) der Dividend.

dividers [di'vaidəz], *s.pl.* der Stechzirkel.

divination [divi'neiʃən], *s.* die Wahrsagung (*prophecy*); die Ahnung.

divine [di'vain], *v.a.* weissagen (*prophesy*); erraten (*guess*). — *adj.* göttlich; (*coll.*) herrlich. —*s.* (*obs.*) der Geistliche (*clergyman*).

divinity [di'viniti], *s.* die Göttlichkeit; die Gottheit (*deity*); die Theologie.

divisibility [divizi'biliti], *s.* (*Maths.*) die Teilbarkeit.

divisible [di'vizibl], *adj.* teilbar.

division [di'viʒən], *s.* (*Maths., Mil.*) die Division; die Teilung (*partition*); die Abteilung (*department*); (*Parl.*) die Abstimmung.

divisor [di'vaizə], *s.* (*Maths.*) der Divisor; der Teiler.

divorce [di'vɔ:s], *s.* (*Law*) die Scheidung; die Trennung (*separation*). — *v.a.* sich von einem scheiden lassen.

divulge [dai'vʌldʒ], *v.a.* ausplaudern; verraten (*betray*); verbreiten (*spread*).

dizziness ['dizinis], *s.* der Schwindel.

dizzy ['dizi], *adj.* schwindlig.

do [du:], *v.a. irr.* tun, machen; — *o.'s duty,* seine Pflicht erfüllen; — *o.'s bit,* das Seinige leisten; — *o.'s homework,* seine Aufgaben machen; — *a favour,* einen Gefallen erweisen; vollbringen (*accomplish*); — *away with,* abschaffen (*Acc.*); einpacken. — *v.n. this will —,* das genügt; *this won't —,* so geht's nicht; — *without,* ohne etwas auskommen; *how — you — ?* sehr angenehm (*on introduction to people*).

docile ['dousail], *adj.* gelehrig, lenksam, fügsam.

docility [do'siliti], *s.* die Gelehrigkeit, die Fügsamkeit.

dock (1) [dɔk], *s.* (*Bot.*) das Ampferkraut; — *leaf,* das Ampferblatt.

dock (2) [dɔk], *s.* (*Naut.*) das Dock; —*yard,* die Schiffswerft; (*Law*) die Anklagebank. — *v.a.* (*Naut.*) ein Schiff ins Dock bringen.

dock (3) [dɔk], *v.a.* stutzen (*clip*); kürzen (*wages*).

docket ['dɔkit], *s.* der Zettel (*chit*); der Lieferschein.

doctor ['dɔktə], *s.* (*Med.*) der Arzt, der Doktor. — *v.a.* operieren, kastrieren (*a cat etc.*).

doctorate ['dɔktərit], *s.* das Doktorat, die Doktorwürde.

doctrinaire [dɔktri'nɛə], *s.* der Doktrinär. — *adj.* doktrinär.

doctrinal [dɔk'trainəl], *adj.* Lehr-.

doctrine ['dɔktrin], *s.* die Lehre, die Doktrin.

document ['dɔkjumənt], *s.* das Dokument, die Urkunde.

documentary [dɔkju'mentəri], *adj.* Dokumentar- (*film*); dokumentarisch (*evidence*).

documentation [dɔkjumen'teiʃən], *s.* die Dokumentation, Heranziehung von Dokumenten.

dodge [dɔdʒ], *v.a.* ausweichen (*Dat.*). — *s.* der Kniff.

dodger ['dɔdʒə], *s.* der Schwindler.

doe [dou], *s.* (*Zool.*) das Reh.

doeskin ['douskin], *s.* das Rehleder.

doff [dɔf], *v.a.* abnehmen, ablegen (*clothes*).

dog [dɔg], *s.* der Hund; —*'s ear,* das Eselsohr (*in book*). — *v.a.* verfolgen, auf Schritt und Tritt folgen (*Dat.*) (*follow closely*).

dogfish ['dɔgfiʃ], *s.* (*Zool.*) der Dornhai.

dogged ['dɔgid], *adj.* unverdrossen, zäh.

doggedness ['dɔgidnis], *s.* die Zähigkeit.

doggerel ['dɔgərəl], *s.* der Knüttelvers.

dogma ['dɔgmə], *s.* das Dogma, der Glaubenssatz.

dogmatic [dɔg'mætik], *adj.* dogmatisch.
dogmatism ['dɔgmətizm], *s.* der Dogmatismus.
dogmatize ['dɔgmətaiz], *v.n.* dogmatisieren.
doldrums ['douldrəmz], *s. pl.* die Schwermut, die Depression; (*Naut.*) die Windstillen, *f.pl.*
dole [doul], *s.* das Almosen; die Arbeitslosenunterstützung (*unemployment benefit*); *be on the* —, stempeln gehen, Arbeitslosenunterstützung beziehen. — *v.a.* — *out*, austeilen, verteilen.
doleful ['doulful], *adj.* traurig, bekümmert.
doll [dɔl], *s.* die Puppe.
dollar ['dɔlə], *s.* der Dollar.
dolman ['dɔlmən], *s.* der Dolman.
dolorous ['dɔlərəs], *adj.* (*Lit.*) schmerzlich, schmerzhaft.
dolphin ['dɔlfin], *s.* (*Zool.*) der Delphin.
dolt [doult], *s.* der Tölpel.
doltish ['doultiʃ], *adj.* tölpelhaft.
doltishness ['doultiʃnis], *s.* die Tölpelhaftigkeit.
domain [do'mein], *s.* das Gebiet, der Bereich.
dome [doum], *s.* (*Archit.*) die Kuppel, die Wölbung; der Dom.
domed [doumd], *adj.* gewölbt.
domestic [do'mestik], *adj.* Haus-, häuslich; — *animal*, das Haustier.
domesticate [do'mestikeit], *v.a.* zähmen (*tame*), zivilisieren.
domesticity [domes'tisiti], *s.* die Häuslichkeit.
domicile ['dɔmisail], *s.* das Domizil; der Wohnort.
domiciled ['dɔmisaild], *adj.* wohnhaft (*at*, in, *Dat.*).
dominant ['dɔminənt], *adj.* vorherrschend. — *s.* (*Mus.*) die Dominante.
dominate ['dɔmineit], *v.a.* beherrschen. — *v.n.* herrschen.
domination [dɔmi'neiʃən], *s.* die Herrschaft.
domineer [dɔmi'niə], *v.n.* tyrannisieren.
domineering [dɔmi'niəriŋ], *adj.* überheblich, gebieterisch.
Dominican [do'minikən], *s.* der Dominikaner (*friar*).
dominion [do'minjən], *s.* die Herrschaft (*rule*); das Dominion (*Br. Commonwealth*).
domino ['dɔminou], *s.* (*pl.* —**noes**) der Domino (*mask*); (*pl.*) das Domino (*game*).
don (1) [dɔn], *s.* der Universitätsgelehrte, Universitätsdozent (*scholar*); Don (*Spanish nobleman*).
don (2) [dɔn], *v.a.* anziehen.
donate [do'neit], *v.a.* schenken, stiften.
donation [do'neiʃən], *s.* die Schenkung, die Stiftung; die Gabe (*gift*).
donkey ['dɔŋki], *s.* (*Zool.*) der Esel; — *engine*, die Hilfsmaschine.
donor ['dounə], *s.* der Spender, der Stifter; *blood* —, der Blutspender.

doom [du:m], *s.* die Verurteilung (*judgment*); der Untergang; das jüngste Gericht.
doomed [du:md], *adj.* verurteilt, verdammt (*to*, zu, *Dat.*).
Doomsday ['du:msdei], der jüngste Tag, der Tag des jüngsten Gerichtes.
door [dɔ:], *s.* die Tür(e); *next* —, nebenan; *out of* —*s*, draußen, im Freien; —*bell*, die Türklingel; — *latch*, die Klinke.
doorman ['dɔ:mæn], *s.* der Türsteher, der Pförtner.
dormant ['dɔ:mənt], *adj.* schlafend; unbenutzt.
dormer window ['dɔ:mə 'windou], *s.* das Dachfenster.
dormitory ['dɔ:mitri], *s.* der Schlafsaal.
dormouse ['dɔ:maus], *s.* (*Zool.*) die Haselmaus.
dose [dous], *s.* (*Med.*) die Dosis. — *v.a.* dosieren.
dot [dɔt], *s.* der Punkt, das Tüpfel. — *v.a.* punktieren; *sign on the* —*ted line*, unterschreiben; — *the i's and cross the t's*, äußerst genau sein.
dotage ['doutidʒ], *s.* die Altersschwäche, das Greisenalter.
dotard ['doutəd], *s.* der alte Dummkopf.
dote [dout], *v.n.* vernarrt sein (*on*, in, *Acc.*).
double [dʌbl], *adj.* (*Maths.*) doppelt; zweideutig (*meaning*); falsch (*false*); — *entry book-keeping*, doppelte Buchführung. — *s.* der Doppelgänger, die Doppelgängerin; *at the* —, im Sturmschritt. — *v.a.* (*Maths.*) verdoppeln; zusammenlegen (*fold in two*). — *v.n.* — *up with pain*, sich vor Schmerzen winden *or* krümmen.
doublet ['dʌblit], *s.* der Wams; — *and hose*, Wams und Hosen; der Pasch (*dice*); (*Ling.*) die Dublette, Doppelform.
doubt [daut], *s.* der Zweifel. — *v.a.* zweifeln (an, *Dat.*); bezweifeln.
doubtful ['dautful], *adj.* zweifelhaft, fraglich (*uncertain*).
doubtless ['dautlis], *adj.* zweifellos, ohne Zweifel.
douche [du:ʃ], *s.* die Dusche.
dough [dou], *s.* der Teig.
doughnut ['dounʌt], *s.* der Krapfen, Pfannkuchen.
doughy ['doui], *adj.* weich, teigig.
douse [daus], *v.a.* begießen, mit Wasser beschütten.
dove [dʌv], *s.* (*Orn.*) die Taube.
dovecote ['dʌvkɔt], *s.* der Taubenschlag.
dovetail ['dʌvteil], *v.a., v.n.* einpassen; fügen; —*ing*, die Einpassung, die Verzinkung.
dowager ['dauədʒə], *s.* die Witwe (*of noble family*, von Stande).
dowdy ['daudi], *adj.* schlampig, unordentlich, unelegant.
dower ['dauə], *s.* die Mitgift, die Ausstattung.

down

down (1) [daun], *s.* der Flaum, die Daune.

down (2) [daun], *s.* das Hügelland.

down (3) [daun], *adv.* hinunter, herunter; nieder; unter; hinab. — *prep.* herab; hinunter. — *adj. the — train,* der Zug aus London. — *v.a.* niederzwingen, hinunterstürzen.

downcast ['daunkɑːst], *adj.* niedergeschlagen.

downfall ['daunfɔːl], *s.* der Sturz.

downhill [daun'hil], *adv.* bergab. — ['daunhil], *adj.* abschüssig.

downpour ['daunpɔː], *s.* der Platzregen.

downright ['daunrait], *adj.* völlig. — *adv.* geradezu.

downward ['daunwəd], *adj.* abschüssig. — *adv. (also* downwards) *see* down.

dowry ['dauri] *see* dower.

doze [douz], *v.n.* dösen, schlummern.

dozen [dʌzn], *s.* das Dutzend.

drab [dræb], *adj.* eintönig; langweilig (*boring*).

draft [drɑːft], *s. (Comm.)* die Tratte; der Entwurf (*sketch*); (*Mil.*) das Detachement. — *v.a.* entwerfen (*sketch*); (*Mil.*) abordnen; (*Am.*) einziehen.

drag [dræg], *v.a.* schleppen. — *s. (Engin.)* die Schleppbremse, der Dregghaken; der Hemmschuh (*wedge*); —*net,* das Schleppnetz; —*wheel,* das Schlepprad.

dragoman ['drægomən], *s.* der Dolmetscher.

dragon ['drægən], *s.* der Drache.

dragonfly ['drægənflai], *s. (Ent.)* die Libelle.

dragoon [drə'guːn], *v.a.* unterdrücken. — *s. (Mil.)* der Dragoner.

drain [drein], *v.a.* entwässern, austrocknen; trockenlegen. — *v.n.* ablaufen, abfließen, auslaufen. — *s.* der Abguß, Abzug, die Gosse (*in street*); (*Engin.*) die Dränage; —*ing board,* das Ablauf- *or* Abwaschbrett; (*Phot.*) —*ing rack,* der Trockenständer; *a — on o.'s income,* eine Belastung des Einkommens.

drainage ['dreinidʒ], *s.* die Trockenlegung, die Kanalisierung.

drainpipe ['dreinpaip], *s.* das Abflußrohr; — *trousers,* die Röhrenhosen, *f. pl.*

drake [dreik], *s. (Orn.)* der Enterich.

dram [dræm], *s.* der Trunk; Schluck (*spirits*).

drama ['drɑːmə], *s.* das Drama, das Schauspiel.

dramatic [drə'mætik], *adj.* dramatisch.

dramatist ['drɑːm- *or* 'dræmətist], *s.* der Dramatiker.

dramatize ['dræmətaiz], *v.a.* dramatisieren.

drape [dreip], *v.a.* drapieren, bedecken; einhüllen (*wrap*). — *s. (Am.)* der Vorhang.

draper ['dreipə], *s.* der Stoffhändler, der Tuchhändler.

drapery ['dreipəri], *s.* — *department,* die Stoff- *or* Tuchabteilung; die Tuchhandlung (*shop*).

drastic ['drɑːstik *or* 'dræstik], *adj.* drastisch, radikal.

draught [drɑːft], *s.* der Zug (*air*); der Tiefgang (— *of ship*); der Schluck (*drink*); der Schlaftrunk (*sleeping* —); — *horse,* das Zugpferd; — *beer,* das Faßbier; —*board,* das Damespielbrett; (*pl.*) das Damespiel.

draw [drɔː], *v.a. irr.* ziehen (*pull*); zeichnen (*sketch*); anlocken (*attract*); ausschreiben (*cheque*); —*well,* der Ziehbrunnen. — *s.* das Los, die Verlosung (*lottery*); (*Sport*) das Unentschieden.

drawback ['drɔːbæk], *s.* der Nachteil, die Schattenseite.

drawbridge ['drɔːbridʒ], *s.* die Zugbrücke.

drawer ['drɔːə], *s.* die Schublade; *chest of* —*s,* die Kommode; (*pl.*) die Unterhosen, *f. pl.*

drawing ['drɔːiŋ], *s. (Art)* die Zeichnung; —*board,* das Reißbrett; —*office,* das Zeichenbüro, der Zeichensaal.

drawing room ['drɔːiŋ rum], *s.* das Wohnzimmer, der Salon.

drawl [drɔːl], *v.n.* gedehnt sprechen. — *s.* die gedehnte Sprechweise.

drawn [drɔːn], *adj.* (*Sport*) unentschieden.

dray [drei], *s.* der Rollwagen, der Karren; —*man,* der Kutscher, der Fuhrmann.

dread [dred], *s.* der Schrecken. — *adj.* schrecklich. — *v.a.* fürchten. — *v.n.* sich fürchten (vor, *Dat.*).

dreadful ['dredful], *adj.* schrecklich, furchtbar.

dreadnought ['drednɔːt], *s. (Naut.)* das große Schlachtschiff.

dream [driːm], *s.* der Traum. — *v.n. irr.* träumen; *I would not* — *of it,* es würde mir nicht im Traum einfallen, ich denke nicht daran.

dreamt [dremt] *see* dream.

dreamy ['driːmi], *adj.* verträumt, träumerisch.

dreariness ['driərinis], *s.* die Öde.

dreary ['driəri], *adj.* traurig, öde.

dredge [dredʒ], *s.* das Schleppnetz. — *v.a.* (*Engin.*) ausbaggern; (*Naut.*) dreggen.

dredger ['dredʒə], *s.* der Bagger, das Baggerschiff; (*Cul.*) die Streubüchse.

dregs [dregz], *s. pl.* der Bodensatz (*in cup etc.*); die Hefe (*yeast*).

drench [drentʃ], *v.a.* durchnässen, tränken.

Dresden ['drezdən], (*china*) das Meißner Porzellan.

dress [dres], *s.* das Kleid; die Kleidung; *evening* —, die Abendkleidung; *full* —, die Gala(kleidung); — *circle,* erster Rang; —*maker,* die Schneiderin; — *rehearsal,* die Generalprobe; — *shirt,* das Frackhemd; — *suit,* der Frackanzug. — *v.a., v.n.* (sich) anziehen.

ductile

dresser ['dresə], s. der Ankleider (*valet*); der Anrichtetisch (*table*).

dressing ['dresiŋ], s. (*Build.*) die Verkleidung; der Verband (*bandage*); der Verputz (*interior decoration*); — *gown*, der Schlafrock, Bademantel; (*Theat.*) — *room*, das Künstlerzimmer; Ankleidezimmer; — *table*, der Toilettentisch.

dressy ['dresi], adj. elegant; modesüchtig.

dribble [dribl], v.n. tröpfeln (*trickle*); geifern (*slaver*); (*Footb.*) dribbeln.

driblet ['driblit], s. die Kleinigkeit, die Lappalie.

drift [drift], s. die Richtung (*direction*); die Strömung (*stream*); das Treiben; Gestöber (*snow*). — v.a. treiben. — v.n. dahintreiben.

drill (1) [dril], v.a. drillen, bohren (*bore*); (*Mil.*) exerzieren; (*Agr.*) eine Furche ziehen; einstudieren (*coach*). — s. (*Mil.*) das Exerzieren; (*Agr.*) die Furche; der Bohrer (*tool*); — *hall*, die Übungs- or Exerzierhalle.

drill (2) [dril], s. der Drillich (*textile*).

drily ['draili], adv. trocken.

drink [driŋk], v.a., v.n. irr. trinken. — s. das Getränk, der Trank (*potion*); etwas zum Trinken (a —); *come, have a* —, trinken wir ein Glas (zusammen); *strong* —, geistiges Getränk.

drinkable ['driŋkəbl], adj. trinkbar; zum Trinken.

drinker ['driŋkə], s. der Trinker, Säufer; der Zecher; der Trunkenbold (*drunkard*).

drip [drip], v.n. tröpfeln. — s. das Tröpfeln.

dripping ['dripiŋ], s. (*Cul.*) das Bratenfett, das Schmalz.

drive [draiv], v.a. irr. treiben (*sheep etc.*); fahren (*a car*). — v.n. fahren; dahinfahren (— *along*). — s. die Ausfahrt, Fahrt (*trip*); die Einfahrt (*approach to house*).

driving ['draiviŋ], s. das Fahren; — *licence*, der Führerschein; — *school*, die Fahrschule; — *test*, die Fahrprüfung.

drivel [drivl], s. der Geifer; der Unsinn (*nonsense*). — v.n. Unsinn reden.

driver ['draivə], s. der Fahrer, der Chauffeur; (*Railw.*) Führer; (*Hunt.*) der Treiber.

drizzle [drizl], v.n. rieseln; leicht regnen. — s. das Rieseln, der feine Regen, der Sprühregen.

droll [droul], adj. drollig, possierlich.

drollery ['drouləri], s. die Possierlichkeit; die Schnurre.

dromedary ['drʌmədəri or 'drɔm-], s. (*Zool.*) das Dromedar.

drone (1) [droun], s. das Gedröhn, das Gesumme (*noise*). — v.n. dröhnen, summen (*hum loudly*).

drone (2) [droun], s. (*Ent.*) die Drohne; der Faulpelz (*lazybones*).

droop [dru:p], v.a. hängen lassen. — v.n. herabhängen; verwelken (*flowers*); ermatten (*tire*).

drop [drɔp], s. der Tropfen (*liquid*); das Fallen (*fall*). — v.a. fallen lassen; — *a brick*, eine taktlose Bemerkung machen; — *a hint*, andeuten, auf etwas hindeuten. — v.n. fallen.

droppings ['drɔpiŋz], s. pl. der Mist, Dünger (*of animals*).

dropsical ['drɔpsikəl], adj. (*Med.*) wassersüchtig.

dropsy ['drɔpsi], s. (*Med.*) die Wassersucht.

dross [drɔs], s. (*Metall.*) die Schlacke; der Unrat, das wertlose Zeug.

drought [draut], s. die Dürre, die Trockenheit.

drove [drouv], s. die Herde, die Trift (*cattle*).

drover ['drouvə], s. der Viehtreiber.

drown [draun], v.a. ertränken; überschwemmen (*flood*); übertönen (*noise*). — v.n. ertrinken.

drowse [drauz], v.n. schlummern, schläfrig sein.

drowsy ['drauzi], adj. schläfrig.

drub [drʌb], v.a. prügeln.

drudge [drʌdʒ], s. das Packtier; der Sklave, der Knecht.

drudgery ['drʌdʒəri], s. die Plackerei, die Plagerei (*hard toil*).

drug [drʌg], s. die Droge; die Medizin; das Rauschgift. — v.a. betäuben.

drugget ['drʌgit], s. der (grobe) Wollstoff.

drum [drʌm], s. die Trommel. — v.n. trommeln, austrommeln.

drunk [drʌŋk], adj. betrunken.

drunkard ['drʌŋkəd], s. der Trunkenbold.

drunkenness ['drʌŋkənnis], s. die Trunkenheit.

dry [drai], adj. trocken, dürr; ausgetrocknet, durstig (*thirsty*). — v.a. austrocknen, trocken machen, dörren. — v.n. trocken werden, trocknen.

dryad ['draiæd], s. die Baumnymphe Dryade.

dryness ['drainis], s. die Trockenheit, die Dürre.

dual ['dju:əl], adj. doppelt; Zwei-.

dub (1) [dʌb], v.a. zum Ritter schlagen; nennen (*name*).

dub (2) [dʌb], v.a. (*Films*) synchronisieren.

dubious ['dju:bjəs], adj. zweifelhaft.

ducal ['dju:kəl], adj. herzoglich.

duchess ['dʌtʃis], s. die Herzogin.

duchy ['dʌtʃi], s. das Herzogtum.

duck (1) [dʌk], s. (*Orn.*) die Ente.

duck (2) [dʌk], v.n. sich ducken, sich bücken; untertauchen (*in water*). — v.a. untertauchen, ins Wasser tauchen.

duckling ['dʌkliŋ], s. (*Orn.*) das Entchen.

duct [dʌkt], s. (*Anat.*) der Kanal; die Röhre.

ductile ['dʌktail], adj. dehnbar; fügsam.

375

dud [dʌd], *s.* (*Mil.*) der Blindgänger; der Fehlschlag.

dude [dju:d], *s.* (*Am.*) der Geck.

dudgeon [ˈdʌdʒən], *s.* der Groll, der Unwille; *in high* —, sehr aufgebracht.

due [dju:], *adj.* gebührend, fällig, schuldig (*to*, *Dat.*); angemessen, recht; *this is* — *to carelessness*, das ist auf Nachlässigkeit zurückzuführen. — *adv.* direkt, gerade. — *s.* (*pl.*) die Gebühren.

duel [ˈdju:əl], *s.* das Duell. — *v.n.* sich duellieren (mit, *Dat.*).

duet [dju:ˈet], *s.* (*Mus.*) das Duett.

duffer [ˈdʌfə], *s.* der Tölpel; (*obs.*) der Hausierer.

duffle, duffel [dʌfl], *s.* der Düffel, das Düffeltuch.

dug [dʌg], *s.* die Zitze.

dug-out [ˈdʌg-aut], *s.* der Unterstand, der Bunker.

duke [dju:k], *s.* der Herzog; *Grand Duke*, der Großherzog.

dukedom [ˈdju:kdəm], *s.* das Herzogtum.

dull [dʌl], *adj.* fade, langweilig (*boring*); träge, schwerfällig (*slow to grasp*); stumpfsinnig (*obtuse*); schal, abgeschmackt (*tasteless*); schwach (*perception*); dumpf (*thud*, *noise*); matt (*colour*); trüb, überwölkt (*weather*); flau (*trade*). — *v.a.* abstumpfen (*senses*).

dullness [ˈdʌlnis], *s.* die Stumpfheit (*senses*); die Langweile (*boredom*); die Schwerfälligkeit (*stolidity*); die Schwäche (*vision etc.*); die Stumpfsinnigkeit (*stupidity*).

dumb [dʌm], *adj.* stumm; (*sl.*) dumm; —*founded*, verblüfft; — *show*, die Pantomime; —*bell* (*Gymn.*) die Hantel.

dumbness [ˈdʌmnis], *s.* die Stummheit.

dummy [ˈdʌmi], *s.* der Strohmann (*cards*); die Kleiderpuppe (*wax figure*); der Blindgänger (*dud shell*); der Schnuller (*baby's*).

dump [dʌmp], *v.a.* kippen, abladen; —*ing ground*, der Abladeplatz. — *s.* (*Am. coll.*) das Bumslokal.

dumpling [ˈdʌmpliŋ], *s.* der Kloß, (*Austr.*) der Knödel.

dumps [dʌmps], *s. pl.* der Unmut, der Mißmut, die Depression.

dumpy [ˈdʌmpi], *adj.* untersetzt, kurz und dick.

dun (1) [dʌn], *adj.* schwarzbraun.

dun (2) [dʌn], *s.* der Gläubiger. — *v.a.* energisch mahnen.

dunce [dʌns], *s.* der Dummkopf.

dune [dju:n], *s.* die Düne.

dung [dʌŋ], *s.* der Dünger. —*v.n.* düngen.

dungeon [ˈdʌndʒən], *s.* der Kerker.

dupe [dju:p], *s.* der Betrogene. — *v.a.* betrügen.

duplicate [ˈdju:plikeit], *v.a.* verdoppeln; doppelt schreiben *or* ausfüllen (*write twice*); vervielfältigen (*stencil*). — [-kit], *s.* das Duplikat.

duplicity [dju:ˈplisiti], *s.* die Falschheit, die Doppelzüngigkeit.

durability [djuərəˈbiliti], *s.* die Dauerhaftigkeit.

durable [ˈdjuərəbl], *adj.* dauerhaft.

duration [djuəˈreiʃən], *s.* die Dauer, die Länge (*time*).

duress [djuəˈres], *s.* der Zwang; *under* —, zwangsweise.

during [ˈdjuəriŋ], *prep.* während.

dusk [dʌsk], *s.* die Dämmerung.

dusky [ˈdʌski], *adj.* dunkel, trüb; düster.

dust [dʌst], *s.* der Staub. — *v.a.* abstauben (*clean*); bestäuben (*pollinate*); bestreuen.

dustbin [ˈdʌstbin], *s.* der Mülleimer.

dusty [ˈdʌsti], *adj.* staubig; *not so* —, (*coll.*) nicht so übel.

Dutch [dʌtʃ], *adj.* holländisch; niederländisch; — *treat*, auf getrennte Kosten; *double* —, Kauderwelsch, Unsinn.

Dutchman [ˈdʌtʃmən], *s.* der Holländer, der Niederländer.

dutiful [ˈdju:tiful], *adj.* gehorsam, pflichttreu, pflichtbewußt.

duty [ˈdju:ti], *s.* die Pflicht; die Abgabe (*tax*); *customs* —, der Zoll; *be on* —, Dienst haben; (*being*) *on* —, diensthabend; *off* —, dienstfrei; —*free*, zollfrei; *in* — *bound*, von Rechts wegen, pflichtgemäß.

dwarf [dwɔ:f], *s.* der Zwerg. — *v.a.* am Wachstum hindern (*stunt*); klein erscheinen lassen (*overshadow*).

dwell [dwel], *v.n. irr.* wohnen (*be domiciled*); verweilen (*remain*).

dwelling [ˈdweliŋ], *s.* die Wohnung; —*place*, der Wohnort.

dwindle [dwindl], *v.n.* abnehmen, kleiner werden.

dye [dai], *v.a.* färben. — *s.* die Farbe; (*Chem.*) der Farbstoff.

dyeing [ˈdaiiŋ], *s.* das Färben; Färbereigewerbe.

dyer [ˈdaiə], *s.* der Färber.

dying [ˈdaiiŋ], *s.* das Sterben; *the* —, (*pl.*) die Sterbenden, *pl.* — *adj.* sterbend.

dynamic [daiˈnæmik], *adj.* dynamisch.

dynamics [daiˈnæmiks], *s. pl.* die Dynamik.

dynamite [ˈdainəmait], *s.* das Dynamit.

dynamo [ˈdainəmou], *s.* der Dynamo, die Dynamomaschine.

dynasty [ˈdinəsti], *s.* die Dynastie.

dysentery [ˈdisəntri], *s.* (*Med.*) die Ruhr.

dyspepsia [disˈpepsiə], *s.* (*Med.*) die Magenverstimmung.

dyspeptic [disˈpeptik], *adj.* mit verstimmtem Magen; schlecht aufgelegt (*grumpy*).

E

E [i:]. das E (*also Mus.*); *E flat*, Es; *E sharp*, Eis; *E minor*, E-moll.

each [i:tʃ], *adj.*, *pron.* jeder, jede, jedes;
— *other*, einander; — *one*, jeder
einzelne.

eager ['i:gə], *adj.* eifrig, begierig.

eagerness ['i:gənis], *s.* der Eifer, die
Begierde.

eagle [i:gl], *s.* (*Orn.*) der Adler; (*Am.*)
das Zehndollarstück.

ear [iə], *s.* das Ohr; —*lap*, das Ohrläppchen; —*phones*, die Kopfhörer; — -
piece, die Hörmuschel; —*drum*, das
Trommelfell; — *of corn*, die Ähre.

earl [ə:l], *s.* der Graf.

earldom ['ə:ldəm], *s.* die (englische)
Grafschaft.

early ['ə:li], *adj.* früh, frühzeitig.

earmark ['iəmɑ:k], *v.a.* kennzeichnen,
bezeichnen.

earn [ə:n], *v.a.* verdienen; erwerben.

earnest ['ə:nist], *s.* der Ernst; der
ernste Beweis, das Handgeld; (*Comm.*)
die Anzahlung; (*fig.*) der Vorgeschmack. — *adj.* ernst, ernsthaft.

earnings ['ə:niŋz], *s.* das Einkommen.

earshot ['iəʃɔt], *s.* die Hörweite.

earth [ə:θ], *s.* die Erde; der Erdboden
(*soil*); der Fuchsbau (*of fox*); *down to*
—, praktisch denkend; *move heaven
and* —, alles daransetzen; *where on* —,
wo in aller Welt.

earthen ['ə:θən], *adj.* irden, aus Erde;
—*ware*, das Steingut.

earthquake ['ə:θkweik], *s.* das Erdbeben.

earthly ['ə:θli], *adj.* irdisch.

earthworm ['ə:θwə:m], *s.* (*Zool.*) der
Regenwurm.

earthy ['ə:θi], *adj.* erdig; irdisch.

earwig ['iəwig], *s.* (*Ent.*) der Ohrwurm.

ease [i:z], *s.* die Leichtigkeit (*facility*);
die Bequemlichkeit (*comfort*); *feel at*
—, sich wie zu Hause fühlen; (*Mil.*)
stand at —*!* rührt euch! *ill at* —,
unbehaglich. — *v.a.* erleichtern,
leichter machen; lindern (*pain*). —
v.n. — *off*, (*Mil.*) sich auflockern.

easel [i:zl], *s.* das Gestell; die Staffelei.

easiness ['i:zinis], *s.* die Leichtigkeit,
die Ungezwungenheit.

east [i:st], *adj.*, *adv.* Ost-, ostwärts
(*direction*). — *s.* der Osten, der
Orient.

Easter ['i:stə]. das *or* (*n.* or *f. pl.*) die
Ostern.

eastern ['i:stən], *adj.* östlich; morgen-
genländisch, orientalisch (*oriental*).

easy ['i:zi], *adj.* leicht, frei; — *chair*, der
Lehnstuhl, Sessel; *stand* —*!* rührt
Euch! *take it* —, nimm's nicht so
ernst; es sich (*Dat.*) bequem machen
(*make o.s. comfortable*); (*Comm.*) —
terms, Zahlungserleichterungen; —
-going, gemütlich.

eat [i:t], *v.a.*, *v.n. irr.* essen, speisen
(*dine*); fressen (*of animals*); —
humble pie, sich demütigen; — *o.'s hat*,
einen Besen fressen; — *o.'s words*
seine Worte bereuen.

eatable ['i:təbl], *adj.* genießbar, eßbar.

eaves [i:vz], *s. pl.* die Dachrinne, die
Traufe.

eavesdrop ['i:vzdrɔp], *v.n.* belauschen
(*on s.o.*, *Acc.*).

eavesdropper ['i:vzdrɔpə], *s.* der
Lauscher.

ebb [eb], *s.* die Ebbe. — *v.n.* nachlassen,
abebben, abfließen.

ebonize ['ebənaiz], *v.a.* wie Ebenholz
or schwarz beizen.

ebony ['ebəni], *s.* das Ebenholz.

ebullient [i'bʌljənt], *adj.* aufwallend.

eccentric [ik'sentrik], *adj.* exzentrisch,
überspannt, wunderlich.

eccentricity [eksen'trisiti], *s.* die
Exzentrizität, die Überspanntheit.

ecclesiastic [ikli:zi'æstik], *s.* der Geistliche. — *adj.* (*also* -**ical**) geistlich,
kirchlich.

echo ['ekou], *s.* das Echo, der Widerhall.
— *v.a.*, *v.n.* widerhallen (*resound*);
wiederholen (*repeat*).

eclectic [i'klektik], *adj.* eklektisch. — *s.*
der Eklektiker.

eclecticism [i'klektisizm], *s.* (*Phil.*) der
Eklektizismus.

eclipse [i'klips], *s.* die Verfinsterung,
Finsternis (*darkness*); die Verdunk-
lung (*darkening*). — *v.a.* verdunkeln.

ecliptic [i'kliptik], *s.* die Ekliptik, die
Sonnenbahn.

economic [i:kə'nɔmik], *adj.* ökonomisch,
wirtschaftlich.

economical [i:kə'nɔmikl], *adj.* (*frugal*)
sparsam, wirtschaftlich.

economics [i:kə'nɔmiks], *s.* (*pl.*) die
Wirtschaftslehre, die Ökonomie.

economist [i'kɔnəmist], *s.* der Ökonom
der Wirtschaftsfachmann.

economize [i'kɔnəmaiz], *v.n.* sparen (*on*,
mit, *Dat.*); sparsam sein mit (*Dat.*).

economy [i'kɔnəmi], *s.* die Wirtschaft;
political —, die Nationalökonomie,
Staatswirtschaftslehre.

ecstasy ['ekstəsi], *s.* die Ekstase, die
Entzückung, die Verzückung.

ecstatic [iks'tætik], *adj.* ekstatisch,
verzückt; entzückt (*delighted*).

Ecuadorean [ekwə'dɔ:riən], *adj.* ekua-
dorianisch. — *n.* der Ekuadorianer.

ecumenical [i:kju'menikəl], *adj.* ökume-
nisch.

eddy ['edi], *s.* der Wirbel, Strudel. —
v.n. wirbeln.

edge [edʒ], *s.* die Schärfe, die Schneide
(*blade*); die Kante (*ledge*); der Rand
(*brink*); der Saum (*border*); die Ecke
(*corner*); der Schnitt (*book*); die
Schärfe (*wit*, *keenness*); *put an* — *on*,
schärfen; *be on* —, nervös sein. —
v.a. besetzen (*decorate*); umgeben;
double- —*d*, zweischneidig; *two*- —*d*,
zweischneidig, zweikantig; —*d with
lace*, mit Spitze eingefaßt. — *v.n.* sich
bewegen; — *forward*, langsam vorrücken; — *off*, sich abseits halten,
sich drücken; — *away from*, abrücken.

edgy ['edʒi], *adj.* kantig, eckig; (*fig.*)
nervös, reizbar.

edible ['edibl], *adj.* eßbar.

edict

edict ['i:dikt], s. die Verordnung.
edification [edifi'keiʃən], s. die Erbauung.
edifice ['edifis], s. der Bau, das Gebäude.
edify ['edifai], v.a. erbauen.
edit ['edit], v.a. herausgeben (book etc.).
edition [i'diʃən], s. die Ausgabe.
editor ['editə], s. der Herausgeber, der Schriftleiter; (newspaper) der Redakteur.
editorial [edi'tɔ:riəl], adj. Redaktions-. — s. der Leitartikel.
editorship ['editəʃip], s. die Redaktion; die Schriftleitung.
educate ['edjukeit], v.a. erziehen, (heran)bilden.
education [edju'keiʃən], s. die Erziehung (upbringing); die Bildung (general culture); das Bildungswesen, das Schulwesen (educational system); primary —, die Grundschulung, das Volksschulwesen; secondary —, das Mittelschulwesen, das höhere Schulwesen; university —, das Hochschulwesen (system), die Universitätsbildung (of individual); local — authority, das Schulamt, die Schulbehörde; Professor of Education, Professor der Pädagogik; further —, adult —, weitere Ausbildung, Erwachsenenbildung.
educational [edju'keiʃənəl], adj. erzieherisch (educative); Bildungs-, Unterrichts- (for education); — attainment, der Bildungsgrad, die Schulstufe (grade); — facilities, die Lehrmittel, Bildungs- or Schulungsmöglichkeiten, f. pl.
education(al)ist [edju'keiʃən(əl)ist], s. der Erzieher, der Pädagoge; der Erziehungsfachmann (theorist).
eel [i:l], s. (Zool.) der Aal.
eerie ['iəri], adj. gespenstisch, unheimlich.
efface [i'feis], v.a. auslöschen, austilgen.
effacement [i'feismənt], s. die Austilgung; self- —, die Selbstaufopferung.
effect [i'fekt], s. die Wirkung; die Folge, das Ergebnis (consequence); der Eindruck (impression); of no —, ohne jede Wirkung; carry into —, ausführen; take — from, vom . . . in Kraft treten. — v.a. bewirken (bring about).
effective [i'fektiv], adj. wirksam (having an effect); gültig (in force); dienstfähig (usable); wirklich (actual).
effectual [i'fektjuəl], adj. wirksam (effective); kräftig, energisch (strong).
effectuate [i'fektjueit], v.a. bewerkstelligen (get done); bewirken (bring about).
effeminacy [i'feminəsi], s. die Verweichlichung.
effeminate [i'feminit], adj. weichlich, verweichlicht.
effervescence [efə'vesəns], s. das Aufbrausen, Schäumen.
effervescent [efə'vesənt], adj. aufbrausend, aufschäumend.

effete [i'fi:t], adj. abgenutzt, erschöpft.
efficacious [efi'keiʃəs], adj. wirksam. energisch.
efficacy ['efikəsi], s. die Wirksamkeit, die Energie.
efficiency [i'fiʃənsi], s. die Tüchtigkeit (of person); die Wirksamkeit; die Leistung.
efficient [i'fiʃənt], adj. tüchtig; leistungsfähig; wirksam (drug etc.).
effigy ['efidʒi], s. das Bild, das Abbild.
efflorescent [eflɔ:'resənt], adj. aufblühend.
effluent ['efluənt], adj. ausfließend.
effluvium [i'flu:viəm], s. die Ausdünstung.
effort ['efət], s. die Anstrengung, die Bemühung; make an —, sich bemühen, sich anstrengen; make every —, alle Kräfte anspannen.
effrontery [i'frʌntəri], s. die Frechheit (cheek); die Unverschämtheit (impertinence).
effortless ['efətlis], adj. mühelos.
effulgence [i'fʌldʒəns], s. der Glanz, das Strahlen.
effulgent [i'fʌldʒənt], adj. schimmernd, strahlend.
effusion [i'fju:ʒən], s. die Ausgießung; der Erguß (verse etc.); der Überschwang.
effusive [i'fju:ziv], adj. überschwenglich.
egg [eg], s. das Ei; fried —, das Spiegelei; scrambled —, das Rührei; — flip, der Eierpunsch; —shell, die Eierschale. — v.a. — on, anspornen, anreizen.
eglantine ['eglantain], s. (Bot.) die wilde Rose.
egoism ['egouizm], s. der Egoismus.
ego(t)ist ['ego(t)ist], s. der Egoist.
egregious [i'gri:dʒəs], adj. ungeheuer-(lich).
egress ['i:gres], s. der Ausgang, der Ausfluß (water etc.).
Egyptian [i'dʒipʃən], adj. ägyptisch. — s. der Ägypter.
eiderdown ['aidədaun], s. die Daunendecke, Steppdecke.
eiderduck ['aidədʌk], s. (Orn.) die Eidergans.
eight [eit], num. adj. acht.
eighteen [ei'ti:n], num. adj. achtzehn.
eighty ['eiti], num. adj. achtzig.
either ['aiðə], adj., pron. einer von beiden. — conj. entweder (or, oder).
ejaculate [i'dʒækjuleit], v.a., v.n. ausstoßen.
eject [i'dʒekt], v.a. hinauswerfen; ausstoßen.
ejection [i'dʒekʃən], s. die Ausstoßung.
eke [i:k], v.a. — out, verlängern, ergänzen; — out an existence, ein spärliches Auskommen finden.
elaborate [i'læbəreit], v.a. ausarbeiten, im einzelnen ausarbeiten. — [-rit], adj. detailliert, ausgearbeitet; kunstvoll (intricate); umständlich (involved).

elaboration [ilæbə'reiʃən], s. die Ausarbeitung (im einzelnen); die Detailarbeit.

elapse [i'læps], v.n. verstreichen, verfließen (time).

elastic [i'læstik], adj. elastisch. — s. das Gummiband.

elasticity [elæs'tisiti], s. (Phys.) die Elastizität.

elate [i'leit], v.a. stolz machen; ermutigen.

elated [i'leitid], adj. in gehobener Stimmung.

elation [i'leiʃən], s. der Stolz; die Begeisterung.

elbow ['elbou], s. (Anat.) der Ellenbogen; at o.'s —, bei der Hand; — room, der Spielraum. — v.a. — o.'s way through, sich durchdrängen.

elder (1) ['eldə], comp. adj. älter. — s. der Alte, der Älteste; Kirchenälteste.

elder (2) ['eldə], s. (Bot.) der Holunder.

elderly ['eldəli], adj. älter; alt; ältlich.

elect [i'lekt], v.a. erwählen (to, zu, Dat.); auswählen (choose). — adj. erwählt, auserwählt; chairman —, der gewählte Vorsitzende.

election [i'lekʃən], s. die Auswahl (selection); (Pol.) die Wahlen, f. pl.; die Wahl (choice); by(e) —, die Bezirkswahl, die Neuwahl; — broadcast, eine Radiowahlrede.

electioneering [ilekʃən'iəriŋ], s. das Wahlmanöver, die Wahlpropaganda, der Wahlkampf.

elective [i'lektiv], adj. durch Wahl bestimmt; Wahl-.

elector [i'lektə], s. (Pol.) der Wähler; das Mitglied eines Wahlausschusses (academic etc.); der Kurfürst (prince).

electorate [i'lektərit], s. die Wählerschaft.

electress [i'lektrəs], s. die Kurfürstin (princess).

electric(al) [i'lektrik(əl)], adj. elektrisch; electrical engineer, der Elektrotechniker; der Student der Elektrotechnik (trainee); electric switch, der elektrische Schalter; — razor, der elektrische Rasierapparat.

electrician [elek'triʃən], s. der Elektriker.

electricity [ilek- or elek'trisiti], s. die Elektrizität.

electrocution [ilektro'kju:ʃən], s. die Hinrichtung or der Unfall (accidental) durch Elektrizität.

electron [i'lektrɔn], s. das Elektron.

electroplate [i'lektropleit], v.a. galvanisch versilbern.

electrotype [i'lektrotaip], s. der galvanische Abdruck, die Galvanographie.

elegance ['eligəns], s. die Eleganz.

elegant ['eligənt], adj. elegant, fein.

elegy ['elidʒi], s. (Lit.) die Elegie.

element ['elimənt], s. das Element; der Bestandteil (component).

elemental [eli'mentl], adj. elementar.

elementary [eli'mentri], adj. einfach (simple); elementar (for beginners).

elephant ['elifənt], s. (Zool.) der Elefant.

elevate ['eliveit], v.a. erheben, erhöhen.

elevation [eli'veiʃən], s. die Erhebung (lifting); (Geom.) die Elevation; die Erhöhung (rise); der Aufriß (Engin. drawing).

elevator ['eliveitə], s. (Am.) der Lift, der Aufzug, der Fahrstuhl; (Agr.) der Getreideheber.

eleven [i'levn], num. adj. elf.

elf [elf], s. der Elf, der Kobold.

elfin ['elfin], adj. Elfen-, elfenhaft.

elicit [i'lisit], v.a. herauslocken, entlocken.

eligibility [elidʒi'biliti], s. die Wählbarkeit.

eligible ['elidʒibl], adj. wählbar, passend.

eliminate [i'limineit], v.a. ausschalten, ausscheiden, eliminieren.

elimination [ilimi'neiʃən], s. die Ausschaltung, die Ausscheidung.

elision [i'liʒən], s. (Phonet.) die Auslassung, die Weglassung.

elixir [i'liksə], s. das Elixier.

elk [elk], s. (Zool.) der Elch.

ell [el], s. die Elle.

ellipse [i'lips], s. (Geom.) die Ellipse.

ellipsis [i'lipsis], s. (Gram.) die Ellipse.

elliptic(al) [i'liptik(əl)], adj. (Gram., Geom.) elliptisch.

elm [elm], s. (Bot.) die Ulme.

elocution [elə'kju:ʃən], s. der Vortrag (delivery); die Vortragskunst.

elocutionist [elə'kju:ʃənist], s. der Vortragskünstler.

elongate ['i:lɔŋgeit], v.a. verlängern.

elongation [i:lɔŋ'geiʃən], s. die Verlängerung.

elope [i'loup], v.n. entlaufen, von zu Hause fliehen.

elopement [i'loupmənt], s. das Entlaufen, die Flucht von zu Hause.

eloquence ['eləkwəns], s. die Beredsamkeit.

eloquent ['eləkwənt], adj. beredt, redegewandt.

else [els], adv. sonst, außerdem, anders; or —, sonst . . .; how — ? wie denn sonst? nobody —, sonst niemand; anyone — ? sonst noch jemand? — conj. sonst.

elsewhere [els'wɛə], adv. anderswo; anderswohin.

Elsinore ['elsinɔ:]. Helsingör, n.

elucidate [i'lju:sideit], v.a. erläutern, erklären (to s.o., Dat.).

elucidation [ilju:si'deiʃən], s. die Erläuterung, die Erklärung.

elude [i'lju:d], v.a. ausweichen, entgehen (Dat.).

elusive [i'lju:siv], adj. schwer faßbar, täuschend.

Elysian [i'liziən], adj. elysisch.

emaciate [i'meiʃieit], v.a. abmagern, dünn werden.

emaciation [imeiʃi'eiʃən], s. die Abmagerung.

emanate

emanate ['emǝneit], *v.n.* ausgehen, herrühren (*derive*); ausstrahlen (*radiate*).

emancipate [i'mænsipeit], *v.a.* befreien, emanzipieren.

emancipation [imænsi'peiʃǝn], *s.* die Emanzipation.

embalm [im'bɑːm], *v.a.* einbalsamieren.

embankment [im'bæŋkmǝnt], *s.* der Flußdamm, der Eisenbahndamm; die Eindämmung.

embarcation *see* **embarkation.**

embargo [im'bɑːgou], *s.* die Handelssperre.

embark [im'bɑːk], *v.a.* einschiffen. — *v.n.* sich einschiffen; — *upon s.th.*, an etwas herangehen, unternehmen.

embarkation [embɑː'keiʃǝn], *s.* die Einschiffung.

embarrass [im'bærǝs], *v.a.* verlegen machen, in Verlegenheit bringen.

embarrassment [im'bærǝsmǝnt], *s.* die Verlegenheit.

embassy ['embǝsi], *s.* (*Pol.*) die Botschaft, die Gesandtschaft.

embed [im'bed], *v.a.* einbetten.

embellish [im'beliʃ], *v.a.* verschönern, ausschmücken; ausmalen (*story*).

embers ['embǝz], *s. pl.* die glühende Asche; die Kohlen, *f. pl.*; *Ember Days,* (*Eccl.*) die Quatembertage, *m. pl.*

embezzle [im'bezl], *v.a.* veruntreuen, unterschlagen.

embitter [im'bitǝ], *v.a.* verbittern.

emblazon [im'bleizn], *v.a.* ausmalen, auf ein Schild setzen.

emblem ['emblǝm], *s.* das Emblem, das Abzeichen.

emblematic(al) [emblǝ'mætik(ǝl)], *adj.* sinnbildlich, symbolisch.

embodiment [im'bɔdimǝnt], *s.* die Verkörperung.

embody [im'bɔdi], *v.a.* verkörpern.

embolden [im'bouldn], *v.a.* erkühnen, anfeuern, anspornen; *be emboldened,* sich erkühnen.

emboss [im'bɔs], *v.a.* in getriebener Arbeit verfertigen, prägen.

embossed [im'bɔst], *adj.* getrieben, in erhabener Arbeit; gestanzt.

embrace [im'breis], *v.a.* (*fig.*) umarmen, umfassen. — *s.* die Umarmung.

embrasure [im'breiʒǝ], *s.* die Schießscharte.

embrocation [embro'keiʃǝn], *s.* die Einreibung (*act*); (*Pharm.*) die Einreibsalbe.

embroider [im'brɔidǝ], *v.a.* sticken; verzieren, ausschmücken (*adorn*).

embroidery [im'brɔidǝri], *s.* die Stickerei; die Verzierung, Ausschmückung (*of story etc.*).

embroil [im'brɔil], *v.a.* verwickeln.

embryo ['embriou], *s.* der Keim; Embryo.

embryonic [embri'ɔnik], *adj.* im Embryostadium, im Werden.

emend [i'mend], *v.a.* verbessern (*text*), berichtigen.

emendation [iːmen'deiʃǝn], *s.* die Textverbesserung.

emendator ['iːmendeitǝ], *s.* der Berichtiger.

emerald ['emǝrǝld], *s.* der Smaragd.

emerge [i'mǝːdʒ], *v.n.* auftauchen, hervortreten, an den Tag kommen.

emergence [i'mǝːdʒǝns], *s.* das Auftauchen, das Hervortreten.

emergency [i'mǝːdʒǝnsi], *s.* der Notfall; die kritische Lage; *in case of —,* im Notfalle; — *exit,* der Notausgang; — *landing,* die Notlandung; — *measures,* Notmaßnahmen; — *brake,* die Notbremse.

emery ['emǝri], *s.* — *paper,* das Schmirgelpapier.

emetic [i'metik], *s.* das Brechmittel.

emigrant ['emigrǝnt], *s.* der Auswanderer.

emigrate ['emigreit], *v.n.* auswandern.

emigration [emi'greiʃǝn], *s.* die Auswanderung.

eminence ['eminǝns], *s.* die Anhöhe; die Eminenz, der hohe Ruf (*fame*); die eminente Stellung, die Autorität (*authority*); *Your Eminence,* Eure Eminenz.

eminent ['eminǝnt], *adj.* eminent, hervorragend.

emissary ['emisǝri], *s.* der Abgesandte, der Sendbote.

emission [i'miʃǝn], *s.* die Aussendung (*sending out*); die Ausstrahlung (*radiation*).

emit [i'mit], *v.a.* aussenden; ausstrahlen; ausströmen.

emolument [i'mɔljumǝnt], *s.* das (Neben)einkommen, das Zusatzgehalt, das Honorar (*fee*).

emotion [i'mouʃǝn], *s.* die Rührung, die Bewegung, das Gefühl, die Gemütsbewegung.

emotional [i'mouʃǝnǝl], *adj.* gefühlvoll.

emperor ['empǝrǝ], *s.* der Kaiser.

emphasis ['emfǝsis], *s.* der Nachdruck.

emphasize ['emfǝsaiz], *v.a.* betonen.

empire ['empaiǝ], *s.* das Reich, das Kaiserreich.

empiric(al) [em'pirik(ǝl)], *adj.* (*Phil.*) empirisch.

empiricism [em'pirisizm], *s.* (*Phil.*) der Empirizismus.

employ [im'plɔi], *v.a.* benutzen (*thing*); beschäftigen, anstellen (*person*).

employee [im'plɔiiː], *s.* der Angestellte.

employer [im'plɔiǝ], *s.* der Arbeitgeber.

employment [im'plɔimǝnt], *s.* die Beschäftigung, die Arbeit.

emporium [em'pɔːriǝm], *s.* der Handelsplatz; (*Naut.*) der Stapelplatz; das Warenhaus (*stores*).

empower [em'pauǝ], *v.a.* bevollmächtigen.

empress ['empres], *s.* die Kaiserin.

emptiness ['emptinis], *s.* die Leere, die Öde.

empty ['empti], *adj.* leer; *-headed,* geistlos.

emulate ['emjuleit], *v.a.* nacheifern (*Dat.*).

emulation [emju'leiʃən], *s.* der Wetteifer, das Nacheifern.

emulous ['emjuləs], *adj.* nacheifernd, wetteifernd; eifersüchtig (*jealous*).

emulsion [i'mʌlʃən], *s.* (*Pharm.*) die Emulsion.

enable [i'neibl], *v.a.* befähigen; ermächtigen (*empower*).

enact [i'nækt], *v.a.* (*Pol.*) verordnen; verfügen (*order*); darstellen, aufführen (*on stage*).

enactment [i'næktmənt], *s.* die Verordnung.

enamel [i'næml], *v.a.* emaillieren. — *s.* die Emaille; (*Med.*) der Schmelz.

enamour [i'næmə], *v.a.* verliebt machen.

encamp [in'kæmp], *v.n.* (sich) lagern, das Lager aufschlagen.

encampment [in'kæmpmənt], *s.* das Lager.

encase [in'keis], *v.a.* einschließen, in ein Gehäuse schließen.

encashment [in'kæʃmənt], *s.* (*Comm.*) das Inkasso, die Einkassierung.

enchain [in'tʃein], *v.a.* in Ketten legen, anketten.

enchant [in'tʃɑːnt], *v.a.* bezaubern.

enchantment [in'tʃɑːntmənt], *s.* die Bezauberung; der Zauber (*spell*).

encircle [in'səːkl], *v.a.* umringen, umkreisen; (*Mil.*) einkreisen.

encirclement [in'səːklmənt], *s.* die Einkreisung.

enclose [in'klouz], *v.a.* einschließen; einlegen (*in letter*).

enclosure [in'klouʒə], *s.* die Einfriedigung; die Beilage, Einlage (*in letter*).

encompass [in'kʌmpəs], *v.a.* umfassen, umspannen (*comprise*).

encore ['ɔŋkɔː, ɔŋ'kɔː], *int.* noch einmal! — *s.* die Wiederholung, Zugabe.

encounter [in'kauntə], *v.a.* treffen; begegnen (*Dat.*). — *s.* das Zusammentreffen.

encourage [in'kʌridʒ], *v.a.* ermutigen; anspornen.

encouragement [in'kʌridʒmənt], *s.* die Ermutigung; die Förderung (*promotion*).

encroach [in'kroutʃ], *v.n.* eingreifen (*interfere*); übergreifen.

encroachment [in'kroutʃmənt], *s.* der Eingriff, der Übergriff.

encrust [in'krʌst], *v.a.* inkrustieren; verkrusten.

encumber [in'kʌmbə], *v.a.* belasten.

encumbrance [in'kʌmbrəns], *s.* die Belastung, das Hindernis.

encyclical [en'siklikl], *s.* das (päpstliche) Rundschreiben, die Enzyklika.

encylopaedia [insaiklo'piːdjə], *s.* das Lexikon, die Enzyklopädie.

encyclopaedic [insaiklo'piːdik], *adj.* enzyklopädisch.

end [end], *s.* das Ende; der Schluß; das Ziel (*aim*); die Absicht (*intention*); *in the* —, am Ende, letzten Endes; *to*

that —, zu dem Zweck; *put an* — *to*, einer Sache ein Ende machen; *make* —*s meet*, sein Auskommen finden; *burn the candle at both* —*s*, seine Kräfte verschwenden. — *v.a.* beenden. — *v.n.* enden, Schluß machen.

ending ['endiŋ], *s.* das Ende (*of play etc.*); (*Gram.*) die Endung.

endanger [in'deindʒə], *v.a.* gefährden, in Gefahr bringen.

endear [in'diə], *v.a.* beliebt machen. — *v.r.* — *o.s. to*, sich lieb Kind machen bei.

endearment [in'diəmənt], *s. term of* —, ein Kosewort.

endeavour [in'devə], *v.n.* sich bemühen, sich bestreben. — *s.* das Streben, die Bestrebung, die Bemühung.

endemic(al) [en'demik(əl)], *adj.* einheimisch; endemisch.

endive ['endiv], *s.* (*Bot.*) die Endivie.

endless ['endlis], *adj.* unendlich, endlos.

endorse [in'dɔːs], *v.a.* bestätigen (*confirm*); beipflichten; (*Fin.*) indossieren (*cheque*).

endorsement [in'dɔːsmənt], *s.* die Bestätigung (*confirmation*); (*Fin.*) das Indossament (*cheque*).

endow [en'dau], *v.a.* begaben (*talents*); ausstatten (*equip*).

endowment [en'daumənt], *s.* die Begabung (*talents*); die Stiftung; — *policy*, die abgekürzte Lebensversicherung.

endurable [in'djuərəbl], *adj.* erträglich.

endurance [in'djuərəns], *s.* die Ausdauer (*toughness*); die Dauer, Fortdauer (*time*); das Ertragen (*suffering*); — *test*, die Dauerprüfung; (*fig.*) die Geduldsprobe (*patience*).

endure [in'djuə], *v.a.* aushalten, ertragen; leiden (*suffer*).

endways, endwise ['endweiz, -waiz], *adv.* mit dem Ende nach vorne; aufrecht (*vertical*).

enemy ['enəmi], *s.* der Feind, der Gegner.

energetic [enə'dʒetik], *adj.* energisch, tatkräftig.

energy ['enədʒi], *s.* die Energie, die Tatkraft; der Nachdruck (*vehemence*).

enervate ['enəːveit], *v.a.* entkräften, schwächen.

enervation [enəː'veiʃən], *s.* die Entkräftigung, die Schwächung.

enfeeble [in'fiːbl], *v.a.* entkräften, schwächen.

enfold [in'fould], *v.a.* umschließen, umfassen; einhüllen (*veil*).

enforce [in'fɔːs], *v.a.* erzwingen, durchsetzen.

enforcement [in'fɔːsmənt], *s.* die Erzwingung, die Durchsetzung.

enfranchise [in'fræntʃaiz], *v.a.* freilassen, befreien (*emancipate*); (*Pol.*) das Stimmrecht geben.

enfranchisement [in'fræntʃizmənt], *s.* die Befreiung, die Gewährung des Stimmrechts.

engage

engage [in'geidʒ], *v.a.* verpflichten, engagieren (*pledge, bind*); anstellen (*employ*); verwickeln (*in conversation*); *become —d*, sich verloben. — *v.n.* *in*, sich einlassen in (*Acc.*), sich befassen mit (*Dat.*).

engagement [in'geidʒmənt], *s.* die Verpflichtung (*pledge*); die Verlobung (*betrothal*); die Verabredung (*appointment*); das Gefecht (*with enemy*).

engaging [in'geidʒiŋ], *adj.* freundlich, verbindlich (*smile etc.*); einnehmend.

engender [in'dʒendə], *v.a.* erzeugen, hervorrufen (*cause*).

engine ['endʒin], *s.* die Maschine; der Motor; (*Railw.*) die Lokomotive; *fire —*, die Feuerspritze; *— driver*, (*Railw.*) der Lokomotivführer.

engineer [endʒi'niə], *s.* der Ingenieur (*professional*); der Techniker (*technician*); (*Am.*) der Lokomotivführer (*engine driver*).

engineering [endʒi'niəriŋ], *s.* das Ingenieurwesen; der Maschinenbau; *chemical —*, die chemische Technik *or* Technologie; *civil —*, das Zivilingenieurwesen; *electrical —*, die Elektrotechnik *or* die Elektrotechnologie; *mechanical —*, der Maschinenbau, die Strukturtechnik; *— laboratory*, das technische Labor; *— workshop*, die technische Werkstatt.

English ['iŋgliʃ], *adj.* englisch; britisch. — *s.* die englische Sprache, das Englisch; (*pl.*) *the —*, die Engländer, *m. pl.*

Englishman ['iŋgliʃmən], *s.* der Engländer.

Englishwoman ['iŋgliʃwumən], *s.* die Engländerin.

engrain [in'grein], *v.a.* tief einprägen.

engrave [in'greiv], *v.a.* gravieren, eingravieren (*art*); einprägen (*impress*).

engraver [in'greivə], *s.* der Graveur, der Kupferstecher.

engraving [in'greiviŋ], *s.* der Kupferstich.

engross [in'grous], *v.a.* ganz in Anspruch nehmen, gefangen halten (*mind*).

engulf [in'gʌlf], *v.a.* verschlingen.

enhance [in'hɑ:ns], *v.a.* erhöhen (*raise*); steigern (*increase*).

enhancement [in'hɑ:nsmənt], *s.* die Erhöhung (*pleasure*); die Steigerung (*growth*).

enigma [i'nigmə], *s.* das Rätsel.

enigmatic(al) [enig'mætik(əl)], *adj.* rätselhaft (*puzzling*); dunkel (*obscure*).

enjoin [in'dʒɔin], *v.a.* (an)befehlen (*s.o., Dat.*), einschärfen (*s.o., Dat.*).

enjoy [in'dʒɔi], *v.a.* genießen (*Acc.*); sich freuen (über, *Acc.*). — *v.r. —o.s.,* sich amüsieren.

enjoyable [in'dʒɔiəbl], *adj.* erfreulich, angenehm, genießbar.

enjoyment [in'dʒɔimənt], *s.* der Genuß, die Freude (*of*, an, *Dat.*).

enlarge [in'lɑ:dʒ], *v.a.* vergrößern (*premises etc.*); erweitern (*expand*). —

v.n. sich verbreiten (*on* or *upon,* über, *Acc.*).

enlargement [in'lɑ:dʒmənt], *s.* die Vergrößerung (*also Phot.*).

enlighten [in'laitn], *v.a.* erleuchten, aufklären (*explain to*).

enlightenment [in'laitnmənt], *s.* (*Eccl.*) die Erleuchtung;(*Phil.*)die Aufklärung.

enlist [in'list], *v.a.* anwerben (*Mil.*); gewinnen (*cooperation*). — *v.n.* (*Mil.*) sich anwerben lassen.

enliven [in'laivn], *v.a.* beleben, aufmuntern.

enmity ['enmiti], *s.* die Feindschaft.

ennoble [i'noubl], *v.a.* adeln; veredeln.

enormity [i'nɔ:miti], *s.* die Ungeheuerlichkeit.

enormous [i'nɔ:məs], *adj.* ungeheuer; ungeheuerlich.

enough [i'nʌf], *adj., adv.* genug; ausreichend; *sure —,* gewiß!; *well —,* ziemlich gut.

enquire *see under* **inquire**.

enquiry *see under* **inquiry**.

enrage [in'reidʒ], *v.a.* wütend machen.

enraged [in'reidʒd], *adj.* wütend, entrüstet.

enrapture [in'ræptʃə], *v.a.* in Entzückung versetzen, entzücken (*delight*).

enrich [in'ritʃ], *v.a.* bereichern; (*Chem.*) verbessern.

enrol [in'roul], *v.a.* einschreiben (*inscribe*); (*Mil.*) anwerben. — *v.n.* sich einschreiben; beitreten (*Dat.*).

enrolment [in'roulmənt], *s.* die Einschreibung; *— form,* das Einschreibeformular.

ensconce [in'skɔns], *v.r. — o.s.,* sich niederlassen.

enshrine [in'ʃrain], *v.a.* umhüllen, einschließen; in einem Schrein aufbewahren.

enshroud [in'ʃraud], *v.a.* einhüllen.

ensign ['ensin *or* 'enzən, 'ensain], *s.* (*Naut.*) die Fahne, die Flagge; (*Mil. rank*) der Fähnrich.

enslave [in'sleiv], *v.a.* unterjochen, versklaven.

ensnare [in'snɛə], *v.a.* umgarnen, verführen (*seduce*).

ensue [in'sju:], *v.n.* folgen.

ensure [in'ʃuə], *v.a.* versichern (*assure*); sicherstellen (*make sure*).

entail [in'teil], *v.a.* zur Folge haben, mit sich bringen.

entangle [in'tæŋgl], *v.a.* verwickeln, verwirren (*confuse*).

entanglement [in'tæŋglmənt], *s.* die Verwicklung; die Verwirrung (*confusion*).

enter ['entə], *v.a.* betreten; eintreten; *— o.'s name,* seinen Namen einschreiben. — *v.n.* eintreten (*in,* in, *Acc.*); *— into agreement,* einen Vertrag eingehen; *— on,* sich einlassen in (*Acc.*); *— upon a career,* eine Laufbahn antreten.

enterprise ['entəpraiz], *s.* das Unternehmen; das Wagnis (*daring*); *private —,* das Privatunternehmen; (*Econ.*)

die freie Wirtschaft; *public* —, das staatliche *or* Staatsunternehmen.

enterprising ['entəpraiziŋ], *adj.* unternehmungslustig.

entertain [entə'tein], *v.a.* unterhalten (*amuse*); zu Tisch haben (*person*); hegen (*opinion*).

entertaining [entə'teiniŋ], *adj.* amüsant, unterhaltend.

entertainment [entə'teinmənt], *s.* die Unterhaltung, Vergnügung.

enthral [in'θrɔ:l], *v.a.* fesseln, bannen.

enthrone [in'θroun], *v.a.* auf den Thron bringen *or* setzen.

enthusiasm [in'θju:ziæzm], *s.* die Begeisterung; die Schwärmerei.

enthusiast [in'θju:ziæst], *s.* der Enthusiast, der Schwärmer.

enthusiastic [inθju:zi'æstik], *adj.* enthusiastisch, begeistert, schwärmerisch.

entice [in'tais], *v.a.* locken, anlocken, verlocken (*lure*).

enticement [in'taismənt], *s.* die Lockung.

entire [in'taiə], *adj.* gesamt, ganz; völlig; vollständig (*complete*).

entirety [in'taiəriti], *s.* die Gesamtheit (*totality*); das Ganze (*total*).

entitle [in'taitl], *v.a.* berechtigen; betiteln (*title*).

entitlement [in'taitlmənt], *s.* die Berechtigung.

entity ['entiti], *s.* das Wesen.

entomb [in'tu:m], *v.a.* begraben.

entomologist [entə'mɔlədʒist], *s.* der Entomologe.

entomology [entə'mɔlədʒi], *s.* die Entomologie.

entrails ['entreilz], *s. pl.* die Eingeweide, *n.pl.*

entrain [in'trein], *v.a.* (*Railw., Mil.*) einsteigen lassen. — *v.n.* (*Railw.*) (in den Zug) einsteigen.

entrance (1) [in'entrəns], *s.* der Eingang (*door*); — *fee*, der Eintritt; — *hall*, der Hausflur, die Vorhalle; *university* —, Zulassung zur Universität.

entrance (2) [in'tra:ns], *v.a.* entzücken, hinreißen.

entrant ['entrənt], *s.* (*to school, university etc.*) der (neu) Zugelassene; Teilnehmer.

entrap [in'træp], *v.a.* fangen, verstricken.

entreat [in'tri:t], *v.a.* anflehen, ersuchen.

entreaty [in'tri:ti], *s.* die flehentliche *or* dringende Bitte, (*obs.*) das Ansuchen.

entrench [in'trentʃ], *v.a.* verschanzen, festsetzen.

entrenchment [in'trentʃmənt], *s.* (*Mil.*) die Verschanzung.

entrust [in'trast], *v.a.* anvertrauen (*s. th.*); betreuen (*s.o. with,* mit, *Dat.*).

entry ['entri], *s.* das Eintreten, der Eintritt; der Eingang (*house*); (*Comm.*) die Eintragung (*book-keeping*); *double* —, doppelte Buchführung; die Einfuhr (*import*); — *permit*, die

Einreisebewilligung; *no* —, Eintritt verboten!

entwine [in'twain], *v.a.* verflechten, herumwickeln.

enumerate [i'nju:məreit], *v.a.* aufzählen.

enumeration [inju:mə'reiʃən], *s.* die Aufzählung.

enunciate [i'nʌnsieit], *v.a.* aussprechen.

enunciation [inʌnsi'eiʃən], *s.* (*Phonet.*) die Aussprache; die Kundgebung (*declaration*).

envelop [in'veləp], *v.a.* einhüllen, umhüllen.

envelope ['enviloup, 'ɔnvəloup], *s.* die Hülle; der Umschlag, Briefumschlag (*letter*).

enviable ['enviəbl], *adj.* beneidenswert.

envious ['enviəs], *adj.* neidisch (*of s.o.,* auf, *Acc.*).

environment [in'vaiərnmənt], *s.* die Umgebung; (*Geog., Zool.*) die Umwelt.

environs [in'vairənz], *s. pl.* die Umgebung, die Umgegend.

envisage [in'vizidʒ], *v.a.* sich vorstellen.

envoy ['envɔi], *s.* (*Pol.*) der Gesandte, der Bote.

envy ['envi], *s.* der Neid. — *v.a.* beneiden.

epaulette [epɔ:'let], *s.* (*Mil.*) das Achselstück, die Epaulette.

ephemeral [i'femərəl], *adj.* Eintags-, Tages-; eintägig, vergänglich (*transient*).

epic ['epik], *adj.* episch. — *s.* das Epos.

epicure ['epikjuə], *s.* der Epikureer, der Feinschmecker, der Genießer.

epidemic [epi'demik], *s.* die Epidemie.

epigram ['epigræm], *s.* das Epigramm.

epigrammatic [epigrə'mætik], *adj.* epigrammatisch, kurz; treffend (*apt*).

epilepsy ['epilepsi], *s.* (*Med.*) die Epilepsie, die Fallsucht.

epileptic [epi'leptik], *s.* (*Med.*) der Epileptiker.

epilogue ['epilɔg], *s.* der Epilog.

Epiphany [i'pifəni], *s.* (*Eccl.*) das Fest der heiligen drei Könige, Epiphanias.

episcopal [i'piskəpəl], *adj.* bischöflich.

episcopate [i'piskəpit], *s.* die Bischofswürde, das Episkopat (*collective*).

episode ['episoud], *s.* die Episode.

epistle [i'pisl], *s.* die Epistel, das Sendschreiben.

epistolary [i'pistələri], *adj.* brieflich, Brief-.

epitaph ['epita:f], *s.* die Grabschrift.

epithet ['epiθet], *s.* das Beiwort, die Benennung.

epitome [i'pitəmi], *s.* die Epitome, der Auszug; der Abriß (*summary*).

epitomize [i'pitəmaiz], *v.a.* kürzen; einen Auszug machen von (*Dat.*).

epoch ['i:pɔk], *s.* die Epoche; — *-making,* bahnbrechend.

equable ['ekwəbl], *adj.* gleich, gleichmäßig; gleichmütig (*tranquil*).

equal ['i:kwəl], *adj.* gleich, ebenbürtig (*to, Dat.*).

equality

equality [i'kwɔliti], s. die Gleichheit, Ebenbürtigkeit.
equalization [i:kwəlai'zeiʃən], s. der Ausgleich; — *of burdens*, der Lastenausgleich.
equalize ['i:kwəlaiz], *v.a.* gleichmachen. — *v.n.* (*Footb.*) ausgleichen.
equanimity [i:kwə'nimiti], s. der Gleichmut.
equate [i'kweit], *v.a.* (*Maths.*) gleichsetzen.
equation [i'kweiʃən], s. die Gleichung.
equator[i'kweitə], *s.* (*Geog.*)der Äquator.
equatorial [ekwə'tɔ:riəl], *adj.* (*Geog.*) äquatorial.
equerry ['ekwəri], s. der Stallmeister; diensttuender Kammerherr (*of King*).
equestrian [i'kwestriən], *adj.* beritten; Reit-; — *art*, die Reitkunst.
equidistant [i:kwi'distənt], *adj.* gleich weit entfernt.
equilateral [i:kwi'lætərəl], *adj.* gleichseitig.
equilibrium [i:kwi'libriəm], s. das Gleichgewicht.
equine ['i:kwain], *adj.* Pferd-, pferdeartig.
equinoctial [i:kwi'nɔkʃəl], *adj.* äquinoktial.
equinox ['i:kwinɔks], s. die Tag- und Nachtgleiche.
equip [i'kwip], *v.a.* (*Mil.*) ausrüsten; ausstatten (*furnish*).
equipment [i'kwipmənt], s. die Ausrüstung, die Ausstattung; das Zeug.
equitable ['ekwitəbl], *adj.* unparteiisch, gerecht, billig.
equity ['ekwiti], s. die Billigkeit, die Unparteilichkeit.
equivalence [i'kwivələns], s. die Gleichwertigkeit, die Gleichheit.
equivalent [i'kwivələnt], *adj.* gleichwertig. — *s.* das Äquivalent, der gleiche Wert, der Gegenwert.
equivocal [i'kwivəkəl], *adj.* zweideutig, doppelsinnig, zweifelhaft.
era ['iərə], s. die Ära, die Zeitrechnung.
eradicate [i'rædikeit], *v.a.* ausrotten, austilgen, vertilgen.
eradication [irædi'keiʃən], s. die Ausrottung, die Vertilgung.
erase [i'reiz], *v.a.* ausradieren.
eraser [i'reizə], s. der Radiergummi (*India rubber*).
erasure [i'reiʒə], s. die Ausradierung; die Auskratzung (*scratching*).
ere [ɛə], *prep.* (*obs.*) vor. — *conj.* (*obs.*) ehe, bevor.
erect [i'rekt], *adj.* aufrecht, gerade. — *v.a.* aufrichten; errichten (*build*).
erection [i'rekʃən], s. die Errichtung (*structure*); die Aufrichtung (*putting up*).
ermine ['ə:min], s. der *or* das Hermelin.
erode [i'roud], *v.a.* (*Geog., Geol.*) ausfressen.
erosion [i'rouʒən], s. die Erosion.
erotic [i'rɔtik], *adj.* erotisch.
err [ə:], *v.n.* irren.
errand ['erənd], s. der Auftrag, Gang;

der Botengang; — *boy*, der Laufbursche.
errant ['erənt], *adj.* herumstreifend; *knight* —, fahrender Ritter.
errata *see under* **erratum**.
erratic [i'rætik], *adj.* regellos, unberechenbar, ohne Verlaß.
erratum [e'reitəm, e'rɑ:təm], s. (*pl.* **errata** [e'reitə, e'rɑ:tə]) der Druckfehler.
erroneous [i'rouniəs], *adj.* irrig, irrtümlich.
error ['erə], s. der Irrtum, der Fehler.
erudite ['erudait], *adj.* gelehrt.
erudition [eru'diʃən], s. die Gelehrsamkeit.
erupt [i'rʌpt], *v.n.* ausbrechen.
eruption [i'rʌpʃən], s. der Ausbruch.
eruptive [i'rʌptiv], *adj.* Ausbruchs-, ausbrechend.
escalator ['eskəleitə], s. die Rolltreppe.
escapade [eskə'peid], s. der Streich (*prank*).
escape [is'keip], *v.a., v.n.* entkommen, entgehen, entfliehen.
escapism [is'keipizm], s. die Philosophie der Weltflucht.
escapist [is'keipist], s. der Weltflüchtling.
escarpment [is'kɑ:pmənt], s. die Böschung.
eschew [is'tʃu:], *v.a.* vermeiden.
escort [is'kɔ:t], *v.a.* geleiten; decken (*cover*). — ['eskɔ:t], *s.* (*Mil.*) die Garde, die Deckung; Begleitung (*persons*); (*Mil.*) das Geleit (*conduct*).
escutcheon [is'kʌtʃən], s. das Wappenschild.
esoteric [eso'terik], *adj.* (*Phil.*) esoterisch, geheim, dunkel.
espalier [es'pæljə], s. (*Mil.*) das Spalier.
especial [is'peʃəl], *adj.* besonder, außergewöhnlich.
espionage ['espiənɑ:ʒ *or* -nidʒ], s. die Spionage, das Spionieren.
espouse [is'pauz], *v.a.* (ver-)heiraten; (*fig.*) eintreten (für, *Acc.*).
espy [is'pai], *v.a.* ausspähen, erspähen.
essay [e'sei], *v.a.* versuchen, probieren. — ['esei], s. der Versuch; der Aufsatz, Essay (*composition*).
essayist ['eseiist], s. der Essayist.
essence ['esəns], s. (*Phil., Chem.*) die Essenz.
essential [i'senʃəl], *adj.* wesentlich; wichtig (*important*).
establish [is'tæbliʃ], *v.a.* feststellen, (*ascertain*); gründen (*found*); —*ed Church*, die englische Staatskirche.
establishment [is'tæbliʃmənt], s. die Feststellung (*ascertainment*); die Gründung (*foundation*); die Unternehmung, das Geschäft (*business*); (*Mil.*) die Aufstellung, der Bestand; (*Eccl.*) die Staatskirche.
estate [is'teit], s. (*Pol.*) der Stand; das Vermögen, das Gut; (*property*) — *duty*, die Vermögenssteuer; — *manager*, der Gutsverwalter; — *agent*, der

Grundstückmakler; *real* —, der Grundbesitz; (*pl.*) Immobilien, *pl.*

esteem [is'ti:m], *v.a.* schätzen (*value*); achten (*respect*). — *s.* die Wertschätzung, die Achtung.

estimable ['estiməbl], *adj.* schätzenswert.

estimate ['estimeit], *v.a.* schätzen (*evaluate*); berechnen (*calculate*). — ['estimit], *s.* die Schätzung, der Voranschlag.

estimation [esti'meiʃən], *s.* die Wertschätzung; die Achtung (*respect*).

Estonian [es'touniən], *adj.* estnisch, estländisch. — *s.* der Este, Estländer.

estrange [is'treindʒ], *v.a.* entfremden.

estrangement [is'treindʒmənt], *s.* die Entfremdung.

estuary ['estjuəri], *s.* die Mündung (*river*); der Meeresarm (*bay*).

etch [etʃ], *v.a.* (*Metall.*) ätzen; (*Art*) radieren.

etching ['etʃiŋ], *s.* (*Art*) die Radierung.

eternal [i'tə:nl], *adj.* ewig; immerwährend.

eternity [i'tə:niti], *s.* die Ewigkeit.

ether ['i:θə], *s.* der Äther.

ethereal [i'θiəriəl], *adj.* ätherisch, luftig.

ethical ['eθikl], *adj.* ethisch, sittlich.

ethics ['eθiks], *s. pl.* die Ethik, die Sittenlehre; *professional* —, das Berufsethos.

Ethiopian [i:θi'oupiən], *adj.* äthiopisch. — *s.* der Äthiopier.

ethnography [eθ'nɔɡrəfi], *s.* die Ethnographie, die Völkerkunde.

etymology [eti'mɔlədʒi], *s.* die Etymologie, die Wortableitung.

eucharist ['ju:kərist], *s.* (*Eccl.*) die Eucharistie; das heilige Abendmahl.

eulogize ['ju:lədʒaiz], *v.a.* loben, preisen.

euphonium [ju'founiəm], *s.* (*Mus.*) das Bombardon, Baritonhorn.

euphony ['ju:fəni], *s.* der Wohlklang.

European [juərə'piən], *adj.* europäisch. — *s.* der Europäer.

euphemism ['ju:fimizm], *s.* der Euphemismus.

euphuism ['ju:fjuizm], *s.* (*Lit.*) die gezierte Stilart.

evacuate [i'vækjueit], *v.a.* evakuieren, räumen.

evacuation [ivækju'eiʃən], *s.* die Evakuierung, die Räumung.

evade [i'veid], *v.a.* ausweichen (*Dat.*); entgehen (*escape, Dat.*).

evanescent [evæ'nesənt], *adj.* verschwindend.

evangelical [i:væn'dʒelikəl], *adj.* evangelisch.

evangelist [i'vændʒəlist], *s.* der Evangelist.

evangelize [i'vændʒəlaiz], *v.a., v.n.* das Evangelium lehren *or* predigen.

evaporate [i'væpəreit], *v.a.* verdunsten lassen, verdampfen lassen. — *v.n.* (*Chem.*) verdunsten.

evaporation [ivæpə'reiʃən], *s.* die Verdampfung, die Verdunstung.

evasion [i'veiʒən], *s.* die Flucht (*escape*) (*from*, von, *Dat.*); die Ausflucht, das Ausweichen.

evasive [i'veiziv], *adj.* ausweichend.

eve, even (1) [i:v, i:vn], *s.* (*Poet.*) der Vorabend; Abend.

even (2) [i:vn], *adj.* eben, glatt (*smooth*); gerade (*number*); quitt (*quits*); gelassen (*temper*); gleich (*equal*). — *v.a.* — *out*, gleichmachen, ebnen.

even (3) [i:vn], *adv.* gerade, selbst, sogar (*emphatic*); *not* —, nicht einmal; — *though*, obwohl.

evening ['i:vniŋ], *s.* der Abend; — *gown*, das Abendkleid; — *dress*, der Abendanzug; der Smoking (*dinner jacket*); der Frack (*tails*).

evenness ['i:vənnis], *s.* die Ebenheit (*of surface*); die Gelassenheit (*of temper*).

event [i'vent], *s.* die Begebenheit, der Vorfall (*happening*); das (große) Ereignis (*state occasion*); *at all* —*s*, auf alle Fälle; *in the* —, im Falle, daß.

eventful [i'ventful], *adj.* ereignisreich.

eventual [i'ventjuəl], *adj.* schließlich, endlich.

ever ['evə], *adv.* je; immer, stets; nur, überhaupt; *for* —, für immer; — *so*, so sehr, sehr; — *since*, seitdem.

evergreen ['evəɡri:n], *adj.* immergrün. —*'s.* (*Bot.*) der Immergrün.

everlasting [evə'la:stiŋ], *adj.* ewig; dauernd; fortwährend (*continual*).

every ['evri], *adj.* jeder, jeder einzelne (*pl.* alle); — *one*, jeder einzelne; — *now and then*, dann und wann; — *other day*, jeden zweiten Tag; — *day*, alle Tage.

everybody, everyone ['evribɔdi, 'evriwʌn], *s.* jedermann, ein jeder.

everyday ['evridei], *adj.* alltäglich.

everyone *see under* **everybody**.

everything ['evriθiŋ], *s.* alles.

everywhere ['evrihwɛə], *adv.* überall.

evict [i'vikt], *v.a.* vertreiben (*eject*); (*Law*) (gerichtlich) kündigen (*Dat.*).

eviction [i'vikʃən], *s.* die Kündigung, die Vertreibung.

evidence ['evidəns], *s.* der Beweis (*proof*); (*Law*) das Zeugnis; *documentary* —, (*Law*) das Beweisstück; (*Law*) *give* —, eine Zeugenaussage machen.

evident ['evidənt], *adj.* klar, deutlich (*obvious*); augenscheinlich (*visible*); *self-* —, selbstverständlich.

evil ['i:vil], *s.* das Übel, das Böse. — *adj.* übel, böse; — *speaking*, die üble Nachrede.

evildoer ['i:vildu:ə], *s.* der Übeltäter.

evince [i'vins], *v.a.* zeigen, dartun, an den Tag legen.

evocation [i:vo'keiʃən], *s.* die Beschwörung (*magic*); das Hervorrufen.

evocative [i'vɔkətiv], *adj.* hervorrufend, voll Erinnerungen (*of*, Genit.).

evoke [i'vouk], *v.a.* hervorrufen (*call forth*); beschwören (*conjure up*).

evolution [i:və'lju:ʃən, ev-], *s.* die Entwicklung, Evolution.

evolutionary [i:və'lju:ʃənri], *adj.* Evolutions-, Entwicklungs-.

evolve [i'vɔlv], *v.a.* entwickeln. — *v.n.* sich entwickeln.

ewe [ju:], *s.* (*Zool.*) das Mutterschaf.

ewer ['juə], *s.* die Wasserkanne.

exact [ig'zækt], *adj.* genau, gewissenhaft, exakt. — *v.a.* fordern; erpressen; eintreiben (*dept.*).

exacting [ig'zæktiŋ], *adj.* genau, anspruchsvoll.

exactitude [ig'zæktitju:d], *s.* die Genauigkeit.

exactly [ig'zæktli], *adv.* (*coll.*) ganz richtig!

exactness [ig'zæktnis], *s.* die Genauigkeit.

exaggerate [ig'zædʒəreit], *v.a.* übertreiben.

exaggeration [igzædʒə'reiʃən], *s.* die Übertreibung.

exalt [ig'zɔ:lt], *v.a.* erhöhen, erheben.

exaltation [egzɔ:l'teiʃən], *s.* die Erhöhung, die Erhebung.

exalted [ig'zɔ:ltid], *adj.* erhaben, hoch.

examination [igzæmi'neiʃən], *s.* die Prüfung; (*Med.*) die Untersuchung; (*Law*) das Verhör, das Untersuchungsverhör; die Ausfragung (*scrutiny*); — *board*, die Prüfungskommission.

examine [ig'zæmin], *v.a.* prüfen; (*Med.*) untersuchen; (*Law*) verhören; ausfragen.

examiner [ig'zæminə], *s.* der Examinator.

example [ig'zɑ:mpl], *s.* das Beispiel; *for* —, zum Beispiel; *set an* —, ein Beispiel geben.

exasperate [ig'zæspəreit], *v.a.* aufreizen; ärgern, aufbringen.

exasperation [igzæspə'reiʃən], *s.* die Entrüstung, die Erbitterung.

excavate ['ekskəveit], *v.a.* ausgraben.

excavation [ekskə'veiʃən], *s.* die Ausgrabung.

exceed [ik'si:d], *v.a.* überschreiten (*go beyond*); übertreffen (*surpass*). — *v.n.* zu weit gehen.

exceeding [ik'si:diŋ], *adj.* (*obs.*) übermäßig, übertrieben.

exceedingly [ik'si:diŋli], *adv.* außerordentlich; äußerst.

excel [ik'sel], *v.a.* übertreffen. — *v.n.* sich auszeichnen (*in*, in, *Dat.*).

excellence ['eksələns], *s.* die Vortrefflichkeit.

excellent ['eksələnt], *adj.* ausgezeichnet, hervorragend.

except [ik'sept], *v.a.* ausnehmen, ausschließen. — *conj.* außer (es sei denn) daß. — *prep.* ausgenommen, mit Ausnahme von (*Dat.*).

exception [ik'sepʃən], *s.* die Ausnahme (*exemption*); der Einwand, Einwurf (*objection*).

exceptionable [ik'sepʃənəbl], *adj.* anfechtbar (*disputable*); anstößig.

exceptional [ik'sepʃənəl], *adj.* außergewöhnlich.

exceptionally [ik'sepʃənəli], *adv.* ausnahmsweise.

excerpt [ik'sə:pt], *v.a.* ausziehen, exzerpieren. — ['eksə:pt], *s.* der Auszug, das Exzerpt.

excess [ik'ses], *s.* das Übermaß; *carry to* —, übertreiben; — *fare*, der Zuschlag; — *luggage*, das Übergewicht.

excessive [ik'sesiv], *adj.* übermäßig, allzuviel.

exchange [iks'tʃeindʒ], *s.* der Austausch; *stock* —, die Börse; *rate of* —, der Kurs; *bill of* —, der Wechsel; der Tausch (*barter*). — *v.a.* wechseln; tauschen (*barter*) (*against*, für, *Acc.*); austauschen (*messages etc.*).

exchangeable [iks'tʃeindʒəbl], *adj.* (*Comm.*) austauschbar.

exchequer [iks'tʃekə], *s.* die Staatskasse; das Finanzamt (*office*); *Chancellor of the Exchequer*, der Schatzkanzler.

excise (1) ['eksaiz], *s.* die Akzise; *customs and* —, das Zollamt, der Zoll; — *officer*, der Zollbeamte, Steuerbeamte.

excise (2) [ek'saiz], *v.a.* (her)ausschneiden.

excision [ek'siʒən], *s.* das Ausschneiden, die Entfernung.

excitable [ik'saitəbl], *adj.* erregbar, reizbar.

excitation [eksi'teiʃən], *s.* (*Phys.*, *Chem.*) die Erregung.

excitement [ik'saitmənt], *s.* die Erregung, Aufregung (*mood*).

exciting [ik'saitiŋ], *adj.* erregend, aufregend, packend (*thrilling*).

exclaim [iks'kleim], *v.a.* ausrufen.

exclamation [eksklə'meiʃən], *s.* der Ausruf (*interjection*); das Geschrei (*shouting*).

exclude [iks'klu:d], *v.a.* ausschließen.

exclusion [iks'klu:ʒən], *s.* der Ausschluß.

exclusive [iks'klu:siv], *adj.* ausschließlich (*sole*); exklusiv (*select*).

exclusiveness [iks'klu:sivnis], *s.* der exklusive Charakter, die Exklusivität.

excommunicate [ekskə'mju:nikeit], *v.a.* (*Eccl.*) von der Kirchengemeinde ausschließen, bannen, exkommunizieren.

excommunication [ekskəmju:ni'keiʃən], *s.* (*Eccl.*) die Exkommunikation, der Bann.

excoriate [eks'kɔ:rieit], *v.a.* häuten; abschälen (*peel*).

excrement ['ekskrimənt], *s.* das Exkrement, der Kot.

excrescence [iks'kresəns], *s.* der Auswuchs.

excretion [eks'kri:ʃən], *s.* die Ausscheidung, der Auswurf.

excruciate [iks'kru:ʃieit], *v.a.* martern, peinigen; *excruciatingly funny*, furchtbar komisch.

exculpate ['ekskʌlpeit], *v.a.* rechtfertigen, entschuldigen.

exculpation [ekskʌl'peiʃən], *s.* die Entschuldigung, die Rechtfertigung.

excursion [iks'kə:ʃən], *s.* der Ausflug, die Exkursion (*outing*); die Digression (*irrelevance*); der Abstecher (*deviation*).

excusable [iks'kju:zəbl], *adj.* entschuldbar, verzeihlich.

excuse [iks'kju:s], *s.* die Entschuldigung. — [-'kju:z], *v.a.* entschuldigen (*Acc.*), verzeihen (*Dat.*).

execrable ['eksikrəbl], *adj.* abscheulich.

execrate ['eksikreit], *v.a.* verfluchen, verwünschen.

execute ['eksikju:t], *v.a.* ausführen (*carry out*); (*Law*) hinrichten (*kill*).

execution [eksi'kju:ʃən], *s.* die Ausführung (*of an order*); (*Law*) die Hinrichtung; die Pfändung (*official forfeit*).

executioner [eksi'kju:ʃənə], *s.* der Henker, der Scharfrichter.

executive [ik'sekjutiv], *adj.* ausübend, vollziehend (*of power etc.*). — *s.* (*Pol.*) die Exekutive; (*Comm.*) das Direktionsmitglied.

executor [ik'sekjutə], *s.* der Testamentsvollstrecker (*of a will*).

exemplar [ig'zemplə], *s.* das Muster, das Beispiel.

exemplary [ig'zempləri], *adj.* musterhaft, vorbildlich.

exemplify [ig'zemplifai], *v.a.* durch Beispiel(e) erläutern.

exempt [ig'zempt], *v.a.* ausnehmen, befreien, verschonen (*spare*).

exemption [ig'zempʃən], *s.* die Ausnahme.

exequies ['eksikwiz], *s. pl.* das Leichenbegängnis, die Totenfeier.

exercise ['eksəsaiz], *s.* die Übung (*practice*); die körperliche Betätigung (*exertion*). — *v.a.* üben; — *o.'s rights*, von seinen Rechten Gebrauch machen; — *discretion*, Diskretion walten lassen; (*Mil.*) — *troops*, exerzieren.

exert [ig'zə:t], *v.a.* ausüben; — *pressure*, Druck ausüben (*upon*, auf, *Acc.*). — *v.r.* — *o.s.*, sich anstrengen.

exertion [ig'zə:ʃən], *s.* die Anstrengung, die Bemühung.

exhale [eks'heil], *v.a.* ausatmen; aushauchen; ausdünsten.

exhalation [ekshə'leiʃən], *s.* die Ausatmung, die Ausdünstung.

exhaust [ig'zə:st], *v.a.* erschöpfen. — *s.* (*Motor.*) der Auspuff.

exhaustible [ig'zə:stibl], *adj.* erschöpflich.

exhaustion [ig'zə:stʃən], *s.* die Erschöpfung.

exhibit [ig'zibit], *v.a.* ausstellen (*display*); zeigen (*demonstrate*). — ['eksibit], *s.* das Ausstellungsobjekt; (*Law*) das Beweisstück.

exhibition [eksi'biʃən], *s.* die Ausstellung (*display*); (*Films*) die Vorführung (*showing*); das Stipendium (*scholarship*).

exhibitioner [eksi'biʃənə], *s.* der Stipendiat.

exhilarate [ig'ziləreit], *v.a.* aufheitern.

exhilaration [igzilə'reiʃən], *s.* die Aufheiterung.

exhort [ig'zə:t], *v.a.* ermahnen.

exhortation [egzə:'teiʃən], *s.* die Ermahnung.

exigence, exigency ['eksidʒəns, -si], *s.* das Bedürfnis, Erfordernis (*necessity*); der dringende Notfall (*emergency*).

exigent ['eksidʒənt], *adj.* dringend.

exile ['eksail], *s.* der Verbannte (*person*); das Exil, die Verbannung (*state*). — *v.a.* verbannen; des Landes verweisen.

exist [ig'zist], *v.n.* existieren.

existence [ig'zistəns], *s.* das Dasein, die Existenz.

existent [ig'zistənt], *adj.* seiend, wirklich, existierend.

existentialism [egzis'tenʃəlizm], *s.* der Existentialismus.

exit ['eksit], *s.* der Ausgang; (*Theat.*) der Abgang.

exonerate [ig'zɔnəreit], *v.a.* entlasten.

exorbitant [ig'zɔ:bitənt], *adj.* übertrieben, übermäßig.

exorcise ['eksɔ:saiz], *v.a.* bannen, beschwören.

exorcism ['eksɔ:sizm], *s.* die Geisterbeschwörung.

exotic [ig'zɔtik], *adj.* exotisch.

expand [iks'pænd], *v.a.* erweitern, ausbreiten, ausdehnen. — *v.n.* sich erweitern (*broaden*); sich ausdehnen (*stretch*).

expansion [iks'pænʃən], *s.* die Ausdehnung, die Ausbreitung.

expansive [iks'pænsiv], *adj.* ausgedehnt; Ausdehnungs- (*forces*); (*fig.*) mitteilsam.

expatiate [iks'peiʃieit], *v.n.* sich verbreiten (*on*, über, *Acc.*).

expatriate [eks'peitrieit], *v.a.* verbannen.

expect [iks'pekt], *v.a.* erwarten (*wait for*); glauben (*believe*); hoffen (*hope for*); — *a baby*, ein Kind erwarten.

expectant [iks'pektənt], *adj.* schwanger (*with child*); voll Erwartung.

expectation [ekspek'teiʃən], *s.* die Erwartung, die Hoffnung.

expedience, expediency [iks'pi:diəns, -si], *s.* die Zweckmäßigkeit, die Schicklichkeit.

expedient [iks'pi:diənt], *adj.* zweckmäßig, schicklich, ratsam. — *s.* das Mittel; der Ausweg.

expedite ['ekspidait], *v.a.* beschleunigen.

expedition [ekspi'diʃən], *s.* (*Mil. etc.*) die Expedition; die schnelle Abfertigung.

expeditious [ekspi'diʃəs], *adj.* schleunig, schnell.

expel [iks'pel], *v.a.* vertreiben, austreiben; (*Sch.*) verweisen (*from*, von, aus).

expend [iks'pend], *v.a.* ausgeben.

expenditure [iks'penditʃə], *s.* (*Comm.*) die Ausgabe; der Aufwand (*of energy*).

expense

expense [iks'pens], s. die Ausgabe; (pl.)
die Kosten, Auslagen, Spesen, f. pl.
expensive [iks'pensiv], adj. teuer,
kostspielig.
experience [iks'piəriəns], s. die Erfahrung, das Erlebnis. — v.a. erfahren.
experienced [iks'piəriənsd], adj. erfahren.
experiment [iks'perimənt], s. das
Experiment, der Versuch. — v.n.
experimentieren, Versuche machen.
experimental [iksperi'mentl], adj.
Probe-, probeweise, experimentell.
expert ['ekspə:t], s. der Fachmann; der
Sachverständige.
expertise [ekspə'ti:z], s. die Expertise,
die Fachkenntnis.
expertness [iks'pə:tnis], s. die Gewandtheit.
expiable ['ekspiəbl], adj. sühnbar.
expiation [ekspi'eiʃən], s. die Sühnung,
die Sühne.
expiration [ekspi'reiʃən], s. das Ausatmen; (fig.) der Tod; der Ablauf
(time); die Verfallszeit (lapse of
validity).
expire [iks'paiə], v.n. aushauchen
(breathe); ablaufen (run out); sterben
(die).
expiry [iks'pairi], s. die Ablaufsfrist
(of papers).
explain [iks'plein], v.a. erklären, erläutern.
explanation [eksplə'neiʃən], s. die
Erklärung, Erläuterung.
expletive [iks'pli:tiv], s. das Fluchwort,
der Kraftausdruck.
explicable ['eksplikəbl], adj. erklärlich,
erklärbar.
explication [ekspli'keiʃən], s. die
Erklärung.
explicit [iks'plisit], adj. ausdrücklich,
deutlich.
explicitness [iks'plisitnis], s. die
Deutlichkeit, die Bestimmtheit.
explode [iks'ploud], v.n. explodieren;
(Mil.) platzen (of a shell). — v.a. explodieren lassen.
exploit [iks'plɔit], v.a. ausbeuten;
ausnützen (utilize). — ['eksplɔit], s.
die Heldentat, die Großtat.
exploitation [eksplɔi'teiʃən], s. die
Ausbeutung, die Ausnützung.
exploration [eksplɔ:'reiʃən], s. die
Erforschung.
explore [iks'plɔ:], v.a. erforschen,
untersuchen (investigate).
explosion [iks'plouʒən], s. die Explosion.
explosive [iks'plousiv], adj. explosiv.
— s. der Sprengstoff.
exponent [iks'pounənt], s. (Maths.) der
Exponent; der Vertreter (of a theory).
export [eks'pɔ:t], v.a. ausführen,
exportieren. — ['ekspɔ:t], s. der
Export, die Ausfuhr.
exporter [eks'pɔ:tə], s. der Exporteur,
der Ausfuhrhändler, der Export-
kaufmann.

expose [iks'pouz], v.a. entblößen;
aussetzen (to cold etc.); bloßstellen
(display); (Phot.) belichten; darlegen
(set forth); ausstellen (exhibit).
exposition [ekspo'ziʃən], s. die Aussetzung; die Auslegung (interpretation); die Darlegung (deposition, declaration); die Ausstellung (exhibition).
exposure [iks'pouʒə], s. die Aussetzung
(to cold etc.); die Bloßstellung; (Phot.)
die Belichtung.
expostulate [iks'pɔstjuleit], v.n. zur
Rede stellen.
expound [iks'paund], v.a. auslegen,
darlegen.
express [iks'pres], v.a. ausdrücken;
zum Ausdruck bringen. — adj. ausdrücklich, eilig, Eil-; besonder; —
letter, der Eilbrief; — train, der
Schnellzug. — s. der Eilzug.
expression [iks'preʃən], s. der Ausdruck.
expressive [iks'presiv], adj. ausdrucks-
voll.
expressly [iks'presli], adv. ausdrücklich, besonders.
expropriate [eks'prouprieit], v.a. enteignen.
expropriation [eksproupri'eiʃən], s.
die Enteignung.
expulsion [iks'pʌlʃən], s. die Ausstoßung; der Ausschluß; die Vertreibung
(of a large number).
expunge [iks'pʌndʒ], v.a. austilgen,
auslöschen.
expurgate ['ekspə:geit], v.a. reinigen.
exquisite ['ekskwizit], adj. auserlesen,
vortrefflich.
extant ['ekstənt, ek'stænt], adj. noch
vorhanden, existierend.
extempore [eks'tempəri], adv. aus dem
Stegreif, extemporiert.
extemporize [eks'tempəraiz], v.a. ex-
temporieren, improvisieren.
extend [iks'tend], v.a. ausdehnen
(boundaries etc.); ausstrecken (a
helping hand); verlängern (time);
bieten (a welcome); erweitern (enlarge).
— v.n. sich erstrecken, sich ausdehnen; dauern (time).
extensible [iks'tensibl], adj. ausdehn-
bar.
extension [iks'tenʃən], s. die Ausdehnung; die Verlängerung (time);
university — classes, Abendkurse, m.pl.
(der Erwachsenenbildung); (Telephone)
der Apparat.
extensive [iks'tensiv], adj. ausgedehnt,
umfassend.
extent [iks'tent], s. die Ausdehnung,
die Weite; die Größe (size); to a
certain —, bis zu einem gewissen
Grade; to the — of £x, bis zu einem
Betrage von x Pfund.
extenuate [iks'tenjueit], v.a. beschönigen; mildern; extenuating circumstances, (Law) mildernde Umstände, m. pl.
extenuation [ikstenju'eiʃən], s. die
Beschönigung, die Abschwächung.

factor

exterior [eks'tiəriə], *adj.* äußerlich. — *s.* das Äußere.

exterminate [iks'tə:mineit], *v.a.* ausrotten, vertilgen.

extermination [ikstə:mi'neiʃən], *s.* die Ausrottung, die Vertilgung.

external [eks'tə:nl], *adj.* äußerlich; auswärtig.

extinct [iks'tiŋkt], *adj.* ausgestorben.

extinction [iks'tiŋkʃən], *s.* das Erlöschen (*dying*); die Vernichtung (*annihilation*); das Aussterben.

extinguish [iks'tiŋgwiʃ], *v.a.* auslöschen; vernichten (*annihilate*). — *v.n.* auslöschen, ausgehen (*of fire or life*).

extirpate ['ekstə:peit], *v.a.* ausrotten.

extol [iks'toul], *v.a.* preisen, erheben.

extort [iks'tɔ:t], *v.a.* erpressen.

extortion [iks'tɔ:ʃən], *s.* die Erpressung.

extortionate [iks'tɔ:ʃənit], *adj.* erpresserisch.

extra ['ekstrə], *adj.* zusätzlich. — *s.* (*pl.*) die Nebenausgaben, *f. pl.*

extract [iks'trækt], *v.a.* (aus)ziehen (*pull out*). — ['ekstrækt], *s.* (*Chem.*) der Extrakt; der Auszug (*book*).

extraction [iks'trækʃən], *s.* das Ausziehen (*pulling out*); das Zahnziehen (*tooth*); das Verfertigen eines Auszuges (*book*); die Herkunft (*origin*).

extradite ['ekstrədait], *v.a.* (*Pol.*) ausliefern.

extradition [ekstrə'diʃən], *s.* (*Pol.*) die Auslieferung.

extraneous [eks'treiniəs], *adj.* nicht zur Sache gehörig, unwesentlich.

extraordinary [iks'trɔ:dnəri], *adj.* außerordentlich.

extravagance [iks'trævəgəns], *s.* die Extravaganz; die Verschwendung (*waste*).

extravagant [iks'trævəgənt], *adj.* extravagant; verschwenderisch.

extravaganza [ikstrævə'gænzə], *s.* fantastisches Werk, die Burleske, Posse.

extreme [iks'tri:m], *adj.* äußerst (*uttermost*); höchst (*highest*); extrem (*stringent*); letzt (*last*); — *unction*, (*Eccl.*) die Letzte Ölung; *in the* —, äußerst.

extremity [iks'tremiti], *s.* die äußerste Grenze (*limit*); die Notlage (*straits, emergency*); (*pl.*) die Extremitäten, *f. pl.*

extricate ['ekstrikeit], *v.a.* herauswinden, herauswickeln (*disentangle*), befreien.

extrude [eks'tru:d], *v.a.* ausstoßen, (*Metall.*) ausziehen.

extrusion [eks'tru:ʒən], *s.* die Ausstoßung; die Ausziehung (*of steel etc.*).

exuberant [ig'zju:bərənt], *adj.* überschwenglich, überschäumend.

exude [ik'sju:d], *v.a.* ausschwitzen; von sich geben (*give out*).

exult [ig'zʌlt], *v.n.* frohlocken.

exultant [ig'zʌltənt], *adj.* triumphierend.

exultation [egzʌl'teiʃən], *s.* das Frohlocken, der Jubel.

eye [ai], *v.a.* anschen, betrachten. — *s.* das Auge; — *of a needle*, das Nadelöhr; *an* — *for an* —, Aug' um Auge; — *witness*, der Augenzeuge.

eyeball ['aibɔ:l], *s.* der Augapfel.

eyebrow ['aibrau], *s.* die Augenbraue.

eyeglass ['aigla:s], *s.* der Zwicker, Klemmer.

eyelash ['ailæʃ], *s.* die Augenwimper.

eyelid ['ailid], *s.* das Augenlid.

eyesight ['aisait], *s.* die Sehkraft, das Augenlicht.

eyrie ['ɛəri, 'iəri], *s.* der Adlerhorst.

F

F [ef].das F (*also Mus.*).

fable [feibl], *s.* die Fabel; das Märchen.

fabric ['fæbrik], *s.* das Gewebe, der Stoff.

fabricate ['fæbrikeit], *v.a.* herstellen; (*fig.*) fabrizieren; erfinden.

fabrication [fæbri'keiʃən], *s.* (*fig.*) die Erdichtung, die Erfindung.

fabulous ['fæbjuləs], *adj.* fabelhaft; wunderbar.

façade [fə'sa:d], *s.* die Fassade.

face [feis], *v.a.* jemandem ins Gesicht sehen (*s.o.*); gegenüberstehen, gegenüberliegen (*lie opposite, Dat.*); — *west*, nach Westen gehen (*of house, window*). — *v.n.* — *about*, sich umdrehen. — *s.* das Gesicht, (*Poet.*) das Angesicht; — *to* — *with*, gegenüber (*Dat.*); *on the* — *of it*, auf den ersten Blick; *lose* —, sich blamieren; *have the* — *to*, die Frechheit haben etwas zu tun.

facet ['fæsit], *s.* die Facette; der Zug (*feature*).

facetious [fə'si:ʃəs], *adj.* scherzhaft.

facetiousness [fə'si:ʃəsnis], *s.* die Scherzhaftigkeit, die Witzigkeit.

facile ['fæsail], *adj.* leicht.

facilitate [fə'siliteit], *v.a.* erleichtern, leicht machen.

facility [fə'siliti], *s.* die Leichtigkeit (*ease*); die Gewandtheit (*deftness*); die Möglichkeit (*possibility*); (*pl.*) die Einrichtungen, die Möglichkeiten, *f. pl.* (*amenities*).

facing ['feisiŋ], *s.* (*Tail.*) der Besatz, der Aufschlag; (*Build.*) die Verkleidung; (*Mil.*) die Schwenkung, die Wendung.

facsimile [fæk'simili], *s.* das Faksimile.

fact [fækt], *s.* die Tatsache; *as a matter of* —, tatsächlich, in Wirklichkeit; —*s and figures*, der Bericht mit Tatsachen und Zahlen; *in* —, tatsächlich; *in point of* —, in der Tat, in Wirklichkeit.

faction ['fækʃən], *s.* (*Pol.*) die Partei, die Faktion.

factitious [fæk'tiʃəs], *adj.* nachgemacht, künstlich.

factor ['fæktə], *s.* der Faktor; (*Comm.*) der Agent; der Umstand (*fact*).

factory

factory ['fæktəri], s. die Fabrik; — *hand*, der Fabrikarbeiter.
factual ['fæktjuəl], *adj.* Tatsachen-, tatsächlich.
faculty ['fækəlti], *s.* (*Univ.*) der Fakultät; die Fähigkeit (*sense*); (*pl.*) die Talente, *n. pl.*, die Begabung; Kräfte *f. pl.*
fad [fæd], *s.* die Grille, die Laune; die Marotte.
faddy ['fædi], *adj.* schrullig.
fade [feid], *v.n.* verschießen (*colour*); verwelken (*flower*); vergehen.
fag [fæg], *v.a.* ermüden. — *v.n.* (*Sch.*) Dienste tun, Diener sein (*for*, für). — *s.* die Plackerei; (*coll.*) die Zigarette; (*Sch.*) der Fuchs, der neue Schüler; — *end*, der Zigarettenstummel; (*Naut.*) das offene Tauende; der letzte Rest (*remnant*).
faggot ['fægət], *s.* das Reisigbündel.
fail [feil], *v.a.* im Stiche lassen (*let down*); (*Sch.*) durchfallen (*an examination*, in einer Prüfung. — *v.n.* — *to do*, etwas nicht tun, fehlgehen, scheitern; versagen.
failing ['feiliŋ], *adj.* schwach, versagend. — *s.* der Mangel, Fehler.
failure ['feiljə], *s.* der Fehlschlag; das Versagen (*weakness*); das Nichteinhalten (*non-compliance*); das Durchfallen (*in examinations*); der Versager (*person*).
fain [fein], *adv.* (*obs.*) gern, gerne.
faint [feint], *v.n.* in Ohnmacht fallen, ohnmächtig werden. — *adj.* leise, schwach (*noise etc.*); — *hearted*, kleinmütig.
fair (1) [fɛə], *adj.* hübsch, schön (*beautiful*); unparteiisch, fair (*impartial*); anständig, angemessen (*equitable*); blond.
fair (2) [fɛə], *s.* der Jahrmarkt (*market*); (*Comm.*) die Messe, die Handelsmesse.
fairness ['fɛənis], *s.* die Schönheit (*beauty*); die Unparteilichkeit, Fairneß (*objectivity*); die Sportlichkeit (*sportsmanship*); die Anständigkeit (*equity*).
fairy ['fɛəri], *s.* die Fee.
faith [feiθ], *s.* der Glaube; die Treue (*loyalty*); das Vertrauen (*trust*).
faithful ['feiθful], *adj.* (*Rel.*) gläubig; treu (*loyal*); ergeben (*devoted*).
faithless ['feiθlis], *adj.* (*Rel.*) ungläubig; treulos, untreu (*disloyal*).
fake [feik], *s.* der Schwindel.
falcon ['fɔ:(l)kən], *s.* (*Orn.*) der Falke.
falconer ['fɔ:(l)knə], *s.* der Falkner.
falconry ['fɔ:(l)kənri], *s.* die Falknerei.
fall [fɔ:l], *v.n.* *irr.* fallen, abfallen (*leaves*); einbrechen (*night*); sich legen (*wind*); heruntergehen, sinken (*price*); geboren werden (*pigs, lambs*); — *through*, mißlingen, zunichte werden. — *s.* der Fall; (*Am.*) der Herbst (*autumn*); der Abhang (*precipice*); der Verfall(*decay*);der Untergang(*decline*).
fallacious [fə'leifəs], *adj.* trügerisch, trüglich, falsch (*assumption etc.*).

fallacy ['fæləsi], *s.* die Täuschung, der Irrtum, Trugschluß.
fallible ['fælibl], *adj.* fehlbar.
falling ['fɔ:liŋ], *s.* das Fallen; — *sickness*, die Fallsucht; — *off*, das Abnehmen (*decrease*); — *out*, der Zwist, der Streit (*disunity*). — *adj.* — *star*, die Sternschnuppe.
fallow ['fælou], *adj.* brach, fahl.
false [fɔ:ls], *adj.* falsch, unrichtig (*untrue*); — *alarm*, der blinde Alarm; — *bottom*, der Doppelboden; — *start*, der Fehlstart; — *step*, der Fehltritt; — *verdict*, das Fehlurteil; — *pretences*, die Vorspiegelung falscher Tatsachen.
falsehood ['fɔ:lshud], *s.* die Lüge, die Unwahrheit.
falseness ['fɔ:lsnis], *s.* die Falschheit; die Unaufrichtigkeit (*insincerity*).
falsify ['fɔ:lsifai], *v.a.* fälschen, verfälschen.
falsity ['fɔ:lsiti] *see* **falseness**.
falter ['fɔ:ltə], *v.n.* straucheln (*stumble*); stammeln (*stammer*).
fame [feim], *s.* der Ruhm; der Ruf; *ill* —, der üble Ruf.
familiar [fə'miljə], *adj.* vertraut, wohlbekannt, intim; gewohnt (*habitual*); *be on*—*terms*, auf vertrautem Fuß stehen.
familiarity [fəmili'æriti], *s.*die Vertrautheit, die Vertraulichkeit (*intimacy*).
familiarize [fə'miljəraiz], *v.a.* vertraut machen, bekannt machen.
family ['fæmili], *s.* die Familie; — *doctor*, der Hausarzt; (*Chem.*) die Gruppe; *be in the* — *way*, in anderen Umständen sein, guter Hoffnung sein, schwanger sein; — *tree*, der Stammbaum.
famine ['fæmin], *s.* die Hungersnot; — *relief*, Hilfe für die Hungernden.
famish ['fæmiʃ], *v.n.* verhungern, hungern; verschmachten.
famous ['feiməs], *adj.* berühmt, wohlbekannt (*for*, wegen).
fan [fæn], *s.* der Fächer (*lady's*); der Ventilator; (*sl.*) der leidenschaftliche Anhänger, der Fan; (*coll.*) Fanatiker (*admirer*). — *v.a.* fächeln; anfachen (*flames*); entfachen (*hatred*). — *v.n.* (*Mil.*) — *out*, sich ausbreiten, ausschwärmen.
fanatic [fə'nætik], *s.* der Fanatiker.
fanatical [fə'nætikəl], *adj.* fanatisch.
fanaticism [fə'nætisizm], *s.* der Fanatismus, die Schwärmerei.
fancier ['fænsiə], *s. pigeon* —, der Taubenzüchter; *bird* —, der Vogelzüchter.
fanciful ['fænsiful], *adj.* schwärmerisch, wunderlich.
fancy ['fænsi], *s.* die Vorliebe (*preference*); die Phantasie; die Laune (*whim*); *take a* — *to*, liebgewinnen. — *adj.* — *dress*, der Maskenanzug, das Kostüm; — *goods*, Galanteriewaren; — *cakes*, Torten, *f.pl.*; das Feingebäck. — *v.a.* denken, gern haben; (*coll.*) — *oneself as*, sich einbilden, man sei; *just*—*!* denk doch mal; denk mal an!

favourable

fanfare ['fænfɛə], s. (Mus.) die Fanfare, der Tusch.
fang [fæŋ], s. (Zool.) der Hauzahn, der Giftzahn (of snake); (Engin.) der Zapfen. — v.a. (Engin.) vollpumpen, aufpumpen und in Tätigkeit setzen.
fanlight ['fænlait], s. die Lünette, das Lichtfenster.
fantastic(al) [fæn'tæstik(əl)], adj. fantastisch.
fantasy ['fæntəsi], s. (Poet., Mus.) die Phantasie; das Hirngespinst (chimæra).
far [fɑː], adj. weit; fern, entfernt (distant). — adv. — and wide, weit und breit; by —, bei weitem; go too —, zu weit gehen; he will go —, er wird seinen Weg machen; — sighted, weitsichtig.
farce [fɑːs], s. die Farce, die Posse.
fare [fɛə], s. das Fahrgeld; der Fahrpreis (of taxi etc.); der Fahrgast (one travelling in taxi); — stage, die Fahror Teilstrecke; das Essen, die Kost (food); bill of —, die Speisekarte. — v.n. ergehen (Dat.), daran sein.
farewell [fɛə'wel], interj. lebewohl! — dinner, das Abschiedsessen; — party, die Abschiedsgesellschaft.
farinaceous [færi'neiʃəs], adj. mehlig, aus Mehl.
farm [fɑːm], s. der Pachthof, der Bauernhof; die Farm; — hand, der Landarbeiter, der Farmarbeiter; — bailiff, der Gutsverwalter. — v.a. bebauen; — out, verpachten. — v.n. Landwirt sein.
farmer ['fɑːmə], s. der Bauer, Landwirt; der Pächter (tenant).
farmland ['fɑːmlænd], s. das Ackerland.
farmyard ['fɑːmjɑːd], s. der Bauernhof, Gutshof.
farrier ['færiə], s. der Hufschmid.
farrow ['færou], s. der Wurf (pigs). — v.n. ferkeln, Junge haben.
farther ['fɑːðə], comp. adj., adv. ferner, weiter.
farthest ['fɑːðist], superl. adj., adv. fernst, weitest.
farthing ['fɑːðiŋ], s. der Farthing, der Heller.
fascinate ['fæsineit], v.a. bezaubern, faszinieren.
fascination [fæsi'neiʃən], s. die Bezauberung; der Reiz, der Zauberbann (spell).
fascism ['fæʃizm], s. (Pol.) der Faschismus.
fashion ['fæʃən], s. die Mode; out of —, außer Mode; die Art und Weise (manner). — v.a. gestalten, bilden (shape); fully —ed, vollgeformt or geformt, angepaßt.
fashionable ['fæʃnəbl], adj. modisch, modern; elegant.
fast (1) [fɑːst], adj. schnell (runner); fest (firm); my watch is —, meine Uhr geht vor; a — woman, eine leichtlebige Frau; — train, der Schnellzug; — and furious, schnell wie der Wind. — adv. fest.

fast (2) [fɑːst], v.n. (Rel.) fasten; (Rel.) — day, der Fasttag.
fasten [fɑːsn], v.a. festbinden, festmachen (fix). — v.n. sich festhalten (on to, an, Dat.).
fastidious [fæs'tidiəs], adj. wählerisch, anspruchsvoll.
fastidiousness [fəs'tidiəsnis], s. die anspruchsvolle Art.
fat [fæt], adj. fett; dick (person). — s. das Fett; (Cul.) das Speisefett.
fatal ['feitəl], adj. tödlich (lethal); verhängnisvoll.
fatalism ['feitəlizm], s. der Fatalismus.
fatality [fə'tæliti], s. das Verhängnis; der Todesfall; der tödliche Unfall.
fate [feit], s. das Schicksal, Geschick; das Verhängnis (doom, destiny).
fated ['feitid], adj. dem Verderben (Untergang) geweiht.
fateful ['feitful], adj. verhängnisvoll, unselig.
father ['fɑːðə], s. der Vater; (Eccl.) Pater; — -in-law, der Schwiegervater. — v.a. Vater sein or werden von (Dat.); zeugen (procreate).
fatherland ['fɑːðəlænd], s. das Vaterland.
fatherly ['fɑːðəli], adj. väterlich; wie ein Vater.
fathom ['fæðəm], s. die Klafter. — v.a. ergründen, erforschen.
fatigue [fə'tiːg], s. die Ermüdung, die Erschöpfung; (Mil.) der Arbeitsdienst. — v.a. ermüden, erschöpfen.
fatling ['fætliŋ], s. (Agr.) das Mastvieh.
fatness ['fætnis], s. die Beleibtheit (person); die Fettheit (animals).
fatten [fætn], v.a. — up, mästen (animals); fett werden lassen. — v.n. fett werden, sich mästen (an, Dat.).
fatty ['fæti], adj. (Chem.) fett, fettig. — s. (coll.) der Dickwanst.
fatuity [fə'tjuːiti], s. die Albernheit, die Dummheit.
fatuous ['fætjuəs], adj. albern, dumm, nichtssagend.
faucet ['fɔːsit], s. der Zapfen, der Hahn.
fault [fɔːlt], s. der Fehler; die Schuld; find — with, etwas kritisieren; tadeln; it is my —, es ist meine Schuld; at —, im Irrtum.
faultless ['fɔːltlis], adj. fehlerlos, fehlerfrei.
faultlessness ['fɔːltlisnis], s. die Fehlerlosigkeit, die fehlerlose Ausführung.
faulty ['fɔːlti], adj. fehlerhaft, mangelhaft.
faun [fɔːn], s. (Myth.) der Faun.
fauna ['fɔːnə], s. die Fauna, die Tierwelt.
favour ['feivə], s. die Gunst, das Wohlwollen; (Comm.) in — of, zugunsten; do a —, einen Gefallen tun or erweisen; be in —, sehr begehrt sein, in hoher Gunst stehen. — v.a. bevorzugen, begünstigen, wohlwollend gegenüberstehen (Dat.).
favourable ['feivərəbl], adj. günstig, vorteilhaft.

391

favourite ['feivərit], s. der Favorit, der Liebling; der Günstling (of kings). — adj. Lieblings-, bevorzugt.

fawn (1) [fɔ:n], s. (Zool.) das junge Reh, das Rehkalb; — coloured, rehfarben. — adj. rehfarben, hellbraun.

fawn (2) [fɔ:n], v.n. schmeicheln, kriecherisch sein ((up)on, Dat.).

fawning ['fɔ:niŋ], adj. kriecherisch, kriechend.

fear [fiə], s. die Furcht, die Angst; stand in — of s.o., sich vor jemandem fürchten; for — of, aus Angst vor (Dat.). — v.a. fürchten, befürchten.

fearful ['fiəful], adj. furchtsam (full of fear); furchtbar (causing fear).

fearless ['fiəlis], adj. furchtlos (of, vor, Dat.).

fearlessness ['fiəlisnis], s. die Furchtlosigkeit.

feasibility [fi:zi'biliti], s. die Tunlichkeit, die Möglichkeit.

feasible ['fi:zibl], adj. tunlich, möglich.

feast [fi:st], s. das Fest, der Festtag; der Schmaus (good meal). — v.n. schmausen (upon, von, Dat.). — v.a. festlich bewirten.

feat [fi:t], s. die Tat, die Heldentat; das Kunststück.

feather ['feðə], s. die Feder; show the white —, Feigheit an den Tag legen; — bed, das Federbett. — v.a. federn; — o.'s nest, sein Schäfchen ins Trockene bringen.

feature ['fi:tʃə], s. der Zug (characteristic); der Gesichtszug (facial). — v.a. charakterisieren; (Film) in der Hauptrolle zeigen.

February ['februəri], der Februar.

feckless ['feklis], adj. hilflos, unfähig.

feculence ['fekjuləns], s. (Chem.) der Bodensatz, der Hefesatz.

fecund ['fekənd], adj. fruchtbar.

fecundate ['fekəndeit], v.a. fruchtbar machen, befruchten.

fecundity [fi'kʌnditi], s. die Fruchtbarkeit.

federacy ['fedərəsi], s. der Bund, die Föderation.

federal ['fedərəl], adj. Bundes-, föderativ.

federalism ['fedərəlizm], s. der Föderalismus.

federalize ['fedərəlaiz], v.a. verbünden.

federation [fedə'reiʃən], s. die Föderation, die Verbündung (Pol.) der Bund.

fee [fi:], s. die Gebühr (official dues); das Honorar (of doctor etc.); (pl.) (Sch.) das Schulgeld.

feeble ['fi:bl], adj. schwach, matt; — minded, schwachsinnig.

feed [fi:d], v.a. irr. füttern; verköstigen (humans); unterhalten (maintain); zuführen (into machine, Dat.); be fed up with, etwas satt haben; — pipe, die Speiseröhre. — v.n. sich nähren (on, von, Dat.); weiden (graze).

feeder ['fi:də], s. der Kinderlatz (bib); (Tech.) der Zubringer.

feel [fi:l], v.n. irr. sich fühlen (sense); meinen (think). — v.a. berühren, betasten (touch); empfinden (be aware of).

feeler ['fi:lə], s. der Fühler; put out a —, die Fühler ausstrecken.

feeling ['fi:liŋ], s. das Gefühl; with —, bewegt, gerührt (moved); grimmig (in anger).

feign [fein], v.a. vortäuschen, heucheln.

feint [feint], s. die Verstellung (disguise); die Finte (fencing).

felicitate [fi'lisiteit], v.a. Glück wünschen (upon, zu, Dat.), beglückwünschen (Acc.).

felicitation [filisi'teiʃən], s. die Beglückwünschung, der Glückwunsch.

felicitous [fi'lisitəs], adj. glücklich ausgedrückt, gut gesagt (in speaking).

felicity [fi'lisiti], s. die Glückseligkeit; die glückliche Ausdruckweise (style).

feline ['fi:lain], adj. Katzen-, katzenartig.

fell (1) [fel], adj. grausam; at one — swoop, mit einem wilden Schwung.

fell (2) [fel], v.a. fällen (timber); töten (kill).

fell (3) [fel], s. das Gebirge, das Felsengelände.

fell (4) [fel], s. das Fell, die Haut (skin).

fellow ['felou], s. der Gefährte, Genosse (companion); das Mitglied eines College or einer Universität; (coll.) der Kerl; queer —, seltsamer Kauz; — feeling, das Mitgefühl; — traveller, der Weggenosse; (Pol.) der Mitläufer.

fellowship ['felouʃip], s. die Mitgliedschaft (einer Hochschule etc.) (membership); die Freundschaft (friendship); good —, die Geselligkeit.

felly, felloe ['feli, 'felou], s. die Radfelge.

felon ['felən], s. der Verbrecher.

felonious [fi'louniəs], adj. verbrecherisch.

felt [felt], s. der Filz.

female ['fi:meil], adj. weiblich. — s. (Zool.) das Weibchen.

feminine ['feminin], adj. weiblich. — s. (Gram.) das weibliche Geschlecht; das Weibliche.

fen [fen], s. das Moor, das Marschland.

fence [fens], s. der Zaun, das Staket. — v.a. umzäunen, einzäunen (enclose). — v.n. fechten (fight with rapiers).

fencing ['fensiŋ], s. die Einzäunung (fence); das Fechten (with rapiers); — master, der Fechtmeister.

fend [fend], v.a. — off, abwehren, parieren. — v.n. — for oneself, sich allein behelfen.

fennel [fenl], s. (Bot.) der Fenchel.

ferment [fə:'ment], v.a. zur Gärung bringen. — v.n. gären, fermentieren. — ['fə:ment], s. das Gärmittel (also fig.); (Chem.) das Gärungsprodukt.

fermentation [fə:men'teiʃən], s. die Gärung.

fern [fə:n], s. (Bot.) das Farnkraut.

ferocious [fə'rouʃəs], adj. wild, grimmig.

ferocity [fəˈrɔsiti], *s.* die Wildheit.
ferret [ˈferit], *s.* (*Zool.*) das Frett, das Frettchen. — *v.a.* — *out*, ausspüren.
ferry [ˈferi], *s.* die Fähre. — *v.a.* — *across*, hinüberrudern, hinüberfahren, übersetzen.
fertile [ˈfəːtail], *adj.* fruchtbar.
fertility [fəˈtiliti], *s.* die Fruchtbarkeit.
fertilize [ˈfəːtilaiz], *v.a.* befruchten.
fertilizer [ˈfəːtilaizə], *s.* das Düngemittel, der Dünger.
fervent [ˈfəːvənt], *adj.* inbrünstig (*prayer*); heiß (*wish*).
fervid [ˈfəːvid], *adj.* glühend, heiß (*with zeal*).
fervour [ˈfəːvə], *s.* die Inbrunst (*prayer*); die Sehnsucht (*wish*).
fester [ˈfestə], *v.n.* schwären, eitern.
festival [ˈfestivəl], *s.* das Fest, die Festspiele, *n. pl.*
festive [ˈfestiv], *adj.* festlich, Fest-.
festivity [fesˈtiviti], *s.* die Festlichkeit.
festoon [fesˈtuːn], *s.* die Girlande. — *v.a.* behängen, mit Girlanden verzieren, schmücken.
fetch [fetʃ], *v.a.* holen, bringen.
fetching [ˈfetʃiŋ], *adj.* einnehmend.
fetter [ˈfetə], *v.a.* fesseln, binden. — *s.* (*pl.*) die Fesseln, *f. pl.*
feud [fjuːd], *s.* die Fehde.
feudal [ˈfjuːdl], *adj.* feudal, Lehns-.
fever [ˈfiːvə], *s.* das Fieber.
few [fjuː], *adj.* einige; wenige; *a* —, ein paar.
fiancé [fiˈɔːnsei], *s.* der Verlobte, Bräutigam.
fiancée [fiˈɔːnsei], *s.* die Verlobte, Braut.
fib [fib], *s.* (*coll.*) die Lüge. — *v.n.* (*coll.*) lügen.
fibre [ˈfaibə], *s.* die Fiber, Faser.
fibrous [ˈfaibrəs], *adj.* faserartig.
fickle [fikl], *adj.* unbeständig, wankelmütig.
fiction [ˈfikʃən], *s.* die Erdichtung (*figment*); (*Lit.*) die Romanliteratur.
fictitious [fikˈtiʃəs], *adj.* erdichtet, in der Phantasie.
fiddle [fidl], *s.* (*coll.*) die Geige, Fiedel, Violine. — *v.n.* (*coll., Mus.*) geigen; schwindeln (*cheat*).
fiddlesticks! [ˈfidlstiks], *int.* Unsinn!
fidelity [fiˈdeliti], *s.* die Treue (*loyalty*); Genauigkeit; (*Engin.*) high —, Präzision, High Fidelity.
fidget [ˈfidʒit], *v.n.* unruhig sein.
fidgety [ˈfidʒiti], *adj.* nervös.
fie! [fai], *int.* pfui!
field [fiːld], *s.* das Feld; (*fig.*) das Gebiet; — *glass*, der Feldstecher; (*Hunt.*) — *sports*, die Feldübungen, der Jagdsport. — *v.a., v.n.* abfangen, abpassen (*cricket*).
fiend [fiːnd], *s.* der Unhold, böse Geist; *fresh air* —, ein Freund der frischen Luft.
fiendish [ˈfiːndiʃ], *adj.* teuflisch, boshaft.
fierce [fiəs], *adj.* wild, wütend (*beast*); — *weather*, — *cold*, die grimmige Kälte, der grimmige Winter.

fiery [ˈfaiəri], *adj.* feurig; hitzig.
fife [faif], *s.* (*Mus.*) die Querpfeife.
fifteen [fifˈtiːn], *num. adj.* fünfzehn.
fifth [fifθ], *num. adj.* der fünfte.
fifty [ˈfifti], *num. adj.* fünfzig.
fig [fig], *s.* (*Bot.*) die Feige.
fight [fait], *v.a., v.n. irr.* kämpfen, bekämpfen (*in battle*); raufen (*of boys*). — *s.* der Kampf; die Rauferei.
figment [ˈfigmənt], *s.* die Erdichtung.
figurative [ˈfigjuərətiv], *adj.* bildlich (*style*).
figure [ˈfigə], *s.* die Figur (*body*); die Gestalt, Form (*shape*); (*Maths.*) die Zahl, die Ziffer; *cut a* —, einen Eindruck machen; *a fine* — *of a man!* ein fabelhafter Kerl! — *v.a.* — *out*, ausdenken, ausrechnen. — *v.n.* eine Rolle spielen, rangieren.
figured [ˈfigəd], *adj.* figuriert.
figurehead [ˈfigəhed], *s.* der scheinbare Leiter, die Repräsentationsfigur.
filament [ˈfiləmənt], *s.* der Faden, der Glühfaden (*bulb*).
filbert [ˈfilbəːt], *s.* (*Bot.*) die Haselnuß.
filch [filtʃ], *v.a.* stehlen, klauen.
file [fail], *s.* (*Engin.*) die Feile; (*Mil.*) die Reihe; (*Comm.*) der Aktenstoß, das Aktenbündel, der Ordner; (*pl.*) die Akten, *f. pl.*; *single* —, im Gänsemarsch; *rank and* —, die große Masse; *on the* —, in den Akten. — *v.a.* feilen (*metal*); zu den Akten legen (*papers*); einreichen (*petition*).
filial [ˈfiliəl], *adj.* kindlich.
filibuster [ˈfilibʌstə], *s.* der Freibeuter; (*Am.*) (*Pol.*) die Obstruktion.
filigree [ˈfiligriː], *s.* die Filigranarbeit.
filing [ˈfailiŋ], *s.* (*pl.*) die Feilspäne; das Einheften (*of papers*); — *cabinet*, die Kartei.
fill [fil], *v.a.* füllen; ausfüllen (*place, job*); plombieren (*tooth*); — *up*, tanken (*with petrol*). — *s.* das volle Maß; *eat o.'s* —, sich satt essen.
fillet [ˈfilit], *s.* das Filet (*meat*); das Band, die Binde (*band*).
filling [ˈfiliŋ], *s.* die Plombe (*in tooth*); — *station*, die Tankstelle.
filly [ˈfili], *s.* das Füllen.
film [film], *s.* der Film (*cinema, Phot.*); die Haut, das Häutchen (*skin*); der Belag (*coating*). — *v.a.* aufnehmen, verfilmen, filmen (*photograph*).
filter [ˈfiltə], *v.a.* filtrieren, filtern. — *v.n.* durchfiltern. — *s.* das Filter.
filth [filθ], *s.* der Schmutz.
filthy [ˈfilθi], *adj.* schmutzig.
filtration [filˈtreiʃən], *s.* das Filtrieren, das Durchsickern.
fin [fin], *s.* (*Zool.*) die Finne, die Flosse.
final [fainl], *adj.* letzt, endlich; endgültig. — *s.* (*Sport*) die Endrunde, das Endspiel.
finale [fiˈnɑːli], *s.* (*Mus.*) das Finale.
finality [faiˈnæliti], *s.* die Endgültigkeit.
finance [fiˈnæns *or* ˈfai-], *s.* die Finanz, das Finanzwesen. — *v.a.* finanzieren.

393

financial

financial [fi'nænʃəl], *adj.* finanziell, Geld-, Finanz-.

finch [fintʃ], *s.* (*Orn.*) der Fink.

find [faind], *v.a. irr.* finden; — *fault with*, jemanden kritisieren; *all found*, volle Verpflegung (inbegriffen). — *s.* der Fund.

finding ['faindiŋ], *s.* das Finden, der Befund; (*Law*) der Wahrspruch.

fine (1) [fain], *adj.* fein (*delicate*); dünn (*thin*); schön (*beautiful*); scharf (*distinct*); großartig(*splendid*).

fine (2) [fain], *v.a.* zu einer Geldstrafe verurteilen. — *s.* die Geldstrafe.

finery ['fainəri], *s.* der Putz; (*Engin.*) der Frischofen.

finger ['fiŋgə], *s.* der Finger; *have a — in the pie*, die Hand im Spiel haben. — *v.a.* berühren, antasten.

finish ['finiʃ], *v.a.* beenden, fertig machen, vollenden; —*ing touch*, die lezte Hand. — *v.n.* aufhören, enden. — *s.* das Ende (*end*); der letzte Schliff; die Appretur, die Fertigung.

finite ['fainait],*adj.* endlich.

Finn [fin], *s.* der Finne.

Finnish ['finiʃ], *adj.* finnisch.

fir [fə:], *s.* (*Bot.*) die Föhre, die Tanne; — *cone*, der Tannenzapfen.

fire [faiə], *s.* das Feuer; — *brigade*, die Feuerwehr; — *damp*, (*Min.*) schlagende Wetter, *n.pl.*; — *engine*, die Feuerspritze; — *extinguisher*, der Löschapparat, Feuerlöscher; — *escape*, die Rettungsleiter. — *v.a.* brennen (*clay*); anzünden, in Gang setzen (*furnace*); ansporen (*enthuse*); (*coll.*) entlassen (*dismiss*). — *v.n.* feuern (*at*, auf, *Acc.*).

firebrand ['faiəbrænd], *s.* der Aufwiegler.

fireman ['faiəmən], *s.* der Heizer.

fireplace ['faiəpleis], *s.* der Kamin.

fireproof ['faiəpru:f], *adj.* feuerfest.

fireside ['faiəsaid], *s.* der (häusliche) Herd, der Kamin.

firewood ['faiəwud], *s.* das Brennholz.

firework ['faiəwə:k], *s.* (*usually pl.*) das Feuerwerk.

firm [fə:m], *adj.* fest, hart (*solid*); entschlossen (*decided*). — *s.* die Firma.

firmament ['fə:məmənt], *s.* das Firmament, Himmelsgewölbe; der Sternenhimmel.

firmness ['fə:mnis], *s.* die Festigkeit, Entschlossenheit.

first [fə:st], *num. adj., adv.* erst; zuerst; — *of all*, zuallererst; — *born*, erstgeboren; — *rate*, erstklassig. — *s. from the* —, von Anfang an.

fiscal ['fiskəl], *adj.* fiskalisch, von der Staatskasse, Finanz-.

fish [fiʃ], *s.* der Fisch; *like a — out of water*, nicht in seinem Element; *a queer* —, ein seltsamer Kauz; —*bone*, die Gräte. — *v.n.* fischen; — *for compliments*, nach Lob haschen, nach Komplimenten fischen.

fisherman ['fiʃəmən], *s.* der Fischer.

fishery ['fiʃəri], *s.* der Fischfang.

fishing ['fiʃiŋ], *s.* das Fischen, der Fischfang; — *fly*, die Angelfliege; — *line*, die Angelschnur; — *rod*, die Angelrute; — *tackle*, das Angelgerät.

fishy ['fiʃi], *adj.* (*coll.*) anrüchig, verdächtig.

fissile ['fisail], *adj.* (*Phys.*) spaltbar.

fission ['fiʃ(ə)n], *s.* (*Phys.*) die Spaltung.

fist [fist], *s.* die Faust; *hand over* —, im Überfluß; *tight* —*ed*, geizig.

fisticuffs ['fistikʌfs], *s.* die Schlägerei, das Raufen.

fistula ['fistjulə], *s.* (*Anat.*) die Fistel.

fit (1) [fit], *v.a.* passen, anpassen (*Dat.*); einfügen (— *into s.th.*); — *in*, hineinpassen; — *on a suit*, einen Anzug anprobieren (*Dat.*); — *for a career*, zu einer Laufbahn vorbereiten; — *out*, ausrüsten. — *v.n.* passen, sich fügen (— *into*); — *in*, passen (*in*, zu, *Dat.*). — *adj.* geeignet, fähig (*suitable*); — *to drop*, todmüde; gesund, stark (*healthy*); schicklich (*proper*); (*Sport*) in guter Form.

fit (2) [fit], *s.* der Anfall; *by* —*s and starts*, ruckweise.

fitful ['fitful], *adj.* launenhaft; unbeständig.

fitness ['fitnis], *s.* die Tauglichkeit (*health*); die Schicklichkeit (*propriety*); die Fähigkeit (*ability*); (*Sport*) die gute Form.

fitter ['fitə], *s.* der Monteur.

fitting, fitment ['fitiŋ, 'fitmənt], *s.* die Armatur; die Montage. — *adj.* passend (*suitable*); geeignet (*appropriate*).

five [faiv], *num. adj.* fünf.

fiver ['faivə], *s.* (*coll.*) die Fünfpfundnote.

fix [fiks], *v.a.* festmachen, befestigen (*make firm*); festsetzen (*a time*); (*Am.*) herrichten, anrichten (*a meal*); — *with a glare or stare*, mit den Augen fixieren, scharf ansehen; — *up* (*coll.*), etwas erledigen (*something*); bedienen (*serve s.o.*). — *s.* (*coll.*) die Klemme, die Schwierigkeit, das Dilemma.

fixture ['fikstʃə], *s.* (*Sport*) die Veranstaltung; das Inventarstück (*furniture*).

fizz [fiz], *v.n.* brausen (*drink*).

fizzle [fizl], *v.n.* zischen (*flame*); — *out*, verebben, ausgehen, zunichte werden; (*Am., coll.*) durchfallen (*fail in school*).

fizzy ['fizi], *adj.* mit Kohlensäure, sprudelnd.

flabbergast ['flæbəga:st], *v.a.* (*coll.*) verblüffen.

flabby ['flæbi], *adj.* schlaff.

flaccid ['flæksid], *adj.* schlapp, schlaff.

flag (1) [flæg], *s.* (*Mil.*) die Flagge; die Fahne; — *officer*, der Flaggoffizier; —*staff*, die Fahnenstange.

flag (2) [flæg], *v.n.* ermatten, erschlaffen.

flag (3) [flæg], *s.* (—*stone*) der Fliesstein, die Fliese. — *v.a.* mit Fliesen auslegen, mit Fliessteinen pflastern.

flop

flagon ['flægən], *s.* die Doppelflasche.
flagrant ['fleigrənt], *adj.* entsetzlich (*shocking*); schamlos (*impudent*).
flail [fleil], *s.* der Dreschflegel.
flair [flɛə], *s.* der Instinkt; (*coll.*) die Nase (*for*, für, *Acc.*).
flake [fleik], *s.* die Flocke. — *v.n.* — *off*, abblättern.
flame [fleim], *s.* die Flamme; (*coll.*) old —, die (alte) Liebe, Geliebte(r), die Flamme. — *v.n.* flammen, lodern.
flamingo [flə'miŋgou], *s.* (*Orn.*) der Flamingo.
flange [flændʒ], *s.* (*Engin.*) der Flan(t)sch.
flank [flæŋk], *s.* die Flanke, die Seite; die Weiche (*of animal*). — *v.a.* flankieren.
flannel [flænl], *s.* der Flanell.
flap [flæp], *s.* die Klappe; das Ohrläppchen (*earlobe*); der Flügelschlag (— *of wings*).
flare [flɛə], *v.n.* flammen, flackern; — *up*, aufbrausen (*in temper*). — *s.* das Aufflammen, das Aufflackern; die Leuchtkugel.
flash [flæʃ], *s.* der Blitz (*of lightning*); das Aufflammen; (*Phot.*) —*light*, das Blitzlicht. — *v.a.* aufflammen lassen, aufblitzen lassen. — *v.n.* aufflammen, aufblitzen.
flashy ['flæʃi], *adj.* großtuend, angeberisch (*bragging*); buntfarbig (*gaudy*).
flask [flɑːsk], *s.* die kleine Flasche, das Fläschchen.
flat [flæt], *adj.* flach, eben; abgestanden, schal (*drink*); — *footed*, plattfüßig; (*Mus.*) zu tief, vermindert; platt; albern (*conversation*); — *tyre*, die Panne. — *adv.* — *out*, ausgepumpt, erschöpft. — *s.* die Mietwohnung, Wohnung (*lodgings*); (*Mus.*) das B; (*pl.*) das Flachland, (*Theat.*) (*pl.*) die Bühnenbilder.
flatness ['flætnis], *s.* die Flachheit, die Plattheit (*of conversation etc.*).
flatten [flætn], *v.a.* flach machen; glätten (*smooth*).
flatter ['flætə], *v.a.* schmeicheln (*Dat.*).
flattery ['flætəri], *s.* die Schmeichelei.
flaunt [flɔːnt], *v.a.* prahlen, prunken (*s.th.*, mit, *Dat.*).
flavour ['fleivə], *s.* der Geschmack, die Würze; das Aroma; die Blume (*bouquet of wine*). — *v.a.* würzen.
flaw [flɔː], *s.* der Riß (*chink*); der Fehler (*fault*).
flawless ['flɔːlis], *adj.* fehlerlos.
flax [flæks], *s.* (*Bot.*) der Flachs.
flay [flei], *v.a.* schinden, die Haut abziehen (*Dat.*).
flea [fliː], *s.* (*Ent.*) der Floh.
fleck [flek], *v.a.* sprenkeln.
fledge [fledʒ], *v.a.* befiedern; *fully* —*d*, flügge; selbständig.
fledgling ['fledʒliŋ], *s.* der Grünschnabel, der Novize.
flee [fliː], *v.a.*, *v.n.* irr. fliehen, entfliehen (*from*, von, *Dat.*); flüchten (vor, *Dat.*).

fleece [fliːs], *s.* das Vlies. — *v.a.* scheren (*sheep*); ausnützen (*exploit*); berauben.
fleet [fliːt], *s.* die Flotte. — *adj.* (*Poet.*) schnellfüßig.
Fleming ['flemiŋ], *s.* der Flame.
Flemish ['flemiʃ], *adj.* flämisch.
flesh [fleʃ], *s.* das (lebende) Fleisch; die Frucht (*of fruit*).
flex [fleks], *s.* (*Elec.*) die Kontaktschnur.
flexible ['fleksibl], *adj.* biegsam; (*fig.*) anpassungsfähig.
flexion ['flekʃən], *s.* (*Gram.*) die Flexion, die Biegung.
flick [flik], *s.* der leichte Schlag. — *v.a.* leicht schlagen, berühren.
flicker ['flikə], *s.* das Flackern, das Flimmern. — *v.n.* flackern, flimmern.
flight [flait], *s.* (*Aviat.*) der Flug; die Flucht (*escape*); — *of stairs*, die Treppe, Treppenflucht.
flimsy ['flimzi], *adj.* hauchdünn (*material*); schwach (*argument*).
flinch [flintʃ], *v.n.* zurückweichen, zurückzucken (*from*, vor, *Dat.*).
fling [fliŋ], *v.a.* irr. schleudern, werfen. — *s.* der Wurf; *highland* —, schottischer Tanz; *have a last* —, sich zum letzten Mal austoben.
flint [flint], *s.* der Feuerstein.
flippancy ['flipənsi], *s.* die Leichtfertigkeit.
flippant ['flipənt], *adj.* leichtfertig, leichtsinnig, schnippisch.
flirt [fləːt], *v.n.* flirten, liebeln, (*with*, *Dat.*).
flirtation [fləː'teiʃən], *s.* die Liebelei.
flit [flit], *v.n.* hin und her flitzen; huschen.
flitch [flitʃ], *s.* die Speckseite.
flitter ['flitə], *v.n.* flattern.
float [flout], *v.n.* obenauf schwimmen, dahingleiten; —*ing ice*, das Treibeis. — *v.a.* schwimmen lassen; (*Naut.*) flott machen; (*Comm.*) gründen (*a company*); ausgeben (*a loan*). — *s.* das Floß (*raft*); der ausgeschmückte Wagen (*decorated vehicle*).
flock [flɔk], *s.* die Herde (*sheep*). — *v.n.* zusammenlaufen, sich scharen.
floe [flou], *s.* die Eisscholle.
flog [flɔg], *v.a.* peitschen (*whip*); antreiben; — *a dead horse*, sich umsonst bemühen; (*coll.*) verkaufen.
flood [flʌd], *s.* die Flut; das Hochwasser, die Überschwemmung (*flooding*); (*fig.*) die Fülle; — *gate*, die Schleuse. — *v.a.* überfluten, überschütten (*with requests*). — *v.n.* überschwemmen (*of river*).
floodlight ['flʌdlait], *s.* das Flutlicht, Scheinwerferlicht.
floor [flɔː], *s.* der Boden, der Fußboden; das Stockwerk, der Stock (*storey*); *from the* —, aus dem Plenum; — *walker*, die Aufsicht (*in stores*). — *v.a.* zu Boden strecken, überrumpeln (*surprise*).
flop [flɔp], *v.n.* (*coll.*) hinsinken, hinplumpsen; versagen (*fail*). — *s.* das Hinfallen; der Versager (*play, film etc.*).

Florentine

Florentine ['florəntain], adj. florentinisch. — s. der Florentiner.
florid ['florid], adj. blühend; überladen.
florin ['florin], s. das Zweischillingstück.
florist ['florist], s. der Blumenhändler.
flotsam ['flotsəm], s. das Strandgut, Wrackgut.
flounce (1) [flauns], v.n. hastig bewegen.
flounce (2) [flauns], v.a. mit Falbeln besetzen (dress). — s. die Falbel (on dress).
flounder (1) ['flaundə], v.n. umhertappen, unsicher sein.
flounder (2) ['flaundə], s. (Zool.) die Flunder.
flour ['flauə], s. das Mehl.
flourish ['flʌriʃ], v.n. blühen; wirken; gedeihen (thrive); schnörkeln, verzieren (in writing); Fanfaren blasen, schmettern (trumpets). — s. der Schnörkel; der Trompetenstoß, Tusch (of trumpets).
flout [flaut], v.a. verhöhnen, verspotten. — s. der Hohn, der Spott.
flow [flou], v.n. irr. fließen, strömen. — s. der Fluß (of water, goods etc.); — of words, der Redeschwall.
flower ['flauə], s. die Blume; die Blüte (blossom). — v.n. blühen, in Blüte stehen.
flowery ['flauəri], adj. gewählt, umständlich, geziert (style).
fluctuate ['flʌktjueit], v.n. schwanken.
fluctuation [flʌktju'eiʃən], s. das Schwanken.
flue [flu:], s. der Rauchfang (of chimney).
fluency ['flu:ənsi], s. das fließende Sprechen, die Geläufigkeit.
fluent ['flu:ənt], adj. geläufig, fließend.
fluid ['flu:id], adj. fließend, flüssig (liquid). — s. die Flüssigkeit.
fluke [flu:k], s. der glückliche Zufall (chance).
flunkey ['flʌŋki], s. der Diener, der Bediente.
flurry ['flʌri], s. die Unruhe; die Aufregung (excitement).
flush (1) [flʌʃ], s. das Erröten (blushing); die Aufwallung (of anger). — v.a. nachspülen (basin); erröten machen (make blush). — v.n. erröten.
flush (2) [flʌʃ], adj. in gleicher Ebene, eben.
flush (3) [flʌʃ], v.a. (Hunt.) aufscheuchen.
fluster ['flʌstə], v.a. verwirren (muddle); aufregen (excite).
flute [flu:t], s. (Mus.) die Flöte; (Carp.) die Hohlkehle. — v.a. (Carp., Archit.) aushöhlen. — v.n. (Mus.) flöten, Flöte spielen.
flutter ['flʌtə], v.n. flattern, unruhig sein. — s. die Unruhe.
flux [flʌks], s. das Fließen; be in —, in der Schwebe sein.
fly [flai], v.a. irr. wehen lassen, hissen (flag). — v.n. irr. (Aviat.) fliegen;

fliehen (escape); eilen (hurry). — s. (Ent.) die Fliege.
flyleaf ['flaili:f], s. das Vorsatzblatt.
flying ['flaiiŋ], adj. fliegend, Flug-; — squad, das Überfallkommando.
flyover ['flaiouvə], s. die Brückenkreuzung, Überführung.
flywheel ['flaiwi:l], s. das Schwungrad.
foal [foul], s, (Zool.) das Füllen. — v.n. fohlen.
foam [foum], s. der Schaum; — rubber, das Schaumgummi. — v.n. schäumen.
fob [fob], v.a. — off, abfertigen, abspeisen.
focus ['foukəs], s. der Brennpunkt; der Mittelpunkt (of interest). — v.a. (Phot.) einstellen. — v.n. — upon, sich konzentrieren auf (Acc.).
fodder ['fodə], s. das Futter.
foe [fou], s. der Feind.
fog [fog], s. der Nebel.
fogey ['fougi], s. der Kerl, Kauz.
foible ['foibl], s. die Schwäche, die schwache Seite.
foil (1) [foil], v.a. vereiteln. — s. das Florett (fencing rapier).
foil (2) [foil], s. die Folie; der Hintergrund (background).
foist [foist], v.a. aufschwatzen (upon, Dat.).
fold (1) [fould], v.a. falten (clothes etc.); umarmen (in o.'s arms). — v.n. schließen, sich falten. — s. die Falte; (Geol.) die Vertiefung.
fold (2) [fould], s. die Herde (sheep); return to the —, zu den Seinen zurückkehren.
folder ['fouldə], s. die Mappe (papers); das Falzbein.
folding ['fouldiŋ], adj. Klapp-; — chair, der Klappstuhl; — door, die Flügeltür.
foliage ['fouljidʒ], s. (Bot.) das Laub.
folio ['fouliou], s. das Folio, der Foliant.
folk [fouk], s. (also pl.) die Leute; (pl.) (Am.)Freunde (mode of address).
folklore ['fouklɔ:], s. die Volkskunde.
folksong ['fouksɔŋ], s. das Volkslied.
follow ['folou], v.a., v.n. folgen (Dat.); — suit, dasselbe tun, Farbe bekennen.
follower ['folouə], s. der Anhänger (supporter); der Nachfolger (successor); camp —, der Mitläufer.
folly ['foli], s. die Narrheit; die törichte Handlung (action).
foment [fo'ment], v.a. anregen (stimulate); pflegen (cultivate); warm baden.
fond [fond], adj. zärtlich, lieb; be — of, gern haben.
fondle ['fondl], v.a. liebkosen.
fondness ['fondnis], s. die Zärtlichkeit, die (Vor-)liebe.
font [font], s. der Taufstein (baptismal).
food [fu:d], s. die Nahrung, Speise (nourishment); Lebensmittel (n.pl.); das Futter (for animals); some —, etwas zum Essen; — store, das Lebensmittelgeschäft.
fool [fu:l], s. der Narr, Tor. — v.a. zum Narren halten, übertölpeln.

foolish ['fu:liʃ], adj. töricht, albern, närrisch (person); unsinnig (act).

foolscap ['fu:lskæp], s. das Kanzleipapier.

foot [fut], s. der Fuß; on —, zu Fuß; — board, das Trittbrett; put o.'s — in it, eine taktlose Bemerkung fallen lassen, ins Fettnäpfchen treten. — v.a. — the bill, bezahlen.

footage ['futidʒ], s. die Länge in Fuß.

football ['futbɔ:l], s. der Fußball.

footbridge ['futbridʒ], s. der Steg.

footing ['futiŋ], s. die Grundlage, Basis.

footlight ['futlait], s. (usually pl.) die Rampenlichter, n. pl.

footman ['futmən], s. der Bediente.

footprint ['futprint], s. die Fußstapfe.

footstool ['futstu:l], s. der Schemel.

fop [fɔp], s. der Geck.

for [fɔ:], prep. für (Acc.); anstatt (Genit.) (instead of); in exchange —, für, um; — example, zum Beispiel; — heaven's sake, um Himmels willen; — two days, zwei Tage lang; auf zwei Tage; seit zwei Tagen; now you are — it! jetzt has du's! as — me, meinetwegen, was mich anbelangt; — all that, trotz alledem. — conj. denn, weil.

forage ['fɔridʒ], s. das Futter. — v.n. furagieren.

forasmuch [fɔrəz'mʌtʃ], conj. (obs.) — as, insofern als.

foray ['fɔrei], s. der Raubzug.

forbear [fɔ:'bɛə], v.a. irr. vermeiden, unterlassen (avoid); sich enthalten (abstain). — v.n. (geduldig) hinnehmen, ertragen.

forbid [fə'bid], v.a. irr. verbieten; God — ! Gott behüte!

forbidding [fə'bidiŋ], adj. abschreckend.

force [fɔ:s], s. (Phys.) die Kraft; die Macht (might); die Gewalt (brute —); (pl.) die Streitkräfte, f. pl.; (Phys.) die Kräfte. — v.a. zwingen, nötigen.

forceful ['fɔ:sful], adj. kräftig, energisch, kraftvoll.

forceps ['fɔ:seps], s. (Med.) die Zange; die Pinzette.

forcible ['fɔ:sibl], adj. heftig, stark (strong); gewaltsam (violent).

ford [fɔ:d], s. die Furt.

fore- [fɔ:], pref. Vorder-, vorder.

forebear [fɔ:'bɛə], s. der Vorfahre.

forebode [fɔ:'boud], v.a. voraussagen, vorbedeuten.

forecast [fɔ:'kɑ:st], v.a. vorhersagen, voraussagen. — ['fɔ:kɑ:st], s. die Vorhersage.

foreclose [fɔ:'klouz], v.a. ausschließen.

forefather ['fɔ:fɑ:ðə], s. der Ahne, der Vorvater.

forefinger ['fɔ:fiŋgə], s. (Anat.) der Zeigefinger.

forego [fɔ:'gou], v.a. irr. vorhergehen.

foreground ['fɔ:graund], s. der Vordergrund.

forehead ['fɔrid], s. die Stirne.

foreign ['fɔrin], adj. fremd; ausländisch.

foreigner ['fɔrinə], s. der Fremde, der Ausländer.

foreland ['fɔ:lənd], s. das Vorgebirge.

foreman ['fɔ:mən], s. der Werkführer, Vorarbeiter.

foremast ['fɔ:mɑ:st], s. (Naut.) der Fockmast.

foremost ['fɔ:moust], adj. vorderst, vornehmlichst, führend. — adv. zuerst; first and —, zuallererst.

forenoon ['fɔ:nu:n], s. der Vormittag.

forensic [fɔ'rensik], adj. forensisch, gerichtsmedizinisch.

forerunner ['fɔ:rʌnə], s. der Vorläufer.

foresail ['fɔ:seil, 'fɔ:səl], s. (Naut.) das Focksegel.

foresee [fɔ:'si:], v.a. irr. vorhersehen.

foreshadow [fɔ:'ʃædou], v.a. vorher andeuten.

foreshorten [fɔ:'ʃɔ:tn], v.a. verkürzen.

foresight ['fɔ:sait], s. die Vorsorge, der Vorbedacht.

forest ['fɔrist], s. der Wald; der Urwald (jungle).

forestall [fɔ:'stɔ:l], v.a. vorwegnehmen, zuvorkommen (Dat.).

forester ['fɔristə], s. der Förster.

forestry ['fɔristri], s. die Forstwissenschaft (science); das Forstwesen (management).

foretaste ['fɔ:teist], s. der Vorgeschmack.

foretell [fɔ:'tel], v.a. irr. voraussagen.

forethought ['fɔ:θɔ:t], s. der Vorbedacht.

forewarn [fɔ:'wɔ:n], v.a. warnen.

forfeit ['fɔ:fit], s. das Pfand (pledge); die Einbuße (fine); (pl.) das Pfänderspiel. — v.a. verlieren, verwirken.

forfeiture ['fɔ:fitʃə], s. die Verwirkung, die Einbuße, der Verlust.

forge [fɔ:dʒ], v.a. schmieden (iron); fälschen (falsify). — v.n. — ahead, sich vorwärtsarbeiten. — s. die Schmiede (iron); der Eisenhammer (hammer).

forget [fə'get], v.a., v.n. irr. vergessen; — -me-not, das Vergißmeinnicht.

forgetful [fə'getful], adj. vergeßlich.

forgive [fə'giv], v.a., v.n. irr. vergeben, verzeihen.

forgo [fɔ:'gou], v.a. irr. verzichten; aufgeben.

fork [fɔ:k], s. die Gabel; die Abzweigung (road). — v.n. sich gabeln, sich spalten.

forlorn [fɔ:'lɔ:n], adj. verlassen, verloren, elend.

form [fɔ:m], s. die Form, die Gestalt (shape); die Formalität (formality); das Formular (document); in good —, (Sport) in guter Form; bad —, gegen den guten Ton; a matter of —, eine Formsache. — v.a. formen, gestalten (shape); bilden (an association etc. of, über, Acc.).

formal ['fɔ:məl], adj. formal, äußerlich; formell.

formality [fɔ:'mæliti], s. die Formalität.

397

formation

formation [fɔ:'meiʃən], *s.* (*Mil.*) die Formation; (*Geol.*) die Bildung; die Formung; die Aufstellung (*sports team*).

former ['fɔ:mə], *adj.* früher, vorig.

formidable ['fɔ:midəbl], *adj.* schrecklich, furchtbar.

formula ['fɔ:mjulə], *s.* die Formel.

formulate ['fɔ:mjuleit], *v.a.* formulieren.

forsake [fɔ:'seik], *v.a. irr.* verlassen, im Stich lassen.

forsooth [fɔ:'su:θ], *adv.* (*Poet.*) wahrlich, wirklich!

forswear [fɔ:'swɛə], *v.a. irr.* abschwören; — *oneself*, einen Meineid schwören.

fort, fortress [fɔ:t, 'fɔ:tris], *s.* das Fort, die Festung.

forth [fɔ:θ], *adv.* vorwärts; weiter (*further*); *and so* —, und so weiter (u.s.w.); fort (*away*).

forthcoming ['fɔ:θkʌmiŋ], *adj.* bevorstehend.

forthwith [fɔ:θ'wiθ], *adv.* sogleich.

fortieth ['fɔ:tiəθ], *num. adj.* vierzigst. — *s.* der Vierzigste.

fortification [fɔ:tifi'keiʃən], *s.* die Befestigung.

fortify ['fɔ:tifai], *v.a.* befestigen; bestärken.

fortitude ['fɔ:titju:d], *s.* die Tapferkeit.

fortnight ['fɔ:tnait], *s.* vierzehn Tage, *m. pl.*

fortuitous [fɔ:'tju:itəs], *adj.* zufällig.

fortunate ['fɔ:tʃənit], *adj.* glücklich, günstig.

fortune ['fɔ:tju:n], *s.* das Glück, das Schicksal; das Vermögen (*wealth*); — *teller*, die Wahrsagerin.

forty ['fɔ:ti], *num. adj.* vierzig.

forward ['fɔ:wəd], *adj.* vorder (*in front*); voreilig, vorlaut (*rash*); früh (*early*). — *adv.* vorne; — *march!* vorwärts! *carry* —, (*Comm.*) übertragen. — *s.* (*Footb.*) der Stürmer, — line, der Angriff. — *v.a.* weiterleiten, expedieren; (*letter*) *please* —, bitte nachsenden.

forwardness ['fɔ:wədnis], *s.* die Frühreife; die Voreiligkeit, Dreistigkeit.

fossil ['fɔsil], *s.* das Fossil.

foster ['fɔstə], *v.a.* nähren (*feed*); aufziehen (*bring up*); — *a thought*, einen Gedanken hegen; — *mother*, die Pflegemutter; — *brother*, der Pflegebruder.

foul [faul], *adj.* schmutzig; faul (*rotten*). — *v.a.* beschmutzen. — *v.n.* (*Footb.*) einen Verstoß begehen. — *s.* (*Footb.*) der Verstoß.

found (1) [faund], *v.a.* gründen, begründen.

found (2) [faund], *v.a.* (*Metall.*) gießen (*cast*).

foundation [faun'deiʃən], *s.* das Fundament; die Unterlage; die Begründung, die Gründung (*initiation*); die Stiftung (*establishment*); — *stone*, der Grundstein.

founder (1) ['faundə], *s.* der Gründer, Stifter.

founder (2) ['faundə], *v.n.* scheitern, Schiffbruch erleiden (*on*, an, *Dat.*).

foundling ['faundliŋ], *s.* das Findelkind, der Findling.

foundry ['faundri], *s.* (*Metall.*) die Gießerei.

fount (1) [faunt], *s.* (*Typ.*) der Schriftguss.

fount (2) [faunt] (*Poet.*) *see* **fountain**.

fountain ['fauntin], *s.* die Quelle, der Brunnen; der Springbrunnen; — *pen*, die Füllfeder; — *head*, der Urquell.

four [fɔ:], *num. adj.* vier; — *-in-hand*, das Viergespann.

fowl [faul], *s.* (*Orn.*) das Huhn, das Geflügel.

fowler ['faulə], *s.* der Vogelsteller, Vogelfänger.

fox [fɔks], *s.* (*Zool.*) der Fuchs; (*fig.*) der listige Kauz, Schlauberger (*cunning fellow*). — *v.a.* (*coll.*) überlisten, täuschen.

fraction ['frækʃən], *s.* (*Maths.*) der Bruch; (*Mech.*) der Bruchteil.

fractional ['frækʃənəl], *adj.* (*Maths.*) Bruch-, gebrochen.

fractionate ['frækʃəneit], *v.a.* (*Chem.*) fraktionieren (*oil*).

fractious ['frækʃəs], *adj.* zänkisch, streitsüchtig.

fracture ['fræktʃə], *s.* (*Med.*) der Bruch. — *v.a.* brechen; — *o.'s leg*, sich das Bein brechen.

fragile ['frædʒail], *adj.* zerbrechlich; gebrechlich (*feeble*).

fragment ['frægmənt], *s.* das Bruchstück, das Fragment.

fragrance ['freigrəns], *s.* der Wohlgeruch, Duft.

fragrant ['freigrənt], *adj.* wohlriechend, duftend.

frail [freil], *adj.* gebrechlich, schwach (*feeble*).

frailty ['freilti], *s.* die Schwäche.

frame [freim], *s.* der Rahmen (*of picture*); das Gerüst (*scaffold*); die Form (*shape*). — *v.a.* einrahmen (*a picture*); (*Am.*) in die Enge treiben, reinlegen (*get s.o. wrongly blamed*); (*Comm.*) entwerfen (*a letter*).

framework ['freimwə:k], *s.* der Rahmen (*outline*); das Fachwerk (*construction*).

franchise ['fræntʃaiz], *s.* das Wahlrecht.

Franciscan [fræn'siskən], *s.* der Franziskaner (*friar*).

frank [fræŋk], *adj.* offen, aufrichtig. — *v.a.* frankieren (*letter*). — *s.* der Frankovermerk.

frankincense ['fræŋkinsens], *s.* der Weihrauch.

frantic ['fræntik], *adj.* wahnsinnig, außer sich.

fraternal [frə'tə:nəl], *adj.* brüderlich.

fraternity [frə'tə:niti], *s.* die Bruderschaft; (*Am.*) der Studentenbund, -klub.

fraternize ['frætənaiz], *v.n.* sich verbrüdern, fraternisieren.

fraud [frɔːd], *s.* der Betrug.

fraudulent ['frɔːdjulənt], *adj.* betrügerisch.

fraught [frɔːt], *adj.* voll (*with*, von, *Dat.*).

fray (1) [frei], *v.a.* abnutzen; — *the nerves*, auf die Nerven gehen (*Dat.*).

fray (2) [frei], *s.* der Kampf, die Schlägerei.

freak [friːk], *s.* das Monstrum, die Mißgeburt.

freakish ['friːkiʃ], *adj.* seltsam; grotesk.

freckle [frekl], *s.* die Sommersprosse.

freckled [frekld], *adj.* sommersprossig.

free [friː], *adj.* frei; offen (*frank*); — *trade area*, die Freihandelszone; *of my own* — *will*, aus freien Stücken. — *v.a.* befreien.

freebooter ['friːbuːtə], *s.* der Freibeuter.

freedom ['friːdəm], *s.* die Freiheit; — *of a city*, das Ehrenbürgerrecht.

freehold ['friːhould], *s.* der freie Grundbesitz, der Freigrundbesitz.

freeholder ['friːhouldə], *s.* der (freie) Grundbesitzer.

freeman ['friːmən], *s.* der Freibürger, Ehrenbürger.

freemason ['friːmeisn], *s.* der Freimaurer.

freewheel ['friːˈwiːl], *s.* der Freilauf, das Freilaufrad. — *v.n.* mit Freilauf fahren.

freeze [friːz], *v.a. irr.* gefrieren lassen. — *v.n.* frieren, gefrieren; — *up*, zufrieren.

freight [freit], *s.* die Fracht. — *v.a.* verfrachten.

freighter ['freitə], *s.* (*Naut.*) der Frachtdampfer.

French [frentʃ], *adj.* französisch; — *bean*, die Schnittbohne; — *horn*, (*Mus.*) das Horn.

Frenchman ['frentʃmən], *s.* der Franzose.

Frenchwoman ['frentʃwumən], *s.* die Französin.

frenzied ['frenzid], *adj.* wahnsinnig, außer sich.

frequency ['friːkwənsi], *s.* (*Phys.*) die Frequenz; die Häufigkeit (*of occurrence*).

frequent ['friːkwənt], *adj.* häufig. — [friˈkwent], *v.a.* (häufig) besuchen.

fresh [freʃ], *adj.* frisch, neu; ungesalzen (*water*); (*sl.*) frech; — *water*, das Süßwasser.

fresher, freshman ['freʃə, 'freʃmən], *s.* der Neuankömmling; (*Univ.*) der Fuchs, Anfänger.

fret (1) [fret], *s.* (*Carp.*) das Gitterwerk, Laubsägewerk. — *v.a.* (*Carp.*) durchbrochen verzieren.

fret (2) [fret], *s.* der Verdruß, Ärger. — *v.n.* sich Sorgen machen.

fretful ['fretful], *adj.* verdrießlich, ärgerlich, mißmutig.

fretsaw ['fretsɔː], *s.* (*Carp.*) die Laubsäge.

friar ['fraiə], *s.* (*Eccl.*) der Mönch, Bettelmönch.

friction ['frikʃən], *s.* die Reibung; (*fig.*) die Unstimmigkeit.

Friday ['fraid(e)i]. der Freitag; *Good* —, der Karfreitag.

friend [frend], *s.* der (die) Freund(in).

friendly ['frendli], *adj.* freundlich.

friendship ['frendʃip], *s.* die Freundschaft.

frigate ['frigit], *s.* (*Naut.*) die Fregatte.

fright [frait], *s.* die Furcht, der Schreck, das Entsetzen.

frighten [fraitn], *v.a.* erschrecken (*s.o.*).

frightful ['fraitful], *adj.* schrecklich.

frigid ['fridʒid], *adj.* kalt, frostig; kühl.

frill [fril], *s.* die Krause; die Ausschmückung (*style*).

frilly ['frili], *adj.* gekräuselt, geziert.

fringe [frindʒ], *s.* die Franse (*fringed edge*); der Rand (*edge, brink*). — *v.a.* mit Fransen besetzen, einsäumen. — *v.n.* — *on*, grenzen an (*Acc.*).

Frisian ['friːʒən], *adj.* friesisch.

frisk [frisk], *v.a.* (*sl.*) durchsuchen (*search*). — *v.n.* hüpfen (*of animals*). — *s.* der Sprung (*of animals*).

frisky ['friski], *adj.* lebhaft, munter.

fritter ['fritə], *s.* der Pfannkuchen; *apple* —, Äpfel im Schlafrock. — *v.a.* zerstückeln (*cut up*); vertrödeln (*waste*), vergeuden.

frivolity [friˈvɔliti], *s.* der Leichtsinn, die Leichtfertigkeit.

frivolous ['frivələs], *adj.* leichtsinnig, leichtfertig.

fro [frou], *adv. to and* —, auf und ab, hin und her.

frock [frɔk], *s.* der Kittel, das Kleid; (*Eccl.*) die Soutane, Kutte.

frog [frɔg], *s.* (*Zool.*) der Frosch.

frogman ['frɔgmən], *s.* der Tauchschwimmer, Froschmann.

frolic ['frɔlik], *s.* der Scherz; der Spaß. — *v.n.* scherzen, ausgelassen sein.

from [frɔm], *prep.* von; von ... her (*hence*); aus ... heraus (*out of*); von ... an (*starting* —); vor (*in the face of*).

front [frʌnt], *s.* die Stirn; die Vorderseite; (*Mil.*) die Front; *in* — *of*, vor (*Dat.*); — *door*, die Haustür.

frontage ['frʌntidʒ], *s.* die Front, Vorderfront (*of building*).

frontal ['frʌntl], *adj.* Stirn-, Vorder-; (*Mil.*) — *attack*, der Frontalangriff. — *s.* (*Eccl.*) die Altardecke.

frontier ['frʌntjə], *s.* die Grenze; — *police*, die Grenzpolizei.

frontispiece ['frʌntispiːs], *s.* das Titelbild.

frost [frɔst], *s.* der Frost, der Reif.

frostbite ['frɔstbait], *s.* die Frostbeule.

frosted ['frɔstid], *adj.* bereift.

froth [frɔθ], *s.* der Schaum. — *v.n.* schäumen.

frown

frown [fraun], *v.n.* die Stirn runzeln, finster dreinschauen. — *s.* das Stirnrunzeln.

frugal ['fru:gəl], *adj.* frugal, sparsam, einfach.

fruit [fru:t], *s.* die Frucht (*singular*); das Obst (*plural or collective*). — *v.n.* (*Bot.*) Früchte tragen.

frustrate [frʌs'treit], *v.a.* verhindern; vereiteln (*bring to nought*).

fry (1) [frai], *v.a.* braten; *fried potatoes*, Bratkartoffeln, *f. pl.*

fry (2) [frai], *s.* der Rogen (*of fish*); (*fig.*) die Brut, Menge.

frying pan ['fraiŋpæn], *s.* die Bratpfanne; *out of the — into the fire*, vom Regen in die Traufe.

fuchsia ['fju:ʃə], *s.* (*Bot.*) die Fuchsie.

fudge [fʌdʒ], *s.* weiches Zuckerwerk; (*coll.*) Unsinn!

fuel ['fjuəl], *s.* der Brennstoff, Treibstoff; das Heizmaterial. — *v.a.*, *v.n.* tanken.

fugitive ['fju:dʒitiv], *adj.* flüchtig, auf der Flucht. — *s.* der Flüchtling.

fugue [fju:g], *s.* (*Mus.*) die Fuge.

fulcrum ['fʌlkrəm], *s.* der Stützpunkt, Hebelpunkt.

fulfil [ful'fil], *v.a.* erfüllen; — *a requirement*, einem Gesetz genüge tun.

full [ful], *adj.* voll; vollständig (*complete*); *—time*, hauptberuflich.

fuller ['fulə], *s.* der Walker.

fullness ['fulnis], *s.* die Fülle.

fulsome ['fulsəm], *adj.* widerlich, ekelhaft; übermäßig.

fumble [fʌmbl], *v.n.* tappen (*for*, nach, *Dat.*).

fume [fju:m], *s.* der Rauch, Dunst; der Zorn (*anger*). — *v.n.* zornig sein, wüten (*be angered*).

fun [fʌn], *s.* der Spaß, Scherz; *have —*, sich gut unterhalten, sich amüsieren; *make — of*, zum besten haben.

function ['fʌŋkʃən], *s.* (*also Maths.*) die Funktion; das Amt (*office*); die Feier(lichkeit) (*formal occasion*). — *v.n.* funktionieren (*be in working order*); fungieren (*officiate*).

fund [fʌnd], *s.* der Fonds (*financial*); (*fig.*) die Fülle (*of*, an); *public —s*, die Staatsgelder.

fundamental [fʌndə'mentl], *adj.* grundsätzlich, wesentlich. — *s.* (*pl.*) die Grundlagen, *f.pl.*

funeral ['fju:nərəl], *s.* die Bestattung, Beerdigung.

funereal [fju:'niəriəl], *adj.* wie bei einem Begräbnis, betrübt, traurig.

fungus ['fʌŋgəs], *s.* (*Bot.*) der Pilz; der Schwamm (*mushroom*).

funk [fʌŋk], *s.* (*sl.*) die Angst, Panik. — *v.a.* fürchten.

funnel [fʌnl], *s.* der Trichter.

funny ['fʌni], *adj.* spaßhaft, komisch.

fur [fə:], *s.* der Pelz, das Fell (*coat of animal*); (*Med.*) der Belag (*on tongue*).

furbelow ['fə:bilou], *s.* die Falbel.

furbish ['fə:biʃ], *v.a.* aufputzen.

furious ['fjuəriəs], *adj.* wild, rasend, wütend.

furl [fə:l], *v.a.* (zusammen-)rollen; (*Naut.*) aufrollen.

furlong ['fə:lɔŋ], *s.* ein Achtel einer englischen Meile.

furlough ['fə:lou], *s.* der Urlaub.

furnace ['fə:nis], *s.* der Ofen, Hochofen (*steel*); (*Metall.*) der Schmelzofen.

furnish ['fə:niʃ], *v.a.* ausstatten, versehen (*equip*); möblieren (*a room etc.*).

furnisher ['fə:niʃə], *s.* der Möbelhändler; der Lieferant.

furniture ['fə:nitʃə], *s.* die Möbel, *n. pl.*; die Einrichtung.

furrier ['fʌriə], *s.* der Kürschner.

furrow ['fʌrou], *s.* die Furche (*field*); die Runzel (*brow*). — *v.a.* runzeln (*brow*); Furchen ziehen (*plough up*).

further ['fə:ðə], *comp. adj.*, *adv.* see **farther**. — *v.a.* fördern (*advance*).

furtherance ['fə:ðərəns], *s.* die Förderung (*advancement*).

furthermore ['fə:ðəmɔ:], *adv.* ferner.

furthest ['fə:ðist], *superl. adj.*, *adv.* see **farthest**.

furtive ['fə:tiv], *adj.* verstohlen, heimlich.

fury ['fjuəri], *s.* die Wut; (*Myth.*) die Furie.

furze [fə:z], *s.* (*Bot.*) der Stechginster.

fuse [fju:z], *v.a.*, *v.n.* schmelzen (*melt*); vereinigen (*unite*). — *s.* (*Elec.*) die Sicherung; *blow a —*, eine Sicherung durchbrennen; — *box*, der Sicherungskasten; — *wire*, der Schmelzdraht.

fuselage ['fju:zila:ʒ *or* -lidʒ], *s.* (*Aviat.*) der (Flugzeug-)rumpf.

fusible ['fju:zibl], *adj.* schmelzbar.

fusilier [fju:zi'liə], *s.* (*Mil.*) der Füsilier.

fusion ['fju:ʒən], *s.* die Verschmelzung; die Vereinigung.

fuss [fʌs], *s.* das Getue, die Umständlichkeit; *make a — about*, viel Aufhebens machen.

fussy ['fʌsi], *adj.* übertrieben genau; umständlich; geschäftig (*busy*); *about*, genau in (*Dat.*).

fusty ['fʌsti], *adj.* moderig, muffig.

futile ['fju:tail], *adj.* nutzlos, vergeblich.

futility [fju:'tiliti], *s.* die Nutzlosigkeit.

future ['fju:tʃə], *s.* die Zukunft. — *adj.* (zu-)künftig.

fuzzy ['fʌzi], *adj.* kraus.

G

G [dʒi:], das G (*also Mus.*); — *sharp*, das Gis; — *flat*, das Ges; *key of —*, der G Schlüssel, Violinschlüssel.

gavotte

gab [gæb], *s.* das Geschwätz; *the gift of the* —, ein gutes Mundwerk.
gabble [gæbl], *v.n.* schwatzen.
gable [geibl], *s.* der Giebel.
gad [gæd], *v.n.* — *about*, umherstreifen.
gadfly ['gædflai], *s.* (*Ent.*) die Bremse.
gag [gæg], *s.* der Knebel; (*sl.*) der Witz. — *v.a.* knebeln.
gaiety ['geiəti], *s.* die Fröhlichkeit.
gain [gein], *v.a.* gewinnen, erwerben (*earn*); — *possession*, Besitz ergreifen. — *s.* der Gewinn, Vorteil.
gainful ['geinful], *adj.* — *employment*, die einträgliche Beschäftigung.
gainsay ['geinsei *or* gein'sei], *v.a.* widersprechen (*pers.*, *Dat.*).
gait [geit], *s.* das Schreiten, der Schritt, Gang.
gaiter ['geitə], *s.* die Gamasche.
galaxy ['gæləksi], *s.* (*Astron.*) die Milchstraße; (*fig.*) die glänzende Versammlung.
gale [geil], *s.* der Sturm.
gall [gɔːl], *s.* die Galle. — *v.a.* verbittern, ärgern.
gallant ['gælənt], *adj.* tapfer (*of soldier*); gallant, höflich (*polite*).
gallantry ['gæləntri], *s.* die Tapferkeit; die Höflichkeit, Galanterie.
gallery ['gæləri], *s.* die Gallerie.
galley ['gæli], *s.* (*Naut.*) die Galeere; (*Typ.*) — *proof*, der Fahnenabzug.
gallon ['gælən], *s.* die Gallone.
gallop ['gæləp], *v.n.* galoppieren. — *s.* der Galopp.
gallows ['gælouz], *s.* der Galgen.
galosh [gə'lɔʃ], *s.* die Galosche.
galvanic [gæl'vænik], *adj.* galvanisch.
galvanize ['gælvənaiz], *v.a.* galvanisieren.
gamble [gæmbl], *v.n.* um Geld spielen; — *away*, verspielen. — *s.* das Risiko.
gambol [gæmbl], *v.n.* herumspringen.
game [geim], *s.* das Spiel (*play*); das Wild, Wildbret (*pheasants etc.*); *fair* —, Freiwild, *n.*, offene Beute, *f.*
gamecock ['geimkɔk], *s.* (*Orn.*) der Kampfhahn.
gamekeeper ['geimkiːpə], *s.* der Wildhüter.
gammon ['gæmən], *s.* der (geräucherte) Schinken (*bacon*).
gamut ['gæmət], *s.* die Tonleiter.
gander ['gændə], *s.* (*Orn.*) der Gänserich.
gang [gæŋ], *s.* die Bande; die Mannschaft (*workmen*). — *v.n.* — *up*, eine Bande bilden; — *up on s.o.*, sich gegen jemanden verbünden.
gangrene ['gæŋgriːn], *s.* (*Med.*) der Brand; die Fäulnis.
gangway ['gæŋwei], *s.* die Planke, der Laufgang (*on boat*); der Durchgang.
gaol, jail [dʒeil], *s.* das Gefängnis. — *v.a.* einsperren.
gaoler, jailer ['dʒeilə], *s.* der Kerkermeister.
gap [gæp], *s.* die Lücke; die Bresche (*breach*).
gape [geip], *v.n.* gähnen, (*fig.*) klaffen.

garage ['gærɑːʒ *or* 'gæridʒ], *s.* die Garage, die Tankstelle.
garb [gɑːb], *s.* die Tracht, Kleidung.
garbage ['gɑːbidʒ], *s.* der Abfall; (*Am.*) — *can*, der Mülleimer.
garble [gɑːbl], *v.a.* verstümmeln.
garden [gɑːdn], *s.* der Garten. — *v.n.* im Garten arbeiten.
gardener ['gɑːdnə], *s.* der Gärtner.
gargle [gɑːgl], *v.n.* gurgeln, spülen.
gargoyle ['gɑːgɔil], *s.* (*Archit.*) der Wasserspeier.
garish ['gɛəriʃ], *adj.* grell, auffallend.
garland ['gɑːlənd], *s.* der Blumenkranz, die Girlande.
garlic ['gɑːlik], *s.* (*Bot.*) der Knoblauch.
garment ['gɑːmənt], *s.* das Gewand.
garner ['gɑːnə], *v.a.* aufspeichern (*store*).
garnet ['gɑːnit], *s.* der Granat.
garnish ['gɑːniʃ], *v.a.* ausschmücken, verzieren.
garret ['gærət], *s.* die Dachkammer.
garrison ['gærisən], *s.* (*Mil.*) die Garnison. — *v.a.* stationieren.
garrulity [gæ'ruːliti], *s.* die Schwatzhaftigkeit.
garter ['gɑːtə], *s.* das Strumpfband, das Hosenband; *Order of the Garter*, der Hosenbandorden.
gas [gæs], *s.* das Gas; (*Am.*) see **gasoline**.
gaseous ['geisiəs], *adj.* gasförmig, gasartig.
Gascon ['gæskən], *s.* der Gaskogner.
gasoline ['gæsoliːn], *s.* (*Am.*) das Benzin.
gash [gæʃ], *s.* die Schnittwunde.
gasp [gɑːsp], *v.n.* keuchen; nach Luft schnappen. — *s.* das Keuchen, das Luftschnappen.
gastric ['gæstrik], *adj.* (*Anat.*) gastrisch; — *ulcer*, das Magengeschwür.
gate [geit], *s.* das Tor, der Eingang. — *v.a.* einsperren, Hausarrest geben (*Dat.*).
gateway ['geitwei], *s.* die Einfahrt.
gather ['gæðə], *v.a.* sammeln, einsammeln (*collect*); versammeln (*assemble*). — *v.n.* entnehmen, schließen (*infer*); sich versammeln (*come together*); aufziehen (*storm*).
gathering ['gæðəriŋ], *s.* die Versammlung (*meeting*).
gauche [gouʃ], *adj.* linkisch, ungeschickt.
gaudy ['gɔːdi], *adj.* übertrieben, grell, prunkhaft.
gauge [geidʒ], *v.a.* (*Engin.*) ausmessen, kalibrieren; eichen (*officially*). — *s.* der Maßstab (*scale*); (*Railw.*) die Spurweite.
gauger ['geidʒə], *s.* der Eichmeister.
Gaul [gɔːl], *s.* der Gallier.
gaunt [gɔːnt], *adj.* mager; hager.
gauntlet ['gɔːntlit], *s.* der (Panzer)handschuh.
gauze [gɔːz], *s.* die Gaze.
gavotte [gə'vɔt], *s.* (*Mus.*) die Gavotte.

401

gay

gay [gei], *adj.* fröhlich, heiter; bunt (*colour*).

gaze [geiz], *v.n.* starren.

gazelle [gə'zel], *s.* (*Zool.*) die Gazelle.

gazette [gə'zet], *s.* die (amtliche) Zeitung; das Amtsblatt.

gear [giə], *s.* das Gerät; (*Mech.*) das Triebwerk; (*Naut.*) das Geschirr; *switch*—, das Schaltgerät; (*Motor.*) der Gang; — *ratio*, die Übersetzung; *differential* —, der Achsenantrieb; *steering* —, die Lenkung (*of car*); — *box*, das Schaltgetriebe, die Gangschaltung; *out of* —, in Unordnung; *in top* —, mit Höchstgeschwindigkeit; *change to bottom* —, auf erste Geschwindigkeit (*or*, auf langsam) einschalten. — *v.a.* — *down*, herabsetzen; (*Engin.*) — *up*, übersetzen; — *to*, anpassen.

gelatine ['dʒeləti:n], *s.* die Gallerte, die Geleemasse.

gem [dʒem], *s.* die Gemme, der Edelstein.

gender ['dʒendə], *s.* (*Gram.*) das Geschlecht.

gene [dʒi:n], *s.* (*Biol.*) das Gen.

geneaology [dʒi:ni'ælədʒi], *s.* die Genealogie; der Stammbaum (*family tree*).

general ['dʒenərəl], *s.* (*Mil.*) der General; *lieutenant*- —, der Generalleutnant. — *adj.* allgemein, General-; — -*purpose*, für alle Zwecke; Allzweck-.

generalization [dʒenərəlai'zeiʃən], *s.* die Verallgemeinerung.

generalize ['dʒenərəlaiz], *v.a.* verallgemeinern.

generate ['dʒenə'reiʃən], *v.a.* erzeugen; (*Elec.*) Strom erzeugen.

generation [dʒenə'reiʃən], *s.* die Generation (*contemporaries*); das Zeugen (*production*); (*Elec.*) die Stromerzeugung.

generosity [dʒenə'rɔsiti], *s.* die Großmut (*magnanimity*); die Freigebigkeit (*liberality*).

generous ['dʒenərəs], *adj.* großmütig; freigebig (*with gifts*).

Genevan [dʒi'ni:vən], *adj.* genferisch. — *s.* der Genfer.

genitive ['dʒenitiv], *s.* (*Gram.*) der Wesfall, Genitiv.

genial ['dʒi:niəl], *adj.* freundlich, mild.

geniality [dʒi:ni'æliti], *s.* die Freundlichkeit, Leutseligkeit.

genital ['dʒenitəl], *adj.* Zeugungs-. — *s.* (*pl.*) die Geschlechtsteile, Genitalien, *pl.*

genius ['dʒi:niəs], *s.* das Genie; der Genius.

Genoese [dʒenou'i:z], *adj.* genuesisch. — *s.* der Genuese.

Gentile ['dʒentail], *s.* heidnisch; nicht jüdisch.

gentility [dʒen'tiliti], *s.* die Herkunft aus vornehmem Haus, Vornehmheit.

gentle [dʒentl], *adj.* sanft, mild; gelind (*breeze*).

gentlefolk ['dʒentlfouk], *s.* bessere *or* vornehme Leute, *pl.*

gentleman ['dʒentlmən], *s.* der Gentleman, Herr; feiner Herr.

gentleness ['dʒentlnis], *s.* die Milde, Sanftheit.

gentry ['dʒentri], *s.* der niedere Adel.

genuine ['dʒenjuin], *adj.* echt.

genus ['dʒenəs], *s.* (*Biol.*) die Gattung.

geographer [dʒi'ɔgrəfə], *s.* der Geograph.

geographical [dʒi:o'græfikəl], *adj.* geographisch.

geography [dʒi'ɔgrəfi], die Geographie, Erdkunde.

geological [dʒi:o'lɔdʒikəl], *adj.* geologisch.

geologist [dʒi'ɔlədʒist], *s.* der Geologe.

geology [dʒi'ɔlədʒi], *s.* die Geologie.

geometric(al) [dʒi:o'metrik(əl)], *adj.* geometrisch.

geometrist [dʒi'ɔmətrist], *s.* der Geometer.

geometry [dʒi'ɔmətri], *s.* die Geometrie.

geranium [dʒə'reiniəm], *s.* (*Bot.*) die Geranie, das Germaniu.

germ [dʒə:m], *s.* der Keim; (*pl.*) die Bakterien, *f. pl.*

German ['dʒə:mən], *adj.* deutsch. — *s.* der, die Deutsche.

germane [dʒə:'mein], *adj.* zur Sache gehörig, zugehörig.

germinate ['dʒə:mineit], *v.n.* keimen.

Germanic [dʒə:'mænik], *adj.* germanisch.

gerund ['dʒerənd], *s.* (*Gram.*) das Gerundium.

gerundive [dʒe'rʌndiv], *s.* (*Gram.*) das Gerundiv(um).

gesticulate [dʒes'tikjuleit], *v.n.* Gebärden machen, gestikulieren.

gesture ['dʒestʃə], *s.* die Geste; der Gebärde.

get [get], *v.a. irr.* bekommen, (*coll.*) kriegen; erhalten (*receive*); erwischen (*catch up with*); einholen (*fetch*); — *over or across*, klar machen. — *v.n.* gelangen (*arrive*); werden (*become*); — *along*, weiterkommen; — *on or* (*Am.*) *along with s.o.*, mit jemandem auskommen; — *in the world*, Karriere machen; — *away*, entkommen; — *down to it*, zur Sache kommen; — *in*, hineinkommen; — *off*, aussteigen; *show s.o. where he* — *s off*, jemandem seine Meinung sagen; (*Sch.*) — *through*, durchkommen (*in examination*); — *up*, aufstehen.

get-up ['getʌp], *s.* das Kostüm; die Ausstattung (*attire*).

Ghanaian [gɑ:'neiən], *adj.* ghanaisch. — *s.* der Ghanaer.

ghastly ['gɑ:stli], *adj.* furchtbar, schrecklich.

gherkin ['gə:kin], *s.* (*Bot.*) die Essiggurke.

ghost [goust], *s.* der Geist, das Gespenst.

giant ['dʒaiənt], *s.* der Riese.

gibberish ['dʒibəriʃ], *s.* das Kauderwelsch.

gibbet ['dʒibit], *s.* der Galgen.

gibe [dʒaib], *v.n.* spotten, höhnen (*at*, über, *Acc.*). — *s.* der Spott, Hohn; die spöttische Bemerkung (*remark*).

giblets [ˈdʒiblits], *s. pl.* das Gänseklein.

giddiness [ˈgidinis], *s.* das Schwindelgefühl.

giddy [ˈgidi], *adj.* schwindelig.

gift [gift], *s.* die Gabe, das Geschenk.

gifted [ˈgiftid], *adj.* begabt.

gig [gig], *s.* der leichte Wagen; (*Naut.*) der Nachen, das Gig.

gigantic [dʒaiˈgæntik], *adj.* riesig, riesengroß.

giggle [gigl], *v.n.* kichern. — *s.* das Kichern, Gekicher.

gild [gild], *v.a.* vergolden; verschönern; —*ing the pill*, etwas Unangenehmes (die Pille) versüßen.

gill (1) [gil], *s.* (*Biol.*) die Kieme.

gill (2) [dʒil], *s.* das Viertel einer Pinte (0.14 *l.*).

gilt [gilt], *s.* die Vergoldung; — *edged*, mit Goldschnitt; (*Comm.*) hochwertige *or* mündelsichere Staatspapiere.

gimlet [ˈgimlit], *s.* (*Carp.*) der Handbohrer.

gin [dʒin], *s.* der Gin, der Wachholderbranntwein; — *and tonic*, Gin und Tonic.

ginger [ˈdʒindʒə], *s.* der Ingwer; — -*haired*, rothaarig; — *nut*, das Ingweror Pfeffernüßchen, Ingwerkeks; — *beer*, Ingwerbier. — *v.a.* — *up*, aufstacheln, anreizen.

gingerbread [ˈdʒindʒəbred], *s.* der Lebkuchen, Pfefferkuchen.

gipsy [ˈdʒipsi], *s.* der Zigeuner.

giraffe [dʒiˈrɑːf], *s.* (*Zool.*) die Giraffe.

gird [gəːd], *v.a.* reg. & irr. (*Poet.*) gürten.

girder [ˈgəːdə], *s.* der Balken, Träger.

girdle [ˈgəːdl], *v.a.* gürten, umgürten; — *the earth*, die Erde umkreisen.

girl [gəːl], *s.* das Mädchen.

girlhood [ˈgəːlhud], *s.* die Mädchenzeit, die Mädchenjahre, *n. pl.*

girlish [ˈgəːliʃ], *adj.* mädchenhaft, wie ein Mädchen.

gist [dʒist], *s.* das Wesentliche.

give [giv], *v.a.* irr. geben; — *out*, bekanntgeben, bekanntmachen; — *up*, aufgeben; — *way to*, Platz machen. — *v.n.* sich dehnen, sich strecken (*of wood, metal etc.*); — *in*, nachgeben (*to, Dat.*).

glacial [ˈgleiʃəl], *adj.* eisig, Gletscher-.

glacier [ˈglæsiə], *s.* der Gletscher.

glad [glæd], *adj.* froh, erfreut (*at*, über, *Acc.*).

gladden [glædn], *v.a.* erheitern, erfreuen.

glade [gleid], *s.* die Lichtung.

glamorous [ˈglæmərəs], *adj.* bezaubernd, blendend glanzvoll.

glamour [ˈglæmə], *s.* der Zauber; der Glanz.

glance [glɑːns], *s.* der Blick; *at a* —, auf den ersten Blick. — *v.n.* flüchtig blicken.

gland [glænd], *s.* (*Anat.*) die Drüse.

glandular [ˈglændjulə], *adj.* Drüsen-, drüsig.

glare [glɛə], *s.* der blendende Glanz, das Schimmern; der (scharf) durchbohrende Blick (*stare*).

glaring [ˈglɛəriŋ], *adj.* schreiend (*of colour*); auffallend (*obvious*).

glass [glɑːs], *s.* das Glas; der Spiegel (*mirror*); das Wetterglas (*barometer*); (*pl.*) die Brille (*spectacles*).

glassblower [ˈglɑːsblouə], *s.* der Glasbläser.

glassworks [ˈglɑːswəːks], *s.* die Glashütte.

glassy [ˈglɑːsi], *adj.* gläsern.

glaze [gleiz], *s.* die Glasur. — *v.a.* glasieren; verglasen.

glazier [ˈgleiziə], *s.* der Glaser.

gleam [gliːm], *v.n.* strahlen, glänzen (*with*, vor, *Dat.*). — *s.* der Glanz, das Strahlen.

glean [gliːn], *v.a.* auflesen; erfahren (*learn*).

glebe [gliːb], *s.* das Pfarrgut.

glee (1) [gliː], *s.* die Freude, Heiterkeit.

glee (2) [gliː], *s.* (*Mus.*) der Rundgesang; — *club*, die Liedertafel.

glen [glen], *s.* das enge Tal.

glib [glib], *adj.* glatt, geläufig, zungenfertig.

glide [glaid], *v.n.* gleiten. — *s.* das Gleiten.

glider [ˈglaidə], *s.* (*Aviat.*) das Segelflugzeug.

glimmer [ˈglimə], *s.* der Schimmer, Glimmer. — *v.n.* schimmern, glimmen.

glimpse [glimps], *s.* der (flüchtige) Blick; *catch a* —, einen Blick erhaschen. — *v.a.* flüchtig blicken (auf, *Acc.*).

glisten [glisn], *v.n.* glitzern, glänzen.

glitter [ˈglitə], *v.n.* glänzen, schimmern.

gloaming [ˈgloumiŋ], *s.* die Dämmerung.

globe [gloub], *s.* der Globus, der Erdball; die Kugel.

globular [ˈglɔbjulə], *adj.* kugelförmig.

gloom [gluːm], *s.* das Dunkel; der Trübsinn, die Traurigkeit.

gloomy [ˈgluːmi], *adj.* deprimiert, trübsinnig, düster.

glorify [ˈglɔːrifai], *v.a.* verherrlichen.

glorious [ˈglɔːriəs], *adj.* herrlich; (*Mil.*) glorreich.

glory [ˈglɔːri], *s.* die Herrlichkeit, der Ruhm. — *v.n.* frohlocken (*in*, über, *Acc.*).

gloss [glɔs], *s.* der Glanz; (*Lit.*) die Glosse, Anmerkung. — *v.a.* — *over*, beschönigen; (*Lit.*) glossieren, mit Anmerkungen versehen.

glossary [ˈglɔsəri], *s.* das Glossar, die Spezialwörterliste; das Wörterbuch.

glossy [ˈglɔsi], *adj.* glänzend.

glove [glʌv], *s.* der Handschuh.

glow [glou], *v.n.* glühen. — *s.* die Glut, das Glühen; Wohlbehagen.

glower [ˈglauə], *v.n.* — *at*, feindselig ansehen, anstarren.

glue

glue [glu:], s. der Leim. — v.a. leimen, zusammenleimen.
glum [glʌm], adj. mürrisch, finster.
glut [glʌt], s. die Überfülle. — v.a. überladen, überfüllen.
glutinous [ˈgluːtinəs], adj. zähe, klebrig.
glutton [glʌtn], s. der Vielfraß.
gluttony [ˈglʌtəni], s. die Schwelgerei, Gefräßigkeit.
glycerine [ˈglisəriːn], s. das Glyzerin.
gnarled [nɑːld], adj. knorrig.
gnash [næʃ], v.a. knirschen (teeth).
gnat [næt], s. (Ent.) die Mücke.
gnaw [nɔː], v.a., v.n. nagen (an, Dat.), zernagen, zerfressen (at, Acc.).
gnome [noum], s. der Erdgeist, der Zwerg, Gnom.
go [gou], v.n. irr. gehen, fahren, laufen; arbeiten (engine); verlaufen (event); sich erstrecken (distance); — down in the general esteem, in der Achtung sinken; — on, fortfahren; — mad, verrückt werden; — bald, die Haare verlieren; — without, leer ausgehen, entbehren; let —, loslassen; — for, auf jemanden losgehen; — in for, sich interessieren für (Acc.); — all out for, energisch unternehmen; a —ing concern, ein gutgehendes Unternehmen; —ing on for 20, fast 20 Jahre. — s. der Versuch; (coll.) plenty of —, recht lebhaft, voller Schwung.
goad [goud], v.a. anstacheln.
goal [goul], s. das Ziel; (Footb.) das Tor.
goalkeeper [ˈgoulkiːpə], s. der Torwart.
goalpost [ˈgoulpoust], s. der Torpfosten.
goat [gout], s. (Zool.) die Geiß, Ziege; billy —, der Ziegenbock; nanny —, die Geiß.
gobble [gɔbl], v.a. verschlingen, gierig essen.
goblet [ˈgɔblit], s. der Becher.
goblin [ˈgɔblin], s. der Kobold, der Gnom; der Schelm.
go-cart [ˈgoukɑːt], s. der Kinderwagen, Gängelwagen.
God [gɔd], Gott.
god [gɔd], s. der Gott.
godchild [ˈgɔdtʃaild], s. das Patenkind.
goddess [ˈgɔdes], s. die Göttin.
godfather [ˈgɔdfɑːðə], s. der Pate.
godhead [ˈgɔdhed], s. die Gottheit.
godless [ˈgɔdlis], adj. gottlos, ungläubig.
godmother [ˈgɔdmʌðə], s. die Patin.
goggle [gɔgl], v.n. glotzen, starren (stare). — s. (pl.) die Schutzbrille.
going [ˈgouiŋ], s. das Gehen, das Funktionieren (of machinery); while the — is good, zur rechten Zeit.
gold [gould], s. das Gold; (Fin.) — standard, die Goldwährung.
goldfinch [ˈgouldfintʃ], s. (Orn.) der Stieglitz.
goldsmith [ˈgouldsmiθ], s. der Goldschmied.
gondola [ˈgɔndələ], s. die Gondel.

good [gud], adj. gut; artig, brav; for —, auf immer; in — time, rechtzeitig; — and proper, (coll.) wie es sich gehört, anständig; as — as, so gut wie; — looking, hübsch; — natured, gutmütig. — s. for your own —, in Ihrem eigenen Interesse; that's no —, das taugt nichts; (pl.) die Güter, n.pl., Waren, f.pl.; goods station, der Frachbahnhof; goods train, der Güterzug; goods yard, der Güterstapelplatz.
goodbye [gud'bai], interj., s.—! leb wohl! auf Wiedersehen!
goodness [ˈgudnis], s. die Güte.
goodwill [gud'wil], s. das Wohlwollen; (Comm.) die Kundschaft.
goose [guːs], s. (Orn.) die Gans.
gooseberry [ˈguzbəri], s. (Bot.) die Stachelbeere.
gore [gɔː], s. das geronnene Blut. — v.a. durchbohren (pierce, stab).
gorge [gɔːdʒ], s. die Felsenschlucht (ravine); (Anat.) die Kehle. — v.a. gierig verschlingen.
gorgeous [ˈgɔːdʒəs], adj. prachtvoll, prächtig.
gorse [gɔːs], s. (Bot.) der Stechginster.
gory [ˈgɔːri], adj. blutig.
goshawk [ˈgɔshɔːk], s. (Orn.) der Hühnerhabicht.
gosling [ˈgɔzliŋ], s. (Orn.) das Gänschen.
gospel [ˈgɔspəl], s. das Evangelium; the — according to, das Evangelium des . . .
gossamer [ˈgɔsəmə], s. das feine Gewebe; die Sommerfäden.
gossip [ˈgɔsip], v.n. klatschen; schwatzen, plaudern. — der Klatsch; der Schwätzer; die Klatschbase.
Gothic [ˈgɔθik], adj. gotisch.
gouge [gaudʒ], s. der Hohlmeißel. — v.a. aushöhlen, ausstechen.
gourd [ˈguəd], s. der Kürbis.
gout [gaut], s. (Med.) die Gicht.
govern [ˈgʌvən], v.a., v.n. (Pol.) regieren; beherrschen; (fig.) leiten, herrschen.
governable [ˈgʌvənəbl], adj. lenkbar, lenksam.
governess [ˈgʌvənis], s. die Erzieherin, die Gouvernante.
government [ˈgʌvənmənt], s. die Regierung; (Pol.) — benches, die Regierungssitze; — loan, die Staatsanleihe.
governor [ˈgʌvənə], s. der Gouverneur, Statthalter.
gown [gaun], s. das Kleid (lady's); (Univ.) der Talar; (official robe) die Amtstracht.
grab [græb], v.a. packen, ergreifen. — s. der Zugriff.
grace [greis], s. die Gnade; Gunst (favour); die Anmut (gracefulness); Your Grace, Euer Gnaden; das Tischgebet (prayer at table); (Mus.) — note, die Fermate; ten minutes' —, zehn Minuten Aufschub. — v.a. schmücken, zieren, ehren.
graceful [ˈgreisful], adj. anmutig, reizend; graziös (movement).

graceless ['greislis], *adj.* ungraziös.
gracious['greiʃəs],*adj.*gnädig,huldreich.
gradation [grə'deiʃən], *s.* die Abstufung, die Stufenleiter.
grade [greid], *s.* der Grad, Rang (*rank*); (*Am.*) (*Sch.*) die Klasse. — *v.a.* sortieren, ordnen.
gradient ['greidiənt], *s.* (*Geog.*) die Steigung; der Steigungswinkel (*angle*).
gradual ['grædjuəl], *adj.* allmählich.
graduate ['grædjueit], *v.n.* promovieren (*receive degree*); — *as a doctor*, als Doktor promovieren, den Doktor machen. — [-djuit], *s.* der Akademiker, Graduierte.
graft (1) [grɑ:ft], *s.* (*Hort., Med.*) die (Haut)übertragung. — *v.a.* (*Hort., Med.*) übertragen, anheften (*on to*, auf, *Acc.*).
graft (2) [grɑ:ft], *s.* (*Am.*) der unerlaubte Gewinn; das Schmiergeld; der Betrug (*swindle*).
grain [grein], *s.* das Korn, Samenkorn; das Getreide; das Gran (=0·065 *gramme*); die Maserung (*in wood*); *against the* —, gegen den Strich.
grammar ['græmə], *s.* die Grammatik; — *school*, das Gymnasium.
grammatical [grə'mætikəl], *adj.* grammatisch.
gramme [græm], *s.* das Gramm.
gramophone ['græməfoun], *s.* das Grammophon.
granary ['grænəri], *s.* der (Korn)speicher, die Kornkammer.
grand [grænd], *adj.* groß, großartig; wunderbar; *Grand Duke*, der Großherzog. — *s.* (*Am.*) (*sl.*) 1000 Dollar; (*piano*) der Flügel; *baby* —, der Stutzflügel.
grandchild ['grændtʃaild], *s.* der Enkel, die Enkelin.
grandee [græn'di:], *s.* der spanische Grande.
grandeur ['grændjə], *s.* die Größe, Pracht.
grandfather ['grændfɑ:ðə], *s.* der Großvater.
grandiloquent [græn'dilokwənt], *adj.* großsprecherisch.
grandmother ['grændmʌðə], *s.* die Großmutter.
grange [greindʒ], *s.* der Meierhof, das Landhaus.
granite ['grænit], *s.* der Granit.
grannie, granny ['græni], *s.* (*coll.*) die Oma.
grant [grɑ:nt], *s.* die Gewährung (*of permission etc.*); die Zuwendung (*subsidy*); (*Sch.*) das Stipendium. — *v.a.* geben, gewähren; *take for* —*ed*, als selbstverständlich hinnehmen.
granular ['grænjulə], *adj.* körnig.
granulated ['grænjuleitid], *adj.* feinkörnig, Kristall- (*sugar*).
grape [greip], *s.* (*Bot.*) die Weinbeere; die Traube; — *sugar*, der Traubenzucker; *bunch of* —*s*,Weintrauben, *f. pl.*
grapefruit ['greipfru:t], *s.* die Pampelmuse.

graphic ['græfik], *adj.* (*Art*) graphisch; deutlich, bildhaft, anschaulich.
grapnel ['græpnəl], *s.* (*Naut.*) der Dreganker.
grapple [græpl], *v.n.* — *with*, raufen, (miteinander) ringen.
grasp [grɑ:sp], *v.a.* (mit der Hand) ergreifen, erfassen. — *s.* das Fassungsvermögen, die Auffassung; der Griff (*hand*).
grasping ['grɑ:spiŋ], *adj.* habgierig, gewinnsüchtig.
grass [grɑ:s], *s.* (*Bot.*) das Gras; der Rasen (*lawn*); — *widow*, die Strohwitwe.
grasshopper ['grɑ:shɔpə], *s.* (*Ent.*) die Heuschrecke.
grate (1) [greit], *s.* der Feuerrost, der Kamin.
grate (2) [greit], *v.a.* reiben (*cheese*); schaben, kratzen. — *v.n.* knirschen; auf die Nerven gehen.
grateful ['greitful], *adj.* dankbar.
grater ['greitə], *s.* das Reibeisen; die Reibe (*electrical*).
gratification [grætifi'keiʃən], *s.* die Genugtuung, Befriedigung.
gratify ['grætifai], *v.a.* befriedigen, erfreuen.
grating ['greitiŋ], *s.* das Gitter.
gratis ['greitis], *adv.* gratis, umsonst, frei, unentgeltlich.
gratitude ['grætitju:d], *s.* die Dankbarkeit.
gratuitous [grə'tju:itəs], *adj.* frei, freiwillig (*voluntary*); unentgeltlich (*free of charge*); grundlos (*baseless*).
gratuity [grə'tju:iti], *s.* das Trinkgeld (*tip*); die Gratifikation.
grave (1) [greiv], *adj.* schwer, ernst (*serious*); feierlich (*solemn*). —*s.* (*Mus.*) das Grave.
grave (2) [greiv], *s.* das Grab (*tomb*).
gravel [grævl], *s.* der Kies.
graveyard ['greivjɑ:d], *s.* der Friedhof.
gravitate ['græviteit], *v.n.* gravitieren, hinstreben.
gravitation[grævi'teiʃən],*s.* die Schwerkraft.
gravitational [grævi'teiʃənəl], *adj.* (*Phys.*) Schwerkrafts-.
gravity ['græviti], *s.* der Ernst (*seriousness*); (*Phys.*) die Schwere, Schwerkraft.
gravy ['greivi], *s.* die Sauce, Soße; der Saft des Fleisches, des Bratens; — *boat*, die Sauciere.
gray, grey [grei], *adj.* grau.
graze (1) [greiz], *v.n.* weiden.
graze (2) [greiz], *v.a.* streifen (*pass closely*), abschürfen.
grazier ['greiziə], *s.* der Viehzüchter.
grease [gri:s], *s.* das Fett; das Schmieröl (*machine*). — *v.a.* einfetten (*pans*); schmieren, einschmieren (*machinery*).
greasy ['gri:si], *adj.* fett, schmierig, ölig.
great [greit], *adj.* groß, bedeutend, wichtig; (*Am.*) wundervoll, wunderbar.

greatcoat ['greitcout], s. der Wintermantel.

great-grandfather [greit'grændfɑ:ðə], s. der Urgroßvater.

greatly ['greitli], adv. stark, sehr.

greatness ['greitnis], s. die Größe, Bedeutung.

greedy ['gri:di], adj. gierig; gefräßig (eater).

Greek [gri:k], adj. griechisch. — s. der Grieche.

green [gri:n], adj. grün; neu (new), frisch (fresh).

greengage ['gri:ngeidʒ], s. (Bot.) die Reineclaude.

greengrocer ['gri:ngrousə], s. der Grünwarenhändler, Gemüsehändler.

greenhorn ['gri:nhɔ:n], s. der Grünschnabel.

greenhouse ['gri:nhaus], s. das Gewächshaus, Treibhaus.

Greenlander ['gri:nləndə], s. der Grönländer.

greet [gri:t], v.a. grüßen, begrüßen.

greeting ['gri:tin], s. die Begrüßung; (pl.) Grüße, m. pl.

gregarious [gri'gɛəriəs], adj. gesellig.

grenade [gri'neid], s. die Granate.

grey see under **gray**.

greyhound ['greihaund], s. (Zool.) das Windspiel, der Windhund.

grid [grid], s. (Elec.) das Stromnetz; (Phys.) das Gitter.

gridiron ['gridaiən], s. der Bratrost, das Bratrostgitter.

grief [gri:f], s. der Kummer, die Trauer.

grievance ['gri:vəns], s. die Klage, Beschwerde.

grieve [gri:v], v.a. kränken. — v.n. sich grämen, sich kränken (over, über, Acc., wegen, Genit.).

grievous ['gri:vəs], adj. schmerzlich.

grill [gril], s. der Rostbraten, Bratrost. — v.a. grillieren, rösten (meat); verhören (question closely).

grilling ['grilin], s. das Verhör.

grim [grim], adj. grimmig, finster.

grimace [gri'meis], s. die Grimasse, die Fratze.

grime [graim], s. der Schmutz, der Ruß.

grimy ['graimi], adj. schmutzig, rußig.

grin [grin], v.n. grinsen; (coll.) — and bear it, mach gute Miene zum bösen Spiel. — s. das Grinsen.

grind [graind], v.a. irr. zerreiben (rub); schleifen (sharpen); mahlen (pulverize); — o.'s teeth, mit den Zähnen knirschen. — s. (coll.) die ungeheuere Anstrengung, die Plackerei.

grinder ['graində], s. coffee —, die Kaffeemühle; knife —, der Schleifer, Wetzer; der Backzahn (molar).

grindstone ['graindstoun], s. der Schleifstein; keep o.'s nose to the —, fest bei der Arbeit bleiben.

grip [grip], s. der Griff; lose o.'s —, nicht mehr bewältigen können (wie bisher); (Tech.) der Handgriff (handle). — v.a. ergreifen, festhalten.

gripe [graip], v.n. (sl.) meckern.

gripes [graips], s. pl. (Med.) das Bauchgrimmen, die Kolik.

gripping ['gripin], arj. fesselnd (story).

grisly ['grizli], adj. scheußlich, gräßlich.

grist [grist], s. das Mahlgut, Gemahlene; — to o.'s mill, Wasser auf seine Mühle.

gristle [grisl], s. der Knorpel.

grit [grit], s. das Schrot, der Kies; der Mut (courage).

gritty ['griti], adj. körnig, kiesig, sandig.

grizzled [grizld], adj. grau, graumeliert.

groan [groun], v.n. stöhnen.

groats [grouts], s. pl. die Hafergrütze.

grocer ['grousə], s. der Kolonialwarenhändler, Feinkosthändler.

groin [grɔin], s. (Anat.) die Leiste; (Archit.) die Gewölbekante, Rippe.

groom [gru:m], s. der Stallknecht (stables); (obs.) der Junge (inn). — v.a. schniegeln, bürsten; schön machen.

groove [gru:v], s. die Rinne; die Rille (of gramophone record). — v.a. rillen; furchen (dig a furrow).

grope [group], v.n. tappen, tasten (around, umher).

gross [grous], adj. dick (fat); plump (heavy-handed); grob (ill-mannered); — weight, das Bruttogewicht; ungeheuer (error).

grotto ['grɔtou], s. die Grotte.

ground [graund], s. der Grund, Boden (also pl.); die Ursache (cause); — floor, das Erdgeschoß. — v.n. stranden (of ship).

groundwork ['graundwə:k], s. die Grundlagen, f. pl.

group [gru:p], s. die Gruppe. — v.a. gruppieren, anordnen.

grouse (1) [graus], v.n. (coll.) meckern, sich beklagen. — s. der Grund zur Klage, die Beschwerde.

grouse (2) [graus], s. (Orn.) das Birkhuhn, Moorhuhn.

grove [grouv], s. der Hain, das Wäldchen.

grovel [grɔvl], v.n. kriechen, schöntun (Dat.).

grow [grou], v.n. irr. wachsen, sich mehren (increase); werden (become). — v.a. anbauen, anpflanzen.

growl [graul], v.n. brummen, knurren. — s. das Gebrumme, Geknurre.

grown-up [groun'ʌp], s. der Erwachsene. — adj. erwachsen.

growth [grouθ], s. das Anwachsen (increase); das Wachstum (growing).

grub [grʌb], s. (Zool.) die Larve; (coll.) das Essen. — v.n. — about, wühlen.

grudge [grʌdʒ], s. der Groll; Neid (jealousy). — v.a. mißgönnen (envy). — v.n. — doing s.th., etwas ungerne tun.

gruel ['gru:əl], s. der Haferschleim.

gruesome ['gru:səm], adj. schauerlich, schrecklich.

gruff [grʌf], adj. mürrisch.

grumble [grʌmbl], v.n. murren, klagen.

grumbler [ˈgrʌmblə], *s.* der Unzu-
friedene, Nörgler.
grunt [grʌnt], *v.n.* grunzen. — *s.* das
Grunzen.
guarantee [gærənˈtiː], *v.a.* bürgen,
garantieren. — *s.* die Bürgschaft;
(*Comm.*) die Garantie.
guarantor [ˈgærəntɔː], *s.* der Bürge;
(*Comm.*) der Garant.
guard [gaːd], *s.* die Wache (*watch* or
watchman); (*Railw.*) der Schaffner; die
Schutzvorrichtung (*protective device*);
(*fire*) —, das Kamingitter ; (*for
sword*) das Stichblatt. — *v.a.* bewachen; behüten (*protect*). — *v.n.* auf
der Hut sein; — *against*, sich hüten
(vor, *Dat.*); vorbeugen.
guarded [ˈgaːdid], *adj.* behutsam,
vorsichtig.
guardian [ˈgaːdjən], *s.* der Vormund
(*of child*); der Wächter.
guardianship [ˈgaːdjənʃip], *s.* (*Law*)
die Vormundschaft.
Guatemalan [gwætiˈmaːlən], *adj.*
guatemaltekisch. — *s.* der Guatemal-
teke.
Guelph [gwelf], *s.* der Welfe.
guess [ges], *v.a.* raten (*a riddle*). —
v.n. (*Am.*) glauben, meinen. — *s.* die
Vermutung; *have a* —, rate mal!
guest [gest], *s.* der Gast; *paying* —,
der Pensionär.
guffaw [gʌˈfɔː], *s.* das (laute) Gelächter.
guidance [ˈgaidəns], *s.* die Führung,
Anleitung.
guide [gaid], *s.* der Führer, Wegweiser,
Reiseführer; (*Phot.*) die Führung. —
v.a. führen, anleiten.
guided [ˈgaidid], *adj.* gelenkt; —
missile, das Ferngeschoß, die Rakete.
guild [gild], *s.* die Gilde, Zunft, Innung.
guildhall [ˈgildhɔːl], *s.* das Rathaus.
guile [gail], *s.* der Betrug, die Arglist.
guileless [ˈgaillis], *adj.* arglos.
guilt [gilt], *s.* die Schuld.
guilty [ˈgilti], *adj.* schuldig.
guinea [ˈgini], *s.* die Guinee (21 *shillings*); — *fowl*, das Perlhuhn; — *pig*,
das Meerschweinchen.
guise [gaiz], *s.* die Verkleidung (*costume*); die Erscheinung (*appearance*).
guitar [giˈtaː], *s.* (*Mus.*) die Gitarre.
gulf [gʌlf], *s.* der Meerbusen, Golf;
der Abgrund (*abyss*).
gull [gʌl], *s.* (*Orn.*) die Möwe.
gullet [ˈgʌlit], *s.* (*Anat.*) der Schlund,
die Gurgel.
gullible [ˈgʌlibl], *adj.* leichtgläubig.
gully [ˈgʌli], *s.* die Schlucht (*abyss*).
gulp [gʌlp], *v.a.* schlucken. — *s.* der
Schluck, Zug.
gum (1) [gʌm], *s.* (*Bot.*) das Gummi.
— *v.a.* gummieren; (*coll.*) — *up*,
verderben (*spoil*).
gum (2) [gʌm], *s.* (*Anat.*) das Zahnfleisch.
gun [gʌn], *s.* das Gewehr (*rifle*); die
Kanone (*cannon*); — *carriage*, die
Lafette.

gunpowder [ˈgʌnpaudə], *s.* das Schieß-
pulver.
gunsmith [ˈgʌnsmiθ], *s.* der Büchsen-
macher.
gurgle [gəːgl], *v.n.* glucksen.
gush [gʌʃ], *v.n.* sich ergießen; schwärmen.
gusset [ˈgʌsit], *s.* (*Tail.*) der Zwickel.
gust [gʌst], *s.* der Windstoß.
gut [gʌt], *s.* (*Anat.*) der Darm; (*pl.*) die
Eingeweide, *n. pl.*; (*coll.*) der Mut.
— *v.a.* ausnehmen; ausleeren.
gutter [ˈgʌtə], *s.* die Rinne, Gosse.
guttersnipe [ˈgʌtəsnaip], *s.* der
Lausbube.
guttural [ˈgʌtərəl], *adj.* Kehl-. — *s.* (*Phon.*)
der Kehllaut.
guy [gai], *s.* die Vogelscheuche, die
verkleidete Puppe; (*Am.*) der Kerl.
guzzle [gʌzl], *v.n.* schlemmen.
gymnasium [dʒimˈneiziəm], *s.* die
Turnhalle.
gymnastics [dʒimˈnæstiks], *s. pl.* das
Turnen; die Gymnastik.
gypsum [ˈdʒipsəm], *s.* der Gips; der
schwefelsaure Kalk.
gyrate [dʒaiəˈreit], *v.n.* sich im Kreise
bewegen, sich drehen, kreisen.

H

H [eitʃ]. das H.
haberdasher [ˈhæbədæʃə], *s.* der Kurz-
warenhändler.
haberdashery [ˈhæbədæʃəri], *s.* die
Kurzwarenhandlung.
habit [ˈhæbit], *s.* die Gewohnheit
(*custom*); *force of* —, aus Gewohnheit,
die Macht der Gewohnheit; die
Kleidung (*costume*); *riding* —, das
Reitkostüm.
habitable [ˈhæbitəbl], *adj.* bewohnbar.
habitation [hæbiˈteiʃən], *s.* die Wohnung.
habitual [həˈbitjuəl], *adj.* gewohnheitsmäßig.
habituate [həˈbitjueit], *v.a.* gewöhnen.
hack (1) [hæk], *v.a.* hacken (*wood*);
treten.
hack (2) [hæk], *s.* der Lohnschreiber;
der (alte) Gaul, das Mietpferd (*horse*).
hackle [hækl], *v.a.* hecheln.
hackney [ˈhækni], *s.* — *carriage*, die
Mietskutsche; das Taxi.
haddock [ˈhædək], *s.* (*Zool.*) der Schellfisch.
haemorrhage [ˈheməridʒ], *s.* (*Med.*)
die Blutung, der Blutsturz.
haemorrhoids [ˈheməroidz], *s.pl.* (*Med.*)
die Hämorrhoiden, *f. pl.*
hag [hæg], *s.* das alte Weib; die Hexe
(*witch*).

haggard

haggard ['hægəd], *adj.* hager (*lean*); häßlich, abgehärmt.
haggle [hægl], *v.n.* feilschen.
haggler ['hæglə], *s.* der Feilscher.
hail (1) [heil], *s.* der Hagel. — *v.n.* hageln.
hail (2) [heil], *v.a.* (mit einem Ruf) begrüßen; rufen. — *interj.* Heil, willkommen! — *s.* der Zuruf, Gruß.
hair [hɛə], *s.* das Haar; *split* —*s*, Haarspalterei treiben.
haircut ['hɛəkʌt], *s.* der Haarschnitt.
hairdresser ['hɛədresə], *s.* der Friseur.
hale [heil], *adj.* — *and hearty*, frisch und gesund, rüstig.
half [hɑːf], *adj.* halb. — *adv.* — *baked*, unreif; unterentwickelt (*stupid*); (*coll.*) *not* —, und wie! sehr gern. — *s.* die Hälfte; *too clever by* —, allzu gescheit.
halfcaste ['hɑːfkɑːst], *s.* der Mischling.
halfpenny ['heipni], *s.* der halbe Penny.
halfwit ['hɑːfwit], *s.* der Dummkopf.
halibut ['hælibət], *s.* (*Zool.*) der Heilbutt.
hall [hɔːl], *s.* der Saal; die Halle; der Hausflur (*entrance* —); (*Univ.*) — (*of residence*), das Studentenheim; — *porter*, der Portier.
hallmark ['hɔːlmɑːk], *s.* das Kennzeichen.
hallow ['hælou], *v.a.* weihen, heiligen.
Halloween [hælou'iːn]. der Allerheiligenabend.
halo ['heilou], *s.* der Heiligenschein (*of saint*); der Hof (*round the moon*).
hallucination [həluːsiˈneiʃən], *s.* die Halluzination.
halt [hɔːlt], *v.n.* halten, haltmachen; —*!* Halt! zögern (*tarry*); —*ing speech,* die Sprechhemmung. — *v.a.* anhalten, zum Halten bringen. — *s.* (*Railw.*) die (kleine) Haltestelle.
halve [hɑːv], *v.a.* halbieren.
ham [hæm], *s.* (*Cul.*) der Schinken; (*Anat.*) der Schenkel; — *acting,* das Schmierentheater.
hammer ['hæmə], *s.* der Hammer. — *v.a., v.n.* hämmern; — *away at,* an etwas emsig arbeiten; — *out a problem,* ein Problem zur Lösung bringen.
hammock ['hæmək], *s.* die Hängematte.
hamper (1) ['hæmpə], *s.* der Packkorb.
hamper (2) ['hæmpə], *v.a.* behindern.
hand [hænd], *s.* die Hand; *a fair* —, eine gute Handschrift; der Uhrzeiger (*on watch, clock*); die Seite (*right, left* —); die Karten, *f. pl.* (*card game*); *play a strong* —, starke Karten halten *or* spielen; *on* —, vorrätig, auf Lager; *get out of* —, unkontrollierbar werden. — *v.a.* — *in,* einhändigen, einreichen; — *out,* austeilen; — *over,* übergeben, einhändigen.
handbag ['hændbæg], *s.* die Handtasche.
handbill ['hændbil], *s.* der Zettel, Reklamezettel (*advertising*).

handful ['hændful], *s.* die Handvoll; *to be quite a* —, genug zu schaffen geben; das Sorgenkind.
handicap ['hændikæp], *s.* das Hindernis. — *v.a.* hindern, behindern.
handicraft ['hændikrɑːft], *s.* das Handwerk; Kunsthandwerk.
handkerchief ['hæŋkətʃif], *s.* das Taschentuch.
handle [hændl], *s.* der Griff; der Henkel (*pot, vase*). — *v.a.* handhaben (*machine*); behandeln (*person*); anpacken (*problem*).
handlebar ['hændlbɑː], *s.* die Lenkstange (*bicycle*).
handmaid(en) ['hændmeid(n)], *s.* (*obs.*) die Magd.
handrail ['hændreil], *s.* das Geländer.
handshake ['hændʃeik], *s.* der Händedruck.
handsome ['hænsəm], *adj.* hübsch, schön, stattlich.
handy ['hændi], *adj.* geschickt; — *man,* der Gelegenheitsarbeiter, Mann für alles.
hang [hæŋ], *v.a. reg. & irr.* hängen; aufhängen (*suspend*); — *it!* zum Henker; — *paper,* ein Zimmer austapezieren; — *dog expression,* den Kopf hängen lassen, die betrübte Miene. — *v.n.* hängen; (*coll.*) — *on!* warte einen Moment! — *about,* herumstehen; herumlungern (*loiter*).
hanger-on [hæŋərˈɔn], *s.* der Anhänger, Mitläufer.
hangman ['hæŋmən], *s.* der Henker.
hanker ['hæŋkə], *v.n.* sich sehnen.
Hanoverian [hænoˈviəriən], *adj.* hannöversch. — *s.* der Hannoveraner.
hansom ['hænsəm], *s.* die zweirädrige Droschke.
haphazard [hæpˈhæzəd], *s.* der Zufall, das Geratewohl.
hapless ['hæplis], *adj.* unglücklich.
happen [hæpn], *v.n.* sich ereignen, passieren; — *to . . .,* zufällig . . .
happiness ['hæpinis], *s.* das Glück; die Glückseligkeit.
happy ['hæpi], *adj.* glücklich, glückselig.
harangue [həˈræŋ], *s.* die Ansprache. — *v.a.* einsprechen (auf, *Acc.*); anreden.
harass ['hærəs], *v.a.* plagen, quälen.
harbinger ['hɑːbindʒə], *s.* der Vorbote, Bote.
harbour ['hɑːbə], *s.* der Hafen. — *v.a.* beherbergen (*shelter*); hegen (*cherish*).
hard [hɑːd], *adj.* schwer (*difficult*); hart (*tough*); hartherzig (*miserly*); — *up,* in Not, in Geldverlegenheit; — *of hearing,* schwerhörig.
harden [hɑːdn], *v.a.* härten. — *v.n.* hart werden.
hardiness ['hɑːdinis], *s.* die Kraft, Stärke; die Rüstigkeit.
hardly ['hɑːdli], *adv.* kaum.
hardship ['hɑːdʃip], *s.* die Not, Bedrängnis (*need*); die Beschwerde (*complaint*).

hardware ['hɑːdwɛə], *s.* die Eisenware(n).

hardy ['hɑːdi], *adj.* abgehärtet, stark; (*Bot.*) — *annual*, ein widerstandsfähiges Jahresgewächs.

hare [hɛə], *s.* (*Zool.*) der Hase; — *brained*, unbedacht, gedankenlos; — *lip*, die Hasenscharte.

harebell ['hɛəbel], *s.* (*Bot.*) die Glockenblume.

haricot ['hærikou], *s.* (*Bot.*) — *bean*, die welsche Bohne.

hark [hɑːk], *v.n.* horchen.

harlequin ['hɑːlikwin], *s.* der Harlekin.

harlot ['hɑːlət], *s.* die Hure.

harm [hɑːm], *s.* das Leid, Unrecht; *do* — *to*, Schaden zufügen (*Dat.*).— *v.a.* verletzen (*hurt*); schaden (*damage, Dat.*).

harmful ['hɑːmful], *adj.* schädlich.

harmless ['hɑːmlis], *adj.* harmlos.

harmonious [hɑːˈmouniəs], *adj.* harmonisch; einmütig (*of one mind*).

harmonize ['hɑːmənaiz], *v.a.* in Einklang bringen. — *v.n.* harmonieren, in Einklang stehen.

harmony ['hɑːməni], *s.* (*Mus.*) die Harmonie; (*fig.*) der Einklang, die Einmütigkeit.

harness ['hɑːnis], *s.* der Harnisch. — *v.a.* anschirren, anspannen (*horse*); (*fig.*) nutzbar machen.

harp [hɑːp], *s.* (*Mus.*) die Harfe. — *v.n.* (*coll.*) — *upon*, herumreiten auf (*Dat.*).

harpoon [hɑːˈpuːn], *s.* die Harpune. — *v.a.* harpunieren.

harrow ['hærou], *s.* die Egge, Harke. — *v.a.* harken, eggen; quälen.

harry ['hæri], *v.a.* verheeren, quälen.

harsh [hɑːʃ], *adj.* herb, rauh (*rough*); streng (*severe*).

hart [hɑːt], *s.* (*Zool.*) der Hirsch.

harvest ['hɑːvist], *s.* die Ernte; — *home*, das Erntefest.

hash [hæʃ], *v.a.* zerhacken; vermischen (*mix up*). — *s.* das Hackfleisch; *make a — of things*, verpfuschen, alles verderben.

hasp [hæsp *or* hɑːsp], *s.* der Haken, die Spange.

haste [heist], *s.* die Hast, Eile (*hurry*); die Voreiligkeit (*rashness*).

hasten [heisn], *v.n.* eilen, sich beeilen.

hasty ['heisti], *adj.* voreilig.

hat [hæt], *s.* der Hut; (*coll.*) *talk through o.'s* —, Unsinn reden.

hatch (1) [hætʃ], *s.* die Brut (*chickens*). — *v.a., v.n.* (aus-)brüten; aushecken (*cunning*).

hatch (2) [hætʃ], *s.* das Servierfenster (*for serving food*); (*Naut.*) die Luke.

hatch (3) [hætʃ], *v.a.* (*Art*) schraffieren.

hatchet ['hætʃit], *s.* das Beil, die Axt; *bury the* —, das Kriegsbeil begraben.

hate [heit], *v.a., v.n.* hassen; — *to* . . ., nicht . . . wollen. — *s.* der Haß, Widerwille, die Abneigung.

hateful ['heitful], *adj.* verhaßt (*hated*); gehässig (*hating*).

hatred ['heitrid], *s.* der Haß.

hatter ['hætə], *s.* der Hutmacher.

haughty ['hɔːti], *adj.* übermütig (*supercilious*); hochmütig, stolz (*proud*); hochnäsig (*giving o.s. airs*).

haul [hɔːl], *v.a.* schleppen, ziehen. — *s.* das Schleppen; (*coll.*) die Beute.

haulage ['hɔːlidʒ], *s.* der Schleppdienst, die Spedition.

haunch [hɔːntʃ], *s.* (*Anat.*) die Hüfte; der Schenkel (*horse*); die Keule (*venison*).

haunt [hɔːnt], *v.a.* heimsuchen, spuken (in, *Dat.*); *it is* —*ed*, hier spuktes.

have [hæv], *v.a. irr.* haben, besitzen (*possess*); erhalten; lassen; — *to*, müssen; — *s.th. made, done*, etwas machen lassen.

haven [heivn], *s.* der Zufluchtsort.

haversack ['hævəsæk], *s.* der Brotbeutel.

havoc ['hævək], *s.* die Verwüstung, Verheerung.

hawk (1) [hɔːk], *s.* (*Orn.*) der Habicht; der Falke (*falcon*).

hawk (2) [hɔːk], *v.a.* hausieren.

hawker ['hɔːkə], *s.* der Hausierer.

hawthorn ['hɔːθɔːn], *s.* (*Bot.*) der Hagedorn.

hay [hei], *s.* das Heu; — *fever*, der Heuschnupfen; — *loft*, der Heuboden; — *rick*, der Heuschober.

hazard ['hæzəd], *s.* der Zufall (*chance*); die Gefahr (*danger*); das Risiko (*risk*). — *v.a.* aufs Spiel setzen, riskieren.

hazardous ['hæzədəs], *adj.* gefährlich, gewagt.

haze [heiz], *s.* der Dunst, Nebeldunst.

hazel [heizl], *s.* (*Bot.*) die Haselstaude; — *nut*, die Haselnuß.

hazy ['heizi], *adj.* dunstig, nebelig.

he [hiː] *pers. pron.* er; — *who*, derjenige, welcher, wer.

head [hed], *s.* der Kopf; die Spitze (*of arrow*); der Leiter (*of firm*); (*Sch.*) der Direktor; die Überschrift (*heading*); die Krisis (*climax*); (*Pol.*) der Führer, das (Staats-)Oberhaupt. — *v.a.* anführen, führen; (*Mil.*) befehligen: — *v.n.* (*Naut.*) — *for*, Kurs nehmen auf (*Acc.*).

headache ['hedeik], *s.* (*Med.*) die Kopfschmerzen, *m. pl.*

headlamp ['hedlæmp], *s.* der Scheinwerfer.

headphone ['hedfoun], *s.* (*usually pl.*) der Kopfhörer.

headstrong ['hedstrɔŋ], *adj.* halsstarrig.

heady ['hedi], *adj.* hastig, ungestüm; berauschend (*liquor*).

heal [hiːl], *v.a.* heilen. — *v.n.* (zu)heilen, verheilen.

health [helθ], *s.* die Gesundheit; — *resort*, der Kurort; *your* (*good*) —*!* Gesundheit! auf Ihr Wohl! Prosit! (*drinking toast*).

healthy ['helθi], *adj.* gesund.

heap [hiːp], *s.* der Haufen, die Menge. — *v.a.* häufen, aufhäufen.

hear

hear [hiə], *v.a.*, *v.n. irr.* hören; erfahren (*learn*); (*Law*) verhören (*evidence*).

hearing ['hiəriŋ], *s.* das Gehör (*auditory perception*); *within* —, in Hörweite; (*Law*) das Verhör.

hearsay ['hiəsei], *s.* das Hörensagen.

hearse [hɑːs], *s.* der Leichenwagen.

heart [hɑːt], *s.* das Herz; der Mut (*courage*); das Innerste (*core*); *by* —, auswendig; *take to* —, beherzigen; *take* — *from*, Mut fassen (aus, *Dat.*).

heartburn ['hɑːtbəːn], *s.* (*Med.*) das Sodbrennen.

heartfelt ['hɑːtfelt], *adj.* herzlich.

hearth [hɑːθ], *s.* der Herd.

hearty ['hɑːti], *adj.* herzlich; aufrichtig (*sincere*); herzhaft.

heat [hiːt], *s.* die Hitze, Wärme; die Brunst (*animals*). — *v.a.* heizen (*fuel*); erhitzen (*make hot*).

heath [hiːθ], *s.* die Heide.

heathen [hiːðən], *s.* der Heide, Ungläubige.

heather ['heðə], *s.* (*Bot.*) das Heidekraut.

heating ['hiːtiŋ], *s.* die Heizung.

heave [hiːv], *v.a. reg. & irr.* heben, hieben. — *v.n.* sich heben und senken.

heaven [hevn], *s.* der Himmel; *good* —*s!* ach, du lieber Himmel!

heaviness ['hevinis], *s.* die Schwere.

heavy ['hevi], *adj.* schwer; schwerwiegend (*grave*).

Hebrew ['hiːbruː], *adj.* hebräisch. — *s.* der Hebräer, der Jude.

hectic ['hektik], *adj.* hektisch, aufgeregt.

hector ['hektə], *v.a.* tyrannisieren (*bully*). — *v.n.* renommieren, prahlen.

hedge [hedʒ], *s.* die Hecke. — *v.a.* einhegen, einzäunen.

hedgehog ['hedʒhɔg], *s.* (*Zool.*) der Igel.

hedgerow ['hedʒrou], *s.* die Baumhecke.

heed [hiːd], *s.* die Hut, Aufmerksamkeit. — *v.a.* beachten.

heedless ['hiːdlis], *adj.* unachtsam.

heel [hiːl], *s.* die Ferse (*foot*); der Absatz (*shoe*); *take to o.'s* —*s*, die Flucht ergreifen; (*Am. sl.*) der Lump.

heifer ['hefə], *s.* (*Zool.*) die junge Kuh.

height [hait], *s.* die Höhe, Anhöhe; die Größe (*tallness*); der Hügel (*hill*).

heighten [haitn], *v.a.* erhöhen.

heir [ɛə], *s.* der Erbe (*to*, *Genit.*).

heiress ['ɛəres], *s.* die Erbin.

heirloom ['ɛəluːm], *s.* das Erbstück.

helicopter ['helikɔptə], *s.* (*Aviat.*) der Hubschrauber.

hell [hel], *s.* die Hölle. — *interj.* zum Teufel!

hellish ['heliʃ], *adj.* höllisch.

helm [helm], *s.* das Steuer, Steuerruder.

helmet ['helmit], *s.* der Helm.

helmsman ['helmzmən], *s.* (*Naut.*) der Steuermann.

help [help], *v.a.*, *v.n.* helfen (*Dat.*); *I cannot* — *laughing*, ich muß lachen; *I cannot* — *it*, ich kann nichts dafür. — *v.r.* — *o.s.*, sich bedienen. — *s.* die Hilfe, Unterstützung.

helpful ['helpful], *adj.* behilflich, hilfreich.

helping ['helpiŋ], *s.* die Portion.

helpless ['helplis], *adj.* hilflos.

helpmate, helpmeet ['helpmeit, -miːt], *s.* der Gehilfe, die Gehilfin.

helter-skelter ['heltə'skeltə], *adv.* Hals über Kopf.

hem [hem], *s.* der Saum. — *v.a.* (*Tail.*) einsäumen, säumen.

hemisphere ['hemisfiə], *s.* die Halbkugel, Hemisphäre.

hemlock ['hemlɔk], *s.* der Schierling.

hemp [hemp], *s.* der Hanf.

hemstitch ['hemstitʃ], *s.* der Hohlsaum.

hen [hen], *s.* die Henne (*poultry*); das Weibchen (*other birds*).

hence [hens], *adv.* von hier; von jetzt an.

henceforth ['hens'fɔːθ], *adv.* fortan, von nun an.

henpecked ['henpekd], *adj.* unter dem Pantoffel stehend.

her [həː], *pers. pron.* sie (*Acc.*), ihr (*Dat.*). — *poss. adj.* ihr.

herald ['herəld], *s.* der Herold. — *v.a.* ankündigen.

heraldry ['herəldri], *s.* die Wappenkunde.

herb [həːb], *s.* (*Bot.*) das Kraut.

herbaceous [həː'beiʃəs], *adj.* krautartig.

herbage [həː'bidʒ], *s.* das Gras; (*Law*) das Weiderecht.

herbal ['həːbəl], *adj.* krautartig, Kräuter-, Kraut-.

herd [həːd], *s.* die Herde. — *v.n.* sich zusammenrotten.

here [hiə], *adv.* hier.

hereafter [hiər'ɑːftə], *adv.* hernach, künftig. —*s.* die Zukunft; das Jenseits.

hereby [hiə'bai], *adv.* hiermit.

hereditary [hi'reditəri], *adj.* erblich.

heredity [hi'rediti], *s.* (*Biol.*) die Erblichkeit, Vererbung.

heresy ['herisi], *s.* die Ketzerei.

heretic ['heritik], *s.* der Ketzer.

heretofore ['hiətufɔː], *adv.* zuvor, vormals.

heritage ['heritidʒ], *s.* die Erbschaft.

hermetic [həː'metik], *adj.* luftdicht.

hermit ['həːmit], *s.* der Eremit, Einsiedler.

hero ['hiərou], *s.* der Held.

heroic [hi'rouik], *adj.* heldenhaft, heldenmütig.

heroine ['heroin], *s.* die Heldin.

heroism ['heroizm], *s.* der Heldenmut.

heron ['herən], *s.* (*Orn.*) der Reiher.

herring ['heriŋ], *s.* (*Zool.*) der Hering; *red* —, die Ablenkungsfinte, das Ablenkungsmanöver; — *bone*, die Gräte; *pickled* —, der eingemachte Hering.

hers [həːz], *poss. pron.* ihr, der ihre, der ihrige.

herself [həː'self], *pers. pron.* sich; sie selbst.

hesitate ['heziteit], *v.n.* zögern, zaudern; unschlüssig sein (*be undecided*).

410

hesitation [hezi'teiʃən], *s.* das Zögern, Zaudern; das Bedenken (*deliberation*).
Hessian ['heʃən], *adj.* hessisch. — *s.* der Hesse.
hessian ['hesiən], *s.* die Sackleinwand (*textile*).
heterodox ['hetərədɔks], *adj.* irrgläubig.
heterogeneous [hetərə'dʒi:niəs], *adj.* heterogen, ungleichartig.
hew [hju:], *v.a. irr.* hauen.
hexagonal [hek'sægənəl], *adj.* sechseckig.
hiatus [hai'eitəs], *s.* die Lücke.
hibernate ['haibəneit], *v.n.* überwintern.
hibernation [haibə'neiʃən], *s.* der Winterschlaf.
hiccup ['hikʌp], *s.* (*usually pl.*) (*Med.*) der Schlucken, Schluckauf.
hickory ['hikəri], *s.* (*Bot.*) das Hickoryholz.
hide (1) [haid], *v.a. irr.* verstecken, verbergen. — *v.n. irr.* sich verbergen; — *and seek*, das Versteckspiel.
hide (2) [haid], *s.* die Haut (*of animal*), das Fell, (*tanned*) das Leder.
hideous ['hidiəs], *adj.* häßlich, scheußlich, furchtbar.
hiding (1) ['haidiŋ], *s.* das Versteck.
hiding (2) ['haidiŋ], *s.* die Tracht Prügel.
hierarchy ['haiərɑ:ki], *s.* die Hierarchie.
higgle [higl] *see* **haggle**.
higgledy-piggledy ['higldi'pigldi], *adv.* wüst durcheinander.
high [hai], *adj.* hoch; erhaben, vornehm; angegangen (*meat*); — *school*, die höhere Schule; — *time*, höchste Zeit; (*Am.*) vergnügliche Zeit; *High Church*, die Hochkirche. — *s.* (*Meteor.*) das Hoch.
Highness ['hainis], *s.* die Hoheit (*title*).
highroad, highway ['hairoud, 'haiwei], *s.* die Haupt- *or* Landstraße.
highwayman ['haiweimən], *s.* der Straßenräuber.
hike [haik], *v.n.* wandern, einen Ausflug machen. — *s.* die Wanderung, der Ausflug.
hilarious [hi'lɛəriəs], *adj.* fröhlich, lustig, ausgelassen.
hill [hil], *s.* der Hügel, Berg.
hilt [hilt], *s.* der Griff.
him [him], *pers. pron.* ihn, ihm.
himself [him'self], *pers. pron.* sich; er selbst.
hind [haind], *s.* (*Zool.*) die Hirschkuh, Hindin.
hinder ['hində], *v.a.* hindern.
hindmost ['haindmoust], *adj.* hinterst; *the devil take the* —, den letzten hol der Teufel! nach mir die Sintflut!
hindrance ['hindrəns], *s.* das Hindernis; (*Law*) *without let or* —, ohne Hinderung.
Hindu [hin'du:], *s.* der Hindu.
hinge [hindʒ], *s.* die Angel, der Angelpunkt. — *v.n.* sich um etwas drehen; von etwas abhängen (on, *Dat.*).

hint [hint], *v.n.* zu verstehen geben, auf etwas hindeuten (at, auf, *Acc.*), andeuten. — *s.* die Andeutung, der Fingerzeig.
hip (1) [hip], *s.* (*Anat.*) die Hüfte.
hip (2) [hip], *s.* (*Bot.*) die Hagebutte.
hire ['haiə], *v.a.* (ver-)mieten (*car etc.*); anstellen (*man etc.*). — *s.* die Miete; der Lohn (*wage*); — *purchase*, der Abzahlungskauf, die Ratenzahlung.
hireling ['haiəliŋ], *s.* der Mietling.
hirsute ['hə:sju:t], *adj.* behaart, haarig.
his [hiz], *poss. adj.* sein, seine. — *poss. pron.* sein, der seinige, der seine.
hiss [his], *v.n.* zischen (at, auf, *Acc.*). — *s.* das Zischen.
historian [his'tɔ:riən], *s.* der Historiker, der Geschichtsschreiber.
historical [his'tɔrikəl], *adj.* historisch, geschichtlich.
history ['histəri], *s.* die Geschichte, die Geschichtswissenschaft.
histrionic [histri'ɔnik], *adj.* schauspielerisch.
hit [hit], *v.a. irr.* schlagen, stoßen. — *s.* der Schlag, der Treffer (*on the target*); (*Am.*) der Schlager, Erfolg (*success*); — *parade*, die Schlagerparade.
hitch [hitʃ], *v.a.* anhaken (*hook*); anhängen; — *a lift*, — *hike*, per Anhalter fahren. — *s.* der Nachteil, der Haken.
hither ['hiðə], *adv.* hierher.
hitherto [hiðə'tu:], *adv.* bisher.
hive [haiv], *s.* der Bienenkorb; Bienenstock; — *of bees*, der Schwarm.
hoar [hɔ:], *adj.* eisgrau, weißlich; — *frost*, der Reif.
hoard [hɔ:d], *v.a.* hamstern. — *s.* der Vorrat, Schatz.
hoarding ['hɔ:diŋ], *s.* die Umzäunung, die Bretterwand; die Reklamewand.
hoarse [hɔ:s], *adj.* heiser.
hoarseness ['hɔ:snis], *s.* die Heiserkeit.
hoax [houks], *s.* der Betrug, die Irreführung; der Schabernack (*in fun*). — *v.a.* betrügen; foppen (*in fun*).
hobble [hɔbl], *v.n.* humpeln. — *v.a.* an den Füßen fesseln.
hobby ['hɔbi], *s.* das Steckenpferd, Hobby, die Liebhaberei.
hobgoblin [hɔb'gɔblin], *s.* der Kobold.
hobnail ['hɔbneil], *s.* der Hufnagel.
hobnailed ['hɔbneild], *adj.* — *boots*, genagelte Stiefel, *m. pl.*
hobnob [hɔb'nɔb], *v.n.* (*coll.*) vertraulich sein.
hock (1) [hɔk], *s.* (*Anat.*) das Sprunggelenk.
hock (2) [hɔk], *s.* (*wine*) der Rheinwein.
hod [hɔd], *s.* (*Build.*) der Trog; der Eimer (*coal*).
hodge-podge *see under* **hotchpotch**.
hoe [hou], *s.* die Hacke, Harke. — *v.a., v.n.* hacken, harken.
hog [hɔg], *s.* das Schwein. — *v.a.* verschlingen (*food*); an sich reißen (*grasp*).
hogshead ['hɔgzhed], *s.* das Oxhoft.
hoist [hɔist], *v.a.* hissen.

hold

hold [hould], *v.a.*, *v.n. irr.* halten (*keep*); enthalten (*contain*); behaupten (*assert*); meinen (*think*); gelten (*be valid*); — *forth*, deklamieren; — *good*, sich bewähren; — *out*, hinhalten (*hope*); (*endure*) aushalten; —*up*, aufhalten. — *s.* (*Naut.*) der Schiffsraum; die Macht (*power*).

holder ['houldə], *s.* der Inhaber, Besitzer.

holding ['houldiŋ], *s.* das Pachtgut (*farm*); der Besitz (*property*); (*Comm.*) der Trust.

hole [houl], *s.* das Loch; die Höhle (*cavity*). — *v.a.* aushöhlen; (*Golf*) ins Loch spielen.

holiday ['hɔlidei], *s.* der Feiertag; der Urlaub (*vacation*); (*pl.*) die Ferien, *pl.*

holiness ['houlinis], *s.* die Heiligkeit.

hollow ['hɔlou], *adj.* hohl. — *s.* die Höhlung; die Höhle.

holly ['hɔli], *s.* (*Bot.*) die Stechpalme.

hollyhock ['hɔlihɔk], *s.* (*Bot.*) die Stockrose.

holocaust ['hɔlokɔːst], *s.* das Brandopfer; die Katastrophe.

holster ['houlstə], *s.* die Pistolentasche, die Halfter.

holy ['houli], *adj.* heilig; *Holy Week*, die Karwoche.

homage ['hɔmidʒ], *s.* die Huldigung; *pay — to*, huldigen (*Dat.*).

home [houm], *s.* das Heim, die Wohnung; die Heimat; *at —*, zu Hause; *Home Office*, das Innenministerium; — *Rule*, (*Pol.*) die Selbstverwaltung.

homer ['houmə] (*Am.*) *see* **homing pigeon**.

homesick ['houmsik], *adj.* an Heimweh leidend.

homestead ['houmsted], *s.* der Bauernhof.

homicide ['hɔmisaid], *s.* der Mord (*crime*); der Mörder (*killer*).

homily ['hɔmili], *s.* die Predigt; Moralpredigt.

homing pigeon ['houmiŋ'pidʒən], *s.* die Brieftaube.

homogeneous [hɔmə'dʒiːniəs], *adj.* homogen; gleichartig.

hone [houn], *s.* der Wetzstein. — *v.a.* (*blade, knife*) abziehen.

honest ['ɔnist], *adj.* ehrlich, aufrichtig.

honesty ['ɔnisti], *s.* die Ehrlichkeit.

honey ['hʌni], *s.* der Honig; (*Am., coll.*) Liebling!

honeycomb ['hʌnikoum], *s.* die Honigwabe.

honeymoon ['hʌnimuːn], *s.* die Flitterwochen.

honorarium [ɔnə'rɛəriəm], *s.* das Honorar.

honorary ['ɔnərəri], *adj.* Ehren-, ehrenamtlich.

honour ['ɔnə], *s.* die Ehre; *your —*, Euer Ehrwürden, Euer Gnaden (*title*). — *v.a.* ehren, auszeichnen.

honourable ['ɔnərəbl], *adj.* ehrenwert, ehrenvoll; Hochwohlgeboren (*title*).

hood [hud], *s.* die Kapuze; das akademische Gradabzeichen über dem Talar; (*Hunt.*) die Haube; —*ed falcon*, der Jagdfalke (mit Haube).

hoodwink ['hudwiŋk], *v.a.* täuschen.

hoof [huːf *or* huf], *s.* der Huf (*horse*); die Klaue.

hook [huk], *s.* der Haken; *by — or by crook*, mit allen Mitteln. — *v.a.* angeln, fangen.

hooked [hukd], *adj.* gekrümmt, hakenförmig.

hooligan ['huːligən], *s.* der Rowdy.

hoop [huːp], *s.* der Reifen. — *v.a.* (ein Faß) binden.

hooper ['huːpə], *s.* der Böttcher.

hoopoe ['huːpou], *s.* (*Orn.*) der Wiedehopf.

hoot [huːt], *v.n.* schreien (*owl*); ertönen (*siren*); hupen (*car*).

hooter ['huːtə], *s.* die Sirene (*siren*); die Hupe (*car*).

hop (1) [hɔp], *v.n.* hüpfen, tanzen; —*ping mad*, ganz verrückt.

hop (2) [hɔp], *s.* (*Bot.*) der Hopfen. — *v.a.* (*beer*) hopfen, Hopfen zusetzen (*Dat.*). — *v.n.* Hopfen ernten.

hope [houp], *s.* die Hoffnung. — *v.n.* hoffen (*for*, auf, *Acc.*).

hopeless ['houplis], *adj.* hoffnungslos.

horizon [hə'raizən], *s.* der Horizont.

horizontal [hɔri'zɔntl], *adj.* horizontal, waagrecht.

horn [hɔːn], *s.* das Horn; (*Mus.*) *French —*, das Waldhorn, Horn; (*Motor.*) die Hupe.

hornet ['hɔːnit], *s.* (*Ent.*) die Hornisse.

hornpipe ['hɔːnpaip], *s.* (*Mus.*) der Matrosentanz; die Hornpfeife.

horrible ['hɔribl], *adj.* schrecklich.

horrid ['hɔrid], *adj.* abscheulich.

horrific [hɔ'rifik], *adj.* schrecklich, schreckenerregend.

horror ['hɔrə], *s.* der Schrecken, das Entsetzen; (*fig.*) der Greuel.

horse [hɔːs], *s.* das Pferd, Roß; *on —back*, zu Pferd.

horseman ['hɔːsmən], *s.* der Reiter.

horsepower ['hɔːspauə], *s.* die Pferdestärke.

horseradish ['hɔːsrædiʃ], *s.* der Meerrettich.

horseshoe ['hɔːsʃuː], *s.* das Hufeisen.

horticulture ['hɔːtikʌltʃə], *s.* der Gartenbau.

hose [houz], *s.* die Strümpfe, *m. pl.* (*stockings*); der Schlauch (*water pipe*).

hosiery ['houʒəri], *s.* die Strumpfwarenindustrie; die Strumpfwaren.

hospitable [hɔs'pitəbl], *adj.* gastlich, gastfreundlich.

hospital ['hɔspitl], *s.* das Krankenhaus.

hospitality [hɔspi'tæliti], *s.* die Gastlichkeit, Gastfreundschaft.

host (1) [houst], *s.* der Gastwirt (*landlord*); der Gastgeber.

host (2) [houst], *s.* (*Rel.*) *angelic —*, die Engelschar; (*Mil.*) das Heer, die Heerschar.

host (3) [houst], *s.* (*Eccl.*) die Hostie.

hostage ['hɔstidʒ], *s.* die Geisel.
hostess ['houstis *or* –tes], *s.* die Gastgeberin; *air* —, die Stewardeß.
hostile ['hɔstail], *adj.* feindlich; feindselig (*inimical*).
hot [hɔt], *adj.* heiß; hitzig (*temperament*); scharf, gewürzt (*of spices*); (*fig.*) heftig, erbittert.
hotchpotch, hodge-podge ['hɔtʃpɔtʃ, 'hɔdʒpɔdʒ], *s.* das Mischmasch.
hotel [ho(u)'tel],*s.*das Hotel,der Gasthof.
hothouse ['hɔthaus], *s.* das Treibhaus.
hound [haund], *s.* (*Zool.*) der Jagdhund. — *v.a.* hetzen.
hour ['auə], *s.* die Stunde; — *hand,* der Stundenzeiger; *for* —*s,* studenlang; *keep early (late)* —*s,* früh (spät) zu Bett gehen.
hourglass ['auəglɑːs], *s.* die Sanduhr.
hourly ['auəli], *adj., adv.,* stündlich.
house [haus], *s.* das Haus; (*Comm.*) die Firma. — [hauz], *v.a.* beherbergen, unterbringen.
houseboat ['hausbout], *s.* das Wohnboot.
housebreaking ['hausbreikiŋ], *s.* der Einbruch.
household ['haushould], *s.* der Haushalt.
housekeeper ['hauskiːpə], *s.* die Haushälterin.
housewife ['hauswaif], *s.* die Hausfrau.
housing ['hauziŋ], *s.* die Unterbringung; — *department,* das Wohnungsamt.
hovel [hɔvl *or* hʌvl], *s.* die Hütte.
hover ['hɔvə *or* 'hʌvə], *v.n.* schweben, schwanken.
how [hau], *adv.* wie; — *do you do? (in introduction)* sehr angenehm; — *are you?* wie geht es Ihnen, Dir?
however [hau'evə], *adv.* wie immer, wie auch immer, wie sehr auch. — *conj.* doch, jedoch, dennoch.
howl [haul], *v.n.* heulen. — *s.* das Geheul.
hoyden ['hɔidn], *s.* das wilde Mädchen.
hub [hʌb], *s.* die Nabe (am Rad); — *of the universe,* die Mitte der Welt.
hubbub ['hʌbʌb], *s.* der Tumult, Lärm.
huckaback ['hʌkəbæk], *s.* der Zwillich (*textile*).
huckle [hʌkl], *s.* die Hüfte.
huddle [hʌdl], *v.n.* sich drängen, sich zusammenducken. — *s.* das Gedränge.
hue [hjuː], *s.* der Farbton, die Tönung.
huff [hʌf], *s.* die schlechte Laune, die Mißstimmung.
huffy ['hʌfi], *adj.* mißmutig, übel gelaunt.
hug [hʌg], *v.a.* umarmen. — *s.* die Umarmung.
huge [hjuːdʒ], *adj.* riesig, groß, ungeheuer.
Huguenot ['hjuːgənou *or* –nɔt], *s.* der Hugenotte. — *adj.* hugenottisch, Hugenotten-.

hulk [hʌlk], *s.* (*Naut.*) das Schiffsinnere, der Schiffsrumpf; der schwerfällige Mensch.
hull [hʌl], *s.* die Hülse, Schale; (*Naut., Aviat.*) der Rumpf. — *v.a.* (*Engin.*) hülsen.
hullo! [hə'lou], *interj.* hallo!
hum [hʌm], *v.n.* summen, brummen. — *s.* das Summen, Brummen, Gemurmel (*murmuring*).
human ['hjuːmən], *adj.* menschlich. — *s.* der Mensch.
humane [hjuː'mein], *adj.* menschenfreundlich.
humanity [hjuː'mæniti], *s.* die Menschheit (*mankind*); die Menschlichkeit (*compassion*); (*pl.*) die klassischen Fächer, *n. pl.,* die humanistischen Wissenschaften, *f. pl.*
humanize ['hjuːmənaiz], *v.a.* menschlich oder gesittet machen.
humble [hʌmbl], *adj.* demütig; bescheiden (*modest*); unterwürfig (*servile*). — *v.a.* erniedrigen (*humiliate*).
humbug ['hʌmbʌg], *s.* die Schwindelei (*swindle*); der Schwindler (*crook*); der Unsinn (*nonsense*).
humdrum ['hʌmdrʌm], *adj.* langweilig, eintönig.
humid ['hjuːmid], *adj.* feucht.
humidity [hjuː'miditi], *s.* die Feuchtigkeit.
humiliate [hjuː'milieit], *v.a.* erniedrigen.
humility [hjuː'militi], *s.* die Demut.
humming-bird ['hʌmiŋbəːd], *s.* (*Orn.*) der Kolibri.
humming-top ['hʌmiŋtɔp], *s.* der Brummkreisel.
humorous ['hjuːmərəs], *adj.* humoristisch, spaßhaft, komisch.
humour ['hjuːmə], *s.* der Humor, die (gute) Laune. — *v.a.* in guter Laune erhalten, gut stimmen; willfahren (*Dat.*).
hump [hʌmp], *s.* der Buckel, der Höcker.
hunch [hʌntʃ], *s.* der Buckel; *have a* —, das Gefühl haben.
hunchback ['hʌntʃbæk], *s.* der Bucklige.
hundred ['hʌndrəd], *num. adj. a* —, hundert.
hundredweight ['hʌndrədweit], *s.* der (englische) Zentner.
Hungarian [haŋ'gɛəriən],*adj.*ungarisch. — *s.* der Ungar.
hunger ['hʌŋgə], *s.* der Hunger.
hungry ['hʌŋgri], *adj.* hungrig.
hunt [hʌnt], *s.* die Jagd. — *v.a., v.n.* jagen.
hunter ['hʌntə], *s.* der Jäger.
hurdle [həːdl], *s.* die Hürde.
hurdy-gurdy ['həːdiɡəːdi], *s.* der Leierkasten.
hurl [həːl], *v.a.* schleudern, werfen.
hurly-burly ['həːliːbəːli], *s.* der Wirrwarr.
hurricane ['hʌrikin], *s.* der Orkan; — *lamp,* die Sturmlaterne.
hurried ['hʌrid], *adj.* eilig, hastig.

hurry

hurry ['hʌri], *v.n.* eilen, sich beeilen; — *to do*, eiligst tun. — *v.a.* beschleunigen. — *s.* die Eile, Hast, Beschleunigung.

hurt [hə:t], *v.a. irr.* verletzen; wehetun (*Dat.*); (*verbally*) kränken. — *s.* die Verletzung, Kränkung.

hurtful ['hə:tful], *adj.* schädlich, kränkend.

husband ['hʌzbənd], *s.* der Mann, Ehemann, Gemahl. — *v.a.* verwalten, sparsam verfahren mit (*Dat.*).

husbandman ['hʌzbəndmən], *s.* der Landwirt.

husbandry ['hʌzbəndri], *s.* die Landwirtschaft.

hush [hʌʃ], *v.a.* zum Schweigen bringen. — *s.* die Stille; — *money*, das Schweigegeld.

husky (1) ['hʌski], *adj.* heiser (*voice*).

husky (2) ['hʌski], *s.* (*Zool.*) der Eskimohund.

hussy ['hʌzi], *s.* (*coll.*) das Frauenzimmer.

hustings ['hʌstiŋz], *s.* die Wahltribüne.

hustle [hʌsl], *v.a.* drängen, stoßen. — *s.* das Gedränge.

hut [hʌt], *s.* die Hütte, Baracke.

hutch [hʌtʃ], *s.* der Trog, Kasten (*chest*).

hybrid ['haibrid], *adj.* Bastard-. — *s.* der Bastard.

hydraulic [hai'drɔ:lik], *adj.* hydraulisch.

hydrogen ['haidrədʒən], *s.* der Wasserstoff.

hydroelectric [haidroui'lektrik], *adj.* hydroelektrisch.

hyena [hai'i:nə], *s.* (*Zool.*) die Hyäne.

hygiene ['haidʒi:n], *s.* die Hygiene, Gesundheitslehre.

hymn [him], *s.* die Hymne, das Kirchenlied.

hymnal ['himnəl], *s.* das Gesangbuch.

hyper- ['haipə], *prefix.* über-.

hyperbole [hai'pə:bəli], *s.* die Übertreibung.

hyphen ['haifən], *s.* der Bindestrich.

hypnosis [hip'nousis], *s.* die Hypnose.

hypochondriac [haipo'kɔndriæk], *adj.* hypochondrisch. — *s.* der Hypochonder.

hypocrisy [hi'pɔkrisi], *s.* die Heuchelei.

hypocrite ['hipəkrit], *s.* der Heuchler.

hypothesis [hai'pɔθisis], *s.* die Hypothese.

hypothetical [haipə'θetikəl], *adj.* hypothetisch, angenommen.

hysteria [his'tiəriə], *s.* die Hysterie.

I

I [ai]. das I.
I [ai], *pers. pron.* ich.

ice [ais], *s.* das Eis; — *bound*, eingefroren; (*Naut.*) — *breaker*, der Eisbrecher; (*Am.*) — *box*, der Kühlschrank; — *cream*, das Eis; das Gefrorene. — *v.a.* (*confectionery*) verzuckern; (*cake*) glasieren.

Icelander ['aislændə], *s.* der Isländer.

Icelandic [ais'lændik], *adj.* isländisch.

icicle ['aisikl], *s.* der Eiszapfen.

icy ['aisi], *adj.* eisig.

idea [ai'diə], *s.* die Idee.

ideal [ai'diəl], *adj.* ideal. — *s.* das Ideal.

idealize [ai'diəlaiz], *v.a.* idealisieren.

identical [ai'dentikəl], *adj.* identisch, gleich.

identification [aidentifi'keiʃən], *s.* die Gleichsetzung, Identifizierung.

identify [ai'dentifai], *v.a.* identifizieren, gleichsetzen.

identity [ai'dentiti], *s.* die Identität, Gleichheit.

idiocy ['idiəsi], *s.* der Blödsinn.

idiom ['idiəm], *s.* das Idiom, die sprachliche Eigentümlichkeit.

idiomatic [idio'mætik], *adj.* idiomatisch.

idiosyncrasy [idio'siŋkrəsi], *s.* die Empfindlichkeit, die Abneigung (gegen, *Acc.*); die Idiosynkrasie.

idle [aidl], *adj.* unnütz (*useless*); müßig, faul (*lazy*). — *v.n.* träge sein.

idleness ['aidlnis], *s.* der Müßiggang, die Faulheit.

idiot ['idiət], *s.* der Idiot.

idol [aidl], *s.* das Götzenbild; das Idol.

idolatry [ai'dɔlətri], *s.* die Götzenverehrung.

idolize ['aidolaiz], *v.a.* vergöttern, abgöttisch lieben.

idyll ['aidil *or* 'idil], *s.* die Idylle, das Idyll.

idyllic [ai'dilik *or* i'dilik], *adj.* idyllisch.

if [if], *conj.* wenn, falls (*in case*); ob (*whether*).

igneous ['igniəs], *adj.* feurig.

ignite [ig'nait], *v.a.* entzünden. — *v.n.* zur Entzündung kommen, sich entzünden.

ignition [ig'niʃən], *s.* die Zündung.

ignoble [ig'noubl], *adj.* unedel, gemein.

ignominious [igno'miniəs], *adj.* schimpflich, schmählich.

ignominy ['ignomini], *s.* die Schande, Schmach.

ignoramus [ignə'reiməs], *s.* der Unwissende.

ignorance ['ignərəns], *s.* die Unwissenheit, Unkenntnis.

ignorant ['ignərənt], *adj.* unwissend.

ignore [ig'nɔ:], *v.a.* ignorieren, nicht beachten.

ill [il], *adj.* böse, schlimm (*bad*); krank (*sick*); — *feeling*, die Verstimmung. — *adv.* — *at ease*, unbequem, verlegen; *can* — *afford*, kann sich kaum leisten …; —*timed*, zu unrechter Zeit.

illbred [il'bred], *adj.* ungezogen.

illegal [i'li:gəl], *adj.* illegal, ungesetzlich.

illegibility [iledʒi'biliti], *s.* die Unleserlichkeit.

illegible [iˈledʒibl], *adj.* unleserlich.
illegitimacy [iliˈdʒitiməsi], *s.* die Unehelichkeit, Illegitimität.
illegitimate [iliˈdʒitimit], *adj.* illegitim, unehelich.
illicit [[iˈlisit], *adj.* unerlaubt.
illiteracy [iˈlitərəsi], *s.* die Unkenntnis des Schreibens und Lesens, das Analphabetentum.
illiterate [iˈlitərit], *s.* der Analphabet.
illness [ˈilnis], *s.* die Krankheit.
illogical [iˈlɔdʒikəl], *adj.* unlogisch.
illuminate [iˈljuːmineit], *v.a.* erleuchten; (*fig.*) aufklären.
illuminating [iˈljuːmineitiŋ], *adj.* aufschlußreich.
illumination [iljuːmiˈneiʃən], *s.* die Erleuchtung; die Erklärung (*explanation*).
illusion [iˈljuːʒən], *s.* die Illusion, Täuschung.
illusive, illusory [iˈljuːziv, iˈljuːzəri], *adj.* trügerisch, täuschend.
illustrate [ˈiləstreit], *v.a.* erläutern; illustrieren (*with pictures*).
illustration [iləsˈtreiʃən], *s.* die Illustration (*pictorial*); Erläuterung, Erklärung; das Beispiel (*instance*).
illustrious [iˈlʌstriəs], *adj.* glänzend, berühmt.
image [ˈimidʒ], *s.* das Bild; das Ebenbild; die Erscheinung (*appearance*).
imagery [ˈimidʒəri], *s.* der Gebrauch von Stilbildern (*style*), die Bildersprache.
imaginable [iˈmædʒinəbl], *adj.* denkbar.
imaginary [iˈmædʒinəri], *adj.* eingebildet, nicht wirklich, vermeintlich.
imagination [imədʒiˈneiʃən], *s.* die Einbildung; die Vorstellung; die Phantasie.
imaginative [iˈmædʒinətiv], *adj.* erfinderisch, voll Phantasie.
imagine [iˈmædʒin], *v.a.* sich vorstellen, sich denken.
imbecile [ˈimbisail *or* ˈimbisiːl], *adj.* schwachsinnig. — *s.* der Idiot.
imbecility [imbiˈsiliti], *s.* der Schwachsinn.
imbibe [imˈbaib], *v.a.* trinken; (*fig.*) in sich aufnehmen.
imbroglio [imˈbrouliou], *s.* die Verwicklung.
imbue [imˈbjuː], *v.a.* erfüllen, sättigen (*fig.*).
imitate [ˈimiteit], *v.a.* nachahmen, imitieren.
imitation [imiˈteiʃən], *s.* die Nachahmung, Imitation; — *leather*, das Kunstleder.
immaculate [iˈmækjulit], *adj.* unbefleckt, makellos.
immaterial [iməˈtiəriəl], *adj.* unwesentlich, unwichtig.
immature [iməˈtjuə], *adj.* unreif.
immeasurable [iˈmeʒərəbl], *adj.* unermeßlich.
immediate [iˈmiːdjit], *adj.* unmittelbar, direkt, sofortig.

immediately [iˈmiːdjətli], *adv.* sofort.
immemorial [imiˈmɔːriəl], *adj.* undenklich, ewig.
immense [iˈmens], *adj.* unermeßlich, ungeheuer.
immerse [iˈməːs], *v.a.* eintauchen.
immersion [iˈməːʃən], *s.* das Eintauchen, die Versenkung; — *heater*, der Tauchsieder.
immigrant [ˈimigrənt], *s.* der Einwanderer.
imminent [ˈiminənt], *adj.* bevorstehend.
immobile [iˈmoubail], *adj.* unbeweglich.
immoderate [iˈmɔdərit], *adj.* unmäßig.
immodest [iˈmɔdist], *adj.* unbescheiden; unsittlich, unanständig (*immoral*).
immodesty [iˈmɔdisti], *s.* die Unanständigkeit (*indecency*); Unbescheidenheit (*presumption*).
immolate [ˈiməleit], *v.a.* opfern.
immoral [iˈmɔrəl], *adj.* unsittlich, unmoralisch.
immortal [iˈmɔːtl], *adj.* unsterblich.
immortalize [iˈmɔːtəlaiz], *v.a.* verewigen, unsterblich machen.
immovable [iˈmuːvəbl], *adj.* unbeweglich (*fig.*).
immunity [iˈmjuːniti], *s.* die Freiheit, Straffreiheit; Immunität.
immutable [iˈmjuːtəbl], *adj.* unabänderlich; unveränderlich.
imp [imp], *s.* der Knirps, Kobold, kleine Schelm.
impair [imˈpɛə], *v.a.* beeinträchtigen; vermindern (*reduce*).
impale [imˈpeil], *v.a.* aufspießen; durchbohren.
impalpable [imˈpælpəbl], *adj.* unfühlbar, unmerklich.
impart [imˈpaːt], *v.a.* erteilen; verleihen (*confer*); mitteilen (*inform*).
impartial [imˈpaːʃəl], *adj.* unparteiisch.
impartiality [impaːʃiˈæliti], *s.* die Unparteilichkeit, Objektivität.
impassable [imˈpaːsəbl], *adj.* unwegsam, unpassierbar.
impasse [imˈpæs], *s.* der völlige Stillstand.
impassioned [imˈpæʃənd], *adj.* leidenschaftlich.
impassive [imˈpæsiv], *adj.* unempfindlich.
impatience [imˈpeiʃəns], *s.* die Ungeduld.
impatient [imˈpeiʃənt], *adj.* ungeduldig.
impeach [imˈpiːtʃ], *v.a.* anklagen.
impeachment [imˈpiːtʃmənt], *s.* die Anklage.
impecunious [impiˈkjuːniəs], *adj.* unbemittelt, mittellos.
impede [imˈpiːd], *v.a.* behindern, verhindern.
impediment [imˈpedimənt], *s.* das Hindernis.
impel [imˈpel], *v.a.* antreiben; zwingen (*force*).

impending

impending [im'pendiŋ], *adj.* bevorstehend, drohend.

impenetrable [im'penitrəbl], *adj.* undurchdringlich, unerforschlich.

impenitent [im'penitənt], *adj.* reuelos,
unbußfertig.

imperative [im'perətiv], *adj.* zwingend
(*cogent*); dringend notwendig. — *s.*
(*Gram.*) der Imperativ, die Befehls-
form.

imperceptible [impə'septibl], *adj.* unmerklich.

imperfect [im'pə:fikt], *adj.* unvollständig, unvollkommen; fehlerhaft
(*goods etc.*). — *s.* (*Gram.*) das Imperfekt.

imperial [im'piəriəl], *adj.* kaiserlich,
Kaiser-, Reichs-.

imperil [im'peril], *v.a.* gefährden; in
Gefahr bringen, einer Gefahr aussetzen.

imperious [im'piəriəs], *adj.* gebieterisch.

imperishable [im'periʃəbl], *adj.* unverwüstlich, unvergänglich.

impermeable [im'pə:miəbl], *adj.* undurchdringlich.

impersonal [im'pə:sənəl], *adj.* unper-
sönlich.

impersonate [im'pə:səneit], *v.a.* verkörpern, darstellen; sich ausgeben als.

impertinence [im'pə:tinəns], *s.* die
Anmaßung, Frechheit, Unverschämtheit.

impertinent [im'pə:tinənt], *adj.* anmaßend, frech, unverschämt.

imperturbable [impə'tə:bəbl], *adj.*
unerschütterlich, ruhig, gelassen.

impervious [im'pə:viəs], *adj.* unwegsam, undurchdringlich.

impetuous [im'petjuəs], *adj.* ungestüm, heftig.

impetus ['impitəs], *s.* die Triebkraft,
der Antrieb.

impinge [im'pindʒ], *v.n.* verstoßen
(*on,* gegen); übergreifen (*on,* in).

implacable [im'plækəbl], *adj.* unversöhnlich.

implement ['implimənt], *s.* das Gerät.
— [impli'ment], *v.a.* (*Law*) erfüllen,
in Wirkung setzen, in Kraft treten
lassen.

implementation [implimen'teiʃən], *s.*
das Inkrafttreten, die Erfüllung,
Ausführung.

implicate ['implikeit], *v.a.* verwickeln.

implicit [im'plisit], *adj.* unbedingt;
einbegriffen.

implore [im'plɔ:], *v.a.* anflehen.

imply [im'plai], *v.a.* besagen, meinen;
andeuten.

impolite [impə'lait], *adj.* unhöflich,
grob.

impolitic [im'pɔlitik], *adj.* unklug, un-
politisch, undiplomatisch.

imponderable [im'pɔndərəbl], *adj.* unwägbar. — *s. pl.* unwägbare, unvor-
hersehbare Umstände, *m.pl.*

import [im'pɔ:t], *v.a.* einführen, im-
portieren; bedeuten, besagen. —

['impɔ:t], *s.* (*Comm.*) die Einfuhr, der
Import; die Bedeutung (*importance,
meaning*), Wichtigkeit (*significance*);
(*Comm.*) — *licence,* die Einfuhrgeneh-
migung.

importance [im'pɔ:təns], *s.* die Bedeutung, Wichtigkeit.

important [im'pɔ:tənt], *adj.* bedeutend,
wichtig.

importation [impɔ:'teiʃən], *s.* die
Einfuhr.

importune [impɔ:'tju:n], *v.a.* belästigen, angehen, dringend bitten.

impose [im'pouz], *v.a.* aufbürden,
auferlegen. — *v.n.* — *upon s.o.,* einen
belästigen.

imposition [impə'ziʃən], *s.* die Belästigung; (*Sch.*) die Strafarbeit.

impossible [im'pɔsibl], *adj.* unmöglich.

impostor [im'pɔstə], *s.* der Schwindler,
Betrüger.

impotent ['impətənt], *adj.* schwach,
machtlos; impotent (*sexually*).

impound [im'paund], *v.a.* beschlagnahmen, in Beschlag nehmen.

impoverish [im'pɔvəriʃ], *v.a.* arm
machen.

impoverished [im'pɔvəriʃd], *adj.* ver-
armt, armselig.

impracticability [impræktikə'biliti], *s.*
die Unmöglichkeit, Unausführbarkeit.

impracticable [im'præktikəbl], *adj.*
unausführbar.

imprecate ['imprikeit], *v.a.* verwünschen.

impregnable [im'pregnəbl], *adj.* uneinnehmbar, unbezwinglich.

impregnate [im'pregneit], *v.a.* impregnieren; (*Chem.*) sättigen.

impress [im'pres], *v.a.* beeindrucken,
imponieren (*fig.*); einprägen, ein-
pressen (*print*). — ['impres], *s.* der
Eindruck, (*Typ.*) Abdruck.

impression [im'preʃən], *s.* (*fig.*) der
Eindruck; die Auflage (*books*).

impressionable [im'preʃənəbl], *adj.*
eindrucksfähig, empfänglich.

impressive [im'presiv], *adj.* ergreifend, eindrucksvoll.

imprint ['imprint], *s.* der Name des
Verlags oder Druckers. — [im'print],
v.a. drucken.

imprison [im'prizn], *v.a.* gefangen-
setzen, in Haft nehmen.

imprisonment [im'priznmənt], *s.* die
Haft; (*Law*) der Arrest.

improbability [imprɔbə'biliti], *s.* die
Unwahrscheinlichkeit.

improbable [im'prɔbəbl], *adj.* unwahrscheinlich.

improbity [im'proubiti], *s.* die Unred-
lichkeit.

impromptu [im'prɔmptju:], *adj., adv.*
aus dem Stegreif, unvorbereitet.

improper [im'prɔpə], *adj.* unpassend;
unanständig (*indecent*).

impropriety [impro'praiiti], *s.* die
Unanständigkeit (*indecency*); die Un-
gehörigkeit.

improve [im'pru:v], *v.a.* verbessern; (*Hort.*) veredeln. — *v.n.* besser werden, sich bessern; (*Med.*) sich erholen.

improvement [im'pru:vmənt], *s.* die Verbesserung; (*Med.*) die Besserung, der Fortschritt.

improvident [im'prɔvidənt], *adj.* unvorsichtig, nicht auf die Zukunft bedacht.

improvise ['imprəvaiz], *v.a.* improvisieren.

imprudent [im'pru:dənt], *adj.* unklug, unvorsichtig.

impudent ['impjudənt], *adj.* unverschämt.

impugn [im'pju:n], *v.a.* anfechten, angreifen.

impulse ['impʌls], *s.* der Impuls; der Anstoß.

impulsive [im'pʌlsiv], *adj.* impulsiv.

impunity [im'pju:niti], *s.* die Straffreiheit.

impure [im'pjuə], *adj.* (*also Metall., Chem.*) unrein, unedel; unsauber.

impute [im'pju:t], *v.a.* beimessen; zurechnen, die Schuld geben für.

in [in], *prep.* in; an; zu, auf; bei; nach, unter; über; von; mit; — *the morning,* vormittags; — *case,* falls; — *any case,* auf jeden Fall; — *German,* auf deutsch; — *my opinion,* meiner Meinung nach; — *the street,* auf der Straße; — *time,* rechtzeitig. — *adv.* drinnen, innen; herein, hinein; zu Hause.

inability [inə'biliti], *s.* die Unfähigkeit.

inaccessible [inæk'sesibl], *adj.* unzugänglich.

inaccurate [in'ækjurit], *adj.* ungenau.

inaction [i'nækʃən], *s.* die Untätigkeit.

inactive [i'næktiv], *adj.* untätig.

inadequate [i'nædikwit], *adj.* unzulänglich.

inadmissible [inəd'misibl], *adj.* unzulässig.

inadvertent [inəd'və:tənt], *adj.* unbeabsichtigt; unachtsam.

inadvertently [inəd'və:təntli], *adv.* unversehens; versehentlich.

inalienable [in'eiliənəbl], *adj.* unveräußerlich.

inane [i'nein], *adj.* hohl, leer, sinnlos.

inanimate [i'nænimit], *adj.* unbeseelt, leblos.

inanity [i'næniti], *s.* die Leere, Nichtigkeit.

inapplicable [in'æplikəbl], *adj.* unanwendbar; unzutreffend.

inappropriate [inə'proupriit], *adj.* unpassend.

inarticulate [ina:'tikjulit], *adj.* unartikuliert.

inasmuch [inəz'mʌtʃ], *adv.* insofern (als).

inattentive [inə'tentiv], *adj.* unaufmerksam.

inaudible [i'nɔ:dibl], *adj.* unhörbar.

inaugural [i'nɔ:gjurəl], *adj.* Inaugural-, Eröffnungs-, Antritts-.

inaugurate [i'nɔ:gjureit], *v.a.* einweihen, eröffnen.

inauspicious [inɔ:'spiʃəs], *adj.* ungünstig.

inborn ['inbɔ:n], *adj.* angeboren.

inbred ['inbred], *adj.* in Inzucht geboren; angeboren, ererbt.

inbreeding ['inbri:din], *s.* die Inzucht.

incalculable [in'kælkjuləbl], *adj.* unberechenbar.

incandescence [inkæn'desəns], *s.* die Weißglut.

incandescent [inkæn'desənt], *adj.* weißglühend.

incantation [inkæn'teiʃən], *s.* die Beschwörung.

incapable [in'keipəbl], *adj.* unfähig (*of doing s.th.*, etwas zu tun).

incapacitate [inkə'pæsiteit], *v.a.* unfähig machen.

incapacity [inkə'pæsiti], *s.* die Unfähigkeit.

incarcerate [in'ka:səreit], *v.a.* einkerkern, einsperren.

incarnate [in'ka:nit], *adj.* eingefleischt; (*Theol.*) verkörpert.

incarnation [inka:'neiʃən], *s.* die Verkörperung; (*Theol.*) Menschwerdung.

incautious [in'kɔ:ʃəs], *adj.* unvorsichtig.

incendiary [in'sendjəri], *adj.* Brand-, brennend. — *s.* der Brandstifter.

incense [in'sens], *v.a.* aufregen, erzürnen (*make angry*); (*Eccl.*) beweihräuchern. — ['insens], *s.* (*Eccl.*) der Weihrauch.

incentive [in'sentiv], *adj.* Ansporn-, Anreiz-. — *s.* der Ansporn, Anreiz; (*Comm.*) — *scheme,* das Inzentivsystem, Akkordsystem.

incessant [in'sesənt], *adj.* unaufhörlich, ununterbrochen.

incest ['insest], *s.* die Blutschande.

incestuous [in'sestjuəs], *adj.* blutschänderisch.

inch [intʃ], *s.* der Zoll. — *v.n.* — *away,* abrücken.

incident ['insidənt], *s.* der Vorfall, Zwischenfall; das Ereignis.

incidental [insi'dentl], *adj.* zufällig. — *s.* (*pl.*) zufällige Ausgaben, *f. pl.*; das Zusätzliche, Nebenausgaben, *f. pl.*

incipient [in'sipiənt], *adj.* beginnend, anfangend.

incise [in'saiz], *v.a.* einschneiden, (*Med.*) einen Einschnitt machen.

incision [in'siʒən], *s.* der Einschnitt.

incisive [in'saisiv], *adj.* einschneidend; energisch (*person*).

incite [in'sait], *v.a.* aufreizen, anspornen.

incivility [insi'viliti], *s.* die Unhöflichkeit.

inclement [in'klemənt], *adj.* unfreundlich (*weather, climate*).

inclination [inkli'neiʃən], *s.* die Neigung (*also fig.*).

incline [in'klain], *v.n.* neigen, sich neigen. — *v.a.* neigen, *s.* der Neigungswinkel; der Abhang.

include [in'klu:d], *v.a.* einschließen (*contain*); umfassen (*enclose*).

including

including [in'klu:diŋ], *prep.* einschließlich.

inclusive [in'klu:siv], *adj.* einschließlich, mitgerechnet.

incoherent [inko'hiərənt], *adj.* unzusammenhängend.

incombustible [inkəm'bʌstibl], *adj.* unverbrennbar.

income ['inkʌm], *s.* das Einkommen.

incommensurable, incommensurate [inkə'menʃərəbl, inkə'menʃərit], *adj.* unvereinbar, unmeßbar.

incomparable [in'kɔmpərəbl], *adj.* unvergleichlich.

incompatible [inkəm'pætibl], *adj.* unvereinbar.

incompetence, incompetency [in'kɔmpitəns, -tənsi], *s.* die Inkompetenz; Unzulänglichkeit.

incompetent [in'kɔmpitənt], *adj.* unzuständig, inkompetent; unzulänglich.

incomplete [inkəm'pli:t], *adj.* unvollständig.

incomprehensible [inkɔmpri'hensibl], *adj.* unverständlich.

inconceivable [inkən'si:vəbl], *adj.* unbegreiflich.

inconclusive [inkən'klu:siv], *adj.* unvollständig (*incomplete*); unüberzeugend; ergebnislos.

incongruity [inkɔŋ'gru:iti], *s.* (*Maths.*) die Inkongruenz; (*fig.*) die Unangemessenheit.

incongruous [in'kɔŋgruəs], *adj.* inkongruent; unangemessen.

inconsequent [in'kɔnsikwənt], *adj.* folgewidrig.

inconsequential [inkɔnsi'kwenʃəl], *adj.* inkonsequent (*inconsistent*); unzusammenhängend.

inconsiderate [inkən'sidərit], *adj.* rücksichtslos, unbedachtsam.

inconsistent [inkən'sistənt], *adj.* inkonsequent.

inconsolable [inkən'souləbl], *adj.* untröstlich.

inconstancy [in'kɔnstənsi], *s.* die Unbeständigkeit; Untreue (*fickleness*).

incontestable [inkən'testəbl], *adj.* unanfechtbar, unbestreitbar.

incontinent [in'kɔntinənt], *adj.* unenthaltsam.

incontrovertible [inkɔntro'və:tibl], *adj.* unstreitig, unanfechtbar.

inconvenience [inkən'vi:niəns], *s.* die Unbequemlichkeit, Unannehmlichkeit.

inconvenient [inkən'vi:niənt], *adj.* unangenehm, unpassend.

inconvertible [inkən'və:tibl], *adj.* unveränderlich; (*Comm.*) unumsetzbar.

incorporate [in'kɔ:pəreit], *v.a.* einverleiben (*Dat.*), eingliedern (*Acc.*).

incorporated [in'kɔ:pəreitid], *adj.* (*Am.*) eingetragene Körperschaft, eingetragener Verein.

incorrect [inkə'rekt], *adj.* unrichtig, fehlerhaft; unschicklich, unpassend.

incorrigible [in'kɔridʒibl], *adj.* unverbesserlich.

incorruptible [inkə'rʌptibl], *adj.* unbestechlich.

increase [in'kri:s], *v.a.* vermehren, vergrößern (*size, volume*); steigern (*heat, intensity*); erhöhen (*price*). — *v.n.* sich vermehren, sich erhöhen; wachsen (*grow*). — ['inkri:s], *s.* die Zunahme; der Zuwachs (*family*); die Erhöhung.

incredible [in'kredibl], *adj.* unglaublich.

incredulity [inkre'dju:liti], *s.* die Ungläubigkeit, der Unglaube.

incredulous [in'kredjuləs], *adj.* ungläubig, schwer zu überzeugen.

increment ['inkrimənt], *s.* (*Comm.*) die Zulage, Gehaltserhöhung.

incriminate [in'krimineit], *v.a.* beschuldigen, inkriminieren.

incubate ['inkjubeit], *v.a.* brüten, ausbrüten. — *v.n.* brüten.

incubator ['inkjubeitə], *s.* der Brutapparat.

inculcate ['inkʌlkeit], *v.a.* einprägen.

inculpate ['inkʌlpeit], *v.a.* beschuldigen.

incumbent [in'kʌmbənt], *adj.* (*upon, Dat.*) obliegend, nötig. — *s.* der Pfründner, Amtsinhaber.

incur [in'kə:], *v.a.* auf sich laden, sich zuziehen.

incurable [in'kjuərəbl], *adj.* unheilbar.

incursion [in'kə:ʃən], *s.* der Einfall, Streifzug.

indebted [in'detid], *adj.* verpflichtet, dankbar (*grateful*); verschuldet (*in debt*).

indecent [in'di:sənt], *adj.* unschicklich, unanständig.

indecision [indi'siʒən], *s.* die Unentschlossenheit.

indecisive [indi'saisiv], *adj.* unentschlossen.

indeclinable [indi'klainəbl], *adj.* (*Gram.*) undeklinierbar.

indecorous [indi'kɔ:rəs *or* in'dekərəs], *adj.* unrühmlich, unanständig.

indeed [in'di:d], *adv.* in der Tat, tatsächlich.

indefatigable [indi'fætigəbl], *adj.* unermüdlich.

indefensible [indi'fensibl], *adj.* unhaltbar; unverzeihlich (*unforgivable*).

indefinable [indi'fainəbl], *adj.* unbestimmbar, undefinierbar.

indefinite [in'definit], *adj.* unbestimmt.

indelible [in'delibl], *adj.* unauslöschlich.

indelicate [in'delikit], *adj.* unfein.

indemnify [in'demnifai], *v.a.* entschädigen.

indemnity [in'demniti], *die* Entschädigung.

indent [in'dent], *v.a.* auszacken, einschneiden.

indenture [in'dentʃə], *s.* der Lehrbrief (*apprentice*); Vertrag.

independence [indi'pendəns], *s.* die Unabhängigkeit, Freiheit.

independent [indi'pendənt], *adj.* unabhängig, frei.

inexhaustible

indescribable [indi'skraibəbl], *adj.* unbeschreiblich.

indestructible [indi'strʌktibl], *adj.* unverwüstlich; unzerstörbar.

indeterminable [indi'tə:minəbl], *adj.* unbestimmbar.

indeterminate [indi'tə:minit], *adj.* unbestimmt.

index ['indeks], *s.* (*pl.* **indexes**) das Inhaltsverzeichnis; (*pl.* **indices**) (*Maths.*) der Exponent; — *finger*, der Zeigefinger; (*pl.*) die Finger, Zeiger, *m. pl.* (*pointers*).

India ['indjə], das Indien; — *paper*, das Dünnpapier.

Indian ['indjən], *adj.* indisch; — *ink*, die Tusche. — *s.* der Ind(i)er.

indiarubber ['indjə'rʌbə], *s.* der Radiergummi.

indicate ['indikeit], *v.a.* anzeigen, angeben.

indication [indi'keiʃən], *s.* das Anzeichen, Merkmal, der Hinweis.

indicative [in'dikətiv], *adj.* bezeichnend (für, *Acc.*). — *s.* (*Gram.*) der Indikativ.

indict [in'dait], *v.a.* anklagen.

indictment [in'daitmənt], *s.* die Anklage.

indifference [in'difrəns], *s.* die Gleichgültigkeit.

indifferent [in'difrənt], *adj.* gleichgültig.

indigence ['indidʒəns], *s.* die Armut.

indigenous [in'didʒinəs], *adj.* eingeboren, einheimisch.

indigent ['indidʒənt], *adj.* arm, dürftig.

indigestible [indi'dʒestibl], *adj.* unverdaulich.

indigestion [indi'dʒestʃən], *s.* die Magenbeschwerden, *f. pl.*; die Magenverstimmung.

indignant [in'dignənt], *adj.* empört, unwillig, entrüstet.

indignation [indig'neiʃən], *s.* die Entrüstung, der Unwille.

indignity [in'digniti], *s.* die Schmach, der Schimpf.

indirect [indi'rekt], *adj.* indirekt, mittelbar.

indiscreet [indis'kri:t], *adj.* indiskret, unvorsichtig; unbescheiden (*immodest*); taktlos.

indiscretion [indis'kreʃən], *s.* die Indiskretion, Taktlosigkeit.

indiscriminate [indis'kriminit], *adj.* ohne Unterschied, wahllos, kritiklos.

indispensable [indis'pensəbl], *adj.* unerläßlich, unentbehrlich.

indisposed [indis'pouzd], *adj.* unwohl (*health*); unwillig (*unwilling*).

indisposition [indispə'ziʃən], *s.* das Unwohlsein (*health*); das Abgeneigtsein (*disinclination*).

indisputable [indis'pju:təbl], *adj.* unbestreitbar.

indissoluble [indi'sɔljubl], *adj.* unauflöslich.

indistinct [indis'tiŋkt], *adj.* undeutlich.

indistinguishable [indis'tiŋgwiʃəbl], *adj.* nicht zu unterscheiden, ununterscheidbar.

individual [indi'vidjuəl], *adj.* individuell, persönlich; einzeln (*single*). — *s.* das Individuum, Einzelwesen.

individuality [individju'æliti], *s.* die Individualität.

indivisible [indi'vizibl], *adj.* unteilbar.

Indo-Chinese [indotʃai'ni:z], *adj.* hinterindisch. — *s.* der Hinterind(i)er.

indolent ['indəlɔnt], *adj.* indolent, träge.

Indonesian [indo'ni:ʒən], *adj.* indonesisch. — *s.* der Indonesier.

indoor ['indɔ:], *adj.* im Haus; drinnen (*inside*).

indoors [in'dɔ:z], *adv.* im Hause, zu Hause.

indubitable [in'dju:bitəbl], *adj.* zweifellos, unzweifelhaft.

induce [in'dju:s], *v.a.* veranlassen, bewegen, verleiten (*incite*).

inducement [in'dju:smənt], *s.* der Beweggrund (*cause*); der Anlaß (*reason*); die Verleitung (*incitement*).

induction [in'dʌkʃən], *s.* die Einführung; (*Elec.*) die Induktion.

inductive [in'dʌktiv], *adj.* (*Log.*, *Elec.*) induktiv.

indulge [in'dʌldʒ], *v.a.* nachgeben (*Dat.*); verwöhnen. — *v.n.* — *in*, frönen (*Dat.*).

indulgence [in'dʌldʒəns], *s.* die Nachsicht; das Wohlleben; (*Eccl.*) der Ablaß.

industrial [in'dʌstriəl], *adj.* industriell, Industrie-.

industrious [in'dʌstriəs], *adj.* fleißig, arbeitsam.

industry ['indəstri], *s.* die Industrie (*production*); der Fleiß (*industriousness*).

inebriate [i'ni:brieit], *v.a.* berauschen. — [–iit], *adj.* berauscht.

ineffable [i'nefəbl], *adj.* unaussprechlich.

ineffective, ineffectual [ini'fektiv, ini'fektjuəl], *adj.* unwirksam, wirkungslos; unfähig.

inefficiency [ini'fiʃənsi], *s.* die Erfolglosigkeit, Untauglichkeit.

inefficient [ini'fiʃənt], *adj.* untauglich, untüchtig.

ineligible [in'elidʒibl], *adj.* nicht wählbar.

inept [i'nept], *adj.* untüchtig, albern, dumm.

ineptitude [i'neptitju:d], *s.* die Unfähigkeit; die Dummheit (*stupidity*).

inequality [ini'kwɔliti], *s.* die Ungleichheit.

inert [i'nə:t], *adj.* träg.

inestimable [in'estiməbl], *adj.* unschätzbar.

inevitable [in'evitəbl], *adj.* unumgänglich, unvermeidlich.

inexcusable [iniks'kju:zəbl], *adj.* unverzeihlich, unentschuldbar.

inexhaustible [inig'zɔ:stibl], *adj.* unerschöpflich.

inexpedient

inexpedient [iniks'pi:djənt], adj. un-zweckmäßig, unpraktisch, unpassend.

inexpensive [iniks'pensiv], adj. billig, nicht kostspielig.

inexperience [iniks'piəriəns], s. die Unerfahrenheit, Naivität.

inexpert [iniks'pə:t], adj. ungeübt, unerfahren.

inexpiable [i'nekspiəbl], adj. unsühn-bar, nicht wieder gut zu machen.

inexplicable [i'neksplikəbl], adj. un-erklärlich.

inexpressible [iniks'presibl], adj. un-aussprechlich.

inexpressive [iniks'presiv], adj. aus-druckslos.

inextinguishable [iniks'tiŋgwiʃəbl], adj. unauslöschlich.

inextricable [i'nekstrikəbl], adj. un-entwirrbar.

infallible [in'fælibl], adj. unfehlbar.

infamous ['infəməs], adj. verrufen, abscheulich, berüchtigt.

infamy ['infəmi], s. die Schande; Ehrlosigkeit (dishonour).

infancy ['infənsi], s. die Kindheit, Un-mündigkeit; (fig.) der Anfang.

infant ['infənt], s. das Kind; (Law) der Unmündige, das Mündel.

infantry ['infəntri], s. die Infanterie.

infatuate [in'fætjueit], v.a. betören.

infect [in'fekt], v.a. anstecken, infizie-ren.

infection [in'fekʃən], s. (Med.) die Ansteckung, Infektion.

infectious [in'fekʃəs], adj. (Med.) an-steckend.

infer [in'fə:], v.a. schließen, herleiten, folgern.

inference ['infərəns], s. die Folge-rung.

inferior [in'fiəriə], comp. adj. geringer; untergeordnet (subordinate); schlech-ter (worse).

inferiority [infiəri'oriti], s. die In-feriorität, Minderwertigkeit.

infernal [in'fə:nəl], adj. höllisch.

infest [in'fest], v.a. heimsuchen, plagen.

infidel ['infidəl], adj. ungläubig. — s. der Heide, Ungläubige.

infiltrate ['infiltreit], v.n. durchsickern, durchdringen, infiltrieren.

infinite ['infinit], adj. unendlich.

infinitive [in'finitiv], s. (Gram.) der Infinitiv, die Nennform.

infirm [in'fə:m], adj. gebrechlich, schwach; siech (sick).

infirmary [in'fə:məri], s. das Kranken-haus.

infirmity [in'fə:miti], s. die Schwäche, Gebrechlichkeit.

inflame [in'fleim], v.a. entzünden.

inflammation [inflə'meiʃən], s. die Entzündung.

inflate [in'fleit], v.a. aufblasen, auf-blähen; (Comm.) künstlich erhöhen (values).

inflation [in'fleiʃən], s. die Aufblähung; (Comm.) die Inflation.

inflect [in'flekt], v.a. (Gram.) biegen, flektieren, deklinieren, konjugieren.

inflection [in'flekʃən], s. (Gram.) die Biegung; (Phonet.) der Tonfall.

inflexible [in'fleksibl], adj. unbiegsam.

inflexion see inflection.

inflict [in'flikt], v.a. auferlegen (im-pose); beibringen (administer).

infliction [in'flikʃən], s. die Ver-hängung, das Beibringen.

influence ['influəns], v.a. beeinflussen. — s. der Einfluß.

influential [influ'enʃəl], adj. einfluß-reich.

influenza [influ'enzə], s. (Med.) die Grippe.

inform [in'fɔ:m], v.a., v.n. informieren, benachrichtigen; — against, jemanden denunzieren.

informal [in'fɔ:məl], adj. nicht formell; ungezwungen, zwanglos.

informant [in'fɔ:mənt], s. der Angeber.

information [infə'meiʃən], s. die In-formation, Nachricht, Auskunft.

infrequent [in'fri:kwənt], adj. selten.

infringe [in'frindʒ], v.a. übertreten.

infuriate [in'fjuərieit], v.a. wütend machen.

infuse [in'fju:z], v.a. einflößen, auf-gießen, begießen.

infusion [in'fju:ʒən], s. die Eingießung; der Aufguß (tea); (Chem.) die In-fusion.

ingenious [in'dʒi:niəs], adj. geistreich, genial.

ingenuity [indʒi'nju:iti], s. der Scharf-sinn.

ingenuous [in'dʒenjuəs], adj. offen, unbefangen, arglos.

ingot ['iŋgət], s. der Barren.

ingrained [in'greind], adj. eingefleischt.

ingratiate [in'greiʃieit], v.r. — o.s., sich beliebt machen, sich einschmeicheln (with, bei).

ingratitude [in'grætitju:d], s. die Un-dankbarkeit.

ingredient [in'gri:diənt], s. der Be-standteil; die Zutat.

inhabit [in'hæbit], v.a. bewohnen.

inhabitant [in'hæbitənt], s. der Be-wohner; Einwohner.

inhale [in'heil], v.a. einatmen.

inherent [in'hiərənt], adj. eigen, an-geboren (innate); in der Sache selbst (intrinsic).

inherit [in'herit], v.a. erben.

inheritance [in'heritəns], s. die Erb-schaft, das Erbgut (patrimony); (fig.) das Erbe.

inhibit [in'hibit], v.a. hindern; —ing factor, der Hemmfaktor.

inhibition [ini'biʃən], s. (Psych.) die Hemmung.

inhospitable [inhos'pitəbl], adj. un-gastlich, ungastfreundlich.

inhuman [in'hju:mən], adj. unmensch-lich.

inhume [in'hju:m], v.a. beerdigen.

inimical [i'nimikəl], adj. feindlich (gesinnt), feindselig.

inimitable [i'nimitəbl], *adj.* unnachahmlich.

iniquitous [i'nikwitəs], *adj.* ungerecht, schlecht, boshaft.

iniquity [i'nikwiti], *s.* die Ungerechtigkeit (*injustice*); die Schändlichkeit (*shame*).

initial [i'niʃəl], *adj.* anfänglich. — *s.* (*Typ.*) der Anfangsbuchstabe.

initiate [i'niʃieit], *v.a.* einweihen, anfangen.

initiative [i'niʃiətiv], *s.* die Initiative; der erste Anstoß (*impulse*).

injection [in'dʒekʃən], *s.* (*Med.*) die Einspritzung, Injektion.

injudicious [indʒu'diʃəs], *adj.* unbedacht, unbesonnen; übereilt (*rash*).

injunction [in'dʒʌŋkʃən], *s.* die Vorschrift, (*Law*) die gerichtliche Verfügung.

injure [in'dʒə], *v.a.* verletzen.

injurious [in'dʒuəriəs], *adj.* verletzend; schädlich (*harmful*).

injury [in'dʒəri], *s.* die Verletzung, Verwundung; der Schaden (*damage*).

injustice [in'dʒʌstis], *s.* die Ungerechtigkeit.

ink [iŋk], *s.* die Tinte.

inkling [iŋkliŋ], *s.* die Ahnung.

inkstand ['iŋkstænd], *s.* das Schreibzeug.

inlaid [in'leid], *adj.* eingelegt.

inland [in'lənd], *adj.* inländisch, Binnen-; — *revenue office*, das Steueramt, Finanzamt.

inlet ['inlit], *s.* (*Geog.*) die kleine Bucht.

inmate ['inmeit], *s.* der Insasse, Bewohner.

inmost ['inmoust], *adj.* innerst.

inn [in], *s.* der Gasthof, das Wirtshaus; *Inns of Court*, die Londoner Rechtskammern, *f. pl.*

innate [i'neit], *adj.* angeboren.

inner ['inə], *adj.* inner; geheim (*secret*).

innings ['iniŋz], *s.* das Daransein (*in Cricket*); die Reihe.

innocence ['inəsəns], *s.* die Unschuld.

innocuous [i'nɔkjuəs], *adj.* unschädlich.

innovate ['inoveit], *v.a., v.n.* als Neuerung einführen, Neuerungen machen.

innovation [ino'veiʃən], *s.* die Neuerung.

innuendo [inju'endou], *s.* das Innuendo, die Anspielung.

innumerable [i'nju:mərəbl], *adj.* unzählig, unzählbar.

inoculate [i'nɔkjuleit], *v.a.* impfen.

inoffensive [ino'fensiv], *adj.* harmlos, unschädlich.

inopportune [in'ɔpətju:n], *adj.* ungelegen.

inordinate [i'nɔ:dinit], *adj.* unmäßig.

inorganic [inɔː'gænik], *adj.* anorganisch.

inquest ['inkwest], *s.* die gerichtliche Untersuchung (*Law*); *coroner's* —, die Leichenschau.

inquire, enquire [in'kwaiə], *v.n.* sich erkundigen (*after*, nach, *Dat.*), nachfragen.

inquiry, enquiry [in'kwaiəri], *s.* die Nachfrage; — *office*, die Auskunftsstelle.

inquisition [inkwi'ziʃən], *s.* (*Eccl.*) die Inquisition; die gerichtliche Untersuchung.

inquisitive [in'kwizitiv], *adj.* neugierig.

inquisitiveness [in'kwizitivnis], *s.* die Neugier(de).

inroad ['inroud], *s.* der Eingriff, Überfall.

insane [in'sein], *adj.* wahnsinnig.

insanity [in'sæniti], *s.* der Wahnsinn.

insatiable [in'seiʃəbl], *adj.* unersättlich.

inscribe [in'skraib], *v.a.* einschreiben (*enrol*); widmen (*book*).

inscription [in'skripʃən], *s.* die Inschrift.

inscrutable [in'skru:təbl], *adj.* unergründlich, unerforschlich.

insect ['insekt], *s.* das Insekt, Kerbtier.

insecure [insi'kjuə], *adj.* unsicher.

insensate [in'sensit], *adj.* unsinnig (*senseless*); gefühllos..

insensible [in'sensibl], *adj.* unempfindlich; gefühllos.

insensitive [in'sensitiv], *adj.* ohne feineres Gefühl, unempfindlich.

inseparable [in'sepərəbl], *adj.* unzertrennlich, untrennbar.

insert [in'sə:t], *v.a.* einsetzen, einschalten (*add*); inserieren (*in newspaper*).

insertion [in'sə:ʃən], *s.* die Einschaltung (*addition*); die Annonce, das Inserat (*press*).

inside [in'said], *adj.* inner. — *adv.* im Innern. — *prep.* innerhalb. — *s.* das Innere.

insidious [in'sidiəs], *adj.* heimtückisch.

insight ['insait], *s.* der Einblick.

insignia [in'signiə], *s., pl.* die Insignien.

insignificance [insig'nifikəns], *s.* die Geringfügigkeit, Bedeutungslosigkeit.

insignificant [insig'nifikənt], *adj.* unbedeutend, geringfügig.

insincere [insin'siə], *adj.* unaufrichtig.

insincerity [insin'seriti], *s.* die Unaufrichtigkeit.

insinuate [in'sinjueit], *v.a.* zu verstehen geben, andeuten, anspielen auf (*Acc.*).

insinuation [insinju'eiʃən], *s.* der Wink, die Andeutung, Anspielung.

insipid [in'sipid], *adj.* schal, geschmacklos.

insist [in'sist], *v.n.* bestehen (*upon*, auf, *Dat.*).

insistence [in'sistəns], *s.* das Bestehen, Beharren.

insolence ['insələns], *s.* die Frechheit.

insolent ['insələnt], *adj.* frech, unverschämt.

insoluble [in'sɔljubl], *adj.* unlösbar; (*Chem.*) unlöslich.

insolvent [in'sɔlvənt], *adj.* insolvent, zahlungsunfähig, bankrott.

inspect [in'spekt], *v.a.* inspizieren; besichtigen.

inspection [in'spekʃən], s. die Inspektion; Besichtigung.

inspiration [inspi'reiʃən], s. die Inspiration, Erleuchtung, Begeisterung.

inspire [in'spaiə], v.a. inspirieren, begeistern.

instability [instə'biliti], s. die Unbeständigkeit, Labilität.

install [in'stɔ:l], v.a. einsetzen (in office); einbauen.

installation [instə'leiʃən], s. die Einsetzung (inauguration); die Installation.

instalment [in'stɔ:lmənt], s. die Rate; by —s, auf Abzahlung; die Fortsetzung (serial).

instance [in'stəns], s. das Beispiel (example); (Law) die Instanz; at my —, auf meine dringende Bitte; for —, zum Beispiel. — v.a. als Beispiel anführen.

instant ['instənt], s. der Augenblick. — adj. gegenwärtig; sofortig; laufend (current month).

instantaneous [instən'teiniəs], adj. augenblicklich, sofortig.

instead [in'sted], adv. dafür, stattdessen; — of, (an)statt (Genit.).

instep ['instep], s. (Anat.) der Rist.

instigate ['instigeit], v.a. aufhetzen, anreizen, anstiften.

instil [in'stil], v.a. einflößen.

instinct [in'stinkt], s. der Instinkt, Naturtrieb.

institute [in'stitju:t], s. das Institut. — v.a. einrichten (install); stiften (found).

institution [insti'tju:ʃən], s. die Stiftung (foundation); die Anstalt (establishment).

instruct [in'strʌkt], v.a. unterrichten, unterweisen.

instruction [in'strʌkʃən], s. der Unterricht (in schools etc.); (pl.) die Instruktionen, f. pl.; die Direktive.

instructive [in'strʌktiv], adj. instruktiv, lehrreich.

instrument ['instrumənt], s. das Instrument; Werkzeug (tool).

insubordination [insəbɔ:di'neiʃən], s. der Ungehorsam.

insufferable [in'sʌfərəbl], adj. unerträglich.

insufficient [insə'fiʃənt], adj. ungenügend, unzulänglich.

insular ['insjulə], adj. Insel-; insular (narrow-minded).

insulate ['insjuleit], v.a. absondern (separate); (Elec.) isolieren; insulating tape, das Isolierband.

insult [in'sʌlt], v.a. beleidigen.

insuperable [in'sju:pərəbl], adj. unüberwindlich.

insupportable [insə'pɔ:təbl], adj. unhaltbar (argument); unerträglich (insufferable).

insurance [in'ʃuərəns], s. die Versicherung; — policy, die Police; — premium, die Prämie; — broker, der Versicherungsmakler.

insure [in'ʃuə], v.a. versichern.

insurgent [in'sə:dʒənt], s. der Aufständische, Aufrührer.

insurmountable [insə'mauntəbl], adj. unüberwindlich.

insurrection [insə'rekʃən], s. der Aufstand, Aufruhr; die Empörung.

intact [in'tækt], adj. unversehrt, intakt.

intangible [in'tændʒibl], adj. unberührbar (untouchable); (Log.) abstrakt. — s. pl. (Log.) die Intangibilien, pl.

integer ['intidʒə], s. (Maths.) das Ganze, die ganze Zahl.

integral ['intigrəl], adj. wesentlich; vollständig. — s. (Maths.) das Integral.

integrate ['intigreit], v.a. (Maths.) integrieren.

integration [inti'greiʃən], s. (Maths.) die Integrierung; (fig.) die Integration, das völlige Aufgehen.

integrity [in'tegriti], s. die Rechtschaffenheit, Redlichkeit (probity).

intellect ['intilekt], s. der Geist, Intellekt, Verstand.

intellectual [inti'lektjuəl], adj. intellektuell. — s. der Intellektuelle.

intelligence [in'telidʒəns], s. die Intelligenz; die Nachricht (news).

intelligent [in'telidʒənt], adj. intelligent.

intelligible [in'telidʒibl], adj. verständlich.

intemperance [in'tempərəns], s. die Unmäßigkeit.

intemperate [in'tempərit], adj. unmäßig.

intend [in'tend], v.a. beabsichtigen, vorhaben.

intendant [in'tendənt], s. der Intendant, Verwalter.

intense [in'tens], adj. intensiv, heftig.

intent [in'tent], adj. gespannt, begierig; bedacht (on, auf, Acc.). — s. die Absicht.

intention [in'tenʃən], s. die Absicht.

intentioned [in'tenʃənd], adj. well- —, wohlgesinnt.

inter [in'tə:], v.a. beerdigen.

intercede [intə'si:d], v.n. vermitteln (between); sich verwenden (on behalf of, für, Acc.).

intercept [intə'sept], v.a. abfangen, auffangen, hemmen.

intercession [intə'seʃən], s. die Vermittlung, Fürsprache, Fürbitte.

interchange [intətʃeindʒ], s. der Austausch. — [-'tʃeindʒ], v.a. austauschen.

intercourse ['intəkɔ:s], s. der Verkehr, Umgang.

interdict [intə'dikt], v.a. untersagen, verbieten.

interest ['intrəst], s. das Interesse; die Beteiligung; (Comm.) die Zinsen, m. pl.; compound —, die Zinseszinsen, m. pl. — v.a. interessieren.

interested ['intrəstid], adj. (in, an, Dat.) interessiert; be — in, sich interessieren für.

interesting ['intrəstiŋ], *adj.* interessant.

interfere [intə'fiə], *v.n.* sich einmischen, eingreifen (*in*, in, *Acc.*)

interference [intə'fiərəns], *s.* die Einmischung; (*Rad.*) die Störung.

interim ['intərim], *adj.* vorläufig, Zwischen-.

interior [in'tiəriə], *adj.* innerlich. — *s.* das Innere; das Binnenland; — *decorator*, der Innenraumgestalter, der Innenarchitekt; *Ministry of the Interior*, das Innenministerium.

interjection [intə'dʒekʃən], *s.* die Interjektion; der Ausruf.

interlace [intə'leis], *v.a.* einflechten.

interleave [intə'li:v], *v.a.* durchschießen (*a book*).

interlinear [intə'liniə], *adj.* zwischenzeilig.

interlocutor [intə'lɔkjutə], *s.* der Gesprächspartner.

interloper ['intəloupə], *s.* der Eindringling.

interlude ['intəlju:d], *s.* das Zwischenspiel.

intermarry [intə'mæri], *v.n.* untereinander heiraten.

intermediate [intə'mi:diit],*adj.* Mittel-; (*Sch.*) — *certificate*, das Mittelstufenzeugnis.

interment [in'tə:mənt], *s.* die Beerdigung.

interminable [in'tə:minəbl], *adj.* endlos, langwierig.

intermingle [intə'miŋgl], *v.n.* sich vermischen.

intermission [intə'miʃən], *s.* die Pause, Unterbrechung.

intermit [intə'mit], *v.a.* unterbrechen.

intermittent [intə'mitənt], *adj.* Wechsel-, aussetzend.

internal [in'tə:nl], *adj.* intern, innerlich.

international [intə'næʃənəl], *adj.* international; — *law*, das Völkerrecht.

interpolate [in'tə:poleit], *v.a.* interpolieren, einschalten.

interpose [intə'pouz], *v.a.* dazwischenstellen. — *v.n.* vermitteln (*mediate*).

interpret [in'tə:prit], *v.a.* verdolmetschen; erklären (*explain*); auslegen, interpretieren.

interpretation [intə:pri'teiʃən], *s.* die Auslegung, Interpretation.

interpreter [in'tə:pritə], *s.* der Dolmetscher.

interrogate [in'terogeit], *v.a.* ausfragen, befragen, vernehmen.

interrogation [intero'geiʃən], *s.* die Befragung; (*Law*) das Verhör, die Vernehmung.

interrogative [intə'rɔgətiv], *adj.* (*Gram.*) Frage-, Interrogativ-.

interrupt [intə'rʌpt], *v.a.* unterbrechen; stören (*disturb*).

interruption [intə'rʌpʃən], *s.* die Unterbrechung; Störung (*disturbance*).

intersect [intə'sekt], *v.a.* durchschneiden.

intersperse [intə'spə:s], *v.a.* untermengen, vermischen, einstreuen.

intertwine [intə'twain], *v.a.*, *v.n.* (sich) durchflechten.

interval ['intəvəl], *s.* der Zwischenraum; die Pause; (*Mus.*) das Interval.

intervene [intə'vi:n], *v.n.* eingreifen; als Vermittler dienen (*act as mediator*).

intervention [intə'venʃən], *s.* die Vermittlung, Intervention.

interview ['intəvju:], *v.a.* zur Vorsprache einladen (*a candidate*); interviewen. — *s.* die Vorsprache, das Interview.

intestate [in'testit], *adj.* ohne Testament.

intestines [in'testinz], *s. pl.* (*Anat.*) die Eingeweide, *n. pl.*

intimacy ['intiməsi], *s.* die Vertraulichkeit, Intimität.

intimate ['intimit], *adj.* intim, vertraut, vertraulich. — [-meit], *v.a.* andeuten, zu verstehen geben.

intimation [inti'meiʃən], *s.* der Wink, die Andeutung.

intimidate [in'timideit], *v.a.* einschüchtern.

into ['intu), *prep.* (*Acc.*) in, in ... hinein (*towards*).

intolerable [in'tɔlərəbl], *adj.* unerträglich.

intolerance [in'tɔlərəns], *s.* die Unduldsamkeit, Intoleranz.

intonation [into'neiʃən], *s.* (*Phonet.*) die Intonation; (*Mus.*) das Anstimmen, der Tonansatz (*of instruments*).

intoxicate [in'tɔksikeit], *v.a.* berauschen.

intractable [in'træktəbl], *adj.* unbändig, unlenksam.

intransitive [in'trænsitiv or in'trɑ:ns-], *adj.* (*Gram.*) intransitiv.

intrepid [in'trepid], *adj.* unerschrocken, furchtlos.

intricacy ['intrikəsi], *s.* die Verwicklung (*tangle*), Schwierigkeit (*difficulty*).

intricate ['intrikit], *adj.* verwickelt, schwierig.

intrigue [in'tri:g], *s.* die Intrige. — *v.n.* intrigieren.

intrinsic [in'trinsik], *adj.* wesentlich; innerlich (*inner*).

introduce [intrə'dju:s], *v.a.* einführen, einleiten (*book etc.*); vorstellen (*person*).

introduction [intrə'dʌkʃən], *s.* die Einführung, das Bekanntmachen; die Einleitung (*preface*); die Vorstellung (*presentation to s.o.*, *Dat.*).

introductory [intrə'dʌktəri], *adj.* einführend.

introspection [intrə'spekʃən], *s.* die Selbstbetrachtung, Introspektion.

introspective [intrə'spektiv], *adj.* nachdenklich, beschaulich.

intrude [in'tru:d], *v.n.* eindringen, sich eindrängen; stören (*be in the way*).

intrusion [in'tru:ʒən], *s.* das Eindringen.

intuition

intuition [intju'iʃən], s. die Intuition, Eingebung.
intuitive [in'tju:itiv], adj. intuitiv, gefühlsmäßig.
inundate ['inʌndeit], v.a. überschwemmen.
inure [i'njuə], v.a. gewöhnen; abhärten (harden).
invade [in'veid], v.a. angreifen, einfallen (in, Dat.).
invalid [in'vælid], adj. ungültig (void); ['invəlid] krank (sick). — s. der Kranke, Invalide.
invalidate [in'vælideit], v.a. ungültig machen, für ungültig erklären.
invalidity [invə'liditi], s. die Ungültigkeit.
invaluable [in'væljuəbl], adj. von hohem Wert, wertvoll, unschätzbar.
invariable [in'vɛəriəbl], adj. unveränderlich. — s. (Maths.) die unveränderliche Größe, die Konstante, Unveränderliche.
invasion [in'veiʒən], s. die Invasion, der Einfall; Angriff (of, auf, Acc.).
invective [in'vektiv], adj. schmähend. — s. die Schmähung.
inveigh [in'vei], v.n. schmähen, losziehen (gegen); schimpfen (auf, Acc.).
inveigle [in'veigl], v.a. verleiten, verführen.
invent [in'vent], v.a. erfinden.
invention [in'venʃən], s. die Erfindung.
inventor [in'ventə], s. der Erfinder.
inventory ['invəntri], s. der Bestand, das Inventar; die Liste (list).
inverse [in'vəːs, 'invəːs], adj. umgekehrt.
inversion [in'vəːʃən], s. die Umkehrung; (Gram., Maths.) die Inversion.
invert [in'vəːt], v.a. umstellen, umkehren. — ['invəːt], s. (Chem.) — sugar, der Invertzucker.
invest [in'vest], v.a. bekleiden; bedecken; (Comm.) investieren, anlegen.
investigate [in'vestigeit], v.a. untersuchen, erforschen.
investiture [in'vestitʃə], s. die Investitur; die Belehnung.
investment [in'vestmənt], s. die Investierung, Kapitalanlage.
inveterate [in'vetərit], adj. eingewurzelt, eingefleischt.
invidious [in'vidiəs], adj. neiderregend, verhaßt.
invigorate [in'vigəreit], v.a. stärken, beleben.
invincible [in'vinsibl], adj. unbesiegbar, unüberwindlich.
inviolable [in'vaiələbl], adj. unverletzlich.
invisible [in'vizibl], adj. unsichtbar.
invitation [invi'teiʃən], s. die Einladung.
invite [in'vait], v.a. einladen.
invocation [invo'keiʃən], s. die Anrufung.
invoice ['invɔis], s. die Rechnung, Faktura. — v.a. fakturieren.
invoke [in'vouk], v.a. anrufen.
involuntary [in'vɔləntri], adj. unfreiwillig (unwilling); unwillkürlich (reflex).

involve [in'vɔlv], v.a. verwickeln.
involved [in'vɔlvd], adj. schwierig, verwickelt, kompliziert.
invulnerable [in'vʌlnərəbl], adj. unverwundbar, unverletzlich.
inward ['inwəd], adj. inner(lich). — adv. (also inwards) einwärts, nach innen, ins Innere.
iodine ['aiədain or 'aiədi:n], s. (Chem.) das Jod.
Iraki, Iraqi [i'rɑːki], adj. irakisch. — s. der Iraker.
Iranian [i'reinjən], adj. iranisch. — s. der Iranier.
irascible [i'ræsibl], adj. jähzornig, aufbrausend.
irate [ai'reit], adj. erzürnt, zornig.
ire [aiə], s. (Poet.) der Zorn.
iridescent [iri'desənt], adj. irisierend, schillernd.
iris ['aiəris], s. (Anat.) die Regenbogenhaut; (Bot.) die Schwertlilie.
Irish ['airiʃ], adj. irisch, ersisch. — s. (pl.) the —, die Irländer, Iren, pl.
Irishman ['airiʃmən], s. der Irländer, Ire.
irk [əːk], v.a. verdrießen, verärgern.
irksome ['əːksəm], adj. lästig, ärgerlich.
iron ['aiən], s. (Metall.) das Eisen; (pl.) die eisernen Fesseln. — adj. eisern, Eisen-. — v.a. bügeln, plätten; — out, schlichten, beilegen.
ironical [ai'rɔnikəl], adj. ironisch.
ironmonger ['aiənmʌngə], s. der Eisenhändler.
ironmould ['aiənmould], s. der Rostfleck.
irony ['aiərəni], s. die Ironie.
irradiate [i'reidieit], v.a. bestrahlen.
irrational [i'ræʃənəl], adj. (Log., Maths.) irrational; unvernünftig (without reason).
irreconcilable [irekən'sailəbl], adj. unversöhnlich; unvereinbar (incompatible).
irregular [i'regjulə], adj. unregelmäßig, gegen die Regel.
irrelevant [i'reləvənt], adj. belanglos.
irremediable [iri'miːdiəbl], adj. unheilbar; nicht wieder gut zu machen.
irreparable [i'repərəbl], adj. unersetzlich.
irrepressible [iri'presibl], adj. nicht zu unterdrücken, unbezähmbar.
irreproachable [iri'proutʃəbl], adj. untadelhaft, tadellos.
irresistible [iri'zistibl], adj. unwiderstehlich.
irresolute [i'rezolju:t], adj. unschlüssig, unentschlossen.
irrespective [iris'pektiv], adj. ohne Rücksicht (of, auf, Acc.).
irresponsible [iris'pɔnsibl], adj. unverantwortlich.
irretrievable [iri'tri:vəbl], adj. unersetzlich, unwiederbringlich.
irreverent [i'revərənt], adj. unehrerbietig.
irrevocable [i'revəkəbl], adj. unwiderruflich.

irrigate ['irigeit], *v.a.* bewässern.
irritable ['iritəbl], *adj.* reizbar.
irritant ['iritənt], *s.* das Reizmittel.
irritation [iri'teiʃən], *s.* die Reizung, das Reizen; die Erzürnung.
irruption [i'rʌpʃən], *s.* der Einbruch.
island ['ailənd], *s.* die Insel.
isle [ail], *s.* (*Poet.*) die Insel.
isolate ['aisəleit], *v.a.* (*Med.*) isolieren; absondern; (*Chem.*) darstellen.
isolation [aisə'leiʃən], *s.* die Absonderung, Isolierung.
Israeli [iz'reili], *adj.* den Staat Israel betreffend. — *s.* der Israeli.
Israelite ['izreiəlait], *adj.* israelitisch. — *s.* der Israelit.
issue ['isju: *or* 'iʃu:], *s.* der Ausgang, Erfolg (*result*); main —, der Hauptpunkt; die Nachkommenschaft (*children*); die Ausgabe (*edition*); Herausgabe (*publication*). — *v.a.* herausgeben; erlassen (*proclaim*); veröffentlichen (*publish*). — *v.n.* herrühren, stammen (*from*).
isthmus ['isθməs], *s.* die Landenge.
it [it], *pron.* es; *with* —, damit.
Italian [i'tæljən], *adj.* italienisch. — *s.* der Italiener.
italics [i'tæliks], *s. pl.* (*Typ.*) der Kursivdruck, die Kursivschrift.
itch [itʃ], *s.* das Jucken. — *v.n.* jucken; — *to do s.th.*, (*coll.*) darauf brennen, etwas zu tun.
item ['aitəm], *s.* der Posten (*in bill*); der Programmpunkt (*agenda*); die Einzelheit.
itemize ['aitəmaiz], *v.a.* (*Comm.*) aufführen; verzeichnen.
iterate ['itəreit], *v.a.* wiederholen.
itinerant [i'tinərənt], *adj.* wandernd.
its [its], *poss. adj.* sein, ihr; dessen, deren.
itself [it'self], *pron.* selber, sich; *of* —, von selbst.
ivory ['aivəri], *s.* das Elfenbein. — *adj.* aus Elfenbein, elfenbeinern.
ivy ['aivi], *s.* (*Bot.*) der Efeu.

J

J [dʒei]. das J.
Jabber ['dʒæbə], *v.n.* schnattern.
Jack [dʒæk]. Hans; *Union* —, die britische Flagge; (*Cards*) der Bube.
jack [dʒæk], *s.* (*Motor.*) der Wagenheber. — *v.a.* — *up*, (*Motor.*) hochwinden.
jackal ['dʒækɔ:l], *s.* (*Zool.*) der Schakal.
jackass ['dʒækæs], *s.* (*Zool.*) der Esel.
jackdaw ['dʒækdɔ:], *s.* (*Orn.*) die Dohle.
jacket ['dʒækit], *s.* das Jackett, die Jacke; *dinner* —, der Smoking;

potatoes in their —s, Kartoffeln in der Schale, *f. pl.*
jade [dʒeid], *s.* der Nierenstein.
jaded ['dʒeidid], *adj.* abgeplagt, abgehärmt, ermüdet.
jag [dʒæg], *s.* die Kerbe. — *v.a.* kerben, zacken.
jagged ['dʒægid], *adj.* zackig.
jail *see under* **gaol**.
jailer *see under* **gaoler**.
jam (1) [dʒæm], *s.* die Marmelade, Konfitüre.
jam (2) [dʒæm], *s. traffic* —, die Verkehrsstauung; (*coll.*) *in a* —, in der Klemme. — *v.a.* zusammenpressen (*press together*); (*Rad.*) stören.
Jamaican [dʒə'meikən], *adj.* jamaikanisch. — *s.* der Jamaikaner.
jamb [dʒæm], *s.* der Türpfosten.
jangle [dʒæŋgl], *v.n.* klirren, rasseln. — *s.* das Geklirr, Gerassel.
janitor ['dʒænitə], *s.* der Portier.
January ['dʒænjuəri]. der Januar.
japan [dʒə'pæn], *s.* lakierte Arbeit. — *v.a.* lackieren.
Japanese [dʒæpə'ni:z], *adj.* japanisch. — *s.* der Japaner.
jar (1) [dʒɑ:], *s.* der Topf, das Glas (*preserves*).
jar (2) [dʒɑ:], *v.n.* offenstehen (*door*); mißtönen, knarren.
jargon ['dʒɑ:gən], *s.* der Jargon.
jasmine ['dʒæzmin], *s.* (*Bot.*) der Jasmin.
jasper ['dʒæspə], *s.* der Jaspis.
jaundice ['dʒɔ:ndis], *s.* (*Med.*) die Gelbsucht; (*fig.*) der Neid (*envy*); —*d outlook*, die Verbitterung, Mißstimmung.
jaunt [dʒɔ:nt], *s.* der Ausflug, Spaziergang. — *v.n.* herumstreifen, spazieren.
jaunty ['dʒɔ:nti], *adj.* leicht, munter, lebhaft.
jaw [dʒɔ:], *s.* (*Anat.*) der Kinnbacken; der Rachen (*animals*).
jay [dʒei], *s.* (*Orn.*) der Häher.
jazz [dʒæz], *s.* die Jazzmusik.
jealous ['dʒeləs], *adj.* eifersüchtig.
jealousy ['dʒeləsi], *s.* die Eifersucht.
jeer ['dʒiə], *v.a.*, *v.n.* spotten, verhöhnen.
jejune [dʒi'dʒu:n], *adj.* nüchtern, trocken.
jelly ['dʒeli], *s.* das Gelee.
jellyfish ['dʒelifiʃ], *s.* (*Zool.*) die Qualle.
jeopardize ['dʒepədaiz], *v.a.* gefährden.
jeopardy ['dʒepədi], *s.* die Gefahr.
jerk [dʒə:k], *v.a.* rucken, stoßen (*push*); plötzlich bewegen (*move suddenly*). — *v.n.* zusammenzucken. — *s.* (*Am. coll.*) der Kerl; der Ruck, Stoß.
jersey ['dʒə:zi], *s.* die Wolljacke.
jessamine ['dʒesəmin], *s.* (*Bot.*) der Jasmin.
jest [dʒest], *s.* der Spaß, Scherz. — *v.n.* scherzen.
jester ['dʒestə], *s.* der Spaßmacher, Hofnarr.

jet

jet (1) [dʒet], *s.* der Strahl, Wasserstrahl; (*Aviat.*) die Düse; — *engine*, der Düsenmotor; — *plane*, das Düsenflugzeug. — *v.n.* hervorspringen.

jet (2) [dʒet], *s.* der Gagat; — *black*, pechschwarz.

jetsam [ˈdʒetsəm], *s.* das Strandgut.

jetty [ˈdʒeti], *s.* der Hafendamm, die Landungsbrücke (*landing stage*).

Jew [dʒuː], *s.* der Jude.

jewel [ˈdʒuəl], *s.* das Juwel, der Edelstein.

jewel(le)ry [ˈdʒuəlri], *s.* der Schmuck; die Juwelen, *n. pl.*

Jewish [ˈdʒuːiʃ], *adj.* jüdisch.

Jewry [ˈdʒuəri], *s.* die Judenschaft, das Judentum.

jiffy [ˈdʒifi], *s.* (*coll.*) der Augenblick.

jig (1) [dʒig], *s.* die Gigue (*dance*).

jig (2) [dʒig], *s.* das Werkzeug (*tool*); —*saw*, die Säge; —*saw puzzle*, das Zusammenlegspiel, -setzspiel.

jilt [dʒilt], *v.a.* sitzen lassen.

jingle [dʒiŋgl], *v.a.* klimpern, klimpern lassen (*coins etc.*). — *s.* das Geklimper.

job [dʒɔb], *s.* die Arbeit, Anstellung; die Stellung; das Geschäft; — *in hand*, die Beschäftigung.

jobber [ˈdʒɔbə], *s.* der Makler, Spekulant (*stock exchange*).

jockey [ˈdʒɔki], *s.* der Jockei, Reiter.

jocular [ˈdʒɔkjulə], *adj.* scherzhaft, lustig.

jocund [ˈdʒɔkənd], *adj.* munter, heiter.

jog [dʒɔg], *v.a.* stoßen, antreiben. — *v.n.* gemächlich traben, trotten. — *s.* der Trott.

join [dʒɔin], *v.a.* verbinden, zusammenfügen; (*club etc.*) beitreten (*Dat.*). — *v.n.* (*rivers*) zusammenfließen (mit, *Dat.*); (*Comm.*) sich vereinigen (mit, *Dat.*).

joiner [ˈdʒɔinə], *s.* der Tischler, Schreiner.

joint [dʒɔint], *s.* (*Anat.*) das Gelenk; das Stück Fleisch, der Braten (*meat*); (*sl.*) das Lokal, die Spelunke. — *adj.* vereint, gemeinsam; (*Comm.*) — *stock company*, die Aktiengesellschaft; — *heir*, der Miterbe.

joist [dʒɔist], *s.* (*Carp.*) der Querbalken.

joke [dʒouk], *s.* der Scherz, Witz.

jollity [ˈdʒɔliti], *s.* die Heiterkeit.

jolly [ˈdʒɔli], *adj.* fröhlich, heiter, lustig.

jolt [dʒoult], *v.a.* schütteln, erschüttern (*shake up*). — *s.* der Stoß.

jostle [dʒɔsl], *v.a.* stoßen, drängen. — *v.n.* drängeln.

jot [dʒɔt], *s.* der Punkt, das Iota. — *v.a.* — (*down*), notieren, niederschreiben.

journal [ˈdʒəːnəl], *s.* die Zeitschrift (*periodical*).

journalism [ˈdʒəːnəlizm], *s.* das Zeitungswesen, der Journalistenberuf.

journalist [ˈdʒəːnəlist], *s.* der Journalist.

journey [ˈdʒəːni], *s.* die Reise.

joust [dʒuːst], *s.* das Turnier.

jovial [ˈdʒouviəl], *adj.* jovial, freundlich; lustig (*gay*).

joy [dʒɔi], *s.* die Freude.

jubilant [ˈdʒuːbilənt], *adj.* frohlockend.

jubilation [dʒuːbiˈleiʃən], *s.* der Jubel.

jubilee [ˈdʒuːbiliː], *s.* das Jubiläum.

Judaism [dʒuˈdeiizm], *s.* das Judentum.

judge [dʒʌdʒ], *s.* der Richter. — *v.a.* richten, beurteilen, entscheiden.

judgment [ˈdʒʌdʒmənt], *s.* das Urteil; das Urteilsvermögen (*discretion*), die Urteilskraft.

judicial [dʒuːˈdiʃəl], *adj.* richterlich, gerichtlich.

judicious [dʒuːˈdiʃəs], *adj.* klug, scharfsinnig.

jug [dʒʌg], *s.* der Krug.

juggle [dʒʌgl], *v.n.* jonglieren, gaukeln.

juggler [ˈdʒʌglə], *s.* der Jongleur.

Jugoslav *see* **Yugoslav.**

jugular [ˈdʒuːg- *or* ˈdʒʌgjulə], *adj.* Kehl-, Hals-, Gurgel-. — *s.* (*vein*) die Halsader.

juice [dʒuːs], *s.* der Saft.

July [dʒuˈlai], *s.* der Juli.

jumble [dʒʌmbl], *v.a.* zusammenmischen, vermischen. — *s.* das gemischte Zeug; — *sale*, der Verkauf, Ausverkauf gebrauchter Dinge, Ramschverkauf.

jump [dʒʌmp], *v.n.* springen. — *s.* der Sprung.

junction [ˈdʒʌŋkʃən], *s.* (*Railw.*) der Knotenpunkt; die Kreuzung.

juncture [ˈdʒʌŋktʃə], *s.* der (kritische) Zeitpunkt.

June [dʒuːn]. der Juni.

jungle [dʒʌŋgl], *s.* der Dschungel.

junior [ˈdʒuːnjə], *adj.* jünger; Unter-.

juniper [ˈdʒuːnipə], *s.* (*Bot.*) der Wacholder.

junk [dʒʌŋk], *s.* (*coll.*) das alte Zeug, alte Möbelstücke, *n. pl.*

junket [ˈdʒʌŋkit], *s.* der Schmaus, das Fest; (*Cul.*) dicke Milch mit Sahne. — *v.n.* schmausen, feiern (*celebrate*).

juridical [dʒuəˈridikəl], *adj.* rechtlich; gerichtlich (*in Court*).

jurisdiction [dʒuəriːˈdikʃən], *s.* die Gerichtsbarkeit.

juror [ˈdʒuərə], *s.* der, die Geschworene.

jury [ˈdʒuəri], *s.* die Jury, das Geschworenengericht.

just [dʒʌst], *adj.* gerecht; rechtschaffen (*decent*); gehörig (*proper*). — *adv.* soeben, eben; —*as*, eben als, gerade wie.

justice [ˈdʒʌstis], *s.* die Gerechtigkeit; der Richter (*judge*).

justifiable [ˈdʒʌstifaiəbl], *adj.* zu rechtfertigen, berechtigt.

justify [ˈdʒʌstifai], *v.a.* rechtfertigen.

jut [dʒʌt], *v.n.* — (*out*), hervorragen. — *s.* der Vorsprung.

jute [dʒuːt], *s.* die Jute.

juvenile [ˈdʒuːvənail], *adj.* jugendlich, unreif.

juxtaposition [dʒʌkstəpəˈziʃən], *s.* die Nebeneinanderstellung, Gegenüberstellung.

K

K [kei]. das K.

kale [keil], s. (*Bot.*) der Krauskohl.

kaleidoscope [kə'laidəskoup], s. das Kaleidoskop.

kangaroo [kæŋgə'ru:], s. (*Zool.*) das Känguruh.

keel [ki:l], s. der Kiel; *on an even —*, bei ruhiger See; (*also fig.*) ruhig. — *v.n. — over*, umkippen.

keen [ki:n], *adj.* eifrig (*intent*); scharfsinnig (*perspicacious*); scharf (*blade*).

keenness ['ki:nnis], s. der Eifer; Scharfsinn; die Schärfe (*blade*).

keep [ki:p], *v.a. irr.* halten (*hold*); behalten (*retain*); führen (*a shop*); hüten (*gate, dog etc.*). — *v.n. — doing, in* etwas fortfahren; — *going*, weitergehen; — *away*, sich fernhalten; — *in, indoors*, zu Hause bleiben; — *off*, abhalten; sich fernhalten; — *out*, draußen bleiben; — *up*, aufrechterhalten. — *s.* das Burgverlies; der Unterhalt.

keeper ['ki:pə], s. der Hüter, Wärter; Museumsbeamte.

keeping ['ki:piŋ], s. die Verwahrung; *in safe —*, in guten Händen, in guter Obhut.

keepsake ['ki:pseik], s. das Andenken.

keg [keg], s. das Fäßchen.

ken [ken], s. die Kenntnis; *in my —*, meines Wissens. — *v.a.* (*Scottish*) kennen.

kennel [kenl], s. die Hundehütte.

kerb(stone) ['kə:b(stoun)], s. der Prellstein.

kerchief ['kə:tʃif], s. das Kopftuch, Halstuch.

kernel [kə:nl], s. der Kern.

kettle [ketl], s. der Kessel; — *drum*, die Kesselpauke.

key [ki:], s. der Schlüssel; (*Mus.*) die Tonart; die Taste (*on piano etc.*); — *man*, eine wichtige Person, Person in einer Schlüsselstellung. — *v.a. — (in)*, einfügen, befestigen.

keyboard ['ki:bɔ:d], s. die Klaviatur; Tastatur (*typewriter*); — *instrument*, das Tasteninstrument.

keyhole ['ki:houl], s. das Schlüsselloch.

keystone ['ki:stoun], s. der Schlußstein.

kick [kik], *v.a., v.n.* mit dem Fuße stoßen *or* treten; — *against s.th.*, sich wehren; — *s.* der Fußstoß, Tritt; (*Footb.*) — *off*, der Ankick; *free —*, der Freistoß; *penalty —*, der Strafstoß, der Elfmeterstoß.

kid (1) [kid], s. (*Zool.*) das Geißlein, Zicklein; *with — gloves*, mit Glacéhandschuhen; (*coll.*) das Kind.

kid (2) [kid], *v.a.* (*Am. coll.*) zum Narren haben, aufziehen (*tease*).

kidnap ['kidnæp], *v.a.* entführen.

kidney ['kidni], s. (*Anat.*) die Niere; — *bean*, die französische Bohne.

kill [kil], *v.a.* töten; schlachten (*animal*).

kiln [kiln], s. der Darrofen; der Ziegelofen (*tiles, bricks*).

kilt [kilt], s. der Schottenrock.

kin [kin], s. die Verwandtschaft; *kith and —*, die Verwandten, *m. pl.*

kind [kaind], s. die Art, Gattung, Art und Weise. — *adj.* freundlich, gütig, liebenswürdig.

kindle [kindl], *v.a.* anzünden, anfachen.

kindliness, kindness ['kaindlinis, 'kaindnis], s. die Güte, Freundlichkeit.

kindred ['kindrid], *adj.* verwandt.

king [kiŋ], s. der König.

kingdom ['kiŋdəm], s. das Königreich.

kink [kiŋk], s. der Knoten; (*coll.*) der Vogel, die Grille (*obsession etc.*).

kinship ['kinʃip], s. die Sippe, Verwandtschaft.

kipper ['kipə], s. der geräucherte Hering.

kiss [kis], *v.a.* küssen. — *s.* der Kuß.

kit [kit], s. (*Mil.*) die Ausrüstung.

kitbag ['kitbæg], s. der Tornister.

kitchen ['kitʃən], s. die Küche; — *garden*, der Gemüsegarten.

kite [kait], s. der Drache, Papierdrache; *fly a —*, einen Drachen steigen lassen; (*Orn.*) der Gabelweih, der (rote) Milan; (*sl.*) der Schwindler.

kith [kiθ], s. now only in *— and kin*, die Verwandten, *m. pl.*

kitten [kitn], s. das Kätzchen.

knack [næk], s. der Kniff, Kunstgriff.

knacker ['nækə], s. der Abdecker (*horse*).

knapsack ['næpsæk], s. der Rucksack, Tornister.

knave [neiv], s. der Kerl, Schurke; Bube (*cards*).

knead [ni:d], *v.a.* kneten.

knee [ni:], s. (*Anat.*) das Knie.

kneel [ni:l], *v.n. irr.* knien, niederknien.

knell [nel], s. die Totenglocke.

knick-knack ['niknæk], s. die Nippsache.

knife [naif], s. das Messer. — *v.a.* erstechen.

knight [nait], s. der Ritter; der Springer (*chess*).

knit [nit], *v.a., v.n. reg. & irr.* stricken; *knitting needle*, die Stricknadel.

knob [nɔb], s. der (Tür)knopf, die Türklinke; der Knorren (*wood*).

knock [nɔk], *v.n.* klopfen, schlagen. — *s.* der Schlag, Stoß.

knoll [noul], s. der kleine Hügel.

knot [nɔt], s. der Knoten; die Schwierigkeit (*difficulty*).

know [nou], *v.a. irr.* kennen (*be acquainted with*); wissen (*possess knowledge (of)*).

knowing ['nouiŋ], *adj.* wissend.

knowledge ['nɔlidʒ], s. die Kenntnis (*acquaintance with*); das Wissen (*by*

427

knuckle

study, information etc.); die Kenntnisse (*of language etc.*).
knuckle [nʌkl], *s.* (*Anat.*) der Knöchel.
— *v.n.* — *under*, sich fügen.
Kremlin ['kremlin], *s.* der Kreml.
kudos ['kju:dɔs], *s.* der Ruhm, das Ansehen.

L

L [el]. das L.
label [leibl], *s.* die Etikette, das Schildchen.
labial ['leibiəl], *adj.* (*Phonet.*) labial, Lippen-. — *s.* (*Phonet.*) der Lippenlaut.
laboratory [lə'bɔrətəri, (*Am.*) 'læbərətəri], *s.* das Laboratorium, (*coll.*) das Labor.
laborious [lə'bɔ:riəs], *adj.* mühsam.
labour ['leibə], *s.* die Arbeit, Mühe; *Labour Party*, die Arbeiterpartei; (*Med.*) die Geburtswehen, *f. pl.* — *v.n.* sich abmühen, leiden; sich anstrengen.
labourer ['leibərə], *s.* der Arbeiter, Taglöhner.
lace [leis], *s.* die Spitze, Tresse. — *v.a.* verbrämen (*trim with lace*); zuschnüren (*shoe*); stärken (*coffee with rum etc.*).
lacerate ['læsəreit], *v.a.* zerreißen.
lack [læk], *v.a.* ermangeln (*Genit.*). — *v.n.* fehlen (an, *Dat.*). — *s.* der Mangel, das Fehlen.
lackadaisical [lækə'deizikəl], *adj.* schlaff, (*coll.*) schlapp, unbekümmert.
lackey ['læki], *s.* der Lakai, Diener, Bediente.
laconic [lə'kɔnik], *adj.* lakonisch.
lacquer ['lækə], *s.* der Lack. — *v.a.* lackieren.
lad [læd], *s.* der Bursche, Junge.
ladder ['lædə], *s.* die Leiter.
lading ['leidiŋ], *s.* (*Comm.*) das Laden; die Fracht; *bill of* —, der Frachtbrief.
ladle [leidl], *s.* der Schöpflöffel, Suppenlöffel; die Kelle. — *v.a.* ausschöpfen, austeilen.
lady ['leidi], *s.* die Dame; — *-in-waiting*, die Hofdame.
ladybird ['leidibə:d], *s.* (*Ent.*) der Marienkäfer.
ladyship ['leidiʃip], *s.* (*Title*) gnädige Frau.
lag [læg], *v.n.* zurückbleiben. — *v.a.* verkleiden, isolieren (*tank*).
laggard ['lægəd], *s.* der Zauderer. — *adj.* zögernd, zaudernd.
lagoon [lə'gu:n], *s.* die Lagune.
lair [lɛə], *s.* das Lager (*of animal*).
laird [lɛəd], *s.* der schottische Gutsherr.

laity ['leiiti], *s.* die Laien, *m. pl.*
lake [leik], *s.* der See.
lamb [læm], *s.* (*Zool.*) das Lamm. — *v.n.* lammen.
lambent ['læmbənt], *adj.* brennend, lodernd, strahlend.
lame [leim], *adj.* lahm. — *v.a.* lähmen.
lament [lə'ment], *v.a.*, *v.n.* betrauern, beweinen. — *s.* das Klagelied, die Wehklage.
lamp [læmp], *s.* die Lampe; — *-post*, der Laternenpfahl.
lampoon [læm'pu:n], *v.a.* schmähen, lächerlich machen. — *s.* die Schmähschrift.
lamprey ['læmpri], *s.* (*Zool.*) das Neunauge.
lance [lɑːns], *s.* (*Mil.*) die Lanze. — *v.a.* durchbohren; (*Med.*) lancieren.
lancer ['lɑːnsə], *s.* (*Mil.*) der Ulan.
lancet ['lɑːnsit], *s.* (*Med.*) die Lanzette.
land [lænd], *s.* das Land; das Grundstück (*plot*); — *tax*, die Grundsteuer. — *v.a.* ans Land bringen, fangen (*fish*). — *v.n.* landen.
landlord ['lændlɔːd], *s.* der Eigentümer, der Hausherr; Wirt (*pub*).
landmark ['lændmɑːk], *s.* der Grenzstein, das Wahrzeichen.
landscape ['lændskeip], *s.* die Landschaft.
landslide, landslip ['lændslaid, 'lændslip], *s.* der Erdrutsch.
lane [lein], *s.* der Heckenweg, Pfad; die Gasse; (*Motor.*) die Fahrbahn.
language ['læŋgwidʒ], *s.* die Sprache.
languid ['læŋgwid], *adj.* flau, matt.
languor ['læŋgə], *s.* die Mattigkeit, Flauheit.
lank [læŋk], *adj.* mager, schlank.
lantern ['læntən], *s.* die Laterne.
Laotian ['lauʃən], *adj.* laotisch. — *s.* der Laote.
lap (1) [læp], *s.* der Schoß.
lap (2) [læp], *s.* das Plätschern (*of waves*). — *v.a.* auflecken (*lick up*). — *v.n.* plätschern.
lapel [lə'pel], *s.* der Aufschlag (*of jacket*).
lapidary ['læpidəri], *adj.* lapidarisch, wuchtig.
lapse [læps], *v.n.* gleiten, fallen; verlaufen (*time*). — *s.* der Verlauf (*time*); der Fehler (*mistake*); das Verfallen (*into laziness etc.*).
lapwing ['læpwiŋ], *s.* (*Orn.*) der Kiebitz.
larceny ['lɑːsəni], *s.* der Diebstahl.
larch [lɑːtʃ], *s.* (*Bot.*) die Lärche.
lard [lɑːd], *s.* das Schweinefett, Schweineschmalz.
larder ['lɑːdə], *s.* die Speisekammer.
large [lɑːdʒ], *adj.* groß; weit; dick, stark.
largesse [lɑː'dʒes], *s.* die Freigebigkeit (*generosity*); die Schenkung (*donation*).
lark (1) [lɑːk], *s.* (*Orn.*) die Lerche.
lark (2) [lɑːk], *s.* (*coll.*) der Scherz. — *v.n.* scherzen.
larkspur ['lɑːkspə:], *s.* (*Bot.*) der Rittersporn.
larva ['lɑːvə], *s.* (*Zool.*) die Larve.

larynx ['lærinks], *s.* (*Anat.*) der Kehlkopf.

lascivious [lə'siviəs], *adj.* wollüstig.

lash [læʃ], *s.* die Wimper (*eye*); die Peitschenschnur (*whip*), der Peitschenhieb (*stroke of whip*). — *v.a.* peitschen.

lass [læs], *s.* (*coll.*) das Mädchen.

lassitude ['læsitju:d], *s.* die Mattigkeit.

lasso [lə'su: or 'læsou], *s.* das Lasso. — *v.a.* mit einem Lasso fangen.

last (1) [lɑːst], *adj.* letzt, vorig, äußerst; *at long —,* endlich.

last (2) [lɑːst], *s.* der Leisten (*shoe-making*).

last (3) [lɑːst], *v.n.* dauern, anhalten; hinreichen (*be sufficient*).

lastly ['lɑːstli], *adv.* zuletzt.

latch [lætʃ], *v.a.* verschließen.

latchkey ['lætʃkiː], *s.* der Hausschlüssel.

late [leit], *adj.* spät; verspätet; verstorben, selig (*deceased*); neulich (*recent*); *the train is —,* der Zug hat Verspätung; *of late,* jüngst.

latent ['leitənt], *adj.* (*Med.*) latent; verborgen.

lateral ['lætərəl], *adj.* seitlich, Seiten-.

lath [lɑːθ], *s.* die Latte.

lathe [leiδ], *s.* die Drehbank.

lather ['læδə], *s.* der Seifenschaum. — *v.n., v.a.* (sich) einseifen.

Latin ['lætin], *adj.* lateinisch. — *s.* das Latein, die lateinische Sprache.

latitude ['lætitjuːd], *s.* die geographische Breite; die Weite (*width*); (*fig.*) der Spielraum (*scope*).

latter ['lætə], *adj.* letzter; später (*later*). — *s.* der Letztere.

latterly ['lætəli], *adv.* neulich, neuerdings.

lattice ['lætis], *s.* das Gitter. — *v.a.* vergittern.

Latvian ['lætviən], *adj.* lettisch. — *s.* der Lette.

laud [lɔːd], *v.a.* loben, preisen.

laudable ['lɔːdəbl], *adj.* lobenswert.

laudatory ['lɔːdətəri], *adj.* belobend.

laugh [lɑːf], *v.n.* lachen; *—ing stock,* der Gegenstand des Gelächters.

laughter ['lɑːftə], *s.* das Lachen, Gelächter.

launch [lɔːntʃ], *s.* die Barkasse. — *v.a.* vom Stapel lassen.

launching ['lɔːntʃiŋ], *s.* der Stapellauf.

laundress ['lɔːndris], *s.* die Wäscherin.

laundry ['lɔːndri], *s.* die Wäsche (*clothes*); Wäscherei (*place*).

laureate ['lɔːriit], *s.* der Hofdichter.

laurel ['lɔrəl], *s.* (*Bot.*) der Lorbeer.

lavatory ['lævətri], *s.* das W.C., der Abort, Waschraum; die Toilette; *public —,* die Bedürfnisanstalt.

lavender ['lævəndə], *s.* (*Bot.*) der Lavendel.

lavish ['læviʃ], *adj.* freigebig, verschwenderisch. — *v.a.* vergeuden.

lavishness ['læviʃnis], *s.* die Freigebigkeit, Verschwendung.

law [lɔː], *s.* das Gesetz (*statute*); das Recht (*justice*); die Jura, Jurisprudenz (*subject of study*).

lawful ['lɔːful], *adj.* gesetzlich, gesetzmäßig.

lawless ['lɔːlis], *adj.* gesetzlos; unrechtmäßig (*illegal*).

lawn (1) [lɔːn], *s.* der Rasen.

lawn (2) [lɔːn], *s.* der Batist.

lawsuit ['lɔːsuːt], *s.* der Prozeß.

lawyer ['lɔːjə], *s.* der Advokat, Rechtsanwalt, Jurist.

lax [læks], *adj.* locker, lax.

laxative ['læksətiv], *s.* das Abführmittel.

laxity ['læksiti], *s.* die Schlaffheit, Lockerheit (*of rope etc.*).

lay (1) [lei], *v.a. irr.* legen; setzen (*put*); stellen (*place*); bannen (*ghost*); — *up,* sammeln. — *v.n.* legen (*eggs*); wetten (*wager*); — *about one,* um sich schlagen.

lay (2) [lei], *s.* (*Poet.*) das Lied.

lay (3) [lei], *adj.* Laien-.

layer ['leiə], *s.* die Schicht; — *cake,* die Cremetorte.

layman ['leimən], *s.* der Laie.

laziness ['leizinis], *s.* die Faulheit.

lazy ['leizi], *adj.* faul, träge.

lea [liː], *s.* (*Poet.*) die Aue.

lead (1) [liːd], *v.a., v.n. irr.* führen, leiten; ausspielen (*cards*). — *s.* die Führung; (*Elec.*) Leitung.

lead (2) [led], *s.* das Blei; Bleilot (*plumb-line*).

leader ['liːdə], *s.* der Führer; (*Mus.*) der Konzertmeister; der Leitartikel (*leading article*).

leaf [liːf], *s.* (*Bot.*) das Blatt; (*Build.*) der Türflügel. — *v.a.* (*coll.*) — *through,* durchblättern.

leafy ['liːfi], *adj.* belaubt.

league (1) [liːg], *s.* drei englische Meilen, *f.pl.*

league (2) [liːg], *s.* das Bündnis (*pact*); *be in —,* verbündet sein; *League of Nations,* der Völkerbund.

leak [liːk], *v.n.* lecken, ein Loch haben. — *s.* das Loch; (*Naut.*) das Leck.

leaky ['liːki], *adj.* leck.

lean (1) [liːn], *v.n. irr.*(sich)lehnen (an, *Acc.*), stützen (auf, *Acc.*).

lean (2) [liːn], *adj.* mager, hager.

leap [liːp], *v.n. irr.* springen. — *s.* der Sprung; — *year,* das Schaltjahr.

learn [ləːn], *v.a. irr.* lernen, erfahren.

learned ['ləːnid], *adj.* gelehrt.

learning ['ləːniŋ], *s.* die Gelehrsamkeit.

lease [liːs], *s.* die Pacht, der Mietvertrag (*of house*). — *v.a.* (ver)pachten.

leasehold ['liːshould], *s.* die Pachtung.

leash [liːʃ], *v.a.* koppeln, anbinden. — *s.* die Koppel.

least [liːst], *adj.* wenigst, geringst, mindest, kleinst. — *s. at (the) —,* wenigstens, mindestens.

leather ['leδə], *s.* das Leder. — *adj.* Leder-, ledern.

leave [liːv], *v.a. irr.* verlassen (*quit*); lassen (*let*); hinterlassen (*bequeath*). — *v.n.* Abschied nehmen, abreisen. — *s.* der Urlaub; der Abschied (*farewell*); die Erlaubnis (*permission*).

leaven

leaven [levn], *s.* der Sauerteig. — *v.a.* säuern.

Lebanese [lebə'ni:z], *adj.* libanesisch. — *s.* der Libanese.

lecture ['lektʃə], *s.* die Vorlesung; der Vortrag.

lecturer ['lektʃərə], *s.* (*Univ.*) der Dozent; der Vortragende (*speaker*).

ledge [ledʒ], *s.* der Sims (*window*).

ledger ['ledʒə], *s.* (*Comm.*) das Hauptbuch.

lee [li:], *s.* die Leeseite (*shelter*).

leech [li:tʃ], *s.* (*Zool.*) der Blutegel.

leek [li:k], *s.* (*Bot.*) der Lauch.

leer ['liə], *s.* das Starren; der Seitenblick. — *v.n.* schielen (*at*, auf, nach); starren.

lees [li:z], *s. pl.* der Bodensatz, die Hefe.

left [left], *adj.* link. — *adv.* inks. — *s.* die linke Seite.

leg [leg], *s.* (*Anat.*) das Bein; der Schaft.

legacy ['legəsi], *s.* das Vermächtnis, das Erbe, Erbgut.

legal ['li:gəl], *adj.* gesetzlich.

legality [li'gæliti], *s.* die Gesetzlichkeit.

legatee [legə'ti:], *s.* (*Law*) der Erbe, die Erbin.

legation [li'geiʃən], *s.* die Gesandtschaft.

legend ['ledʒənd], *s.* die Legende, Sage; die Inschrift (*inscription*).

legendary ['ledʒəndəri], *adj.* legendär, sagenhaft.

leggings ['leginz], *s. pl.* die Gamaschen.

legible ['ledʒibl], *adj.* leserlich.

legislation [ledʒis'leiʃən], *s.* die Gesetzgebung.

legislative ['ledʒislətiv], *adj.* gesetzgebend.

legislator ['ledʒisleitə], *s.* der Gesetzgeber.

legitimacy [li'dʒitiməsi], *s.* die Gesetzmäßigkeit; (*Law*) die eheliche Geburt (*of birth*).

legitimate [li'dʒitimit], *adj.* gesetzmäßig; (*Law*) ehelich (*child*). — [-meit], *v.a.* für gesetzlich erklären.

legitimize [li'dʒitimaiz], *v.a.* legitimieren.

leguminous [li'gju:minəs], *adj.* Hülsen—; hülsentragend.

leisure ['leʒə], *s.* die Freizeit, Muße.

leisurely ['leʒəli], *adj., adv.* gelassen, gemächlich.

lemon ['lemən], *s.* (*Bot.*) die Zitrone.

lemonade [lemən'eid], *s.* die Limonade.

lend [lend], *v.a. irr.* leihen; —*ing library*, die Leihbibliothek.

length [leŋθ], *s.* die Länge (*extent*); die Dauer (*duration*); *at* —, ausführlich.

lengthen ['leŋθən], *v.a., v.n.* (sich) verlängern.

lengthy ['leŋθi], *adj.* langwierig, lang.

lenient ['li:niənt], *adj.* nachsichtig, milde.

lens [lenz], *s.* die Linse (*optics*); das Objektiv.

Lent [lent], die Fastenzeit.

lentil ['lentil], *s.* (*Bot.*) die Linse.

leprosy ['leprəsi], *s.* der Aussatz, die Leprakrankheit.

leprous ['leprəs], *adj.* aussätzig.

lesion ['li:ʒən], *s.* die Verletzung.

less [les], *comp. adj., adv.* weniger, kleiner.

lessee [le'si:], *s.* der Pächter, Mieter.

lessen [lesn], *v.a., v.n.* (sich) verringern, vermindern.

lesser ['lesə], *comp. adj.* geringer; kleiner.

lesson [lesn], *s.* die Lehrstunde, Lektion; (*pl.*) der Unterricht; (*Rel.*) der Bibeltext.

lessor ['lesə], *s.* der Eigentümer, Vermieter.

lest [lest], *conj.* damit nicht; aus Furcht, daß.

let [let], *v.a. irr.* lassen; zulassen; vermieten; (*room*); — *down*, blamieren, enttäuschen; *off*, abschießen. — *s. without* — *or hindrance*, ohne Hinderung.

lethal ['li:θəl], *adj.* tödlich.

letter ['letə], *s.* der Brief; der Buchstabe (*character*); — *box*, der Briefkasten; (*pl.*) die Literatur.

letterpress ['letəpres], *s.* die Kopierpresse.

lettuce ['letis], *s.* (*Bot.*) der Salat.

level [levl], *adj.* eben, gleich. — *s.* die Ebene; das Niveau. — *v.a.* ebnen, ausgleichen; (*Build.*) planieren.

lever ['li:və], *s.* der Hebel.

levity ['leviti], *s.* der Leichtsinn.

levy ['levi], *v.a.* erheben (*tax*); auferlegen (*penalty*). — *s.* die Steuer.

lewd [lju:d *or* lu:d], *adj.* liederlich, gemein, unzüchtig.

liability [laiə'biliti], *s.* die Verantwortlichkeit; *limited* —, beschränkte Haftung; die Steuerpflichtigkeit (*to tax*), Zollpflichtigkeit (*to duty*).

liable ['laiəbl], *adj.* haftbar, zahlungspflichtig.

liar ['laiə], *s.* der Lügner.

libel ['laibəl], *s.* die Verleumdung. — *v.a.* verleumden, schmähen.

libellous ['laibələs], *adj.* verleumderisch.

liberal ['libərəl], *adj.* (*Pol.*) liberal; freigebig (*generous*); — *arts*, Geisteswissenschaften, *f. pl.*

liberate ['libəreit], *v.a.* befreien, freisetzen; (*Law*) in Freiheit setzen.

Liberian [lai'bi:riən], *adj.* liberisch. — *s.* der Liberier.

libertine ['libəti:n], *s.* der Wüstling.

liberty ['libəti], *s.* die Freiheit; die Erlaubnis (*permission*).

librarian [lai'brɛəriən], *s.* der Bibliothekar, die Bibliothekarin.

library ['laibrəri], *s.* die Bibliothek.

Libyan ['libjən], *adj.* libysch. — *s.* der Libyer.

licence ['laisəns], *s.* die Genehmigung, Erlaubnis (*permit*); *driving* —, der Führerschein; die Zügellosigkeit (*licentiousness*).

license ['laisəns], *v.a.* genehmigen, bewilligen; *licensing laws*, Ausschanksgesetze, *n. pl.* (*for alcohol*).

liquidate

licentiate [lai'senʃiit], s. der Lizenziat (degree).

licentious [lai'senʃəs], adj. ausschweifend, liederlich, locker (in morals).

lichen ['laikən, 'litʃən], s. (Bot.) die Flechte.

lichgate ['litʃgeit], s. das Friedhofstor.

lick [lik], v.a. lecken; (Am.) prügeln, verhauen.

lid [lid], s. das Augenlid; der Deckel.

lie [lai], (1) v.n. lügen. — s. die Lüge (untruth).

lie [lai], (2) v.n. irr. liegen; — down, sich legen, hinlegen; sich fügen (fig.).

lieu [lju:], s. in —, an Stelle, anstatt (Genit.).

lieutenant [lef'tenənt], s. der Leutnant.

life [laif], s. das Leben.

lifebelt ['laifbelt], s. der Rettungsgürtel.

lifeboat ['laifbout], s. das Rettungsboot.

lifetime ['laiftaim], s. die Lebenszeit, Zeit seines Lebens.

lift [lift], s. der Aufzug, Fahrstuhl; (coll.) give a —, mitnehmen (im Auto). — v.a. heben; aufheben (abolish); (coll.) klauen, stehlen.

ligament ['ligəmənt], s. das Band; (Anat.) die Flechse, die Sehne.

ligature ['ligətʃə], s. (Typ.) die Ligatur; die Verbindung.

light [lait], adj. hell, licht; blond (hair); leicht (weight). — s. das Licht; give a —, ein Streichholz geben, Feuer geben. — v.a. irr. beleuchten (room); anzünden (fire). — v.n. irr. — (up), hell werden, leuchten; (fig.) aufleuchten.

lighten [laitn], v.a. erhellen (brighten); erleichtern (ease).

lighter ['laitə], s. das Feuerzeug (smoker's); (Naut.) das Lichterschiff.

lighthouse ['laithaus], s. der Leuchtturm.

lightning ['laitniŋ], s. der Blitz; — conductor, der Blitzableiter; — speed, die Blitzesschnelle.

ligneous ['ligniəs], adj. holzig.

lignite ['lignait], s. die Braunkohle.

like (1) [laik], v.a. gern haben; I — to sing, ich singe gern. — v.n. belieben, wollen; as you —, wie Sie wollen. — s. his —s and dislikes, seine Wünsche und Abneigungen.

like (2) [laik], adj. gleich, ähnlich. — s. his —, seinesgleichen. — prep. gleich, wie; just — him! das sieht ihm ähnlich! feel —, möchte gern; what is it —? wie sieht es aus?

likelihood ['laiklihud], s. die Möglichkeit; Wahrscheinlichkeit (probability).

likely ['laikli], adj. möglich; wahrscheinlich (probable).

liken ['laikən], v.a. vergleichen.

likeness ['laiknis], s. die Ähnlichkeit.

likewise ['laikwaiz], adv. ebenso, gleichfalls, auch.

liking ['laikiŋ], s. die Vorliebe (for, für, Acc.); Neigung (for, zu, Dat.); to my

—, nach meinem Geschmack or Wunsch.

lilac ['lailək], s. (Bot.) der Flieder.

lilt [lilt], v.a., v.n. trällern, summen. — s. die Melodie, Weise.

lily ['lili], (Bot.) s. die Lilie; — of the valley, das Maiglöckchen.

limb [lim], s. das Glied.

limber ['limbə], adj. geschmeidig.

lime (1) [laim], s. der Leim, Kalk (chalk).

lime (2) [laim], s. (Bot.) die Linde (tree); die Limone (fruit); — juice, der Limonensaft.

limestone ['laimstoun], s. der Kalkstein.

limit ['limit], s. die Grenze, das Ende. — v.a. begrenzen, beschränken.

limitation [limi'teiʃən], s. die Begrenzung.

limn [lim], v.a. (Art.) zeichnen, malen.

limp [limp], v.n. hinken. — adj. müde, schlaff.

limpid ['limpid], adj. klar, durchsichtig.

linden ['lindən], s. (Bot.) die Linde.

line (1) [lain], s. die Linie, Eisenbahnlinie (Railw.); die Zeile; der Strich; (Mil.) die Reihe; — of business, die Geschäftsbranche; (Genealogy) die Abstammung; take a strong —, entschlossen auftreten.

line (2) [lain], v.a. füttern (a garment).

lineage ['liniidʒ], s. die Abstammung.

lineament ['liniəmənt], s. der Gesichtszug.

linear ['liniə], adj. linear, geradlinig.

linen ['linin], s. die Leinwand; bed —, die Laken, Bettwäsche. — adj. leinen.

liner ['lainə], s. (Naut.) das Passagierschiff.

linger ['liŋgə], v.n. zögern; verweilen.

lingerie ['lɛ̃ʒəri:], s. die Damenunterwäsche.

linguist ['liŋgwist], s. der Sprachkundige, Philologe, Linguist.

liniment ['linimənt], s. (Med.) die Salbe.

lining ['lainiŋ], s. das Futter (of garment).

link [liŋk], s. das Glied (in chain); die Verbindung (connexion). — v.a. verbinden, verknüpfen.

linnet ['linit], s. (Orn.) der Hänfling.

linseed ['linsi:d], s. der Leinsamen; — oil, das Leinöl.

lint [lint], s. die Scharpie, das Verbandzeug.

lion ['laiən], s. (Zool.) der Löwe.

lioness ['laiənes], s. (Zool.) die Löwin.

lip [lip], s. (Anat., Bot.) die Lippe (mouth); der Rand (of jug).

lipstick ['lipstik], s. der Lippenstift.

liquefy ['likwifai], v.a., v.n. flüssig machen or werden.

liqueur [li'kjuə], s. der Likör.

liquid ['likwid], adj. flüssig. — s. die Flüssigkeit.

liquidate ['likwideit], v.a. liquidieren; (Comm.) flüssig machen (assets); bezahlen (pay off).

liquor

liquor ['likə], *s.* der Alkohol.
liquorice ['likəris], *s.* die Lakritze.
lisp [lisp], *v.n.* lispeln. — *s.* der Sprachfehler, das Anstoßen, Lispeln.
list [list], *s.* die Liste, das Verzeichnis; (*Naut.*) die Schlagseite.
listen [lisn], *v.n.* horchen, zuhören.
listless ['listlis], *adj.* teilnahmslos.
litany ['litəni], *s.* (*Eccl.*) die Litanei.
literal ['litərəl], *adj.* buchstäblich.
literary ['litərəri], *adj.* literarisch, Literatur-.
literature ['litrətʃə], *s.* die Literatur.
lithe [laið], *adj.* geschmeidig.
Lithuanian [liθju'einiən], *adj.* litauisch. — *s.* der Litauer.
litigate ['litigeit], *v.n.* einen Prozeß anstrengen, litigieren, prozessieren.
litigation [liti'geiʃən], *s.* die Litigation, der Prozeß.
litter ['litə], *s.* (*Zool.*) die Jungen, *n. pl.*; die Brut; die Sänfte (*carriage*); der Abfall, die Abfälle (*waste paper etc.*). — *v.n.* (*Zool.*) Junge haben, werfen. — *v.a.* Abfälle wegwerfen, unsauber machen.
little [litl], *adj.* klein (*size*, *value*); gering (*value*); — *by* —, nach und nach.
liturgy ['litədʒi], *s.* (*Eccl.*) die Liturgie.
live [liv], *v.n.* leben; wohnen (*dwell*).
livelihood ['laivlihud], *s.* der Lebensunterhalt.
liveliness ['laivlinis], *s.* die Lebhaftigkeit.
lively ['laivli], *adj.* lebhaft.
liven [laivn], *v.a.* — *up*, beleben.
liver ['livə], *s.* (*Anat.*) die Leber.
livery ['livəri], *s.* die Livree (*uniform*); — *company*, die Zunftgenossenschaft.
livid ['livid], *adj.* bleich, blaß.
living ['liviŋ], *s.* das Auskommen, der Unterhalt; die Lebensweise; (*Eccl.*) die Pfründe, Pfarrstelle.
lizard ['lizəd], *s.* (*Zool.*) die Eidechse.
lo! [lou], *excl.* (*obs.*) sieh, da! siehe!
load [loud], *s.* die Last, Belastung. — *v.a.* beladen, belasten. — *v.n.* laden, aufladen.
loadstone see **lodestone**.
loaf [louf], *s.* der Laib (*bread*); *sugar* —, der Zuckerhut. — *v.n.* herumlungern, nichts tun.
loafer ['loufə], *s.* der Faulenzer, Drückeberger.
loam [loum], *s.* der Lehm.
loan [loun], *s.* die Anleihe. — *v.a.* leihen.
loath [louθ], *adj.* unwillig, abgeneigt.
loathe [louð], *v.a.* verabscheuen, hassen.
loathing ['louðiŋ], *s.* der Abscheu, Ekel.
loathsome ['louθsəm], *adj.* abscheulich, ekelhaft.
lobby ['lɔbi], *s.* die Vorhalle. — *v.a.* (*Pol.*) einen beeinflussen.
lobe [loub], *s.* das Läppchen.
lobster ['lɔbstə], *s.* (*Zool.*) der Hummer.
local ['loukəl], *adj.* lokal, örtlich. — *s.* (*coll.*) das Stammgasthaus (*pub*).

locality [lo'kæliti], *s.* die Lokalität, die Örtlichkeit, der Ort.
localize ['loukəlaiz], *v.a.* lokalisieren, auf einen Ort beschränken.
locate [lo'keit], *v.a.* finden (*find*); ausfindig machen.
location [lo'keiʃən], *s.* die Plazierung (*position*); die Lage; der Standort; *on* —, auf dem Gelände, auf Außenaufnahme (*film*).
loch [lɔx], *s.* (*Scot.*) der See.
lock [lɔk], *s.* das Schloß (*on door*); die Schleuse (*on waterway*); die Locke (*hair*). — *v.a.* schließen, abschließen (*door*); hemmen (*wheel*). — *v.n.* sich schließen; — *in*, ineinandergreifen (*cogs*).
locker ['lɔkə], *s.* der Schließschrank, das Schließfach.
locket ['lɔkit], *s.* das Medaillon.
locksmith ['lɔksmiθ], *s.* der Schlosser.
lock-up ['lɔkʌp], *s.* der Arrest, die Haftzelle; (*coll.*) die Garage.
locust ['loukəst], *s.* (*Ent.*) die Heuschrecke.
lodestone ['loudstoun], *s.* der Magnetstein, Magnet.
lodge [lɔdʒ], *v.n.* wohnen; logieren (*temporary*). — *v.a.* beherbergen (*accommodate*); einbringen (*a complaint*, *protest*). — *s.* das Haus, das Häuschen; die Loge (*Freemasons*).
lodger ['lɔdʒə], *s.* der (Unter)mieter.
lodgings ['lɔdʒiŋz], *s. pl.* das möblierte Zimmer, die Wohnung.
loft [lɔft], *s.* der Boden, Dachboden.
lofty ['lɔfti], *adj.* hoch; erhaben; stolz (*proud*).
log [lɔg], *s.* der Holzklotz, das Scheit; —*cabin*, —*house*, das Blockhaus; (*Naut.*) das Log, das Schiffstagebuch. — *v.a.* (*Naut.*) eintragen.
loggerheads ['lɔgəhedz], *s. pl.* at —, in Widerspruch, Widerstreit, im Konflikt.
logic ['lɔdʒik], *s.* die Logik.
logical ['lɔdʒikəl], *adj.* logisch.
loin [lɔin], *s.* (*Anat.*) die Lende.
loincloth ['lɔinklɔθ], *s.* der Lendenschurz.
loiter ['lɔitə], *v.n.* herumlungern; bummeln.
loiterer ['lɔitərə], *s.* der Lungerer, Faulenzer.
loitering ['lɔitəriŋ], *s.* das Herumlungern, Herumstehen, Faulenzen.
loll [lɔl], *v.n.* herumlungern.
lollipop ['lɔlipɔp], *s.* das Zuckerwerk, die Süßigkeit; (*fig.*) der Leckerbissen.
loneliness ['lounlinis], *s.* die Einsamkeit.
lonely, (*Am.*) **lonesome** ['lounli, 'lounsəm], *adj.* einsam.
long [lɔŋ], *adj.* lang. — *adv.* — *ago*, vor langer Zeit; before —, in kurzer Zeit. — *v.n.* sich sehnen (*for*, nach, *Dat.*).
longitude ['lɔndʒitjuːd], *s.* die Länge; (*Geog.*) der Längengrad.

longitudinal [lɔndʒi'tju:dinəl], *adj.* in der geographischen Länge, Längen-.

look [luk], *v.n.* blicken, sehen, schauen (*at*, auf, *Acc.*); — *to it*, dafür sorgen; — *out for*, Ausschau halten nach (*Dat.*); — *out!* paß auf! — *after s.o.*, sich um jemanden kümmern; — *into*, prüfen, untersuchen; — *forward to*, sich freuen (auf, *Acc.*); — *over*, durchsehen. — *s.* der Blick (*glance*); das Aussehen (*appearance*).

looking-glass ['lukiŋglɑːs], *s.* der Spiegel.

look-out ['lukaut], *s.* der Ausblick; die Ausschau.

loom [lu:m], *s.* der Webstuhl. — *v.n.* in der Ferne auftauchen (*emerge*).

loon [lu:n], *s.* (*Orn.*) der Eisvogel, Eistaucher; (*coll.*) der Narr.

loony ['lu:ni], *adj.* (*coll.*) wahnsinnig, närrisch.

loop [lu:p], *s.* die Schlinge, das Schlingband; (*Railw.*) — *line*, die Schleife.

loophole ['lu:phoul], *s.* der Ausweg, die Hintertür.

loose [lu:s], *adj.* locker, lose; liederlich (*morals*). — *v.a.* lösen.

loosen [lu:sn], *v.a.* auflockern, locker machen.

lop [lɔp], *v.a.* stutzen (*trees*).

lopsided [lɔp'saidid], *adj.* einseitig.

loquacious [lo'kweifəs], *adj.* geschwätzig.

loquacity [lo'kwæsiti], *s.* die Schwatzhaftigkeit.

Lord [lɔ:d], *s.* (*Rel.*) the —, Gott der Herr; der Lord (*nobleman's title*); — *Mayor*, der Oberbürgermeister.

lord [lɔ:d], *s.* der Herr.

lordly ['lɔ:dli], *adj.* vornehm, stolz.

lore [lɔ:], *s.* die Kunde.

lose [lu:z], *v.a., v.n. irr.* verlieren; nachgehen (*of timepiece*).

loser ['lu:zə], *s.* der Verlierende.

loss [lɔs], *s.* der Verlust.

lot [lɔt], *s.* das Los; der Anteil (*share*); die Menge (*quantity*); die Partie (*auction*); (*Am.*) das Stück Land.

loth *see* loath.

lotion ['loufən], *s.* das Waschmittel, das Wasser.

loud [laud], *adj.* laut; grell (*colour*).

lounge [laundʒ], *s.* der Gesellschaftsraum; (*Obs.*) die Chaiselongue; — *suit*, der Straßenanzug. — *v.n.* nichts tun, herumlungern, herumsitzen.

louse [laus], *s.* (*Zool.*) die Laus.

lout [laut], *s.* der Tölpel.

lovable ['lʌvəbl], *adj.* liebenswürdig, liebenswert.

love [lʌv], *s.* die Liebe; *for the — of God*, um Gottes Willen; *for —*, um nichts; *not for — nor money*, weder für Geld noch gute Worte, auf keinen Fall. — *v.a., v.n.* lieben; — *to*, gern tun.

lover ['lʌvə], *s.* der Liebhaber, der *or* die Geliebte.

low [lou], *adj.* niedrig; nieder, tief; leise; (*Mus.*) tief; (*spirits*) niedergeschlagen. — *v.n.* muhen (*of cattle*).

lowlands ['loulændz], *s. pl.* die Niederungen, *f.pl.*; die Ebene; das Unterland.

lowliness ['loulinis], *s.* die Demut, Bescheidenheit.

lowness ['lounis], *s.* die Niedrigkeit; Tiefe.

loyal ['lɔiəl], *adj.* treu, ergeben, loyal.

loyalty ['lɔiəlti], *s.* die Treue, Ergebenheit, Loyalität.

lozenge ['lɔzindʒ], *s.* die Pastille; (*Geom.*) die Raute.

lubricant ['lu:brikənt], *s.* das Schmiermittel, Schmieröl.

lubricate ['lu:brikeit], *v.a.* ölen, schmieren.

lucid ['lu:sid], *adj.* klar, deutlich.

lucidity [lu:'siditi], *s.* die Klarheit.

luck [lʌk], *s.* das Glück, der Glücksfall.

luckily ['lʌkili], *adv.* glücklicherweise.

lucky ['lʌki], *adj.* mit Glück gesegnet, glücklich.

lucrative ['lu:krətiv], *adj.* einträglich.

lucre ['lu:kə], *s.* der Gewinn.

ludicrous ['lu:dikrəs], *adj.* lächerlich, komisch.

lug [lʌg], *v.a.* schleifen, zerren; (*burden*) schleppen.

luggage ['lʌgidʒ], *s.* das Gepäck.

lugger ['lʌgə], *s.* (*Naut.*) der Logger, Lugger.

lugubrious [lu:'gju:briəs], *adj.* traurig.

lukewarm ['lu:kwɔ:m], *adj.* lauwarm.

lull [lʌl], *s.* die (Wind)stille. — *v.a.* einlullen, beschwichtigen.

lullaby ['lʌləbai], *s.* das Wiegenlied.

lumbago [lʌm'beigou], *s.* (*Med.*) der Hexenschuß.

lumbar ['lʌmbə], *adj.* (*Anat.*) zu den Lenden gehörig, Lenden-.

lumber ['lʌmbə], *s.* der Kram, das alte Zeug; (*timber*) das Bauholz; — *room*, die Rumpelkammer.

luminous ['lu:minəs], *adj.* leuchtend, Leucht-.

lump [lʌmp], *s.* der Klumpen, Haufen; — *sugar*, der Würfelzucker; — *sum*, die Pauschalsumme. — *v.a.* — (*together*), zusammenwerfen.

lumpy ['lʌmpi], *adj.* klumpig.

lunacy ['lu:nəsi], *s.* der Wahnsinn.

lunatic ['lu:nətik], *adj.* wahnsinnig. — *s.* der Wahnsinnige; — *asylum*, das Irrenhaus, die Irrenanstalt.

lunch [lʌntf], *v.n.* zu Mittag essen. — *s.* (*also* **luncheon** ['lʌntfən]) das Mittagessen.

lung [lʌŋ], *s.* (*Anat.*) die Lunge.

lunge [lʌndʒ], *v.n.* stoßen, stürzen. — *s.* der Stoß.

lurch [lə:tf], *s. leave in the —*, im Stiche lassen. — *v.n.* taumeln.

lure [luə], *v.a.* locken, ködern (*bait*). — *s.* der Köder (*bait*), die Lockung.

lurid ['ljuərid], *adj.* unheimlich, grell.

lurk [lə:k], *v.n.* lauern.

luscious ['lʌfəs], *adj.* saftig, süß.

lush [lʌf], *adj.* üppig (*vegetation*); übermäßig.

lust [lʌst], *s.* die Wollust, Sucht. — *v.n.* gelüsten (*for*, nach, *Dat.*).
lustre [ˈlʌstə], *s.* der Glanz.
lusty [ˈlʌsti], *adj.* kräftig, laut.
lute [luːt], *s.* (*Mus.*) die Laute.
lutanist [ˈluːtənist], *s.* (*Mus.*) der Lautenspieler.
Lutheran [ˈluːθərən], *adj.* lutherisch. — *s.* der Lutheraner.
luxuriate [lʌgˈzjuərieit, lʌkˈsjuə-], *v.n.* schwelgen; (*Bot.*) üppig wachsen.
luxurious [lʌgˈzjuəriəs, lʌkˈsjuə-], *adj.* üppig; (*rich*) reich ausgeschmückt, prächtig, luxuriös.
luxury [ˈlʌkʃəri], *s.* der Luxus, Aufwand.
lymph [limf], *s.* die Lymphe.
lynx [links], *s.* (*Zool.*) der Luchs.
lyric [ˈlirik], *s.* die Lyrik.
lyrical [ˈlirikəl], *adj.* lyrisch.

M

M [em]. das M.
macaroon [mækəˈruːn], *s.* die Makrone.
mace [meis], *s.* das Zepter.
macerate [ˈmæsəreit], *v.a.* abzehren.
machination [mækiˈneiʃən], *s.* die Machenschaft, Ränke, *m.pl.*
machine [məˈʃiːn], *s.* die Maschine.
mackerel [ˈmækərəl], *s.* (*Zool.*) die Makrele.
mackintosh [ˈmækintɔʃ], *s.* der Regenmantel.
mad [mæd], *adj.* verrückt, wahnsinnig.
madam [ˈmædəm], *s.* (*addr.*) gnädige Frau.
madden [mædn], *v.a.* verrückt machen.
madman [ˈmædmən], *s.* der Wahnsinnige.
madness [ˈmædnis], *s.* der Wahnsinn.
magazine [mægəˈziːn], *s.* die (illustrierte) Zeitschrift; (*gun*) der Ladestock; der Lagerraum (*storeroom*).
maggot [ˈmægət], *s.* (*Ent.*) die Made. —
magic [ˈmædʒik], *adj.* zauberhaft; — *lantern*, die Laterna Magica. — *s.* der Zauber; die Magie, Zauberei.
magician [məˈdʒiʃən], *s.* der Zauberer.
magistracy [ˈmædʒistrəsi], *s.* die Obrigkeit (*authority*).
magistrate [ˈmædʒistr(e)it], *s.* der Richter.
magnanimity [mægnəˈnimiti], *s.* der Großmut.
magnanimous [mægˈnæniməs], *adj.* großmütig.
magnate [ˈmægneit], *s.* der Magnat, Großunternehmer.
magnet [ˈmægnit], *s.* der Magnet.
magnetic [mægˈnetik], *adj.* magnetisch.
magnetize [ˈmægnitaiz], *v.a.* magnetisieren.

magnificence [mægˈnifisəns], *s.* die Herrlichkeit.
magnificent [mægˈnifisənt], *adj.* herrlich, großartig.
magnify [ˈmægnifai], *v.a.* vergrößern (*make larger*); (*Rel.*) verherrlichen.
magnitude [ˈmægnitjuːd], *s.* die Größe; *order of* —, die Größenordnung.
magpie [ˈmægpai], *s.* (*Orn.*) die Elster.
Magyar [ˈmægjɑː], *adj.* madjarisch. — *s.* der Magyar, Madjar.
mahogany [məˈhɔgəni], *s.* das Mahagoni(holz).
maid [meid], *s.* (*Poet.*) das Mädchen; das Stubenmädchen (*servant*).
maiden [meidn], *s.* (*Poet.*) die Jungfrau, das Mädchen; — *aunt*, die unverheiratete Tante.
mail (1) [meil], *s.* die Post. — *v.a.* aufgeben, mit der Post senden.
mail (2) [meil], *s.* (*Mil.*) der Panzer.
maim [meim], *v.a.* verstümmeln, lähmen.
main (1) [mein], *adj.* hauptsächlich, Haupt-; (*Railw.*) — *line*, die Hauptstrecke. — *s.* der Hauptteil; *in the* —, hauptsächlich; (*Poet.*) das Weltmeer; (*pl.*) das Hauptrohr, die Hauptleitung.
main (2) [mein], *s. with might and* —, mit allen Kräften.
mainstay [ˈmeinstei], *s.* die Hauptgrundlage, Hauptstütze.
maintain [meinˈtein], *v.a.* erhalten, unterhalten (*keep*); behaupten (*assert*).
maintenance [ˈmeintənəns], *s.* der Unterhalt, die Unterhaltskosten, *pl.* die Erhaltung.
maize [meiz], *s.* (*Bot.*) der Mais.
majestic [məˈdʒestik], *adj.* majestätisch, prunkvoll.
majesty [ˈmædʒəsti], *s.* die Majestät.
major [ˈmeidʒə], *adj.* größer, älter (*elder brother*); wichtig (*more important*). — *s.* (*Mil.*) der Major; (*Law*) der Mündige. — *v.n.* (*Am.*) sich spezialisieren.
majority [məˈdʒɔriti], *s.* die Mehrheit (*in numbers*); (*Law*) die Mündigkeit; (*Mil.*) der Majorsrang.
make [meik], *v.a. irr.* machen, schaffen, herstellen (*produce*); (*coll.*) verdienen (*money*); *he has made it!* (*coll.*) er hat's geschafft!; — *out*, ausfüllen (*cheque etc.*); entziffern (*decipher*); — *up*, erfinden (*invent*); schminken (*o.'s face*). — *v.n. what do you* — *of him?* was halten Sie von ihm? — *s.* die Marke.
make-believe [ˈmeikbəliːv], *s.* der Vorwand. — *adj.* vorgeblich.
maladjustment [mæləˈdʒʌstmənt], *s.* die Unfähigkeit sich anzupassen; die falsche Einstellung; das Missverhältnis.
maladroit [mæləˈdrɔit], *adj.* ungeschickt, ungewandt.
malady [ˈmælədi], *s.* das Leiden, die Krankheit.

Malagasy [mælə'gæsi], *adj.* madagassisch. — *s.* der Madagasse.
Malaysian [mə'leiziən], *adj.* malaysisch. — *s.* der Malaysier.
malcontent ['mælkəntent], *adj.* mißvergnügt.
male [meil], *adj.* männlich; — *screw*, die Schraubenspindel. — *s.* der Mann; (*Zool.*) das Männchen.
malefactor ['mælifæktə], *s.* der Übeltäter.
malice ['mælis], *s.* die Bosheit.
malicious [mə'liʃəs], *adj.* boshaft, böswillig.
malign [mə'lain], *v.a.* lästern, verleumden.
malignant [mə'lignənt], *adj.* bösartig.
malignity [mə'ligniti], *s.* die Bösartigkeit.
malinger [mə'lingə], *v.n.* sich krank stellen.
malleable ['mæliəbl], *adj.* (*Metall.*) leicht zu hämmern; (*fig.*) geschmeidig.
mallet ['mælit], *s.* der Schlegel, Holzhammer.
mallow ['mælou], *s.* (*Bot.*) die Malve.
malpractice [mæl'præktis], *s.* das gesetzwidrige Handeln, der Mißbrauch; die Amtsvergehung.
malt [mɔ:lt], *s.* das Malz.
Maltese [mɔ:l'ti:z], *adj.* maltesisch. — *s.* der Malteser.
maltreat [mæl'tri:t], *v.a.* mißhandeln.
mammal ['mæməl], *s.* (*Zool.*) das Säugetier.
man [mæn], *s.* der Mann (*adult male*); der Mensch (*human being*); — *of war*, das Kriegschiff. — *v.a.* bemannen.
manacle ['mænəkl], *s.* die Handschelle. — *v.a.* fesseln.
manage ['mænidʒ], *v.a.* leiten, handhaben, verwalten; *how did you — it?* wie haben Sie's fertiggebracht?
management ['mænidʒmənt], *s.* die Leitung, Führung.
manager ['mænədʒə], *s.* der Leiter, Geschäftsführer, Manager.
mandatary *see* **mandatory**.
mandate ['mændeit], *s.* das Mandat.
mandatory ['mændətəri], *adj.* befehlend, bevollmächtigt, beauftragt. — *s.* der Bevollmächtigte, Beauftragte.
mandrake ['mændreik], *s.* der Alraun.
mane [mein], *s.* die Mähne.
manganese ['mæŋgəni:z], *s.* (*Chem.*) das Mangan.
mange [meindʒ], *s.* die Räude.
manger ['meindʒə], *s.* die Krippe.
mangle (1) [mæŋgl], *s.* die Mangel. — *v.a.* rollen; mangeln (*laundry*).
mangle (2) [mæŋgl], *v.a.* verstümmeln (*disfigure*).
mango ['mæŋgou], *s.* (*Bot.*) die Mangofrucht.
manhood ['mænhud], *s.* die Mannbarkeit, das Mannesalter.
mania ['meiniə], *s.* der Wahnsinn, die Manie.
maniac ['meiniæk], *s.* der Wahnsinnige. — *adj.* wahnsinnig.

manifest ['mænifest], *adj.* deutlich, klar, offenbar.
manifestation [mænifes'teiʃən], *s.* die Offenbarung.
manifesto [mæni'festou], *s.* das Manifest.
manifold ['mænifould], *adj.* mannigfach.
manipulate [mə'nipjuleit], *v.a.* manipulieren, handhaben.
mankind [mæn'kaind], *s.* die Menschheit.
manly ['mænli], *adj.* mannhaft, männlich.
manner ['mænə], *s.* die Art, Sitte (*custom*); die Manier (*bearing*); das Benehmen (*behaviour*); (*pl.*) gute Sitten.
mannered ['mænəd], *adj.* gesittet, geartet; manieriert, gekünstelt (*artificial*).
manor ['mænə], *s.* — *house*, das Herrenhaus, Schloß.
manorial [mə'nɔ:riəl], *adj.* des Herrenhauses, herrschaftlich.
manservant ['mænsə:vənt], *s.* der Bediente, Diener.
mansion ['mænʃən], *s.* das (herrschaftliche) Wohnhaus, Herrenhaus.
manslaughter ['mænslɔ:tə], *s.* der Totschlag.
mantelpiece ['mæntlpi:s], *s.* der Kaminsims.
mantle [mæntl], *s.* (*gas*) der Glühstrumpf; (*Tail.*) der Mantel. — *v.a.* verhüllen (*cloak*).
manual ['mænjuəl], *s.* das Handbuch; (*Mus.*) das Handregister. — *adj.* Hand-.
manufacture [mænju'fæktʃə], *s.* die Herstellung, Erzeugung (*production*); (*Comm.*) das Fabrikat (*product*).
manufacturer [mænju'fæktʃərə], *s.* der Fabrikant, Erzeuger.
manure [mə'njuə], *s.* der Dünger; der Mist. — *v.a.* düngen.
manuscript ['mænjuskript], *s.* die Handschrift, das Manuskript.
many ['meni], *adj.* viele; *as — as*, ganze . . . (*emphatically*); — *a*, mancher.
map [mæp], *s.* die Landkarte. — *v.a.* —(*out*), nach der Karte planen.
maple [meipl], *s.* (*Bot.*) der Ahorn.
mar [ma:], *v.a.* verderben.
marauder [mə'rɔ:də], *s.* der Plünderer.
marble [ma:bl], *s.* der Marmor (*rock*); (*pl.*) die Murmel (*game*). — *adj.* marmorn.
March [ma:tʃ], der März.
march [ma:tʃ], *s.* der Marsch. — *v.n.* marschieren; *steal a — on s.o.*, jemandem zuvorkommen.
marchioness [ma:ʃə'nes], *s.* die Marquise.
mare [meə], *s.* (*Zool.*) die Stute.
margin ['ma:dʒin], *s.* der Rand.
marginal ['ma:dʒinəl], *adj.* Rand-, am Rande gelegen.
marigold ['mærigould], *s.* (*Bot.*) die Dotterblume.

marine

marine [mə'ri:n], *adj.* Marine-, See-. — *s.* (*Mil.*) der Seesoldat; *tell that to the Marines!* der Großmutter erzählen.
mariner ['mærinə], *s.* der Seemann.
marital ['mæritəl], *adj.* ehelich.
maritime ['mæritaim], *adj.* Meeres-, See-.
mark [mɑːk], *s.* das Zeichen (*sign*); (*Sch.*) die Zensur, Note; (*Comm.*) die Marke; *wide of the* —, auf dem Holzwege. — *v.a.* markieren (*make sign on*); — *my words*, merk dir das! paß auf! (*Comm.*) — *down*, den Preis heruntersetzen; ins Auge fassen (*observe closely*); *a* —*ed man*, ein Gezeichneter.
market ['mɑːkit], *s.* der Markt. — *v.a.* auf den Markt bringen.
marksman ['mɑːksmən], *s.* der Schütze.
marl [mɑːl], *s.* der Mergel.
marmalade ['mɑːməleid], *s.* die Orangenmarmelade.
marmot ['mɑːmət], *s.* (*Zool.*) das Murmeltier.
maroon (1) [mə'ruːn], *adj.* kastanienbraun, rotbraun.
maroon (2) [mə'ruːn], *v.a.* aussetzen.
marquee [mɑː'kiː], *s.* das große Zelt.
marquess, marquis ['mɑːkwis], *s.* der Marquis.
marriage ['mæridʒ], *s.* die Ehe, Heirat; die Hochzeit (*wedding*).
marriageable ['mæridʒəbl], *adj.* heiratsfähig.
married ['mærid], *adj.* verheiratet.
marrow ['mærou], *s.* . (*Anat.*) das Mark; (*Bot.*) der Kürbis.
marry ['mæri], *v.a.* heiraten; trauen (*perform marriage ceremony*); — *off*, verheiraten (*o.'s daughter*). — *v.n.* sich verheiraten.
marsh [mɑːʃ], *s.* der Morast, Sumpf.
marshal ['mɑːʃəl], *s.* der Marschall.
marshy ['mɑːʃi], *adj.* morastig, sumpfig.
marten ['mɑːtin], *s.* (*Zool.*) der Marder.
martial ['mɑːʃəl], *adj.* Kriegs-, kriegerisch.
martin ['mɑːtin], *s.* (*Orn.*) die Mauerschwalbe.
martyr ['mɑːtə], *s.* der Märtyrer.
martyrdom ['mɑːtədəm], *s.* das Märtyrertum, der Märtyrertod.
marvel [mɑːvl], *v.n.* staunen (*at*, über, *Acc.*).
marvellous ['mɑːv(ə)ləs], *adj.* wunderbar, erstaunlich.
masculine ['mæskjulin], *adj.* männlich. — *s.* (*Gram.*) das Maskulinum, das männliche Geschlecht.
mash [mæʃ], *v.a.* zerquetschen, zerdrücken. — *s.* der Brei.
mask [mɑːsk], *v.a.*, *v.n.* maskieren, sich vermummen. — *s.* die Maske.
mason ['meisən], *s.* der Maurer.
masonic [mə'sɔnik], *adj.* freimaurerisch.
masonry ['meisənri], *s.* das Mauerwerk.
masquerade [mæskə'reid], *s.* der Mummenschanz, die Maskerade.
Mass [mæs, mɑːs], *s.* (*Eccl.*) die Messe; *Low Mass*, die stille Messe; *High Mass*, das Hochamt; *Requiem Mass*, die Seelenmesse.
mass [mæs], *s.* die Masse; die Menge. — *v.a.*, *v.n.* (sich) massen, ansammeln.
massacre ['mæsəkə], *s.* das Blutbad.
massive ['mæsiv], *adj.* massiv, schwer.
mast [mɑːst], *s.* der Mast. — *v.a.* (*Naut.*) bemasten.
Master ['mɑːstə], *s.* (*Univ.*) der Magister; der junge Herr (*before boy's name*).
master ['mɑːstə], *s.* der Meister (*of a craft*); der Herr, Arbeitgeber (*employer*); — *key*, der Hauptschlüssel. — *v.a.* meistern, beherrschen.
masticate ['mæstikeit] *v.a.* kauen.
mastiff ['mæstif], *s.* (*Zool.*) der Kettenhund, Mastiff.
mat [mæt], *s.* die Matte.
match (1) [mætʃ], *s.* das Streichholz, Zündholz.
match (2) [mætʃ], *s.* der ebenbürtige Partner (*suitable partner*); *find o.'s* —, seinesgleichen finden; (*Sport*) das Wettspiel, der Wettkampf; Fußballkampf; (*Cricket*) das Cricketspiel. — *v.a.*, *v.n.* passen zu, anpassen; ebenbürtig sein (*be equal*).
matchless ['mætʃlis], *adj.* unvergleichlich, ohnegleichen.
mate (1) [meit], *s.* der Gefährte, Genosse; (*Naut.*) der Maat, Steuermann; (*coll.*) Freund. — *v.n.* sich paaren, sich verheiraten.
mate (2) [meit], *v.a.* (*Chess*) matt setzen.
material [mə'tiəriəl], *s.* das Material, der Stoff. — *adj.* wesentlich (*essential*); materiell (*tangible*).
materialism [mə'tiəriəlizm], *s.* der Materialismus.
maternal [mə'tə:nəl], *adj.* mütterlich.
maternity [mə'tə:niti], *s.* die Mutterschaft; — *ward*, die Geburtsklinik.
mathematical [mæθə'mætikəl], *adj.* mathematisch.
mathematics [mæθə'mætiks], *s.* die Mathematik.
matins ['mætinz], *s.* (*Eccl.*) die Frühmette.
matriculate [mə'trikjuleit], *v.n.* immatrikulieren (*lassen*).
matrimonial [mætri'mouniəl], *adj.* Ehe-, ehelich.
matrimony ['mætrimoni], *s.* die Ehe.
matron ['meitrən], *s.* die Oberschwester, Oberin (*in hospital etc.*); die Matrone (*older woman*).
matter ['mætə], *s.* der Stoff (*substance*); die Sache, der Gegenstand (*subject*); die Angelegenheit (*case*); *printed* —, Drucksache; *what is the* —*?* was ist los?; *the heart of the* —, des Pudels Kern; *as a* — *of fact*, tatsächlich, ernst gesprochen. — *v.n.* bedeutsam sein, wichtig sein.
mattock ['mætək], *s.* die Haue.
mattress ['mætrəs], *s.* die Matratze.
mature [mə'tjuə], *adj.* reif; (*fig.*) gereift. — *v.a.*, *v.n.* reifen, zur Reife bringen; (*Comm.*) fällig werden.

memorial

matured [mə'tjuəd], *adj.* abgelagert.
maturity [mə'tjuəriti], *s.* die Reife; (*Comm.*) die Fälligkeit.
maudlin ['mɔːdlin], *adj.* rührselig, sentimental.
maul [mɔːl], *v.a.* mißhandeln.
Maundy Thursday ['mɔːndi'θəːzd(e)i]. der Gründonnerstag.
mauve [mouv], *adj.* malvenfarbig; violett.
maw [mɔː], *s.* (*Zool.*) der Magen.
mawkish ['mɔːkiʃ], *adj.* abgeschmackt, sentimental, rührselig.
maxim ['mæksim], *s.* der Grundsatz.
May [mei]. der Mai.
may (1) [mei], *v.n. aux. irr.* mögen, können; (*permissive*) dürfen.
may (2) [mei], *s.* (*Bot.*) der Weißdorn.
mayor [mɛə], *s.* der Bürgermeister.
maypole ['meipoul], *s.* der Maibaum.
maze [meiz], *s.* das Labyrinth.
me [miː], *pers. pron.* (*Acc.*) mich; (*Dat.*) mir.
mead [miːd], *s.* der Met.
meadow ['medou], *s.* die Wiese.
meagre ['miːgə], *adj.* mager, karg (*lean, poor*); dürftig.
meal (1) [miːl], *s.* das Mahl, Essen, die Mahlzeit.
meal (2) [miːl], *s.* das Mehl (*flour*).
mealy ['miːli], *adj.* mehlig; — -*mouthed*, frömmelnd; kleinlaut (*shy*).
mean (1) [miːn], *v.a. irr.* bedeuten (*signify*); meinen (*wish to express*); vorhaben (*intend*).
mean (2) [miːn], *adj.* mittelmäßig, Mittel– (*average*). — *s.* die Mitte.
mean (3) [miːn], *adj.* gemein, niedrig (*despicable*); geizig.
meander [mi'ændə], *s.* die Windung, das Wellenmuster. — *v.n.* sich winden, sich schlängeln.
meaning ['miːniŋ], *s.* die Bedeutung (*significance, connotation*); der Sinn.
meaningless ['miːniŋlis], *adj.* bedeutungslos.
means [miːnz], *s.* das Mittel; *by all* —, auf jeden Fall, unbedingt; *by no* —, keinesfalls; *by—of*, mittels (*Genit.*).
meantime, meanwhile ['miːntaim, 'miːnwail], *s.* die Zwischenzeit.— *adv.* in der Zwischenzeit, indessen.
measles [miːzlz], *s.* (*Med.*) die Masern, *f. pl.*; *German* —, die Röteln, *m. pl.*
measurable ['meʒərəbl], *adj.* meßbar.
measure ['meʒə], *s.* das Maß; der Maßstab (*scale*); (*Mus.*) der Takt; das Zeitmaß.— *v.a.* messen, abmessen.
meat [miːt], *s.* das Fleisch.
mechanic [mi'kænik], *s.* der Mechaniker.
mechanical [mi'kænikəl], *adj.* mechanisch, automatisch; — *engineering*, der Maschinenbau.
mechanics [mi'kæniks], *s.* die Mechanik.
medal [medl], *s.* die Medaille, der Orden.
meddle [medl], *v.n.* sich einmischen (in, *in*, *Acc.*).

mediæval, medieval [medi'iːvəl], *adj.* mittelalterlich.
mediate ['miːdieit], *v.n.* vermitteln, intervenieren. — *adj.* mittelbar.
mediator ['miːdieitə], *s.* der Vermittler.
medical ['medikəl], *adj.* medizinisch, ärztlich; — *orderly*, der Krankenwärter.
medicate ['medikeit], *v.a.* medizinisch behandeln.
medicine ['medsən], *s.* die Medizin, Arznei.
medieval *see* **mediæval**.
mediocre ['miːdioukə], *adj.* mittelmäßig.
mediocrity [miːdi'ɔkriti], *s.* die Mittelmäßigkeit.
meditate ['mediteit], *v.n.* nachdenken, sinnen.
meditation [medi'teiʃən], *s.* das Sinnen, Nachdenken.
Mediterranean [medita'reiniən], *adj.* mittelländisch. — *s.* das Mittelmeer, mittelländische Meer.
medium ['miːdjəm], *s.* das Medium; das Mittel (*means*). — *adj.* mittelgroß.
medlar ['medlə], *s.* (*Bot.*) die Mispel.
medley ['medli], *s.* (*Mus.*) das Potpourri; das Gemisch (*mixture*).
meek [miːk], *adj.* sanft, mild.
meet [miːt], *v.a., v.n. irr.* treffen (*Acc.*), sich treffen (mit, *Dat.*), begegnen (*Dat.*). — *s.* (*Hunt.*) die Jagd.
meeting ['miːtiŋ], *s.* das Zusammentreffen; die Tagung, Sitzung (*conference*).
melancholy ['melənkɔli], *adj.* melancholisch, schwermütig. — *s.* die Melancholie, die Schwermut.
mellifluous [me'lifluəs], *adj.* lieblich, süß (*of sounds*).
mellow ['melou], *adj.* mild, weich, mürbe (*fruit etc.*); freundlich (*mood*). — *v.a.* mürbe machen, reifen lassen. — *v.n.* weich werden.
melodious [mə'loudiəs], *adj.* klangvoll, wohlklingend, melodisch.
melodrama ['melədrɑːmə], *s.* das Melodrama.
melody ['melədi], *s.* die Melodie.
melon ['melən], *s.* (*Bot.*) die Melone.
melt [melt], *v.a., v.n. reg. & irr.* schmelzen.
member ['membə], *s.* das Mitglied (*of club*); (*Parl.*) der Abgeordnete, das Glied.
membrane ['membrein], *s.* die Membran; (*Anat.*) das Häutchen.
memento [mi'mentou], *s.* das Andenken.
memoir ['memwɑː], *s.* die Denkschrift; (*pl.*) die Memoiren, *n. pl.*
memorable ['memərəbl], *adj.* denkwürdig.
memorandum [memə'rændəm], *s.* das Memorandum, die Denkschrift.
memorial [mi'mɔːriəl], *s.* das Denkmal (*monument*). — *adj.* Gedenk-, zum Gedenken, Gedächtnis-.

memory

memory ['meməri], s. die Erinnerung; das Gedächtnis (*faculty*); das Andenken (*remembrance*).

menace ['menis], s. die Drohung. — *v.a.* bedrohen.

mend [mend], *v.a.* reparieren; verbessern, ausbessern. — *v.n.* sich bessern.

mendacious [men'deiʃəs], *adj.* lügnerisch, verlogen (*lying*).

mendacity [men'dæsiti], s. die Lügenhaftigkeit, Verlogenheit.

mendicant ['mendikənt], *adj.* bettlerisch. — s. der Bettler.

mendicity [men'disiti], s. die Bettelei.

menial ['mi:niəl], *adj.* gemein, grob (*job*).

mental [mentl], *adj.* geistig; (*coll.*) geisteskrank.

mention ['menʃən], *v.a.* erwähnen; *don't* — *it*, gern geschehen! — s. die Erwähnung.

mentor ['mentə], s. der Ratgeber.

menu ['menju:], s. die Speisekarte.

mercantile ['mə:kəntail], *adj.* Handels-, kaufmännisch.

mercenary ['mə:sənəri], *adj.* für Geld zu haben, käuflich, feil; materiell eingestellt. — s. der Söldner.

mercer ['mə:sə], s. der Seidenhändler.

mercerised ['mə:səraizd], *adj.* (*Textile*) merzerisiert.

merchandise ['mə:tʃəndaiz], s. die Ware.

merchant ['mə:tʃənt], s. der Kaufmann.

merchantman ['mə:tʃəntmən], s. (*Naut.*) das Handelsschiff, Frachtschiff.

merciful ['mə:siful], *adj.* barmherzig, gnädig.

Mercury ['mə:kjuəri]. (*Myth.*) Merkur, *m.*

mercury ['mə:kjuəri], s. (*Chem.*) das Quecksilber.

mercy ['mə:si], s. die Barmherzigkeit, Gnade.

mere (1) [miə], *adj.* bloß, allein.

mere (2) [miə], s. der Teich.

meretricious [meri'triʃəs], *adj.* falsch, täuschend.

merge [mə:dʒ], *v.n.* aufgehen lassen, verschmelzen (*combine*).

merger ['mə:dʒə], s. (*Comm.*) die Fusion, Vereinigung, Zusammenlegung.

meridian [mə'ridiən], s. der Meridian; (*fig.*) der Gipfel.

merit ['merit], s. das Verdienst, der Wert. — *v.a.* verdienen.

meritorious [meri'tɔ:riəs], *adj.* verdienstlich.

mermaid ['mə:meid], s. die Wasserjungfer, Nixe.

merriment ['merimənt], s. die Belustigung, das Fröhlichsein, die Fröhlichkeit.

merry ['meri], *adj.* froh, fröhlich; — *go-round*, das Karussell.

mesh [meʃ], s. das Netz; die Masche (*knitting*). — *v.a.* einfangen.

mess (1) [mes], s. (*Mil.*) die Offiziersmesse.

mess (2) [mes], s. die Unordnung (*disorder*).

message ['mesidʒ], s. die Nachricht, Mitteilung, Botschaft.

messenger ['mesindʒə], s. der Bote.

Messiah [mi'saiə], s. der Messias.

metal [metl], s. das Metall.

metallurgy ['metələ:dʒi], s. die Metallurgie, Hüttenkunde.

metaphor ['metəfə:], s. die Metapher.

metaphorical [metə'fɔrikəl], *adj.* bildlich.

meter ['mi:tə], s. der Messer, Zähler (*gauge*); (*Am.*) see **metre** (1).

methinks [mi'θiŋks], *v. impers.* (*obs.*) mich dünkt, ich meine, mir scheint.

method ['meθəd], s. die Methode.

methodical [mi'θɔdikəl], *adj.* methodisch, systematisch.

methylate ['meθileit], *v.a.* (*Chem.*) denaturieren.

metre (1) ['mi:tə], s. der *or* das Meter (*unit of measurement*).

metre (2) ['mi:tə], s. (*Poet.*) das Versmaß.

metric ['metrik], *adj.* metrisch (*system of measurement*).

metrical ['metrikəl], *adj.* (*Poet.*) im Metrum, metrisch, Vers–.

metropolis [mi'trɔpəlis], s. die Metropole.

metropolitan [metrə'pɔlitən], *adj.* hauptstädtisch. — s. (*Eccl.*) der Erzbischof.

mettle [metl], s. der Mut (*courage*); *put s.o. on his* —, einen anspornen.

mew [mju:], s. das Miauen (*of cat*). — *v.n.* miauen.

mews [mju:z], s. *pl.* die Stallung.

Mexican ['meksikən], *adj.* mexikanisch. — s. der Mexikaner.

microphone ['maikrəfoun], s. das Mikrophon.

mid- [mid], *prefix.* mittel, Mittel-, mittler.

midday [mid'dei], s. der Mittag.

middle [midl], s. die Mitte, das Zentrum.

middling ['midliŋ], *adj.* (*coll.*) mittelmäßig.

midget ['midʒit], s. der Zwerg (*dwarf*).

midnight ['midnait], s. die Mitternacht.

midriff ['midrif], s. das Zwerchfell.

midshipman ['midʃipmən], s. (*Naut.*) der Seekadett.

midwife ['midwaif], s. die Hebamme.

mien [mi:n], s. die Miene.

might [mait], s. die Macht, Gewalt.

mighty ['maiti], *adj.* mächtig, stark.

mignonette [minjə'net], s. (*Bot.*) die Reseda.

migrate [mai'greit], *v.n.* wandern, migrieren; (*birds*) ziehen.

migratory ['maigrətəri], *adj.* Zug-, Wander-.

Milanese [milə′n:iz], *adj.* mailändisch. — *s.* der Mailänder.

mild [maild], *adj.* mild, sanft.

mildew [′mildju:], *s.* der Meltau.

mile [mail], *s.* die (englische) Meile.

mileage [′mailidʒ], *s.* die Meilenzahl.

milfoil [′milfoil], *s.* (*Bot.*) die Schafgarbe (*yarrow*).

military [′militəri], *adj.* militärisch. — *s.* das Militär.

militia [mi′lifə], *s.* die Miliz.

milk [milk], *v.a.* melken. — *s.* die Milch.

milksop [′milksɔp], *s.* die Memme.

milky [′milki], *adj.* milchig; *Milky Way*, die Milchstraße.

mill [mil], *s.* die Mühle; die Spinnerei (*textile*); *rolling* —, das Walzwerk; *run of the* —, gewöhnlich; *through the* —, wohl erfahren, lebenserfahren. — *v.a.* mahlen (*flour*); rollen, walzen (*steel*); rändern (*coins*); —*ed edge*, die Rändelkante. —*v.n.* — (*around*), sich drängen.

miller [′milə], *s.* der Müller.

millet [′milit], *s.* die Hirse.

milliner [′milinə], *s.* die Modistin, Putzmacherin.

millinery [′milinəri], *s.* die Putzwaren, Modewaren, *f. pl.*

million [′miljən], *s.* die Million.

milt [milt], *s.* die Fischmilch; (*Anat.*) die Milz.

mimic [′mimik], *s.* der Mimiker. — *v.a.* nachahmen.

mimicry [′mimikri], *s.* die Nachahmung; (*Zool.*) die Anpassung (*in colour*).

mince [mins], *v.a.* kleinhacken (*meat*); — *o.'s words*, affektiert sprechen; *not* — *o.'s words*, kein Blatt vor den Mund nehmen. — *s.* gehacktes Fleisch; — *pie*, die Dörrobstpastete.

mincemeat [′minsmi:t], *s.* die (gehackte) Dörrobstmischung.

mincing [′minsiŋ], *adj.* affektiert; — *steps*, trippelnde Schritte.

mind [maind], *s.* der Geist, das Gemüt; die Meinung; der Sinn; der Verstand; *what is on your* —? was bedrückt Sie?; *bear in* —, daran denken; *have a* —, Lust haben; *make up o.'s* —, sich entschließen; *with an open* —, unparteiisch. — *v.a.* beachten, achten (auf, *Acc.*). — *v.n. do you* —? macht es Ihnen etwas aus? *never* —, macht nichts; *I don't* —, mir ist's recht, meinetwegen.

minded [′maindid], *adj.* gesinnt, eingestellt.

mine (1) [main], *poss. pron.* mein, meinig.

mine (2) [main], *s.* das Bergwerk (*general*), die Grube (*coal*). — *v.a.* abbauen, graben (*Acc.*, nach, *Dat.*).

miner [′mainə], *s.* der Bergmann, Bergarbeiter; (*coll.*) der Kumpel.

mineral [′minərəl], *s.* das Mineral; (*pl.*) Mineralwasser.

mingle [miŋgl], *v.a.*, *v.n.* (sich) mischen.

minimize [′minimaiz], *v.a.* (möglichst) klein machen.

mining [′mainiŋ], *s.* die Hüttenkunde (*theory*); der Bergbau.

minion [′minjən], *s.* der Liebling.

minister [′ministə], *s.* (*Pol.*) der Minister; *Prime Minister*, der Ministerpräsident; (*Eccl.*) der Geistliche, Pfarrer. — *v.n.* einen Gottesdienst abhalten; dienen (*to*, *Dat.*).

ministration [minis′treifən], *s.* der Dienst, die Dienstleistung.

ministry [′ministri], *s.* das Ministerium (*department of state*); (*Eccl.*) der Beruf *or* das Amt des Geistlichen.

minnow [′minou], *s.* (*Zool.*) die Elritze.

minor [′mainə], *adj.* kleiner, geringer; (*Sch.*) jünger (*after boy's name*). — *s.* (*Law*) der Minderjährige, Unmündige.

minority [mai′nɔriti], *s.* die Minorität (*in numbers*); (*Law*) die Unmündigkeit.

minster [′minstə], *s.* (*Eccl.*) das Münster.

minstrel [′minstrəl], *s.* der Spielmann.

mint (1) [mint], *s.* (*Bot.*) die Minze.

mint (2) [mint], *s.* die Münzstätte. — *v.a.* münzen.

minuet [minju′et], *s.* (*Mus.*) das Menuett.

minute (1) [′minit], *s.* die Minute (*time*); (*pl.*) das Protokoll (*of meeting*). — *v.a.* zu Protokoll nehmen, protokollieren.

minute (2) [mai′nju:t], *adj.* winzig, klein.

minutiae [mi′nju:fii], *s. pl.* die Details, *n. pl.*, die Einzelheiten, *f. pl.*

miracle [′mirəkl], *s.* das Wunder.

miraculous [mi′rækjuləs], *adj.* wunderbar; wundertätig.

mirage [mi′rɑ:ʒ], *s.* die Luftspiegelung, die Fata Morgana.

mire [maiə], *s.* der Schlamm, Kot.

mirror [′mirə], *s.* der Spiegel. — *v.a.* reflektieren, spiegeln.

mirth [mə:θ], *s.* der Frohsinn.

misadventure [misəd′ventʃə], *s.* das Mißgeschick.

misalliance [misə′laiəns], *s.* die Mißheirat, Mesalliance.

misapply [misə′plai], *v.a.* falsch anwenden.

misapprehend [misæpri′hend], *v.a.* mißverstehen.

misapprehension [misæpri′henfən], *s.* das Mißverständnis.

misappropriate [misə′prouprieit], *v.a.* unrechtmäßig erwerben, unterschlagen.

misbehave [misbi′heiv], *v.n.* sich schlecht benehmen.

miscalculate [mis′kælkjuleit], *v.a.*, *v.n.* sich verrechnen.

miscarriage [mis′kæridʒ], *s.* das Mißlingen; (*Med.*) die Fehlgeburt.

miscarry [mis′kæri], *v.n.* mißlingen; (*Med.*) fehlgebären.

miscellaneous [misə′leiniəs], *adj.* vermischt.

miscellany

miscellany [mi'seləni], *s.* der Sammelband (*of writers*); die Mischung, das Gemisch.

mischief ['mistʃif], *s.* der Unfug; *out to make —*, darauf aus, Unfug zu stiften; — *maker*, der Unheilstifter.

mischievous ['mistʃivəs], *adj.* boshaft.

misconceive [miskən'si:v], *v.a.* mißverstehen.

misconception [miskən'sepʃən], *s.* das Mißverständnis.

misconduct [mis'kɔndʌkt], *s.* das unkorrekte Verhalten; der Fehltritt.

misconstruction [miskən'strʌkʃən], *s.* die Mißdeutung.

misconstrue [miskən'stru:], *v.a.* mißdeuten.

misdeed [mis'di:d], *s.* die Missetat.

misdemeanour [misdi'mi:nə], *s.* (*Law.*) das Vergehen; die Missetat.

miser ['maizə], *s.* der Geizhals.

miserable ['mizərəbl], *adj.* elend, kläglich (*wretched*); nichtswürdig (*base*).

miserly ['maizəli], *adj.* geizig.

misery ['mizəri], *s.* das Elend, die Not.

misfortune [mis'fɔ:tʃən], *s.* das Unglück.

misgiving [mis'givin], *s.* die Befürchtung, der Zweifel (*doubt*).

misguide [mis'gaid], *v.a.* irreführen, verleiten.

mishap [mis'hæp], *s.* der Unfall.

misinform [misin'fɔ:m], *v.a.* falsch informieren, falsch unterrichten.

misinterpret [misin'tə:prit], *v.a.* mißdeuten.

misjudge [mis'dʒʌdʒ], *v.a.* falsch beurteilen.

mislay [mis'lei], *v.a. irr.* verlegen.

mislead [mis'li:d], *v.a. irr.* verführen, irreführen.

misnomer [mis'noumə], *s.* der falsche Name.

misogynist [mi'sɔdʒinist], *s.* der Weiberfeind.

misplace [mis'pleis], *v.a.* übel anbringen (*remark*); verlegen (*thing*).

misprint [mis'print], *v.a.* verdrucken, falsch drucken. — ['misprint], *s.* der Druckfehler.

misquote [mis'kwout], *v.a.* falsch zitieren.

misrepresent [misrepri'zent], *v.a.* falsch darstellen.

misrule [mis'ru:l], *s.* die schlechte Regierung; die Unordnung (*disorder*).

miss (1) [mis], *s.* das Fräulein.

miss (2) [mis], *v.a.* vermissen (*yearn for*); versäumen (*a train, lesson etc.*); verfehlen (*target*); — *the boat*, den Anschluß verpassen; *be missing*, fehlen.

missal [misl], *s.* (*Eccl.*) das Meßbuch.

misshapen [mis'ʃeipən], *adj.* mißgestaltet.

missile ['misail], *s.* das Geschoß; *ballistic —*, das Raketengeschoß; *guided —*, ferngesteuertes Raketengeschoss.

mission ['miʃən], *s.* die Mission; Sendung; der Auftrag (*task*).

missionary ['miʃənəri], *adj.* Missions-. — *s.* der Missionar.

missive ['misiv], *s.* das Sendschreiben.

misspell [mis'spel], *v.a.* falsch buchstabieren, falsch schreiben.

mist [mist], *s.* der Dunst; Nebel (*fog*).

mistake [mis'teik], *s.* der Fehler. — *v.a. irr.* verkennen.

mistaken [mis'teikn], *adj.* im Unrecht; irrig; *be —*, sich irren.

mistimed [mis'taimd], *adj.* zur Unzeit, unzeitig.

mistletoe ['misltou], *s.* (*Bot.*) die Mistel, der Mistelzweig.

mistress ['mistrəs], *s.* die Herrin; Hausfrau; Geliebte (*paramour*); Lehrerin (*Sch.*).

mistrust [mis'trʌst], *v.a.* mißtrauen.

misunderstand [misʌndə'stænd], *v.a. irr.* mißverstehen.

misuse [mis'ju:z], *v.a.* mißbrauchen.

mite (1) [mait], *s.* (*Zool.*) die Milbe.

mite (2) [mait], *s.* das Scherflein (*coin*); (*coll.*) das Kindchen, das Kerlchen.

mitigate ['mitigeit], *v.a.* mildern.

mitre ['maitə], *s.* die Bischofsmütze, Mitra.

mitten [mitn], *s.* der Fäustling, Fausthandschuh.

mix [miks], *v.a.* mischen, vermischen. — *v.n.* verkehren.

mixed [mikst], *adj. a — blessing*, eine fragliche Wohltat.

mizzle [mizl], *v.n.* sprühen, rieseln.

mnemonics [ni'mɔniks], *s.* die Gedächtniskunst.

moan [moun], *v.n.* stöhnen (*wail*); klagen (*complain*). — *s.(coll.)* die Klage.

moat [mout], *s.* der Burggraben, Wassergraben.

mob [mɔb], *s.* der Pöbel.

mobility [mo'biliti], *s.* die Beweglichkeit.

mobilize ['moubilaiz], *v.a.* mobilisieren.

mock [mɔk], *v.a.* verspotten (*tease*); täuschen (*mislead*). — *v.n.* spotten. — *s.* der Spott, die Täuschung. — *adj.* Schein-; — *heroic*, komischheroisch.

modal [moudl], *adj.* (*Gram.*) modal, der Aussageweise nach; (*Mus.*) dem Modus nach.

mode [moud], *s.* (*Mus.*) der Modus, die Art; die Mode (*fashion*).

model [mɔdl], *s.* das Modell; das Muster (*pattern*). — *v.a., v.n.* modellieren.

moderate ['mɔdərit], *adj.* mäßig; (*climate*) gemäßigt. — [-reit], *v.a.* mäßigen; abändern.

modern ['mɔdən], *adj.* modern.

modernize ['mɔdənaiz], *v.a.* modernisieren.

modest ['mɔdist], *adj.* bescheiden.

modesty ['mɔdisti], *s.* die Bescheidenheit.

modify ['mɔdifai], *v.a.* abändern, modifizieren.

modish ['moudiʃ], *adj.* nach der neuesten Mode, modisch.
modulate ['mɔdjuleit], *v.a.* modulieren.
moil [mɔil], *v.n.* sich plagen.
moist [mɔist], *adj.* feucht.
moisten [mɔisn], *v.a.* befeuchten.
moisture ['mɔistʃə], *s.* die Feuchtigkeit.
molasses [mo'læsiz], *s.* die Melasse.
mole (1) [moul], *s.* (*Zool.*) der Maulwurf.
mole (2) [moul], *s.* das Muttermal (*skin mark*).
mole (3) [moul], *s.* der Seedamm, Hafendamm.
molecular [mo'lekjulə], *adj.* molekular.
molecule ['mɔl-, 'moulikju:l], *s.* das Molekül.
molest [mo'lest], *v.a.* belästigen.
mollify ['mɔlifai], *v.a.* besänftigen.
mollusc ['mɔləsk], *s.* (*Zool.*) die Molluske.
molt *see under* **moult**.
molten ['moultən], *adj.* geschmolzen.
moment ['moumənt], *s.* der Augenblick, Moment (*instant*); die Wichtigkeit (*importance*).
momentary ['mouməntəri], *adj.* momentan, einen Augenblick lang.
momentum [mo'mentəm], *s.* das Moment, die Triebkraft.
monarch ['mɔnək], *s.* der Monarch.
monarchy ['mɔnəki], *s.* die Monarchie.
monastery ['mɔnəstri], *s.* das (Mönchs-)kloster.
monastic [mə'næstik], *adj.* klösterlich.
Monday ['mʌndi]. der Montag.
money ['mʌni], *s.* das Geld; *ready* —, bares Geld; *make* —, Geld verdienen; — *order*, die Postanweisung.
Mongolian [mɔŋ'goulian], *adj.* mongolisch. — *s.* der Mongole.
mongrel ['mʌŋɡrəl], *s.* (*Zool.*) der Mischling.
monitor ['mɔnitə], *s.* der Ermahner; (*Rad.*) der Abhörer.
monitoring ['mɔnitəriŋ], *adj.* — *service*, der Abhördienst.
monk [mʌŋk], *s.* (*Eccl.*) der Mönch.
monkey ['mʌŋki], *s.* (*Zool.*) der Affe.
monomania [mɔno'meiniə], *s.* die Monomanie, fixe Idee.
monopolize [mə'nɔpəlaiz], *v.a.* monopolisieren.
monopoly [mə'nɔpəli], *s.* das Monopol.
monosyllabic [mɔnəsi'læbik], *adj.* einsilbig.
monotonous [mə'nɔtənəs], *adj.* monoton, eintönig.
monsoon [mɔn'su:n], *s.* der Monsun.
monster ['mɔnstə], *s.* das Ungeheuer.
monstrance ['mɔnstrəns], *s.* (*Eccl.*) die Monstranz.
monstrosity [mɔns'trɔsiti], *s.* die Ungeheuerlichkeit.
monstrous ['mɔnstrəs], *adj.* ungeheuerlich.
month [mʌnθ], *s.* der Monat.
monthly ['mʌnθli], *adj.* monatlich, Monats-.

mood [mu:d], *s.* die Stimmung, Laune; (*Gram., Mus.*) der Modus.
moodiness ['mu:dinis], *s.* die Launenhaftigkeit.
moody ['mu:di], *adj.* launenhaft.
moon [mu:n], *s.* der Mond.
moonlight ['mu:nlait], *s.* das Mondlicht, der Mondschein.
moonshine ['mu:nʃain], *s.* der Mondschein; (*fig.*) Unsinn.
moonstruck ['mu:nstrʌk], *adj.* mondsüchtig; verliebt.
Moor [muə], *s.* der Mohr.
moor [muə], *s.* das Moor, Heideland.
moorage ['muəridʒ], *s.* der Ankerplatz.
moorhen ['mɔ:hen], *s.* (*Orn.*) das Moorhuhn, Wildhuhn.
moorish ['muəriʃ], *adj.* maurisch.
moot [mu:t], *v.a.* erörtern, besprechen. — *adj. a* — *point*, ein strittiger Punkt.
mop [mɔp], *s.* der Wischlappen, Mop. — *v.a.* aufwischen (*floor*), wischen (*brow*).
mope [moup], *v.n.* traurig sein.
moral ['mɔrəl], *adj.* moralisch (*high principled*); sittlich (*decent*). — *s.* die Moral (*precept*); (*pl.*) die Sitten, *f. pl.*; die Sittlichkeit.
moralize ['mɔrəlaiz], *v.n.* moralisieren, Moral predigen (*Dat.*).
morass [mo'ræs], *s.* der Morast.
morbid ['mɔ:bid], *adj.* krankhaft.
more [mɔ:], *comp. adj., adv.* mehr; *once* —, noch einmal; *all the* —, umso mehr; *the* — *the better*, je mehr desto besser.
moreover [mɔ:'rouvə], *adv.* zudem, überdies, weiterhin.
morning ['mɔ:niŋ], *s.* der Morgen, Vormittag; — *coat*, der Cutaway, Frack.
Moroccan [mə'rɔkən], *adj.* marokkanisch. — *s.* der Marokkaner.
Morocco [mə'rɔkou]. Marokko, *n.*
morocco [mə'rɔkou], *s.* der Saffian, das Maroquinleder.
moron ['mɔ:rɔn], *s.* der Schwachsinnige.
morose [mə'rous], *adj.* mürrisch.
morrow ['mɔrou], *s.* (*Poet.*) der Morgen.
morsel [mɔ:sl], *s.* der Bissen, das Stück.
mortal [mɔ:tl], *adj.* sterblich, tödlich; — *sin*, die Todsünde. — *s.* der Sterbliche, der Mensch.
mortality [mɔ:'tæliti], *s.* die Sterblichkeit.
mortar ['mɔ:tə], *s.* (*Build.*) der Mörtel; (*Mil.*) der Mörser.
mortgage ['mɔ:gidʒ], *s.* die Hypothek. — *v.a.* verpfänden; eine Hypothek aufnehmen (auf, *Acc.*).
mortgagee [mɔ:gi'dʒi:], *s.* der Hypothekengläubiger.
mortician [mɔ:'tiʃən], *s.* (*Am.*) *see* **undertaker**.
mortify ['mɔ:tifai], *v.a.* kasteien (*chasten*); kränken (*humiliate*).
mortise ['mɔ:tis], *s.* (*Build.*) das Zapfenloch.

mortuary ['mɔ:tjuəri], s. die Leichenhalle.

mosque [mɔsk], s. (Rel.) die Moschee.

mosquito [mɔs'ki:tou], s. (Ent.) der Moskito.

moss [mɔs], s. (Bot.) das Moos.

most [moust], superl. adj. meist; (pl.) die meisten. — adv. meist, meistens; höchst (before adjectives).

mostly ['moustli], adv. meistenteils.

mote [mout], s. das Stäubchen.

moth [mɔθ], s. (Ent.) die Motte.

mother ['mʌðə], s. die Mutter; — -in-law, die Schwiegermutter; —-of-pearl, die Perlmutter.

motherly ['mʌðəli], adj. mütterlich.

motion ['mouʃən], s. die Bewegung, der Gang; (Parl., Rhet.) der Antrag. — v.a. bewegen. — v.n. zuwinken (Dat.).

motive ['moutiv], s. das Motiv, der Beweggrund.

motley ['mɔtli], adj. scheckig, bunt.

motor ['moutə], s. der Motor.

motoring ['moutəriŋ], s. das Autofahren, der Autosport.

mottled [mɔtld], adj. gescheckt, gesprenkelt.

motto ['mɔtou], s. das Motto, der Wahlspruch.

mould (1) [mould], s. die Form; Gußform (casting); die Schablone. — v.a. formen; (Metall.) gießen, formen.

mould (2) [mould], s. der Schimmel (fungus); (Hort.) die Gartenerde. — v.n. schimmeln.

moulder (1) ['mouldə], s. der Bildner; (Metall.) der Gießer.

moulder (2) ['mouldə], v.n. vermodern.

mouldy ['mouldi], adj. moderig, schimmelig.

moult, (Am.) **molt** [moult], v.n. (Zool.) sich mausern.

mound [maund], s. der Erdhügel.

mount [maunt], v.a. besteigen (horse, hill); montieren, anbringen (apparatus). — v.n. sich belaufen (bill), betragen. — s. (Poet.) der Berg.

mountain ['mauntin], s. der Berg.

mountaineer [maunti'niə], s. der Bergsteiger.

mountainous ['mauntinəs], adj. gebirgig.

mourn [mɔ:n], v.a., v.n. (be)trauern.

mourner ['mɔ:nə], s. der Leidtragende.

mournful ['mɔ:nful], adj. traurig.

mourning ['mɔ:niŋ], s. die Trauer.

mouse [maus], s. (Zool.) die Maus.

moustache [məs'ta:ʃ], s. der Schnurrbart.

mouth [mauθ], s. (Anat.) der Mund; (Geog.) die Mündung.

movable ['mu:vəbl], adj. beweglich, verschiebbar.

move [mu:v], v.a. bewegen (emotionally) rühren; den Antrag stellen (a motion). — v.n. umziehen; übersiedeln (change residence).

movement ['mu:vmənt], s. die Bewegung (motion); (Mus.) der Satz; das Gehwerk (mechanism).

movies ['mu:viz], s. pl. (coll.) das Kino, der Film.

mow [mou], v.a. irr. mähen.

much [mʌtʃ], adj. viel. — adv. sehr, bei weitem; as — as, ganze ...; as — again, noch einmal so viel.

mud [mʌd], s. der Schmutz, Schlamm.

muddle [mʌdl], v.a. verwirren. — s. die Verwirrung.

muff (1) [mʌf], s. der Muff.

muff (2) [mʌf], v.a. verderben (mar).

muffin ['mʌfin], s. der dünne Kuchen, der Butterkuchen.

muffle [mʌfl], v.a. umwickeln; dämpfen (a sound).

muffler ['mʌflə], s. das Halstuch; (Motor.) der Schalldämpfer.

mug [mʌg], s. der Krug; (coll.) der Tölpel.

muggy ['mʌgi], adj. schwül; feucht (humid).

mulatto [mju'lætou], s. der Mulatte.

mulberry ['mʌlbəri], s. (Bot.) die Maulbeere.

mule [mju:l], s. (Zool.) das Maultier, der Maulesel.

muleteer [mju:li'tiə], s. der Mauleseltreiber.

mulish ['mju:liʃ], adj. störrisch.

mull (1) [mʌl], v.a. würzen (add spices to); mulled wine, der Glühwein.

mull (2) [mʌl], v.a., v.n. — over, überlegen, überdenken.

multifarious [mʌlti'fɛəriəs], adj. mannigfaltig.

multiple ['mʌltipl], s. das Vielfache. — adj. vielfach.

multiply ['mʌltiplai], v.a., v.n. multiplizieren, (sich) vervielfachen.

multitude ['mʌltitju:d], s. die Menge.

multitudinous [mʌlti'tju:dinəs], adj. zahlreich, massenhaft.

mumble [mʌmbl], v.a., v.n. murmeln.

mummery ['mʌməri], s. der Mummenschanz.

mummy (1) ['mʌmi], s. die Mumie.

mummy (2) ['mʌmi], s. (coll.) die Mutti.

mumps [mʌmps], s. (Med.) der Ziegenpeter.

munch [mʌntʃ], v.a., v.n. kauen.

mundane ['mʌndein], adj. weltlich.

municipal [mju'nisipəl], adj. städtisch.

municipality [mjunisi'pæliti], s. die Stadtgemeinde.

munificence [mju'nifisəns], s. die Freigebigkeit.

munificent [mju'nifisənt], adj. freigebig.

mural ['mjuərəl], s. die Wandmalerei; das Wandgemälde. — adj. Wand-.

murder ['mə:də], s. der Mord. — v.a. ermorden, morden.

murderer ['mə:dərə], s. der Mörder.

murderous ['mə:dərəs], adj. mörderisch.

murky ['mə:ki], adj. trübe, unklar.

murmur ['mə:mə], s. das Gemurmel.

muscle [mʌsl], s. (Anat.) der Muskel.

muscular ['mʌskjulə], adj. (Anat.) muskulös, Muskel-.

muse (1) [mju:z], v.n. nachdenken, sinnen.
muse (2) [mju:z], s. (Myth.) die Muse.
museum [mju:'ziəm], s. das Museum.
mushroom ['mʌʃrum], s. (Bot.) der (eßbare) Pilz.
music ['mju:zik], s. die Musik; — stand, das Notenpult.
musician [mju:'ziʃən], s. der Musiker.
musk [mʌsk], s. der Moschus, Bisam.
musket ['mʌskit], s. die Muskete, Flinte.
muslin ['mʌzlin], s. der Musselin.
mussel [mʌsl], s. (Zool.) die Muschel.
must [mʌst], v. aux. irr. müssen; (with neg.) dürfen.
mustard ['mʌstəd], s. der Senf.
muster ['mʌstə], v.a. mustern. — v.n. sich sammeln. — s. die Musterung; pass —, die Prüfung bestehen.
musty ['mʌsti], adj. dumpf, dumpfig, muffig.
mutable ['mju:təbl], adj. veränderlich.
mutation [mju'teiʃən], s. die Veränderung; (Maths., Genetics) die Mutation.
mute [mju:t], adj. stumm. — v.a. (Mus.) dämpfen. — s. (Mus.) der Dämpfer.
mutilate ['mju:tileit], v.a. verstümmeln.
mutinous ['mju:tinəs], adj. aufrührerisch.
mutiny ['mju:tini], s. die Meuterei.
mutter ['mʌtə], v.a., v.n. murmeln.
mutton [mʌtn], s. das Hammelfleisch; — chop, das Hammelkotelett.
mutual ['mju:tjuəl], adj. gegenseitig.
muzzle [mʌzl], s. der Maulkorb (of dog); die Mündung (of rifle).
my [mai], poss. adj. mein.
myrrh [mə:], s. die Myrrhe.
myrtle [mə:tl], s. (Bot.) die Myrte.
myself [mai'self], pron. ich selbst; (refl.) mir, mich.
mysterious [mis'tiəriəs], adj. geheimnisvoll.
mystery ['mistəri], s. das Geheimnis.
mystic ['mistik], s. der Mystiker.
mystic(al) ['mistik(əl)], adj. mystisch, geheimnisvoll, dunkel.
mystification [mistifi'keiʃən], s. die Täuschung, Irreführung.
mystify ['mistifai], v.a. täuschen, verblüffen.
myth [miθ], s. der Mythos, die Mythe, Sage.

N

N [en], das N.
nag (1) [næg], v.a. nörgeln.
nag (2) [næg], s. der Gaul.
nail [neil], s. der Nagel. — v.a. annageln.

naïve ['naii:v], adj. naiv.
naïveté, naïvety [nai'i:vti], s. die Naivität, Einfalt.
naked ['neikid], adj. nackt.
name [neim], s. der Name. — v.a. nennen, heißen.
nameless ['neimlis], adj. namenlos.
namely ['neimli], adv. nämlich.
namesake ['neimseik], s. der Namensvetter.
nap [næp], s. das Schläfchen. — v.n. schlummern, einnicken.
nape [neip], s. (Anat.) das Genick.
napkin ['næpkin], s. die Serviette; Windel (baby's).
narrate [nə'reit], v.a. erzählen.
narrative ['nærətiv], s. die Erzählung, Geschichte.
narrator [nə'reitə], s. der Erzähler; (Rad.) der Sprecher.
narrow ['nærou], adj. eng, schmal; — gauge, die Schmalspur; — minded, engstirnig.
nasty ['na:sti], adj. widerlich, unangenehm.
natal [neitl], adj. Geburts-.
nation ['neiʃən], s. die Nation, das Volk.
nationality [næʃə'næliti], s. die Staatsangehörigkeit, Nationalität.
native ['neitiv], adj. einheimisch, eingeboren. — s. der Eingeborene.
natural ['nætʃərəl], adj. natürlich.
naturalist ['nætʃərəlist], s. der Naturforscher.
naturalization [nætʃərəlai'zeiʃən], s. die Naturalisierung, Einbürgerung.
naturalize ['nætʃərəlaiz], v.a., v.n. naturalisieren, einbürgern.
nature ['neitʃə], s. die Natur, das Wesen.
naught [nɔ:t], s. die Null.
naughty ['nɔ:ti], adj. unartig.
nausea ['nɔ:siə], s. (Med.) der Brechreiz, das Erbrechen.
nautical ['nɔ:tikəl], adj. nautisch, Schiffs-.
naval ['neivəl], adj. Marine-.
nave [neiv], s. (Archit.) das Schiff.
navigable ['nævigəbl], adj. schiffbar.
navigate ['nævigeit], v.a., v.n. steuern.
navigation [nævi'geiʃən], s. die Schifffahrt (shipping); das Steuern, die Navigation.
navy ['neivi], s. die Flotte, Marine.
Neopolitan [niə'politən], adj. neapolitanisch. — s. der Neapolitaner.
near [niə], adj., adv. nahe, in der Nähe. — prep. nahe (an or bei).
nearly ['niəli], adv. beinahe, fast.
nearness ['niənis], s. die Nähe.
neat [ni:t], adj. nett, sauber (tidy); rein, unvermischt, pur (unmixed).
neatness ['ni:tnis], s. die Sauberkeit.
necessary ['nesəsəri], adj. notwendig.
necessity [ni'sesiti], s. die Not, Notwendigkeit; (pl.) das zum Leben Nötige.
neck [nek], s. (Anat.) der Hals; stick o.'s — out, es riskieren. — v.n. (Am. sl.) knutschen.

necklace

necklace ['neklis], *s.* das Halsband, die Halskette.
necktie ['nektai], *s.* der Schlips, die Krawatte.
need [ni:d], *s.* die Not, der Bedarf. — *v.a.* brauchen, nötig haben.
needful ['ni:dful], *adj.* notwendig.
needle [ni:dl], *s.* die Nadel. — *v.a.* (*coll.*) sticheln, ärgern (*annoy*).
needy ['ni:di], *adj.* in Not befindlich, arm, bedürftig.
nefarious [ni'fɛəriəs], *adj.* nichtswürdig, schändlich.
negative ['negətiv], *adj.* negativ, verneinend. — *s.* (*Phot.*) das Negativ; die Verneinung (*denial*); *in the* —, verneinend.
neglect [ni'glekt], *v.a.* vernachlässigen, außer acht lassen. — *s.* die Vernachlässigung.
neglectful [ni'glektful], *adj.* nachlässig.
negligence ['neglidʒəns], *s.* die Nachlässigkeit.
negotiate [ni'gouʃieit], *v.a.*, *v.n.* verhandeln, unterhandeln.
negotiation [nigouʃi'eiʃən], *s.* die Unterhandlung.
Negro ['ni:grou], *s.* der Neger.
neigh [nei], *v.n.* wiehern.
neighbour ['neibə], *s.* der Nachbar.
neighbourhood ['neibəhud], *s.* die Nachbarschaft, Umgebung.
neighbouring ['neibəriŋ], *adj.* Nachbar-, benachbart.
neighbourliness ['neibəlinis], *s.* das gute nachbarliche Verhältnis, die Geselligkeit.
neither ['naiðə *or* 'ni:ðə], *adj.*, *pron.* keiner (von beiden). — *conj.* auch nicht; — . . . *nor*, weder . . . noch.
Nepalese [nepə'li:z], *adj.* nepalesisch. — *s.* der Nepalese.
nephew ['nefju *or* 'nevju], *s.* der Neffe.
nerve [nə:v], *s.* der Nerv; der Mut (*courage*); die Frechheit (*impudence*); (*pl.*) die Angst, Nervosität.
nervous ['nə:vəs], *adj.* nervös; — *of*, furchtsam vor (*Dat.*), ängstlich wegen (*Genit.*).
nest [nest], *s.* das Nest; (*fig.*) — *egg*, die Ersparnisse, *f.pl.* — *v.n.* nisten.
nestle [nesl], *v.n.* sich anschmiegen.
net (1) [net], *s.* das Netz. — *v.a.* (Fische) fangen, ins Netz bekommen.
net (2) [net], *adj.* netto; ohne Verpackung; — *weight*, das Nettogewicht.
nettle [netl], *s.* (*Bot.*) die Nessel. — *v.a.* sticheln, ärgern.
neurosis [njuə'rousis], *s.* (*Med.*) die Neurose.
neutrality [nju:'træliti], *s.* die Neutralität.
never ['nevə], *adv.* nie, niemals; — *mind*, mach Dir (machen Sie sich) nichts draus!
nevertheless [nevəðə'les], *conj.* trotzdem, nichtsdestoweniger.
new [nju:], *adj.* neu; *New Year's Day*, der Neujahrstag; *New Zealander*, der

Neuseeländer. — *s.* (*pl.*) die Nachrichten, *f. pl.*
newspaper ['nju:speipə], *s.* die Zeitung.
next [nekst], *adj.* nächst. — *adv.* danach.
nib [nib], *s.* die Spitze (*of pen*).
nibble [nibl], *v.a.*, *v.n.* knabbern, nagen (*at*, *an*, *Dat.*).
nice [nais], *adj.* fein (*scrupulous*); nett, angenehm (*pleasant*).
nicety ['naisəti], *s.* die Feinheit (*of distinction etc.*).
nickel [nikl], *s.* das Nickel; (*Am.*) das Fünfcentstück.
nickname ['nikneim], *s.* der Spitzname.
niece [ni:s], *s.* die Nichte.
Nigerian [nai'dʒiəriən], *adj.* nigerisch. — *s.* der Nigerier.
niggardly ['nigədli], *adj.* geizig.
nigh [nai], *adj.*, *adv.* (*Poet.*) nahe.
night [nait], *s.* die Nacht; *last* —, gestern abend; *the* — *before last*, vorgestern abend; *at* —, nachts.
nightingale ['naitiŋgeil], *s.* (*Orn.*) die Nachtigall.
nightmare ['naitmɛə], *s.* der Alpdruck.
nimble [nimbl], *adj.* flink; geschickt (*deft*).
nine [nain], *num. adj.* neun.
nineteen [nain'ti:n], *num. adj.* neunzehn.
ninety ['nainti], *num. adj.* neunzig.
ninth [nainθ], *num. adj.* neunte.
nip [nip], *v.a.* zwicken.
nipple [nipl], *s.* (*Anat.*) die Brustwarze.
nitrogen ['naitrədʒən], *s.* (*Chem.*) der Stickstoff.
no [nou], *part.* nein. — *adj.* kein. — *adv.* nicht; — *one*, niemand.
nobility [no'biliti], *s.* der Adel.
noble [noubl], *adj.* edel; großmütig (*magnanimous*); adlig (*well born*).
nobody ['noubədi], *pron.* niemand.
nod [nɔd], *v.n.* nicken.
noise [nɔiz], *s.* der Lärm, das Geräusch.
noiseless ['nɔizlis], *adj.* geräuschlos.
noisy ['nɔizi], *adj.* laut, lärmend.
nominal ['nɔminəl], *adj.* nominell.
nominate ['nɔmineit], *v.a.* nennen (*name*); ernennen (*appoint*).
nomination [nɔmi'neiʃən], *s.* die Nennung, Ernennung.
none [nʌn], *pron.* keiner, niemand.
nonsense ['nɔnsəns], *s.* der Unsinn.
nook [nuk], *s.* die Ecke, der Winkel.
noon [nu:n], *s.* der Mittag.
noose [nu:s], *s.* die Schlinge.
nor [nɔ:], *conj.* auch nicht; *neither* . . . —, weder . . . noch.
normal [nɔ:məl], *adj.* normal.
normalize ['nɔ:məlaiz], *v.a.* normalisieren.
Norman ['nɔ:mən], *adj.* normannisch. — *s.* der Normanne.
north [nɔ:θ], *s.* der Norden. — *adj.* nördlich.
northerly, northern ['nɔ:ðəli, 'nɔ:ðən], *adj.* nördlich, von Norden.
Norwegian [nɔ:'wi:dʒən], *adj.* norwegisch. — *s.* der Norweger.
nose [nouz], *s.* (*Anat.*) die Nase; — *dive*, der Sturzflug.

nosey ['nouzi], *adj.* (*coll.*) neugierig.
nostalgia [nɔs'tældʒə], *s.* das Heimweh, die Sehnsucht.
nostril ['nɔstril], *s.* (*Anat.*) das Nasenloch.
not [nɔt], *adv.* nicht; — *at all*, keineswegs.
notable ['noutəbl], *adj.* berühmt, wohlbekannt; bemerkenswert.
notary ['noutəri], *s.* der Notar.
notch [nɔtʃ], *s.* die Kerbe. — *v.a.* kerben, einkerben.
note [nout], *s.* die Notiz, der Zettel; (*Mus.*) die Note; die Bedeutung; *take* —*s*, Notizen machen; *take* — *of*, zur Kenntnis nehmen. — *v.a.* notieren, aufzeichnen.
notepaper ['noutpeipə], *s.* das Briefpapier.
noteworthy ['noutwə:ði], *adj.* beachtenswert.
nothing ['nʌθiŋ], *pron. s.* nichts; *for* —, umsonst; *good for* —, der Taugenichts.
notice ['noutis], *s.* die Kenntnis (*attention*); die Anzeige (*in press etc.*); Notiz; Bekanntmachung; *give* —, kündigen. — *v.a.* bemerken.
noticeable ['noutisəbl], *adj.* bemerkbar.
notification [noutifi'keiʃən], *s.* die Benachrichtigung, Bekanntmachung.
notify ['noutifai], *v.a.* benachrichtigen, informieren.
notion ['nouʃən], *s.* der Begriff (*concept*); die Idee (*idea*); die Meinung (*opinion*).
notoriety [noutə'raiiti], *s.* der üble Ruf.
notorious [no'tɔ:riəs], *adj.* berüchtigt.
notwithstanding [nɔtwið'stændiŋ], *prep.* ungeachtet (*Genit.*). — *adv.* trotzdem, dennoch. — *conj.* — *that*, obgleich.
nought [nɔ:t], *s.* die Null (*figure 0*); nichts (*nothing*).
noun [naun], *s.* (*Gram.*) das Hauptwort, Substantiv.
nourish ['nʌriʃ], *v.a.* nähren; ernähren.
nourishment ['nʌriʃmənt], *s.* die Nahrung.
Nova Scotian ['nouvə'skouʃən], *adj.* neuschottisch. [Neuschottland]
novel [nɔvl], *s.* (*Lit.*) der Roman. — *adj.* neu; neuartig (*modern*).
novelty ['nɔvlti], *s.* die Neuheit.
November [no'vembə], *s.* der November.
novice ['nɔvis], *s.* der Neuling (*greenhorn*); (*Eccl.*) der, die Novize.
novitiate [no'viʃiit], *s.* die Lehrzeit; (*Eccl.*) das Noviziat.
now [nau], *adv.* nun, jetzt; — *and then*, dann und wann, hin und wieder. — *conj.* — (*that*), da nun.
nowadays ['nauədeiz], *adv.* heutzutage.
nowhere ['nouhwɛə], *adv.* nirgends.
noxious ['nɔkʃəs], *adj.* (*Med., Bot.*) schädlich.
nozzle [nɔzl], *s.* die Düse; (*sl.*) die Schnauze.
nuclear ['nju:kliə], *adj.* (*Phys.*) nuklear, Kern-.
nucleus ['nju:kliəs], *s.* der Kern.

nude [nju:d], *adj.* nackt, bloß.
nudge [nʌdʒ], *v.a.* leicht anstoßen.
nudity ['nju:diti], *s.* die Nacktheit.
nugget ['nʌgit], *s.* der Klumpen.
nuisance ['nju:səns], *s.* die Plage, Lästigkeit; das Ärgernis (*annoyance*).
null [nʌl], *adj.* null und nichtig; ungültig.
nullify ['nʌlifai], *v.a.* annullieren, ungültig machen.
nullity ['nʌliti], *s.* die Ungültigkeit.
numb [nʌm], *adj.* erstarrt, gefühllos. — *v.a.* erstarren lassen.
number ['nʌmbə], *s.* die Zahl, Nummer (*telephone etc.*); die Anzahl (*quantity*); *cardinal* —, die Grundzahl; *ordinal* —, die Ordnungszahl. — *v.a.* nummerieren; zählen (*count*).
numbness ['nʌmnis], *s.* die Erstarrung.
numeral ['nju:mərəl], *s.* (*Gram.*) das Zahlwort.
numerical [nju:'merikəl], *adj.* (*Maths.*) Zahlen-, numerisch.
numerous ['nju:mərəs], *adj.* zahlreich.
numismatics [nju:miz'mætiks], *s.* die Münzkunde.
numskull ['nʌmskʌl], *s.* der Dummkopf.
nun [nʌn], *s.* (*Eccl.*) die Nonne.
nunnery ['nʌnəri], *s.* (*Eccl.*) das Nonnenkloster.
nuptials ['nʌpʃəlz], *s. pl.* (*Lit., Poet.*) die Hochzeit, das Hochzeitsfest.
nurse [nə:s], *s.* die Krankenschwester, Pflegerin; die Amme (*wet nurse*). — *v.a.* pflegen.
nursery ['nə:səri], *s.* das Kinderzimmer; (*Bot.*) die Pflanzschule, Baumschule (*for trees*); — *school*, der Kindergarten.
nurture ['nə:tʃə], *v.a.* nähren, aufziehen.
nut [nʌt], *s.* (*Bot.*) die Nuß; (*Tech.*) die Schraubenmutter; (*Am. coll.*) *nuts*, verrückt.
nutcracker ['nʌtkrækə], *s.* (*usually pl.*) der Nußknacker.
nutmeg ['nʌtmeg], *s.* (*Cul.*) die Muskatnuß.
nutriment ['nju:trimənt], *s.* die Nahrung; (*animals*) das Futter.
nutrition [nju:'triʃən], *s.* die Ernährung.
nutritious [nju:'triʃəs], *adj.* nahrhaft.
nutshell ['nʌtʃel], *s.* die Nußschale; (*fig.*) *put in a* —, kurz ausdrücken.
nymph [nimf], *s.* (*Myth.*) die Nymphe.

O

O [ou], das O. — *int.* oh!
oaf [ouf], *s.* der Tölpel.
oak [ouk], *s.* (*Bot.*) die Eiche.
oaken ['oukən], *adj.* eichen, aus Eichenholz.

oar

oar [ɔː], *s.* das Ruder; *put o.'s — in*, sich einmengen.

oasis [ouˈeisis], *s.* die Oase.

oath [ouθ], *s.* der Eid; der Fluch (*curse*); *commissioner for —s*, der öffentliche Notar; *take an —*, einen Eid schwören *or* leisten.

oats [outs], *s. pl.* (*Bot.*) der Hafer; *sow o.'s wild —s*, sich austoben, sich die Hörner ablaufen.

obdurate [ˈɔbdjurit], *adj.* halsstarrig.

obedience [oˈbiːdjəns], *s.* der Gehorsam.

obedient [oˈbiːdjənt], *adj.* gehorsam.

obeisance [oˈbeisəns], *s.* die Verbeugung, Ehrfurchtsbezeigung.

obese [oˈbiːs], *adj.* fettleibig, beleibt.

obey [oˈbei], *v.a., v.n.* gehorchen (*Dat.*).

obituary [oˈbitjuəri], *s.* der Nachruf, der Nekrolog.

object [ˈɔbdʒikt], *s.* der Gegenstand (*thing*); (*Gram.*) das Objekt; der Zweck (*objective, purpose*). — [əbˈdʒekt], *v.n.* — *to*, einwenden (*gainsay*); vorhalten (*remonstrate*).

objection [əbˈdʒekʃən], *s.* der Einwand.

objectionable [əbˈdʒekʃənəbl], *adj.* anstößig.

objective [əbˈdʒektiv], *adj.* objektiv, unparteiisch. — *s.* das Ziel (*aim*).

obligation [ɔbliˈgeiʃən], *s.* die Verpflichtung.

obligatory [oˈbligətəri, ˈɔblig-], *adj.* verbindlich, obligatorisch.

oblige [oˈblaidʒ], *v.a.* verpflichten; *much obliged*, vielen Dank; *can you — me?* können Sie mir aushelfen?

obliging [oˈblaidʒiŋ], *adj.* gefällig, zuvorkommend.

oblique [oˈbliːk], *adj.* schräg, schief; (*fig.*) indirekt.

obliterate [oˈblitəreit], *v.a.* auslöschen (*extinguish*); vertilgen (*destroy*).

oblivion [oˈbliviən], *s.* die Vergessenheit.

oblivious [oˈbliviəs], *adj.* vergeßlich.

oblong [ˈɔblɔŋ], *adj.* länglich. — *s.* das Rechteck.

obloquy [ˈɔbləkwi], *s.* die Schmähung, Schande.

obnoxious [ɔbˈnɔkʃəs], *adj.* verhaßt, scheußlich.

obscene [ɔbˈsiːn], *adj.* anstößig, obszön.

obscenity [ɔbˈsen-, ɔbˈsiːniti], *s.* die Obszönität.

obscure [əbˈskjuə], *adj.* dunkel (*dark*); unbekannt (*unknown*).

obscurity [əbˈskjuəriti], *s.* die Dunkelheit (*darkness*); die Unbekanntheit.

obsequies [ˈɔbsikwiz], *s. pl.* das Leichenbegängnis.

obsequious [əbˈsiːkwiəs], *adj.* unterwürfig.

observance [əbˈzəːvəns], *s.* die Befolgung, Beobachtung, das Einhalten (*Law etc.*).

observant [əbˈzəːvənt], *adj.* aufmerksam; achtsam.

observation [ɔbzəˈveiʃən], *s.* die Beobachtung (*watching*); die Bemerkung (*remark*).

observatory [əbˈzəːvətri], *s.* die Sternwarte.

observe [əbˈzəːv], *v.a.* beobachten (*watch*); bemerken (*notice, remark on*).

obsession [əbˈseʃən], *s.* die Besessenheit, fixe Idee.

obsolete [ˈɔbsəliːt], *adj.* veraltet.

obstacle [ˈɔbstəkl], *s.* das Hindernis.

obstinacy [ˈɔbstinəsi], *s.* die Hartnäckigkeit.

obstinate [ˈɔbstinit], *adj.* hartnäckig.

obstruct [əbˈstrʌkt], *v.a.* hemmen, hindern.

obstruction [əbˈstrʌkʃən], *s.* das Hindernis, die Hemmung, Verstopfung.

obtain [əbˈtein], *v.a.* erhalten, erlangen; bekommen (*get*).

obtrude [əbˈtruːd], *v.n.* sich aufdrängen. — *v.a.* aufdrängen.

obtrusive [əbˈtruːsiv], *adj.* aufdringlich.

obtuse [əbˈtjuːs], *adj.* stumpf; dumm (*stupid*).

obviate [ˈɔbvieit], *v.a.* vorbeugen (*Dat.*).

obvious [ˈɔbviəs], *adj.* klar, offenbar, selbstverständlich.

occasion [oˈkeiʒən], *s.* die Gelegenheit (*chance*); der Anlaß; die Veranlassung (*cause*). — *v.a.* veranlassen; verursachen (*cause*).

occasional [oˈkeiʒənəl], *adj.* gelegentlich.

occident [ˈɔksidənt], *s.* das Abendland, der Westen.

occult [ɔˈkʌlt], *adj.* geheim, Okkult-.

occupancy [ˈɔkjupənsi], *s.* der Besitz, das Innehaben (*holding*).

occupant [ˈɔkjupənt], *s.* der Inhaber; der Bewohner (*of house*), Insasse.

occupation [ɔkjuˈpeiʃən], *s.* die Besetzung; (*Mil.*) *army of —*, die Besatzung; der Beruf, die Beschäftigung (*job*); *— with*, das Befassen mit (*Dat.*).

occupy [ˈɔkjupai], *v.a.* (*Mil.*) besetzen, in Besitz nehmen; beschäftigen (*engage*); bekleiden (*office*).

occur [əˈkəː], *v.n.* geschehen, sich ereignen; *— to s.o.*, jemandem einfallen.

occurrence [əˈkʌrəns], *s.* das Geschehen, Ereignis, der Vorfall.

ocean [ˈouʃən], *s.* der Ozean, die See, das Meer. — *adj.* Meeres-.

octagon [ˈɔktəgən], *s.* das Achteck.

octagonal [ɔkˈtægənəl], *adj.* achteckig.

October [ɔkˈtoubə], *s.* der Oktober.

octogenarian [ɔktodʒiˈnɛəriən], *s.* der Achtzigjährige.

ocular [ˈɔkjulə], *adj.* Augen-.

oculist [ˈɔkjulist], *s.* (*Med.*) der Augenarzt.

odd [ɔd], *adj.* ungerade; seltsam (*queer*); einzeln (*solitary*). — *s.* (*pl.*) die Wahrscheinlichkeit.

oddity [ˈɔditi], *s.* die Seltenheit, Sonderbarkeit.

oddment [ˈɔdmənt], *s.* (*pl.*) die Reste, *m. pl.*

ode [oud], *s.* (*Poet.*) die Ode.

odious [ˈoudiəs], *adj.* verhaßt, widerwärtig.

operatic

odium ['oudiəm], *s.* der Haß.
odorous ['oudərəs], *adj.* duftend, duftig.
odour ['oudə], *s.* der Geruch, Duft.
of [ɔv], *prep.* von (*Dat.*); aus (*out of*) (*Dat.*); — *course*, natürlich.
off [ɔf, ɔːf], *adv.* fort, weg; entfernt; *make* —, sich davonmachen; *far* —, weit weg; — *and on*, ab und zu; *well* —, wohlhabend. — *prep.* von (*from*); fort von; entfernt von (*distant from*).
offal [ɔfl], *s.* der Abfall.
offence [o'fens], *s.* (*Law*) das Vergehen; die Beleidigung (*insult*).
offend [o'fend], *v.a.* beleidigen (*insult*). — *v.n.* (*Law*) sich vergehen (gegen, *Acc.*).
offensive [o'fensiv], *adj.* beleidigend (*insulting*); anstößig (*indecent*). — *s.* die Offensive, der Angriff (*against*, auf, *Acc.*).
offer ['ɔfə], *v.a.* bieten (*auction*); anbieten (*hold out*). — *s.* das Anerbieten; (*Comm.*) das Angebot, der Antrag.
offering ['ɔfəriŋ], *s.* das Opfer.
office ['ɔfis], *s.* das Amt; die Stellung (*position*); die Funktion (*duties*); das Büro; (*Eccl.*) der Gottesdienst; *high* —, das hohe Amt; — *bearer*, der Amtswalter.
officer ['ɔfisə], *s.* (*Mil.*) der Offizier; der Beamte (*functionary*); *honorary* —, der ehrenamtliche Beamte, der Beamte im Ehrenamt.
official [o'fiʃəl], *adj.* offiziell, amtlich. — *s.* der Beamte.
officiate [o'fiʃieit], *v.n.* amtieren; fungieren.
officious [o'fiʃəs], *adj.* zudringlich, (übertrieben) dienstfertig.
offing ['ɔfiŋ], *s.* (*Naut.*) die hohe See; *in the* —, bevorstehend.
offset [ɔf'set], *v.a.* (*Comm.*) ausgleichen; (*Typ.*) offset drucken, im Offset drucken; (*fig.*) unschädlich machen, wettmachen. — ['ɔfset], *s.* (*Comm.*) die Gegenrechnung, der Ausgleich; (*Typ.*) der Offsetdruck.
offshoot ['ɔfʃuːt], *s.* der Sprößling.
offspring ['ɔfspriŋ], *s.* die Nachkommenschaft.
often, (*Poet.*) **oft** [ɔfn,ɔft], *adv.* oft, häufig.
ogle [ougl], *v.a.*, *v.n.* äugeln, beäugeln, glotzen, anglotzen.
ogre ['ougə], *s.* der Menschenfresser.
oil [ɔil], *s.* das Öl. — *v.a.* einölen, einschmieren.
oilcloth ['ɔilklɔθ], *s.* das Wachstuch.
ointment ['ɔintmənt], *s.* die Salbe.
old [ould], *adj.* alt; —*fashioned*, altmodisch.
olive ['ɔliv], *s.* (*Bot.*) die Olive; *the Mount of Olives*, der Ölberg.
Olympic [o'limpik], *adj.* olympisch; *the* — *Games*, die Olympischen Spiele.
omelette ['ɔmlit], *s.* (*Cul.*) das Omelett, der Eierkuchen.
omen ['oumən], *s.* das (böse) Vorzeichen, das Omen.

ominous ['ɔminəs], *adj.* von schlimmer Vorbedeutung, ominös.
omission [o'miʃən], *s.* die Unterlassung; (*Typ.*) die Auslassung.
omit [o'mit], *v.a.* unterlassen (*leave undone*); auslassen (*leave out*).
omnibus ['ɔmnibəs], *s.* der Omnibus, der Autobus.
omnipotent [ɔm'nipətənt], *adj.* allmächtig.
omniscient [ɔm'nisiənt], *adj.* allwissend.
on [ɔn], *prep.* an; auf; über; vor; bei; zu; nach; um; call — (*s.o.*), vorsprechen (bei, *Dat.*); — *fire*, in Flammen; — *condition*, unter der Bedingung (*Comm.*); — *account*, a Konto; — *high*, hoch oben; — *my honour*, auf mein Ehrenwort; — *purpose*, absichtlich; — *sale*, zum Verkauf. — *adv.* weiter, fort (*forward*); gültig, zutreffend (*correct*, *valid*); *get* —, vorwärtskommen; *get* — *with s.th.*, weitermachen; *get* — *with s.o.*, auskommen (mit, *Dat.*).
once [wʌns], *adv.* einmal; einst (*long ago*); — *more*, nochmals, noch einmal; — *and for all*, ein für alle Mal; *at* —, sogleich; — *in a while*, ab und zu. — *conj.* sobald.
one [wʌn], *num. adj.* ein, eine, ein; — *way street*, die Einbahnstraße. — *pron.* man (*impersonal*); — *s. little* —, der Kleine; — *by* —, eins nach dem anderen, einzeln.
onerous ['ɔnərəs], *adj.* beschwerlich.
onion ['ʌnjən], *s.* (*Bot.*) die Zwiebel.
onlooker ['ɔnlukə], *s.* der Zuschauer.
only ['ounli], *adj.* einzig, allein. — *adv.* nur, bloß. — *conj.* jedoch.
onset ['ɔnset], *s.* der Angriff (*attack*); der Anfang (*beginning*).
onslaught ['ɔnslɔːt], *s.* der Angriff, Überfall.
onward ['ɔnwəd], *adj.* fortschreitend. — *adv.* (*also* **onwards**) vorwärts.
ooze [uːz], *s.* der Schlamm. — *v.n.* träufeln, sickern.
opacity [o'pæsiti], *s.* (*Phys.*) die Dunkelheit, Undurchsichtigkeit.
opal [oupl], *s.* der Opal.
opaque [o'peik], *adj.* (*Phys.*) dunkel, undurchsichtig.
open [oupn], *adj.* offen; offenherzig (*frank*); — *to suggestions*, einem Vorschlag zugänglich. — *v.a.* öffnen; eröffnen (*start*); — *an account*, ein Konto eröffnen. — *v.n.* sich öffnen, sich auftun.
opening ['oupniŋ], *s.* das Öffnen; die freie Stelle; die Gelegenheit (*opportunity*). — *adj.* einleitend; — *gambit*, (*Chess*) der Eröffnungszug.
openness ['oupənnis], *s.* die Offenheit, Ehrlichkeit (*frankness*).
opera ['ɔpərə], *s.* (*Mus.*) die Oper; *comic* —, die komische Oper; — *hat*, der Zylinderhut, Klapphut.
operatic [ɔpə'rætik], *adj.* (*Mus.*) Opern-.

447

operate

operate [ˈɔpəreit], v.a., v.n. (Engin.) bedienen; (Med.) operieren (on, Acc.).
operation [ɔpəˈreiʃən], s. (Med., Mil.) die Operation; die Bedienung (of engine etc.).
operative [ˈɔpərətiv], adj. wirksam (effective). — s. der Arbeiter.
opiate [ˈoupiit], s. das Schlafmittel. — adj. einschläfernd.
opine [oˈpain], v.n. meinen.
opinion [oˈpinjən], s. die Meinung; in my —, meiner Meinung nach.
opinionated [oˈpinjəneitid], adj. von sich eingenommen, selbstgefällig.
opium [ˈoupjəm], s. das Opium.
opponent [əˈpounənt], s. der Gegner.
opportune [ˈɔpətjuːn], adj. gelegen, günstig.
opportunity [ɔpəˈtjuːniti], s. die Gelegenheit, Chance; die Möglichkeit.
oppose [əˈpouz], v.a. bekämpfen; widerstehen, entgegentreten (Dat.).
opposite [ˈɔpəzit], adj. entgegengesetzt; gegenüberliegend; gegensätzlich (contrary). — prep. gegenüber (Dat.). — s. das Gegenteil.
opposition [ɔpəˈziʃən], s. (Parl.) die Opposition; der Widerstand.
oppress [əˈpres], v.a. unterdrücken.
oppression [əˈpreʃən], s. die Unterdrückung.
oppressive [əˈpresiv], adj. drückend, tyrannisch.
opprobrious [əˈproubriəs], adj. schändlich, schimpflich.
opprobrium [əˈproubriəm], s. die Schande.
optician [ɔpˈtiʃən], s. der Optiker.
optics [ˈɔptiks], s. die Optik.
optimism [ˈɔptimizm], s. der Optimismus.
option [ˈɔpʃən], s. die Wahl.
optional [ˈɔpʃənəl], adj. Wahl-, frei, beliebig.
opulence [ˈɔpjuləns], s. der Reichtum (an, Dat.), die Üppigkeit.
opulent [ˈɔpjulənt], adj. reich, üppig.
or [ɔː], conj. oder; noch (after neg.); either . . . —, entweder . . . oder.
oracle [ˈɔrəkl], s. das Orakel.
oral [ˈɔːrəl], adj. mündlich. — s. die mündliche Prüfung.
orange [ˈɔrindʒ,] s. (Bot.) die Orange, Apfelsine.
oration [ɔˈreiʃən], s. die feierliche Rede, Ansprache.
orator [ˈɔrətə], s. der Redner.
oratorio [ɔrəˈtɔːriou], s. (Mus.) das Oratorium.
oratory [ˈɔrətəri], s. (Eccl.) die Kapelle; (Rhet.) die Redekunst.
orb [ɔːb], s. die Kugel; der Reichsapfel; (Poet.) der Himmelskörper.
orbit [ˈɔːbit], s. (Astron.) die Bahn (der Gestirne), Planetenbahn.
orchard [ˈɔːtʃəd], s. der Obstgarten.
orchestra [ˈɔːkistrə], s. (Mus.) das Orchester.
ordain [ɔːˈdein], v.a. ordinieren, anordnen; (Eccl.) zum Priester weihen.

ordeal [ˈɔːdiəl], s. die Feuerprobe; Heimsuchung.
order [ˈɔːdə], s. die Ordnung (system); die Verordnung (command etc.); (Mil.) der Befehl; (Comm.) die Bestellung; (Biol.) die Ordnung; der Orden (Eccl.; also decoration); take (holy) —s, ordiniert werden, Priester werden; in — to, um zu; in — that, so daß; by —, auf (den) Befehl. — v.a. befehlen, verordnen, anordnen: (Comm.) bestellen.
orderly [ˈɔːdəli], adj. ordentlich, ruhig. —s. (Mil.) der Ordonanz; (Med.) der Gehilfe, Krankenwärter.
ordinal [ˈɔːdinl], adj., s. (number) die Ordnungszahl.
ordinance [ˈɔːdinəns], s. die Verordnung.
ordinary [ˈɔːdinəri], adj. gewöhnlich.
ordnance [ˈɔːdnəns], s. das schwere Geschütz; (Mil., Geog.) — survey, die Landesvermessung.
ore [ɔː], s. das Erz, Metall.
organ [ˈɔːgən], s. das Organ; (Mus.) die Orgel; — grinder, der Leierkastenmann.
organic [ɔːˈgænik], adj. organisch.
organisation [ɔːgənaiˈzeiʃən], s. die Organisation.
organise [ˈɔːgənaiz], v.a. organisieren.
organism [ˈɔːgənizm], s. (Biol.) der Organismus.
organist [ˈɔːgənist], s. (Mus.) der Organist.
orgy [ˈɔːdʒi], s. die Orgie.
oriel [ˈɔːriəl], s. der Erker; — window, das Erkerfenster.
orient [ˈɔːriənt], s. der Orient, Osten.
oriental [ɔːriˈentl], adj. östlich.
orifice [ˈɔrifis], s. die Öffnung, Mündung.
origin [ˈɔridʒin], s. der Ursprung, die Herkunft.
original [əˈridʒinl], adj. Ursprungs-, ursprünglich; originell (creative). — s. das Original.
originality [əridʒiˈnæliti], s. die Originalität.
originate [əˈridʒineit], v.n. entstehen, entspringen. — v.a. hervorbringen, entstehen lassen.
ornament [ˈɔːnəmənt], s. das Ornament; die Verzierung (decoration).
ornate [ɔːˈneit], adj. geziert, geschmückt.
orphan [ˈɔːfən], s. der, die Waise.
orphanage [ˈɔːfənidʒ], s. das Waisenhaus.
orthodoxy [ˈɔːθədɔksi], s. die Orthodoxie, die Rechtgläubigkeit.
orthography [ɔːˈθɔgrəfi], s. die Rechtschreibung.
orthopaedic [ɔːθəˈpiːdik], adj. orthopädisch.
oscillate [ˈɔsileit], v.n. oszillieren, schwingen.
oscillatory [ˈɔsileitəri], adj. schwingend, oszillierend.
osier [ˈouʒiə], s. (Bot.) die Korbweide.
osprey [ˈɔsprei], s. (Orn.) der Seeadler.

ossify ['ɔsifai], *v.a.* verknöchern lassen; versteinern lassen (*stone*). — *v.n.* verknöchern; versteinern (*stone*).

ostensible [ɔs'tensibl], *adj.* scheinbar, anscheinend, vorgeblich.

ostentation [ɔsten'teiʃən], *s.* die Großtuerei, der Prunk.

ostentatious [ɔsten'teiʃəs], *adj.* großtuerisch, prahlerisch, protzig.

ostler ['ɔslə], *s.* (*obs.*) der Stallknecht.

ostracize ['ɔstrəsaiz], *v.a.* verbannen, ausschließen.

ostrich ['ɔstritʃ], *s.* (*Orn.*) der Strauß.

other ['ʌðə], *adj.* ander. — *pron.*, *s.* the —, der, die, das andere.

otherwise ['ʌðəwaiz], *conj.* sonst. — *adv.* andernfalls.

otter ['ɔtə], *s.* (*Zool.*) die Otter.

ought [ɔ:t], *v. aux. defect.* sollte, müßte.

ounce [auns], *s.* die Unze.

our ['auə], *poss. adj.* unser, uns(e)re, unser.

ours ['auəz], *poss. pron.* unsrig, unser, uns(e)re, unser.

ourselves [auə'selvz], *pers. pron.* wir, wir selbst, uns selbst; (*refl.*) uns.

ousel [u:zl], *s.* (*Orn.*) die Amsel.

out [aut], *adv.* aus; draußen (*outside*); außerhalb (*outside, externally*); heraus; hinaus (*outward, away from the speaker*). —*prep.—of*, aus, von (*Dat.*).

outer ['autə], *adj.* äußer.

outfit ['autfit], *s.* die Ausrüstung.

outing ['autiŋ], *s.* der Ausflug.

outhouse ['authaus], *s.* das Nebengebäude, der Anbau.

outlaw ['autlɔ:], *s.* der Verbannte, der Vogelfreie.

outlay ['autlei], *s.* (*Comm.*) die Auslagen, die Spesen, *f. pl.*

outlet ['autlit], *s.* der Ausfluß, Abfluß; (*fig.*) das Ventil.

outline ['autlain], *s.* der Umriß, Entwurf. — [aut'lain], *v.a.* skizzieren, umreißen, kurz beschreiben.

outlive [aut'liv], *v.a.* überleben.

outlook ['autluk], *s.* die Aussicht, der Ausblick; die Weltanschauung (*philosophy*).

outlying ['autlaiiŋ], *adj.* außenliegend, außerhalb liegend, entlegen.

outnumber [aut'nʌmbə], *v.a.* an Zahl übertreffen.

outpatient ['autpeiʃənt], *s.* der ambulante Patient.

outrage ['autreidʒ], *s.* die Beleidigung (*insult*); die Gewalttat. — [aut'reidʒ], *v.a.* verletzen, beleidigen, schänden.

outrageous [aut'reidʒəs], *adj.* schändlich, schimpflich, unerhört; übertrieben (*exaggerated*).

outright ['autrait], *adj.* völlig. — [aut'rait], *adv.* gerade heraus, gänzlich.

outrun [aut'rʌn], *v.a. irr.* überholen, einholen.

outset ['autset], *s.* der Anfang.

outshine [aut'ʃain], *v.a. irr.* übertreffen.

outside [aut'said], *adv.* außen, draußen. — ['autsaid], *prep.* außerhalb (*Genit.*).

— *adj.* äußere, außenstehend. — *s.* das Äußere, die Außenseite.

outskirts ['autskə:ts], *s. pl.* die Umgebung, Vorstadt.

outstanding [aut'stændiŋ], *adj.* hervorragend (*excellent*); noch unbeglichen (*unpaid*); unerledigt (*undone*).

outstay [aut'stei], *v.a.* länger bleiben, zu lange bleiben.

outvote [aut'vout], *v.a.* überstimmen.

outward ['autwəd], *adj.* äußere, äußerlich, außerhalb befindlich. — *adv.* (*also* **outwards**) auswärts, nach außen.

outweigh [aut'wei], *v.a.* schwerer wiegen als, überwiegen.

outwit [aut'wit], *v.a.* überlisten.

oval [ouvl], *adj.* oval. — *s.* das Oval.

ovary ['ouvəri], *s.* (*Anat.*) der Eierstock.

ovation [o'veiʃən], *s.* die Huldigung, Ovation.

oven [ʌvn], *s.* der Backofen; (kleine) Schmelzofen.

over ['ouvə], *prep.* über; oberhalb. — *adv.* über; herüber; drüben; — there, drüben; hinüber (*across*); vorüber (*past*).

overact [ouvər'ækt], *v.n.* übertreiben.

overawe [ouvər'ɔ:], *v.a.* einschüchtern.

overbalance [ouvə'bæləns], *v.a.* überwiegen. — *v.n.* überkippen.

overbear [ouvə'bɛə], *v.a. irr.* überwältigen.

overbearing [ouvə'bɛəriŋ], *adj.* anmaßend.

overboard ['ouvəbɔ:d], *adv.* über Bord.

overburden [ouvə'bə:dn], *v.a.* überlasten.

overcast [ouvə'ka:st], *adj.* bewölkt.

overcharge [ouvə'tʃa:dʒ], *v.a.* zu viel berechnen (*pers., Dat.*), übervorteien; überladen (*overload*). — *s.* die Übervorteilung; (*Tech.*) der Überdruck.

overcoat ['ouvəkout], *s.* der Mantel; light —, der Überzieher.

overcome [ouvə'kʌm], *v.a., v.n. irr.* überwinden.

overdo [ouvə'du:], *v.a. irr.* übertreiben.

overdone [ouvə'dʌn], *adj.* übergar, zu lange gekocht.

overdrive [ouvə'draiv], *v.a. irr.* abhetzen, zu weit treiben. — ['ouvədraiv] *s.* (*Motor.*) der Schnellgang.

overdue [ouvə'dju:], *adj.* überfällig, verfallen.

overflow [ouvə'flou], *v.a., v.n.* überfließen; überfluten (*banks*). — ['ouvəflou], *s.* der Überfluß (*flood*); die Überschwemmung.

overgrow [ouvə'grou], *v.a. irr.* überwachsen, überwuchern. — *v.n.* zu groß werden.

overhang [ouvə'hæŋ], *v.a. irr.* überhängen.

overhaul [ouvə'hɔ:l], *v.a.* überholen. — ['ouvəhɔ:l], *s.* die Überholung.

overhead [ouvə'hed], *adv.* droben; oben (*above*). — ['ouvəhed], (*pl.*) (*Comm.*) laufende Unkosten, *pl.*

overhear [ouvə'hiə], *v.a. irr.* zufällig hören.

overjoyed [ouvə'dʒɔid], *adj.* entzückt.

overlap [ouvə'læp], *v.n.* überschneiden, zusammenfallen *(dates etc.).* — ['ouvə-læp], *s.* die Überschneidung, das Zusammenfallen.

overload [ouvə'loud], *v.a.* überlasten; *(Elec.)* überladen.

overlook [ouvə'luk], *v.a.* übersehen; verzeihen *(disregard).*

overmuch [ouvə'mʌtʃ], *adv.* allzusehr.

overpay [ouvə'pei], *v.a., v.n.* zu viel bezahlen.

overpopulated [ouvə'pɔpjuleitid], *adj.* übervölkert.

overpower [ouvə'pauə], *v.a.* überwältigen.

overrate [ouvə'reit], *v.a.* überschätzen.

overreach [ouvə'ri:tʃ], *v.a.* übervorteilen.

override [ouvə'raid], *v.a. irr.* überreiten; unterdrücken *(suppress).*

overrule [ouvə'ru:l], *v.a.* nicht gelten lassen, verwerfen.

overseer ['ouvəsiə], *s.* der Aufseher.

oversleep [ouvə'sli:p], *v.n. irr.* sich verschlafen.

overstep [ouvə'step], *v.a.* überschreiten.

overstrain [ouvə'strein], *v.a., v.n.* (sich) zu sehr anstrengen, überanstrengen.

overt ['ouvə:t], *adj.* offenkundig; öffentlich *(public).*

overtake [ouvə'teik], *v.a. irr.* einholen; *(Mot.)* überholen.

overtax [ouvə'tæks], *v.a.* zu hoch besteuern; *(fig.)* überanstrengen *(strain).*

overthrow [ouvə'θrou], *v.a. irr.* umstürzen; *(Pol.)* stürzen. — ['ouvəθrou], *s.* der Sturz.

overtime ['ouvətaim], *s.* Überstunden, *f. pl.*

overture ['ouvətjuə], *s.* die Ouvertüre.

overturn [ouvə'tə:n], *v.a.* umstürzen. — *v.n.* überschlagen.

overweening [ouvə'wi:niŋ], *adj.* eingebildet.

overweight [ouvə'weit], *s.* das Übergewicht.

overwhelm [ouvə'welm], *v.a.* überwältigen.

overwork [ouvə'wə:k], *v.n.* sich überarbeiten.

overwrought [ouvə'rɔ:t], *adj.* übermäßig erregt, aufgeregt, überreizt.

owe [ou], *v.a.* schulden. — *v.n.* verdanken *(be in debt).*

owing ['ouiŋ], *pred. adj.* — *to,* dank *(Dat.),* zufolge *(Dat.).*

owl [aul], *s. (Orn.)* die Eule.

own (1) [oun], *v.a.* besitzen *(possess).* — *adj.* eigen.

own (2) [oun], *v.a.* anerkennen *(acknowledge).*

owner ['ounə], *s.* der Besitzer, Eigentümer.

ox [ɔks], *s. (Zool.)* der Ochse.

oxidate ['ɔksideit] *see* **oxidise.**

oxide ['ɔksaid], *s. (Chem.)* das Oxyd.

oxidise ['ɔksidaiz], *v.a., v.n. (Chem.)* oxydieren.

oxtail ['ɔksteil], *s.* der Ochsenschwanz.

oxygen ['ɔksidʒən], *s. (Chem.)* der Sauerstoff.

oyster ['ɔistə], *s. (Zool.)* die Auster.

ozone ['ouzoun], *s. (Chem.)* das Ozon.

P

P [pi:]. das P.

pa [pɑː], *s. (coll.)* Papa, der Vater.

pace [peis], *s.* der Gang, Schritt *(step);* das Tempo *(rate).* — *v.n.* — *up and down,* auf- und abschreiten. — *v.a.* einschulen *(horse).*

Pacific, The [pə'sifik, θə]. der Stille Ozean.

pacific [pə'sifik], *adj.* friedlich, still.

pacify ['pæsifai], *v.a.* Frieden stiften, beruhigen.

pack [pæk], *s.* das *or* der Pack; der Ballen *(bale);* das Rudel *(wolves);* das Spiel *(cards);* das Paket, die Packung. — *v.a.* packen *(a case);* parteiisch zusammensetzen; die Karten schlecht mischen *(cheat at cards); packed like sardines,* dichtgedrängt, eingepfercht. — *v.n.* packen; seine Sachen einpacken.

package ['pækidʒ], *s.* der Ballen *(bale);* das Gepäckstück, Paket.

packet ['pækit], *s.* das Paket; *(Naut.)* — *boat,* das Paketboot, Postschiff.

pact [pækt], *s.* der Pakt, Vertrag.

pad [pæd], *s.* das Polster, Kissen; der Notizblock *(writing block).* — *v.a.* auspolstern; *padded cell,* die Gummizelle.

padding ['pædiŋ], *s. (Tail.)* das Futter; *(fig.)* die (nichtssagende) Ausfüllung, das leere Geschwätz.

paddle [pædl], *v.a., v.n.* rudern, paddeln. — *s.* das Paddel, (Doppel)ruder, das Schaufelruder; — *steamer,* der Raddampfer.

paddock ['pædək], *s.* der Sattelplatz; das Gehege.

padlock ['pædlɔk], *s.* das Vorhängeschloß, Vorlegeschloß.

pagan ['peigən], *adj.* heidnisch. — *s.* der Heide.

paganism ['peigənizm], *s.* das Heidentum.

page (1) [peidʒ], *s.* der Page *(court attendant);* Hoteljunge *(hotel boy).* — *v.a.* durch Pagen suchen lassen.

page (2) [peidʒ], die Seite *(of book).* — *v.a.* paginieren *(book).*

pageant ['pædʒənt], *s.* der Aufzug, der Prunkzug; das Schaustück *(dramatic).*

pail [peil], *s.* der Eimer.

pain [pein], *s.* der Schmerz, die Pein; (*pl.*) die Mühe; *go to a lot of* —*s*, sich große Mühe geben. — *v.a.* schmerzen; bekümmern (*mentally*).

paint [peint], *s.* die Farbe (*dye*); die Schminke (*make-up*). — *v.a.* anstreichen, malen.

painter ['peintə], *s.* der Maler.

painting ['peintiŋ], *s.* das Gemälde.

pair [pɛə], *s.* das Paar; *two* —*s of shoes*, zwei Paar Schuhe; *a* — *of spectacles*, die Brille; *a* — *of scissors*, die Schere. — *v.a.* paaren. — *v.n.* sich paaren.

pajamas [pə'dʒɑ:məz] *see under* **pyjamas**.

Pakistani [pɑ:ki'stɑ:ni], *adj.* pakistanisch. — *s.* der Pakistaner.

palace ['pæləs], *s.* der Palast.

palatable ['pælətəbl], *adj.* schmackhaft.

palatal ['pælətl], *adj.* (*Phonet.*) palatal, Gaumen-, Vordergaumen-. — *s.* (*Phonet.*) der Gaumenlaut.

palate ['pælit], *s.* der Gaumen.

Palatinate, The [pə'lætinit, ðə]. die Pfalz, Pfalzgrafschaft.

palaver [pə'lɑ:və], *s.* die Unterredung; das Palaver.

pale (1) [peil], *adj.* blaß, bleich.

pale (2) [peil], *s.* der Pfahl; *beyond the* —, unkultiviert.

Palestinian [pælis'tiniən], *adj.* palästinisch. — *s.* der Palästiner.

palette ['pælit], *s.* die Palette (*see also* **pallet** (1)).

paling ['peiliŋ], *s.* der Lattenzaun; (*pl.*) der Pfahlbau.

pall (1) [pɔ:l], *s.* das Leichentuch.

pall (2) [pɔ:l], *v.n.* schal werden (*become stale*).

pallet (1) ['pælit], *s.* die Palette (*painter's*); — *knife*, das Streichmesser (*potter's etc.*).

pallet (2) ['pælit], *s.* der Strohsack.

palliative ['pæliətiv], *s.* linderndes Mittel; (*fig.*) die Beschönigung.

pallid ['pælid], *adj.* blaß, bleich.

pallor ['pælə], *s.* die Blässe.

palm (1) [pɑ:m], *s.* die Handfläche. — *v.a.* — (*off*) *on to s.o.*, an jemanden loswerden, jemandem etwas andrehen.

palm (2) [pɑ:m], *s.* (*Bot.*) die Palme; *Palm Sunday*, Palmsonntag.

palmer ['pɑ:mə], *s.* (*obs.*) der Pilger (*pilgrim*).

palmist ['pɑ:mist], *s.* der Handleser, Wahrsager.

palmistry ['pɑ:mistri], *s.* die Handwahrsagerei.

palmy ['pɑ:mi], *adj.* glorreich.

palpable ['pælpəbl], *adj.* handgreiflich, greifbar, klar.

palpitate ['pælpiteit], *v.n.* klopfen (*of heart*).

palsied ['pɔ:lzid], *adj.* (*Med.*) gelähmt.

palsy ['pɔ:lzi], *s.* (*Med.*) die Lähmung.

paltry ['pɔ:ltri], *adj.* erbärmlich, armselig.

pamper ['pæmpə], *v.a.* verwöhnen.

pan (1) [pæn], *s.* die Pfanne. — *v.n.* —

out, sich ausbreiten, sich weiten.

pan (2) [pæn], *v.a.* (*Phot.*) kreisen, im Bogen führen.

panacea [pænə'siə], *s.* das Universalmittel.

pancake ['pænkeik], *s.* der Pfannkuchen.

pander ['pændə], *v.n.* fröhnen (*Dat.*), nachgeben.

pane [pein], *s.* die Glasscheibe.

panel ['pænl], *s.* die Holzfüllung, Täfelung (*in room*); die Liste; die Kommission (*of experts etc.*).

pang [pæŋ], *s.* die Angst, Pein; der Schmerz, Stich (*stab of pain*).

panic ['pænik], *s.* die Panik, der Schrecken.

panoply ['pænəpli], *s.* (*Poet.*) die Rüstung.

pansy ['pænzi], *s.* (*Bot.*) das Stiefmütterchen; (*sl.*) der Weichling, Feigling.

pant [pænt], *v.n.* keuchen, schwer atmen.

pantaloons [pæntə'lu:nz] (*usually abbr.* **pants** [pænts]), *s. pl.* die Unterhosen, Hosen, *f.pl.*

panther ['pænθə], *s.* (*Zool.*) der Panther.

pantomime ['pæntəmaim], *s.* die Pantomime, das Weihnachtsstück.

pantry ['pæntri], *s.* die Speisekammer.

pap [pæp], *s.* der Kinderbrei.

papacy ['peipəsi], *s.* das Papsttum.

papal ['peipəl], *adj.* päpstlich.

paper ['peipə], *s.* das Papier (*material*); die Zeitung (*daily* —); die Abhandlung (*essay*); — *knife*, der Brieföffner. — *v.a.* tapezieren (*a room*).

paperhanger ['peipəhæŋə], *s.* der Tapezierer.

paperweight ['peipəweit], *s.* der Briefbeschwerer.

par [pɑ:], *s.* die Gleichheit, das Pari.

parable ['pærəbl], *s.* die Parabel, das Gleichnis.

parabola [pə'ræbələ], *s.* (*Geom.*) die Parabel.

parabolic [pærə'bɔlik], *adj.* parabolisch, gleichnishaft.

parachute ['pærəʃu:t], *s.* (*Aviat.*) der Fallschirm.

parade [pə'reid], *s.* die Parade, der Aufmarsch. — *v.a.* herausstellen; zur Schau tragen (*show off*). — *v.n.* (*Mil.*) vorbeimarschieren.

paradise ['pærədais], *s.* das Paradies.

paraffin ['pærəfin], *s.* das Paraffin.

paragon ['pærəgən], *s.* das Musterkind, Musterbeispiel, Vorbild.

paragraph ['pærəgrɑ:f], *s.* der Abschnitt, Absatz, Paragraph.

Paraguayan [pærə'gwaiən], *adj.* paraguayisch. — *s.* der Paraguayer.

parallel ['pærəlel], *adj.* parallel. — *s.* die Parallele.

paralyse ['pærəlaiz], *v.a.* lähmen.

paralysis [pə'rælisis], *s.* die Lähmung.

paramount ['pærəmaunt], *adj.* oberst.

paramour ['pærəmuə], *s.* der *or* die Geliebte.

parapet

parapet ['pærəpit], *s.* das Geländer, die Brüstung.

paraphrase ['pærəfreiz], *s.* die Umschreibung. — *v.a.* umschreiben.

parasite ['pærəsait], *s.* der Schmarotzer, Parasit.

parasol ['pærəsɔl], *s.* der Sonnenschirm.

parboil ['pɑːbɔil], *v.a.* aufkochen lassen.

parcel [pɑːsl], *s.* das Paket; Bündel (*bundle*). — *v.a.* — *up,* einpacken.

parch [pɑːtʃ], *v.a.* austrocknen.

parchment ['pɑːtʃmənt], *s.* das Pergament.

pardon [pɑːdn], *v.a.* vergeben, verzeihen (*Dat.*); begnadigen (*Acc.*) (*give amnesty*). — *s.* der Pardon, die Verzeihung; — *!, I beg your* — *!* bitte um Entschuldigung; *I beg your* —? wie bitte?

pare [pɛə], *v.a.* beschneiden (*nails*); schälen (*fruit*).

parent ['pɛərənt], *s.* der Vater, die Mutter, (*pl.*) die Eltern, *pl.*

parentage ['pɛərəntidʒ], *s.* die Abkunft, Herkunft.

parenthesis [pə'renθisis], *s.* die Parenthese, die Klammer.

parish ['pæriʃ], *s.* das Kirchspiel, die Gemeinde, die Pfarre.

parishioner [pə'riʃənə], *s.* das Gemeindemitglied.

Parisian [pə'riziən], *adj.* parisisch. — *s.* der Pariser.

park [pɑːk], *s.* der Park; (*Motor.*) der Wagenpark, Parkplatz. — *v.a., v.n.* parken.

parking ['pɑːkiŋ], *s.* (*Motor.*) das Parken; — *meter,* die Parkuhr, der Parkometer.

parley ['pɑːli], *s.* die Unterredung, Verhandlung. — *v.n.* verhandeln.

parliament ['pɑːləmənt], *s.* das Parlament.

parlour ['pɑːlə], *s.* das Wohnzimmer, die gute Stube; —*maid,* die Dienstmädchen; — *trick,* das Kunststück.

parochial [pə'roukiəl], *adj.* Pfarr-, Gemeinde-; (*fig.*) engstirnig.

parody ['pærədi], *s.* die Parodie. — *v.a.* parodieren.

parole [pə'roul], *s.* das Ehrenwort; (*Mil.*) das Losungswort.

paroxysm ['pærəksizm], *s.* der heftige Anfall.

parquet ['pɑːki], *s.* das Parkett; — *floor,* der Parkettfußboden.

parrot ['pærət], *s.* (*Orn.*) der Papagei.

parry ['pæri], *v.a.* parieren, abwehren.

parse [pɑːs, pɑːz], *v.a.* (*Gram.*) analysieren.

parsimony ['pɑːsiməni], *s.* die Sparsamkeit.

parsley ['pɑːsli], *s.* (*Bot.*) die Petersilie.

parson [pɑːsn], *s.* der Pastor, Pfarrer.

parsonage ['pɑːsənidʒ], *s.* das Pfarrhaus.

part [pɑːt], *s.* der Teil; Anteil (*share*); (*Theat.*) die Rolle; (*Mus.*) die Stimme;

(*Geog.*) die Gegend; *for his* —, seinerseits. — *v.n.* — (*with*), sich trennen (von, *Dat.*); — *company,* auseinandergehen.

partake [pɑː'teik], *v.n.* teilnehmen, teilhaben (*in,* an, *Dat.*).

partial [pɑːʃl], *adj.* Teil-; parteiisch (*subjective*); — *to,* eingenommen für.

participate [pɑː'tisipeit], *v.n.* teilnehmen (*in,* an, *Dat.*).

participation [pɑːtisi'peiʃən], *s.* die Teilnahme.

participle ['pɑːtisipl], *s.* (*Gram.*) das Mittelwort, Partizip(ium).

particle ['pɑːtikl], *s.* die Partikel, das Teilchen.

particular [pə'tikjulə], *adj.* besonder (*special*); einzel (*individual*); sonderbar (*queer*); ungewöhnlich; genau. — *s.* (*pl.*) die Details, *n. pl.,* Einzelheiten, *f. pl.*

parting ['pɑːtiŋ], *s.* der Abschied (*taking leave*); der Scheitel (*hair*).

partisan [pɑːti'zæn], *s.* der Partisane, Parteigänger.

partition [pɑː'tiʃən], *s.* die Teilung (*division*); die Scheidewand (*dividing wall*). — *v.a.* teilen; aufteilen (*divide up*).

partly ['pɑːtli], *adv.* zum Teil, teils.

partner ['pɑːtnə], *s.* der Partner; Teilhaber (*in business etc.*).

partnership ['pɑːtnəʃip], *s.* die Partnerschaft.

partridge ['pɑːtridʒ], *s.* (*Orn.*) das Rebhuhn.

party ['pɑːti], *s.* (*Pol.*) die Partei; (*Law*) die Partei, Seite; die Gesellschaft, die Party (*social gathering*); *throw* or *give a* —, einen Gesellschaftsabend (*or* eine Party) geben; *guilty* —, der schuldige Teil; (*Build.*) — *wall,* die Brandmauer.

Paschal ['pɑːskəl], *adj.* Oster-.

pass [pɑːs], *v.a.* passieren; vorbeigehen (an, *Dat.*); durchlassen (*let through*); (*Law*) — *sentence,* das Urteil fällen. — *v.n.* fortgehen, vergehen, geschehen (*happen*); vorübergehen (*of time*); — *for,* gelten; (*Sch.*) durchkommen (*exam*); *come to* —, sich ereignen. — *s.* der Paß; (*Theat.*) die Freikarte.

passable ['pɑːsəbl], *adj.* gangbar; (*fig.*) leidlich, erträglich.

passage ['pæsidʒ], *s.* der Durchgang (*thoroughfare*); das Vergehen (*of time*); die Seereise; die Stelle (*book*).

passenger ['pæsindʒə], *s.* der Reisende, Passagier; — *train,* der Personenzug.

passer-by ['pɑːsəbai], *s.* der Passant, Vorübergehende.

passing ['pɑːsiŋ], *s.* das Vorbeigehen, das Vorübergehen; (*Parl.*) das Durchgehen; das Hinscheiden (*death*). — *adj.* vorübergehend, zeitweilig.

Passion ['pæʃən], *s.* (*Eccl.*) das Leiden; (*Mus.*) die Passion; — *Week,* die Karwoche; — *flower,* die Passionsblume.

passion ['pæʃən], *s.* die Leidenschaft;

fly into a —, aufbrausen.

passive ['pæsiv], *adj.* passiv. — *s.* (*Gram.*) das Passiv(um).

Passover ['pɑːsouvə], *s.* (*Rel.*) das Passahfest.

passport ['pɑːspɔːt], *s.* der Reisepaß.

past [pɑːst], *adj.* vergangen. — *adv.* vorbei. — *prep.* nach (*time*). — *s.* die Vergangenheit; (*Gram.*) das Imperfekt, Präteritum.

paste [peist], *s.* die Paste, der Brei; der Kleister (*glue*). — *v.a.* kleben, kleistern.

pasteboard ['peistbɔːd], *s.* die Pappe.

pastime ['pɑːstaim], *s.* der Zeitvertreib.

pastor ['pɑːstə], *s.* (*Rel.*) der Seelsorger, Pfarrer.

pastoral ['pɑːstərəl], *adj.* Hirten-, pastoral. — *s.* (*Poet.*) das Hirtengedicht.

pastry ['peistri], *s.* (*Cul.*) die Pastete; das Gebäck; — *cook*, der Konditor, Zuckerbäcker.

pasture ['pɑːstʃə], *s.* die Weide, das Grasland. — *v.n.* weiden, grasen.

pasty ['pɑːsti, 'pæsti], *s.* (*Cul.*) die Pastete. — ['peisti], *adj.* teigig.

pat [pæt], *s.* der Klaps; der Schlag (*slap*). — *v.a.* leicht schlagen, streicheln (*gently*).

patch [pætʃ], *v.a.* flicken, ausbessern. — *s.* der Fleck (*mending material*); der Flecken (*land*); (*coll.*) *no* — *on him*, kein Vergleich mit ihm; nicht zu vergleichen mit ihm.

patent ['peitənt *or* 'pætənt], *adj.* offen, klar, patent; — *leather*, das Glanzleder. — *s.* das Patent.

patentee [peitən'tiː], *s.* der Patentinhaber.

paternal [pə'təːnəl], *adj.* väterlich.

path [pɑːθ], *s.* der Pfad, Weg, Fußsteig.

pathetic [pə'θetik], *adj.* pathetisch, rührend; armselig.

pathology [pə'θɔlədʒi], *s.* (*Med.*) die Pathologie.

pathway ['pɑːθwei], *s.* der Fußweg, Fußsteig.

patience ['peiʃəns], *s.* die Geduld; die Patience (*card game*).

patient ['peiʃənt], *adj.* geduldig. — *s.* (*Med.*) der Patient.

patrician [pə'triʃən], *adj.* patrizisch. — *s.* der Patrizier.

patrimony ['pætriməni], *s.* das (väterliche) Erbgut.

patriot ['peitriət, 'pætriət], *s.* der Patriot.

patriotism ['peitriətizm, 'pæt-], *s.* die Vaterlandsliebe, der Patriotismus.

patrol [pə'troul], *s.* die Patrouille, Streife. — *v.n.* auf Patrouille gehen.

patron ['peitrən], *s.* der Schutzherr, der Gönner; (*Comm.*) der Kunde; — *saint*, der Schutzheilige.

patronage ['pætrənidʒ], *s.* die Gönnerschaft, Huld.

patronize ['pætrənaiz], *v.a.* besuchen (*frequent*); begünstigen (*favour*).

patronizing ['pætrənaiziŋ], *adj.* herablassend.

patten [pætn], *s.* (*Archit.*) der Sockel; der Holzschuh (*clog*).

patter (1) ['pætə], *s.* das Geplätscher (*rain etc.*). — *v.n.* plätschern.

patter (2) ['pætə], *s.* das Geplauder (*chatter*). — *v.n.* schwätzen.

pattern ['pætən], *s.* das Muster; die Schablone (*in material*).

paucity ['pɔːsiti], *s.* die geringe Anzahl, der Mangel.

paunch [pɔːntʃ], *s.* der Wanst.

pauper ['pɔːpə], *s.* der Arme.

pauperize ['pɔːpəraiz], *v.a.* arm machen, verarmen lassen.

pause [pɔːz], *s.* die Pause. — *v.n.* innehalten.

pave [peiv], *v.a.* pflastern.

pavement ['peivmənt], *s.* das Pflaster; der Bürgersteig, Gehsteig.

pavilion [pə'viljən], *s.* das Gartenhaus; der Pavillon.

paw [pɔː], *s.* die Pfote; die Tatze. — *v.a.* streicheln, betasten.

pawn (1) [pɔːn], *s.* das Pfand. — *v.a.* verpfänden.

pawn (2) [pɔːn], *s.* (*Chess*) der Bauer.

pawnbroker ['pɔːnbroukə], *s.* der Pfandleiher.

pay [pei], *v.a. irr.* zahlen; bezahlen, begleichen (*bill*); — *attention*, aufpassen, Aufmerksamkeit schenken; — *o.'s respects*, Respekt zollen. — *v.n. irr.* sich bezahlt machen, sich lohnen (*it* —*s to* . . .). — *s.* (*Mil.*) der Sold; (*Comm.*) der Lohn (*wage*), die Bezahlung (*payment*).

payable ['peiəbl], *adj.* zahlbar, zu bezahlen.

payee [pei'iː], *s.* der Empfänger, Präsentant.

payer ['peiə], *s.* der Zahler; (*Comm.*) der Trassat.

payment ['peimənt], *s.* die Bezahlung, Begleichung (*of sum*).

pea [piː], *s.* (*Bot.*) die Erbse (*see also* **peas(e)**).

peace [piːs], *s.* der Friede(n); die Ruhe (*restfulness*).

peaceable ['piːsəbl], *adj.* friedlich; friedliebend.

peaceful ['piːsful], *adj.* friedlich, ruhig (*restful*).

peach [piːtʃ], *s.* (*Bot.*) der *or* (*Austr.*) die Pfirsich.

peacock ['piːkɔk], *s.* (*Orn.*) der Pfau.

peahen ['piːhen], *s.* (*Orn.*) die Pfauhenne.

peak [piːk], *s.* der Gipfel, die Spitze; der Schirm (*of cap*); — *hour*, die Stunde des Hochbetriebs, Hauptverkehrsstunde.

peal [piːl], *v.a.* läuten. — *v.n.* erschallen. — *s.* das Läuten, Geläute.

peanut ['piːnʌt], *s.* (*Bot.*) die Erdnuß.

pear [pɛə], *s.* (*Bot.*) die Birne.

pearl [pəːl], *s.* die Perle; — *barley*, die Perlgraupen, *f. pl.*; *mother of* —, die Perlmutter.

peasant ['pezənt], s. der Bauer.
peasantry ['pezəntri], s. das Bauernvolk, die Bauernschaft.
peas(e) [pi:z], s. pl. pease pudding, der Erbsenbrei, das Erbsenpüree.
peat [pi:t], s. der Torf.
pebble [pebl], s. der Kiesel(stein).
peck (1) [pek], s. der Viertelscheffel (=9 litres.)
peck (2) [pek], s. das Picken (of hen); (coll.) der Kuß. — v.a. hacken, hauen.
pecker ['pekə], s. die Picke, Haue; keep your — up! Mut bewahren!
peckish ['pekiʃ], adj. hungrig.
pectoral ['pektərəl], adj. Brust-. — s. das Brustmittel.
peculiar [pi'kju:liə], adj. eigenartig, eigentümlich (strange); — to, eigen (Dat.); besonder (special).
peculiarity [pikju:li'æriti], s. die Eigentümlichkeit, Eigenartigkeit.
pecuniary [pi'kju:niəri], adj. Geld-, geldlich, finanziell, pekuniär.
pedagogue ['pedəgɔg], s. der Pädagog(e), Erzieher.
pedal [pedl] s. das Pedal; (Motor.) der Fußhebel. — v.n. radfahren; (coll.) radeln.
pedant ['pedənt], s. der Pedant.
pedantic [pi'dæntik], adj. pedantisch.
pedantry ['pedəntri], s. die Pedanterie.
peddle [pedl], v.a. hausieren.
peddling ['pedliŋ], adj. kleinlich, unbedeutend.
pedestal ['pedistl], s. der Sockel.
pedestrian [pi'destriən], s. der Fußgänger. — adj. Fuß-, Fußgänger-.
pedigree ['pedigri:], s. der Stammbaum.
pediment ['pedimənt], s. (Archit.) der Ziergiebel.
pedlar ['pedlə], s. der Hausierer.
peel [pi:l], s. die Schale (of fruit). — v.a. schälen. — v.n. sich schälen.
peep [pi:p], v.n. gucken. — s. der (schnelle) Blick, das Gucken; — show, der Guckkasten.
peer (1) [piə], s. (Parl.) der Pair, Lord; der Ebenbürtige (equal).
peer (2) [piə], v.n. gucken, blicken, schauen.
peerage ['piəridʒ], s. der (Reichs)adel.
peeress ['piəres], s. die Gattin eines Pairs.
peerless ['piəlis], adj. unvergleichlich.
peevish ['pi:viʃ], adj. mürrisch.
pe(e)wit ['pi:wit], s. (Orn.) der Kiebitz.
peg ['peg], s. der Pflock (stake); der Holzstift (in wall); clothes —, die Wäscheklammer. — v.a. anpflocken (to ground).
pelican ['pelikən], s. (Orn.) der Pelikan.
pellet ['pelit], s. das Kügelchen.
pell-mell ['pel'mel], adv. durcheinander.
pelt (1) [pelt], v.a. — with, bewerfen mit, — a person with, werfen nach einem (Acc.). — v.n. strömen (rain etc.); rennen (hasten).
pelt (2) [pelt], s. der Pelz (of animal).

pen (1) [pen], s. quill —, die Feder; fountain —, die Füllfeder; ballpoint —, der Kugelschreiber. — v.a. schreiben; verfassen (compose).
pen (2) [pen], s. das Gehege. — v.a. einschliessen (sheep).
penal ['pi:nəl], adj. Straf-; — servitude, die Zuchthausstrafe.
penalize ['pi:nəlaiz], v.a. bestrafen.
penalty ['penəlti], s. die Strafe.
penance ['penəns], s. die Buße.
pence [pens] see under **penny**.
pencil ['pensl], s. der Bleistift; der Stift; (Geom.) der Strahl. — v.a. niederschreiben, notieren.
pendant ['pendənt], s. das Ohrgehänge; (fig.) das Gegenstück.
pendent ['pendənt], adj. hängend, schwebend.
pending ['pendiŋ], adj. in der Schwebe; unentschieden (undecided). — prep. während (during); bis (zu) (until).
pendulum ['pendjuləm], s. das Pendel.
penetrate ['penitreit], v.a. durchdringen.
peninsula [pi'ninsjulə], s. die Halbinsel.
penitent ['penitənt], s. der Büßer. — adj. bußfertig.
penitentiary [peni'tenʃəri], s. (Am.) das Zuchthaus (prison).
penknife ['pennaif], s. das Taschenmesser.
pennant ['penənt], s. der Wimpel, das Fähnchen.
penniless ['penilis], adj. mittellos, ohne einen Heller Geld, arm.
pennon ['penən] see **pennant**.
penny ['peni], s. (pl. pence [pens], pennies ['peniz]) der Penny; (Am.) das Centstück; — farthing, das Hochrad; — whistle, die Blechpfeife; a pretty —, hübsches Geld.
pension ['penʃən], s. die Pension; das Ruhegehalt. — v.a. (off) pensionieren, in den Ruhestand versetzen.
pensive ['pensiv], adj. nachdenklich.
Pentecost ['pentikɔst]. das or (pl.) die Pfingsten.
penthouse ['penthaus], s. das Wetterdach.
penurious [pi'njuəriəs], adj. unbemittelt, arm (poor); dürftig, karg (meagre).
penury ['penjuəri], s. die Not, Armut.
peony ['piəni], s. (Bot.) die Päonie, Pfingstrose.
people [pi:pl], s. pl. das Volk (nation); die Leute, Menschen (pl.). — v.a. bevölkern.
pepper ['pepə], s. der Pfeffer. — v.a. pfeffern.
per [pə:], prep. pro; per; durch; as — account, laut Rechnung.
peradventure [pə:rəd'ventʃə], adv. (obs.) von ungefähr; vielleicht (perhaps).
perambulator [pə'ræmbjuleitə] (abbr. coll.) **pram** [præm]), s. der Kinderwagen.

perceive [pə'si:v], *v.a.* wahrnehmen, merken.
percentage [pə'sentidʒ], *s.* der Prozentsatz (*of interest*); Prozente, *n. pl.*
perceptible [pə'septibl], *adj.* wahrnehmbar, merklich.
perception [pə'sepʃən], *s.* die Wahrnehmung, Empfindung.
perch (1) [pə:tʃ], *v.n.* aufsitzen; sitzen (*of birds*). — *s.* die Stange.
perch (2) [pə:tʃ], *s.* (*Zool.*) der Barsch.
perchance [pə'tʃɑ:ns], *adv.* vielleicht.
percolate ['pə:kəleit], *v.n.* durchsickern, durchtröpfeln.
percolator ['pə:kəleitə], *s.* die Kaffeemaschine.
percussion [pə'kʌʃən], *s.* (*Mus.*) das Schlagzeug.
peremptory ['perəmptəri, pə'remptəri], *adj.* entschieden, bestimmt (*decided*); absprechend.
perennial [pə'reniəl], *adj.* (*Bot.*) perennierend; Dauer-.
perfect ['pə:fikt], *adj.* vollkommen, vollendet, perfekt. — *s.* (*tense*) (*Gram.*) das Perfekt(um). — [pə'fekt], *v.a.* vollenden.
perfection [pə'fekʃən], *s.* die Vollendung, Vollkommenheit; *to* —, vollkommen.
perfidious [pə'fidiəs], *adj.* treulos, untreu; tückisch.
perfidy ['pə:fidi], *s.* die Treulosigkeit.
perforate ['pə:fəreit], *v.a.* durchlöchern, perforieren (*paper*); durchbohren (*pierce*).
perforce [pə'fɔ:s], *adv.* mit Gewalt, notgedrungen.
perform [pə'fɔ:m], *v.a.* ausführen (*carry out*); (*Theat.*) aufführen. — *v.n.* spielen, auftreten (*of actor*).
performance [pə'fɔ:məns], *s.* die Ausführung; Verrichtung (*execution of duty etc.*); (*Theat.*) die Aufführung.
perfume ['pə:fju:m], *s.* das Parfüm; der Duft (*scent*). — *v.a.* parfümieren.
perfunctory [pə'fʌŋktəri], *adj.* nachlässig, oberflächlich, flüchtig.
perhaps [pə'hæps], *adv.* vielleicht.
peril ['peril], *s.* die Gefahr.
period ['piəriəd], *s.* die Periode (*time*); der Zeitraum (*span*); (*Am.*) der Punkt (*full stop*).
periodical [piəri'ɔdikəl], *adj.* periodisch. — *s.* die Zeitschrift.
perish ['periʃ], *v.n.* zugrunde gehen, umkommen.
perishable ['periʃəbl], *adj.* vergänglich; (leicht) verderblich (*of food*).
periwig ['periwig], *s.* die Perücke.
periwinkle (1) ['periwiŋkl], *s.* (*Zool.*) die Uferschnecke.
periwinkle (2) ['periwiŋkl], (*Bot.*) das Immergrün.
perjure ['pə:dʒə], *v.r.* meineidig werden.
perjurer ['pə:dʒərə], *s.* der Meineidige.
perjury ['pə:dʒəri], *s.* der Meineid.
permanence, permanency ['pə:mə-nəns, 'pə:mənənsi], *s.* die Dauer, Beständigkeit.
permanent ['pə:mənənt], *adj.* Dauer-, dauerhaft, beständig; — *wave,* die Dauerwelle.
permeability [pə:miə'biliti], *s.* die Durchdringbarkeit, Durchlässigkeit.
permeable ['pə:miəbl], *adj.* durchdringlich.
permeate ['pə:mieit], *v.a.* durchdringen.
permissible [pə'misibl], *adj.* zulässig, statthaft.
permission [pə'miʃən], *s.* die Erlaubnis.
permit [pə'mit], *v.a.* zulassen, erlauben. — ['pə:mit], *s.* die Erlaubnis; (*official*) die Genehmigung.
permutation [pə:mju'teiʃən], *s.*(*Maths.*) die Permutation.
pernicious [pə'niʃəs], *adj.* verderblich, schädlich, bösartig.
perorate ['perəreit], *v.n.* eine (lange) Rede beschließen.
perpendicular [pə:pən'dikjulə], *adj.* senkrecht. — *s.* die Senkrechte.
perpetrate ['pə:pitreit], *v.a.* begehen (*commit*).
perpetration [pə:pi'treiʃən], *s.* die Verübung, Begehung.
perpetrator ['pə:pitreitə], *s.* der Begeher, Täter.
perpetual [pə'petjuəl], *adj.* (an-) dauernd; ewig.
perpetuate [pə'petjueit], *v.a.* verewigen.
perpetuity [pə:pi'tju:iti], *s.* die Ewigkeit.
perplex [pə'pleks], *v.a.* bestürzen, verblüffen.
perplexity [pə'pleksiti], *s.* die Bestürzung, Verwirrung.
persecute ['pə:sikju:t], *v.a.* verfolgen.
persecution [pə:si'kju:ʃən], *s.* die Verfolgung.
perseverance [pə:si'viərəns], *s.* die Ausdauer, Beharrlichkeit.
persevere [pə:si'viə], *v.n.* beharren (*in,* bei, *Dat.*).
Persian ['pə:ʃən], *adj.* persisch. — *s.* der Perser.
persist [pə'sist], *v.n.* beharren (*in,* auf, *Dat.*).
persistence [pə'sistəns], *s.* die Beharrlichkeit.
person ['pə:sən], *s.* die Person; *in* —, persönlich.
personal ['pə:sənəl], *adj.* persönlich.
personality [pə:sə'næliti], *s.* die Persönlichkeit.
personify [pə'sɔnifai], *v.a.* verkörpern.
personnel [pə:sə'nel], *s.* das Personal; (*Comm.*) — *manager,* der Personalchef.
perspective [pə'spektiv], *s.* die Perspektive. — *adj.* perspektivisch.
perspicacious [pə:spi'keiʃəs], *adj.* scharfsichtig, scharfsinnig.
perspicacity [pə:spi'kæsiti], *s.* der Scharfblick, Scharfsinn.
perspicuity [pə:spi'kju:iti], *s.* die Durchsichtigkeit, Klarheit.

perspicuous

perspicuous [pə'spikjuəs], *adj.* deutlich, klar.
perspiration [pə:spi'reiʃən], *s.* der Schweiß.
perspire [pə'spaiə], *v.n.* schwitzen.
persuade [pə'sweid], *v.a.* überreden.
persuasion [pə'sweiʒən], *s.* die Überredung.
persuasive [pə'sweiziv], *adj.* überzeugend, überredend.
pert [pə:t], *adj.* naseweis, keck.
pertain [pə'tein], *v.n.* (an)gehören (*to Dat.*).
pertinacious [pə:ti'neiʃəs], *adj.* beharrlich, halsstarrig.
pertinacity [pə:ti'næsiti], *s.* die Beharrlichkeit, Halsstarrigkeit.
pertinence, pertinency ['pə:tinəns, 'pə:tinənsi], *s.* die Angemessenheit.
pertinent ['pə:tinənt], *adj.* angemessen, passend.
pertness ['pə:tnis], *s.* die Keckheit, der Vorwitz.
perturb [pə'tə:b], *v.a.* verwirren, stören, beunruhigen.
perturbation [pə:tə'beiʃən], *s.* die Verwirrung, Störung, Beunruhigung.
peruke [pə'ru:k], *s.* die Perücke.
peruse [pə'ru:z], *v.a.* durchlesen.
Peruvian [pə'ru:viən], *adj.* peruanisch.
— *s.* der Peruaner.
pervade [pə'veid], *v.a.* durchdringen.
perverse [pə'və:s], *adj.* verkehrt.
perversion [pə'və:ʃən],*s.* die Perversion.
perversity [pə'və:siti], *s.* die Verdorbenheit, Widernatürlichkeit.
pervert [pə'və:t], *v.a.* verkehren, verderben. — ['pə:və:t], *s.* der Verdorbene, der perverse Mensch.
perverted [pə'və:tid], *adj.* pervers (*sexually*).
pervious ['pə:viəs], *adj.* zugänglich, passierbar; durchlässig.
pessimist ['pesimist], *s.* der Pessimist.
pest [pest], *s.* (*Med.*) die Pest; (*fig.*) die Plage.
pester ['pestə], *v.a.* quälen, auf die Nerven gehen (*Dat.*).
pestiferous [pes'tifərəs], *adj.* verpestend.
pestilence ['pestiləns], *s.* (*Med.*) die Pest, Seuche.
pestle [pesl], *s.* die Mörserkeule.
pet [pet], *s.* das Haustier; der Liebling; — *name*, der Kosename. — *v.a.* liebkosen, streicheln.
petition [pi'tiʃən], *s.* die Bittschrift. — *v.a.* mit einer Bittschrift herantreten an (*Acc.*).
petrel ['petrəl], *s.* (*Orn.*) der Sturmvogel.
petrification [petrifi'keiʃən], *s.* die Versteinerung.
petrify ['petrifai], *v.a.* versteinern; (*fig.*) starr machen, bestürzen; *petrified with fright*, starr vor Entsetzen. — *v.n.* zu Stein werden.
petrol ['petrəl], *s.* das Benzin; (*crude oil*) das Petroleum; — *station*, die Tankstelle.

petticoat ['petikout], *s.* der Unterrock.
pettifogging ['petifɔgiŋ], *adj.* Winkel-, kleinlich, schikanös (*petty*).
pettiness ['petinis], *s.* die Kleinlichkeit.
pettish ['petiʃ], *adj.* verdrießlich.
petty ['peti], *adj.* klein, gering, kleinlich.
petulance ['petjuləns], *s.* die Launenhaftigkeit, Gereiztheit.
petulant ['petjulənt], *adj.* launenhaft.
pew [pju:], *s.* (*Eccl.*) der Kirchensitz; (*coll.*) der Sitz, Stuhl.
pewit ['pi:wit] *see* pe(e)wit.
pewter ['pju:tə], *s.* das Zinn; die Zinnwaren, *f. pl.* (*wares*).
pewterer ['pju:tərə], *s.* der Zinngießer.
phantom ['fæntəm], *s.* das Phantom, Trugbild; das Gespenst (*ghost*).
Pharisee ['færisi:], *s.* der Pharisäer.
pharmaceutical [fɑ:mə'sju:tikəl], *adj.* pharmazeutisch.
pharmacy ['fɑ:məsi], *s.* die Apothekerkunst (*dispensing*); die Apotheke (*dispensary*); die Pharmazeutik (*discipline*).
phase [feiz], *s.* die Phase.
pheasant ['fezənt], *s.* (*Orn.*) der Fasan.
phenomenal [fi'nɔminəl], *adj.* außerordentlich, phänomenal.
phenomenon [fi'nɔminən], *s.* das Phänomen.
phial ['faiəl], *s.* die Phiole, das Fläschchen.
philanthropist [fi'lænθrəpist], *s.* der Philanthrop.
philanthropy [fi'lænθrəpi], *s.* die Philanthropie.
philatelist [fi'lætəlist], *s.* der Philatelist, Markensammler.
philately [fi'lætəli], *s.* das Markensammeln, die Philatelie, Briefmarkenkunde.
Philippine ['filipi:n], *adj.* philippinisch.
Philistine ['filistain], *s.* der Philister; (*fig.*) der Spießbürger.
philologist [fi'blədʒist], *s.* der Philologe.
philology [fi'blədʒi], *s.* die Philologie.
philosopher [fi'lɔsəfə], *s.* der Philosoph.
philosophize [fi'lɔsəfaiz], *v.n.* philosophieren.
philosophy [fi'lɔsəfi], *s.* die Philosophie.
phlegm [flem], *s.* das Phlegma (*mood*); (*Med.*) der Schleim.
phlegmatic [fleg'mætik], *adj.* phlegmatisch, gelassen.
phone [foun] *see under* telephone.
phonetics [fə'netiks], *s.* die Phonetik.
phosphorescent [fɔsfə'resənt], *adj.* phosphoreszierend, leuchtend.
phosphorus ['fɔsfərəs], *s.* (*Chem.*) der Phosphor.
photograph ['foutəgræf *or* -grɑ:f], *s.* die Photographie, das Lichtbild (*picture*). — *v.a.* photographieren, aufnehmen, (*coll.*) knipsen.
photographer [fə'tɔgrəfə], *s.* der Photograph.

photography [fə'tɔgrəfi], s. die Photographie.

phrase [freiz], s. die Phrase. — v.a. phrasieren, fassen, ausdrücken.

phrenology [fre'nɔlədʒi], s. die Phrenologie, Schädellehre.

phthisis ['θaisis], s. (Med.) die Schwindsucht.

physic ['fizik], s. (obs.) die Medizin, Arznei.

physical ['fizikəl], adj. körperlich (bodily); physikalisch (of physics).

physician [fi'ziʃən], s. der Arzt.

physics ['fiziks], s. die Physik.

physiognomy [fizi'ɔnəmi or -'ɔgnəmi], s. die Physiognomie, die Gesichtsbildung.

physiologist [fizi'ɔlədʒist], s. der Physiolog.

physiology [fizi'ɔlədʒi], s. die Physiologie.

piano(forte) ['pjænou('fɔ:ti)], s. das Klavier.

pick [pik], v.a. pflücken (flowers); hacken (hack); — up, auflesen; auswählen (select); gewaltsam öffnen (a lock); anfangen (a quarrel). — v.n. why — on me? warum gerade mich auswählen? — s. die Picke, Spitzhacke (axe); — the Auswahl; — of the bunch, (coll.) das Beste von allen.

picket ['pikit], s. die Wache; der Streikposten (of strikers); der Pflock (wood). — v.a. bewachen. — v.n. Wache stehen.

pickle [pikl], s. (Cul.) der Pökel, das Gepökelte; (coll.) die unangenehme Lage (calamity). — v.a. einpökeln.

pickpocket ['pikpɔkit], s. der Taschendieb.

picnic ['piknik], s. das Picknick. — v.n. picknicken.

pictorial [pik'tɔ:riəl], adj. illustriert.

picture ['piktʃə], s. das Bild; — book, das Bilderbuch; — postcard, die Ansichtskarte; pretty as a —, bildhübsch; der Film; (pl.) das Kino. — v.a. sich vorstellen.

picturesque [piktʃə'resk], adj. pittoresk, malerisch.

pie [pai], s. (Cul.) die Pastete (savoury); das Törtchen (sweet).

piebald ['paibɔ:ld], adj. scheckig. — s. der Schecke (horse).

piece [pi:s], s. das Stück. — v.a. — together, zusammenflicken (mend), zusammensetzen (compose).

piecemeal ['pi:smi:l], adv. stückweise.

pied [paid] see piebald.

pier [piə], s. der Hafendamm; der Pfeiler (column).

pierce [piəs], v.a. durchstechen, durchbohren.

pierglass ['piəglɑ:s], s. der Pfeilerspiegel.

piety ['paiəti], s. die Pietät, Frömmigkeit.

pig [pig], s. (Zool.) das Schwein.

pigeon ['pidʒən], s. (Orn.) die Taube.

pigeonhole ['pidʒənhoul], s. das Fach.

pigheaded [pig'hedid], adj. starrköpfig, dickköpfig.

piglet ['piglit], s. (Zool.) das Ferkel.

pigment ['pigmənt], s. das Pigment, der (natürliche) Farbstoff.

pigtail ['pigteil], s. der Haarzopf.

pike [paik], s. (Zool.) der Hecht; die Pike (weapon).

pile (1) [pail], s. der Haufen, Stoß (paper). — v.a. aufhäufen.

pile (2) [pail], s. (Archit.) der Pfahl; Pfeiler (stone).

pile (3) [pail], s. (Text.) der Teppichflausch (carpet), die Noppe (cloth).

piles [pailz], s. pl. (Med. coll.) die Haemorrhoiden, (pl.).

pilfer ['pilfə], v.a. stehlen, mausen.

pilferer ['pilfərə], s. der Dieb.

pilgrim ['pilgrim], s. der Pilger.

pill [pil], s. (Med.) die Pille.

pillage ['pilidʒ], s. die Plünderung. — v.a. ausplündern.

pillar ['pilə], s. der Pfeiler, die Säule; — box, der Briefkasten.

pillion ['piljən], s. der zweite Sitz, Sozius (motorcycle).

pillory ['pilɔri], s. der Pranger. — v.a. anprangern.

pillow ['pilou], s. das Kopfkissen.

pilot ['pailət], s. der Pilot; (Naut.) der Lotse. — v.a. (Aviat.) steuern, (Naut.) lotsen.

pimento [pi'mentou], s. (Bot.) der Jamaikapfeffer.

pimp [pimp], s. der Kuppler.

pimple [pimpl], s. der Pickel; (pl.) der Ausschlag.

pin [pin], s. die Stecknadel; (Engin.) der Bolzen, Stift; (skittles) der Kegel. — v.a. — down, festlegen.

pinafore ['pinəfɔ:], s. die Schürze, Kinderschürze.

pincers ['pinsəz], s. pl. die Kneifzange, Zange.

pinch [pintʃ], v.a. kneifen, zwicken; (coll.) klauen, stehlen. — v.n. sparen, darben. — s. die Prise (tobacco); at a —, wenn es sein muß.

pine (1) [pain], s. (Bot.) die Kiefer, Föhre.

pine (2) [pain], v.n. — for, schmachten (nach, Dat.), sich sehnen.

pineapple ['painæpl], s. (Bot.) die Ananas.

pinion ['pinjən], s. der Flügel (wing); (Poet.) die Schwinge; (Mech.) das Zahnrad; — shaft, die Ritzelwelle; — spindle, die Zahnradwelle. — v.a. binden, fesseln.

pink [pink], adj. rosa. — s. (Bot.) die (rosa) Nelke; (Hunt.) der (rote) Jagdrock; in the — (of condition), in bester Gesundheit, in bester Form.

pinnacle ['pinəkl], s. die Zinne, Spitze; (fig.) der Gipfel.

pint [paint], s. die Pinte (0.57 litre); (beer) der Schoppen.

pioneer [paiə'niə], s. der Pionier. — v.a. bahnbrechend sein, bahnen.

pious ['paiəs], adj. fromm.

pip

pip [pip], s. der Obstkern; (*Mil. coll.*) der Leutnantsstern.

pipe [paip], s. die Pfeife; (*Engin.*) das Rohr; die Röhre; (*Mus.*) die Pfeife. — *v.a.* pfeifen; durch Rohre leiten.

piping ['paipiŋ], *adj.* — *hot*, kochend heiß.

pipkin ['pipkin], s. das Töpfchen.

piquant ['pi:kənt], *adj.* pikant; scharf (*taste*).

pique [pi:k], s. der Groll. — *v.a.* reizen.

piracy ['pairəsi], s. die Seeräuberei.

pirate ['pairit], s. der Pirat, Seeräuber. — [pai'reit], *v.a.* (*fig.*) plagiieren, ohne Erlaubnis drucken (*books*).

pistil ['pistil], s. (*Bot.*) der Stempel.

pistol ['pistəl], s. die Pistole.

piston ['pistən], s. (*Mech.*) der Kolben.

pit [pit], s. die Grube; (*Min.*) der Schacht, das Bergwerk; (*Theat., Mus.*) der Orchesterraum; (*Theat.*) das Parterre.

pitch (1) [pitʃ], s. der Grad, Gipfel (*height*); (*Mus.*) der Ton, die Tonhöhe (*level*); (*Sport*) das Spielfeld. — *v.a.* werfen; feststecken; (*Mus.*) stimmen; befestigen; (*tent*) (ein Zelt) aufschlagen; — *in*, sich ins Zeug legen.

pitch (2) [pitʃ], s. das Pech (*tar*); — *dark*, pechschwarz.

pitchblende ['pitʃblend], s. die Pechblende.

pitcher ['pitʃə], s. der Krug.

pitchfork ['pitʃfɔ:k], s. die Heugabel.

piteous ['pitiəs], *adj.* erbärmlich.

pitfall ['pitfɔ:l], s. die Falle.

pith [piθ], s. das Mark; (*fig.*) der Kern, das Wesentliche; die Kraft (*strength*).

pithy ['piθi], *adj.* markig, kräftig; prägnant.

pitiable ['pitiəbl], *adj.* erbärmlich.

pitiful ['pitiful], *adj.* erbärmlich (*pitiable*); mitleidig (*sympathetic*).

pitiless ['pitilis], *adj.* erbarmungslos, grausam.

pittance ['pitəns], s. der Hungerlohn, das Bißchen, die Kleinigkeit.

pity ['piti], s. das Mitleid. — *v.a.* bemitleiden, bedauern.

pivot ['pivət], s. (*Mech.*) der Drehpunkt, Zapfen; (*fig.*) der Mittelpunkt, Angelpunkt. — *v.n.* zum Mittelpunkt haben, sich drehen (um).

placard ['plækɑ:d], s. das Plakat.

placate [plə'keit], *v.a.* versöhnen.

place [pleis], s. der Platz, Ort, die Stelle; — *name*, der Ortsname; (*rank*) der Rang, die Rangstufe. — *v.a.* plazieren (*in a job*); legen, setzen, stellen; — *an order*, einen Auftrag geben.

placid ['plæsid], *adj.* gelassen, sanft, gutmütig.

plagiarism ['pleidʒiərizm], s. das Plagiat, das Plagiieren.

plague [pleig], s. (*Med.*) die Pest, Seuche; (*fig.*) die Plage. — *v.a.* belästigen, plagen.

plaice [pleis], s. (*Zool.*) die Scholle.

plain [plein], s. die Ebene, Fläche. — *adj.* eben, flach (*even*); schlicht, einfach, klar; — *dealing*, ehrliche Handlungsweise; — *speaking*, offenes Sprechen, aufrichtiges Reden; (*Mus.*) — *song*, der einstimmige Chorgesang, die gregorianische Kirchenmusik.

plaintiff ['pleintif], s. (*Law*) der Kläger.

plaintive ['pleintiv], *adj.* klagend.

plait [plæt], s. der Zopf, die Flechte. — *v.a.* flechten (*hair*); falten.

plan [plæn], s. der Plan, Grundriß. — *v.a.* planen, entwerfen.

plane (1) [plein], *v.a.* hobeln (*wood*). — s. die Fläche (*surface*); die Stufe (*level*); (*coll.*) das Flugzeug (*aeroplane*).

plane (2) *see* **plane-tree**.

planet ['plænit], s. (*Astron.*) der Planet.

plane-tree ['pleintri:], s. (*Bot.*) die Platane.

planish ['plæniʃ], *v.a.* (*woodwork*) polieren, glätten.

plank [plæŋk], s. die Planke; (*Pol.*) der Programmpunkt.

plant [plɑ:nt], s. (*Bot.*) die Pflanze; (*Ind.*) die Anlage, der Betrieb. — *v.a.* anpflanzen, anlegen; — *suspicion*, Verdacht einflößen (*of, against*, gegen, *Acc.*).

plantain ['plæntein], s. (*Bot.*) der Wegerich; (*fruit*) der Pisang.

plantation [plæn'teiʃən], s. die Pflanzung, Plantage.

plaster ['plɑ:stə], s. das Pflaster (*adhesive*); (*Build.*) der Mörtel, der Mauerbewurf; — *cast*, der Gipsabdruck; — *of Paris*, der Stuck, der feine Gipsmörtel. — *v.a.* bepflastern, verputzen; (*fig.*) dick auftragen.

plastic ['plæstik], *adj.* plastisch; (*malleable*) formbar; — *surgery*, plastische Chirurgie. — s. der Kunststoff.

Plate, River [pleit, 'rivə]. der La Plata Strom.

plate [pleit], s. der Teller (*dish*), die Platte, Scheibe; (*coll.*) — *glass*, das Spiegelglas; das Geschirr (*service of crockery*); *gold* —, das Goldgeschirr. — *v.a.* überziehen, versilbern, verchromen.

platform ['plætfɔ:m], s. (*Railw.*) der Bahnsteig; die Bühne, das Podium.

platinum ['plætinəm], s. das Platin.

platitude ['plætitju:d], s. die Plattheit, der Gemeinplatz.

platitudinous [plæti'tju:dinəs], *adj.* nichtssagend.

platoon [plə'tu:n], s. (*Mil.*) der Zug.

plaudit ['plɔ:dit], s. der Beifall.

plausible ['plɔ:zibl], *adj.* wahrscheinlich, glaubwürdig, einleuchtend.

play [plei], s. das Spiel (*game*); (*Theat.*) das Stück. — *v.a., v.n.* spielen.

player ['pleiə], s. der Spieler; (*Theat.*) der Schauspieler.

playful ['pleiful], *adj.* spielerisch, spielend.

playground ['pleigraund], s. der Spielplatz.

playhouse ['pleihaus], s. das Schauspielhaus.

playmate ['pleimeit], *s.* der Spielgefährte.

playwright ['pleirait], *s.* der Dramatiker, Schauspieldichter.

plea [pli:], *s.* die Bitte; das Gesuch; der Vorwand.

plead [pli:d], *v.a., v.n.* plädieren, sich berufen auf; vorschützen (*claim*).

pleasant ['plezənt], *adj.* angenehm, freundlich.

pleasantry ['plezəntri], *s.* das freundliche Wort, der Scherz (*joke*).

please [pli:z], *v.a., v.n.* gefallen; einen Gefallen tun (*do a favour*); —! bitte, haben Sie die Güte!; *if you* —, wenn Sie nichts dagegen haben.

pleasing ['pli:ziŋ], *adj.* einnehmend, angenehm.

pleasure ['pleʒə], *s.* das Vergnügen; *at your* —, nach Belieben; *take* — *in*, Vergnügen finden an (*Dat.*).

pleat [pli:t], *v.a.* plissieren. — *s.* die Falte, das Plissee.

pledge [pledʒ], *s.* das Pfand, die Bürgschaft (*guarantee*); das Versprechen (*promise*). — *v.a.* sich verbürgen, versprechen; zutrinken (*drink to*).

plenary ['pli:nəri], *adj.* Plenar-, vollständig.

plenipotentiary [plenipo'tenʃəri], *s.* der Bevollmächtigte.

plenitude ['plenitju:d], *s.* die Fülle.

plenteous, plentiful ['plentiəs, 'plentiful], *adj.* reichlich, in Fülle.

plenty ['plenti], *s.* die Fülle.

pleurisy ['pluərəsi], *s.* (*Med.*) die Brustfellentzündung.

pliable, pliant ['plaiəbl, 'plaiənt], *adj.* geschmeidig, biegsam.

pliers ['plaiəz], *s. pl.* die Drahtzange.

plight (1) [plait], *s.* die Notlage.

plight (2) [plait], *v.a.* feierlich versprechen.

plod [plɔd], *v.n.* schwerfällig gehen (*walk*); sich plagen (*work hard*).

plot (1) [plɔt], *s.* das Stück Land, der Bauplatz.

plot (2) [plɔt], *s.* das Komplott, die Verschwörung; die Handlung (*book, play etc.*). — *v.a.* aushecken (*ambush etc.*), planen.

plough, plow [plau], *s.* der Pflug. — *v.a.* pflügen; (*coll.*) *be* —*ed*, durchfallen (*in*, in, *Dat.*).

ploughshare ['plauʃeə], *s.* die Pflugschar.

plover ['plʌvə], *s.* (*Orn.*) der Kiebitz, Regenpfeifer.

plow *see under* **plough.**

pluck (1) [plʌk], *v.a.* pflücken (*flowers*); rupfen (*feathers*); — *up courage*, Mut fassen.

pluck (2) [plʌk], *s.* (*coll.*) der Mut.

plucky ['plʌki], *adj.* mutig.

plug [plʌg], *s.* (*Elec.*) der Stecker; der Stöpsel (*stopper*); *sparking* —, (*Motor.*) die Zündkerze. — *v.a.* stöpseln, zustopfen (*block*); (*fig.*) betonen, herausstellen (*repeat for advertisement*).

plum [plʌm], *s.* (*Bot.*) die Pflaume; (*coll.*) das Beste.

plumage ['plu:midʒ], *s.* (*Orn.*) das Gefieder.

plumb [plʌm], *s.* das Senkblei, Lot; — *-rule*, die Senkwaage. — *adv.* senkrecht, gerade, lotrecht.

plume [plu:m], *s.* die (Schmuck)feder.

plump [plʌmp], *adj.* dick, drall.

plunder ['plʌndə], *v.a., v.n.* plündern. — *s.* die Beute, der Raub.

plunge [plʌndʒ], *v.a., v.n.* untertauchen, stoßen, hinabstürzen.

plunger ['plʌndʒə], *s.* der Taucher; (*Engin.*) der Tauchkolben.

pluperfect [plu:'pə:fikt], *s.* (*Gram.*) das Plusquamperfektum.

plural ['pluərəl], *s.* (*Gram.*) der Plural, die Mehrzahl.

plurality [pluə'ræliti], *s.* die Mehrzahl, der Plural.

plus [plʌs], *prep.* plus, zuzüglich.

plush [plʌʃ], *s.* (*Text.*) der Plüsch.

ply [plai], *s.* die Falte (*fold*), Lage (*layer*). — *v.a.* ausüben (*trade*).

plywood ['plaiwud], *s.* das Sperrholz, die Sperrholzplatte.

pneumonia [nju'mouniə], *s.* (*Med.*) die Lungenentzündung.

poach (1) [poutʃ], *v.n.* wildern; — *on*, übergreifen auf.

poach (2) [poutʃ], *v.a.* ohne Schale kochen; *poached eggs*, verlorene Eier, *n. pl.*

poacher ['poutʃə], *s.* der Wilderer, Wilddieb.

pocket ['pɔkit], *s.* die Tasche; — *book*, die Brieftasche; das Taschenbuch; — *money*, das Taschengeld.

pod [pɔd], *s.* (*Bot.*) die Schote.

poem ['pouim], *s.* das Gedicht.

poet ['pouit], *s.* der Dichter.

poetic(al) [pou'etik(l)], *adj.* dichterisch.

poignancy ['pɔinjənsi], *s.* die Schärfe.

poignant ['pɔinjənt], *adj.* scharf, beißend, schmerzlich.

point [pɔint], *s.* der Punkt (*of remark, sentence*); die Sache; der Zweck; die Spitze (*of pencil etc.*); *make a* —, es sich zur Aufgabe machen; *in* — *of fact*, tatsächlich; *come to the* —, zur Sache kommen. — *v.a., v.n.* spitzen, zuspitzen (*pencil*); — *out*, zeigen, (hin)deuten, — *to*, hinweisen auf; — *the moral*, die Moral erklären.

pointblank ['pɔint'blæŋk], *adj., adv.* schnurgerade, direkt.

pointed ['pɔintid], *adj.* scharf, spitzig, deutlich (*remark*).

pointer ['pɔintə], *s.* der Zeiger; (*fig.*) der Fingerzeig (*hint*).

poise [pɔiz], *s.* das Gleichgewicht; (*fig.*) angemessenes Benehmen, die Grazie. — *v.a.* abwägen; im Gleichgewicht halten. — *v.n.* schweben; —*d for action*, tatbereit.

poison [pɔizn], *s.* das Gift. — *v.a.* vergiften.

poke

poke (1) [pouk], *v.a.* schüren (*fire*); stoßen; — *fun at*, sich lustig machen über. — *s.* der Stoß; — *in the ribs*, ein Rippenstoß.

poke (2) [pouk], *s.* der Sack; *a pig in a* —, die Katze im Sack.

poker (1) ['poukə], *s.* der Schürhaken, das Schüreisen.

poker (2) ['poukə], *s.* (*Cards*) das Pokerspiel.

polar ['poulə], *adj.* (*Geog.*) Polar-; (*Phys.*) polar.

polarity [po'læriti], *s.* die Polarität.

Pole [poul], *s.* der Pole.

pole (1) [poul], *s.* (*Geog.*) der Pol.

pole (2) [poul], *s.* die Stange (*rod*); der Pfahl (*upright*).

poleaxe ['poulæks], *s.* die Streitaxt.

polecat ['poulkæt], *s.* (*Zool.*) der Iltis.

polemic [pɔ'lemik], *s.* die Polemik, der Streit.

police [pə'li:s], *s.* die Polizei. — *v.a.* polizeilich beaufsichtigen.

policeman [pə'li:smən], *s.* der Polizist.

policy (1) ['pɔlisi], *s.* die Politik.

policy (2) ['pɔlisi], *s.* (*Insurance*) die Police.

Polish ['pouliʃ], *adj.* polnisch.

polish ['pɔliʃ], *v.a.* polieren. — *s.* die Politur, der Glanz.

polished ['pɔliʃd], *adj.* glatt (*smooth*); (*fig.*) wohlerzogen, fein (*manners*).

polite [pə'lait], *adj.* höflich.

politeness [pə'laitnis], *s.* die Höflichkeit.

politic ['pɔlitik], *adj.* politisch; schlau (*cunning*).

political [pə'litikəl], *adj.* politisch; staatskundig.

politician [pɔli'tiʃən], *s.* der Politiker, Staatsmann.

politics ['pɔlitiks], *s.* (*sometimes pl.*) die Politik, politische Gesinnung.

poll [poul], *s.* die Wahl (*election*). — *v.n.* abstimmen, wählen, seine Stimme abgeben.

pollard ['pɔləd], *s.* (*Bot.*) der gekappte Baum; (*Zool.*) das hornlose Tier.

pollen ['pɔlən], *s.*(*Bot.*) der Blütenstaub.

pollinate ['pɔlineit], *v.a.* (*Bot.*) bestäuben.

polling ['pouliŋ], *s.* die Wahl, der Wahlgang (*election*); — *station*, das Wahllokal.

pollute [pə'lju:t], *v.a.* verunreinigen.

pollution [pə'lju:ʃən], *s.* die Verunreinigung.

poltroon [pɔl'tru:n], *s.* die Memme.

poly- ['pɔli], *pref.* viel-.

Polynesian [pɔli'ni:ziən], *adj.* polynesisch. — *s.* der Polynesier.

polytechnic [pɔli'teknik], *s.* das Technikum; polytechnische Fachschule.

pomegranate ['pɔm-, 'pʌmgrænit], *s.* (*Bot.*) der Granatapfel.

Pomeranian [pɔmə'reiniən], *adj.* pommerisch. — *s.* der Pommer; der Spitz (*dog*).

pommel [pʌml], *s.* der Sattelknopf; der Knauf (*sword*). — *v.a.* schlagen.

pomp [pɔmp], *s.* der Pomp, das Gepränge.

pompous ['pɔmpəs], *adj.* hochtrabend, prahlerisch; (*manner*) schwerfällig, wichtigtuerisch.

pond [pɔnd], *s.* der Teich.

ponder ['pɔndə], *v.a.*, *v.n.* bedenken, überlegen.

ponderous ['pɔndərəs], *adj.* schwer, schwerfällig.

pontiff ['pɔntif], *s.* der Hohepriester; der Papst.

pontifical [pɔn'tifikəl], *adj.* bischöflich, päpstlich. — *s. pl.* die bischöfliche Amtstracht.

pontificate [pɔn'tifikit], *s.* das (*or* der) Pontifikat. — [-keit], *v.n.* (*coll.*) predigen.

pontoon (1) [pɔn'tu:n], *s.* die Schiffsbrücke, der Brückenkahn.

pontoon (2) [pɔn'tu:n], *s.* (*cards*) das Einundzwanzig, Vingt-et-un.

pony ['pouni], *s.* (*Zool.*) der *or* das Pony.

poodle [pu:dl], *s.* (*Zool.*) der Pudel.

pooh-pooh [pu:'pu:], *v.a.* verspotten.

pool (1) [pu:l], *s.* die Lache, der Pfuhl.

pool (2) [pu:l], *s.* (*fig.*) der gemeinsame Einsatz (*money, forces etc.*). — *v.a.* zusammenschließen.

poop [pu:p], *s.* (*Naut.*) das Heck, Hinterteil.

poor [puə], *adj.* arm, dürftig; *in* — *health*, bei schwacher Gesundheit; (*fig.*) armselig, schlecht.

pop [pɔp], *v.n.* knallen, explodieren. — *v.a.* (*coll.*) schnell versetzen, verpfänden.

Pope [poup], *s.* (*Eccl.*) der Papst.

poplar ['pɔplə], *s.* (*Bot.*) die Pappel.

poppy ['pɔpi], *s.* (*Bot.*) der Mohn.

populace ['pɔpjulis], *s.* der Pöbel.

popular ['pɔpjulə], *adj.* volkstümlich, beliebt.

popularity [pɔpju'læriti], *s.* die Beliebtheit.

populate ['pɔpjuleit], *v.a.* bevölkern.

population [pɔpju'leiʃən], *s.* die Bevölkerung.

populous ['pɔpjuləs], *adj.* dicht bevölkert.

porcelain ['pɔ:slin], *s.* das Porzellan, das Geschirr.

porch [pɔ:tʃ], *s.* die Eingangshalle, Vorhalle.

porcupine ['pɔ:kjupain], *s.* (*Zool.*) das Stachelschwein.

pore (1) [pɔ:], *s.* die Pore.

pore (2) [pɔ:], *v.n.* sich vertiefen (*over, in*), brüten (*über*).

pork [pɔ:k], *s.* das Schweinefleisch.

porosity [pɔ:'rɔsiti], *s.* die Porosität.

porous ['pɔ:rəs], *adj.* porös.

porpoise ['pɔ:pəs], *s.* (*Zool.*) der Tümmler, das Meerschwein.

porridge ['pɔridʒ], *s.* (*Cul.*) der Haferbrei.

porringer ['pɔrindʒə], *s.* (*Cul.*) der Napf.

port (1) [pɔ:t], *s.* der Hafen.

port (2) [pɔ:t], *s.* der Portwein (*wine*).

portable ['pɔ:təbl], *adj.* tragbar; Koffer- (*radio etc.*).
portcullis [pɔ:'tkʌlis], *s.* das Fallgatter.
portend [pɔ:'tend], *v.a.* vorbedeuten, ahnen lassen.
portent ['pɔ:tent], *s.* die Vorbedeutung.
porter ['pɔ:tə], *s.* (*Railw.*) der Gepäckträger; der Pförtner, Portier (*caretaker, janitor*); das Porterbier (*beer*).
porterage ['pɔ:təridʒ], *s.* der Trägerlohn, die Zustellkosten, *f.pl.*
portfolio [pɔ:t'fouliou], *s.* die Mappe; (*Pol.*) das Ressort; das Portefeuille.
portico ['pɔ:tikou], *s.* (*Archit.*) die Säulenhalle.
portion ['pɔ:ʃən], *s.* die Portion, der Anteil. — *v.a.* aufteilen, austeilen (*share out*).
portliness ['pɔ:tlinis], *s.* die Stattlichkeit (*dignity*); Behäbigkeit (*corpulence*).
portly ['pɔ:tli], *adj.* stattlich (*dignified*); behäbig (*corpulent*).
portmanteau [pɔ:t'mæntou], *s.* der Handkoffer.
portrait ['pɔ:trit], *s.* (*Art*) das Bildnis, Porträt.
portray [pɔ:'trei], *v.a.* im Bilde darstellen, porträtieren; (*fig.*) schildern, darstellen (*describe*).
Portuguese [pɔ:tju'gi:z], *adj.* portugiesisch. — *s.* der Portugiese.
pose [pouz], *s.* die Haltung, Stellung (*of model etc.*). — *v.a.* in Pose stellen; aufwerfen (*question*). — *v.n.* (*as model*) stehen, sitzen; — *as*, posieren, sich ausgeben als (*pretend to be*).
poser ['pouzə], *s.* die schwierige Frage.
position [pə'ziʃən], *s.* die Lage (*situation*); die Stellung (*job*); der Stand, Rang (*rank*); (*Astron., Mil.*) die Position.
positive ['pɔzitiv], *adj.* positiv; (*fig.*) ausdrücklich, sicher (*sure*).
possess [pə'zes], *v.a.* besitzen.
possession [pə'zeʃən], *s.* der Besitz, Besitztum.
possessive [pə'zesiv], *adj.* (*Gram.*) besitzanzeigend, possessiv; (*fig.*) besitzgierig.
possibility [pɔsi'biliti], *s.* die Möglichkeit.
possible ['pɔsibl], *adj.* möglich.
post (1) [poust], *s.* der Pfosten (*pillar*).
post (2) [poust], *s.* die Post (*mail*); der Posten (*job*). — *v.a.* zur Post geben; (*coll.*) einstecken (*letter*).
postage ['poustidʒ], *s.* das Porto; — *stamp*, die Briefmarke.
postal [poustl], *adj.* Post-.
poster ['poustə], *s.* das Plakat.
posterity [pɔs'teriti], *s.* die Nachwelt.
posthumous ['pɔstjuməs], *adj.* hinterlassen, nach dem Tode, postum.
postman ['poustmən], *s.* der Briefträger.
postmark ['poustmɑ:k], *s.* der Poststempel.
post-mortem [poust'mɔ:təm], *s.* — — —

(*examination*), die Obduktion, Leichenschau.
post-office ['poustɔfis], *s.* das Postamt.
postpone [poust'poun], *v.a.* verschieben, aufschieben.
postscript ['poustskript], *s.* die Nachschrift.
postulate ['pɔstjuleit], *v.a.* postulieren, voraussetzen.
posture ['pɔstʃə], *s.* die Positur, Haltung (*of body*).
pot [pɔt], *s.* der Topf; die Kanne (*beer*); (*coll.*) *go to* —, zugrunde gehen. — *v.a.* einkochen, einmachen; (*fig.*) kürzen.
potash ['pɔtæʃ], *s.* (*Chem.*) die Pottasche.
potassium [pə'tæsiəm], *s.* (*Chem.*) das Kalium.
potato [pə'teitou], *s.* (*Bot.*) die Kartoffel.
potent ['poutənt], *adj.* kräftig, stark, wirksam.
potential [pə'tenʃəl], *s.* das Potential. — *adj.* möglich, potentiell (*possible*).
potter ['pɔtə], *s.* der Töpfer.
pottery ['pɔtəri], *s.* die Töpferei; die Töpferwaren, Tonwaren, *f. pl.* (*goods*).
pouch [pautʃ], *s.* der Beutel.
poulterer ['poultərə], *s.* der Geflügelhändler.
poultice ['poultis], *s.* der Umschlag.
poultry ['poultri], *s.* das Geflügel.
pounce (1) [pauns], *s.*(*obs.*) die Klaue. — *v.n.* — *upon*, herfallen (über, *Acc.*).
pounce (2) [pauns], *s.* das Bimssteinpulver. — *v.a.* (mit Bimsstein) abreiben.
pound (1) [paund], *s.* das Pfund; das Pfund Sterling.
pound (2) [paund], *v.a.* zerstoßen.
poundage ['paundidʒ], *s.* das Pfundgeld, die Gebühr pro Pfund.
pour [pɔ:], *v.a.* gießen, schütten, einschenken. — *v.n.* strömen.
pout [paut], *v.n.* schmollen.
poverty ['pɔvəti], *s.* die Armut.
powder ['paudə], *s.* (*Mil.*) das Pulver; der Puder (*face etc.*). — *v.a.* zu Pulver machen, stoßen; (*face*) pudern.
power [pauə], *s.* die Macht, Gewalt; Kraft; Fähigkeit; — *of attorney*, die Vollmacht; (*Maths.*) die Potenz; (*Elec.*) der Strom; — *house*, — *station*, das Elektrizitätswerk; — *cut*, die Stromstörung.
powerful ['pauəful], *adj.* kräftig, mächtig, einflußreich.
powerless ['pauəlis], *adj.* kraftlos, machtlos.
pox [pɔks], *s.* (*Med.*) die Pocken, *f. pl.*; die Syphilis.
practicable ['præktikəbl], *adj.* ausführbar, tunlich.
practical ['præktikəl], *adj.* praktisch.
practice ['præktis], *s.* die Ausübung (*doing, carrying out*); die Praxis.
practise ['præktis], *v.a.* ausführen, ausüben (*a profession etc.*); üben (*rehearse*). — *v.n.* sich üben.

practised

practised ['præktisd], *adj.* geübt, geschult (in).
practitioner [præk'tiʃənə], *s.* (*Med.*) praktischer Arzt; (*Law*) Advokat.
pragmatic [præg'mætik], *adj.* pragmatisch.
prairie ['prɛəri], *s.* die Prärie.
praise [preiz], *v.a.* preisen, loben. — *s.* das Lob.
pram *see under* **perambulator.**
prance [prɑːns], *v.n.* sich bäumen; (*fig.*) sich brüsten (*brag*).
prank [præŋk], *s.* der Streich.
prate [preit], *v.n.* plappern, schwatzen.
prattle [prætl], *v.n.* plaudern, schwatzen. — *s.* das Geschwätz.
prawn [prɔːn], *s.* (*Zool.*) die Steingarnele.
pray [prei], *v.n.* beten. — *v.a.* bitten, ersuchen (*beseech*).
prayer [prɛə], *s.* das Gebet.
preach [priːtʃ], *v.a., v.n.* predigen.
preacher ['priːtʃə], *s.* der Prediger.
preamble [priː'æmbl], *s.* die Vorrede, der Einleitungsparagraph.
precarious [pri'kɛəriəs], *adj.* unsicher, prekär.
precaution [pri'kɔːʃən], *s.* die Vorsichtsmaßregel.
precede [pri'siːd], *v.a., v.n.* vorausgehen, den Vortritt haben.
precedence ['priːsidəns *or* pri'siːdəns], *s.* der Vortritt, Vorrang.
precedent ['prisidənt], *s.* der Präzedenzfall.
precept ['priːsept], *s.* die Vorschrift, Regel.
preceptor [pri'septə], *s.* der Lehrer, Lehrmeister.
precinct ['priːsiŋkt], *s.* das Gebiet, der Bezirk; (*pl.*) die Grenzen, *f. pl.*
precious ['preʃəs], *adj.* wertvoll, kostbar; — *metal*, das Edelmetall.
precipice ['presipis], *s.* der Abgrund.
precipitous [pri'sipitəs], *adj.* jäh, abschüssig.
precise [pri'sais], *adj.* genau, bestimmt.
precision [pri'siʒən], *s.* die Präzision, Genauigkeit; (*Engin.*) — *tool*, das Präzisionswerkzeug.
preclude [pri'kluːd], *v.a.* ausschließen.
precocious [pri'kouʃəs], *adj.* frühreif.
preconceive [priːkən'siːv], *v.a.* vorher denken.
preconceived [priːkən'siːvd], *adj.* vorgefaßt.
preconception [priːkən'sepʃən], *s.* das Vorurteil.
precursor [pri'kəːsə], *s.* der Vorläufer.
predatory ['predətəri], *adj.* räuberisch, Raub-.
predecessor ['priːdisesə], *s.* der Vorgänger.
predestin(at)e [priː'destin(eit)], *v.a.* vorher bestimmen; (*Theol.*) prädestinieren.
predicament [pri'dikəmənt], *s.* die Verlegenheit.
predicate ['predikit], *s.* (*Gram.*) das Prädikat. — [-keit], *v.a.* behaupten.

predict [pri'dikt], *v.a.* voraussagen, vorhersagen.
prediction [pri'dikʃən], *s.* die Vorhersage (*weather etc.*); die Weissagung (*prophecy*).
predilection [priːdi'lekʃən], *s.* die Vorliebe.
predispose [priːdis'pouz], *v.a.* vorbereiten; empfänglich machen.
predominant [pri'dɔminənt], *adj.* vorherrschend.
predominate [pri'dɔmineit], *v.n.* vorherrschen.
pre-eminence [priː'eminəns], *s.* der Vorrang.
prefabricate [priː'fæbrikeit], *v.a.* vorfabrizieren, als Fertigteil herstellen, in der Fabrik herstellen.
prefabrication [priːfæbri'keiʃən], *s.* die Vorfabrizierung.
preface ['prefis], *s.* das Vorwort.
prefatory ['prefətəri], *adj.* einleitend.
prefect ['priːfekt], *s.* der Präfekt.
prefer [pri'fəː], *v.a.* vorziehen.
preference ['prefərəns], *s.* der Vorzug (*Comm.*) — *share*, die Vorzugsaktie.
preferment [pri'fəːmənt], *s.* die Beförderung.
prefix ['priːfiks], *s.* die Vorsilbe. — [priː'fiks], *v.a.* vorsetzen.
pregnancy ['pregnənsi], *s.* die Schwangerschaft.
pregnant ['pregnənt], *adj.* schwanger.
prejudge [priː'dʒʌdʒ], *v.a.* vorher urteilen, voreilig urteilen.
prejudice ['predʒudis], *s.* das Vorurteil. — *v.a.* beeinträchtigen.
prejudicial [predʒu'diʃəl], *adj.* schädlich.
prelate ['prelit], *s.* (*Eccl.*) der Prälat.
preliminary [pri'liminəri], *adj.* vorläufig, Präliminar-. —*s.* (*pl.*) die Vorbereitungen, *f. pl.*
prelude ['preljuːd], *s.* das Vorspiel.
premature ['premətʃə], *adj.* vorschnell, übereilt, vorzeitig.
premeditate [priː'mediteit], *v.a.* (*Law*) vorher überlegen.
Premier ['premiə], *s.* der Premierminister.
premise (1) ['premis], *s.* (*Log.*) die Prämisse; (*pl.*) das Haus, Grundstück; die Stätte, der Ort; das Lokal (*inn etc.*).
premise (2) [priː'maiz], *v.a.* vorausschicken.
premium ['priːmiəm], *s.* die Prämie.
premonition [priːmə'niʃən], *s.* die Vorahnung.
preoccupation [priːɔkju'peiʃən], *s.* die Zerstreutheit.
preoccupied [priː'ɔkjupaid], *adj.* besorgt; zerstreut (*absent-minded*).
preparation [prepə'reiʃən], *s.* die Vorbereitung; Zubereitung (*of meals*).
preparatory [pri'pærətri], *adj.* vorbereitend; — *school*, die Vorschule.
prepare [pri'pɛə], *v.a., v.n.* vorbereiten (*for, auf*); zubereiten (*meals*).
prepay [priː'pei], *v.a. irr.* vorausbezahlen; (*post*) frankieren.

preponderant [pri'pɔndərənt], *adj.* überwiegend.

preponderate [pri'pɔndəreit], *v.a., v.n.* überwiegen.

preposition [prepə'ziʃən], *s.* (*Gram.*) die Präposition.

prepossess [pri:pə'zes], *v.a.* einnehmen, beeindrucken.

preposterous [pri'pɔstərəs], *adj.* töricht, lächerlich, unerhört.

prerogative [pri'rɔgətiv],*s.*das Vorrecht.

presage [pri'seidʒ], *v.a.* prophezeien. — ['presidʒ], *s.* die Prophezeiung.

prescient ['preʃiənt, 'pri:–], *adj.* vorahnend, vorherwissend.

prescribe [pri'skraib], *v.a., v.n.* vorschreiben; (*Med.*) verschreiben, verordnen.

prescription [pri'skripʃən], *s.* die Vorschrift(*precept*); (*Med.*) das Rezept.

presence ['prezəns], *s.* die Gegenwart, Anwesenheit (*attendance*); das Äußere (*appearance*); — *of mind*, die Geistesgegenwart.

present (1) ['prezənt], *adj.* anwesend, gegenwärtig; jetzig. — *s.* (*Gram.*) das Präsens, die Gegenwart; (*time*) die Gegenwart, heutige Zeit.

present (2) [pri'zənt], *v.a.* darstellen (*on stage*); vorstellen (*introduce*); präsentieren (*arms*); schenken, geben (*gifts*). — ['prezənt], *s.* das Geschenk (*gift*).

presentation [prezən'teiʃən], *s.* die Darstellung (*stage, art*); die Vorstellung (*introduction*); die Überreichung (*of gift*).

presentiment [pri'zentimənt], *s.* das Vorgefühl, die Vorahnung.

presently ['prezəntli], *adv.* bald, sogleich.

preservation [prezə'veiʃən], *s.* die Erhaltung, Bewahrung.

preservative [pri'zə:vətiv], *s.* das Konservierungsmittel.

preserve [pri'zə:v], *v.a.* bewahren, erhalten; (*fruit*) einmachen. — *s.* (*Hunt.*) das Jagdgehege, Jagdrevier, (*pl.*) die Konserven, *f. pl.*

preside [pri'zaid], *v.n.* (*over*) den Vorsitz führen.

president ['prezidənt], *s.* der Präsident.

press [pres], *v.a., v.n.* drücken (*push*); bügeln, plätten (*iron*); nötigen (*force*); dringend bitten (*entreat*). — *s.* die Presse (*newspapers, printing*); der Schrank (*cupboard*); das Gedränge (*crowd*).

pressing ['presiŋ], *adj.* dringend.

pressure ['preʃə], *s.* der Druck.

prestige [pres'ti:ʒ], *s.* das Prestige, Ansehen.

presumable [pri'zju:məbl], *adj.* mutmaßlich, vermutlich.

presume [pri'zju:m], *v.a., v.n.* vermuten; — *on*, sich anmaßen.

presumption [pri'zʌmpʃən], *s.* die Annahme; die Anmaßung (*arrogance*).

presumptive [pri'zʌmptiv], *adj.* mutmaßlich.

presumptuous [pri'zʌmptjuəs], *adj.* anmaßend, dreist, vermessen.

presuppose [pri:sə'pouz], *v.a.* voraussetzen.

pretence [pri'tens], *s.* der Vorwand.

pretend [pri'tend], *v.a., v.n.* vortäuschen, vorgeben.

pretension [pri'tenʃən], *s.* die Anmaßung, der Anspruch (*to, auf*).

pretentious [pri'tenʃəs], *adj.* anspruchsvoll.

preterite ['pretərit], *s.* (*Gram.*) das Präteritum.

pretext ['pri:tekst], *s.* der Vorwand.

pretty ['priti], *adj.* hübsch, nett. — *adv.* (*coll.*) ziemlich.

prevail [pri'veil], *v.n.* vorherrschen, die Oberhand gewinnen.

prevalence ['prevələns], *s.* das Vorherrschen.

prevaricate [pri'værikeit], *v.n.* Ausflüchte machen.

prevent [pri'vent], *v.a.* verhindern.

prevention [pri'venʃən], *s.* die Verhinderung.

preventive [pri'ventiv],*adj.*vorbeugend.

previous ['pri:viəs], *adj.* vorhergehend.

prey [prei], *s.* die Beute, der Raub. — *v.n.* rauben, nachstellen.

price [prais], *s.* der Preis, Wert.

priceless ['praislis], *adj.* unschätzbar, unbezahlbar.

prick [prik], *s.* der Stachel, Stich (*stab*). — *v.a.* stechen (*stab*); punktieren (*puncture*).

prickle [prikl], *s.* (*Bot.*) der Stachel.

pride [praid], *s.* der Stolz. — *v.r.* — *o.s.*, sich brüsten, stolz sein (*on, auf, Acc.*).

priest [pri:st], *s.* (*Eccl.*) der Priester.

prig [prig], *s.* der eingebildete Tropf; Tugendheld.

priggish ['prigiʃ], *adj.* dünkelhaft, selbstgefällig.

prim [prim], *adj.* steif, spröde.

primacy ['praiməsi], *s.* der, das Primat.

primæval [prai'mi:vəl], *adj.* Ur-, anfänglich, ursprünglich.

primary ['praiməri], *adj.* erst, ursprünglich; Haupt- (*main*). — *s.* (*pl.*) (*Am.*) die Vorwahlen, *f. pl.* (*Presidential elections*).

prime [praim], *adj.* erst, wichtigst. — *s.* die Blüte, Vollendung, Vollkraft.

primer ['praimə], *s.* das Elementarbuch, die Fibel.

primitive ['primitiv], *adj.* primitiv; ursprünglich (*original*).

primness ['primnis], *s.* die Geziertheit, Steifheit.

primrose ['primrouz], *s.* (*Bot.*) die Primel.

prince [prins], *s.* der Prinz; Fürst (*rank*).

princess [prin'ses], *s.* die Prinzessin.

principal ['prinsipl], *s.* der Direktor (*business*); Rektor (*school etc.*); (*Comm.*) das Kapital; (*Mus.*) der erste Spieler. — *adj.* erst, Haupt-.

principality [prinsi'pæliti], *s.* das Fürstentum.

principle

principle ['prinsipl], s. das Prinzip, der Grundsatz.
print [print], v.a. drucken, abdrucken. — s. (Typ., Art) der Druck; out of —, vergriffen.
printer ['printə], s. der (Buch-)drucker.
prior [praiə], adj. früher, eher; — to, vor (Dat.). — s. (Eccl.) der Prior.
priority [prai'ɔriti], s. die Priorität, der Vorrang.
prise [praiz], v.a. — open, gewaltsam öffnen, aufbrechen.
prism [prizm], s. das Prisma.
prison [prizn], s. das Gefängnis.
prisoner ['prizənə], s. der Gefangene, Sträfling.
pristine ['pristain], adj. ehemalig, vormalig, ursprünglich.
privacy ['praivəsi or 'privəsi], s. die Zurückgezogenheit, Stille.
private ['praivit], adj. privat, persönlich, vertraulich (confidential). — s. (Mil.) der Gemeine, Landser.
privation [prai'veiʃən], s. der Mangel, die Entbehrung (lack); die Beraubung (deprivation).
privilege ['privilidʒ], s. das Privileg, Vorrecht. — v.a. ausnehmen, privilegieren.
privy ['privi], s. der Abtritt, Abort. — adj. — to, mitwissend; Privy Council, der Staatsrat.
prize [praiz], s. der Preis, die Belohnung; — v.a. hochschätzen.
prizewinner ['praizwinə], s. der Preisträger; Nobel —, der Nobelpreisträger.
probability [prɔbə'biliti], s. die Wahrscheinlichkeit.
probable ['prɔbəbl], adj. wahrscheinlich.
probate ['proubeit], s. (Law) die Testamentsbestätigung.
probation [pro'beiʃən], s. die Bewährung, Bewährungsfrist (period).
probationary [pro'beiʃənəri], adj. Bewährungs-.
probe [proub], v.a. sondieren, untersuchen. — s. die Sonde, Prüfung.
probity ['proubiti], s. die Redlichkeit, Anständigkeit.
problem ['prɔbləm], s. das Problem.
problematic [prɔblə'mætik], adj. zweifelhaft, problematisch.
proboscis [prɔ'bɔsis],s.(Ent.) der Rüssel.
procedure [prə'si:dʒə], s. der Vorgang, das Verfahren.
proceed [prə'si:d], v.n. vorgehen, verfahren.
proceeds ['prousi:dz], s. pl. der Ertrag.
process (1) ['prouses], s. der Vorgang, Prozeß. — v.a. verarbeiten, fertigen.
process (2) [pro'ses], v.n. in einem Zuge gehen.
procession [prə'seʃən], s. der (feierliche) Umzug, die Prozession.
proclaim [prə'kleim], v.a. (Pol.) proklamieren, ausrufen.
proclamation [prɔklə'meiʃən], s. (Pol.)

die Ausrufung, Proklamation.
proclivity [prə'kliviti], s. der Hang, die Neigung (tendency).
procrastinate [prə'kræstineit], v.a. aufschieben. — v.n. zögern, zaudern.
procreate ['proukrieit], v.a. zeugen, hervorbringen.
procurable [prə'kjuərəbl], adj. zu verschaffen, erhältlich.
procure [prə'kjuə], v.a. verschaffen, besorgen.
prod [prɔd], v.a. stoßen.
prodigal ['prɔdigəl], adj. verschwenderisch, vergeudend; — son, der verlorene Sohn.
prodigious [prə'didʒəs], adj. erstaunlich, ungeheuer.
prodigy ['prɔdidʒi], s. das Wunderkind.
produce [prə'dju:s], v.a. erzeugen, produzieren. — ['prɔdju:s], s. das Produkt, Erzeugnis.
producer [prə'dju:sə], s. der Erzeuger; (Theat., Cinema) der Regisseur.
product ['prɔdʌkt], s. das Produkt, Erzeugnis.
production [prə'dʌkʃən], s. die Produktion; die Erzeugung (industrial); das Zeigen, Vorweisen (of documents); (Theat.) die Regie.
productive [prə'dʌktiv], adj. produktiv, schöpferisch (mind); fruchtbar (soil).
profane [prə'fein], adj. profan; ruchlos.
profanity [prə'fæniti], s. die Profanierung; das Lästern.
profess [prə'fes], v.a., v.n. bekennen, erklären, sich bekennen zu.
profession [prə'feʃən], s. der (höhere) Beruf; (Eccl.) das Bekenntnis; die Beteuerung (protestation).
professional [prə'feʃənəl], adj. beruflich, berufsmäßig.
professor [prə'fesə], s. der (Universitäts) Professor.
professorship [prə'fesəʃip], s. die Professur.
proffer ['prɔfə], v.a. anbieten (offer).
proficiency [prə'fiʃənsi], s. die Tüchtigkeit; (skill) die Beherrschung.
proficient [prə'fiʃənt], adj. bewandert, tüchtig; (in language) fließend.
profile ['proufail], s. das Profil.
profit ['prɔfit], s. der Profit, Gewinn, Nutzen. — v.n. Nutzen ziehen. — v.a. von Nutzen sein (Dat.).
profound [prə'faund], adj. tief; gründlich (thorough).
profuse [prə'fju:s], adj. reichlich, verschwenderisch.
profusion [prə'fju:ʒen], s. der Überfluß.
progeny ['prɔdʒəni], s. der Nachkomme; die Nachkommenschaft.
prognosticate [prɔg'nɔstikeit], v.a. vorhersagen.
prognostication [prɔgnɔsti'keiʃən], s. die Voraussage.
programme, (Am.) program ['prougræm], s. das Programm.
progress ['prougres], s. der Fortschritt. — [prou'gres], v.n. fortschreiten, Fortschritte machen.

464

progression [proˈgreʃən], s. (Maths.) die Reihe, Progression.

progressive [proˈgresiv], adj. fortschrittlich (modern); fortschreitend (continuous); progressiv.

prohibit [prouˈhibit], v.a. verbieten.

prohibition [prouiˈbiʃən], s. das Verbot.

project [prəˈdʒekt], v.a. projizieren; entwerfen. — [ˈprɔdʒekt], s. das Projekt, der Plan.

projectile [prəˈdʒektail], s. das Geschoß.

projection [prəˈdʒekʃən], s. die Projektion (film); der Entwurf (plan); der Vorsprung (jutting out).

proletarian [prouliˈtɛəriən], adj. proletarisch. — s. der Prolet(arier).

prolific [prəˈlifik], adj. fruchtbar.

prolix [ˈprouliks], adj. weitschweifig.

prologue [ˈproulɔg], s. der Prolog.

prolong [prəˈlɔŋ], v.a. verlängern, prolongieren.

prominent [ˈprɔminənt], adj. prominent, hervorragend.

promiscuous [prəˈmiskjuəs], adj. unterschiedslos (indiscriminate); vermischt (mixed).

promise [ˈprɔmis], v.a. versprechen. — v.n. Erwartungen erwecken. — s. das Versprechen.

promissory [ˈprɔmisəri], adj. versprechend; (Comm.) — note, der Schuldschein.

promontory [ˈprɔməntəri], s. das Vorgebirge.

promote [prəˈmout], v.a. befördern; fördern (foster).

promotion [prəˈmouʃən], s. die Beförderung (advancement); Förderung (fostering); (Am.) die Reklame (publicity).

prompt [prɔmpt], adj. prompt, pünktlich. — v.a. (Theat.) soufflieren; treiben (inspire).

prompter [ˈprɔmptə], s. (Theat.) der Souffleur.

promptitude [ˈprɔmptitjuːd], s. die Promptheit, Pünktlichkeit.

promulgate [ˈprɔmelgeit], v.a. bekanntmachen, verbreiten.

prone [proun], adj. geneigt, neigend.

prong [prɔŋ], s. die Zinke, Gabel.

pronominal [proˈnɔminəl], adj. (Gram.) pronominal.

pronoun [ˈprounaun], s. das Fürwort, Pronomen.

pronounce [prəˈnauns], v.a., v.n. aussprechen (words); feierlich erklären (proclaim).

pronunciation [prənʌnsiˈeiʃən], s. die Aussprache.

proof [pruːf], s. der Beweis, die Probe; (Typ.) der Korrekturbogen. — v.a. (Engin., Chem.) impregnieren.

prop [prɔp], s. die Stütze, der Stützpfahl. — v.a. stützen.

propaganda [prɔpəˈgændə], s. die Propaganda, Reklame.

propagate [ˈprɔpəgeit], v.a. propagieren; (Bot.) fortpflanzen.

propel [prəˈpel], v.a. forttreiben, vorwärtstreiben.

propeller [prəˈpelə], s. der Propeller, die Schraube.

propensity [prəˈpensiti], s. die Neigung, der Hang.

proper [ˈprɔpə], adj. schicklich (manners); eigentümlich, eigen (peculiar).

property [ˈprɔpəti], s. das Eigentum (possession); die Eigenschaft (quality).

prophecy [ˈprɔfisi], s. die Prophezeiung, Weissagung.

prophesy [ˈprɔfisai], v.a. prophezeien.

propitiate [prəˈpiʃieit], v.a. versöhnen.

propitiation [prəpiʃiˈeiʃən], s. die Versöhnung.

propitious [prəˈpiʃəs], adj. gnädig, günstig, geneigt.

proportion [prəˈpɔːʃən], s. das Verhältnis; die Proportion; der Anteil (portion); das Ebenmaß (in art).

proportionate [prəˈpɔːʃənit], adj. im Verhältnis, verhältnismäßig, proportioniert.

proposal [prəˈpouzəl], s. der Vorschlag, Antrag.

propose [prəˈpouz], v.a. antragen, beantragen, vorschlagen. — v.n. — to a lady, einen Heiratsantrag machen.

proposition [prɔpəˈziʃən], s. der Vorschlag, Antrag; die Idee.

propound [prəˈpaund], v.a. vorlegen, vorbringen (a theory etc.).

proprietor [prəˈpraiətə], s. der Eigentümer.

propriety [prəˈpraiəti], s. die Schicklichkeit.

propulsion [prəˈpʌlʃən], s. der Antrieb.

prorogue [prəˈroug], v.a. vertagen.

prosaic [prəˈzeiik], adj. prosaisch, nüchtern.

proscribe [proˈskraib], v.a. verbieten, ächten.

proscription [proˈskripʃən], s. die Verbannung, das Verbot.

prose [prouz], s. die Prosa.

prosecute [ˈprɔsikjuːt], v.a. verfolgen; (Law) gerichtlich verfolgen, anklagen.

prosecutor [ˈprɔsikjuːtə], s. (public) der Staatsanwalt; der Kläger.

proselyte [ˈprɔsəlait], s. der Neubekehrte, Proselyt.

prospect [ˈprɔspekt], s. die Aussicht; (pl.) die Aussichten, Chancen, f.pl. — [prɔsˈpekt], v.n. suchen (for, nach, Dat.).

prospectus [prəˈspektəs], s. der Prospekt.

prosper [ˈprɔspə], v.n. gedeihen, blühen. — v.a. segnen.

prosperity [prɔsˈperiti], s. der Wohlstand; der Reichtum; das Gedeihen (thriving).

prosperous [ˈprɔspərəs], adj. glücklich, wohlhabend.

prostitute [ˈprɔstitjuːt], s. die Prostituierte, Dirne. — v.a. erniedrigen.

prostrate [ˈprɔstreit], adj. hingestreckt, niedergeworfen, fußfällig. — [prɔsˈtreit], v.a. niederwerfen.

465

prosy

prosy ['prouzi], *adj.* prosaisch, weitschweifig, langweilig.

protect [prə'tekt], *v.a.* beschützen.

protection [prə'tekʃən], *s.* der Schutz; die Protektion (*favour*).

protective [prə'tektiv], *adj.* Schutz-, schützend.

protector [prə'tektə], *s.* der Beschützer; (*Engin.*) der Schutz.

protest [prə'test], *v.a.,v.n.* protestieren, einwenden. — ['proutest], *s.* der Protest, Einspruch.

Protestant ['prɔtistənt], *adj.* protestantisch. — *s.* der Protestant.

protestation [prɔtes'teiʃən], *s.* die Beteuerung, Verwahrung.

protocol ['proutəkɔl], *s.* das Protokoll.

prototype ['proutotaip], *s.* das Urbild, Modell, der Prototyp.

protract [prə'trækt], *v.a.* in die Länge ziehen; hinausziehen.

protractor [prə'træktə], *s.* der Winkelmesser, Transporteur, die Schmiege.

protrude [prə'tru:d], *v.n.* herausragen, hervorstehen, vordringen.

protuberance [prə'tju:bərəns], *s.* der Höcker, der Auswuchs, die Protuberanz.

proud [praud], *adj.* stolz (*of*, auf, *Acc.*).

prove [pru:v], *v.a.* beweisen. — *v.n.* sich erweisen (*turn out*).

provender ['provində], *s.* das Viehfutter.

proverb ['provə:b], *s.* das Sprichwort.

proverbial [prə'və:biəl], *adj.* sprichwörtlich.

provide [prə'vaid], *v.a., v.n.* vorsehen, versorgen, verschaffen.

provided [prə'vaidid], *conj.* vorausgesetzt.

providence ['providəns], *s.* die Vorsehung.

provident ['providənt], *adj.* vorsorglich.

providential [provi'denʃəl], *adj.* von der Vorsehung bestimmt.

province ['provins], *s.* die Provinz, das Gebiet (*also fig.*).

provincial [prə'vinʃəl], *adj.* ländlich, Provinz-; provinziell.

provision [prə'viʒən], *s.* die Versorgung (*supply*); der Vorrat (*stock*); (*pl.*) die Lebensmittel (*victuals*).

provisional [prə'viʒənəl], *adj.* vorläufig.

proviso [prə'vaizou], *s.* der Vorbehalt.

provocation [provə'keiʃən], *s.* die Herausforderung.

provoke [prə'vouk], *v.a.* herausfordern, provozieren.

prow [prau], *s.* (*Naut.*) der Bug.

prowess ['praues], *s.* die Stärke (*physical*); die körperliche Tüchtigkeit; Tapferkeit.

prowl [praul], *v.n.* herumstreichen.

proximity [prɔk'simiti], *s.* die Nähe.

proxy ['prɔksi], *s.* der Stellvertreter.

prudence ['pru:dəns], *s.* die Klugheit, Vorsicht.

prudent ['pru:dənt], *adj.* klug, vorsichtig.

prudery ['pru:dəri], *s.* die Sprödigkeit.

prudish ['pru:diʃ], *adj.* prüde, spröde, zimperlich.

prune (1) [pru:n], *s.* (*Cul.*) die Backpflaume.

prune (2) [pru:n], *v.a.* beschneiden, stutzen.

Prussian ['prʌʃən], *adj.* preußisch; — *blue*, das Berlinerblau. — *s.* der Preuße.

prussic ['prʌsik], *adj.* blausauer; — *acid*, die Blausäure.

pry [prai], *v.n.* spähen, ausforschen.

psalm [sɑ:m], *s.* der Psalm.

psychology [sai'kɔlədʒi], *s.* die Psychologie.

pub [pʌb], *s.* das Wirtshaus, die Kneipe.

puberty ['pju:bəti], *s.* die Pubertät, Mannbarkeit.

public ['pʌblik], *adj.* öffentlich. — *s.* das Publikum; die Öffentlichkeit.

publican ['pʌblikən], *s.* der Gastwirt.

publication [pʌbli'keiʃən], *s.* die Veröffentlichung, Herausgabe.

publicity [pʌb'lisiti], *s.* die Werbung, die Reklame; — *manager*, der Reklamechef, Werbeleiter.

publicize ['pʌblisaiz], *v.a.* weithin bekannt machen, publizieren.

publish ['pʌbliʃ], *v.a.* veröffentlichen; verlegen (*books*); — *ing house*, der Verlag.

publisher ['pʌbliʃə], *s.* der Verleger.

pucker ['pʌkə], *v.a.* falten; runzeln (*wrinkle*). — *s.* die Falte.

pudding ['pudiŋ], *s.* der Pudding.

puddle [pʌdl], *s.* die Pfütze. — *v.a.* puddeln (*iron*).

puerile ['pjuərail], *adj.* kindisch, knabenhaft.

puff [pʌf], *v.a., v.n.* puffen, paffen, blasen; —*ed-up*, aufgebläht, stolz. — *s.* der Windstoß; — *pastry*, der Blätterteig.

pug [pʌg], *s.* (*Zool.*) der Mops.

pugnacious [pʌg'neiʃəs], *adj.* kampfsüchtig, kampflustig.

puisne ['pju:ni], *adj.* (*Law*) jünger, Unter-.

puissant ['pwi:sənt], *adj.* mächtig, stark.

puke [pju:k], *v.n.* sich erbrechen.

pull [pul], *v.a., v.n.* ziehen, reißen; zerren. — *s.* der Zug, Ruck.

pullet ['pulit], *s.* (*Orn.*) das Hühnchen.

pulley ['puli], *s.* der Flaschenzug.

pulmonary, pulmonic ['pʌlmənəri, pʌl'mɔnik], *adj.* Lungen-.

pulp [pʌlp], *s.* der Brei; das Fleisch (*of fruit*); das Mark (*marrow*); die Pulpa (*tooth*). — *v.a.* zerstampfen, zu Brei stampfen.

pulpit ['pulpit], *s.* (*Eccl.*) die Kanzel.

pulsate [pʌl'seit], *v.n.* pulsieren, schlagen.

pulse (1) [pʌls], *s.* der Puls.

pulse (2) [pʌls], *s.* (*Bot.*) die Hülsenfrüchte, *f. pl.*

pulverize ['pʌlvəraiz], *v.a.* zu Pulver stoßen, zerstoßen.

pumice ['pʌmis], *s.* der Bimsstein.
pump (1) [pʌmp], *s.* die Pumpe. — *v.a.,*
v.n. pumpen; ausfragen (*question*).
pump (2) [pʌmp], *s.* der Tanzschuh
(*dancing shoe*).
pumpkin ['pʌmpkin], *s.* (*Bot.*) der
Kürbis.
pun [pʌn], *s.* das Wortspiel. — *v.n.*
Wortspiele machen.
Punch [pʌntʃ], *s.* das Kasperle; — *and*
Judy, Hanswurst und seine Frau.
punch (1) [pʌntʃ], *v.a.* schlagen,
boxen (*box*). — *s.* der Schlag (*hit*);
der Faustschlag (*boxing*).
punch (2) [pʌntʃ], *v.a.* lochen (*card*). —
s. der Pfriem (*tool*).
punch (3) [pʌntʃ], *s.* der Punsch (*drink*).
punchy ['pʌntʃi], *adj.* kurz, dick,
untersetzt.
punctilious [pʌŋk'tiliəs], *adj.* sorgfältig, spitzfindig.
punctual ['pʌŋktjuəl], *adj.* pünktlich.
punctuate ['pʌŋktjueit], *v.a.* (*Gram.*)
interpunktieren; (*fig.*) betonen.
punctuation [pʌŋktjuˈeiʃən], *s.* (*Gram.*)
die Interpunktion.
puncture ['pʌŋktʃə], *s.* (*Motor.*) der
Reifendefekt, die Panne; (*Med.*) die
Punktur, der Einstich. — *v.a.* (*Med.*)
punktieren.
pungent ['pʌndʒənt], *adj.* scharf,
stechend.
punish [pʌniʃ], *v.a.* bestrafen (*s.o.*);
strafen.
punishable ['pʌniʃəbl], *adj.* strafbar.
punishment ['pʌniʃmənt], *s.* die Strafe,
Bestrafung.
punt [pʌnt], *s.* das kleine Boot, Flachboot.
puny ['pjuːni], *adj.* schwach, winzig.
pup [pʌp], *s.* der junge Hund; *be*
sold a —, einen schlechten Kauf
machen. — *v.n.* Junge werfen.
pupil (1) ['pjuːpil], *s.* der Schüler.
pupil (2) ['pjuːpil], *s.* die Pupille (*eye*).
pupil(l)age ['pjuːpilidʒ], *s.* die Minder-
jährigkeit (*of minor*).
puppet ['pʌpit], *s.* die Puppe, Marionette; der Strohmann (*human tool*).
puppy ['pʌpi] *see* **pup.**
purblind ['pəːblaind], *adj.* halbblind.
purchase ['pəːtʃis], *s.* der Kauf, Einkauf. — *v.a.* kaufen.
pure ['pjuə], *adj.* pur, rein.
purge [pəːdʒ], *v.a.* reinigen. — *s.* die
Reinigung; (*Pol.*) die Säuberung.
purify ['pjuərifai], *v.a.* läutern, reinigen.
purl (1) [pəːl], *s.* die Borte; (*knitting*)
die Häkelkante.
purl (2) [pəːl], *v.n.* sich drehen,
wirbeln; (*sl.*) umkippen.
purl (3) [pəːl], *s.* das Murmeln, Rieseln
(*of brook*). — *v.n.* murmeln, rieseln.
purloin [pəːˈlɔin], *v.a.* stehlen.
purple [pəːpl], *adj.* purpurn; — *patch,*
die Glanzstelle. — *s.* der Purpur.
purport [pəːˈpɔːt], *v.a.* bedeuten, Sinn
haben. — ['pəːpət], *s.* der Sinn, die
Bedeutung.
purpose ['pəːpəs], *s.* die Absicht, der
Zweck.

purposeful ['pəːpəsful], *adj.* zweck-
bewußt, energisch, zielbewußt.
purr [pəː], *v.n.* schnurren (*of cat*).
purse [pəːs], *s.* die Börse, Geldtasche;
das Portemonnaie.
pursuance [pəˈsjuːəns], *s.* (*Law*) die
Verfolgung, Ausführung.
pursuant [pəˈsjuːənt], *adj.* (*Law*)
zufolge, gemäß (*to, Dat.*).
pursue [pəˈsjuː], *v.a.* verfolgen.
pursuit [pəˈsjuːt], *s.* die Verfolgung;
(*pl.*) die Geschäfte, *n. pl.*; Beschäftigung.
purvey [pəˈvei], *v.a.* versorgen, liefern.
purview ['pəːvjuː], *s.* der Spielraum;
das Blickfeld.
push [puʃ], *v.a.* stoßen, drücken,
schieben, drängen; *be —ed for,* in der
Klemme sein. — *s.* der Stoß, Schub,
das Drängen; *at a —,* wenn absolut
nötig.
pusillanimous [pjuːsiˈlæniməs], *adj.*
kleinmütig.
puss, pussy [pus, 'pusi], *s.* (*coll.*) die
Katze, das Kätzchen, Miezchen.
put [put], *v.a. irr.* setzen (*set*),legen(*lay*),
stellen (*stand*); — *off,* aufschieben,
aus der Fassung bringen (*deflect*); —
on, anziehen, auflegen; — *it on thickly,*
es dick auftragen. — *v.n.* (*Naut.*) —
in, anlegen.
putrefy ['pjuːtrifai], *v.a., v.n.* faul
werden (*rot*), verwesen.
putrid ['pjuːtrid], *adj.* faul (*rotten*).
puttee ['pʌtiː], *s.* (*Mil.*) die Wickel-
gamasche.
putty ['pʌti], *s.* der Kitt.
puzzle [pʌzl], *s.* das Rätsel. — *v.a.* zu
denken geben (*Dat.*).
pygmy ['pigmi], *s.* der Pygmäe.
pyjamas, (*Am.*) **pajamas** [piˈdʒɑːməz,
pə-], *s. pl.* der Schlafanzug.
pyramid ['pirəmid], *s.* die Pyramide.
pyre [paiə], *s.* der Scheiterhaufen.
pyrotechnics [paiərəˈtekniks], *s. pl.*
das Feuerwerk, die Feuerwerkskunst.
python ['paiθən], *s.* (*Zool.*) die Riesenschlange.

Q

Q [kjuː]. das Q.
qua [kwei], *conj.* als.
quack [kwæk], *v.n.* quaken; (*coll.*)
quacksalbern. — *s.* der Quacksalber.
quadrangle ['kwɔdræŋgl], *s.* (*abbr.*
quad [kwɔd]), das Viereck; der Hof
(*in college etc.*).
quadrant ['kwɔdrənt], *s.* der Quadrant,
Viertelkreis; (*Engin.*) der Winkelmesser.
quadrille [kwɔˈdril], *s.* die Quadrille,
der Kontertanz.

quadruped

quadruped ['kwɔdruped], *s.* (*Zool.*) das vierfüßige Tier.

quadruple ['kwɔdrupl], *adj.* vierfach.

quaff [kwæf], *v.a.* schlucken. — *v.n.* zechen (*drink heavily*).

quagmire ['kwægmaiə], *s.* der Sumpf.

quail (1) [kweil], *s.* (*Orn.*) die Wachtel.

quail (2) [kweil], *v.n.* verzagen.

quaint [kweint], *adj.* seltsam, wunderlich, eigenartig.

quake [kweik], *v.n.* erzittern, beben.

Quaker ['kweikə], *s.* der Quäker.

qualification [kwɔlifi'keiʃən], *s.* die Befähigung, Qualifikation (*ability*); die Einschränkung (*proviso*).

qualify ['kwɔlifai], *v.a.* befähigen (*make able*); beschränken, mäßigen, qualifizieren (*modify*). — *v.n.* sich qualifizieren, das Studium abschließen.

qualitative ['kwɔlitətiv], *adj.* qualitätsmäßig, Wert-, qualitativ.

quality ['kwɔliti], *s.* die Qualität (*high class*); der Wert (*standard*).

qualm [kwɑ:m], *s.* der Skrupel.

quantitative ['kwɔntitətiv], *adj.* quantitativ.

quantity ['kwɔntiti], *s.* die Quantität, Menge.

quantum ['kwɔntəm], *s.* die Menge; das Quantum; — *theory*, die Quantentheorie.

quarantine ['kwɔrənti:n], *s.* die Quarantäne.

quarrel ['kwɔrəl], *s.* der Streit, Zwist. — *v.n.* streiten, zanken.

quarry (1) ['kwɔri], *s.* der Steinbruch.

quarry (2) ['kwɔri], *s.* die Beute (*prey*).

quart [kwɔ:t], *s.* das Viertelmaß (*1.15 litre*).

quarter ['kwɔ:tə], *s.* das Viertel (jahr); (*Arith.*) das Viertel (*also of town*); (*pl.*) das Quartier.

quartermaster ['kwɔ:təmɑ:stə], *s.* (*Mil.*) der Feldzeugmeister.

quartet(te) [kwɔ:'tet], *s.* das Quartett.

quarto ['kwɔ:tou], *s.* das Quartformat.

quartz [kwɔ:ts], *s.* der Quartz.

quash [kwɔʃ], *v.a.* unterdrücken (*suppress*); (*Law*) annullieren.

quaver ['kweivə], *s.* (*Mus.*) die Achtelnote; der Triller (*trill*). — *v.n.* tremolieren, trillern.

quay [ki:], *s.* der Kai, Hafendamm.

queen [kwi:n], *s.* die Königin.

queer [kwiə], *adj.* seltsam, sonderlich.

quell [kwel], *v.a.* unterdrücken.

quench [kwentʃ], *v.a.* löschen; stillen (*thirst*).

querulous ['kweruləs], *adj.* mürrisch, jämmerlich; zänkisch.

query ['kwiəri], *s.* die Frage. — *v.a.* in Frage stellen.

quest [kwest], *s.* das Suchen, Streben; die Suche.

question ['kwestʃən], *s.* die Frage; — *mark*, das Fragezeichen. — *v.a.* fragen, in Frage stellen; ausfragen (*s.o.*).

questionable ['kwestʃənəbl], *adj.* zweifelhaft, fraglich, bedenklich.

queue [kju:], *s.* die Schlange, das Anstellen. — *v.n.* Schlange stehen.

quibble [kwibl], *s.* die Ausflucht. — *v.n.* um Worte streiten.

quick [kwik], *adj.* schnell (*fast*); lebendig (*live*).

quicken ['kwikən], *v.a.* beleben, anfeuern.

quicklime ['kwiklaim], *s.* der ungelöschte Kalk.

quicksand ['kwiksænd], *s.* der Flugsand.

quicksilver ['kwiksilvə], *s.* (*Chem.*) das Quecksilber.

quid (1) [kwid], *s.* (*sl.*) das Pfund Sterling.

quid (2) [kwid], *s.* (*Lat.*) etwas; — *pro quo*, Gleiches mit Gleichem.

quiescence [kwi'esəns], *s.* die Ruhe.

quiet ['kwaiət], *adj.* ruhig.

quietism ['kwaiətizm], *s.* der Quietismus.

quietness ['kwaiətnis], *s.* die Ruhe, Stille.

quill [kwil], *s.* der Federkiel, die Feder. — *v.a.* falten, fälteln.

quilt [kwilt], *s.* die Steppdecke.

quince [kwins], *s.* (*Bot.*) die Quitte.

quinine [kwi'ni:n], *s.* (*Med.*) das Chinin.

quinquennial [kwiŋ'kweniəl], *adj.* fünfjährig, fünfjährlich, alle fünf Jahre.

quinsy ['kwinzi], *s.* (*Med.*) die Bräune.

quint [kwint], *s.* (*Mus.*) die Quinte.

quintessence [kwin'tesəns], *s.* die Quintessenz, der Kern, der Inbegriff.

quintuple ['kwintjupl], *adj.* fünffach.

quip [kwip], *s.* die Stichelei; die witzige Bemerkung.

quire [kwaiə], *s.* das Buch Papier.

quirk [kwə:k], *s.* die (unerwartete) Wendung; Spitzfindigkeit.

quit [kwit], *v.a., v.n.* verlassen; weggehen; (*Am.*) aufhören. — *adj.* (*pl.*) (**quits**) quitt, bezahlt.

quite [kwait], *adv.* ganz, völlig.

quiver (1) ['kwivə], *s.* der Köcher.

quiver (2) ['kwivə], *v.n.* erzittern, schauern.

quiz [kwiz], *s.* das Fragespiel, Quizprogramm (*Radio etc.*).

quoit [kɔit], *s.* die Wurfscheibe.

quorum ['kwɔ:rəm], *s.* die beschlußfähige Anzahl.

quota ['kwoutə], *s.* die Quote.

quotation [kwo'teiʃən], *s.* das Zitat; (*Comm.*) der Kostenanschlag, die Notierung.

quote [kwout], *v.a.* zitieren; (*Comm.*) einen Preis zitieren, notieren.

R

R [ɑ:(r)]. das R.

rabbet ['ræbit], *s.* die Fuge, Nute. — *v.a.* einfugen.

ransom

rabbi ['ræbai], s. (Rel.) der Rabbiner.
rabbit ['ræbit], s. (Zool.) das Kaninchen.
rabble [ræbl], s. der Pöbel.
rabid ['ræbid], adj. wütend, rasend.
race (1) [reis], s. die Rasse; das Geschlecht (stock).
race (2) [reis], s. das Rennen (horses etc.); der Wettlauf (run); — course, die Rennbahn. — v.a., v.n. um die Wette laufen.
racial ['reiʃəl], adj. rassisch.
raciness ['reisinis], s. das Rassige, die Urwüchsigkeit.
rack [ræk], s. die Folterbank; das Reck (gymnasium); (Railw.) das Gepäcknetz. — v.a. recken, strecken; — o.'s brains, sich den Kopf zerbrechen.
racket (1), racquet ['rækit], s. der Tennisschläger.
racket (2) ['rækit], s. der Lärm (noise, din).
racket (3) ['rækit], s. (coll.) der Schwindel.
racketeer [ræki'tiə], s. der Schwindler.
racy ['reisi], adj. stark; pikant.
radar, ['reida:], s. das Radar.
radiance ['reidiəns], s. der Glanz, das Strahlen.
radiant ['reidiənt], adj. strahlend.
radiate ['reidieit], v.a., v.n. strahlen, ausstrahlen.
radiator ['reidieitə], s. der Heizapparat, Heizkörper; (Motor.) der Kühler.
radical ['rædikəl], adj. (Pol.) radikal; gründlich (thorough). — s. (Pol.) der Radikale; (Phonet.) der Grundlaut, Wurzellaut.
radio ['reidiou], s. das Radio, der Rundfunk.
radioactive [reidiou'æktiv], adj. radioaktiv.
radish ['rædiʃ], s. (Bot.) der Rettich.
radius ['reidiəs], s. der Radius, Halbmesser; (Phys., Maths.) der Strahl (line).
raffle [ræfl], s. die Auslosung. — v.a. auslosen, ausspielen.
raft [ra:ft], s. das Floß.
rafter ['ra:ftə], s. der Dachsparren.
rag (1) [ræg], s. der Lumpen.
rag (2) [ræg], v.a. necken, zum Besten haben (tease).
ragamuffin ['rægəmʌfin], s. der Lumpenkerl.
rage [reidʒ], s. die Wut, Raserei; die Manie, Mode (fashion). — v.n. wüten, rasen.
ragged ['rægid], adj. zerlumpt; zackig, rauh (rough).
ragout [ra'gu:], s. (Cul.) das Ragout.
raid [reid], s. der Streifzug, die Razzia; der Angriff. — v.a. überfallen.
rail (1) [reil], s. (Railw.) die Schiene; by —, mit der Eisenbahn.
rail (2) [reil], v.n. schmähen; spotten (Genit.).
railing ['reiliŋ], s. das Geländer, Gitter.
raillery ['reiləri], s. die Spöttelei, das Schmähen.

railway, (Am.) railroad ['reilwei, 'reilroud], s. die Eisenbahn.
raiment ['reimənt], s. (Poet.) die Kleidung.
rain [rein], s. der Regen. — v.n. regnen.
rainbow ['reinbou], s. der Regenbogen.
raincoat ['reinkout], s. der Regenmantel.
raise [reiz], v.a. heben (lift); steigern (prices); aufbringen (army, money); züchten (breed); aufziehen (children). — s. (Am.) die Steigerung, Erhöhung (salary).
raisin ['reizin], s. (Bot.) die Rosine.
rake (1) [reik], s. der Rechen (tool). — v.a. zusammenrechen, harken; bestreichen (fire at).
rake (2) [reik], s. der Schlemmer (roué).
rakish ['reikiʃ], adj. liederlich.
rally ['ræli], v.a. sammeln, versammeln. — v.n. sich versammeln, sich scharen. — s. die Massenversammlung, Kundgebung; das Treffen.
ram [ræm], s. der Widder; (Mil.) die Ramme. — v.a. rammen.
ramble [ræmbl], v.n. (im Grünen) wandern; herumschweifen; einen Ausflug machen. — s. der Ausflug.
rambler ['ræmblə], s. der Wanderer (hiker); (Bot.) die Heckenrose.
ramification [ræmifi'keiʃən], s. die Verzweigung, Verästelung (also fig.); (pl.) Zweige, m. pl. (also fig.).
ramp [ræmp], v.n. sich ranken (of plants). — s. die Rampe.
rampant ['ræmpənt], adj. zügellos, grassierend (wild); (Her.) sich bäumend.
rampart ['ræmpa:t], s. der Wall.
ramshackle ['ræmʃækl], adj. wackelig, baufällig.
rancid ['rænsid], adj. ranzig.
rancour ['ræŋkə], s. der Groll, die Erbitterung.
random ['rændəm], s. at —, aufs Geratewohl. — adj. zufällig, Zufalls-.
range [reindʒ], s. die Reihe (row, series); (Geog.) die Bergkette; der Küchenherd (stove); (Mil.) die Schießstätte (shooting ground); die Schußweite, Reichweite (distance). — v.n. sich reihen; sich erstrecken (stretch). — v.a. rangieren, anordnen, durchstreifen.
rangefinder ['reindʒfaində], s. (Phot.) der Entfernungsmesser.
ranger ['reindʒə], s. der Förster, Forstgehilfe; (Mil.) der leichte Reiter.
rank (1) [ræŋk], s. die Klasse; der Rang (order); — and file, die Mannschaft (of members); die Mitgliedschaft, Masse. — v.n. sich reihen; gelten.
rank (2) [ræŋk], adj. übermäßig, üppig, allzu stark; ranzig (of fat etc.).
rankle [ræŋkl], v.n. nagen.
ransack ['rænsæk], v.a. plündern.
ransom ['rænsəm], s. das Lösegeld; hold to —, (gegen Lösegeld) gefangen halten. — v.a. loskaufen.

469

rant

rant [rænt], *v.n.* wüten; großtun; groß-sprechen.

rap [ræp], *v.a., v.n.* schlagen, klopfen.

rapacious [rə'peiʃəs], *adj.* raubgierig.

rape (1) [reip], *v.a.* vergewaltigen. — *s.* die Vergewaltigung.

rape (2) [reip], *s.* (*Bot.*) der Raps.

rapid ['ræpid], *adj.* rasch, schnell, reißend (*river*). — *s.* (*pl.*) die Strom-schnelle.

rapier ['reipiə], *s.* der Degen; (*fencing*) das Rapier.

rapine ['ræpain], *s.* (*Poet.*) der Raub.

rapt [ræpt], *adj.* entzückt; versunken.

rapture ['ræptʃə], *s.* das Entzücken.

rare (1) [rɛə], *adj.* selten.

rare (2) [rɛə], *adj.* (*meat*) rar.

rarity ['rɛəriti], *s.* die Seltenheit.

rascal ['rɑːskəl], *s.* der Schurke.

rash (1) [ræʃ], *adj.* unbesonnen.

rash (2) [ræʃ], *s.* der Ausschlag (*skin*).

rasher ['ræʃə], *s.* die Speckschnitte.

rasp [rɑːsp], *s.* die Raspel, Feile. — *v.a., v.n.* raspeln; heiser sein (*speech*).

raspberry ['rɑːzbəri], *s.* (*Bot.*) die Himbeere.

rat [ræt], *s.* (*Zool.*) die Ratte; (*fig.*) der Verräter.

ratable ['reitəbl], *adj.* steuerpflichtig.

rate (1) [reit], *s.* das Mass; der Tarif; die Geschwindigkeit (*speed*); Gemein-deabgabe (*tax*); das Verhältnis (*pro-portion*). — *v.a.* schätzen (*estimate*); (*Am.*) einschätzen, halten für.

rate (2) [reit], *v.a.* schelten (*berate*).

rather ['rɑːðə], *adv.* vielmehr, eher, lieber (*in comparisons*); — *good*, ziem-lich gut.

ratification [rætifi'keiʃən], *s.* die Be-stätigung; (*Pol.*) die Ratifizierung.

ratify ['rætifai], *v.a.* bestätigen; (*Pol.*) ratifizieren.

ratio ['reiʃiou], *s.* das Verhältnis.

ration ['ræʃən], *s.* die Ration.

rational ['ræʃənəl], *adj.* Vernunfts-, rationell, vernunftgemäß.

rattle [rætl], *s.* das Geklapper (*noise*); die Klapper (*toy etc.*); *death* —, das Todesröcheln. — *v.a.* klappern, Lärm machen; (*fig.*) aus der Fassung bringen; — *off*, herunterleiern. — *v.n.* rasseln, klappern.

raucous ['rɔːkəs], *adj.* heiser, rauh.

ravage ['rævidʒ], *v.a.* verheeren. — *s.* (*pl.*) die Verheerung, Verwüstung.

rave [reiv], *v.n.* vernarrt sein (*about*, in); schwärmen (*für*).

raven [reivn], *s.* (*Orn.*) der Rabe.

ravenous ['rævənəs], *adj.* gefräßig, gierig.

ravine [rə'viːn], *s.* die Schlucht.

ravish ['ræviʃ], *v.a.* schänden, enteh-ren; (*delight*) entzücken.

raw [rɔː], *adj.* rauh (*rough*); roh (*meat*); jung, grün (*novice*); *a — deal*, die unfaire Behandlung.

ray (1) [rei], *s.* (*Phys.*) der Strahl. — *v.n.* strahlen.

ray (2) [rei], *s.* (*Zool.*) der Rochen.

raze [reiz], *v.a.* radieren (*erase*); zer-stören (*destroy*).

razor ['reizə], *s.* der Rasierapparat; — *strop*, der Streichriemen.

re* [riː], *pref.* wieder —, noch einmal, zurück-.

* In the following pages, only those compounds are listed in which the meaning is different from the root word or where no simple stem exists.

reach [riːtʃ], *v.a.* reichen, erlangen (*attain*); reichen (*hand*); erreichen. — *s.* der Bereich, (*fig.*) die Weite.

react [ri'ækt], *v.n.* reagieren (*to*, auf, *Acc.*).

read (1) [riːd], *v.a., v.n. irr.* lesen; an-zeigen (*meter etc.*); — *for a degree*, studieren.

read (2) [red], *adj. well—*, belesen.

readable ['riːdəbl], *adj.* gut zu lesen, lesenswert; leserlich (*legible*).

reader ['riːdə], *s.* der Leser; (*Univ.*) der außerordentliche Professor; (*fig.*) das Lesebuch.

readiness ['redinis], *s.* die Bereitschaft, Bereitwilligkeit.

ready ['redi], *adj.* bereit, fertig; prompt; — *money*, das Bargeld.

real [riəl], *adj.* wirklich, wahr, tatsäch-lich; echt; — *estate*, der Grundbesitz.

realistic [riə'listik], *adj.* realistisch.

reality [ri'æliti], *s.* die Wirklichkeit.

realize ['riəlaiz], *v.a.* (*understand*) be-greifen; (*sell*) veräußern; verwirklichen.

realm [relm], *s.* das Reich.

reap [riːp], *v.a.* ernten.

rear (1) [riə], *adj.* hinter, nach-. — *s.* der Hintergrund; (*Mil.*) die Nachhut.

rear (2) [riə], *v.a.* aufziehen, erziehen (*bring up*). — *v.n.* sich bäumen.

reason ['riːzən], *s.* die Ursache, der Grund (*cause*); die Vernunft (*reason-ableness*). — *v.n.* argumentieren, debattieren.

reasonable ['riːzənəbl], *adj.* vernünftig; verständig.

reasonably ['riːzənəbli], *adv.* ziemlich, verhältnismäßig.

rebate ['riːbeit], *s.* der Rabatt.

rebel [rebl], *s.* der Rebell. — [ri'bel], *v.n.* sich empören.

rebound [ri:'baund], *v.n.* zurückprallen. —['riːbaund], *s.* der Rückprall.

rebuff [ri'bʌf], *s.* die Abweisung. — *v.a.* abweisen, zurückweisen.

rebuke [ri'bjuːk], *v.a.* zurechtweisen, tadeln. — *s.* der Tadel, die Kritik (an).

rebut [ri'bʌt], *v.a.* zurückweisen.

rebuttal [ri'bʌtl], *s.* die Widerlegung.

recalcitrant [ri'kælsitrənt], *adj.* wider-spenstig, störrisch.

recall [ri'kɔːl], *v.a.* zurückrufen; (*re-member*) sich erinnern.

recant [ri'kænt], *v.a., v.n.* widerrufen.

recapitulate [riːkə'pitjuleit], *v.a.* re-kapitulieren, wiederholen.

recast [riː'kɑːst], *v.a.* neu fassen, umar-beiten.

recede [ri'siːd], *v.n.* zurückgehen; heruntergehen (*prices etc.*).

refine

receipt [ri'si:t], s. die Empfangsbestäti-
gung, Quittung. — v.a. quittieren.
receive [ri'si:v], v.a. erhalten, empfangen; (Law) Diebesgut annehmen.
receiver [ri'si:və], s. der Empfänger;
(Law) der Hehler; (Telephone) der
Hörer; (Rad.) der Apparat.
recent ['ri:sənt], adj. jüngst, neuest.
recently ['ri:səntli], adv. vor kurzem.
reception [ri'sepʃən], s. der Empfang.
receptive [ri'septiv], adj. empfänglich.
recess [ri'ses], s. (Parl.) die Ferien, pl.;
die Pause; die Nische (nook).
recession [ri'seʃən], s. (Econ.) die
Rezession, die Baisse.
recipe ['resipi], s. (Cul.) das Rezept.
recipient [ri'sipiənt], s. der Empfänger
(of donation etc.).
reciprocal [ri'siprəkəl], adj. gegenseitig,
wechselseitig.
reciprocate [ri'siprəkeit], v.a., v.n. erwidern, vergelten.
recital [ri'saitl], s. der Vortrag; (Mus.)
das Solokonzert, Kammerkonzert.
recite [ri'sait], v.a. vortragen; (story)
erzählen, aufsagen.
reckless ['reklis], adj. leichtsinnig.
reckon ['rekən], v.n. rechnen (on, mit,
Dat.); dafür halten, denken (think).
reclamation [reklə'meiʃən], s. (Agr.)
die Urbarmachung; (fig.) die Beschwerde, Reklamation.
recline [ri'klain], v.n. sich zurücklehn-
nen.
recluse [ri'klu:s], s. der Einsiedler.
recognition [rekəg'niʃən], s. die Anerkennung.
recognize ['rekəgnaiz], v.a. anerkennen
(als) (acknowledge); erkennen (know
again).
recoil [ri'kɔil], v.n. zurückprallen,
zurückfahren.
recollect [rekə'lekt], v.a. sich erinnern
(an, Acc.).
recollection [rekə'lekʃən], s. die Erinnerung, das Gedächtnis.
recommend [rekə'mend], v.a. empfehlen.
recompense ['rekəmpens], v.a. vergelten, entschädigen, belohnen.
reconcile ['rekənsail], v.a. versöhnen.
reconciliation [rekənsili'eiʃən], s. die
Versöhnung.
recondite ['rekəndait], adj. dunkel,
verborgen, wenig bekannt.
reconnoitre [rekə'nɔitə], v.a. auskundschaften.
record [ri'kɔ:d], v.a. notieren, eintragen
(enter), festhalten; aufnehmen (tape
etc.). — ['rekɔ:d], s. die Aufzeichnung
(in writing); die Schallplatte (gramophone); (Sports) der Rekord.
recorder [ri'kɔ:də], s. der Protokollführer; (Law) der Richter; Syndikus,
Registrator; (Mus.) die Blockflöte.
recount [ri'kaunt], v.a. erzählen
recourse [ri'kɔ:s], s. die Zuflucht.
recover [ri'kʌvə], v.a. wiedererlangen.
— v.n. sich erholen.

recovery [ri'kʌvəri], s. die Wiederer-
langung (regaining); (Med.) die
Genesung, Erholung.
recreation [rekri'eiʃən], s. die Erholung.
recrimination [rekrimi'neiʃən], s. die
Gegenklage.
recruit [ri'kru:t], v.a. rekrutieren, anwerben. — s. der Rekrut.
rectangle ['rektæŋgl], s. das Rechteck.
rectify ['rektifai], v.a. richtigstellen;
(Elec.) gleichrichten, umformen.
rectilinear [rekti'liniə], adj. geradlinig.
rectitude ['rektitju:d], s. die Aufrichtigkeit.
rector ['rektə], s. (Eccl.) der Pfarrer;
der Rektor, Vorstand (institution).
recuperate [ri'kju:pəreit], v.n. sich
erholen.
recur [ri'kə:], v.n. sich wieder ereignen,
sich wiederholen.
recurrence [ri'kʌrəns], s. die Wiederholung.
red [red], adj. rot; — hot, glühend heiß.
redbreast ['redbrest], s. (Orn.) das
Rotkehlchen.
redeem [ri'di:m], v.a. erlösen.
redemption [ri'dempʃən], s. die Erlösung.
redolent ['redolənt], adj. duftend.
redound [ri'daund], v.n. gereichen, sich
erweisen.
redress [ri'dres], v.a. abhelfen (Dat.);
wieder herstellen. — s. die Abhilfe.
reduce [ri'dju:s], v.a. vermindern,
herabsetzen; (fig.) degradieren. —
v.n. (weight) abnehmen.
reduction [ri'dʌkʃən], s. die Herabsetzung (price etc.); die Verminderung
(decrease); (Chem.) die Reduktion.
redundant [ri'dʌndənt], adj. überflüssig.
reduplicate [ri:'dju:plikeit], v.a. verdoppeln.
reed [ri:d], s. (Bot.) das Schilfrohr;
(Mus.) die Rohrpfeife.
reef [ri:f], s. das Riff, Felsenriff; (Naut.)
das Reff.
reek [ri:k], v.n. rauchen, dampfen,
riechen. — s. der Rauch, Dampf, der
Gestank.
reel [ri:l], s. die Spule, Rolle, Haspel.
— v.a. — off, abrollen; (fig.) mechanisch hersagen. — v.n. taumeln.
refectory [ri'fektəri], s. der Speisesaal;
das Refektorium (in monastery etc.).
refer [ri'fə:], v.n. — to s.th., weiterleiten; überweisen; — to, sich beziehen (auf, Acc.).
referee [refə'ri:], s. der Referent;
(Sport) der Schiedsrichter.
reference ['refərəns], s. with — to, in
or mit Bezug auf; die Referenz,
Empfehlung; Verweisung (to, auf); —
library, die Nachschlagebibliothek; —
index, das (Nachschlags)verzeichnis.
refine [ri'fain], v.a. (Chem.) raffinieren;
(manners) verfeinern; (products) läutern, veredeln.

471

reflect

reflect [ri'flekt], *v.a.* widerspiegeln (*mirror*); ein Licht werfen (auf, *Acc.*). — *v.n.* — *on*, überlegen (*think over*).

reflection, reflexion [ri'flekʃən], *s.* die Überlegung, das Nachdenken; die Spiegelung, Reflexion.

reform [ri:'fɔ:m], *s.* die Reform, Verbesserung. — *v.a.* reformieren; ['ri:'fɔ:m] (sich) neu bilden. — *v.n.* sich bessern.

refractory [ri'fræktəri], *adj.* widerspenstig.

refrain (1) [ri'frein], *v.n.* — *from*, sich enthalten (*Genit.*); absehen von (*Dat.*).

refrain (2) [ri'frein], *s.* (*Mus., Poet.*) der Kehrreim.

refresh [ri'freʃ], *v.a.* erfrischen.

refrigerator [ri'fridʒəreitə], *s.* der Kühlschrank.

refuge ['refju:dʒ], *s.* die Zuflucht.

refugee [refju'dʒi:], *s.* der Flüchtling. — *adj.* Flüchtlings-.

refund [ri:'fʌnd], *v.a.* ersetzen, zurückzahlen. — ['ri:fʌnd], *s.* die Rückvergütung.

refusal [ri'fju:zəl], *s.* die Verweigerung.

refuse [ri'fju:z], *v.a.* verweigern, abschlagen. — *v.n.* — *to*, sich weigern. — ['refju:s], *s.* der Müll.

refute [ri'fju:t], *v.a.* widerlegen.

regal ['ri:gəl], *adj.* königlich.

regale [ri'geil], *v.a.* bewirten.

regalia [ri'geiliə], *s. pl.* die Kronjuwelen, *pl.*; (*fig.*) die Amtstracht, der Amtsschmuck.

regard [ri'ga:d], *v.a.* ansehen (*as*, als); beachten (*heed*); *as* —*s*, was ... betrifft. — *s.* die Hochachtung, Achtung (*esteem*); (*pl.*) die Grüsse, *m.pl.* with —, mit Bezug auf.

regarding [ri'ga:diŋ], *prep.* bezüglich, mit Bezug auf.

regardless [ri'ga:dlis], *adj.* rücksichtslos, ohne Rücksicht auf.

regency ['ri:dʒənsi], *s.* die Regentschaft.

regent ['ri:dʒənt], *s.* der Regent.

regiment ['redʒimənt], *s.* (*Mil.*) das Regiment. — [-ment], *v.a.* (*fig.*) regimentieren.

region ['ri:dʒən], *s.* die Gegend.

regional ['ri:dʒənəl], *adj.* örtlich, lokal, Bezirks-.

register ['redʒistə], *s.* das Register, die Liste. — *v.n.* sich eintragen.

registrar ['redʒistra:], *s.* der Registrator; der Standesbeamte (*births etc.*); der Kanzleidirektor (*institution*).

registry ['redʒistri], *s.* die Registratur.

regret [ri'gret], *v.a.* bereuen, bedauern. — *s.* die Reue; das Bedauern (*in formal apology*); *with* —, mit Bedauern.

regular ['regjulə], *adj.* regelmäßig; (*Am.*) anständig. — *s.* (*Mil.*) der Berufssoldat.

regulate ['regjuleit], *v.a.* regulieren, regeln.

regulation [regju'leiʃən], *s.* die Regelung; die Anordnung (*order*).

rehabilitate [ri:hə'biliteit], *v.a.* rehabilitieren.

rehearsal [ri'hə:sl], *s.* (*Theat., Mus.*) die Probe.

rehearse [ri'hə:s], *v.a.* proben, wiederholen.

reign [rein], *v.n.* herrschen, regieren. — *s.* die Herrschaft, Regierung.

rein [rein], *s.* der Zügel, der Zaum.

reindeer ['reindiə], *s.* (*Zool.*) das Ren, Rentier.

reinforce [ri:in'fɔ:s], *v.a.* betonen, verstärken.

reinforced [ri:in'fɔ:sd], *adj.* verstärkt; — *concrete*, der Eisenbeton.

reject [ri'dʒekt], *v.a.* ausschlagen, verwerfen.

rejection [ri'dʒekʃən], *s.* die Ablehnung, Verwerfung.

rejoice [ri'dʒɔis], *v.n.* sich freuen.

rejoin ['ri:'dʒɔin], *v.a.* wiedervereinigen. — [ri'dʒɔin], *v.n.* erwidern.

rejoinder [ri'dʒɔində], *s.* die Erwiderung.

relapse [ri'læps], *s.* der Rückfall. — *v.n.* fallen, zurückfallen.

relation [ri'leiʃən], *s.* die Beziehung (*connexion*); der, die Verwandte (*relative*); (*pl.*) die Verwandtschaft (*family*).

relative ['relətiv], *adj.* relativ; verhältnismäßig (*in proportion*). — *s.* der, die Verwandte.

relax [ri'læks], *v.n.* sich ausruhen; nachlassen. — *v.a.* entspannen.

relay [ri'lei], *v.a.* (*Rad.*) übertragen. — ['ri:lei], *s.* — *race*, der Staffellauf.

release [ri'li:s], *v.a.* freilassen, freisetzen (*prisoner*); freigeben (*news*). — *s.* die Freigabe (*news etc.*); die Freisetzung (*liberation*).

relegate ['religeit], *v.a.* verweisen, zurückweisen.

relent [ri'lent], *v.n.* nachgeben.

relentless [ri'lentlis], *adj.* unerbittlich, unnachgiebig.

relevance ['reləvəns], *s.* die Wichtigkeit.

relevant ['reləvənt], *adj.* wichtig, sachdienlich.

reliable [ri'laiəbl], *adj.* verläßlich, zuverlässig.

reliance [ri'laiəns], *s.* das Vertrauen.

relic ['relik], *s.* das Überbleibsel; das Andenken; (*Eccl.*) die Reliquie.

relief (1) [ri'li:f], *s.* die Erleichterung, Linderung, (*easement*); die Ablösung (*guard etc.*); die Aushilfe (*extra staff etc.*).

relief (2) [ri'li:f], *s.* (*Art*) das Relief.

relieve [ri'li:v], *v.a.* erleichtern; lindern (*pain*); ablösen (*from duty*).

religion [ri'lidʒən], *s.* die Religion.

religious [ri'lidʒəs], *adj.* religiös, gläubig, fromm.

relinquish [ri'liŋkwiʃ], *v.a.* verlassen, aufgeben.

relish ['reliʃ], *v.a.* Geschmack finden an. — *v.n.* schmecken. — *s.* der Geschmack, die Würze.

reluctance [ri'lʌktəns], *s.* der Widerwille, das Zögern.

reluctant [ri'lʌktənt], *adj.* widerwillig, widerstrebend.

rely [ri'lai], *v.n.* sich verlassen (*on*, auf); vertrauen (auf).

remain [ri'mein], *v.n.* bleiben, zurückbleiben, übrigbleiben.

remainder [ri'meində], *s.* der Rest.

remand [ri'mɑ:nd], *v.a.* — *in custody*, in die Untersuchungshaft zurückschicken. — *s.* — *home*, die Besserungsanstalt.

remark [ri'mɑ:k], *s.* die Bemerkung. — *v.a.* bemerken.

remarkable [ri'mɑ:kəbl], *adj.* bemerkenswert, außerordentlich.

remedial [rə'mi:diəl], *adj.* Heil-, abhelfend.

remedy ['remədi], *s.* das Heilmittel, Hilfsmittel. — *v.a.* abhelfen (*Dat.*).

remember [ri'membə], *v.a.* sich erinnern an; — *s.o. to s.o. else*, jemanden von jemandem grüßen lassen.

remembrance [ri'membrəns], *s.* die Erinnerung.

remind [ri'maind], *v.a.* erinnern (*of*, an), mahnen.

reminiscence [remi'nisəns], *s.* die Erinnerung.

remiss [ri'mis], *adj.* nachlässig.

remission [ri'miʃən], *s.* der Nachlaß; (*Rel.*) die Vergebung (*of sins*).

remit [ri'mit], *v.a.* (*Comm.*) überweisen, einsenden; erlassen (*forgive*).

remittance [ri'mitəns], *s.* (*Comm.*) die Rimesse, die Überweisung.

remnant ['remnənt], *s.* der Überrest.

remonstrate ['remənstreit], *v.n.* Vorstellungen machen.

remorse [ri'mɔ:s], *s.* die Reue.

remote [ri'mout], *adj.* fern, entlegen.

removal [ri'mu:vəl], *s.* das Wegschaffen (*taking away*); die Übersiedlung, der Umzug.

remove [ri'mu:v], *v.a.* entfernen. — *v.n.* umziehen. — *s.* (*Sch.*) die Versetzungsklasse; der Verwandtschaftsgrad (*relationship*).

removed [ri'mu:vd], *adj.* entfernt; *cousin once* —, der Vetter ersten Grades.

remuneration [rimju:nə'reiʃən], *s.* die Besoldung, Entlöhnung.

rend [rend], *v.a.* reißen, zerreißen.

render ['rendə], *v.a.* leisten (*service*); übersetzen (*translate*); wiedergeben; (*Comm.*) — *account*, Rechnung vorlegen.

rendering ['rendəriŋ], *s.* die Wiedergabe, der Vortrag (*of song etc.*); (*Comm.*) die Vorlage; die Übersetzung (*translation*).

renegade ['renigeid], *s.* der Abtrünnige.

renewal [ri'nju:əl], *s.* die Erneuerung; die Verlängerung (*extension*).

rennet ['renit], *s.* das Lab.

renounce [ri'nauns], *v.a.* entsagen (*Dat.*), verzichten auf (*Acc.*).

renown [ri'naun], *s.* der Ruhm.

rent (1) [rent], *v.a.* mieten, pachten. — *s.* die Miete, Pacht (*of land, farm*).

rent (2) [rent], *s.* der Riß (*tear*).

rental [rentl], *s.* die Miete.

renunciation [rinʌnsi'eiʃən], *s.* die Entsagung, der Verzicht.

repair [ri'pɛə], *v.a.* ausbessern, reparieren. — *s.* die Reparatur; *beyond* —, nicht reparierbar.

reparations [repə'reiʃənz], *s. pl.* (*Pol.*) die Reparationen, Wiedergutmachungskosten, *f. pl.*

repartee [repɑ:'ti:], *s.* die treffende Antwort.

repast [ri'pɑ:st], *s.* die Mahlzeit.

repeal [ri'pi:l], *v.a.* (*Parl.*) aufheben, widerrufen. — *s.* die Aufhebung.

repeat [ri'pi:t], *v.a.* wiederholen.

repent [ri'pent], *v.a.* bereuen.

repercussion [ri:pə'kʌʃən], *s.* der Rückstoß, die Rückwirkung.

repertory ['repətəri], *s.* (*Theat. etc.*) das Repertoire, der Spielplan.

repetition [repi'tiʃən], *s.* die Wiederholung.

replace [ri:'pleis], *v.a.* ersetzen.

replete [ri'pli:t], *adj.* voll, angefüllt.

reply [ri'plai], *v.n.* antworten, erwidern. — *s.* die Antwort.

report [ri'pɔ:t], *v.a., v.n.* berichten. — *s.* der Bericht; (*Sch.*) das Zeugnis; der Knall (*of explosion*).

repose [ri'pouz], *v.n.* ruhen. — *v.a.* setzen (*in*, auf). — *s.* die Ruhe, der Friede.

repository [ri'pɔzitəri], *s.* die Niederlage, Aufbewahrungsstätte, Fundstätte.

reprehensible [repri'hensibl], *adj.* tadelnswert.

represent [repri'zent], *v.a.* repräsentieren, vertreten.

representative [repri'zentətiv], *adj.* repräsentativ, typisch. — *s.* der Stellvertreter; (*Pol.*) der Repräsentant.

repress [ri'pres], *v.a.* unterdrücken.

reprieve [ri'pri:v], *v.a.* begnadigen. — *s.* die Gnadenfrist.

reprimand [repri'mɑ:nd], *v.a.* verweisen, tadeln. — *s.* der Tadel.

reprint [ri:'print], *v.a.* neu drucken. — ['ri:print], *s.* der Neudruck.

reprisal [ri'praizəl], *s.* die Vergeltungsmaßregel; (*pl.*) die Repressalien, *f. pl.*

reproach [ri'proutʃ], *v.a.* vorwerfen (*Dat.*), tadeln. — *s.* der Vorwurf, Tadel.

reprobate ['reprəbeit], *adj.* ruchlos, verworfen.

reproduce [ri:prə'dju:s], *v.a.* reproduzieren, erzeugen.

reproof [ri'pru:f], *s.* der Vorwurf, Tadel.

reprove [ri'pru:v], *v.a.* tadeln, rügen (*a person*), mißbilligen (*a practice*).

473

republic

republic [ri'pʌblik], s. die Republik.
repudiate [ri'pju:dieit], v.a. zurückweisen, verwerfen.
repugnant [ri'pʌgnənt], adj. widerwärtig, ekelhaft.
repulse [ri'pʌls], v.a. (Mil.) zurückschlagen; abweisen (s.o.). — s. (Mil.) das Zurückschlagen; (fig.) die Zurückweisung.
repulsive [ri'pʌlsiv], adj. widerwärtig.
reputation [repju'teiʃən], s. der (gute) Ruf.
request [ri'kwest], v.a. ersuchen. — s. das Ersuchen, Ansuchen, die Bitte.
requiem ['rekwiəm], s. (Eccl.) das Requiem, die Totenmesse.
require [ri'kwaiə], v.a. fordern, verlangen, brauchen.
requirement [ri'kwaiəmənt], s. die Anforderung, das Erfordernis.
requisite ['rekwizit], adj. erforderlich.
requisition [rekwi'ziʃən], s. (Mil.) die Requisition; die Forderung.
requite [ri'kwait], v.a. vergelten.
rescind [ri'sind], v.a. für ungültig erklären, aufheben.
rescue ['reskju:], v.a. retten. — s. die Rettung.
research [ri'sə:tʃ], v.n. forschen, Forschung treiben. — s. die Forschung.
resemble [ri'zembl], v.a. ähnlich sein (Dat.), gleichen (Dat.).
resent [ri'zent], v.a. übelnehmen.
resentful [ri'zentful], adj. nachträgerisch; empfindlich (over-sensitive).
resentment [ri'zentmənt], s. die Empfindlichkeit; der Groll (spite).
reservation [rezə'veiʃən], s. die Reservierung (of seat); der Vorbehalt (doubt).
reserve [ri'zə:v], v.a. reservieren, belegen (seat); (fig.) vorbehalten (o.'s position). — s. die Reserve, die Verschlossenheit (shyness); die Einschränkung (limitation); die Reserven, s. pl. (money).
reside [ri'zaid], v.n. wohnen.
resident ['rezidənt], adj. wohnhaft. — s. der Ansässige.
residual [ri'zidjuəl], adj. übrig bleibend.
residue ['rezidju:], s. der Rückstand, Rest.
resign [ri'zain], v.a. abtreten, aufgeben; (ein Amt) niederlegen. — v.n. abdanken. — v.r. — o.s. to, sich in etwas fügen, zurücktreten.
resignation [rezig'neiʃən], s. die Resignation, der Rücktritt (from office); die Fügung, Resignation (attitude).
resin ['rezin], s. das Harz.
resist [ri'zist], v.a., v.n. widerstehen, Widerstand leisten (Dat.).
resistance [ri'zistəns], s. der Widerstand.
resolute ['rezəlju:t], adj. entschlossen.
resolution [rezə'lju:ʃən], s. die Entschlossenheit (determination); die Entscheidung (decision); der Vorsatz, Entschluß (vow).

resolve [ri'zɔlv], v.a. auflösen (solve); beschließen (conclude). — v.n. entscheiden (decide). — s. der Beschluß, die Entscheidung.
resonance ['rezənəns], s. die Resonanz.
resort [ri'zɔ:t], v.n. — to, seine Zuflucht nehmen (zu). — s. seaside —, das Seebad, health —, der Kurort (spa).
resound [ri'zaund], v.n. widerhallen.
resource [ri'sɔ:s], s. das Hilfsmittel; (pl.) die Mittel, n. pl.
respect [ri'spekt], v.a. respektieren, achten; berücksichtigen (have regard to). — s. der Respekt, die Achtung; with — to, mit Bezug auf; in — of, bezüglich (Genit.).
respectability [rispektə'biliti], s. die Anständigkeit; Achtbarkeit.
respective [ris'pektiv], adj. respektiv.
respectively [ris'pektivli], adv. beziehungsweise.
respiration [respi'reiʃən], s. die Atmung.
respiratory [ris'paiərətri or 'respireitəri], adj. Atmungs-.
respire [ris'paiə], v.a. atmen.
respite ['respit], s. die Frist, der Aufschub.
resplendent [ri'splendənt], adj. glänzend.
respond [ri'spɔnd], v.n. antworten, eingehen (to, auf).
respondent [ri'spɔndənt], s. (Law) der Beklagte.
response [ri'spɔns], s. die Antwort, Aufnahme, Reaktion; (fig.) der Widerhall.
responsibility [rispɔnsi'biliti], s. die Verantwortung, Verantwortlichkeit.
responsible [ri'spɔnsibl], adj. verantwortlich.
responsive [ri'spɔnsiv], adj. empfänglich, zugänglich.
rest (1) [rest], v.n. ruhen, rasten. — s. die Ruhe, Rast; (Mus.) die Pause.
rest (2) [rest], v.n. bleiben (stay); — assured, sei (seien Sie) versichert. — s. der Rest; die übrigen, pl.
restaurant ['restərā], s. das Restaurant.
restful ['restful], adj. ruhig.
restitution [resti'tju:ʃən], s. die Wiedergutmachung.
restive ['restiv], adj. unruhig, ruhelos.
restless ['restlis], adj. rastlos, unruhig.
restoration [restɔ:'reiʃən], s. die Wiederherstellung; (Hist.) die Restauration.
restore [ri'stɔ:], v.a. wiederherstellen.
restrain [ri'strein], v.a. zurückhalten, einschränken.
restraint [ri'streint], s. die Zurückhaltung.
restrict [ri'strikt], v.a. beschränken.
restriction [ri'strikʃən], s. die Einschränkung.
restrictive [ri'striktiv], adj. einschränkend.

result [ri'zʌlt], *v.n.* folgen, sich ergeben; (*come about*) erfolgen. — *s.* das Ergebnis, Resultat; (*consequence*) die Folge.

resume [ri'zju:m], *v.a.* wiederaufnehmen; (*narrative*) fortsetzen. — *v.n.* fortfahren.

résumé ['rezjumei], *s.* das Resümee, die Zusammenfassung.

resumption [ri'zʌmpʃən], *s.* die Wiederaufnahme.

resurrection [rezə'rekʃən], *s.* (*Rel.*) die Auferstehung.

resuscitate [ri'sʌsiteit], *v.a.* wiederbeleben.

retail ['ri:teil], *s.* der Kleinhandel, Einzelhandel. — [ri'teil], *v.a.* im Detail handeln, verkaufen.

retain [ri'tein], *v.a.* behalten.

retainer [ri'teinə], *s.* der Diener; Gefolgsmann; der Vorschuß (*fee*).

retake [ri:'teik], *v.a. irr.* (*Mil.*) wieder erobern; (*Phot., Film*) noch einmal aufnehmen. — *s.* (*Am.*) die Neuaufnahme (*Phot., Film*).

retaliate [ri'tælieit], *v.n.* sich rächen, vergelten.

retard [ri'tɑ:d], *v.a.* verzögern, verlangsamen.

retch [retʃ], *v.n.* sich erbrechen.

retentive [ri'tentiv], *adj.* behaltend, gut (*memory*).

reticent ['retisənt], *adj.* schweigsam, einsilbig.

retina ['retinə], *s.* (*Anat.*) die Netzhaut.

retinue ['retinju:], *s.* das Gefolge.

retire [ri'taiə], *v.n.* sich zurückziehen (*withdraw*); in den Ruhestand treten (*from work*). — *v.a.* pensionieren.

retirement [ri'taiəmənt], *s.* die Pension, der Ruhestand; die Zurückgezogenheit (*seclusion*).

retort [ri'tɔ:t], *s.* (*Chem.*) die Retorte; die scharfe Antwort (*debate*). — *v.n.* scharf erwidern.

retouch [ri:'tʌtʃ], *v.a.* (*Phot.*) retouchieren.

retrace [ri:'treis], *v.a.* zurückverfolgen.

retreat [ri'tri:t], *v.n.* sich zurückziehen. — *s.* der Rückzug (*Mil.*); Zufluchtsort.

retrench [ri'trentʃ], *v.a.* einschränken (*restrict*); verkürzen (*shorten*). — *v.n.* sich einschränken.

retribution [retri'bju:ʃən], *s.* die Vergeltung.

retrieve [ri'tri:v], *v.a.* wieder bekommen, wieder gewinnen.

retriever [ri'tri:və], *s.* (*Zool.*) der Apportierhund, Stöberhund.

retrograde ['retrogreid], *adj.* rückgängig, rückwärts.

retrospect ['retrospekt], *s.* der Rückblick.

retrospective [retro'spektiv], *adj.* rückblickend.

return [ri'tə:n], *v.a.* zurückgeben; erwidern (*reciprocate*); abordnen, entsenden (*to Parl.*); (*figures*) einsenden. — *v.n.* zurückkehren, zurückkommen.

reunion [ri:'ju:niən], *s.* die Wiedervereinigung.

reveal [ri'vi:l], *v.a.* enthüllen, offenbaren (*show*); verraten (*betray*).

reveille [ri'væli], *s.* (*Mil.*) das Wecken, Wecksignal.

revel [revl], *v.n.* schwelgen.

revelation [revə'leiʃən], *s.* die Offenbarung.

revelry ['revəlri], *s.* die Schwelgerei.

revenge [ri'vendʒ], *s.* die Rache, Revanche. — *v.r.* (*also be revenged*) sich rächen (*on, an, Dat.*).

revenue ['revənju:], *s.* das Einkommen; *Inland* —, die Steuereinnahmen.

reverberate [ri'və:bəreit], *v.n.* widerhallen.

revere [ri'viə], *v.a.* verehren.

reverence ['revərəns], *s.* die Ehrerbietung, der Respekt; *show* —, Ehrerbietung zollen.

Reverend ['revərənd], *adj.* (*abbr.* **Rev.**) (*Eccl.*) *The* —, Seine Ehrwürden; *The Very* —, Seine Hochwürden.

reverent, reverential ['revərənt, revə'renʃəl], *adj.* ehrerbietig.

reverie ['revəri], *s.* die Träumerei.

reversal [ri'və:səl], *s.* die Umkehrung, Umstoßung.

reverse [ri'və:s], *v.a., v.n.* umkehren, umdrehen. — *s.* das Gegenteil (*contrary*); die Kehrseite (*of coin*).

revert [ri'və:t], *v.a., v.n.* umkehren, zurückkehren.

review [ri'vju:], *v.a.* durchsehen, prüfen (*examine*); rezensieren (*book etc.*). — *s.* die Revision; (*Mil.*) die Parade, Truppenmusterung; die Rezension, Besprechung (*book etc.*).

revile [ri'vail], *v.a., v.n.* schmähen.

revise [ri'vaiz], *v.a.* korrigieren (*correct*); wiederholen (*recapitulate*); umarbeiten (*modify*).

revision [ri'viʒən], *s.* die Revision; Korrektur; Umarbeitung; Wiederholung (*recapitulation*).

revolt [ri'voult], *v.n.* sich empören, revoltieren. — *v.a.* empören. — *s.* die Empörung.

revolting [ri'voultin], *adj.* ekelhaft, empörend.

revolution [revə'lju:ʃən], *s.* (*Pol.*) die Revolution; (*Motor.*) die Umdrehung.

revolve [ri'vɔlv], *v.n.* rotieren, sich drehen.

revolver [ri'vɔlvə], *s.* der Revolver.

revue [ri'vju:], *s.* (*Theat.*) die Revue.

revulsion [ri'vʌlʃən], *s.* der Ekel; der Umschwung.

reward [ri'wɔ:d], *v.a.* belohnen (*person*); vergelten (*deed*). — *s.* die Belohnung.

rheumatic [ru:'mætik], *adj.* (*Med.*) rheumatisch.

rheumatism

rheumatism [ˈruːmətizm], *s.* (*Med.*) der Rheumatismus.

rhetoric [ˈretərik], *s.* die Redekunst.

Rhodesian [roˈdiːʃən, -ˈdiːʒən], *adj.* rhodesisch. — *s.* der Rhodesier.

rhododendron [roudoˈdendrən], *s.* (*Bot.*) die Alpenrose.

rhubarb [ˈruːbɑːb], *s.* (*Bot.*) der Rhabarber.

rhyme [raim], *s.* der Reim; *no — nor reason*, sinnlos.

rhythm [riðm], *s.* der Rhythmus.

rib [rib], *s.* (*Anat.*) die Rippe.

ribald [ˈribəld], *adj.* liederlich; (*joke*) unanständig.

ribbon [ˈribən], *s.* das Band.

rice [rais], *s.* der Reis.

rich [ritʃ], *adj.* reich; fruchtbar (*fertile*).

rick [rik], *s.* der Schober.

rickets [ˈrikits], *s.* (*Med.*) die englische Krankheit, die Rachitis.

rickety [ˈrikiti], *adj.* gebrechlich, wackelig, baufällig.

rid [rid], *v.a. irr.* befreien, freimachen (*of*, von); — *o.s.*, sich entledigen (*of*, *Genit.*); *get — of*, loswerden (*Acc.*); *be — of*, los sein (*Acc.*).

riddance [ˈridəns], *s.* die Befreiung, das Loswerden.

riddle (1) [ridl], *s.* das Rätsel (*puzzle*).

riddle (2) [ridl], *s.* das grobe Sieb (*sieve*). — *v.a.* sieben (*sieve*); durchlöchern.

ride [raid], *v.a., v.n. irr.* reiten (*on horse*), fahren (*on bicycle etc.*); — *at anchor*, vor Anker liegen. — *s.* der Ritt (*on horse*), die Fahrt (*in vehicle*).

rider [ˈraidə], *s.* der Reiter (*horseman*); der Fahrer (*cyclist etc.*); der Zusatz (*addition*).

ridge [ridʒ], *s.* der Rücken (*edge*); die Bergkette; die Furche (*furrow*). — *v.a.* furchen.

ridicule [ˈridikjuːl], *s.* der Spott. — *v.a.* lächerlich machen.

ridiculous [riˈdikjuləs], *adj.* lächerlich.

rife [raif], *adj.* häufig, weitverbreitet.

rifle (1) [raifl], *s.* die Büchse, das Gewehr.

rifle (2) [raifl], *v.a.* ausplündern.

rift [rift], *s.* der Riß, Spalt, die Spalte. — *v.a.* spalten.

rig [rig], *s.* (*Naut.*) die Takelung; (*fig.*) — *out*, die Ausstattung. — *v.a.* (*Naut.*) (auf)takeln; (*Am.*) fälschen (*fake*); — *out*, ausstatten.

right [rait], *adj.* recht; richtig; wahr; gesund; korrekt; — *hand*, rechtsseitig; *you are —*, Sie haben recht; *that's —*, das stimmt. — *s.* das Recht; *by right(s)*, rechtmäßig; *drive on the —*, rechts fahren.

righteous [ˈraitʃəs], *adj.* rechtschaffen, aufrecht.

rightful [ˈraitful], *adj.* rechtmäßig.

rigid [ˈridʒid], *adj.* steif; unbeugsam; streng (*severe*).

rigidity [riˈdʒiditi], *s.* die Steifheit, Unnachgiebigkeit; die Strenge.

rigmarole [ˈrigməroul], *s.* die Salbaderei, das Gewäsch.

rigorous [ˈrigərəs], *adj.* streng; genau.

rigour [ˈrigə], *s.* die Strenge; die Härte.

rill [ril], *s.* (*Poet.*) das Bächlein.

rim [rim], *s.* der Rand, die Felge.

rime [raim], *s.* (*Poet.*) der Reif.

rind [raind], *s.* die Rinde.

ring (1) [riŋ], *s.* der Ring.

ring (2) [riŋ], *s.* der Schall, das Läuten (*bell*); der Anruf (*telephone*); das Geläute (*bells*). — *v.a. irr.* läuten, klingeln (*bell*). — *v.n.* läuten; ertönen, tönen (*call, voice*).

ringleader [ˈriŋliːdə], *s.* der Rädelsführer.

rink [riŋk], *s.* die Eisbahn; Rollschuhbahn.

rinse [rins], *v.a.* spülen, waschen. — *s.* das Abspülen.

riot [ˈraiət], *s.* der Aufruhr. — *v.n.* Aufruhr stiften; meutern.

rip [rip], *v.a.* reißen, aufreißen. — *s.* der Riß.

ripe [raip], *adj.* reif.

ripen [ˈraipən], *v.n.* reifen. — *v.a.* reifen lassen.

ripple [ripl], *s.* die Welle, Kräuselwelle (*water*). — *v.n.* kräuseln (*water*); (*Bot.*) riffeln.

rise [raiz], *v.n. irr.* aufstehen (*get up*); aufsteigen (*ascend*); anschwellen (*swell*); steigen (*price*). — *s.* die Erhöhung; (*Comm.*) der Anstieg; die Steigerung; Erhöhung (*salary*); der Ursprung (*origin*).

rising [ˈraiziŋ], *s.* der Aufstand (*rebellion*).

risk [risk], *s.* das Risiko. — *v.a.* wagen, riskieren.

rite [rait], *s.* der Ritus.

ritual [ˈritjuəl], *s.* das Ritual.

rival [raivl], *s.* der Rivale, Nebenbuhler. — *adj.* nebenbuhlerisch, konkurrierend. — *v.a.* konkurrieren, wetteifern.

river [ˈrivə], *s.* der Fluß.

rivet [ˈrivit], *s.* die Niete. — *v.a.* nieten.

roach [routʃ], *s.* (*Zool.*) die Plötze.

road [roud], *s.* die Straße; der Weg.

roam [roum], *v.n.* herumstreifen.

roan [roun], *s.* der Rotschimmel (*horse*).

roar [rɔː], *v.n.* brüllen (*animals*); brausen (*storm*). — *s.* das Gebrüll (*animal*); das Getöse, Brausen, Rauschen.

roast [roust], *v.a., v.n.* braten, rösten. — *s.* der Braten.

rob [rɔb], *v.a.* berauben.

robbery [ˈrɔbəri], *s.* der Raub, die Räuberei.

robe [roub], *s.* die Robe.

robin [ˈrɔbin], *s.* (*Orn.*) das Rotkehlchen.

rock [rɔk], *s.* der Felsen, die Klippe. — *v.a.* schaukeln, wiegen. — *v.n.* wackeln, taumeln.

rocket [ˈrɔkit], *s.* die Rakete; (*sl.*) die Rüge. — *v.n.* hochfliegen; hochgehen (*prices*).

rocky [ˈrɔki], *adj.* felsig.

476

rod [rɔd], *s.* die Rute; (*fishing*) die Angelrute; die Stange (*pole*).
rodent [ˈroudənt], *s.* (*Zool.*) das Nagetier.
roe (1) [rou], *s.* der Fischrogen.
roe (2) [rou], *s.* (*Zool.*) das Reh, die Hirschkuh.
rogation [roˈgeiʃən], *s.* das Gebet, die Litanei; *Rogation Sunday*, der Sonntag Rogate.
rogue [roug], *s.* der Schelm.
role [roul]. *s.* (*Theat., fig.*) die Rolle.
roll [roul], *s.* — *call*, der Aufruf, die Parade; die Rolle; die Semmel, das Brötchen (*bread*). — *v.a.* rollen; wälzen. — *v.n.* rollen; sich wälzen; sich drehen; schlingen (*ship*); schlenkern (*person*).
roller [ˈroulə], *s.* die Rolle; — *bandage*, das Wickelband; — *skates*, die Rollschuhe.
rollick [ˈrɔlik], *v.n.* herumtollen, lustig sein.
rolling stock [ˈrouliŋ stɔk], *s.* (*Railw.*) der Wagenbestand.
romance [rouˈmæns], *s.* die Romanze.
romantic [rouˈmæntik], *adj.* romantisch.
romp [rɔmp], *s.* der Wildfang, das Tollen. — *v.n.* toben.
roof [ru:f], *s.* das Dach. — *v.a.* decken.
rook (1) [ruk], *s.* (*Orn.*) die Saatkrähe.
rook (2) [ruk], *s.* (*Chess*) der Turm.
room [ru:m, rum], *s.* der Raum, das Zimmer. — *v.n.* (*Am.*) ein Zimmer teilen (*with*, mit).
roomy [ˈru:mi], *adj.* geräumig.
roost [ru:st], *s.* der Hühnerstall. — *v.n.* aufsitzen, schlafen.
root [ru:t], *s.* die Wurzel. — *v.n.* wurzeln.
rooted [ˈru:tid], *adj.* eingewurzelt.
rope [roup], *s.* das Seil. — *v.a.* anseilen (*in climbing*); (*coll.*) — *in*, verwickeln, hereinziehen.
rosary [ˈrouzəri], *s.* (*Rel.*) der Rosenkranz.
rose [rouz], *s.* (*Bot.*) die Rose.
Rosemary [ˈrouzməri]. Rosemarie.
rosemary [ˈrouzməri], *s.* (*Bot.*) der Rosmarin.
rosin [ˈrɔzin] *see* **resin**.
rosy [ˈrouzi], *adj.* rosig.
rot [rɔt], *v.n.* faulen, modern. — *s.* die Fäulnis, Verwesung; (*coll.*) der Unsinn.
rotate [roˈteit], *v.a., v.n.* (sich) drehen, rotieren.
rote [rout], *s.* by — *, mechanisch, auswendig.
rotten [rɔtn], *adj.* faul, verdorben, schlecht.
rotund [roˈtʌnd], *adj.* rundlich, rund.
rough [rʌf], *adj.* rauh, grob; flüchtig, ungefähr (*approximate*); ungehobelt (*ill-mannered*).
roughshod [ˈrʌfʃɔd], *adj.* rücksichtslos.
round [raund], *adj.* rund. — *s.* die Runde. — *prep.* (rund) um; um . . . herum. — *adv.* (rings)herum; (*around*) ungefähr; etwa (*approximately*).

roundabout [ˈraundəbaut], *s.* das Karussel. — *adj.* umständlich.
Roundhead [ˈraundhed], *s.* (*Eng. Hist.*) der Puritaner.
rouse [rauz], *v.a.* erwecken.
rout [raut], *s.* (*Mil.*) die wilde Flucht. — *v.a.* in die Flucht jagen.
route [ru:t], *s.* der Weg; die Route.
rover [ˈrouvə], *s.* der Wanderer, ältere Pfadfinder (*scout*); der Seeräuber (*pirate*).
row (1) [rou], *s.* die Reihe.
row (2) [rau], *s.* der Lärm, Streit. — *v.n.* (*coll.*) lärmen streiten, zanken.
row (3) [rou], *v.n.* rudern.
rowdy [ˈraudi], *s.* der Raufbold. — *adj.* laut, lärmend.
royal [ˈrɔiəl], *adj.* königlich.
royalty [ˈrɔiəlti], *s.* das Mitglied des Königshauses, die königliche Hoheit; (*pl.*) (*Law*) die Tantieme.
rub [rʌb], *v.a., v.n.* (sich) reiben. — *s.* die Reibung; die heikle Stelle, das Problem.
rubber (1) [ˈrʌbə], *s.* der Gummi; Radiergummi.
rubber (2) [ˈrʌbə], *s.* (*Whist*) der Robber.
rubbish [ˈrʌbiʃ], *s.* der Abfall, Mist; (*fig.*) der Schund (*book*), der Unsinn (*nonsense*).
ruby [ˈru:bi], *s.* der Rubin.
rudder [ˈrʌdə], *s.* das Steuerruder.
ruddy [ˈrʌdi], *adj.* rötlich.
rude [ru:d], *adj.* roh; grob; ungebildet; unhöflich.
rudiment [ˈru:dimənt], *s.* die Anfangsgründe, die Grundlage.
rue (1) [ru:], *s.* (*Bot.*) die Raute.
rue (2) [ru:], *v.a.* beklagen, bereuen.
ruff [rʌf], *s.* die Halskrause.
ruffian [ˈrʌfiən], *s.* der Raufbold.
ruffle [rʌfl], *v.a.* zerzausen (*hair*); verwirren (*muddle*). — *s.* die Krause (*on dress*); die Aufregung.
rug [rʌg], *s.* die Wolldecke, der Vorleger.
rugged [ˈrʌgid], *adj.* rauh; uneben.
ruin [ˈru:in], *s.* die Ruine; (*fig.*) der Zusammenbruch. — *v.a.* ruinieren.
rule [ru:l], *s.* die Regel, Vorschrift; die Herrschaft; *slide* —, der Rechenschieber. — *v.a.* beherrschen; regeln; lin(i)ieren (*draw lines* —). — *v.n.* herrschen (*reign*; *be valid*); lin(i)ieren (*draw lines*); entscheiden (*decide*).
ruling [ˈru:liŋ], *s.* die Regelung, Entscheidung.
rum (1) [rʌm], *s.* der Rum.
rum (2) [rʌm], *adj.* (*sl.*) seltsam.
Rumanian [ru:ˈmeinien], *adj.* rumänisch. — *s.* der Rumäne.
rumble [rʌmbl], *v.n.* poltern, rasseln, rumpeln; (*stomach*) knurren.
ruminate [ˈru:mineit], *v.n.* wiederkäuen; nachsinnen.
rummage [ˈrʌmidʒ], *v.a., v.n.* durchstöbern.
rumour [ˈru:mə], *s.* das Gerücht.
rump [rʌmp], *s.* der Rumpf, Steiß; — *steak*, das Rumpsteak.

run

run [rʌn], *v.n. irr.* laufen, rennen; eilen; verkehren (*bus*); fließen (*flow*); (*Theat.*) gegeben werden; lauten (*text*). — *s.* der Lauf, das Rennen; (*Theat.*) die Spieldauer; *in the long —,* am Ende, auf die Dauer.

runaway ['rʌnəwei], *adj.* entlaufen. — *s.* der Ausreißer.

rung [rʌn], *s.* die Sprosse.

runway ['rʌnwei], *s.* (*Aviat.*) die Rollbahn, Startbahn, Landebahn.

rupture ['rʌptʃə], *s.* (*Med.*) der Leistenbruch.

rural ['ruərəl], *adj.* ländlich.

rush (1) [rʌʃ], *s.* (*Bot.*) die Binse.

rush (2) [rʌʃ], *s.* der Ansturm, Andrang; die Hetze; der Hochbetrieb. — *v.n.* stürzen, in Eile sein.

Russian ['rʌʃən], *adj.* russisch. — *s.* der Russe.

rust [rʌst], *s.* der Rost. — *v.n.* verrosten.

rustic ['rʌstik], *adj.* ländlich.

rut (1) [rʌt], *s.* die Spur; das Geleise.

rut (2) [rʌt], *s.* (*animals*) die Brunst.

ruthless ['ruːθlis], *adj.* grausam, rücksichtslos.

rye [rai], *s.* (*Bot.*) der Roggen.

S

S [es], das S.

sable [seibl], *s.* der Zobel. — *adj.* schwarz.

sabotage ['sæbotɑːʒ], *s.* die Sabotage. — *v.a.* sabotieren.

sabre ['seibə], *s.* der Säbel.

sack (1) [sæk], *s.* der Sack; (*coll.*) die Entlassung (*get the —*). — *v.a.* (*coll.*) entlassen.

sack (2) [sæk], *v.a.* plündern (*pillage*).

sack (3) [sæk], *s.* (*obs.*) der Weißwein.

sacrament ['sækrəmənt], *s.* das Sakrament.

sacred ['seikrid], *adj.* heilig.

sacrifice ['sækrifais], *s.* das Opfer. — *v.a.* opfern.

sacrilege ['sækrilidʒ], *s.* das Sakrileg, der Frevel.

sad [sæd], *adj.* traurig.

sadden [sædn], *v.a.* betrüben.

saddle [sædl], *s.* der Sattel. — *v.a.* satteln; (*coll.*) — *s.o. with s.th.,* einem etwas aufhalsen.

safe [seif], *adj.* sicher (*secure*); wohlbehalten (*arrival etc.*). — *s.* der Geldschrank, das Safe.

safeguard ['seifgɑːd], *v.a.* beschützen, garantieren. — *s.* der Schutz, die Sicherheit.

safety ['seifti], *s.* die Sicherheit.

saffron ['sæfrən], *s.* der Safran. — *adj.* safrangelb.

sagacious [sə'geiʃəs], *adj.* scharfsinnig.

sagacity [sə'gæsiti], *s.* der Scharfsinn.

sage (1) [seidʒ], *s.* (*Bot.*) der, die Salbei.

sage (2) [seidʒ], *s.* der Weise. — *adj.* weise, klug.

sail [seil], *s.* das Segel. — *v.n.* segeln, (*Naut.*) fahren.

sailor ['seilə], *s.* der Matrose, Seemann.

Saint [seint, sənt]. (*abbr.* **S.** *or* **St.**) Sankt (*before name*).

saint [seint], *s.* der *or* die Heilige.

sake [seik], *s. for my son's —,* um meines Sohnes willen; *for the — of peace,* um des Friedens willen.

salacious [sə'leiʃəs], *adj.* geil; zotig (*joke*).

salad ['sæləd], *s.* der Salat.

salary ['sæləri], *s.* das Gehalt.

sale [seil], *s.* der Verkauf; *annual —,* (*Comm.*) der Ausverkauf.

salesman ['seilzmən], *s.* der Verkäufer.

salient ['seiliənt], *adj.* hervorspringend, wichtig, Haupt-.

saline ['seilain], *s.* die Salzquelle. — *adj.* salzhaltig.

saliva [sə'laivə], *s.* der Speichel.

sallow ['sælou], *adj.* blaß, bleich.

sally ['sæli], *s.* der Ausfall, (*fig.*) der komische Einfall. — *v.n.* ausfallen; — *forth,* losgehen.

salmon ['sæmən], *s.* (*Zool.*) der Lachs.

saloon [sə'luːn], *s.* der Salon; (*Am.*) das Wirtshaus, die Kneipe.

salt [sɔːlt], *s.* das Salz; — *cellar,* das Salzfäßchen; (*coll.*) *old —,* der alte Matrose. — *v.a.* salzen.

saltpetre [sɔːlt'piːtə], *s.* der Salpeter.

salubrious [sə'ljuːbriəs], *adj.* gesund (*climate, neighbourhood*).

salutary ['sæljutəri], *adj.* heilsam (*lesson, experience*).

salute [sə'ljuːt], *v.a.* grüßen. — *s.* der Gruß, (*Mil.*) Salut.

salvage ['sælvidʒ], *s.* die Bergung, Rettung; das Bergegut. — *v.a.* retten, bergen.

salvation [sæl'veiʃən], *s.* die Rettung; (*Rel.*) die Erlösung, das Heil.

salve [sælv, sɑːv], *v.a.* einsalben; heilen. — *s.* die Salbe.

salver ['sælvə], *s.* der Präsentierteller.

salvo ['sælvou], *s.* (*Mil.*) die Salve.

Samaritan [sə'mæritən], *s.* der Samariter; (*fig.*) der Wohltäter.

same [seim], *adj.* der-, die-, dasselbe.

sample [sɑːmpl], *s.* die Probe, das Muster (*test, pack etc.*). — *v.a.* probieren; kosten (*food*).

sampler ['sɑːmplə], *s.* das Stickmuster.

sanctify ['sæŋktifai], *v.a.* heiligen.

sanctimonious [sæŋkti'mouniəs], *adj.* scheinheilig.

sanction ['sæŋkʃən], *s.* (*Pol.*) die Sanktion; (*fig.*) Genehmigung. — *v.a.* genehmigen, sanktionieren.

sanctuary ['sæŋktjuəri], *s.* das Heiligtum.

sand [sænd], *s.* der Sand. — *v.a.* sanden, bestreuen; (*floors*) abreiben.

sandal [sændl], *s.* die Sandale.

sandwich ['sænwitʃ], *s.* das belegte (Butter)brot.

sane [sein], *adj.* gesund (*mind*); vernünftig.

sanguine ['sæŋgwin], *adj.* optimistisch.

sanitary ['sænitəri], *adj.* Gesundheits-, Sanitäts-; — *towel,* die (Damen)binde.

sanity ['sæniti], *s.* die Vernunft, der gesunde Menschenverstand; (*Law*) die Zurechnungsfähigkeit.

Santa Claus [sæntə'klɔːz]. der heilige Nikolaus, Knecht Ruprecht.

sap (1) [sæp], *s.* der Saft; (*fig.*) die Lebenskraft.

sap (2) [sæp], *v.a.* untergraben, schwächen.

sapling ['sæpliŋ], *s.* (*Bot.*) das Bäumchen, der junge Baum.

sapper ['sæpə], *s.* (*Mil.*) der Sappeur; der Schanzgräber, Pionier.

sapphire ['sæfaiə], *s.* der Saphir.

sarcasm ['sɑːkæzm], *s.* der Sarkasmus.

sarcastic [sɑːˈkæstik], *adj.* sarkastisch.

sash (1) [sæʃ], *s.* die Schärpe.

sash (2) [sæʃ], *s.* — *window,* das Schiebefenster; — *cord,* die Fensterschnur.

Satan ['seitən]. der Satan.

satchel ['sætʃəl], *s.* die Leder(schul)-tasche.

sate [seit], *v.a.* sättigen.

satellite ['sætəlait], *s.* der Satellit, Trabant.

satin ['sætin], *s.* (*Text.*) der Atlas.

satire ['sætaiə], *s.* die Satire.

satisfaction [sætisˈfækʃən], *s.* die Befriedigung, Zufriedenheit.

satisfactory [sætisˈfæktri], *adj.* befriedigend, genügend; zufriedenstellend.

satisfy ['sætisfai], *v.a.* befriedigen, sättigen; (*fig.*) zufriedenstellen.

saturate ['sætʃureit], *v.a.* (*Chem.*) saturieren, sättigen.

Saturday ['sætədei]. der Samstag, Sonnabend.

sauce [sɔːs], *s.* (*Cul.*) die Sauce, Tunke; (*coll.*) die Unverschämtheit.

saucepan ['sɔːspæn], *s.* (*Cul.*) der Kochtopf.

saucer ['sɔːsə], *s.* die Untertasse.

saucy ['sɔːsi], *adj.* (*coll.*) unverschämt, frech.

saunter ['sɔːntə], *v.n.* schlendern, spazieren.

sausage ['sɔsidʒ], *s.* die Wurst.

savage ['sævidʒ], *adj.* wild. — *s.* der Wilde.

save [seiv], *v.a.* retten (*life*); (*Theol.*) erlösen; sparen (*money*); sich ersparen (*trouble, labour*); aufheben (*keep*). — *v.n.* sparen, sparsam sein. — *prep., conj.* außer, außer daß, ausgenommen.

saving ['seiviŋ], *s.* die Ersparnis; *savings bank,* die Sparkasse.

saviour ['seivjə], *s.* der Retter; (*Rel.*) der Heiland.

savour ['seivə], *s.* der Geschmack; die Würze. — *v.n.* schmecken (*of,* nach, *Dat.*).

savoury ['seivəri], *adj.* schmackhaft. — *s.* pikantes Vor- *or* Nachgericht.

saw (1) [sɔː], *v.a.* sägen. — *s.* die Säge.

saw (2) [sɔː], *s.* (*obs.*) das Sprichwort.

sawyer ['sɔːjə], *s.* der Sägearbeiter, Säger.

Saxon ['sæksən], *adj.* sächsisch. — *s.* der Sachse.

say [sei], *v.a. irr.* sagen; (*lines, prayer*) hersagen. — *v.n.* (*Am. coll.*) —! sagen Sie mal! — *s.* das entscheidende Wort.

saying ['seiiŋ], *s.* das Sprichwort, der Spruch.

scab [skæb], *s.* der Schorf, die Krätze.

scabbard ['skæbəd], *s.* die Degenscheide.

scaffold ['skæfəld], *s.* (*Build.*) das Gerüst; das Schafott (*place of execution*).

scald [skɔːld], *v.a.* verbrühen; —*ing hot,* brühheiß.

scale (1) [skeil], *s.* die Waagschale (*balance*).

scale (2) [skeil], *s.* (*Mus.*) die Skala, Tonleiter.

scale (3) [skeil], *s.* (*Geog. etc.*) die Skala, das Ausmaß, der Maßstab; *on a large* —, im großen (Maßstabe). — *v.a.* erklettern (*climb*); — *down,* im Maßstab verringern.

scale (4) [skeil], *s.* (*fish etc.*) die Schuppe. — *v.a.* schuppen, abschälen (*remove* —*s*).

scallop ['skɔləp], *s.* (*Zool.*) die Kammuschel.

scalp [skælp], *s.* (*Anat.*) die Kopfhaut. — *v.a.* skalpieren, die Kopfhaut abziehen.

scamp [skæmp], *s.* (*coll.*) der Taugenichts.

scan [skæn], *v.a.* (*Poet.*) skandieren; (*Rad.*) absuchen.

scandalize ['skændəlaiz], *v.a.* empören, verärgern.

scant [skænt], *adj.* selten; knapp, sparsam.

Scandinavian [skændiˈneivjən], *adj.* skandinavisch. — *s.* der Skandinavier.

scanty ['skænti], *adj.* spärlich, knapp.

scapegoat ['skeipgout], *s.* der Sündenbock.

scar [skɑː], *s.* die Narbe.

scarce [skɛəs], *adj.* selten, spärlich.

scarcely ['skɛəsli], *adv.* kaum.

scarcity ['skɛəsiti], *s.* die Seltenheit, Knappheit.

scare [skɛə], *v.a.* erschrecken, ängstigen. — *s.* der Schreck.

scarecrow ['skɛəkrou], *s.* die Vogelscheuche.

scarf [skɑːf], *s.* der Schal, das Halstuch.

scarlet ['skɑːlit], *adj.* scharlachrot. — *s.* der Scharlach.

scarp [skɑːp], *s.* die Böschung.

scatter ['skætə], *v.a., v.n.* (sich) zerstreuen, (sich) verbreiten; streuen.

scavenge ['skævindʒ], *v.a.* ausreinigen, auswaschen; säubern.

scavenger ['skævindʒə], *s.* der Straßenkehrer; Aasgeier.

scene

scene [si:n], *s.* die Szene, der Schauplatz; *behind the —s,* hinter den Kulissen; — *shifter,* der Kulissenschieber.

scenery ['si:nəri], *s.* die Landschaft (*nature*); (*Theat.*) das Bühnenbild, die Kulissen, *f. pl.*

scent [sent], *s.* der Geruch, Duft, das Parfüm (*perfume*); die Witterung, Fährte (*trail of hunted animal*).

sceptic ['skeptik], *s.* der Skeptiker.

sceptre ['septə], *s.* das Zepter.

schedule ['ʃedju:l, (*Am.*) 'ske-], *s.* der Plan; die Liste; der (Fahr-, Stunden-) plan; (*Law*) der Zusatz (*in documents*). — *v.a.* (*Am.*) einteilen, zuteilen (*apportion*); aufzeichnen.

scheme [ski:m], *s.* das Schema; der Plan; — *of things,* in der Gesamtplanung. — *v.n.* aushecken; Ränke schmieden.

scholar ['skɔlə], *s.* der Gelehrte, der Wissenschaftler; der Schuljunge, Schüler; (*Univ.*) der Stipendiat.

scholarly ['skɔləli], *adj.* gelehrt.

scholarship ['skɔləʃip], *s.* die Gelehrsamkeit (*learning*); das Stipendium (*award*).

scholastic [skoˈlæstik], *adj.* scholastisch. — *s.* der Scholastiker.

school [sku:l], *s.* die Schule. — *v.a.* abrichten; schulen; erziehen.

schoolboy ['sku:lbɔi], *s.* der Schüler.

schoolgirl ['sku:lgə:l], *s.* die Schülerin.

schoolmaster ['sku:lma:stə], *s.* der Lehrer.

schoolmistress ['sku:lmistrəs], *s.* die Lehrerin.

schooner ['sku:nə], *s.* (*Naut.*) der Schoner.

science ['saiəns], *s.* die Wissenschaft, Naturwissenschaft (*natural — s*).

scientific [saiənˈtifik], *adj.* wissenschaftlich, naturwissenschaftlich.

scientist ['saiəntist], *s.* der Gelehrte; Naturwissenschaftler, Naturforscher.

scintillate ['sintileit], *v.n.* funkeln, glänzen.

scion ['saiən], *s.* der Sprößling.

scissors ['sizəz], *s. pl.* die Schere.

scoff [skɔf], *v.a.* verspotten, verhöhnen. — *v.n.* spotten. —*s.* der Spott, Hohn.

scold [skould], *v.a.* schelten. — *v.n.* zanken.

scoop [sku:p], *v.a.* aushöhlen (*hollow out*); ausschöpfen (*ladle out*). — *s.* die Schippe, Schöppkelle; (*fig.*) die Sensation, Erstmeldung.

scope [skoup], *s.* der Wirkungskreis, Spielraum.

scooter ['sku:tə], *s.* der (Motor)roller.

scorch [skɔ:tʃ], *v.a.* versengen, verbrennen. — *v.n.* versengt werden; (*coll.*) dahinrasen (*speed*).

score [skɔ:], *s.* die Zwanzig; die Rechnung; (*Mus.*) die Partitur; das Spielergebnis (*in game*).

scorn [skɔ:n], *v.a.* verachten. — *s.* der Spott (*scoffing*); die Geringschätzung, Verachtung.

Scot, Scotsman [skɔt, 'skɔtsmən], *s.* der Schotte.

Scotch [skɔtʃ], *s.* der Whisky.

scotch [skɔtʃ], *v.a.* ritzen; (*fig.*) vernichten.

Scotswoman ['skɔtswumən], *s.* die Schottin.

Scottish ['skɔtiʃ], *adj.* schottisch.

scoundrel ['skaundrəl], *s.* der Schurke.

scour ['skauə], *v.a.* scheuern, reinigen.

scourge [skə:dʒ], *s.* die Geißel. — *v.a.* geißeln.

scout [skaut], *s.* der Kundschafter; (*Boy Scout*) der Pfadfinder.

scowl [skaul], *v.n.* finster dreinsehen. — *s.* das finstere Gesicht.

scraggy ['skrægi], *adj.* hager, dürr.

scramble ['skræmbl], *v.n.* klettern. — *v.a.* verrühren; *scrambled eggs,* das Rührei.

scrap [skræp], *s.* das Stückchen, der Brocken, Fetzen; — *merchant,* der Altwarenhändler. — *v.a.* zum alten Eisen werfen, verschrotten.

scrapbook ['skræpbuk], *s.* das Sammelbuch, Bilderbuch.

scrape [skreip], *v.a., v.n.* (sich) schaben, kratzen; (*coll.*) — *up,* auflesen. — *s.* (*coll.*) die Klemme (*difficulty*).

scraper ['skreipə], *s.* der Fußabstreifer.

scratch [skrætʃ], *v.a., v.n.* kratzen; sich kratzen; (*Sport*) zurückziehen. — *s.* der Kratzer; *come up to —,* seinen Mann stellen.

scrawl [skrɔ:l], *v.a., v.n.* kritzeln (*scribble*); (*coll.*) unleserlich schreiben. — *s.* das Gekritzel.

scream [skri:m], *v.n.* schreien; kreischen. — *s.* der Schrei; (*coll.*) zum Schreien, zum Lachen.

screech [skri:tʃ], *v.n.* schreien, kreischen (*hoarsely*). — *s.* das Gekreisch.

screen [skri:n], *s.* der Schirm (*protection*); (*Cinema*) die Leinwand. — *v.a.* abschirmen (*shade*); (*Film*) durchspielen, vorführen; (*question*) untersuchen; ausfragen.

screening ['skri:niŋ], *s.* (*Cinema*) die Vorführung; (*Pol.*) die Befragung, Untersuchung.

screw [skru:], *v.a.* schrauben. — *s.* die Schraube.

screwdriver ['skru:draivə], *s.* der Schraubenzieher.

scribble [skribl], *v.a., v.n.* kritzeln, (unleserlich) schreiben. — *s.* das Gekritzel.

scribe [skraib], *s.* der Schreiber.

script [skript], *s.* das Manuskript; (*Film*) das Drehbuch.

scripture ['skriptʃə], *s.* die Heilige Schrift.

scroll [skroul], *s.* die Schriftrolle; (*Typ.*) der Schnörkel; die Urkunde (*document etc.*).

scrub [skrʌb], *v.a.* schrubben, reiben, scheuern.

scruff [skrʌf], *s.* (*of the neck*) das Genick.

scruple ['skru:pl], *s.* der Skrupel.

scrupulous ['skru:pjuləs], *adj.* genau, gewissenhaft; azllu bedenklich.

self

scrutinize ['skru:tinaiz], *v.a.* genau prüfen, untersuchen.
scrutiny ['skru:tini], *s.* die genaue Prüfung; die Untersuchung.
scuffle [skʌfl], *v.n.* sich raufen. — *s.* die Balgerei, Rauferei.
scull [skʌl], *s.* das kurze Ruder.
scullery ['skʌləri], *s.* die Abwaschküche.
scullion ['skʌliən], *s.* (*obs.*) der Küchenjunge.
sculptor ['skʌlptə], *s.* der Bildhauer.
sculpture ['skʌlptʃə], *s.* die Bildhauerei (*activity*); die Skulptur (*piece*).
scum [skʌm], *s.* der Abschaum.
scurf [skə:f], *s.* der Schorf, Grind.
scurrilous ['skʌriləs], *adj.* gemein.
scurvy ['skə:vi], *s.* (*Med.*) der Skorbut. — *adj.* niederträchtig.
scutcheon ['skʌtʃən] *see* escutcheon.
scuttle (1) [skʌtl], *s.* (*Naut.*) die Springluke. — *v.a.* (*Naut.*) ein Schiff zum Sinken bringen, versenken.
scuttle (2) [skʌtl], *s.* der Kohleneimer.
scuttle (3) [skʌtl], *v.n.* eilen (*hurry*).
scythe [saið], *s.* die Sense.
sea [si:], *s.* die See, das Meer.
seal (1) [si:l], *s.* das Siegel, Petschaft. — *v.a.* (be)siegeln.
seal (2) [si:l], *s.* (*Zool.*) der Seehund, die Robbe.
seam [si:m], *s.* der Saum; die Naht; (*Min.*) die Ader, das Flöz; (*Metall.*) die Naht. — *v.a.* einsäumen.
seamstress ['si:mstrəs], *s.* die Näherin.
sear [siə], *v.a.* sengen (*burn*); trocknen; verdorren. — *adj. see* sere.
search [sə:tʃ], *v.n.* suchen (*for, nach, Dat.*); forschen (*for, nach, Dat.*). — *v.a.* untersuchen, durchsuchen (*house, case etc.*). — *s.* die Suche (*for person*); die Untersuchung (*of house etc.*).
searchlight ['sə:tʃlait], *s.* der Scheinwerfer.
seasick ['si:sik], *adj.* seekrank.
seaside ['si:said], *s.* die Küste, der Strand.
season [si:zn], *s.* die Jahreszeit, Saison; — *ticket*, die Dauerkarte. — *v.a.* würzen (*spice*). — *v.n.* reifen (*mature*).
seasoning ['si:zniŋ], *s.* die Würze.
seat [si:t], *s.* der Sitz, Sitzplatz, Stuhl. — *v.a.* setzen; fassen (*of room capacity*); *be —ed*, Platz nehmen.
seaweed ['si:wi:d], *s.* (*Bot.*) der Seetang.
secession [si'seʃən], *s.* die Loslösung, Trennung, Spaltung.
seclude [si'klu:d], *v.a.* abschließen, absondern.
seclusion [si'klu:ʒn], *s.* die Abgeschlossenheit.
second ['sekənd], *num. adj.* zweit; (*repeat*) noch ein. — *s.* die Sekunde (*time*); (*Sport*) der Sekundant. — *v.a.* sekundieren (*Dat.*), beipflichten; [si'kɔnd] abkommandieren (zu).
secondary ['sekəndri], *adj.* zweitrangig, sekundär.
secondhand ['sekəndhænd], *adj.* antiquarisch, gebraucht.

secrecy ['si:krəsi], *s.* die Heimlichkeit; *pledge to —*, die Verschwiegenheit.
secret ['si:krit], *s.* das Geheimnis. — *adj.* geheim.
secretary ['sekrətəri], *s.* der Sekretär, die Sekretärin.
secrete [si'kri:t], *v.a.* ausscheiden, absondern.
secretion [si'kri:ʃən], *s.* die Ausscheidung; (*Med.*) das Sekret.
sect [sekt], *s.* die Sekte.
section ['sekʃən], *s.* die Sektion, Abteilung (*department*); der Teil (*part*); Abschnitt (*in book etc.*).
secular ['sekjulə], *adj.* weltlich, säkulär.
secure [sə'kjuə], *adj.* sicher, gesichert. — *v.a.* sichern (*make safe*); besorgen (*obtain*).
security [sə'kjuəriti], *s.* die Sicherheit; (*Comm.*) die Garantie, Bürgschaft; (*pl.*) die Staatspapiere, Wertpapiere, *n. pl.*, Aktien, *f. pl.*
sedate [si'deit], *adj.* gesetzt, ruhig (*placid*).
sedative ['sedativ], *adj.* beruhigend. — *s.* das Beruhigungsmittel.
sedentary ['sedəntri], *adj.* sitzend, Sitz-.
sediment ['sedimənt], *s.* der Bodensatz; (*Geol.*) das Sediment.
sedition [si'diʃən], *s.* der Aufstand.
seditious [si'diʃəs], *adj.* aufrührerisch.
seduce [si'dju:s], *v.a.* verführen.
sedulous ['sedjuləs], *adj.* emsig, fleißig.
see (1) [si:], *s.* (*Eccl.*) das (Erz)bistum; *Holy See*, der Heilige Stuhl.
see (2) [si:], *v.a., v.n. irr.* sehen; einsehen, verstehen (*understand*).
seed [si:d], *s.* die Saat; der Same (*grain*). — *v.a.* (*Sport*) aussetzen, setzen.
seediness ['si:dinis], *s.* die Schäbigkeit; Armseligkeit, das Elend.
seedy ['si:di], *adj.* elend; schäbig.
seeing ['si:iŋ], *conj.* — *that*, da doch.
seek [si:k], *v.a. irr.* suchen (*object*). — *v.n.* trachten (*to, infin.*).
seem [si:m], *v.n.* scheinen, erscheinen.
seemly ['si:mli], *adj.* schicklich, anständig.
seer [siə], *s.* der Prophet.
seesaw ['si:sɔ:], *s.* die Schaukel.
seethe [si:ð], *v.n.* kochen, (*fig.*) sieden.
segment ['segmənt], *s.* (*Geom.*) der Abschnitt.
segregate ['segrigeit], *v.a.* absondern.
segregation [segri'geiʃən], *s. racial —*, die Rassentrennung.
seize [si:z], *v.a.* ergreifen, packen (*arrest, grasp*); beschlagnahmen (*impound*).
seizure ['si:ʒə], *s.* die Beschlagnahme (*of goods*); (*Med.*) der Anfall.
seldom ['seldəm], *adv.* selten.
select [si'lekt], *v.a.* auswählen, auslesen. — *adj.* auserlesen.
selection [si'lekʃən], *s.* die Wahl, Auswahl.
self [self], *s.* das Selbst; — — *consciousness*, die Befangenheit; — — *denial*, die Selbstverleugnung, Selbstaufopferung.

481

selfish

selfish ['selfiʃ], adj. egoistisch, selbstsüchtig.
sell [sel], v.a. irr. verkaufen; (sl.) —
(s.o.) out, jemanden verraten.
semblance ['sembləns], s. der Anschein,
die Ähnlichkeit.
semi- ['semi], pref. halb.
semibreve ['semibri:v], s. (Mus.) die
ganze Note.
semicircle ['semisə:kl], s. der Halb-
kreis.
semicolon ['semikoulən], s. der Strichpunkt.
semiquaver ['semikweivə], s. (Mus.)
die Sechzehntelnote.
senate ['senit], s. der Senat.
send [send], v.a. irr. senden, schicken;
— for, holen lassen; — -off, die
Abschiedsfeier.
Senegalese [senigə'li:z], adj. senegal-.
— s. der Senegalese.
senile ['si:nail], adj. altersschwach.
senior ['si:njə], adj. älter; dienstälter
(in position).
seniority [si:ni'ɔriti], s. der Rangvor-
tritt, das Dienstalter.
sensation [sen'seiʃən], s. die Empfindung; Sensation.
sensational [sen'seiʃənəl], adj. sensationell.
sense [sens], v.a. fühlen, empfinden.
— s. der Sinn; das Empfinden,
Gefühl; common —, gesunder Menschenverstand.
senseless ['senslis], adj. sinnlos.
sensibility [sensi'biliti], s. die Empfindlichkeit.
sensible ['sensibl], adj. vernünftig.
sensitive ['sensitiv], adj. feinfühlend,
empfindlich.
sensitize ['sensitaiz], v.a. (Phot. etc.)
empfindlich machen.
sensual ['sensjuəl], adj. sinnlich, wollüstig.
sensuous ['sensjuəs], adj. sinnlich.
sentence ['sentəns], s. (Gram.) der
Satz; (Law) das Urteil. — v.a. verurteilen.
sententious [sen'tenʃəs], adj. spruch-
reich; affektiert.
sentiment ['sentimənt], s. die Empfindung, das Gefühl; die Meinung
(opinion).
sentimental [senti'mentl], adj. sentimental, gefühlvoll; empfindsam.
sentinel ['sentinəl], s. (Mil.) die Schildwache, Wache.
separable ['sepərəbl], adj. trennbar.
separate ['sepəreit], v.a. trennen. —
[-rit], adj. getrennt.
separation [sepə'reiʃən], s. die Trennung.
September [sep'tembə]. der September.
sequel ['si:kwəl], s. die Folge, Fortsetzung (serial).
sequence ['si:kwəns], s. die Ordnung,
Reihenfolge, Aufeinanderfolge.
sequester [si'kwestə], v.a. absondern,
entfernen.

sere [siə], adj. trocken, dürr.
serene [si'ri:n], adj. heiter; gelassen,
ruhig (quiet).
serf [sə:f], s. der Leibeigene.
sergeant ['sɑ:dʒənt], s. (Mil.) der
Feldwebel.
series ['siəri:z or 'siərii:z], s. die Reihe.
serious ['siəriəs], adj. ernst, seriös.
sermon ['sə:mən], s. die Predigt.
serpent ['sə:pənt], s. (Zool.) die
Schlange.
serpentine ['sə:pəntain], adj. schlangenartig, sich schlängelnd.
serrated [se'reitid], adj. (Bot., Engin.)
zackig, gezackt.
serried ['serid], adj. dichtgedrängt.
servant ['sə:vənt], s. der Bediente,
Diener; die Magd, das Mädchen,
Dienstmädchen.
serve [sə:v], v.a., v.n. dienen (Dat.);
(Law) abbüßen, absitzen (sentence);
servieren (food); (Tennis) angeben.
service ['sə:vis], s. der Dienst, die
Bedienung; (Mil.) der Militärdienst;
das Service, Geschirr, Porzellan
(china).
serviceable ['sə:visəbl], adj. brauchbar, dienlich, benutzbar.
servile ['sə:vail], adj. knechtisch.
servility [sə:'viliti], s. die Kriecherei.
servitude ['sə:vitju:d], s. die Knechtschaft.
session ['seʃən], s. die Sitzung; das
Studienjahr, Hochschuljahr.
set [set], v.a. irr. setzen; stellen (stand);
legen (lay); ordnen (— out); — a
saw, eine Säge schärfen, wetzen;
fassen (stone); — fire to, in Brand
setzen; — aside, beiseitelegen; — to
music, vertonen; — about, anfangen,
sich anschicken; herfallen über (s.o.);
— up, einrichten. — v.n. — forth,
forward, aufbrechen; — out to, streben, trachten; (sun) untergehen; fest
werden (solidify). — s. der Satz (complete collection); die Garnitur (gar-
ments); der Kreis, die Clique (circle
of people); (Theat.) das Bühnenbild.
settee [se'ti:], s. das Sofa.
setter ['setə], s. (Zool.) der Vorsteh-
hund; red —, der Hühnerhund.
setting ['setiŋ], s. das Setzen; die
Szene (of play etc.); der Sonnenuntergang (of the sun); (Typ.) — up, die
Auslegung, Aufstellung.
settle (1) [setl], v.a. ordnen, schlichten;
(Comm.) begleichen, bezahlen. —
v.n. sich niederlassen, siedeln; (weather) sich aufklären.
settle (2) [setl], s. der Ruhesitz.
settlement ['setlmənt], s. (Comm.) die
Begleichung; die Siedlung (habitation).
seven [sevn], num. adj. sieben.
seventeen ['sevnti:n], num. adj. siebzehn.
seventh [sevnθ], num. adj. siebente.
seventy ['sevnti], num. adj. siebzig.
sever ['sevə], v.a. trennen.
several ['sevərəl], adj. pl. verschiedene,
mehrere.

482

severance ['sevərəns], s. die Trennung.
severe [si'viə], adj. streng.
severity [si'veriti], s. die Strenge.
sew [sou], v.a., v.n. nähen.
sewage ['sju:idʒ], s. das Abfuhrwasser, Kloakenwasser, Kanalwasser.
sewer (1) ['sjuə], s. die Kanalanlage, der Abzugskanal.
sewer (2) ['souə], s. der Näher, die Näherin.
sewing ['souiŋ], s. das Nähen; — machine, die Nähmaschine.
sex [seks], s. das Geschlecht.
sexagenarian [seksədʒə'neəriən], s. der Sechzigjährige.
sextant ['sekstənt], s. der Sextant.
sexton ['sekstən], s. (Eccl.) der Küster, Totengräber.
sexual ['seksuəl], adj. geschlechtlich, sexuell.
shabby ['ʃæbi], adj. schäbig; (fig.) erbärmlich.
shackle [ʃækl], v.a. fesseln. — s. (usually pl.) die Fesseln, f. pl.
shade [ʃeid], s. der Schatten; (pl.) (Am.) die Jalousien, f. pl. (blinds). — v.a. beschatten; (Art) schattieren, verdunkeln.
shadow ['ʃædou], s. der Schatten. — v.a. verfolgen.
shady ['ʃeidi], adj. schattig; (fig.) verdächtig.
shaft [ʃɑ:ft], s. der Schaft (handle); (Min.) der Schacht; die Deichsel (cart); der Pfeil (arrow).
shag [ʃæg], s. der Tabak.
shaggy ['ʃægi], adj. zottig.
shake [ʃeik], v.a. irr. schütteln; rütteln; (fig.) erschüttern. — v.n. zittern (tremble); wanken (waver). — s. das Zittern, Beben; (Mus.) der Triller.
shaky ['ʃeiki], adj. zitternd, wankend; rissig, wackelig (wobbly); (fig.) unsicher (insecure).
shall [ʃæl], v. aux. sollen (be supposed to); werden (future).
shallow ['ʃælou], adj. flach, seicht. — s. die Untiefe (sea).
sham [ʃæm], adj. falsch, unecht. — v.a. vortäuschen.
shambles [ʃæmblz], s. die Unordnung; (fig.) das Schlachtfeld.
shame [ʃeim], s. die Scham (remorse); die Schande (dishonour); what a —! wie schade! — v.a. beschämen.
shamefaced ['ʃeimfeisd], adj. verschämt.
shameful ['ʃeimful], adj. schändlich (despicable).
shampoo [ʃæm'pu:], s. das Haarwaschmittel. — v.a. das Haar waschen.
shamrock ['ʃæmrɔk], s. (Bot.) der irische Klee.
shank [ʃæŋk], s. der Unterschenkel; (coll.) on Shanks's pony, zu Fuß.
shanty (1) ['ʃænti], s. die Hütte.
shanty (2) ['ʃænti], s. sea —, das Matrosenlied.
shape [ʃeip], s. die Gestalt, Figur, Form. — v.a. gestalten, formen. — v.n. Gestalt annehmen.

shapely ['ʃeipli], adj. wohlgestaltet, schön gestaltet.
share [ʃeə], v.a., v.n. (sich) teilen. — s. der Teil, Anteil; (Comm.) die Aktie (in company).
shareholder ['ʃeəhouldə], s. der Aktionär.
shark [ʃɑ:k], s. (Zool.) der Haifisch, Hai; (fig.) der Wucherer (profiteer), Hochstapler.
sharp [ʃɑ:p], adj. scharf; (fig.) intelligent. — s. (Mus.) das Kreuz.
sharpen [ʃɑ:pn], v.a. schärfen; spitzen (pencil).
sharpener ['ʃɑ:pnə], s. pencil —, der Bleistiftspitzer.
shatter ['ʃætə], v.a. zerschmettern. — v.n. zerbrechen.
shave [ʃeiv], v.a., v.n. (sich) rasieren; abschaben (pare). — s. die Rasur, das Rasieren.
shavings ['ʃeivinz], s. pl. die Hobelspäne, m. pl.
shawl [ʃɔ:l], s. der Schal, das Umschlagetuch.
she [ʃi:], pers. pron. sie.
sheaf [ʃi:f], s. die Garbe.
shear [ʃiə], v.a. irr. scheren (sheep etc.).
shears [ʃiəz], s. pl. die Schere.
sheath [ʃi:θ], s. die Scheide.
sheathe [ʃi:ð], v.a. in die Scheide stecken.
shed (1) [ʃed], s. der Schuppen.
shed (2) [ʃed], v.a. irr. vergießen (blood, tears); ausschütten.
sheen [ʃi:n], s. der Glanz.
sheep [ʃi:p], s. (Zool.) das Schaf.
sheer (1) [ʃiə], adj. rein, lauter; senkrecht.
sheer (2) [ʃiə], v.n. (Naut.) gieren, abgieren.
sheet [ʃi:t], s. das Bettuch; das Blatt, der Bogen (paper); die Platte (metal); — metal, — iron, das Eisenblech; — lightning, das Wetterleuchten.
shelf [ʃelf], s. das Brett, Regal; der Sims (mantel); (Geog.) die Sandbank; (coll.) on the —, sitzengeblieben.
shell [ʃel], s. die Schale (case); die Muschel (mussel); (Mil.) die Bombe, Granate. — v.a. schälen (peas); bombardieren, beschiessen (town).
shelter ['ʃeltə], s. das Obdach (lodging); der Unterstand, Schuppen; der Schutz (protection). — v.a. Obdach gewähren (Dat.); beschützen (protect). — v.n. sich schützen, unterstellen.
shelve [ʃelv], v.a. auf ein Brett legen; (fig.) aufschieben (postpone).
shelving ['ʃelvin], s. das Regal.
shepherd ['ʃepəd], s. der Schäfer, Hirt.
sheriff ['ʃerif], s. der Sheriff.
shew [ʃou] see show.
shield [ʃi:ld], s. der Schild. — v.a. schützen.
shift [ʃift], v.a. verschieben. — v.n. die Lage ändern. — s. die Veränderung, der Wechsel; (Industry) die Schicht.
shifty ['ʃifti], adj. unstet; durchtrieben.

shin [ʃin], s. (*Anat.*) das Schienbein.
shindy [ʃindi], s. der Lärm.
shine [ʃain], v.n. irr. scheinen (*sun*); glänzen. — s. der Glanz.
shingle (1) [ʃingl], s. (*Build.*) die Schindel; (*Hair*) der Herrenschnitt.
shingle (2) [ʃingl], s. (*Geol.*) der Kiesel.
shingles [ʃinglz], s. pl. (*Med.*) die Gürtelrose.
ship [ʃip], s. das Schiff. — v.a. verschiffen, (*Comm.*) versenden.
shipping [ʃipin], s. die Schiffahrt; (*Comm.*) der Versand, die Verfrachtung, Verschiffung.
shire [ʃaiə], s. die Grafschaft.
shirk [ʃə:k], v.a. vermeiden, sich drücken (vor, *Dat.*).
shirt [ʃə:t], s. das Hemd.
shirting [ʃə:tin], s. der Hemdenstoff.
shiver [ʃivə], v.n. zittern, beben. — s. der Schauer, Schauder.
shoal [ʃoul], s. der Schwarm; (*Naut.*) die Untiefe.
shock (1) [ʃɔk], v.a. entsetzen; erschrecken; schockieren. — s. der Schock, das Entsetzen.
shock (2) [ʃɔk], s. — of hair, zottiges Haar.
shoddy [ʃɔdi], adj. schlecht, wertlos.
shoe [ʃu:], s. der Schuh. — v.a. beschuhen; (*horse*) beschlagen.
shoelace, shoestring [ʃu:leis, ʃu:strin], s. der Schuhsenkel, (*Austr.*) das Schuhschnürl; on a shoestring, fast ohne Geld.
shoeshine [ʃu:ʃain], s. (*Am.*) der Schuhputzer.
shoestring see under **shoelace**.
shoot [ʃu:t], v.a. irr. schießen. — v.n. sprossen, hervorschießen; (*film*) aufnehmen. — s. (*Bot.*) der Sproß.
shooting [ʃu:tin], s. das Schießen; — range, der Schießstand. — adj. — star, die Sternschnuppe.
shop [ʃɔp], s. der Laden, das Geschäft; (*work*) die Werkstatt; talk —, fachsimpeln; — window, das Schaufenster. — v.n. einkaufen.
shopkeeper [ʃɔpki:pə], s. der Kaufmann, Krämer.
shoplifter [ʃɔpliftə], s. der Ladendieb.
shore [ʃɔ:], s. das Gestade, die Küste; die Stütze. — v.a. — up, stützen.
short [ʃɔ:t], adj. kurz, klein, knapp; (*curt*) kurz angebunden; — of money, in Geldnot; run —, knapp werden; — sighted, kurzsichtig; be on — time working, kurz arbeiten. — s. (*Elect.*) (*coll.*) der Kurzschluß (short circuit); (*pl.*) die Kniehose, kurze Hose.
shortcoming [ʃɔ:tkʌmin], s. der Fehler, Mangel.
shorten [ʃɔ:tn], v.a. verkürzen, abkürzen. — v.n. kürzer werden.
shorthand [ʃɔ:thænd], s. die Stenographie; — typist, die Stenotypistin.
shot [ʃɔt], s. der Schuß; (*man*) der Schütze.

shoulder [ʃouldə], s. (*Anat.*) die Schulter. — v.a. schultern, auf sich nehmen, auf die Achsel nehmen.
shout [ʃaut], v.n. schreien, rufen. — s. der Schrei, Ruf.
shove [ʃʌv], v.a. schieben, stoßen. — s. der Schub, Stoß.
shovel [ʃʌvl], s. die Schaufel. — v.a. schaufeln.
show [ʃou], v.a. irr. zeigen; (*fig.*) dartun. — v.n. sich zeigen, zu sehen sein; — off, prahlen, protzen. — v.r. — o.s. to be, sich erweisen als. — s. (*Theat.*) die Schau, Aufführung.
shower [ʃauə], s. der Schauer (*rain*); (*fig.*) die Fülle, der Überfluß; — (*bath*), die Dusche; take a — (*bath*), brausen. — v.a., v.n. herabregnen; überschütten.
showing [ʃouin], s. die Vorführung, der Beweis.
showy [ʃoui], adj. protzig, angeberisch.
shred [ʃred], s. der Fetzen; (*fig.*) die Spur (*of evidence*). — v.a. zerreißen, zerfetzen.
shrew [ʃru:], s. die Spitzmaus; (*fig.*) das zänkische Weib.
shrewd [ʃru:d], adj. schlau, verschlagen, listig.
shriek [ʃri:k], v.n. kreischen. — s. der Schrei, das Gekreisch.
shrift [ʃrift], s. give s.o. short —, mit einem kurzen Prozeß machen.
shrill [ʃril], adj. schrill, gellend, durchdringend.
shrimp [ʃrimp], s. (*Zool.*) die Garnele.
shrine [ʃrain], s. der (Reliquien-)schrein; der Altar.
shrink [ʃrink], v.n. irr. eingehen, einschrumpfen. — v.a. eingehen lassen.
shrinkage [ʃrinkidʒ], s. das Eingehen (*fabric*); (*Geol.*) die Schrumpfung.
shrivel [ʃrivl], v.n. einschrumpfen, sich runzeln.
shroud [ʃraud], s. das Leichentuch. — v.a. einhüllen.
Shrove [ʃrouv] **Tuesday**, die Fastnacht.
shrub [ʃrʌb], s. (*Bot.*) der Strauch, die Staude.
shrug [ʃrʌg], v.a. (*shoulders*) die Achseln zucken. — s. das Achselzucken.
shudder [ʃʌdə], s. der Schauder. — v.n. schaudern.
shuffle [ʃʌfl], v.a. (*cards*) mischen. — v.n. schlürfen, schleppend gehen.
shun [ʃʌn], v.a. meiden.
shunt [ʃʌnt], v.a., v.n. rangieren.
shut [ʃʌt], v.a. irr. schließen. — v.n. sich schließen, zugehen; (*coll.*) — up! halt's Maul!
shutter [ʃʌtə], s. der Fensterladen.
shuttle [ʃʌtl], s. (*Mech.*) das Weberschiff.
shuttlecock [ʃʌtlkɔk], s. der Federball.
shy (1) [ʃai], adj. scheu, schüchtern. — v.n. scheuen (*of horses*).
shy (2) [ʃai], s. der Wurf.
sick [sik], adj. krank; unwohl, übel; leidend (*suffering*); (*fig.*) — of, überdrüssig (*Genit.*).

sicken [sikn], *v.n.* krank werden *or* sein; sich ekeln (*be nauseated*). — *v.a.* anekeln.
sickle [sikl], *s.* die Sichel.
sickness ['siknis], *s.* die Krankheit.
side [said], *s.* die Seite. — *v.n.* — *with*, Partei ergreifen für.
sideboard ['saidbɔ:d], *s.* das Büffet, die Anrichte.
sidereal [sai'diəriəl], *adj.* (*Maths., Phys.*) Sternen-, Stern-.
sidewalk ['saidwɔ:k] (*Am.*) *see* **pavement**.
siding ['saidiŋ], *s.* (*Railw.*) das Nebengleis.
sidle [saidl], *v.n.* — *up to*, sich heranmachen.
siege [si:dʒ], *s.* die Belagerung.
sieve [siv], *s.* das Sieb. — *v.a.* sieben.
sift [sift], *v.a.* sieben; (*fig.*) prüfen.
sigh [sai], *v.n.* seufzen. — *s.* der Seufzer.
sight [sait], *s.* die Sicht (*view*); die Sehkraft (*sense of*); der Anblick; *at* —, auf den ersten Blick; *out of* —, *out of mind*, aus den Augen, aus dem Sinn; (*pl.*) die Sehenswürdigkeiten, *f. pl.*; —*seeing*, die Besichtigung (der Sehenswürdigkeiten). — *v.a.* sichten.
sign [sain], *s.* das Zeichen; der Wink (*hint*); das Aushängeschild (*of pub, shop etc*). — *v.a.* unterschreiben, unterzeichnen. — *v.n.* winken.
signal ['signəl], *s.* das Signal.
signboard ['sainbɔ:d], *s.* das Aushängeschild.
signet ['signit], *s.* das Siegel; — *ring*, der Siegelring.
significance [sig'nifikəns], *s.* die Bedeutung, der Sinn.
significant [sig'nifikənt], *adj.* bedeutend, wichtig.
signify ['signifai], *v.a.* bedeuten (*mean*); anzeigen (*denote*).
silence ['sailəns], *s.* das Schweigen, die Ruhe.
silent ['sailənt], *adj.* still; schweigsam (*taciturn*).
Silesian [sai'li:ʃən], *adj.* schlesisch. — *s.* der Schlesier.
silk [silk], *s.* (*Text.*) die Seide.
silkworm ['silkwə:m], *s.* (*Ent.*) die Seidenraupe.
sill [sil], *s.* die Schwelle; *window* —, das Fensterbrett.
silly ['sili], *adj.* albern, dumm.
silver ['silvə], *s.* das Silber. — *v.a.* versilbern. — *adj.* silbern.
similar ['similə], *adj.* ähnlich.
simile ['simili], *s.* (*Lit.*) das Gleichnis.
simmer ['simə], *v.n., v.a.* langsam kochen.
simper ['simpə], *v.n.* lächeln, grinsen.
simple [simpl], *adj.* einfach; (*fig.*) einfältig.
simpleton ['simpltən], *s.* der Einfaltspinsel, Tor.
simplicity [sim'plisiti], *s.* die Einfachheit; (*fig.*) die Einfalt.
simplify ['simplifai], *v.a.* vereinfachen.
simulate ['simjuleit], *v.a.* nachahmen, heucheln, vortäuschen.

simultaneous [siməl'teinjəs], *adj.* gleichzeitig.
sin [sin], *s.* die Sünde. — *v.n.* sündigen.
since [sins], *prep.* seit (*Dat.*). — *conj.* seit (*time*); weil, da (*cause*). — *adv.* seither, seitdem.
sincere [sin'siə], *adj.* aufrichtig.
sincerely [sin'siəli], *adv. yours* —, Ihr ergebener (*letters*).
sincerity [sin'seriti], *s.* die Aufrichtigkeit.
sine [sain], *s.* (*Maths.*) der Sinus, die Sinuskurve.
sinecure ['sainikjuə], *s.* der Ruheposten, die Sinekure.
sinew ['sinju:], *s.* (*Anat.*) die Sehne, der Nerv.
sinful ['sinful], *adj.* sündig, sündhaft.
sing [siŋ], *v.a., v.n. irr.* singen; — *of*, besingen.
singe [sindʒ], *v.a.* sengen.
Singhalese [siŋɡa'li:z], *adj.* singhalesisch. — *s.* der Singhalese, die Singhalesin.
single [siŋgl], *adj.* einzeln; ledig (*unmarried*; *single-handed*, allein. — *v.a.* — *out*, auswählen.
singlet ['siŋglit], *s.* die Unterjacke.
singly ['siŋgli], *adv.* einzeln (*one by one*).
singular ['siŋgjulə], *adj.* einzigartig, einzig. — *s.* (*Gram.*) die Einzahl.
sinister ['sinistə], *adj.* böse, unheimlich, finster.
sink [siŋk], *v.a. irr.* versenken; (*fig.*) (*differences etc.*) begraben. — *v.n.* versinken; (*Naut.*) sinken, versinken. — *s.* das Abwaschbecken, Ausgußbecken.
sinker ['siŋkə], *s.* der Schachtarbeiter (*man*); (*Naut.*) das Senkblei.
sinuous ['sinjuəs], *adj.* gewunden.
sinus ['sainəs], *s.* (*Anat.*) die Knochenhöhle; die Bucht.
sip [sip], *v.a.* schlürfen, nippen. — *s.* das Schlückchen.
siphon ['saifən], *s.* (*Phys.*) der Heber; die Siphonflasche. — *v.a.* auspumpen.
Sir (1) [sə:] (*title preceding Christian name*) Herr von... (*baronet or knight*).
sir (2) [sə:], *s.* Herr (*respectful form of address*); *dear* —, sehr geehrter Herr (*in letters*).
sire [saiə], *s.* der Ahnherr, Vater. — *v.a.* zeugen (*horses etc.*).
siren ['saiərən], *s.* die Sirene.
sirloin ['sə:lɔin], *s.* das Lendenstück.
siskin ['siskin], *s.* (*Orn.*) der Zeisig.
sister ['sistə], *s.* die Schwester; (*Eccl.*) Nonne; —*in-law*, die Schwägerin.
sit [sit], *v.n. irr.* sitzen. — *v.a.* — *an examination*, eine Prüfung machen.
site [sait], *s.* die Lage, der Platz.
sitting ['sitiŋ], *s.* die Sitzung; — *room*, das Wohnzimmer.
situated ['sitjueitid], *adj.* gelegen.
situation [sitju'eiʃən], *s.* die Lage, Situation; der Posten, die Stellung (*post*).

485

six

six [siks], *num. adj.* sechs; *be at —es and sevens*, durcheinander, uneinig sein.

sixteen [siks'ti:n], *num. adj.* sechzehn.

sixth [siksθ], *num. adj.* sechste.

sixty ['siksti], *num. adj.* sechzig.

size [saiz], *s.* die Größe, das Maß; (*fig.*) der Umfang.

skate (1) [skeit], *s.* der Schlittschuh. — *v.n.* Schlittschuh laufen.

skate (2) [skeit], *s.* (*Zool.*) der Glattrochen.

skeleton ['skelitən], *s.* das Skelett, Knochengerüst; — *key*, der Dietrich.

sketch [sketʃ], *s.* die Skizze, der Entwurf. — *v.a.* skizzieren, entwerfen. — *v.n.* Skizzen entwerfen.

sketchy ['sketʃi], *adj.* flüchtig.

skew [skju:], *adj.* schief, schräg.

skewer [skju:ə], *s.* der Fleischspieß.

ski [ski:], *s.* der Schi.

skid [skid], *v.n.* gleiten, schleudern, rutschen. — *v.a.* hemmen, bremsen (*wheel*). — *s.* der Hemmschuh, die Bremse (*of wheel*).

skiff [skif], *s.* (*Naut.*) der Nachen, Kahn.

skilful ['skilful], *adj.* geschickt, gewandt; (*fig.*) erfahren.

skill [skil], *s.* die Geschicklichkeit, Gewandtheit; (*fig.*) die Erfahrung.

skim [skim], *v.a.* abschöpfen, abschäumen.

skimp [skimp], *v.a.* knausern, sparsam sein (mit, *Dat.*).

skimpy ['skimpi], *adj.* knapp.

skin [skin], *s.* die Haut; die Schale (*fruit*); — *deep*, oberflächlich. — *v.a.* häuten, schinden.

skinflint ['skinflint], *s.* der Geizhals.

skinner ['skinə], *s.* der Kürschner.

skip [skip], *v.n.* springen, hüpfen. — *v.a.* (*coll.*) auslassen, überspringen. — *s.* der Sprung.

skipper ['skipə], *s.* (*Naut.*) der Kapitän; (*coll.*) der Chef.

skipping rope ['skipiŋ roup], *s.* das Springseil.

skirmish ['skə:miʃ], *s.* das Scharmützel. — *v.n.* scharmützeln.

skirt [skə:t], *s.* der Rock, Rockschoß (*woman's garment*); der Saum (*edge*). — *v.a.* einsäumen (*seam, edge*); grenzen, am Rande entlang gehen.

skirting (board) ['skə:tiŋ (bɔ:d)], *s.* die Fußleiste.

skit [skit], *s.* die Stichelei, die Parodie, Satire.

skittish ['skitiʃ], *adj.* leichtfertig.

skulk [skʌlk], *v.n.* lauern, herumlungern.

skull [skʌl], *s.* der Schädel; — *and crossbones*, der Totenkopf.

skunk [skʌŋk], *s.* (*Zool.*) das Stinktier; (*coll.*) der Schuft.

sky [skai], *s.* der (sichtbare) Himmel.

skylark ['skaila:k], *s.* (*Orn.*) die Feldlerche.

skylarking ['skaila:kiŋ], *s.* das Possenreißen, die Streiche.

skyline ['skailain], *s.* der Horizont.

skyscraper ['skaiskreipə], *s.* der Wolkenkratzer.

slab [slæb], *s.* die Platte (*stone*); die Tafel, das Stück.

slack [slæk], *adj.* schlaff (*feeble*); locker (*loose*). — *s.* der Kohlengrus. — *v.n.* nachlassen, locker werden, faulenzen.

slacken [slækn], *v.a., v.n.* locker werden, nachlassen.

slackness ['slæknis], *s.* die Schlaffheit, Faulheit.

slag [slæg], *s.* die Schlacke.

slake [sleik], *v.a.* dämpfen, löschen, stillen.

slam (1) [slæm], *v.a.* zuwerfen, zuschlagen (*door*). — *s.* der Schlag.

slam (2) [slæm], *v.a.* (*Cards*) Schlemm ansagen, Schlemm machen. — *s.* (*Cards*) der Stich.

slander ['sla:ndə], *v.a.* verleumden. — *s.* die Verleumdung.

slanderer ['sla:ndərə], *s.* der Verleumder.

slang [slæŋ], *s.* der Slang.

slant [sla:nt], *s.* die schräge Richtung, der Winkel (*angle*).

slap [slæp], *v.a.* schlagen. — *s.* der Klaps, Schlag.

slapdash ['slæpdæʃ], *adj.* oberflächlich.

slash [slæʃ], *v.a.* schlitzen, aufschlitzen; (*coll.*) (*Comm.*) herunterbringen (*prices*). — *s.* der Hieb, Schlag.

slate [sleit], *s.* der Schiefer. — *v.a.* mit Schiefer decken; (*fig.*) ankreiden, ausschelten (*scold*).

slattern ['slætə:n], *s.* die Schlampe.

slaughter ['slɔ:tə], *v.a.* schlachten; niedermetzeln. — *s.* das Schlachten; das Gemetzel.

slave [sleiv], *s.* der Sklave; — *driver*, der Sklavenaufseher. — *v.n.* — (*away*), sich placken, sich rackern.

slavery ['sleivəri], *s.* die Sklaverei.

slavish ['sleiviʃ], *adj.* sklavisch.

slay [slei], *v.a.* erschlagen, töten.

sled, sledge [sled, sledʒ], *s.* der Schlitten.

sleek [sli:k], *adj.* glatt. — *v.a.* glätten.

sleep [sli:p], *v.n. irr.* schlafen. — *s.* der Schlaf.

sleeper ['sli:pə], *s.* der Schläfer; (*Railw.*) die Bahnschwelle; der Schlafwagen (*sleeping car*).

sleepwalker ['sli:pwɔ:kə], *s.* der Nachtwandler.

sleet [sli:t], *s.* der Graupelregen.

sleeve [sli:v], *s.* der Ärmel; der Umschlag (*of record*); *have up o.'s* —, eine Überraschung bereithalten; *laugh in o.'s* —, sich ins Fäustchen lachen.

sleigh [slei], *s.* der Schlitten; — *ride*, die Schlittenfahrt.

sleight [slait], *s.—of hand*, der Taschenspielerstreich; der Trick.

slender ['slendə], *adj.* schlank, dünn, gering.

slice [slais], *s.* die Schnitte, Scheibe. — *v.a.* in Scheiben schneiden.

slick [slik], *adj.* glatt.

slide [slaid], *v.n. irr.* gleiten, rutschen (*glide*). — *v.a.* einschieben. — *s.* die Rutschbahn; (*Phot.*) das Dia, Diapositiv; — *rule*, der Rechenschieber.

slight [slait], *adj.* leicht (*light*), gering (*small*); (*fig.*) schwach, dünn(*weak*). — *s.* die Geringschätzung, Respektlosigkeit. — *v.a.* mißachten, geringschätzig behandeln.

slim [slim], *adj.* schlank.

slime [slaim], *s.* der Schleim (*phlegm*); der Schlamm (*mud*).

sling [sliŋ], *v.a.* irr. schleudern, werfen. — *s.* die Schleuder; (*Med.*) die Binde; der Wurf (*throw*).

slink [sliŋk], *v.n.* irr. schleichen.

slip [slip], *v.n.* ausgleiten; — *away*, entschlüpfen; — *up*, einen Fehltritt begehen (*err*). — *v.a.* gleiten lassen, schieben. — *s.* das Ausgleiten; (*fig.*) der Fehltritt; der Fehler (*mistake*); der Unterrock (*petticoat*); give s.o. the —, einem entgehen, entschlüpfen.

slipper ['slipə], *s.* der Pantoffel, Hausschuh.

slippery ['slipəri], *adj.* schlüpfrig, glatt.

slipshod ['slipʃɔd], *adj.* nachlässig.

slit [slit], *v.a.* schlitzen, spalten. — *s.* der Schlitz, Spalt.

slither ['sliðə], *v.n.* gleiten, rutschen.

sloe [slou], *s.* (*Bot.*) die Schlehe.

slogan ['slougən], *s.* das Schlagwort.

sloop [slu:p], *s.* (*Naut.*) die Schaluppe.

slop [slɔp], *s.* das Spülicht, Spülwasser.

slope [sloup], *s.* der Abhang, die Abdachung. — *v.n.* sich neigen. — *v.a.* abschrägen.

sloppy ['slɔpi], *adj.* unordentlich, nachlässig.

slot [slɔt], *s.* der Spalt, Schlitz (*slit*); die Kerbe (*notch*); — *machine*, der Automat.

sloth [slouθ], *s.* die Trägheit; (*Zool.*) das Faultier.

slouch [slautʃ], *v.n.* umherschlendern; sich schlaff halten.

slough [slau], *s.* der Morast, Sumpf.

slovenly ['slʌvnli], *adj.* schlampig, schmutzig.

slow [slou], *adj.* langsam; (*Phot.*) — *motion*, die Zeitlupenaufnahme. — *v.n.* — *down*, langsamer fahren or laufen.

slow-worm ['slouwə:m], *s.* (*Zool.*) die Blindschleiche.

sludge [slʌdʒ], *s.* der Schlamm, Schmutz.

slug [slʌg], *s.* (*Zool.*) die Wegschnecke; (*Am.*) die Kugel.

sluggish ['slʌgiʃ], *adj.* träg(e).

sluice [slu:s], *s.* die Schleuse. — *v.a.* ablassen (*drain*); begießen (*water*).

slum [slʌm], *s.* das Elendsviertel; Haus im Elendsviertel.

slumber ['slʌmbə], *s.* der Schlummer. — *v.n.* schlummern.

slump [slʌmp], *s.* (*Comm.*) der Tiefstand der Konjunktur; der Preissturz. — *v.n.* stürzen.

slur [slə:], *v.a.* undeutlich sprechen. — *s.* der Schandfleck, die Beleidigung; das Bindezeichen.

slush [slʌʃ], *s.* der Matsch, Schlamm; (*Lit.*) der Kitsch, die Schundliteratur.

slut [slʌt], *s.* die Schlampe.

sly [slai], *adj.* schlau, listig.

smack [smæk], *v.n.* schmecken (*of*, nach, *Dat.*). — *v.a.* schmatzen, lecken. — *s.* der Klaps. — *adv.* (*coll.*) — *in the middle*, gerade in der Mitte.

small [smɔ:l], *adj.* klein; (*fig.*) kleinlich (*petty*); — *talk*, das Geplauder.

smallpox ['smɔ:lpɔks], *s.* (*Med.*) die Blattern, *f. pl.*

smart [smɑ:t], *adj.* schneidig; elegant, schick (*well-dressed*). — *v.n.* schmerzen. — *s.* der Schmerz.

smash [smæʃ], *v.a.* zertrümmern, in Stücke schlagen.— *v.n.* zerschmettern; (*fig.*) zusammenbrechen. — *s.* der Krach.

smattering ['smætəriŋ], *s.* die oberflächliche Kenntnis.

smear [smiə], *v.a.* beschmieren; (*Am. coll.*) den Charakter angreifen, verleumden. — *s.* die Beschmierung, Befleckung.

smell [smel], *v.a.* irr. riechen. — *v.n.* riechen (nach, *Dat.*). — *s.* der Geruch.

smelt (1) [smelt], *v.a.* (*Metall.*) schmelzen.

smelt (2) [smelt], *s.* (*Zool.*) der Stintfisch.

smile [smail], *v.n.* lächeln. — *s.* das Lächeln.

smirk [smə:k], *v.n.* grinsen. — *s.* das Grinsen, die Grimasse.

smite [smait], *v.a.* irr. treffen, schlagen.

smith [smiθ], *s.* der Schmied.

smitten [smitn], *adj.* verliebt.

smock [smɔk], *s.* der Arbeitskittel.

smoke [smouk], *v.a.*, *v.n.* rauchen; räuchern (*fish etc.*). — *s.* der Rauch.

smoked [smoukd], *adj.* — *ham*, der Räucherschinken.

smooth [smu:ð], *adj.* glatt, sanft (*to touch*); (*fig.*) glatt, geschmeidig, wendig. — *v.a.* glätten, ebnen.

smother ['smʌðə], *v.a.* ersticken.

smoulder ['smouldə], *v.n.* schwelen.

smudge [smʌdʒ], *v.a.* beschmutzen. — *v.n.* schmieren, schmutzen. — *s.* der Schmutzfleck, Schmutz.

smug [smʌg], *adj.* selbstgefällig.

smuggle [smʌgl], *v.a.* schmuggeln.

smuggler ['smʌglə], *s.* der Schmuggler.

smut [smʌt], *v.a.*, *v.n.* beschmutzen. — *s.* (*fig.*) der Schmutz.

snack [snæk], *s.* der Imbiß.

snaffle [snæfl], *s.* die Trense.

snag [snæg], *s.* die Schwierigkeit; der Haken.

snail [sneil], *s.* (*Zool.*) die Schnecke.

snake [sneik], *s.* (*Zool.*) die Schlange.

snap [snæp], *v.n.* schnappen (*at*, nach, *Dat.*); (*fig.*) einen anfahren (*shout at s.o.*). — *v.a.* (er)schnappen; (*Phot.*) knipsen. — *s.* (*abbr. for* **snapshot** ['snæpʃɔt]) (*Phot.*) das Photo.

snare [snɛə], *s.* die Schlinge. — *v.a. see* **ensnare.**

snarl [snɑ:l], *v.n.* knurren (*dog*); — *at s.o.*, einen anfahren, anschnauzen.

snatch

snatch [snætʃ], *v.a.* erschnappen, erhaschen.
sneak [sni:k], *v.n.* kriechen, schleichen. — *s.* der Kriecher.
sneer [sniə], *v.n.* höhnen, verhöhnen (*at*, *Acc.*). — *s.* der Spott.
sneeze [sni:z], *v.n.* niesen. — *s.* das Niesen.
sniff [snif], *v.a.*, *v.n.* schnüffeln.
snigger [ˈsnigə], *v.n.* kichern. — *s.* das Kichern.
snip [snip], *v.a.* schneiden, schnippeln.
snipe (1) [snaip], *s.* (*Orn.*) die Schnepfe.
snipe (2) [snaip], *v.n.* schießen.
snivel [snivl], *v.n.* schluchzen (*from weeping*); verschnupft sein (*with a cold*).
snob [snɔb], *s.* der Snob.
snobbish [ˈsnɔbiʃ], *adj.* vornehm tuend; protzig, snobistisch.
snooze [snu:z], *s.* das Schläfchen. — *v.n.* einschlafen, ein Schläfchen machen.
snore [snɔ:], *v.n.* schnarchen. — *s.* das Schnarchen.
snort [snɔ:t], *v.n.* schnaufen; schnarchen (*snore*).
snout [snaut], *s.* die Schnauze, der Rüssel.
snow [snou], *s.* der Schnee. — *v.n.* schneien.
snowdrift [ˈsnoudrift], *s.* das Schneegestöber.
snowdrop [ˈsnoudrɔp], *s.* (*Bot.*) das Schneeglöckchen.
snub [snʌb], *v.a.* kurz abfertigen; (*fig.*) schneiden (*ignore*). — *adj.* — *nosed*, stumpfnasig. — *s.* die Geringschätzung, das Ignorieren.
snuff [snʌf], *s.* der Schnupftabak. — *v.a.* ausblasen (*candle*).
snug [snʌg], *adj.* behaglich; geborgen (*protected*).
so [sou], *adv.* so, also; *not — as*, nicht so wie. — *conj.* so.
soak [souk], *v.a.* einweichen, durchtränken. — *v.n.* weichen, durchsickern (*in*(*to*), in, *Acc.*). — *s.* der Regenguß.
soap [soup], *s.* die Seife. — *v.a.* einseifen.
soar [sɔ:], *v.n.* sich aufschwingen, schweben.
sob [sɔb], *v.n.* schluchzen. — *s.* das Schluchzen.
sober [ˈsoubə], *adj.* nüchtern. — *v.a.*, *v.n.* — (*down*), (sich) ernüchtern.
sobriety [soˈbraiəti], *s.* die Nüchternheit.
soccer [ˈsɔkə], *s.* (*Sport*) das Fußballspiel.
sociable [ˈsouʃəbl], *adj.* gesellig.
social [ˈsouʃəl], *adj.* sozial, gesellschaftlich. — *s.* die Gesellschaft (*party*).
socialism [ˈsouʃəlizm], *s.* (*Pol.*) der Sozialismus.
socialist [ˈsouʃəlist], *adj.* (*Pol.*) sozialistisch, Sozial-. — *s.* der Sozialist.
society [səˈsaiəti], *s.* die Gesellschaft (*human —*); der Verein (*association*); (*Comm.*) die (Handels)gesellschaft.

sock (1) [sɔk], *s.* der Strumpf.
sock (2) [sɔk], *v.a.* (*sl.*) schlagen, boxen.
socket [ˈsɔkit], *s.* *eye —*, die Augenhöhle; (*Elec.*) die Steckdose.
sod [sɔd], *s.* der Rasen, die Erde.
sodden [sɔdn], *adj.* durchweicht.
sofa [ˈsoufə], *s.* das Sofa.
soft [sɔft], *adj.* weich, sanft; einfältig (*stupid*).
soften [sɔfn], *v.a.* weich machen, erweichen. — *v.n.* weich werden, erweichen.
soil [sɔil], *s.* der Boden, die Erde. — *v.a.* beschmutzen.
sojourn [ˈsʌdʒən *or* ˈsɔdʒən], *s.* der Aufenthalt. — *v.n.* sich aufhalten.
solace [ˈsɔlis], *s.* der Trost.
solar [ˈsoulə], *adj.* Sonnen-.
solder [ˈsɔldə *or* ˈsɔ:də], *v.a.* löten. — *s.* das Lötmittel.
soldier [ˈsouldʒə], *s.* der Soldat. — *v.n.* dienen, Soldat sein.
sole (1) [soul], *s.* (*Zool.*) die Seezunge.
sole (2) [soul], *s.* die Sohle (*foot*).
sole (3) [soul], *adj.* allein, einzig.
solecism [ˈsɔlisizm], *s.* der Sprachschnitzer.
solemn [ˈsɔləm], *adj.* feierlich.
solemnize [ˈsɔləmnaiz], *v.a.* feiern, feierlich begehen.
solicit [səˈlisit], *v.a.* direkt erbitten, angehen, anhalten (*for*, um).
solicitor [səˈlisitə], *s.* (*Law*) der Anwalt, Rechtsanwalt.
solicitous [səˈlisitəs], *adj.* besorgt.
solid [ˈsɔlid], *adj.* fest; solide; (*fig.*) gediegen; massiv (*bulky*).
solidify [səˈlidifai], *v.a.* verdichten, fest machen. — *v.n.* sich verfestigen.
soliloquy [səˈliləkwi], *s.* das Selbstgespräch, der Monolog.
solitaire [sɔliˈteə], *s.* der Solitär; (*Am.*) die Patience.
solitary [ˈsɔlitəri], *adj.* einzeln (*single*); einsam (*lonely*).
solitude [ˈsɔlitju:d], *s.* die Einsamkeit.
solstice [ˈsɔlstis], *s.* die Sonnenwende.
soluble [ˈsɔljubl], *adj.* (*Chem.*) löslich; lösbar.
solution [səˈlju:ʃən], *s.* die Lösung.
solvable [ˈsɔlvəbl], *adj.* (auf)lösbar (*problem, puzzle*).
solve [sɔlv], *v.a.* lösen (*problem, puzzle*).
solvent [ˈsɔlvənt], *adj.* (*Chem.*) auflösend; (*Comm.*) zahlungsfähig. — *s.* das Lösungsmittel.
sombre [ˈsɔmbə], *adj.* düster; schwermütig, traurig.
some [sʌm], *adj.* irgend ein, etwas; (*pl.*) einige, manche; etliche.
somebody [ˈsʌmbɔdi], *s.* jemand.
somersault [ˈsʌməsɔ:lt], *s.* der Purzelbaum.
sometimes [ˈsʌmtaimz], *adv.* manchmal, zuweilen.
somewhat [ˈsʌmwɔt], *adv.* etwas, ziemlich.
somewhere [ˈsʌmweə], *adv.* irgendwo(hin).

speculate

somnambulist [sɔm'næmbjulist], *s.* der Nachtwandler.

somnolent ['sɔmnələnt], *adj.* schläfrig, schlafsüchtig.

son [sʌn], *s.* der Sohn; —*-in-law*, der Schwiegersohn.

song [sɔŋ], *s.* (*Mus.*) das Lied; der Gesang; *for a* —, spottbillig.

sonnet ['sɔnit], *s.* (*Poet.*) das Sonett.

sonorous ['sɔnərəs], *adj.* wohlklingend.

soon [suːn], *adv.* bald.

sooner ['suːnə], *comp. adv.* lieber (*rather*); früher, eher (*earlier*), *no* — *said than done*, gesagt, getan.

soot [sut], *s.* der Ruß.

soothe [suːð], *v.a.* besänftigen.

soothsayer ['suːθseiə], *s.* der Wahrsager.

sop [sɔp], *s.* der eingetunkte Bissen; (*fig.*) die Bestechung (*bribe*).

soporific [sɔpə'rifik], *adj.* einschläfernd.

soprano [sə'prɑːnou], *s.* (*Mus.*) der Sopran.

sorcerer ['sɔːsərə], *s.* der Zauberer.

sorceress ['sɔːsəres], *s.* die Hexe.

sorcery ['sɔːsəri], *s.* die Zauberei, Hexerei.

sordid ['sɔːdid], *adj.* schmutzig; gemein.

sore [sɔː], *adj.* wund, schmerzhaft; empfindlich. — *s.* die wunde Stelle.

sorrel (1) ['sɔrəl], *s.* (*Bot.*) der Sauerampfer.

sorrel (2) ['sɔrəl], *s.* (*Zool.*) der Rotfuchs.

sorrow ['sɔrou], *s.* der Kummer, das Leid, der Gram.

sorry ['sɔri], *adj.* traurig; *I am* —, es tut mir leid.

sort [sɔːt], *s.* die Art, Gattung, Sorte. — *v.a.* aussortieren.

sortie ['sɔːtiː], *s.* (*Mil.*) der Ausfall.

sot [sɔt], *s.* der Trunkenbold.

soul [soul], *s.* die Seele; *not a* —, niemand, keine Menschenseele.

sound (1) [saund], *v.n.*, *v.a.* tönen, klingen, erklingen lassen. — *s.* der Klang, Ton, Laut.

sound (2) [saund], *adj.* gesund; (*fig.*) vernünftig (*plan etc.*); solide.

soup [suːp], *s.* die Suppe.

sour [sauə], *adj.* sauer; (*fig.*) mürrisch.

source [sɔːs], *s.* die Quelle; der Ursprung (*origin*).

souse [saus], *v.a.* einpökeln, einsalzen.

south [sauθ], *s.* der Süden.

South African [sauθ 'æfrikən], *adj.* südafrikanisch. — *s.* der Südafrikaner.

southern ['sʌðən], *adj.* südlich, Süd-.

sou(th)-wester [sau(θ)'westə], *s.* (*Naut.*) der Südwester.

souvenir ['suːvəniə], *s.* das Andenken.

sovereign ['sɔvrin], *s.* der Herrscher (*ruler*); das Goldstück (£1 *coin*). — *adj.* allerhöchst, souverän.

Soviet ['souviːt], *adj.* sowjetisch. — *s.* der Sowjet.

sow (1) [sau], *s.* (*Zool.*) die Sau.

sow (2) [sou], *v.a. irr.* säen, ausstreuen (*cast*).

spa [spɑː], *s.* das Bad; der Kurort.

space [speis], *s.* der Zwischenraum (*interval*); der Raum, das Weltall, der Kosmos (*interplanetary*); der Platz (*room*). — *v.a.* sperren, richtig plazieren.

spacious ['speiʃəs], *adj.* geräumig.

spade [speid], *s.* der Spaten; *call a* — *a* —, das Kind beim rechten Namen nennen; (*Cards*) das Pik.

span [spæn], *s.* die Spanne (*time*); die Spannweite. — *v.a.* überspannen (*bridge*); ausmessen.

spangle [spæŋgl], *s.* der Flitter. — *v.a.* beflittern, schmücken.

Spaniard ['spænjəd], *s.* der Spanier.

spaniel ['spænjəl], *s.* (*Zool.*) der Wachtelhund.

Spanish ['spæniʃ], *adj.* spanisch.

spanner ['spænə], *s.* der Schraubenschlüssel.

spar (1) [spɑː], *s.* (*Naut.*) der Sparren.

spar (2) [spɑː], *s.* (*Geol.*) der Spat.

spar (3) [spɑː], *v.n.* boxen.

spare [spɛə], *v.a.* schonen (*save*); sparsam sein; übrig haben. — *v.n.* sparen; sparsam sein. — *adj.* übrig (*extra*); mager, hager (*lean*); Reserve- (*tyre etc.*).

sparing ['spɛəriŋ], *adj.* sparsam, karg.

spark [spɑːk], *s.* der Funken; (*fig.*) der helle Kopf.

sparkle [spɑːkl], *v.n.* glänzen, funkeln. — *s.* das Funkeln.

sparrow ['spærou], *s.* (*Orn.*) der Sperling.

sparrowhawk ['spærouhɔːk], *s.* (*Orn.*) der Sperber.

sparse [spɑːs], *adj.* spärlich, dünn.

spasm [spæzm], *s.* der Krampf.

spasmodic [spæz'mɔdik], *adj.* krampfhaft; (*fig.*) ab und zu auftretend.

spats [spæts], *s. pl.* die Gamaschen, *f. pl.*

spatter ['spætə], *v.a.* bespritzen, besudeln.

spatula ['spætjulə], *s.* der Spachtel.

spawn [spɔːn], *s.* der Laich, die Brut.

speak [spiːk], *v.a.*, *v.n. irr.* sprechen, reden; — *out*, frei heraussprechen.

speaker ['spiːkə], *s.* der Sprecher.

spear [spiə], *s.* der Spieß, Speer, die Lanze. — *v.a.* aufspießen.

special [speʃl], *adj.* besonder, speziell, Sonder-.

specific [spi'sifik], *adj.* spezifisch, eigentümlich.

specify ['spesifai], *v.a.* spezifizieren.

specimen ['spesimən], *s.* die Probe; (*Comm.*) das Muster.

specious ['spiːʃəs], *adj.* bestechend, trügerisch.

speck [spek], *s.* der Fleck.

speckle [spekl], *s.* der Tüpfel, Sprenkel. — *v.a.* sprenkeln.

spectacle ['spektəkl], *s.* das Schauspiel, der Anblick; (*pl.*) die Brille.

spectator [spek'teitə], *s.* der Zuschauer.

spectre ['spektə], *s.* das Gespenst.

speculate ['spekjuleit], *v.n.* nachsinnen, grübeln (*ponder*); spekulieren.

489

speculative

speculative ['spekjulətiv], *adj.* speku-
lativ; sinnend.
speech [spi:tʃ], *s.* die Rede, Ansprache;
das Sprechen (*articulation*); *figure of*
—, die Redewendung; *make a* —,
eine Rede halten.
speechify ['spi:tʃifai], *v.n.* viele Worte
machen, unermüdlich reden.
speed [spi:d], *s.* die Eile; die Geschwindigkeit (*velocity*); (*Mus.*) das Tempo.
— *v.a.* (eilig) fortschicken. — *v.n.*
eilen, schnell fahren; — *up*, sich
beeilen.
spell (1) [spel], *s.* der Zauber (*enchantment*). — *v.a.* buchstabieren (*verbally*);
richtig schreiben (*in writing*).
spell (2) [spel], *s.* die Zeitlang, Zeit
(*period*).
spellbound ['spelbaund], *adj.* bezau-
bert, gebannt.
spend [spend], *v.a. irr.* ausgeben
(*money*); verbringen (*time*); aufwenden (*energy*); erschöpfen (*exhaust*).
spendthrift ['spendθrift], *s.* der Ver-
schwender.
spew [spju:], *v.a.* speien; ausspeien.
sphere [sfiə], *s.* die Sphäre (*also fig.*);
(*Geom.*) die Kugel.
spice [spais], *s.* die Würze (*seasoning*);
das Gewürz (*herb*). — *v.a.* würzen.
spider ['spaidə], *s.* (*Zool.*) der Spinne.
spigot ['spigət], *s.* (*Mech.*) der Zapfen.
spike [spaik], *s.* die Spitze, der lange
Nagel; (*fig.*) der Dorn. — *v.a.* durchbohren, spießen; (*Mil.*) vernageln
(*a gun*).
spill (1) [spil], *v.a. irr.* ausschütten,
vergießen; (*Am. coll.*) — *the beans*,
mit der Sprache herausrücken, alles
verraten; *it's no good crying over spilt
milk*, was geschehen ist, ist geschehen.
spill (2) [spil], *s.* der Fidibus.
spin [spin], *v.a. irr.* spinnen, drehen,
wirbeln. — *v.n.* wirbeln, sich schnell
drehen; — *dry*, schleudern. — *s.* die
schnelle Drehung; — *drier*, die
Wäscheschleuder.
spinach ['spinidʒ], *s.* (*Bot.*) der Spinat.
spinal ['spainəl], *adj.* Rückgrats-.
spine [spain], *s.* (*Anat.*) die Wirbelsäule;
der Rücken (*of book*).
spinney ['spini], *s.* das Gestrüpp.
spinster ['spinstə], *s.* die (alte) Jungfer;
die unverheiratete Dame.
spiral ['spaiərəl], *adj.* Spiral-, gewunden. — *s.* (*Geom.*) die Spirale.
spirant ['spaiərənt], *s.* (*Phonet.*) der
Spirant.
spire [spaiə], *s.* (*Archit.*) die Turmspitze.
spirit ['spirit], *s.* der Geist; das Gespenst (*ghost*); der Mut (*courage*); die
Stimmung, Verfassung (*mood*); das
geistige Getränk (*drink*), (*pl.*) Spirituosen, *pl.*; *in high* —*s*, in guter Stimmung, Laune. — *v.a.* — *away*, entführen, verschwinden lassen.
spiritual ['spiritjuəl], *adj.* geistig (*mental*); (*Rel.*) geistlich. — *s.* (*Mus.*) das
Negerlied.

spit (1) [spit], *s.* der Spieß, Bratspieß.
— *v.a.* aufspießen.
spit (2) [spit], *v.n. irr.* ausspucken. — *s.*
die Spucke.
spite [spait], *s.* der Groll; *in* — *of*, trotz
(*Genit.*). — *v.a.* ärgern.
spiteful ['spaitful], *adj.* boshaft.
spittle [spitl], *s.* der Speichel.
spittoon [spi'tu:n], *s.* der Spucknapf.
splash [splæʃ], *s.* der Spritzer; *make a*
—, Aufsehen erregen. — *v.a., v.n.*
spritzen; (*fig.*) um sich werfen
(*money etc.*).
splay [splei], *v.a.* ausrenken, verrenken.
spleen [spli:n], *s.* (*Anat.*) die Milz;
(*fig.*) der Spleen, die Laune, Marotte.
splendour ['splendə], *s.* die Pracht, der
Glanz.
splice [splais], *v.a.* splissen; (*Naut.*) —
the mainbrace, das Hauptfaß öffnen.
splint [splint], *s.* (*Med.*) die Schiene.
splinter ['splintə], *s.* der Span; der
Splitter (*fragment*).
split [split], *v.a. irr.* spalten; (*fig.*)
verteilen, teilen (*divide*). — *v.n.* sich
trennen; (*coll.*) — *on s.o.*, einen
verraten. — *adj.* — *second timing*, auf
den Bruchteil einer Sekunde. — *s.*
die Spaltung.
splutter ['splʌtə], *v.n.* sprudeln. — *s.*
das Sprudeln.
spoil [spɔil], *v.a. irr.* verderben; (*child*)
verwöhnen; (*Mil.*) plündern, berau-
ben. — *v.n.* verderben. — *s.* (*pl.*) die
Beute.
spoilsport ['spɔilspɔ:t], *s.* der Spielverderber.
spoke [spouk], *s.* die Speiche; die
Sprosse.
spokesman ['spouksmən], *s.* der Wortführer, Sprecher.
sponge [spʌndʒ], *s.* der Schwamm; —
cake, die Sandtorte. — *v.a.* mit dem
Schwamm wischen. — *v.n.* (*coll.*)
schmarotzen (*on*, bei, *Dat.*).
sponger ['spʌndʒə], *s.* (*coll.*) der
Schmarotzer (*parasite*).
sponsor ['spɔnsə], *s.* der Bürge (*guarantor*); der Förderer; Pate. — *v.a.*
fördern, unterstützen.
spontaneous [spɔn'teiniəs], *adj.* spontan, freiwillig.
spook [spuk], *s.* der Spuk, Geist, das
Gespenst.
spool [spu:l], *s.* die Spule. — *v.a.* auf-
spulen.
spoon [spu:n], *s.* der Löffel. — *v.a.* mit
dem Löffel essen, löffeln.
sport [spɔ:t], *s.* der Sport; (*fig.*) der
Scherz. — *v.a.* tragen (*wear*). — *v.n.*
scherzen.
spot [spɔt], *s.* die Stelle, der Ort, Platz;
(*stain*) der Fleck; (*fig.*) der Schandfleck (*on o.'s honour*); *on the* —,
sogleich; auf der Stelle; *in a* —, (*Am.
coll.*) in Verlegenheit; — *cash*, Barzahlung, *f.* — *v.a.* entdecken, finden.
spotted ['spɔtid], *adj.* fleckig, gefleckt;
befleckt; pickelig.
spouse [spauz], *s.* der Gatte; die Gattin.

spout [spaut], *v.a.*, *v.n.* ausspeien, sprudeln, sprudeln lassen; (*sl.*) predigen, schwatzen. — *s.* die Tülle (*teapot etc.*); die Abflußröhre.

sprain [sprein], *v.a.* (*Med.*) verrenken. — *s.* die Verrenkung.

sprat [spræt], *s.* (*Zool.*) die Sprotte.

sprawl [sprɔːl], *v.n.* sich spreizen, ausbreiten.

spray [sprei], *v.a.*, *v.n.* sprühen spritzen. — *s.* die Sprühe; der Sprühregen.

spread [spred], *v.a.*, *v.n. irr.* ausbreiten; verbreiten (*get abroad*); streichen (*overlay with*). — *s.* die Ausbreitung; Verbreitung.

spree [spriː], *s.* das Vergnügen, der lustige Abend, Bummel.

sprig [sprig], *s.* der Zweig, Sprößling.

sprightly [ˈspraitli], *adj.* munter, lebhaft.

spring [spriŋ], *s.* die Quelle (*water*); der Ursprung (*origin*); der Frühling (*season*); (*Mech.*) die Feder, Sprungfeder, Spirale. — *v.n. irr.* springen (*jump*); entspringen (*originate*). — *v.a.* — *a surprise,* eine Überraschung bereiten.

springe [sprindʒ], *s.* der Sprenkel.

sprinkle [spriŋkl], *v.a.* (be)sprengen; (*Hort.*) berieseln.

sprint [sprint], *s.* der Kurzstreckenlauf, Wettlauf.

sprite [sprait], *s.* der Geist, Kobold.

sprout [spraut], *s.* (*Bot.*) die Sprosse, der Sprößling; *Brussels —s,* der Rosenkohl.

spruce (1) [spruːs], *adj.* sauber, geputzt; schmuck.

spruce (2) [spruːs], *s.* (*Bot.*) die Fichte, Rottanne.

spume [spjuːm], *s.* der Schaum.

spur [spəː], *s.* der Sporn (*goad*); (*fig.*) der Stachel; der Ansporn, Antrieb; (*Geog.*) der Ausläufer (*of range*). — *v.a.* anspornen.

spurious [ˈspjuəriəs], *adj.* unecht, falsch.

spurn [spəːn], *v.a.* verschmähen, verachten.

spurt [spəːt], *v.a.* spritzen. — *v.n.* sich anstrengen. — *s.* die Anstrengung.

sputter [ˈspʌtə], *v.a.* herausprudeln. — *v.n.* sprühen, sprudeln.

spy [spai], *s.* der Spion. — *v.n.* spionieren (*on,* bei, *Dat.*).

squabble [skwɔbl], *v.n.* zanken. — *s.* der Zank, Streit.

squad [skwɔd], *s.* der Trupp.

squadron [ˈskwɔdrən], *s.* die Schwadron, das Geschwader.

squalid [ˈskwɔlid], *adj.* schmutzig, elend, eklig.

squall [skwɔːl], *s.* der Windstoß.

squalor [ˈskwɔlə], *s.* der Schmutz.

squander [ˈskwɔndə], *v.a.* verschwenden, vergeuden.

square [skwɛə], *s.* das Quadrat; der Platz; (*coll.*) der Philister, Spießer. — *v.a.* ausrichten; (*coll.*) ins Reine bringen. — *adj.* viereckig; quadratisch; redlich (*honest*); quitt (*quits*).

squash (1) [skwɔʃ], *v.a.* zerquetschen, zerdrücken (*press together*). — *s.* das Gedränge (*crowd*); der Fruchtsaft (*drink*).

squash (2) [skwɔʃ], *s.* (*Sport*) eine Art Racketspiel.

squat [skwɔt], *v.n.* kauern; sich niederlassen. — *adj.* stämmig, untersetzt.

squatter [ˈskwɔtə], *s.* der Ansiedler.

squaw [skwɔː], *s.* die Indianerfrau.

squeak [skwiːk], *v.n.* quieken, quietschen. — *s.* das Gequiek.

squeal [skwiːl], *v.n.* quieken; (*Am. coll.*) verraten, preisgeben.

squeamish [ˈskwiːmiʃ], *adj.* empfindlich, zimperlich.

squeeze [skwiːz], *v.a.* drücken, quetschen. — *s.* das Gedränge.

squib [skwib], *s.* der Frosch (*firework*); (*Lit.*) das Spottgedicht.

squint [skwint], *v.n.* schielen. — *s.* das Schielen.

squire [skwaiə], *s.* der Landedelmann, Junker.

squirrel [ˈskwirəl], *s.* (*Zool.*) das Eichhörnchen.

squirt [skwəːt], *v.a.* spritzen. — *s.* der Spritzer, Wasserstrahl; (*sl.*) der Wicht.

stab [stæb], *v.a.* erstechen, erdolchen. — *s.* der Dolchstich, Dolchstoß.

stability [stəˈbiliti], *s.* die Beständigkeit, Stabilität.

stable (1) [steibl], *adj.* fest, beständig; (*Phys.*) stabil.

stable (2) [steibl], *s.* der Stall.

stack [stæk], *s.* der Stoß (*pile*); der Schornstein (*chimneys*). — *v.a.* aufschichten.

staff [stɑːf], *s.* der Stab, Stock; (*Mil.*) der Stab, Generalstab; (*Sch.*) der Lehrkörper; das Personal. — *v.a.* besetzen.

stag [stæg], *s.* (*Zool.*) der Hirsch; — *party,* die Herrengesellschaft.

stage [steidʒ], *s.* (*Theat.*) die Bühne; die Stufe, das Stadium (*phase*); (*fig.*) der Schauplatz; *fare —,* die Teilstrecke. — *v.a.* (*Theat.*) inszenieren, abhalten (*hold*).

stagecoach [ˈsteidʒkoutʃ], *s.* die Postkutsche.

stagger [ˈstægə], *v.n.* schwanken, wanken, taumeln. — *v.a.* (*coll.*) verblüffen (*astonish*); staffeln (*graduate*).

stagnate [stægˈneit], *v.n.* stocken, stillstehen.

staid [steid], *adj.* gesetzt, gelassen.

stain [stein], *s.* der Fleck, Makel. — *v.a.* beflecken; beizen; färben (*dye*).

stained [steind], *adj.* — *glass window,* buntes Fenster.

stainless [ˈsteinlis], *adj.* rostfrei.

stair [stɛə], *s.* die Stufe, Stiege.

staircase [ˈstɛəkeis], *s.* das Treppenhaus; die Treppe.

stake [steik], *s.* der Pfahl, Pfosten; Scheiterhaufen; (*Gambling*) der Einsatz; *at —,* auf dem Spiel. — *v.a.* aufs Spiel setzen.

stale [steil], *adj.* abgestanden, schal.

stalemate ['steilmeit], *s.* (*Chess*) das Patt; der Stillstand.

stalk (1) [stɔ:k], *s.* (*Bot.*) der Stengel, Halm.

stalk (2) [stɔ:k], *v.n.* stolzieren, steif gehen. — *v.a.* pirschen (*hunt*).

stall [stɔ:l], *s.* die Bude (*booth*), der Stand (*stand*); (*Eccl.*) der Chorstuhl; (*Theat.*) der Sperrsitz; Parterresitz. — *v.n.* (*Motor.*) stehenbleiben.

stallion ['stæljən], *s.* (*Zool.*) der Hengst.

stalwart ['stɔ:lwət], *adj.* kräftig, stark, verläßlich.

stamina ['stæminə], *s.* die Ausdauer, Widerstandskraft.

stammer ['stæmə], *v.n.* stammeln, stottern.

stamp [stæmp], *s.* der Stempel (*rubber* —); die Marke (*postage*); die Stampfe, Stanze (*die* —). — *v.a.* stempeln; (*Mech.*) stanzen; frankieren (*letters*). — *v.n.* stampfen.

stampede [stæm'pi:d], *s.* die wilde Flucht. — *v.n.* in wilder Flucht davonlaufen.

stand [stænd], *v.n. irr.* stehen. — *v.a.* aushalten, standhalten (*Dat.*). — *s.* der Ständer (*hats etc.*); der Stand (*stall*); (*fig.*) die Stellung.

standard ['stændəd], *s.* der Standard (*level*); (*Mil.*) die Standarte; der Maßstab (*yardstick*). — *adj.* normal.

standing ['stændin], *s.* der Rang, das Ansehen. — *adj.* — *orders*, die Geschäftsordnung; (*Mil.*) die Vorschriften, *f. pl.*, Dauerbefehle, *m. pl.*

standpoint ['stændpoint], *s.* der Standpunkt (*point of view*).

standstill ['stændstil], *s.* der Stillstand.

stanza ['stænzə], *s.* (*Poet.*) die Stanze, Strophe.

staple [steipl], *s.* das Haupterzeugnis; der Stapelplatz. — *adj.* Haupt-. — *v.a.* stapeln; heften (*paper*).

stapler ['steiplə], *s.* die Heftmaschine.

star [stɑ:], *s.* der Stern; (*Theat. etc.*) der Star. — *v.n.* (*Theat. etc.*) die Hauptrolle spielen.

starboard ['stɑ:bəd], *s.* das Steuerbord.

starch [stɑ:tʃ], *s.* die Stärke (*laundry*). — *v.a.* stärken.

stare [steə], *v.n.* starren. — *s.* der starre Blick, das Starren.

stark [stɑ:k], *adj.* völlig, ganz.

starling ['stɑ:lin], *s.* (*Orn.*) der Star.

start [stɑ:t], *v.n.* anfangen; aufbrechen; auffahren, aufspringen; stutzen (*jerk*); abfahren (*depart*). — *v.a.* starten (*car etc.*), in Gang setzen. — *s.* der Anfang; (*Sport*) der Start, Anlauf; der Aufbruch (*departure*); *by fits and* —*s*, ruckweise.

starter ['stɑ:tə], *s.* (*Sport*) der Starter, Teilnehmer (*participant*); das Rennpferd (*horse*); (*Motor.*) der Anlasser.

startle [stɑ:tl], *v.a.* erschrecken.

starve [stɑ:v], *v.n.* verhungern, hungern. — *v.a.* aushungern.

state [steit], *s.* der Zustand, die Lage; (*Pol.*) der Staat; (*personal*) der Stand (*single etc.*). — *v.a.* erklären, darlegen.

stately ['steitli], *adj.* stattlich, prachtvoll.

statement ['steitmənt], *s.* die Feststellung; *bank* —, der Kontoauszug.

statesman ['steitsmən], *s.* der Staatsmann, Politiker.

statics ['stætiks], *s.* die Statik.

station ['steiʃən], *s.* (*Railw.*) die Station; der Bahnhof; die Stellung, der Rang (*position*); (*Mil.*) die Stationierung. — *v.a.* (*Mil.*) aufstellen, stationieren; (*fig.*) hinstellen.

stationary ['steiʃənri], *adj.* stationär, stillstehend.

stationer ['steiʃənə], *s.* der Papierhändler.

stationery ['steiʃənri], *s.* das Briefpapier, Schreibpapier; die Papierwaren, *f. pl.*

statuary ['stætjuəri], *s.* die Bildhauerkunst.

statue ['stætju:], *s.* das Standbild.

status ['steitəs], *s.* die Stellung (*rank, position*).

statute ['stætju:t], *s.* das Statut; — *law*, das Landesrecht, Gesetzesrecht.

staunch [stɔ:ntʃ], *adj.* zuverlässig.

stave [steiv], *s.* die Faßdaube (*of vat*); (*Poet.*) die Strophe; (*Mus.*) die Linie. — *v.a.* — *off*, abwehren.

stay [stei], *v.n.* bleiben, verweilen, wohnen. — *v.a.* hindern, aufhalten. — *s.* der Aufenthalt; (*pl.*) das Korsett.

stead [sted], *s.* die Stelle; *in his* —, an seiner Statt.

steadfast ['stedfɑ:st], *adj.* standhaft, fest.

steadiness ['stedinis], *s.* die Beständigkeit.

steady ['stedi], *adj.* fest, sicher; beständig, treu.

steak [steik], *s.* das Steak.

steal [sti:l], *v.a. irr.* stehlen. — *v.n.* sich stehlen, schleichen.

stealth [stelθ], *s.* die Heimlichkeit.

stealthy ['stelθi], *adj.* heimlich, verstohlen.

steam [sti:m], *s.* der Dampf; *get up* —, in Gang bringen *or* kommen; — *boiler*, der Dampfkessel. — *v.n.* dampfen; davondampfen. — *v.a.* dämpfen, (*Cul.*) dünsten.

steed [sti:d], *s.* das Schlachtroß.

steel [sti:l], *s.* der Stahl. — *adj.* stählern. — *v.n.* — *o.s.*, sich stählen.

steep (1) [sti:p], *adj.* steil; (*fig.*) hoch; (*coll.*) gesalzen (*price*).

steep (2) [sti:p], *v.a.* einweichen, sättigen.

steeple [sti:pl], *s.* (*Archit.*) der Kirchturm.

steeplechase ['sti:pltʃeis], *s.* das Hindernisrennen.

steeplejack ['sti:pldʒæk], *s.* der Turmdecker.

steer (1) [stiə], *s.* (*Zool.*) der junge Stier.

steer (2) [stiə], *v.a.* steuern (*guide*).

steerage ['stiəridʒ], *s.* die Steuerung; (*Naut.*) das Zwischendeck.

stellar ['stelə], *adj.* Stern-, Sternen-.

stem (1) [stem], *s.* der Stamm; (*Phonet.*) der Stamm; der Stiel, die Wurzel. — *v.n.* — *from*, kommen von, abstammen.

stem (2) [stem], *v.a.* sich entgegenstemmen (*Dat.*); (*fig.*) eindämmen.

stench [stentʃ], *s.* der Gestank.

stencil ['stensil], *s.* die Schablone, Matrize; *cut a* —, auf Matrize schreiben.

step [step], *s.* der Schritt, Tritt; (*of ladder*) die Sprosse; (*of stairs*) die Stufe. — *v.n.* treten, schreiten (*stride*). — *v.a.* (*coll.*) — *up*, beschleunigen.

step- [step], *pref.* Stief- (*brother, mother etc.*).

stereo- ['stiəriou], *pref.* Stereo-.

sterile ['sterail], *adj.* steril.

sterling ['stəːliŋ], *adj.* echt, vollwertig; *pound* —, ein Pfund Sterling.

stern (1) [stəːn], *adj.* streng.

stern (2) [stəːn], *s.* (*Naut.*) das Heck.

stevedore ['stiːvədɔː], *s.* der Hafenarbeiter.

stew [stjuː], *s.* (*Cul.*) das Schmorfleisch, das Gulasch.

steward ['stjuːəd], *s.* der Verwalter; der Haushofmeister; (*Naut.*) der Steward.

stick [stik], *s.* der Stock, Stecken. — *v.a.* stecken (*insert*); kleben (*glue*). — *v.n.* stecken, haften bleiben; (*fig., coll.*) — *to s.o.*, zu jemandem halten (*be loyal*).

sticky ['stiki], *adj.* klebrig; (*fig.*) prekär, schwierig (*difficult*); *come to a* — *end*, ein böses Ende nehmen.

stiff [stif], *adj.* steif; schwer, schwierig (*examination*); formell (*manner*).

stiffen [stifn], *v.a.* steifen, versteifen. — *v.n.* steif werden, sich versteifen.

stifle [staifl], *v.a., v.n.* ersticken; (*fig.*) unterdrücken.

stigmatize ['stigmətaiz], *v.a.* stigmatisieren, brandmarken.

stile [stail], *s.* der Zauntritt, Übergang.

still (1) [stil], *adj.* still, ruhig. — *adv.* immer noch. — *conj.* doch, dennoch. — *v.a.* stillen, beruhigen.

still (2) [stil], *s.* die Destillierflasche, der Destillierkolben.

stilt [stilt], *s.* die Stelze.

stilted ['stiltid], *adj.* auf Stelzen; (*fig.*) hochtrabend, geschraubt.

stimulant ['stimjulənt], *s.* das Reizmittel. — *adj.* anreizend, anregend.

stimulate ['stimjuleit], *v.a.* anreizen, stimulieren, anregen.

stimulus ['stimjuləs], *s.* der Reiz, die Anregung.

sting [stiŋ], *v.a. irr.* stechen; (*fig.*) kränken, verwunden. — *v.n.* irr. stechen, brennen, schmerzen. — *s.* der Stachel (*prick*); der Stich (*stab*).

stink [stiŋk], *v.n. irr.* stinken. — *s.* der Gestank.

stint [stint], *s.* die Einschränkung (*limit*); das Maß, Tagespensum. — *v.a.* beschränken, einschränken.

stipend ['staipend], *s.* die Besoldung, das Gehalt.

stipendiary [stai'pendiəri], *adj.* besoldet, bezahlt.

stipulate ['stipjuleit], *v.a.* festsetzen, ausbedingen.

stir [stəː], *v.a.* rühren, bewegen. — *v.n.* sich rühren. — *s.* die Aufregung; *cause a* —, Aufsehen erregen.

stirrup ['stirəp], *s.* der Steigbügel.

stitch [stitʃ], *v.a.* sticken, nähen. — *s.* der Stich; der stechende Schmerz, der Seitenstich (*pain*).

stoat [stout], *s.* (*Zool.*) das Hermelin.

stock [stɔk], *s.* das Lager; *in* —, auf Lager; vorrätig; der Stamm, die Familie; (*Fin.*) das Kapital; *exchange*, die Börse; (*pl.*) die Börsenpapiere, *n. pl.*, Aktien, *f. pl.* — *v.a.* halten, führen.

stockade [stɔ'keid], *s.* das Staket.

stockbroker ['stɔkbroukə], *s.* (*Fin.*) der Börsenmakler.

stockholder ['stɔkhouldə], *s.* (*Fin., Am.*) der Aktionär.

stocking ['stɔkiŋ], *s.* der Strumpf.

stocktaking ['stɔkteikiŋ], *s.* die Inventuraufnahme.

stoical ['stouikəl], *adj.* stoisch.

stoke [stouk], *v.a.* schüren.

stoker ['stoukə], *s.* der Heizer.

stole [stoul], *s.* (*Eccl.*) die Stola; der Pelzkragen (*fur*).

stolid ['stɔlid], *adj.* schwerfällig, gleichgültig.

stomach ['stʌmək], *s.* der Magen; (*fig.*) der Appetit.

stone [stoun], *s.* der Stein; der Kern (*fruit*). — *v.a.* steinigen (*throw* —*s at*); entsteinen (*fruit*).

stony ['stouni], *adj.* steinig; (*sl.*) — *broke*, pleite.

stool [stuːl], *s.* der Schemel, Hocker; (*Med.*) der Stuhlgang.

stoop [stuːp], *v.n.* sich bücken; (*fig.*) sich herablassen.

stooping ['stuːpiŋ], *adj.* gebückt.

stop [stɔp], *v.a.* halten, stoppen; aufhören; aufhalten (*halt*); — *up*, verstopfen, versperren (*block*); (*tooth*) plombieren. — *v.n.* stehen bleiben (*stand*); sich aufhalten (*stay*). — *s.* der Halt, die Haltestelle (*of bus etc.*); das Aufhalten, Innehalten (*stoppage*); das Register (*organ*); (*Gram.*) der Punkt.

stoppage ['stɔpidʒ], *s.* die Stockung, Hemmung (*hindrance*); die Arbeitseinstellung (*strike*).

stopper ['stɔpə], *s.* der Stöpsel.

storage ['stɔːridʒ], *s.* das Lagern.

store [stɔː], *s.* der Vorrat, das Lagerhaus, Magazin; (*Am.*) das Kaufhaus; (*fig.*) die Menge (*of anecdotes etc.*). — *v.a.* lagern.

storey ['stɔːri], *s.* das Stockwerk.

stork [stɔːk], *s.* (*Orn.*) der Storch.

storm [stɔːm], *s.* der Sturm, das Gewitter.

story ['stɔːri], *s.* die Geschichte, Erzählung (*narrative*).

stout

stout [staut], *adj.* fest; stark, kräftig. — *s.* das starke Bier.
stove [stouv], *s.* der Ofen.
stow [stou], *v.a.* verstauen, packen. — *v.n.* — *away*, als blinder Passagier fahren.
stowaway [´stouəwei], *s.* der blinde Passagier.
straddle [strædl], *v.n.* rittlings sitzen.
straggle [strægl], *v.n.* umherschweifen, streifen; (*Bot.*) wuchern.
straight [streit], *adj.* gerade, offen. — *adv.* — *away*, sofort, sogleich.
straighten [streitn], *v.a.* ausrichten, gerade richten. — *v.n.* sich ausrichten.
strain [strein], *s.* die Anstrengung, Anspannung; (*Mus.*) der Ton, Stil; der Hang. — *v.a.* anstrengen, filtrieren; seihen. — *v.n.* sich anstrengen.
strainer [´streinə], *s.* der Seiher, der Filter, das Sieb.
strait [streit], *adj.* eng. — *s.* (*usually pl.*) die Enge, Meerenge.
strand (1) [strænd], *s.* der Strand.
strand (2) [strænd], *s.* die Litze (*of rope, string*).
strange [streindʒ], *adj.* fremd (*unknown*); seltsam (*queer*).
stranger [´streindʒə], *s.* der Fremdling, Fremde; der Unbekannte.
strangle [stræŋgl], *v.a.* erdrosseln, erwürgen.
strangulation [stræŋgju´leiʃən], *s.* die Erdrosselung, Erwürgung.
strap [stræp], *v.a.* festschnallen, anschnallen. — *s.* der Gurt, Riemen.
strapping [´stræpiŋ], *adj.* stark, stämmig.
strata *see under* **stratum**.
stratagem [´strætədʒəm], *s.* die List; (*Mil.*) der Plan.
strategy [´strætədʒi], *s.* die Strategie.
stratification [strætifi´keiʃən], *s.* die Schichtung; (*Geol.*) die Lagerung.
stratum [´streitəm], *s.* (*pl.* **strata** [´streitə]) die Schicht, Lage.
straw [strɔ:], *s.* das Stroh; *that's the last* —, das ist die Höhe!
strawberry [´strɔ:bəri], *s.* (*Bot.*) die Erdbeere.
stray [strei], *v.n.* irregehen, schweifen; sich verirren. — *adj.* irr, verirrt.
streak [stri:k], *s.* der Strich; der Streifen; (*fig.*) der Anflug.
streaky [´stri:ki], *adj.* gestreift; (*bacon*) durchwachsen.
stream [stri:m], *v.n.* strömen, wehen (*in the wind*). — *s.* die Strömung (*flow*); der Bach (*brook*), der Strom (*river*).
streamer [´stri:mə], *s.* der Wimpel, das Band, die Papierschlange.
street [stri:t], *s.* die Straße; —*s ahead*, weit voraus.
streetcar [´stri:tka:], *s.* (*Am.*) *see* **tram**.
streetlamp [´stri:tlæmp], *s.* die Straßenlaterne.
strength [streŋθ], *s.* die Stärke; die Kraft.

strengthen [´streŋθən], *v.a.* stärken; (*fig.*) bekräftigen (*support*).
strenuous [´strenjuəs], *adj.* anstrengend.
stress [stres], *v.a.* (*Phonet.*) betonen; (*fig.*) hervorheben. — *s.* die Betonung (*emphasis*); der Druck (*pressure*).
stretch [stretʃ], *v.a.* spannen; strecken, ausstrecken; — *a point*, eine Ausnahme machen. — *s.* die Strecke (*distance*); (*coll.*) die Zuchthausstrafe (*penal sentence*).
stretcher [´stretʃə], *s.* die Tragbahre.
strew [stru:], *v.a.* streuen, ausstreuen.
strict [strikt], *adj.* streng (*severe*); genau (*exact*).
stricture [´striktʃə], *s.* der Tadel, die Kritik; (*pl.*) die kritische Rede.
stride [straid], *v.n. irr.* schreiten. — *s.* der Schritt; *take in o.'s* —, leicht bewältigen.
strident [´straidənt], *adj.* laut, lärmend; grell.
strife [straif], *s.* der Streit, Zank.
strike [straik], *v.a., v.n. irr.* schlagen; abmachen (*bargain*); (*Mus.*) — *up*, anstimmen (*song*), aufspielen (*instrument*); beginnen; — *the eye*, auffallen; streiken, in Streik treten. — *s.* der Streik, die Arbeitseinstellung.
striking [´straikiŋ], *adj.* auffallend.
string [striŋ], *s.* die Schnur; (*Mus.*) die Saite; — *quartet*, das Streichquartett; die Reihe (*series*). — *v.a.* anreihen (*beads etc.*); — *together*, verbinden. — *v.n.* — *along*, sich anschließen.
stringency [´strindʒənsi], *s.* die Strenge (*severity*); die Knappheit (*shortage*).
stringent [´strindʒənt], *adj.* streng (*severe*); knapp (*short*).
strip [strip], *s.* der Streifen. — *v.a., v.n.* abstreifen, (sich) entkleiden; (sich) entblößen.
stripe [straip], *s.* der (Farb)streifen; die Strieme (*mark on body*). — *v.a.* streifen, bestreifen.
strive [straiv], *v.n. irr.* sich bemühen (*for*, um, *Acc.*), streben (*for*, nach, *Dat.*).
stroke (1) [strouk], *v.a.* streicheln.
stroke (2) [strouk], *s.* der Strich (*brush*); der Streich (*sword*), der Stoß (*blow*); (*Med.*) der Schlaganfall.
stroll [stroul], *v.n.* schlendern.
strolling [´stroulin], *adj.* — *players*, die Wandertruppe.
strong [strɔŋ], *adj.* stark.
strongbox [´strɔŋbɔks], *s.* die Geldkassette.
strongroom [´strɔŋrum], *s.* der Geldtresor.
strop [strɔp], *s.* der Streichriemen.
structure [´strʌktʃə], *s.* der Bau, Aufbau; die Struktur.
struggle [strʌgl], *s.* der Kampf, das Ringen. — *v.n.* kämpfen, ringen.
strut [strʌt], *v.n.* stolzieren.
stub [stʌb], *s.* der Stumpf, Stummel (*cigarette*). — *v.a.* — *out*, ausmachen, auslöschen (*cigarette etc.*).

494

stubble ['stʌbl], s. die Stoppel, das Stoppelfeld; die (Bart)stoppeln, f. pl. (beard).
stubborn ['stʌbən], adj. eigensinnig, hartnäckig.
stucco ['stʌkou], s. die Stuckarbeit.
stud (1) [stʌd], s. der Hemdenknopf, Kragenknopf (collar —). — v.a. beschlagen (nail); besetzen (bejewel).
stud (2) [stʌd], s. das Gestüt (horses).
student ['stju:dənt], s. der Student.
studied ['stʌdid], adj. geziert, absichtlich (deliberate); gelehrt (learned).
studio ['stju:diou], s. (Phot.) das Atelier; (Film, Rad.) das Studio.
studious ['stju:diəs], adj. beflissen, fleißig; lernbegierig.
study ['stʌdi], v.a., v.n. studieren. — s. das Studium; das Arbeitszimmer (room); (Mus. etc.) die Studie; (Art) der Entwurf; die Untersuchung (investigation).
stuff [stʌf], s. der Stoff, das Material; (coll.) das Zeug (rubbish). — v.a. stopfen, ausstopfen (animals); (Cul.) füllen.
stuffing ['stʌfiŋ], s. die Füllung, das Füllsel.
stultify ['stʌltifai], v.a. dumm machen.
stumble [stʌmbl], v.n. stolpern; — upon, zufällig stoßen (auf, Acc.).
stumbling ['stʌmbliŋ], s. das Stolpern; — block, das Hindernis, der Stein des Anstoßes.
stump [stʌmp], s. der Stumpf. — v.a. verblüffen; abstumpfen. — v.n. schwerfällig gehen.
stun [stʌn], v.a. betäuben, verdutzen.
stunning ['stʌniŋ], adj. betörend, fabelhaft, überwältigend.
stunt (1) [stʌnt], v.a. am Wachstum behindern, klein halten.
stunt (2) [stʌnt], s. der Trick, das Kunststück; (Aviat.) der Kunstflug.
stupefy ['stju:pifai], v.a. betäuben.
stupendous [stju:'pendəs], adj. erstaunlich.
stupid ['stju:pid], adj. dumm.
stupor ['stju:pə], s. die Erstarrung, Lähmung (of mind).
sturdy ['stə:di], adj. derb, stark, stämmig.
sturgeon ['stə:dʒən], s. (Zool.) der Stör.
stutter ['stʌtə], v.n. stottern.
sty [stai], s. der Schweinestall.
sty(e) [stai], s. (Med.) das Gerstenkorn (on eyelid).
style [stail], s. (Lit.) der Stil; der Griffel (stylus); die Mode (fashion); die Anrede (address). — v.a. anreden.
stylish ['stailiʃ], adj. elegant, modern.
suave [sweiv, swa:v], adj. höflich, gewinnend.
sub- [sʌb], pref. Unter-.
subaltern ['sʌbəltən], s. (Mil.) der Leutnant, Oberleutnant.
subject ['sʌbdʒikt], s. (Gram.) das Subjekt; (Pol.) der Untertan; der Gegenstand. — adj. untertan (to,

Dat.); — to, abhängig von. — [səb'dʒekt], v.a. unterwerfen (to, Dat.); aussetzen (Dat.).
subjunctive [səb'dʒʌŋktiv], s. (Gram.) der Konjunktiv.
sublet [sʌb'let], v.a. in Untermiete vermieten, untervermieten.
sublimate ['sʌblimeit], v.a. sublimieren.
submarine ['sʌbməri:n], s. das Unterseeboot.
submission [səb'miʃən], s. die Unterwerfung (subjection); der Vorschlag (suggestion).
submit [səb'mit], v.a. unterwerfen (subjugate); vorlegen. — v.n. sich beugen (to, Dat.).
suborn [sʌ'bɔ:n], v.a. anstiften; bestechen (corrupt).
subpoena [sʌb'pi:nə], s. (Law) die Vorladung.
subscribe [səb'skraib], v.a. unterschreiben. — v.n. abonnieren (to, zu); abonnieren (paper).
subscription [səb'skripʃən], s. das Abonnement (to, Genit.); (club) der Beitrag.
subsequent ['sʌbsikwənt], adj. folgend.
subservient [sʌb'sə:viənt], adj. unterwürfig.
subside [səb'said], v.n. sinken; abnehmen (decrease).
subsidence [sʌb'saidəns, 'sʌbsidəns], s. das Sinken, Sichsetzen.
subsidiary [sʌb'sidjəri], adj. Hilfs-, Neben-.
subsidize ['sʌbsidaiz], v.a. unterstützen (with money), subventionieren.
subsidy ['sʌbsidi], s. die Unterstützung, Subvention.
subsist [səb'sist], v.n. leben, existieren.
subsistence [səb'sistəns], s. das Dasein, Auskommen; der Lebensunterhalt.
substance ['sʌbstəns], s. das Wesen, der Stoff, die Substanz.
substantial [səb'stænʃəl], adj. wesentlich, beträchtlich.
substantiate [səb'stænʃieit], v.a. dartun, nachweisen, bestätigen.
substantive ['sʌbstəntiv], s. (Gram.) das Substantiv, Hauptwort. — adj. (Mil.) effektiv, wirklich.
substitute ['sʌbstitju:t], v.a. ersetzen, an die Stelle setzen. — s. der Ersatzmann, Vertreter.
subterfuge ['sʌbtəfju:dʒ], s. die Ausflucht.
subtle [sʌtl], adj. fein, schlau, subtil.
subtract [səb'trækt], v.a. abziehen; (Maths.) subtrahieren.
suburb ['sʌbə:b], s. die Vorstadt, der Vorort.
subversion [səb'və:ʃən], s. (Pol.) der Umsturz.
subversive [səb'və:siv], adj. umstürzlerisch, umstürzend.
subway ['sʌbwei], s. die Unterführung; (Am.) die Untergrundbahn.
succeed [sək'si:d], v.n. erfolgreich sein, Erfolg haben. — v.a. nachfolgen (Dat.) (follow).

success [sək'ses], s. der Erfolg.
successful [sək'sesful], adj. erfolgreich.
succession [sək'sefən], s. die Nachfolge.
successive [sək'sesiv], adj. der Reihe nach, aufeinanderfolgend.
succinct [sək'siŋkt], adj. bündig, kurz.
succour ['sʌkə], v.a. beistehen (Dat.), helfen (Dat.).
succulent ['sʌkjulənt], adj. saftig.
succumb [sə'kʌm], v.n. unterliegen (to, Dat.).
such [sʌtʃ], adj. solch, derartig. — pron. ein solcher; — as, diejenigen, alle die.
suchlike ['sʌtʃlaik], pron. (coll.) dergleichen.
suck [sʌk], v.a., v.n. saugen.
suckle [sʌkl], v.a. säugen, stillen.
suction ['sʌkʃən], s. das Saugen; (Engin.) Saug-.
Sudanese [su:də'ni:z], adj. sudanisch, sudanesisch. — s. der Sudan(es)er.
sudden [sʌdn], adj. plötzlich.
suds [sʌdz], s. pl. das Seifenwasser.
sue [sju:], v.a. gerichtlich belangen, verklagen.
suède [sweid], s. das Wildleder.
suet ['su:it], s. das Nierenfett.
suffer ['sʌfə], v.a. ertragen, dulden. — v.n. leiden (from, an).
sufferance ['sʌfərəns], s. die Duldung; on —, nur widerwillig.
suffice [sə'fais], v.n. genügen, langen, (aus)reichen.
sufficient [sə'fiʃənt], adj. genügend, hinreichend.
suffocate ['sʌfəkeit], v.a., v.n. ersticken.
suffragan ['sʌfrəgən], s. (Eccl.) der Weihbischof.
suffrage ['sʌfridʒ], s. das Wahlrecht, Stimmrecht.
suffuse [sə'fju:z], v.a. übergießen, überfließen.
sugar ['ʃugə], s. der Zucker; — basin, die Zuckerdose.
suggest [sə'dʒest], v.a. vorschlagen, anregen.
suggestion [sə'dʒestʃən], s. der Vorschlag.
suggestive [sə'dʒestiv], adj. zweideutig.
suicide ['sju:isaid], s. der Selbstmord, Freitod.
suit [su:t], s. das Gesuch, die Bitte (request); die Farbe (cards); (Law) der Prozeß; der Anzug (clothes). — v.n. passen (Dat.) (be convenient) ; passen zu (look well with). — v.a. anpassen (match).
suitcase ['su:tkeis], s. der Handkoffer.
suitable ['su:təbl], adj. passend.
suite [swi:t], s. das Gefolge (following); die Zimmerflucht (rooms); die Reihe (cards).
suitor ['su:tə], s. der Brautwerber, Freier.
sulk [sʌlk], v.n. schmollen.
sullen ['sʌlən], adj. düster, mürrisch.
sully ['sʌli], v.a. beschmutzen.
sulphur ['sʌlfə], s. (Chem.) der Schwefel.

Sultan ['sʌltən], s. der Sultan.
Sultana [sʌl'ta:nə], s. die Sultanin.
sultana [sʌl'ta:nə], s. (Bot.) die Sultanine.
sultry ['sʌltri], adj. schwül.
sum [sʌm], s. die Summe; (fig.) der Inbegriff. — v.a., v.n. — up, zusammenfassen.
summary ['sʌməri], s. die Zusammenfassung, der Auszug. — adj. summarisch.
summer ['sʌmə], s. der Sommer; Indian —, der Spätsommer, Altweibersommer, Nachsommer.
summit ['sʌmit], s. der Gipfel, die Spitze.
summon(s) ['sʌmən(z)], v.a. (Law) vorladen. — s. (**summons**) die Vorladung.
sump [sʌmp], s. (Motor.) die Ölwanne.
sumptuous ['sʌmptjuəs], adj. prächtig, mit Aufwand, kostbar.
sun [sʌn], s. die Sonne. — v.r. sich sonnen.
sunburn ['sʌnbə:n], s. der Sonnenbrand.
Sunday ['sʌnd(e)i]. der Sonntag.
sundial ['sʌndaiəl], s. die Sonnenuhr.
sundown ['sʌndaun] see **sunset**.
sundry ['sʌndri], adj. mehrere, verschiedene. — s. (pl.) Gemischtwaren, f. pl.
sunny ['sʌni], adj. sonnig.
sunrise ['sʌnraiz], s. der Sonnenaufgang.
sunset ['sʌnset], s. der Sonnenuntergang.
sunshade ['sʌnʃeid], s. das Sonnendach, der Sonnenschirm (parasol).
super ['su:pə], s. (Theat.) der Statist. — adj. (coll.) fein, genos.
super- ['su:pə], pref. über-, hinzu-.
superannuation [su:pərænju'eiʃən], s. die Pensionierung.
superb [su'pə:b], adj. hervorragend, herrlich.
supercilious [su:pə'siliəs], adj. hochmütig, anmaßend.
superficial [su:pə'fiʃəl], adj. oberflächlich.
superfluous [su:'pə:fluəs], adj. überflüssig.
superintendent [su:pərin'tendənt], s. der Oberaufseher.
superior [su:'piəriə], adj. ober, höher. — s. der Vorgesetzte.
superiority [su:piəri'oriti], s. die Überlegenheit.
superlative [su:'pə:lətiv], s. (Gram.) der Superlativ. — adj. ausnehmend gut.
supermarket ['su:pəma:kit], s. das Selbstbedienungsgeschäft, SB-Geschäft, der grosse Lebensmittelladen.
supersede [su:pə'si:d], v.a. verdrängen.
superstition [su:pə'stiʃən], s. der Aberglaube.
superstitious [su:pə'stiʃəs], adj. abergläubisch.
supervise ['su:pəvaiz], v.a. beaufsichtigen, überwachen.

sway

supine [su'pain], *adj.* auf dem Rücken liegend. — ['su:pain], *s.* (*Gram.*) das Supinum.

supper ['sʌpə], *s.* das Abendessen; *Last Supper*, das Heilige Abendmahl.

supplant [sə'plɑ:nt], *v.a.* verdrängen.

supple [sʌpl], *adj.* geschmeidig, biegsam.

supplement ['sʌplimənt], *s.* die Beilage (*paper*); der Zusatz.

supplementary [sʌpli'mentri], *adj.* zusätzlich.

supplier [sə'plaiə], *s.* der Lieferant.

supply [sə'plai], *v.a.* liefern (*s. th.*); beliefern, versorgen (*s.o.*). — *s.* die Versorgung.

support [sə'pɔ:t], *v.a.* unterstützen. — *s.* die Stütze (*prop*); die Unterstützung (*financial etc.*).

suppose [sə'pouz], *v.a.* annehmen, vermuten.

supposition [sʌpə'ziʃən], *s.* die Annahme, Vermutung, Voraussetzung.

suppress [sə'pres], *v.a.* unterdrücken.

suppurate ['sʌpjureit], *v.n.* eitern.

supremacy [su'preməsi], *s.* die Überlegenheit (*pre-eminence*); Obergewalt (*power*).

supreme [su'pri:m], *adj.* höchst, oberst.

surcharge [sə:'tʃɑ:dʒ], *s.* die Sonderzahlung, der Aufschlag, Zuschlag.

sure [ʃuə], *adj.* sicher; *to be —*, sicherlich; *make —*, sich überzeugen.

surety ['ʃuəti], *s.* (*Law*) die Kaution.

surf [sə:f], *s.* die Brandung.

surface ['sə:fis], *s.* die Oberfläche.

surfeit ['sə:fit], *s.* die Übersättigung, das Übermaß. — *v.a.* übersättigen.

surge [sə:dʒ], *v.n.* wogen, rauschen. — *s.* die Woge, das Aufwallen.

surgeon ['sə:dʒən], *s.* (*Med.*) der Chirurg.

surgery ['sə:dʒəri], *s.* (*Med.*) die Chirurgie (*subject*); — *hours*, die Sprechstunde.

surgical ['sə:dʒikəl], *adj.* chirurgisch.

surly ['sə:li], *adj.* mürrisch.

surmise [sə:'maiz], *v.a.* mutmaßen, vermuten. — *s.* die Mutmaßung, Vermutung.

surmount [sə'maunt], *v.a.* übersteigen; überwinden (*overcome*).

surname ['sə:neim], *s.* der Zuname.

surpass [sə'pɑ:s], *v.a.* übertreffen.

surplice ['sə:plis], *s.* das Chorhemd.

surplus ['sə:pləs], *s.* der Überfluß.

surprise [sə'praiz], *s.* die Überraschung. — *v.a.* überraschen.

surrender [sə'rendə], *v.a.* übergeben, aufgeben. — *v.n.* sich ergeben. — *s.* die Waffenstreckung, Kapitulation.

surreptitious [sʌrəp'tiʃəs], *adj.* heimlich.

surround [sə'raund], *v.a.* umgeben, einschließen.

surroundings [sə'raundiŋz], *s. pl.* die Umgegend, Umgebung.

survey ['sə:vei], *s.* die Übersicht; die Vermessung. — [sə'vei], *v.a.* überblicken; vermessen.

surveyor [sə'veiə], *s.* der Vermesser, Feldmesser.

survival [sə'vaivəl], *s.* das Überleben.

survive [sə'vaiv], *v.a.*, *v.n.* überleben, überstehen.

susceptibility [səsepti'biliti], *s.* die Empfänglichkeit.

susceptible [sə'septibl], *adj.* empfänglich, empfindlich.

suspect [səs'pekt], *v.a.* verdächtigen. — ['sʌspekt], *adj.* verdächtig. — *s.* die Verdachtsperson, der Verdächtigte.

suspend [səs'pend], *v.a.* aufhängen; unterbrechen (*procedure*); einstellen (*work*).

suspense [səs'pens], *s.* die Spannung (*tension*); Ungewißheit (*uncertainty*).

suspension [səs'penʃən], *s.* (*Law*) die Suspension; die Einstellung (*stoppage*); die Aufhängung, Suspension; (*Motor.*) die Federung; — *bridge*, die Kettenbrücke, Hängebrücke.

suspicion [səs'piʃən], *s.* der Verdacht, Argwohn.

suspicious [səs'piʃəs], *adj.* verdächtig; argwöhnisch.

sustain [səs'tein], *v.a.* erleiden (*suffer*); ertragen (*bear*); aufrechterhalten (*maintain*).

sustenance ['sʌstinəns], *s.* der Unterhalt (*maintenance*); die Nahrung (*food*).

suture ['sju:tʃə], *s.* (*Med.*) die Naht.

suzerain ['sju:zərein], *s.* der Oberherr, Oberlehnsherr.

swab [swɔb], *s.* (*Med.*) die Laborprobe, der Abstrich; der Schrubber (*scrubber*). — *v.a.* (*Med.*) eine Probe entnehmen; schrubben (*scrub*).

swaddle [swɔdl], *s.* die Windel.

swaddling ['swɔdliŋ], *adj.* — *clothes*, die Windeln, *f. pl.*

swagger ['swægə], *v.n.* großtun. — *s.* das Großtun, Renommieren.

swallow (1) ['swɔlou], *s.* (*Orn.*) die Schwalbe.

swallow (2) ['swɔlou], *v.a.* schlucken; verschlingen (*devour*).

swamp [swɔmp], *s.* der Sumpf. — *v.a.* versenken; (*fig.*) überschütten.

swan [swɔn], *s.* (*Orn.*) der Schwan.

swank [swæŋk], *v.n.* großtun, angeben, aufschneiden. — *s.* der Großtuer.

swap, swop [swɔp], *v.a.* eintauschen, tauschen. — *v.n.* tauschen. — *s.* der Tausch.

sward [swɔ:d], *s.* (*Poet.*) der Rasen.

swarm [swɔ:m], *v.n.* schwärmen. — *s.* der Schwarm.

swarthy ['swɔ:ði], *adj.* dunkel, dunkelbraun.

swashbuckler ['swɔʃbʌklə], *s.* der Aufschneider, Angeber, Renommist.

swastika ['swɔstikə], *s.* das Hakenkreuz.

swathe [sweið], *v.a.* einhüllen, einwickeln.

sway [swei], *v.a.* schwenken; beeinflußen. — *v.n.* schwanken, sich schwingen. — *s.* der Einfluß, die Macht.

swear

swear [swɛə], *v.a.*, *v.n. irr.* schwören
(*an oath*); fluchen (*curse*).

sweat [swet], *v.n.* schwitzen. — *s.* der
Schweiß.

Swede [swi:d], *s.* der Schwede.

Swedish ['swi:diʃ], *adj.* schwedisch.

sweep [swi:p], *v.a.*, *v.n. irr.* fegen,
kehren; *a new broom —s clean*, neue
Besen kehren gut. — *s.* der Schornsteinfeger (*chimney —*).

sweet [swi:t], *adj.* süß. — *s.* der Nachtisch; (*pl.*) Süßigkeiten, *f. pl.*

swell [swel], *v.a. irr.* anschwellen lassen.
— *v.n.* anschwellen. — *adj.*, *adv.*
(*Am. sl.*) ausgezeichnet. — *s.* (*sl.*) der
feine Kerl.

swelter ['sweltə], *v.n.* vor Hitze vergehen.

swerve [swə:v], *v.n.* abschweifen, ab-
biegen.

swift (1) [swift], *adj.* schnell, behende,
rasch.

swift (2) [swift], *s.* (*Orn.*) die Turm-
schwalbe.

swill [swil], *v.a.* spülen (*rinse*); (*sl.*)
saufen (*drink heavily*). — *s.* das
Spülicht (*dishwater*); (*coll.*) das Gesöff.

swim [swim], *v.n. irr.* schwimmen. —
s. das Schwimmen.

swindle [swindl], *v.a.* beschwindeln.
— *s.* der Schwindel.

swine [swain], *s. pl.* die Schweine;
(*sing.*) der Schweinehund, das
Schwein.

swing [swiŋ], *v.a.*, *v.n. irr.* schwingen,
schaukeln. — *s.* der Schwung; die
Schaukel.

swipe [swaip], *v.a.* schlagen; (*fig.*)
stehlen. — *s.* der Schlag.

swirl [swə:l], *v.a.*, *v.n.* wirbeln (*in air*).
— *s.* der Wirbel.

Swiss [swis], *s.* der Schweizer. — *adj.*
schweizerisch, Schweizer-.

switch [switʃ], *v.a.* (*Elec.*) — *on*, andrehen, einschalten; — *off*, abschalten;
(*fig.*) wechseln, vertauschen (*change*).
— *v.n.* umstellen, umschalten. —
s. (*Elec.*) der Schalter.

switchboard ['switʃbɔ:d], *s.* die Tele-
phonzentrale, das Schaltbrett.

switchgear ['switʃgiə], *s.* (*Elec.*) das
Schaltgerät, die Schaltung.

swivel [swivl], *v.n.* drehen. — *s.* der
Drehring; — *chair*, der Drehstuhl.

swoon [swu:n], *v.n.* in Ohnmacht fallen.
— *s.* die Ohnmacht.

swoop [swu:p], *s.* der Stoß. — *v.n.*
(herab)stoßen; stürzen; (nieder)-
schießen.

swop *see* **swap.**

sword [sɔ:d], *s.* das Schwert.

syllable ['silabl], *s.* die Silbe.

syllabus ['siləbəs], *s.* das Verzeichnis,
der Lehrplan.

symbol ['simbəl], *s.* das Symbol,
Sinnbild.

sympathetic [simpə'θetik], *adj.* mitfüh-
lend, teilnehmend; sympathisch.

sympathy ['simpəθi], *s.* die Sympathie,
das Mitgefühl.

symphony ['simfəni], *s.* (*Mus.*) die
Symphonie.

synchronize ['siŋkrənaiz], *v.a.* synchronisieren.

syndicate ['sindikit], *s.* die Arbeits-
gruppe, das Syndikat.

synod ['sinəd], *s.* die Synode, Kirchen-
tagung.

synonymous [si'nɔniməs], *adj.* syn-
onym.

synopsis [si'nɔpsis], *s.* die Zusammenfassung, Übersicht.

Syrian ['siriən], *adj.* syrisch. — *s.* der
Syrer.

syringe ['sirindʒ], *s.* die Spritze.

syrup ['sirəp], *s.* der Sirup.

system ['sistəm], *s.* das System.

systematize ['sistəmətaiz], *v.a.* ordnen, in ein System bringen.

T

T [ti:]. das T.

tab [tæb], *s.* das Schildchen, der Streifen.

tabard ['tæbəd], *s.* der Wappenrock,
Heroldsrock.

tabby ['tæbi], *s.* (*cat*) die getigerte
Katze.

table [teibl], *s.* der Tisch; (*Maths.*) die
Tabelle, das Einmaleins. — *v.a.*
(*Parl.*) einen Entwurf einbringen;
(*Am.*) auf die lange Bank schieben.

tablecloth ['teiblklɔθ], *s.* das Tischtuch.

tablemat ['teiblmæt], *s.* der Untersatz.

tablenapkin ['teiblnæpkin], *s.* die Serviette.

tablespoon ['teiblspu:n], *s.* der Eßlöffel.

tablet ['tæblit], *s.* die Tablette (*pill*);
die Schreibtafel, der Block (*writing*).

taboo [tə'bu:], *s.* das Verbot, Tabu.

tabular ['tæbjulə], *adj.* tabellarisch;
wie eine Tafel.

tacit ['tæsit], *adj.* stillschweigend.

taciturn ['tæsitə:n], *adj.* schweigsam,
einsilbig.

tack [tæk], *s.* der Stift; der Stich
(*sewing*). — *v.a.* nageln; heften (*sew*).

tackle [tækl], *v.a.* (*Naut.*) takeln;
(*Footb.*, *fig.*) angreifen; anpacken. —
s. (*Naut.*) das Takel; (*fig.*) das Zeug;
(*Footb.*) das Angreifen.

tact [tækt], *s.* der Takt; das Zartgefühl.

tactics ['tæktiks], *s. pl.* die Taktik.

tadpole ['tædpoul], *s.* (*Zool.*) die Kaulquappe.

taffeta ['tæfitə], *s.* (*Text.*) der Taft.

tag [tæg], *s.* der Anhängezettel; das
Sprichwort (*saying*). — *v.a.* anhängen. — *v.n.* — *on to*, sich anschließen.

tail [teil], *s.* der Schwanz; (*fig.*) das Ende; (*pl.*) der Frack (*tailcoat*). — *v.a.* (*Am.*) folgen (*Dat.*).

tailor ['teilə], *s.* der Schneider; —*made*, geschneidert, nach Maß gemacht. — *v.a.* schneidern.

taint [teint], *v.a.* beflecken; verderben (*corrupt*). — *s.* der Fleck.

take [teik], *v.a. irr.* nehmen; bringen, ergreifen (*seize*); erfordern (*require*); — *up*, aufnehmen, beginnen; ertragen (*suffer*, *tolerate*); — *breath*, Atem holen; — *care*, sich in acht nehmen; — *offence at*, Anstoß nehmen an; — *place*, stattfinden; — *for*, halten für. — *v.n.* wirken (*be effective*); — *to*, Gefallen finden (an, *Dat.*); — *to flight* or *à.'s heels*, sich aus dem Staube machen; — *after*, ähnlich sein.

takings ['teikiŋz], *s.* (*pl.*) die Einnahmen, *f. pl.*

tale [teil], *s.* das Märchen, die Geschichte.

talent ['tælənt], *s.* das Talent, die Begabung.

talented ['tæləntid], *adj.* talentiert, begabt.

talk [tɔ:k], *v.a., v.n.* reden, sprechen. — *s.* das Gespräch (*discussion*); der Vortrag (*lecture*); das Reden, Gerede (*speaking*).

talkative ['tɔ:kətiv], *adj.* geschwätzig, redselig, gesprächig.

tall [tɔ:l], *adj.* hoch (*high*); groß (*grown high*); *a — order*, eine schwierige Aufgabe; *a — story*, eine Aufschneiderei, das Seemannsgarn.

tallow ['tælou], *s.* der Talg.

tally ['tæli], *v.n.* passen (*match*); stimmen (*be correct*).

talon ['tælən], *s.* die Klaue, Kralle.

tame [teim], *adj.* zahm. — *v.a.* zähmen.

tamper ['tæmpə], *v.n.* hineinpfuschen (*with*, in, *Acc.*).

tan [tæn], *s.* die Lohe; die braune Farbe; der Sonnenbrand (*sun*). — *v.a.* bräunen; (*leather*) gerben; (*fig.*) verbleuen (*beat*).

tang [tæŋ], *s.* der Seetang; (*fig.*) der Beigeschmack.

tangible ['tændʒibl], *adj.* greifbar.

tangle [tæŋgl], *v.a.* verwickeln (*entangle*). — *s.* die Verwirrung, Verwicklung.

tank [tæŋk], *s.* der Tank; (*Mil.*) der Panzer; der Wasserspeicher (*cistern*). — *v.a., v.n.* tanken.

tankard ['tæŋkəd], *s.* der Maßkrug, Bierkrug.

tanner (1) ['tænə], *s.* der Gerber.

tanner (2) ['tænə], *s.* (*sl.*) das Sechspencestück.

tantalize ['tæntəlaiz], *v.a.* quälen.

tantamount ['tæntəmaunt], *adj.* gleich, gleichwertig.

tap [tæp], *v.a.* anzapfen (*barrel*); klopfen; tippen (*on shoulder etc.*); (*fig.*) anpumpen (*for money*). — *s.* der Hahn; der Zapfen (*barrel*); der leichte Schlag (*on shoulder etc.*).

tape [teip], *s.* das Band; *red* —, die Bürokratie, der Bürokratismus; — *measure*, das Bandmaß; — *recorder*, das Tonbandgerät.

taper ['teipə], *v.n.* spitz zulaufen. — *v.a.* spitzen. — *s.* die (spitze) Kerze.

tapestry ['tæpistri], *s.* die Tapete, der Wandteppich.

tapeworm ['teipwə:m], *s.* der Bandwurm.

taproot ['tæpru:t], *s.* die Pfahlwurzel, Hauptwurzel.

tar [tɑ:], *s.* der Teer; (*Naut. sl.*) der Matrose. — *v.a.* teeren.

tardy ['tɑ:di], *adj.* träge (*sluggish*), langsam.

tare (1) [tɛə], *s.* das Taragewicht, die Tara (*weight*). — *v.a.* auswägen, tarieren.

tare (2) [tɛə], *s.* (*Bot.*) die Wicke.

target ['tɑ:git], *s.* das Ziel; die Zielscheibe (*board*).

tariff ['tærif], *s.* der Tarif.

tarnish ['tɑ:niʃ], *v.a.* trüben. — *v.n.* anlaufen.

tarpaulin [tɑ:'pɔ:lin], *s.* die Persenning.

tarry (1) ['tæri], *v.n.* zögern (*hesitate*); warten (*wait*).

tarry (2) ['tɑ:ri], *adj.* teerig.

tart (1) [tɑ:t], *s.* die Torte.

tart (2) [tɑ:t], *adj.* herb, sauer.

tart (3) [tɑ:t], *s.* (*sl.*) die Dirne.

Tartar ['tɑ:tə], *s.* der Tatar; (*fig.*) der Tyrann.

tartar ['tɑ:tə], *s.* (*Chem.*) der Weinstein.

task [tɑ:sk], *s.* die Aufgabe, das Tagewerk; *take to* —, zur Rechenschaft ziehen.

tassel [tæsl], *s.* die Quaste.

taste [teist], *v.a.* schmecken; versuchen, kosten. — *s.* die Probe (*tasting*); der Geschmack (*flavour*).

tasteful ['teistful], *adj.* geschmackvoll.

tasteless ['teistlis], *adj.* geschmacklos.

tasty ['teisti], *adj.* schmackhaft.

tatter ['tætə], *s.* der Lumpen. — *v.a.* in Fetzen reißen, zerfetzen.

tattle [tætl], *v.n.* schwatzen. — *s.* das Geschwätz.

tattoo (1) [tə'tu:], *s.* (*Mil.*) der Zapfenstreich, das militärische Schaustück, die Parade.

tattoo (2) [tə'tu:], *v.a.* tätowieren. — *s.* die Tätowierung.

taunt [tɔ:nt], *v.a.* höhnen, schmähen. — *s.* der Hohn, Spott.

tavern ['tævən], *s.* die Schenke.

tawdry ['tɔ:dri], *adj.* kitschig, flitterhaft.

tawny ['tɔ:ni], *adj.* braungelb, lohfarbig.

tax [tæks], *s.* die Abgabe, Steuer; Besteuerung (*taxation*). — *v.a.* besteuern; (*fig.*) anstrengen, ermüden (*strain*).

taxi ['tæksi], *s.* das Taxi.

tea [ti:], *s.* der Tee.

teach [ti:tʃ], *v.a., v.n. irr.* lehren, unterrichten.

teacher ['ti:tʃə], *s.* der Lehrer, die Lehrerin.

team

team [ti:m], *s.* (*Sport*) die Mannschaft;
das Gespann (*horses*); (*fig.*) der Stab;
— *spirit*, der Korpsgeist.
tear (1) [tɛə], *s.* der Riß (*rent*). — *v.a. irr.*
zerreißen (*rend*).
tear (2) [tiə], *s.* die Träne.
tearing ['tɛəriŋ], *adj.* — *hurry*, rasende
Eile.
tease [ti:z], *v.a.* necken (*mock*); auf-
rauhen (*roughen*).
teat [ti:t], *s.* die Brustwarze, Zitze.
technical ['teknikəl], *adj.* technisch.
technique [tek'ni:k], *s.* die Technik,
Methode.
techy *see* **tetchy**.
tedious ['ti:diəs], *adj.* langweilig,
lästig.
tedium ['ti:diəm], *s.* der Überdruß, die
Langeweile.
tee [ti:], *s.* (*Sport*) der Golfballhalter.
teem [ti:m], *v.n.* wimmeln.
teenager ['ti:neidʒə], *s.* der, die Jugendliche; Teenager.
teeth *see under* **tooth**.
teethe [ti:ð], *v.n.* Zähne bekommen,
zahnen.
teetotal [ti:'toutl], *adj.* abstinent, anti-
alkoholisch.
teetotaller [ti:'toutlə], *s.* der Antialkoholiker.
telegram ['teligræm], *s.* das Telegramm.
telephone ['telifoun], *s.* (*abbr.* **phone**)
das Telephon; – *booth*, die Fernsprech-
zelle; — *exchange*, das Fernsprechamt.
television [teli'viʒən], *s.* das Fernsehen; — *set*, der Fernsehapparat.
tell [tel], *v.a. irr.* erzählen, berichten
(*relate*); verraten (*reveal*).
tell-tale ['telteil], *s.* der Angeber,
Zuträger. — *adj.* sprechend; War-
nungs-.
teller ['telə], *s.* der Zähler; der Kassier
(*cashier*).
temerity [ti'meriti], *s.* die Verwegenheit, Tollkühnheit.
temper ['tempə], *v.a.* vermischen
(*mix*); mäßigen (*moderate*); (*Metall.*)
härten. — *s.* die üble Stimmung, Wut,
Laune; (*Metall.*) die Härte.
temperance ['tempərəns], *s.* die Mäßigkeit, Enthaltsamkeit.
temperate ['tempərit], *adj.* gemäßigt,
temperiert.
temperature ['temprətʃə], *s.* die Temperatur.
tempest ['tempist], *s.* der Sturm.
tempestuous [tem'pestjuəs], *adj.* stürmisch.
temple (1) [templ], *s.* der Tempel.
temple (2) [templ], *s.* (*Anat.*) die
Schläfe (*side of brow*).
temporal ['tempərəl], *adj.* weltlich,
zeitlich.
temporary ['tempərəri], *adj.* zeitweilig,
vorläufig, provisorisch.
temporize ['tempəraiz], *v.n.* zögern,
Zeit zu gewinnen suchen.
tempt [tempt], *v.a.* versuchen.
temptation [temp'teiʃən], *s.* die Versuchung.

ten [ten], *num. adj.* zehn.
tenth [tenθ], *num. adj.* zehnte. — *s.* der
Zehnte.
tenable ['tenəbl], *adj.* haltbar.
tenacious [ti'neiʃəs], *adj.* zähe, festhal-
tend, hartnäckig.
tenacity [ti'næsiti], *s.* die Zähigkeit,
Ausdauer.
tenancy ['tenənsi], *s.* das Mietver-
hältnis; die Mietdauer.
tenant ['tenənt], *s.* der Mieter, Pächter.
tench [tentʃ], *s.* (*Zool.*) die Schleie.
tend (1) [tend], *v.a., v.n.* warten,
pflegen (*nurse*).
tend (2) [tend], *v.n.* neigen, gerichtet
sein (*be inclined*).
tendency ['tendənsi], *s.* die Tendenz,
Neigung.
tender (1) ['tendə], *s.* das Angebot
(*offer*); *legal* —, das Zahlungsmittel.
— *v.a.* einreichen.
tender (2) ['tendə], *adj.* sanft (*affectionate*); zart, zärtlich, weich (*delicate*).
tender (3) ['tendə], *s.* (*Railw.*) der
Tender.
tendon ['tendən], *s.* (*Anat.*) die Sehne,
Flechse.
tendril ['tendril], *s.* (*Bot.*) die Ranke.
tenement ['tenimənt], *s.* die Miets-
wohnung, die Mietskaserne.
tenet ['tenit], *s.* der Grundsatz (*principle*); die Lehre (*doctrine*).
tenfold ['tenfould], *adj.* zehnfach.
tennis ['tenis], *s.* das Tennis.
tenor ['tenə], *s.* (*Mus.*) der Tenor; der
Sinn, Inhalt (*meaning*).
tense (1) [tens], *adj.* gespannt; straff
(*taut*).
tense (2) [tens], *s.* (*Gram.*) die Zeitform.
tension ['tenʃən], *s.* die Spannung.
tent [tent], *s.* das Zelt.
tentacle ['tentəkl], *s.* (*Zool.*) das Fühlhorn, der Fühler.
tentative ['tentətiv], *adj.* versuchend,
vorsichtig; (*fig.*) vorläufig.
tenterhooks ['tentəhuks], *s. pl.* die
Spannhaken, *m. pl.*; *be on* —, in
größter Spannung sein.
tenuous ['tenjuəs], *adj.* dünn, fadenscheinig, spärlich.
tenure ['tenjuə], *s.* der Mietbesitz, die
Mietvertragslänge, das Mietrecht; —
of office, die Amtsdauer.
tepid ['tepid], *adj.* lau, lauwarm.
term [tə:m], *s.* der Ausdruck (*expression*); die Bedingung (*condition*); der
Termin, die Frist (*period*); (*Sch.*) das
Semester, Trimester; *be on good —s
with* (*s.o.*), auf gutem Fuß stehen mit.
— *v.a.* benennen, bezeichen.
terminate ['tə:mineit], *v.a.* beenden,
zu Ende bringen. — *v.n.* zu Ende
kommen.
terminus ['tə:minəs], *s.* die Endstation.
terrace ['teris], *s.* die Terrasse.
terrestrial [tə'restriəl], *adj.* irdisch.
terrible ['teribl], *adj.* schrecklich,
furchtbar.
terrific [tə'rifik], *adj.* fürchterlich;
(*coll.*) ungeheuer.

terrify ['terifai], *v.a.* erschrecken.
territory ['teritəri], *s.* das Gebiet.
terror ['terə], *s.* der Schrecken.
terse [tə:s], *adj.* bündig, kurz.
tertiary ['tə:ʃəri], *adj.* tertiär.
test [test], *s.* die Prüfung; (*Chem.*) die Probe; — -*tube*, das Reagensglas *or* Reagenzglas. — *v.a.* prüfen.
testament ['testəmənt], *s.* das Testament.
testator [tes'teitə], *s.* der Erblasser.
testicle ['testikl], *s.* (*Anat.*) die Hode.
testify ['testifai], *v.a.* bezeugen.
testimonial [testi'mouniəl], *s.* das Zeugnis.
testimony ['testiməni], *s.* das Zeugnis, die Zeugenaussage (*oral*).
testiness ['testinis], *s.* die Verdrießlichkeit.
testy ['testi], *adj.* verdrießlich, reizbar.
tetanus ['tetənəs], *s.* (*Med.*) der Starrkrampf.
tetchy, techy ['tetʃi], *adj.* mürrisch, reizbar.
tether ['teðə], *s.* das Spannseil; (*fig.*) *at the end of o.'s —*, am Ende seiner Geduld. — *v.a.* anbinden.
text [tekst], *s.* der Text, Wortlaut.
textile ['tekstail], *s.* die Textilware, der Webstoff.
textual ['tekstjuəl], *adj.* textlich, Text-.
texture ['tekstʃə], *s.* das Gewebe, die Struktur.
Thai [tai], *adj.* Thai-, siamesisch. — *s. pl.* die Thaivölker, *pl.*
than [ðæn], *conj.* als (*after comparatives*).
thank [θæŋk], *v.a.* danken (*Dat.*). — *s.* (*pl.*) der Dank.
that [ðæt], *dem. adj.* der, die, das, jener. — *dem. pron.* der, die, das; (*absolute, no pl.*) das. — *rel. pron.* der, die, das, welcher, was. — *conj.* daß; damit (*in order —*).
thatch [θætʃ], *v.a.* decken (mit Stroh). — *s.* das Strohdach.
thaw [θɔ:], *v.n.* tauen; auftauen. — *s.* das Tauwetter.
the [ðə, *before vowel* ði], *def. art.* der, die, das. — *adv.* — *bigger* — *better*, je grösser desto *or* umso besser.
theatre ['θiətə], *s.* das Theater; (*fig.*) der Schauplatz.
theatrical [θi'ætrikəl], *adj.* bühnenhaft (*of the stage*); theatralisch; Bühnen-, Theater-.
theft [θeft], *s.* der Diebstahl.
their [ðeə], *poss. adj.* ihr.
theirs [ðeəz], *poss. pron.* der, die, das ihrige, der, die, das ihre.
them [ðem], *pers. pron.* sie, ihnen.
theme [θi:m], *s.* das Thema; (*Mus.*) das Thema, Motiv.
then [ðen], *adv.* dann, damals; *by —*, *till —*, bis dahin. — *conj.* dann, denn. — *adj.* damalig.
thence [ðens], *adv.* von da; daher.
theology [θi'ɔlədʒi], *s.* die Theologie.
theorem ['θiərəm], *s.* (*Maths.*) der Lehrsatz, Grundsatz.
theorize ['θiəraiz], *v.n.* theoretisieren.

therapeutics [θerə'pju:tiks], *s. pl.* die Heilkunde.
therapy ['θerəpi], *s.* die Therapie.
there [ðɛə], *adv.* dort, da; dorthin, dahin (*thereto*); — *is*, — *are*, es gibt; *here and —*, hier und da.
thereabout(s) [ðɛərəbaut(s)], *adv.* ungefähr, da herum.
thereafter [ðɛər'ɑ:ftə], *adv.* hernach, danach.
thereby [ðɛə'bai], *adv.* dadurch.
therefore ['ðɛəfɔ:], *adv.* darum, deshalb.
thermal, thermic ['θə:məl, 'θə:mik], *adj.* thermisch; warm; Wärme-.
thermometer [θə'mɔmitə], *s.* das Thermometer.
these [ði:z], *dem. adj. & pron. pl.* diese.
thesis ['θi:sis], *s.* die These; die Dissertation.
they [ðei], *pers. pron. pl.* sie.
thick [θik], *adj.* dick; dicht; (*fig.*) dick befreundet; — *as thieves*, wie eine Diebsbande.
thicken ['θikən], *v.a.* verdicken. — *v.n.* dick werden.
thicket ['θikit], *s.* das Dickicht.
thickness ['θiknis], *s.* die Dicke.
thief [θi:f], *s.* der Dieb.
thieve [θi:v], *v.n.* stehlen.
thigh [θai], *s.* (*Anat.*) der Oberschenkel.
thimble [θimbl], *s.* der Fingerhut.
thin [θin], *adj.* dünn. — *v.a., v.n.* (sich) verdünnen.
thine [ðain], *poss. pron.* (*Poet.*) dein, der, die, das deinige.
thing [θiŋ], *s.* das Ding; die Sache (*matter*).
think [θiŋk], *v.a., v.n. irr.* denken; meinen, glauben.
thinker ['θiŋkə], *s.* der Denker.
third [θə:d], *num. adj.* der, die, das dritte. — *s.* das Drittel.
thirdly ['θə:dli], *adv.* drittens.
thirst [θə:st], *s.* der Durst (*for*, nach). — *v.n.* dürsten.
thirsty ['θə:sti], *adj.* durstig; *be —*, Durst haben.
thirteen [θə:'ti:n], *num. adj.* dreizehn.
thirty ['θə:ti], *num. adj.* dreißig.
this [ðis], *dem. adj.* dieser, diese, dieses. — *dem. pron.* dieser, diese, dieses; dies.
thistle [θisl], *s.* (*Bot.*) die Distel.
thither [ðiðə], *adv.* dahin, dorthin.
tho' [ðou] *see under* **though.**
thong [θɔŋ], *s.* der Riemen (*strap*); die Peitschenschnur.
thorn [θɔ:n], *s.* (*Bot.*) der Dorn.
thorough ['θʌrə], *adj.* gründlich; völlig (*complete*).
thoroughbred ['θʌrəbred], *s.* das Vollblut, der Vollblüter. — *adj.* Vollblut-.
thoroughfare ['θʌrəfɛə], *s.* der Durchgang (*path*); die Durchfahrt.
those [ðouz], *dem. adj. pl.* die, jene. — *dem. pron. pl.* jene, diejenigen.
thou [ðau], *pers. pron.* (*Poet.*) du.
though [ðou], *conj.* (*abbr.* tho') obgleich, obwohl, wenn auch (*even if*). — *adv.* doch, zwar.

thought

thought [θɔ:t], s. der Gedanke; *also past tense and participle of* think *q.v.*

thoughtful ['θɔ:tful], *adj.* rücksichtsvoll, nachdenklich.

thoughtless ['θɔ:tlis], *adj.* gedankenlos.

thousand ['θauzənd], *num. adj.* a —, tausend. — *s.* das Tausend.

thrash [θræʃ], *v.a.* dreschen (*corn*); prügeln (*s.o.*).

thread [θred], *s.* der Faden. — *v.a.* einfädeln. — *v.n.* sich schlängeln, sich winden.

threadbare ['θredbɛə], *adj.* fadenscheinig.

threat [θret], *s.* die Drohung.

threaten [θretn], *v.a.* drohen, androhen (*Dat.*).

three [θri:], *num. adj.* drei.

threescore ['θri:skɔ:], *num. adj.* sechzig.

thresh [θreʃ], *v.a.* dreschen (*corn*). — *See also* thrash.

threshold ['θreʃould], *s.* die Schwelle (*of door*).

thrice [θrais], *num. adv.* dreimal.

thrift [θrift], *s.* die Sparsamkeit; (*Bot.*) die Grasnelke, Meernelke.

thrill [θril], *v.a.* packen (*grip*). — *v.n.* erschauern, zittern (vor, *Dat.*). — *s.* der Schauer; die Spannung.

thriller ['θrilə], *s.* der Thriller, der spannende Roman *or* Film etc.

thrive [θraiv], *v.n.* gedeihen (*also fig.*); (*fig.*) gut weiterkommen, Glück haben.

thriving ['θraiviŋ], *adj.* blühend, (*Comm.*) gut gehend.

throat [θrout], *s.* (*Anat.*) der Schlund, die Kehle.

throb [θrɔb], *v.n.* pochen, klopfen.

throes [θrouz], *s. pl.* die Wehen, *f. pl.*; die Schmerzen, *m. pl.*

throne [θroun], *s.* der Thron.

throng [θrɔŋ], *s.* die Menge, das Gedränge. — *v.a., v.n.* (sich) drängen.

throttle [θrɔtl], *s.* die Kehle, Luftröhre; (*Mech.*) das Drosselventil; (*Motor.*) open the —, Gas geben.

through [θru:], *prep.* durch (*Acc.*); mittels (*Genit.*) (*by means of*). — *adv.* (mitten) durch.

throughout [θru:'aut], *prep.* ganz (hin)durch (*space*); während, hindurch (*time*). — *adv.* durchaus, in jeder Beziehung.

throw [θrou], *v.a. irr.* werfen; — *open*, eröffnen. — *s.* der Wurf.

thrush [θrʌʃ], *s.* (*Orn.*) die Drossel.

thrust [θrʌst], *v.a.* stoßen, drücken. — *v.n.* stoßen (*at*, nach); sich drängen. — *s.* der Stoß, Angriff; *cut and* —, Hieb und Gegenhieb.

thud [θʌd], *s.* der Schlag, das Dröhnen, der dumpfe Ton. — *v.n.* dröhnen, aufschlagen.

thumb [θʌm], *s.* (*Anat.*) der Daumen; *rule of* —, die Faustregel; (*Am.*) *tack* see **drawing pin**. — *v.a.* durchblättern (*book*); — *a lift*, per Anhalter fahren.

thump [θʌmp], *v.a.* schlagen, puffen. —

v.n. schlagen (*on, auf*; *against*, gegen). — *s.* der Schlag, Stoß.

thunder ['θʌndə], *s.* der Donner. — *v.n.* donnern.

thunderstruck ['θʌndəstrʌk], *adj.* wie vom Donner gerührt.

Thursday ['θə:zdi]. der Donnerstag.

Thuringian [θuə'rindʒiən], *adj.* thüringisch. — *s.* der Thüringer.

thus [ðʌs], *adv.* so, auf diese Weise (*in this way*).

thwart [θwɔ:t], *v.a.* vereiteln, durchkreuzen.

thy [ðai], *poss. adj.* (*Poet.*) dein, deine, dein.

thyme [taim], *s.* (*Bot.*) der Thymian.

tic [tik], *s.* (*Med.*) das Zucken.

tick (1) [tik], *s.* das Ticken (*watch*). — *v.n.* ticken.

tick (2) [tik], *s.* (*coll.*) der Kredit, Borg.

ticket ['tikit], *s.* die Fahrkarte (*travel*); die Eintrittskarte (*entry*); (*Am.*) der Strafzettel (*driving*).

ticking (1) ['tikiŋ], *s.* das Ticken (*of watch*).

ticking (2) ['tikiŋ], *s.* (*Text.*) der Zwillich.

tickle [tikl], *v.a., v.n.* kitzeln. — *s.* das Kitzeln.

ticklish ['tikliʃ], *adj.* kitzlig.

tidal [taidl], *adj.* Gezeiten-, Ebbe-, Flut-.

tide [taid], *s.* die Gezeiten, *f.pl.*, die Ebbe und Flut. — *v.a.* — *over*, hinweghelfen (über, *Acc.*).

tidiness ['taidinis], *s.* die Sauberkeit, Ordnung.

tidings ['taidiŋz], *s. pl.* (*Poet.*) die Nachricht.

tidy ['taidi], *adj.* nett, sauber, ordentlich. — *v.a.* — *up*, sauber machen.

tie [tai], *v.a.* binden, knüpfen. — *v.n.* (*Sport*) unentschieden sein. — *s.* die Binde, Krawatte; (*Sport*) das Unentschieden.

tier [tiə], *s.* der Rang, die Reihe, Sitzreihe.

tiger ['taigə], *s.* (*Zool.*) der Tiger.

tight [tait], *adj.* fest, eng, dicht (*close*); (*coll.*) betrunken (*drunk*); — *fisted*, geizig (*stingy*). — *s. pl.* die Trikothosen, *f.pl.*

tighten [taitn], *v.a.* festziehen.

tile [tail], *s.* der Ziegel (*roof etc.*); die Kachel (*glazed*). — *v.a.* kacheln, ziegeln.

till (1) [til], *prep., conj.* bis.

till (2) [til], *v.a.* aufbauen, beackern (*land*).

till (3) [til], *s.* die Ladenkasse.

tilt [tilt], *v.a.* kippen, neigen, umschlagen (*tip over*). — *v.n.* sich neigen, kippen, kentern. — *s.* die Neigung.

timber ['timbə], *s.* das Holz, Bauholz.

time [taim], *s.* die Zeit; (*Mus.*) das Tempo, Zeitmaß; *in* —, zur rechten Zeit; *every* —, jedesmal; *what is the* —? wieviel Uhr ist es? — *v.a.* zeitlich messen, rechtzeitig einrichten.

timely ['taimli], *adj.* rechtzeitig.

timetable ['taimteibl], *s. (Railw.)* der Fahrplan; *(Sch.)* der Stundenplan.

timid ['timid], *adj.* furchtsam.

timpani ['timpəni], *s. pl. (Mus.)* die Kesselpauken, *f. pl.*

tin [tin], *s.* das Zinn, Weißblech; die Dose, Büchse *(preserved foods)*; — *opener,* der Büchsenöffner.

tincture ['tiŋktʃə], *s.* die Tinktur, das Färbungsmittel.

tinder ['tində], *s.* der Zunder.

tinfoil ['tinfɔil], *s.* das Stanniol.

tinge [tindʒ], *v.a.* färben, anfärben. — *s.* die Färbung, leichte Farbe; *(fig.)* die Spur.

tingle [tiŋgl], *v.n.* klingen *(bells)*; *(Anat.)* prickeln. — *s.* das Klingen; Prickeln.

tinker ['tiŋkə], *s.* der Kesselflicker. — *v.n.* basteln.

tinkle [tiŋkl], *v.a.* klingeln.

tinsel ['tinsəl], *s.* das Lametta, Flittergold.

tint [tint], *v.a.* färben. — *s.* die Farbe; der Farbton.

tiny ['taini], *adj.* winzig.

tip (1) [tip], *v.a.* kippen; *(coll.)* ein Trinkgeld geben *(Dat.)*. — *s. (Sport etc.) (coll.)* der Tip; das Trinkgeld *(gratuity)*.

tip (2) [tip], *s.* die Spitze; das Mundstück *(cigarette)*.

tipple [tipl], *v.n.* (viel) trinken, zechen.

tipsy ['tipsi], *adj.* beschwipst.

tiptoe ['tiptou], *s. on* —, auf Zehenspitzen.

tiptop ['tiptɔp], *adj. (coll.)* erstklassig.

tirade [ti'reid *or* tai'reid], *s.* der Wortschwall, die Tirade.

tire (1) [taiə], *v.a., v.n.* ermüden.

tire (2) *see under* **tyre**.

tired ['taiəd], *adj.* müde.

tiresome ['taiəsəm], *adj.* langweilig *(boring)*; auf die Nerven gehend *(annoying)*.

tissue ['tiʃju:], *s.* das Gewebe; — *paper,* das Seidenpapier.

titbit ['titbit], *s.* der Leckerbissen.

tithe [taið], *s.* der Zehnte.

title [taitl], *s.* der Titel, die Überschrift; *(fig.)* der Anspruch *(claim)*.

titmouse ['titmaus], *s. (Orn.)* die Meise.

titter ['titə], *v.n.* kichern. — *s.* das Kichern.

tittle [titl], *s.* das Tüpfelchen; — *tattle,* das Geschwätz.

titular ['titjulə], *adj.* Titular-.

to [tu], *prep.* zu *(Dat.)*, gegen *(Acc.)*; bis *(until, as far as)*, nach, an, auf; *in order* —, um zu. — [tu:], *adv.* zu; — *and fro,* hin und her.

toad [toud], *s. (Zool.)* die Kröte.

toadstool ['toudstu:l], *s. (Bot.)* der Giftpilz.

toady ['toudi], *v.n.* kriechen. — *s.* der Kriecher.

toast [toust], *s.* der Toast, das Röstbrot; der Trinkspruch. — *v.a.* toasten, rösten; trinken auf; — *s.o.,* einen Trinkspruch ausbringen auf einen.

tobacco [tə'bækou], *s.* der Tabak.

toboggan [tə'bɔgən], *s.* der Rodel, der Schlitten. — *v.n.* rodeln, Schlitten fahren.

tocsin ['tɔksin], *s.* die Sturmglocke.

today [tə'dei], *adv.* heute.

toddle [tɔdl], *v.n.* watscheln; abschieben (— *off*).

toddler ['tɔdlə], *s. (coll.)* das kleine Kind (das gehen lernt).

toe [tou], *s. (Anat.)* die Zehe.

toffee ['tɔfi], *s.* der Sahnebonbon.

together [tə'geðə], *adv.* zusammen.

toil [tɔil], *v.n.* hart arbeiten. — *s.* die schwere, harte Arbeit.

toilet ['tɔilit], *s.* das Anziehen, Ankleiden; die Toilette, der Abort, das Klosett *(lavatory)*.

token ['toukən], *s.* das Zeichen *(sign)*; der Beweis *(proof)*; das Andenken *(keepsake)*.

tolerable ['tɔlərəbl], *adj.* erträglich, leidlich.

tolerance ['tɔlərəns], *s.* die Toleranz, Duldsamkeit; *(Tech.)* die Toleranz.

tolerant ['tɔlərənt], *adj.* tolerant, duldsam.

tolerate ['tɔləreit], *v.a.* ertragen, dulden.

toll [toul], *v.a., v.n.* läuten. — *s.* der Zoll; — *gate,* — *bar,* der Schlagbaum.

tomato [tə'mɑ:tou], *s. (Bot.)* die Tomate.

tomb [tu:m], *s.* das Grab, Grabmal.

tomboy ['tɔmbɔi], *s.* der Wildfang.

tomcat ['tɔmkæt], *s. (Zool.)* der Kater.

tome [toum], *s.* der große Band, *(coll.)* der Wälzer.

tomfoolery [tɔm'fu:ləri], *s.* die Narretei.

Tommy ['tɔmi], *s. (Mil.) (coll.)* der englische Soldat.

tomorrow [tə'mɔrou], *adv.* morgen; — *morning,* morgen früh; *the day after* —, übermorgen.

ton [tʌn], *s.* die Tonne.

tone [toun], *s.* der Ton, Klang; *(fig.)* die Stimmung *(mood)*. — *v.a.* — *down,* abtönen, abstimmen.

tongs [tɔŋz], *s. pl.* die Zange.

tongue [tʌŋ], *s. (Anat.)* die Zunge.

tonic ['tɔnik], *s.* das Stärkungsmittel. — *adj.* tonisch, stärkend.

tonight [tu'nait], *adv.* heute abend, heute nacht.

tonnage ['tʌnidʒ], *s.* die Tonnage, das Tonnengeld.

tonsil ['tɔnsil], *s. (Anat.)* die Mandel.

tonsilitis [tɔnsi'laitis], *s. (Med.)* die Mandelentzündung.

tonsure ['tɔnʃə], *s.* die Tonsur.

too [tu:], *adv.* allzu, zu, allzusehr; auch *(also)*.

tool [tu:l], *s.* das Werkzeug, das Gerät; *machine* —, die Werkzeugmaschine.

tooth [tu:θ], *s. (pl. teeth* [ti:θ]) der Zahn.

toothache ['tu:θeik], *s.* das Zahnweh.

toothbrush ['tu:θbrʌʃ], *s.* die Zahnbürste.

toothpaste

toothpaste ['tu:θpeist], *s.* die Zahnpaste.

top (1) [tɔp], *s.* die Spitze; der Gipfel (*mountain*); der Wipfel (*tree*); der Giebel (*house*); die Oberfläche (*surface*); big —, das Zirkuszeltdach; — *hat*, der Zylinder. — *v.a.* übertreffen (*surpass*); bedecken (*cover*).

top (2) [tɔp], *s.* der Kreisel (*spinning* —).

topaz ['toupæz], *s.* der Topas.

tope [toup], *v.n.* zechen, saufen.

toper ['toupə], *s.* der Zecher.

topic ['tɔpik], *s.* das Thema, der Gegenstand.

topical ['tɔpikəl], *adj.* aktuell (*up to date*).

topmost ['tɔpmoust], *adj.* höchst, oberst.

topsy-turvy ['tɔpsi 'tə:vi], *adv.* durcheinander, auf den Kopf gestellt.

torch [tɔ:tʃ], *s.* die Fackel; (*Elec.*) die Taschenlampe.

torment ['tɔ:mənt], *s.* die Qual, Marter. — [tɔ:'ment], *v.a.* quälen, martern, peinigen.

tornado [tɔ:'neidou], *s.* der Wirbelsturm.

torpid ['tɔ:pid], *adj.* starr, betäubt; (*fig.*) stumpfsinnig.

torpor ['tɔ:pə], *s.* die Starre; die Stumpfheit, Stumpfsinnigkeit.

torrent ['tɔrənt], *s.* der Gießbach, der (reißende) Strom.

torrid ['tɔrid], *adj.* brennend heiß, verbrannt.

torsion ['tɔ:ʃən], *s.* die Drehung, Windung.

tortoise ['tɔ:təs], *s.* (*Zool.*) die Schildkröte.

tortoiseshell ['tɔ:təʃel], *s.* das Schildpatt.

tortuous ['tɔ:tjuəs], *adj.* gewunden.

torture ['tɔ:tʃə], *s.* die Folter; (*fig.*) die Folterqualen, *f. pl.* — *v.a.* foltern.

Tory ['tɔ:ri], *s.* (*Pol.*) der englische Konservative.

toss [tɔs], *s.* der Wurf (*of coin, etc.*); *argue the* —, sich streiten. — *v.a.* werfen. — *v.n.* — *up*, losen.

total [toutl], *adj.* ganz, gänzlich, total. — *s.* die Gesamtsumme. — *v.a.* sich (im ganzen) belaufen auf.

totality [tou'tæliti], *s.* die Gesamtheit.

totter ['tɔtə], *v.n.* wanken, schwanken, torkeln.

touch [tʌtʃ], *v.a.* berühren; anfassen; (*coll.*) anpumpen (*for money*); — *up*, auffrischen. — *s.* die Berührung (*contact*); (*Mus.*) der Anschlag.

touching ['tʌtʃiŋ], *adj.* rührend, ergreifend.

touchline ['tʌtʃlain], *s.* (*Sport*) der Rand des Spielfeldes, die Seitenlinie.

touchy ['tʌtʃi], *adj.* empfindlich.

tough [tʌf], *adj.* zäh, widerstandsfähig (*resistant*); *get* —, grob werden; — *luck*, Pech! — *s.* (*Am. coll.*) der Grobian.

tour [tuə], *s.* die Tour, Reise; (*Theat.*) die Tournee. — *v.a., v.n.* touren, bereisen.

tourist ['tuərist], *s.* der Tourist.

tournament ['tuə- *or* 'tə:nəmənt], *s.* der Wettkampf, das Turnier.

tout [taut], *v.n.* Kunden suchen, anlocken. — *s.* der Kundenfänger.

tow [tou], *s.* das Schlepptau. — *v.a.* ziehen, schleppen.

toward(s) [tu'wɔ:d(z), tɔ:d(z)], *prep.* gegen; gegenüber; zu . . . hin; auf . . . zu; für.

towel ['tauəl], *s.* das Handtuch.

towelling ['tauəliŋ], *s.* der Handtuchdrell; *Turkish* —, das Frottiertuch.

tower [tauə], *s.* der Turm, Zwinger. — *v.n.* emporragen, hervorragen (über).

towing path ['tou(iŋ) pɑ:θ] *see* **towpath**.

town [taun], *s.* die Stadt; — *crier*, der Ausrufer; — *hall*, das Rathaus (*offices*).

townsman ['taunzmən], *s.* der Städter.

towpath ['toupɑ:θ], *s.* der Treidelpfad.

toy [tɔi], *s.* das Spielzeug; (*pl.*) Spielsachen, Speilwaren, *f. pl.*; — *shop*, der Speilwarenladen. — *v.n.* spielen.

trace [treis], *s.* die Spur. — *v.a.* suchen, aufspüren; pausen (*through paper*).

track [træk], *s.* die Spur, Fährte (*path*); (*Railw.*) das Geleis(e).

tract [trækt], *s.* der Traktat (*pamphlet*); die Strecke (*stretch*).

traction ['trækʃən], *s.* das Ziehen (*pulling*); (*Tech.*) der Zug.

tractor ['træktə], *s.* der Traktor.

trade [treid], *s.* der Handel (*commerce*); das Gewerbe (*craft*); — *wind*, der Passatwind; — *union*, die Gewerkschaft. — *v.a.* — *in*, in Zahlung geben. — *v.n.* handeln, Handel treiben; — *in*, eintauschen.

trademark ['treidmɑ:k], *s.* die (Schutz)-marke, das Warenzeichen.

tradesman ['treidzmən], *s.* der Lieferant.

traduce [trə'dju:s], *v.a.* verleumden.

traffic ['træfik], *s.* der Verkehr; (*Comm.*) der Handel; — *light*, die Verkehrsampel.

trafficator ['træfikeitə], *s.* (*Motor.*) der Winker.

tragedy ['trædʒədi], *s.* die Tragödie, das Trauerspiel.

tragic ['trædʒik], *adj.* tragisch.

tradition [trə'diʃən], *s.* die Tradition.

traditional [trə'diʃənəl], *adj.* traditionell.

trail [treil], *s.* die Spur, Fährte; (*Am.*) der Pfad. — *v.a.* nach sich ziehen, schleppen; (*Am.*) nachfolgen (*Dat.*).

trailer ['treilə], *s.* (*Motor.*) der Anhänger; (*Film*) die Voranzeige.

train [trein], *v.a.* ausbilden; (*Sport*) trainieren, abrichten, dressieren (*animal*). — *v.n.* (*Sport*) sich vorbereiten; sich ausbilden (*for profession*). — *s.* (*Railw.*) der Zug; (*Mil.*) der Zug, Transport; die Schleppe (*bridal gown, etc.*); — *of thought*, die Gedankenfolge.

training ['treiniŋ], *s.* die Erziehung; Ausbildung; — *college*, das Lehrerseminar, die pädagogische Hochschule.

trait [trei, treit], *s.* der Zug, Wesenszug.

traitor ['treita], *s.* der Verräter.

tram(car) ['træm(kɑ:)], *s.* die Straßenbahn, der Strassenbahnwagen.

trammelled [træmld], *adj.* gebunden, gefesselt.

tramp [træmp], *s.* der Landstreicher, Strolch. — *v.n.* trampeln; (zu Fuß) wandern.

trample ['træmpl], *v.a.* niedertrampeln. — *v.n.* trampeln, treten.

tramway ['træmwei], *s.* die Strassenbahn.

trance [trɑ:ns], *s.* die Verzückung.

tranquil ['træŋkwil], *adj.* ruhig, still, friedlich.

tranquillizer ['træŋkwilaizə], *s.* (*Med.*) das Beruhigungsmittel.

transact [træn'zækt], *v.a.* abmachen; verrichten (*conclude*), erledigen.

transaction [træn'zækʃən], *s.* die Verhandlung, Abmachung, Durchführung.

transcend [træn'send], *v.a.* übersteigen.

transcendental [trænsen'dentl], *adj.* transzendental.

transcribe [træn'skraib], *v.a.* übertragen; umschreiben (*cipher etc.*); abschreiben.

transcription [træn'skripʃən], *s.* die Umschrift; die Abschrift (*copy*).

transept ['trænsept], *s.* (*Archit.*) das Querschiff.

transfer [træns'fə:], *v.a.* versetzen, überführen; übertragen; überweisen (*money*). — *v.n.* verlegt werden. — ['trænsfə:], *s.* der Wechsel, Transfer; die Versetzung; Überweisung.

transfigure [træns'figə], *v.a.* verklären.

transfix [træns'fiks], *v.a.* durchbohren.

transform [træns'fɔ:m], *v.a.* verändern, umwandeln. — *v.r.* sich verwandeln.

transgress [træns'gres], *v.a.* überschreiten (*trespass on*). — *v.n.* sich vergehen.

transient ['trænsiənt], *adj.* vergänglich.

transit ['trænsit, 'trænzit], *s.* der Durchgang; die Durchfahrt, Durchfuhr (*travel*); (*Comm.*) der Transit. — *v.n.* (*Am.*) durchfahren (*of goods*).

transitive ['trænsitiv], *adj.* (*Gram.*) transitiv.

transitory ['trænsitəri], *adj.* vergänglich, flüchtig.

translate [træns'leit], *v.a.* übersetzen; versetzen (*office*).

translation [træns'leiʃən], *s.* die Übersetzung, die Übertragung.

translucent [trænz'lju:sənt], *adj.* durchscheinend.

transmission [trænz'miʃən], *s.* die Übersetzung, Übermittlung; (*Rad.*) die Sendung; (*Motor.*) die Transmission.

transmit [trænz'mit], *v.a.* übersenden,

übermitteln; (*Rad.*, *T.V.*) übertragen, senden.

transmutation [trænzmju'teiʃən], *s.* die Verwandlung.

transparent [træns'pɛərənt], *adj.* durchsichtig.

transpire [træns'paiə, trænz–], *v.n.* bekannt werden.

transplant [træns'plɑ:nt, trænz–], *v.a.* verpflanzen; (*Med.*) übertragen.

transport [træns'pɔ:t], *v.a.* transportieren; (*fig.*) entzücken. — ['trænspɔ:t], *s.* der Transport; die Versendung (*sending*); (*fig.*) die Entzückung.

transpose [træns'pouz], *v.a.* (*Mus.*) transponieren.

transverse [trænz'və:s], *adj.* quer; schräg (*oblique*).

trap [træp], *v.a.* in eine Falle führen; ertappen (*detect*). — *s.* die Falle; der Einspänner (*gig*).

trapeze [trə'pi:z], *s.* das Trapez.

trapper ['træpə], *s.* der Fallensteller.

trappings ['træpiŋz], *s.pl.* der Schmuck; (*fig.*) die Äußerlichkeiten, *f.pl.*

trash [træʃ], *s.* (*Lit.*) der Schund; der Kitsch; das wertlose Zeug.

trashy ['træʃi], *adj.* wertlos, kitschig.

travail ['træveil], *s.* die Wehen, Sorgen, die Mühe.

travel [trævl], *v.n.* reisen. — *v.a.* bereisen. — *s.* das Reisen; — *agency*, das Reisebüro.

traveller ['trævələ], *s.* der Reisende; (*Comm.*) der Handelsreisende, Vertreter.

traverse ['trævə:s], *adj.* quer. — *s.* die Traverse, der Querbalken. — [trə-'və:s], *v.a.* durchqueren; (*fig.*) durchwandern.

trawl [trɔ:l], *v.n.* (mit Schleppnetz) fischen.

trawler ['trɔ:lə], *s.* das Fischerboot, der Fischdampfer.

tray [trei], *s.* das Tablett.

treacherous ['tretʃərəs], *adj.* verräterisch; (*fig.*) gefährlich.

treachery ['tretʃəri], *s.* der Verrat.

treacle [tri:kl], *s.* der Sirup.

tread [tred], *v.a.*, *v.n.* *irr.* (be)treten, auftreten. — *s.* der Tritt, Schritt; die Lauffläche (*of a tyre*).

treason [tri:zn], *s.* der Verrat.

treasure ['treʒə], *s.* der Schatz.

treasurer ['treʒərə], *s.* der Schatzmeister.

treasury ['treʒəri], *s.* die Schatzkammer; (*U.K.*) *the Treasury*, das Schatzamt, Finanzministerium.

treat [tri:t], *v.a.* behandeln; bewirten (*as host*). — *v.n.* (*Pol.*) unterhandeln (*negotiate*). — *s.* der Genuß (*pleasure*).

treatise ['tri:tis], *s.* die Abhandlung.

treatment ['tri:tmənt], *s.* die Behandlung.

treaty ['tri:ti], *s.* der Vertrag.

treble [trebl], *s.* (*Mus.*) die Sopranstimme, Knabenstimme, der Diskant; (*Maths.*) das Dreifache. — *v.a.* verdreifachen.

tree

tree [tri:], s. (*Bot.*) der Baum.
trefoil ['tri:fɔil], s. (*Bot.*) der dreiblätt(e)rige Klee; das Dreiblatt.
trellis ['trelis], s. das Gitter.
tremble [trembl], v.n. zittern. — s. das Zittern.
tremendous [tri'mendəs], adj. ungeheuer (groß); schrecklich.
tremor ['tremə], s. das Zittern; (*Geol.*) das Beben; (*Med.*) das Zucken.
trench [trentʃ], s. der Graben.
trenchant ['trentʃənt], adj. einschneidend, scharf.
trend [trend], s. die Tendenz; (*Comm.*) der Trend.
trepidation [trepi'deiʃən], s. die Angst, das Zittern.
trespass ['trespəs], v.n. sich vergehen, übertreten (*law*); — *on*, unbefugt betreten. — s. die Übertretung.
tress [tres], s. die Flechte, Haarlocke.
trestle [tresl], s. das Gestell; — *table*, der Klapptisch.
trial ['traiəl], s. die Probe, der Versuch; (*Law*) die Verhandlung, der Prozeß, das Verhör.
triangle ['traiæŋgl], s. das Dreieck; (*Mus.*) der Triangel.
tribe [traib], s. der Stamm.
tribulation [tribju'leiʃən], s. die Trübsal, Drangsal.
tribunal [trai'bju:nəl], s. das Tribunal, der Gerichtshof.
tributary ['tribjutəri], adj. Neben-. — s. der Nebenfluß.
tribute ['tribju:t], s. der Tribut.
trice [trais], s. *in a —*, im Nu.
trick [trik], s. der Kniff, Trick. — v.a. betrügen.
trickery ['trikəri], s. der Betrug.
trickle [trikl], v.n. tröpfeln, sickern. — s. das Tröpfeln.
tricky ['triki], adj. verwickelt; (*fig.*) bedenklich, heikel.
tricycle ['traisikl], s. das Dreirad.
tried [traid], adj. erprobt, bewährt.
triennial [trai'eniəl], adj. dreijährlich.
trifle [traifl], v.n. scherzen, spielen. — s. die Kleinigkeit; (*Cul.*) der süße Auflauf.
trigger ['trigə], s. der Drücker. — v.a. — *off*, auslösen.
trilateral [trai'lætərəl], adj. dreiseitig.
trill [tril], s. (*Mus.*) der Triller. — v.a., v.n. trillern.
trim [trim], adj. niedlich, schmuck; nett (*dress*). — v.a. beschneiden; (*Naut.*) — *sails*, einziehen. — s. die Ausrüstung; (*Naut.*) das Gleichgewicht.
trimmer ['trimə], s. die Putzmacherin; (*fig.*) der Opportunist.
trimmings ['triminz], s. *pl.* (*fig.*) der Kleinkram; (*Tail.*) der Besatz.
Trinity ['triniti], s. (*Theol.*) die Dreifaltigkeit, Dreieinigkeit.
trinket ['triŋkit], s. das Geschmeide; (*pl.*) Schmucksachen, *f. pl.*
trip [trip], s. der Ausflug, die Reise. —

v.a. — *up*, ein Bein stellen (*Dat.*). — v.n. stolpern.
tripe ['traip], s. die Kaldaunen, *f. pl.*; (*fig.*) der Unsinn.
triple [tripl], adj. dreifach.
triplet ['triplit], s. der Drilling; (*Mus.*) die Triole; (*Poet.*) der Dreireim.
tripod ['traipɔd], s. der Dreifuß.
tripos ['traipɔs], s. das Schlußexamen (*Cambridge Univ.*).
trite [trait], adj. abgedroschen.
triumph ['traiʌmf], s. der Triumph. — v.n. triumphieren.
triumphant [trai'ʌmfənt], adj. triumphierend.
trivial ['triviəl], adj. trivial, platt, alltäglich.
troll (1) [troul], v.n. trällern (*hum*); fischen. — s. der Rundgesang (*song*).
troll (2) [troul], s. der Kobold (*gnome*).
trolley ['trɔli], s. der Teewagen (*furniture*); (*Tech.*) die Dräsine, der Karren.
trollop ['trɔləp], s. die Schlampe.
trombone [trɔm'boun], s. (*Mus.*) die Posaune.
troop [tru:p], s. der Haufe; (*Mil.*) die Truppe, der Trupp. — v.n. sich sammeln. — v.a. *Trooping the Colour*, die Fahnenparade.
trophy ['troufi], s. die Trophäe, das Siegeszeichen.
tropic ['trɔpik], s. (*Geog.*) der Wendekreis; (*pl.*) die Tropen, *f. pl.*
tropical ['trɔpikəl], adj. tropisch.
trot [trɔt], v.n. traben. — s. der Trab, Trott.
troth [trouθ], s. (*obs.*) die Treue; *pledge o.'s —*, Treue geloben.
trouble [trʌbl], s. die Mühe, Sorge (*worry*); der Kummer (*sadness*); die Störung (*disturbance*). — v.a. bemühen (*ask favour of*); bekümmern (*worry*); stören (*disturb*).
troublesome ['trʌblsəm], adj. ärgerlich, schwierig, unangenehm.
trough [trɔf], s. der Trog; (*Met.*) das Tief.
trounce [trauns], v.a. verprügeln.
trouncing ['traunsiŋ], s. die Tracht Prügel.
trousers ['trauzəz], s. *pl.* die Hosen, *f.pl.*
trout [traut], s. (*Zool.*) die Forelle.
trowel ['trauəl], s. die Kelle.
troy(weight) ['trɔi(weit)], s. das Troygewicht.
truant ['tru:ənt], s. (*Sch.*) der Schulschwänzer; *play —*, die Schule schwänzen.
truce [tru:s], s. der Waffenstillstand.
truck (1) [trʌk], s. (*Rail.*) der Güterwagen; (*Am.*) see **lorry**.
truck (2) [trʌk], s. *have no — with*, nichts zu tun haben mit.
truculent ['trʌkjulənt], adj. streitsüchtig.
trudge [trʌdʒ], v.n. sich schleppen.
true [tru:], adj. wahr; treu (*faithful*); echt (*genuine*); richtig (*correct*).

twelfth

truffle [trʌfl], *s.* die Trüffel.
truism ['truːizm], *s.* der Gemeinplatz, die Binsenwahrheit.
truly ['truːli], *adv. yours* —, Ihr ergebener.
trump [trʌmp], *s.* der Trumpf; — *card,* die Trumpfkarte. — *v.a.* — *up,* erfinden, erdichten.
trumpery ['trʌmpəri], *s.* der Plunder, Schund. — *adj.* wertlos, belanglos.
trumpet ['trʌmpit], *s.* (*Mus.*) die Trompete. — *v.a.* stolz austrompeten, ausposaunen. — *v.n.* trompeten.
truncate [trʌŋ'keit], *v.a.* verstümmeln, stutzen.
truncheon ['trʌnʃən], *s.* der Knüppel. — *v.a.* durchprügeln.
trundle [trʌndl], *v.n.* trudeln; sich wälzen. — *v.a.* — *a hoop,* Reifen schlagen.
trunk [trʌŋk], *s.* der Stamm (*tree*); der Rüssel (*of elephant*); der (große) Koffer (*chest*); — *call,* das Ferngespräch.
truss [trʌs], *s.* das Band, Bruchband. — *v.a.* zäumen, stützen; aufschürzen.
trust [trʌst], *v.a., v.n.* trauen (*Dat.*), vertrauen (*Dat.*); anvertrauen (*Dat., Acc.*). — *s.* das Vertrauen; *in* —, zu treuen Händen, als Treuhänder; (*Comm.*) der Trust.
trustworthy ['trʌstwəːði], *adj.* zuverlässig.
truth [truːθ], *s.* die Wahrheit.
truthful ['truːθful], *adj.* wahrhaftig.
try [trai], *v.a. irr.* versuchen (*s. th.*); (*Law*) verhören; — *on* (*clothes*), anprobieren; — *out,* ausprobieren. — *v.n.* versuchen, sich bemühen. — *s.* der Versuch (*attempt*); (*Rugby*) der Try.
Tsar [zɑː], *s.* der Zar.
tub [tʌb], *s.* die Kufe; die Wanne (*bath*); (*Naut.*) das Übungsboot.
tube [tjuːb], *s.* die Tube (*paste etc.*); die Röhre (*pipe, also Elec.*); der Schlauch (*tyre*); das Rohr (*tubing*); (*Transport*) die Londoner Untergrundbahn.
tuberous ['tjuːbərəs], *adj.* knollenartig, knollig.
tubular ['tjuːbjulə], *adj.* röhrenförmig.
tuck [tʌk], *s.* (*Tail.*) die Falte; (*Sch. sl.*) der Leckerbissen. — *v.a.* — *up,* zudecken; — *in,* einschlagen. — *v.n.* (*sl.*) — *in,* tüchtig zugreifen.
tucker ['tʌkə], *s.* (*sl.*) das Essen.
tuckshop ['tʌkʃɔp], *s.* der Schulladen.
Tuesday ['tjuːzdi], der Dienstag.
tuft [tʌft], *s.* der Büschel.
tug [tʌg], *v.a.* ziehen, zerren. — *s.* (*Naut.*) der Schlepper; — *of war,* das Tauziehen.
tuition [tjuː'iʃən], *s.* der Unterricht, Privatunterricht.
tulip ['tjuːlip], *s.* (*Bot.*) die Tulpe.
tumble [tʌmbl], *v.n.* purzeln. — *s.* der Sturz, Fall.
tumbril ['tʌmbril], *s.* der Karren.
tumid ['tjuːmid], *adj.* geschwollen.
tumour ['tjuːmə], *s.* (*Med.*) die Geschwulst, der Tumor.

tumult ['tjuːmʌlt], *s.* der Tumult, Auflauf; der Lärm (*noise*).
tun [tʌn], *s.* die Tonne, das Faß.
tune [tjuːn], *s.* die Melodie. — *v.a.* stimmen; (*Rad.*) — *in (to),* einstellen (auf).
tuneful ['tjuːnful], *adj.* melodisch.
tuner ['tjuːnə], *s.* der (Klavier)stimmer.
tunic ['tjuːnik], *s.* der Kittel.
tuning ['tjuːniŋ], *s.* das Stimmen; die Abstimmung (*also Rad.*); — *fork,* die Stimmgabel.
tunnel [tʌnl], *s.* der Tunnel. — *v.n.* graben, einen Tunnel bauen.
turbid ['təːbid], *adj.* trüb, dick.
turbot ['təːbət], *s.* (*Zool.*) der Steinbutt.
turbulence ['təːbjuləns], *s.* der Sturm, das Ungestüm; (*Aviat.*) die Turbulenz.
tureen [tjuə'riːn], *s.* die Suppenterrine, Suppenschüssel.
turf [təːf], *s.* der Rasen; (*Sport*) die Rennbahn, der Turf. — *v.a.* mit Rasen belegen; (*sl.*) — *out,* hinausschmeißen.
turgid ['təːdʒid], *adj.* schwülstig (*style*).
Turk [təːk], *s.* der Türke.
turkey ['təːki], *s.* (*Orn.*) der Truthahn.
Turkish ['təːkiʃ], *adj.* türkisch.
turmoil ['təːmɔil], *s.* die Unruhe, der Aufruhr.
turn [təːn], *v.a.* wenden, drehen, kehren (*to*); — *down,* ablehnen; (*coll.*) — *in,* abgeben (*hand over*); — *on,* andrehen (*tap etc.*); — *off,* ausdrehen; — *out,* produzieren; — *v.n.* sich drehen, sich ändern; werden; — *on s.o.,* jemanden verraten; (*coll.*) — *out,* ausrücken; (*coll.*) — *up,* auftauchen. — *s.* die Drehung, Windung; der Hang; die Reihe; die Nummer (*act*); *it is my* —, ich bin an der Reihe.
turncoat ['təːnkout], *s.* der Überläufer.
turner ['təːnə], *s.* der Drechsler.
turnip ['təːnip], *s.* (*Bot.*) die Rübe.
turnpike ['təːnpaik], *s.* der Schlagbaum.
turnstile ['təːnstail], *s.* das Drehkreuz.
turntable ['təːnteibl], *s.* die Drehscheibe.
turpentine ['təːpəntain], *s.* der *or* das Terpentin.
turquoise ['təːkwɔiz *or* 'təːkɔiz], *s.* der Türkis.
turret ['tʌrit], *s.* (*Archit.*) der Turm, das Türmchen.
turtle [təːtl], *s.* (*Zool.*) die Schildkröte; (*Orn.*) — *-dove,* die Turteltaube.
tusk [tʌsk], *s.* (*Zool.*) der Stoßzahn.
tussle [tʌsl], *s.* der Streit, die Rauferei.
tutelage ['tjuːtilidʒ], *s.* die Vormundschaft.
tutor ['tjuːtə], *s.* der Privatlehrer; der Tutor, Studienleiter. — *v.a.* unterrichten.
twaddle [twɔdl], *s.* das Geschwätz. — *v.n.* schwätzen.
twang [twæŋ], *s.* der scharfe Ton. — *v.n.* scharf klingen.
tweed [twiːd], *s.* (*Text.*) der Tweed.
twelfth [twelfθ], *num.adj.* zwölft; *Twelfth Night,* das Fest der Heiligen Drei Könige (*6th January*).

507

twelve

twelve [twelv], *num. adj.* zwölf.

twenty ['twenti], *num. adj.* zwanzig.

twice [twais], *num. adv.* zweimal, doppelt.

twig [twig], *s.* (*Bot.*) der Zweig, die Rute.

twilight ['twailait], *s.* das Zwielicht, die Dämmerung.

twill [twil], *s.* (*Text.*) der Köper. — *v.a.* köpern.

twin [twin], *s.* der Zwilling.

twine [twain], *s.* der Bindfaden, die Schnur. — *v.a.* drehen, zwirnen. — *v.n.* sich verflechten; sich winden (*plant*).

twinge [twindʒ], *s.* der Zwick, Stich.

twinkle ['twiŋkl], *v.n.* blinzeln, blinken. — *s.* das Zwinkern, der Blick.

twirl [twə:l], *s.* der Wirbel. — *v.a.* schnell drehen, wirbeln.

twist [twist], *v.a.* flechten, drehen; verdrehen. — *s.* die Drehung, Krümmung; das Geflecht; (*fig.*) die Wendung (*sudden change*).

twitch [twitʃ], *v.a.* zupfen, zucken. — *v.n.* zucken. — *s.* das Zucken, der Krampf.

twitter ['twitə], *v.n.* zwitschern; (*fig.*) zittern. — *s.* das Gezwitscher; (*fig.*) die Angst.

two [tu:], *num. adj.* zwei; — -faced, falsch.

twofold ['tu:fould], *adj.* zweifach.

tympanum ['timpənəm], *s.* (*Med.*) das Trommelfell.

type [taip], *s.* (*Typ.*) die Type; (*Psych.*) der Typ, Typus. — *v.a.*, *v.n.* tippen; mit der Maschine schreiben.

typewriter ['taipraitə], *s.* die Schreibmaschine.

typhoid ['taifɔid], *s.* (*Med.*) der (Unterleibs)typhus. — *adj.* typhusartig.

typist ['taipist], *s.* der (die) Maschinenschreiber(in).

typhoon [tai'fu:n], *s.* der Taifun.

typical ['tipikəl], *adj.* typisch, charakteristisch.

typography [tai'pɔgrəfi], *s.* die Typographie, Buchdruckerkunst.

tyrannical [ti'rænikəl], *adj.* tyrannisch.

tyranny ['tirəni], *s.* die Tyrannei.

tyrant ['taiərənt], *s.* der Tyrann.

tyre, (*Am.*) tire [taiə], *s.* der Reifen.

tyro ['taiərou], *s.* der Anfänger.

Tyrolese [tiro'li:z], *adj.* tirolisch, Tiroler-. — *s.* der Tiroler.

U

U [ju:], das U.

ubiquitous [ju'bikwitəs], *adj.* überall da, überall zu finden.

udder ['ʌdə], *s.* (*Zool.*) das Euter.

ugly ['ʌgli], *adj.* häßlich.

Ukrainian [ju:'kreiniən], *adj.* ukrainisch. — *s.* der Ukrainer.

ulcer ['ʌlsə], *s.* (*Med.*) das Geschwür.

ulcerate ['ʌlsəreit], *v.n.* (*Med.*) schwären.

ulcerous ['ʌlsərəs], *adj.* (*Med.*) geschwürig.

ulterior [ʌl'tiəriə], *adj.* weiter, ferner, weiterliegend.

ultimate ['ʌltimit], *adj.* letzt, endlich, äußerst.

ultimatum [ʌlti'meitəm], *s.* das Ultimatum.

umbrage ['ʌmbridʒ], *s.* der Schatten; *take* —, Anstoß nehmen (an, *Dat.*).

umbrella [ʌm'brelə], *s.* der Schirm, Regenschirm.

umpire ['ʌmpaiə], *s.* (*Sport*) der Schiedsrichter.

umpteen ['ʌmpti:n], *adj.* zahlreiche, verschiedene.

un- [ʌn], *negating pref.* un-, nicht-; with *verbs*, auf-, ent-, los-, ver-; *where a word is not given, see the simple form.*

unable [ʌn'eibl], *adj.* unfähig; *be* —, nicht können.

unaccustomed [ʌnə'kʌstəmd], *adj.* ungewohnt.

unaided [ʌn'eidid], *adj.* allein, ohne Hilfe.

unaware [ʌnə'wɛə], *adj.* unbewußt.

uncertain [ʌn'sə:tin], *adj.* unsicher.

uncle [ʌŋkl], *s.* der Onkel.

unconscious [ʌn'kɔnʃəs], *adj.* bewußtlos; unbewusst.

uncouth [ʌn'ku:θ], *adj.* ungehobelt, roh.

unction ['ʌŋkʃən], *s.* die Salbung (*anointing*); die Salbe; *Extreme Unction,* (*Eccl.*) die Letzte Ölung.

unctuous ['ʌŋktjuəs], *adj.* salbungsvoll.

under ['ʌndə], *prep.* unter. — *adv.* darunter, unten (*underneath*); *pref.* (*compounds*) unter-.

undercarriage ['ʌndəkæridʒ], *s.* (*Aviat.*) das Fahrwerk.

underfed [ʌndə'fed], *adj.* unterernährt.

undergo [ʌndə'gou], *v.a. irr.* durchmachen, erdulden.

undergraduate [ʌndə'grædjuit], *s.* (*Univ.*) der Student.

underground ['ʌndəgraund], *adj.* unterirdisch; — *railway* die Untergrundbahn; — [ʌndə'graund], *adv.* unterirdisch.

underhand [ʌndə'hænd], *adj.* heimlich, hinterlistig.

underline [ʌndə'lain], *v.a.* unterstreichen.

undermine [ʌndə'main], *v.a.* untergraben.

underneath [ʌndə'ni:θ], *adv.* unten, darunter. — ['ʌndəni:θ], *prep.* unter.

undersigned ['ʌndəsaind], *adj.* unterzeichnet. —*s.* der Unterzeichnete.

understand [ʌndə'stænd], *v.a. irr.* verstehen, begreifen.

understatement ['ʌndəsteitmənt], *s.* die zu bescheidene Festellung, Unterbewertung.

508

undertaker [ˈʌndəteikə], s. der Leichenbestatter.
undertaking [ʌndəˈteikiŋ], s. das Unternehmen (*business*); das Versprechen (*promise*).
undertone [ˈʌndətoun], s. der Unterton.
underwrite [ʌndəˈrait], v.a. irr. (*Comm.*) versichern.
underwriter [ˈʌndəraitə], s. (*Comm.*) der Assekurant, Versicherer, Mitversicherer.
undeserved [ʌndiˈzəːvd], adj. unverdient.
undeserving [ʌndiˈzəːviŋ], adj. unwürdig.
undignified [ʌnˈdignifaid], adj. würdelos.
undiscerning [ʌndiˈzəːniŋ], adj. geschmacklos.
undiscriminating [ʌndisˈkrimineitiŋ], adj. unterschiedslos, unkritisch.
undisputed [ʌndisˈpjuːtid], adj. unbestritten.
undo [ʌnˈduː], v.a. irr. zerstören (*destroy*); öffnen (*open*).
undoubted [ʌnˈdautid], adj. zweifellos.
undress [ʌnˈdres], v.a., v.n. — (sich)ausziehen. — [ˈʌndres], s. das Hauskleid.
undue [ʌnˈdjuː], adj. unangemessen.
undulate [ˈʌndjuleit], v.n. wallen, Wellen schlagen.
unduly [ʌnˈdjuːli], adv. ungebührlich, übermäßig.
unearth [ʌnˈəːθ], v.a. ausgraben.
unearthly [ʌnˈəːθli], adj. überirdisch.
uneasy [ʌnˈiːzi], adj. unruhig, unbehaglich.
unemployed [ʌnimˈplɔid], adj. arbeitslos.
unemployment [ʌnimˈplɔimənt], s. die Arbeitslosigkeit.
unending [ʌnˈendiŋ], adj. endlos.
uneven [ʌnˈiːvən], adj. uneben; ungerade.
unexceptionable [ʌnikˈsepʃənəbl], adj. tadellos.
unexpired [ʌniksˈpaiəd], adj. noch nicht abgelaufen, noch gültig.
unfair [ʌnˈfɛə], adj. unfair; unehrlich.
unfeeling [ʌnˈfiːliŋ], adj. gefühllos.
unfit [ʌnˈfit], adj. (*Mil.*, *Med.*) untauglich, schwach; (*food etc.*) ungenießbar.
unfold [ʌnˈfould], v.a. entfalten.
unforeseen [ʌnfɔːˈsiːn], adj. unerwartet.
unfounded [ʌnˈfaundid], adj. grundlos.
unfurnished [ʌnˈfəːniʃd], adj. unmöbliert.
ungrudging [ʌnˈgrʌdʒiŋ], adj. bereitwillig.
unhappy [ʌnˈhæpi], adj. unglücklich.
unhinge [ʌnˈhindʒ], v.a. aus den Angeln heben.
unicorn [ˈjuːnikɔːn], s. (*Myth.*) das Einhorn.
uniform [ˈjuːnifɔːm], s. die Uniform. — adj. gleichförmig, einförmig.
union [ˈjuːniən], s. die Vereinigung; trade —, die Gewerkschaft; *Union Jack*, die britische Nationalflagge.

unique [juˈniːk], adj. einzigartig.
unison [ˈjuːnisən], s. (*Mus.*) der Einklang, die Harmonie.
unit [ˈjuːnit], s. die Einheit (*measure etc.*).
unite [juˈnait], v.a. vereinen. — v.n. sich vereinen, verbünden.
unity [ˈjuːniti], s. die Einigkeit.
universal [juːniˈvəːsəl], adj. allgemein.
universe [ˈjuːnivəːs], s. das Weltall.
university [juːniˈvəːsiti], s. die Universität, Hochschule; — degree, der akademische Grad.
unkempt [ʌnˈkempt], adj. ungekämmt, ungepflegt.
unleavened [ʌnˈlevənd], adj. ungesäuert.
unless [ʌnˈles], conj. außer, wenn nicht, es sei denn.
unlettered [ʌnˈletəd], adj. ungebildet.
unlicensed [ʌnˈlaisənsd], adj. nicht (für Alkoholverkauf) lizenziert.
unlike [ʌnˈlaik], adj. ungleich. — [ˈʌnlaik], prep. anders als, verschieden von.
unlikely [ʌnˈlaikli], adj., adv. unwahrscheinlich.
unlock [ʌnˈlɔk], v.a. aufschließen.
unmask [ʌnˈmɑːsk], v.a. entlarven.
unpack [ʌnˈpæk], v.a., v.n. auspacken.
unpleasant [ʌnˈpleznt], adj. unangenehm.
unreliable [ʌnriˈlaiəbl], adj. unzuverlässig.
unremitting [ʌnriˈmitiŋ], adj. unablässig.
unrepentant [ʌnriˈpentənt], adj. reuelos.
unrest [ʌnˈrest], s. die Unruhe.
unsafe [ʌnˈseif], adj. unsicher.
unscathed [ʌnˈskeiðd], adj. unversehrt.
unscrew [ʌnˈskruː], v.a. abschrauben.
unscrupulous [ʌnˈskruːpjuləs], adj. skrupellos, gewissenlos.
unseat [ʌnˈsiːt], v.a. aus dem Sattel heben; absetzen.
unselfish [ʌnˈselfiʃ], adj. selbstlos.
unsettle [ʌnˈsetl], v.a. verwirren; (*fig.*) aus dem Konzept bringen.
unsew [ʌnˈsou], v.a. auftrennen.
unshrinking [ʌnˈʃrinkiŋ], adj. unverzagt.
unsophisticated [ʌnsəˈfistikeitid], adj. naiv, natürlich.
unsparing [ʌnˈspɛəriŋ], adj. schonungslos.
unstable [ʌnˈsteibl], adj. unsicher; labil.
unstitch [ʌnˈstitʃ], v.a. auftrennen.
unstop [ʌnˈstɔp], v.a. aufstöpseln, öffnen (*a bottle*).
unstudied [ʌnˈstʌdid], adj. ungekünstelt.
unsuccessful [ʌnsəkˈsesful], adj. erfolglos.
unsuspecting [ʌnsəˈspektiŋ], adj. arglos.
untie [ʌnˈtai], v.a. losbinden.
until [ʌnˈtil], prep., conj. bis.

untimely [ʌn'taimli], *adj.* vorzeitig, unzeitig.
untiring [ʌn'taiəriŋ], *adj.* unermüdlich.
unto ['ʌntu], *prep.* (*Poet.*) zu.
untold [ʌn'tould], *adj.* ungezählt, unermeßlich.
untoward [ʌn'tɔːd *or* ʌn'touəd], *adj.* unangenehm; widerspenstig (*recalcitrant*).
untrustworthy [ʌn'trʌstwəːði], *adj.* unzuverlässig.
unveil [ʌn'veil], *v.a.* enthüllen.
unwieldy [ʌn'wiːldi], *adj.* sperrig, schwerfällig.
unwind [ʌn'waind], *v.a.* abwickeln.
unwitting [ʌn'witiŋ], *adj.* unwissentlich, unbewusst.
unwonted [ʌn'wountid], *adj.* ungewohnt.
unwrap [ʌn'ræp], *v.a.* auspacken, auswickeln.
unyielding [ʌn'jiːldiŋ], *adj.* unnachgiebig; hartnäckig.
unyoke [ʌn'jouk], *v.a.* ausspannen.
up [ʌp], *adv.* auf, aufwärts (*upward*); aufgestanden (*out of bed*); — (*there*), oben; *what's up?* was ist los? — *to*, bis zu; *be* — *to s.th.*, auf etwas aus sein, etwas im Schilde führen; *it's* — *to you*, es liegt an dir. — *prep.* auf, hinauf. — *s. ups and downs*, das wechselnde Schicksal, Auf und Ab.
upbraid [ʌp'breid], *v.a.* tadeln.
upheaval [ʌp'hiːvl], *s.* das Chaos, Durcheinander, die Umwälzung.
uphill [ʌp'hil], *adv.* bergauf(wärts). — ['ʌphil], *adj.* (an)steigend; (*fig.*) mühsam.
uphold [ʌp'hould], *v.a.* aufrechterhalten.
upholster [ʌp'houlstə], *v.a.* polstern.
upholstery [ʌp'houlstəri], *s.* die Polsterung.
upon [ʌ'pɔn] *see on.*
upper ['ʌpə], *adj.* ober, höher; — *hand*, die Oberhand.
uppish ['ʌpiʃ], *adj.* anmaßend.
upright ['ʌprait], *adj.* aufrecht, gerade; (*fig.*) aufrichtig, rechtschaffen.
uproar ['ʌprɔː], *s.* der Lärm, Aufruhr.
uproot [ʌp'ruːt], *v.a.* entwurzeln.
upset [ʌp'set], *v.a.* umwerfen; (*fig.*) aus der Fassung bringen. — ['ʌpset], *s.* das Umwerfen; (*fig.*) die Bestürzung.
upshot ['ʌpʃɔt], *s.* der Ausgang, das Ergebnis.
upside ['ʌpsaid], *s.* die Oberseite; — *down*, auf den Kopf gestellt.
upstairs [ʌp'stɛəz], *adv.* oben, nach oben.
upstart ['ʌpstaːt], *s.* der Parvenü, Emporkömmling.
upward ['ʌpwəd], *adj.* steigend, aufwärtsgehend. — *adv.* (*also* **upwards**) aufwärts; — *of*, mehr als.
urban ['əːbən], *adj.* städtisch.
urbane [əː'bein], *adj.* zivilisiert.
urbanity [əː'bæniti], *s.* die Bildung, der Schliff.
urchin ['əːtʃin], *s.* der Schelm; (*Zool.*) *sea* —, der Seeigel.

urge [əːdʒ], *v.a.* drängen. — *s.* der Drang.
urgent ['əːdʒənt], *adj.* dringend, drängend, dringlich.
urine ['juərin], *s.* der Urin.
urn [əːn], *s.* die Urne.
Uruguayan [ju:ru'gwaiən], *adj.* uruguayisch. — *s.* der Uruguayer.
us [ʌs], *pers. pron.* uns.
usage ['juːsidʒ], *s.* der (Sprach)gebrauch; die Sitte.
use [juːz], *v.a.* gebrauchen, benutzen. — [juːs], *s.* der Gebrauch, die Benutzung; der Nutzen (*usefulness*).
usher ['ʌʃə], *s.* der Türhüter, Platzanweiser. — *v.a.* — *in*, anmelden, einführen.
usherette [ʌʃə'ret], *s.* die Platzanweiserin, Programmverkäuferin.
usual ['juːʒuəl], *adj.* gewöhnlich, üblich.
usurer ['juːʒərə *or* 'juːzjuərə], *s.* der Wucherer.
usurp [juː'zəːp], *v.a.* an sich reißen, usurpieren.
usury ['juːʒuari], *s.* der Wucher.
utensil [juː'tensil], *s.* das Gerät, Werkzeug.
utility [juː'tiliti], *s.* die Nützlichkeit (*usefulness*); der Nutzen; *public* —, (die) öffentliche Einrichtung.
utilize ['juːtilaiz], *v.a.* nutzbar machen, ausbeuten, ausnützen.
utmost ['ʌtmoust], *adj.* äußerst, weitest, höchst. — *s.* das Höchste, Äußerste.
utter ['ʌtə], *adj.* äußerst, gänzlich. — *v.a.* äußern, aussprechen.
utterly ['ʌtəli], *adv.* äußerst, völlig.
uvula ['juːvjulə], *s.* (*Anat.*) das Zäpfchen.

V

V [viː], das V.
vacancy ['veikənsi], *s.* die freie Stelle, die Vakanz.
vacant ['veikənt], *adj.* frei; leer.
vacate [və'keit], *v.a.* frei machen.
vacation [və'keiʃən], *s.* die Niederlegung (*of a post*); die Ferien, *pl.* (*school*); der Urlaub (*holiday*).
vaccinate ['væksineit], *v.a.* (*Med.*) impfen.
vaccine ['væksiːn], *s.* (*Med.*) der Impfstoff.
vacillate ['væsileit], *v.n.* schwanken.
vacuity [væ'kjuːiti], *s.* die Leere.
vacuous ['vækjuəs], *adj.* leer.
vacuum ['vækjuəm], *s.* das Vakuum; — *cleaner*, der Staubsauger.
vagabond ['vægəbɔnd], *s.* der Landstreicher.
vagary [və'gɛəri], *s.* die Laune, Grille.

vagrant ['veigrənt], *adj.* herumstreichend. — *s.* der Landstreicher.
vague [veig], *adj.* vage, unbestimmt, unklar.
vain [vein], *adj.* nichtig, vergeblich, eitel; *in* —, vergebens, umsonst.
vale [veil], *s.* (*Poet.*) das Tal.
valerian [və'liəriən], *s.* (*Bot.*) der Baldrian.
valet ['vælei, 'vælit], *s.* der Diener.
valiant ['væljənt], *adj.* mutig, tapfer.
valid ['vælid], *adj.* gültig, stichhaltig.
valley ['væli], *s.* das Tal.
valuable ['væljuəbl], *adj.* wertvoll, kostbar.
valuation [vælju'eiʃən], *s.* die Schätzung.
value ['vælju:], *s.* der Wert. — *v.a.* wertschätzen, schätzen.
valve [vælv], *s.* (*Mech.*) das Ventil; (*Rad.*) die Röhre.
vamp (1) [væmp], *s.* das Oberleder.
vamp (2) [væmp], *s.* (*Am. coll.*) der Vamp.
vampire ['væmpaiə], *s.* der Vampir.
van [væn], *s.* der Lieferwagen.
vane [vein], *s.* die Wetterfahne.
vanguard ['vænga:d], *s.* die Vorhut, der Vortrupp.
vanilla [və'nilə], *s.* die Vanille.
vanish ['væniʃ], *v.n.* verschwinden.
vanity ['væniti], *s.* die Nichtigkeit; die Eitelkeit (*conceit*).
vanquish ['væŋkwiʃ], *v.a.* besiegen.
vantage ['va:ntidʒ], *s.* der Vorteil; — *point*, die günstige Position.
vapid ['væpid], *adj.* leer, schal.
vapour ['veipə], *s.* der Dunst; (*Chem.*) der Dampf.
variable ['vɛəriəbl], *adj.* variabel, veränderlich.
variance ['vɛəriəns], *s.* die Uneinigkeit.
variation [vɛəri'eiʃən], *s.* die Variation; die Veränderung, Abweichung.
varicose ['værikəs], *adj.* Krampf-, krampfaderig.
variegated ['vɛərigeitid], *adj.* bunt, vielfarbig.
variety [və'raiəti], *s.* die Mannigfaltigkeit; (*Bot.*) die Varietät, Abart; (*Theat.*) das Varieté, das Varietétheater.
various ['vɛəriəs], *adj.* verschieden; mannigfaltig.
varnish ['va:niʃ], *s.* der Firnis, der Lack. — *v.a.* mit Firnis anstreichen, lackieren.
vary ['vɛəri], *v.a.* abändern. — *v.n.* sich ändern, variieren.
vase [va:z], *s.* die Vase.
vassal ['væsl], *s.* der Vasall, Lehnsmann.
vast [va:st], *adj.* ungeheuer, groß.
vat [væt], *s.* die Kufe, das große Faß.
vault [vɔ:lt], *s.* das Gewölbe; die Gruft (*grave*); (*Sport*) der Sprung, *pole* —, der Stabhochsprung. — *v.n.* springen.
vaunt [vɔ:nt], *v.a.* rühmen. — *v.n.* prahlen, sich rühmen. — *s.* die Prahlerei.
veal [vi:l], *s.* das Kalbfleisch.

veer [viə], *v.n.* sich drehen.
vegetable ['vedʒitəbl], *s.* das Gemüse.
vegetarian [vedʒi'tɛəriən], *adj.* vegetarisch. — *s.* der Vegetarier.
vegetate ['vedʒiteit], *v.n.* vegetieren.
vehemence ['vi:əməns], *s.* die Vehemenz, Heftigkeit.
vehicle ['vi:ikl], *s.* das Fahrzeug, Fuhrwerk; (*Motor.*) der Wagen.
veil [veil], *s.* der Schleier. — *v.a.* verschleiern.
vein [vein], *s.* die Ader.
vellum ['veləm], *s.* das feine Pergamentpapier.
velocity [vi'lɔsiti], *s.* die Geschwindigkeit, Schnelligkeit.
velvet ['velvit], *s.* (*Text.*) der Samt.
venal ['vi:nəl], *adj.* käuflich.
vend [vend], *v.a.* verkaufen; —*ing machine*, der Automat.
veneer [və'niə], *s.* das Furnier. — *v.a.* furnieren.
venerable ['venərəbl], *adj.* ehrwürdig.
venerate ['venəreit], *v.a.* verehren.
venereal [və'niəriəl], *adj.* Geschlechts-.
Venezuelan [veni'zweilən], *adj.* venezolanisch. — *s.* der Venezolaner.
vengeance ['vendʒəns], *s.* die Rache.
venison ['venizn *or* venzn], *s.* das Wildpret.
venom ['venəm], *s.* das Gift.
vent [vent], *v.a.* Luft machen (*Dat.*). — *s.* das Luftloch, die Öffnung.
ventilate ['ventileit], *v.a.* ventilieren, lüften.
ventricle ['ventrikl], *s.* (*Anat.*) die Herzkammer.
ventriloquist [ven'triləkwist], *s.* der Bauchredner.
venture ['ventʃə], *s.* das Wagnis, Unternehmen. — *v.a.* wagen, riskieren. — *v.n.* sich erlauben, (sich) wagen.
venue ['venju:], *s.* der Treffpunkt, Versammlungsort.
veracity [və'ræsiti], *s.* die Glaubwürdigkeit, Wahrhaftigkeit.
verbose [və:'bous], *adj.* wortreich, weitschweifig.
verdant ['və:dənt], *adj.* grünend, grün.
verdict ['və:dikt], *s.* das Urteil, die Entscheidung.
verdigris ['və:digri:s], *s.* der Grünspan.
verdure ['və:djə], *s.* das Grün.
verge [və:dʒ], *s.* der Rand, die Einfassung. — *v.n.* grenzen (*on*, an, *Acc.*).
verify ['verifai], *v.a.* bestätigen; (*Law*) beglaubigen.
verily ['verili], *adv.* (*Bibl.*) wahrlich.
veritable ['veritəbl], *adj.* wahr, echt.
vermicelli [və:mi'seli], *s.* die Nudeln, *f. pl.*
vermilion [və'miljən], *s.* das Zinnober (*paint*).
vermin ['və:min], *s. pl.* das Ungeziefer.
vermouth ['və:mu:θ, -mu:t], *s.* der Wermut.
vernacular [və'nækjulə], *s.* die Landessprache. — *adj.* einheimisch.
vernal ['və:nəl], *adj.* frühlingsartig, Frühlings-.

versatile

versatile ['vɔ:sɔtail], *adj.* gewandt; vielseitig.
verse [vɔ:s], *s.* der Vers; (*Poet.*) die Strophe.
versed [vɔ:sd], *adj.* bewandert.
version ['vɔ:ʃən], *s.* die Version, Fassung, Lesart; (*fig.*) die Darstellung.
vertebrate ['vɔ:tibrɔt], *s.* (*Zool.*) das Wirbeltier. — *adj.* mit Rückenwirbeln versehen.
vertex ['vɔ:teks], *s.* der Zenit.
vertigo ['vɔ:tigou], *s.* (*Med.*) der Schwindel, das Schwindelgefühl.
verve [vɔ:v], *s.* die Schwung.
very ['veri], *adv.* sehr. — *adj.* echt, wirklich, wahrhaftig.
vespers ['vespɔz], *s. pl.* (*Eccl.*) der Abendgottesdienst, die Vesper.
vessel [vesl], *s.* das Gefäß (*container*); (*Naut.*) das Fahrzeug, Schiff.
vest [vest], *s.* das Gewand; (*Tail.*) die Weste; das Unterhemd (*undergarment*). — *v.a.* übertragen.
vested ['vestid], *adj.* — *interests*, das Eigeninteresse.
vestige ['vestidʒ], *s.* die Spur.
vestment ['vestmɔnt], *s.* (*Eccl.*) das Meßgewand.
vestry ['vestri], *s.* (*Eccl.*) die Sakristei.
vetch [vetʃ], *s.* (*Bot.*) die Wicke.
veterinary ['vetɔrinri], *adj.* tierärztlich; — *surgeon*, der Tierarzt.
veto ['vi:tou], *s.* (*Pol.*) der Einspruch, das Veto.
vex [veks], *v.a.* quälen, plagen.
vexation [vek'seiʃən], *s.* die Plage, der Verdruß.
via [vaiɔ], *prep.* über.
vibrate [vai'breit], *v.n.* schwingen, vibrieren.
vicar ['vikɔ], *s.* (*Eccl.*) der Pfarrer, Vikar.
vicarious [vi'kɛɔriɔs], *adj.* stellvertretend.
vice (1) [vais], *s.* das Laster (*immorality*).
vice (2) [vais], *s.* (*Mech.*) der Schraubstock.
vice- [vais], *pref.* Vize-, zweiter (*chairman etc.*).
vicinity [vi'siniti], *s.* die Nachbarschaft, Nähe.
vicious ['viʃɔs], *adj.* böse, bösartig.
vicissitude [vi'sisitju:d], *s.* der Wechsel, Wandel; (*pl.*) Wechselfälle, *m. pl.*
victim ['viktim], *s.* das Opfer.
victuals [vitlz], *s. pl.* die Lebensmittel, *n. pl.*
vie [vai], *v.n.* wetteifern.
Vietnamese [vjetnɔ'mi:z], *adj.* vietnamesisch. — *s.* der Vietnamese.
view [vju:], *s.* der Anblick, die Aussicht (*panorama*); die Ansicht (*opinion*); die Absicht (*intention*). — *v.a.* betrachten; besichtigen (*inspect*).
vigil ['vidʒil], *s.* die Nachtwache.
vigilance ['vidʒilɔns], *s.* die Wachsamkeit.
vigorous ['vigɔrɔs], *adj.* kräftig, rüstig, energisch.
vigour ['vigɔ], *s.* die Kraft, Energie.
vile [vail], *adj.* schlecht, niedrig.

vilify ['vilifai], *v.a.* beschimpfen, erniedrigen.
villa ['vilɔ], *s.* das Landhaus, die Villa.
village ['vilidʒ], *s.* das Dorf.
villain ['vilɔn], *s.* der Schurke.
villainous ['vilɔnɔs], *adj.* niederträchtig.
villainy ['vilɔni], *s.* die Niedertracht, Schändlichkeit.
vindicate ['vindikeit], *v.a.* behaupten, verteidigen; rechtfertigen (*justify*).
vindictive [vin'diktiv], *adj.* rachsüchtig.
vine [vain], *s.* (*Bot.*) der Weinstock, die Rebe.
vinegar ['vinigɔ], *s.* der Essig.
vintage ['vintidʒ], *s.* die Weinernte; der Jahrgang (*also fig.*).
vintner ['vintnɔ], *s.* der Weinbauer, Winzer.
viola [vi'oulɔ], *s.* (*Mus.*) die Viola, Bratsche.
violate ['vaiɔleit], *v.a.* verletzen, schänden.
violence ['vaiɔlɔns], *s.* die Gewalt; die Gewalttätigkeit.
violent ['vaiɔlɔnt], *adj.* gewalttätig (*brutal*); heftig (*vehement*).
violet ['vaiɔlit], *s.* (*Bot.*) das Veilchen. — *adj.* veilchenblau, violett.
violin [vaiɔ'lin], *s.* (*Mus.*) die Violine, Geige.
viper ['vaipɔ], *s.* (*Zool.*) die Viper, Natter.
virago [vi'rɑ:gou], *s.* das Mannweib.
virgin ['vɔ:dʒin], *s.* die Jungfrau.
virile ['virail], *adj.* männlich, kräftig.
virtual ['vɔ:tjuɔl], *adj.* eigentlich.
virtue ['vɔ:tju:], *s.* die Tugend; *by* — *of*, kraft (*Genit.*).
virtuoso [vɔ:tju'ousou], *s.* der Virtuose.
virtuous ['vɔ:tjuɔs], *adj.* tugendhaft.
virulent ['virulɔnt], *adj.* bösartig, giftig.
virus ['vaiɔrɔs], *s.* (*Med.*) das Gift, Virus.
viscosity [vis'kɔsiti], *s.* die Zähigkeit, Zähflüssigkeit.
viscount ['vaikaunt], *s.* der Vicomte.
viscous ['viskɔs], *adj.* zähflüssig, klebrig.
visibility [vizi'biliti], *s.* die Sichtbarkeit, Sicht.
visible ['vizibl], *adj.* sichtbar.
vision ['viʒɔn], *s.* die Sehkraft; (*fig.*) die Vision (*dream*); die Erscheinung (*apparition*).
visionary ['viʒɔnri], *s.* der Träumer, (*Poet.*) der Seher. — *adj.* visionär, phantastisch, seherisch.
visit ['vizit], *s.* der Besuch. — *v.a.* besuchen.
visitation [vizi'teiʃɔn], *s.* die Heimsuchung.
visor ['vaizɔ], *s.* das Visier.
vista ['vistɔ], *s.* (*Art*) die Aussicht, der Ausblick.
visual ['viʒuɔl], *adj.* visuell, Seh-.
vital [vaitl], *adj.* lebenswichtig; (*fig.*) wesentlich.
vitality [vai'tæliti], *s.* die Lebenskraft, Vitalität.

512

vitiate ['viʃieit], *v.a.* verderben, umstoßen.
vitreous ['vitriəs], *adj.* gläsern, glasartig.
vitrify ['vitrifai], *v.a.* verglasen.
vivacious [vi'veiʃəs], *adj.* lebhaft, munter.
viva (voce) ['vaivə ('vousi)], *s.* die mündliche Prüfung.
vivacity [vi'væsiti], *s.* die Lebhaftigkeit.
vivid ['vivid], *adj.* lebhaft.
vixen ['viksən], *s.* (*Zool.*) die Füchsin; (*fig.*) das zänkische Weib.
vizier [vi'ziə], *s.* der Wesir.
vocabulary [vo'kæbjuləri], *s.* das Vokabular; der Wortschatz.
vocal ['voukəl], *adj.* laut; (*Mus.*) Stimm-, Sing-.
vocation [vo'keiʃən], *s.* die Berufung (*call*); der Beruf (*occupation*).
vociferous [vo'sifərəs], *adj.* schreiend, laut.
vogue [voug], *s.* die Mode.
voice [vɔis], *s.* die Stimme.
void [vɔid], *adj.* leer (*empty*); ungültig, (*invalid*); *null and* —, null und nichtig. — *s.* die Leere.
volatile ['vɔlətail], *adj.* flüchtig.
volcanic [vɔl'kænik], *adj.* vulkanisch.
volcano [vɔl'keinou], *s.* der Vulkan.
volition [vo'liʃən], *s.* der Wille.
volley ['vɔli], *s.* (*Mil.*) die Salve; (*Footb.*) der Volleyschuß; (*Tennis*) der Flugball.
volt [voult], *s.* (*Elec.*) das Volt.
voltage ['voultidʒ], *s.* die Spannung.
voluble ['vɔljubl], *adj.* gesprächig, zungenfertig.
volume ['vɔlju:m], *s.* (*Phys.*) das Volumen; der Band (*book*); (*fig.*) der Umfang.
voluminous [və'lju:minəs], *adj.* umfangreich.
voluntary ['vɔləntri], *adj.* freiwillig. — *s.* (*Mus.*) das Orgelsolo.
volunteer [vɔlən'tiə], *s.* der Freiwillige. — *v.n.* sich freiwillig melden.
voluptuous [və'lʌptjuəs], *adj.* wollüstig, lüstern.
vomit ['vɔmit], *v.a.*, *v.n.* (sich) erbrechen, übergeben.
voracious [vɔ'reiʃəs], *adj.* gierig, gefräßig.
vortex ['vɔ:teks], *s.* der Wirbel, Strudel.
vote [vout], *v.n.* (*Pol.*) wählen, abstimmen, die Stimme abgeben. — *s.* (*Pol.*) die Stimme.
voter ['voutə], *s.* der Wähler.
votive ['voutiv], *adj.* (*Eccl.*) geweiht, gelobt; Votiv-.
vouch [vautʃ], *v.a.*, *v.n.* (sich) verbürgen, einstehen(für).
voucher ['vautʃə], *s.* der Beleg; (*Comm.*) der Gutschein.
vouchsafe [vautʃ'seif], *v.a.* bewilligen, gewähren. — *v.n.* geruhen, sich herablassen.
vow [vau], *s.* das Gelübde. — *v.a.* schwören, geloben.

vowel ['vauəl], *s.* der Vokal.
voyage ['vɔiidʒ], *s.* die Seereise. — *v.n.* zur See reisen.
vulcanize ['vʌlkənaiz], *v.a.* vulkanisieren.
vulgar ['vʌlgə], *adj.* gemein, pöbelhaft, ordinär, vulgär.
vulnerable ['vʌlnərəbl], *adj.* verwundbar, verletzbar.
vulture ['vʌltʃə], *s.* (*Orn.*) der Geier.

W

W ['dʌblju:]. das W.
wabble *see* **wobble.**
wad [wɔd], *s.* das Bündel (*notes*); der Bausch (*cotton wool*).
waddle [wɔdl], *v.n.* watscheln.
wade [weid], *v.n.* waten, durchwaten.
wafer ['weifə], *s.* die Oblate, die Waffel; (*Eccl.*) die Hostie.
waffle [wɔfl], *s.* (*Cul.*) die Waffel. — *v.n.* (*coll.*) schwafeln.
waft [wæft], *v.a.* wegwehen.
wag (1) [wæg], *v.a.* wedeln, schütteln.
wag (2) [wæg], *s.* der Spaßvogel.
wage (1) [weidʒ], *v.a.* unternehmen; — *war*, Krieg führen.
wage (2) ['weidʒ], *s.* (*often in pl.*) der Lohn.
wager ['weidʒə], *v.a.* wetten. — *s.* die Wette.
waggish ['wægiʃ], *adj.* spaßhaft, mutwillig, schelmisch.
wag(g)on ['wægən], *s.* der Wagen, Güterwagen.
wagtail ['wægteil], *s.* (*Orn.*) die Bachstelze.
waif [weif], *s.* das verwahrloste Kind; das herrenlose Gut.
wail [weil], *v.n.* wehklagen. — *s.* das Wehklagen, die Klage.
waist [weist], *s.* (*Anat.*) die Taille.
waistcoat ['weiskout, 'weskət], *s.* die Weste, das Wams.
wait [weit], *v.n.* warten; — *for*, warten auf; — *upon*, bedienen. — *v.a.* erwarten.
waiter ['weitə], *s.* der Kellner; *head* —, der Oberkellner, (*coll.*) der Ober.
waiting room ['weitiŋ rum], *s.* das Wartezimmer; (*Railw.*) der Wartesaal.
waive [weiv], *v.a.* aufgeben, verzichten (auf, *Acc.*).
wake (1) [weik], *v.n.* *irr.* wachen, aufwachen, wach sein. — *v.a.* aufwecken.
wake (2) [weik], *s.* (*Naut.*) das Kielwasser; (*fig.*) die Spur; *in the* — *of*, in den Fußstapfen (*Genit.*).
waken ['weikən], *v.a.* aufwecken. — *v.n.* aufwachen.
walk [wɔ:k], *v.n.* (zu Fuß) gehen. — *s.* der Gang (*gait*); der Spaziergang.

wall

wall [wɔ:l], s. die Wand, Mauer.
wallet ['wɔlit], s. die Brieftasche.
wallflower ['wɔ:lflauə], s. (Bot.) der Goldlack; (fig.) das Mauerblümchen.
wallow ['wɔlou], v.n. schwelgen; sich wälzen.
walnut ['wɔ:lnʌt], s. (Bot.) die Walnuß.
walrus ['wɔ:lrəs], s. (Zool.) das Walroß.
waltz [wɔ:lts], s. der Walzer.
wan [wɔn], adj. blaß, bleich.
wand [wɔnd], s. der Stab.
wander ['wɔndə], v.n. wandern, durchwandern; (fig.) — from the subject, vom Thema abkommen.
wane [wein], v.n. abnehmen, verfallen.
want [wɔnt], v.a. brauchen, wollen, nötig haben, wünschen. — v.n. mangeln, fehlen. — s. die Not.
wanton ['wɔntən], adj. mutwillig, ausgelassen.
war [wɔ:], s. der Krieg.
warble [wɔ:bl], v.a., v.n. singen; (Mus.) trillern.
warbler ['wɔ:blə], s. (Orn.) der Singvogel.
ward [wɔ:d], s. die Verwahrung; das or der Mündel (child in care); (Pol.) der Wahlbezirk; die Station (hospital). — v.a. — off, abwehren.
warden [wɔ:dn], s. der Vorstand, Vorsteher; Rektor.
warder ['wɔ:də], s. der Wächter; (in prison) der Wärter, Gefängniswärter.
wardrobe ['wɔ:droub], s. der Kleiderschrank.
ware [wɛə], s. die Ware.
warehouse ['wɛəhaus], s. das Warenlager.
warfare ['wɔ:fɛə], s. der Krieg, die Kriegsführung.
warlike ['wɔ:laik], adj. kriegerisch.
warm [wɔ:m], adj. warm.
warn [wɔ:n], v.a. warnen, ermahnen.
warning ['wɔ:niŋ], s. die Warnung.
warp [wɔ:p], v.a. krümmen, verziehen (of wood); (fig.) verderben; verzerren, verdrehen. — v.n. sich werfen, krümmen.
warrant ['wɔrənt], s. (Law) der Haftbefehl; — officer, der Unteroffizier; (Comm.) die Vollmacht, Bürgschaft. — v.a. garantieren (vouch for); versichern (assure).
warranty ['wɔrənti], s. (Law) die Gewähr; Garantie.
warren ['wɔrən], s. das Gehege.
warrior ['wɔriə], s. der Krieger.
wart [wɔ:t], s. (Med.) die Warze.
wary ['wɛəri], adj. vorsichtig, achtsam (careful).
wash [wɔʃ], v.a., v.n. (sich) waschen; — up, spülen, abwaschen. — s. die Wäsche (laundry).
wasp [wɔsp], s. (Ent.) die Wespe.
waspish ['wɔspiʃ], adj. reizbar, zänkisch, bissig.
wassail [wɔsl], s. das Trinkgelage. — v.n. zechen.
waste [weist], v.a. zerstören, verwüsten;

verschwenden. — adj. wüst, öde. — s. die Verschwendung (process); der Abfall (product); — paper, die Makulatur; — paper basket, der Papierkorb.
wasteful ['weistful], adj. verschwenderisch.
watch [wɔtʃ], v.a. bewachen; beobachten (observe); hüten (guard). — s. die Wache (guard); die Uhr, Taschenuhr (time-piece).
watchful ['wɔtʃful], adj. wachsam.
watchman ['wɔtʃmən], s. der Nachtwächter.
water ['wɔ:tə], s. das Wasser; (pl.) Kur; — colour, das Aquarell; — gauge, der Pegel. — v.a. wässern; begießen (flowers).
watercress ['wɔ:təkres], s. (Bot.) die Brunnenkresse.
waterproof ['wɔ:təpru:f], adj. wasserdicht.
watt [wɔt], s. (Elec.) das Watt.
wattle [wɔtl], s. (Bot.) die Hürde.
wave [weiv], s. die Welle; permanent —, die Dauerwelle. — v.n. zuwinken (Dat.); wehen; winken. — v.a. schwenken (handkerchief).
waver ['weivə], v.n. schwanken, unentschlossen sein.
wax [wæks], s. das Wachs, der Siegellack. — v.a. wachsen, bohnern.
waxen [wæksn], adj. aus Wachs, wächsern.
way [wei], s. der Weg (road etc.); die Strecke; Richtung; in no —, keineswegs; (pl.) die Art und Weise; Milky Way, die Milchstraße.
wayward ['weiwəd], adj. eigensinnig.
we [wi:], pers. pron. wir.
weak [wi:k], adj. schwach, kraftlos.
weaken ['wi:kən], v.a. schwächen. — v.n. schwach werden.
weakling ['wi:kliŋ], s. der Schwächling.
wealth [welθ], s. der Wohlstand, Reichtum.
wealthy ['welθi], adj. wohlhabend, reich.
wean [wi:n], v.a. entwöhnen.
weapon ['wepən], s. die Waffe.
wear [wɛə], v.a. irr. tragen (clothes). — v.n. — off, sich abtragen, schäbig werden; — out, sich erschöpfen. — s. die Abnutzung.
weariness ['wiərinis], s. die Müdigkeit, der Überdruß.
weary ['wiəri], adj. müde, überdrüssig.
weasel [wi:zl], s. (Zool.) das Wiesel.
weather ['wɛðə], s. das Wetter. — v.a. überstehen. — v.n. (Geol.) verwittern.
weatherbeaten ['wɛðəbi:tn], adj. abgehärtet, wetterhart.
weathercock ['wɛðəkɔk], s. der Wetterhahn; (fig.) wetterwendischer Mensch.
weave [wi:v], v.a. irr. (Text.) weben. — s. das Gewebe.
web [web], s. das Gewebe.
wed [wed], v.a. heiraten; trauen (a couple). — v.n. (sich ver)heiraten.
wedding ['wediŋ], s. die Hochzeit; Trauung (ceremony).

wedge [wedʒ], *s.* der Keil. — *v.a.* keilen.

wedlock ['wedlɔk], *s.* die Ehe.

Wednesday ['wenzd(e)i]. der Mittwoch.

wee [wi:], *adj.* (*Scot.*) winzig, klein.

weed [wi:d], *s.* das Unkraut. — *v.a.* ausjäten, jäten.

week [wi:k], *s.* die Woche.

weep [wi:p], *v.n. irr.* weinen; —*ing willow*, die Trauerweide.

weigh [wei], *v.a.* wiegen, wägen; (*fig.*) abwägen, beurteilen; (*Naut.*) — *anchor*, den Anker lichten. — *v.n.* wiegen.

weighing machine ['weiiŋ məˈʃi:n], *s.* die Waage.

weight [weit], *s.* das Gewicht; *gross* —, das Bruttogewicht; *net* —, das Nettogewicht.

weighty ['weiti], *adj.* (ge)wichtig; (*fig.*) schwer.

weir [wiə], *s.* das Wehr.

weird [wiəd], *adj.* unheimlich.

welcome ['welkəm], *adj.* willkommen. — *s.* der *or* das Willkommen. — *v.a.* willkommen heißen, begrüßen.

weld [weld], *v.a.* schweißen.

welfare ['welfeə], *s.* die Wohlfahrt, soziale Fürsorge.

well (1) [wel], *s.* der Brunnen. — *v.n.* hervorsprudeln.

well (2) [wel], *adv.* gut, wohl; durchaus; — *bred*, wohlerzogen. — *pred. adj.* gesund, wohl.

Welsh [welʃ], *adj.* walisisch. — *s. pl.* die Waliser, *m.pl.*

Welshman ['welʃmən], *s.* der Waliser.

welt [welt], *s.* der Rand, die Einfassung.

welter ['weltə], *s.* die Masse, das Chaos. — *v.n.* sich wälzen.

wen [wen], *s.* (*Med.*) die Schwellung.

wench [wentʃ], *s.* die Magd, das Mädchen.

west [west], *s.* der Westen. — *adj.* (*also* **westerly, western** ['westəli, 'westən]) westlich.

Westphalian [westˈfeiliən], *adj.* westfälisch. — *s.* der Westfale.

wet [wet], *adj.* naß, feucht; — *paint*, frisch gestrichen. — *v.a.* anfeuchten, benetzen, naß machen.

whack [hwæk], *v.a.* durchprügeln. — *s.* die Tracht Prügel, der Schlag.

whale [hweil], *s.* (*Zool.*) der Walfisch.

whalebone ['hweilboun], *s.* das Fischbein.

wharf [hwɔ:f], *s.* der Kai.

wharfinger ['hwɔ:findʒə], *s.* der Kaimeister.

what [hwɔt], *rel. & interr. pron.* was; welcher, welche, welches; was für.

what(so)ever [hwɔt(sou)ˈevə], *rel. pron.* was auch immer. — *adj.* einerlei welche-r, -s, -n.

wheat [hwi:t], *s.* (*Bot.*) der Weizen.

wheedle ['hwi:dl], *v.a.* beschwatzen.

wheel [hwi:l], *s.* das Rad; die Umdrehung, Drehung. — *v.a., v.n.* drehen, sich drehen, schieben.

wheelbarrow ['hwi:lbærou], *s.* der Schubkarren.

wheeze [hwi:z], *v.n.* keuchen, schnaufen. — *s.* das Keuchen.

whelp [hwelp], *s.* (*Zool.*) das Junge, der junge Hund. — *v.n.* Junge werfen.

when [hwen], *adv.* (*interr.*) wann? — *conj.* als (*in past*), wenn, während.

whence [hwens], *adv.* woher, von wo.

where [hweə], *adv.* wo, wohin; (*interr.*) wo? wohin?

whereabout(s) ['hwɛərəbaut(s)], *adv.* wo, wo etwa. — *s.* (**whereabouts**) der zeitweilige Aufenthalt *or* Wohnort.

whereas [hwɛərˈæz], *conj.* wohingegen, während.

whereupon [hwɛərəˈpɔn], *conj.* woraufhin.

wherewithal ['hwɛəwiðɔ:l], *s.* die gesamte Habe, das Nötige. — *adv.* (*obs.*) womit.

whet [hwet], *v.a.* wetzen, schleifen.

whether ['hweðə], *conj.* ob.

whey [hwei], *s.* die Molke.

which [hwitʃ], *rel. & interr. pron.* welcher, welche, welches; der, die, das.

whiff [hwif], *s.* der Hauch, Luftzug.

while [hwail], *s.* die Weile, Zeit. — *v.a.* — *away the time*, dahinbringen, vertreiben. — *conj.* (*also* **whilst**) während, so lange als.

whim [hwim], *s.* die Laune, Grille.

whimper ['hwimpə], *v.n.* winseln.

whimsical ['hwimzikəl], *adj.* grillenhaft.

whine [hwain], *v.n.* weinen, wimmern, klagen. — *s.* das Gewimmer, Gejammer.

whinny ['hwini], *v.n.* wiehern.

whip [hwip], *s.* die Peitsche; (*Pol.*) der Einpeitscher. — *v.a.* peitschen.

whir [hwə:], *v.n.* schwirren. — *s.* das Schwirren.

whirl [hwə:l], *s.* der Wirbel, Strudel. — *v.a., v.n.* wirbeln.

whirligig ['hwə:ligig], *s.* der Karussel.

whirlpool ['hwə:lpu:l], *s.* der Strudel.

whirr *see* whir.

whisk [hwisk], *v.a.* fegen; schlagen; — *away* or *off*, schnell wegtun (*a th.*), schnell fortnehmen (*a p.*). — *v.n.* — *away*, dahinhuschen. — *s.* der Schläger.

whiskers ['hwiskəz], *s.* der Backenbart, Bart.

whisky ['hwiski], *s.* der Whisky.

whisper ['hwispə], *s.* das Geflüster. *v.a., v.n.* flüstern.

whistle [hwisl], *s.* die Pfeife (*instrument*); der Pfiff (*sound*). — *v.a., v.n.* pfeifen.

whit [hwit], *s.* die Kleinigkeit; *not a* —, nicht im geringsten.

white [hwait], *adj.* weiß; — *lead*, das Bleiweiß; — *lie*, die Notlüge.

whitebait ['hwaitbeit], *s.* (*Zool.*) der Breitling.

whiten ['hwaitn], *v.a.* weißen, bleichen.

whitewash ['hwaitwɔʃ], *s.* die Tünche. — *v.a.* reinwaschen.

whither [ˈhwiðə], adv. wohin; dahin wo.

whiting [ˈhwaitiŋ], s. (Zool.) der Weißfisch; die Schlämmkreide (chalk).

whitlow [ˈhwitlou], s. (Med.) das Nagelgeschwür.

Whitsun(tide) [ˈhwitsən(taid)], s. (das) Pfingsten; Whit Sunday, der Pfingstsonntag.

whittle [hwitl], v.a. schnitzen, abschaben.

whiz [hwiz], v.n. zischen; (fig.) vorbeiflitzen.

who [hu:], interr. pron. wer?, welcher?, welche? — rel. pron. welcher, welche, welches, der, die, das.

whoever [hu:ˈevə], rel. pron. wer auch immer.

whole [houl], adj. ganz, völlig. — s. das Ganze.

wholesale [ˈhoulseil], adv. im Engros. — adj. Engros-, Großhandels-.

wholesome [ˈhoulsəm], adj. gesund.

whoop [hu:p], s. das Geschrei; — v.n. laut keuchen; —ing cough, der Keuchhusten.

whortleberry [ˈhwə:tlbəri], s. (Bot.) die Heidelbeere.

whose [hu:z], pron. wessen, dessen, deren.

whosoever [hu:souˈevə] see whoever.

why [hwai], rel. & interr. adv. warum?

wick [wik], s. der Docht.

wicked [ˈwikid], adj. böse, schlecht.

wicker [ˈwikə], adj. Rohr-, geflochten.

wicket [ˈwikit], s. das Pförtchen.

wide [waid], adj. weit, breit; (fig.) umfangreich, groß, reich(experience).— adv. far and —, weit und breit; — awake, völlig wach.

widen [waidn], v.a., erweitern.

widgeon [ˈwidʒən], s. die Pfeifente.

widow [ˈwidou], s. die Witwe.

widower [ˈwidouə], s. der Witwer.

width [widθ], s. die Weite, Breite.

wield [wi:ld], v.a. schwingen; —power, die Macht ausüben.

wife [waif], s. die Frau, Gattin.

wig [wig], s. die Perücke.

wild [waild], adj. wild.

wilderness [ˈwildənis], s. die Wildnis.

wildfire [ˈwaildfaiə], s. das Lauffeuer.

wilful [ˈwilful], adj. absichtlich; vorsätzlich.

wiliness [ˈwailinis], s. die Schlauheit, Arglist.

will [wil], s. der Wille; (Law) der letzte Wille, das Testament. — v.n. wollen. — v.a. (Law) vermachen, hinterlassen.

willing [ˈwiliŋ], adj. bereitwillig.

will-o'-the-wisp [wiləðəˈwisp], s. das Irrlicht.

willow [ˈwilou], s. (Bot.) die Weide.

wily [ˈwaili], adj. schlau, verschmitzt.

wimple [wimpl], s. der Schleier.

win [win], v.a., v.n. irr. gewinnen, siegen, erringen.

wince [wins], v.n. zucken, zusammenzucken.

winch [wintʃ], s. die Kurbel, Winde.

wind (1) [wind], s. der Wind; der Atem (breath); get — of s.th., von etwas hören.

wind (2) [waind], v.a. irr. winden; wenden, drehen (turn); —(up), aufziehen (timepiece); — up, (business, debate) beenden. — v.n. sich schlängeln, winden.

windfall [ˈwindfɔ:l], s. das Fallobst (fruit); (fig.) der Glücksfall.

windlass [ˈwindləs], s. die Winde.

window [ˈwindou], s. das Fenster; — sill, das Fensterbrett.

windpipe [ˈwindpaip], s. (Anat.) die Luftröhre.

windscreen [ˈwindskri:n], s. (Motor.) die Windschutzscheibe.

windshield [ˈwindʃi:ld] (Am.) see windscreen.

windy [ˈwindi], adj. windig.

wine [wain], s. der Wein; — merchant, der Weinhändler.

wing [wiŋ], s. der Flügel; (Poet.) die Schwinge.

wink [wiŋk], s. das Zwinkern; der Augenblick.— v.n. blinzeln, zwinkern.

winner [ˈwinə], s. der Sieger, Gewinner.

winning [ˈwiniŋ], adj. einnehmend.

winsome [ˈwinsəm], adj. reizend, einnehmend.

winter [ˈwintə], s. der Winter.

wintry [ˈwintri], adj. winterlich.

wipe [waip], v.a. wischen, abwischen.

wire [waiə], s. der Draht; (coll.) das Telegramm; barbed —, der Stacheldraht. — v.a. verbinden; (fig.) telegraphieren. — v.n. telegraphieren.

wireless [ˈwaiəlis], s. das Radio. — adj. drahtlos.

wirepuller [ˈwaiəpulə], s. der Puppenspieler; (fig.) der Intrigant.

wiry [ˈwaiəri], adj. zäh, stark.

wisdom [ˈwizdəm], s. die Weisheit.

wise [waiz], adj. weise, verständig, klug.

wiseacre [ˈwaizeikə], s. der Allzuschlaue, Naseweis.

wish [wiʃ], v.a., v.n. wünschen. — s. der Wunsch.

wistful [ˈwistful], adj. nachdenklich (pensive); wehmütig (sad).

wit [wit], s. der Witz; Geist; Verstand; der witzige Mensch; der Witzbold.

witch [witʃ], s. die Hexe, Zauberin.

witchcraft [ˈwitʃkrɑːft], s. die Zauberkunst, Hexerei.

with [wið], prep. mit, mitsamt, bei, durch, von.

withal [wiˈðɔ:l], adv. obendrein.

withdraw [wiðˈdrɔ:], v.a., v.n. irr. (sich) zurückziehen; widerrufen; abheben (money from bank).

withdrawal [wiðˈdrɔ:əl], s. der Rückzug; (Comm. etc.) die Widerrufung; Abhebung (bank).

wither [ˈwiðə], v.a. welk machen. — v.n. verwelken; ausdorren, verdorren (dry up); (fig.) vergehen.

withhold [wiðˈhould], v.a. irr. zurückhalten, vorenthalten.

within [wi'ðin], *prep.* innerhalb; (*time*) binnen (*Genit.*). — *adv.* darin, drinnen.

without [wi'ðaut], *prep.* ohne; (*obs.*) außerhalb (*outside*); *do* —, entbehren. — *adv.* draußen, außen.

withstand [wið'stænd], *v.a. irr.* widerstehen (*Dat.*).

withy ['wiði], *s.* der Weidenzweig.

witless ['witlis], *adj.* einfältig.

witness ['witnis], *s.* der Zeuge. — *v.a.* bezeugen, Zeuge sein von. — *v.n.* zeugen, Zeuge sein.

witticism ['witisizm], *s.* das Bonmot, die witzige Bemerkung.

witty ['witi], *adj.* witzig, geistreich.

wizard ['wizəd], *s.* der Zauberer.

wizened ['wizənd], *adj.* verwelkt, vertrocknet, runzlig.

wobble [wɔbl], *v.n.* wackeln.

woe [wou], *s.* (*Poet.*) das Weh, Leid.

wolf [wulf], *s.* (*Zool.*) der Wolf.

woman ['wumən], *s.* die Frau, das Weib.

womanly ['wumənli], *adj.* weiblich.

womb [wu:m], *s.* der Mutterleib, Schoß; (*Anat.*) die Gebärmutter.

wonder ['wʌndə], *s.* das Wunder. — *v.n.* sich wundern (*be amazed*); gern wissen mögen (*like to know*); sich fragen.

wonderful ['wʌndəful], *adj.* wunderbar.

wondrous ['wʌndrəs], *adj.* (*Poet.*) wunderbar.

wont [wount], *s.* die Gewohnheit. — *pred. adj.* gewohnt.

won't [wount] = **will not**.

woo [wu:], *v.a.* freien, werben (um).

wood [wud], *s.* das Holz (*timber*); der Wald (*forest*).

woodbine ['wudbain], *s.* das Geißblatt.

woodcock ['wudkɔk], *s.* (*Orn.*) die Waldschnepfe.

woodcut ['wudkʌt], *s.* (*Art*) der Holzschnitt.

wooded ['wudid], *adj.* bewaldet.

wooden [wudn], *adj.* hölzern, Holz–.

woodlark ['wudlɑ:k], *s.* (*Orn.*) die Heidelerche.

woodpecker ['wudpekə], *s.* (*Orn.*) der Specht.

woodruff ['wudrʌf], *s.* (*Bot.*) der Waldmeister.

woof [wu:f], *s.* (*Text.*) der Einschlag, das Gewebe.

wool [wul], *s.* die Wolle; — *gathering*, zerstreut.

woollen ['wulən], *adj.* wollen, aus Wolle.

woolly ['wuli], *adj.* wollig; (*fig.*) unklar, verschwommen.

word [wə:d], *s.* das Wort; *send* —, Botschaft senden. — *v.a.* ausdrücken.

wording ['wə:diŋ], *s.* die Fassung, der Stil.

work [wə:k], *s.* die Arbeit; *out of* —, arbeitslos; das Werk (*opus*); (*pl.*) (der Fabrik. — *v.a., v.n.* arbeiten, bearbeiten; (*engine*) funktionieren.

worker ['wə:kə], *s.* der Arbeiter.

workhouse ['wə:khaus], *s.* das Armenhaus.

workshop ['wə:kʃɔp], *s.* die Werkstatt.

world [wə:ld], *s.* die Welt.

worldly ['wə:ldli], *adj.* weltlich, zeitlich.

worm [wə:m], *s.* (*Zool.*) der Wurm. — *v.a.* — *o.'s way*, sich einschleichen. — *v.n.* sich einschleichen.

wormeaten ['wə:mi:tn], *adj.* wurmstichig.

worry ['wʌri], *v.a., v.n.* plagen, quälen, sorgen, ängstigen; sich beunruhigen; *don't* —, bitte machen Sie sich keine Mühe. — *s.* die Plage, Mühe, Qual, Sorge (*about*, um, *Acc.*).

worse [wə:s], *comp. adj., adv.* schlechter, schlimmer.

worship ['wə:ʃip], *s.* die Verehrung; der Gottesdienst (*divine* —).

worst [wə:st], *superl. adj.* schlechtest, schlimmst. — *adv.* am schlimmsten *or* schlechtesten. — *s.* das Schlimmste.

worsted ['wustid], *s.* (*Text.*) das Kammgarn.

worth [wə:θ], *adj.* wert. — *s.* der Wert.

worthy ['wə:ði], *adj.* würdig, wert, verdient.

would [wud] *past tense of* **will**, *q.v.*

wound [wu:nd], *s.* die Wunde. — *v.a.* verwunden.

wraith [reiθ], *s.* das Gespenst.

wrangle [ræŋgl], *v.n.* zanken, streiten. — *s.* der Zank, Streit.

wrap [ræp], *v.a.* einwickeln, einhüllen. — *s.* (*Am.*) der Mantel (*coat*), Pelz (*fur*), Schal (*stole*).

wrapper ['ræpə], *s.* der Umschlag, die Hülle.

wrath [rɔ:θ], *s.* der Zorn, Grimm.

wreak [ri:k], *v.a.* (*Lit.*) auslassen, üben.

wreath [ri:θ], *s.* der Kranz.

wreathe [ri:ð], *v.a.* winden, bekränzen.

wreck [rek], *s.* der Schiffbruch; das Wrack (*debris*). — *v.a.* zerstören, zertrümmern, (*fig.*) verderben.

wren [ren], *s.* (*Orn.*) der Zaunkönig.

wrench [rentʃ], *v.a.* entreißen (*tear from*); verdrehen. — *s.* heftiger Ruck; (*fig.*) der (Trennungs)schmerz.

wrest [rest], *v.a.* zerren.

wrestle [resl], *v.n.* ringen, im Ringkampf kämpfen.

wrestling ['resliŋ], *s.* der Ringkampf.

wretch [retʃ], *s.* der Schuft, Lump (*scoundrel*).

wretched ['retʃid], *adj.* elend.

wriggle [rigl], *v.n.* sich winden, schlängeln.

wring [riŋ], *v.a. irr.* auswinden, ausringen.

wrinkle [riŋkl], *s.* die Hautfalte, Runzel. — *v.a.* runzeln (*brow*); rümpfen (*nose*).

wrist [rist], *s.* (*Anat.*) das Handgelenk.

wristwatch ['ristwɔtʃ], *s.* die Armbanduhr.

writ [rit], *s.* die Schrift; (*Law*) die Vorladung.

write [rait], *v.a.*, *v.n. irr.* schreiben, verfassen.

writer ['raitə], *s.* der Schreiber; (*Lit.*) der Schriftsteller.

writhe [raið], *v.n.* sich winden.

writing ['raitiŋ], *s.* die Schrift; der Stil (*style*).

wrong [rɔŋ], *adj.* falsch, verkehrt; *to be —*, unrecht haben. — *s.* das Unrecht. — *v.a.* Unrecht *or* Schaden tun (*Dat.*).

wrongful ['rɔŋful], *adj.* unrechtmäßig.

wrongheaded [rɔŋ'hedid], *adj.* querköpfig.

wroth [rouθ], *adj.* (*Lit.*) zornig.

wrought [rɔːt], *adj.* (*work*) gearbeitet; *— iron*, das Schmiedeeisen.

wry [rai], *adj.* verkehrt, krumm, schief, verdreht.

X

X [eks]. das X.

X-ray ['eksrei], *s.* (der) Röntgenstrahl.

xylophone ['zailəfoun], *s.* (*Mus.*) das Xylophon.

Y

Y [wai]. das Y, Ypsilon.

yacht [jɔt], *s.* (*Naut.*) die Jacht.

yachtsman ['jɔtsmən], *s.* (*Naut.*) der Segelsportler.

yap [jæp], *v.n.* kläffen.

yard (1) [jɑːd], *s.* der Hof.

yard (2) [jɑːd], *s.* die englische Elle, der Yard.

yarn [jɑːn], *s.* das Garn; (*coll.*) die Geschichte (*tale*).

yarrow ['jærou], *s.* (*Bot.*) die Schafgarbe.

yawl [jɔːl], *s.* (*Naut.*) die Yawl.

yawn [jɔːn], *v.n.* gähnen. — *s.* das Gähnen.

ye [jiː], *pron.* (*obs.*) *see* you.

year [jə *or* jiə], *s.* das Jahr; *every other —*, alle zwei Jahre.

yearly ['jiəli], *adj.*, *adv.* jährlich.

yearn [jəːn], *v.n.* sich sehnen (nach, *Dat.*).

yeast [jiːst], *s.* die Hefe.

yell [jel], *v.n.* gellen, schreien. — *s.* der Schrei.

yellow ['jelou], *adj.* gelb; (*sl.*) feige.

yelp [jelp], *v.n.* kläffen, bellen. — *s.* das Gebelle.

yeoman ['joumən], *s.* der Freisasse; (*Mil.*) der Leibgardist (*Yeoman of the Guard*).

yes [jes], *adv.* ja; jawohl.

yesterday ['jestəd(e)i], *adv.* gestern; *the day before —*, vorgestern.

yet [jet], *conj.* doch, dennoch. — *adv.* noch, außerdem; *as —*, bisher; *not —*, noch nicht.

yew [juː], *s.* (*Bot.*) die Eibe.

yield [jiːld], *v.a.* hervorbringen, ergeben; abwerfen (*profit*). — *v.n.* nachgeben (*to, Dat.*). — *s.* der Ertrag.

yoke [jouk], *s.* das Joch (Ochsen). — *v.a.* einspannen, anspannen.

yolk [jouk], *s.* das Eidotter.

yon, yonder [jɔn, 'jɔndə], *dem. adj.* (*obs.*) jener, jene, jenes; der *or* die *or* das da drüben.

yore [jɔː], *adv.* (*obs.*) *of —*, von damals; ehedem.

you [juː], *pers. pron.* du, dich, ihr, euch; (*formal*) sie (*in letters*, Du, Dich etc.).

young [jʌŋ], *adj.* jung. — *s.* (*Zool.*) das Junge.

your [juə], *poss. adj.* dein, deine, dein; euer, eure, euer; (*formal*) ihr, ihre, ihr (*in letters* Dein, Euer etc.).

yours [jɔːz], *poss. pron.* deinig, eurig; der, die *or* das ihrige (*in letters* Deinig, der Ihrige etc.).

yourself [juə'self], *pers. pron.* du selbst, Sie selbst; ihr selbst; dich (selbst), euch (selbst) (*in letters* Du selbst; Dich (selbst) etc.).

youth [juːθ], *s.* die Jugend.

youthful ['juːθful], *adj.* jugendlich.

Yugoslav [juːgo'slɑːv], *adj.* jugoslawisch. — *s.* der Jugoslawe.

Yule, Yuletide [juːl, 'juːltaid], *s.* das Julfest, die Weihnachtszeit.

Z

Z [zed, (*Am.*) ziː]. das Z.

zany ['zeini], *s.* der Hanswurst.

zeal [ziːl], *s.* der Eifer.

zealous ['zeləs], *adj.* eifrig.

zebra ['ziːbrə], *s.* (*Zool.*) das Zebra.

zenith ['zeniθ], *s.* der Zenit, Scheitelpunkt.

zero ['ziərou], *s.* der Nullpunkt, die (Ziffer) Null; *— hour*, die festgesetzte Stunde; festgesetzter Zeitpunkt.

zest [zest], *s.* die Lust; den Genuß; die Würze.

zigzag ['zigzæg], *s.* der Zickzack. — *adj.* Zickzack-.

zinc [ziŋk], *s.* das Zink.

zip(per) ['zip(ə)], *s.* der Reißverschluß (*zip fastener*).

zone [zoun], *s.* die Zone.

zoological gardens [zouə'lɔdʒikəl gɑːdnz], *s.* (*abbr.* **zoo** [zuː]) zoologischer Garten, der Zoo, Tiergarten.

German Irregular Verbs

Note: *Where a compound irregular verb is not given, its forms are identical with those of the simple irregular verb as listed.*

Infin.	Pres. Indic. 3rd Pers. Sing.	Imperf. Indic.	Imperf. Subj.
backen	bäckt	backte (buk)	backte
befehlen	befiehlt	befahl	beföhle
beginnen	beginnt	begann	begönne
beißen	beißt	biß	bisse
bergen	birgt	barg	bürge
bersten	birst	barst	börste
bewegen	bewegt	bewog	bewöge
biegen	biegt	bog	böge
bieten	bietet	bot	böte
binden	bindet	band	bände
bitten	bittet	bat	bäte
blasen	bläst	blies	bliese
bleiben	bleibt	blieb	bliebe
braten	brät	briet	briete
brechen	bricht	brach	bräche
brennen	brennt	brannte	brennte
bringen	bringt	brachte	brächte
denken	denkt	dachte	dächte
dreschen	drischt	drosch	dräsche
dringen	dringt	drang	dränge
dürfen	darf	durfte	dürfte
empfangen	empfängt	empfing	empfinge
empfehlen	empfiehlt	empfahl	empföhle
empfinden	empfindet	empfand	empfände
erlöschen	erlischt	erlosch	erlösche

German Irregular Verbs

Imper.	Past Participle	English
backe	gebacken	bake
befiehl	befohlen	order, command
beginn(e)	begonnen	begin
beiß(e)	gebissen	bite
birg	geborgen	save, conceal
birst	geborsten	burst
beweg(e)	bewogen	induce
bieg(e)	gebogen	bend
biet(e)	geboten	offer
bind(e)	gebunden	tie, bind
bitte	gebeten	request
blas(e)	geblasen	blow
bleib(e)	geblieben	remain
brat(e)	gebraten	roast
brich	gebrochen	break
brenne	gebrannt	burn
bring(e)	gebracht	bring
denk(e)	gedacht	think
drisch	gedroschen	thrash
dring(e)	gedrungen	press forward
	gedurft	be permitted
empfang(e)	empfangen	receive
empfiehl	empfohlen	(re)commend
empfind(e)	empfunden	feel, perceive
erlisch	erloschen	extinguish

German Irregular Verbs

Infin.	Pres. Indic. 3rd Pers. Sing.	Imperf. Indic.	Imperf. Subj.
erschrecken (*v.n.*)	erschrickt	erschrak	erschräke
essen	ißt	aß	äße
fahren	fährt	fuhr	führe
fallen	fällt	fiel	fiele
fangen	fängt	fing	finge
fechten	ficht	focht	föchte
finden	findet	fand	fände
flechten	flicht	flocht	flöchte
fliegen	fliegt	flog	flöge
fliehen	flieht	floh	flöhe
fließen	fließt	floß	flösse
fressen	frißt	fraß	fräße
frieren	friert	fror	fröre
gebären	gebiert	gebar	gebäre
geben	gibt	gab	gäbe
gedeihen	gedeiht	gedieh	gediehe
gehen	geht	ging	ginge
gelingen (*impers.*)	(mir) gelingt	gelang	gelänge
gelten	gilt	galt	gälte
genesen	genest	genas	genäse
genießen	genießt	genoß	genösse
geschehen (*impers.*)	(mir) geschieht	geschah	geschähe
gewinnen	gewinnt	gewann	gewönne
gießen	gießt	goß	gösse
gleichen	gleicht	glich	gliche
gleiten	gleitet	glitt	glitte
graben	gräbt	grub	grübe
greifen	greift	griff	griffe

German Irregular Verbs

Imper.	Past Participle	English
erschrick	erschrocken	be frightened
iß	gegessen	eat
fahr(e)	gefahren	travel
fall(e)	gefallen	fall
fang(e)	gefangen	catch
ficht	gefochten	fight
find(e)	gefunden	find
flicht	geflochten	twine together
flieg(e)	geflogen	fly
flieh(e)	geflohen	flee
fließ(e)	geflossen	flow
friß	gefressen	eat (of animals)
frier(e)	gefroren	freeze
gebier	geboren	give birth to
gib	gegeben	give
gedeih(e)	gediehen	thrive
geh(e)	gegangen	go
geling(e)	gelungen	succeed
gilt	gegolten	be worth, be valid
genese	genesen	recover
genieß(e)	genossen	enjoy
	geschehen	happen
gewinn(e)	gewonnen	win
gieß(e)	gegossen	pour
gleich(e)	geglichen	equal, resemble
gleit(e)	geglitten	glide
grab(e)	gegraben	dig
greif(e)	gegriffen	grasp

German Irregular Verbs

Infin.	Pres. Indic. 3rd Pers. Sing.	Imperf. Indic.	Imperf. Subj.
haben	hat	hatte	hätte
halten	hält	hielt	hielte
hangen (v.n.)	hängt	hing	hinge
heben	hebt	hob	höbe
heißen	heißt	hieß	hieße
helfen	hilft	half	hülfe
kennen	kennt	kannte	kennte
klimmen	klimmt	klomm	klömme
klingen	klingt	klang	klänge
kneifen	kneift	kniff	kniffe
kommen	kommt	kam	käme
können	kann	konnte	könnte
kriechen	kriecht	kroch	kröche
laden	lädt	lud	lüde
lassen	läßt	ließ	ließe
laufen	läuft	lief	liefe
leiden	leidet	litt	litte
leihen	leiht	lieh	liehe
lesen	liest	las	läse
liegen	liegt	lag	läge
lügen	lügt	log	löge
mahlen	mahlt	mahlte	mahlte
meiden	meidet	mied	miede
messen	mißt	maß	mäße
mißlingen (impers.)	(mir) mißlingt	mißlang	mißlänge
mögen	mag	mochte	möchte
müssen	muß	mußte	müßte
nehmen	nimmt	nahm	nähme

German Irregular Verbs

Imper.	Past Participle	English
habe	gehabt	have
halt(e)	gehalten	hold
häng(e)	gehangen	hang
hebe	gehoben	lift
heiß(e)	geheißen	be called
hilf	geholfen	help
kenn(e)	gekannt	know
klimm(e)	geklommen	climb
kling(e)	geklungen	ring, sound
kneif(e)	gekniffen	pinch
komm(e)	gekommen	come
	gekonnt	be able
kriech(e)	gekrochen	creep
lad(e)	geladen	load
laß	gelassen	let
lauf(e)	gelaufen	run
leid(e)	gelitten	suffer
leih(e)	geliehen	lend
lies	gelesen	read
lieg(e)	gelegen	lie
lüg(e)	gelogen	lie, be untruthful
mahle	gemahlen	grind
meid(e)	gemieden	avoid
miß	gemessen	measure
	mißlungen	fail
	gemocht	wish, be willing
	gemußt	have to
nimm	genommen	take

German Irregular Verbs

Infin.	Pres. Indic. 3rd Pers. Sing.	Imperf. Indic.	Imperf. Subj.
nennen	nennt	nannte	nennte
pfeifen	pfeift	pfiff	pfiffe
preisen	preist	pries	priese
quellen (*v.n.*)	quillt	quoll	quölle
raten	rät	riet	riete
reiben	reibt	rieb	riebe
reißen	reißt	riß	risse
reiten	reitet	ritt	ritte
rennen	rennt	rannte	rennte
riechen	riecht	roch	röche
ringen	ringt	rang	ränge
rinnen	rinnt	rann	rönne
rufen	ruft	rief	riefe
saufen	säuft	soff	söffe
saugen	saugt	sog	söge
schaffen	schafft	schuf	schüfe
scheiden	scheidet	schied	schiede
scheinen	scheint	schien	schiene
schelten	schilt	schalt	schölte
schieben	schiebt	schob	schöbe
schießen	schießt	schoß	schösse
schinden	schindet	schund	schünde
schlafen	schläft	schlief	schliefe
schlagen	schlägt	schlug	schlüge
schleichen	schleicht	schlich	schliche
schleifen	schleift	schliff	schliffe
schließen	schließt	schloß	schlösse
schlingen	schlingt	schlang	schlänge

Imper.	Past Participle	English
nenne	genannt	name
pfeif(e)	gepfiffen	whistle
preis(e)	gepriesen	praise
quill	gequollen	spring
rat(e)	geraten	counsel
reib(e)	gerieben	rub
reiß(e)	gerissen	tear
reit(e)	geritten	ride
renn(e)	gerannt	run
riech(e)	gerochen	smell
ring(e)	gerungen	struggle
rinn(e)	geronnen	flow
ruf(e)	gerufen	call
sauf(e)	gesoffen	drink (to excess)
saug(e)	gesogen	suck
schaff(e)	geschaffen	create
scheid(e)	geschieden	separate
schein(e)	geschienen	appear
schilt	gescholten	scold
schieb(e)	geschoben	shove
schieß(e)	geschossen	shoot
schind(e)	geschunden	skin
schlaf(e)	geschlafen	sleep
schlag(e)	geschlagen	beat
schleich(e)	geschlichen	slink, creep
schleif(e)	geschliffen	slide, polish
schließ(e)	geschlossen	shut, close
schling(e)	geschlungen	wind, devour

German Irregular Verbs

Infin.	Pres. Indic. 3rd Pers. Sing.	Imperf. Indic.	Imperf. Subj.
schmeißen	schmeißt	schmiß	schmisse
schmelzen (v.n.)	schmilzt	schmolz	schmölze
schneiden	schneidet	schnitt	schnitte
schrecken (v.n.)	schrickt	schrak	schräke
schreiben	schreibt	schrieb	schriebe
schreien	schreit	schrie	schriee
schreiten	schreitet	schritt	schritte
schweigen	schweigt	schwieg	schwiege
schwellen	schwillt	schwoll	schwölle
schwimmen	schwimmt	schwamm	schwömme
schwinden	schwindet	schwand	schwände
schwingen	schwingt	schwang	schwänge
schwören	schwört	schwur	schwüre
sehen	sieht	sah	sähe
sein	ist	war	wäre
senden	sendet	sandte or sendete	sendete
singen	singt	sang	sänge
sinken	sinkt	sank	sänke
sinnen	sinnt	sann	sänne
sitzen	sitzt	saß	säße
sollen	soll	sollte	sollte
speien	speit	spie	spiee
spinnen	spinnt	spann	spönne
sprechen	spricht	sprach	spräche
sprießen	sprießt	sproß	sprösse
springen	springt	sprang	spränge
stechen	sticht	stach	stäche
stehen	steht	stand	stände

German Irregular Verbs

Imper.	Past Participle	English
schmeiß(e)	geschmissen	hurl
schmilz	geschmolzen	melt
schneid(e)	geschnitten	cut
schrick	(erschrocken)	frighten
schreib(e)	geschrieben	write
schrei(e)	geschrien	cry
schreit(e)	geschritten	stride
schweig(e)	geschwiegen	be silent
schwill	geschwollen	swell
schwimm(e)	geschwommen	swim
schwind(e)	geschwunden	vanish
schwing(e)	geschwungen	swing
schwör(e)	geschworen	swear
sieh	gesehen	see
sei	gewesen	be
send(e)	gesandt *or* gesendet	send
sing(e)	gesungen	sing
sink(e)	gesunken	sink
sinn(e)	gesonnen	meditate
sitz(e)	gesessen	sit
	gesollt	be obliged
spei(e)	gespieen	spit
spinn(e)	gesponnen	spin
sprich	gesprochen	speak
sprieß(e)	gesprossen	sprout
spring(e)	gesprungen	leap
stich	gestochen	prick
steh(e)	gestanden	stand

German Irregular Verbs

Infin.	Pres. Indic. 3rd Pers. Sing.	Imperf. Indic.	Imperf. Subj.
stehlen	stiehlt	stahl	stöhle
steigen	steigt	stieg	stiege
sterben	stirbt	starb	stürbe
stinken	stinkt	stank	stänke
stoßen	stößt	stieß	stieße
streichen	streicht	strich	striche
streiten	streitet	stritt	stritte
tragen	trägt	trug	trüge
treffen	trifft	traf	träfe
treiben	treibt	trieb	triebe
treten	tritt	trat	träte
trinken	trinkt	trank	tränke
trügen	trügt	trog	tröge
tun	tut	tat	täte
verderben	verdirbt	verdarb	verdürbe
verdrießen	verdrießt	verdroß	verdrösse
vergessen	vergißt	vergaß	vergäße
verlieren	verliert	verlor	verlöre
wachsen	wächst	wuchs	wüchse
wägen	wägt	wog	wöge
waschen	wäscht	wusch	wüsche
weichen	weicht	wich	wiche
weisen	weist	wies	wiese
werben	wirbt	warb	würbe
werden	wird	wurde	würde
werfen	wirft	warf	würfe
wiegen	wiegt	wog	wöge
winden (v.a.)	windet	wand	wände

German Irregular Verbs

Imper.	Past Participle	English
stiehl	gestohlen	steal
steig(e)	gestiegen	climb
stirb	gestorben	die
stink(e)	gestunken	stink
stoß(e)	gestoßen	push
streich(e)	gestrichen	stroke, touch
streit(e)	gestritten	quarrel, fight
trag(e)	getragen	carry
triff	getroffen	meet
treib(e)	getrieben	drive
tritt	getreten	step
trink(e)	getrunken	drink
trüg(e)	getrogen	deceive
tu(e)	getan	do
verdirb	verdorben (and verderbt)	spoil
verdrieß(e)	verdrossen	grieve
vergiß	vergessen	forget
verlier(e)	verloren	lose
wachs(e)	gewachsen	grow
wäg(e)	gewogen	weigh
wasch(e)	gewaschen	wash
weich(e)	gewichen	yield
weis(e)	gewiesen	show
wirb	geworben	court
werde	geworden	become
wirf	geworfen	throw
wieg(e)	gewogen	weigh
wind(e)	gewunden	wind

German Irregular Verbs

Infin.	Pres. Indic. 3rd. Pers. Sing.	Imperf. Indic.	Imperf. Subj.
wissen	weiß	wußte	wüßte
wollen	will	wollte	wollte
zeihen	zeiht	zieh	ziehe
ziehen	zieht	zog	zöge
zwingen	zwingt	zwang	zwänge

German Irregular Verbs

Imper.	Past Participle	English
wisse	gewußt	know
wolle	gewollt	wish, want
zeih(e)	geziehen	accuse
zieh(e)	gezogen	draw, pull
zwing(e)	gezwungen	force, compel

English Irregular Verbs

Infin.	Past Indic.	Past Participle	German
abide	abode	abode	bleiben
arise	arose	arisen	aufstehen
awake	awoke	awoke	aufwecken
be	was, were	been	sein
bear	bore	borne	tragen
beat	beat	beaten	schlagen
become	became	become	werden
beget	begot	begotten	zeugen
begin	began	begun	beginnen
bend	bent	bent	biegen
bereave	bereaved, bereft	bereaved, bereft	berauben
beseech	besought	besought	bitten
bid	bade, bid	bidden, bid	gebieten
bide	bided, bode	bided	verbleiben
bind	bound	bound	binden
bite	bit	bitten	beißen
bleed	bled	bled	bluten
blow	blew	blown	blasen
break	broke	broken	brechen
breed	bred	bred	zeugen
bring	brought	brought	bringen
build	built	built	bauen
burn	burnt, burned	burnt, burned	brennen
burst	burst	burst	bersten
buy	bought	bought	kaufen

English Irregular Verbs

Infin.	Past Indic.	Past Participle	German
can (*pres. indic.*)	could	—	können
cast	cast	cast	werfen
catch	caught	caught	fangen
chide	chid	chidden, chid	schelten
choose	chose	chosen	wählen
cleave	cleft, clove	cleft, cloven	spalten
cling	clung	clung	sich anklammern
clothe	clothed, clad	clothed, clad	kleiden
come	came	come	kommen
cost	cost	cost	kosten
creep	crept	crept	kriechen
crow	crowed, crew	crowed	krähen
cut	cut	cut	schneiden
dare	dared, durst	dared	wagen
deal	dealt	dealt	austeilen, handeln
dig	dug	dug	graben
do	did	done	tun
draw	drew	drawn	ziehen
dream	dreamt, dreamed	dreamt, dreamed	träumen
drink	drank	drunk	trinken
drive	drove	driven	treiben
dwell	dwelt	dwelt	wohnen
eat	ate	eaten	essen
fall	fell	fallen	fallen
feed	fed	fed	füttern
feel	felt	felt	fühlen
fight	fought	fought	kämpfen
find	found	found	finden

English Irregular Verbs

Infin.	Past Indic.	Past Participle	German
flee	fled	fled	fliehen
fling	flung	flung	schleudern
fly	flew	flown	fliegen
forbid	forbad(e)	forbidden	verbieten
forget	forgot	forgotten	vergessen
forgive	forgave	forgiven	vergeben
forsake	forsook	forsaken	verlassen
freeze	froze	frozen	frieren
get	got	got	bekommen
gird	girded, girt	girden, girt	gürten
give	gave	given	geben
go	went	gone	gehen
grind	ground	ground	mahlen
grow	grew	grown	wachsen
hang	hung	hung	hängen
have	had	had	haben
hear	heard	heard	hören
heave	heaved, hove	heaved, hove	heben
hew	hewed	hewn, hewed	hauen
hide	hid	hidden, hid	verstecken
hit	hit	hit	schlagen
hold	held	held	halten
hurt	hurt	hurt	verletzen
keep	kept	kept	halten
kneel	knelt	knelt	knien
knit	knitted, knit	knitted, knit	stricken
know	knew	known	kennen, wissen
lay	laid	laid	legen

English Irregular Verbs

Infin.	Past Indic.	Past Participle	German
lead	led	led	führen
lean	leant, leaned	leant, leaned	lehnen
leap	leaped, leapt	leaped, leapt	springen
learn	learned, learnt	learned, learnt	lernen
leave	left	left	lassen
lend	lent	lent	leihen
let	let	let	lassen
lie (= recline)	lay	lain	liegen
light	lit, lighted	lit, lighted	beleuchten
lost	lost	lost	verlieren
make	made	made	machen
may (*pres. indic.*)	might	—	mögen
mean	meant	meant	meinen
meet	met	met	treffen, begegnen
melt	melted	melted, molten	schmelzen
mow	mowed	mown	mähen
must (*pres. indic.*)	—	—	müssen
pay	paid	paid	zahlen
put	put	put	stellen
quit	quit(ted)	quit(ted)	verlassen
—	quoth	—	sagte
read	read	read	lesen
rend	rent	rent	reissen
rid	rid	rid	befreien
ride	rode	ridden	reiten, fahren
ring	rang	rung	klingeln
rise	rose	risen	aufstehen
run	ran	run	laufen

English Irregular Verbs

Infin.	Past Indic.	Past Participle	German
saw	sawed	sawn	sägen
say	said	said	sagen
see	saw	seen	sehen
seek	sought	sought	suchen
sell	sold	sold	verkaufen
send	sent	sent	senden
set	set	set	setzen
shake	shook	shaken	schütteln
shall (*pres. indic.*)	should	—	werden, sollen
shape	shaped	shaped, shapen	formen
shear	sheared	shorn	scheren
shed	shed	shed	vergiessen
shine	shone	shone	scheinen
shoe	shod	shod	beschuhen
shoot	shot	shot	schiessen
show	showed	shown	zeigen
shrink	shrank	shrunk	schrumpfen
shut	shut	shut	schliessen
sing	sang	sung	singen
sink	sank	sunk	sinken
sit	sat	sat	sitzen
slay	slew	slain	erschlagen
sleep	slept	slept	schlafen
slide	slid	slid	gleiten
sling	slung	slung	schleudern
slink	slunk	slunk	schleichen
slit	slit	slit	schlitzen
smell	smelt, smelled	smelt, smelled	riechen

English Irregular Verbs

Infin.	Past Indic.	Past Participle	German
smit	smote	smitten	schlagen
sow	sowed	sown, sowed	säen
speak	spoke	spoken	sprechen
speed	sped, speeded	sped, speeded	eilen
spell	spelt, spelled	spelt, spelled	buchstabieren
spend	spent	spent	ausgeben
spill	spilled, spilt	spilled, spilt	verschütten
spin	spun, span	spun	spinnen
spit	spat	spat	speien
split	split	split	spalten
spread	spread	spread	ausbreiten
spring	sprang	sprung	springen
stand	stood	stood	stehen
steal	stole	stolen	stehlen
stick	stuck	stuck	stecken
sting	stung	stung	stechen
stink	stank, stunk	stunk	stinken
strew	strewed	strewed, strewn	streuen
stride	strode	stridden	schreiten
strike	struck	struck, stricken	schlagen
string	strung	strung	(auf)reihen
strive	strove	striven	streben
swear	swore	sworn	schwören
sweep	swept	swept	kehren
swell	swelled	swollen, swelled	schwellen
swim	swam	swum	schwimmen
swing	swung	swung	schwingen
take	took	taken	nehmen

English Irregular Verbs

Infin.	Past Indic.	Past Participle	German
teach	taught	taught	lehren
tear	tore	torn	zerreißen
tell	told	told	erzählen
think	thought	thought	denken
thrive	thrived, throve	thrived, thriven	gedeihen
throw	threw	thrown	werfen
thrust	thrust	thrust	stoßen
tread	trod	trodden	treten
wake	woke, waked	waked, woken woke	wachen
wear	wore	worn	tragen
weave	wove	woven	weben
weep	wept	wept	weinen
will	would	—	wollen
win	won	won	gewinnen
wind	wound	wound	winden
work	worked, wrought	worked, wrought	arbeiten
wring	wrung	wrung	ringen
write	wrote	written	schreiben

Numerical Tables

Cardinal Numbers

0	nought, zero	null
1	one	eins
2	two	zwei
3	three	drei
4	four	vier
5	five	fünf
6	six	sechs
7	seven	sieben
8	eight	acht
9	nine	neun
10	ten	zehn
11	eleven	elf
12	twelve	zwölf
13	thirteen	dreizehn
14	fourteen	vierzehn
15	fifteen	fünfzehn
16	sixteen	sechzehn
17	seventeen	siebzehn
18	eighteen	achtzehn
19	nineteen	neunzehn
20	twenty	zwanzig
21	twenty-one	einundzwanzig
22	twenty-two	zweiundzwanzig
25	twenty-five	fünfundzwanzig
30	thirty	dreißig
36	thirty-six	sechsunddreißig
40	forty	vierzig
50	fifty	fünfzig
60	sixty	sechzig
70	seventy	siebzig
80	eighty	achtzig
90	ninety	neunzig
100	(one)hundred	hundert
101	(a)hundred and one	hundert(und)eins
102	(a)hundred and two	hundert(und)zwei
200	two hundred	zweihundert
300	three hundred	dreihundert
600	six hundred	sechshundert
625	six hundred and twenty-five	sechshundertfünf-undzwanzig
1000	(a)thousand	tausend
1965	nineteen hundred and sixty-five	neunzehnhundert-fünfundsechzig
2000	two thousand	zweitausend
1,000,000	a million	eine Million
2,000,000	two million	zwei Millionen

Various suffixes may be added to German numerals, the commonest of which are cited in the following examples:

zehnfach	tenfold
dreisilbig	trisyllabic
vierstimmig	four-part (*i.e.* for four voices)
sechsteilig	in six parts

Ordinal Numbers

1st	first	erste (abbr. 1.)
2nd	second	zweite (abbr. 2.)
3rd	third	dritte (abbr. 3.)
4th	fourth	vierte
5th	fifth	fünfte
6th	sixth	sechste
7th	seventh	siebte
8th	eighth	achte
9th	ninth	neunte
10th	tenth	zehnte
11th	eleventh	elfte
12th	twelfth	zwölfte
13th	thirteenth	dreizehnte
14th	fourteenth	vierzehnte
15th	fifteenth	fünfzehnte
16th	sixteenth	sechzehnte
17th	seventeenth	siebzehnte
18th	eighteenth	achtzehnte
19th	nineteenth	neunzehnte
20th	twentieth	zwanzigste
21st	twenty-first	einundzwanzigste
22nd	twenty-second	zweiundzwanzigste
25th	twenty-fifth	fünfundzwanzigste
30th	thirtieth	dreißigste
40th	fortieth	vierzigste
50th	fiftieth	fünfzigste
60th	sixtieth	sechzigste
70th	seventieth	siebzigste
80th	eightieth	achtzigste
90th	ninetieth	neunzigste
100th	hundredth	hundertste
102nd	hundred and second	hundert(und)zweite
200th	two hundredth	zweihundertste
300th	three hundredth	dreihundertste
625th	six hundred and twenty-fifth	sechshundertfünf-undzwanzigste
1000th	thousandth	tausendste
2000th	two thousandth	zweitausendste
1,000,000th	millionth	millionste

Fractions etc.

$\frac{1}{4}$	a quarter	ein Viertel
$\frac{1}{3}$	a third	ein ·Drittel
$\frac{1}{2}$	a half	(ein)halb
$\frac{2}{3}$	two thirds	zwei Drittel
$\frac{3}{4}$	three quarters	drei Viertel
$1\frac{1}{4}$	one and a quarter	ein ein Viertel
$1\frac{1}{2}$	one and a half	anderthalb
$5\frac{1}{2}$	five and a half	fünfeinhalb
$7\frac{2}{5}$	seven and two-fifths	sieben zwei Fünftel
$\frac{15}{20}$	fifteen-twentieths	fünfzehn Zwanzigstel
.7	point seven	0,7 Null Komma sieben